CME PROJECT

Algebra 2

TEACHER'S EDITION

PEARSON

Boston, Massachusetts
Chandler, Arizona
Glenview, Illinois
Shoreview, Minnesota
Upper Saddle River, New Jersey

EDC

Education Development Center, Inc.
Center for Mathematics Education
Newton, Massachusetts

Acknowledgments appear on page T870, which constitutes an extension of this copyright page.

PEARSON

13-digit ISBN 978-0-13-350023-3
10-digit ISBN 0-13-350023-3

1 2 3 4 5 6 7 8 9 10 12 11 10 09 08

Algebra 2
Teacher's Edition Contents

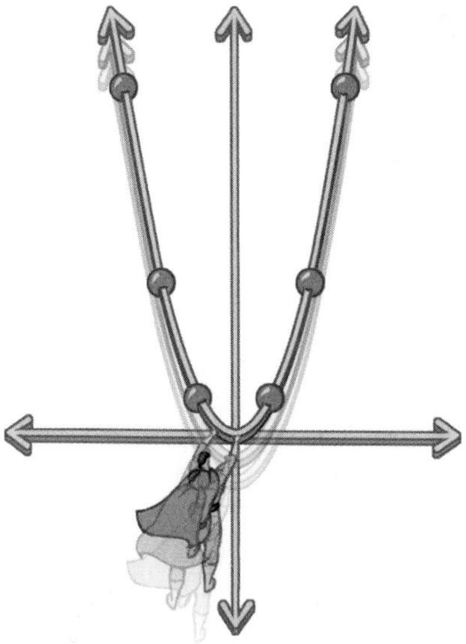

Student Edition With Teacher Notes

The Center for Mathematics Education Project was developed at Education Development Center, Inc. (EDC) within the Center for Mathematics Education (CME), with partial support from the National Science Foundation.

Education Development Center, Inc.
Center for Mathematics Education
Newton, Massachusetts

This material is based upon work supported by the National Science Foundation under Grant No. ESI-0242476, Grant No. MDR-9252952, and Grant No. ESI-9617369. Any opinions, findings, and conclusions or recommendations expressed in this material are those of the author(s) and do not necessarily reflect the views of the National Science Foundation.

CME Project Development Team

Lead Developer: Al Cuoco

Core Development Team: Anna Baccaglini-Frank, Jean Benson, Nancy Antonellis D'Amato, Daniel Erman, Brian Harvey, Wayne Harvey, Bowen Kerins, Doreen Kilday, Ryota Matsuura, Stephen Maurer, Sarah Sword, Audrey Ting, and Kevin Waterman

Others who contributed include Steve Benson, Paul D'Amato, Robert Devaney, Andrew Golay, Paul Goldenberg, Jane Gorman, C. Jud Hill, Eric Karnowski, Helen Lebowitz, Joseph Leverich, Melanie Palma, Mark Saul, Nina Shteingold, and Brett Thomas.

Acknowledgments appear on page 878 , which constitutes an extension of this copyright page.

PEARSON

13-digit ISBN 978-0-13-350019-6
10-digit ISBN 0-13-350019-5

1 2 3 4 5 6 7 8 9 10 12 11 10 09 08

Introduction to the CME Project

CME PROJECT

The CME Project, developed by EDC's Center for Mathematics Education, is a new NSF-funded high school program, organized around the familiar courses of algebra 1, geometry, algebra 2, and precalculus. The CME Project provides teachers and schools with a third alternative to the choice between traditional texts driven by basic skill development and more progressive texts that have unfamiliar organizations. This program gives teachers the option of a problem-based, student-centered program, organized around the mathematical themes with which teachers and parents are familiar. Furthermore, the tremendous success of NSF-funded middle school programs has left a need for a high school program with similar rigor and pedagogy. The CME Project fills this need.

The goal of the CME Project is to help students acquire a deep understanding of mathematics. Therefore, the mathematics here is rigorous. We took great care to create lesson plans that, while challenging, will capture and engage students of all abilities and improve their mathematical achievement. Independent research confirms that we achieved this goal in diverse classrooms around the country.

The Program's Approach

The organization of the CME Project provides students the time and focus they need to develop fundamental mathematical ways of thinking. Its primary goal is to develop in students robust mathematical proficiency.

- The program employs innovative instructional methods, developed over decades of classroom experience and informed by research, that help students master mathematical topics.
- One of the core tenets of the CME Project is to focus on developing students' Habits of Mind, or ways in which students approach and solve mathematical challenges.
- The program builds on lessons learned from high-performing countries: develop an idea thoroughly and then revisit it only to deepen it; organize ideas in a way that is faithful to how they are organized in mathematics; and reduce clutter and extraneous topics.
- It also employs the best American models that call for grappling with ideas and problems as preparation for instruction, moving from concrete problems to abstractions and general theories, and situating mathematics in engaging contexts.
- The CME Project is a comprehensive curriculum that meets the dual goals of mathematical rigor and accessibility for a broad range of students.

About CME

EDC's Center for Mathematics Education, led by mathematician and teacher **Al Cuoco**, brings together an eclectic staff of mathematicians, teachers, cognitive scientists, education researchers, curriculum developers, specialists in educational technology, and teacher educators, internationally known for leadership across the entire range of K–16 mathematics education. We aim to help students and teachers in this country experience the thrill of solving problems and building theories, understand the history of ideas behind the evolution of mathematical disciplines, and appreciate the standards of rigor that are central to mathematical culture.

Contributors to the CME Project

National Advisory Board The National Advisory Board met early in the project, providing critical feedback on the instructional design and the overall organization. Members include

Richard Askey, University of Wisconsin
Edward Barbeau, University of Toronto
Hyman Bass, University of Michigan
Carol Findell, Boston University
Arthur Heinricher, Worcester Polytechnic Institute
Roger Howe, Yale University
Barbara Janson, Janson Associates
Kenneth Levasseur, University of Massachusetts, Lowell
James Madden, Louisiana State University, Baton Rouge
Jacqueline Miller, Education Development Center
James Newton, University of Maryland
Robert Segall, Greater Hartford Academy of Mathematics and Science
Glenn Stevens, Boston University
Herbert Wilf, University of Pennsylvania
Hung-Hsi Wu, University of California, Berkeley

Core Mathematical Consultants **Dick Askey, Ed Barbeau,** and **Roger Howe** have been involved in an even more substantial way, reviewing chapters and providing detailed and critical advice on every aspect of the program. Dick and Roger spent many hours reading and criticizing drafts, brainstorming with the writing team, and offering advice on everything from the logical organization to the actual numbers used in problems. We can't thank them enough.

Teacher Advisory Board The Teacher Advisory Board for the CME Project was essential in helping us create an effective format for our lessons that embodies the philosophy and goals of the program. Their debates about pedagogical issues and how to develop mathematical topics helped to shape the distinguishing features of the curriculum so that our lessons work effectively in the classroom. The advisory board includes

Jayne Abbas, Richard Coffey, Charles Garabedian, Dennis Geller, Eileen Herlihy, Doreen Kilday, Gayle Masse, Hugh McLaughlin, Nancy McLaughlin, Allen Olsen, Kimberly Osborne, Brian Shoemaker, and **Benjamin Sinwell**

Field-Test Teachers Our field-test teachers gave us the benefit of their classroom experience by teaching from our draft lessons and giving us extensive, critical feedback that shaped the drafts into realistic, teachable lessons. They shared their concerns, questions, challenges, and successes and kept us focused on the real world. Some of them even welcomed us into their classrooms as co-teachers to give us the direct experience with students that we needed to hone our lessons. Working with these expert professionals has been one of the most gratifying parts of the development—they are "highly qualified" in the most profound sense.

California **Barney Martinez**, Jefferson High School, Daly City; **Calvin Baylon** and **Jaime Lao**, Bell Junior High School, San Diego; **Colorado** **Rocky Cundiff**, Ignacio High School, Ignacio; **Illinois** **Jeremy Kahan, Tammy Nguyen**, and **Stephanie Pederson**, Ida Crown Jewish Academy, Chicago; **Massachusetts** **Carol Martignette, Chris Martino,** and **Kent Werst**, Arlington High School, Arlington; **Larry Davidson**, Boston University Academy, Boston; **Joe Bishop** and **Carol Rosen**, Lawrence High School, Lawrence; **Maureen Mulryan**, Lowell High School, Lowell; **Felisa Honeyman**, Newton South High School, Newton Centre; **Jim Barnes** and **Carol Haney**, Revere High School, Revere; **New Hampshire** **Jayne Abbas** and **Terin Voisine,** Cawley Middle School, Hooksett; **New Mexico** **Mary Andrews**, Las Cruces High School, Las Cruces; **Ohio** **James Stallworth**, Hughes Center, Cincinnati; **Texas** **Arnell Crayton**, Bellaire High School, Bellaire; **Utah** **Troy Jones**, Waterford School, Sandy; **Washington** **Dale Erz, Kathy Greer, Karena Hanscom**, and **John Henry**, Port Angeles High School, Port Angeles; **Wisconsin** **Annette Roskam**, Rice Lake High School, Rice Lake.

Special thanks go to our colleagues at Pearson, most notably Elizabeth Lehnertz, Joe Will, and Stewart Wood. The program benefits from their expertise in every way, from the actual mathematics to the design of the printed page.

This Pacing Guide can help you customize your course.

It accounts for 111 standard class periods. If you allow one day for each of the 26 exploratory Getting Started lessons, you can average about 1.5 days for each of the teaching lessons and still have adequate time for assessment. A Daily Planner precedes each chapter and gives lesson-by-lesson suggestions for that chapter.

Chapter 1 *Fitting Functions to Tables* — **12 Days**

DAY	LESSON	DAY	LESSON
1	1.1 Getting Started	7	1.7 Fitting Lines to Data
2	1.2 Two Types of Definitions—Closed-Form and Recursive Function Definitions	8	1.8 The Line of Best Fit, Part 1
3	1.3 Constant Differences	9	1.9 The Line of Best Fit, Part 2
4	1.4 Tables and Slope	10	1.10 Getting Started
5	1.5 Deeper Differences—Difference Tables for Polynomial Functions	11	1.11 Monthly Payments
6	1.6 Getting Started	12	1.12 The Factorial Function

Chapter 2 *Functions and Polynomials* — **16 Days**

DAY	LESSON	DAY	LESSON
1	2.0 Polynomial Basics—Optional Review	9	2.8 Getting Started
2	2.1 Getting Started	10	2.9 Polynomial Division
3	2.2 Getting Precise About Functions	11	2.10 The Factor Theorem
4	2.3 Algebra With Functions	12	2.11 Getting Started
5	2.4 Inverses: Doing and Undoing	13	2.12 Quadratics
6	2.5 Getting Started	14	2.13 Factoring Cubics
7	2.6 Lagrange Interpolation—Fitting Polynomial Functions to Tables	15	2.14 Pippins and Cheese—More Factoring Techniques
8	2.7 Agreeing to Disagree—Finding Functions with Specific Values	16	2.15 Rational Expressions

Chapter 3 *Complex Numbers*			**13 Days**
DAY	**LESSON**	**DAY**	**LESSON**
1	3.1 Getting Started	**8**	3.8 Arithmetic in the Complex Plane
2	3.2 Extending Number Systems	**9**	3.9 Magnitude and Direction
3	3.3 Making the Extension: $\sqrt{-1}$	**10**	3.10 Getting Started
4	3.4 Extension to Complex Numbers	**11**	3.11 Multiplying Complex Numbers
5	3.5 Reciprocals and Division	**12**	3.12 Conjugates and Roots
6	3.6 Getting Started	**13**	3.13 Roots of Unity
7	3.7 Graphing Complex Numbers		

Chapter 4 *Linear Algebra*			**13 Days**
DAY	**LESSON**	**DAY**	**LESSON**
1	4.1 Getting Started	**8**	4.8 Matrix Inverses
2	4.2 Solving Systems Systematically	**9**	4.9 Matrix Properties
3	4.3 Solving Again, in Matrix Form	**10**	4.10 Getting Started
4	4.4 Getting Started	**11**	4.11 Geometric Transformations
5	4.5 Basic Matrix Operations—Addition, Subtraction, and Scalar Multiplication	**12**	4.12 Transition Matrices
6	4.6 Dot Products	**13**	4.13 Probability Models
7	4.7 Matrix Multiplication		

Chapter 5 *Exponential and Logarithmic Functions*			**15 Days**
DAY	**LESSON**	**DAY**	**LESSON**
1	5.1 Getting Started	**9**	5.9 Properties of Exponential Functions
2	5.2 Laws of Exponents	**10**	5.10 Exponential Functions, One-to-One
3	5.3 Zero and Negative Exponents	**11**	5.11 Getting Started
4	5.4 Sequences and Operations	**12**	5.12 Defining Logarithms
5	5.5 Defining Rational Exponents	**13**	5.13 Laws of Logarithms
6	5.6 Getting Started	**14**	5.14 Graphing Logarithmic Functions
7	5.7 Graphs of Exponential Functions	**15**	5.15 The Logarithmic Scale
8	5.8 Tables of Exponential Functions		

Chapter 6 *Graphs and Transformations*			**10 Days**
DAY	**LESSON**	**DAY**	**LESSON**
1	6.1 Getting Started	**6**	6.6 Introducing Affine Transformations
2	6.2 More Basic Graphs—$x^2 + y^2 = 1$, $y = x^3 \pm x$	**7**	6.7 Transforming Equations
3	6.3 Translating Graphs	**8**	6.8 Getting Started
4	6.4 Scaling and Reflecting Graphs	**9**	6.9 Replacing the Axes
5	6.5 Getting Started	**10**	6.10 Advanced Affine Transformations

Chapter 7 *Sequences and Series*			**17 Days**
DAY	**LESSON**	**DAY**	**LESSON**
1	7.1 Getting Started	**10**	7.10 Arithmetic Sequences and Series
2	7.2 Gauss's Method and Euclid's Method	**11**	7.11 Geometric Sequences and Series—Day 1
3	7.3 Ways to Visualize Sums	**12**	7.11 Geometric Sequences and Series—Day 2
4	7.4 The Σ Notation	**13**	7.12 Limits
5	7.5 Getting Started	**14**	7.13 Repeating Decimals
6	7.6 Definite and Indefinite Sums	**15**	7.14 Getting Started
7	7.7 Σ Identities	**16**	7.15 Pascal's Triangle
8	7.8 Tables and Figurate Numbers	**17**	7.16 The Binomial Theorem
9	7.9 Getting Started		

Chapter 8 *Introduction to Trigonometry*			**15 Days**
DAY	**LESSON**	**DAY**	**LESSON**
1	8.0 Right Triangle Trigonometry	**9**	8.8 Graphing the Tangent Function
2	8.1 Getting Started	**10**	8.9 The Angle-Sum Identities
3	8.2 Extending the Domain, Part 1—0° to 360°	**11**	8.10 Getting Started
4	8.3 Extending the Domain, Part 2—All Real Numbers	**12**	8.11 The Area of a Triangle
5	8.4 The Pythagorean Identity	**13**	8.12 The Law of Sines
6	8.5 Solving Trigonometric Equations	**14**	8.13 The Law of Cosines
7	8.6 Getting Started	**15**	8.14 Heron's Formula—Using Side Lengths to Find the Area of a Triangle
8	8.7 Graphing Cosine and Sine		

1 Fitting Functions to Tables

2 Functions and Polynomials

3 Complex Numbers

4 Linear Algebra

Exponential and Logarithmic Functions

6 Graphs and Transformations

7 Sequences and Series

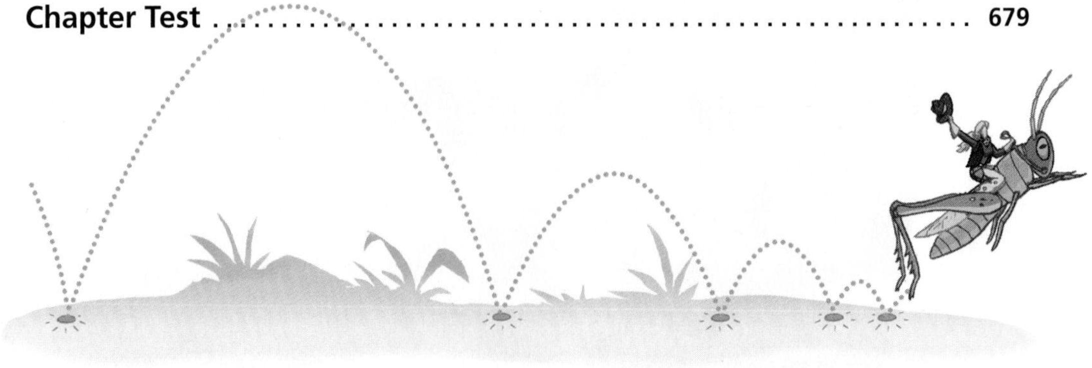

8 Introduction to Trigonometry

CME Project
Student Handbook

What Makes CME Different

Welcome to the CME Project! The goal of this program is to help you develop a deep understanding of mathematics. Throughout this book, you will engage in many different activities to help you develop that deep understanding. Some of these instructional activities may be different from ones you are used to. Below is an overview of some of these elements and why they are an important part of the CME Project.

The Habits of Mind Experience

Mathematical Habits of Mind are the foundation for serious questioning, solid thinking, good problem solving, and critical analysis. These Habits of Mind are what will help you become a mathematical thinker. Throughout the CME Project, you will focus on developing and refining these Habits of Mind.

Developing Habits of Mind

Develop thinking skills. This feature provides you with various methods and approaches to solving problems.

You will develop, use, and revisit specific Habits of Mind throughout the course. These include

- **Process** (how you work through problems)
- **Visualization** (how you "picture" problems)
- **Representation** (what you write down)
- **Patterns** (what you find)
- **Relationships** (what you find or use)

Developing good habits will help you as problems become more complicated.

Habits of Mind

Think. These special margin notes highlight key thinking skills and prompt you to apply your developing Habits of Mind.

You can find Developing Habits of Mind **on pages** 8, 9, 17, 23, 47, 48, 62, 77, 78, 104, 105, 110, 118, 120, 141, 150, 152, 157, 166, 172, 201, 207, 218, 220, 229, 238, 243, 258, 271, 295, 308, 309, 325, 327, 343, 347, 348, 361, 402, 419, 431, 438, 452, 465, 471, 515, 524, 536, 537, 551, 599, 657, 669, 695, 699, 710, 719, 722, 742, 748, 760.

Minds in Action

Discussion of mathematical ideas is an effective method of learning. The Minds in Action feature exposes you to ways of communicating about mathematics.

Join Sasha, Tony, Derman, and others as they think, calculate, predict, and discuss their way towards understanding.

Minds in Action prologue

Sasha, Tony, and Derman have just skimmed through their CME Project Algebra 2 *book.*

Sasha Did you notice the student dialogs throughout the book?

Derman Sure did!

Tony They talk and think just the way we do.

Sasha I know! And they even make mistakes sometimes, the way we do.

Tony But I like how they help each other to learn from those mistakes. I bet they use the Habits of Mind I saw all over the book, too.

Sasha That's great! They should help a lot.

You can find Minds in Action on pages 16, 32, 60, 115, 131, 139, 157, 173, 179, 207, 235, 256, 271, 287, 317, 337, 344, 406, 418, 437, 439, 478, 505, 513, 522, 539, 546, 548, 550, 562, 572, 593, 609, 611, 632, 650, 709, 754.

Exploring Mathematics

Throughout the CME Project, you will engage in activities that extend your learning and allow you to explore the concepts you learn in greater depth. Two of these activities are In-Class Experiments and Chapter Projects.

In-Class Experiment

In-Class Experiments allow you to explore new concepts and apply the Habits of Mind.

You will explore math as mathematicians do. You start with a question and develop answers through experimentation.

You can find In-Class Experiments on pages 55, 115, 237, 429, 436, 444, 484, 571, 597, 598, 639, 649, 724.

Chapter Projects

Chapter Projects allow you to apply your Habits of Mind to the content of the chapter. These projects cover many different topics and allow you to explore and engage in greater depth.

Chapter Projects
Using Mathematical Habits

Here is a list of the Chapter Projects and page numbers.

Using Your CME Book

To help you make the most of your CME experience, we are providing the following overview of the organization of your book.

Focusing Your Learning

In *Algebra 2*, there are 8 chapters, with each chapter devoted to a mathematical concept. With only 8 chapters, your class will be able to focus on these core concepts and develop a deep understanding of them.

Within each chapter, you will explore a series of Investigations. Each Investigation focuses on an important aspect of the mathematical concept for that chapter.

The CME Investigation

The goal of each mathematical Investigation is for you to formalize your understanding of the mathematics being taught. There are some common instructional features in each Investigation.

Getting Started

You will launch into each Investigation with a Getting Started lesson that activates prior knowledge and explores new ideas. This lesson provides you the opportunity to grapple with ideas and problems. The goal of these lessons is for you to explore—not all your questions will be answered in these lessons.

2.1 Getting Started

Activating Prior Knowledge
Exploring New Ideas

By now, you have some idea of what a function is. Here are a few functions.

SQRT(x) = the square root of a real number x
SQR(x) = the square of a real number x
REC(n) = the reciprocal of a real number n
BD(p) = the birthday of a person p
SUM(a, b) = the sum of two numbers a and b
PR(a, b) = the product of two numbers a and b
$Q(a, b)$ = the quotient of two numbers a and b

Here is a formula for Q.
$Q(a, b) = \frac{a}{b}$
Not all functions have formulas. For example, BD does not have one.

For You to Explore

1. If possible, find the value of each expression. If an expression cannot be evaluated, explain why not.
   a. PR(3, 4)
   b. Q(3, 4)
   c. Q(6, 8)
   d. Q(0, 23)
   e. Q(23, 0)
   f. SQR(SQRT(5))
   g. SQRT(SQR(5))
   h. SQR(SQRT(−5))
   i. SQRT(SQR(−5))
   j. Q(P(3, 4), P(2, 6))
   k. BD(Pierre Fermat)
   l. BD(3)
   m. SQRT(SUM(9, 16))
   n. SUM(SQRT(9), SQRT(16))
   o. SQRT(BD(Isaac Newton))
   p. SQRT(PR(−2, $\frac{1}{3}$))
   q. REC(2)
   r. REC(REC(2))
   s. REC(REC(REC(2)))
   t. REC(0)
2. A mystery function $m(x)$ has the inputs and outputs below. How can you define the function?
   $m(\pi) = 3, m(2.9) = 2, m(5) = 5, m(11.6) = 11, m(-1.3) = -2$
3. Consider the func... SQ...

Learning the Mathematics

You will engage in, learn, and practice the mathematics in a variety of ways. The types of learning elements you will find throughout this course include

- **Worked-Out Examples** that model how to solve problems
- **Definitions and Theorems** to summarize key concepts
- **In-Class Experiments** to explore the concepts
- **For You to Do** assignments to check your understanding
- **For Discussion** questions to encourage communication
- **Minds in Action** to model mathematical discussion

Communicating the Mathematics

Minds in Action

Student dialogs

By featuring dialogs between characters, the CME Project exposes you to a way of communicating about mathematics. These dialogs will then become a real part of your classroom!

2.7 Agreeing to Disagree

More than one polynomial function can agree with the inputs and outputs in a table.

Minds in Action episode 6

Tony and Sasha are looking at Table A.

Table A

Input	Output
1	4
2	6
3	8
4	10

Tony Sure, $h(x) = 2x + 2$ is a polynomial function that works. But I think there are other functions that agree with the table. I couldn't write down a rule, but I can draw a graph. Look.

Tony draws on the board.

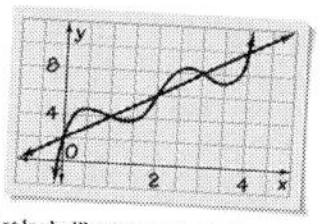

Sasha Well, that looks like the graph of a function all right, but how do you know it's the graph of a *polynomial* function? Can you find a polynomial that's not linear and that goes through the points you get from the table?

Why might Sasha say this "looks like the graph of a function"?

Tony Hmm . . . sure! I just add another input to the table. Let's say 5. Then I make the output something other than $2 \cdot 5 + 2$. I'll make it 13.

Table A

Input	Output
1	4
2	6
3	8
4	10
5	13

2.7 Agreeing to Disagree 139

Reflecting on the Mathematics

At the end of each Investigation, Mathematical Reflections give you an opportunity to put ideas together. This feature allows you to demonstrate your understanding of the Investigation and reflect on what you learn.

Practice

The CME Project views extensive practice as a critical component of a mathematics curriculum. You will have daily opportunities to practice what you learn.

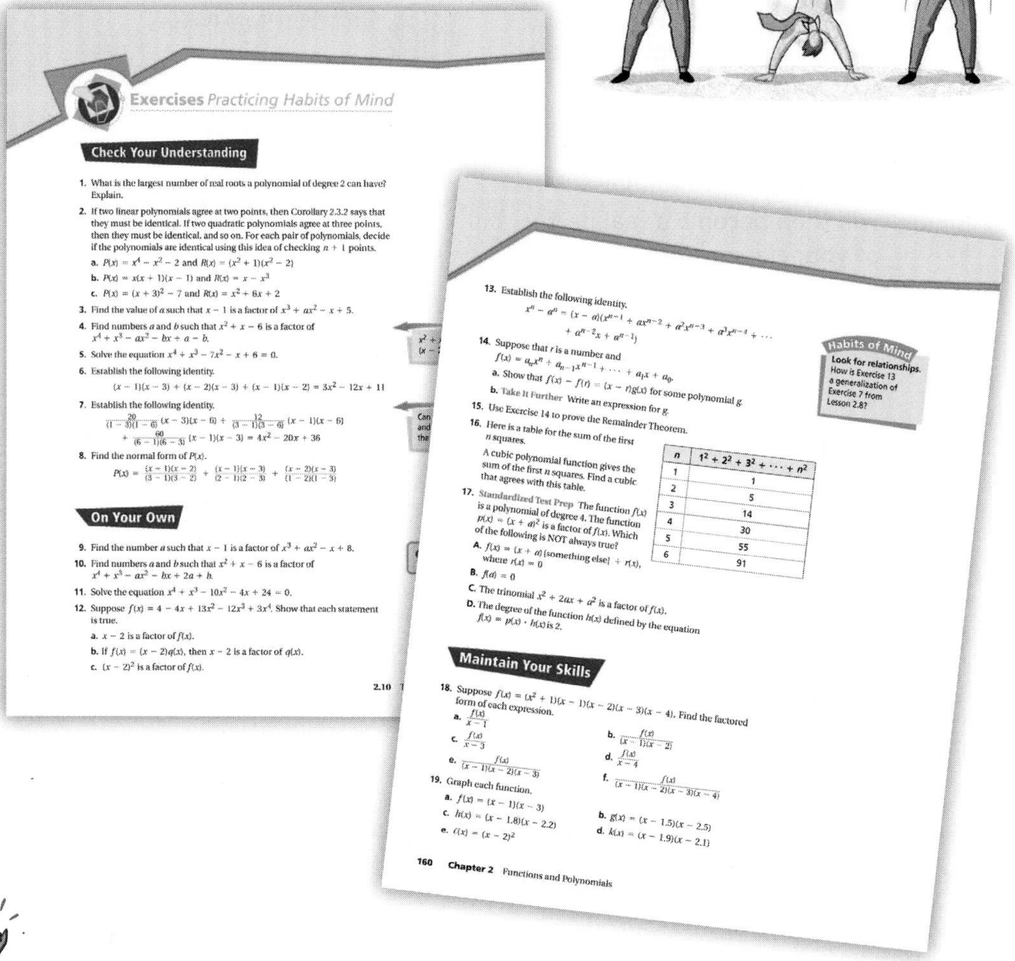

Exercises *Practicing Habits of Mind*

Check Your Understanding

1. What is the largest number of real roots a polynomial of degree 2 can have? Explain.
2. If two linear polynomials agree at two points, then Corollary 2.3.2 says that they must be identical. If two quadratic polynomials agree at three points, then they must be identical, and so on. For each pair of polynomials, decide if the polynomials are identical using this idea of checking $n + 1$ points.
   a. $P(x) = x^4 - x^2 - 2$ and $R(x) = (x^2 + 1)(x^2 - 2)$
   b. $P(x) = x(x + 1)(x - 1)$ and $R(x) = x - x^3$
   c. $P(x) = (x + 3)^2 - 7$ and $R(x) = x^2 + 6x + 2$
3. Find the value of a such that $x - 1$ is a factor of $x^3 + ax^2 - x + 5$.
4. Find numbers a and b such that $x^2 + x - 6$ is a factor of $x^4 + x^3 - ax^2 - bx + a - b$.
5. Solve the equation $x^4 + x^3 - 7x^2 - x + 6 = 0$.
6. Establish the following identity.
   $(x - 1)(x - 3) + (x - 2)(x - 3) + (x - 1)(x - 2) = 3x^2 - 12x + 11$
7. Establish the following identity.
   $\frac{20}{(1 - 3)(1 - 6)}(x - 3)(x - 6) + \frac{12}{(3 - 1)(3 - 6)}(x - 1)(x - 6) + \frac{60}{(6 - 1)(6 - 3)}(x - 1)(x - 3) = 4x^2 - 20x + 36$
8. Find the normal form of $P(x)$.
   $P(x) = \frac{(x - 1)(x - 2)}{(3 - 1)(3 - 2)} + \frac{(x - 1)(x - 3)}{(2 - 1)(2 - 3)} + \frac{(x - 2)(x - 3)}{(1 - 2)(1 - 3)}$

On Your Own

9. Find the number a such that $x - 1$ is a factor of $x^3 + ax^2 - x + 8$.
10. Find numbers a and b such that $x^2 + x - 6$ is a factor of $x^4 + x^3 - ax^2 - bx + 2a + b$.
11. Solve the equation $x^4 + x^3 - 10x^2 - 4x + 24 = 0$.
12. Suppose $f(x) = 4 - 4x + 13x^2 - 12x^3 + 3x^4$. Show that each statement is true.
   a. $x - 2$ is a factor of $f(x)$.
   b. If $f(x) = (x - 2)q(x)$, then $x - 2$ is a factor of $q(x)$.
   c. $(x - 2)^2$ is a factor of $f(x)$.

2.10

13. Establish the following identity.
   $x^n - a^n = (x - a)(x^{n-1} + ax^{n-2} + a^2x^{n-3} + a^3x^{n-4} + \cdots + a^{n-2}x + a^{n-1})$
14. Suppose that r is a number and
   $f(x) = a_nx^n + a_{n-1}x^{n-1} + \cdots + a_1x + a_0$.
   a. Show that $f(x) - f(r) = (x - r)g(x)$ for some polynomial g.
   b. Take It Further Write an expression for g.
15. Use Exercise 14 to prove the Remainder Theorem.
16. Here is a table for the sum of the first n squares.
   A cubic polynomial function gives the sum of the first n squares. Find a cubic that agrees with this table.

n	$1^2 + 2^2 + 3^2 + \cdots + n^2$
1	1
2	5
3	14
4	30
5	55
6	91

17. Standardized Test Prep The function $f(x)$ is a polynomial of degree 4. The function $p(x) = (x + a)^2$ is a factor of $f(x)$. Which of the following is NOT always true?
   A. $f(x) = (x + a)$ (something else) $+ r(x)$, where $r(x) = 0$
   B. $f(a) = 0$
   C. The trinomial $x^2 + 2ax + a^2$ is a factor of $f(x)$.
   D. The degree of the function $h(x)$ defined by the equation $f(x) = p(x) \cdot h(x)$ is 2.

Habits of Mind
Look for relationships. How is Exercise 13 a generalization of Exercise 7 from Lesson 2.8?

Maintain Your Skills

18. Suppose $f(x) = (x^2 + 1)(x - 1)(x - 2)(x - 3)(x - 4)$. Find the factored form of each expression.
   a. $\frac{f(x)}{x - 1}$
   b. $\frac{f(x)}{(x - 1)(x - 2)}$
   c. $\frac{f(x)}{x - 3}$
   d. $\frac{f(x)}{x - 4}$
   e. $\frac{f(x)}{(x - 1)(x - 2)(x - 3)}$
   f. $\frac{f(x)}{(x - 1)(x - 2)(x - 3)(x - 4)}$
19. Graph each function.
   a. $f(x) = (x - 1)(x - 3)$
   b. $g(x) = (x - 1.5)(x - 2.5)$
   c. $h(x) = (x - 1.8)(x - 2.2)$
   d. $k(x) = (x - 1.9)(x - 2.1)$
   e. $\ell(x) = (x - 2)^2$

160 **Chapter 2** Functions and Polynomials

Check Your Understanding

Assess your readiness for independent practice by working through these problems in class.

On Your Own

Practice and continue developing the mathematical understanding you learn in each lesson.

Maintain Your Skills

Review and reinforce skills from previous lessons.

Also Available

An additional Practice Workbook is available separately.

Go Online

Throughout this book you will find links to the Prentice Hall Web site. Use the Web Codes provided with each link to gain direct access to online material. Here's how to Go Online.

1. **Go to PHSchool.com.**
2. **Enter the Web Code.**
3. **Click Go!**

Check out the TI-Nspire™ Technology Handbook on p. 778 for examples of how you can use handheld technology with your math learning!

Go Online Lesson Web Codes

Additional Practice Web Codes: For every lesson, (except Getting Started lessons) there is additional practice online. Access this additional practice using the Web Code format at the right.

Additional Practice

Web Code format: bfa-0203
02 = Chapter 2 03 = Lesson 3

Go Online Chapter Web Codes

Chapter	Vocabulary Review	Mid-Chapter Test	Chapter Test
1	bfj-0151	bfa-0152	bfa-0153
2	bfj-0251	bfa-0252	bfa-0253
3	bfj-0351	bfa-0352	bfa-0353
4	bfj-0451	bfa-0452	bfa-0453
5	bfj-0551	bfa-0552	bfa-0553
6	bfj-0651	bfa-0652	bfa-0653
7	bfj-0751	bfa-0752	bfa-0753
8	bfj-0851	bfa-0852	bfa-0853

Go Online Additional Web Codes

Video Tutor

Use **Web Code:** bfe-0775 to access engaging online instructional videos to help bring math concepts to life. See page 6.

Math Background

Use **Web Code:** bfe-8031 to find additional background historical information. See page 205.
Use **Web Code:** bfe-9031 to find additional background information related to the mathematics at hand.
See page 46.

Chapter 1
Fitting Functions to Tables

This chapter reintroduces students to the idea of a function by having them look for mathematical rules, closed form and recursive, that match input-output tables of numbers.

Chapter Overview

INVESTIGATION 1A, *Tables,* has students explore tables that are designed to match simple functions—for the most part linear and quadratic polynomials—and students learn to use difference tables to match a table to a function.

INVESTIGATION 1B, *Fitting and Data,* has students explore the problem of finding functions that approximate tables of data. They learn how to find the line of best fit for a data set.

INVESTIGATION 1C, *More About Recursive Models,* has students work more extensively with recursion, including work with the factorial function and with a function that calculates the balance on a loan.

For more information on the investigations, see

- Chapter Road Map, pp. 2–3
- Investigation Road Maps, pp. 4, 40, 68

PROJECT The Project near the end of the chapter is optional. You can assign the Project at any time during the chapter depending on how often and how long you feel students should work on it.

Pacing Suggestions and Materials

Investigation 1A *Tables*

DAY	LESSON	HOMEWORK
1	1.1 Getting Started Core: 1, 2 Optional: none	Core: 3, 4, 7, 8, 9, 10, 11, 12, 13, 14, 15, 19, 20 Optional: 5, 6, 16, 17, 18, 21, 22, 23
2	1.2 Two Types of Definitions Core: 1, 2, 3, 4, 5, 6, 7, 8 Optional: 9	Core: 10, 11a, 12, 14 Optional: 13, 15; Extension: 11b
3	1.3 Constant Differences Core: 1, 2, 3, 5, 6, 7, 8 Optional: 4, 9	Core: 10, 11, 12, 13, 14, 15, 16 Optional: 17, 19, 20; Extension: 18
4	1.4 Tables and Slope Core: 1, 2, 3, 4, 5, 8, 9 Optional: 6, 7	Core: 10, 12, 13, 14, 15, 18, 19 Optional: 11, 17, 20a–e, 21; Extension: 16, 20f
5	1.5 Deeper Differences Core: 1, 3, 4, 5 Optional: 2, 8, 9, 10, 11; Extension: 6, 7, 12	Core: 13, 14, 15, 17, 18, 20 Optional: 16, 21a–e, 22; Extension: 19, 21f

Investigation 1B *Fitting and Data*

DAY	LESSON	HOMEWORK
1	1.6 Getting Started Core: 1, 2, 3, 4, 5 Optional: 6	Core: 7, 8, 9, 10, 11, 13, 14 Optional: 12, 15, 16, 17
2	1.7 Fitting Lines to Data Core: 1, 2, 3, 4 Optional: 5, 6	Core: 7, 9a–b, 10, 12, 13, 14 Optional: 8, 11, 15, 16, 17, 18; Extension: 9c
3	1.8 The Line of Best Fit, Part 1 Core: 2, 3, 4, 5 Optional: 1	Core: 6, 7, 8, 10, 11, 12 Optional: 9, 14a–b, 15, 16; Extension: 13, 14c–d
4	1.9 The Line of Best Fit, Part 2 Core: 1, 2, 3a Optional: none; Extension: 3b	Core: 4, 5, 6, 7, 8, 9, 10 Optional: 11, 13, 14; Extension: 12

NOTES	MATERIALS
Encourage students to try all the problems.	• CAS (recommended) • geometry software • graph paper • graphing calculators • Blackline Masters MC1, 1.1
	• CAS (recommended) • graph paper • spreadsheet software • Blackline Masters MC1, 1.2A–C
You may skip the For Discussion (or do it very informally) so students have more time to work on exercises in class.	• CAS (recommended) • graph paper • graphing calculators • Blackline Masters MC1, 1.2B
	• CAS (recommended) • graph paper • graphing calculators • spreadsheet software • Blackline Masters MC1, 1.4
	• CAS (recommended) • graphing calculators • spreadsheet software • Blackline Masters 1.5A–C

NOTES	MATERIALS
	• CAS (recommended) • graph paper • graphing calculators • number cubes • spreadsheet software
	• CAS (recommended) • graph paper • graphing calculators • spreadsheet software • Blackline Masters 1.7A–C
Work through the first For You to Do.	• CAS (recommended) • geometry software • graph paper • graphing calculators • spreadsheet software • Blackline Master 1.8
	• CAS (recommended) • graph paper • graphing calculators • Blackline Master 1.9

Mathematics Background

DIFFERENCE TABLES Through the use of difference tables, students are able to fit a function to an input-output table. Many of the tables they see have inputs starting at 0 and increasing by one each time. This special arrangement allows students to see patterns more easily. They quickly learn that if the outputs have a constant difference, the function that matches the table is linear and the constant difference is the coefficient of the x term in the matching linear function.

x	y	Δ
0	4	1
1	5	1
2	6	1
3	7	

In Chapter 2, students will develop a general purpose method, called *Lagrange interpolation*, that is not dependent on a special structure for a function table.

Next in this chapter students experiment with tables that have a constant second difference. In this case, the function that matches the table is quadratic, and the constant difference is equal to twice the coefficient of the x^2 term in the matching quadratic function. Students prove this relationship in an exercise.

x	y	Δ	Δ^2	$y - 3x^2$
0	4	4	6	4
1	8	10	6	5
2	18	16	6	6
3	34	22	6	7
4	56	28		8
5	84			9

Once students know the coefficient of the x^2 term, they subtract this term from their original set of outputs to find the rest of the function. This reduces the problem to that of finding a linear function to match a table with a constant first difference.

As time allows, you can have students experiment with cubic functions. Tables that match cubic functions have a constant third difference equal to six times the coefficient of the x^3 term in the cubic matching function. When this term is subtracted from the original outputs, the problem is reduced to finding a quadratic function to match a table with a constant second difference—a problem your students have already solved.

continued on p. 2c

continued from p. 2b

See the TI-Nspire Technology Handbook on p. 778 for instructions on how to make tables like this.

x	y	Δ	Δ^2	Δ^3	$y - 2x^3$
0	4	6	18	12	4
1	10	24	30	12	8
2	34	54	42	12	18
3	88	96	54		34
4	184	150			56
5	334				84

In CME Project *Precalculus*, students will develop another method for finding a polynomial that matches a table, Newton's Difference Formula, that uses the entries in the first row of the difference table. For example, in this case, the matching function would be:

$$x \mapsto 4 + 6x + \frac{18x(x-1)}{2} + \frac{12x(x-1)(x-2)}{6}$$

LINE OF BEST FIT In this chapter, students learn to find the line of best fit for a table of data. The text asks students to consider how they might choose such a line. The line should minimize error, but what measure of error is the best one to choose? Students consider several measures of error, and they see why minimizing the sum of the squares of the y-differences produces a good line of best fit. Students must then find a series of lines with slopes 3, 2, 1, and 0 that each minimize this error. They notice that all of these lines pass through a single point, and that this point turns out to be the centroid or balance point of the data.

This task verifies their earlier experiences of plotting a data set and its centroid (balance point) on the same graph and noticing that when the data has a linear trend, the centroid appears to lie on the trend line. These results combine to lead to the conjecture that the line of best fit must pass through the centroid of the data. (Students prove this conjecture in the Chapter 7 project.)

Students then have enough information to actually calculate the line of best fit. Since they know that the line of best fit must pass through the centroid of the data, they need only to find the slope that minimizes the error. They find this slope by writing the equation of a line with slope m that passes through the centroid and then calculating the error with this line. This effort leads to a quadratic expression in m, and students know that the minimum value of a quadratic expression occurs at its intersection with its line of symmetry. So, the value of m that minimizes an error of $am^2 + bm + c$ will be $m = \frac{-b}{2a}$.

DAILY PLANNER DAILY PLANNER DAILY PLA

Pacing Suggestions and Materials

Investigation 1C *More About Recursive Models*

DAY	LESSON	HOMEWORK
1	1.10 Getting Started Core: 1, 2, 3, 4, 7, 8 Optional: 5, 6	Core: 9, 10, 11, 13, 15 Optional: 12, 14, 16, 17, 18
2	1.11 Monthly Payments Core: 1, 2, 3, 4 Optional: 5	Core: 6, 7, 8 Optional: 9, 10
3	1.12 The Factorial Function Core: 1, 2, 3, 4 Optional: 5	Core: 6, 7, 8, 10, 12, 13 Optional: 9, 11, 14, 15, 16, 17, 18

	NOTES	MATERIALS
	Encourage students to try all the exercises.	• CAS (recommended) • graphing calculators
		• CAS (recommended) • graphing calculators • spreadsheet software
		• CAS (recommended) • graphing calculators • Blackline Master 1.12

Hand calculation of the line of best fit is practical only for fairly small data sets. Students will also use their calculators to find these lines. By understanding the calculations behind finding a line of best fit, students learn where the numbers come from and why a particular process was chosen.

RECURSION This chapter gives students many opportunities to examine the interplay between recursive definitions and closed-form definitions for functions. Although recursive functions can have restricted domains, they often reveal patterns in the outputs of a function that are less obvious in the closed form. The process of converting between recursive and closed-form definitions helps students see how they are related to each other.

Students are also introduced to the factorial function, which has a simple recursive definition but no simple closed form. They also use a recursively defined function that calculates the balance owed at the end of each month on an interest-bearing loan to work toward a surprising result: the monthly payment on a loan depends linearly on the amount you borrow.

The monthly payment context appears throughout the program. It appears in CME Project *Algebra 1* and in *Precalculus*.

Developing Students' Mathematical Habits

Key mathematical habits of mind in this chapter include

- **TINKERING** with expressions, trying out ideas, and refining guesses. Students call on their memories of previous courses to find functions that behave the way they want them to.
- **REDUCING PROBLEMS TO SIMPLER ONES** by seeing that the differences for outputs in a table that matches a quadratic function vary linearly. Students look at tables of monthly payments for different loan amounts and see the linear relationship embedded in this complex process.
- **GENERALIZING REPEATED CALCULATIONS** into a completely general process helps students see how to convert between recursive and closed-form representations for various functions.

Chapter Vocabulary and Notation

The following list gives key vocabulary and notation used in the chapter. Selected new vocabulary and notation items are shown in boldface on the student page.

- balance point, p. 44
- closed-form definition, p. 9
- cubic function, p. 35
- difference table, p. 10
- factorial function, $n!$, pp. 78, 79
- hockey stick property, p. 17
- line of best fit, p. 62
- mean absolute error, p. 55
- mean squared error, p. 55
- outlier, p. 46
- quadratic function, p. 31
- recursive definition, p. 9
- slope, p. 15
- standard error, p. 55
- up-and-over property, p. 17

Chapter Road Map

INVESTIGATION 1A, *Tables,* has students explore the problem of finding a simple function (a "rule") that matches an input-output table of numbers. "Simple" means something such as a linear, quadratic, or cubic polynomial function. (Students will expand their ideas of what is "simple" as the course progresses.) In this investigation, the input-output tables are mainly made-up sets of numbers, and the goal is for students to develop the habit of finding and describing (with algebra) any patterns that they see. Students learn how to model functions in the function-modeling language on their calculators or computers.

Fitting Functions to Tables

You might buy all of your cars with cash, but most people take out a loan when they buy a car. Shopping for the right car loan is a complicated process, full of choices. The techniques you will learn in this chapter will help you to compare your options.

To buy a car, you need to know how much you can afford as a down payment, what you can afford to pay per month on the loan, the interest rate, and the length of the loan. These variables can depend on the model of car you want to buy, the lender, and your credit rating. You can borrow the money through the car dealer, through a bank, or get a personal loan from a family member.

Sometimes car dealers have special promotional interest rates for certain models. Some dealers offer a rebate that you can use as all or part of your down payment. You are likely to have several different financing offers to consider. The financing might even influence your choice of car.

Vocabulary

- balance point
- closed-form definition
- cubic function
- difference table
- factorial function, n!
- hockey stick property
- line of best fit
- mean absolute error
- mean squared error
- outlier
- quadratic function
- recursive definition
- slope
- standard error
- up-and-over property

INVESTIGATION 1B, *Fitting and Data,* has students consider tables of numbers that are not as neat as the ones used in the first investigation. These types of tables often come from data collected in experiments or surveys. There is usually no useful simple function that fits such data exactly. So in the second investigation, students study functions that approximate data—the graph of the function is "close" to the scatter plot of the data. The lessons elaborate on this point.

INVESTIGATION 1C, *More About Recursive Models,* has students look more carefully at two functions that are defined recursively: a function that determines the balance owed at the end of any month during the term of a loan and the factorial function.

Chapter Technology

CME Project *Algebra 2* assumes that each student has access to a graphing calculator. It also recommends access to a computer algebra system (CAS).

Support for the use of technology is available in the TI-Nspire™ Technology Handbook. See p. 778. The margin notes highlighted in purple in the Student Edition direct students to the handbook.

A list of technology used with important concepts in this chapter appears below. Students will need access to the functionality listed to develop complete understanding of these topics.

Computer Algebra System

LESSON 1.2 Define linear and quadratic functions and ask for $f(x+1) - f(x)$, p. 14.

LESSON 1.4 Make a difference table, p. 28.

LESSON 1.5 Define quadratic and cubic functions and ask for $f(x+1) - f(x)$, pp. 32, 36.

LESSON 1.8 Calculate the sum of the squares of the errors, p. 57.

Function-Modeling Language

LESSON 1.2 Build a model and experiment with it, p. 9. Model a recursively defined function, p. 10.

LESSON 1.3 Model recursive and closed-form definitions of a function, p. 20.

LESSON 1.10 Model a recursive function, pp. 69, 70.

LESSON 1.11 Model a recursive function for a monthly payment, p. 74.

LESSON 1.12 Model a recursive rule for the factorial function, p. 78.

Geometry Software

LESSON 1.8 Make a visual model to calculate the sum of the squares of the errors, p. 55.

Graphing Calculator

LESSON 1.8 Find the best fit quadratic function for a set of data, p. 59.

LESSON 1.12 Find the numerical value of a factorial function, p. 79.

Spreadsheet Software

LESSON 1.2 Tabulate a model for a function, p. 9.

LESSON 1.5 Make a difference table, p. 35.

LESSON 1.11 Make a table for costs, p. 76.

Investigation Overview

This investigation has two goals:

- Students use tables to think about functions.
- Students begin the study of *Algebra 2* in a spirit of mathematical inquiry.

This investigation introduces the thread of "functions and fitting." CME Project *Algebra 1* introduces functions as machines. Although the material in *Algebra 2* continues to draw on this metaphor, this course pushes students to think of functions as objects in themselves and to understand that they can add, multiply, and compose functions.

In this investigation, students investigate the use of constant differences to determine whether a kind of rule (e.g., linear or quadratic) fits a table. Students work with recursive models and closed forms. The theme of fitting functions to tables continues in Chapter 2, where students use Lagrange interpolation to find polynomial rules to fit tables.

Students build on their foundation from *Algebra 1*. For example, the idea that equations are point-testers underlies some of the work of rule-finding in this investigation. This investigation reintroduces slope from *Algebra 1*: the slope between two points on the Cartesian plane is the change in their y-coordinates divided by the change in their x-coordinates.

You may wish to assign Questions 1–3 for students to think and write about during the investigation.

Learning Goals

- Identify and describe specific patterns in input-output tables.
- Determine whether a linear function matches a table.
- Use differences to decide what type of function can fit a table.
- Compare recursive and closed-form rules for functions.
- Understand the relationship between difference tables and slope.

Habits and Skills

- Look for patterns and describe them with algebra.
- "Work like a mathematician"—search for hidden regularities, describe patterns explicitly, and explain inconsistencies.
- Generalize methods so that they work in a greater number of situations.
- Find laws and principles based on patterns in tables.
- Make conjectures using the guess and check method.

Investigation 1A

Tables

In *Tables*, you will use algebra to describe patterns that you see in tables of numbers. You can describe mathematics as the "science of patterns." That is a big oversimplification, but it is true that the ability to find patterns in data is an important skill for mathematicians and people who use mathematical thinking in their work and in their lives.

By the end of this investigation, you will be able to answer questions like these.

1. How can you tell whether there is a linear function that fits a table?
2. How can you use differences to decide what type of function fits a table?
3. What polynomial function agrees with this table?

Input	Output
0	1
1	5
2	11
3	19
4	29
5	41

You will learn how to

- identify and describe specific patterns in input-output tables
- determine whether a linear function matches a table
- use differences to decide what type of function can fit a table
- compare recursive and closed-form rules for functions

You will develop these habits and skills:

- Look for patterns and describe them with algebra.
- "Work like a mathematician"—search for hidden regularities, describe the patterns explicitly, and explain inconsistencies.
- Generalize methods so that they work in a greater number of situations.
- Find laws and principles based on patterns in tables.
- Make conjectures using the guess and check method.

You can record a jumping frog's height in a table. Then you can fit a polynomial function to the table.

Investigation Road Map

LESSON 1.1, *Getting Started,* asks students, using any method they choose, to find rules that would produce the outputs for a given table.

LESSON 1.2, *Two Types of Definitions,* helps students formalize the concepts of recursive and closed-form rules.

LESSON 1.3, *Constant Differences,* introduces the formal notion of constant differences. This lesson also introduces the up-and-over and hockey stick properties of difference tables.

LESSON 1.4, *Tables and Slope,* reviews the concept of the slope between two points and introduces the relationship between difference tables and slope.

LESSON 1.5, *Deeper Differences,* has students investigate what happens when first differences are not constant.

1.1 Getting Started

Activating Prior Knowledge
Exploring New Ideas

You can write a rule for a function based on the input and output values in a table.

For You to Explore

The object of the game is to find a simple function that agrees with each table.

Some examples of simple functions are linear, quadratic, reciprocal, and square-root functions. You can also describe a simple function with words, such as "each output is 2 more than the previous output."

Table A

Input, n	Output, $A(n)$
0	0
1	2
2	4
3	6
4	8

Table B

Input, n	Output, $B(n)$
0	0
1	2
2	6
3	12
4	20

Table C

Input, n	Output, $C(n)$
0	2
1	1
2	0
3	−1
4	−2

Table D

Input, n	Output, $D(n)$
0	0
1	3
2	8
3	15
4	24

1. For each table above, find a rule that produces these outputs. Do not worry about the notation or vocabulary you use to describe the rule. You can use an equation such as

   output = 3 × input

   or a sentence such as "each output is the output above it plus 4."

2. Richard notices there is more than one rule for Table A. He says, "Sure, I can find a rule that works: Double the input. But there are other functions that make that same table from 0 to 4 and produce different outputs for inputs greater than 4."
   a. Draw a graph with the 5 points of Table A. Then draw the graph of the function $n \mapsto 2n$.
   b. **Write About It** Do you agree or disagree with Richard? Explain your answer using additional graphs or tables as needed.
   c. **Take It Further** Find a function that supports Richard's claim. If no such function exists, explain why.

Richard claims that there are many functions that agree with Table A.

Answers

For You to Explore

1. $A(n) = 2n$
   $B(n) = n(n + 1)$
   $C(n) = -n + 2$
   $D(n) = n(n + 2)$
2. a. See back of book.
   b–c. Answers may vary. Samples are given.
   b. Disagree; here is another way to draw the graph:

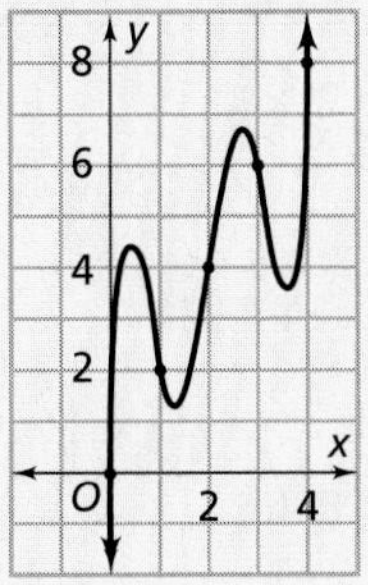

   c. $A(n) = 2n + n(n - 1)(n - 2)(n - 3)(n - 4)$

Lesson Overview

GOAL

- Identify and describe specific patterns in input-output tables.

Students search for and describe possible rules that agree with given tables. Allow students to describe the rules as they wish: using recursive rules, verbal descriptions, or closed forms. This kind of exploratory work is an important part of "working like a mathematician." Try to cover this lesson in one day—there is no need for every student to understand every problem before you move on. In later lessons, you will generalize and formalize the work done here.

FOR YOU TO EXPLORE
- Core: 1, 2
- Optional: none

MATERIALS
- CAS (recommended)
- geometry software
- graph paper
- graphing calculators
- Blackline Masters MC1, 1.1

HOMEWORK
- Core: 3, 4, 7, 8, 9, 10, 11, 12, 13, 14, 15, 19, 20
- Optional: 5, 6, 16, 17, 18, 21, 22, 23

Launch

You may wish to have students work in pairs or in small groups. Have students examine the tables. When you describe the task of finding rules that agree with the tables, emphasize that students can use any description they want for the rules.

You can use Blackline Master 1.1 as a transparency or handout for a classroom activity. You can also use Blackline Master MC1.

Explore

For You to Explore

PROBLEM 1 You might want to point out to students that the 'rule' does not have to relate the output to the corresponding input. It could relate the output to the previous output (or outputs). For example, "To get any output, add two to the previous output." Or, the rule might relate several inputs to get the output. For example, "Multiply each input by the following input to get the correct output."

Circulate as students work on the problems. Ways students might try to find a rule for Table A include:

- Every output is twice the input, so

  output = 2 × input

- Each output is two more than the output above it.

continued on p. 6

continued from p. 5

- $A(n) = 2n$
- The first output is 0. Add 2 for each subsequent output.

For Table B, answers might be even more interesting. For example, a student might say:

- The outputs are a little bit more than the inputs squared. The first output is the input squared, and the second output is one more than the input squared. Each output is just the input squared plus the input.
- The second output is two more than the first output. The third output is four more than the second output. The fourth output is six more than the third output. So the differences in the outputs increase by two each time.
- Each output is 2 times the input plus the last output.
- Each output is equal to the input multiplied by the next input.

You may want to start a class record of student conjectures for rules that fit the tables and ask students to verify each others' rules. Point out the variety of rules that can be used to describe a single table.

If students finish For You to Explore problems early, they can start to work the On Your Own exercises you assign.

Some questions to ask about each table include:

- Which of the functions you found are the same?
- Could there be other, different functions that match this table?

Wrap Up

At the end of this lesson, you might want to allow time to debrief students about their work. Although some of the exercises are "optional," you may want to assign them for some classes. Occasionally, you may want to assign every exercise for a lesson.

Exercises

HOMEWORK

- Core: 3, 4, 7, 8, 9, 10, 11, 12, 13, 14, 15, 19, 20
- Optional: 5, 6, 16, 17, 18, 21, 22, 23

On Your Own

EXERCISE 4 Although students might easily see the rule "Add $\frac{1}{2}$ to the previous output," finding a rule to relate the output to the corresponding input is more challenging. One strategy here is to write each output as a fraction with denominator 2: $\frac{-4}{2}$, $\frac{-3}{2}$, $\frac{-2}{2}$, $\frac{-1}{2}$, $\frac{0}{2}$. The rule $n \mapsto \frac{n-2}{2}$ is now more apparent.

Exercises *Practicing Habits of Mind*

On Your Own

Habits of Mind

Think about it another way. There are many ways to think about these exercises. For example, you can suppose there is a mystery function generating each table. You want to find it.

For Exercises 3–20, find a function that agrees with each table. Keep track of the functions you find, because the solution for one exercise may be useful in a later exercise.

3. Table E

Input	Output
0	3
1	5
2	7
3	9
4	11

4. Table F

Input	Output
0	-2
1	$-1\frac{1}{2}$
2	-1
3	$-\frac{1}{2}$
4	0

5. Table G

Input	Output
0	-7
1	-4
2	-1
3	2
4	5

6. Table H

Input	Output
0	3
1	8
2	13
3	18
4	23

7. Table I

Input	Output
0	0
1	1
2	4
3	9
4	16

8. Table J

Input	Output
0	0
1	2
2	8
3	18
4	32

9. Table K

Input	Output
0	1
1	2
2	5
3	10
4	17

10. Table L

Input	Output
0	-25
1	-24
2	-21
3	-16
4	-9

11. Table M

Input	Output
0	9
1	15
2	21
3	27
4	33

Go Online Video Tutor PHSchool.com

Web Code: bfe-0775

Answers

Exercises

3–20. Answers may vary. Samples are given.

3. $E(n) = 2n + 3$

4. $F(n) = \frac{1}{2}n - 2$

5. $G(n) = 3n - 7$

6. $H(n) = 5n + 3$

7. $I(n) = n^2$

8. $J(n) = 2n^2$

9. $K(n) = n^2 + 1$

10. $L(n) = n^2 - 25$

11. $M(n) = 6n + 9$

12. $N(n) = (n + 3)^2$

13. $O(n) = 5n^2$

14. $P(n) = 4n + 1$

15. $Q(n) = 5n^2 + 4n + 1$

16. $R(n) = n^3$

17. $S(n) = n^3 + 3$

18. $T(n) = 3^n$

19. $U(n) = 2^n$

12. Table N

Input	Output
0	9
1	16
2	25
3	36
4	49

13. Table O

Input	Output
0	0
1	5
2	20
3	45
4	80

14. Table P

Input	Output
0	1
1	5
2	9
3	13
4	17

15. Table Q

Input	Output
0	1
1	10
2	29
3	58
4	97

16. Table R

Input	Output
0	0
1	1
2	8
3	27
4	64

17. Table S

Input	Output
0	3
1	4
2	11
3	30
4	67
5	128

18. Table T

Input	Output
0	1
1	3
2	9
3	27
4	81
5	243

19. Table U

Input	Output
0	1
1	2
2	4
3	8
4	16
5	32

20. Table V

Input	Output
0	0
1	1
2	3
3	7
4	15
5	31

Maintain Your Skills

21. Make a table for the inputs 0 through 5 for each of the following functions.

a. $a(x) = x^2$ **b.** $b(x) = x^2 - 1$ **c.** $c(x) = x^2 - 4$ **d.** $d(x) = x^2 - 9$

22. Find a number c that makes $f(x) = x^2 - c$ equal to zero when $x = 5$.

23. Show that the following identity is true.

$$(x + 1)^2 - x^2 = 2x + 1$$

EXERCISE 7 Point out that students can use exponents in their rules.

EXERCISE 8 Students should notice that the outputs in Table J are double the outputs in Table I, and this explains where the rule comes from.

EXERCISE 9 Table K and Table I are related, and students may notice this as they find the rules.

EXERCISE 10 Notice if students find more than one way to describe this rule.

EXERCISE 13 Elicit the fact that the outputs in Table O are all multiples of 5.

EXERCISE 15 Suggest students look back at previous exercises if they get stuck here.

EXERCISE 18 Students will probably see the rule "Multiply the previous output by 3." They may not realize that the input can actually be the exponent in the rule: 3^{input} = output. You can ask students to extend this table to find 3^{-1}.

EXERCISE 20 Relate this exercise to Table U. Each output is one less than the corresponding output of Table U. So, a rule is: $2^{\text{input}} - 1$. For example, if the input is 3, the output is $2^3 - 1 = 8 - 1 = 7$.

Maintain Your Skills

EXERCISE 21 reminds students about the difference of squares and gives them practice in generating tables from function rules.

20. $V(n) = 2^n - 1$

21. a.

x	$a(x)$
0	0
1	1
2	4
3	9
4	16
5	25

b.

x	$b(x)$
0	−1
1	0
2	3
3	8
4	15
5	24

c.

x	$c(x)$
0	−4
1	−3
2	0
3	5
4	12
5	21

d.

x	$d(x)$
0	−9
1	−8
2	−5
3	0
4	7
5	16

22. 25

23. $$\begin{aligned} 2x + 1 &= (x + 1)^2 - x^2 \\ &= (x + 1)(x + 1) - x^2 \\ &= x^2 + 2x + 1 - x^2 \\ &= 2x + 1 \end{aligned}$$

Lesson Overview

GOAL

- Compare recursive and closed-form rules.

This lesson begins to formalize the work students did in the Getting Started lesson. Students look closely at recursive and closed-form definitions for functions and compare the two types. Students learn to model both recursive and closed-form definitions using the function-modeling language of their calculators or computers. They learn to set up difference tables to help them determine rules for functions.

CHECK YOUR UNDERSTANDING
- Core: 1, 2, 3, 4, 5, 6, 7, 8
- Optional: 9

MATERIALS
- CAS (recommended)
- graph paper
- spreadsheet software
- Blackline Masters MC1, 1.2A–C

HOMEWORK
- Core: 10, 11a, 12, 14
- Optional: 13, 15
- Extension: 11b

VOCABULARY
- closed-form definition
- difference table
- recursive definition
- slope

Launch

As you navigate this lesson, keep in mind some reasons to introduce recursive definitions and to compare them with closed-form definitions:

- Comparing closed and recursive forms leads to questions of domain. The recursive definitions in this lesson can accept only nonnegative integers as inputs. This restriction is highlighted in For You to Do Problem 2.
- Sometimes it is easier to see a recursive pattern than a closed form, and students can then use the recursive pattern to find a closed form for a rule.

One way to begin this lesson is to choose some of the exercises students did for homework in Lesson 1.1 and ask students to share the rules they found. The Getting Started exercises were designed in part to invite questions about recursive and closed-form rules. In order to draw students' attention to these questions, the text focuses on Table H, but Table G and Table E are also good choices.

You may realize that two important words appear without definition: *rule* and *function*. As in *Algebra 1*, a rule is a description of *how* the function computes its output. As for the word *function*, for now you can remind students of the *Algebra 1* definition: you can define a function by a rule that always returns the same output for each valid input. A formal definition of *function* appears in the next chapter after students have had more experience with tables and graphs. As students work through the text, they will find that the word *rule* is used less in this context. Students will begin to think of "defining a function," rather than "writing a rule that defines a function."

1.2 Two Types of Definitions

The table below is from Exercise 6 of Lesson 1.1.

Table H

Input	Output
0	3
1	8
2	13
3	18
4	23

You can describe a function that agrees with this table in more than one way. For example,

- If the input n is zero, the output is 3. To get the next output, add 5 to the previous output.
- $g(n) = 5n + 3$

Developing Habits of Mind

Look for patterns. In Chapter 2, you will learn that Table H itself is a function. The set of possible inputs is $\{0, 1, 2, 3, 4\}$ and nothing else. When you think of the table as a function, you can write $H(2) = 13$, but $H(6)$ is not defined.

In this lesson, you are looking for something different—a way to express some regularity in the table. Finding and describing a pattern can allow you to extend the domain from $\{0, 1, 2, 3, 4\}$ to a larger set of numbers. Both bulleted descriptions above do this. When you match a table with a polynomial or another simple rule, you are uncovering a hidden relationship in the numbers. This is something that mathematicians really prize.

You learned that the domain of a function is *the set of allowable inputs*. You will learn a more precise definition in Chapter 2.

For You to Do

1. When the input is 9, what is the output of each of the two functions described above?
2. Can you use each function to find the output when the input is -2? Explain.

Answers

For You to Do

1. 48
2. No; $g(-2) = 5(-2) + 3 = -10 + 3 = -7$, but the written description works only for finding outputs for nonnegative integer inputs.

Facts and Notation

A function definition such as "$g(n) = 5n + 3$" is a closed-form definition. A closed-form definition lets you find any output $g(n)$ for any input n by direct calculation.

A function definition such as "$f(0) = 3$ and any output is 5 more than the previous output" is a recursive definition. Recursive definitions are useful for expressing patterns in the outputs of a function. The notation below is a useful way to write a recursive definition.

$$f(n) = \begin{cases} 3 & \text{if } n = 0 \\ f(n-1) + 5 & \text{if } n > 0 \end{cases}$$

Notice that f is a recursive function and g is a closed-form function. Do the two definitions give the same function?

Developing Habits of Mind

Use a model. The closed-form definition below matches Table H from Exercise 6 of the Getting Started lesson.

$$g(n) = 5n + 3$$

You can build a computer or calculator model for function g in your function-modeling language. Then you can experiment with the model. You can do the following:

- Evaluate the function.
- Graph the function.
- Make a table of the function in a spreadsheet window.

It is a good habit to build models like these for the functions you use, especially when you want to get a feel for how the functions behave.

How you build a model depends on your computer or calculator. See the TI-Nspire Handbook, p. 778.

The magnifying glass points out giant sequoia rings that formed in the years A.D. 311, 362, and 419. Tree growth is a recursive process that a tree's rings record.

Explore

For You to Do

PROBLEMS 1 AND 2 You can use both functions to find the output when the input is a nonnegative integer. The closed-form function is easier to compute and can accept negative numbers and nonintegers as inputs, but the recursive function expresses a wonderful pattern in the table.

You cannot use the recursive function given for Table H to find the output when the input is -2, since that function is defined in a way that forces the inputs to be integers greater than or equal to 0. Of course, you could redefine the function in such a way as to allow "working the rule backwards," subtracting 5 from any input to find the previous value and adding 5 to any input to find the next value. In this redefinition, you could start at 0 and then subtract 5 from its output to get the output for -1. Then if you subtracted 5 from that output, you would get the output for -2. You will not often use definitions like that in this course, though.

Note that the domain of closed-form rule is the real numbers, and the domain of recursive rule is the positive integers and zero. This distinction will be important in CME Project *Precalculus*.

FACTS AND NOTATION Ask students if there is any input that does *not* give the same output for both definitions.

For You To Do

Blackline Master 1.2A provides a copy of Table H with additional rows for use with Problem 4.

PROBLEMS 3–5 It is worth taking some time here to make sure that each student can perform these tasks, because they will find similar exercises in the homework assignments.

Students may need a little convincing that the starting point matters when they calculate an output. If students do not include a starting point in their descriptions of their recursive rules, you might make a new table from their rule. Suppose the recursive rule for Table H were only "to get the next output, add five to the previous output." If the new output for input 0 happened to be 10, the table would be very different and would look like this.

Input	Output
0	10
1	15
2	20
3	25
4	30

For You to Do

PROBLEM 6 The way that calculators treat recursively defined functions gives students an opportunity to think informally about domain as they explore what the calculator will accept as inputs for recursive definitions. Students will get precise about domain in the next chapter.

DIFFERENCE TABLES This section introduces difference tables. Many textbooks construct difference tables with the differences hovering between the function values. There are several reasons to write differences between function values $f(n)$ and $f(n-1)$ on the same line as $f(n-1)$, including:

- It is easier to think of Δ (and Δ^2, Δ^n) as functions in their own right if it is possible to see the output given an input.
- This table structure will serve students well in CME Project *Precalculus* and beyond. For example, in *Precalculus*, students will use Newton's Difference Method to fit polynomials to tables, so formatting difference tables in this way will be useful.

Blackline Master 1.2B provides a copy of Table H with a blank difference column.

For You to Do

3. Build a model for g in your function-modeling language.

4. Make a table of your model for inputs between 0 and 10.

5. Graph your model in your graphing environment.

A recursive definition lets you calculate any output in terms of previous outputs. The simplest kind of recursive definition for a function f tells you how to compute $f(n)$ for an integer n in terms of $f(n-1)$. You need a place to start. The definition below tells you to start at 3 (when $n = 0$) and to add 5 to get from one output to the next.

$$f(n) = \begin{cases} 3 & \text{if } n = 0 \\ f(n-1) + 5 & \text{if } n > 0 \end{cases}$$

Read the second line as "the current output is the previous output plus five." This recursively defined function fits all the entries in Table H.

- $f(0) = 3$, because $n = 0$
- $f(1) = f(1-1) + 5 = f(0) + 5 = 3 + 5 = 8$
- $f(2) = f(2-1) + 5 = f(1) + 5 = 8 + 5 = 13$

For You to Do

You can use function-modeling language to model a recursive definition. Your technology may even provide a template like the one below. For help, see the TI-Nspire Handbook, p. 778.

$$\text{define } f(n) = \begin{cases} \blacksquare, \blacksquare \\ \blacksquare, \blacksquare \end{cases}$$

You just fill in the boxes.

$$\text{define } f(n) = \begin{cases} 3, & \text{if } n = 0 \\ f(n-1) + 5, & \text{if } n > 0 \end{cases}$$

6. Build a model for f and experiment with it. What numbers will f accept as inputs? Explain. How does g compare to f?

Recursive definitions tell you how the outputs are related. Closed-form definitions tell you how inputs are related to outputs. Each tells you something interesting. In some cases, you can convert one to the other. Later in this investigation you will see how.

Difference Tables

A **difference table** can help you see patterns that lead to recursive definitions. Use Table H from Exercise 6 of Lesson 1.1.

Table H

Input	Output
0	3
1	8
2	13
3	18
4	23

Answers

For You to Do

3. Check students' work.

4.

n	$g(n)$
0	3
1	8
2	13
3	18
4	23
5	28
6	33
7	38
8	43
9	48
10	53

To make a difference table, add a third column marked with the Δ symbol. Write the difference between one output and the next in the third column.

Input	Output	Δ
0	3	8 − 3 = **5**
1	8	13 − 8 = **5**
2	13	18 − 13 = **5**
3	18	23 − 18 = **5**
4	23	

The Δ symbol is the capital Greek letter delta. It represents change or difference.

The differences are exactly what you need to write a recursively defined function that matches Table H. In this case, all the differences are the same number, 5. The following recursive definition fits Table H.

$$f(n) = \begin{cases} 3 & \text{if } n = 0 \\ f(n-1) + 5 & \text{if } n > 0 \end{cases}$$

In some tables the differences are not constant, as in the table below.

Table D

Input, n	Output, $d(n)$	Δ
0	0	3
1	3	5
2	8	7
3	15	9
4	24	11
5	35	13
6	48	

In Lesson 1.5, you will see that you can still use the Δ column to find a recursive function that matches the table. Here is a recursive definition for d.

What function matches the Δ column?

$$d(n) = \begin{cases} 0 & \text{if } n = 0 \\ d(n-1) + 2n + 1 & \text{if } n > 0 \end{cases}$$

For You to Do

7. Show that the function d fits Table D.

For You to Do

PROBLEM 7 You can use Blackline Master 1.2C to fill in Table D using the recursive definition of $d(n)$.

Some students may want to figure out how to define a function recursively when the differences are not constant. First, note that for any n, the value in the Δ column is equal to $2n + 3$. However, in the second line of the definition of the recursive function, you need to know the Δ value for $n - 1$. Substitute $n - 1$ for n in the expression $2n + 3$ to see the value of the difference for $n - 1$:

$$2(n-1) + 3 = 2n - 2 + 3 = 2n + 1$$

Wrap Up

If possible, allow students at least half the class period to work on the Check Your Understanding exercises.

Go over Exercises 2 and 3. Ask students to find a recursive definition that fits Table B. Challenge students to find other closed-form definitions that fit Table B.

Assessment Resources

Lesson Quiz 1.2

1. Complete each difference table.

a.

Input	Output	Δ
0	4	−2
1		
2	3	
3		−1
4	−6	

b.

Input	Output	Δ
0		4
1		4
2	11	
3	6	3
4		

2. Use the recursive definition to find the values of $f(0)$ through $f(5)$.

$$f(n) = \begin{cases} 3 & \text{if } n = 0 \\ 4 \cdot f(n-1) & \text{if } n > 0 \end{cases}$$

3. Decide whether there is a closed-form definition for $f(n)$ in Exercise 2. If so, find the definition.

5.

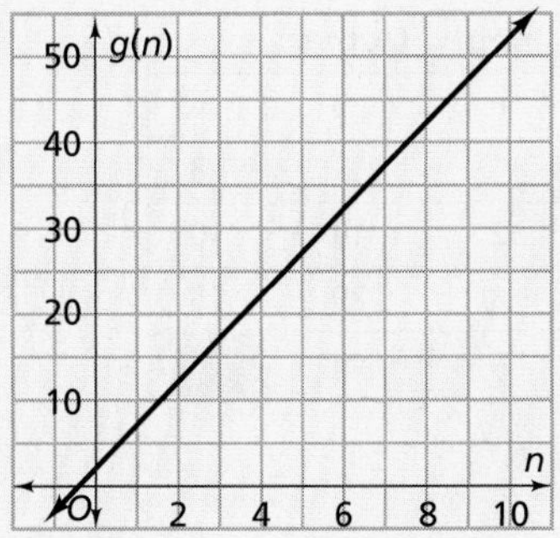

6. Nonnegative integers; $f(n - 1)$ has meaning only if $n - 1$ is a nonnegative integer; g accepts all values of n, including zero, negative, and noninteger values.

7. Using the recursive definition, $d(0) = 0$;
$d(1) = d(0) + 2(1) + 1 = 3$;
$d(2) = d(1) + 2(2) + 1 = 8$;
$d(3) = d(2) + 2(3) + 1 = 15$;
$d(4) = 24$; $d(5) = 35$;
$d(6) = 48$. Those values fit Table D.

Exercises

HOMEWORK
- Core: 10, 11a, 12, 14
- Optional: 13, 15
- Extension: 11b

Check Your Understanding

You can use Blackline Master MC1 to provide students with copies of blank tables for use in the exercises.

EXERCISE 2 You might ask students to find a rule for the Δ column that they wrote in Exercise 1. (Answer: $2n + 2$) Since the rule applies to the previous input, replace n with $n - 1$: $2(n - 1) + 2 = 2n - 2 + 2 = 2n$. So, each output is the previous output $(b(n - 1))$ plus 2 times the input $(2n)$.

EXERCISE 3 Part (d) is a good place to point out that you need to check all the inputs. The rule works for $n = 0$, 1, and 2, but fails to work when $n = 3$ and when $n = 4$.

Exercises *Practicing Habits of Mind*

Check Your Understanding

For Exercises 1–3, use Table B from Lesson 1.1.

Table B

Input, n	Output, $B(n)$
0	0
1	2
2	6
3	12
4	20

1. Make a difference table for Table B.

2. Decide whether each recursive definition fits Table B.

a. $b(n) = \begin{cases} 0 & \text{if } n = 0 \\ b(n-1) + 2 & \text{if } n > 0 \end{cases}$

b. $b(n) = \begin{cases} 0 & \text{if } n = 0 \\ b(n-1) + 2(n-1) & \text{if } n > 0 \end{cases}$

c. $b(n) = \begin{cases} 0 & \text{if } n = 0 \\ b(n-1) + 2n & \text{if } n > 0 \end{cases}$

d. $b(n) = \begin{cases} 2 & \text{if } n = 0 \\ b(n-1) + 2n & \text{if } n > 0 \end{cases}$

3. Decide whether each closed-form definition fits Table B.

a. $b(n) = 2n$

b. $b(n) = n^2 + n$

c. To find each output, take the input and multiply by one more than the input.

d. $b(n) = 2^{n+1} - 2$

Answers

Exercises

1.

Input, n	Output, $B(n)$	Δ
0	0	2
1	2	4
2	6	6
3	12	8
4	20	

2. a. no **b.** no **c.** yes **d.** no

3. a. no **b.** yes **c.** yes **d.** no

4.

Input	Output	Δ
0	5	6
1	11	**8**
2	19	10
3	**29**	15
4	**44**	

For Exercises 4–6, copy and complete each difference table.

4.

Input	Output	Δ
0	5	6
1	11	■
2	19	10
3	■	15
4	■	

5.

Input	Output	Δ
0	■	3
1	■	3
2	■	3
3	■	3
4	18	

6.

Input	Output	Δ
0	5	−3
1	■	■
2	17	■
3	■	−5
4	−1	

7. Use the recursive definition below.

$$f(n) = \begin{cases} 1 & \text{if } n = 0 \\ n \cdot f(n-1) & \text{if } n > 0 \end{cases}$$

a. Find the values of $f(1)$ through $f(6)$ for this function.

b. What preprogrammed function on your calculator agrees with f?

8. The table at the right is an incomplete input-output table for a function.

You can use each rule to complete the table. Make a completed table for each rule.

Input	Output
0	2
1	6
2	■
3	■
4	■

a. To get each output, take the previous output and add four.

b. To get each output, take the previous output and multiply by three.

c. $n \mapsto 2(3^n)$

d. To get each output, take the input, multiply by four, and then add two.

Remember...

$a^0 = 1$ for any nonzero number a, so $3^0 = 1$.

9. **Write About It** Consider the tables in Lesson 1.1. Find three tables that are related. Describe how they are related. You may find it helpful to make difference tables.

EXERCISES 4–6 Ask students why there is no last entry in the Δ column.

EXERCISE 7 Use this exercise to check if students are familiar with the factorial function or to remind students about it. Students will see this function again in Investigation 1C, *More About Recursive Models*.

EXERCISE 8 Ask students: Which of these rules are closed form and which are recursive? Do any rules give the same table?

EXERCISE 9 can lead to a great discussion, but use your discretion about how much time you can spare.

5.

Input	Output	Δ
0	**6**	3
1	**9**	3
2	**12**	3
3	**15**	3
4	18	

6. See back of book.

7. a.
$f(1) = 1 \cdot f(0) = 1 \cdot 1 = 1$
$f(2) = 2 \cdot f(1) = 2 \cdot 1 = 2$
$f(3) = 3 \cdot f(2) = 3 \cdot 2 = 6$
$f(4) = 4 \cdot f(3) = 4 \cdot 6 = 24$
$f(5) = 5 \cdot f(4) = 5 \cdot 24 = 120$
$f(6) = 6 \cdot f(5) = 6 \cdot 120 = 720$

b. $f(n) = n!$

8. See back of book.

9. Answers may vary. Sample: Tables E, F, and G have a constant difference in the difference table. Tables I, J, and K include an x^2 term in the rule.

On Your Own

TRIANGULAR NUMBERS To generate the triangular number spiral shown here, you arrange the counting numbers in a grid like this:

5 4 3
6 1 2
7 8 9...

Then you highlight only the triangular numbers. You can ask students to explore the patterns that result when you highlight other types of numbers, such as primes or square numbers.

EXERCISE 11 For part (b), you can give students the hint that fractions may be involved in the closed-form rule. Ask students if they can find a relationship between this table and Table B on page 12.

On Your Own

The *triangular numbers* are numbers determined by the pattern shown below. The number of dots in a triangular pattern with n dots on a side is the nth triangular number.

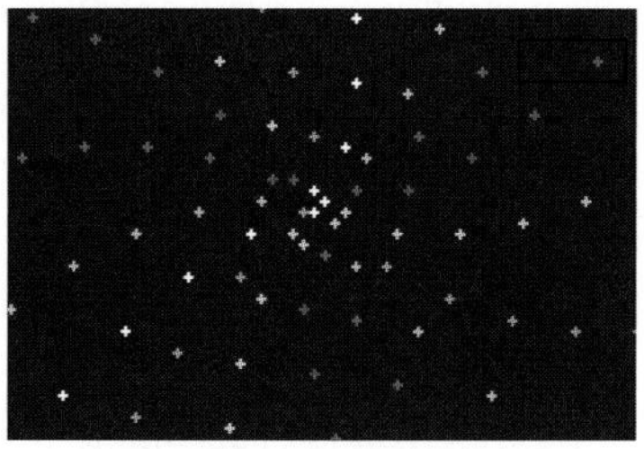

This pattern results when you arrange the counting numbers in a spiral and color the triangular numbers.

Here is a table for the triangular numbers.

Side Length	Number of Dots
0	0
1	1
2	3
3	6
4	10
5	15

10. Make a difference table for the triangular numbers.

11. a. Write a recursive function definition that fits the table of triangular numbers.

b. Take It Further Find a closed-form definition for a function that generates the triangular numbers.

12. a. Copy and complete the difference table below.

Input, x	Output, $ax + b$	Δ
0	b	■
1	$a + b$	■
2	$2a + b$	■
3	$3a + b$	■
4	$4a + b$	■
5	$5a + b$	

b. Find a formula for $f(x + 1) - f(x)$ when $f(x) = ax + b$.

You can define $f(x) = ax + b$ in your computer algebra system (CAS) and ask for $f(x + 1) - f(x)$. Make sure you have not assigned any values to a, b, or x.

Answers

10.

Side Length	Number of Dots	Δ
0	0	**1**
1	1	**2**
2	3	**3**
3	6	**4**
4	10	**5**
5	15	

11. a. $T(n) = \begin{cases} 0 & \text{if } n = 0 \\ T(n-1) + n & \text{if } n > 0 \end{cases}$

b. $T(n) = \dfrac{n(n+1)}{2}$

12. a.

Input, x	Output, $ax + b$	Δ
0	b	**a**
1	$a + b$	**a**
2	$2a + b$	**a**
3	$3a + b$	**a**
4	$4a + b$	**a**
5	$5a + b$	

b. $f(x + 1) - f(x) = a$

13. a. Copy and complete the difference table below.

Input, x	Output, $ax^2 + bx + c$	Δ
0	c	■
1	$a + b + c$	■
2	$4a + 2b + c$	■
3	$9a + 3b + c$	■
4	$16a + 4b + c$	■
5	$25a + 5b + c$	

b. Find a formula for $f(x + 1) - f(x)$ when $f(x) = ax^2 + bx + c$.

Habits of Mind

Look for relationships. What is the connection between the two parts of this exercise?

14. Standardized Test Prep Find the output of the function $g(n)$ below for the input $n = 4$.

$$g(n) = \begin{cases} 1 & \text{if } n = 1 \\ g(n-1) + 2n - 1 & \text{if } n > 1 \end{cases}$$

A. 1 **B.** 4
C. 10 **D.** 16

Go Online PHSchool.com

For additional practice, go to **Web Code:** bfa-0102

Maintain Your Skills

15. In each table below, the input-output pairs represent points on the graph of a linear function. Find the slope of each graph.

a.

Input	Output
0	−7
1	−4
2	−1
3	2
4	5
5	8

b.

Input	Output
0	−7
1	−11
2	−15
3	−19
4	−23
5	−27

c.

Input	Output
0	2
1	$1\frac{1}{2}$
2	1
3	$\frac{1}{2}$
4	0
5	$-\frac{1}{2}$

d. Describe how you can find the slope of a linear function when you have a table for the function in which the inputs are consecutive integers.

Remember...

Slope is the ratio of the change in the y-coordinates to the change in the x-coordinates.

13. a. See back of book.
b. $f(x + 1) - f(x) = 2ax + a + b$
14. D
15. a. 3
b. −4
c. $-\frac{1}{2}$
d. The slope is the constant difference.

EXERCISE 13b Remind students that an entry in the Δ column is the output, $f(x)$, subtracted from the following output, $f(x + 1)$, or $f(x + 1) - f(x)$.

EXERCISE 15d Suggest that students generate a difference table and relate the information in the difference table to the slope of the line.

Additional Resources

PRINT RESOURCES
- Solution Manual
- Practice Workbook
- Assessment Resources
- Teaching Resources

TECHNOLOGY
- Interactive Textbook
- TeacherExpress CD-ROM
- ExamView CD-ROM
- PHSchool.com

Additional Practice

For Exercises 1 and 2, use the difference table.

1. Complete the difference table.
2. Find a formula for $f(x) - f(x - 1)$ when $f(x) = ax + a$.

Input, x	Output, $ax + a$	Δ
0	a	
1	$2a$	
2	$3a$	
3	$4a$	

For Exercises 3–5, use the difference table of perfect squares.

3. Complete the difference table.
4. Write a recursive definition for a function that fits the table of perfect squares.
5. Find a closed-form definition for a function that generates the perfect squares.

Input	Output	Δ
0	0	
1	1	
2	4	
3	9	
4	16	
5	25	

For Exercises 6–9, use Table A.

6. Make a difference table for Table A.
7. How are the differences related to the outputs?
8. Write a recursive definition for a function that fits Table A.
9. Write a closed-form definition for a function that fits Table A.

Table A

n	$h(n)$
0	3
1	6
2	12
3	24
4	48
5	96

10. Describe how to find a recursive definition for a function that fits a table with constant differences. Include an example.
11. A table with integer inputs has constant differences. When the input is 2, the output is −6. When the input is 10, the output is 18. Calculate the constant difference.

Practice: For Lesson 1.2, assign Exercises 1–5.

Lesson Overview

GOALS

- Use differences to decide what type of function can fit a table.
- Determine whether a linear function matches a table.

This lesson introduces two important properties of difference tables: the up-and-over property and the hockey stick property. The up-and-over property relates an output to the previous output and their corresponding difference. The hockey stick property relates an output to previous differences and an initial output. Students find a closed-form rule for a recursive rule that has constant differences.

CHECK YOUR UNDERSTANDING
- Core: 1, 2, 3, 5, 6, 7
- Optional: 4, 8

MATERIALS
- CAS (recommended)
- graph paper
- graphing calculators
- Blackline Masters MC1, 1.2B

HOMEWORK
- Core: 10, 11, 12, 13, 14, 15, 16
- Optional: 17, 19, 20
- Extension: 18

VOCABULARY
- hockey stick property
- up-and-over property

Launch

Use Blackline Master 1.2B to display a transparency of Table H from Exercise 6 of the Getting Started lesson. Start by asking students to find the differences between consecutive outputs. Once the differences are in place, cover up the values of $f(1)$ to $f(4)$. Ask students to find $f(1)$ from $f(0)$ and the differences. Then ask students if they can find $f(4)$ from $f(0)$ and the differences. Students probably will be able to work quickly through the dialog and exposition of this lesson. You may wish to allot much of class time to working on the Check Your Understanding exercises.

Explore

Minds in Action

This is a good place to remind students that a recursive definition requires a starting point. Changing the starting point will change the outputs. For example, if $f(0) = 7$ then $f(4) = f(0) + 4(5) = 7 + 20 = 27$, not 23.

1.3 Constant Differences

In this lesson, you will explore a specific type of difference table. The inputs are consecutive integers and all the differences between the outputs are constant. Here is Table H from Lesson 1.1.

Table H

Input	Output
0	3
1	8
2	13
3	18
4	23

Below is a difference table for Table H.

Input	Output	Δ
0	3	5
1	8	5
2	13	5
3	18	5
4	23	

In Lesson 1.2, you saw that the recursively defined function below fits the table.

$$f(n) = \begin{cases} 3 & \text{if } n = 0 \\ f(n-1) + 5 & \text{if } n > 0 \end{cases}$$

You can use a recursive definition that has constant differences to find a closed form that also fits the table.

Minds in Action — episode 1

Leslie explains how she finds a closed-form definition that fits the table.

Leslie Say I'm looking for $f(4)$ and all I know is the recursive definition.

$$f(4) = f(3) + 5$$

So if I want to know $f(4)$, I just need to know what $f(3)$ was. But $f(3)$ depends on $f(2)$. Oh, I have to use the recursive definition *again*.

$$f(3) = f(2) + 5$$

And I can combine those two: $f(4) = f(2) + 5 + 5$. Two steps, two fives. Every step I take is another five. So if I go all the way back, that's four steps.

$$f(4) = f(0) + 4 \cdot 5$$

The definition tells me $f(0) = 3$, so $f(4)$ is 3 plus 4 fives. What's great about this is there isn't anything special about finding $f(4)$. If I want to find $f(17)$, I add 3 plus 17 fives. If I want to find $f(n)$, I add 3 plus n fives.

$$f(n) = 3 + n \cdot 5$$

I think I'd rather write that as $f(n) = 5n + 3$.

Input	Output	Δ
0	3	5
1	8	5
2	13	5
3	18	5
4	23	

Leslie used the numbers highlighted in this difference table to find $f(4) = f(0) + 4 \cdot 5$.

Developing Habits of Mind

Visualize. The two properties below apply to any difference table, whether or not it has constant differences.

- **Up-and-over property.** An output is the sum of two numbers above it: the output directly above and the difference above and to the right.
- **Hockey stick property.** An output is the sum of all the differences above it to the right and the single output at the top of the table.

When you highlight all the numbers you add up, it looks like a hockey stick. Otherwise, this property has nothing to do with hockey!

The properties are easier to see than to describe. Here is an example of the up-and-over property for Table Q from Lesson 1.1.

Input	Output	Δ
0	1	9
1	10	19
2	29	29
3	58	39
4	97	

$$10 + 19 = 29$$

The output for an input of 2 is the sum of the output for 1 and the difference next to the output for 1.

Here is an example of the hockey stick property for Table Q.

Input	Output	Δ
0	1	9
1	10	19
2	29	29
3	58	39
4	97	

$$1 + (9 + 19 + 29) = 58$$

The output for an input of 3 is the sum of all the differences in the column leading up to $Q(3)$ and the output for 0.

Developing Habits of Mind

Ask students to verify that the two properties apply to a difference table with nonconstant differences. For example, consider the following table.

n	$f(n)$	Δ
0	2	1
1	3	3
2	6	5
3	11	7
4	18	

Up-and-over: $f(3) = 6 + 5 = 11$

Hockey stick: $f(3) = 2 + (1 + 3 + 5) = 2 + 9 = 11$

For Discussion

You can cover these problems as formally as you wish—or even skip so that students have more time to work on the Check Your Understanding exercises.

PROBLEM 3 Your students may know how to "read off" the slope from the equation of a line. If so, they will be able to conclude that the slope is just the coefficient a from the linear equation.

You may also want to show that the slope of the graph of the function $f(x) = \Delta x + f(0)$ is equal to Δ. You know two points on the graph, $(0, f(0))$ and $(1, f(1))$. You also know that the slope of a line is constant and equal to the slope between any two points on the line. In this case, the slope is $\frac{f(1) - f(0)}{1 - 0}$ or just $f(1) - f(0)$. This is how you calculate the difference, so the slope of the line is Δ.

For You to Do

PROBLEM 4 To help students see what they need to do to prove Theorem 1.2, you might suggest that they make a difference table for the function.

Wrap Up

Go over the Check Your Understanding exercises with students. Ask

- How do you find a recursive rule that matches a table with constant differences?
- How do you find a closed-form rule that matches a table with constant differences?
- Can you use your recursive rule to find a closed-form rule?

Assessment Resources

Lesson Quiz 1.3

For Exercises 1–4, use the table.

n	$g(n)$
0	4
1	8
2	16
3	32
4	64
5	128

1. Make a difference table for the table.
2. How are the differences related to the outputs?
3. Write a recursive definition for a function that fits the table.
4. Write a closed-form definition for a function that fits the table.

The hockey stick property leads to Theorem 1.1.

Theorem 1.1

You can match an input-output table with constant differences with a linear function. The slope of the graph of the function is the constant difference in the table.

In this chapter, assume that the inputs in the table are {0, 1, 2, 3, . . . } unless stated otherwise.

For Discussion

1. Show that the up-and-over property is a result of the way you construct difference tables.
2. Show that the hockey stick property is a result of the way you construct difference tables.
3. Use the hockey stick property to prove Theorem 1.1.

Theorem 1.2 is the converse of Theorem 1.1.

Theorem 1.2

If $f(x) = ax + b$ is a linear function, its differences are constant.

Habits of Mind

Detect the key characteristics. What is the value of the constant difference?

For You to Do

4. Prove Theorem 1.2.

You can use the hockey stick property to quickly find a closed-form definition for a function that fits a table with constant differences. Here is Table H again with a hockey stick illustrated.

Input	Output	Δ
0	3	5
1	8	5
2	13	5
3	18	5
4	23	

The output is the number at the tip of the hockey stick plus the sum of the numbers on the handle.

For You to Do

5. Describe how you can find the number 23 using the hockey stick property.
6. How can you use the hockey stick property to find a closed form that agrees with the table?

Answers

For Discussion

1. Let O_n and O_{n+1} represent the outputs in the nth and $(n + 1)$st rows, respectively, and let Δ_n represent the difference in the nth row. Then $\Delta_n = O_{n+1} - O_n$, so $O_{n+1} = \Delta_n + O_n$, which is the up-and-over property.
2. Each output value is the first output value plus the sum of the numbers that get added to the first output. The numbers "that get added" are shown in the Δ column, so "the first output value plus the sum of the numbers" is what is called the hockey stick property.
3. Suppose a difference table has $f(0) = b$ and constant difference a. Then the hockey stick property gives $f(n) = b + n \cdot a = an + b$, a linear function with slope a.

For You to Do

4–6. See back of book.

Exercises *Practicing Habits of Mind*

Check Your Understanding

For Exercises 1–4, use Table G from this investigation's Getting Started lesson.

Table G

Input	Output
0	−7
1	−4
2	−1
3	2
4	5

1. Make a difference table for Table G.

2. Write a recursive definition for a function that fits Table G.

3. Write a closed-form definition for a function that fits Table G.

4. Use the functions from Exercises 2 and 3. What does each function give as output for each input below?

a. 10

b. 10.1

Habits of Mind

Look for relationships. Model your recursive and closed-form rules in your function modeling language. Do they agree for all inputs?

5. **What's Wrong Here?** Leslie built a difference table for the input-output table at the right.

n	$f(n)$
0	11
1	5
2	11
3	5
4	11

Leslie says, "All the differences are 6. So, this table has constant differences. Then the rule for the table is $f(n) = 6n + 11$. Hmm, that doesn't seem right. That rule says $f(4)$ is 35, but it's not."

Find the flaw in Leslie's logic.

6. The table at the right has constant differences. Copy and complete the table.

n	$p(n)$	Δ
0	3	■
1	■	■
2	■	■
3	■	■
4	−4	

7. Suppose the table from Exercise 6 continues with constant differences. Find the values of $p(10)$, $p(100)$, and $p(263)$.

8. **Standardized Test Prep** Suppose you have a table with constant differences. The input 2 gives the output 11. The input 3 gives the output 14. What is the output for the input 7?

A. 10 **B.** 17

C. 21 **D.** 26

Exercises

HOMEWORK

- Core: 10, 11, 12, 13, 14, 15, 16
- Optional: 17, 19, 20
- Extension: 18

Check Your Understanding

You can use Blackline Master MC1 to provide students with copies of blank tables to use in the exercises.

EXERCISE 4 This is an important distinction between closed-form and recursive rules, one which you will revisit when you talk more formally about functions. Effectively, the closed-form and recursive rules are different functions since they have different domains. Closed-form rules can work for any input, while recursive rules are restricted to nonnegative integer inputs and depend on the given starting point.

EXERCISE 6 Ask students to think about the hockey stick property here. Will it help them find the missing numbers? Are any of the missing numbers the same (a constant)?

Exercises

1. See back of book.

2. $g(n) = \begin{cases} -7 & \text{if } n = 0 \\ g(n-1) + 3 & \text{if } n > 0 \end{cases}$

3. $g(n) = 3n - 7$

4. **a.** 23

b. 23.3 for closed-form rule; the recursive rule cannot be applied if n is not a nonnegative integer.

5. The differences are −6, 6, −6, 6, which are not constant.

6.

n	$p(n)$	Δ
0	3	$-\frac{7}{4}$
1	$\frac{5}{4}$	$-\frac{7}{4}$
2	$-\frac{1}{2}$	$-\frac{7}{4}$
3	$-\frac{9}{4}$	$-\frac{7}{4}$
4	−4	

7. $p(10) = -\frac{29}{2}$, $p(100) = -172$, $p(263) = -\frac{1829}{4}$

8. D

EXERCISE 9 As an extension, you can ask students to explain why the Fibonacci pattern would emerge here. The difference rule $F(n) - F(n-1) = F(n-2)$ is the cause.

On Your Own

EXERCISES 10–12 You may wish to use these exercises as an assessment of students' understanding of the lesson.

9. Use the function table for $F(n)$.
   a. Build a difference table for $F(n)$.
   b. How are the differences related to the outputs?
   c. Predict the value of $F(10)$ by extending the pattern in the table.

n	$F(n)$
0	1
1	1
2	2
3	3
4	5
5	8
6	13

Can you model this function in your function-modeling language?

On Your Own

For Exercises 10–12, use Table M from Lesson 1.1.

10. Make a difference table for Table M.
11. Write a recursive definition for a function that fits Table M.
12. Write a closed-form definition for a function that fits Table M.
13. Model your recursive and closed-form definitions from Exercises 10 and 11 in your function-modeling language. Do they agree for all inputs?
14. Use the function table for $D(n)$.
    a. Build a difference table for $D(n)$.
    b. How are the differences related to the outputs?
    c. Predict the value of $D(10)$ by extending the pattern.

Table M

Input	Output
0	9
1	15
2	21
3	27
4	33

n	$D(n)$
0	1
1	2
2	4
3	8
4	16
5	32
6	64

Habits of Mind

Experiment. In Exercise 13, what does each model give as an output when you input 7? What does each model give as an output when you input -7?

You can use a keyboard or voice-recognition software. If the words you input are the same, then the outputs will be the same.

Go Online
PHSchool.com

For additional practice, go to **Web Code:** bfa-0103

Answers

9. **a.** See back of book.
   b. The differences are the same as the outputs except that $\Delta_0 = 0$ and $\Delta_n = F(n-1)$ for $n > 0$.
   c. $F(10) = 89$

10.

Input	Output	Δ
0	9	6
1	15	6
2	21	6
3	27	6
4	33	

11. $M(n) = \begin{cases} 9 & \text{if } n = 0 \\ M(n-1) + 6 & \text{if } n > 0 \end{cases}$

12. $M(n) = 6n + 9$

13. The recursive form and closed form give the same output when n is nonnegative. The recursive form cannot be used when n is negative.

14. **a.** See back of book.
    b. $D(n+1) - D(n) = D(n)$
    c. 1024

15. **Write About It** Describe how to find a closed-form definition for a function that fits a table with constant differences. Include an example.

16. Which of the Tables A–V in Lesson 1.1 have constant differences?

17. A table with integer inputs has constant differences. When the input is 3, the output is 9. When the input is 11, the output is −3. Calculate the constant difference.

18. **Take It Further** Suppose you reverse the inputs and outputs of Table M. You get the input-output table at the right.

Inverse of Table M

Input	Output
9	0
15	1
21	2
27	3
33	4

a. Find a function that fits the table.

b. Using your function, copy and complete the difference table below that has integer inputs from 0 to 4.

Input	Output	Δ
0	■	■
1	■	■
2	■	■
3	■	■
4	■	

c. How is the constant difference in the table from part (b) related to the constant difference in the original Table M?

Habits of Mind

Organize what you know. It may help to make the table, even if you cannot fill in very much of it at first.

Maintain Your Skills

19. The table at the right has constant differences. Copy and complete the table.

Input	Output	Δ
0	■	■
1	■	■
2	−5	■
3	■	■
4	■	■
5	22	■
6	■	

20. Find the slope between each pair of points.

a. $A(2, -5)$ and $B(5, 22)$

b. $C(7, -5)$ and $D(10, 22)$

c. $E(-5, 2)$ and $F(22, 5)$

15. Answers may vary. Sample: If the constant difference is a and the first output is b, then $f(n) = an + b$. Check students' examples.

16. Tables A, C, E, F, G, H, M, P

17. −1.5

18. a. $f(n) = \frac{n}{6} - \frac{3}{2}$

b. See back of book.

c. They are reciprocals.

19.

Input	Output	Δ
0	−23	9
1	−14	9
2	−5	9
3	4	9
4	13	9
5	22	9
6	31	

20. a. 9 **b.** 9 **c.** $\frac{1}{9}$

EXERCISE 16 Completing this exercise will take a while. You could select four or five tables from the Getting Started lesson and ask about those, or you could ask students to find at least three tables which have this property.

EXERCISE 18 previews the concept of an inverse function, which will be explored in Investigation 2A.

Maintain Your Skills

EXERCISE 19 The hockey stick can start anywhere in the table. Here 22 = −5 + ■ + ■ + ■, so 27 = 3 · ■ and ■ = 9.

Additional Resources

PRINT RESOURCES
- Solution Manual
- Practice Workbook
- Assessment Resources
- Teaching Resources

TECHNOLOGY
- Interactive Textbook
- TeacherExpress CD-ROM
- ExamView CD-ROM
- PHSchool.com

Additional Practice

For Exercises 1 and 2, use the difference table.

1. Complete the difference table.

2. Find a formula for $f(x) - f(x - 1)$ when $f(x) = ax + a$.

Input, x	Output, $ax + a$	Δ
0	a	
1	$2a$	
2	$3a$	
3	$4a$	

For Exercises 3–5, use the difference table of perfect squares.

3. Complete the difference table.

4. Write a recursive definition for a function that fits the table of perfect squares.

5. Find a closed-form definition for a function that generates the perfect squares.

Input	Output	Δ
0	0	
1	1	
2	4	
3	9	
4	16	
5	25	

For Exercises 6–9, use Table A.

6. Make a difference table for Table A.

7. How are the differences related to the outputs?

8. Write a recursive definition for a function that fits Table A.

9. Write a closed-form definition for a function that fits Table A.

Table A

n	$h(n)$
0	3
1	6
2	12
3	24
4	48
5	96

10. Describe how to find a recursive definition for a function that fits a table with constant differences. Include an example.

11. A table with integer inputs has constant differences. When the input is 2, the output is −6. When the input is 10, the output is 18. Calculate the constant difference.

Practice: For Lesson 1.3, assign Exercises 6–11.

Lesson Overview

GOAL

- Understand the relationship between difference tables and slope.

In this lesson, students see the relationship between difference tables and slope. Almost all of the tables students see in this investigation (not just in this lesson) are very special: the first input is 0 and the subsequent change in input is always one unit. It is pretty simple to see the slope between two points in such a table, and you will exploit that in this lesson. Class discussion is very important here but it can take a lot of class time. Try to reserve some time for the Check Your Understanding exercises.

CHECK YOUR UNDERSTANDING
- Core: 1, 2, 3, 4, 5, 8, 9
- Optional: 6, 7

MATERIALS
- CAS (recommended)
- graph paper
- graphing calculators
- spreadsheet software
- Blackline Masters MC1, 1.4

HOMEWORK
- Core: 10, 12, 13, 14, 15, 18, 19
- Optional: 11, 17, 20a–e, 21
- Extension: 16, 20f

VOCABULARY
- slope

Launch

Students who remember the lessons on slope in CME Project *Algebra 1* may have already noticed the connection between differences in these tables and slope. If this is the case, you may want to start this lesson by asking students what slope is. Then ask them to make conjectures about the relationship between slope and differences in the tables in this investigation. Challenge students to remember what slope is: a measure of direction for points and lines.

Explore

Example

You can use Blackline Master 1.4 to guide students through the Example.

You could use the hockey stick property to find k, but filling in the table without finding k first emphasizes the relationship between the output when the input is 2 and all the other outputs.

1.4 Tables and Slope

In the last lesson, you saw that you can fit a linear function to a table with constant differences. In this lesson, you will learn the relationship between difference tables and slope.

Example

Problem An input-output table has constant differences. When the input is 2, the output is 9. When the input is 7, the output is −6. Find the constant difference.

Assume that the inputs are consecutive integers.

Solution Suppose the constant difference is k. You can make this difference table.

Input	Output	Δ
0	?	k
1	?	k
2	9	k
3	?	k
4	?	k
5	?	k
6	?	k
7	−6	

Since the table has a constant difference, you can label every entry in the Δ column k.

Now that you have labeled the difference column, you can write other outputs as expressions in terms of k. For example, you can use the up-and-over property of difference tables to find the output when the input is 3.

Input	Output	Δ
0	?	k
1	?	k
2	**9**	$\mathbf{k}$
3	**9 + k**	k
4	?	k
5	?	k
6	?	k
7	−6	

You can calculate the other outputs in the same way. When the input is 4, the output is $9 + 2k$. The completed table at the right shows the outputs written in terms of k.

Input	Output	Δ
0	$9 - 2k$	k
1	$9 - k$	k
2	9	k
3	$9 + k$	k
4	$9 + 2k$	k
5	$9 + 3k$	k
6	$9 + 4k$	k
7	**$9 + 5k$**	

Now you know two expressions for the output when the input is 7. The up-and-over property gives $9 + 5k$, but the output is supposed to be -6. These must be equal.

$$9 + 5k = -6$$

Solve for k to find the constant difference.

$$\begin{aligned} 9 + 5k &= -6 \\ 5k &= -15 \\ k &= -3 \end{aligned}$$

For Discussion

1. Can you use the hockey stick property, instead, to find the constant difference? Explain.
2. Find a linear function that fits the table.

Developing Habits of Mind

Consider more than one strategy. There is another way to find the constant difference.

Theorem 1.1 says that you can match a table with constant differences with a *linear* function. The graph of the function is a line with slope equal to the constant difference in the table.

You can calculate the slope of that line by finding the slope between any two points on the line. Any input-output pair from the table gives the coordinates of a point on that line.

Therefore, you can calculate the constant difference as $\frac{\text{change in output}}{\text{change in input}}$.

Developing Habits of Mind

Ask students to verify that the slope of the linear function that fits the table is k by choosing input-output pairs where the inputs are *not* consecutive integers. For example, they could choose $(3, 9 + k)$ and $(7, 9 + 5k)$. Then,

$$\text{slope} = \frac{(9 + 5k) - (9 + k)}{7 - 3} = \frac{4k}{4} = k$$

Answers

For Discussion

1. Yes; each output is equal to the original output plus the sum of the differences up to that output.
2. $f(n) = 15 - 3n$

For You to Do

Keep focusing students' attention on the relationship between constant differences and slope.

Wrap Up

Go over as many of the Check Your Understanding exercises as time allows. To end the class, ask,

- What is slope?
- What is the relationship between slope and differences?

Assessment Resources

Lesson Quiz 1.4

1. A line contains the points $(-1, 5)$ and $(4, -10)$.
   a. Find the slope of the line.
   b. Find the value of a such that the point $(3, a)$ lies on the line.
   c. Find the value of b such that the point $(b, -4)$ lies on the line.

2. A line connects the points $(-5, 3)$ and $(-1, 6)$.
   a. Draw the line on a coordinate plane.
   b. Find the slope of the line.
   c. Write an equation for the line.

3. A line connects the points $(7, -2)$ and $(7, 4)$.
   a. Draw the line on a coordinate plane.
   b. Describe the slope of the line.
   c. Write an equation for the line.

Exercises

HOMEWORK

- Core: 10, 12, 13, 14, 15, 18, 19
- Optional: 11, 17, 20a–e, 21
- Extension: 16, 20f

Check Your Understanding

You can use Blackline Master MC1 to provide students with copies of blank tables for use in the exercises.

EXERCISE 2 Ask students to compare this exercise to Exercise 1. They should recognize that the two exercises are actually the same problem.

For You to Do

3. A table has constant differences. When the input is 6, the output is 10. When the input is 15, the output is also 15. Find the constant difference.

Exercises *Practicing Habits of Mind*

Check Your Understanding

1. An input-output table has constant differences. When the input is 3, the output is 10. When the input is 7, the output is 24.

a. Find the constant difference.

b. Find the output when the input is 0.

c. Find the linear function that fits the table.

2. A line passes through the points $(3, 10)$ and $(7, 24)$.

a. Find the slope of the line.

b. Find an equation for the line.

3. **Write About It** Is there a line that contains the points $(0, -12)$, $(3, 5)$, and $(4, 10)$? Explain.

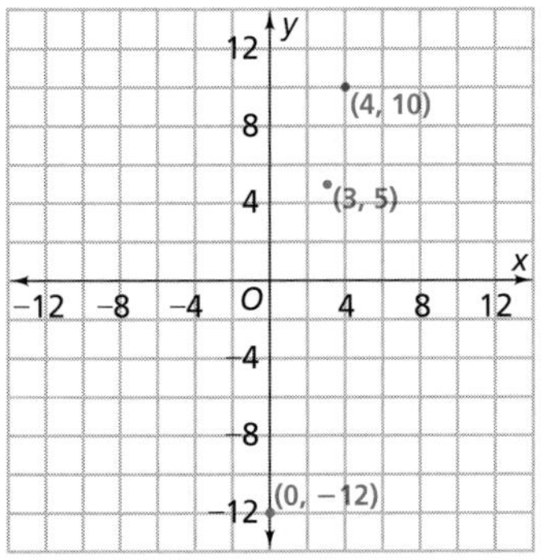

Answers

For You to Do

3. $\frac{5}{9}$

Exercises

1. a. $\frac{7}{2}$

b. $-\frac{1}{2}$

c. $f(n) = \frac{7}{2}n - \frac{1}{2}$

2. a. $\frac{7}{2}$

b. $y = \frac{7}{2}x - \frac{1}{2}$ or $2y = 7x - 1$

3. No; the slope for $(0, -12)$ and $(3, 5)$ is $\frac{17}{3}$ and the slope for $(3, 5)$ and $(4, 10)$ is 5, so one line cannot contain all three points.

4. Some entries are missing from the table below. Can a linear function generate the table? Explain.

Input	Output
0	−12
1	?
2	?
3	5
4	10

5. A linear function generated the table below left. Find the values of *a* and *b*.

Input	Output
0	?
1	4
2	*a*
3	?
4	?
5	?
6	−21
7	*b*

Input	Output
0	−4
1	$-3\frac{1}{2}$
2	−3
3	$-2\frac{1}{2}$
4	−2

6. Find a linear function that agrees with the table above right.

7. An input-output table has constant difference 5. When the input is 6, the output is −3.
   - **a.** Find the output when the input is 7.
   - **b.** Find the output when the input is 3.
   - **c.** Find a linear function that fits the input-output table.

8. Use differences to prove that you cannot find a linear function that matches Table K from Lesson 1.1.

Table K

Input	Output
0	1
1	2
2	5
3	10
4	17

4. No; the difference for the last two outputs is 5, but using that as the constant difference, you would expect the output for 0 to be −10, so the table does not have a constant difference.

5. $a = -1$, $b = -26$

6. $f(n) = \frac{n}{2} - 4$

7. a. 2

b. −18

c. $f(n) = 5n - 33$

8. The differences are 1, 3, 5, 7. Since those differences are not constant, the table cannot match a linear function.

EXERCISE 5 If the output is 4 when the input is 1 and the output is −21 when the input is 6, and if the function is linear, then the slope (and thus the constant difference) must be negative. So, *a* must be less than 4 and *b* must be less than −21. Use the hockey stick property to find the constant difference.

EXERCISE 6 The constant difference here is $\frac{1}{2}$. Students might make an error with the fraction and/or the negative signs.

EXERCISE 8 Point out to students that there is a pattern to the differences. If they construct another column and find the differences of the differences, that column will be constant. They should be able to find the linear function that describes the difference column.

On Your Own

EXERCISE 9 Ask students what they think the constant difference in the Δ^2 column tells them about the function. (Later they will learn that the function that fits the table is quadratic if the Δ^2 column is constant.)

EXERCISE 10 Students may notice the similarity to Exercise 5. The given inputs and outputs in Exercise 5 are (1, 4) and (6, −21). So the two problems involve the same linear function. Furthermore, Exercises 10b and 10c are asking for the outputs when the inputs are 2 and 7. The *a* and *b* in Exercise 10 are the same as the *a* and *b* in Exercise 5. In fact, these two exercises are the same.

EXERCISE 14 Students have already found a quadratic function that agrees with the table in the Getting Started lesson. Ask students what they think might be true about the Δ^2 column. Confirm their conjectures by adding a Δ^2 column. You might ask students in groups to build difference tables for their own quadratic functions to see if the Δ^2 column is always a constant. They will discuss this again in the next lesson.

9. Copy and complete the difference table from Table K. Complete the last column by finding the differences of the numbers in the Δ column.

x	$K(x)$	Δ	Δ^2
0	1	1	2
1	2	3	■
2	5	■	■
3	10	7	
4	17		

The symbol Δ^2 means "Δ of the Δ." Find the differences of the difference column.

On Your Own

10. A line contains the points (1, 4) and (6, −21).

a. Find the slope of the line.

b. Find the value of *a* such that the point (2, *a*) lies on the line.

c. Find the value of *b* such that the point (7, *b*) lies on the line.

Habits of Mind

Look for patterns. What is the value of *c* such that (6, *c*) lies on the line?

11. Write About It Does the table below have constant differences? Explain.

Input, x	Output, y
0	11
1	11
2	11
3	11
4	11

12. A line connects the points (3, 7) and (−2, 7).

a. Draw the line on a coordinate plane.

b. Find the slope of the line.

c. Write an equation for the line.

13. A line connects the points (7, 3) and (7, −2).

a. Draw the line on a coordinate plane.

b. Explain why the slope of this line is undefined.

c. Write an equation for the line.

14. Make a difference table for Table O from Lesson 1.1.

Explain why Table O *cannot* come from a linear function.

Table O

Input	Output
0	0
1	5
2	20
3	45
4	80

Go Online PHSchool.com

For additional practice, go to **Web Code:** bfa-0104

Answers

9.

x	$K(x)$	Δ	Δ^2
0	1	1	2
1	2	3	2
2	5	5	2
3	10	7	
4	17		

10. a. −5 **b.** $a = -1$ **c.** $b = -26$

11. Yes; the differences are 0, 0, 0, and 0, so the differences are constant.

12. a.

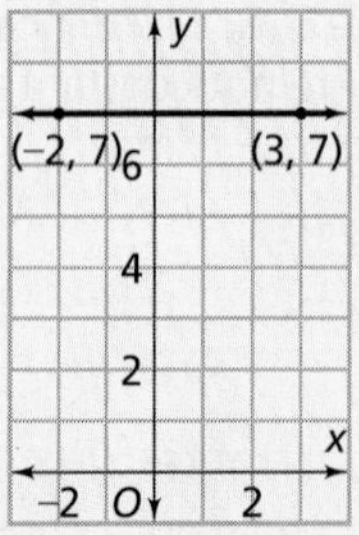

b. 0 **c.** $y = 7$

13. a.

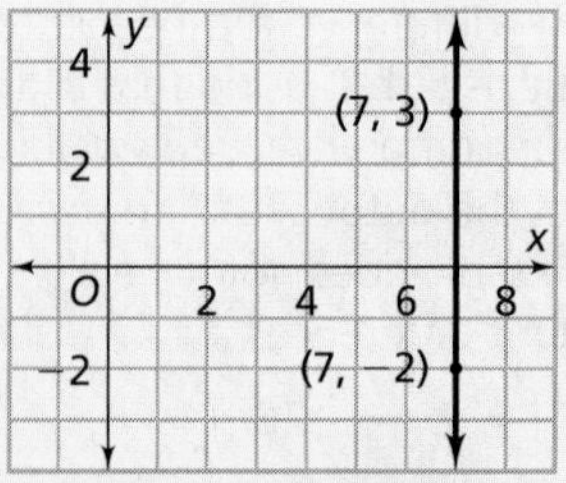

b. One meaning of slope is $\frac{\Delta y}{\Delta x}$. Since $\Delta x = 0$ and division by 0 is undefined, the line has undefined slope.

c. $x = 7$

15. Use differences to find a linear rule that agrees with Table P from Lesson 1.1.

Table P

Input	Output
0	1
1	5
2	9
3	13
4	17

16. **Take It Further** Here is a difference table for Table Q from Lesson 1.1.

a. Describe the relationship between Tables O, P, and Q.

b. Describe the relationship between the difference tables that come from Tables O, P, and Q.

n	$Q(n)$	Δ
0	1	9
1	10	19
2	29	29
3	58	39
4	97	

17. The table below comes from the function $R(w) = w^3$. You can find the entries in the Δ, Δ^2, and Δ^3 difference columns by finding the differences of the numbers in the respective previous columns.

Copy and complete the table.

w	$R(w)$	Δ	Δ^2	Δ^3
0	0	1	6	■
1	1	■	■	■
2	8	19	■	■
3	27	■	24	6
4	64	61	30	■
5	125	91	■	
6	216	■		
7	343			

Each difference column will have one entry fewer than the one before it.

The Sudbury Neutrino Observatory is enclosed in this sphere with a 9-m radius. You can use the cubic function $V = \frac{4}{3}\pi r^3$ to find the volume of the sphere.

EXERCISE 16 Assign this exercise only if you have assigned Exercises 14 and 15.

EXERCISE 17 also appears in the next lesson as Exercise 3. Here it is a preview of tables with more than one difference column. Assign this exercise only once, either here or as a concept review in the next lesson.

14.

Input	Output	Δ
0	0	**5**
1	5	**15**
2	20	**25**
3	45	**35**
4	80	

The differences are not constant, so the function is not linear.

15. $P(b) = 4b + 1$

16. a. The outputs in Table Q are the sums of the outputs in Tables O and P.

b. The differences in Table Q are the sums of the differences in Tables O and P.

17.

w	$R(w)$	Δ	Δ^2	Δ^3
0	0	1	6	**6**
1	1	**7**	**12**	**6**
2	8	19	**18**	**6**
3	27	**37**	24	6
4	64	61	30	**6**
5	125	91	**36**	
6	216	**127**		
7	343			

EXERCISE 18 previews the result from Chapter 2 that two polynomials give equal outputs for a set of inputs if and only if their difference vanishes on that set. Also a polynomial vanishes at a number a if and only if it has $x - a$ as a factor.

EXERCISE 21 Functions $g(x)$, $k(x)$, and $s(x)$ describe the difference columns for functions f, h, and r, respectively. The function g that describes the difference column for the linear function f is a constant. A linear function, k, describes the difference column for the quadratic function h. The function s that describes the difference column for the cubic function r is quadratic. Ask students what kind of function would describe the Δ column for a 4th degree polynomial function.

Additional Resources

PRINT RESOURCES
- Solution Manual
- Practice Workbook
- Assessment Resources
- Teaching Resources

TECHNOLOGY
- Interactive Textbook
- TeacherExpress CD-ROM
- ExamView CD-ROM
- PHSchool.com

Additional Practice

1. A line contains the points $(-2, 3)$ and $(4, -9)$.
   a. Find the slope of the line.
   b. Find the value of a such that the point $(3, a)$ lies on the line.
   c. Find the value of b such that the point $(b, -4)$ lies on the line.

2. A line connects the points $(-5, 3)$ and $(-3, 9)$.
   a Draw the line on a coordinate plane.
   b. Find the slope of the line.
   c. Write an equation for the line.

3. A line connects the points $(3, 11)$ and $(-4, 11)$.
   a. Draw the line on a coordinate plane.
   b. Describe the slope of the line.
   c. Write an equation for the line.

4. Use differences to find a linear rule that agrees with the table.

Input	Output
0	4
1	7
2	10
3	13

For Exercises 5–7, find a function that agrees with each table.

5.

n	$a(n)$
0	12
1	8
2	4
3	0

6.

n	$b(n)$
0	−3
1	0
2	5
3	12

7.

n	$c(n)$
0	1
1	3
2	17
3	55

8. Use the input-output table. Show that the table could not have come from a linear, quadratic, or cubic function.

Input, x	Output, y
1	2
2	2
3	4
4	6
5	10

Practice: For Lesson 1.4, assign Exercises 1–4.

18. Derman is making a table for the function below.

$d(x) = x^4 - 6x^3 + 11x^2 - 4x + 3$

x	$d(x)$	Δ
0	■	■
1	■	■
2	■	■
3	■	

a. Copy and complete Derman's table for him.

b. Derman says, "What? Do I have a linear function?" How can you help Derman figure this out?

19. **Standardized Test Prep** Ramon accidentally shredded his physics homework. He knows the relationship he was graphing is linear. He is able to reconstruct two table values. For the input of 2, the output is 17. For the input of 11, the output is 38. What is the slope of the relationship Ramon was graphing?

A. $\frac{39}{17}$ **B.** $\frac{3}{7}$ **C.** $\frac{7}{3}$ **D.** $\frac{9}{5}$

Maintain Your Skills

20. Make a difference table for each function. Include inputs 0 through 4.

a. $a(x) = x^2$

b. $b(x) = 2x^2$

c. $c(x) = 5x^2$

d. $d(x) = -10x^2$

e. Find a number k such that the function $e(x) = kx^2$ has the number 50 in its difference column.

f. **Take It Further** Find all integers k such that the function $e(x) = kx^2$ has the number 50 in its difference column.

21. Make a difference table for each function. Use inputs 0, 1, 2, 3, and 4.

a. $f(x) = 3x + 2$

b. $g(x) = f(x + 1) - f(x)$

c. $h(x) = x^2 + 3x$

d. $k(x) = h(x + 1) - h(x)$

e. $r(x) = x^3$

f. $s(x) = r(x + 1) - r(x)$

Habits of Mind

Organize what you know. How can you use your CAS for this exercise?

Answers

18. a.

x	$d(x)$	Δ
0	3	2
1	5	2
2	7	2
3	9	

b. The first three differences are 2, but $d(4) = 35$ so the next difference is 26. This means that the function is not linear.

19. C

20. a.

x	$a(x)$	Δ
0	0	1
1	1	3
2	4	5
3	9	7
4	16	

b.

x	$b(x)$	Δ
0	0	2
1	2	6
2	8	10
3	18	14
4	32	

c.

x	$c(x)$	Δ
0	0	5
1	5	15
2	20	25
3	45	35
4	80	

d.

x	$d(x)$	Δ
0	0	−10
1	−10	−30
2	−40	−50
3	−90	−70
4	−160	

1.5 Deeper Differences

Here is a difference table for the function $D(n) = n^2 + 2n$.

You can look at the first and third columns at the right as a new table. You can match this new table with $n \rightarrow 2n + 3$. Then you can make another difference column showing the differences of the new outputs. These "differences of the differences" are second differences.

Input, *n*	Output, *D*(*n*)	Δ
0	0	3
1	3	5
2	8	7
3	15	9
4	24	11
5	35	13
6	48	

So far in this chapter, you have found functions that match a table. In this lesson, you will also start with a function and use it to generate a table.

Here is the table with a second differences column.

You can continue this process to find third differences and even more differences. For the table that comes from $D(n)$, all the third differences are equal to zero. So are any fourth differences, fifth differences, and so on.

Input, *n*	Output, *D*(*n*)	Δ	Δ^2
0	0	3	2
1	3	5	2
2	8	7	2
3	15	9	2
4	24	11	2
5	35	13	
6	48		

Habits of Mind

Understand the notation. The second differences are in the column labeled Δ^2. This notation means you perform the Δ operation twice. It does not mean to square the differences.

Example

Problem Use difference tables to find a recursive definition for a function that matches the following table.

Input	Output
0	−2
1	0
2	16
3	46
4	90

Solution A recursive definition for a function that fits this table might look something like the one below.

$$f(x) = \begin{cases} -2 & \text{if } x = 0 \\ f(x-1) + (\blacksquare) & \text{if } x > 0 \end{cases}$$

e. Answers may vary. Sample: 50

f. $k = 2, 10, \text{ or } 50$

21. a.

x	*f*(*x*)	Δ
0	2	3
1	5	3
2	8	3
3	11	3
4	14	

b.

x	*g*(*x*)	Δ
0	3	0
1	3	0
2	3	0
3	3	0
4	3	

c.

x	*h*(*x*)	Δ
0	0	4
1	4	6
2	10	8
3	18	10
4	28	

d.

x	*k*(*x*)	Δ
0	4	2
1	6	2
2	8	2
3	10	2
4	12	

e.

x	*r*(*x*)	Δ
0	0	1
1	1	7
2	8	19
3	27	37
4	64	

f.

x	*s*(*x*)	Δ
0	1	6
1	7	12
2	19	18
3	37	24
4	61	

Lesson Overview

GOAL

- Use differences to decide what type of function can fit a table.

This lesson extends the work of the previous lesson by having students look at tables in which first differences are not constant. They look at tables in which second differences are constant. They use recursive definitions to generate closed forms for functions that fit the tables with constant second differences. Some challenging problems look at tables with constant third differences and beyond.

Depending on your needs, you may wish to give this lesson a light treatment—for example, covering quadratic functions only rather than quadratics and cubics. The idea of constant *n*th differences will appear in mathematics that students encounter in CME Project *Precalculus* and throughout college. This material can be fun. Covering only parts of this lesson, though, will not prevent students from understanding subsequent material.

CHECK YOUR UNDERSTANDING

- Core: 1, 3, 4, 5
- Optional: 2, 8, 9, 10, 11
- Extension: 6, 7, 12

MATERIALS

- CAS (recommended)
- graphing calculators
- spreadsheet software
- Blackline Masters 1.5A–C

HOMEWORK

- Core: 13, 14, 15, 17, 18, 20
- Optional: 16, 21a–e, 22
- Extension: 19, 21f

VOCABULARY

- cubic function
- quadratic function

Launch

Use Blackline Master 1.5A to display a table for *D*(*n*) with blank columns for the first and second differences. Get students to generate the first differences. Then ask if they can generate the entries in the Δ column by a linear function. When students say they could not, ask why not. Students will probably point out that the differences are not constant. Then ask students to generate second differences and enter them in the last column. They *are* constant, which means that the first differences could be generated by a linear function on the original inputs. Have students explain.

At this point, taking second differences should feel as if it is a natural task to students. Explain that the notation for second differences is Δ^2, and write Δ^2 at the top of the last column.

You may wish to point out that $\Delta^2 \neq \Delta \times \Delta$. Although this notation looks like an exponent, that is not its meaning. In fact, $\Delta^2 = \Delta \circ \Delta$, where $\circ$ indicates function composition—in other words, taking the difference of the differences.

Explore

Example

Blackline Master 1.5B provides a copy of the table, with blank columns added for the first and second differences.

When writing the recursive rule for f, students are using the up-and-over property, which means that they must add on the previous output, $f(x - 1)$, and corresponding difference: $14(x - 1) + 2$. This is often a stumbling block for students.

Here is the difference table. The Δ column tells you what to add to move from one output to the next. So finding a rule for the Δ column gives the missing information for the recursive definition.

Input	Output	Δ
0	−2	2
1	0	16
2	16	30
3	46	44
4	90	

Now you need to find a function that fits the Δ column. Try finding the second differences.

Input	Output	Δ	Δ^2
0	−2	2	14
1	0	16	14
2	16	30	14
3	46	44	
4	90		

The second differences are constant. Therefore, you can find a linear function that gives the first differences in the Δ column as outputs. In this case, a linear function that matches the input column with the Δ column is $x \rightarrow 14x + 2$.

New "Output"

Input	Δ	Δ^2
0	2	14
1	16	14
2	30	14
3	44	
4		

Ignore the output column. Think of the Δ column as a new output column.

Before you write down the recursive definition, you may find it helpful to write out a few specific examples with numbers. This can give you the rhythm of how to produce the outputs.

$$\begin{aligned} f(1) &= f(0) + 14 \cdot 0 + 2 \\ f(2) &= f(1) + 14 \cdot 1 + 2 \\ f(3) &= f(2) + 14 \cdot 2 + 2 \\ f(4) &= f(3) + 14 \cdot 3 + 2 \\ f(5) &= f(4) + 14 \cdot 4 + 2 \\ &\vdots \\ f(175) &= f(174) + 14 \cdot 174 + 2 \end{aligned}$$

The rhythm of the outputs suggests this general definition.

$$f(x) = \begin{cases} -2 & \text{if } x = 0 \\ f(x-1) + 14(x-1) + 2 & \text{if } x > 0 \end{cases}$$

or

$$f(x) = \begin{cases} -2 & \text{if } x = 0 \\ f(x-1) + 14x - 12 & \text{if } x > 0 \end{cases}$$

Where did the expression $14x - 12$ come from?

For You to Do

Derman looks at all this and says, "I have a closed-form definition for a function that matches the table." Here is Derman's definition:

$$f(x) = 7x^2 - 5x - 2$$

1. Does Derman's function match the table?
2. How do you think he found his definition?

"He guessed" is not the best answer to Problem 2.

A **quadratic function** is a function defined by a polynomial of degree 2. For example, $f(x) = 3x^2 + 5x - 7$ is quadratic. But $g(x) = 3x^2 + 5x - 7x^3$ is not quadratic—it has degree 3.

So far, you have seen two quadratic functions in this lesson. The first, $D(n) = n^2 + 2n$, has constant second differences equal to 2. The second, $f(x) = 7x^2 - 5x - 2$, has constant second differences equal to 14. Notice that 14 is twice 7, and 7 is the coefficient of x^2.

Look at another example. Here is a difference table for $s(t) = -16t^2 + 150t$.

The function $s(t)$ gives the height of an object thrown up in the air at 150 feet per second. Here, t is the number of seconds since the throw, and $s(t)$ is the height of the object.

Input, t	Output, $s(t)$	Δ	Δ^2
0	0	134	−32
1	134	102	−32
2	236	70	−32
3	306	38	
4	344		

The leading coefficient is the coefficient of the highest-degree term. For $s(t) = -16t^2 + 150t$, the leading coefficient is −16. The second differences in the table are constant and twice the leading coefficient.

You can use the general quadratic $p(x) = ax^2 + bx + c$ to show that this happens in general. In the table below, note that the second differences are constant and twice the leading coefficient.

Input, x	Output, $ax^2 + bx + c$	Δ	Δ^2
0	c	$a + b$	$2a$
1	$a + b + c$	$3a + b$	$2a$
2	$4a + 2b + c$	$5a + b$	$2a$
3	$9a + 3b + c$	$7a + b$	$2a$
4	$16a + 4b + c$	$9a + b$	
5	$25a + 5b + c$		

This table suggests that the second differences for any quadratic function are constant.

Answers

For You to Do

1. yes
2. Answers may vary. Sample: The constant second difference is 14, so the coefficient of x^2 is 7. The constant is −2 when the input is 0.

For You to Do

PROBLEMS 1 AND 2 Students should be able to answer the first question, but they may have some difficulty figuring out how Derman found his function. Do not spend too much time here. Let students explore some conjectures and then move on to the rest of the development.

As you work through the material following the For You to Do problems, have students experiment with their own quadratic functions. The first line of the difference table, when the input is 0, actually gives them more than just the leading coefficient. Since $f(0) = a(0)^2 + b(0) + c = c$, the output is c. If you know a and c, there are several ways to find b: You can use $f(1) = a + b + c$ or the fact that the first difference is $a + b$ when the input is 0.

PROOF OF THEOREM 1.3 Ask students to explain why $n \mapsto 2an + (a + b)$ is linear. What is the variable? (Answer: n) What is the coefficient of the variable? (Answer: $2a$) Emphasize that a, b, and c are constants.

Theorem 1.3

For any quadratic function $p(x) = ax^2 + bx + c$, the second differences are constant. The constant second difference is $2a$, twice the coefficient of the squared term.

Proof Basically, you want to show that the pattern in the above table continues. First, compute the entry in the Δ column for any input n.

Input	Output	Δ
⋮	⋮	⋮
n	$p(n) = an^2 + bn + c$	?
$n + 1$	$p(n + 1) = a(n + 1)^2 + b(n + 1) + c$	⋮
⋮	⋮	⋮

Use the up-and-over property.

$$\begin{aligned} p(n + 1) - p(n) &= (a(n + 1)^2 + b(n + 1) + c) - (an^2 + bn + c) \\ &= a((n + 1)^2 - n^2) + b((n + 1) - n) + (c - c) \\ &= a(2n + 1) + b = 2an + a + b \end{aligned}$$

Use the identity from Exercise 23 in Lesson 1.1. You can also define $p(x) = ax^2 + bx + c$ in your CAS and ask for $p(n + 1) - p(n)$. Make sure you have not assigned any values to a, b, c, or d.

This gives you a formula for the Δ column. It agrees with the table above for the general quadratic. Also, as predicted, the formula for the Δ column defines a linear function.

$$n \mapsto 2an + (a + b)$$

Here, a and b are constants. By Theorem 1.2, the first differences of this linear function—that is, the second differences of the original function p—are constant. Below, you will finish the proof by finding the value of the constant difference.

For You to Do

3. Finish the proof by showing that the value of the constant second difference is twice the coefficient of x^2.

Minds in Action episode 2

Tony is trying to figure out how Derman got that function in the For You to Do section on the previous page.

Tony Derman's definition is $f(x) = 7x^2 - 5x - 2$. I think I can figure it out for myself. The second differences are constant, so I bet there's a quadratic function that fits the table. And since the second difference is 14, the coefficient of x^2 would be 7.

Answers

For You to Do

3. Since $n \mapsto 2an + (a + b)$, then $n + 1 \mapsto 2a(n + 1) + (a + b)$. The difference $(n + 1) - n$ is equal to $2an + 2a + (a + b) - (2an + (a + b)) = 2a$. Thus, the constant difference is 2 times a or twice the coefficient of x^2.

So now I'm going to make a table with the inputs and outputs for $f(x)$, and an extra column with just the values of $7x^2$.

Input, x	Output, $f(x)$	Output, $7x^2$
0	−2	0
1	0	7
2	16	28
3	46	63
4	90	112

The real rule is $f(x)$ equals $7x^2$ plus something. I can figure out that something by subtracting $7x^2$ from all the outputs of $f(x)$. I'll make a new column for that.

Input, x	Output, $f(x)$	Output, $7x^2$	$f(x) - 7x^2$
0	−2	0	−2
1	0	7	−7
2	16	28	−12
3	46	63	−17
4	90	112	−22

Try using your function-modeling language to do this experiment.

Check it out: −2, −7, −12, −17, and −22. Those numbers can be matched with a linear function, and I know how to find one. The linear function is $x \mapsto -5x - 2$. So the whole thing must be

$$f(x) = 7x^2 + (-5x - 2)$$

And this works! It's like breaking down the problem into a simpler one. Once you subtract $7x^2$, the rest of it has to be linear.

For Discussion

4. Use Tony's ideas to find a closed-form definition for a function that fits Table R from Lesson 1.1.

Table R

Input	Output
0	0
1	1
2	8
3	27
4	64

For Discussion

PROBLEM 4 The function for Table R is cubic, not quadratic. If you assigned Exercise 17 in Lesson 1.4, use the completed table from that exercise as you discuss Problem 4. You may need to help students extend Tony's ideas and apply them to the process of finding a cubic function that fits a table. Or, you can let students explore this process when they do Exercises 3–5, and choose, instead, to use Table Q from Lesson 1.1 in this For Discussion section. In that case, use Blackline Master 1.5C to display Table Q, with blank columns for the first and second differences and the difference between $Q(n)$ and the squared term.

Have students compute the first and second differences for the table. They will discover that the second differences are constant and equal to 10. This tells them that the coefficient of the n^2 term in the function that matches this table must be 5. So the table entries for $Q(n) - 5n^2$ should be matched by a linear function in n.

A useful table might look like this.

Input, n	Output, $Q(n)$	Δ	Δ^2	$Q(n) - 5n^2$
0	1	9	10	1
1	10	19	10	5
2	29	29	10	9
3	58	39		13
4	97			17

The $Q(n) - 5n^2$ column is matched by the linear function $Q(n) - 5n^2 = 4n + 1$, which gives you $Q(n) = 5n^2 + 4n + 1$ as the function that matches the table.

For Discussion

4. $f(n) = n^3$

Wrap Up

Go over as many of the Check Your Understanding exercises as time allows. For Exercise 2, ask questions such as the following: How do you know that a quadratic function fits this table? What is the coefficient of the squared term of that quadratic function?

Before they tackle Exercises 3 and 4, ask students to guess what might be true about the third differences. They will write about this in Exercise 5.

Assessment Resources

Lesson Quiz 1.5

1. Find a function that fits the table.

x	$f(x)$
0	5
1	7
2	9
3	11

2. Is there a quadratic function that fits the table? If so, find one. If not, explain.

x	$f(x)$
0	5
1	7
2	9
3	11

3. Make a difference table for the cubic function $f(x) = 2x^3 - 1$. What is the relationship between the constant difference and the degree of the function?

Exercises

HOMEWORK

- Core: 13, 14, 15, 17, 18, 20
- Optional: 16, 21a–e, 22
- Extension: 19, 21f

Tony suspects that if the second differences are constant, a quadratic function will fit the table.

Theorem 1.4

If a table has constant second differences, there is some quadratic function that agrees with the table.

This is the converse of Theorem 1.3. It is true, and you can use Tony's method to prove it.

Exercises *Practicing Habits of Mind*

Check Your Understanding

1. Is there a quadratic function that fits the table below? If so, find one. If not, explain why.

n	$y(n)$
0	−2
1	6
2	24
3	52
4	90

2. Find a quadratic function that fits the table below.

n	$y(n)$
0	10
1	22
2	28
3	28
4	22

Answers

Exercises

1. yes; $y(n) = 5n^2 + 3n - 2$

2. $y(n) = -3n^2 + 15n + 10$

3.

w	$R(w)$	Δ	Δ^2	Δ^3
0	0	1	6	6
1	1	7	12	6
2	8	19	18	6
3	27	37	24	6
4	64	61	30	6
5	125	91	36	
6	216	127		
7	343			

Check Your Understanding

EXERCISE 3 appeared as a preview in the last lesson (Exercise 17 in Lesson 1.4). If you assigned it for that lesson, do not assign it here.

EXERCISE 5 Have students share their results. Confirm that the third difference is constant and equal to $6a$.

EXERCISE 6 This is an extremely important property of the Δ function: The Δ of the sum of two functions is the sum of their Δ s, and the Δ of kf is k times the Δ of f for all numbers k.

EXERCISE 7 proves the statements made in Exercise 5. Some students may want to try this, or even the general quartic (fourth-power polynomial).

Copy and complete the difference table for each function.

3. $R(w) = w^3$

w	R(w)	Δ	Δ^2	Δ^3
0	0	1	6	■
1	1	■	■	■
2	8	19	■	■
3	27	■	24	6
4	64	61	30	■
5	125	91	■	
6	216	■		
7	343			

4. $m(x) = 5x^3 + 2x^2 - 10x + 4$

x	m(x)	Δ	Δ^2	Δ^3
0	4	■	■	■
1	1	■	■	■
2	32	■	■	■
3	127	■	■	■
4	316	■	■	■
5	629	■	■	
6	1096	■		
7	1747			

Can you use your spreadsheet tool to create the difference table for you?

5. Write About It Make a difference table for a cubic function of your choice. Answer the following questions based on your tables from Exercises 3 and 4.

a. When does a cubic function yield constant differences?

b. What is the relationship between the constant difference and the leading coefficient?

A **cubic function** is a polynomial in which the highest-degree term is cubed. $f(x) = 3x^3 + 5x - 7$ is cubic, while $g(x) = 3x^2 + 5x - 7$ is quadratic.

6. Take It Further Sasha thinks she has an efficient way to do Exercise 4. She says, "I make a record of the formulas for the Δs of the basic powers like x^3, x^2, and so on.

- The Δ for $x \mapsto x^3$ is $x \mapsto 3x^2 + 3x + 1$.
- The Δ for $x \mapsto x^2$ is $x \mapsto 2x + 1$.
- The Δ for $x \mapsto x$ is $x \mapsto 1$.
- The Δ for $x \mapsto 1$ is $x \mapsto 0$.

So, the Δ for $x \mapsto 5x^3 + 2x^2 - 10x + 4$ is

$x \mapsto 5(3x^2 + 3x + 1) + 2(2x + 1) - 10(1) + 4(0)$."

Does Sasha's method work for all cubic functions? Justify your answer with a proof or a counterexample.

7. Take It Further Make a difference table for the general cubic function $f(x) = ax^3 + bx^2 + cx + d$. Include enough inputs and difference columns to show the constant difference.

4.

x	m(x)	Δ	Δ^2	Δ^3
0	4	−3	34	30
1	1	31	64	30
2	32	95	94	30
3	127	189	124	30
4	316	313	154	30
5	629	467	184	
6	1096	651		
7	1747			

5. a. The third differences are constant.

b. The constant third difference is 6 times the leading coefficient.

6. Yes; for any table with constant third differences, calculate $f(x + 1) - f(x)$ and show that the result can be put into Sasha's form.

7. The Δ column begins $a + b + c$, $7a + 3b + c$, $19a + 5b + c$; the Δ^2 column begins $6a + 2b$, $12a + 2b$, $18a + 2b$; the Δ^3 column begins $6a$, $6a$, $6a$.

EXERCISE 8 You may want to have students observe that the leading coefficient is the product of the leading coefficients of each of the factors: $(1)(1)(1) = 1$, and that the constant term is the product of the constant terms of the factors: $(-1)(-3)(-6) = -18$.

EXERCISE 9 Students should be able to fill in the Δ^3 column right away. Since the leading coefficient is 1, the constant third difference is $6(1) = 6$.

EXERCISE 11 This is the Fibonacci sequence. There is no constant difference, but there is a pattern to each difference column.

8. a. Find three values of x that make the following equation true.

$$(x - 3)(x - 5)(x - 6) = 0$$

b. Expand the expression $(x - 3)(x - 5)(x - 6)$ so that it has no parentheses.

9. Copy and complete the difference table for the following function.

$$v(x) = (x - 3)(x - 5)(x - 6)$$

x	$v(x)$	Δ	Δ^2	Δ^3
0	−90	■	■	■
1	−40	■	■	■
2	−12	■	■	■
3	0	■	■	■
4	2	■	■	■
5	0	■	■	
6	0	■		
7	8			

Habits of Mind

Look for patterns. What is the degree of $(x - 1)(x - 3)(x - 6)$? What is the constant term? Can you answer these questions without expanding or using a CAS?

You can define $v(x)$ in your CAS and ask for $v(x + 1) - v(x)$. Make sure you have not assigned any value to x.

10. Find a quadratic function that fits the table below.

Input	Output
0	7
1	−6
2	1
3	28
4	75

11. Use this table for $F(n)$ from Lesson 1.3. Use difference tables to answer the following questions.

a. Could the table have come from a cubic function?

b. Describe any patterns you find in the repeated difference that comes from the function.

n	$F(n)$
0	1
1	1
2	2
3	3
4	5
5	8
6	13

Answers

8. a. $x = 3, x = 5, x = 6$

b. $x^3 - 14x^2 + 63x - 90$

9.

x	$v(x)$	Δ	Δ^2	Δ^3
0	90	50	−22	6
1	−40	28	−16	6
2	−12	12	−10	6
3	0	2	−4	6
4	2	−2	2	6
5	0	0	8	
6	0	8		
7	8			

10. $f(x) = 10x^2 - 23x + 7$

11. a. No, the third differences are not constant.

b. Except for the left column, each entry is equal to the entry that is one to the right and one down.

12. **Take It Further** Find a function that fits the table at the right.

Input	Output
0	−3
1	−5
2	−5
3	9
4	49
5	127

On Your Own

13. Could the table at the right have come from a quadratic function? Explain.

n	$y(n)$
0	−7
1	−5
2	3
3	23
4	61

For Exercises 14 and 15, find a function that agrees with each table.

14.

Input, a	Output, b
0	25
1	11
2	−3
3	−17
4	−31

15.

n	$c(n)$
0	−8
1	0
2	4
3	4
4	0

16. Use the table at the right for $D(n)$ from Lesson 1.3.

Use difference tables to answer these questions.

a. Could the table have come from a cubic function?

b. Describe any patterns you find in the difference table.

n	$D(n)$
0	1
1	2
2	4
3	8
4	16
5	32
6	64

Go Online PHSchool.com

For additional practice, go to Web Code: bfa-0105

EXERCISE 12 requires persistence, attention to detail, and accurate computation, but students may find the process satisfying. You might suggest that students work with a partner. They should check their computations at each step.

On Your Own

EXERCISE 13 Students may note that the table could come from a cubic rule. You might ask them to find the cubic rule as an extension. The rule is $y(n) = n^3 + n - 1$.

EXERCISE 16 The difference column just repeats the original outputs moved up one row. Students might recognize that there is a common ratio $\left(\frac{2}{1} = 2, \frac{4}{2} = 2, \frac{8}{4} = 2, \text{etc.}\right)$, not a common difference. Exponential functions will be discussed in a future chapter.

12. $f(n) = 2n^3 - 5n^2 + n - 3$

13. No; the second differences are not constant.

14. $b = -14a + 25$

15. $c(n) = -2n^2 + 10n - 8$

16. a. No, the third differences are not constant.

b. Each column of differences is 1, 2, 4, 8, 16, . . . , which is the same as the column of output values.

EXERCISE 18 is meant to stimulate ideas in the upcoming investigation on fitting functions to data.

EXERCISE 19 is time-consuming and requires considerable accuracy and attention to detail. Students who can solve this exercise may be able to discover Newton's Difference Formula with a few more examples.

Maintain Your Skills

EXERCISE 21 For two of the items in this exercise, students have the option to choose their own functions. You may want to use your CAS to factor their functions, if they have expanded them, or to check their input-output tables.

EXERCISE 22 previews Investigation 2B on Lagrange interpolation.

Additional Resources

PRINT RESOURCES
- Solution Manual
- Practice Workbook
- Assessment Resources
- Teaching Resources

TECHNOLOGY
- Interactive Textbook
- TeacherExpress CD-ROM
- ExamView CD-ROM
- PHSchool.com

Additional Practice

1. A line contains the points $(-2, 3)$ and $(4, -9)$.
   a. Find the slope of the line.
   b. Find the value of a such that the point $(3, a)$ lies on the line.
   c. Find the value of b such that the point $(b, -4)$ lies on the line.

2. A line connects the points $(-5, 3)$ and $(-3, 9)$.
   a Draw the line on a coordinate plane.
   b. Find the slope of the line.
   c. Write an equation for the line.

3. A line connects the points $(3, 11)$ and $(-4, 11)$.
   a. Draw the line on a coordinate plane.
   b. Describe the slope of the line.
   c. Write an equation for the line.

4. Use differences to find a linear rule that agrees with the table.

Input	Output
0	4
1	7
2	10
3	13

For Exercises 5–7, find a function that agrees with each table.

5.

n	$a(n)$
0	12
1	8
2	4
3	0

6.

n	$b(n)$
0	−3
1	0
2	5
3	12

7.

n	$c(n)$
0	1
1	3
2	17
3	55

8. Use the input-output table. Show that the table could not have come from a linear, quadratic, or cubic function.

Input, x	Output, y
1	2
2	2
3	4
4	6
5	10

Practice: For Lesson 1.5, assign Exercises 5–8.

For Exercises 17–19, use the input-output table below.

Input, x	Output, y
0	1
1	1
2	4
3	7
4	12

17. Show that the table could not have come from a linear, quadratic, or cubic function.

18. None of the rules below exactly matches the input-output table, but which rule is the closest fit? Explain.

Rule 1: $y = 2x - 5$ Rule 2: $y = 2.8x - 0.6$

Rule 3: $y = x^2 - x + 1$ Rule 4: $y = x^3 - 3x^2 - 2x + 1$

19. Take It Further Find a polynomial function that fits the table exactly.

20. Standardized Test Prep What is the value of the constant third differences of the cubic function $f(x) = x^3 + 2x^2 + 7$?

A. 0 **B.** 3

C. 6 **D.** 7

Maintain Your Skills

21. Make an input-output table for each function. Use the inputs 0 through 5.

a. $f(x) = (x - 7)(x - 2)$ **b.** $g(x) = (x - 6)(x - 13)$

c. $h(x) = x(x - 9)$ **d.** $j(x) = 3(x - 1)(x - 3)$

e. a function $k(x)$ for which $k(5)$ and $k(6)$ both equal zero

f. Take It Further a function $m(x)$ for which $m(0) = 0, m(1) = 0, m(2) = 0$, and $m(3) = 24$

22. Make an input-output table for each function. Use the inputs 0 through 4.

a. $f(x) = 3x$ **b.** $g(x) = 3x + x$

c. $h(x) = 3x + x(x - 1)$ **d.** $j(x) = 3x + x(x - 1)(x - 2)$

e. a function $k(x)$ that is different from $f(x)$, but has the same outputs for the inputs 0 through 4 (For example, the two functions might have different outputs for an input of 5.)

Answers

17. None of the first, second, or third differences are constant, so the table is not a linear, quadratic, or cubic function.

18. Answers may vary. Sample: Rule 3; Rules 1 and 2 do not give any y-values that match the table, while Rules 3 and 4 both give three y-values that match the table. For Rule 3, the other two y-values differ from the y-values in the table by 1, while for Rule 4, the other two y-values differ from the y-values in the table by 3 and 13.

19. $y = \frac{5}{24}x^4 - \frac{7}{4}x^3 + \frac{127}{24}x^2 - \frac{15}{4}x + 1$

20. 6

21–22. See back of book.

Mathematical Reflections 1A

In this investigation, you learned how to find closed-form and recursive function definitions that fit tables and how to use difference tables to decide whether a linear or quadratic function fits a given table. These questions will help you summarize what you have learned.

Use Table B for Exercises 1 and 2.

Table B

Input, n	Output, $B(n)$
0	1
1	3
2	7
3	13
4	21

1. Find a recursively defined function g that agrees with Table B.
2. Find a closed-form definition for a function f that agrees with Table B.
3. Find an equation for the line that contains (2, 5) and (−4, 8).
4. How can you tell whether there is a linear function that fits a table?
5. How can you use differences to decide what type of function fits a table?
6. What polynomial function agrees with this table?

Input	Output
0	1
1	5
2	11
3	19
4	29
5	41

You can use the polynomial function that describes the frog's motion to predict the time the frog will land.

Vocabulary

In this investigation, you learned these terms.
Make sure you understand what each one means and how to use it.

- **closed-form definition**
- **cubic function**
- **difference table**
- **hockey stick property**
- **quadratic function**
- **recursive definition**
- **slope**
- **up-and-over property**

Mathematical Reflections

EXERCISES 4–6 At the start of the investigation, you may have assigned these as Questions 1–3 for students to think and write about.

Mathematical Reflections

1. $g(n) = \begin{cases} 1 & \text{if } n = 0 \\ g(n-1) + 2n & \text{if } n > 0 \end{cases}$
2. $f(n) = n^2 + n + 1$
3. $x + 2y = 12$
4. If the first differences are constant, then a linear function fits the table.
5. If the nth differences are constant, then a function of degree n fits the table.
6. $f(x) = x^2 + 3x + 1$

Investigation Overview

This investigation has two major goals:

- Students develop a statistical perspective and think of data in terms of trends, rather than as sets of individual points.
- You can eliminate the "big black box" of statistical calculations. Students learn what the graphing calculator is doing when it performs calculations, as well as determining when those calculations are appropriate.

The investigation continues work in data from *Algebra 1* as well as work from Investigation 1A, in which students were asked to find rules that fit tables. In that investigation, students were looking for exact fits. In this investigation—because they should be more concerned with trends than actual data points—they can think about fitting lines (or curves) that describe the trend efficiently, rather than lines or curves that contain every data point.

Students find lines of best fit and determine when linear fits are appropriate to use. In situations where linear fits are not appropriate to use, students use quadratic and exponential fits. After developing an independent perspective on data analysis, students take a tour of the graphing calculator so that they can use the tool effectively, including use of the formula that the calculator uses to find the line of best fit.

You may wish to assign Questions 1–3 for students to think and write about during the investigation.

Learning Goals

- Decide whether a linear function reasonably represents a data set.
- Calculate the balance point of a data set.
- Estimate the slope of a fitting line.
- Calculate error, given a data set and a fitting function.
- Calculate the mean absolute error, mean squared error, and standard error.
- Use algebra to find the line of best fit for a set of data.

Habits and Skills

- Compare measures of error in data.
- Approximate scatter plots with graphs of simple functions.
- Graph linear equations.
- Evaluate the quality of a function's agreement with data.
- Use absolute value and square roots in calculation of error.

Investigation 1B

Fitting and Data

In *Fitting and Data,* you will learn to analyze data. This includes real data that you quite likely cannot fit with a simple rule. For some types of real data, you will learn how to find a line that best fits the data. You will use the line of best fit to analyze the data and make predictions.

By the end of this investigation, you will be able to answer questions like these:

1. How do you find a line that fits a set of data?
2. What is the definition of the line of best fit?
3. What is the line of best fit for the data in the table at the right?

Men's 1500-meter Olympic Gold Medal Times (seconds)

Year	Time	Year	Time	Year	Time
1896	273.2	1932	231.2	1972	216.3
1900	246.2	1936	227.8	1976	219.2
1904	245.4	1948	229.8	1980	218.4
1908	243.4	1952	225.1	1984	212.5
1912	236.8	1956	221.2	1988	215.96
1920	241.8	1960	215.6	1992	220.12
1924	233.6	1964	218.1	1996	215.78
1928	233.2	1968	214.9	2000	212.07

SOURCE: *2007 ESPN Sports Almanac*

You will learn how to:

- decide whether a linear function reasonably represents a data set
- calculate the balance point of a data set
- estimate the slope of a fitting line
- calculate error, given a data set and a fitting function
- calculate the mean absolute error, mean squared error, and standard error
- use algebra to find the line of best fit for a set of data

You will develop these habits and skills:

- Compare measures of error in data.
- Approximate scatter plots with graphs of simple functions.
- Graph linear equations.
- Evaluate the quality of a function's agreement with data.
- Use absolute value and square roots in calculations of error.

Investigation Road Map

LESSON 1.6, *Getting Started,* involves an experiment with a number cube. Students keep track of the cumulative sum of *n* rolls. The scatter plot of rolls against sum is close to linear, introducing the idea of a fitting line.

LESSON 1.7, *Fitting Lines to Data,* formally introduces the fitting line, including calculation of the balance point of a data set, estimation for the slope of the best fit line, and error, the difference between the data and the expected value from the fitting function.

LESSON 1.8, *The Line of Best Fit, Part 1,* defines various measures of "badness," or error, for a line with respect to a data set.

LESSON 1.9, *The Line of Best Fit, Part 2,* has students continue working with lines of best fit. They see how the calculator determines the line of best fit for a data set.

1.6 Getting Started

Activating Prior Knowledge
Exploring New Ideas

The problems in this lesson are about an experiment with a number cube. You will build a table that shows the number of rolls of the number cube and the cumulative total for all the rolls. For example, your table might look like the one below after 5 rolls.

Rolls	Total
0	0
1	5
2	10
3	14
4	16
5	22
⋮	⋮

Why is the total zero after zero rolls, and not some other number?

For You to Explore

With a partner, roll a number cube 20 times.

1. Record the cumulative totals in a table like the one above. Then make a difference table for your results. It might look like the table below.

Rolls	Total	Δ
0	0	5
1	5	5
2	10	4
3	14	2
4	16	6
5	22	

How do the numbers in the Δ column relate to the results of the rolls?

2. **Write About It** Look at the difference table you made in Problem 1. Is there a linear function that matches the table? Justify your answer.
3. Bethany rolls a number cube 100 times and records the total. Which of these totals is the most likely after 100 rolls? Explain.

A. 98 **B.** 256
C. 354 **D.** 412

Lesson Overview

GOAL

- Decide whether a linear function reasonably represents a data set.

The investigation begins with a variant on the difference tables students learned about in Investigation 1A. Students probably will not expect that the table and scatter plot they are building here will be nearly linear. Students already know how to find the equation of a line when all the points are on the line, but how can they find the equation for a situation where the points approximate a line?

The fact that some of the observations are surprising means that students should compare results often. You might have students report their results to the class or display one large data set that contains the work of all students.

FOR YOU TO EXPLORE
- Core: 1, 2, 3, 4, 5, 6

MATERIALS
- CAS (recommended)
- graph paper
- graphing calculators
- number cubes
- spreadsheet software

HOMEWORK
- Core: 7, 8, 9, 10, 11, 13, 14
- Optional: 12, 15, 16, 17

VOCABULARY
- balance point

Launch

You may wish to have students work in pairs or small groups for this experiment. Partners take turns rolling the number cube and recording the results.

Explore

Check that students are reaching reasonable results. If time is limited, consider stopping the experiment after 10 rolls instead of 20 rolls. Results may not be as clear to students due to random behavior, but it will speed up the experiment.

For You to Explore

PROBLEM 2 serves as a reminder of how you can generate a linear table (constant differences). It also sets up the later problems on expected value and the slope of the line of best fit. This is also a good place for students to catch any errors in their data recording, since the Δ value must always be between 1 and 6. Elicit the fact that one would expect the total to go up about $3\frac{1}{2}$ (the average of the numbers from 1 through 6) with each new roll.

PROBLEM 3 pushes students toward the idea of an expected value. Astute students will recognize here that the expected value for a single roll is the mean of the faces on the number cube. If this topic comes up, you may want to discuss it.

Answers

For You to Explore

1. Answers may vary. The difference column should show the results of the individual rolls.
2. The difference column, which shows the individual rolls, is unlikely to be constant (that would mean the same number was rolled each time), so no linear function will match the table.
3. The average roll is $\frac{1+2+3+4+5+6}{6} = 3.5$, so the expected total after 100 rolls is 350; choice (C) is the most likely total.

PROBLEM 4 Again, this is a good problem for full-class discussion, since one group's findings will be supported by the fact that other groups found similar patterns. It is unlikely that a group's graph will not be close to linear, unless students made mistakes in recording the data.

PROBLEM 5 Asking students to compare answers as a class may be useful here, since it is possible for groups to disagree between parts (c), (d), and (e). Most groups will likely select (d) as the best fit. Some students may think to use a calculator to find the actual best-fit line if they are familiar with the calculator's capabilities.

Wrap Up

For You to Explore Problems 4 and 5 are the most important problems of the lesson. If time allows, go over as much of these two problems as possible. As always in a Getting Started lesson, there is no need to formalize the mathematics. Just get students talking about their own ideas and findings.

4. Draw a scatter plot with the number of rolls r on the horizontal axis and the total T on the vertical axis. Here is a plot for the number cube example on the previous page.

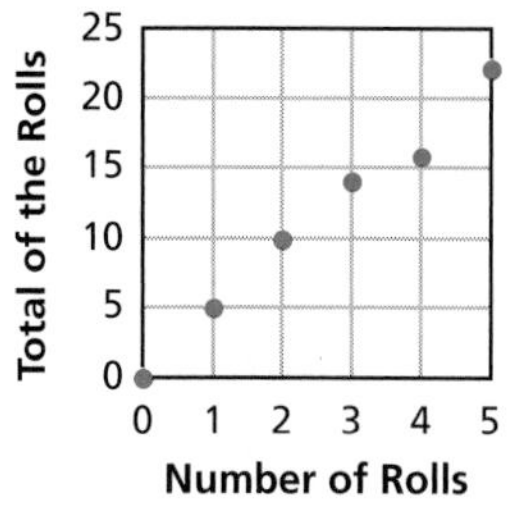

Your graph should go from 0 to 20 on the horizontal axis.

Describe your graph. How does your graph compare with the graphs of other groups?

5. On the same coordinate axes as your data, plot T against r for each of the functions below. Which function best fits the trends in your data? Which fits the worst?

a. $T = r + 30$

b. $T + 3r = 60$

c. $T = 2.5r$

d. $T = 3.5r$

e. $T = 4.5r$

6. Think about a ruler with weights hanging from it.

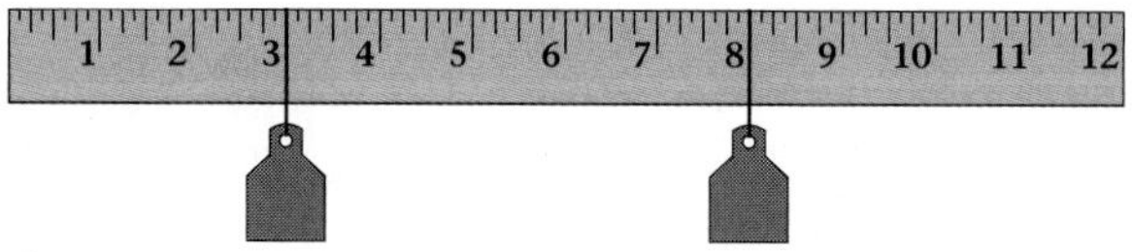

For the purpose of this exercise, assume the ruler is weightless and all the weights are equal.

a. Suppose the ruler has two weights on it, at 3 inches and 8 inches. Where can you place the ruler on your finger to balance the weights?

b. Suppose the two weights are at x inches and y inches. Write a rule that tells you where the ruler's balance point is.

c. Suppose the ruler has three weights on it, at 1 inch, 3 inches, and 8 inches. Where is the ruler's balance point?

Answers

4. Answers may vary, but all the graphs will be nearly linear.

5. best: choice (d); worst: choice (b)

6. a. 5.5 in.

b. $\frac{x + y}{2}$ in.

c. 4 in.

Exercises *Practicing Habits of Mind*

On Your Own

7. **Write About It** There were no Olympic Games held in 1916, 1940, or 1944, due to the two world wars. How can you make a guess about what the winning time would have been for the 1500-meter run in 1944? How can you make the same sort of predictions for Olympic Games in the future?

8. **a.** Lisa takes three tests. She gets scores of 85, 82, and 91. What is her average?

b. A meter stick has three weights on it, at 85 cm, 82 cm, and 91 cm. Where is the ruler's balance point?

> Assume the ruler is weightless and all the weights are equal.

9. Every 10 years, the U.S. Census is taken. One of the reported calculations is the location in the United States that is the center of population. The report says,

> The concept of the center of population as used by the U.S. Census Bureau is that of a balance point. That is, the center of population is the point at which [a map of the country] would balance if weights of identical size were placed on it so that each weight represented the location of one person.

a. According to the Census Bureau, the population center of the U.S. has moved west in every census since its inception in 1790. Give some possible reasons why this has happened.

b. A Census Bureau report explains how to calculate the center.

> [T]he latitude of the center of population was determined by multiplying the population of each unit of area by the latitude of its population center, then adding all these products and dividing this total by the total population of the United States. The result is the latitude of the population center.

What mathematical calculation is the Census Bureau describing?

> **Habits of Mind**
> **Look for relationships.** In geometry, you called balance points *centroids*. Is there a connection here?

10. The table below shows the coordinates of some points (x, y).

x	y
0	4
1	7
2	10
5	19
8	28

a. How do you know that these points lie on a line?

b. Find the equation of the line.

c. Find the balance point for these five points by calculating the mean of the x-coordinates and the mean of the y-coordinates.

d. Show that the balance point is on the line.

> Do not forget about the zero in the input list when calculating the mean of the five inputs.

Exercises

HOMEWORK
- Core: 7, 8, 9, 10, 11, 13, 14
- Optional: 12, 15, 16, 17

On Your Own

EXERCISE 7 will be a focus in Lesson 1.7. Assign this exercise to give students some experience with the topic of approximating a line of best fit and using that line to estimate a missing value.

EXERCISE 8 is intended to draw the connection between the balance point and the calculation of the mean. Most students will know how to calculate Lisa's average, but not every student will see the connection to balance points.

EXERCISE 9 simulates the idea of the mean point $(\bar{x}, \bar{y})$ as the center of data. It helps explain why this point is used as part of the equation for the best fit line.

EXERCISE 10 One goal of this exercise is to introduce the calculation of the balance point $(\bar{x}, \bar{y})$ and to note that if all the points you are balancing lie on a line, this balance point is also on that line. In general, if all points (x_i, y_i) satisfy $y = ax + b$, then $(\bar{x}, \bar{y})$ also satisfies the equation. Proving this is a good exercise in algebra. Suppose, for example, that there are three points (x_1, y_1), (x_2, y_2), (x_3, y_3) that satisfy $y = ax + b$. Then

$$\begin{aligned} a\bar{x} + b &= a\left(\frac{x_1 + x_2 + x_3}{3}\right) + b \\ &= \frac{a(x_1 + x_2 + x_3) + 3b}{3} \\ &= \frac{ax_1 + b + ax_2 + b + ax_3 + b}{3} \\ &= \frac{y_1 + y_2 + y_3}{3} = \bar{y} \end{aligned}$$

Exercises

7. Answers may vary. Sample: Find an equation that fits the given data, and use that equation for the year(s) in question.

8. **a.** 86
b. 86 cm

9. **a.** Answers may vary. Sample: More people are living in the western regions of the country.
b. finding the mean

10. **a.** For each pair of points the slope is 3, so the points lie on a line.
b. $y = 3x + 4$
c. (3.2, 13.6)
d. Answers may vary. Sample: The slope for (3.2, 13.6) and (0, 4) is $\frac{9.6}{3.2} = 3$, so (3.2, 13.6) is on the same line as the points in the table.

EXERCISE 11 Since you will use the balance point in calculating the line of best fit, it is important to recognize that the balance point lies along a linear trend for a data set.

EXERCISE 12 Students will revisit these particular functions in Lesson 1.8, Check Your Understanding, Exercise 4.

Maintain Your Skills

EXERCISES 13–16 This set of exercises helps students understand the meaning of the balance point of a set of data—it *balances* out the differences between individual data points.

11. The table below shows the coordinates of some points (x, y).

x	y
3	2
6	3
8	5
11	5
12	6

a. Plot the five points. How do you know that the points are not collinear?

b. These points follow a linear trend. Estimate the slope of a line that closely approximates the data.

c. Find the balance point for these five points.

d. Plot the balance point on the same graph as the five points. Explain why the balance point might be a good anchor for a line of best fit.

Habits of Mind

Communicate by context. Points are collinear if they lie on the same line. What do you think *linear trend* might mean?

12. Find the value of p that minimizes each function.

a. $p \mapsto 158.86 - 47.2 + 4p^2$ **b.** $p \mapsto 52.26 - 27.2p + 4p^2$

c. $p \mapsto 5.66 - 7.2p + 4p^2$ **d.** $p \mapsto 19.06 + 12.8p + 4p^2$

Maintain Your Skills

The **balance point** $(\bar{x}, \bar{y})$ is the point with x-coordinate that is the average of the x-coordinates in the table and with y-coordinate that is the average of the y-coordinates in the table.

For Exercises 13–16, do the following steps.

Step 1: Compute the balance point $(\bar{x}, \bar{y})$.

Step 2: Build a new table by subtracting $\bar{x}$ from each x-value and subtracting $\bar{y}$ from each y-value.

Step 3: Compute the balance point for the new (x, y) values.

Step 4: Make and justify some conjectures about this process.

13.

x	y
0	4
1	7
2	10
5	19
8	28

→

$x - \bar{x}$	$y - \bar{y}$
■	■
■	■
■	■
■	■
■	■

Answers

11. a.

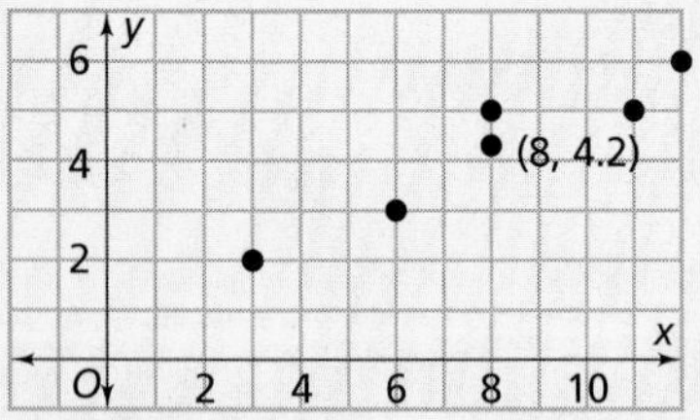

The slopes for pairs of points are not equal, so the points are not collinear.

b. Answers may vary. Sample: $\frac{1}{2}$

c. (8, 4.2)

d. See part (a). The balance point is a good "anchor point" because it is on the line that approximates the data and the sum of the distances from the balance point to the data values on each side of it are equal.

12. a. 5.9 **b.** 3.4

c. 0.9 **d.** −1.6

13. Step 1: (3.2, 13.6)

Step 2:

$x - \bar{x}$	$y - \bar{y}$
−3.2	−9.6
−2.2	−6.6
−1.2	−3.6
1.8	5.4
4.8	14.4

Step 3: about (0, 0)

Step 4: Answers will vary. Sample: The balance points for the tables are the means of the columns.

14.

x	y
3	2
6	3
8	5
11	5
12	6

→

$x-\bar{x}$	$y-\bar{y}$
■	■
■	■
■	■
■	■
■	■

15.

x	y
1900	246.2
1904	245.4
1908	243.4
1912	236.8
1920	241.8
1924	233.6
1928	233.2

→

$x-\bar{x}$	$y-\bar{y}$
■	■
■	■
■	■
■	■
■	■
■	■
■	■

16.

x	y
73	6
22	66
16	54
60	18
6	9
73	13
10	82
6	85
8	73
33	57

→

$x-\bar{x}$	$y-\bar{y}$
■	■
■	■
■	■
■	■
■	■
■	■
■	■
■	■
■	■
■	■

17. Show that the following identity is true.

$$(a-b)^2 = 2(a^2+b^2) - (a+b)^2$$

To slide along a grind rail, a skateboarder finds a balance point. How is a physical balance point related to the balance point of a data set?

EXERCISE 15 Ask students to estimate the balance point before they calculate it. If they know what to expect, they might recognize any possible calculation error.

EXERCISE 17 is a good exercise to strengthen students' algebra skills. They can verify that the two sides of the identity are the same on their CAS, but they should also perform the calculations. Remind them to be careful of the negative sign in front of $(a+b)^2$.

14. Step 1: (8, 4.2)

Step 2:

$x-\bar{x}$	$y-\bar{y}$
−5	−2.2
−2	−1.2
0	0.8
3	0.8
4	1.8

Step 3: (0, 0)

Step 4: Answers will vary. Sample: The balance points for the tables are the means of the columns.

15. Step 1: (1913.7, 240.1)

Step 2:

$x-\bar{x}$	$y-\bar{y}$
−13.7	6.1
−9.7	5.3
−5.7	3.3
−1.7	−3.3
6.3	1.7
10.3	−6.5
14.3	−6.9

Step 3: (0, 0)

Step 4: Answers will vary. Sample: The balance points for the tables are the means of the columns.

16. Step 1: (30.7, 46.3)

Step 2: See back of book.

Step 3: (0, 0)

Step 4: Answers will vary. Sample: The balance points for the tables are the means of the columns.

17. $(a-b)^2 = 2(a^2+b^2) - (a+b)^2$

$= 2a^2 + 2b^2 - (a^2 + 2ab + b^2)$

$= a^2 - 2ab + b^2$

$= (a-b)^2$

The original equation is an identity.

Lesson Overview

GOALS

- Calculate the balance point of a data set.
- Estimate the slope of a fitting line.

The goal of this lesson is to help students understand what a fitting line is, and when a linear fit is appropriate to use for a data set. The development is somewhat unusual: students calculate the balance point (a central point for the data set) and use that to find a fitting line. The actual best fit line for a data set will always pass through the balance point.

Error, the difference between the actual value in data and the value predicted by the fitting function, is also introduced in this lesson. Students will use errors in the next lesson to make decisions about the quality of a fitting function.

CHECK YOUR UNDERSTANDING
- Core: 1, 2, 3, 4
- Optional: 5, 6

MATERIALS
- CAS (recommended)
- graph paper
- graphing calculators
- spreadsheet software
- Blackline Masters 1.7A–C

HOMEWORK
- Core: 7, 9a–b, 10, 12, 13, 14
- Optional: 8, 11, 15, 16, 17, 18
- Extension: 9c

VOCABULARY
- outlier

Launch

Refer to Exercise 7 from Lesson 1.6. This exercise sets up the exposition at the start of this lesson.

Ask students to look at the graph and estimate the coordinates of the balance point without actually doing any calculations. Ask volunteers to explain how they got their answer. The balance point should be about (1950, 230).

You can use Blackline Masters 1.7A and 1.7B to make a transparency of the 1500-meter data table and scatter plot.

1.7 Fitting Lines to Data

The table below shows the winning times for the men's 1500-meter run at each Olympics from 1896 until 2000.

Men's 1500-meter Olympic Gold Medal Times (seconds)

Year	Time	Year	Time	Year	Time
1896	273.2	**1932**	231.2	**1972**	216.3
1900	246.2	**1936**	227.8	**1976**	219.2
1904	245.4	**1948**	229.8	**1980**	218.4
1908	243.4	**1952**	225.1	**1984**	212.5
1912	236.8	**1956**	221.2	**1988**	215.96
1920	241.8	**1960**	215.6	**1992**	220.12
1924	233.6	**1964**	218.1	**1996**	215.78
1928	233.2	**1968**	214.9	**2000**	212.07

SOURCE: *2007 ESPN Sports Almanac*

Go Online PHSchool.com

For more practice with scatter plots, go to **Web Code:** bfe-9031

Here is a scatter plot for the data.

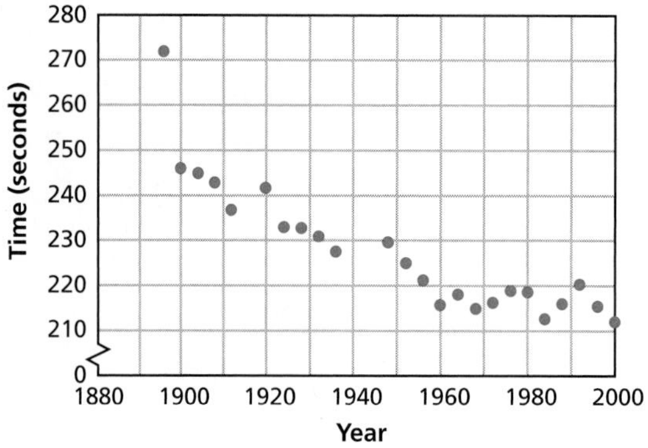

The data point for the 1896 Olympics is far away from the rest. Such a point is an **outlier**. Except for the 1896 data point, there is a general downward trend that seems to follow a straight path. It makes sense to approximate the data with a line.

On the other hand, the trend after 1960 seems to level out. You will investigate this idea in Exercise 6.

In your first-year algebra course, you learned that a line with slope m through the point (h, k) has the following equation.

$$y - k = m(x - h)$$

In order to use this method for finding the equation of a fitting line, you need a point on the line and a slope.

When the data seem to follow a linear trend, a good anchor point for your fitting line is the balance point of the data. For the gold medal data, the balance point is (1949.8, 227.82). Throwing out the 1896 data point gives a slightly different balance point of (1952.2, 225.85).

Right now, you do not have a good definition of the best possible fitting line, so all you can do is approximate the slope of a fitting line that looks good to you. Later in this investigation, you will develop the definition of the line of best fit, and explore the reasons why that definition makes sense.

Remember...

The balance point (or centroid) has x-coordinate equal to the average of the x-coordinates of the data. Its y-coordinate is equal to the average of the y-coordinates of the data.

For You to Do

Copy the scatter plot of the gold medal data.

1. Use the balance point that excludes (1896, 273.2) and a slope that you estimate to draw a fitting line for the 1500-meter data. Find the equation of your line.
2. The Olympic Games were not held in 1944 because of World War II. Use your equation to estimate what a winning time in the 1944 Olympics might have been.

Habits of Mind

Look for relationships. Later in this course, you will do arithmetic and algebra with points. Then the balance point will just be the average of the data points. What would be a good way to add (3, 2) and (5, −1)?

Developing Habits of Mind

Establish a process. Start thinking about how to decide whether one fitting line is better than another. Then you can develop the definition of the best-fit line.

Look at the table of gold medal times. When you plot the data, the vertical axis tells you the outcome of each race. The horizontal axis tells you when each outcome happened. If you want to use a line to predict future outcomes, you want the line's y-height at each year to be close to the y-height for the data point for that year. For example, you want the height of the line at 1920 to be close to 241.8.

You want a line that comes as close as possible to all the outcomes. So, you want to somehow minimize the overall differences between the data and the line's y-values.

Explore

For You to Do

To estimate the slope, students can actually draw a line through the balance point that seems to follow the trend of the data. Point out that the units on the horizontal axis are years and the units on the vertical axis are seconds. So, the slope has seconds/year as units. Ask:

What would a slope of $-\frac{1}{4}$ mean for this problem? (Answer: The time decreases by 1 second every 4 years.)

Developing Habits of Mind

This text introduces the calculation of error in relation to a line of best fit and brings issues of fit quality. These ideas are the focus of the next few lessons, so this is just a preview.

Blackline Master 1.7C provides a copy of the error table shown on the next page.

Answers

For You to Do

1. Answers may vary. Sample: $y - 225.84 = -0.332(x - 1952.2)$
2. Using the equation from Problem 1 above, a value for the winning time is 228.6 seconds.

For Discussion

This brief discussion should lead to a couple of topics: absolute value (very likely to be mentioned right away) and squaring. Squaring is the more important topic, since it supports calculations like variance and standard deviation. If you choose to have this discussion, make sure to elicit both absolute value and squaring.

Developing Habits of Mind

The line actually crosses the x-axis around $x = 2623$. Discuss what might actually happen to this data in the future. Is it really possible that the time for a 1500 m race can even reach 10 seconds? 20 seconds? The students should realize that the improvements in time will probably get smaller and smaller as time nears some limit. What will happen to the slope of the line of best fit? Are there functions that approach a horizontal line as x gets larger, but do not cross that horizontal line? If the line of best fit is locally a good predictor, then would it sometimes be better to calculate the line of best fit as a piecewise function?

Wrap Up

Assessment Resources

Lesson Quiz 1.7

For Exercises 1 and 2, use the table of data at the right.

Input	Output
1	0.5
2	1.3
3	2.1
4	2.8
5	3.5
6	4.3
7	5.1

1. a. Draw a scatter plot for the points in the table.
b. Calculate and plot the balance point.
c. Explain whether it is reasonable to fit a line to the data.

2. a. Find the equation of a line that contains the balance point.
b. Show that the sum of the differences between the data and the corresponding points on your line is 0.

The table below shows the calculation of the errors for one possible fitting line for the 1500-meter data. In the equation, x is the year and y is the time in seconds.

Data vs. Line Fit
$y = -0.34x + 892.1$

Year	Actual Time	Predicted Time	Error: Actual – Predicted
1900	246.2	246.1	0.1
1904	245.4	244.7	0.7
1908	243.4	243.4	0.0
1912	236.8	242.0	−5.2
1920	241.8	239.3	2.5
1924	233.6	237.9	−4.3
⋮	⋮	⋮	⋮
1992	220.12	214.8	5.32
1996	215.78	213.5	2.28
2000	212.07	212.1	−0.03

You often cannot make all the numbers in the error column small with one linear function. A line that makes one error small may make another error large. So you need some idea of overall error. Calculating the overall error is not as simple as just adding all the numbers in the error column, since negative and positive errors can cancel each other.

In fact, for any line that contains the balance point, the total sum of all the errors equals 0. See Exercise 9.

For Discussion

3. Think of a function you can apply to the numbers in the error column so you can add them together to get one measure of total error.

Developing Habits of Mind

Consider more than one strategy. You can always draw a line to approximate the data in a scatter plot. Sometimes, however, curves do a better job of minimizing error.

Even when lines do a good job of approximating the data, they often do it only locally. For example, you cannot use the line for $y = -0.34x + 892.1$ to predict 1500-meter times too far into the future. It would predict negative times. For what year does this first happen?

Answers

For Discussion

3. Answers may vary. Sample: Find the mean of the absolute values of the numbers in the Error column.

Exercises

1. a. Answers may vary. Samples: $y = 2x$, $y = x + 3$, $y = 6$
b. $7x + 5y = 51$

2. a–b.

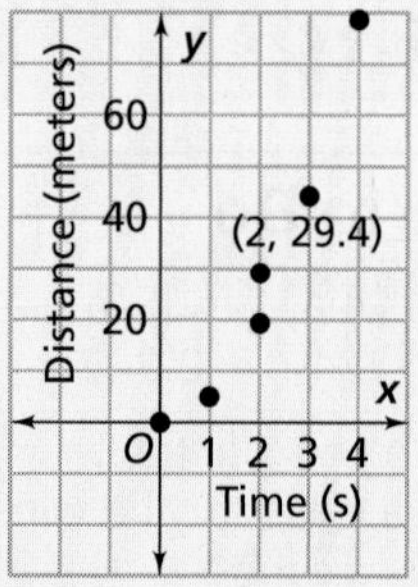

b. (2, 29.4)
c. No; the points seem to lie on a curve, not a line.

Exercises *Practicing Habits of Mind*

Check Your Understanding

1. **a.** Find the equations of three different lines that contain the point (3, 6).

b. Find the equation of the one line that contains (3, 6) and (8, −1).

For Exercises 2 and 3, do parts (a)–(c).

a. Draw a scatter plot for the points in the table.

b. Calculate and plot the balance point.

c. Explain whether it is reasonable to fit a line to the data.

2.

Time (seconds)	Distance (meters)
0	0
1	4.9
2	19.6
3	44.1
4	78.4

3.

Time (seconds)	$\sqrt{\text{Distance}}$ ($\sqrt{\text{meters}}$)
0	0
1	2.21
2	4.43
3	6.64
4	8.85

The numbers in the second column in Exercise 3 are the approximate square roots of the distances in Exercise 2.

4. Use the table of data at the right.

Plot the data points and the four lines given below on the same axes. Which line do you think fits the data best? Explain your choice.

A. $y = x + 1$ **B.** $y = 0.5x + 2.5$

C. $y = 0.9x + 0.9$ **D.** $y = x + 0.5$

Input	Output
1	1.8
2	1.7
3	3.6
5	5.4
6	7.3
7	7.2

3. a–b.

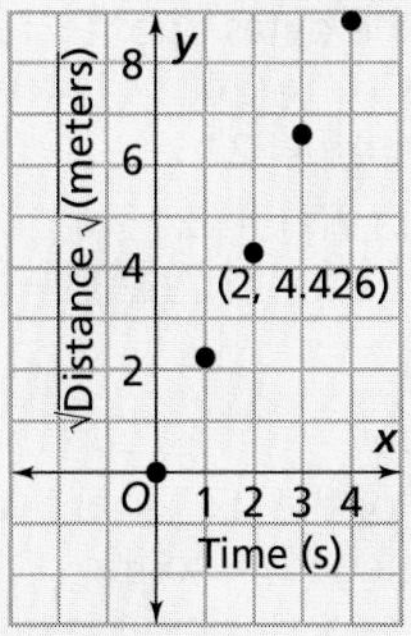

b. (2, 4.426)

c. Yes, the points seem to lie on a line.

4.

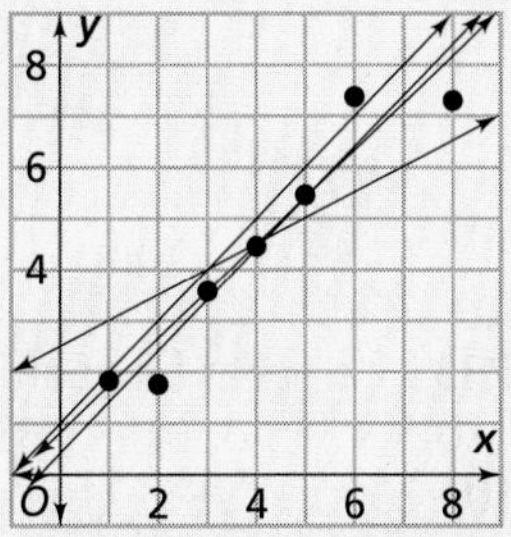

Lines (c) and (d) seem to fit the data.

Exercises

HOMEWORK
- Core: 7, 9a–b, 10, 12, 13, 14
- Optional: 8, 11, 15, 16, 17, 18
- Extension: 9c

Check Your Understanding

EXERCISE 1 is a quick practice exercise to remind students of the util ity of different forms for the equation of a line. Students who are able to write the equation of a line in the form $y - k = m(x - h)$ for a known slope m and a known point (h, k) will find it useful in this exercise. Watch for students who are dependent on a $y = ax + b$ form. Encourage those students to save time by using the more convenient form for the situation.

EXERCISE 2 When determining whether it is reasonable to fit a line to the data, students can look at the graph. They can also look at the table and examine the first differences: (4.9, 14.7, 24.5, 34.3). Although you do not expect them to be constant for a linear fit, they should not be getting increasingly greater as they are here. The second differences here are all close to 10. Does this imply it is reasonable to fit a quadratic to the data?

EXERCISE 5 Students may recall similar calculations from CME Project *Geometry*, where they were asked to find the center of mass for a polygon.

EXERCISE 6 introduces an idea that is useful when you deal with actual data. Sometimes a piecewise linear function gives a much better fit than a single line.

On Your Own

EXERCISE 7 Lesson 1.8 will use this type of table extensively. Be aware that students may accidentally reverse signs on many of the errors. Writing "Error: Actual − Predicted" can help avoid this mistake, since it makes the direction of the calculation clear.

5. On a coordinate plane, City A is at (300, 20), City B is at (700, 100), and City C is at (1000, −400).

a. If the three cities have about the same population, what is a good spot to call the "population center" for the cities?

b. If City A has 100,000 people, City B has 200,000 people, and City C has 50,000 people, what is a good spot to call the population center for the cities?

6. Roger is looking at the gold medal data from the beginning of the lesson. He says, "I disagree with the claim that a single line fits the data. It seems to me, both from the table and the scatter plot, that there is a good fit to a line from 1900 to 1960, decreasing at about $\frac{1}{2}$ second per year. Then times were nearly static from 1960 to 2000."

Divide the data set into two parts. For each part, calculate the balance point and plot a good fitting line. Compare this piecewise fit to the linear fit with equation $y = -0.34x + 892.1$.

Part A: 1900–1960 **Part B:** 1960–2000

a. What does the piecewise fit suggest might have happened in the years when there were no Olympics?

b. What does it predict for the year 2624?

On Your Own

7. The table below shows an analysis of the first fitting line from Exercise 4.

Data vs. Line Fit: $y = x + 1$

Input	Actual	Predicted: $y = x + 1$	Error: Actual – Predicted
1	1.8	2	−0.2
2	1.7	3	−1.3
3	3.6	4	−0.4
5	5.4	6	−0.6
6	7.3	7	0.3
7	7.2	8	−0.8

a. Does the line $y = x + 1$ contain any of the six data points?

b. The error column is negative for some entries. Are those points above or below the line $y = x + 1$?

c. **Write About It** Use the table and the graph from Exercise 4. Decide whether $y = x + 1$ is a good fitting line for the six data points.

Go Online PHSchool.com

For additional practice, go to **Web Code:** bfa-0107

Answers

5. a. (667, −93)

b. (629, 6)

6. For 1900 – 1960: (1929, 233.2); a linear function is $f(x) = -0.5(x - 1929) + 233.3$. For 1960–2000: (1980, 216); a linear function is $f(x) = 216$. The two functions fit the data better than the single function $f(x) = -0.34x + 892.1$.

a. Using $f(x) = -0.5(x - 1929) + 233.3$ for the dates prior to 1960, $f(1916) \approx 240$, $f(1940) \approx 228$, $f(1944) \approx 226$.

b. Using $f(x) = 216$ for dates after 1960, $f(2623) = 216$.

7. a. no

b. below

c. Five of the six "Error" values are negative, so five of the six points are below the graph of $y = x + 1$; the equation is not a good fit.

8. In Exercise 4, there are four fitting lines suggested for a table of data. In Exercise 7, there is a table of errors for the first line, $y = x + 1$.
   a. Build a table of errors for each of the other three lines listed in Exercise 4.
   b. Which line has the fewest errors? c. Which line has the smallest errors?
9. Use the data in Exercise 4.
   a. Find the equation of a line that contains the balance point.
   b. Show that the sum of the differences between the data and the corresponding points on your line is 0.
   c. **Take It Further** Show that the sum of the differences between the data and the corresponding points on any line that contains the balance point is 0.

For part (a), you get to pick the slope.

10. a. Where is the balance point of a ruler?
   b. Where is the balance point of a coin?
   c. **Write About It** Is it possible for an object to have a balance point that is not part of the object? Describe an example, or explain why it is impossible.

A line that contains the balance point has an equation of the form $y - \bar{y} = m(x - \bar{x})$.

11. Harvey rolls a number cube 85 times and writes down the outcomes. He counts 10 ones, 15 twos, 19 threes, 16 fours, and 11 fives.
   a. How many sixes does Harvey roll?
   b. Find the mean, median, and mode for Harvey's 85 rolls.
12. The table of data below comes from an experiment by Tor Carlson in 1913 on *Saccharomyces cerevisiae* (a type of yeast). The data show the number of hours elapsed and the number of yeast cells per square unit of area in a Petri dish.

Hours	Yeast Density
0	9.6
1	18.3
2	29.0
3	47.2
4	71.1
5	119.1
6	174.6
7	257.3

Where is the balance point of the forks and the blue toothpick?

   a. Draw a scatter plot for the eight data points.
   b. Calculate and plot the balance point.
   c. Is using a fitting line reasonable for these data? Explain your reasoning.

8. a. See back of book.
b. line (c)
c. line (d)

9. a. The balance point is (4, 4.5); an equation is $y = x + 0.5$ or $y = 0.9x + 0.9$.
b. For line (c), the sum of the errors is 0 and for line (d) the sum of the errors is 0.
c. Answers may vary. Check that the sum of the errors is 0.

10. a. The balance point is halfway from left to right and halfway from top to bottom.
b. The balance point is at the center of the circular face, halfway between the two parallel circular faces.
c. Yes; examples are a boomerang and a cup.

11. a. 14 sixes
b. mean: 3.5; median; 3; mode: 3

12. a. See back of book.
b. (3.5, 90.8)
c. No, the points do not lie along a line.

EXERCISE 8 gets students thinking about how you calculate the best fit line. Students consider two different lines, one of which has the fewest errors and one of which has the smallest errors. In Lesson 1.9 you will present a method for finding a single number to decide whether line (c) or (d) is, overall, a better fitting line.

EXERCISE 10 gives another connection to the idea that an object (here, a ruler or coin) can have a center of mass that is not part of its body. This is similar to an exponential graph whose balance point is not along a trend line. Compare that to a linear graph (such as a ruler) where the balance point is along the trend.

You might mention here that a linear object must contain its own balance point. This is one way to justify the balance point as a good starting location for a fitting line.

EXERCISE 12 Students might notice that each hour the number of cells multiplies by about 1.5. This suggests an exponential function would fit the data. Exponential functions will be discussed in Chapter 5.

EXERCISE 13 Allow students to use a calculator for the second part of this exercise.

Maintain Your Skills

EXERCISES 15–18 The goal here is for students to recognize that the balance point for a line is on the line, and the balance point for a nonlinear function is not likely to be on the line. It is possible, coincidentally, to pick a nonlinear function whose balance point happens to be on the graph. One example (using a tabulation from 0 to 4) is $f(x) = (x - 2)^3$. The balance point is (2, 0).

If you discuss this set of problems, ask if students noticed what happened to the balance point's x-coordinate. It should always be 2, since the chosen x-values are always the same.

Discuss the fact that between Exercise 15 and Exercise 16, each y-coordinate went up by 3, and the mean $\bar{y}$ also went up by 3. Then discuss the fact that between Exercise 17 and Exercise 18, each y-coordinate went up by 3, and the mean $\bar{y}$ also went up by 3.

Additional Resources

PRINT RESOURCES
- Solution Manual
- Practice Workbook
- Assessment Resources
- Teaching Resources

TECHNOLOGY
- Interactive Textbook
- TeacherExpress CD-ROM
- ExamView CD-ROM
- PHSchool.com

Additional Practice

For Exercises 1–3, use the table of data.

Input	Output
1	3.0
2	3.7
3	4.9
4	5.5
5	6.4
6	7.1

1. Plot the data points and the four lines given below on the same axes. Which line do you think fits the data best? Explain.
   I. $y = x + 2$ **II.** $y = 1.5x + 2.5$
   III. $y = 0.75x + 2.5$ **IV.** $y = x + 3$

2. **a.** Build a table of errors for each of the four lines listed in Exercise 1.
   b. Which lines have the fewest errors?
   c. Which line has the smallest errors?

3. **a.** Calculate the balance point.
   b. Find the equation of a line that contains the balance point.
   c. Show that the sum of the differences between the data and the corresponding points on your line is 0.

4. **a.** Where is the balance point of a closed book? Of an audio CD?
   b. Give an example of an object with a balance point that is part of the object. Give an example of an object with a balance point that is not part of the object.

5. The table of data represents the growth of bacteria in a petri dish. The data show the number of hours elapsed and the number of bacteria cells per square unit of area.

Hours	Bacteria Density
0	10.6
1	15.8
2	23.9
3	35.9
4	54.1
5	80.7
6	119.8

   a. Draw a scatter plot for the data points.
   b. Calculate and plot the balance point.
   c. Is using a fitting line reasonable for these data? Explain your reasoning.
   d. A graphing calculator gives the best-fit line $y = 16.5x - 3.0$. Build a table of errors for this line.

Practice: For Lesson 1.7, assign Exercises 1–5.

13. a. For the table in Exercise 12, a graphing calculator gives the best-fit line $y = 33.4476x - 26.2917$. Copy and complete the table of errors.

Calculate the error as the actual value minus the predicted value.

Data vs. Line Fit: $y = 33.4476x - 26.2917$

Hours, x	Actual Yeast Density	Predicted Yeast Density, y	Error
0	9.6	■	■
1	18.3	■	■
2	29.0	■	■
3	47.2	■	■
4	71.1	■	■
5	119.1	■	■
6	174.6	■	■
7	257.3	■	■

b. Calculate the following numbers and arrange the list of numbers from least to greatest.
- **I.** the average of the absolute values of the errors
- **II.** the average of the errors
- **III.** the average of the squares of the errors

14. Standardized Test Prep Which line contains the point $(-1, 2)$ and has a slope of 4?
A. $y = 4x$ **B.** $y = 2x + 4$
C. $y = 2(2x - 1)$ **D.** $y = 4x + 6$

Maintain Your Skills

For Exercises 15–18, do parts (a)–(d).

a. Make a table of the function for integer inputs from 0 to 4.
b. Make a graph of the five input-output pairs in your table.
c. Find and plot the balance point of the five points in your table.
d. Decide whether the balance point is on the graph of the function.

15. $f(x) = 3x + 1$ **16.** $x \mapsto 3x + 4$
17. $x \mapsto x^2$ **18.** $g(x) = x^2 + 3$

Habits of Mind
Look for relationships. As usual, your job in these exercises is to practice calculations and to look for hidden theorems.

Answers

13. a. See back of book.
b. I. 24.2; **II.** -0.0625 (rounding keeps it from being equal to 0); **III.** 815.1. In order, they are II, I, III.

14. D

15. a. See back of book.

b–c.
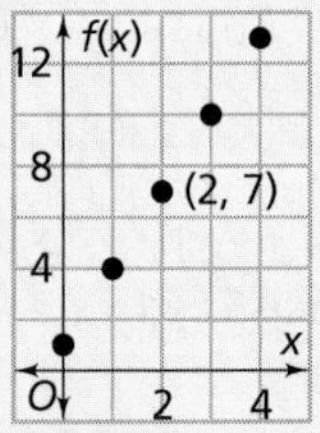

c. (2, 7)
d. (2, 7) is on the graph.

1.8 The Line of Best Fit, Part 1

Some calculators can find a *line of best fit* for any data set with two variables. How exactly do they do it? In this lesson and the next, you will learn what the line of best fit is and how to find it.

The data table below shows the weight losses of ten people on the same diet and the number of months it took them to lose the weight.

Months	Pounds
5	18
2	2
15	54
10	39
18	65
8	25
5	12
13	41
23	72
11	46

The scatter plot below left suggests that a line might approximate the data well. To figure out the best line, you need to measure how good a line is. For example, the scatter plot below right shows the graph of $y = 3x - 1$ and the data.

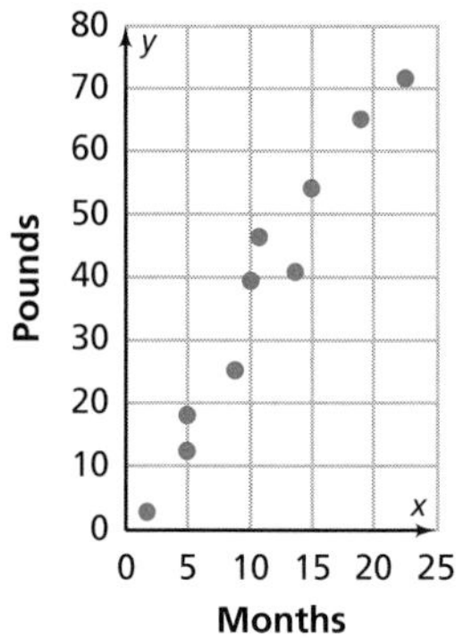

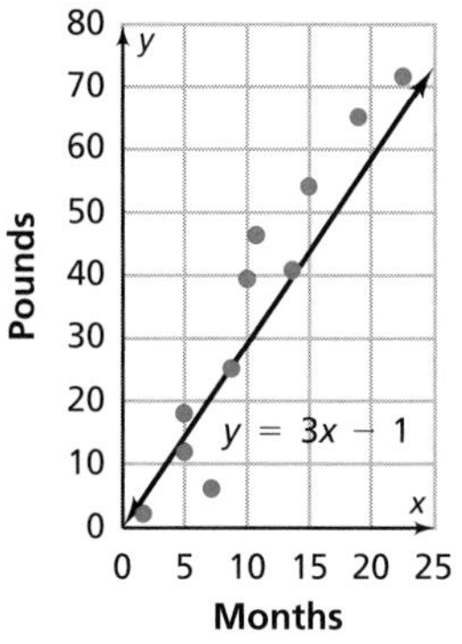

Lesson Overview

GOALS

- Calculate error, given a data set and a fitting function.
- Calculate the mean absolute error, mean squared error, and standard error.

In the previous lesson, students had a lot of practice finding fitting lines. In this lesson, they work to evaluate the fitting lines based on different measures of error. Students see how to make these decisions based on different measures of error. In the next lesson, they will define the line of best fit and learn how to calculate it.

CHECK YOUR UNDERSTANDING

- Core: 2, 4, 5
- Optional: 1, 3

MATERIALS

- CAS (recommended)
- geometry software
- graph paper
- graphing calculators
- spreadsheet software
- Blackline Master 1.8

HOMEWORK

- Core: 6, 7, 10, 11, 12
- Optional: 9, 14a–b, 15, 16
- Extension: 13, 14c–d

VOCABULARY

- mean absolute error
- mean squared error
- standard error

Launch

Present the weight loss data at the beginning of the lesson and proceed quickly through to For You to Do Problem 1. Emphasize the image of the vertical "sticks" from the actual data points to the fitting line as a way to measure the fit of the line.

Blackline Master 1.8 provides a blank error table and a blank graph for the students to complete.

16. a. See back of book.

b–c.

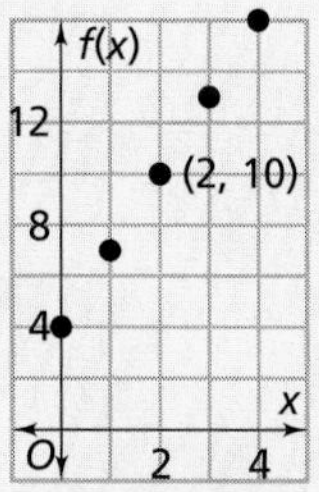

c. (2, 10)

d. (2, 10) is on the graph.

17. a–c. See back of book.

d. (2, 6) is not on the graph.

18. a.

x	$g(x)$
0	3
1	4
2	7
3	12
4	19

b–c. See back of book.

d. (2, 9) is not on the graph.

Explore

Ask students why they cannot think about a difference column for this table. They often have to be reminded that the input column has to increase by the same amount to use a difference table. Also, ask:

Does the data in the table describe a function? Explain.

It is always a good idea to point out what the slope represents. In this case it represents pounds lost/month. Also, point out that each tic mark on the vertical axis represents 10 pounds, while each tic mark on the horizontal axis represents 5 months.

As you did in the previous lesson, you can calculate the errors from the approximating line.

Data vs. Line Fit: $y = 3x - 1$

Months	Pounds	Predicted	Error
5	18	14	4
2	2	5	−3
15	54	44	10
10	39	29	10
18	65	53	12
8	25	23	2
5	12	14	−2
13	41	38	3
23	72	68	4
11	46	32	14

You can show the error column of the table on the graph. Each error is the vertical distance between the actual data and the approximating line.

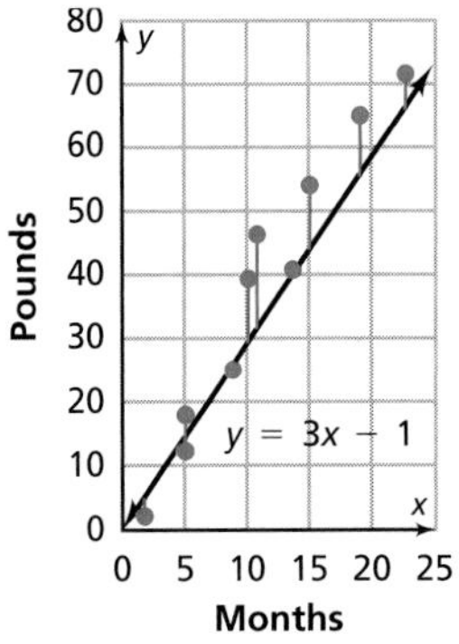

For example, the data point (15, 54) lies above the point (15, 45) on the line. The height of the "stick" from the data to the line is the error, which is 9.

Facts and Notation

One measure of overall error is the average length of the sticks. The lengths are the absolute values of the errors. Their average is the mean absolute error.

A calculator does something different to find the line of best fit. It sums the squares of the lengths of the sticks—the squares of the errors. The average of the squares of the errors is the mean squared error. The line of best fit minimizes the mean squared error.

Another useful measure of error is standard error or *root mean squared error*. **It is just the square root of the mean squared error.**

Why do you take the square root? One reason is that it preserves units. For example, in the weight-loss data, the standard error is a measure of pounds, not pounds^2.

For You to Do

1. Calculate the mean squared error for the graph of $y = 3x - 1$ and the weight loss data. Can you find a line that has a smaller mean squared error?

In-Class Experiment

Here is a useful way to think about finding the line of best fit.

Suppose you have a moveable line on a scatter plot. You also have vertical sticks between the line and the data points. As you move the line, some sticks grow in length, while others shrink. If you keep track of the sums of the squares of the stick lengths, you can fine-tune the line position. You can adjust the line to make the overall error small.

2. You can turn this thought experiment into a real experiment. Use your dynamic geometry software and the data in the table at the beginning of this lesson.

Step 1 Make a scatter plot of the data.

Step 2 Construct a moveable line on the plot. Translating the line keeps the slope the same. Rotating the line changes the slope.

Step 3 Construct a vertical segment from each of the ten data points to the moveable line.

Step 4 Ask the system to calculate the sum of the squares of the vertical segment lengths.

Step 5 Adjust the line. Try to make it so that the sum in Step 4 is as small as possible.

For more details, see the TI-Nspire Handbook, p. 778.

Answers

For You to Do

1. 57.9; answers may vary. Sample: Equation $y = 3.5x - 0.78$ has a mean squared error of 22.4.

In-Class Experiment

2. Check students' work.

FACTS AND NOTATION Have a volunteer read this section aloud and have a class discussion to clarify any misconceptions. Students must differentiate these terms in order to succeed in later lessons.

For You to Do

Ask students:

Do you think $y = 3x - 1$ is the line of best fit for the data? If you could move the line, would you change the slope? Would you move the line up or down?

In–Class Experiment

You might want to go through this step-by-step as a class so that students become comfortable with the technology.

One possible answer is to increase the slope by a small amount. For example, try $y = 3.5x - 1$. Use your spreadsheet to generate a table with $y = 3.5x - 1$ as the "predicted" column. Generate the error column:

Months	Pounds	Predicted $y = 3.5x - 1$	Error
5	18	16.5	1.5
2	2	6	−4
15	54	51.5	2.5
10	39	34	5
18	65	62	3
8	25	27	−2
5	12	16.5	−4.5
13	41	44.5	−3.5
23	72	79.5	−7.5
11	46	37.5	8.5

The lengths of the sticks are the absolute values of the errors. Add these for each error column to see which is smaller. The sum for $y = 3x - 1$ is 63. The sum for $y = 3.5x - 1$ is 42. So, $y = 3.5x - 1$ is a better fit.

THEOREM 1.5 Take two points on the line of best fit, (x_1, y_1) and (x_2, y_2). When you move the points, $(x_1, y_1) \rightarrow (x_1 + a, y_1 + b)$ and $(x_2, y_2) \rightarrow (x_2 + a, y_2 + b)$. The slope is

$$\frac{(y_2 + b) - (y_1 + b)}{(x_2 + a) - (x_1 + a)} = \frac{y_2 - y_1}{x_2 - x_1}$$

which is the slope of the original line of best fit.

For Discussion

If necessary, remind students of the role that the sum of the squares plays in calculating the mean of the squares. Students should realize that the average is the (sum)/(number of data points). Since the number of data points does not change, making the sum as small as possible will make the average as small as possible.

Wrap Up

You may wish to have volunteers make a poster for the classroom that shows the vocabulary terms for the lesson with their definitions. If time allows discuss the core exercises from Check Your Understanding.

Assessment Resources

Lesson Quiz 1.8

The data set at the right follows a linear trend.

1. Find the mean absolute error for the graph of each equation.
   a. $y = x + 3$
   b. $y = 1.5x + 2.5$
   c. $y = 2x + 1.5$

2. Find the standard error for each line in Exercise 1.

3. According to standard error, which line is the best fit?

Input	Output
0	2
1	4
2	5
3	7
4	8
5	10
6	12
7	13

Exercises

HOMEWORK
- Core: 6, 7, 10, 11, 12
- Optional: 9, 14a–b, 15,16
- Extension: 13, 14c–d

Check Your Understanding

EXERCISE 1 Use this exercise for a quick check of understanding. Ask the students:

Is it reasonable to fit a line to the data?

Would the slope of the line be positive or negative?

If the slope is positive, would it be more than 1 or less than 1?

Where would the line cross the *y*-axis (approximately)?

These questions should lead to answer A.

Theorem 1.5 Invariance Under Translation

Suppose *a* and *b* are fixed numbers and you have a set of data labeled (x, y). If you perform the transformation $(x, y) \mapsto (x + a, y + b)$ on the data set, the lines of best fit for the two data sets will have the same slope.

Remember...

The notation $(x, y) \mapsto (x + a, y + b)$ means that you add *a* to all the x-values and add *b* to all the y-values.

For You to Do

3. Write a convincing argument to support Theorem 1.5.

For Discussion

4. The mean squared error is the average of the squares of the errors. Why does making the sum of the squares of the errors as small as possible also minimize the mean squared error?

Exercises *Practicing Habits of Mind*

Check Your Understanding

1. Use the graph of data points at the right. Which line best fits the data in the graph?
   A. $y = 2x + 3$
   B. $y = \frac{1}{2}x + 3$
   C. $y = 2x - 3$
   D. $y = -2x + 3$

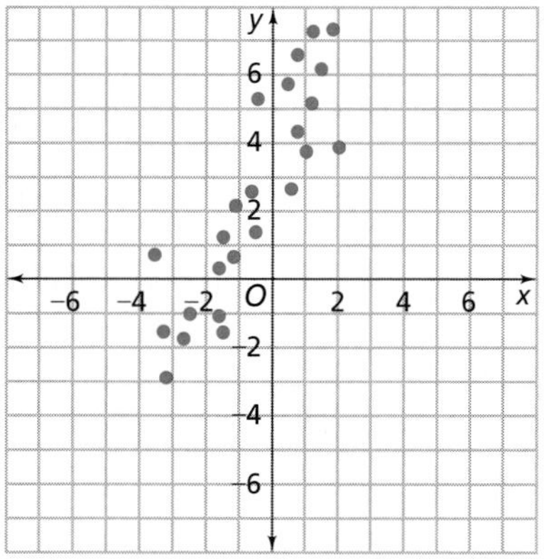

Answers

For You to Do

3. Answers may vary. Sample: Consider any two points (x_1, y_1) and (x_2, y_2) in the original data set and $(x_1 + a, y_1 + b)$ and $(x_2 + a, y_2 + b)$ in the transformed data set. The slope of the line for both sets of points is $\frac{y_2 - y_1}{x_2 - x_1}$, so the lines have the same slope.

For Discussion

4. If the sum of the squares of the errors is minimized, the mean squared error, which is that value divided by *n*, is also minimized.

Exercises

1. A

2. Use the table of data at the right.

Input	Output
1	3
2	4.5
3	8.1
4	8

a. Which equation has a graph that best fits the data?

A. $y = 3x - 1$ B. $y = -x + 8.4$

b. For each equation in part (a), compare the following.

- the sum of the errors
- the mean absolute error
- the mean squared error

3. Tony looks at the data in Exercise 2 and wonders, "If I keep the slope at 3, which line will give me the smallest mean squared error?" Sasha says, "Every line with slope 3 has an equation $y = 3x + b$ for some number b. So, let's keep b variable and calculate the sum of the squares of the errors as a function of b."

a. Copy and complete the following table for Tony and Sasha.

Data vs. Line Fit: $y = 3x + b$

Input	Output	Predicted	Error
1	3	$3 \cdot 1 + b = 3 + b$	$3 - (3 + b) = -b$
2	4.5	■	■
3	8.1	$3 \cdot 3 + b = 9 + b$	■
4	8	■	$-4 - b$

b. What is the sum of the squares of the errors in terms of b?

c. What value of b minimizes the sum in part (b)?

d. What is the equation of the line that Tony wants?

Your CAS can be a great help here.

4. Use the data from Exercise 2 and the method from Exercise 3. Find the equation of the line with the given slope that minimizes the sum of the squares of the errors.

a. slope = 1 b. slope = 2 c. slope = 3

Habits of Mind

Consider more than one strategy. What is the balance point of the data?

5. Make a table like the one below using your solutions to Exercises 3 and 4.

Slope	Equation of Best Line
0	■
1	■
2	■
3	■

How do the coefficients in the equation of the best-fitting line depend on its slope?

EXERCISE 2 Clearly, the graph for equation A is a better fit because the slope is positive and the data support that with an upward trend. In part (b), emphasize again that the sum of the errors is not a good indicator because positives and negatives can cancel each other out.

EXERCISE 4 If you assign this exercise, also assign Exercises 2 and 3.

EXERCISE 5 If you assign this exercise, also assign Exercises 2, 3, and 4.

2. a. A

b. For $y = 3x - 1$: sum of errors is -2.4; mean absolute error is 1.15; mean squared error is 2.565. For $y = -x + 8.4$: sum of errors is 1; mean absolute error is 2.9; mean squared error is 8.855.

3. a. See back of book.

b. $4b^2 + 12.8b + 19.06$

c. -1.6 **d.** $y = 3x - 1.6$

4. a. $y = x + 3.4$

b. $y = 2x + 0.9$

c. $y = 5.9$

5.

Slope	Equation of Best Line
0	$y = 5.9$
1	$y = x + 3.4$
2	$y = 2x + 0.9$
3	$y = 3x - 1.6$

As the slope increases by 1, the constant term decreases by 2.5.

On Your Own

Exercises 6, 7, 9, and 10 also appear as Exercises 5, 6, 8 and 9 in Lesson 1.9. You can choose to assign parts of them now, and use the other parts for Lesson 1.9.

EXERCISE 7 Students should recognize that the balance point lies along the trend line when there is one. In Table 3, there is no trend line, so the balance point does not lie along the (quadratic) trend. You do not have to assign all four tables. Make sure you assign Table 3 and at least one other table.

EXERCISE 8 is a critical result. Because the centroid must lie on the line of best fit, all students need to do now is find the slope of the line that minimizes some measure of the error.

EXERCISE 9 The purpose of this exercise is to note that the mean absolute error can be identical for more than one line. This does not happen with the mean squared error or standard error; there is always one best line with a smallest standard error. For this data set, that line is $y = x + 3$, as Exercise 10 shows. To cut down on time, you could assign only parts (a) and (b) here and in the next exercise.

EXERCISE 10 Use a graphing calculator or a computer if available.

TECHNOLOGY TIP Have students use the calculator or computer to calculate the line of best fit from the data. The best fit line for this data set (returned by calculator) is, perhaps surprisingly, $y = x + 3$.

On Your Own

6. Plot each data set below. Then use the plot to decide whether a line would be a good fit to the data.

Table 1

Input	Output
1	2
2	4
3	7
4	9
5	12

Table 2

Input	Output
2	1
5	3
7	4
10	6
13	8

Table 3

Input	Output
2	0
3	6
4	8
5	6
6	0
7	−10

Table 4

Input	Output
1	−5
2	−1
2	2
3	4
4	9

Go Online PHSchool.com

For additional practice, go to **Web Code:** bfa-0108

7. For each table in Exercise 6, calculate the balance point $(\bar{x}, \bar{y})$. Plot it along with the data.

Remember... $\bar{x}$ is the mean (average) of the x-values.

8. Show that all the lines you found in Exercises 3 and 4 are concurrent. Is their common point significant with respect to the data?

Lines are concurrent if they all intersect in the same point.

9. The data set at the right follows a linear trend. Find the mean absolute error for the graph of each equation.

a. $y = x + 3$ **b.** $y = x + 2$

c. $y = x + 4$ **d.** $y = 2x - 2$

Input	Output
0	4
2	4
4	5
5	7
5	9
6	11
8	12
10	12

10. Find the standard error for the first three lines in Exercise 9. According to standard error, which one is the best fit?

11. Standardized Test Prep What is the balance point of the data set below?

(5, 1), (6, 22), (14, 17), (23, 29), (34, 27), (38, 42)

A. (6, 6) **B.** (20, 30) **C.** (120, 138) **D.** (114, 132)

Answers

6. See back of book. Tables 1, 2, and 4 show a linear trend.

7. a. (3, 6.8)

b. (7.4, 4.4)

c. $\left(4\frac{1}{2}, 1\frac{2}{3}\right)$

d. (2.4, 1.8)

The balance points are shown in the graphs for Exercise 6.

8. The lines are concurrent because they all pass through (2.5, 5.9), which is the balance point.

9. a. 1.25

b. 1.25

c. 1.25

d. 2.5

10. a. 1.32

b. 1.66

c. 1.66

Equation $y = x + 3$ is the best fit.

11. B

12. **Write About It** There is an old saying: The mean squared error downplays small errors and magnifies large ones.

   a. Explain what the statement means and why it is true. (*Hint:* What do you know about the squares of positive numbers less than 1 and greater than 1?)

   b. What are the advantages of a measure of error that downplays small errors and magnifies large ones?

13. **Take It Further** Use Tor Carlson's data from Lesson 1.7, shown below.

   a. Use a graphing calculator to find the best-fit quadratic function of the form $y = Ax^2 + Bx + C$.

   b. Find the best-fit exponential function of the form $y = A \cdot B^x$.

   c. Which function has the smaller standard error?

Hours	Yeast Density
0	9.6
1	18.3
2	29.0
3	47.2
4	71.1
5	119.1
6	174.6
7	257.3

For help, see the TI-Nspire Handbook, p. 778.

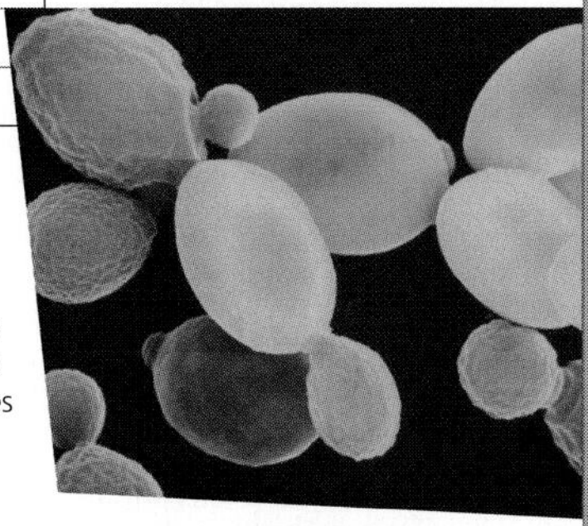

yeast cells magnified 2200 times

Maintain Your Skills

14. a. Find five numbers that have a mean of 23.

   b. Find five numbers that have a mean of 23 and a median of 25.

   c. **Take It Further** Find five numbers that have a mean of 23, a median of 25, and a mode of 27.

   d. **Take It Further** Find a different set of five numbers that also has a mean of 23, a median of 25, and a mode of 27.

15. Consider the five numbers you found in Exercise 13a.

   a. If you increase each number by 7, what is the new mean?

   b. If you double each number, what is the new mean?

   c. Use the five numbers to build a new set that has a mean of 1.

   d. Use the five numbers to build a new set that has a mean of 0.

16. Find the mean, median, and mode for each data set.

   a. 6, 6, 7, 7, 10, 10, 10   b. 4, 5, 6, 7, 10, 10, 14   c. −2, 3, 5, 7, 10, 10, 23

Remember...

The *median* is the middle number in a sorted list of the data. The *mode* is the most common data value.

Go Online
Video Tutor
PHSchool.com

Web Code: bfe-0775

12. a. Squaring a number less than 1 decreases it; squaring a number greater than 1 increases it.
b. It results in a line that is closest to most of the data points.

13. a. $y = 6.104x^2 - 9.277x + 16.433$
b. $y = 10.976(1.590)^x$
c. quadratic

14. a–d. Answers may vary. Samples are given.
a. 23, 23, 23, 23, 23
b. 16, 20, 25, 27, 27
c. 16, 20, 25, 27, 27
d. 15, 21, 25, 27, 27

15. a. 30
b. 46
c–d. Answers may vary. Samples are given.
c. −6, −2, 3, 5, 5
d. −7, −3, 2, 4, 4

16. a. mean: 8: median: 7; mode: 10
b. mean: 8: median: 7; mode: 10
c. mean: 8: median: 7; mode: 10

EXERCISE 13 Students should be comfortable with the first two parts and be able to complete them quickly, as long as they can find the appropriate fitting functions on the calculator. (See the TI-Nspire Handbook, p. 778.)

EXERCISE 14 If students are unsure of how to proceed, you can ask: If the mean of five numbers is 23, what is the sum of the five numbers?

EXERCISE 15 It is important that you increase each number by 7, so that you increase the sum by $(5)(7) = 35$ and the mean by $\frac{35}{5} = 7$.

Additional Resources

PRINT RESOURCES
- Solution Manual
- Practice Workbook
- Assessment Resources
- Teaching Resources

TECHNOLOGY
- Interactive Textbook
- TeacherExpress CD-ROM
- ExamView CD-ROM
- PHSchool.com

Additional Practice

For Exercises 1–3, use the data set.

Input	Output
0	5
1	6
2	8
4	10
4	12
5	13
6	15

1. Find the mean absolute error for the graph of each equation.
   a. $y = x + 4$ b. $y = 2x + 5$ c. $y = 1.5x + 4.5$

2. Find the standard error for each line in Exercise 1. According to standard error, which line is the best fit?

3. a. Use a graphing calculator to find the best-fit quadratic function for the data of the form $y = Ax^2 + Bx + C$.
   b. Find the best-fit exponential function for the data of the form $y = A \cdot B^x$.
   c. Which function has the smaller standard error? Explain.

For Exercises 4–6, use the tables below.

Table 1

Input	Output
0	14
1	17
2	21
3	25

Table 2

Input	Output
1	−2
3	3
5	7
7	12

Table 3

Input	Output
2	1
4	3
7	17
9	25

4. a. Plot each data set. Then use the plot to decide whether a line would be a good fit to the data.
   b. For each table with a linear trend, find the equation of the line of best fit.

5. For each table, calculate the balance point $(\bar{x}, \bar{y})$. Plot it along with the data.

6. For each table with a linear trend, estimate the slope of the trend. Then use the balance point that you found in Exercise 5 to write the equation of the line that best fits the data. Check your answer against the actual slope of the best-fit line in Exercise 4b.

Practice: For Lesson 1.8, assign Exercises 1–3.

Lesson Overview

GOAL

- Use algebra to find the line of best fit for a set of data.

In the previous lesson, students practiced finding a fitting line that would minimize the mean squared error for any given slope. After finding several such lines for different slopes, they saw that all those lines were concurrent and that the point of concurrency was the centroid (balance point) of the data. In this lesson, students start with the assumption that the balance point is on the line of best fit. They will use error calculation to find the slope that minimizes the mean squared error.

CHECK YOUR UNDERSTANDING
- Core: 1, 2, 3

MATERIALS
- CAS (recommended)
- graph paper
- graphing calculators
- Blackline Master 1.9

HOMEWORK
- Core: 4, 5, 6, 7, 8, 10
- Optional: 11, 13, 14
- Extension: 12

VOCABULARY
- mean absolute error

Launch

Have students use their calculators to follow along with the dialog. They should begin by plotting the data and using the calculator to find the equation of the line of best fit for the function.

Explore

Minds in Action

You can tell students to think of the centroid (balance point) as a pivot point. As you rotate the line about the point, you change the slope. You want to find the slope that gives the minimum mean squared error.

1.9 The Line of Best Fit, Part 2

You can use the fact that the line of best fit contains the balance point to develop a definition for the line of best fit.

Minds in Action — episode 3

Tony and Sasha used a calculator to plot the data from Lesson 1.8, shown below left. The trend looked linear, so Tony asked the calculator for the line of best fit. They saw the graphs below right.

Months	Pounds
5	18
2	2
15	54
10	39
18	65
8	25
5	12
13	41
23	72
11	46

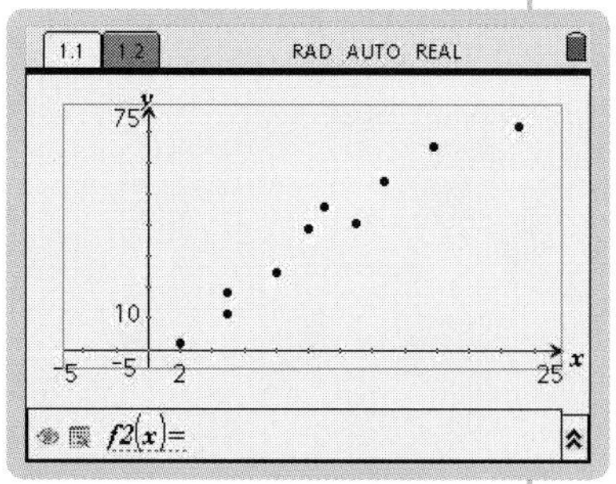

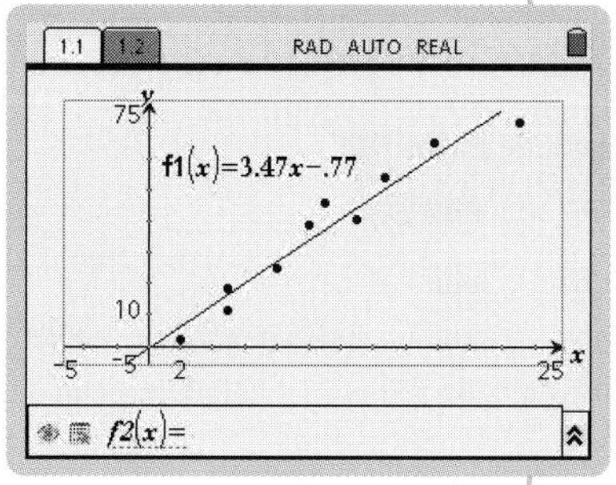

Tony So, the best-fit line has equation $y = 3.47x - 0.77$. How'd it get that?

Sasha The work we've done already makes me think that the line of best fit goes through the centroid. Let's see, the centroid is . . .

They calculate.

Tony The balance point is (11, 37.4). And, yes, (11, 37.4) is on the graph of $y = 3.47x - 0.77$. But (11, 37.4) is on many lines.

How does Tony know that (11, 37.4) is on the graph of $y = 3.47x - 0.77$?

Sasha But all the lines have equations with the same form. The equations of all the lines that go through the balance point look similar.

$$y - 37.4 = m(x - 11)$$

$$\text{or } y = m(x - 11) + 37.4$$

Hey, this is like Exercise 3 in Lesson 1.8. The only unknown is m. Let's go back to our error table and fill in the errors in terms of m. Then we'll calculate the mean squared error as a function of m and see if we can find an m that minimizes the mean squared error.

Tony Sounds tricky, but let's try it and see what we get.

For You to Do

1. Help Tony and Sasha carry out their plan by copying and completing the error table below.

Data vs. Line Fit: $y = m(x - 11) + 37.4$

Months	Pounds	Predicted	Error
5	18	$m(5 - 11) + 37.4 = -6m + 37.4$	$18 - (-6m + 37.4) = 6m - 19.4$
2	2	■	■
15	54	■	■
10	39	$m(10 - 11) + 37.4 = -m + 37.4$	$39 - (-m + 37.4) = m + 1.6$
18	65	■	■
8	25	$m(8 - 11) + 37.4 = -3m + 37.4$	$25 - (-3m + 37.4) = 3m - 12.4$
5	12	■	■
13	41	■	■
23	72	$m(23 - 11) + 37.4 = 12m + 37.4$	$72 - (12m + 37.4) = -12m + 34.6$
11	46	■	■

Some entries are filled in for you.

Sasha and Tony look at the completed table.

Tony See, it *is* tricky. So the sum of the squares of the errors is

$$(6m - 19.4)^2 + (9m - 35.4)^2 + (-4m + 16.6)^2 + (m + 1.6)^2$$
$$+ (-7m + 27.6)^2 + (3m - 12.4)^2 + (6m - 25.4)^2$$
$$+ (-2m + 3.6)^2 + (-12m + 34.6)^2 + (8.6)^2$$

What a mess! What does that tell us?

Sasha It's a mess all right, but look. It is a quadratic expression in m, and we know how to minimize a quadratic. If we have a CAS, we can use it to expand all this and see what we get.

Tony And if we don't have a CAS, we can ask some friends to help—it's only a bunch of squares of binomials to expand.

Sasha uses her CAS to expand the sum of squares expression.

Habits of Mind

Look for relationships. How can you tell from the expression that its normal form is a quadratic in m?

For You to Do

PROBLEM 1 You may wish to have students work in pairs or in small groups to copy and complete the error table. You can use Blackline Master 1.9 to provide students with a copy of the table.

Students (and teachers) can make errors entering long expressions into the calculator. One way to tackle this is to divide up the expression and then combine the results. Another is to have students compare their answers with one another.

Answers

For You to Do

1. See back of book.

DEFINITION Remind students, if a line minimizes the sum of the squares, it must minimize the mean of the sum of the squares, or the mean squared error, because the mean is the sum of squares of errors divided by the number of data points and the number of data points is not changing.

Wrap Up

Go over the Check Your Understanding core exercises with the class. Have students verbalize how they found their answers.

Assessment Resources

Lesson Quiz 1.9

For Exercises 1–5, use the data set at the right.

Input	Output
2	4
3	6
4	9
5	14
6	17
7	20

1. Plot the data set.
2. Calculate the balance point and plot it along with the data.
3. Find the best-fit line.
4. Find the best-fit quadratic and best-fit exponential.
5. Determine which of the three equations you found in Exercises 3 and 4 has the least mean squared error.

Tony Wow, much better. We get $4752.4 - 2610m + 376m^2$.

I know how to minimize that—it's just the vertex result we learned in our first-year algebra course. The vertex of the graph of $x \mapsto ax^2 + bx + c$ has x-coordinate $\frac{-b}{2a}$.

Sasha Right. And $\frac{-(-2610)}{2 \cdot 376}$ is . . .

Sasha types it into the calculator.

Tony The suspense is too much.

Sasha . . . approximately 3.47074. Great! That's where the 3.47 comes from.

Tony And the best-fit line has equation $y = 3.47(x - 11) + 37.4$.

Sure enough, this gives us $y = 3.47x - 0.77$. Very smooth. This method will work for any data set. But even with a CAS, I wouldn't want to try it on sets with huge amounts of data.

Sasha Maybe we can do it in general, once and for all, and get a formula for the best-fit line.

Tony Let's save that for another day. It's lunch time.

Check the answer.

Developing Habits of Mind

Check your assumptions. Tony and Sasha have discovered a method for finding a line that minimizes the sum of the squares of the errors for any data set. Their method rests on one assumption that you have not proved: All best-fit lines contain the balance point (centroid). It is not hard to prove this. In fact, if you try the project in Chapter 7 of this course, you will work through a proof. The proof is a bit technical, so consider it a reasonable but unproved conjecture for now.

Conjecture 1.1

For any set of data, the line of best fit contains the balance point.

Finally, you have a definition of *line of best fit.*

Definition

Given a set of data, the line of best fit is the line that minimizes the sum of the squares of the errors. It minimizes the mean squared error.

For most reasonable sets of data, there is exactly one line that satisfies this definition.

Exercises *Practicing Habits of Mind*

Check Your Understanding

1. Find the equation of the line of best fit for each table.

Table 1

Input	Output
1	−10
2	8
3	12
4	2

Table 2

Input	Output
4	−10
5	8
6	12
7	2

Table 3

Input	Output
1	−22
2	58
3	40
4	24

Table 4

Input	Output
3	−22
4	58
5	40
6	24

Habits of Mind

Look for relationships. Look for connections among your answers. Make conjectures.

2. Find the equation for the line of best fit for the table from Exercise 2 of Lesson 1.8 shown at the right.

Input	Output
1	3
2	4.5
3	8.1
4	8

3. Use the data set at the right.

a. Find the best-fit line.

b. **Take It Further** Find the best-fit quadratic and best-fit exponential. Determine which has the lesser mean squared error.

Input	Output
1	20
2	30
3	50
4	100
5	150
6	200
7	300
8	400

Answers

Exercises

1. Table 1: $y = 4x - 7$;
Table 2: $y = 4x - 19$;
Table 3: $y = 12x - 5$;
Table 4: $y = 12x - 29$

2. $y = 1.86x + 1.25$

3. a. $y = 53.69x - 85.36$

b. quadratic: $y = 7.56x^2 - 14.35x + 28.04$; exponential: $y = 13.9 \cdot 1.55^x$; the quadratic has the smaller mean squared error.

Exercises

HOMEWORK

- Core: 4, 5, 6, 7, 8, 9, 10
- Optional: 11, 13, 14
- Extension: 12

Check Your Understanding

EXERCISE 1 You would expect that the line of best fit for Tables 1 and 2 would have the same slope because the data points are translated to the right 3 units. Similarly, the data points in Table 4 are 2 units to the right of the data points in Table 3. For Tables 1 and 3, have students calculate *m* as they did in For You to Do Problem 1 and write the equation of the line of best fit. They can use the results to find the equations for Table 2 and Table 4 by using translations.

EXERCISE 3 You can find a line of best fit even if it does not fit the data very well. Both the quadratic and the exponential functions are better fits, with the quadratic being the best fit.

On Your Own

EXERCISE 4 After repeated calculations, students who work these exercises by hand will notice the patterns in the tables. Students who are using calculators to compute the line of best fit may have less intuition about why the slope of the line of best fit is the same for these four tables. Encourage these students to look at graphs of the data points with their lines of best fit for more than one table on the same set of axes.

Exercises 5, 6, 8, and 9 also appeared as Exercises 6, 7, 9 and 10 in Lesson 1.8. You may have assigned parts of them for that lesson. The notes about those exercises are repeated here.

EXERCISE 5 Ask students: What kind of function might fit Table 3? (Answer: quadratic)

What do you know about the leading coefficient? (Answer: It is negative.)

On Your Own

Go Online PHSchool.com

For additional practice, go to **Web Code:** bfa-0109

4. Find the equation of the line of best fit for each table.

Table 1

Input	Output
1	0
2	90
3	50
4	60

Table 2

Input	Output
−1	0
0	90
1	50
2	60

Table 3

Input	Output
−1	−1
0	89
1	49
2	59

Table 4

Input	Output
−1.5	−50
−0.5	40
0.5	0
1.5	10

5. Plot the data set in each table below. Then use the plot to decide whether a line would be a good approximation of the data.

Table 1

Input	Output
1	2
2	4
3	7
4	9
5	12

Table 2

Input	Output
2	1
5	3
7	4
10	6
13	8

Table 3

Input	Output
2	0
3	6
4	8
5	6
6	0
7	−10

Table 4

Input	Output
1	−5
2	−1
2	2
3	4
4	9

The relationship between the height and the age of a giant sequoia tree is linear. A plot of height against age will suggest a line.

Answers

4. Table 1: $y = 14x + 15$;
Table 2: $y = 14x + 43$;
Table 3: $y = 14x + 42$;
Table 4: $y = 14x$

5. See back of book.

6. The four balance points are shown in the graphs for Exercise 5.

Table 1: (3, 6.8); Table 2: (7.4, 4.4); Table 3: $\left(4\frac{1}{2}, 1\frac{2}{3}\right)$; Table 4: (2.4, 1.8)

7. Table 1: $y = 2.5x - 0.7$;
Table 2: $y = 0.631x - 0.27$;
Table 4: $y = 4.5x - 9$

8. **a.** 1.25 **b.** 1.25 **c.** 1.25 **d.** 2.5

9. **a.** 1.32 **b.** 1.66 **c.** 1.66
The line $y = x + 3$ is the best fit.

10. C

6. For each table in Exercise 5, calculate the balance point $(\bar{x}, \bar{y})$ and plot it along with the data.

7. For each table in Exercise 5 with a linear trend, estimate the slope of the trend. Then use the balance point you found in Exercise 6 to write the equation of the line that best fits the data. Check your answer against the actual slope of the best-fit line.

8. The data set at the right follows a linear trend. Find the mean absolute error for each line.

   a. $y = x + 3$ b. $y = x + 2$

   c. $y = x + 4$ d. $y = 2x - 2$

Input	Output
0	4
2	4
4	5
5	7
5	9
6	11
8	12
10	12

9. Find the standard error for the first three lines in Exercise 8. Which one is the best fit according to standard error?

Remember...

The standard error is the square root of the mean squared error.

10. **Standardized Test Prep** Which statement about a line of best fit is true?

    A. The line of best fit must contain all the points in the data set.

    B. The line of best fit cannot contain any points in the data set.

    C. The line of best fit contains the balance point of the data set.

    D. The line of best fit contains the origin.

11. Pick one table from Exercise 4. Build a different table that has the same line of best fit.

12. **Take It Further** Find a set of data that has more than one line of best fit.

Find more than one line that satisfies the definition.

Maintain Your Skills

Exercises 13 and 14 lead to an algebraic identity that is useful in many statistical calculations.

13. Establish each algebraic identity.

    a. $(x_1 - x_2)^2 = 2((x_1)^2 + (x_2)^2) - (x_1 + x_2)^2$

    b. $(x_1 - x_2)^2 + (x_1 - x_3)^2 + (x_2 - x_3)^2$
    $= 3((x_1)^2 + (x_2)^2 + (x_3)^2) - (x_1 + x_2 + x_3)^2$

    c. $(x_1 - x_2)^2 + (x_1 - x_3)^2 + (x_1 - x_4)^2 + (x_2 - x_3)^2 + (x_2 - x_4)^2$
    $+ (x_3 - x_4)^2 = 4((x_1)^2 + (x_2)^2 + (x_3)^2 + (x_4)^2) - (x_1 + x_2 + x_3 + x_4)^2$

14. What might the next identity be? What is the general identity?

The name of the general identity is the Lagrange Identity.

11. Answers may vary. Sample: Here is a table for $y = 14x + 15$:

Input	Output
1	29
2	43
3	57
4	71

12. Answers may vary. The data for any vertical line will fit. Sample:

Input	Output
1	4
1	5
1	7
1	8

13–14. See back of book.

EXERCISE 6 Students should recognize that the balance point lies along the trend line when there is one. In Table 3, there is no linear trend, so the balance point does not lie along the (quadratic) trend.

You do not have to assign all four tables. Make sure you assign Table 3 and at least one other table.

EXERCISE 7 You may not need to assign all parts of this exercise. This exercise gives students practice with finding best fit lines on small data sets. Hopefully students will see that they can make good fitting lines without asking the calculator to perform a best fit.

EXERCISE 8 One purpose of this exercise is to note that the mean absolute error can be identical for more than one line. This does not happen with the mean squared error or standard error; there is always one best line with a smallest standard error. For this data set, that line is $y = x + 3$, as Exercise 9 shows. To cut down on time, you could assign only parts (a) and (b) here and in the next exercise.

EXERCISE 9 Use a graphing calculator or a computer if available.

TECHNOLOGY TIP Have students use the calculator or computer to calculate the line of best fit from the data. The best fit line for this data set (returned by calculator) is, perhaps surprisingly, $y = x + 3$.

Additional Resources

PRINT RESOURCES
- Solution Manual
- Practice Workbook
- Assessment Resources
- Teaching Resources

TECHNOLOGY
- Interactive Textbook
- TeacherExpress CD-ROM
- ExamView CD-ROM
- PHSchool.com

Additional Practice

For Exercises 1–3, use the data set.

Input	Output
0	5
1	6
2	8
4	10
4	12
5	13
6	15

1. Find the mean absolute error for the graph of each equation.
   a. $y = x + 4$ b. $y = 2x + 5$ c. $y = 1.5x + 4.5$

2. Find the standard error for each line in Exercise 1. According to standard error, which line is the best fit?

3. a. Use a graphing calculator to find the best-fit quadratic function for the data of the form $y = Ax^2 + Bx + C$.
   b. Find the best-fit exponential function for the data of the form $y = A \cdot B^x$.
   c. Which function has the smaller standard error? Explain.

For Exercises 4–6, use the tables below.

Table 1

Input	Output
0	14
1	17
2	21
3	25

Table 2

Input	Output
1	−2
3	3
5	7
7	12

Table 3

Input	Output
2	1
4	3
7	17
9	25

4. a. Plot each data set. Then use the plot to decide whether a line would be a good fit to the data.
   b. For each table with a linear trend, find the equation of the line of best fit.

5. For each table, calculate the balance point $(\bar{x}, \bar{y})$. Plot it along with the data.

6. For each table with a linear trend, estimate the slope of the trend. Then use the balance point that you found in Exercise 5 to write the equation of the line that best fits the data. Check your answer against the actual slope of the best-fit line in Exercise 4b.

Practice: For Lesson 1.9, assign Exercises 4–6.

Mathematical Reflections

EXERCISES 2–4 At the start of the investigation, you may have assigned these as Questions 1–3 for students to think and write about.

EXERCISE 4 If your students have access to graphing calculators, assign this exercise. However, if your students are finding the line of best fit by hand, they should not use more than about four points. You might choose to have them find the line of best fit for the last four data points in this set, or you might just skip this exercise.

If students find the line of best fit by hand for the last four points, here is the beginning of the solution:

Year	Time
1988	215.96
1992	220.12
1996	215.78
2000	212.07

First find the balance point for the data set.

$$\bar{x} = \frac{1988 + 1992 + 1996 + 2000}{4} = 1994$$

$$\bar{y} = \frac{215.96 + 220.12 + 215.78 + 212.07}{4} \approx 216$$

So the balance point is (1994, 216).

You know that the line of best fit must pass through the balance point, so the equation for the line of best fit must be of the form $y = m(x - 1994) + 216$ for some slope m. Make an error table for this line and minimize the sum of the squares of the error.

Mathematical Reflections 1B

In this investigation, you learned how linear functions can represent some data sets. You calculated the balance point for a data set and found the line of best fit. These questions will help you summarize what you have learned.

1. Find the line of best fit for the data in Table N.

Table N

Input	Output
−1	−2
2	88
5	48
6	58

2. How do you find a line that fits a set of data?

3. What is the definition of the line of best fit?

4. What is the line of best fit for data in the table below?

Men's 1500-meter Olympic Gold Medal Times (seconds)

Year	Time	Year	Time	Year	Time
1896	273.2	1932	231.2	1972	216.3
1900	246.2	1936	227.8	1976	219.2
1904	245.4	1948	229.8	1980	218.4
1908	243.4	1952	225.1	1984	212.5
1912	236.8	1956	221.2	1988	215.96
1920	241.8	1960	215.6	1992	220.12
1924	233.6	1964	218.1	1996	215.78
1928	233.2	1968	214.9	2000	212.07

SOURCE: *2007 ESPN Sports Almanac*

Vocabulary

In this investigation you learned these terms. Make sure you understand what each one means and how to use it.

- **balance point**
- **line of best fit**
- **mean absolute error**
- **mean squared error**
- **outlier**
- **standard error**

Answers

Mathematical Reflections

1. $y = \frac{19}{3}x + 29$

2. Answers may vary. Sample: Use a CAS or use a balance point and a table of errors.

3. It is the line that minimizes the mean squared error.

4. $y = -0.394x + 996$

Chapter 1

Mid-Chapter Test

Go Online PHSchool.com

For a mid-chapter test, go to Web Code: bfa-0152

Multiple Choice

1. A linear function generates the input-output table below. What is the missing output?

Input	Output
1	5
−2	6
7	■

A. 7 **B.** 3 **C.** 4 **D.** 2

2. Which of the following lines best fits the data in the graph below?

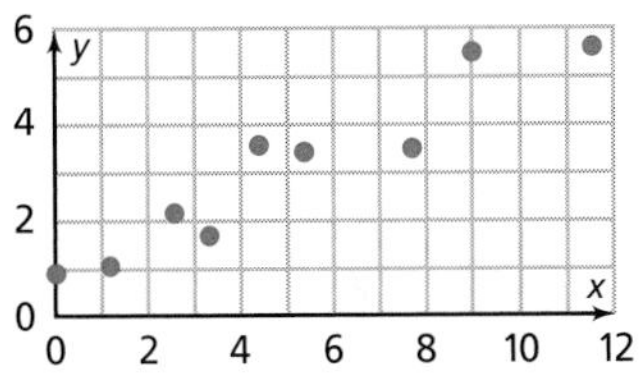

A. $y = \frac{1}{2}x - 1$ **B.** $y = 2x + 1$

C. $y = \frac{1}{2}x + \frac{1}{2}$ **D.** $y = -x + 0.6$

3. Which of the following points is the balance point for the data set below?

x	y
−1	4
2	6
3	−2
8	8

A. (3.5, 5) **B.** (3, 4) **C.** (12, 16) **D.** (2.5, 2)

Open Response

4. Find a closed-form function and a recursive function that match the following table.

n	d(n)
0	−7
1	−4.5
2	−2
3	0.5
4	3

5. Make a difference table for the input-output table below. Include enough columns to show a constant difference. Use your difference table to find a closed-form function that matches the table. Explain how you used the information in the table to find the function.

x	e(x)
0	5
1	10
2	17
3	26
4	37
5	50

6. Find the equation for the line with a slope of 2 that has the least standard error for the data set below.

x	y
0	−4
1	2
2	3
3	5

Does the line you found contain the balance point of the data set?

Mid-Chapter Test

1. B

2. C

3. B

4. $d(n) = 2.5n - 7$

$$d(n) = \begin{cases} -7 & \text{if } n = 0 \\ d(n-1) + 2.5 & \text{if } n > 0 \end{cases}$$

5.

x	e(x)	Δ	Δ²
0	5	5	2
1	10	7	2
2	17	9	2
3	26	11	2
4	37	13	
5	50		

The second differences are constant; $e(x) = x^2 + 4x + 5$.

6. $y = 2x - 1.5$; yes, the balance point is (1.5, 1.5)

Mid-Chapter Test

Assessment Resources

Mid-Chapter Test page 1

Multiple Choice

1. Which table best matches the recursive function $a(n) = \begin{cases} 3 & \text{if } n = 0 \\ 3 \cdot a(n-1) - 1 & \text{if } n > 0 \end{cases}$?

A.

n	a(n)
3	0
4	1
5	16
6	289

B.

n	a(n)
0	3
1	10
2	31
3	94

C.

n	a(n)
0	3
1	10
2	62
3	550

D.

n	a(n)
0	1
1	4
2	25
3	226

2. The table at the right is part of a table that was generated by a linear function. Which of the following statements is false?

A. $b(1) - b(5) = 22$
B. $b(10) = -40$
C. $b(0.5)$ is not defined.
D. The completed table agrees with the function

$$b(n) = \begin{cases} 15 & \text{if } n = 0 \\ b(n-1) - 5.5 & \text{if } n > 0 \end{cases}.$$

n	b(n)
0	
1	
2	4
3	
4	
5	
6	−18

3. Which of the following lines best fits the data in the graph?

A. $y = 2x - 2$ **B.** $y = 2x + 1$
C. $y = \frac{1}{2}x - 2$ **D.** $y = 3x - 1$

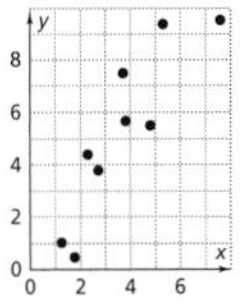

4. The table shows an analysis of the fitting line $y = 2x - 1$ to a data set. Which of the following statements is false?

A. The mean absolute error is 0.175.
B. This fitting line is the line of slope 2 that has the least standard error.
C. The standard error is greater than the mean squared error.
D. The mean squared error is 0.0375.

Data vs. Line Fit: $y = 2x - 1$

Input	Output	Predicted	Error
0	−1.1	−1	−0.1
1	1.2	1	0.2
2	2.9	3	−0.1
3	5.3	5	0.3

Mid-Chapter Test page 2

Open Response

5. a. Complete the difference table.
b. Extend the difference table to include enough columns to show a constant difference. Use your table to find a closed-form function that matches the table. Explain how you used the information in the table to find the function.
c. Find a recursive function definition for the table.

x	b(x)	Δ
0		6
1	10	
2	18	
3		12
4	40	

6. a. Graph the data set at the right.
b. Find the centroid and plot it on your graph.
c. Is the centroid close to the trend of the data?
d. Does the data follow a linear trend?
e. What is your visual estimate of the slope of the line of best fit?
f. From your graph, does the line of best fit for the data intersect the y-axis at a point above or below the x-axis? Explain.

x	y
1.2	9.1
1.8	9.6
2.2	5.8
2.7	6.2
3.8	2.6
3.9	4.3
4.8	4.5
5.1	1
7.6	0.4

7. Find the equation for the line of slope 4 that has the least standard error for this data set.

x	y
0	−6
1	−2
2	1
3	4

8. Find the equation for the line of best fit for this data set.

x	y
2	−1
3	5
5	5
10	3

Also available: Form B

Investigation Overview

This investigation has two goals:

- Explore recursive functions and gain experience with the factorial function, which does not have a closed form definition.
- Investigate monthly payments on a loan through a recursively defined function.

Students will begin this investigation with another look at recursive and closed-form definitions for functions. They will continue to use difference tables to gather information about the functions.

They will be introduced to a recursive function to determine the monthly payment on a loan. They will be able to determine how the cost of the car, the interest rate, and the length of the loan affect the monthly payment, so that they can become informed consumers.

The investigation ends with an exploration of the factorial function. Students will learn to simplify expressions with factorials. They will learn that the recursive definition is the only definition for the factorial function. There is no closed form.

You may wish to assign Questions 1–3 for students to think and write about during the investigation.

Learning Goals

- Find the monthly payment on a loan given the interest rate, term, and amount you borrow.
- Understand how the monthly payment on a loan changes with the amount you borrow.
- Build a recursively defined function that agrees with a table.
- Use the recursive model for the factorial function.

Habits and Skills

- Build and modify recursive definitions for functions.
- Search for hidden regularity in tables of numbers.
- Reason about algebraic forms.
- Build models for recursively defined functions in function-modeling language.

Investigation 1C

More About Recursive Models

In *More About Recursive Models,* you will analyze the following question.

How does a bank figure out the monthly payment on a loan?

You will answer this question with a recursively defined function that calculates the balance you owe in any month of a car loan.

You will also see a function that has no simple closed form—its recursive model is its primary definition. This is the factorial function. Its value at n is the product of all integers between 1 and n.

$$f(n) = 1 \cdot 2 \cdot 3 \cdot \cdots \cdot n$$

By the end of this investigation, you will be able to answer questions like these.

1. What is a recursive definition of a function? When is this type of definition useful?
2. What is the recursive definition of the factorial function?
3. What is the monthly payment on a loan of \$10,000 for 36 months with an interest rate of 5%?

You will learn how to

- find the monthly payment on a loan given the interest rate, term, and amount you borrow
- understand how the monthly payment on a loan changes with the amount you borrow
- build a recursively defined function that agrees with a table
- use the recursive model for the factorial function

You will develop these habits and skills:

- Build and modify recursive definitions for functions.
- Search for hidden regularity in tables of numbers.
- Reason about algebraic forms.
- Build models for recursively defined functions in your function-modeling language.

You have to set the table. There are $3 \cdot 2 \cdot 1$, or 6, possible arrangements of three utensils.

Investigation Road Map

LESSON 1.10, ***Getting Started,*** emphasizes conversion between recursively defined functions and their closed forms. Students examine the interplay between these two types of definition.

LESSON 1.11, ***Monthly Payments,*** introduces a recursively defined function that gives the balance on a loan at the end of any month. The function accepts as input the month you want to know the balance for. Students can change or use a variable for the amount of the loan, the interest rate, the down payment, or the monthly payment. They experiment with the function and discover relationships between the various parameters of the loan.

LESSON 1.12, ***The Factorial Function,*** introduces the factorial function, $n! = n \cdot (n-1) \cdot (n-2) \cdot \cdots \cdot 3 \cdot 2 \cdot 1$. This is a function that has a recursive definition but no simple closed form.

1.10 Getting Started

Activating Prior Knowledge
Exploring New Ideas

You can use a table to help you rewrite a recursive definition for a function as a closed-form definition.

For You to Explore

For Exercises 1–5, make a table of the function values for inputs between 0 and 10. Then find a closed-form definition that agrees with the table. Use your closed-form definition to find the outputs at 103, 104, and 245.

1. $g(n) = \begin{cases} 5 & \text{if } n = 0 \\ g(n-1) + 7 & \text{if } n > 0 \end{cases}$

2. $t(n) = \begin{cases} 1 & \text{if } n = 0 \\ 2 \cdot t(n-1) & \text{if } n > 0 \end{cases}$

3. $j(n) = \begin{cases} 0 & \text{if } n = 0 \\ j(n-1) + 2n - 1 & \text{if } n > 0 \end{cases}$

4. $k(n) = \begin{cases} 0 & \text{if } n = 0 \\ k(n-1) + 2n & \text{if } n > 0 \end{cases}$

5. $\ell(n) = \begin{cases} 0 & \text{if } n = 0 \\ \ell(n-1) + n & \text{if } n > 0 \end{cases}$

You can build models of the functions in your function-modeling language.

For Exercises 6–8, find a recursively defined function that agrees with each table. Make a table of the function values for inputs from 0 to 10.

6.

Input	Output
0	6
1	9
2	12
3	15
4	18
5	21

7.

Input	Output
0	7
1	11
2	15
3	19
4	23
5	27

8.

Input	Output
0	7
1	18
2	33
3	52
4	75
5	102

Answers

For You to Explore

1–8. See back of book.

Lesson Overview

GOAL

- Warm up to the ideas of the investigation.

In this lesson, students practice converting between recursive definitions and closed form definitions for functions. In some cases, the difference table techniques they learned in Investigation 1A will be helpful, but in other cases they may need to look for new techniques. For example, if difference tables do not seem to have a constant difference, it might be useful to look at quotients of successive outputs rather than their differences.

FOR YOU TO EXPLORE
- Core: 1, 2, 3, 4, 7, 8
- Optional: 5, 6

MATERIALS
- CAS (recommended)
- graphing calculators

HOMEWORK
- Core: 9, 10, 11, 13, 15
- Optional: 12, 14, 16, 17, 18

Launch

Before students begin the problems, you can review what you know about the tables for linear (constant first differences) and quadratic (constant second differences) functions. Then let the students work on the problems in groups.

Explore

As you circulate, ask students to verbalize strategies. You might ask them how they can determine whether difference table techniques will be helpful in determining a closed form for a recursive function or table. Have them explain the characteristics that lead to a decision to use difference tables.

For You to Explore

PROBLEM 1 Students can build a difference table as they did in Investigation 1A. If the recursive rule is to add a constant to the previous output, the function will have constant first differences and the function is linear. In this problem and subsequent problems, it is a good idea to connect the form of the recursive rule to the type of function it describes.

PROBLEM 2 You can advise students to try an exponential function if the differences repeat the output column, but move up a row (or rows).

PROBLEM 3 If the recursive rule is to add a linear expression to the previous output, the function is a quadratic.

PROBLEM 8 This table is the running total of the one in Problem 7. Help students notice this fact by reminding them to look at previous exercises for patterns. If they wonder how this information is helpful, you might encourage them to find a closed form for the table in Problem 7.

Wrap Up

At the end of this lesson, you might want to have a class discussion and allow students to share their work. Remember that you do not need to formalize the mathematics at this point; just let the students try out their ideas.

Exercises

HOMEWORK
- Core: 9, 10, 11, 13, 15
- Optional: 12, 14, 16, 17, 18

On Your Own

EXERCISE 12 If you skipped parts of Lesson 1.5 in Investigation 1A due to time constraints, do not assign this exercise as it involves finding a cubic function from a table of values and would require students to use the third difference in a difference table.

EXERCISE 13 If students have trouble, encourage them to write the outputs as products of the inputs.

EXERCISE 14 The Fibonacci sequence again! Make sure that students understand that $f(n-1)$ is the previous output and $f(n-2)$ is the output previous to $f(n-1)$. So, any output is the sum of the two previous outputs.

Exercises *Practicing Habits of Mind*

On Your Own

For Exercises 9–12, make a table of the function values for inputs between 0 and 10. Then find a closed-form definition that agrees with the table. Use your closed-form definition to find the outputs at 103, 104, and 245.

You can build models of the functions in your function language.

9. $g(n) = \begin{cases} 0 & \text{if } n = 0 \\ g(n-1) + 1 & \text{if } n > 0 \end{cases}$

10. $t(n) = \begin{cases} 1 & \text{if } n = 0 \\ 3 \cdot t(n-1) & \text{if } n > 0 \end{cases}$

11. $j(n) = \begin{cases} 1 & \text{if } n = 0 \\ j(n-1) + 2n + 1 & \text{if } n > 0 \end{cases}$

12. $k(n) = \begin{cases} 0 & \text{if } n = 0 \\ k(n-1) + \dfrac{n(n-1)}{2} & \text{if } n > 0 \end{cases}$

13. Find a recursively defined function that agrees with the table below. Make a table of the function values for inputs from 0 to 10.

Input	Output
0	1
1	1
2	2
3	6
4	24
5	120

Go Online
Video Tutor
PHSchool.com
Web Code: bfe-0775

14. Make a table of the function f defined below for inputs from 0 to 10.

$$f(n) = \begin{cases} 1 & \text{if } n = 0 \\ 1 & \text{if } n = 1 \\ f(n-1) + f(n-2) & \text{if } n > 1 \end{cases}$$

For advice on modeling recursive functions, see the TI-Nspire Handbook, p. 778.

Answers

9–14. See back of book.

15. **a.** Use your function-modeling language to model the function b defined below. For what value of n is $b(n)$ closest to 0?

$$b(n) = \begin{cases} 10{,}000 & \text{if } n = 0 \\ \frac{12.05}{12} \cdot b(n-1) - 438.71 & \text{if } n > 0 \end{cases}$$

b. Find the value of x that makes $b(36)$ closest to 0 for the definition of b below.

$$b(n) = \begin{cases} 10{,}000 & \text{if } n = 0 \\ \frac{12.02}{12} \cdot b(n-1) - x & \text{if } n > 0 \end{cases}$$

Maintain Your Skills

16. How many ways are there to arrange the letters in each word?
   - **a.** TO
   - **b.** MOP
   - **c.** FORM
   - **d.** SHOWN
   - **e.** CLOSED
17. How many ways are there to arrange the letters in "ABCDEFHIJ"?
18. Show that the following identity is true.

$$\frac{n(n+1)}{2} - \frac{(n-1)n}{2} = n$$

Recursion Using Mirrors

15. a. 24
b. 286.43

16. a. 2
b. 6
c. 24
d. 120
e. 720

17. 362,880

18. $\frac{n(n+1)}{2} - \frac{(n-1)n}{2} = \frac{n^2 + n - (n^2 - n)}{2} = \frac{n^2 + n - n^2 + n}{2} = \frac{2n}{2} = n$

EXERCISE 15 These recursively defined functions model the balance on a loan. In part (a), $10,000 was borrowed at 5% interest. It is being paid off with a monthly payment of $438.71. $b(n)$ gives the amount still owed on the loan after n months of payments. Students find how many months it would take to pay off this loan, given a monthly payment of $438.71. In part (b), students find the monthly payment required to pay off a $10,000 loan at 2% interest in 36 months.

Maintain Your Skills

EXERCISE 16 The answers in this exercise follow the pattern

(2) (1)

(3) (2) (1)

(4) (3) (2) (1)

Students will examine the factorial function in Lesson 1.12.

Lesson Overview

GOALS

- Find the monthly payment on a loan, given the interest, rate, term, and amount you borrow.
- Understand how the monthly payment on a loan changes with the amount you borrow.
- Build a recursively defined function that agrees with a table.

Students recursively define a function that determines the balance owed at the end of the *n*th month of a loan. They see how to make more efficient the calculations involved in computing the function values. They see the effect of inefficient calculations on a recursive function. Through the exercises, students examine the interplay between all of the variables in this situation: loan amount, term of the loan, interest rate, and monthly payment.

CHECK YOUR UNDERSTANDING
- Core: 1, 2, 3, 4
- Optional: 5

MATERIALS
- CAS (recommended)
- graphing calculators
- spreadsheet software

HOMEWORK
- Core: 6, 7, 8
- Optional: 9, 10

Launch

You might want to begin by having students discuss what they know about monthly payments, compound interest, and similar topics. Then work through For You to Do problems to look at loan balances for a 0% loan.

Explore

For You to Do

Students can define $b(n)$ on their CAS and calculate the balances $b(1)$, $b(2)$, $b(6)$, $b(12)$, and $b(36)$.

1.11 Monthly Payments

Suppose you want to buy a car. You can put \$1000 down and pay \$250 per month. The interest rate is 5%, and the dealer wants the loan paid off in three years. How much can you afford to spend on the car?

A recursive approach lets you experiment using your function modeling language. Can you afford a \$10,000 car? Well, after you pay \$1000 down, you can borrow \$9000. At the end of 36 months, you want the balance to be 0.

Begin with a simpler model, one that would hold in an ideal world where you did not have to pay any interest.

> Every now and then, car dealers offer a 0% interest rate.

- At the end of Month 0, you owe \$9000 (that is how much you borrowed, and Month 0 is when the loan starts).
- For any month after Month 0, you owe \$250 less than the month before (because you paid \$250).

If $b(n)$ is the balance in dollars at the end of the nth month, then

$$b(n) = \begin{cases} 9000 & \text{if } n = 0 \\ b(n-1) - 250 & \text{if } n > 0 \end{cases}$$

For You to Do

For Problems 1–4, find how much you owe after each time span.

1. 1 month
2. 2 months
3. 6 months
4. 1 year
5. Can you pay off your car in 36 months? If not, how much do you still owe?

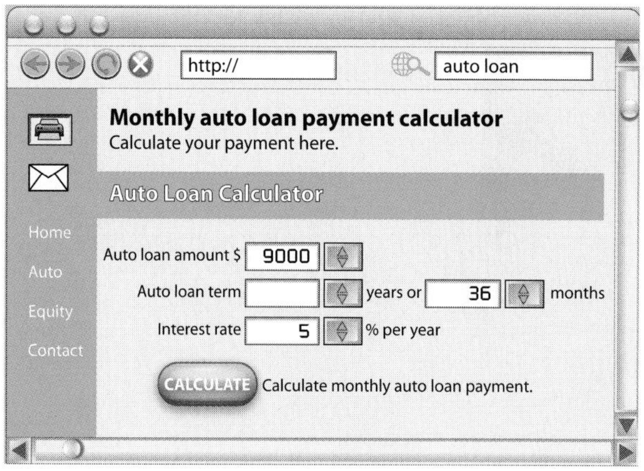

Go Online PHSchool.com

For a project with monthly payments, go to **Web Code:** bfe-9031

Answers

For You to Do

1. \$8750
2. \$8500
3. \$7500
4. \$6000
5. Yes; after 36 months you will have paid the entire \$9000 loan.

For Discussion

6. Find a closed form for the function b on the previous page.

What happens when you take the 5% interest into account?

- Month 0 is when the loan starts. At the end of Month 0, you owe \$9000. That amount is how much you borrowed.
- For any month after Month 0, you owe the balance from the previous month, plus the interest on that balance, minus \$250.

The interest for one month is one twelfth the interest for a whole year. The interest for a year is 5%, so the interest for a month is $\frac{0.05}{12}$ times the balance for that month.

You can now refine the definition of b.

$$b(n) = \begin{cases} \$9000 & \text{if } n = 0 \\ b(n-1) + \frac{0.05}{12} \cdot b(n-1) - \$250 & \text{if } n > 0 \end{cases}$$

At the end of the first month you owe

- \$9000 (what you owed at the beginning of the month)
- plus $\frac{0.05}{12} \cdot \$9000$ (which is \$45.83)
- minus \$250 (your monthly payment)

$$\$9000 + \left(\frac{0.05}{12} \cdot \$9000\right) - \$250 = \$8787.50$$

Banks use the following rule: What you owe at the end of the month is what you owed at the start of the month, plus $\frac{1}{12}$ of the yearly interest on that amount, minus the monthly payment.

For You to Do

7. What do you owe at the end of Month 2?
8. What do you owe at the end of Month 3?

The Memory Error

When you model the new recursive definition for b, your system can quickly run out of memory. Why?

Your calculator may return a message such as "Recursion too deep."

How does a computer find $b(4)$ using this definition? You tell it that $n = 4$, and, as it scans the definition, it notes what it needs to do. It sees two places where it will need to compute $b(3)$.

$$b(4) = b(3) + \frac{0.05}{12} \cdot b(3) - 250$$

$$b(2) + \frac{0.05}{12} \cdot b(2) - 250 \qquad b(2) + \frac{0.05}{12} \cdot b(2) - 250$$

$$? \qquad ? \qquad ? \qquad ?$$

In each of these 2 computations of $b(3)$, the computer needs to compute $b(2)$ twice, for a total of 4 times. Continuing, it computes $b(1)$ 8 times, and

For Discussion

6. $b(n) = 9000 - 250n$

For You to Do

7. \$8574.11
8. \$8359.84

For Discussion

Students should recognize that this recursive definition can be defined by a closed-form linear function since you are adding a constant, -250.

For You to Do

Ask students to calculate the interest paid each month. They often do not realize that more of your payment goes toward interest at the beginning of the loan than at the end of the loan. Discuss why this is true.

The Memory Error

Let students experiment with different values of n. The calculation becomes noticeably slower as n gets larger. For very large values of n there is an error message that may read "Error: Resource Exhaustion."

the base case $b(0)$ 16 times. Then it feeds this information back through three layers of computation to do 1 last calculation to get $b(4)$.

Adding the number of evaluations of b, you have

$$1 + 2 + 4 + 8 + 16 = 31 = 2^{(4+1)} - 1$$

That is how many computations the computer needs to compute $b(4)$. In general, calculating $b(n)$ requires tracking $2^{(n+1)} - 1$ evaluations of b. No wonder your calculator or computer runs into trouble quickly.

But where your calculator sees two calculations to be done separately, a person would notice that they are the same—both $b(n-1)$. You can figure it out once and then plug it in both places.

$$b(4) = b(3) + \frac{0.05}{12} \cdot b(3) - 250$$

$$b(2) + \frac{0.05}{12} \cdot b(2) - 250$$

You can force the computer to do the calculation the smart way as well. If you take the expression $b(n-1) + \frac{0.05}{12} \cdot b(n-1)$ and factor out $b(n-1)$, you get the following expression.

$$\begin{aligned} b(n-1) + \frac{0.05}{12} \cdot b(n-1) &= 1 \cdot b(n-1) + \frac{0.05}{12} \cdot b(n-1) \\ &= b(n-1)\left(1 + \frac{0.05}{12}\right) \end{aligned}$$

Now the computer only needs to track $n + 1$ evaluations of b in order to find $b(n)$. This change makes the computation manageable.

Habits of Mind

Estimate. Estimating shows that $2^{10} > 1000$ and $2^{20} > 1{,}000{,}000$.

Smart calculation does not guarantee you will never get the memory error, just that you will not get it as soon!

For You to Do

9. Build a model in your function-modeling language for the function b below.

$$b(n) = \begin{cases} 9000 & \text{if } n = 0 \\ \left(1 + \frac{0.05}{12}\right) + b(n-1) - 250 & \text{if } n > 0 \end{cases}$$

10. How much do you owe after 6 months? How long does it take you to pay the loan down to $8000?

You can add extra inputs that will let you change the monthly payment, the amount of the loan, or the interest rate on the loan. See the TI-Nspire Handbook, p. 778.

For You to Do

Encourage students to build a spreadsheet on their CAS to answer Problem 10.

Wrap Up

Have students work on the core exercises at the end of class. For Exercise 3, ask students to determine the total amount of interest paid for each amount of time. Could this influence their choice of loans if they were not concerned with the amount of the monthly payment?

Assessment Resources

Lesson Quiz 1.11

1. Suppose you take a $20,000 loan at 4% interest with a $350 monthly payment. How much do you owe at the end of one year?

2. If you can only afford to pay $330 per month, and you must pay your loan off in 48 months at 5% interest, how much money can you borrow?

3. What does the interest rate have to be so that you can afford a $21,000 car with $3000 down and payments of $405 per month for 48 months?

4. A car dealer has an ad each week that offers two deals on its cars.
   - You can get a $2500 rebate on the list price of the car. You then pay off the rest in 48 months at 7.9% interest.
   - Instead of the rebate, you can get a low 0.9% interest rate and then pay off the full list price of the car in 48 months.

   Suppose you want to buy a car with a list price of $33,000. Is it better to take the rebate or the low interest rate deal?

Answers

For You to Do

9. Check students' work.

10. $7711.64; the balance is under $8000 after 5 months.

Exercises *Practicing Habits of Mind*

Check Your Understanding

For Exercises 1–3, suppose you take a \$9000 loan at 5% interest with a \$250 monthly payment.

1. How much do you owe at the end of one year?
2. Can you pay off the loan in 36 months?
3. What monthly payment will let you pay off the loan in each amount of time?
   a. 36 months **b.** 39 months **c.** 48 months
4. If you can only afford to pay \$250 per month, and you must pay your loan off in 36 months at 5% interest, how much money can you borrow?
5. What does the interest rate have to be so that you can afford a \$12,000 car with \$1000 down and payments of \$310 per month for 36 months?

On Your Own

6. Suppose you want to pay off a car loan in 36 months. Pick an interest rate and keep it constant. Investigate how the monthly payment changes with the cost of the car.
   a. Make a table like the one below and complete it.

Cost of Car (thousands of dollars)	Monthly Payment
10	■
11	■
12	■
13	■
14	■
15	■
16	■
⋮	⋮

   b. Find either a closed-form or a recursive definition for a function that agrees with your table. Build a model of your function.
   c. Use your model to find the monthly payment on a \$26,000 car.

Make sure you state what interest rate you are using. You can find a rate in a newspaper car ad.

Go Online
PHSchool.com

For additional practice, go to **Web Code:** bfa-0111

If this function works for all inputs, you can use it to calculate the monthly payment in terms of the cost of the car.

Exercises

HOMEWORK
- Core: 6, 7, 8
- Optional: 9, 10

Check Your Understanding

EXERCISE 2 If $b(36) = 0$ the loan is paid off. If $b(36) > 0$ the loan is not paid off. If $b(36) < 0$, the loan is overpaid.

EXRECISE 3 This is a good exercise to add an extra input:

$$b(n, p) = \begin{cases} 9000, & n = 0 \\ \left(1 + \frac{0.05}{12}\right) \cdot b(n-1, p) - p, & n > 0 \end{cases}$$

Then you can use your CAS. Evaluate solve$(b(36, p) = 0, p)$ to get the correct payment.

On Your Own

EXERCISE 6 You can add a third input for the cost of the car:

$$b(n, p, c) = \begin{cases} c, & n = 0 \\ \left(1 + \frac{0.05}{12}\right) \cdot b(n-1, p, c) - p, & n > 0 \end{cases}$$

Use solve$(b(36, p, 10000) = 0, p)$ to find the first entry in the table. Then change the cost of the car to find other entries. Or, you could build a spreadsheet on your CAS.

Exercises

1. \$6390.74
2. no; \$764.92 remains to be paid
3. **a.** \$269.74
   b. \$250.51
   c. \$207.26
4. \$8341.43
5. about 0.9%
6. **a.** See back of book.
   b. If A = amount borrowed, P = amount of each payment, m is the monthly interest rate $\left(m = \frac{r}{12}\right)$, then here are two closed form equations:
   $$P = \frac{A \cdot m(1+m)^{36}}{(1+m)^{36} - 1} \text{ and } A = \frac{P((1+m)^{36} - 1)}{m(1+m)^{36}}.$$
   c. Answers may vary. Sample: At 7% the monthly payment would be \$798.50.

EXERCISE 7 In Exercise 6 you found a closed-form definition to find the monthly payment. If you multiply the monthly payment by 36, you will get the actual cost of the car. You want to build a similar table for the low interest rate and compare the actual costs.

Maintain Your Skills

EXERCISE 9 Compare the answers to powers of 2. Each sum is one less than a power of 2.

Additional Resources

PRINT RESOURCES
- Solution Manual
- Practice Workbook
- Assessment Resources
- Teaching Resources

TECHNOLOGY
- Interactive Textbook
- TeacherExpress CD-ROM
- ExamView CD-ROM
- PHSchool.com

Additional Practice

For Exercises 1–3, suppose you take a $10,000 loan at 6% interest with a $275 monthly payment.

1. How much do you owe at the end of one year?
2. Can you pay off the loan in 36 months?
3. What monthly payment will let you pay off the loan in each amount of time?
   a. 36 months   b. 39 months   c. 48 months
4. If you can only afford to pay $250 per month, and you must pay your loan off in 48 months at 6% interest, how much money can you borrow?
5. What does the interest rate have to be so that you can afford a $15,000 car with $1000 down and payments of $300 per month for 48 months?
6. Suppose you want to pay off a car loan in 48 months. Pick an interest rate and keep it constant. Investigate how the monthly payment changes with the cost of the car.
   a. Complete the table.
   b. Find either a closed-form or a recursive definition for a function that agrees with your table. Build a model of your function.
   c. Use your model to find the monthly payment on a $25,000 car.

Cost of Car (thousands of dollars)	Monthly Payment
15	
16	
17	
18	
19	
20	
⋮	⋮

7. A car dealer has an ad each week that offers two deals on its cars.
   - You can get a $2500 rebate on the list price of the car. You then pay off the rest in 48 months at 6.9% interest.
   - Instead of the rebate, you can get a low 1.9% interest rate and then pay off the full list price of the car in 48 months.

   Cars on the lot sell at prices between $15,000 and $35,000.
   a. For which cars is it better to take the rebate?
   b. For which cars is it better to take the low interest rate?
   c. For what price are the deals the same?

Practice: For Lesson 1.11, assign Exercises 1–7.

7. A local car dealer has an ad each week that offers two deals on its cars.
- You can get a $2000 rebate on the list price of the car. You then pay off the rest in 36 months at 5% interest.
- Instead of the rebate, you can get a low 0.9% interest rate and then pay off the full list price of the car in 36 months.

Cars on the lot sell at prices between $20,000 and $40,000. For which cars is it better to take the rebate? For which cars is it better to take the low interest rate? For what price are the deals the same?

8. Standardized Test Prep Suppose you take a $10,000 loan at 5% interest. How much do you owe after three monthly payments of $500?

A. $1500.00 **B.** $8500.00 **C.** $8619.25 **D.** $8925.00

Habits of Mind

Organize what you know. Make a table for prices between $20,000 and $40,000 in increments of $1000. Figure out the monthly payment for each price. You can use your function-modeling language and a spreadsheet.

Maintain Your Skills

9. Evaluate each sum.

a. $1 + 2$

b. $1 + 2 + 2^2$

c. $1 + 2 + 2^2 + 2^3$

d. $1 + 2 + 2^2 + 2^3 + 2^4$

e. $1 + 2 + 2^2 + 2^3 + 2^4 + 2^5$

f. $1 + 2 + 2^2 + 2^3 + 2^4 + 2^5 + \cdots + 2^9$

10. Use the description of s below.

$$s(n) = 1 + 2 + 2^2 + 2^3 + \cdots + 2^n$$

a. Find a recursive definition for s.

b. Find a closed form for s.

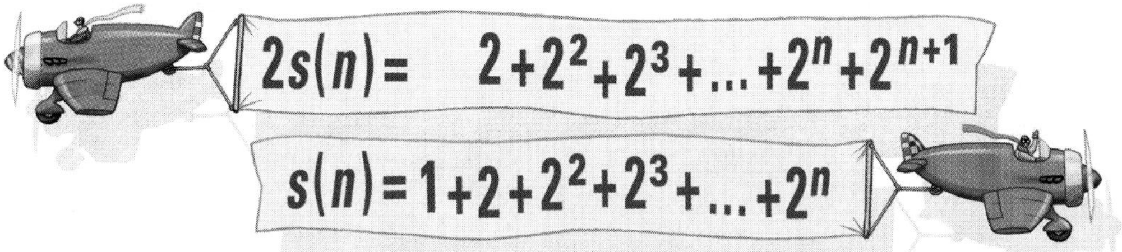

Answers

7. Check students' tables. Answers may vary. Sample: For cars that cost less than $33,200, you would pay less over the life of the loan if you chose the rebate deal. For cars that cost more than $33,200, you would pay less if you chose the low interest rate deal. The deals are the same if the car costs $33,200.

8. C

9. a. 3
b. 7
c. 15
d. 31
e. 63
f. 1023

10. a.
$$s(n) = \begin{cases} 1 & \text{if } n = 0 \\ s(n-1) + 2^n & \text{if } n > 0 \end{cases}$$

b. $s(n) = 2^{n+1} - 1$

1.12 The Factorial Function

Not all useful functions have both closed forms and recursive models. In this lesson, you will study a very useful function that has no simple closed form.

Suppose you have three books, labeled A, B, and C. In how many ways can you arrange them on a shelf? Well, you could make a systematic list.

A B C
A C D
B A C
B C A
C A B
C B A

So there are six arrangements. But what if you have 5 books? Or 8 books? Making a list of all possible arrangements would take a long time.

Developing Habits of Mind

Establish a process. One way to think about the arrangement problem is to model it with a function. Let

$f(n)$ = the number of ways to arrange n books on a shelf

You can think about f and try to get a closed-form or recursive definition for it. For example, since there is one way to arrange a single book, two ways to arrange 2 books, and six ways to arrange 3 books, you have the start of a table for f.

n	$f(n)$
1	1
2	2
3	6

There are many functions that agree with f for inputs 1, 2, and 3. You want one that counts arrangements of any number of books.

Look for a recursive relation. Can you use the fact that there are six ways to arrange 3 books to find how many ways there are to arrange 4 books? Consider the following steps.

Step 1 Suppose your books are labeled A, B, C, and D. First place D. There are four places to do that. Pick one.

Step 2 Now you have three books left and three spots in which you can place them. But you have already solved that problem. There are $f(3)$, or 6, ways to arrange 3 books.

Step 3 So, for each of your four choices for Book D, there are $f(3)$, or 6, ways to arrange the rest of the books. There must be $4 \cdot f(3) = 24$ ways to arrange the four books.

This is an example of a counting problem. In many counting problems, recursive definitions are easier to find than closed forms.

Just for fun, make a table for $g(x) = \frac{5x^2 - 15x + 12}{2}$ with inputs 1, 2, and 3. What is $g(4)$?

Lesson Overview

GOAL

- Use the recursive model for the factorial function.

This lesson introduces students to the *factorial function*—an important and useful function that has no simple closed form but that can be defined recursively. Students see an application of the factorial function in counting the arrangements (more formally called *permutations*) of books on a shelf. Then they experiment with the factorial function.

CHECK YOUR UNDERSTANDING
- Core: 1, 2, 3, 4
- Optional: 5

MATERIALS
- CAS (recommended)
- graphing calculators
- Blackline Master 1.12

HOMEWORK
- Core: 6, 7, 8, 10, 12, 13
- Optional: 9, 11, 14, 15, 16, 17, 18

VOCABULARY
- factorial function, $n!$

Launch

Work through the arrangements of objects with your class, counting the number of possible arrangements of one, two, and three objects. You might wish to have a volunteer model the different arrangements of three books on a shelf.

You can use Blackline Master 1.12 to guide students through the arrangements. You can add letters to the series to represent additional books.

Explore

Developing Habits of Mind

Work through the process with the class. For the nth book there are n spots in which you can place it and there are $n - 1$ books left to place. You can place the $n - 1$ books in $f(n - 1)$ ways. So, there are $n \cdot f(n - 1)$ ways to place n books on the shelf.

For You to Do

Students should have a strategy here. Otherwise, it is easy to miss an arrangement.

For Discussion

PROBLEM 2 Ask students:

What should be the value of $f(1)$?

If there is 1 book, how many ways can you arrange it on a shelf?

PROBLEM 3 Emphasize here that the domain of the recursive function is the set of non-negative integers. Ask students: What does your calculator give if you enter $f(2.5)$?

Wrap Up

If possible, give students some time in class to work on the Check Your Understanding core exercises and share their results.

For You to Do

1. Write out the 24 arrangements of four books in a list. Start by placing D, and then fill out the shelf with all six arrangements of A, B, and C.

For Discussion

2. Come up with an argument to show that $f(n) = n \cdot f(n-1)$ for $n > 1$.

This leads to the definition of a function that appears throughout mathematics.

Definition

The recursive rule below defines the factorial function.

$$f(n) = \begin{cases} 1 & \text{if } n = 0 \\ n \cdot f(n-1) & \text{if } n > 0 \end{cases}$$

In how many ways can you arrange 0 books on a shelf?

For Discussion

3. Build a model for f in your function-modeling language. Make a table of f for inputs between 1 and 6.

Is there a closed form for f? Look at $f(5)$.

$f(5) = 5 \cdot f(4)$	But $f(4) = 4 \cdot f(3)$.
$= 5 \cdot 4 \cdot f(3)$	But $f(3) = 3 \cdot f(2)$.
$= 5 \cdot 4 \cdot 3 \cdot f(2)$	But $f(2) = 2 \cdot f(1)$.
$= 5 \cdot 4 \cdot 3 \cdot 2 \cdot f(1)$	You know $f(1) = 1$.
$= 5 \cdot 4 \cdot 3 \cdot 2 \cdot 1$	Now you can compute.
$= 120$	

You can work out $f(n)$ for other positive integers n. You will see that $f(n)$ is the product of all the integers from 1 to n.

Developing Habits of Mind

Detect the key characteristics. So, is $f(n) = 1 \cdot 2 \cdot 3 \cdot \cdots \cdot n$ a closed-form definition for the factorial function?

It does not seem to use $f(n-1)$. But the dots conceal the true nature of f. You cannot use this equation to build a model for f in your function-modeling language. A machine cannot guess what the missing numbers are.

Answers

For You to Do

1.

DABC	CABD	BACD	ABCD
DACB	CADB	BADC	ABDC
DBAC	CBAD	BCAD	ACBD
DBCA	CBDA	BCDA	ACDB
DCAB	CDAB	BDAC	ADBC
DCBA	CDBA	BDCA	ADCB

For Discussion

2. Answers may vary. Sample: Suppose you have listed all the arrangements of $(n - 1)$ items. If you have another item, you can place it to the left of each of the $(n - 1)$ items or to the right of the last item, so there are $(n - 1) + 1 = n$ different ways to place the nth item. So $f(n) = n \cdot f(n - 1)$.

3.

n	$f(n)$
1	1
2	2
3	6
4	24
5	120
6	720

Can you write a closed-form definition for the factorial function? The answer is no. In a closed-form definition, you can calculate the output of the function at n by a fixed number of operations regardless of the value of n. But computing the factorial function requires more operations for larger values of the input. The factorial function has no simple closed form.

The factorial function is so useful that it has a formal notation. You represent the factorial of n as $n!$. So, $n!$ is the product of all the integers from 1 to n.

Computer scientists use this distinction between closed-form and recursive definitions.

For You to Do

Just to get used to the notation, find the numerical value of each expression.

4. $5!$ **5.** $7!$ **6.** $\frac{7!}{5!}$ **7.** $\frac{100!}{98!}$

Your calculator has a model of the factorial function built in. Or you can use your own recursive model.

Exercises *Practicing Habits of Mind*

Check Your Understanding

1. Use the definition of g below.

$$g(n) = \frac{n!}{(n-1)!}$$

Make a table for g with inputs from 2 to 10. Find a closed form for g.

2. Use the definition of h below.

$$h(n) = \frac{n!}{(n-2)!}$$

Make a table for h with inputs from 3 to 10. Find a closed form for h.

3. Express $k(n) = n(n-1)(n-2)(n-3)$ in terms of factorials.

4. Express $q(n)$ below in terms of $n!$.

$$q(n) = \begin{cases} 1 & \text{if } n = 0 \\ n^2 \cdot q(n-1) & \text{if } n > 0 \end{cases}$$

5. Without computing the numbers exactly, find how many zeros are at the end of each number.

a. $5!$ **b.** $10!$ **c.** $20!$

Assessment Resources

Lesson Quiz 1.12

1. Solve each equation for n.

a. $\frac{(n+4)!}{(n+2)!} = 72$

b. $\frac{(n+1)!}{(n-1)!} = 72$

2. Find a recursively defined function that agrees with the table at the right.

Input	Output
1	5
2	10
3	30
4	120
5	600
6	3000

3. Consider the function $p(n) = 1 + 2 + 2^2 + 2^3 + \cdots + 2^n$.

a. Make an input-output table for whole-number inputs from 1 to 5.

b. Find a recursive model for the function.

c. Decide whether there is a closed-form. Explain.

Exercises

HOMEWORK

- Core: 6, 7, 8, 10, 12, 13
- Optional: 9, 11, 14, 15, 16, 17, 18

For You to Do

4. 120

5. 5040

6. 42

7. 9900

Exercises

1–2. See back of book.

3. $k(n) = \frac{n!}{(n-4)!}$

4. $q(n) = (n!)^2$

5. a. 1

b. 2

c. 4

On Your Own

6. Solve each equation for n.

   a. $\frac{n!}{(n-2)!} = 56$ b. $\frac{(n-1)!}{(n-3)!} = 56$ c. $\frac{(n+1)!}{(n-1)!} = 56$ d. $\frac{(n+1)!}{n!} = 56$

7. Find a recursively defined function that agrees with the table at the right.

Input	Output
1	2
2	4
3	12
4	48
5	240
6	1440

Is there a closed form?

8. **Standardized Test Prep** The formula for the number of possible ways to choose r objects from a set of n objects is $\frac{n!}{r!(n-r)!}$. How many different ways can you choose a group of 3 students from a group of 8 students?

   A. 24 **B.** 56

   C. 120 **D.** 336

9. How many zeros are at the end of 150!?

Go Online PHSchool.com

For additional practice, go to **Web Code:** bfa-0112

For each function in Exercises 10–13, do parts (a)–(c).

a. Make an input-output table for whole-number inputs from 1 to 5.

b. Find a recursive model for the function.

c. Decide whether there is a closed form. Explain.

10. $r(n) = 1 + 2 + \ldots + n$
11. $s(n) = 1 + 3 + 5 + \ldots + (2n + 1)$
12. $t(n) = 1 \cdot 3 \cdot 5 \cdot \ldots \cdot (2n + 1)$
13. $r(n) = 1 + 3 + 3^2 + \ldots + 3^n$
14. **Take It Further** Are there any values of n such that $n! > 100^n$?

Hint: If S is the sum of the powers of 3 from 1 to 3^n, then what is $3S$?

Maintain Your Skills

For the expanded form of each expression, find the coefficient of the second-highest power of x and the constant term.

15. $(x-1)(x-2)$
16. $(x-1)(x-2)(x-3)$
17. $(x-1)(x-2)(x-3)(x-4)$
18. $(x-1)(x-2)(x-3)(x-4)(x-5)(x-6)(x-7)(x-8)$

Additional Resources

PRINT RESOURCES
- Solution Manual
- Practice Workbook
- Assessment Resources
- Teaching Resources

TECHNOLOGY
- Interactive Textbook
- TeacherExpress CD-ROM
- ExamView CD-ROM
- PHSchool.com

Additional Practice

1. Use the definition of k below.

$$k(n) = \frac{(n-1)!}{(n-3)!}$$

Make a table for k with inputs from 3 to 12. Find a closed-form for k.

2. Express $m(n) = (n-1)(n-2)(n-3)(n-4)$ in terms of factorials.

For Exercises 3–6, solve each equation for n.

3. $\frac{(n+2)!}{n!} = 110$
4. $\frac{(n+3)!}{(n+1)!} = 110$
5. $\frac{(n-1)!}{(n-2)!} = 110$
6. $\frac{(n-2)!}{(n-4)!} = 110$
7. Find a recursively-defined function that agrees with the table.

Input	Output
1	6
2	12
3	36
4	144
5	720
6	4320

For Exercises 8–10, do parts (a)–(c).

a. Make an input-output table for whole number inputs from 1 and 5.
b. Find a recursive model for the function.
c. Decide whether there is a closed-form. Explain.

8. $p(n) = 2 + 4 + 6 + \cdots + (2n + 2)$
9. $r(n) = 2 \cdot 4 \cdot 6 \cdot \cdots \cdot (2n + 2)$
10. $s(n) = 1 + 4 + 4^2 + \cdots + 4^n$

Practice: For Lesson 1.12, assign Exercises 1–10.

Answers

6. a. 8 **b.** 9 **c.** 7 **d.** 55

7. $f(n) = \begin{cases} 2 & \text{if } n = 1 \\ n \cdot f(n-1) & \text{if } n > 1 \end{cases}$

8. B

9. 37

10. a.

n	$r(n)$
1	1
2	3
3	6
4	10
5	15

b. $r(n) = \begin{cases} 1 & \text{if } n = 1 \\ r(n-1) + n & \text{if } n > 1 \end{cases}$

c. $r(n) = \frac{n(n+1)}{2}$

11. a.

n	$s(n)$
1	4
2	9
3	16
4	25
5	36

b. $s(n) = \begin{cases} 4 & \text{if } n = 1 \\ s(n-1) + 2n + 1 & \text{if } n > 1 \end{cases}$

c. $s(n) = (n+1)^2$

12. a.

n	$t(n)$
1	3
2	15
3	105
4	945
5	10,395

b. $t(n) = \begin{cases} 3 & \text{if } n = 1 \\ t(n-1) \cdot (2n+1) & \text{if } n > 1 \end{cases}$

c. No; this function is related to the factorial function, which has no closed form.

Mathematical Reflections 1C

In this investigation, you learned to evaluate recursive functions, including the factorial function. You calculated the balance on a loan and solved for an unknown variable in a monthly payment situation. These questions will help you summarize what you have learned.

1. Find a closed form for the following function.

$$k(n) = \begin{cases} 0 & \text{if } n = 0 \\ k(n-1) + 4n & \text{if } n > 0 \end{cases}$$

For Exercises 2 and 3, find a recursively defined function that agrees with each table. Make a table of the function for inputs from 1 to 10.

2.

Input	Output
0	3
1	8
2	13
3	18
4	23
5	28

3.

Input	Output
0	3
1	11
2	24
3	42
4	65
5	93

There are 4!, or 24, possible arrangements of four utensils.

4. Make a table for the function b below with inputs from 1 to 10.

$$b(n) = \begin{cases} 12{,}000 & \text{if } n = 0 \\ \frac{12.06}{12} \cdot b(n-1) - 400 & \text{if } n > 0 \end{cases}$$

a. Suppose $b(n)$ is a model for the balance on a loan at the end of month n. What is the amount of the loan? What is the interest rate?

b. For what value of n is $b(n)$ closest to 0?

5. What is a recursive definition of a function? When is this type of definition useful?

6. What is the recursive definition of the factorial function?

7. What is the monthly payment on a loan of $10,000 for 36 months with an interest rate of 5%?

Vocabulary and Notation

In this investigation, you learned this term and symbol. Make sure you understand what each one means and how to use it.

- **factorial function, $n!$**

Mathematical Reflections

EXERCISES 5–7 At the start of the investigation, you may have assigned these as Questions 1–3 for students to think and write about.

Mathematical Reflections

1. $k(n) = 2n(n + 1)$

2–4. See back of book.

5. In a recursive function, each value after the first one(s) is defined in terms of the previous one(s). They are useful for expressing patterns in the outputs of a function.

6. $f(n) = \begin{cases} 1 & \text{if } n = 0 \\ f(n-1) \cdot n & \text{if } n > 0 \end{cases}$

7. $299.71

13. a.

n	$r(n)$
1	4
2	13
3	40
4	121
5	364

b. $r(n) = \begin{cases} 4 & \text{if } n = 1 \\ r(n-1) + 3^n & \text{if } n > 1 \end{cases}$

c. $r(n) = \frac{3^{n+1} - 1}{2}$

14. $n \geq 269$

15. The coefficient of x is -3; the constant term is 2.

16. The coefficient of x^2 is -6; the constant term is -6.

17. The coefficient of x^3 is -10; the constant term is 24.

18. The coefficient of x^7 is -36; the constant term is 40,320.

Project

This project gives students a closer look at the function that determines the balance on a loan given the original loan amount, the interest rate, the monthly payment, and the term of the loan (the number of months it takes to pay it off).

Although students have already worked fairly extensively with this monthly payment situation, they have not as yet done a general mathematical investigation of this function and how all of the variables interact. By keeping two of the variables constant, they will be able to see how the remaining quantities affect each other. Their goal is to express this relationship as a closed-form and/or recursive function.

If you like, you can have students work with a partner. The project becomes more personal if the students look in newspapers or online to find a car they would be interested in buying and use that in their project.

You might consider asking for preliminary drafts so that you can give students early feedback and make sure that they are progressing. Although evaluating these drafts creates more work for you, giving feedback on early drafts will lead to better final write-ups.

After students have completed the project, you might ask several students to present their results for each of the exercises. Students should be aware that no matter what constant values were chosen, the type of relationship for the remaining variables is unchanged. For example, in the first exercise no matter what interest rate was chosen for a 36-month loan, the relationship between the monthly payment and the cost of the car will be linear. Point out the type of relationship found in each of the other exercises.

EXERCISE 1 Students should pick a reasonable interest rate. They can find this information online, at their local bank, or in ads in the newspaper. They should complete the table using their monthly payment function and enter it as a spreadsheet on their calculator or computer. Graphing the data will give them a good idea what kind of function they are looking for. They can find that function on their own, or use the calculator to find the regression equation.

Project: Using Mathematical Habits

More On Monthly Payments

You need to consider several variables when you use a loan to buy a car:

- the cost of the car
- the interest rate
- the monthly payment
- the number of months that you will take to pay off the loan

The general function *b* below relates these variables. It gives the balance at the end of *n* months on a loan amount of *c* dollars at an interest rate of *i*% (represented by a decimal) with a monthly payment of *m* dollars.

$$b(n, c, i, m) = \begin{cases} c & \text{if } n = 0 \\ (1 + i)b(n - 1, c, i, m) - m & \text{if } n > 0 \end{cases}$$

In this project, you will look at the effects of two of the variables on the rest.

- If *i* and *n* are constant, how does *c* depend on *m*?
- If *c* and *n* are constant, how does *m* depend on *i*?
- If *i* and *c* are constant, how does *m* depend on *n*?

If you finance $9000 at 5% interest for 36 months to buy this car, you will pay $9710.57 in all.

Cost and Monthly Payment

1. Pick an interest rate and keep it constant. Suppose you want to pay off a car loan in 36 months. Investigate how much you can spend on a car for a given monthly payment.

   a. Make a table like the one below.

Monthly Payment	Cost of Car
200	■
210	■
220	■
230	■
240	■
250	■
260	■
270	■
280	■
⋮	⋮

   b. Find either a closed-form or a recursive definition that lets you calculate the cost of the car in terms of the monthly payment. Build a model for your function.

   c. Use your model from part (b) to find the cost of a car you can afford with a $360 monthly payment. Check your result with the original model for *b*.

Answers

Project

1. Check students' work.

Interest Rate and Monthly Payment

2. Investigate the effect of interest on the monthly payment. Pick a car price and keep it constant. Suppose you want to pay off a car in 36 months. The interest rate might range from 0% to 15%.

a. Make a table like the one below.

Interest Rate (%)	Monthly Payment
0	■
1	■
2	■
3	■
4	■
5	■
6	■
7	■
8	■
⋮	⋮

b. Find the monthly payment on the car when the interest rate is 13%.

c. **Take It Further** Find either a closed-form or a recursive definition that lets you calculate the monthly payment in terms of the interest rate. Express the interest rate as a decimal or a percent. Build a model for your function.

d. **Take It Further** Use the model you wrote in part (c) to find the monthly payment on your car when the interest rate is 13%. Check your result with the original model for *b*.

Length of Loan and Monthly Payment

3. Investigate the effect of the length of the loan on the monthly payment. Pick a car price and keep it constant. Find the monthly payment on the car as the number of months varies.

a. Make a table like the one below.

Term (months)	Monthly Payment
24	■
28	■
32	■
36	■
40	■
44	■
48	■
52	■
56	■
⋮	⋮

b. Find the monthly payment on the car when the term of the loan is five years.

c. **Take It Further** Find either a closed-form or a recursive definition that lets you calculate the monthly payment in terms of the length of the loan. Build a model for your function.

d. **Take It Further** Use the model you wrote in part (c) to find the monthly payment on the car when the length of the loan is five years. Check your result with the original model for *b*.

2–3. Check students' work.

EXERCISE 2 Students can search for a car that they would like to buy online or in the newspaper. They can fill in the table and enter the data in a spreadsheet. Have them graph the data and determine the type of function they are looking for. Ask: Does the monthly payment increase by some constant amount as the interest rate increases?

EXERCISE 3 When students graph the data for this exercise, they will see that it is not linear. They should use their calculator to find different regression equations and determine whether quadratic, power, or exponential gives the best fit.

This is a good exercise to talk about the total interest paid. Ask students: Do you pay the same total amount when the term is 24 months as when the term is 48 months? You might want to talk about being an informed consumer.

Answers

Chapter Review

1. $a(n) = 5^n$, $a(n) = \begin{cases} 1 & \text{if } n = 0 \\ a(n-1) \cdot 5 & \text{if } n > 0 \end{cases}$;

$a(15) = 30{,}517{,}578{,}125$

2.

x	$b(x)$	Δ	Δ^2
0	1	2	3
1	3	5	3
2	8	8	3
3	16	11	3
4	27	14	
5	41		

The second differences are constant, so a quadratic equation will agree with this table. The equation is $b(n) = 1.5n^2 + 0.5n + 1$.

3.

x	$c(x)$	Δ	Δ^2
0	−3	7	4
1	4	11	4
2	15	15	4
3	30	19	
4	49		

The second differences are constant, so a quadratic equation will agree with this table. The second differences are 4 so the coefficient of the x^2 term is 2. Using a CAS, an equation is $c(x) = 2x^2 + 5x - 3$.

4.

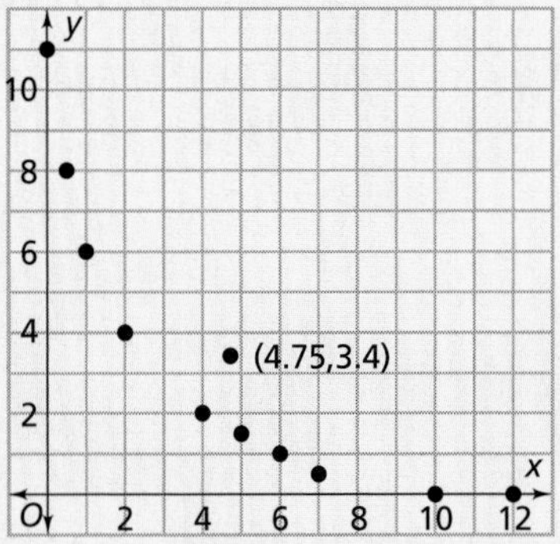

The balance point is (4.75, 3.4); the points do not lie on a line, so a linear function would not be a good representation for the data.

Chapter 1 Review

Go Online PHSchool.com

For additional practice, go to **Web Code:** bfj-0151

In **Investigation 1A,** you learned how to

- find closed-form and recursive functions to fit input-output tables
- use difference tables to determine whether a linear or a quadratic function will fit a given table
- use the up-and-over and hockey stick properties of difference tables

The following questions will help you check your understanding.

1. Write a closed-form and a recursive rule to match the table below. Use either rule to find $a(15)$.

n	$a(n)$
0	1
1	5
2	25
3	125
4	625
5	3125

2. Copy and complete the difference table below.

x	$b(x)$	Δ	Δ^2
0	1	2	3
1	■	■	■
2	■	8	■
3	■	■	3
4	■	■	
5	■		

What kind of function agrees with the inputs and outputs in the table?

3. Make a difference table for the input-output table below. Include enough columns to show a constant difference. Use your difference table to find a closed-form function that matches the table. Explain how you used the information in the table to find the function.

x	$c(x)$
0	−3
1	4
2	15
3	30
4	49

In **Investigation 1B,** you learned how to

- decide whether a linear function can reasonably represent a data set
- calculate error measures for a given data set and fitting line
- find the balance point and line of best fit for a data set

The following questions will help you check your understanding.

4. Graph the data in the following data set.

Find the balance point for the data set. Include it in your graph. Would a linear function be a good fit for the data?

x	y
0	11
0.5	8
1	6
2	4
4	2
5	1.5
6	1
7	0.5
10	0
12	0

5. Find the mean absolute error, mean squared error, and standard error for the data in the following table and the fitting line $y = 3x - 2$.

x	y
1	0.2
4	8.8
6	17
7	21.1

6. Calculate the line of best fit for the following data set.

x	y
1	−6
2	2
3	8
4	12

In **Investigation 1C,** you learned how to

- define, identify, and evaluate recursive functions including the factorial function
- calculate the balance on a loan given a loan amount, interest rate, length, and monthly payment
- solve for an unknown variable in a monthly payment situation

The following questions will help you check your understanding.

7. Make a table of the function $g(n) = \frac{n!}{(n-2)!2!}$ with inputs from 3 to 10.

8. Find recursive and closed-form functions that agree with your table from Exercise 7.

9. Suppose that you can afford to pay $1000 down and $300 per month. You can get a 36-month loan at 3%. What is the maximum price of a car that you can buy in this situation?

10. The car Maya wants to buy costs $12,000. The dealer offers her a choice of loans. She can get a $1000 rebate that she can use as her down payment. She can then take out a loan at 5% interest for 36 months to pay off the loan. Or, she can choose a zero down payment option with a 0.9% interest rate for 36 months. Which loan has the lower monthly payment?

5. m.a.e. = 1.275;
m.s.e. = 1.8725;
s.e. ≈ 1.368

6. $y = 6x - 11$

7.

n	$g(n)$
3	3
4	6
5	10
6	15
7	21
8	28
9	36
10	45

8. $g(n) = \begin{cases} 3 & \text{if } n = 3 \\ g(n-1) + n-1 & \text{if } n > 3 \end{cases};$

$g(n) = \frac{n(n-1)}{2}$ for $n \geq 3$

9. about $11,316

10. The 5% loan has a lower payment by $8.30 per month ($329.68 for the 5% loan, $337.98 for the 0.9% loan).

Chapter Test

Assessment Resources

Chapter Test page 1 of 3

Multiple Choice

1. Which of the following recursive functions best fits the table?

n	$a(n)$
0	2
1	−1
2	−2
3	−1
4	2

A. $a(n) = \begin{cases} 2 & \text{if } n = 0 \\ a(n-1) - 3 & \text{if } n > 0 \end{cases}$

B. $a(n) = \begin{cases} 2 & \text{if } n = 0 \\ 2 \cdot a(n-1) - 5 & \text{if } n > 0 \end{cases}$

C. $a(n) = \begin{cases} 2 & \text{if } n = 0 \\ a(n-1) + 2n - 5 & \text{if } n > 0 \end{cases}$

D. $a(n) = \begin{cases} 0 & \text{if } n = 2 \\ a(n-1) + 4n - 3 & \text{if } n > 2 \end{cases}$

2. The table at the right is part of a difference table for a function $b(n)$. The table has constant first differences. Find $b(100)$.

A. −257 **B.** −272
C. −300 **D.** not enough information

n	$b(n)$
0	28
1	
2	
3	
4	
5	13

3. Which of the following lines best fits the data in the graph?

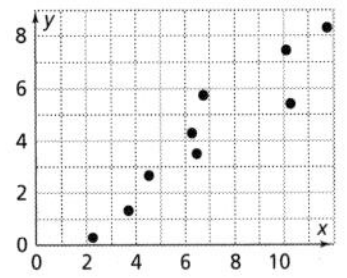

A. $y = -\frac{1}{2}x + 2$ **B.** $y = x - 2$ **C.** $y = 2x - 1$ **D.** $y = \frac{1}{3}x - \frac{1}{3}$

4. Sasha graphs a set of data points that appear to follow a linear trend. She visually estimates the slope of the trend to be 2. The line with slope 2 that minimizes the sum of the squares of the error has equation $y = 2x - 3$. Which of the following statements must be true?

A. The line with equation $y = 2x - 3$ is the line of best fit for this data set.
B. The line with equation $y = 2x - 3$ passes through the balance point of the data set.
C. If the sum of the error terms for this line is negative, then Sasha chose a slope that was too steep.
D. The line with equation $y = 2x - 3$ has the least possible mean absolute error for any fitting line with this data set.

Chapter 1 Test

Go Online PHSchool.com

For additional practice, go to Web Code: bfa-0153

Multiple Choice

1. Which of the following recursive functions best fits the table below?

Input, n	Output, $a(n)$
0	2
1	−1
2	−7
3	−19
4	−43

A. $a(n) = \begin{cases} 2 & \text{if } n = 0 \\ a(n-1) - 3 & \text{if } n > 0 \end{cases}$

B. $a(n) = \begin{cases} 2 & \text{if } n = 0 \\ 2 \cdot a(n-1) - 5 & \text{if } n > 0 \end{cases}$

C. $a(n) = \begin{cases} 2 & \text{if } n = 0 \\ a(n-1) + 2n - 5 & \text{if } n > 0 \end{cases}$

D. $a(n) = \begin{cases} 2 & \text{if } n = 0 \\ a(n-1) - 2n - 2 & \text{if } n > 0 \end{cases}$

2. Which of the following lines best fits the data in the graph below?

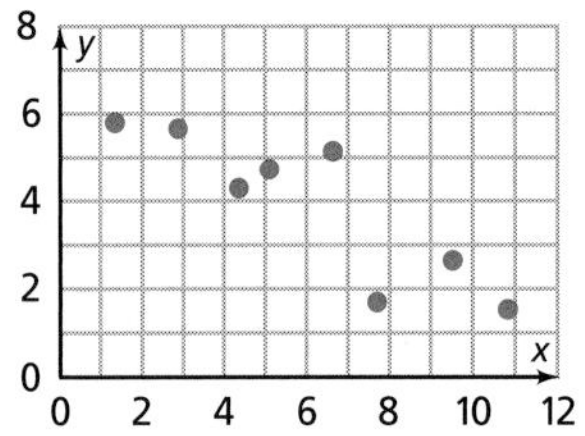

A. $y = -\frac{1}{2}x - 2$ **B.** $y = -2x + 6$
C. $y = -0.6x + 7$ **D.** $y = x - 3$

3. The table below is part of a difference table for a function $b(n)$. The table has constant first differences. Find $b(20)$.

Input, n	Output, $b(n)$
0	■
1	−3
2	■
3	■
4	24

A. 168
B. 177
C. 180
D. You cannot determine the value of $b(20)$ from the information given.

4. Which of the following statements about the line of best fit for a table of data is false?

A. The line of best fit contains the centroid of the data.
B. The line of best fit is the line with the least possible standard error.
C. The line of best fit must contain at least two data points.
D. The line of best fit may not have the least mean absolute error of any fitting line.

5. Solve the equation below for n.

$$\frac{(n+1)!}{(n-1)!} = 72$$

A. $n = 7$ **B.** $n = 8$
C. $n = 9$ **D.** $n = 10$

6. Dana bought a car for $12,000. She put $1000 down and got a 36-month loan at 4% interest. How much is her car payment each month?

A. $305.56 **B.** $324.76
C. $329.68 **D.** $359.62

Answers

Chapter Test

1. B
2. C
3. A
4. C
5. B
6. B

Open Response

7. Make a table of the following recursive function with inputs from 0 to 10.

$$m(n) = \begin{cases} 4 & \text{if } n = 0 \\ 2 \cdot m(n-1) + 3n - 10 & \text{if } n > 0 \end{cases}$$

Find a closed-form function that agrees with your table. Use it to find $m(80)$.

8. Find a recursive function definition and a closed-form function definition that agree with the table below.

n	$p(n)$
0	−8
1	−5
2	−2
3	1
4	4

9. Copy and complete the difference table below.

x	$g(x)$	Δ	Δ^2
0	4		
1	7		
2	8		
3	7		
4	4		

Find a closed-form function definition that agrees with the table. Explain how you can find the coefficients of the function from the difference table.

Use Table R for Exercises 10 and 11.

Table R

Input	Output
−2.1	−8.2
1.3	−0.6
4	4.8
5.2	7.4

10. Calculate the mean absolute error, the mean squared error, and the standard error for the data in Table R and the fitting line $y = 2x - 3$.

11. Find the balance point for the data in Table R. Does the line with equation $y = 2x - 3$ pass through the balance point? Is the line with equation $y = 2x - 3$ the line of slope 2 that minimizes the standard error for Table R?

12. Find an equation for the line of best fit for the following set of data.

x	y
5	18
2	12
8	23
5	12

13. Use your knowledge of the factorial function to show that the following equation is true.

$$\frac{n!}{(n-1)! \cdot 1!} + \frac{n!}{(n-2)! \cdot 2!} = \frac{(n+1)!}{(n-1)! \cdot 2!}$$

14. Shawn can put \$1200 down and pay \$300 a month on a loan. He can get a 36-month loan at 5% interest. How much can Shawn afford to pay for a car?

15. Shawn found a car for the exact price you calculated in Exercise 14. How much will Shawn pay over the life of the loan? If Shawn pays \$350 each month instead of \$300 with the same loan, how many months will it take him to pay off the loan? How much will he save over the life of the loan?

Assessment Resources

Chapter Test page 2 of 3

5. Evaluate $\frac{n!}{(n-2)!2!}$ for $n = 1000$.

A. 249,750 **B.** 499,500 **C.** 999,000
D. The recursion is too deep, so it cannot be evaluated.

6. Oscar took out a loan for a car and is making more than the minimum monthly payment each month. Oscar's car cost \$11,000 and he made a \$1000 down payment. His interest rate is 4% and he pays \$500 per month. How long will it take Oscar to pay off the loan?

A. 15 months **B.** 21 months
C. 23 months **D.** 32 months

Open Response

7. Complete the difference table at the right.

x	$w(x)$	Δ	Δ^2
0		6	2
1	10		2
2			2
3			
4			

8. Make a difference table of the following function with inputs from 0 to 4.

$$d(n) = \begin{cases} 1 & \text{if } n = 0 \\ d(n-1) + 4n - 5 & \text{if } n > 0 \end{cases}$$

Include enough columns to show a constant difference. Then find a closed-form function that agrees with your table.

9. Find a recursive function definition that agrees with the table.

x	$f(x)$
2	4
3	12
4	48
5	240
6	1440

10. Calculate the mean absolute error, the mean squared error, and the standard error for the data in the table and the fitting line $y = -3x + 1$.

Input	Output
−3	10
1	−3
5	−12
8	−20

Also available: Form B

7. See back of book.

8. $p(n) = \begin{cases} -8 & \text{if } n = 0 \\ p(n-1) + 3 & \text{if } n > 0 \end{cases}$,

$p(n) = 3n - 8$

9.

x	$g(x)$	Δ	Δ^2
0	4	3	−2
1	7	1	−2
2	8	−1	−2
3	7	−3	
4	4		

$g(x) = -x^2 + 4x + 4$; the coefficient of x^2 is half the constant second difference and the constant term is the value of $g(0)$.

10. m.a.e. = 0.35, m.s.e. = 0.27, s.e. ≈ 0.520

11. (2.1, 0.85); no; yes

12. $y = \frac{11}{6}x + \frac{85}{12}$

13. On the left side, $\frac{n!}{(n-1)!1!} + \frac{n!}{(n-2)!2!} = n + \frac{n(n-1)}{2} = \frac{2n}{2} + \frac{n^2 - n}{2} = \frac{n^2 + n}{2}$.
The right side is $\frac{(n+1) \cdot n}{2} = \frac{n^2 + n}{2}$.
So the original equation is an identity.

14. about \$11,210

15. about \$12,000; 31 months (actually, 30.5 months); about \$120

Chapter 2
Functions and Polynomials

This chapter reviews and extends students' experience with the idea of *function*. Students learn more strategies and techniques for exploring polynomial functions. They continue their work in matching functions to tables with Lagrange interpolation, a technique that can help them find a polynomial function to match any table that defines a function. Students cover traditional topics, such as factoring and solving polynomial equations, in depth but with a slightly different focus. Students learn to choose and write the form of a polynomial that best serves their purpose and to recognize classes of polynomials that respond to different factoring techniques.

Chapter Overview

INVESTIGATION 2A, ***About Functions,*** develops students' understanding of functions.

INVESTIGATION 2B, ***Making It Fit,*** has students use Lagrange interpolation to find a polynomial function to match any table that defines a function.

INVESTIGATION 2C, ***Factors, Roots, and Zeros,*** has students prove the Remainder Theorem and the Factor Theorem.

INVESTIGATION 2D, ***Advanced Factoring,*** has students practice factoring polynomials, with emphasis on quadratics.

For more information on the investigations, see

- Chapter Road Map, pp. 88–89
- Investigation Road Maps, pp. 96, 126, 146, 162

PROJECT The Project near the end of the chapter is optional. You can assign the Project at any time during the chapter depending on how often and how long you feel students should work on it.

Pacing Suggestions and Materials

Reviewing Key Ideas

DAY	LESSON	HOMEWORK
1	2.0 Polynomial Basics Core: 1, 2, 4, 5 Optional: 3	Core: 6, 7, 8, 9, 10, 11, 12, 13 Optional: 14, 15, 16, 17

Investigation 2A *About Functions*

DAY	LESSON	HOMEWORK
1	2.1 Getting Started Core: 1, 2, 4, 5 Optional: 3a; Extension: 3b	Core: 6, 7, 8a–e, 11 Optional: 9, 10, 12, 13; Extension: 8f
2	2.2 Getting Precise About Functions Core: 1, 2, 3, 4, 5 Optional: 6, 7, 8, 9	Core: 10, 11, 12a–d, 14, 16, 17, 19, 23a–d Optional: 13, 15, 18, 20, 21 Extension: 12e, 23e, 24
3	2.3 Algebra With Functions Core: 1, 2, 3, 4, 5, 6 Optional: 7; Extension: 8, 9	Core: 10, 11, 13, 16, 17, 18 Optional: 12, 14, 15, 20, 21; Extension: 19
4	2.4 Inverses: Doing and Undoing Core: 1, 2, 3, 4, 5, 7 Optional: 6, 8; Extension: 9	Core: 10, 11, 13, 14, 15, 19 Optional: 12, 16, 18, 20; Extension: 17

Investigation 2B *Making It Fit*

DAY	LESSON	HOMEWORK
1	2.5 Getting Started Core: 1, 2, 4, 5, 6, 9 Optional: 3, 7, 8	Core: 10, 11, 12 Optional: 13, 14a–c, 15a–c, 16a–c, 17a–c, 18a–c; Extension: 14d, 15d, 16d, 17d, 18d
2	2.6 Lagrange Interpolation Core: 1, 2, 3 Optional: 4, 5, 6	Core: 8, 9, 10, 11, 12, 13 Optional: 7, 14, 16a–c, 17a–c Extension: 15, 16d, 17d
3	2.7 Agreeing to Disagree Core: 1, 2, 3, 4 Optional: 5	Core: 6, 7, 10, 11, 13 Optional: 8, 9, 12, 14, 15

NOTES	MATERIALS
This lesson reviews polynomial basics and is optional.	• CAS (recommended)

NOTES	MATERIALS
Encourage students to try all the problems.	• graph paper • graphing calculators
	• CAS (recommended) • graph paper • graphing calculators • Blackline Master 2.2
	• CAS (recommended) • graph paper • graphing calculators • Blackline Master 2.3
	• graph paper • graphing calculators • Blackline Master 2.4

NOTES	MATERIALS
	• CAS (recommended) • graph paper • graphing calculators • Blackline Master 2.5
	• CAS (recommended) • graph paper • graphing calculators • Blackline Master 2.6
	• CAS (recommended) • graph paper • graphing calculators • Blackline Master 2.7

Mathematics Background

COMPOSITION OF FUNCTIONS You will see composition of functions as a computational challenge for students, or as a way of expressing a multi-step calculation. However, composition is also an operation on the set of functions, just as addition is an operation on a set of numbers. In *Algebra 2,* you will expose students to the notation and calculation of composition. Students will begin to think more like algebraists—thinking of composition and functions abstractly.

When an algebraist encounters an operation on a set, some questions immediately arise. Is this set "closed" on this operation? Is there an identity element for this operation? Is this operation associative? Commutative? Are there inverses under this operation? During the course of their study of composition of functions, students encounter and investigate these questions. They extend their understanding of functions so that functions are no longer just a way to express a complicated operation on an input but also are objects in their own right.

MATCHING A FUNCTION TO A TABLE In Chapter 1, students learned to match a polynomial to a table using difference tables. This technique required the tables to be specially constructed with inputs increasing by 1 in each new row. In this chapter, students learn a completely general technique, Lagrange interpolation, which allows them to match any input-output table to a polynomial function, as long as the table meets the requirements for a function. As long as there is no instance where more than one output is given for a single input, Lagrange interpolation will produce a polynomial that agrees with the table. Students also learn how to find classes of functions that agree with a table but do not agree everywhere.

FACTORING You can factor by hand only a few specially constructed polynomials out of the infinite set of polynomials, so why is it important for students to learn to factor? Students who learn to factor polynomials are certainly capable computationally, but that is not the only goal. By factoring polynomials, students learn to exploit the different forms of the polynomials for different purposes. They also come to understand the correspondence between the linear factors of a polynomial and its roots. They see the utility of "lumping," making a substitution in order to see a simpler relationship embedded in a more complex form. Although students can use a computer algebra system (CAS) to factor a polynomial, their own factoring experience will help them understand how to evaluate and use those results.

Pacing Suggestions and Materials

Investigation 2C *Factors, Roots, and Zeros*

DAY	LESSON	HOMEWORK
1	2.8 Getting Started Core: 1, 2, 3, 5, 6, 7 Optional: 4	Core: 9, 12, 13, 14 Optional: 8, 10, 11
2	2.9 Polynomial Division Core: 1, 2, 3, 4, 5, 6 Optional: none	Core: 7, 8, 9, 11, 14 Optional: 10, 13, 16, 17; Extension: 12, 15
3	2.10 The Factor Theorem Core: 1, 2, 3, 6 Optional: 4, 5, 7, 8	Core: 9, 10, 16, 17 Optional: 11, 12, 13, 14a, 15, 18, 19 Extension: 14b

Investigation 2D *Advanced Factoring*

DAY	LESSON	HOMEWORK
1	2.11 Getting Started Core: 1, 2, 3 Optional: 4	Core: 5, 6, 9, 11 Optional: 7, 8, 10, 12
2	2.12 Quadratics Core: 1, 2 Optional: none	Core: 3, 4, 6, 8, 9 Optional: 5, 7
3	2.13 Factoring Cubics Core: 1, 2 Optional: 3	Core: 4, 8, 9 Optional: 5, 6; Extension: 7
4	2.14 Pippins and Cheese Core: 1, 2, 3a–b, 4 Optional: none; Extension: 3c	Core: 5, 7, 8 Optional: 6a–d, 10; Extension: 6e, 9
5	2.15 Rational Expressions Core: 1, 2 Optional: 3, 4, 5	Core: 9, 10 Optional: 6, 7; Extension: 8, 11

NOTES	MATERIALS
Encourage students to try all the exercises.	
	• CAS (recommended) • Blackline Master 2.9
	• CAS (recommended) • graph paper • graphing calculators • Blackline Master 2.10

NOTES	MATERIALS
Encourage students to try all the exercises.	• CAS (recommended)
	• CAS (recommended)
	• CAS (recommended) • Blackline Master 2.13
	• CAS (recommended)
This lesson is optional.	• CAS (recommended) • graph paper • graphing calculators • Blackline Master 2.15

Developing Students' Mathematical Habits

In this chapter, students will develop key mathematical habits of mind. They will learn to

- write, compose, and invert functions
- model functions in function-modeling language
- develop an algebraic perspective in functions
- "work like a mathematician"—search for hidden regularity, describe patterns explicitly, and explain inconsistencies
- establish perspectives of functions through their formal perspectives

Chapter Vocabulary and Notation

The following list gives key vocabulary and notation used in the chapter. Selected new vocabulary and notation items are shown in boldface on the student page.

- additive inverse, p. 120
- binary operation, p. 110
- composite function, $g \circ f$, p. 110
- difference of cubes, p. 169
- domain, p. 104
- equal functions, p. 105
- Euclidean Property, p. 150
- function, p. 104
- identity function, p. 119
- inverse function, f^{-1}, p. 119
- Lagrange interpolation, p. 135
- monic, p. 124
- multiplicative inverse, p. 120
- natural domain, p. 97
- normal form, p. 107
- one-to-one, p. 117
- opposite, p. 120
- potato-and-arrow diagram, p. 104
- quadratic formula, p. 169
- quotient, p. 150
- range, p. 104
- rational expression, p. 183
- reciprocal, p. 120
- remainder, p. 150
- sum of cubes, p. 169
- target, p. 104
- zeros of a function, p. 123
- $f : A \rightarrow B$, p. 104
- $x \mapsto y$ (x maps to y), p. 100
- $\mathbb{R}$ (the real numbers), p. 102
- $\mathbb{Z}$ (the integers), p. 163
- $\mathbb{Q}$ (the rational numbers), p. 181

Chapter Road Map

INVESTIGATION 2A, *About Functions,* develops students' understanding of functions, including domain, target, and range of a function. Students represent functions with algebraic notation, graphs, and tables. They explore the properties of function composition and practice finding inverses of one-to-one functions.

INVESTIGATION 2B, *Making It Fit,* extends ideas from Chapter 1. Rather than relying on a special kind of table, such as the difference table work in the previous chapter, students learn to use Lagrange interpolation to find a polynomial function to match any table that defines a function. Through this work, students deepen their understanding of the Zero Product Property and begin to develop the idea that $n + 1$ data points are enough to completely determine a polynomial of degree n.

Functions and Polynomials

Mathematics has a remarkable relationship with the natural world. Often a table of observations of two related quantities matches a mathematical function. Examination of this function can reveal the relationship between the two quantities.

Suppose you throw a ball up into the air and measure its height at different times. Suppose further that you make a table with columns for the time elapsed since the throw and the height observed at that time. There is a quadratic function that matches this table.

If you measure the velocity of the ball at several times and make a table of time and the ball's velocity, a linear function matches the table. The linear function shows that the upward velocity of the ball decreases at a constant rate, eventually becoming negative as the ball stops rising and begins to fall back down.

The functions tell you what is happening to the ball. A scientific explanation tells why the function has the structure it does and what the coefficients and roots of the polynomial mean.

Vocabulary and Notation

- **composite function, $g \circ f$**
- **difference of cubes**
- **domain**
- **equal functions**
- **function**
- **identity function**
- **inverse function, f^{-1}**
- **Lagrange interpolation**
- **one-to-one**
- **quadratic formula**
- **quotient**
- **range**
- **rational expression**
- **remainder**
- **sum of cubes**
- **target**
- **$x \mapsto y$ (x maps to y)**
- **$\mathbb{R}$ (the real numbers)**
- **$\mathbb{Z}$ (the integers)**
- **$\mathbb{Q}$ (the rational numbers)**

INVESTIGATION 2C, ***Factors, Roots, and Zeros,*** has students prove the Remainder Theorem and the Factor Theorem. Students come to understand the correspondence between the roots of a polynomial and its linear factors. This understanding allows students to prove their intuition about the number of points required to completely determine a polynomial of degree n.

INVESTIGATION 2D, ***Advanced Factoring,*** has students practice factoring polynomials, with emphasis on quadratics. They will learn to scale a quadratic equation in order to write a new equation that is simpler to factor, and they learn techniques such as grouping and lumping.

Chapter Technology

CME Project *Algebra 2* assumes that each student has access to a graphing calculator. It also recommends access to a computer algebra system (CAS).

Support for the use of technology is available in the TI-Nspire™ Technology Handbook. See p. 778.

A list of technology used with important concepts in this chapter appears below. Students will need access to the functionality listed to develop complete understanding of these topics.

Computer Algebra System

LESSON 2.6 Use LaGrange interpolation to determine the next term in a sequence, p. 136.

LESSON 2.7 Find a polynomial function that agrees with the extension of a table, p. 140.

LESSON 2.9 Do polynomial division, p. 149.

LESSON 2.12 Factor a polynomial, p. 167.

Function-Modeling Language

LESSON 2.2 Experiment with $g(x) = \frac{1}{x} + 1$, p. 101. Build models defined by function machine networks, tabulate them, and graph them, p. 103.

LESSON 2.3 Build models for three functions and compose them, p. 111.

Graphing Calculator

LESSON 2.2 Experiment with the square root function, p. 101.

Lesson Overview

This lesson is special in the sense that it does not introduce new material to students, but reviews polynomials from *Algebra 1*. Use as much of this lesson as you feel you need to with your students. In any case, this should be a fairly quick review to remind students about polynomials. The problems and exercises in this lesson serve as a kind of general "Getting Started" for the rest of the chapter.

Students can do much of the reading for this lesson on their own, but make sure they remember the Zero Product Property (ZPP). Students will use it frequently for the rest of the chapter.

As students work on the problems and exercises in this review and in subsequent lessons, keep in mind the two ways of thinking of polynomials:

- You can think about them as *expressions*—things you can factor, simplify, or combine.
- You can think about them as *functions*—machines that take inputs and turn them into outputs.

The work that follows, and indeed, much of the subject of algebra, involves thinking about polynomials in both of these ways.

CHECK YOUR UNDERSTANDING
- Core: 1, 2, 4, 5
- Optional: 3

MATERIALS
- CAS (recommended)

HOMEWORK
- Core: 6, 7, 8, 9, 10, 11, 12, 13
- Optional: 14, 15, 16, 17

VOCABULARY
- coefficient
- degree of a monomial
- degree of a polynomial
- identity
- monomial
- normal form
- polynomial
- terms of a monomial
- terms of a polynomial

2.0 Polynomial Basics

Activating Prior Knowledge
Reviewing Key Ideas

In your first-year algebra course, you studied the basic facts about polynomials—what they are, how to talk about them, and how to calculate with them. This lesson reviews that material.

Start by reviewing some vocabulary.

First, pick a set of variables. The variables are just placeholders, and their meaning does not matter at the moment. The variables can be letters or expressions, such as x, y, $\sqrt{x}$, $\frac{1}{z}$, or more complicated expressions.

A **monomial** is an expression that you can write as a product of a nonzero number (this is the **coefficient**), and one or more variables, each raised to a nonnegative integer exponent.

The **degree of a monomial** is the sum of the exponents of each variable in the monomial.

When you want to specify the variables, you say that a monomial is a "monomial in something." For example, $4x^2y^3$ is a monomial in x and y.

A **polynomial** is a sum of monomials. The monomials are the **terms** of the polynomial.

The **degree of a polynomial** is the degree of all of its terms.

Here are a few examples:

- $3x^2$ is a monomial in x of degree 2. Its coefficient is 3.
- The monomial $7x^2y^3$ has coefficient 7, variables x and y, and degree 5.
- $7x^6 + 5x^3 - 3$ is a polynomial in x of degree 6.
- $7x^6 + 5x^3 - 3$ is also polynomial in x^3 of degree 2, because you can rewrite it as $7(x^3)^2 + 5(x^3) - 3$.
- The monomial b^3 has coefficient 1, variable b, and degree 3.
- The monomial $-\frac{1}{2}$ has coefficient $-\frac{1}{2}$ and degree 0. One way to think about this is that $x^0 = 1$, so $-\frac{1}{2}$ is equivalent to $-\frac{1}{2}x^0$.
- You can say that $3a + a^2b + 2ab^3 + 9b + 3$ is a polynomial in a and b. You can also say it is a quadratic polynomial in a with coefficients that are polynomials in b.
$$(9b + 3) + (3 + 2b^3)a + ba^2$$
You can also say that $3a + a^2b + 2ab^3 + 9b + 3$ is a cubic polynomial in b with coefficients that are polynomials in a.
$$(3a + 3) + (a^2 + 9)b + 2ab^3$$

$b^3 = 1b^3$

For You to Do

Consider the polynomial $\frac{1}{x^2} + \frac{3}{x^6}$.

1. Explain why it is not a polynomial in x.
2. It is a polynomial in $\frac{1}{x}$. What is its degree?
3. It is also a polynomial in $\frac{1}{x^2}$. What is its degree?

Answers

For You to Do

1. $\frac{1}{x^2} + \frac{3}{x^6}$ is not a polynomial because the variable appears in a denominator.
2. $\frac{1}{x^2} + \frac{3}{x^6} = \left(\frac{1}{x}\right)^2 + 3\left(\frac{1}{x}\right)^6$; the degree is 6.
3. $\frac{1}{x^2} + \frac{3}{x^6} = \left(\frac{1}{x^2}\right) + 3\left(\frac{1}{x^2}\right)^3$; the degree is 3.

Facts and Notation

There are several points to remember.

- **Two polynomials are equivalent if you can transform one into another with the basic rules of algebra. These rules include the commutative properties for addition and multiplication, the associative properties for addition and multiplication, and the Distributive Property.**
- **An *identity* is a statement that two polynomials are equivalent. For example, $x(x - 1) = x^2 - x$ is an identity. You can transform one side of the equation into the other using the basic rules of algebra.**
- **The form implies function principle says that if two polynomials are equivalent, then they define equal functions. They produce the same output for the same input. For example, $f(x) = x(x - 1)$ and $g(x) = x^2 - x$ produce the same output for any given input.**
- **The normal form of a polynomial in one variable is what you get when you apply the basic rules of algebra, collect like terms, and write the terms from highest to lowest degree. For example, the normal form of $f(x) = (x - 2)(x - 1)$ is $f(x) = x^2 - 3x + 2$.**

You may have learned the commutative and associative properties as the any-order-any-grouping principle. What are the other basic rules?

You can define normal form for polynomials in more than one variable, too. Each CAS has its own way of doing this.

For Discussion

4. Determine whether each expression is a polynomial in x. For expressions that are not polynomials in x, explain how they fail to meet the definition. For those that are polynomials in x, give the degree.

a. $5x$	b. $\frac{5}{x}$	c. $\frac{x}{5}$
d. $x + \sqrt{5}$	e. $5 + \sqrt{x}$	f. $xyz - z^{1999} - 0.093$
g. $(x^2 + x + 1)(y - 1)$	h. $x^{2.5} - 1.414$	i. $x^3 + 3^x$

For You to Do

5. Explain why two polynomials are equivalent if they have the same normal form.

Calculations with Polynomials

There are two ways to think about polynomials.

- You can think about them as formal expressions, in which the variables have no particular meaning.
- You can think about them as functions, in which the variables are placeholders for inputs.

Algebra involves thinking about polynomials in both ways. When you calculate with polynomials, you often think about them as expressions. The variables help you to keep the terms straight in your mind. When you substitute a number for the variable, you are thinking of the polynomial as a function.

Calculate here means to apply the basic rules of algebra.

Launch

Begin with For Discussion and then move on to the Examples.

Explore

For You to Do

This is an instance of the transitive property of equivalence. If two things are each equivalent to the same thing, they must be equivalent to each other. Another way that students might think about this is that they can transform each of the original polynomials into its normal form through a series of applications of the basic rules of algebra. Each of these rules is a "two-way street," so you could follow a path from one of the original polynomials to its normal form and then backward through the rules to the second original polynomial.

For You to Do

This is an identity that students will see again and again.

$$(x - 1)(1 + x + x^2 + x^3) = 1 - x^4$$

After a while, it will become as familiar to them as $(x - 1)(x + 1) = x^2 - 1$.

For Discussion

4. **a.** Yes; degree is 1.
   b. No; the variable is in a denominator.
   c. Yes; the degree is 1.
   d. Yes; the degree is 1.
   e. No; the variable appears inside a radical.
   f. No; there are 3 variables.
   g. No; there are 2 variables.
   h. No; the power of the variable is not a nonnegative integer.
   i. No; the variable appears in an exponent.

For You to Do

5. Answers may vary. Sample: If two polynomials (of degree n) have the same normal form, then they can be compared term by term. If each term of both polynomials is equal, then the polynomials are equal.

THEOREM Students should be convinced this is true before the proof. An alternate proof uses the fact that a number is either positive, negative, or zero, and there are nine possible outcomes when multiplying two numbers if you consider only the sign of the number. Every time $ab = 0$, one of a or b must be zero.

Wrap Up

Ask students to give an example in which they might use the Zero Product Property to solve an equation. Students should provide a quadratic equation such as $(x - 4)(x + 3) = 0$.

Example 1

Problem Find the normal form of $(1 - x)(1 + x + x^2)$.

Solution
$$\begin{aligned}(1 - x)(1 + x + x^2) &= 1 \cdot (1 + x + x^2) - x(1 + x + x^2)\\ &= 1 + x + x^2 + (-x - x^2 - x^3)\\ &= 1 - x^3\end{aligned}$$

For You to Do

6. Find the normal form of $(x - 1)(1 + x + x^2 + x^3)$.

One kind of polynomial identity results from factoring a polynomial. You can use this kind of identity in conjunction with the following property of real numbers to solve equations.

For example, $2x^2 + x - 1 = (2x + 3)(x - 1)$ is an identity. What numbers make $2x^2 + x - 1$ equal to 0?

Theorem 2.0 The Zero Product Property

If a and b are real numbers with a product of 0, then either a or b (or both) must be 0.

Put another way, the Zero Product Property (ZPP) says that if $ab = 0$, then at least one of the numbers a and b has to be 0.

Proof Suppose $ab = 0$.

If $a = 0$, you are done.

Suppose $a \neq 0$. Then by the basic rules of arithmetic, a has a reciprocal, $\frac{1}{a}$.

Multiply both sides of the equation $ab = 0$ by $\frac{1}{a}$. You find that $b = 0$.

So, if a is not 0, then b must be 0.

Example 2

Problem Find the solutions of each equation.

a. $x^2 - 5x + 6 = 0$

b. $x^2 - 10x + 10 = -14$

Solution

a. To solve the equation $x^2 - 5x + 6 = 0$, factor the polynomial.

$$x^2 - 5x + 6 = (x - 2)(x - 3)$$

Answers

For You to Do

6. $x^4 - 1$

So you can rewrite the equation as $(x-2)(x-3)=0$. By the ZPP, either

$$x-2=0 \text{ or } x-3=0$$

So $x=2$ or $x=3$.

b. To solve the equation $x^2-10x+10=-14$ with the ZPP, you cannot just factor. If $ab=-14$, you cannot conclude that $a=-14$ or $b=-14$. You need to use basic moves of algebra to rewrite the equation.

$$x^2-10x+24=0$$

Then you factor.

$$x^2-10x+24=(x-6)(x-4)$$

So $x=6$ or $x=4$.

If you substitute 2 or 3 into the original equation, you get $0=0$.

For You to Do

Solve each equation.

7. $(5x-3)(x^2-5x+6)=0$

8. $x^2-15x+30=-26$

Exercises *Practicing Habits of Mind*

Check Your Understanding

1. Determine which of these equations are identities.

a. $x^3-27=(x-3)(x^2+3x+9x)$

b. $x^2-16=(x-4)(x-4)$

c. $x^2-16=(4-x)(-4-x)$

d. $4x^2-16=(2x-4)(2x+4)$

e. $(2x-5)(4x+3)=10x^2-14x-15$

2. Without expanding, find the coefficient of x^{11} in the normal form of each polynomial.

a. $(x+x^2+x^3+x^4+x^5+x^6)^2$

b. $(x+x^2+x^3+x^4+x^5+x^6)^3$

For You to Do

7. $\frac{3}{5}$, 2, 3

8. 7, 8

Exercises

1. a. no **b.** no **c.** yes
d. yes **e.** no

2. a. 2 **b.** 27

Exercises

HOMEWORK

- Core: 6, 7, 8, 9, 10, 11, 12, 13
- Optional: 14, 15, 16, 17

Check Your Understanding

EXERCISE 2 Part (b) is much more elaborate than part (a). Encourage your students to do this without a CAS, as the intent of this exercise is to spark thoughts about how the terms in the normal form come about.

The polynomial $(x+x^2+x^3+x^4+x^5+x^6)$ represents the toss of one number cube. Chapter 6 explores more about this connection.

EXERCISE 3 Students who struggle with fractions (adding and multiplying them) may have difficulty here. Try to steer students away from expanding the product. Instead, they should expand the numerators and add or subtract the fractions, and then multiply the results. This method makes the computation much simpler.

GOING FURTHER The function at the beginning of this exercise simplifies to n^3, a very common function. This exercise presents a very interesting identity about perfect cubes. If students are familiar with triangular numbers, they might recognize the forms $\frac{n(n+1)}{2}$ and $\frac{n(n-1)}{2}$ as triangular numbers. They may also recognize the factored form as a difference of perfect squares:

$$\left(\frac{n(n+1)}{2}\right)^2 - \left(\frac{n(n-1)}{2}\right)^2$$

So, the identity is that you can express every perfect cube as a difference of squares of triangular numbers:

$$n^3 = \left(\frac{n(n+1)}{2}\right)^2 - \left(\frac{n(n-1)}{2}\right)^2$$

As always, to give this identity meaning, you might have students produce examples and then try to predict what the triangular numbers are for a given perfect cube.

EXERCISE 4 There is a proof of this exercise in the Solution Manual. The proof is an extension you should do only if time permits.

On Your Own

EXERCISES 6 AND 7 preview the Factor Theorem, which students will see in Lesson 2.10. Be sure to assign Exercise 6 and to review it as needed.

EXERCISE 10 If time permits, you might show the relationship between this exercise and Exercise 2. In fact, the answer to 10b is the same as the answer to 2b, because you can factor an x from each term in Exercise 2.

3. Consider the function below.

$$g(n) = \left(\frac{n(n+1)}{2} + \frac{n(n-1)}{2}\right)\left(\frac{n(n+1)}{2} - \frac{n(n-1)}{2}\right)$$

Find a much simpler expression that defines g.

4. Expand each product and combine like powers of x.

a. $(1 + x)(1 + x^2)$

b. $(1 + x)(1 + x^2)(1 + x^4)$

c. $(1 + x)(1 + x^2)(1 + x^4)(1 + x^8)$

d. $(1 + x)(1 + x^2)(1 + x^4)(1 + x^8)(1 + x^{16})$

5. Solve each equation.

a. $x^2 - 7x + 12 = 0$ **b.** $x^2 + 16x - 30 = 50$

c. $x^2 + 9 = 10x - 33$

On Your Own

6. Consider the polynomial $f(x) = x^2 + 4x - 5$.

a. Find $f(1)$.

b. Show that $(x - 1)$ is a factor of $f(x)$.

7. Consider the polynomial $g(x) = x^2 - 14x - 51$.

a. Find $g(17)$.

b. Show that $(x - 17)$ is a factor of $g(x)$.

8. Consider the polynomial $f(x) = x^2 + 4x - 5$.

a. Find $f(3)$. **b.** Find $f(x) - f(3)$.

c. Show that $(x - 3)$ is a factor of the polynomial $h(x) = f(x) - f(3)$.

9. Consider the polynomial $g(x) = x^2 - 14x - 51$.

a. Find $g(5)$. **b.** Find $g(x) - g(5)$.

c. Show that $(x - 5)$ is a factor of the polynomial $m(x) = g(x) - g(5)$.

10. a. Without expanding, find the coefficient of x^8 in the normal form of $(1 + x + x^2 + x^3 + x^4 + x^5)^2$.

b. Without expanding, find the coefficient of x^8 in the normal form of $(1 + x + x^2 + x^3 + x^4 + x^5)^3$.

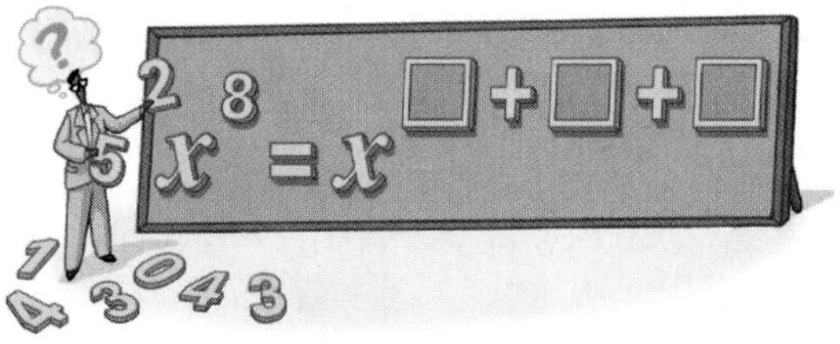

Answers

3. $g(n) = n^3$

4. a. $x^3 + x^2 + x + 1$

b. $x^7 + x^6 + x^5 + x^4 + x^3 + x^2 + x + 1$

c. $x^{15} + x^{14} + \cdots + x^2 + x + 1$

d. $x^{31} + x^{30} + \cdots + x^2 + x + 1$

5. a. 3, 4 **b.** −20, 4 **c.** 4, 6

6. a. 0

b. $f(1) = 0$, so $(x - 1)$ is a factor of $f(x)$.

7. a. $g(17) = 0$

b. $g(17) = 0$, so $(x - 17)$ is a factor of $g(x)$.

8. a. $f(3) = 16$

b. $x^2 + 4x - 21$

c. $f(x) - f(3) = x^2 + 4x - 21 = (x + 7)(x - 3)$, and $(x - 3)$ is a factor of that expression.

11. Let deg p be the degree of a polynomial p. Suppose f and g are arbitrary polynomials in x. For each part, find a relationship among the given values.

a. deg fg, deg f, and deg g

b. deg $2g$ and deg g

c. deg $(f + g)$, deg f, and deg g

12. If possible, find two polynomials, each of degree 6, such that the degree of their sum is 4.

13. If possible, find two polynomials, each of degree 6, such that the degree of their sum is 8.

14. Find the normal form for $(r + s)^3 - 3rs(r + s)$.

Habits of Mind

Experiment. Try some concrete examples. What are the polynomials of degree 0?

This is a polynomial in two variables. Think of it as a polynomial in one of the variables.

Maintain Your Skills

15. Find the degree of each polynomial.

a. $(x - 2)$

b. $(x - 2)(x + 3)$

c. $(x - 2)(x + 3)(x - 4)$

d. $(x - 2)(x + 3)(x - 4)(x - 5)$

e. $(x - 2)(x + 3)(x - 4)(x - 5)(x - 6)(x - 12)(x - 15)$

f. $(x - 2)(x + 3)^2$

g. $(x - 2)(x + 3)^2(x - 4)^3(x - 5)$

h. $(x - 2)^{20}$

16. Expand each product.

a. $(a - b)(a + b)$

b. $(a - b)(a^2 + ab + b^2)$

c. $(a - b)(a^3 + a^2b + ab^2 + b^3)$

d. $(a - b)(a^4 + a^3b + a^2b^2 + ab^3 + b^4)$

e. What is the pattern?

17. Expand each product.

a. $(1 + x)(1 - x)$

b. $(1 + x)(1 - x + x^2)$

c. $(1 + x)(1 - x + x^2 - x^3)$

d. What is the pattern?

EXERCISE 11 In part (c), students may not be able to express the relationship mathematically, but may be able to describe it well with a sentence. Many students will think that $\deg(f + g) = \deg f + \deg g$. Or they will miss the possibility that the sum of two polynomials may have a lower degree than each of the addends.

This exercise previews some findings in the lesson on Lagrange interpolation, in which the sum of several polynomials may be a polynomial of lesser degree.

9. a. $g(5) = -96$

b. $x^2 - 14x + 45$

c. $g(x) - g(5) = x^2 - 14x + 45 = (x - 9)(x - 5)$, and $(x - 5)$ is a factor of that expression.

10. a. 3 **b.** 27

11. a. $\deg(fg) = \deg(f) + \deg(g)$

b. $\deg(2g) = \deg(g)$

c. $\deg(f + g)$ is the greater of $\deg(f)$ and $\deg(g)$; if the degrees are equal, and if the leading coefficients are opposites, then $\deg(f + g)$ is less than $\deg(f)$ or $\deg(g)$.

12. Answers may vary. Sample: $f(x) = x^6 + x^4$ and $g(x) = -x^6 + x^4$

13. Not possible; the degree of the sum is less than or equal to that of the greater-degree polynomial.

14. $r^3 + s^3$

15. a. 1 **b.** 2 **c.** 3 **d.** 4 **e.** 7 **f.** 3 **g.** 7 **h.** 20

16–17. See back of book.

Investigation Overview

This investigation continues work in functions from *Algebra 1* as well as work from the previous investigations in this course. *Algebra 1* introduced the function as a machine. Although the machine metaphor can be useful, the previous investigations' focus on finding rules to fit tables and on graphing gets students beyond that metaphor into thinking of functions as objects in their own right.

In adopting this perspective, you want students to think like "algebraists." The set of functions has an operation, composition, under which

- The set is closed. The composition of two functions is a function.
- There is an identity element. For any function $f(x)$, you know $f \circ x = x \circ f = f$.
- The set is associative. For any three functions $f(x)$, $g(x)$, and $h(x)$, you know $f \circ (g \circ h) = (f \circ g) \circ h$.
- Some elements have inverses. One-to-one functions are invertible.

Other properties do not necessarily hold. For example, the set is not commutative, because it is not always true that $f \circ g = g \circ f$.

You want to emphasize that you are not formally focusing on algebraic structure here. You just want students to get used to thinking this way, to smooth the way for future work. For example, this perspective will be invaluable when students work with matrices in Chapter 4. The set of matrices with multiplication is another set that is closed, has identity and associativity, partial inverses, and no commutativity.

You may wish to assign Questions 1–3 for students to think and write about during the investigation.

Learning Goals

- Decide whether a table, graph, or closed-form rule is a function.
- Use function notation.
- Decide whether two rules define the same function.
- Determine the domain, target, and range of a function.
- Compose functions.
- Decide whether a given function has an inverse.
- Find the inverse of a one-to-one function.

Habits and Skills

- Write, compose, and invert functions.
- Model functions in a function-modeling language.
- Develop an algebraic perspective on functions.
- "Work like a mathematician"—search for hidden regularities, describe the patterns explicitly, and explain inconsistencies.
- Establish properties of functions.

Investigation 2A

About Functions

In *About Functions*, you will build on your understanding of functions as machines that accept inputs and produce outputs. You will also see that the definition of a function is not complete unless you specify the set of allowable inputs.

By the end of this investigation, you will be able to answer questions like these.

1. What is a function?
2. How do you compose two functions to make a new function?
3. What function undoes $x \mapsto 3x + 7$?

You will learn how to

- decide whether a table, graph, or closed-form rule is a function
- use function notation
- decide whether two rules define the same function
- determine the domain, target, and range of a function
- compose functions
- decide whether a given function has an inverse
- find the inverse of a one-to-one function

You will develop these habits and skills:

- Write, compose, and invert functions.
- Model functions in a function-modeling language.
- Develop an algebraic perspective on functions.
- "Work like a mathematician"—search for hidden regularities, describe the patterns explicitly, and explain inconsistencies.
- Establish properties of functions.

A function machine can double the size of the input.

Investigation Road Map

LESSON 2.1, ***Getting Started,*** gets students thinking about functions, including ideas about domain and range.

LESSON 2.2, ***Getting Precise About Functions,*** reminds students of the *Algebra 1* perspective and builds the formal definitions of *function, domain, target,* and *range* on that perspective.

LESSON 2.3, ***Algebra With Functions,*** introduces students to composition.

LESSON 2.4, ***Inverses: Doing and Undoing,*** introduces one-to-one functions and inverse functions.

2.1 Getting Started

Activating Prior Knowledge
Exploring New Ideas

By now, you have some idea of what a function is. Here are a few functions.

SQRT(x) = the square root of a real number x
SQR(x) = the square of a real number x
REC(n) = the reciprocal of a real number n
BD(p) = the birthday of a person p
SUM(a, b) = the sum of two numbers a and b
PR(a, b) = the product of two numbers a and b
QUO(a, b) = the quotient of two numbers a and b

Here is a formula for QUO.
QUO(a, b) $= \frac{a}{b}$
Not all functions have formulas. For example, BD does not have one.

For You to Explore

1. If possible, find the value of each expression. If an expression cannot be evaluated, explain why not.
   - a. PR(3, 4)
   - b. QUO(3, 4)
   - c. QUO(6, 8)
   - d. QUO(0, 23)
   - e. QUO(23, 0)
   - f. SQR(SQRT(5))
   - g. SQRT(SQR(5))
   - h. SQR(SQRT(−5))
   - i. SQRT(SQR(−5))
   - j. QUO(P(3,4), P(2,6))
   - k. BD(Pierre Fermat)
   - l. BD(3)
   - m. SQRT(SUM(9, 16))
   - n. SUM(SQRT(9), SQRT(16))
   - o. SQRT(BD(Isaac Newton))
   - p. SQRT(PR$\left(-2, \frac{1}{3}\right)$)
   - q. REC(2)
   - r. REC(REC(2))
   - s. REC(REC(REC(2)))
   - t. REC(0)
2. A mystery function $m(x)$ has the inputs and outputs below. How can you define the function?

   $m(\pi) = 3 \quad m(2.9) = 2 \quad m(5) = 5 \quad m(11.6) = 11 \quad m(-1.3) = -2$
3. Consider the function SQRT.
   - a. Is the following equation true?

     SQRT($a + b$) = SUM(SQRT(a), SQRT(b))
   - b. **Take It Further** If the equation above is true for all numbers, prove it. If it is not, find the conditions on a and b that make it true.

SQRT(Joseph Louis Lagrange) does not make sense. The largest set of inputs for which a function produces an output is the function's natural domain.

You can restrict the domain even further. For example, the function $A(r) = \pi r^2$ gives the area of a circle with radius r. You want to restrict the domain to positive numbers.

4. Find the natural domain of each function. Describe the domain in detail.
   - a. QUO
   - b. SQRT
   - c. QUO
   - d. REC
   - e. $f(x) = \frac{\sqrt{x}}{x-2}$

Answers

For You to Explore

1. See back of book.
2. Answers may vary. Sample: $m(x)$ is the greatest integer less than or equal to x.
3. **a–b.** This is true if $a = 0$ or if $b = 0$, but not true otherwise.
4. **a.** The domain consists of all persons or animals.

   b. The domain is all nonnegative numbers.

   c. The domain is all real numbers, as long as the second number is not 0.

   d. The domain is all real numbers except 0.

   e. The domain is all nonnegative real numbers except 2.

Lesson Overview

GOAL

- Warm up to the ideas of the investigation.

In this lesson, students encounter functions by evaluating a number of expressions. This work introduces several ideas such as

- In evaluating expressions PR(3, 4), where PR(a, b) is the product of the two numbers a and b, students encounter functions of two variables.
- Inverse functions get a nod when students evaluate SQR(SQRT(5)), where SQR(x) is the square of x and SQRT(x) is the square root of x.
- This lesson introduces composition with expressions such as SQRT(SUM(9,16)), where SUM(a, b) is the sum of the two numbers a and b, and SQRT is the square root function.
- This lesson introduces ideas of domain when students try to evaluate BD(3), where BD(p) is the birthday of a person p.

As always in a Getting Started lesson, there is no need to formalize these ideas today. Students encounter these ideas again throughout the investigation.

FOR YOU TO EXPLORE
- Core: 1, 2, 4, 5
- Optional: 3a
- Extension: 3b

HOMEWORK
- Core: 6, 7, 8a–e, 11
- Optional: 9, 10, 12, 13
- Extension: 8f

MATERIALS
- graph paper
- graphing calculators

VOCABULARY
- natural domain

Launch

Discuss the functions shown at the beginning of the lesson. Some of these functions have a familiar mathematical form. Students should see that SQR(x) is the same as x^2 and REC(n) is the same as $\frac{1}{n}$. A function, however, does not have to be mathematical. For example, BD(p) returns the birthday of the person p. You might ask, "What is BD(a student in your class)?" Once students are comfortable with the notation, let them get started on the For You to Explore problems.

Explore

For You to Explore

As students work, have them verbalize their idea of "function." Are students thinking in terms of the machine metaphor? Are they noticing relationships between functions? How comfortable are they with composition and function notation?

continued on p. 98

continued from p. 97

PROBLEMS 1–5 Let students work freely on these problems, which stress order of functions and raise some issues of domain, such as when functions are undefined.

PROBLEM 3 Students may get stuck on part (b). It is not critical that they complete the problem right now. Encourage them to give it a try. If a solution does not come easily, go on to the rest of the problems and come back to this problem later.

Wrap Up

Go over selected parts of Problems 1, 4, and 5. Discuss *natural domain*.

Exercises

HOMEWORK

- Core: 6, 7, 8a–e, 11
- Optional: 9, 10, 12, 13
- Extension: 8f

On Your Own

EXERCISE 7 In part (b), you might have two students in your class with the same birthday. If not, ask if students know of friends, relatives, or famous people who share their birthdays. For example, BD(James Polk) = BD(Warren Harding) = November 2.

EXERCISE 9 In part (f), ask students to write an equation for $B(x, y, z)$ that does not contain $D(x, y)$. (Answer: $B(x, y, z) = \sqrt{x^2 + y^2} + z$) If $\sqrt{x^2 + y^2} + z = 0$, what is the sign of z? (Answer: negative)

The key property of a function is that it turns each input into a well-defined output. The inputs are members of the domain. The set of all outputs is the *range* of the function.

5. For each function in Problem 4, you defined a domain. Using that domain, describe each function's range.

Exercises *Practicing Habits of Mind*

On Your Own

6. Suppose each function gives an output of 9. Do you have enough information to determine the input? Explain.

a. PR **b.** SQRT **c.** SQR

7. If possible, find two different inputs for each function that give the same output.

a. SQR **b.** BD **c.** QUO

d. SQRT **e.** REC

8. Use the definition of function D below.

$$D(x, y) = \sqrt{x^2 + y^2}$$

Find each value.

a. $D(0, 0)$ **b.** $D(3, 4)$ **c.** $D(-3, 4)$ **d.** $D(4, 3)$

e. Find another input that makes $D(x, y) = 5$.

f. **Take It Further** Draw a graph of all the coordinate pairs (x, y) that make $D(x, y) = 5$.

What is the natural domain of D?

Can you find a pair of irrational numbers (x, y) that makes $D(x, y) = 5$?

9. Suppose you define the function $B(x, y, z)$ in terms of $D(x, y)$ from Exercise 8 as follows.

$$B(x, y, z) = D(x, y) + z$$

For example, $B(3, 4, 10) = 15$, since $D(3, 4) = 5$.

Find each value.

a. $B(0, 0, 0)$ **b.** $B(3, 4, 5)$ **c.** $B(4, 3, 5)$ **d.** $B(-3, 4, -5)$

e. Find the value of z such that $B(5, 12, z) = 7$.

f. Find all triples (x, y, z) such that $B(x, y, z) = 0$.

Answers

5. a. The range is any day of the year.
b. The range is any nonnegative number.
c. The range is all real numbers.
d. The range is all real numbers except 0.
e. The range is all real numbers.

Exercises

6. a. no **b.** yes; 81 **c.** no

7. a. Answers may vary. Sample: −3 and 3
b. Answers may vary. Sample: almost all twins
c. Answers may vary. Sample: (3, 6) and (4, 8)
d. impossible
e. impossible

8. a. 0 **b.** 5 **c.** 5 **d.** 5
e. Answers may vary. Sample: (−3, −4)
f. See back of book.

9. See back of book.

10. a. Is it possible for the output of $D(x, y)$ to be negative? Explain.
b. Is it possible for the output of $B(x, y, z)$ to be negative? Explain.

Maintain Your Skills

11. Use the definitions of functions f and g below.

$f(x) = 3x - 7$

$g(x) = \frac{x+7}{3}$

Find each value.

a. $f(10)$ b. $g(23)$
c. $f(f(0))$ d. $g(g(-28))$
e. $f(g(172))$ f. $g(f(0.27))$
g. $f(g(f(g(1000))))$

12. Use the definitions of functions h and j below.

$h(x) = (x - 1)^2$

$j(x) = \sqrt{x} + 1$

Find each value.

a. $h(4)$ b. $j(9)$
c. $h(h(3))$ d. $j(j(16))$
e. $j(h(5))$ f. $j(h(-5))$
g. $h(j(-3))$

What are the natural domains of h and j?

13. Suppose $f(x) = x + 4$. Find each value.

a. $f(3)$ b. $f(f(3))$
c. $f(f(f(3)))$ d. $f(f(f(f(3))))$
e. $\underbrace{f(f(\ldots(f(3)))))))))))}_{12\ f\text{'s}}$

14. Suppose $g(x) = \frac{x+1}{x}$. Find each value.

a. $g(1)$ b. $g(g(1))$
c. $g(g(g(1)))$ d. $g(g(g(g(1))))$
e. $g(g(g(g(g(1)))))$ f. $\underbrace{g(g(\ldots(g(1))))))))))}_{10\ g\text{'s}}$

10. a. No, $D(x, y) = \sqrt{x^2 + y^2}$, and since $x^2 \geq 0$ and $y^2 \geq 0$, $D(x, y) \geq 0$.
b. If $z < -\sqrt{a^2 + b^2}$, then $B(x, y, z) < 0$. Answers may vary. Sample: $B(3, 4, -6) = 5 - 6 = -1$

11. a. 23 b. 10 c. -28
d. 0 e. 172 f. 0.27
g. 1000

12. a. 9 b. 4 c. 9
d. $\sqrt{5} + 1$ e. 5 f. 7
g. undefined

13. a. 7 b. 11 c. 15
d. 19 e. 51

14. a. 2 b. $\frac{3}{2}$ c. $\frac{5}{3}$
d. $\frac{8}{5}$ e. $\frac{13}{8}$ f. $\frac{144}{89}$

Maintain Your Skills

EXERCISE 11 is an important preview of the concept and relationships of inverse functions. Be sure to assign it and check for students' understanding.

EXERCISE 12 Students may get the wrong answer for part (g) because they are using the results from earlier computations. They may not yet be considering the domain and range of functions. Functions h and j are not complete inverses for this reason: both functions have only positive outputs, so although h can accept negative inputs, you will never get a negative output from any composition of these functions. You might ask students to compute $j(h(-3))$, which is not equal to -3.

EXERCISE 13 Students may notice that this repeated application of the same function to an input reminds them of the recursive functions with w hich they have already worked. It is like computing $r(12)$ for this function:

$$r(n) = \begin{cases} 3 & \text{if } n = 0 \\ r(n-1) + 4 & \text{if } n > 0 \end{cases}$$

Lesson Overview

GOALS

- Use function notation.
- Determine whether two rules define the same function.
- Determine the domain, target, and range of a function.
- Compose functions.

This lesson has two main components: to review the *Algebra 1* notion of functions and to introduce the formal definition of a function.

If students are comfortable with the idea that a function takes an input to a single consistent output, you can go through the introductory material in the chapter quickly. This is also a good place to check that students know that for a function f and input a, the output is $f(a)$.

It is important that the formal notion is built on the intuition about functions that students have built up through work in *Algebra 1* and previous investigations in *Algebra 2*. You want the formal ideas to be sensible to students. To that end, this lesson introduces two concepts:

- The domain of a function is part of its definition.

When thinking about domain, students are building on the work they did in Lesson 2.1: It just is not sensible to evaluate BD(3) (What is 3's birthday?). 3 is not in the domain of the function BD(p). Similarly, if the volume of a box is given by a particular function, the only sensible inputs are those that could be possible to form a box.

- Functions are determined by their behavior.

In a machine model of a function, you can think of the functions $x \mapsto x^2 + x$ and $x \mapsto x(x + 1)$ as very different "machines." But from the functional perspective, these are the same function, because they refer to the same input-output pairings.

After you introduce these ideas, you give the formal definition of a function along with two ways to think about the definition in the context of representations of functions.

CHECK YOUR UNDERSTANDING
- Core: 1, 2, 3, 4, 5
- Optional: 6, 7, 8, 9

MATERIALS
- CAS (recommended)
- graph paper
- graphing calculators
- Blackline Master 2.2

HOMEWORK
- Core: 10, 11, 12a–d, 14, 16, 17, 19, 23a–d
- Optional: 13, 15, 18, 20, 21
- Extension: 12e, 23e, 24

VOCABULARY
- domain
- equal functions
- function
- normal form
- range
- target
- $f : A \mapsto B$

2.2 Getting Precise About Functions

The algebra 1 point of view

You may think of functions as machines that take inputs and produce outputs.

The function is the machine. An input is anything you pass into a function, and the corresponding output is whatever the machine produces. You can define many functions with rules or algorithms, sets of instructions about what to do to an input to produce an output.

You put in x.

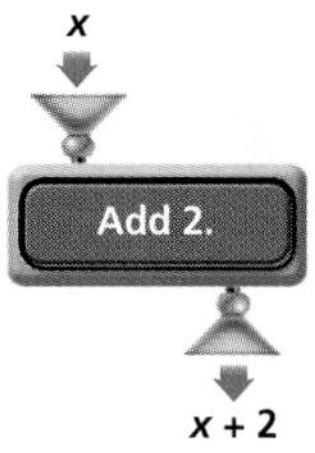

Out comes $x + 2$.

The function is the machine.

The rule is what the machine does to the input to get the output.

Remember...
An algorithm or rule is a recipe. Two kinds of rules are especially useful in algebra: polynomial rules and recursive rules.

You can use arrow notation to write a function.

$$x \mapsto \frac{1}{x}$$

You say "x maps to 1 over x."

For this function, the input is a nonzero number x and the output at x is the reciprocal of x.

You put in 2. You put in 9. You put in $-\frac{1}{3}$.

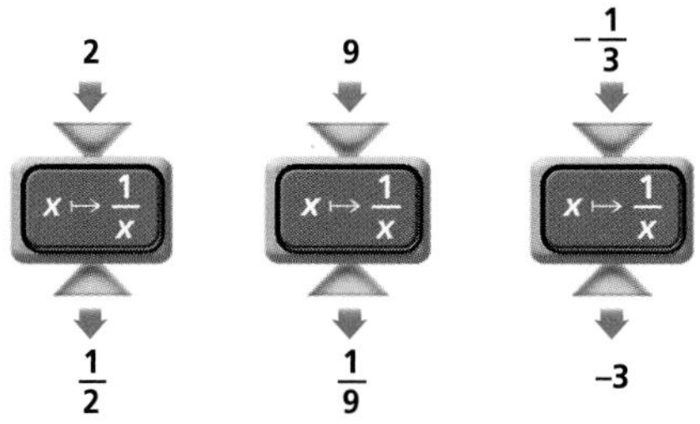

Out comes $\frac{1}{2}$. Out comes $\frac{1}{9}$. Out comes −3.

Habits of Mind
Detect the key characteristics. Why does the input have to be a nonzero number?

Another way to describe functions is to name the machine, usually with a letter, such as f, or a shorthand, such as ABS. Then you can use the name of the function to describe the output. If you call a function f and you give it an input of 3, the output is $f(3)$.

If the input is x and the function is f, then the output is $f(x)$.

Not every rule gives a function. The rule "to find $f(x)$, flip a coin; if it comes up heads, output $x + 2$; otherwise output $x + 3$" does not define a function.

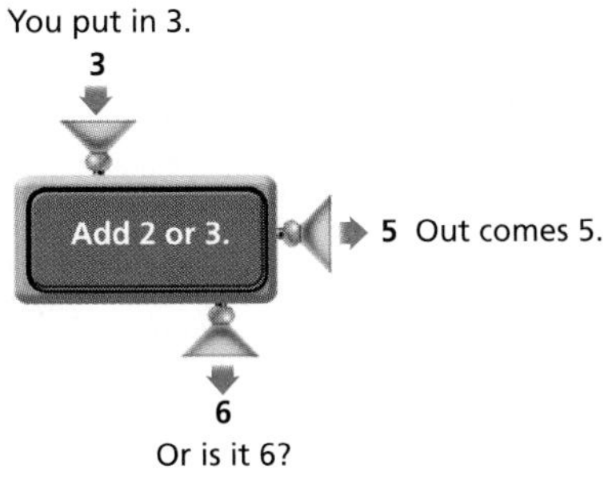

A good example of a function on your calculator is the square root function. You give it an input, and it gives you exactly one output.

Remember...

In mathematics, it is customary to name a function with a single letter. In computer science, it is customary to name a function with a short abbreviation for what it does. So, ABS might stand for absolute value. How does your calculator name functions?

For You to Do

1. Experiment with the square root function on your calculator. Find the outputs for the inputs 4, 8, and −4. What numbers are their own square roots?
2. Pick a positive number. Take its square root. Take the square root of the result. Keep going. What happens?

You can also define your own function in a function-modeling language. You give the function a name and a rule for finding outputs.

$$\text{define } g(x) = \frac{1}{x} + 1$$

You can then use this model just like a built-in function—give it inputs, tabulate it, graph it, and experiment with it.

Try evaluating 5 + 2*g(6).

For You to Do

3. Pick a positive number. Take g of it. Take g of the result. Keep going. What happens?

Launch

Depending on students' previous experience with functions, either spend some time on the machine metaphor in Problems 1–3 or move quickly to "Building on the Algebra 1 point of view."

Explore

Discuss the machine that uses the coin-flipping rule. Suppose you input 4 and the coin comes up heads, making the output 6. Suppose you input 4 again, and this time the coin comes up tails. Now the output is 7. The same input produced two *different* outputs, so the rule does not define a function.

For You to Do

PROBLEMS 1–3 Several ideas come up here: domain, composition, and functional notation. For Problem 3, when students choose a positive number and apply g repeatedly, their answer tends to the number $1.6180\ldots = \frac{1 + \sqrt{5}}{2}$, one of the fixed points of the function g. The goal here is not to get distracted by this fixed point, but it is intriguing. If students' interest is piqued, they might use a graph to explore what is happening.

Answers

For You to Do

1. $4 \to 2$; $8 \to 2.828$; $-4 \to$ "error;" 1 and 0
2. Answers may vary. Sample: The result gets closer and closer to 1.
3. Answers may vary. Sample: The result gets closer and closer to 1.62.

For You to Do

PROBLEM 4 Blackline Master 2.2 provides a copy of the box.

When students graph this function, you might ask whether the domain they have chosen for their graphs makes sense. This is an important example of the importance of domain: you want to make sure students are using functions sensibly. Because this function is associated with a real problem, the domain is restricted to "sensible" values of x.

If students graph the function $V(x) = x(5 - 2x)(8 - 2x)$, the domain appears to be all real numbers. But volume is only nonnegative for $0 \leq x \leq 2.5$ and $4 \leq x$. Furthermore, x cannot be more than 2.5, because one side of the box has length 5. So, the sensible domain for the function (and for the graph of the function) is $0 \leq x \leq 2.5$.

Some students may argue that $x = 0$ and $x = 2.5$ are invalid inputs as well because they do not lead to an actual box. This is acceptable, but do not spend time debating it.

In your first-year algebra course, you may have learned that the set of all possible inputs that cause a function to produce an output is the domain of the function.

The calculator model of $g(x) = \frac{1}{x} + 1$ can take any input except 0. Asking for $g(0)$ generates an error. This means that 0 is not in the domain of g.

You put in 0.

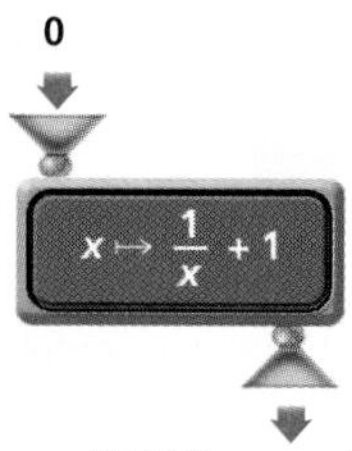

ERROR: no reciprocal.

Building on the algebra 1 point of view

In this course, it is essential to make some finer distinctions about functions and to state things in a more precise way. Here, you will revisit the working definitions of *function* and *domain*. You will talk about the collection of outputs for a function. This discussion focuses on two of the finer distinctions about functions.

In the next lesson, you will do a kind of algebra with functions. You will need a better and more precise language for talking about functions.

The domain of a function is part of its definition. Take a piece of paper, say 5 inches × 8 inches. Cut a little square out of each corner. Fold up the sides to make a box.

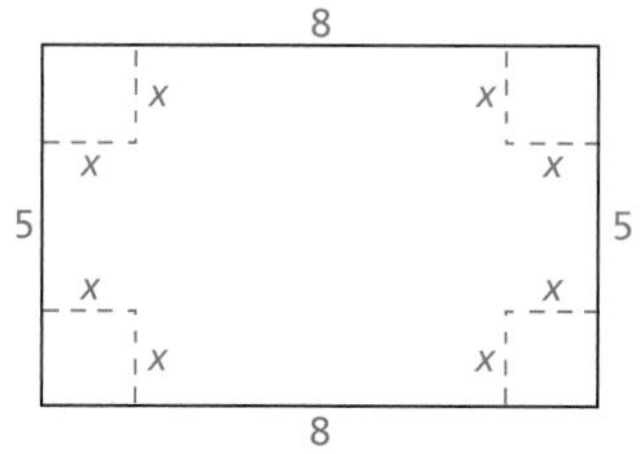

If the side length of the cutout is x, the volume V of the box is a function of x.

For You to Do

4. Let $V(x)$ be the volume of the box when a square of side length x is cut from each corner. Show that $V(x) = x(5 - 2x)(8 - 2x)$.

There is a problem here. The natural domain for V is all real numbers, $\mathbb{R}$. But, in terms of the box, an input of -2 makes no sense. You cannot cut -2 inches from the corners of the rectangle. In fact, the only numbers that make sense for the size of a cutout are $0 \leq x \leq \frac{5}{2}$. So, a complete definition of V is

Besides, $V(-2) = -216$.

> V is the function defined on the domain $0 \leq x \leq \frac{5}{2}$ such that $V(x) = x(5 - 2x)(8 - 2x)$.

Answers

For You to Do

4. After cutting out 4 squares of side x for the corners and folding the open box, the dimensions are x, $5 - 2x$, and $8 - 2x$. So the volume is $x(5 - 2x)(8 - 2x)$.

Functions on different domains are different functions, even if they share the same formula. The function defined on all of $\mathbb{R}$ by

$$f(x) = x(5 - 2x)(8 - 2x)$$

is different from V. In fact, since the domain for f contains the domain for V, you call V a restriction of f and you call f an extension of V.

Habits of Mind

Consider the context. Sometimes you use the same expression to define a function on different domains. The appropriate domain depends on the context.

Functions are determined by their behavior. Look at these machine models for two functions.

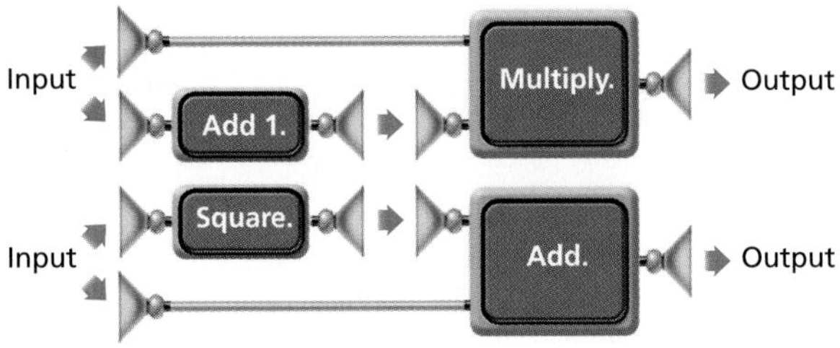

The domain for both functions is all of $\mathbb{R}$. These networks look as if they do very different things to their inputs. But if you build models for the functions in a function-modeling language and display tables of them side by side, you cannot tell them apart.

For You to Do

5. Try it. Build a model for each network above. Call the models f and g. Make a table for f and g. Then graph them. Do you see any difference? Can you prove that the two functions act the same for all inputs?

For advice on modeling, graphing, and making tables of functions, see the TI-Nspire Handbook, p. 778.

For all practical purposes, these two functions are the same. This point of view—two functions are the same if they give the same outputs for all inputs is—is the one that people use in most parts of mathematics and science today. As long as two functions refer to the same input-output pairings, it does not matter how the rule works on the inside.

For You to Do

6. Suppose f has domain $\mathbb{R}^+$ and the rule $f(x) = 3x + 7$. Show that the two functions below agree with f on its domain.

- $x \mapsto 3|x| + 7$
- $x \mapsto |3x + 7|$

Does either of them agree with f on all of $\mathbb{R}$?

In this course, $\mathbb{R}^+$ stands for the nonnegative real numbers.

For You to Do

5. The first model is $f(x) = (x + 1)x$ and the second model is $g(x) = x^2 + x$. Since $(x + 1)x = x^2 + x$, the two functions always give the same output for a given input.

6. If x is a nonnegative real number, then $3x + 7$ is nonnegative, so $|3x + 7| = 3x + 7$.
No; sample: If $x = -5$, then $3x + 7 = -8$, $3|x| + 7 = 22$, and $|3x + 7| = 8$.

For You to Do

PROBLEM 6 You might want to ask students to find the largest domain on which each function agrees with f. (Answer: $x \mapsto 3|x| + 7$ agrees with f when $x \geq 0$. $x \mapsto |3x + 7|$ agrees with f when $x \geq -\frac{7}{3}$.)

NOTE ON NOTATION Throughout the book you will use the notation $\mathbb{R}^+$ to stand for nonnegative real numbers. While this is a standard notation for this set, some books refer to $\mathbb{R}^+$ as positive real numbers (not including zero). Decide which notation you would prefer to use: if you decide to use $\mathbb{R}^+$ to represent positive real numbers, then the notation for nonnegative numbers is

$$\mathbb{R}^+ \cup \{0\}$$

Developing Habits of Mind

Ask students to visualize a potato-and-arrow diagram that does not represent a function.

To define a function, you must first specify two sets: a *domain* A and a *target* B. Then a function from A to B is a recipe that produces, for each member of A, a unique member of B.

Definitions

Suppose A and B are two sets of objects. A function from A to B is a pairing between A and B such that each element in A pairs with exactly one element of B.

This notation denotes a function f from set A to set B:

$$f : A \rightarrow B$$

A is the domain of f. B is the target of f. The set of objects in B that are paired with objects in A is the range of f.

Remember...

A and *B* can be sets of numbers, points, people, triangles, and so on. Any pairing between *A* and *B* is a *relation*, while a *function* is a pairing that involves each element of *A* exactly once.

If the domain of a function is not stated explicitly, assume that its domain is as large as possible. This is the natural domain of a function. For example, the natural domain of $f(x) = \frac{1}{x} + 1$ is all real numbers other than 0.

Developing Habits of Mind

Visualize. The key idea here is that a function assigns each object in A to exactly one object in B. Here is a picture of a function from A to B.

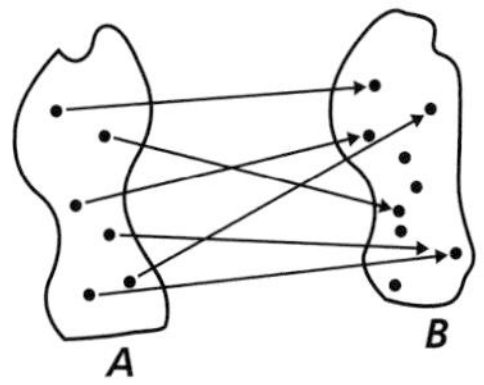

This is a "potato-and-arrow" diagram.

Each element of A is paired with exactly one element of B.
Note the following:

- Not every element of B is an output. The range (things that are outputs) does not have to match the entire target (things that might be outputs).
- Two elements of A can be paired with the same element of B. The definition of a function only prohibits one element of A from being paired with more than one element of B.

Think about the birthday function from Lesson 2.1. One possible domain (Set A) might be the students in your class. The target (Set B) is the days of the year. The range is not all days in the year, however. It is only those days that actually get paired. The range for that domain is the days of the year that are birthdays for at least one person in your class.

Note that it is still a function if two students in the same class have the same birthday. It would not be a function if one student had two birthdays!

Example

Problem Find the domain, target, and range for the function $f: \mathbb{R} \to \mathbb{R}$, where $f(x) = x^2$.

Solution The domain and target are given by the function statement. The domain is $\mathbb{R}$, and so is the target.

The rule $f(x) = x^2$ determines the range. This function produces squares. No squares are negative. So the range is the set of all nonnegative real numbers, $\mathbb{R}^+$.

Remember...

The domain is the first set, and the target is the second.

So, when are two functions the same? You now have the language to talk about this.

Definition

Two functions *f* and *g* are equal functions if both these conditions are satisfied.

- **f and g have the same domain.**
- **$f(a) = g(a)$ for every a in the common domain.**

If f and g are equal functions, you write $f = g$. This means the functions satisfy the conditions in this definition.

Developing Habits of Mind

Look for relationships. Two functions may be different (not equal) on their natural domains and yet be equal if you restrict their domains to some smaller set. For example, the two functions below are not equal.

$$f: \mathbb{R} \to \mathbb{R}, \text{ where } f = 2x + 1$$

$$g: \mathbb{R} \to \mathbb{R}, \text{ where } g(x) = 2x + 1 + (x-1)(x-2)(x-3)$$

For example, $f(5) = 11$ and $g(5) = 35$. But f and g are equal if you restrict the domain to the numbers 1, 2, and 3. So you can say $f = g$ on the domain $\{1, 2, 3\}$.

For You to Do

7. Suppose you have the following function.

$$f(x) = \begin{cases} 3 & \text{if } x = 0 \\ f(x-1) + 5 & \text{if } x > 0 \end{cases}$$

What is the natural domain of f? Find a function $g: \mathbb{R} \to \mathbb{R}$ that is equal to f on the natural domain of f.

For You to Do

7. The natural domain is all nonnegative integers; $g(x) = 5x + 3$.

For You to Do

PROBLEM 7 Students could work on this problem before beginning the Check Your Understanding exercises, but since they probably do not have much experience thinking about the target, you might want to do this problem with the Check Your Understanding exercises together as a class. You might also start with the Example. The target can be any set that contains the range. So in the Example, you could also write the function as

$$f: \mathbb{R} \to \mathbb{R}^+, \text{ where } f(x) = x^2$$

in which case the target would be $\mathbb{R}^+$. Or you could write the function as

$$f: \mathbb{R} \to \mathbb{R}^+ \cup \{-2\}, \text{ where } f(x) = x^2$$

in which case the target would be $\mathbb{R}^+ \cup \{-2\}$. In other words, there is not necessarily a single correct answer for how to write the function in the form $f: A \to B$, and there is not necessarily a single correct target space. The target has to match B and has to contain the range.

Call attention to the fact that domain and range are the important considerations here.

Wrap Up

To conclude this lesson, make sure students can identify functions. For a given function, students should be able to identify the domain and the range of the function. To assess this, go over one of the Check Your Understanding core exercises.

Assessment Resources

Lesson Quiz 2.2

1. Consider the function $f(x) = (\sqrt[4]{x})^3$.
   a. What is the natural domain of f?
   b. Find the range of f using the natural domain.

2. For each function, find the natural domain, target, and range.
   a. $f(x) = -4x^2 + 8x - 3$
   b. $f(x) = \sqrt{x-4} + 3$
   c. $f(x, y) = 2x - 3y$
   d. $f(x, y) = (-x, -y)$

3. Suppose $f: \mathbb{R} \to \mathbb{R}$ and $f(x) = 2x - 1$. Find the value of a in each case.
   a. $2f(4) + 1 = 6a$
   b. $f(a + 2) = 6$
   c. $f(a + 2) = 3a - 4$

4. For each function, find all values of x such that $f(x) = 1890$.
   a. $f(x) = 8x + 6$
   b. $f(x) = 8x^2 + 6$
   c. $f(x) = 8x^3 + 6$

Exercises

HOMEWORK

- Core: 10, 11, 12a–d, 14, 16, 17, 19, 23a–d
- Optional: 13, 15, 18, 20, 21
- Extension: 12e, 23e, 24

Check Your Understanding

EXERCISES 1–6 elicit an intuitive understanding of domain and range coming from a situation. You should assign these exercises as a follow-up to Problem 4 in this lesson about the volume function.

EXERCISE 2 In part (b), you may want to point out how the physical properties of the rectangle restrict the domain of A. Because the length of a side of the rectangle cannot be less than or equal to zero, $x > 0$. To help students place an upper limit on the value of x, ask them to think about what the sum of the rectangle's base and height must be if its perimeter is 144. (Answer: 72)

EXERCISE 4 Point out the connection to Chapter 1 and the differences between a recursive and closed-form definition of a rule.

EXERCISE 5 You might have students compare the natural domain and range of h with the natural domain and range of the function $g(x) = \sqrt{x^2}$. Like h, g has $\mathbb{R}$ as its natural domain, but its range is $\mathbb{R}^+$, instead of $\mathbb{R}$. This comparison may help students understand Exercise 13.

Exercises *Practicing Habits of Mind*

Check Your Understanding

1. Let $f : \mathbb{R} \to \mathbb{R}$ and $f(x) = 72x - x^2$.

a. What is the range of f?

b. Graph f over its domain.

2. There are many rectangles with perimeter 144. Let x be the length of such a rectangle and let $A(x)$ be the area of the rectangle in terms of x.

a. Express $A(x)$ as a function of x.

b. What is the domain of A?

c. What is the range of A?

d. Graph A over its domain.

3. Write About It Are the functions in Exercises 1 and 2 equal? Explain.

> Use the definition of equal functions from this lesson.

4. Here are two functions.

$$H(n) = 3 + 5n$$

$$K(n) = \begin{cases} 3 & \text{if } n = 0 \\ K(n-1) + 5 & \text{if } n > 0 \end{cases}$$

a. Make a table of values for H and K that includes inputs from 0 to 5.

b. What is the natural domain of H? What is the natural domain of K?

c. Are H and K equal functions? Explain.

5. Consider the function $h(x) = \sqrt{x^3}$.

a. What is the natural domain of h?

b. Find the range of h using the natural domain.

6. Let $f : \mathbb{R}^2 \to \mathbb{R}$ and $f(a, b) = 2a + 3b$.

a. Find the domain and target of f.

b. Find some pairs (x, y) that make $f(x, y) = 12$.

c. Graph the set of all points (x, y) for which $f(x, y) = 12$.

> $\mathbb{R}^2$ means that the function takes two real numbers as inputs. The SUM, PR, and QUO functions from the Getting Started lesson have $\mathbb{R}^2$ as their domains.

7. Let $f : \mathbb{R} \to \mathbb{R}$ and $f(x) = 3x^2$.

a. Calculate $f(3)$ and $f(-3)$.

b. Find all values of x for which $f(x) = 12$.

c. Calculate $f(11) - f(10)$.

d. Show that you can write $f(x + 1)$ as $f(x + 1) = 3x^2 + 6x + 3$.

e. Write a simplified expression for $f(x + 1) - f(x)$.

f. If $g(x) = f(x + 1) - f(x)$, what is $g(10)$?

Answers

Exercises

1. a. all real numbers ≤ 36

b.

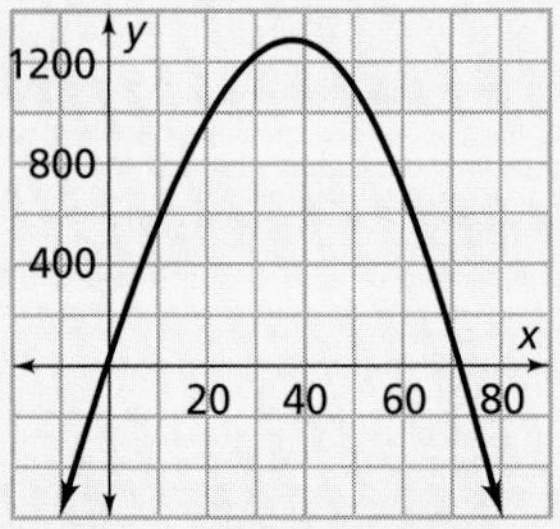

2. a. $A(x) = x(72 - x)$

b. positive numbers less than 72

c. positive numbers less than or equal to 1296

d.

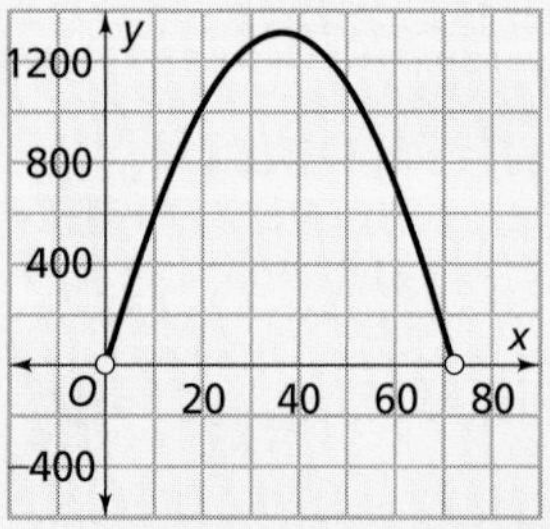

3. No; they have different domains and ranges.

4. a.

Input	Output
0	3
1	8
2	13
3	18
4	23
5	28

b. H: all real numbers; K: all nonnegative integers

c. No; they have different domains and ranges.

8. Suppose $g(x) = f(x + 1) - f(x)$, where f is another function. For each $f(x)$, find a polynomial formula in normal form for $g(x)$.

a. $f(x) = 5x$ **b.** $f(x) = 5x + 7$
c. $f(x) = 10x - 12$ **d.** $f(x) = Ax + B$
e. $f(x) = x^2$ **f.** $f(x) = 3x^2$
g. $f(x) = 10x^2$ **h.** $f(x) = x^2 + 10x - 12$
i. $f(x) = 3x^2 + 10x - 12$

Remember...
A polynomial is in normal form if it contains no parentheses, like terms have been combined, and the degrees of the terms go from highest to lowest.

9. Suppose you define function f in two pieces.

$$f(x) = \begin{cases} x & \text{if } x < 0 \\ 2x & \text{if } 0 \le x \le 6 \end{cases}$$

a. What is the natural domain of f? **b.** Sketch the graph of f.

On Your Own

10. Consider the function $j(x) = (\sqrt{x})^3$.
   a. What is the natural domain of j?
   b. Find the range of j using the natural domain.

11. A recipe takes a date as input, such as May 12. The output is the day of the week (Sunday, Monday, and so on) on which that date next occurs.
   a. Find the output for your birthday.
   b. Find the output for the day after your birthday.
   c. Does this recipe define a function? Explain.

12. Suppose $N: \mathbb{R}^2 \to \mathbb{R}$ and $N(a, b) = a^2 + b^2$.
   a. Find the domain and target of N.
   b. Find some pairs (x, y) that make $N(x, y) = 25$.
   c. Find all pairs (x, y) that make $N(x, y) = 0$.
   d. Graph the set of all points (x, y) that make $N(x, y) = 25$.
   e. **Take It Further** What is the range of N? Explain.

13. **What's Wrong Here?** While using a calculator, Derman noticed that $(\sqrt{3})^2 = 3$ and $(\sqrt{9})^2 = 9$ and $(\sqrt{10})^2 = 10$. He says that the function $t(x) = (\sqrt{x})^2$ is the same function as $f(x) = x$. Why is this incorrect?

14. For each function, find the natural domain, target, and range.
   a. $f(x) = 6x^2 - x - 2$ **b.** $f(x) = \sqrt{x - 3}$ **c.** $f(x) = \dfrac{1}{\sqrt{x - 3}}$
   d. $f(x) = \frac{1}{x} + 1$ **e.** $f(x, y) = x + 3y$ **f.** $f(x) = (x, x^3)$
   g. $f(x, y) = (y, x)$

On Your Own

EXERCISE 8 relates to the analysis of differences in Chapter 1. The function $g(x) = f(x + 1) - f(x)$ is similar to the operation of taking common differences.

EXERCISE 11 Some students may argue this is not a function because the outputs change every year. This is a fine objection and not really something intended in this problem. If this comes up, acknowledge it, but then move on.

EXERCISE 12 You may not want to assign anything further than part (c) here. Part (d) asks about the graph of a circle, while part (e) asks about what outputs are possible from N.

Function N will come up in Chapter 3. It is the norm function, the square of the magnitude of complex number $a + bi$.

EXERCISE 14 You could ask students for just the domain or just the domain and target. Some of the ranges are difficult to find completely.

5. a. all nonnegative real numbers
b. all nonnegative real numbers

6. a. domain: all real numbers; target: all nonnegative real numbers
b. Answers may vary. Sample: (0, 4), (6, 0), (3, 2), or any solution of $b = \frac{12 - 2a}{3}$
c.

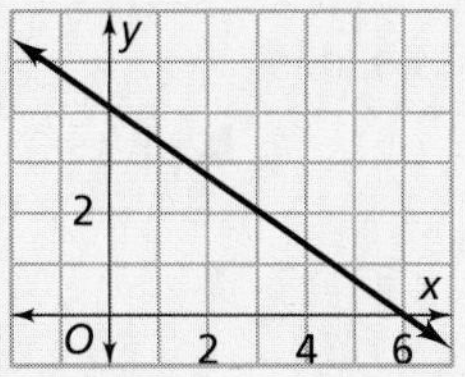

7. a. $f(3) = 27$, $f(-3) = 27$
b. 2, −2
c. 63
d. $f(x + 1) = 3(x + 1)^2 = 3(x^2 + 2x + 1) = 3x^2 + 6x + 3$
e. $6x + 3$
f. 63

8. a. 5 **b.** 5
c. 10 **d.** A
e. $2x + 1$ **f.** $6x + 3$
g. $20x + 10$ **h.** $2x + 11$
i. $6x + 13$

9. a. all real numbers ≤6
b.

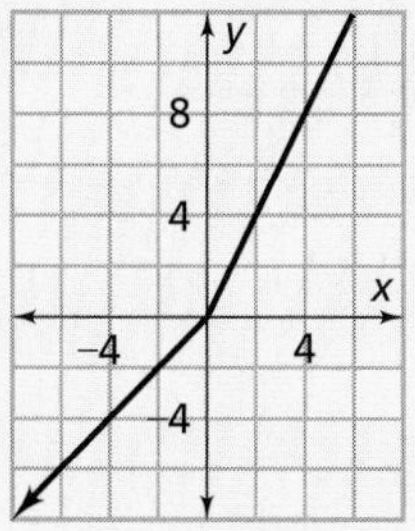

10. a. all nonnegative real numbers
b. all nonnegative real numbers

11–14. See back of book.

EXERCISE 15 You may want to skip part (g), since students may expect real answers where there are none. The graphs of $f(x)$ and $g(x)$ also provide this information.

EXERCISE 20 Spiro's trick is a composition of functions. Some students may conjecture a generalization from this that the inverse of a composition of functions is the composition of the inverses of the functions in reverse order.

EXERCISE 22 Equally important here is to show that this is not always true. The functions in the previous exercise do not behave this way, and neither do most functions.

Maintain Your Skills

EXERCISE 24 The form of g is the slope formula, and g measures the slope between two points on the graph of the function f. If f is a linear function, g is constant. If f is not linear, g is not constant.

Additional Resources

PRINT RESOURCES
- Solution Manual
- Practice Workbook
- Assessment Resources
- Teaching Resources

TECHNOLOGY
- Interactive Textbook
- TeacherExpress CD-ROM
- ExamView CD-ROM
- PHSchool.com

Additional Practice

1. Consider the function $f(x) = (\sqrt[3]{x})^2$.
   a. What is the natural domain of f?
   b. Find the range of f using the natural domain.

2. Suppose $N: \mathbb{R}^3 \to \mathbb{R}$ and $N(a, b) = a^3 + b^3$.
   a. Find the domain and target of N.
   b. Find some pairs (x, y) that make $N(x, y) = 35$.
   c. Find all pairs (x, y) that make $N(x, y) = 0$.
   d. Graph the set of all points (x, y) that make $N(x, y) = 35$.

3. For each function, find the natural domain, target, and range.
   a. $f(x) = 3x^2 - 6x + 9$ b. $f(x) = \sqrt{x+4} - 2$
   c. $f(x) = \frac{2}{x+4}$ d. $f(x) = (x, x^2)$
   e. $f(x, y) = 2x + y$ f. $f(x, y) = (-y, -x)$

4. Suppose $f: \mathbb{R} \to \mathbb{R}$ and $f(x) = -4x + 1$. Find the value of a in each case.
   a. $2f(4) + 2 = 8a$ b. $f(3a - 1) = 6$
   c. $f(3a - 1) = a + 4$

5. Find all values of x such that $f(x) = 2338$.
   a. $f(x) = 5x + 8$ b. $f(x) = 5x^2 + 8$
   c. $f(x) = 5x^3 + 8$

6. Consider the functions $f(x) = 2x^2 + 1$ and $g(x) = 4x - 3$. Find each value.
   a. $f(-2)$ b. $g(-2)$ c. $f(-2) \cdot g(-2)$
   d. $f(g(-2))$ e. $f \circ g(-2)$ f. $g \circ f(-2)$

7. Suppose $f(x) = 2x^2 + 4x - 1$, $g(x) = -3x + 5$, and $h(x) = 2x - 4$. Find a formula for each composition.
   a. $h \circ (g \circ f)(x)$ b. $(h \circ g) \circ f(x)$

8. Suppose $a(x) = 4x + 3$, $b(x) = x^2 + 5$, and $c(x) = -x + 6$. Find a formula for each composition.
   a. $a \circ b$ b. $b \circ c$ c. $(a \circ b) \circ c$ d. $a \circ (b \circ c)$

Practice: For Lesson 2.2, assign Exercises 1–5.

15. Suppose $f(x) = x^2 - 4x$ and $g(x) = x - 6$. Find each value.
    a. $f(g(2))$ b. $g(f(2))$ c. $f(g(z))$
    d. $g(f(z))$ e. $f(f(z))$ f. $g(g(z))$
    g. Find all numbers a such that $f(a) = g(a)$.
    h. Find all numbers b such that $f(g(b)) = g(f(b))$.

Go Online PHSchool.com

For additional practice, go to **Web Code:** bfa-0202

16. Suppose $f: \mathbb{R} \to \mathbb{R}$ and $f(x) = 3x + 2$. Find the value of a in each case.
    a. $2f(a) + 3 = 5$ b. $f(2a + 3) = 5$ c. $f(2a + 3) = a + 3$

17. For each function, find all values of x such that $f(x) = 12{,}290$.
    a. $f(x) = 3x + 2$ b. $f(x) = 3x^2 + 2$
    c. $f(x) = 3x^3 + 2$ d. $f(x) = 3x^6 + 2$

18. Derman says that for any function $f: \mathbb{R} \to \mathbb{R}$, if $f(r) = f(s)$, then $r = s$. Check Derman's conjecture for each function.
    a. $f(x) = 3x + 2$ b. $f(x) = 3x^2 + 2$
    c. $f(x) = 3x^3 + 2$ d. $f(x) = 3x^6 + 2$

19. **Standardized Test Prep** What is the natural domain of the function $f(x) = \frac{1}{x^2 - 5x + 4}$?
    A. $x \geq -3$ B. $x > 5$
    C. $x > 4$ D. $x \neq 1$ and $x \neq 4$

20. Spiro the Spectacular has a number trick: A player picks a number, adds 3, divides by 2, subtracts 3, and multiplies by 4. Find the inverse of Spiro's trick.

The inverse of Spiro's trick lets you figure out what number the player picked.

21. Suppose $f: \mathbb{R} \to \mathbb{R}$ and $f(3a + 1) = a - 2$. Find each value.
    a. $f(7)$ b. $f(14)$ c. $f(16)$ d. $f(z)$ (in terms of z)

22. Find two different functions f and g such that $f(g(x)) = g(f(x))$ for every number x.

Maintain Your Skills

23. Each of these functions has a domain of $\mathbb{R}$. Which functions have a range of $\mathbb{R}$?
    a. $f(x) = x^2$ b. $g(x) = x^3$ c. $h(x) = x^4$ d. $j(x) = x^5$
    e. **Take It Further** $k(x) = x^3 - 4x$

24. **Take It Further** Suppose $g: \mathbb{R}^2 \to \mathbb{R}$ and $g(x, y) = \dfrac{f(x) - f(y)}{x - y}$.
    For each function f, find $g(x, y)$.
    a. $f(x) = 3x + 5$ b. $f(x) = 5x + 5$ c. $f(x) = 12x + 5$
    d. $f(x) = x^2$ e. $f(x) = x^2 + x$ f. $f(x) = 3x^2 + 2x - 1$

Answers

15. a. 32 **b.** −10
c. $z^2 - 16z + 60$
d. $z^2 - 4z - 6$
e. $z^4 - 8z^3 + 12z^2 + 16z$
f. $z - 12$
g. 2 or 3 **h.** 5.5

16. a. $-\frac{1}{3}$ **b.** −1 **c.** $\frac{-8}{5}$

17. a. 4096 **b.** ±64 **c.** 16 **d.** ±4

18. a. true **b.** false
c. true **d.** false

19. D

20. Take the final number, add 6, and then divide by 2 to get the original number.

21. a. 0 **b.** $\frac{7}{3}$ **c.** 3 **d.** $\frac{z-7}{3}$

22. Answers may vary. Sample: $f(x) = x + 5$, $g(x) = x - 3$

23. functions b, d, e

24. a. 3 **b.** 5
c. 12 **d.** $x + y$
e. $x + y + 1$ **f.** $3x + 3y + 2$

2.3 Algebra With Functions

The basic rules of algebra tell you how the operations of addition and multiplication behave. Addition and multiplication are operations that combine numbers. In this lesson, you will learn about an operation that combines functions. Here are two functions.

- $B(p)$ is the birthday of person p. The domain is all people, and the target is the days of the year.
- $W(d)$ is the day of the week on which a date d will occur next year. The domain is the days of the year, and the target is the seven days of the week.

So B(Carl Gauss) = April 30.

You can compose these two functions to form a third function.

- $C(p)$ is the day of the week of person p's birthday next year. The domain is all people, and the target is the seven days of the week.

C is a composition of functions W and B. To find $C(p)$, you start with the person, find that person's birthday, and then find the day of the week of that date next year. In other words, C is the result of running an input through B, taking the output, and running that output through W.

For You to Do

Find each value.

1. B(you) **2.** W(you) **3.** C(you)

You can express the relationship between these functions with the equation

$$C(p) = W(B(p))$$

This tells you how to compute the output of C for any input. If you just want to say that C is the composition of W and B, you write it as $C = W \circ B$.

Composing functions together by using the output of one as the input of the next is very common. You can do this with any two functions for which the domain of one function contains the target of another. If $f : A \to B$ and $g : B \to C$, you can define a new function that maps inputs in A to outputs in C with the following rule.

$$x \mapsto g(f(x))$$

This new function has domain A and target C. Instead of using a new letter to name it, you can just call the composition $g \circ f$. You read $g \circ f$ as "g circle f" or "g composed with f."

Remember...

When you evaluate $g(f(x))$, first you do f and then you do g.

For You to Do

1–3. Check students' work.

Lesson Overview

GOALS

- Compose functions.
- Decide whether a given function has an inverse.

This lesson is about composition. There are two principal emphases here.

THINK ABOUT COMPOSITION OF FUNCTIONS There is a clear emphasis on mathematical habits of mind in this lesson: thinking about composition as an operation on two functions (f and g) that outputs a third function ($f \circ g$). For this reason, CME Project *Algebra 2* tends to emphasize the $f \circ g$ notation, rather than the $f(g(x))$ notation, although you want to make sure that students feel comfortable with both. This lesson offers students an opportunity to think about questions such as:

- Is there an identity function when doing composition; in other words, is there some function f so that for any function g, $f \circ g = g \circ f = g$? (There is: $f(x) = x$.)
- Are there inverses when doing composition? In other words, for a given function g, is there some function h so that $g \circ h = h \circ g = x$? In this lesson, look for conjectures. Students will see in the next lesson that some functions have inverses, but others do not.
- Is this operation commutative? In other words, for any two functions m and n, is it always true that $m \circ n = n \circ m$? (No. For example, let $m(x) = 2x + 1$ and $n = x^2$.)

COMPUTE COMPOSITIONS OF FUNCTIONS There is also an emphasis on being able to compute compositions of functions.

CHECK YOUR UNDERSTANDING
- Core: 1, 2, 3, 4, 5, 6
- Optional: 7
- Extension: 8, 9

MATERIALS
- CAS (recommended)
- graph paper
- graphing calculators
- Blackline Master 2.3

HOMEWORK
- Core: 10, 11, 13, 16, 17, 18
- Optional: 12, 14, 15, 20, 21
- Extension: 19

VOCABULARY
- binary operation
- composite function, $g \circ f$

Launch

Begin this lesson with For You to Do Problems 1–3, which introduce composition of functions. When you discuss the function W, note that for dates before February 29, the day of the week moves ahead by *two* days during a leap year.

Explore

Developing Habits of Mind

You can use Blackline Master 2.3 to help introduce composite functions.

Ask students to describe what each of the three bulleted statements about addition and multiplication means for composition of functions:

- An identity element for composition would be a function that returned the original function when composed with that function. Using symbols: if f is an identity function, then $(g \circ f)(x) = g(f(x)) = g(x)$ and $(f \circ g)(x) = f(g(x)) = g(x)$.
- An inverse function would, when composed with the original function, take the output of that function and return the original input. Using symbols: if g is the inverse of f, then $(g \circ f)(x) = g(f(x)) = x$.
- If composition of functions were commutative, then the order of the composition would not change the result; that is, $(g \circ f)(x)$ and $(f \circ g)(x)$ would always be equal. Note that, in general, this is not true, as students will see in For You to Do Problem 7.

Developing Habits of Mind

Look for relationships. You can think of functions as objects on which you can perform operations, just as you do with numbers.

- $g \circ f$ is a function.
- $g(f(x))$ is the output of that function for input x.

Composition takes two functions and produces a third function. The concept of an operation with two inputs and one output is very common in algebra. Composition of functions is another example.

Operations that take two inputs and produce one output are binary operations. They are functions, too, as long as they always produce the same output given the same two inputs.

The addition and the multiplication of two numbers are two more examples of a binary operation. Some of the concepts that apply to addition and multiplication may carry over to composition. Here are some questions to consider.

- Addition and multiplication have identity elements. You can add 0 to a number and it does not change. You can multiply a number by 1 and it does not change. Is there an identity function for composition?
- Addition and multiplication have inverses (with one exception). All numbers have opposites that sum to 0, the identity. All numbers other than 0 have reciprocals. Do compositions of functions have inverses?
- Addition and multiplication are commutative. You can add or multiply in either order: $3 + 5 = 5 + 3$ and $3 \cdot 5 = 5 \cdot 3$. Is composition commutative?

When you work on these questions, you are thinking about functions as objects rather than machines. Composition is an operation on these objects, just as addition and multiplication are operations on numbers.

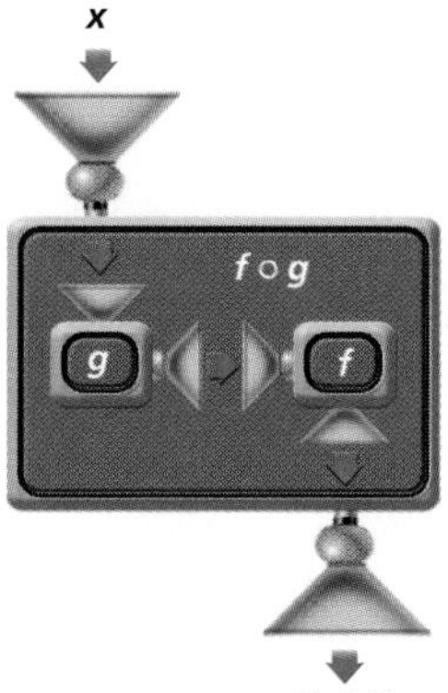

Artist's rendition of $f \circ g$

Here is the formal definition of composition.

Definition

For two functions $f : A \to B$ and $g : B \to C$, the composite function $g \circ f$ meets the following conditions.

- $g \circ f : A \to C$
- $g \circ f(x) = g(f(x))$

For You to Do

Suppose $f, g, h : \mathbb{R} \rightarrow \mathbb{R}$ and

$$f(x) = 2x^2 - 1$$
$$g(x) = x + 1$$
$$h(x) = 4x^3 - 3x$$

4. Build models for the three functions in your function-modeling language.

5. Show that $f \circ g(5) = 71$.

6. Find $g \circ f(5)$, $f \circ h(5)$, and $h \circ f(5)$.

7. Find formulas for $f \circ g$ and $g \circ f$. Are these functions the same?

The notation $f, g, h : \mathbb{R} \rightarrow \mathbb{R}$ means that f, g, and h all have domain $\mathbb{R}$ and target $\mathbb{R}$.

Historical Perspective

Algebra began as a collection of methods for finding unknown numbers—for solving equations. The object was to find general formulas, like the quadratic formula, that provided recipes for solving a class of equations. Mathematicians stated the recipes in terms of the operations of arithmetic. (Take the *negative* of the coefficient of x, *add* it to the *square root* of the *square* of that coefficient *minus*. . .) The goal was to make the recipe independent of the actual numbers in the equations. Over time, mathematicians began to look for similar formulas in systems other than numbers that had different operations. Gradually, the focus shifted from the formulas to the operations themselves. This systems approach to algebra led people to investigate properties of operations and to make lists of the properties that are useful in calculating—properties that are very similar to the basic rules of arithmetic.

Algebra today deals with all kinds of systems—numbers, polynomials, matrices, functions, and more exotic objects. Each system has one or more operations that allow for calculations. One such system is the set of functions, all with the same domain and target, in which the operation is composition.

The output is dependent on the input, but the recipe itself is independent of both.

Answers

For You to Do

4. Check students' work.

5. $f \circ g(5) = f(g(5)) = f(5 + 1) = 2 \cdot 6^2 - 1 = 71$

6. 50; 470,449; 470,449

7. $f \circ g(x) = 2x^2 + 4x + 1$; $g \circ f(x) = 2x^2$; they are not the same function.

For You to Do

This section serves two purposes. First, students get some practice composing functions. Second, students may start thinking about whether composition is a commutative operation. If students are having trouble understanding the $f \circ g$ notation, rewriting $f \circ g(x)$ as $f(g(x))$ may help. It is worth going over these problems before beginning the exercises, because students often have trouble with the mechanics of composition. For You to Do gives students an opportunity to self-correct before beginning the Check Your Understanding exercises. It is important that students understand that $f \circ g$ is a function, and $f \circ g(x)$ is a number—the final output of the composition for the input x.

Historical Perspective

Although students may not be familiar with some of the systems mentioned, they should be able to discuss the algebra of numbers, polynomials, and functions.

Wrap Up

To wrap up this lesson, you might want to go over Check Your Understanding Exercises 5 and 6, which set up the next lesson on inverse functions.

Assessment Resources

Lesson Quiz 2.3

1. Consider the functions $f(x) = 3x^2 - 2$ and $g(x) = -x + 2$. Find each value.
a. $f(-1) \cdot g(-1))$ **b.** $f \circ g(-1)$ **c.** $g \circ f(-1)$

2. Suppose $f(x) = 2x^2 - 6x + 1$, $g(x) = -4x + 2$, and $h(x) = 3x - 5$. Find a formula for each composition.
a. $h \circ (g \circ f)(x)$ **b.** $(h \circ g) \circ f(x)$

3. Suppose $a(x) = 4x + 3$, $b(x) = x^2 + 5$, and $c(x) = -x + 6$. Find a formula for each composition.
a. $a \circ b$ **b.** $b \circ c$ **c.** $(a \circ b) \circ c$ **d.** $a \circ (b \circ c)$

Exercises

HOMEWORK
- Core: 10, 11, 13, 16, 17, 18
- Optional: 12, 14, 15, 20, 21
- Extension: 19

Check Your Understanding

EXERCISE 1 is for students to recognize that $f \cdot g$ and $f \circ g$ are not the same thing, and that $f(g(x))$ and $f \circ g(x)$ are.

EXERCISE 2 Students should notice that the results of $f \circ g$ and $g \circ f$ are not the same.

EXERCISE 3 Students may do this exercise without recognizing they are doing composition of functions, so point that out if you have the time to go over this exercise in class.

EXERCISE 5 targets an understanding of inverse functions. See if you can get students to describe f and g as reversing or "undoing" one another.

EXERCISE 6 Some students may have learned a method of switching variables (swapping y for x and then solving for y) that they want to use to find inverse functions. If they are having success with this method, it is not necessary for them to do things differently. If they are having trouble, you might try emphasizing the process described in the solution: think about what the original function is doing, and find a function that undoes that process.

Exercises *Practicing Habits of Mind*

Check Your Understanding

Unless otherwise stated, all functions in these exercises have domain $\mathbb{R}$ and target $\mathbb{R}$.

1. Consider the functions $f(x) = 2x + 3$ and $g(x) = 5x + 1$. Find each value.
   a. $f(3)$ b. $g(3)$ c. $f(g(3))$
   d. $f \circ g(3)$ e. $g \circ f(3)$ f. $f(3) \cdot g(3)$
2. Let $f(x) = 2x + 3$ and $g(x) = 5x + 1$.
   a. Find a formula for $g \circ f(x)$.
   b. Find a formula for $f \circ g(x)$.
3. Suppose you drop a stone into a pond. It makes concentric circular ripples. The radius of a ripple as a function of time is $r = 4t$, where r is the radius in inches and t is the time in seconds.
   a. Express the area of a ripple as a function of its radius.
   b. Express the area of a ripple as a function of time.

4. Suppose $f : \mathbb{R} \to \mathbb{R}$ and $f(x) = x$. For each definition of g, find formulas for $f \circ g(x)$ and $g \circ f(x)$.
   a. $g(x) = x^2 + 3$
   b. $g(x) = 2x - 7$
   c. $g(x) = (x - 4)^3$
   d. **Write About It** Explain what it might mean to say that the function f is the identity function on $\mathbb{R}$.
5. Suppose $f(x) = 3x - 1$. If possible, find a function g such that $f \circ g(x) = x$.
6. Suppose $f(x) = 2x + 3$. If possible, find a function g such that $g \circ f(x) = x$.
7. Suppose $f(x) = 2x + 5$. If possible, find a function g that makes each equation true.
   a. $f \circ g(x) = 4x^2 + 1$
   b. $g \circ f(x) = 4x^2 + 1$
8. **Take It Further** Let $f(x) = ax + b$ and $g(x) = cx + d$.
   a. Find formulas for $f \circ g(x)$ and $g \circ f(x)$.
   b. Find conditions on a, b, c, and d that make $f \circ g = g \circ f$.
9. **Take It Further** Find a linear function $f(x) = ax + b$ such that $f \circ f(x) = 4x + 9$.

Go Online PHSchool.com

For more information about composite functions, go to **Web Code:** bfe-9031

Answers

Exercises

1. a. 9 **b.** 16 **c.** 35
d. 35 **e.** 46 **f.** 144

2. a. $g \circ f(x) = 10x + 16$
b. $f \circ g(x) = 10x + 5$

3. a. $A = \pi r^2$ **b.** $A = 16\pi t^2$

4. a. $f \circ g(x) = x^2 + 3$; $g \circ f(x) = x^2 + 3$
b. $f \circ g(x) = 2x - 7$; $g \circ f(x) = 2x - 7$
c. $f \circ g(x) = (x - 4)^3$; $g \circ f(x) = (x - 4)^3$
d. Answers may vary. Sample: The function takes any input and produces that same value as the output.

5. $g(x) = \frac{x + 1}{3}$

6. $g(x) = \frac{x - 3}{2}$

7. a. $g(x) = 2x^2 - 2$
b. $g(x) = x^2 - 10x + 26$

8. a. $f \circ g(x) = acx + ad + b$, $g \circ f(x) = acx + bc + d$
b. $ad + b = bc + d$ or $\frac{a}{c} = \frac{b - 1}{d - 1}$

9. $f(x) = 2x + 3$ or $f(x) = -2x - 9$

On Your Own

10. Consider the functions $f(x) = x^2 - 1$ and $g(x) = 3x + 1$. Find each value.
   a. $f(4)$ b. $g(4)$
   c. $f(4) \cdot g(4)$ d. $f(g(4))$
   e. $f \circ g(4)$ f. $g \circ f(4)$
11. Suppose $h : \mathbb{R} \to \mathbb{R}$ and $h(x) = \sqrt{x^2}$. Show that $h = a$, where $a(x) = |x|$.
12. Suppose $f(x) = x^2 - 5x + 6$ and $g(x) = x - 2$. Find each value.
   a. $f \circ g(3)$ b. $g \circ f(3)$
   c. $f \circ g(a)$ d. $g \circ f(a)$
   e. $(f \circ g) \circ f(a)$ f. $f \circ (g \circ f)(a)$
   g. Find all numbers a such that $f \circ g(a) = 0$.
   h. Find all numbers a such that $g \circ f(a) = 0$.
13. Use the functions below.

$$f(x) = x^2 - 6x + 8$$
$$g(x) = x + 3$$
$$h(x) = x + 1$$

   Find a formula for each composition.
   a. $h \circ (f \circ g)(x)$ b. $(h \circ f) \circ g(x)$
14. Suppose $f(x) = x^2 - 10x + 21$. If possible, find linear functions g and h that make each equation true.
   a. $f \circ g(x) = x^2 - 4$ b. $h \circ (f \circ g)(x) = x^2$
15. If $f(x) = x^2$, find a function g, that is not equal to f, such that $f \circ g = g \circ f$.
16. **Standardized Test Prep** Suppose $f(x) = x - 5$. Find a function g such that $g \circ f(x) = 3x^2 - 11x - 20$.
   A. $g(x) = 3x^2 + 19x$
   B. $g(x) = 3x^2 + 4$
   C. $g(x) = (3x - 4)$
   D. $g(x) = (3x + 4)$

Go Online PHSchool.com

For additional practice, go to **Web Code:** bfa-0203

Remember...

A linear function is a function in the form $x \mapsto ax + b$ for some numbers a and b. Why do you call it linear?

On Your Own

EXERCISE 11 Here is one place to bring up the argument about equal functions: if $h(x)$ has the same domain and outputs as the absolute value function, then it is the same function regardless of how it is originally defined.

EXERCISE 12 Parts (e) and (f) are time-consuming. If you assign these exercises, see if students notice that the two results are equal. Without expanding to normal form, most students would not notice these are identical. The goal of these two questions is to give an example of associativity of functions under composition.

EXERCISE 14 If students have trouble beginning part (a), suggest that they write $f(g(x)) = f(ax + b) = (ax + b)^2 - 10(ax + b) + 21$. Most students will see that for this expression to equal $x^2 - 4$, a must be 1 or -1. Students can then substitute one of these a-values and solve for b.

EXERCISE 15 If students have trouble beginning this exercise, suggest that they use the fact that $f(x) = x^2$ to rewrite $f(g(x)) = g(f(x))$ as $(g(x))^2 = g(x^2)$.

EXERCISE 17 is another example of associativity of composition.

10. a. 15
b. 13
c. 195
d. 168
e. 168
f. 46

11. Since $\sqrt{x^2} = |x|$ for all real numbers, then if $h(x) = \sqrt{x^2}$ and $a(x) = |x|$, $h = a$.

12. a. 2
b. -2
c. $a^2 - 9a + 20$
d. $a^2 - 5a + 4$
e. $(a^2 - 5a + 6)^2 - 9(a^2 - 5a + 6) + 20$ or $a^4 - 10a^3 + 28a^2 - 15a + 2$
f. $(a^2 - 5a + 4)^2 - 5(a^2 - 5a + 4) + 6$ or $a^4 - 10a^3 + 28a^2 - 15a + 2$
g. 4 or 5
h. 1 or 4

13. a. x^2 **b.** x^2

14. a. $g(x) = x + 5$ or $g(x) = -x - 5$
b. Let $g(x) = x + 5$ as in part (a). Then $h(x) = x + 4$ yields $h \circ (f \circ g)(x) = x^2$.

15. Answers may vary. Sample: $g(x) = x$

16. A

Maintain Your Skills

EXERCISES 20 AND 21 Assign these exercises before talking about inverse functions. The goal is for students to recognize that $f \circ g(x) = x$ when f and g are inverse functions *before* the formal definition of inverse is given in the next lesson.

Additional Resources

PRINT RESOURCES
- Solution Manual
- Practice Workbook
- Assessment Resources
- Teaching Resources

TECHNOLOGY
- Interactive Textbook
- TeacherExpress CD-ROM
- ExamView CD-ROM
- PHSchool.com

Additional Practice

1. Consider the function $f(x) = (\sqrt[3]{x})^2$.
a. What is the natural domain of f?
b. Find the range of f using the natural domain.

2. Suppose $N: \mathbb{R}^3 \rightarrow \mathbb{R}$ and $N(a, b) = a^3 + b^3$.
a. Find the domain and target of N.
b. Find some pairs (x, y) that make $N(x, y) = 35$.
c. Find all pairs (x, y) that make $N(x, y) = 0$.
d. Graph the set of all points (x, y) that make $N(x, y) = 35$.

3. For each function, find the natural domain, target, and range.
a. $f(x) = 3x^2 - 6x + 9$
b. $f(x) = \sqrt{x + 4} - 2$
c. $f(x) = \frac{2}{x + 4}$
d. $f(x) = (x, x^2)$
e. $f(x, y) = 2x + y$
f. $f(x, y) = (-y, -x)$

4. Suppose $f: \mathbb{R} \rightarrow \mathbb{R}$ and $f(x) = -4x + 1$. Find the value of a in each case.
a. $2f(4) + 2 = 8a$
b. $f(3a - 1) = 6$
c. $f(3a - 1) = a + 4$

5. Find all values of x such that $f(x) = 2338$.
a. $f(x) = 5x + 8$
b. $f(x) = 5x^2 + 8$
c. $f(x) = 5x^3 + 8$

6. Consider the functions $f(x) = 2x^2 + 1$ and $g(x) = 4x - 3$. Find each value.
a. $f(-2)$
b. $g(-2)$
c. $f(-2) \cdot g(-2)$
d. $f(g(-2))$
e. $f \circ g(-2)$
f. $g \circ f(-2)$

7. Suppose $f(x) = 2x^2 + 4x - 1$, $g(x) = -3x + 5$, and $h(x) = 2x - 4$. Find a formula for each composition.
a. $h \circ (g \circ f)(x)$
b. $(h \circ g) \circ f(x)$

8. Suppose $a(x) = 4x + 3$, $b(x) = x^2 + 5$, and $c(x) = -x + 6$. Find a formula for each composition.
a. $a \circ b$
b. $b \circ c$
c. $(a \circ b) \circ c$
d. $a \circ (b \circ c)$

Practice: For Lesson 2.3, assign Exercises 6–8.

17. Consider these three functions.

$$a(x) = 3x + 1$$
$$b(x) = x^2 - 7$$
$$c(x) = x - 5$$

Find a formula for each composition.

a. $a \circ b$

b. $b \circ c$

c. $(a \circ b) \circ c$

d. $a \circ (b \circ c)$

18. Suppose $a, b, c: \mathbb{R} \rightarrow \mathbb{R}$. Show that $(a \circ b) \circ c = a \circ (b \circ c)$.

19. **Take It Further** Suppose $f(x) = 2x + 3$ and $g(x) = x^2$. Find a way to construct the graph of $f \circ g$ from the graphs of f and g.

In arithmetic, addition is associative. For any numbers a, b, and c, $(a + b) + c = a + (b + c)$.

Maintain Your Skills

20. For each function f, find a function g such that $f \circ g(x) = x$.

a. $f(x) = x + 3$

b. $f(x) = x - 3$

c. $f(x) = 3x + 5$

d. $f(x) = 3x - 5$

e. $f(x) = 2x + 5$

f. $f(x) = Ax + B$, where $A \neq 0$

21. For each function f, find a function g such that $g \circ f(x) = x$.

a. $f(x) = x + 3$

b. $f(x) = x - 3$

c. $f(x) = 3x + 5$

d. $f(x) = 3x - 5$

e. $f(x) = 2x + 5$

f. $f(x) = Ax + B$, where $A \neq 0$

Go Online
Video Tutor
PHSchool.com
Web Code: bfe-0775

Answers

17. a. $3x^2 - 20$
b. $x^2 - 10x + 18$
c. $3x^2 - 30x + 55$
d. $3x^2 - 30x + 55$

18. Answers may vary. Sample: Set up two "potato-and-arrow diagrams," one for $(a \circ b) \circ c$ and the other for $a \circ (b \circ c)$, and show that the arrow chains through the diagrams are equivalent.

19. Answers may vary. Sample: The exercise asks how to find the ordered pairs $(x, f(g(x)))$ or $(x, 2x^2 + 3)$. For each x-value, find the $g(x)$ value x^2 on the graph. Then find that x^2-value in the domain of f and use that to find the corresponding range value, $2x^2 + 3$.

20–21. See back of book.

2.4 Inverses: Doing and Undoing

Suppose you have an output and you want to find the input that generated it. Can you always find it?

In-Class Experiment

Have everyone think of an integer from 1 to 20. Then, follow these steps:

- Subtract 10 from your number.
- Square the result.
- Add 7 to the squared result to get an ending number.

List everyone's starting and ending numbers.

1. Did any students get the same ending number? More important, did any two students who got the same ending number start with different numbers?
2. If a student gives you an ending number, can you always find the starting number? Explain.

Try the experiment again. This time, cube the number in the second step.

3. Did any students get the same ending number this time? Did any two students who got the same ending number start with different numbers?
4. If a student gives you an ending number, can you always find the starting number? Explain.

Minds in Action

episode 4

Sasha and Derman are looking at the results from the In-Class Experiment.

Derman Tony and Michelle got the same number at the end, and they started with different numbers: Tony had 13 and Michelle had 7.

Sasha Maybe we should look at what they did with their numbers.

	Tony	Michelle
Starting number	13	7
After subtracting 10	3	−3
After squaring	9	9
After adding 7	16	16

In Class Experiment

1. The starting numbers 1 and 19, 2 and 18, 3 and 17, . . . , 9 and 11 give the same ending number, so students with the same ending number can have different starting numbers.
2. no, because the same ending number, say 88, can come from two starting numbers (here, 1 or 19)
3. Answers may vary. Sample: In cubing, each different input value goes to a different output value.
4. Answers may vary. Sample: Yes, because every ending number comes from only one starting number.

Lesson Overview

GOAL

- Find the inverse of a one-to-one function.

This lesson begins with an In-Class Experiment that highlights the differences between one-to-one functions and functions that are not one-to-one. (A function that is not one-to-one is often called "many-to-one.") In Problem 1 of the In-Class Experiment, students use the function $x \mapsto (x - 10)^2 + 7$. In this experiment, students may have started with different numbers and ended up with the same number. (If you have a very small class, you may need to repeat the experiment several times.) In Problem 2, students use the function $x \mapsto (x - 10)^3 + 7$, and no matter how many times you repeat the experiment, students who start with different numbers will end up with different numbers, because this function is one-to-one.

You want students to understand (not just memorize)

- why a one-to-one function has an inverse, and a function that is not one-to-one does not have an inverse
- what the limitations of the horizontal line test are
- how to find the inverse of a function

CHECK YOUR UNDERSTANDING

- Core: 1, 2, 3, 4, 5, 7
- Optional: 6, 8
- Extension: 9

MATERIALS

- graph paper
- graphing calculators
- Blackline Master 2.4

HOMEWORK

- Core: 10, 11, 13, 14, 15, 19
- Optional: 12, 16, 18, 20
- Extension: 17

VOCABULARY

- additive inverse
- identity function
- inverse function
- monic
- multiplicative inverse
- one-to-one
- opposite
- potato-and-arrow diagram
- reciprocal
- zeros of a function

Launch

Start with the In-Class Experiment. You can use Blackline Master 2.4 as a transparency or a handout.

Explore

In-Class Experiment

Ask students how they would "undo" each step. In what order would they undo the steps? They may remember using backtracking to solve equations.

continued on p. 116

continued from p. 115

PROBLEM 1 If no two students come up with the same ending number from different starting numbers, ask the students to try doing the experiment using the numbers 13 and 7.

After your class has discussed Problem 3, ask if there are *any* two starting numbers that could yield the same ending number. Give students a moment to work on this question. Collect conjectures.

Minds in Action

Ask students how they would choose the starting numbers to be sure they had the same ending number. They should be able to see that if a and b are the starting numbers, then $|a - 10| = |b - 10|$.

Derman Either way, they end up with 16. I wonder if we can retrace the steps from the output 16.

	Tony	Michelle
Ending number	16	16
After undoing addition by 7	9	9
After undoing squaring	???	???

Derman Hmm. We can't undo the squaring. If $x^2 = 9$, then x could be 3 or -3.

Sasha It looks like there's no way to decide. If you only told me Tony and Michelle ended up with 16, I couldn't figure out what their original numbers were.

Derman It's weird. That didn't happen the second time we ran the experiment. If two people started with different numbers, they always got different results. That time, Tony started with 5 and Michelle started with 12.

	Tony	Michelle
Starting number	5	12
After subtracting 10	−5	2
After cubing	−125	8
After adding 7	−118	15

Sasha What happens if we try to undo the operations?

	Tony	Michelle
Ending number	−118	15
After undoing addition by 7	−125	8
After undoing cubing	−5	2
After undoing subtraction by 10	5	12

Derman No problems this time. We found their starting numbers. I think you could do this with any ending number.

Sasha To go from the ending number back to the starting number, we should start with the last operation. So we have these steps:

- Subtract seven from the ending number.
- Take the cube root of that.
- Add ten to *that.*

We *will* be able to get back the starting number!

Why can Sasha and Derman undo cubing but not squaring?

Derman As long as all the steps can be undone. I wonder how we can decide whether or not a step can be undone.

For Discussion

5. In the second experiment, why can Sasha and Derman always derive the starting number from the ending number?
6. Change the first experiment in some way to make its process reversible.

The second In-Class Experiment amounted to evaluating the function $f(x) = (x - 10)^3 + 7$ for different starting values of x. When your class evaluated this function in the In-Class Experiment, you found that, if two students got the same output, they must have started with the same input. When a function has this behavior, it is *one-to-one*.

Definition

A function is one-to-one if its ouputs are unique. That is, a function f is one-to-one if $f(r) = f(s)$ only when $r = s$.

The function from the first In-Class Experiment is not one-to-one, since the different inputs 13 and 7 both give the same output, 16. That is, $f(13) = f(7)$. But $13 \neq 7$.

Habits of Mind

Establish a process. To check if a function f is one-to-one, assume that $f(r) = f(s)$ and try to show that $r = s$.

For You to Do

7. Which of these functions are one-to-one?

$P(x) = x^2$ $\quad Q(x) = x^3$ $\quad R(x) = |x - 10|$ $\quad S(x) = \sqrt{x + 15}$

Is P one-to-one? That is, if $P(r) = P(s)$, does r have to equal s? If $r^2 = s^2$, does $r = s$? No, not necessarily!

You can sometimes tell that a function from $\mathbb{R}$ to $\mathbb{R}$ is not one-to-one from its graph. Here is the graph of a function $g: \mathbb{R} \to \mathbb{R}$.

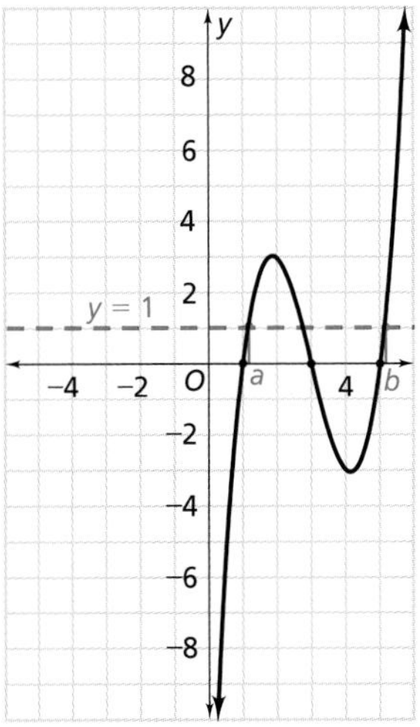

From the graph, you can see that there are different inputs that give the same output. If two points on the graph have the same y-height, they correspond to different inputs that produce the same output. This graph shows two different inputs a and b with $g(a) = g(b)$.

If a horizontal line crosses the graph of a function in more than one place, the function cannot be one-to-one.

Habits of Mind

Be careful. The graph of an $\mathbb{R}$-to-$\mathbb{R}$ function cannot tell you with certainty that a function *is* one-to-one, because you can never see the complete graph. For example, suppose $f(x) = x^3 - x$ and $g(x) = f(x - 20)$. Graph g over the interval $-10 \leq x \leq 10$. No horizontal line cuts the graph twice. But is g one-to-one? Check out the graph over the interval $-10 \leq x \leq 30$.

DEFINITION OF ONE-TO-ONE FUNCTION Draw a potato-and-arrow diagram of a one-to-one function. The diagram will show each element of the domain paired with exactly one element of the range, and each element of the range paired with exactly one element of the domain.

Answers

For Discussion

5. Check students' work.
6. Check students' work.

For You to Do

7. $P(x) = x^2$ and $S(x) = \sqrt{x + 15}$ are one-to-one functions.

For You to Do

PROBLEM 13 Students may not see that the function F is one-to-one. Remind them that the radical symbol represents the positive square root.

Developing Habits of Mind

Ask students to find two ordered pairs that show that the squaring function is *not* one-to-one. (Answer: For example, $(3, 9)$ and $(-3, 9)$.)

For You to Do

Use graphs to determine which functions are not one-to-one. Which functions are one-to-one? Explain.

8. $A(x) = x$

9. $B(x) = x^2$

10. $C(x) = x^3$

11. $D(x) = \frac{1}{x}$

12. $E(x) = |x|$

13. $F(x) = \sqrt{x}$

14. $G(x) = x^3 - x$

15. $H(x) = x^3 + x$

Developing Habits of Mind

Visualize. Here is a potato-and-arrow diagram for a one-to-one function.

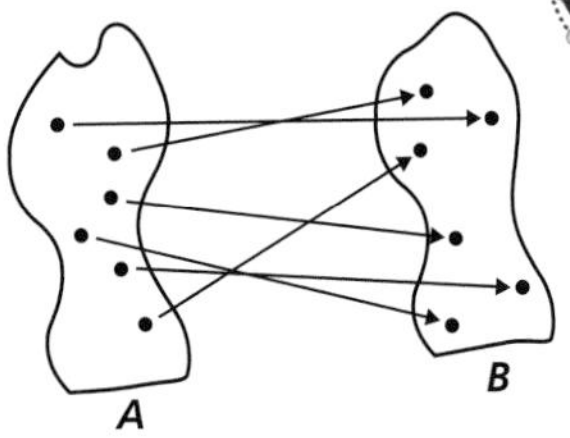

Any two arrows from A end at different objects in B. Only a one-to-one function has this property.

One important fact about one-to-one functions is that they are reversible, as Derman and Sasha noticed. In the diagram, if you pick any output in Set B, it is always possible to determine where it came from.

This means there is another function, an *inverse function*, from Set B to Set A. In a potato-and-arrow diagram, the inverse function looks similar, but all the arrows reverse direction.

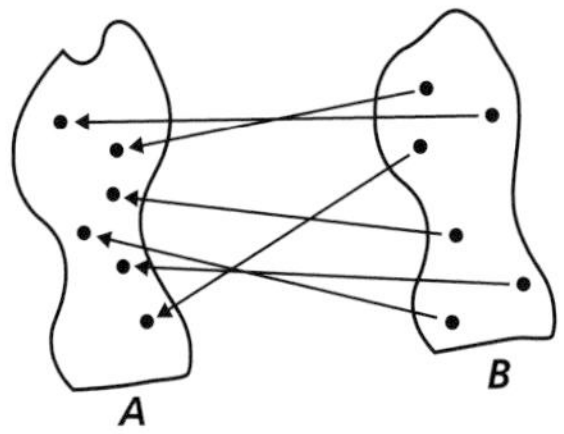

The domain and range switch. If you follow an arrow in the original function and then the corresponding arrow of the inverse function, you are back where you started.

You will see the formal definition of an inverse function in a moment. Derman and Sasha used inverse functions in their dialog.

- The function "add 7" has an inverse: "subtract 7."
- The function "cube the number" has an inverse: "take the cube root."
- The function "subtract 10" has an inverse: "add 10."

It might appear that the squaring and square root functions are inverses, but they are not. When the domain is $\mathbb{R}$, the squaring function is not one-to-one, so the squaring step cannot be inverted. What do you find if the domain is different?

See Exercise 4.

Answers

For You to Do

8. Yes; every horizontal line crosses the graph in exactly one place.

9. No; some horizontal lines cross the graph in two places.

10. Yes; every horizontal line crosses the graph in exactly one place.

11. Yes; every horizontal line (except $y = 0$) crosses the graph in exactly one place.

12. No; some horizontal lines cross the graph in two places.

13. Yes; every horizontal line $y = a$, where $a > 0$, crosses the graph in exactly one place.

14. No; some horizontal lines (such as $y = 0$) cross the graph in more than one place.

15. Yes; every horizontal line crosses the graph in exactly one place.

You can write the inverse of f as f^{-1}. Here is the formal definition.

Definition

Suppose f is a one-to-one function with domain A and range B. The inverse function f^{-1} is a function with these properties:

- **f^{-1} has domain B and range A.**
- **For all x in B, $f(f^{-1}(x)) = x$.**

There is another way to state this definition that puts the emphasis on the function rather than on its output. The **identity function** on a set is the function id that simply returns its input.

$$\text{id}(x) = x$$

There is an identity function for each domain, but they all behave the same way: They do nothing to an input. What is the graph of id : $\mathbb{R} \rightarrow \mathbb{R}$?

Definition

(Alternate Version) Suppose f is a one-to-one function with domain A and range B. The inverse function f^{-1} is a function with these properties:

- **f^{-1} has domain B and range A.**
- **For all x in B, $f \circ f^{-1} = \text{id}$.**

Derman's description of the function $f(x) = (x - 10)^3 + 7$ refers to f as a composition of three simpler functions, in this order.

- Subtract 10.
- Cube.
- Add 7.

Sasha and Derman then describe how to recover the original input from the output.

- Subtract 7.
- Take the cube root.
- Add 10.

This process describes the inverse function of $f(x) = (x - 10)^3 + 7$. You can build the inverse function by starting with x and applying the three reversing rules in the order above.

$$f^{-1}(x) = \sqrt[3]{x - 7} + 10$$

The original function f is the composition $f = c \circ b \circ a$ of the steps listed. Then the inverse f^{-1} is $f^{-1} = a^{-1} \circ b^{-1} \circ c^{-1}$. You invert each function and reverse their order.

When an inverse function exists, you can often find it by describing the steps to reverse the process.

DEFINITION OF AN INVERSE FUNCTION Point out that the -1 in f^{-1} is *not* an exponent. The context will always make it clear whether the -1 is an exponent or indicates an inverse function.

After discussing the definition, you may want to ask students this question: If the point (12, 15) is on the graph of f, what point is on the graph of f^{-1}?

Example

Sometimes students are careless with parentheses in this type of exercise. For Method 1, note that to show that you subtract 5 *before* you multiply by 2, you need to put $x - 5$ in parentheses. Likewise, for Method 2, to show that you are multiplying the expression $x - 5$ by 2, you must put $x - 5$ in parentheses.

For You to Do

PROBLEM 16 Students should note that $f^{-1}(x)$ in the Example is $g(x)$ here. The method of the Example should yield $g^{-1} = \frac{x}{2} + 5$.

For Discussion

PROBLEM 17 Note the connection to the original In-Class Experiment function here. If you try the method for finding the inverse of $h(x) = (x - 10)^2 + 7$, you end up with something that is not a function. Any $x > 7$ will return two different outputs.

$$h(h^{-1}(x)) = x$$
$$(h^{-1}(x) - 10)^2 + 7 = x$$
$$(h^{-1}(x) - 10)^2 = x - 7$$
$$h^{-1}(x) - 10 = \pm\text{SQRT}(x - 7)$$

Developing Habits of Mind

Ask students to give examples of each type of inverse. They should be able to give simple examples for inverse functions. For example, if f is the function that adds 5 to x, then f^{-1} is the function that subtracts 5 from x:

$$f^{-1}(f(x)) = f^{-1}(x + 5) = x + 5 - 5 = x$$

Example

Problem Find the inverse function of $f(x) = \frac{x}{2} + 5$.

Solution

Method 1 One way to do this is to describe $f(x)$ as steps: Divide by 2 and then add 5. The inverse function f^{-1} takes an input, subtracts 5, and then multiplies by 2.

$$f^{-1}(x) = 2(x - 5)$$

Method 2 The other way to find an inverse function is to use the definition.

$$f(f^{-1}(x)) = x$$

If $f(x) = \frac{x}{2} + 5$, then

$$f(f^{-1}(x)) = \frac{f^{-1}(x)}{2} + 5$$

Since $x = f(f^{-1}(x))$, you have

$$x = \frac{f^{-1}(x)}{2} + 5$$

Solve for $f^{-1}(x)$ as you would for any variable. You can subtract 5 from each side and then multiply by 2.

$$x = \frac{f^{-1}(x)}{2} + 5$$
$$x - 5 = \frac{f^{-1}(x)}{2}$$
$$2(x - 5) = f^{-1}(x)$$

Habits of Mind

Represent a function. You can think of this equation as $f(\text{anything}) = \frac{\text{anything}}{2} + 5$.

For You to Do

16. Find the inverse of $g(x) = 2(x - 5)$.

For Discussion

17. What happens when you try to find the inverse of $h(x) = (x - 10)^2 + 7$?

Developing Habits of Mind

Look for relationships. In arithmetic, numbers have additive inverses. When you add a number to its additive inverse, you get 0, the identity for addition. The additive inverse of a number is its opposite.

Nonzero numbers have multiplicative inverses. When you multiply a number by its multiplicative inverse, you get 1, the identity for multiplication. The multiplicative inverse of a number is its reciprocal.

Answers

For You to Do

16. $g^{-1}(x) = \frac{x}{2} + 5$

For Discussion

17. The inverse operations are "subtract 7, take the square root, and add 10," but "take the square root" is not a one-to-one relationship.

One-to-one functions have inverses with respect to composition. When you compose a function with its inverse, you get id, the identity for composition. There is one hitch: composition, unlike addition and multiplication, is not commutative. $f \circ g \neq g \circ f$ unless f and g are special functions. For a function and its inverse, though, the story is much simpler, thanks to the following theorem.

Remember...

The functions $f \circ g$ and $g \circ f$ do not necessarily have the same domain.

Theorem 2.1

Suppose $f: A \rightarrow B$ is one-to-one. Then

- **$f^{-1}: B \rightarrow A$ is one-to-one**
- **$(f^{-1})^{-1} = f$**

Proof

- Suppose $f^{-1}(r) = f^{-1}(s)$. Take f of each side to conclude that $r = s$.
- For f to be the inverse of f^{-1} (that is, $f = (f^{-1})^{-1}$), f must have a domain A and range B (which it does).

  Also, $f^{-1}(f(a))$ must equal a for all a in A.

  You know $f \circ f^{-1}$ is the identity, so

  $$f(f^{-1}(f(a)) = f \circ f^{-1}(f(a)) = \text{id}(f(a) = f(a).$$

  The fact that f is one-to-one and $f(f^{-1}(f(a)) = f(a)$ means that

  $$f^{-1}(f(a)) = a.$$

  Thus f fits the definition of the inverse of f^{-1}. So, $f = (f^{-1})^{-1}$.

Habits of Mind

Detect the key characteristics. Study the two characteristics of f proved in the second part. They meet the requirements for f to be the inverse of f^{-1}. That is why you can conclude $f = (f^{-1})^{-1}$.

Exercises *Practicing Habits of Mind*

Check Your Understanding

1. The basic functions below are all from $\mathbb{R}$ to $\mathbb{R}$. For each function, determine whether the function has an inverse. If it does, find the inverse function. If it does not, explain why not.

   a. $f(x) = x$ **b.** $g(x) = \frac{1}{x}$ **c.** $h(x) = x^2$

   d. $k(x) = x^3$ **e.** $\ell(x) = x^3 - x$ **f.** $m(x) = \sqrt{x}$

   g. $n(x) = |x|$

Exercises

1. a. Yes; $f^{-1}(x) = x$

b. Yes; $g^{-1}(x) = \frac{1}{x}$

c. No; $h(x) = x^2$ is not one-to-one.

d. Yes; $k^{-1}(x) = x^{\frac{1}{3}}$

e. No; $1(x) = x^3 - x$ is not one-to-one.

f. Yes; $m^{-1}(x) = x^2$

g. No; $n(x) = |x|$ is not one-to-one.

THEOREM 2.1 In the second-to-last sentence of the proof, emphasize the expressions that must be equal in the equation $f(f^{-1}(f(a))) = f(a)$:

$$f(f^{-1}(f(a)) = f(a)$$

This will help students recognize that $f^{-1}(f(a)) = a$.

Wrap Up

To end this lesson, you might go back to the In-Class Experiment. Ask students to give examples of several possible experiments. For each experiment students give, ask whether the experiment is reversible—if they could guess the starting number from the ending number. Ask how they could tell, in general, whether an experiment is reversible.

Assessment Resources

Lesson Quiz 2.4

1. Function $g(x)$ is one-to-one with $g(4) = 9$ and $g(-1) = 3$. Which equations must be true?

   I. $f^{-1}(4) = \frac{1}{9}$ **II.** $f^{-1}(-1) = 3$

   III. $f^{-1}(9) = 4$ **IV.** $f^{-1}(3) = -1$

2. Each function below has an inverse function. Find the inverse of each.

   a. $f(x) = 2x + 6$ **b.** $f(x) = -5x + 7$

   c. $f(x) = \frac{1}{4}x + 8$ **d.** $f(x) = 0.5x + 0.8$

3. Let $f(x) = 4x + 7$. Find each value.

   a. $f(8)$ **b.** $f^{-1}(87)$

   c. $f(f(0))$ **d.** $f^{-1}(f^{-1}((19))$

Exercises

HOMEWORK

- Core: 10, 11, 13, 14, 15, 19
- Optional: 12, 16, 18, 20
- Extension:17

EXERCISE 2 Have students copy the graph and add the graph of the line $y = x$. The graph of the inverse of a function is the reflection of the graph of the function over the line $y = x$. The coordinates of a point where the graphs of a function and its inverse intersect must be in the form (a, a).

EXERCISE 4 Most students will restrict the domain to the set of nonnegative real numbers. Ask them if there is more than one way to restrict the domain. The function is also one-to-one if you restrict the domain to the set of nonpositive real numbers, in which case the inverse is $x \mapsto -\sqrt{x}$.

Check Your Understanding

EXERCISE 5 Some texts just reverse the arrows in the potato-and-arrow diagram to make the "inverse of a relation." This inverse relation is not a function unless the original function was one-to-one. You can try reversing the arrows, but you need to look closely at the resulting diagram. If the original function had two or more inputs that had the same output, this "inverse" will have at least one input that produces two or more outputs. This means this "inverse" is not a function, and therefore is not a true inverse.

EXERCISE 6 will be much simpler if you use y or some other variable in place of $f^{-1}(x)$.

EXERCISE 7 Note that $h(x) = x^2$ would not be the inverse function because it is not one-to-one.

2. Use the graph of a function and its inverse at the right.

a. The point (1, 5) is on the graph of the function. What point must be on the graph of the inverse function?

b. If $f : \mathbb{R} \to \mathbb{R}$, describe how you get the graph of f^{-1} from the graph of f.

c. How does this graph connect to the statement of Theorem 2.1?

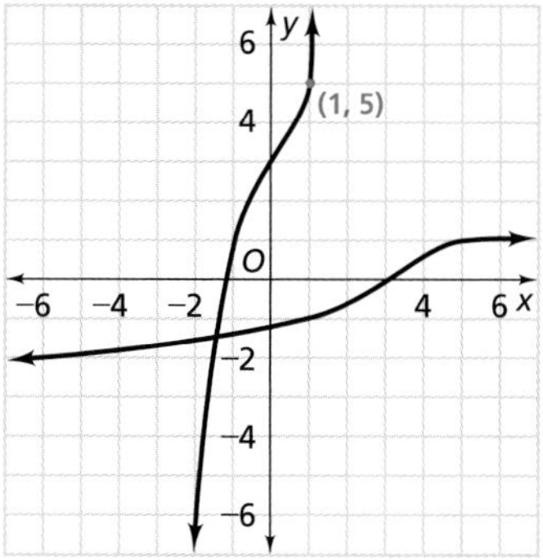

3. Use the definition of f below.

$$f(x) = \begin{cases} x & \text{if } x < 0 \\ 2x & \text{if } 0 \le x \le 6 \end{cases}$$

This is the function from Exercise 9 in Lesson 2.2.

a. What is the natural domain of f?

b. Sketch the graph of f.

c. Extend the definition of f so that its domain is all of $\mathbb{R}$ and f is one-to-one.

d. Extend the definition of f so that its domain is all of $\mathbb{R}$ and f is not one-to-one.

4. The function $x \mapsto x^2$ is not one-to-one on its natural domain.

a. Restrict its domain to a set on which the function is one-to-one.

b. On this restricted domain, what is the inverse of $x \mapsto x^2$?

5. The table at the right defines the function t.

a. What is the domain of t?

b. Draw a potato-and-arrow diagram that illustrates $t(x)$.

c. Why is t a function?

d. Does t have an inverse? If so, give the table for t^{-1}. If not, change the table to make a new function that is one-to-one.

x	$t(x)$
1	3
5	7
9	11
13	11

Remember...
In exercises like this, the table is the entire function. If an input is not in the table, then it is not in the domain of t.

6. Find the inverse of $f(x) = \frac{x}{x-1}$, where $x \neq 1$.

7. Functions h and j are defined on $\mathbb{R}^+$.

$$h(x) = x^2$$
$$j(x) = \sqrt{x}$$

Graph $h(x)$ and $j(x)$. Is h equal to j^{-1}?

Answers

2. a. (5, 1)

b. Answers may vary. Sample: Reflect the graph over the line $y = x$.

c. Answers may vary. Sample: Each graph represents a one-to-one function, and if you reflect either graph over the line $y = x$, you get the other graph.

3. a. $x \le 6$

b.

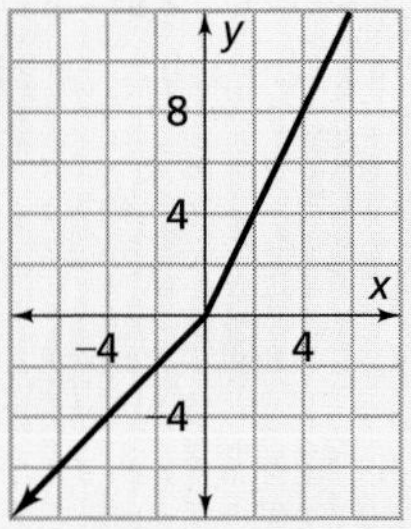

c. Answers may vary. Sample:

$$f(x) = \begin{cases} x & \text{if } x < 0 \\ 2x & \text{if } x \ge 0 \end{cases}$$

d. Answers may vary. Sample:

$$f(x) = \begin{cases} x & \text{if } x < 0 \\ 2x & \text{if } 0 \le x \le 6 \\ -x & \text{if } x > 6 \end{cases}$$

4. a. Answers may vary. Sample: $x > 0$

b. $f^{-1}(x) = \sqrt{x}$

5. a. the numbers 1, 5, 9, 13

b.

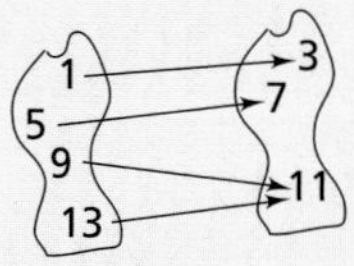

c. Each input is matched to a unique output.

d. $t(x)$ does not have an inverse because it contains (9, 11) and (13, 11). To make it a function, change one of the output 11's to a number other than 3, 7, or 11.

8. Suppose $f, g : \mathbb{R} \to \mathbb{R}$, with $f(x) = 5x^2 - 17x + 6$ and $g(x) = 5x$.

   a. Find a formula for $g \circ f(x)$.

   b. Find a formula for $h(x) = g \circ f \circ g^{-1}(x)$.

   c. Draw the graphs of f and h on the same axes.

   d. Find the zeros of h and the zeros of f.

Remember...

The zeros of a function j are the numbers a that make $j(a) = 0$.

9. **Take It Further** Prove or disprove the following statement. If $f(x) = f^{-1}(x)$ for an input x, then $f(x) = x$.

On Your Own

10. Here are the graphs of four functions. Which functions are definitely not one-to-one?

a.

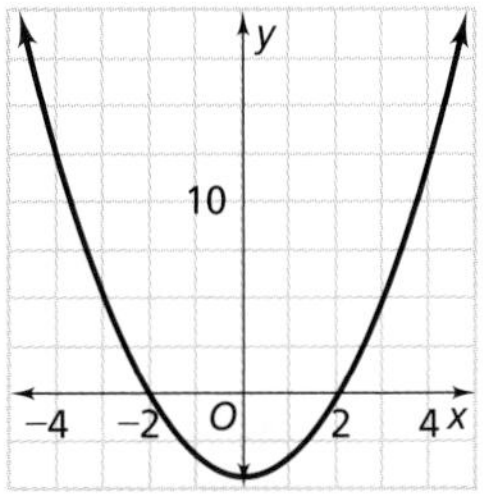

b.

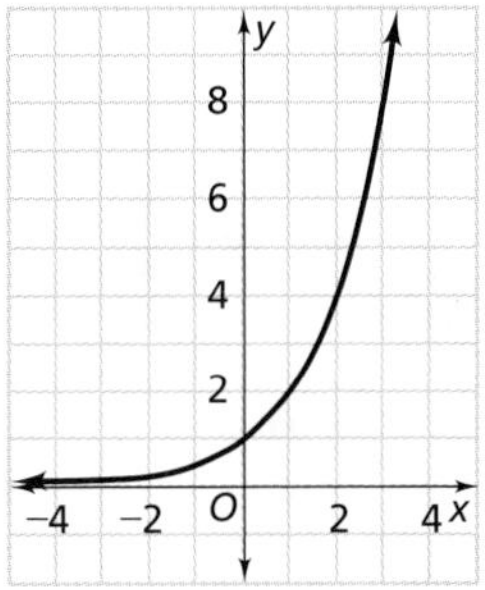

c.

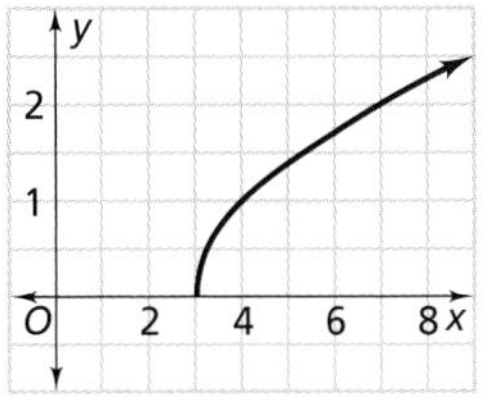

d.

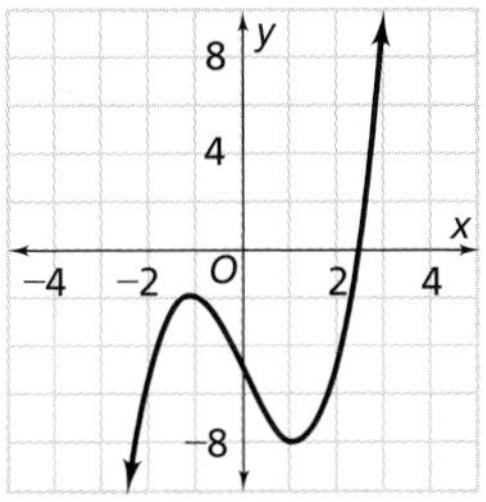

Habits of Mind

Visualize. Some of these functions may be one-to-one. Think about how the graph may extend for $x > 4$ if the function really is one-to-one. How might it look if the function is not one-to-one?

11. **Standardized Test Prep** Function $f(x)$ is one-to-one, with $f(3) = 7$ and $f(7) = 5$. Which equation must be true?

   A. $f^{-1}(3) = \frac{1}{7}$ B. $f^{-1}(3) = 7$

   C. $f^{-1}(7) = 5$ D. $f^{-1}(7) = 3$

Go Online PHSchool.com

For additional practice, go to **Web Code** bfa-0204

12. Prove that, if functions $f, g : \mathbb{R} \to \mathbb{R}$ are one-to-one, then $f \circ g$ is one-to-one.

On Your Own

EXERCISE 9 is subtle. If $f(x) = f^{-1}(x)$, then the graph of f is also the graph of f^{-1}. Because the graph of f^{-1} is the reflection of the graph of f over the line $y = x$, the graph of f must be symmetric with respect to the line $y = x$. Any function (not just $f(x) = x$) with a graph that is symmetric with respect to the line $y = x$ will have the property that $f(x) = f^{-1}(x)$. One example is $f(x) = \frac{1}{x}$.

EXERCISE 10 should be a quick skill exercise. Some students will argue that (b) or (c) are not one-to-one because of the flatness of the graph. This especially applies to (b), so it might be worth discussing how a graph can look as though it is very close to being horizontal but still be one-to-one. You could use the graph of $y = \frac{1}{x}$ as another example.

EXERCISE 11 Suggest to students that they use each of the given equations to write an ordered pair for the function f. This will allow them to determine two ordered pairs of the inverse function.

6. $f^{-1}(x) = \frac{x}{x - 1}$

7. Yes, $h = j^{-1}$.

8. a. $g \circ f(x) = 25x^2 - 85x + 30$

b. $5x^2 - 17x + 6$

c. The graphs are identical parabolas.

d. The zeros of each are $\frac{2}{5}$ and 3.

9. False; answers may vary. Sample: See Exercise 6, in which $f(x) = f^{-1}(x) = \frac{x}{x - 1}$.

10. a and d

11. D

12. Answers may vary. Samples: $f \circ g(a) = f(g(a))$. Since g is one-to-one, $g(a)$ is unique for a given a. And since f is one-to-one, $f(g(a))$ is unique for a given $g(a)$. So $f \circ g$ is one-to-one.

EXERCISE 13 If students have trouble here, appeal to their intuitive notion of inverses. It may be helpful to suggest that students refer to their experience in the In-Class Experiment.

EXERCISE 14 Note that *m* and *q* are inverses. Some students may not catch this.

EXERCISE 15 Students could look at the results in Exercise 14 to get ideas for part (b).

Maintain Your Skills

EXERCISE 19 mirrors earlier exercises in the investigation. Some students will do this exercise by finding a rule for $f^{-1}(x)$, while others will use the definition of inverse to help them do those parts. These are both excellent methods to use and are worth discussing.

Additional Resources

PRINT RESOURCES
- Solution Manual
- Practice Workbook
- Assessment Resources
- Teaching Resources

TECHNOLOGY
- Interactive Textbook
- TeacherExpress CD-ROM
- ExamView CD-ROM
- PHSchool.com

Additional Practice

1. Below are the graphs of three functions. Which functions are one-to-one, if any?

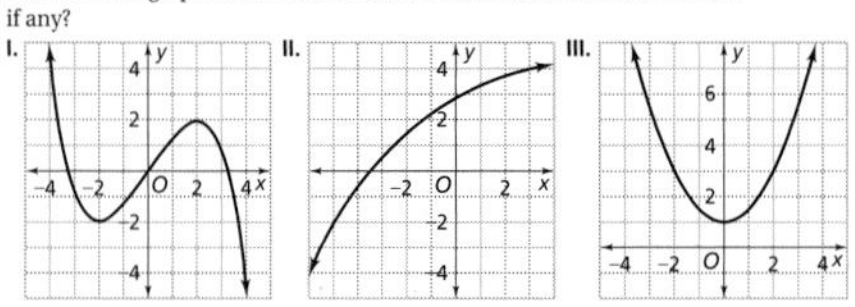

2. Function $g(x)$ is one-to-one with $g(2) = 8$ and $g(5) = 12$. Which equations must be true?
   I. $g^{-1}(2) = \frac{1}{8}$ II. $g^{-1}(5) = 12$
   III. $g^{-1}(8) = 2$ IV. $g^{-1}(12) = 5$

3. **Multiple Choice** Functions *h* and *j* are one-to-one. Which function is the inverse function of $h \circ j$?
   A. $h^{-1} \circ j^{-1}$ B. $h^{-1} \circ j$ C. $j^{-1} \circ h^{-1}$ D. $j \circ h^{-1}$

For Exercises 4–7, each function has an inverse function. Find the inverse for each.

4. $f(x) = 4x - 5$

5. $g(x) = -3x + 9$

6. $h(x) = \frac{1}{2}x + 8$

7. $j(x) = 0.3x - 0.7$

8. Let $f(x) = 5x + 1$. Find each value.
   a. $f(9)$ b. $f^{-1}(61)$
   c. $f(f(0))$ d. $f^{-1}(f^{-1}(16))$
   e. $f(f^{-1}(101))$ f. $f^{-1}(f(-17))$
   g. $f(f^{-1}(f(25)))$

Practice: For Lesson 2.4, assign Exercises 1–8.

13. Functions *f* and *g* are one-to-one. Which function is the inverse function of $f \circ g$?
A. $f^{-1} \circ g^{-1}$ B. $g^{-1} \circ f^{-1}$
C. $f^{-1} \circ g$ D. $g^{-1} \circ f$

14. Find the inverse of each function.
a. $m(x) = 5x + 3$ b. $n(x) = 2x - 11$
c. $p(x) = -3x + 4$ d. $q(x) = \frac{x}{5} - 0.6$

The domain of each function is $\mathbb{R}$.

15. The graph of the function $f(x) = ax + b$ is a line with slope *a*.
a. If $a \neq 0$, show that *f* is one-to-one.
b. Find a formula for $f^{-1}(x)$.
c. Find the slope of the graph of the inverse function f^{-1}.
d. Find three linear functions *g*, *h*, and *j* such that each is its own inverse.

16. Suppose $f, g, k: \mathbb{R} \rightarrow \mathbb{R}$, $f(x) = 5x^3 - 12x^2 - 11x + 6$, $g(x) = 25x$, and $k(x) = 5x$.
a. Find a formula for $g \circ f(x)$.
b. Find a formula for $h(x) = g \circ f \circ k^{-1}(x)$.
c. Draw the graphs of *f* and *h* on the same axes.
d. Find the zeros of *f* and the zeros of *h*.

17. Take It Further Suppose $f: \mathbb{R} \rightarrow \mathbb{R}$ and $f(x) = 7x^2 - 15x + 2$. Find a linear function *g* such that $g \circ f \circ g^{-1}$ is a monic quadratic polynomial.

A quadratic is monic if the coefficient of x^2 is 1.

18. Write About It The graph of function $f: \mathbb{R} \rightarrow \mathbb{R}$ is increasing, which means that as *x* increases, $f(x)$ also increases.
a. Draw a possible graph of function *f*.
b. Roy says that any increasing function, no matter what its graph looks like, must be one-to-one. Do you agree? Explain.

Maintain Your Skills

19. Let $f(x) = 4x + 3$. Find each value.
a. $f(10)$ b. $f^{-1}(43)$ c. $f(f(0))$
d. $f^{-1}(f^{-1}(15))$ e. $f(f^{-1}(289))$ f. $f^{-1}(f(-162.3))$
g. $f(f^{-1}(f(10)))$

20. Let $f(x) = 4x + 3$. Find each value in terms of *r*.
a. $f(r)$ b. $f(f(r))$ c. $f(f(f(r)))$
d. $f(f(f(f(r))))$ e. $f(f(f(f(f(r)))))$ f. $f^{12}(r)$

The notation $f^{12}(r)$ means "compose 12 copies of *f* and apply the composition to *r*."

Answers

13. B

14. a. $m^{-1}(x) = \frac{x - 3}{5}$

b. $n^{-1}(x) = \frac{x + 11}{2}$

c. $p^{-1}(x) = \frac{-x + 4}{3}$

d. $q^{-1}(x) = 5(x + 0.6) = 5x + 3$

15. a. Solving for $f(x) = y$, $x = \frac{y - b}{a}$, so each value of *y* generates a unique value of *x*.

b. $f^{-1}(x) = \frac{y - b}{a}$

c. $\frac{1}{a}$

d. Answers may vary. Samples: $f(x) = x$, $g(x) = -x$, $h(x) = -x + 3$

16. a. $g \circ f(x) = 125x^3 - 300x^2 - 275x + 150$

b. $x^3 - 12x^2 - 55x + 150$

c. Check students' graphs.

d. *f* has zeros of about −1, 0.4, and 3; *h* has zeros of about −5, 2, and 15.

17–20. See back of book.

Mathematical Reflections 2A

In this investigation, you learned how to determine whether a table, graph, or closed-form rule is a function; compose functions; and find the inverse of a function if it exists. These exercises will help you summarize what you have learned.

1. Suppose $f : \mathbb{R} \rightarrow \mathbb{R}$ and $f(x) = 3x^2 - 6x + 1$.

a. Calculate $f(3)$ and $f(-3)$.

b. Find all values of x for which $f(x) = 12$.

c. Calculate $f(11) - f(10)$.

d. Show that you can write $f(x + 1)$ as $f(x + 1) = 3x^2 - 2$.

e. Write a simplified expression for $f(x + 1) - f(x)$.

f. If $g(x) = f(x + 1) - f(x)$, what is $g(10)$?

2. Consider the functions $f(x) = 3x + 2$ and $g(x) = x + 5$. Calculate each value.

a. $f(3)$ **b.** $g(3)$ **c.** $f(g(3))$ **d.** $f \circ g(3)$ **e.** $g \circ f(3)$ **f.** $f(3) \cdot g(3)$

3. Consider the function $f(x) = 3x + 2$. Find a function g that makes each equation true.

a. $f \circ g(x) = x$ **b.** $g \circ f(x) = x$ **c.** $f \circ g(x) = x^2$

d. $g \circ f(x) = x^2$ **e.** $g \circ f(x) = f(x)$ **f.** $f \circ g(x) = f(x)$

4. Suppose $f, g, k : \mathbb{R} \rightarrow \mathbb{R}$, $f(x) = -3 + x + 8x^2 + 4x^3$, $g(x) = 16x$, and $k(x) = 4x$.

a. Find a formula for $g \circ f(x)$.

b. Find a formula for $h(x) = g \circ f \circ k^{-1}(x)$.

c. Draw the graphs of f and h on the same axes.

d. Find the zeros of h and the zeros of f.

5. What is a function?

6. How do you compose two functions to make a new function?

7. What function undoes $x \mapsto 3x + 7$?

Vocabulary and Notation

In this investigation you learned these terms and symbols. Make sure you understand what each one means and how to use it.

- **composite function, $g \circ f$**
- **domain**
- **equal functions**
- **function**
- **identity function**
- **inverse function, f^{-1}**
- **one-to-one**
- **range**
- **target**
- **$x \mapsto y$ (x maps to y)**
- **$\mathbb{R}$ (the real numbers)**

Mathematical Reflections

EXERCISES 5–7 At the start of the investigation, you may have assigned these as Questions 1–3 for students to think and write about.

Mathematical Reflections

1. a. $f(3) = 10$, $f(-3) = 46$

b. $x = \dfrac{3 \pm \sqrt{42}}{3}$

c. 57

d. $f(x + 1) = 3(x + 1)^2 - 6(x + 1) + 1 = 3x^2 + 6x + 3 - 6x - 6 + 1 = 3x^2 - 2$

e. $6x - 3$ **f.** 57

2. a. $f(3) = 11$ **b.** $g(3) = 8$

c. $f(g(3)) = 26$ **d.** $f \circ g(3) = 26$

e. 16 **f.** 88

3. a. $g(x) = \dfrac{x - 2}{3}$

b. $g(x) = \dfrac{x - 2}{3}$

c. $g(x) = \dfrac{x^2 - 2}{3}$

d. $g(x) = \left(\dfrac{x - 2}{3}\right)^2$

e. $g(x) = x$ **f.** $g(x) = x$

4. a. $g \circ f(x) = -48 + 16x + 128x^2 + 64x^3$

b. $-48 + 4x + 8x^2 + x^3$

c–d. See back of book.

5–7. See back of book.

Investigation Overview

In Chapter 1, students found polynomials to match tables with inputs that started with 0 and increased by 1. This investigation introduces Lagrange interpolation, a general method, so that given *any* table, students can find a polynomial that matches the table.

This investigation is technical and requires a certain flexibility with polynomials. So why teach Lagrange interpolation? Students develop the flexibility they need while engaging in work around Lagrange interpolation, and this work also brings several major algebraic concepts to the fore.

Approach Lagrange interpolation with several goals in mind. You want students to have enough experience working with polynomials that theorems about polynomials seem natural.

- This investigation is an important review of the Zero Product Property from *Algebra 1* and a preview of the Factor Theorem, which appears in the next investigation.
- Students begin to develop an intuition that n points uniquely define a polynomial of degree $n - 1$.
- Students get used to operating with polynomials and begin to develop intuition about degrees of sums and products of polynomials.

Students work with one of the most fundamental concepts of algebra: linear combinations. Students use linear combinations of polynomials to find polynomials that interpolate tables.

This investigation also provides a connection to Chapter 4, where students learn how to find these polynomials using systems of linear equations.

Although computer algebra systems (CAS) are not necessary to solve most of the exercises in this investigation, they will help. Some exercises are marked to indicate they require a CAS.

You may wish to assign Questions 1–3 for students to think and write about during the investigation.

Learning Goals

- Fit polynomials to tables.
- Work with linear combinations.

Habits and Skills

- Use linear combinations of polynomials to determine new polynomials.
- Use zeros of polynomials to determine factors of polynomials.
- Find several functions that agree with a given table.
- Predict the result of calculations without having to carry them out.

Investigation 2B

Making It Fit

In Chapter 1, you learned how to find a simple function that fits a table if the inputs increase in a regular way. In *Making It Fit,* you will learn a general-purpose technique called Lagrange interpolation. You can use this technique to fit a polynomial function to any table.

By the end of this investigation, you will be able to answer questions like these.

1. How can you find a polynomial that agrees with a table?
2. How can you find two different functions that agree with the same table?
3. What number comes next in the sequence 1, 4, 9, . . . ?

You will learn how to

- fit polynomials to tables
- work with linear combinations

You will develop these habits and skills:

- Use linear combinations of polynomials to determine new polynomials.
- Use zeros of polynomials to determine factors of polynomials.
- Find several functions that agree with a given table.
- Predict the results of calculations without having to carry them out.

In this latticework, pairs of apple-tree branches suggest polynomial-function graphs that agree at one point.

Investigation Road Map

LESSON 2.5, *Getting Started,* has students find polynomials that match tables of values. They see an informal development of Lagrange interpolation.

LESSON 2.6, *Lagrange Interpolation,* shows students a complete development of Lagrange interpolation.

LESSON 2.7, *Agreeing to Disagree,* shows students that there are many possible rules that fit a given table. Students see a first introduction to the general form of polynomials that fit a particular table.

2.5 Getting Started

Activating Prior Knowledge
Exploring New Ideas

In Chapter 1, you learned some techniques for finding polynomial functions that agree with tables. Usually the tables started with 0 and had inputs that increased by 1. How do you handle inputs that are not arranged that way? What do you do if the inputs do not follow a simple pattern? Suppose you have to work with a graph like this.

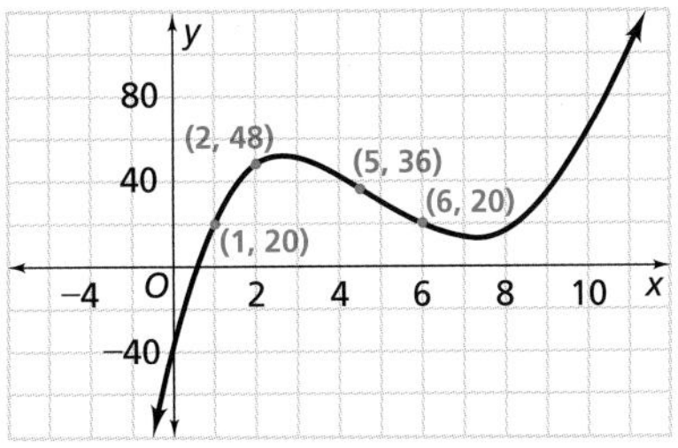

In this investigation, you will learn *Lagrange interpolation*. This technique will handle any data set that can come from a polynomial function.

For You to Explore

In Problems 1–3, find a polynomial function that agrees with each table.

How can you check that the functions you find actually agree with the tables?

1.

n	$f(n)$
2	5
5	11
7	15

2.

n	$g(n)$
2	6
5	30
7	56

3.

x	$h(x)$
2	10
5	55
7	105

4. a. Find a quadratic function that agrees with the following table.

x	$k(x)$
1	0
3	0

b. Is the function you found the only quadratic function that agrees with the table? If it is, explain why. If not, find another one.

Answers

For You to Explore

1. $f(n) = 2n + 1$

2. $g(n) = n(n + 1)$

3. $h(x) = 2x^2 + x$

4. a. Answers may vary. Sample:
$k(x) = (x - 1)(x - 3)$
$= x^2 - 4x + 3$

b. Another quadratic function is
$k(x) = 2(x - 1)(x - 3)$
$= 2x^2 - 8x + 6.$

Lesson Overview

GOAL

- Fit polynomials to tables.

In this Getting Started lesson, students encounter Lagrange interpolation. In Investigation 1A, students found polynomials that matched tables, so the problems and exercises in this lesson should look familiar. Students can solve the first three problems with tables as they did in the previous chapter. Subsequent problems push students to generate polynomials with zeros at particular *x* values.

As always in a Getting Started lesson, there is no need to formalize these ideas today. Students meet all the ideas again throughout the investigation.

FOR YOU TO EXPLORE
- Core: 1, 2, 4, 5, 6, 9
- Optional: 3, 7, 8

MATERIALS
- CAS (recommended)
- graph paper
- graphing calculator
- Blackline Master 2.5

HOMEWORK
- Core: 10, 11, 12
- Optional: 13, 14a–c, 15a–c, 16a–c, 17a–c, 18a–c
- Extension: 14d, 15d, 16d, 17d, 18d

Launch

Begin the lesson by reviewing techniques students have used in the past to find a function that agrees with a table. How are the tables in the For You to Explore problems different? Students should see that a difference table makes no sense when the inputs do not increase by a set amount. Ask students to think about what other tools they have to determine a function that agrees with a table: look at a graph, factor the outputs, look for relationships. Then, let the students work cooperatively on the For You To Explore problems.

Explore

For You to Explore

These problems are not easy, so give students plenty of time to struggle with them. Students may not be able to solve these problems today. These will all be easier to solve after the next lesson.

PROBLEM 1 Students might graph the points given by the table and notice that they seem to be collinear.

PROBLEMS 2 AND 3 are difficult. Lagrange interpolation provides a method to solve these problems. Let students work for a while, but part of the purpose here is for some students not to make progress, so they can devise a better method.

PROBLEM 3 is a good example of a problem in which solving a linear system of equations is helpful.

PROBLEMS 5 AND 6 You can use Blackline Master 2.5 as a transparency.

PROBLEM 6 follows up on Problem 5. Give students an opportunity to see the connection. If they grasp this connection, Lagrange interpolation will be a natural next step.

PROBLEM 7 Before you simplify, write this on the board:

$$3(x-1)(x-3) - 2(x-1)(x-6) + 1(x-3)(x-6)$$

Ask: what is the value when $x = 1$? When $x = 3$? When $x = 6$? Then change the coefficients in front of each "term" and do it again. Then put letters in from of each term and figure out the values of the letters if you want the expression to be 20 when $x = 1$, 12 when $x = 3$, and 60 when $x = 6$. This discovery is another track to Lagrange interpolation.

Wrap Up

Have students verbalize how they solved Problems 4–6.

5. Find a quadratic function that agrees with each table.

a.

x	$j(x)$
1	20
3	0
6	0

b.

x	$n(x)$
1	0
3	12
6	0

c.

x	$m(x)$
1	0
3	0
6	60

d. Copy and complete the following table.

x	$j(x) + n(x) + m(x)$
1	■
3	■
6	■

6. Find a quadratic function f that agrees with this table.

x	$f(x)$
1	20
3	12
6	60

7. Find a polynomial function k that agrees with this table.

x	$k(x)$
1	10
3	12
6	45

8. Find a polynomial function t that agrees with this table.

x	$t(x)$
1	84
5	48
8	42

9. Find a quadratic function f such that the graph of f contains the points in the graph.

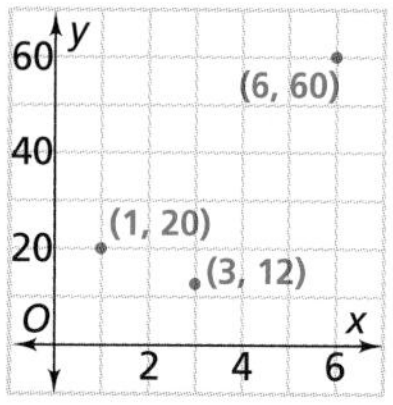

Answers

5. a. $j(x) = 2(x-3)(x-6)$
$= 2x^2 - 18x + 36$

b. $n(x) = -2(x-1)(x-6)$
$= -2x^2 + 14x - 12$

c. $m(x) = 4(x-1)(x-3)$
$= 4x^2 - 16x + 12$

d. The values in the second column are 20, 12, 60.

6. $f(x) = 4x^2 - 20x + 36$

7. $k(x) = 2x^2 - 7x + 15$

8. $f(t) = t^2 - 15t + 98$

9. $f(x) = 4x^2 - 20x + 36$

Exercises

10. a. $A = 6$, $B = -2$, $C = 3$

b. $f(x) = 7x^2 - 46x + 84$

11. $r(x) = 7x^2 - 46x + 84$

12. a. The $f(x)$ values are -5, -2, 1, 4, 7, 10, 13, and 16; the $g(x)$ values are 499, -2, -55, 4, 7, -46, 13, and 520.

Exercises *Practicing Habits of Mind*

On Your Own

10. Suppose $f(x) = A(x-1)(x-4) + B(x-1)(x-6) + C(x-4)(x-6)$ for some numbers A, B, and C.

Sketch the graph of f.

a. Find the numbers A, B, and C such that the graph of f contains the points $(1, 45)$, $(4, 12)$, and $(6, 60)$.

b. Find the normal form of the polynomial that defines f.

11. Find a function that agrees with this table.

x	$r(x)$
1	45
4	12
6	60

12. Consider these two functions.

$f(x) = 3x + 1$
$g(x) = 3x + 1 + 7(x-1)(x-2)(x-4)(x+1)$

a. Copy and complete the following table.

x	$f(x)$	$g(x)$
−2	■	■
−1	■	■
0	■	■
1	■	■
2	■	■
3	■	■
4	■	■
5	■	■

b. On which inputs do f and g agree?

c. Are the inputs you found in part (a) the only inputs on which f and g agree? Explain.

d. Find the normal form of the polynomial that defines g.

e. Sketch the graphs of f and g.

b. −1, 1, 2, and 4

c. Yes; sample: if $f(x) = g(x)$, then $3x + 1 = 3x + 1 + 7(x-1)(x-2)(x-4)(x+1)$ or $7(x-1)(x-2)(x-4)(x+1) = 0$. That is true only for the values $x = 1, 2, 4,$ or -1.

d. $g(x) = 7x^4 - 42x^3 + 49x^2 + 45x - 55$

e.

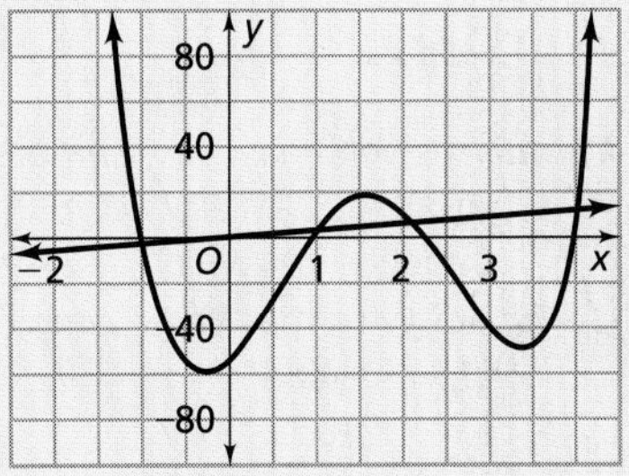

Exercises

HOMEWORK

- Core: 10, 11, 12
- Optional: 13, 14a–c, 15a–c, 16a–c, 17a–c, 18a–c
- Extension: 14d, 15d, 16d, 17d, 18d

On Your Own

EXERCISE 12 Later, you will prove that any two polynomials that agree on a large-enough set of inputs are equiva lent. "Large-enough" means $n + 1$ inputs for a polynomial of degree n. The proof comes out of this method: the difference between the two polynomials vanishes on the given set of inputs. This is also an opportunity to review and remind students of the Zero Product Property. In this case, $7(x-1)(x-2)(x-4)(x+1) = 0$ if and only if one of the factors is 0, *i.e.* if and only if $x = -1, 1, 2,$ or 4.

EXERCISE 13 In part (a), students should realize that there are many functions that agree with f only for $x = 2$. Graph f and show that there are many lines that pass through the point (2, 5). Challenge students to find a nonlinear function that agrees with f only for $x = 2$. (Answer: For example, $g(x) = 4x - 3 + (x - 2)(x^2 + 1) = x^3 - 2x^2 + 5x - 5$.)

EXERCISES 14–18 Point out to students that these exercises are related to Problem 5. Some students will be more comfortable breaking the equation for $f(x)$ into three functions and then adding them together. They will see this method again in the next lesson.

EXERCISES 16 AND 17 Before they find the polynomials that define these functions, ask students to plot the points and make conjectures about the functions. From their work on Exercises 14 and 15, students should recognize that both functions are quadratic. The leading coefficient of the function in Exercise 16 is positive and the leading coefficient of the function in Exercise 17 is negative.

13. Let $f(x) = 4x - 3$.

a. Find a polynomial function that agrees with f for the input 2 but differs from it for every other input.

b. Find a polynomial function that agrees with f for the inputs 2, 5, and 7 but differs from f for every other input.

Maintain Your Skills

Suppose $f(x) = A(x - 1)(x - 4) + B(x - 1)(x - 6) + C(x - 4)(x - 6)$ for some numbers A, B, and C. For Exercises 14–18, use the information given about f to do parts (a)–(d).

a. Find A, B, and C.

b. Find the normal form of the polynomial that defines f.

c. Sketch the graph of f.

d. **Take It Further** Find the minimum or maximum output of f.

14.

x	$f(x)$
1	60
4	−18
6	20

15.

x	$f(x)$
1	60
4	−18
6	10

16. The graph of f contains (1, 0), (4, 6), and (6, 30).

17. The graph of f contains (1, 0), (4, 6), and (6, −30).

18.

x	$f(x)$
1	30
4	−6
6	−30

The cars are approaching the roller coaster's maximum.

Answers

13. a. Answers may vary. Sample: $g(x) = 5$ (or any polynomial function for which $g(2) = 5$).

b. Answers may vary. Sample: $h(x) = 4x - 3 + (x - 2)(x - 5)(x - 7)$

14. a. $A = 2, B = 3, C = 4$

b. $f(x) = 9x^2 - 71x + 122$

c.

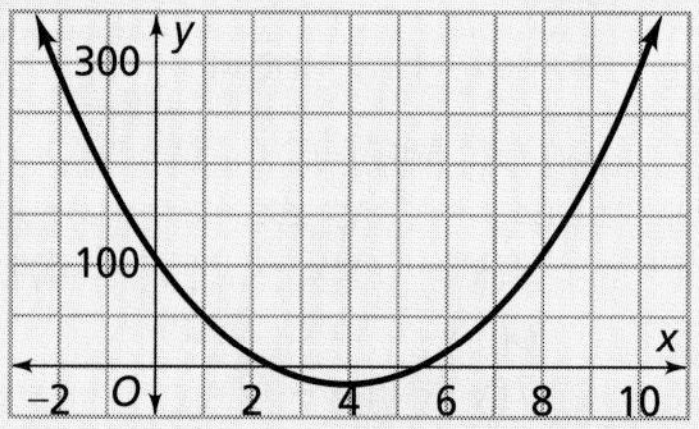

d. minimum $= -\frac{649}{18}$; no maximum

2.6 Lagrange Interpolation

In Chapter 1, you found rules to match the entries in tables. You developed some methods for fitting functions to tables. The methods were not general for two reasons.

- Most of the tables in Chapter 1 had inputs that started with 0 and increased by 1 in each row.
- The methods relied on your ability to spot patterns.

You learned that a constant first difference means there is an exact linear fit. A constant nonzero second difference means there is an exact quadratic fit.

In this lesson you will develop a way of matching the values in a table for any n distinct points using a polynomial of degree less than n. If you just rely on cleverness, it can be hard to find a function that agrees with a table (very hard for some tables), so it is very useful to have a method that will work for all tables.

The polynomial you get using this method may not be the simplest function that matches the n values in your table. It may look so messy that you want to use a computer or calculator to simplify it. But the method always works. Given a table, you will be able to find a function every time. And if the simplest function that matches the table is a polynomial, the method gives you the unique simplest rule for the table.

You will prove that the rule you get is unique in a later lesson.

Minds in Action episode 5

Derman and Sasha are working on Problem 6 from the Getting Started lesson.

Table A

Input, x	Output, f(x)
1	20
3	12
6	60

Derman I wish a couple of these outputs were 0. Then this would be easy.

Sasha Derman, that gives me an idea. We could split up Table A this way.

Sasha writes the following three tables on the board.

x	g(x)
1	20
3	0
6	0

+

x	h(x)
1	0
3	12
6	0

+

x	j(x)
1	0
3	0
6	60

15. a. $A = 1, B = 3, C = 4$

b. $f(x) = 8x^2 - 66x + 188$

c.

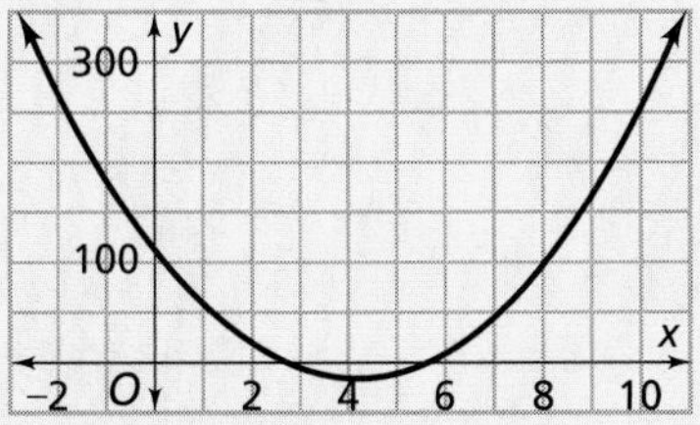

d. minimum $= -\frac{145}{8}$; no maximum

16–18. See back of book.

Lesson Overview

GOAL

- Fit polynomials to tables.

This lesson introduces Lagrange interpolation formally. By the end of the lesson, students should be able to find a polynomial that agrees with any table they encounter. In fact, the polynomial given by Lagrange interpolation is the polynomial of the *least degree* that agrees with the table.

CHECK YOUR UNDERSTANDING
- Core: 1, 2, 3
- Optional: 4, 5, 6

MATERIALS
- CAS (recommended)
- graph paper
- graphing calculators
- Blackline Master 2.6

HOMEWORK
- Core: 8, 9, 10, 11, 12, 13
- Optional: 7, 14, 16a–c, 17a–c
- Extension: 15, 16d, 17d

VOCABULARY
- Lagrange interpolation

Launch

If your students had no trouble with Lesson 2.5, go straight to the Minds in Action dialog that opens this lesson. If students struggled with the Getting Started problems, ask students how they would find a quadratic function that agrees with the following table (see Blackline Master 2.6):

x	$s(x)$
1	0
3	0

Students will probably answer $s(x) = (x - 1)(x - 3)$. Ask how they would find a quadratic function that agrees with this table (see Blackline Master 2.6):

x	$t(x)$
1	0
3	0
6	60

Now $s(x) = (x - 1)(x - 3)$ will not work, but $t(x) = M(x - 1)(x - 3)$ for some constant M will. You can find M by using the point (6, 60).

$$60 = M(6 - 1)(6 - 3)$$
$$4 = M$$

So $t(x) = 4(x - 1)(x - 3)$ is a quadratic function that agrees with the table. You might point out that $t(x)$ also agrees with the previous table. Once students have worked on these two tables, move on to the dialog that opens the chapter.

Explore

Minds in Action

Some students will prefer this method of writing three simpler functions and then adding them together. They can even write each of the three functions in normal form before they add them together. Students who use a CAS to find the normal form should enter the expression(s) carefully. A small error is often difficult to find and will prove frustrating. Students should always check that their functions actually fit the tables.

Sasha I can find polynomials that fit these tables. Look what happens if we add $g(x) + h(x) + j(x)$.

x	g(x) + h(x) + j(x)
1	20 + 0 + 0 = 20
3	0 + 12 + 0 = 12
6	0 + 0 + 60 = 60

We're back to Table A. So if we can figure out polynomials that fit the three simpler tables, we can get a polynomial that fits Table A. Let's look at the first table.

x	g(x)
1	20
3	0
6	0

Let's start with $x \mapsto (x - 3)(x - 6)$. At least that agrees with our table for $x = 3$ and $x = 6$.

Derman Well, in that function, $1 \mapsto 10$, so that doesn't agree with the table.

Sasha OK, what about a multiple of that function? Try $g(x) = A(x - 3)(x - 6)$ for some A. Let's figure out what A has to be in order for $g(1)$ to be 20.

$$20 = g(1) = A(1 - 3)(1 - 6)$$
$$20 = A(-2)(-5)$$
$$20 = 10A$$
$$A = 2$$

So $g(x) = 2(x - 3)(x - 6) = 2x^2 - 18x + 36$.

Derman OK, that works. And $h(x)$ could be $B(x - 1)(x - 6)$ for some number B. Then I can figure out what B is.

$$12 = h(3) = B(3 - 1)(3 - 6)$$
$$12 = B(2)(-3)$$
$$12 = -6B$$
$$B = -2$$

So $h(x) = -2(x - 1)(x - 6) = -2x^2 + 14x - 12$.

Habits of Mind

Determine the process. How might Sasha have known that $x \mapsto (x - 3)(x - 6)$ agrees with their table for $x = 3$ and $x = 6$? How does Derman know that $1 \mapsto 10$?

Do you agree with Derman that $g(x) = 2(x - 3)(x - 6)$ works?

Sasha While you were doing that, I figured out a function for the last table.

$$j(x) = 4(x - 1)(x - 3) = 4x^2 - 16x + 12$$

Derman Adding $g(x) + h(x) + j(x)$, we get $f(x) = 4x^2 - 20x + 36$.

And here is its graph.

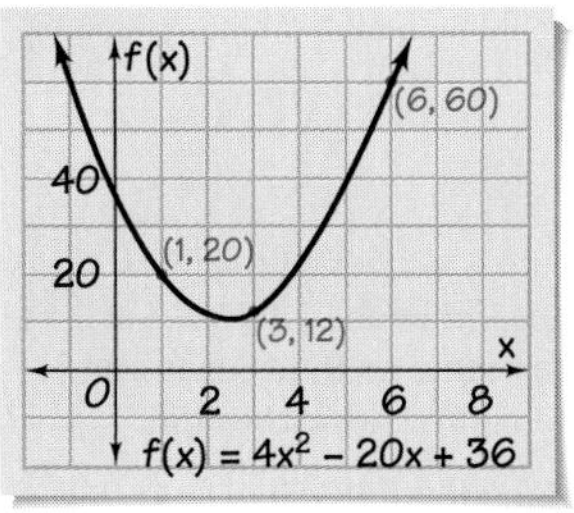

Sasha Hey, if we write $f(x)$ without expanding all the pieces, we can see more.

Sasha writes an equation on the board.

$$f(x) = 2(x - 3)(x - 6) - 2(x - 1)(x - 6) + 4(x - 1)(x - 3)$$

Derman That looks much more complicated.

Sasha Yes, but it lets you see the way it all works. Look what happens if you replace x with 1.

Derman Oh yeah—everything disappears except the first bit.

Sasha So, if we had another table with inputs 1, 3, and 6, and if the output for 1 were 30, I could change the $2(x - 3)(x - 6)$ to $3(x - 3)(x - 6)$.

Derman And you could adjust the other numbers to make this expression work for any table with inputs 1, 3, and 6. So I guess the complicated form is pretty useful.

Habits of Mind

Establish a process. How can you check that the function $f(x)$ fits the original table?

Why would Sasha change the 2 to a 3?

For You to Do

1. Find a polynomial function with a graph that contains (1, 80), (3, 36), and (6, 30).

Remember to check that the polynomial you find actually agrees with the input-output pairs.

For You to Do

PROBLEM 1 To check that $g(x) + h(x) + j(x)$ gives the correct function, students can test the points they know. Have students make an input-ouput table similar to the one in Minds in Action.

Answers

For You to Do

1. $f(x) = 4x^2 - 38x + 114$

Example

Some students might find it easier to use the approach demonstrated in Minds in Action, episode 5. They can break up $f(x)$ into four simpler functions.

Example

Problem Suppose you have the following table.

Input, x	Output, $f(x)$
1	20
2	48
5	36
6	20

If you graph the data, you can determine that there is neither a linear nor a quadratic fit. So, you are looking for a polynomial function—of degree at least 3—that agrees with the table. You can use the same method Sasha and Derman used. Here is a somewhat streamlined version of what they did.

Solution Suppose the following strange rule gives a function $f(x)$. You will determine the numbers A, B, C, and D later.

$$f(x) = A(x-1)(x-2)(x-5) + B(x-1)(x-2)(x-6) + C(x-1)(x-5)(x-6) + D(x-2)(x-5)(x-6)$$

Notice that, no matter what the values for A, B, C, and D are, this function cannot have degree greater than 3.

Why would anyone write a function this way? This is just a sum of functions, like the sum of functions Sasha and Derman found. Now you can find expressions for $f(1)$, $f(2)$, $f(5)$, and $f(6)$.

$$\begin{aligned} f(1) &= A(1-1)(1-2)(1-5) + B(1-1)(1-2)(1-6) \\ &\quad + C(1-1)(1-5)(1-6) + D(1-2)(1-5)(1-6) \\ &= 0 + 0 + 0 + D(1-2)(1-5)(1-6) \\ &= D(-1)(-4)(-5) \\ &= -20D \end{aligned}$$

In the same way, you can find $f(2)$, $f(5)$, and $f(6)$.

$$f(2) = C(2-1)(2-5)(2-6) = 12C$$
$$f(5) = B(5-1)(5-2)(5-6) = -12B$$
$$f(6) = A(6-1)(6-2)(6-5) = 20A$$

But you know $f(1)$, $f(2)$, $f(5)$, and $f(6)$. They are in the table.

$$f(1) = 20 = -20D, \text{ so } D = -1$$
$$f(2) = 48 = 12C, \text{ so } C = 4$$
$$f(5) = 36 = -12B, \text{ so } B = -3$$
$$f(6) = 20 = 20A, \text{ so } A = 1$$

By substituting in these values, you find a formula for $f(x)$.

$$f(x) = (x-1)(x-2)(x-5) - 3(x-1)(x-2)(x-6) + 4(x-1)(x-5)(x-6) - 1(x-2)(x-5)(x-6)$$

Too messy, you say. But a CAS can simplify this with no trouble. You could too, if you needed to. The formula simplifies to

$$f(x) = x^3 - 16x^2 + 69x - 34$$

This is a well-behaved cubic that agrees with the table. How is this similar to the method Sasha and Derman used?

$y = x^3 - 16x^2 + 69x - 34$

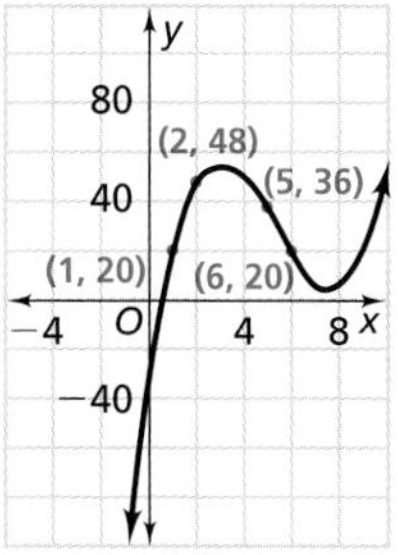

Here is the graph.

This method of finding a polynomial to agree with a table is **Lagrange interpolation.**

For You to Do

2. Use Lagrange interpolation to find a polynomial function with a graph that contains (1, 20), (2, 48), and (5, 36).

Historical Perspective

Joseph-Louis Lagrange was born in Turin, Italy, in 1736, and died in Paris, France, in 1813. His interest in advanced mathematics began when he read a calculus book by Edmond Halley (of Halley's comet fame).

Lagrange was a professor of geometry at the Royal Artillery School in Turin from 1755 (at age 19) to 1766 and helped to found the Royal Academy of Sciences there in 1757. In 1766, when Leonhard Euler left his post as director of the Berlin Academy of Sciences, Lagrange succeeded him. In 1787, Lagrange left Berlin to become a member of the French Academy of Sciences, where he remained for the rest of his career.

Lagrange contributed many results and techniques to the field of algebra. Lagrange interpolation is one of these contributions. Another contribution was a new proof that every integer is the sum of the squares of at most four integers. His interest in physics and mechanics led him to devise a new way of writing down Newton's laws of motion.

Joseph-Louis Lagrange

Answers

For You to Do

2. $f(x) = -8x^2 + 52x - 24$

For You to Do

PROBLEM 2 Using the method in the Example, students set up a polynomial $f(x) = A(x - 1)(x - 2) + B(x - 1)(x - 5) + C(x - 2)(x - 5)$ and solve for A, B, and C. Have students check that their answers work by testing the points they know.

Historical Perspective

There are fifteen positive integers less than 100 that cannot be written as the sum of three squares. One of them is 47. The others are 7, 15, 23, 28, 31, 39, 55, 60, 63, 71, 79, 87, 92, and 95.

Wrap Up

If time permits, go over Check Your Understanding Exercises 1–3.

Assessment Resources

Lesson Quiz 2.6

For Exercises 1 and 2, find a polynomial function that agrees with each table.

1.

Input	Output
1	5
2	10
3	17
4	26
5	37

2.

Input	Output
1	5
2	15
3	37
4	77
5	141

3. Find a nonconstant polynomial function r such that $r(1) = r(2) = r(3) = 0$.

4. Find a nonconstant polynomial function f such that $f(1) = f(2) = f(3) = f(4) = 6$.

Exercises

HOMEWORK
- Core: 8, 9, 10, 11, 12, 13
- Optional: 7, 14, 16a–c, 17a–c
- Extension: 15, 16d, 17d

Check Your Understanding

EXERCISE 2 Let students use Lagrange interpolation here. It is important to see that Lagrange interpolation still gives the correct fit.

EXERCISE 4 You may not wish to ask students to expand this expression without a CAS. However, they should be able to get the Lagrange form of $f(x)$.

EXERCISE 5 is a general method, different from Lagrange interpolation. To find a matching function with this method, set up an initial expression for the function as is done in this exercise. The initial function should have one term that is zero for all but one input, one that is zero for all but two inputs, another that is zero for all but three inputs, and so on. Each term has a coefficient that you can find by substituting the points you know in an order that works for the set-up you used.

You might also note that it is not necessary for the inputs to increase by 1 each time (as it was for the difference table methods in Chapter 1), even though the inputs do follow that pattern in this exercise. This method, like Lagrange interpolation, produces a function that agrees with any number of given points. As with Lagrange interpolation, though, the more points there are, the more complex the calculations.

On Your Own

EXERCISE 7 Students will need access to a computer algebra system (CAS) to solve this exercise.

Exercises *Practicing Habits of Mind*

Check Your Understanding

In Exercises 1–4, find a polynomial function that agrees with each table.

1.

Input	Output
1	12
2	8
4	36

2.

Input	Output
1	2
2	11
3	20

3.

Input	Output
1	2
2	11
3	28

4.

Input	Output
1	1
2	22
3	61
4	124

5. Sasha has a method for solving Exercise 4. She writes
$f(x) = A + B(x - 1) + C(x - 1)(x - 2) + D(x - 1)(x - 2)(x - 3)$.
Then she uses $f(1) = 1$ to find A, $f(2) = 22$ to find B, and so on.

a. Find A, B, C, and D using Sasha's method.

b. Do you get the same rule for f as you got in Exercise 4?

6. **Write About It** Sometimes, when you might expect a cubic, Lagrange interpolation produces a polynomial of lesser degree. How might this happen? (*Hint:* You can use Exercise 2 as an example.)

A curved underground hose joining 4 sprinkler heads could suggest a unique polynomial function of degree 3 or less.

On Your Own

7. A radio show offers a prize to the first caller who can predict the next term in this sequence.

$\{1, 2, 4, 8, 16\}$

a. What do you get if you use common sense?

b. What do you get if you use Lagrange interpolation? (You will need a CAS for this one.)

Answers

Exercises

1. $f(x) = 6x^2 - 22x + 28$

2. $f(x) = 9x - 7$

3. $f(x) = 4x^2 - 3x + 1$

4. $f(x) = x^3 + 3x^2 + 5x - 8$

5. a. $A = 1, B = 21, C = 9, D = 1$
b. yes

6. Answers may vary. Sample: As in Exercise 18 in Lesson 2.5, when $A = -3$, $B = 1$, and $C = 2$, the final coefficient of x^2 was 0, so the equation was linear. Whenever the coefficient of the leading term is 0, the degree will be lower than expected.

7. a. 32
b. 31

EXERCISE 8 shows that Lagrange interpolation always works.

EXERCISE 10 previews the fact that a unique polynomial of degree less than or equal to n is determined by $(n + 1)$ points; here, $n = 4$ for five points.

EXERCISE 11 previews the Factor Theorem.

EXERCISE 12 Discuss the fact that every polynomial that has this property is a multiple of $(x - 1)(x - 2)(x - 3)$, plus 3.

8. Find a polynomial function that agrees with this table.

Input	Output
1	−6
3	166
6	7159
8	31,291
9	56,938
12	243,787

9. **Write About It** Explain Lagrange interpolation in your own words.

10. Suppose you have a table that has five entries. What is the greatest possible degree of polynomial that you would need to match the table using Lagrange interpolation? What is the least possible degree of polynomial that you would need?

For Exercises 11 and 12, sketch the graphs!

11. Find a nonconstant polynomial function h such that

$$h(1) = h(2) = h(3) = h(4) = 0$$

12. Find a nonconstant polynomial function j such that

$$j(1) = j(2) = j(3) = 3$$

13. **Standardized Test Prep** Tony has the graph of an unknown function and four points on the graph. He has written the following equation to approximate the function.

$$f(x) = A(x - 1)(x - 3) + B(x + 2)(x - 1)(x - 3) + C(x + 2)(x - 3) + D(x + 2)(x - 1)$$

If the value of C is 2 and the value of D is 1, what are the values of A and B?

A. $A = -1, B = 0$ **B.** $A = 0, B = -1$

C. $A = 1, B = -1$ **D.** $A = 1, B = 1$

14. You may know a formula for the sum of the numbers from 1 to n. If you do not know it, you can figure it out. You can model the sum of the first n numbers with a recursively defined function s.

$$s(n) = \begin{cases} 1 & \text{if } n = 1 \\ s(n-1) + n & \text{if } n > 1 \end{cases}$$

a. Explain why the recursion above yields the following sum.

$$s(n) = 1 + 2 + 3 + \cdots + (n - 1) + n$$

This is the sum of the integers between 1 and n.

b. Make a table of $s(n)$. Find a simple polynomial function S that agrees with s for all values in your table.

8. $f(x) = x^5 - 3x^3 + x^2 - 5$

9. Answers may vary. Sample: You can identify a polynomial function for a table by creating a function that uses $(x - a)$, where a is an input value, and undetermined values of $A, B, C, \ldots$, and then using the given ordered pairs to find the values of $A, B, C, \ldots$

10. greatest degree: 4; least degree: 0

11. Answers may vary. Sample: $h(x) = (x - 1)(x - 2)(x - 3)(x - 4) = x^4 - 10x^3 + 35x^2 - 50x + 24$

12. Answers may vary. Sample: $j(x) = (x - 1)(x - 2)(x - 3) + 3 = x^3 - 6x^2 + 11x - 3$

13. B

14. a. Answers may vary. Sample: The recursion formula results in a sum where you start with 1 for $n = 1$ and then add the current value of n to the previous sum. So the sum is $1 + 2 + 3 + \cdots + n$.

b. $S(n) = \dfrac{n(n + 1)}{2}$

EXERCISE 15 Calculating $q(n)$ is pretty difficult without a CAS to help. If you did not cover finding cubics with difference table techniques in Chapter 1, students will not be able to use that method either.

Maintain Your Skills

EXERCISE 16 asks students to use Lagrange interpolation to find a line through two given points. The general case in the last part of the exercise involves some complex algebraic manipulation and attention to detail. Some students might enjoy seeing this result through the lens of Lagrange interpolation. A CAS would make this part more accessible.

EXERCISE 17 gives a general method for finding a quadratic function through three points. The general case requires access to a CAS. The algebraic simplification is time-consuming if students attempt to do it by hand.

TECHNOLOGY TIP Many calculators can accept "a1" as a variable name, so students can work with subscripted variables if they choose.

Additional Resources

PRINT RESOURCES
- Solution Manual
- Practice Workbook
- Assessment Resources
- Teaching Resources

TECHNOLOGY
- Interactive Textbook
- TeacherExpress CD-ROM
- ExamView CD-ROM
- PHSchool.com

Additional Practice

For Exercises 1–4, find a polynomial function that agrees with each table.

1.

Input	Output
1	7
2	19
3	31
4	43
5	55

2.

Input	Output
1	3
2	7
3	13
4	21
5	31

3.

Input	Output
1	4
2	18
3	48
4	100
5	180

4.

Input	Output
1	−6
3	84
5	750
7	2856
9	7650

5. Suppose you have a table that has six entries. What is the greatest possible degree of polynomial that you would need to match the table using Lagrange interpolation? What is the least possible degree of polynomial that you would need?

6. Find a nonconstant polynomial function f such that $f(1) = f(2) = f(3) = f(4) = 1$.

7. Find a nonconstant polynomial function r such that $r(1) = r(2) = r(3) = 5$.

8. Suppose $f(x) = \frac{3}{8-4}(x-4) + \frac{1}{4-8}(x-8)$.

a. Find $f(4)$ and $f(8)$.
b. Write f in normal form.

Practice: For Lesson 2.6, assign Exercises 1–8.

15. Take It Further Use the method in Exercise 14 to find a formula for the sum of the squares between 1 and n. The recursive function below gives the sum of the squares of the numbers from 1 to n.

$$q(n) = \begin{cases} 1 & \text{if } n = 1 \\ q(n-1) + n^2 & \text{if } n > 1 \end{cases}$$

Find a closed-form polynomial function Q that agrees with q.

Maintain Your Skills

16. For each function f, find $f(5)$ and $f(7)$. Then write f in normal form.

a. $f(x) = \frac{6}{7-5}(x-5) + \frac{3}{5-7}(x-7)$

b. $f(x) = \frac{12}{7-5}(x-5) + \frac{-20}{5-7}(x-7)$

c. $f(x) = \frac{b_2}{7-5}(x-5) + \frac{b_1}{5-7}(x-7)$

d. Take It Further Suppose $f(x) = \frac{b_2}{a_2-a_1}(x-a_1) + \frac{b_1}{a_1-a_2}(x-a_2)$. Find $f(a_1)$ and $f(a_2)$. Write f in normal form.

17. For each function f, find $f(3)$, $f(5)$, and $f(7)$. Then write f in normal form.

a. $f(x) = \frac{6}{(7-3)(7-5)}(x-3)(x-5) + \frac{4}{(5-3)(5-7)}(x-3)(x-7) + \frac{9}{(3-5)(3-7)}(x-5)(x-7)$

b. $f(x) = \frac{16}{(7-3)(7-5)}(x-3)(x-5) + \frac{-9}{(5-3)(5-7)}(x-3)(x-7) + \frac{29}{(3-5)(3-7)}(x-5)(x-7)$

c. $f(x) = \frac{b_3}{(7-3)(7-5)}(x-3)(x-5) + \frac{b_2}{(5-3)(5-7)}(x-3)(x-7) + \frac{b_1}{(3-5)(3-7)}(x-5)(x-7)$

d. Take It Further Suppose $f(x) = \frac{b_3}{(a_3-a_1)(a_3-a_2)}(x-a_1)(x-a_2) + \frac{b_2}{(a_2-a_1)(a_2-a_3)}(x-a_1)(x-a_3) + \frac{b_1}{(a_1-a_2)(a_1-a_3)}(x-a_2)(x-a_3)$. Find $f(a_1)$, $f(a_2)$, and $f(a_3)$.

Write f in normal form.

Answers

15. $Q(n) = \frac{n(n+1)(2n+1)}{6}$

16. a. (i) $f(5) = 3$, $f(7) = 6$
(ii) $f(x) = 1.5x - 4.5$

b. (i) $f(5) = -20$, $f(7) = 12$
(ii) $f(x) = 16x - 100$

c. (i) $f(5) = b_1$, $f(7) = b_2$
(ii) $f(x) = \frac{b_2 - b_1}{2}x + \frac{7b_1 - 5b_2}{2}$

d. (i) $f(a_1) = b_1$, $f(a_2) = b_2$
(ii) $f(x) = \frac{b_2 - b_1}{a_2 - a_1}x + \frac{a_2b_1 - a_1b_2}{a_2 - a_1}$

17. a. (i) $f(3) = 9$, $f(5) = 4$, $f(7) = 6$
(ii) $f(x) = \frac{7}{8}x^2 - \frac{19}{2}x + \frac{237}{8}$

b. (i) $f(3) = 29$, $f(5) = -9$, $f(7) = 16$
(ii) $f(x) = \frac{63}{8}x^2 - 82x + \frac{1633}{8}$

2.7 Agreeing to Disagree

More than one polynomial function can agree with the inputs and outputs in a table.

Minds in Action episode 6

Tony and Sasha are looking at Table A.

Table A

Input	Output
1	4
2	6
3	8
4	10

Tony Sure, $h(x) = 2x + 2$ is a polynomial function that works. But I think there are other functions that agree with the table. I couldn't write down a rule, but I can draw a graph. Look.

Tony draws on the board.

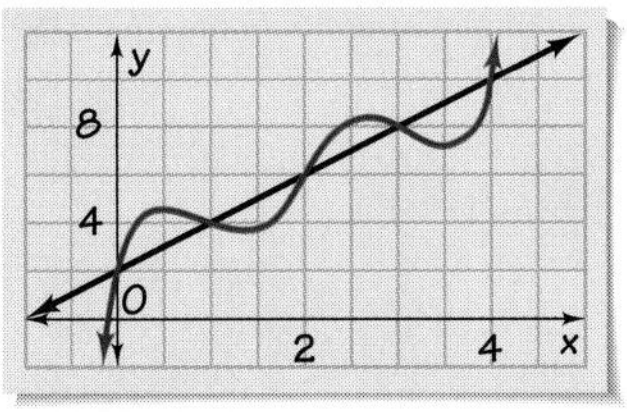

Sasha Well, that looks like the graph of a function, all right, but how do you know it's the graph of a *polynomial* function? Can you find a polynomial that's not linear and that goes through the points you get from the table?

Why might Sasha say this "looks like the graph of a function"?

Tony Hmm . . . sure! I just add another input to the table. Let's say 5. Then I make the output something other than $2 \cdot 5 + 2$. I'll make it 13.

Table A

Input	Output
1	4
2	6
3	8
4	10
5	13

17. c. (i) $f(3) = b_1$, $f(5) = b_2$, $f(7) = b_3$

(ii) $$f(x) = \frac{b_1 - 2b_2 + b_3}{8}x^2 + \frac{-3b_1 + 5b_2 - 2b_3}{2}x + \frac{35b_1 - 42b_2 + 15b_3}{8}$$

d. (i) $f(a_1) = b_1$, $f(a_2) = b_2$, $f(a_3) = b_3$

(ii) $$f(x) = \left[\frac{b_3}{(a_3 - a_1)(a_3 - a_2)} + \frac{b_2}{(a_2 - a_1)(a_2 - a_3)} + \frac{b_1}{(a_1 - a_2)(a_1 - a_3)}\right]x^2 + \left[-\frac{b_3(a_1 + a_2)}{(a_3 - a_1)(a_3 - a_2)} - \frac{b_2(a_1 + a_3)}{(a_2 - a_1)(a_2 - a_3)} - \frac{b_1(a_2 + a_3)}{(a_1 - a_2)(a_1 - a_3)}\right]x + \left[\frac{b_3a_1a_2}{(a_3 - a_1)(a_3 - a_2)} + \frac{b_2a_1a_3}{(a_2 - a_1)(a_2 - a_3)} + \frac{b_1a_2a_3}{(a_1 - a_2)(a_1 - a_3)}\right]$$

Lesson Overview

GOALS

- Fit polynomials to tables.
- Work with linear combinations.

By the end of this lesson, students should have these two ideas in mind.

- Given a table, there are many rules that agree with the table. Similarly, given a pattern, any number could be "the next number" in the pattern.
- Polynomial rules that fit tables have particular forms. The next lesson develops this concept, but the idea appears here for students to consider.

CHECK YOUR UNDERSTANDING
- Core: 1, 2, 3, 4
- Optional: 5

MATERIALS
- CAS (recommended)
- graph paper
- graphing calculators
- Blackline Master 2.7

HOMEWORK
- Core: 6, 7, 10, 11, 13
- Optional: 8, 9, 12, 14, 15

Launch

You might begin this lesson with the question:

What is the next number in this sequence? 2, 4, 6, 8, . . .

If students say "10", ask: "Could 0 be the next number in this sequence?" Lagrange interpolation gives students a way to prove that 0 could be the next number in this sequence; indeed, any number could be.

Minds in Action

Because Lagrange interpolation always gives you the simplest polynomial function that fits a table, using Lagrange interpolation on Table A as it appears at the beginning of the dialog gives the linear function $h(x) = 2x + 2$. In order to find a polynomial of higher degree that fits the table, you must follow Tony's advice and add another input.

Explore

For You to Do

PROBLEM 1 If you are pressed for time, simply ask students what the form of the function is.

If students solve this problem, ask them to check their answers by using the extended Table A.

Tony and Sasha . . . and then use Lagrange interpolation!

Sasha So, all those problems on the standardized tests that ask you to find the next term in a sequence are misleading—*any* number could be the next term in a sequence.

Tony The test writers must not know about Lagrange interpolation.

For You to Do

1. Find a polynomial function that agrees with Tony's extension of Table A.

A CAS might be helpful here.

Tony and Sasha are still thinking about the original Table A.

Sasha I think I have another way to trick the table, a way that might be easier than Lagrange interpolation. We know that $x \mapsto 2x + 2$ fits what we have. If I add to that another polynomial that outputs zero for the inputs 1, 2, 3, and 4, the result will still produce the outputs of Table A.

Tony How are you going to find a function like that?

Sasha I remember we did that a few days ago.

Sasha thumbs through her notebook.

Sasha Here it is: Exercise 11 from Lesson 2.6. This will do the trick.

$$x \mapsto (x - 1)(x - 2)(x - 3)(x - 4)$$

Tony So $r(x) = 2x + 2 + (x - 1)(x - 2)(x - 3)(x - 4)$ will agree with Table A. And it is not linear—it has degree 4.

Why does Tony's polynomial have degree 4?

Sasha So will $t(x) = 2x + 2 + 3(x - 1)(x - 2)(x - 3)(x - 4)$ and $q(x) = 2x + 2 + 275(x - 1)(x - 2)(x - 3)(x - 4)$.

For that matter,
$x \mapsto 2x + 2 + (\text{any polynomial}) \cdot (x - 1)(x - 2)(x - 3)(x - 4)$
will work.

Tony I think we're onto something. I wonder if every polynomial function that agrees with the table can be built by this method.

Sasha We need to think about that.

For Discussion

2. Can you write the polynomial Tony got using Lagrange interpolation in Sasha's form below? Explain.

$x \mapsto 2x + 2 + (\text{any polynomial}) \cdot (x - 1)(x - 2)(x - 3)(x - 4)$

Answers

For You to Do

1. Answers may vary. Sample:
$f(x) = 2x + 2 + \frac{1}{24}(x - 1) \cdot (x - 2)(x - 3)(x - 4)$

For Discussion

2. Yes; $x \to 2x + 2 + g(x) \cdot (x - 1)(x - 2) \cdot (x - 3)(x - 4)$ when $f(x) = \frac{1}{24}$.

Developing Habits of Mind

Establish a process. You can use Tony and Sasha's new method to find a polynomial that agrees with a given function on any finite set of inputs but that takes on a different specific value at some other input. For example, suppose you want a function f that agrees with $x \mapsto 3x$ for x-values of 1, 3, and 4, but you want $f(2)$ to be 12. Start with the following equation.

$$f(x) = 3x + A(x - 1)(x - 3)(x - 4)$$

This function agrees with $x \mapsto 3x$ for x-values of 1, 3, and 4. Then you can figure out A from the equation below.

$$12 = f(2) = 3 \cdot 2 + A(2 - 1)(2 - 3)(2 - 5)$$

For You to Do

3. Find the value of A.
4. Find a function that agrees with $x \mapsto 3x$ at 1, 3, and 5 but that takes on the value 21 at $x = 2$.

Exercises *Practicing Habits of Mind*

Check Your Understanding

1. Graph the functions f and h with equations $f(x) = 2x + 2 + 3(x - 1)(x - 2)(x - 3)$ and $h(x) = 2x + 2$. List the points where the graphs intersect.
2. Find and graph two different functions j and k that agree with $h(x) = 2x + 2$ for x-values of 1, 2, and 3. How can you produce more functions like these?
3. Consider the function with outputs 1, 3, and 5 for $x = 1, 2, 3$.
   a. If someone asked you to come up with the next term, what would you say? What simple rule could define this function?
   b. Give another possible next term and the rule that produces it.
   c. Find a rule that gives 19 as the next term.
   d. Find a rule that gives 1 as the next term.

For You to Do

3. $A = 2$
4. $f(x) = 3x + 5(x - 1)(x - 3)(x - 5)$ or $f(x) = 5x^3 - 45x^2 + 118x - 75$

Exercises

1. (1, 4), (2, 6), and (3, 8)
2. $j(x) = 2x + 2 + T(x - 1)(x - 2) \cdot (x - 3)$, where T is a polynomial or a constant. Check students' graphs.
3. **a.** $f(x) = 2x - 1$; the next term is 7.
   b. Answers may vary. Sample: For the rule $g(x) = 2x - 1 + (x - 1)(x - 2)(x - 3)$, the next term, $g(4)$, is 13.
   c. $g(x) = 2x - 1 + 2(x - 1) \cdot (x - 2)(x - 3)$ or $g(x) = 2x^3 - 12x^2 + 24x - 13$
   d. $g(x) = 2x - 1 - (x - 1) \cdot (x - 2)(x - 3)$ or $g(x) = -x^3 + 6x^2 - 9x + 5$

Wrap Up

To finish the class, go back to the question you posed at the beginning of class:

What is the next number in this sequence? 2, 4, 6, 8, ...

Students should see that any number could be the next number in the sequence.

Assessment Resources

Lesson Quiz 2.7

1. Graph the functions f and g with equations $f(x) = x - 1 + 4(x - 1)(x - 2)(x - 3)$ and $g(x) = x - 1$. List the points where the graphs intersect.

For Exercises 2 and 3, find a function that agrees with the given function for the given inputs but is not equal to the given function. Graph your function and the given function on the same set of axes. Identify the points where the graphs intersect.

2. $x \mapsto 3x - 3$; $x = 0, 1, 2$, and 3
3. $x \mapsto 3x - 3$; $x = 0, 1, 2, 3$, and 4
4. Is there another linear function that agrees with $x \mapsto 3x - 3$ at the inputs 1 and 2? Explain.

Exercises

HOMEWORK

- Core: 6, 7, 10, 11, 13
- Optional: 8, 9, 12, 14, 15

Check Your Understanding

EXERCISE 2 A proof of this result comes in the next investigation, using the Factor Theorem.

EXERCISE 4 is a good exercise to talk about in detail as a summary of this investigation. Students who can follow the reasoning here have a good understanding of how Lagrange interpolation works.

EXERCISE 5 Blackline Master 2.7 provides a scorecard for the Polynomial Game. Students should play this game. No part of the exercise says that. The goal of this game is not for students to prove that a polynomial of degree n is uniquely determined by $n + 1$ points but for them to become convinced that this is so. This exercise really requires a computer algebra system (CAS). Otherwise, the computations slow the game down too much for students to see the pattern.

On Your Own

EXERCISES 6–9 Students can do Exercise 6 without a CAS, but they will need a graphing calculator to see the comparative graphs for this and for the next three exercises. You should consider Exercises 8 and 9 extra practice with the techniques from Exercises 6 and 7. You may not need to assign all four of these exercises.

4. Suppose you see the following problem on a multiple-choice test.

What is the next number in the sequence?

2, 4, 6, . . .

A. 0 **B.** 8 **C.** 10 **D.** 80

Show that any of these answers could be correct. To do this, you may want to set up tables like the one at the right.

Input	Output
1	2
2	4
3	6
4	■

5. Use the following rules to play the Polynomial Game. This game requires at least three players.

- Choose one player to be the Polynomial Keeper. The other players are the Finders.
- The Polynomial Keeper writes down a (secret) polynomial function and gives one input-output pair to the Finders.
- The Finders guess a polynomial function. If they are successful, the Keeper gets one point. If they are not successful, the Keeper gives them another input-output pair.
- The Keeper continues to give out pairs until the Finders figure out the polynomial. The Keeper scores one point for every pair the Finders need to figure out the polynomial. Then the Keeper becomes a Finder and a new Keeper is chosen.
- The player with the most points at the end of the game wins.

a. How many points is a Keeper likely to get for a quadratic function?

b. How many points is a Keeper likely to get for a quintic function? A quintic function is a polynomial of degree 5.

c. How many points is a Keeper likely to get for a polynomial of degree n?

On Your Own

For Exercises 6–9, find a function that agrees with the given function for the given inputs but is not equal to the given function. Graph your function and the given function on the same set of axes. Identify the points where the graphs intersect.

Go Online PHSchool.com

For additional practice, go to **Web Code:** bfa-0207

6. $x \mapsto 3x - 1$; $x = 0, 1, 2, 3$

7. $x \mapsto 3x - 1$; $x = 0, 1, 2, 3, 4$

8. $x \mapsto 4 - x^2$; $x = 0, 1, 2, 3$

9. $x \mapsto 4 - x^2$; $x = 0, 1, 2, 3, 4$

Answers

4. Answers may vary. Samples are given.

a. $f(4) = 0$ if $f(x) = 2x - \frac{4}{3}(x - 1)(x - 2)(x - 3)$

b. $f(4) = 8$ if $f(x) = 2x$

c. $f(4) = 10$ if $f(x) = 2x + \frac{1}{3}(x - 1)(x - 2)(x - 3)$ or $f(x) = \frac{x^3}{3} - 2x^2 + \frac{17}{3}x - 2$

d. $f(4) = 80$ if $f(x) = 2x + 12(x - 1)(x - 2)(x - 3)$ or $f(x) = 12x^3 - 72x^2 + 134x - 72$

5. a. 3 points **b.** 6 points

c. $(n + 1)$ points

6. Answers may vary. Sample: $f(x) = 3x - 1$ and $p(x) = 3x - 1 + 2x(x - 1) \cdot (x - 2)(x - 3)$

The graphs intersect at $(0, -1)$, $(1, 2)$, $(2, 5)$, and $(3, 8)$.

7–9. See back of book.

10. Is there another linear function that agrees with $x \mapsto 3x - 1$ at the inputs 1 and 2? Explain.

11. **a.** Is there another quadratic function that agrees with $x \mapsto 4 - x^2$ at the inputs 1 and 2? Explain.

    b. Is there another quadratic function that agrees with $x \mapsto 4 - x^2$ at the inputs 1, 2, and 3? Explain.

12. **Write About It** Describe two methods for finding a function that agrees with $x \mapsto x^2$ at $x = 1, 2,$ and 3 and that takes on the value 7 at $x = 4$.

13. **Standardized Test Prep** You are given three points on a line. You wish to find a function that has the same values as the linear function at those three points but is different everywhere else. What is the least possible degree of a polynomial function through those points?

    A. 2 **B.** 3

    C. 4 **D.** 5

14. **Write About It** Is there a nonconstant polynomial that takes on the value 0 at every integer? Explain.

Maintain Your Skills

15. Expand each product. Describe and explain at least two patterns among the coefficients in the collection of answers.

    a. $(x - 1)(x - 2)$

    b. $(x - 1)(x - 2)(x - 3)$

    c. $(x - 1)(x - 2)(x - 3)(x - 4)$

    d. $(x - 1)(x - 2)(x - 3)(x - 4)(x - 5)$

    e. $(x - 1)(x - 2)(x - 3)(x - 4)(x - 5)(x - 6)$

    f. $(x - 1)(x - 2)(x - 3)(x - 4)(x - 5)(x - 6)(x - 7)$

    g. $(x - 1)(x - 2)(x - 3)(x - 4)(x - 5)(x - 6)(x - 7)(x - 8)$

Use each answer to help you get the next one.

Go Online
Video Tutor
PHSchool.com

Web Code: bfe-0775

10. No; exactly one line goes through the two points (1, 2) and (2, 5).

11. a. Yes; sample : $f(x) = 3(x - 2)^2$

b. No; there is only one quadratic function that contains any three (noncollinear) points.

12. Answers may vary. Sample: (1) Use the Lagrange method on (1, 1), (2, 4), (3, 9), and (4, 7); (2) Use the equation $g(x) = x^2 + A(x - 1)(x - 2)(x - 3)$ with $g(4) = 7$ and find the value of A.

13. B

14. No; the only nonconstant expression would have to include the nonterminating expression $\ldots(x - (-2))(x - (-1))(x - 0) \cdot (x - 1)\ldots$, and that expression is not a polynomial.

15. a. $x^2 - 3x + 2$

b. $x^3 - 6x^2 + 11x - 6$

c. $x^4 - 10x^3 + 35x^2 - 50x + 24$

d. $x^5 - 15x^4 + 85x^3 - 225x^2 + 274x - 120$

e–g. See back of book.

EXERCISE 10 is a quick question for which students can use common sense. They need not use Lagrange interpolation.

EXERCISE 12 asks students to describe how they would proceed, not to actually find the function. Some students may have trouble thinking of a second way, especially if they see Lagrange interpolation and the "disagreeing" method in the same light.

Maintain your Skills

EXERCISE 15 Assign only as many parts of this exercise as you feel will be appropriate. A CAS is helpful.

Additional Resources

PRINT RESOURCES
- Solution Manual
- Practice Workbook
- Assessment Resources
- Teaching Resources

TECHNOLOGY
- Interactive Textbook
- TeacherExpress CD-ROM
- ExamView CD-ROM
- PHSchool.com

Additional Practice

1. Graph the functions f and g with equations $f(x) = 3x + 1 + 2(x - 1)(x - 2)(x - 3)$ and $g(x) = 3x + 1$. List the points where the graphs intersect.

2. Consider the function with outputs 6, 8, 10 for $x = 1, 2, 3$.
   a. If someone asked you to come up with the next term, what would you say? What simple rule could define this function?
   b. Give another possible next term and the rule that produces it.
   c. Find a rule that gives 24 as the next term.
   d. Find a rule that gives 6 as the next term.

For Exercises 3–6, find a function that agrees with the given function for the given inputs but is not equal to the given function. Graph your function and the given function on the same set of axes. Identify the points where the graphs intersect.

3. $x \mapsto 2x - 2; x = 0, 1, 2, 3$

4. $x \mapsto 2x - 2; x = 0, 1, 2, 3, 4$

5. $x \mapsto 3 - x^2; x = 0, 1, 2, 3$

6. $x \mapsto 3 - x^2; x = 0, 1, 2, 3, 4$

7. Is there another linear function that agrees with $x \mapsto 2x - 2$ at the inputs 1 and 2? Explain.

8. **a.** Is there another quadratic function that agrees with $x \mapsto 3 - x^2$ at the inputs 1 and 2? Explain.
   b. Is there another quadratic function that agrees with $x \mapsto 3 - x^2$ at the inputs 1, 2, and 3? Explain.

9. Describe two methods for finding a function that agrees with $x \mapsto 2x^2$ at $x = 1, 2,$ and 3 and that takes on the value 20 at $x = 3$.

10. Is there a nonconstant polynomial that takes on the value 2 at every integer? Explain.

Practice: For Lesson 2.7, assign Exercises 1–10.

Mathematical Reflections

EXERCISES 6–8 At the start of the investigation, you may have assigned these as Questions 1–3 for students to think and write about.

Mathematical Reflections 2B

In this investigation, you learned how to use linear combinations of polynomials to determine new polynomials and find polynomials that agree with a given table. These exercises will help you summarize what you have learned.

In Exercises 1 and 2, find a polynomial function that agrees with each table.

1.

Input	Output
1	3
2	7
4	21

2.

Input	Output
1	4
3	40
5	156

3. Find a nonconstant polynomial h such that $h(1) = h(2) = h(4) = 7$.

4. Find a polynomial function that agrees with $x \rightarrow x^3 - x$ at $x = 1, 2,$ and 3 but has the value 0 at $x = 4$.

5. **Take It Further** Suppose you define the function q for nonnegative integers using the following rule.

$$q(x) = \begin{cases} 1 & \text{if } x = 0 \\ q(x-1) + 3x^2 - x + 1 & \text{if } x > 0 \end{cases}$$

Find a polynomial function that agrees with q on its domain.

6. How can you find a polynomial that agrees with a table?

7. How can you find two different functions that agree with the same table?

8. What number comes next in the sequence 1, 4, 9, . . . ?

Vocabulary

In this investigation, you learned this term. Make sure you understand what it means and how to use it.

- **Lagrange interpolation**

Through any three noncollinear points there is a unique polynomial of degree 2 with a graph that fits the points.

Answers

Mathematical Reflections

1. $g(x) = x^2 + x + 1$

2. $f(x) = 10x^2 - 22x + 16$

3. $h(x) = 7 + (x - 1)(x - 2)(x - 4)$

4. $f(x) = x^3 - x - 10(x - 1)(x - 2) \cdot (x - 3)$ or $f(x) = -9x^3 + 60x^2 - 111x - 60$

5. $q(x) = x^3 + x^2 + x + 1$

6. You can use Lagrange interpolation to find a polynomial that agrees with a function.

7. Answers may vary. Sample: After you find one function, add an expression that is zero for all the values in the table but nonzero for other values.

8. The simplest answer is 16, but you can find a cubic polynomial that has *any* desired value for the fourth term.

Chapter 2

Mid-Chapter Test

Go Online PHSchool.com

For a mid-chapter test, go to Web Code: bfa-0252

Multiple Choice

1. Suppose f and g are functions with $f(x) = 3x$ and $g(x) = f(x + 1) - f(x)$. Which expression is equal to $g(x)$?
   - A. 1
   - B. 3
   - C. x
   - D. $2x + 1$

2. Suppose $N: \mathbb{R}^2 \to \mathbb{R}$ and $N(a, b) = a^2 + b^2$. Which of the following ordered pairs does NOT give an output of 169?
   - A. $(-5, 12)$
   - B. $(12, 5)$
   - C. $(1, 12)$
   - D. $(-5, -12)$

3. Let $f(x) = 3x - 4$ and $g(x) = 2x + 5$. Which value is equal to $f \circ g(2)$?
   - A. 9
   - B. 11
   - C. 18
   - D. 23

4. Let $m(x) = 2x - 7$. Which expression is equal to $m^{-1}(x)$?
   - A. $2x + 7$
   - B. $-2x + 7$
   - C. $\frac{x + 7}{2}$
   - D. $\frac{1}{2}x + 7$

5. Let $f(x) = 3x - 5 + 4(x - 1)(x - 6)$ and $g(x) = 3x - 5$. Find the x-coordinates of the points at which the graphs of f and g intersect.
   - A. 1, 4, or 6
   - B. $\frac{5}{3}$
   - C. 0, 1, or 6
   - D. 1 or 6

Open Response

6. Suppose $f: \mathbb{R} \to \mathbb{R}$ and $f(x) = 3x^2 + 1$.
   - a. Calculate $f(2)$ and $f(-2)$.
   - b. Find all values of x that make $f(x) = 49$.
   - c. Calculate $f(5) - f(4)$.
   - d. Show that you can write $f(x + 1)$ as $f(x + 1) = 3x^2 + 6x + 4$.
   - e. Write a simplified expression for $f(x + 1) - f(x)$.
   - f. If $g(x) = f(x + 1) - f(x)$, what is $g(4)$?

7. Suppose $f(x) = 3x + 4$. If possible, find a function g such that $g \circ f(x) = x$.

8. Use the definition of function f below.

$$f(x) = \begin{cases} 2x & \text{if } x < 0 \\ x^2 & \text{if } 0 \le x \le 2 \end{cases}$$

   - a. What is the natural domain of f?
   - b. Sketch a graph of f.
   - c. Extend the definition of f so that its domain is all of $\mathbb{R}$ and f is one-to-one.
   - d. Extend the definition of f so that its domain is all of $\mathbb{R}$ and f is not one-to-one.

9. Suppose $f(x) = \frac{1}{x + 2}$, where $x \ne -2$. Find the inverse of f.

10. Find a polynomial function f that agrees with this table.

Input	Output
1	6
2	15
3	36

11. What is a function?

Mid-Chapter Test

Assessment Resources

Mid-Chapter Test page 1 of 2

Multiple Choice

1. Suppose f and g are functions with $f(x) = 2x + 3$ and $g(x) = f(x + 1) - f(x)$. Which expression is equal to $g(x)$?
   A. 1
   B. 2
   C. 3
   D. $2x + 2$

2. Suppose $N: \mathbb{R}^2 \to \mathbb{R}$ and $N(a, b) = (a + b)^2$. Which ordered pair gives an output of 49?
   A. $(3, -4)$
   B. $(3, 4)$
   C. $(-4, 3)$
   D. $(7, 7)$

3. Let $s(x) = 2x + 7$ and $t(x) = 3x + 1$. Which value is equal to $s \circ t(4)$?
   A. 7
   B. 33
   C. 46
   D. 195

4. Let $m(x) = 3x + 1$. Which expression is equal to $m^{-1}(x)$?
   A. $3x - 1$
   B. $-3x - 1$
   C. $\frac{x + 1}{3}$
   D. $\frac{x - 1}{3}$

5. If $f(x) = 2x - 5(x - 2)(x + 3)$ and $g(x) = 2x$, then at which x-coordinates do the graphs of f and g intersect?
   A. 2, 3, or 5
   B. 2 or -3
   C. -2 or 3
   D. 0

Also available: Form B

Mid-Chapter Test

1. B **2.** C **3.** D **4.** C

5. D

6. a. $f(2) = 13$, $f(-2) = 13$

b. 4 or -4

c. 27

d. $f(x + 1) = 3(x + 1)^2 + 1 = 3(x^2 + 2x + 1) + 1 = 3x^2 + 6x + 3 + 1 = 3x^2 + 6x + 4$

e. $6x + 3$

f. 27

7. $g(x) = \frac{x - 4}{3}$

8. a. The domain is $x \le 2$.

b.

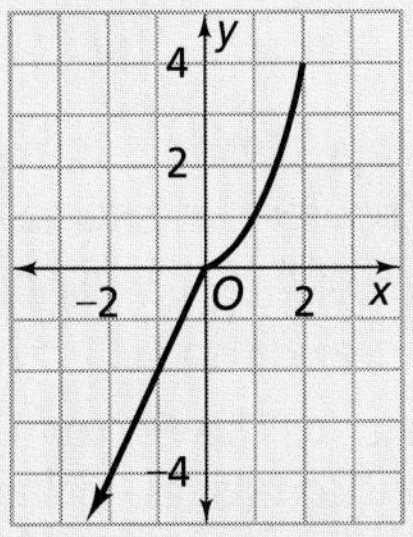

c. Answers may vary. Sample:

$$f(x) = \begin{cases} 2x & \text{if } x < 0 \\ x^2 & \text{if } x > 0 \end{cases}$$

d. Answers may vary. Sample:

$$f(x) = \begin{cases} 2x & \text{if } x < 0 \\ x^2 & \text{if } 0 \le x \le 2 \\ -2x + 8 & \text{if } 2 < x \end{cases}$$

9. $f^{-1}(x) = \frac{1}{x} - 2$

10. $f(x) = 6x^2 - 9x + 9$

11. Answers may vary. Sample: A function is a correspondence between two sets such that each element of the first set is paired with exactly one element of the second set.

Investigation Overview

This investigation teaches two important theorems: the Factor Theorem and the Remainder Theorem.

Students should be familiar with the relationships among factors, roots and zeros. It will be no surprise that if, for example, $f(5) = 0$ or $(5, 0)$ is a point on the graph, then $(x - 5)$ is a factor of $f(x)$. After this investigation, students will be able to express this relationship as "the remainder when $x^5 - 25$ is divided by $(x - 5)$ is 0."

This lesson focuses on the importance of the two perspectives on polynomials:

When you think of $f(x) = x^2 - 1$, where x is a variable, and this function generates a table and a graph, you are thinking of $x^2 - 1$ as a function.

When you divide $x^2 - 1$ by $x - 1$, you are not usually thinking of either polynomial as a function; you think rather, of each as a "form." In this situation, you do not think of x as a variable but as an indeterminate.

These are special results that apply only to polynomials.

- The Factor Theorem holds only for polynomials, not for other functions. For example, if $h(x) = \sqrt{x - 3}$, then $h(3) = 0$ but $h(x)$ is not divisible by $(x - 3)$.
- If two polynomials are the same on a sufficiently large number of points, you can prove them to be the same everywhere. This does not apply to functions in general. For example, take $f(x) = x$ and $g(x) = |x|$. They agree on an infinite number of points, but they are not the same function.

You may wish to assign Questions 1–3 for students to think and write about during the investigation.

Learning Goals

- Understand the relationship between roots and factors of a polynomial.
- Divide polynomials by monic linear polynomials.
- State and use the Remainder Theorem and the Factor Theorem.
- Check that two polynomials of degree n are equivalent by checking $n + 1$ function values.
- Write the general form of a function that fits a table.

Habits and Skills

- Make conjectures and write proofs.
- Formalize previous experiences.
- Connect the algebra in this investigation to Lagrange interpolation.

Investigation 2C

Factors, Roots, and Zeros

In *Factors, Roots, and Zeros*, you will discover some important facts about polynomials and polynomial functions. You will study the connection between the zeros of a polynomial function and the factors of the polynomial. In your first-year algebra course, you may have learned the "form-implies-function" principle:

> **If you can transform one polynomial into another with the basic rules of algebra, the polynomials define the same function.**

In this investigation, you will see a partial converse:

> **If two polynomial functions agree for enough inputs (depending on their degree), then they are equivalent under the basic rules of algebra.**

By the end of this investigation, you will be able to answer questions like these.

1. How are the zeros of a polynomial related to its factors?
2. How can you tell if two polynomials are equivalent without using the form-implies-function principle?
3. What is the greatest-degree polynomial you need to fit a table with four inputs?

You will learn how to

- understand the relationship between roots and factors of a polynomial
- divide polynomials by monic linear polynomials
- state and use the Remainder Theorem and the Factor Theorem
- check that two polynomials of degree n are equivalent by checking $n + 1$ function values
- write the general form of a function that fits a table

You will develop these habits and skills:

- Make conjectures and create proofs.
- Formalize previous experiences.
- Connect the algebra in this investigation to Lagrange interpolation.

A blacksmith puts specific points of iron stock into place along a bending jig. Identical curves result.

Investigation Road Map

LESSON 2.8, *Getting Started,* gives students an opportunity to work with the Factor Theorem, the Remainder Theorem, and polynomial division.

LESSON 2.9, *Polynomial Division,* is an introduction to polynomial division by monic linear divisors. It formally introduces the Remainder Theorem.

LESSON 2.10, *The Factor Theorem,* introduces the Factor Theorem and several important corollaries, including the one that states that a polynomial of degree n is uniquely determined by its values at $n + 1$ inputs. In this investigation, students also see the general form of a polynomial that agrees with a table.

2.8 Getting Started

Activating Prior Knowledge
Exploring New Ideas

These exercises look like ordinary calculations, but they give a preview of some important themes in this investigation.

For You to Explore

1. Suppose $f(x) = (x - 5)(x - 3)(x^2 - 1) + 219$.
   a. Find $f(5)$.
   b. List four values of x for which $f(x) = 219$.
2. a. Find a nonconstant polynomial that agrees with the table at the right. You do not need to find the normal form.

x	$q(x)$
1	0
3	0

   b. What is the degree of the polynomial you found in part (a)?
   c. Find a nonconstant polynomial that agrees with the table at the right. You do not need to find the normal form.

x	$r(x)$
1	0
3	0
5	0
7	0
9	0

   d. What is the degree of the polynomial you found in part (c)?
3. a. Find two different polynomials $j(x)$ and $g(x)$ such that the degree of each polynomial is greater than 1 and $j(5) = g(5) = 0$.
   b. Suppose $h(x) = j(x) - g(x)$. What is $h(5)$?
4. Use the three functions below. Find the degree of each polynomial.
   $t(x) = x^5 - 1$ $u(x) = x^5 + x^2 + 3$ $v(x) = x^4 + 7$
   a. $t(x) + u(x)$
   b. $t(x) - u(x)$
   c. $t(x) + v(x)$
   d. $t(x) - v(x)$
   e. $t(x) \cdot u(x)$
5. Find k if $m(x) = (x - 8)\left(7x^3 + 12x^2 - 13x + \frac{22}{5}\right) + 7(k + 1)$ and $m(8) = 21$.
6. Find a polynomial $g(x)$ such that $x^3 - 1 = (x - 1)g(x)$.
7. Show that if n is a positive integer,
   $x^n - 1 = (x - 1)(x^{n-1} + x^{n-2} + \cdots + x^2 + x + 1)$.

This is an important identity that you will use throughout this course.

Answers

For You to Explore

1. a. 219
   b. −1, 1, 3, 5
2. a. $q(x) = (x - 1)(x - 3)$
   b. 2
   c. $r(x) = (x - 1)(x - 3)(x - 5) \cdot (x - 9)$
   d. 5
3. a. Answers may vary. Sample: $j(x) = x(x - 5)$; $g(x) = x^2(x - 5)$
   b. 0
4. a. 5 b. 2 c. 5
   d. 5 e. 10
5. 2
6. $g(x) = x^2 + x + 1$
7. Answers may vary. Sample: Distributing x from $(x - 1)$ gives $x^n + x^{n-1} + \cdots + n$, and distributing -1 from $(x - 1)$ gives $-x^{n-1} - x^{n-2} - \cdots - n - 1$. Adding like terms gives $x^n - 1$.

Lesson Overview

GOAL

- Warm up to the ideas of the investigation.

In this Getting Started lesson, students encounter ideas they have seen before, but the exercises drive students toward formalizing their ideas.

For example, in the For You to Explore problems, students encounter a polynomial written in the form $f(x) = (x - 5)(x - 3)(x^2 - 1) + 219$, and they are asked to find $f(5)$. This serves as a preview of the Remainder Theorem.

One important set of ideas comes up. In the For You to Explore problems, students find the normal form of $(x - 1)(x^4 + x^3 + x^2 + x + 1)$. Then in the On Your Own exercises, students find

$$\frac{x^5 - 1}{x - 1}$$

The idea is for students to start thinking about polynomial division before they encounter the formal introduction.

Here the two perspectives on polynomials ("polynomials as functions" and "polynomials as forms") become important. From a "polynomials as functions" perspective, dividing by $x^5 - 1$ by $x - 1$ requires care, because x is a variable and x could equal 1. From a "polynomials as forms" perspective, the fact that $x^5 - 1 = (x - 1)(x^4 + x^3 + x^2 + x + 1)$ means $\frac{x^5 - 1}{x - 1} = (x^4 + x^3 + x^2 + x + 1)$.

As always in a Getting Started lesson, there is no need to formalize these ideas today. Students meet all the ideas again throughout the investigation.

FOR YOU TO EXPLORE
- Core: 1, 2, 3, 5, 6, 7
- Optional: 4

HOMEWORK
- Core: 9, 12, 13, 14
- Optional: 8, 10, 11

Launch

Begin with a quick vocabulary review. Students should be familiar with *degree of a polynomial, zero of a function, factor,* and *normal form*. They can then begin to work on the For You To Explore problems. You may want to have them work in groups to share their ideas.

Explore

For You to Explore

EXERCISE 1 previews the Remainder Theorem. Ask students if there are any other values of x for which $f(x)$ can be found quickly.

EXERCISE 3 Watch to see whether students identify that $(x - 5)$ is a factor of these polynomials. This is a key concept in this investigation.

EXERCISE 5 previews the Remainder Theorem. Here, $7(k + 1)$ is the remainder when dividing by $(x - 8)$.

EXERCISES 6 AND 7 is a specific instance of the identity that students will prove in Exercise 7.

Wrap Up

If time permits, go over Exercise 1 in order to preview the Remainder Theorem. Exercise 6 sets students up to begin polynomial division in the next lesson.

Exercises

HOMEWORK
- Core: 9, 12, 13, 14
- Optional: 8, 10, 11

On Your Own

EXERCISE 8 Some students may notice that it is also possible to evaluate $h(-1)$ quickly, since the factors of the expression $x^5 + x^4 + x^3 + x^2 + x + 1$ include $(x + 1)$.

EXERCISE 9 is the "difference of cubes" factoring form. Students should be comfortable with it by the end of the chapter.

EXERCISE 11 If students have trouble, ask them to rewrite this exercise in a form without a fraction. To do this, multiply both sides of the equation by $x - 1$. Then it becomes the same type of expression as those in earlier exercises.

Maintain Your Skills

EXERCISES 12–14 suggest a general form:

$$(x^n - 1)(x^{2n} + x^n + 1) = x^{3n} - 1$$

This is really the difference of cubes identity. Students who are comfortable with the idea of lumping will see the pattern quickly. Each exercise takes the form

$$(M - 1)(M^2 + M + 1) = M^3 - 1$$

with $M = x^2$ in Exercise 12, $M = x^3$ in Exercise 13, and $M = x^4$ in Exercise 14.

Exercises *Practicing Habits of Mind*

On Your Own

8. Suppose $h(x) = (x - 1)(x + 3)(x^5 + x^4 + x^3 + x^2 + x + 1) + 5x - 2$.

a. For what inputs a can you easily find $h(a)$ without using a calculator?

b. Find the output of h for each of your answers to part (a).

9. If a is some fixed number, find the normal form of $(x - a)(x^2 + ax + a^2)$.

10. If a is some fixed number, find the normal form of $(x - a)(x^3 + ax^2 + a^2x + a^3)$.

11. Find a polynomial $g(x)$ such that $\frac{x^5 - 1}{x - 1} = g(x)$.

Habits of Mind

Look for patterns. What is a general result suggested by Exercises 9 and 10?

Maintain Your Skills

In Exercises 12–14, expand each expression and write the result in normal form.

12. $(x^2 - 1)(x^4 + x^2 + 1)$

13. $(x^3 - 1)(x^6 + x^3 + 1)$

14. $(x^4 - 1)(x^8 + x^4 + 1)$

Go Online
Video Tutor
PHSchool.com

Web Code: bfe-0775

Answers

Exercises

8. a. 1 and -3

b. $h(1) = 3$, $h(-3) = -17$

9. $x^3 - a^3$

10. $x^4 - a^4$

11. $g(x) = x^4 + x^3 + x^2 + x + 1$

12. $x^6 - 1$

13. $x^9 - 1$

14. $x^{12} - 1$

2.9 Polynomial Division

After you learned to multiply numbers, you learned to "undo" multiplication with division. The same thing can be done with polynomials. If you know that $x^3 + 10x^2 + 18x - 35 = (x + 5)(x^2 + 5x + 7)$, then you also know that $\frac{x^3 + 10x^2 + 18x - 35}{x + 5} = x^2 + 5x - 7$.

When you divide one polynomial by another, you get a quotient and a remainder. In the example above, the quotient is $x^2 + 5x - 7$ and the remainder is 0.

Example

Problem Find the quotient and the remainder when you divide $x^3 + 2x^2 + 4x + 6$ by $x - 2$.

Solution You can do a calculation that looks just like long division.

$$
\begin{array}{r|l}
 & x^2 + 4x + 12 \\
\hline
x - 2 & x^3 + 2x^2 + 4x + 6 \\
 & x^3 - 2x^2 \\
\hline
 & 4x^2 + 4x + 6 \\
 & 4x^2 - 8x \\
\hline
 & 12x + 6 \\
 & 12x - 24 \\
\hline
 & 30
\end{array}
$$

So, the quotient is $x^2 + 4x + 12$ and the remainder is 30.

For information on dividing polynomials, see the TI-Nspire Handbook, p. 778.

Habits of Mind

Establish a process. In the long division process, how do you know when to stop?

For You to Do

1. Find the quotient and the remainder when you divide $x^3 + 2x^2 + 4x + 10$ by $x - 2$.
2. If $g(x) = x^3 + 2x^2 + 4x + 10$, what is $g(2)$?
3. Find a polynomial $q(x)$ and a number r such that $x^3 + 2x^2 + 4x + 10 = (x - 2)q(x) + r$.

When you divide 37 by 7, the quotient is 5 and the remainder is 2.

$$
\begin{array}{r|l}
 & 5 \\
\hline
7 & 37 \\
 & 35 \\
\hline
 & 2
\end{array}
$$

You can summarize the division by writing $37 = 7 \cdot 5 + 2$.

You could also say $37 = 7 \cdot 4 + 9$.

$$
\begin{array}{r|l}
 & 4 \\
\hline
7 & 37 \\
 & 28 \\
\hline
 & 9
\end{array}
$$

For You to Do

1. $x^2 + 4x + 12 + \frac{34}{x - 2}$
2. 34
3. $q(x) = x^2 + 4x + 12$; $r = 34$

Lesson Overview

GOALS

- Understand the relationship between roots and factors of a polynomial.
- Divide polynomials by monic linear polynomials.
- State and use the Remainder Theorem and the Factor Theorem.

Asking students who are having trouble with polynomial division to work a parallel problem with numbers is helpful. The emphasis in the lesson is on reasoning about the division process rather than on the technical computation. To this end, you will introduce the Euclidean Property.

The proof of this theorem develops the habit of rooting formal mathematics in experience: when faced with some abstract theorem, you check to see if it makes sense for examples. In this case, that very checking is generalized to the proof.

CHECK YOUR UNDERSTANDING
- Core: 1, 2, 3, 4, 5, 6
- Optional: none

MATERIALS
- CAS (recommended)
- Blackline Master 2.9

HOMEWORK
- Core: 7, 8, 9, 11, 14
- Optional: 10, 13, 16, 17
- Extension: 12, 15

VOCABULARY
- Euclidean Property
- quotient
- remainder

Launch

Review the Maintain Your Skills exercises from Lesson 2.8. Then ask, "If you do not allow x to equal 1, does it make sense to divide the polynomial $x^2 - 1$ by $x - 1$?"

When you begin this lesson, you may want to use Blackline Master 2.9 to guide students through the Example.

Explore

Example

You can do a side-by-side example to compare and contrast this long division problem and a numerical long division problem, such as $24\overline{)36{,}795}$. Students should be aware that the algorithm is the same.

For You to Do

Students may make some conjectures here about $f(a)$ and the remainder when $f(x)$ is divided by $x - a$.

For You to Do

Some students will want to evaluate $h(2)$ using the normal form for $h(x)$. Point out that using the form given in Problem 4 will result in fewer calculations.

Developing Habits of Mind

Have students look back at the Example. Ask them, What are $g(x)$, $q(x)$, and $r(x)$ in the Example? The single term $g(x) \cdot q(x)$ represents several lines in the Example.

While $37 = 7 \cdot 4 + 9$ is correct, this is not standard division. When you divide, the remainder must be less than the divisor (less than 7, in this example). In general, an important property of integers is the Euclidean Property.

It is called the Euclidean Property because it was first stated as a property of integers in Euclid's *Elements* around 300 B.C. In advanced courses in arithmetic, you prove it as a theorem. One proof uses a careful analysis of long division.

Property *Euclidean Property*

Given positive integers a and b, there are unique nonnegative integers q (the quotient) and r (the remainder) such that

- $b = a \cdot q + r$
- $0 \le r < a$

In the example above, $b = 37$, $a = 7$, $q = 5$, and $r = 2$.

There is a Euclidean Property for polynomials, too. It comes from the fact that you can divide and get a remainder with degree less than the degree of the divisor. In the example, the result is an identity.

$$x^3 + 2x^2 + 4x + 6 = (x - 2)(x^2 + 4x + 12) + 30$$

For You to Do

4. Use the basic rules of algebra to show that $(x - 2)(x^2 + 4x + 12) + 30$ is, in fact, equal to $x^3 + 2x^2 + 4x + 6$.

5. If $h(x) = x^3 + 2x^2 + 4x + 6$, find $h(2)$.

Property *Euclidean Property for Polynomials*

Given polynomials $f(x)$ and $g(x)$, there are unique polynomials $q(x)$ (the quotient) and $r(x)$ (the remainder) such that

- $f(x) = g(x) \cdot q(x) + r(x)$
- $\deg(r(x)) < \deg(g(x))$

Developing Habits of Mind

Use an equation to represent a process. The identity $f(x) = g(x) \cdot q(x) + r(x)$ is just another way to state the division.

$$\begin{array}{r|l} & q(x) \\ \hline g(x) & f(x) \\ & \underline{g(x) \cdot q(x)} \\ & r(x) \end{array}$$

The polynomial $g(x)$ is the divisor. It is what gets divided into $f(x)$. The condition $\deg(r(x)) < \deg(g(x))$ guarantees that the degree of the remainder is less than the degree of the divisor.

Answers

For You to Do

4. $(x - 2)(x^2 + 4x + 12) + 30 = x^3 + 4x^2 + 12x - 2x^2 - 8x - 24 + 30 = x^3 + 2x^2 + 4x + 6$

5. 30

For You to Do

6. Using the above notation, find $q(x)$ and $r(x)$ if $f(x) = 2x^3 - 7x^2 - 8x - 34$ and $g(x) = x - 5$.

The most important case for this investigation is when the divisor is of the form $x - a$ for some number a. Suppose $f(x)$ is a polynomial and you divide it by $x - a$. Then the remainder has degree less than 1, so it must be a constant. The constant turns out to be very useful. It is equal to $f(a)$. Here are the details.

Working with greater-degree divisors is important, especially in calculus. In general, though, it is more important to be able to reason about the division process than to be skilled at carrying it out.

Theorem 2.2 The Remainder Theorem

If you divide a polynomial $f(x)$ by $x - a$, where a is a number, the remainder is the number $f(a)$.

Proof First look at a concrete example. Use the polynomial from the example at the beginning of the lesson. Suppose $f(x) = x^3 + 2x^2 + 4x + 6$ and you divide it by $x - 2$.

$$\begin{array}{r|l} & x^2 + 4x + 12 \\ x - 2 & x^3 + 2x^2 + 4x + 6 \\ & x^3 - 2x^2 \\ \hline & 4x^2 + 4x + 6 \\ & 4x^2 - 8x \\ \hline & 12x + 6 \\ & 12x - 24 \\ \hline & 30 \end{array}$$

So you can summarize the division by writing

$$f(x) = x^3 + 2x^2 + 4x + 6 = (x - 2)(x^2 + 4x + 12) + 30$$

Use the far right side as the form that defines f.

$$\begin{aligned} f(2) &= (2 - 2)(2^2 + 2x + 12) + 30 \\ &= 0 \cdot (\text{some number}) + 30 \\ &= 30 \end{aligned}$$

The proof amounts to carrying out this argument generally, without using specific polynomials. It goes this way.

Suppose you divide $f(x)$ by $x - a$. The remainder is a number, because you are dividing by $x - a$. You cannot stop until you get a polynomial of degree less than 1 (that is, a constant). Call the remainder r. The main point of the theorem is that the remainder r is the same as $f(a)$. So the division looks like this.

$$\begin{array}{r|l} & q(x) \\ x - a & f(x) \\ & (x - a)q(x) \\ \hline & r \end{array}$$

Go Online PHSchool.com

For more information about polynomial division, go to Web Code: bfe-9031

For You To Do

Students can perform this division on their CAS if they are comfortable doing the long division by hand.

THEOREM 2.2 THE REMAINDER THEOREM When teaching the proof; consider giving the students an overview of the process in words.

$f(x)$ = divisor · quotient + remainder

When the divisor is $(x - a)$, you have

$f(x) = (x - a)$ · quotient + remainder

and therefore

$f(a) = (a - a)$ · quotient + remainder
= remainder

For You to Do

6. $q(x) = 2x^2 + 3x + 7,\ r(x) = 1$

Developing Habits of Mind

So, $f(a)$ is the remainder when you divide $f(x)$ by $(x - a)$.

Wrap Up

To end this class, discuss the first exercise. Emphasize the relationship between the remainder when you divide $h(x)$ by $(x + 2)$ and $h(-2)$. Have students do Exercises 2, 3, and 4 to solidify what they have learned.

Assessment Resources

Lesson Quiz 2.9

1. Suppose $(x + 1)$ divides evenly into some polynomial $P(x)$. What is $P(-1)$?
2. Suppose $P(x) = 4x^3 + x^2 - 3x + 1$. Use the Remainder Theorem to show that $P(x) - P(2)$ is divisible by $x - 2$.
3. **a.** Find the quotient and the remainder when you divide $f(x) = x^4 + 2x^2 - x + 3$ by $x - 1$.
   b. Find $f(1)$.
4. Find the remainders when you divide each polynomial by $x + 5$.
   a. $x^4 - 2$
   b. $x + 1$
   c. $x^5 - x^3 - x - 1$
   d. $(x^2 + 3x - 3)(x + 2)$

Exercises

HOMEWORK

- Core: 7, 8, 9, 11, 14
- Optional: 10, 13, 16, 17
- Extension: 12, 15

Check Your Understanding

EXERCISE 2 is an important exercise. Students who do this exercise quickly know the Remainder Theorem well. Let other students work for a while, and then show them the way out.

EXERCISE 3 After students learn how to do Exercise 2, this exercise is a natural next step. However, some students may miss the connection between $(x + 1)$ and $f(-1)$. If you need to make this connection explicit, you could rewrite $(x + 1)$ as $(x - (-1))$.

You can summarize the division by writing $f(x) = (x - a)q(x) + r$.

Now replace x with a.

$$f(a) = (a - a) \cdot q(a) + r$$
$$= 0 \cdot (\text{some number}) + r$$
$$= r$$

So, $f(a) = r$.

The remainder r is a number, so it does not change when you replace x with a.

Developing Habits of Mind

Think about it another way. You can restate the Remainder Theorem this way.

If $f(x)$ is a polynomial and a is a number, then there exists a polynomial $q(x)$ such that $f(x) = (x - a)q(x) + f(a)$.

For You to Do

7. Find the quotient and the remainder when you divide $f(x) = x^3 + x^2 + x$ by $x - 2$.
8. Find $f(2)$.
9. What are the zeros of f?

Remember...

The zeros of f are the numbers a that make $f(a) = 0$.

Exercises *Practicing Habits of Mind*

Check Your Understanding

1. **a.** Find the quotient and the remainder when you divide $h(x) = x^3 + 2x^2 - 3x - 6$ by $x + 2$.
   b. Use your result to find $h(-2)$.
2. Find the remainder of $x^{105} + x + 1$ divided by $x - 1$.
3. Find the remainder of $x^{105} + x + 1$ divided by $x + 1$.

Long division takes too long in these cases. Some CAS systems will have trouble, too.

Answers

For You to Do

7. quotient: $x^2 + 3x + 7$; remainder: 14
8. 14
9. 0

Exercises

1. **a.** quotient: $x^2 - 3$; remainder: 0
   b. 0
2. 3
3. -1

4. Suppose $(x - 10)$ divides evenly into some polynomial $P(x)$. What is $P(10)$?

5. At Sasha's party, Tony presents the following puzzle: "I'm thinking of a number. If I divide it by 3, the remainder is 2. If I divide it by 5, the remainder is 3. If I divide it by 7, the remainder is 1. What's my number?"
   a. What number might Tony be thinking of?
   b. Is there more than one integer that fits Tony's puzzle? If so, name two of them. If not, explain why.

6. Later that night, Derman takes the floor and presents the following puzzle: "I'm thinking of a polynomial. If I divide it by $x - 3$, the remainder is 16. If I divide it by $x - 5$, the remainder is 42. If I divide it by $x - 7$, the remainder is 84. What's my polynomial?"
   a. What polynomial might Derman be thinking of?
   b. Is there more than one polynomial that fits Derman's puzzle? If so, name two of them. If not, explain why.

On Your Own

7. a. Find the quotient and the remainder when you divide $f(x) = x^3 + x^2 + x$ by $x + 2$.
   b. Find $f(-2)$.

8. Find the remainders when you divide each polynomial by $x - 3$.
   a. $x^3 - 1$
   b. $x - 1$
   c. $x^2 + x + 1$
   d. $x^4 + x^2 + 1$
   e. $(x^4 + x^2 + 1)(x - 1)$
   f. $x^4 + x^3 + x^2$

Habits of Mind

Consider more than one strategy. Is long division really necessary?

9. Suppose that f and g are polynomials and that $f(2) = 5$ and $g(2) = -4$. Find the remainder when you divide each polynomial by $x - 2$.
   a. $3f + g$
   b. fg^2
   c. $(x^2 + x + 1)f(x) + g(x)$

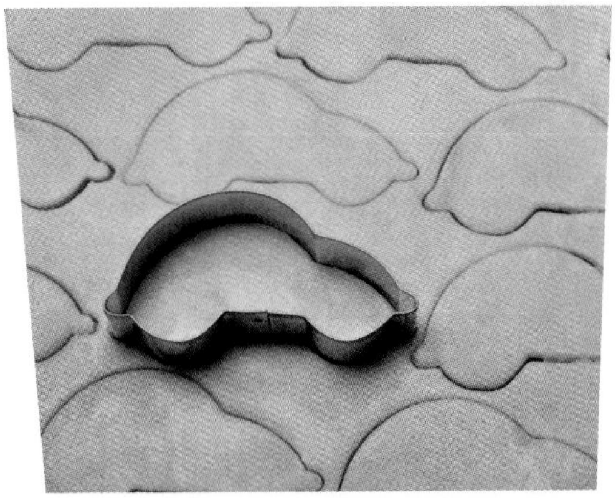

The leftover dough between the cookies is the remainder.

4. 0

5. a. Answers may vary. Sample: 8

b. Answers may vary. Samples: 113, 218, or any number of the form $8 + 105n$, where n is a nonnegative integer

6. a. Answers may vary. Sample: $f(x) = 2x^2 - 3x + 7$

b. Answers may vary. Sample: any polynomial of the form $g(x) = 2x^2 - 3x + 7 + p(x)(x - 3)(x - 5)(x - 7)$, where $p(x)$ is a polynomial

7. a. quotient: $x^2 - x + 3$; remainder: -6

b. -6

8. a. 26
b. 2
c. 13
d. 91
e. 182
f. 117

9. a. 11
b. 80
c. 31

On Your Own

EXERCISE 5 This is a challenging problem for students, and they will probably try integers until they find a pattern. They will quickly find that 8 works, but the next integer that works is 113, and the one after that is 218. Once they have found these, they might conjecture that $n(x) = 105x + 8$. Once they have written the function, they should see that $105 = (3)(5)(7)$ and 8 was the least nonnegative integer that worked. Challenge them to write their own "game" following Tony's example and play it with other students in the class.

EXERCISE 6 This problem can be solved using Lagrange interpolation. The remainder when you divide $p(x)$ by $(x - 3)$ is 16, so you know that $p(3) = 16$. Similarly, you know that $p(5) = 42$ and $p(7) = 84$. Since you know three input/output pairs, you can use Lagrange interpolation. You can find other polynomials by adding a fourth input/output pair and using Lagrange interpolation again.

EXERCISE 8 Students who are successful with this exercise have a good understanding of the Remainder Theorem.

EXERCISE 10 can be conceptually challenging, but students who solve it will have an understanding of the utility of using other variables as bases.

EXERCISE 13 Some students will use the method from Exercise 10, but others may not realize they can. Suggest to struggling students that they look back to Exercise 10.

Maintain Your Skills

EXERCISE 16 Once students have recognized the pattern, you might ask them to use it to factor $x^3 - 1$ and $x^4 - 1$. This works nicely for $x^3 - 1 = (x - 1)(x^2 + x + 1)$, but $x^4 - 1 = (x - 1)(x^3 + x^2 + x + 1)$ is not completely factored. They will probably see that $x^4 - 1 = (x - 1)(x + 1)(x^2 + 1)$. You can ask the students to verify that $x^3 + x^2 + x + 1 = (x + 1)(x^2 + 1)$.

EXERCISE 17 One goal of this exercise is to help students see that $f(x) - f(a)$ is always divisible by $(x - a)$, regardless of what polynomial $f(x)$ is or what value a is chosen.

Additional Resources

PRINT RESOURCES
- Solution Manual
- Practice Workbook
- Assessment Resources
- Teaching Resources

TECHNOLOGY
- Interactive Textbook
- TeacherExpress CD-ROM
- ExamView CD-ROM
- PHSchool.com

Additional Practice

1. a. Find the quotient and the remainder when you divide $f(x) = 2x^3 + 4x^2 + x - 1$ by $x + 3$.
   b. Find $f(-3)$.

2. a. Find the quotient and the remainder when you divide $f(x) = 3x^4 + 2x^2 - 6x + 5$ by $x - 1$.
   b. Find $f(1)$.

3. Find the remainders when you divide each polynomial by $x - 4$.
   a. $x^4 - 2$ b. $x + 1$
   c. $x^2 + 2x + 3$ d. $x^5 + x^3 + x$
   e. $x^5 + x^4 + x^3$ f. $(x^2 + 2x + 3)(x + 1)$

4. Suppose f and g are polynomials and that $f(3) = 6$ and $g(3) = -1$. Find the remainder when you divide each polynomial by $x - 3$.
   a. $2f + g$ b. f^2g
   c. $(x^2 + 2x + 3)f(x) + g(x)$

5. Suppose f and g are polynomials and that $f(1) = 8$ and $g(1) = -3$. Find the remainder when you divide each polynomial by $x - 1$.
   a. $f + 2g$ b. f^2g^2
   c. $(x^2 + x + 1)f(x) + g(x)$

6. Suppose $P(x) = x^3 - 2x^2 + 3x - 4$. Use the Remainder Theorem to show that $P(x) - P(5)$ is divisible by $x - 5$.

7. Suppose $(x + 11)$ divides evenly into some polynomial $P(x)$. What is $P(-11)$?

8. Suppose $f(x) = 6(x + 3)^3 - 2(x + 3)^2 + 3(x + 3) - 5$.
   a. What is $f(-3)$?
   b. What is the remainder when you divide $f(x)$ by $x + 3$?
   c. Suppose $g(x)$ is the quotient when you divide $f(x)$ by $x + 3$. What is $g(-3)$?

Practice: For Lesson 2.9, assign Exercises 1–8.

10. Suppose $f(x) = 5(x - 2)^3 + 3(x - 2)^2 - 6(x - 2) + 8$.
   a. What is $f(2)$?
   b. What is the remainder when you divide $f(x)$ by $x - 2$?
   c. Suppose $g(x)$ is the quotient when you divide $f(x)$ by $x - 2$. What is $g(2)$?
   d. What is the remainder when you divide $g(x)$ by $x - 2$?
   e. Suppose $h(x)$ is the quotient when you divide $g(x)$ by $x - 2$. What is $h(2)$?
   f. What is the remainder when you divide $h(x)$ by $x - 2$?
   g. Suppose $m(x)$ is the quotient when you divide $h(x)$ by $x - 2$. What is $m(2)$?
   h. What is the remainder when you divide $m(x)$ by $x - 2$?

Go Online PHSchool.com
For additional practice, go to Web Code: bfa-0209

11. **Standardized Test Prep** Let $g(x) = x^3 - 12x^2 + 21x + 98$ and $g(-2) = 0$. Find the roots of $g(x)$.
   A. -2 and -7
   B. -2 and 7
   C. 2 and -7
   D. 2 and 7

12. **Take It Further** Suppose $f(x)$ is a polynomial such that $f(2) = 5$ and $f(3) = 7$. What is the remainder when you divide $f(x)$ by $(x - 2)(x - 3)$?

13. Find numbers B, C, and D such that
$x^3 + x^2 - 8x + 13 = (x - 1)^3 + B(x - 1)^2 + C(x - 1) + D$.

14. Suppose $P(x) = x^3 - 3x^2 + 2x + 5$. Use the Remainder Theorem to show that $P(x) - P(7)$ is divisible by $x - 7$.

15. **Take It Further** Suppose $P(x)$ is any polynomial and a is a number. Use the Remainder Theorem to show that $P(x) - P(a)$ is divisible by $x - a$.

Maintain Your Skills

16. Find each quotient.
   a. $\frac{x^2 - 1}{x - 1}$ b. $\frac{x^3 - 1}{x - 1}$ c. $\frac{x^4 - 1}{x - 1}$ d. $\frac{x^5 - 1}{x - 1}$ e. $\frac{x^{12} - 1}{x - 1}$

17. Suppose $f(x) = 2x^2 + 5x - 1$. Simplify each expression.
   a. $\frac{f(x) - f(1)}{x - 1}$ b. $\frac{f(x) - f(2)}{x - 2}$ c. $\frac{f(x) - f(3)}{x - 3}$
   d. $\frac{f(x) - f(4)}{x - 4}$ e. $\frac{f(x) - f(5)}{x - 5}$ f. $\frac{f(x) - f(6)}{x - 6}$

What is the pattern?

Answers

10. a. 8 **b.** 8 **c.** -6
d. -6 **e.** 3 **f.** 3
g. 5 **h.** 5

11. B **12.** $2x + 1$

13. $B = 4, C = -3, D = 7$

14. Answers may vary. Sample: Since $P(x) = (x - 7) \cdot Q(x) + R$, then $P(7) = R$. So $P(x) - P(7) = (x - 7) \cdot Q(x) + R - R = (x - 7) \cdot Q(x)$, and $(x - 7)$ is a factor of $P(x) - P(7)$.

15. Use a method similar to Exercise 13: $P(x) = (x - a) \cdot Q(x) + R$ so $P(a) = R$. Then $P(x) - P(a) = (x - a) \cdot Q(x)$ or $(x - a)$ is a factor of $P(x) - P(a)$.

16. a. $x + 1$ **b.** $x^2 + x + 1$
c. $x^3 + x^2 + x + 1$
d. $x^4 + x^3 + x^2 + x + 1$
e. $x^{11} + x^{10} + \cdots + x^2 + x + 1$

17. a. $2x + 7$ **b.** $2x + 9$
c. $2x + 11$ **d.** $2x + 13$
e. $2x + 15$ **f.** $2x + 17$

2.10 The Factor Theorem

Suppose you want to find all roots of the equation below.

$$x^3 + 4x^2 - 9x - 36 = 0$$

You can start by factoring the left side of the equation.

$$x^3 + 4x^2 - 9x - 36 = (x^2 - 9)(x + 4) = (x - 3)(x + 3)(x + 4)$$

Suppose a is a root of the equation. Then $a^3 + 4a^2 - 9a - 36 = 0$.

By the form-implies-function principle, $(a - 3)(a + 3)(a + 4) = 0$.

By the Zero Product Property, one of the factors must be 0.

$$a - 3 = 0 \text{ or } a + 3 = 0 \text{ or } a + 4 = 0$$

If $a - 3 = 0$, then $a = 3$. If $a + 3 = 0$, then $a = -3$. If $a + 4 = 0$, then $a = -4$. So, the roots of the equation are 3, -3, and -4. Notice that each root a of the equation corresponds to a factor $(x - a)$ of the polynomial on the left side. This happens for any root.

Remember...

The form-implies-function principle says that if two expressions are the same under the basic rules of algebra, then they define functions that produce the same output for the same input.

The Zero Product Property states that if $ab = 0$, then at least one of the numbers a and b has to be zero.

Theorem 2.3 The Factor Theorem

Suppose $f(x)$ is a polynomial. Then the number a is a root of the equation $f(x) = 0$ if and only if $x - a$ is a factor of $f(x)$.

For Discussion

1. Use the Remainder Theorem to prove the Factor Theorem.

For You to Do

2. Suppose $p(x)$ is a polynomial of degree 3 with three zeros at $x = 1, 2,$ and 3. Find $p(x)$ if $p(5) = 48$.

For Discussion

1. The Remainder Theorem is $f(x) = (x - a) \cdot q(x) + f(a)$. So $(x - a)$ is a factor of $f(x)$ if and only if $f(a) = 0$.

For You to Do

2. $P(x) = 2(x - 1)(x - 2)(x - 3)$

Lesson Overview

GOALS

- Understand the relationship between roots and factors of a polynomial.
- State and use the Remainder Theorem and the Factor Theorem.
- Check that two polynomials of degree n are equivalent by checking $n + 1$ function values.
- Write the general form of a function that fits a table.

The Factor Theorem is one of the most important theorems of high school algebra. Students use the Remainder Theorem to prove the Factor Theorem in this lesson. They also look at several very important corollaries. The last dialog serves as a way to bring all these ideas together to characterize all polynomials that fit a particular table.

Students have seen the "Form Implies Function" concept in *Algebra 1*, and earlier in this chapter: if the normal form of two polynomials is the same, then the polynomials define the same function. Now students see the "Function Implies Form" theorem for polynomials: if two polynomials output the same functional values for enough inputs (and "enough" depends on the degree of the polynomials in question), their forms must be the same.

CHECK YOUR UNDERSTANDING
- Core: 1, 2, 3, 6
- Optional: 4, 5, 7, 8

MATERIALS
- CAS (recommended)
- graph paper
- graphing calculators
- Blackline Master 2.10

HOMEWORK
- Core: 9, 10, 16, 17
- Optional: 11, 12, 13, 14a, 15, 18, 19
- Extension: 14b

Launch

Ask students to find the roots of the polynomial equation $x^6 + 4x^5 - 3x^4 - 12x^3 = 0$. Ask how they know they have found all the roots.

Explore

For Discussion

If $x - a$ is a factor of $f(x)$, then $f(x) = (x - a)g(x)$ for some polynomial g. So $f(a) = (a - a)g(x) = 0$. To see the other direction, use the Remainder Theorem, which states:

If a polynomial $f(x)$ is divided by $x - a$ (where a is a number), the remainder is the number $f(a)$.

If $f(a) = 0$, then by the Remainder Theorem, the remainder when $f(x)$ is divided by $x - a$ is 0; in other

continued on p. 156

continued from p. 155

words, $f(x) = (x - a)g(x)$, so $x - a$ is a factor of $f(x)$.

For You To Do

Use the Factor Theorem to find three factors of the polynomial. Since the degree of $p(x)$ is 3, k must be a constant.

(Answer: Because you know three zeros of the polynomial, you know three factors of the polynomial. So, $p(x) = k(x - 1)(x - 2)(x - 3)$ for some polynomial k.
$p(5) = k(5 - 1)(5 - 2)(5 - 3) = k \cdot 4 \cdot 3 \cdot 2 = 48$, so $k = 2$. Therefore, the polynomial is $p(x) = 2(x - 1)(x - 2)(x - 3)$, or $p(x) = 2x^3 - 12x^2 + 22x - 12$.)

For You to Do

You can skip this For You to Do problem if you are pressed for time. If you decide to do it, look for the following elements in students' arguments.

The polynomial $f(x)$ has degree 3. Suppose $f(x)$ has a zero at $x = a$. Then by the Factor Theorem,

$$f(x) = (x - a)q(x)$$

for some polynomial $q(x)$. And the degree of $q(x)$ has to be 2. Suppose b is another zero of $f(x)$, different from a. Then using the above identity,

$$0 = f(b) = (b - a)q(b)$$

Since $b - a \neq 0$ (because b was chosen to be different from a), you have that $q(b) = 0$ by the Zero Product Property. Applying the factor theorem again, there is a polynomial $p(x)$ of degree 1 such that

$$q(x) = (x - b)p(x)$$

But $p(x)$ has to be linear. And since the original polynomial $f(x)$ is monic, $p(x)$ must be monic, so

$$p(x) = x - c$$

for some constant c. So $f(x)$ can have at most three zeros.

Students can check this result: $f(x)$ has only one zero, and it is not a rational number, so students will not find it if they just try to factor $f(x)$ using a CAS. They can see one root exists by graphing $f(x)$ or by keying "solve $(x^3 - 2x^2 - x + 2 = 0, x)$" into a graphing calculator.

There are many corollaries to the Factor Theorem that have a wide range of applications in algebra. Here are a few.

Corollary 2.3.1

A polynomial of degree n can have at most n distinct real-number zeros.

Proof Suppose $f(x)$ is a polynomial of degree n and a is a zero. Then, by the Factor Theorem, there is a polynomial $q(x)$ such that

$$f(x) = (x - a)q(x)$$

Because the degree of a product is the sum of the degrees (see Problem 4 from Lesson 2.8), the degree of $q(x)$ has to be $n - 1$.

Suppose b is another zero of $f(x)$, different from a. Then, using the above equation,

$$0 = f(b) = (b - a)q(b)$$

Since $b - a \neq 0$, $q(b) = 0$ by the Zero Product Property. Apply the Factor Theorem and the result of Problem 4 from Lesson 2.8. There is a polynomial $p(x)$ of degree $n - 2$ such that

$$q(x) = (x - b)p(x)$$

Substituting $f(x) = (x - a)q(x)$, you have

$$f(x) = (x - a)(x - b)p(x)$$

Keep doing this until you run out of real zeros.

$$f(x) = (x - a)(x - b)(x - c)\ldots \ell(x)$$

The polynomial $\ell(x)$ has no real zeros. Since the degree of $f(x)$ is n, the sum of the degrees on the right side must be n. Since each zero of $f(x)$ contributes 1 to this sum, there can be at most n of them.

For You to Do

3. Carefully write out the steps for applying this proof to $f(x) = x^3 - 2x^2 - x + 2$.

Corollary 2.3.2

If two polynomials of degree n agree at $n + 1$ inputs, they are identical.

For Discussion

4. Prove Corollary 2.3.2. Why might you call Corollary 2.3.2 the "function-implies-form" principle?

Answers

For You to Do

3. Answers may vary. Sample: Suppose $f(x) = x^3 - 2x^2 - x + 2$. You know $(x + 1)(x^2 - 3x + 2) = x^3 - 2x^2 - x + 2$, so $f(x) = (x + 1) \cdot (x^2 - 3x + 2)$. Also, $x^2 - 3x + 2 = (x - 1)(x - 2)$, so $f(x) = (x + 1)(x - 1)(x - 2)$. Therefore $f(x)$ has three zeros, and 3 is the degree of $f(x)$.

For Discussion

4. Answers may vary. Sample: The Lagrange method would give the same polynomial function for the two sets of $n + 1$ ordered pairs. Since both polynomials have degree n, the polynomials must be identical.

Developing Habits of Mind

Use a different process to get the same answer. Corollary 2.3.2 will save you time and effort. It provides an alternative to the form-implies-function principle.

For example, suppose you have two polynomials of degree 5. You want to show that they will always give the same output for a given input. One way to do that is to show that they are equivalent under the basic rules of algebra. Another way is to show that they agree at six inputs. Corollary 2.3.2 says that, if two fifth-degree polynomials agree for six inputs, they are automatically identical. That is, they are equivalent under the basic rules.

So, to check that two polynomial functions are equal for all real inputs, all you have to do is to show that they agree on enough inputs. *Enough* means 1 more than their degree. This is quite a remarkable fact. It is not often that only a few checks of a result guarantee the result for infinitely many other cases.

Corollary 2.3.3

A polynomial of degree n is completely determined by its output values for $n + 1$ inputs.

Minds in Action

episode 7

Tony and Sasha are picking up where they left off in Lesson 2.7.

Tony So, we have a way to build as many polynomials as we want that agree with this table for $f(x) = 2x + 2$.

x	f(x)
1	4
2	6
3	8
4	10

Sasha Right. We just take another function of the form

$$r(x) = 2x + 2 + (\text{something}) \cdot (x - 1)(x - 2)(x - 3)(x - 4).$$

And I think this is the only way to get such a function.

Tony Me too, but I don't see why.

For Discussion

To prove Corollary 2.3.1, note that every root produces a linear factor, and as in the proof of the Factor Theorem, every linear factor increases the degree of the product of factors by 1. So, if $f(x)$ is not equal to zero and $f(x)$ has more than n factors, then the degree of $f(x)$ has to be more than n. So, if $f(x)$ has more roots than its degree, $f(x) = 0$.

Corollary 2.3.2 is easier to prove than the previous one. Suppose $f(x)$ and $g(x)$ are polynomials of degree n that agree on $n + 1$ outputs. Then $f(x) - g(x)$ is a polynomial of degree at most n that has $n + 1$ roots. By the previous corollary, $f(x) - g(x) = 0$, or $f(x) = g(x)$.

You call Corollary 2.3.2 the Function Implies Form Theorem because if you can show that two polynomials of degree $\leq n$ have the same values for $n + 1$ inputs, they are the same. So if two polynomials are the same when you see them from the functional perspective, they are the same from the formal perspective. You may want to use Blackline Master 2.10 to illustrate this corollary.

Corollary 2.3.3

You might want to relate this to the work students have done with Lagrange interpolation: when an input-output table has four input-output pairs, the polynomial function that fits the table is of at most degree 3.

Minds in Action

The "something" that Sasha talks about cannot have any zeros if $r(x)$ is to agree with $f(x)$ only at $x = 1, 2, 3, 4$ and nowhere else.

For You to Do

There is a theorem that states that if $f = g$ for inputs $a_1, \dots, a_n$, then there is a polynomial h such that

$$f(x) = g(x) + h(x)(x - a_1) \dots (x - a_n)$$

$h(x)$ is multiplied by a string of factors that guarantee that the product it is part of will equal zero for any of the inputs on which the two functions agree, so it will only impact this equation for some other input.

Another way to state this theorem is, If f and g agree for n outputs, then their difference vanishes at these inputs and so has degree n or more.

Wrap Up

To end the lesson, go over Exercises 1, 2, 3, and 6. In Exercises 1 and 3, students should apply the Factor Theorem. In Exercises 2 and 6, they should use Corollary 2.3.3.

Assessment Resources

Lesson Quiz 2.10

1. What is the greatest number of real roots a polynomial of degree 5 can have? Explain.

2. Find the value of a such that $x + 3$ is a factor of $x^3 + ax^2 - 2x - 6$.

3. Find the numbers a and b such that $x^2 + x - 4$ is a factor of $x^4 + ax^3 - bx^2 - ax + 4$.

4. Find a cubic polynomial function that agrees with the table.

x	$f(x)$
1	6
2	15
3	36
4	75
5	138
6	231

Sasha Suppose we have a function $g(x)$ that agrees with f on the table. Then if I subtract $g(x)$ from $f(x)$, I get a polynomial that outputs zero for all the input values in the table.

x	f(x)	g(x)	f(x) − g(x)
1	4	4	0
2	6	6	0
3	8	8	0
4	10	10	0

What do we know about a polynomial that has 1, 2, 3, and 4 as zeros?

Tony We know it looks like

$$(\text{something}) \cdot (x - 1)(x - 2)(x - 3)(x - 4)$$

Why do they know this?

Sasha Right. So,

$$f(x) - g(x) = (\text{something}) \cdot (x - 1)(x - 2)(x - 3)(x - 4)$$

So . . .

Tony Oh.

$$f(x) = g(x) + (\text{something}) \cdot (x - 1)(x - 2)(x - 3)(x - 4)$$

and $g(x)$ comes from our method. Very smooth.

Derman enters the discussion.

Derman But I have another function that agrees with f at 1, 2, 3, and 4. Look.

$$d(x) = 338 - 698x + 490x^2 - 140x^3 + 14x^4$$

For You to Do

5. Write Derman's function in a way that shows how it comes from Tony and Sasha's method.

Answers

For You to Do

5. Check students' work.

Exercises *Practicing Habits of Mind*

Check Your Understanding

1. What is the greatest number of real roots a polynomial of degree 2 can have? Explain.
2. If two linear polynomials agree at two points, then Corollary 2.3.2 says that they must be identical. If two quadratic polynomials agree at three points, then they must be identical, and so on. For each pair of polynomials, decide if the polynomials are identical using this idea of checking $n + 1$ points.
   a. $P(x) = x^4 - x^2 - 2$ and $R(x) = (x^2 + 1)(x^2 - 2)$
   b. $P(x) = x(x + 1)(x - 1)$ and $R(x) = x - x^3$
   c. $P(x) = (x + 3)^2 - 7$ and $R(x) = x^2 + 6x + 2$
3. Find the value of a such that $x - 1$ is a factor of $x^3 + ax^2 - x + 5$.
4. Find numbers a and b such that $x^2 + x - 6$ is a factor of $x^4 + x^3 - ax^2 - bx + a - b$.
5. Solve the equation $x^4 + x^3 - 7x^2 - x + 6 = 0$.
6. Establish the following identity.
   $$(x - 1)(x - 3) + (x - 2)(x - 3) + (x - 1)(x - 2) = 3x^2 - 12x + 11$$
7. Establish the following identity.
   $$\frac{20}{(1 - 3)(1 - 6)}(x - 3)(x - 6) + \frac{12}{(3 - 1)(3 - 6)}(x - 1)(x - 6) + \frac{60}{(6 - 1)(6 - 3)}(x - 1)(x - 3) = 4x^2 - 20x + 36$$
8. Find the normal form of $P(x)$.
   $$P(x) = \frac{(x - 1)(x - 2)}{(3 - 1)(3 - 2)} + \frac{(x - 1)(x - 3)}{(2 - 1)(2 - 3)} + \frac{(x - 2)(x - 3)}{(1 - 2)(1 - 3)}$$

$x^2 + x - 6 = (x - 2)(x + 3)$

Can you do Exercises 6 and 7 without expanding the left sides?

On Your Own

9. Find the number a such that $x - 1$ is a factor of $x^3 + ax^2 - x + 8$.
10. Find numbers a and b such that $x^2 + x - 6$ is a factor of $x^4 + x^3 - ax^2 - bx + 2a + b$.
11. Solve the equation $x^4 + x^3 - 10x^2 - 4x + 24 = 0$.
12. Suppose $f(x) = 4 - 4x + 13x^2 - 12x^3 + 3x^4$. Show that each statement is true.
    a. $x - 2$ is a factor of $f(x)$.
    b. $(x - 2)^2$ is a factor of $f(x)$.
    c. If $f(x) = (x - 2)q(x)$, then $x - 2$ is a factor of $q(x)$.

Go Online PHSchool.com

For additional practice, go to **Web Code**: bfa-0210

Exercises

HOMEWORK
- Core: 9, 10, 16, 17
- Optional: 11, 12, 13, 14a, 15, 18, 19
- Extension: 14b

Check Your Understanding

EXERCISES 2 AND 3 Students may want to work on Exercise 2 in a different way. They may even be able to say the expressions are identical (or not) without this work. Still, encourage the work. Exercise 3 gives a more direct example where evaluation is simpler than expansion.

EXERCISE 5 Students should recognize the polynomial as the one they found in Exercise 4. So, they know two solutions already: $x = 2$ and $x = -3$. To find the other two solutions, suggest they use their CAS to divide and then factor the resulting quadratic.

EXERCISE 6 is a situation where testing for 3 points is faster than expansion, although some students will still solve by expansion.

EXERCISE 12 This is an example of a polynomial with a factor of multiplicity 2. Since $f(x) = (x - 2)^2(3x^2 + 1)$, this is a good example to discuss zeros (only $x = 2$), domain (all real numbers), and range (all real numbers greater than or equal to 2).

Exercises

1. By Corollary 2.3.1, a polynomial of degree 2 can have at most two real roots.
2. **a.** Checking any five values, $P(0) = R(0) = -2$, $P(1) = R(1) = -2$, $P(-1) = R(-1) = -2$, $P(\sqrt{2}) = R(\sqrt{2}) = 0$, and $P(-\sqrt{2}) = R(-\sqrt{2}) = 0$. So $P(x) = R(x)$.
   b. Checking any four values, $P(1) = R(1) = 0$, $P(0) = R(0) = 0$, $P(-1) = R(-1) = 0$, but $P(2) \neq R(2)$. So $P(x) \neq R(x)$.
   c. Checking any three values, $P(-3) = R(-3) = -7$, $P(0) = R(0) = 2$, $P(-2) = R(-2) = -6$. So $P(x) = R(x)$.
3. -5
4. $a = 7, b = 1$
5. $-3, -1, 1, 2$

6–12. See back of book.

EXERCISE 13 To see the relationship with Exercise 7 from Lesson 2.8, let $a = 1$. Or you might want to give a concrete example:

$$x^5 - 32 = (x^5 - x^2)$$
$$= (x - 2)(x^4 + 2x^3 + 4x^2 + 8x + 16)$$

EXERCISE 16 This is a good place to emphasize Corollary 2.3.3. Since the polynomial is a cubic, you only need four inputs. If the students use Lagrange interpolation to find the cubic, they can use any four of the given input/output pairs. The resulting cubic will fit the entire table.

EXERCISE 19 In parts (a)–(d), the two zeros get closer together and closer to 2. No matter how close together they are, however, the range of the function still includes some negative numbers. In part (e), there is only one zero, namely 2, and the range is nonnegative real numbers. Have students look at the graphs of these functions on their graphing calculators. They should zoom in until they can distinguish among the graphs of c, d, and e.

Additional Resources

PRINT RESOURCES
- Solution Manual
- Practice Workbook
- Assessment Resources
- Teaching Resources

TECHNOLOGY
- Interactive Textbook
- TeacherExpress CD-ROM
- ExamView CD-ROM
- PHSchool.com

Additional Practice

1. What is the greatest number of real roots a polynomial of degree 4 can have? Explain.

2. Find the number a such that $x + 2$ is a factor of $x^3 + ax^2 + x - 6$.

3. Find the number b such that $x^2 + x - 3$ is a factor of $x^4 + bx^3 - 5x - b$.

4. Find the numbers a and b such that $x^2 + x + 1$ is a factor of $x^4 + ax^3 + bx^2 + 4x + 3$.

5. Solve the equation $x^4 + 3x^3 - 15x^2 - 19x + 30 = 0$.

6. Suppose $f(x) = x^4 + 4x^3 + 3x^2 - 4x - 4$. Show that each statement is true.
a. $x + 2$ is a factor of $f(x)$.
b. If $f(x) = (x + 2)s(x)$, then $x + 2$ is a factor of $s(x)$.
c. $(x + 2)^2$ is a factor of $f(x)$.

7. Find a cubic polynomial function that agrees with the table.

x	f(x)
1	−1
2	3
3	17
4	47
5	99
6	179

8. Suppose $f(x) = (x^2 + 2)(x + 1)(x + 3)(x - 5)(x - 7)$. Find the factored form of each expression.
a. $\frac{f(x)}{x + 1}$
b. $\frac{f(x)}{(x + 1)(x + 3)}$
c. $\frac{f(x)}{x - 5}$
d. $\frac{f(x)}{x - 7}$
e. $\frac{f(x)}{(x + 1)(x + 3)(x - 5)}$
f. $\frac{f(x)}{(x + 1)(x + 3)(x - 5)(x - 7)}$

Practice: For Lesson 2.10, assign Exercises 1–8.

13. Establish the following identity.

$$x^n - a^n = (x - a)(x^{n-1} + ax^{n-2} + a^2x^{n-3} + a^3x^{n-4} + \cdots + a^{n-2}x + a^{n-1})$$

Habits of Mind
Look for relationships. How is Exercise 13 a generalization of Exercise 7 from Lesson 2.8?

14. Suppose that r is a number and $f(x) = a_nx^n + a_{n-1}x^{n-1} + \cdots + a_1x + a_0$.
a. Show that $f(x) - f(r) = (x - r)g(x)$ for some polynomial g.
b. Take It Further Write an expression for g.

15. Use Exercise 14 to prove the Remainder Theorem.

16. Here is a table for the sum of the first n squares.

A cubic polynomial function gives the sum of the first n squares. Find a cubic that agrees with this table.

n	$1^2 + 2^2 + \cdots + n^2$
1	1
2	5
3	14
4	30
5	55
6	91

17. Standardized Test Prep The function $f(x)$ is a polynomial of degree 4. The function $p(x) = (x + a)^2$ is a factor of $f(x)$. Which of the following is NOT always true?
A. $f(x) = (x + a) \cdot$ (something else) $+ r(x)$, where $r(x) = 0$
B. $f(a) = 0$
C. The trinomial $x^2 + 2ax + a^2$ is a factor of $f(x)$.
D. The degree of the function $h(x)$ defined by the equation $f(x) = p(x) \cdot h(x)$ is 2.

Maintain Your Skills

18. Suppose $f(x) = (x^2 + 1)(x - 1)(x - 2)(x - 3)(x - 4)$. Find the factored form of each expression.
a. $\frac{f(x)}{x - 1}$
b. $\frac{f(x)}{(x - 1)(x - 2)}$
c. $\frac{f(x)}{x - 3}$
d. $\frac{f(x)}{x - 4}$
e. $\frac{f(x)}{(x - 1)(x - 2)(x - 3)}$
f. $\frac{f(x)}{(x - 1)(x - 2)(x - 3)(x - 4)}$

19. Graph each function.
a. $f(x) = (x - 1)(x - 3)$
b. $g(x) = (x - 1.5)(x - 2.5)$
c. $h(x) = (x - 1.8)(x - 2.2)$
d. $k(x) = (x - 1.9)(x - 2.1)$
e. $\ell(x) = (x - 2)^2$

Answers

13. Distributing x from the factor $(x - a)$ gives $x^n + ax^{n-1} + a^2x^{n-2} + \cdots + a^{n-2}x^2 + a^{n-1}x$, and distributing $-a$ from $(x - a)$ gives $-ax^{n-1} - a^2x^{n-2} - \cdots - a^{n-2}x^2 - a^{n-1}x - a^n$. Adding those terms results in pairs of additive inverses and $x^n - a^n$.

14. See back of book.

15. The Remainder Theorem states that if $f(x)$ is divided by $(x - a)$, the remainder is $f(a)$. From Exercise 14, $f(x) - f(a) = g(x) \cdot (x - a)$, so $f(x) = g(x) \cdot (x - a) + f(a)$. This is the format that a dividend is equal to a factor times the quotient, plus a remainder, and $f(a)$ is the remainder.

16. $S(n) = \frac{n(n + 1)(2n + 1)}{6}$

17. B

18–19. See back of book.

Mathematical Reflections 2C

In this investigation, you learned how to divide polynomials by linear polynomials and how to use the Remainder Theorem and the Factor Theorem. You also learned about the relationship between roots and factors of polynomials. These exercises will help you summarize what you have learned.

1. Find the polynomial $g(x)$ such that $x^8 - 1 = (x - 1)g(x)$.
2. Find the polynomial $g(x)$ such that $x^8 - 1 = (x - 1)(x + 1)g(x)$.
3. Find the remainder of $x^{105} - 3x + 1$ divided by $x + 1$.
4. Find numbers B and C such that $x^2 + 2x = (x - 1)^2 + B(x - 1) + C$.
5. **Take It Further** Find numbers r and s if $(x - 2)^2$ is a factor of $2x^3 + rx^2 + sx + 4$.
6. How are the zeros of a polynomial related to its factors?
7. How can you tell if two polynomials are equal without using the form-implies-function principle?
8. What is the greatest-degree polynomial you need to fit a table with four inputs?

Vocabulary

In this investigation, you learned these terms. Make sure you understand what each one means and how to use it.

- **quotient**
- **remainder**

The posts determine a unique fence line. A set of points can determine a unique function.

Mathematical Reflections

EXERCISES 6–8 At the start of the investigation, you may have assigned these as Questions 1–3 for students to think and write about.

Mathematical Reflections

1. $g(x) = x^7 + x^6 + x^5 + x^4 + x^3 + x^2 + x + 1$
2. $g(x) = x^6 + x^4 + x^2 + 1$
3. 3
4. $B = 4, C = 3$
5. $r = -7, s = 4$
6. If a is a zero or root, then $x - a$ is a factor.
7. Answers may vary. Sample: You can use Corollary 2.3.2, which states that if two polynomials of degree n agree at $n + 1$ inputs, they are equivalent.
8. degree 3 or less

Investigation Overview

This investigation is about more than factoring. There is the hope that students revisit some of the algebraic ideas that are embedded in the work of factoring, such as, the correspondence between linear factors of a polynomial and roots.

There is a mix of techniques available for solving polynomial equations: using an analytic technique or graphing and approximating a root. Here you want to nail down the algebraic technique of factoring so that when students see the more analytic techniques in *Precalculus*, they understand how solving polynomial equations is one place in which analytic techniques and algebraic techniques come together.

The investigation presents a short review of the quadratic formula. Quickly, the investigation moves to factoring nonmonic polynomials by scaling. Students then see sums and differences of squares and cubes, factoring by grouping, and the method of finding factors by finding roots. An optional lesson, *Pippins and Cheese*, looks at "quadratic-like" and "cubic-like" polynomials. Students also get a hint of complex numbers in this lesson. The final lesson of this investigation introduces rational expressions and uses the work of the previous investigations to simplify rational expressions.

Although the subject matter, factoring, is absolutely traditional, the approach here is not. The hope is that students will engage in the work, take on some of the more demanding exercises, and enjoy the challenge.

You may wish to assign Questions 1–3 for students to think and write about during the investigation.

Learning Goals

- Factor polynomials by scaling.
- Factor polynomials using the differences and sums of squares.
- Factor polynomials using the differences and sums of cubes.
- Factor polynomials using grouping.
- Factor polynomials by identifying quadratic-like or cubic-like polynomials.
- Factor polynomials by finding roots.
- Factor polynomials to solve polynomial equations.

Habits and Skills

- Rearrange polynomials into more useful forms. Sometimes a factored form of a polynomial is more useful than an expanded form.
- Use several techniques for factoring polynomials.

Investigation 2D

Advanced Factoring

In *Advanced Factoring*, you will develop some advanced factoring methods. Many of them depend on the connection between roots and factors. Factoring a polynomial is important because it simplifies the problem of finding the zeros of the polynomial.

By the end of this investigation, you will be able to answer questions like these.

1. How do you factor nonmonic quadratics?
2. How do you factor differences and sums of cubes?
3. Does $x^4 + 4$ factor over $\mathbb{Z}$?

You will learn how to

- factor polynomials by scaling
- factor polynomials using the differences and sums of squares
- factor polynomials using the differences and sums of cubes
- factor polynomials using grouping
- factor polynomials by identifying quadratic-like or cubic-like polynomials
- factor polynomials by finding roots

You will develop these habits and skills:

- Rearrange polynomials into more useful forms. Sometimes a factored form of a polynomial is more useful than an expanded form.
- Use several techniques for factoring polynomials.

Breaking a house into parts makes it easier to move. Breaking a polynomial into factors makes it easier to identify roots.

Investigation Road Map

LESSON 2.11, *Getting Started,* reviews factoring.

LESSON 2.12, *Quadratics,* reviews the quadratic formula and introduces techniques for factoring nonmonic quadratics.

LESSON 2.13, *Factoring Cubics,* presents differences of squares and cubes, sums of squares and cubes, factoring by grouping, and the method of finding a root to find a factor.

LESSON 2.14, *Pippins and Cheese,* is optional. It introduces factoring "quadratic-like" and "cubic-like" expressions.

LESSON 2.15, *Rational Expressions,* is an optional lesson. It introduces rational expressions and uses the work of previous lessons to simplify them.

2.11 Getting Started

Activating Prior Knowledge
Exploring New Ideas

The following problems and exercises ask you to review some ideas from your first-year algebra course and to preview some ideas from this investigation.

You can decide if a problem or exercise is a review, a preview, or both.

For You to Explore

1. Factor each quadratic polynomial over $\mathbb{Z}$. If a polynomial does not factor, explain why not.
   - **a.** $x^2 + 10x + 25$
   - **b.** $x^2 + 10x + 24$
   - **c.** $z^2 + 10z + 23$
   - **d.** $u^2 + 10u + 21$
   - **e.** $y^2 + 10y + 26$

The symbol $\mathbb{Z}$ means the integers.

2. Factor each polynomial over $\mathbb{Z}$. If a polynomial does not factor, explain why not.
   - **a.** $x^2 + 18x + 45$
   - **b.** $4x^2 + 36x + 45$
   - **c.** $(x - 3)^2 + 18(x - 3) + 45$
   - **d.** $z^2 - 121$
   - **e.** $9u^2 - 121$
   - **f.** $(y + 5)^2 - 121$
   - **g.** $y^2(y + 5) - 4(y + 5)$
   - **h.** $y^2(y + 5) - 3(y + 5)$
3. Suppose α and β are roots of this equation.
   $$x^2 - 6x + 5 = 0$$
   Find each value.
   - **a.** $\alpha + \beta$
   - **b.** $\alpha\beta$
4. Suppose α and β are two numbers with a sum of 6 and a product of -3. Show that α and β are roots of the equation $x^2 - 6x - 3 = 0$.

Answers

For You to Explore

1. **a.** $(x + 5)(x + 5)$
   b. $(x + 6)(x + 4)$
   c. It doesn't factor; there are no rational numbers with sum 10 and product 23.
   d. $(u + 7)(u + 3)$
   e. It doesn't factor; there are no rational (or real) numbers with sum 10 and product 26.
2. **a.** $(x + 3)(x + 15)$
   b. $(2x + 3)(2x + 15)$
   c. $x(x + 12)$
   d. $(z + 11)(z - 11)$
   e. $(3u + 11)(3u - 11)$
   f. $(y + 16)(y - 6)$
   g. $(y + 2)(y - 2)(y + 5)$
   h. $(y^2 - 3)(y + 5)$
3. **a.** 6
   b. 5
4. See back of book.

Lesson Overview

GOAL

- Warm up to the ideas of the investigation.

In this lesson, students spend time factoring quadratics. Some are straightforward and others are more difficult. Encourage students to do what they can. As always in a Getting Started lesson, there is no need to formalize these ideas today. Students meet all the ideas again throughout the investigation.

FOR YOU TO EXPLORE
- Core: 1, 2, 3
- Optional: 4

MATERIALS
- CAS (recommended)

HOMEWORK
- Core: 5, 6, 9, 11
- Optional: 7, 8, 10, 12

VOCABULARY
- $\mathbb{Z}$ (the integers)

Launch

Have students work cooperatively to factor as many of the polynomials as they can in For You To Explore Problems 1 and 2. Then bring the class together to go over their results. Point out the relationship between the forms of 2a and 2c, and between the forms of 2d, 2e, and 2f.

Explore

In addition to previewing the rest of this investigation, these problems serve as an assessment of prior work in *Algebra 1*. Use this time to see how much review students need of the quadratic formula and the process of factoring straightforward monic quadratics.

For You to Explore

PROBLEM 1 Here is a chance to remind students of what it means to factor over $\mathbb{Z}$. Students will probably factor over $\mathbb{Z}$ without even thinking about it.

PROBLEM 2 The solutions for this exercise describe some of the techniques that students can use to factor these polynomials. Of course, if a student's method results in a correct factoring, they have solved the problem correctly. However, some students will benefit from a brief reminder of these factoring techniques so they are not dependent on a single strategy.

PROBLEMS 3 AND 4 remind students of another way to think about the problem of factoring a monic quadratic expression. If the coefficient of the x^2 term is 1, the sum of the roots is the opposite of the coefficient of the x term and their product is the constant term.

Wrap Up

Go over a few of the For You to Explore problems, focusing on any that students had trouble with. Demonstrate how some of the quadratics in Exercise 7 (such as parts (a) and (i)) relate to the identity in Exercise 13 of Lesson 2.10.

Exercises

HOMEWORK
- Core: 5, 6, 9, 11
- Optional: 7, 8, 10, 12

On Your Own

EXERCISE 6 asks students to find the rules for sum and difference of cubes. This is also the first of many exercises requiring students to work with $x^n - 1$ and $x^n + 1$. Make sure students are comfortable with this exercise, even though it amounts to only an expansion.

EXERCISE 7 Students may have some trouble with any of the parts of this exercise beyond part (b). This exercise previews material that comes later in this investigation. Assign at least parts (a) and (b), and perhaps include the others as optional, depending on the ability level of your class and their confidence about approaching new problems. You could also let students know that in this lesson, as in any Getting Started lesson, they may be asked to attempt things they have not seen before. Encourage them to give these exercises a try and see what they can do.

EXERCISES 8 AND 9 If students are struggling with Exercise 9, suggest they look back at Exercise 8.

Maintain Your Skills

EXERCISE 12 The last two parts of this exercise are a difference of cubes. Your students will not be as familiar with these forms as they are with the difference of squares forms used in the earlier parts of this exercise. You may want to make the last two parts optional or remind students that they will use these forms throughout the investigation.

Exercises *Practicing Habits of Mind*

On Your Own

5. Factor these quadratic polynomials over $\mathbb{Z}$. If a polynomial does not factor, explain why not.

a. $x^2 + 6x + 5$ **b.** $x^2 - 6x + 9$ **c.** $x^2 + 12x + 20$
d. $x^2 + 10x - 20$ **e.** $x^2 - 5x - 24$ **f.** $x^2 + 10x + 30$

Habits of Mind
Look for patterns. Generalize the identities you find.

6. Find the normal form for each polynomial.

a. $(x - 1)(x^2 + x + 1)$ **b.** $(x + 1)(x^2 - x + 1)$

7. Factor each polynomial over $\mathbb{Z}$.

a. $x^3 - 1$ **b.** $x^3 + 1$ **c.** $x^3 - 8$
d. $x^3 + 8$ **e.** $8x^3 - 1$ **f.** $8x^3 + 1$
g. $x^3 - a^3$ **h.** $x^3 + a^3$ **i.** $(x + 1)^3 - 1$
j. $(x - 1)^3 + 1$

In parts (g) and (h), *a* stands for an integer.

8. Show that if the equation $x^2 - 10x + 7 = 0$ has roots p and q, then the following statement must be true.

$$p + q = 10 \quad \text{and} \quad pq = 7$$

Is the converse true?

9. Find a quadratic equation with solutions $3 + \sqrt{7}$ and $3 - \sqrt{7}$.

10. Find A, B, C, and D such that

$$-37 + 40x - 18x^2 + 3x^3 = A(x - 2)^3 + B(x - 2)^2 + C(x - 2) + D$$

Maintain Your Skills

11. Find the normal form for each polynomial.

a. $x^2 - 9$ **b.** $(2x)^2 - 9$
c. $9 - x^2$ **d.** $(x + 1)^2 - 9$
e. $(x + 1)^2 - x^2$ **f.** $(x^2 + 1)^2 - x^2$
g. $(x^2 + 1)^3 - x^3$ **h.** $(x^2 + 1)^3 - x^6$

12. Factor each polynomial over $\mathbb{Z}$.

a. $x^2 - 9$ **b.** $(2x)^2 - 9$
c. $9 - x^2$ **d.** $(x + 1)^2 - 9$
e. $(x + 1)^2 - x^2$ **f.** $(x^2 + 1)^2 - x^2$
g. $(x^2 + 1)^3 - x^3$ **h.** $(x^2 + 1)^3 - x^6$

Answers

Exercises

5. a. $(x + 1)(x + 5)$
b. $(x - 3)(x - 3)$
c. $(x + 2)(x + 10)$
d. It doesn't factor; there are no rational numbers with sum 10 and product −20.
e. $(x - 8)(x + 3)$
f. It doesn't factor; there are no rational (or real) numbers with sum 10 and product 30.

6. a. $x^3 - 1$ **b.** $x^3 + 1$

7–8. See back of book.

9. $x^2 - 6x + 2 = 0$

10. $A = 3, B = 0, C = 4, D = -5$

11. a. $x^2 - 9$
b. $4x^2 - 9$
c. $-x^2 + 9$
d. $x^2 + 2x - 8$
e. $2x + 1$
f. $x^4 + x^2 + 1$
g. $x^6 + 3x^4 - x^3 + 3x^2 + 1$
h. $3x^4 + 3x^2 + 1$

12. See back of book.

2.12 Quadratics

In your first-year algebra course, you learned to factor quadratic polynomials in order to solve quadratic equations. Most of the quadratics you factored were monic—the coefficient of x^2 was 1. In this lesson, you will build on the methods you used to factor monics to find the factors of any quadratic polynomial. The new methods will extend to polynomials of higher degrees.

Factoring to solve was the original motivation for factoring, but, like most topics in mathematics, factoring has become an interesting problem in its own right.

First, you will quickly review the basic factoring techniques for monic quadratics. If you want to factor $x^2 - 7x + 12$, you look for two numbers with sum of 7 and a product of 12. To understand why you do this, suppose the equation is in factored form.

$$x^2 - 7x + 12 = (x - r)(x - s)$$

If you multiply out the right side, you get

$$x^2 - 7x + 12 = x^2 - (r + s)x + rs$$

So, in this case, $r + s = 7$ and $rs = 12$.

Make sure you know how to multiply out the right side.

For You to Do

1. Factor $x^2 - 7x + 12$.

Now, what can you do if the quadratic is not monic? A good mathematical habit is to make use of something you already know how to do. The scaling method is a good example of this habit.

You can scale up to make a process—such as removing bunny ears—easier to do. After you have fixed the problem, you can scale back down.

Lesson Overview

GOAL

- Factor polynomials by scaling.

This lesson reviews the process of factoring quadratics from *Algebra 1* and introduces new methods of factoring nonmonic quadratics. In particular, you introduce the useful method of scaling nonmonic quadratics so that they "look" monic. This is the first of a series of transformation methods that are introduced in this investigation.

CHECK YOUR UNDERSTANDING
- Core: 1, 2
- Optional: none

MATERIALS
- CAS (recommended)

HOMEWORK
- Core: 3, 4, 6, 8, 9
- Optional: 5, 7

Launch

Begin this lesson with the For You to Do. Then read the preceding text together and discuss how it applies to the For You to Do. Students should recognize the quadratic as $x^2 - (\text{sum})x + (\text{product})$. As a class, continue with the Example. As an additional example, you can have students factor $2x^2 + 11x + 12$.

For You to Do

Have students list pairs of integers with a product of 12. Then have them identify the pair with a sum of 7. Ask the students the following questions: If you change the problem to "Factor $x^2 - x - 12$," how does your list of integers change? What pair gives a sum of 1? What are the factors of $x^2 - x - 12$?

For You to Do

1. $(x - 4)(x - 3)$

Explore

Developing Habits of Mind

Ask students to factor $(x - 3)^2 + 18(x - 3) + 45$ first by lumping and then by expanding and factoring. Do they get the same result? Which method do they prefer?

For You to Do

Note that this quadratic has rational roots, not integer ones. This is fine, unless you want to factor over $\mathbb{Z}$, in which case you will need some adjustment. Discuss this. In any case, the goal is not for students to be too attached to either method; both are useful in different circumstances.

For Discussion

Let students find their own words and descriptions for this algorithm, if you choose to make this discussion part of your class. You might leave this as a writing assignment for homework or save it for the Wrap Up of the class.

Wrap Up

Have students do the For You to Do. Then, as a class, write the algorithm requested in the For Discussion.

Assessment Resources

Lesson Quiz 2.12

1. Factor each polynomial.
   a. $5x^2 + 22x + 21$
   b. $5x^2 + 32x - 21$
   c. $5x^2 + 8x - 21$
   d. $5(x - 1)^2 + 8(x - 1) - 21$
   e. $5x^4 + 38x^2 + 21$
   f. $5(x + 1)^4 + 38(x + 1)^2 + 21$

2. Solve $7x - \frac{9}{x} = 2$ for x.

3. Solve each pair of equations and compare the roots.
   a. $x^2 + 5x + 6 = 0$ and $x^2 - 15x + 54 = 0$
   b. $2x^2 + 9x - 35 = 0$ and $x^2 + 18x - 280 = 0$

Example

Problem Factor $6x^2 + 11x - 10$.

Solution You can use the scaling method to transform nonmonic polynomials into monic ones. Here are the steps.

Step 1 Multiply the polynomial by 6 to make the leading coefficient a perfect square.

$$6(6x^2 + 11x - 10) = 36x^2 + 11 \cdot 6x - 60 = (6x)^2 + 11(6x) - 60$$

Step 2 Think of $6x$ as the variable. Let $z = 6x$.

$$z^2 + 11z - 60$$

Step 3 This expression factors.

$$z^2 + 11z - 60 = (z + 15)(z - 4)$$

Step 4 Replace z with $6x$.

$$(6x + 15)(6x - 4)$$

So

$$\begin{aligned} 6(6x^2 + 11x - 10) &= (6x + 15)(6x - 4) \\ &= 3(2x + 5) \cdot 2(3x - 2) \\ &= 6(2x + 5)(3x - 2) \end{aligned}$$

Step 5 Divide both sides by 6 to obtain the factored form.

$$6x^2 + 11x - 10 = (2x + 5)(3x - 2)$$

Habits of Mind

Look for relationships. Dividing by 6 undoes the multiplication by 6 that you did in Step 1.

Developing Habits of Mind

Change variables. This idea of lumping part of an expression into one unit is very useful in mathematics. You can say that $(2x)^2 + 18(2x) + 45$ is a monic quadratic in $2x$. This means that if you think of $2x$ as the variable instead of x, the quadratic looks monic.

For You to Do

2. Factor $6x^2 - 31x + 35$.

For Discussion

3. State the scaling method as an algorithm, a sequence of steps that describes exactly what to do.

Answers

For You to Do

2. $(3x - 5)(2x - 7)$

For Discussion

3. Answers may vary. Sample: Multiply each term of the polynomial by a number that makes the leading coefficient a perfect square. Rewrite the polynomial as $(ax)^2 + ax \cdot m + b$, and factor that polynomial. For the last step, divide both sides by the factor you used in the first step.

Exercises Practicing Habits of Mind

Check Your Understanding

1. Factor each polynomial.
   a. $9x^2 + 18x - 7$
   b. $6x^2 - 31x + 35$
   c. $15x^2 + 16x - 7$
   d. $9x^2 + 62x - 7$
   e. $-18x^2 - 65x - 7$
   f. $-18x^2 + 61x + 7$
   g. $9x^4 + 62x^2 - 7$
   h. $25 - 4x^2$
   i. $18x^3 - 61x^2 - 7x$

For more on factoring polynomials, see the TI-Nspire Handbook, p. 778.

2. Factor each polynomial.
   a. $9x^2 + 18xy - 7y^2$
   b. $6x^2 - 31xy + 35y^2$
   c. $15x^2 + 16xa - 7a^2$
   d. $9x^2 + 62xb - 7b^2$
   e. $-18x^2 - 65xa - 7a^2$
   f. $-18x^2 + 61xy + 7y^2$
   g. $25y^2 - 4x^2$
   h. $18x^3 - 61x^2y - 7xy^2$

On Your Own

3. Factor each polynomial.
   a. $4x^2 - 13x + 3$
   b. $4x^2 - 8x + 3$
   c. $4x^2 + 4x - 3$
   d. $4(x + 1)^2 + 4(x + 1) - 3$
   e. $4x^4 - 13x^2 + 3$
   f. $4(x - 1)^4 - 13(x - 1)^2 + 3$
   g. $4(x - 1)^{12} - 13(x - 1)^6 + 3$
   h. $(x^2 + 1)^2 - x^2$

Go Online PHSchool.com

For additional practice, go to **Web Code:** bfa-0212

4. Solve $2x - \frac{3}{x} = 5$ for x.
5. In the equation $x^2 - 6x + 7 = 0$, let $z = x - 3$.
   a. Express the equation in terms of z.
   b. Solve the equation for z.
   c. Use the result from part (b) to solve the original equation.

If $z = x - 3$, then $x = z + 3$.

Exercises

HOMEWORK
- Core: 3, 4, 6, 8, 9
- Optional: 5, 7

Check Your Understanding

EXERCISE 1 Students often neglect the linear term when using the scaling method. If the quadratic term is $(6x^2)$, emphasize that the linear term must be in the form $k \cdot (6x)$ where k is some constant.

EXERCISES 1 AND 2 Consider which parts of Exercise 1 you would like to assign, since some are more challenging than others. Also, since the factorings in Exercise 2 are closely related to those in Exercise 1 (except for part (g)), you should assign only corresponding parts from each of these exercises.

EXERCISE 2 If students are having trouble, ask them to expand some related expressions such as $(x + 3)(x - 5)$ and $(x + 3k)(x - 5k)$.

On Your Own

EXERCISE 3 As with other exercises, choose strategically what parts to assign. The last part is challenging conceptually, but it is accessible once students apply the methods they know.

EXERCISE 4 Some students may have trouble getting started here, so ask them how they might deal with the fractions. It is okay to give the $x \neq 0$ issue a light treatment, because it will be explored in more detail later.

EXERCISE 5 helps students see that a change of variable makes it easier to solve an equation. The equation in terms of z is much simpler, and they can solve it without using the quadratic formula.

Exercises

1. a. $(3x + 7)(3x - 1)$
b. $(2x - 7)(3x - 5)$
c. $(3x - 1)(5x + 7)$
d. $(9x - 1)(x + 7)$
e. $-(9x + 1)(2x + 7)$
f. $-(9x + 1)(2x - 7)$
g. $(3x + 1)(3x - 1)(x^2 + 7)$
h. $(5 - 2x)(5 + 2x)$
i. $x(9x + 1)(2x - 7)$

2. a. $(3x + 7y)(3x - y)$
b. $(2x - 7y)(3x - 5y)$
c. $(3x - a)(5x + 7a)$
d. $(9x - b)(x + 7b)$
e. $-(9x + a)(2x + 7a)$
f. $-(9x + y)(2x - 7y)$
g. $(5y + 2x)(5y - 2x)$
h. $x(9x + y)(2x - 7y)$

3. See back of book.

4. $-\frac{1}{2}, 3$

5. a. $z^2 = 2$
b. $z = \pm\sqrt{2}$
c. $x = 3 \pm \sqrt{2}$

Maintain Your Skills

EXERCISE 8 The parts of this exercise are independent, so you do not have to assign them all unless you feel your students need the practice. However, the more exercises they do, the more likely they are to see a pattern.

Additional Resources

PRINT RESOURCES	TECHNOLOGY
• Solution Manual	• Interactive Textbook
• Practice Workbook	• TeacherExpress CD-Rom
• Assessment Resources	• ExamView CD-ROM
• Teaching Resources	• PHSchool.com

Additional Practice

1. Factor each polynomial.
   - a. $8x^2 + 22x + 5$
   - b. $8x^2 + 14x + 5$
   - c. $8x^2 - 6x - 5$
   - d. $8(x - 1)^2 - 6(x - 1) - 5$
   - e. $4x^4 - 19x^2 - 5$
   - f. $4(x + 1)^4 - 19(x + 1)^2 - 5$
   - g. $4(x + 1)^{10} - 19(x + 1)^5 - 5$
   - h. $(x^2 - 1)^2 - 2x^2 + 3$
2. Solve $5x - \frac{7}{x} = 2$ for x.
3. Solve each pair of equations and compare the roots.
   - a. $x^2 + 4x + 3 = 0$ and $x^2 + 12x + 27 = 0$
   - b. $2x^2 + 10x + 12 = 0$ and $2x^2 + 20x + 48 = 0$
   - c. $3x^2 + 18x + 24 = 0$ and $2x^2 + 3x + 1 = 0$
   - d. $5x^2 + 6x - 27 = 0$ and $x^2 + 6x - 135 = 0$
4. Find an equation with roots scaled in each of the following ways.
   - a. 2 times the roots of $6x^2 + 9x - 6 = 0$
   - b. 3 times the roots of $3x^2 + 13x - 10 = 0$
   - c. 5 times the roots of $5x^2 - 17x + 6 = 0$
   - d. 4 times the roots of $4x^2 - 3x - 7 = 0$
5. Factor each polynomial over $\mathbb{Z}$.
   - a. $x^3 - 8$
   - b. $x^3 + 8$
   - c. $125x^3 - 8$
   - d. $125x^3 + 8$
   - e. $(x - 2)^3 - 64$
   - f. $(2x + 1)^3 + 64$
   - g. $x^3 + 6x^2 + 12x + 8$
   - h. $4x^3 + x^2 + x - 3$
   - i. $y^4 - (2x - 1)^4$
   - j. $x^4 - y^2 - 4yz - 2z^2$
   - k. $(y + 2)^3 + z^3$
   - l. $x^3 + 3x^2 + 3x + 1$
6. Find the normal form of each polynomial.
   - a. $x + 2$
   - b. $(x + 2)^2$
   - c. $(x + 2)^3$
   - d. $(x + 2)^4$
   - e. $(x + 2)^5$

Practice: For Lesson 2.12, assign Exercises 1–4.

6. **Standardized Test Prep** Sasha has a number of rules for factoring quadratic polynomial of the form $ax^2 + bx + c$. Which of the following is NOT always true?
   - **A.** If $a > 0$ and $c > 0$, then one real root is positive and one real root is negative.
   - **B.** If $a = 1$ and $b < 0$ and d and e are the roots, with $|d| > |e|$, then $(x - d)$ is a factor of the polynomial.
   - **C.** If a is an integer greater than 1, then multiplying c by a^2 converts the polynomial into a monic polynomial.
   - **D.** If a, b, and c are integers and all are greater than zero, then any real roots, if they exist, are less than zero.
7. Derman wants to use the scaling method to factor $18x^2 + 7x - 1$. He multiplies the polynomial by 2 to make 18 a perfect square. Will this work?

Maintain Your Skills

8. Solve each pair of equations and compare the solutions.
   - **a.** $x^2 - 8x + 7 = 0$ and $x^2 - 24x + 63 = 0$
   - **b.** $2x^2 + 11x - 21 = 0$ and $2x^2 + 22x - 84 = 0$
   - **c.** $2x^2 + 11x - 21 = 0$ and $2x^2 + 33x - 189 = 0$
   - **d.** $2x^2 + 11x - 21 = 0$ and $2x^2 + 55x - 525 = 0$
   - **e.** $2x^2 + 11x - 21 = 0$ and $x^2 + 11x - 42 = 0$
   - **f.** $3x^2 + 16x - 35 = 0$ and $x^2 + 16x - 105 = 0$
   - **g.** $3x^2 + 16x - 32 = 0$ and $x^2 + 16x - 96 = 0$

How are the equations in each pair related?

9. Find an equation with solutions scaled in each of the following ways.
   - **a.** 7 times the solutions of $x^2 - 8x + 7 = 0$
   - **b.** 7 times the solutions of $2x^2 + 11x - 21 = 0$
   - **c.** 2 times the solutions of $2x^2 + 11x - 21 = 0$
   - **d.** 3 times the solutions of $3x^2 + 11x - 21 = 0$
   - **e.** 5 times the solutions of $5x^2 + 11x - 21 = 0$

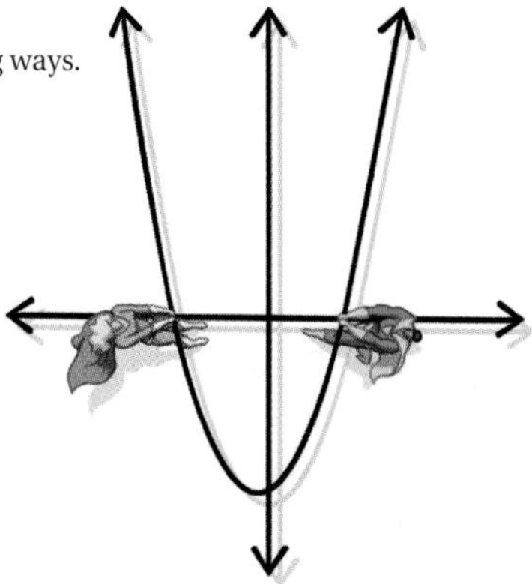

Answers

6. C
7. Yes, $36x^2 + 14x - 2$ can be factored, but it will have fractional coefficients.
8. **a.** 1 and 7; 3 and 21; the second roots are 3 times the first roots.
   b. -7 and $\frac{3}{2}$; -14 and 3; the second roots are 2 times the first roots.
   c. -7 and $\frac{3}{2}$; -21 and $\frac{9}{2}$; the second roots are 3 times the first roots.
   d. -7 and $\frac{3}{2}$; -35 and $\frac{15}{2}$; the second roots are 5 times the first roots.
   e. -7 and $\frac{3}{2}$; -14 and 3; the second roots are 2 times the first roots.
   f. -7 and $\frac{5}{3}$; -21 and 5; the second roots are 3 times the first roots.
   g. $\frac{-16 \pm \sqrt{640}}{6}$; $\frac{-16 \pm \sqrt{640}}{2}$; the second roots are 3 times the first roots.
9. See back of book.

2.13 Factoring Cubics

In your first-year algebra course, you learned some basic identities that allow you to factor most quadratics that factor over $\mathbb{Z}$. Some of these identities included

- the difference-of-squares identity

  $x^2 - y^2 = (x - y)(x + y)$

- the perfect-square identities

  $x^2 + 2xy + y^2 = (x + y)^2$

  $x^2 - 2xy + y^2 = (x - y)^2$

- the sum-and-product identity

  $x^2 - (a + b)x + ab = (x - a)(x - b)$

Only one of these perfect-square identities is really necessary.

Equipped with these identities, the **quadratic formula,** the Factor Theorem, and the scaling method, you can tackle any quadratic, often in more than one way.

If all else fails, you can use the quadratic formula to get the roots.

$$x = \frac{-b \pm \sqrt{b^2 - 4ac}}{2a}$$

If the roots are rational numbers, you can factor the quadratic over $\mathbb{Z}$.

But how can you handle cubics?

In this lesson, you will learn some methods for factoring certain cubics. There is a formula, similar to the quadratic formula, that you can use to find the roots, and therefore the factors, of any cubic. But this cubic formula often leads to solutions that are in such an unrecognizable form that they are useless, so factoring special cubics is still worthwhile. Besides, it is fun.

Sums and Differences of Cubes

By now, you have seen the following theorem several times in exercises.

Theorem 2.4

The following identities show the factoring for the difference of cubes and the sum of cubes.

- $x^3 - y^3 = (x - y)(x^2 + xy + y^2)$
- $x^3 + y^3 = (x + y)(x^2 - xy + y^2)$

Habits of Mind

Look for relationships. You need only one of these identities.

For Discussion

1. Prove Theorem 2.4.

For Discussion

1. Distributing the x term from $(x + y)$ or $(x - y)$ gives $x^3 + x^2y + xy^2$ or $x^3 - x^2y + y^3$; distributing the $-y$ or y gives $x^2y + xy^2 + y^3$ or $-x^2y + xy^2 - y^3$. Combining the appropriate partial products gives the desired results.

Lesson Overview

GOALS

- Factor polynomials using the differences and sums of squares.
- Factor polynomials using the differences and sums of cubes.
- Factor polynomials using groupings.

This lesson introduces factoring cubic polynomials. Students learn to apply the identities for the difference of cubes and sum of cubes that they first encountered in Exercises 6 and 7 of Lesson 2.11. They learn to factor cubic polynomials that are in the form of a difference or sum of cubes by lumping. Other cubic polynomials can be factored by grouping or by finding a root of the function and using the root to find a factor.

CHECK YOUR UNDERSTANDING
- Core: 1, 2
- Optional: 3

MATERIALS
- CAS (recommended)
- Blackline Master 2.13

HOMEWORK
- Core: 4, 8, 9
- Optional: 5, 6
- Extension: 7

VOCABULARY
- difference of cubes
- quadratic formula
- sum of cubes

Launch

You might ask students to try factoring $x^2 - 4$ to remind them of the difference of squares form that they saw often in *Algebra 1*. Then invite them to try factoring $x^3 - 8$ and $x^3 + 8$. If students are not sure where to start, ask them to find one root of the expression. Then they can use polynomial division to find its other factor. This will be quadratic, so students should be able to determine whether this new factor is also factorable.

Once students have solved this specific case, introduce the general identities for differences and sums of cubes.

Use Blackline Master 2.13 as a transparency or a handout.

Explore

For Discussion

Simply expanding the left side of the equations yields the right side. For example:

$$(x - y)(x^2 + xy + y^2) = x^3 + x^2y + y^2x - yx^2 - xy^2 - y^3$$
$$= x^3 - y^3$$

For You to Do

Have students try these problems before they see the worked-out examples in the text. After they do this, the examples should go quickly.

EXAMPLE 1 Caution students to be careful with parentheses in Method 1 and to remember to take out the common factor of *x* in Method 2.

For You to Do

2. Factor $x^3 - 27$ and $8x^3 + 27$ over $\mathbb{Z}$.

Example 1

Problem Factor $(x + 1)^3 - 1$ over $\mathbb{Z}$.

Solution You can look at this two different ways.

Method 1 Difference of Cubes

If you lump things together and think of $x + 1$ as z, you get

$$z^3 - 1 = z^3 - 1^3$$

By Theorem 2.4, you can factor this as a difference of cubes.

$$z^3 - 1^3 = (z - 1)(z^2 + z + 1)$$

Now replace z with $(x + 1)$ and simplify.

$$\begin{aligned}(z - 1)(z^2 + z + 1) &= ((x + 1) - 1)((x + 1)^2 + (x + 1) + 1)\\ &= x((x^2 + 2x + 1) + (x + 1) + 1)\\ &= x(x^2 + 3x + 3)\end{aligned}$$

Since $x^2 + 3x + 3$ does not factor over $\mathbb{Z}$, this is the factored form.

Method 2 Expand and Simplify

For this method, you just expand $(x + 1)^3$, subtract 1, simplify, and factor the result.

$$\begin{aligned}(x + 1)^3 &= (x + 1)(x + 1)^2\\ &= (x + 1)(x^2 + 2x + 1)\\ &= x^3 + 2x^2 + x + x^2 + 2x + 1\\ &= x^3 + 3x^2 + 3x + 1\end{aligned}$$

So

$$(x + 1)^3 - 1 = (x^3 + 3x^2 + 3x + 1) - 1 = x^3 + 3x^2 + 3x$$

Now factor out the common factor of x.

$$x^3 + 3x^2 + 3x = x(x^2 + 3x + 3)$$

Habits of Mind

Check your work. It is a good thing that both methods give the same answer, because there is only one factorization of a polynomial over $\mathbb{Z}$.

Answers

For You to Do

2. $x^3 - 27 = x^3 - 3^3 = (x - 3) \cdot (x^2 + 3x + 9)$;
$8x^3 + 27 = (2x)^3 + 3^3 = (2x + 3)(4x^2 - 6x + 9)$

For You to Do

3. Factor $(3x + 2)^3 + 8$ over $\mathbb{Z}$.

Grouping

Grouping is a technique in which you lump a few terms of a polynomial together so that you can factor that piece. Sometimes the factors of that piece are also factors of the whole polynomial.

You can apply grouping to any polynomial. Cubics with four terms are convenient because sometimes you can group them in pairs.

Example 2

Problem Factor the following two polynomials over $\mathbb{Z}$.

a. $x^3 - 8x^2 + 4x - 32$

b. $x^3 - 2x^2 + x - 2$

Solution

a. Factor $x^3 - 8x^2 + 4x - 32$.

Group the first two terms and the last two terms together.

$$x^3 - 8x^2 + 4x - 32 = (x^3 - 8x^2) + (4x - 32)$$

Factor out the common factor in each group.

$$(x^3 - 8x^2) + (4x - 32) = x^2(x - 8) + 4(x - 8)$$

Each group has a factor of $x - 8$, so you can pull it out.

$$x^2(x - 8) + 4(x - 8) = (x - 8)(x^2 + 4)$$

The polynomial $x^2 + 4$ does not factor over $\mathbb{Z}$, so you are done.

If $f(x) = x^3 - 8x^2 + 4x - 32$, what is $f(8)$?

b. Factor $x^3 - 2x^2 + x - 2$.

Just for variety, group the first and third terms together, and then the second and fourth terms.

$$x^3 - 2x^2 + x - 2 = (x^3 + x) + (-2x^2 - 2)$$

Factor out the common factor in each group.

$$(x^3 + x) + (-2x^2 - 2) = x(x^2 + 1) - 2(x^2 + 1)$$

Each group has a factor of $x^2 + 1$, so you can pull it out.

$$x(x^2 + 1) - 2(x^2 + 1) = (x - 2)(x^2 + 1)$$

The polynomial $x^2 + 1$ does not factor over $\mathbb{Z}$, so you are done.

If $f(x) = x^3 - 2x^2 + x - 2$, what is $f(2)$?

For You to Do

3. $(3x + 2)^3 + 2^3 = (3x + 4) \cdot (9x^2 + 6x + 4)$

EXAMPLE 2 In part (a), you could also group the first and third terms together and the second and fourth terms together. However, grouping the first and the fourth terms together will not work.

For Discussion

This For Discussion is optional. This is not a classic factoring-by-grouping problem—it is really just using the Distributive Property. One way to solve it is to see that

$$\begin{aligned}(r+s)^3 - 3rs(r+s) &= (r+s)((r+s)^2 - 3rs)\\ &= (r+s)r^2 + 2rs + s^2 - 3rs)\\ &= (r+s)(r^2 - rs + s^2)\\ &= r^3 + s^3\end{aligned}$$

Since

$$(r+s)^3 - 3rs(r+s) = r^3 + s^3$$

you know

$$(r+s)^3 - 3rs(r+s) - (r^3 + s^3) = 0$$

Developing Habits of Mind

Students should learn to use a variety of methods for factoring. If they have trouble, suggest that one method they should try is graphing the polynomial function to look for zeros. Keep in mind that the zero they are looking for must be in the form $\frac{p}{q}$, where p is a factor of the constant and q is a factor of the leading coefficient.

For You to Do

4. Factor $x^3 - 2x^2 + x - 2$ another way: Group the first two terms together and the last two terms together.

For Discussion

5. Factor the expression $(r+s)^3 - 3rs(r+s)$ by grouping.
6. Use your factoring to establish the identity below.

$$(r+s)^3 - 3rs(r+s) - (r^3 + s^3) = 0$$

Developing Habits of Mind

Consider more than one strategy. Some warnings:

- Not all cubics can be factored by grouping, but they may still factor. For example, you can try every grouping combination for $2x^3 - 13x^2 + x + 21$ and nothing will work, but it still factors.

$$2x^3 - 13x^2 + x + 21 = (2x - 3)(x^2 - 5x - 7)$$

- Sometimes a combination of methods can be useful. For example, look at the following polynomial.

$$27x^3 + 27x^2 + 9x + 1$$

Grouping the first and second terms looks promising, but it does not lead anywhere. You can group the first and last terms, factor that pair as a sum of cubes, and then factor out the common factor from the middle two terms.

$$\begin{aligned}27x^3 + 27x^2 + 9x + 1 &= (27x^3 + 1) + 27x^2 + 9x\\ &= (3x+1)((3x)^2 - (3x) + 1) + 9x(3x+1)\\ &= (3x+1)(9x^2 - 3x + 1) + 9x(3x+1)\\ &= (3x+1)(9x^2 - 3x + 1 + 9x)\\ &= (3x+1)(9x^2 + 6x + 1)\\ &= (3x+1)(3x+1)^2\\ &= (3x+1)^3\end{aligned}$$

If $f(x) = 2x^3 - 13x^2 + x = 21$, what is a zero of $f(x)$?

So $27x^3 + 27x^2 + 9x + 1$ is a perfect cube.

Answers

For You to Do

4. $(x^3 - 2x^2) + (x - 2) = x^2(x - 2) + 1(x - 2) = (x^2 + 1)(x - 2)$

For Discussion

5. $$\begin{aligned}(r+s)^3 - 3rs(r+s) &= (r+s)((r+s)^2 - 3rs)\\ &= (r+s)(r^2 + 2rs + s^2 - 3rs)\\ &= (r+s)(r^2 - rs + s^2)\end{aligned}$$
6. Using the results and the pattern for factoring from Problem 5, the sum of two cubes, $(r+s)^3 = (r+s)(r^2 - rs + s^2) = r^3 + s^3$, so $(r+s)^3 - 3rs(r+s) - (r^3 + s^3) = 0$.

Find a Root, Find a Factor

The Factor Theorem sets up a correspondence between roots and factors. For cubics, if you can find a root a of the equation $f(x) = 0$, you have found a factor of $f(x)$, namely $x - a$. So, you know $f(x) = (x - a)g(x)$, where $g(x)$ is a quadratic. And you know how to handle quadratics.

Minds in Action — episode 8

Sasha and Tony are trying to factor $x^3 - 8x^2 + 22x - 21$ over $\mathbb{Z}$.

Tony We can factor $x^3 - 8x^2 + 22x - 21$ if we can solve the equation $x^3 - 8x^2 + 22x - 21 = 0$. Do you have any ideas about roots? They could be anything.

Sasha Let's use the trick of working backward. Suppose we have a root a. Then $x - a$ is a factor, so we'd get something like

$$x^3 - 8x^2 + 8x + 21 = (x - a)(rx^2 + sx + t)$$

for integers r, s, and t.

Tony I know that r would have to be 1, because if you multiplied it back out, the leading term would be rx^3. May be we could figure out the other coefficients in the same way.

Sasha I'm looking at the constant term. It would have to be $-at$. So, $-at = 21$, and $at = -21$.

> Why does the constant term have to be $-at$?

Derman joins the discussion.

Derman Well, there are millions of pairs of numbers with a product of -21. Like -100 and $\frac{21}{100}$, for example. Or $\frac{21}{\sqrt{2}}$ and $\sqrt{2}$.

Sasha Yes, Derman, but a and t have to be integers. That narrows the field.

Tony Right. We're basically looking at factors of 21. So a can only be 1, 3, or 7.

Sasha Or their opposites. So, we only have six numbers to try. Let's do it.

They split up the numbers—three for Sasha, two for Tony, and one for Derman.

Tony I've got it: 3 is a root. So, $x - 3$ is a factor. Now we can either figure out s from $x^3 - 8x^2 + 8x + 21 = (x - 3)(x^2 + sx - 7)$, or we can use long division.

> Why is the second factor $x^2 + sx - 7$?

They try it both ways and get the same answer.

Tony So here's how it factors.

$$x^3 - 8x^2 + 8x + 21 = (x - 3)(x^2 - 5x - 7)$$

Derman Does the quadratic factor some more?

Minds in Action

Tony gives three factors: 1, 3, or 7. Sasha says they have six numbers to try. Be sure students realize that they should also try -1, -3, and -7.

For You to Do

Unless otherwise stated, you are factoring over $\mathbb{Z}$. If you do not restrict the factors to integer coefficients, you can factor the quadratic:

$$x^2 - 5x - 7 = \left(x - \frac{5 + \sqrt{53}}{2}\right)\left(x - \frac{5 - \sqrt{53}}{2}\right).$$

For Discussion

This is an optional discussion.

You can write $(2x)^3 - 13(2x)^2 + 2(2x) + 84$ after multiplying through by a factor of 4. Substituting $M = 2x$ and using "find a root, find a factor" you get

$$(M)^3 - 13(M)^2 + 2(M) + 84 = (M - 3)(M^2 - 10M - 28)$$

or

$$(2x)^3 - 13(2x)^2 + 2(2x) + 84 = ((2x - 3)((2x)^2 - 10(2x) - 28)$$

And now you have to factor out the 4 you multiplied through in the beginning:

$$2x^3 - 13x^2 + x + 21 = (2x - 3)(x^2 - 5x - 7)$$

For You to Do

This problem is optional. If you have done the For Discussion, however, you might want to complete the problem by finding the factors. Look at factors of 84 to find possible factors of the polynomial.

Wrap Up

Choose several problems from Check Your Understanding Exercise 2 to highlight the different methods students can use to factor cubic polynomials. Exercise 3 is a good review of the scaling method.

Assessment Resources

Lesson Quiz 2.13

1. Factor each polynomial over $\mathbb{Z}$.
   - a. $x^3 - 64$
   - b. $x^3 + 64$
   - c. $27x^3 - 64$
   - d. $27x^3 + 64$
   - e. $(x - 1)^3 - 8$
   - f. $(2x + 3)^3 + 8$
   - g. $x^3 + 12x^2 + 48x + 64$
   - h. $3x^3 - 5x^2 + 8x - 4$
   - i. $y^4 - (3x + 2)^4$
   - j. $x^6 - y^2 - 8yz - 16z^2$
   - k. $(2y + 1)^3 + z^3$
   - l. $x^3 + 6x^2 + 12x + 8$
2. Find the normal form of each polynomial.
   - a. $(x - 2)^2$
   - b. $(x - 2)^3$
   - c. $(x - 2)^4$
   - d. $(x - 2)^5$

Exercises

HOMEWORK

- Core: 4, 8, 9
- Optional: 5, 6
- Extension: 7

For You to Do

7. What are the roots of $x^2 - 5x - 7$?
8. Answer Derman's question from the dialog.

For Discussion

9. Can you use the scaling method to turn nonmonic cubics into monic cubics? Try it with $2x^3 - 13x^2 + x + 21$.

For You to Do

10. Find all real roots of $2x^3 - 13x^2 + x + 21$.

Exercises *Practicing Habits of Mind*

Check Your Understanding

1. Prove the following theorem that shows how to cube a binomial.

Theorem 2.5

The following are identities.

- $(x + y)^3 = x^3 + 3x^2y + 3xy^2 + y^3$
- $(x - y)^3 = x^3 - 3x^2y + 3xy^2 - y^3$

2. Factor each polynomial over $\mathbb{Z}$.
   - a. $x^3 - 64$
   - b. $x^3 + 64$
   - c. $27x^3 - 64$
   - d. $27x^3 + 64$
   - e. $(x + 1)^3 - 64$
   - f. $(2x - 3)^3 + 64$
   - g. $x^3 + 3x^2 - 9x - 27$
   - h. $x^3 + ax^2 - a^2x - a^3$
   - i. $x^2 - (3x + 1)^2$
   - j. $x^2 - y^2 + 2yz - z^2$
   - k. $x^3 - 4x^2 - 31x + 70$
   - l. $x^3 - 4x^2y - 31xy^2 + 70y^3$
   - m. $(x + 1)^3 - 3x(x + 1)$

Answers

For You to Do

7. $x = \frac{5 \pm \sqrt{53}}{2}$

8. yes, $x^2 - 5x - 7 = \left(x - \frac{5 + \sqrt{53}}{2}\right)\left(x - \frac{5 - \sqrt{53}}{2}\right)$

For Discussion

9. Answers may vary. Sample: Multiply each term by 4 to get $8x^3 - 52x^2 + 4x + 84 = (2x)^3 - 13(2x)^2 + 2(2x) + 84$, which is a monic polynomial in $(2x)$.

For You to Do

10. $2x^3 - 13x^2 + x + 21 = (2x - 3)(x^2 - 5x - 7)$; the roots of $(2x - 3)(x^2 - 5x - 7)$ are $\frac{3}{2}$ and $\frac{5 \pm \sqrt{53}}{2}$.

Exercises

1–2. See back of book.

3. Use the scaling method to transform $5x^2 + 3x^2 + 3x - 2$ into a monic cubic. Then use the transformed cubic to factor $5x^3 + 3x^2 + 3x - 2$.

On Your Own

4. Factor each polynomial over $\mathbb{Z}$.
   - **a.** $x^3 - 27$
   - **b.** $x^3 + 27$
   - **c.** $64x^3 - 27$
   - **d.** $64x^3 + 27$
   - **e.** $(x - 1)^3 - 125$
   - **f.** $(2x - 3)^3 + 125$
   - **g.** $x^3 + 5x^2 - 25x - 125$
   - **h.** $5x^3 - 7x^2 + 7x - 2$
   - **i.** $x^4 - (3x + 1)^4$
   - **j.** $x^2 - y^2 - 2yz - z^2$
   - **k.** $(x + 1)^3 + x^3$
   - **l.** $x^3 - 3x^2 + 3x - 2$
   - **m.** $x^3 - 3x^2z + 3xz^2 - 2z^3$
   - **n.** $x^3 - 12x^2 + 48x - 64$

Go Online PHSchool.com

For additional practice, go to **Web Code:** bfa-0213

5. Factor $x^3 - 15x - 4$ over $\mathbb{Z}$.

6. Factor $(x - 1)^3 - 15(x - 1) - 4$ over $\mathbb{Z}$.

7. **Take It Further** Factor $x^4 - x^3 - 2x^2 + x + 1$ over $\mathbb{Z}$.

8. **Standardized Test Prep** What is the difference $(x + 4)^3 - (x^3 + 4^3)$?
   - **A.** $x^2 - 4x + 4$
   - **B.** $x^2 - 4x + 16$
   - **C.** $3x^2 + 48$
   - **D.** $12x^2 + 48x$

Maintain Your Skills

9. Find the normal form of each polynomial.
   - **a.** $x + 1$
   - **b.** $(x + 1)^2$
   - **c.** $(x + 1)^3$
   - **d.** $(x + 1)^4$
   - **e.** $(x + 1)^5$

What patterns do you see?

3. See back of book.

4. a. $(x - 3)(x^2 + 3x + 9)$
b. $(x + 3)(x^2 - 3x + 9)$
c. $(4x - 3)(16x^2 + 12x + 9)$
d. $(4x + 3)(16x^2 - 12x + 9)$
e. $(x - 6)(x^2 + 3x + 21)$
f. $2(x + 1)(4x^2 - 22x + 49)$
g. $(x + 5)(x - 5)(x + 5)$
h. $(5x - 2)(x^2 - x + 1)$
i. $(4x + 1)(-2x - 1)(10x^2 + 6x + 1)$
j. $(x + y + z)(x - y - z)$
k. $(2x + 1)(x^2 + x + 1)$
l. $(x - 2)(x^2 - x + 1)$
m. $(x - 2z)(x^2 - xz + z^2)$
n. $(x - 4)(x - 4)(x - 4)$

5. $(x - 4)(x^2 + 4x + 1)$

6. $(x - 5)(x^2 + 2x - 2)$

7. $(x + 1)(x - 1)(x^2 - x - 1)$

8. D

9. a. $x + 1$
b. $x^2 + 2x + 1$
c. $x^3 + 3x^2 + 3x + 1$
d. $x^4 + 4x^3 + 6x^2 + 4x + 1$
e. $x^5 + 5x^4 + 10x^3 + 10x^2 + 5x + 1$

Check Your Understanding

EXERCISE 1 You may want to use Blackline Master 2.13 again here.

EXERCISE 2 You may want to read through the solutions before deciding which parts of this exercise to assign. The parts of this exercise have differing levels of complexity, so assign strategically. Consider this exercise to be practice, so you can skip any or all parts. Since students will be working on this exercise in class, you might want to let students solve what they can and then share results.

EXERCISE 3 is a sophisticated application of the grouping method. If your students have had trouble with grouping during the lesson, you may not wish to assign this exercise. Or, do the exercise as a whole class.

On Your Own

EXERCISE 7 If students have trouble beginning this exercise, remind them of this saying: "Find a root, find a factor." The only possible rational roots are $x = 1$ and $x = -1$.

Additional Resources

PRINT RESOURCES
- Solution Manual
- Practice Workbook
- Assessment Resources
- Teaching Resources

TECHNOLOGY
- Interactive Textbook
- TeacherExpress CD-Rom
- ExamView CD-ROM
- PHSchool.com

Additional Practice

1. Factor each polynomial.
   - **a.** $8x^2 + 22x + 5$
   - **b.** $8x^2 + 14x + 5$
   - **c.** $8x^2 - 6x - 5$
   - **d.** $8(x - 1)^2 - 6(x - 1) - 5$
   - **e.** $4x^4 - 19x^2 - 5$
   - **f.** $4(x + 1)^4 - 19(x + 1)^2 - 5$
   - **g.** $4(x + 1)^{10} - 19(x + 1)^5 - 5$
   - **h.** $(x^2 - 1)^2 - 2x^2 + 3$

2. Solve $5x - \frac{7}{x} = 2$ for x.

3. Solve each pair of equations and compare the roots.
   - **a.** $x^2 + 4x + 3 = 0$ and $x^2 + 12x + 27 = 0$
   - **b.** $2x^2 + 10x + 12 = 0$ and $2x^2 + 20x + 48 = 0$
   - **c.** $3x^2 + 18x + 24 = 0$ and $2x^2 + 3x + 1 = 0$
   - **d.** $5x^2 + 6x - 27 = 0$ and $x^2 + 6x - 135 = 0$

4. Find an equation with roots scaled in each of the following ways.
   - **a.** 2 times the roots of $6x^2 + 9x - 6 = 0$
   - **b.** 3 times the roots of $3x^2 + 13x - 10 = 0$
   - **c.** 5 times the roots of $5x^2 - 17x + 6 = 0$
   - **d.** 4 times the roots of $4x^2 - 3x - 7 = 0$

5. Factor each polynomial over $\mathbb{Z}$.
   - **a.** $x^3 - 8$
   - **b.** $x^3 + 8$
   - **c.** $125x^3 - 8$
   - **d.** $125x^3 + 8$
   - **e.** $(x - 2)^3 - 64$
   - **f.** $(2x + 1)^3 + 64$
   - **g.** $x^3 + 6x^2 + 12x + 8$
   - **h.** $4x^3 + x^2 + x - 3$
   - **i.** $y^4 - (2x - 1)^4$
   - **j.** $x^4 - y^2 - 4yz - 2z^2$
   - **k.** $(y + 2)^3 + z^3$
   - **l.** $x^3 + 3x^2 + 3x + 1$

6. Find the normal form of each polynomial.
   - **a.** $x + 2$
   - **b.** $(x + 2)^2$
   - **c.** $(x + 2)^3$
   - **d.** $(x + 2)^4$
   - **e.** $(x + 2)^5$

Practice: For Lesson 2.13, assign Exercises 5–6.

Lesson Overview

GOALS

- Factor polynomials by identifying quadratic-like or cubic-like polynomials.
- Factor polynomials by finding roots.

This challenging lesson is optional. This lession covers some of the main ideas described in the Investigation Overview. Students transform hard-to-factor polynomials into familiar quadratics and cubics. They will learn to recognize and factor polynomials that are in quadratic or cubic form, to rewrite some quadratics as the difference of two squares by adding and subtracting a perfect square, and to factor over $\mathbb{R}$ using the quadratic formula. The lesson ends with a dialog that previews the next chapter on complex numbers.

CHECK YOUR UNDERSTANDING

- Core: 1, 2, 3a–b, 4
- Optional: none
- Extension: 3c

MATERIALS

- CAS (recommended)

HOMEWORK

- Core: 5, 7, 8
- Optional: 6a–d, 10
- Extension: 6e, 9

VOCABULARY

- $\mathbb{Q}$ (the rational numbers)

Launch

You might ask students to think about how to factor the polynomial $9x^4 - 37x^2 + 4$ in For You to Do Problem 1.

For You to Do

Students should rewrite this as a quadratic in x^2. They can use the scaling method to factor the quadratic, if necessary.

2.14 Pippins and Cheese

There are many more methods of factoring, some of them quite involved. You will learn about a few more very beautiful ones later. For now, you will look at three more topics to round out the discussion.

> I will make an end of my dinner; there's pippins and cheese to come.
> —William Shakespeare

Quadratic-like and Cubic-like Polynomials

In Exercise 3a from Lesson 2.12, you factored this quadratic.

$$4x^2 - 13x + 3 = (4x - 1)(x - 3)$$

Then in Exercise 3e, you factored this fourth-degree polynomial.

$$4x^4 - 13x^2 + 3$$

One way to factor is to notice that this is a quadratic in x^2.

$$4x^4 - 13x^2 + 3 = 4(x^2)^2 - 13(x^2) + 3$$

So, if you let $z = x^2$, you have the same form as in Exercise 3a.

$$4z^2 - 13z + 3 = (4z - 1)(z - 3)$$

Now $z = x^2$, so you can convert to a polynomial in x.

$$4x^4 - 13x^2 + 3 = (4x^2 - 1)(x^2 - 3)$$

Then $4x^2 - 1$ factors some more over $\mathbb{Z}$, but $x^2 - 3$ does not.

> **Remember...**
> A fourth-degree polynomial is a quartic. Some people call a quartic that is a quadratic in x^2 a biquadratic.

For You to Do

1. Factor $9x^4 - 37x^2 + 4$ over $\mathbb{Z}$.

There are other kinds of quadratic-like polynomials—polynomials that are quadratic in some power of x.

Example 1

Problem Factor $x^6 - 7x^3 - 8$ over $\mathbb{Z}$.

Solution Is it a sixth degree polynomial? Well, yes, but it is a quadratic in x^3.

$$x^6 - 7x^3 - 8 = (x^3)^2 - 7(x^3) - 8$$

This is like $z^2 - 7z - 8$, where $z = x^3$. Write $z^2 - 7z - 8 = (z - 8)(z + 1)$.

For You to Do

2. Finish the example. Replace z with x^3 and finish the factorization.

Answers

For You to Do

1. $(3x + 1)(3x - 1)(x + 2)(x - 2)$
2. $(x - 2)(x^2 + 2x + 4)(x + 1) \cdot (x^2 - x + 1)$

So, some polynomials are quadratic-like. And some are cubic-like.

Example 2

Problem Factor $x^9 - 8x^6 + 4x^3 - 32$ over $\mathbb{Z}$.

Solution This is a cubic in x^3.

$$x^9 - 8x^6 + 4x^3 - 32 = (x^3)^3 - 8(x^3)^2 + 4(x^3) - 32$$

Let $z = x^3$. Then you get $x^9 - 8x^6 + 4x^3 - 32 = z^3 - 8z^2 + 4z - 32$.

In Example 2 from Lesson 2.13, you factored this cubic by grouping.

$$z^3 - 8z^2 + 4z - 32 = (z - 8)(z^2 + 4)$$

Now replace z with x^3.

$$(z - 8)(z^2 + 4) = (x^3 - 8)((x^3)^2 + 4) = (x^3 - 8)(x^6 + 4)$$

The polynomial $x^3 - 8$ factors as a difference of cubes.

$$(x^3 - 8) = (x - 2)(x^2 + 2x + 4)$$

So you have $x^9 - 8x^6 + 4x^3 - 32 = (x - 2)(x^2 + 2x + 4)(x^6 + 4)$.

Well, in Lesson 2.13 it was a different variable.

For Discussion

3. Are you done? Does either $x^2 + 2x + 4$ or $x^6 + 4$ factor over $\mathbb{Z}$?

Difference of Squares in Disguise

There is a class of biquadratics that you can factor as the difference of two squares if you add and subtract a perfect square. Here is how it works.

Example 3

Problem Factor $x^4 - 7x^2 + 9$ over $\mathbb{Z}$.

Solution This is a quadratic in x^2, but if you let $z = x^2$, you get $z^2 - 7z + 9$. This does not factor over $\mathbb{Z}$. But $x^4 - 7x^2 + 9$ almost looks like a perfect square. If only the $-7x^2$ were $-6x^2$, you could do something like this.

$$x^4 - 6x^2 + 9 = (x^2 - 3)^2$$

Well, you can make the middle term $-6x^2$ by adding and subtracting x^2.

$$x^4 - 7x^2 + 9 = x^4 - 6x^2 + 9 - x^2 = (x^2 - 3)^2 - x^2$$

That did it. This is a difference of squares, so now you can factor it.

$$x^4 - 7x^2 + 9 = (x^2 - 3)^2 - x^2 = (x^2 - 3 - x)(x^2 - 3 + x)$$

You can write each factor in normal form.

$$x^4 - 7x^2 + 9 = (x^2 - x - 3)(x^2 + x - 3)$$

Can you factor either of these factors any more?

For Discussion

3. Neither expression factors further.

Explore

EXAMPLE 2 This is a good place to point out that you need to check each factor to make sure it cannot be factored any further.

For Discussion

PROBLEM 3 You are not done. Students can check the quadratic with the quadratic formula. The polynomial $x^6 + 4$ also does not factor over $\mathbb{Z}$. If your calculator has a factoring capability, you can also use it to check on polynomials that you do not think will factor over $\mathbb{Z}$. For example,

$$\begin{aligned} x^4 + 4 &= x^4 + 4x^2 + 4 - 4x^2 \\ &= (x^2 + 2)^2 - 4x^2 \\ &= (x^2 + 2 - 2x)(x^2 + 2 + 2x) \\ &= (x^2 - 2x + 2)(x^2 + 2x + 2) \end{aligned}$$

These do not factor further. This is an example of a polynomial for which the "find a root, find a factor" method does not work.

EXAMPLE 3 This method only works if the term you need to add and subtract is a perfect square, making the expression a difference of squares.

For You to Do

You might give the students a hint by writing on the board: $x^4 + 4 = (x^2)^2 + 0 \cdot x^2 + 4$.

For Discussion

PROBLEM 5 These are not two different factorizations because

$$(x^4 + x^2 + 1) = (x^2 + x + 1)(x^2 - x + 1)$$

The second factorization is not in simplest form. To factor $x^4 + x^2 + 1$, add and subtract x^2 to get the difference of two squares.

For You to Do

4. Factor $x^4 + 4$ over $\mathbb{Z}$.

For Discussion

5. Suppose you want to factor $x^6 - 1$ over $\mathbb{Z}$. You have at least two ways to do it:

- as a difference of squares

$$\begin{aligned} x^6 - 1 &= (x^3)^2 - 1 \\ &= (x^3 - 1)(x^3 + 1) \\ &= (x - 1)(x^2 + x + 1)(x + 1)(x^2 - x + 1) \end{aligned}$$

- as a difference of cubes

$$\begin{aligned} x^6 - 1 &= (x^2)^3 - 1 \\ &= (x^2 - 1)((x^2)^2 + (x^2) + 1) \\ &= (x - 1)(x + 1)(x^4 + x^2 + 1) \end{aligned}$$

These look like two different factorizations. Are they?

Factoring Over Extensions

Throughout this investigation, the verb *factor* has meant "to factor over $\mathbb{Z}$." If you allow for polynomials with real-number coefficients, some polynomials that do not factor over $\mathbb{Z}$ will factor over $\mathbb{R}$. For example, $x^2 - 3$ is irreducible over $\mathbb{Z}$, but if you "move up" to $\mathbb{R}$, you can factor it.

$$x^2 - 3 = (x - \sqrt{3})(x + \sqrt{3})$$

Factoring over $\mathbb{R}$ is often the right setting for applying the Factor Theorem.

Another way to say that a polynomial does not factor over $\mathbb{Z}$ is to say that a polynomial is *irreducible* over $\mathbb{Z}$.

Sometimes you have to search a larger set of objects to find what you are looking for.

Answers

For You to Do

4. $(x^2 + 2x + 2)(x^2 - 2x + 2)$

For Discussion

5. They are the same because $(x^2 + x + 1)(x^2 - x + 1) = x^4 + x^2 + 1$.

Example 4

Problem Factor $x^2 - 14x + 1$ over $\mathbb{R}$.

Solution The polynomial does not factor over $\mathbb{Z}$. In fact, the quadratic formula shows that its two roots are $7 + 4\sqrt{3}$ and $7 - 4\sqrt{3}$.

The Factor Theorem says that if $7 + 4\sqrt{3}$ is a root, $(x - (7 + 4\sqrt{3}))$, or $(x - 7 - 4\sqrt{3})$, must be a factor.

Similarly, another factor must be

$$(x - (7 - 4\sqrt{3})) = (x - 7 + 4\sqrt{3})$$

Since the original is a monic quadratic, the factorization must be

$$x^2 - 14x + 1 = (x - 7 - 4\sqrt{3})(x - 7 + 4\sqrt{3})$$

Check that the quadratic formula gives these roots.

For You to Do

6. Expand the product $(x - 7 - 4\sqrt{3})(x - 7 + 4\sqrt{3})$. (*Hint:* Why is this equal to $(x - 7)^2 - 48$?)

For Discussion

7. Find real numbers a and b such that $(a + b\sqrt{3})^2 = 7 + 4\sqrt{3}$.

8. Find four real roots for the equation $x^4 - 14x^2 + 1 = 0$.

Factoring over the real numbers can sometimes lead to puzzling situations.

Minds in Action episode 9

Tony and Sasha are discussing Exercise 5 from Lesson 2.13.

Tony We want to factor $x^3 - 15x - 4$. Well, I know that 4 is a root of $x^3 - 15x - 4 = 0$, so $(x - 4)$ is a factor.

Sasha And I can use polynomial division to find that the other factor is $x^2 + 4x + 1$.

Tony If we apply the quadratic formula to $x^2 + 4x + 1 = 0$, we get the roots $2 + \sqrt{3}$ and $2 - \sqrt{3}$. So, the factorization over $\mathbb{R}$ is

$$(x - 4)(x - 2 - \sqrt{3})(x - 2 + \sqrt{3})$$

How did Tony get this factorization?

For You to Do

6. $((x - 7) - 4\sqrt{3})((x - 7) + 4\sqrt{3})$
$= (x - 7)^2 - (4\sqrt{3})^2$
$= x^2 - 14x + 49 - 48$
$= x^2 - 14x + 1$

For Discussion

7. $a = 2, b = 1$; $a = -2, b = -1$;
$a = \sqrt{3}, b = \frac{2\sqrt{3}}{3}$;
$a = -\sqrt{3}, b = \frac{-2\sqrt{3}}{3}$

8. $\pm\sqrt{7 + 4\sqrt{3}}, \pm\sqrt{7 - 4\sqrt{3}}$

For You to Do

Some students might discover that they could have factored the original polynomial by adding and subtracting 48:

$$\begin{aligned} x^2 - 14x + 1 &= x^2 - 14x + 1 + 48 - 48 \\ &= (x^2 - 14x + 49) - 48 \\ &= (x - 7)^2 - 48 \\ &= (x - 7 + \sqrt{48})(x - 7 - \sqrt{48}) \\ &= (x - 7 + 4\sqrt{3})(x - 7 - 4\sqrt{3}) \end{aligned}$$

For Discussion

PROBLEM 7 $(2 + \sqrt{3})^2 = 7 + 4\sqrt{3}$

PROBLEM 8 Using Example 4, you get:

$$\begin{aligned} x^4 - 14x^2 + 1 &= (x^2)^2 - 14(x^2) + 1 \\ &= (x^2 - 7 - 4\sqrt{3})(x^2 - 7 + 4 - 3) \end{aligned}$$

So you solve

$$x^2 - 7 - 4 - \sqrt{3} = 0$$

and

$$x^2 - 7 + 4\sqrt{3} = 0.$$

Minds in Action

This is another example of "Find a root, find a factor." Make sure that students are careful with parentheses:

$$(x - (2 + \sqrt{3})) = x - 2 - \sqrt{3}$$

and

$$(x - (2 - \sqrt{3})) = x - 2 + \sqrt{3}.$$

Minds in Action

Review Sasha's favorite identity. Remember that this is a preview of topics that will be covered in the next chapter, so students will not be able to find $r + s$ (yet).

For You to Do

PROBLEM 9 foreshadows operations with complex numbers.

Wrap Up

As a class, discuss what methods students could use to factor each of the polynomials in Exercises 1 and 2. Then let students work together to find the factors.

Assessment Resources

Lesson Quiz 2.14

1. Factor each polynomial over $\mathbb{Z}$.
   a. $x^4 - 18x^2 + 32$
   b. $x^6 - 10x^3 + 25$
   c. $x^6 - 64$
   d. $x^6 + 5x^3 + 9$
2. Factor each polynomial over $\mathbb{R}$.
   a. $x^2 - 8x - 12$
   b. $x^2 + 6x + 3$
3. Find a polynomial with integer coefficients that has a zero for each given value.
   a. $4 + \sqrt{7}$
   b. $4 - \sqrt{7}$
   c. $\sqrt{7} + \sqrt{5}$

Sasha I've been thinking. I wonder if we could find the roots of the cubic $x^3 - 15x - 4$ another way. Let's use my favorite identity from the For Discussion Problem 6 in Lesson 2.13.

Sasha writes $(r + s)^3 - 3rs(r + s) - (r^3 + s^3) = 0$ *on the board.*

Tony Huh?

Sasha My idea is to think of the root as $r + s$—call this z. So the identity is

$$z^3 - 3rs \cdot z - (r^3 + s^3) = 0$$

Now match this up with the equation

$$x^3 - 15x - 4 = 0$$

I want to find numbers r and s such that

$$3rs = 15 \text{ and } r^3 + s^3 = 4$$

or

$$rs = 5 \text{ and } r^3 + s^3 = 4$$

Tony I get it. This almost looks like a sum-and-product problem. So, let's cube the first equation.

$$r^3s^3 = 125 \text{ and } r^3 + s^3 = 4$$

Now we can find r^3 and s^3, since we know their sum and product. When we're done, we just need to take the cube roots of the answers and we'll have r and s. And then we should be able to recover our three roots: 4 and $2 \pm \sqrt{3}$.

Sasha Well, by the sum-and-product identity, r^3 and s^3 are roots of $x^2 - 4x + 125 = 0$.

So we can apply the quadratic formula and get

$$r^3 = \frac{4 + \sqrt{16 - 500}}{2} \text{ and } r^3 = \frac{4 - \sqrt{16 - 500}}{2}$$

When we simplify r and s, we get something very odd.

$$r^3 = \frac{4 + \sqrt{-484}}{2} \text{ and } r^3 = \frac{4 - \sqrt{-484}}{2}$$

How can this be? We know the roots, and they are all real.

Tony I have no idea. The next chapter in this book is "Complex Numbers." Well, $\frac{4 + \sqrt{-484}}{2}$ is certainly as complex as they come. Let's wait until Chapter 3 and then come back to this.

Sasha agrees, very reluctantly.

For You to Do

9. Suppose that $\frac{4 + \sqrt{-484}}{2}$ and $\frac{4 - \sqrt{-484}}{2}$ actually exist and that they obey the basic rules of algebra. What are their sum and their product?

Answers

For You to Do

9. sum: 4, product: 125

Exercises *Practicing Habits of Mind*

Check Your Understanding

1. Factor each polynomial over $\mathbb{Z}$.
   a. $x^4 - x^2 - 6$
   b. $x^6 - 9x^3 + 8$
   c. $x^4 - 16$
   d. $x^6 - 8$
   e. $x^4 - 16y^4$
   f. $x^6 + 8$
   g. $x^4 - 9x^2 + 16$
   h. $x^4 + x^2 + 1$
2. Factor each polynomial over $\mathbb{R}$.
   a. $x^2 - 2x - 4$
   b. $x^2 - x - 1$
3. Find a polynomial with integer coefficients that has a zero for each given value.
   a. $2 + \sqrt{3}$
   b. $2 - \sqrt{3}$
   c. **Take It Further** $\sqrt{2} + \sqrt{3}$
4. Can a polynomial be irreducible over $\mathbb{Z}$ but factor over $\mathbb{Q}$? Explain.

Think of quadratics, for example. The symbol $\mathbb{Q}$ means the rational numbers.

On Your Own

5. Factor each polynomial over $\mathbb{Z}$.
   a. $x^4 - 11x^2 + 28$
   b. $x^6 - 6x^3 + 9$
   c. $x^6 - 27$
   d. $x^6 + 3x^4 + 3x^2 + 1$
   e. $x^4 + 9x^2 + 25$
   f. $x^4 - 3a^2x^2 + a^4$
   g. $x^6 - 1$
   h. $x^8 - 1$
6. Solve each equation.
   a. $\sqrt{x} = 7$
   b. $\sqrt{x - 3} = 7$
   c. $\sqrt{x - 3} = \sqrt{78}$
   d. $\sqrt{x - 3} = \sqrt{x^2 - 15}$
   e. **Take It Further** $\sqrt{2x - 5} - \sqrt{x - 2} = 2$

Exercises

HOMEWORK
- Core: 5, 7, 8
- Optional: 6a–d, 10
- Extension: 6e, 9

Check Your Understanding

EXERCISE 1 As with the factoring exercises in the previous lesson, you should carefully decide which problems you would like to assign. The solutions indicate which parts are related.

EXERCISE 2 The roots of the second expression are the golden ratio and its opposite reciprocal.

EXERCISE 3 The last part of this exercise is more involved than the others. A goal for students is to recognize that if $a + \sqrt{b}$ is a root of a polynomial with integer coefficients, $a - \sqrt{b}$ must also be a root.

On Your Own

EXERCISE 5 As with other factoring, you should check in advance to see if there are techniques that your class needs more experience with before they can complete certain parts of this exercise. Consider assigning exercises based on what students worked on in the lesson.

EXERCISE 6 The last two parts of this exercise include some false answers that result from squaring both sides of the equation in order to solve it. Whenever students square both sides, they should remember to check their answers.

Exercises

1. a. $(x^2 + 2)(x^2 - 3)$
b. $(x - 1)(x^2 + x + 1)(x - 2) \cdot (x^2 + 2x + 4)$
c. $(x^2 + 4)(x + 2)(x - 2)$
d. $(x^2 - 2)(x^4 + 2x^2 + 4)$
e. $(x^2 + 4y^2)(x + 2y)(x - 2y)$
f. $(x^2 + 2)(x^4 - 2x^2 + 4)$
g. $(x^2 + x - 4)(x^2 - x - 4)$
h. $(x^2 + x + 1)(x^2 - x + 1)$

2. a. $(x - 1 - \sqrt{5})(x - 1 + \sqrt{5})$
b. $\left(x - 0.5 - \frac{\sqrt{5}}{2}\right)\left(x - 0.5 + \frac{\sqrt{5}}{2}\right)$

3. a. Answers may vary. Sample: $x^2 - 4x + 1$
b. Answers may vary. Sample: $x^2 - 4x + 1$
c. $x^4 - 10x^2 + 1 = 0$

4. Yes; sample: $x^2 - \frac{1}{4} = \left(x - \frac{1}{2}\right)\left(x + \frac{1}{2}\right)$

5. a. $(x^2 - 7)(x + 2)(x - 2)$
b. $(x^3 - 3)(x^3 - 3)$
c. $(x^2 - 3)(x^4 + 3x^2 + 9)$
d. $(x^2 + 1)(x^2 + 1)(x^2 + 1)$
e. $(x^2 - x + 5)(x^2 + x + 5)$
f. $(x^2 + ax - a^2)(x^2 - ax - a^2)$
g. $(x + 1)(x^2 - x + 1)(x - 1) \cdot (x^2 + x + 1)$
h. $(x^4 + 1)(x^2 + 1)(x + 1)(x - 1)$

6. a. 49
b. 52
c. 81
d. 4
e. 27

EXERCISE 9 This is a challenging problem. Expand the right side $x^4 + (a + b)x^3 + (2 + ab)x^2 + (a + b)x + 1$ and set up a system of equations to solve for a and b: $a + b = 1$ and $2 + ab = 1$.

Maintain Your Skills

EXERCISE 10 Some of these polynomials can be challenging for students to factor by hand, but the factorings are accessible if they use a CAS.

Additional Resources

PRINT RESOURCES
- Solution Manual
- Practice Workbook
- Assessment Resources
- Teaching Resources

TECHNOLOGY
- Interactive Textbook
- TeacherExpress CD-Rom
- ExamView CD-ROM
- PHSchool.com

Additional Practice

1. Factor each polynomial over $\mathbb{Z}$.

a. $x^4 - 12x^2 + 35$ **b.** $x^6 - 8x^3 + 16$
c. $x^6 - 8$ **d.** $x^6 + 2x^5 + 3x^4 + 2x^3 + x^2$
e. $x^4 + 11x^2 + 36$ **f.** $x^6 - 3a^3x^3 + a^6$
g. $x^6 - 64$ **h.** $x^8 - 64$

2. Factor each polynomial over $\mathbb{R}$.

a. $x^2 - 8x - 5$
b. $2x^2 + 4x - 8$

3. Find a polynomial with integer coefficients that has a zero for each given value.

a. $3 + \sqrt{5}$
b. $3 - \sqrt{5}$
c. $\sqrt{3} + \sqrt{5}$

4. Solve each equation.

a. $\sqrt{x} = 11$ **b.** $\sqrt{x - 2} = 11$
c. $\sqrt{x - 2} = \sqrt{53}$ **d.** $\sqrt{x - 2} = \sqrt{x^2 - 8}$

5. Simplify each rational expression.

a. $\frac{x^2 - 4}{x + 2}$ **b.** $\frac{x^3 - 8}{x - 2}$
c. $\frac{x^4 - 16}{(x + 2)(x - 2)}$ **d.** $\frac{x^5 - 32}{x - 2}$
e. $\frac{x^6 - 64}{(x + 2)(x - 2)}$ **f.** $\frac{x^8 - 256}{(x + 2)(x - 2)(x^2 + 4)}$
g. $\frac{x^9 - 64}{(x + 2)(x - 2)(x^3 - 4)}$ **h.** $\frac{x^{12} - 64}{(x + 2)(x - 2)(x^2 - 2)}$

6. Let $f(x) = \frac{2x^2 - 3x - 9}{3x^2 - 7x - 6}$.

Suppose you define $g(x)$ as the same fraction, except it is in simplest form. What is $g(x)$? How do the graphs of $f(x)$ and $g(x)$ compare?

7. Find numbers A and B such that $\frac{1}{(x + 1)(x + 2)} = \frac{A}{x + 1} + \frac{B}{x + 2}$.

Practice: For Lesson 2.14, assign Exercises 1–4.

7. Derman is thinking about For Discussion Problem 5. He says, "I have a third way to factor $x^6 - 1$. I remember it from a homework problem a long time ago.

$$x^6 - 1 = (x - 1)(x^5 + x^4 + x^3 + x^2 + x + 1)$$

This is different from both answers."

Is Derman's factorization really different?

8. Standardized Test Prep What is the greatest number of binomial factors over $\mathbb{Z}$ that you can use in a product to get $x^4 - 1$?

A. 2
B. 3
C. 4
D. 5

9. Take It Further Find real numbers a and b such that

$$x^4 + x^3 + x^2 + x + 1 = (x^2 + ax + 1)(x^2 + bx + 1)$$

Go Online PHSchool.com
For additional practice, go to **Web Code:** bfa-0214

Maintain Your Skills

10. Factor each polynomial over $\mathbb{Z}$.

a. $1 + x + x^2 + x^3$
b. $1 + x + x^2 + x^3 + x^4 + x^5$
c. $1 + x + x^2 + x^3 + x^4 + x^5 + x^6 + x^7$
d. $1 + x + x^2 + x^3 + x^4 + x^5 + x^6 + x^7 + x^8 + x^9$

Is there a general method here?

Answers

7. No, the second term in Derman's factoring can be further factored as $(x + 1)(x^2 - x + 1)(x^2 + x + 1)$, so the total factorings are the same.

8. B

9. $a = \frac{1 + \sqrt{5}}{2}$, $b = \frac{1 - \sqrt{5}}{2}$

10. a. $(x + 1)(x^2 + 1)$
b. $(x + 1)(x^2 - x + 1)(x^2 + x + 1)$
c. $(x + 1)(x^2 + 1)(x^4 + 1)$
d. $(x + 1)(x^4 - x^3 + x^2 - x + 1) \cdot (x^4 + x^3 + x^2 + x + 1)$

2.15 Rational Expressions

Polynomials have an arithmetic that is similar to the arithmetic of ordinary integers. In both systems, you can add, subtract, multiply, and divide, and these operations obey the same basic rules. You also have long division in both systems. You can use these facts to show that you can factor anything (into primes for an integer and into irreducibles for a polynomial) in exactly one way.

There may be more than one way to carry out the factorization, but there will only be one final result.

Factoring polynomials is useful when you want to solve polynomial equations. Factoring integers is useful when you want to do arithmetic with fractions. That is, when you want to simplify a fraction and when you want to add two fractions.

For You to Do

1. Just for old-time's sake, simplify $\frac{25{,}725}{86{,}625}$.
2. Find the sum $\frac{18}{49} + \frac{5}{21}$.

Because polynomials have an arithmetic (the basic rules of algebra) that is so much like the arithmetic of $\mathbb{Z}$, you can do arithmetic with fractions of polynomials.

Example 1

Problem Simplify $\frac{x^2 - 5x + 6}{x^2 - 9}$.

Solution

$$\begin{aligned}\frac{x^2 - 5x + 6}{x^2 - 9} &= \frac{(x-3)(x-2)}{(x-3)(x+3)} \\ &= \frac{\cancel{(x-3)}(x-2)}{\cancel{(x-3)}(x+3)} \\ &= \frac{(x-2)}{(x+3)}\end{aligned}$$

Notice that this expression is equivalent to the original everywhere except at $x = 3$. At $x = 3$, the original rational expression was undefined, but this new expression is equal to $\frac{1}{6}$ at $x = 3$.

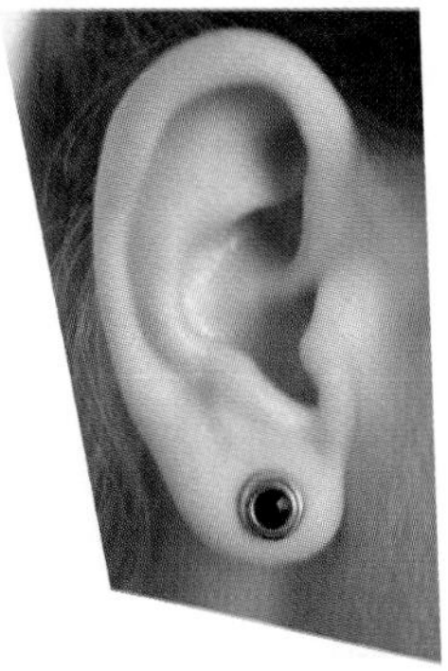

When you get your ear pierced, your ear remains the same everywhere except at one point.

For You to Do

1. $$\begin{aligned}\frac{25{,}725}{86{,}625} &= \frac{3 \cdot 5 \cdot 5 \cdot 7 \cdot 7 \cdot 7}{3 \cdot 3 \cdot 5 \cdot 5 \cdot 5 \cdot 7 \cdot 11} \\ &= \frac{7 \cdot 7}{3 \cdot 5 \cdot 11} \\ &= \frac{49}{165}\end{aligned}$$

2. $\frac{18}{49} + \frac{5}{21} = \frac{54}{147} + \frac{35}{147} = \frac{89}{147}$

Lesson Overview

GOAL

- Factor polynomials to solve polynomial equations.

This lesson is optional and is included for those who need or want to teach this material in *Algebra 2*. Rational expressions are introduced, and techniques from previous lessons are used to simplify them and to perform the basic operations of addition and subtraction, paying attention to restrictions on the domain. Exercises also include some work with partial fractions.

CHECK YOUR UNDERSTANDING
- Core: 1, 2
- Optional: 3, 4
- Extension: 5

MATERIALS
- CAS (recommended)
- graph paper
- graphing calculators
- Blackline Master 2.15

HOMEWORK
- Core: 9, 10
- Optional: 6, 7
- Extension: 8, 11

VOCABULARY
- rational expression

Launch

Begin this lesson with For You to Do Problems 1 and 2.

Explore

For You to Do

PROBLEM 2 is the place to draw parallels between the work of this section with polynomials and the familiar work with numbers. Have students complete this work without a calculator. Remind students that simplifying a fraction or finding the least common denominator is easier when you look at the factored form of the numbers.

EXAMPLE 1 The graph of $y = \frac{x^2 - 5x + 6}{x^2 - 9}$ will be identical to the graph of $y = \frac{x-2}{x+3}$, *except* there will be a "hole" at the point $\left(3, \frac{1}{6}\right)$.

For You to Do

Emphasize that students should factor first.

EXAMPLE 2 Refer to For You to Do Problem 2 for parallels to arithmetic. It might help to write $x^2 - 1$ in factored form.

For You to Do

Warn students to be careful of the subtraction sign in front of the second fraction. They want to subtract the entire expression in the numerator.

Wrap Up

If time allows, go over Exercise 1 to review simplifying fractions and Exercise 4 to review adding and subtracting fractions.

Assessment Resources

Lesson Quiz 2.15

1. Simplify each rational expression.

a. $\frac{x^2 - 9}{x + 3}$

b. $\frac{x^3 - 27}{x - 3}$

c. $\frac{x^4 - 81}{(x + 3)(x - 3)}$

d. $\frac{x^6 - 1}{x^4 - 1}$

e. $\frac{x^8 - 81}{(x + 3)(x - 3)(x^2 + 3)}$

f. $\frac{2x^2 + 5x - 12}{3x^2 + 7x - 20}$

2. Find numbers A and B such that $\frac{1}{(x - 2)(x + 3)} = \frac{A}{x - 2} + \frac{B}{x + 3}$.

3. Write each sum as a single rational expression.

a. $\frac{x}{x + y} + \frac{y}{x - y}$

b. $\frac{x + 2}{2x - 2} + \frac{x - 3}{x^2 - 6x + 5}$

For You to Do

3. Simplify $\frac{x^3 - 1}{x^2 - 1}$.

Example 2

Problem Write this sum as a single rational expression.

$$\frac{5x + 1}{x^2 - 1} + \frac{3}{x - 1} + \frac{2}{x + 1}$$

Solution Just as with integers, you need to find a common denominator. Since $x^2 - 1 = (x - 1)(x + 1)$, all three denominators are factors of $x^2 - 1$. You can use that expression as the denominator. Multiply each fraction by a form of 1 that makes its denominator $x^2 - 1$.

$$\begin{aligned}\frac{5x + 1}{x^2 - 1} + \frac{3}{x - 1} + \frac{2}{x + 1} &= \frac{5x + 1}{x^2 - 1} + \frac{3}{x - 1} \cdot \frac{(x + 1)}{(x + 1)} + \frac{2}{x + 1} \cdot \frac{(x - 1)}{(x - 1)} \\ &= \frac{5x + 1}{x^2 - 1} + \frac{3(x + 1)}{x^2 - 1} + \frac{2(x - 1)}{x^2 - 1} \\ &= \frac{(5x + 1) + 3(x + 1) + 2(x - 1)}{x^2 - 1} \\ &= \frac{10x + 2}{x^2 - 1} \\ &= \frac{2(5x + 1)}{x^2 - 1}\end{aligned}$$

Habits of Mind

Think about it more than one way. If you are thinking of the polynomials as expressions, you call fractions like these **rational expressions.** If you are thinking of the polynomials as functions, you call them rational functions.

For You to Do

4. Write this difference as a single rational expression.

$$\frac{10}{x + 2} - \frac{6}{x - 2}$$

Answers

For You to Do

3. $\frac{x^2 + x + 1}{x + 1}; x \neq -1$

4. $\frac{4x - 32}{(x + 2)(x - 2)}$

Exercises *Practicing Habits of Mind*

Check Your Understanding

1. Simplify each rational expression.

a. $\frac{15x}{5x^2}$ **b.** $\frac{x^2 - y^2}{(x + y)}$

c. $\frac{x^2 - y^2}{(x + y)^2}$ **d.** $\frac{x^2 - 1}{x^4 - 1}$

e. $\frac{2x^2 + x - 6}{3x^2 + 4x - 4}$ **f.** $\frac{3 - x - 3x^4 + x^5}{3 - x - 3x^3 + x^4}$

2. Let $f(x) = \frac{2x^2 + x - 6}{3x^2 + 4x - 4}$.

Suppose you define $g(x)$ by the same fraction, except the fraction is in simplest form. How do the graphs of $f(x)$ and $g(x)$ compare?

3. Write each sum as a single rational expression.

a. $\frac{b}{b - a} + \frac{a}{a - b}$

b. $\frac{1}{(x - a)(a - b)} + \frac{1}{(x - b)(b - a)}$

4. Write each sum as a single rational expression.

a. $\frac{1 + 2x}{3x - 3} + \frac{5 - x}{x^2 - 5x + 4}$

b. $\frac{2}{x - 3} - \frac{2}{x + 3} - \frac{1}{x}$

c. $\frac{1}{(a - b)(b - c)} + \frac{1}{(b - c)(c - a)} + \frac{1}{(c - a)(a - b)}$

5. Take It Further Find numbers A and B such that

$$\frac{1}{(x - 1)(x - 3)} = \frac{A}{(x - 1)} + \frac{B}{(x - 3)}$$

On Your Own

6. Simplify each rational expression.

a. $\frac{x^2 - 1}{x - 1}$ **b.** $\frac{x^4 - 1}{x^2 - 1}$ **c.** $\frac{x^6 - 1}{x^3 - 1}$

d. $\frac{x^8 - 1}{x^4 - 1}$ **e.** $\frac{x^{10} - 1}{x^5 - 1}$

Exercises

HOMEWORK
- Core: 9, 10
- Optional: 6, 7
- Extension: 8, 11

Check Your Understanding

EXERCISE 1 The parts of this exercise increase in complexity. Encourage students to stick with the more complicated parts and to share strategies. You may want to use Blackline Master 2.15 here.

EXERCISE 2 The expression here is the same one from Exercise 1 part (e).

EXERCISE 4 As with earlier exercises, these parts increase in complexity. Use your judgment to decide how many of the parts to assign.

EXERCISE 5 This type of calculation comes in handy when students learn the partial fractions method of integration in a calculus course.

Exercises

1. a. $\frac{3}{x}$ **b.** $x - y$ **c.** $\frac{x - y}{x + y}$

d. $\frac{1}{x^2 + 1}$ **e.** $\frac{2x - 3}{3x - 2}$

f. $\frac{(x + 1)(x^2 + 1)}{x^2 + x + 1}$

2. $f(x) = \frac{(2x - 3)(x + 2)}{(3x - 2)(x + 2)}$ and $g(x) = \frac{2x - 3}{3x - 2}$. The graph of $f(x)$ will have a "hole" at $f(-2)$, or $(-2, 0.875)$, since $f(-2)$ is undefined. The graph of $g(x)$ will not have a hole, since $g(-2)$ is defined.

3. a. 1 **b.** $\frac{1}{(x - a)(x - b)}$

4. a. $\frac{2x^2 - 10x + 11}{3(x - 1)(x - 4)}$

b. $\frac{-x^2 + 12x + 9}{x(x - 3)(x + 3)}$

c. 0

5. $A = -\frac{1}{2}, B = \frac{1}{2}$

6. a. $x + 1$ **b.** $x^2 + 1$

c. $x^3 + 1$ **d.** $x^4 + 1$

e. $x^5 + 1$

On Your Own

EXERCISE 8 is another example of the partial fractions method. Students will use this when they study calculus. The idea is to write the fraction as the sum of two or more simpler fractions—sort of addition in "reverse." Partial fractions are an integration tool in calculus.

Maintain Your Skills

EXERCISE 10 The parts involving $x^9 - 1$ and $x^{10} - 1$ are especially complex to factor by hand. See how students fare with the other parts first or suggest they use their CAS to do some of the factoring.

Additional Resources

PRINT RESOURCES
- Solution Manual
- Practice Workbook
- Assessment Resources
- Teaching Resources

TECHNOLOGY
- Interactive Textbook
- TeacherExpress CD-Rom
- ExamView CD-ROM
- PHSchool.com

Additional Practice

1. Factor each polynomial over $\mathbb{Z}$.
   a. $x^4 - 12x^2 + 35$ b. $x^6 - 8x^3 + 16$
   c. $x^6 - 8$ d. $x^6 + 2x^5 + 3x^4 + 2x^3 + x^2$
   e. $x^4 + 11x^2 + 36$ f. $x^6 - 3a^3x^3 + a^6$
   g. $x^6 - 64$ h. $x^8 - 64$

2. Factor each polynomial over $\mathbb{R}$.
   a. $x^2 - 8x - 5$
   b. $2x^2 + 4x - 8$

3. Find a polynomial with integer coefficients that has a zero for each given value.
   a. $3 + \sqrt{5}$
   b. $3 - \sqrt{5}$
   c. $\sqrt{3} + \sqrt{5}$

4. Solve each equation.
   a. $\sqrt{x} = 11$ b. $\sqrt{x - 2} = 11$
   c. $\sqrt{x - 2} = \sqrt{53}$ d. $\sqrt{x - 2} = \sqrt{x^2 - 8}$

5. Simplify each rational expression.
   a. $\frac{x^2 - 4}{x + 2}$ b. $\frac{x^3 - 8}{x - 2}$
   c. $\frac{x^4 - 16}{(x + 2)(x - 2)}$ d. $\frac{x^5 - 32}{x - 2}$
   e. $\frac{x^6 - 64}{(x + 2)(x - 2)}$ f. $\frac{x^8 - 256}{(x + 2)(x - 2)(x^2 + 4)}$
   g. $\frac{x^9 - 64}{(x + 2)(x - 2)(x^3 - 4)}$ h. $\frac{x^{12} - 64}{(x + 2)(x - 2)(x^2 - 2)}$

6. Let $f(x) = \frac{2x^2 - 3x - 9}{3x^2 - 7x - 6}$.

   Suppose you define $g(x)$ as the same fraction, except it is in simplest form. What is $g(x)$? How do the graphs of $f(x)$ and $g(x)$ compare?

7. Find numbers A and B such that $\frac{1}{(x + 1)(x + 2)} = \frac{A}{x + 1} + \frac{B}{x + 2}$.

Practice: For Lesson 2.15, assign Exercises 5–7.

7. Write each expression as the quotient of two polynomials.

a. $1 + \frac{1}{x - 1} - \frac{1}{1 + x}$ b. $1 - \frac{2}{1 + x^2}$

c. $\frac{1}{x - 2} - \frac{1}{x - 1}$ d. $\frac{1}{2(x - 3)} - \frac{1}{x - 2} + \frac{1}{2(x - 1)}$

e. $\frac{2}{(x - 1)^2} + \frac{1}{x - 1} - \frac{1}{x - 2}$

Go Online PHSchool.com
For additional practice, go to **Web Code:** bfa-0215

8. Take It Further Find numbers A and B such that

$$\frac{1}{(x - 1)(x - 2)} = \frac{A}{x - 1} + \frac{B}{x - 2}$$

9. Standardized Test Prep What is $\frac{x^2 - 9x + 20}{-x^2 + 6x - 8}$ written in lowest terms?

A. $\frac{x - 5}{2 - x}$ B. $\frac{x - 5}{x - 2}$

C. $\frac{x - 4}{x - 2}$ D. $\frac{x - 5}{x - 4}$

Maintain Your Skills

10. Simplify each rational expression.

a. $\frac{x^3 - 1}{x - 1}$ b. $\frac{x^4 - 1}{(x - 1)(x + 1)}$

c. $\frac{x^5 - 1}{x - 1}$ d. $\frac{x^6 - 1}{(x - 1)(x + 1)(x^2 + x + 1)}$

e. $\frac{x^8 - 1}{(x - 1)(x + 1)(x^2 + 1)}$ f. $\frac{x^9 - 1}{(x - 1)(x^2 + x + 1)}$

g. $\frac{x^{10} - 1}{(x - 1)(x + 1)(x^4 + x^3 + x^2 + x + 1)}$

h. $\frac{x^{12} - 1}{(x - 1)(x + 1)(x^2 + x + 1)(x^2 + 1)(x^2 - x + 1)}$

Go Online Video Tutor PHSchool.com
Web Code: bfe-0775

11. Take It Further Suppose that $f(x) = \frac{1}{(x - 1)(x - 2)}$. Find each value.

a. $f(3) + f(4) + f(5)$

b. $f(3) + f(4) + f(5) + f(6)$

c. $f(3) + f(4) + f(5) + f(6) + f(7)$

d. $f(3) + f(4) + f(5) + f(6) + f(7) + \cdots + f(23)$

e. $f(3) + f(4) + f(5) + f(6) + f(7) + \cdots + f(n)$ (in terms of n)

Answers

7. a. $\frac{x^2 + 1}{x^2 - 1}$

b. $\frac{x^2 - 1}{x^2 + 1}$

c. $\frac{1}{(x - 1)(x - 2)}$

d. $\frac{1}{(x - 3)(x - 2)(x - 1)}$

e. $\frac{x - 3}{(x - 1)^2(x - 2)}$

8. $A = -1$, $B = 1$

9. A

10. a. $x^2 + x + 1$

b. $x^2 + 1$

c. $x^4 + x^3 + x^2 + x + 1$

d. $x^2 - x + 1$

e. $x^4 + 1$

f. $x^6 + x^3 + 1$

g. $x^4 - x^3 + x^2 - x + 1$

h. $x^4 - x^2 + 1$

11. a. $\frac{3}{4}$ **b.** $\frac{4}{5}$ **c.** $\frac{5}{6}$

d. $\frac{21}{22}$ **e.** $\frac{n - 2}{n - 1}$

Mathematical Reflections 2D

In this investigation, you learned to factor polynomials by scaling, by finding roots, by using the sums and differences of squares and cubes, by grouping, and by identifying quadratic-like or cubic-like polynomials. These questions will help you summarize what you have learned.

1. Factor each polynomial.
   a. $6x^2 - x - 15$
   b. $6x^2 + x - 15$
   c. $35x^2 + 79x + 42$

2. Factor each polynomial over $\mathbb{Z}$.
   a. $x^3 - 125$
   b. $x^3 + 125$
   c. $27x^3 - 64$
   d. $27x^3 + 64$
   e. $(x - 1)^3 - 27$
   f. $(2x - 3)^3 + 27$
   g. $x^3 + 3x^2 - 9x - 27$
   h. $x^3 - 4x^2 + 4x - 3$
   i. $x^4 - (2x + 1)^4$
   j. $x^2 - y^2 + 2yz - z^2$

3. Factor each polynomial over $\mathbb{Z}$.
   a. $35x^4 + 79x^2 + 42$
   b. $6x^6 + x^3 - 15$
   c. $x^4 - 81$
   d. $x^6 - 27$
   e. $4x^4 - 5x^2 + 1$
   f. $x^4 + 5x^2 + 9$

4. For each number, find an equation with integer coefficients that has that number as a solution.
   a. $\sqrt{5}$
   b. $\sqrt{5} + \sqrt{7}$
   c. **Take It Further** $3 + \sqrt{5} + \sqrt{7}$

5. Write each expression as a single rational expression.
   a. $1 - \frac{x + 2}{x^2 + x + 1}$
   b. $1 - \frac{2}{3(1 + x)} + \frac{2(x - 2)}{3(1 - x + x^2)}$

6. How do you factor nonmonic quadratics?

7. How do you factor differences and sums of cubes?

8. Does $x^4 + 4$ factor over $\mathbb{Z}$?

Vocabulary and Notation

In this investigation, you learned these terms and symbols. Make sure you understand what each one means and how to use it.

- **difference of cubes**
- **quadratic formula**
- **rational expression**
- **sum of cubes**
- **$\mathbb{Z}$ (the integers)**
- **$\mathbb{Q}$ (the rational numbers)**

Mathematical Reflections

1. a. $(3x - 5)(2x + 3)$
   b. $(3x + 5)(2x - 3)$
   c. $(7x + 6)(5x + 7)$

2–3. See back of book.

4. a. $x^2 - 5 = 0$
   b. $x^4 - 24x^2 + 4 = 0$
   c. $x^4 - 12x^3 + 30x^2 + 36x - 131 = 0$

5. a. $\frac{x^2 - 1}{x^2 + x + 1}$
   b. $\frac{x^3 - 1}{x^3 + 1}$

6. You can take out common factors, use special patterns (difference of two squares, perfect square trinomial), use the quadratic formula, or use scaling.

7. Use the patterns $x^3 - y^3 = (x - y)(x^2 + xy + y^2)$ or $x^3 + y^3 = (x + y)(x^2 - xy + y^2)$.

8. $(x^2 + 2x + 2)(x^2 - 2x + 2)$

Mathematical Reflections

EXERCISES 6–8 At the start of the investigation, you may have assigned these as Questions 1–3 for students to think and write about.

Project

This project asks students to read through a mathematical proof and make it their own. By supplying details not in the text, students come to understand the reasons behind each step in the proof. An early step in learning to write original proofs is this process of reading and working through a piece of mathematical exposition.

Project Using Mathematical Habits

Heron's Formula

One of the most beautiful theorems in geometry is named after Heron of Alexandria, who lived about A.D. 62. It gives a formula for finding the area of a triangle in terms of the lengths of its three sides. The purpose of this project is to derive Heron's formula by using the ideas of this chapter.

Heron's Formula

If the sides of a triangle have lengths a, b, and c, the area of the triangle is

$$\sqrt{s(s-a)(s-b)(s-c)}$$

where $s = \frac{1}{2}(a+b+c)$.

Before you look at the proof, you can look at some reasons that the formula makes sense.

1. Show that you can also write Heron's formula as $\frac{1}{4}\sqrt{(a+b+c)(a+b-c)(a+c-b)(b+c-a)}$
2. Use Heron's formula to find the area of an equilateral triangle with side length 8. Check this against the result of the formula $A = \frac{1}{2}bh$.
3. What is the area of a "triangle" with sides of length 4, 5, and 9? What happens when you apply Heron's formula to these numbers?
4. Under what conditions on a, b, and c will the output of Heron's formula be 0? What kinds of triangles give these inputs?
5. You can think of Heron's formula as a function of three inputs.

   $H(a, b, c) =$
   $\frac{1}{4}\sqrt{(a+b+c)(a+b-c)(a+c-b)(b+c-a)}$

   Show that $H(a, b, c) = H(a, c, b) = H(b, a, c) = H(b, c, a) = H(c, a, b) = H(c, b, a)$. Why does this make sense geometrically?
6. From the formula

   $H(a, b, c) =$
   $\frac{1}{4}\sqrt{(a+b+c)(a+b-c)(a+c-b)(b+c-a)}$

   you can conclude that

   $16(H(a, b, c))^2 =$
   $(a+b+c)(a+b-c)(a+c-b)(b+c-a)$

   a. Expand the right side, removing the parentheses.

   b. Show that $H(a, b, c)^2 = H(\pm a, \pm b, \pm c)$.

   c. If $c^2 = a^2 + b^2$, the triangle is a right triangle. How does the expression for $16(H(a, b, c))^2$ simplify if $c^2 = a^2 + b^2$?

Answers

Project

1. Substituting $\frac{1}{2}(a+b+c)$ for s, the radical becomes $\sqrt{\left(\frac{1}{2}\right)^4(a+b+c)(a+b-c)} \cdot \sqrt{(a+c-b)(b+c-a)}$

   Then rewrite $\sqrt{\left(\frac{1}{2}\right)^4} = \frac{1}{16}$.
2. $16\sqrt{3}$
3. Heron's formula gives the value 0 (the three lengths cannot form a triangle).
4. If the sum of any two sides is equal to the third side, the output is 0. These "triangles," where $a + b = c$, are called *degenerate triangles*.
5. Answers may vary. Sample: Thinking of $H(a, b, c)$ as a function of "side a, side b, and side c," it doesn't matter which order you use for the sides; the area of the triangle is not affected.
6. **a.** Think of the expression in the right side as $H(a, b, c) = \frac{1}{4}\sqrt{F}$.

   Then $H(a, b, c) = \frac{1}{16}F$ and $16[H(a, b, c)]^2 = F$. Removing parentheses from F results in $-a^4 - 2a^2b^2 + 2a^2c^2 + 2b^2c^2 - c^4 + 4a^2b^2$.

   b. Since each of a, b, and c appears to an even power, $H(\pm a, \pm b, \pm c) = H(a, b, c)$.

   c. $16[H(a, b, c)]^2 = 4a^2b^2$

Now try the proof. Suppose you label the triangle this way, where h is the altitude from side c.

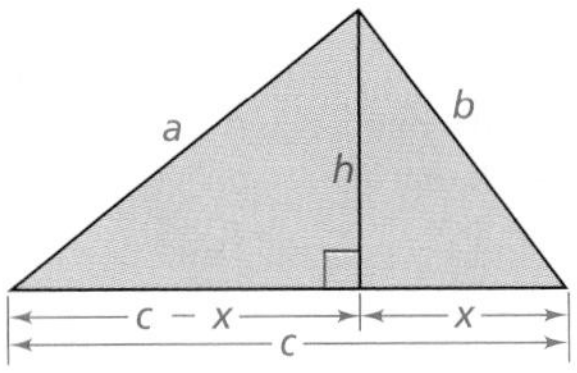

The area of the triangle is $\frac{1}{2}ch$. So, you need to find an expression for h in terms of a, b, and c. Apply the Pythagorean Theorem to the two right triangles in the figure.

$$h^2 + x^2 = b^2$$
$$h^2 + (c - x)^2 = a^2$$

Expand the second equation.

$$h^2 + c^2 - 2cx + x^2 = a^2$$

7. Show that this implies that $x = \frac{c^2 + b^2 - a^2}{2c}$.

Since $h^2 + x^2 = b^2$,

$$h^2 = b^2 - x^2$$
$$= b^2 - \left(\frac{c^2 + b^2 - a^2}{2c}\right)^2$$

8. Show that this implies that
$h^2 = \frac{1}{4c^2}(4b^2c^2 - (c^2 + b^2 - a^2)^2)$

The expression inside the parentheses is a difference of squares.

$$h^2 = \frac{1}{4c^2}\left(2bc - \left(c^2 + b^2 - a^2\right)\right) \cdot \left(2bc + \left(c^2 + b^2 - a^2\right)\right)$$
$$= \frac{1}{4c^2}(a^2 - (c^2 - 2bc + b^2)) \cdot ((c^2 + 2bc + b^2) - a^2)$$

9. Finish the factorization to show that $h^2 = \frac{1}{4c^2} \cdot$
$(a - c + b)(a + c - b)(c + b - a)(c + b + a)$

10. Finally, use the previous exercises to derive Heron's formula. Write up your solutions and derivations as a report.

You can use Heron's formula to find the areas of the roof sections of this theater.

7. In the equation $h^2 + c^2 - 2cx + x^2 = a^2$, substitute $h^2 + x^2$ with b^2 to get $b^2 + c^2 - 2cx = a^2$ or $b^2 + c^2 - a^2 = 2cx$. Then divide both sides by $2c$ to get $x = \frac{b^2 + c^2 - a^2}{2c}$.

8. From Exercise 7, $h^2 = b^2 - \left(\frac{c^2 + b^2 - a^2}{2c}\right)^2 = b^2 - \frac{1}{4c^2} \cdot (c^2 + b^2 - a^2)^2 = \frac{4b^2c^2}{4c^2} - \frac{1}{4c^2}(c^2 + b^2 - a^2)^2 = \frac{1}{4c^2} \cdot (4b^2c^2 - (c^2 + b^2 - a^2)^2)$.

9. From the last line of Exercise 8, $h^2 = \frac{1}{4c^2}(a - (c - b)) \cdot (a + (c - b))((c + b) - a) \cdot ((c + b) + a) = \frac{1}{4c^2} \cdot (a - c + b)(a + c - b) \cdot (c + b - a)(c + b + a)$.

10. From the last line of Exercise 9, multiply both sides by $4c^2$ and take the square root of each side to get $2ch = \sqrt{(a - c + b)(a + c - b)} \cdot \sqrt{(c - b - a)(c + b + a)}$.

Since $A = \frac{1}{2}ch$, then $2ch$ is $4A$ and $A = \frac{1}{4}\sqrt{(a - c + b)(a + c - b)} \cdot \sqrt{(c + b - a)(c + b + a)}$.

Answers

Chapter Review

1. a. 13

b. 1

c. 10

d. $4\frac{1}{3}$

e. 10

f. 13

2. a. $f \circ g\,(x) = x^2 + 4x - 1$

b. $g \circ f\,(x) = x^2 - 3$

3. a.

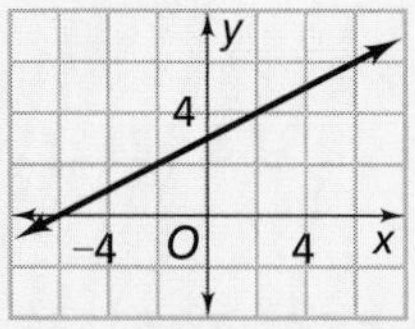

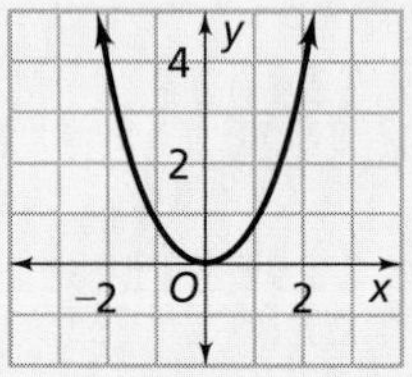

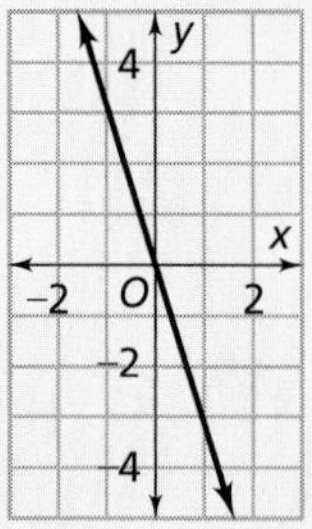

b. Functions f and h are one-to-one; function g is not.

c. $f^{-1}(x) = 2x - 6$; $h^{-1}(x) = -\frac{x}{3}$

4. Answers may vary. Sample:
$h(x) = (x - 1)(x - 3)(x - 4)$
$= x^3 - 8x^2 + 19x - 12$

5. $f(x) = x^3 - 17x^2 + 75x - 83$

6. a. Answers may vary. Sample:
$g(x) = 3x - 5 + (x + 1)(x - 2)$

b.

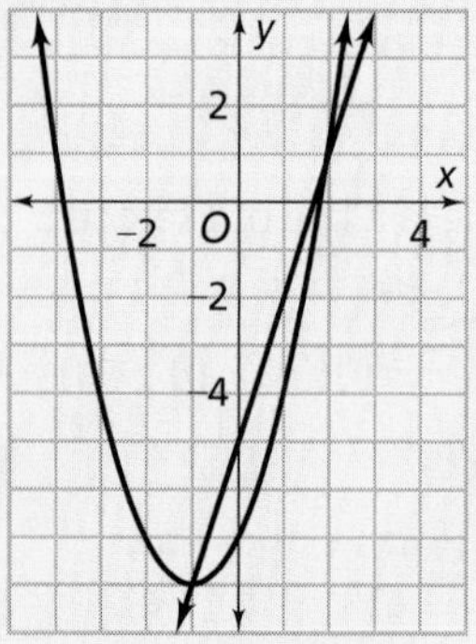

Chapter 2 Review

Go Online PHSchool.com — For vocabulary review, go to **Web Code**: bfj-0251

In **Investigation 2A,** you learned how to

- determine whether a table, graph, or closed-form rule is a function
- compose functions
- find the inverse of a function, if it exists

The following questions will help you check your understanding.

1. Consider the functions f and g.

$f(x) = 3x + 7$

$g(x) = \frac{x + 1}{3}$

Calculate each value.

a. $f(2)$ **b.** $g(2)$

c. $f(g(2))$ **d.** $g(f(2))$

e. $f \circ g(2)$ **f.** $f(2) \cdot g(2)$

2. Use the definitions of functions f and g below.

$f(x) = x - 2$

$g(x) = x^2 + 4x + 1$

a. Find a formula for $f \circ g(x)$.

b. Find a formula for $g \circ f(x)$.

3. Use the definitions of functions f, g, and h below.

$f(x) = \frac{x}{2} + 3$

$g(x) = x^2$

$h(x) = -3x$

a. Sketch the graph of each function.

b. Determine whether each function is one-to-one.

c. For each function that is one-to-one, find the inverse function.

In **Investigation 2B,** you learned how to

- use linear combinations of polynomials to determine new polynomials
- use zeros of polynomials to determine factors of polynomials
- find polynomials that agree with a given table

The following questions will help you check your understanding.

4. Find a nonconstant polynomial function h such that $h(1) = h(3) = h(4) = 0$.

5. Find a polynomial function f in normal form that agrees with this table.

Input	Output
1	−24
3	16
4	9
5	−8

6. a. Find a quadratic function g that agrees with $f: x \mapsto 3x - 5$ only at inputs $x = -1$ and $x = 2$.

b. Sketch the graphs of f and g on the same set of axes.

In **Investigation 2C,** you learned how to

- understand the relationship between roots and factors of polynomials
- divide polynomials by monic linear polynomials
- state and use the Remainder Theorem and the Factor Theorem
- write the general form of a function that fits a table

The following questions will help you check your understanding.

7. a. Find the quotient and remainder when you divide $p(x) = x^3 - 8x^2 + 3x - 5$ by $x + 3$.

b. Use your answer to find $p(-3)$.

8. Find the number a such that $x - 2$ is a factor of $p(x) = x^3 + 3x^2 + 4x + a$.

9. Find the numbers B and C such that $x^2 - 8x = (x - 1)^2 + B(x - 1) + C$.

In **Investigation 2D,** you learned how to

- factor polynomials by scaling and by finding roots
- factor polynomials using the sums and differences of squares and cubes
- factor polynomials by grouping and by identifying quadratic-like or cubic-like polynomials

The following questions will help you check your understanding.

10. Factor each polynomial over $\mathbb{Z}$.

a. $4x^2 + 4x - 3$

b. $6x^2 + 23x + 21$

c. $36x^2 - 49y^2$

d. $3(x - 2)^2 + 5(x - 2) + 2$

e. $x^3 + 8$

f. $x^3 - 2x^2 + 3x - 6$

11. Factor each polynomial over $\mathbb{R}$.

a. $x^4 - 2x^2 + 1$

b. $x^2 - x - 4$

12. Write each expression as a single rational expression.

a. $\frac{2}{x - 4} + \frac{x}{x + 4}$

b. $2 - \frac{x + 3}{x - 2}$

7. a. quotient: $x^2 - 11x + 36$; remainder: -113

b. -113

8. $a = -28$

9. $B = -6, C = -7$

10. a. $(2x - 1)(2x + 3)$

b. $(3x + 7)(2x + 3)$

c. $(6x + 7y)(6x - 7y)$

d. $(3x - 4)(x - 1)$

e. $(x + 2)(x^2 - 2x + 4)$

f. $(x^2 + 3)(x - 2)$

11. a. $(x + 1)(x - 1)(x + 1)(x - 1)$

b. $\left(x - 0.5 - \frac{\sqrt{17}}{2}\right) \cdot \left(x - 0.5 + \frac{\sqrt{17}}{2}\right)$

12. a. $\frac{x^2 - 2x + 8}{(x + 4)(x - 4)}$

b. $\frac{x - 7}{x - 2}$

Chapter Test

Assessment Resources

Chapter Test — page 1

Multiple Choice

1. Suppose $f(x) = x + 3$ and $g(x) = x^2$. Which value is equal to $f \circ g(4)$?
   A. 9
   B. 13
   C. 19
   D. 25

2. Suppose $f(x) = 2x + 3$. Which expression is equal to $f^{-1}(x)$?
   A. $2x - 3$
   B. $-2x - 3$
   C. $\frac{x-3}{2}$
   D. $\frac{x}{2} - 3$

3. Suppose the graph of $f: x \mapsto A(x - 1)(x + 2)$ contains the points $(-2, 0)$, $(1, 0)$, and $(3, 5)$. What is the value of A?
   A. 2
   B. $\frac{1}{2}$
   C. -5
   D. cannot be determined

4. When you divide $p(x) = x^3 + 5x^2 - x + 3$ by $x - 1$, what is the remainder?
   A. -3
   B. 2
   C. 4
   D. 8

5. Which expression is the factored form of $8x^3 + 125$?
   A. $(2x + 5)(4x^2 - 10x + 25)$
   B. $(2x + 5)^3$
   C. $(2x + 5)(4x^2 + 20x + 25)$
   D. $(2x + 5)(4x^2 + 10x + 25)$

Chapter Test — page 2

Open Response

6. The functions f and g are defined as $f(x) = 3x + 1$ and $g(x) = 4x - 7$.
   a. Find $f \circ g(x)$.
   b. Find $g \circ f(x)$.
   c. Find the inverse of f. Show that $f \circ f^{-1}(x) = x$.

7. Find a polynomial function in normal form that agrees with the table.

Input, x	Output, $f(x)$
1	0
3	−6
6	60

8. a. Find the quotient and remainder when you divide $f(x) = x^3 + 5x^2 + 3x - 10$ by $x + 2$.
   b. Use your answer to find $f(-2)$.

9. Factor each polynomial over $\mathbb{Z}$.
   a. $15x^2 - 7x - 2$
   b. $x^6 - 9x^3 + 8$

10. Find the sum $\frac{2x}{x+6} + 1$.

11. Does $x^4 + 4$ factor over $\mathbb{Z}$? Show your work.

Also available: Form B

Chapter 2

Chapter Test

Go Online PHSchool.com — For a chapter test, go to **Web Code:** bfa-0253

Multiple Choice

1. Use functions f and g below.
   $f(x) = 2x - 3$
   $g(x) = 4x + 1$
   Which value is equal to $f \circ g(3)$?
   A. 3
   B. 13
   C. 23
   D. 39

2. Suppose $f(x) = \sqrt[3]{x} + 1$. Which expression is equal to $f^{-1}(x)$?
   A. $x^3 - 1$
   B. $(x - 1)^3$
   C. $-\sqrt[3]{x} - 1$
   D. $(x + 1)^3$

3. Suppose the graph of $f: x \mapsto A(x - 2)(x - 3)$ contains the points $(2, 0)$, $(3, 0)$, and $(2, 0)$, $(3, 0)$, and $(4, -6)$. What is the value of A?
   A. -6
   B. -3
   C. $-\frac{1}{3}$
   D. 3

4. When you divide $p(x) = 2x^3 - 3x^2 + 5x - 1$ by $x - 2$, what is the remainder?
   A. -1
   B. 0
   C. 13
   D. 36

5. Which expression is the factored form of $x^3 - 8$?
   A. $(x + 2)(x^2 + 2x + 4)$
   B. $(x - 2)^3$
   C. $(x - 2)(x^2 + 2x + 4)$
   D. $(x - 2)(x^2 + 4x + 4)$

Open Response

6. The functions f and g are defined as
   $f(x) = \frac{2x+1}{3}$
   $g(x) = x^2 - 1$
   a. Find $f \circ g(x)$.
   b. Find $g \circ f(x)$.
   c. Find the inverse of f. Show that $f \circ f^{-1}(x) = x$.

7. Find a polynomial function in normal form that agrees with the table.

Input, x	Output, $f(x)$
1	4
2	−2
3	20

8. **a.** Find the quotient and remainder when you divide $f(x) = 2x^3 + 4x^2 - 5x + 6$ by $x - 3$.
   b. Use your answer to find $f(3)$.

9. Factor each polynomial over $\mathbb{Z}$.
   a. $8x^2 + 22x + 15$
   b. $x^4 - 13x^2 + 36$
   c. $x^3 + 1$

10. Find the difference.
    $\frac{x}{x+3} - \frac{3}{x-2}$

11. How are the zeros of a polynomial related to its factors?

Answers

Chapter Test

1. C
2. B
3. B
4. C
5. C
6. a. $\frac{2x^2 - 1}{3}$
   b. $\frac{4x^2 + 4x - 8}{9}$
   c. $f^{-1}(x) = \frac{3x - 1}{2}$;
   $$f \circ f^{-1}(x) = f\left(\frac{3x-1}{2}\right) = \frac{2\left(\frac{3x-1}{2}\right) + 1}{3} = \frac{3x - 1 + 1}{3} = \frac{3x}{3} = x$$
7. $f(x) = 14x^2 - 48x + 38$
8. a. quotient: $2x^2 + 10x + 25$; remainder: 81
   b. 81

Chapter 2

Cumulative Review

1. Which of the following recursive functions best fits the data in the table?

Input, n	Output, $a(n)$
0	3
1	5
2	7
3	9
4	11

A. $a(n) = \begin{cases} 3 & \text{if } n = 0 \\ 2(n-1) & \text{if } n > 0 \end{cases}$

B. $a(n) = \begin{cases} 0 & \text{if } n = 0 \\ 2(n-1)+5 & \text{if } n > 0 \end{cases}$

C. $a(n) = \begin{cases} 3 & \text{if } n = 0 \\ 2(n-1)+2 & \text{if } n > 0 \end{cases}$

D. $a(n) = \begin{cases} 3 & \text{if } n = 0 \\ 3(n-1)+2 & \text{if } n > 0 \end{cases}$

2. The input-output table below models a function with a constant first difference. Find $a(50)$ and $a(100)$.

Input, n	Output, $a(n)$
0	58
1	■
2	■
3	■
4	■
5	−22

3. Which line best fits the data in the graph?

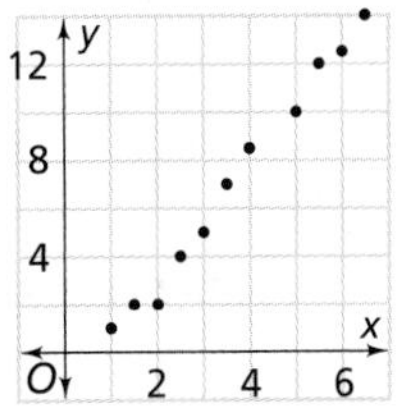

A. $y = \frac{3}{2}x - 1$

B. $y = 2x + 1$

C. $y = 2.5x - 2$

D. $y = x - 3$

4. Evaluate $\frac{2n!}{(n-1)!}$ for each value.

a. $n = 100$

b. $n = 500$

5. Molly took out a loan for college and is making more than the minimum monthly payment each month. Molly's loan was for \$20,000. Her interest rate is 3.5% and she pays \$400 per month. How long will it take Molly to pay off the loan?

A. 50 months

B. 52 months

C. 54 months

D. 60 months

6. Copy and complete the difference table.

Input, n	Output, $a(n)$	Δ	Δ^2
0	■	8	3
1	12	■	3
2	■	■	3
3	■	■	■
4	■	■	■

9. a. $(4x + 5)(2x + 3)$
   b. $(x + 2)(x - 2)(x + 3)(x - 3)$
   c. $(x + 1)(x^2 - x + 1)$

10. $\frac{x^2 - 5x - 9}{(x + 3)(x - 2)}$

11. If a is a root or zero, then $(x - a)$ is a factor.

Cumulative Review

1. B

2. $a(50) = -742$; $a(100) = -1542$

3. C

4. a. 200
   b. 1000

5. B

6. first-column values: 0, 1, 2, 3, 4
   second-column values: 4, 12, 33, 57, 74
   third-column values: 8, 11, 14, 17
   fourth-column values: 3, 3, 3

Cumulative Review

Assessment Resources

Quarter Test page 1

Multiple Choice

1. The table at the right is part of a table that was generated by a linear function. Which of the following statements is false?

n	$a(n)$
0	
1	−2
2	
3	
4	7
5	

A. $a(2) - a(5) = -9$
B. $a(0)$ is not defined.
C. $a(-6) = -23$
D. The completed table agrees with the function $a(n) = \begin{cases} -5 & \text{if } n = 0 \\ a(n-1) + 3 & \text{if } n > 0 \end{cases}$.

2. Evaluate $\frac{2(n+1)!}{n(n-1)!}$ for $n = 100$.

A. 101 B. 202
C. 10,100 D. 20,200

3. Anne took out a loan for a car. Her car cost \$16,000 and she made a \$1500 down payment. Her interest rate is 5% and she pays \$450 per month. How long will it take Anne to pay off the loan?

A. 33 months B. 35 months
C. 36 months D. 38 months

4. Let $f(x) = -2x + 5$ and $g(x) = -3x^2$. Which value is equal to $f \circ g(-2)$?

A. −19 B. −12
C. 19 D. 29

5. Let $f(x) = -9x + 3$. Which expression is equal to $f^{-1}(x)$?

A. $9x - 3$ B. $-9x - 3$
C. $-\frac{1}{9}x + \frac{1}{3}$ D. $\frac{1}{9}x - \frac{1}{3}$

6. When you divide $p(x) = 2x^3 + 5x^2 - x + 4$ by $x - 3$, what is the remainder?

A. −3 B. −2
C. 3 D. 100

Quarter Test page 2

Open Response

7. Find a closed-form function that agrees with the table at the right.

n	$f(n)$
1	2
2	6
3	12
4	20
5	30

8. Calculate the mean absolute error, the mean squared error, and the standard error for the data in the table and the fitting line $y = 3x + 1$.

Input	Output
−1	−3
1	3
4	11
5	17

9. Find the line of slope 2 that minimizes the standard error for the data set at the right. Does your line pass through the balance point?

Input	Output
0	−3
1	−1
2	2
3	5
4	7

10. The functions f and g are defined as $f(x) = -2x + 3$ and $g(x) = 5x - 1$.
   a. Find $f \circ g(x)$.
   b. Find $g \circ f(x)$.
   c. Find the inverse of f. Show that $f \circ f^{-1}(x) = x$.

11. Factor each polynomial over $\mathbb{Z}$.
   a. $6x^2 - 11x - 10$ b. $x^4 - 6x^2 + 5$

12. Find the sum $\frac{2x}{x+1} + 3$.

13. Does $x^6 - 64$ factor over $\mathbb{Z}$? Show your work.

7. Make a difference table for the following function from $n = 0$ to $n = 4$. Include enough columns to show a constant difference. Use your table to find a closed-form function that agrees with the inputs and outputs in the table.

$$f(n) = \begin{cases} 1 & \text{if } n = 0 \\ f(n-1) + 2n + 1 & \text{if } n > 0 \end{cases}$$

8. Find a recursive function that agrees with the following table.

Input, n	Output, $a(n)$
0	2
1	4
2	12
3	48
4	240

9. Find the mean absolute error, mean squared error, and standard error for this data set, using the line with equation $y = x - 1$.

x	y
0	−3
1	−1
2	2
3	4
4	5

10. Find the line of slope 2 that has the least standard error for the data set below.

x	y
2	3
5	7
8	12
11	15
14	19

11. Find the line of best fit for the data set below.

x	y
3	48
7	27
9	15
14	9
20	1

12. Make a table for this function for $n = 1$ to $n = 10$. Then find closed-form and recursive functions that agree with your table.

$$r(n) = \frac{(n+1)!}{2(n-1)!}$$

13. Joan took out a loan for $12,000 from her parents to buy a used car. She agreed to pay back the loan over 4 years.

a. At first, Joan's parents do not want to charge interest. What would be her monthly payment on a 0% interest loan?

b. Joan feels she should pay some interest. After discussing it, her parents decide that 5% interest is reasonable. What are Joan's monthly payments under this agreement?

c. How much interest in all will Joan pay?

14. Thomas can put $2500 down and pay $450 per month for a new car. He has qualified for a four-year, 3% loan. What is the most expensive car he can afford?

15. Use functions f and g below to find each value.

$$f(x) = x^2 + 1$$
$$g(x) = 2x - 3$$

a. $f(-1)$

b. $f \circ g(4)$

c. $g \circ f(x)$

d. $g^{-1}(x)$

16. The graph of $f: x \mapsto A(x+2)(x-3)$ passes through points $(0, -18)$, $(1, -12)$ and $(3, 0)$. Find the value of A.

Answers

7. $f(n) = n^2 + 2n + 1$

8. $a(n) = \begin{cases} 2 & \text{if } n = 0 \\ 2(n+1)! & \text{if } n > 0 \end{cases}$

9. The mean absolute error is 1.6. The mean squared error is 2.8. The standard error is 1.67332.

10. $y = 2x - 4$

11. $y = -2.6x + 47.3$

12. A closed-form function is $f(n) = 0.5n^2 + 0.5n$. A recursive function is

$$f(n) = \begin{cases} 1 & \text{if } n = 1 \\ f(n-1) + n & \text{if } n > 1 \end{cases}$$

13. a. $250 per month
b. $276.35 per month
c. $1264.80 of interest

14. $22,830

15. a. $f(-1) = 2$
b. $f \circ g(4) = 26$
c. $g \circ f(x) = 2x^2 - 1$
d. $g^{-1}(x) = \frac{1}{2}x + \frac{3}{2}$

16. 0

17. What is the remainder when you divide $p(x) = 2x^3 - 3x^2 + x - 2$ by $x + 2$?

18. Factor each expression.

a. $27x^3 - 64$

b. $125x^3 + 8x^3$

19. Given the function $f(x) = -3x + 1$, find its inverse and show that $f \circ f^{-1}(x) = x$.

20. Find a polynomial function in normal form that agrees with the following table.

Input, x	Output, f(x)
0	58
1	7
2	15

21. Use the polynomial $p(x) = -x^3 + 2x^2 + 3x - 1$.

a. Find the quotient and remainder when $p(x)$ is divided by $x + 3$.

b. Use your answer to find $p(-3)$.

22. Factor each polynomial over $\mathbb{Z}$.

a. $12x^2 - 3x - 9$

b. $10x^2 + 11x + 3$

c. $x^8 - 5x^4 + 4$

23. Does $x^6 + 64$ factor over $\mathbb{Z}$? Explain.

24. Find each sum or difference.

a. $2 + \frac{x-1}{x+1}$

b. $\frac{3x}{2x+3} - 1$

17. -32

18. a. $(3x - 4)(9x^2 + 12x + 16)$

b. $(5x + 2y)(25x^2 - 10xy + 4y^2)$

19. $f^{-1}(x) = -\frac{1}{3}x + \frac{1}{3}$;
$f \circ f^{-1}(x) = x = -3\left(-\frac{1}{3}x + \frac{1}{3}\right) +$ 1 when simplified.

20. $p(x) = 2x^2 + 2x + 3$

21. a. Quotient is $-x^2 + 5x - 12$. Remainder is 35.

b. 35

22. a. $3(4x + 3)(x - 1)$

b. $(2x + 1)(5x + 3)$

c. $(x + 1)(x - 1)(x^2 + 1) \cdot (x^2 + 2)(x^2 - 2)$

23. Yes, it factors into $(x^2 + 4)(x^4 - 4x^2 + 16)$.

24. a. $\frac{3x + 1}{x + 1}$

b. $\frac{x - 3}{2x + 3}$

Chapter 3 Complex Numbers

This chapter introduces the complex numbers of the form $a + bi$ where a and b are real numbers and $i^2 = -1$. Students learn to compute in this new domain and to visualize complex numbers and operations on them in the complex plane.

Chapter Overview

INVESTIGATION 3A, *Introduction to Complex Numbers,* has students extend the real numbers and work with this new set of complex numbers.

INVESTIGATION 3B, *The Complex Plane,* introduces students to the complex plane and gives them insight into properties of complex numbers.

INVESTIGATION 3C, *Complex Numbers, Geometry, and Algebra,* has students explore the synergy between algebraic computations with complex numbers and the geometric representation of the complex plane.

For more information on the investigations, see

- Chapter Road Map, pp. 196–197
- Investigation Road Maps, pp. 198, 224, 252

PROJECT The Project near the end of the chapter is optional. You can assign the Project at any time during the chapter depending on how often and how long you feel students should work on it.

Pacing Suggestions and Materials

Investigation 3A *Introduction to Complex Numbers*

DAY	LESSON	HOMEWORK
1	3.1 Getting Started Core: 1, 2, 3, 4a, 6, 8 Optional: 5; Extension: 4b, 7	Core: 9, 11, 12, 14a–d Optional: 10, 15, 16, 17 Extension: 13, 14e
2	3.2 Extending Number Systems Core: 1, 5, 6, 8 Optional: 2, 3, 4, 7, 9, 10a–e, 11a–c; Extension: 10f, 11d	Core: 12, 13, 14, 16, 17 Optional: 15, 18
3	3.3 Making the Extension: $\sqrt{-1}$ Core: 1, 2, 3, 4, 6 Optional: 5, 7, 8	Core: 9, 11, 12, 13, 16, 17 Optional: 10, 14; Extension: 15
4	3.4 Extension to Complex Numbers Core: 1, 2, 3, 4, 6 Optional: 5, 7; Extension: 8	Core: 9, 10a–d, 11, 12, 13, 14 Optional: 15, 17, 18, 19 Extension: 10e, 16
5	3.5 Reciprocals and Division Core: 1, 2, 3, 5a–e, 6, 7, 8, 9 Optional: 4; Extension: 5f	Core: 10, 11, 12, 13a, 14, 15 Optional: 16, 17, 18, 19, 20a–c Extension: 13b, 20d

Investigation 3B *The Complex Plane*

DAY	LESSON	HOMEWORK
1	3.6 Getting Started Core: 1, 2, 3, 5, 6 Optional: 4	Core: 7, 9, 10, 12 Optional: 8, 11, 13, 14, 15
2	3.7 Graphing Complex Numbers Core: 1, 2, 3, 4, 6 Optional: 5	Core: 7, 8, 9, 10, 14 Optional: 11, 12, 13, 16, 17 Extension: 15
3	3.8 Arithmetic in the Complex Plane Core: 1, 2a–e, 3, 6, 7, 8 Optional: 4, 5, 9; Extension: 2f	Core: 10, 11, 13, 14, 18 Optional: 12, 15, 16a, 17 Extension: 16b
4, 5	3.9 Magnitude and Direction Core: 1, 3, 4, 6, 7, 8 Optional: 2, 5, 9, 10	Core: 11, 12, 13, 14, 16 Optional: 15, 17, 18a, 19, 20 Extension: 18b

NOTES	MATERIALS
	• Blackline Master 3.1
	• graph paper • graphing calculators • Blackline Master 3.2
	• graph paper • graphing calculators • Blackline Master 3.3
	• CAS (recommended) • graphing calculators
	• CAS (recommended) • graphing calculators • Blackline Master 3.5

NOTES	MATERIALS
	• CAS (recommended) • graph paper • graphing calculators • protractors • Blackline Master 3.6
	• CAS (recommended) • graph paper • graphing calculators • Blackline Master MC2
You may want to spend two days on this lesson. See the lesson notes for suggestions.	• graph paper • graphing calculators • Blackline Master 3.8
You may want to spend two days on this lesson. See the lesson notes for suggestions.	• CAS (recommended) • graph paper • graphing calculators • Blackline Masters MC2, 3.9

Mathematics Background

COMPLEX NUMBERS Many courses wait to cover complex numbers until after students have studied more trigonometry, but CME Project *Algebra 2* covers complex numbers just after the study of functions and polynomials. There are some solid reasons behind this choice, having to do with the mathematics embedded in the topic of complex numbers. Most texts introduce the symbol *i* as a way to solve quadratic equations with no real roots. The first example is invariably $x^2 + 1 = 0$. This masks the history a bit. In fact, complex numbers emerged in mathematics as algebraic objects, useful in finding solutions to *cubic* equations.

When mathematicians applied a general method for solving cubic equations to certain cubic polynomials, they could arrive only at the real number solutions of those equations by "passing through" some expressions involving square roots of negative numbers. Later, they found that every polynomial of degree *n* with real coefficients has exactly *n* roots in the complex numbers. This amazing fact—that the complex numbers are all you need to solve any polynomial with real coefficients—is known as the Fundamental Theorem of Algebra.

So you will introduce a new kind of number into the mix. If you need complex numbers to solve polynomials with real coefficients, you probably need some other kind of number to solve polynomials with complex coefficients. Right? Amazingly, no! Even if you allow the coefficients of a polynomial to be complex numbers, you still have exactly *n* roots for a polynomial of degree *n*, and those roots can all be found in the complex number system. Later in the chapter, you will use the Fundamental Theorem of Algebra to prove this generalized result. In spite of its name, every proof of the Fundamental Theorem must use results that are strictly outside algebra.

VISUALIZING COMPLEX NUMBERS Often in mathematics, the significance of new findings is not immediately clear. Complex numbers helped solve many problems in algebra, but including a geometric interpretation of these numbers allowed for new insights into other fields of study as well. The geometric interpretation of complex numbers as points on the plane is a true mathematical *representation*—not only can you assign complex numbers to points, you can also interpret the operations (addition and multiplication) geometrically.

The geometric interpretation of multiplication is usually reserved until students have studied trigonometry, because the classical way to make

continued on p. 196c

continued from p. 196b

the interpretation is to use the addition formulas for sine and cosine. But in the summer of 2002, teachers at the Park City Mathematics Institute in Utah discovered a way to get the geometry of multiplication without using anything more than right triangle trigonometry. You develop their discovery in Investigation 3C. It has huge consequences for high school mathematics. It is another important reason to introduce complex numbers now, because it allows you to use the geometry of complex multiplication to derive the addition formulas for sine and cosine as well as many other basic trigonometric identities. This will save your class time and help make some central mathematical connections.

Another benefit for students in thinking of the complex numbers as either points or vectors in the complex plane is that it provides a new and relevant context in which to review basic graphing skills and right triangle trigonometry. This allows you to assess your students in these important skills from prior courses without redoing the work of those courses. Your students are covering new material and making the new complex number computations more concrete through visualization.

MOVING ON FROM HERE By visualizing complex numbers as vectors in the complex plane, your students prepare themselves to extend the right triangle trigonometry they have learned to include the entire unit circle. Vectors representing complex numbers occur in all four quadrants of the complex plane, and students develop the idea of a "reference" angle as a means of finding the direction of such vectors naturally out of necessity. They see the coordinates of points in the complex plane with relation to the sines and cosines of these reference angles, and they make sense of the sign of each coordinate from its context. This experience lays the groundwork for extending the domain of the trigonometric functions. The geometric connections they have learned in this chapter will also be useful as they expand their knowledge of trigonometry. In precalculus, students will exploit the arithmetic and geometry of complex numbers to make a complete analysis of the equation $x^n - 1 = 0$. This "cyclotomic connection," first developed by Gauss, allows students to connect algebra, arithmetic, and geometry in an extremely elegant suite of results. It allows students to bring some coherence to the topics surrounding DeMoivre's theorem. Students will have a brief introduction to this topic in Lesson 3.13, *Roots of Unity*.

Pacing Suggestions and Materials

Investigation 3C *Complex Numbers, Geometry, and Algebra*

DAY	LESSON	HOMEWORK
1	3.10 Getting Started Core: 1, 2a–b, 3, 6 Optional: 4, 5; Extension: 2c, 7	Core: 8, 9a–c, 10, 11 Optional: 12; Extension: 9d
2	3.11 Multiplying Complex Numbers Core: 1, 2, 3, 6, 8 Optional: 4, 5, 7	Core: 9, 10, 11a, 12, 13, 14, 16 Optional: 15, 17a, 19, 20 Extension: 11b, 17b, 18, 21
3	3.12 Conjugates and Roots Core: 1, 2, 3, 5 Optional: 4; Extension: 6	Core: 7, 8, 9, 10, 11, 12 Optional: 13, 14a–c, 15, 16 Extension: 14d
4	3.13 Roots of Unity Core: 1, 2, 3, 4, 5, 8 Optional: 6, 7; Extension: 9	Core: 10, 11, 12, 13 Optional: 15, 16; Extension: 14

NOTES	MATERIALS
	• graph paper • graphing calculators • Blackline Master MC2
	• graph paper • graphing calculators • Blackline Masters MC2, 3.11
	• graph paper • graphing calculators
	• graph paper • graphing calculators • Blackline Master 3.13

Developing Students' Mathematical Habits

These key habits are developed in this chapter.

EXTENSION Students see the decisions made in deciding how to calculate with complex numbers as an extension from the real numbers in such a way as to preserve the basic rules. They make sense of the behavior of these new numbers and clearly see distinctions between matters of convention and matters of mathematics.

VISUALIZATION By operating on complex numbers visually in the complex plane, students make connections between the results of their calculations as numbers and as geometric objects. They see conjugation as a reflection over the real axis, addition as making parallelograms by translating vectors, and multiplication as scaling and rotation of vectors.

DEDUCTIVE REASONING This chapter challenges students to make conjectures about complex numbers and to prove them through deductive reasoning or to follow the arguments in a presented proof.

Chapter Vocabulary and Notation

The following list gives key vocabulary and notation used in the chapter. Selected new vocabulary and notation items are shown in boldface on the student page.

- Argand plane, p. 229
- argument, arg z, p. 247
- circumcenter, p. 226
- complex numbers, $\mathbb{C}$, p. 212
- complex plane, p. 229
- conjugate, $\overline{z}$, p. 218
- dilation, p. 236
- direction, p. 244
- exact, p. 227
- Fundamental Theorem of Algebra, p. 215
- hypotenuse, p. 225
- intercept, p. 203
- irrational numbers, p. 201
- legs, p. 228
- magnitude, $|z|$, p. 242
- natural numbers, $\mathbb{N}$, p. 201
- roots of unity, p. 271
- i, $\sqrt{-1}$, p. 204
- $a + bi$ (complex number), p. 212

Chapter Road Map

INVESTIGATION 3A, *Introduction to Complex Numbers,* has students extend the real numbers by including a new number, $\sqrt{-1}$, later written as i. They work in this new set of complex numbers, $\mathbb{C}$. This extension is done with careful attention to the basic rules, and students see how allowing square roots of negative numbers changes what they know. For example, the identity $\sqrt{a}\sqrt{b} = \sqrt{ab}$ no longer holds in the complex numbers, but quadratic equations that had no solutions in the real numbers do have solutions in the complex numbers.

INVESTIGATION 3B, *The Complex Plane,* introduces students to the complex plane, which is a representation that allows students to visualize complex numbers as geometric objects and to see operations on them as transformations in the complex plane. By looking at computations with complex numbers in this new way, students gain insight into their properties and develop new results.

Complex Numbers

Fractals are self-similar geometric objects. This means that if you zoom in on a picture of a fractal, you will see small-scale details similar to the large-scale characteristics of the whole shape. Fractals have incredibly complex boundaries that reveal even more complexity under magnification.

One particularly beautiful and famous fractal is the Mandelbrot set. This set develops from a series of repeated calculations with complex numbers. Images of the Mandelbrot set often have color. The shading assigned to each point is based on the number of repeated calculations at that point required to achieve a particular goal.

Vocabulary

- **argument, arg z**
- **complex numbers, $\mathbb{C}$**
- **complex plane**
- **conjugate, $\bar{z}$**
- **direction**
- **Fundamental Theorem of Algebra**
- **irrational numbers**
- **magnitude, $|z|$**
- **natural numbers, $\mathbb{N}$**
- **roots of unity**
- **i ($\sqrt{-1}$)**
- **$a + bi$ (complex number)**

Chapter Technology

CME Project *Algebra 2* assumes that each student has access to a graphing calculator. It also recommends access to a computer algebra system (CAS).

Support for the use of technology is available in the TI-Nspire™ Technology Handbook. See p. 778.

A list of technology used with important concepts in this chapter appears below. Students will need access to the functionality listed to develop complete understanding of these topics.

Computer Algebra System

LESSON 3.8 Find complex solutions to equations, p. 241.

LESSON 3.10 Expand a product of polynomials, p. 253.

LESSON 3.12 Find complex roots of a polynomial equation, p. 266.

Geometry Software

LESSON 3.9 Calculate the magnitude of a complex number, pp. 242, 243.

Graphing Calculator

LESSON 3.6 Find the value of an inverse tangent function, p. 225.

LESSON 3.9 Calculate the magnitude of a complex number, pp. 242, 243. Calculate the argument of a complex number, p. 247.

LESSON 3.11 Use the complex number function to find the direction, p. 255.

INVESTIGATION 3C, ***Complex Numbers, Geometry, and Algebra,*** has students explore the synergy between algebraic computations with complex numbers and the geometric representation of the complex plane. They use the connection to establish identities and prove theorems and eventually visualize the roots of an equation of the form $x^n - 1 = 0$ as the vertices of a regular n-gon in the complex plane.

Investigation Overview

This investigation serves as an introduction to complex numbers. Complex numbers first came about in the context of solving cubic equations using a method that came to be known as Cardano's formula. A mathematician named Bombelli applied Cardano's formula to the cubic equation $x^3 - 15x - 4 = 0$ and found a root of the strange form $\sqrt[3]{2 + \sqrt{-121}} + \sqrt[3]{2 - \sqrt{-121}}$. Bombelli knew that his polynomial had a "nice" root; in fact, 4 is one of the roots. He was able to complete calculations like this by pretending that things like $\sqrt{-121}$ "exist" and working with them.

Square roots of negative numbers arise naturally when using the quadratic formula for solving quadratic equations, and students are accustomed to writing "no real solution" when the discriminant is negative. But if you "pretend" that things like $\sqrt{-121}$ exist, as Bombelli did, you can find solutions to any polynomial equation. In fact, the Fundamental Theorem of Algebra states that a polynomial of degree $n \geq 1$ has exactly n roots in the complex numbers.

The work of this investigation is the work of extending the real numbers to the complex numbers. You begin by asking students to think about familiar extensions: extending from the natural numbers to include zero, and then extending that number system to the integers and beyond to the rational numbers, irrational numbers, and real numbers. You then introduce square roots of negative numbers and engage students in a careful exploration of the extension. For example: What properties of real numbers also hold for complex numbers? How does arithmetic work?

You may wish to assign Questions 1–3 for students to think and write about during the investigation.

Learning Goals

- Understand the set of complex numbers as an extension of the real numbers.
- Use complex numbers as tools for solving equations.
- Be fluent in complex number arithmetic.

Habits and Skills

- Think like an algebraist by examining extensions of number systems.
- Work with properties of complex numbers.
- Prove facts about operations of complex numbers and their conjugates.

Investigation 3A

Introduction to Complex Numbers

In *Introduction to Complex Numbers*, you will begin your exploration of complex numbers. When you solve a quadratic equation, you sometimes end up with the square root of a negative number in your solution. In the past, you have interpreted this to mean that there are no real-number solutions to the equation. That is true. However, if you expand your set of allowable solutions beyond the real numbers to the complex numbers, you can find solutions to all quadratic equations.

By the end of this investigation, you will be able to answer questions like these.

1. What are complex numbers?
2. What two numbers have a sum of 20 and a product of 109?
3. How can you use complex numbers to solve any quadratic equation?

You will learn how to

- understand the set of complex numbers as an extension of the real numbers
- use complex numbers as tools for solving equations
- be fluent in complex number arithmetic

You will develop these habits and skills:

- Think like an algebraist by examining extensions of number systems.
- Work with properties of complex numbers.
- Prove facts about operations on complex numbers and their conjugates.

In the Flammarion woodcut, a man peers beyond the familiar world. In this chapter, you will explore beyond ℝ.

Investigation Road Map

LESSON 3.1, *Getting Started,* gets students started thinking about square roots of negative numbers.

LESSON 3.2, *Extending Number Systems,* reminds students of the work of extending number systems.

LESSON 3.3, *Making the Extension:* $\sqrt{-1}$, introduces square roots of negative numbers. Students see the definition of $\sqrt{-1}$ and then, for positive real numbers n, the definition of $\sqrt{n}$.

LESSON 3.4, *Extension to Complex Numbers,* introduces the definition of the complex numbers, including the definition of i. Students learn to add, subtract, and multiply complex numbers.

LESSON 3.5, *Reciprocals and Division,* presents division of complex numbers.

3.1 Getting Started

Activating Prior Knowledge
Exploring New Ideas

You can construct a quadratic equation by using the sum and product of its roots.

For You to Explore

1. **a.** Is there a real number with a square -16? Explain.
   b. Is there a real number with a square -1? Explain.
2. The quadratic equation $x^2 - 12x + 27 = 0$ has two roots.
   a. What is the sum of the roots?
   b. What is the product of the roots?
   c. What is the sum of the squares of the roots?
3. The quadratic equation $x^2 - 12x + 34 = 0$ has two roots.
   a. What is the sum of the roots?
   b. What is the product of the roots?
   c. What is the sum of the squares of the roots?
4. **a.** Show that the identity $x^2 + y^2 = (x + y)^2 - 2xy$ is true.
   b. **Take It Further** Write $x^3 + y^3$ in terms of the expressions $(x + y)$ and xy.
5. For each quadratic equation, find the sum of the roots, the product of the roots, and the sum of the squares of the roots.
   a. $x^2 - 12x + 35 = 0$
   b. $x^2 - 12x + 32 = 0$
   c. $x^2 - 12x + 33 = 0$
   d. $x^2 + 12x + 32 = 0$
   e. $x^2 - 25 = 0$
   f. $x^2 - 10 = 0$
   g. $x^2 + 8x - 33 = 0$
6. For the general monic quadratic $x^2 + bx + c$, find each quantity in terms of the coefficients b and c.
   a. the sum of the roots
   b. the product of the roots
   c. the sum of the squares of the roots
7. **Take It Further** For each quadratic equation, find the sum of the cubes of the roots.
   a. $x^2 - 12x + 35 = 0$
   b. $x^2 - 12x + 32 = 0$
   c. $x^2 - 12x + 33 = 0$
8. Consider the quadratic $x^2 - 14x + 50$.
   a. If two real numbers sum to 14, what is their largest possible product?
   b. What happens if you use the quadratic formula to solve $x^2 - 14x + 50 = 0$?

Habits of Mind

Establish a process. Can you find the sum of the cubes of the roots without finding the roots?

Answers

For You to Explore

1. **a.** No; the square of any real number is nonnegative.
   b. No; the square of any real number is nonnegative.
2. **a.** 12 **b.** 27 **c.** 90
3. **a.** 12 **b.** 34 **c.** 76
4. **a.** Expand the right side to get $x^2 + 2xy + y^2 - 2xy$, which is equal to the left side.
   b. $x^3 + y^3 = (x + y)^3 - 3xy(x + y)$
5. See back of book.
6. **a.** $-b$ **b.** c **c.** $b^2 - 2c$
7. **a.** 468 **b.** 576 **c.** 540
8. **a.** 49
   b. Answers may vary. Sample: The roots are not real numbers.

Lesson Overview

GOALS

- Warm up to the ideas of the investigation.
- Understand the set of complex numbers as an extension of the real numbers.

This lesson sets up sum-product problems, which form a backbone of the whole investigation. For a monic quadratic $x^2 + bx + c$, the sum of the roots is $-b$, and the product of the roots is c—even if the roots are not real.

FOR YOU TO EXPLORE
- Core: 1, 2, 3, 4a, 6, 8
- Optional: 5
- Extension: 4b, 7

MATERIALS
- Blackline Master 3.1

HOMEWORK
- Core: 9, 11, 12, 14a–d
- Optional: 10, 15, 16, 17
- Extension: 13, 14e

Launch

Have students start on the For You to Explore problems right away.

Explore

For You to Explore

You can use Blackline Master 3.1 for Problems 2, 3, 5, and 6.

PROBLEM 1 The result of this exercise comes up in several places in this chapter, so make sure that all students understand the conclusion. Most students likely have an informal understanding that the function $y = x^2$ has positive outputs and that the function $y = \sqrt{x}$ requires positive inputs.

PROBLEMS 2 AND 3 Point out that you do not need to know the roots to find their sum and product. You might ask students to establish this identity: $(x - r)(x - s) = x^2 - (r + s)x + rs$. Also, if you expand $(r + s)^2$, an expression for the square of the sum of the roots, you can get this expression for the sum of the squares of the roots: $r^2 + s^2 = (r + s)^2 - 2rs$.

PROBLEM 4 The first part of this exercise will be referred to in Lesson 3.2, so it is important to assign it. If a student has trouble getting started, ask them to expand the right side.

PROBLEM 5 This optional exercise provides extra practice for students who do not see (or have not learned) the sum-product connection in Problems 2 and 3. You might ask for just the sum and product here, rather than the sum of squares, in order to save time.

PROBLEM 7 Assign this extra exercise only if students finish the others.

Wrap Up

It is worth doing Problem 6 as a class to make sure that all the students have a chance to see the relationship between the sum and product of the roots and the coefficients of the quadratic with those roots.

A good wrap up for the day might be to write down the quadratic from Problem 8. Ask: If this quadratic has roots, what would the sum of the roots be? (Answer: 14) What would the product of the roots be? (Answer: 50) Can two real numbers add up to 14 and have a product of 50? Explain. Then go over the rest of the problem. This kind of problem shows up again throughout the investigation.

Exercises

HOMEWORK
- Core: 9, 11, 12, 14a–d
- Optional: 10, 15, 16, 17
- Extension: 13, 14e

Check Your Understanding

EXERCISE 9 The point of this exercise is that part (a) is much simpler than part (b). You could assign just part (a) and demonstrate part (b). Part (b) is a good exercise in radical arithmetic, but it is more difficult and time-consuming than part (a).

EXERCISE 12 The two roots are imaginary (they are $5 \pm 2i$), but the sum of squares formula still works, since the sum and product of the imaginaries are real. Make sure you assign this exercise, since it is referenced as one of the examples in Lesson 3.2.

EXERCISE 13 As a teaser, you can tell students that it is possible to answer this question without using radicals or finding the two roots of the original quadratic. While this exercise is difficult, it is an example of a place where the sum-of-squares calculation proves very helpful.

EXERCISE 14 Help students see the connection between this question and finding the roots of a quadratic equation.

Maintain Your Skills

EXERCISE 15 shows students an analog to a new operation that they will learn about in this investigation—taking the complex conjugate of a number. Students are going to be seeing this form a lot in the course of this investigation. This review experience with computations of square roots should help them feel comfortable with complex conjugates when they encounter them.

Exercises *Practicing Habits of Mind*

On Your Own

9. Suppose $a + b = 14$ and $ab = 47$. Find the value of $a^2 + b^2$ in two ways.
a. Use the identity from Problem 4. **b.** Find a and b first.

10. Write About It Decide whether each statement is true or false. Explain.
a. If $r + s$ is an integer, and rs is an integer, then $r^2 + s^2$ is an integer.
b. If $r + s$ and rs are integers, then r and s are integers.

11. Explain why the graph of $y = x^2 - 10x + 29$ cannot cross the x-axis.

> What happens if you use the quadratic formula to find the roots of $x^2 - 10x + 29 = 0$?

12. Suppose $a + b = 10$ and $ab = 29$.
a. Find the value of $a^2 + b^2$. Use the identity from Problem 4.
b. What happens if you try to find $a^2 + b^2$ by finding a and b first?

13. Take It Further The quadratic $x^2 - 10x + 22$ has two roots. Find a quadratic with roots that are the *squares* of the roots of $x^2 - 10x + 22$.

14. Find two numbers with sum p and product q.
a. $p = 7, q = 10$ **b.** $p = 2, q = -15$ **c.** $p = 2, q = \frac{3}{4}$ **d.** $p = 2, q = -1$
e. Take It Further Express the two numbers in terms of p and q.

> These problems are all sum-and-product problems. However, you need different types of numbers for each one. Can you determine which type of numbers you need in each case?

Maintain Your Skills

15. Expand each expression.
a. $(\sqrt{7} + \sqrt{3})(\sqrt{7} - \sqrt{3})$
b. $(\sqrt{5} + \sqrt{2})(\sqrt{5} - \sqrt{2})$
c. $(3 + \sqrt{7})(3 - \sqrt{7})$
d. $(2\sqrt{3} + \sqrt{5})(2\sqrt{3} - \sqrt{5})$
e. $(\sqrt{m} + \sqrt{n})(\sqrt{m} - \sqrt{n})$
f. $(a + \sqrt{b})(a - \sqrt{b})$

> Give exact answers, not decimal approximations.

16. Rewrite each fraction so that it has an integer denominator.
a. $\frac{1}{\sqrt{7} + \sqrt{3}}$
b. $\frac{1}{\sqrt{5} + \sqrt{2}}$

17. Simplify each expression without using a calculator.
a. $(\sqrt{2})^2 + (-\sqrt{2})^2$
b. $(1 + \sqrt{2})^2 + (1 - \sqrt{2})^2$
c. $\sqrt{2} \cdot \sqrt{5}$
d. $\sqrt{3} \cdot \sqrt{5}$
e. $\sqrt{7} \cdot \sqrt{7}$
f. $(b\sqrt{2}) \cdot (b\sqrt{2})$
g. $\sqrt{a} \cdot \sqrt{b}$
h. $\sqrt{k} \cdot \sqrt{k}$

Answers

Exercises

9. a. 102 **b.** 102

10. a. True; answers may vary. Sample: Using the identity in Exercise 4(a), $r^2 + s^2 = (r + s)^2 - 2rs$, if $r + s$ and rs are integers, then $r^2 + s^2$ is an integer.

b. False; answers may vary. Sample: If $r = 2 + \sqrt{2}$ and $s = 2 - \sqrt{2}$, then $r + s = 4$ and $rs = 2$ are integers, but r and s are not integers.

11. The roots are not real numbers, so there are no x-intercepts.

12. a. 42

b. Answers may vary. Sample: The given values of $a + b$ and ab correspond with the quadratic $x^2 - 10x + 29$, which has no real-number roots.

3.2 Extending Number Systems

The set of complex numbers is a number system that is an extension of the real numbers. In this lesson, you will examine why and how such extensions come about.

The earliest records of mathematics point to the system of counting numbers (1, 2, 3, . . .) and the operations of addition and multiplication. This system of counting numbers is referred to as the **natural numbers,** $\mathbb{N}$.

This system is closed under addition and multiplication. If you add or multiply two counting numbers, the result is a counting number. The counting numbers are not closed under other operations, but the results may still have meaning. This leads to extensions of $\mathbb{N}$.

- Consider $3 - 5 + 8$. The result is 6, but $3 - 5$ is not a counting number. So, you must "dip into" negative numbers in the middle of this calculation. However, the original expression and its result are both in $\mathbb{N}$. This type of calculation leads to the system of integers, $\mathbb{Z}$.
- Consider $28 \div 5 \times 10$. The result is 56, but $28 \div 5$, or $\frac{28}{5}$, is not an integer. This leads to the system of rational numbers, $\mathbb{Q}$. The rational numbers are closed under addition, subtraction, multiplication, and division (except division by 0).

$\mathbb{Q}$ stands for "quotient." $\mathbb{Q}$ consists of all numbers $\frac{p}{q}$ where p and q are integers and $q \neq 0$.

Developing Habits of Mind

Experiment. You can define new numbers and incorporate them into an existing number system by extending the rules of calculation.

For example, start with $\mathbb{N}$ and extend to include 0, the identity for addition. Now you can define other numbers by how they operate under addition and multiplication.

- -5 is a new number defined by the fact that when you add it to 5, you get 0.
- $\frac{1}{5}$ is a new number defined by the fact that when you multiply it by 5, you get 1.

A number is something you can point to on the number line. The number line is a representation of all real numbers. Real numbers contain the rational numbers $\mathbb{Q}$ and **irrational numbers** that you cannot express as a quotient of integers. Irrational numbers include numbers such as $\sqrt{2}$ and π.

Remember...
Use $\mathbb{R}$ to represent the real numbers. So, you have $\mathbb{N}$, $\mathbb{Z}$, $\mathbb{Q}$, and $\mathbb{R}$.

You have already seen problems where even real numbers are not enough. Take a closer look at Exercise 12 in Lesson 3.1.

13. $x^2 - 56x + 484 = 0$

14. a. 5 and 2
b. 5 and -3
c. $\frac{3}{2}$ and $\frac{1}{2}$
d. $1 + \sqrt{2}$ and $1 - \sqrt{2}$
e. $\frac{p + \sqrt{p^2 - 4q}}{2}$ and $\frac{p - \sqrt{p^2 - 4q}}{2}$

15. a. 4 **b.** 3 **c.** 2 **d.** 7
e. $m - n$
f. $a^2 - b$

16. a. $\frac{\sqrt{7} - \sqrt{3}}{4}$ **b.** $\frac{\sqrt{5} - \sqrt{2}}{3}$

17. a. 4 **b.** 6 **c.** $\sqrt{10}$
d. $\sqrt{15}$ **e.** 7 **f.** $2b^2$
g. $\sqrt{ab}$ **h.** k

Lesson Overview

GOALS

- Understand the set of complex numbers as an extension of the real numbers.
- Use complex numbers as tools for solving equations.

This lesson should go quickly, with students spending most of their time on the exercises. The general idea of the lesson is very simple: number systems get extended when they need to be. The lesson opens with two examples of problems stated with counting numbers whose solutions are counting numbers. The work to find those solutions, though, requires "dipping into" extensions of the system of counting numbers. The Example is a first hint that the real numbers may also be extended.

CHECK YOUR UNDERSTANDING
- Core: 1, 5, 6, 8
- Optional: 2, 3, 4, 7, 9, 10a–e, 11a–c
- Extension: 10f, 11d

MATERIALS
- graph paper
- graphing calculators
- Blackline Master 3.2

HOMEWORK
- Core: 12, 13, 14, 16, 17
- Optional: 15, 18

VOCABULARY
- intercept
- irrational numbers
- natural numbers, $\mathbb{N}$
- i, $\sqrt{-1}$

Launch

Open this lesson by reminding students what the counting numbers are. Ask: If you add two counting numbers, will you get a counting number? What about multiplying? What about subtracting? Dividing? These facts are sometimes described by saying the counting numbers are closed under addition and multiplication, but they are not closed under subtraction and division.

You can use Blackline Master 3.2 as a transparency to review the definition of each set of numbers. Placing the answers to calculations can help students see that the counting numbers are not closed under all operations.

Explore

Example

This is the first example of square roots of negative numbers. It is worth your while to work with the class to show that $a^2 + b^2 = 42$. The explanation is technical and requires making plenty of assumptions about how $\sqrt{-16}$ behaves. That is the whole point. It took a long time to get used to the idea that using the usual rules on complex numbers would not result in nonsense. This is a good place to help your students as they start down that path.

To finish the Example, assuming these numbers obey the usual rules of arithmetic, you can square each and add the answers:

$$a^2 = \left(\frac{10 + \sqrt{-16}}{2}\right)^2$$
$$= \frac{(10 + \sqrt{-16})^2}{4}$$
$$= \frac{100 + 2 \cdot 10\sqrt{-16} + (\sqrt{-16})^2}{4}$$
$$= \frac{100 + 20\sqrt{-16} + (-16)}{4}$$

(after all, $(\sqrt{-16})^2$ should equal -16)

$$= \frac{84 + 20\sqrt{-16}}{4}$$

Using the same reasoning, b^2 should equal $\frac{84 - 20\sqrt{-16}}{4}$. So, assume that arithmetic acts the way you want it to.

$$a^2 + b^2 = \frac{84 + 20\sqrt{-16}}{4} + \frac{84 - 20\sqrt{-16}}{4}$$
$$= \frac{84 + 20\sqrt{-16} + 84 - 20\sqrt{-16}}{4}$$
$$= \frac{84 + 84 + 20\sqrt{-16} - 20\sqrt{-16}}{4}$$
$$= \frac{168}{4} = 42$$

If you "make believe" that square roots of negative numbers exist and calculate as if they obey the rules of arithmetic, the "imaginary" numbers drop out at the end, and you are left with 42.

Wrap Up

To wrap this lesson up, you might choose one or two polynomial equations and look at the solutions. One interesting choice might be $x^3 = 1$. After students find the solution $x = 1$, you might ask students to use the quadratic formula to find the other solutions. This will foreshadow Lesson 3.3.

Example

Problem Suppose $a + b = 10$ and $ab = 29$. Find the value of $a^2 + b^2$.

Solution 1 Use the identity $x^2 + y^2 = (x + y)^2 - 2xy$.

If $a + b = 10$ and $ab = 29$, then

$$a^2 + b^2 = (a + b)^2 - 2ab$$
$$= 10^2 - 2 \cdot 29$$
$$= 100 - 58$$
$$= 42$$

The value of $a^2 + b^2$ is 42.

Solution 2 Another idea is to find a and b first. Think of it as a sum-and-product problem. If $a + b = 10$ and $ab = 29$, then a and b are the two roots of the equation $x^2 - 10x + 29 = 0$.

To find a and b, use the quadratic formula. This results in two strange-looking roots.

$$\frac{10 \pm \sqrt{100 - 4 \cdot 29}}{2} = \frac{10 \pm \sqrt{100 - 116}}{2} = \frac{10 \pm \sqrt{-16}}{2}$$

The expression $\sqrt{-16}$ seems to make no sense because there is no real number with square -16. But suppose that the roots are numbers. So, there are two numbers a and b.

$$a = \frac{10 + \sqrt{-16}}{2} \text{ and } b = \frac{10 - \sqrt{-16}}{2}$$

There are still several steps to do to show that $a^2 + b^2 = 42$. Consider this method a work in progress.

Remember...

An *identity* is an equation that is true for any substitution for its variables.

In algebra, you sometimes make believe certain numbers exist to help you solve problems.

For Discussion

1. What steps might you try next to show that $a^2 + b^2 = 42$? Do you have to make any assumptions about how $\sqrt{-16}$ behaves?

Often a problem and its solution are in the same number system, but the process of solving the problem requires you to leave the system. Sometimes you must invent new objects that cancel out at the end of the process.

Gradually, mathematicians regarded numbers such as $\sqrt{-16}$ as more than just convenient devices that might cancel out in a calculation. Mathematicians found more and more uses for such numbers. These types of numbers fill in many of the algebraic holes in $\mathbb{R}$, in a way similar to how the numbers in $\mathbb{R}$ fill in the geometric holes in $\mathbb{Q}$.

In this chapter you will work with square roots of negative numbers until you begin to feel comfortable working with them. Then you can use them to solve problems in algebra and geometry.

Habits of Mind

Look for relationships. Sometimes, you get answers that are familiar, but the computations go through unfamiliar territory. Other times, you get answers that come from unfamiliar territory.

Answers

For Discussion

1. Answers may vary. Sample: You have to assume that $a\sqrt{-n} + b\sqrt{-n} = (a + b)\sqrt{-n}$ and that $\left(\sqrt{-n}\right)^2 = -n$. Then

$$a^2 + b^2 = \left(\frac{10 + \sqrt{-16}}{2}\right)^2 + \left(\frac{10 - \sqrt{-16}}{2}\right)^2$$
$$= \frac{100 + 20\sqrt{-16} + (-16)}{4} + \frac{100 - 20\sqrt{-16} + (-16)}{4}$$
$$= \frac{100 - 16 + 100 - 16}{4} = 42$$

Exercises *Practicing Habits of Mind*

Check Your Understanding

1. For each equation, find the solutions, if any, that are in $\mathbb{N}$ (the natural numbers).

   a. $x^2 + 24 = 10x$ b. $x^2 = 10x$

   c. $x^2 + 10x + 24 = 0$ d. $24x^2 + 1 = 10x$

   e. $x^2 = 10$ f. $x^2 + 10 = 0$

   g. $x^2 + x + 1 = 0$ h. $x^3 = 1$

2. For each equation in Exercise 1, find the solutions, if any, that are in $\mathbb{Z}$ (the integers) but not in $\mathbb{N}$.

3. For each equation in Exercise 1, find the solutions, if any, that are in $\mathbb{Q}$ (the rational numbers) but not in $\mathbb{Z}$.

4. For each equation in Exercise 1, find the solutions, if any, that are in $\mathbb{R}$ (the real numbers) but not in $\mathbb{Q}$.

5. For each equation in Exercise 1, find the solutions, if any, that are not in $\mathbb{R}$.

6. For each equation, determine the number of real solutions.

   a. $x^2 + 4x + 3 = 0$ b. $x^2 + 4x + 4 = 0$

   c. $x^2 + 4x + 5 = 0$ d. $3x^2 - 10x + 8 = 0$

7. Graph each equation. Find the coordinates of all intercepts.

   a. $y = x^2 + 4x + 3$ b. $y = x^2 + 4x + 4$

   c. $y = x^2 + 4x + 5$ d. $y = 3x^2 - 10x + 8$

Remember...

An intercept is a point where a graph crosses either the *x*- or *y*-axis.

8. Suppose there is a number i with square -1.

   a. Simplify $(1 + i)^2 - 2(1 + i) + 2$.

   b. Explain why the number $1 + i$ is a solution of the equation $x^2 - 2x + 2 = 0$.

Every time you see an i^2, replace it with -1.

9. Use the function $a(n)$. The domain is the whole numbers $\{0, 1, 2, 3, \ldots\}$.

$$a(n) = (\sqrt{3})^n + (-\sqrt{3})^n$$

   a. Find $a(n)$ for $n = 0$ through $n = 6$.

   b. Find $a(10)$ and $a(101)$.

   c. Is there a polynomial that agrees with this function a on all of $\mathbb{N}$? Explain.

Assessment Resources

Lesson Quiz 3.2

1. For each equation, find the solutions, if any, that are in $\mathbb{N}$.

   a. $x^2 + 11x + 10 = 0$ b. $x^2 + 10 = 11x$

   c. $x^2 + 3x = -7$ d. $x^2 - 3 = 6$

   e. $x^2 = 17$ f. $3x^2 + 8 = 10x$

2. For each equation in Exercise 1, find the solutions, if any, that meet the given conditions.

   I. in $\mathbb{Z}$ but not in $\mathbb{N}$ II. in $\mathbb{Q}$ but not in $\mathbb{Z}$

   III. in $\mathbb{R}$ but not in $\mathbb{Q}$ IV. not in $\mathbb{R}$

3. Decide whether each calculation results in a real number. Explain.

   a. $(7 + 2\sqrt{-1}) + (7 - 2\sqrt{-1})$ b. $(8 + \sqrt{-1}) - (8 - \sqrt{-1})$

   c. $(3 + \sqrt{-1})(3 + \sqrt{-1})$ d. $(3 + \sqrt{-1})(3 - \sqrt{-1})$

Exercises

HOMEWORK

- Core: 12, 13, 14, 16, 17
- Optional: 15, 18

Check Your Understanding

EXERCISES 2–5 You may wish to assign only parts of the series of exercises from Exercises 2–5. Either ask students to follow only some of the quadratics through the whole series of extended allowable solutions, or ask them to follow all of the quadratics through some of the extensions for allowable solutions. Make your choice based on where you feel students need the most practice.

The concept in this series of exercises is that the number system drives the number and type of solutions. In this chapter, you seek to expand students' knowledge of number systems to $\mathbb{C}$, while reminding them that it is sometimes still appropriate to think about other systems.

EXERCISES 6 AND 7 Exercise 6 is connected to Exercise 7, but they are independent. You can assign one or the other or both, as you wish.

EXERCISE 7 Students should use a graphing calculator for this exercise. If students are not using graphing calculators, you may want to skip it.

Exercises

1. **a.** 4, 6
   b. 10
   c–g. no solution
   h. 1
2. **a.** no additional solutions
   b. 0
   c. $-6, -4$
   d–h. no additional solutions
3. **a–c.** no additional solutions
   d. $\frac{1}{4}, \frac{1}{6}$
   e–h. no additional solutions
4. **a–d.** no additional solutions
   e. $\sqrt{10}, -\sqrt{10}$
   f–h. no additional solutions
5. **a–e.** no additional solutions
   f. $\sqrt{-10}, -\sqrt{-10}$
   g. $\frac{-1 \pm \sqrt{-3}}{2}$ **h.** $\frac{-1 \pm \sqrt{-3}}{2}$
6. **a.** 2 **b.** 1 **c.** 0 **d.** 2
7. See back of book.
8. **a.** 0
   b. If $f(x) = x^2 - 2x + 2$, then $f(1 + i) = 0$ (by Exercise 8a).
9. See back of book.

EXERCISE 10 Use of a calculator is fine here, but expect students to be surprised that $f(n)$ produces integers. The last two parts are more theoretical and you can skip them if you are focusing on basic calculation at this stage. If students have not yet found a method for producing an equation with a given root, you might want to go over the solution to that part with your class.

The final part does involve some subtle factoring techniques, and some students may need support.

Although this exercise includes irrational numbers rather than complex numbers, many of the techniques for computing with irrational numbers are parallel to techniques students will use with complex numbers. See Exercise 11.

EXERCISE 11 Students should use a calculator that recognizes imaginary numbers or has the capability of a computer algebra system (CAS) to evaluate expressions including an unknown.

Encourage students to approach the exercise by thinking of $\sqrt{-1}$ as some constant i, and leave it as an unknown in their equations. They then need to make substitutions for terms such as i^2 and i^3 in a way that makes sense.

On Your Own

EXERCISE 12 gets students thinking about the relationships between different systems of numbers and how elements of a system can be operated on to obtain elements of another. You may wish to review this exercise to generate a lot of different student examples.

EXERCISE 13 Students may be able to find solutions that work for more than one of the cases.

EXERCISE 14 is designed as an independent followup to Exercises 1–5 from the Check Your Understanding exercises. You may wish to assign it to reinforce the concept of extending the range of acceptable solutions for a quadratic equation. Solving all parts for every equation in Exercise 13 may be more than your students need, so assign strategically.

10. Use the function $f(n)$. The domain is the whole numbers $\{0, 1, 2, 3, \ldots\}$.

$$f(n) = (1 + \sqrt{2})^n + (1 - \sqrt{2})^n$$

Determine whether each number is rational or irrational.

a. $(1 + \sqrt{2})^0$ **b.** $(1 + \sqrt{2})^1$ **c.** $(1 + \sqrt{2})^2$

d. Find $f(n)$ for $n = 0$ through $n = 6$.

e. Find an equation with integer coefficients that has $1 + \sqrt{2}$ as a solution.

f. **Take It Further** Show that $f(n) = 2f(n-1) + f(n-2)$ for any positive integer $n > 2$.

11. Suppose there is a number $\sqrt{-1}$, with square -1, that obeys the basic rules of arithmetic. The domain of the function $g(n)$ below is the whole numbers.

$$g(n) = (2 + \sqrt{-1})^n + (2 - \sqrt{-1})^n$$

a. Find $g(n)$ for $n = 0$ through $n = 6$.

b. Show that $(2 + \sqrt{-1})^2 = 3 + 4\sqrt{-1}$.

c. Find an equation with integer coefficients that has $2 + \sqrt{-1}$ as a root.

d. **Take It Further** Show that $g(n) = 4g(n-1) - 5g(n-2)$ for any positive integer $n > 2$.

For convenience, you might use some letter instead of $\sqrt{-1}$. Many people use i.

On Your Own

12. For each case, give two examples of a calculation with two numbers.

a. The inputs are not positive integers, but the result is a positive integer.

b. The inputs are not integers, but the result is an integer.

c. The inputs are not rational numbers, but the result is a rational number.

d. The inputs are not real numbers, but the result is a real number.

e. The inputs are positive integers, but the result is not a positive integer.

f. The inputs are integers, but the result is not an integer.

g. The inputs are rational numbers, but the result is not a rational number.

h. The inputs are real numbers, but the result is not a real number.

13. For each equation, find the solutions, if any, that are in $\mathbb{N}$.

a. $x^2 + 5 = 6x$ **b.** $x^2 + 6x + 5 = 0$ **c.** $x^2 + 4x = -2$

d. $5x^2 + x = 6$ **e.** $x^2 = 5$ **f.** $x^2 + 11 = 6x$

14. For each equation in Exercise 13, find the solutions, if any, that meet the given condition.

a. in $\mathbb{Z}$ but not in $\mathbb{N}$ **b.** in $\mathbb{Q}$ but not in $\mathbb{Z}$

c. in $\mathbb{R}$ but not in $\mathbb{Q}$ **d.** not in $\mathbb{R}$

Go Online
PHSchool.com

For additional practice, go to **Web Code:** bfa-0302

Answers

10–11. See back of book.

12. Answers may vary. Samples are given.

a. $(-10) - (-20) = 10$, $(-10)(-20) = 200$

b. $\frac{5}{4} \cdot \frac{4}{5} = 1$, $\frac{5}{4} + \frac{3}{4} = 2$

c. $\frac{5\sqrt{3}}{\sqrt{3}} = 5$, $\sqrt{2} \cdot \sqrt{8} = 4$

d. $(1 + \sqrt{-2}) + (1 - \sqrt{-2}) = 2$, $\sqrt{-1} \cdot \sqrt{-1} = -1$

e. $4 - 10 = -6$, $\frac{15}{25} = \frac{3}{5}$

f. $\frac{-6}{8} = \frac{-3}{4}$, $1 \div 2 = 0.5$

g. $\sqrt{\frac{1}{2}} = \frac{\sqrt{2}}{2}$, $\sqrt{\frac{50}{10}} = \sqrt{5}$

h. $\sqrt{4 - 8} = \sqrt{-4}$, $\sqrt{5 - 7} = \sqrt{-2}$

13. a. 1, 5 **b–c.** no solution
d. 1 **e–f.** no solution

14. a. Exercise 13b: $-1, -5$
b. Exercise 13d: $-\frac{6}{5}$
c. Exercise 13c: $-2 \pm \sqrt{2}$
Exercise 13e: $\pm\sqrt{5}$
d. Exercise 13f: $3 \pm \sqrt{-2}$

15. Calculate the sum and product of each pair of numbers.

a. 13 and −23 b. $1 + 3$ and $1 - 3$

c. $1 + \sqrt{3}$ and $1 - \sqrt{3}$ d. $1 + \sqrt{n}$ and $1 - \sqrt{n}$

e. $1 + \sqrt{-3}$ and $1 - \sqrt{-3}$

You should give the answers for Exercise 15d in terms of *n*.

16. **Standardized Test Prep** What is the product of $3 + \sqrt{-2}$ and $3 - \sqrt{-2}$?

A. 1 B. 7 C. 9 D. 11

Maintain Your Skills

17. Decide whether each calculation results in a real number. Explain.

a. $(2 + \sqrt{-1}) + (2 - \sqrt{-1})$ b. $(2 + \sqrt{-1}) - (2 - \sqrt{-1})$

c. $(2 + \sqrt{-1})(2 + \sqrt{-1})$ d. $(2 + \sqrt{-1})(2 - \sqrt{-1})$

e. $\dfrac{2 + \sqrt{-1}}{2 + \sqrt{-1}}$

Again, assume you have a number $\sqrt{-1}$ that obeys the basic rules of arithmetic.

18. Suppose $x^2 = -1$. Write each expression in the form $A + Bx$, for real numbers A and B.

a. $(2 + 3x) + (5 + 6x)$ b. $(2 + 3x) + (2 - 3x)$ c. $(2 + 3x) - (2 - 3x)$

d. $(2 + 3x)(5 + 6x)$ e. $(2 + 3x)^2$ f. $(2 + 3x)(2 - 3x)$

Go Online
PHSchool.com

For more information about complex numbers, go to **Web Code:** bfe-0831

Historical Perspective

Square roots of negative numbers were first studied in the early 1500s. Mathematicians wanted to find a formula, similar to the quadratic formula, to solve cubic equations. Girolamo Cardano (1501–1576), Nicolo Tartaglia (1500–1557), and others developed and refined such a formula.

When they applied the formula to cubic functions with real roots, such as $x^3 - 15x - 4$, they ended up with expressions involving square roots of negative numbers.

The mathematicians did not let this strange result stop them. They imagined that they could calculate with these expressions, using the basic rules and the theorems of algebra.

Girolamo Cardano Nicolo Tartaglia

15. a. The sum is −10, and the product is −299.
b. The sum is 2, and the product is −8.
c. The sum is 2, and the product is −2.
d. The sum is 2, and the product is $1 - n$.
e. The sum is 2, and the product is 4.

16. D

17. a. Yes; the $\sqrt{-1}$ terms cancel each other, so the result is real.
b. No; there will be a $\sqrt{-1}$ term in the result, so it is not real.
c. No; there will be a $\sqrt{-1}$ term in the result, so it is not real.
d. Yes; the $\sqrt{-1}$ terms cancel each other, so the result is real.
e. Yes; there will be no $\sqrt{-1}$ term in the result, so it is real.

18. a. $7 + 9x$ b. $4 + 0x$
c. $0 + 6x$ d. $-8 + 27x$
e. $-5 + 12x$ f. $13 + 0x$

Maintain Your Skills

EXERCISE 17 The hope is that students will be surprised by the possibility that operations on complex numbers can result in real numbers, but recognize that this result can occur with other systems.

EXERCISE 18 is a good practice exercise for helping students get used to the idea of working with *i*.

Additional Resources

PRINT RESOURCES
- Solution Manual
- Practice Workbook
- Assessment Resources
- Teaching Resources

TECHNOLOGY
- Interactive Textbook
- TeacherExpress CD-ROM
- ExamView CD-ROM
- PHSchool.com

Additional Practice

1. For each equation, find the solutions, if any, that are in $\mathbb{N}$.
a. $x^2 + 7x + 6 = 0$ b. $x^2 + 6 = 7x$
c. $x^2 + 7x = 6$ d. $x^2 - 4 = 12$
e. $x^2 = 3$ f. $7x^2 - 1 = 6x$

2. For each equation in Exercise 1, find the solutions, if any, that meet the given conditions.
I. in $\mathbb{Z}$ but not in $\mathbb{N}$
II. in $\mathbb{Q}$ but not in $\mathbb{Z}$
III. in $\mathbb{R}$ but not in $\mathbb{Q}$
IV. not in $\mathbb{R}$

3. Decide whether each calculation results in a real number. Explain.
a. $(5 + \sqrt{-1}) + (5 - \sqrt{-1})$ b. $(5 + \sqrt{-1})(5 + \sqrt{-1})$
c. $\dfrac{5 - \sqrt{-1}}{-5 + \sqrt{-1}}$ d. $(5 + \sqrt{-1})(5 - \sqrt{-1})$

4. Simplify each product.
a. $\sqrt{-2} \cdot \sqrt{-8}$ b. $\sqrt{-3} \cdot \sqrt{-3}$
c. $\sqrt{-16} \cdot \sqrt{-4}$ d. $\sqrt{-4} \cdot \sqrt{-16}$
e. $(3 - \sqrt{-5}) \cdot \sqrt{-5}$ f. $\sqrt{-6} \cdot (1 + \sqrt{-6})$

5. Write each expression in the form $a + b\sqrt{-1}$, where a and b are real numbers.
a. $(5 + 3\sqrt{-1}) + (7 + 4\sqrt{-1})$ b. $(6 + \sqrt{-9}) + (2 + 4\sqrt{-81})$
c. $(5 + 3\sqrt{-1})(5 + \sqrt{-1})$ d. $(7 - 4\sqrt{-1}) + (7 + 4\sqrt{-1})$

6. The equation $x^3 - 27 = 0$ has one solution in $\mathbb{R}$, $x = 3$.
a. Factor $x^3 - 27$.
b. Use the factored form to find all three solutions to the equation.

7. Simplify each expression.
a. $(5 + \sqrt{-2})(5 - \sqrt{-2})$ b. $\sqrt{-1} \cdot (\sqrt{-1} \cdot \sqrt{-1})$
c. $(\sqrt{-1})^5$ d. $(x + y\sqrt{-4})(x - y\sqrt{-4})$
e. $(6 + 3\sqrt{-1})(6 - 3\sqrt{-1})$ f. $(\sqrt{-1})^7$

Practice: For Lesson 3.2, assign Exercises 1–3.

Lesson Overview

GOALS

- Understand the set of complex numbers as an extension of the real numbers.
- Use complex numbers as tools for solving equations.

At this point in the investigation, students equations should have a clear idea that the goal is to extend the real numbers to another system. The point of this investigation is that such an extension has to be carried out with care. The For Discussion problems that ask students to find the value of $\sqrt{-12}\sqrt{-3}$ and $\sqrt{-12}\sqrt{-12}$ are important because:

- This alerts students that the rules for calculation may break when a system is extended. Here, the rule $\sqrt{a}\sqrt{b} = \sqrt{ab}$ breaks down in the extension.
- This alerts students to the need for a definition of the square root of a negative number and to the need for a convention to use in assigning a meaning to $\sqrt{-n}$. In fact, the square root symbol was defined to mean the positive square root of a positive number. Now the symbol has no meaning for negative numbers. If you try to use this symbol by extending its multiplicative property, you get into trouble with the basic rules.
- You want students to be fluent at computation with complex numbers.

CHECK YOUR UNDERSTANDING
- Core: 1, 2, 3, 4, 6
- Optional: 5, 7, 8

MATERIALS
- graph paper
- graphing calculators
- Blackline Master 3.3

HOMEWORK
- Core: 9, 11, 12, 13, 16, 17
- Optional: 10, 14
- Extension: 15

Launch

Launch this lesson with the example in the opening paragraph: $x^2 - 4x + 16 = 0$. Then move straight into For You to Do.

Explore

For You to Do

PROBLEMS 1 AND 2 If students do not notice the relationship between these answers and the coefficients of the polynomial $x^2 - 4x + 16 = 0$, point it out.

Example

This example reviews simplifying radicals. Some students may not know how to begin.

3.3 Making the Extension: $\sqrt{-1}$

To find two numbers with a sum of 4 and a product of 16, you can solve the quadratic equation $x^2 - 4x + 16 = 0$. Use the quadratic formula to find the two solutions.

$$x = \frac{4 \pm \sqrt{4^2 - 4 \cdot 16}}{2} = \frac{4 \pm \sqrt{-48}}{2}$$

Because you cannot take the square root of a negative number in the real number system, no real solutions exist for the equation. So you cannot find two real numbers with a sum of 4 and a product of 16. However, if you allow for square roots of negatives, the two roots you found with the quadratic formula may solve the problem.

For You to Do

Evaluate each expression.

1. $\frac{4 + \sqrt{-48}}{2} + \frac{4 - \sqrt{-48}}{2}$
2. $\frac{4 + \sqrt{-48}}{2} \cdot \frac{4 - \sqrt{-48}}{2}$

Assume that the basic rules for calculating with numbers still work, and that $(\sqrt{-48})^2 = -48$.

Example

Problem Rewrite $\frac{4 + \sqrt{-48}}{2}$ as an expression without a denominator.

Solution Note that $-48 = 16 \cdot -3$.

$$\sqrt{-48} = \sqrt{16 \cdot -3} = \sqrt{16} \cdot \sqrt{-3} = 4\sqrt{-3}$$

Rewrite $\sqrt{-48}$ to simplify the expression.

$$\frac{4 + \sqrt{-48}}{2} = \frac{4 + 4\sqrt{-3}}{2}$$
$$= \frac{2(2 + 2\sqrt{-3})}{2}$$
$$= 2 + 2\sqrt{-3}$$

Answers

For You to Do

1. 4
2. 16

Developing Habits of Mind

Check your work. Look more carefully at the calculation below.

$$\sqrt{-48} \overset{(1)}{=} \sqrt{16 \cdot -3} \overset{(2)}{=} \sqrt{16} \cdot \sqrt{-3} \overset{(3)}{=} 4\sqrt{-3}$$

Step (1) and Step (3) seem fine. But is Step (2) legitimate? Is the square root of a product always equal to the product of the square roots? It is true when the numbers are positive, but that is because of a convention. There are two numbers with a square 9, but we defined the symbol $\sqrt{9}$ to mean the positive number with a square 9.

You can use the "duck principle" to see if the ends of the calculation agree. Do you get -48 when you square $4\sqrt{-3}$?

$$(4\sqrt{-3})^2 = 4\sqrt{-3} \cdot 4\sqrt{-3} = 16 \cdot \sqrt{-3} \cdot \sqrt{-3} = 16 \cdot (-3) = -48$$

Since $\sqrt{-3} \cdot \sqrt{-3} = -3$, it seems reasonable for you to say that $\sqrt{-48} = 4\sqrt{-3}$. But what happens when both square roots are of negative numbers?

The duck principle: If it walks like a duck and quacks like a duck, then it probably is a duck.

For Discussion

3. Find the value of $\sqrt{-12} \cdot \sqrt{-3}$.

4. Find the value of $\sqrt{-12} \cdot \sqrt{-12}$.

Minds in Action

episode 10

Tony and Sasha debate their answers to the For Discussion problems.

Tony I solved the first one. It's 6.

Sasha I solved it too. It's -6.

Tony Well, then you're wrong. It can't be both 6 *and* -6.

Sasha No, you're wrong. I replaced $\sqrt{-12}$ with $2\sqrt{-3}$ and calculated.

$$\sqrt{-12}\sqrt{-3} = \sqrt{4 \cdot -3}\sqrt{-3} = \sqrt{4}\sqrt{-3}\sqrt{-3} = 2\sqrt{-3} \cdot \sqrt{-3}$$

The square roots $\sqrt{-3}$ and $\sqrt{-3}$ multiply to make -3. Then 2 times -3 is -6, and that's the answer.

Tony Hmm. That looks pretty solid, actually.

Sasha As I said, I'm right and you're wrong. What did you do?

Tony I used the fact that $\sqrt{a}$ times $\sqrt{b}$ is $\sqrt{ab}$. So, $\sqrt{-12} \cdot \sqrt{-3}$ is the same as $\sqrt{-12 \cdot -3}$. I multiplied and got $\sqrt{36}$. Then $\sqrt{36}$ is 6, and that's my answer.

For Discussion

3. $\sqrt{123}\sqrt{-12} \cdot \sqrt{-3}$
$= \sqrt{12}\sqrt{-1} \cdot \sqrt{3}\sqrt{-1}$
$= \sqrt{36}(\sqrt{-1})^2$
$= 6 \cdot (-1)$
$= -6$

4. $\sqrt{-12} \cdot \sqrt{-12}$
$= \sqrt{12}\sqrt{-1} \cdot \sqrt{12}\sqrt{-1}$
$= (\sqrt{12})^2 \cdot (\sqrt{-1})^2$
$= 12 \cdot -1$
$= -12$

Developing Habits of Mind

This section encourages students to be skeptical of the idea of simply extending rules to a larger number system. Instead of simply stating what rules work, students should question each rule, and special cases of each rule, before deciding whether it makes sense to extend the rule.

For Discussion

With any luck, students will come up with different answers to these questions. For Problem 3, the answer could be 6 or -6. For Problem 4, the answer could be 12 or -12.

Let students argue for a few moments. You can use Blackline Master 3.3 to illustrate various methods for solving Problems 3 and 4. It shows the convention for taking the square root of negative numbers so that students can agree on the correct answers. Without a convention in place, there is no way of "deciding" which answer is correct. If the discussion is good enough, skip the dialog (you might mention that Tony and Sasha go through the same complexities) and go straight to the convention. Otherwise, the dialog may be useful in bringing the argument to the classroom. The correct answers, by convention, are -6 and -12.

Minds in Action

Tony and Sasha model what could be the discussion in your class. If you find students are not coming up with conflicting possibilities for the For Discussion problems, you can simply continue on to this dialog.

Once the dialog is complete, continue the discussion with students. See if they have a particular feeling as to which answer should be the convention.

NOTE ON NOTATION The second margin note suggests using i to represent $\sqrt{-1}$. The next lesson formalizes the definition, so there is no need to make an issue of it at this time. Advanced students may want to make the jump right to using i, while other students may be more comfortable working through the exercises using $\sqrt{-1}$.

Sasha Hmm. That looks pretty solid too. That's trouble. Did you get -12 for the second one?

Tony Sure. That one was easier, $\sqrt{x} \cdot \sqrt{x}$ is just x, no matter what x is.

Sasha Why didn't you use the rule you used for the first one?

Tony I don't know, I guess I could have. Then $\sqrt{-12} \cdot \sqrt{-12}$ is the same as $\sqrt{-12 \cdot -12}$. That's . . . uh oh, that's $\sqrt{144}$ which is 12, not -12.

Sasha Maybe you can't trust that $\sqrt{ab}$ rule after all . . .

Sasha and Tony's discussion leads to an important consequence. Known rules for calculation may no longer work in an extended system. The rule $\sqrt{a} \cdot \sqrt{b} = \sqrt{ab}$ works for nonnegative real numbers, but leads to a contradiction when both a and b are negative. Sasha and Tony discovered this contradiction when they compared their answers to Problem 3. Both 6 and -6 seem to make sense as values of $\sqrt{-12} \cdot \sqrt{-3}$. You need a more precise rule for handling square roots of negative numbers.

Think about the square roots of positive numbers. What does $\sqrt{49}$ mean? Your answer may be "a number with a square of 49," but there are two of these, 7 and –7. By convention, people decided that $\sqrt{49}$ represents the positive square root. Once you accept this convention, you can use it to prove theorems such as $\sqrt{a} \cdot \sqrt{b} = \sqrt{ab}$ (when a and b are nonnegative).

What does this use of *convention* mean?

You need a similar convention for negative numbers in order to avoid Tony and Sasha's contradiction. The following definition does the trick.

- Start with the real numbers, $\mathbb{R}$. $\mathbb{R}$ already contains the square roots of positive numbers.
- Introduce one new number, $\sqrt{-1}$. This is just a symbol. The only property of $\sqrt{-1}$ is that its square is –1.
- If n is positive, define $\sqrt{n}$ as $\sqrt{-n} = \sqrt{n} \cdot \sqrt{-1}$.

Remember...

You can use the letter i to represent $\sqrt{-1}$.

The following are some examples of numbers using this definition of $\sqrt{-n}$.

$$\sqrt{-4} = \sqrt{4} \cdot \sqrt{-1} = 2\sqrt{-1}$$
$$\sqrt{-6} = \sqrt{6} \cdot \sqrt{-1}$$
$$\sqrt{-100} = 10 \cdot \sqrt{-1}$$

This convention takes care of Tony and Sasha's contradiction. There is only one value for $\sqrt{-12} \cdot \sqrt{-3}$.

$$\begin{aligned}\sqrt{-12} \cdot \sqrt{-3} &= (\sqrt{12} \cdot \sqrt{-1}) \cdot (\sqrt{3} \cdot \sqrt{-1}) \\ &= (\sqrt{12} \cdot \sqrt{3}) \cdot (\sqrt{-1} \cdot \sqrt{-1}) \\ &= (\sqrt{12 \cdot 3}) \cdot (-1) \\ &= 6 \cdot -1 \\ &= -6\end{aligned}$$

For You to Do

Simplify. Each product is an integer.

5. $\sqrt{-2} \cdot \sqrt{-8}$
6. $\sqrt{-9} \cdot \sqrt{-1}$
7. $\sqrt{-18} \cdot \sqrt{-8}$

The convention eliminates the ambiguity in multiplying square roots of negative numbers. Clearly the theorem $\sqrt{ab} = \sqrt{a} \cdot \sqrt{b}$ stops working in this new system. Moving forward, you will work with *complex numbers.* Complex numbers are expressions of the form

$$a + b\sqrt{-1}$$

where a and b are real numbers.

You will explore a more formal definition of the complex numbers in the next lesson.

In some of the exercises that follow, you will test whether other basic results extend to complex numbers. In others, you will investigate the nature of this new arithmetic.

Exercises *Practicing Habits of Mind*

Check Your Understanding

1. Expand each expression.
   a. $(a + b)(a - b)$
   b. $(a + b\sqrt{2})(a - b\sqrt{2})$
   c. $(a + b\sqrt{3})(a - b\sqrt{3})$
   d. $(a + b\sqrt{c})(a - b\sqrt{c})$
   e. $(a + b\sqrt{-1})(a - b\sqrt{-1})$
2. Sketch the graphs of $y = x^2$ and $y = 6x - 11$. How many times do the graphs intersect?
3. When you include square roots of negative numbers, the equation $x^2 = 6x - 11$ has two solutions.
   a. Find the solutions. Express the solutions without denominators.
   b. Find the sum and the product of the solutions.

For You to Do

Even if your students do not have difficulty with these calculations, it is still good reinforcement for them to practice a few calculations.

Wrap Up

You might wrap up this day asking students to share their solutions to the equation $x^3 - 8 = 0$ from On Your Own Exercise 13. Have them compare the results with the previous lesson's Wrap Up, in which they found the solutions to the equation $x^3 = 1$.

Assessment Resources

Lesson Quiz 3.3

1. Simplify each expression. When possible, write your result in the form $a + b\sqrt{-1}$, where a and b are real numbers.
   a. $\sqrt{-5} \cdot \sqrt{-20}$
   b. $\sqrt{-11} \cdot \sqrt{-11}$
   c. $3(-2 + \sqrt{-1})$
   d. $(2 - \sqrt{-3})\sqrt{-3}$
   e. $\sqrt{-5}(2 + \sqrt{-5})$
   f. $2(\sqrt{-1})^4$
   g. $(7 + 3\sqrt{-1}) + (4 + \sqrt{-1})$
   h. $(3 + \sqrt{-16}) + (2 - 3\sqrt{-25})$
   i. $(6 + 3\sqrt{-1})(6 - \sqrt{-1})$
   j. $(11 - \sqrt{-1}) + (11 + \sqrt{-1})$
   k. $(12 + \sqrt{-2})(12 - \sqrt{-2})$
   l. $(6 + 3\sqrt{-1})(6 - 3\sqrt{-1})$
   m. $(x - y\sqrt{-9})(x + y\sqrt{-9})$
   n. $(2x + \sqrt{-4})(2x - \sqrt{-4})$
2. Factor each equation. Then use the factored form to find all three solutions to each equation.
   a. $x^3 - 125 = 0$
   b. $8x^3 - 1 = 0$

Exercises

HOMEWORK

- Core: 9, 11, 12, 13, 16, 17
- Optional: 10, 14
- Extension: 15

Check Your Understanding

EXERCISE 1 should be straightforward practice. Each part results in a difference of squares. For part (e), encourage students to be careful about their signs. The pattern is the same for each part, but for part (e), they end up with a sum of squares.

EXERCISES 2 AND 3 are connected. There are no intersections because there are no real solutions to $x^2 = 6x - 11$.

Answers

For You to Do

5. -4
6. -3
7. -12

Exercises

1. a. $a^2 - b^2$ b. $a^2 - 2b^2$
   c. $a^2 - 3b^2$ d. $a^2 - cb^2$
   e. $a^2 + b^2$

2.

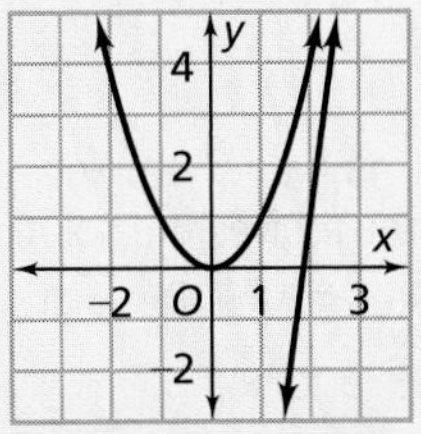

The graphs do not intersect.

3. a. $3 \pm \sqrt{-2}$
   b. The sum is 6, and the product is 11.

EXERCISES 7 AND 8 go together, so assign both or neither. Exercise 8 gets at the nature of the relationship between roots and coefficients in the cubic. You can read the three answers to this exercise from the coefficients. Hope that students will notice the connection either during or after the exercise. If no one notices the connection to the coefficients, point it out.

On Your Own

EXERCISE 9 The purpose of this exercise is for students to recognize that the commutative property still holds after extending the real numbers to include square roots of negative numbers.

EXERCISE 10 Encourage students to include all the critical details that constitute a formal mathematical proof, paying attention to the reasons they give for any step they take in calculation.

EXERCISE 11 Do not worry about the notation here. 6 is just as correct an answer as $6 + 0\sqrt{-1}$.

4. Does every quadratic equation with real coefficients have a solution if you include square roots of negative numbers? Explain.

5. What two numbers have squares of 34? Provide approximations rounded to the nearest hundredth for these two numbers.

6. Decide whether the following statement is true. Explain.

For every nonnegative real number a, there are two numbers with squares equal to a.

7. Show that the equation $x^3 - 5x^2 + 8x - 6 = 0$ has the following solutions.

$$x = 3, x = 1 + \sqrt{-1}, x = 1 - \sqrt{-1}$$

8. Simplify each expression.

a. $3 + (1 + \sqrt{-1}) + (1 - \sqrt{-1})$

b. $3(1 + \sqrt{-1}) + 3(1 - \sqrt{-1}) + (1 + \sqrt{-1})(1 - \sqrt{-1})$

c. $3(1 + \sqrt{-1})(1 - \sqrt{-1})$

On Your Own

9. Simplify each product.

a. $\sqrt{-4} \cdot \sqrt{-9}$ **b.** $\sqrt{-9} \cdot \sqrt{-4}$

c. $\sqrt{-3} \cdot \sqrt{-27}$ **d.** $\sqrt{-27} \cdot \sqrt{-3}$

e. $(2 + \sqrt{-3}) \cdot \sqrt{-3}$ **f.** $\sqrt{-3} \cdot (2 + \sqrt{-3})$

10. **Write About It** Does the Commutative Property of Multiplication apply to this new arithmetic? Explain. Use examples or proof.

11. Write each expression in the form $a + b\sqrt{-1}$, where a and b are real numbers.

a. $(3 + 4\sqrt{-1}) + (4 + 5\sqrt{-1})$ **b.** $(3 + \sqrt{-16}) + (4 + \sqrt{-25})$

c. $(5 + \sqrt{-1})(5 + 2\sqrt{-1})$ **d.** $(3 + \sqrt{-2}) + (3 - \sqrt{-2})$

e. $(3 + \sqrt{-2})(3 - \sqrt{-2})$

12. **Standardized Test Prep** What are the solutions to $x^2 - 10x + 26 = 0$?

A. $x = 5$ and $x = -5$

B. $x = 5 + \sqrt{2}$ and $x = 5 - \sqrt{2}$

C. $x = 5 + \sqrt{-1}$ and $x = 5 - \sqrt{-1}$

D. $x = 5 + \sqrt{-2}$ and $x = 5 - \sqrt{-2}$

Go Online
PHSchool.com

For additional practice, go to **Web Code: bfa-0303**

Answers

4. Yes; answers may vary. Sample: The quadratic formula gives the solutions to any quadratic equation.

5. $\sqrt{34} = 5.83$ and $-\sqrt{34} = -5.83$

6. No; 0 is nonnegative and has only one number whose square is 0.

7. Answers may vary. Sample: $x^3 - 5x^2 + 8x - 6 = (x - 3)(x^2 - 2x + 2) = 0$, and the solutions to $x^2 - 2x + 2 = 0$ are $1 + \sqrt{-1}$ and $1 - \sqrt{-1}$.

8. a. 5 **b.** 8 **c.** 6

9. a. −6 **b.** −6 **c.** −9 **d.** −9

e. $-3 + 2\sqrt{-3}$

f. $-3 + 2\sqrt{-3}$

10. Yes; answers may vary. Sample: The examples in Exercise 9 indicate that the Commutative Property of Multiplication applies.

13. The equation $x^3 - 8 = 0$ has one solution in $\mathbb{R}$, $x = 2$.

When you include square roots of negative numbers, the equation has three solutions.

a. Factor $x^3 - 8$.

b. Use the factored form to find all three solutions to the equation $x^3 - 8 = 0$.

c. Find the three solutions to $x^3 - 1 = 0$.

14. a. Use factoring to find the solutions to the equation $x^3 - 64 = 0$.

b. Compare the solutions with the solutions to $x^3 - 8 = 0$ and $x^3 - 1 = 0$.

15. Take It Further Find all six solutions to the equation $x^6 - 64 = 0$.

You can start by factoring the left side as a difference of squares.

Maintain Your Skills

16. Simplify each expression.

a. $(3 + 4\sqrt{-1})(3 - 4\sqrt{-1})$

b. $(12 + 5\sqrt{-1})(12 - 5\sqrt{-1})$

c. $(7 + \sqrt{-1})(7 - \sqrt{-1})$

d. $(x + y\sqrt{-1})(x - y\sqrt{-1})$

17. Simplify each expression.

a. $\sqrt{-1} \cdot \sqrt{-1}$

b. $\sqrt{-1} \cdot \sqrt{-1} \cdot \sqrt{-1} \cdot \sqrt{-1}$

c. $(\sqrt{-1})^6$

d. $(\sqrt{-1})^8$

e. $(\sqrt{-1})^9$

Go Online
Video Tutor
PHSchool.com

Web Code: bfe-0775

11. a. $7 + 9\sqrt{-1}$
b. $7 + 9\sqrt{-1}$
c. $23 + 15\sqrt{-1}$
d. $6 + 0\sqrt{-1}$
e. $11 + 0\sqrt{-1}$

12. C

13. a. $x^3 - 8 = (x - 2)(x^2 + 2x + 4)$
b. $2, -1 \pm \sqrt{-3}$
c. $1, \dfrac{-1 \pm \sqrt{-3}}{2}$

14. a. $4, -2 \pm 2\sqrt{-3}$
b. The solutions are 2 times the solutions to $x^3 - 8 = 0$ and 4 times the solutions to $x^3 - 1 = 0$.

15. $2, -2, 1 \pm \sqrt{-3}, -1 \pm \sqrt{-3}$

16. a. 25 b. 169
c. 50 d. $x^2 + y^2$

17. a. -1 b. 1
c. -1 d. 1
e. $\sqrt{-1}$

EXERCISE 13 asks students to be persistent in their factoring, so encourage students to keep looking for ways to factor more. Some students may choose to approach the exercise first as a difference of two cubes. They may have trouble factoring the resulting quadratic, which has a fairly complicated factoring.

$$
\begin{aligned}
x^6 - 64 &= 0 \\
(x^2)^3 - (4)^3 &= 0 \\
(x^2 - 4)(x^4 + 4x^2 + 16) &= 0 \\
(x + 2)(x - 2)(x^4 + 4x^2 + 16 + 4x^2 - 4x^2) &= 0 \\
(x + 2)(x - 2)[(x^4 + 8x^2 + 16) - 4x^2] &= 0 \\
(x + 2)(x - 2)[(x^2 + 4)^2 - (2x)^2] &= 0 \\
(x + 2)(x - 2)(x^2 + 4 + 2x)(x^2 + 4 - 2x) &= 0 \\
(x + 2)(x - 2)(x^2 + 2x + 4)(x^2 - 2x + 4) &= 0
\end{aligned}
$$

Maintain Your Skills

EXERCISE 16 is another place for students to learn the difference of squares factoring associated with conjugate pairs. In the next lesson, students will perform similar calculations using the notation i in place of $\sqrt{-1}$.

Additional Resources

PRINT RESOURCES
- Solution Manual
- Practice Workbook
- Assessment Resources
- Teaching Resources

TECHNOLOGY
- Interactive Textbook
- TeacherExpress CD-ROM
- ExamView CD-ROM
- PHSchool.com

Additional Practice

1. For each equation, find the solutions, if any, that are in $\mathbb{N}$.
a. $x^2 + 7x + 6 = 0$ b. $x^2 + 6 = 7x$
c. $x^2 + 7x = 6$ d. $x^2 - 4 = 12$
e. $x^2 = 3$ f. $7x^2 - 1 = 6x$

2. For each equation in Exercise 1, find the solutions, if any, that meet the given conditions.
I. in $\mathbb{Z}$ but not in $\mathbb{N}$
II. in $\mathbb{Q}$ but not in $\mathbb{Z}$
III. in $\mathbb{R}$ but not in $\mathbb{Q}$
IV. not in $\mathbb{R}$

3. Decide whether each calculation results in a real number. Explain.
a. $(5 + \sqrt{-1}) + (5 - \sqrt{-1})$ b. $(5 + \sqrt{-1})(5 + \sqrt{-1})$
c. $\dfrac{5 - \sqrt{-1}}{-5 + \sqrt{-1}}$ d. $(5 + \sqrt{-1})(5 - \sqrt{-1})$

4. Simplify each product.
a. $\sqrt{-2} \cdot \sqrt{-8}$ b. $\sqrt{-3} \cdot \sqrt{-3}$
c. $\sqrt{-16} \cdot \sqrt{-4}$ d. $\sqrt{-4} \cdot \sqrt{-16}$
e. $(3 - \sqrt{-5}) \cdot \sqrt{-5}$ f. $\sqrt{-6} \cdot (1 + \sqrt{-6})$

5. Write each expression in the form $a + b\sqrt{-1}$, where a and b are real numbers.
a. $(5 + 3\sqrt{-1}) + (7 + 4\sqrt{-1})$ b. $(6 + \sqrt{-9}) + (2 + 4\sqrt{-81})$
c. $(5 + 3\sqrt{-1})(5 + \sqrt{-1})$ d. $(7 - 4\sqrt{-1}) + (7 + 4\sqrt{-1})$

6. The equation $x^3 - 27 = 0$ has one solution in $\mathbb{R}$, $x = 3$.
a. Factor $x^3 - 27$.
b. Use the factored form to find all three solutions to the equation.

7. Simplify each expression.
a. $(5 + \sqrt{-2})(5 - \sqrt{-2})$ b. $\sqrt{-1} \cdot (\sqrt{-1} \cdot \sqrt{-1})$
c. $(\sqrt{-1})^5$ d. $(x + y\sqrt{-4})(x - y\sqrt{-4})$
e. $(6 + 3\sqrt{-1})(6 - 3\sqrt{-1})$ f. $(\sqrt{-1})^7$

Practice: For Lesson 3.3, assign Exercises 4–7.

Lesson Overview

GOALS

- Use complex numbers as tools for solving equations.
- Be fluent in complex number arithmetic.

In this lesson, you introduce students formally to the arithmetic of complex numbers. They also see that the complex numbers are closed under addition, subtraction, and multiplication. Division of complex numbers is introduced in the next lesson.

CHECK YOUR UNDERSTANDING
- Core: 1, 2, 3, 4, 6
- Optional: 5, 7
- Extension: 8

MATERIALS
- CAS (recommended)
- graphing calculators

HOMEWORK
- Core: 9, 10a–d, 11, 12, 13, 14
- Optional: 15, 17, 18, 19
- Extension: 10e, 16

VOCABULARY
- complex numbers, $\mathbb{C}$
- Fundamental Theorem of Algebra
- $a + bi$ (complex number)

Launch

The solutions to the exercises in the previous lessons use a shorthand for $\sqrt{-1}$. At this point, students may also be glad to know they can write just *i*. Introduce the definition of the complex numbers.

Explore

For Discussion

PROBLEM 1 Refer students back to Problem 1b in Lesson 3.1 for this discussion. If *i* were a real number, then i^2 would have to be -1. But students know that real numbers have positive squares. Since this number has a negative square, it is not real.

Students may have other interesting answers. For example: If $a^2 = -1$, then *a* is a root of the equation $x^2 + 1 = 0$. But the roots of the equation have sum 0 and product 1. If the roots were real, they would have to be additive inverses (since their sum is zero), and they would have to be reciprocals (since their product is 1). But this cannot happen with real numbers because reciprocals always have the same sign, so reciprocals cannot be additive inverses.

PROBLEM 2 speaks to the definition and closure of complex numbers.

3.4 Extension to Complex Numbers

Lesson 3.3 introduced the number $\sqrt{-1}$ to allow you to work with square roots of negative numbers. This number is just a symbol defined by its behavior.

$$(\sqrt{-1})^2 = -1$$

Rather than writing $\sqrt{-1}$, you can use the letter *i*. Again, this is just a symbol defined by its behavior.

If *a* and *b* are real numbers, a number written in the form $a + bi$ is a *complex number*. Here is the formal definition.

Definition

The system of complex numbers $\mathbb{C}$ consists of all expressions in the form $a + bi$ with the following properties.

- **a and b are real numbers.**
- **$i^2 = -1$**
- **You can use addition and multiplication as if $a + bi$ were a polynomial.**

A real number is also a complex number. For example, $3 = 3 + 0i$.

For Discussion

1. Explain how you know that *i* is not a real number.
2. Is $(2 + 3i)(5 - 4i)$ a complex number? Explain.

The following examples show that calculating with complex numbers is very similar to calculating with polynomials.

Example 1

Problem Write each expression as a complex number in the form $a + bi$.

a. $(3 + 2i) + (2 - 5i)$ **b.** $(3 + 2i) - (2 - 5i)$ **c.** $(3 + 2i)(2 - 5i)$

Solution

a. Use the associative and commutative properties of addition. Then combine like terms.

$$\begin{aligned}(3 + 2i) + (2 - 5i) &= 3 + 2 + 2i - 5i \\ &= 5 + (2 - 5)i \\ &= 5 - 3i\end{aligned}$$

Answers

For Discussion

1. The symbol *i* represents $\sqrt{-1}$, and the square root of a negative number is not part of the real number system.
2. $(2 + 3i)(5 - 4i) = 22 + 7i$, which is a complex number.

b. Distribute the negative. Then combine like terms.

$$(3 + 2i) - (2 - 5i) = 3 + 2i - 2 + 5i$$
$$= 1 + 2i + 5i$$
$$= 1 + 7i$$

c. Multiply. Then combine like terms.

$$(3 + 2i)(2 - 5i) = 6 - 15i + 4i - 10i^2$$
$$= 6 - 11i - 10i^2$$
$$= 6 - 11i - 10(-1)$$
$$= 6 - 11i + 10$$
$$= 16 - 11i$$

Habits of Mind

Establish a process. Treat the expressions as polynomials. Use the basic rules.

Remember...

Replace i^2 with -1.

For You to Do

Write each expression as a complex number in the form $a + bi$.

3. $(10 - 11i) + (3 - 2i)$ **4.** $(5 + 7i) - (5 - 3i)$ **5.** $(3 - 2i)(2 + 5i)$

You can represent a generic complex number with a single letter. So, if $z = 3 + 2i$ and $w = -1 + i$, you can think about the expressions $z + w$, which equals $(2 + 3i)$, and zw, which equals $(-5 + i)$.

But, how do you know that there is only one way you can write a complex number in the form $a + bi$ with a and b real? Maybe you can find other real numbers x and y such that $x + yi$ is equal to $3 + 2i$. The following theorem and proof show that you cannot find such numbers.

Theorem 3.1

If a, b, c, and d are real numbers, then $a + bi = c + di$ only when $a = c$ and $b = d$.

Proof Suppose $a + bi = c + di$. Prove that $a = c$ and $b = d$. You can prove this with indirect reasoning. Suppose $b \neq d$. Then solve the equation for i.

$$a + bi = c + di$$
$$bi - di = c - a$$
$$i = \frac{c - a}{b - d}$$

The expression $\frac{c - a}{b - d}$ represents a real number. This is a contradiction because i is not a real number. Therefore, b must equal d.

Since $b = d$, then $bi = di$. You can subtract terms bi and di from each side of the original equation. This leaves $a = c$. So, if $a + bi = c + di$, then $a = c$ and $b = d$.

Example 1

You may wish to demonstrate this example with a calculator as well as by hand.

For You to Do

These problems have students perform simple arithmetic with complex numbers. Encourage them to follow the convention of writing the answer in the $a + bi$ form where a and b are real numbers.

Theorem 3.1, which follows, ensures that the convention uniquely represents a complex number.

The problems provide an opportunity to make sure that students are comfortable with computation before beginning the Check Your Understanding exercises.

For You to Do

3. $13 - 13i$

4. $0 + 10i$

5. $16 + 11i$

Example 2

Before sharing the solution to this problem, you might ask students how they would solve it. A natural approach is to divide by z. It may be worth having students try to divide by z to get $z = \frac{21 - i}{2 - i}$. Ask: Is this fraction a complex number? If so, how can we write this complex number in the form $a + bi$?

When students get to the next lesson, the method of using conjugates to divide should seem a lot simpler than solving a system of equations.

You may wish to demonstrate how to do these calculations with calculators as well as by hand. Students should have an opportunity to be comfortable with both methods.

Wrap Up

Students should have a good handle on the arithmetic of complex numbers. If students are having difficulty, encourage them to think of i as just another variable and perform polynomial arithmetic on the expressions. Then, when they are done and they cannot simplify the expression any more, they can replace i^2 with -1 and simplify further.

Exercise 4 checks that students understand the $a + bi$ definition of complex numbers. Exercise 3, with examples chosen from Exercise 2, is a good preview of the upcoming lesson.

Assessment Resources

Lesson Quiz 3.4

1. Write each expression in simplest form without using an exponent.
   a. $i^4 \cdot i^6$ b. $i(i^2)^3$ c. $i^4(i^3 \cdot i^5)$

2. Solve each equation. The solutions are complex numbers.
   a. $-3z + (3 + i) = -6 + 4i$
   b. $2x + 3 = -7 - 2i$
   c. $x^2 - 12 = -28$
   d. $z^2 = 2z - 5$

3. Find a complex number z such that the product $z \cdot (-3 + 5i)$ is a real number.

4. Show that you can factor $x^2 + 81$ over $\mathbb{C}$, but not over $\mathbb{R}$.

Facts and Notation

Because of Theorem 3.1, there is only one way you can write a complex number as $a + bi$, where a and b are real. So, every complex number is determined by two numbers—its real part and its imaginary part. Using this language, you can state Theorem 3.1 as follows.

Two complex numbers are equal if and only if their real parts are equal and their imaginary parts are equal.

When you write a complex number in the form $a + bi$, you are expressing the number in standard form.

Example 2

Problem Find the complex number z that satisfies the equation below.

$$z \cdot (2 - i) = 21 + i$$

Solution Write $z = a + bi$ and multiply.

$$\begin{aligned}(a + bi)(2 - i) &= 2a - ai + 2bi - bi^2 \\ &= 2a - ai + 2bi + b \\ &= (2a + b) + (-a + 2b)i\end{aligned}$$

So, $2a + b = 21$, and $-a + 2b = 1$. Now you have a system of two equations and two unknowns.

$$\begin{aligned}2a + b &= 21 \\ -a + 2b &= 1\end{aligned}$$

Complex numbers have two parts, the real part and the imaginary part. So, equations with complex numbers may result in two equations and two unknowns.

You can solve this system of equations in several ways. One way is to multiply each side of the second equation by 2 and then add.

$$\begin{aligned}2a + b &= 21 \\ + \quad -2a + 4b &= 2 \\ \hline 5b &= 23 \\ b &= \tfrac{23}{5}\end{aligned}$$

You can substitute to find the value $a = \frac{41}{5}$. The complex number z is $\frac{41}{5} + \frac{23}{5}i$.

For You to Do

6. Find the complex number w that satisfies the equation $w + (3 - i) = 4i$.

You have extended $\mathbb{R}$ to include the square roots of all real numbers, keeping the basic rules intact. But you discovered that not all familiar properties hold true in this new number system. For example, you gave up $a^2 \geq 0$. This is similar to giving up the idea that multiplication makes things bigger in passing from $\mathbb{N}$ to $\mathbb{Z}$.

Answers

For You to Do

6. $-3 + 5i$

By extending $\mathbb{R}$ to $\mathbb{C}$, you now have a system in which all quadratic equations with real coefficients have roots. Over the centuries, mathematicians discovered that even more is true. $\mathbb{C}$ not only contains all roots of any quadratic equation, it also contains all roots of any polynomial equation with real coefficients. This was a big discovery, and it took mathematicians generations to fully understand its meaning. It is now called the **Fundamental Theorem of Algebra**. It was first proved by Carl Friedrich Gauss in the 1800s.

Go Online
PHSchool.com

For more information about the Fundamental Theorem of Algebra, go to Web Code: bfe-9031

Exercises *Practicing Habits of Mind*

Check Your Understanding

1. Simplify each expression. Write your answer in the form $a + bi$, where a and b are real numbers.
   - **a.** $(3 + 2i) + (9 - i)$
   - **b.** $(3 + 2i)(9 + i)$
   - **c.** $(5 + 2i) + (5 - 2i)$
   - **d.** $(5 + 2i)(5 - 2i)$
   - **e.** $(4 + 2i) + (2 + 4i)$
   - **f.** $(4 + 2i)(2 + 4i)$
2. The complex number $3 - 5i$ is the *conjugate* of $3 + 5i$. Simplify each expression involving conjugates.
   - **a.** $(3 + 5i) + (3 - 5i)$
   - **b.** $(3 + 5i)(3 - 5i)$
   - **c.** $(-7 + 2i) + (-7 - 2i)$
   - **d.** $(-7 + 2i)(-7 - 2i)$
   - **e.** $(12 + 5i) + (12 - 5i)$
   - **f.** $(12 + 5i)(12 - 5i)$
3. **a.** What is the conjugate of $(a + bi)$?
   - **b.** Show that when you add a complex number and its conjugate, the result is a real number.
   - **c.** Show that when you multiply a complex number by its conjugate, the result is a real number.
   - **d.** When is the sum of a number and its conjugate 0?
   - **e.** When is the product of a number and its conjugate 0?
4. **What's Wrong Here?** Derman does not think that if two complex numbers are equal, their parts must be equal.

   Derman says, "I've got a really simple counterexample. If $a = i$ and $b = i$, it's the same as having $c = -1$ and $d = 1$. Try it, and you'll see. If $a + bi = c + di$, it doesn't mean $a = c$ and $b = d$."

   What happened? Is Derman correct? Explain.

Exercises

1. **a.** $12 + i$ **b.** $25 + 21i$ **c.** $10 + 0i$ **d.** $29 + 0i$ **e.** $6 + 6i$ **f.** $0 + 20i$
2. **a.** 6 **b.** 34 **c.** −14 **d.** 53 **e.** 24 **f.** 169
3. **a.** $(a - bi)$
   b. $(a + bi) + (a - bi) = a + a + (b - b)i = 2a$, and if a is real, $2a$ is also real.
   c. $(a + bi)(a - bi) = a^2 - b^2i^2 + abi - abi = a^2 + b^2$, and if a and b are real, $a^2 + b^2$ is also real.
   d. when $a = 0$ in $a + bi$ and $a - bi$
   e. when $a = 0$ and $b = 0$
4. No; Derman is wrong because a and b must be real numbers in $a + bi$.

Exercises

HOMEWORK
- Core: 9, 10a–d, 11, 12, 13, 14
- Optional: 15, 17, 18, 19
- Extension: 10e, 16

Check Your Understanding

EXERCISES 2 AND 3 Assign these exercises. Both are core exercises, and students should leave the lesson with the understanding that a pair of conjugates has a real number sum and a *positive* real number product.

EXERCISE 3 is core because it helps students realize that any complex roots of equations with coefficients in $\mathbb{R}$ must come in complex conjugate pairs. This result is analogous to the situation in which an equation with integer coefficients can have irrational roots only in conjugate pairs. For example, $x^2 - 6x - 11$ has roots $x = 3 + 2\sqrt{5}$ and $3 - 2\sqrt{5}$.

The fact that the sum and product of a complex conjugate pair is a real number is critical in understanding how you divide complex numbers, so make sure you assign and review this exercise.

EXERCISE 4 is a quick exercise that you can skip if time is limited. The most important Check Your Understanding exercises in this set are the first three.

EXERCISE 5 You will revisit this exercise in the next lesson once students learn how to divide complex numbers using conjugates.

EXERCISE 6 can be a useful exercise to show students another of the properties of $\mathbb{R}$ that carries over into $\mathbb{C}$.

On Your Own

EXERCISE 10 You will revisit powers of i when students learn about the complex plane. There, multiplying by i corresponds to a 90° rotation, so $i^4 = 1$ can have a second interpretation there.

EXERCISE 11 is a good practice exercise. Some students may not notice the second solution to $x^2 = -9$. Point out that this type of equation has just as many solutions as $x^2 = 9$ has.

5. Find the complex number $a + bi$ that satisfies the following equation.

$$(a + bi)(1 + i) = 11 - 3i$$

6. Every real number x has an opposite, a number that when added to x results in a sum of 0.

a. Does $2 + 3i$ have an opposite? Explain.

b. What complex numbers have opposites?

7. The conjugate of z is represented by $\overline{z}$. Show that if z and $\overline{z}$ are conjugates, then $z^2 + (\overline{z})^2$ is a real number.

8. **Take It Further** For each part, find an equation with real coefficients that has the listed numbers among its roots. Remember that when you add or multiply a complex number and its conjugate, the result is real.

a. $3 + 2i$

b. $3 - 2i$

c. $1 + 5i$ and $3 + 2i$

d. $1 + 5i$ and $-1 + 5i$

e. $1 + i\sqrt{3}$

f. $\sqrt{2} + \sqrt{3}$

g. $\sqrt{2} + i\sqrt{3}$

On Your Own

9. **Standardized Test Prep** If a and b are real numbers, what is the product $(a + bi)(b - ai)$?

A. $(b^2 - a^2)i$

B. 0

C. $2ab$

D. $2ab + (b^2 - a^2)i$

10. You can use the rule $i^2 = -1$ to simplify other powers of i.

a. Express i^3 in simplest form without using an exponent.

b. Express i^4 in simplest form without using an exponent.

c. Simplify i^5, i^6, i^7, and i^8.

d. What is i^{210}?

e. **Take It Further** Express $\frac{1}{i}$ without a denominator.

11. Solve each equation. The solutions are complex numbers.

a. $z + (3 - i) = 6 + 2i$

b. $w - 3 = 6 + i$

c. $x^2 = -9$

d. $z^2 = 6z - 34$

Go Online PHSchool.com

For additional practice, go to **Web Code:** bfa-0304

Answers

5. $4 - 7i$

6. a. Yes; the opposite of $2 + 3i$ is $-2 - 3i$.

b. All complex numbers have opposites.

7. If $z = a + bi$, then $z^2 + (\overline{z})^2 = (a + bi)^2 + (a - bi)^2 = (a^2 + 2abi - b^2) + (a^2 - 2abi - b^2) = 2a^2 - 2b^2$, which is a real number.

8. a. $x^2 - 6x + 13 = 0$

b. $x^2 - 6x + 13 = 0$

c. $(x^2 - 6x + 13)(x^2 - 2x + 26) = 0$

d. $(x^2 - 2x + 26)(x^2 + 2x + 26) = 0$

e. $x^2 - 2x + 4 = 0$

f. $x - (\sqrt{2} + \sqrt{3}) = 0$, or $x^4 - 10x^2 + 1 = 0$

g. $x^2 - (2\sqrt{2})x + 5 = 0$

9. D

10–11. See back of book.

12. Answers may vary. Sample: $z = 3 - 2i$

12. Find a complex number z such that the product $z \cdot (3 + 2i)$ is a real number.

13. Find a number that meets each set of given conditions. If no such number exists, explain why.
   - **a.** a complex number that is not real
   - **b.** a rational number that is also real
   - **c.** a real number that is not rational
   - **d.** a rational number that is not complex
   - **e.** a real number that is also complex

14. **a.** Show that $x^2 + 1 = (x + i)(x - i)$.

    b. **Write About It** You may have learned in a previous course that $x^2 + 1$ does not factor. Does this statement contradict part (a)? Explain.

15. **a.** Use the quadratic formula to find the two solutions to the equation $x^2 - 10x + 34 = 0$.

    b. Find the sum and product of the solutions.

    c. Find the sum of the squares of the solutions.

16. **Take It Further** Find all complex numbers $a + bi$ that satisfy this equation.

$$(a + bi)^2 = -11 + 60i$$

Maintain Your Skills

17. Find each sum or difference.
   - **a.** $(2 + i) + (3 + i)$
   - **b.** $(3 + i) + (2 + i)$
   - **c.** $(5 + i) - (4 + 3i)$
   - **d.** $(4 + 3i) - (5 + i)$
   - **e.** $(5 + 3i) + (8 - 3i)$
   - **f.** $(3 + i\sqrt{2}) + (3 - i\sqrt{2})$

18. Find each product.
   - **a.** $(2 + i)(3 + i)$
   - **b.** $(3 + i)(2 + i)$
   - **c.** $(5 + i)(5 - i)$
   - **d.** $(2 + i)^2$
   - **e.** $(3 + 2i)^2$
   - **f.** $(4 + i)^2$

19. Find the complex number z that satisfies each equation.
   - **a.** $z \cdot (2 - i) = 3 + i$
   - **b.** $z \cdot (2 - i) = 6 + 2i$
   - **c.** $z \cdot (2 - i) = 9 + 3i$
   - **d.** $z \cdot (2 - i) = 5$
   - **e.** $z \cdot (2 - i) = 10$
   - **f.** $z \cdot (2 - i) = 15$

13. Answers may vary. Samples are given.

a. $1 + i$ **b.** $\frac{1}{2}$ **c.** $\sqrt{2}$

d. Not possible; any rational number a can be written as $a + 0i$.

e. $1 + 0i$

14. a. $(x + i)(x - i) =$
$x^2 - i^2 + xi - xi$
$= x^2 - (-1) = x^2 + 1$

b. No; $x^2 + 1$ does not factor in the real number system, but it does factor in the complex number system.

15. a. $5 \pm 3i$

b. The sum is 10. The product is 34.

c. 32

16. $5 + 6i$ and $-5 - 6i$

17. a. $5 + 2i$ **b.** $5 + 2i$

c. $1 - 2i$ **d.** $-1 + 2i$

e. 13 **f.** 6

18. a. $5 + 5i$ **b.** $5 + 5i$

c. 26 **d.** $3 + 4i$

e. $5 + 12i$ **f.** $15 + 8i$

19. a. $1 + i$ **b.** $2 + 2i$

c. $3 + 3i$ **d.** $2 + i$

e. $4 + 2i$ **f.** $6 + 3i$

EXERCISE 13 If you review this exercise in class, give special emphasis to the last two parts: any rational or real number is also complex.

EXERCISE 15 If you review this exercise in class, point out the connection to the identity in the Getting Started exercises.

EXERCISE 16 Students may try to calculate $\sqrt{-11 + 60i}$ and not know what the next step should be. Suggest that they first expand the left side and then compare the real and imaginary parts of the resulting expression to the real and imaginary parts of the number $-11 + 60i$. They will end up with two equations in two real unknowns, which they have the tools to solve.

Maintain Your Skills

EXERCISE 19 An additional point here is that students can use the solution from one part to help in another. The z in the second equation must be double the z from the first equation. You might also consider revisiting this exercise after students learn how to divide using conjugates.

Additional Resources

PRINT RESOURCES
- Solution Manual
- Practice Workbook
- Assessment Resources
- Teaching Resources

TECHNOLOGY
- Interactive Textbook
- TeacherExpress CD-ROM
- ExamView CD-ROM
- PHSchool.com

Additional Practice

1. Write each expression in simplest form without using an exponent.
   a. $i^3 \cdot i^5$ **b.** $i^2(i^3)^3$ **c.** $i(i^3 \cdot i^2)$

2. Solve each equation. The solutions are complex numbers.
   a. $2z - (4 + i) = 8 + i$ **b.** $x + 5 = -7 - i$
   c. $x^2 = -25$ **d.** $z^2 = 4z - 13$

3. Find a complex number z such that the product $z \cdot (4 - 5i)$ is a real number.

4. Find a number that meets each set of conditions. If no such number exists, explain why.
   a. a complex number that is real
   b. a rational number that is not real
   c. a real number that is rational
   d. a rational number that is complex
   e. a real number that is not complex

5. Show that $x^2 + 4 = (x + 2i)(x - 2i)$.

6. Write each expression in the form $a + bi$.
   a. $(-4 + 3i) + (7 - 6i)$ **b.** $(-3 + 4i) - (-7 - 5i)$
   c. $(4 + 2i)(-5 - 3i)$ **d.** $\frac{1}{2 + i}$
   e. $\frac{1}{3 - 2i}$ **f.** $\frac{1}{4 + 5i}$

7. Consider the function $f(x) = 2x^2 + 1$, where the domain is $\mathbb{C}$. Write each output in the form $a + bi$.
   a. $f(i)$ **b.** $f(-i)$
   c. $f(1 + i)$ **d.** $f(1 - i)$
   e. $f(5 + i)$ **f.** $f(5 - i)$
   g. $f(-3 + 2i)$ **h.** $f(-3 - 2i)$

8. Write each complex number in the form $a + bi$.
   a. $\frac{5 + i}{5 - i}$ **b.** $\frac{4 + 7i}{4 - 7i}$ **c.** $\frac{x + yi}{x - yi}$

Practice: For Lesson 3.4, assign Exercises 1–5.

Lesson Overview

GOAL

- Be fluent in complex number arithmetic.

In this lesson students learn about complex conjugates. They use them to divide complex numbers. They also prove statements about operations with conjugate pairs.

The pairing of the operation of conjugation and the set of complex numbers is interesting. With the extra simplification rule, $i^2 = -1$, you can guarantee that every nonzero complex number has a reciprocal that is also a complex number. And the mapping $z \mapsto \overline{z}$ maps $\mathbb{C}$ to $\mathbb{C}$ in a way that preserves the structure of the set—distances between points are unchanged, and no elements are added or removed from the set. Conjugation is additive and multiplicative: $\overline{z} + \overline{w} = \overline{z + w}$ and $\overline{z} \cdot \overline{w} = \overline{zw}$.

CHECK YOUR UNDERSTANDING
- Core: 1, 2, 3, 5a–e, 6, 7, 8, 9
- Optional: 4
- Extension: 5f

MATERIALS
- CAS (recommended)
- graphing calculators
- Blackline Master 3.5

HOMEWORK
- Core: 10, 11, 12, 13a, 14, 15
- Optional: 16, 17, 18, 19, 20a–c
- Extension: 13b, 20d

VOCABULARY
- conjugate, $\overline{z}$

Launch

Students may need reminders about what the words *commutativity, associativity, identities,* and *inverses* mean, so you may want to begin by reviewing these terms. Students who used CME Project *Algebra 1* may recall the commutative and associative properties as the any order, any grouping properties.

Explore

Developing Habits of Mind

This section formalizes the idea that arithmetic of complex numbers is nearly identical to arithmetic of polynomials, with some additional substitutions as mentioned in the previous lesson. For students struggling with the arithmetic, this is another opportunity to point out the relationship.

3.5 Reciprocals and Division

Addition and multiplication of complex numbers share the following important properties with addition and multiplication of polynomials. Let z, w, and u be complex numbers.

Distributive Property: $z(w + u) = zw + zu$

Properties of Addition and Multiplication

Addition	Property	Multiplication
$z + w = w + z$	Commutative	$zw = wz$
$z + (w + u) = (z + w) + u$	Associative	$z(wu) = (zw)u$
$z + 0 = z$	Identity	$z \cdot 1 = z$
z has an opposite in $\mathbb{C}$.	Inverse	You will explore this now.

Developing Habits of Mind

Look for relationships. The fact that these properties hold for complex numbers is not anything magical. Remember the following from the definition of complex numbers in Lesson 3.4.

You can use addition and multiplication as if $a + bi$ were a polynomial.

This more or less forces complex numbers to obey the rules for calculating that hold for polynomials.

Complex numbers have the structure of polynomials and the extra rule $i^2 = -1$. This is enough extra structure to guarantee that every nonzero complex number has a reciprocal. The following definition explains why.

Every complex number $a + bi$ has a **conjugate** $a - bi$. The product of a complex number and its conjugate is a real number. "Taking the conjugate" is the key operation that will allow you to divide complex numbers and to find their reciprocals.

When you extend the playing field, you have to adjust the rules to cover new situations.

Example 1

Problem Find the complex number z that satisfies $z \cdot (2 - i) = 21 + i$.

Solution In Lesson 3.4, you solved the same problem using a system of equations. It is simpler to solve using conjugates. Multiply the left and right sides of the equation by the conjugate of $(2 - i)$, which is $(2 + i)$.

$$z \cdot (2 - i) = 21 + i$$

$$z \cdot (2 - i)(2 + i) = (21 + i)(2 + i)$$

$$z \cdot 5 = 41 + 23i$$

The reason you want to multiply by $2 + i$ is that the product $(2 - i)(2 + i)$ is the real number 5. To solve the new equation $5z = 41 + 23i$, you just divide each side by 5.

$$z = \frac{41 + 23i}{5}$$

You can also express this number as $\frac{41}{5} + \frac{23}{5}i$.

Multiplying a complex number by its conjugate always results in a real number. This property is the key to simplifying fractions involving complex numbers.

Example 2

Problem Express $\frac{18 + i}{3 - 4i}$ in the form $a + bi$.

Solution The denominator is a complex number. If you multiply the denominator by its conjugate, $3 + 4i$, the result is a real number. Since you do not want to affect the value of the original fraction, multiply both the numerator and the denominator by $3 + 4i$.

$$\frac{18 + i}{3 - 4i} \cdot \frac{3 + 4i}{3 + 4i} = \frac{50 + 75i}{25} = 2 + 3i$$

The fraction simplifies to $2 + 3i$. You can multiply to check the result.

$$(2 + 3i)(3 - 4i) = 6 - 8i + 9i - 12i^2 = 18 + i$$

Since $(2 + 3i)(3 - 4i) = 18 + i$, it is also true that $\frac{18 + i}{3 - 4i} = 2 + 3i$.

Remember...

When you multiply the numerator and denominator of a fraction by the same number, you are multiplying the fraction by 1.

For You to Do

1. Find the reciprocal of $2 + 3i$.

Example 1

When students see a problem such as this one, their first instinct may be to divide both sides by $2 - i$. This example shows the idea of multiplying by the conjugate first to avoid the more difficult idea of division. However, either method that students choose is fine.

Example 2

After completing this example, you may want to revisit Example 1. This time, solve by dividing both sides by $2 - i$ and then doing the division as explained in Example 2. You can then ask students which method they find easier.

For You to Do

This problem asks students to express $\frac{1}{2 + 3i}$ as a complex number. They could also approach it by solving for the complex number $a + bi$ in the equation $(a + bi)(2 + 3i) = 1$. Either method will work.

Answers

For You to Do

1. $\frac{2}{13} - \frac{3}{13}i$

For Discussion

Suppose z is some nonzero complex number. Its reciprocal is $\frac{1}{z}$. If you multiply the top and bottom of this fraction by the conjugate $\overline{z}$, the denominator of the resulting fraction will be a positive real number, and you will have expressed the reciprocal of z as a complex number. (If $z = a + bi$, then $\overline{z} = a - bi$ and $z \cdot \overline{z} = a^2 + b^2$. The reciprocal of z is then $\frac{a}{a^2 + b^2} - \frac{b}{a^2 + b^2}i$. This means that the complex numbers are closed under division, excepting division by zero, which is undefined.

Zero does not have a reciprocal. $\frac{1}{0}$ is still undefined in the complex numbers. The reason that division by 0 is undefined is that there is no number a so that $0 \cdot a = 1$, because any number multiplied by 0 gives a product of 0.

Wrap Up

It is crucial that students understand why the conjugate of the sum of two complex numbers is equal to the sum of the conjugates, and, similarly, why the conjugate of the product of two complex numbers is equal to the product of the conjugates.

You can use Blackline Master 3.5 as a transparency to summarize the properties of complex numbers. You can encourage students to add any other useful observations they have made.

Assessment Resources

Lesson Quiz 3.5

1. Write each expression in the form $a + bi$.
   a. $(-5 + i) + (9 - 6i)$ b. $(-2 + 5i) - (6 - 5i)$ c. $(3 - 2i)(-5 + 4i)$
   d. $\frac{1}{-3 + i}$ e. $\frac{1}{5 - 4i}$ f. $\frac{1}{5 + 4i}$

2. Consider the function $f(x) = x^2 - 1$, where the domain is $\mathbb{C}$. Write each output in the form $a + bi$.
   a. $f(i)$ b. $f(-i)$ c. $f(1 + i)$ d. $f(1 - i)$
   e. $f(6 + i)$ f. $f(6 - i)$ g. $f(-2 + 5i)$ h. $f(-2 - 5i)$

3. Write each complex number in the form $a + bi$.
   a. $\frac{9 + i}{9 - i}$ b. $\frac{4 + 3i}{4 - 3i}$

Developing Habits of Mind

Represent conjugates. The symbol $\overline{z}$ represents the conjugate of z. This notation helps you to describe more simply the relationships between complex numbers and their conjugates. For example, you can state the multiplication property from this lesson in an abbreviated manner.

$z\overline{z}$ is a real number.

Conjugation is a function in which the input is a complex number and the output is a complex number. Here is a statement you will prove in the exercises.

$$\overline{z + w} = \overline{z} + \overline{w}$$

This statement illustrates the order of operations. The left side is the result of adding two complex numbers and then taking the conjugate. The right side is the result of taking both conjugates and adding them together.

Some of the exercises ask you to find or prove other statements about conjugation.

$z\overline{z}$ is the product of a complex number and its conjugate.

For Discussion

2. Suppose z is some nonzero complex number. Show that z has a reciprocal in $\mathbb{C}$. Does 0 have a reciprocal? Explain.

You can now complete the Properties of Addition and Multiplication table from the beginning of the lesson. For the Inverse Property under multiplication, you can include the following statement.

If $z \neq 0$, then z has a reciprocal in $\mathbb{C}$.

Exercises *Practicing Habits of Mind*

Check Your Understanding

1. Rewrite the following statement using z and $\overline{z}$.
   The sum of a complex number and its conjugate is a real number.

Answers

For Discussion

2. If $z = a + bi$, then $\frac{1}{z} = \frac{1}{a + bi} = \frac{a - bi}{(a + bi)(a - bi)} = \frac{a - bi}{a^2 + b^2} = \frac{a}{a^2 + b^2} - \frac{b}{a^2 + b^2}i$; no; if $a + bi = 0$, then $a = b = 0$ and $\frac{1}{a + bi} = \frac{1}{0}$, which is undefined.

Exercises

1. $z + \overline{z}$ is a real number.
2. a. $-2i$
   b. 7
   c. $\overline{z + w} = \overline{7 + 2i} = 7 - 2i$, and $\overline{z} + \overline{w} = -2i + 7 = 7 - 2i$, so they are equal.
3. a. $\overline{z} = a - bi$, and $\overline{w} = c - di$
   b. $\overline{z + w} = \overline{(a + c) + (b + d)i} = (a + c) - (b + d)i$; $\overline{z} + \overline{w} = (a - bi) + (c - di) = (a + c) - (b + d)i$

2. a. What is the conjugate of $2i$? b. What is the conjugate of 7?

c. Show that the statement $\overline{z + w} = \overline{z} + \overline{w}$ is true when $z = 2i$ and $w = 7$.

Remember... A real number is also a complex number.

3. Suppose $z = a + bi$ and $w = c + di$.

a. Write expressions for $\overline{z}$ and $\overline{w}$.

b. Prove that $\overline{z + w} = \overline{z} + \overline{w}$ is true for any complex numbers z and w.

4. Suppose $z = 3 + 2i$ and $w = 4 - 5i$. Write each of the following as $r + si$, where r and s are real numbers.

a. $\overline{z}$ b. $\overline{(\overline{z})}$ c. $\overline{z + w}$ d. $\overline{z} + \overline{w}$

e. $\overline{zw}$ f. $(\overline{z})(\overline{w})$ g. $z + \overline{z}$ h. $w\overline{w}$

5. Express each fraction in the form $a + bi$.

a. $\frac{11 - 3i}{1 + i}$ b. $\frac{4 + i}{2 - i}$

c. $\frac{8 + 4i}{2 + i}$ d. $\frac{3 + i}{3 - i}$

e. $\frac{3 - i}{3 + i}$ f. **Take It Further** $\frac{c + di}{a + bi}$

6. Find each product.

a. $(3 + 4i)(5 + 6i)$ b. $(3 - 4i)(5 - 6i)$

c. $(2 + 7i)(8 - 3i)$ d. $(2 - 7i)(8 + 3i)$

e. $(-10 + 3i)(2 - 7i)$ f. $(-10 - 3i)(2 + 7i)$

7. The results in Exercise 6 suggest the following relationship for conjugates.

$$\overline{zw} = (\overline{z})(\overline{w})$$

Prove that this statement is true for any complex numbers z and w.

8. Let $z = a + bi$. Show that each statement is true.

a. $z + \overline{z} = 2a$ b. $z\overline{z} = a^2 + b^2$

9. a. Find two real numbers a and b such that $2a = 14$ and $a^2 + b^2 = 74$.

b. Find two complex numbers with a sum of 14 and a product of 74.

These results prove that the sum and the product of conjugates are always real numbers.

On Your Own

10. Express each quotient in the form $a + bi$.

a. $\frac{1}{1 + i}$ b. $\frac{1}{1 - i}$ c. $\frac{1}{2 + 3i}$ d. $\frac{1}{5 + 6i}$

11. Suppose $z = a + bi$, where a and b are real numbers, and $z \neq 0$. Write $\frac{1}{z}$ in the form $c + di$ for real numbers c and d.

4. a. $3 - 2i$ **b.** $3 + 2i$
c. $7 + 3i$ **d.** $7 + 3i$
e. $22 + 7i$ **f.** $22 + 7i$
g. 6 **h.** 41

5. a. $4 - 7i$ **b.** $\frac{7}{5} + \frac{6}{5}i$
c. $4 + 0i$ **d.** $\frac{4}{5} + \frac{3}{5}i$
e. $\frac{4}{5} - \frac{3}{5}i$
f. $\frac{ac + bd}{a^2 + b^2} + \frac{ad - bc}{a^2 + b^2}i$

6. a. $-9 + 38i$ **b.** $-9 - 38i$
c. $37 + 50i$ **d.** $37 - 50i$
e. $1 + 76i$ **f.** $1 - 76i$

7. If $z = a + bi$ and $w = c + di$, then $\overline{zw} = \overline{(ac - bd) + (ad + bd)i} = (ac - bd) - (ad + bc)i$, and $(\overline{z})(\overline{w}) = (a - bi)(c - di) = (ac - bd) + (-ad - bc)i = (ac - bd) - (ad + bc)i$.

8–10. See back of book.

11. $\frac{a}{a^2 + b^2} - \frac{b}{a^2 + b^2}i$

Exercises

HOMEWORK
- Core: 10, 11, 12, 13a, 14, 15
- Optional: 16, 17, 18, 19, 20a–c
- Extension: 13b, 20d

Check Your Understanding

EXERCISES 2 AND 3 Use Exercise 2 to preview Exercise 3, which asks students to prove that this property holds for all complex numbers.

EXERCISE 5 The general case in part (f) requires fairly strong algebra skills.

EXERCISES 6 AND 7 Practice Exercise 6 leads into Exercise 7 as the general case. Exercise 7 is an important property. Be sure students understand what the property means.

EXERCISES 8 AND 9 Exercise 9 follows up on Exercise 8. Do not assign Exercise 9 without also assigning Exercise 8.

On Your Own

EXERCISES 12 AND 13 Practice Exercise 12 leads into the generalization in Exercise 13.

EXERCISE 14 Assign this as extra practice if students need more work dividing complex numbers.

EXERCISE 16 Students may not recognize the numbers as the side lengths of a 5-12-13 right triangle. Point out that the second statement is about the sum of two squares equaling another square, which is the basis for Pythagorean triples.

This exercise shows a correspondence between Pythagorean triples and the complex numbers. Students will explore this topic a little more in the chapter and revisit the connection explicitly later.

EXERCISE 18 The steps in this exercise are fairly subtle for students just beginning to be comfortable with the properties of complex conjugates. This concept will be revisited later in the chapter.

Maintain Your Skills

EXERCISE 19 suggests that:

$$\frac{\overline{z}}{\overline{w}} = \overline{\left(\frac{z}{w}\right)}$$

Additional Resources

PRINT RESOURCES
- Solution Manual
- Practice Workbook
- Assessment Resources
- Teaching Resources

TECHNOLOGY
- Interactive Textbook
- TeacherExpress CD-ROM
- ExamView CD-ROM
- PHSchool.com

Additional Practice

1. Write each expression in simplest form without using an exponent.
   a. $i^3 \cdot i^5$ b. $i^2(i^3)^3$ c. $i(i^3 \cdot i^2)$

2. Solve each equation. The solutions are complex numbers.
   a. $2z - (4 + i) = 8 + i$ b. $x + 5 = -7 - i$
   c. $x^2 = -25$ d. $z^2 = 4z - 13$

3. Find a complex number z such that the product $z \cdot (4 - 5i)$ is a real number.

4. Find a number that meets each set of conditions. If no such number exists, explain why.
   a. a complex number that is real
   b. a rational number that is not real
   c. a real number that is rational
   d. a rational number that is complex
   e. a real number that is not complex

5. Show that $x^2 + 4 = (x + 2i)(x - 2i)$.

6. Write each expression in the form $a + bi$.
   a. $(-4 + 3i) + (7 - 6i)$ b. $(-3 + 4i) - (-7 - 5i)$
   c. $(4 + 2i)(-5 - 3i)$ d. $\frac{1}{2 + i}$
   e. $\frac{1}{3 - 2i}$ f. $\frac{1}{4 + 5i}$

7. Consider the function $f(x) = 2x^2 + 1$, where the domain is $\mathbb{C}$. Write each output in the form $a + bi$.
   a. $f(i)$ b. $f(-i)$
   c. $f(1 + i)$ d. $f(1 - i)$
   e. $f(5 + i)$ f. $f(5 - i)$
   g. $f(-3 + 2i)$ h. $f(-3 - 2i)$

8. Write each complex number in the form $a + bi$.
   a. $\frac{5 + i}{5 - i}$ b. $\frac{4 + 7i}{4 - 7i}$ c. $\frac{x + yi}{x - yi}$

Practice: For Lesson 3.5, assign Exercises 6–8.

12. Consider the function $f(x) = x^2$, where the domain is $\mathbb{C}$. Write each output in the form $a + bi$.
    a. $f(i)$ b. $f(-i)$ c. $f(2 + i)$
    d. $f(2 - i)$ e. $f(3 + i)$ f. $f(3 - i)$
    g. $f(-5 + 4i)$ h. $f(-5 - 4i)$

13. The results in Exercise 12 suggest the relationship $\overline{z^2} = (\overline{z})^2$.
    a. Prove that this statement is true for any complex number z.
    b. **Take It Further** Explain how this relationship is a consequence of the result in Exercise 7.

14. Write each complex number in the form $r + si$.
    a. $\frac{4 + i}{4 - i}$ b. $\frac{2 + 3i}{2 - 3i}$ c. $\frac{a + bi}{a - bi}$

15. **Standardized Test Prep** Complex number w is the reciprocal of complex number z. If $z = x + yi$ and $w = u + vi$, what are the values of u and v in terms of x and y?
    A. $u = x$ and $v = y$
    B. $u = \frac{x}{x^2 + y^2}$ and $v = \frac{-y}{x^2 + y^2}$
    C. $u = \frac{x}{x^2 - y^2}$ and $v = \frac{-y}{x^2 - y^2}$
    D. $u = \frac{x}{x^2 + y^2}$ and $v = \frac{y}{x^2 + y^2}$

16. a. Show that $(a + bi)^2 = (a^2 - b^2) + (2ab)i$.
    b. Show that $(a^2 + b^2)^2 = (a^2 - b^2)^2 + (2ab)^2$.
    c. Let $a = 3$ and $b = 2$ in the equation from part (b). What are the values of $a^2 + b^2$, $a^2 - b^2$, and $2ab$?

17. List three quadratic equations with real coefficients and roots that are nonreal complex numbers. Then find the roots for each equation.

18. Prove that if z is a root of a quadratic polynomial with real coefficients, then $\overline{z}$ is also a root.

Maintain Your Skills

19. Express each quotient in the form $a + bi$.
    a. $\frac{8 + i}{2 + i}$ b. $\frac{8 - i}{2 - i}$ c. $\frac{3 + 5i}{2 - 3i}$
    d. $\frac{3 - 5i}{2 + 3i}$ e. $\frac{17 - 4i}{6 - 5i}$ f. $\frac{17 + 4i}{6 + 5i}$

20. Simplify each expression.
    a. $\frac{1}{1 + i} + \frac{1}{1 - i}$ b. $\frac{1}{2 + 3i} + \frac{1}{2 - 3i}$ c. $\frac{1}{5 + i} + \frac{1}{5 - i}$
    d. **Take It Further** Prove that if z is a nonzero complex number, then $\frac{1}{z} + \frac{1}{\overline{z}}$ is a real number.

Answers

12. a. -1 **b.** -1
c. $3 + 4i$ **d.** $3 - 4i$
e. $8 + 6i$ **f.** $8 - 6i$
g. $9 - 40i$ **h.** $9 + 40i$

13. a. Let $z = a + bi$ and $\overline{z} = a - bi$. So, $z^2 = (a^2 - b^2) + 2abi$, $\overline{z^2} = (a^2 - b^2) - 2abi$, and $(\overline{z})^2 = (a^2 - b^2) - 2abi$.

b. The result proved in Exercise 7 is $\overline{zw} = (\overline{z})(\overline{w})$. Substitute z for w to get $\overline{z \cdot z} = (\overline{z})(\overline{z})$, or $\overline{z^2} = (\overline{z})^2$.

14. a. $\frac{15}{17} + \frac{8}{17}i$ **b.** $-\frac{5}{13} + \frac{12}{13}i$
c. $\frac{a^2 - b^2}{a^2 + b^2} + \frac{2ab}{a^2 + b^2}i$

15. B

16. See back of book.

17. Answers may vary. Sample: For $x^2 + 1 = 0$, $x = i$ or $x = -i$; for $x^2 + x + 1 = 0$, $x = \frac{-1 \pm i\sqrt{3}}{2}$; for $x^2 + 2 = 0$, $x = \pm i\sqrt{2}$.

18–20. See back of book.

Mathematical Reflections 3A

In this investigation, you explored the set of complex numbers. You learned to calculate with complex numbers and you used complex numbers as tools to solve equations. These exercises will help you summarize what you have learned.

1. Find the solutions, if they exist, to $x^4 - 121 = 0$ that meet each of the following conditions.
   a. The solution is in $\mathbb{N}$.
   b. The solution is in $\mathbb{Z}$ but not in $\mathbb{N}$.
   c. The solution is in $\mathbb{Q}$ but not in $\mathbb{Z}$.
   d. The solution is in $\mathbb{R}$ but not in $\mathbb{Q}$.
   e. The solution is not in $\mathbb{R}$.
2. Use the quadratic polynomial $x^2 - 4x + 13$.
   a. Find its roots.
   b. Find the sum of its roots.
   c. Find the product of its roots.
   d. Find the sum of the squares of its roots.
3. Find all roots of the polynomial $x^3 - 64$.
4. Find a complex number $z = a + bi$, with a and b real numbers, that satisfies each equation.
   a. $z + (4 - 3i) = 6 + 8i$
   b. $z \cdot (4 - 3i) = 6 + 8i$
5. Given two complex numbers, $z = 2 - 5i$ and $w = -3 + 7i$, show that $\overline{zw} = (\overline{z})(\overline{w})$.
6. What are complex numbers?
7. What two numbers have a sum of 20 and a product of 109?
8. How can you use complex numbers to solve any quadratic equation?

Vocabulary and Notation

In this investigation, you learned these terms and symbols. Make sure you understand what each one means and how to use it.

- **complex numbers, $\mathbb{C}$**
- **conjugate, $\overline{z}$**
- **Fundamental Theorem of Algebra**
- **irrational numbers**
- **natural numbers, $\mathbb{N}$**
- **i ($\sqrt{-1}$)**
- **$a + bi$ (complex number)**

Mathematical Reflections

EXERCISES 6–8 At the start of the investigation, you may have assigned these as Questions 1–3 for students to think and write about.

Mathematical Reflections

1. **a–c.** no solutions
   d. $\pm\sqrt{11}$ **e.** $\pm i\sqrt{11}$
2. **a.** $2 \pm 3i$ **b.** 4
   c. 13 **d.** -10
3. $4, -2 + 2i\sqrt{3}, -2 - 2i\sqrt{3}$
4. **a.** $2 + 11i$ **b.** $2i$
5. $\overline{zw} = \overline{(2 - 5i)(-3 + 7i)} = \overline{29 + 29i} = 29 - 29i$; $(\overline{z})(\overline{w}) = (2 + 5i)(-3 - 7i) = 29 - 29i$
6. The complex numbers are numbers of the form $a + bi$, where $i = \sqrt{-1}$, and a and b are real numbers.
7. $10 \pm 3i$
8. You can use the quadratic formula to solve any quadratic equation. When the discriminant is negative, you can find a solution by replacing $\sqrt{-1}$ with i and writing the solution as a complex number.

Investigation Overview

This investigation continues the extension of the real numbers into the complex numbers much as the story continued historically. Mathematicians up until the 19th century did not accept complex numbers as having any actual usefulness as numbers in themselves but rather as a troublesome intermediate step in calculation. However, when the idea of visualizing the complex numbers as points (and as vectors) in a coordinate plane—with the horizontal axis measuring the real part and the vertical axis measuring the imaginary part of the complex number—the process of visualizing both the complex numbers themselves and calculations involving them suddenly became more concrete.

You may wish to assign Questions 1–3 for students to think and write about during the investigation.

Learning Goals

- Graph complex numbers on the complex plane.
- Visualize operations on complex numbers as transformations on the complex plane.
- Develop greater fluency with complex number calculations, which include finding magnitude and direction.

Habits and Skills

- Extend the concept of absolute value in the real numbers to magnitude in the complex numbers.
- Visualize complex numbers and operations on them in the context of the complex plane.
- Represent complex numbers as points or as vectors, depending upon the context.

Investigation 3B

The Complex Plane

In *The Complex Plane*, you will visualize complex numbers as points or vectors on a coordinate plane. This visual representation of complex numbers will help you develop new insights into addition, multiplication, and conjugation of complex numbers. By translating algebraic calculations into geometric operations, you can form a new understanding of the algebraic calculations.

By the end of this investigation, you will be able to answer questions like these.

1. How do you represent a complex number graphically?
2. What is the graphical effect of adding two complex numbers?
3. What is the graphical effect of multiplying a complex number by i?

You will learn how to

- graph complex numbers on the complex plane
- visualize operations on complex numbers as transformations on the complex plane
- develop greater fluency with complex number calculations, which include finding magnitude and direction

You will develop these habits and skills:

- Extend the concept of absolute value in the real numbers to magnitude in the complex numbers.
- Visualize complex numbers and operations on them in the context of the complex plane.
- Represent complex numbers as points or as vectors, depending upon the context.

a Julia set fractal on the complex plane

Investigation Road Map

LESSON 3.6, *Getting Started,* has students review the distance formula and the process of using trigonometric functions to find unknown lengths or unknown angles in the coordinate plane.

LESSON 3.7, *Graphing Complex Numbers,* has students come to see the coordinate plane as a visual representation of complex numbers. Each number $a + bi$ is mapped to a point (a, b) on the coordinate plane.

LESSON 3.8, *Arithmetic in the Complex Plane,* has students use their new representation of the complex numbers to visualize the results of operations on complex numbers.

LESSON 3.9, *Magnitude and Direction,* has students extend the idea of absolute value in the real numbers to magnitude in the complex numbers.

3.6 Getting Started

Activating Prior Knowledge
Exploring New Ideas

You can use properties of geometry and trigonometry to find angle measures and segment lengths on the coordinate plane.

For You to Explore

1. A triangle on the coordinate plane has vertices $O(0, 0)$, $A(4, 0)$, and $B(4, 3)$.

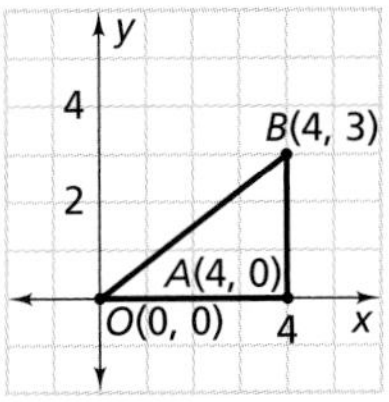

   a. Explain why this is a right triangle.
   b. Find the length of the hypotenuse.
   c. Angle B has a measure of approximately $53.13°$. Find the approximate measure of angle O.
   d. Use a calculator in degree mode to find the value of $\tan^{-1}\left(\frac{3}{4}\right)$ to two decimal places.

2. A triangle has vertices $O(0, 0)$, $P(\sqrt{3}, 1)$, and $Q(\sqrt{3}, -1)$.

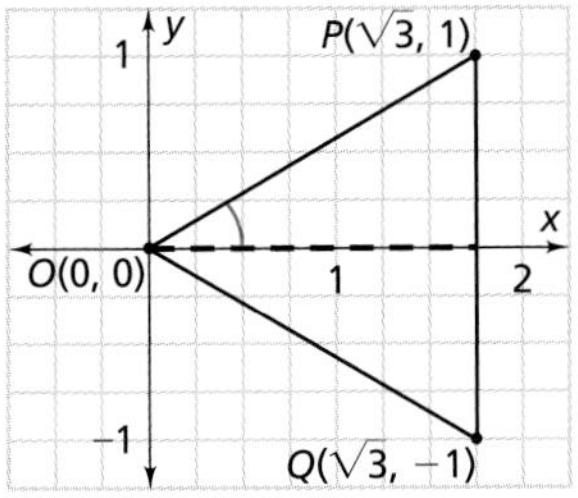

   a. Show that all three sides have the same length.
   b. Find the measure of the marked angle between $\overline{OP}$ and the x-axis.

3. A line segment on the coordinate plane has endpoints at $(0, 0)$ and $(7, 24)$.

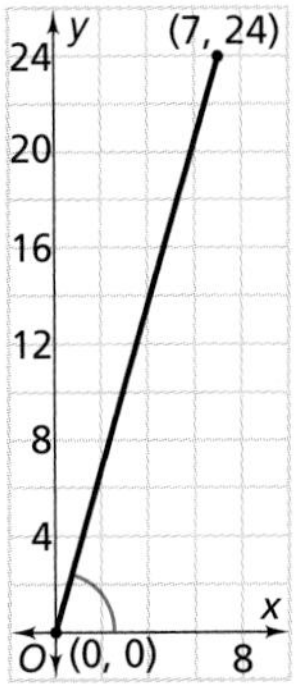

   a. Find the slope of the line segment.
   b. Find the length of the line segment.
   c. Estimate the measure of the marked angle.
   d. Use a calculator in degree mode to find the value of $\tan^{-1}\left(\frac{24}{7}\right)$ to two decimal places.

Remember...

The hypotenuse of a right triangle is the side opposite the right angle.

Habits of Mind

Look for relationships. What does part (d) have to do with the other parts of this problem?

Answers

For You to Explore

1. a. Answers may vary. Sample: Vertical line $\overline{AB}$ is perpendicular to horizontal line $\overline{OA}$.
   b. 5 units
   c. 36.87°
   d. 36.87°
2. a. $OP = 2$, $OQ = 2$, $PQ = 2$
   b. 30°
3. a. $\frac{24}{7}$
   b. 25
   c. Answers may vary. Sample: about 75°
   d. 73.74°

Lesson Overview

GOAL

- Warm up to the ideas of the investigation.

As always in a Getting Started lesson, there is no need to formalize these ideas today. Students will meet all the ideas again throughout the investigation.

FOR YOU TO EXPLORE
- Core: 1, 2, 3, 5, 6
- Optional: 4

MATERIALS
- CAS (recommended)
- graph paper
- graphing calculators
- protractors
- Blackline Master 3.6

HOMEWORK
- Core: 7, 9, 10, 12
- Optional: 8, 11, 13, 14, 15

VOCABULARY
- circumcenter
- exact
- hypotenuse
- legs

Launch

The For You to Explore problems review coordinate geometry, including the distance formula and basic trigonometry. As your students work on the problems, watch for any key gaps in their knowledge of these topics. Take time to review the concepts of

- distance formula
- using trigonometric functions to find unknown lengths, unknown angle measures, and side ratios in special right triangles.

Explore

For You to Explore

You can use Blackline Master 3.6 for Problems 1 and 2.

PROBLEM 1 reviews a few results from geometry, including the distance formula and how to use the inverse trigonometric functions to determine an angle measure. Students should realize that the inverse tangent function gives an estimate of the measure of an angle that is as accurate as they need.

PROBLEM 2 Use this problem as a review of the side ratios in a 30°-60°-90° right triangle.

PROBLEM 3 If protractors are available, students may want to use them to estimate the angle's measure. Point out that a calculator can give the angle measure to any reasonable level of accuracy.

PROBLEM 5 reviews the process of finding unknown side lengths in 30°-60°-90° triangles.

PROBLEM 6 In the complex plane, these four points represent the powers of i, or the fourth roots of unity—the solutions to the equation $x^4 = 1$. To find those solutions, you can factor the equation over the complex numbers:

$$x^4 = 1$$
$$x^4 - 1 = 0$$
$$(x^2 - 1)(x^2 + 1) = 0$$
$$(x - 1)(x + 1)(x - i)(x + i) = 0$$

So the solutions are 1, -1, i, and $-i$. A number of geometric properties arise when you look at the roots of unity and their relationship with regular polynomials. Students will explore roots of unity further in Lesson 3.13 and in CME Project *Precalculus*.

4. A triangle has vertices $A(2, 0)$, $P(-1, \sqrt{3})$, and $Q(-1, -\sqrt{3})$. Its circumcenter is $O(0, 0)$.

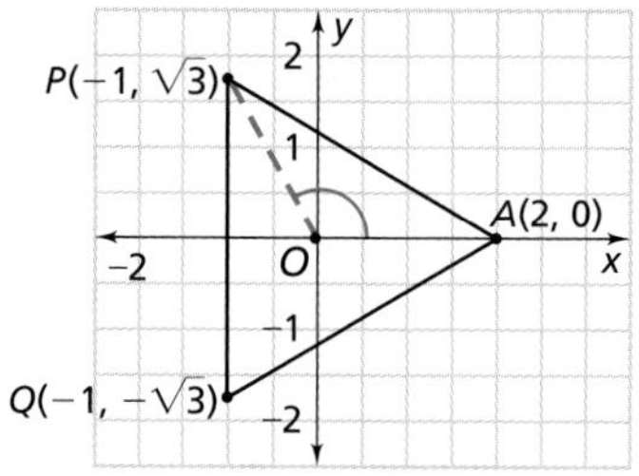

a. Show that all three sides have the same length.

b. Find the measure of the marked angle between $\overline{OP}$ and the x-axis.

5. For each triangle, find the coordinates of points A and B.

a.

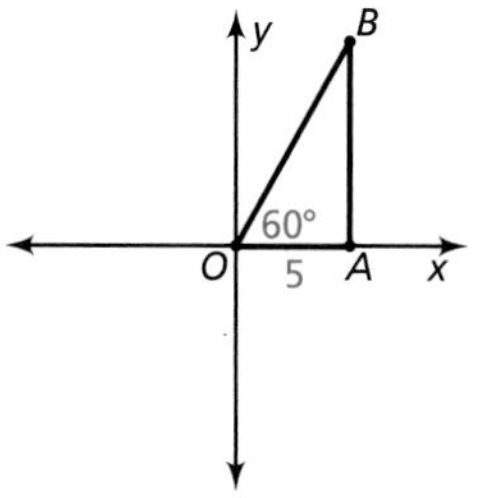

b.

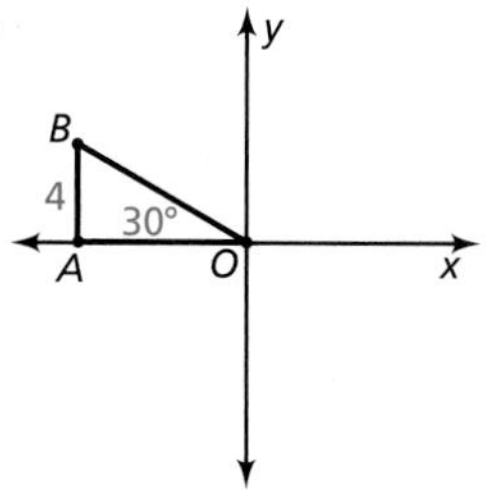

c.

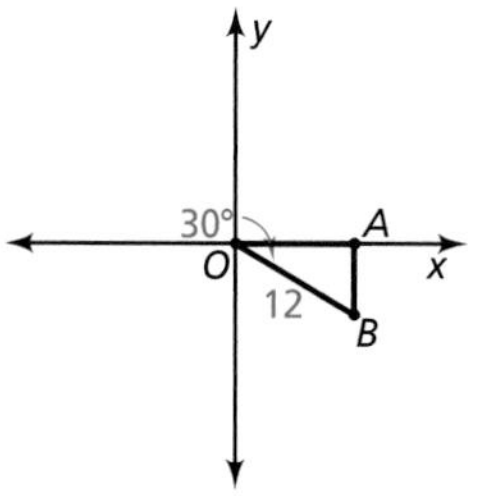

6. A square has a vertex at $(1, 0)$. The circumcenter of the square is at the origin. Find the coordinates of the other three vertices of the square.

Remember...

The circumcenter of a polygon is the center of the circle that contains the vertices of the polygon.

Answers

4. $AP = 2\sqrt{3}$, $PQ = 2\sqrt{3}$, $AQ = 2\sqrt{3}$
b. 120°

5. a. $A(5, 0)$, $B(5, 5\sqrt{3})$
b. $A(-4\sqrt{3}, 0)$, $B(-4\sqrt{3}, 4)$
c. $A(6\sqrt{3}, 0)$, $B(6\sqrt{3}, -6)$

6. $(0, 1)$, $(-1, 0)$, $(0, -1)$

Exercises *Practicing Habits of Mind*

On Your Own

7. Graph each line segment. Then find the exact length of each segment.

a. endpoints at (0, 0) and (4, 1)

b. endpoints at (0, 0) and (2, 1)

c. endpoints at (0, 0) and (7, 6)

d. endpoints at (0, 0) and (3, 4)

e. endpoints at (0, 0) and (6, 8)

f. endpoints at (0, 0) and $(1, \sqrt{3})$

8. Find each product.

a. $(4 + i)(4 - i)$

b. $(2 + i)(2 - i)$

c. $(4 + i)(2 + i)$

d. $(7 + 6i)(7 - 6i)$

e. $(3 + 4i)(3 - 4i)$

f. $(1 + i\sqrt{3})(1 - i\sqrt{3})$

9. Use the inverse tangent function on a calculator. Find the measure of each marked angle to two decimal places.

a.

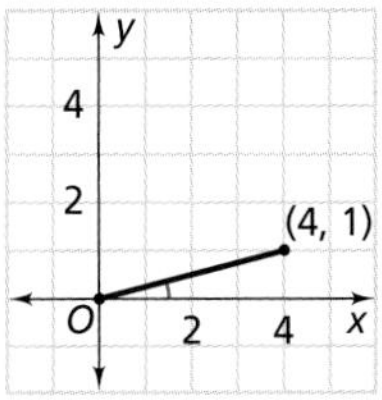

b.

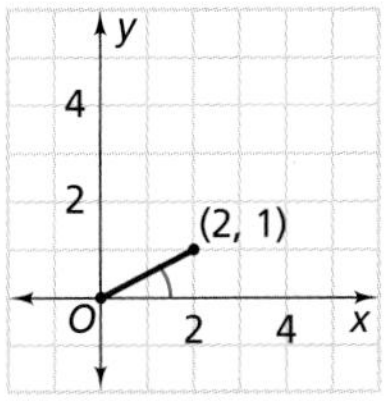

c.

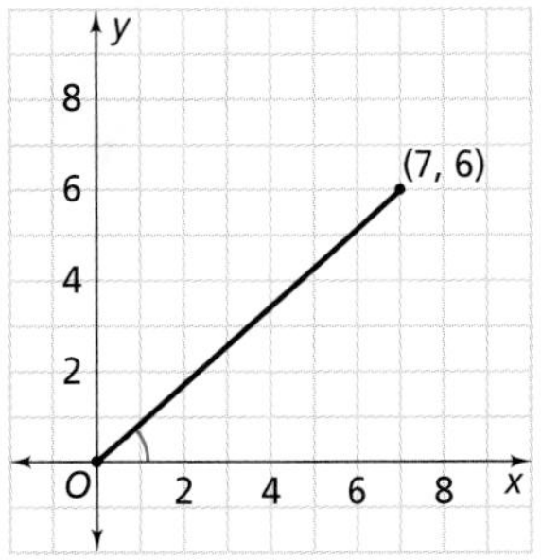

d.

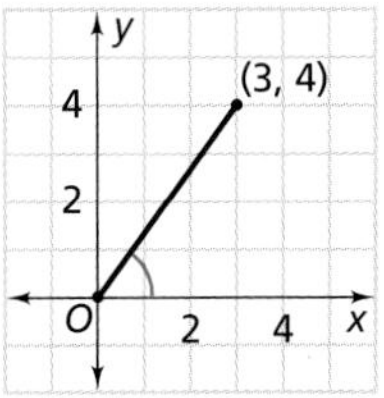

Remember...

Exact means no approximations. For example, $\sqrt{13}$ is exact, but 3.60555 is an approximation to $\sqrt{13}$.

Wrap Up

You might end this class by going over some of the core For You to Explore problems.

Exercises

HOMEWORK

- Core: 7, 9, 10, 12
- Optional: 8, 11, 13, 14, 15

On Your Own

EXERCISE 7 Some students may do this exercise without drawing the projection segments, and that approach is fine.

EXERCISES 7 AND 8 Most students probably will not see the connection between Exercise 8 and Exercise 7. See if you can lead them to the connection, but there is no need to spend much time on this.

EXERCISE 9 Make sure students know how to get their calculators into degree mode. In the review, you might point out the relationship between the angle measures. You will pick up on these relationships later: the inverse tangent of $\frac{6}{7}$ is exactly the sum of those for $\frac{1}{4}$ and $\frac{1}{2}$. This turns out to be related to the complex multiplication: $(4 + i)(2 + i) = 7 + 6i$, since complex multiplication adds angles. (This concept is covered later in the chapter.) Also, the angle for $\frac{4}{3}$ is exactly twice the angle for $\frac{1}{2}$, which is related to the complex calculation $(2 + i)^2 = 3 + 4i$.

Exercises

7. a. $\sqrt{17}$ **b.** $\sqrt{5}$

c. $\sqrt{85}$ **d.** 5

e. 10 **f.** 2

8. a. 17 **b.** 5

c. $7 + 6i$ **d.** 85

e. 25 **f.** 4

9. a. 14.04° **b.** 26.57°

c. 40.60° **d.** 53.13°

EXERCISES 10 AND 11 These exercises review another special triangle, the 45°-45°-90° triangle. The 30°-60°-90° and 45°-45°-90° triangles, along with Pythagorean triple triangles such as the 3-4-5 right triangle, are the basis for the bulk of students' early work with complex numbers.

Maintain Your Skills

EXERCISE 13 $-1 + i\sqrt{3}$, $-1 - i\sqrt{3}$, and 2 are the cube roots of 8. Students will revisit roots of unity in Investigation 3C. If you are skipping roots of unity, skip this exercise. Students can use a CAS to work on this exercise, as long as it is set up to work with complex numbers.

EXERCISE 14 The intent of these exercises is to get students to develop the conjecture that rotating by 90° is akin to multiplying by *i*. Students will see this specific theorem later in the investigation.

10. An isosceles right triangle has a right angle and two 45° angles.

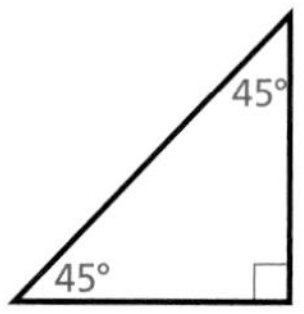

a. If one leg has length 4, find the length of the hypotenuse.
b. If one leg has length 10, find the length of the hypotenuse.
c. If one leg has length *a*, find the length of the hypotenuse.
d. If the hypotenuse has length 4, find the length of each leg.
e. If the hypotenuse has length 10, find the length of each leg.
f. If the hypotenuse has length *b*, find the length of each leg.

Remember...
The legs in a right triangle are the sides adjacent to the right angle.

11. For each triangle, find the coordinates of points *A* and *B*.

a.

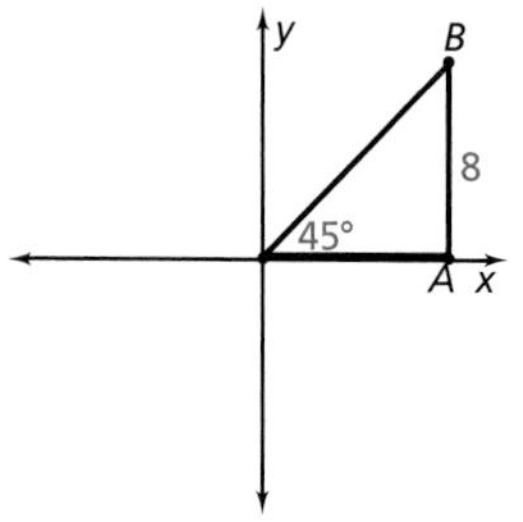

b.

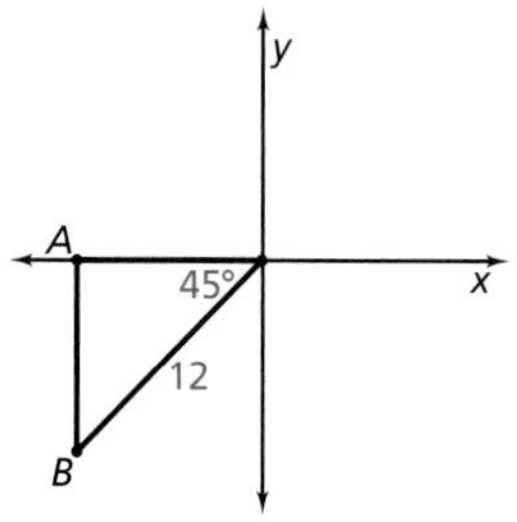

12. An equilateral triangle has a vertex at $(1, 0)$. The circumcenter of the triangle is at the origin. Find the exact coordinates of the other two vertices.

Maintain Your Skills

Go Online
Video Tutor
PHSchool.com
Web Code: bfe-0775

13. Evaluate each expression.

a. $(-1 + i\sqrt{3})^3$ **b.** $(-1 - i\sqrt{3})^3$ **c.** 2^3
d. $2(-1 + i\sqrt{3})(-1 - 1i\sqrt{3})$ **e.** $2 + (-1 + i\sqrt{3}) + (-1 - i\sqrt{3})$

14. For each point *A*, find the coordinates of point *A′*, which you locate by rotating *A* 90° counterclockwise about the origin.

a. $A(1, 0)$ **b.** $A(0, -1)$ **c.** $A(3, 5)$ **d.** $A(6, -1)$

15. Write each complex number in the form $a + bi$, where *a* and *b* are real numbers.

a. $(3 + 4i)^2$ **b.** $(3 + 4i)^3$ **c.** $(3 + 4i)^4$ **d.** $(3 + 4i)^5$

Answers

10. a. $4\sqrt{2}$ **b.** $10\sqrt{2}$ **c.** $a\sqrt{2}$
d. $2\sqrt{2}$ **e.** $5\sqrt{2}$ **f.** $\frac{b\sqrt{2}}{2}$

11. a. $A(8, 0)$, $B(8, 8)$
b. $A(-6\sqrt{2}, 0)$, $B(-6\sqrt{2}, -6\sqrt{2})$

12. $\left(-\frac{1}{2}, \frac{\sqrt{3}}{2}\right), \left(-\frac{1}{2}, -\frac{\sqrt{3}}{2}\right)$

13. a–d. 8
e. 0

14. a. $(0, 1)$ **b.** $(1, 0)$
c. $(-5, 3)$ **d.** $(1, 6)$

15. a. $-7 + 24i$
b. $-117 + 44i$
c. $-527 - 336i$
d. $-237 - 3116i$

3.7 Graphing Complex Numbers

Throughout the 1600s and 1700s, mathematicians used "imaginary" numbers as tools to solve problems involving real numbers. However, they did not feel that these numbers had any existence on their own.

Around 1800, mathematicians invented a geometric representation for numbers like $2 + i$. This graphic representation of complex numbers led to an explosion of activity in mathematics—many new fields were born.

The geometric representation, along with the use of *i*, was made popular by Gauss in the early 1800s.

On the number line, you represent real numbers as points. For example, here is how you represent 5 on the number line.

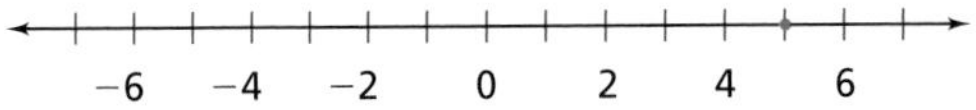

And here is -3.

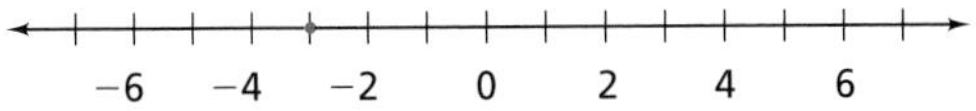

Developing Habits of Mind

Look for relationships. How do you represent a complex number geometrically? To know a complex number, you need to know two numbers—the real part and the imaginary part.

Two complex numbers are equal if and only if both their real and imaginary parts are equal by Theorem 3.1. So there is a one-to-one correspondence between complex numbers and pairs of real numbers. And how do you represent ordered pairs of real numbers? You represent ordered pairs as points on the coordinate plane.

So, take the number line and make a second axis, perpendicular to the first, to record multiples of *i*. This is the **complex plane**. Each complex number $a + bi$ is represented on the complex plane by a point at the coordinates (a, b).

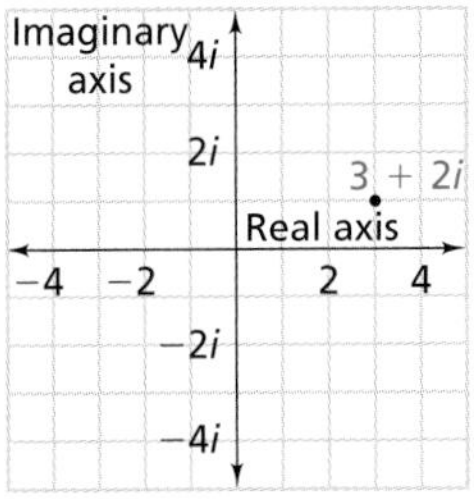

The complex plane is sometimes called the *Argand plane* in honor of Jean Argand, the author of one of the first papers about it.

Lesson Overview

GOALS

- Graph complex numbers on the complex plane.
- Visualize operations on complex numbers as transformations on the complex plane.

This lesson introduces students to the complex plane. The primary message from this lesson is that there is little difference between thinking about an ordered pair of numbers, such as (a, b), and the complex number $a + bi$. In CME Project *Geometry,* students learn to add points by adding their corresponding coordinates. Addition of complex numbers works exactly the same way—you add the corresponding real and imaginary parts separately. In a way, the complex plane allows mathematicians to extend the arithmetic of the coordinate plane by introducing multiplication, as students will see in the next lesson.

CHECK YOUR UNDERSTANDING

- Core: 1, 2, 3, 4, 6
- Optional: 5

MATERIALS

- CAS (recommended)
- graph paper
- graphing calculators
- Blackline Master MC2

HOMEWORK

- Core: 7, 8, 9, 10, 14
- Optional: 11, 12, 13, 16, 17
- Extension: 15

VOCABULARY

- Argand plane
- complex plane

Launch

Discuss the Developing Habits of Mind section with your class. You can use Blackline Master MC2 to demonstrate graphing complex numbers.

Explore

As students begin graphing on the complex plane, see if any review of basic coordinate graphing is necessary. Ensure that they have made the transition from graphing ordered pairs of real numbers to graphing complex numbers.

Developing Habits of Mind

The key idea students should get from this section is that there is a one-to-one correspondence between ordered pairs in the coordinate plane and complex numbers. That is, the ordered pair (2, 3) uniquely identifies a point on the coordinate plane, just as $2 + 3i$ uniquely identifies a complex number. If $a + bi = 2 + 3i$, then $a = 2$ and $b = 3$.

Students may also notice that addition of points and addition of complex numbers are the same.

Wrap Up

You might go over Exercises 3 and 4. It is also valuable to see what students notice about the geometric transformations that result as i is taken to various powers in Exercise 6.

Assessment Resources

Lesson Quiz 3.7

For Exercises 1 and 2, graph and label the four complex numbers on the same complex plane.

1. a. $4 + 5i$ **b.** $4 - 5i$ **c.** $-4 + 5i$ **d.** $-4 - 5i$

2. a. $1 + i$ **b.** $(1 + i)^2$ **c.** $(1 + i)^3$ **d.** $(1 + i)^4$

3. Solve each equation. Then graph the solutions on the complex plane.
a. $x^2 + 5x + 6 = 0$ **b.** $x^2 + 5x + 4 = 0$
c. $x^2 + 8x + 20 = 0$ **d.** $x^2 + 8x + 25 = 0$

4. Solve the equation $x^4 + 81 = 0$. Then graph the solutions on the complex plane.

Example

Problem Graph each complex number.

- $3i$
- $2 + i$
- $4 - 3i$
- -3

Solution The complex plane below shows the four points that correspond to the given numbers.

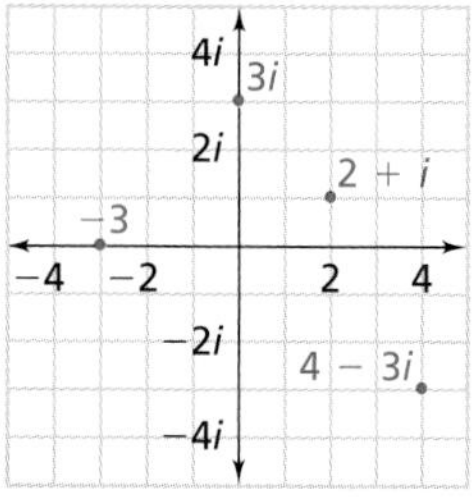

Note that you still represent a real number as a point on the real number line.

Remember... Any real number is also a complex number.

For You to Do

1. Identify the complex number represented by each point.

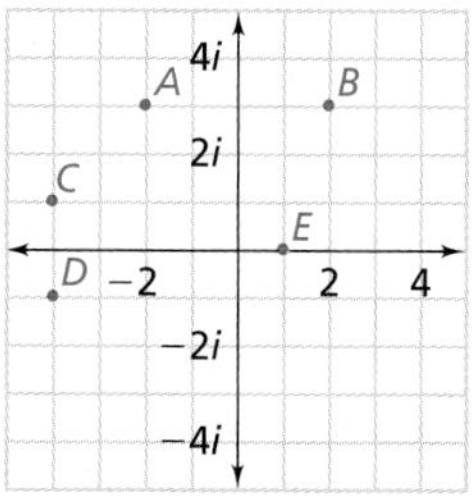

2. Which two points on the complex plane above are conjugates of each other?
3. If z is a complex number, compare the locations of z and $-z$ on the complex plane.

Answers

For You to Do

1. $A(-2 + 3i)$, $B(2 + 3i)$, $C(-4 + i)$
$D(-4 - i)$, $E(1 + 0i)$

2. C and D

3. Answers may vary. Sample: $-z$ is a rotation of z by 180° about the origin.

Exercises

1. a–d.

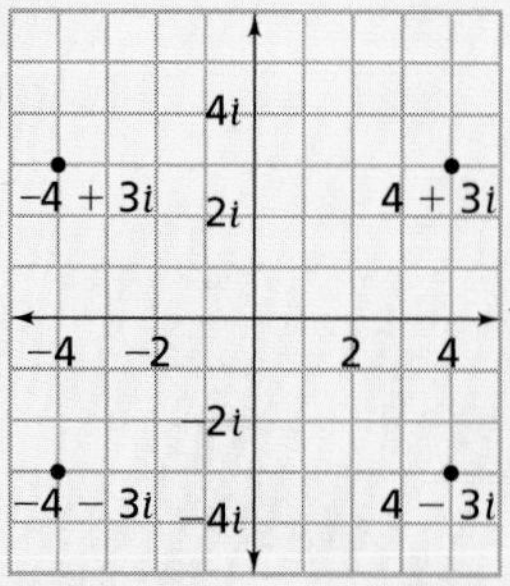

2. a. $a > 0, b > 0$ **b.** $a < 0, b > 0$
c. $a < 0, b < 0$ **d.** $a > 0, b < 0$

3. a.

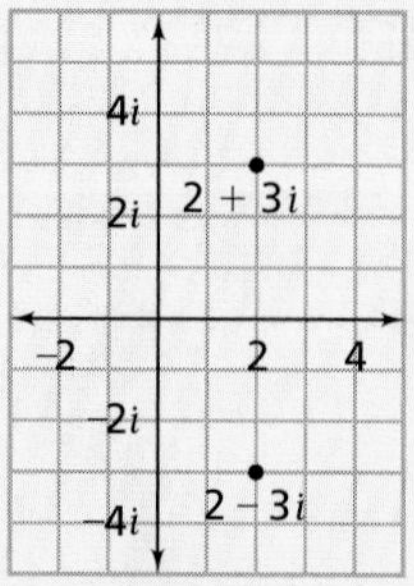

b. The sum is 4, and the product is 13.

Exercises Practicing Habits of Mind

Check Your Understanding

1. Graph and label each complex number on the same complex plane.

   a. $4 + 3i$ b. $4 - 3i$
   c. $-4 + 3i$ d. $-4 - 3i$

2. You can write a complex number as $z = a + bi$. What can you say about a and b if z is located in the given quadrant?

   a. Quadrant I b. Quadrant II
   c. Quadrant III d. Quadrant IV

3. a. Graph both solutions to the equation $x^2 + 13 = 4x$ on the complex plane.
   b. Compute the sum and product of the two solutions.

Habits of Mind
Look for relationships. How are the graphs of the solutions related?

4. a. Graph all three solutions to the equation $x^3 - 8 = 0$ on the complex plane.
   b. The roots lie on the vertices of a triangle. Is this triangle equilateral, isosceles, or scalene? Justify your answer.
   c. Compute the sum and product of the three solutions.

5. Find four complex numbers that lie on the vertices of a square on the complex plane.

6. Graph and label each complex number on the same complex plane.

   a. i^0 b. i^1 c. i^2
   d. i^3 e. i^4 f. i^5

On Your Own

For Exercises 7 and 8, graph and label the four complex numbers on a single complex plane.

7. a. $3 + 2i$ b. $3 - 2i$
   c. $-3 - 2i$ d. $-3 + 2i$

8. a. $2 + i$ b. $(2 + i)^2$
   c. $(2 + i)^3$ d. $(2 + i)^4$

Go Online PHSchool.com
For additional practice, go to **Web Code:** bfa-0307

Exercises

HOMEWORK
- Core: 7, 8, 9, 10, 14
- Optional: 11, 12, 13, 16, 17
- Extension: 15

Check Your Understanding

EXERCISE 2 The purpose of this exercise is for students to associate the real part of a complex number with the horizontal coordinate and the complex part with the vertical. It also serves as a review of quadrants, which will be useful later in this investigation for the definition of *direction*.

EXERCISE 4 If you assigned Exercise 13 from Maintain Your Skills in Lesson 3.6, reference it here. Students probably would not recognize they have already found the sum and product of the three solutions. Students are much less familiar with the complex cube roots of 8 and much less likely to recognize them.

EXERCISE 6 Students should already know $i^4 = 1$ from Investigation 3A, but this exercise gives a graphical method for understanding it. Students who completed Exercise 5 may also notice that the four points are the vertices of a square.

On Your Own

EXERCISE 8 You will talk about these powers of $2 + i$ later in the investigation, so keep this exercise in mind as the investigation continues.

4. a.

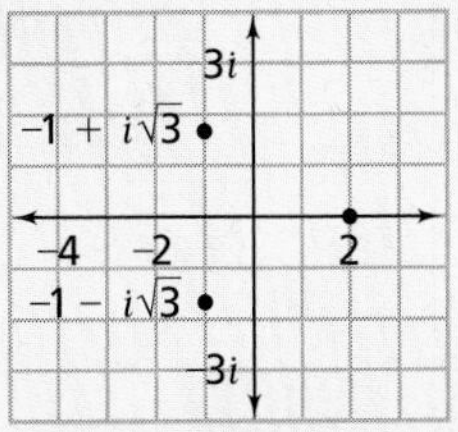

b. Equilateral; the length of each side of the triangle is $2\sqrt{3}$.
c. The sum is 0, and the product is 8.

5. Answers may vary. Sample: $1 + i$, $1 - i$, $-1 - i$, $-1 + i$

6. a–f.

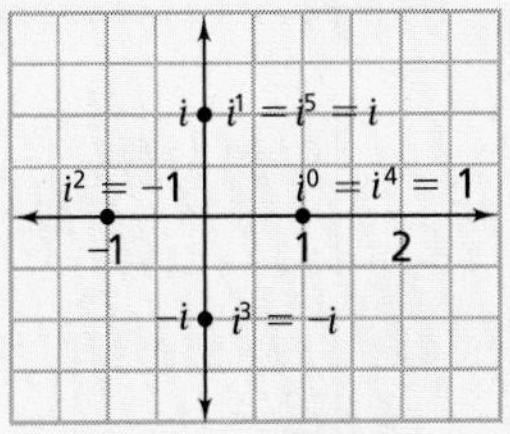

7. a–d.

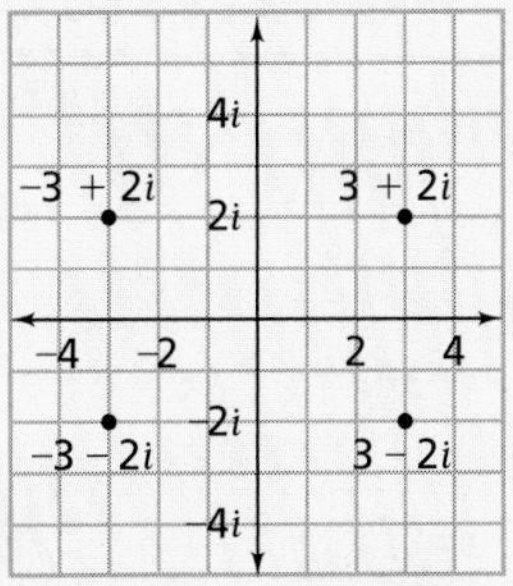

8. a–d.

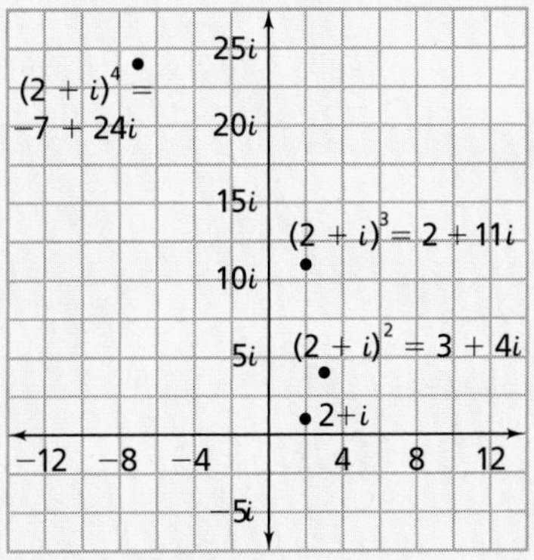

EXERCISE 9 In later lessons, students will have more opportunities to think about how to visualize complex sums graphically, so do not worry if this is not clear yet.

EXERCISE 11 You might assign only part (b) of this exercise, since all parts are very similar. This exercise relies on students' factoring ability.

EXERCISE 13 Students should notice that the numbers in each part are collinear, and they may notice the relationship between complex numbers and their conjugates. This exercise is also intended as practice for graphing in the complex plane.

9. Suppose a and b are positive real numbers.

a. Graph what $a + bi$ and $a - bi$ might look like on the same complex plane.

b. Graph the sum of $z = a + bi$ and $\overline{z} = a - bi$.

c. Describe how the sum $z + \overline{z}$ is geometrically related to z and $\overline{z}$.

d. Describe how the difference $z - \overline{z}$ is geometrically related to z and $\overline{z}$.

In Exercises 10 and 11, solve each equation. Then graph the solutions on the complex plane.

10. **a.** $x^2 + 6x + 5 = 0$

b. $x^2 + 6x + 8 = 0$

c. $x^2 + 6x + 10 = 0$

d. $x^2 + 6x + 13 = 0$

e. $x^2 + 6x + 18 = 0$

11. **a.** $x^4 - 1 = 0$

b. $x^4 - 16 = 0$

c. $x^4 - 81 = 0$

d. $x^4 - 256 = 0$

12. Graph each complex number on the same complex plane.

a. i^{10} **b.** i^{11} **c.** i^{243}

d. i^{-1} **e.** i^{-11} **f.** i^{-243}

13. Suppose $z = 3 + i$ and $w = 2 - i$. Graph each group of numbers on the complex plane.

a. $w, 2w, 3w$

b. $z + w, z + 2w, z + 3w$

c. $\overline{w}, \overline{2w}, \overline{3w}$

d. $\overline{z + w}, \overline{z + 2w}, \overline{z + 3w}$

Answers

9. a.

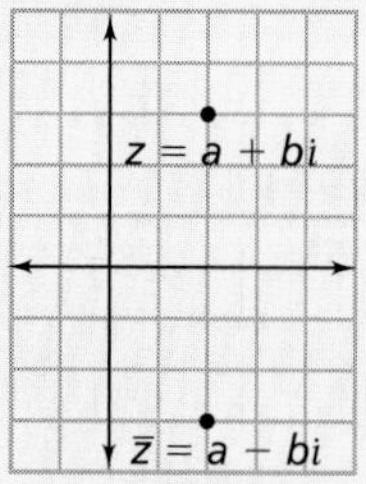

9. b.

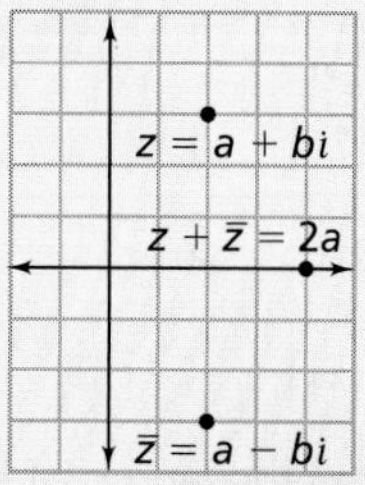

c. $z + \overline{z}$ corresponds to the point $2a$, which is on the positive real axis.

d. $z - \overline{z}$ corresponds to the point $0 + 2bi$, which is on the positive imaginary axis.

14. Standardized Test Prep Suppose $z = 5 + i$ and $w = 4 - i$. Which of the following numbers is NOT in Quadrant IV on the complex plane?

A. zw **B.** w^2

C. $\bar{z}$ **D.** $3z + 2w$

15. Take It Further Suppose $z = \frac{\sqrt{2}}{2} + \frac{\sqrt{2}}{2}i$. Simplify each expression. Then graph all the numbers on the same complex plane.

a. z^0 **b.** z^1 **c.** z^2 **d.** z^3

e. z^4 **f.** z^8 **g.** z^{27} **h.** z^{275}

Maintain Your Skills

16. Graph and label each complex number on the same complex plane.

a. $-3 + i$

b. $2(-3 + i)$

c. $3(-3 + i)$

d. $4(-3 + i)$

e. $-1(-3 + i)$

17. Write each expression as a complex number $a + bi$. Then graph and label each complex number on the same complex plane.

a. $3 + 5i$

b. $(3 + 5i) \cdot i$

c. $(3 + 5i) \cdot i^2$

d. $(3 + 5i) \cdot i^3$

e. $(3 + 5i) \cdot i^4$

10–13. See back of book.

14. D

15.

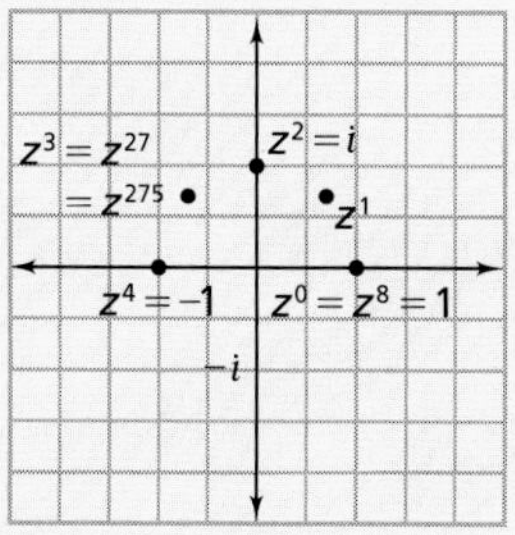

a. 1

b. $\frac{\sqrt{2}}{2} + \frac{\sqrt{2}}{2}i$

c. i

d. $-\frac{\sqrt{2}}{2} + \frac{\sqrt{2}}{2}i$

e. -1

f. 1

g. $-\frac{\sqrt{2}}{2} + \frac{\sqrt{2}}{2}i$

h. $-\frac{\sqrt{2}}{2} + \frac{\sqrt{2}}{2}i$

16–17. See back of book.

EXERCISE 15 Use of a CAS can make this exercise a lot easier, but take care that students look for patterns among the powers of z. They will revisit this topic in Lesson 3.13 *Roots of Unity*. If you are skipping that lesson, consider skipping this exercise, especially if students do not have access to a CAS.

Maintain Your Skills

EXERCISE 16 Students should notice that all the points are collinear.

EXERCISE 17 Students should recognize that multiplying by i^4 does not change the point, since $i^4 = 1$, and that the points are rotating through the quadrants as they are multiplied by the different powers of i. If time permits, you might ask students whether the points are the vertices of a square (they are), but this discussion is time-consuming.

Additional Resources

PRINT RESOURCES
- Solution Manual
- Practice Workbook
- Assessment Resources
- Teaching Resources

TECHNOLOGY
- Interactive Textbook
- TeacherExpress CD-ROM
- ExamView CD-ROM
- PHSchool.com

Additional Practice

For Exercises 1 and 2, graph and label the four complex numbers on a single complex plane.

1. a. $5 + 3i$ **b.** $5 - 3i$ **c.** $-5 + 3i$ **d.** $-5 - 3i$

2. a. $3 + i$ **b.** $(3 + i)^2$ **c.** $(3 + i)^3$ **d.** $(3 + i)^4$

3. Suppose x and y are positive real numbers.
a. Graph what $x + yi$ and $x - yi$ might look like on the same complex plane.
b. Let $z = x + yi$ and $\bar{z} = x - yi$. Graph the sum $z + \bar{z}$ and the difference $z - \bar{z}$ on the same complex plane.
c. Describe how the sum $z + \bar{z}$ is related geometrically to z and $\bar{z}$.
d. Describe how the difference $z - \bar{z}$ is related geometrically to z and $\bar{z}$.

4. Solve each equation. Then graph the solutions on the complex plane.
a. $x^2 + 4x + 3 = 0$ **b.** $x^2 + 4x + 4 = 0$
c. $x^2 + 4x + 5 = 0$ **d.** $x^2 + 4x + 8 = 0$

5. Illustrate the following equation graphically.
$$(2 - i) + (2 - i) + (2 - i) = 6 - 3i$$

6. For each complex number, find its distance from the origin on the complex plane.
a. $4 + i$ **b.** $5 - i$
c. $(4 + i)(5 - i)$ **d.** $(3 + i)^3$

7. Order the following complex numbers from least to greatest, based on how far each number is from the origin.
$3 - 2i$ $4 + 5i$ $-6 + i$ -5

8. Suppose $z = 2 - i$. For each value of w, draw a diagram that shows z, w, and zw.
a. $w = 4 + 5i$ **b.** $w = -4 + 5i$
c. $w = -1 + 3i$ **d.** $w = 5$
e. $w = -6i$ **f.** $w = 2 + i$

Practice: For Lesson 3.7, assign Exercises 1–4.

Lesson Overview

GOALS

- Visualize operations on complex numbers as transformations on the complex plane.
- Develop greater fluency with complex number calculations, which include finding magnitude and direction.

This lesson demonstrates geometric representations of arithmetic operations of complex numbers. Students will

- look at complex numbers as vectors.
- see how they can add two complex numbers by drawing a parallelogram.
- see how they can multiply two complex numbers using geometric transformations (rotation and dilation) on one vector. The real and imaginary parts of the other complex number will define the transformation rules.

CHECK YOUR UNDERSTANDING
- Core: 1, 2a–e, 3, 6, 7, 8
- Optional: 4, 5, 9
- Extension: 2f

MATERIALS
- graph paper
- graphing calculators
- Blackline Master 3.8

HOMEWORK
- Core: 10, 11, 13, 14, 18
- Optional: 12, 15, 16a, 17
- Extension: 16b

VOCABULARY
- dilation

Launch

To begin class, you might ask students to think about their answers for the opening questions.

One approach to this lesson is to spend two classes covering it. For the first class have students investigate these questions and develop a list of conjectures. Then in the second class, start with the addition section and gradually develop answers to all the questions.

If you can not afford to spend two days on this lesson, keep the preliminary discussion brief so that students have time to work on the development of the answers in the rest of the lesson.

3.8 Arithmetic in the Complex Plane

Once mathematicians realized that there is a one-to-one correspondence between points on a plane and complex numbers, they started asking questions about visualizing operations on complex numbers.

Suppose z and w are complex numbers, represented as points on the complex plane. How can you locate the following numbers?

- $z + w$
- $3z$
- zw
- $\overline{z}$
- $-z$

You have already explored some of these questions. In this lesson, you will focus on addition, and you will begin to explore multiplication.

Addition

The graph below shows $z = 2 + 3i$, $w = 6 + i$, and the sum $z + w = 8 + 4i$ on the complex plane.

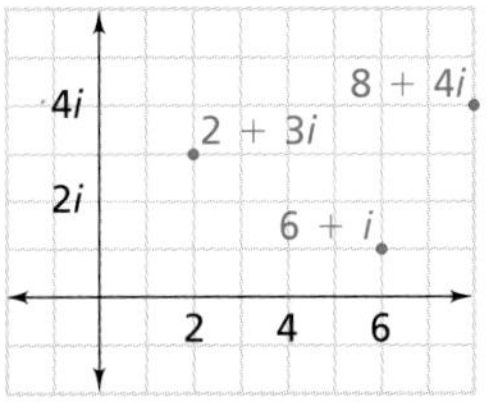

These may look like three random points, but if you draw vectors from the origin to z and w, you see more structure.

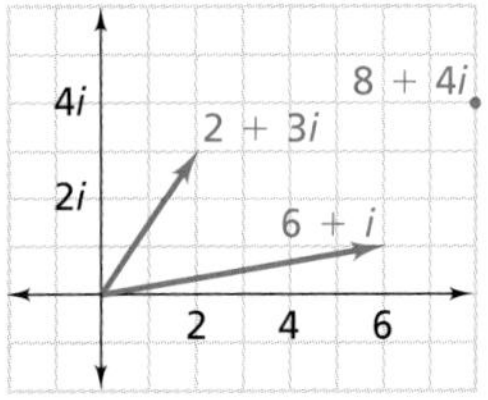

Remember...

A vector is an arrow from the origin to a point. You can use vectors to bring clarity to figures like this one.

Minds in Action episode 11

Tony draws the vector for the sum $8 + 4i$.

Tony Hey, look, Sasha. If I draw in the vector for the sum, I get this.

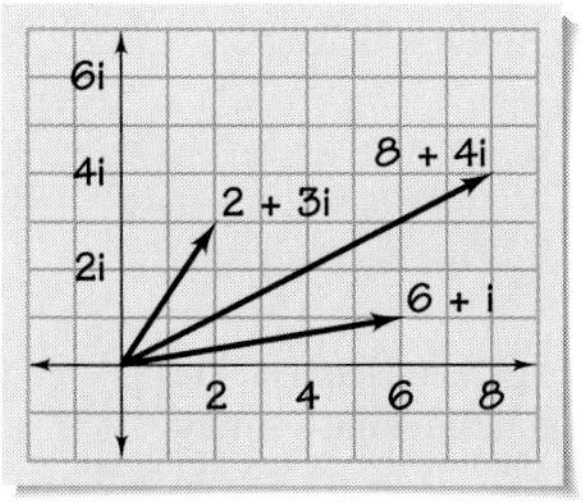

Sasha draws on Tony's graph.

Sasha And if I connect the dots, it looks like a parallelogram.

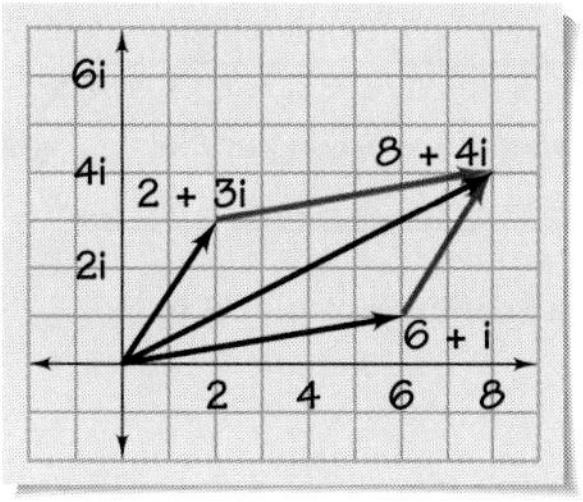

For You to Do

1. Prove Sasha correct. Show that if $z = 2 + 3i$ and $w = 6 + i$, then 0, z, w, and $z + w$ are the vertices of a parallelogram.

The following theorem shows that Sasha's parallelogram law always works. The proof is just a general version of what you did above with $2 + 3i$ and $6 + i$.

Theorem 3.2

Suppose $z = a + bi$ and $w = c + di$ are complex numbers. Then, on the complex plane, the numbers 0, z, w, and $z + w$ form the vertices of a parallelogram.

Explore

For You to Do

The key to the proof is to remind students that if two lines (or line segments) have the same slope, then they are either parallel or collinear. In this case, it is easy to show that two line segments with the same slope are not collinear, since no three of the points are collinear.

You could explore this part further by picking two complex numbers that have the same direction. Ask how the parallelogram law applies to their addition. (Answer: You simply line up the two vectors head-to-tail. Two angles in this devolved parallelogram measure 180°, and two measure 0°.)

To demonstrate this case, show how to add $1 + 2i$ and $2 + 4i$. To demonstrate another devolved case, show the addition of $2 - 3i$ and $-6 + 9i$. In this case, the two vectors are collinear, but in opposite directions. When you arrange the two vectors head-to-tail, the second turns back onto the first.

Answers

For You to Do

1. Answers may vary. Sample: Think of the quadrilateral on a real coordinate plane with vertices (0, 0), (2, 3), (8, 4), and (6, 1). Prove that opposite sides of the quadrilateral are parallel by showing that their slopes are equal. The slope between (0, 0) and (2, 3) is $\frac{3}{2}$, which is the same as the slope between (6, 1) and (8, 4). The slope between (2, 3) and (8, 4) is $\frac{1}{6}$, which is the same as the slope between (0, 0) and (6, 1). The slopes of opposite sides of the quadrilateral are equal, so the quadrilateral is a parallelogram.

MULTIPLICATION: FIRST STEPS This section begins the discussion of multiplying two complex numbers with two special cases:

- multiplying a complex number by a real number.
- multiplying a complex number by i.

These two special cases can be combined to give a geometric interpretation of multiplying any two complex numbers. This is discussed in Lesson 3.11.

For Discussion

If z is a complex number $a + bi$, then $4z = 4(a + bi) = 4a + 4bi$. If $4z$, z and 0 are collinear, any pair of points among the three must have the same slope between them.

The slope between points (0, 0) and (a, b) is $\frac{b}{a}$. The slope between points (0, 0) and $(4a, 4b)$ is $\frac{4b}{4a} = \frac{b}{a}$. You now have enough evidence to prove that the three points are collinear, but you can also show that the slope between (a, b) and $(4a, 4b)$ is $\frac{4b - b}{4a - a} = \frac{3b}{3a} = \frac{b}{a}$.

Proof $z + w = (a + c) + (b + d)i$, so the coordinates of the point corresponding to $z + w$ are $(a + c, b + d)$.

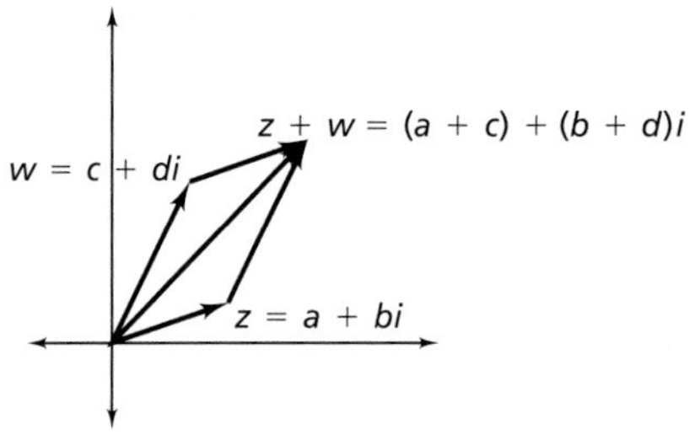

A figure is a parallelogram if its opposite sides are parallel. Parallel lines have the same slope. The slope from 0 to w is $\frac{d}{c}$, and the slope from z to $z + w$ is

$$\frac{(b + d) - b}{(a + c) - a} = \frac{d}{c}$$

So these two sides are parallel.

For You to Do

2. Complete the proof by showing that the other two sides are also parallel.

Or you can show that the sides you proved parallel are also congruent.

You can also use the parallelogram law to subtract complex numbers by adding the opposite.

Multiplication: First Steps

How do you visualize multiplication? This is more difficult. Given z and w on the complex plane, can you locate zw? In this lesson, you will look at two special cases: when w is a real number, and when $w = i$.

You can visualize multiplication of a complex number z by a positive real number k as stretching or shrinking the vector by a factor of k. For example, for $z = -3 + i$, the graph below shows vectors for z and $4z$.

Stretches and shrinks by a factor of k are dilations.

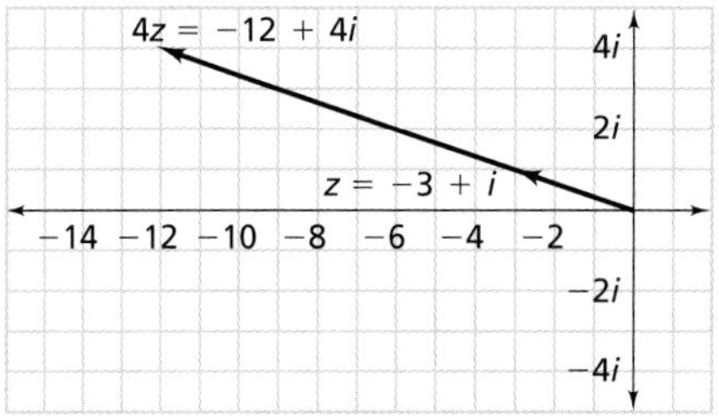

Answers

For You to Do

2. The slope from O to z is $\frac{b}{a}$, and the slope from w to $(z + w)$ is $\frac{(b + d) - d}{(a + c) - c} = \frac{b}{a}$, so the sides are parallel.

For Discussion

3. Answers may vary. Sample: The slope from $4z$ to z is $\frac{4 - 1}{-12 - (-3)} = \frac{3}{-9} = -\frac{1}{3}$, and the slope from z to 0 is $\frac{1 - 0}{-3 - 0} = -\frac{1}{3}$. The slopes are the same, so $4z$, z, and 0 are collinear.

For Discussion

3. In the graph, $4z$, z, and 0 appear to be collinear. Prove that this is, in fact, true.

How do you prove that three points are collinear?

You can multiply z by a negative real number $-k$ by graphing $-z$ and then scaling that vector by k. For example, the graph below shows $-3 + i$ and $-2 \cdot (-3 + i)$ drawn as vectors.

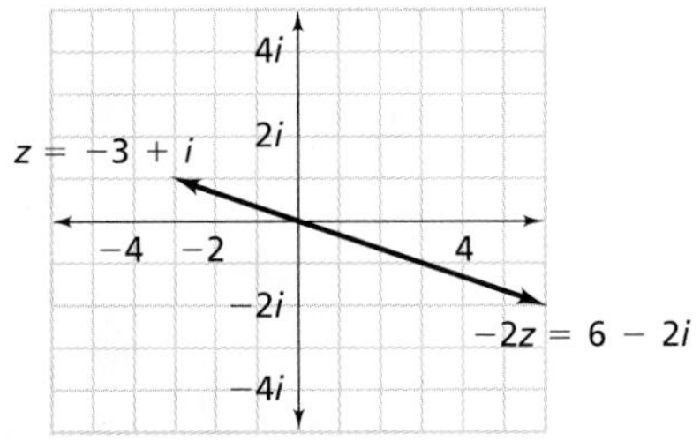

This works since $z \cdot (-k) = (-z) \cdot k$.

In-Class Experiment

For each z, graph z and iz as vectors on the same complex plane.

4. $z = 3 + 5i$

5. $z = -2 + i$

6. $z = -3 - 4i$

Describe how the graph of iz compares to the graph of z in the complex plane.

Habits of Mind

Experiment. Try more examples if you need to. Choose other complex numbers for z.

The In-Class Experiment above suggests the following relationship.

Theorem 3.3 Multiplication by i

If z is a complex number, iz is obtained from z by rotating it 90° counterclockwise about the origin.

The fact that the rotation is counterclockwise instead of clockwise is surprisingly technical. Ask your teacher if you are curious about the details.

In-Class Experiment

In general, you graph a complex number $z = a + bi$ as (a, b). $iz = i(a + bi) = -b + ai$, so you graph the product iz as $(-b, a)$. This is the image of (a, b) after a rotation of 90° counterclockwise around the origin. If your students have difficulty visualizing this rotation, you might show them a transparency overlay of the rotation.

Sketch a vector for a complex number z on two transparencies, showing the coordinate grid (or at least the axes) on the bottom transparency. You might choose one of the specific examples from the experiment, or just a general vector. Then, keeping the origins of the two transparencies together, rotate the top copy of the vector until its arrowhead is at $(-b, a)$. Now the top copy is the image of the original complex number after multiplication by i. Students should be able to see that it can also be seen as the image after rotation around the origin by 90° counterclockwise.

To explain to a curious student why this rotation *must* be counterclockwise, take a quadrant-by-quadrant look at the signs of the real and imaginary parts of the resulting vector iz.

- If z is in the first quadrant, then it has a positive real and imaginary part. iz with real part $-b$ and imaginary part a will have a negative real part and a positive imaginary part, placing it in Quadrant II. The 90° rotation was counterclockwise.
- If z is in the second quadrant, then it has a negative real and a positive imaginary part. iz with real part $-b$ and imaginary part a will have a negative real part and a negative imaginary part, placing it in Quadrant III. Again, the 90° rotation was counterclockwise.
- If z is in the third quadrant, then it has a negative real and imaginary part. iz with real part $-b$ and imaginary part a will have a positive real part and a negative imaginary part, placing it in Quadrant IV. The 90° rotation was counterclockwise.
- Finally, with z is in the fourth quadrant, it has a positive real and a negative imaginary part. iz with real part $-b$ and imaginary part a will have a positive real part and a positive imaginary part, placing it in Quadrant I. The 90° rotation was also counterclockwise.

In-Class Experiment

4. $z = 3 + 5i$, $iz = -5 + 3i$

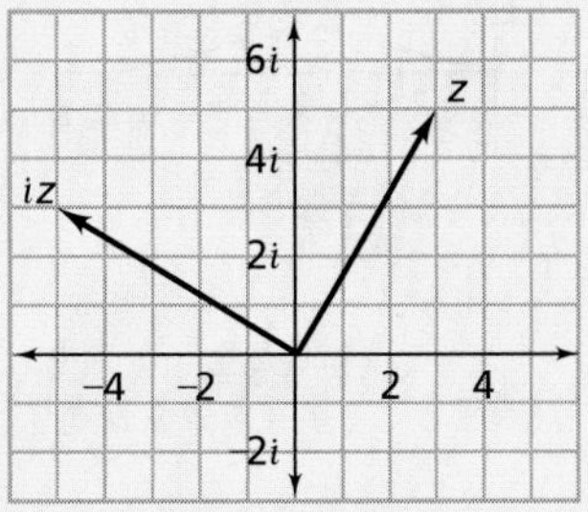

5. $z = -2 + i$, $iz = -1 - 2i$

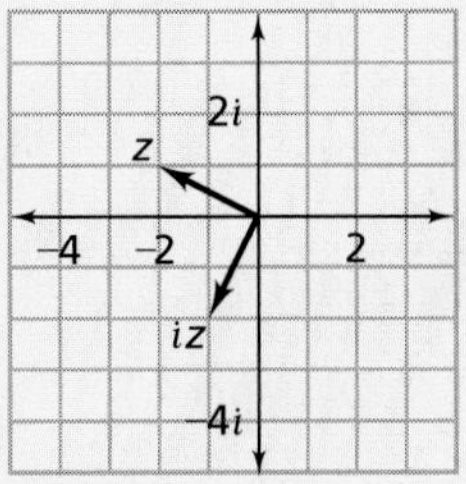

6. See back of book.

Wrap Up

Have students look again at Tony's and Sasha's final diagram in Minds in Action episode 11. Because the figure is a parallelogram, the blue arrow from $2 + 3i$ to $8 + 4i$ is parallel and congruent to the vector for $6 + i$. So, you can find the location of the sum $(2 + 3i) + (6 + i)$ by beginning at the end of the $2 + 3i$ vector and drawing an arrow parallel and congruent to the $6 + i$ vector. The answer graphs for Exercises 1 and 2 show this method of illustrating complex number addition. The vector for the second addend is grey, with its parallel and congruent arrow drawn in black from the end of the first addend's vector to the location of the sum.

Assessment Resources

Lesson Quiz 3.8

1. Illustrate the equation $(1 + 2i) + (1 + 2i) + (1 + 2i) = 3 + 6i$ graphically.

2. Order the following complex numbers from least to greatest, based on how far each number is from the origin.

   $-3 + 2i \qquad 4 - 5i \qquad -7 - i \qquad 5$

3. Suppose $z = 3 + i$. For each value of w, draw a diagram that shows z, w, and zw.
   a. $w = 1 + 3i$ b. $w = -1 + 3i$ c. $w = -7 + 3i$
   d. $w = -2$ e. $w = -4i$ f. $w = 3 - i$

4. For each complex number, find its distance from the origin on the complex plane.
   a. $6 + 2i$ b. $-3 - i$ c. $(6 + 2i)(-3 - i)$ d. $(5 + i)^3$

Proof Show that the vectors representing iz and z are perpendicular and are the same distance from the origin. Then you obtain iz from z by a 90° rotation.

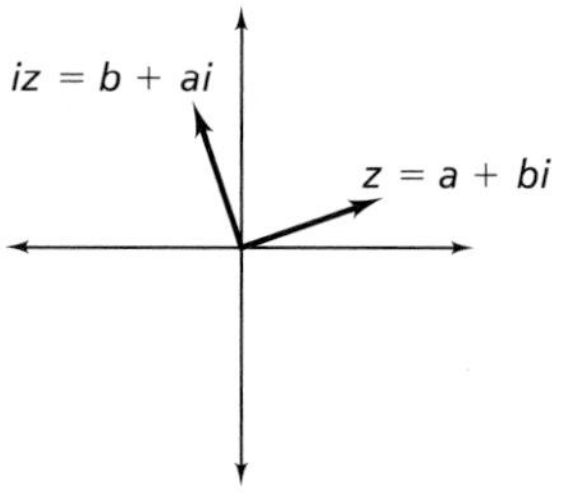

Start by writing $z = a + bi$. Then $iz = -b + ai$.

You can use slope to prove that the two vectors are perpendicular. The slope of the vector representing z is $\frac{b}{a}$. The slope of the vector representing iz is $\frac{a}{-b}$. These slopes are negative reciprocals.

$$\frac{b}{a} \cdot \frac{a}{-b} = -1$$

Therefore, the vectors are perpendicular, and the angle between z and iz is 90°.

In the exercises, you will prove that $z = a + bi$ and $iz = -b + ai$ are the same distance from the origin.

You can use vectors to describe the magnitude and direction of the wind, currents, and movement of the ship.

Developing Habits of Mind

Represent complex numbers graphically. You can think about a complex number graphically in two ways: as a point and as a vector. By thinking about complex numbers as points, you can apply all the machinery of geometry. This representation helps you perform algebraic tasks, such as solving equations.

By thinking about complex numbers as vectors, you can visualize operations, such as adding or multiplying by i. Vectors also help you compare the relative sizes of complex numbers.

It is important that you become comfortable with both representations and that you develop a sense of when it is appropriate to "think point" or to "think vector."

You use vectors extensively in navigation and physics. Complex numbers are also key in analyzing signals, such as radio waves or electric current.

For You to Do

7. Which of these four complex numbers has the longest vector?

$$-5 - 6i \qquad 6 + i \qquad 4 + 5i \qquad 8$$

Answers

For You to Do

7. 8

Exercises

1. a.

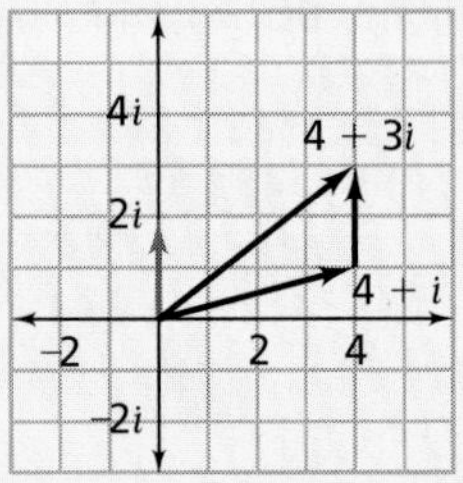

b.

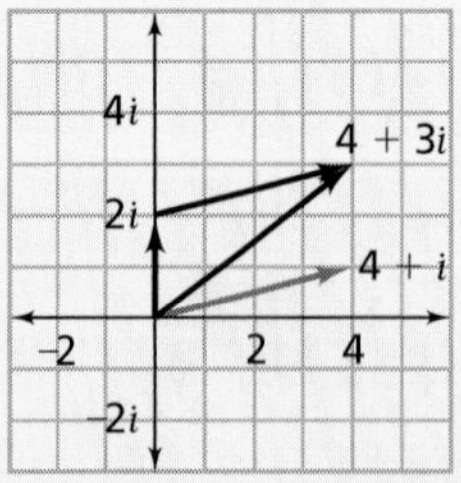

c.

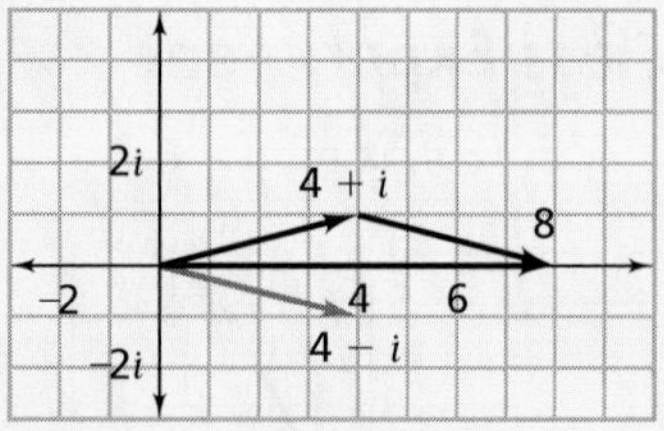

Exercises *Practicing Habits of Mind*

Check Your Understanding

1. Illustrate each addition equation on the complex plane.
   - **a.** $(4 + i) + (2i) = 4 + 3i$
   - **b.** $(2i) + (4 + i) = 4 + 3i$
   - **c.** $(4 + i) + (4 - i) = 8$
   - **d.** $(4 + i) + (-3 + i) = 1 + 2i$
   - **e.** $-8 + 3 = -5$

2. The graph below shows two complex numbers z and w.

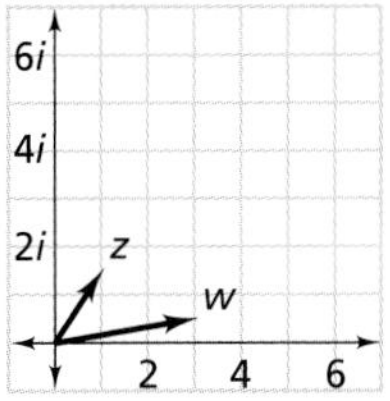

Graph each expression.

- **a.** $z + w$
- **b.** $2z$
- **c.** $-w$
- **d.** $2z + 2w$
- **e.** $2z - w$
- **f. Take It Further** $z + wi$

3. If $z = a + bi$ is a complex number, show that z and iz are the same distance from the origin.

4. For each complex number, find the distance to the origin on the complex plane.
   - **a.** $4 + i$
   - **b.** $2 + i$
   - **c.** $3 - 2i$
   - **d.** $6 + 5i$

5. Find each product.
   - **a.** $(4 + i)(4 - i)$
   - **b.** $(2 + i)(2 - i)$
   - **c.** $(3 - 2i)(3 + 2i)$
   - **d.** $(6 + 5i)(6 - 5i)$

Go Online PHSchool.com

For more information about multiplying complex numbers, go to **Web Code:** bfe-9031

Exercises

HOMEWORK
- Core: 10, 11, 13, 14, 18
- Optional: 12, 15, 16a, 17
- Extension: 16b

Check Your Understanding

EXERCISE 1 Note that parts (a) and (b) form an example of the "parallelogram law."

EXERCISE 2 is a good exercise to see if students understand conceptually how to add vectors. Watch for students trying to write z and w in $a + bi$ form: that is not the goal of this exercise. The last part is more difficult than the others. Blackline Master 3.8 corresponds to this exercise.

EXERCISES 4 AND 5 Assign Exercise 4 along with Exercise 5. Discuss the similarity in the results. Make the connection explicit by pointing out that the magnitude calculated for $a + bi$ in Exercise 4 was $\sqrt{a^2 + b^2}$. In Exercise 5, the result of the multiplication $(a + bi)(a - bi)$ is $a^2 + b^2$.

Students will revisit this topic in the next lesson on magnitude and direction, since one potential definition of magnitude is $\sqrt{z\bar{z}}$.

d.

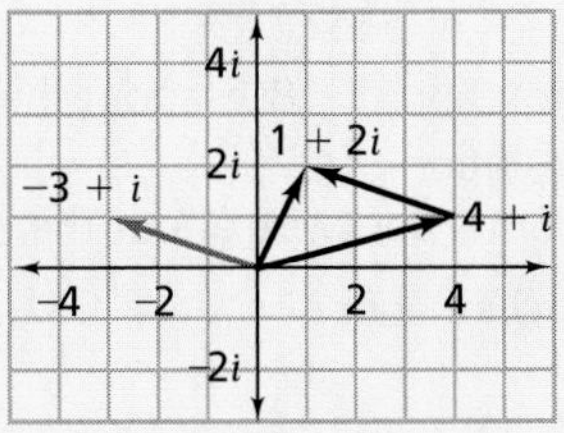

e.

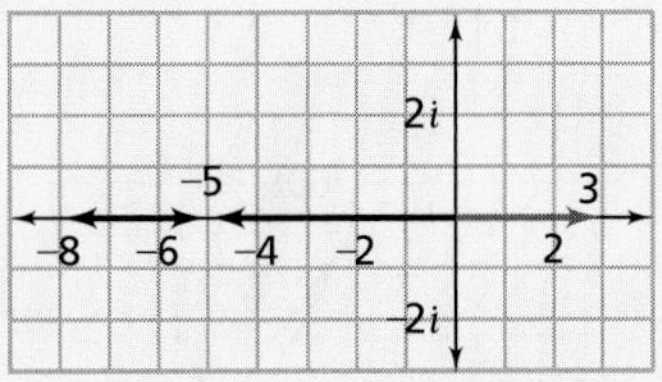

2. See back of book.

3. $z = a + bi$ is $\sqrt{a^2 + b^2}$ units from the origin, and $iz = -b + ai$ is $\sqrt{b^2 + a^2}$ units from the origin. The distances are equal.

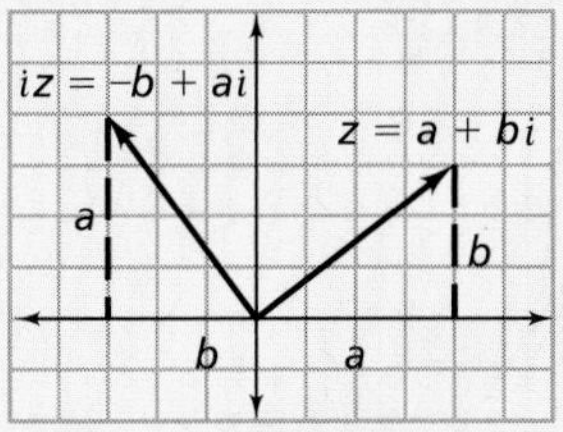

4. a. $\sqrt{17}$ **b.** $\sqrt{5}$ **c.** $\sqrt{13}$ **d.** $\sqrt{61}$

5. a. 17 **b.** 5 **c.** 13 **d.** 61

EXERCISE 6 is optional. It relates to later work but is time-consuming. You might break up the calculations among groups of students. Note that the triangle is not a right triangle, but all its side lengths and vertices are integers—this is rare.

EXERCISE 7 reinforces the idea that multiplying by i gives a 90° rotation in the complex plane.

On Your Own

EXERCISE 9 One important habit of mind students should develop is the ability to decide when a particular representation is helpful, and when it is not. This exercise encourages students to choose between the two geometric forms of a complex number (a point or a vector), and to explain why one representation is better than the other. (In each part, there is clearly a better choice.)

An answer can be short but should include a clear argument as to why the representation the student chose is more helpful than the one not chosen.

EXERCISE 11 You might point out here that the magnitude of $(3 + i)(4 - i)$ is the product of the magnitudes of $3 + i$ and $4 - i$, and that the magnitude of $(2 + i)^2$ is the square of the magnitude of $2 + i$. Students will explore this in detail in Investigation 3C.

EXERCISES 15 AND 16 are connected. They extend of the concept of "multiplying by i" to another complex number that is a lot harder to work with algebraically.

6. Consider the triangle with the following vertices.

$$-18 + 49i \qquad 15 - 7i \qquad 30 - 15i$$

a. Find the lengths of the sides of the triangle.

b. If you multiply each vertex by -1, what is the position of the resulting triangle compared to the original triangle in the complex plane? Draw a picture to support your answer.

c. If you multiply each vertex by i, what is the position of the resulting triangle compared to the original triangle in the complex plane? Draw a picture to support your answer.

7. For each complex number z, graph z and iz as vectors on the same complex plane.

a. $z = 3 + 2i$ **b.** $z = -1 + 4i$

c. $z = -1 - 3i$ **d.** $z = 2 - 3i$

8. **a.** Describe the effect, in the complex plane, of multiplying a complex number by i^2.

b. Describe the effect, in the complex plane, of multiplying a complex number by $-i$.

9. **Write About It** For each statement, decide whether you would represent the complex numbers as points or as vectors. Give reasons for your choice. Then draw a diagram.

a. The numbers 1, i, -1, and $-i$ lie on the vertices of a square on the complex plane.

b. You can use the parallelogram law to visualize the sum $(3 + 2i) + (7 - 6i)$.

c. If you multiply the vertices of a triangle by i, the new triangle is congruent to the original.

d. The distance from $5 + 12i$ to the origin is greater than the distance from $3 + 4i$ to the origin.

On Your Own

10. Illustrate the following equation graphically.

$$(3 - i) + (3 - i) + (3 - i) = 9 - 3i$$

11. For each complex number, find its distance from the origin on the complex plane.

a. $3 + i$ **b.** $4 - i$ **c.** $(3 + i)(4 - i)$

d. $(2 + i)^2$ **e.** $(2 + i)^3$

Go Online PHSchool.com

For additional practice, go to **Web Code:** bfa-0308

Answers

6. a. 65, 17, 80

b. rotated 180°

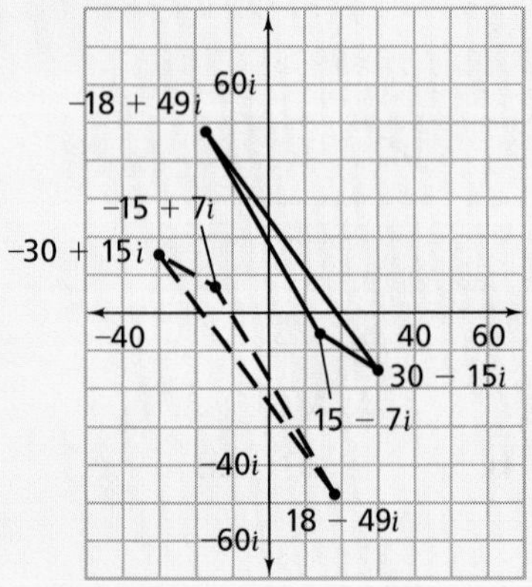

c. rotated 90°

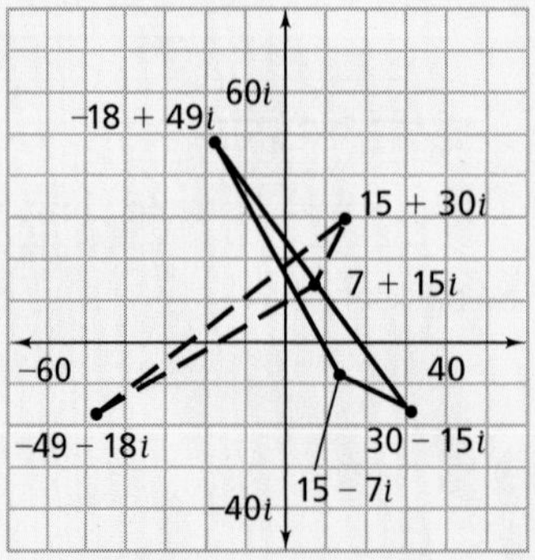

7. See back of book.

8. a. a rotation of 180° about the origin

b. a rotation of 270° counterclockwise about the origin

9. See back of book.

12. Does Theorem 3.2 work for two real numbers? Explain.

13. Order the following complex numbers from least to greatest, based on how far each number is from the origin.

$5 + 3i \qquad 2 - 7i \qquad 8 \qquad -6 - 4i$

14. **Standardized Test Prep** Below is a graph of $2iz$, for a complex number z, on the complex plane. Which of the following numbers is z?

A. $-3 + 2i$

B. $2 + 3i$

C. $3 - 2i$

D. $4 + 6i$

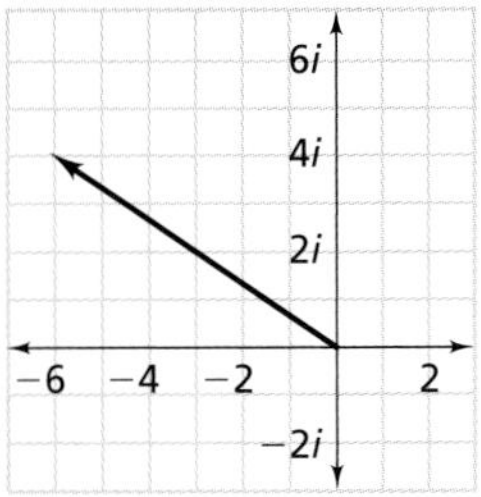

15. Suppose $z = \frac{\sqrt{2}}{2} + \frac{\sqrt{2}}{2}i$. Graph each pair of complex numbers.

a. $1 + i$ and $(1 + i) \cdot z$

b. $3 + 5i$ and $(3 + 5i) \cdot z$

c. $-2 + i$ and $(-2 + i) \cdot z$

d. $-3 - 4i$ and $(-3 - 4i) \cdot z$

16. a. **Write About It** Describe the effect, in the complex plane, of multiplying by $z = \frac{\sqrt{2}}{2} + \frac{\sqrt{2}}{2}i$ in Exercise 15.

b. **Take It Further** Describe the effect, in the complex plane, of multiplying by $z^2 = \left(\frac{\sqrt{2}}{2} + \frac{\sqrt{2}}{2}i\right)^2$.

Maintain Your Skills

17. Solve each equation.

a. $x^3 - 1 = 0$

b. $x^3 - 8 = 0$

c. $x^3 = 27$

d. $x^3 = 64$

e. Find an equation with integer coefficients having solutions that include 8 and $-4 + 4i\sqrt{3}$.

18. Suppose $z = 1 + i$. For each value of w, draw a diagram that shows z, w, and zw.

a. $w = 3 + 4i$

b. $w = -3 + 4i$

c. $w = -5 + 12i$

d. $w = 7$

e. $w = 3i$

For Exercise 17 help, see the TI-Nspire Handbook, p. 778.

Habits of Mind

Make strategic choices. You can represent complex numbers as vectors or as points. Decide which form is most helpful to you in each case.

Additional Resources

PRINT RESOURCES
- Solution Manual
- Practice Workbook
- Assessment Resources
- Teaching Resources

TECHNOLOGY
- Interactive Textbook
- TeacherExpress CD-ROM
- ExamView CD-ROM
- PHSchool.com

Additional Practice

For Exercises 1 and 2, graph and label the four complex numbers on a single complex plane.

1. a. $5 + 3i$ b. $5 - 3i$ c. $-5 + 3i$ d. $-5 - 3i$

2. a. $3 + i$ b. $(3 + i)^2$ c. $(3 + i)^3$ d. $(3 + i)^4$

3. Suppose x and y are positive real numbers.
   a. Graph what $x + yi$ and $x - yi$ might look like on the same complex plane.
   b. Let $z = x + yi$ and $\overline{z} = x - yi$. Graph the sum $z + \overline{z}$ and the difference $z - \overline{z}$ on the same complex plane.
   c. Describe how the sum $z + \overline{z}$ is related geometrically to z and $\overline{z}$.
   d. Describe how the difference $z - \overline{z}$ is related geometrically to z and $\overline{z}$.

4. Solve each equation. Then graph the solutions on the complex plane.
   a. $x^2 + 4x + 3 = 0$ b. $x^2 + 4x + 4 = 0$
   c. $x^2 + 4x + 5 = 0$ d. $x^2 + 4x + 8 = 0$

5. Illustrate the following equation graphically.
   $(2 - i) + (2 - i) + (2 - i) = 6 - 3i$

6. For each complex number, find its distance from the origin on the complex plane.
   a. $4 + i$ b. $5 - i$
   c. $(4 + i)(5 - i)$ d. $(3 + i)^3$

7. Order the following complex numbers from least to greatest, based on how far each number is from the origin.
   $3 - 2i \qquad 4 + 5i \qquad -6 + i \qquad -5$

8. Suppose $z = 2 - i$. For each value of w, draw a diagram that shows z, w, and zw.
   a. $w = 4 + 5i$ b. $w = -4 + 5i$
   c. $w = -1 + 3i$ d. $w = 5$
   e. $w = -6i$ f. $w = 2 + i$

Practice: For Lesson 3.8, assign Exercises 5–8.

10.

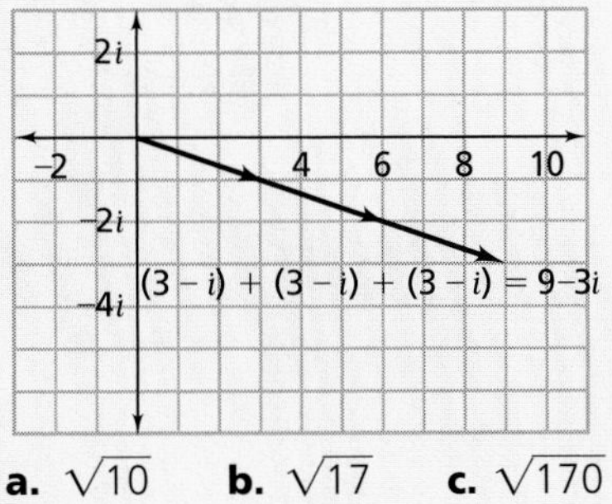

11. a. $\sqrt{10}$ **b.** $\sqrt{17}$ **c.** $\sqrt{170}$ **d.** 5 **e.** $5\sqrt{5}$

12. Yes; the ordered pairs (0, 0), (a, b), (c, d), and ($a + c$, $b + d$) form the vertices of a parallelogram.

13. $5 + 3i$, $-6 - 4i$, $2 - 7i$, 8

14. B

15. See back of book.

16. a. The effect is to rotate the vector 45° counterclockwise about the origin, with no change to the magnitude.

b. The effect is to rotate the vector 90° counterclockwise about the origin, with no change to the magnitude.

17. a. $1, -\frac{1}{2} \pm \frac{\sqrt{3}}{2}i$

b. $2, -1 \pm i\sqrt{3}$

c. $3, -\frac{3}{2} \pm \frac{3\sqrt{3}}{2}i$

d. $4, -2 \pm 2i\sqrt{3}$

e. Answers may vary. Sample: $x^3 - 512 = 0$

18. See back of book.

Lesson Overview

GOAL

- Develop greater fluency with complex number calculations, which include finding magnitude and direction.

This lesson formalizes two key attributes of complex numbers: magnitude (or absolute value) and direction (or argument). Although students will not formally consider "cis" notation until CME Project *Precalculus,* they will use magnitude and direction to explore a number of ideas in complex arithmetic. This will include how to represent multiplication of two vectors by dilating and rotating one of the vectors based on the magnitude and direction of the other.

CHECK YOUR UNDERSTANDING
- Core: 1, 3, 4, 6, 7, 8
- Optional: 2, 5, 9, 10

MATERIALS
- CAS (recommended)
- graph paper
- graphing calculators
- Blackline Masters MC2, 3.9

HOMEWORK
- Core: 11, 12, 13, 14, 16
- Optional: 15, 17, 18a, 19, 20
- Extension: 18b

VOCABULARY
- argument, arg z
- direction
- magnitude, $|z|$

Launch

You may want to split this lesson over two days. Start the first class by reading the definition of *magnitude.* Have students work on For You to Do Problems 1–5.

Begin the second class for this lesson by going over the definition of *direction* with students. Have them work through Example 2.

Explore

Theorem 3.4 If students have a difficult time with the proof, have them work through one or two numerical examples first. An interesting (and useful) factoring idea that emerges here is that you can factor the sum of squares using complex numbers. That is,

$$a^2 + b^2 = (a + bi)(a - bi)$$

The key idea is that you can rewrite $a^2 + b^2$ as $a^2 - (bi)^2$, since $i^2 = -1$.

3.9 Magnitude and Direction

In the last lesson, you represented complex numbers as vectors. Now you will focus on two properties of vectors, *magnitude* and *direction.*

Definition

The magnitude of the complex number z, denoted by $|z|$, is the distance between the complex number and (0, 0) in the complex plane. In other words, $|z|$ is the length of the vector that represents z.

If $z = a + bi$, the magnitude is the length of the line segment connecting $(0, 0)$ and (a, b) in the coordinate plane.

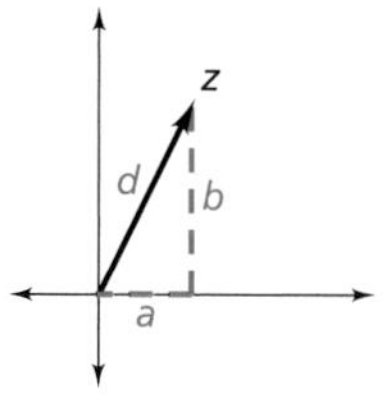

$d^2 = a^2 + b^2$

For You to Do

1. Find $|-3 + 5i|$.
2. Find a complex number in the fourth quadrant with magnitude 5.
3. Show that the magnitude of $z = a + bi$ is $|z| = \sqrt{a^2 + b^2}$.

To calculate magnitude, see the TI-Nspire Handbook, p. 778.

Theorem 3.4 Magnitude and Conjugates

The magnitude $|z|$ of a complex number is given by

$$|z| = \sqrt{z\bar{z}}$$

The product of a number and its conjugate $z\bar{z}$ is the *norm* of z. So, $|z|$ is the square root of the norm of z.

Proof Let $z = a + bi$. The conjugate is $\bar{z} = a - bi$. Find $\sqrt{z\bar{z}}$.

$$\sqrt{z\bar{z}} = \sqrt{(a + bi)(a - bi)} = \sqrt{a^2 + b^2}$$

This is the same as the expression for magnitude that you verified in Problem 3. So, $|z| = \sqrt{z\bar{z}}$.

Answers

For You to Do

1. $\sqrt{34}$
2. Answers may vary. Sample: $3 - 4i$
3. If $z = a + bi$, then

$$|z| = \sqrt{(a - 0)^2 + (b - 0)^2} = \sqrt{a^2 + b^2}$$

Developing Habits of Mind

Look for relationships. The symbol for magnitude is the same as the symbol for absolute value. There are at least two reasons that this makes sense.

- Find the magnitude of a real number $a + 0i$.

$$|a + 0i| = \sqrt{a^2 + 0^2} = \sqrt{a^2}$$

  This satisfies one definition of absolute value: $|a| = \sqrt{a^2}$. For real numbers, magnitude and absolute value are equal.

- The absolute value of a real number is its distance from (0, 0) on a number line. Magnitude is also distance from (0, 0), but on the complex plane.

By defining $|z|$ as the distance between z and (0, 0), you extend the definition of absolute value from $\mathbb{R}$ to $\mathbb{C}$.

Remember...

Real numbers are still complex numbers. They have imaginary parts equal to 0.

For You to Do

4. Find as many complex numbers as you can with magnitude 5. Are any of them also real numbers?

Example 1

Problem Graph each complex number as a vector and find its magnitude.

a. $(2 + i)^0$

b. $(2 + i)^1$

c. $(2 + i)^2$

d. $(2 + i)^3$

e. $(2 + i)^4$

Solution Evaluate each expression to find the real and imaginary parts of each number.

a. A number raised to the zero power is 1, so $(2 + i)^0 = 1$.

b. A number raised to the first power is itself, so $(2 + i)^1 = 2 + i$.

c. $(2 + i)^2 = 3 + 4i$

d. $(2 + i)^3 = (3 + 4i)(2 + i) = 2 + 11i$

e. $(2 + i)^4 = (2 + 11i)(2 + i) = -7 + 24i$

For help with the calculations, see the TI-Nspire Handbook, p. 778.

For You to Do

4. Answers may vary. Samples: $\pm 5 \pm 0i$, $0 \pm 5i$, $\pm 3 \pm 4i$, $\pm 4 \pm 3i$, and $\pm\sqrt{p} \pm \sqrt{q}i$, where $p + q = 25$; 5 and -5.

Developing Habits of Mind

In CME Project *Algebra 1,* students developed the definition of absolute value specifically as the distance between two points on the number line (defining $|a - b|$ first). Then they defined the absolute value of a single number ($|a|$) as its distance from 0. This choice of development may have been unusual at the time, but it was intentional in order to make the concept extendable here to complex numbers.

Example 1

This example demonstrates part of De Moivre's Theorem, which states that

$$(r(\cos\theta + i\sin\theta))^n = r^n(\cos n\theta + i\sin n\theta)$$

Although students will not see the representation of a complex number using trigonometric functions until CME Project *Precalculus,* they will start working toward De Moivre's Theorem in Lesson 3.13. In effect, the theorem says that when you raise a complex number to the power n, you raise its magnitude to the nth power and you multiply the size of its angle from the x-axis by n.

Here in Example 1, students consider only the relationship of the magnitudes of the complex numbers z and z^n. You may want to use Blackline Master 3.9 to guide students through Example 1.

For You to Do

This is a good place to end the first class if you plan to take two days for this lesson. If you do, assign the magnitude parts of the Check Your Understanding core exercises as homework.

This plot shows all five complex numbers drawn as vectors.

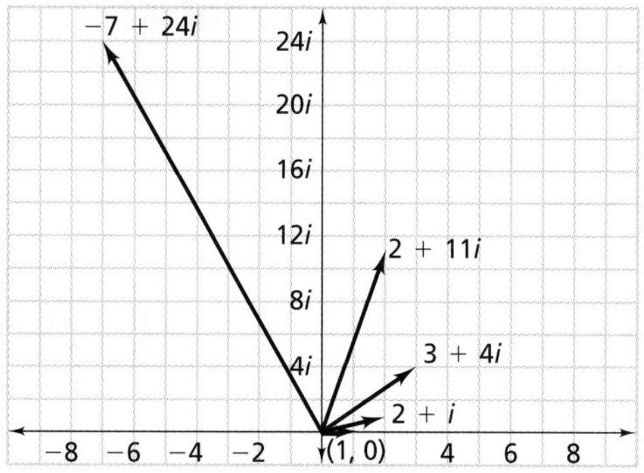

To find the magnitude of each number, use the expression $\sqrt{a^2 + b^2}$ or the Pythagorean Theorem.

a. $|1| = 1$

b. $|2 + i| = \sqrt{2^2 + 1^2} = \sqrt{5}$

c. $|3 + 4i| = \sqrt{3^2 + 4^2} = \sqrt{25} = 5$

d. $|2 + 11i| = \sqrt{2^2 + 11^2} = \sqrt{125} = 5\sqrt{5}$

e. $|-7 + 24i| = \sqrt{(-7)^2 + 24^2} = \sqrt{625} = 25$

For You to Do

5. Find the magnitude of $2 + 3i$ and $(2 + 3i)^2$.

A complex number has magnitude. But, if you think of a complex number as a vector, it also has a specific direction. How should you define direction? You can define direction by using the counterclockwise angle measured from the positive real axis.

A compass measures direction with respect to Earth's magnetic field.

Definition

The direction of the complex number *z* is the angle measured from the positive real axis in a counterclockwise direction.

Generally, you express direction with a measure between 0° and 360°. What does a direction of 450° mean?

Answers

For You to Do

5. $\sqrt{13}$; 13

Example 2

Problem Find the magnitude and direction of each complex number.

a. $-2i$

b. $-1 + i$

c. $1 + 3i$

d. $(1 + 3i)^2 = -8 + 6i$

Solution

a. The magnitude of $-2i$ is 2. Since $-2i$ lies directly along the negative imaginary axis, its direction angle is three fourths of a full circle. The direction is 270°.

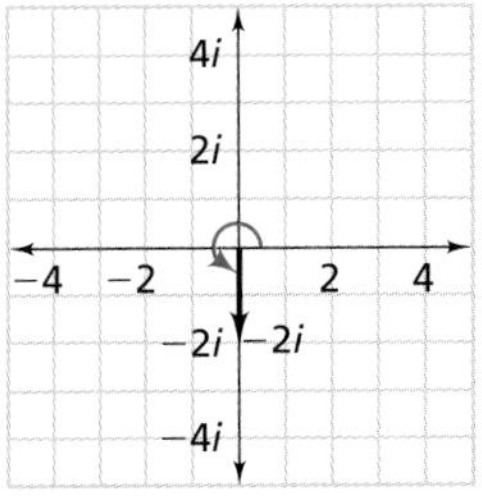

b. $|-1 + i| = \sqrt{2}$ because

$$|-1 + i| = \sqrt{(-1 + i)(-1 - i)} = \sqrt{(-1)^2 + 1^2} = \sqrt{2}.$$

By dropping an altitude from the point $(-1, 1)$, you make an isosceles right triangle. The measures of the angles in this triangle are 45°, 45°, and 90°.

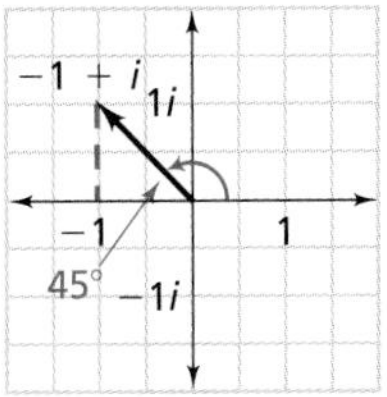

The direction angle is supplementary to the angle in the isosceles right triangle. Therefore, the direction is 135°.

Habits of Mind

Visualize. Graphing a complex number as a vector helps to illustrate its magnitude and direction.

Where is $|-1 + i|$ in this picture?

Example 2

a. If your students do not see why the magnitude is 2, note that each axis has the same unit length (that is, the plane has a square grid). If you count down 2 along the imaginary axis, the length is 2.

b. The magnitude of $-1 + i$ is the length of the vector drawn from the origin to the point $-1 + i$.

c. All of the angles in this chapter are expressed in degrees, so make sure your students' calculators are in degree mode.

d. Part (d) provides reinforcement that the signs of the real and imaginary parts have no relationship to the length. You might want to demonstrate that $-8 + 6i$ has the same length as $8 + 6i$, $8 - 6i$, and $-8 - 6i$. Make sure students notice that the direction of $(1 + 3i)^2$ is twice that of $1 + 3i$. Some students may conjecture that the direction of the square of a complex number is *always* twice that of the original complex number.

After students have had a chance to work through the Example, have them express the relationship between the direction of $(1 + 3i)^2$ and the direction of $1 + 3i$. Challenge students to use that relationship to predict the direction of $(1 + 3i)^3$.

Wrap Up

If time allows, go over Check Your Understanding core exercises.

Assessment Resources

Lesson Quiz 3.9

1. Find the magnitude and direction of each complex number.
   a. $3 + 4i$ b. $3 - 4i$
   c. $-3 + 4i$ d. $-3 - 4i$

2. A complex number z has magnitude 4 and direction 60°.
   a. Graph z as a vector on the complex plane.
   b. Graph the conjugate $\overline{z}$ on the same complex plane.
   c. Find the magnitude and direction of $\overline{z}$.

3. For each complex number z, graph z and $\frac{1}{z}$ on the same complex plane.
   a. $z = 1 - i$ b. $z = 2 - i$
   c. $z = 1 - i\sqrt{3}$ d. $z = 3 - i$

c. The magnitude of $1 + 3i$ is $\sqrt{10}$ because $\sqrt{1^2 + 3^2} = \sqrt{10}$. By dropping an altitude from the point $(1, 3)$, you make a right triangle.

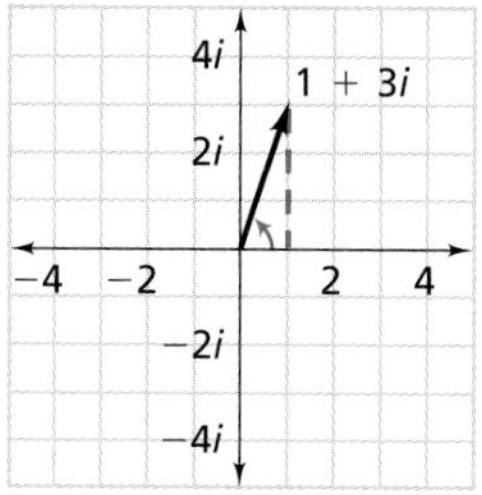

This triangle is not a special right triangle. So use trigonometry to approximate the measure of the marked angle. Since you know the lengths of all the sides, you can use any of the trigonometric ratios. For example, find the angle measure by using tangent.

$$\tan x = \frac{3}{1}$$
$$x = \tan^{-1}\left(\frac{3}{1}\right)$$
$$x \approx 71.565°$$

So, 71.565° is the approximate direction.

d. The magnitude of $-8 + 6i$ is 10 because $\sqrt{(-8)^2 + 6^2} = 10$. Drop an altitude from the point $(-8, 6)$ to make a right triangle.

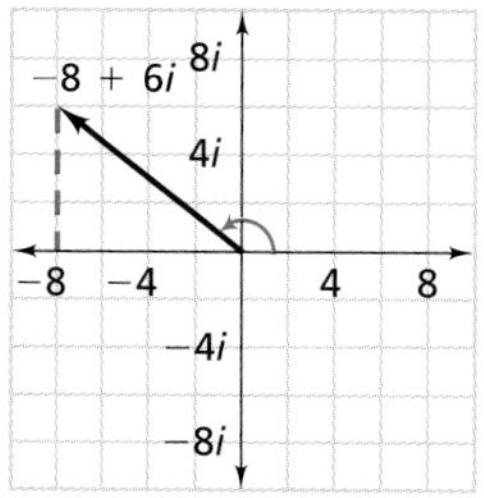

This triangle is not a special right triangle. So use trigonometry to approximate the angle formed by the hypotenuse and the negative real axis.

$$\tan x = \frac{6}{8}$$
$$x = \tan^{-1}\left(\frac{6}{8}\right)$$
$$x \approx 36.870°$$

The direction angle is supplementary to this angle. Therefore, the direction angle is approximately $180° - 36.870° = 143.130°$.

Habits of Mind

Make strategic choices. Always look for exact values first. In some cases, such as for algebraic calculations and theoretical purposes, you may find expressions like $\tan^{-1}\left(\frac{3}{1}\right)$ more useful than approximations. Deciding which form to use is an important skill.

Why should you use tangent? The numbers involved in the tangent calculation come directly from the original complex number. Still, you could use sine, cosine, or tangent.

Facts and Notation

You will typically use the word *direction* when referring to vectors. However, when the vectors stand for complex numbers, it is more conventional to use the older term **argument** and the notation "arg." Below are some examples.

- $\arg -2i = 270°$
- $\arg(-1 + i) = 135°$
- $\arg(1 + 3i) \approx 71.565°$

For help calculating the argument of a complex number, see the TI-Nspire Handbook, p. 778

For You to Do

Find $|z|$ and $\arg z$ for each complex number z.

6. $z = 2 + 2i$
7. $z = (1 + 3i)^3$
8. $z = 3$
9. $z = 1 - i\sqrt{3}$

Exercises *Practicing Habits of Mind*

Check Your Understanding

1. Find the magnitude and direction of each complex number.
   a. $4 + 3i$ b. $4 - 3i$
   c. $-4 + 3i$ d. $-4 - 3i$
2. Find $|w|$ and $\arg w$ for each complex number w.
   a. $w = 2 + 2i$ b. $w = 2 - 2i$
   c. $w = -2 + 2i$ d. $w = -2 - 2i$
3. Without using a calculator, estimate the direction of each complex number to within 10°.
   a. $5 + 4i$ b. $-5 + 4i$
   c. $5 - 4i$ d. $-5 - 4i$

Throughout these exercises, calculate the direction to the nearest degree if you cannot find the exact angle.

Answers

For You to Do

6. $|z| = 2\sqrt{2}$, $\arg z = 45°$
7. $|z| = 10\sqrt{10}$; $\arg z \approx 214.695°$
8. $|z| = 3$; $\arg z = 0°$
9. $|z| = 2$; $\arg z = 300°$

Exercises

1. **a.** 5, 37° **b.** 5, 323°
   c. 5, 143° **d.** 5, 217°
2. **a.** $|w| = 2\sqrt{2}$, $\arg w = 45°$
   b. $|w| = 2\sqrt{2}$, $\arg w = 315°$
   c. $|w| = 2\sqrt{2}$, $\arg w = 135°$
   d. $|w| = 2\sqrt{2}$, $\arg w = 225°$
3. Answers may vary. Samples are given.
   a. 40° **b.** 140°
   c. 320° **d.** 220°

FACTS AND NOTATION While *direction* is the natural word to use in most cases, *argument* is the generally accepted term to use for complex numbers. It is the name of most calculator functions that determine the angle of a complex number. In this course, using either term is fine, but students should be familiar and comfortable with both.

Similarly, *magnitude* and *absolute value* both connote the same property of a number. Both you and your students may find it easier to read "$|a|$" as "the magnitude of a," whether a is a real or complex number.

Exercises

HOMEWORK

- Core: 11, 12, 13, 14, 16
- Optional: 15, 17, 18a, 19, 20
- Extension: 18b

Check Your Understanding

EXERCISE 1 These are the same numbers as those in Lesson 3.7 Exercise 1. See if you can develop students' understanding of the related angles: x, $180° - x$, $180° + x$, and $360° - x$. The more groundwork you do here, the less trouble students will have when doing similar work with sine and cosine later in this course and in precalculus.

EXERCISES 1 AND 2 Some students will note that these numbers are "halfway" through the quadrant and should therefore make a 45° angle with the real axis. It is probably not as easy for your students to recognize $30° - 60° - 90°$ triangles in this way. Try to stress the notion of related angles here. Also point out that the results for this exercise are *exact* angles, not approximate.

EXERCISE 3 You might give a second, similar exercise to see whether students grasp quickly how to find the related angles. You have not explicitly given students a method for computing these angles yet. You are relying on students to see the right triangles formed by the vector and the real axis. These exercises are designed to help lead students to see these angles as related to each other in this way: θ, $180° - \theta$, $180° + \theta$, and $360° - \theta$.

EXERCISE 5 In Investigation 3C, students prove this result in general as a theorem that makes use of the fact that $|z| = \sqrt{z \cdot \bar{z}}$.

EXERCISE 6 You could follow up this exercise by asking students to describe the relationship between z and z^2. They will see this again at the start of Investigation 3C.

EXERCISE 8 You might ask for a generalization after this exercise. Knowing a relationship between the magnitude and direction of a complex number and its reciprocal is not as central a result as the generalizations for the product of two complex numbers and for the square (or other power) of a complex number.

EXERCISES 9 AND 10 Exercise 10 is the generalization of Exercise 9. The concept here is that any complex number (other than 0) can be related to a "unit" complex number. Students will explore this connection in depth when they study the unit circle in trigonometry.

On Your Own

EXERCISE 15 The second part offers a good opportunity to discuss the possibility and use of directions larger than 360°. Here, most students will say "add 90° to the direction" without much thought as to what happens in Quadrant IV. Still, this description works as long as it allows directions larger than 360°. Then it makes sense to do so.

EXERCISE 16 has an unexpected result. If you discuss it with your class, make sure to bring up the relationship between these directions (they are multiples). Use this exercise as a bridge to Investigation 3C.

Students will revisit this topic in *Precalculus* as "DeMoivre's Theorem," which applies to both complex numbers and expressions in trigonometry. One of the goals in this investigation is to ask some of the questions students will answer in trigonometry, both to ease the transition to trigonometry and to establish an important relationship between trigonometry and complex numbers that becomes prominent in later mathematics courses.

4. Describe what happens to the magnitude and direction of a complex number when you double the complex number.

5. For real numbers x and y, absolute value is multiplicative.

$$|xy| = |x| \cdot |y|$$

With a partner, test two examples to see if $|zw| = |z| \cdot |w|$ is true when z and w are complex numbers.

6. For each complex number z, find the magnitude and direction of z and of z^2.

a. $z = 2i$ **b.** $z = -1 + i$

c. $z = 4 + i$ **d.** $z = -4 + i$

7. For each complex number z, plot z and $\frac{1}{z}$ on the same complex plane.

a. $z = 1 + i$ **b.** $z = 2 + i$

c. $z = 1 + i\sqrt{3}$ **d.** $z = -1 - i$

Remember...

The expression $\frac{1}{z}$ is the reciprocal of a complex number z. You worked with reciprocals in Lesson 3.5.

8. For each complex number z in Exercise 7, find the magnitude and direction of z and of $\frac{1}{z}$.

9. Write each complex number as a product of a positive real number and a complex number of magnitude 1.

a. $4 + 3i$ **b.** $5 + 12i$ **c.** $1 + i$

d. $1 - i$ **e.** $2 + 3i$ **f.** $-1 + i\sqrt{3}$

10. Show that you can write any nonzero complex number as the product of a positive real number and a complex number of magnitude 1.

On Your Own

11. Find the magnitude and direction of each complex number.

a. $3 + 2i$ **b.** $3 - 2i$

c. $-3 - 2i$ **d.** $-3 + 2i$

12. Find $|z|$ and $\arg z$ for each complex number z.

a. $z = 1 + i\sqrt{3}$ **b.** $z = 1 - i\sqrt{3}$

c. $-z = 1 + i\sqrt{3}$ **d.** $z = (1 + i\sqrt{3})(1 - i\sqrt{3})$

Go Online PHSchool.com

For additional practice, go to **Web Code:** bfa-0309

Answers

4. The magnitude is doubled, and the direction stays the same.

5. Check students' work (the property holds for complex numbers).

6. a. $|z| = 2$; $\arg z = 90°$
$|z^2| = 4$; $\arg z^2 = 180°$

b. $|z| = \sqrt{2}$; $\arg z = 135°$
$|z^2| = 2$; $\arg z^2 = 270°$

c. $|z| = \sqrt{17}$; $\arg z \approx 14°$
$|z^2| = 17$; $\arg z^2 \approx 28°$

d. $|z| = \sqrt{17}$; $\arg z \approx 166°$
$|z^2| = 17$; $\arg z^2 \approx 332°$

7–10. See back of book.

11. a. $\sqrt{13}$, 33.69°
b. $\sqrt{13}$, 326.31°
c. $\sqrt{13}$, 213.69°
d. $\sqrt{13}$, 146.31°

12. a. 2, 60°
b. 2, 300°
c. 2, 240°
d. 4, 0°

13. Standardized Test Prep To the nearest degree, arg $(-2 + 5i)$ is 112°. Which is the direction of $-2 - 5i$?

A. 202° B. 224° C. 248° D. 292°

14. A complex number z has magnitude 5 and direction 50°.

a. Graph z as a vector on the complex plane.

b. Graph the conjugate $\overline{z}$ on the same complex plane.

c. Find the magnitude and direction of $\overline{z}$.

15. Describe what happens to the magnitude and direction of a complex number when you multiply the number by i.

16. Find the direction of each of these complex numbers from Example 1.

a. $(2 + i)^0$ b. $(2 + i)^1$

c. $(2 + i)^2$ d. $(2 + i)^3$

e. $(2 + i)^4$

Use approximations if necessary.

17. For each pair of complex numbers, calculate $|z|$, $|w|$, and $|zw|$.

a. $z = 2 + i$ and $w = 3 + i$

b. $z = 2 + i$ and $w = 3 + 2i$

c. $z = 5i$ and $w = 3i$

d. $z = 2 + i$ and $w = \frac{2 - i}{5}$

18. a. Based on your results from Exercise 17, make a conjecture about the relationship between $|z|$, $|w|$, and $|zw|$.

b. Take It Further Prove your conjecture.

Maintain Your Skills

19. Find the magnitude of each complex number.

a. $(1 + i)^2$ b. $(2 + i)^2$

c. $(3 + i)^2$ d. $(7 + i)^2$

e. $(2 + 3i)^2$

f. Find a complex number $a + bi$, with nonzero a and b, that has magnitude 29.

20. For each equation, find the magnitude and direction of all the solutions.

a. $x^2 - 1 = 0$ b. $x^3 - 1 = 0$ c. $x^4 - 1 = 0$

The equation $x^4 - 1 = 0$ has four solutions in $\mathbb{C}$.

13. C

14. a–b.

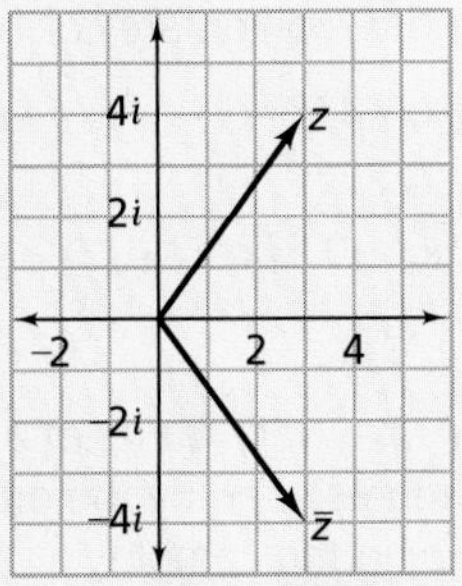

c. 5, 310°

15. The magnitude is not changed, and the direction is increased by 90°.

16. a. 0°
b. 26.565°
c. 53.13°
d. 79.695°
e. 106.26°

17–19. See back of book.

20. a. magnitude 1; direction 0°, 180°
b. magnitude 1; direction 0°, 120°, 240°
c. magnitude 1; direction 0°, 90°, 180°, 270°

EXERCISES 17 AND 18 preview the upcoming lesson on general complex multiplication.

EXERCISE 18 Help students see that although $\sqrt{ab} = \sqrt{a}\sqrt{b}$ is not always true in the complex numbers, it is used here on real numbers where it is always true.

Maintain Your Skills

EXERCISE 19 If time permits, make the connection to Pythagorean triples. The numbers used here are: 3-4-5, 8-6-10, 48-14-50, 5-12-13, 21-20-29. All are Pythagorean triples. In general, this method with $(m + ni)$ leads to the formula for generating triples: $(m^2 - n^2, 2mn, m^2 + n^2)$ is a Pythagorean triple Here, $(m + ni)^2 = (m^2 - n^2) + (2mn)i$, and the magnitude is $m^2 + n^2$...

EXERCISE 20 serves as extra practice, but students will revisit this topic in the next Investigation. These solutions are referred to as "roots of unity" and are always equally spaced.

Additional Resources

PRINT RESOURCES
- Solution Manual
- Practice Workbook
- Assessment Resources
- Teaching Resources

TECHNOLOGY
- Interactive Textbook
- TeacherExpress CD-ROM
- ExamView CD-ROM
- PHSchool.com

Additional Practice

1. Find the magnitude and direction of each complex number.
a. $5 + 4i$ b. $5 - 4i$
c. $-5 + 4i$ d. $-5 - 4i$

2. For each complex number z, find $|z|$ and arg z.
a. $z = 2 + 4i$ b. $z = 2 - 4i$
c. $-z = 2 - 4i$ d. $z = -2 - 4i$

3. For each complex number z in Exercise 2, find $|z^2|$ and arg z^2.

4. A complex number z has magnitude 2 and direction 45°.
a. Graph z as a vector on the complex plane.
b. Graph the conjugate $\overline{z}$ on the same complex plane.
c. Find the magnitude and direction of $\overline{z}$.

5. Describe what happens to the magnitude and direction of a complex number when you multiply the number by $2i$.

6. Find the direction of each complex number.
a. $(3 + i)^0$ b. $(3 + i)^1$
c. $(3 + i)^2$ d. $(3 + i)^3$
e. $(3 + i)^4$

7. For each complex number z, graph z and $\frac{1}{z}$ as vectors on the same complex plane.
a. $z = -1 - i$ b. $z = -2 - i$
c. $z = 2 - i\sqrt{3}$ d. $z = 3 + i$

8. For each pair of complex numbers, calculate $|z|$, $|w|$, and $|zw|$.
a. $z = 3 + i$ and $w = 4 + i$
b. $z = 3 + i$ and $w = 4 + 2i$
c. $z = -4i$ and $w = 5i$
d. $z = 3 + i$ and $w = \frac{3 + i}{4}$

Practice: For Lesson 3.9, assign Exercises 1–8.

Mathematical Reflections

EXERCISES 6–8 At the start of the investigation, you may have assigned these as Questions 1–3 for students to think and write about.

Mathematical Reflections 3B

In this investigation, you graphed complex numbers as points and as vectors on the complex plane. You also calculated magnitude and direction of complex numbers. These exercises will help you summarize what you have learned.

1. Graph and label each pair of numbers on the same complex plane.
   a. $u = 2 - 3i$ and $\overline{u}$
   b. $v = -2$ and $\overline{v}$
   c. $w = 4i$ and $\overline{w}$
   d. $z = -3 + i$ and $\overline{z}$
2. For $z = -1 + i$ and $w = 4 + 2i$, graph and label z, w, $z + w$, $-w$, iw, zw, and z^2 on the same complex plane.
3. Prove that, for any nonzero real number r and nonzero complex number z, the product rz is collinear with 0 and z on the complex plane.
4. Find the magnitude and direction of each complex number.
   a. $1 + 2i$
   b. $(1 + 2i)^2$
   c. $(1 + 2i)^3$
5. A complex number has magnitude 4 and direction $120°$. Write this complex number in the form $a + bi$, where a and b are exact real numbers.
6. How do you represent a complex number graphically?
7. What is the graphical effect of adding two complex numbers?
8. What is the graphical effect of multiplying a complex number by i?

Vocabulary and Notation

In this investigation, you learned these terms and symbols. Make sure you understand what each one means and how to use it.

- **argument, arg *z***
- **complex plane**
- **direction**
- **magnitude, |*z*|**

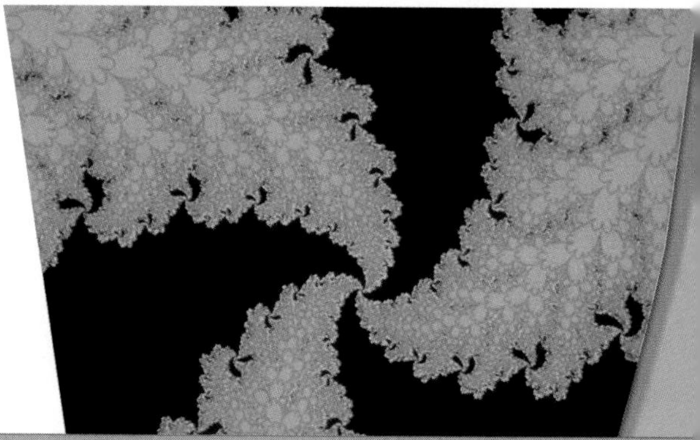

another Julia set fractal

Answers

Mathematical Reflections

1.

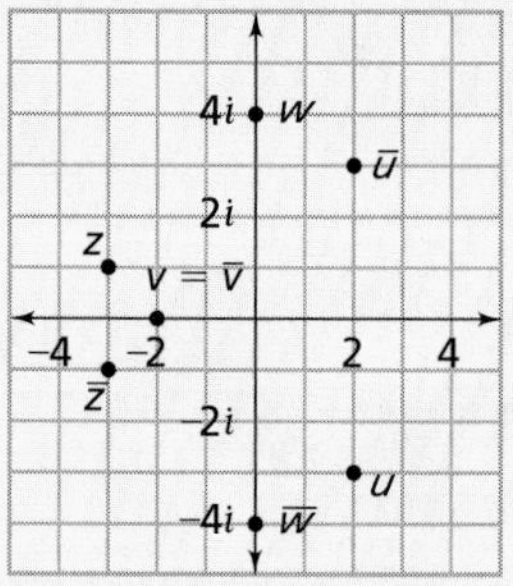

$\overline{u} = 2 + 3i$, $\overline{v} = -2$, $\overline{w} = -4i$, $\overline{z} = -3 - i$

2.

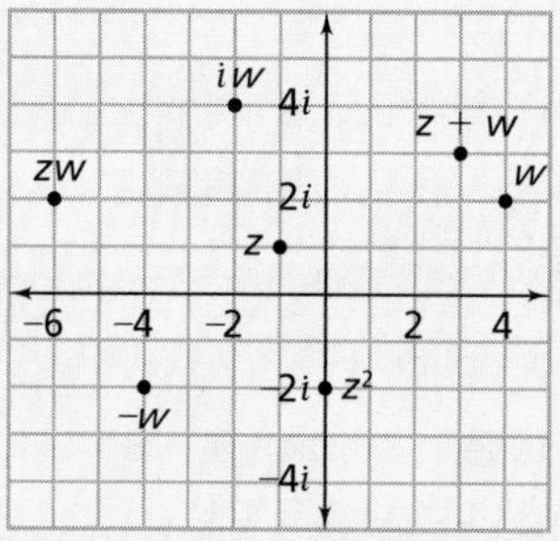

$z + w = 3 + 3i$, $-w = -4 - 2i$, $iw = -2 + 4i$, $zw = -6 + 2i$, $z^2 = -2i$

3. Let $z = a + bi$. Then $rz = ar + bri$. The slope for (0, 0) and z is $\frac{b}{a}$ and the slope for (0, 0) and rz is $\frac{br}{ar} = \frac{b}{a}$. So z, rz, and the origin are collinear.

4. a. $\sqrt{5}$, 63.43°
b. 5, 126.87°
c. $5\sqrt{5}$, 190.30°

5. $-2 + 2\sqrt{3}i$

6. Answers may vary. Sample: $a + bi$ can be represented by the ordered pair (a, b) in the complex plane or as a vector from the origin to (a, b).

7. Answers may vary. Sample: It is the fourth vertex of the parallelogram whose other three vertices are the

Mid-Chapter Test

Go Online PHSchool.com — For a mid-chapter test, go to **Web Code:** bfa-0352

Multiple Choice

1. What is the value of $\sqrt{-5} \cdot \sqrt{-20}$?

A. -5 **B.** -10 **C.** $10\sqrt{-1}$ **D.** 10

2. What is the value of $2(1 + \sqrt{-1}) + 2(-\sqrt{-1}) + (1 + \sqrt{-1})(1 - \sqrt{-1})$?

A. 4 **B.** $6\sqrt{-1}$ **C.** 6 **D.** $4\sqrt{-1}$

3. Which of the following is a complex number, but NOT a real number?

A. 2 **B.** $3i^2$ **C.** $4 - 2i$ **D.** 0

4. What is the magnitude of $2 + 3i$?

A. $\sqrt{5}$ **B.** $\sqrt{13}$ **C.** 4 **D.** $2 - 3i$

5. Which is the approximate argument of $2 + 3i$?

A. $33.7°$ **B.** $56.3°$ **C.** $26.2°$ **D.** $0.011°$

Open Response

6. Use the equation $x^2 + 2x + 5 = 0$.

a. Find the solutions of the equation.

b. Find the sum of the solutions of the equation.

c. Find the product of the solutions of the equation.

d. Find the sum of the squares of the solutions of the equation.

7. a. What are the three solutions to $x^3 + 27 = 0$?

b. Graph the solutions on the complex plane.

8. Simplify each expression. Write your answer in the form $a + bi$.

a. $(3 + 4i) + (3 - 4i)$

b. $(3 + 4i) - (3 - 4i)$

c. $(3 + 4i)(3 - 4i)$

d. $\frac{3 + 4i}{3 - 4i}$

e. $\frac{3 - 4i}{3 + 4i}$

9. Solve each equation. The solutions are complex numbers.

a. $z + (3 - 2i) = 5 - 8i$

b. $x^2 = -25$

c. $2x^2 + 3x = -5$

d. $z \cdot (3 + i) = 4 - i$

10. Use the complex number $z = 1 + i\sqrt{3}$.

a. Find $\bar{z}$.

b. Find $2z$.

c. Find z^2.

d. Graph z, $\bar{z}$, $2z$, and z^2 on the complex plane.

e. Copy and complete this table.

Vector	Magnitude	Direction
z	■	■
$\bar{z}$	■	■
$2z$	■	■
z^2	■	■

11. Describe the set of complex numbers.

Mid-Chapter Test

Assessment Resources

Mid-Chapter Test page 1 of 2

Multiple Choice

1. What is the value of $\sqrt{-2} \cdot \sqrt{200}$?
A. -400
B. -20
C. 20
D. $20\sqrt{-1}$

2. What is the value of $3(2 + \sqrt{-1}) + 3(2 - \sqrt{-1}) + (3 + \sqrt{-1})(3 - \sqrt{-1})$?
A. 20
B. 22
C. $22\sqrt{-1}$
D. $20\sqrt{-1}$

3. Which of the following is a complex number and a real number, but NOT a rational number?
A. $3i^2$
B. 0
C. $\frac{3}{4}$
D. $\sqrt{2}$

4. What is the magnitude of $4 - 3i$?
A. $4 + 3i$
B. $\sqrt{5}$
C. $\sqrt{7}$
D. 5

5. What is the argument of $3i$?
A. $0°$
B. $90°$
C. $180°$
D. $270°$

Also available: Form B

origin and the two given complex numbers.

8. Answers may vary. Sample: The effect is to rotate the point (or vector) by 90° counterclockwise about the origin.

Mid-Chapter Test

1. B

2. A

3. C

4. B

5. B

6. a. $-1 \pm 2i$ **b.** -2

c. 5 **d.** -6

7. a. $-3, \frac{3}{2} \pm \frac{3\sqrt{3}}{2}i$

b.

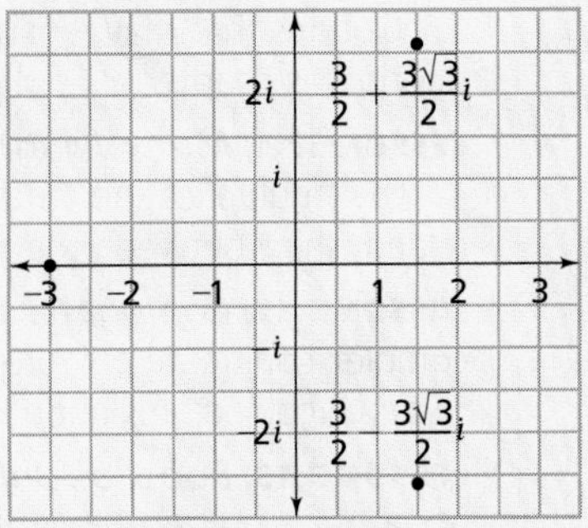

8. a. $6 + 0i$

b. $0 + 8i$

c. $25 + 0i$

d. $-\frac{7}{25} + \frac{24}{25}i$

e. $-\frac{7}{25} - \frac{24}{25}i$

9. a. $2 - 6i$

b. $\pm 5i$

c. $\frac{-3 \pm i\sqrt{31}}{4}$

d. $\frac{11 - 7i}{10}$

10. See back of book.

11. The complex numbers are numbers of the form $a + bi$, where a and b are real numbers and $i = \sqrt{-1}$.

Investigation Overview

This investigation delves more deeply into connections between geometry, algebra, and the complex numbers. In the previous investigation, students found that the magnitude of the product of two complex numbers is equal to the product of their magnitudes. Here they prove that the argument of the product of two complex numbers is equal to the sum of their arguments. They also show that if you input a complex number and its conjugate into a polynomial function with real coefficients, the resulting outputs will be conjugates of each other. A consequence of this result is that if a complex number is a solution to a polynomial equation with real coefficients, its conjugate is also a solution. Although students believed this earlier, here they prove it. Students also begin their study of roots of unity, a study that will continue into precalculus.

This investigation gives students more experience with complex number calculation and graphing, and with proof. The topics covered here are not strictly necessary for the further development of this course. Your course syllabus may require you to emphasize other topics, but this investigation is very important as a preparation for what is coming in *Precalculus.*

You may wish to assign Questions 1–3 for students to think and write about during the investigation.

Learning Goals

- Describe relationships between magnitudes and arguments of factors and products.
- Prove the relationship between the function values of complex conjugates.
- Find and graph the roots of equations of the form $x^n - 1 = 0$ in the complex plane.

Habits and Skills

- Visualize algebraic calculations as geometric transformations.
- Tinker with complex number calculations to find patterns and develop conjectures.
- Reason deductively to prove conjectures about the complex numbers.

Investigation 3C

Complex Numbers, Geometry, and Algebra

In *Complex Numbers, Geometry, and Algebra,* you will connect many of the results you have proved about complex numbers and develop them further. You will also prove some conjectures you made in previous investigations.

By the end of this investigation, you will be able to answer questions like these.

1. How are the magnitude and argument of the product of two complex numbers related to the magnitude and argument of the original numbers?
2. If $-2 + i$ is a root of the polynomial $x^3 + 7x^2 + 17x + 15$, what is another root?
3. How can you graph the solutions to the equation $x^{10} - 1 = 0$ on the complex plane without doing many calculations?

You will learn how to

- describe relationships between magnitudes and arguments of factors and products
- prove the relationship between the function values of complex conjugates
- find and graph the roots of equations of the form $x^n - 1 = 0$ on the complex plane

You will develop these habits and skills:

- Visualize algebraic calculations as geometric transformations.
- Tinker with complex number calculations to find patterns and develop conjectures.
- Reason deductively to prove conjectures about the complex numbers.

An artist used algorithms for approximating the roots of a complex polynomial to render this polynomiograph.

Investigation Road Map

LESSON 3.10, *Getting Started,* provides practice with complex number calculations that may remind students of conjectures that they have developed during this chapter.

LESSON 3.11, *Multiplying Complex Numbers,* continues work with complex number multiplication, and leads students to a fuller understanding of the relationships between the magnitudes and arguments of factors and products.

LESSON 3.12, *Conjugates and Roots,* uncovers that the function values of a complex conjugate pair are also conjugates of each other. Students use this result to prove conjectures about polynomial solutions and their conjugates.

LESSON 3.13, *Roots of Unity,* explores solutions to equations of the form $x^n - 1 = 0$, also called roots of unity, and their location in the complex plane.

3.10 Getting Started

Activating Prior Knowledge
Exploring New Ideas

You can find relationships between the magnitudes and directions of two complex numbers and the magnitude and direction of their product.

For You to Explore

1. For each complex number, find the exact magnitude and the direction to the nearest tenth of a degree.

   a. $3 + i$ b. $2 + i$ c. $(3 + i)(2 + i)$
   d. $4 + 3i$ e. $1 + 2i$ f. $(4 + 3i)(1 + 2i)$

2. Complex number z has magnitude 5 and direction 60°.
   Complex number w has magnitude 2 and direction 150°.

   a. Graph z and w on the complex plane.
   b. Estimate the magnitude and direction of the product zw.
   c. **Take It Further** Determine zw and write it in the form $a + bi$.

3. Graph each complex number on the complex plane. Then find its direction.

   a. $1 + i\sqrt{3}$ b. $-1 + i\sqrt{3}$ c. $-1 - i\sqrt{3}$ d. $1 - i\sqrt{3}$

4. Establish the following identity.

   $$(ac - bd)^2 + (bc + ad)^2 = (a^2 + b^2)(c^2 + d^2)$$

5. You can write a cubic with three roots in either expanded or factored form, where r, s, and t are the roots.

   $$x^3 + ax^2 + bx + c = (x - r)(x - s)(x - t)$$

   a. Expand the right side of the equation.
   b. Write a in terms of r, s, and t.
   c. Write b in terms of r, s, and t.
   d. Write c in terms of r, s, and t.

6. For $f(x) = x^3 - 4x^2 - 2x + 20$, how are the following outputs related?

   a. $f(2 + i)$ and $f(2 - i)$ b. $f(4 + i)$ and $f(4 - i)$
   c. $f(-1 + 3i)$ and $f(-1 - 3i)$
   d. Evaluate $f(3 + i)$ and use it to calculate $f(3 - i)$.

7. **Take It Further** Find two complex numbers with the indicated sum and product. Graph them on the coordinate plane

   a. sum $\frac{-1 + \sqrt{5}}{2}$, product 1 b. sum $\frac{-1 - \sqrt{5}}{2}$, product 1
   c. Expand the following product.

   $$(x - 1)\left(x^2 + \frac{1 + \sqrt{5}}{2}x + 1\right)\left(x^2 + \frac{1 - \sqrt{5}}{2}x + 1\right)$$

What is the magnitude of each number?

Remember...
What does the Factor Theorem say?

For expansion help, see the TI-Nspire Handbook, p. 778.

Answers

For You to Explore

1. a. $\sqrt{10}$, 18.4°
   b. $\sqrt{5}$, 26.6°
   c. $5\sqrt{2}$, 45°
   d. 5, 36.9°
   e. $\sqrt{5}$, 63.4°
   f. $5\sqrt{5}$, 100.3°

2. a.

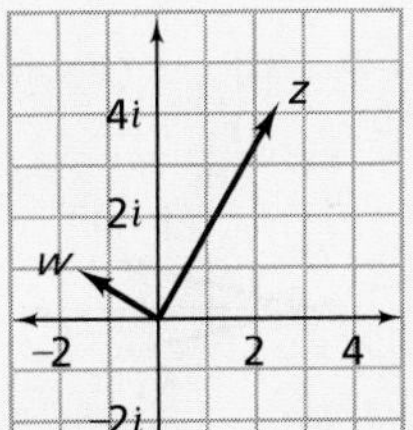

   b. magnitude 10, direction 210°
   c. $-5\sqrt{3} - 5i$

3–7. See back of book.

Lesson Overview

GOAL

- Warm up to the ideas of the investigation.

This lesson reviews the ideas of magnitude and direction from the previous investigation. It also reviews factoring polynomials. Magnitude and direction have roles in the multiplication of complex numbers. Also, students will think about factoring over $\mathbb{C}$ when they explore roots of unity.

As always in a Getting Started lesson, there is no need to formalize these ideas today. Students will meet all of the ideas again throughout the investigation.

FOR YOU TO EXPLORE
- Core: 1, 2a–b, 3, 6
- Optional: 4, 5
- Extension: 2c, 7

HOMEWORK
- Core: 8, 9a–c, 10, 11
- Optional: 12
- Extension: 9d

MATERIALS
- graph paper
- graphing calculators
- Blackline Master MC2

Launch

Students can begin work on the For You to Explore problems. Ask students to keep track of any conjectures they develop.

Explore

Circulate among the students while they work and make a note of any results that you would like to discuss with the class.

For You to Explore

PROBLEM 1 Encourage students to find the direction of $5 + 5i$ without using a calculator, since it forms an angle with the real axis that is part of one of the special right triangles. If time permits, you might ask about the relationship between the directions of $2 + i$ and $1 + 2i$, which are complementary.

PROBLEM 4 shows one way to prove that the magnitude of a product equals the product of the magnitudes.

PROBLEM 5 You may wish to point out that these rules are the analog of the "sum-wish product" rules for quadratics. Help students to note especially that a is the negative of the sum and c is the negative of the product. This is different than the sum-product rule for quadratics. You will use these properties in Lesson 3.12 on complex roots of polynomials.

PROBLEM 6 Use this exercise to convince students that "conjugate input gives conjugate output" for a polynomial with real coefficients.

PROBLEM 7 The five numbers (the four solutions found in the first part plus $x = 1$) are the fifth roots of unity. They form a regular pentagon when you plot them together in the complex plane.

This is a way to find an exact expression for the value of cos 72° because the x-coordinate of the solution to $x^5 - 1$ that lies in Quadrant I is cos 72°. The Technology Appendix demonstrates how to factor expressions such as $x^5 - 1$ over the real numbers, which can allow you to find exact expressions for trigonometric functions of even more angles.

Wrap Up

Have students share their conjectures. Some possible conjectures include:

- The magnitude of a product is the product of the magnitudes (from Problems 1 and 2).
- The direction of a product is the sum of the directions (from Problems 1 and 2).
- The directions of complex numbers $a + bi$ and $-a - bi$ have a difference of 180° (from Problem 3).
- The directions of conjugates sum to 360° (from Problem 3).
- If f is a polynomial function, then $f(\overline{z}) = \overline{f(z)}$ (from Problem 6).

Remember: there is no need to force any conjectures. They will come out throughout the investigation.

Exercises

HOMEWORK
- Core: 8, 9a–c, 10, 11
- Optional: 12
- Extension: 9d

On Your Own

EXERCISE 9 If students do not bring up solution methods that use the multiplication or squaring properties, do not force it on them. You can always revisit this exercise after the next lesson if you choose.

EXERCISE 10 lets students see when the order of operations on complex numbers makes a difference to the result. For example, in part (b) students first take the conjugate of each number and then multiply. In part (c), they multiply first and then find the conjugate of the product. The results are the same.

Maintain Your Skills

EXERCISE 12 Using either points or vectors is fine here, since the exercise does not specify, and each has a visual advantage.

Exercises *Practicing Habits of Mind*

On Your Own

8. Graph each complex number. Then calculate its direction to the nearest degree.

a. $4 + i$ **b.** $4 - i$

c. $-4 + i$ **d.** $-4 - i$

9. Find the direction of each complex number.

a. $\sqrt{3} + i$

b. $\sqrt{2} + i\sqrt{2}$

c. $\left(\sqrt{3} + i\right)\left(\sqrt{2} + i\sqrt{2}\right)$

d. **Take It Further** $\left(\sqrt{3} + i\right)^2\left(\sqrt{2} + i\sqrt{2}\right)^2$

10. Use the complex numbers $z = 2 + 3i$ and $w = 1 + i$. Find each of the following.

a. $\overline{z}$ **b.** $\overline{z} \cdot \overline{w}$ **c.** $\overline{zw}$

d. z^2 **e.** $\overline{z^2}$ **f.** $(\overline{z})^2$

11. If w and z are any two complex numbers, then $\overline{z} \cdot \overline{w} = \overline{zw}$.

a. Express the statement in words.

b. Prove that the statement is true.

Remember...

$\overline{z}$ is the conjugate of the complex number z. The conjugate of $a + bi$ is $a - bi$.

Maintain Your Skills

12. Use the complex number $w = \frac{1 + i\sqrt{3}}{2}$. Graph each of the following on the same complex plane.

a. w **b.** w^2 **c.** w^3 **d.** w^4

e. w^5 **f.** w^6 **g.** w^7 **h.** w^{12}

Answers

8.

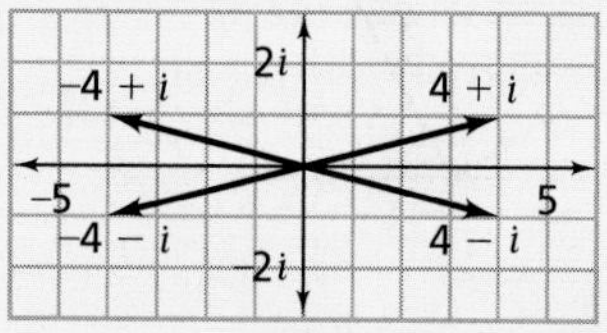

a. 14° **b.** 346°

c. 166° **d.** 194°

9. a. 30° **b.** 45°

c. 75° **d.** 150°

10. a. $2 - 3i$ **b.** $-1 - 5i$

c. $-1 - 5i$ **d.** $-5 + 12i$

e. $-5 - 12i$ **f.** $-5 - 12i$

11. a. The product of two conjugates is equal to the conjugate of the product.

b. Answers may vary. Sample: If $z = a + bi$ and $w = c + di$, then $\overline{z} \cdot \overline{w} = (a - bi)(c - di) = (ac - bd) - (ad + bc)i$. Since $zw = (a + bi)(c + di) = (ac - bd) + (ad + bc)i$, then $\overline{z \cdot w} = (ac - bd) - (ad + bc)i$, so $\overline{z} \cdot \overline{w} = \overline{z \cdot w}$.

3.11 Multiplying Complex Numbers

In the last investigation, you learned that representing a complex number as a vector helps to show three operations.

Remember...

The other way to represent a complex number is as a point.

- Add two numbers by completing the parallelogram.

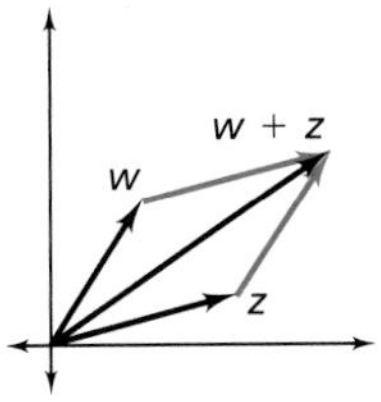

- Multiply a complex number by a real number k by dilating the vector for the complex number by a factor of k.

If $k > 0$, the head of the vector is k times as far from the origin in the same direction. If $k < 0$, the head of the vector is k times as far from the origin in the opposite direction.

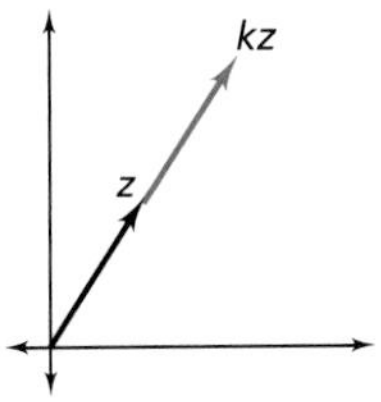

- Multiply a complex number by i by rotating the complex number 90° counterclockwise.

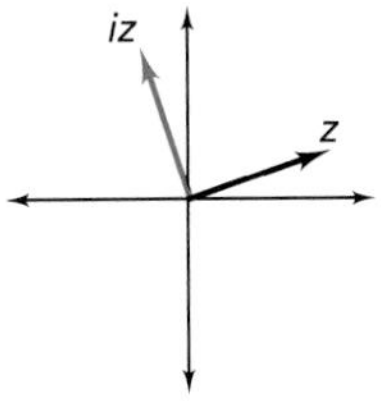

Some of the questions in Lesson 3.10 asked you to look at the relationship between the magnitude and direction of complex numbers and their products. Here is an example, using the product of $1 + 2i$ and $1 + 3i$.

$$(1 + 2i)(1 + 3i) = -5 + 5i$$

Number z	Magnitude $\|z\|$	Direction: arg z (within 0.001°)
$1 + 2i$	$\sqrt{5}$	63.435°
$1 + 3i$	$\sqrt{10}$	71.565°
$-5 + 5i$	$\sqrt{50}$	135.000°

Habits of Mind

Establish a process. To find the direction, first build a right triangle. Then use trigonometry, geometry, or the complex number functions on your calculator.

Lesson Overview

GOAL

- Describe relationships between magnitudes and arguments of factors and products.

This lesson formalizes a geometric interpretation of the product of complex numbers. Students use the pieces they developed in the last investigation, as well as in Lesson 3.10, to build these ideas. In the end, students meet a precursor to De Moivre's Theorem, along with a proof. A key idea here is that complex multiplication provides a way to transform vectors: to multiply a complex number z by another, w, you scale z by the factor $|w|$, and you rotate z by arg w.

CHECK YOUR UNDERSTANDING

- Core: 1, 2, 3, 6, 8
- Optional: 4, 5, 7

MATERIALS

- graph paper
- graphing calculators
- Blackline Masters MC2, 3.11

HOMEWORK

- Core: 9, 10, 11a, 12, 13, 14, 16
- Optional: 15, 17a, 19, 20
- Extension: 11b, 17b, 18, 21

Launch

Start the class by working through the figures and calculations leading to Theorem 3.5.

12.

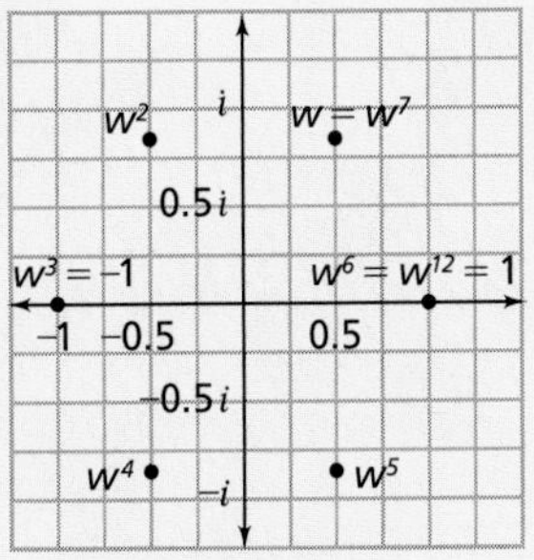

a–h. $w = \dfrac{1 + i\sqrt{3}}{2}$; $w^2 = \dfrac{-1 + i\sqrt{3}}{2}$; $w^3 = -1$; $w^4 = \dfrac{-1 - i\sqrt{3}}{2}$; $w^5 = \dfrac{1 - i\sqrt{3}}{2}$; $w^6 = 1$; $w^7 = \dfrac{1 + i\sqrt{3}}{2}$; $w^{12} = 1$

Explore

THEOREM 3.5 Theorem 3.5 is a precursor to De Moivre's Theorem:

$$(r(\cos \theta + i \sin \theta))^n = r^n(\cos n\theta + i \sin n\theta)$$

Students explore this theorem more completely in CME Project *Precalculus.*

For Discussion

If you start at the positive real axis and rotate 460°, you will pass the positive real axis again with 100° left to go, so a direction of 460° is the same as a direction of 100° and the complex number is in Quadrant II.

Minds in Action

As Tony and Sasha work through this geometric method for multiplying complex numbers, they stumble upon the start of a proof for part of Theorem 3.5 (that the argument of the product is the sum of the arguments).

The magnitude of the product is the product of the magnitudes.

$$\sqrt{5} \cdot \sqrt{10} = \sqrt{50}$$

The direction of the product is the sum of the directions.

$$63.435° + 71.565° = 135°$$

This suggests the following theorem about the magnitude and direction of products.

Habits of Mind

Experiment. If you are not convinced it works, try another example.

Theorem 3.5

Given complex numbers *z* and *w*, the following statements are true.

- $|zw| = |z| \cdot |w|$
- $\arg zw = \arg z + \arg w$.

In other words, magnitudes multiply and directions add when you consider the product of two complex numbers.

Remember...

The terms *argument* and *direction* have the same meaning when you refer to a complex number vector.

For Discussion

1. The argument of the product is the sum of the arguments. If $\arg z = 150°$ and $\arg w = 310°$, $\arg zw = 460°$. What does it mean to have an argument of 460°? In what quadrant is zw?

You can prove Theorem 3.5 using the properties of addition and multiplication you learned in the last lesson.

Minds in Action episode 12

Sasha helps Tony prove Theorem 3.5.

Tony Let's say I want to multiply $(4 + 3i)$ and $(1 + 2i)$. I can find the product $-2 + 11i$. Then I can graph the two numbers and their product. Now what do I do?

Sasha We know how to add, so let's break it up.

$$(4 + 3i)(1 + 2i) = 4(1 + 2i) + 3i(1 + 2i)$$

That's four $(1 + 2i)$'s and $3i$ more $(1 + 2i)$'s. Well, I can make $4(1 + 2i)$ by extending $1 + 2i$ to four times its original size.

Answers

For Discussion

1. Having an argument of 460° is the same as having an argument of $460° - 360° = 100°$; zw would be in Quadrant II.

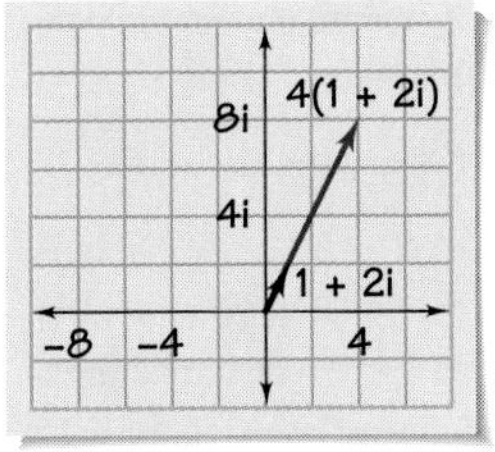

Now I need $3i(1 + 2i)$'s. I multiply by i by rotating 90° counterclockwise. So multiplying by $3i$ is rotating 90° and scaling by 3.

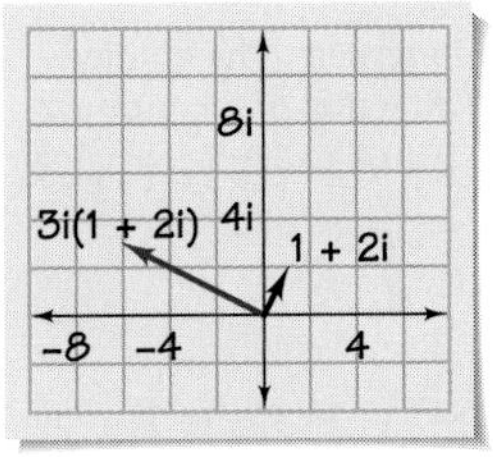

Then I can use the parallelogram law to add. I've got it.

The parallelogram law is Theorem 3.2 from Lesson 3.8.

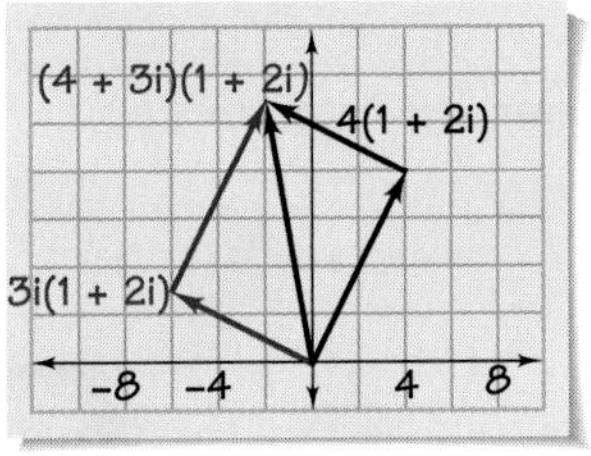

This dark triangle looks a lot like the triangle I drew in Lesson 3.10 to measure $4 + 3i$. Here, I'll show you what I mean.

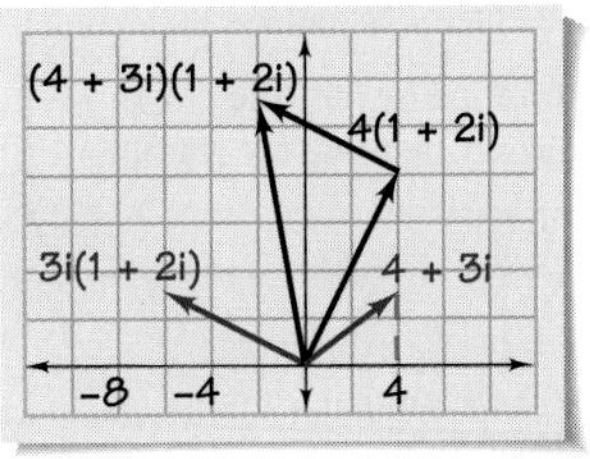

The big triangle for $(4 + 3i)(1 + 2i)$ looks just like the smaller triangle for $4 + 3i$. It's just larger and rotated a little. I'll bet I can prove those triangles are similar. Then I'll have enough evidence to prove Theorem 3.5.

For You to Do

You may want to use Blackline Master 3.11 to illustrate the consequences from the dialog.

For You to Do

2. Explain why the two drawn triangles both have a 90° angle.
3. Explain why each leg in the larger triangle is $\sqrt{5}$ times as long as each leg in the smaller triangle.
4. Explain why the two right triangles are similar.

The triangle similarity in the dialog above has two important consequences.

- The sides in similar triangles are proportional. Each side in the larger triangle is $\sqrt{5}$ times as long as the corresponding side in the smaller triangle. The magnitude of the product is $5\sqrt{5}$. This is also the product of the magnitudes of the original numbers $4 + 3i$ and $1 + 2i$.
- Corresponding angles in similar triangles are congruent. The marked angles on the graph below are congruent. The direction of the product is the sum of the two original angles.

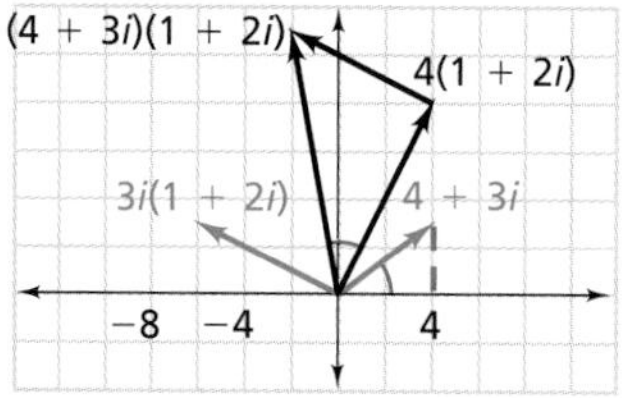

A formal proof of Theorem 3.5 uses the generic complex numbers $(a + bi)$ and $(c + di)$, but the ideas are the same.

Developing Habits of Mind

Visualize. The magnitude of a product is the product of the magnitudes. The argument of a product is the sum of the arguments.

If z and w are complex numbers, you obtain zw from z by a rotation and a scaling. The angle of rotation is arg w and the scale factor is $|w|$.

For example, if you multiply by $(1 + i)$, you are rotating by 45° (the argument of $1 + i$) and scaling by $\sqrt{2}$. If you multiply by i, you are rotating by 90° and scaling by 1.

You can also use algebra to prove that the magnitude of a product is the product of the magnitudes. The product of $a + bi$ and $c + di$ is $(ac - bd) + (bc + ad)i$. Find the magnitude of the product.

$$\sqrt{(ac - bd)^2 + (bc + ad)^2}$$

Then find the product of the magnitudes.

$$\sqrt{a^2 + b^2} \cdot \sqrt{c^2 + d^2}$$

Answers

For You to Do

2. Answers may vary. Sample: For the smaller triangle, one leg is horizontal and the other is vertical, which means there is a 90° angle between them. In the larger triangle, one leg is $4(1 + 2i)$ and the other is parallel to $3i(1 + 2i)$. Multiplying a complex number by i results in a rotation of 90° counterclockwise, so $3i(1 + 2i)$ (and any vector parallel to it) is perpendicular to $4(1 + 2i)$. So, both triangles are right.
3. Answers may vary. Sample: because each leg of the smaller triangle is multiplied by $1 + 2i$ to get the larger triangle, and the magnitude of $1 + 2i$ is $\sqrt{5}$.
4. Answers may vary. Sample: The two legs of one triangle are proportional to the two corresponding legs of the other triangle, and the included angles are congruent, so the triangles are similar.

The numbers under the square roots are not negative. Rewrite the expression above as $\sqrt{(a^2 + b^2)(c^2 + d^2)}$.

The result follows from an identity you established in Lesson 3.10.

Another algebraic method is to use the fact that the magnitude equals $\sqrt{z\overline{z}}$, where $\overline{z}$ is the conjugate.

$$
\begin{aligned}
|zw| &= \sqrt{zw\,\overline{zw}} \\
&= \sqrt{zw\,\overline{z}\,\overline{w}} \\
&= \sqrt{z\overline{z}\,w\overline{w}} \\
&= \sqrt{z\overline{z}}\sqrt{w\overline{w}} = |z||w|
\end{aligned}
$$

Remember...

$\sqrt{r}\sqrt{s} = \sqrt{rs}$ when r and s are nonnegative real numbers.

For Discussion

5. Give reasons for every step in the calculation above. At one point, a square root becomes the product of two square roots. Is that a legal step? Explain.

For You to Do

6. Describe multiplication by each number, in terms of rotation and scaling.

$2 + i \qquad -i \qquad -1$

Exercises Practicing Habits of Mind

Check Your Understanding

1. Complex number z has magnitude 3 and direction 120°.
   a. Find the magnitude and direction of z^2.
   b. Find the magnitude and direction of z^3.
   c. Find an equation with integer coefficients such that z is a solution of the equation.
2. **Write About It** Suppose you know the magnitude and direction of complex number z. Describe how to find the magnitude and direction of z^2, z^3, and the general number z^n.

For Discussion

5. $|zw| = \sqrt{zw\overline{zw}}$ Theorem 3.4

$= \sqrt{zw\overline{z}\overline{w}}$ The conjugate of a product is the product of the conjugates.

$= \sqrt{z\overline{z}w\overline{w}}$ Commutative and Associative Properties

$= \sqrt{z\overline{z}} \cdot \sqrt{w\overline{w}}$ For positive real numbers, the root of a product is the product of the roots.

$= |z| \cdot |w|$ Theorem 3.4;

It is legal to rewrite $\sqrt{z\overline{z}w\overline{w}}$ as $\sqrt{z\overline{z}} \cdot \sqrt{w\overline{w}}$ because the product of a complex number and its conjugate is a real number, so $z\overline{z}$ and $w\overline{w}$ are real numbers.

For You to Do

6. See back of book.

Exercises

1–2. See back of book.

Wrap Up

The For You to Do and For Discussion problems summarize the ideas discussed in the lesson. Make sure students work through to both problems before starting the exercises.

Assessment Resources

Lesson Quiz 3.11

1. Complex number z has magnitude 3 and direction 150°.
   a. Find the magnitude and direction of z^2.
   b. Find the magnitude and direction of z^3.
   c. Find an equation with integer coefficients such that z is a solution of the equation.

2. a. Graph the triangle with vertices $3 + 4i$, $2 - 3i$, and $-2 - 2i$.
   b. Graph the triangle that results if you multiply each vertex by i.
   c. Graph the triangle that results if you add $2 - i$ to each vertex.

3. The graph shows two complex numbers z and w. Estimate the magnitude and direction of zw.

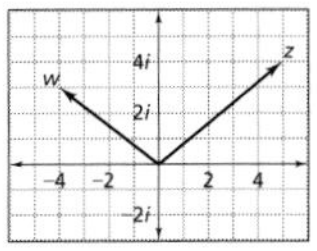

Exercises

HOMEWORK

- Core: 9, 10, 11a, 12, 13, 14, 16
- Optional: 15, 17a, 19, 20
- Extension: 11b, 17b, 18, 21

Check Your Understanding

EXERCISE 1 Encourage students to use the rules developed in this lesson to find the magnitude and direction of the various powers of z. However, to find the equation with integer roots that has z as a solution, $a + bi$ form is useful. If students have trouble finding this form, have them draw a sketch showing z in the complex plane.

EXERCISE 2 Students who were successful with Exercise 1 will also be able to work this exercise. This property comes up again in the lesson on roots of unity.

EXERCISE 3 Many students will answer only (b), not recognizing that there can be more than one correct statement. These properties are important to the understanding of roots of unity, but they are not as central in this lesson. You can relate the situation in this exercise to the fact that $x^2 = 9$ has two solutions, and only one of those is the number you think of as $\sqrt{9}$.

EXERCISE 6 Encourage students to use the multiplication properties rather than writing z and w in $a + bi$ form and computing.

EXERCISE 7 A student might answer here that a direction greater than 360° is correct, and that is acceptable.

EXERCISE 8 If you do not assign all parts of this exercise, assign at least one conjugate pair. For example, you might have students find the powers of i and $-i$. This conjugate pair is the most important because it is a foundation for all the others.

3. A complex number z^3 has magnitude 27 and direction 180°. Which of the following statements could be true about z?

A. z has magnitude 9 and direction 60°.

B. z has magnitude 3 and direction 60°.

C. z has magnitude 3 and direction 180°.

D. z has magnitude 3 and direction 300°.

For Exercises 4 and 5, use the following complex numbers.

- w, with magnitude 5 and direction 40°
- $x = 1 - i$
- $y = -w$
- $z = -x$

4. Sketch w, $\overline{w}$, y, and $\overline{y}$ on the same complex plane. Label each vector with its magnitude and direction.

5. a. Find the exact magnitude and direction of wx.

b. Find the exact magnitude and direction of yz.

c. Use algebra to show that $wx = yz$.

6. The graph below shows two complex numbers z and w. Estimate the magnitude and direction of zw.

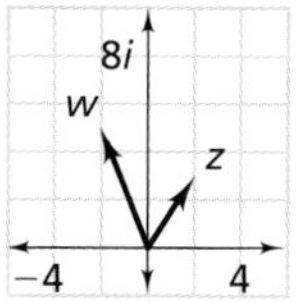

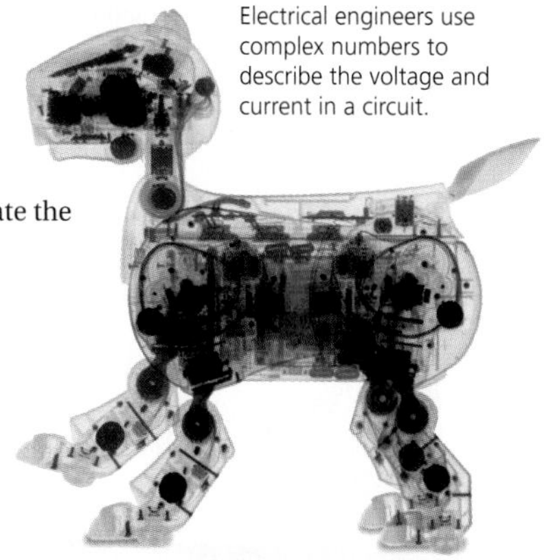

Electrical engineers use complex numbers to describe the voltage and current in a circuit.

7. **Write About It** Suppose you have two complex numbers with directions that add to more than 360°. Describe how to find the magnitude and direction of their product.

8. For each z, graph the first few powers of z ($z^0, z^1, z^2, \ldots$). Describe what happens if you graph higher powers of z. Explain why.

a. $z = i$ **b.** $z = -i$

c. $z = 1 + i$ **d.** $z = 1 - i$

e. $z = 2 + i$ **f.** $z = 2 - i$

Answers

3. B, C, D

4.

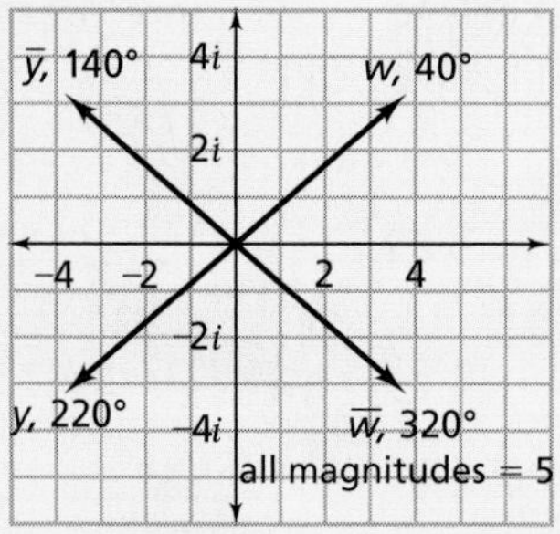

5. a. magnitude $5\sqrt{2}$, direction 355°

b. magnitude $5\sqrt{2}$, direction 355°

c. $yz = (-w)(-x) = wx$

6. Answers may vary. Sample: The magnitude is about $(3.5)(5.5) \approx 19$, and the direction is about $50° + 110° = 160°$

7. The magnitude of the product is the product of the magnitudes. The direction of the product is the sum of the directions, but subtract 360° if necessary to express the angle between 0° and 360°.

8. See back of book.

9. a, c, d, and e must have magnitude 1.

10. See back of book.

11. a. Answers may vary. Sample: $1 + i$, $5 + 5i$

b. Answers may vary. Sample: If $zw = 10i$, then $w = \frac{10i}{z}$. To divide, multiply by the conjugate $w = \frac{(10i)(\overline{z})}{z\overline{z}}$.

12. Answers may vary. Sample: $|zw| \approx 3 \cdot 2.5 = 7.5$; $\arg zw \approx 200° + 50° = 250°$

On Your Own

9. Suppose z and w are complex numbers with magnitude 1. Determine whether each number must also have magnitude 1.

   a. zw b. $z + w$ c. $\overline{w}$
   d. $\frac{1}{z}$ e. z^2 f. $2z$

Go Online PHSchool.com

For additional practice, go to **Web Code:** bfa-0311

10. a. Graph the triangle with vertices $2 + 3i$, $4 + 6i$, and $7 - i$.
    b. Graph the triangle that results if you multiply each vertex by i.
    c. Graph the triangle that results if you multiply each vertex by $1 + i$.
    d. Graph the triangle that results if you add $1 + i$ to each vertex.

11. Two complex numbers have product $10i$. Neither number is a real number.
    a. Find one possible pair of numbers that fits this description.
    b. **Take It Further** Given any nonzero complex number z, explain how to find w such that $zw = 10i$.

12. The graph below shows two complex numbers z and w. Estimate the magnitude and direction of zw.

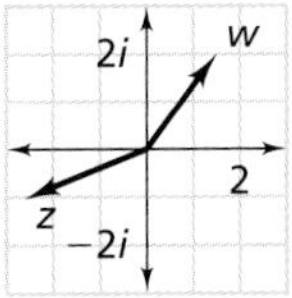

13. a. On the complex plane, graph, as points, four different numbers with direction 210°.
    b. Graph the set of all points with direction 210°.
    c. What complex number has magnitude 10 and direction 210°?

14. **Standardized Test Prep** Which of the following describes multiplication by $4 + 4i$?

    A. Rotate by 90° and scale by $4\sqrt{2}$.
    B. Rotate by 45° and scale by $2\sqrt{2}$.
    C. Rotate by 45° and scale by $4\sqrt{2}$.
    D. Rotate by 90° and scale by 4.

15. Use the complex numbers $z = 3 - 2i$ and $w = 1 + 3i$.
    a. Graph z and w as vectors. Determine the magnitude and direction of each.
    b. Find the magnitude and direction of zw.
    c. Find the magnitude and direction of $\overline{zw}$ and $\frac{1}{zw}$.

On Your Own

EXERCISE 12 Encourage students to use the multiplication properties from the lesson rather than writing z and w in $a + bi$ form and computing.

EXERCISE 16 Not every student will notice the relationship. In the end, this is not a critical relationship, but it is tied to the fact that $\frac{z}{w} = z \cdot \frac{1}{w}$.

13. a. Answers may vary. Sample:

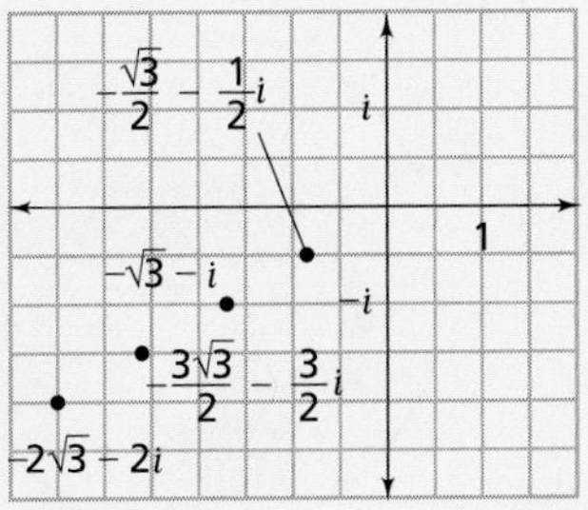

b.

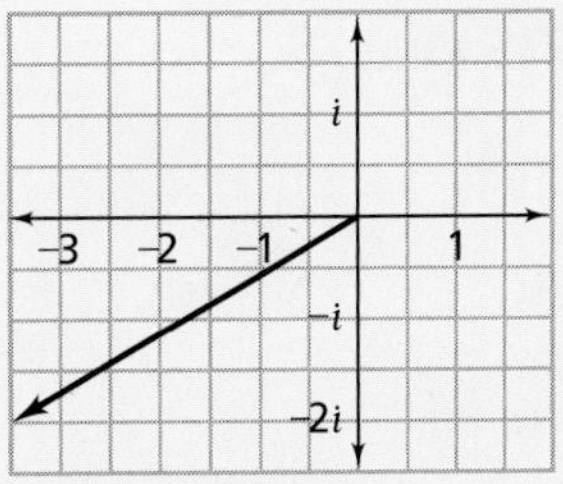

c. $-5\sqrt{3} - 5i$

14. C

15. a.

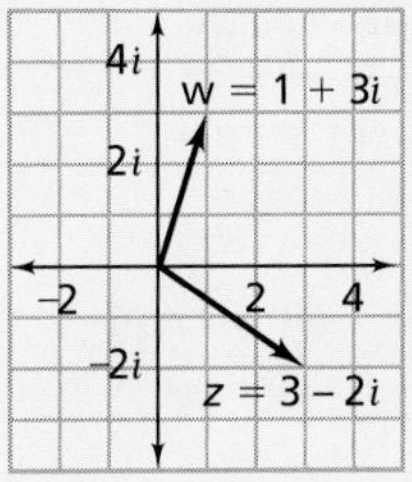

$|z| = \sqrt{13}$, $\arg z \approx 326.3°$; $|w| = \sqrt{10}$, $\arg w \approx 71.6°$

b. $|zw| = \sqrt{130}$, $\arg zw \approx 37.9°$

c. $|\overline{zw}| = \sqrt{130}$, $\arg \overline{zw} \approx 322.1°$;
$\left|\frac{1}{zw}\right| = \frac{\sqrt{130}}{130}$, $\arg \frac{1}{zw} = 322.1°$

EXERCISE 17 With discussion, students may develop an intuition for why $|z| = 13$ has the graph it does. This helps cement students' understanding of magnitude as distance in the complex plane.

EXERCISE 18 ties into the CME Project model of graphs as "point-testers."

Maintain Your Skills

EXERCISE 19 helps students recognize the relationship between the function that outputs the conjugate of a complex number—$c(z) = \overline{z}$, and other functions. Specifically, $f(\overline{z}) = \overline{f(z)}$. As a consequence, if $f(z) = 0$, then $f(\overline{z}) = 0$ too.

EXERCISE 21 The most familiar root of unity is i—a fourth root of unity. The next most familiar one is w—a cube root of unity. Like i, w is a root of a quadratic equation $x^2 + x + 1 = 0$. In addition to the role of w in the theory of regular polygons, students will see in CME Project *Precalculus* how w enters in a central way in the general formula for solving any cubic equation. A special property of any set of roots of unity is that the sum of all the roots of unity is 0. (For instance, the sum of the four fourth roots of unity is $i + (-1) + (-i) + 1 = 0$.)

Additional Resources

PRINT RESOURCES
- Solution Manual
- Practice Workbook
- Assessment Resources
- Teaching Resources

TECHNOLOGY
- Interactive Textbook
- TeacherExpress CD-ROM
- ExamView CD-ROM
- PHSchool.com

Additional Practice

1. Complex number z has magnitude 4 and direction 60°.
   a. Find the magnitude and direction of z^2.
   b. Find the magnitude and direction of z^3.
   c. Find an equation with integer coefficients such that z is a solution of the equation.

2. A complex number z^3 has magnitude 8 and direction 90°. Which of the following statements could be true about z?
   I. z has magnitude 8 and direction 90°.
   II. z has magnitude 4 and direction 90°.
   III. z has magnitude 2 and direction 90°.
   IV. z has magnitude 2 and direction 30°.

3. Suppose you know the magnitude and direction of complex number z^2. Describe in words how to find the magnitude and direction of z, z^3, and the general number z^n.

4. Suppose z and w are complex numbers with magnitude 3. Determine whether each given number must also have magnitude 3.
   a. zw b. $z + w$ c. $\overline{w}$
   d. $\frac{1}{z}$ e. z^2 f. $2z$

5. a. Graph the triangle with vertices $4 + 3i$, $3 - 2i$, and $-1 + 2i$.
   b. Graph the triangle that results if you multiply each vertex by $-i$.
   c. Graph the triangle that results if you multiply each vertex by $2 + i$.
   d. Graph the triangle that results if you add $2 + i$ to each vertex.

6. The graph shows two complex numbers z and w.

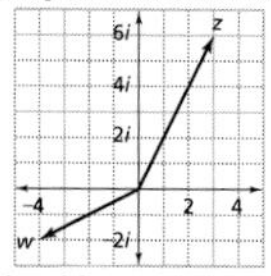

Estimate the magnitude and direction of zw.

Practice: For Lesson 3.11, assign Exercises 1–6.

16. You learned how to find the magnitude and direction of the product of two complex numbers, but how do you find the quotient? Use the complex numbers $z = 4 + 2i$ and $w = 3 + i$.
    a. Write $\frac{z}{w}$ in the form $a + bi$, where a and b are in $\mathbb{R}$.
    b. Find the magnitude and direction of $\frac{z}{w}$.
    c. Describe the relationship between the magnitude and direction of z, w, and $\frac{z}{w}$.

17. a. Find five complex numbers with magnitude 13.
    b. **Take It Further** Graph the set of all complex numbers z such that $|z| = 13$.

18. **Take It Further** For each equation or inequality, graph the set of all complex numbers that satisfy the equation or inequality.
    a. $|z| = 3$ b. $|z| = 1$ c. $|z| < 1$ d. $|z| > 1$
    e. $|z| = \left|\frac{1}{z}\right|$ f. $z^2 = z$ g. $\overline{z} = z$ h. $|z^2| = |z|$

Maintain Your Skills

19. For each polynomial $p(x)$, calculate $p(2 + i)$ and $p(2 - i)$.
    a. $p(x) = x^2$ b. $p(x) = x^2 + 5x + 7$
    c. $p(x) = x^3$ d. $p(x) = x^3 + x^2$
    e. $p(x) = x^3 + x^2 - 15x + 25$ f. $p(x) = x^3 - 3x^2 + x + 5$

Is $x^2 - 4x + 5$ a factor of any these polynomials?

20. Write each sum in the form $a + bi$, where a and b are in $\mathbb{R}$.
    a. $1 + i + i^2$ b. $1 + i + i^2 + i^3$
    c. $1 + i + i^2 + i^3 + i^4$ d. $1 + i + i^2 + i^3 + i^4 + i^5$
    e. $1 + i + i^2 + i^3 + i^4 + i^5 + i^6$
    f. $1 + i + i^2 + i^3 + i^4 + i^5 + i^6 + i^7 + \cdots + i^{67}$

21. **Take It Further** Suppose that $w = -\frac{1}{2} + \frac{\sqrt{3}}{2}i$. Write each sum in the form $a + bi$, where a and b are in $\mathbb{R}$.
    a. $1 + w + w^2$
    b. $1 + w + w^2 + w^3$
    c. $1 + w + w^2 + w^3 + w^4$
    d. $1 + w + w^2 + w^3 + w^4 + w^5$
    e. $1 + w + w^2 + w^3 + w^4 + w^5 + w^6$
    f. $1 + w + w^2 + w^3 + w^4 + w^5 + w^6 + w^7 + \cdots + w^{67}$

Answers

16. a. $\frac{7}{5} + \frac{1}{5}i$

b. $\left|\frac{z}{w}\right| = \sqrt{2}$, $\arg \frac{z}{w} \approx 8.13°$

c. $\left|\frac{z}{w}\right| = \frac{|z|}{|w|}$;
$\arg \frac{z}{w} = \arg z - \arg w$

17. a. Answers may vary. Sample: $13 + 0i$, $5 + 12i$, $5 - 12i$, $-5 + 12i$, $-5 - 12i$

b.

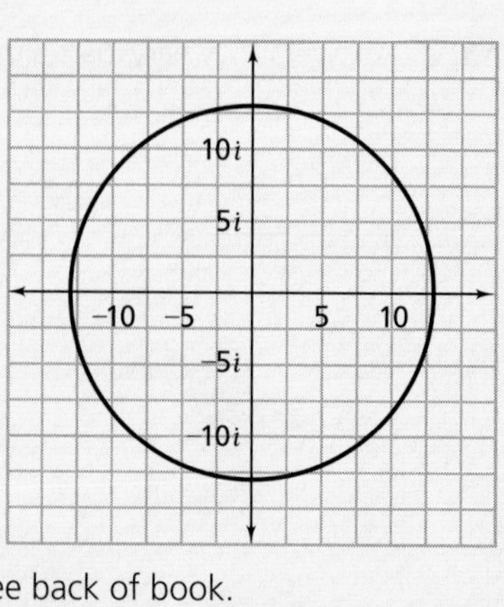

18. See back of book.

3.12 Conjugates and Roots

One focus of this chapter is the properties of the conjugate of a complex number. This lesson explores an important property of conjugates that you can apply to find the roots of polynomials. In Exercise 18 of Lesson 3.5, you showed that if z is a root of a quadratic polynomial with real coefficients, so is $\overline{z}$. This result holds for higher-degree polynomials as well.

Theorem 3.6 lists the main algebraic properties of conjugation.

One root of $x^2 - 4x + 5$ is $2 + i$. The other root is $2 - i = \overline{2 + i}$.

Theorem 3.6

Suppose that z and w are complex numbers. Then the following statements are true.

- $\overline{z} + \overline{w} = \overline{z + w}$

  When you add conjugates, the result is the conjugate of the sum of the original numbers.
- $\overline{z} \cdot \overline{w} = \overline{zw}$

  When you multiply conjugates, the result is the conjugate of the product of the original numbers.
- $(\overline{z})^2 = \overline{z^2}$

  When you square a conjugate, the result is the conjugate of the square of the original number.
- **If z is a real number, then $\overline{z} = z$.**

Remember...

The sum of the conjugates is the conjugate of the sum. And the product of the conjugates is the conjugate of the product.

For Discussion

1. Why does $(\overline{z})^2 = \overline{z^2}$ follow from $\overline{z} \cdot \overline{w} = \overline{zw}$?
2. Explain why $(\overline{z})^3 = \overline{z^3}$.

In the exercises, you will explain why $(\overline{z})^k = \overline{z^k}$ for any positive integer k. This fact leads to the following theorem about conjugates.

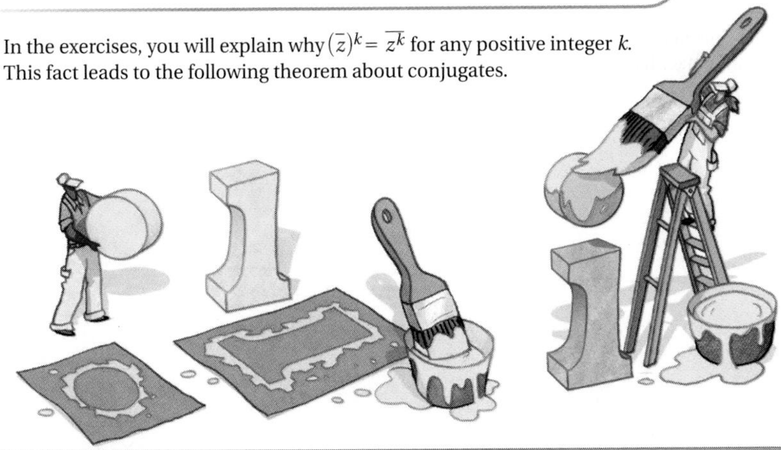

19. a. $3 + 4i$, $3 - 4i$
b. $20 + 9i$, $20 - 9i$
c. $2 + 11i$, $2 - 11i$
d. $5 + 15i$, $5 - 15i$
e. 0, 0
f. 0, 0

20. a. $0 + i$ **b.** $0 + 0i$
c. $1 + 0i$ **d.** $1 + i$
e. $0 + i$ **f.** $0 + 0i$

21. a. 0 **b.** 1
c. $\frac{1}{2} + \frac{\sqrt{3}}{2}i$ **d.** 0
e. 1 **f.** $\frac{1}{2} + \frac{\sqrt{3}}{2}i$

For Discussion

1. If $w = z$, then $\overline{z} \cdot \overline{w} = \overline{z \cdot w}$ becomes $\overline{z} \cdot \overline{z} = \overline{z \cdot z}$ or $(\overline{z})^2 = \overline{z^2}$.
2. $(\overline{z})^3 = (\overline{z})^2 \cdot \overline{z} = \overline{z^2} \cdot \overline{z} = \overline{z^2 \cdot z} = \overline{z^3}$

Lesson Overview

GOAL

- Prove the relationship between the function values of complex conjugates.

In this lesson, students explore complex roots of polynomials. When they learned the Factor Theorem, they discovered that the number of real roots is less than or equal to the degree of the polynomial. When considering complex roots, the number of roots is equal to the degree of the polynomial. This lesson formalizes the fact that these complex roots always come in pairs (conjugate pairs, for that matter).

CHECK YOUR UNDERSTANDING
- Core: 1, 2, 3, 5
- Optional: 4
- Extension: 6

MATERIALS
- graph paper
- graphing calculators

HOMEWORK
- Core: 7, 8, 9, 10, 11, 12
- Optional: 13, 14a–c, 15, 16
- Extension: 14d

Launch

Review Problem 5 from Lesson 3.10. You might also want to review Corollary 2.3.1 from Lesson 2.10, which states:

A polynomial of degree n can have at most n distinct real zeros.

Throughout this lesson, you can extend this corollary to make a statement about how many complex zeros a polynomial of degree n can have:

A polynomial (of a single variable with complex coefficients) of degree n has exactly n complex zeros (including multiplicities).

"Including multiplicities" means that if, for example, a polynomial has a factor of $(x - 3)^2$, then the 3 counts twice as a zero of that polynomial.

Explore

For Discussion

PROBLEM 1 Part 3 of Theorem 3.6 is just a specific case of part 2. Substitute z for w in the statement in part 2 and you get the statement in part 3.

PROBLEM 2 $(\overline{z})^3 = (\overline{z})^2(\overline{z}) = (\overline{z^2})(\overline{z})$. Then, using part 2 again, this is equal to $\overline{z^3}$.

Theorem 3.7 *Polynomials and Conjugates*

For any polynomial f with real coefficients and any complex number z, $\overline{f(z)} = f(\overline{z})$.

Proof Consider the case in which f is a cubic polynomial.

$$\begin{aligned} f(x) &= ax^3 + bx^2 + cx + d \\ \overline{f(z)} &= \overline{az^3 + bz^2 + cz + d} \\ &= \overline{az^3} + \overline{bz^2} + \overline{cz} + \overline{d} \\ &= \overline{a} \cdot \overline{z^3} + \overline{b} \cdot \overline{z^2} + \overline{c} \cdot \overline{z} + \overline{d} \\ &= a\overline{z^3} + b\overline{z^2} + c\overline{z} + d \\ &= a(\overline{z})^3 + b(\overline{z})^2 + c\overline{z} + d \\ &= f(\overline{z}) \end{aligned}$$

So $\overline{f(z)} = f(\overline{z})$. The proof of the general case involves the same ideas.

For Discussion

3. Theorem 3.7 states that the polynomial has real coefficients. Which step of the proof uses this requirement?

Corollary 3.7.1 *Conjugate Pairs*

If f is a polynomial with real coefficients, and $f(z) = 0$, then $f(\overline{z}) = 0$.

For Discussion

4. Prove Corollary 3.7.1 using Theorem 3.7.

Corollary 3.7.1 says that complex roots come in conjugate pairs. If $2 + i$ is a root of a polynomial with real coefficients, then $2 - i$ must be another root.

Answers

For Discussion

3. The third step, where $\overline{a} \cdot \overline{z^3} + \overline{b} \cdot \overline{z^2} + \overline{c} \cdot \overline{z} + \overline{d}$ is rewritten as $a\overline{z^3} + b\overline{z^2} + c\overline{z} + d$; a, b, c, and d must be real numbers because only real numbers are equal to their conjugates.

For Discussion

4. Answers may vary. Sample: If $f(z) = 0$, then $\overline{f(z)} = 0$. Using Theorem 3.7, $\overline{f(z)} = f(\overline{z})$. So $f(\overline{z}) = 0$.

Example 1

Problem Use the polynomial $f(x) = x^3 - 2x^2 - 14x + 40$.

a. Show that $z = 3 + i$ is a root of f. **b.** Find the other two roots.

Solution

a. Let $x = 3 + i$ in $f(x)$.

$$\begin{aligned} f(3+i) &= (3+i)^3 - 2(3+i)^2 - 14(3+i) + 40 \\ &= (18+26i) - 2(8+6i) - 14(3+i) + 40 \\ &= (18+26i) + (-16-12i) + (-42-14i) + 40 \\ &= (18-16-42+40) + (26-12-14)i \\ &= 0 \end{aligned}$$

Since $f(3 + i) = 0$, then $3 + i$ is a root of f.

b. Since f has real coefficients, the conjugate is also a root. So, $3 - i$ is a root.

There are a few ways to find the third root. One is to use the sum property. The sum of the three roots is 2. If the third root is r, then $(3 + i) + (3 - i) + r = 2$.

Combine like terms and solve to get $r = -4$. So, -4 is the third root.

You can confirm this by showing that $f(3 - i) = 0$.

For You to Do

5. How do you solve the equation $x^3 - 5x^2 + 11x - 15 = 0$ if you do not know any of the roots of the polynomial $x^3 - 5x^3 + 11x - 15$?

For this polynomial, the sum of the three roots is 5 and the product is 15.

Example 2

Problem Find a polynomial with real coefficients and $1 - 2i$ and -4 as roots.

Solution Since $1 - 2i$ is a root, $1 + 2i$ must also be a root.

$$f(x) = (x - (1 - 2i))(x - (1 + 2i))(x + 4)$$

Multiply the first two terms. The sum of $1 - 2i$ and $1 + 2i$ is 2, and the product is 5.

$$(x - (1 - 2i))(x - (1 + 2i)) = x^2 - 2x + 5$$

To find $f(x)$, expand the entire expression.

$$\begin{aligned} f(x) &= (x^2 - 2x + 5)(x + 4) \\ &= x^3 + 2x^2 - 3x + 20 \end{aligned}$$

Note that this is not the only possible polynomial with these roots, but it is the polynomial with the least possible degree.

For You to Do

5. Answers may vary. Check students' work.

Example 2

For advanced classes, you may want to ask students to find a polynomial with complex coefficients that has the given numbers as roots. Then ask why Corollary 3.7.1 does not apply to polynomials with complex coefficients.

Wrap Up

The key idea from this lesson is that, for polynomials with real coefficients, any complex roots come in pairs, with the conjugate of a complex root also being a root. This property stems from the "distributive" nature of conjugation—the conjugate of a sum is the sum of the conjugates, and the conjugate of a product is the product of the conjugates.

You can wrap up today's lesson by discussing how the rules found for complex polynomials extend the rules with which students are already familiar:

- The extension of Corollary 2.4 (see Launch notes).
- The extension of the "sums and products" theorem from CME Project *Algebra 1*, which states that the coefficient of the x-term is the sum of the roots, and the coefficient of the constant term is the product. Now you see that for a polynomial of degree n, the coefficient of the term of degree $n - 1$ is the sum of the roots, and the coefficient of the constant term is the product of the roots. (There is also a predictable pattern for determining each of the other coefficients as a combination of sums and products of the roots, taken some number at a time.)

Assessment Resources

Lesson Quiz 3.12

1. Use the complex numbers $z = 6 + 3i$ and $w = 1 - 2i$.
a. Find the magnitude and direction of z and w.
b. Find the magnitude and direction of zw without finding zw.
c. Find the magnitude and direction of z^2 and w^2.

2. a. Show that $2 + i$ is a root of $x^3 - 7x^2 + 17x - 15 = 0$.
b. Find the other two roots.
c. Graph the three roots as points on the complex plane.

3. Suppose $f(x)$ is a polynomial with real coefficients and z is a complex number. Find $f(\overline{z})$ for each value of $f(z)$.
a. $f(z) = 0$
b. $f(z) = -4i$
c. $f(z) = 2 + i$
d. $f(z) = 4 - 3i$

Exercises

HOMEWORK

- Core: 7, 8, 9, 10, 11, 12
- Optional: 13, 14a–c, 15, 16
- Extension: 14d

Check Your Understanding

EXERCISE 4 Other methods for finding the third root include the product property, polynomial long division, and graphing $g(x)$ on a calculator.

EXERCISE 6 If you assign this exercise, you may wish to review the solution in class as students may not have found a complete proof on their own. Students will appreciate this proof even if they did not discover it.

On Your Own

EXERCISE 7 Check to ensure students are comfortable with this exercise. It is a checkpoint for the previous lesson.

EXERCISES 8 AND 9 Some students may notice the relationship to the Exercise 9 roots in Exercise 8. This occurs since $p(x)$ is a translation 3 units to the right, so all its roots will translate the same way.

Exercises *Practicing Habits of Mind*

Check Your Understanding

1. At the right is the graph of $f(x) = x^3 + 6x + 20$.
   a. Use the graph to find a root of $f(x)$.
   b. Find the other two roots.

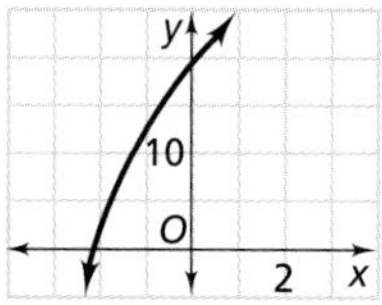

2. Find a polynomial equation with real coefficients that has $4 - i$ as one of its solutions.
3. Find a polynomial equation with real coefficients that has $4 - i$ and 7 as solutions.
4. a. Show that $-1 + 2i$ is a root of $g(x) = x^3 - 4x^2 - 7x - 30$.
   b. Find the other two roots.
5. a. Show that $3 + i$ is a solution to the equation $x^2 - (8 + 6i) = 0$.
   b. **What's Wrong Here?** Gina says that because $3 + i$ is a solution, then $3 - i$ must also be a solution. Is Gina correct? Explain.
6. **Take It Further** Given p is a polynomial with real coefficients, prove the following statement.

   The product of all the roots of p is positive if and only if the product of all the real roots of p is positive.

On Your Own

7. Use the complex numbers $z = 5 + i$ and $w = 2 + 3i$.
   a. Find the magnitude and direction of z and w.
   b. Find the magnitude and direction of zw without finding zw.
   c. Find the magnitude and direction of z^2 and w^2.

Give the exact magnitude and approximate the direction to the nearest degree.

8. a. Show that $4 - i$ is a root of $x^3 - 5x^2 - 7x + 51 = 0$.
   b. Find the other two roots.
   c. Graph the three roots as points on the complex plane.

To find complex roots, see the TI-Nspire Handbook, p. 778.

9. Use the function $p(x) = (x - 3)^3 - 5(x - 3)^2 - 7(x - 3) + 51$.
   a. Show that $7 - i$ is a root of $p(x)$.
   b. Find the other two roots.
   c. Plot the three roots as points on the complex plane.

Answers

Exercises

1. a. $x = -2$

b. $x = 1 \pm 3i$

2. $x^2 - 8x + 17 = 0$

3. $x^3 - 15x^2 + 73x - 119 = 0$

4. a. $g(-1 + 2i) = (-1 + 2i)^3 - 4(-1 + 2i)^2 - 7(-1 + 2i) - 30$
$= (11 - 2i) - (-12 - 16i) - (-7 + 14i) - 30$
$= 0$

So $(-1 + 2i)$ is a root of $g(x)$.

b. $-1 - 2i, 6$

5. a. $f(3 + i) = (3 + i)^2 - (8 + 6i) = (8 + 6i) - (8 + 6i) = 0$,, so $3 + i$ is a solution.

b. No; the equation does not have real coefficients, which is a requirement for the conjugate to be a root. When you test $x = 3 - i$, it does not make the equation true.

6. All the complex roots come in pairs, $a + bi$ and $a - bi$, and the product of each pair of complex roots is $a^2 + b^2$, which is positive. Since the product of all the roots is the product of the complex roots and the real roots, then that product is positive if and only if the product of the real roots is positive.

7. a. $|z| = \sqrt{26}$, $\arg z \approx 11°$; $|w| = \sqrt{13}$, $\arg w \approx 56°$

b. $|zw| = |z| \cdot |w| = \sqrt{26} \cdot \sqrt{13} = \sqrt{338} = 13\sqrt{2}$;
$\arg zw = \arg z + \arg w \approx 11° + 56° = 67°$

c. $|z^2| = 26$, $\arg z^2 \approx 22°$; $|w^2| = 13$, $\arg w^2 \approx 112°$

EXERCISE 10 should be a review, but if students are not getting the correct conjugate, ask them to write numbers in $a + bi$ form.

10. Suppose $f(x)$ is a polynomial with real coefficients and z is a complex number. Find $f(\overline{z})$ for each value of $f(z)$.

a. $f(z) = 0$ **b.** $f(z) = 7$

c. $f(z) = 1 + 3i$ **d.** $f(z) = -5i$

11. Find a polynomial function with real coefficients that has $4 - i$ and -5 as roots.

Go Online PHSchool.com

For additional practice, go to **Web Code:** bfa-0312

Historical Perspective

Complex numbers first emerged in mathematics as algebraic objects, useful in solving cubic equations. Once mathematicians got used to them as numbers, they realized that they could solve every quadratic equation with real coefficients in the complex numbers.

Not only does every quadratic equation with real coefficients have all its roots in $\mathbb{C}$, every polynomial of any degree n with real coefficients has exactly n roots in $\mathbb{C}$. This fact is the Fundamental Theorem of Algebra. The first rigorous proof of the theorem was given by Gauss in his doctoral thesis in 1799.

This important development in mathematics history is still relevant today. Of course, if you need complex numbers to solve polynomial equations with real coefficients, you probably think you need some other kind of number to solve polynomial equations with complex coefficients. Amazingly, this is not the case. Even if you allow the coefficients of a polynomial to be complex numbers, you still have exactly n roots for a polynomial of degree n, and you can find all those roots in the complex number system.

This number system, in which any polynomial with coefficients from the system has all its roots in the system, is considered algebraically closed. So, the Fundamental Theorem of Algebra states that $\mathbb{C}$ is algebraically closed.

The Fundamental Theorem of Algebra is an existence theorem. It states that an nth-degree polynomial has all its roots in $\mathbb{C}$, but it does not tell you how to find them. In fact, for polynomials of degree five or more, there is no analog to the quadratic formula that allows you to solve all polynomials of a given degree.

The packaging is like the Fundamental Theorem of Algebra. It tells you how many cards you get, but not what they are.

10. a. 0

b. 7

c. $1 - 3i$

d. $5i$

11. Answers may vary. Sample: $x^3 - 3x^2 - 23x + 85 = 0$

8. a. $(4 - i)^3 - 5(4 - i)^2 - 7(4 - i) + 51$

$= (52 - 47i) - 5(15 - 8i) - 7(4 - i) + 51$

$= 52 - 47i - 75 + 40i - 28 + 7i + 51$

$= 0$

So $(4 - i)$ is a root.

b. $4 + i, -3$

c.

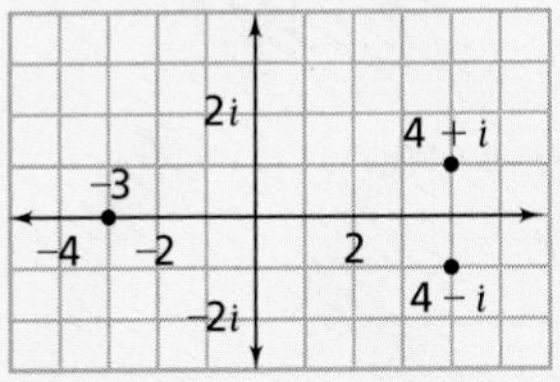

9. a. $p(7 - i)$

$= (7 - i - 3)^3 - 5(7 - i - 3)^2 - 7(7 - i - 3) + 51$

$= (4 - i)^3 - 5(4 - i)^2 - 7(4 - i) + 51$

$= 0$ (from Exercise 8)

So $(7 - i)$ is a root of $p(x)$.

b. $7 + i, 0$

c.

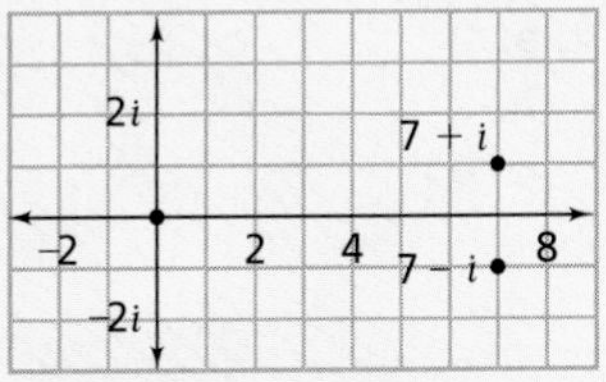

EXERCISE 13 You can use this exercise as a followup to Example 2.

EXERCISE 14 Students should use a calculator for the questions involving i, since it can be difficult to calculate these by hand. Alternately, students who calculate the magnitude and direction for w and w^2 may find the answer without any difficult computation.

This exercise is a transition into the next lesson on roots of unity. The graph shows the sixth roots of unity.

Maintain Your Skills

EXERCISE 15 shows that all these numbers have the same result for z^4 (specifically, -4). That means the equation $z^4 = -4$ has four solutions.

EXERCISE 16 Some students may notice that one other answer is possible, direction 288°. If you assign this exercise, you may wish to revisit it in the next lesson when the fifth roots of unity are plotted.

Additional Resources

PRINT RESOURCES
- Solution Manual
- Practice Workbook
- Assessment Resources
- Teaching Resources

TECHNOLOGY
- Interactive Textbook
- TeacherExpress CD-ROM
- ExamView CD-ROM
- PHSchool.com

Additional Practice

1. Consider the complex numbers $z = 3 + i$ and $w = 4 + 2i$.
   a. Find the magnitude and direction of z and w.
   b. Find the magnitude and direction of zw without finding zw.
   c. Find the magnitude and direction of z^2 and w^2.

2. a. Show that $-3 + i$ is a root of $x^3 + 4x^2 - 2x - 20 = 0$.
   b. Find the other two roots.
   c. Graph the three roots as points on the complex plane.

3. Suppose $f(x)$ is a polynomial with real coefficients and z is a complex number. Find $f(\overline{z})$ for each value of $f(z)$.
   a. $f(z) = 1$ b. $f(z) = 3i$
   c. $f(z) = 1 + 2i$ d. $f(z) = 3 + 4i$

4. Find a polynomial equation with real coefficients that has $3 + i$ and -4 as roots.

5. A complex number z has magnitude 3 and direction 18°. The powers of z are the vertices of a regular polygon on the complex plane. How many sides does this polygon have?

6. Consider the complex number $z = \frac{\sqrt{3} + i}{2}$.
   a. Find the magnitude and direction of z.
   b. Find a power n such that $z^n = 1$.
   c. Graph the powers of z as points on the complex plane.

7. The graph shows the six solutions to $x^6 = 1$.

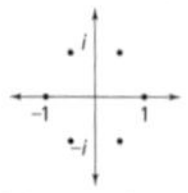

   a. Find the magnitude and direction of each solution.
   b. Write each complex number in $a + bi$ form. Use radicals where needed.

8. Graph the eight solutions to $x^8 = 1$ on the complex plane.

Practice: For Lesson 3.12, assign Exercises 1–4.

12. **Standardized Test Prep** If $3 + 4i$ is a root of $f(x) = x^3 - 2x^2 + x + 100$, which are the other two roots?
    A. $3 - 4i$ and 4 **B.** $3 - 5i$ and -4
    C. $-3 - 5i$ and 8 **D.** $3 - 4i$ and -4

13. **a.** Find a cubic function with real coefficients for which one root is $2 + 7i$ and the sum of the roots is 0.
    b. Find a cubic function with real coefficients for which one root is $2 + 7i$ and the product of the roots is 106.

14. Use the function $g(x) = x^6 - 1$. Calculate each value.
    a. $g(-1)$
    b. $g(w)$, where $w = \frac{1 + i\sqrt{3}}{2}$
    c. $g(w^2)$
    d. **Take It Further** Plot all six complex numbers that make $g(x) = 0$.

Maintain Your Skills

15. For each complex number z, calculate the magnitude and direction of z^4.
    a. $z = 1 + i$ **b.** $z = 1 - i$
    c. $z = -1 + i$ **d.** $z = -1 - i$

16. Suppose z^5 has magnitude 1 and direction 0°. Determine whether each statement could be true about z.
    a. $z = 1$
    b. z has magnitude 1 and direction 72°.
    c. z has magnitude 1 and direction 120°.
    d. z has magnitude 1 and direction 144°.
    e. $z = -1$
    f. z has magnitude 1 and direction 216°.

This is a more complicated way to say $z^5 = 1$.

Answers

12. D

13. a. Answers may vary. Sample: $x^3 + 37x + 212 = 0$
b. Answers may vary. Sample: $x^3 - 6x^2 + 61x - 106 = 0$

14. a. 0
b. 0
c. 0
d.

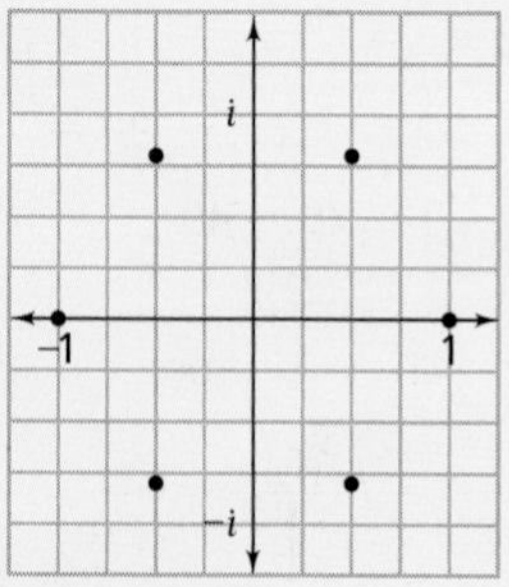

15. a–d. 4, 180°

3.13 Roots of Unity

In Chapter 2, you learned how to factor polynomials of the form $x^n - 1$. This lesson focuses on the roots of those polynomials.

Example

Problem Find and graph all solutions to each equation as points on the complex plane.

a. $x^2 = 1$

b. $x^3 = 1$

c. $x^4 = 1$

d. $x^6 = 1$

Solution Set each equation equal to zero and then factor it. Use the Zero-Product Property to find the solutions.

a. Solve $x^2 - 1 = (x - 1)(x + 1)$ using difference of squares. The two roots are $x = 1$ and $x = -1$.

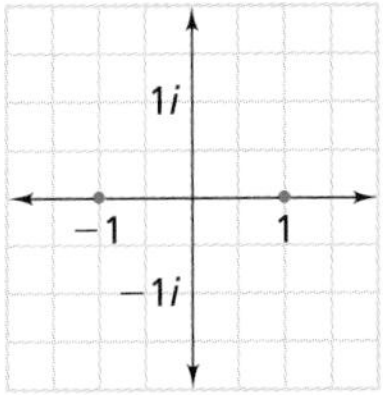

The Ferris wheel cars suggest the roots of $x^{12} - 1$.

b. Solve $x^3 - 1 = (x - 1)(x^2 + x + 1)$ using difference of cubes. The first factor gives the root $x = 1$. Use the quadratic formula with the second factor to find the other roots.

$$x = \frac{-1 \pm \sqrt{1 - 4}}{2} = \frac{-1 \pm i\sqrt{3}}{2}$$

The other two roots are complex conjugates with magnitude 1 and directions 120° and 240°.

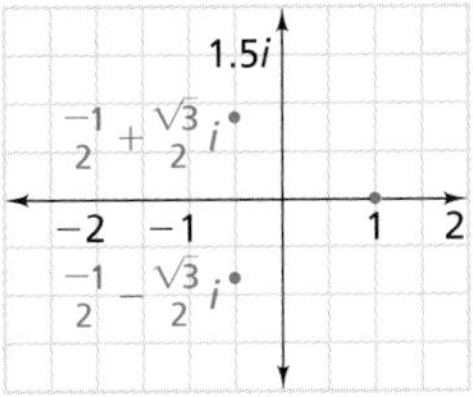

Lesson Overview

GOAL

- Find and graph the roots of equations of the form $x^n - 1 = 0$ on the complex plane.

In this lesson, students consider the roots of 1 (unity). This lesson is optional. Roots of unity are covered in more detail in CME Project *Precalculus.*

When *square root* was first defined, a convention was chosen to define $\sqrt{n}$ to be the positive square root of the number, even though there is a second choice. Without that convention, you could say $\sqrt{1}$ has two possible values, 1 and −1, because if you square either number, you get 1.

Similarly, you think of $\sqrt[3]{1}$ to have one value: 1. It is true that there is only one real number whose cube is 1, but there are, in fact, 2 other complex numbers whose cubes are 1.

Finding the roots of unity is the same process as finding roots of equations of the form $x^n - 1 = 0$, where n is a positive integer. In the previous lesson, you discussed that there are exactly n roots to such an equation, so, for any value of n, there are exactly n possible values for $\sqrt[n]{1}$. These roots become more interesting as you graph them, and see that their geometry forms vertices of a regular polygon of n sides.

CHECK YOUR UNDERSTANDING

- Core: 1, 2, 3, 4, 5, 8
- Optional: 6, 7
- Extension: 9

MATERIALS

- graph paper
- graphing calculators
- Blackline Master 3.13

HOMEWORK

- Core: 10, 11, 12, 13
- Optional: 15, 16
- Extension: 14

VOCABULARY

- roots of unity

Launch

Begin this lesson by introducing the Example. You may want to use Blackline Master 3.13 to guide students through this.

16. a. could be true

b. could be true

c. could not be true (z cannot have direction 120°)

d. could be true

e. could not be true (z cannot have direction 180°)

f. could be true

Explore

For You to Do

You may wish to have students work in pairs or in small groups. Circulate while students work.

PROBLEM 2 gets at the idea that if z is a root of $x^n = 1$, then z is also a root of $x^{kn} = 1$ for any integer values of k and n.

Have students verbalize how they found the answers to Problems 1 and 2.

c. Solve $x^4 - 1 = \left(x^2 - 1\right)\left(x^2 + 1\right)$ using difference of squares. Use difference of squares again to factor $x^2 - 1$.

$$x^4 - 1 = (x - 1)(x + 1)(x^2 + 1)$$

The first two factors give the roots $x = 1$ and $x = -1$. Use the quadratic formula with the third factor to find the other roots.

$$x = \frac{0 \pm \sqrt{-4}}{2} = \frac{0 \pm 2i}{2} = \pm i$$

The four roots are 1, i, -1, and $-i$.

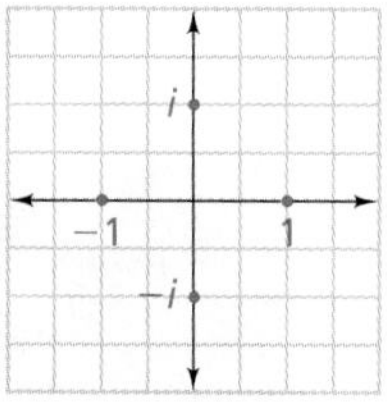

d. Solve $x^6 - 1 = (x^3 - 1)(x^3 + 1)$ using difference of squares. Use sum and difference of cubes to factor $x^3 - 1$ and $x^3 + 1$.

$$x^6 - 1 = (x - 1)(x^2 + x + 1)(x + 1)(x^2 - x + 1)$$

The first and third factors give the roots $x = 1$ and $x = -1$. Use the quadratic formula for the quadratic factors. The six roots are 1, -1, $\frac{-1 \pm i\sqrt{3}}{2}$, and $\frac{1 \pm i\sqrt{3}}{2}$.

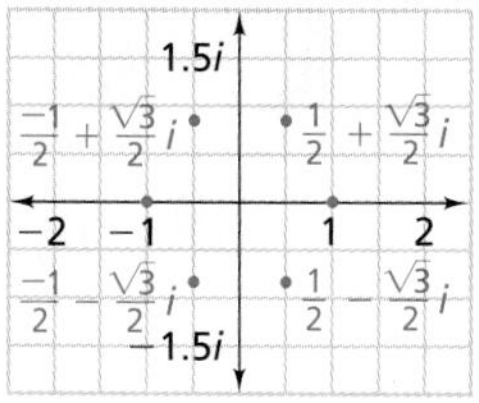

For You to Do

1. Find the magnitude and direction for each of the six solutions to $x^6 = 1$.
2. Show that all the complex numbers in the above example are also solutions of $x^{12} - 1 = 0$.

Answers

For You to Do

1. The solutions are 1, -1, $\frac{-1 + i\sqrt{3}}{2}$, $\frac{-1 - i\sqrt{3}}{2}$, $\frac{1 + i\sqrt{3}}{2}$, and $\frac{1 - i\sqrt{3}}{2}$. All magnitudes are 1, and the directions are 0°, 180°, 120°, 240°, 60°, and 300°, respectively.
2. Answers may vary. Sample: $x^{12} - 1 = (x^6 - 1)(x^6 + 1)$, so all the solutions of $x^6 - 1 = 0$ will also be solutions of $x^{12} - 1 = 0$.

Developing Habits of Mind

Look for relationships. The solutions to $x^n = 1$ are **roots of unity.** Solving the equation involves taking a root of 1.

$$x^n = 1 \text{ or } x = \sqrt[n]{1}$$

In the real numbers, the only possible solutions to such an equation are $x = 1$ and $x = -1$. But there are many other complex numbers with magnitude 1, and there are many other ways for x^n to equal 1.

Think about how you represent 1 on the complex plane. It has magnitude 1 and direction 0°. But you can also think of 1 as having magnitude 1 and direction 360°, by going all the way around. Or you can think of the direction as 720°, or 1080°, and so on.

In an exercise in Lesson 3.11, you found that the direction of z^3 is three times the direction of z. If $z^3 = 1$, then three times the direction of z must be a multiple of 360°.

$x = 1$ is always a solution. When is $x = -1$ a solution?

Minds in Action episode 13

Tony is trying to find the solutions to $x^5 = 1$.

Tony The example skips right over $x^5 = 1$, but I can find those solutions by magnitude and direction. If $x^5 = 1$, then x has to have magnitude 1. So now I just need to know the directions. The direction of x^5 is five times the direction of x. That means I know one possible direction for x.

$$\frac{360°}{5} = 72°$$

Five times at 72° is one trip all the way around and back to 1. The next one is two trips all the way around, which is 720°. So I divide by 5 to find the direction.

$$\frac{720°}{5} = 144°$$

They just come equally spaced like that. The directions are all the multiples of 72° and the magnitudes are always 1. Here's what it looks like in the complex plane.

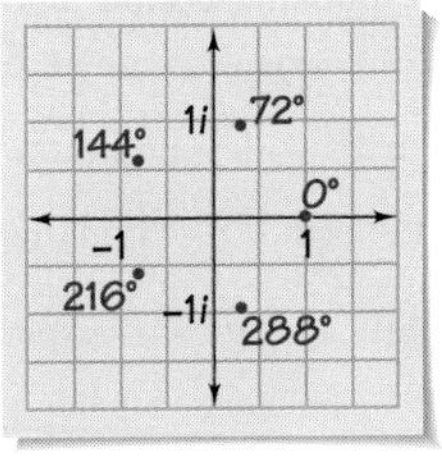

If I connect the points, I make a regular pentagon. The others from the example all work that way, too. The point at 1 is always going to be a vertex, since $1^n = 1$ for any power. I like this because I don't have to factor. This even works for stuff that doesn't factor.

Developing Habits of Mind

The idea hinted at in the margin note is that when n is odd, -1 is not a root of $x^n = 1$. The method that Tony describes in Minds in Action that follows gives a rational reason for this fact: let $n = 2k - 1$, where k is a positive integer (and thus, n is odd). If the roots are evenly spaced and there are an odd number, then -1 cannot be one of the roots.

For more detail, you can prove this fact algebraically. If $x^{2k-1} = 1$, the angles for each of the root vectors will be

$$\frac{360j}{2k - 1}$$

where j, an integer, goes from 1 to $2k - 2$ (since the next integer, $2k - 1$, cycles back around). So suppose

$$\frac{360m}{2k - 1} = 180$$

Then

$$\begin{aligned} 360m &= 180(2k - 1) \\ 360m &= 360k - 180 \\ 360k - 360m &= 180 \\ 360(k - m) &= 180 \\ k - m &= \frac{1}{2} \end{aligned}$$

But since both k and m are integers, their difference cannot be a fraction. So there is no m, and thus, -1 is not a root.

Wrap Up

As time allows, go over the Check Your Understanding core exercises with your class.

Assessment Resources

Lesson Quiz 3.13

1. A complex number z has magnitude 5 and direction 72°. The powers of z are the vertices of a regular polygon on the complex plane. How many sides does this polygon have?

2. Consider the complex number $z = \frac{\sqrt{2} + i\sqrt{2}}{2}$.
   a. Find the magnitude and direction of z.
   b. Find a power n such that $z^n = 1$.
   c. Graph the powers of z as points on the complex plane.

3. Graph the eight solutions to $x^8 = 1$ as points on the complex plane.

4. Find the sum of the eighth roots of unity.

Exercises

HOMEWORK
- Core: 10, 11, 12, 13
- Optional: 15, 16
- Extension: 14

For You to Do

By now, students should readily accept that the magnitude of all roots of unity is 1. It makes logical sense by the first part of Theorem 3.5, which states "$|zw| = |z| \cdot |w|$." For z^n, you have the special case that $|z^n| = (|z|)^n$.

So, if z is an nth root of unity, then $z^n = 1$, and $|z^n| = |1| = 1$. But if $|z^n| = (|z|)^n$, then $(|z|)^n = 1$. Since $|z|$ must be a positive real number, the only positive real number whose nth root is 1 is 1.

The fact that all the roots have magnitude 1 reinforces a geometric fact: you can always circumscribe a regular polygon with a circle.

Check Your Understanding

EXERCISE 1 As the callout box explains, this proof ensures that once you find the basic (principal) root of unity you can find all the roots of unity.

For You to Do

3. Find the magnitude and direction of all solutions to $x^9 = 1$.

Tony's method works in general. For example, below are the seventh roots of unity, which all satisfy $x^7 = 1$.

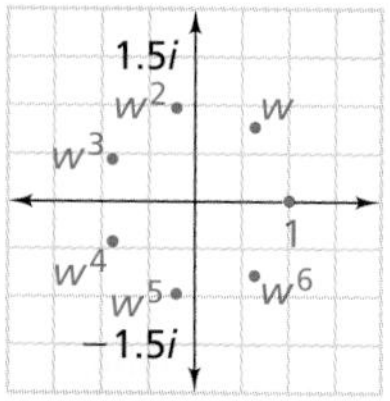

You can call the equation $x^n - 1 = 0$ the *cyclotomic* equation. This means that the roots of the equation divide a circle of radius 1 in the complex plane into n congruent arcs.

These seven numbers are all solutions to $x^7 - 1 = 0$. Since this equation can have at most seven solutions, this is the entire list of the solutions to the equation. And these seven roots of unity form a regular 7-gon in the complex plane.

Exercises *Practicing Habits of Mind*

Check Your Understanding

1. Suppose $w^n = 1$.
   a. Use the properties of exponents to show that $(w^2)^n = 1$.
   b. Show that for any positive integer k, $(w^k)^n = 1$.

This proves that if w is a root of unity, then w^k is also a root of unity.

2. Graph the ten solutions to $x^{10} = 1$ as points on the complex plane.
3. a. Graph the twelve solutions to $x^{12} = 1$ on the complex plane.
   b. Is $x = \frac{-1}{2} - \frac{\sqrt{3}}{2}i$ a solution to $x^{12} = 1$? Explain.

Answers

For You to Do

3. The magnitudes are 1, and the directions are 0°, 40°, 80°, 120°, 160°, 200°, 240°, 280°, 320°.

Exercises

1. a. $(w^2)^n = w^{2n} = (w^n)^2 = 1^2 = 1$

b. $(w^k)^n = w^{nk} = (w^n)^k = 1^k = 1$

2.

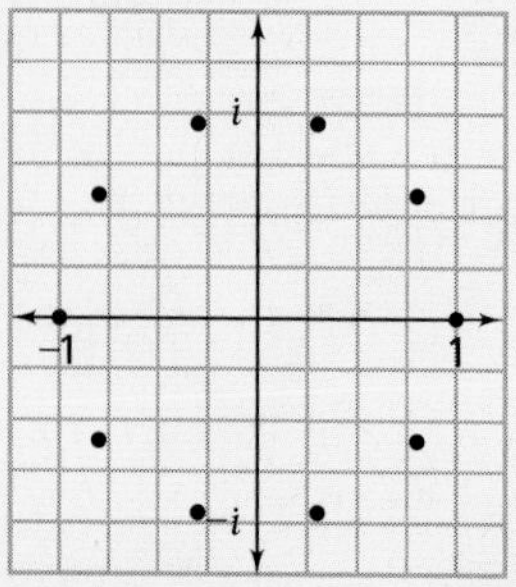

3. a.

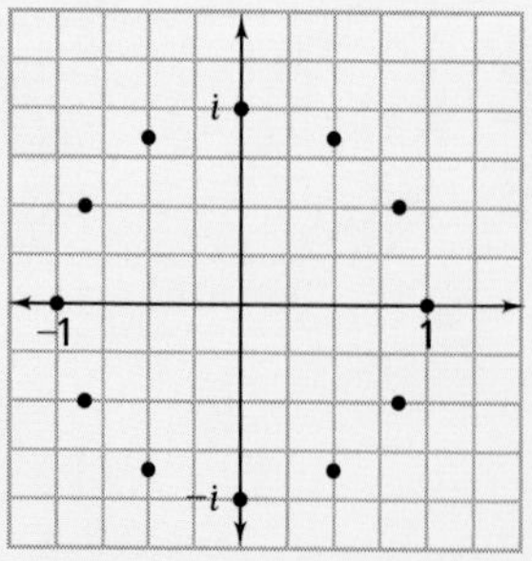

b. Yes; answers may vary. Sample: the magnitude of $-\frac{1}{2} - \frac{\sqrt{3}}{2}i$ is $\sqrt{\frac{1}{4} + \frac{3}{4}} = 1$ and the direction is 240°, and that is one of the solutions shown in part (a).

4. a.

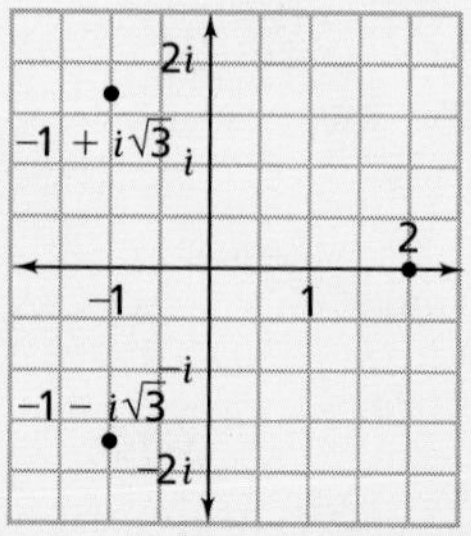

b. Each solution to $x^3 = 8$ is doubled in magnitude.

4. **a.** Find the three solutions to $x^3 = 8$. Then graph them on the complex plane.

b. Describe how the solutions to $x^3 = 8$ are related to the solutions to $x^3 = 1$.

5. Use magnitude and direction to find two complex numbers z such that $z^2 = i$.

These numbers are the square roots of i.

6. **a.** Find a complex number z such that $z^3 = i$.

b. Find all three complex numbers that are solutions to $x^3 = i$. Then plot them as points on the complex plane.

c. Describe how the solutions to $x^3 = i$ are related to the solutions to $x^3 = 1$.

7. Find the sum of the sixth roots of unity.

8. Sasha says that if w is a fifth root of unity, so is $\overline{w}$. Is she correct? Explain.

9. **Take It Further** Some roots of unity repeat. For example, the cube roots of unity (solutions to $x^3 = 1$) are also sixth roots of unity (solutions to $x^6 = 1$). Also, $x = 1$ always repeats. But some roots of unity are new for a particular power. For example, i and $-i$ are solutions to $x^4 = 1$, but not of any lower-degree equations.

a. Copy and complete the table below with the number of new roots of unity for each equation.

Equation	Number of New Roots
$x = 1$	1
$x^2 = 1$	1
$x^3 = 1$	2
$x^4 = 1$	2
$x^5 = 1$	■
$x^6 = 1$	■
$x^7 = 1$	■
$x^8 = 1$	■
$x^9 = 1$	■
$x^{10} = 1$	■

b. Describe any relationships you notice in the table. Describe a rule for the number of new roots of unity for $x^n = 1$.

EXERCISE 4 As a followup, you might ask students to plot the solutions to $x^3 = 64$ without doing extensive calculations. The three complex solutions to $x^3 = 64$ must each have magnitude 4, and their directions will be evenly spaced around the origin—0°, 120°, and 240°. You do not need the exact coordinates to plot these points.

EXERCISE 7 If students discover different methods to find the sum, you may wish to have them present their solutions to the class.

EXERCISE 8 Point out to students that the algebraic method here generalizes to any degree.

EXERCISE 9 This function (of the power) is called Euler's "phi" function $\phi(n)$, and counts the number of integers less than n that are relatively prime to n; that is, they share no common factor with n. The phi function is very prominent in number theory.

EXERCISE 14 Use this exercise to note that the "first" root of unity—that is, the root z with smallest argument greater than 0—forms a basis for all the other roots, so that the nth roots of unity are $z, z^2, z^3, \ldots, z^n$. If the roots evenly divide the unit circle into equally-sized arcs, then the angles of those arcs are also equal. If the angle to the first root is k, then the angle to the second is $2k$, to the third is $3k$, and so on. From Theorem 3.5, $\arg zw = \arg z + \arg w$. In this case, $\arg z^n = n \arg z$. So if $\arg z$ is the first angle, $2 \arg z = \arg z^2$ is the second. Similarly, $3 \arg z = \arg z^3$ is the third, and so forth.

Maintain Your Skills

EXERCISE 15 gives students another chance to notice the Pythagorean relationship that comes when complex numbers (with integer parts) are squared.

5. $\frac{\sqrt{2}}{2} + \frac{\sqrt{2}}{2}i, -\frac{\sqrt{2}}{2} - \frac{\sqrt{2}}{2}i$

6. a. Answers may vary. Sample: $\frac{\sqrt{3}}{2} + \frac{1}{2}i$

b. $-i, \frac{\sqrt{3}}{2} + \frac{1}{2}i, -\frac{\sqrt{3}}{2} + \frac{1}{2}i$

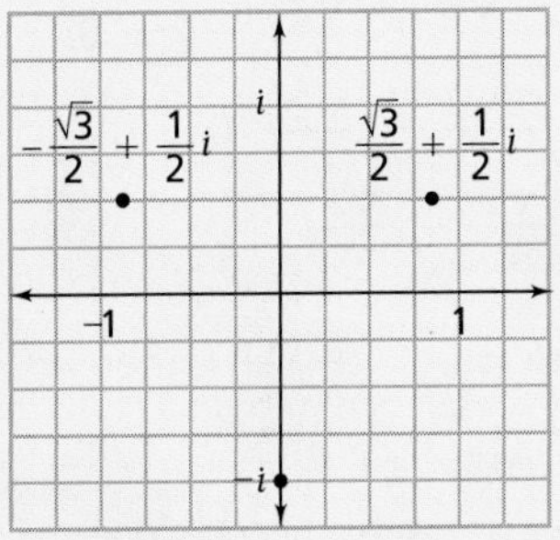

c. Rotate the solutions to $x^3 = 1$ by 270° counterclockwise to get the solutions to $x^3 = i$.

7. 0

8. Yes; complex roots of polynomials come in conjugate pairs.

9. a.

Equation	Number of New Roots
$x = 1$	1
$x^2 = 1$	1
$x^3 = 1$	2
$x^4 = 1$	2
$x^5 = 1$	4
$x^6 = 1$	2
$x^7 = 1$	6
$x^8 = 1$	4
$x^9 = 1$	6
$x^{10} = 1$	4

b. Answers may vary. Sample: Beginning with $x^3 = 1$, the number of new roots is even.

Additional Resources

PRINT RESOURCES
- Solution Manual
- Practice Workbook
- Assessment Resources
- Teaching Resources

TECHNOLOGY
- Interactive Textbook
- TeacherExpress CD-ROM
- ExamView CD-ROM
- PHSchool.com

Additional Practice

1. Consider the complex numbers $z = 3 + i$ and $w = 4 + 2i$.
  a. Find the magnitude and direction of z and w.
  b. Find the magnitude and direction of zw without finding zw.
  c. Find the magnitude and direction of z^2 and w^2.

2. a. Show that $-3 + i$ is a root of $x^3 + 4x^2 - 2x - 20 = 0$.
  b. Find the other two roots.
  c. Graph the three roots as points on the complex plane.

3. Suppose $f(x)$ is a polynomial with real coefficients and z is a complex number. Find $f(\overline{z})$ for each value of $f(z)$.
  a. $f(z) = 1$ **b.** $f(z) = 3i$
  c. $f(z) = 1 + 2i$ **d.** $f(z) = 3 + 4i$

4. Find a polynomial equation with real coefficients that has $3 + i$ and -4 as roots.

5. A complex number z has magnitude 3 and direction 18°. The powers of z are the vertices of a regular polygon on the complex plane. How many sides does this polygon have?

6. Consider the complex number $z = \frac{\sqrt{3} + i}{2}$.
  a. Find the magnitude and direction of z.
  b. Find a power n such that $z^n = 1$.
  c. Graph the powers of z as points on the complex plane.

7. The graph shows the six solutions to $x^6 = 1$.

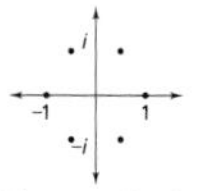

  a. Find the magnitude and direction of each solution.
  b. Write each complex number in $a + bi$ form. Use radicals where needed.

8. Graph the eight solutions to $x^8 = 1$ on the complex plane.

Practice: For Lesson 3.13, assign Exercises 5–8.

On Your Own

10. **Standardized Test Prep** Which angle is the difference in direction between consecutive solutions to $x^9 = 1$?

A. 20° **B.** 30° **C.** 40° **D.** 45°

11. A complex number z has magnitude 1 and direction 20°. The powers of z are the vertices of a regular polygon on the complex plane. How many sides does this polygon have?

12. Consider the complex number $z = \frac{1 + i\sqrt{3}}{2}$.
  a. Find the magnitude and direction of z.
  b. Find a power n such that $z^n = 1$.
  c. Graph the powers of z as points on the complex plane.

13. The graph below shows the eight solutions to $x^8 = 1$.

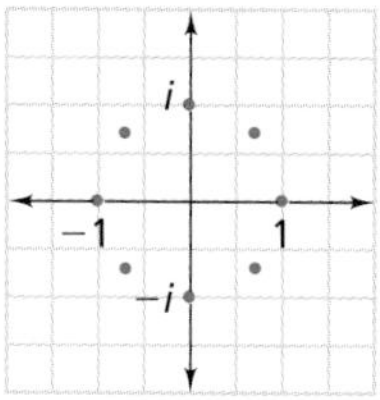

  a. Find the magnitude and direction of each solution.
  b. Write each complex number in the form $a + bi$. Use radicals where needed.

14. **Take It Further** Show that all eight numbers in Exercise 13 are powers of the same number.

Go Online PHSchool.com
For additional practice, go to **Web Code:** bfa-0313

Maintain Your Skills

15. For each complex number z, calculate z^2. Then find the magnitude of z^2.
  a. $z = 2 + i$ **b.** $z = 3 + 2i$ **c.** $z = 4 + i$
  d. $z = 4 + 3i$ **e.** $z = m + ni$

16. a. Find $1 + i + i^2 + i^3 + i^4$. Justify your answer.
  b. If $w^3 = 1$, find $1 + w + w^2$. Justify your answer.
  c. If $z^5 = 1$, find $1 + z + z^2 + z^3 + z^4$. Justify your answer.
  d. If $w^6 = 1$, find $1 + w + w^2 + w^3 + w^4 + w^5$. Justify your answer.

Answers

10. C

11. 18 sides

12. a. $|z| = 1$, $\arg z = 60°$
  b. $n = 6$
  c.

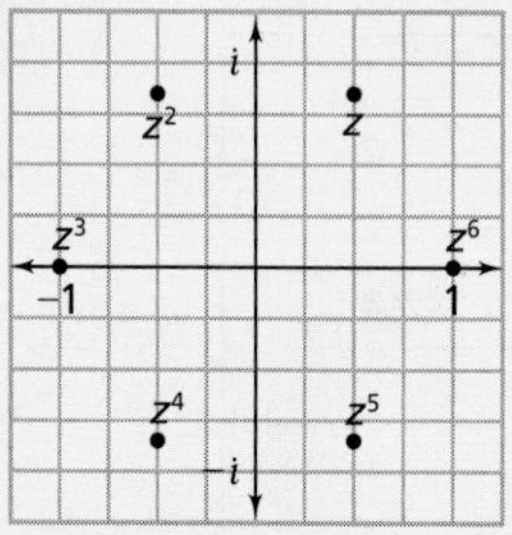

13. a. The magnitudes are 1, and the directions are 0°, 45°, 90°, 135°, 180°, 225°, 270°, 315°.
  b. $1 + 0i$, $\frac{\sqrt{2}}{2} + \frac{\sqrt{2}}{2}i$, $0 + i$, $-\frac{\sqrt{2}}{2} + \frac{\sqrt{2}}{2}i$, $-1 + 0i$, $-\frac{\sqrt{2}}{2} - \frac{\sqrt{2}}{2}i$, $0 - i$, $\frac{\sqrt{2}}{2} - \frac{\sqrt{2}}{2}i$

14. If $w = \frac{\sqrt{2}}{2} + \frac{\sqrt{2}}{2}i$, then $w^2 = i$, $w^3 = -\frac{\sqrt{2}}{2} + \frac{\sqrt{2}}{2}i$, $w^4 = -1$, $w^5 = -\frac{\sqrt{2}}{2} - \frac{\sqrt{2}}{2}i$, $w^6 = -i$, $w^7 = \frac{\sqrt{2}}{2} - \frac{\sqrt{2}}{2}i$, which are the 8 values listed in Exercise 13(b).

15. a. $z^2 = 3 + 4i$, $|z^2| = 5$
  b. $z^2 = 5 + 12i$, $|z^2| = 13$
  c. $z^2 = 15 + 8i$, $|z^2| = 17$
  d. $z^2 = 7 + 24i$, $|z^2| = 25$
  e. $z^2 = (m^2 - n^2) + (2mn)i$, $|z^2| = m^2 + n^2$

16. a. 1; $1 + i + i^2 + i^3 + i^4 = 1 + i - 1 - i + 1 = 1$
  b. 0, 3; If $w^3 = 1$, then $w^3 - 1 = 0$ and $(w - 1)(w^2 + w + 1) = 0$. Then either $w - 1 = 0$, in which case $w = 1$ and $1 + w + w^2 = 3$, or $1 + w + w^2 = 0$.

Mathematical Reflections 3C

In this investigation, you found relationships between magnitudes and arguments of factors and products. You also graphed the solutions to equations in the form $x^n - 1 = 0$. These exercises will help you summarize what you have learned.

1. Use $z = 1 - \sqrt{3}i$. Find the magnitude and direction for each power of z.
   a. z b. z^2 c. z^3 d. z^4
   e. Which, if any, of the powers of z that you found is a real number? Explain.
2. A complex number z has magnitude 6 and direction 135°. A complex number w has magnitude 2 and direction 240°.
   a. Find the magnitude and direction of the product zw.
   b. Find the magnitude and direction of v such that zv has magnitude 3 and direction 30°.
3. Find a polynomial with real coefficients that has $2 - i$ and 3 among its roots. Is your polynomial the only possible polynomial? If so, explain why. If not, find another polynomial.
4. Show that $6i$ is a root of the polynomial $x^3 + 2x^2 + 36x + 72$. Then find the other roots.
5. Find the magnitude and direction of all solutions to the equation $x^5 - 1 = 0$. If there are any solutions in Quadrant II, express them in the form $a + bi$, where a and b are real numbers. Approximate to the nearest hundredth if you cannot find an exact answer.
6. How are the magnitude and argument of the product of two complex numbers related to the magnitude and argument of the original numbers?
7. If $-2 + i$ is a root of the polynomial $x^3 + 7x^2 + 17x + 15$, what is another root?
8. How can you graph the solution to the equation $x^{10} - 1 = 0$ on the complex plane without doing many calculations?

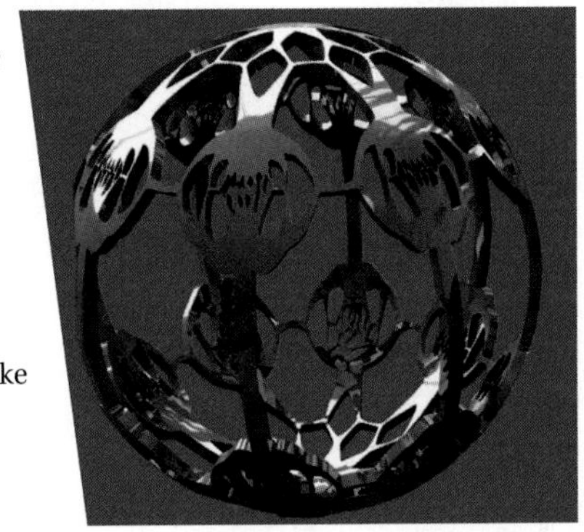

This sculpture is based on the polynomiograph on p. 252.

Vocabulary

In this investigation, you learned this term. Make sure you understand what it means and how to use it.

- **roots of unity**

Mathematical Reflections

EXERCISES 6–8 At the start of the investigation, you may have assigned these as Questions 1–3 for students to think and write about.

c. 0, 5; If $z^5 = 1$, then $z^5 - 1 = 0$ and $(z - 1)(z^4 + z^3 + z^2 + z + 1) = 0$. Then either $z - 1 = 0$, in which case $z = 1$ and $1 + z + z^2 + z^3 + z^4 = 5$, or $1 + z + z^2 + z^3 + z^4 = 0$.

d. 0, 6; If $w^6 = 1$ then $w^6 - 1 = 0$ and $(w - 1)(w^5 + w^4 + w^3 + w^2 + w + 1) = 0$. Then either $w - 1 = 0$, in which case $w = 1$ and $1 + w + w^2 + w^3 + w^4 + w^5 = 6$, or $1 + w + w^2 + w^3 + w^4 + w^5 = 0$.

Mathematical Reflections

1. a. $|z| = 2$, $\arg z = 300°$
b. $|z^2| = 4$, $\arg z^2 = 240°$
c. $|z^3| = 8$, $\arg z^3 = 180°$
d. $|z^4| = 16$, $\arg z^4 = 120°$
e. $z^3 = -8 + 0i$; its direction is 180° so it lies on the real axis.

2. a. $|zw| = 12$, $\arg zw = 15°$
b. $|v| = \frac{1}{2}$, $\arg v = 255°$

3. $x^3 - 7x^2 + 17x - 15 = 0$; no; other polynomials are $p(x) \cdot (x^3 - 7x^2 + 17x - 15) = 0$, where $p(x)$ is any polynomial.

4. $(6i)^3 + 2(6i)^2 + 36(6i) + 72 = -216i - 72 + 216i + 72 = 0$, so $6i$ is a root. The other roots are $-6i$ and -2.

5. All magnitudes are 1, and the directions are 0°, 72°, 144°, 216°, 288°; the solution in Quadrant II is $-0.81 + 0.59i$.

6. The magnitude of the product is the product of the magnitudes, and the direction of the product is the sum of the directions (subtracting 360° if necessary).

7. $-2 - i$

8. There are 10 solutions, each on a circle of radius 1 centered at the origin. The directions are multiples of $\frac{360°}{10}$, which are 36°, 72°, 108°, 144°, 180°, 216°, 252°, 288°, 324°, and 360°.

Project

The ultimate goal of this project is to demonstrate the relationship between cyclotomic polynomials (in the form $x^n - 1$) and integers. As students build the table, hope that they will see that the number of factors of $x^n - 1$ when factored over $\mathbb{Z}$ is the same as the number of factors of n. Students will revisit this concept in CME Project *Precalculus.*

You can either do this project as a class or allow individual students to do the project independently. In either case, you may want to provide students with an opportunity to present their results, either in a paper or as a presentation to the class. If you do this project as a class, you might want to begin by making a class table and having students work in groups to fill it in and check each other's work. A CAS is extremely helpful here.

Give students a chance to present any conjectures they have developed, such as these:

- If n is prime, the answer is 2.
- If n is the square of a prime, the answer is 3.
- If n is a product of two primes, the answer is 4.

It is fun to write these on the board and then, when the general conjecture emerges that the number of factors of $x^n - 1$ over $\mathbb{Z}$ is the number of factors of n, show how it implies all the conjectures on the board. The general conjecture may come from the students, but it can also come from you.

The proof of this general result is hard. In *Precalculus,* students will prove that if n is a factor of m, then $x^n - 1$ is a factor of $x^m - 1$. Proving the converse requires the factorization into linear factors in $\mathbb{C}$.

Project: Using Mathematical Habits

Factoring a Sequence of Polynomials

Consider the following polynomials.

$$\{x^2 - 1, x^3 - 1, x^4 - 1, x^5 - 1, \ldots, x^n - 1, \ldots\}$$

For this project, you are to investigate how these polynomials factor over $\mathbb{Z}$.

Factor over $\mathbb{Z}$ means that the factors have integer coefficients. Integers are probably what your CAS gives by default when you tell it to factor things.

Note that not all the factors will be linear polynomials. You could have a factor like $(x^2 + x + 1)$, which does not factor further in $\mathbb{Z}$.

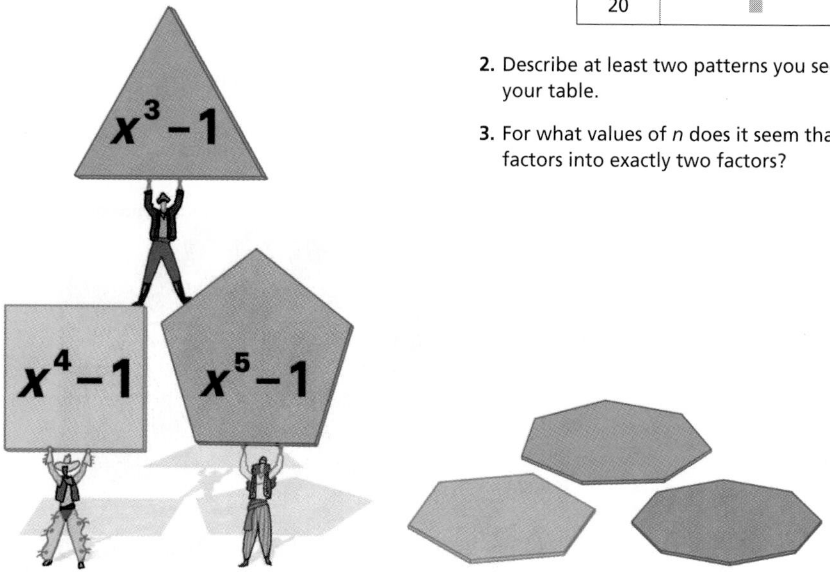

1. Make a table like the one below and complete it.

n	Number of Factors of $x^n - 1$
1	■
2	■
3	■
4	■
5	■
6	■
⋮	■
20	■

2. Describe at least two patterns you see in your table.

3. For what values of n does it seem that $x^n - 1$ factors into exactly two factors?

Answers

Project

1. The entries in the second column are 1, 2, 2, 3, 2, 4, 2, 4, 3, 4, 2, 6, 2, 4, 4, 5, 2, 6, 2, and 6.

2. Answers may vary. Sample: When n is a square the number of factors is odd; when n is prime the number of factors is 2.

3. when n is prime

Chapter Review

1. a. none **b.** 0
 c. none **d.** $\pm\sqrt{6}$
 e. $\pm i\sqrt{6}$

2. a. $\frac{1 \pm i\sqrt{39}}{4}$ **b.** $-5 - 4i$
 c. $\frac{3}{2} + \frac{3}{2}i$

3. a. $3 + 5i$ **b.** $4 - 2i$
 c. $-10 + 10i$ **d.** $4 + 28i$
 e. $-8 - 6i$ **f.** $-\frac{1}{10} - \frac{3}{10}i$

4. a.

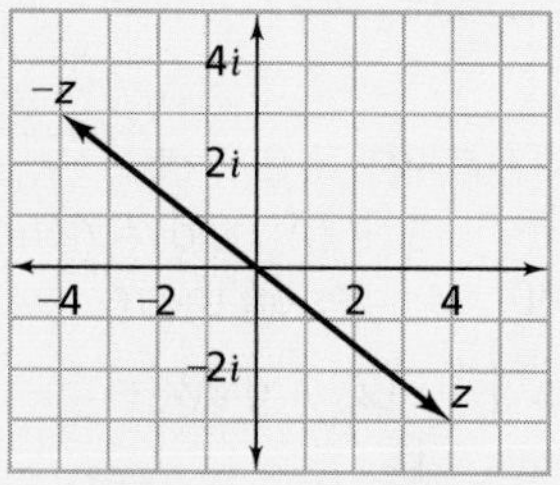

b.

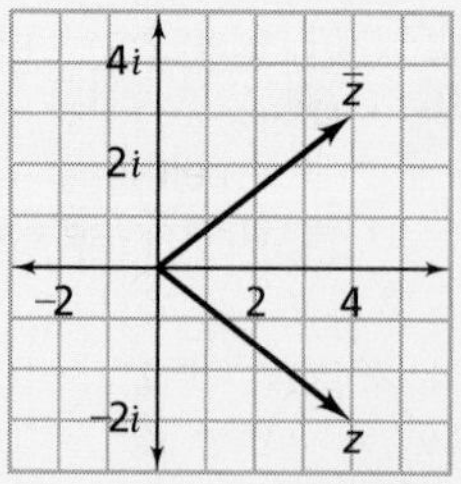

c.

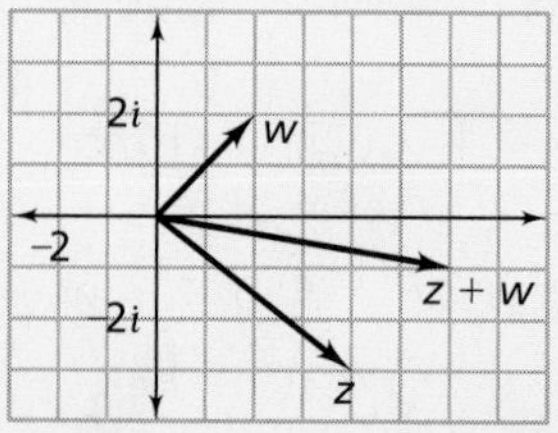

Chapter 3 Review

Go Online PHSchool.com

For vocabulary review, go to **Web Code:** bfj-0351

In **Investigation 3A,** you learned how to

- understand complex numbers as an extension of the real numbers
- use complex numbers as tools for solving equations
- be fluent in complex-number arithmetic

The following questions will help you check your understanding.

1. Use the equation $x^5 - 36x = 0$. Find the solutions, if they exist, that meet each of the following conditions.
   a. The solution is in $\mathbb{N}$.
   b. The solution is in $\mathbb{Z}$ but not in $\mathbb{N}$.
   c. The solution is in $\mathbb{Q}$ but not in $\mathbb{Z}$.
   d. The solution is in $\mathbb{R}$ but not in $\mathbb{Q}$.
   e. The solution is not in $\mathbb{R}$.

2. a. Solve $2x^2 - x + 5 = 0$ over $\mathbb{C}$.
   b. Find a complex number $z = a + bi$, where a and b are real numbers, that satisfies $z + (3 - 7i) = -2 - 11i$.
   c. Find a complex number $z = a + bi$, where a and b are real numbers, that satisfies $(1 - i) \cdot z = 3$.

3. Given two complex numbers $z = -1 + 3i$ and $w = 4 + 2i$, find each of the following.
   a. $z + w$ b. $\overline{w}$
   c. $z \cdot w$ d. $2z \cdot \overline{w}$
   e. z^2 f. $\frac{1}{z}$

In **Investigation 3B,** you learned how to

- graph complex numbers on the complex plane
- visualize operations on complex numbers as transformations on the complex plane
- develop greater fluency with complex number calculations, which include finding magnitude and direction

The following questions will help you check your understanding.

4. For $z = 4 - 3i$ and $w = 2 + 2i$, graph and label each on the complex plane.
   a. z and $-z$ b. z and $\overline{z}$
   c. z, w, and $z + w$ d. w and $2w$
   e. w, $i \cdot w$ f. z, w, and $z \cdot w$

5. Graph $2i$, $(2i)^2$, and $(2i)^3$ on the same complex plane.

6. Let $z = -1 + i$. Copy and complete the following table.

	$a - bi$	Magnitude	Direction
z	$-1 + i$	■	■
$-z$	■	■	■
$\overline{z}$	■	■	■
$i \cdot z$	■	■	■
$3z$	■	■	■
z^2	■	■	■

d.

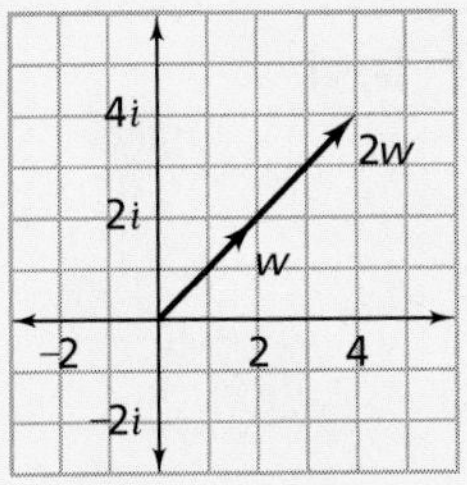

e.

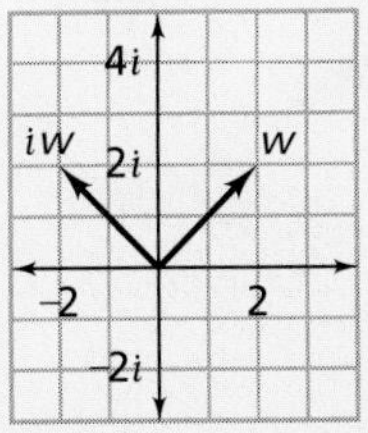

f.

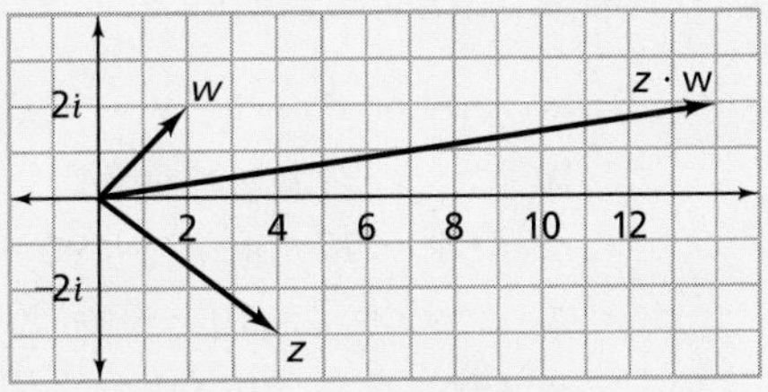

5.

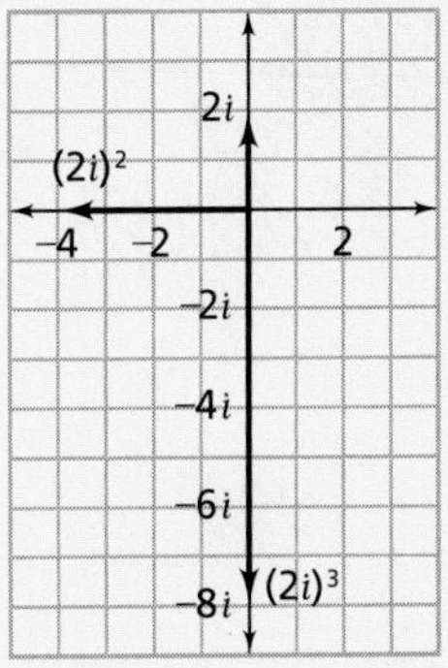

6.

	$a - bi$	Magnitude	Direction
z	$-1 + i$	$\sqrt{2}$	135°
$-z$	$1 - i$	$\sqrt{2}$	315°
$\overline{z}$	$-1 - i$	$\sqrt{2}$	225°
$i \cdot z$	$-1 - i$	$\sqrt{2}$	225°
$3z$	$-3 + 3i$	$3\sqrt{2}$	135°
z^2	$-2i$	2	270°

In **Investigation 3C,** you learned how to

- describe relationships between magnitudes and arguments of factors and products
- prove the relationship between the function values of complex conjugates
- find and graph the solutions to equations of the form $x^n - 1 = 0$ on the complex plane

The following questions will help you check your understanding.

7. Complex number z has magnitude 3 and direction 30°. Complex number w has magnitude 2 and direction 120°.

Find the magnitude and direction of each number.

a. zw **b.** z^2

c. z^3 **d.** $-w$

e. $4w$ **f.** $\bar{z}$

8. Find a quadratic equation with real coefficients that has $2 + 3i$ as one of its solutions.

9. Without actually solving the equation, find the magnitude and direction of all solutions to the equation $x^6 - 1 = 0$.

Answers

7. a. $|zw| = 6$, $\arg zw = 150°$

b. $|z^2| = 9$, $\arg z^2 = 60°$

c. $|z^3| = 27$, $\arg z^3 = 90°$

d. $|-w| = 2$, $\arg -w = 300°$

e. $|4w| = 8$, $\arg 4w = 120°$

f. $|\bar{z}| = 3$, $\arg \bar{z} = 330°$

8. $x^2 - 4x + 13 = 0$

9. All magnitudes are 1, and the directions are 0°, 60°, 120°, 180°, 240°, and 300°.

Chapter Test

1. B

2. C

3. D

4. C

5. D

6. a. none

b. $1 \pm 3i$

7. a. $6 - 6i$

b. $2 - i$

8. a. -4

Chapter 3 Test

Go Online PHSchool.com

For a chapter test, go to **Web Code:** bfa-0353

Multiple Choice

1. What is the value of $\sqrt{-4} \cdot \sqrt{-9}$?
   - A. 6
   - B. −6
   - C. $6i$
   - D. $-6i$
2. If $z = 4 + 6i$, what is $z - \bar{z}$?
   - A. 0
   - B. 8
   - C. $12i$
   - D. $8 + 12i$
3. If $z = a + bi$ is in Quadrant III, then $i \cdot z$ is in which quadrant?
   - A. I
   - B. II
   - C. III
   - D. IV
4. What is the value of $|5 - 12i|$?
   - A. $\sqrt{119}$
   - B. 7
   - C. 13
   - D. 17
5. One solution of $ax^2 + bx + c = 0$ is $4 - 6i$. Which of the following is another solution?
   - A. $-4 + 6i$
   - B. $\sqrt{52}$
   - C. $-4 - 6i$
   - D. $4 + 6i$

Open Response

6. Find the solutions of $x^2 - 2x + 10 = 0$ that are in each number system.
   - a. $\mathbb{R}$
   - b. $\mathbb{C}$
7. Solve each equation over $\mathbb{C}$. Express your answer in the form $a + bi$, where a and b are real numbers.
   - a. $z + 4i = 2(3 - i)$
   - b. $z \cdot (5 + i) = 11 - 3i$
8. Use $z = -2 + 2i$ and $w = 1 + i$.
   - a. Find $z \cdot w$.
   - b. On the complex plane, graph z, w, and $z \cdot w$.
   - c. Copy and complete the table below.

	$a + bi$	Magnitude	Direction
z	$-2 + 2i$	■	■
w	$1 + i$	■	■
$z \cdot w$	■	■	■

9. A complex number z has magnitude 4 and direction 30°. Find the magnitude and direction of each power of z.
   - a. z^2
   - b. z^3
   - c. z^4
10. Find a cubic equation with real coefficients that has $3 - i$ and 1 as two of its solutions.

---

b.

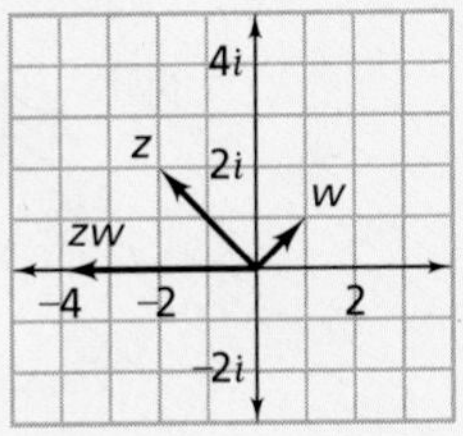

c.

	$a + bi$	Magnitude	Direction
z	$-2 + 2i$	$2\sqrt{2}$	135°
w	$1 + i$	$\sqrt{2}$	45°
$z \cdot w$	−4	4	180°

9. a. $|z^2| = 16$, $\arg z^2 = 60°$
b. $|z^3| = 64$, $\arg z^3 = 90°$
c. $|z^4| = 256$, $\arg z^4 = 120°$

10. Answers may vary. Sample: $x^3 - 7x^2 + 16x - 10 = 0$

Chapter Test

Assessment Resources

Chapter Test — page 1 of 2

Multiple Choice

1. What is the value of $\sqrt{-2} \cdot \sqrt{8}$?
   - A. 4
   - B. −4
   - C. $4i$
   - D. $-4i$
2. If $z = -2 + 5i$, what is $z + \bar{z}$?
   - A. −4
   - B. 0
   - C. $10i$
   - D. $-4 + 10i$
3. If $z = a + bi$ is in Quadrant III, then $-z$ is in which quadrant?
   - A. I
   - B. II
   - C. III
   - D. IV
4. What is the value of $|4 + 3i|$?
   - A. $\sqrt{7}$
   - B. 5
   - C. 7
   - D. 25
5. One solution of $ax^2 + bx + c = 0$ is $1 + 4i$. Which of the following is another solution?
   - A. $-1 - 4i$
   - B. $\sqrt{17}$
   - C. $-1 + 4i$
   - D. $1 - 4i$

Chapter Test — page 2 of 2

Open Response

6. Find the solutions of $x^4 - 16 = 0$ that meet each given condition.
   - a. in $\mathbb{R}$
   - b. in $\mathbb{C}$ but not in $\mathbb{R}$
7. Solve each equation over $\mathbb{C}$. Express your answer in the form $a + bi$, where a and b are real numbers.
   - a. $z + (-1 + 7i) = -4 - 5i$
   - b. $z \cdot (8 + 6i) = 1$
8. Use $z = 1 + \sqrt{3} \cdot i$ and $w = 2i$.
   - a. Find $z \cdot w$.
   - b. On the complex plane, graph z, w, and $z \cdot w$ as vectors.
   - c. Complete the table below.

	$a + bi$	Magnitude	Direction
z	$1 + \sqrt{3} \cdot i$		
w	$2i$		
$z \cdot w$			

9. A complex number z has magnitude 2 and direction 60°. Find the magnitude and direction of each power of z.
   - a. z^2
   - b. z^3
   - c. z^4
10. Find the magnitude and direction of all solutions to the equation $x^8 - 1 = 0$. If there are any solutions in Quadrant I, express them in the form $a + bi$, where a and b are real numbers.
11. If $-2 + i$ is a root of the polynomial $x^3 + 7x^2 + 17x + 15 = 0$, what is another root?

Also available: Form B

Chapter 4 Linear Algebra

This chapter introduces matrices both as shorthand (to record all the information in a system of linear equations) and as mathematical objects in their own right. Students learn to translate between systems of linear equations and matrix notation, and they use Gaussian Elimination to solve a system of equations. Then they learn to do other computations with matrices, exploring their algebraic structure and finding meaning for each calculation in context. Finally, students dip their toes in to the applications of linear algebra by looking at geometric transformations in the plane, transition matrices for dynamic systems, and probability matrices.

Chapter Overview

INVESTIGATION 4A, *Gaussian Elimination,* introduces students to matrices and to Gaussian Elimination.

INVESTIGATION 4B, *Matrix Algebra,* introduces students to definitions and properties of operations defined on matrices.

INVESTIGATION 4C, *Applications of Matrix Multiplication,* introduces students to some applications of linear algebra.

For more information on the investigations, see

- Chapter Road Map, p. 280
- Investigation Road Maps, pp. 282, 302, 354

PROJECT The Project near the end of the chapter is optional. You can assign the Project at any time during the chapter depending on how often and how long you feel students should work on it.

Pacing Suggestions and Materials

Investigation 4A *Gaussian Elimination*

DAY	LESSON	HOMEWORK
1	4.1 Getting Started Core: 1, 2, 3, 6 Optional: 4, 5	Core: 7, 9, 10, 13, 14, 15 Optional: 8, 12, 16, 17, 18, 19; Extension: 11
2	4.2 Solving Systems Systematically Core: 1, 3, 4, 5 Optional: 2	Core: 6, 7, 9, 12, 14, 15 Optional: 8, 13; Extension: 10, 11
3	4.3 Solving Again, in Matrix Form Core: 1, 2, 3, 4, 5, 6, 8a–b Optional: 7; Extension: 8c	Core: 9, 10, 11, 13, 14, 15, 19, 22, 26, 27 Optional: 12, 16, 18, 21, 23, 24, 25; Extension: 17, 20

Investigation 4B *Matrix Algebra*

DAY	LESSON	HOMEWORK
1	4.4 Getting Started Core: 1, 2, 3, 4, 5 Optional: 6	Core: 7, 8, 9, 10, 11, 12, 14 Optional: 13, 15a–b; Extension: 15c
2	4.5 Basic Matrix Operations Core: 1, 2, 4, 5, 6, 7 Optional: 3	Core: 8, 9, 10, 11, 12, 13, 14, 16, 17, 18, 19 Optional: 15, 20, 21
3	4.6 Dot Products Core: 1, 2, 4, 5, 7, 9, 10 Optional: 3, 6, 8	Core: 11, 12, 13, 14, 17, 18, 19, 20 Optional: 16a–c, 21, 22, 23, 24, 25, 26, 27, 28, 29; Extension: 15, 16d
4	4.7 Matrix Multiplication Core: 1, 2, 3, 4, 5, 6, 7, 13, 14 Optional: 8, 9, 10, 11, 12	Core: 15, 17, 18, 19, 21, 23, 25, 31, 32 Optional: 16, 20, 22, 24, 26, 27, 28, 30, 33, 34, 35, 36, 37, 38, 39, 40; Extension: 29
5	4.8 Matrix Inverses Core: 1, 3, 4, 5, 7, 8 Optional: 2, 6	Core: 9, 10, 12, 13, 15 Optional: 11, 14, 17, 18; Extension: 16
6	4.9 Matrix Properties Core: 2, 3, 4, 5, 6 Optional: 1, 7, 8	Core: 9, 10, 12, 14, 17, 18 Optional: 11, 13, 15, 16, 19, 20

NOTES	MATERIALS
	• graph paper • graphing calculators
	• graph paper • graphing calculators
	• CAS (recommended) • graphing calculators • Blackline Master 4.3

NOTES	MATERIALS
	• graphing calculators • spreadsheet software
	• graphing calculators • Blackline Master 4.5
	• graphing calculators
You may wish to spend two days on this lesson. See the Lesson Overview and Wrap Up.	• graph paper • graphing calculators • Blackline Masters 4.7A, 4.7B
	• graphing calculators
This lesson is optional.	• graphing calculators • Blackline Master 4.9

Mathematics Background

ALGORITHM Your students may find the task of using matrices to solve systems of linear equations the most natural and familiar material in this chapter. In CME Project *Algebra 1,* students learned the techniques of substitution and elimination to solve two linear equations in two unknowns. They apply these techniques to larger systems, but students soon see that it is difficult to keep track of the process and be certain of moving productively toward a solution.

Matrix notation eliminates a lot of writing by using position to associate a particular coefficient with a particular variable. This by itself it is not enough to make the task of solving a large system of linear equations practical. To do that, you need to systemize the solution process through the algorithm of Gaussian Elimination. This algorithm describes a small series of steps that you can apply to any system of linear equations, no matter how large. Gaussian Elimination removes human choice and intervention from the process, so although you may not reach a solution to your system in the most efficient way, you will always get to a solution by the end of the algorithm. If you follow the algorithm exactly, you cannot take a clever shortcut that eliminates a lot of steps, but you also cannot accidentally end up going around in a circle and not making progress. The other benefit to systematizing the solution process is that you can turn it over to a computer to do. If there is no choice involved, it is easy to program.

Matrix notation has other advantages. For example, once you have used Gaussian Elimination to get a coefficient matrix into row-reduced echelon form, you can tell how many solutions it will have for any column of constants. This process reveals an interesting property of systems of linear equations. They can have one solution, infinitely many solutions, or no solutions. That is it. The row-reduced echelon form tells you which of these options holds.

UTILITY As students learn to operate on matrices as mathematical objects in their own right, students make connections to real-world applications of matrix operations. They see situations in which they can use matrix addition and subtraction to calculate cost or profit in a table of values. They can also see situations in which it is necessary to multiply a matrix by a scalar. Students see how they can use dot product to calculate a total cost of a series of purchases, so dot product begins to make sense as a sensible thing to do. And finally, students see situations in which linear substitutions of variables require a definition of matrix multiplication they may not have expected.

Mathematicians could have chosen to define matrix multiplication in a more intuitive way (similar to the way in which they define matrix addition and subtraction). Take two matrices that are the same size. Their product is the new matrix that has as each of its entries the product of the corresponding entries from the factor matrices. However, that is not how mathematicians define matrix multiplication. Instead, it is a much more complex definition involving the dot products of rows from the left factor and columns from the right factor. Why? Because this version is how linear substitutions are solved.

Pacing Suggestions and Materials

Investigation 4C *Applications of Matrix Multiplication*

DAY	LESSON	HOMEWORK
1	4.10 Getting Started Core: 1, 2, 4, 5, 6, 8 Optional: 3, 7	Core: 9, 10, 11, 13 Optional: 12, 14, 15, 16
2	4.11 Geometric Transformations Core: 1, 2, 3, 5, 6, 7, 9, 12 Optional: 8, 10, 11; Extension: 4, 13, 14	Core: 15, 17, 18, 19, 22, 23, 29, 30 Optional: 16, 24, 25, 26, 27, 31 Extension: 20, 21, 28
3	4.12 Transition Matrices Core: 1, 3, 4, 5 Optional: 2, 6	Core: 7, 8, 9, 11, 12, 13, 14 Optional: 15; Extension: 10
4	4.13 Probability Models Core: 1, 2, 4, 5, 7 Optional: 3, 6	Core: 8, 13, 14, 15, 16 Optional: 9, 10; Extension: 11, 12

	NOTES	MATERIALS
		• CAS (recommended) • graph paper • graphing calculators • Blackline Master 4.10
		• CAS (recommended) • geometry software • graph paper • graphing calculators • paper for folding • Blackline Masters MC2, 4.11
		• graphing calculators
		• graphing calculators • Blackline Masters 4.13A, 4.13B

ALGEBRAIC STRUCTURE As with the complex numbers in Chapter 3, matrices have their own algebraic structure. This means that students need to investigate how these new mathematical objects and new operations interact. Is matrix addition commutative and associative? What is the zero matrix? What are the properties of dot product? Is $A \cdot B = B \cdot A$? How does multiplication by a scalar fit in with matrix addition and dot product?

It is especially interesting to investigate matrix multiplication because it is not commutative. In fact, unless A and B are the right size, one or both of the products AB and BA may not even be defined. Because matrix multiplication is not commutative, students have to pay attention to which side they multiply on for the first time, leading to the terms *pre-multiply* for multiplying on the left and *post-multiply* for multiplying on the right. Since it is possible to express a series of linear equations as a matrix equation $AX = b$, students could solve such an equation by multiplying each side on the left by the inverse of the matrix A. Because calculators can compute matrix inverses, using a calculater can provide a quick way to solve a system of equations without having to go through the process of Gaussian Elimination, but only certain matrices have inverses.

Developing Students' Mathematical Habits

Key mathematical habits in this chapter include:

EXTENSION Students see how to extend the ideas of substitution and elimination to make the algorithm for Gaussian Elimination. They can systematically apply the methods they used to solve small systems of two linear equations in two unknowns to solve larger systems.

LOGICAL REASONING By proving properties of matrix calculation, students develop their ability to reason logically and to think algebraically.

MAKING CONNECTIONS As students translate back and forth between real-world contexts and matrix calculations, they see why you define matrix operations as they are.

Chapter Vocabulary and Notation

The following list gives key vocabulary and notation used in the chapter. Selected new vocabulary and notation items are shown in boldface on the student page.

- absorbing state, p. 381
- augmentation line, p. 292
- augmented matrix, p. 292
- coefficient matrix, p. 292
- determinant, p. 340
- diagonal matrices, p. 351
- dimension, p. 292
- dot product, p. 315
- eigenvalue, p. 364
- eigenvector, p. 364
- elementary row operations, p. 295
- elimination, p. 286
- equation labels, p. 286
- Gaussian Elimination, p. 294
- identity matrix, I, pp. 296, 338
- indices, p. 310
- inverse, A^{-1}, p. 339
- linear combination, p. 323
- Markov chain, p. 384
- matrix, p. 292
- matrix multiplication, p. 324
- matrix transformation, p. 360
- n-tuple, p. 315
- probability transition matrix, p. 379
- row-reduced echelon form (rref), p. 295
- scalar multiplication, p. 309
- sequence, p. 355
- steady state, p. 373
- substitution, p. 286
- transition matrix, p. 373
- triangular form, p. 294
- triangular system, p. 290
- vector representation, p. 371
- zero matrix, 0, p. 329
- Zero Product Property, p. 347

Chapter Road Map

INVESTIGATION 4A, *Gaussian Elimination,* introduces students to matrices as a shorthand way to write a system of linear equations and to Gaussian Elimination as a systematic algorithm to solve such a system.

INVESTIGATION 4B, *Matrix Algebra,* has students work to understand the definitions of the various matrix operations and to reason about the properties of these operations.

INVESTIGATION 4C, *Applications of Matrix Multiplication,* has students explore some of the applications of linear algebra, including geometric transformations, modeling dynamic systems, and computing probabilities.

Linear Algebra

The World Wide Web consists of hundreds of millions of pages of content. New pages are added at any time without notice. How does anyone ever find anything he or she wants? One popular search engine determined that text matching alone would not be enough to help people find relevant information quickly. Its developers decided to rank pages by importance as well as using text matching techniques.

You can determine the importance of a Web page with an equation that counts contributions from every other page on the Web. To find the importance of a particular page, look at every page that links to it. Each linking page contributes the amount of its own importance divided by the number of pages it links to. This means that links from more important pages carry greater weight. To keep track of all these equations, one for every page, each with millions of terms, you can use a gigantic matrix. Then, every time a search engine crawls the Web to rebuild its index, it can use sophisticated linear algebra techniques to recalculate the matrix.

Vocabulary and Notation

- absorbing state
- determinant
- dimension
- dot product
- elimination
- Gaussian Elimination
- identity matrix, I
- inverse, A^{-1}
- linear combination
- matrix
- matrix multiplication
- matrix transformation
- n-tuple
- probability transition matrix
- row-reduced echelon form (rref)
- scalar multiplication
- steady state
- substitution
- transition matrix
- zero matrix, 0

Chapter Technology

CME Project *Algebra 2* assumes that each student has access to a graphing calculator. It also recommends access to a computer algebra system (CAS).

Support for the use of technology is available in the TI-Nspire™ Technology Handbook. See p. 778.

A list of technology used with important concepts in this chapter appears below. Students will need access to the functionality listed to develop complete understanding of these topics.

Computer Algebra System

LESSON 4.3 Input matrices and find row-reduced echelon form, pp. 296, 300. Find the unique polynomial of degree 3 or less that passes through four given points, p. 299.

Function-Modeling Language

LESSON 4.10 Model a sequence, p. 355. Model rental car inventories, p. 357.

Geometry Software

LESSON 4.11 Experiment with transformations, p. 360.

Graphing Calculator

LESSON 4.3 Input matrices and find row-reduced echelon form, pp. 296, 300. Find the unique polynomial of degree 3 or less that passes through four given points, p. 299.

LESSON 4.7 Perform matrix and n-tuple operations, p. 328. Multiply matrices, p. 330.

LESSON 4.8 Find matrix inverses and solve matrix equations, p. 339.

Investigation Overview

In this investigation, students begin by solving systems of two equations in two unknowns. They review the solution techniques of substitution and elimination that they learned in CME Project *Algebra 1*. Then they extend this work to solve systems of three equations in three unknowns, eventually developing and describing ways to solve these systems systematically. Along the way, they realize that the variables in these equations do not really have an effect on the solution techniques except as identifiers for the coefficients. If students use position to keep track of which coefficient goes along with which variable, they will have much less writing to do and will be able to further systematize their work. The last lesson of this investigation describes Gaussian Elimination, which reduces the solution of a system of equations into a series of steps that students can program into a computer. Students learn to use the technique by hand as well as with technology so that they can better understand the results they get.

You may wish to assign Questions 1–3 for students to think and write about during the investigation.

Learning Goals

- Solve a system of three equations in three unknowns.
- Write a system of linear equations in matrix form or translate a matrix into a system of equations.
- Describe and apply the process of Gaussian Elimination and apply it both by hand and with technology to solve a system.

Habits and Skills

- Connect the results from substitution and elimination methods and show that the methods are equivalent.
- Strategize to solve a system of equations systematically.
- Reason about how to describe an algorithm generally as a series of steps that you can apply to any situation.

Investigation 4A

Gaussian Elimination

In *Gaussian Elimination*, you will review several methods for solving systems of equations. You will also learn about matrices and how to use them to solve systems of equations.

By the end of this investigation, you will be able to answer questions like these.

1. Why is it possible to solve systems of linear equations in matrix form?
2. What is the process of Gaussian Elimination?
3. Find x, y, and z such that

$$\begin{aligned} 4x - y + 4z &= 1 \\ 2x - y + 8z &= 11 \\ 2x - 2y + 4z &= 0 \end{aligned}$$

You will learn how to

- solve a system of three equations in three unknowns
- write a system of linear equations in matrix form or translate a matrix into a system of equations
- describe and apply the process of Gaussian Elimination and apply it both by hand and with technology to solve a system

You will develop these habits and skills:

- Connect the results from substitution and elimination methods and show that the methods are equivalent.
- Strategize to solve a system of equations systematically.
- Reason about how to describe an algorithm generally as a series of steps that you can apply to any situation.

The scoreboard shows the score of the baseball game in matrix form.

Investigation Road Map

LESSON 4.1, *Getting Started,* has students solve systems of two equations in two unknowns by using what they remember from CME Project *Algebra 1*. Two key techniques they review are substitution and elimination. They begin to think about how to extend the solution process to systems involving more equations and more unknowns.

LESSON 4.2, *Solving Systems Systematically,* has students begin to work formally with systems of three equations in three unknowns and to strategize about ways to solve these systems productively, making progress toward a solution rather than going in circles. Students compare the techniques of substitution and elimination.

LESSON 4.3, *Solving Again, in Matrix Form,* has students represent a system of equations with an augmented matrix and operate directly on the matrix in order to solve the system through Gaussian Elimination.

4.1 Getting Started

Activating Prior Knowledge
Exploring New Ideas

In your first-year algebra course, you learned several ways to solve a system of equations.

For You to Explore

1. Solve the following system in at least two ways.

$$x + y = 4$$
$$2x - y = -1$$

2. Solve the following system.

$$2x + y = 1$$
$$3x + 2y = 1$$

3. Find the point where the lines given by the following equations intersect.

$$y = 3x + 2$$
$$y = -2x + 1$$

4. Find an x-value for which these two functions have the same output.

$$f(x) = 3x + 2$$
$$g(x) = -2x + 1$$

5. In Chapter 2, you learned how to use Lagrange Interpolation to find a polynomial that fits a set of data points. Find a polynomial $p(x)$ with a graph that passes through the points $(0, 1)$, $(1, -1)$, and $(3, 1)$.

6. Another way to find a polynomial with a graph that passes through the points $(0, 1)$, $(1, -1)$, and $(3, 1)$ is to first realize that the highest-degree polynomial you need to fit these three points is a quadratic. Then you can begin with a general form of a quadratic function, $q(x) = ax^2 + bx + c$. Use the data points to write a system of equations for finding the coefficients a, b, and c.
   a. Explain why $q(3) = 1$ implies that $9a + 3b + c = 1$.
   b. Find two more equations involving a, b, and c using the other data points.
   c. Find an equation for the polynomial.

Habits of Mind

Detect the key characterisitics. Why do three points determine a quadratic?

Answers

For You to Explore

1. $x = 1, y = 3$
2. $x = 1, y = -1$
3. $\left(-\frac{1}{5}, \frac{7}{5}\right)$
4. $x = -\frac{1}{5}$
5. $p(x) = x^2 - 3x + 1$
6. a. If $q(x) = ax^2 + bx + c$, then $q(3) = 9a + 3b + c$. Since $q(3) = 1$, then $9a + 3b + c = 1$.
   b. $q(0) = 1$, so $c = 1$; $q(1) = -1$ so $a + b + c = -1$.
   c. $a = 1, b = -3, c = 1$ so $q(x) = x^2 - 3x + 1$.

Lesson Overview

GOAL

- Warm up to the ideas of the investigation.

This lesson introduces systems of linear equations in more than two variables. It gives your students an opportunity to review the methods they used for two equations in two unknowns in CME Project *Algebra 1,* while they also review some contexts in which solving systems of equations is useful. You will get an opportunity to assess how much students have retained and how easily they come up with ideas for handling more equations and variables. The lesson also introduces, without fanfare, the idea of triangular systems of equations—the key intermediate stage for solving more general systems. Finally, this lesson gives some hints about what is involved when a system does not have a unique solution, for instance, when there are more variables than equations.

FOR YOU TO EXPLORE
- Core: 1, 2, 3, 6
- Optional: 4, 5

MATERIALS
- graph paper
- graphing calculators

HOMEWORK
- Core: 7, 9, 10, 13, 14, 15
- Optional: 8, 12, 16, 17, 18, 19
- Extension: 11

Launch

Start right in with the For You to Explore problems.

Explore

The most important goal of this lesson is to bring your students back up to speed on what they once knew about solving systems of two linear equations in two unknowns. As students are working, see if you can spot any areas that might require a quick review with the whole class.

For You to Explore

PROBLEM 3 This geometry problem reduces to the same sort of algebraic system as the previous problems.

You can also solve the problem by graphing the two lines. This will give only an approximate answer, but it is an excellent check on the algebra.

PROBLEM 4 This is Problem 3 in disguise. Recognizing different representations of the same underlying situation is a key mathematical skill. Looking for different representations is an important habit of mind.

PROBLEM 6 The point to this problem is that students can solve fitting a quadratic to data by turning it into a question of solving three linear equations in three unknowns. For now, this is a harder way for your students to do it. However, once students learn how to solve standard linear systems with technology, this approach is one of the standard ways to fit polynomials to data.

What other approaches did your students come up with? Did they use tables? Did anyone notice that because the y-values for $x = 0$ and $x = 3$ are the same, that $x = \frac{3}{2}$ must be the axis of symmetry? They use this fact to write the equation in the form $y = \left(x - \frac{3}{2}\right)^2 + d$ and then solve for d to find the equation of the parabola.

Wrap Up

The key goal is for students to complete this initial set of problems with a clear reconstruction of the methods they used to solve two equations in two unknowns, specifically substitution and elimination. So, have a thorough discussion of Problems 1 and 2.

Exercises

HOMEWORK

- Core: 7, 9, 10, 13, 14, 15
- Optional: 8, 12, 16, 17, 18, 19
- Extension: 11

On Your Own

EXERCISE 8 The point of this exercise is that neither line is described in the "right" format for solving the problem using a system of equations.

EXERCISE 9 Students may want to find the line by other methods they know, but ask them to try reducing the situation to a system of linear equations.

EXERCISE 10 is the main example problem of the next section. Having students struggle with it now, before they have any systematic methods, may be valuable. For now, students who solve it can try to identify a method in what they have done, and you can try to elicit general solution principles from them.

EXERCISE 11 For part (e), all that is actually shown by these manipulations is that the values of (x, y, z) displayed above are the only candidates for solutions. In a real problem situation, some of these solutions might be extraneous. Indeed, this has been a (deliberate) failing of all the discussion and solutions so far. Later students see how all steps needed to solve linear systems are reversible; as long as no arithmetic mistakes are made, all solutions found by working forward are guaranteed to be correct.

Exercises *Practicing Habits of Mind*

On Your Own

7. Solve the following system.

$$2x + 3y = 1$$
$$\frac{1}{2}x + \frac{1}{3}y = 1$$

8. Find the point of intersection of the line with equation $\frac{y-1}{x-1} = 2$ and the line with slope -1 and x-intercept 3.

Remember...

If a line has x-intercept a, that means that the graph of the line intersects the x-axis at the point $(a, 0)$.

9. The simplest graph that goes through two points is a line. You know many ways to find an equation for this line. Here is a technique that uses a system of equations. Suppose the two points are (1, 4) and (3, 2). The polynomial must be of the form $p(x) = ax + b$. Use the two points to find two equations in a and b. Then solve them to find the polynomial.

10. Solve the following system.

$$x + y + z = 2$$
$$2x - y + z = 5$$
$$x + 2y + 3z = 5$$

Habits of Mind

Use a consistent process. Exercise 9 is like Problem 6. To understand a method, one good habit is to apply it in simpler situations.

11. Take It Further The system below has more unknowns than equations. However, you can still use the methods for solving two equations in two unknowns to find all the solutions.

$$x + 2y + 3z = 4$$
$$2x + y - z = -2$$

a. Solve the first equation for x and substitute into the second equation, eliminating x.

b. Eliminate x from the second equation another way: by subtracting a multiple of the first equation.

c. After using either method, solve the new second equation for y in terms of z.

d. Substitute your result from part (c) into the original first equation to eliminate y. Then express x in terms of z.

e. Explain why there is one solution (x, y, z) of the original system of equations for each value of z.

The solutions to part (e) form a *one-parameter family*. You can express all the solutions in terms of the single variable z. This gives you a way to manage an infinite set of solutions.

Answers

Exercises

7. $x = \frac{16}{5}, y = -\frac{9}{5}$

8. $\left(\frac{4}{3}, \frac{5}{3}\right)$

9. $p(1) = 4$ so $a + b = 4$; $p(3) = 2$ so $3a + b = 2$; $a = -1$ and $b = 5$ so $p(x) = -x + 5$.

10. $(1, -1, 2)$

11. a. $x = 4 - 2y - 3z$; $-3y - 7z = -10$

b. $-3y - 7z = -10$

c. $y = \frac{10-7z}{3}$

d. $x = -\frac{8}{3} + \frac{5}{3}z$

e. $(x, y, z) = \left(-\frac{8}{3} + \frac{5}{3}z, \frac{10-7z}{3}, z\right)$, so each value of z generates exactly one value of the ordered triple (x, y, z).

12. Solve each system. What new situations arise? How would you describe each solution?

a. $x + 2y = 3$
$2x + 4y = 6$

b. $x + 2y = 3$
$2x + 4y = 7$

Habits of Mind

Consider more than one strategy. Along with the algebraic solution methods you have been reviewing, you might want to solve these systems graphically, too.

Maintain Your Skills

Solve each system.

13. $x + 2y + 3z = 1$
$3y - z = 4$
$2z = -2$

14. $2x - 3y + 5z - 2t = 9$
$5y - z + 3t = 1$
$7z - t = 3$
$2t = 8$

15. 4×4 systems (four equations in four unknowns) are usually quite difficult to solve by hand, but the one in Exercise 14 is not. Explain.

Solve each system.

16. $2x = 4$
$x - y = 3$
$-x + 2y + z = 2$

17. $x + 2z = 4$
$3z = -3$
$x + 2y - z = 1$

18. Consider the following system.

$$x + 2y + 3z = 4$$
$$-3y - 7z = -10$$

You can rewrite it with z's on the right side.

$$x + 2y = 4 - 3z$$
$$-3y = -10 + 7z$$

a. What does this new system now have in common with other Maintain Your Skills exercises?

b. Use this similarity to solve for x and y in terms of z.

19. Solve the following system.

$$x - 2y + z = 7$$
$$2x - y + 4z = 17$$
$$3x - 2y + 2z = 14$$

Go Online
Video Tutor
PHSchool.com
Web Code: bfe-0775

12. a. The two equations represent the same line, so any point on $x + 2y = 3$ is a solution to the system.

b. The two equations represent parallel lines, so the system has no solution.

13. (2, 1, −1)

14. (3, −2, 1, 4)

15. Answers may vary. Sample: The fourth equation is easily solved, giving a system of three equations and three unknowns.

16. (2, −1, 6)

17. (6, −3, −1)

18. a. The new system is in "triangular form" on the left side.

b. $x = -\frac{8}{3} + \frac{5}{3}z$, $y = \frac{10}{3} - \frac{7}{3}z$

19. (2, −1, 3)

Maintain Your Skills

EXERCISES 13 AND 14 The main idea of this set of exercises is *triangular form.* The nice thing about all linear systems in triangular form is that students can solve them easily by a process called *backsubstitution.* The last variable is in an equation by itself, so you can immediately solve for it. Then substitute its value into the next to last equation, and you can solve for the next to last variable. And so on. The students do not reflect on why triangular form is so useful until Exercise 14.

The backsubstitution method does not require the last variable (that is, the rightmost) to be the one you solve for first. (See Exercises 16 and 17.) However, the way the general solution method is usually carried out leads to exactly the triangular form you see in Exercise 13. This exercise reappears as Exercise 14 in Lesson 4.2. There students solve the system by adding and subtracting equations instead of by substitution, in preparation for the backsubstitution part of Gaussian Elimination.

EXERCISE 14 Three variables, four variables, five variables . . . if a system is triangular, solving it does not really get more difficult.

Like Exercise 13, this exercise also reappears later as preparation for Gaussian Elimination. (See Exercise 15 in Lesson 4.2.)

EXERCISE 16 is similar to triangular form, but the "triangle" is arranged differently.

EXERCISE 17 is similar to triangular form in that one equation has one variable, another has two variables, and the third has all three. If you rewrite the equations with the variables in the order *y, x, z,* and then change the order among the equations, the triangle appears, just as in the first few exercises in this exercise set.

EXERCISE 18 is just Exercise 11, picked up after *x* was eliminated from the second equation. It is reformatted to reveal the triangular form on the left-hand side. It turns out that you can solve all linear systems by making use of triangular form, but sometimes one or more variables have to be "free." If a variable is "free," that means that it can take on any value. Such variables are often put on the right-hand side of a system.

EXERCISE 19 The next lesson is about how to solve this kind of linear system without going around in circles.

Lesson Overview

GOAL

- Solve a system of three equations in three unknowns.

The title says it all: there is a systematic method for solving systems of linear equations, and following this method avoids a lot of flailing around.

The text introduces the method in two stages. In this lesson, students extend the substitution and elimination approaches from CME Project *Algebra 1* to larger systems of equations. The key technique that makes either method work in larger systems is to pick one variable and eliminate it from all but one of the equations. This gives a reduced system with one fewer variable and one fewer equation. This method is often the best to use by hand and should seem like a natural extension for your students.

In the next lesson students go a step further and learn how to carry out solutions in matrix form, following the process of Gaussian Elimination.

For the most part, students see systems where there are as many equations as unknowns and for which there is a unique solution. However, some of the exercises begin to explore the more general situation—more than one solution, no solutions, or systems with a different number of equations than unknowns.

CHECK YOUR UNDERSTANDING
- Core: 1, 3, 4, 5
- Optional: 2

MATERIALS
- graph paper
- graphing calculators

HOMEWORK
- Core: 6, 7, 9, 12, 14, 15
- Optional: 8, 13
- Extension: 10, 11

VOCABULARY
- elimination
- equation labels
- substitution
- triangular system

Launch

Your students should be well primed from the Getting Started lesson to launch right into systems of three equations in three unknowns. Have them go right to work on the 3×3 system that is the main example of the lesson.

4.2 Solving Systems Systematically

Exercise 10 in Lesson 4.1 asked you to solve the system

$$x + y + z = 2 \quad (1)$$

$$2x - y + z = 5 \quad (2)$$

$$x + 2y + 3z = 5 \quad (3)$$

The numbers in parentheses are equation labels. They are helpful when you want to discuss several equations at once, or describe operations involving two equations. Remember to distinguish the number 2 from the equation (2).

This is a 3×3 system—three linear equations in three unknowns. It is natural to try the methods you used on two equations in two unknowns. The two main methods were *substitution* and *elimination.* In **substitution,** you solve one equation for one variable and substitute that solution into the other equation. Then you have an equation in the other variable alone, which you can solve. In **elimination,** you add or subtract the two equations so that one variable cancels out, again resulting in an equation in the other variable alone.

In a 3×3 system, both methods allow many more choices. Say you solve Equation (1) for x and substitute the result into (2). That still gives an equation in two unknowns, y and z, so what do you do next? You can do another substitution, but if you are not careful you may go in circles. The way to succeed is to substitute the same expression for x into the third equation. That gives you two equations in the same two unknowns, which you know how to solve.

Habits of Mind

Make strategic choices. Going from three equations in three unknowns to two equations in two unknowns is an instance of *reducing a problem to a simpler case.*

Specifically, solving (1) for x gives

$$x = 2 - y - z \quad (4)$$

Substituting into (2) gives

$$2(2 - y - z) - y + z = 5$$

$$4 - 2y - 2z - y + z = 5$$

$$-3y - z = 1$$

Substituting (4) into (3) gives

$$(2 - y - z) + 2y + 3z = 5$$

$$2 + y + 2z = 5$$

$$y + 2z = 3$$

Substitution has given you a 2×2 system.

$$-3y - z = 1$$

$$y + 2z = 3$$

For You to Do

1. Solve the 2×2 system above.

Once you solve the 2×2 system, substitute the values of y and z into (4) to find x. In this problem, the final result is $x = 1,\ y = -1$, and $z = 2$.

You can also write $(x, y, z) = (1, -1, 2)$.

Minds in Action episode 14

Sasha and Derman are trying to solve the same system (1)–(3) using the elimination method.

Sasha I think this will be easiest if we follow the method just shown as closely as possible.

Derman How can it be close? In elimination, you add and subtract equations, you don't substitute.

Sasha Right, but I mean let's use the same equations in the same order. I think that's our best chance to get down to two equations in y and z.

Derman I don't think it would have to be y and z, but yeah, let's do that. In the substitution method, we solved Equation (1) for x and substituted the result into Equations (2) and (3).

Sasha So let's try adding or subtracting (1) from (2) and (1) from (3) to eliminate x twice.

Derman But we've got to eliminate $2x$ from (2).

Sasha So let's multiply (1) by 2 and then subtract the result from (2).

$$\begin{array}{r} 2x - y + z = 5 \\ \underline{(-)2x + 2y + 2z = 4} \\ -3y - z = 1 \end{array}$$

Derman It's easier to eliminate x from (3)—just subtract (1) as it is.

$$\begin{array}{r} x + 2y + 3z = 5 \\ \underline{(-)x + y + z = 2} \\ y + 2z = 3 \end{array}$$

Derman So the reduced system we get is

$$-3y - z = 1$$
$$y + 2z = 3$$

It's the same as before. Hmm.

Sasha That's good. We'll get the same solution as before, and we should.

Derman But lots of 2×2 systems have the same solution $y = -1,\ z = 2$. Do the two methods always give the same reduced system?

Answers

For You to Do

1. $y = -1, z = 2$

Explore

For You to Do

Students will solve this problem in lots of orders, probably preferring substitution to elimination, especially since the text has so far shown the substitution method only. When you get to Gaussian Elimination you will see that the formal version of the algorithm always uses elimination, not substitution, and always eliminates variables from left to right except when that is impossible.

Minds in Action

As Derman notes, elimination does not at first seem much like substitution, but Sasha figures out how they correspond. You work with the same pairs of equations in the same order, whether you are doing elimination or substitution.

The elimination method uses addition and subtraction, but as Sasha notes, sometimes you have to multiply an equation first. (Or, you might have to divide.)

Note the notation here. A minus sign in parentheses applies to the whole equation, not just to the closest term. Thus you "subtract" the whole equation $2x + 2y + 2z = 4$ from the equation $2x - y + z = 5$.

Wrap Up

The first few Check Your Understanding exercises give students practice using the techniques of this section—elimination especially, but also substitution—in a context where they already know the answers. The exercises also make the point that there is freedom to solve for the variables in different orders.

Make sure that students see the key point: the substitution and elimination methods they learned for 2×2 systems extend easily to 3×3 systems, so long as they start by removing the same variable from all but one of the equations. Perhaps you can make this clear by picking one of the exercises in the Check Your Understanding set and pointing out specifically how this approach was used.

Assessment Resources

Lesson Quiz 4.2

1. Solve the following system by elimination.

$$-2x + 4y - z = 7$$
$$5x - 3y + 2z = -3$$
$$x + 3y - 7z = 14$$

2. Solve the following system by substitution.

$$-2x + y - z = -1$$
$$3x - 2y + z = 0$$
$$-8z = 4x$$

3. Try using both substitution and elimination to solve the following system. What happens?

$$3x - y = 5$$
$$-6x + 2y = 9$$

For Discussion

2. Think about Derman's question. Can you explain why the substitution and elimination methods ended up with the same 2×2 reduced system? Look carefully at the work shown in the text for solving the system (1)–(3).

This lesson has been about extending the methods you know for solving two equations in two unknowns to larger systems. It is time to put the pieces together and do one example from start to finish.

Example

Problem Solve the following system.

$$x - y + z = 0 \qquad (5)$$
$$x + y + 2z = 1 \qquad (6)$$
$$-x + 2y - 3z = 3 \qquad (7)$$

Solution This solution uses the elimination method. Subtract (5) from (6) and add (5) to (7). You get

$$2y + z = 1 \qquad (8)$$
$$y - 2z = 3 \qquad (9)$$

Now subtract (9) multiplied by 2 from (8).

$$5z = -5$$

So $z = -1$. Substitute this value into (9).

$$y + 2 = 3 \quad \text{so} \quad y = 1$$

Substituting into (8) would also work.

Now substitute the y- and z-values into any one of the original equations, for example (5).

$$x - 1 - 1 = 0 \quad \text{so} \quad x = 2$$

Conclusion: $(x, y, z) = (2, 1, -1)$

You can describe this process by saying that you solved the system by eliminating x first and then y.

Answers

For Discussion

2. Answers may vary. Sample: Both methods of substitution and elimination give equations that are equivalent to the original equations.

Exercises *Practicing Habits of Mind*

Check Your Understanding

Consider the system (5)–(7) from the Example.

1. Solve the system again, this time eliminating y first by adding or subtracting (5) from (6) and (5) from (7).
2. Solve the system again, this time eliminating z first.
3. Solve the system again, this time by the substitution method. Solve for x from (5) and substitute into the other equations. Do you get the same 2×2 reduced system as in the solution by elimination in the Example?
4. Solve the system again, this time by the substitution method. Solve for y from (5) and substitute into the other equations. Do you get the same 2×2 reduced system as in Exercise 1? Can you explain why?
5. A quadratic function $f(x) = ax^2 + bx + c$ passes through the points (1, 1), (2, 3), and (3, 6). Find a, b, and c.

On Your Own

6. **Standardized Test Prep** Which is the solution to the system of equations at the right?

$$x - 3y + 6z = 2$$
$$-2x + 2y + z = 9$$
$$-x + 3y - 7z = -3$$

A. $(-7, 1, 2)$ **B.** $(-7.75, -3.25, 0)$
C. $(-4, 0, 1)$ **D.** $(5, 7.8, 3.4)$

7. Consider the 4×4 system at the right.

$$x + y + z - w = -1$$
$$x + y - z + w = 0$$
$$x - y + z + w = 1$$
$$-x + y + z + w = 2$$

a. Reduce this system to a 3×3 system by elimination, eliminating x.
b. Reduce this system to a 3×3 system by substitution, again eliminating x.
c. Solve the 3×3 system you got in part (a).
d. Solve the original 4×4 system.

You may have gotten different systems for parts (a) and (b). Do the two systems have the same solution?

8. Solve the 4×4 system at the right.

$$u + 2x - y + z = 1$$
$$x + y + z = 2$$
$$2x - y + z = 5$$
$$x + 2y + 3z = 5$$

Exercises

1–4. $(2, 1, -1)$

5. $a = \frac{1}{2}, b = \frac{1}{2}, c = 0$

6. C

7. a. Answers may vary. Sample: $-2z + 2w = 1$, $-2y + 2w = 2$, $2y + 2z = 1$
b. Answers may vary. Sample: $2y + 2z = 1$, $2y + 2w = 2$, $2z + 2w = 3$
c. $\left(0, \frac{1}{2}, 1\right)$
d. $\left(-\frac{1}{2}, 0, \frac{1}{2}, 1\right)$

8. $(-4, 1, -1, 2)$

Exercises

HOMEWORK
- Core: 6, 7, 9, 12, 14, 15
- Optional: 8, 13
- Extension: 10, 11

Check Your Understanding

EXERCISES 3 AND 4 If you would like students to reflect on why the elimination and substitution methods give the same reduced system, you can assign Exercise 4.

EXERCISE 4 Your students may have different ways to explain why substitution and elimination always lead to the same equations. Have them share their strategies with the class.

EXERCISE 5 Maybe the formula is familiar if students use n instead of x. Have they seen the formula for the sum $1 + 2 + \cdots + n$?

In any event, they will do this exercise again with Gaussian Elimination in Exercise 18 in Lesson 4.3.

On Your Own

EXERCISE 7 is the first example of a 4×4 system that is not in triangular form, but the numbers are such that it is not that bad to do by hand.

As for the sidenote, the 3×3 systems in (a) and (b) will always have the same solution (if the algebra is done right) because any solution must give the y, z, w values of the (in this case unique) solution to the original 4×4 system.

EXERCISE 8 If you strip off the first equation (the only one that contains u), you have Sasha and Derman's problem. So, you already know that $x = 1$, $y = -1$, and $z = 2$. Substitute these values in the first equation to get $u = -4$.

Of course, students may not notice that they have solved the 3×3 system before, which is fine; they get good practice solving it. Since u appears only in the first equation, there is no work to reduce to a 3×3 system.

EXERCISE 9 If your students have not yet seen equations or systems of equations with no solutions, then it is well worth having a discussion about it. The usual way to determine that there is no solution is to deduce a contradiction, such as $0 = -2$.

Maintain Your Skills

EXERCISE 12 Students might be able to see that (0, 0, 0) is a solution just by looking at the equations. But they will need to do the work to show that it is the only solution.

This exercise takes more setup to rewrite it in the form for the elimination method.

EXERCISE 13 In both parts, the solution is the same as for Sasha and Derman, $x = 1$, $y = -1$, $z = 2$. Just as adding and subtracting equations can lead to solutions, so can they lead to related systems with the same solutions. Challenge students to figure out how these systems came from Sasha and Derman's original system.

Additional Resources

PRINT RESOURCES
- Solution Manual
- Practice Workbook
- Assessment Resources
- Teaching Resources

TECHNOLOGY
- Interactive Textbook
- TeacherExpress CD-ROM
- ExamView CD-ROM
- PHSchool.com

Additional Practice

1. Use elimination to solve the following system.

$$\begin{aligned} 2x - 3y &= 4 \\ 3x + y &= 6 \end{aligned}$$

2. Use substitution to solve the following system.

$$\begin{aligned} 2x + y - z &= 5 \\ -3y + z &= 3 \\ 2z &= -6 \end{aligned}$$

3. Solve the following system.

$$\begin{aligned} x &= 2y + z \\ y &= 2z + x \\ z &= 2x + y \end{aligned}$$

4. Solve the following system using addition and subtraction.

$$\begin{aligned} x - y + 2z - w &= 6 \\ -3y + z - 2w &= 8 \\ 2z - w &= 1 \\ 3w &= 9 \end{aligned}$$

5. Consider the system below.

$$\begin{aligned} -x + y + z + w &= 1 \\ x - y + z + w &= 2 \\ x + y - z + w &= 0 \\ x + y + z - w &= -1 \end{aligned}$$

a. Reduce this system to a 3×3 system by elimination, eliminating x.
b. Reduce this system to a 3×3 system by substitution, again eliminating x.
c. Solve the 3×3 system you got in part (a).
d. Solve the original 4×4 system.

6. A quadratic function $f(x) = ax^2 + bx + c$ passes through the points $(0, -3)$, $(-1, -6)$, and $(2, -9)$. Find a, b, and c.

7. Try using both substitution and elimination to solve the following system. What happens?

$$\begin{aligned} 3x - y &= 5 \\ -6x + 2y &= 9 \end{aligned}$$

Practice: For Lesson 4.2, assign Exercises 1–7.

9. Try using both substitution and elimination to solve the following system. What happens?

$$\begin{aligned} x + 2y &= 3 \\ 2x + 4y &= 4 \end{aligned}$$

10. Take It Further Consider this system.

$$\begin{aligned} x + 2y + z &= 2 \\ 2x + 4y + 3z &= 5 \end{aligned}$$

The last time you had two equations in three unknowns (see Lesson 4.1, Exercise 18), there was one solution for every value of z. What happens for this system?

11. Take It Further You write the equation for the graph of a circle in the form $(x - a)^2 + (y - b)^2 = r^2$, where (a, b) is the center and r is the radius.

a. By solving a system of equations, find the center and radius of the circle that goes through the points $(-4, 0)$, $(0, 2)$, and $(4, 0)$.

b. Find the center and radius using geometric methods.

Go Online PHSchool.com
For additional practice, go to **Web Code:** bfa-0402

These equations are not linear equations, but the method of adding and subtracting equations still works.

Maintain Your Skills

12. Solve this system.

$$\begin{aligned} x &= y + z \\ y &= x + z \\ z &= x + y \end{aligned}$$

13. Solve each system. Compare the solutions to the ones from the dialog.

a.
$$\begin{aligned} x + y + z &= 2 \\ 2x - y + z &= 5 \\ 3x + y + 4z &= 10 \end{aligned}$$

b.
$$\begin{aligned} x + y + z &= 2 \\ 2x - y + z &= 5 \\ 2x + 3y + 4z &= 7 \end{aligned}$$

14. In Exercise 13 from Lesson 4.1, you solved the following system.

$$\begin{aligned} x + 2y + 3z &= 1 \\ 3y - z &= 4 \\ 2z &= -2 \end{aligned}$$

The natural way to solve such a triangular system is to solve for z and then substitute. However, you have learned that adding and subtracting equations can accomplish the same thing as substitution. Solve this system again without any substitutions.

15. Solve this system using addition and subtraction.

$$\begin{aligned} 2x - 3y + 5z - 2t &= 9 \\ 5y - z + 3t &= 1 \\ 7z - t &= 3 \\ 2t &= 8 \end{aligned}$$

It is more work to add and subtract equations, but there is a reason for doing it. Stay tuned for the next lesson.

Answers

9. The system has no solution.

10. Answers may vary. Sample: Every triple of the form $(1 - 2y, y, 1)$ is a solution.

11. a. center $(0, -3)$; radius 5
b. center $(0, -3)$, radius 5

12. $(0, 0, 0)$

13. a. $(1, -1, 2)$
b. $(1, -1, 2)$
Answers may vary. Sample: The first two equations are the same, and the third equations are different 3-variable equations that contain the triple $(1, -1, 2)$.

14. $(2, 1, -1)$

15. $(x, y, z, t) = (3, -2, 1, 4)$

4.3 Solving Again, in Matrix Form

Substitution and elimination are effectively the same—if you apply them to the equations in the same order, you get the same key equations along the way. So, is there any reason to recommend one method over the other?

For large systems, it is much easier to implement elimination. You can describe elimination as a consistent series of steps that you always apply in the same order.

You can more easily implement elimination methods with technology.

In the elimination method, you can consistently put each variable in the same place. For instance, you can always make the x's be first and the y's second. Also, the variables play almost no role! Only the coefficients and the constants on the right side of the equations change. The only role the variables play is as labels for the coefficients. For instance, if you subtract $2x + 4y = 6$ from $2x + 5y = 2$, the y's tell you that the 4 and the 5 both belong to the same variable and you can subtract them from each other.

But if the variables are always in the same place, then the position alone determines which coefficient goes with which variable. You do not need to write the variables at all! For instance, consider again Sasha and Derman's old friend.

$$x + y + z = 2 \quad (1)$$

$$2x - y + z = 5 \quad (2)$$

$$x + 2y + 3z = 5 \quad (3)$$

You can instead write

$$A = \left(\begin{array}{ccc|c} 1 & 1 & 1 & 2 \\ 2 & -1 & 1 & 5 \\ 1 & 2 & 3 & 5 \end{array}\right)$$

Now, instead of subtracting 2 times (1) from (2), multiply row 1 of A by 2 and subtract the result from row 2, entry by entry. Instead of writing a new system of equations with a new second equation, write a new matrix A' with a new second row.

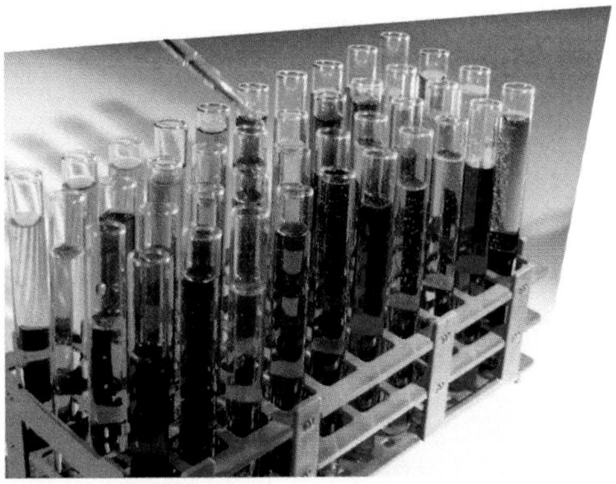

Sometimes it makes sense to record data from experiments in matrix form.

Lesson Overview

GOALS

- Write a system of linear equations in matrix form or translate a matrix into a system of equations.
- Describe and apply the process of Gaussian Elimination and apply it both by hand and with technology to solve a system.

This lesson introduces Gaussian Elimination, in which the equations are represented in matrix form and then one variable at a time is eliminated until there is only one left. At that point backsubstitution determines the other variables. This method is really the same as the elimination method in Lesson 4.2, but it is usually called *Gaussian Elimination* when you write it in matrix form.

Several aspects of this method may seem foreign, for instance, the insistence that you work with a full set of equations at each stage. However, this is necessary in order for the systems to be equivalent—no solutions are gained or lost in the solution process.

You can do Gaussian Elimination on calculators that handle matrices, using the rref command. Students should do the exercises in this section mostly by hand, to get a feel for what is going on.

CHECK YOUR UNDERSTANDING

- Core: 1, 2, 3, 4, 5, 6, 8a–b
- Optional: 7
- Extension: 8c

MATERIALS

- CAS (recommended)
- graphing calculators
- Blackline Master 4.3

HOMEWORK

- Core: 9, 10, 11, 13, 14, 15, 19, 22, 26, 27
- Optional: 12, 16, 18, 21, 23, 24, 25
- Extension: 17, 20

VOCABULARY

- augmentation line
- augmented matrix
- coefficient matrix
- dimension
- elementary row operations
- Gaussian Elimination
- identity matrix, *I*
- matrix
- row-reduced echelon form (rref)
- triangular form

Launch

Begin by talking about the key idea necessary for solving equations in matrix form. You can translate equations into matrices because the variables do not really play a part in the solution strategy. The variables serve only as identifiers of the coefficients, and as long as you keep all of the coefficients for any one variable in the same column as you calculate, you do not need to write the variable at all.

Show how to write Sasha and Derman's system as an augmented matrix. Then show what it looks like when you operate on the rows of the matrix rather than on equations.

You can use Blackline Master 4.3 to show how to use matrices to solve by elimination.

Explore

FACTS AND NOTATION You may wish to make these points:

- If students say "matrixes" for the plural, point out the margin note.
- When writing matrices, it is good to get in the habit of lining up the rows and columns, as in the text.
- Instead of saying that A has dimension 3×4 ("3 by 4"), you can say that A has dimensions 3×4, or size 3×4, or that A is a 3×4 matrix. In any case, you always mention the number of rows first.
- When the number of rows and columns are equal, you say that the matrix is *square*.
- The phrase "coefficient matrix" is important and will reoccur.

Look at the process up close.

$$\left(\begin{array}{ccc|c} 1 & 1 & 1 & 2 \\ 2 & -1 & 1 & 5 \\ 2 & 2 & 2 & 4 \\ 1 & 2 & 3 & 5 \end{array}\right) \longrightarrow A' = \left(\begin{array}{ccc|c} 1 & 1 & 1 & 2 \\ 0 & -3 & -1 & 1 \\ 1 & 2 & 3 & 5 \end{array}\right)$$

In the diagram, you see matrix A in black. Then, two times row 1 is shown in blue below row 2. Subtract term by term and replace row 2 with the result. The new resulting row is shown in blue in the second matrix.

To continue, instead of subtracting (1) from (3), subtract row 1 from row 3 to make a new row that replaces row 3.

$$A' = \left(\begin{array}{ccc|c} 1 & 1 & 1 & 2 \\ 0 & -3 & -1 & 1 \\ 1 & 2 & 3 & 5 \\ 1 & 1 & 1 & 2 \end{array}\right) \longrightarrow A'' = \left(\begin{array}{ccc|c} 1 & 1 & 1 & 2 \\ 0 & -3 & -1 & 1 \\ 0 & 1 & 2 & 3 \end{array}\right)$$

The bottom two rows now correspond to

$$-3y - z = 1$$

$$y + 2z = 3$$

These are the same equations as before.

Facts and Notation

A rectangular array like A is a matrix. This matrix has 3 rows (the horizontals) and 4 columns (the verticals). The vertical bar is an augmentation line. The whole matrix A is an augmented matrix. The thing that is augmented in A is the coefficient matrix of the linear system (1)–(3). The matrix below shows what that coefficient matrix looks like by itself.

$$B = \begin{pmatrix} 1 & 1 & 1 \\ 2 & -1 & 1 \\ 1 & 2 & 3 \end{pmatrix}$$

Matrix B does not have an augmentation line. In fact, even in an augmented matrix, the augmentation line is just a convenient reminder. Some books do not use them. (You cannot usually use them on a calculator.) The augmented matrix A has dimension 3×4 (3 rows, 4 columns). The coefficient matrix B has dimension 3×3.

The plural of *matrix* is *matrices.*

This book shows matrices enclosed by parentheses. In some books they are enclosed in square brackets, [ ].

For You to Do

1. Write down (but do not solve) the coefficient matrix and the augmented matrix for the linear system below.

$$x - 2y + z = 7$$
$$2x - y + 4z = 17$$
$$3x - 2y + 2z = 14$$

2. Write down (but do not solve) the system of equations corresponding to matrix M below. Let the variables be x, y, z in that order.

$$M = \left(\begin{array}{ccc|c} 1 & 2 & -3 & 2 \\ 2 & 0 & -1 & 4 \\ -3 & 1 & 2 & -5 \end{array}\right)$$

3. Start with matrix M from Problem 2. Make a new matrix M' by subtracting 2 times row 1 from row 2. (The row you subtract from is always the one you change.) Then, from M', make M'' by adding 3 times row 1 to row 3.

Now you have reduced Sasha and Derman's problem to a 2×2 system. You can continue to solve it in matrix form starting from

$$C = \left(\begin{array}{cc|c} -3 & -1 & 1 \\ 1 & 2 & 3 \end{array}\right)$$

Remember, the variables here are y and z. Eliminate y by adding 3 times the second row of C to the first row. You get

You could also say that you subtracted -3 times the second row from the first row. Why be so complicated? Because in some contexts it is cleaner to always solve systems with the same operation.

$$D = \left(\begin{array}{cc|c} 0 & 5 & 10 \\ 1 & 2 & 3 \end{array}\right)$$

The first row of D says that $5z = 10$, so $z = 2$. You can now substitute in the equation for the second row to find y. Then you can substitute in the original equation (1) to find x.

There is just one problem with this method. You deal partly with matrices and partly with equations. You jump around picking information from different matrices and different equations. Also, you use matrices of different sizes. None of this is good for calculators or computers. For them, it is much easier and more efficient if all matrices for a given situation are the same size, operations are always done in the same order, and all the information ever needed is kept in the current matrix (so they can discard any earlier matrices).

Answers

For You to Do

1. $\begin{pmatrix} 1 & -2 & 1 \\ 2 & -1 & 4 \\ 3 & -2 & 2 \end{pmatrix}$, $\left(\begin{array}{ccc|c} 1 & -2 & 1 & 7 \\ 2 & -1 & 4 & 17 \\ 3 & -2 & 2 & 14 \end{array}\right)$

2. $x + 2y - 3z = 2$, $2x - z = 4$, $-3x + y + 2z = -5$

3. $M' = \left(\begin{array}{ccc|c} 1 & 2 & -3 & 2 \\ 0 & -4 & 5 & 0 \\ -3 & 1 & 2 & -5 \end{array}\right)$,

$M'' = \left(\begin{array}{ccc|c} 1 & 2 & -3 & 2 \\ 0 & -4 & 5 & 0 \\ 0 & 7 & -7 & 1 \end{array}\right)$

For You to Do

You might have students carry out Problem 3 in equation form as well, doing steps in parallel to the matrix steps.

The exposition following the For You to Do section raises the question, "Why is one matrix of a fixed size better for computers?" This is because there is overhead (extra calculations) involved for the computer to figure out where in memory to store and find each matrix entry.

Each time a matrix is resized, there is more overhead.

NOTE ON NOTATION It probably is best for students to discuss what the notation over the arrows means the very first time they see it. You might ask them to speak the instructions out loud, proposing interpretations as they go.

The term *switch* appears for the first time here. It means to switch two rows. The final coefficient matrix on the page is an identity matrix, a term introduced shortly. Make sure students come to understand that when they reach an identity matrix, they are done. In this case, $x = 1$, $y = -1$, and $z = 2$.

For Discussion

You do not need to belabor this explanation if all the students seem to get the notation. If they do not, it is worth spending time on it, because the operations being described are fundamental. They are the *elementary row operations* discussed in the next Developing Habits of Mind.

You can solve Sasha and Derman's problem entirely in the matrix world. The expressions over the arrows summarize what steps you take. You will learn their meaning shortly. The first half goes like this.

$$A = \left(\begin{array}{ccc|c} 1 & 1 & 1 & 2 \\ 2 & -1 & 1 & 5 \\ 1 & 2 & 3 & 5 \end{array}\right) \xrightarrow{(2)\,-\,2(1)} \left(\begin{array}{ccc|c} 1 & 1 & 1 & 2 \\ 0 & -3 & -1 & 1 \\ 1 & 2 & 3 & 5 \end{array}\right)$$

$$\xrightarrow{(3)\,-\,(1)} \left(\begin{array}{ccc|c} 1 & 1 & 1 & 2 \\ 0 & -3 & -1 & 1 \\ 0 & 1 & 2 & 3 \end{array}\right) \xrightarrow{\text{Switch }(2),\,(3)} \left(\begin{array}{ccc|c} 1 & 1 & 1 & 2 \\ 0 & 1 & 2 & 3 \\ 0 & -3 & -1 & 1 \end{array}\right)$$

$$\xrightarrow{(3)+3(2)} \left(\begin{array}{ccc|c} 1 & 1 & 1 & 2 \\ 0 & 1 & 2 & 3 \\ 0 & 0 & 5 & 10 \end{array}\right) \xrightarrow{(3)\div 5} \left(\begin{array}{ccc|c} 1 & 1 & 1 & 2 \\ 0 & 1 & 2 & 3 \\ 0 & 0 & 1 & 2 \end{array}\right)$$

Now the third row says that $z = 2$. You can begin the process of substitution. Both the matrix and the corresponding equations are in triangular form, so you could easily solve for z, y, and x in that order by returning to equations and using substitution.

But you have already learned that you can accomplish substitution by elimination—adding and subtracting equations. So you can also carry out the substitution in matrix form. Machines do that easily. So continue.

$$\left(\begin{array}{ccc|c} 1 & 1 & 1 & 2 \\ 0 & 1 & 2 & 3 \\ 0 & 0 & 1 & 2 \end{array}\right) \xrightarrow{(2)-2(3)} \left(\begin{array}{ccc|c} 1 & 1 & 1 & 2 \\ 0 & 1 & 0 & -1 \\ 0 & 0 & 1 & 2 \end{array}\right) \underset{(1)-(3)}{\xrightarrow{(1)-(2)}} \left(\begin{array}{ccc|c} 1 & 0 & 0 & 1 \\ 0 & 1 & 0 & -1 \\ 0 & 0 & 1 & 2 \end{array}\right)$$

This final matrix corresponds to the three equations $x = 1$, $y = -1$, and $z = 2$, so you have solved the original problem by using only matrices.

Can you figure out the expressions over and under the arrows? For instance, between matrix A and the next one, you see the expression $(2) - 2(1)$. This means replace row 2 of A with row 2 minus two times row 1.

For Discussion

4. Figure out the meanings of all the other expressions over and under the arrows.

This solution method is called **Gaussian Elimination**. Gaussian Elimination is an algorithm that transforms the matrix of any given system of linear equations through a sequence of other matrices. It ends in a final matrix from which the solution to the corresponding system is obvious. You call it Gaussian Elimination because the first stage (the reduction to triangular form) corresponds on the equation level to eliminating the variables one at a time.

Answers

For Discussion

4. Answers may vary. Sample: $(m) - a(n)$ means replace row m with the result of subtracting a times row n from row m.

Developing Habits of Mind

Experiment. Is this pure matrix approach an improvement? Some people like the time saving from not having to write variables and equations. However, they do not like the extra work of keeping all the rows and columns. But remember, this is not a method intended for humans, except for small examples. So why take you through it? Because, like most good algorithms, it can tell you a lot. For instance, thinking about the patterns that could appear in the final matrix can lead to insights about the theory of solutions to equations. But you cannot think about what the final form might look like without understanding the algorithm. So, the point of the following exercises is to help you develop a feel for the algorithm.

In Gaussian Elimination, the transformations from one system of equations (or one matrix) to another use only three kinds of steps:

- *Scaling.* Replace one equation (row) with a multiple of itself.
- *Switching.* Switch the order of two equations (rows).
- *Subtracting.* Subtract or add a multiple of one equation (row) from another and replace the other equation with the result.

Not only do these steps allow you to go forward, they allow you to go backward: You can reverse every step. For instance, if you subtract three times (1) from (2), you can reverse this by adding three times (1) to the new (2). This means that you can always get from the last system back to the first.

Facts and Notation

Since you can get from the first system of equations to the last, any solution to the first system is a solution to the last. Since you can get from the last system to the first, any solution to the last system is a solution to the first. This means that the first and last systems are equivalent. They have the same solutions. Usually the last system has exactly one solution—for instance, in Sasha and Derman's example $(x, y, z) = (1, -1, 2)$. In that case, Gaussian Elimination has revealed for us the one and only solution to the original system.

Each step you take preserves the solution set.

This situation is like the situation with basic moves for equations in one variable: You can reverse a basic move, and a basic move preserves the solution set. Therefore, you might call scaling, switching, and subtracting the basic moves for linear systems. The formal name is *elementary row operations.*

The final matrix you get to in Gaussian Elimination is in row-reduced echelon form, abbreviated *rref*. For instance, the last matrix in Sasha and Derman's example is

$$\left(\begin{array}{ccc|c} 1 & 0 & 0 & 1 \\ 0 & 1 & 0 & -1 \\ 0 & 0 & 1 & 2 \end{array}\right)$$

You can call row-reduced echelon form just "row-reduced form." You can describe a matrix as "row reduced."

Developing Habits of Mind

Here is a convention that might make students more at ease with the extra work of keeping all the rows and columns: let a blank space correspond to a 0. For this to work, you must line up the rows and columns very straight or else you will not be sure where the missing 0's go.

For now, the final form that appears in the coefficient matrix is almost always an identity matrix. After doing several examples, students may begin to verbalize why an identity matrix shows up, and what can happen to keep it from showing up.

FACTS AND NOTATION There is a very important but subtle fact stated very succinctly here: whenever you can reverse a set of calculations, then the initial and final equations have the same solution set. When a set of calculations goes only one way (for instance, squaring), then the solution set to the final equation can be larger (never smaller) than the solution set to the initial equation.

For instance, squaring $x = y$ leads to $x^2 = y^2$. The latter equation includes $x = 1$, $y = -1$ in its solution set, but the former equation does not. When you can reverse calculations, each solution set is contained in the other, so they are equal.

Should you try to clarify this subtlety with your class? It depends on the students, their curiosity about this issue, and their readiness for it.

Row-reduced form, rref, is a key concept. You can pronounce it "ref," with a longer, drawn-out r.

Wrap Up

Make sure the students really understand how Gaussian Elimination works. You may want to go over Problem 1 again, or do another straightforward 3×3 system such as Exercise 9 from the On Your Own exercises.

Assessment Resources

Lesson Quiz 4.3

For Exercises 1 and 2, solve each system by Gaussian Elimination in matrix form.

1. $2x + 5y = 12$
$-3x + 2y = 1$

2. $-x + 2y - z = -7$
$2x + 3y + 2z = 7$
$-3x - y + z = -2$

3. Thomas is thinking of four numbers. He says, "The third number is twice the second number. The average of the first three numbers is 2. The average of the last three numbers is 1. The average of all four numbers is 0." What are Thomas's numbers?

Exercises

HOMEWORK
- Core: 9, 10, 11, 13, 14, 15, 19, 22, 26, 27
- Optional: 12, 16, 18, 21, 23, 24, 25
- Extension: 17, 20

Check Your Understanding

EXERCISE 1 Hopefully, some student will complain, "How do I know what the variables are?" They do not have to be x, y, and z. However, what they are called does not really make a difference. The same ordered triple is the solution.

EXERCISE 2 For this exercise, only the substitution part of the algorithm is needed, or rather, the elementary row operations that correspond to substitution. This is because the matrix corresponding to these equations is already in triangular form.

Most graphing calculators are also matrix calculators. They can store matrices and do many matrix computations, such as finding row-reduced echelon form. Look for an **rref** command in the matrix menus. Find out how to input matrices and how to get your calculator to display their row-reduced forms. You cannot input the augmentation line, but you know where it goes.

For instructions for using the rref command, see the TI-Nspire Handbook, p. 778.

In the example, the part of the row-reduced echelon form before the augmentation line is an **identity matrix**: a square matrix with all entries 0 except for 1's along the main diagonal from top left to lower right. This always happens when there is a unique solution. However, not every linear system has a unique solution, so the row-reduced form is not always so simple.

Some of the exercises will illustrate what happens when there is not a unique solution and begin to hint at the general pattern.

Exercises *Practicing Habits of Mind*

Check Your Understanding

1. Consider this augmented matrix.

$$\left(\begin{array}{ccc|c} 1 & -1 & 2 & 5 \\ 2 & -3 & 1 & 3 \\ 1 & 0 & 7 & 16 \end{array}\right)$$

a. What system of equations does it correspond to?

b. Solve this system in matrix form.

2. Solve the following system using Gaussian Elimination on matrices.

$$\begin{aligned} x + y + z &= 1 \\ 2y + z &= 2 \\ 3z &= 3 \end{aligned}$$

Answers

Exercises

1. a. $x - y + 2z = 5$, $2x - 3y + z = 3$, $x + 7z = 16$

b. $\left(\begin{array}{ccc|c} 1 & 0 & 0 & 2 \\ 0 & 1 & 0 & 1 \\ 0 & 0 & 1 & 2 \end{array}\right)$ or $(x, y, z) = (2, 1, 2)$

2. $\left(\begin{array}{ccc|c} 1 & 0 & 0 & -\frac{1}{2} \\ 0 & 1 & 0 & \frac{1}{2} \\ 0 & 0 & 1 & 1 \end{array}\right)$

3. Yes, $\left(\begin{array}{ccc|c} 1 & 0 & 0 & 1 \\ 0 & 1 & 0 & -1 \\ 0 & 0 & 1 & 2 \end{array}\right)$ represents the same solution.

4. $\left(\begin{array}{ccc|c} 1 & 0 & 0 & 1 \\ 0 & 1 & 0 & -1 \\ 0 & 0 & 1 & 2 \end{array}\right) \xrightarrow[(1)+(3)]{(1)+(2)} \left(\begin{array}{ccc|c} 1 & 1 & 1 & 2 \\ 0 & 1 & 0 & -1 \\ 0 & 0 & 1 & 2 \end{array}\right) \xrightarrow{(2)+2(3)} \left(\begin{array}{ccc|c} 1 & 1 & 1 & 2 \\ 0 & 1 & 2 & 3 \\ 0 & 0 & 1 & 2 \end{array}\right)$;

then reverse the steps shown at the top of page 294 to get $A = \left(\begin{array}{ccc|c} 1 & 1 & 1 & 2 \\ 2 & -1 & 1 & 5 \\ 1 & 2 & 3 & 5 \end{array}\right)$.

3. Go back to the complete matrix solution of system (1)–(3) to the point where the system was

$$\left(\begin{array}{ccc|c} 1 & 1 & 1 & 2 \\ 0 & -3 & -1 & 1 \\ 0 & 1 & 2 & 3 \end{array}\right)$$

Instead of then switching the last two rows, add or subtract a multiple of the second row from the third to eliminate y. Then continue with the type of steps shown in the lesson until you reach a matrix in the form below.

$$\left(\begin{array}{ccc|c} 1 & 0 & 0 & \blacksquare \\ 0 & 1 & 0 & \blacksquare \\ 0 & 0 & 1 & \blacksquare \end{array}\right)$$

Do you get the same solution you got before?

4. Illustrate the claim that you can reverse every step in a matrix solution. Reverse every step in the complete matrix solution of Sasha and Derman's problem. That is, show that using just scaling, switching, and subtracting, you can get from the matrix form of the final system back to the matrix form of the original system.

$$\begin{array}{c} x = 1 \\ y = -1 \\ z = 2 \end{array} \longrightarrow \begin{array}{r} x + y + z = 2 \\ 2x - y + z = 5 \\ x + 2y + 3z = 5 \end{array}$$

5. **Write About It** Subtracting a multiple of one equation from another is a basic move for systems. Yet sometimes it would be best to add a multiple of one equation to another. Explain why you do not have to list adding as a fourth basic move.

6. Solve this system by Gaussian Elimination in matrix form.

$$x + 2y = -3$$
$$2x - y = 4$$

7. The function $f(n) = a2^n + b3^n$, where a and b are constants, satisfies the conditions $f(1) = 1$ and $f(2) = 10$. Find a and b.

8. If you think of equations representing lines in the plane, you have a geometric interpretation for 2×2 systems. This interpretation helps explain why the solution to most, but not all, 2×2 systems is a single pair (x, y).

   a. How can you interpret the solution of a 2×2 system geometrically?

   b. Use that interpretation to help you to conjecture what can happen with $m \times 2$ systems. Remember, an $m \times 2$ system has m equations and two unknowns.

   c. **Take It Further** Make a conjecture about a geometric interpretation for $m \times 3$ systems.

Habits of Mind

Check your method. When mathematicians come up with a new approach, one of the things they do to test it out is to try it on a simpler system that they already know how to solve by other methods.

You might want to make a table for f and apply the methods of Chapter 1. Can you find any patterns? Your main task here, however, is to determine the function by the methods of the current chapter.

EXERCISE 3 justifies allowing students to vary their solution procedures to make the algebra easier to do by hand. So long as every step they do is a basic move (elementary row operation), they will get to the same solution(s) that you get to by following Gaussian Elimination in order. Still, as the text notes, for calculations it is better to follow a fixed order.

EXERCISE 4 Of course, nobody ever has to reverse the steps in practice, but this is a core exercise because, by doing it once or twice, students should internalize that the steps are always reversible.

EXERCISE 6 Try to keep students from reverting to familiar nonmatrix methods for solving 2×2 systems. Not because Gaussian Elimination in matrix form is easier; it is not. One way to really learn a new method is to force yourself to use it and understand how it works in a situation where your natural inclination is to do it a more familiar way. For larger systems, and with technology, Gaussian Elimination really is the way to go.

5. Answers may vary. Sample: Adding a positive multiple is the same as subtracting the same multiple with the opposite sign(s).

6. $\left(\begin{array}{cc|c} 1 & 0 & 1 \\ 0 & 1 & -2 \end{array}\right)$

7. $a = -\frac{7}{2}, b = \frac{8}{3}$

8. a. Each equation in the system is a line in the xy-plane, and the intersection of the lines is the solution to the system.

b. The solution represents m lines in the xy-plane; if the lines have point(s) in common, that point or points is the solution to the system.

c. Each equation represents a plane in 3-space; the common intersection of the m planes (if it exists) is the solution to the system.

On Your Own

EXERCISE 10 See if the students notice that the steps they take to solve this system are exactly the same as for Sasha and Derman's—same multiples of one equation subtracted, and so on. Only the constants on the right of the equations change. That suggests that students can solve both exercises simultaneously with a considerable saving of work. Do your students have any suggestions for how to do that? However, suppose that you give them the first exercise today and tell them to solve it now, and then give them the second exercise tomorrow. Is there still a way for them to save a record of the steps they took to solve the first so that they do not have to do it all over for the second? Many college linear algebra courses answer this question.

EXERCISE 11 makes the same point as Exercise 4. You direct the calculations you do to solve a system of equations entirely by the coefficients of the unknowns, not by the constants. Indeed, the sequence of Gaussian Elimination steps in parts (a) and (b) are exactly the same, since the coefficients in (a) and (b) are the same, and the solution shows how to solve the two systems simultaneously.

EXERCISE 13 You may find that many students accidentally convert this to a 3 × 2 matrix, as if there were only two unknowns.

EXERCISE 14 is a core exercise because it is one of the few "word problems" in this section. But it also involves an interesting observation: this exercise reduces to Exercise 13. You can put this observation in the format of Gaussian Elimination. Just make the first step scaling each row by 2:

$$\left(\begin{array}{ccc|c} \frac{1}{2} & \frac{1}{2} & 0 & 1 \\ 0 & \frac{1}{2} & \frac{1}{2} & 2 \\ \frac{1}{2} & 0 & \frac{1}{2} & 2 \end{array}\right) \rightarrow \left(\begin{array}{ccc|c} 1 & 1 & 0 & 2 \\ 0 & 1 & 1 & 4 \\ 1 & 0 & 1 & 6 \end{array}\right)$$

This, however, is not the standard order in Gaussian Elimination; usually (that is, when computers do it) variables are eliminated before scaling.

EXERCISE 16 Draw students' attention to the margin notes on this page. Students will discover that having the same constants as another system does not lead to any similarity in carrying out the solution. This is quite different from when the coefficient matrices of two systems are the same, as in Exercise 11.

On Your Own

9. Standardized Test Prep In Gaussian Elimination, which of the following transformations can you NOT use?

A. scaling **B.** subtracting
C. switching columns **D.** switching rows

10. Solve the following system.

$$\begin{aligned} x + y + z &= 3 \\ 2x - y + z &= 2 \\ x + 2y + 3z &= 6 \end{aligned}$$

Notice that this system is the same as Sasha and Derman's problem (1)–(3) except that the constants on the right are different.

11. Solve each system.

a. $$\begin{aligned} x + y + z &= 1 \\ 2x - y + z &= -2 \\ x + 2y + 3z &= 4 \end{aligned}$$

b. $$\begin{aligned} x + y + z &= 1 \\ 2x - y + z &= 3 \\ x + 2y + 3z &= -1 \end{aligned}$$

12. Find the unique linear function that goes through the points (2, 2) and (5, 8). You know several ways to solve this type of problem. Use Gaussian Elimination in matrix form.

Go Online PHSchool.com
For additional practice, go to **Web Code:** bfa-0403

13. Solve the following system by matrix methods.

$$\begin{aligned} x + y &= 2 \\ y + z &= 4 \\ z + x &= 6 \end{aligned}$$

14. Derman is thinking of three numbers. He says, "The average of the first two numbers is 1. The average of the last two numbers is 2. The average of the first number and last number is 3." What are Derman's numbers?

15. Rewrite the following system in a form to which you can apply Gaussian Elimination. You do not need to solve the system.

$$\begin{aligned} x + y + 2(y + z) &= 3 \\ x &= \tfrac{1}{2}(y + z + 2) \\ x + \frac{y + \frac{1}{2}z}{3} &= 1 \end{aligned}$$

16. Solve the following system.

$$\begin{aligned} x + y + 2z &= 2 \\ x - y + z &= 5 \\ 2x + 2y + 3z &= 5 \end{aligned}$$

Notice that this problem has the same constants on the right as Sasha and Derman's problem (1)–(3), but the rest is different.

Answers

9. C

10. (1, 1, 1)

11. a. (−1, 1, 1) **b.** (2, 0, −1)

12. $f(x) = 2x - 2$

13. (2, 0, 4)

14. $x = 2, y = 0, z = 4$

15. $x + 3y + 2z = 3,\ x - \frac{1}{2}y - \frac{1}{2}z = 1,\ x + \frac{1}{3}y + \frac{1}{6}z = 1$

16. (5, −1, −1)

17. The value of each of the four variables is −1.

18. For $f(x) = ax^2 + bx + c$, $f(1) = a + b + c = 1$, $f(2) = 4a + 2b + c = 3$, and $f(3) = 9a + 3b + c = 6$. The initial matrix is $\left(\begin{array}{ccc|c} 1 & 1 & 1 & 1 \\ 4 & 2 & 1 & 3 \\ 9 & 3 & 1 & 6 \end{array}\right)$ and the final matrix is $\left(\begin{array}{ccc|c} 1 & 0 & 0 & \frac{1}{2} \\ 0 & 1 & 0 & \frac{1}{2} \\ 0 & 0 & 1 & 0 \end{array}\right)$.

17. **Take It Further** Solve the system represented by the following augmented matrix without using a calculator. Even though it is 4×4, you can solve it by hand with Gaussian Elimination.

$$\left(\begin{array}{cccc|c} 1 & -1 & -1 & 0 & 1 \\ 0 & 1 & -1 & -1 & 1 \\ -1 & 0 & 1 & -1 & 1 \\ -1 & -1 & 0 & 1 & 1 \end{array}\right)$$

18. Do Exercise 5 from Lesson 4.2 in matrix form.

19. A rectangular box has six sides that come in three congruent pairs. Suppose the perimeters of the three different rectangular sides are 20 in., 24 in., and 28 in., respectively. What are the dimensions (length, width, and height) of the box?

20. **Take It Further** Consider another rectangular box. Suppose that the perimeters of all six sides of the box are the same. Does the box have to be a cube? Explain.

21. Find the unique polynomial of degree 3 or less that goes through the points (1, 1), (2, 3), (3, 6), and (4, 10).

Solve this exercise using the rref command. See the TI-Nspire Handbook, p. 778.

22. Solve each system. If you use Gaussian Elimination, what situations arise?

a. $x + 2y = 3$
$2x + 4y = 6$

b. $x + 2y = 3$
$2x + 4y = 7$

Maintain Your Skills

23. What is the system of equations associated with the following augmented matrix? Assume the variables are x and y.

$$\left(\begin{array}{cc|c} 1 & 3 & 5 \\ 2 & 4 & 6 \end{array}\right)$$

24. Use Gaussian Elimination to solve the system from Exercise 23.

25. Do Exercise 12 from Lesson 4.2 again, this time in matrix form.

19. 4 in. by 6 in. by 8 in.

20. Yes, the box must be a cube.

21. $p(x) = \frac{1}{2}x^2 + \frac{1}{2}x$

22. a. The row-reduced matrix is $\left(\begin{array}{cc|c} 1 & 2 & 3 \\ 0 & 0 & 0 \end{array}\right)$, so the solution is all points on the line $x + 2y = 3$.

b. The row-reduced matrix is $\left(\begin{array}{cc|c} 1 & 2 & 3 \\ 0 & 0 & 1 \end{array}\right)$; the second row says $0 = 1$, which is false, so the system has no solution.

23. $x + 3y = 5$, $2x + 4y = 6$

24. The row-reduced matrix is $\left(\begin{array}{cc|c} 1 & 0 & -1 \\ 0 & 1 & 2 \end{array}\right)$, or $x = -1$, $y = 2$.

25. Rewriting the system as $x - y - z = 0$, $-x + y - z = 0$, $-x - y + z = 0$, the initial matrix is $\left(\begin{array}{ccc|c} 1 & -1 & -1 & 0 \\ -1 & 1 & -1 & 0 \\ -1 & -1 & 1 & 0 \end{array}\right)$ and the row-reduced matrix is $\left(\begin{array}{ccc|c} 1 & 0 & 0 & 0 \\ 0 & 1 & 0 & 0 \\ 0 & 0 & 1 & 0 \end{array}\right)$.

EXERCISE 17 For this exercise it is possible to figure out the answer by symmetry. Because of the cyclical nature of the equations, you treat all the variables the same. This means that there should be a solution in which they are all equal. If they are all equal, then each equation says $-1x = 1$, where x is any of the variables. So, all variables equal to -1 should be a solution, and this is easily checked. What this argument does not prove, is that this is the only solution. Gaussian Elimination does prove that.

Symmetry is always worth pointing out, and cyclical symmetry is one of the more common forms. However, it is probably not worth pushing this observation on students if they do not see it themselves.

EXERCISE 20 Method 1 of the solution does not show the steps of the reduction. This is because you can prove without doing it that the final matrix must be what is claimed. Why? Because only the coefficients to the left of the augmentation line matter in determining what steps to do and what the rref is. So from the solution to Exercise 19 you know that the rref is the identity matrix. That means there is a unique solution. Since $l = w = h = \frac{p}{4}$ is one solution (by symmetry), now you know it is the only solution.

Perhaps one of your students will suggest this reasoning. If not, you might try to elicit it. State that you know the final matrix is correct without computing it and see what students say.

EXERCISE 21 is most practical to do with technology. Performing Gaussian Elimination on a general 4×4 is usually a long process. You can, as you have done in earlier exercises, find some 4×4 matrices that are reasonable to solve by hand, but it is also valuable for students to be comfortable with the technology.

EXERCISE 22 continues the theme from Exercise 11 that only the coefficients matter, but it adds several new issues. It is helpful that they first appear in a context (two equations, two unknowns) where students should already be able to draw the right conclusions from previous methods. Then they can make a connection with how to read off the same conclusions from Gaussian Elimination.

Maintain Your Skills

EXERCISE 25 There are several interesting issues here. The first is that linear problems do not always come in the form where you can immediately apply Gaussian Elimination. Sometimes you first have to work them into that form. Second, whenever all the constants in a linear system are 0, then setting all the variables to 0 is a solution. (Such a matrix is called homogeneous.) However, you still have to solve to

continued on p. 300

continued from p. 299

find out if there are other solutions. For instance, the system $x + y = 0$ and $2x + 2y = 0$ has every pair $(x, -x)$ as a solution.

Third is the observation that you need not write the augmentation column at all for homogeneous systems; it will never change from all 0's.

EXERCISE 26 The usual convention in Gaussian Elimination is to clear out only columns in the coefficient matrix. Most tests say that the rref for the matrix in part (f) is $\left(\begin{array}{ccc|c} 1 & 0 & -1 & 1 \\ 0 & 1 & 2 & 2 \\ 0 & 0 & 0 & 1 \end{array}\right)$ because you should not reduce the constant column. But calculators do not know how to handle an augmentation column differently. They show the last column of the rref of part (f) to be $\begin{pmatrix} 0 \\ 0 \\ 1 \end{pmatrix}$. This disagreement makes no difference in reading off the solutions. Notice that for both versions of the rref of part (f), the third equation is $0 = 1$, so there are no solutions. Indeed, the only time the augmentation column gets cleared to 0's and a 1 by your calculator is when there is no solution.

Additional Resources

PRINT RESOURCES
- Solution Manual
- Practice Workbook
- Assessment Resources
- Teaching Resources

TECHNOLOGY
- Interactive Textbook
- TeacherExpress CD-ROM
- ExamView CD-ROM
- PHSchool.com

Additional Practice

For Exercises 1–4, solve each system by Gaussian Elimination in matrix form.

1. $x - 2y = -8$
$2x - y = -7$

2. $3x + 2y = 6$
$-2x + 2y = 6$

3. $2x + y + 3z = 0$
$5x - 2y + z = 11$
$6x - 2y - 2z = 16$

4. $-x + 6y + z = 18$
$x - 3y - 2z = -16$
$7x + 5y + z = 0$

5. Kylie is thinking of three numbers. She says, "The average of the first two numbers is 2. The average of the last two numbers is 4. The average of all three numbers is 5." What are Kylie's numbers?

6. Rewrite the following system in a form to which you can apply Gaussian Elimination. Do not solve the system.

$$2x + 3(y - 2z) - 4 = 1$$
$$y = \tfrac{1}{4}(x + y - z)$$
$$3x + \frac{2y - z}{2} = -1$$

7. Solve the system represented by the following augmented matrix. Do not use a calculator.

$$\left(\begin{array}{cccc|c} 1 & -1 & 1 & 0 & 1 \\ 0 & 1 & -1 & 1 & 1 \\ -1 & 0 & 1 & -1 & 1 \\ 1 & -1 & 0 & 1 & 1 \end{array}\right)$$

8. Solve each system. If you use Gaussian Elimination, what types of situations arise? Explain.

a. $3x + 8y = 4$
$\frac{3}{2}x + 4y = 2$

b. $-2x + 6y = 1$
$x - 3y = 5$

Practice: For Lesson 4.3, assign Exercises 1–8.

26. Use your calculator to compute the rref of each matrix below. Divide up the work with your friends so that no one has many to do. Describe any patterns you discover about the form of rrefs. Randomly create some more matrices and find their rrefs with your calculator. Do the rrefs of these matrices confirm the patterns you have found?

a. $\left(\begin{array}{cc|c} 1 & -2 & -8 \\ -3 & 5 & 21 \end{array}\right)$

b. $\left(\begin{array}{cc|c} 1 & -2 & -8 \\ -3 & 6 & 21 \end{array}\right)$

c. $\left(\begin{array}{cc|c} 1 & -2 & -2 \\ -3 & 6 & 6 \end{array}\right)$

d. $\left(\begin{array}{ccc|c} 1 & 2 & 3 & 5 \\ 2 & 3 & 4 & 8 \\ 3 & 2 & 1 & 7 \end{array}\right)$

e. $\left(\begin{array}{ccc|c} 3 & 1 & -1 & 5 \\ 1 & -4 & -9 & -7 \\ 4 & 0 & -4 & 4 \end{array}\right)$

f. $\left(\begin{array}{ccc|c} 1 & 2 & 3 & 8 \\ 2 & 3 & 4 & 12 \\ 3 & 2 & 1 & 6 \end{array}\right)$

g. $\left(\begin{array}{ccc|c} 3 & 1 & -1 & 4 \\ 1 & -4 & -9 & 2 \\ 4 & 0 & -4 & 3 \end{array}\right)$

h. $\left(\begin{array}{ccc|c} 1 & -2 & 2 & 4 \\ 2 & -4 & 3 & 5 \\ 3 & -6 & 2 & 0 \end{array}\right)$

i. $\left(\begin{array}{ccc|c} 3 & -6 & 1 & -3 \\ 1 & -2 & -4 & -14 \\ 4 & -8 & 0 & -8 \end{array}\right)$

j. $\left(\begin{array}{ccc|c} 1 & 3 & 2 & 4 \\ 2 & 6 & 3 & 5 \\ 3 & 9 & 2 & 0 \end{array}\right)$

k. $\left(\begin{array}{ccc|c} 3 & 9 & 1 & -3 \\ 1 & 3 & -4 & -14 \\ 4 & 12 & 0 & -8 \end{array}\right)$

l. $\left(\begin{array}{ccc|c} 1 & 2 & -2 & 8 \\ 2 & 3 & -3 & 13 \\ 3 & 2 & -2 & 12 \end{array}\right)$

m. $\left(\begin{array}{ccc|c} 3 & 1 & -1 & 9 \\ 1 & -4 & 4 & -10 \\ 4 & 0 & 0 & 8 \end{array}\right)$

n. $\left(\begin{array}{ccc|c} 1 & 2 & 3 & 9 \\ 2 & 3 & 4 & 13 \\ 3 & 2 & -1 & 1 \end{array}\right)$

o. $\left(\begin{array}{ccc|c} 3 & 1 & -1 & 2 \\ 1 & -4 & 9 & 33 \\ 4 & 0 & -1 & 5 \end{array}\right)$

p. $\left(\begin{array}{cccc|c} 1 & 2 & 9 & 3 & 14 \\ 2 & 3 & 15 & 4 & 20 \\ 3 & 2 & 15 & -1 & 4 \\ 3 & 1 & 12 & 2 & 11 \end{array}\right)$

q. $\left(\begin{array}{cccc|c} 1 & 2 & 3 & -5 & -6 \\ 2 & 3 & 4 & -5 & -8 \\ 3 & 2 & -1 & 9 & 0 \\ 3 & 1 & 2 & 4 & -1 \end{array}\right)$

r. $\left(\begin{array}{ccccc|c} 1 & -2 & 3 & 0 & 1 & 4 \\ 0 & 0 & 0 & 1 & 3 & 5 \end{array}\right)$

27. For parts (d), (f), (h), and (j) of Exercise 26, write down the equations that the original matrix represents and the equations that the rref represents. In what sense do the equations represented by the rref solve the problem?

Answers

26. See back of book.

27. d. $x + 2y + 3z = 5$, $2x + 3y + 4z = 8$, $3x + 2y + z = 7$; $x - z = 1$, $y + 2z = 2$; this is a system of two equations in three variables, and from any value of z you can generate an (x, y, z) solution.

f. $x + 2y + 3z = 8$, $2x + 3y + 4z = 12$, $3x + 2y + z = 6$; the last equation of the row-reduced matrix is $0 = 1$, so the system has no solution.

h. $x - 2y + 2z = 4$, $2x - 4y + 3z = 5$, $3x - 6y + 2z = 0$; the equations $x = -2 + 2y$ and $z = 3$ indicate that for any value of y you can generate an (x, y, z) solution.

j. $x + 3y + 2z = 4$, $2x + 6y + 3z = 5$, $3x + 9y + 2z = 0$; the equations $x + 3y = -2$, $z = 3$ indicate that for any value of y you can generate an (x, y, z) solution.

Mathematical Reflections 4A

In this investigation, you learned how to solve a system of three equations in three unknowns. You also learned how to use matrices and Gaussian Elimination to solve systems. These questions will help you summarize what you have learned.

You can use a matrix to organize a large amount of information, such as a bus schedule.

1. Show how to solve this system using each technique.

$$2x - y = 3$$
$$x + 3y = 5$$

a. substitution **b.** elimination

2. Solve this system.

$$3x - y + 2z = 4$$
$$4y - 3z = 3$$
$$6z = -6$$

3. Write the following system of equations as an augmented matrix.

$$x - 3z = 5$$
$$6y = 7 - z$$
$$2y + 6 = x$$

4. Find the row-reduced echelon form for this matrix. $\left(\begin{array}{ccc|c} 1 & 1 & 1 & 1 \\ 0 & 1 & 2 & 4 \\ 3 & 0 & 2 & 6 \end{array}\right)$

5. Sasha used Gaussian Elimination to solve a system of equations. She ended up with the following matrix. How should she interpret these results? $\left(\begin{array}{ccc|c} 1 & 0 & 0 & -2 \\ 0 & 1 & 0 & 4 \\ 0 & 0 & 0 & 3 \end{array}\right)$

6. Why is it possible to solve systems of linear equations in matrix form?

7. What is the process of Gaussian Elimination?

8. Find x, y, and z such that

$$4x - y + 4z = 1$$
$$2x - y + 8z = 11$$
$$2x - 2y + 4z = 0$$

Vocabulary

In this investigation, you learned these terms. Make sure you understand what each one means and how to use it.

- **dimension**
- **elimination**
- **Gaussian Elimination**
- **matrix**
- **row-reduced echelon form (rref)**
- **substitution**

Mathematical Reflections

EXERCISES 6–8 At the start of the investigation, you may have assigned these as Questions 1–3 for students to think and write about.

Mathematical Reflections

1. a. Using the first equation, $y = 2x - 3$, the second equation can be rewritten $x + 3(2x - 3) = 5$ and so $x = 2$. Then $y = 2x - 3 = 1$.

b. Multiply the first equation by 3 to get $6x - 3y = 9$; adding that to the second equation gives $7x = 14$ or $x = 2$; replace x in either equation to get $y = 1$.

2. $(x, y, z) = (2, 0, -1)$

3. $\left(\begin{array}{ccc|c} 1 & 0 & -3 & 5 \\ 0 & 6 & 1 & 7 \\ 1 & -2 & 0 & 6 \end{array}\right)$

4. $\left(\begin{array}{ccc|c} 1 & 0 & 0 & 0 \\ 0 & 1 & 0 & -2 \\ 0 & 0 & 1 & 3 \end{array}\right)$

5. The original system has no solution.

6. Answers may vary. Sample: The matrix serves to keep the coefficients associated with the appropriate variables.

7. Answers may vary. Sample: You write a series of equivalent augmented matrices until you get one that is in row-reduced echelon form.

8. $(x, y, z) = (-1, 3, 2)$

Investigation Overview

Matrices are much more than tables. They have a mathematical life of their own. They can be added, subtracted, multiplied, and multiplied by scalars (real numbers). The algebra of matrices is similar to the algebra of numbers students already know, but not the same. The most significant difference is that multiplication is not commutative: in general $AB \neq BA$.

Since matrices have not traditionally been part of the high school curriculum, matrix algebra is not either. But for the CME Project, this algebra has many advantages. To understand the general structure of algebra, it is valuable to see alternative algebras. To learn to think of mathematical entities as objects and to be open-minded about the properties they might have helps students see many varieties of objects with different properties.

Finally, matrices have a myriad of applications. They have the advantage that they can encapsulate a tremendous amount of information in single symbols, and they can encapsulate many numerical calculations as single matrix calculations. The economy of thought from such economy of notation keeps guiding principles from being lost in a sea of data.

The hardest matrix operation to understand is matrix multiplication. The definition of matrix multiplication is complicated and may be nonintuitive. This text makes an effort to explain where this definition of matrix multiplication comes from and tries to make its introduction more natural.

You may wish to assign Questions 1–3 for students to think and write about during the investigation.

Learning Goals

- Communicate and prove results about matrices, including the ideas of rows and columns and indices.
- Compute sums, differences, dot products, products, and inverses of matrices.
- Interpret and solve problems using matrix calculations.

Habits and Skills

- Visualize an operation on a matrix as a product.
- Explore the algebraic structure of matrices and n-tuples.
- Reason deductively to prove properties about matrices or find counterexamples.

Investigation 4B

Matrix Algebra

In *Matrix Algebra*, you will learn how to perform basic operations with matrices. You will explore and prove properties of matrix algebra. You will compare matrix properties to the properties of real numbers.

By the end of this investigation, you will be able to answer questions like these.

1. What is a dot product? How can you represent matrix multiplication using dot products?
2. What are some special cases in which $AB = BA$ is true for matrices A and B?
3. How can you solve this system of equations using matrix inverses? What is the solution?

$$\begin{aligned} x + 4y - z &= -3 \\ 2x - 2y + z &= 0 \\ 3x + y - 3z &= -9 \end{aligned}$$

You will learn how to

- communicate and prove results about matrices, including the ideas of rows and columns and indices
- compute sums, differences, dot products, products, and inverses of matrices
- interpret and solve problems using matrix calculations

You will develop these habits and skills:

- Visualize an operation on a matrix as a product.
- Explore the algebraic structure of matrices and n-tuples.
- Reason deductively to prove properties about matrices or find counterexamples.

What is the sum of the different colors at each point on the cover?

Investigation Road Map

LESSON 4.4, *Getting Started,* motivates the learning of definitions to come.

LESSON 4.5, *Basic Matrix Operations,* gives the definition of matrix addition and scalar multiplication.

LESSON 4.6, *Dot Products,* introduces dot products as a way-station to the definition of matrix product.

LESSON 4.7, *Matrix Multiplication,* introduces matrix multiplication in general, starting with applied examples of linear substitutions.

LESSON 4.8, *Matrix Inverses,* introduces the matrix inverse.

LESSON 4.9, *Matrix Properties,* looks at the structure of matrix algebra. Students discover which rules of number algebra continue to hold.

4.4 Getting Started

Activating Prior Knowledge
Exploring New Ideas

You can use tables to organize data.

For You to Explore

1. On the side of a box of cereal, there is a table that shows what percent of recommended daily food values are provided by 1 ounce of the cereal.

Daily Value

Carbohydrates	7%
Vitamin A	10%
Vitamin B_{12}	25%

Suppose for breakfast you eat 3 ounces of the cereal. Make your own personal table of the percent of your daily value you have met.

2. Cereal boxes usually give two columns in their daily percents table: one column for a standard serving of the cereal alone, and the other for the cereal and a standard amount of milk. Suppose the standard serving is 1 ounce of cereal, with or without one half cup of milk, and the table looks like this

	Cereal	Cereal With Milk
Carbohydrates	7%	9%
Vitamin A	10%	15%
Vitamin B_{12}	25%	35%

Make a bigger table with a column showing the percents for the one half cup of milk alone.

3. The weather bureau collects climate data for many U.S. cities. One set of data concerns cloudiness. Each day is classified as clear, partly cloudy, or cloudy. In an average year, Boston has 98 clear days and 164 cloudy days. On the other hand, Philadelphia has 93 clear days and 160 cloudy days, while San Francisco has 160 clear days and only 105 cloudy days.

Determine the average annual number of partly cloudy days in each of these cities. (Assume there are 365 days in a year.)

Put the given information and the information you compute into a labeled table.

4. Return to the data in Problem 3. Suppose you want to determine the average number of clear, partly cloudy, and cloudy days for each of the three cities for

- two years
- the first half of the year (January to June)

Can you use the results of Problem 3 to calculate these numbers? If so, explain how. If not, explain why not.

Lesson Overview

GOALS

- Warm up to the ideas of the investigation.
- Communicate about matrices.

This lesson may not seem very mathematical; it includes mostly a lot of data manipulation in tables. There is a point, though, which becomes clearer in later lessons. The For You to Explore problems and On Your Own exercises introduce matrix operations through examples. Later it should seem natural for students to define the operations they have already used. Through the Maintain Your Skills exercises, students should come to realize they need a systematic way to refer to entries in matrices. This motivates the double subscript notation that comes in Lesson 4.5.

FOR YOU TO EXPLORE
- Core: 1, 2, 3, 4, 5
- Optional: 6

MATERIALS
- graphing calculators
- spreadsheet software

HOMEWORK
- Core: 7, 8, 9, 10, 11, 12, 14
- Optional: 13, 15a–b
- Extension: 15c

Launch

Just have the students jump right into the For You to Explore problems.

Explore

As students are working, listen to their descriptions of the operations they are performing. Later, when you formalize these operations as operations on matrices, you can use some of the students' own vocabulary when you describe the processes.

For You to Explore

PROBLEM 1 In the next lesson, students see that this problem is an instance of multiplying a matrix by a scalar.

PROBLEM 2 If you think of each column of the table as a 3×1 matrix, this problem is an instance of matrix subtraction.

PROBLEM 4 Students must not only do a calculation on a table of data, but they must decide whether the obvious calculation would produce good results. In the second part of the problem, students should consider dividing each entry by 2, but they should also realize that weather is not evenly distributed over a given year.

Answers

For You to Explore

1. carbohydrates: 21%; vitamin A: 30%; vitamin B_{12}: 75%
2. carbohydrates: 7%, 9%, 2%; vitamin A: 10%, 15%, 5%; vitamin B_{12}: 25%, 35%, 10%
3. Boston: 103; Philadelphia: 112; San Francisco: 100
4. Answers may vary. Sample: Multiply the data values in Exercise 3 by the appropriate fraction of a year.

PROBLEM 5 With this problem students begin to see dot products. You have to multiply the number of each type of item (women's suits, men's suits, and goggles) by the price for each type of item and then add the products. This is a dot product.

PROBLEM 6 is another dot product problem. You have to multiply the number of pounds of each type of food (beef, pork, chicken, and fish) by the price for each type of food and then add the products.

Wrap Up

Go over the For You to Explore core problems as time allows.

5. The swim team buys swimsuits and goggles for its members. The team is going to buy 30 women's suits, 25 men's suits, and 55 pairs of goggles. The prices per item are $20 for a woman's suit, $15 for a man's, and $8 for a pair of goggles. You can display this information in a table.

	W	M	G
Number	30	25	55
Price ($)	20	15	8

What is the total amount the swim team will spend buying these things? Does the format of the table make it easy to describe the calculation?

6. The school cafeteria buys food wholesale. The following table shows a typical order.

	Beef	Pork	Chicken	Fish
Weight (lb)	200	50	250	100
Price ($/lb)	3.50	2.00	1.50	3.00

How much will the order cost?

Exercises *Practicing Habits of Mind*

On Your Own

7. The following table shows passenger car sales for various auto companies during a certain year.

Passenger Car Sales (millions of cars)

	Company A	Company B	Company C	Company D	Company E
Europe	0.4	0.2	0.2	0.2	1
United States	2	1.5	0.6	1	0.3
Asia	0.2	0.1	0.8	3.5	0.1

Answers

5. $1415; multiply the two numbers in each column and then add the three products.

6. $1475

Exercises

7. See back of book.

The table below shows the year's sales for other personal motor vehicles, including SUVs, vans, and light trucks.

Other Vehicle Sales (millions of vehicles)

	Company A	Company B	Company C	Company D	Company E
Europe	0.2	0.05	0.1	0.1	0.3
United States	2.6	1.8	0.8	1.2	0.1
Asia	0.1	0.05	0.5	1	0

Make a table of all personal motor vehicle sales for the year.

8. Here are tables of revenue (total money taken in) and expenditures (total money paid out) for the same auto companies during the same year.

Revenue (billions of dollars)

	Company A	Company B	Company C	Company D	Company E
Europe	18	7.5	9	10	38
United States	129	92.5	37	70	12
Asia	8	4.5	40	131	3

Expenditures (billions of dollars)

	Company A	Company B	Company C	Company D	Company E
Europe	17	7	9	9	32
United States	127	93	35	67	12
Asia	9	5	32	120	4

a. Mark a table for profit (revenues minus expenditures).

b. For each company, calculate the total profit for all regions combined.

c. For each region of the world, calculate the total profit of all the companies combined.

Habits of Mind

Make strategic choices. For parts (b) and (c), what is a good way to display the results? In terms of the table, what are you doing?

8. a. Profit (billions of dollars)

	A	B	C	D	E
Europe	1	0.5	0	1	6
United States	2	−0.5	2	3	0
Asia	−1	−0.5	8	11	−1

b. Company A: 2; Company B: −0.5; Company C: 10; Company D: 15; Company E: 5

c. Europe: 8.5; US: 6.5; Asia: 16.5

Exercises

HOMEWORK

- Core: 7, 8, 9, 10, 11, 12, 14
- Optional: 13, 15a–b
- Extension: 15c

On Your Own

EXERCISE 7 is another example of matrix addition. For each company and location, you have to add the number of passenger car sales to the number of other vehicle sales to obtain the total number of personal motor vehicle sales. Thus, you add corresponding entries of the two matrices to obtain a new matrix of the same size.

EXERCISE 8 Part (a) is an example of matrix subtraction. To compute the profit by company and location, subtract the expenditures from the revenues for that combination. Thus, you subtract corresponding entries of the two matrices to obtain a new matrix of the same size.

In part (b) you use the matrix you found in part (a) and add down each column.

In part (c) you use the matrix you found in part (a) and add across each row.

EXERCISE 9 Part (a) of this exercise is an example of multiplying a matrix by a scalar. In the other parts of the exercise, you scale rows and columns by different factors.

EXERCISE 10 is another example of dot product. For each truck you multiply the number of gallons in the tank by the mileage per gallon to get how far that truck can travel. Then you add these distances for all the trucks.

EXERCISE 11 The tables help students distinguish between matrix and column multiplication. In part (b) they see that different orders of computation result in different amounts of work. With vector and dot product notation (not introduced until later), you can think of N_1 and N_2 as the two rows of numbers of items and P as the column of prices. Then the computation $N_1 \cdot P + N_2 \cdot P$ takes five additions and six multiplications, whereas the computation $(N_1 + N_2) \cdot P$ takes five additions and only three multiplications. The equality

$$N_1 \cdot P + N_2 \cdot P = (N_1 + N_2) \cdot P$$

is a true statement, but it only means equality of value, not of effort. One of the reasons for seeking identities is precisely because one side may be easier to compute than the other.

9. Use the data from Exercise 7.

a. Suppose experts predict that sales of passenger cars will increase across the board by 5% in the following year. Make a table of predicted passenger car sales for the following year. How did you get it?

b. Suppose it turns out that only Company D's sales increased by 5%. Company B's sales increased 3%, Company E's sales 2%, and the others had no change. Make a table for the actual sales. How did you get it?

c. Suppose it turned out that growth is regional: All companies had 6% growth in Asia, but only 1% growth in the U.S., and a 1% decline in Europe. Make a table for the actual sales. How did you get it?

10. A local bakery has four trucks of different sizes. Their gas tanks hold different amounts of gas, and they get different miles per gallon, as shown in the table below.

	Trucks			
Tank Size (gal)	15	18	20	25
mi/gal	20	18	12	15

If the bakery fills up all the tanks, how many miles of driving can it get from its fleet of trucks?

11. Return to the swim team from Problem 5. That table was just for the varsity squad. The team also buys suits and goggles for the JV squad at the same prices. These tables present the data a somewhat different way.

	W	M	G
Varsity Numbers	30	25	55
JV Numbers	25	22	47

20
15
8

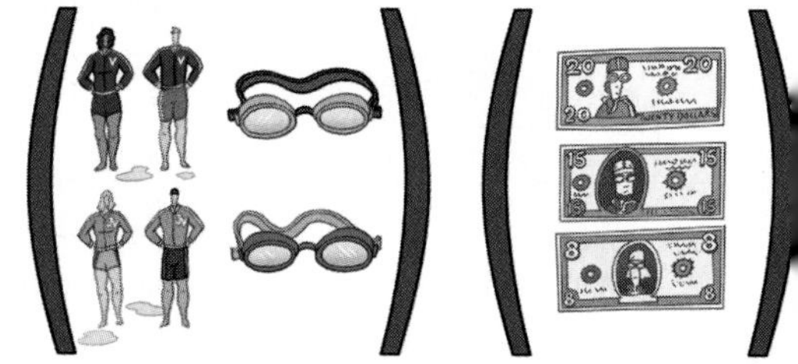

a. What is the total amount the swim team will spend buying these things? Does the format of the tables make it easy to describe the calculation?

b. There are at least two methods to calculate the answer to part (a). You can compute the cost for varsity and JV separately, or you can add the numbers in each category (women's suits, men's suits, goggles) first. Repeat part (a) using each method. Which method feels like less work? Explain.

Answers

9. See back of book.

10. 1239 mi

11. a. \$2621; the format does make it easy to describe the calculation.

b. Answers may vary. Sample: It is less work to add the numbers in each category because that calls for just three multiplications.

12. a. Answers may vary. Sample: Tell the row and column for each value.

b. $\begin{pmatrix} 1 & 2 & 3 & 4 \\ 2 & 3 & 4 & 5 \\ 3 & 4 & 5 & 6 \\ 4 & 5 & 6 & 7 \end{pmatrix}$

c. $\begin{pmatrix} \text{1 through 12} \\ \text{2 through 13} \\ \vdots \\ \text{10 through 21} \end{pmatrix}$

d. Answers may vary. Sample: The entry in row r, column c is $r + c - 1$.

Maintain Your Skills

For the matrices in Exercises 12 and 13, do parts (a)–(d).

a. Suppose you had to describe the matrix to a friend over the phone. How would you do it?

b. Write down or describe a 4×4 matrix that follows the same pattern as the given matrix.

c. Repeat part (b), but describe a 10×12 matrix.

d. You may have used many words to describe the general pattern in parts (a), (b), and (c). Can you think of a way to use symbols to be just as precise without as much explanation?

12. $M = \begin{pmatrix} 1 & 2 & 3 \\ 2 & 3 & 4 \\ 3 & 4 & 5 \end{pmatrix}$

13. $N = \begin{pmatrix} 1 & 1 & 1 \\ 2 & 4 & 8 \\ 3 & 9 & 27 \end{pmatrix}$

14. Consider the matrix below.

$$I = \begin{pmatrix} 1 & 0 & 0 \\ 0 & 1 & 0 \\ 0 & 0 & 1 \end{pmatrix}$$

This is the 3×3 identity matrix.

a. Suppose you had to describe this matrix to a friend over the phone. How would you do it?

b. Write down or describe a 6×6 matrix that follows the same pattern as the one you described for I.

c. If n is an unknown positive integer, how would you describe an $n \times n$ matrix with the same pattern?

15. Consider this 1×20 matrix.

$$A = (10 \quad 7 \quad 4 \quad 1 \quad -2 \quad -5 \quad \dots)$$

a. What might be the last entry in the matrix? Explain.

b. How would you describe this matrix to a friend without showing it? Can you do this with symbols?

c. Take It Further Now consider this 1×20 matrix.

$$B = (2 \quad 4 \quad 6 \quad 8 \quad \dots)$$

Suppose you wanted to combine these two matrices in the same way you combined the two rows in Exercise 11. How would you describe to a friend what you need to do without showing the calculations? Can you do this with symbols?

13. a. Answers may vary. Sample: There are three columns, and the entries in row r are r, r^2, r^3.

b. $\begin{pmatrix} 1 & 1 & 1 & 1 \\ 2 & 4 & 8 & 16 \\ 3 & 9 & 27 & 81 \\ 4 & 16 & 64 & 256 \end{pmatrix}$

c. There are ten rows, twelve elements per row. The first entry in row n is n, and each subsequent entry is the row number times the entry to its left.

d. Answers may vary. Sample: The entry in row r, column c is r^c.

14. a. Answers may vary. Sample: The main diagonal has 1's, each other entry is 0.

b. Answers may vary. Sample: The main diagonal has 1's, each other entry is 0.

c. Answers may vary. Sample: The main diagonal has 1's, each other entry is 0.

15. See back of book.

Maintain Your Skills

EXERCISES 12 AND 13 The purpose of these exercises is to get students to realize that there needs to be some systematic algebraic way to describe entries in matrices; writing the whole matrix out is not reasonable as the matrices get large. The standard way is to use doubly subscripted variables, which you introduce in the next lesson. This notation can be a bit overwhelming for students who may not have even seen single subscript notation often. So it will be better if they discover the notation (or something like it) beforehand, or at least recognize the need for some such notation. This text uses the notation a_{ij}, but if students come up with something like $a(i, j)$ or $a(x, y)$, that is great, too.

For Exercise 12c mathematicians would write: $M = [a_{ij}]$ is the 10×12 matrix with $a_{ij} = i + j - 1$. Probably your students will not come up with this, but see how close they get, either here or in later exercises in this set.

EXERCISE 14 Students may remember the term *identity* as being associated with a particular operation. For example, the additive identity for real numbers is 0, and the multiplicative identity is 1. They may be curious at this stage to know for what operation this kind of matrix is an identity. The other interesting feature for students to notice is that all of these identities are square matrices; they have the same number of rows as columns.

EXERCISE 15 Students learn techniques for finding the sum of a series like the one in part (c) in Chapter 7. For now, they will probably have to work the sum out by finding the actual terms and adding them, or by using a spreadsheet or similar application.

Lesson Overview

GOAL

- Communicate and prove results about matrices, including the ideas of rows and columns and indices.

In this lesson, students see that they can view the data tables from the Getting Started lesson as matrices. This gives them a different use for matrices than in the previous investigation. The operations on tables from the Getting Started lesson become matrix sums and scalar multiplication. Also, you introduce double index notation. This notation presents a powerful way to describe matrix operations or indeed to discuss anything about matrices and their entries.

CHECK YOUR UNDERSTANDING
- Core: 1, 2, 4, 5, 6, 7
- Optional: 3

MATERIALS
- graphing calculators
- Blackline Master 4.5

HOMEWORK
- Core: 8, 9, 10, 11, 12, 13, 14, 16, 17, 18, 19
- Optional: 15, 20, 21

VOCABULARY
- indices
- scalar multiplication

Launch

Start with the idea of matrix sum from the opening of the lesson. Move on to the For Discussion. Expect the definitions in this lesson to seem very reasonable to students. You may end up spending most of your class time helping students get comfortable with the new double subscript notation.

4.5 Basic Matrix Operations

You call the data displays in Lesson 4.4 tables, or sometimes two-way tables, but to mathematicians they are just matrices with labels! Indeed, you can show such tables with all sorts of formatting.

Passenger Car Sales (millions of cars)

	Company A	Company B	Company C	Company D	Company E
Europe	0.4	0.2	0.2	0.2	1
United States	2	1.5	0.6	1	0.3
Asia	0.2	0.1	0.8	3.5	0.1

But the tables are still just matrices. So you can write them as such.

$$\begin{pmatrix} 0.4 & 0.2 & 0.2 & 0.2 & 1 \\ 2 & 1.5 & 0.6 & 1 & 0.3 \\ 0.2 & 0.1 & 0.8 & 3.5 & 0.1 \end{pmatrix}$$

Or, if it is helpful, you can keep the labels.

$$\begin{array}{r} \\ \text{Europe} \\ \text{U.S.} \\ \text{Asia} \end{array} \begin{array}{c} \begin{array}{ccccc} \text{A} & \text{B} & \text{C} & \text{D} & \text{E} \end{array} \\ \begin{pmatrix} 0.4 & 0.2 & 0.2 & 0.2 & 1 \\ 2 & 1.5 & 0.6 & 1 & 0.3 \\ 0.2 & 0.1 & 0.8 & 3.5 & 0.1 \end{pmatrix} \end{array}$$

Developing Habits of Mind

Look for relationships. The tables help organize calculations people want to do. This means useful mathematical definitions are lurking! Try to identify the kinds of calculations that seem to be useful. See if you can define them for matrices independent of their particular use. Then you probably have concepts that will be useful in many places you have not yet imagined.

Consider Exercise 7 in Lesson 4.4, where you combined tables of passenger car sales with other vehicle sales to get total sales of all personal motor vehicles. Abstractly, what did you do? You started with two matrices.

$$\begin{pmatrix} 0.4 & 0.2 & 0.2 & 0.2 & 1 \\ 2 & 1.5 & 0.6 & 1 & 0.3 \\ 0.2 & 0.1 & 0.8 & 3.5 & 0.1 \end{pmatrix} \text{ and } \begin{pmatrix} 0.2 & 0.05 & 0.1 & 0.1 & 0.3 \\ 2.6 & 1.8 & 0.8 & 1.2 & 0.1 \\ 0.1 & 0.05 & 0.5 & 1 & 0 \end{pmatrix}$$

You got the matrix below.

$$\begin{pmatrix} 0.6 & 0.25 & 0.3 & 0.3 & 1.3 \\ 4.6 & 3.3 & 1.4 & 2.2 & 0.4 \\ 0.3 & 0.15 & 1.3 & 4.5 & 0.1 \end{pmatrix}$$

So, mathematically, you took two matrices of the same size and added the corresponding entries. The result was another matrix of the same size.

The entries of a matrix are the numbers inside it.

To make an algebra out of this, you need to use symbols. The sum $A + B$ of matrices A and B is the matrix you get by adding the corresponding entries.

For Discussion

1. Consider Exercise 8 from Lesson 4.4. Define another matrix operation based on this exercise.

Exercise 9a in Lesson 4.4 suggests another operation that takes one matrix and returns another matrix of the same size. You increase each entry by 5%. You can represent a percent increase as multiplication, in this case by 1.05. Since each entry of the matrix is multiplied by 1.05, the matrix is scaled. If you call the original matrix A, you can call the result $1.05A$. The process is **scalar multiplication.**

Scalar is another word for a number that you use when working with matrices. The product kA, where k is a number and A is a matrix, is another matrix you can get from A by multiplying each of its entries by k.

For You to Do

2. Use the matrices below.

$$A = \begin{pmatrix} 1 & 2 & 3 \\ 4 & 5 & 6 \end{pmatrix} \quad B = \begin{pmatrix} 1 & 0 & 1 \\ 0 & -1 & 0 \end{pmatrix} \quad C = \begin{pmatrix} 1 & 3 \\ 2 & 4 \end{pmatrix}$$

Compute $A + B$, $A - B$, $A + C$, $2A$, and $(-1)A$. Some of these expressions may be undefined.

Developing Habits of Mind

Detect the key characteristics. The definition of $A + B$ talks about "corresponding entries." In some cases, this may be clear. In other cases, such as in the definition of matrix multiplication, "corresponding entries" may not be clear. While it may be evident that you cannot add A and C in For You to Do Problem 2, shouldn't a good definition say something about that instead of leaving it for you to figure out? To address such clarity issues, you need more notation.

Explore

For Discussion

In this problem, you subtracted corresponding entries. It makes sense to think of this as *matrix subtraction.* The *difference* $A - B$ of matrices A and B is the matrix you get by subtracting the corresponding entry from B from each entry of A.

DEFINITION OF SCALAR MULTIPLICATION Discuss the definition of scalar multiplication with your class. In addition to Exercise 9a mentioned in the exposition, Problems 1 and 4 in Lesson 4.4 provide even clearer instances where you want to multiply a matrix by a scalar. In Problem 1, you want to multiply the matrix by 3. In Problem 4, you want to multiply the matrix by 2 and then by $\frac{1}{2}$.

For You to Do

Students have seen that matrix addition, matrix subtraction, and scalar multiplication arise naturally. Now, can they deal with these operations at the abstract level of algebraic symbolism? And do they recognize that to add or subtract matrices, the matrices must have the same dimension? Thus $A + C$ is not defined.

Developing Habits of Mind

There are two issues here, a general one and a specific one.

The general issue is that notation can be good. When you find yourself using a broad word (here *corresponding*) to describe something, you may find that a good notation can be more precise and more succinct. One of the great powers of mathematical language is its receptiveness to new notation.

The specific issue is the double subscript notation. Students have probably never seen it before. Some people will write it with a comma, as in $a_{2,3}$ instead of a_{23}. Indeed, a comma is necessary if there is any chance of confusion. Several later exercises allow students to practice with this notation until they get comfortable with it.

Answers

For Discussion

1. The difference $A - B$ of matrices A and B is the matrix you get by subtracting the corresponding entries.

For You to Do

2. $A + B = \begin{pmatrix} 2 & 2 & 4 \\ 4 & 4 & 6 \end{pmatrix}$;

$A - B = \begin{pmatrix} 0 & 2 & 2 \\ 4 & 6 & 6 \end{pmatrix}$;

$A + C$ is not defined;

$2A = \begin{pmatrix} 2 & 4 & 6 \\ 8 & 10 & 12 \end{pmatrix}$;

$(-1)A = \begin{pmatrix} -1 & -2 & -3 \\ -4 & -5 & -6 \end{pmatrix}$

For Discussion

Indices are like coordinates in that they locate the item in two dimensions. They are different, though, because the first index marks vertical location, and positive is in the down direction; the second index marks horizontal location. It is almost as if you replace coordinates (x, y) with indices $-y, x$.

You can use Blackline Master 4.5 as a transparency to introduce how to read double subscript notation.

First, the size of matrix A is the number of its rows and its columns. Matrices A and B are the same size if they both have the same number of rows, m, and the same number of columns, n. More briefly, A and B are the same size if they are both $m \times n$. Two matrices must be the same size in order for you to add or subtract them.

Second, you need a way to talk about specific entries. Entries in a matrix need two coordinates—their row number and their column number. These numbers are listed as subscripts, called indices. So a 3×4 matrix A might be

$$A = \begin{pmatrix} a_{11} & a_{12} & a_{13} & a_{14} \\ a_{21} & a_{22} & a_{23} & a_{24} \\ a_{31} & a_{32} & a_{33} & a_{34} \end{pmatrix}$$

The singular of *indices* is *index*.

The first number in the subscript is the row number and the second is the column number. So, more generally, an $m \times n$ matrix could be

column 3

$$\begin{pmatrix} a_{11} & a_{12} & a_{13} & \cdots & a_{1n} \\ a_{21} & a_{22} & a_{23} & \cdots & a_{2n} \\ \vdots & \vdots & \vdots & & \vdots \\ a_{m1} & a_{m2} & a_{m3} & \cdots & a_{mn} \end{pmatrix} \leftarrow \text{row 2}$$

the entry in row 2 and column 3

For Discussion

3. Indices are like coordinates, in a way. How are they similar to coordinates? How are they different?

With this index notation comes a nice shorthand. You can write

$$\text{Let } A = (a_{ij}).$$

This notation tells us two things:

- The entries of A will all be a-something.
- For this matrix, i will be the index of the rows and j will be the index of the columns. That is, you will use i when referring to a typical row of A and j when referring to a typical column.

With this notation, you can indicate the size of A at the same time. You can write

$$\text{Let } A \text{ be the } 3 \times 5 \text{ matrix } (a_{pq}).$$

or

$$\text{Let } A = (a_{pq}),\ p = 1, 2, 3, \text{ and } q = 1, 2, 3, 4, 5.$$

You do not always have to use i and j as your indices. Sometimes there is a good reason not to.

Answers

For Discussion

3. Answers may vary. Sample: They are like coordinates in that they are ordered ($a_{ij} \neq a_{ji}$); they are different in that i and j must be positive integers.

For You to Do

4. If $B = b_{ij}$ is a 3×2 matrix, then the matrix is $B = \begin{pmatrix} b_{11} & b_{12} \\ b_{21} & b_{22} \\ b_{31} & b_{32} \end{pmatrix}$.

Given only that $b_{ij} = i^j$, then
$b_{11} = 1$ and $b_{12} = 1^2 = 1$;
$b_{21} = 2$ and $b_{22} = 2^2 = 4$;
$b_{31} = 3$ and $b_{32} = 3^2 = 9$.

The matrix is $\begin{pmatrix} 1 & 1 \\ 2 & 4 \\ 3 & 9 \end{pmatrix}$.

For You to Do

4. Define $B = (b_{ij})$ to be the 3×2 matrix in which $b_{ij} = i^j$. Explain why this means that B is the matrix below.

$$B = \begin{pmatrix} 1 & 1 \\ 2 & 4 \\ 3 & 9 \end{pmatrix}$$

So what good is all this? The subscript notation is good for at least two reasons. First, it allows you to define matrices, even very big ones, without listing all the entries. Second, it allows you to give precise definitions of matrix operations such as sum and scalar product.

For instance, with this notation you can feed large matrices into calculators and computers without a huge number of keystrokes.

Definition

If $A = (a_{ij})$ and $B = (b_{ij})$ are both $m \times n$ matrices, then their sum $A + B$ is defined to be the $m \times n$ matrix with ij entry $a_{ij} + b_{ij}$. In other words, if $C = A + B$, then $c_{ij} = a_{ij} + b_{ij}$.

In such definitions, it is understood that any statement about entry ij is true for every such entry, but you can also be explicit and say $c_{ij} = a_{ij} + b_{ij}$ for all i from 1 to m and all j from 1 to n.

$$c_{ij} = a_{ij} + b_{ij},\ i = 1, 2, \ldots, m \text{ and } j = 1, 2, \ldots, n$$

For You to Do

5. Give similarly precise definitions for $A - B$ and kA.

Exercises *Practicing Habits of Mind*

Check Your Understanding

1. Identify each value for the matrix A.

$$A = (a_{ij}) = \begin{pmatrix} 1 & 2 & 3 \\ 4 & 5 & 6 \end{pmatrix}$$

a. the size of A **b.** a_{12} **c.** a_{21}
d. a_{23} **e.** a_{32}

5. If $A = (a_{ij})$ and $B = (b_{ij})$ are both $m \times n$ matrices, then their difference $A - B$ is defined to be the $m \times n$ matrix for which entry ij is $a_{ij} - b_{ij}$, and the scalar multiple $k \cdot A$ is the $m \times n$ matrix for which entry ij is $k \cdot a_{ij}$.

Exercises

1. a. 2×3
b. 2
c. 4
d. 6
e. There is no 3rd row.

For You to Do

PROBLEM 4 Alternative answer: For column $j = 1$, $i^j = i$, so the column is 1, 2, 3. For column $j = 2$, the column is i^2 or 1, 4, 9.

PROBLEM 5 Alternative answer: if A and B are two matrices of the same size, then their difference $A - B = C$ is also that size, and $c_{ij} = a_{ij} - b_{ij}$. If $A = (a_{ij})$ and $C = kA$, then C is the same size as A and $c_{ij} = ka_{ij}$.

Wrap Up

If the students are having trouble using index notation easily, it might be best to finish with a discussion about this. Otherwise an applied problem serves as a reminder that the definitions of matrix sum and scalar product were made up with a purpose.

Assessment Resources

Lesson Quiz 4.5

1. Define the 3×4 matrix $D = (d_{jk})$ by $d_{jk} = k^2 - j$. Write out D.

2. **a.** Suppose $z = -y_1 + 2y_2 - 3y_3$ and $y_1 = -x$, $y_2 = 2x$, $y_3 = -4x$

   Express z in terms of x.

   b. Now suppose that $y_1 = -3$, $y_2 = 2$, and $y_3 = -4$. Evaluate z.

3. On the side of a box of granola bars, there is a table that shows what percent of daily food recommended values are provided by one granola bar.

   Fat 5% Carbohydrates 9% Protein 5%

   If you eat 3 granola bars in one day, what percents do you get? What matrix and what matrix operation were involved in your calculations?

Exercises

HOMEWORK
- Core: 8, 9, 10, 11, 12, 13, 14, 16, 17, 18, 19
- Optional: 15, 20, 21

Check Your Understanding

EXERCISE 1 Students practice using double index notation with specific indices.

EXERCISE 2 Students practice using index notation with a shorthand formula for all of the entries of a matrix at once.

EXERCISE 3 is the reverse of Exercise 2 and thus much harder. Students must find an indices-based shorthand formula that fits the given entries.

EXERCISE 4 presents an opportunity to fall back to single indices, which students may find more comfortable. For instance, you could say, let $A = (a_j)$ and $B = (b_j)$ be $1 \times m$ matrices. Then $A + B = C$, where $c_j = a_j + b_j$. In the next lesson, one-row and one-column matrices play an important role, and you call them *n*-tuples.

EXERCISE 5 is Problem 1 of Lesson 4.4 repeated, but now you can express it using matrix concepts. It is a straightforward example of the naturalness of scalar multiplication.

2. Let $E = (e_{pq})$ with $e_{pq} = p^2 + 2^q$.

a. Write out E if it is 4×1.
b. Write out E if it is 1×4.

3. Come up with formulas for the entries of each matrix.

a. $A = \begin{pmatrix} 2 & 3 & 4 \\ 3 & 4 & 5 \end{pmatrix}$
b. $B = \begin{pmatrix} 1 & 2 & 3 \\ 3 & 4 & 5 \end{pmatrix}$
c. $C = \begin{pmatrix} 1 & 2 & 3 & 4 \\ 4 & 9 & 16 & 25 \end{pmatrix}$

4. Suppose you want to add single-row matrices such as (1, 2, 3, 4, 5) and (1, 4, 9, 16, 25). You do not need two indices to define addition.

a. Give a definition of $A + B$ for single-row matrices.
b. Give a definition of $A - B$ for single-row matrices.
c. Give a definition of scalar multiplication for single-row matrices.

Of course, the same approach works for single-column matrices.

5. On the side of a box of cereal, there is a table that shows what percent of recommended daily food values are provided by 1 ounce of the cereal.

Carbohydrates 7%   Vitamin A 10%   Vitamin B_{12} 25%

If you eat 3 ounces, what percents do you get? What matrix and what matrix operation are involved in your calculation?

6. A mathematics teacher keeps a record of each student's points on homework and points on tests. For three students, here are the homework points and test points for the first and second marking periods.

Of course, you can do this calculation without thinking about matrices. The point here is to illustrate that matrices are everywhere and, in some sense, you have been using them all your life.

First Marking Period Points

	Tony	Sasha	Derman
Homework	127	143	107
Tests	181	170	165

Second Marking Period Points

	Tony	Sasha	Derman
Homework	144	139	126
Tests	184	192	175

The teacher now wants to compute the homework points and test points for both marking periods combined. Help the teacher and do the computations. What matrix operation do you use?

Answers

2. a. $\begin{pmatrix} 3 \\ 6 \\ 11 \\ 18 \end{pmatrix}$

b. $(3 \quad 5 \quad 9 \quad 17)$

3. a. $a_{ij} = i + j$
b. $b_{ij} = 2(i - 1) + j$
c. $c_{ij} = (i + j - 1)^i$

4. a. $A + B = (c_{ij})$, where $c_{ij} = a_{ij} + b_{ij}$.
b. $A - B = (c_{ij})$, where $c_{ij} = a_{ij} - b_{ij}$.
c. $k \cdot A = (c_{ij})$, where $c_{ij} = k \cdot a_{ij}$.

5. carbohydrates: 21%, vitamin A: 30%, vitamin B_{12}: 75%; $3 \cdot \begin{pmatrix} 7 \\ 10 \\ 25 \end{pmatrix} = \begin{pmatrix} 21 \\ 30 \\ 75 \end{pmatrix}$ or $3 \cdot (7 \quad 10 \quad 25) = (21 \quad 30 \quad 75)$, scalar multiplication

6. $\begin{pmatrix} 271 & 282 & 233 \\ 365 & 362 & 340 \end{pmatrix}$; matrix addition

7. Another mathematics teacher keeps records as percents. For three students, here are the homework percents and test percents for the first and second marking periods.

Tony, Sasha, and Derman take more than one mathematics course.

First Marking Period Percents

	Sasha	Tony	Derman
Homework	94	98	85
Tests	95	91	83

Second Marking Period Percents

	Sasha	Tony	Derman
Homework	95	96	89
Tests	94	92	85

The teacher now wants to compute the homework percents and test percents for both marking periods combined. Can you compute this information from these tables? Explain.

On Your Own

8. Suppose $D = (d_{ij})$ is 3×3 and $d_{ij} = 2j$. Write out D.

9. Define the 2×4 matrix $C = (c_{jk})$ as $c_{jk} = k^j$. Write out C.

10. Define a matrix $M = (m_{ij})$ as $m_{ij} = \begin{cases} 1 & \text{if } i = j \\ 0 & \text{otherwise} \end{cases}$

For each size, write out the matrix M.

a. 4×4 b. 2×2 c. 4×3

This is your first example of a case statement defining a matrix. This type of definition is quite common.

11. **Standardized Test Prep** Define $D = (d_{jk})$ to be the 3×3 matrix in which $d_{jk} = (-j)^{(j+k)}$. Define $F = (f_{jk})$ to be the 3×3 matrix in which $f_{jk} = (2)^{(j-k)}$. If $G = D + F$, which is the entry in the second column of the third row of G?

A. −241 B. −31.5 C. 85 D. 730

12. In Exercise 7 of Lesson 4.4, you got one table about auto sales from two others. Viewing the tables as matrices, what matrix operation did you use?

13. In Exercise 8 of Lesson 4.4, you got one table about auto industry finances from two others. Viewing the tables as matrices, what matrix operation did you use?

14. In Problem 4 of Lesson 4.4, you got one table about weather from another. Viewing the tables as matrices, what matrix operation did you use?

Go Online PHSchool.com

For additional practice, go to **Web Code:** bfa-0405

EXERCISE 7 is the first of a few exercises that show you cannot go on automatic when combining matrices. Yes, the matrices in Exercise 6 should be added, but not the matrices in Exercise 7.

On Your Own

EXERCISES 8 AND 9 As in For You to Do Problem 4, these exercises provide basic practice in using double index notation.

EXERCISE 10 To make sure that students really understand case notation, it may be useful to have students explain one of the answers out loud, entry by entry. For instance, the answer for part (b) is $M = \begin{pmatrix} 1 & 0 \\ 0 & 1 \end{pmatrix}$. Make sure they can they explain why $m_{11} = 1$, why $m_{12} = 0$, and how exactly this follows from the meaning of the case statement.

EXERCISES 12–14 The purpose here is to make sure the students are consciously aware that the definitions in Lesson 4.5 have merely codified the natural operations in Lesson 4.4.

7. No; an average of percents is not necessarily the correct percentage of the whole. 47 of 50 is 94%. 190 of 200 is 95%, but 237 of 250 is 94.8%, not 94.5%.

8. $\begin{pmatrix} 2 & 4 & 6 \\ 2 & 4 & 6 \\ 2 & 4 & 6 \end{pmatrix}$ **9.** $\begin{pmatrix} 1 & 2 & 3 & 4 \\ 1 & 4 & 9 & 16 \end{pmatrix}$

10. a. $\begin{pmatrix} 1 & 0 & 0 & 0 \\ 0 & 1 & 0 & 0 \\ 0 & 0 & 1 & 0 \\ 0 & 0 & 0 & 1 \end{pmatrix}$

b. $\begin{pmatrix} 1 & 0 \\ 0 & 1 \end{pmatrix}$

c. $\begin{pmatrix} 1 & 0 & 0 \\ 0 & 1 & 0 \\ 0 & 0 & 1 \\ 0 & 0 & 0 \end{pmatrix}$

11. A

12. matrix addition

13. matrix subtraction

14. scalar multiplication

EXERCISE 15 Make sure all students have a basic understanding of these baseball statistics.

Maintain Your Skills

EXERCISE 16 For the next several lessons, the Maintain Your Skills exercises lead into the next lesson. In this set, all the exercises motivate the definition of dot product in the next lesson. Every exercise in this set is a linear substitution—one variable is a linear combination of several others and those others are all multiples of yet another variable. The formula for expressing the first variable in terms of the last variable always involves a sum of products—a dot product.

Additional Resources

PRINT RESOURCES
- Solution Manual
- Practice Workbook
- Assessment Resources
- Teaching Resources

TECHNOLOGY
- Interactive Textbook
- TeacherExpress CD-ROM
- ExamView CD-ROM
- PHSchool.com

Additional Practice

1. Identify each value for the matrix B.

$$B = (b_{ij}) = \begin{pmatrix} 1 & 3 & 5 \\ 2 & 4 & 6 \end{pmatrix}$$

a. the size of B
b. b_{12} **c.** b_{23} **d.** b_{13} **e.** b_{21}

2. Let $A = (a_{ij})$ with $a_{ij} = 2i^2 + j$.
a. Write out A if it is 3×2.
b. Write out A if it is 2×4.

3. Define the 2×4 matrix $D = (d_{jk})$ by $d_{jk} = k^j$. Write out D.

4. Define a matrix $K = (k_{ij})$ by $k_{ij} = \begin{cases} -1 & \text{if } i=j \\ 1 & \text{otherwise} \end{cases}$
For each size, write out the matrix K.
a. 4×4
b. 2×2
c. 3×3

5. Suppose $z = 4y_1 - 3y_2$ and $y_1 = -2x$, $y_2 = 5x$
Express z in terms of x.

6. Suppose $z = 2y_1 + 3y_2 - y_3$ and $y_1 = -2x$, $y_2 = 5x$, $y_3 = -3x$
Express z in terms of x.

7. Suppose again that $z = 2y_1 + 3y_2 - y_3$, but now $y_1 = -5$, $y_2 = 1$, and $y_3 = -3$. Evaluate z.

8. While traveling in Europe, Ian spends 200 pounds in England, 320 euros in France, and 275 francs in Switzerland. At the time, a pound was worth \$1.75, a euro was worth \$1.15, and a Swiss franc was worth \$.80.
a. In dollars, how much does Ian spend?
b. How does this exercise connect to the previous ones?

Practice: For Lesson 4.5, assign Exercises 1–8.

15. For three baseball players, Andre, Bobby, and Carlos, here are the RBIs and BAs for the first half and the second half of last season.

First Half of Season

	A	B	C
RBI	31	37	42
BA	.263	.294	.283

Second Half of Season

	A	B	C
RBI	26	36	53
BA	.243	.291	.314

Suppose you want to know their RBIs and BAs for the entire season. Can you get them from these tables? Explain.

RBI is the total number of runs batted in. BA, or batting average, is the ratio $\frac{\text{total hits}}{\text{total at bats}}$.

Maintain Your Skills

16. Suppose $z = 2y_1 + 5y_2$ and $y_1 = 3x$, $y_2 = -x$

Express z in terms of x.

17. Suppose

$$z = 2y_1 + 5y_2 - 3y_3 \quad \text{and} \quad \begin{aligned} y_1 &= 3x \\ y_2 &= -x \\ y_3 &= 4x \end{aligned}$$

Express z in terms of x. Is there a common pattern in this exercise and in Exercise 16? Explain.

18. Suppose again that $z = 2y_1 + 5y_2 - 3y_3$, but now $y_1 = 3$, $y_2 = -1$, and $y_3 = 4$. Evaluate z.

19. On a shopping spree in Europe, Bob spends 100 pounds in England, 150 euros in France, and 200 francs in Switzerland. At the time, a pound is worth \$1.80, a euro is worth \$1.25 and a Swiss franc is worth \$.75.

a. In dollars, how much does Bob spend?

b. How does this exercise connect to Exercises 16–18?

20. Suppose

$$z = a_1y_1 + a_2y_2 + a_3y_3 \quad \text{and} \quad \begin{aligned} y_1 &= b_1x \\ y_2 &= b_2x \\ y_3 &= b_3x \end{aligned}$$

Express z in terms of x.

21. Suppose

$$\begin{aligned} z &= a_1y_1 + a_2y_2 + a_3y_3 \\ w &= b_1y_1 + b_2y_2 + b_3y_3 \end{aligned} \quad \text{and} \quad \begin{aligned} y_1 &= c_1x \\ y_2 &= c_2x \\ y_3 &= c_3x \end{aligned}$$

Express the matrix $\begin{pmatrix} z \\ w \end{pmatrix}$ in terms of x.

Habits of Mind

Look for relationships. Exercise 20 is meant to give you a general statement of something you have done several times already in this investigation. What is it?

Answers

15. For the full-season RBI, add the corresponding elements. For the full-season batting average, "weight" the data in each table by multiplying the BA by the number of at-bats, then divide the total of the two corresponding products by the total number of at-bats.

16. $z = x$

17. $z = 11x$

18. $z = -11$

19. a. \$517.50

b. $S = 100p + 150e + 200f$ where $p = 1.8d$, $e = 1.25d$, and $f = 0.75d$

20. $z = (a_1b_1 + a_2b_2 + a_3b_3)x$

21. $\begin{pmatrix} z \\ w \end{pmatrix} = \begin{pmatrix} a_1c_1 + a_2c_2 + a_3c_3 \\ b_1c_1 + b_2c_2 + b_3c_3 \end{pmatrix}x$

4.6 Dot Products

The exercises in the Maintain Your Skills section in Lesson 4.5 led to this general result in Exercise 20.

If

$$z = a_1y_1 + a_2y_2 + b_3y_3 \text{ and } \begin{aligned} y_1 &= b_1x \\ y_2 &= b_2x \\ y_3 &= b_3x \end{aligned}$$

then

$$z = (a_1b_1 + a_2b_2 + a_3b_3)x$$

When there are just two intermediate variables y_1 and y_2, the result is $z = (a_1b_1 + a_2b_2)x$. (This is the result in Exercise 16. What are the values of a_1, a_2, b_1, and b_2 there?)

If there are n intermediate variables y_1 through y_n, then the result is

$$z = (a_1b_1 + a_2b_2 + \cdots + a_{n-1}b_{n-1} + a_nb_n)x$$

So what should you make of all this? You can write some definitions!

First, a string of n numbers, say $(a_1, a_2, \ldots, a_n)$, is an **n-tuple**. Second, given two n-tuples $A = (a_1, a_2, \ldots, a_n)$ and $B = (b_1, b_2, \ldots, b_n)$, define their **dot product** $A \cdot B$ to be the number

$$a_1b_1 + a_2b_2 + \cdots + a_nb_n$$

This is exactly the expression you got for the coefficient of x in Exercise 20, with $n = 3$. Dot products have plenty of uses, as you will soon see. In fact, you have already seen dot products in some word problems, such as Exercise 19 in Lesson 4.5.

Remember...

The most common name mathematicians use for an n-tuple is *vector*. The algebra of n-tuples is *vector algebra*. However, you are used to thinking of vectors as geometric objects—ordered pairs of points in a coordinate system.

Note that when $n = 2$, you have another geometric interpretation of n-tuples as points on the plane or as complex numbers represented as points on the complex plane. Also, when $n = 2$, you usually say "ordered pair" instead of "2-tuple."

For You to Do

Find each dot product, or explain why the calculation does not make sense.

1. $(1, 2) \cdot (-3, 4)$
2. $(2, 3) \cdot (-3, 2)$
3. $(1, 0, -1, 2) \cdot (3, 2, 1, x)$
4. $(1, 2) \cdot (2, -3, 4)$

You can view n-tuples as special thin matrices, either single rows or single columns, whichever seems more appropriate. For instance, the format of Exercise 20 suggests that you write the following.

$$\begin{pmatrix} y_1 \\ y_2 \\ y_3 \end{pmatrix} = \begin{pmatrix} b_1 \\ b_2 \\ b_3 \end{pmatrix} x$$

For You to Do

1. 5
2. 0
3. $2 + 2x$
4. Not defined; the n-tuples have different values of n.

Lesson Overview

GOAL

- Compute sums, differences, dot products, products, and inverses of matrices.

Based on the Maintain Your Skills exercises from the previous lesson, students know that expressions like $a_1b_1 + a_2b_2 + \cdots + a_nb_n$ show up repeatedly in calculations with matrices. So it should not seem surprising to give this calculation a name and study its properties. Actually, you give names to both the components: $= (a_1, \ldots, a_n)$ and $= (b_1, \ldots, b_n)$ you call *n-tuples;* the result: $a_1b_1 + a_2b_2 + \cdots + a_nb_n$ you call the *dot product* and you write $A \cdot B$. (In CME Project *Precalculus,* the text calls these n-tuples *vectors,* because that is what most mathematicians call them. However, for now that word *vectors* is not used, because students are more used to vectors as geometric objects—ordered pairs of points in a coordinate system.)

The amount of time and effort devoted to notation and properties of dot products may be heavy going for some, but there are several reasons for it. First, n-tuples continue to show up in several contexts. Second, dot products make the transition to matrix product much easier. Matrix product is defined in terms of dot products in the next lesson, and this definition turns out to be much simpler than defining matrix multiplication in terms of individual matrix entries. Second, justifications of the properties of matrix operations are much easier for students after they have done such justifications in the simpler domain of dot products. Finally, one of the habits of mind for students to develop is that many kinds of things, not just numbers, can be mathematical objects with properties.

CHECK YOUR UNDERSTANDING

- Core: 1, 2, 4, 5, 7, 9, 10
- Optional: 3, 6, 8

MATERIALS

- graphing calculators

HOMEWORK

- Core: 11, 12, 13, 14, 17, 18, 19, 20
- Optional: 16a–c, 21, 22, 23, 24, 25, 26, 27, 28, 29
- Extension: 15, 16d

VOCABULARY

- dot product
- *n*-tuple

Launch

You may decide to spend two days on this lesson if you cover all of the more theoretical aspects on the algebraic structure of dot product. In that case, break before the final dialog. On the second day, after going through the dialog in class, have students work through some of the optional exercises from the On Your Own set in class. The Maintain Your Skills exercises preview the next lesson and would be a good homework assignment for this second day.

continued on p. 316

continued from p. 315

Develop the definition of dot product right away and go to For You to Do.

Explore

Get students comfortable with the basic dot product calculation early on. Then the more abstract discussions about dot product properties will be easier to follow.

Dot product is probably the first operation students have seen where you multiply two objects and produce a *different* kind of object—the dot product of two n-tuples is a number. Keep reminding students of this fact. It helps them avoid trying to compute something like $A \cdot B \cdot C$.

For You to Do

In each set, the answers are the same. Hope that students will decide that these exercises illustrate general rules and that they will be able to formulate the rules, namely, for n-tuples of the same size.

Also note that if your goals for the treatment of matrices are less theoretical and more focused on calculation, you may wish to skip the remainder of this lesson and the exercises associated with it. You might also choose to come back to this material before you do the last lesson of this investigation on matrix properties.

Do you see how viewing (y_1, y_2, y_3) as a matrix allows you to regard the x as a scalar and put it on the outside? In Exercise 20, if you regard $A = (a_1, a_2, a_3)$ as a row, then the expression $a_1b_1 + a_2b_2 + a_3b_3$ is the dot product of a row and a column. For dot products, it does not matter whether you think of the n-tuples as rows or as columns, so long as they both have the same number of elements.

Not only do dot products show up in several places in this chapter, but they will show up in later math courses.

When you multiply two n-tuples together, you do not get another n-tuple, you get a number. Usually, when you combine two things, you get the same sort of thing. For example, when you add two matrices, you get a matrix. When you multiply two complex numbers, you get a complex number. However, this is not the case for dot products.

For You to Do

Do each set of computations. For each set, what is the relationship? How can you express the pattern?

5. $(1, 2, 3) \cdot (4, 5, 6)$ and $(4, 5, 6) \cdot (1, 2, 3)$

6. $(1, 0, 2) \cdot (x(1, -2, 2)), (x(1, 0, 2)) \cdot (1, -1, 2)$, and $x((1, 0, 2) \cdot (1, -1, 2))$

7. $(2, 3, 4) \cdot (c_1, c_2, c_3) + (3, 4, 5) \cdot (c_1, c_2, c_3)$ and $((2, 3, 4) + (3, 4, 5)) \cdot (c_1, c_2, c_3)$

Go back to the equations from Exercise 20 of Lesson 4.5. You can think of this in terms of the following matrices.

$$A = (a_1, a_2, a_3)$$
$$B = (b_1, b_2, b_3)$$
$$Y = (y_1, y_2, y_3)$$

The exercise says

$$z = A \cdot Y,\ Y = Bx, \text{ and } z = A \cdot (Bx)$$

The solution to Exercise 20 is $z = (a_1 b_1 + a_2 b_2 + a_3 b_3)x$, which you can write as

$$z = (A \cdot B)x$$

So in this case, $A \cdot (Bx) = (A \cdot B)x$. A similar equality showed up in Problem 6 above.

You can also write $x(A \cdot B)$. Since both x and $(A \cdot B)$ are numbers, they commute.

Is the following statement a rule about dot products?

$$(kA) \cdot B = A \cdot (kB) = (A \cdot B)k$$

Yes, this is a rule, or theorem, about dot products. And it is easy to remember because it looks similar to one of the basic rules of algebra. Although, if it is so familiar, what is left to prove? In the following dialog, Tony and Sasha grapple with some of these basic rules. In the exercises, you will discover and explain several other basic rules about n-tuples and dot products.

Answers

For You to Do

5. 32, 32; dot products are commutative.

6. $5x$, $5x$; you can take out a factor from either n-tuple or take the factor all the way out, as a scalar.

7. $5c_1 + 7c_2 + 9c_3$, $5c_1 + 7c_2 + 9c_3$; you can distribute an n-tuple over a sum of matrices.

Minds in Action episode 15

Tony and Sasha have been asked to justify, or find counterexamples to, two proposed rules for n-tuples.

$$(kA) \cdot B = k(A \cdot B) \text{ and } A + B = B + A$$

Tony Hey, Sasha, what's there to show? This is just basic algebra. Everybody knows that $(ka)b = k(ab)$ and $a + b = b + a$. These are just the basic rules of associativity and commutativity.

Sasha Yes, we already know them for real-number addition and multiplication, but here we have n-tuples and dot products.

Tony Ugh! If all the rules are the same and we know them, I don't see why we should have to show them again.

Sasha Well, they aren't really the same, because n-tuples aren't numbers, so their sum isn't quite a number sum. Maybe the rules aren't even true. Though I hope they are, because their form is so familiar—something we would want to use. So how should we start?

Tony I still don't get it. What do you mean that the sum isn't a number sum?

Sasha Well, when we say $a + b = b + a$ for numbers, we are saying $3 + 7 = 7 + 3$ and old stuff like that. But when we say $A + B = B + A$ for n-tuples, we are saying $(1, 2, 3) + (2, 4, 1) = (2, 4, 1) + (1, 2, 3)$ and new stuff like that. This is a new use of the plus sign, so we've got to think about whether it's right. So the first issue is, what does the plus sign mean for n-tuples? Our teacher never really told us.

Tony If they're just thin matrices, then it should be the same meaning as for matrices: Add corresponding entries.

Sasha So A and B would have to be the same size, say $1 \times n$, and we could write

$$A = (a_1, a_2, \ldots, a_n)$$
$$B = (b_1, b_2, \ldots, b_n)$$

Those old indices again, but only one at a time, thank goodness.

Tony $A + B$ is $(a_1 + b_1, a_2 + b_2, \ldots)$. Each entry is $a_i + b_i$.

Sasha Hey, each entry of $B + A$ is $b_i + a_i$. I think we're done, because $a_i + b_i = b_i + a_i$.

Tony No way! You're going in circles. You're saying that A and B commute because a_i and b_i commute.

Minds in Action

This dialog addresses several issues.

One is, why is there anything to prove? Sasha is right in explaining that n-tuples are not numbers, so our knowledge of numbers does not automatically transfer to knowledge of n-tuples.

A second issue: All right, maybe there is something to prove, but if all the same rules turn out to be true, why should people bother? One answer is that the usual rules do not all turn out to be true, but that fact does not come out in this dialog. (For instance, the Associative Property fails for dot products; see Exercise 13.) A better answer for now is that the method of proof illustrates an important principle in mathematics—how you use knowledge of simpler systems to develop knowledge of more complicated systems. In this case, you use knowledge of properties of numbers to develop knowledge of n-tuples of numbers.

A third issue: Note Tony's comment, "You're going in circles." It is great that Tony has heard of circular reasoning, but Sasha's reasoning only looks circular if you think that A and a_i mean the same sort of thing, that is, that you use different notations arbitrarily and they denote no difference. But mathematics notation is deliberately case-sensitive (and even font sensitive). Throughout this chapter capital letters are matrices (of which n-tuples are examples) and lowercase letters are numbers.

For Discussion

The expressions are not the same, but they are equal (they have the same value), which is what you need. They are equal because the letters represent numbers, so the rules of number algebra hold. For instance, by the Associative Property of multiplication, $(ka_i)b_i = k(a_ib_i)$, and likewise for the other summands in the first expression. Then, by the Distributive Property, $k(a_1b_1) + k(a_2b_2) + k(a_3b_3) = k(a_1b_1 + a_2b_2 + a_3b_3)$.

Wrap Up

Wrap up the lesson by going over the Check Your Understanding core exercises as time allows.

Assessment Resources

Lesson Quiz 4.6

1. Find each dot product.
   a. $(-1, 3, -5) \cdot (2, -4, 6)$
   b. $(1, -3) \cdot (2, 0, 6)$
   c. $(-1, -3, 1) \cdot (x, y, z)$
   d. $(1, 5, 9) \cdot (-1, -5, -9)$
   e. $(3, 7) \cdot (7, -3)$
   f. $(-2, 6) \cdot (12, 4)$

2. Find an n-tuple W that satisfies each equation.
   a. $(3, 6) + W = (0, 0)$
   b. $(-a, b) + W = 0$
   c. $(-2, 0, 3) + W = 0$
   d. $(-3, 0, 1, 3) + W = (-3, 0, 1, 3)$

3. Determine whether each statement is *true* or *false*. Explain.
   a. $(A \cdot B) \cdot C = A \cdot (B \cdot C)$
   b. $A \cdot (-B) = (-A) \cdot B$
   c. $A \cdot (kB) = k(A \cdot B)$
   d. $(A + B) \cdot (A - B) = A \cdot A - B \cdot B$

Sasha No, I'm not going in circles, because A and B are n-tuples and a_i and b_i are numbers. We already know that numbers commute. We've reduced it to the previous case!

Tony Okay, I see what you mean. I guess they are different. It still feels like we're just doing the same thing, but let's go on to the other rule.

Sasha Well, I see an important difference here. Both sides of $(kA) \cdot B = k(A \cdot B)$ are numbers. Both sides of $A + B = B + A$ are thin matrices.

Tony Good news. To show that two matrices are equal, we had to show that they were equal entry by entry. Now we just have two numbers that have to be equal.

Sasha Yeah, but each number is constructed in a complicated way. On the left, $(kA) \cdot B$, we start with A. Suppose $A = (a_1, a_2, a_3)$. Then we multiply by some number k. Then we dot with some other 3-tuple B. Let's say $B = (b_1, b_2, b_3)$.

Tony Who says these vectors are 3-tuples?

Sasha No one, but if we see what is going on for 3-tuples, maybe the general pattern won't be much different. Try it. You compute $(kA) \cdot B$.

Tony All right. $kA = (ka_1, ka_2, ka_3)$, so then $(kA) \cdot B$ would be

$$(ka_1)b_1 + (ka_2)b_2 + (ka_3)b_3$$

Sasha Thanks. Now the right side of the rule, $k(A \cdot B)$, is

$$k(a_1b_1 + a_2b_2 + a_3b_3)$$

So are the two sides the same or not?

For Discussion

8. Are the two expressions that Tony and Sasha found actually the same?

Go Online PHSchool.com

For a project using linear algebra, go to **Web Code:** bfe-0931

Answers

For Discussion

8. yes

Exercises *Practicing Habits of Mind*

Check Your Understanding

1. There were several dot-product exercises in Lesson 4.4—you just did not know they were dot products. Which exercises involved dot products? Explain.

2. Find each dot product.

   a. $(1, 2, 3) \cdot (4, 5, 6)$ **b.** $(4, 5, 6) \cdot (1, 2, 3)$

   c. $(1, 2, 3) \cdot \begin{pmatrix} 4 \\ 5 \\ 6 \end{pmatrix}$ **d.** $\begin{pmatrix} 3 \\ 2 \\ 1 \end{pmatrix} \cdot \begin{pmatrix} 6 \\ 5 \\ 4 \end{pmatrix}$

   e. $\begin{pmatrix} 1 \\ 2 \\ 3 \end{pmatrix} \cdot (4, 5, 6)$ **f.** $(1, 2) \cdot (3, 4, 5)$

3. Find each dot product.

   a. $(3, 4) \cdot (3, 4)$

   b. $(a, b) \cdot (a, b)$

   c. $(2, 3, 4) \cdot (2, 3, 4)$

4. Find an n-tuple Z that satisfies each equation.

   a. $(1, 2) + Z = (1, 2)$

   b. $(x, y) + Z = (x, y)$

   c. $(1, 2, -3, \pi) + Z = (1, 2, -3, \pi)$

5. Generalize from Exercise 4. Show that for each n-tuple X, there is another n-tuple Z such that $X + Z = X$.

Not surprisingly, you call such a Z a zero.

6. **a.** Compute $(1, 0, 1) \cdot (x, y, z) + (0, 2, 1) \cdot (x, y, z) - (1, 2, 2) \cdot (x, y, z)$.

   b. Without actually computing any dot product, explain why the answer to part (a) has to be 0.

7. The Distributive Property of dot products says

$$A \cdot (B \pm C) = A \cdot B \pm A \cdot C$$

and

$$(A \pm B) \cdot C = A \cdot C \pm B \cdot C$$

That is, the dot product distributes over n-tuple addition and subtraction. You worked out a specific example of this property in Problem 5 in the For You to Do section.

Assuming this property, show that

$$(A + B) \cdot (A + B) = A \cdot A + 2A \cdot B + B \cdot B$$

The sign $\pm$ means "plus or minus." When it appears more than once in an equation, you must make the same choice in every case. For instance, in the equation to the left, either use plus both times or use minus both times.

Exercises

HOMEWORK

- Core: 11, 12, 13, 14, 17, 18, 19, 20
- Optional: 16a–c, 21, 22, 23, 24, 25, 26, 27, 28, 29
- Extension: 15, 16d

Check Your Understanding

EXERCISE 2 The most important points are that dot product commutes, and that it does not matter whether n-tuples are written as rows or columns. For part (f) the answer is *undefined* because you can only dot two n-tuples of the same length (same n).

EXERCISE 3 Do students see, and can they verbalize, that the dot product of an n-tuple with itself always produces a sum of squares?

EXERCISE 4 gets at the question of whether there is an additive identity for n-tuples. There is, but it must have the same size as the n-tuple to which it is being added. Of course, Z is chosen to suggest zero. Sometimes the number zero is used too, but only if it is clear from context that you mean an n-tuple $(0, 0, \ldots, 0)$, not the single number 0. To avoid any such confusion, many books write boldface 0, or (for handwriting) use an overbar, as in $\overline{0}$.

EXERCISE 5 helps, in a nondirective way, plant the idea that n-tuple algebra (vector algebra), like number algebra, has special elements.

EXERCISE 7 Here students are not to prove the Distributive Property. Rather, they are to assume it is true and show some consequences. They prove the Distributive Property in Exercise 20.

Exercises

1. Exercises 5, 6, 10, and 11; each solution is the sum of the element-wise products of the table entries.

2. **a.** 32 **b.** 32 **c.** 32
   d. 32 **e.** 32
   f. The dot product is not defined.

3. **a.** 25 **b.** $a^2 + b^2$ **c.** 29

4. **a.** (0, 0)
   b. (0, 0)
   c. (0, 0, 0, 0)

5. For any n-tuple X, there is a unique n-tuple $Z = (0, 0, \ldots, 0)$ such that $X + Z = X$.

6. **a.** 0
   b. Answers may vary. Sample: Rewrite the expression as $(1 + 0 - 1, 0 + 2 - 2, (1 + 1 - 2) \cdot (x, y, z) = (0, 0, 0) \cdot (x, y, z) = 0$.

7. $(A + B) \cdot (A + B)$
   $= (A + B) \cdot A + (A + B) \cdot B$
   $= A \cdot A + B \cdot A + A \cdot B + B \cdot B$
   $= A \cdot A + A \cdot B + A \cdot B + B \cdot B$
   $= A \cdot A + 2A \cdot B + B \cdot B$

EXERCISE 9 is supported by information in Exercises 18 and 19. So you may choose not to assign it until you have assigned those. This exercise says that $-X$ is defined a certain way that is different from $(-1)X$. But why should it be? The answer is: to parallel the difference in number algebra between $-x$ (the additive inverse of x) and $(-1)x$. Exercises 18 and 19 help make it clear that n-tuples *have* additive inverses and what they should be.

Thus this exercise may be especially hard for students. The calculation is easy enough (except perhaps for subscripts and the general value of n), but the reason for doing it is subtle. Nonetheless, it is worth addressing subtleties occasionally. An important point is that each mathematical object, such as $-X$ or kx, is defined a certain way, and in mathematics you cannot say it means something else or write it another way without justification, even if it is only a bit different.

On Your Own

EXERCISE 12 n-tuples such as (1, 0, 0) and (0, 0, 0, 1, 0) are called standard unit vectors. Here students see, in the case $n = 3$, that standard unit vectors can be used with dot products to identify coordinates.

EXERCISE 13 No, there is not an associative property. Neither side of the proposed equation even makes sense! Here students begin to see that dot product algebra does differ from number algebra.

EXERCISE 14 may be a surprise for students. Since so many of the properties of real number multiplication have worked, they may not expect to find that the Zero Product Property does not hold.

EXERCISE 15 You might need to jog some of your students' memories by asking a question such as, "How would you decide whether two vectors are perpendicular?" Once they have decided to test the lines containing the vectors, they will likely remember how to tell whether two lines are perpendicular. If not, it is something they can look up or that you can choose to review with your class.

8. Again assuming the Distributive Property, show that

$$(A + B) \cdot (A - B) = A \cdot A - B \cdot B$$

9. Show that, for all n-tuples X (actually, for all matrices X), $(-1)X = -X$. While this should be true if matrix algebra is to behave properly, note that it is not automatically true, because the two sides mean entirely different things. The left side means the result of multiplying X by the scalar -1. The right side means whatever n-tuple W satisfies $X + W = (0, 0, \dots)$.

10. Use Exercise 9 to show that $A \cdot (-B) = -(A \cdot B) = (-A) \cdot B$ is a special case of the general rule $A \cdot (kB) = k(A \cdot B) = (kA) \cdot B$.

On Your Own

11. **Standardized Test Prep** Find the following dot product.

$$(3, -5, 4) \cdot (2, 6, 7)$$

A. (5, 1, 11) **B.** (6, −30, 28) **C.** 4 **D.** 17

12. Find each dot product.

a. $(1, 0, 0) \cdot (x, y, z)$ **b.** $(0, 1, 0) \cdot (x, y, z)$ **c.** $(x, y, z) \cdot (0, 0, 1)$

13. Is there an associative property for dot products? That is, is the statement below true? Explain.

$$A \cdot (B \cdot C) = (A \cdot B) \cdot C$$

14. In parts (a)–(d), find each dot product.

a. $(3, 4) \cdot (4, -3)$ **b.** $(3, 4) \cdot (-4, 3)$

c. $(3, 4) \cdot (8, -6)$ **d.** $(a, b) \cdot (b, -a)$

e. In your first-year algebra class, you learned the Zero Product Property. If $ab = 0$, then what can you conclude? What does this exercise have to do with the Zero Product Property?

15. **Take It Further** For parts (a)–(d) of Exercise 14, represent each ordered pair as a point on the plane and draw the vectors from the origin to those points. Do you notice anything? Pick some other pairs of ordered pairs, compute their dot products, and draw the associated vectors. Report on your findings.

16. **a.** Find A such that $A \cdot (1, 2) = 5$.

b. Check that this same A satisfies $A \cdot (3, 6) = 15$.

c. Find B such that $B \cdot (2, 4) = 10$.

d. **Take It Further** Classify all A such that $A \cdot (1, 2) = 5$.

Go Online PHSchool.com

For additional practice, go to **Web Code**: bfa-0406

Answers

8. $(A + B) \cdot (A - B)$
$= A \cdot (A - B) + B \cdot (A - B)$
$= A \cdot A - A \cdot B + B \cdot A - B \cdot B$
$= A \cdot A - A \cdot B + A \cdot B - B \cdot B$
$= A \cdot A - B \cdot B$

9. If X is the n-tuple $(x_1, x_2, \dots, x_n)$, then $(-1)X = (-1)\,(x_1, x_2, \dots, x_n) = (-x_1, -x_2, \dots, -x_n)$. Then $X + (-1)X = (0, 0, \dots, 0)$, so $-1(X) = -X$.

10. We know that $A \cdot (kB) = k(A \cdot B) = (kA) \cdot B$, so $A \cdot ((-1)B) = A \cdot (-B)$ by Exercise 9, and $A \cdot (-B) = -(A \cdot B) = (-A) \cdot B$.

11. C

12. **a.** x **b.** y **c.** z

13. no

14–16. See back of book.

17. The dot product satisfies the commutative property:

$$A \cdot B = B \cdot A$$

Explain why. Perhaps you can begin with $A = (a_1, a_2)$ and $B = (b_1, b_2)$ and work up to $A = (a_1, a_2, \ldots, a_n)$ and $B = (b_1, b_2, \ldots, b_n)$.

18. Find an n-tuple W that satisfies each equation.

a. $(1, 2) + W = (0, 0)$

b. $(x, y) + W = 0$

c. $(1, 2, -3, \pi) + W = 0$

19. Every number x has an additive inverse $-x$, which satisfies the property $x + (-x) = 0$. Generalize from Exercise 17 to define an additive inverse $-X$ for every n-tuple X. Show that $-X$ exists for every X. That is, for $X = (x_1, x_2, \ldots, x_n)$, find the coordinates of $-X$.

20. Show that the dot product distributes over n-tuple addition and subtraction.

$$A \cdot (B \pm C) = A \cdot B \pm A \cdot C$$

21. For real-number multiplication, there is an inverse, so you can solve $ax = b$ for x by multiplying both sides by a^{-1} to get $x = a^{-1}b$, assuming that $a \neq 0$, of course. Do n-tuples have dot-product inverses? That is, can you solve the equation $A \cdot X = b$ by taking the dot product with some n-tuple A^{-1}? Explain.

22. **Write About It** To what extent are dot-product rules the same as number rules? Is there a pattern to which rules are the same and which are not?

Habits of Mind

Try a specific case. You might set $n = 3$. If you can answer the question in a way that does not use any particular property of 3, your argument is correct for any n.

Maintain Your Skills

23. Consider the linear system below. Show how to represent z_1 and z_2 as a dot product using the vector $Y = (y_1, y_2, y_3)$.

$$z_1 = 2y_1 + 3y_2 + 4y_3$$
$$z_2 = 3y_1 - 2y_2 + 5y_3$$

24. Use the equations below.

$$\begin{aligned} z_1 &= 2y_1 + 5y_2 - 3y_3 \\ z_2 &= 3y_1 - y_2 + y_3 \end{aligned} \quad \text{and} \quad \begin{aligned} y_1 &= 3x \\ y_2 &= -x \\ y_3 &= 4x \end{aligned}$$

Express z_1 and z_2 in terms of x. What is the common pattern in this exercise and in Exercises 16 and 17 of Lesson 4.5? Can you use dot products to do this exercise? Explain.

17. If $A = (a_1, a_2)$ and $B = (b_1, b_2)$, then $A \cdot B = (a_1, a_2) \cdot (b_1, b_2) = a_1b_1 + a_2b_2 = b_1a_1 + b_2a_2 = B \cdot A$.

18. a. $(-1, -2)$

b. $(-x, -y)$

c. $(-1, -2, 3, -\pi)$

19. If $X = (x_1, x_2, \ldots, x_n)$, then $-X = (-x_1, -x_2, \ldots, -x_n)$.

20. See back of book.

21. No; if $A \cdot X = b$, then the left side is a number and the expression $A^{-1} \cdot (A \cdot X)$, which would be the dot product of a matrix and a number, has no meaning.

22. Answers may vary. Sample: Dot products involving one dot have properties similar to properties of numbers; an exception is the Zero Product Property.

23. $z_1 = (2, 3, 4) \cdot Y$, $z_2 = (3, -2, 5) \cdot Y$

24. $z_1 = -11x$, $z_2 = 14x$; there is another y_i term; yes; $z_1 = (2, 5, -3) \cdot (y_1, y_2, y_3)$, $z_2 = (3, -1, 1) \cdot (y_1, y_2, y_3)$

EXERCISE 17 is another example of a proof in which students may not understand what they can and cannot use as results. The distinction between n-tuples and real numbers is a subtle one, and it can take a while for students to get the hang of the fact that although n-tuples are not real numbers, they do have real numbers as their coordinates. Especially when you are using variables, it may be difficult for students to spot the moment when they begin to work with numbers rather than n-tuples.

EXERCISES 18 AND 19 Just as Exercises 4 and 5 suggest that, for each n, there is a zero in n-tuple algebra, Exercises 18 and 19 suggest that there are also additive inverses. Once an operation has a zero, you can always ask if it has additive inverses.

Maintain Your Skills

This set of exercises shows that systems of linear equations can be written as dot product equations. This insight will lead, in the next lesson, to writing each system of linear equations as a single matrix equation. Students have already represented systems of linear equations with a matrix, but they did not do any algebra between matrices (adding them or multiplying them) either to represent the systems or to describe Gaussian Elimination. This is coming.

For now, the goal is for students, now that they have seen so many computations that amount to matrix multiplications, either to come up with the abstract definition themselves or at least to regard the definition as natural when you present it in the next lesson. This is an important goal, because matrix multiplication seems really strange to most people when they first see it, like some mad mathematician's idea of pointless torture.

To accomplish this goal, it is important that the students work through all the Maintain Your Skills exercises and discuss where the exercises seem to be going.

EXERCISE 23 continues the theme of linear substitutions from the previous lesson. In the previous Maintain Your Skills most of the substitutions were of the 1, n, 1 variety: one variable (say z) you defined as a linear combination of n variables, say $y_1, \ldots, y_n$, and you defined all n of these you defined in terms of one further variable, say x. You asked students to express z in terms of x. Now you generalize that idea, one step at a time, to m, n, p substitutions: $z_1, \ldots, z_m$ in terms of $y_1, \ldots, y_n$, which in turn you express in terms of $x_1, \ldots, x_p$. You ask students to express the z's in terms of the x's.

EXERCISE 28 The message should be becoming clear. When you combine sets of linear equations by substitution, in matrix form you go across rows on the left and columns on the right, dotting as you go. This concept is made explicit in the next lesson.

Additional Resources

PRINT RESOURCES
- Solution Manual
- Practice Workbook
- Assessment Resources
- Teaching Resources

TECHNOLOGY
- Interactive Textbook
- TeacherExpress CD-ROM
- ExamView CD-ROM
- PHSchool.com

Additional Practice

1. Find each dot product.
a. $(1, 3, 5) \cdot (2, 4, 6)$ **b.** $(1, 3) \cdot (2, 4, 6)$ **c.** $(1, 0, 1) \cdot (x, y, z)$
d. $(3, 5, 7) \cdot (3, 5, 7)$ **e.** $(2, 5) \cdot (5, -2)$ **f.** $(2, 5) \cdot (10, -4)$

2. Find an n-tuple W that satisfies each equation.
a. $(2, 3) + W = (0, 0)$ **b.** $(a, -b) + W = 0$
c. $(-1, 0, 1) + W = 0$ **d.** $(0, 1, 2, 3) + W = (0, 1, 2, 3)$

3. a. Show that the dot product satisfies the Commutative Property.
$$A \cdot B = B \cdot A$$
b. Show that the dot product satisfies the Distributive Property.
$$A \cdot (B + C) = A \cdot B + A \cdot C \quad \text{and} \quad (A + B) \cdot C = A \cdot C + B \cdot C$$

4. Use the matrices below to compute each expression.
$$A = \begin{pmatrix} -1 & 2 \\ -3 & 4 \end{pmatrix} \quad B = \begin{pmatrix} 1 & -2 \\ 0 & -1 \end{pmatrix} \quad C = \begin{pmatrix} -3 & 5 \end{pmatrix}$$
a. AB **b.** BA **c.** $AB - BA$
d. $C(AB)$ **e.** $C(A + B)$

5. Use the matrices below. Compute AB, AC, and AD.
$$A = \begin{pmatrix} 0 & -3 \\ -1 & 2 \\ 3 & 1 \end{pmatrix} \quad B = \begin{pmatrix} 2 \\ -5 \end{pmatrix} \quad C = \begin{pmatrix} -4 \\ 3 \end{pmatrix} \quad D = \begin{pmatrix} 2 & 0 \\ -5 & 4 \end{pmatrix}$$

6. The table shows the number of students in each class year by letter grade received at a local high school.

	A	B	C	D	F
6th Grade	16	24	20	6	2
7th Grade	13	18	28	9	3
8th Grade	18	26	16	7	1

a. Compute the total number of students in each year. Show how you can express this computation as matrix multiplication.
b. Compute the total number of students who received each letter grade. Show how you can express this computation as matrix multiplication.
c. Use parts (a) and (b) to compute the total enrollment two ways. Show how you can express each way as matrix multiplication.

Practice: For Lesson 4.6, assign Exercises 1–3.

25. Suppose $a = 3p + 7q$ and $p = 2x - 3y$, $q = 5x + 4y$

Express a in terms of x and y. Can you express your calculation using dot products? Explain.

26. Suppose $a = 3p + 7q$, $b = p - 2q$ and $p = 2x - 3y$, $q = 5x + 4y$

Express a and b in terms of x and y. Look for dot products again.

27. Exercise 24 gave you two sets of equations and asked you to find a third set by substitution. Suppose you represent each given set of equations with its matrix of coefficients. Putting the two matrices side by side, they are
$$\begin{pmatrix} 2 & 5 & -3 \\ 3 & -1 & 1 \end{pmatrix} \begin{pmatrix} 3 \\ -1 \\ 4 \end{pmatrix}$$
The solution to Exercise 24 is the set of equations
$$z_1 = -11x$$
$$z_2 = 14x$$
You can represent this solution with the matrix
$$\begin{pmatrix} -11 \\ 14 \end{pmatrix}$$
Can you explain a method for getting the final matrix directly from the two given matrices?

28. Exercise 25 gave you two sets of equations and asked you to find another equation by substitution. Suppose you represent each given set of equations with its matrix of coefficients. Putting the two matrices side by side, they are
$$\begin{pmatrix} 3 & 7 \end{pmatrix} \begin{pmatrix} 2 & -3 \\ 5 & 4 \end{pmatrix}$$
The resulting equation was $a = 41x + 19y$, so the resulting matrix is the row matrix $(41 \ 19)$. Can you explain a method for getting this row matrix directly from the two given matrices?

29. Exercise 26 gave you two sets of equations and asked you to find a third set by substitution. Suppose you represent each given set of equations with its matrix of coefficients. Putting the two matrices side by side, they are
$$\begin{pmatrix} 3 & 7 \\ 1 & -2 \end{pmatrix} \begin{pmatrix} 2 & -3 \\ 5 & 4 \end{pmatrix}$$
a. Write the matrix of coefficients of the resulting set of equations.

b. Can you explain a method for getting the final matrix directly from the two given matrices? Try to be as general as you can.

Answers

25. $a = 41x + 19y$; one way to use dot products for the calculation is to let $a = (3, 7) \cdot \begin{pmatrix} p \\ q \end{pmatrix}$ where $\begin{pmatrix} p \\ q \end{pmatrix} = x\begin{pmatrix} 2 \\ 5 \end{pmatrix} + y\begin{pmatrix} -3 \\ 4 \end{pmatrix}$.

26. $a = 41x + 19y$, $b = -8x - 11y$

27. Answers may vary. Sample: Find the dot products of the rows of the matrix on the left with the column of the matrix on the right.

28. Answers may vary. Sample: If you find the dot products of the row of the matrix on the left with the columns of the matrix on the right, you get (41, 19), which are the coefficients of x and y.

29. a. $\begin{pmatrix} 41 & 19 \\ -8 & -11 \end{pmatrix}$

b. Answers may vary. Sample: To find each entry p_{ij} of the final matrix, form the dot product of row i from the left matrix and column j of the right matrix.

4.7 Matrix Multiplication

Matrix addition is defined by adding corresponding entries. It might make sense to define *matrix multiplication* the same way, entry-wise. It would be easy, but it is not done that way. Why not? A different, much less obvious definition turns out to be much more valuable. You will begin to see how valuable it is in this lesson, and you will see even more uses later as the chapter continues. Of course, historically it took time for mathematicians to realize which definition would be the most useful.

The "correct" definition grew out of the problem of linear substitutions. All the Maintain Your Skills exercises in the last two lessons were about linear substitutions. Consider Exercise 25 from Lesson 4.6. The variables a and b are linear in p and q. That is, a and b are both sums of multiples of p and q. There are no squares, square roots, exponentials, or constant terms. Moreover, the variables p and q are linear in x and y. What are a and b when expressed directly in terms of x and y? In Exercise 25, you substituted the expressions for p and q into the equations for a and b and got the answer. In particular, a and b turned out to be linear in x and y as well. And the computation involved dot products. For instance, in Exercise 25, a turned out to equal $41x + 19y$, where

Another way to say this is to say a and b are **linear combinations** of p and q.

$$41 = (3, 7) \cdot (2, 5) \quad \text{and} \quad 19 = (3, 7) \cdot (-3, 4)$$

If linear substitutions occurred rarely, then each time you could do the work from scratch, as in Exercise 25. But, in fact, linear substitutions occur quite frequently in applications (see Example 2), so it is worth finding a time saver. Exercise 28 from Lesson 4.6 suggests how. Just as you can speed up solving linear systems by writing matrices instead of equations, you can speed up substitutions by getting the final matrix directly from the two original matrices, as in Exercise 28. The method is to dot rows of the first matrix with columns of the second. This result is defined to be the matrix product.

For instance, continuing with Exercise 25, the matrices associated with the two sets of equations (a and b in terms of p and q and then p and q in terms of x and y) are

$$A = \begin{pmatrix} 3 & 7 \\ 1 & -2 \end{pmatrix} \quad \text{and} \quad B = \begin{pmatrix} 2 & -3 \\ 5 & 4 \end{pmatrix}$$

The matrix associated with the resulting set of equations (a and b in terms of x and y) is

$$C = \begin{pmatrix} 41 & 19 \\ -8 & -11 \end{pmatrix}$$

Note that the dot product of the first row of A with the first column of B is $(3, 7) \cdot (2, 5) = 41$, which is the coefficient of x in $a = 41x + 19y$ and the top left entry of C. Then note that $19 = (3, 7) \cdot (-3, 4)$, which is the dot product of the first row of A and the second column of B, and 19 is the top right entry of C. In all four cases, the dot product of the ith row of A and the jth column of B results in the ij entry of C. (Check this!) So taking the dot product of rows of the left matrix with columns of the right matrix does seem to be the thing to do.

Lesson Overview

GOALS

- Compute sums, differences, dot products, and products of matrixes.
- Interpret and solve problems using matrix calculations.

In Investigation 4A, students learned how to solve linear systems solely at the matrix level with Gaussian Elimination. The goal here is to do linear substitutions completely at the matrix level as well. The payoff is even greater, because it leads to an algebra of matrices—a definition of matrix multiplication.

This is an essential lesson. Matrix multiplication is what makes matrices more than mere tables. There are three main focus points for students.

1. The definition of matrix multiplication is natural extrinsically in that it captures the idea of linear substitution in several variables; put differently, there are multistage linear processes, where one set of variables depends on a second set, and that second set depends on a third.
2. The definition of matrix multiplication is natural intrinsically in that by turning any system of linear equations into a single equation $AX = B$, you develop an algebra of systems.
3. The definition of matrix multiplication allows multiplication to be a versatile operation. You can do many things to n-tuples and matrices by multiplying them by other matrices. For instance, it turns out (as seen in Investigation 4C) that you can describe all sorts of geometric transformations by matrix multiplication.

You may wish to spend at least two days on this lesson. The exercise sets are very long; there is much to practice. The practice will pay off if students develop a feel for how matrix multiplication works.

CHECK YOUR UNDERSTANDING

- Core: 1, 2, 3, 4, 5, 6, 7, 13, 14
- Optional: 8, 9, 10, 11, 12

MATERIALS

- graph paper
- graphing calculators
- Blackline Masters 4.7A, 4.7B

HOMEWORK

- Core: 15, 17, 18, 19, 21, 23, 25, 31, 32
- Optional: 16, 20, 22, 24, 26, 27, 28, 30, 33, 34, 35, 36, 37, 38, 39, 40
- Extension: 29

VOCABULARY

- linear combination
- matrix multiplication
- zero matrix, 0

Launch

Start with information on and the definition of matrix multiplication. Then cover Example 1. The Maintain Your Skills exercises from the previous

continued on p. 324

continued from p. 323

lesson should have given students enough experience, that the definition is plausible. Once students have worked with the definition for a while, they can come back to Example 1 and solidify their understanding of how matrix multiplication is applicable. Applied examples raise all sorts of additional complications—gleaning the mathematics from all the words, and deciding the order in which to multiply the matrices.

Explore

Students will use most of the time in the lesson getting used to the asymmetric nature of matrix multiplication—rows on the left versus columns on the right. You might have students explain their ways of thinking about matrix multiplication to each other.

DEFINITION Tactile strategy: To find the row-2 column-3 entry of AB, you run your left-hand index finger across the second row of A while, at the same speed, you run your right-hand index finger down the third column of B. You multiply numbers that your fingers cross at the same time and keep a running sum.

Example 1

You can use Blackline Master 4.7A as a transparency to guide students through this example.

For You to Do

You can compute a product if the width of the left matrix is the same as the depth of the right matrix. This condition holds in Problems 1 and 2 (the left matrix is 2 wide and the right matrix is 2 deep) but not in Problem 3.

Here is the definition of **matrix multiplication.**

Definition

Let A have as many columns as B has rows. Suppose A is $m \times n$ and B is $n \times p$. Let the rows of A be called $R_1, R_2, \dots, R_m$. Let the columns of B be called $C_1, C_2, \dots, C_p$. The product AB is defined to be the $m \times p$ matrix with an ij entry that is the number $R_i \cdot C_j$.

$$AB = \begin{pmatrix} R_1 \cdot C_1 & R_1 \cdot C_2 & \dots & R_1 \cdot C_p \\ R_2 \cdot C_1 & R_2 \cdot C_2 & \dots & R_2 \cdot C_p \\ \vdots & \vdots & \ddots & \vdots \\ R_m \cdot C_1 & R_m \cdot C_2 & \dots & R_m \cdot C_p \end{pmatrix}$$

Example 1

Problem Let $A = \begin{pmatrix} 1 & 2 & 3 \\ 2 & 3 & 4 \end{pmatrix}$ and $B = \begin{pmatrix} 1 \\ -1 \\ 2 \end{pmatrix}$. Compute AB.

Solution A is 2×3 with rows $R_1 = (1, 2, 3)$ and $R_2 = (2, 3, 4)$.

B is 3×1 with the one column

$$C_1 = \begin{pmatrix} 1 \\ -1 \\ 2 \end{pmatrix}$$

So,

$$AB = \begin{pmatrix} R_1 \cdot C_1 \\ R_2 \cdot C_1 \end{pmatrix} = \begin{pmatrix} 5 \\ 7 \end{pmatrix}$$

In terms of the letters in the definition, $m = 2$, $n = 3$, and $p = 1$.

Go Online
PHSchool.com

For a demonstration of matrix multiplication, go to Web Code: bfe-9031

For You to Do

Compute each product, or explain why it cannot be computed.

1. $\begin{pmatrix} 1 & 2 \\ 2 & 3 \\ 3 & 4 \end{pmatrix}\begin{pmatrix} 1 & -2 \\ -3 & 4 \end{pmatrix}$
2. $\begin{pmatrix} 1 & 2 \end{pmatrix}\begin{pmatrix} 1 & -2 & 1 & 2 \\ 2 & 1 & -1 & 3 \end{pmatrix}$
3. $\begin{pmatrix} 1 & -2 & 1 & 2 \\ 2 & 1 & -1 & 3 \end{pmatrix}\begin{pmatrix} 1 & -2 \\ -3 & 4 \end{pmatrix}$

Answers

For You to Do

1. $\begin{pmatrix} -5 & 6 \\ -7 & 8 \\ -9 & 10 \end{pmatrix}$
2. $\begin{pmatrix} 5 & 0 & -1 & 8 \end{pmatrix}$
3. The product is not defined because the number of columns of the left matrix is not equal to the number of rows of the right matrix.

Developing Habits of Mind

Visualize. Some people think about the matrix product AB as shown in the figure below. A is on the left and B is on top. The matrix that just fits on the bottom right between them is AB. The size is correct. To compute any entry in the product (represented by the large dot), you multiply the row in A directly to its left (represented by a segment) by the column in B directly above it. As usual, multiplying a row by a column means finding the dot product.

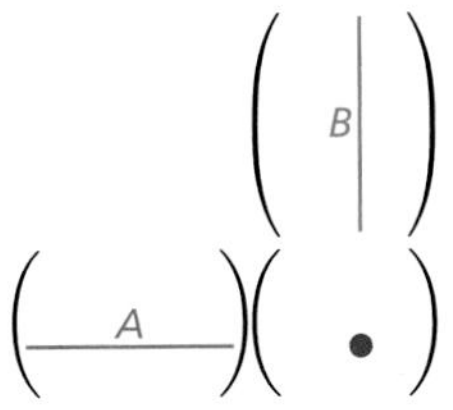

For Discussion

4. Why is A required to have as many columns as B has rows?

Mathematicians wrote the definition of a matrix product to mimic exactly what happens when you summarize the results of linear substitutions with matrices. So the following theorem should not be a surprise. In fact, the definition is constructed to make this theorem true!

Theorem 4.1

Suppose matrix A represents a system where the z's are linear combinations of y's. Suppose matrix B represents a system where these y's are linear combinations of x's.

Then, by substitution, the z's are linear combinations of the x's, and the matrix that represents this system is the product AB.

Make sure you understand what it means to *represent* a linear system with a matrix. Write the system in the usual way in rows.

$$y_1 = 2x_1 + 3x_2 - 4x_3$$
$$y_2 = -5x_1 + x_2 + 8x_3$$

Then the matrix is $\begin{pmatrix} 2 & 3 & -4 \\ -5 & 1 & 8 \end{pmatrix}$.

You take the coefficients from the equations and arrange them in the matrix in the same order they appear, one row for each equation.

Habits of Mind

Make strategic choices. In mathematics, you can pick your definition in order to make a theorem. As Georg Cantor said, "The essence of mathematics lies in its freedom."

For Discussion

4. Answers may vary. Sample: In order to calculate a dot product, the number of entries in a row of the left matrix (which is how many *columns* it has) must equal the number of entries in a column of the right matrix (which is how many *rows* it has).

Developing Habits of Mind

The visual display here affords another opportunity to demonstrate moving the left hand horizontally across a row of matrix A while moving the right hand vertically down a column of matrix B.

Example 2

Example 2 is an immediate illustration of Theorem 4.1.

Like any example that shows the applicability of matrix multiplication, it is quite long. So you might want to take your students through a purely numerical example. For one such example, see Exercise 11 in Check Your Understanding.

Here is another, which has a special relevance. Let $A = \begin{pmatrix} 120 & 95 \\ 20 & 52 \end{pmatrix}$ and $B = \begin{pmatrix} 1.1 & 1.3 \\ 0.5 & 0.3 \end{pmatrix}$.

a. Suppose A represents a linear system where the z's are linear combinations of the y's. Write out this system.

b. Suppose B represents a linear system where the y's are linear combinations of the x's. Write out this system.

c. Compute $C = AB$.

d. Write out the linear system that C represents, assuming it represents z's in terms of x's.

e. According to Theorem 4.1, the system from part (d) is the very system you would get by substituting the equations from part (b) into the equations from part (a) and simplifying. Verify this.

Of course, the numerical system above is not randomly picked. It is exactly the system of Example 2, with the story stripped off!

Example 2

Problem A steel company makes stainless steel and tempered steel. For either type, the raw ingredients are iron and coal, but in different amounts. The table below shows how many tons of iron and how many tons of coal the company needs to produce each ton of steel.

Tons of Raw Material per Ton of Steel

	Stainless Steel	Tempered Steel
Iron	1.1	1.3
Coal	0.5	0.3

In turn, there are costs associated with these raw goods. There is the cost of buying them, and there is also the cost of storing them. The table below shows the costs and the amount of space needed to store 1 ton of each raw good. The price is given in dollars and the space is given in cubic yards.

	Iron	Coal
Cost ($)	120	95
Space (yd^3)	20	52

a. Turn the first table into a system of linear equations. Let s and t be the amounts in tons of stainless and tempered steel, respectively. The other two variables are i and c. What do they stand for?

b. Similarly, turn the second table into a linear system.

c. What the steel company would really like to know is the direct relationship among how much steel they produce, how much money they need to spend, and how much space they need. Figure this out. Express it as a table.

Solution

a. Let i be the number of tons of iron and c be the number of tons of coal. Then

$$\begin{aligned} i &= 1.1s + 1.3t \\ c &= 0.5s + 0.3t \end{aligned} \tag{10}$$

Notice you can read these equations from the rows of the table.

b. Let p be the cost in dollars and q be the number of cubic yards of space needed. You get

$$\begin{aligned} p &= 120i + 95c \\ q &= 20i + 52c \end{aligned} \tag{11}$$

c. To find the direct relationship between steel amounts and cost, you need to eliminate the intermediate variables i and c. As shown in parts (a) and (b), the dollar cost p and amount of space q are linear combinations of the amounts of iron i and coal c. Also, i and c are linear combinations of amounts of steel s and t. You could do the elimination by substitution, but Theorem 4.1 says you can do it by matrix multiplication instead.

A real steel company would make many more types of steel and would use many more raw ingredients. But the form of the example is real. The main difference in actual practice is that the matrices are much bigger. Linear substitutions arise in real life whenever one set of things (here steel outputs) determines a second set (raw goods required) and that second set determines a third (costs).

The theorem says to compute AB, where A is the matrix of p and q in terms of i and c, and B is the matrix for i and c in terms of s and t. From system (11),

$$A = \begin{pmatrix} 120 & 95 \\ 20 & 52 \end{pmatrix}$$

From system (10),

$$B = \begin{pmatrix} 1.1 & 1.3 \\ 0.5 & 0.3 \end{pmatrix}$$

According to the definition of matrix multiplication,

$$AB = \begin{pmatrix} 120 \cdot 1.1 + 95 \cdot 0.5 & 120 \cdot 1.3 + 95 \cdot 0.3 \\ 20 \cdot 1.1 + 52 \cdot 0.5 & 20 \cdot 1.3 + 52 \cdot 0.3 \end{pmatrix} = \begin{pmatrix} 179.5 & 184.5 \\ 48 & 41.6 \end{pmatrix}$$

So

$$p = 179.5s + 184.5t$$
$$q = 48s + 41.6t$$

The table below shows the information the company wants to use.

	Stainless Steel	Tempered Steel
Cost ($)	179.5	184.5
Space (yd³)	48	41.6

Habits of Mind

Detect the key characteristics. Notice the order of multiplication is opposite from the order in which the data were introduced. It is natural to introduce the information top-down—you produced the final products from intermediate material, which you have to buy and store. But, once again, the order is reversed in terms of substituting equations.

For Discussion

5. Why is there such a fuss about which set of equations became matrix A on the left in the product? Is it true for matrices that $AB = BA$?

Developing Habits of Mind

Detect the key characteristics. To get the correct matrices when using Theorem 4.1, you must write the equations in rows. But not every table translates to row equations. For instance, the steel company could have represented the original data about raw goods with this table.

Raw Materials per Ton of Steel

	Iron	Coal
Stainless Steel	1.1	0.5
Tempered Steel	1.3	0.3

If you then used the matrix $\begin{pmatrix} 1.1 & 0.5 \\ 1.3 & 0.3 \end{pmatrix}$, you would be in trouble! Always make sure you know which way the equations go before converting to matrices. If the equations correspond to the columns, as in the table above, you have to first flip them into rows.

Answers

For Discussion

5. Matrix multiplication is not commutative (in general, $AB \neq BA$), so it is important to be clear which set of equations becomes matrix A and which information becomes matrix B.

For Discussion

For Problem 6, if you multiply the matrices on the right, you get

$$\begin{pmatrix} x \\ y \\ z \end{pmatrix} = \begin{pmatrix} u + 2v \\ 3u + 4v \\ 5u + 6v \end{pmatrix}$$

which you can write quite naturally as

$$x = u + 2v$$
$$y = 3u + 4v$$
$$x = 5u + 6v$$

For Problem 7, if you multiply the matrices on the left, you get the row matrix equation

$$(x + 2y + 3z, 2x + 3y + 4z, -3x - 4y - 5z) = (3, 5, 7)$$

which is harder to read. But you can "unpack" and write the equations vertically.

$$x + 2y + 3z = 3$$
$$2x + 3y + 4z = 5$$
$$-3x - 4y - 5z = 7$$

So writing variables in columns instead of rows allows matrix multiplication to better capture the usual vertical format for systems of equations, although either way works.

MATRIX OPERATIONS ON CALCULATORS For the most part, students should not do the exercises in this lesson using a calculator to do the matrix products. The goal here is for students to internalize how matrix multiplication works; for that they need to think about it, and pushing the pencil helps. Also, the numbers stay manageable for most of these exercises. Of course, for large matrices and matrices with messy numbers, you should turn to a calculator or even more powerful computer programs. Exercise 7 is the first place where students should use a calculator in the exercises. This exercise also gives you an opportunity to stop the class and make sure everyone learns how to do matrix multiplication on their calculators. But you might choose to do that check earlier.

Wrap Up

Go over the Check Your Understanding core exercises as time allows. If you find that students have difficulty doing matrix multiplication, it might be worthwhile to have them continue working on these exercises as homework and spend a second day discussing strategies for organizing the work of matrix multiplication. If you do, you will also have more time to work on translating applications into matrix multiplication as in Exercises 12, 13, and 14.

Matrix Equations

So far in this investigation, you have used matrices to represent the coefficients of equations but not the equations themselves. But with matrix multiplication, you can also easily represent systems of equations.

$$\begin{aligned} 4x - 5y &= 3 \\ 3x + y &= -1 \end{aligned} \quad \text{becomes} \quad \begin{pmatrix} 4 & -5 \\ 3 & 1 \end{pmatrix}\begin{pmatrix} x \\ y \end{pmatrix} = \begin{pmatrix} 3 \\ -1 \end{pmatrix}$$

$$\begin{aligned} z_1 &= 2y_1 + 5y_2 - 3y_3 \\ z_2 &= 3y_1 - y_2 + y_3 \end{aligned} \quad \text{becomes} \quad \begin{pmatrix} z_1 \\ z_2 \end{pmatrix} = \begin{pmatrix} 2 & 5 & 3 \\ 3 & -1 & 1 \end{pmatrix}\begin{pmatrix} y_1 \\ y_2 \\ y_3 \end{pmatrix}$$

When equations have numbers on one side, you usually write the numbers on the right. When equations have single variables on one side, you usually write the variables on the left.

For Discussion

Go the other way: Translate each equation into a linear system. Were you more comfortable with one translation than the other? Explain.

6. $\begin{pmatrix} x \\ y \\ z \end{pmatrix} = \begin{pmatrix} 1 & 2 \\ 3 & 4 \\ 5 & 6 \end{pmatrix}\begin{pmatrix} u \\ v \end{pmatrix}$

7. $(x\ y\ z)\begin{pmatrix} 1 & 2 & 3 \\ 2 & 3 & 4 \\ -3 & -4 & -5 \end{pmatrix} = (3\ 5\ 7)$

In short, if you allow yourself to put variables as well as constants into matrices and make use of single columns (or, less conveniently, single rows), you can express any linear system, no matter how big, as a single matrix equation. For instance, $Y = AX$.

It is cute, but does it really help? Time will tell.

And by the way, what happened to Gaussian Elimination? Matrices started out as a shorthand for solving linear systems, but solving systems has not played a role since Investigation 4A.

Matrix Operations on Calculators

Your calculator can do all the matrix and n-tuple operations discussed so far and more. See the TI-Nspire Handbook on p. 778 to find out how. Mathematicians and scientists routinely use calculators (or, more likely, computers) to do any matrix calculations bigger than about three rows or columns. For now, do all calculations by hand except where a calculator is requested. It takes a while to get a feel for all the things matrix multiplication can do, and the best way to get that feel is through hands-on practice.

Answers

For Discussion

6. $x = u + 2v$, $y = 3u + 4v$, $z = 5u + 6v$

7. $x + 2y - 3z = 3$, $2x + 3y - 4z = 5$, $3x + 4y - 5z = 7$
Answers may vary. Sample: Translation 2 is easier because it involves just one set of variables rather than two sets.

Exercises *Practicing Habits of Mind*

The text has explained where matrix multiplication comes from. In this exercise set, you will begin to get a feel for all the things matrix multiplication can do. As always, look for patterns.

Check Your Understanding

1. Compute each product.

a. $\begin{pmatrix} a & b \\ c & d \end{pmatrix}\begin{pmatrix} 1 & 0 \\ 0 & 1 \end{pmatrix}$ **b.** $\begin{pmatrix} 1 & 0 \\ 0 & 1 \end{pmatrix}\begin{pmatrix} a & b \\ c & d \end{pmatrix}$

c. $\begin{pmatrix} a & b \\ c & d \end{pmatrix}\begin{pmatrix} 2 & 0 \\ 0 & -3 \end{pmatrix}$ **d.** $\begin{pmatrix} 2 & 0 \\ 0 & -3 \end{pmatrix}\begin{pmatrix} a & b \\ c & d \end{pmatrix}$

2. You can think of ordered pairs as representing points on the plane. Here you will begin to investigate what matrix multiplication does to points. You will return to this idea in Investigation 4C.

Throughout this exercise, let

$$U = \begin{pmatrix} 1 \\ 0 \end{pmatrix},\ V = \begin{pmatrix} 1 \\ 3 \end{pmatrix},\ W = \begin{pmatrix} 2 \\ 6 \end{pmatrix},\ X = \begin{pmatrix} -1 \\ -3 \end{pmatrix},\ Y = \begin{pmatrix} 3 \\ 4 \end{pmatrix}, \text{ and } Z = \begin{pmatrix} -1 \\ 1 \end{pmatrix}.$$

a. Plot $U, \dots, Z$ as points on the plane.

b. Let $A = \begin{pmatrix} 1 & 0 \\ 0 & -1 \end{pmatrix}$. Compute $AU, \dots, AZ$.

c. Plot the points in part (b) on the plane. Match the pairs U and AU, then V and AV, and so on. How is each point related to its match?

d. Now let $B = \begin{pmatrix} 0 & -1 \\ 1 & 0 \end{pmatrix}$. Compute $BU, \dots, BZ$. Plot the results on the plane.

Match the pairs U and BU, then V and BV, and so on. How is each point related to its match?

3. Compute each product.

a. $\begin{pmatrix} 1 & 2 & 3 \\ 4 & 5 & 6 \\ 5 & 3 & 1 \end{pmatrix}\begin{pmatrix} 0 \\ 1 \\ 0 \end{pmatrix}$ **b.** $\begin{pmatrix} 1 & 2 & 3 \\ 4 & 5 & 6 \\ 5 & 3 & 1 \end{pmatrix}\begin{pmatrix} 1 \\ 1 \\ 1 \end{pmatrix}$

c. $\begin{pmatrix} 0 & 0 & 1 \end{pmatrix}\begin{pmatrix} 1 & 2 & 3 \\ 4 & 5 & 6 \\ 5 & 3 & 1 \end{pmatrix}$ **d.** $\begin{pmatrix} 1 & 0 & -1 \end{pmatrix}\begin{pmatrix} 1 & 2 & 3 \\ 4 & 5 & 6 \\ 5 & 3 & 1 \end{pmatrix}$

e. $\begin{pmatrix} 1 & 2 \\ 4 & 5 \\ 5 & 3 \end{pmatrix}\begin{pmatrix} 0 & 0 \\ 0 & 0 \end{pmatrix}$ **f.** $\begin{pmatrix} 0 & 0 \\ 0 & 0 \\ 0 & 0 \end{pmatrix}\begin{pmatrix} 3 & 5 \\ -2 & 6 \end{pmatrix}$

Any matrix with all entries 0 is a **zero matrix.** You usually call it 0.

Assessment Resources

Lesson Quiz 4.7

1. Use the matrices below to compute each expression.

$$A = \begin{pmatrix} -2 & 4 \\ 0 & -5 \\ 3 & 1 \end{pmatrix} \quad B = \begin{pmatrix} 1 & -2 \\ 0 & -1 \end{pmatrix} \quad C = \begin{pmatrix} -3 & 5 \end{pmatrix} \quad D = \begin{pmatrix} 2 & -1 \\ 3 & 4 \end{pmatrix}$$

a. BD **b.** DB **c.** $DB - BD$ **d.** $(AB)D$
e. $C(B + D)$ **f.** AC **g.** $CD + C$

2. The table shows the number of students who scored a certain grade by gender in a math class.

	A	B	C	D	F
Female	16	21	14	11	1
Male	15	23	16	12	3

a. Compute the total number of students of each gender. Show how you can express this computation as matrix multiplication.
b. Compute the total number of students earning each grade. Show how you can express this computation as matrix multiplication.
c. Use parts (a) and (b) to compute the total enrollment two ways. Show how you can express each way as matrix multiplication.

Exercises

HOMEWORK
- Core: 15, 17, 18, 19, 21, 23, 25, 31, 32
- Optional: 16, 20, 22, 24, 26, 27, 28, 30, 33, 34, 35, 36, 37, 38, 39, 40
- Extension: 29

Check Your Understanding

EXERCISE 1 Parts (a) and (b) suggest, correctly, that multiplication by an identity matrix on either side has no effect. Parts (c) and (d) show, however, that multiplication involving other simple matrices—here diagonal matrices—does not commute.

EXERCISE 2 will be a welcome change for visual learners and should lead to some good class discussion.

EXERCISE 3 suggests that the matrix on the right in the multiplication determines the number of columns in the product. The matrix on the left determines the number of rows in the product.

Exercises

1. a. $\begin{pmatrix} a & b \\ c & d \end{pmatrix}$

b. $\begin{pmatrix} a & b \\ c & d \end{pmatrix}$

c. $\begin{pmatrix} 2a & -3b \\ 2c & -3d \end{pmatrix}$

d. $\begin{pmatrix} 2a & 2b \\ -3c & -3d \end{pmatrix}$

2. See back of book.

3. a. $\begin{pmatrix} 2 \\ 5 \\ 3 \end{pmatrix}$ **b.** $\begin{pmatrix} 6 \\ 15 \\ 9 \end{pmatrix}$

c. $\begin{pmatrix} 5 & 3 & 1 \end{pmatrix}$ **d.** $\begin{pmatrix} -4 & -1 & 2 \end{pmatrix}$

e. $\begin{pmatrix} 0 & 0 \\ 0 & 0 \\ 0 & 0 \end{pmatrix}$ **f.** $\begin{pmatrix} 0 & 0 \\ 0 & 0 \\ 0 & 0 \end{pmatrix}$

EXERCISE 5 As shown by For Discussion Problems 6 and 7, the translation will work best if students make *x*, *y*, *z* into a column, and likewise for *u*, *v*, *w*.

EXERCISE 6 You can tell a lot about matrix operations just by looking at the shapes of the matrices. In answering this exercise, students are forced not to think mindlessly about numerical calculations but to concentrate on the type of matrix operation.

EXERCISE 7 is here to allow you to designate a time when everyone will get up to speed on using calculators to do matrix multiplication. There are differences in what calculators can do with matrix multiplication and how you format the commands. Also, there may be special shortcuts for doing very common matrix products.

4. Translate each equation into a system of linear equations.

a. $\begin{pmatrix} p \\ q \end{pmatrix} = \begin{pmatrix} 1 & -1 \\ 3 & -2 \end{pmatrix}\begin{pmatrix} x \\ y \end{pmatrix}$ **b.** $\begin{pmatrix} 2 & 1 \\ 4 & 3 \\ 0 & 6 \end{pmatrix}\begin{pmatrix} a \\ b \end{pmatrix} = \begin{pmatrix} 3 \\ 5 \\ 7 \end{pmatrix}$

5. Translate each system into matrix form with the variables in a column.

a. $x = 2u - 3v + 4w$
$y = -u + 2v + \pi w$
$z = 7u - 4v - 2w$

b. $p = 2x + 3y - 4z$
$q = x - 3y$

c. $y_1 = 3x$
$y_2 = -x$
$y_3 = 4x$

6. Which of the following matrix operations are possible? Since only shape matters for this question, actual entries are not shown.

a. $\begin{pmatrix} \blacksquare & \blacksquare \\ \blacksquare & \blacksquare \end{pmatrix} + \begin{pmatrix} \blacksquare & \blacksquare \\ \blacksquare & \blacksquare \end{pmatrix}$ **b.** $\begin{pmatrix} \blacksquare \\ \blacksquare \end{pmatrix} + \begin{pmatrix} \blacksquare & \blacksquare \\ \blacksquare & \blacksquare \end{pmatrix}$

c. $k\begin{pmatrix} \blacksquare & \blacksquare & \blacksquare \\ \blacksquare & \blacksquare & \blacksquare \end{pmatrix}$ **d.** $\begin{pmatrix} \blacksquare \\ \blacksquare \end{pmatrix}\begin{pmatrix} \blacksquare & \blacksquare \\ \blacksquare & \blacksquare \end{pmatrix}$

e. $\begin{pmatrix} \blacksquare & \blacksquare \\ \blacksquare & \blacksquare \end{pmatrix}\begin{pmatrix} \blacksquare \\ \blacksquare \end{pmatrix}$ **f.** $\begin{pmatrix} \blacksquare & \blacksquare \\ \blacksquare & \blacksquare \end{pmatrix}\begin{pmatrix} \blacksquare & \blacksquare \end{pmatrix}$

g. $\begin{pmatrix} \blacksquare & \blacksquare \end{pmatrix}\begin{pmatrix} \blacksquare & \blacksquare \\ \blacksquare & \blacksquare \end{pmatrix}$ **h.** $\begin{pmatrix} \blacksquare & \blacksquare & \blacksquare \end{pmatrix}\begin{pmatrix} \blacksquare & \blacksquare \\ \blacksquare & \blacksquare \end{pmatrix}$

Sometimes dimensions are importan

7. Your calculator knows how to multiply matrices. See the TI-Nspire Handbook on p. 778 for advice on doing matrix multiplication.

- Use your calculator to check your work on Exercise 3.
- Create a matrix multiplication problem that would be difficult to do by hand but that a calculator can handle. Do the multiplication with your calculator.

Anyone can make a mistake when entering a problem into a calculator. What are some ways you can check the calculator's result without doing the entire calculation by hand?

Answers

4. a. $p = x - y$, $q = 3x - 2y$

b. $2a + b = 3$, $4a + 3b = 5$, $6b = 7$

5. a. $\begin{pmatrix} x \\ y \\ z \end{pmatrix} = \begin{pmatrix} 2 & -3 & 4 \\ -1 & 2 & \pi \\ 7 & -4 & -2 \end{pmatrix}\begin{pmatrix} u \\ v \\ w \end{pmatrix}$

b. $\begin{pmatrix} p \\ q \end{pmatrix} = \begin{pmatrix} 2 & 3 & -4 \\ 1 & -3 & 0 \end{pmatrix}\begin{pmatrix} x \\ y \\ z \end{pmatrix}$

c. $\begin{pmatrix} y_1 \\ y_2 \\ y_3 \end{pmatrix} = x\begin{pmatrix} 3 \\ -1 \\ 4 \end{pmatrix}$

6. a. possible
b. not possible
c. possible
d. not possible
e. possible
f. not possible
g. possible
h. not possible

7. Answers may vary. Check students' work.

8. Matrices A and B are *conformable* for multiplication in the order AB if the product AB is defined. Suppose $A = \begin{pmatrix} 1 & 3 & 5 \\ 2 & 4 & 6 \end{pmatrix}$.

a. What size matrices B are conformable for multiplication with A in the order AB?

b. What size matrices B are conformable for multiplication with A in the order BA?

c. What size matrices B are conformable for multiplication with A in either order?

9. For what size matrix A is it true that whenever B is the same size as A, then AB exists?

10. For what size matrix A is it true that whenever B is the same size as A, then BA exists?

11. Consider the equations below.

$$z_1 = y_1 + 2y_2 \qquad y_1 = 2x_1 - x_2$$
$$z_2 = 3y_1 - 4y_2 \qquad y_2 = 3x_1 + x_2$$

Use matrix multiplication (not direct substitution) to find formulas for z_1 and z_2 in terms of x_1 and x_2.

12. Return to Exercise 8 in Lesson 4.4 and regard the profit table from part (a) as a matrix. How could you add down columns as in part (b) by matrix multiplication? How could you add across rows as in part (c) by matrix multiplication?

13. For fundraisers, Local High School has a car wash and a play. All students are encouraged to sell tickets at \$5 for a car wash and \$10 for the play. The bordered matrix below shows how many tickets each class has sold.

	Sr	Jr	Soph
Car	200	150	50
Play	100	100	85

a. Copy and complete the following matrix. Use a matrix product to compute the entries.

	Sr	Jr	Soph
Revenue	■	■	■
Total tickets	■	■	■

b. Use another matrix product to determine the total revenue and total ticket sales for all three classes together.

You may be able to easily compute the entries in this matrix in your head, but the point is to recognize how you can use matrix multiplication in this situation.

EXERCISES 8–10 Like Exercise 6, these exercises force students to think about the matrix operations because there are no actual numerical calculations to get in the way.

EXERCISE 11 You could assign this exercise to be done right after Theorem 4.1 and before Example 2, as it provides a purely numerical, and hence much shorter, illustration of the theorem.

EXERCISE 13 might be worth a class discussion. How do you decide when to multiply the given matrix on the left? On the right? How do you decide the coefficients of the multiplier? You sometimes call matrices used to manipulate data by multiplying on the left *pre-multipliers.* You call those used on the right *post-multipliers.*

8. a. Matrix B must have 3 rows.
b. Matrix B must have 2 columns.
c. Matrix B must have 3 rows and 2 columns.

9. any square matrix

10. any square matrix

11. $z_1 = 8x_1 + x_2$, $z_2 = -6x_1 - 7x_2$

12. To add down the columns, you can multiply on the left by a 1×3 matrix of 1's. To add across columns, you can multiply on the right by a 5×1 matrix of 1's.

13. a. $\begin{pmatrix} 5 & 10 \\ 1 & 1 \end{pmatrix}\begin{pmatrix} 200 & 150 & 50 \\ 100 & 100 & 85 \end{pmatrix} = \begin{pmatrix} 2000 & 1750 & 1100 \\ 300 & 250 & 135 \end{pmatrix}$

b. $\begin{pmatrix} 2000 & 1750 & 1100 \\ 300 & 250 & 135 \end{pmatrix}\begin{pmatrix} 1 \\ 1 \\ 1 \end{pmatrix} = \begin{pmatrix} 4850 \\ 685 \end{pmatrix}$

EXERCISE 14 You may wish to use Blackline Master 4.7B with this exercise. It may seem like a cheap trick to use the sizes of the matrices to decide in which order to multiply them. Also, sometimes this trick is not available. For instance, this is the exercise closest to Example 2 in the text about the steel company, and there students could multiply the matrices in either order. Here, as there, the matrices have to be multiplied in the opposite order from the order in which they were mentioned. That order was natural in that it was "top down;" you started with the final product and work back to basic components. The advice there about how to decide the correct multiplication order applies here, too, and a class discussion about how to decide may be worthwhile. Recall, you look for the quantities that index both matrices. Here they are the grains wheat, rice, and oats. The left matrix is the one in which the common quantities are on the right-hand side of the equations (equivalently, label the columns).

Here is yet another way to look at it. Multiplied in the order *BA*, the grains "line up." For instance, in computing the row-1, column-2 entry of *BA*, the calculation is $2 \cdot 0.5 + 1 \cdot 0.2 + 3 \cdot 0.3$. Both factors in $2 \cdot 0.5$ concern wheat; both in $1 \cdot 0.2$ concern rice, and both in $3 \cdot 0.3$ concern oats. If you try to multiply *BA*, the units do not line up even if the multiplication is possible.

On Your Own

EXERCISES 15 AND 16 show the action of an identity matrix. In Exercise 16, students see how, for a nonsquare matrix, the size of the identity depends upon in which order the multiplication is performed.

EXERCISE 18 makes the same point as For Discussion Problem 5: matrix multiplication does not commute. If students did not pick this up in Problem 5, it should be impressed on them here. An important consequence is that matrix algebra does not satisfy all the rules of number algebra, a point discussed at more length in a later lesson.

14. Cereals A and B are multigrain cereals. The table below left shows how many ounces of certain grains are in one ounce of each cereal. The table on the right shows how many grams of vitamins X, Y and Z are in one ounce of those same grains.

	A	B
Wheat	0.3	0.5
Rice	0.3	0.2
Oats	0.3	0.3

	Wheat	Rice	Oats
Vitamin X	2	1	3
Vitamin Y	3	4	2
Vitamin Z	2	2	1

Use matrix multiplication to devise a table that shows how many grams of each vitamin is in one ounce of each cereal. That is, copy and complete the following table using matrix algebra.

	A	B
Vitamin X	■	■
Vitamin Y	■	■
Vitamin Z	■	■

On Your Own

For Exercises 15 and 16, compute each pair of matrix products.

15. $\begin{pmatrix} a & b & c \\ d & e & f \\ g & h & i \end{pmatrix}\begin{pmatrix} 1 & 0 & 0 \\ 0 & 1 & 0 \\ 0 & 0 & 1 \end{pmatrix}$ and $\begin{pmatrix} 1 & 0 & 0 \\ 0 & 1 & 0 \\ 0 & 0 & 1 \end{pmatrix}\begin{pmatrix} a & b & c \\ d & e & f \\ g & h & i \end{pmatrix}$

16. $\begin{pmatrix} 1 & 0 & 0 \\ 0 & 1 & 0 \\ 0 & 0 & 1 \end{pmatrix}\begin{pmatrix} a_1 & a_2 \\ b_1 & b_2 \\ c_1 & c_2 \end{pmatrix}$ and $\begin{pmatrix} a_1 & a_2 \\ b_1 & b_2 \\ c_1 & c_2 \end{pmatrix}\begin{pmatrix} 1 & 0 \\ 0 & 1 \end{pmatrix}$

17. Standardized Test Prep Suppose A is a 3×2 matrix, B is a 2×4 matrix, and C is a 4×3 matrix. What are the dimensions of $B(CA)$?

A. 2×2 **B.** 3×3

C. 4×4 **D.** $B(CA)$ is not possible.

18. Use the matrices below. Compute AB and BA.

$$A = \begin{pmatrix} 3 & 4 \\ 1 & -2 \end{pmatrix} \quad B = \begin{pmatrix} 2 & -3 \\ 3 & 4 \end{pmatrix}$$

Go Online PHSchool.com

For additional practice, go to **Web Code:** bfa-0407

Answers

14. $BA = \begin{pmatrix} 2 & 1 & 3 \\ 3 & 4 & 2 \\ 2 & 2 & 1 \end{pmatrix}\begin{pmatrix} 0.3 & 0.5 \\ 0.3 & 0.2 \\ 0.3 & 0.3 \end{pmatrix} = \begin{pmatrix} 1.8 & 2.1 \\ 2.7 & 2.9 \\ 1.5 & 1.7 \end{pmatrix}$

15. $\begin{pmatrix} a & b & c \\ d & e & f \\ g & h & i \end{pmatrix}, \begin{pmatrix} a & b & c \\ d & e & f \\ g & h & i \end{pmatrix}$

16. $\begin{pmatrix} a_1 & a_2 \\ b_1 & b_2 \\ c_1 & c_2 \end{pmatrix}, \begin{pmatrix} a_1 & a_2 \\ b_1 & b_2 \\ c_1 & c_2 \end{pmatrix}$

17. A

18. $AB = \begin{pmatrix} 18 & 7 \\ -4 & -11 \end{pmatrix}$, $BA = \begin{pmatrix} 3 & 14 \\ 13 & 4 \end{pmatrix}$

19. Use the matrices below.

$$A = \begin{pmatrix} 1 & 2 \\ 3 & 4 \end{pmatrix} \quad B = \begin{pmatrix} 2 \\ -1 \end{pmatrix} \quad C = \begin{pmatrix} 3 \\ 4 \end{pmatrix}$$

a. Compute $AB + AC$. Compute it exactly as it is written. Find AB first, then AC, and then add.

b. Compute $A(B + C)$. Again, do the computation exactly as written.

20. Use the matrices below.

$$A = \begin{pmatrix} 1 & 3 \\ 2 & 4 \end{pmatrix} \quad B = (2 \ \ -1) \quad C = (3 \ \ 4)$$

a. Compute $BA + CA$. Compute it exactly as it is written. Find BA first, then find CA, and then add.

b. Compute $(B + C)A$. Again, do the computation exactly as written.

21. Use the matrices below to compute each product.

$$A = \begin{pmatrix} 1 & 2 \\ 3 & 4 \end{pmatrix} \quad B = \begin{pmatrix} 2 & 3 \\ 4 & 5 \end{pmatrix} \quad C = \begin{pmatrix} 1 & 0 \\ -1 & -2 \end{pmatrix}$$

a. $A(BC)$ **b.** $(AB)C$

22. Do part (c) of the steel company example in this lesson again, but this time do it by substitution, not matrix multiplication. Which method do you prefer?

23. The following table shows the enrollments last year by gender at Local High School.

	Sophomores	Juniors	Seniors
Male	154	148	136
Female	162	155	150

a. Compute the total number of students per class. Show how you can express this computation as matrix multiplication.

b. Compute the total number of males and the total number of females in the high school. Show how you can express this computation as matrix multiplication.

c. Use parts (a) and (b) to compute the total enrollment two ways. Show how you can express each way as matrix multiplication.

Matrix multiplication is not necessarily the best way to do this calculation, but it is valuable to realize that you can use matrix multiplication to do it. You can use matrix multiplication for an amazing number of calculations.

EXERCISES 19 AND 20 Students who are really getting the hang of matrix calculations will be expecting Exercise 19. Exercise 19 shows an instance of distribution of matrix multiplication over a sum where the sum is on the right. Exercise 20 shows an instance of distribution of matrix multiplication over a sum where the sum is on the left. Neither Exercise 19 nor 20 constitutes a proof of the Distributive Property, though. Such a proof requires general matrices.

Perhaps students will notice another point to the pairing of Exercises 19 and 20. All the given matrices in Exercise 20 are the same as those in Exercise 19 except that you have switched rows and columns. The resulting matrices (resulting from addition and multiplication) turn out to be the same also, except for the same switch. This was not an accident and perhaps somebody will be curious enough to try to explain it.

EXERCISE 21 You can use this exercise to help students make the connection with the Associative Property of Multiplication for real numbers. Given that the Commutative Property of Multiplication fails for matrices, it is hardly obvious that the Associative Property should be true. Indeed, students earlier saw that the Associative Property is false for dot products. Students may not believe (or want to assume) that association works for matrix multiplication, but they may choose to experiment with more matrices to see if this example was just a fluke.

EXERCISE 23 The goal of part (c) is to see that the Associative Property of Multiplication shows up naturally. From examples like this, students should begin to believe that the Associative Property must be true, in general. However, complete proofs are either complicated or subtle, so students will have to accept associativity of matrix multiplication as a conjecture.

19. a. $AB + AC = \begin{pmatrix} 0 \\ 2 \end{pmatrix} + \begin{pmatrix} 11 \\ 25 \end{pmatrix} = \begin{pmatrix} 11 \\ 27 \end{pmatrix}$

b. $A(B + C) = \begin{pmatrix} 1 & 2 \\ 3 & 4 \end{pmatrix}\begin{pmatrix} 5 \\ 3 \end{pmatrix} = \begin{pmatrix} 11 \\ 27 \end{pmatrix}$

20. a. $BA + CA = (0 \ \ 2) + (11 \ \ 25) = (11 \ \ 27)$

b. $(B + C)A = (5 \ \ 3)\begin{pmatrix} 1 & 2 \\ 3 & 4 \end{pmatrix} = (11 \ \ 27)$

21. a. $\begin{pmatrix} -3 & -26 \\ -7 & -58 \end{pmatrix}$

b. $\begin{pmatrix} -3 & -26 \\ -7 & -58 \end{pmatrix}$

22. $p = 179.5s + 184.5t$, $q = 48s + 41.6t$; the substitution method involves many more steps than matrix multiplication.

23. See back of book.

EXERCISE 24 The first point here is that scalar multiplication is not powerful enough to produce all the new matrices, but matrix multiplication is. You can do only part (a) by scalar multiplication. You can do part (b) by matrix multiplication on the right by a diagonal matrix. You can do part (c) by matrix multiplication on the left by a diagonal matrix.

EXERCISES 27–29 As practice translating systems of linear equations into matrix equations, you could place Exercises 27 and 28 anywhere in this lesson. However, they are placed here to lead up to Exercise 29. They illustrate concretely the general result in Exercise 29. There you define matrix multiplication in a way that automatically makes it associative.

24. Return to Exercise 7 in Lesson 4.4 and regard each table as a matrix. Explain how to get each matrix for the following year by using matrix operations on the matrix for the original year.

25. Assume that the following table shows the number of grams of nutrients in one ounce of food indicated.

	Meat	Potato	Cabbage
Protein	5.5	0.5	3
Fat	5.5	0.03	0.02
Carbohydrates	0.1	6	1.5

a. If you eat a meal consisting of 9 ounces of meat, 20 ounces of potatoes, and 5 ounces of cabbage, how many grams of each nutrient do you get?

b. Why is this exercise in an investigation on matrices?

26. Continuing with the data from Exercise 25, suppose the military wants to use these same foods to feed new recruits a dinner providing 45 grams of protein, 35 grams of fat, and 100 grams of carbohydrates.

a. Write a system of equations, in traditional form, with a solution that would determine how much of each food the military should prepare for each recruit.

b. Rewrite your system of equations as a single matrix equation.

Do not solve the system right now. The calculations are messy. Later you will learn some methods for solving systems like this. See Exercise 9 in Lesson 4.8.

27. Consider again Exercise 24 in Lesson 4.6. Translate both sets of given equations into matrix equations. Translate the solution set of equations into a matrix equation.

28. Consider again Exercise 26 in Lesson 4.6. Translate both sets of given equations into matrix equations. Translate the solution set of equations into a matrix equation.

29. Take It Further Suppose you have z's that equal linear expressions in y and y's that equal linear expressions in x. You know you can write the first linear system as $Z = AY$ and the second as $Y = BX$. Furthermore, you know from Theorem 4.1 that the matrix for the z's in terms of the x's is AB. That is,

$$Z = (AB)X$$

But wait a minute. Now that you have matrix equations, you can just substitute $Y = BX$ into $Z = AY$. The result is

$$Z = A(BX)$$

Compare the two equations for Z in terms of A, B, and X. What do you conclude? Is this a proof of something?

Answers

24–26. See back of book.

27. $\begin{pmatrix} z_1 \\ z_2 \end{pmatrix} = \begin{pmatrix} 2 & 5 & -3 \\ 3 & -1 & 1 \end{pmatrix}\begin{pmatrix} y_1 \\ y_2 \\ y_3 \end{pmatrix}$;

$\begin{pmatrix} y_1 \\ y_2 \\ y_3 \end{pmatrix} = \begin{pmatrix} 3 \\ -1 \\ 4 \end{pmatrix}x$;

$\begin{pmatrix} z_1 \\ z_2 \end{pmatrix} = \left(\begin{pmatrix} 2 & 5 & -3 \\ 3 & -1 & 1 \end{pmatrix}\begin{pmatrix} 3 \\ -1 \\ 4 \end{pmatrix}\right)x = \begin{pmatrix} -11 \\ 14 \end{pmatrix}x$

28. $\begin{pmatrix} a \\ b \end{pmatrix} = \begin{pmatrix} 3 & 7 \\ 1 & -2 \end{pmatrix}\begin{pmatrix} p \\ q \end{pmatrix}$,

$\begin{pmatrix} p \\ q \end{pmatrix} = \begin{pmatrix} 2 & -3 \\ 5 & 4 \end{pmatrix}\begin{pmatrix} x \\ y \end{pmatrix}$;

$\begin{pmatrix} a \\ b \end{pmatrix} = \begin{pmatrix} 41 & 19 \\ -8 & -11 \end{pmatrix}\begin{pmatrix} x \\ y \end{pmatrix} = \left(\begin{pmatrix} 3 & 7 \\ 1 & -2 \end{pmatrix}\begin{pmatrix} 2 & -3 \\ 5 & 4 \end{pmatrix}\right)\begin{pmatrix} x \\ y \end{pmatrix}$

29. $(AB)X = A(BX)$; this suggests that the Associative Property of Multiplication holds for matrix multiplication.

30. Use the matrices below.

$$A = \begin{pmatrix} 1 & 2 & 1 \\ 2 & 5 & 1 \\ -1 & 1 & 2 \end{pmatrix} \quad B = \begin{pmatrix} 1 & 0 & 0 \\ -2 & 1 & 0 \\ 1 & 0 & 1 \end{pmatrix} \quad C = \begin{pmatrix} 1 & 0 & 0 \\ 0 & 1 & 0 \\ 0 & -3 & 1 \end{pmatrix}$$

a. Compute $D = BA$.

b. Compute $E = C(BA)$.

c. Compute $(CB)A$.

d. Do you recognize D and E? Explain.

Maintain Your Skills

31. Use matrix A below. Compute AB for each matrix B.

$$A = \begin{pmatrix} 1 & 2 & 3 \\ 4 & 5 & 6 \\ 7 & 8 & 9 \end{pmatrix}$$

a. $B = \begin{pmatrix} 0 \\ 1 \\ 0 \end{pmatrix}$ **b.** $B = \begin{pmatrix} 0 \\ 0 \\ -1 \end{pmatrix}$

c. $B = \begin{pmatrix} 0 & 0 & 0 \\ 0 & 0 & 1 \\ 0 & 0 & 0 \end{pmatrix}$ **d.** $B = \begin{pmatrix} 0 & 0 & 1 \\ 0 & 1 & 0 \\ 1 & 0 & 0 \end{pmatrix}$

32. Use the matrices below. Compute AB, AC, and AD.

$$A = \begin{pmatrix} 1 & 2 \\ 3 & 4 \\ 5 & 6 \end{pmatrix} \quad B = \begin{pmatrix} 2 \\ -3 \end{pmatrix} \quad C = \begin{pmatrix} 0 \\ 1 \end{pmatrix} \quad D = \begin{pmatrix} 2 & 0 \\ -3 & 1 \end{pmatrix}$$

33. Use matrix A below. Compute CA for each matrix C.

$$A = \begin{pmatrix} 1 & 2 & 3 \\ 4 & 5 & 6 \\ 7 & 8 & 9 \end{pmatrix}$$

a. $C = \begin{pmatrix} 0 & 1 & 0 \end{pmatrix}$ **b.** $C = \begin{pmatrix} 0 & 0 & -1 \end{pmatrix}$

c. $C = \begin{pmatrix} 0 & 0 & 0 \\ 0 & 0 & 0 \\ 0 & 1 & 0 \end{pmatrix}$ **d.** $C = \begin{pmatrix} 0 & 0 & 1 \\ 0 & 1 & 0 \\ 1 & 0 & 0 \end{pmatrix}$

34. Use the matrices below. Compute EA, FA, and GA.

$$A = \begin{pmatrix} 1 & 2 \\ 3 & 4 \\ 5 & 6 \end{pmatrix} \quad E = \begin{pmatrix} 1 & 0 & -1 \end{pmatrix} \quad F = \begin{pmatrix} -1 & 2 & -1 \end{pmatrix} \quad G = \begin{pmatrix} 1 & 0 & -1 \\ -1 & 2 & -1 \end{pmatrix}$$

Go Online
Video Tutor
PHSchool.com

Web Code: bfe-0775

30. a. $\begin{pmatrix} 1 & 2 & 1 \\ 0 & 1 & -1 \\ 0 & 3 & 3 \end{pmatrix}$

b. $\begin{pmatrix} 1 & 2 & 1 \\ 0 & 1 & -1 \\ 0 & 0 & 6 \end{pmatrix}$

c. $\begin{pmatrix} 1 & 2 & 1 \\ 0 & 1 & -1 \\ 0 & 0 & 6 \end{pmatrix}$

d. Answers may vary. Sample: Matrices D and E are the results of two steps of Gaussian Elimination on matrix A.

31. a. $\begin{pmatrix} 2 \\ 5 \\ 8 \end{pmatrix}$ **b.** $\begin{pmatrix} -3 \\ -6 \\ -9 \end{pmatrix}$

c. $\begin{pmatrix} 0 & 0 & 2 \\ 0 & 0 & 5 \\ 0 & 0 & 8 \end{pmatrix}$ **d.** $\begin{pmatrix} 3 & 2 & 1 \\ 6 & 5 & 4 \\ 9 & 8 & 7 \end{pmatrix}$

32. $AB = \begin{pmatrix} -4 \\ -6 \\ -8 \end{pmatrix}$, $AC = \begin{pmatrix} 2 \\ 4 \\ 6 \end{pmatrix}$,

$AD = \begin{pmatrix} -4 & 2 \\ -6 & 4 \\ -8 & 6 \end{pmatrix}$

33–34. See back of book.

EXERCISE 30 begins to get at the dangling issue—what does matrix multiplication have to do with Gaussian Elimination? The key observation is that, by pre-multiplication by a special sort of matrix you can accomplish every step of Gaussian Elimination, that is, every elementary row operation. So, the whole sequence of steps in any Gauss reduction. By pre-multiplication by a single matrix, You can accomplish the matrix you create by the product of the special matrices for individual steps.

Maintain Your Skills

Unlike in the last two lessons, the Maintain Your Skills exercises here mostly do not look ahead to the next lesson. Rather they continue consolidation of a computational feel for what matrices can do.

EXERCISE 31 The point here is that you can use post-multiplication (multiplying a matrix A on the right by B) to extract or manipulate the columns of A. Each column of B can do a different manipulation, and which column of A it manipulates depends on which entries of that B column are nonzero. If the second entry is nonzero, the second column of A is manipulated.

EXERCISE 32 Each column of AX is computed independently. The first column of AX depends only on the first column of X (and all of A). The second column of AX depends only on the second column of X (and all of A).

EXERCISE 33 The point here is that you can use pre-multiplication (multiplying a matrix A on the left by C) to extract or manipulate the rows of A. Each row of C can do a different manipulation, and which row of A it manipulates depends on which entries of that C row are nonzero. If the second entry is nonzero, the second row of A is manipulated.

EXERCISE 34 Each row of YA is computed independently. The first row of YA depends only on the first row of Y (and all of A). The second row of YA depends only on the second row of Y (and all of A).

Also, the fact that $FA = \begin{pmatrix} 0 & 0 \end{pmatrix}$ looks ahead to the idea of linear dependence of vectors.

EXERCISE 35 looks ahead to the idea of the inverse of a matrix. Namely, if AB is the product in part (a), then $AB = BA = (ad - bc)I$, where I is the 2×2 identity matrix. Thus B almost inverts A, and a scalar multiple of B inverts A exactly. In Lesson 4.8, students will see that matrix inverses have the same usefulness as number inverses.

EXERCISE 36 Both products exist, but they are very different!

EXERCISE 37 The Zero Product Property fails miserably!

EXERCISE 38 In number algebra there is (almost always) a cancellation property: If $ab = ac$, then $b = c$. Ask students if the same holds for matrix algebra.

EXERCISE 40 Real numbers have at most two square roots. In this problem, students discover that the situation for matrices is very different.

By the end of this string of exercises, students should be very wary of assuming that a number-algebra property automatically holds for matrix algebra. Maybe they will develop some respect for the need for proof.

Additional Resources

PRINT RESOURCES
- Solution Manual
- Practice Workbook
- Assessment Resources
- Teaching Resources

TECHNOLOGY
- Interactive Textbook
- TeacherExpress CD-ROM
- ExamView CD-ROM
- PHSchool.com

Additional Practice

1. Find each dot product.
   a. $(1, 3, 5) \cdot (2, 4, 6)$ b. $(1, 3) \cdot (2, 4, 6)$ c. $(1, 0, 1) \cdot (x, y, z)$
   d. $(3, 5, 7) \cdot (3, 5, 7)$ e. $(2, 5) \cdot (5, -2)$ f. $(2, 5) \cdot (10, -4)$

2. Find an n-tuple W that satisfies each equation.
   a. $(2, 3) + W = (0, 0)$ b. $(a, -b) + W = 0$
   c. $(-1, 0, 1) + W = 0$ d. $(0, 1, 2, 3) + W = (0, 1, 2, 3)$

3. a. Show that the dot product satisfies the Commutative Property.
$$A \cdot B = B \cdot A$$
   b. Show that the dot product satisfies the Distributive Property.
$$A \cdot (B + C) = A \cdot B + A \cdot C \quad \text{and} \quad (A + B) \cdot C = A \cdot C + B \cdot C$$

4. Use the matrices below to compute each expression.
$$A = \begin{pmatrix} -1 & 2 \\ -3 & 4 \end{pmatrix} \quad B = \begin{pmatrix} 1 & -2 \\ 0 & -1 \end{pmatrix} \quad C = \begin{pmatrix} -3 & 5 \end{pmatrix}$$
   a. AB b. BA c. $AB - BA$
   d. $C(AB)$ e. $C(A + B)$

5. Use the matrices below. Compute AB, AC, and AD.
$$A = \begin{pmatrix} 0 & -3 \\ -1 & 2 \\ 3 & 1 \end{pmatrix} \quad B = \begin{pmatrix} 2 \\ -5 \end{pmatrix} \quad C = \begin{pmatrix} -4 \\ 3 \end{pmatrix} \quad D = \begin{pmatrix} 2 & 0 \\ -5 & 4 \end{pmatrix}$$

6. The table shows the number of students in each class year by letter grade received at a local high school.

	A	B	C	D	F
6th Grade	16	24	20	6	2
7th Grade	13	18	28	9	3
8th Grade	18	26	16	7	1

   a. Compute the total number of students in each year. Show how you can express this computation as matrix multiplication.
   b. Compute the total number of students who received each letter grade. Show how you can express this computation as matrix multiplication.
   c. Use parts (a) and (b) to compute the total enrollment two ways. Show how you can express each way as matrix multiplication.

Practice: For Lesson 4.7, assign Exercises 4–6.

35. Compute each product.

a. $\begin{pmatrix} a & b \\ c & d \end{pmatrix}\begin{pmatrix} d & -b \\ -c & a \end{pmatrix}$ **b.** $\begin{pmatrix} d & -b \\ -c & a \end{pmatrix}\begin{pmatrix} a & b \\ c & d \end{pmatrix}$

36. Use the matrices below.
$$A = \begin{pmatrix} a_1 & a_2 & a_3 \end{pmatrix} \qquad B = \begin{pmatrix} b_1 \\ b_2 \\ b_3 \end{pmatrix}$$

a. Compute AB or explain why it does not exist.

b. Compute BA or explain why it does not exist.

37. Compute $\begin{pmatrix} 1 & 3 \\ 2 & 6 \end{pmatrix}\begin{pmatrix} 3 & -6 \\ -1 & 2 \end{pmatrix}$. Do you notice anything surprising about the result? Explain.

38. Check the following equation.
$$\begin{pmatrix} 1 & 3 \\ 2 & 6 \end{pmatrix}\begin{pmatrix} 2 \\ 3 \end{pmatrix} = \begin{pmatrix} 1 & 3 \\ 2 & 6 \end{pmatrix}\begin{pmatrix} 5 \\ 2 \end{pmatrix}$$
Do you notice anything surprising about this equation? Explain.

39. Use the matrices below.
$$A = \begin{pmatrix} 1 & 2 \\ 3 & 4 \end{pmatrix} \qquad B = \begin{pmatrix} -1 \\ 1 \end{pmatrix}$$
Compute $A(AB)$ and $(AA)B$. Are the answers the same? Was the amount of work the same?

Just as in real-number algebra, you can write AA as A^2.

40. Square each matrix.

a. $I = \begin{pmatrix} 1 & 0 \\ 0 & 1 \end{pmatrix}$ **b.** $B = \begin{pmatrix} 1 & 0 \\ 0 & -1 \end{pmatrix}$

c. $C = \begin{pmatrix} 0 & 1 \\ 1 & 0 \end{pmatrix}$ **d.** $D = \begin{pmatrix} \frac{\sqrt{2}}{2} & \frac{\sqrt{2}}{2} \\ \frac{\sqrt{2}}{2} & -\frac{\sqrt{2}}{2} \end{pmatrix}$

e. $E = \begin{pmatrix} \frac{1}{2} & \frac{\sqrt{3}}{2} \\ \frac{\sqrt{3}}{2} & -\frac{1}{2} \end{pmatrix}$

Answers

35. a. $\begin{pmatrix} ad - bc & 0 \\ 0 & ad - bc \end{pmatrix}$

b. $\begin{pmatrix} ad - bc & 0 \\ 0 & ad - bc \end{pmatrix}$

36. a. $a_1b_1 + a_2b_2 + a_3b_3$

b. $\begin{pmatrix} a_1b_1 & a_2b_1 & a_3b_1 \\ a_1b_2 & a_2b_2 & a_3b_2 \\ a_1b_3 & a_2b_3 & a_3b_3 \end{pmatrix}$

37. $\begin{pmatrix} 0 & 0 \\ 0 & 0 \end{pmatrix}$; the product of two matrices is the zero matrix, but neither matrix factor is a zero matrix.

38. $\begin{pmatrix} 1 & 3 \\ 2 & 6 \end{pmatrix}\begin{pmatrix} 2 \\ 3 \end{pmatrix} = \begin{pmatrix} 11 \\ 22 \end{pmatrix}$ and $\begin{pmatrix} 1 & 3 \\ 2 & 6 \end{pmatrix}\begin{pmatrix} 5 \\ 2 \end{pmatrix} = \begin{pmatrix} 11 \\ 22 \end{pmatrix}$; for matrices A, B, and C, $AB = AC$ but $B \neq C$.

39. $A(AB) = \begin{pmatrix} 3 \\ 7 \end{pmatrix}$; $(AA)B = \begin{pmatrix} 3 \\ 7 \end{pmatrix}$; the result shows that $A(AB) = (AA)B$, but it takes more steps to calculate $(AA)B$ than to calculate $A(AB)$.

4.8 Matrix Inverses

Matrix notation gives you another way to solve systems of equations.

Minds in Action episode 16

Sasha is doing her matrix homework in the cafeteria when Xavier wanders up and looks over her shoulder. Xavier is taking first-year algebra.

Xavier Hey Sasha, that looks pretty hard.

Sasha That's what I thought. We're solving several equations at the same time, with several variables. But at least now we've learned a shorthand for writing it. We can write a system of equations of any size as simple as this: $AX = B$.

Xavier I don't know anything about that several-equations stuff, but come on, $AX = B$ is easy.

Sasha What do you mean?

Xavier Just divide by A. We learned that in first-year algebra. So $X = \frac{B}{A}$.

Sasha Nice try, Xavier, but you don't understand. We're not talking about $ax = b$ where a, b, and x are numbers. Why do you think I wrote capital letters? A and B are matrices.

Xavier So what? Just do a basic move and divide by A.

Sasha You can't divide by matrices. It hasn't been defined.

Xavier Well, can you multiply by matrices, whatever they are?

Sasha Yes.

Xavier You can undo multiplication by using the inverse. Multiplying by 5 is undone by multiplying by $\frac{1}{5}$. So find the inverse A^{-1}.

Sasha Who says there's an inverse matrix?

Xavier Well, every number a has an inverse a^{-1}, where $a^{-1}a = 1$. So if you multiply both sides of $ax = b$ by a^{-1}, you get $1x = x = a^{-1}b$. Just do the same with your matrices, whatever they are—you still haven't told me.

Well, 0 does not have a multiplicative inverse.

Sasha Look, they're these two-way tables on my paper. They're not numbers and you can't multiply them to get numbers, so there's no way there's going to be some A^{-1} that you can multiply by A to get 1. You've got to do a lot more, like row reduce or add and subtract equations.

Xavier Sorry! But it looked so simple, written $AX = B$.

40. a. $\begin{pmatrix} 1 & 0 \\ 0 & 1 \end{pmatrix}$

b. $\begin{pmatrix} 1 & 0 \\ 0 & 1 \end{pmatrix}$

c. $\begin{pmatrix} 1 & 0 \\ 0 & 1 \end{pmatrix}$

d. $\begin{pmatrix} 1 & 0 \\ 0 & 1 \end{pmatrix}$

e. $\begin{pmatrix} 1 & 0 \\ 0 & 1 \end{pmatrix}$

Lesson Overview

GOALS

- Compute sums, differences, dot products, products, and inverses of matrices.
- Interpret and solve problems using matrix calculations.

The method developed in this lesson is to solve $AX = B$ in the form $X = A^{-1}B$ by using the inverse key on a graphing calculator. That focus could make this section short and fun, in the sense that it provides some relief from heavy calculation.

However, the very ease of the method means there are some important mathematical points that should not get lost. First is the beautiful idea that there should be inverses: it is not only numbers that might have multiplicative inverses but also objects in any mathematical system with multiplication and an identity. Furthermore, thinking in terms of inverses makes it possible to think about solving complicated matrix systems.

Second, there is a danger students might treat inverses as a black box. They will move to using inverses on the calculator to solve square systems because the amount of work needed to compute the inverse by hand is significant except in the smallest cases. However, it is important for students to see that they can compute inverses by hand using a method they have already learned—Gaussian Elimination.

It is also important for students to know that inverses are not a panacea. Yes, students can use them to solve the most common sort of linear system, those with as many equations as unknowns and a unique solution. However, inverses are not available for other linear systems, and they are not even the most efficient method for these common systems. This is not a point that students are likely to understand deeply, because this text only treats other linear systems lightly and does almost nothing with questions of algorithmic efficiency. However, students should at least hear this point.

CHECK YOUR UNDERSTANDING
- Core: 1, 3, 4, 5, 7, 8
- Optional: 2, 6

MATERIALS
- graphing calculators

HOMEWORK
- Core: 9, 10, 12, 13, 15
- Optional: 11, 14, 17, 18
- Extension: 16

VOCABULARY
- determinant
- identity matrix, I
- inverse, A^{-1}

Launch

Have the class read the dialog between Sasha and Xavier and then try out calculator solutions with the inverse key.

Explore

Minds in Action, p. 337

This is an example of the power of simple reasoning. Do not confuse it with simplistic reasoning.

Near the end of the dialog, perhaps Xavier's reasoning would seem clearer if he just says, "So if you multiply both sides of $ax = b$ by a^{-1}, you get $x = a^{-1}b$." However, the 1 is there because only by understanding the role it plays does it become clear that I works as well in the matrix context. Here is the full deduction.

$$\begin{aligned} ax &= b \\ a^{-1}(ax) &= a^{-1}b \\ (a^{-1}a)x &= a^{-1}b \\ 1x &= a^{-1}b \\ x &= a^{-1}b \end{aligned}$$

All of these steps work with matrices A, A^{-1}, X, and B, as long as you replace 1 by I.

Using good notation has several advantages. Yes, it makes complicated things easier to write, but it also suggests a way to think about an idea. The matrix equation notation made Xavier think about solving equations as in first-year algebra. As it turns out, he is right!

This was his argument: You solve $ax = b$ by multiplying both sides by a^{-1} to get $x = a^{-1}b$. Sasha objected because she thinks there is no matrix C such that $CA = 1$, so there cannot be a matrix that deserves to be called A^{-1}.

There is a matrix I such that $IX = X$. Such a matrix is an **identity matrix**, because multiplying by it gives you back what you start with identically.

What does I look like? Perhaps you know from earlier exercises. Consider the following equations.

$$\begin{pmatrix} 1 & 0 \\ 0 & 1 \end{pmatrix}\begin{pmatrix} x \\ y \end{pmatrix} = \begin{pmatrix} x \\ y \end{pmatrix} \qquad \begin{pmatrix} 1 & 0 & 0 \\ 0 & 1 & 0 \\ 0 & 0 & 1 \end{pmatrix}\begin{pmatrix} x \\ y \\ z \end{pmatrix} = \begin{pmatrix} x \\ y \\ z \end{pmatrix}$$

If X is $m \times 1$, then I is the $m \times m$ matrix with 0's everywhere except for 1's along the main diagonal. You denote all these matrices as I and call each one an identity matrix. If it is important to indicate the size, you can write I_2, I_3, etc.

So, Sasha was mistaken. You do not need the number 1. You need something that serves the same function as 1 in the matrix context. It exists: I.

If there is a matrix M such that $MA = I$, then M will serve the same role as a^{-1}, and Xavier's method for solving matrix equations will work. Starting with $AX = B$, multiply on the left by M, you get

$$X = IX = MAX = MB$$

Example

Problem See if Xavier's method works for the following system.

$$\begin{aligned} s + 2t &= 5 \\ 3s + 4t &= 6 \end{aligned}$$

Solution First, rewrite the system in matrix form.

$$\begin{pmatrix} 1 & 2 \\ 3 & 4 \end{pmatrix}\begin{pmatrix} s \\ t \end{pmatrix} = \begin{pmatrix} 5 \\ 6 \end{pmatrix} \qquad (12)$$

Now you need a 2×2 matrix M such that

$$M\begin{pmatrix} 1 & 2 \\ 3 & 4 \end{pmatrix} = \begin{pmatrix} 1 & 0 \\ 0 & 1 \end{pmatrix}$$

$\begin{pmatrix} 1 & 0 \\ 0 & 1 \end{pmatrix}$ is the 2×2 identity matrix.

In Exercise 12, you will show that there is such a matrix.

$$M = \begin{pmatrix} -2 & 1 \\ \frac{3}{2} & -\frac{1}{2} \end{pmatrix}$$

Therefore, multiply both sides of (12) by M, just as you would to solve a real-number equation.

$$\begin{pmatrix} 1 & 2 \\ 3 & 4 \end{pmatrix}\begin{pmatrix} s \\ t \end{pmatrix} = \begin{pmatrix} 5 \\ 6 \end{pmatrix}$$

$$\begin{pmatrix} -2 & 1 \\ \frac{3}{2} & -\frac{1}{2} \end{pmatrix}\begin{pmatrix} 1 & 2 \\ 3 & 4 \end{pmatrix}\begin{pmatrix} s \\ t \end{pmatrix} = \begin{pmatrix} -2 & 1 \\ \frac{3}{2} & -\frac{1}{2} \end{pmatrix}\begin{pmatrix} 5 \\ 6 \end{pmatrix}$$

$$\begin{pmatrix} 1 & 0 \\ 0 & 1 \end{pmatrix}\begin{pmatrix} s \\ t \end{pmatrix} = \begin{pmatrix} -2 & 1 \\ \frac{3}{2} & -\frac{1}{2} \end{pmatrix}\begin{pmatrix} 5 \\ 6 \end{pmatrix} = \begin{pmatrix} -4 \\ \frac{9}{2} \end{pmatrix}$$

$$\begin{pmatrix} s \\ t \end{pmatrix} = \begin{pmatrix} -4 \\ \frac{9}{2} \end{pmatrix}$$

The solution is $s = -4$ and $t = 4\frac{1}{2}$.

For You to Do

1. It is often easier to check a possible solution than to find it. In the example above, check that M really is the inverse of $A = \begin{pmatrix} 1 & 2 \\ 3 & 4 \end{pmatrix}$ by computing MA.

   Then check that $\begin{pmatrix} s \\ t \end{pmatrix} = \begin{pmatrix} -4 \\ 4\frac{1}{2} \end{pmatrix}$ really does solve the original equations.

When a matrix A has a companion matrix M such that $MA = I$, this companion matrix is the **inverse**. You write it as A^{-1}.

Good news and bad news The good news is that your calculator knows how to find matrix inverses. Therefore, your calculator provides a quick way to solve the matrix system $AX = B$.

Step 1 Input A.

Step 2 Press one or more keys to get A^{-1}.

Step 3 Compute the product $A^{-1}B$.

The answer appears on your screen.

The bad news is that the inverse method does not always work, because A^{-1} does not always exist. The inverse never exists if A is not square, and it often does not exist even if A is square. This is quite different from the situation with real numbers, where only 0 has no multiplicative inverse. In contrast, Gaussian Elimination always works when solving the system $AX = B$ for any matrix A. It turns out A^{-1} exists precisely when the system $AX = B$ has a unique solution. Gaussian Elimination handles those systems, as well as systems with no solution or many solutions. On the other hand, in this course, you will mostly consider systems with unique solutions, so the inverse matrix method will generally work for you.

Habits of Mind

Check your definition. This is a working definition. As you will see in Exercise 5, you have to say a little more.

You can always press the exponent key (^) followed by -1. On some calculators, there is an x^{-1} button that allows you to find inverses with a single keystroke. See the TI-Nspire Handbook, p. 778.

For You to Do

Just as in number algebra, to check a solution you "plug it in." Substitute it and verify that the equation is true. So here students multiply out MA, or have their calculators do it, and verify that $MA = I_2$. Similarly, they substitute $s = -4$ and $t = 4\frac{1}{2}$ into the linear equations at the start of the Example and check that the equations are true. Better yet, students can verify the solution at the matrix level by using Equation (12). Multiply $\begin{pmatrix} 1 & 2 \\ 3 & 4 \end{pmatrix}\begin{pmatrix} -4 \\ 4\frac{1}{2} \end{pmatrix}$ and obtain $\begin{pmatrix} 5 \\ 6 \end{pmatrix}$.

GOOD NEWS AND BAD NEWS Even for systems with a unique solutions, the inverse method is slower than Gaussian Elimination, generally by a factor of 3.

Gaussian Elimination is faster because it figures out the solution (that is, $A^{-1}B$) without ever figuring out A^{-1}. For systems of the size you would enter into a calculator, the work gets done so fast that you would not notice the difference in speed, so the inverse method is fine. But companies solve linear systems with thousands or even millions of variables, and then the difference is substantial, even on the fastest computers.

Answers

For You to Do

1. $MA = \begin{pmatrix} -2 & 1 \\ \frac{3}{2} & -\frac{1}{2} \end{pmatrix}\begin{pmatrix} 1 & 2 \\ 3 & 4 \end{pmatrix} = \begin{pmatrix} -2+3 & -4+4 \\ \frac{3}{2}-\frac{3}{2} & 3-2 \end{pmatrix} = \begin{pmatrix} 1 & 0 \\ 0 & 1 \end{pmatrix}$; if $s = -4$ and $t = \frac{9}{2}$, then $s + 2t = -4 + 2(\frac{9}{2}) = 5$ and $3s + 4t = 3(-4) + 4(\frac{9}{2}) = -12 + 18 = 6$, so the solution checks.

THE 2 × 2 CASE It may not be important for your students to memorize the formula for the inverse of a 2 × 2 matrix, especially with access to technology. However, it is important for them to know how to determine whether a 2 × 2 matrix has an inverse.

Also, the 2 × 2 inverse formula is not hard to learn and many students enjoy using it. For 2 × 2 examples, it is often easier to do them by hand than to take out a calculator, and you can do them by hand if you can compute $ad - bc$ quickly.

Wrap Up

As time allows go over some of the Check Your Understanding core exercises. You may want to emphasize the distinction between matrix inverses and real number inverses in Exercise 4. Also, draw students' attention to the more complete definition of matrix inverse by discussing Exercise 5. Their calculators may not be able to find a one-sided inverse like M directly.

Assessment Resources

Lesson Quiz 4.8

1. Attempt to solve the system $\begin{pmatrix} 2 & -1 \\ 1 & 2 \end{pmatrix}\begin{pmatrix} x \\ y \end{pmatrix} = \begin{pmatrix} 2 \\ 6 \end{pmatrix}$ by each method. What happens?
   - **a.** geometrically, by graphing the line corresponding to each equation
   - **b.** Gaussian Elimination
   - **c.** inverse method
2. Is there a matrix $\begin{pmatrix} a & b \\ c & d \end{pmatrix}$ that solves $\begin{pmatrix} a & b \\ c & d \end{pmatrix}\begin{pmatrix} -1 & 2 \\ -3 & 4 \end{pmatrix} = \begin{pmatrix} 1 & 0 \\ 0 & 1 \end{pmatrix}$?
3. Compute the inverse of each matrix.
   a. $\begin{pmatrix} 1 & 0 \\ -1 & 3 \end{pmatrix}$ **b.** $\begin{pmatrix} 0 & 2 \\ -2 & 1 \end{pmatrix}$ **c.** $\begin{pmatrix} 3 & 2 & 1 \\ 0 & 2 & 1 \\ 0 & 0 & 1 \end{pmatrix}$

Exercises

HOMEWORK
- Core: 9, 10, 12, 13, 15
- Optional: 11, 14, 17, 18
- Extension: 16

Check Your Understanding

EXERCISE 1 Of course, students better get the same answer! If they do not, they may be having trouble inputting data or carrying out the matrix operations on their calculators. If so, have them stop and get their calculator procedures straight before going on. It is always good to try a new method (in this case, the inverse method with a calculator) on a known example first.

EXERCISE 2 Exercise 21 from Lesson 4.3 is a particularly tedious exercise to do by hand.

The 2 × 2 case In general, there is no simple formula for A^{-1} in terms of A, although there is a straightforward algorithm to determine whether A has an inverse and to find A^{-1} when it does—a variant of Gaussian Elimination! However, in the 2 × 2 case, there is a nice formula, which is worth knowing. Recall the result you discovered in Exercise 34 of Lesson 4.7.

If $A = \begin{pmatrix} a & b \\ c & d \end{pmatrix}$ and $B = \begin{pmatrix} d & -b \\ -c & a \end{pmatrix}$, then $BA = AB = (ad - bc)I$.

Therefore, as long as $ad - bc \neq 0$,

$$A^{-1} = \frac{1}{ad - bc}\begin{pmatrix} d & -b \\ -c & a \end{pmatrix}$$

What can you do if $ad - bc = 0$? It turns out there is never an inverse when $ad - bc = 0$, so the 2 × 2 case is completely resolved: A^{-1} exists if and only if $ad - bc \neq 0$, in which case you use the formula above for A^{-1}. See Exercise 14.

Habits of Mind

Detect the key characteristics. Here is one way to think about 2 × 2 inverses: To get A^{-1} you switch the entries on the main diagonal of A and switch the signs of the other two entries. Then you divide by the scalar $ad - bc$. This scalar shows up in many other contexts. It is the **determinant** of A.

Exercises *Practicing Habits of Mind*

Check Your Understanding

1. Return again to Sasha and Derman's favorite problem.
$$\begin{aligned} x + y + z &= 2 \\ 2x - y + z &= 5 \\ x + 2y + 3z &= 5 \end{aligned}$$
Solve this system using inverses.
2. Solve Exercise 21 from Lesson 4.3 again, this time using the inverse.
3. Consider the system below.
$$\begin{pmatrix} 1 & 2 \\ 2 & 4 \end{pmatrix}\begin{pmatrix} x \\ y \end{pmatrix} = \begin{pmatrix} 1 \\ 1 \end{pmatrix}$$
   - **a.** Attempt to solve it geometrically, that is, by graphing the line corresponding to each equation. What happens?
   - **b.** Attempt to solve it by Gaussian Elimination. What happens?
   - **c.** Attempt to solve it by the inverse method. What happens?

There is one matrix equation here, but there are two linear equations.

4. **Write About It** In proposing how to solve $AX = B$, Xavier initially wrote $\frac{1}{A}$ and put the A directly under the B, as in $\frac{B}{A}$. Why does the book only show the notation A^{-1}, and why always on the left, as in $A^{-1}B$, instead of BA^{-1} or $\frac{B}{A}$?

Answers

Exercises

1. $\begin{pmatrix} x \\ y \\ z \end{pmatrix} = \begin{pmatrix} 1 \\ -1 \\ 2 \end{pmatrix}$
2. $\begin{pmatrix} a \\ b \\ c \\ d \end{pmatrix} = \begin{pmatrix} 0 \\ \frac{1}{2} \\ \frac{1}{2} \\ 0 \end{pmatrix}$
3. **a.** The two lines $x + 2y = 1$ and $2x + 4y = 1$ are parallel, so the system has no solution.
   b. Gaussian Elimination results in $\left(\begin{array}{cc|c} 1 & 2 & 1 \\ 0 & 0 & -1 \end{array}\right)$, and the second row indicates that the system has no solution.
   c. The inverse does not exist ($ad - bc = 0$).
4. Answers may vary. Sample: To solve $AX = B$, find A^{-1} and write $A^{-1}AX = A^{-1}B$ or $X = A^{-1}B$.

5. Let $A = \begin{pmatrix} 1 & 0 \\ 3 & 4 \\ 0 & 1 \end{pmatrix}$ and $M = \begin{pmatrix} 1 & 0 & 0 \\ 0 & 0 & 1 \end{pmatrix}$.

Check that $MA = I$ and $AM \neq I$. So M is only a one-sided inverse of A, something that does not happen with number multiplication.

6. In the example, you showed that $M = \begin{pmatrix} -2 & 1 \\ \frac{3}{2} & -\frac{1}{2} \end{pmatrix}$ is the inverse of $A = \begin{pmatrix} 1 & 2 \\ 3 & 4 \end{pmatrix}$ in the sense that $MA = I$. Check whether $AM = I$.

7. Xavier said that every real number a has an inverse $\frac{1}{a}$. Is his statement true or false? Explain.

8. Consider the following equation: $\begin{pmatrix} 3 & -1 \\ -2 & 2 \end{pmatrix}\begin{pmatrix} 1 \\ 2 \end{pmatrix} = \begin{pmatrix} 1 \\ 2 \end{pmatrix}$

Does this mean that $\begin{pmatrix} 3 & -1 \\ -2 & 2 \end{pmatrix}$ is also an identity matrix? Explain.

Habits of Mind

Detect the key characteristics. As it turns out, the correct definition of an inverse for matrices is that M is an inverse of A if $MA = AM = I$. The working definition in the lesson was incomplete. The complete definition implies that only square matrices can have inverses, but a matrix being square is not sufficient.

On Your Own

9. Use inverses to solve the system of equations you set up for Exercise 26 of Lesson 4.7.

10. Suppose in Exercise 26 of Lesson 4.7 the military wants each meal to have 120 grams of carbohydrates instead of 150, but otherwise everything else stays the same. How many ounces of each food should the military now prepare for each recruit?

11. Show that the only matrix $\begin{pmatrix} a & b \\ c & d \end{pmatrix}$ that satisfies $\begin{pmatrix} a & b \\ c & d \end{pmatrix}\begin{pmatrix} x \\ y \end{pmatrix} = \begin{pmatrix} x \\ y \end{pmatrix}$ for all x and y is the 2×2 identity matrix $\begin{pmatrix} 1 & 0 \\ 0 & 1 \end{pmatrix}$.

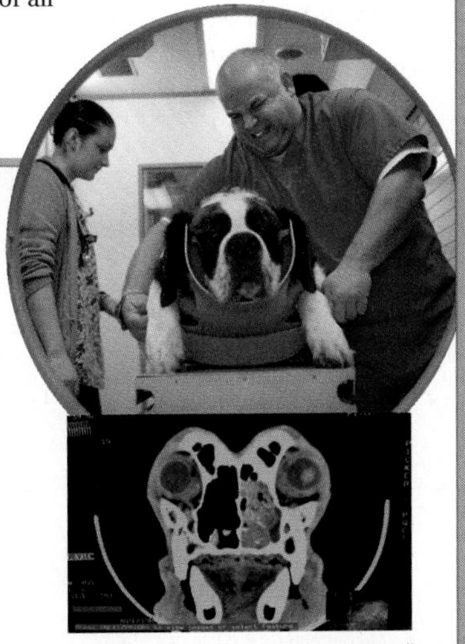

Historical Perspective
Linear Equations and CAT Scans

When you get a CAT scan, the machine shoots X-rays through a slice of you from various angles. The strength of each beam when it comes out the other side reports the sum of the densities of matter along the ray. But your doctor is not interested in sums of densities. Your doctor wants to know the density at each point in the slice. The density indicates what sort of tissue, bone, or tumor is there. So, the software that creates the picture from the CAT scan essentially has to solve a system of summation equations similar to the one in Exercise 15, only much bigger.

5. $MA = \begin{pmatrix} 1 & 0 & 0 \\ 0 & 0 & 1 \end{pmatrix}\begin{pmatrix} 1 & 0 \\ 3 & 4 \\ 0 & 1 \end{pmatrix} = \begin{pmatrix} 1 & 0 \\ 0 & 1 \end{pmatrix}$ and

$AM = \begin{pmatrix} 1 & 0 \\ 3 & 4 \\ 0 & 1 \end{pmatrix}\begin{pmatrix} 1 & 0 & 0 \\ 0 & 0 & 1 \end{pmatrix} = \begin{pmatrix} 1 & 0 & 0 \\ 3 & 0 & 4 \\ 0 & 0 & 1 \end{pmatrix}$, so $MA \neq AM$.

6. $AM = \begin{pmatrix} 1 & 2 \\ 3 & 4 \end{pmatrix}\begin{pmatrix} -2 & 1 \\ \frac{3}{2} & -\frac{1}{2} \end{pmatrix} = \begin{pmatrix} -2+3 & 1-1 \\ -6+6 & 3-2 \end{pmatrix} = \begin{pmatrix} 1 & 0 \\ 0 & 1 \end{pmatrix} = I$

7. No, zero is a real number but it does not have an inverse.

8–11. See back of book.

EXERCISE 3 This exercise brings home the point that the inverse method does not always work—inverses do not always exist—and simultaneously reminds students of the interplay between algebra and geometry.

EXERCISE 4 is worth emphasizing because students will not be used to the idea that it makes a difference which side you multiply on. Indeed, they will not have the concepts "multiply on the left" and "multiply on the right;" they will have just the concept "multiply." You can introduce the terms *pre-multiply* and *post-multiply.*

EXERCISE 7 may lead students to raise the question, "Which matrices have inverses and which do not?" It is not just matrices of 0's that do not have inverses, as you showed in Exercise 5. Even for square matrices there are many noninvertible matrices. Finding nice characterizations of the noninvertible matrices (also called *singular* matrices) is one of the goals of a college linear algebra course.

On Your Own

EXERCISES 9 AND 10 There are several valuable lessons embedded in Exercises 9 and 10.

- Some problems, even medium-sized ones, are really best done by machine. The hand-algebra here gets very messy, but the amount of button pushing is reasonable.
- It often happens that you have to solve $AX = B$ several times, for the same A but different B. In real-life examples, where the matrices may be very big, it turns out to be efficient to save intermediate results, for instance, A^{-1}. In this case, the students who store (or know how to retrieve) A will save a lot of time. It would be tedious to input it again.
- In many real-world problems, only nonnegative solutions count.

EXERCISE 11 The method of proof here may be completely new to your students, though they may find it easy and fun (because they get to pick the really useful values). Emphasize that this sort of exercise is different from equations where the constants are fixed.

EXERCISES 12 AND 13 The equations to solve in these exercises are quite different, and yet the solution is the same. Hope that some student will wonder about this.

EXERCISE 16 shows that it is often possible to find out something about expressions in unknowns without solving for the unknowns, especially when there is symmetry.

EXERCISE 17 looks very much like Exercise 15, so students might expect a similar solution. However, in this case, there is no solution at all.

Maintain Your Skills

EXERCISE 18 The inverses all include the same pattern of **0**'s as the original. This does not always happen. An inverse can have many fewer **0**'s than the original. Let the students explore and state their observations and conjectures.

Additional Resources

PRINT RESOURCES
- Solution Manual
- Practice Workbook
- Assessment Resources
- Teaching Resources

TECHNOLOGY
- Interactive Textbook
- TeacherExpress CD-ROM
- ExamView CD-ROM
- PHSchool.com

Additional Practice

1. Consider the system $\begin{pmatrix} 2 & -3 \\ 1 & 2 \end{pmatrix}\begin{pmatrix} x \\ y \end{pmatrix} = \begin{pmatrix} 8 \\ -3 \end{pmatrix}$.

a. Attempt to solve it geometrically, that is, by graphing the line corresponding to each equation. What happens?
b. Attempt to solve it by Gaussian Elimination. What happens?
c. Attempt to solve it by the inverse method. What happens?

For Exercises 2 and 3, determine whether there is a matrix $\begin{pmatrix} a & b \\ c & d \end{pmatrix}$ that solves the equation.

2. $\begin{pmatrix} a & b \\ c & d \end{pmatrix}\begin{pmatrix} 1 & 3 \\ 2 & 4 \end{pmatrix} = \begin{pmatrix} 1 & 0 \\ 0 & 1 \end{pmatrix}$

3. $\begin{pmatrix} 1 & 3 \\ 2 & 4 \end{pmatrix}\begin{pmatrix} a & b \\ c & d \end{pmatrix} = \begin{pmatrix} 1 & 0 \\ 0 & 1 \end{pmatrix}$

4. Suppose a_1 is the sum of x_1 and x_2, a_2 is the sum of x_2 and x_3, and a_3 is the sum of x_3 and x_1. If $(a_1, a_2, a_3) = (3, 4, 5)$, what are x_1, x_2, and x_3?

5. Let $B = \begin{pmatrix} -1 & 2 \\ 3 & -6 \end{pmatrix}$.

a. Find all 2×1 columns A such that $BA = 0$.
b. Find all 2×2 matrices A such that $BA = 0$.

6. Is $A + A + A = 3A$ true for all matrices? You can use the definitions of *sum* and *scalar multiple* for matrices. You can also use the basic rules for matrices.

7. Consider the special binomial expansion $(X - I)^2 = X^2 - 2IX + I^2$. Is this special binomial expansion correct for all matrices? Explain.

8. a. Is there a matrix $\begin{pmatrix} a & b \\ c & d \end{pmatrix}$ that solves the following equation?

$$\begin{pmatrix} -2 & 3 \\ 4 & -5 \end{pmatrix}\begin{pmatrix} a & b \\ c & d \end{pmatrix} = \begin{pmatrix} -2 & 3 \\ 4 & -5 \end{pmatrix}$$

b. Find all matrices that commute under multiplication with $\begin{pmatrix} 1 & \\ & 1 \end{pmatrix}$.

Practice: For Lesson 4.8, assign Exercises 1–4.

12. Is there a matrix $\begin{pmatrix} x & y \\ z & w \end{pmatrix}$ that solves the following equation?

$$\begin{pmatrix} x & y \\ z & w \end{pmatrix}\begin{pmatrix} 1 & 2 \\ 3 & 4 \end{pmatrix} = \begin{pmatrix} 1 & 0 \\ 0 & 1 \end{pmatrix}$$

Write this single matrix equation as four ordinary equations. This gives you four linear equations in four unknowns. However, if you look at it carefully, you will see that this particular system is not hard to solve even by hand. Do it.

13. Is there a matrix $\begin{pmatrix} x & y \\ z & w \end{pmatrix}$ that solves the following equation?

$$\begin{pmatrix} 1 & 2 \\ 3 & 4 \end{pmatrix}\begin{pmatrix} x & y \\ z & w \end{pmatrix} = \begin{pmatrix} 1 & 0 \\ 0 & 1 \end{pmatrix}$$

Find out by converting this single matrix equation into four ordinary equations.

14. You already know that if $ad - bc \neq 0$, then $M = \begin{pmatrix} a & b \\ c & d \end{pmatrix}$ has the inverse $\frac{1}{ad - bc}\begin{pmatrix} d & -b \\ -c & a \end{pmatrix}$. Now show that you have not missed any matrices. Prove that M has an inverse only if $ad - bc \neq 0$.

15. **Standardized Test Prep** Suppose a_1 is the sum of x_1 and x_2, a_2 is the sum of x_2 and x_3, and a_3 is the sum of x_3 and x_1. If $(a_1, a_2, a_3) = (1, 2, 3)$, what are x_1, x_2, and x_3?

A. (1, 2, 2) **B.** (1, 2, 3) **C.** (1, 0, 2) **D.** (0, 1, 2)

16. **Take It Further** Continuing with Exercise 15, forget all the work to find the individual x values. Is it possible to find the sum $x_1 + x_2 + x_3$ by adding the given equations? Explain.

17. Suppose b_1 is the sum of x_1 and x_2, b_2 is the sum of x_2 and x_3, b_3 is the sum of x_3 and x_4, and b_4 is the sum of x_4 and x_1. If $(b_1, b_2, b_3, b_4) = (1, 2, 3, 4)$, what are x_1, x_2, x_3, and x_4?

Go Online PHSchool.com
For additional practice, go to **Web Code: bfa-0408**

Remember...
The system
$ax + by = e$
$ax + dy = f$
where a, b, c, d, e and f are known constants, has the unique solution $(x, y) = \left(\frac{de - bf}{ad - bc}, \frac{af - ce}{ad - bc}\right)$

Maintain Your Skills

18. Compute the inverse of each matrix.

a. $\begin{pmatrix} 1 & 0 & 0 \\ 0 & 2 & 0 \\ 0 & 0 & \frac{1}{3} \end{pmatrix}$ **b.** $\begin{pmatrix} 1 & 1 \\ 0 & 1 \end{pmatrix}$ **c.** $\begin{pmatrix} 1 & 2 & 3 \\ 0 & 4 & 5 \\ 0 & 0 & 6 \end{pmatrix}$ **d.** $\begin{pmatrix} 1 & 0 & 0 \\ 2 & 1 & 0 \\ 2 & 1 & 2 \end{pmatrix}$

e. $\begin{pmatrix} 1 & 2 & 0 & 0 \\ 3 & 4 & 0 & 0 \\ 0 & 0 & 1 & 2 \\ 0 & 0 & 3 & 4 \end{pmatrix}$ **f.** $\begin{pmatrix} 1 & \frac{1}{2} \\ \frac{1}{2} & \frac{1}{3} \end{pmatrix}$ **g.** $\begin{pmatrix} 1 & \frac{1}{2} & \frac{1}{3} \\ \frac{1}{2} & \frac{1}{3} & \frac{1}{4} \\ \frac{1}{3} & \frac{1}{4} & \frac{1}{5} \end{pmatrix}$

Answers

12. $\begin{pmatrix} x & y \\ z & w \end{pmatrix} = \begin{pmatrix} -2 & 1 \\ \frac{3}{2} & -\frac{1}{2} \end{pmatrix}$

13. $\begin{pmatrix} x & y \\ z & w \end{pmatrix} = \begin{pmatrix} -2 & 1 \\ \frac{3}{2} & -\frac{1}{2} \end{pmatrix}$

14. Suppose M has an inverse, M^{-1}. Let $M^{-1} = \begin{pmatrix} x & y \\ z & w \end{pmatrix}$.

Then $I = M \cdot M^{-1} = \begin{pmatrix} a & b \\ c & d \end{pmatrix} \cdot \begin{pmatrix} x & y \\ z & w \end{pmatrix} = \begin{pmatrix} 1 & 0 \\ 0 & 1 \end{pmatrix}$.

This implies that $1 = ax + bz$, $0 = cx + dz$, and $1 = cy + dw$. The first two equations yield $d = adx + b(dz) = adx + b(-cx) = (ad - bc)x$. If $d \neq 0$, then $ad - bc \neq 0$. If $d = 0$, then the third equation implies $c \neq 0$, so by the second equation $x = 0$. Thus $b \neq 0$ from the first equation. Finally $ad - bc = -bc \neq 0$.

15. C

16. Adding the left and right sides of $a_1 = x_1 + x_2$, $a_2 = x_2 + x_3$, and $a_3 = x_1 + x_3$ gives $a_1 + a_2 + a_3 =$

4.9 Matrix Properties

With addition and multiplication of matrices defined, there is a whole algebra of matrices. You can write expressions such as $(X + Y)^2$, equations such as $X^2 + 3X = B$, and even systems of matrix equations such as

$$AX + BY = C$$
$$DX + EY = F$$

Do the rules of ordinary algebra apply? For instance, are the following equations true?

$$(3X + 4Y) - 2(X - Y) = X + 6Y$$
$$(X + Y)^2 = X^2 + 2XY + Y^2$$

Also, does $AB = 0$ imply $A = 0$ or $B = 0$?

If the usual rules do apply, that would make it much easier to do matrix algebra.

Remember...

The notation 0 stands for a matrix with all entries equaling zero.

Developing Habits of Mind

Make strategic choices. There are many moves you can make in ordinary algebra. Do you have to verify each of them from scratch to apply them to matrices? No, not necessarily. Instead, you can find a few basic rules and deduce the other valid rules from them. This deductive approach is one of the great achievements of mathematics. You have probably already used it in your first-year algebra course to prove properties of real numbers. First, you can identify some key properties as basic rules, for instance, the commutative properties of addition and multiplication and the Distributive Property.

$$a + b = b + a \text{ and } ab = ba \quad \text{for all real numbers } a \text{ and } b$$
$$a(b + c) = ab + ac \quad \text{for all real numbers } a, b, \text{ and } c$$

Then you can show that many other properties followed from the full set of basic rules. For instance, you can prove the expansion principle: To multiply two sums, multiply each term in the first sum by each term in the second sum and add the results.

$$(x + y + z)(a + b) = xa + xb + ya + yb + za + zb$$

Similarly, if all the same basic rules held for matrix algebra, then so would the expansion principle.

It turns out that most, but not all, of the basic rules for real numbers hold for matrices as well. You will see the consequences shortly.

$2(x_1 + x_2 + x_3)$. So if $a_1 + a_2 + a_3 = 3 + 2 + 3 = 6$, then $x_1 + x_2 + x_3 = \frac{6}{2} = 3$.

17. no solution

18. a. $\begin{pmatrix} 1 & 0 & 0 \\ 0 & \frac{1}{2} & 0 \\ 0 & 0 & 3 \end{pmatrix}$

b. $\begin{pmatrix} 1 & -1 \\ 0 & 1 \end{pmatrix}$

c. $\begin{pmatrix} 1 & -\frac{1}{2} & -\frac{1}{12} \\ 0 & \frac{1}{4} & -\frac{5}{24} \\ 0 & 0 & \frac{1}{6} \end{pmatrix}$

d. $\begin{pmatrix} 1 & 0 & 0 \\ -2 & 1 & 0 \\ 0 & -\frac{1}{2} & \frac{1}{2} \end{pmatrix}$

e. $\begin{pmatrix} -2 & 1 & 0 & 0 \\ \frac{3}{2} & -\frac{1}{2} & 0 & 0 \\ 0 & 0 & -2 & 1 \\ 0 & 0 & \frac{3}{2} & -\frac{1}{2} \end{pmatrix}$

f. $\begin{pmatrix} 4 & -6 \\ -6 & 12 \end{pmatrix}$

g. $\begin{pmatrix} 9 & -36 & 30 \\ -36 & 192 & -180 \\ 30 & -180 & 180 \end{pmatrix}$

Lesson Overview

GOAL

- Interpret and solve problems using matrix calculations.

There is a structure to matrix algebra. You do not have to remember an endless list of correct and incorrect manipulations. You just have to know the basic rules and everything else that is legitimate follows from them. This is the same situation as holds in traditional (number) algebra. That point was made in Lesson 2.5, *Rephrasing the Basic Rules* in CME Project *Algebra 1*. There the basic rules of traditional algebra were laid out, and you saw how other properties followed. This lesson plays the same role for matrix algebra. There are two differences, however.

First, the basic rules for matrix algebra are not quite the same as the basic rules for number algebra. There are some rules that have no direct analog in number algebra, because number algebra has only one sort of multiplication while matrix algebra has two (scalar multiplication and matrix multiplication). More confusing for students is the fact that there are some rules of number algebra that are false in matrix algebra, most notably, the commutative property $ab = ba$.

Second, the students had lots of experience with number algebra before reaching the lesson on the deductive structure. For matrix algebra, they have this chapter only. So this lesson on deductive structure may be too early for some. If so, it is certainly optional material. The actual proofs of some of the basic matrix rules will be hard for all students, and indeed, the lesson goes lightly on these proofs.

If you do cover this lesson, the most important point for students to come away with is that matrix algebra does have an organized structure, but certain algebra rules that students might want to apply automatically from past experience are false. The text states explicitly the most important examples in the Facts and Notation section. Because some familiar number algebra rules are false, students need to understand that they cannot run on automatic when doing matrix algebra.

CHECK YOUR UNDERSTANDING
- Core: 2, 3, 4, 5, 6
- Optional: 1, 7, 8

MATERIALS
- graphing calculators
- Blackline Master 4.9

HOMEWORK
- Core: 9, 10, 12, 14, 17, 18
- Optional: 11, 13, 15, 16, 19, 20

VOCABULARY
- diagonal matrices
- Zero Product Property

Launch

Work through the dialog between Tony and Sasha, perhaps prefaced by some remarks as to what the lesson is all about. You may want to remind students about how they investigated the algebraic structure of the compound numbers in Chapter 3 and let them know that they will do a similar thing here for matrices.

Explore

Minds in Action

Sasha raises an important point about understanding why a claim is false, which is overlooked in superficial discussions of what mathematicians do. Yes, it is often said that, to disprove something, it suffices to find just one counterexample. But mathematicians are rarely satisfied with that. If a claim is plausible enough to conjecture that it is true, then why is it not true? The dialog shows one way to explore such questions.

Minds in Action **episode 17**

Tony and Sasha have been asked to justify, or find counterexamples to, the matrix versions of the two commutative properties.

Tony We're half done, because we have already seen in Exercise 17 from Lesson 4.7 that $AB \neq BA$. So let's consider $A + B = B + A$. That's always been true in all the examples I've seen.

Sasha But that's not a proof.

Tony True, but I've caught on to how this is done. We already worked this out for n-tuples. Matrices $A + B$ and $B + A$ will be equal if the real numbers inside them are equal entry by entry. So consider a typical entry.

Sasha I see. For the typical entry of $A + B$, you add the A-entry and the B-entry. For $B + A$, you add the B-entry and the A-entry. Since these entries are numbers, and we already know that number addition commutes, we're done.

Tony It helps me to build an example. Let $A = \begin{pmatrix} 1 & 2 \\ 3 & 4 \end{pmatrix}$ and $B = \begin{pmatrix} 5 & 6 \\ 7 & 8 \end{pmatrix}$. The row-1, column-2 entry of $A + B$ is $2 + 6$. The row-1, column-2 entry of $B + A$ is $6 + 2$. But good old number addition commutes.

Sasha I like that. And since there was nothing special about the row-1, column-2 entry, we've shown that corresponding entries agree in all cases, so $A + B$ and $B + A$ are equal.

Tony Great! Now we're done, because we already know that matrix multiplication doesn't commute.

Sasha Yes, we have a specific example where $AB \neq BA$, but I'm not happy with that.

Tony Why not? A claim is false if there is even just one counterexample.

Sasha Yes, but I don't think I understand yet why order matters for matrix multiplication. I don't know whether failure to commute is rare or common.

Tony Let's look at the definition of matrix multiplication and see if it gives us any clues.

Sasha I like to think about the definition with the dot product of rows and columns. So I think of the ij entry of AB this way.

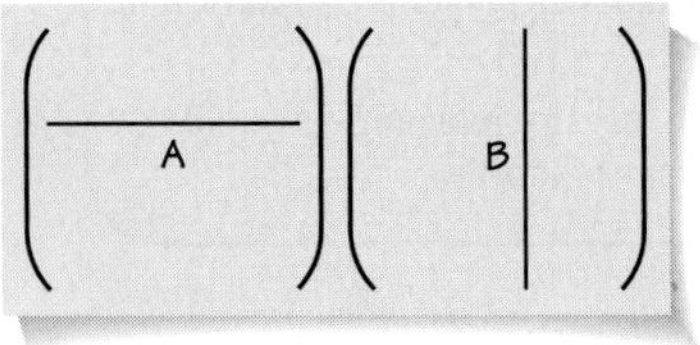

The horizontal and vertical lines I drew show how to compute a typical element of A times B: a dot product of the ith row of A and the jth column of B.

Tony Looks good.

Sasha Let's find the same entry of B times A.

Tony OK, now the picture looks like this.

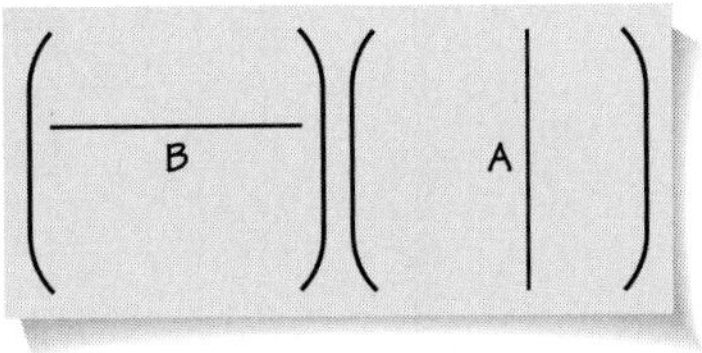

It looks about the same.

Sasha It only looks the same if you ignore that the matrices have been switched! See, the numbers that you multiply are all different. Here, let me draw in the row and column of numbers that we took the dot product of when the product was AB.

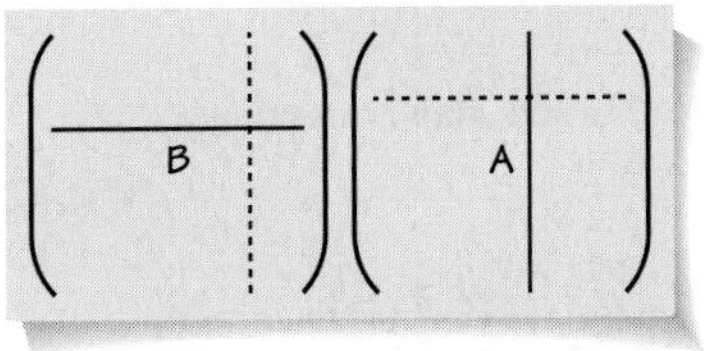

Look, they're almost completely different from the solid line entries that we used to compute BA. No wonder it is different!

Tony Hmm. Now I'm surprised that AB ever equals BA in any entry!

Sasha But we know it sometimes does, as in $AI = IA$ for an identity matrix. I guess those must be rare exceptions.

Tony I wonder if we can explain with your pictures why I commutes with other matrices.

You will give an explanation in Exercise 8.

For Discussion

1. While thinking about why $AB \neq BA$, Sasha drew a picture with square matrices. If you look at nonsquare matrices, you can argue just from the sizes and the products that you cannot have equality. Explain.

Answers

For Discussion

1. Answers may vary. Sample: The product $(a \quad b)\begin{pmatrix} c & d \\ e & f \end{pmatrix}$ exists, but the product $\begin{pmatrix} c & d \\ e & f \end{pmatrix}(a \quad b)$ does not exist.

FACTS AND NOTATION This section provides a good opportunity for your students to refamiliarize themselves with the standard number properties and their names. What they should not do is memorize this page. In any event, the properties that hold for matrix algebra (most of them) will probably be common knowledge from the number world, so students will not have to learn them. The important new pieces of information to note are the number properties that are not true in the matrix world. It is also valuable for students to note how some number properties split into several versions because there are two types of matrix multiplication.

Facts and Notation

You can now summarize the properties of matrix algebra, as compared to the properties of real numbers.

Commutative Properties:

- $A + B = B + A$ **True**
- $AB = BA$ **False (It is not true for all A and B.)**

Associative Properties:

- $(A + B) + C = A + (B + C)$ **True**
- $(AB)C = A(BC)$ **True**

Distributive Property:

- $A(B + C) = AB + AC$ **and** $(B + C)A = BA + CA$ **True**

Because matrix algebra has both matrix multiplication and scalar multiplication, some of the basic rules of real numbers split into several matrix rules. Consider the Distributive Property. Along with the version above, there are also two scalar versions:

- $a(B + C) = aB + aC$ **True**
- $(a + b)C = aC + bC$ **True**

Again, because there are two types of multiplication, some rules may look like associative properties, but they are not.

- $a(BC) = (aB)C = B(aC)$ **True**
- $a(bC) = (ab)C = b(aC)$ **True**

Additive Identity:

- **For each matrix A, there exists a matrix 0 of the same size such that $A + 0 = A$. The matrix 0 has the number 0 in every entry. True**

Additive Inverse:

- **For every matrix A there exists another matrix $-A$ of the same size such that $A + (-A) = 0$. In fact, if $A = (a_{ij})$, then $-A = (-a_{ij})$. True**

Multiplicative Identity:

- **For each square matrix A, there exists a matrix I such that $AI = IA = A$. If A is $m \times n$, and I_k is the $k \times k$ identity matrix, with 1's on the main diagonal and 0's elsewhere, then $I_mA = AI_n = A$. True**

Multiplicative Inverses:

- **For each matrix A, where $A \neq 0$, there exists a matrix A^{-1} such that $AA^{-1} = A^{-1}A = I$. False**

When you consider a property with a sum like $A + B$ or a product like AB, you may assume that A and B are of the appropriate sizes for the operation.

Habits of Mind

Experiment. Where have you already seen examples for which the last rule is false?

Developing Habits of Mind

Look for relationships. As Tony and Sasha noted, for those rules that are true, there are proofs. For those that are false, there are counterexamples and maybe some sort of intuitive way to see that there should be counterexamples.

But what do the proofs look like? The proof Tony and Sasha found for $A + B = B + A$ uses one standard matrix technique: Look at a typical entry (the *ij* entry). See whether the matrix identity reduces to a known numeric identity. In a similar way, proofs of facts about scalar multiplication often work out to be proofs about sums. See, for instance, Exercise 9.

Claims involving matrix multiplication are much more complicated to prove or disprove. This is because the formula for the typical entry of a product matrix is complicated.

Perhaps the most difficult basic rule to justify is the associative property of multiplication. Some earlier exercises illustrated instances of this property. They explained that the definition of matrix multiplication was tailored to make $A(BX) = (AB)X$ true, at least when X is a single column. You can accept the associative property of matrix multiplication as a working conjecture.

In particular, Exercise 26 in Lesson 4.6

You will explore some of the multiplication rules in the exercises.

Beyond the Basics

Any matrix claim that just involves addition, subtraction, and scalar multiplication is correct if the basic algebra version of it is correct. But claims that involve matrix multiplication may be wrong.

For instance, the matrix equation

$$a(X + Y) - b(X + 2Y) = (a - b)X + (a - 2b)Y \qquad (13)$$

corresponds to the number equation

$$a(x + y) - b(x + 2y) = (a - b)x + (a - 2b)y \qquad (14)$$

Equation (13) uses just matrix addition and subtraction and scalar multiplication. Equation (14) is correct, therefore (13) is correct. Why is it? The basic rules for matrix addition, subtraction, and scalar multiplication are the same as the basic rules for number addition, subtraction, and multiplication. So however you justify (14) from the basic algebra rules, exactly the same justification works for (13) using the basic matrix rules.

However, the following matrix-product statement is false even though the corresponding statement for real numbers is true.

If $AB = 0$, then $A = 0$ or $B = 0$.

If $ab = 0$, then $a = 0$ or $b = 0$. (Zero Product Property)

BEYOND THE BASICS The text gives a good explanation of why you can be confident that the matrix properties that involve addition, subtraction, and scalar multiplication are just like the corresponding number-algebra properties: the basic rules about these operations are the same in both worlds.

The text is less convincing that you ought to be suspicious of any claim involving matrix multiplication. Why not just be suspicious of claims involving the Commutative Property of Multiplication and multiplicative inverses? The reason you should be more generally suspicious is that the Commutative Property and multiplicative inverses often play roles in disguise, especially inverses.

For instance, as shown on the next page, the proof of the Zero Product Property for numbers relies on the existence of inverses, even though the statement of this property does not mention inverses at all.

Developing Habits of Mind

The text makes an important point: random searching for counterexamples is not likely to succeed, unless the conjecture is wildly wrong. The best way to find counterexamples is to try to prove the conjecture and find where you get stuck. This focuses the mind on where to look for a counterexample.

For You to Do

PROBLEM 2 If the students need a hint, tell them to figure out B one column at a time. In fact, every B is of the form $\begin{pmatrix} 2k & 2j \\ -k & -j \end{pmatrix}$ where k and j are arbitrary.

PROBLEM 3 If students have trouble, suggest that they try some specific examples. From the hint, they can write $AB - AC = A(B - C) = 0$. They know from Problem 2 that both A and $B - C$ can be nonzero. For instance, set $A = \begin{pmatrix} 1 & 2 \\ 3 & 6 \end{pmatrix}$ and $B - C = D = \begin{pmatrix} -2 & 6 \\ 1 & -3 \end{pmatrix}$. Now let C be any 2×2 matrix you want and set $B = C + D$. Then $AB = A(C + D) = AC + AD = AC + 0 = AC$ and yet $B \neq C$.

Wrap Up

Have a class discussion about the expansion principle for matrix algebra, based on Exercise 6.

Assessment Resources

Lesson Quiz 4.9

1. Let $B = \begin{pmatrix} 1 & 3 \\ 2 & 6 \end{pmatrix}$.
   a. Find all 2×1 columns A such that $BA = 0$.
   b. Find all 2×2 matrices A such that $BA = 0$.

2. Is $A + A + A = A^3$ true for all matrices? You can use the definitions of *sum* and *scalar multiple* for matrices. You can also use the basic rules for matrices.

3. Let $A = \begin{pmatrix} 0 & 2 & 4 \\ 1 & 3 & 5 \end{pmatrix}$.
   a. Find a matrix I such that $IA = A$.
   b. Find a matrix I such that $AI = A$.

Developing Habits of Mind

Consider more than one strategy. How can you determine whether a suspect claim is false? Sometimes you are lucky and you already have a counterexample that you discovered while doing something else. For instance, you discovered in Exercise 13 of Lesson 4.6 that the Zero Product Property is false for dot products, and dot products are a special sort of matrix product. If you are not lucky, you should probably not start by trying random examples. If the first example or two shows the claim to be false, you have your answer, but you do not know why. On the other hand, if the claim works for the first five examples, were you lucky, or was this because the claim is true? There is no way to be sure.

A better approach is to try to prove the claim from the basic rules and any other known truths. Either you will succeed, in which case no search for counterexamples is necessary, or else you will discover how the proof breaks down. That will probably suggest how to find a counterexample.

A good navigation system will help you find what you are looking for.

How do you prove the Zero Product Property for real numbers? One proof goes this way.

Assume $ab = 0$. Either $a = 0$ or not. If it does, you are done. If it does not, multiply $ab = 0$ by $\frac{1}{a}$, getting $b = 0$. So, $a = 0$ or $b = 0$.

Aha! The proof uses the existence of a^{-1}, which works for numbers so long as $a \neq 0$. But it does not work for most matrices, so you might suspect that the Zero Product Property for matrices will fail when A is not invertible.

Habits of Mind

Make strategic choices. The Zero Product Property will not necessarily fail for matrices. There might be a proof that does not use inverses and still works. But you should be very suspicious that the property will fail for matrices. It is now worth looking for a counterexample.

For You to Do

2. According to Exercise 14 in Lesson 4.8, $A = \begin{pmatrix} 1 & 2 \\ 3 & 6 \end{pmatrix}$ is not invertible, because $1 \cdot 6 - 3 \cdot 2 = 0$. Find a nonzero 2×2 matrix B such that $AB = 0$.

The Zero Product Property is a property that eliminates a product. You go from a statement about ab to a statement about a or b. All such properties involve inverses somewhere, and all are suspect (and usually false) in matrix algebra. The following problem gives one more property that would be useful if it were true for matrices, but it is not.

For You to Do

3. One of the cancellation laws of number algebra is

If $ab = ac$, then $b = c$ (unless $a = 0$).

Show that the corresponding matrix statement is false.

If $AB = AC$, then $B = C$ (unless $A = 0$).

(*Hint:* Subtract AC from both sides and set up a zero product.)

Answers

For You to Do

2. Answers may vary. Sample:

$B = \begin{pmatrix} 2 & 2 \\ -1 & -1 \end{pmatrix}$

3. Answers may vary. Sample: Suppose $A \neq 0$, $B \neq 0$, $C \neq 0$, and $B \neq C$. Then if $AB = AC$, you can subtract AC from each side to get $AB - AC = AC - AC$. This can be rewritten as $A(B - C) = 0$. So the product of A and $(B - C)$ is zero, but $A \neq 0$ and $B - C \neq 0$ (because $B \neq C$).

Exercises

1. a. $I = \begin{pmatrix} 1 & 0 \\ 0 & 1 \end{pmatrix}$

b. $I = \begin{pmatrix} 1 & 0 & 0 \\ 0 & 1 & 0 \\ 0 & 0 & 1 \end{pmatrix}$

2. If $A = B$, then by substitution $AB = AA = BA$, so square matrices commute with themselves under multiplication. Also,

Exercises Practicing Habits of Mind

The exercises give some more examples of rules involving multiplication that break down. Be prepared for them to break down every time, except if special matrices like I are involved.

Check Your Understanding

1. Let $A = \begin{pmatrix} 1 & 2 & 3 \\ 4 & 5 & 6 \end{pmatrix}$.
   a. Find a matrix I such that $IA = A$.
   b. Find a matrix I such that $AI = A$.

This exercise confirms the fact that a matrix can have different identities on the left and the right.

2. Show that every square matrix A commutes under multiplication with itself. Does A also commute with A^2? Explain.

3. You usually state the Distributive Property for number algebra in just one equation.
$$a(b + c) = ab + ac$$
Explain why the Distributive Property for matrices was stated in two equations.
$$A(B + C) = AB + AC \text{ and } (B + C)A = BA + CA$$

4. Let $A = \begin{pmatrix} 1 & 2 \\ 3 & 6 \end{pmatrix}$.
   a. Find all 2×1 columns B such that $AB = 0$.
   b. Find all 2×2 matrices B such that $AB = 0$.

5. **What's Wrong Here?** In number algebra,
$$(x + y)^2 = x^2 + 2xy + y^2$$
Below is a proposed proof that the statement is also true for matrices. For each line that is correct, explain why. For each line that is wrong, explain why.
$$\begin{aligned}(X + Y)^2 &= (X + Y)(X + Y) \\ &= X(X + Y) + Y(X + Y) \\ &= (XX + XY) + (YX + YY) \\ &= X^2 + (XY + YX) + Y^2 \\ &= X^2 + 2XY + Y^2\end{aligned}$$

6. Does the expansion principle hold for matrix algebra?

7. Show that the following revised cancellation law is valid for matrix algebra: If A is invertible and $AB = AC$, then $B = C$.

See the first Developing Habits of Mind section in this lesson for an explanation of the expansion principle.

$AA^2 = AAA = A^2A$ because matrix multiplication is associative.

3. Answers may vary. Sample: Matrix multiplication is not always commutative, so $A(B + C) \neq (B + C)A$. Therefore, you need a Distributive Property for $A(B + C)$ and another Distributive Property for $(B + C)A$.

4. a. $B = \begin{pmatrix} -2c \\ c \end{pmatrix}$ for any value of c.
   b. $B = \begin{pmatrix} -2c & -2d \\ c & d \end{pmatrix}$ for any values of c and d.

5. Line 1: OK, by the definition of squaring; Line 2: OK; distribute the second factor $(X + Y)$ over the two terms of the first factor; Line 3: OK; Distributive Property; Line 4: OK, by the definition of squaring; Line 5: wrong because $XY \neq YX$. The last line should be $X^2 + XY + YX + Y^2$.

6. yes

7. Since A^{-1} exists and $AB = AC$, then $A^{-1}(AB) = A^{-1}(AC)$. Then $(A^{-1}A)B = (A^{-1}A)C$ or $B = C$.

Exercises

HOMEWORK
- Core: 9, 10, 12, 14, 17, 18
- Optional: 11, 13, 15, 16, 19, 20

Check Your Understanding

EXERCISE 2 A consequence of this result, very useful in advanced work, is this: even though matrix algebra is highly noncommutative, for any square matrix A, the subalgebra consisting of polynomials in A (e.g., such matrices as $A^2 - 3A$ and $A^3 - 2A^2 + 6I$) is commutative; all matrices in such a subset commute.

EXERCISE 4 Most of the work occurs in part (a). In any product AB, each column of B works independently of the others in the sense that the jth column of AB depends on all of A but only on column j of B. Similarly (but not of use in this exercise), all the rows of A work independently in determining the product AB.

EXERCISE 5 Blackline Master 4.9 provides a copy of this exercise. Some students think the property $(x + y)^2 = x^2 + 2xy + y^2$ ("squaring a binomial") is a free-standing fact having nothing to do with basic rules of algebra. These students are likely to assume that the matrix version is also a free-standing fact. But if, as in this exercise, students take the time to see how squaring a binomial is a consequence of the basic number-algebra rules, they are also likely to see that it is probably false for matrices.

EXERCISE 6 and its conclusion—the expansion principle, suitably stated, holds for matrix algebra—are well worth a class discussion. Encourage students to present examples in case their explanations are too vague to be helpful. Make sure everyone understands the need, absent in number algebra, *not* to rewrite the terms in an "alphabetically pleasing" order.

On Your Own

EXERCISE 10 This expansion is correct so long as you use only X and I, which commute with each other and of course with powers of themselves. In this case, you are in a commutative world. All number-algebra facts that depend on the Commutative Property will also hold for your matrices. See the Exercise 2 note about polynomial subalgebras.

EXERCISE 12 It is sufficient at this stage for students to give an example proof, as long as they can explain how they know it is a general example.

EXERCISE 13 shows that there are lots of matrices without multiplicative inverses, whereas there is only one number without a multiplicative inverse. However, in another sense, noninvertible square matrices turn out to be rare. If, for instance, you pick each entry in a 2×2 matrix at random, say from -10 to 10, almost every matrix you devise would be invertible. Have students think about why this is so. One approach: review the facts about 2×2 determinants at the end of Lesson 4.8.

EXERCISE 15 The result here is the same as for Exercise 10. The scalar b makes no difference, because scalars "pass through" (commute with) matrices, as shown in Exercise 14.

8. Follow up on Tony's thought at the end of the dialog. Can you use Sasha's pictures to explain why AI is equal to IA? Explain.

As Sasha did, assume that A is a square matrix.

On Your Own

9. Is $A + A = 2A$ true for all matrices? You can use the definitions of *sum* and *scalar multiple* for matrices. However, if you note that $1A = A$, then you can also use one of the basic rules for matrices.

10. Consider the special binomial expansion $(X + I)^2 = X^2 + 2X + I$. This is the matrix version of $(x + 1)^2 = x^2 + 2x + 1$. Is this special matrix binomial expansion correct for all square matrices?

Habits of Mind

Detect the key characteristics. Here, the matrix X must be square. Explain

11. Show that $(X + Y)^2 = X^2 + 2XY + Y^2$ if and only if X and Y commute.

12. Explain why $A(B + C) = AB + AC$. That is, justify the Distributive Property for matrix algebra.

13. a. Show that the all-0's matrix Z never has a multiplicative inverse, no matter what its size.

b. Show that there exist infinitely many 2×2 matrices A that do not have an inverse. In fact, show that there are infinitely many 2×2 matrices in which all four entries are nonzero and yet A^{-1} does not exist.

14. Consider again one of the basic rules of matrix algebra.

$$a(BC) = (aB)C = B(aC)$$

This rule says that three different computations give the same result. You can describe the first computation as, "First you multiply the two matrices and then you scale." Describe in your own words the three different computations.

15. Show that the claim $(X + bI)^2 = X^2 + 2bX + b^2I$ is correct for any square matrix X and scalar b.

16. **Write About It** What have you learned in this lesson about rules for matrix algebra?

17. **Standardized Test Prep** Suppose X is a 2×2 matrix. Cynthia has a system for constructing a 2×2 matrix Y such that $XY = YX$. She says if $X = \begin{pmatrix} a & b \\ c & d \end{pmatrix}$, then $Y = \begin{pmatrix} f & kb \\ kc & f - k(a - d) \end{pmatrix}$.

Suppose $X = \begin{pmatrix} 5 & 2 \\ 1 & 4 \end{pmatrix}$, $y_{11} = 4$, and $y_{12} = 6$. What is YX?

A. $\begin{pmatrix} 4 & 6 \\ 3 & 1 \end{pmatrix}$ **B.** $\begin{pmatrix} 20 & 12 \\ 3 & 4 \end{pmatrix}$ **C.** $\begin{pmatrix} 26 & 32 \\ 16 & 10 \end{pmatrix}$ **D.** $\begin{pmatrix} 26 & 54 \\ 16 & 54 \end{pmatrix}$

Go Online PHSchool.com

For additional practice, go to **Web Code**: bfa-0409

Answers

8. Answers may vary. Sample: When you multiply a square matrix M by its appropriate identity matrix, there is only one element in each row of M that results in a nonzero term, and that is the same whether the identity is to the left or to the right of M.

9. Answers may vary. Sample: $A + A = 1A + 1A = (1 + 1)A = 2A$

10. Yes; from Exercise 5, $(X + Y)^2 = X^2 + XY + YX + Y^2$. Substituting I for Y gives $(X + I)^2 = X^2 + XI + IX + I^2 = X^2 + 2X + I$.

11. Exercise 5 shows that $(X + Y)^2 = X^2 + XY + YX + Y^2$. That is equal to $X^2 + 2XY + Y^2$ if and only if $XY = YX$, which is another way of saying that X and Y commute.

12. Let R_i denote the ith row of A, while B_j and C_j denote the jth columns of B and C, respectively. Then entry ij of $A(B + C)$ is $R_i \cdot (B_j + C_j)$. Using the distributive property of dot products (see Exercise 7 of lesson 4.6), this is the same as $R_i \cdot B_j + R_i \cdot C_j$, which is entry ij of AB plus entry ij of AC. This says that $A(B + C)$ and $AB + AC$ have all the same entries, so they are equal.

13. a. For a zero matrix Z and another matrix B, $ZB = Z$. Since $ZB \neq I$ for any B, matrix Z cannot have an inverse.

b. We know that $\begin{pmatrix} a & b \\ c & d \end{pmatrix}$ *does not* have an inverse if $ad - bc = 0$, or if $ad = bc$. So matrices such as $\begin{pmatrix} 1 & 2 \\ 2 & 4 \end{pmatrix}$, $\begin{pmatrix} 3 & 6 \\ 2 & 4 \end{pmatrix}$, or $\begin{pmatrix} 1 & \pi \\ 7 & 7\pi \end{pmatrix}$ do not have an inverse.

14. Answers may vary. Sample: The product of two matrices times a scalar is equal to the product (in the same order) of either matrix and the scalar multiple of the other matrix.

Maintain Your Skills

18. The multiplication formula for 1×1 matrices is especially simple. What is it? Are there any pairs of 1×1 matrices that do not commute?

19. Use the matrices A and D below.

$$A = \begin{pmatrix} a & 0 & 0 \\ 0 & b & 0 \\ 0 & 0 & c \end{pmatrix} \qquad D = \begin{pmatrix} d & 0 & 0 \\ 0 & e & 0 \\ 0 & 0 & f \end{pmatrix}$$

Compute AD and DA. What do you notice?

20. a. Find all matrices that commute under multiplication with $\begin{pmatrix} 0 & \\ & 1 \end{pmatrix}$.

b. Find all matrices that commute under multiplication with $\begin{pmatrix} 0 & & \\ & 0 & \\ & & 1 \end{pmatrix}$.

c. Expand $(X + I)^3$.

d. Expand $(X + I)^4$.

e. Expand $(X + Y)^3$. Compare this expansion with the expansion of $(X + Y)^2$ in Exercise 5. See if you can find a pattern.

f. Expand $(X + Y + Z)^2$. Compare this expansion with the expansion of $(X + Y)^2$ in Exercise 5. See if you can find a pattern.

The nonzero entries in A and D are on the main diagonal. Matrices with nonzero entries only along the main diagonal are *diagonal matrices.* You can display them with spaces instead of 0's to avoid visual clutter.

$$A = \begin{pmatrix} a & & \\ & b & \\ & & c \end{pmatrix}$$

Additional Resources

PRINT RESOURCES
- Solution Manual
- Practice Workbook
- Assessment Resources
- Teaching Resources

TECHNOLOGY
- Interactive Textbook
- TeacherExpress CD-ROM
- ExamView CD-ROM
- PHSchool.com

Additional Practice

1. Consider the system $\begin{pmatrix} 2 & -3 \\ 1 & 2 \end{pmatrix}\begin{pmatrix} x \\ y \end{pmatrix} = \begin{pmatrix} 8 \\ -3 \end{pmatrix}$.

a. Attempt to solve it geometrically, that is, by graphing the line corresponding to each equation. What happens?

b. Attempt to solve it by Gaussian Elimination. What happens?

c. Attempt to solve it by the inverse method. What happens?

For Exercises 2 and 3, determine whether there is a matrix $\begin{pmatrix} a & b \\ c & d \end{pmatrix}$ that solves the equation.

2. $\begin{pmatrix} a & b \\ c & d \end{pmatrix}\begin{pmatrix} 1 & 3 \\ 2 & 4 \end{pmatrix} = \begin{pmatrix} 1 & 0 \\ 0 & 1 \end{pmatrix}$

3. $\begin{pmatrix} 1 & 3 \\ 2 & 4 \end{pmatrix}\begin{pmatrix} a & b \\ c & d \end{pmatrix} = \begin{pmatrix} 1 & 0 \\ 0 & 1 \end{pmatrix}$

4. Suppose a_1 is the sum of x_1 and x_2, a_2 is the sum of x_2 and x_3, and a_3 is the sum of x_3 and x_1. If $(a_1, a_2, a_3) = (3, 4, 5)$, what are x_1, x_2, and x_3?

5. Let $B = \begin{pmatrix} -1 & 2 \\ 3 & -6 \end{pmatrix}$.

a. Find all 2×1 columns A such that $BA = 0$.

b. Find all 2×2 matrices A such that $BA = 0$.

6. Is $A + A + A = 3A$ true for all matrices? You can use the definitions of *sum* and *scalar multiple* for matrices. You can also use the basic rules for matrices.

7. Consider the special binomial expansion $(X - I)^2 = X^2 - 2IX + I^2$. Is this special binomial expansion correct for all matrices? Explain.

8. a. Is there a matrix $\begin{pmatrix} a & b \\ c & d \end{pmatrix}$ that solves the following equation?

$$\begin{pmatrix} -2 & 3 \\ 4 & -5 \end{pmatrix}\begin{pmatrix} a & b \\ c & d \end{pmatrix} = \begin{pmatrix} -2 & 3 \\ 4 & -5 \end{pmatrix}$$

b. Find all matrices that commute under multiplication with $\begin{pmatrix} 1 & \\ & 1 \end{pmatrix}$.

Practice: For Lesson 4.9, assign Exercises 5–8.

15. Answers may vary. Sample: Using Exercise 5, $(X + Y)^2 = X^2 + XY + YX + Y^2$. Using bI for Y, then $(X + bI)^2 = X^2 + XbI + bIX + (bI)^2$. Using Exercise 14 and the fact that $IX = XI = X$, the product can be written as $X^2 + 2bX + (bI)^2$; using the property that $(bI)^2 = bIbI = b^2I^2 = b^2I$, the product can be written as $X^2 + 2bX + b^2I$.

16. Answers may vary. Students should be able to describe matrix properties that are similar to number properties, such as the associative properties for addition and for multiplication, the Distributive Property, the existence of an additive identity, an additive inverse, a multiplicative identity, and when a matrix has a multiplicative inverse. Also, students should be able to describe matrix properties that are different from number properties, such as there are two Distributive Properties, that matrix multiplication is not necessarily commutative, and there is no Zero Product Property for matrices.

17. C

18. Multiplying 1×1 matrices is multiplying numbers, so all 1×1 matrices commute.

19. $AD = \begin{pmatrix} ad & 0 & 0 \\ 0 & be & 0 \\ 0 & 0 & cf \end{pmatrix} = DA$; all square "diagonal matrices" commute.

20. a. any matrix of the form $\begin{pmatrix} a & 0 \\ 0 & d \end{pmatrix}$

b. any matrix of the form $\begin{pmatrix} a & b & 0 \\ d & e & 0 \\ 0 & 0 & i \end{pmatrix}$

c. $(X + I)^3 = X^3 + 3X^2 + 3X + I$

d. $(X + I)^4 = X^4 + 4X^3 + 6X^2 + 4X + I$

e. $(X + Y)^3 = X^3 + X^2Y + XYX + YX^2 + XY^2 + YXY + Y^2X + Y^3$

f. $(X + Y + Z)^2 = X^2 + Y^2 + Z^2 + XY + YX + XZ + ZX + YZ + ZY$

Mathematical Reflections

EXERCISES 6–8 At the start of the investigation, you may have assigned these as Questions 1–3 for students to think and write about.

Mathematical Reflections 4B

In this investigation, you learned how to compute sums, differences, dot products, products, and inverses of matrices. You also explored the properties of matrix algebra. These questions will help you summarize what you have learned.

1. Use the following matrices.

$$A = \begin{pmatrix} 3 & 1 \\ -1 & 0 \end{pmatrix} \quad B = \begin{pmatrix} 4 & 2 \end{pmatrix} \quad C = \begin{pmatrix} 0 \\ -2 \end{pmatrix} \quad D = \begin{pmatrix} 5 & 0 \\ 1 & -2 \end{pmatrix}$$

For each part, either do the calculation or explain why it does not make sense.

a. $3D$ **b.** $A + B$ **c.** $A - D$ **d.** $B \cdot C$

e. $A \cdot C$ **f.** AB **g.** AC **h.** AD

2. Find a 3-tuple $E = (a \;\; b \;\; c)$ such that $E \cdot (-2 \;\; 1 \;\; 4) = 0$. Is the E you found the only possible answer? If so, explain why. If not, give another example.

3. For the following matrices, show that $F(G + H) = FG + FH$.

$$F = \begin{pmatrix} 1 & -1 \\ 2 & 0 \end{pmatrix} \quad G = \begin{pmatrix} -3 & 1 \\ 0 & 4 \end{pmatrix} \quad H = \begin{pmatrix} 0 & 1 \\ -2 & 0 \end{pmatrix}$$

4. Use the following matrices.

$$J = \begin{pmatrix} 1 & -1 \\ 0 & 2 \\ 3 & 1 \end{pmatrix} \quad K = \begin{pmatrix} 2 & -1 & 0 \\ 0 & -2 & 1 \end{pmatrix}$$

Is JK equal to KJ? Make a prediction and then find both products to check.

5. Give an example of a 2×2 matrix that does not have an inverse. Explain how you know.

6. What is a dot product? How can you represent matrix multiplication using dot products?

7. What are some special cases in which $AB = BA$ is true for matrices A and B?

8. How can you solve this system of equations using matrix inverses? What is the solution?

$$\begin{aligned} x + 4y - z &= -3 \\ 2x - 2y + z &= 0 \\ 3x + y - 3z &= -9 \end{aligned}$$

The final color at each point on the cover is the sum of the individual colors at that point.

Vocabulary and Notation

In this investigation, you learned these terms and symbols. Make sure you understand what each one means and how to use it.

- **determinant**
- **dot product**
- **identity matrix, *I***
- **inverse, A^{-1}**
- **linear combination**
- **matrix multiplication**
- ***n*-tuple**
- **scalar multiplication**
- **zero matrix, 0**

Answers

Mathematical Reflections

1. a. $3D = \begin{pmatrix} 15 & 0 \\ 3 & -6 \end{pmatrix}$

b. $A + B$ does not exist.

c. $A - D = \begin{pmatrix} -2 & 1 \\ -2 & 2 \end{pmatrix}$

d. $B \cdot C = (4)(0) + (2)(-2) = -4$

e. $A \cdot C$ does not exist because A and C have different n-tuples.

f. AB does not exist.

g. $AC = \begin{pmatrix} -2 \\ 0 \end{pmatrix}$

h. $AD = \begin{pmatrix} 16 & -2 \\ -5 & 0 \end{pmatrix}$

2. Answers may vary. Sample: $(0 \;\; 0 \;\; 0)$, $(2 \;\; 0 \;\; 1)$, or any triple $(a \;\; b \;\; c)$ such that $-2a + b + 4c = 0$

3–4. See back of book.

5. Answers may vary. Sample: $\begin{pmatrix} 1 & 2 \\ 2 & 4 \end{pmatrix}$, or any 2×2 matrix $\begin{pmatrix} a & b \\ c & d \end{pmatrix}$ where $ad - bc = 0$

6. For two n-tuples $(a_1, a_2, \dots, a_n)$ and $(b_1, b_2, \dots, b_n)$, the dot product is the number $a_1b_1 + a_2b_2 + \cdots + a_nb_n$. To multiply two matrices, where the left one has n columns and the right one has n rows, entry ij of the product matrix is the dot product of the ith row of the left matrix by the jth column of the right matrix.

7. If $AB = BA$, then A and B are both same-size square matrices.

8. Rewrite the system as $\begin{pmatrix} 1 & 4 & -1 \\ 2 & -2 & 1 \\ 3 & 1 & -3 \end{pmatrix}\begin{pmatrix} x \\ y \\ z \end{pmatrix} = \begin{pmatrix} -3 \\ 0 \\ -9 \end{pmatrix}$. For each side, multiply on the left by the inverse of the coefficients matrix to get $\begin{pmatrix} x \\ y \\ z \end{pmatrix} = \begin{pmatrix} -1 \\ 0 \\ 2 \end{pmatrix}$.

Mid-Chapter Test

Go Online PHSchool.com — For a mid-chapter test, go to Web Code: bfa-0452

Multiple Choice

1. What is the solution to the following system?

$$2x - 5y = 1$$
$$3x - 4y = 5$$

A. $(-7, 3)$ B. $(3, 1)$
C. $(1, 3)$ D. $(-2, -1)$

2. A local soccer team placed the following order at their favorite restaurant.

Item	Hot Dog	Hamburger	Drink
Cost ($)	3.00	4.00	1.50
Number Ordered	5	6	11

What is the cost of the entire order?

A. $8.50 B. $22.00
C. $50.55 D. $55.50

3. Find the dot product $(-1, 3, 5) \cdot (2, -4, 6)$.

A. 11 B. 16 C. 20 D. 240

4. After using Gaussian Elimination to solve a system of equations, you get this matrix.

$$\left(\begin{array}{ccc|c} 1 & 0 & 2 & 3 \\ 0 & 1 & 0 & 7 \\ 0 & 0 & 0 & 0 \end{array}\right)$$

What can you conclude?

A. The only solution is $(2, 4, 0)$.
B. One possible solution is $(-1, 7, 2)$.
C. One possible solution is $(3, 0, 0)$.
D. There is no solution.

5. Suppose $A = (a_{ij})$, as shown below.

$$A = \begin{pmatrix} 4 & 3 & -1 & 2 \\ 1 & 5 & 0 & 8 \\ 7 & 11 & -3 & 10 \end{pmatrix}$$

Find a_{32}.

A. -3 B. 0 C. 8 D. 11

Open Response

6. The graph of a quadratic function $f(x) = ax^2 + bx + c$ passes through the points $(-2, 21)$, $(1, 6)$, and $(2, 9)$. Find a, b, and c.

7. Consider the augmented matrix below.

$$\left(\begin{array}{ccc|c} 1 & -2 & 1 & -9 \\ 2 & 1 & -3 & 7 \\ 1 & 2 & 4 & -3 \end{array}\right)$$

a. To what system of equations does this matrix correspond?
b. Solve the system in matrix form.

8. Let $A = (a_{ij})$ be a 2×3 matrix where $a_{ij} = i + 2j$.

a. Find A.
b. Find $2A$.
c. Find AB, where $B = \begin{pmatrix} 2 \\ -3 \\ 0 \end{pmatrix}$.

9. Use the following matrices.

$$A = \begin{pmatrix} 3 & -1 \\ 2 & 0 \\ -4 & 5 \end{pmatrix} \quad B = \begin{pmatrix} 2 & -5 & 4 \\ 6 & -4 & -2 \\ 3 & 0 & 8 \\ 4 & 6 & -2 \end{pmatrix}$$

$$C = \begin{pmatrix} 3 & 1 \\ 6 & -2 \\ 0 & 4 \end{pmatrix}$$

Find each matrix, if possible.

a. $A + C$ b. $-B$
c. AB d. BA

10. Let $D = \begin{pmatrix} 2 & 1 \\ 8 & 3 \end{pmatrix}$.

a. Find D^{-1}.
b. Suppose $\begin{pmatrix} 2 & 1 \\ 8 & 3 \end{pmatrix}\begin{pmatrix} x \\ y \end{pmatrix} = \begin{pmatrix} 2 \\ 4 \end{pmatrix}$. Find x and y.
c. Write the system of equations that you just solved.

11. Why is it possible to solve systems of linear equations in matrix form?

Mid-Chapter Test

Assessment Resources

Mid-Chapter Test page 1 of 2

Multiple Choice

1. What is the solution to the following system?

$$3x + 2y = 8$$
$$4x - y = 7$$

A. $(8, 7)$ B. $(4, -2)$
C. $(2, 1)$ D. $(-2, -15)$

2. A local theater group sold the following tickets to their next performance.

	Orchestra	Mezzanine	Balcony
Cost ($)	20	15	10
Number Sold	70	50	80

How much money did they collect for their next performance?

A. $200 B. $2500
C. $2950 D. $9000

3. Find the dot product $(2, -3, 1) \cdot (-4, 0, 5)$.

A. -6 B. -3 C. 0 D. 36

4. After using Gaussian Elimination to solve a system of equations, you get this matrix.

$$\left(\begin{array}{ccc|c} 1 & 0 & 0 & -2 \\ 0 & 1 & 0 & 3 \\ 0 & 0 & 1 & 5 \end{array}\right)$$

What can you conclude?

A. The only solution is $(-2, 3, 5)$.
B. One possible solution is $(1, 1, 1)$.
C. One possible solution is $(0, 0, 5)$.
D. There is no solution.

5. Suppose $A = (a_{ij})$ as shown below.

$$A = \begin{pmatrix} -2 & 1 & -4 & 0 \\ 4 & 9 & 2 & 5 \\ 12 & 11 & 2 & -9 \end{pmatrix}$$

Find a_{12}.

A. -9 B. 1 C. 4 D. 9

Also available: Form B

Mid-Chapter Test

1. B
2. D
3. B
4. B
5. D
6. $f(x) = 2x^2 - 3x + 7$
7. a. $x - 2y + z = -9$, $2x + y - 3z = 7$, $x + 2y + 4z = -3$
   b. $(x, y, z) = (-1, 3, -2)$
8. a. $A = \begin{pmatrix} 3 & 5 & 7 \\ 4 & 6 & 8 \end{pmatrix}$
   b. $2A = \begin{pmatrix} 6 & 10 & 14 \\ 8 & 12 & 16 \end{pmatrix}$
   c. $AB = \begin{pmatrix} -9 \\ -10 \end{pmatrix}$
9. a. $A + C = \begin{pmatrix} 6 & 0 \\ 8 & -2 \\ -4 & 9 \end{pmatrix}$
   b. $-B = \begin{pmatrix} -2 & 5 & -4 \\ -6 & 4 & 2 \\ -3 & 0 & -8 \\ -4 & -6 & 2 \end{pmatrix}$
   c. AB is not defined.
   d. $BA = \begin{pmatrix} -20 & 18 \\ 18 & -16 \\ -23 & 37 \\ 32 & -14 \end{pmatrix}$
10. a. $D^{-1} = \begin{pmatrix} -\frac{3}{2} & \frac{1}{2} \\ 4 & -1 \end{pmatrix}$
    b. $x = -1$, $y = 4$
    c. $2x + y = 2$, $8x + 3y = 4$
11. Answers may vary. Sample: Matrices let you keep the coefficients associated with the appropriate variables.

Investigation Overview

This investigation is an introduction to the power of using matrix multiplication to model all sorts of multivariate phenomena in a way that is conceptually and notationally simple.

Basically, whenever you have a linear system with a lot of variables, then you can model the system with a single matrix equation. Moreover, if the system evolves over time in a series of steps where you can express the new values of the variables in terms of the old values, using the same linear equations at each step, then matrix powers apply. You can model each step by a single matrix multiplication by some square matrix M, and you can model the effect of n steps by multiplying by M^n.

Serious applications use very large matrices, but you can explain the basic idea with small matrices. Using small matrices, students do some simple geometric transformation problems, some population growth models, and finally some probability models.

Often you want to learn about long-term behavior, that is, what happens in the limit. For this, advanced methods (eigentheory) are best. This theory is hinted at in some examples, but your students are not ready to address it in a systematic way. However, modern technology allows students to see and believe the long-term behavior by allowing calculations (M to high powers) that were not possible before.

Calculators (or software) that can do matrix multiplication and matrix powers are essential for this investigation. Preferably the calculator will compute any integer power with a limited number of button pushes.

You may wish to assign Questions 1–3 for students to think and write about during the investigation.

Learning Goals

- Flexibly transition between systems of real-variable equations and matrices.
- Model the evolution of a system over time.
- Analyze sequences of repeated probabilities.

Habits and Skills

- Reason about matrices as mathematical objects, like numbers, with which you can compute.
- Analyze a multistep process in several variables as a series of transition steps expressed as matrix multiplication.
- Visualize the result of matrix multiplication as a geometric transformation in the coordinate plane.

Investigation 4C

Applications of Matrix Multiplication

In *Applications of Matrix Multiplication*, you will use matrices and matrix multiplication to model various situations, such as geometric transformations, transition problems, and probability problems.

By the end of this investigation, you will be able to answer questions like these.

1. Is it true that a matrix associated with a reflection must be its own inverse? If so, what are some relationships that must hold for the entries a, b, c, and d in a 2×2 reflection matrix $R = \begin{pmatrix} a & b \\ c & d \end{pmatrix}$?
2. What is an absorbing state, and what does such a state look like in a transition matrix?
3. A transition matrix for a fixed population of 150 is $\begin{pmatrix} 0.2 & 0.7 \\ 0.8 & 0.3 \end{pmatrix}$. Does this matrix have a steady state? If so, what is it? If not, why not?

You will learn how to

- flexibly transition between systems of real-variable equations and matrices
- model the evolution of a system over time
- analyze sequences of repeated probabilities

You will develop these habits and skills:

- Reason about matrices as mathematical objects, like numbers, that you can compute with.
- Analyze a multistep process in several variables as a series of transition steps expressed as matrix multiplication.
- Visualize the result of matrix multiplication as a geometric transformation in the coordinate plane.

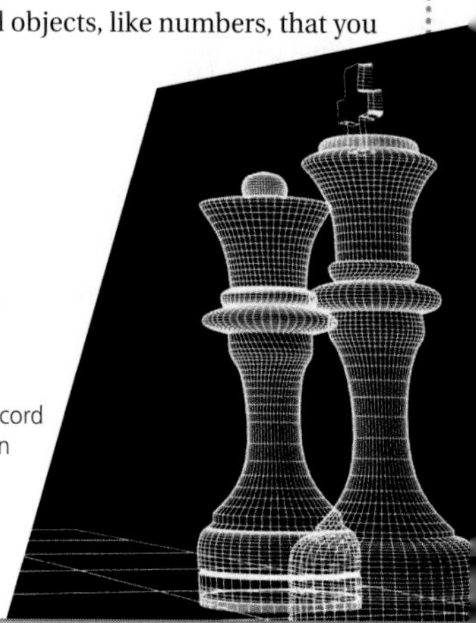

You can use matrices to record the coordinates of points in computer graphics.

Investigation Road Map

LESSON 4.10, *Getting Started,* introduces the general approach of this investigation through examples of geometric transformations of the plane, iteration through matrix powers, and population models.

LESSON 4.11, *Geometric Transformations,* shows that you can use matrices to understand and study most of the geometric transformations students have seen in earlier courses.

LESSON 4.12, *Transition Matrices,* examines real-world population models. The first example is the movement of rental cars between rental locations. The next example is of an insect life cycle model.

LESSON 4.13, *Probability Models,* discusses how to use matrices to analyze sequences of repeated probabilities.

4.10 Getting Started

Activating Prior Knowledge
Exploring New Ideas

Look for patterns as you complete the following problems.

For You to Explore

1. Consider two sequences s and t, defined as follows.

$$s(0) = t(0) = 1$$
$$s(n) = s(n-1) + t(n-1) \quad \text{for } n \geq 1 \quad (15)$$
$$t(n) = s(n-1) - t(n-1) \quad \text{for } n \geq 1$$

a. Compute several terms of each sequence until you see a pattern. You might want to line up the two sequences this way.

$s(0) \quad s(1) \quad s(2) \quad s(3) \ldots$
$t(0) \quad t(1) \quad t(2) \quad t(3) \ldots$

b. Since the equations that define the sequences are all linear, you can replace them with a single matrix equation. Let $S(n) = \begin{pmatrix} s(n) \\ t(n) \end{pmatrix}$ and $M = \begin{pmatrix} 1 & 1 \\ 1 & -1 \end{pmatrix}$.

Verify that you can rewrite (15) as

$$S(n) = \begin{cases} \begin{pmatrix} 1 \\ 1 \end{pmatrix} & \text{if } n = 0 \\ MS(n-1) & \text{if } n > 0 \end{cases}$$

c. Note that $S(2) = MS(1) = M(MS(0)) = M^2S(0)$, since matrix multiplication is associative. Explain why $S(n) = M^nS(0)$.

d. Compute $M, M^2, M^3, \ldots$ until you see a pattern. For as far as you computed powers of M, verify that $S(n) = M^nS(0)$.

2. Let $A = \begin{pmatrix} 1 & 1 \\ 0 & 1 \end{pmatrix}$. Compute powers of A until you can make a conjecture about a pattern.

3. Consider two sequences $u_0, u_1, \ldots$ and $v_0, v_1, \ldots$, defined as follows.

$$u(0) = v(0) = 1$$
$$u(n+1) = u(n) + v(n) \quad \text{for } n \geq 0$$
$$v(n+1) = v(n) \quad \text{for } n \geq 0$$

a. Compute several terms of each sequence until you see a pattern.

b. You can replace the system of equations that defines these sequences with a single matrix equation. Define $U(n) = \begin{pmatrix} u(n) \\ v(n) \end{pmatrix}$ and find the matrix M such that $U(n+1) = MU(n)$.

c. Compute $M, M^2, M^3, \ldots$ until you see a pattern. For the powers n that you computed, verify that $U(n) = M^nU(0)$.

A *sequence* is a function with a domain that is the nonnegative integers.

Model the sequence S. See the TI-Nspire Handbook, p. 778.

Answers

For You to Explore

1. See back of book.

2. If $A = \begin{pmatrix} 1 & 1 \\ 0 & 1 \end{pmatrix}$ then $A^2 = \begin{pmatrix} 1 & 2 \\ 0 & 1 \end{pmatrix}$, $A^3 = \begin{pmatrix} 1 & 3 \\ 0 & 1 \end{pmatrix}$, $A^4 = \begin{pmatrix} 1 & 4 \\ 0 & 1 \end{pmatrix}$, $A^5 = \begin{pmatrix} 1 & 5 \\ 0 & 1 \end{pmatrix}, \ldots, A^n = \begin{pmatrix} 1 & n \\ 0 & 1 \end{pmatrix}$.

3. **a.** $u(n) = n + 1$, $v(n) = 1$

b. $M = \begin{pmatrix} 1 & 1 \\ 0 & 1 \end{pmatrix}$

c. $M^n = \begin{pmatrix} 1 & n \\ 0 & 1 \end{pmatrix}$; $M^nU(0) = \begin{pmatrix} 1 & n \\ 0 & 1 \end{pmatrix}\begin{pmatrix} 1 \\ 1 \end{pmatrix} = \begin{pmatrix} n+1 \\ 1 \end{pmatrix} = U(n)$

Lesson Overview

GOAL

- Warm up to the ideas of the investigation.

This lesson introduces most of the topics in the next three lessons of the investigation: geometric mappings via matrix multiplication, iteration of mappings via powers of matrices, and population transition problems. Make sure students work on at least some problems of each type.

FOR YOU TO EXPLORE
- Core: 1, 2, 4, 5, 6, 8
- Optional: 3, 7

MATERIALS
- CAS (recommended)
- graph paper
- graphing calculators
- Blackline Master 4.10

HOMEWORK
- Core: 9, 10, 11, 13
- Optional: 12, 14, 15, 16

VOCABULARY
- sequence

Launch

Have the students jump right into the For You to Explore problems.

Explore

As students are working, notice how they are describing the patterns they find. If they describe a pattern in words, encourage them to find a symbolic description or to predict a large power of a matrix. By now, you have established some classroom policy about technology use, but consider whether you would like students to do some of these calculations by hand.

For You to Explore

PROBLEM 1 is actually the most challenging problem in this For You to Explore, because the pattern is somewhat complicated to see and describe. But students are freshest at the beginning, and the problem also shows them the matrix that allows the intertwined sequences to be described by a single matrix equation. It is your choice whether to have students do this problem first.

PROBLEM 2 Here you only have to deal with powers of a matrix. The pattern is easy to discover.

PROBLEM 3 In this problem, students have to determine the right matrix themselves. Once they do, they will find that they already know most of the answers from Problem 2.

PROBLEM 4 Blackline Master 4.10 provides a coordinate plane to show the mappings. This problem is similar to the first For Discussion in Lesson 4.11. So, it is worth spending time on this problem, and hopefully students will remember it later. Also, this is the first geometric activity in this problem set. Lesson 4.11 is entirely about geometric examples of matrix multiplication.

PROBLEMS 5 AND 6 continue with geometry and introduce in that context the interpretation of powers of the transformation matrix. For the earlier sequence problems, powers of the matrix were introduced right away.

A geometric mapping is a function that maps points in the plane to other points in the plane in some organized way. One of the topics in this investigation is to understand what sorts of mappings of the plane you can describe with matrix multiplication.

For Exercises 4 and 5, let $M = \begin{pmatrix} -1 & 0 \\ 0 & 1 \end{pmatrix}$. If you think of $\begin{pmatrix} x \\ y \end{pmatrix}$ as a point in the plane, you can think of the following mapping as a geometric mapping.

$$X = \begin{pmatrix} x \\ y \end{pmatrix} \mapsto X' = M\begin{pmatrix} x \\ y \end{pmatrix} = \begin{pmatrix} -x \\ y \end{pmatrix}$$

You usually write points as horizontal ordered pairs (x, y). If you want to multiply them by a matrix on the left, then you must write them as columns. Doing so ensures that the matrix multiplication is defined.

4. One way to find out how a particular matrix M maps the plane is to choose several points $X_1, X_2, \ldots$ that form a nice pattern and then see what patterns $X'_1 = MX_1, X'_2 = MX_2, \ldots$ exhibit.

Consider the following points. These are the integer points on the sides of a certain rectangle.

$$\begin{pmatrix} 0 \\ 0 \end{pmatrix}, \begin{pmatrix} 1 \\ 0 \end{pmatrix}, \begin{pmatrix} 1 \\ 1 \end{pmatrix}, \begin{pmatrix} 1 \\ 2 \end{pmatrix}, \begin{pmatrix} 0 \\ 2 \end{pmatrix}, \begin{pmatrix} 0 \\ 1 \end{pmatrix}$$

a. Plot each point.

b. For each point X you plotted, compute and plot MX as well. Indicate which points pair up. You can draw an arrow from X to MX.

c. What does the mapping seem to do to lines? To polygons?

d. Describe what you think M does to the whole plane.

e. Plot a few more points X that form a nice pattern. What do you think M will do to this pattern? Plot MX for your points and see if you are right.

5. If $X \mapsto MX$ maps the plane to itself, you can repeat the mapping.

$$X \mapsto MX \mapsto M(MX) = M^2X \mapsto M(M^2X) = M^3X$$

a. Consider M again. In Exercise 4, you probably decided that M reflects the plane over a certain line. If so, what should be the net effect if you repeat the mapping a second time?

b. Compute M^2 and M^2X, where $X = \begin{pmatrix} x \\ y \end{pmatrix}$. Did you confirm your answer to part (a)?

Habits of Mind

Look for relationships. This repetition is the same function iteration that you have seen many times for numerical functions.

6. Now consider the x-axis as a line and reflect points of the plane over that line.

a. What are the images of the points $\begin{pmatrix} 2 \\ 1 \end{pmatrix}$, $\begin{pmatrix} -1 \\ -2 \end{pmatrix}$, and $\begin{pmatrix} 0 \\ 0 \end{pmatrix}$?

What is the image of the generic point $\begin{pmatrix} x \\ y \end{pmatrix}$?

b. Find a matrix M such that $X' = MX$ is the image of X after reflection over the x-axis for every point X.

c. Determine, with and without matrices, the effect of doing this reflection twice.

Answers

4. See back of book.

5. a. After reflecting over the y-axis two times, the result is the original preimage.

b. If $M = \begin{pmatrix} -1 & 0 \\ 0 & 1 \end{pmatrix}$, then $M^2 = \begin{pmatrix} -1 & 0 \\ 0 & 1 \end{pmatrix}\begin{pmatrix} -1 & 0 \\ 0 & 1 \end{pmatrix} = \begin{pmatrix} 1 & 0 \\ 0 & 1 \end{pmatrix}$ and $M^2X = \begin{pmatrix} 1 & 0 \\ 0 & 1 \end{pmatrix}\begin{pmatrix} x \\ y \end{pmatrix} = \begin{pmatrix} x \\ y \end{pmatrix}$, which is the preimage.

6. a. The images are $\begin{pmatrix} 2 \\ -1 \end{pmatrix}$, $\begin{pmatrix} -1 \\ 2 \end{pmatrix}$, and $\begin{pmatrix} 0 \\ 0 \end{pmatrix}$, respectively; the image of $\begin{pmatrix} x \\ y \end{pmatrix}$ is $\begin{pmatrix} x \\ -y \end{pmatrix}$.

b. $M = \begin{pmatrix} 1 & 0 \\ 0 & -1 \end{pmatrix}$

c. After reflecting over the x-axis two times, the result is the original preimage.

7. Now consider points in space and reflect them over the *xy*-plane.

a. What are the images of the points $(1, 2, 3)$, $(1, 2, -3)$, $(2, -1, 4)$, $(0, 0, 0)$, and (x, y, z)?

b. State how to express this reflection as a matrix multiplication. As usual, you will have to write points as columns. This time they are 3-tuple columns.

c. Determine, with and without matrices, the effect of doing this reflection twice.

8. A certain car rental agency has two locations, one in Boston and one in Cambridge. All rentals are for one week, and the agency allows cars from both locations to be returned to either location. Experience shows that 80% of the cars rented in Boston return there, but only 50% of the cars rented in Cambridge return there. At the start of a certain month, the agency has 70 cars in each location. What will be the situation one week later? Two weeks later? Three weeks later? What happens many weeks into the future?

Model the rental car inventories problem. See the TI-Nspire Handbook, p. 778.

Exercises *Practicing Habits of Mind*

On Your Own

9. Let $M = \begin{pmatrix} 3 & 0 \\ 0 & 3 \end{pmatrix}$. Consider the mapping $X = \begin{pmatrix} x \\ y \end{pmatrix} \mapsto X' = M\begin{pmatrix} x \\ y \end{pmatrix} = \begin{pmatrix} 3x \\ 3y \end{pmatrix}$.

Think of $\begin{pmatrix} x \\ y \end{pmatrix}$ as a point in the plane and $X \mapsto MX$ as a geometric mapping.

As in Problem 4, consider the points $\begin{pmatrix} 0 \\ 0 \end{pmatrix}, \begin{pmatrix} 1 \\ 0 \end{pmatrix}, \begin{pmatrix} 1 \\ 1 \end{pmatrix}, \begin{pmatrix} 1 \\ 2 \end{pmatrix}, \begin{pmatrix} 0 \\ 2 \end{pmatrix}$, and $\begin{pmatrix} 0 \\ 1 \end{pmatrix}$.

a. Plot each point.

b. For each point X you plotted, compute and plot MX as well. Indicate which points pair up. You can draw an arrow from X to MX.

c. What does the mapping seem to do to lines? To polygons?

d. Describe what you think M does to the whole plane.

e. Plot a few more points X that form a nice pattern. What do you think M will do to this pattern? Plot MX for your points and see if you are right.

f. Explain why you might call this mapping $X \mapsto MX$ a scaling mapping with scale factor 3.

PROBLEM 7 Three-dimensional geometry is much more difficult than plane geometry, but reflection in the *xy*-plane is perhaps the simplest three-dimensional case.

PROBLEM 8 becomes the first Example in Lesson 4.12, Transition Matrices. With all the words, students may not have much of an idea how to algebraicize the problem. The key is to generate two sequences $b_0, b_1, b_2, \ldots$ (the number of cars at the Boston location initially and then at the end of each week) and $c_0, c_1, c_2, \ldots$ (same for the Cambridge location). The problem tells them b_0, c_0 and how to describe b_{n+1} and c_{n+1} in terms of b_n and c_n. These are linear equations, so you can replace them by a single matrix equation. The process parallels what happened in Problems 1 and 3. Maybe, with a hint to review these problems, students can make progress on the auto rental problem.

In this problem and in any of the following problems that ask students to predict behavior far into the future, students should model the problem on their calculators. If your class does not have access to technology, you may wish to ask students to predict the behavior of the system, because doing hand-calculation of large matrix powers is not a reasonable approach.

Wrap Up

As time allows, go over the For You to Explore core problems with your class. See what students remember about geometric transformations from previous courses and help them standardize their language. For example, if they mention that a transformation is a dilation, ask for the scale factor and the center of dilation.

Exercises

HOMEWORK

- Core: 9, 10, 11, 13
- Optional: 12, 14, 15, 16

On Your Own

EXERCISE 9 is a warmup for scaling mappings in the first Example of Lesson 4.11.

7. a. The images are $(1, 2, -3)$, $(1, 2, 3)$, $(2, -1, -4)$, $(0, 0, 0)$, and $(x, y, -z)$, respectively.

b. Using $M = \begin{pmatrix} 1 & 0 & 0 \\ 0 & 1 & 0 \\ 0 & 0 & -1 \end{pmatrix}$ gives

$$M\begin{pmatrix} x \\ y \\ z \end{pmatrix} = \begin{pmatrix} x \\ y \\ -z \end{pmatrix}.$$

c. After reflecting over the *xy*-plane twice, the result is the original preimage.

8. After 1 week, there will be 91 cars in the Boston lot and 49 cars in the Cambridge lot. After 2 weeks, there will be approximately 98 and 42 cars in the respective lots. After 3 weeks, 99 and 41. After many weeks, the number of cars in each lot will remain steady at 100 and 40 respectively.

9. See back of book.

EXERCISES 10–12 concern what happens when you apply a geometric transformation twice, or transform with the square of the matrix. The questions are equivalent, because $M^2X = (MM)X = M(MX)$, so the mapping $X \mapsto M^2X$ is the same as the repeated mapping $X \mapsto MX \mapsto M(MX)$.

EXERCISE 13 Problem 8 showed that matrix multiplication can model moving cars. Now students see that matrix multiplication can model moving people. Population problems (cars, people, bugs, and so on) are the primary examples of Lesson 4.12.

10. **a.** Consider again M from Exercise 9. What do you expect the net effect to be if you repeat the mapping a second time?

b. Compute M^2 and M^2X, where $X = \begin{pmatrix} x \\ y \end{pmatrix}$. Did you confirm your answer to part (a)?

c. What do you expect the net effect to be if you repeat the mapping a third time? Compute M^3 and then M^3X to confirm your answer.

11. Consider rotation of the plane by 180° counterclockwise around the origin.

a. What are the images of the points $\begin{pmatrix} 2 \\ 1 \end{pmatrix}, \begin{pmatrix} -1 \\ -2 \end{pmatrix}$, and $\begin{pmatrix} 0 \\ 0 \end{pmatrix}$?

What is the image of the generic point $\begin{pmatrix} x \\ y \end{pmatrix}$?

b. Find M such that this rotation is the mapping $X \mapsto MX$.

c. Determine, with and without matrices, the effect of doing this rotation twice.

12. Suppose there is a matrix M such that the mapping of the plane $X \mapsto MX$ is a 30° counterclockwise rotation around the origin. What would the mapping $X \mapsto M^2X$ accomplish?

There is such a matrix, but do not worry for now what it is. This exercise is meant to be a thought experiment.

13. Suppose that in a certain developing country, 35% of the people in the countryside move to the cities each year, and only 5% of the people in the cities move to the countryside. Assume there are no births and deaths, and nobody moves to or from other countries. If there were 8 million people in the countryside and 4 million in the cities at the beginning of 2007, what will be the situation at the start of 2008? At the start of 2009? At the start of 2010? What will happen many years into the future?

These assumptions are unreasonable, but it is always a good idea to start with a simple model and, once you understand that model, later build in more complications.

Answers

10. a. The result is a dilation by a factor of 9, centered at the origin.

b. $M = \begin{pmatrix} 3 & 0 \\ 0 & 3 \end{pmatrix}$, $M^2 = \begin{pmatrix} 9 & 0 \\ 0 & 9 \end{pmatrix}$, $M^2X = \begin{pmatrix} 9x \\ 9y \end{pmatrix}$

c. $M^3 = \begin{pmatrix} 27 & 0 \\ 0 & 27 \end{pmatrix}$, $M^3X = \begin{pmatrix} 27x \\ 27y \end{pmatrix}$

11. a. The images are $\begin{pmatrix} -2 \\ -1 \end{pmatrix}, \begin{pmatrix} 1 \\ 2 \end{pmatrix}, \begin{pmatrix} 0 \\ 0 \end{pmatrix}$, and $\begin{pmatrix} -x \\ -y \end{pmatrix}$, respectively.

b. $M = \begin{pmatrix} -1 & 0 \\ 0 & -1 \end{pmatrix}$

c. After performing the rotation twice, the result is the original image.

12. The result is a 60° counterclockwise rotation around the origin.

13. After 1 year, there will be 5.4 million people in the country and 6.6 million people in the city. After 2 years, there will be 3.8 million people in the country and 8.2 million people in the city. After 3 years, there will be 2.9 million people in the country and 9.1 million people in the city. After many years, the population of the country and city will level off at 1.5 million and 10.5 million respectively.

14. a. $X(1) = \begin{pmatrix} 2 + \sqrt{2} \\ \sqrt{2} \end{pmatrix}$, $X(2) = \begin{pmatrix} 2 + 2\sqrt{2} \\ 2 \end{pmatrix}$, $X(3) = \begin{pmatrix} 4 + 2\sqrt{2} \\ 2\sqrt{2} \end{pmatrix}$, $X(4) = \begin{pmatrix} 4 + 4\sqrt{2} \\ 4 \end{pmatrix}$

b. $Y(1) = \begin{pmatrix} 2 + \sqrt{2} \\ \sqrt{2} \end{pmatrix}$, $Y(2) = \begin{pmatrix} 2 + 2\sqrt{2} \\ 2 \end{pmatrix}$, $Y(3) = \begin{pmatrix} 4 + 2\sqrt{2} \\ 2\sqrt{2} \end{pmatrix}$, $Y(4) = \begin{pmatrix} 4 + 4\sqrt{2} \\ 4 \end{pmatrix}$

Maintain Your Skills

14. Use matrix M from For You to Explore Problem 1. Let $X(0) = \begin{pmatrix} 1+\sqrt{2} \\ 1 \end{pmatrix}$, $X(1) = MX(0)$, $X(2) = MX(1)$, and so on.

a. Compute $X(1)$, $X(2)$, $X(3)$, and $X(4)$.

b. Now define $Y(0) = X(0)$, $Y(1) = \sqrt{2}Y(0)$, $Y(2) = \sqrt{2}Y(1)$, and so on. Compute $Y(1)$, $Y(2)$, $Y(3)$, and $Y(4)$.

c. Now define $Z(0) = \begin{pmatrix} 1-\sqrt{2} \\ 1 \end{pmatrix}$, $Z(1) = MZ(0)$, $Z(2) = MZ(1)$, and so on. Compute $Z(1)$, $Z(2)$, $Z(3)$, and $Z(4)$.

d. Now define $W(0) = Z(0)$, $W(1) = -\sqrt{2}W(0)$, $W(2) = -\sqrt{2}W(1)$, and so on. Compute $W(1)$, $W(2)$, $W(3)$, $W(4)$.

15. Use the following matrices.

$$D = \begin{pmatrix} \frac{\sqrt{2}}{2} & -\frac{\sqrt{2}}{2} \\ \frac{\sqrt{2}}{2} & \frac{\sqrt{2}}{2} \end{pmatrix} \qquad P = \begin{pmatrix} 1 \\ 0 \end{pmatrix} \qquad Q = \begin{pmatrix} 2 \\ 1 \end{pmatrix}$$

Compute and plot $DP, D^2P, D^3P, \dots$ and $DQ, D^2Q, D^3Q, \dots$ until you see from your plot what is happening. What is the pattern?

16. Let $B = \begin{pmatrix} 1 & 1 \\ 1 & 0 \end{pmatrix}$.

a. Compute B^2.

b. Compute B^3.

c. Compute several more powers. What patterns do you see?

d. Define a sequence of column vectors $S(n) = \begin{pmatrix} s(n) \\ t(n) \end{pmatrix}$ as

$$S(n) = \begin{cases} \begin{pmatrix} 2 \\ 1 \end{pmatrix} & \text{if } n = 0 \\ BS(n-1) & \text{if } n > 0 \end{cases}$$

Compute several terms of the sequence. What patterns do you see?

e. Find a system of nonmatrix equations for finding the next pair of values $s(n)$ and $t(n)$ from the previous values.

This is the reverse of For You to Explore Problem 1.

Maintain Your Skills

EXERCISE 14 is the first appearance of eigenvalues and eigenvectors. These concepts occur again in the exposition of Lesson 4.11, but the topics are left mostly for a linear algebra course, where they are major considerations. A more mundane purpose of this exercise is to provide practice with radicals, which have not appeared previously in the chapter. As the solution to this exercise hints, radicals show up naturally when you consider matrix transformations.

EXERCISE 15 appears at first to be nothing but messy algebraic work with radicals. It ends up, however, having a simple geometric interpretation.

EXERCISE 16 Even if students have not seen, or do not recognize, the Fibonacci numbers, there are many partial patterns for them to see. For instance, the first column of B^n is the second column of B^{n+1}.

c. $Z(1) = \begin{pmatrix} 2-\sqrt{2} \\ -\sqrt{2} \end{pmatrix}$,

$Z(2) = \begin{pmatrix} 2-2\sqrt{2} \\ 2 \end{pmatrix}$,

$Z(3) = \begin{pmatrix} 4-2\sqrt{2} \\ -2\sqrt{2} \end{pmatrix}$,

$Z(4) = \begin{pmatrix} 4-4\sqrt{2} \\ 4 \end{pmatrix}$

d. $W(1) = \begin{pmatrix} 2-\sqrt{2} \\ -\sqrt{2} \end{pmatrix}$,

$W(2) = \begin{pmatrix} 2-2\sqrt{2} \\ 2 \end{pmatrix}$,

$W(3) = \begin{pmatrix} 4-2\sqrt{2} \\ -2\sqrt{2} \end{pmatrix}$,

$W(4) = \begin{pmatrix} 4-4\sqrt{2} \\ 4 \end{pmatrix}$

15. $DP = \begin{pmatrix} \frac{\sqrt{2}}{2} \\ \frac{\sqrt{2}}{2} \end{pmatrix}$, $D^2P = \begin{pmatrix} 0 \\ 1 \end{pmatrix}$,

$D^3P = \begin{pmatrix} -\frac{\sqrt{2}}{2} \\ \frac{\sqrt{2}}{2} \end{pmatrix}$, $D^4P = \begin{pmatrix} -1 \\ 0 \end{pmatrix}$,

$D^5P = \begin{pmatrix} -\frac{\sqrt{2}}{2} \\ -\frac{\sqrt{2}}{2} \end{pmatrix}$; $DQ = \begin{pmatrix} \frac{\sqrt{2}}{2} \\ \frac{3\sqrt{2}}{2} \end{pmatrix}$, $D^2Q = \begin{pmatrix} -1 \\ 2 \end{pmatrix}$,

$D^3Q = \begin{pmatrix} -\frac{3\sqrt{2}}{2} \\ \frac{\sqrt{2}}{2} \end{pmatrix}$, $D^4Q = \begin{pmatrix} -2 \\ -1 \end{pmatrix}$,

$D^5Q = \begin{pmatrix} -\frac{\sqrt{2}}{2} \\ -\frac{3\sqrt{2}}{2} \end{pmatrix}$

D rotates points by 45° counterclockwise about the origin.

16. See back of book.

Lesson Overview

GOAL

- Flexibly transition between systems of real-variable equations and matrices.

This lesson focuses on several topics. The first focus is for students to understand that each 2×2 matrix A is associated with a mapping $X \mapsto AX$ and that they can view this mapping geometrically.

The next focus is for students to be able to go back and forth easily in simple cases. Given a particularly simple matrix, students should learn to identity the geometric transformation. Given a simple transformation, such as scaling or reflection over the axes, they should learn to figure out the associated matrix.

The next focus is to begin to get some "respect" for the vast variety of transformations that represent matrices. Not all of the transformations have simple geometric interpretations, at least not interpretations that students can discover easily. Actually, all matrices of any size do have geometric interpretations. This is the great achievement of the theory of *eigenvalues* and *eigenvectors*. There is no way you can cover this theory at this level, but you can give students a glimpse. That is precisely what the final, ambitious Example does.

This is the longest lesson in this investigation, mainly because it has a much longer problem section. This lesson continues the mission of having students get a feel for matrix multiplication. This takes some doing, as matrix multiplication has a much richer variety of behaviors than number multiplication. Most of the work in the lesson is experimental and exploratory. The students will not be able to prove many of the properties that they will discover.

CHECK YOUR UNDERSTANDING

- Core: 1, 2, 3, 5, 6, 7, 9, 12
- Optional: 8, 10, 11
- Extension: 4, 13, 14

MATERIALS

- CAS (recommended)
- geometry software
- graph paper
- graphing calculators
- paper for folding
- Blackline Masters MC2, 4.11

HOMEWORK

- Core: 15, 17, 18, 19, 22, 23, 29, 30
- Optional: 16, 24, 25, 26, 27, 31
- Optional: 20, 21, 28

VOCABULARY

- eigenvalue
- eigenvector
- matrix transformation
- vector representation

Launch

Introduce the basic move from A to the mapping $X \rightarrow AX$. You may need to review this notation. Then set the students free to work on the problems.

4.11 Geometric Transformations

In Lesson 4.10, you studied geometric transformations, where each point in the plane gets mapped to another. For instance, the mapping $(x, y) \mapsto (x + 1, y)$ translates points in the plane (shifts everything over) one unit in the positive x-direction.

You can express many geometric transformations (mappings) with matrix multiplication. A transformation is a **matrix transformation** if you can express it in the form $X \mapsto AX$, where A is a 2×2 matrix and a point X is represented as a column vector $\begin{pmatrix} x \\ y \end{pmatrix}$. You use column vectors so that you can multiply them by matrices on the left. You say this mapping is associated with the matrix A.

In this lesson, you will get a feel for what matrices can do geometrically. The work will be exploratory. You will do examples, often by plotting many points.

> There are also geometric transformations of three-dimensional space, or even higher dimensions, using bigger matrices. Indeed, with the right methods, every matrix of any size can be analyzed geometrically!

Example 1

Problem Let $A = \begin{pmatrix} 2 & 0 \\ 0 & 2 \end{pmatrix}$. What does the map $X \mapsto AX$ do?

Solution Let $X = \begin{pmatrix} x \\ y \end{pmatrix}$. Then

$$AX = \begin{pmatrix} 2 & 0 \\ 0 & 2 \end{pmatrix} \begin{pmatrix} x \\ y \end{pmatrix} = \begin{pmatrix} 2x \\ 2y \end{pmatrix} = 2X$$

This map scales everything by the factor 2 with the dilation centered at the origin. Every point moves twice as far from the origin. As a consequence, every length doubles in size as well, since every length is a distance between points. For instance, look at the graph below. When you dilate all the points in the small triangle by 2, the result is the large triangle. The lower left vertex (2, 1) of the smaller triangle maps to (4, 2), which is the lower left vertex of the larger triangle. The point (4, 2) is twice as far as (2, 1) from the origin. Similarly, the small quarter circle maps to the larger quarter circle.

> Experimenting with transformations can help you understand the effects of mappings. See the TI-Nspire Handbook, p. 778.

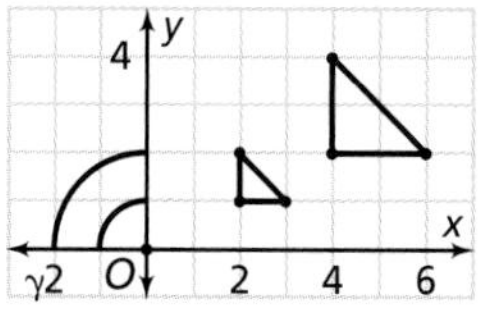

Developing Habits of Mind

Experiment. Other matrix transformations in this lesson may be harder to interpret geometrically. How do you figure them out? Experiment! Start with several points in some sort of familiar shape. Plot them and plot all their images. You may need to use more than one figure and more than one shape.

For Discussion

1. Let $B = \begin{pmatrix} 1 & 0 \\ 0 & -1 \end{pmatrix}$. What does the map $X \mapsto BX$ do?

Example 2

Problem Let $R = \begin{pmatrix} 0 & -1 \\ 1 & 0 \end{pmatrix}$. What does the map $X \mapsto RX$ do?

Solution First, let $X = \begin{pmatrix} x \\ y \end{pmatrix}$. Then $RX = \begin{pmatrix} 0 & -1 \\ 1 & 0 \end{pmatrix}\begin{pmatrix} x \\ y \end{pmatrix} = \begin{pmatrix} -y \\ x \end{pmatrix}$.

You can rewrite the map $X \mapsto RX$ as $(x, y) \mapsto (-y, x)$. But it is still not so obvious what is going on. Plot some points and their images. Call the original points A, B, C, and D and their images A', B', C', and D'.

Original

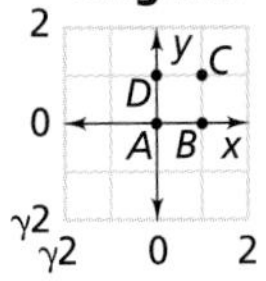

Image

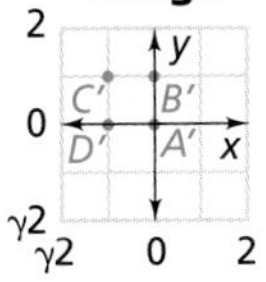

It seems the unit square has been rotated 90° counterclockwise around the origin $A = A'$. You could check this out with more points, for example, the points on the line with equation $x = 2$ or the points on the unit circle. Here is the result for the line with equation $x = 2$.

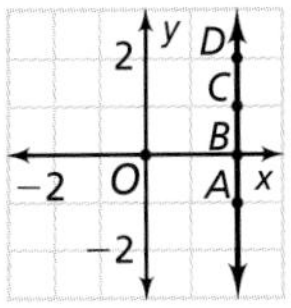

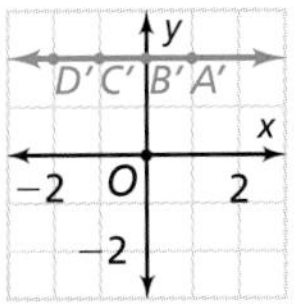

Indeed, the points on the line have been rotated, too.

Answers

For Discussion

1. $\begin{pmatrix} 1 & 0 \\ 0 & -1 \end{pmatrix}\begin{pmatrix} x \\ y \end{pmatrix} = \begin{pmatrix} x \\ -y \end{pmatrix}$, so B reflects points over the y-axis.

Explore

The main way to get students started on how to interpret any given mapping $X \to AX$ is to plot a lot of points X and their images AX. This can be quite tedious if students have to compute each product AX by hand. Technology can help.

You can use Blackline Master MC2 to guide students through the examples in this lesson.

For Discussion

Plotting a few points should convince students that this mapping reflects points over the x-axis. The general formula is $(x, y) \mapsto (x, -y)$, or written in column form, $xy \mapsto x - y$. It is easy to draw pictures to see that this mapping takes points to their mirror image after reflection over the x-axis. Indeed, this example is very similar to Exercise 4 in Lesson 4.10.

Example 2

You can use Blackline Master 4.11 with this example.

Note that students are supposed to finish the argument. How formal their argument will be depends on what sort of geometry studies they have done before. The key step is that $\alpha = \gamma$ by congruent triangles. Since $\alpha + \beta = 90°$, then $90° = \beta + \gamma$, which is the angle by which you to take the original point.

Does your argument depend on (x, y) being in the first quadrant, as shown in the figure in the text? If students refer to x as a length, it does.

MORE ON REFLECTIONS AND ROTATIONS Here is the outline of an explanation for you the teacher as to why all such reflections and rotations can be done by matrix multiplication. You construct the matrix M as follows. In the first column you put the point that (1, 0) is mapped to, and in the second column the point that (0, 1) is mapped to. It turns out that any linear transformation in the plane is uniquely determined by where it maps (1, 0) and (0, 1), and that $X \mapsto MX$ with this M is a formula for it. Since reflections and rotations through the origin are linear transformations, this matrix M must be the right one.

However, you need a general argument to show that every point (x, y) is rotated 90° counterclockwise around the origin when it is mapped to $(-y, x)$. The next figure should help. What can you say about angles α, β, and γ?

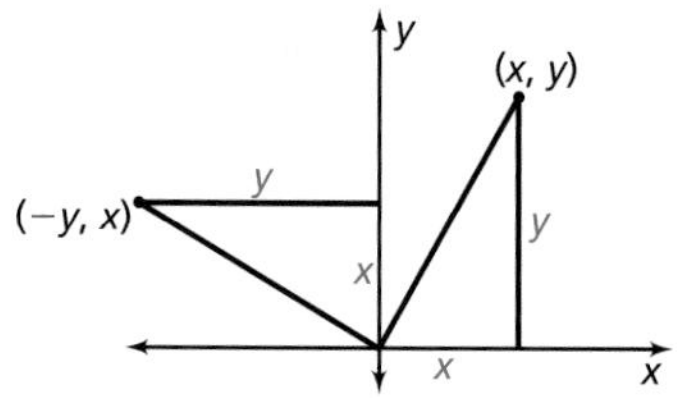

More on Reflections and Rotations

Any reflection over a line through the origin can be done by matrix multiplication. Any rotation around the origin can also be done by matrix multiplication. It is complicated to prove this with what you know, but the following examples illustrate it.

Example 3

Problem Use the matrix below.

$$M = \frac{1}{5}\begin{pmatrix} 3 & 4 \\ 4 & -3 \end{pmatrix} = \begin{pmatrix} \frac{3}{5} & \frac{4}{5} \\ \frac{4}{5} & -\frac{3}{5} \end{pmatrix}$$

It turns out that the mapping $X \mapsto MX$ is a reflection. Find the line of reflection.

Solution Any reflection in the plane has a line of reflection, also called the axis of reflection. You can visualize this by thinking of folding the plane along this line and mapping each point to the point it touches when you fold the plane. Another way to visualize it is by thinking of the line of reflection as a two-sided mirror. Then each point in the plane is mapped to its reflection in that mirror.

A reflection fixes a point if and only if the point is on the line of reflection. Assuming this mapping $X \mapsto MX$ is a reflection, a point $X = (x, y)$ is on the line of reflection if and only if $MX = X$. So write out this matrix equation as two real-number equations and solve them.

If you fold a piece of paper, points on the fold do not touch other points. Only points not on the fold line will touch different points on the paper.

$$\begin{aligned} \tfrac{3}{5}x + \tfrac{4}{5}y &= x \\ \tfrac{4}{5}x - \tfrac{3}{5}y &= y \end{aligned} \quad \Rightarrow \quad \begin{aligned} 3x + 4y &= 5x \\ 4x - 3y &= 5y \end{aligned} \quad \Rightarrow \quad \begin{aligned} -2x + 4y &= 0 \\ 4x - 8y &= 0 \end{aligned}$$

The bottom equation on the right is a multiple of the top equation. They are equivalent equations, so you can write them both as $y = \frac{1}{2}x$. This is the equation of the line of slope $\frac{1}{2}$ through the origin.

For You to Do

2. Let $N = \frac{1}{2}\begin{pmatrix} 1 & \sqrt{3} \\ -\sqrt{3} & 1 \end{pmatrix}$.

It turns out (though it is not obvious) that N is the matrix of a rotation around the origin. Plot some points to convince yourself it is a rotation and to discover the angle of rotation.

(*Hint:* Every point X will be rotated by the same angle, so you do not need to solve for X as in the last example. Instead, just pick some points X, compute NX, and see how much the original points are rotated.)

Example 2 suggests some points to pick, but you can also choose other points. You also need to check that NX is the same distance from the origin as X. Otherwise, the mapping is doing more than just rotating.

In fact, you only need one point X, but just to confirm that this mapping really is a rotation, and to catch any arithmetic errors, use several points.

Other Matrix Transformations

Matrices can do much more than scaling, reflecting, and rotating. For example, they can do scaling by different factors in different directions.

For Discussion

3. Let $A = \begin{pmatrix} 3 & 0 \\ 0 & 2 \end{pmatrix}$. Predict what A does to the plane. Then show that you are right by computing what A does to the corners of the unit square. The unit square is the square with corners at (0, 0), (1, 0), (1, 1) and (0, 1).

Many matrices do this sort of multiple stretching, but not always in an obvious way.

Example 4

Problem Analyze the transformation $X \mapsto AX$, where

$$A = \begin{pmatrix} -2.7 & 1.4 \\ -2.1 & 2.2 \end{pmatrix}$$

Solution A few points may not make the pattern clear, but it gets clearer as you show more points. The graph on the left shows the original points and the graph on the right shows their images. Rather than label so many dots, a few of them are made different sizes. The biggest dot in the figure on the left maps to the biggest dot in the figure on the right.

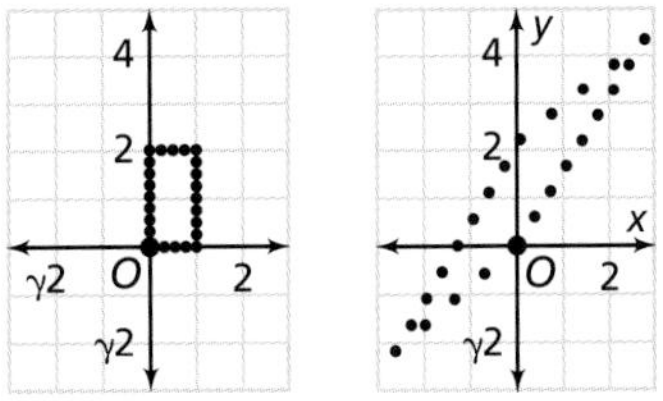

For Discussion

The map $X \mapsto AX$ stretches the plane by the factor 3 in the horizontal direction and the factor 2 in the vertical direction. The unit square becomes the rectangle with corners at (0, 0), (3, 0), (3, 2) and (0, 2).

Example 4

On this and the next page, there are two original-and-image pairs of figures. This is done, rather than having the students compute all the images for themselves as in some problems, because there are a lot of points to compute to get the picture.

To understand what is going on, students have to think sequentially. As suggested by the text at the start of the next page, they can take the original points one at a time, starting at the origin. They can move along one of the edges of the original rectangle, and think about the images of the points one at a time.

Have them do this for a few points. Using matrix A at the start of the example, they could compute

$$A\begin{pmatrix} 0 \\ 0 \end{pmatrix}, A\begin{pmatrix} 0.1 \\ 0 \end{pmatrix}, A\begin{pmatrix} 0.2 \\ 0 \end{pmatrix}, \ldots$$

and

$$A\begin{pmatrix} 0 \\ 0.1 \end{pmatrix}, A\begin{pmatrix} 0 \\ 0.2 \end{pmatrix}, A\begin{pmatrix} 0 \\ 0.3 \end{pmatrix}, \ldots$$

Have them talk about what they glean from this.

Answers

For You to Do

2. Answers may vary. Sample:

$$N\begin{pmatrix} 1 \\ 0 \end{pmatrix} = \frac{1}{2}\begin{pmatrix} 1 & \sqrt{3} \\ -\sqrt{3} & 1 \end{pmatrix}\begin{pmatrix} 1 \\ 0 \end{pmatrix} =$$

$\begin{pmatrix} \frac{1}{2} \\ -\frac{\sqrt{3}}{2} \end{pmatrix}$, so N is a rotation of 60° clockwise about the origin.

For Discussion

3. A is a dilation by a factor of 3 horizontally and a factor of 2 vertically, centered at the origin.

$$\begin{pmatrix} 3 & 0 \\ 0 & 2 \end{pmatrix}\begin{pmatrix} 0 & 1 & 1 & 0 \\ 0 & 0 & 1 & 1 \end{pmatrix} =$$

$\begin{pmatrix} 0 & 3 & 3 & 0 \\ 0 & 0 & 2 & 2 \end{pmatrix}$, so the images of (0, 0), (1, 0), (1, 1), and (0, 1) are (0, 0), (3, 0), (3, 2), and (0, 2), respectively.

WHAT IS COMMON TO ALL THESE TRANSFORMATIONS? Basically, matrix transformations are linear transformations. As such they preserve all linear structure (as well as the origin). Lines map to lines, planes to planes, segments to segments, polygons to polygons, convex sets to convex sets.

If a linear transformation is not one-to-one, it can reduce dimensionality, but it still maps linear structures to linear structures. That is, a line might map to a point, a plane to a line, and parallel lines to the same line or a point.

All of the transformations studied so far have been both one-to-one and onto; they map the plane to the whole plane with no overlaps. Some examples of many-to-one matrix transformations appear in the exercises.

Wrap Up

Be sure to elicit the basic fact that matrix multiplication can represent simple geometric transformations that leave the origin fixed. As time allows, go over the Check Your Understanding core exercises with your class.

Assessment Resources

Lesson Quiz 4.11

1. Let $A = \begin{pmatrix} 3 & 0 \\ 0 & 5 \end{pmatrix}$.
   a. What does the mapping $X \mapsto AX$ do in the x-direction and the y-direction?
   b. What does the mapping $X \mapsto A^{-1}X$ do? Confirm your conjecture by computing A^{-1} and then calculating a few pairs X and $A^{-1}X$.

2. Determine what each matrix does.
   a. $A = \begin{pmatrix} 0 & 0 \\ 0 & 1 \end{pmatrix}$ b. $B = \begin{pmatrix} -1 & 0 \\ 0 & 0 \end{pmatrix}$ c. $C = \begin{pmatrix} 5 & 0 \\ 0 & 5 \end{pmatrix}$

3. Consider the lines with the equations below.
   $L_1: x = -2$ $L_2: y = 3$ $L_3: y = x$ $L_4: y = x + 3$
   Find the image of each line under multiplication by the following matrix in Exercise 2.
   a. A b. B

You can see that the segments of the rectangle get stretched, but the directions also get changed. For instance, take a sequence of points in the left figure starting at the origin and moving along the positive x-axis. The images of these points in the right figure get flipped over and move down and left from the origin.

It turns out that the original shape does not clearly show what is happening. Look what happens to the parallelogram in the graph below. The parallelogram on the right is its image, using the same matrix A.

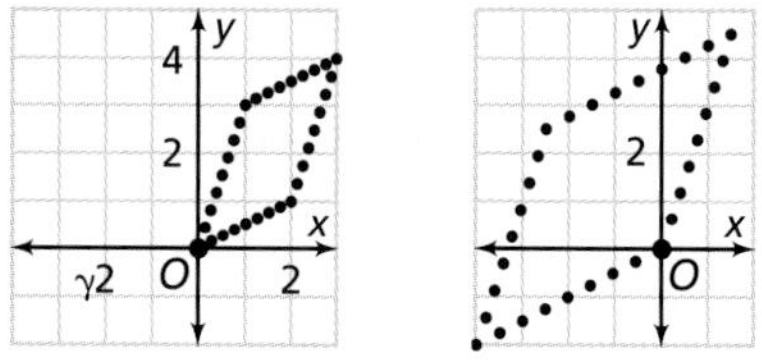

So the stretching is in a direction parallel to the sides of the parallelogram, with either a positive or negative scaling factor. For instance, the point (2, 1) on the left parallelogram gets mapped to $(-4, -2) = -2(2, 1)$ on the right. On the left side of the left parallelogram, the point (1, 3) gets mapped to $(1.5, 4.5) = \frac{3}{2}(1, 3)$ on the right.

When $AX = kX$, X is an *eigenvector* for A and k is its *eigenvalue*. This is an important concept in more advanced matrix algebra. It is the basis on which you can give every matrix a geometric interpretation.

How do you find these special directions, in which the map $X \mapsto AX$ just stretches? It turns out that most matrix transformations have them. You will be able to find them for many 2×2 matrices. See Exercises 10, 11, and 21.

Matrices can do all sorts of things geometrically. You will explore this more in the exercises. Perhaps the important thing to remember is that you can use matrices to describe several key geometric transformations: scaling, reflection, and rotation.

Can matrices describe translations? Well, see below.

What is common to all these transformations?

It is impressive, if confusing, that matrices can do all these different transformations. Fortunately, there are some common aspects to all the transformations $X \mapsto AX$. Have you noticed that, in all the matrix transformations so far, lines get mapped to lines and parallel lines get mapped to parallel lines? Some of the exercises address the reasons for this fact.

The fact that lines map to lines can save you time when you are plotting points to see what a matrix transformation does. Just find the image of two distinct points. The image is the line through the two image points.

Another common aspect of all matrix transformations is that the origin gets mapped to the origin.

You can prove this with what you know. If $X \mapsto AX$, then substitute $\begin{pmatrix} 0 \\ 0 \end{pmatrix}$ for X and simply note that $A\begin{pmatrix} 0 \\ 0 \end{pmatrix} = \begin{pmatrix} 0 \\ 0 \end{pmatrix}$ for any 2×2 matrix A.

Answers

Exercises

1. a. $(x, y) \mapsto (-x, y)$, which is a reflection over the y-axis.
b. $(x, y) \mapsto (y, x)$, which is a reflection over the line $y = x$.

The fact that (0, 0) always gets mapped to itself is an important restriction. The first geometric transformation mentioned in this lesson, $(x, y) \mapsto (x + 1, y)$, is a translation, and it maps (0, 0) to (1, 0). So translations are not matrix transformations. In fact, neither are rotations if they are not centered at the origin. Think about it—in such a rotation, the origin will be rotated to somewhere else. Reflections are not matrix transformations either, unless the line of reflection goes through the origin.

So, are matrix methods in geometry only of limited use? No! You can fix this problem. One way is to shift coordinates so that a rotation, for instance, is centered at the origin. Another way avoids shifting coordinates by using 3×3 matrices.

See Exercise 23.

Exercises *Practicing Habits of Mind*

Check Your Understanding

1. Determine what each matrix does. That is, describe the geometric transformation associated with it.

   a. $A = \begin{pmatrix} -1 & 0 \\ 0 & 1 \end{pmatrix}$ b. $B = \begin{pmatrix} 0 & 1 \\ 1 & 0 \end{pmatrix}$

2. Let $A = \begin{pmatrix} 2 & 0 \\ 0 & 2 \end{pmatrix}$. In Example 1, you showed that the mapping $X \mapsto AX$ scales every point by the factor 2. What do you think the mapping $X \mapsto A^{-1}X$ does? Confirm your conjecture by computing A^{-1} and then plotting a few pairs X and $A^{-1}X$.

3. Use matrix A from Exercise 2. What does the mapping $X \mapsto A^2X$ do? What does the mapping $X \mapsto A^{-2}X$ do? (As with numbers, A^{-2} means $(A^{-1})^2$.)

4. **Take It Further** Now think of each ordered pair $\begin{pmatrix} a \\ b \end{pmatrix}$ as representing a point $a + bi$ on the complex plane. Let $M = \begin{pmatrix} c & -d \\ d & c \end{pmatrix}$. Use your knowledge of complex plane geometry to describe geometrically what the mapping $X \mapsto MX$ does. Begin by computing $M\begin{pmatrix} a \\ b \end{pmatrix}$.

2. $A^{-1} = \begin{pmatrix} \frac{1}{2} & 0 \\ 0 & \frac{1}{2} \end{pmatrix}$; $A^{-1}\begin{pmatrix} x \\ y \end{pmatrix} = \begin{pmatrix} \frac{1}{2} & 0 \\ 0 & \frac{1}{2} \end{pmatrix}\begin{pmatrix} x \\ y \end{pmatrix} = \begin{pmatrix} \frac{1}{2}x \\ \frac{1}{2}y \end{pmatrix}$; scales by a factor of $\frac{1}{2}$.

3. $A^2 = \begin{pmatrix} 4 & 0 \\ 0 & 4 \end{pmatrix}$, so $A^2\begin{pmatrix} x \\ y \end{pmatrix} = \begin{pmatrix} 4x \\ 4y \end{pmatrix}$, scales by the factor 4.

$A^{-2} = \begin{pmatrix} \frac{1}{4} & 0 \\ 0 & \frac{1}{4} \end{pmatrix}$, so $A^{-2}\begin{pmatrix} x \\ y \end{pmatrix} = \begin{pmatrix} \frac{1}{4}x \\ \frac{1}{4}y \end{pmatrix}$, scales by a factor of $\frac{1}{4}$.

4. $M\begin{pmatrix} a \\ b \end{pmatrix} = \begin{pmatrix} c & -d \\ d & c \end{pmatrix}\begin{pmatrix} a \\ b \end{pmatrix} = \begin{pmatrix} ac - bd \\ ad + bc \end{pmatrix}$, or M maps the point $a + bi$ to $ac - bd + (ad + bc)i = (a + bi)(c + di)$.

Exercises

HOMEWORK

- Core: 15, 17, 18, 19, 22, 23, 29, 30
- Optional: 16, 24, 25, 26, 27, 31
- Extension: 20, 21, 28

Check Your Understanding

EXERCISES 2 AND 3 The idea here is to show that geometric ideas (reversing a process, repeating a process) and algebraic ideas (inverting a matrix, squaring a matrix, respectively) run in parallel.

EXERCISE 4 shows that you can accomplish complex number multiplication by matrix multiplication. Students have already learned that complex number multiplication rotates and scales on the complex plane. In this lesson they learn that matrix multiplication rotates and scales on the coordinate plane. So it is reasonable to expect that in some sense the two operations are the same.

EXERCISE 7 Students may be surprised that a "complicated" matrix like M can be its own inverse. After all, the only numbers that are their own multiplicative inverses are 1 and -1. Students might expect that the only matrices satisfying $A = A^{-1}$ are I and $-I$. However, any geometric reflection is always its own inverse, so the parallel between geometric inverses and matrix inverses (as discussed in several earlier problems) reveals that many matrices must be their own inverses.

EXERCISE 8 The underlying geometric observation is this: For any reflection in a line through the origin, the perpendicular line through the origin is also special. The reflection maps that line to itself by sending each point X on it to $-X$. In sophisticated language, for any such reflection, both $+1$ and -1 are eigenvalues ($+1$ for points on the axis of symmetry, -1 for points on the perpendicular line).

EXERCISE 9 If matrix squaring corresponds to doing a geometric operation twice, then cubing corresponds to doing it three times, and so on.

5. Example 3 claimed that $M = \frac{1}{5}\begin{pmatrix} 3 & 4 \\ 4 & -3 \end{pmatrix}$ is the matrix of a reflection over the line with equation $y = \frac{1}{2}x$. Plot this line and several points off the line. Pick points on either side of the line. For each of these points X, compute and plot MX. Are they reflections as claimed?

6. Continue with Example 3. If the mapping $X \mapsto MX$ reflects over the line with equation $y = \frac{1}{2}x$, what do you think the mapping $X \mapsto M^{-1}X$ does? How should M and M^{-1} be related? Confirm your conjectures by computing M^{-1}.

7. If $M = \frac{1}{5}\begin{pmatrix} 3 & 4 \\ 4 & -3 \end{pmatrix}$ is the matrix of a reflection, then it turns out there are points X such that $MX = -X$.

a. Use the method of Example 3, where this matrix was introduced, to find all such points X. Plot several of them and their images MX.

b. Let X be any one of the points you just plotted. Draw the vector to it from the origin.

Let Y be any of the points on the line of reflection. Draw the vector to it from the origin. What is the angle between these two vectors? Why does this make sense?

c. Take the dot product of your two points X and Y from part (b).

8. In light of Exercises 5 and 7, explain why reflections are examples of transformations that scale, but by different factors in different directions.

9. The text showed that you can represent a 90° rotation counterclockwise around the origin as

$$\begin{pmatrix} x' \\ y' \end{pmatrix} = \begin{pmatrix} 0 & -1 \\ 1 & 0 \end{pmatrix}\begin{pmatrix} x \\ y \end{pmatrix}$$

where (x, y) is the original point and (x', y') is the resulting point.

If you can rotate once, you can rotate twice. Call the original point X, the new point X', and the rotation matrix R. Then, to rotate twice, compute

$$X'' = RX' = R(RX) = (RR)X = R^2X$$

In this exercise, *rotate* always means counterclockwise around the origin.

a. Without any use of matrices, determine the result if the point (x, y) is rotated by 90° twice.

b. Confirm that you get the same answer as in part (a) using the matrix R^2.

c. Without any use of matrices, determine the result if the point (x, y) is rotated by 90° three times.

d. Determine how to do part (c) again with a power of R. Confirm that you get the same answer.

e. Determine, with and without R, the result of rotating the point (x, y) by 90° four times.

Answers

5. The result of the matrix is to reflect each point over the line $y = \frac{1}{2}x$.

6. The mapping $X \mapsto M^{-1}X$ reflects a preimage over the line $y = \frac{1}{2}x$; $M^{-1} = \begin{pmatrix} \frac{3}{5} & \frac{4}{5} \\ \frac{4}{5} & -\frac{3}{5} \end{pmatrix}$ so $M^{-1} = M$.

7. a. If a point is on the line $y = -2x$, then its image is also on that line.

b. 90°

c. $(2t)s + t(-2s) = 0$

8. A reflection scales by 1 in the direction of the line of reflection (points on this line are not moved) and scales by -1 in the perpendicular direction identified in Exercise 7.

9. a. 180° (counterclockwise) rotation

b. $R^2 = \begin{pmatrix} -1 & 0 \\ 0 & -1 \end{pmatrix}$, so $R^2\begin{pmatrix} x \\ y \end{pmatrix} = \begin{pmatrix} -x \\ -y \end{pmatrix}$.

c. 270° counterclockwise rotation

d. $R^3 = \begin{pmatrix} 0 & 1 \\ -1 & 0 \end{pmatrix}$, so $R^3\begin{pmatrix} x \\ y \end{pmatrix} = \begin{pmatrix} y \\ -x \end{pmatrix}$.

e. $R^4 = \begin{pmatrix} 1 & 0 \\ 0 & 1 \end{pmatrix}$, which is the same as a (clockwise) rotation of 360°.

10. This exercise shows, given a 2×2 matrix A, how to find scalars k and vectors X such that $AX = kX$. Use the matrix A below.

$$A = \begin{pmatrix} 1 & 1 \\ 2 & 0 \end{pmatrix}$$

a. Write out the equation $AX = kX$ as two real-number equations and rewrite them so that both equations equal 0. Your equations will involve three unknowns, the unknown coordinates x and y and the unknown scalar k.

b. In general, two linear equations in x and y equaling 0 will have only one solution $(x, y) = (0, 0)$. However, if the two equations turn out to be different equations for the same line, then there will be other solutions. When are two equations in the form below just different equations for the same line?

$$ax + by = 0$$
$$cx + dy = 0$$

The first equation describes the line with equation $y = (-\frac{a}{b})x$ and the second equation describes the line with equation $y = (-\frac{c}{d})x$, so set $\frac{a}{b} = \frac{c}{d}$. Plug in the values of a, b, c, and d you found in part (a). Then solve the equation for k. The equation is quadratic, so you will get two solutions.

Assume $b \neq 0$ and $d \neq 0$.

c. Now, for each value of k, solve $AX = kX$ for x and y.

11. In Example 4, you were given the matrix below.

$$A = \begin{pmatrix} -2.7 & 1.4 \\ -2.1 & 2.2 \end{pmatrix}$$

The text made the claim that A stretches (2, 1) by the factor −2 and stretches (1, 3) by the factor 1.5 without any explanation. These claims were easy enough to check, but where did they come from? Using the method of Exercise 10, discover these facts for yourself.

12. Figure out the matrix that represents reflection over the line with equation $y = -x$.

(*Hint:* Figure out what the reflection does to a few points that are easy to compute with, such as $\begin{pmatrix} 1 \\ 0 \end{pmatrix}$ and $\begin{pmatrix} 0 \\ 1 \end{pmatrix}$. Then find a matrix that accomplishes the same thing by multiplication.)

13. **Take It Further** The design at the right was made using 45° counterclockwise rotations. Figure out the matrix for 45° rotation counterclockwise around the origin.

EXERCISE 10 The method in part (b) is the standard linear algebra textbook method for finding eigenvalues, but in disguise. The exercise asks students to find the roots of the determinant polynomial $|A - kI|$. But the directions avoid this terminology here because students so far have met determinants only in passing. Also, this determinant method is not the method used in real-world problems because it is terribly inefficient for larger matrices. See the Project at the end of the chapter for a brief introduction to determinants (not in the context of eigenvalues).

EXERCISE 12 The idea introduced here (without proof) is that you can find the matrix of a transformation by determining what the transformation does to two points. Students can use the method again in Exercise 13.

10. a. $x + y = kx$, $2x = ky$; $(1 - k)x + y = 0$, $2x - ky = 0$

b. $k = 2$, $k = -1$

c. If $k = 2$, the equations are $-x + y = 0$ and $2x - 2y = 0$; the solution to that system is any point on the line $y = x$. If $k = -1$, the equations are $2x + y = 0$ and $2x + y = 0$; the solution to that system is any point on the line $y = -2x$.

11. Answers may vary. Sample: Using the technique from Exercise 10 results in the proportion $\frac{-2.7 - k}{-1.4} = \frac{2.1}{2.2 - k}$; solving that proportion gives $k = -2$ or $k = \frac{3}{2}$. The value $k = -2$ results in a system of equations with a solution of all points on the line $y = \frac{1}{2}x$. The value $k = \frac{3}{2}$ results in a system of equations with a solution of all points on the line $y = 3x$.

12. $M = \begin{pmatrix} 0 & -1 \\ -1 & 0 \end{pmatrix}$

13. $M = \begin{pmatrix} \frac{\sqrt{2}}{2} & -\frac{\sqrt{2}}{2} \\ \frac{\sqrt{2}}{2} & \frac{\sqrt{2}}{2} \end{pmatrix}$

EXERCISE 14 The easy proof alluded to—using lines in matrix form—occurs in Exercise 28. Such a proof is more commonly called a vector-algebra proof.

On Your Own

EXERCISE 15 extends the connection between matrix inverses and geometric inverses to slightly more complicated geometric situations.

EXERCISE 17 Finally, here are some matrix transformations that map the plane to a line and some lines to a point. Which lines? Exercise 18 investigates that question.

Also, part (b) will probably be difficult for students, but encourage them to graph many examples of points and their images to get a sense of what is going on.

14. **Take It Further** If the 2×2 matrix M is invertible, then the geometric mapping $X \mapsto MX$ maps lines to lines and parallel lines to parallel lines. (Even if M is not invertible, M generally maps lines to lines, but it maps some lines to points and some parallel lines to the same line or to a point.) It is easy to prove these facts once you describe lines in matrix form, but you have not done that yet. So here is the outline of a proof using what you know.

You know that a set of points (x, y) form a line if they are the solutions to an equation $ax + by = c$, where a and b are not both 0.

Now, if $\begin{pmatrix} x' \\ y' \end{pmatrix} = M\begin{pmatrix} x \\ y \end{pmatrix}$ is the typical point in the image set of the line and M is invertible, then $\begin{pmatrix} x \\ y \end{pmatrix} = M^{-1}\begin{pmatrix} x' \\ y' \end{pmatrix}$.

Also, M^{-1} is some matrix $\begin{pmatrix} p & q \\ r & s \end{pmatrix}$ and $\begin{matrix} x = px' + qy' \\ y = rx' + sy' \end{matrix}$

Substitute these expressions into $ax + by = c$ and regroup until you have something of the form $a'x' + b'y' = c'$. At that point, you have shown that the points (x', y') also form a line. (You also have to argue that a' and b' are not both 0.)

And you also need to show that any point satisfying $a'x' + b'y' = c'$ is in the image set.

On Your Own

15. Let $A = \begin{pmatrix} 3 & 0 \\ 0 & 2 \end{pmatrix}$. In Problem 3, you showed that the mapping $X \mapsto AX$ stretches the plane by the factor 3 in the x-direction and by the factor 2 in the y-direction. What do you think the mapping $X \mapsto A^{-1}X$ does? Confirm your conjecture by computing A^{-1} and then plotting a few pairs X and $A^{-1}X$.

16. Continue with Example 2. If this mapping is indeed associated with rotation by 90° counterclockwise around the origin, then, for every point X, its image ought to be the same distance from the origin. Pick some points and compare the distances of X and AX from the origin.

17. Determine what each matrix does.

a. $B = \begin{pmatrix} 1 & 0 \\ 0 & 0 \end{pmatrix}$ **b.** $C = \begin{pmatrix} \frac{1}{2} & \frac{1}{2} \\ \frac{1}{2} & \frac{1}{2} \end{pmatrix}$

These transformations are different from all those discussed in the text, because they are not one-to-one. That is, $X \mapsto AX$ maps many points to the same point.

Answers

14. Check students' work.

15. $X \mapsto A^{-1}X$ dilates the plane by a factor of $\frac{1}{3}$ horizontally and by a factor of $\frac{1}{2}$ vertically; $A^{-1} = \begin{pmatrix} \frac{1}{3} & 0 \\ 0 & \frac{1}{2} \end{pmatrix}$.

16. Answers may vary. Sample: Using the general point $\begin{pmatrix} x \\ y \end{pmatrix}$, $\begin{pmatrix} 0 & -1 \\ 1 & 0 \end{pmatrix}\begin{pmatrix} x \\ y \end{pmatrix} = \begin{pmatrix} -y \\ x \end{pmatrix}$, and the distance from the origin to $\begin{pmatrix} x \\ y \end{pmatrix}$ or to $\begin{pmatrix} -y \\ x \end{pmatrix}$ is $\sqrt{x^2 + y^2}$.

17. a. $\begin{pmatrix} 1 & 0 \\ 0 & 0 \end{pmatrix}\begin{pmatrix} x \\ y \end{pmatrix} = \begin{pmatrix} x \\ 0 \end{pmatrix}$; every point (x, y) is moved vertically to the point $(x, 0)$ on the x-axis.

b. $\begin{pmatrix} \frac{1}{2} & \frac{1}{2} \\ \frac{1}{2} & \frac{1}{2} \end{pmatrix}\begin{pmatrix} x \\ y \end{pmatrix} = \begin{pmatrix} \frac{1}{2}(x + y) \\ \frac{1}{2}(x + y) \end{pmatrix}$; every point (x, y) is moved to the midpoint of the segment whose endpoints are $(0, 0)$ and $(x + y, x + y)$.

18. Continue with the transformations associated with matrices B and C from Exercise 17. Also consider the lines with the following equations.

L_1: $x = 1$ L_2: $x = 2$ L_3: $y = 1$

L_4: $y = -1$ L_5: $y = x$ L_6: $y = x + 2$

a. Find the image of each line under multiplication by B.

b. Find the image of each line under multiplication by C.

19. Suppose all you know about the matrix transformation $X \mapsto AX$ is that $(2, 1) \mapsto (-4, -2)$ and $(1, 3) \mapsto (1.5, 4.5)$. That is, you know only that

$$A\begin{pmatrix} 2 \\ 1 \end{pmatrix} = \begin{pmatrix} -4 \\ -2 \end{pmatrix} \quad \text{and} \quad A\begin{pmatrix} 1 \\ 3 \end{pmatrix} = \begin{pmatrix} 1.5 \\ 4.5 \end{pmatrix}$$

a. What does (6, 3) map to? (*Hint:* What properties do you know about the matrix product $A(kB)$?)

b. What does $(2, 1) + (1, 3) = (3, 4)$ map to?

c. What does $(-1, 2)$ map to?

d. Explain why you can figure out what any point (x, y) maps to.

e. In fact, you know all about this matrix transformation. It is the mapping from Example 4 and $A = \begin{pmatrix} -2.7 & 1.4 \\ -2.1 & 2.2 \end{pmatrix}$. Confirm your answers to parts (a)–(c) by direct multiplication.

20. **Take It Further** Consider A from Exercise 19 again. Suppose there is another matrix B such that $B\begin{pmatrix} 2 \\ 1 \end{pmatrix} = \begin{pmatrix} -4 \\ -2 \end{pmatrix}$ and $B\begin{pmatrix} 1 \\ 3 \end{pmatrix} = \begin{pmatrix} 1.5 \\ 4.5 \end{pmatrix}$. How are A and B related? Explain your reasoning.

21. **Take It Further** Let $R = \begin{pmatrix} 0 & -1 \\ 1 & 0 \end{pmatrix}$. This is the matrix from Example 2. Using the method of Exercise 10, find scalars k and points X such that $RX = kX$.

22. This lesson began with the mapping $(x, y) \mapsto (x + 1, y)$, which shifts everything over by one unit in the x-direction. It is not a matrix multiplication transformation because $(0, 0) \mapsto (1, 0)$. However, it is still a transformation that uses matrix algebra, because you can write it in the form $X \mapsto MX + B$, where $M = I$ and $B = \begin{pmatrix} 1 \\ 0 \end{pmatrix}$.

Show how to write the geometric transformation below in the form $X \mapsto MX + B$.

$$\begin{pmatrix} x \\ y \end{pmatrix} \mapsto \begin{pmatrix} x + 2y + 3 \\ 3x + 4 \end{pmatrix}$$

Go Online PHSchool.com

For additional practice, go to **Web Code:** bfa-0411

You may think that because the transformation associated with this matrix is a 90° rotation, there is no point X that is scaled by any scalar k. Do the algebra and see what happens.

EXERCISE 18 Matrix B projects any point onto a point somewhere on the x-axis, and also projects any line perpendicular to the x-axis onto a single point—the intersection of the two perpendicular lines. Any other line has the entire x-axis as its image.

Matrix C projects any point onto a point somewhere on the line with equation $y = x$, and also projects any line perpendicular to the line with equation $y = x$ onto a single point—the intersection of the two perpendicular lines. Any other line has the entire line with equation $y = x$ as its image. These cases are not all shown in the exercise, but interested students might want to find examples that demonstrate these situations.

EXERCISE 19 begins, without fanfare, to get at the idea that you know all about a matrix transformation as soon as you know what it does to a "basis," which on the plane means two points not on the same line through the origin.

EXERCISE 21 There are points that rotation scales if you allow ordered pairs with complex number entries. What does this mean? Note that this is not the same as representing the real-number ordered pair (a, b) as $a + bi$. Now a and b themselves can be complex numbers. This question is left unanswered, but maybe some students will think about it. It turns out that this exercise is really about two-dimensional complex space, which is somewhat like four-dimensional real space. In any event, the claim in the text that most square matrices have eigenvalues is true only if you allow complex eigenvalues. In that case, every square matrix has at least one eigenvalue.

21. $k = i$ and $X = \begin{pmatrix} -i \\ 1 \end{pmatrix}$, or $k = -i$ and $X = \begin{pmatrix} i \\ 1 \end{pmatrix}$

22. $\begin{pmatrix} x + 2y + 3 \\ 3x + 4 \end{pmatrix} = \begin{pmatrix} 1 & 2 \\ 3 & 0 \end{pmatrix}\begin{pmatrix} x \\ y \end{pmatrix} + \begin{pmatrix} 3 \\ 4 \end{pmatrix}$

18. a. The mapping $X \mapsto BX$ projects lines L_1 and L_2 to the points (1, 0) and (2, 0), respectively, and projects each of lines L_3 through L_6 to the line $y = 0$.

b. The mapping $X \mapsto CX$ projects each of the lines to the line $y = x$.

19. a. $(-12, -6)$

b. $(-2.5, 2.5)$

c. $(5.5, 6.5)$

d. Answers may vary. Sample: Every point (x, y) can be represented by $a(2, 1) + b(1, 3)$ for particular values of a and b, so the image of (x, y) is $a(-4, -2) + b(1.5, 4.5)$ for those values of a and b.

e. Answers may vary. Sample:

$$\begin{pmatrix} -2.7 & 1.4 \\ -2.1 & 2.2 \end{pmatrix}\begin{pmatrix} 2 & 1 & 6 \\ 1 & 3 & 3 \end{pmatrix} = \begin{pmatrix} -4 & 1.5 & -12 \\ -2 & 4.5 & -6 \end{pmatrix}$$, which checks with the given and part (a).

20. Matrices A and B must be the same.

EXERCISE 24 You may wish to note that it is always the case that a rotation followed by a reflection is equivalent to a reflection, even if you do not restrict the rotations to those centered at the origin and reflections to those over lines through the origin. With the restrictions—the rotation is centered at the origin so that it is a matrix transformation and the reflection is over a line through the origin so that it is also a matrix transformation—their composition must fix the origin, too, and so be a matrix transformation itself.

EXERCISES 25 AND 26 The results from Exercises 25 and 26 are both true in any number of dimensions. The proof given for Exercise 25 is good in any number of dimensions, but you need a better method to prove Exercise 26 in general.

EXERCISE 27 Invertibility (the existence of an inverse) plays just the role Xavier proposed: You can multiply by the inverse to solve the equation. The solution shows why the final definition of M^{-1} requires that both $M^{-1}M$ and MM^{-1} be I.

Maintain Your Skills

EXERCISE 30 takes the parallel between algebra and geometry yet another step. The product of two different matrices now runs parallel to doing one geometric transformation after a different one (composition). This parallel also gives another explanation of why matrix multiplication is not commutative.

23. You can often handle transformations that do not fix the origin with matrix multiplication methods by using the following method of adding a dimension. It works this way:

$$\begin{pmatrix} x \\ y \end{pmatrix} \rightarrow \begin{pmatrix} x \\ y \\ 1 \end{pmatrix} \rightarrow A\begin{pmatrix} x \\ y \\ 1 \end{pmatrix} = \begin{pmatrix} x' \\ y' \\ 1 \end{pmatrix} \rightarrow \begin{pmatrix} x' \\ y' \end{pmatrix}$$

You insert a third component in your starting point. Typically you insert 1. Then, you act on your new point with a 3×3 matrix A. Finally, you strip off the third component to get the final transformation.

Show that if you use this method on (x, y) with the matrix A below, then (x, y) maps to $(x, y) + (a, b)$. That is, show that the matrix A represents the translation by (a, b).

$$A = \begin{pmatrix} 1 & 0 & a \\ 0 & 1 & b \\ 0 & 0 & 1 \end{pmatrix}$$

The method of adding a dimension is used in computer graphics routines. Computer graphics routines need to handle motions like translations and rotations around arbitrary points in space. So you can start with 3×3 matrices and add a dimension to get 4×4 matrices.

24. Imagine rotating the xy-plane 90° counterclockwise through the origin and then reflecting over the x-axis.

a. Without any use of matrices, determine where the following points end up.

$$(1, 0),\ (0, 1),\ (1, 1),\ (-1, 1),\ (x, y)$$

b. Find a matrix M such that the mapping $X \mapsto MX$ accomplishes what you did in part (a).

c. Using your knowledge of matrices for rotations and reflections, find a matrix R for the rotation part of this exercise. Find another matrix R' for the reflection part.

d. Verify that $M = R'R$. Explain why this makes sense.

e. Express this transformation (the rotation followed by the reflection) as a single geometric action. It might be a rotation or a reflection.

25. Prove that if M is invertible (meaning the inverse M^{-1} exists), then the mapping of the plane $X \mapsto MX$ is one-to-one. That is, show that if $MX = MY$, then $X = Y$.

26. Prove the inverse of Exercise 25: If M is not invertible, then the mapping of the plane $X \mapsto MX$ is not one-to-one. (*Hint:* If $M = \begin{pmatrix} p & q \\ r & s \end{pmatrix}$ is not invertible, then you know that $ps - qr = 0$.)

A mapping is not one-to-one if you can find two points x_1 and x_2 such that $x_1 \neq x_2$ but $Mx_1 = Mx_2$.

27. Prove that, if M is invertible, then the mapping of the plane $X \mapsto MX$ is *onto*. A mapping is onto if for every X', there exists some X such that $MX = X'$. In other words, some point X is mapped to X'.

Answers

23. Start with $\begin{pmatrix} 1 & 0 & a \\ 0 & 1 & b \\ 0 & 0 & 1 \end{pmatrix}\begin{pmatrix} x \\ y \\ 1 \end{pmatrix} = \begin{pmatrix} x+a \\ y+b \\ 1 \end{pmatrix}$.
Then use only the first two rows to write $(x, y) \mapsto (x + a, y + b)$ or $(x, y) \mapsto (x, y) + (a, b)$.

24. a. The images are $(0, -1)$, $(-1, 0)$, $(-1, -1)$, $(-1, 1)$, $(-y, -x)$.

b. $\begin{pmatrix} 0 & -1 \\ -1 & 0 \end{pmatrix}$

c. The rotation matrix R is $\begin{pmatrix} 0 & -1 \\ 1 & 0 \end{pmatrix}$; the reflection matrix R' is $\begin{pmatrix} 1 & 0 \\ 0 & -1 \end{pmatrix}$.

d. $R'R = \begin{pmatrix} 1 & 0 \\ 0 & -1 \end{pmatrix}\begin{pmatrix} 0 & -1 \\ 1 & 0 \end{pmatrix} = \begin{pmatrix} 0 & -1 \\ -1 & 0 \end{pmatrix}$, which is M.

e. It is a reflection over the line $y = -x$.

25. If $MX = MY$, then $M^{-1}MX = M^{-1}MY$. That can be rewritten as $IX = IY$ or $X = Y$.

26. Answers may vary. Sample:
Suppose $M = \begin{pmatrix} p & q \\ r & s \end{pmatrix}$ does not have an inverse. Then $M\begin{pmatrix} q \\ -p \end{pmatrix} = \begin{pmatrix} p & q \\ r & s \end{pmatrix}\begin{pmatrix} q \\ -p \end{pmatrix} = \begin{pmatrix} pq - qp \\ rq - sp \end{pmatrix} = 0$;
If M is one-to-one, then $p = q = 0$, in which case $M\begin{pmatrix} s \\ -r \end{pmatrix} = \begin{pmatrix} p & q \\ r & s \end{pmatrix}\begin{pmatrix} s \\ -r \end{pmatrix} = \begin{pmatrix} 0 \\ 0 \end{pmatrix} = 0$. But then $r = s = 0$. So M is identically 0. Contradiction.

27. Given X', we want to find X so that $MX = X'$. That would mean $M^{-1}MX = M^{-1}X'$, or $X = M^{-1}X'$.

28. **Take It Further** A set of points forms a line if and only if you can represent the points on the line in the form $X = P + tD$, with P any point on the line, D a nonzero ordered pair called the direction vector for the line, and t a parameter that can be any real number. Two lines are parallel if you can represent them in this form using the same D but different matrices P.

So if a set of points forms a line, then you can represent the set of images under M as the set with points that have the form $MX = M(P + tD)$.

But $P + tD$ is a matrix, so you can apply the Distributive Property, $MX = MP + t(MD)$.

Why does this identity prove that the set of image points MX forms a line?

For each line, P and D are fixed. This way of thinking about lines is *vector representation*. This representation works just as well in three dimensions, or in any number of dimensions.

29. **Standardized Test Prep** Which of the following statements is NOT true?

A. The sum of the squares of the elements of each row of a 2×2 matrix is 1 for a rotation with no dilation.

B. The square of a reflection matrix is the identity matrix. $(AA = I)$

C. Divide 360° by the angle of rotation. If the remainder is 0, then you must raise the transformation matrix to that quotient to get an identity matrix.

D. For a rotation, the inverse of a matrix must equal itself. $(M^{-1} = M)$

Maintain Your Skills

30. Use the following matrix descriptions.

R = the matrix for rotation 90° counterclockwise around the origin
F = the matrix for reflection over the x-axis
S_{-1} = the matrix for dilating by $k = -1$ around the origin
S_2 = the matrix for dilating by $k = 2$ around the origin

$(S_2R)X$ first rotates X by 90° and then scales by 2.

Describe a geometric transformation for each product matrix.

a. R^2 **b.** R^3 **c.** R^4 **d.** R^5 **e.** $(S_2)^2$
f. $S_{-1}S_2$ **g.** S_2S_{-1} **h.** $(S_{-1})^2$ **i.** F^2 **j.** S_2R
k. RS_2 **l.** FR **m.** RF

31. Many transformations of 3-dimensional space are matrix transformations. Points have the form $X = (x, y, z)$ and the matrices are 3×3. For each matrix M, figure out what the transformation $X \mapsto MX$ does.

a. $M = \begin{pmatrix} 2 & 0 & 0 \\ 0 & 2 & 0 \\ 0 & 0 & 2 \end{pmatrix}$ **b.** $M = \begin{pmatrix} 1 & 0 & 0 \\ 0 & 2 & 0 \\ 0 & 0 & 3 \end{pmatrix}$ **c.** $M = \begin{pmatrix} 1 & 0 & 0 \\ 0 & 1 & 0 \\ 0 & 0 & -1 \end{pmatrix}$

d. $M = \begin{pmatrix} 0 & -1 & 0 \\ 1 & 0 & 0 \\ 0 & 0 & 1 \end{pmatrix}$ **e.** $M = \begin{pmatrix} -1 & 0 & 0 \\ 0 & 1 & 0 \\ 0 & 0 & -1 \end{pmatrix}$ **f.** $M = \begin{pmatrix} 0 & 0 & 1 \\ 1 & 0 & 0 \\ 0 & 1 & 0 \end{pmatrix}$

Additional Resources

PRINT RESOURCES
- Solution Manual
- Practice Workbook
- Assessment Resources
- Teaching Resources

TECHNOLOGY
- Interactive Textbook
- TeacherExpress CD-ROM
- ExamView CD-ROM
- PHSchool.com

Additional Practice

1. Let $A = \begin{pmatrix} 2 & 0 \\ 0 & 4 \end{pmatrix}$.
   a. What does the mapping $X \mapsto AX$ do in the x-direction and the y-direction?
   b. What does the mapping $X \mapsto A^{-1}X$ do? Confirm your conjecture by computing A^{-1} and then plotting a few pairs X and $A^{-1}X$.

For Exercises 2 and 3, use the matrices below.

$A = \begin{pmatrix} -1 & 0 \\ 0 & -1 \end{pmatrix}$ $B = \begin{pmatrix} 0 & 1 \\ 0 & 0 \end{pmatrix}$ $C = \begin{pmatrix} 0.25 & 0 \\ 0 & 0.25 \end{pmatrix}$

2. Determine what each matrix does.
   a. A b. B c. C

3. Consider the lines with the equations below.
   $L_1: x = -1$ $L_2: x = 0$ $L_3: y = 2$
   $L_4: y = -3$ $L_5: y = -x$ $L_6: y = -x + 1$
   Find the image of each line under multiplication by each matrix.
   a. A b. B c. C

4. Suppose all you know about the matrix transformation $X \mapsto AX$ is that $(3, -1) \mapsto (-9, 3)$ and $(-2, -6) \mapsto (-1, -3)$. That is, you only know that
   $$A\begin{pmatrix} 3 \\ -1 \end{pmatrix} = \begin{pmatrix} -9 \\ 3 \end{pmatrix} \text{ and } A\begin{pmatrix} -2 \\ -6 \end{pmatrix} = \begin{pmatrix} -1 \\ -3 \end{pmatrix}$$
   a. What does $(1, 3)$ map to?
   b. What does $(3, -1) + (-2, -6) = (1, -7)$ map to?
   c. What does $(1, -3)$ map to?

5. Write the geometric transformation below in the form $X \mapsto MX + B$.
   $$\begin{pmatrix} x \\ y \end{pmatrix} \mapsto \begin{pmatrix} 2x + y + 2 \\ 5x + 1 \end{pmatrix}$$

6. Let R = the matrix for rotation 180° counterclockwise around the origin
   F = the matrix for reflection over the y-axis
   S = the matrix for dilating by $k = 3$ around the origin
   Describe a geometric transformation for each product matrix.
   a. R^2 b. SR
   c. FR d. SRF

Practice: For Lesson 4.11, assign Exercises 1–6.

28. MP is a point and MD is a nonzero ordered pair, so $MX = MP + MD$ is a line.

29. A

30. a. 180° (counterclockwise) rotation
b. 270° counterclockwise rotation
c. 360° (counterclockwise) rotation
d. 450° (or 90°) counterclockwise rotation
e. dilation by $k = 4$
f. dilation by $k = -2$
g. dilation by $k = -2$
h. dilation by 1 (no change)
i. no change (reflection over x-axis, then reflection back over x-axis)
j. $(x, y) \mapsto (-2y, 2x)$
k. $(x, y) \mapsto (-2y, 2x)$
l. $(x, y) \mapsto (-y, -x)$
m. $(x, y) \mapsto (y, x)$

31. a. dilation by 2
b. dilation by 1, 2, and 3 in the x, y, and z directions, respectively
c. reflection over the xy-plane
d. $(x, y, z) \mapsto (-y, x, z)$; that is a rotation of 90° counterclockwise around the z-axis.
e. $(x, y, z) \mapsto (-x, y, -z)$
f. $(x, y, z) \mapsto (z, x, y)$

Lesson Overview

GOAL

- Model the evolution of a system over time.

Matrices have tremendous power to encapsulate complicated situations into simple algebraic expressions. Situations may have many variables, but if the same type of changes happen over and over again, you can describe the whole process as a sequence of matrix powers. This is the great payoff of this lesson.

The downside is that it takes a while to digest all the information in a realistic application and to get used to formulating it as a matrix powers problem. That is one reason this chapter starts with geometric transformations; the situations you model there are easier to grasp. So you have planted the idea of using matrices. The hard part is to make the transition to more complicated situations.

This lesson, indeed this investigation, is experimental, in the sense that whenever you ask students to find a pattern or a long-term limit, they can report only what they see; they do not have the tools to prove it. There are more advanced methods that allow proofs and, in many cases, simpler computations to get the numerical limits. This is the theory of eigenvalues and eigenvectors.

CHECK YOUR UNDERSTANDING

- Core: 1, 3, 4, 5
- Optional: 2, 6

MATERIALS

- graphing calculators

HOMEWORK

- Core: 7, 8, 9, 11, 12, 13, 14
- Optional: 15
- Extension: 10

VOCABULARY

- steady state
- transition matrix

Launch

Start right in on the car rental example. Your class may already have discussed this situation in the Getting Started lesson and, if so, you may want to remind the class of some of their early conjectures about the situation.

Explore

Circulate as students work and gather any questions or comments for a class discussion.

4.12 Transition Matrices

There are many situations where you want to study what happens when something happens over and over again—an object rotates again and again, a rental car agency has its cars move between locations week after week, and so on. You would like to know what happens after any number of iterations into the future. And if there is a long-term pattern, you would like to know that, too.

In the past, you may have looked at an iteration when there was one variable.

For instance, if you iterate $x \rightarrow 1.01x + 50$, you learn what happens when you add \$50 to your bank account each month and the money already there grows by 1% monthly interest.

Now, with the help of matrices, you will analyze iteration with more variables.

Example 1

Return to Problem 8 from Lesson 4.10, about the car rental company with locations in Boston and Cambridge. They wanted to know where their cars would be at the end of each week. Solve their problem with matrices.

Solution Let $b(n)$ be the number of the company's cars in Boston at the end of week n. Similarly, let $c(n)$ be the number in Cambridge at the end of week n. Since each location has 70 cars to start, you have $b(0) = c(0) = 70$. In symbols, this is what the problem says about how cars move around each week:

$$b(n) = 0.8b(n-1) + 0.5c(n-1)$$
$$c(n) = 0.2b(n-1) + 0.5c(n-1)$$

The problem does not say 20% of cars in Boston at the start of one week are returned to Cambridge at the end of the week, but, since there are only two locations, that is where the rest of the cars have to go.

So what are the matrices? Well, the equations are linear. Define $A(n)$ (A for auto) by

$$A(n) = \begin{pmatrix} b(n) \\ c(n) \end{pmatrix}$$

The system above becomes

$$A(n) = \begin{pmatrix} 0.8 & 0.5 \\ 0.2 & 0.5 \end{pmatrix} A(n-1)$$

You are assuming there are no new cars, no crashes, and no thefts. It is also unrealistic to assume that all rentals are for one week. However, more realistic models can be built using larger matrices.

Answers

For Discussion

1. Answers may vary. Sample: Round each decimal to the nearest whole number.

2. Answers may vary. Sample: Once you reach the point that there are 100 cars in Boston and 40 cars in Cambridge, those numbers will not change after each subsequent week.

So, if you let $M = \begin{pmatrix} 0.8 & 0.5 \\ 0.2 & 0.5 \end{pmatrix}$, then the information in the problem boils down to this:

$$A(n) = \begin{cases} \begin{pmatrix} 70 \\ 70 \end{pmatrix} & \text{if } n = 0 \\ MA(n-1) & \text{if } n > 0 \end{cases}$$

Therefore,

$A(1) = MA(0)$ (Substitute 0 for n.)

$A(2) = MA(1) = M(MA(0)) = M^2A(0)$ (Substitute 1 for n.)

$A(3) = MA(2) = M(M^2A(0)) = M^3A(0)$ (Substitute 2 for n.)

In general, $A(n) = M^nA(0)$.

This is a simple equation for a complicated situation. Matrix notation is powerful because of its simplicity.

Because you use the same matrix M to transition from each time period to the next (you multiply by M one more time), M is a **transition matrix.**

Using technology, you can compute the following values.

$$A(1) = \begin{pmatrix} 91 \\ 49 \end{pmatrix} \quad A(2) = \begin{pmatrix} 97.3 \\ 42.7 \end{pmatrix} \quad A(3) = \begin{pmatrix} 99.19 \\ 40.81 \end{pmatrix}$$

Do you have a conjecture about what is happening? Check out $A(10)$. To four decimal places, it is

$$\begin{pmatrix} 99.9998 \\ 40.0002 \end{pmatrix}$$

It seems that as the weeks go by, the distribution of cars is stabilizing, with 100 cars in Boston and 40 cars in Cambridge. When this happens, you call it a **steady state.**

For Discussion

Example 1 raises more questions than it answers. Here are a few. You may have more.

1. What do you make of these decimal values? You cannot have decimal numbers of cars!

2. What does it mean to say "stabilizing with 100 in Boston"? There cannot be 100 cars that always stay in Boston.

For You to Do

3. What happens if the company starts with 30 cars in Boston and 110 in Cambridge?

4. What happens if the company starts with 100 cars in Boston and 40 in Cambridge?

5. Consider the matrices M^2, M^3, and so on. Describe what happens to M^n for greater and greater values of n.

Example 1

The notation in the definitions of $b(n)$ and $c(n)$ (on p. 372) may be confusing due to the spacing. Some students may read the first term on the right as $0.8b$ times $n - 1$. The correct reading is 0.8 times the $(n-1)$st value of b. It is partly to avoid such ambiguity that many students prefer subscript notation for sequences. Here that would give you $0.8b_{n-1}$. However, sequences are functions from the domain of nonnegative integers, and using standard function notation such as $b(n)$ and $b(n-1)$ emphasizes that fact.

For You to Do

3. Each week the two locations will get closer to 100 cars in Boston and 40 cars in Cambridge.

4. They would always have 100 cars in Boston and 40 cars in Cambridge.

5. $M^2 = \begin{pmatrix} 0.74 & 0.65 \\ 0.26 & 0.35 \end{pmatrix}$, $M^3 = \begin{pmatrix} 0.722 & 0.695 \\ 0.278 & 0.305 \end{pmatrix}$, $M^4 = \begin{pmatrix} 0.7166 & 0.7085 \\ 0.2834 & 0.2915 \end{pmatrix}$; as the power of M gets larger, the entries in the matrix stabilize.

Example 2

Again in this example, a problem about a set of linked sequences is turned into a problem about a single matrix equation. This method permeates this lesson and the next. Almost all the problems in this lesson and the next are like this. The only variation, and the variation is slight, occurs when a problem about a single sequence with several terms (e.g., the Fibonacci sequence) is turned into a matrix problem.

The rental example is about a fixed population of cars in which the total number does not change. Another use for repeated transition matrices is to model changes in living populations.

Example 2

Problem A certain beetle has three life stages: egg, larva, and adult. During each time period, each adult alive at the start of the period lays 15 eggs and then dies, 80% of the live eggs at the start of the period hatch into larvae, and 20% of the larvae alive at the start of the period survive and become adults. The remaining eggs never hatch and the rest of the larvae die.

Actually, each female adult lays 30 eggs and each male lays 0, but the average works fine in this model. Sometimes scientists just model the female population and use the fact that the male population is some constant multiple of the female population.

Suppose a certain garden initially harbors 50 eggs, 20 larvae, and 10 adults. What will be the situation at the end of one time period? At the end of two time periods? At the end of three time periods?

Solution First define the functions.

$e(n)$ = number of eggs at the end of time period n

$l(n)$ = number of larvae at the end of time period n

$a(n)$ = number of adults at the end of time period n

The given information is

$$e(0) = 50 \qquad e(n) = 15a(n-1)$$

$$l(0) = 20 \quad \text{and} \quad l(n) = 0.8e(n-1)$$

$$a(0) = 10 \qquad a(n) = 0.2l(n-1)$$

You can turn this into a matrix equation.

$$P(n) = \begin{pmatrix} e(n) \\ l(n) \\ a(n) \end{pmatrix} \qquad M = \begin{pmatrix} 0 & 0 & 15 \\ 0.8 & 0 & 0 \\ 0 & 0.2 & 0 \end{pmatrix}$$

$$P(n) = \begin{cases} \begin{pmatrix} 50 \\ 20 \\ 10 \end{pmatrix} & \text{if } n = 0 \\ MP(n-1) & \text{if } n > 0 \end{cases}$$

Use the matrix M to calculate $P(n)$ for a few iterations.

$$P(1) = MP(0) = \begin{pmatrix} 150 \\ 40 \\ 4 \end{pmatrix}$$

$$P(2) = MP(1) = M\big(MP(0)\big) = M^2P(0) = \begin{pmatrix} 60 \\ 120 \\ 8 \end{pmatrix}$$

$$P(3) = M^3P(0) = \begin{pmatrix} 120 \\ 48 \\ 24 \end{pmatrix}$$

It is instructive to look at the powers of M.

$$M^2 = \begin{pmatrix} 0 & 3 & 0 \\ 0 & 0 & 12 \\ 0.16 & 0 & 0 \end{pmatrix} \quad M^3 = \begin{pmatrix} 2.4 & 0 & 0 \\ 0 & 2.4 & 0 \\ 0 & 0 & 2.4 \end{pmatrix}$$

What do these equations tell you?

M^3 tells us that every three periods, the beetle population grows by 2.4 times in every category. In other words, the population is cyclical. Every three periods it returns to the ratio of eggs to larvae to adults that it had three periods ago, but at 2.4 times the population. You call this a periodic growth cycle. You can check it out by actually computing $P(4)$, $P(5)$, . . . and comparing. For instance, at the end of periods 1, 4, 7, . . . the ratio of larvae to adults is always 10 to 1, whereas after periods 3, 6, 9, . . . it is always just 2 to 1.

Actually, some factor you have not been told about, such as crowding or insecticide, must take over. Otherwise, with its population more than doubling every three time periods, these beetles are going to take over the world, not just this garden. This raises an important point. Transition models rarely model the real world forever.

For You to Do

6. You do not really need matrices to solve the problem in the example. Show that the equations

$$e(n) = 15a(n-1) \qquad (16)$$

$$l(n) = 0.8e(n-1) \qquad (17)$$

$$a(n) = 0.2l(n-1) \qquad (18)$$

lead directly to

$$e(n+3) = 2.4e(n)$$

$$l(n+3) = 2.4l(n)$$

$$a(n+3) = 2.4a(n)$$

For instance, here is most of the calculation for $e(n+3)$.

$$e(n+3) = 15a(n+2) \qquad \text{from (16)}$$

$$= 15(0.2l(n+1)) \qquad \text{from (17)}$$

$$= 15(0.2(0.8e(n))) \qquad \text{from (18)}$$

However, for populations where there is not such a rigid separation between life-cycle stages, the matrix approach is much easier.

You can use transition matrices to model the population cycles of sea turtles.

Answers

For You to Do

6. $e(n+3) = 15a(n+2) = 15(0.2l(n+1)) = 15(0.2)(0.8e(n)) = 2.4e(n)$
$l(n+3) = 0.8e(n+2) = 0.8(15a(n+1)) = (0.8)(15)(0.2l(n)) = 2.4l(n)$
$a(n+3) = 0.2l(n+2) = (0.2)(0.8)e(n+1) = (0.2)(0.8)15a(n) = 2.4a(n)$

Wrap Up

You might have students explain to each other one more time how they derived the matrix equations from the data in the two examples in this lesson. Or have them suggest variations on these examples and derive the new matrices. Some of the Check Your Understanding core exercises treat variations, so work on these as time allows.

Assessment Resources

Lesson Quiz 4.12

1. Suppose that each year, in a particular country, 5% of the people east of the river move west and 3% of the people west of the river move east. Assume that initially there are 1,000,000 people on each side of the river. Find the transition matrix and figure out what happens in the long run.

2. A certain species of caterpillar has three life stages: egg, larva, and adult. During each time period, each adult alive at the start of the period lays 12 eggs and then dies, 75% of the live eggs at the start of the period hatch into larvae, and 25% of the larvae alive at the start of the period survive and become adults. The remaining eggs never hatch and the rest of the larvae die. Assume that initially there are 60 eggs, 25 larvae, and 15 adults in a garden. Find the transition matrix and find a pattern in the three life stages in the long run.

3. Consider the transition matrix $M = \begin{pmatrix} 0.8 & 0.35 \\ 0.2 & 0.65 \end{pmatrix}$. For a fixed population of 750, find the steady state $X = (x, y)$ such that $MX = X$.

Exercises

HOMEWORK
- Core: 7, 8, 9, 11, 12, 13, 14
- Optional: 15
- Extension: 10

Check Your Understanding

EXERCISE 1 From a more advanced perspective, what is going on here is this: For the transition matrix M you are assuming that $k = 1$ is an eigenvalue and are proceeding by the standard approach to find an associated eigenvector. This rental car problem is a Markov Chain problem (see the margin note on page 384). It is a theorem that $k = 1$ is always an eigenvalue for a Markov Chain.

EXERCISE 2 Students may need a hint. Point out that M is a square matrix and $A(0)$ is merely a column. So while $(MM)(A(0)) = M(MA(0))$, the left side involves one product of square matrices and the right side does not. What other sizes of matrix multiplications appear on the two sides?

TECHNOLOGY TIP If students are not able to enter something like $M \times$ **Ans** into their calculators because **Ans** must be the first entry in a new expression, it may be useful to show them how to use the transpose M^T of a matrix M. You get the transpose of a matrix by flipping M over its main diagonal—switching its rows and columns. If you transpose everything in sight, so that $A(k)^T$ is a row vector, then the calculation you want is $A(k + 1)^T = (k)^T M^T$.

Exercises *Practicing Habits of Mind*

Check Your Understanding

1. In Example 1, suppose you assumed there was a steady state $A = (b, c)$, but you did not know what it was. That is, suppose you assumed there was a way to divide the 140 cars, b in Boston and c in Cambridge, so that $MA = A$. Use this matrix equation to solve for A.

2. Consider again Example 1. Given M and $A(0)$, one way to compute $A(1)$, $A(2)$, $A(3)$, . . . is to compute M, M^2, M^3, . . . and then multiply each of them by $A(0)$. But note that $M^2A(0) = M(MA(0))$, $M^3A(0) = M(M(MA(0)))$, and so on. Explain how this allows you to compute $A(1)$, $A(2)$, $A(3)$, . . . with fewer multiplications.

3. Another auto rental company has three locations A, B, and C. Let $a(n)$ be the number of cars at A at the end of week n, $b(n)$ be the number at B, and $c(n)$ be the number at C. Suppose the following equations describe the movement of cars.

$$a(n) = 0.7a(n-1) + 0.2b(n-1) + 0.3c(n-1)$$
$$b(n) = 0.2a(n-1) + 0.5b(n-1) + 0.1c(n-1)$$
$$c(n) = 0.1a(n-1) + 0.3b(n-1) + 0.6c(n-1)$$

a. Describe this situation in words. (*Hint*: It is similar to the situation in Example 1.)

b. Find the transition matrix.

c. Initially, the company has 100 cars in each location. How many cars are in each location two weeks later? Three weeks later? In the long run?

4. You can turn recurrences involving several terms into transition matrix problems with a nice method. Consider the Fibonacci sequence.

$$f(n) = \begin{cases} 1 & \text{if } n = 0 \text{ or } 1 \\ f(n-1) + f(n-2) & \text{if } n \geq 2 \end{cases}$$

a. Let $X(n) = \begin{pmatrix} f(n) \\ f(n-1) \end{pmatrix}$. Show that $X(n) = \begin{pmatrix} 1 & 1 \\ 1 & 0 \end{pmatrix} X(n-1)$.

b. Use your result from part (a) to compute $f(10)$.

By using this method, you turn a second-order recurrence for a sequence of numbers (f_n) into a first-order recurrence for a sequence of ordered pairs (the X_n).

5. Use the method in Exercise 4 to turn the second-order recurrence below into a matrix equation.

$$g(n) = 3g(n-1) - 4g(n-2)$$

Answers

Exercises

1. Rewriting $MA = A$ as $\begin{pmatrix} 0.8 & 0.5 \\ 0.2 & 0.5 \end{pmatrix}\begin{pmatrix} b \\ c \end{pmatrix} = \begin{pmatrix} b \\ c \end{pmatrix}$, then $A = \begin{pmatrix} 100 \\ 40 \end{pmatrix}$.

2. $A(n) = M(A(n-1))$

3. a. For the cars that start at location A, 70% of them are returned to A, 20% are returned to B, and 10% are returned to C. For the cars that start at location B, 20% of them are returned to A, 50% are returned to B, and 30% are returned to C. For the cars that start at location C, 30% of them are returned to A, 10% are returned to B, and 60% are returned to C.

b. $M = \begin{pmatrix} 0.7 & 0.2 & 0.3 \\ 0.2 & 0.5 & 0.1 \\ 0.1 & 0.3 & 0.6 \end{pmatrix}$

c. $P(2) = \begin{pmatrix} 130 \\ 74 \\ 96 \end{pmatrix}$, $P(3) = \begin{pmatrix} 134.6 \\ 72.6 \\ 92.8 \end{pmatrix}$; the distribution seems to settle at about $\begin{pmatrix} 138 \\ 73 \\ 89 \end{pmatrix}$.

4. a. Answers may vary. Sample: We know that $X(n) = \begin{pmatrix} f(n) \\ f(n-1) \end{pmatrix}$. Also, $\begin{pmatrix} 1 & 1 \\ 1 & 0 \end{pmatrix}\begin{pmatrix} f(n-1) \\ f(n-2) \end{pmatrix} = \begin{pmatrix} f(n-1) + f(n-2) \\ f(n-1) \end{pmatrix}$. But $f(n-1) + f(n-2) = f(n)$ by definition, so $\begin{pmatrix} f(n-1) + f(n-2) \\ f(n-1) \end{pmatrix} = \begin{pmatrix} f(n) \\ f(n-1) \end{pmatrix}$. So the

6. Now reverse the process of Exercises 4 and 5. Turn the following matrix equation into a third-order recurrence for the sequence h_n.

$$\begin{pmatrix} h(n) \\ h(n-1) \\ h(n-2) \end{pmatrix} = \begin{pmatrix} 2 & -3 & 4 \\ 1 & 0 & 0 \\ 0 & 1 & 0 \end{pmatrix} \begin{pmatrix} h(n-1) \\ h(n-2) \\ h(n-3) \end{pmatrix}$$

On Your Own

7. Suppose, each year, 3% of the people east of the Mississippi move west and 2% of the people west of the Mississippi move east. Assume initially there are 150 million people on each side. Find the transition matrix and figure out what happens in the long run.

This is not a very realistic problem about American population because it is a closed system: There is no flow in or out of the whole country, and the total population of the country is fixed. But it is always a good idea to start with a simple model. You can set up more realistic models with bigger matrices.

8. Another species of beetle, related to the one in Example 2, also has three life stages: egg, larva, and adult. The reproduction and survival rates for each time period are also the same, with one exception. Instead of 80% of eggs surviving to larvae in one period, 70% of the eggs hatch out as larvae, 2% of the eggs mature so quickly that they emerge as adults at the end of the period, and the rest do not survive.

   a. What is the transition matrix M for this beetle?

   b. Compute M^2, M^3, and so on. Can you find any patterns or stability in long-term growth for this second kind of beetle? Explain. How does the pattern compare with the pattern for the first kind of beetle?

9. Let $M = \begin{pmatrix} 0.6 & 0.25 \\ 0.4 & 0.75 \end{pmatrix}$.

   a. Come up with a scenario involving a fixed population that uses M as the transition matrix.

   b. Suppose that the total population is 260. Assuming that your scenario has a steady state $X = (x, y)$, find it using the method from Exercise 1.

10. **Take It Further** Consider the translation on the line with equation $f(x) = x + 1$. You cannot represent this directly with a transition matrix because of the constant term. But note that

$$\begin{pmatrix} 1 & 1 \\ 0 & 1 \end{pmatrix} \begin{pmatrix} x \\ 1 \end{pmatrix} = \begin{pmatrix} x+1 \\ 1 \end{pmatrix}$$

Then $f(x)$ is the first coordinate of TX, where T is the 2×2 matrix above, and $X = \begin{pmatrix} x \\ 1 \end{pmatrix}$. Therefore $f(f(x))$ is the first coordinate of T^2X, and so on.

   a. Without any use of matrices, determine what 10 iterations of $f(x)$ do to x.

   b. Verify your result with the matrix method.

Habits of Mind

Consider more than one strategy. By going up one dimension, a problem with constant terms becomes a matrix problem. For more explanation of this method, see Exercise 23 in Lesson 4.11.

EXERCISE 5 In Chapter 7 students learn how to find a closed form for a function defined in this way.

EXERCISE 6 As this exercise suggests, every linear recurrence corresponds to a matrix problem. If the recurrence is kth order, then the transition matrix is $k \times k$.

On Your Own

EXERCISE 8 Your students may have a difficult time coming up with predictions about the future behavior of this system by experimentation alone, although it is possible.

Unlike for the previous beetle problem, there is no recurrent diagonal matrix, and unlike for the rental car problem, the matrices do not converge to a limit as the power n increases. Instead the numbers of beetles keep growing. In fact, the ratio of populations in the three life stages do approach a limit, and the ratio of population growth per period also approaches a limit. So, if your students do not discover any patterns by themselves, ask them to look at $\frac{a(n+1)}{a(n)}$ and $\frac{a(n)}{l(n)}$ for increasing values of n. Once students learn the theory of eigenvalues and eigenvectors in a more advanced course, they will not have to try *ad hoc* methods to discover what is going on. The standard procedures of the theory will reveal the limit patterns.

transitive property of equality lets us conclude that

$X(n) = \begin{pmatrix} 1 & 1 \\ 1 & 0 \end{pmatrix} \begin{pmatrix} f(n-1) \\ f(n-2) \end{pmatrix}$ or

$X(n) = \begin{pmatrix} 1 & 1 \\ 1 & 0 \end{pmatrix} X(n-1)$.

b. Let $M = \begin{pmatrix} 1 & 1 \\ 1 & 0 \end{pmatrix}$. Then

$X(9) = \begin{pmatrix} f(10) \\ f(9) \end{pmatrix} =$

$M^9X(0) = \begin{pmatrix} 55 & 34 \\ 34 & 31 \end{pmatrix} \begin{pmatrix} 1 \\ 1 \end{pmatrix} =$

$\begin{pmatrix} 89 \\ 55 \end{pmatrix}$, or $f(10) = 89$.

5. For $n > 1$, $Y(n) = \begin{pmatrix} g(n) \\ g(n-1) \end{pmatrix}$;

$Y(n+1) = \begin{pmatrix} 3 & -4 \\ 1 & 0 \end{pmatrix} Y(n)$.

6. $h(n+1) = 2h(n) - 3h(n-1) + 4h(n-2)$

7. The transition matrix is $\begin{pmatrix} 0.97 & 0.02 \\ 0.03 & 0.98 \end{pmatrix}$; the migrations stabilize with 120 million people in the east and 180 million people in the west.

8. a. $M = \begin{pmatrix} 0 & 0 & 15 \\ 0.7 & 0 & 0 \\ 0.02 & 0.2 & 0 \end{pmatrix}$

b. Answers may vary. Sample: There is no simple pattern, such as M being a diagonal matrix for the first beetle. Pretty soon all entries of the matrix are nonzero, because the generations get "mixed up."

9. a. Answers may vary. Sample: A car rental agency has 2 locations. For cars rented at A, 60% return to A and 40% return to B. For cars rented at B, 25% return to A and 75% return to B.

b. $X = (100, 160)$

10. a. $x \mapsto x + 10$

b. $\begin{pmatrix} 1 & 1 \\ 0 & 1 \end{pmatrix}^{10} \begin{pmatrix} x \\ 1 \end{pmatrix} = \begin{pmatrix} 1 & 10 \\ 0 & 1 \end{pmatrix} \begin{pmatrix} x \\ 1 \end{pmatrix} = \begin{pmatrix} x+10 \\ 1 \end{pmatrix}$

Maintain Your Skills

EXERCISES 12–15 These bugs will be the main subject matter of the next lesson, so students should do all or most of these exercises. Students are likely to go about these exercises in an *ad hoc* manner, not thinking in terms of matrices at all. They are likely to think in terms of cases.

For instance, for all the part (b)'s they may think the bug can go clockwise each time, or can stay put one minute and move the next, and so forth. And of course this approach can work. But get them to ask themselves, first, what more general questions might they want to know about the movements of these bugs, and second, would an *ad hoc* method still work well?

If you analyze completely what can happen in one minute—and this information goes in a single transition matrix—then what happens in n minutes is merely the composition, that is, matrix power. If your students do not get to this sophisticated approach now, they will see it in the next lesson. For a simple hint, ask them now, what do these bug problems have to do with matrices?

Additional Resources

PRINT RESOURCES
- Solution Manual
- Practice Workbook
- Assessment Resources
- Teaching Resources

TECHNOLOGY
- Interactive Textbook
- TeacherExpress CD-ROM
- ExamView CD-ROM
- PHSchool.com

Additional Practice

1. Suppose that each year in a particular city, 4% of the people north of the downtown area move south and 6% of the people south of the downtown area move north. Assume that initially there are 200,000 people on each side of the downtown area. Find the transition matrix and figure out what happens in the long run.

2. A moving truck rental company has three locations A, B, and C. Let $a(n)$ be the number of trucks at A at the end of week n, $b(n)$ be the number at B, and $c(n)$ be the number at C. Suppose the following equations describe the movement of trucks.

$$a(n) = 0.6a(n-1) + 0.25b(n-1) + 0.2c(n-1)$$
$$b(n) = 0.3a(n-1) + 0.45b(n-1) + 0.15c(n-1)$$
$$c(n) = 0.1a(n-1) + 0.3b(n-1) + 0.65c(n-1)$$

a. Describe this situation in words. Then find the transition matrix.
b. Initially, the company has 50 trucks at each location. How many trucks are at each location after two weeks? After three weeks? In the long run?

3. a. Let $M = \begin{pmatrix} 0.85 & 0.25 \\ 0.15 & 0.75 \end{pmatrix}$. Come up with a scenario involving a fixed population that uses M as the transition matrix.

b. Suppose that the total population is 500. Find the steady state $X = (x, y)$ such that $MX = X$.

4. John and Molly take turns tossing a fair coin. The first player to toss tails loses the game. Set up a matrix to find the probability of each event.
a. John loses right away.
b. The game ends in six or fewer moves.
c. Molly loses on the fifth toss.

5. John and Molly decide to use a number cube. The first player to toss a multiple of 3 loses. The first person to toss a 2 wins. Find the probability for each event in this variation.
a. The game ends on the third toss.
b. John loses the game on the fourth toss.
c. Molly wins the game on the fifth toss.

6. Let $A = \begin{pmatrix} 0 & 1 \\ 3 & 5 \end{pmatrix}$ and $B = \begin{pmatrix} 2 & 4 \\ 6 & 0 \end{pmatrix}$. Compute each determinant.
a. $\det(A)$ **b.** $\det(B)$ **c.** $\det(AB)$ **d.** $\det(A^{-1})$ **e.** $\det(B^{-1})$

Practice: For Lesson 4.12, assign Exercises 1–3.

11. Standardized Test Prep A store has two hat displays: a bin and a table. Each day, customers move 15% of the hats from the bin to the table and 65% of the hats from the table to the bin. If each display starts with 200 hats, how many hats are in the bin after 10 days?

A. 76 **B.** 200 **C.** 300 **D.** 324

Go Online PHSchool.com
For additional practice, go to Web Code: bfa-0412

Maintain Your Skills

In Exercises 12–15, you will consider several bugs, each constrained to sit at one vertex of an equilateral triangle. Each minute, each bug either moves to another vertex or stays put, according to certain probabilities.

12. Bug 1 is antsy and does not like to stay put.

No matter where she is now, in one minute she will move with equal probability to one of the other two vertices.

Find the probability of each event.

a. During the next two minutes, she moves clockwise both times.

b. Two minutes from now, she will be one vertex counterclockwise from where she is now.

c. Two minutes from now, she will be back to where she is now.

13. Bug 2 is also antsy, but favors the top vertex. When at vertices L or R, he will go to T $\frac{2}{3}$ of the time and to the other vertex $\frac{1}{3}$ of the time. From T, he will head to L or R with equal probability. The figure summarizes this information.

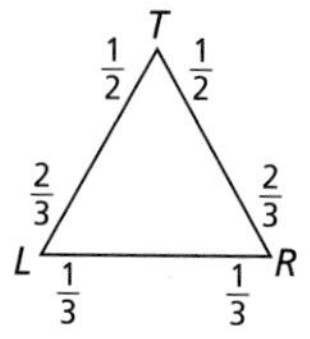

Assume Bug 2 is currently at T. Find the probability of each event.

a. In the next two minutes, Bug 2 moves clockwise both times.

b. Two minutes from now, Bug 2 will be back to where he is now.

c. Same as part (a), but assume Bug 2 starts at L.

d. Same as part (b), but assume Bug 2 starts at L.

14. Bug 3 is lazy and prefers to stay put. No matter where he is now, at the next stage, he will stay put with probability $\frac{1}{2}$ and move to either of the other vertices with probability $\frac{1}{4}$. Find the probability of each event described in exercise 12, parts (a)–(c).

15. Bug 4 prefers to move clockwise. No matter where she is now, she will move one vertex clockwise with probability $\frac{3}{6}$, will stay put with probability $\frac{2}{6}$, and will move one vertex counterclockwise with probability $\frac{1}{6}$. Find the probability of each event described in Exercise 12, parts (a)–(c).

Why is it convenient to call this $\frac{3}{6}$ instead of $\frac{1}{2}$?

Answers

11. D

12. a. $\frac{1}{4}$ **b.** $\frac{1}{4}$ **c.** $\frac{1}{2}$

13. a. $\frac{1}{6}$ **b.** $\frac{2}{3}$ **c.** $\frac{1}{3}$ **d.** $\frac{4}{9}$

14. a. $\frac{1}{16}$ **b.** $\frac{5}{16}$ **c.** $\frac{3}{8}$

15. a. $\frac{1}{4}$ **b.** $\frac{13}{36}$ **c.** $\frac{5}{18}$

4.13 Probability Models

Consider all those bugs from the Lesson 4.12 Maintain Your Skills exercises. They all were moving around among the three corners of a triangle, named T, L, and R. The bugs had different probabilities for the direction of their moves in the next minute. For each bug, you used his or her transition probabilities to figure out the probabilities for his or her location after two minutes. There was nothing special about the number two. You could do it for 10 minutes or 100 minutes, although the calculations would get much longer.

The bug problems are multistep transition problems, just as the other problems in Lesson 4.12 are. Only now the questions are about probabilities instead of numbers of things. So matrix methods ought to work equally well to simplify the notation and the calculations, for any number of minutes.

To see this, here is notation that works for all the bugs at once. Let p_{AB} be the probability of moving to position A from position B in one minute. So, for each bug you have a **probability transition matrix.**

$$M = \begin{array}{c} \\ T \\ L \\ R \end{array} \begin{array}{c} \begin{array}{ccc} T & L & R \end{array} \\ \begin{pmatrix} p_{TT} & p_{TL} & p_{TR} \\ p_{LT} & p_{LL} & p_{LR} \\ p_{RT} & p_{RL} & p_{RR} \end{pmatrix} \end{array}$$

The columns represent where the bug was and the rows represent where the bug goes.

For instance, for Bug 1 the probability transition matrix is

$$M = \begin{array}{c} \\ T \\ L \\ R \end{array} \begin{array}{c} \begin{array}{ccc} T & L & R \end{array} \\ \begin{pmatrix} 0 & \frac{1}{2} & \frac{1}{2} \\ \frac{1}{2} & 0 & \frac{1}{2} \\ \frac{1}{2} & \frac{1}{2} & 0 \end{pmatrix} \end{array}$$

For You to Do

1. Determine the transition matrix for Bug 2 from Exercise 12 of Lesson 4.12.

Now suppose at some time (not necessarily the start), a bug has probabilities p_T, p_L, and p_R of being at T, L, and R, respectively. Note that you are using just one subscript now. You want to figure out the probabilities of the bug being at T, L, and R one minute later. Call these probabilities p'_T, p'_L, and p'_R.

For You to Do

1. $M = \begin{pmatrix} 0 & \frac{1}{2} & \frac{1}{2} \\ \frac{2}{3} & 0 & \frac{1}{3} \\ \frac{2}{3} & \frac{1}{3} & 0 \end{pmatrix}$

Lesson Overview

GOAL

- Analyze sequences of repeated probabilities.

The previous lesson dealt with modeling the change in counts (how many cars in Boston this week; how many cars in Cambridge this week). This lesson deals with modeling change in probabilities (what the probability the bug is at L this minute; what is the probability the bug is at R this minute). The sort of equations you get for the transition from one time period to the next are algebraically the same as before—dot products—so the same matrix-powers method applies.

The application to games, starting with coin tossing between Alice and Bob in Example 2, may interest the students more than the bug problems. The games do add an additional complication: modeling the end of games with *terminal states*. One or more such states need to be in the model, since these models are supposed to be closed—every probability option needs to be considered. In the course of the lesson and the problems, you model this same game with three different matrices of different sizes. What you count as a state depends on what you want to analyze.

Finally, the exercises consider some applications to weather prediction and predicting someone's bad moods. These models are very simple (too simple to be realistic), but they have the advantage of resulting in 2 × 2 matrices. The hard part of this topic is coming up with the transition matrix; this is much easier when there are only two states.

CHECK YOUR UNDERSTANDING
- Core: 1, 2, 4, 5, 7
- Optional: 3, 6

MATERIALS
- graphing calculators
- Blackline Masters 4.13A, 4.13B

HOMEWORK
- Core: 8, 13, 14, 15, 16
- Optional: 9, 10
- Extension: 11, 12

VOCABULARY
- absorbing state
- Markov chain
- probability transition matrix

Launch

This lesson starts more abstractly than the previous lesson. You introduce general formulas rather than numerical examples rather quickly. The Maintain Your Skills exercises with the bugs from Lesson 4.12 should have given the students the context to appreciate these formulas. It is essential that they have done these bug exercises first. Still, you may wish to start more concretely, working out the equations for p'_T, p'_L, and p'_R with numerical examples first. You can use Blackline Master 4.13A to introduce transition matrices.

Explore

For You to Do, p. 379

The zeroes along the main diagonal show that Bug 2 never stays put and always moves. In each case, that represents a probability of staying on the same vertex. In the left column, Bug 2 is starting from the top vertex, and the probabilities of his going to either of the other two vertices are equal. However, in the next two columns, he is starting at either the left vertex or the right vertex. Since he prefers the top vertex, he will go there twice as often, so $p_{TL} = p_{TR} = \frac{2}{3}$. In other words, the probability of going to the tip from the left vertex is equal to the probability of going to the top from the right vertex, and both are equal to $\frac{2}{3}$.

If your students have not studied much probability, you may wish to remind them that there are only three possible events for each starting state. The bug can move to vertex *T*, *L*, or *R*. The probabilities for those three events must sum to 1 for any starting state, so each of the columns in the probability transition matrix must sum to 1.

For Discussion

The reasoning is similar to that in the three-choice display in the text before this section. For instance, the bug can get to *L* one minute later by either coming from *T*, by already being at *L* and staying there, or by coming from *R*.

Example 1

You can use Blackline Master 4.13A to guide students through this example. It is instructive to compare the solution given in this example for parts (b) and (d) of Exercise 13 with the solution students may have used in Lesson 4.12. Perhaps the students will now note that the calculations in Exercise 13 were in the form of dot products and correspond to certain of the calculations used to compute M^2.

To see how these probabilities are related, ask, How can Bug 1 get to, say, vertex *T* one minute later? There are three ways: During that minute she could either stay put if she was at *T* already, she could move there from *L*, or she could move there from *R*. Therefore p'_T is the sum of three terms:

- the probability she stays put at *T* for the minute times the probability she was already at *T*
- the probability she moves to *T* from *L* times the probability she was already at *L*
- the probability she moves to *T* from *R* times the probability she was already at *R*

Therefore, $p'_T = p_{TT}p_T + p_{TL}p_L + p_{TR}p_R$.

Remember...

To find the probability of a compound event, where first one event happens and then another event happens, you multiply the probability of the first event by the probability of the second event.

For Discussion

2. Come up with similar formulas for p'_L and p'_R.

You can write the three equations for p'_T, p'_L, and p'_R as one matrix equation:

$$\begin{pmatrix} p'_T \\ p'_L \\ p'_R \end{pmatrix} = \begin{pmatrix} p_{TT} & p_{TL} & p_{TR} \\ p_{LT} & p_{LL} & p_{LR} \\ p_{RT} & p_{RL} & p_{RR} \end{pmatrix} \begin{pmatrix} p_T \\ p_L \\ p_R \end{pmatrix}$$

If you let P' stand for the column of probabilities on the left and P for the column of probabilities on the right, you get $P' = MP$.

By the same reasoning as in the previous lesson, $P(1) = MP(0)$ and $P(2) = MP(1) = M(MP(0)) = M^2P(0)$.

In general, $P(n) = M^nP(0)$. $P(n)$ is the column of probabilities that the bug is at *T*, *L*, or *R* after *n* minutes.

Example 1

Problem Exercise 13 from Lesson 4.12 was about Bug 2, who prefers vertex *T* of the triangle. Use matrix methods to solve parts (b) and (d) of this exercise again. Then take it further: What can you say about Bug 2's location 3 minutes from now? 4 minutes from now? In the long run?

Solution In part (b), Bug 2 starts at *T*, so

$$P(0) = \begin{pmatrix} 1 \\ 0 \\ 0 \end{pmatrix}$$

The probability transition matrix for Bug 2 is

$$M = \begin{pmatrix} 0 & \frac{2}{3} & \frac{2}{3} \\ \frac{1}{2} & 0 & \frac{1}{3} \\ \frac{1}{2} & \frac{1}{3} & 0 \end{pmatrix}$$

Answers

For Discussion

2. $p'_L = p_{LL}p_L + p_{LT}p_T + p_{LR}p_R$,
$p'_R = p_{RR}p_R + p_{RT}p_T + p_{RL}p_L$

Therefore

$$P(2) = \begin{pmatrix} p_T(2) \\ p_L(2) \\ p_R(2) \end{pmatrix} = M^2 \begin{pmatrix} 1 \\ 0 \\ 0 \end{pmatrix} = \begin{pmatrix} \frac{2}{3} & \frac{2}{9} & \frac{2}{9} \\ \frac{1}{6} & \frac{4}{9} & \frac{1}{3} \\ \frac{1}{6} & \frac{1}{3} & \frac{4}{9} \end{pmatrix} \begin{pmatrix} 1 \\ 0 \\ 0 \end{pmatrix} = \begin{pmatrix} \frac{2}{3} \\ \frac{1}{6} \\ \frac{1}{6} \end{pmatrix}$$

So, the answer to part (b) is $\frac{2}{3}$.

To answer part (d), you compute $M^2 \begin{pmatrix} 0 \\ 1 \\ 0 \end{pmatrix}$. But note that this is just the second column of M^2, which you have already computed. You want the middle entry of that column. So the answer is $\frac{4}{9}$.

To take the problem further, you just need to compute M^3, M^4, and enough higher powers to look for a pattern.

$$M^3 = \begin{pmatrix} \frac{2}{9} & \frac{14}{27} & \frac{14}{27} \\ \frac{7}{18} & \frac{2}{9} & \frac{7}{27} \\ \frac{7}{18} & \frac{7}{27} & \frac{2}{9} \end{pmatrix} \qquad M^4 = \begin{pmatrix} \frac{14}{27} & \frac{26}{81} & \frac{26}{81} \\ \frac{13}{54} & \frac{28}{81} & \frac{1}{3} \\ \frac{13}{54} & \frac{1}{3} & \frac{28}{81} \end{pmatrix}$$

For instance, if Bug 2 starts at T, the probability of his being at T after 3 minutes is $\frac{2}{9}$, and his probability of being at R after 4 minutes is $\frac{13}{54}$. If he starts at L, his probability of being at R after 4 minutes is $\frac{1}{3}$.

This is about as far as you will want to take exact fractions. The denominators are getting too big. The next computation is approximated to three decimal places.

For a long-term pattern, you can compute higher powers of M.

$$M^{10} = \begin{pmatrix} 0.410 & 0.393 & 0.393 \\ 0.295 & 0.303 & 0.303 \\ 0.295 & 0.303 & 0.303 \end{pmatrix} \qquad M^{100} = \begin{pmatrix} 0.400 & 0.400 & 0.400 \\ 0.300 & 0.300 & 0.300 \\ 0.300 & 0.300 & 0.300 \end{pmatrix}$$

It seems that in the long run, Bug 2 has probabilities of 0.4, 0.3, and 0.3 of being at T, L, and R, regardless of where he starts, because the columns of M^{100} are the same.

For Discussion

3. Does this matrix method also answer parts (a) and (c) of Exercise 12 from Lesson 4.12?

For You to Do

4. Figure out where Bug 1 will be after 3 minutes. That is, figure out the probabilities, depending on where she starts. Do the same thing for 10 minutes.

In the examples so far, the moves could go on forever, but many situations have rules that tell you when to stop. These are taken care of in matrix models by **absorbing states.**

For Discussion

3. yes

For You to Do

4. $M^3 = \begin{pmatrix} \frac{1}{4} & \frac{3}{8} & \frac{3}{8} \\ \frac{3}{8} & \frac{1}{4} & \frac{3}{8} \\ \frac{3}{8} & \frac{3}{8} & \frac{1}{4} \end{pmatrix}$;

$$M^{10} = \begin{pmatrix} 0.334 & 0.333 & 0.333 \\ 0.333 & 0.334 & 0.333 \\ 0.333 & 0.333 & 0.334 \end{pmatrix}$$

For Discussion

Parts (a) and (c) are about a specific way to make a transition. For instance, (a) is about one way to go from T to L in two moves. But the matrix model is set up to give only the total probability of moving from T to L in two moves.

Now, for Bug 2, it turns out that two clockwise moves is the only way to get from T to L in two moves, because Bug 2 never stays put. The row-2, column-1 entry of M^2 is $\frac{1}{6}$, which is the correct answer for (a). Likewise, the row-3, column-2 entry of M^2, which is $\frac{1}{3}$, is the correct answer for (c).

Example 2

In all previous transition problems, something was actually moving—bugs, cars, people—or something was changing physically, say eggs into larvae. Here the change is abstract; you change from one state of a game to another. The same mathematics applies!

Harder perhaps for the students is this: it is not so obvious now what the set of states should be. There has got to be some state or states for the game ending, but why not a state "the game just ended," or two end states depending on who won? This issue may come up in class discussion.

In fact, as the rest of the lesson shows, there is no one right model for this game; you use different sorts of endgame states depending on what you want to compute. Tell the students this if they question the model used in Example 2, but also ask them to go with the flow for the moment.

Every problem in this lesson is an example of a Markov chain. One thing is absolutely necessary about the states in order to make a Markov chain matrix: the set of states must be closed, that is, everything that can happen must be covered by some state. Only if this is true will the sum of the probabilities in each column be 1, part of the definition of a Markov chain.

Example 2

Problem Alice and Bob play the following game. They take turns tossing a number cube. The first person to toss a 6 loses. Alice goes first. Find the probability of each event.

a. Alice loses right away.

b. The game ends in 5 or fewer moves.

c. Bob loses on the fourth toss.

Solution To model this problem with a probability transition matrix, you need to identify the states. What happens next depends on who is tossing, but to cover all possibilities, you also need an absorbing state. So, let the three states be

A. Alice is about to toss.

B. Bob is about to toss.

E. The game has ended (just a moment ago or earlier).

Each toss marks a transition. The probability transition matrix is

$$G = \begin{array}{c} \\ A \\ B \\ E \end{array}\begin{array}{c} \begin{array}{ccc} A & B & E \end{array} \\ \begin{pmatrix} 0 & \frac{5}{6} & 0 \\ \frac{5}{6} & 0 & 0 \\ \frac{1}{6} & \frac{1}{6} & 1 \end{pmatrix} \end{array}$$

Take time to make sense of this matrix before you move on.

Consider the first column (the A column), for instance. If Alice is about to toss, either she does toss a 6, with probability $\frac{1}{6}$, and the game passes to the end state, or she does not toss a 6. So with probability $\frac{5}{6}$, the game passes to the state where Bob is about to toss.

Notice that E is an absorbing state. Once the game has ended, it remains ended. It never gets out of state E. Mathematically, this is represented by the fact that the E column is all 0's except for a 1 on the main diagonal.

Think of the game as having infinitely many rounds, but nothing happens in any round after someone tosses a 6.

Let $P(n)$ be the column of probabilities that states A, B, and E occur after n tosses. Then you have

$$P(n) = G^n P(0) \text{ with } P(0) = \begin{pmatrix} 1 \\ 0 \\ 0 \end{pmatrix}$$

The entries in $P(0)$ reflect the fact that Alice goes first. Therefore, $P(n)$ is given by the first column (the A column) of G^n.

a. You have already found the probability of the first event. The probability that Alice loses right away is the probability that the game passes in one step to the E state. This probability is $\frac{1}{6}$.

b. This probability is the entry in column A and row E of G^5.

$$G^5 = \begin{pmatrix} 0 & 0.402 & 0 \\ 0.402 & 0 & 0 \\ 0.598 & 0.598 & 1 \end{pmatrix}$$

Column A says that there is a 0% chance it is Alice's turn, about a 40% chance it is Bob's turn, and about a 60% chance the game is over.

You find that the game ends on or before the fifth toss with probability 0.598.

c. You cannot find this probability directly from any power of G because there is no state for "just lost" (but see Exercise 10). However, for Bob to lose on the fourth toss, he must get the fourth toss and then toss a 6. The probability that he is about to toss in round 4 is the entry in the A column and B row of G^3. Compute G^3, and you will find that this entry is 0.579. Multiply by $\frac{1}{6}$ and you get the probability 0.097.

For You to Do

In the game above, what is the probability that Alice loses?

This is not a question that you can answer with the matrix you used above, because that matrix lumps all losses together into one state, E. So, separate the states. Turn the state E into two absorbing states, "Alice lost" (not necessarily on the most recent toss) and "Bob lost." Now the probability transition matrix is

$$M = \begin{array}{c} \\ \text{A} \\ \text{B} \\ \text{AL} \\ \text{BL} \end{array} \begin{array}{c} \begin{array}{cccc} \text{A} & \text{B} & \text{AL} & \text{BL} \end{array} \\ \begin{pmatrix} 0 & \frac{5}{6} & 0 & 0 \\ \frac{5}{6} & 0 & 0 & 0 \\ \frac{1}{6} & 0 & 1 & 0 \\ 0 & \frac{1}{6} & 0 & 1 \end{pmatrix} \end{array}$$

Explain the entries in this new matrix. Use it to determine the probability of each of the following events. Continue to assume that Alice goes first.

5. Alice loses on or before the fifth toss.
6. Bob loses on or before the tenth toss.
7. Bob loses on the tenth toss.
8. Alice loses.

Answers

For You to Do

5. about 0.363
6. about 0.381
7. about 0.032
8. $\frac{6}{11}$

For You to Do

PROBLEMS 5–8 Blackline Master 4.13B provides a copy of this transition matrix.

Wrap Up

You can use For You to Do Problems 5–8 as a wrap up. However, you may wish to go on to some of the simpler exercises with the whole class, such as Exercise 1 or Exercise 5.

Assessment Resources

Lesson Quiz 4.13

1. Katy and Molly take turns tossing a coin 3 times in a row. The first player to toss heads 3 times in a row loses the game. Set up a matrix to find the probability of each event.
   a. Either Katy or Molly loses after only one turn.
   b. Molly loses on the fifth toss.

2. Katy and Molly decide to use a number cube. The first person to toss a 1 loses. If a person tosses a 3, she gets to toss again right away. Find the probability of each event in this variation.
   a. The game ends on or before the third toss.
   b. Katy loses the game on the fourth toss.

3. Let $A = \begin{pmatrix} -1 & 0 \\ 3 & -3 \end{pmatrix}$ and $B = \begin{pmatrix} -2 & 3 \\ 0 & -1 \end{pmatrix}$. Compute each determinant.
   a. $\det(A)$ b. $\det(B)$ c. $\det(AB)$ d. $\det(A^{-1})$ e. $\det(B^{-1})$

Exercises

HOMEWORK

- Core: 8, 13, 14, 15, 16
- Optional: 9, 10
- Extension: 11, 12

Check Your Understanding

EXERCISES 1–3 Remind students that if M is a transition matrix, then entry pq of M^k is the total probability of all ways to get to state p in k steps from state q. Thus, if an exercise part is about only some of the ways to get in two steps from state p to state q, that question cannot be answered directly by the matrix computation—unless you can argue those are the only ways to get from p to q.

EXERCISE 5 provides an opportunity to save time through clever calculation. For example, once a student has computed M^5, they could simply square that matrix to find M^{10} rather than multiplying by M five more times.

EXERCISE 6 For part (c), ask: what is the probability Bob is in the *same* bad mood 12 hours later, that is, that he never changed his mood? This question is easy to answer, but not by the Markov chain method.

EXERCISE 7 You might ask students to go further and figure out the total probability that Alice loses. This coin game turns out to be unfair. That the game is unfair may surprise some students. If so, get a discussion going.

Exercises Practicing Habits of Mind

Check Your Understanding

Use probability transition matrices to solve the following exercises from Lesson 4.12 again. If you cannot answer some parts of each exercise using matrix methods, explain why.

1. Exercise 12 **2.** Exercise 14 **3.** Exercise 15

4. **Write About It** In every probability transition matrix in this lesson, each column had only nonnegative entries and they summed to 1. Explain why.

Any transition problem in which the matrix has nonnegative entries and each column sums to 1 is a *Markov chain*. Probability transition problems are automatically Markov chains.

5. The weather tomorrow is influenced by the weather today. If it is sunny today, suppose the probability is 0.6 that it will be sunny tomorrow. If it is rainy today, suppose the probability is only 0.3 that it will be rainy tomorrow. Assume that the only choices are sunny or rainy.

Set up this situation as a matrix transition problem: Assume it is sunny today. Find the probabilities of sun and rain at each time.

a. 2 days from now **b.** 5 days from now

c. 10 days from now **d.** in the long run

e. If it is rainy today, find the probability of sunny weather 5 days from now.

6. Everyone has good moods and bad moods. Some people have a very hard time getting out of a bad mood.

Suppose Bob has thought a lot about his mental state and has made the following observations. If he is in a good mood now, the probability he will still be in a good mood in an hour is 0.8. But if he is in a bad mood now, the probability that he will still be in a bad mood in an hour is 0.9.

Assume that Bob has only two moods, good or bad.

a. Describe Bob's moods with a probability transition matrix.

b. Suppose Bob wakes up in a good mood. What is the probability he will be in a good mood 12 hours later?

c. Suppose Bob wakes up in a bad mood. What is the probability he will be in a bad mood 12 hours later?

7. Suppose Alice and Bob take turns tossing a fair coin instead of a number cube. Again Alice goes first. The first player to toss heads loses the game. Set up a matrix. Find the probability of each event you found in Example 2.

Answers

Exercises

1. a. $\frac{1}{4}$ **b.** $\frac{1}{4}$ **c.** $\frac{1}{2}$

2. a. This cannot be answered using a matrix because the matrix does not describe how to get to one vertex counterclockwise in 2 steps.

b. $\frac{5}{16}$

c. $\frac{3}{8}$

3. a. This cannot be answered using a matrix because the matrix does not describe how to get one vertex counterclockwise in 2 steps.

b. $\frac{13}{36}$

c. $\frac{5}{18}$

4. Answers may vary. Sample: Probabilities cannot be negative; each column represents all the possibilities for a particular situation, so the sum of the entries in a column must be 1.

5. The weather transition matrix is $\begin{pmatrix} 0.6 & 0.7 \\ 0.4 & 0.3 \end{pmatrix}$.

a. 0.64; 0.36

b. 0.636; 0.364

c. 0.636; 0.364

d. 0.636; 0.364

e. 0.636; 0.364

6. a. $\begin{pmatrix} 0.8 & 0.1 \\ 0.2 & 0.9 \end{pmatrix}$

b. 0.343

c. 0.671

7. The matrix is $\begin{pmatrix} 0 & \frac{1}{2} & 0 \\ \frac{1}{2} & 0 & 0 \\ \frac{1}{2} & \frac{1}{2} & 1 \end{pmatrix}$.

(1) $\frac{1}{2}$

(2) 0.969 or $\frac{31}{32}$

(3) $\frac{1}{16}$

On Your Own

8. Return to Bug 3 from Exercise 13 of Lesson 4.12. What are the probabilities of where he will be after three moves? After four? In the long run? Do the answers depend on the vertex at which he starts?

9. Return to Bug 4 from Exercise 14 of Lesson 4.12. What are the probabilities of where she will be after three moves? After four? In the long run? Do the answers depend on the vertex at which she starts?

10. Redo Example 2 with five states: Alice about to toss, Bob about to toss, Alice just lost, Bob just lost, and the game ended earlier. Use this matrix to determine the probability that Bob loses in the 4th round and the probability that he loses in the 8th round. Explain why you do not need the five-state matrix to find the probability that Bob loses in the 9th round.

So now you have modeled this same situation with a 3×3 matrix, a 4×4 matrix, and a 5×5 matrix. Depending on what you want to find, different models may work best, even for the same problem.

11. **Take It Further** Alice and Bob slightly change the rules to their number-cube tossing game. If you toss a 6, you still lose. But if you toss a 1, you must toss again right away. In all other cases, the number cube passes to the other player, as before. Find the probability for each event in this variation. Before you compute, decide what matrix model will give you all the answers you want. (Recall that you have used three different models for the original game between Alice and Bob.)
    a. The game ends on or before the fifth toss.
    b. The game ends on or before the fifth toss, and Alice loses.
    c. Bob makes the fifth toss.
    d. Bob loses the game on the fifth toss.
    e. Alice loses the game.

12. **Take It Further** Change the rules for Alice and Bob again.
    - If you toss a 1, you get to toss again right away.
    - If you toss a 2 or a 3, you win.
    - If you toss a 4 or a 5, you pass the number cube to the other player.
    - If you toss a 6, you lose.

    Use these rules to find the probability of each event below. Before computing, decide what matrix model will give you all the answers you want.
    a. The game ends on or before the fifth toss.
    b. The game ends on or before the fifth toss, and Alice loses.
    c. There is a fifth toss, and Bob makes it.
    d. Bob loses the game on the fifth toss.
    e. Alice loses the game.

On Your Own

EXERCISES 8 AND 9 Both Bugs 3 and 4 are equally likely, in the long run, to be anywhere. This was also true of Bug 1, but not of Bug 2. In none of these games are the probabilities symmetric (there is not a $\frac{1}{3}$ chance of going each place the next time). Can students propose reasons why the long-run probabilities were nonetheless sometimes symmetric?

EXERCISES 11–13 Remind students that the more complicated the situation, the more thought they need to give to choosing the states, and the more care they need to give in determining the transition probabilities for the fundamental matrix.

8. $M^3 = \begin{pmatrix} 0.344 & 0.328 & 0.328 \\ 0.328 & 0.344 & 0.328 \\ 0.328 & 0.328 & 0.344 \end{pmatrix}$, $M^4 = \begin{pmatrix} 0.336 & 0.332 & 0.332 \\ 0.332 & 0.336 & 0.332 \\ 0.332 & 0.332 & 0.336 \end{pmatrix}$; in the long run, all the entries will be 0.333, regardless of the starting vertex.

9. $M^3 = \begin{pmatrix} 0.333 & 0.319 & 0.347 \\ 0.347 & 0.333 & 0.319 \\ 0.319 & 0.347 & 0.333 \end{pmatrix}$, $M^4 = \begin{pmatrix} 0.338 & 0.331 & 0.331 \\ 0.331 & 0.338 & 0.331 \\ 0.331 & 0.331 & 0.338 \end{pmatrix}$; in the long run, all the entries will be 0.333, regardless of the starting vertex.

10. P(Bob loses in 4th round) = 0.096; P(Bob loses in 8th round) = 0.047; Bob cannot lose in the 9th round because Alice would be tossing in that round.

11. a. 0.598
b. 0.356
c. 0.311
d. 0.052
e. $\frac{5}{9}$

12. a. 0.969
b. 0.413
c. 0.031
d. 0.005
e. $\frac{3}{7}$

Maintain Your Skills

EXERCISE 15 From this exercise, students may conjecture that, for 2×2 matrices, the product of the determinants is the determinant of the product.

EXERCISE 16 Students may conjecture that the inverse of the determinant is the determinant of the inverse.

Additional Resources

PRINT RESOURCES
- Solution Manual
- Practice Workbook
- Assessment Resources
- Teaching Resources

TECHNOLOGY
- Interactive Textbook
- TeacherExpress CD-ROM
- ExamView CD-ROM
- PHSchool.com

Additional Practice

1. Suppose that each year in a particular city, 4% of the people north of the downtown area move south and 6% of the people south of the downtown area move north. Assume that initially there are 200,000 people on each side of the downtown area. Find the transition matrix and figure out what happens in the long run.

2. A moving truck rental company has three locations A, B, and C. Let $a(n)$ be the number of trucks at A at the end of week n, $b(n)$ be the number at B, and $c(n)$ be the number at C. Suppose the following equations describe the movement of trucks.
$$a(n) = 0.6a(n-1) + 0.25b(n-1) + 0.2c(n-1)$$
$$b(n) = 0.3a(n-1) + 0.45b(n-1) + 0.15c(n-1)$$
$$c(n) = 0.1a(n-1) + 0.3b(n-1) + 0.65c(n-1)$$
   a. Describe this situation in words. Then find the transition matrix.
   b. Initially, the company has 50 trucks at each location. How many trucks are at each location after two weeks? After three weeks? In the long run?

3. **a.** Let $M = \begin{pmatrix} 0.85 & 0.25 \\ 0.15 & 0.75 \end{pmatrix}$. Come up with a scenario involving a fixed population that uses M as the transition matrix.
   b. Suppose that the total population is 500. Find the steady state $X = (x, y)$ such that $MX = X$.

4. John and Molly take turns tossing a fair coin. The first player to toss tails loses the game. Set up a matrix to find the probability of each event.
   a. John loses right away.
   b. The game ends in six or fewer moves.
   c. Molly loses on the fifth toss.

5. John and Molly decide to use a number cube. The first player to toss a multiple of 3 loses. The first person to toss a 2 wins. Find the probability for each event in this variation.
   a. The game ends on the third toss.
   b. John loses the game on the fourth toss.
   c. Molly wins the game on the fifth toss.

6. Let $A = \begin{pmatrix} 0 & 1 \\ 3 & 5 \end{pmatrix}$ and $B = \begin{pmatrix} 2 & 4 \\ 6 & 0 \end{pmatrix}$. Compute each determinant.
   a. $\det(A)$ **b.** $\det(B)$ **c.** $\det(AB)$ **d.** $\det(A^{-1})$ **e.** $\det(B^{-1})$

Practice: For Lesson 4.13, assign Exercises 4–6.

13. Alice gets tired of playing these games with Bob, so she decides to play alone. If she tosses a 2 or 3, she wins. If she tosses a 6, she loses. For any other toss, she tosses again.
   a. What is the probability that Alice wins in four or fewer tosses?
   b. What is the probability that Alice loses in four or fewer tosses?
   c. What is the probability that the game never ends?
   d. What is the probability that Alice wins?

Go Online PHSchool.com

For additional practice, go to Web Code: bfa-0413

14. **Standardized Test Prep** Suppose A and B are both 2×2 invertible matrices, and I is the 2×2 identity matrix. Let $\det A$ represent the determinant of matrix A. Which of the following statements is NOT true?
   A. $\det A = \det A^{-1}$ for all A in which $\det A \neq 0$.
   B. $\det A \cdot \det A^{-1} = 1$ for all A in which $\det A \neq 0$.
   C. $\det B = -1$ if B is a transformation matrix for a reflection over a line that passes through the origin.
   D. $\det I = 1$

Maintain Your Skills

15. Recall that the determinant of a 2×2 matrix $A = \begin{pmatrix} a & b \\ c & d \end{pmatrix}$ is given by $\det(A) = ad - bc$.

   For each pair of matrices, compute

   $\det(A)$ $\det(B)$ $\det(AB)$

   a. $A = \begin{pmatrix} 1 & 2 \\ 3 & 4 \end{pmatrix}, B = \begin{pmatrix} 5 & 6 \\ 7 & 8 \end{pmatrix}$
   b. $A = \begin{pmatrix} -2 & 1 \\ 5 & -3 \end{pmatrix}, B = \begin{pmatrix} 7 & 1 \\ 4 & -2 \end{pmatrix}$
   c. $A = \begin{pmatrix} 6 & 2 \\ 3 & 1 \end{pmatrix}, B = \begin{pmatrix} 4 & 1 \\ 8 & 3 \end{pmatrix}$
   d. $A = \begin{pmatrix} 1 & 2 \\ 2 & 4 \end{pmatrix}, B = \begin{pmatrix} x & y \\ z & w \end{pmatrix}$

Go Online Video Tutor PHSchool.com

Web Code: bfe-0775

16. Recall that if $A = \begin{pmatrix} a & b \\ c & d \end{pmatrix}$ with $\det(A) \neq 0$, then its inverse is
$$A^{-1} = \frac{1}{\det(A)} \begin{pmatrix} d & -b \\ -c & a \end{pmatrix}.$$
   For each matrix, compute $\det(A)$ and $\det(A^{-1})$.

   a. $A = \begin{pmatrix} 3 & 1 \\ 4 & 2 \end{pmatrix}$
   b. $A = \begin{pmatrix} 3 & 10 \\ 1 & 5 \end{pmatrix}$
   c. $A = \begin{pmatrix} 2 & 1 \\ 1 & 2 \end{pmatrix}$
   d. $A = \begin{pmatrix} x & 0 \\ 0 & 1 \end{pmatrix}$ with $x \neq 0$

Answers

13. a. 0.625
b. 0.312
c. 0
d. $\frac{2}{3}$

14. A

15. a. $\det(A) = -2$, $\det(B) = -2$, $\det(AB) = 4$
b. $\det(A) = 1$, $\det(B) = -18$, $\det(AB) = -18$
c. $\det(A) = 0$, $\det(B) = 4$, $\det(AB) = 0$
d. $\det(A) = 0$, $\det(B) = xw - yz$, $\det(AB) = 0$

16. a. $\det(A) = 2$, $\det(A^{-1}) = \frac{1}{2}$
b. $\det(A) = 5$, $\det(A^{-1}) = \frac{1}{5}$
c. $\det(A) = 3$, $\det(A^{-1}) = \frac{1}{3}$
d. $\det(A) = x$, $\det(A^{-1}) = \frac{1}{x}$

Mathematical Reflections

4C

In this investigation, you used matrix multiplication to describe geometric transformations. You also used matrices and matrix multiplication to model situations that change over time. These exercises will help you summarize what you have learned.

1. Use the matrix transformation $X \to AX$ with the matrix $A = \begin{pmatrix} 0 & 1 \\ 1 & 0 \end{pmatrix}$.
   a. Graph the triangle with vertices (2, 1), (4, 1), and (2, 0). Find the image of this triangle after the transformation.
   b. Describe what this transformation does to any point (x, y) in the plane, both algebraically and geometrically.
2. Find a matrix B such that the mapping $X \to BX$ is a 90° clockwise rotation around the origin. Graph the three points from Exercise 1 both before and after this mapping to show the effect of your matrix.
3. Tori sets up a mountain bike rental business with stations at the north and south ends of the town forest. She starts with 50 bikes at each location. She notices that 90% of the bikes that start at the south end and 60% of the bikes that start at the north end are returned to the north station.
   a. Set up a transition matrix for this situation.
   b. How many bikes would you predict to be at each station after 2 weeks?
   c. How many bikes would you predict to be at each station after 4 weeks?
   d. Will this situation settle down in the long term? If so, what number of bikes will be at each station in the steady state?
4. A beetle passes through the life stages of egg, larva, and adult. In any one time period, an adult alive at the beginning of the time period will lay 100 eggs and die. 40% of eggs that are alive at the beginning of a time period will hatch into larvae. The rest will die. 10% of larvae alive at the beginning of a time period will survive to become adults. The rest will die.
   a. Set up a transition matrix for this beetle population.
   b. One adult beetle brings 10 larvae and 20 eggs and colonizes Derman's locker. After 6 time periods, what will Derman find when he opens his locker door?

You can use matrix multiplication to describe the translation of a chess piece across the board.

Mathematical Reflections

1–2. See back of book

3. a. $\begin{pmatrix} 0.6 & 0.9 \\ 0.4 & 0.1 \end{pmatrix}$

b. 67 or 68 bikes at the north end, 32 or 33 bikes at the south end

c. about 69 bikes at the north end, 31 bikes at the south end

d. about 69 bikes at the north end, 31 bikes at the south end

4. a. $\begin{pmatrix} 0 & 0 & 100 \\ 0.4 & 0 & 0 \\ 0 & 0.1 & 0 \end{pmatrix}$

b. 320 eggs, 160 larvae, 16 adult beetles

Mathematical Reflections

EXERCISES 6–8 At the start of the investigation, you may have assigned these as Questions 1–3 for students to think and write about.

5. Wrongway Wainwright plays for the Hapless Losers baseball team. He stands still in the batter's box and earns a walk every time he is at bat. When this happens, the first base coach calls to him until he makes it to first base. From there, however, he is on his own.

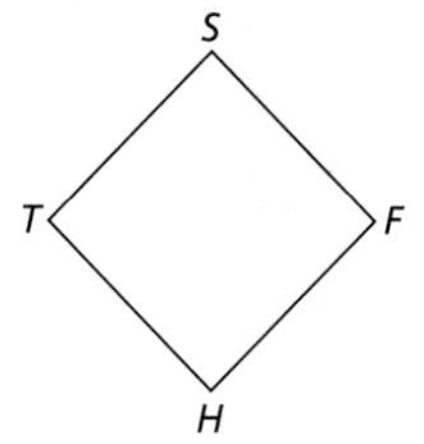

Wrongway prefers to run to the next base in a counterclockwise direction (which is also what his team prefers) and does so 80% of the time. However, the other 20% of the time, he runs clockwise. He will move to a new base each time one of his teammates gets a hit or a walk. Once he gets to home plate (from either direction), he will return to the dugout.

a. Set up a transition matrix for Wrongway that you can use to compute his probability of being at any of the four bases.

b. What are the probabilities for Wrongway being at each of the four bases after two of his teammates have gotten hits?

c. What is the probability that he has reached home plate (one way or another) after three of his teammates have gotten hits?

d. What is the probability that he still has not it made it home after six of his teammates have gotten hits?

6. Is it true that a matrix associated with a reflection must be its own inverse? If so, what are some relationships that must hold for the entries a, b, c, and d in a 2×2 reflection matrix $R = \begin{pmatrix} a & b \\ c & d \end{pmatrix}$?

7. What is an absorbing state, and what does such a state look like in a transition matrix?

8. A transition matrix for a fixed population of 150 is $\begin{pmatrix} 0.2 & 0.7 \\ 0.8 & 0.3 \end{pmatrix}$.

Does this matrix have a steady state? If so, what is it? If not, why not?

Vocabulary

In this investigation, you learned these terms. Make sure you understand what each one means and how to use it.

- **absorbing state**
- **matrix transformation**
- **probability transition matrix**
- **steady state**
- **transition matrix**

Answers

5. a. $\begin{pmatrix} 0 & 0.2 & 0 & 0 \\ 0.8 & 0 & 0.2 & 0 \\ 0 & 0.8 & 0 & 0 \\ 0.2 & 0 & 0.8 & 1 \end{pmatrix}$

b. $P(\text{F}) = 0.16$, $P(\text{T}) = 0.64$, $P(\text{H}) = 0.2$

c. 0.744

d. 0.08192

6. Yes, reflecting over *any* line, and then over that line again, results in the original preimage. If $R = \begin{pmatrix} a & b \\ c & d \end{pmatrix}$ and $R^2 = \begin{pmatrix} 1 & 0 \\ 0 & 1 \end{pmatrix}$, then $a^2 + bc = bc + d^2$ and $|a| = |b|$.

7. Answers may vary. Sample: An absorbing state is a state that ends a game. Its transformation matrix has 0 in every entry except one, which has a 1.

8. The steady state is $\begin{pmatrix} 70 \\ 80 \end{pmatrix}$ because $\begin{pmatrix} 0.2 & 0.7 \\ 0.8 & 0.3 \end{pmatrix}\begin{pmatrix} 70 \\ 80 \end{pmatrix} = \begin{pmatrix} 70 \\ 80 \end{pmatrix}$.

Project: Using Mathematical Habits

More Matrix Operations

In this chapter, you looked at several applications of matrix algebra, including Gaussian Elimination, matrix addition, and matrix multiplication. There are several other operations on matrices that have proved very useful in mathematics and other disciplines. In this project, you will look at three of these operations: determinant, trace, and transpose. First, you will look at the definitions of these operations. In the problems, you will look at some of their properties.

You can carry out each of the three operations on a matrix of any size. They are functions that take a matrix as input and produce either a number or a matrix as output. In this project, you will only worry about 2×2 matrices. Here are the definitions.

Suppose $A = \begin{pmatrix} a & b \\ c & d \end{pmatrix}$.

- The determinant of A, written either as det A or $|A|$, is the number defined by

$$\det A = \begin{vmatrix} a & b \\ c & d \end{vmatrix} = ad - bc$$

- The trace of A, written as Tr(A), is the number defined by

$$\text{Tr}(A) = \text{Tr}\begin{pmatrix} a & b \\ c & d \end{pmatrix} = a + d$$

  Tr(A) is the sum of the diagonal entries in A.

- The transpose of A, written as ${}^tA$, is the matrix defined by

$${}^tA = {}^t\begin{pmatrix} a & b \\ c & d \end{pmatrix} = \begin{pmatrix} a & c \\ b & d \end{pmatrix}$$

  ${}^tA$ is the matrix you get by "flipping" A over its main diagonal.

1. Consider the following system of linear equations.

$$x + 2y = 4$$
$$3x - y = -7$$

Show that

$$x = \frac{\begin{vmatrix} 4 & 2 \\ -7 & -1 \end{vmatrix}}{\begin{vmatrix} 1 & 2 \\ 3 & -1 \end{vmatrix}} \text{ and } y = \frac{\begin{vmatrix} 1 & 4 \\ 3 & -7 \end{vmatrix}}{\begin{vmatrix} 1 & 2 \\ 3 & -1 \end{vmatrix}}$$

2. Consider the following system of linear equations.

$$ax + by = e$$
$$cx + dy = f$$

If $\begin{vmatrix} a & b \\ c & d \end{vmatrix} \neq 0$, show that

$$x = \frac{\begin{vmatrix} e & b \\ f & d \end{vmatrix}}{\begin{vmatrix} a & b \\ c & d \end{vmatrix}} \text{ and } y = \frac{\begin{vmatrix} a & e \\ c & f \end{vmatrix}}{\begin{vmatrix} a & b \\ c & d \end{vmatrix}}$$

3. Consider the parallelogram below with vertices $(0, 0)$, (a, b), (c, d), and $(a + c, b + d)$.

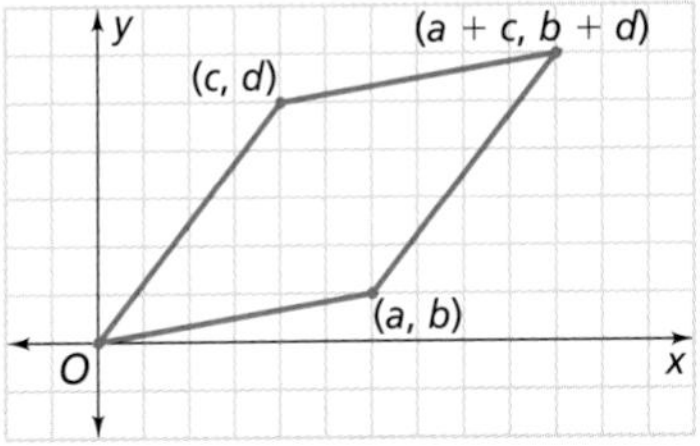

Show that the area of the parallelogram is $\begin{vmatrix} a & b \\ c & d \end{vmatrix}$.

Project

It would be possible to dedicate a whole chapter to covering this material. There are much more conceptual ways to derive most of the solutions to the exercises here. The exercises in this project are special cases of more general results. Here though, your students will develop only the properties of determinant, trace, and transpose that are needed in *Precalculus.* They will do this using 2×2 matrices and algebraic calculations.

You may want to use this project as a take-home assignment. Let students work on the exercises for a few weeks. Then they can carefully write up their results and pass in their reports. After reviewing the reports, you may want to discuss them in class. As extra credit, you might ask students to extend the ideas beyond 2×2 matrices. For trace and transpose, it is pretty clear what to do. For the determinant, students will likely need to do a little investigating, or get some help from you.

EXERCISE 2 This is the 2×2 version of Cramer's Rule. It holds for any square system. The general proof makes use of the multilinear properties of determinant, some of which are developed in this project for 2×2 matrices.

EXERCISE 3 There is a close connection between determinant and area. This exercise is just the beginning. For another way to think about the connection, notice that if a matrix A is applied to the square with vertices $(0, 0)$, $(1, 0)$, $(0, 1)$, and $(1, 1)$, the resulting parallelogram has area that is the area of the square multiplied by det A. In fact, this is true for any polygon (not just the unit square).

Project

1. $x = -\frac{10}{7}$; $y = \frac{19}{7}$

2. $\begin{pmatrix} 1 & 0 & \frac{ed - bf}{ad - bc} \\ 0 & 1 & \frac{af - ec}{ad - bc} \end{pmatrix} = \begin{pmatrix} 1 & 0 & \frac{\begin{vmatrix} e & b \\ f & d \end{vmatrix}}{\begin{vmatrix} a & b \\ c & d \end{vmatrix}} \\ 0 & 1 & \frac{\begin{vmatrix} a & e \\ c & f \end{vmatrix}}{\begin{vmatrix} a & b \\ c & d \end{vmatrix}} \end{pmatrix}$

3. Take the area of the rectangle that the parallelogram fits inside, and subtract off the area of two triangles and two trapezoids. You obtain $(a + c)(b + d) - \frac{1}{2}ab - \frac{1}{2}cd - \left(\frac{b + b + d}{2}\right)c - \left(\frac{c + a + c}{2}\right)b$, which simplifies to $ad - bc = \begin{vmatrix} a & c \\ b & d \end{vmatrix}$.

EXERCISE 4 You may want to encourage students to relate this exercise to Exercise 3. Here is another opportunity to show the connection between determinant and area. If you transform by A and then B, the scale change to the area is the same as if you transform by B and then A.

EXERCISE 6 It is possible to multiply out each product and then take the determinant. Encourage students, though, to use the results of the previous exercises to find these values. It is easier (and more fun).

EXERCISE 9 For a 2×2 matrix with determinant 1, the inverse has the same trace as the original matrix. This, however, is not always true. The trace of a square matrix of any size is the sum of its diagonal entries.

EXERCISE 10 is a special case of the more general theorem that "similar" matrices have the same trace.

This square dance suggests how to find the transpose of a 2×2 matrix.

4. Suppose that A and B are 2×2 matrices. Show that

$$\det(AB) = \det(A)\det(B)$$

5. Suppose P is a matrix that has an inverse. By Exercise 14 from Lesson 4.8, $\det(P) \neq 0$. Show that

$$\det(P^{-1}) = \frac{1}{\det(P)}$$

6. Use the following matrices.

$$A = \begin{pmatrix} 3 & 4 \\ 3 & 8 \end{pmatrix} \quad B = \begin{pmatrix} 3 & 4 \\ 1 & 2 \end{pmatrix} \quad C = \begin{pmatrix} 3 & 4 \\ 6 & 8 \end{pmatrix}$$

Find each value.

a. $\det(AB)$
b. $\det(B^{-1})$
c. $\det(AB^{-1})$
d. $\det(BAB^{-1})$
e. $\det(B^5)$
f. $\det(C^5)$
g. $\det(A^2B^3C)$

7. Suppose A and B are 2×2 matrices and $\det(B) \neq 0$. Show that

$$\det(BAB^{-1}) = \det A$$

8. Suppose A is a 2×2 matrix. Show that

$$\det(A) = \det({}^tA)$$

9. **Write About It** Suppose that A and B are 2×2 matrices. Which of the following statements are true? For those that are true, state the result as a theorem and prove it. For those that are not true, explain why.

a. $\text{Tr}(A + B) = \text{Tr}(A) + \text{Tr}(B)$
b. $\text{Tr}(AB) = \text{Tr}(A)\text{Tr}(B)$
c. $\text{Tr}(AB) = \text{Tr}(BA)$
d. ${}^t(A^{-1}) = ({}^tA)^{-1}$
e. $\text{Tr}(A^{-1}) = \frac{1}{\text{Tr}(A)}$

10. Suppose A and B are 2×2 matrices and $\det(B) \neq 0$. Show that

$$\text{Tr}(BAB^{-1}) = \text{Tr}(A)$$

11. **Take It Further** Use the matrices below.

$$A = \begin{pmatrix} 19 & -12 \\ 20 & -12 \end{pmatrix} \text{ and } P = \begin{pmatrix} 4 & -3 \\ -5 & 4 \end{pmatrix}$$

Find PA^6P^{-1}.

Answers

4. $\det(AB) = (ae + bg)(cf + dh) - (af + bh)(ce + dg) = aecf + aedh + bgcf + bgdh - afce - afdg - bhce - bhdg = ad(eh - fg) - bc(-fg + eh) = (ad - bc)(eh - fg) = \det(A)\det(B)$

5. Since $PP^{-1} = \begin{pmatrix} 1 & 0 \\ 0 & 1 \end{pmatrix}$, $\det(PP^{-1}) = \det\begin{pmatrix} 1 & 0 \\ 0 & 1 \end{pmatrix} = 1$. By Exercise 4, $\det(PP^{-1}) = \det(P)\det(P^{-1})$. Therefore $1 = \det(P)\det(P^{-1})$ and the result follows.

6. **a.** $\det(AB) = \det(A) \cdot \det(B) = 12 \cdot 2 = 24$
b. $\det(B^{-1}) = \frac{1}{\det(B)} = \frac{1}{2}$
c. $\det(AB^{-1}) = \det(A) \cdot \det(B^{-1}) = 12 \cdot \frac{1}{2} = 6$
d. $\det(BAB^{-1}) = \det(B) \cdot \det(A) \cdot \det(B^{-1}) = 2 \cdot 12 \cdot \frac{1}{2} = 12$
e. $\det(B^5) = \det(B)^5 = 2^5 = 64$
f. $\det(C^5) = \det(C)^5 = 0^5 = 0$
g. $\det(A^2B^3C) = \det(A^2) \cdot \det(B^3) \cdot \det(C) = \det(A)^2 \cdot \det(B)^3 \cdot 0 = 0$

7. $\det(BAB^{-1}) = \det(B) \cdot \det(A) \cdot \det(B^{-1}) = \det(B) \cdot \det(A) \cdot \frac{1}{\det(B)} = \det(A)$

8. Let $A = \begin{pmatrix} a & b \\ c & d \end{pmatrix}$. Then $\det(A) = ad - bc$, and $\det({}^tA) = \det\begin{pmatrix} a & c \\ b & d \end{pmatrix} = ad - bc$.

9. **a.** True. Adding matrices is done entry by entry. So, the sum of the diagonal entries of $A + B$ is just a rearranged sum of all four of the diagonal entries of A and B.
b. False. This does not work if $A = \begin{pmatrix} 1 & 2 \\ 3 & 4 \end{pmatrix}$ and $B = \begin{pmatrix} 3 & 2 \\ 3 & 4 \end{pmatrix}$.
c. True. Suppose $A = \begin{pmatrix} a & b \\ c & d \end{pmatrix}$ and $B = \begin{pmatrix} e & f \\ g & h \end{pmatrix}$. Then $AB = \begin{pmatrix} ae + bg & af + bh \\ ce + dg & cf + dh \end{pmatrix}$ and

Chapter 4

Review

Go Online PHSchool.com For vocabulary review, go to Web Code: bfj-0451

In **Investigation 4A,** you learned how to

- solve a system of three equations in three unknowns
- write a system of linear equations in matrix form or translate a matrix into a system of equations
- describe the process of Gaussian Elimination and apply it both by hand and with technology to solve a system

The following questions will help you check your understanding.

1. Solve the following system of equations.

$$\begin{aligned} x - y + 4z &= 7 \\ 2x + 3y - 2z &= 4 \\ x + 2y + 8z &= 6 \end{aligned}$$

2. a. Write the following system of equations as an augmented matrix.

$$\begin{aligned} 2x + 3y + z &= 5 \\ x - y &= 7 \\ x + 2z &= 16 \end{aligned}$$

b. Solve the system using Gaussian Elimination.

3. Find the row-reduced echelon form of this matrix.

$$\left(\begin{array}{ccc|c} 2 & 5 & -3 & -8 \\ 1 & -4 & 0 & 9 \\ 3 & -2 & 1 & 7 \end{array}\right)$$

In **Investigation 4B,** you learned how to

- communicate and prove results about matrices
- compute dot products, sums, differences, products, and inverses of matrices
- interpret and solve problems using matrix calculations

The following questions will help you check your understanding.

4. Various clubs at a high school are selling boxes of cookies for a fundraiser. They are reporting their weekly sales in tables.

Week 1

	Chocolate Chip	Sugar	Oatmeal
Art Club	10	12	5
Spanish Club	8	8	3
Math Club	15	12	10
Science Club	14	8	9

Week 2

	Chocolate Chip	Sugar	Oatmeal
Art Club	18	10	7
Spanish Club	12	9	5
Math Club	19	13	4
Science Club	15	8	11

$BA = \begin{pmatrix} ea + fc & eb + fd \\ ga + hc & gb + hd \end{pmatrix}$. So, $\text{Tr}(AB) = (ae + bg) + (cf + dh)$ and $\text{Tr}(BA) = (ea + fc) + (gb + hd)$.

d. True. ${}^t(A^{-1}) = {}^t\left[\frac{1}{ad - bc}\begin{pmatrix} d & -b \\ -c & a \end{pmatrix}\right] = \frac{1}{ad - bc}\begin{pmatrix} d & -c \\ -b & a \end{pmatrix} = \begin{pmatrix} a & c \\ b & d \end{pmatrix}^{-1} = ({}^tA)^{-1}$.

e. False. For example, if $A = \begin{pmatrix} 1 & 1 \\ 1 & 0 \end{pmatrix}$, then $A^{-1} = \begin{pmatrix} 0 & 1 \\ 1 & -1 \end{pmatrix}$. So $\text{Tr}(A^{-1}) = -1$ and $\frac{1}{\text{Tr}(A)} = 1$.

10. $\text{Tr}(BAB^{-1}) = \text{Tr}((BA)(B^{-1})) = \text{Tr}((B^{-1})(BA)) = \text{Tr}((B^{-1}B)(A)) = \text{Tr}(IA) = \text{Tr}(A)$

11. $\begin{pmatrix} 4096 & 0 \\ 0 & 729 \end{pmatrix}$

Chapter Review

1. $(x, y, z) = \left(4, -1, \frac{1}{2}\right)$

2. a. $\left(\begin{array}{ccc|c} 2 & 3 & 1 & 5 \\ 1 & -1 & 0 & 7 \\ 1 & 0 & 2 & 16 \end{array}\right)$

b. $(x, y, z) = (4, -3, 6)$

3. $\left(\begin{array}{ccc|c} 1 & 0 & 0 & 1 \\ 0 & 1 & 0 & -2 \\ 0 & 0 & 1 & 0 \end{array}\right)$

4. a. The totals, as a matrix, are $\begin{pmatrix} 28 & 22 & 12 \\ 20 & 17 & 8 \\ 34 & 25 & 14 \\ 29 & 16 & 20 \end{pmatrix}$.

b. The Revenue column, as a matrix, is $\begin{pmatrix} 220 \\ 159 \\ 260 \\ 234 \end{pmatrix}$.

a. Copy and complete the following table showing the total sales after two weeks. Use matrix algebra.

Total

	Chocolate Chip	Sugar	Oatmeal
Art Club	■	■	■
Spanish Club	■	■	■
Math Club	■	■	■
Science Club	■	■	■

b. Suppose chocolate chip cookies are $4 per box, sugar cookies are $3 per box, and oatmeal cookies are $3.50 per box. Copy and complete the following table. Use a matrix product to find the entries.

	Revenue ($)
Art Club	■
Spanish Club	■
Math Club	■
Science Club	■

5. Let A be a 2×2 matrix where $a_{ij} = i + j$, B be a 2×3 matrix where $b_{ij} = 2j$, and C be a 3×1 matrix where $c_{ij} = (2i - j)^2$. Find each matrix, if possible.

a. A, B, and C **b.** AB

c. BC **d.** $A + B$

e. $3B$ **f.** A^{-1}

6. Use the following matrix equation.

$$\begin{pmatrix} 3 & 2 \\ 5 & 6 \end{pmatrix}\begin{pmatrix} x \\ y \end{pmatrix} = \begin{pmatrix} 4 \\ 20 \end{pmatrix}$$

a. Find x and y.

b. Translate the matrix equation into a system of linear equations.

In **Investigation 4C,** you learned how to

- make transitions between systems of equations and matrices
- use matrices to model the evolution of a system over time
- analyze sequences of repeated probabilities

The following questions will help you check your understanding.

7. Let $A = \begin{pmatrix} -1 & 0 \\ 0 & 1 \end{pmatrix}$, $B = \begin{pmatrix} 0 & -2 \\ 2 & 0 \end{pmatrix}$, and $C = \begin{pmatrix} 0 & 1 \\ 1 & 0 \end{pmatrix}$.

a. Find $A \cdot \begin{pmatrix} 2 \\ -3 \end{pmatrix}$. What does matrix A do?

b. Find $B \cdot \begin{pmatrix} 2 \\ -3 \end{pmatrix}$. What does matrix B do?

c. Find $C \cdot \begin{pmatrix} 2 \\ -3 \end{pmatrix}$. What does matrix C do?

8. Suppose that the following matrix is a transition matrix for a fixed population.

$$M = \begin{pmatrix} 0.7 & 0.4 \\ 0.3 & 0.6 \end{pmatrix}$$

Assume that the total population is 700 and that there is a steady state $X = (x, y)$. Find X.

9. Marcie baby-sits for a very temperamental toddler named Joey. She has noticed that if Joey is happy when she arrives, the probability that he will still be happy in one hour is 0.6. If he is unhappy when she arrives, the probability that he will still be unhappy in one hour is 0.9.

a. Describe Joey's temperament with a probability transition matrix.

b. If Joey is happy when Marcie arrives, what is the probability that he will still be happy when his parents come home in 4 hours?

Answers

5. a. $A = \begin{pmatrix} 2 & 3 \\ 3 & 4 \end{pmatrix}$, $B = \begin{pmatrix} 2 & 4 & 6 \\ 2 & 4 & 6 \end{pmatrix}$, $C = \begin{pmatrix} 1 \\ 9 \\ 25 \end{pmatrix}$

b. $AB = \begin{pmatrix} 10 & 20 & 30 \\ 14 & 28 & 42 \end{pmatrix}$

c. $BC = \begin{pmatrix} 188 \\ 188 \end{pmatrix}$

d. $A + B$ is not defined.

e. $3B = \begin{pmatrix} 6 & 12 & 18 \\ 6 & 12 & 18 \end{pmatrix}$

f. $A^{-1} = \begin{pmatrix} -4 & 3 \\ 3 & -2 \end{pmatrix}$

6. a. $x = -2$, $y = 5$

b. $3x + 2y = 4$, $5x + 6y = 20$

7. a. $\begin{pmatrix} -2 \\ -3 \end{pmatrix}$; $(x, y) \mapsto (-x, y)$, which is a reflection over the y-axis.

b. $\begin{pmatrix} 6 \\ 4 \end{pmatrix}$; $(x, y) \mapsto (-2y, 2x)$; this is a rotation of 90° counterclockwise and a dilation by the factor 2.

c. $\begin{pmatrix} -3 \\ 2 \end{pmatrix}$; $(x, y) \mapsto (y, x)$; this is a reflection over the line $y = x$.

8. (400, 300)

9. a. $\begin{pmatrix} 0.6 & 0.1 \\ 0.4 & 0.9 \end{pmatrix}$

b. 0.25

Chapter 4 Test

Go Online PHSchool.com — For a chapter test, go to Web Code: bfa-0453

Multiple Choice

1. Which matrix is the row-reduced echelon form of the following matrix?

$$\left(\begin{array}{cc|c} 1 & 2 & 4 \\ 2 & -1 & 3 \end{array}\right)$$

A. $\left(\begin{array}{cc|c} 1 & 0 & 1 \\ 0 & 1 & 1 \end{array}\right)$ **B.** $\left(\begin{array}{cc|c} 1 & 2 & 4 \\ 0 & -5 & -5 \end{array}\right)$

C. $\left(\begin{array}{cc|c} 1 & 0 & 2 \\ 0 & 1 & 1 \end{array}\right)$ **D.** $\left(\begin{array}{cc|c} 1 & 1 & 2 \\ 1 & 1 & 1 \end{array}\right)$

2. Use the following matrix.

$$A = (a_{ij}) = \begin{pmatrix} 4 & -9 & 8 \\ -2 & 7 & 5 \\ 1 & -3 & 0 \end{pmatrix}$$

Find a_{12}.

A. 0 **B.** -9

C. -2 **D.** -36

3. Find the following dot product.

$$(2, 0, 0) \cdot (a, b, c)$$

A. $2a + b + c$ **B.** $2a$

C. 0 **D.** $2(a + b + c)$

4. Translate the following matrix equation into a linear system.

$$\begin{pmatrix} a \\ b \end{pmatrix} = \begin{pmatrix} 7 & 2 \\ -5 & 3 \end{pmatrix}\begin{pmatrix} x \\ y \end{pmatrix}$$

A. $7x - 5y = a$, $2x + 3y = b$ **B.** $7a - 5b = x$, $2a + 3b = y$

C. $7x + 2y = a$, $-5x + 3y = b$ **D.** $7a + 2b = x$, $-5a + 3b = y$

5. Which matrix results in a reflection across the y-axis?

A. $\begin{pmatrix} -1 & 0 \\ 0 & 1 \end{pmatrix}$ **B.** $\begin{pmatrix} 1 & 0 \\ 0 & -1 \end{pmatrix}$

C. $\begin{pmatrix} 0 & 1 \\ 1 & 0 \end{pmatrix}$ **D.** $\begin{pmatrix} 0 & 1 \\ -1 & 0 \end{pmatrix}$

Open Response

6. Solve the following system using Gaussian Elimination.

$$\begin{aligned} x - y + z &= 8 \\ 2y + z &= -12 \\ x + 4z &= 12 \end{aligned}$$

7. Use the matrices below.

$$A = \begin{pmatrix} 4 & -1 \\ 0 & 3 \\ 6 & 5 \end{pmatrix} \quad B = \begin{pmatrix} 10 & -4 \\ 3 & 2 \\ -5 & -20 \end{pmatrix} \quad C = \begin{pmatrix} 1 & 4 \\ -5 & 6 \end{pmatrix}$$

Find each value or matrix, if possible.

a. the size of A **b.** $A + 2B$

c. BC **d.** CB **e.** C^2 **f.** C^{-1}

8. Solve the following matrix equation for x and y.

$$\begin{pmatrix} 3 & -2 \\ 6 & 5 \end{pmatrix}\begin{pmatrix} x \\ y \end{pmatrix} = \begin{pmatrix} 24 \\ 21 \end{pmatrix}$$

9. Let $X \mapsto AX = X'$ and $X = \begin{pmatrix} -2 \\ 5 \end{pmatrix}$. For each matrix A, describe the geometric transformation and find X'.

a. $A = \begin{pmatrix} 0 & 1 \\ 1 & 0 \end{pmatrix}$ **b.** $A = \begin{pmatrix} 1 & 0 \\ 0 & -1 \end{pmatrix}$

c. $A = \begin{pmatrix} 2 & 0 \\ 0 & 2 \end{pmatrix}$ **d.** $A = \begin{pmatrix} -\frac{1}{2} & 0 \\ 0 & \frac{1}{2} \end{pmatrix}$

10. There are two different routes from a certain town into the city. If Stella chooses the first route today, there is a 0.8 probability she will choose the first route tomorrow. If she chooses the second route today, there is a 0.4 probability that she will choose the first route tomorrow.

a. Express this situation as a transition matrix.

b. If Stella chooses the first route Monday, what is the probability that she will choose the second route Friday? Assume she goes to the city each weekday.

c. What can you say about Stella's choice of routes in the long run?

11. What is the process of Gaussian Elimination?

Chapter Test

Assessment Resources

Chapter Test Form A page 1 of 2

Multiple Choice

1. Which matrix is the row-reduced echelon form of the following matrix?

$$\left(\begin{array}{cc|c} 3 & -2 & 0 \\ -1 & 5 & 13 \end{array}\right)$$

A. $\left(\begin{array}{cc|c} 1 & 0 & 2 \\ 0 & 1 & 3 \end{array}\right)$ **B.** $\left(\begin{array}{cc|c} 3 & -2 & 0 \\ -1 & 5 & 13 \end{array}\right)$

C. $\left(\begin{array}{cc|c} 1 & 0 & 3 \\ 0 & 1 & 2 \end{array}\right)$ **D.** $\left(\begin{array}{cc|c} 1 & 1 & 2 \\ 1 & 1 & 3 \end{array}\right)$

2. Use the following matrix.

$$A = (a_{ij}) = \begin{pmatrix} -4 & 0 & 3 \\ -1 & 11 & 15 \\ 10 & -5 & 8 \end{pmatrix}$$

Find a_{23}.

A. -5 **B.** 0 **C.** 8 **D.** 15

3. Find the following dot product.

$$(-2, 3, 1) \cdot (a, b, c)$$

A. $-2a + 3b + c$ **B.** $-6abc$

C. $-6a + b + c$ **D.** $-6(a + b + c)$

4. Translate the following matrix equation into a linear system.

$$\begin{pmatrix} 2a \\ 5b \end{pmatrix} = \begin{pmatrix} 3 & 1 \\ -4 & 7 \end{pmatrix}\begin{pmatrix} x \\ y \end{pmatrix}$$

A. $3x - 4y = 2a$, $x + 7y = 5b$ **B.** $3a + 5b = x$, $-4a + 35b = y$

C. $3x + y = 2a$, $-4x + 7y = 5b$ **D.** $2a + 5b = 4x$, $5a + 2b = 3y$

5. Which matrix results in a reflection across the x-axis?

A. $\begin{pmatrix} -1 & 0 \\ 0 & 1 \end{pmatrix}$ **B.** $\begin{pmatrix} 1 & 0 \\ 0 & -1 \end{pmatrix}$

C. $\begin{pmatrix} 0 & 1 \\ 1 & 0 \end{pmatrix}$ **D.** $\begin{pmatrix} 0 & 1 \\ -1 & 0 \end{pmatrix}$

Also available: Form B

Chapter Test

1. C

2. B

3. B

4. C

5. A

6. $(x, y, z) = (-4, -8, 4)$

7. a. 3×2

b. $\begin{pmatrix} 24 & -9 \\ 6 & 7 \\ -4 & -35 \end{pmatrix}$

c. $\begin{pmatrix} 30 & 16 \\ -7 & 24 \\ 95 & -140 \end{pmatrix}$

d. CB does not exist.

e. $\begin{pmatrix} -19 & 28 \\ -35 & 16 \end{pmatrix}$

f. $\begin{pmatrix} \frac{3}{13} & -\frac{2}{13} \\ \frac{5}{26} & \frac{1}{26} \end{pmatrix}$

8. $x = 6$, $y = -3$

9. a. A reflects a point over the line given by $y = x$; $X' = \begin{pmatrix} 5 \\ -2 \end{pmatrix}$

b. A reflects a point over the x-axis; $X' = \begin{pmatrix} -2 \\ -5 \end{pmatrix}$

c. A dilates a figure by the factor 2; $X' = \begin{pmatrix} -4 \\ 10 \end{pmatrix}$

d. A reflects a figure over the y-axis and dilates it by the factor $\frac{1}{2}$; $X' = \begin{pmatrix} 1 \\ \frac{5}{2} \end{pmatrix}$

10. a. $M = \begin{pmatrix} 0.8 & 0.4 \\ 0.2 & 0.6 \end{pmatrix}$

b. 0.325

c. In the long run, the commuter will choose the first route 66.7% of the time and will choose the second route 33.3% of the time.

11. Answers may vary. Sample: You make an augmented matrix, then perform operations on rows to produce the row-reduced echelon form of the augmented matrix.

Cumulative Review

Assessment Resources

Quarter Test — page 1 of 2

Multiple Choice

1. What is the value of $(5 + \sqrt{-2})(5 - \sqrt{-2})$?
   A. 21 B. 23 C. 25 D. $25\sqrt{2}$

2. Which complex number z makes the product $z(-4 - 2i)$ a real number?
   A. $-4 + 2i$ B. $-4 - 2i$ C. $-2i$ D. $2i$

3. Which of the following complex numbers is equivalent to $\frac{5 + 4i}{5 - 4i}$?
   A. $\frac{5 + 4i}{41}$ B. $\frac{25 - 4i}{-41}$ C. $\frac{9 + 40i}{9}$ D. $\frac{9 + 40i}{41}$

4. What is the solution to the following system?
   $$5x + 4y = 8$$
   $$-x + 2y = -10$$
   A. $(-3, 1)$ B. $(1, -2)$ C. $(4, -3)$ D. $(8, 5)$

5. Find the dot product $(2, -5, 3) \cdot (x, y, z)$.
   A. $2x - 5y + 3z$ B. $3x - 5y + 2z$
   C. $-10(xyz)$ D. 0

6. There are two different routes to get out of a city. If Sally chooses the first route today, there is a 0.8 probability she will choose the first route tomorrow. If Sally chooses the second route today, there is a 0.4 probability she will choose the first route tomorrow. Which of the following matrices is the transition matrix for this situation?
   A. $(0.8 \quad 0.4)$ B. $\begin{pmatrix} 0.8 & 0.4 \\ 0.2 & 0.6 \end{pmatrix}$ C. $\begin{pmatrix} 0.8 & 0.4 \\ 0.8 & 0.4 \end{pmatrix}$ D. $\begin{pmatrix} 0.2 & 0.8 \\ 0.4 & 0.6 \end{pmatrix}$

Open Response

7. Let $z = 4 + i$ and $w = 2 - 3i$.
   a. Find $z \cdot w$.
   b. On the complex plane, graph z, w, and $z \cdot w$ as vectors.
   c. Complete the table at the right.

	$a + bi$	Magnitude	Direction
z	$4 + i$		
w	$2 - 3i$		
$z \cdot w$			

Chapter 4

Cumulative Review

Multiple Choice

1. Simplify $\sqrt{3} \cdot \sqrt{-27}$.
   A. 9 **B.** -9 **C.** $9i$ **D.** $-9i$

2. Suppose $z = -3 + 2i$. Find $z - \overline{z}$.
   A. $-6 + 4i$ **B.** $4i$
   C. 0 **D.** $-12i$

3. If $z = a + bi$ is in Quadrant II, then $-z$ is in which quadrant?
   A. I **B.** II **C.** III **D.** IV

4. Simplify $|-5 + 4i|$.
   A. 4 **B.** 5 **C.** $\sqrt{41}$ **D.** -1

5. If one solution of a quadratic equation is $3 - 4i$, which of the following numbers must be the other solution?
   A. $3 + 4i$ **B.** $-3 + 4i$
   C. $-3 - 4i$ **D.** 5

Open Response

6. **a.** Find the solutions of $x^4 - 81 = 0$ that are in $\mathbb{R}$.
   b. Find the solutions of $x^4 - 81 = 0$ that are in $\mathbb{C}$ but not in $\mathbb{R}$.

7. Solve each equation over $\mathbb{C}$. Express your answer in the form $a + bi$, where a and b are real numbers.
   a. $z + (3 - 5i) = -9 + 2i$
   b. $z \cdot (6 - 4i) = 1$

8. Let $z = \sqrt{3} + i$ and $w = 4i$.
   a. Find $z \cdot w$.
   b. On the complex plane, graph z, w, and $z \cdot w$.
   c. Find the magnitude and direction of z, w, and $z \cdot w$.

9. A complex number z has magnitude 3 and direction 120°. Find the magnitude and direction of each number.
   a. z^2 **b.** z^3 **c.** z^4

10. Find the magnitude and direction of all the solutions to the equation $x^4 - 16 = 0$.

11. Rewrite the matrix $\left(\begin{array}{cc|c} 2 & -1 & 5 \\ 1 & 3 & 8 \end{array}\right)$ in row-reduced echelon form.

12. Let $A = (a_{ij}) = \begin{pmatrix} 3 & 2 & 0 \\ -4 & 6 & -1 \\ 1 & 5 & 2 \end{pmatrix}$. Find a_{13} and a_{21}.

13. Simplify $(5, 7, -1) \cdot (a, b, c)$.

14. Rewrite each matrix equation as a linear system of equations.
    a. $\begin{pmatrix} 3a \\ 7b \end{pmatrix} = \begin{pmatrix} 2 & 5 \\ -1 & 4 \end{pmatrix}\begin{pmatrix} x \\ y \end{pmatrix}$
    b. $\begin{pmatrix} -a \\ 2b \\ 5c \end{pmatrix} = \begin{pmatrix} 4 & 3 & -1 \\ 2 & 8 & 5 \\ 6 & -3 & 1 \end{pmatrix}\begin{pmatrix} x \\ y \\ z \end{pmatrix}$

15. What matrix results in a reflection across the y-axis?

16. What matrix results in a counterclockwise rotation of 90°?

17. Solve the following system using Gaussian Elimination.
    $$4x + 8z = 0$$
    $$3x - 2y + z = 0$$
    $$-2x + y - z = -1$$

18. Use the following matrices.
    $A = \begin{pmatrix} 3 & -2 & 1 \\ 5 & 0 & 4 \end{pmatrix}$ $B = \begin{pmatrix} -4 & 2 \\ 0 & 3 \end{pmatrix}$ $C = \begin{pmatrix} 5 & -6 \\ 9 & 2 \end{pmatrix}$
    Find each matrix, if possible.
    a. $B + C$ **b.** AC **c.** CB
    d. A^{-1} **e.** B^{-1}

Answers

Cumulative Review

1. C **2.** B **3.** D **4.** C **5.** A

6. a. The real solutions are $x = 3$ and $x = -3$.
b. The solutions that are in $\mathbb{C}$ but not in $\mathbb{R}$ are $x = 3i$ and $x = -3i$.

7. a. $z = -12 + 7i$ **b.** $z = \frac{3}{26} + \frac{1}{13}i$

8. See back of book.

9. a. z^2: magnitude = 9, direction = 240°
b. z^3: magnitude = 27, direction = 360°
c. z^4: magnitude = 81, direction = 480°

10. The solutions all lie on a circle of radius 4 in the complex plane. They are equally spaced around the origin. Since the polynomial is degree 4, it has 4 solutions. All 4 have magnitude of 4 and their directions are 0°, 90°, 180° and 270°. None lie within Quadrant I.

11. $\begin{pmatrix} 1 & 0 & 3.286 \\ 0 & 1 & 1.571 \end{pmatrix}$

12. $a_{13} = 0$, $a_{21} = -4$

13. $5a + 7b - c$

14. a. $3a = 2x + 5y$
$7b = -x + 4y$
b. $-a = 4x + 3y - z$
$2b = 2x + 8y + 5z$
$5c = 6x - 3y + z$

15. $\begin{pmatrix} -1 & 0 \\ 0 & 1 \end{pmatrix}$ **16.** $\begin{pmatrix} 0 & -1 \\ 1 & 0 \end{pmatrix}$

17. The solution is $(4, 5, -2)$.

18. a. $\begin{pmatrix} 1 & -4 \\ 9 & 5 \end{pmatrix}$
b. not possible
c. $\begin{pmatrix} -20 & -8 \\ -36 & 24 \end{pmatrix}$
d. not possible
e. $\begin{pmatrix} -\frac{1}{4} & \frac{1}{6} \\ 0 & \frac{1}{3} \end{pmatrix}$

19. $x = 2$, $y = 8$

19. Solve the following equation for x and y.

$$\begin{pmatrix} y \\ y-3 \end{pmatrix} = \begin{pmatrix} 4x \\ 2x+1 \end{pmatrix}$$

20. Let $X \mapsto AX = X'$ and $X = \begin{pmatrix} 5 \\ -2 \end{pmatrix}$. For each matrix A, describe the geometric transformation and find X'.

a. $A = \begin{pmatrix} 0 & -1 \\ -1 & 0 \end{pmatrix}$ b. $A = \begin{pmatrix} 1 & 0 \\ 0 & -1 \end{pmatrix}$

c. $A = \begin{pmatrix} -4 & 0 \\ 0 & 4 \end{pmatrix}$ d. $A = \begin{pmatrix} 3 & 0 \\ 0 & 5 \end{pmatrix}$

21. There are only two exits that buses can take to leave a college campus. Suppose each bus driver leaves the campus once per day. If a driver chooses the first exit today, there is a 0.3 probability she will choose the first exit tomorrow. If a driver chooses the second exit today, there is a 0.6 probability that she will choose the first exit tomorrow.

a. Express this situation as a probability transition matrix.

b. If a driver chooses the first exit Monday, what is the probability that she will choose the first exit again on Thursday?

c. What can you determine about a driver's choice of exits in the long run?

22. Copy and complete this difference table.

Input, n	Output, $a(n)$	Δ	Δ^2
0	■	4	1
1	9	■	1
2	■	■	1
3	■	■	
4	■		

23. Use the input-output table for the function $a(n)$. The function has a constant first difference. Find $a(50)$ and $a(100)$.

Input, n	Output, $a(n)$
0	83
1	■
2	■
3	■
4	■
5	−2

24. Find a recursive function that agrees with the following table of values.

Input, n	Output, $a(n)$
0	−1
1	4
2	9
3	14
4	19

25. Find the mean absolute error, mean squared error, and standard error for this data set, using the line with equation $y = 2x + 5$.

x	y
0	4
1	5
2	6
3	7
4	8

26. Use the following function definitions.

$f(x) = 2x^2 - 3$

$g(x) = -5x + 1$

Find each value.

a. $f(-2)$ b. $f \circ g(3)$

c. $g \circ f(x)$ d. $g^{-1}(x)$

27. Factor each polynomial.

a. $81x^2 - 49y^2$ b. $64x^3 + 27y^3$

28. Let $f(x) = 4x + 1$. Find the inverse of f and show that $f \circ f^{-1}(x) = x$.

29. Let $p(x) = 2x^3 - x^2 + 4x - 1$.

a. Find the quotient and remainder when you divide $p(x)$ by $x + 1$.

b. Use your answer from part (a) to find $p(-1)$.

30. Factor each polynomial over $\mathbb{Z}$.

a. $5x^2 - 16x + 12$

b. $6x^2 + 21x + 9$

c. $9x^4 - 35x^2 - 4$

Assessment Resources

Midyear Test — page 1 of 2

Multiple Choice

1. Which line best fits the data in the graph?

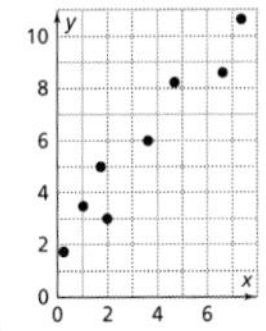

A. $y = 2x + 2$ B. $y = x + 4$
C. $y = 2x + 5$ D. $y = 1.5x + 3$

2. When you divide $p(x) = 2x^3 - 4x^2 - 3x + 1$ by $x - 3$, what is the remainder?
A. −8 B. −3
C. 10 D. 12

3. If $3 + i$ is a root of the polynomial $x^3 + 6x^2 + 12x + 9 = 0$, which is another root?
A. $-3 + i$ B. $3 - i$ C. $-3i$ D. $3i$

4. What is the value of $\sqrt{-8} \cdot \sqrt{50}$?
A. 20 B. −20 C. $20i$ D. $-20i$

5. Suppose $z = 4y_1 - 3y_2$ and $y_1 = -2x$, $y_2 = 5x$

Express z in terms of x.
A. $7x$ B. $3x$ C. $-11x$ D. $-23x$

6. What is the solution to the following system?

$$-2x + y = 4$$
$$3x - 2y = 6$$

A. (4, 6) B. (−14, −24) C. (3, 12) D. (−2, 3)

Open Response

7. Make a difference table of the following function with inputs from 0 to 4.

$$a(n) = \begin{cases} 5 & \text{if } n = 0 \\ a(n-1) + 3n - 2 & \text{if } n > 0 \end{cases}$$

Include enough columns to show a constant difference. Then find a closed-form function that agrees with your table.

8. Lou can put $1500 down and pay $520 per month on a car loan. He can get a 4-year loan at 5% interest. How much can Lou afford to pay for a car?

Also available: Form B

20. a. $AX = \begin{pmatrix} 2 \\ -5 \end{pmatrix}$; this is a reflection over the line $y = -x$.

b. $AX = \begin{pmatrix} 5 \\ 2 \end{pmatrix}$; this is a reflection over the x-axis.

c. $AX = \begin{pmatrix} -20 \\ -8 \end{pmatrix}$; this is a dilation by the factor 4 and reflects over the y-axis.

d. $AX = \begin{pmatrix} 15 \\ -10 \end{pmatrix}$; this matrix scales x by the factor 3 and y by the factor 5.

21. a. $M = \begin{pmatrix} 0.3 & 0.6 \\ 0.7 & 0.4 \end{pmatrix}$

b. $M^2 = \begin{pmatrix} 0.51 & 0.42 \\ 0.49 & 0.58 \end{pmatrix}$; therefore, the probability is 0.49.

c. The probabilities within the matrix stabilize. In the long run a driver will chose the first exit 46.7% of the time and the second exit 53.3% of the time.

22. See back of book.

23. $a(50) = -767$; $a(100) = -1617$

24. The recursive function that agrees with the table's values is $a(n) = \begin{cases} -1 & \text{if } n = 0 \\ a(n-1) + 5 & \text{if } n > 0 \end{cases}$

25. The mean absolute error is 3.0
The mean squared error is 1.0.
The standard error is 1.0.

26. a. $f(-2) = 5$

b. $f \circ g(3) = 389$

c. $g \circ f(x) = -10x^2 + 16$

d. $g^{-1}(x) = -\frac{1}{5}x + \frac{1}{5}$

27. See back of book.

28. Given the function $f(x) = 4x + 1$, you have $f^{-1}(x) = \frac{1}{4}x - \frac{1}{4}$. Therefore, $f \circ f^{-1}(x) = 4\left(\frac{1}{4}x - \frac{1}{4}\right) + 1 = x$.

29. a. The quotient is $2x^2 - 3x + 7$ and the remainder is $\frac{-8}{x+1}$.

b. $p(-1) = -8$

30. See back of book.

Chapter 5 Exponential and Logarithmic Functions

In this chapter, students extend the definition of exponents to include rational and real-valued exponents. They make this extension in a way that preserves the laws of exponents. Along the way they review properties of exponential functions that they learned in CME Project *Algebra 1*. Students also graph and tabulate exponential functions, eventually proving that such functions are one-to-one and, therefore, have inverse functions. Finally, they investigate the inverse functions of exponential functions, logarithms, learn to evaluate logarithms in any base, to use logarithms to solve problems, and to understand the properties of logarithms.

Chapter Overview

INVESTIGATION 5A, *Working with Exponents,* has students extend the set of allowable exponents to all real numbers.

INVESTIGATION 5B, *Exponential Functions,* has students work with exponential functions.

INVESTIGATION 5C, *Logarithmic Functions,* has students investigate logarithmic functions and their relationship to exponential functions.

For more information on the investigations, see

- Chapter Road Map, pp. 396–397
- Investigation Road Maps, pp. 398, 424, 460

PROJECT The Project near the end of the chapter is optional. You can assign the Project at any time during the chapter depending on how often and how long you feel students should work on it.

DAILY PLANNER DAILY PLANNER DAILY PL

Pacing Suggestions and Materials

Investigation 5A *Working with Exponents*

DAY	LESSON	HOMEWORK
1	5.1 Getting Started Core: 1, 2, 4, 5 Optional: 3	Core: 6, 7, 8, 9 Optional: 11; Extension: 10
2	5.2 Laws of Exponents Core: 1, 2, 3, 4, 7, 8, 9, 11 Optional: 5, 6, 10, 12	Core: 13, 14, 15, 18, 21, 22, 23 Optional: 16, 17, 19, 20, 24
3	5.3 Zero and Negative Exponents Core: 1, 2, 3, 4a–e, 7, 8, 9 Optional: 5, 6; Extension: 4f	Core: 10, 11, 13, 15, 17, 18, 19, 21 Optional: 12, 14, 16, 20, 22, 23, 24
4	5.4 Sequences and Operations Core: 1, 2, 3, 4, 5, 8, 9 Optional: 6a, 7; Extension: 6b	Core: 10, 11, 12, 13, 15, 17 Optional: 14a, 16, 19, 20, 21 Extension: 14b, 18
5	5.5 Defining Rational Exponents Core: 1, 2, 3, 4, 6 Optional: 7; Extension: 5	Core: 9, 10, 11, 13, 14, 15, 16 Optional: 8, 17, 18; Extension: 12

Investigation 5B *Exponential Functions*

DAY	LESSON	HOMEWORK
1	5.6 Getting Started Core: 1, 2, 3, 4, 5, 6, 7, 8, 9 Optional: none; Extension: 10	Core: 11, 12, 13, 14, 15, 16, 18 Optional: 17, 19
2	5.7 Graphs of Exponential Functions Core: 1, 2, 3a, 5, 6, 7, 8, 9 Optional: 4, 10; Extension: 3b	Core: 11, 12, 13, 14, 15, 16, 17, 18, 20 Optional: 21, 22; Extension: 19
3	5.8 Tables of Exponential Functions Core: 1, 2, 3, 4, 5, 6, 7 Optional: none; Extension: 8	Core: 9, 10, 11, 12, 13, 14 Optional: 15, 16, 17, 18
4	5.9 Properties of Exponential Functions Core: 1, 2, 3, 4, 5, 6, 7 Optional: 8; Extension: 9	Core: 10, 11, 12, 13, 14, 17, 19 Optional: 15, 16, 20, 21 Extension: 18
5	5.10 Exponential Functions, One-to-One Core: 1, 2, 3, 4, 6, 7 Optional: 5, 8; Extension: 9	Core: 10, 11, 12, 13, 15, 16, 17 Optional: 18, 19; Extension: 14

NOTES	MATERIALS
	• graphing calculators • Blackline Master 5.1
Depending on students' backgrounds, you may be able to combine this lesson and the next.	• CAS (recommended) • graphing calculators
	• graphing calculators • Blackline Master 5.3
	• graphing calculators
	• graph paper • graphing calculators

NOTES	MATERIALS
	• graph paper • graphing calculators • Blackline Master MC1
	• graph paper • graphing calculators • Blackline Masters 5.7A, 5.7B
	• CAS (recommended) • graph paper • graphing calculators
	• graph paper • graphing calculators • spreadsheet software • Blackline Master 5.9
	• CAS (recommended) • graph paper • graphing calculators

Mathematics Background

APPLICATIONS One reason that it is important to study exponential and logarithmic functions is that functions of these two types are useful in describing many commonly-occurring situations. Some examples of exponential models include population growth, radioactive decay, electrical charge in a capacitor, temperature change, finding effective dosages for medication, and compound interest. Of course, there are also many mathematical applications of exponential functions.

The inverse of an exponential function is a logarithmic function, so logarithms are immediately useful when students solve exponential equations where the exponent is unknown. Without logarithms, you can solve this type of equation only through trial and error. Logarithmic scales, such as the Richter scale for earthquake magnitude, make widely ranging values easier to understand and compare. The nature of the logarithmic scale means that numbers that vary from 1 to 1,000,000, for example, are collapsed down to a range from 0 to 6. Graphing data on graph paper where you measure one or both axes in a logarithmic scale is useful in determining whether the data follows an exponential trend and for finding the particular exponential function that best matches the data.

EXTENSION In this chapter, students use mathematical extension again to extend the set of numbers that you can use as exponents. In CME Project *Algebra 1*, students worked through the process of extending from allowing only positive integers as exponents to allowing any integer, including zero. In this course, students review that process and extend the set to include rational numbers and, then, all real numbers.

Students extend to the rational numbers with the same goal as the extension to all integers—by making choices for definitions that preserve the laws of exponents. Students see that they should define $x^{\frac{1}{2}}$ in such a way as to make $x^{\frac{1}{2}} \cdot x^{\frac{1}{2}} = x^{\frac{1}{2}+\frac{1}{2}} = x^1 = x$. In other words, $x^{\frac{1}{2}}$ has to be an expression that, when squared, is equal to x. Students have already encountered an expression that behaves in this way. Since $(\sqrt{x})^2 = x$, it makes sense to define $x^{\frac{1}{2}} = \sqrt{x}$. Similar logic allows students to interpret any expression of the form $b^{\frac{p}{q}}$ where p and q are integers with $q \neq 0$ and b is a positive real number.

To think about how to evaluate expressions with irrational exponents, however, students must stretch their thinking about limits. To make sense of an expression such as $5^{\sqrt{3}}$, you ask students to think about rational numbers on either side of

continued on p. 396c

continued from p. 396b

$\sqrt{3}$. For example, $\sqrt{3}$ is between 1.7 and 1.8. This means that, because the function $f(x) = 5^x$ is strictly increasing—a fact that is later proven in the chapter—$5^{1.7} < 5^{\sqrt{3}} < 5^{1.8}$.

Terminating decimals are good rational numbers to use in this context, because students can use their calculator's decimal approximation of $\sqrt{3}$ to make appropriate choices.

As students use closer and closer rational number approximations p and q to "surround" $\sqrt{3}$, they will see the values of 5^p and 5^q get closer to each other. However, it is still a big step in intuition to say, "As the approximations p and q get closer to each other and to $\sqrt{3}$, the values of 5^p and 5^q are both approaching some number. This is the number chosen as the value of $5^{\sqrt{3}}$." As students gain experience with numerical examples, and with using their calculators to compute expressions with irrational exponents, this idea will feel natural. They have, after all, been using decimal approximations like these to represent irrational numbers such as $\sqrt{3}$ and π for a long time.

THE NATURAL LOGARITHM In CME Project *Precalculus*, students continue their study of exponential and logarithmic functions to include the natural logarithm, which has as its base the Euler constant, $e \approx 2.7182818\ldots$, and its inverse function $y = e^x$. These two functions are extremely interesting mathematically, as is the number e, especially as students approach the study of calculus. $\ln a$, the natural logarithm of a constant $a > 0$ is equal to the area under the curve (the integral) of the graph of $y = \frac{1}{x}$ from $x = 1$ to $x = a$. You can also express the natural logarithm simply as a Taylor series. The function e^x is its own derivative, which means that the slope of the graph of the curve $y = e^x$ at any point is equal to the y-coordinate of that point. And, surprisingly, e pops up in one of the most astounding identities in all of mathematics—the Euler identity, $e^{i\pi} + 1 = 0$.

Pacing Suggestions and Materials

Investigation 5C *Logarithm Functions*

DAY	LESSON	HOMEWORK
1	5.11 Getting Started Core: 1, 2, 3, 4, 5, 6, 7, 9 Optional: 8; Extension: 10	Core: 11, 12, 13, 14, 15, 16, 17, 18 Optional: 19
2	5.12 Defining Logarithms Core: 1, 2, 3, 4, 5, 6, 7, 8, 9 Optional: none; Extension: 10	Core: 11, 12, 13, 14, 15, 16, 17, 20 Optional: 18, 21, 22; Extension: 19
3	5.13 Laws of Logarithms Core: 1, 2, 3, 4, 5, 6, 7, 12 Optional: 8, 9, 10, 11; Extension: 13, 14	Core: 15, 16, 17, 18, 19, 20, 21, 22, 23, 26, 28 Optional: 24, 25a–b, 29; Extension: 25c, 27
4	5.14 Graphing Logarithmic Functions Core: 1, 2, 3, 4, 6 Optional: 5; Extension: 7	Core: 8, 9, 10, 11, 13, 15 Optional: 12, 16; Extension: 14
5	5.15 The Logarithmic Scale Core: 1, 2, 3, 4, 5, 7 Optional: 6	Core: 8, 10, 11 Optional: 9a–b, 12, 14, 15, 16 Extension: 9c, 13

NOTES	MATERIALS
	• graph paper • graphing calculators • Blackline Master 5.11
	• graph paper • graphing calculators • Blackline Master 5.12
	• graphing calculators • Blackline Master 5.13
	• CAS (recommended) • graph paper • graphing calculators • Blackline Master 5.14
	• graph paper • graphing calculators • log-log graph paper • semilog graph paper • Blackline Masters 5.15A–D

Developing Students' Mathematical Habits

Key mathematical habits in this chapter include:

EXTENSION By making strategic choices that preserve the laws of exponents, students extend the set of numbers that can be used as exponents to include all real numbers.

VISUALIZATION Students use the graphs of exponential and logarithm functions to conjecture critical properties of these functions.

LOGICAL REASONING To solve problems, students reason about exponential and logarithmic functions using the laws of exponents and the laws of logarithms.

Chapter Vocabulary and Notation

The following list gives key vocabulary and notation used in the chapter. Selected new vocabulary and notation items are shown in boldface on the student page.

- arithmetic sequence, p. 412
- b^n, p. 402
- base, p. 428
- change-of-base rule, p. 466
- closed-form definition, p. 438
- common logarithm, $\log x$, p. 464
- exponent, p. 401
- exponential decay, p. 436
- exponential function, p. 428
- exponential growth, p. 436
- extension by continuity, p. 430
- functional equation, p. 445
- geometric sequence, p. 413
- inverse function, p. 452
- laws of exponents, p. 401
- laws of logarithms, p. 470
- linear scale, p. 484
- log-log graph paper, p. 487
- logarithmic function, $x \mapsto \log_b x$, p. 463
- logarithmic scale, p. 484
- monotonic, p. 446
- negative exponent, a^{-m}, p. 407
- one-to-one, p. 451
- product model, p. 401
- rational exponent, $a^{\frac{p}{q}}$, p. 420
- real nth root, $\sqrt[n]{r}$, p. 419
- recursive definition, p. 438
- semilog graph paper, p. 487
- strictly decreasing, p. 430
- strictly increasing, p. 429
- unit fraction exponent, $a^{\frac{1}{n}}$, p. 419
- zero exponent, a^0, p. 407

Chapter Road Map

INVESTIGATION 5A, ***Working with Exponents,*** has students review the basic laws of exponents for integer exponents and extend the set of allowable exponents to all real numbers in such a way as to preserve the laws of exponents.

INVESTIGATION 5B, ***Exponential Functions,*** introduces students to how exponential functions are graphed and tabulated. Students write closed-form and recursive definitions of exponential functions to agree with given data. They eventually prove that exponential functions are one-to-one, which means that they have inverses.

INVESTIGATION 5C, ***Logarithmic Functions,*** has students investigate logarithms, the inverses of exponential functions. They develop the laws of logarithms to parallel the laws of exponents. They also graph logarithmic functions and investigate the logarithmic scale.

Exponential and Logarithmic Functions

In the 1930s, Charles Richter developed the Richter scale at the California Institute of Technology. The Richter scale measures the magnitude of earthquakes. Earthquake magnitudes vary widely, from tiny microearthquakes that only sensitive seismographs can detect to catastrophic events that cause widespread destruction.

The wide variation of magnitude led Richter and his colleagues to use the base-10 logarithm in their formula. This limits the possible values of the magnitude to a more manageable and understandable range.

To calculate the magnitude M_L of an earthquake, you measure the maximum amplitude A of the wave pattern that your seismograph records. Richter used the formula $M_L = \log_{10} A - \log_{10} A_0$, where A_0 is a correction value based on the seismograph's distance from the earthquake and local conditions.

A small earthquake can have a negative magnitude. The largest magnitude ever recorded was 9.5, during the Great Chilean Earthquake on May 22, 1960. Instruments detect over a million earthquakes every year. Humans can only feel about one third of these.

Vocabulary and Notation

- base
- common logarithm, $\log x$
- exponential decay
- exponential function
- exponential growth
- logarithm function, $x \mapsto \log_b x$
- logarithmic scale
- negative exponent, a^{-m}
- nth root, $\sqrt[n]{r}$
- zero exponent, a^0

Chapter Technology

CME Project *Algebra 2* assumes that each student has access to a graphing calculator. It also recommends access to a computer algebra system (CAS).

Support for the use of technology is available in the TI-Nspire™ Technology Handbook. See p. 778.

A list of technology used with important concepts in this chapter appears below. Students will need access to the functionality listed to develop complete understanding of these topics.

Computer Algebra System

LESSON 5.10 Model an exponential function, p. 457.

LESSON 5.12 Use the logarithm template to evaluate logarithms in bases other than 10, p. 465.

Function-Modeling Language

LESSON 5.8 Model a recursively-defined exponential function, p. 436

Graphing Calculator

LESSON 5.5 Solve exponential equations, p. 422.

LESSON 5.7 Find an intersection point of two exponential graphs, p. 433.

LESSON 5.11 Find the log of a number, pp. 461, 462.

LESSON 5.12 Find the log (in bases other than 10) of a number, p. 468.

LESSON 5.13 Use the change-of-base formula and work with a base-3 logarithm, p. 475. Order six numbers expressed as logarithms, p. 476.

LESSON 5.14 Find ln 1 and ln 0, p. 480. Find intersection points, p. 480. Graph the inverse of an exponential function, p. 482.

Investigation Overview

This investigation reintroduces the laws of exponents as defined for positive integer exponents. It asks students to use those laws as the basis for deciding how to extend the definition to zero, negative, and rational exponents. As with any mathematical extension, encourage students to make sense of the choices made in the extended definition and to understand why the choices are inevitable given the goal of retaining the laws of exponents.

You may wish to assign Questions 1–3 for students to think and write about during the investigation.

Learning Goals

- Review the laws of exponents.
- Evaluate expressions involving exponents, including zero, negative, and rational exponents.
- Find missing terms in a geometric sequence and generate sequences to interpret expressions involving rational exponents.
- Convert between exponential and radical forms for rational exponents.

Habits and Skills

- Extend the laws of exponents to allow evaluation of zero, negative, and rational exponents.
- Reason logically to verify that a particular interpretation of an exponent follows the laws of exponents.
- Generalize from specific examples to develop and verify identities.

Investigation 5A

Working with Exponents

In *Working with Exponents*, you will use the basic rules of algebra to discover the laws of exponents. You will learn how to extend the rules to work with zero, negative, and rational exponents.

By the end of this investigation, you will be able to answer questions like these.

1. What is the Fundamental Law of Exponents? What are some of its corollaries?
2. How do you extend the laws of exponents to define zero, negative, and rational exponents?
3. What are the simplified forms of the expressions 4^0, 7^{-2} and $5^{\frac{27}{3}}$?

You will learn how to

- evaluate expressions involving exponents, including zero, negative, and rational exponents
- find missing terms in a geometric sequence and generate geometric sequences to interpret expressions involving rational exponents
- convert between exponential and radical forms for rational exponents

You will develop these habits and skills:

- Extend the laws of exponents to allow evaluation of zero, negative, and rational exponents.
- Reason logically to verify that a particular interpretation of an exponent follows the laws of exponents.
- Generalize from specific examples to develop and verify identities.

Radiographers use X-rays for medical imaging. X-rays have wavelengths between 10^{-7} and 10^{-10} cm.

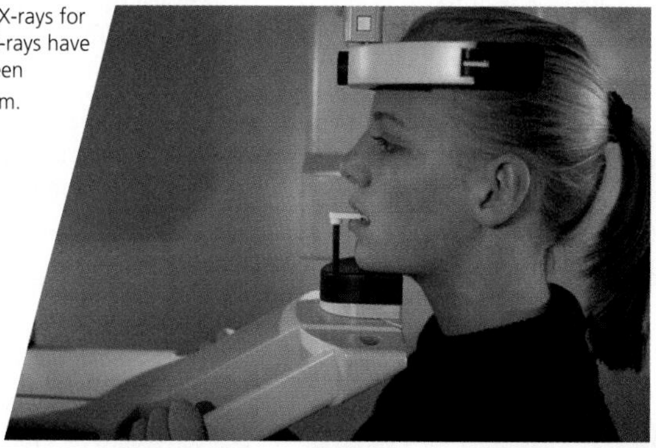

Investigation Road Map

LESSON 5.1, *Getting Started,* has students refresh their memories about the laws of exponents.

LESSON 5.2, *Laws of Exponents,* is a review of the laws of exponents.

LESSON 5.3, *Zero and Negative Exponents,* goes through the process of extending the definition of exponent to include zero and negative exponents.

LESSON 5.4, *Sequences and Operations,* prepares students to define rational exponents formally.

LESSON 5.5, *Defining Rational Exponents,* formally extends the definition of exponent to include rational numbers.

5.1 Getting Started

Activating Prior Knowledge
Exploring New Ideas

Expressions or equations may contain variables as exponents.

For You to Explore

1. Copy and complete this table for the function $f(n) = 2^n$.

Input, n	Output, $f(n)$
6	64
5	32
4	16
3	8
2	■
1	■
0	■
−1	■
−2	■
−3	■

2. Solve each equation.
   a. $2^3 \cdot 2^5 = 2^a$
   b. $2^b \cdot 2^8 = 2^{14}$
   c. $3^c \cdot 3^c = 3^{12}$
   d. $(3^d)^2 = 3^8$
   e. $\frac{5^7}{5^f} = 5^6$
   f. $3^g = 9^5$
   g. $5^{3h} = 5^7$
   h. $(5^k)^3 = 5^4$
3. **Write About It** What are some rules of exponents? Give examples.

A *geometric sequence* is a list of numbers in which you get each term by multiplying the previous one by a constant. For example, the sequence below is a geometric sequence, since each term is three times as great as the previous term.

4, 12, 36, 108, 324, . . .

For Problems 4 and 5, find the missing terms in each geometric sequence.

4. a. 4, 8, 16, ■, ■, ■, . . .
   b. 4, −8, 16, ■, ■, ■, . . .
   c. $2, 2\sqrt{3}$, ■, ■, ■, ■, . . .
   d. $a, 2a$, ■, ■, ■, ■, . . .
   e. $k, 3k$, ■, ■, ■, ■, . . .
5. a. 1, ■, ■, 8, ■, ■, . . .
   b. ■, ■, 1, $\frac{1}{2}$, ■, ■, . . .
   c. 2, ■, 18, ■, ■, ■, . . .
   d. 1, ■, ■, ■, 9, ■, . . .

Habits of Mind

Look for relationships. What is a closed form for the function g with this sequence of outputs?

Input	Output
0	4
1	12
2	36
3	108
4	324

Answers

For You to Explore

1. See back of book.
2. **a.** 8 **b.** 6 **c.** 6 **d.** 4
   e. 1 **f.** 10 **g.** $\frac{7}{3}$ **h.** $\frac{4}{3}$
3. Answers may vary. Sample:
   $a^b \cdot a^c = a^{b+c}$, $\frac{a^b}{a^c} = a^{b-c}$,
   $(a^b)^c = a^{bc}$
4. **a.** 4, 8, 16, 32, 64, 128, . . .
   b. 4, −8, 16, −32, 64, −128, . . .
   c. $2, 2\sqrt{3}, 6, 6\sqrt{3}, 18, 18\sqrt{3}, \ldots$
   d. $a, 2a, 4a, 8a, 16a, 32a, \ldots$
   e. $k, 3k, 9k, 27k, 81k, 243k, \ldots$
5. **a.** 1, 2, 4, 8, 16, 32, . . .
   b. $4, 2, 1, \frac{1}{2}, \frac{1}{4}, \frac{1}{8}, \ldots$
   c. 2, 6, 18, 54, 162, 486, . . .
   d. $1, \sqrt{3}, 3, 3\sqrt{3}, 9, 9\sqrt{3}, \ldots$ or $1, -\sqrt{3}, 3, -3\sqrt{3}, 9, -9\sqrt{3}, \ldots$

Lesson Overview

GOALS

- Warm up to the ideas of the investigation.
- Review the laws of exponents.

The exercises in this lesson give you a chance to evaluate your students' memory of the laws of exponents so you will be able to judge how much you need to cover in the review lesson that follows. Students get an opportunity to think about zero and negative exponents as continuing a pattern. As always in a Getting Started lesson, there is no need to formalize these ideas today. Students will meet all the ideas again throughout the investigation.

Clarify for your students when they can use a calculator. The text occasionally encourages students to try an exercise without a calculator or it will suggest that a calculator might be helpful for a particular exercise. Set the calculator policy for your class.

FOR YOU TO EXPLORE
- Core: 1, 2, 4, 5
- Optional: 3

MATERIALS
- graphing calculators
- Blackline Master 5.1

HOMEWORK
- Core: 6, 7, 8, 9
- Optional: 11
- Extension: 10

Launch

Have students get started on the For You to Explore problems right away. Although Problem 3 is not listed as a core problem you may wish to assign it or at least to encourage students to be thinking about this question as they work. Blackline Master 5.1 provides a blank copy of the table to be completed in Problem 1.

Explore

As students are working, keep track of questions, conjectures, or disagreements to discuss.

For You to Explore

PROBLEM 1 The goal of this exercise is for students to come upon $2^0 = 1$ and $2^{-n} = \frac{1}{2^n}$ with little help. Students should not use a calculator for this exercise, but they should use their own understanding of the situation to decide how to fill in the table. It is acceptable if students are incorrect or if they disagree, because the real point is for students to make a choice of what to do. This exercise opens questions such as "What does it mean to raise two to the power zero?" for scrutiny. If students struggle, ask them to look for a pattern in the table of inputs and outputs.

PROBLEM 2 Encourage students to try to complete this without a calculator or to use it as a check. See if students notice the underlying assumption they need to make to solve these equations: if you have exponential expressions on either side of the equals sign, their exponents must also be equal.

PROBLEM 3 is a focus for discussion. Ask students to pay special attention to the kinds of numbers that are acceptable as bases and exponents in an exponential expression.

PROBLEMS 4 AND 5 Students may just be following a pattern, but in doing so, they are also working to evaluate an exponential function that determines the *n*th term in each sequence.

Wrap Up

Go over the For You to Explore core problems. Give students a chance to explain their work. Make a class list of students' memory of the laws of exponents, paying special attention to the restrictions on the numbers that they can use as exponents or as bases for exponents.

Exercises

HOMEWORK

- Core: 6, 7, 8, 9
- Optional: 11
- Extension: 10

On Your Own

EXERCISE 6 Encourage students to think about what restrictions might be necessary beyond the given restriction that *a*, *b*, and *c* must be positive integers.

EXERCISE 7 reviews the basics of exponential expressions. Have your students complete it without a calculator, and have them justify their answers. Although they could just multiply out 2^{12} and each of the expressions, it is more efficient to think about the basic rules.

EXERCISE 8 It is preferable for students to complete this exercise without a calculator to help them examine any assumptions they make (or memories they have) about how to deal with zero and negative exponents.

EXERCISE 9 is designed to help students remember the rule $a^n \cdot b^n = (ab)^n$.

EXERCISE 10 The first part of this exercise amounts to a proof that *x* and *y* cannot be rational numbers. Students will visit this later in the investigation.

Maintain Your Skills

EXERCISE 11 These questions are similar to ones from CME Project *Algebra 1*. Our hope is that students will solve by "backtracking," learning that whatever is in the exponent must equal 4.

Exercises *Practicing Habits of Mind*

On Your Own

6. Decide whether each equation is true for all positive integers *a*, *b*, and *c*.

a. $a^b \stackrel{?}{=} b^a$ **b.** $a^{b+c} \stackrel{?}{=} a^b + a^c$ **c.** $a^{b+c} \stackrel{?}{=} a^b \cdot a^c$
d. $a^b \cdot a^c \stackrel{?}{=} a^{bc}$ **e.** $(a^b)^c \stackrel{?}{=} a^{bc}$ **f.** $(a^b)^c \stackrel{?}{=} a^{(b^c)}$
g. $\frac{a^b}{a^c} \stackrel{?}{=} a^{b-c}$ **h.** $(ab)^c \stackrel{?}{=} a(b^c)$

Habits of Mind
Experiment. If the equation is not true for all positive integers, is it true for some values of a, b, and c?

7. Determine whether each expression is equal to 2^{12}. Explain.

a. $2^{10} + 2^2$ **b.** $(2^4)(2^4)(2^4)$ **c.** $2^6 \cdot 2^6$
d. $2^9 + 2^3$ **e.** $(2^{10})(2^2)$ **f.** $2^{11} + 2^{11}$
g. $(2^4)(2^3)$ **h.** $4(2^{10})$

Try this without a calculator.

8. Copy and complete the table for the function $g(n) = 3^n$.

Input, *n*	Output, *g*(*n*)
5	243
4	81
3	27
2	■
1	■
0	■
−1	■
−2	■
−3	■

9. Problem 1 shows a table for $f(n) = 2^n$. Exercise 8 shows a table for $g(n) = 3^n$. Consider the function $h(n) = f(n) \cdot g(n)$.

a. Calculate $h(3)$.
b. Use the completed tables to calculate $h(0)$, $h(1)$, and $h(2)$.
c. Find a simple rule for $h(n)$.

10. Take It Further

a. Explain why there are no positive integers *a* and *b* such that $2^a = 5^b$.
b. Find the number *x* that makes $2^x = 5$. Round to four decimal places.
c. Find the number *y* that makes $2 = 5^y$. Round to four decimal places.
d. What is the relationship between *x* and *y*?

Maintain Your Skills

11. Solve each equation.

a. $3^x = 81$ **b.** $3^{x+1} = 81$ **c.** $3^{2x} = 81$
d. $3^{-x} = 81$ **e.** $3^{4x-1} = 81$ **f.** $3^{x^2} = 81$

Answers

Exercises

6. a. no **b.** no **c.** yes **d.** no
e. yes **f.** no **g.** yes **h.** no

7. a. No; $2^{10} + 2^2 \neq 2^{10+2}$. This sum cannot be written as a single power of 2.
b. Yes; $2^4 \cdot 2^4 \cdot 2^4 = 2^{4+4+4} = 2^{12}$
c. Yes; $2^6 \cdot 2^6 = 2^{6+6} = 2^{12}$
d. No; $2^9 + 2^3 \neq 2^{9+3}$. This sum cannot be written as a single power of 2.
e. Yes; $2^{10} \cdot 2^2 = 2^{10+2} = 2^{12}$
f. Yes; $2^{11} + 2^{11} = 2 \cdot 2^{11} = 2^1 \cdot 2^{11} = 2^{1+11} = 2^{12}$
g. No; $2^4 \cdot 2^3 = 2^{4+3} = 2^7 \neq 2^{12}$
h. Yes; $4 \cdot 2^{10} = 2^2 \cdot 2^{10} = 2^{2+10} = 2^{12}$

8. See back of book.

9. a. 216
b. $h(0) = 1$, $h(1) = 6$, $h(2) = 36$
c. $h(n) = 6^n$

5.2 Laws of Exponents

If n is a positive integer, then a^n (read as "a to the n") is the product of n factors of a.

$$a^n = \underbrace{a \cdot a \cdot a \cdot \cdots \cdot a}_{n \text{ factors of } a}$$

This lesson develops the rules for working with expressions in the form a^n. These rules are built on the basic rules for multiplication and division.

For You to Do

1. Use a product model like the one above to demonstrate that $a^3 \cdot a^5 = a^8$.
2. How can you use a product model to write out $(a^2)^5$? What is the result?

Multiplication has the any-order, any-grouping properties, but not all operations do. Division and subtraction do not have either property. Neither does exponentiation.

$$2^{20} \neq 20^2 \text{ and } (2^3)^4 \neq 2^{(3^4)}$$

You will review some of the rules for calculating with exponents and look at why they work.

Remember...

Another name for the any-order property is the commutative property: $3 \cdot 5 = 5 \cdot 3$. Another name for the any-grouping property is the associative property: $(3 \cdot 5) \cdot 7 = 3 \cdot (5 \cdot 7)$.

Theorem 5.1 The Fundamental Law of Exponents

If b and c are positive integers, then

$$a^b \cdot a^c = a^{b+c}$$

Proof Use a product model to expand a^b and a^c.

$$(a^b)(a^c) = \underbrace{(a \cdot a \cdot \cdots \cdot a)}_{b \text{ factors}} \cdot \underbrace{(a \cdot a \cdot \cdots \cdot a)}_{c \text{ factors}} = \underbrace{(a \cdot a \cdot \cdots \cdot a)}_{(b+c) \text{ factors}} = a^{b+c}$$

Habits of Mind

Experiment. It may help to work out this proof with numbers. For example, suppose a is 5, b is 3 and c is 7.

It is important to notice that you can use Theorem 5.1 only if the base numbers are the same.

$$7^3 \cdot 7^8 = 7^{3+8} = 7^{11} \text{ but } 6^3 \cdot 7^8 \neq (6 \cdot 7)^{3+8}$$

For Discussion

3. Use Theorem 5.1 to prove that $a^b \cdot a^c \cdot a^d = a^{b+c+d}$.

10. a. Answers may vary. Sample: For any positive integers a and b, 2^a is even and 5^b is odd, so $2^a \neq 5^b$.

b. 2.3219

c. 0.4307

d. $xy = 1$ or $\frac{1}{x} = y$

11. a. 4 **b.** 3 **c.** 2

d. -4 **e.** $\frac{5}{4}$ **f.** ± 2

For You to Do

1. $a^3 \cdot a^5 = (a \cdot a \cdot a) \cdot (a \cdot a \cdot a \cdot a \cdot a) = a^8$

2. $(a^2)^5 = a^2 \cdot a^2 \cdot a^2 \cdot a^2 \cdot a^2$
$= (a \cdot a) \cdot (a \cdot a) \cdot (a \cdot a) \cdot (a \cdot a) \cdot (a \cdot a)$
$= a^{10}$

For Discussion

3. $a^b \cdot a^c \cdot a^d = a^b \cdot (a^c \cdot a^d) = a^b \cdot a^{c+d} = a^{b+c+d}$

Lesson Overview

GOALS

- Review the laws of exponents.
- Evaluate expressions involving exponents.

During your discussion in the Getting Started lesson, you probably learned a lot about how much your students remember of the laws of exponents. This lesson gives a brief review, so you can go through it quickly. Emphasize that if students do not remember one of the laws, they can always use the product model of the exponential expressions to figure it out.

CHECK YOUR UNDERSTANDING
- Core: 1, 2, 3, 4, 7, 8, 9, 11
- Optional: 5, 6, 10, 12

MATERIALS
- CAS (recommended)
- graphing calculators

HOMEWORK
- Core: 13, 14, 15, 18, 21, 22, 23
- Optional: 16, 17, 19, 20, 24

VOCABULARY
- b^n
- base
- exponent
- laws of exponents
- product model

Launch

Start this lesson with a brief reminder of the product model for exponential expressions. Then have students complete For You to Do.

Explore

THEOREM 5.1 Note that this theorem is limited to positive integers b and c, since students have not yet defined the values of bases raised to exponents that are not positive integers. As this investigation continues, this theorem is restated as the set of values that are allowable as *exponents* is expanded to include zero, negative, and rational exponents.

For Discussion

Use the any-grouping property of multiplication to rewrite $a^b \cdot a^c \cdot a^d$ as $(a^b \cdot a^c) \cdot a^d$. Theorem 5.1 lets you simplify the expression in the parentheses to get $(a^{b+c}) \cdot a^d$. Then apply it again to get a^{b+c+d}.

Developing Habits of Mind

In this Developing Habits of Mind, students see a way to rebuild the law of exponents and its corollaries. So, for example, if a student forgets whether $a^{3^4} = a^7$ or a^{12}, encourage him or her to write the expression a^{3^4} as $aaa \cdot aaa \cdot aaa \cdot aaa$. The rule makes more sense after doing a calculation like this, and students can have confidence that they are using the right rules. Students can see that new rules match the rules they learned in first-year algebra. In this instance, students may remember the rule, but this is a good tool to use to resolve issues such as why $b^{\frac{1}{2}}$ has the same meaning as $\sqrt{b}$.

Wrap Up

If time allows, go over the Check Your Understanding core exercises.

Assessment Resources

Lesson Quiz 5.2

1. Simplify each expression.
   a. $5^4 \cdot 8^2$ b. $9^5 \cdot \left(\frac{1}{9}\right)^5$ c. $\left(\frac{9}{8}\right)^3 \cdot \left(\frac{16}{3}\right)^3$
2. Decide whether each expression equals 5^5. Explain.
   a. $5^2 + 5^3$ b. $(5^3)(5^2)$ c. $5 \cdot 5^4$
   d. $\frac{5^{20}}{5^4}$ e. $\frac{5^9}{5^4}$ f. $\left(\frac{5^3}{5}\right)^2$
3. Write each expression as a single power of x.
   a. $x^3 \cdot x^2 \cdot x$ b. $x^3 \cdot (x^3)^3$ c. $(x^7)^3$
   d. $\frac{x^{12}}{x^6}$ e. $\frac{x^8}{x^5}$ f. $x^{14} \cdot \left(\frac{1}{x^2}\right)^5$

A second law of exponents follows from Theorem 5.1.

Corollary 5.1.1

If b and c are positive integers such that $b > c$ and $a \neq 0$, then

$$\frac{a^b}{a^c} = a^{b-c}$$

> Later in this investigation, you will find a way to remove the restriction $b > c$.

Proof By Theorem 5.1, you have

$$a^c \cdot a^{b-c} = a^{c+(b-c)} = a^b$$

Note that $b - c$ is positive, which allows you to use Theorem 5.1. Since $a^c \neq 0$, you can divide each side by a^c.

$$a^{b-c} = \frac{a^b}{a^c}$$

A third law of exponents applies when you raise an expression with an exponent to another power.

Corollary 5.1.2

For all numbers a and positive integers b and c,

$$(a^b)^c = a^{bc}$$

Proof Write c copies of a^b and then use Theorem 5.1.

$$(a^b)^c = \underbrace{(a^b)(a^b) \cdot \cdots \cdot (a^b)}_{c \text{ factors of } a^b}$$
$$= a^{(b+b+\cdots+b)}$$
$$= a^{bc}$$

> In the expression $a^{(b+b+\cdots+b)}$, the exponent is the sum of c values of b.

Developing Habits of Mind

Use a different process to get the same result. These three laws come from the properties you learned for multiplication and division. So, if you are unsure about the rules of exponents while doing calculations, you can rewrite the expressions as products of factors. For example, you can rewrite

$$\frac{(b^4)^2}{b^7} \text{ as } \frac{(b \cdot b \cdot b \cdot b) \cdot (b \cdot b \cdot b \cdot b)}{b \cdot b \cdot b \cdot b \cdot b \cdot b \cdot b}$$

Then, you can cancel the factors of b to get the answer: b^1, or just b.

> **Remember...**
> The expression $(b^4)^2$ means b^4 times itself. So, $(b^4)^2 = (b^4)(b^4)$.

For now, these rules apply only to positive integer exponents. The rest of this investigation will focus on how to extend the definition of exponents to zero, negative integers, rational numbers, and real numbers. Some of the exercises in this lesson ask you to work with exponents that are not positive integers. Try them and see what happens.

Answers

Exercises

1. $(ab)^n = \underbrace{(ab) \cdot (ab) \cdot \cdots \cdot (ab)}_{n \text{ copies of } ab} =$

$\underbrace{(a \cdot a \cdot \cdots \cdot a)}_{n \text{ copies of}}\underbrace{(b \cdot b \cdot \cdots \cdot b)}_{n \text{ copies of } b} =$

$a^n \cdot b^n$

2. $\frac{3^{11}}{3^5} =$

$\frac{3 \cdot 3 \cdot 3 \cdot 3 \cdot 3 \cdot 3 \cdot 3 \cdot 3 \cdot 3 \cdot 3 \cdot 3}{3 \cdot 3 \cdot 3 \cdot 3 \cdot 3} =$

$\frac{3 \cdot 3 \cdot 3 \cdot 3 \cdot 3}{3 \cdot 3 \cdot 3 \cdot 3 \cdot 3} \cdot \frac{3 \cdot 3 \cdot 3 \cdot 3 \cdot 3 \cdot 3}{1} =$

$1 \cdot 3^6 = 3^6$

3. See back of book.

4. a. Yes; $3^{14} + 3^{14} + 3^{14} = 3 \cdot 3^{14} = 3^1 + 3^{14} = 3^{1+14} = 3^{15}$

b. No; $(3^6)^9 = 3^{6 \cdot 9} = 3^{54} \neq 3^{15}$

c. Yes; $(3^{10})(3^5) = 3^{10+5} = 3^{15}$

d. No; $(3^3)(3^5) = 3^{3+5} = 3^8 \neq 3^{15}$

e. No; $(3^{15})(3^1) = 3^{15+1} = 3^{16} \neq 3^{15}$

f. Yes; $(3^5)(3^5)(3^5) = 3^{5+5+5} = 3^{15}$

Exercises *Practicing Habits of Mind*

Check Your Understanding

1. Explain why $(ab)^n = a^n b^n$. It may help to make models similar to the ones at the beginning of this lesson.
2. Use a product model to show that $\frac{3^{11}}{3^5} = 3^6$.
3. Use a product model to prove Corollaries 5.2 and 5.3.
4. Decide whether each expression equals 3^{15}. Explain.
   - **a.** $3^{14} + 3^{14} + 3^{14}$
   - **b.** $(3^6)^9$
   - **c.** $(3^{10})(3^5)$
   - **d.** $(3^3)(3^5)$
   - **e.** $(3^{15})(3^1)$
   - **f.** $(3^5)(3^5)(3^5)$
   - **g.** $3^9 + 3^6$
   - **h.** $(3^5)^3$
   - **i.** $(3^3)^5$
   - **j.** $9(3^{13})$
   - **k.** $(3^5)^{10}$
   - **l.** $(3^1)^{15}$
5. Suppose $M = c^4$ and $N = c^3$. Find at least two different ways to write c^{15} in terms of M and N.
6. **Write About It** Describe how you can use the Fundamental Law of Exponents (Theorem 5.1) to expand the product $(x^7 - 3x^2 + 6)(x^5 + 2x^3 + 3)$.
7. Write the following expression as a single power of 3.
   $$3 \cdot 3^2 \cdot 3^4 \cdot 3^8 \cdot 3^{16}$$
8. Solve each equation.
   - **a.** $2^x = 8$
   - **b.** $2^{y-1} = 16$
   - **c.** $2^{5z} = 64$
   - **d.** $(2^w)(2^w) = 64$
9. Find a function that fits this table.

Input	Output
0	3
1	15
2	75
3	375
4	1875

Habits of Mind

Look for a relationship. Your calculator will just slow you down in exercises like this one.

g. No; $3^9 + 3^6 \neq 3^{9+6}$. This sum cannot be written as a single power of 3.
h. Yes; $(3^5)^3 = 3^{5 \cdot 3} = 3^{15}$
i. Yes; $(3^3)^5 = 3^{3 \cdot 5} = 3^{15}$
j. Yes; $9(3^{13}) = (3^2)(3^{13}) = 3^{2+13} = 3^{15}$
k. No; $(3^5)^{10} = 3^{5 \cdot 10} = 3^{50} \neq 3^{15}$
l. Yes; $(3^1)^{15} = 3^{1 \cdot 15} = 3^{15}$

5. Answers may vary. Sample: M^3N, $\frac{M^6}{N^3}$

6. Each time you multiply a power of x from the first factor by a power of x from the second factor, you can use the Fundamental Law of Exponents to find the exponent to place on x in the resulting term of the product.

7. 3^{31}

8. a. 3 **b.** 5
c. $\frac{6}{5}$ **d.** 3

9. $f(n) = 3 \cdot 5^n$

Exercises

HOMEWORK
- Core: 13, 14, 15, 18, 21, 22, 23
- Optional: 16, 17, 19, 20, 24

Check Your Understanding

EXERCISE 5 Different students will tackle this exercise differently. If students are having trouble getting started, give them some examples using M and N that do not work out to c^{15} but can help them get going. So, for example, ask questions like these: What does $M \cdot N$ equal? What does $M \cdot N^2$ equal? What does $\frac{M}{N}$ equal? You can make this exercise more difficult for advanced students by encouraging them to find more than two ways to write c^{15}, or even a generalization of all the ways $M^a \cdot N^b$ could equal c^{15}, which comes from the linear equation $4a + 3b = 15$.

EXERCISE 8 These equations are meant to review the powers of 2 and the basics of exponents and exponential expressions. Since students do not know logarithms, there is no systematic way to solve problems of this type. They need to remember facts about powers of 2, such as $2^6 = 64$, and then work backwards from there.

EXERCISE 9 Point out to students that they could use Lagrange interpolation to find a polynomial through these same five points and that there are infinitely many such polynomials. If, however, they use the pattern of multiplication by 5 in the table to define the function, they can get a simpler function defined either recursively or as an exponential function. Also, the table implies the knowledge $5^0 = 1$, since 0 is used as an input. You can use this type of table to justify why it makes sense to define $a^0 = 1$ for a non-zero a.

EXERCISE 10 illustrates one of the advantages of scientific notation—it is easy to see the magnitude of numbers (and so it is easier to calculate the median).

EXERCISE 11 Watch for different answers to the last part; see if any students come up with the result 2^{-3}. If no one does, bring up that as a possible answer and as a connection to the next lesson.

On Your Own

EXERCISE 14 You can use the given statement to explain why, when you extend the allowable values for exponents to include 0 and negative numbers, a^0 should be 1 and a^{-1} should be $\frac{1}{a}$.

EXERCISE 15 Some students may choose to provide a recursive definition for this function.

EXERCISE 16 An interesting question to ask your students is: "By adding just 2s and/or 3s, how can you get a sum of 8?" Students may find this question easier to answer than to solve the exercise as it is stated, but it is essentially the same question.

EXERCISE 19 should be done without a calculator. If students must use a calculator, you might modify the exercise in the following way: the units digit of 2^{508} is 6. What are the units digits of 2^{509}, 2^{510}, 2^{1016}, and 2^{507}? Students should realize that they only need the units digit to find the units digit for parts (a) through (c). In part (c), watch for students who double the units digit over and over. They will get the correct answer, but they may not have noticed that they can use the corollary that $2^{16} = (2^8)^2$. In part (d), the units digit could be 3 or 8, but students should recognize that a power of 2 cannot end in 3.

10. Find the mean and the median of the following list of numbers.

$5 \cdot 10^4 \quad 5 \cdot 10^3 \quad 5 \cdot 10^2 \quad 5 \cdot 10^1 \quad 5$

11. Compute each quotient.

a. $\frac{10^9}{10^8}$

b. $\frac{3^2y^8}{(2y)^3}$

c. $\frac{6^3x^9}{3^32^2x^5}$

d. $\frac{2^2}{2^5}$

12. Solve each equation for x.

a. $(x - 1)(x + 1) = 15$

b. $(2^x - 1)(2^x + 1) = 15$

On Your Own

13. Simplify each expression.

a. $5^3 \cdot 2^3$

b. $4^6 \cdot 25^6$

c. $9^{10} \cdot \left(\frac{1}{9}\right)^{10}$

d. $20^4 \cdot \left(\frac{1}{10}\right)^4$

e. $20^4 \cdot 5^4$

f. $\left(\frac{4}{3}\right)^4 \cdot \left(\frac{15}{2}\right)^4$

14. Use each method to prove the following statement.

If $n > 1$ is a positive integer and $a \neq 0$, then $\frac{a^n}{a} = a^{n-1}$.

a. The Fundamental Law of Exponents (Theorem 5.1)

b. a product model

15. Find a function that fits this table.

Input	Output
0	5
1	15
2	45
3	135
4	405

16. Suppose $A = c^3$ and $B = c^2$. Find two different ways to write c^8 in terms of A and B.

17. The number 2^{10} is close to 1000. Use this fact to estimate the value of 2^{21}.

Go Online PHSchool.com

For additional practice, go to Web Code: bfa-0502

Answers

10. mean: 11,111; median: $5 \cdot 10^2$ or 500

11. a. 10 **b.** $\frac{9y^5}{8}$ **c.** $2x^4$ **d.** $\frac{1}{8}$

12. a. ± 4 **b.** 2

13. a. 1000 **b.** 1,000,000,000,000
c. 1 **d.** 16
e. 100,000,000 **f.** 10,000

14. a. By Theorem 5.1, $a^n = a^{n-1} \cdot a^1$, or $a^n = a^{n-1} \cdot a$. Dividing each side of this equation by a gives $\frac{a^n}{a} = \frac{a^{n-1} \cdot a}{a}$. Simplifying the right side of this equation gives $\frac{a^n}{a} = a^{n-1}$.

b. $\frac{a^n}{a} = \frac{\overbrace{(a \cdot a \cdot \ldots \cdot a)}^{n \text{ copies of } a}}{a} = \frac{a \cdot \overbrace{(a \cdot a \cdot \ldots \cdot a)}^{(n-1) \text{ copies of } a}}{a}$

$= \overbrace{(a \cdot a \cdot \ldots \cdot a)}^{(n-1) \text{ copies of } a} = a^{n-1}$

15. $g(n) = 5 \cdot 3^n$

16. Answers may vary. Sample: $A^2 \cdot B$, B^4

17. about 2,000,000

18. a. No; $\frac{2^6}{2^2} = 2^{6-2} = 2^4 \neq 2^3$

b. Yes; $\frac{2^6}{2^3} = 2^{6-3} = 2^3$

c. No; $(2^2)^1 = 2^{2 \cdot 1} = 2^2 \neq 2^3$

d. Yes; $\frac{(2^2)^5}{2^7} = \frac{2^{2 \cdot 5}}{7} = \frac{2^{10}}{2^7} = 2^{10-7} = 2^3$

e. Yes; $\frac{2^9}{2^6} = 2^{9-6} = 2^3$

f. No; $\frac{2^9}{2^3} = 2^{9-3} = 2^6 \neq 2^3$

g. No; $\frac{2^7 \cdot 2^8}{2^5} = \frac{2^{7+8}}{2^5} = \frac{2^{15}}{2^5} = 2^{15-5} = 2^{10} \neq 2^3$

19. a. 2 **b.** 4 **c.** 6 **d.** 8

20. 9

21. a. Yes; $5 \cdot 5 \cdot 5 \cdot 5 \cdot 5 \cdot 5 = 5^6$

b. Yes; $5^4 \cdot 5^2 = 5^{4+2} = 5^6$

c. No; because $5^3 \cdot 3^5$ has five factors of 3, it cannot be written as the product of only factors of 5.

18. Decide whether each expression equals 2^3. Explain.

a. $\frac{2^6}{2^2}$ **b.** $\frac{2^6}{2^3}$ **c.** $(2^2)^1$ **d.** $\frac{(2^2)^5}{2^7}$

e. $\frac{2^9}{2^6}$ **f.** $\frac{2^9}{2^3}$ **g.** $\frac{2^7 2^8}{2^5}$

19. Use the fact $2^8 = 256$ to find the units digit of each number.

a. 2^9 **b.** 2^{10} **c.** 2^{16} **d.** 2^7

20. Find the units digit of $(2^5)^2 + (5^2)^2$.

21. Decide whether each expression equals 5^6. Explain.

a. $5 \cdot 5 \cdot 5 \cdot 5 \cdot 5 \cdot 5$ **b.** $5^4 5^2$

c. $(5^3)(3^5)$ **d.** $\frac{5^{15}}{5^9}$

e. $\frac{(5^2)(5^2)(5^3)}{5}$ **f.** $5^5 + 5$

g. $\frac{5^{18}}{5^{12}}$ **h.** $(5^2)^3$

i. $(5^6)^1$ **j.** $(5^3)^3$

k. $\frac{(5^3)^3}{5^3}$ **l.** $5 + 5 + 5 + 5 + 5 + 5$

22. Write each expression as a single power of x.

a. $(x^2)^6$ **b.** $(x^2)^5$ **c.** $(x^3)^9$ **d.** $(x^{10})^{10}$

e. $\frac{x^8}{x^2}$ **f.** $\frac{x^9}{x^7}$ **g.** $\frac{1}{x^6}(x^{14})$

23. **Standardized Test Prep** Which value of x satisfies the equation $6^{x-1} = \frac{3}{2} \cdot 12^2$?

A. 2 **B.** 3 **C.** 4 **D.** 5

Remember...

The units digit is the rightmost digit of an integer. For example, the units digit of 256 is 6.

Habits of Mind

Look for relationships. Try it without a calculator.

Maintain Your Skills

24. Determine whether each relationship is an identity.

a. $(-x)^1 \stackrel{?}{=} -x^1$ **b.** $(-x)^2 \stackrel{?}{=} -x^2$

c. $(-x)^3 \stackrel{?}{=} -x^3$ **d.** $(-x)^4 \stackrel{?}{=} -x^4$

e. $(-x)^5 \stackrel{?}{=} -x^5$ **f.** $(-x)^{13} \stackrel{?}{=} -x^{13}$

Remember...

An identity must be true for every possible choice of variable: positive, negative, zero, rational, irrational, etc.

Additional Resources

PRINT RESOURCES
- Solution Manual
- Practice Workbook
- Assessment Resources
- Teaching Resources

TECHNOLOGY
- Interactive Textbook
- TeacherExpress CD-ROM
- ExamView CD-ROM
- PHSchool.com

Additional Practice

1. Simplify each expression.

a. $2^4 \cdot 5^4$ **b.** $3^5 \cdot 12^5$

c. $\left(\frac{3}{2}\right)^3 \cdot \left(\frac{8}{15}\right)^3$ **d.** $15^3 \cdot \left(\frac{1}{15}\right)^3$

2. Decide whether each expression equals 3^4. Explain.

a. $3 \cdot 3 \cdot 3 \cdot 3$ **b.** $3^3 \cdot 3$

c. $3^2 + 3^2$ **d.** $\left(\frac{3^{12}}{3^3}\right)$

e. $\left(\frac{3^9}{3^5}\right)$ **f.** $(3^2)(2^3)$

g. $\frac{(3^3)^2}{3^2}$ **h.** $\left(\frac{3^2}{3}\right)^4$

3. Write each expression as a single power of x.

a. $x \cdot x^2 \cdot x \cdot x^2$ **b.** $x^2(x^2)^2$ **c.** $(x^5)^3$

d. $\left(\frac{x^9}{x^3}\right)$ **e.** $\left(\frac{x^{12}}{x^5}\right)$ **f.** $x^{24}\left(\frac{1}{x^4}\right)^5$

4. Find each variable.

a. $3^5 \cdot 3^{-3} = 3^a$ **b.** $\frac{5^5}{5^{-2}} = 5^b$ **c.** $\frac{4^6}{4^c} = 4^{10}$

5. Write each expression as a single power of y.

a. $y^2 y^{-3} y^5$ **b.** $\left((y^2)^2\right)^{-2}$

c. $(y^5)^0$ **d.** $\left(\frac{y^9}{y^3}\right)^0$

e. $\left(\frac{y^{12}}{y^5}\right)^{-1}$ **f.** $y^4\left(\frac{1}{y^4}\right)^{-5}$

6. Complete each table.

a.

x	$f(x) = 3^x$
−2	
−1	
0	
1	
2	9

b.

x	$g(x) = \left(\frac{1}{3}\right)^x$
−2	9
−1	
0	
1	
2	

Practice: For Lesson 5.2, assign Exercises 1–3.

d. Yes; $\frac{5^{15}}{5^9} = 5^{15-9} = 5^6$

e. Yes; $\frac{(5^2)(5^2)(5^3)}{5} = \frac{5^{2+2+3}}{5} = \frac{5^7}{5^1} = 5^{7-1} = 5^6$

f. No; $5^5 + 5 \neq 5^{5+1}$

g. Yes; $\frac{5^{18}}{5^{12}} = 5^{18-12} = 5^6$

h. Yes; $(5^2)^3 = 5^{2 \cdot 3} = 5^6$

i. Yes; $(5^6)^1 = 5^{6 \cdot 1} = 5^6$

j. No; $(5^3)^3 = 5^{3 \cdot 3} = 5^9 \neq 5^6$

k. Yes; $\frac{(5^3)^3}{5^3} = \frac{5^{3 \cdot 3}}{5^3} = \frac{5^9}{5^3} = 5^{9-3} = 5^6$

l. No; $5 + 5 + 5 + 5 + 5 + 5 = 5 \cdot 6 \neq 5^6$

22. a. x^{12} **b.** x^{10} **c.** x^{27} **d.** x^{100} **e.** x^6 **f.** x^2 **g.** x^8

23. C

24. a. yes **b.** no **c.** yes **d.** no **e.** yes **f.** yes

Lesson Overview

GOAL

- Evaluate expressions involving exponents, including zero and negative exponents.

In this lesson, students examine the consequences of various choices for how to define the value of a term raised to a zero or negative exponent. They see that if their goal is to retain the laws of exponents, there is only one choice they could make in each case. $b^0 = 1$ and $b^{-n} = \frac{1}{b^n}$. Other choices are plausible, but they lead to a breakdown in the laws of exponents.

CHECK YOUR UNDERSTANDING
- Core: 1, 2, 3, 4a–e, 7, 8, 9
- Optional: 5, 6
- Extension: 4f

MATERIALS
- graphing calculators
- Blackline Master 5.3

HOMEWORK
- Core: 10, 11, 13, 15, 17, 18, 19, 21
- Optional: 12, 14, 16, 20, 22, 23, 24

VOCABULARY
- negative exponent, a^{-m}
- zero exponent, a^0

Launch

Start this lesson by reviewing the laws of exponents and asking students how they would choose to extend the laws for zero and negative exponents. Accept any reasonable answer for now. As you proceed through the lesson, test each idea with the laws of exponents.

Explore

For Discussion

Mathematical definitions are not arbitrary. You want students to realize how mathematicians create new mathematical knowledge by extending old mathematical knowledge. Here, students extend the basic rules of exponents in order to find a coherent definition of 2^0. If they want their definition of 2^0 to continue to obey the basic rules, then the basic rules force the definition upon them. $2^0 = 1$ is the only choice that matches the basic rules.

Minds in Action

Again, the idea here is to show that the basic rules force the definitions for negative exponents upon students. The dialog focuses on a single example, which is meant to illustrate the general case. For example, if 2^{-3} is going to continue to follow the basic rules of exponents, then 2^{-3} must equal $\frac{1}{2^3}$.

For You to Do and For Discussion, which follow this dialog, are meant to emphasize this point.

You may want to remind students of the work they did in CME Project *Algebra 1*, where they extended the tables of arithmetic.

5.3 Zero and Negative Exponents

In the last lesson, you studied the three basic rules for working with exponents.

Laws of Exponents

Let $a \neq 0$ and let b and c be positive integers.

The Fundamental Law of Exponents

- $a^b \cdot a^c = a^{b+c}$

Corollaries

- $\frac{a^b}{a^c} = a^{b-c}$, provided $b > c$
- $(a^b)^c = a^{bc}$

These rules apply when b and c are positive integers. However, you can extend the definition to allow for other numbers as exponents. Each equation below uses a law of exponents in a way that was not defined in the last lesson.

$$2^5 \cdot 2^0 = 2^5 \qquad \frac{3^5}{3^7} = 3^{-2} \qquad \left(7^{\frac{1}{3}}\right)^3 = 7^1$$

You must define symbols, such as 2^0, 3^{-2}, and $7^{\frac{1}{3}}$, in a way that is consistent with the rules. In this lesson, you will find that there is only one way to define zero and negative integral exponents that is consistent with these rules.

You will explore rational exponents, such as $7^{\frac{1}{3}}$, later in this investigation.

For Discussion

1. Tony thinks that he should define 2^0 to equal 0. Use the laws of exponents to explain why this cannot work.
2. Explain why the equation $2^5 \cdot 2^0 = 2^5$ suggests that you should define 2^0 to equal 1.

Minds in Action — episode 18

Tony wants to make up his own definition of negative exponents.

Tony We're learning the definitions for zero and negative exponents, but why can't I make up my own definition?

Nina Like what?

Tony Well, the calculator says 10^{-2} is 0.01, which is $\frac{1}{100}$, but I think that's confusing. I think a negative exponent should give a negative answer, so 10^{-2} should be -100, the opposite of 10^2.

Answers

For Discussion

1. Answers may vary. Sample: If $2^0 = 0$, then $2^5 \cdot 2^0$ would be $2^5 \cdot 0 = 0$. But $2^5 \cdot 2^0 = 2^{5+0} = 2^5$, so $2^0 \neq 0$.
2. The equation $2^5 \cdot 2^0 = 2^5$ suggests that 2^0 is the number that you multiply 2^5 by to get 2^5, which can only be the number 1. So, 2^0 should be defined to be 1.

Nina All right, but it better work.

Tony What do you mean? I just defined it, so it must work.

Nina I mean it has to be consistent with other exponents. All right, let's check it. What's 10^{-2} times 10^3?

Tony I use the Fundamental Law of Exponents for that.

$$10^{-2} \cdot 10^3 = 10^{(-2+3)} = 10^1$$

The answer is 10.

Nina Wait a second! What number did you define 10^{-2} to be?

Tony -100.

Nina I'm going to fill in your number for 10^{-2} and see what happens. If I use your number for 10^{-2}, I get $10^{-2} \cdot 10^3 = (-100) \cdot (1000) = -100{,}000$.

If I use your definition, the product is $-100{,}000$! You said it should be 10.

Tony It should be 10. That's what the Fundamental Law of Exponents gives. Fine, I guess 10^{-2} can't be -100.

For You to Do

3. Use the example $10^{-2} \cdot 10^3 = 10^1$ to explain why 10^{-2} should equal $\frac{1}{100}$.

The following definitions allow the laws of exponents to work for any integer exponents, positive, negative, or zero.

Definitions

Zero exponent: If $a \neq 0$, then $a^0 = 1$.

Negative exponent: If $a \neq 0$ and m is a positive integer, then $a^{-m} = \frac{1}{a^m}$.

For Discussion

4. Here is a statement that uses both negative and zero exponents. Is it true? Explain.

$$a^b \cdot a^{-b} = a^0$$

For You to Do

The Minds in Action dialog shows why 10^{-2} cannot be defined to be -100. You might encourage students to pick other wrong answers for 10^{-2} and then track the process of why those cannot be right either. For example, you might ask a student to convince you and classmates that 10^{-2} cannot be 5 (or 0, or -2), using the dialog as a way to model the argument. If $10^{-2} = M$, then $M \cdot 10^3 = 10$; solve this equation to see that $10^{-2} = \frac{1}{100}$.

Wrap Up

Finish today's lesson by reiterating that the laws of exponents are now considered true for all integer exponents. Go over as many of the Check Your Understanding core exercises as time allows.

Assessment Resources

Lesson Quiz 5.3

1. Find each variable.
   a. $2^5 \cdot 2^{-8} = 2^a$
   b. $\frac{4^7}{4^{-2}} = 4^b$
   c. $\frac{7^9}{7^c} = 7^{12}$

2. Write each expression as a single power of x.
   a. $x^2 \cdot x^{-3} \cdot x^{-1}$
   b. $\left((x^3)^2\right)^{-1}$
   c. $(x^9)^0$
   d. $\left(\frac{x^9}{x^6}\right)^0$
   e. $\left(\frac{x^{14}}{x^8}\right)^{-1}$
   f. $x^3 \cdot \left(\frac{1}{x^3}\right)^{-4}$

3. Explain why $\left(\frac{2}{3}\right)\left(\frac{2}{3}\right)^{-1} = 1$.

4. Describe a relationship between the functions $f(x) = 5^x$ and $g(x) = \left(\frac{1}{5}\right)^x$. Explain why the relationship holds.

For You to Do

3. Write the equation $10^{-2} \cdot 10^3 = 10^1$ as $10^{-2} \cdot 1000 = 10$. This implies that 10^{-2} is the number you multiply 1000 by to get 10, which is the number $\frac{1}{100}$. So, 10^{-2} should equal $\frac{1}{100}$.

For Discussion

4. Yes; $a^b \cdot a^{-b} = a^b \cdot \frac{1}{a^b} = \frac{a^b}{a^b} = 1 = a^0$

Exercises

HOMEWORK
- Core: 10, 11, 13, 15, 17, 18, 19, 21
- Optional: 12, 14, 16, 20, 22, 23, 24

Check Your Understanding

EXERCISE 1 Encourage students to do this exercise without a calculator. Blackline Master 5.3 can be used here.

EXERCISE 2 Some students will try to directly apply the product rule for exponents $a^b \cdot a^c = a^{b+c}$. This is not appropriate for this exercise. What it asks students to do is to test the definition to make sure that it obeys the laws of exponents. If they use the product rule, they are assuming that the laws of exponents hold.

EXERCISE 3 Encourage students to attempt to write general proofs here, instead of just giving numerical examples.

EXERCISE 4 Some students may try to solve for a in order to complete this exercise. It is not only unnecessary, it is counter-productive, so try to prevent this by suggesting they use the laws of exponents.

With the proper definitions of zero and negative exponents, you can extend the laws of exponents to include all integer exponents.

Laws of Exponents

Let $a \neq 0$ and let b and c be integers.

The Fundamental Law of Exponents
- $a^b \cdot a^c = a^{b+c}$

Corollaries
- $\frac{a^b}{a^c} = a^{b-c}$
- $(a^b)^c = a^{bc}$

Some of the exercises that follow ask you to justify extending the laws in this fashion.

There are still other exponents unaccounted for. Why is $9^{\frac{1}{2}}$ equal to 3, for example? The next two lessons look at how you can make the extension to include these exponents.

Exercises *Practicing Habits of Mind*

Check Your Understanding

1. Decide whether each expression equals 7^{-10}. Explain.

a. $\left(\frac{1}{7}\right)^{10}$ **b.** $7^{-4} \cdot 7^{-3}$ **c.** $(7^{13})(7^{-6})$ **d.** $\frac{7^3}{7^{13}}$

e. $\frac{7^2}{7^3 7^4 7^4}$ **f.** $\left(\frac{1}{7^{-10}}\right)$ **g.** $7^5 \cdot 7^{-2}$ **h.** $\left(\frac{1}{7^2}\right)^5$

i. $(7^5)^{-15}$ **j.** $(7^5)^{-2}$ **k.** $(7^{-2})^5$ **l.** $\left(\frac{1}{7^{10}}\right)$

2. Use the definition of a negative exponent to show that $10^{-2} \cdot 10^3 = 10^1$.

3. Write About It Show that each of the three laws of exponents continues to work when one of the exponents is zero.

4. Suppose a is a number that satisfies the equation $3^a = 2$. Use the laws of exponents to simplify each expression.

a. 3^{a+1} **b.** 3^{a-1} **c.** 3^{2a} **d.** 3^{3a} **e.** 3^{0a}

f. Take It Further $3^{\frac{a}{2}}$

5. Find the units digit of $13^9 10^3 + (117 + 921)^0$.

Answers

Exercises

1. a. Yes; $\left(\frac{1}{7}\right)^{10} = (7^{-1})^{10} = 7^{-1 \cdot 10} = 7^{-10}$

b. No; $7^{-4} \cdot 7^{-3} = 7^{-4+(-3)} = 7^{-7} \neq 7^{-10}$

c. No; $(7^{13})(7^{-6}) = 7^{13+(-6)} = 7^7 \neq 7^{-10}$

d. Yes; $\frac{7^3}{7^{13}} = 7^{3-13} = 7^{-10}$

e. No; $\frac{7^2}{7^3 \cdot 7^4 \cdot 7^4} = \frac{7^2}{7^{3+4+4}} = \frac{7^2}{7^{11}} = 7^{2-11} = 7^{-9} \neq 7^{-10}$

f. No; $\frac{1}{7^{-10}} = 7^{-(-10)} = 7^{10} \neq 7^{-10}$

g. No; $7^5 \cdot 7^{-2} = 7^{5+(-2)} = 7^3 \neq 7^{-10}$

h. Yes; $\left(\frac{1}{7^2}\right)^5 = (7^{-2})^5 = 7^{(-2) \cdot 5} = 7^{-10}$

i. No; $(7^5)^{-15} = 7^{5 \cdot (-15)} = 7^{-75} \neq 7^{-10}$

j. Yes; $(7^5)^{-2} = 7^{5 \cdot (-2)} = 7^{-10}$

k. Yes; $(7^{-2})^5 = 7^{-2 \cdot 5} = 7^{-10}$

l. Yes; $\frac{1}{7^{10}} = 7^{-10}$

2. $10^{-2} \cdot 10^3 = \frac{1}{10^2} \cdot \frac{10^3}{1} = \frac{10^3}{10^2} = 10^{3-2} = 10^1$

3. $a^b \cdot a^c = a^{b+c}$: If $b = 0$, then $a^b \cdot a^c = a^0 \cdot a^c = a^c$ and $a^{b+c} = a^{0+c} = a^c$.

$\frac{a^b}{a^c} = a^{b-c}$ $(b > c)$: If $c = 0$, then $\frac{a^b}{a^c} = \frac{a^b}{a^0} = \frac{a^b}{1} = a^b$ and $a^{b-c} = a^{b-0} = a^b$.

$(a^b)^c = a^{bc}$: If $b = 0$, then $(a^b)^c = (a^0)^c = 1^c = 1$ and $a^{bc} = a^{0 \cdot c} = a^0 = 1$.

4. a. 6

b. $\frac{2}{3}$

c. 4

d. 8

e. 1

f. $2^{\frac{1}{2}}$ or $\sqrt{2}$

5. 1

6. The table below gives the minimum distance from the Earth to some astronomical objects.

Object	Distance From Earth (miles)
Moon	2.25×10^5
Mars	3.46×10^7
Pluto	2.66×10^9

A garden snail can move at the rate of 3×10^{-2} miles per hour. If a garden snail could fly through space at that rate, how many hours would it take to reach the Moon? To reach Mars? To reach Pluto?

7. Find the missing terms in each geometric sequence.

a. 16, 8, 4, ■, ■, ■, . . .
b. 2, ■, 18, ■, ■, ■, . . .
c. 1, a, a^2, ■, ■, ■, . . .
d. b^6, b^3, 1, ■, ■, ■, . . .
e. c^{10}, ■, ■, c^4, ■, ■, . . .

8. Here is a table for a function $h(x)$.

a. Find a rule $h(x)$ in the form $h(x) = c \cdot a^x$ that matches the table.

b. Copy and complete the table using this rule.

x	$h(x)$
−3	■
−2	■
−1	■
0	2
1	10
2	50
3	250
4	1250

9. Explain why $(2^3)(2^{-3}) = 1$.

On Your Own

10. Find each variable.

a. $2^5 \cdot 2^{-3} = 2^a$
b. $2^5 \cdot 2^{-7} = 2^b$
c. $\frac{2^5}{2^7} = 2^c$
d. $\frac{2^5}{2^{-7}} = 2^d$
e. $\frac{2^5}{2^f} = 2^8$

11. Decide whether each expression is equal to 5^3. Explain.

a. $\left(\frac{1}{5}\right)^{-3}$
b. $5^{-3} \cdot 5^3$
c. $(5^8)(5^{-2})$
d. $\frac{5^6}{5^9}$
e. $\frac{5^{10}}{5^2 5^3 5^2}$
f. $\left(\frac{1}{5^3}\right)$
g. $5^5 \cdot 5^{-2}$
h. $\left(\frac{1}{5^3}\right)^{-1}$
i. $(5^{15})^{\frac{1}{5}}$
j. $(5^2)^1$
k. $(5^4)^{-1}$
l. $\left(\frac{1}{5^{-3}}\right)$

Go Online PHSchool.com

For additional practice, go to **Web Code:** bfa-0503

EXERCISE 6 Although scientific notation is not covered in this lesson, this exercise is an opportunity to bring it up with your students. Stress the division with exponents in any discussion of this exercise. Also, decide whether you would like to talk about the different ways to write a number in scientific notation. This text does not include much about scientific notation for class-time considerations.

As an extension, you might ask students how many years the number of hours translates to, perhaps using scientific notation to represent the 8760 hours per calendar year.

On Your Own

EXERCISE 10 continues to use the underlying assumption that if $b^m = b^n$, then $m = n$. Students will prove this assumption later in the investigation. If some of your students are aware of this assumption and that it has not been proven yet, they are showing some real mathematical thinking.

EXERCISE 11 Watch for students doing this exercise by calculator only. The answer is $5^3 = 125$ so that students could check work with a calculator, but make sure students can explain why each answer works or does not work.

6. 0.75×10^7 h; 1.153×10^9 h; 0.89×10^{11} h

7. a. 16, 8, 4, 2, 1, $\frac{1}{2}$, . . .
b. 2, 6, 18, 54, 162, 486, . . . or 2, −6, 18, −54, 162, −486, . . .
c. 1, a, a^2, a^3, a^4, a^5, . . .
d. b^6, b^3, 1, b^{-3}, b^{-6}, b^{-9}, . . .
e. c^{10}, c^8, c^6, c^4, c^2, 1, . . .

8. a. $h(x) = 2 \cdot 5^x$
b. See back of book.

9. $(2^3)(2^{-3}) = 2^{3+(-3)} = 2^0 = 1$

10. a. 2
b. −2
c. −2
d. 12
e. −3

11. a. Yes; $\left(\frac{1}{5}\right)^{-3} = (5^{-1})^{-3} = 5^{-1 \cdot (-3)} = 5^3$
b. No; $5^{-3} \cdot 5^3 = 5^{-3+3} = 5^0 \neq 5^3$
c. No; $(5^8)(5^{-2}) = 5^{8+(-2)} = 5^6 \neq 5^3$
d. No; $\frac{5^6}{5^9} = 5^{6-9} = 5^{-3} \neq 5^3$
e. Yes; $\frac{5^{10}}{5^2 \cdot 5^3 \cdot 5^2} = \frac{5^{10}}{5^{2+3+2}} = \frac{5^{10}}{5^7} = 5^3$
f. No; $\frac{1}{5^3} = 5^{-3} \neq 5^3$
g. Yes; $5^5 \cdot 5^{-2} = 5^{5+(-2)} = 5^3$
h. Yes; $\left(\frac{1}{5^3}\right)^{-1} = (5^{-3})^{-1} = 5^{-3 \cdot (-1)} = 5^3$
i. Yes; $(5^{15})^{\frac{1}{5}} = 5^{15 \cdot \frac{1}{5}} = 5^3$
j. No; $(5^2)^1 = 5^{2 \cdot 1} = 5^2 \neq 5^3$
k. No; $(5^4)^{-1} = 5^{4 \cdot (-1)} = 5^{-4} \neq 5^3$
l. Yes; $\frac{1}{5^{-3}} = 5^{-(-3)} = 5^3$

EXERCISE 12 At the beginning of this chapter, the laws of exponents only applied to positive integer exponents. This exercise asks students to be specific about exactly how the laws have been extended. The most important reason to focus on this is that later in this chapter, the laws will be extended to rational and then real exponents. Beyond the scope of this book, these laws are further expanded to include complex number exponents and even matrix exponents.

EXERCISE 16 You may find some students performing illegal steps here, such as $3^{x^2} = (3^x)^2 = 3^{2x}$. Stop right there and use a numerical example to show that these illegal ideas do not work. For example $3^{4^2} = 3^{16} = 43{,}046{,}721$, but $(3^4)^2 = 81^2 = 6561$. There is no "any-grouping" property for exponents. Remind students to apply the laws as written in the text and not to write their own rules.

Maintain Your Skills

EXERCISE 23 is a follow-up question to Exercise 22, so elicit the connection between the two.

EXERCISE 24 previews the idea of finding the sum of a geometric series that students study in Chapter 7.

12. **Write About It** This lesson lists the laws of exponents twice, at the beginning and at the end of the lesson. Describe the differences between the first list and the second list.

13. Find the normal form of this polynomial.

$$(4x + 5y - 6z)^0 + (3xy^2 - 5z)^1$$

14. Expand each expression.

a. $(3^x + 3^{-x})^2$ **b.** $(3^x - 3^{-x})^2$ **c.** $(3^x + 3^{-x})^2 - (3^x - 3^{-x})^2$

15. Write each expression as a single power of z.

a. $(z^{-2})(z^4)$ **b.** $((z^3)^3)^{-3}$ **c.** $\frac{(z^2)(z^{-4})}{z^2}$

d. $\frac{(z^0)^4}{z^{10}}$ **e.** $\frac{(z^7)^0}{(z^0)(z^{11})}$

16. Suppose $f(x) = 3^x$ and $g(x) = x^2$. Find each value.

a. $(g \circ f)(1)$ **b.** $(g \circ f)(-1)$ **c.** $(g \circ f)(2)$

d. $(g \circ f)(x)$ **e.** $(f \circ g)(1)$ **f.** $(f \circ g)(-1)$

g. $(f \circ g)(2)$ **h.** $(f \circ g)(x)$

17. Copy and complete this table for $f(x) = 2^x$.

Input	Output
−3	■
−2	■
−1	■
0	■
1	■
2	4
3	■

18. Copy and complete this table for $g(x) = \left(\frac{1}{2}\right)^x$.

Input	Output
−3	■
−2	4
−1	■
0	■
1	■
2	■
3	■

19. Describe a relationship between the two tables in Exercises 17 and 18. Explain why the relationship holds.

Answers

12. Answers may vary. Sample: At the beginning of the lesson, the rules are given for positive integer exponents only, and the second law applies only when $b > c$. At the end of the lesson, these restrictions have been removed. The laws apply to all integer exponents, and the second law can also be used when $b \leq c$.

13. $3xy^2 - 5z + 1$

14. **a.** $3^{2x} + 2 + 3^{-2x}$
b. $3^{2x} - 2 + 3^{-2x}$
c. 4

15. **a.** z^2 **b.** z^{-27}
c. z^{-4} **d.** z^{-10}
e. z^{-11}

16. **a.** 9 **b.** $\frac{1}{9}$
c. 81 **d.** 3^{2x} or 9^x
e. 3 **f.** 3
g. 81 **h.** 3^{x^2}

17.

Input	Output
−3	$\frac{1}{8}$
−2	$\frac{1}{4}$
−1	$\frac{1}{2}$
0	1
1	2
2	4
3	8

18.

Input	Output
−3	8
−2	4
−1	2
0	1
1	$\frac{1}{2}$
2	$\frac{1}{4}$
3	$\frac{1}{8}$

20. Copy and complete this table for $w(x) = \left(\frac{-1 + i\sqrt{3}}{2}\right)^x$.

Input	Output
−3	■
−2	■
−1	■
0	■
1	■
2	■
3	1
4	■
5	■

Knowing that $w(3) = 1$ will help.

21. **Standardized Test Prep** Simplify $\frac{5^2 \cdot (5^{-3})^0}{5^{-6}}$.

A. 5^{-4} **B.** 5^5 **C.** 5^6 **D.** 5^8

Maintain Your Skills

22. Find the missing values in each geometric sequence.

a. 1, ■, ■, 125, . . .
b. 1, ■, ■, 27, ■, . . .
c. 1, ■, 64, . . .
d. 1, ■, ■, 64, . . .
e. 1, ■, ■, ■, ■, ■, 64, . . .

23. Solve each equation.

a. $x^3 = 125$
b. $x^3 = 27$
c. $x^2 = 64$
d. $x^3 = 64$
e. $x^6 = 64$

24. Calculate each sum. Express each result as a mixed number, such as $1\frac{2}{3}$.

a. 2^0
b. $2^0 + 2^{-1}$
c. $2^0 + 2^{-1} + 2^{-2}$
d. $2^0 + 2^{-1} + 2^{-2} + 2^{-3}$
e. $2^0 + 2^{-1} + 2^{-2} + 2^{-3} + 2^{-4}$
f. What is the sum if this pattern continues forever? Explain.

A dust mite is about 4.5×10^{-2} cm long.

Additional Resources

PRINT RESOURCES
- Solution Manual
- Practice Workbook
- Assessment Resources
- Teaching Resources

TECHNOLOGY
- Interactive Textbook
- TeacherExpress CD-ROM
- ExamView CD-ROM
- PHSchool.com

Additional Practice

1. Simplify each expression.

a. $2^4 \cdot 5^4$
b. $3^5 \cdot 12^5$
c. $\left(\frac{3}{2}\right)^3 \cdot \left(\frac{8}{15}\right)^3$
d. $15^3 \cdot \left(\frac{1}{15}\right)^3$

2. Decide whether each expression equals 3^4. Explain.

a. $3 \cdot 3 \cdot 3 \cdot 3$
b. $3^3 \cdot 3$
c. $3^2 + 3^2$
d. $\left(\frac{3^{12}}{3^3}\right)$
e. $\left(\frac{3^9}{3^5}\right)$
f. $(3^2)(2^3)$
g. $\frac{(3^3)^2}{3^2}$
h. $\left(\frac{3^2}{3}\right)^4$

3. Write each expression as a single power of x.

a. $x \cdot x^2 \cdot x \cdot x^2$
b. $x^2(x^2)^2$
c. $(x^5)^3$
d. $\left(\frac{x^9}{x^3}\right)$
e. $\left(\frac{x^{12}}{x^5}\right)$
f. $x^{24}\left(\frac{1}{x^4}\right)^5$

4. Find each variable.

a. $3^5 \cdot 3^{-3} = 3^a$
b. $\frac{5^5}{5^{-2}} = 5^b$
c. $\frac{4^6}{4^c} = 4^{10}$

5. Write each expression as a single power of y.

a. $y^2y^{-3}y^5$
b. $\left((y^2)^2\right)^{-2}$
c. $(y^5)^0$
d. $\left(\frac{y^9}{y^3}\right)^0$
e. $\left(\frac{y^{12}}{y^5}\right)^{-1}$
f. $y^4\left(\frac{1}{y^4}\right)^{-5}$

6. Complete each table.

a.

x	$f(x) = 3^x$
−2	
−1	
0	
1	
2	9

b.

x	$g(x) = \left(\frac{1}{3}\right)^x$
−2	9
−1	
0	
1	
2	

Practice: For Lesson 5.3, assign Exercises 4–6.

19. Answers may vary. Sample: The output for a given x-value in the second table is equal to the output for $-x$ in the first table; because $\frac{1}{2} = 2^{-1}$, $g(x) = \left(\frac{1}{2}\right)^x = (2^{-1})^x = 2^{-x} = f(-x)$.

20.

Input	Output
−3	1
−2	$\frac{-1 + i\sqrt{3}}{2}$
−1	$\frac{-1 - i\sqrt{3}}{2}$
0	1
1	$\frac{-1 + i\sqrt{3}}{2}$
2	$\frac{-1 - i\sqrt{3}}{2}$
3	1
4	$\frac{-1 + i\sqrt{3}}{2}$
5	$\frac{-1 - i\sqrt{3}}{2}$

21. D

22. a. 1, 5, 25, 125, . . .
b. 1, 3, 9, 27, 81, . . .
c. 1, 8, 64, . . . or 1, −8, 64, . . .
d. 1, 4, 16, 64, . . .
e. 1, 2, 4, 8, 16, 32, 64, . . . or 1, −2, 4, −8, 16, −32, 64, . . .

23. a. 5 **b.** 3 **c.** ±8
d. 4 **e.** ±2

24. a. 1 **b.** $1\frac{1}{2}$ **c.** $1\frac{3}{4}$
d. $1\frac{7}{8}$ **e.** $1\frac{15}{16}$
f. The sum gets closer and closer to 2.

Lesson Overview

GOAL

- Find missing terms in a geometric sequence and generate geometric sequences to interpret expressions involving rational exponents.
- Evaluate expressions involving rational exponents.

This lesson helps students see a concrete, but informal, way to calculate fractional powers, as a preparation for extending the set of allowable exponents to include all rational numbers. By relating multiplication to repeated addition of a number, developing an arithmetic sequence of that number's multiples, students see that multiplication by a fraction is the same as filling in missing terms in this arithmetic sequence. Similarly, exponentiation is related to repeated multiplication of the base, creating a geometric sequence of the base's powers. Raising a base to a fractional power is the same as filling in missing terms in this geometric sequence. In the lesson that follows, students confirm that this way of thinking about fractional exponents preserves the laws of exponents, and they will also define fractional exponents formally.

CHECK YOUR UNDERSTANDING
- Core: 1, 2, 3, 4, 5, 8, 9
- Optional: 6a, 7
- Extension: 6b

MATERIALS
- graphing calculators

HOMEWORK
- Core: 10, 11, 12, 13, 15, 17
- Optional: 14a, 16, 19, 20, 21
- Extension: 14b, 18

VOCABULARY
- arithmetic sequence
- geometric sequence

Launch

Start this lesson by defining *arithmetic sequence*. Make sure that students are able to connect multiplication by a fraction to filling in missing terms in an arithmetic sequence with For You to Do.

Explore

Circulate as students work. Have students verbalize their thinking as they complete the For You to Do problems.

5.4 Sequences and Operations

So far, the laws and definitions about exponents apply only to integer exponents—expressions like 5^{-2} or $(-3)^0$. An expression like $8^{\frac{2}{3}}$ is still undefined. This lesson seeks to build a conceptual understanding of how you can define expressions like $8^{\frac{2}{3}}$. One way to approach this is to look at the connections between repeated addition and repeated multiplication.

$$3 + 3 + 3 + 3 + 3 = 3 \cdot 5 \qquad 3 \cdot 3 \cdot 3 \cdot 3 \cdot 3 = 3^5$$

You can apply these types of calculations to fractions.

Repeated Addition

If you start with a number and keep adding the same quantity, you get a sequence with constant differences. Such a sequence is an arithmetic sequence.

Definition

A list of numbers is an arithmetic sequence if the difference *d* between any two consecutive terms is constant.

The following lists are examples of arithmetic sequences.

$1, 4, 7, 10, \ldots$
$5, 1, -3, -7, \ldots$
$3, 3 + 2i, 3 + 4i, \ldots$
$a, a + d, a + 2d, a + 3d, \ldots$

Chapter 7 will deal with these sequences in depth.

You can use an arithmetic sequence to list the integer multiples of any number by starting with 0 and repeatedly adding that number. Here are the multiples of 27.

$$0, 27, 54, 81, 108, 135, \ldots$$

If you add 27 five times, you get 135, so $27 \cdot 5 = 135$. But what is $27 \cdot \frac{2}{3}$? The result is 18, but how can you add something $\frac{2}{3}$ of one time?

One way is to insert extra terms in the arithmetic sequence between 0 and 27.

$$0, \blacksquare, \blacksquare, 27, \blacksquare, \blacksquare, 54, \blacksquare, \ldots$$

Start with 0, the identity for addition.

Since it remains an arithmetic sequence, you can replace the first blank with *d*. Then you can find the others in terms of *d*.

$$0, d, 2d, 3d, 4d, 5d, 6d, 7d, \ldots$$

Find *d* by setting up the equation $3d = 27$. So, *d* must be 9. Then you know that the sequence is

$$0, 9, 18, 27, 36, 45, 54, 63, \ldots$$

You get the result $27 \cdot \frac{2}{3} = 18$, since 18 is two thirds of the way from 0 to 27 in an arithmetic sequence.

For You to Do

1. Build an arithmetic sequence that shows that $16 \cdot \frac{3}{4} = 12$.

Answers

For You to Do

1. 0, 4, 8, 12, 16, . . .

Repeated Multiplication

When you start with a number and keep multiplying by the same quantity, you get a sequence with constant ratios. This sequence is a *geometric sequence.*

Definition

A list of numbers is a geometric sequence if the ratio r between any two consecutive terms is constant.

The following lists are examples of geometric sequences.

$1, 4, 16, 64, \ldots$

$2, 1, \frac{1}{2}, \frac{1}{4}, \ldots$

$-3, -6, -12, \ldots$

$a, ar, ar^2, ar^3, \ldots$

You can use a geometric sequence to list the integer powers of any number by starting with 1 and repeatedly multiplying by that number. Here are the powers of 27.

$$1;\ 27;\ 729;\ 19{,}683;\ 531{,}441, \ldots$$

If you multiply 1 by 27 four times, or multiply 4 factors of 27, you get 531,441. So, $27^4 = 531{,}441$. But what is $27^{\frac{2}{3}}$? How can you multiply 1 by something $\frac{2}{3}$ of one time?

One way is to insert extra terms in the geometric sequence between 1 and 27.

$$1, \blacksquare, \blacksquare, 27, \blacksquare, \blacksquare, 729, \blacksquare, \ldots$$

Assume it remains a geometric sequence. If you replace the first blank with r, you can find the other numbers in the sequence in terms of r.

$$1, r, r^2, r^3, r^4, r^5, r^6, r^7, \ldots$$

Find r by setting up the equation $r^3 = 27$. So, one possible value of r is 3. Then the sequence is

$$1, 3, 9, 27, 81, 243, 729, 2187, \ldots$$

Look at the sequence. The number 9 is two thirds of the way from 1 to 27. Then it makes sense to say that $27^{\frac{2}{3}} = 9$.

For You to Do

2. What is $27^{\frac{1}{3}}$? $27^{\frac{4}{3}}$? $27^{\frac{3}{3}}$?
3. Build a geometric sequence that shows that $16^{\frac{3}{4}} = 8$.

For Discussion

4. For $r^3 = 27$, the text says "one possible value of r is 3." Are there other possible values of r? Why does it make sense to pick $r = 3$ instead of the others?

The concept set forth here is an informal way of working with rational exponents. You will find a more formal definition in the next lesson. For the exercises that follow, use the laws of exponents or a geometric sequence model to work with expressions like $8^{\frac{2}{3}}$.

Habits of Mind

Check your method. You need to make sure that this way of thinking about fractional exponents is consistent with the laws of exponents.

For You to Do

PROBLEM 3 asks students to build a sequence that has 16 in it. Beware of students writing the sequence 1, 4, 16, . . . rather than 1, 2, 4, 8, 16, ... Another possible issue here is that some students may not want to start the sequence with 1. Remind students that 1 is the identity for multiplication. If students want to start with 0, remind them that since this is a geometric sequence, if the first term is 0, then all the terms are 0.

For You to Do

2. 3; 81; 27
3. 1, 2, 4, 8, 16, . . .

For Discussion

4. Answers may vary. Sample: If $r^3 = 27$, then $r^3 - 27 = 0$ and so $(r - 3)(r^2 + 3r + 9) = 0$. The solutions to this equation are $r = 3$ and $r = \frac{-3 \pm 3i\sqrt{3}}{2}$. It makes sense to pick $r = 3$ because it is the only real value of r.

Example 1

As a class, you could actually approximate the cube root of 17 by choosing different starting points for your sequence. Example 1 shows that the cube root of 17 is between 2 and 3, but how do you know if it is greater or less than 2.5? One method is to build a geometric sequence that begins 1, 2.5, 6.25, 15.625. . . . Since 15.625 is less than 17, you know that 2.5 is less than the cube root of 17. Try 2.6. The geometric sequence is then 1, 2.6, 6.76, 17.576. . . .

From these two examples, students know that $17^{\frac{1}{3}}$ is between 2.5 and 2.6 and that it is probably closer to 2.6, judging from the approximations.

Wrap Up

Work through as many of the Check Your Understanding core exercises as time allows. Exercises 2 and 4 may prove to be good indicators of students' understanding of the techniques shown in the lesson.

Assessment Resources

Lesson Quiz 5.4

1. Simplify each expression.
   - a. $26^{\frac{1}{2}} \cdot 26^{\frac{1}{2}}$
   - b. $8^{\frac{1}{3}} \cdot 8^{\frac{5}{3}}$
   - c. $\left(16^{\frac{1}{6}}\right)^3$
2. Find each value to the nearest integer. Do not use a calculator.
   - a. $11^{\frac{1}{2}}$
   - b. $61^{\frac{1}{3}}$
   - c. $16^{\frac{3}{4}}$
3. Solve each equation.
   - a. $4^x = 32$
   - b. $9^{x-2} = 27^{2x}$
   - c. $4^{2x+1} = 64$

Example 1

Problem Between what two integers is $17^{\frac{1}{3}}$?

Solution Build a geometric sequence starting with 1 and with the fourth term equal to 17.

$$1, ■, ■, 17, ■, ■, 289, ■, \ldots$$

The number for the first blank is $17^{\frac{1}{3}}$, the next is $17^{\frac{2}{3}}$, and so on.

If the ratio from one term to the next is r, the terms are

$$1, r, r^2, r^3, \ldots$$

If you match the two sequences, you can see that r equals $17^{\frac{1}{3}}$.

Since $2^3 = 8$ and $3^3 = 27$, the value of r is between 2 and 3. You can find a more accurate answer by solving $r^3 = 17$. Take the cube root:

$$r = \sqrt[3]{17} \approx 2.5713$$

For You to Do

5. Use the value of $17^{\frac{1}{3}}$ to find $17^{\frac{2}{3}}$ to three decimal places.
6. Between what two integers is $39^{\frac{1}{2}}$?

Example 2

Problem Solve $16^x = 32$ for x.

Solution Note that 16 and 32 are both powers of 2.

$$16^x = 32$$
$$(2^4)^x = 2^5$$
$$2^{4x} = 2^5$$
$$4x = 5$$
$$x = \frac{5}{4}$$

Another method is to write the geometric sequence of powers of 2, starting with $2^0 = 1$.

$$1, 2, 4, 8, 16, 32, 64, 128, \ldots$$

16 is 2^4. Counting by one-fourth powers, $16^{\frac{1}{4}} = 2$ and $16^{\frac{5}{4}} = 32$.

Habits of Mind

Use a key characteristic. To deduce $4x = 5$ from $2^{4x} = 2^5$, you can use the fact that the function $f(x) = 2^x$ is one-to-one. You will prove this later.

Answers

For You to Do

5. 6.612
6. 6 and 7

For You to Do

7. Solve $32^y = 16$ for y.

This lesson gives some ideas about the meaning of symbols like $27^{\frac{1}{3}}$. A big question remains: Does this method of extending the use of exponents still preserve the important laws of exponents? That question, along with the formal definition of rational exponents, is the subject of the next lesson.

Exercises *Practicing Habits of Mind*

Check Your Understanding

1. Find the missing terms in each arithmetic sequence.
   a. 0, 3, 6, ■, ■, ■, . . .
   b. 0, ■, ■, ■, ■, 30, . . .
   c. 1, ■, ■, ■, 81, ■, . . .
   d. 5, ■, ■, −7, ■, ■, ■, . . .
2. **Write About It** Describe how you can use the arithmetic sequence in Exercise 1b to show that $30 \cdot \frac{3}{5} = 18$.
3. Find the missing terms in each geometric sequence.
   a. 2, −6, 18, ■, ■, ■, . . .
   b. 1, i, −1, ■, ■, ■, . . .
   c. 1, ■, 5, ■, ■, ■, . . .
   d. 1, ■, ■, 125, ■, . . .
   e. 1, ■, ■, ■, 9, ■, ■, . . .
4. **Write About It** Describe how you can use the geometric sequence in Exercise 3d to show that $125^{\frac{2}{3}} = 25$.
5. Let $a, b > 0$. For each type of sequence, find an expression in terms of a and b for the missing number in the sequence below.

   $$a, ■, b$$

   a. arithmetic sequence
   b. geometric sequence

For You to Do

7. $\frac{4}{5}$

Exercises

1. a. 0, 3, 6, **9, 12, 15,** . . .
   b. 0, **6, 12, 18, 24,** 30, . . .
   c. 1, **21, 41, 61,** 81, **101,** . . .
   d. 5, **1, −3,** −7, **−11, −15, −19,** . . .
2. There are five "steps" from 0 to 30, so the third step, 18, is three-fifths of the way from 0 to 30.
3. a. 2, −6, 18, **−54, 162, −486,** . . .
   b. 1, i, −1, **$-i$, 1, i,** . . .
   c. 1, **$\sqrt{5}$,** 5, **$5\sqrt{5}$, 25, $25\sqrt{5}$,** . . .
   d. 1, **5, 25,** 125, **625,** . . .
   e. 1, **$\sqrt{3}$, 3, $3\sqrt{3}$,** 9, **$9\sqrt{3}$. 27,** . . .
4. There are three "steps" from 1 to 125, so the second step, 25, is two-thirds of the way from 1 to 125.
5. a. $\frac{a+b}{2}$ b. $\sqrt{ab}$

Exercises

HOMEWORK
- Core: 10, 11, 12, 13, 15, 17
- Optional: 14a, 16, 19, 20, 21
- Extension: 14b, 18

Check Your Understanding

EXERCISE 1 It may help some students to represent the unknown difference as d and use the sequence as a way to write an equation in d. For example, in part (b), they could write $0, d, 2d, 3d, 4d, 5d = 30$. Then, since $5d = 30$, $d = 6$.

EXERCISE 3 Some students may find it helpful to write the sequence in terms of r, the common ratio. This helps them generate an equation to solve for the ratio and find the missing terms.

EXERCISE 4 By drawing parallels to the (perhaps) more familiar arithmetic sequence and fractional multiplication, this method for finding rational powers of a number may make the process more concrete for your students. Some may still want to use a calculator to check their work, knowing that their calculators can compute fractional powers perfectly well, but encourage all of your students to try working these problems by hand.

EXERCISE 5 is an important reminder to students that they have to know what kind of a sequence they are working with before they can find missing terms. You might remind them of their work in Chapter 2 in which they used Lagrange interpolation. In that chapter, they showed that no matter how many initial terms they had in a table for a sequence of numbers, they could find a function that would generate the table but still make the next term be any number they wanted it to be.

EXERCISE 6 Students proved the arithmetic-geometric mean inequality in CME Project *Algebra 1* and *Geometry*. This table may suggest that the inequality holds, but to conclude that it is actually true for any positive a and b, students need to supply a general proof.

EXERCISE 7 Students have seen the alternating sign pattern that results from a negative ratio in earlier exercises, but they may not think of it right away. If they cannot think of another way to complete the sequence, suggest they look back at Exercise 3.

EXERCISE 8 In the next lesson, students prove that the way they have been thinking of rational exponents—as missing terms in a geometric sequence—allows them to rely on the laws of exponents to calculate the value of an expression with a rational exponent. Suzanne is taking the step of assuming that the laws should hold.

EXERCISE 9 Students who have not yet made connections between expressions such as $17^{\frac{1}{2}}$ and $\sqrt{17}$ may find this exercise challenging. Encourage them to think of the geometric sequence and to guess at the "step" they will need to take to get to their goal. For example, if they try a ratio of 3 for part (a), they did get the sequence 1, 3, 9. The third step needs to be 17, so they should try a greater step. With a ratio of 4, the sequence is 1, 4, 16. They are almost there, but not quite. With a ratio of 5, the sequence is 1, 5, 25, and that is too far. So you can conclude that the ratio that would get you to 17 on the third step must be between 4 and 5 and much closer to 4 than to 5.

On Your Own

EXERCISE 10 The hope here is that students recognize that they can apply the laws of exponents to expressions like the ones in this exercise. They can calculate each part using the geometric sequence methods described in the lesson to evaluate each term, but students will find the exercise simpler if they use the laws of exponents.

EXERCISE 11 is another exercise designed to encourage students to take the step of using the laws of exponents on expressions with rational exponents.

6. a. Copy and complete the following table.

(a, b)	$\frac{a+b}{2}$	$\sqrt{ab}$
(1, 2)	1.5	1.4142
(2, 5)	■	■
(4, 1)	■	■
(3, 3)	■	■
(6, 9)	■	■
(8, 10)	■	■
(7, 7)	■	■

Approximate the square roots to 4 decimal places.

b. **Take It Further** Let $a > 0$ and $b > 0$. Which is greater, $\frac{a+b}{2}$ or $\sqrt{ab}$? Explain your reasoning.

7. Here is a geometric sequence with three missing terms.

1, ■, ■, ■, 16, ...

Alan says that there is more than one possible way to fill in the missing terms. Is he right? Find as many ways as you can to fill in the missing terms.

8. Suzanne has another method for calculating expressions like $81^{\frac{3}{4}}$. She says, "The Fundamental Law of Exponents says that I add exponents when I multiply, so I write down as many $81^{\frac{3}{4}}$ terms as I need to get rid of the denominator. The number of terms is always whatever the denominator is. So here it's 4 of them.

$$81^{\frac{3}{4}} \cdot 81^{\frac{3}{4}} \cdot 81^{\frac{3}{4}} \cdot 81^{\frac{3}{4}}$$

"The result is 81^3. So I have to multiply it four times. If we let x denote $81^{\frac{3}{4}}$, then $x^4 = 81^3$.

"Then I find the root on the calculator, if it's too big for me to figure out in my head: $x = \sqrt[4]{81^3} = 27$."

Use Suzanne's method to calculate $64^{\frac{2}{3}}$ and $625^{\frac{1}{4}}$.

9. Find each value to the nearest integer. Do not use a calculator.

a. $17^{\frac{1}{2}}$ **b.** $25^{\frac{1}{3}}$ **c.** $84^{\frac{1}{4}}$ **d.** $32^{\frac{4}{5}}$

On Your Own

10. Simplify each expression.

a. $81^{\frac{1}{2}} \cdot 81^{\frac{1}{2}}$ **b.** $(27^{\frac{1}{3}})^3$ **c.** $16^{\frac{3}{4}} \cdot 16^{\frac{1}{4}}$ **d.** $(9^{\frac{1}{2}})^3$

11. Find each value to the nearest integer. Do not use a calculator.

a. $27^{\frac{1}{2}}$ **b.** $7^{\frac{1}{3}}$ **c.** $64^{\frac{5}{6}}$ **d.** $117^{\frac{1}{3}}$

Answers

6. See back of book.

7. Yes; the missing terms could be 2, 4, 8, or −2, 4, −8.

8. $64^{\frac{2}{3}} = 16$, $625^{\frac{1}{4}} = 5$

9. a. 4 **b.** 3 **c.** 3 **d.** 16

10. a. 81 **b.** 27 **c.** 16 **d.** 27

11. a. 5 **b.** 2 **c.** 32 **d.** 5

12. a. See back of book.
b. Geometric; the ratio of each balance to the previous balance is 1.03.

13. a. 5 **b.** 10 **c.** 7
d. 1 **e.** 4

14. a. $f(x) = \sqrt{x}$
b. $g(x) = x^{\frac{1}{4}}$ or $g(x) = \sqrt[4]{x}$

15. C

12. Sarah invests \$500 in a savings account that grows by 3% per year.

a. Copy and complete the table. Round to the nearest cent.

b. Does the balance follow an arithmetic or a geometric sequence? Explain.

Years	Balance (dollars)
0	500.00
1	515.00
2	530.45
3	■
4	■
5	■
6	■

Go Online PHSchool.com

For additional practice, go to **Web Code:** bfa-0504

13. Suppose $f(x) = x^{\frac{1}{2}}$. Calculate each value.

a. $f(25)$ **b.** $f(100)$ **c.** $f(49)$ **d.** $f(1)$ **e.** $f(f(256))$

14. a. Based on your work in Exercise 13, write another function rule that could be equivalent to $f(x) = x^{\frac{1}{2}}$.

b. **Take It Further** Write a function rule that could be equivalent to $f(f(x))$.

15. **Standardized Test Prep** What is the next term in the geometric sequence 4, 6, 9, . . . ?

A. $\frac{3}{2}$ **B.** 12 **C.** $\frac{27}{2}$ **D.** 15

16. Are there any sequences that are both arithmetic and geometric? Explain.

17. Solve each equation.

a. $8^x = 4$ **b.** $5^x = 25^{x-3}$ **c.** $3^{2x-1} = 9^{x+1}$

d. $8^{2x} = 4^{x-1}$ **e.** $8^x = 3^x$

18. **Take It Further** Find all solutions to each equation.

a. $4^x + 2^x - 6 = 0$ **b.** $9^x - 12 \cdot 3^x + 27 = 0$

c. $16^x - 6 \cdot 4^x + 8 = 0$

Maintain Your Skills

19. Simplify each expression.

a. $\frac{8^{\frac{4}{3}}}{8^{\frac{1}{3}}}$ **b.** $\frac{27}{27^{\frac{2}{3}}}$ **c.** $\frac{125^{\frac{1}{3}}}{125^{\frac{2}{3}}}$ **d.** $\frac{49^{\frac{1}{2}}}{49^{\frac{3}{2}}}$ **e.** $\frac{17^{\frac{7}{5}}}{17^{\frac{2}{5}}}$

20. Find the number of real solutions to each equation.

a. $x^3 = 8$ **b.** $x^4 = 16$ **c.** $x^3 = 7$

d. $x^5 = -32$ **e.** $x^4 = -4$ **f.** $x^3 = -27$

21. Given a real number $a \neq 0$ and a positive integer n, how many real solutions does $x^n = a$ have? Explain.

Go Online Video Tutor PHSchool.com

Web Code: bfe-0775

16. Yes; the sequence $a, a, a, \ldots$ is an arithmetic sequence with common difference $d = 0$, and is a geometric sequence with common ratio $r = 1$.

17. a. $\frac{2}{3}$

b. 6

c. no solution

d. $-\frac{1}{2}$

e. 0

18. a. 1 **b.** 1, 2 **c.** 1, $\frac{1}{2}$

19. a. 8 **b.** 3

c. $\frac{1}{5}$ **d.** $\frac{1}{49}$

e. 17

20. a. 1 **b.** 2 **c.** 1

d. 1 **e.** 0 **f.** 1

21. 0, 1, or 2; if n is odd, then the equation has one real solution, which is negative if $a < 0$ and is positive if $a > 0$. If n is even, then the equation has two solutions if $a > 0$ and has no solutions if $a < 0$.

EXERCISES 13 AND 14 If students have not yet made the connection between $x^{\frac{1}{2}}$ and $\sqrt{x}$, Exercises 13 and 14 may help. If you assign Exercise 14, you should also assign Exercise 13.

EXERCISE 17 is another instance in which students must assume that if $b^m = b^n$, then $m = n$. Later in the chapter, students prove that the function $y = a \cdot b^x$ is one-to-one, and this assumption is a consequence of that fact.

Maintain Your Skills

EXERCISE 19 The calculations go much faster if students recognize that the quotient rule for exponents should still apply to rational exponents. Consider doing the exercise two different ways. First, use the quotient rule to subtract the exponents. For example, part (a) gives $8^{\frac{4}{3} - \frac{1}{3}} = 8^1 = 8$. Second, evaluate each numerator and denominator and then divide. Once again, you will get 8, of course. The second way gives more practice with fractional exponents, but the exercise is constructed so that the first method is more efficient and convinces students that the laws of exponents that they already know are still valid. The last part tests whether this pattern has been learned, since otherwise students must approximate the values on a calculator.

Additional Resources

PRINT RESOURCES
- Solution Manual
- Practice Workbook
- Assessment Resources
- Teaching Resources

TECHNOLOGY
- Interactive Textbook
- TeacherExpress CD-ROM
- ExamView CD-ROM
- PHSchool.com

Additional Practice

1. Simplify each expression.

a. $16^{\frac{1}{2}} \cdot 16^{\frac{1}{2}}$ **b.** $64^{\frac{1}{3}} \cdot 64^{\frac{2}{3}}$ **c.** $(32^{\frac{1}{5}})^{10}$

2. Find each value to the nearest integer. Do not use a calculator.

a. $20^{\frac{1}{2}}$ **b.** $15^{\frac{1}{3}}$ **c.** $81^{\frac{3}{4}}$

3. Lauren invests \$1000 in a savings account that grows by 4% per year.

a. Complete the table. Round to the nearest cent.

Years	Balance (dollars)
0	
1	
2	
3	
4	
5	

b. Does the balance follow an arithmetic or a geometric sequence? Explain.

4. Suppose $f(x) = x^{\frac{1}{3}}$. Calculate each value.

a. $f(8)$ **b.** $f(125)$ **c.** $f(1000)$

5. Find all four solutions to the equation $x^4 = 16$.

6. a. What number is defined to be $16^{\frac{1}{4}}$?

b. What is $16^{-\frac{1}{4}}$? Use a law of exponents.

7. Show that $27^{\frac{1}{6}} = \sqrt{3}$.

8. Here is a geometric sequence.

$1, \square, \square, \square, x^3, \square, \square, \square, \square, \ldots \square$

Write the missing terms as expressions of x.

Practice: For Lesson 5.4, assign Exercises 1–4.

Lesson Overview

GOALS

- Evaluate expressions involving rational exponents.
- Convert between exponential and radical forms for rational exponents.

Now that students have some experience in computing rational exponents as missing terms in a geometric sequence, they will need to examine whether that interpretation is consistent with the laws of exponents. They consider this algebraic extension carefully, and their work leads to a more exact definition of rational exponents.

CHECK YOUR UNDERSTANDING
- Core: 1, 2, 3, 4, 6
- Optional: 7
- Extension: 5

MATERIALS
- graph paper
- graphing calculators

HOMEWORK
- Core: 9, 10, 11, 13, 14, 15, 16
- Optional: 8, 17, 18
- Extension: 12

VOCABULARY
- rational exponent
- real *n*th root, $\sqrt[n]{r}$
- rational exponent, $a^{\frac{p}{q}}$
- unit fraction exponent, $a^{\frac{1}{n}}$

Launch

Begin today's lesson with the For You to Do Problems 1 and 2.

Explore

For You to Do

In Problem 1, students should use the fact that $8^{\frac{1}{3}} = 2$ and write $8^{\frac{2}{3}}$ as $(8^{\frac{1}{3}})^2$. This is not the only way to do this problem, however. For example, students could also write $8^{\frac{2}{3}}$ as $8^{1-\frac{2}{3}}$ or as $8^{\frac{1}{3}+\frac{1}{3}}$.

In Problem 2, students can rewrite the expression as $(8^{\frac{2}{3}})^{-1} = 4^{-1}$, or they can use the definition of a negative exponent from the last lesson to write the expression as $\frac{1}{8^{\frac{2}{3}}}$. Encourage students to be creative and find more than one way to solve these problems.

Have students share their thinking for how they worked For You to Do Problems 3–5.

5.5 Defining Rational Exponents

The previous lesson introduced a way of thinking about rational exponents. This lesson focuses on rational exponents from an algebraic perspective. It also covers how you should define rational exponents for the laws of exponents to apply. This idea of extension is extremely important in algebra. You will extend the set of possible exponents from integers to rational numbers in a way that ensures the laws of exponents and the related formulas still hold.

Consider the expression $8^{\frac{1}{3}}$. Corollary 5.1.2 says,

$$(a^b)^c = a^{bc}$$

Suppose you apply this rule to $8^{\frac{1}{3}}$. Try cubing it.

$$(8^{\frac{1}{3}})^3 = 8^{\left(\frac{1}{3}\cdot 3\right)} = 8^1 = 8$$

So, if $8^{\frac{1}{3}}$ means anything at all, it has to be a number with a cube that is 8. There is only one real number with a cube that is 8. Therefore, it makes sense to define

$$8^{\frac{1}{3}} = 2$$

For You to Do

1. Use Corollary 5.1.2 to determine what $8^{\frac{2}{3}}$ should mean.
2. What should $8^{-\frac{2}{3}}$ mean? Explain.

What is $7^{\frac{1}{3}}$? The same reasoning tells you that it should mean a number with a cube that is 7. The only real number with a cube that is 7 is $\sqrt[3]{7}$, so it makes sense to define

$$7^{\frac{1}{3}} = \sqrt[3]{7}$$

In general, if *a* is any real number, then $a^{\frac{1}{3}}$ is equal to $\sqrt[3]{a}$.

Minds in Action — episode 19

Tony wonders what to do when there is more than one real-number choice for a root.

Tony So I realize I should pick the real number when I can. What can I do about $16^{\frac{1}{4}}$? It's a number with fourth power 16. But there's more than one choice.

$$2^4 = 16 \quad (-2)^4 = 16 \quad (2i)^4 = 16 \quad (-2i)^4 = 16$$

There are four numbers with a fourth power of 16. So now I have to pick one. I know I should pick a real number, but then I still have to decide between 2 and −2. I'll just pick 2. It's the positive one. Besides, it's the one I get when I type $16^{\frac{1}{4}}$ into a calculator.

Answers

For You to Do

1. 4
2. $\frac{1}{4}$; answers may vary. Sample: If $8^{\frac{1}{3}} = 2$, then $8^{-\frac{2}{3}} = (8^{\frac{1}{3}})^{-2} = 2^{-2} = \frac{1}{2^2} = \frac{1}{4}$.

Developing Habits of Mind

Establish a process. Consider the expression $a^{\frac{1}{n}}$. If $a^{\frac{1}{n}}$ equals a number x, then you can use Corollary 5.1.2 to remove the fraction.

$$x = a^{\frac{1}{n}}$$
$$x^n = \left(a^{\frac{1}{n}}\right)^n$$
$$x^n = a$$

The value of x comes from the equation $x^n = a$. This equation has n complex solutions, and either 0, 1, or 2 of these solutions are real numbers.

Tony had to make a choice when there were two real solutions. He picked the one that is commonly used. The choice is arbitrary. It makes just as much sense to let $16^{\frac{1}{4}}$ equal -2. In general, you use the positive solution.

Overall, to find the value of an expression like $a^{\frac{1}{n}}$, look at the real solutions to $x^n = a$.

- If there is one real solution to the equation $x^n = a$, use it. For example, $(-8)^{\frac{1}{3}} = -2$.
- If there are two real solutions to the equation $x^n = a$, use the positive solution. For example, $9^{\frac{1}{2}}$ is 3 and not -3.
- If there are no real solutions to the equation $x^n = a$, then $a^{\frac{1}{n}}$ is left undefined in this course. For example, $(-4)^{\frac{1}{4}}$ is undefined.

There is more to the story. In later courses, you will learn that you can choose one of the n roots in the complex plane. For example, you can define $(-4)^{\frac{1}{4}}$ to be equal to $1 + i$.

Definitions

Unit fraction exponent: The expression $a^{\frac{1}{n}}$ is defined, when possible, as the real ***n*th root** of a.

$$a^{\frac{1}{n}} = \sqrt[n]{a}$$

If there is no real nth root of a, then $a^{\frac{1}{n}}$ is undefined in this course.

Most scientific calculators have a square root key. Some have a cube root key. A few have keys for fourth roots or larger roots. This definition of rational exponents explains why: you can always evaluate $\sqrt[6]{5}$ on a calculator as $5^{\frac{1}{6}}$.

Calculators may give different answers to some expressions with fractional exponents, depending on what mode they are in. For example, a calculator may say $(-4)^{\frac{1}{2}}$ is an error in normal mode, but is equal to $2i$ when the calculator is in complex mode.

What is $8^{\frac{2}{3}}$? Use the laws of exponents. The rule $a^b \cdot a^c = a^{b+c}$ gives

$$8^{\frac{2}{3}} = 8^{\frac{1}{3}} \cdot 8^{\frac{1}{3}} = \sqrt[3]{8} \cdot \sqrt[3]{8} = \left(\sqrt[3]{8}\right)^2$$

You can also use the rule $(a^b)^c = a^{bc}$.

$$8^{\frac{2}{3}} = \left(8^{\frac{1}{3}}\right)^2 = \left(\sqrt[3]{8}\right)^2$$

Applying this logic to the general case gives the following definition.

Developing Habits of Mind

The discussion here is similar to the discussion students saw in CME Project *Algebra 1* about the definition of the square root symbol. Students should know from *Algebra 1* that $\sqrt{9} = 3$, and not -3. With other fractional exponents, there is not the same ambiguity in the real numbers. For example, $16^{\frac{1}{3}}$ can only be defined as a real number in one way. That is, there is only one real number that solves the equation $x^3 = 16$.

Wrap Up

Go over as many of the Check Your Understanding core exercises as time allows.

Assessment Resources

Lesson Quiz 5.5

1. Simplify each expression.
   a. $9^{\frac{1}{4}} \cdot 9^{\frac{1}{4}}$
   b. $8^{-\frac{2}{3}}$
   c. $\left(16^{\frac{3}{2}}\right)^{\frac{2}{3}}$
   d. $\left(27^{\frac{3}{2}}\right)^{-\frac{4}{9}}$

2. a. Find all four solutions to the equation $x^4 = 256$.
   b. What number is defined to be $256^{\frac{1}{4}}$?
   c. What is $256^{\frac{1}{4}}$? Use a law of exponents.

3. Show that $8^{\frac{1}{6}} = \sqrt{2}$.

Exercises

HOMEWORK
- Core: 9, 10, 11, 13, 14, 15, 16
- Optional: 8, 17, 18
- Extension: 12

Check Your Understanding

EXERCISE 1 If students are to get the full benefit of this exercise, they should complete it without a calculator.

EXERCISE 2 Students can do all of these parts without a calculator. Encourage students to reason out the results first, using the laws of exponents.

EXERCISE 3 The step of "raising each side of the equation to the nth power" is part of the proof that the number a making $10^a = 2$ (for example) is irrational.

Definition

Rational exponent: For integers p and q with $q > 0$, if $a^{\frac{1}{q}}$ is a real number, then

$$a^{\frac{p}{q}} = \left(a^{\frac{1}{q}}\right)^p = \left(\sqrt[q]{a}\right)^p$$

So, $a^{\frac{1}{2}} = \sqrt{a}$,
$a^{\frac{2}{3}} = (a^{\frac{1}{3}})^2 = (\sqrt[3]{a})^2$,
and $a^{\frac{3}{3}} = \sqrt[3]{a^3} = a$.

For You to Do

Simplify each expression in two different ways. Evaluate the rational exponents and use the laws of exponents.

3. $27^{\frac{2}{3}} \cdot 27^{\frac{1}{3}}$ **4.** $\dfrac{64^{\frac{1}{2}}}{64^{\frac{1}{3}}}$ **5.** $\left(16^{\frac{3}{4}}\right)^2$

The laws of exponents leave little choice for these definitions. If $9^{\frac{1}{2}}$ means anything at all, it must satisfy the equation

$$\left(9^{\frac{1}{2}}\right)^2 = 9$$

The only decision left is whether to let this expression equal 3 or -3. You learned to use the positive value when there is an option.

In the next investigation, you will see a few examples that the rules still do not cover. For example, how should you define $3^{\sqrt{2}}$?

Exercises *Practicing Habits of Mind*

Check Your Understanding

1. a. Give an approximation for $37^{\frac{1}{2}}$.
b. Give an approximation for $37^{\frac{3}{2}}$.

2. Simplify each expression.
a. $3^{\frac{1}{3}} \cdot 9^{\frac{1}{3}}$ **b.** $64^{\frac{5}{6}}$ **c.** $\left(7^{\frac{1}{3}}\right)^6$ **d.** $81^{\frac{1}{3}} \cdot 81^{\frac{1}{6}}$

3. Suppose two numbers a and b satisfy this relationship.

$$a^{\frac{2}{5}} = b$$

a. Find possible values for a and b, not including $a = b = 1$ or $a = b = 0$.
b. Is the equation $a^2 = b^5$ true for all numbers a and b that satisfy the equation $a^{\frac{2}{5}} = b$? Explain.

Answers

For You to Do

3. $27^{\frac{2}{3}} \cdot 27^{\frac{1}{3}} = 3^2 \cdot 3 = 9 \cdot 3 = 27$;
$27^{\frac{2}{3}} \cdot 27^{\frac{1}{3}} = 27^{\frac{2}{3}+\frac{1}{3}} = 27^1 = 27$

4. $\dfrac{64^{\frac{1}{2}}}{64^{\frac{1}{3}}} = \dfrac{8}{4} = 2$; $\dfrac{64^{\frac{1}{2}}}{64^{\frac{1}{3}}} = 64^{\frac{1}{2}-\frac{1}{3}} = 64^{\frac{1}{6}} = 2$

5. $\left(16^{\frac{3}{4}}\right)^2 = (2^3)^2 = 8^2 = 64$;
$\left(16^{\frac{3}{4}}\right)^2 = 16^{\frac{3}{2}} = 4^3 = 64$

Exercises

1. a. a little more than 6
b. Answers may vary. Sample: a little more than 222

2. a. 3 **b.** 32
c. 49 **d.** 9

3. a. Answers may vary. Sample: $a = 32$, $b = 4$
b. Yes; if $a^{\frac{2}{5}} = b$, then $\left(a^{\frac{2}{5}}\right)^5 = b^5$, which simplifies to $a^2 = b^5$.

4. $1^{\frac{p}{q}} = (1^p)^{\frac{1}{q}} = 1^{\frac{1}{q}} = \sqrt[q]{1} = 1$

5. The graph is made up of points from the horizontal lines $y = 1$ and $y = -1$. It consists of the points $(x, 1)$ when x is an even integer and $(x, -1)$ when x is an odd integer. If x is not an integer, the output is sometimes defined (for example, $(-1)^{\frac{1}{3}} = -1$) and sometimes not defined (for example, $(-1)^{\frac{1}{2}}$ is not a real number).

4. Use the definition of a rational exponent to prove that $1^{\frac{p}{q}} = 1$ for any integers p and q, with $q > 0$.

5. **Take It Further** The graph of $f(x) = 1^x$ is a horizontal line. Describe the graph of $g(x) = (-1)^x$.

6. Consider the functions $a(x) = x^2$ and $b(x) = x^{\frac{1}{2}}$.
   a. Calculate $a(b(9))$ and $b(a(7))$.
   b. Are $a(x)$ and $b(x)$ inverse functions? Explain.

7. Prove this statement.
   If $a, b, c, d, \ldots$ is an arithmetic sequence, then $10^a, 10^b, 10^c, 10^d, \ldots$ is a geometric sequence.

On Your Own

8. **Write About It** Explain why $(-25)^{\frac{1}{2}}$ is undefined in this course.

9. Simplify each expression.
   a. $7^{\frac{1}{3}} \cdot 7^{-\frac{1}{3}}$
   b. $27^{-\frac{2}{3}}$
   c. $\left(9^{\frac{2}{3}}\right)^{\frac{3}{4}}$
   d. $\left(62^{\frac{a}{3}}\right)^{\frac{3}{a}}$

10. Find all four solutions to the equation $x^4 = 81$.

11. a. What number is defined to be $81^{\frac{1}{4}}$?
    b. What is $81^{-\frac{1}{4}}$? Use a law of exponents.

12. **Take It Further** Suppose a function $E(x)$ is defined for all real numbers x. Let $E(1) = 3$. The function follows the rule below for any numbers a and b.

$$E(a + b) = E(a) \cdot E(b)$$

   a. Show that $E(0) = 1$.
   b. Find $E(4)$.
   c. Show that $E(n) = 3 \cdot E(n - 1)$ for any n.
   d. Write a function rule for $E(x)$.

13. Show that $8^{\frac{1}{6}} = \sqrt{2}$.

14. Here is a geometric sequence.

$$1, ■, ■, a^2, ■, ■, ■, ■, \ldots$$

   Write the missing terms as expressions of a.

Go Online PHSchool.com

For additional practice, go to **Web Code:** bfa-0505

EXERCISE 5 is one function for which a graphing calculator will not be able to give students a good idea of what the graph looks like. Encourage students to plot points and think about the overall picture.

EXERCISE 6 may help students remember that for a function to have an inverse it must be one-to-one. If you restrict the domain of $a(x)$ to nonnegative real numbers, that piece of the function is one-to-one, and the two functions are inverses.

EXERCISE 7 Students who are able to solve this exercise demonstrate a solid understanding of the definitions of both arithmetic and geometric sequences.

On Your Own

EXERCISE 8 reminds students that the definition of *rational exponent* in this course does not allow for a complex solution.

EXERCISES 10 AND 11 Make sure that students notice the difference between solving Exercise 10 and Exercise 11, in which they are asked to evaluate $81^{\frac{1}{4}}$.

EXERCISE 14 The expectation here is that students will use rational exponents rather than expressions such as $\sqrt[3]{a^2}$. However, both ways of solving the problem are correct.

6. a. $a(b(9)) = 9,\ b(a(7)) = 7$
b. No; answers may vary. Sample: It is not always true that $b(a(x)) = x$. For example, $b(a(-7)) = b(49) = 7$.

7. If $a, b, c, d, \ldots$ is an arithmetic sequence, then $b = a + k$, $c = a + 2k$, $d = a + 3k, \ldots$, for some number k. Then $10^b = 10^{a+k} = 10^a \cdot 10^k$, $10^c = 10^{a+2k} = 10^a \cdot 10^{2k}$, and $10^d = 10^{a+3k} = 10^a \cdot 10^{3k}$. Thus $10^a, 10^b, 10^c, 10^d, \ldots$ is a geometric sequence with the common ratio 10^k.

8. Using our definition of a rational exponent would mean that $(-25)^{\frac{1}{2}}$ is the real number that is the square root of -25, which does not exist.

9. a. 1
b. $\frac{1}{9}$
c. 3
d. 62

10. $\pm 3, \pm 3i$

11. a. 3
b. $\frac{1}{3}$

12. a. $E(1) = E(0 + 1) = E(0) \cdot E(1)$ so $3 = E(0) \cdot 3$ and $E(0) = 1$.
b. 81
c. $E(n) = E(1 + n - 1) = E(1) \cdot E(n - 1) = 3 \cdot E(n - 1)$
d. $E(x) = 3^x$

13. $8^{\frac{1}{6}} = (2^3)^{\frac{1}{6}} = 2^{\frac{3}{6}} = 2^{\frac{1}{2}} = \sqrt{2}$

14. $1, a^{\frac{2}{3}}, a^{\frac{4}{3}}, a^2, a^{\frac{8}{3}}, a^{\frac{10}{3}}, a^4, a^{\frac{14}{3}}, \ldots$

EXERCISE 15 Elicit the fact that $f(x)$ and $g(x)$ are inverse functions, since it will be a good reminder as students head toward exponential and logarithm functions later in this chapter. Students are not expected to use a graphing calculator here, but many probably will. They will need a scientific calculator for some of the calculations.

Maintain Your Skills

EXERCISE 17 Ask students how they could build the number 4 using only 10^a. Unfortunately, they may say $10^a + 10^a$. If so, ask them how to build 8 or 16 using only 10^a. At some point, they should realize they will be better off writing $10^a \cdot 10^a$ or just $(10^a)^2$ for 4. This will help students see why the relationships among parts (a), (b), (c), and (d) hold. You might point out that $b = 2a$, $c = 3a$, and $d = 4a$.

EXERCISE 18 Use the same idea as in Exercise 17. Start by asking, "How could I build 6 using only 10^a and 10^b?" You might point out that $a = b = c$, $a + c = d$, and $b + d = f$.

Additional Resources

PRINT RESOURCES
- Solution Manual
- Practice Workbook
- Assessment Resources
- Teaching Resources

TECHNOLOGY
- Interactive Textbook
- TeacherExpress CD-ROM
- ExamView CD-ROM
- PHSchool.com

Additional Practice

1. Simplify each expression.
a. $16^{\frac{1}{2}} \cdot 16^{\frac{1}{2}}$ **b.** $64^{\frac{1}{3}} \cdot 64^{\frac{2}{3}}$ **c.** $(32^{\frac{1}{5}})^{10}$

2. Find each value to the nearest integer. Do not use a calculator.
a. $20^{\frac{1}{2}}$ **b.** $15^{\frac{1}{3}}$ **c.** $81^{\frac{3}{4}}$

3. Lauren invests \$1000 in a savings account that grows by 4% per year.
a. Complete the table. Round to the nearest cent.

Years	Balance (dollars)
0	
1	
2	
3	
4	
5	

b. Does the balance follow an arithmetic or a geometric sequence? Explain.

4. Suppose $f(x) = x^{\frac{1}{3}}$. Calculate each value.
a. $f(8)$ **b.** $f(125)$ **c.** $f(1000)$

5. Find all four solutions to the equation $x^4 = 16$.

6. a. What number is defined to be $16^{\frac{1}{4}}$?
b. What is $16^{-\frac{1}{4}}$? Use a law of exponents.

7. Show that $27^{\frac{1}{6}} = \sqrt{3}$.

8. Here is a geometric sequence.
$1, \square, \square, \square, x^3, \square, \square, \square, \square, \ldots \square$
Write the missing terms as expressions of x.

Practice: For Lesson 5.5, assign Exercises 5–8.

15. Consider the functions $f(x) = x^3$ and $g(x) = x^{\frac{1}{3}}$.

a. Copy and complete this table. Round to three decimal places.

x	$f(x) = x^3$	$g(x) = x^{\frac{1}{3}}$
-8	■	■
-2	■	■
-1	■	■
$-\frac{1}{2}$	■	■
$-\frac{1}{8}$	■	■
0	■	■
$\frac{1}{8}$	■	■
$\frac{1}{2}$	■	■
1	■	■
2	■	■
8	■	■

b. Using the table, sketch the graphs of $f(x) = x^3$ and $g(x) = x^{\frac{1}{3}}$ on the same axes.

Use the same scale on both axes.

c. How are the two graphs related to each other?

d. How many solutions are there to the equation $f(x) = g(x)$?

16. Standardized Test Prep Which expression is equal to $x^{\frac{2}{3}}$?

A. $\frac{2}{3}x^{-1}$ **B.** $\frac{1}{x^{\frac{1}{3}}}$ **C.** $\sqrt{x^3}$ **D.** $\sqrt[3]{x^2}$

Maintain Your Skills

For Exercises 17 and 18, use a calculator to find each solution. Round to three decimal places.

17. a. $10^a = 2$ **b.** $10^b = 4$ **c.** $10^c = 8$ **d.** $10^d = 16$

18. a. $10^a = 2$ **b.** $10^b = 3$ **c.** $10^c = 6$ **d.** $10^d = 12$ **e.** $10^f = 36$

Answers

15. See back of book.

16. D

17. a. 0.301 **b.** 0.602
c. 0.903 **d.** 1.204

18. a. 0.301 **b.** 0.477
c. 0.778 **d.** 1.079
e. 1.556

Mathematical Reflections

1. $\frac{b^6}{b^2} = \frac{b \cdot b \cdot b \cdot b \cdot b \cdot b}{b \cdot b}$
$= \frac{b \cdot b}{b \cdot b} \cdot \frac{b \cdot b \cdot b \cdot b}{1}$
$= 1 \cdot b^4 = b^{6-2}$

2. a. 1 **b.** $q^{\frac{65}{8}}$ **c.** r^{-4} or $\frac{1}{r^4}$
d. s **e.** t^7 **f.** $u^{\frac{17}{3}}$

3. a. 6 **b.** 27
c. $\frac{3}{2}$ **d.** 9

Mathematical Reflections

5A

In this investigation, you evaluated and simplified exponents. You developed the laws of exponents by extending exponents from positive integers to include zero, negative, and rational numbers. You also used sequences to explore exponents. These exercises will help you summarize what you have learned.

1. Use a product model to show why $\frac{b^6}{b^2} = b^{6-2}$.

2. Simplify each expression given $p, q, r, s, t, u \neq 0$.

a. $p^6 \cdot p^{-6}$ **b.** $q^8 \cdot q^{\frac{1}{8}}$ **c.** $(r^2)^{-2}$

d. $(s^4)^{\frac{1}{4}}$ **e.** $\frac{t^5}{t^{-2}}$ **f.** $\frac{u^6}{u^{\frac{1}{3}}}$

3. Suppose m is a number that satisfies the equation $2^m = 3$. Use the laws of exponents to find each value.

a. 2^{m+1} **b.** 2^{3m}

c. 2^{m-1} **d.** $(2^2)^m$

4. a. Build a geometric sequence that shows that $64^{\frac{2}{3}} = 16$. Show at least six terms of the sequence.

b. What is the ratio between successive terms in your sequence? Why did you choose that ratio?

c. Find $64^{\frac{4}{3}}$. Explain your method.

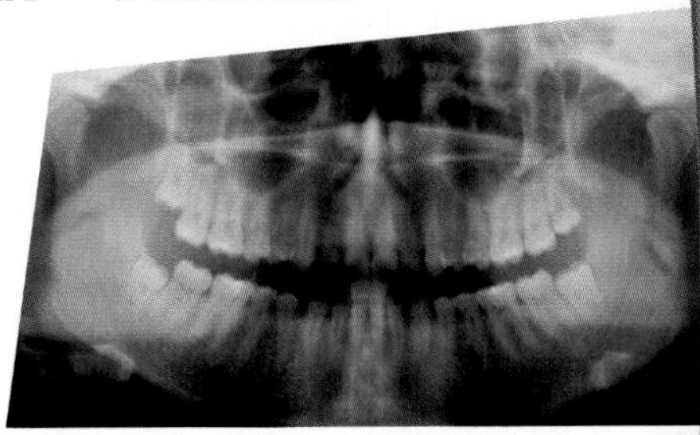

X-rays with wavelengths between 10^{-9} cm and 5×10^{-9} cm are used in dental radiography.

5. Simplify each expression.

a. $81^{\frac{3}{4}}$ **b.** $32^{\frac{4}{5}}$

c. $(11^4)^{\frac{1}{2}}$ **d.** $(\sqrt[3]{64})^2$

6. What is the Fundamental Law of Exponents? What are some of its corollaries?

7. How do you extend the laws of exponents to define zero, negative, and rational exponents?

8. Simplify the expressions 4^0, 7^{-2}, and $5^{\frac{2}{3}}$.

Vocabulary and Notation

In this investigation, you learned these terms and symbols. Make sure you understand what each one means and how to use it.

- **arithmetic sequence**
- **geometric sequence**
- **negative exponent, a^{-m}**
- ***n*th root, $\sqrt[n]{r}$**
- **rational exponent, $a^{\frac{p}{q}}$**
- **unit fraction exponent, $a^{\frac{1}{n}}$**
- **zero exponent, a^0**

Mathematical Reflections

EXERCISES 6–8 At the start of the investigation, you may have assigned these as Questions 1–3 for students to think and write about.

4. a. 1, 4, 16, 64, 256, 1024, . . .

b. 4; to get from 1 to 64 in 3 steps, $r^3 = 64$. So, $r = 4$.

c. 256; answers may vary. Sample:

$$64^{\frac{4}{3}} = \left(64^{\frac{2}{3}}\right)^2 = 16^2 = 256$$

5. a. 27 **b.** 16

c. 121 **d.** 16

6. If $a \neq 0$ and b and c are rational numbers, then $a^b \cdot a^c = a^{b+c}$; $\frac{a^b}{a^c} = a^{b-c}$ and $(a^b)^c = a^{bc}$.

7. Answers may vary. Sample: The definitions of zero, negative, and rational exponents are chosen so that the Fundamental Law of Exponents and its corollaries work with zero, negative, and rational exponents.

8. $4^0 = 1$, $7^{-2} = \frac{1}{49}$, $5^{\frac{2}{3}} = \sqrt[3]{25}$

Investigation Overview

In this investigation, the exponential function is defined, and students examine its graph and investigate its properties. In order to graph an exponential function, students have to further extend the definition of exponent to include all real numbers. This is done through an informal argument involving reasoning by continuity and limits of closer and closer approximations. Students look at the tables generated by exponential functions and realize that such a table will always have a constant ratio between successive terms. Students will be able to identify a table that can be matched by an exponential function and use the entries in the table to build either a closed-form or recursive definition of the exponential function that matches the table. Finally, students will prove that exponential functions are one-to-one, which implies that they have inverses. They will begin to think about the properties of these inverse functions, motivating the next investigation on logarithms.

You may wish to assign Questions 1–3 for students to think and write about during the investigation.

Learning Goals

- Graph an exponential function and determine the equation of an exponential function given two points on its graph.
- Identify an exponential function from the table it generates and use the table to create a closed-form or recursive definition of the function.
- Extend the laws of exponents to include all real-number exponents and express the laws as function equations.
- Evaluate the inverse of the function $y = b^x$ either exactly or by approximation.

Habits and Skills

- Reason by continuity to extend the definition of exponent to include all real numbers.
- Visualize exponential growth by examining graphs and tables of exponential functions.
- Draw logical conclusions from the laws of exponents and properties of exponential functions to solve problems and prove conjectures.

Investigation 5B

Exponential Functions

In *Exponential Functions*, you will use the laws of exponents to explore exponential functions. You will sketch the graphs of exponential functions and write exponential function rules from tables and points on graphs. You will also explore the properties of the inverse of the function $y = b^x$.

By the end of this investigation, you will be able to answer questions like these.

1. For $f(x) = b^x$, why is it true that $f(m) \cdot f(n) = f(m + n)$?
2. Why must an exponential function have an inverse function?
3. If you invest \$1000 in an account at 6% interest, compounded annually, how much money will you have after 30 years?

You will learn how to

- graph an exponential function and determine the equation of an exponential function given two points on its graph
- identify an exponential function from the table it generates and use the table to create a closed-form or recursive definition of the function
- evaluate the inverse of the function $y = b^x$ either exactly or by approximation

You will develop these habits and skills:

- Reason by continuity to extend the definition of exponent to include all real numbers.
- Visualize exponential growth by examining graphs and tables of exponential functions.
- Draw logical conclusions from the laws of exponents and properties of exponential functions to solve problems and prove conjectures.

Archaeologists use exponential functions that model radioactive decay to determine the age of objects.

Investigation Road Map

LESSON 5.6, *Getting Started,* gives students a quick review of difference tables and introduces ratio tables.

LESSON 5.7, *Graphs of Exponential Functions,* formally defines *exponential functions* and has students investigate graphs of these functions.

LESSON 5.8, *Tables of Exponential Functions,* has students examine the tables generated by exponential functions and challenges them to create closed-form and recursive definitions of an exponential function from its table.

LESSON 5.9, *Properties of Exponential Functions,* has students use the laws of exponents to solve equations.

LESSON 5.10, *Exponential Functions, One-to-One,* has students prove that exponential functions are one-to-one.

5.6 **Getting Started**

Activating Prior Knowledge
Exploring New Ideas

A difference table can help you find a function rule that fits a table. For some tables, a ratio table will help you find a rule that fits the table.

For You to Explore

For each function in Problems 1–5, make a difference table. Show the outputs for the inputs 0 through 5 and the differences between terms.

1. $a(x) = 3x + 1$
2. $b(x) = x^2 - x + 1$
3. $c(x) = 3^x$
4. $d(x) = 3 \cdot 5^x$
5. $f(x) = \left(\frac{1}{2}\right)^x$
6. Find a function $g(x)$ for which the difference column is equal to the output column.

Input	Output	Δ
0	■	■
1	■	■
2	■	■
3	■	■
4	■	■
5	■	

Note that $d(x)$ is not equal to 15^x, since only the 5 is raised to the xth power.

Instead of calculating the difference between one term and the next, it sometimes makes sense to calculate the ratio of one term to the next.

7. a. Copy and complete this ratio table for $a(x) = 3x + 1$. Round to the nearest hundredth.

   b. What happens to the numbers in the ratio column if you continue the table for larger inputs? Explain.

Input	Output	÷
0	1	4
1	4	■
2	7	■
3	10	1.3
4	13	■
5	16	

8. For each function from Problems 2–5, build a ratio table with the inputs from 0 to 5.
9. **Write About It** Suppose you have an input-output function table with integer inputs from 0 to 5.
   a. Describe how to find a rule that fits the table if the table has constant differences.
   b. Describe how to find a rule that fits the table if the table has constant ratios.
10. **Take It Further** Find a function $h(x)$ for which the ratio column is equal to the output column.

Answers

For You to Explore

1–5. See back of book.

6. $g(x) = 2^x$, $g(x) = 0$

7–8. See back of book.

9. a. Answers may vary. Sample: The output values are a, $a + k$, $a + 2k$, $a + 3k$, . . . , so a rule is $f(n) = f(0) + nk$, where $f(0)$ is the first output and k is the constant difference.

b. Answers may vary. Sample: The output values are $f(0)$, $r \cdot f(0)$, $r^2 \cdot f(0)$, . . . , so a rule is $f(n) = r^n \cdot f(0)$, where $f(0)$ is the first output and r is the constant ratio.

10. Answers may vary. Sample: $f(x) = k^{(2^x)}$, where k is a real number.

Lesson Overview

GOAL

- Build a ratio table for a function.

Through the exercises in this lesson, students are reintroduced to the idea of building a ratio table for a function. This type of table is particularly useful for analyzing exponential functions.

FOR YOU TO EXPLORE
- Core: 1, 2, 3, 4, 5, 6, 7, 8, 9
- Optional: none
- Extension: 10

HOMEWORK
- Core: 11, 12, 13, 14, 15, 16, 18
- Optional: 17, 19

MATERIALS
- graph paper
- graphing calculators
- Blackline Master MC1

Launch

Have students get started on the For You to Explore problems right away. Blackline Master MC1 can be used for Problems 1–7.

Explore

Many For You to Explore problems may seem to be computational practice, but they remind students of what the input-output tables for exponential functions look like and how to define a closed-form function that matches such a table.

For You to Explore

PROBLEM 2 Students see that every function that does not show a constant difference is not an exponential function. The differences for this quadratic function grow in a linear pattern.

PROBLEMS 3–5 The explosive growth of the differences seen in Problems 3 and 4 is a marker that a table may match an exponential function and that a ratio table is helpful in determining the function. In Problem 5, students see an "implosive" decrease in the differences between terms, marking an exponential function with a base less than one.

PROBLEM 7 The second part of this problem asks students to informally take the limit as x approaches infinity of $\frac{f(x + 1)}{f(x)}$. Thought experiments like this one will help students when they begin their formal study of limits.

PROBLEM 8 confirms that exponential functions have constant ratios.

Wrap Up

You may want to end today's class with a discussion of Problem 9.

Exercises

HOMEWORK

- Core: 11, 12, 13, 14, 15, 16, 18
- Optional: 17, 19

On Your Own

EXERCISE 11 reminds students that they have not yet found a good way to solve equations of the form $5 = 2^x$ except by closer and closer approximations.

EXERCISE 12 Expect students to do this exercise by finding several input-output pairs, but many may use a graphing calculator. The sketches should be similar, but check to see that students understand how to calculate $c(-1)$ or $c\left(\frac{1}{2}\right)$.

EXERCISE 13 The idea of continuity may not mean much to your students at this point, but they may say things such as "smooth" and "doesn't have any holes" if they are thinking informally about continuity.

EXERCISE 14 Once students see that they can use their calculators to evaluate expressions such as $3^{\sqrt{2}}$ (which may have happened quite a while ago), it may be difficult for them to see why they still need to formalize their results mathematically. Emphasize that, although their calculators can give them an approximation for such an expression, their current mathematical definition does not cover the situation.

EXERCISE 15 Exercises like this one give your students more experience with the behavior of exponential functions, and it helps them recognize these functions and define them in the future.

Exercises *Practicing Habits of Mind*

On Your Own

11. Solve each equation any way you choose. Then, decide which equation was the most difficult for you to solve. Explain.

a. $5 = x^2$ **b.** $5 = 2^x$

c. $x = 5^2$ **d.** $8 = 2^x$

12. Sketch the graph of $c(x) = 3^x$.

You will need more input-output pairs than the ones you found in Problem 3.

The expression $3^{\sqrt{2}}$ is undefined so far, since you cannot write $\sqrt{2}$ as a rational number.

13. Use your graph of $c(x) = 3^x$ to explain why $3^{\sqrt{2}}$ should be between 3 and 9.

14. **Write About It** Describe how you can make a more accurate estimate of $3^{\sqrt{2}}$.

15. Copy and complete the table of values for each exponential function.

a. $f(a) = 3 \cdot 2^a$

Input, *a*	Output, *f*(*a*)
−2	■
−1	■
0	■
1	■
2	■

b. $g(a) = 30 \cdot 2^a$

Input, *a*	Output, *g*(*a*)
−2	■
−1	■
0	■
1	■
2	■

c. $h(a) = \frac{1}{5} \cdot 5^a$

Input, *a*	Output, *h*(*a*)
0	■
1	■
2	■
3	■
4	■

d. $j(a) = 27 \cdot \left(\frac{1}{3}\right)^a$

Input, *a*	Output, *j*(*a*)
−1	■
0	■
1	■
2	■
3	■

Answers

Exercises

11. a. $\pm\sqrt{5}$

b. 2.32

c. 25

d. 3

12.

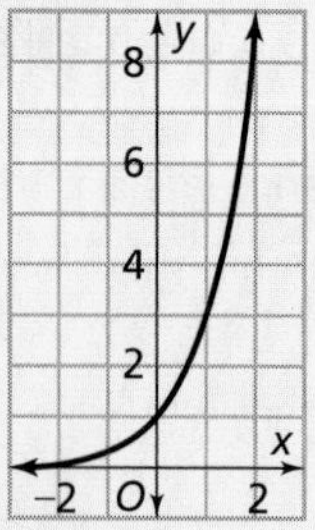

13. $1 < \sqrt{2} < 2$, so $3^1 < 3^{\sqrt{2}} < 3^2$ or $3 < 3^{\sqrt{2}} < 9$.

14. Answers may vary. Sample: Use the graph in Exercise 12 to find the *y*-value of the point whose *x*-value is $\sqrt{2} \approx 1.414$.

15. a.

Input, *a*	Output, *f*(*a*)
−2	$\frac{3}{4}$
−1	$\frac{3}{2}$
0	3
1	6
2	12

b–d. See back of book.

16. Find an exponential function that agrees with each table.

a.

Input, a	Output, $k(a)$
0	4
1	12
2	36
3	108
4	324

b.

Input, h	Output, $L(h)$
0	100
1	50
2	25
3	12.5
4	6.25

c.

Input, x	Output, $p(x)$
0	2
1	$\frac{1}{2}$
2	$\frac{1}{8}$
3	$\frac{1}{32}$
4	$\frac{1}{128}$

d.

Input, n	Output, $Q(n)$
0	8
1	12
2	18
3	27
4	40.5

An exponential function is a function that you can write in the form $f(x) = a \cdot b^x$.

17. Copy and complete this input-output table for $f(x) = 2^x$. Round to three decimal places.

x	$f(x) = 2^x$
0	1
1	■
1.4	■
1.41	■
1.414	■
1.4142	■
1.41421	■
1.414213	■

18. a. Explain why there are no integers a and b other than $a = b = 0$ that satisfy the equation $2^a = 5^b$.

b. Determine whether there are integers c and d other than $c = d = 0$ that satisfy the equation $4^c = 8^d$. If so, what are c and d?

Maintain Your Skills

19. Consider the function $f(x) = 2^x$. State whether you believe each value is a rational number. Find each rational value exactly, without using a calculator.

a. $f(0)$
b. $f\left(\frac{1}{2}\right)$
c. $f(\pi)$
d. $f(f(2))$
e. all values of a such that $f(a) = \frac{1}{8}$
f. all values of a such that $f(a) = 7$
g. all values of a such that $f(a) = -1$

EXERCISE 16 It might be helpful to remind students to think about the ratio between terms, although they do not need to complete a ratio table for any of these functions.

EXERCISE 17 This table is seen again in the upcoming lesson, so it is worth assigning this exercise if you plan to talk about irrational exponents. You might ask students to calculate $2^{\sqrt{2}}$ and compare the answer to the numbers here. The success of this exercise relies on students recognizing the inputs as closer and closer approximations to $\sqrt{2}$. Make sure that connection is clear if you ask about $2^{\sqrt{2}}$ here.

EXERCISE 18 You may wish to emphasize that the reason the first part has no solution is that you are considering only integer solutions.

16. a. $k(a) = 4 \cdot 3^a$

b. $L(h) = 100 \cdot \left(\frac{1}{2}\right)^h$

c. $p(x) = 2 \cdot \left(\frac{1}{4}\right)^x$

d. $Q(n) = 8 \cdot \left(\frac{3}{2}\right)^n$

17.

x	$f(x) = 2^x$
0	1
1	**2**
1.4	**2.639**
1.41	**2.657**
1.414	**2.665**
1.4142	**2.665**
1.41421	**2.665**
1.414213	**2.665**

18. a. Answers may vary. Sample: 2^a is even and 5^b is odd, so $2^a \neq 5^b$ except for $a = b = 0$.

b. Yes; answers may vary. Sample: $c = 3$, $d = 2$

19. a. yes; 1

b. no

c. no

d. yes; 16

e. yes; $a = -3$

f. no

g. no solution

Lesson Overview

GOAL

- Graph an exponential function and determine the equation of an exponential function given two points on its graph.

In this lesson, students experiment with the graphs of exponential functions. As they work, they develop many conjectures that they prove later in the investigation. Key conjectures include:

- Exponential functions are either strictly increasing or strictly decreasing.
- If the base is less than one, the function decreases. If it is greater than one, the function increases.
- Exponential functions are one-to-one.

CHECK YOUR UNDERSTANDING

- Core: 1, 2, 3a, 5, 6, 7, 8, 9
- Optional: 4, 10
- Extension: 3b

MATERIALS

- graph paper
- graphing calculators
- Blackline Masters 5.7A, 5.7B

HOMEWORK

- Core: 11, 12, 13, 14, 15, 16, 17, 18, 20
- Optional: 21, 22
- Extension: 19

VOCABULARY

- base
- exponential function
- extension by continuity
- strictly increasing
- strictly decreasing

Launch

Start this lesson by going over the definition of *exponential functions.* The For Discussion problem that follows the definition should help students understand the reasons for some of the restrictions in the definition.

5.7 Graphs of Exponential Functions

Several of the functions in the Getting Started lesson of this investigation are *exponential functions.*

Definitions

An exponential function is a function f that you can write in the form $f(x) = a \cdot b^x$, where $a \neq 0$, $b > 0$, and $b \neq 1$. The number b is the base.

The function $d(x) = 3 \cdot 5^x$ is exponential. What is its domain?

For Discussion

1. What happens if $a = 0$? What happens if $b = 1$?

Here are the graphs of $f(x) = 2^x$ and $g(x) = 5^x$.

Both graphs have their y-intercept at (0, 1). Both graphs pass through Quadrants I and II. Both functions are increasing. The greater x is, the greater the corresponding y is.

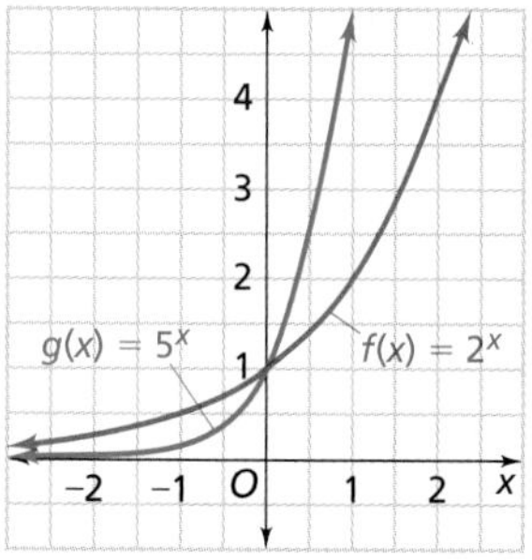

Habits of Mind

Establish a process. How can you decide whether the point (−3.5, 0.1) is on the graph of $f(x)$?

For You to Do

2. According to the graphs, for what values of x is $2^x > 5^x$?

Here are the graphs of $h(x) = \left(\frac{1}{2}\right)^x$ and $j(x) = \left(\frac{1}{5}\right)^x$.

Both graphs have their y-intercept at (0, 1). Both graphs pass through Quadrants I and II. Both functions are decreasing. The greater x is, the less the corresponding y is.

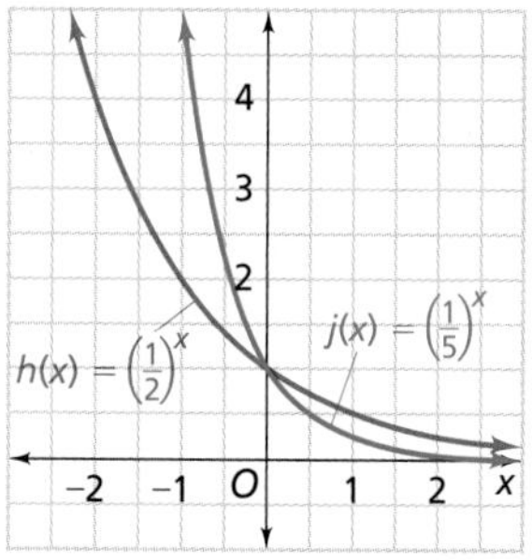

Habits of Mind

Establish a process. How can you decide whether the point (3.5, 0.1) is on the graph of $h(x)$?

Answers

For Discussion

1. If $a = 0$, then $f(x) = 0$, a linear function (the x-axis). If $b = 1$, then $f(x) = a$, a linear function (the horizontal line $y = a$).

For You to Do

2. $x < 0$

In-Class Experiment

3.

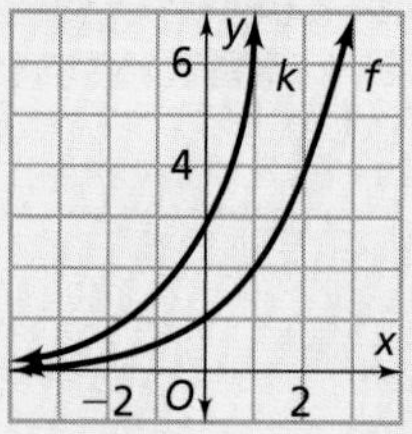

The graph of k is a vertical stretching of the graph of f.

In-Class Experiment

3. Graph $f(x) = 2^x$ and $k(x) = 3 \cdot 2^x$. How are the graphs related?

4. Graph $k(x) = 3 \cdot 2^x$ and $m(x) = -3 \cdot 2^x$. How are the graphs related?

5. Graph $f(x) = 2^x$ and $h(x) = \left(\frac{1}{2}\right)^x$. How are the graphs related?

Monotonic Functions

As you have seen, the graph of $f(x) = 2^x$ seems to indicate that this function is **strictly increasing.** In other words, if $s > t$, then $f(s) > f(t)$. You will now verify this observation.

Lemma 5.1

Let $b > 1$ and let x be a positive rational number. Then $b^x > 1$.

Proof Since x is positive and rational, you can write $x = \frac{p}{q}$ for some positive integers p and q. First, use the following fact about power functions.

Let $g(x) = x^n$, where n is a positive integer. Then $g(x)$ is strictly increasing on nonnegative inputs. In other words, if s and t are nonnegative, then $s^n > t^n$ if and only if $s > t$.

Now, let $s = b^{\frac{1}{q}}$, $t = 1$, and $n = q$. By the above fact,

$$(b^{\frac{1}{q}})^q > 1^q \Leftrightarrow b^{\frac{1}{q}} > 1$$

But $(b^{\frac{1}{q}})^q = b$, so

$$b > 1 \Leftrightarrow b^{\frac{1}{q}} > 1$$

Since $b > 1$ is given, then $b^{\frac{1}{q}} > 1$.

Now use the above fact again, with $n = p$.

$$(b^{\frac{1}{q}})^p > 1^p \Leftrightarrow (b)^{\frac{1}{q}} > 1$$

Therefore $b^{\frac{p}{q}} > 1$ for any positive integers p and q.

So $b^x > 1$, as desired.

Theorem 5.2

If $b > 1$, then the function $f(x) = b^x$ is strictly increasing on rational-number inputs. In other words, if s and t are rational numbers such that $s > t$, then $f(s) > f(t)$.

Remember...

A function of the form $y = x^n$ is a polynomial function and not an exponential function.

4.

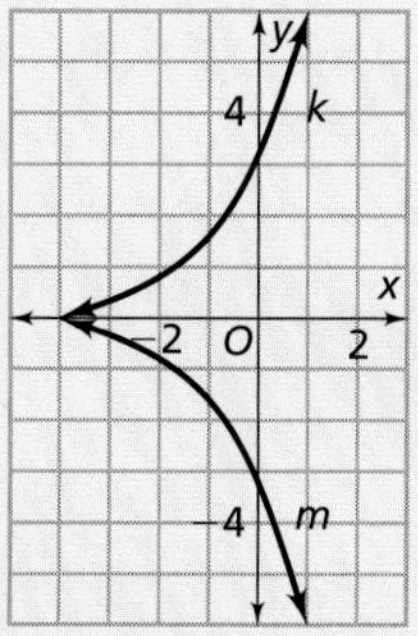

The graphs are reflections of each other over the x-axis.

5.

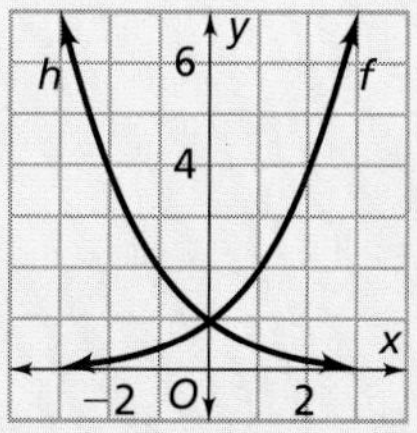

The graphs are reflections of each other over the y-axis.

Explore

In-Class Experiment

Ask students to talk about the graphs in terms of transformations: stretching or shrinking, reflecting. The graphs in Problem 3 are related by a vertical stretch. The graphs in Problem 4 are related by a vertical reflection (or a reflection over the x-axis), and the graphs in Problem 5 are related by a horizontal reflection (or a reflection over the y-axis). Transformation rules will become more prominent in Chapter 6. Later in this chapter, students will see that, for an exponential function, a vertical stretch has the same effect as a horizontal translation. To see this algebraically, note that $2^{x+1} = 2 \times 2^x$.

DOMAIN AND RANGE When you draw a smooth curve for the graph of $f(x) = 2x$, you make the assumption that any real number is a valid input for x. Up to this point, any graph technically should have been drawn with gaps (although in practice, we recognize that students do not usually do this). It may be useful to point out that the work in this lesson closes those gaps.

Proof Suppose s and t are rational numbers such that $s > t$. Then $s - t > 0$, so Lemma 5.4 gives

$$b^{s-t} > 1$$

You know b^t is positive. You can multiply each side of the inequality by b^t.

$$b^{s-t} \cdot b^t > 1 \cdot b^t$$

$$b^{s-t+t} > b^t \quad \text{using Theorem 5.1}$$

$$b^s > b^t$$

$$f(s) > f(t)$$

This is the desired result.

Similarly, you have observed from its graph that the function $h(x) = \left(\frac{1}{2}\right)^x$ is **strictly decreasing.** In general, if $0 < b < 1$, the function $g(x) = b^x$ is strictly decreasing on rational number inputs. See Exercise 4 for the proof.

Domain and Range

You can draw the graph of $f(x) = 2^x$ without any gaps. This suggests that its domain should be the set of all real numbers, $\mathbb{R}$, but the work in Investigation 5A only defines exponents for integers and rational numbers. The real numbers include irrational numbers such as $\sqrt{2}$ and π. How should you define $2^{\sqrt{2}}$?

You want to define $2^{\sqrt{2}}$ in such a way that the function $f(x) = 2^x$ is increasing on all real-number inputs. For example, since

$$1 < \sqrt{2} < 2$$

you must have

$$2^1 < 2^{\sqrt{2}} < 2^2$$

Thus, you must define $2^{\sqrt{2}}$ to be a number between 2 and 4. In fact, the graph suggests $2^{\sqrt{2}}$ should be between 2 and 3.

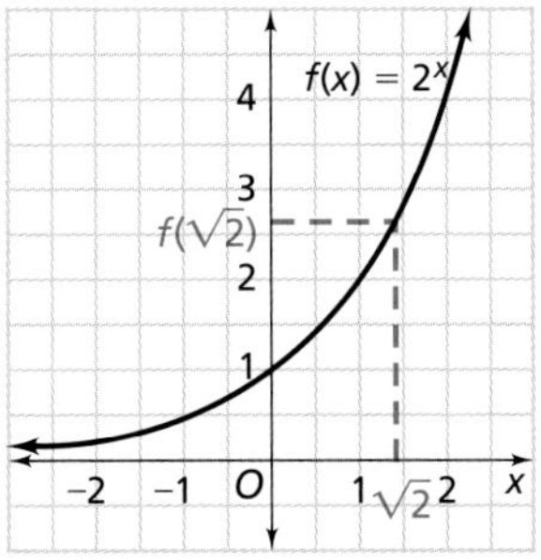

The key to defining irrational exponents is that, even though $\sqrt{2}$ is irrational, you can pick rational numbers that are as close to $\sqrt{2}$ as desired. As the rational numbers on either side get closer to $\sqrt{2}$, the outputs of $f(x) = 2^x$ get closer to a specific real number. You use this number for $2^{\sqrt{2}}$.

Habits of Mind

Extend what you know. This type of reasoning is *extension by continuity*. You can often use it to take things that work for integers or rational numbers and apply them to real numbers.

Developing Habits of Mind

Establish a process. Evaluate $2^{\sqrt{2}}$ by approximating it with nearby rational exponents. Terminating decimals work well, since they are all rational numbers. Since $\sqrt{2} \approx 1.41421356$, you can get a good estimate for $2^{\sqrt{2}}$ by finding $2^{1.41}$ and $2^{1.42}$.

$$2^{1.41} < 2^{\sqrt{2}} < 2^{1.42}$$

You can do even better using better approximations.

$$2^{1.414} < 2^{\sqrt{2}} < 2^{2.415}$$

This table shows how you can approximate $2^{\sqrt{2}}$ by using decimals close to $\sqrt{2}$ as inputs to the function $f(x) = 2^x$, with outputs rounded to five decimal places.

Input, x	Output, $f(x) = 2^x$
1.41	2.65737
1.414	2.66475
1.4142	2.66512
1.41421	2.66514
1.414213	2.66514
1.4142135	2.66514

The value of $2^{\sqrt{2}}$ to five decimal places is 2.66514. As the inputs get closer to $\sqrt{2}$, the outputs get closer to a number, and you take that number as the value of $2^{\sqrt{2}}$. It is possible to approximate any irrational number with rational numbers. Therefore, it is possible to define $f(x) = 2^x$ for any real number x. So, the domain of f is the set of all real numbers.

This limiting process only works for positive bases. Therefore, you cannot define expressions like $(-2)^{\sqrt{2}}$ in a reasonable way.

Habits of Mind

Make strategic choices. In Chapter 7, you will explore further this concept of calculating a result as a limit of other results.

Based on this extension, the domain of an exponential function is the set of all real numbers. The range of $f(x) = b^x$ is restricted to positive numbers as long as $b > 0$ (see Exercise 20). Then the value of a determines whether the range of $f(x) = a \cdot b^x$ is all positive numbers or all negative numbers.

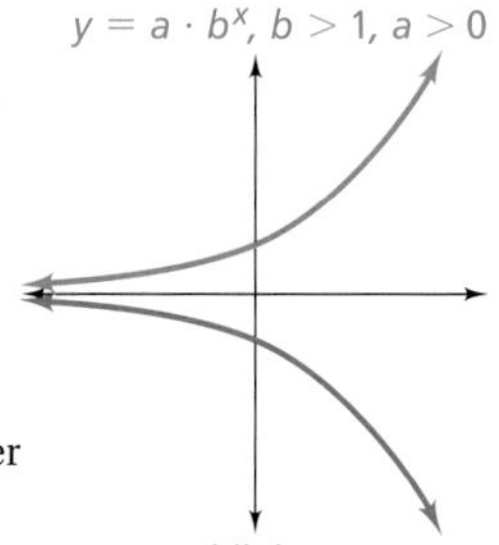

As the input x becomes more negative, the corresponding output y approaches but never reaches 0. This behavior—approaching but not reaching $f(x) = 0$—is very different from the behavior of any polynomial function.

Developing Habits of Mind

Students may not have realized that the graphs of polynomials will always approach $\pm\infty$ as x approaches $\pm\infty$, so they may not be aware that the behavior of the exponential functions—that the function value can approach, but never reach, zero—is different. Other students may be so comfortable with the graph of $y = \frac{1}{x}$ that they are used to this idea and do not see it as different, but then $y = \frac{1}{x}$ is not a polynomial function.

You may wish to remind students about how useful the zeros of polynomials were, both in sketching their graphs and factoring, to bring out this difference between polynomial functions and exponential functions a bit more. Exponential functions do not have zeros.

Blackline Master 5.7A can be used as a transparency here.

Wrap Up

Take a moment to go through the Properties of Exponential Functions and answer any questions students may have. Then let students work on and discuss the Check Your Understanding core exercises as time allows.

Assessment Resources

Lesson Quiz 5.7

1. What is the y-intercept of the graph of $f(x) = 8 \cdot 2^x$?

2. **Multiple Choice** Which of the following points is on the graph of $f(x) = 12 \cdot \left(\frac{1}{2}\right)^x$?

   A. (0, 12) **B.** (3, 4) **C.** (−1, −24) **D.** (2, 6)

3. Due to inflation, the cost of Harry's Hot Wings grows by 4% every year. This year, a dozen Hot Wings cost $5.99.
   a. How much will a dozen Hot Wings cost next year and the year after that?
   b. How can you find the cost of a dozen Hot Wings 15 years from now?
   c. Will a dozen Hot Wings ever cost more that $20? Explain.

4. Explain why $4^{\sqrt{11}}$ must be greater than 64 and less than 256.

Exercises

HOMEWORK
- Core: 11, 12, 13, 14, 15, 16, 17, 18, 20
- Optional: 21, 22
- Extension: 19

Check Your Understanding

EXERCISE 1 An exponential function $f(x) = a \cdot b^x$ can have $a > 0$ or $a < 0$ and $b > 1$ or $b < 1$. These four graphs show all possible combinations of these variations. Blackline Master 5.7B can be used as a transparency here.

Summary ***Properties of Exponential Functions***

An exponential function $f : \mathbb{R} \mapsto \mathbb{R}$ is defined as $f(x) = a \cdot b^x$.

- **The value of a cannot be zero, and b must be positive and not 1.**
- **The domain of f is $\mathbb{R}$.**
- **The range of f is all positive real numbers if $a > 0$, and all negative real numbers if $a < 0$.**
- **The graph of $y = f(x)$ has one y-intercept at $(0, a)$ and no x-intercepts.**
- **If $a > 0$, the graph of $y = f(x)$ is strictly increasing when $b > 1$ and strictly decreasing when $0 < b < 1$.**

Exercises *Practicing Habits of Mind*

Check Your Understanding

1. Match each graph with its equation.

$f(x) = 3 \cdot 2^x$ $f(x) = 3 \cdot \left(\frac{1}{2}\right)^x$ $f(x) = 3 \cdot 5^x$ $f(x) = -3 \cdot 2^x$

a.

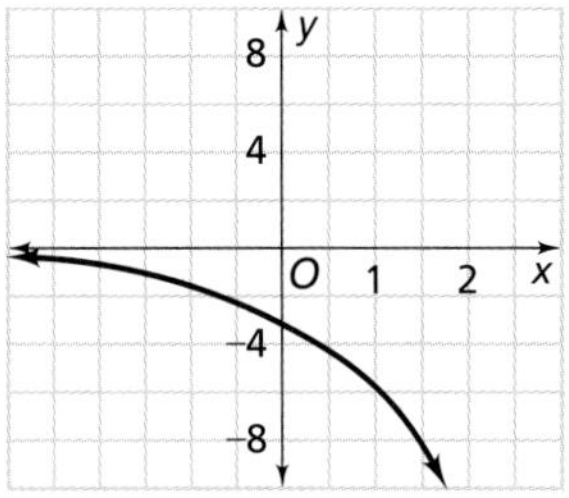

b.

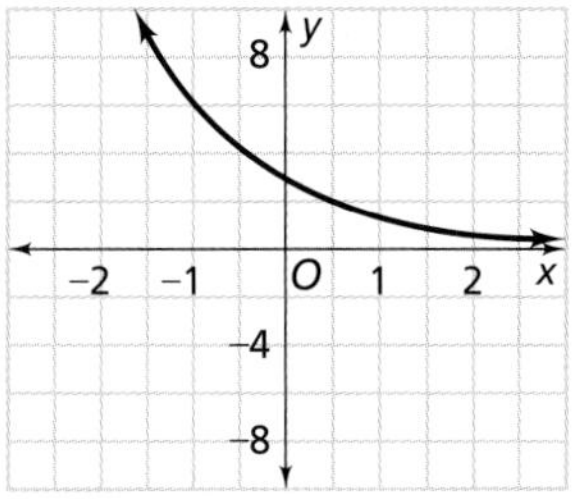

c.

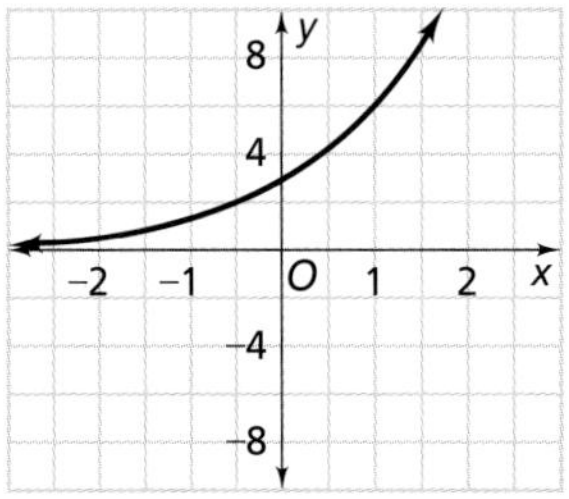

d.

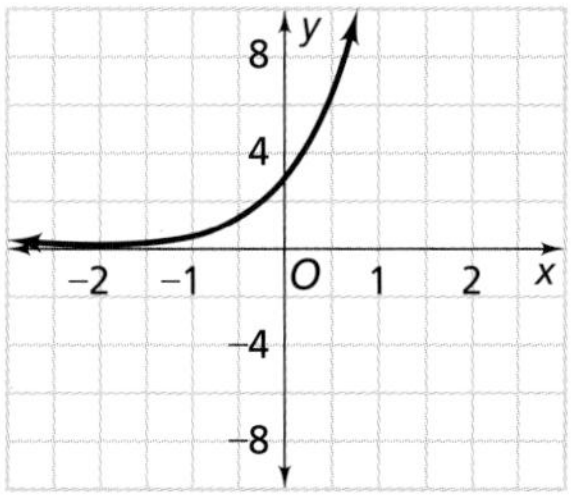

Answers

Exercises

1. a. $f(x) = -3 \cdot 2^x$

b. $f(x) = 3 \cdot \left(\frac{1}{2}\right)^x$

c. $f(x) = 3 \cdot 2^x$

d. $f(x) = 3 \cdot 5^x$

2. a. $f(x) = 12 \cdot \left(\frac{1}{2}\right)^x$

b. $f(x) = 48 \cdot \left(\frac{1}{2}\right)^x$

3. a. Answers may vary. Sample: $f(x) = 2 \cdot 6^x$, $g(x) = 8 \cdot 3^x$

b. $f(x) = a \cdot \left(\sqrt{\frac{72}{a}}\right)^x$

4. Lemma: The proof uses the fact that b^x is strictly decreasing for nonnegative integer inputs. Let $x = \frac{p}{q}$ for some positive integers p and q, and then suppose that $b^{\frac{1}{q}} \geq 1$. Then $b = \left(b^{\frac{1}{q}}\right)^q \geq 1^q = 1$, which implies $b \geq 1$. But this contradicts the hypothesis of the lemma that $b < 1$. Thus $b^{\frac{1}{q}} < 1$, and therefore

2. a. The graph of an exponential function contains the points (0, 12) and (2, 3). Find its equation.

   b. The graph of an exponential function contains the points (2, 12) and (4, 3). Find its equation.

3. a. Write the equations for at least two exponential functions with graphs that contain the point (2, 72).

   b. **Take It Further** Write the general form for any exponential function with a graph that contains the point (2, 72).

4. Prove the following lemma and theorem.

Lemma 5.2

Let $0 < b < 1$ and let x be a positive rational number. Then $b^x < 1$.

Theorem 5.3

Let $0 < b < 1$. Then the function $f(x) = b^x$ is strictly decreasing on rational-number inputs.

5. The graphs of $f(x) = 2^x$ and $g(x) = \left(\frac{1}{2}\right)^x$ are reflections of each other in the y-axis.

   Explain why this reflection property makes sense, using the definition of a negative exponent.

$$b^{-x} = \frac{1}{b^x}$$

If $f(x) = 2^x$ is increasing and $g(x) = \left(\frac{1}{2}\right)^x$ is its reflection over the y-axis, what can you say about $g(x)$?

For Exercises 6 and 7, estimate the solution to each equation.

6. $2^x = 7$

7. $2^x = \frac{1}{7} \cdot 4^x$

8. a. Sketch the graph of each function for $-10 \le x \le 10$ and $-10 \le y \le 10$.

$$f(x) = 5 \cdot (1.07)^x$$
$$g(x) = (1.12)^x$$

   Do the graphs intersect in this window?

   b. Determine the total number of intersections of the two graphs.

For advice on how to find an intersection point, see the TI-Nspire Handbook, p. 778.

9. In the lesson, you learned that $2^{\sqrt{2}}$ is a number $a \approx 2.66514$.

   a. Calculate $a^{\sqrt{2}}$.

   b. Is there a way to directly calculate $(2^{\sqrt{2}})^{\sqrt{2}}$? Explain.

10. Try to use the method in the Developing Habits of Mind section to define $(-2)^{\sqrt{2}}$. What happens?

$b^x = b^{\frac{p}{q}} = \left(b^{\frac{1}{q}}\right)^p < 1^p = 1.$
So, $b^x < 1$.
Theorem: Let s and t be rational numbers such that $s > t$. Then $s - t > 0$, so (using the Lemma) $b^{s-t} < 1$. Since $b^t > 0$, multiplying both sides of the inequality does not reverse the inequality symbol. So,

$$b^{s-t} \cdot b^t < 1 \cdot b^t$$
$$b^{s-t+t} < b^t$$
$$b^s < b^t$$

Thus, if $s > t$, then $f(s) < f(t)$, which means that f is strictly decreasing on rational-number inputs.

5. Answers may vary. Sample: If $f(x) = 2^x$, then $f(-x) = 2^{-x} = \frac{1}{2^x} = \left(\frac{1}{2}\right)^x = g(x)$.

6. 2.807

7. 2.807

8. a–b. See back of book.

9. a. 4

b. Yes; $\left(2^{\sqrt{2}}\right)^{\sqrt{2}} = 2^{\sqrt{2}\cdot\sqrt{2}} = 2^2 = 4$

10. Answers may vary. Sample: A calculator gives error messages because b^a is not defined for $b < 0$.

EXERCISE 2 Students can solve the second part of this exercise by extending the pattern. For example, when the input decreases by 2, the output is multiplied by 4. This means that if they were to decrease the output by 2 again to 0, the new output would be 4 times 12 or 48, giving the point (0, 48).

Another option is to use the given points to write equations in a and b for the function $y = a \cdot b^x$. Then students can divide one equation by the other to get an equation in b alone, which is easier to solve.

EXERCISE 3 As with linear equations, two points are necessary to completely determine the exponential function whose graph passes through both. If you know only one point, the graphs of infinitely many exponential functions pass through that point.

EXERCISE 5 Assign this exercise only if students have worked on the appropriate material in Chapter 2.

EXERCISE 6 Expect students to do this by using the graph of $f(x) = 2^x$ and looking for the x-coordinate of the intersection with the horizontal line $y = 7$. Any method of numeric approximation is fine, but if you discuss this exercise with your class, use the graphs and bring back the "point-tester" theme.

EXERCISE 10 For this equation, it is actually possible to build a limiting sequence of all positive results and a second limiting sequence of all negative results. The fact that both sequences exist means that you cannot define $(-2)^{\sqrt{2}}$ well. Overall this situation is just a mess, and one reason why exponential functions b^x are restricted to $b > 0$.

Another way to think about this situation is to realize that if the function values of a continuous function change sign, you must be able to trace the graph of the function without lifting your pencil, so you will somehow have to cross the x-axis. But b^x cannot equal 0 unless $b = 0$. That means that for $b < 0$, the function b^x cannot be continuous. This is another way to say that this situation is a mess.

On Your Own

EXERCISE 12 reminds students to use the "point-tester" idea. The equation for a graph is a point-tester for the graph. Only points that satisfy the equation are on the graph.

EXERCISE 13 assumes a constant rate of inflation over nearly 60 years, which is not the case in the real world. However, it may help students get a feel for exponential growth.

EXERCISE 14 may make the idea of "approaching, but never reaching, zero" more concrete. Students could choose any positive number, no matter how small, and find the value at which the exponential function is closer to zero than that small number. But, since there is no number that is the least number greater than zero, you can always choose a lesser number, and the exponential function can get closer to zero than that number, too.

EXERCISE 16 is a proof that most solutions to equations such as $2^x = 7$ or $10^x = 3$ are irrational. Later, it means that numbers like $\log_2 7$ are irrational.

EXERCISE 18 Expect different answers to the second part. If students are confused about how to add more points, that is encouraging since it means they do not want to use a negative base. You can encourage students to build a table with smaller steps, such as steps of $\frac{1}{3}$, and ask why steps of $\frac{1}{2}$ would not work. This should be enough to show students that $f(x) = (-2)^x$ is not well-defined in general.

On Your Own

Go Online
PHSchool.com

For additional practice, go to Web Code: bfa-0507

11. Explain why the y-intercept of the graph of $f(x) = a \cdot b^x$ is $(0, a)$.

12. **Standardized Test Prep** Which of these points is on the graph of $f(x) = -3 \cdot 2^x$?

A. (0, 1) **B.** (−1, 6)

C. (−2, −0.75) **D.** (2, 36)

13. Due to inflation, the cost of a Big Burger grows by 3% every year. This year a Big Burger costs $3.99.

a. How much will a Big Burger cost next year and the year after that?

b. How can you find the cost of a Big Burger ten years from now?

c. Will a Big Burger ever cost more than $20? Explain.

d. Find a rule for the function $C(n)$, with an output that is the cost of a Big Burger n years from now.

14. **What's Wrong Here?** Cody says, "The graph of $y = 2^x$ can't get to *every* positive number if it doesn't make it to zero. It has to stop somewhere. I'll bet it never gets below one millionth."

Show that Cody is mistaken by finding a number x such that 2^x is positive but less than $\frac{1}{1{,}000{,}000}$.

15. Explain why $3^{\sqrt{6}}$ must be greater than 9 and less than 27.

16. Dorris claims the solution x in Exercise 6 must be an irrational number. She says, "If $2^x = 7$ is solved by a fraction, then it looks like $2^{\frac{p}{q}} = 7$. Then I raise both sides to a power of q.

$$2^{\frac{p}{q}} = 7$$
$$\left(2^{\frac{p}{q}}\right)^q = 7^q$$
$$2^p = 7^q$$

"And p and q have to be integers. I'm pretty sure that can't happen unless p and q are both zero."

Is it possible for $2^p = 7^q$ if p and q are nonzero integers? Explain.

17. Dorris's explanation above shows that the solution to $2^x = 7$ must be irrational. How does her argument break down if you try to apply it to the equation $2^x = 8$?

Answers

11. $f(0) = a \cdot b^0 = a \cdot 1 = a$, so the graph contains $(0, a)$.

12. C

13. a. \$4.11, \$4.23

b. Calculate $3.99 \cdot 1.03^{10}$.

c. Yes; 55 years from now the cost will be $3.99 \cdot (1.03)^{55} = \$20.28$.

d. $C(n) = 3.99 \cdot (1.03)^n$

14. Answers may vary. Sample: −20

15. $2 < \sqrt{6} < 3$, so $3^2 < 3^{\sqrt{6}} < 3^3$ or $9 < 3^{\sqrt{6}} < 27$.

16. No; if p and q are positive integers, 2^q is even and 7^q is odd, so $2^q \neq 7^q$. If p and q are negative integers, the denominator of $\frac{1}{2^p}$ is even and the denominator of $\frac{1}{7^q}$ is odd, so $\frac{1}{2^p} \cdot \frac{1}{7^q}$.

17. If $2^{\frac{p}{q}} = 8$, then $2^{\frac{p}{q}} = 2^3$, so $2^p = 2^{3q}$. Then $p = 3q$, which is true for values of p and q other than 0.

18. a.

Input	Output
−2	$\frac{1}{4}$
−1	$-\frac{1}{2}$
0	1
1	−2
2	4
3	−8

18. **a.** Copy and complete this table for $f(x) = (-2)^x$.

b. What happens if you try to make a smooth graph for $f(x) = (-2)^x$?

Input	Output
−2	■
−1	■
0	■
1	■
2	■
3	■

19. **Take It Further** The equation

$$a \cdot b^x = c \cdot d^x$$

may have a different number of solutions, depending on the values of a, b, c, and d. Describe the conditions on these parameters that make the equation have each number of solutions.

- exactly one
- none
- more than one

20. **a.** If $b > 0$ and x is an integer, explain why b^x must be positive.

b. If $b > 0$ and x is rational, use the definition of rational exponent to explain why b^x must be positive.

Maintain Your Skills

21. Simplify each expression.

a. $\left(3^{\sqrt{2}}\right)^{\sqrt{2}}$ **b.** $\left(3^{\sqrt{2}}\right)^{2}$ **c.** $\left(3^{-\sqrt{2}}\right)^{-1}$

d. $\left(3^{\sqrt{8}}\right)^{\sqrt{2}}$ **e.** $3^{\sqrt{2}} \cdot 3^{-\sqrt{2}}$ **f.** $\left(3^{-\sqrt{2}}\right)^{-\sqrt{2}}$

g. $3^{\sqrt{2}} \cdot 5^{\sqrt{2}}$ **h.** $\left(3^{\sqrt[3]{2}}\right)^{\sqrt[3]{2}}$ **i.** $\left(3^{\sqrt[3]{2}}\right)^{\sqrt[3]{4}}$

Decide for yourself what *simplify* means, but your answer cannot be identical to the given expression.

22. Graph each function on the same set of axes. Let $-10 \le x \le 10$ and let $0 \le y \le 10$.

- $a(x) = 3^x$
- $b(x) = 3 \cdot 3^x$
- $c(x) = 9 \cdot 3^x$
- $d(x) = 27 \cdot 3^x$
- $f(x) = 81 \cdot 3^x$

How are these graphs related?

The logarithmic spiral is the graph of $r = ae^{b\theta}$ in polar coordinates. The arrangement of seeds in a sunflower approximates the logarithmic spiral.

Additional Resources

PRINT RESOURCES
- Solution Manual
- Practice Workbook
- Assessment Resources
- Teaching Resources

TECHNOLOGY
- Interactive Textbook
- TeacherExpress CD-ROM
- ExamView CD-ROM
- PHSchool.com

Additional Practice

1. What is the y-intercept of the graph of $f(x) = a \cdot b^x$?

2. **Multiple Choice** Which of these points is on the graph of $f(x) = -5 \cdot 3^x$?
A. (0, −5) **B.** (2, 45) **C.** $\left(-1, -\frac{5}{3}\right)$ **D.** (3, −135)

3. Due to inflation, the cost of a Perfect Pizza grows by 2% every year. This year a Perfect Pizza costs $8.99.
a. How much will a Perfect Pizza cost next year and the year after that?
b. How can you find the cost of a Perfect Pizza 20 years from now?
c. Will a Perfect Pizza ever cost more than $25? Explain.
d. Find a rule for the $C(n)$ function, with an output that is the cost of a Perfect Pizza n years from now.

4. Explain why $5^{\sqrt{5}}$ must be greater than 25 and less than 125.

5. Here are the graphs of two exponential functions. Find a closed-form rule that defines each function.

a.
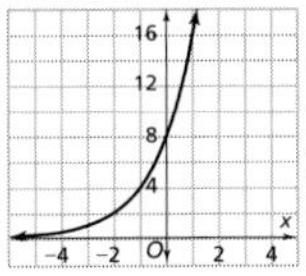

b.
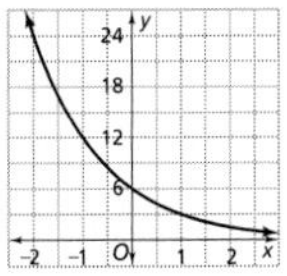

6. **a.** Complete each table.

I.

n	$f(n)$	÷
0	18	$\frac{2}{3}$
1		$\frac{2}{3}$
2		$\frac{2}{3}$
3		$\frac{2}{3}$
4		

II.

n	$f(n)$	÷
0	−1	−4
1		−4
2		−4
3		−4
4		

b. Find both a closed-form rule and a recursive rule that matches each table.
c. Describe how to calculate $f(12)$ for each table if the pattern in the ratio column continues.

Practice: For Lesson 5.7, assign Exercises 1–4.

21. a. 9 **b.** $3^{2\sqrt{2}}$
c. $3^{\sqrt{2}}$ **d.** 81
e. 1 **f.** 9
g. $15^{\sqrt{2}}$ **h.** $3^{\sqrt[3]{4}}$
i. 9

22.
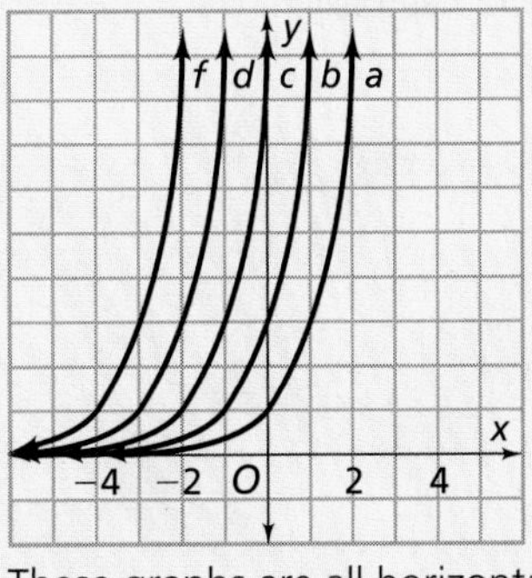

These graphs are all horizontal translations of each other.

b. The outputs in the table are alternately positive and negative, so a smooth curve drawn through the points from the table would cross the x-axis. But $f(x)$ is never 0, so the curve cannot cross the axis, and thus it is impossible to connect all the points with a smooth curve.

19. Exactly one: $b \ne d$, a and c have the same sign. None: a and c have opposite signs, or $b = d$ and $a \ne c$. More than one: $b = d$ and $a = c$.

20. a. By definition, b^x is the product of x factors of b, and the product of positive factors must be positive.

b. Write the rational number x as $\frac{p}{q}$ where p and q are positive integers. Then $b^x = b^{\frac{p}{q}} = \sqrt[q]{b^p}$, which is positive because b^q is positive (see part (a)) and the qth root of a positive number is positive.

Lesson Overview

GOAL

- Identify an exponential function from the table it generates and use the table to create a closed-form or recursive definition of the function.

Students examine input-output tables generated by exponential functions, and they match the tables to recursive rules. Looking at recursive definitions of linear functions sharpened students' understanding of the role of slope. The recursive definitions of exponential functions make the role of the base and the coefficient clearer.

CHECK YOUR UNDERSTANDING
- Core: 1, 2, 3, 4, 5, 6, 7
- Optional: none
- Extension: 8

MATERIALS
- CAS (recommended)
- graph paper
- graphing calculators

HOMEWORK
- Core: 9, 10, 11, 12, 13, 14
- Optional: 15, 16, 17, 18

VOCABULARY
- closed-form definition
- exponential decay
- exponential growth
- recursive definition

Launch

Start this lesson with the In-Class Experiment.

Explore

In-Class Experiment

If students are having trouble getting started, ask them to write out the answers without calculating. For example, they could write $B(1) = 1.06 \times 500$. Then $B(2) = 1.06 \times 1.06 \times 500$. If students write the expressions out this way, eventually they will decide to use an exponent. After all, it is much more efficient to write $(1.06)^{10} \times 500$ than it is to write the factor 1.06 ten times. The strategy here is to write down what your calculation would be, rather than just working out the value. Students will then see what the calculation actually is.

5.8 Tables of Exponential Functions

This lesson focuses on exponential functions from a tabular perspective. It also focuses on how recursive rules can generate exponential functions.

In-Class Experiment

Consider this function defined on nonnegative integers.

$$B(n) = \begin{cases} 500 & \text{if } n = 0 \\ 1.06 \cdot B(n-1) & \text{if } n > 0 \end{cases}$$

This recursive function can be modeled. See the TI-Nspire Handbook, p. 778.

1. Use the definition to calculate $B(10)$. Then figure out a more direct way to get $B(10)$.
2. Calculate $B(50)$.
3. Find the smallest integer n such that $B(n) > 4000$.

The exponential function $L(h) = 100 \cdot \left(\frac{1}{2}\right)^h$ is decreasing. If $h = 0$, $L = 100$.

If the base b is between 0 and 1, it is an **exponential decay** function. If the base is greater than 1, it is an **exponential growth** function.

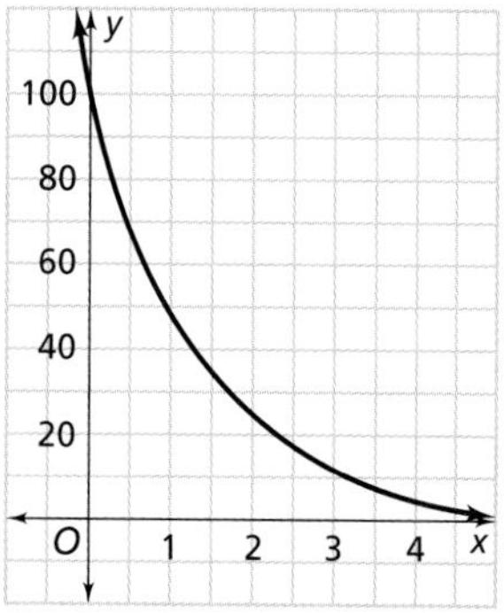

Here is a table for $L(h)$ for integer values of h from 0 to 4.

h	$L(h)$
0	100
1	50
2	25
3	12.5
4	6.25

Answers

In-Class Experiment

1. about 895.42; $B(10) = 500 \cdot 1.06^{10} \approx 895.42$
2. about 9210.08
3. 36

Minds in Action episode 20

Tony thinks he can start with the table and find an exponential function rule.

Tony If you just gave me that table, I could find an exponential function that matches it. There's an exponential that matches the table, since it has a constant ratio between any pair of successive terms. Here's a ratio table.

h	L(h)	÷
0	100	$\frac{1}{2}$
1	50	$\frac{1}{2}$
2	25	$\frac{1}{2}$
3	12.5	$\frac{1}{2}$
4	6.25	

You calculate the ÷ column by computing ratios of successive terms. $\frac{50}{100} = \frac{1}{2}$

And I know $L(0) = 100$, so $L(h)$ is 100 times one half to the h. Now, that's not the only function that matches the table, but it's probably the simplest one. And I can describe $L(h)$ term by term. Start with 100 and divide by 2 each time the input increases by 1.

For You to Do

4. Find a rule that fits this table.

x	$f(x)$
0	12
1	18
2	27

For You to Do

4. Answers may vary. Sample:

$f(x) = 12 \cdot \left(\frac{3}{2}\right)^x$

Minds in Action

Tony builds a ratio table, similar to the ones students built in Investigation 1A at the beginning of this course. A ratio table could be used to show that a function is not exponential if any of the ratios of successive terms were different.

For You to Do

Note that the question does not specify an exponential rule, so students may use difference tables to find a quadratic function that matches the table, or use even Lagrange interpolation to find a polynomial fit.

Example

Method 2 is similar to the methods students use when solving systems of two equations in two unknowns. The difference is that these are exponential, not linear, equations. Typical linear system strategies such as adding or subtracting equations are not useful here, but dividing equations is useful. After dividing, students get an equation with only one variable, and then they can use back-substitution, just as they would in the linear context. This will help students develop a sense of thinking "multiplicatively" in these exponential contexts, just as they have developed thinking "additively" in linear contexts.

Developing Habits of Mind

Make strategic choices. Tony describes $L(h)$ using a recursive rule: Start with $L(0) = 100$ and divide by 2 each time. You can describe any exponential function $f(x) = a \cdot b^x$ in this way. In this case, the value of a is 100 and the base b is $\frac{1}{2}$, since dividing by 2 is the same as multiplying by one half.

Exponential functions arise naturally in situations like the following.

- the number of teams in an elimination tournament (Half of the teams move on to the next round.)
- the growth of money in a bank account (with 6% interest compounded annually)
- the growth of a population over time (The population doubles every 50 years.)

The function L is connected to the concept of a half-life in biology. Specifically, $L(h)$ outputs the percentage remaining of an element after h half-lives.

The recursive definition for $L(h)$ looks like this.

$$L(h) = \begin{cases} 100 & \text{if } h = 0 \\ 0.5 \cdot L(h-1) & \text{if } h > 0 \end{cases}$$

There is an important concern about domain here. The recursive rule for $L(h)$ limits its domain to nonnegative integers, since it fails to give a value for something like $L(1.5)$ or $L(-2)$. In some situations, it may make sense to use only nonnegative integers as inputs. However, remember that there is a difference between this version of $L(h)$ and the closed-form definition $L(h) = 100 \cdot \left(\frac{1}{2}\right)^h$, which has all real numbers as its domain.

Habits of Mind

Experiment. Build a model for L in your function-modeling language.

If you have a table for an exponential function, but the inputs do not start at 0 or they have gaps, you can still find the function using algebra if you know at least two input-output pairs.

Example

Problem An exponential function P defined as $P(x) = a \cdot b^x$ has this table of inputs and outputs. Find the values of a and b.

x	$P(x)$
−2	108
−1	36
2	$\frac{4}{3}$

The outputs are positive and decreasing, so it must be exponential decay. The base b must be between 0 and 1.

Solution

Method 1 When two terms have inputs that differ by 1, you can calculate the base b directly as the ratio between these successive terms.

$$b = \frac{36}{108} = \frac{1}{3}$$

Then $P(x) = a \cdot \left(\frac{1}{3}\right)^x$. You can find a using any of the input-output pairs. Use $(-1, 36)$.

$$\begin{aligned} P(x) &= a \cdot \left(\tfrac{1}{3}\right)^x \\ 36 &= a \cdot \left(\tfrac{1}{3}\right)^{-1} \\ 36 &= a \cdot 3 \\ 12 &= a \end{aligned}$$

The function is $P(x) = 12 \cdot \left(\frac{1}{3}\right)^x$.

Method 2 Pick any two points and set up the equation $P(x) = a \cdot b^x$ for each. For example, take $(-1, 36)$ and $\left(2, \frac{4}{3}\right)$.

$$\begin{aligned} 36 &= a \cdot b^{-1} \\ \tfrac{4}{3} &= a \cdot b^2 \end{aligned}$$

Then divide to build an equation for b.

$$\begin{aligned} \frac{36}{\frac{4}{3}} &= \frac{a \cdot b^{-1}}{a \cdot b^2} \\ 27 &= b^{-3} \end{aligned}$$

Solve for b. If $b^{-3} = 27$, then $b^3 = \frac{1}{27}$ and $b = \frac{1}{3}$. Then find a.

For You to Do

5. Find the exponential function with a graph that contains the points $(1, 36)$ and $(2, 108)$.

Minds in Action episode 21

Tony has another way to think about finding an exponential function from two points on its graph.

Tony I guess the example does the same thing, but I like to think of it as how far apart the points are in a geometric sequence. Say the points are $(-3, 10)$ and $(2, 20)$. The x-values have a difference of 5, so it's a geometric sequences with five steps from 10 to 20.

10, ■, ■, ■, ■, 20

So whatever the base is, the output doubles from 10 to 20 in five terms. That means the base has to solve the equation $b^5 = 2$. And once you find b, you can use either point to find a.

Answers

For You to Do

5. $f(x) = 12 \cdot 3^x$

Minds in Action

Tony's description follows the geometric sequences introduced in Investigation 5A. Some students may latch onto this concept better than other solution methods. The additive reasoning students might use in a linear context can help them build multiplicative reasoning that can be applied to exponential situations. If this were a linear situation, a student might ask, "What do I have to add to 10 five times in order to get 20?" In this exponential situation, the student might ask, "What do I have to multiply 10 by five times in order to get 20?"

Wrap Up

As time allows, go over the Check Your Understanding core exercises.

Assessment Resources

Lesson Quiz 5.8

1. The table has the first output and the ratio column completed.
   a. Complete the table.
   b. Is $f(x)$ an exponential function? Explain.
   c. Find a closed-form rule that defines $f(x)$.
   d. Describe how to calculate $f(20)$ if the pattern in the ratio column continues.

x	$f(x)$	÷
−2	$\frac{16}{9}$	$\frac{3}{2}$
−1		$\frac{3}{2}$
0		$\frac{3}{2}$
1		$\frac{3}{2}$
2		$\frac{3}{2}$
3		$\frac{3}{2}$

2. Cecily has a money market account that grows by 5% per year. Her account has \$3000 in it.
   a. Find the amount of money in Cecily's account after 1 year, 2 years, and 3 years.
   b. Find a rule for $B(n)$, the balance after n years.
   c. Find the amount of money in Cecily's account after 25 years.

3. Find two functions for which $f(-3) = 1$ and $f(1) = 16$.

Exercises

HOMEWORK

- Core: 9, 10, 11, 12, 13, 14
- Optional: 15, 16, 17, 18

Check Your Understanding

EXERCISE 1 Be sure that your students recognize the constant ratio between successive terms as the marker that points to an exponential function.

EXERCISE 4 Make sure that students follow the restrictions outlined in the definition of an exponential functions. Be sure that they can distinguish between finding an exponential function through these two points and finding any function between these two points or finding a value of b to solve the equation $b^2 = \frac{1}{25}$ when b is not considered as the base of an exponential function.

EXERCISE 5 Students might get confused by the open-ended nature of this exercise, so if they get stuck, you might suggest they find a linear function and an exponential. Also, students will probably approximate a rather than use the exact value of $10 \cdot 2^{\frac{3}{5}}$, and that's fine.

Exercises *Practicing Habits of Mind*

Check Your Understanding

1. For each table, find the exponential function that matches the table or explain how you know that an exponential function cannot fit the table.

a.

n	$A(n)$
0	18
1	6
2	2
3	$\frac{2}{3}$

b.

x	$B(x)$
0	−2
1	−8
2	−32
3	−128

c.

t	$C(t)$
0	4
1	6
2	9
3	12

d.

z	$D(z)$
1	2
2	12
3	72
4	432

2. For each exponential function in Exercise 1, build a recursive model in your function-modeling language.

3. Suppose q is an exponential function with $q(3) = 100$ and $q(5) = 4$. Find $q(x)$.

4. **What's Wrong Here?** George says there are two possible values of the base b for the exponential function in Exercise 3.

George says, "The function goes from 100 to 4 in two steps, which means dividing by 25. So $b^2 = \frac{1}{25}$. But then there are two possible values of b. It could be either $\frac{1}{5}$ or $\frac{-1}{5}$. Either could be right."

Do you agree or disagree with George's statement? Explain.

5. Find two functions for which $f(-3) = 10$ and $f(2) = 20$.

The function $f(x)$ does not need to be an exponential function.

Answers

Exercises

1. a. $A(n) = 18 \cdot \left(\frac{1}{3}\right)^n$

b. $B(x) = -2 \cdot (4)^x$

c. No exponential function fits the table because the ratio between consecutive outputs is not constant.

d. $D(z) = \frac{1}{3} \cdot 6^z$

2. a. $A(n) = \begin{cases} 18 & \text{if } n = 0 \\ \frac{1}{3} \cdot A(n-1) & \text{if } n > 0 \end{cases}$

b. $B(x) = \begin{cases} -2 & \text{if } x = 0 \\ 4 \cdot B(x-1) & \text{if } x > 0 \end{cases}$

c. not an exponential function

d. $D(z) = \begin{cases} \frac{1}{3} & \text{if } z = 0 \\ 6 \cdot D(z-1) & \text{if } z > 0 \end{cases}$

3. $q(x) = 12{,}500 \cdot \left(\frac{1}{5}\right)^x$

4. Disagree; a value of $-\frac{1}{5}$ for b is not possible because the base of an exponential function must be positive.

5. Answers may vary.
Sample: $f(x) = 2x + 16$;
$f(x) = \left(10 \cdot 2^{\frac{3}{5}}\right)\left(2^{\frac{1}{5}}\right)^x$

6. T is an exponential function with this table.

a. If $T(x) = a \cdot b^x$, find a and b.

b. Copy and complete the table.

x	$T(x)$	÷
0	100	▪
1	▪	▪
2	▪	▪
3	▪	▪
4	▪	▪
5	300	

7. Suppose a new car that costs $20,000 depreciates in value about 20% each year.

a. How much will the car be worth after 1 year? After 2 years? After 3 years?

b. Find a rule for $V(n)$, the value of the car after n years of driving.

c. Will the car ever be worth less than $1000? Explain.

Most cars actually depreciate more than 20% the first year.

8. **Take It Further** The graph of an exponential function passes through the points (x_1, y_1) and (x_2, y_2). Find the function in terms of these coordinates.

Habits of Mind

Generalize. Exercise 8 is a generalization of the type of problem found in Exercises 3 and 12.

On Your Own

9. **Standardized Test Prep** Suppose f is an exponential function $f(x) = a \cdot b^x$ with $f(0) = 4$ and $f(2) = 25$. What are the values of a and b?

A. $a = 1, b = 5$ B. $a = 1, b = 10$

C. $a = 4, b = 2.5$ D. $a = 4, b = 5$

10. The ratio column of this table is filled in.

n	$M(n)$	÷
0	16	1.5
1	▪	1.5
2	▪	1.5
3	▪	1.5
4	▪	

Copy and complete the table. Define $M(n)$ with both a closed-form rule and a recursive rule.

EXERCISE 8 If you assign this exercise, make sure that students know that memorizing the general form for an exponential function between two points is not likely to be very useful to them. However, being able to derive this general form shows an admirable command of algebraic simplification and an understanding of the process of finding such a function.

On Your Own

EXERCISE 10 One feature of this exercise is that it may help students discover a quick way to generate points on an exponential function. This idea comes in handy when you plot an exponential function by hand.

6. a. $a = 100$, $b = 3^{\frac{1}{5}}$

b.

x	$T(x)$	÷
0	100	**≈1.246**
1	**≈124.57**	**≈1.246**
2	**≈155.18**	**≈1.246**
3	**≈193.32**	**≈1.246**
4	**≈240.82**	**≈1.246**
5	300	

7. a. $16,000; $12,800; $10,240

b. $V(n) = 20{,}000 \cdot (0.8)^n$

c. Yes; $V(14) = 879.61$, so after 14 years the car will be worth less than $1000.

8.

$$y = y_1^{\frac{-x_2}{x_1 - x_2}} \cdot y_2^{\frac{x_1}{x_1 - x_2}} \cdot \left(\left(\frac{y_1}{y_2}\right)^{\frac{1}{x_1 - x_2}}\right)^x$$

9. C

10.

n	$M(n)$	÷
0	16	1.5
1	**24**	1.5
2	**36**	1.5
3	**54**	1.5
4	**81**	

$M(n) = 16 \cdot \left(\frac{3}{2}\right)^n$,

$$M(n) = \begin{cases} 16 & \text{if } n = 0 \\ \frac{3}{2} \cdot M(n-1) & \text{if } n > 0 \end{cases}$$

EXERCISE 11 Students may recognize the factorial function from Chapter 1.

EXERCISE 12 is really equivalent to finding an exponential function given two points, but some students may find the graphs helpful in confirming their results. For example, in part (b), when the coefficient a in the form $a \cdot b^x$ turns out to be negative, some students might be worried that they have made a mistake in calculation without being able to see the graph.

EXERCISE 14 If you go over this exercise with your class, you might wish to ask them how long it would take to completely pay off the balance if the 0% interest rate were to continue. You could also extend the exercise by asking how much the card company would charge in interest the first month after the 0% rate were to stop in the original statement of the problem. (Students could look at some credit card offers to find a standard interest rate for a credit card or you could give them a particular value to use.) A few calculations like this might help students see why paying only the minimum balance is not a particularly good strategy with a credit card balance.

11. This table has the first output and the ratio column filled in.

Go Online PHSchool.com

For additional practice, go to **Web Code:** bfa-0508

n	$F(n)$	$\div$
0	1	1
1	■	2
2	■	3
3	■	4
4	■	5
5	■	6
6	■	

a. Copy and complete the table.

b. Is F an exponential function? Explain.

c. Describe how to calculate $F(10)$ if the pattern in the ratio column continues.

12. Here are the graphs of three exponential functions. Find a closed-form rule that defines each function.

a.

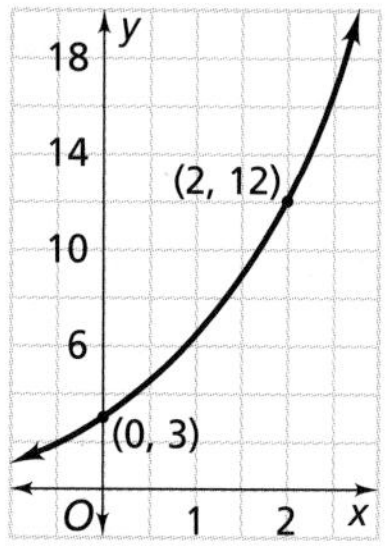

b.

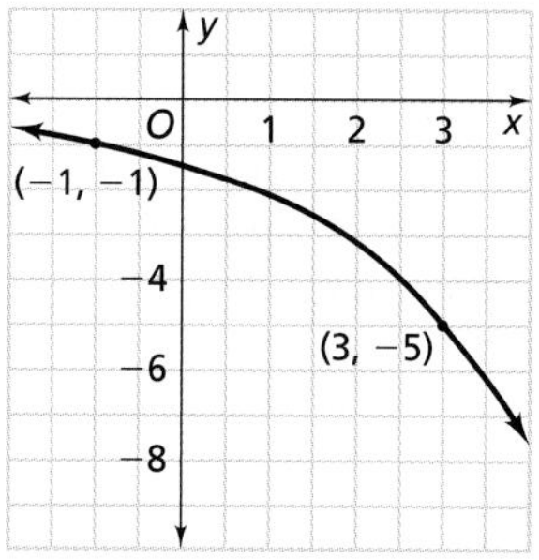

c.

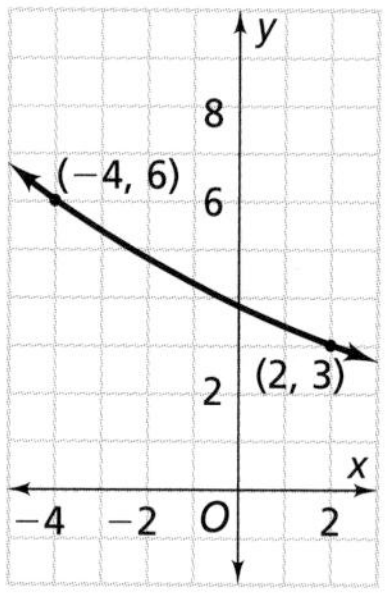

Answers

11. a.

n	$F(n)$	$\div$
0	1	1
1	**1**	2
2	**2**	3
3	**6**	4
4	**24**	5
5	**120**	6
6	**720**	7

b. No; the ratio of successive outputs is not constant.

c. Find the product of the first 10 positive integers.

12. a. $y = 3 \cdot 2^x$

b. $y = -5^{\frac{1}{4}} \cdot \left(5^{\frac{1}{4}}\right)^x$ or $y = -5^{\frac{x+1}{4}}$

c. $y = 3 \cdot 2^{\frac{1}{3}} \cdot \left(\frac{1}{2}\right)^{\frac{x}{6}}$ or $y = 3 \cdot 2^{\frac{2-x}{6}}$

13. Money in a savings account typically grows by about 3% per year. Kara's savings account has $1000 in it.

a. Find the amount of money in Kara's account after 1 year, 2 years, and 3 years.

b. Find the amount of money in Kara's account after 20 years.

14. Some credit cards offer 0% interest on their balance for 12 months, as long as you make a required monthly payment of at least 2% of the balance. Suppose you owe $2000 on one of these cards and make only the minimum payment each month.

a. Find the balance after 1 month, 2 months, and 3 months.

b. Find a rule for $B(n)$, the balance after n months.

c. What is the domain of $B(n)$? Explain.

15. Suppose you have the credit card in Exercise 14, but want to be sure to pay off half the total balance by the end of the first year. If you plan to pay the same percentage of the remaining balance each month, about what percent of the balance do you need to pay?

16. **Write About It** Use the two function definitions below.

$$f(x) = 5 \cdot 2^x$$

$$g(x) = \begin{cases} 5 & \text{if } x = 0 \\ 2 \cdot g(x-1) & \text{if } x > 0 \end{cases}$$

Explain why the graphs of these functions do not look the same.

So, Kara will earn $30 (3% of $1000) interest during the first year. Why will she earn more than $30 interest during the second year?

Maintain Your Skills

17. Suppose $b(x) = 3^x$. Calculate each value.

a. $b(5)$ **b.** $b(3) \cdot b(2)$ **c.** $b(1)$

d. $\frac{b(3)}{b(2)}$ **e.** $b(6)$ **f.** $(b(2))^3$

18. Suppose $f(x) = b^x$ for $b > 0$ with $f(3) = p$ and $f(5) = q$. Find each value in terms of p and q.

a. $f(0)$ **b.** $f(-3)$ **c.** $f(8)$

d. $f(6)$ **e.** $f(15)$

Habits of Mind

Look for relationships. How is $f(8)$ related to $f(3)$ and $f(5)$? Use the fact that $f(x) = b^x$.

13. a. $1030; $1060.90; $1092.73
b. $1806.11

14. a. $1960; $1920.80; $1882.38
b. $B(n) = 2000 \cdot 0.98^n$
c. {0, 1, 2, . . . , 10, 11, 12}; you make a payment each month for 12 months.

15. about 5.6%

16. The domain of f is all real numbers, but g is defined only for nonnegative integers.

17. a. 243
b. 243
c. 3
d. 3
e. 729
f. 729

18. a. 1
b. $\frac{1}{p}$
c. pq
d. p^2
e. p^5 or q^3

EXERCISE 15 To extend this exercise, ask students to compute the payments for a few months, based on the idea of paying 5.6% of the remaining balance each month. They will see that, over time, the payments decrease.

Maintain Your Skills

EXERCISE 17 The answers to the parts of this exercise come in equal pairs, and this results from and reinforces the Laws of Exponents.

EXERCISE 18 Students may get stuck on $f(8)$ and $f(6)$. Asking them to write out that $f(8) = b^8$ may be helpful here, since it may prompt them to realize that $f(8) = f(3) \cdot f(5)$. Referring to Exercise 17 may also help.

Additional Resources

PRINT RESOURCES
- Solution Manual
- Practice Workbook
- Assessment Resources
- Teaching Resources

TECHNOLOGY
- Interactive Textbook
- TeacherExpress CD-ROM
- ExamView CD-ROM
- PHSchool.com

Additional Practice

1. What is the y-intercept of the graph of $f(x) = a \cdot b^x$?

2. Multiple Choice Which of these points is on the graph of $f(x) = -5 \cdot 3^x$?
A. (0, −5) **B.** (2, 45) **C.** $\left(-1, -\frac{5}{3}\right)$ **D.** (3, −135)

3. Due to inflation, the cost of a Perfect Pizza grows by 2% every year. This year a Perfect Pizza costs $8.99.
a. How much will a Perfect Pizza cost next year and the year after that?
b. How can you find the cost of a Perfect Pizza 20 years from now?
c. Will a Perfect Pizza ever cost more than $25? Explain.
d. Find a rule for the $C(n)$ function, with an output that is the cost of a Perfect Pizza n years from now.

4. Explain why $5^{\sqrt{5}}$ must be greater than 25 and less than 125.

5. Here are the graphs of two exponential functions. Find a closed-form rule that defines each function.

a.
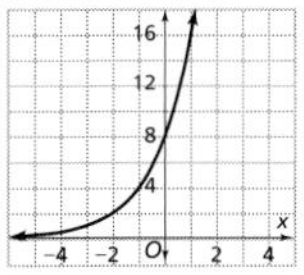

b.
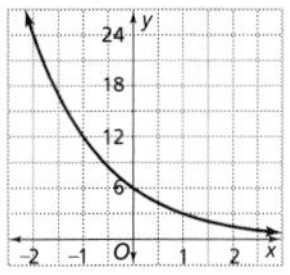

6. a. Complete each table.

I.

n	$f(n)$	÷
0	18	$\frac{2}{3}$
1		$\frac{2}{3}$
2		$\frac{2}{3}$
3		$\frac{2}{3}$
4		

II.

n	$f(n)$	÷
0	−1	−4
1		−4
2		−4
3		−4
4		

b. Find both a closed-form rule and a recursive rule that matches each table.
c. Describe how to calculate $f(12)$ for each table if the pattern in the ratio column continues.

Practice: For Lesson 5.8, assign Exercises 5 and 6.

Lesson Overview

GOAL

- Extend the laws of exponents to include all real-number exponents and express the laws as function equations.

This lesson formally extends the laws of exponents to include all real-number exponents and expresses the laws as function equations as well as with exponential expressions. Students see how to approximate the solution to an exponential equation where the exponent is unknown. Then they see how to derive more points that solve an exponential equation from a small number of given points.

CHECK YOUR UNDERSTANDING
- Core: 1, 2, 3, 4, 5, 6, 7
- Optional: 8
- Extension: 9

MATERIALS
- graph paper
- graphing calculators
- spreadsheet software
- Blackline Master 5.9

HOMEWORK
- Core: 10, 11, 12, 13, 14, 17, 19
- Optional: 15, 16, 20, 21
- Extension: 18

VOCABULARY
- functional equation
- monotonic

Launch

Begin today's lesson with the In-Class Experiment.

5.9 Properties of Exponential Functions

This lesson explores several properties of exponential functions that are dictated by the laws of exponents.

In-Class Experiment

1. Sketch the graph of $f(x) = 2^x$. Then sketch the graphs of each pair of functions.
   - $f(x + 1)$ and $2 \cdot f(x)$
   - $f(x - 2)$ and $\frac{f(x)}{4}$
2. How are the graphs of each pair related?

You can now apply the laws of exponents to any real-number exponent.

Laws of Exponents

Let base $b > 0$ and let x and y be real numbers.

The Fundamental Law of Exponents

- $b^{x+y} = b^x \cdot b^y$

Corollaries

- $b^{x-y} = \frac{b^x}{b^y}$
- $b^{xy} = (b^x)^y$

See the discussion on how you extend exponents from rational numbers to real numbers in the Developing Habits of Mind section in Lesson 5.7.

The graphs for each pair of functions in the In-Class Experiment were identical. A similar example is the graph of $f(x) = 3^x$. The graphs of $f(x + 1)$ and $3 \cdot f(x)$ are identical.

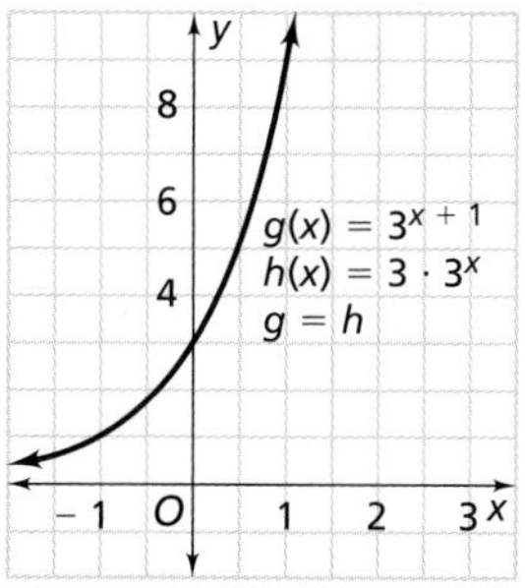

This is not a coincidence. It is a consequence of the Fundamental Law of Exponents. If $f(x) = 3^x$, then

$$f(x + 1) = 3^{x+1} = 3^x \cdot 3^1 = 3 \cdot 3^x = 3f(x)$$

Answers

In-Class Experiment

1. 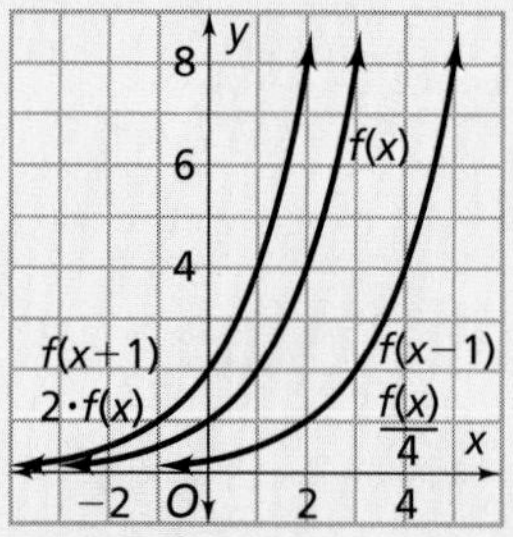

2. For each pair of functions, the two graphs are identical.

You can rewrite the laws of exponents using function notation. It is important to note that none of the results below is new. They are just written using the language of functions.

Laws of Exponents *Function Version*

Let $f(x) = b^x$ with $b > 0$ and domain $\mathbb{R}$.

The Fundamental Law of Exponents

- $f(x + y) = f(x) \cdot f(y)$

Corollaries

- $f(x - y) = \frac{f(x)}{f(y)}$
- $f(xy) = (f(x))^y$

The definitions for zero and negative exponents give these equations.

- $f(0) = 1$
- $f(-x) = \frac{1}{f(x)}$

A **functional equation** is an equation that relates some values of a function to other values of the function. For example, $g(n) = g(n - 1) + 3$ is a functional equation for a linear function with a slope of 3. This list of functional equations relates values of the function $f(x) = b^x$.

For Discussion

3. Let $f(x) = b^x$ with $b > 0$. Prove that $f(x + y) = f(x) \cdot f(y)$.

The statement that $f(x + 1) = 3 \cdot f(x)$ for $f(x) = 3^x$ is the Fundamental Law of Exponents, with 1 replacing y.

Example

Problem Let $g(x) = 4^x$. Solve each equation exactly, if possible. Otherwise, round to four decimal places.

a. $g(a) = 5$ **b.** $g(b) = 8$ **c.** $g(c) = 40$

Solution

a. You cannot find the solution $g(a) = 5$ exactly as an integer or as a fraction. The exact solution to $4^x = 5$ is irrational. Approximate the solution by successive guesses at a. Use the fact that $g(x) = 4^x$ is increasing.

Guess, a	$g(a) = 4^a$	The next guess should be . . .
1	4	Higher
1.2	5.2780	Lower
1.15	4.9246	Higher
1.16	4.9933	Higher (close!)

Successive approximations give the value $a \approx 1.1610$ to four decimal places.

If the solution is rational, then $4^{\frac{p}{q}} = 5$, and $4^p = 5^q$. This is impossible if p and q are nonzero integers.

For Discussion

3. $f(x + y) = b^{x+y} = b^x \cdot b^y = f(x) \cdot f(y)$

Explore

LAWS OF EXPONENTS Some students will have trouble understanding the meaning of a functional equation such as $f(x + y) = f(x) \cdot f(y)$. If they do, encourage them to generate specific examples (a good habit of mind!). For example, let $b = 2$, $x = 3$, and $y = 4$. Then students should be able to verify any of the properties listed. In verifying the properties, students should realize that each boils down to the Fundamental Law of Exponents or a corollary. In the end, each of these functional equations is just a restatement of a fact that students have already seen in another form.

For Discussion

You can also prove the corollaries in class. The proofs are fairly accessible, so you may wish to have students do the work.

Example

In parts (a) and (c), the Example makes use of the fact that the function g is monotonic: if $g(1) = 4$, then the x-value for which $g(x) = 5$ must be greater than 1. This kind of argument only works for monotonic functions. (And to say that x must be greater than 1, you must also know that the function is increasing.) If you are doing this example in class, students may come up with the final observation, which is that $g(c) = g(a) \cdot g(b)$.

For You to Do

The last part may seem like a trick to your students, but you can actually use the division rule or the power rule (with the power equal to zero).

Wrap Up

As time allows, go over the Check Your Understanding core exercises with your class. Exercises 1 through 4 can give you a baseline assessment of whether students are able to solve exponential equations. This set of exercises can also serve as a motivation for the study of logarithms in the next investigation, because the most difficult type of exponential equation to solve is one where the exponent is unknown.

Assessment Resources

Lesson Quiz 5.9

1. Using $g(x) = 3^x$, solve each equation for x.
   a. $g(x) = 27$
   b. $g(x) = 3^{-7}$
   c. $g(x) = 81^3$
   d. $g(x) = 0$

2. Thomas deposits \$1500 in an investment account that earns 5% interest per year. The amount of money that Thomas can withdraw after x years is given by the exponential function $f(x) = 1500(1.05)^x$. How long will it take for Thomas's money to double in value? To triple in value?

3. Sketch the graph of each function.
   a. $a(x) = 5^x$
   b. $b(x) = 5 \cdot 5^x$
   c. $c(x) = 25 \cdot 5^x$
   d. How are these graphs related? Explain.

b. The solution to $g(b) = 8$ is exactly $\frac{3}{2}$. Both 8 and 4 are powers of 2, so you can solve $4^b = 8$ by rewriting each number as a power of 2.

$$(2^2)^b = 2^3$$

Then $2b = 3$ and $b = \frac{3}{2}$.

c. The solution to $g(c) = 40$ is irrational, since you cannot write 40 as a rational power of 2. Approximate the solution by successive guesses at c.

Guess, c	$g(c) = 4^c$	The next guess should be . . .
2	16	Higher
2.5	32	Higher
2.7	42.2243	Lower
2.65	39.3966	Higher
2.66	39.9466	Higher (close!)

Successive approximations give the value $c \approx 2.6610$ to four decimal places.

You can find the value of c more quickly by using the Fundamental Law of Exponents. It says that the following equation is true for any choices of a and b.

$$g(a + b) = g(a) \cdot g(b)$$

If $g(a) = 5$ and $g(b) = 8$, then $g(a + b) = 40$, which is exactly what you need for this problem. Then $c = a + b \approx 2.6610$ is the solution.

For You to Do

Use the information that $g(1.1610) \approx 5$ and $g(1.5) = 8$ to solve each equation.

4. $g(m) = 25$

5. $g(n) = 1.6$

6. $g(p) = 200$

7. $g(q) = 0.2$

8. $g(r) = 1$

In the next lesson, you will look at another important property of exponential functions: They are one-to-one, and therefore have inverse functions. An inverse function for something like $g(x) = 4^x$ is very useful, since it allows you to solve equations such as $g(x) = 5$ more quickly.

$$g(x) = 5$$
$$g^{-1}(g(x)) = g^{-1}(5)$$
$$x = g^{-1}(5)$$

For now, that inverse function is unknown, but you will study its properties in the next investigation.

Exponential functions are one-to-one because they are **monotonic**. This means these functions are either increasing for all inputs or decreasing for all inputs.

Answers

For You to Do

4. 2.3220

5. 0.3390

6. 3.8220

7. −1.1610

8. 0

Exercises

1. Multiply a by the power b^x.

2. Divide C by the power b^x.

3. Find the $\frac{1}{x}$ power of the quotient $C \div a$.

4. Find $C \div a$, and then find the power of b that results in the value $C \div a$.

Exercises *Practicing Habits of Mind*

Check Your Understanding

For Exercises 1–4, use the equation $C = a \cdot b^x$. This equation has four variables. If you know three of them, you can find the fourth.

1. Describe how to find C if you know a, b, and x.
2. Describe how to find a if you know C, b, and x.
3. Describe how to find b if you know C, a, and x.
4. Describe how to find x if you know C, a, and b.
5. Let $f(x) = 2^x$. The solution of $f(a) = 3$ is approximately 1.5850. The solution to $f(b) = 5$ is approximately 2.3219.
   a. You can use the information above and the properties of exponents to find all but one of this table's missing entries. Copy and complete the table, except for that entry. Give all answers to four decimal places.
   b. Find the last missing entry by approximating it to four decimal places.

x	$f(x) = 2^x$
0	1
1	2
1.5850	3
■	4
2.3219	5
■	6
■	7
■	8
■	9
■	10

6. The function versions of the laws of exponents work only for functions in the form $f(x) = b^x$. Other exponential functions have the form $f(x) = a \cdot b^x$. How do the rules change if $f(x) = a \cdot b^x$ instead? For example, is it still true that $f(x + y) = f(x) \cdot f(y)$? If not, what adjustments can you make?

5. a.

x	$f(x) = 2^x$
0	1
1	2
1.5850	3
2	4
2.3219	5
2.5850	6
■	7
3	8
3.1700	9
3.3219	10

b. 2.8074

6. a. $f(x + y) = \dfrac{f(x) \cdot f(y)}{a}$

b. $f(x - y) = a \cdot \dfrac{f(x)}{f(y)}$

c. $f(xy) = a^{1-y} \cdot (f(x))^y$

Exercises

HOMEWORK
- Core: 10, 11, 12, 13, 14, 17, 19
- Optional: 15, 16, 20, 21
- Extension: 18

Check Your Understanding

EXERCISES 1–4 These exercises motivate the need for an inverse function for exponential functions. This inverse function leads to a more efficient way of determining an unknown exponent—the case outlined in Exercise 4.

EXERCISE 4 It is important for students to recognize that this exercise is far more difficult than Exercises 1–3, even though it is phrased almost identically. In fact, they may not be able to find an answer, which will provide a motivation for the next investigation!

EXERCISE 5 The exponent that solves $2^x = 7$ is the only entry in the table that you cannot derive from the values for $2^x = 3$ and $2^x = 5$, because 7 is not a multiple of 3 or 5. Blackline Master 5.9 provides a copy of the table.

EXERCISE 6 gives students a chance to work through an argument like those presented in class to prove the laws of exponents. Students may not be able to predict the final result before they begin.

EXERCISE 8 Students should be able to complete the table with j and j^2, which should lead them to the equation $j^3 = 10$. If students are having trouble getting started, encourage them to use the guess-check-generalize method: Students can guess a value for j and figure out how to check if the guess is correct. This should also lead to the equation $j^3 = 10$.

EXERCISE 9 It can be a challenge for students to find all of the cases. Many may not consider the case where $x = -1$ because they have grown used to the definition of exponential function, which does not allow for negative bases.

On Your Own

EXERCISE 10 A similar equation is solved at the beginning of the next lesson, so this is an important exercise to assign. Until now, you have used an underlying assumption in solving exponential equations. You have assumed that $a^x = a^y$ implies $x = y$. You will prove this property formally in the next lesson.

7. Binh tells you that by investing, he expects to have ten times as much money in 30 years as he has now. He expects his investment to grow by about the same percentage every year. He says he can break the 30 years into 15-year halves, where each half has the same proportional growth.

Earnings per Dollar Invested

Years Invested	Earnings	÷
0	\$1	k
15	■	k
30	\$10	

a. Find k to three decimal places.

b. Find the exact value of k using a radical or rational exponent.

c. If Binh invests \$1500, how much money does he expect to have after 15 years?

8. Binh goes on to explain that he can also break the 30 years of investing into three groups of 10 years each.

Earnings per Dollar Invested

Years Invested	Earnings	÷
0	\$1	j
10	■	j
20	■	j
30	\$10	

a. Find j to three decimal places.

b. Find the exact value of j using a radical or rational exponent.

c. If Binh invests \$1500, how much money does he expect to have after 20 years?

Financial analysts use exponential functions to model the growth of investments.

9. **Take It Further** Find all real numbers x and y for which $x^y = 1$.

On Your Own

10. Using $g(x) = 5^x$, solve each equation for x.

a. $g(x) = 25$ b. $g(x) = 5^{-11}$ c. $g(x) = 25^3$ d. $g(x) = 0$

Answers

7. a. 3.162
b. $\sqrt{10}$
c. \$4743.42

8. a. 2.154
b. $\sqrt[3]{10}$
c. \$6962.38

9. If $x = 1$, then $x^y = 1$ for all real-number values of y; if $x = -1$, then $x^y = 1$ for all even values of y, or for all fractions $\frac{p}{q}$ where p and q are relatively prime and p is even; if $y = 0$, then $x^y = 1$ for all values of x except $x = 0$.

10. a. 2
b. -11
c. 6
d. no solution

11. Answers may vary. Samples are given.
$f(x + y) = f(x) \cdot f(y)$:
If $x = 2$ and $y = 3$, then
$f(x + y) = f(2 + 3) = f(5) = 10^5 = 10^2 \cdot 10^3 = f(x) \cdot f(y)$;
$f(x - y) = \frac{f(x)}{f(y)}$: If $x = 4$ and $y = 3$, then $f(x - y) = f(4 - 3) = f(1) = 10^1 = \frac{10^4}{10^3} = \frac{f(x)}{f(y)}$;
$f(xy) = (f(x))^y$: If $x = 3$ and $y = 2$, then $f(xy) = f(3 \cdot 2) = f(6) = 10^6 = 10^{3 \cdot 2} = (10^3)^2 = (f(x))^y$.

12. a. 11.9 yr
b. 18.85 yr
c. 30.75 yr

11. Let $f(x) = 10^x$. Give examples to verify the function version of each law of exponents for this particular function.

12. Sophie has made a deal with her father. She can deposit any amount of money with him, and he will guarantee her 6% interest per year. She deposits \$100. The amount of money she can withdraw from the Bank of Dad after x years is given by the exponential function $f(x) = 100(1.06)^x$.

 a. How long will it take for Sophie's money to double in value?

 b. How long will it take for Sophie's money to triple in value?

 c. How long will it take for Sophie's money to sextuple in value, or in other words, for her original deposit to be worth \$600?

13. Sketch the graph of each function.

- $a(x) = 3^x$
- $b(x) = 3 \cdot 3^x$
- $c(x) = 9 \cdot 3^x$
- $d(x) = 27 \cdot 3^x$
- $f(x) = 81 \cdot 3^x$

 How are these graphs related? Explain.

14. The table in Exercise 5 stops when the output is 10. Give three other examples of outputs N for which you can solve $f(x) = N$ by using the solutions to $f(a) = 3$ and $f(b) = 5$.

15. If x is an integer, $f(x) = i^x$ is a function that calculates the powers of the imaginary unit $i = \sqrt{-1}$.

 a. Calculate $f(2)$, $f(3)$, and $f(5)$. Is it true that $f(2) \cdot f(3) = f(5)$?

 b. Do all the laws of exponents work for this function f?

16. Alicia gets her first full-time job with a starting salary of \$25,000. She is offered two compensation plans for the future.

 Plan 1: Alicia will earn a raise of \$3000 every year.

 Plan 2: Alicia will earn an 8% raise every year.

 Determine how many years it will take for Alicia's salary to reach each amount under the two plans.

 a. at least \$30,000 b. at least \$40,000

 c. at least \$50,000 d. at least \$100,000

Go Online PHSchool.com

For additional practice, go to **Web Code:** bfa-0509

See Exercise 22 in Lesson 5.7.

EXERCISE 11 For some students, working through a numerical verification like this can make the laws of exponents more concrete.

EXERCISE 12 The purpose of this exercise is for students to notice the relationship between the three results—the third is the sum of the previous two. This relationship bears itself out in logarithms with the rule $\log 2 + \log 3 = \log 6$.

EXERCISE 14 Encourage students to do this exercise without referring to the graph of the function $y = 2^x$. They should use the given values to generate others through the laws of exponents.

EXERCISE 15 Students explore powers of complex numbers and powers of negative numbers in much greater detail in CME Project *Precalculus*.

EXERCISE 16 Some students may not recognize that they need to round up any answer they find for Plan 2, because Alicia gets only one raise a year. Students might also use a table or spreadsheet to solve this exercise, generating Alicia's salary for each year and then reading the answers to the questions from the table.

13.

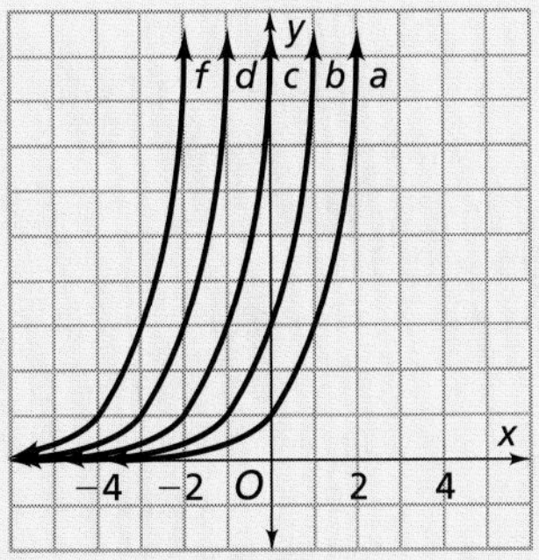

The graphs are all horizontal translations of each other; answers may vary. Sample: Each function can be written in the form $f(x) = 3^{x+n}$, which represents a horizontal translation of $a(x) = 3^x$. For example, $c(x) = 9 \cdot 3^x = 3^2 + 3^x = 3^{2+x}$, so the graph of $c(x) = 3^{x+2}$ is a horizontal translation of two units to left of the graph of $a(x) = 3^x$.

14. Answers may vary. Sample: 12, 15, and 18

15. a. $f(2) = -1$, $f(3) = -i$, $f(5) = i$; yes

 b. yes

16. a. Plan 1: 2 yr, Plan 2: 3 yr

 b. Plan 1: 5 yr, Plan 2: 7 yr

 c. Plan 1: 9 yr, Plan 2: 10 yr

 d. Plan 1: 25 yr, Plan 2: 19 yr

EXERCISE 17 involves a common error that many students make when considering the laws of exponents.

EXERCISE 18 $L(x)$ is the logarithm function base 2.

Maintain Your Skills

EXERCISE 20 Students should be able to answer the last part of this exercise far more quickly if they notice the pattern. Some students may not recognize 1024 as a power of 2. It is 2^{10}.

EXERCISE 21 The pattern to recognize in this exercise is that the two solutions to $a^x = b$ and $b^x = a$ are reciprocals. This may be difficult to notice, which is why the first pair's answers are nearly 2, then just over 0.5. Once students learn logarithms, you will revisit this question, and the reciprocal relationship between the two solutions will be clearer. The solution to the first pair is $x = \frac{\log 35}{\log 6}$, then $x = \frac{\log 6}{\log 35}$. The last pair can be answered more quickly using the pattern from the previous exercise.

Additional Resources

PRINT RESOURCES
- Solution Manual
- Practice Workbook
- Assessment Resources
- Teaching Resources

TECHNOLOGY
- Interactive Textbook
- TeacherExpress CD-ROM
- ExamView CD-ROM
- PHSchool.com

Additional Practice

1. Using $g(x) = 4^x$, solve each equation for x.
   a. $g(x) = 16$
   b. $g(x) = 4^{-9}$
   c. $g(x) = 64^2$
   d. $g(x) = 0$

2. Jeff's grandmother wants to help him save money for college. Jeff can deposit any amount of money with her, and she will guarantee him 7% interest per year. He deposits \$500. The amount of money he can withdraw from Grandma's Bank after x years is given by the exponential function $m(x) = 500(1.07)^x$.
   a. How long will it take for Jeff's money to double in value?
   b. How long will it take for Jeff's money to triple in value?
   c. How long will it take for Jeff's money to be worth \$2500?

3. Sketch the graph of each function.
   a. $a(x) = 2^x$
   b. $b(x) = 2 \cdot 2^x$
   c. $c(x) = 4 \cdot 2^x$
   d. $d(x) = 8 \cdot 2^x$
   e. How are these graphs related? Explain.

4. Suppose $L_b(x)$ is the inverse of $f(x) = b^x$.
   a. Is $L_3(x)$ a one-to-one function? Explain.
   b. The value of $L_3(23)$ is between what two integers?
   c. Complete the table for $L_3(x)$. Give approximations to four decimal places.

x	$L_3(x)$
1	0
2	0.6309
3	1
4	
5	
6	
7	
8	
9	

5. Simon puts \$750 in an investment account. He earns 4.9% interest per year.
   a. After how many years will Simon be closest to doubling his starting investment?
   b. After how many years will Simon be closest to doubling his starting investment if the account earns 5.9% interest per year? 6.9% interest per year?

6. a. Describe the Rule of 72 using sentences.
   b. According to the Rule of 72, how long will it take an investment's value to double if the interest rate is 8% APR?

Practice: For Lesson 5.9, assign Exercises 1–3.

17. What's Wrong Here? Stacy says the function versions of the laws of exponents do not always work. "Here's one example. I take an exponential function $f(x) = x^3$. It says $f(x)$ times $f(y)$ equals $f(x + y)$, but that doesn't work. Take $x = 1$ and $y = 2$, for example: $f(x)$ times $f(y)$ is 8, but $f(x + y)$ is 27. I've got plenty of these."

What is wrong with Stacy's reasoning?

18. Take It Further Suppose a one-to-one function $L(x)$ has $L(2) = 1$ and follows the rule below for any positive numbers a and b.

$$L(a) + L(b) = L(ab)$$

a. Show that $L(4) = 2$ and $L(1) = 0$.

b. Find x if $L(x) = 6$.

c. Show that if n is an integer, then $L(a^n) = n \cdot L(a)$.

d. Find x if $L(x) = \frac{1}{2}$.

19. Standardized Test Prep Suppose a restaurant's sales increase 15% each year for 8 years. Use the approximations $(1.15)^3 \approx 1.521$ and $(1.15)^8 \approx 3.059$. What is the ratio of the restaurant's sales in the fifth year to the restaurant's sales in the first year?

A. 1.538 **B.** 2.011 **C.** 2.136 **D.** 4.580

Maintain Your Skills

20. Solve each equation. Round to three decimal places.

a. $2^x = 7$ **b.** $4^x = 7$

c. $8^x = 7$ **d.** $16^x = 7$

e. $1024^x = 7$

21. Solve each equation. Round to three decimal places.

a. $6^x = 35$ **b.** $35^x = 6$

c. $3^x = 28$ **d.** $28^x = 3$

e. $9^x = 28$ **f.** $28^x = 9$

Go Online
Video Tutor
PHSchool.com

Web Code: bfe-0775

Answers

17. $f(x) = x^3$ is not an exponential function.

18. a. $L(4) = L(2 \cdot 2) = L(2) + L(2) = 1 + 1 = 2$; since $L(1) + L(2) = L(1 \cdot 2) = L(2)$, it follows that $L(1) = 0$.

b. 64

c. If $n > 0$, then $L(a^n) = L(\underbrace{a \cdot a \cdot \dots \cdot a}_{n \text{ copies of } a}) = \underbrace{L(a) + L(a) + \dots + L(a)}_{n \text{ copies of } L(a)} = n \cdot L(a)$. If $n = 0$, then $L(a^n) = L(a^0) = L(1) = 0 = 0 \cdot L(a) = n \cdot L(a)$.
If $n < 0$, let $n = -m$ where $m > 0$. Then

$$L(a^m \cdot a^{-m}) = L(a^m) + L(a^{-m})$$
$$L(a^0) = m \cdot L(a) + L(a^{-m})$$
$$L(1) = m \cdot L(a) + L(a^{-m})$$
$$0 = m \cdot L(a) + L(a^{-m})$$
$$-m \cdot L(a) = L(a^{-m})$$
$$n \cdot L(a) = L(a^n)$$

d. $\sqrt{2}$

19. B

5.10 Exponential Functions, One-to-One

Consider the equation $8^x = 32$. You can solve this equation by writing 8 and 32 as powers of 2.

$$8^x = 32$$
$$(2^3)^x = 2^5$$
$$2^{3x} = 2^5$$
$$3x = 5$$
$$x = \frac{5}{3}$$

The step that removes the exponent is an interesting one. If $2^x = 2^y$, is it always true that $x = y$? This has been an assumption throughout the chapter. This lesson provides a proof, as well as some initial exploration of the inverse functions of exponential functions.

Recall the definition of *one-to-one* from Chapter 2: A function is one-to-one if there is a unique input that produces a given output. Algebraically, a function f is one-to-one if $f(a) = f(b)$ only when $a = b$.

The graph of a function can suggest whether it is one-to-one. For example, $f(x) = x^3 - 4x$ is not one-to-one. You can see this from its graph.

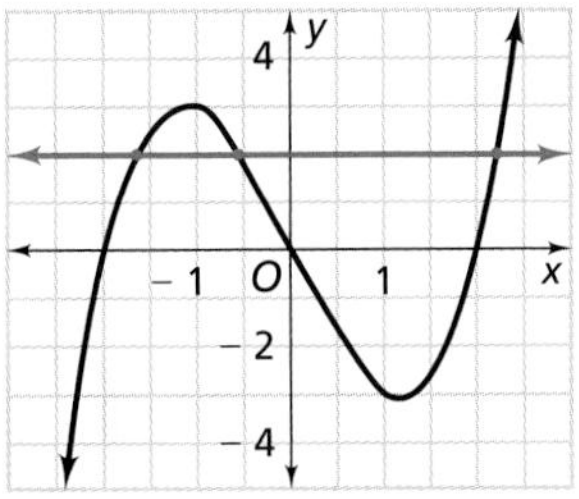

This function cannot be one-to-one since there is more than one input that gives the output $y = 2$. However, the graph of $f(x) = 2^x$ suggests that this function is one-to-one.

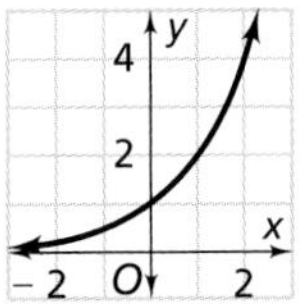

Remember...

Since you use a horizontal line to find such counterexamples, this is the horizontal-line test. A function is not one-to-one if a horizontal line intersects the graph more than once.

20. a. 2.807
b. 1.404
c. 0.936
d. 0.702
e. 0.281
21. a. 1.984
b. 0.504
c. 3.033
d. 0.330
e. 1.517
f. 0.659

Lesson Overview

GOAL

- Evaluate the inverse of the function $y = b^x$ either exactly or by approximation.

Students make the connection between the monotonicity of the exponential function—it is always either strictly increasing or strictly decreasing—and the fact that it must be one-to-one. This guarantees that there is an inverse function for any exponential function. Students experiment with these inverse functions and, in the next investigation, they study these functions and their properties under their formal names, *logarithms*.

CHECK YOUR UNDERSTANDING
- Core: 1, 2, 3, 4, 6, 7
- Optional: 5, 8
- Extension: 9

MATERIALS
- CAS (recommended)
- graph paper
- graphing calculators
- Blackline Master 5.10

HOMEWORK
- Core: 10, 11, 12, 13, 15, 16, 17
- Optional: 18, 19
- Extension: 14

VOCABULARY
- inverse function
- one-to-one

Launch

Start this lesson by reviewing the definition of *one-to-one* from Chapter 2 and discussing ways to prove that exponential functions are one-to-one. Blackline Master 5.10 can be used here.

Explore

THEOREM 5.4 Some students may be uncomfortable assuming that exponential functions are strictly increasing or strictly decreasing. The only evidence they have of this property is the graphs they have seen of exponential functions, and they might be concerned about making an assumption from that evidence alone. Here is a way to show, without using that assumption, that exponential functions must be one-to-one.

If $f(m) = f(n)$, then $\frac{f(m)}{f(n)} = 1$. (You know that since $f(x)$ is an exponential function, $f(n) \neq 0$, so it is okay to divide by it.)

$$\frac{f(m)}{f(n)} = \frac{ab^m}{ab^n} = b^{m-n}$$

If $b^{m-n} = 1$, then, since $b \neq 1$ by the definition of exponential function, $m - n = 0$ and $m = n$. You can also use the definition of the function to show that if $m = n$, then $f(m) = ab^m = ab^n = f(n)$.

You can state the fact that all exponential functions are one-to-one as a theorem.

Theorem 5.4 *One-to-One Property for Exponential Functions*

If f is an exponential function, then f is one-to-one.

Proof Suppose that $f(a) = f(b)$, where a and b are real numbers. Recall from Lesson 5.7 that an exponential function is either strictly increasing or strictly decreasing. Assume that f is strictly increasing. If $a < b$, you have $f(a) < f(b)$, which contradicts the assumption that $f(a) = f(b)$. You get a similar contradiction if $a > b$. Thus, $a = b$. The proof is almost identical for the case in which f is strictly decreasing.

You must show that $a = b$.

For Discussion

1. Complete the missing cases in the proof.

The fact that exponential functions are one-to-one provides an algebraic corollary. The algebraic step of "undoing the exponent" is valid as long as the base is positive and not equal to 1.

Corollary 5.4.1

If $b > 0$, $b \neq 1$, and $b^x = b^y$, then $x = y$.

Developing Habits of Mind

Detect the key characteristics. One other important property of a one-to-one function is that it has an inverse function. That means that any exponential function has an inverse function.

So, consider this table for the function $f(x) = 2^x$.

x	$f(x)$
−1	$\frac{1}{2}$
0	1
1	2
2	4
3	8
4	16

Answers

For Discussion

1. Proof of second case for the assumption that f is strictly increasing: If $a > b$, then $f(a) > f(b)$, which contradicts the original assumption that $f(a) = f(b)$.

   Proof for the assumption that f is strictly decreasing: If $a < b$, then $f(a) > f(b)$, which contradicts the original assumption that $f(a) = f(b)$. If $a > b$, then $f(a) < f(b)$, which contradicts the original assumption that $f(a) = f(b)$.

There is another function, which you can call $L_2(x)$, that is the inverse function. So its table would include these input-output pairs.

x	$L_2(x)$
$\frac{1}{2}$	-1
1	0
2	1
4	2
8	3
16	4

The use of the subscript 2 helps remind you that the original function had base 2. So, you could give the inverse function of $f(x) = 10^x$ the name $L_{10}(x)$. You will learn the more standard notation for this function in Investigation 5C.

Note that these are the same pairs listed for $f(x) = 2^x$ with the inputs and outputs switched.

But what can you do for other inputs to $L_2(x)$? For example, what is $L_2(3)$? The value of $L_2(3)$ is the number that solves $2^x = 3$, since 3 would appear as the output in the 2^x table. That value is an irrational number, about 1.5850 (see Exercise 5 in Lesson 5.9). So $L_2(3)$ is about 1.5850, which seems reasonable, given the table. You expect it to be somewhere between 1 and 2.

For You to Do

2. What two integers is $L_2(9)$ between? Find its value to three decimal places.

Any one-to-one function has an inverse function. If the point (x, y) is on the graph of the function f, then the point (y, x) is on the graph of the inverse f^{-1}. You can draw the graph of the inverse by reflecting the graph of the function across the line $y = x$.

As in Chapter 2, the -1 in the notation $f^{-1}(x)$ means "inverse with respect to function composition."

Here are the graphs of $f(x) = 2^x$ and its inverse function, which you will temporarily call $L_2(x)$.

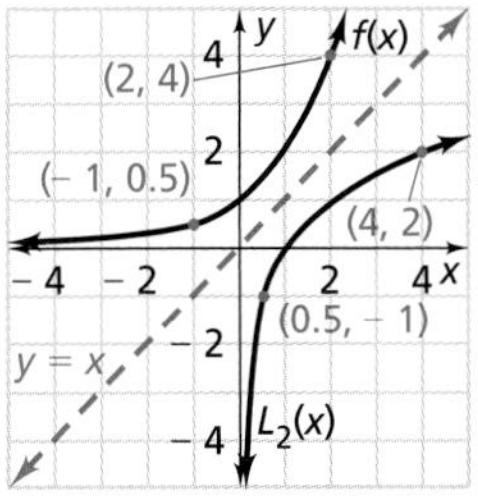

The next investigation focuses on functions such as $L_2(x)$, their properties, and how they are used to solve equations in algebra.

For You to Do

2. 3 and 4; 3.170

Developing Habits of Mind

Although this function can be written as $f(x) = \log_2(x)$, this book deliberately avoids the use of the notation here. This gives students a chance to discover the properties of these functions and focus as closely as possible on the inverse relationship with exponential functions. Many of the questions asked in this lesson can only be answered by looking at the inverse relationship.

For You to Do

9 is chosen as the input since it is 3^2, so the answer will be exactly double $L_2(3)$. You are really asking students here to estimate $\log_2 9$ from an estimate of $\log_2 3$.

Wrap Up

As time allows, have students work on the Check Your Understanding core exercises and share their solutions.

Assessment Resources

Lesson Quiz 5.10

1. Let $L_b(x)$ be the inverse function of $f(x) = b^x$.
  a. Is $L_5(x)$ a one-to-one function? Explain.
  b. The value of $L_5(49)$ is between what two integers?
  c. Complete the table. Approximate to four decimal places.

x	$L_5(x)$
1	0
2	0.4307
3	
4	
5	1
6	
7	
8	
9	

2. Sandy puts \$1200 into a bank account that earns 4.5% interest per year.
  a. After how many years will Sandy be closest to doubling her starting investment?
  b. After how many years will Sandy be closest to doubling her starting investment if the account earns 5.5% interest per year? 6.5% per year?

3. Use the Rule of 72 to calculate how long it takes to double the value of an investment account with an interest rate of 5% APR.

Exercises

HOMEWORK
- Core: 10, 11, 12, 13, 15, 16, 17
- Optional: 18, 19
- Extension: 14

Check Your Understanding

EXERCISE 2 Even after students begin working with logarithms more formally, it will be useful to rewrite an expression involving a logarithm in an exponential form and vice versa. Emphasize this "change of form" as a useful technique.

EXERCISE 3 Students may not recognize this as the same question from the Example in Lesson 5.9, so you may want to point this out. One purpose of this exercise is to give students an opportunity to recognize that $L_4(5) + L_4(8) = L_4(40)$, which is an example of one of the logarithm laws they encounter in the next investigation.

EXERCISE 6 In this exercise, students discover that exponential functions will eventually take on greater values than polynomial functions. Over time, exponential growth beats polynomial growth.

Exercises *Practicing Habits of Mind*

Check Your Understanding

Throughout these exercises, $L_b(x)$ refers to the inverse of $f(x) = b^x$.

1. Based on what you know about $f(x) = 2^x$, find the domain and range of the inverse function $L_2(x)$.

2. Find each value. Each result is an integer.

a. $L_5(25)$ **b.** $L_7(1)$ **c.** $L_{11}(11^6)$
d. $L_{0.1}(0.001)$ **e.** $L_3(\frac{1}{9})$

3. Find each value, either exactly or to four decimal places.

a. $L_4(5)$ **b.** $L_4(8)$ **c.** $L_4(40)$ **d.** $L_4(\frac{8}{5})$

4. Copy the graph below of $f(x) = (0.5)^x$. Sketch the graph of the inverse function.

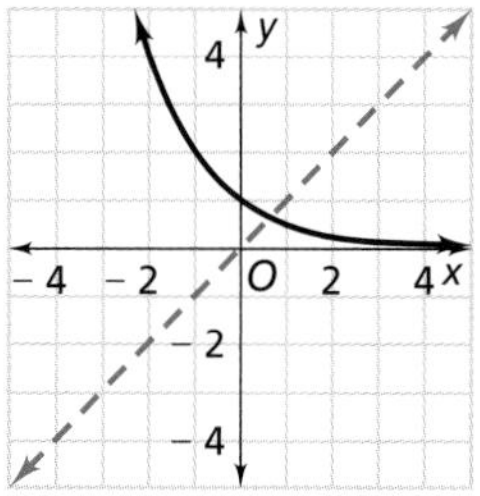

5. Let $f(x) = 2^x$. Determine which value in each pair is greater. (*Hint:* Use the graph of $f(x) = 2^x$.)

a. the mean of $f(3)$ and $f(5)$ $f(4)$
b. the mean of $f(5)$ and $f(7)$ $f(6)$
c. the mean of $f(-4)$ and $f(-2)$ $f(-3)$
d. the mean of $f(x)$ and $f(y)$ $f(\frac{x+y}{2})$

6. a. Sketch the graphs of $y = 2^x$ and $y = x^2$.
b. How many numbers x satisfy $2^x = x^2$?

Answers

Exercises

1. domain: positive real numbers; range: all real numbers

2. a. 2 **b.** 0
c. 6 **d.** 3
e. −2

3. a. 1.1610
b. 1.5
c. 2.6610
d. 0.3390

4.

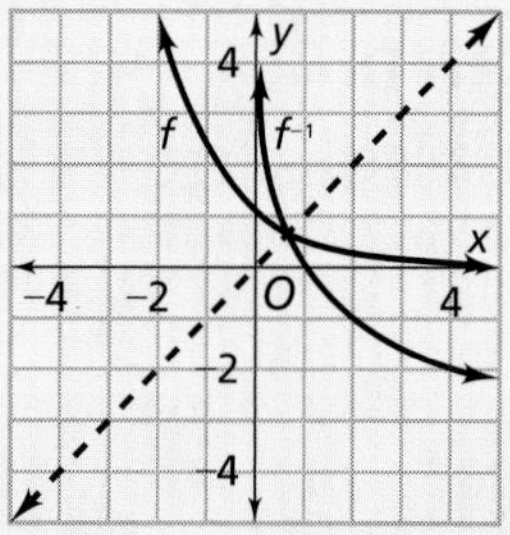

5. a. the mean of $f(3)$ and $f(5)$
b. the mean of $f(5)$ and $f(7)$
c. the mean of $f(-4)$ and $f(-2)$
d. the mean of $f(x)$ and $f(y)$

7. As x increases, 2^x becomes greater than x^2. Consider the values of 1.06^x. Use the graphs of $y = x^2$ and $y = 1.06^x$.

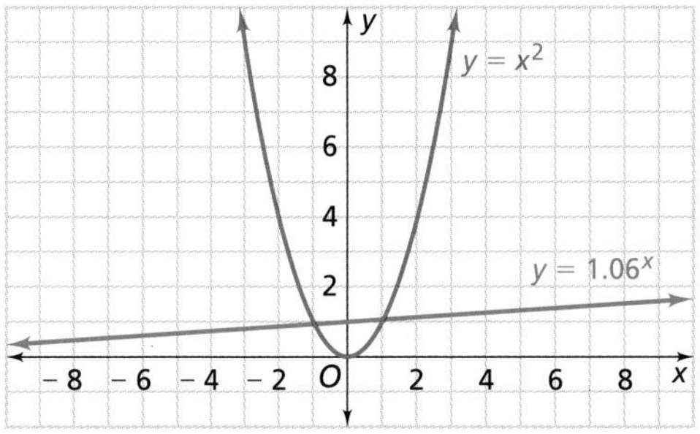

As x increases, will x^2 always be greater than 1.06^x?

8. As x increases, 2^x becomes greater than x^2. Consider the values of x^{10}. Use the graphs of $y = x^{10}$ and $y = 2^x$.

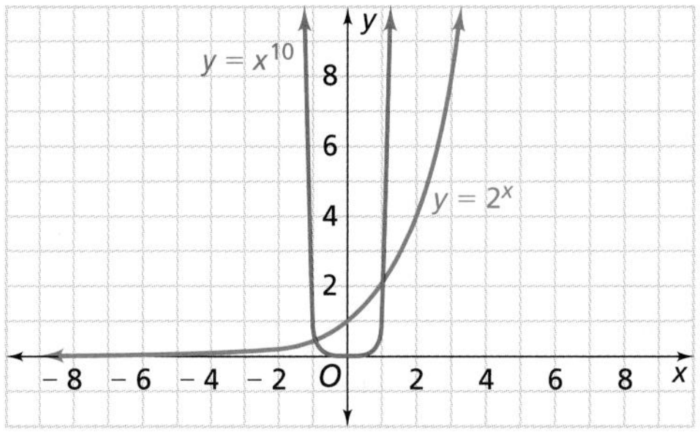

a. As x increases, will x^{10} always be greater than 2^x?

b. As x increases, will x^{10} always be greater than 1.06^x?

c. As x increases, will 2^x always be greater than 1.06^x?

9. **Take It Further** The graph of $y = 2^x$ does not intersect the graph of $y = x$. The graph of $y = 1.06^x$ intersects the graph of $y = x$ in two places. Approximate the greatest number b such that the graph of $y = b^x$ intersects the graph of $y = x$. Approximate the coordinates of the one point at which $y = b^x$ intersects $y = x$.

6. a. See back of book.
b. 3 solutions
7. no
8. a. no
b. no
c. yes
9. $b \approx 1.4$; about (2.7, 2.7)

EXERCISE 7 At the scales shown here, the graph of $y = 1.06x$ looks nearly linear. Students should have an inkling that this function is not going to look linear for very long. Encourage them to look again with a different x-axis scale—for example, a scale −50 to 50 instead of −10 to 10. This should help students see why x^2 will not always be greater than 1.06^x.

EXERCISE 9 Students will likely respond with decimal approximations for these intersection points, but the exact value of b is $e^{\frac{1}{e}}$, and the coordinates of the point are (e, e), where e is the Euler constant, the base of the natural logarithm.

On Your Own

EXERCISE 12 can be time-consuming, until students realize this is the same table from Exercise 5 in Lesson 5.9. Even if they do not recognize the table, they can use the same techniques they used to complete the table before. $L_2(6) = 2 \cdot L_2(3)$, and so on. The goal of the exercise is for students to recognize how to calculate an output for this function by following it back through $f(x) = 2^x$.

EXERCISE 13 Expect students to find the missing entries by approximating solutions to exponential equations with missing exponents by using trial and error rather than by using logarithms. As a consequence, this exercise can be time-consuming. However, that may motivate students to notice patterns in the entries, which prepares them for the next investigation.

EXERCISE 14 If necessary, suggest to students that they convert this equation in L functions into exponential form.

On Your Own

Go Online PHSchool.com
For additional practice, go to **Web Code:** bfa-0510

10. Is $L_2(x)$ a one-to-one function? Explain.

11. **Standardized Test Prep** The value of $L_3(28)$ is between what two integers?

A. 1 and 2 **B.** 2 and 3 **C.** 3 and 4 **D.** 4 and 5

12. Copy and complete this table for $L_2(x)$. Give approximations to four decimal places.

x	$L_2(x)$
1	0
2	1
3	1.5850
4	■
5	■
6	■
7	■
8	■
9	■

13. **a.** Explain why $L_8(8) = 1$.

b. Explain why $L_8(2) = \frac{1}{3}$.

c. Copy and complete this table for $L_8(x)$. Give approximations to four decimal places.

x	$L_8(x)$
1	0
2	0.3333
3	0.5283
4	■
5	■
6	■
7	■
8	1
9	■

14. **Take It Further** Prove that $L_2(x) = 3 \cdot L_8(x)$ for any positive real number x.

15. Ariela puts \$500 in an investment account. She earns 9% interest per year. After how many years will she be closest to doubling her starting investment?

Answers

10. Yes; $L_2(x)$ is the inverse of $f(x) = 2^x$. Since $f(x)$ is one-to-one, its inverse is one-to-one.

11. C

12. See back of book.

13. **a.** $8^1 = 8$, so $L_8(8) = 1$.

b. $8^{\frac{1}{3}} = 2$, so $L_8(2) = \frac{1}{3}$.

c. See back of book.

14. Let $L_2(x) = a$, which means $x = 2^a$, and let $3 \cdot L_8(x) = b$, which means $L_8(x) = \frac{b}{3}$ or $x = 8^{\frac{b}{3}} = (2^3)^{\frac{b}{3}} = 2^b$. Since $x = 2^a$ and $x = 2^b$, $2^a = 2^b$. So, by Corollary 5.7, $a = b$. Thus, $L_2(x) = 3 \cdot L_8(x)$.

15. 8 yr

16. Ariela wonders what will happen with higher or lower interest rates. Copy the table at the right. For each interest rate, find out after how many years Ariela will be closest to doubling her starting $500 investment.

Doubling Time

APR	Years to Double
3%	■
4%	■
5%	■
6%	12
7%	■
8%	■
9%	■
10%	■
11%	■
12%	■

Any APR will show exponential growth. See the TI-Nspire Handbook, p. 778.

Remember...

APR stands for "annual percentage rate."

17. Many financial advisors use the Rule of 72 when offering advice about long-term investments.

Rule of 72 To find the number of years it takes to double an investment's value, divide 72 by the annual percentage rate.

a. Recopy the table from Exercise 16 and use the Rule of 72 to complete it. How do your results using the Rule of 72 compare to the results you found in Exercise 16?

b. According to the Rule of 72, how long will it take a credit card balance to double if the interest rate is 18% APR?

c. If Ariela invests $500 in an account at 9% APR for 40 years, how many times will her money double in value? How much money does the Rule of 72 suggest she will have after 40 years?

Go Online PHSchool.com

For more information on the Rule of 72, go to **Web Code:** bfe-9031

Maintain Your Skills

In Exercises 18 and 19, find each value to four decimal places.

18. a. $L_5(3)$ **b.** $L_5(9)$ **c.** $L_5(27)$ **d.** $L_5(81)$

19. a. $L_2(7)$ **b.** $L_4(7)$ **c.** $L_8(7)$ **d.** $L_{16}(7)$ **e.** $L_{1024}(7)$

16. See back of book.

17. a. The table is the same as the table in Exercise 16 except for the result for 3%. The Rule of 72 gives a value of 24 years instead of 23 years.

b. 4 yr

c. 5 times; $16,000

18. a. 0.6826

b. 1.3652

c. 2.0478

d. 2.7304

19. a. 2.8074

b. 1.4037

c. 0.9358

d. 0.7018

e. 0.2807

EXERCISE 16 Encourage students to model the function on their calculators for quicker calculations.

EXERCISE 17 Consider asking students to investigate the Rule of 72 online, where it is also sometimes called "the rule of 71," or "the rule of 70," or even "the rule of 69.3." The rule of 72 is a good way for students to get a feel for the long-term growth of an account, especially the difference in growth between a savings account earning 2% and a credit card balance accruing 18%. By the way, this rule gives an accurate-enough estimate that bankers and investment bankers use it.

Maintain Your Skills

EXERCISE 18 Some students may recognize $L_5(9) = 2 \cdot L_5(3)$, and so on.

EXERCISE 19 is actually the same question as Exercise 20 in Lesson 5.9, rephrased using the function notation. The goal here, as in many of these exercises, is to get students used to logarithms as a function before they are formally introduced to logarithm notation and properties.

Additional Resources

PRINT RESOURCES
- Solution Manual
- Practice Workbook
- Assessment Resources
- Teaching Resources

TECHNOLOGY
- Interactive Textbook
- TeacherExpress CD-ROM
- ExamView CD-ROM
- PHSchool.com

Additional Practice

1. Using $g(x) = 4^x$, solve each equation for x.
   a. $g(x) = 16$
   b. $g(x) = 4^{-9}$
   c. $g(x) = 64^2$
   d. $g(x) = 0$

2. Jeff's grandmother wants to help him save money for college. Jeff can deposit any amount of money with her, and she will guarantee him 7% interest per year. He deposits $500. The amount of money he can withdraw from Grandma's Bank after x years is given by the exponential function $m(x) = 500(1.07)^x$.
   a. How long will it take for Jeff's money to double in value?
   b. How long will it take for Jeff's money to triple in value?
   c. How long will it take for Jeff's money to be worth $2500?

3. Sketch the graph of each function.
   a. $a(x) = 2^x$
   b. $b(x) = 2 \cdot 2^x$
   c. $c(x) = 4 \cdot 2^x$
   d. $d(x) = 8 \cdot 2^x$
   e. How are these graphs related? Explain.

4. Suppose $L_b(x)$ is the inverse of $f(x) = b^x$.
   a. Is $L_3(x)$ a one-to-one function? Explain.
   b. The value of $L_3(23)$ is between what two integers?
   c. Complete the table for $L_3(x)$. Give approximations to four decimal places.

x	$L_3(x)$
1	0
2	0.6309
3	1
4	
5	
6	
7	
8	
9	

5. Simon puts $750 in an investment account. He earns 4.9% interest per year.
   a. After how many years will Simon be closest to doubling his starting investment?
   b. After how many years will Simon be closest to doubling his starting investment if the account earns 5.9% interest per year? 6.9% interest per year?

6. **a.** Describe the Rule of 72 using sentences.
   b. According to the Rule of 72, how long will it take an investment's value to double if the interest rate is 8% APR?

Practice: For Lesson 5.10, assign Exercises 4–6.

Mathematical Reflections

EXERCISES 6–8 At the start of the investigation, you may have assigned these as Questions 1–3 for students to think and write about.

Mathematical Reflections 5B

In this investigation, you graphed exponential functions. You wrote rules for exponential functions, given a table of inputs and outputs or two points on the graph of the function. These exercises will help you summarize what you have learned.

1. Give the definition of *exponential function.* Pay special attention to any restrictions on the variables in your definition. Give an example of an exponential function and describe its domain and range. Describe where your function is increasing and where it is decreasing.

2. Use this table for the exponential function $g(x)$.

a. Write a recursive definition for $g(x)$.

b. Write a closed-form definition for $g(x)$.

c. Do your answers for parts (a) and (b) define the same function? Explain.

x	$g(x)$
0	−5
1	−10
2	−20
3	−40
4	−80

3. a. Copy and complete this ratio table for $h(x)$.

b. Find $h(23)$ to four decimal places.

c. Could $h(x)$ be an exponential function? Explain.

x	$h(x)$	÷
0	■	$\frac{2}{3}$
1	6	$\frac{2}{3}$
2	■	$\frac{2}{3}$
3	■	$\frac{2}{3}$
4	■	

4. Find the exact values of x that solve each equation.

a. $12 = 3x^2$

b. $x = 5 \cdot 4^{-\frac{1}{2}}$

c. $16 = 4 \cdot 32^x$

d. $-5 = x \cdot 27^{\frac{2}{3}}$

5. $L_3(x)$ is the inverse of the function $f(x) = 3^x$.

a. Find $L_3(1)$.

b. Find $L_3(81)$.

c. If $L_3(2) \approx 0.6309$, find $L_3(4)$ and $L_3(8)$.

d. Approximate $L_3(5)$ to four decimal places.

6. For $f(x) = b^x$, why is it true that $f(m) \cdot f(n) = f(m + n)$?

7. Why must an exponential function have an inverse function?

8. If you invest $1000 in an account at 6% interest, compounded annually, how much money will you have in 30 years?

Vocabulary

In this investigation, you learned these terms. Make sure you understand what each one means and how to use it.

- **base**
- **exponential decay**
- **exponential function**
- **exponential growth**
- **functional equation**
- **monotonic**
- **strictly decreasing**
- **strictly increasing**

Answers

Mathematical Reflections

1. An exponential function is a function of the form $f(x) = a \cdot b^x$, where a and b are real numbers, $a \neq 0$, $b > 0$, $b \neq 1$; answers may vary.
Sample: $f(x) = -2 \cdot \left(\frac{1}{3}\right)^x$, domain: all real numbers, range: all negative numbers; increasing for all x

2. a. $g(x) = \begin{cases} -5 & \text{if } x = 0 \\ 2 \cdot g(x-1) & \text{if } x > 0 \end{cases}$

b. $g(x) = -5 \cdot 2^x$

c. No; the domain for the recursive definition is nonnegative integers, while the domain for the closed form definition is all real numbers.

3. a.

x	$h(x)$	÷
0	9	$\frac{2}{3}$
1	6	$\frac{2}{3}$
2	4	$\frac{2}{3}$
3	$\frac{8}{3}$	$\frac{2}{3}$
4	$\frac{16}{9}$	

b. 0.0008

c. Yes; the ratio of successive terms is constant.

4. a. ± 2

b. $\frac{5}{2}$

c. $\frac{2}{5}$

d. $-\frac{5}{9}$

5. a. 0

b. 4

c. $L_3(4) = 1.2618$, $L_3(8) = 1.8928$

d. 1.4650

6. $f(m) \cdot f(n) = b^m \cdot b^n = b^{m+n} = f(m + n)$

Chapter 5

Mid-Chapter Test

Go Online PHSchool.com — For a mid-chapter test, go to Web Code: bfa-0552

Multiple Choice

1. Which of the following expressions is NOT equal to 5^{12}?
   - A. $(5^6)^2$
   - B. $(5^3)(5^4)$
   - C. $\frac{5^{24}}{5^{12}}$
   - D. $(5^{10})(5^2)$
2. Simplify $((x^{-2})^2)^2$.
   - A. x^{-8}
   - B. x^{-6}
   - C. x^2
   - D. x^{16}
3. Simplify $64^{\frac{3}{2}}$.
   - A. 16
   - B. 96
   - C. 512
   - D. 32,768
4. Which of these points is NOT on the graph of $f(x) = 4 \cdot \left(\frac{1}{2}\right)^x$?
   - A. $(-2, 16)$
   - B. $(0, 4)$
   - C. $\left(1, \frac{1}{2}\right)$
   - D. $(2, 1)$
5. Let $L_4(x)$ be the inverse of the function $f(x) = 4^x$. What is the value of $L_4(16)$?
   - A. -4
   - B. -2
   - C. 2
   - D. 4

Open Response

6. Use this table of the function $h(x)$.

x	$h(x)$	÷
0	3	■
1	6	■
2	12	■
3	■	■
4	■	■
5	■	

   a. Find a rule for $h(x)$ in the form $h(x) = c \cdot a^x$ that matches the table.
   b. Copy and complete the table.
   c. Find a recursive definition for $h(x)$.

7. Use the sequence below.

   3, 6, ■, ■, ■, . . .

   a. Find the missing terms if the sequence is arithmetic.
   b. Find the missing terms if the sequence is geometric.

8. Simplify each expression. Assume $x, y, z \neq 0$.
   a. $x^{-4} \cdot x^6$
   b. $\left(y^{\frac{1}{3}}\right)^3$
   c. $\frac{x^{-2}}{x^6}$
   d. $z^{-7} \cdot z^7$
   e. $x^{\frac{1}{2}} \cdot x^2$
   f. $(x^{-6})^{-5}$

9. a. Suppose q is an exponential function with $q(2) = 9$ and $q(3) = 27$. Find $q(x)$.
   b. Sketch the graph of $q(x)$.
   c. Let $t(x) = -2 \cdot q(x)$. Find a rule for $t(x)$. Find $t(2)$ and $t(3)$.
   d. Sketch the graph of $t(x)$.

10. Find the exact values of x that solve each equation.
    a. $16 = 4x^2$
    b. $16 = 4 \cdot 2^x$
    c. $x = 4 \cdot 16^{-\frac{1}{2}}$

11. Simplify the expressions 4^0, 7^{-2}, and $5^{\frac{2}{3}}$.

Mid-Chapter Test

Assessment Resources

Mid-Chapter Test — page 1 of 2

Multiple Choice

1. Which of the following expressions is NOT equal to 3^{24}?
   A. $(3^6)^4$
   B. $(3^{12})(3^{12})$
   C. $\frac{3^{24}}{3^0}$
   D. $(3^{12})(3^2)$
2. Simplify $\frac{x^{-12}}{x^{-6}}$.
   A. x^{-18}
   B. x^{-6}
   C. x^2
   D. x^6
3. Simplify $27^{-\frac{2}{3}}$.
   A. -18
   B. $\frac{1}{18}$
   C. $\frac{1}{9}$
   D. 9
4. Which of these points is on the graph of $f(x) = -2 \cdot 3^x$?
   A. $(-1, 6)$
   B. $(0, -2)$
   C. $\left(1, \frac{2}{3}\right)$
   D. $(2, 3)$
5. Let $L_3(x)$ be the inverse of the function $y = 3^x$. Between which two integers does $L_3(16)$ lie?
   A. 1 and 2
   B. 2 and 3
   C. 3 and 4
   D. 4 and 5

Also available: Form B

7. Exponential functions are strictly increasing or strictly decreasing, so every exponential function is one-to-one and has an inverse function.
8. $5743.49

Mid-Chapter Test

1. B
2. A
3. C
4. C
5. C
6. a. $h(x) = 3 \cdot 2^x$
   b. See back of book.
   c. $h(x) = \begin{cases} 3 & \text{if } x = 0 \\ 2 \cdot h(x-1) & \text{if } x > 0 \end{cases}$
7. a. 3, 6, 9, 12, 15, . . .
   b. 3, 6, 12, 24, 48, . . .
8. a. x^2
   b. y
   c. x^{-8} or $\frac{1}{x^8}$
   d. 1
   e. $x^{\frac{5}{2}}$
   f. x^{30}
9. a. $q(x) = 3^x$
   b. See back of book.
   c. $t(x) = -2 \cdot 3^x$; $t(2) = -18$, $t(3) = -54$
   d. See back of book.
10. a. ± 2
    b. 2
    c. 1
11. $4^0 = 1$, $7^{-2} = \frac{1}{49}$, $5^{\frac{2}{3}} = \sqrt[3]{25} \approx 2.92$

Investigation Overview

Throughout this chapter, students have studied exponential functions. In the last lesson of Investigation 5B, students proved that exponential functions are one-to-one, so they must have inverses. In this investigation, students study the inverses of exponential functions, logarithms. Students begin by converting expressions involving logarithms into equations involving exponents and solving these equations by hand, where possible. Then they learn to use their calculators to compute base-10 logarithms, and with the change-of-base rule, to compute logarithms of any base, even if their calculator shows only logarithms with base 10 and base e. Along the way, students use logarithms to solve exponential equations with unknown exponents. Students also use the laws of exponents to develop corresponding laws of logarithms, and they graph logarithmic functions and think about their properties. Finally, students explore graphing functions on logarithmic scales and see when such scales are helpful.

You may wish to assign Questions 1–3 for students to think and write about during the investigation.

Learning Goals

- Evaluate logarithms of any base using a calculator.
- Use logarithms to solve exponential equations.
- Graph logarithmic functions.
- Graph functions using a logarithmic scale.

Habits and Skills

- Reason logically from the definition of a logarithmic function and from the laws of exponents to develop the laws of logarithms.
- Visualize the graph of a logarithmic function from the graph of the corresponding exponential function.
- Convert flexibly and strategically between logarithmic form and exponential form, and choose the best form to solve problems.

Investigation 5C

Logarithmic Functions

In *Logarithmic Functions*, you will learn that logarithms are the inverses of exponential functions. You will use logarithms to solve exponential equations.

By the end of this investigation, you will be able to answer questions like these.

1. What are some reasons to use logarithms?
2. What is a logarithmic scale and when do you use it?
3. If you invest \$1000 at 6% interest, compounded annually, how many years will it take until your money grows to \$10,000?

You will learn how to

- evaluate logarithms of any base using a calculator
- use logarithms to solve exponential equations
- graph logarithmic functions

You will develop these habits and skills:

- Reason logically from the definition of a logarithmic function and the laws of exponents to develop the laws of logarithms.
- Visualize the graph of a logarithmic function from the graph of the corresponding exponential function.
- Convert flexibly and strategically between logarithmic form and exponential form, and choose the best form to solve problems.

The Krumbein scale is a logarithmic scale used to classify the size of particles. A boulder with diameter 256 mm or greater has a scale value of −8 or less.

Investigation Road Map

LESSON 5.11, *Getting Started,* has students explore the effect of the LOG button on their calculators and begin to see some of the laws of logarithms in action.

LESSON 5.12, *Defining Logarithms,* has students convert between logarithmic notation and exponential notation.

LESSON 5.13, *Laws of Logarithms,* has students use the laws of exponents to develop the corresponding laws of logarithms.

LESSON 5.14, *Graphing Logarithmic Functions,* has students graph logarithmic functions and think about the domains and ranges of these functions.

LESSON 5.15, *The Logarithmic Scale,* has students experiment with graphing using graph paper that has a logarithmic scale on one or both axes.

5.11 Getting Started

Activating Prior Knowledge
Exploring New Ideas

In this lesson, you will investigate a function on your calculator called LOG. There may be a LOG key on your calculator. If there is not, look in your calculator's function library. You use the notation $\log x$ for this function.

Although you use parentheses in $f(x)$ function notation, the parentheses are optional for the log function. You can write $\log(x)$ or $\log x$. You still must use parentheses when needed to avoid confusion, for example in expressions such as $\log(x + 1)$.

For You to Explore

1. Use your calculator to find the output when you use the LOG key for each integer input from 0 to 10. Copy and complete the table below. Record each output to four decimal places.

x	$\log x$
0	■
1	■
2	■
3	■
4	■
5	■
6	■
7	■
8	■
9	■
10	■

2. Find the value of $\log 2 + \log 3$ to four decimal places.
3. **a.** Calculate $\log 2 + \log 6$.
   b. Calculate $\log 3 + \log 4$.
   c. Calculate $\log 3 + \log 2 + \log 2$.
   d. Find the number x such that $\log x = \log 2 + \log 6$.
4. Estimate each result using the table from Problem 1 and any patterns you have seen so far. Then use a calculator to confirm the answer.
   a. $\log 15$ **b.** $\log 24$ **c.** $\log 36$ **d.** $\log 63$
5. Find a rule for calculating $\log MN$ in terms of $\log M$ and $\log N$. (*Hint:* Refer to the results from Problem 4.)
6. Estimate each result using the table from Problem 1 and any patterns you have seen so far. Then use a calculator to confirm the answer.
   a. $\log 16$ **b.** $\log 32$ **c.** $\log 64$ **d.** $\log 2^{10}$ **e.** $\log 3^5$
7. Find a rule for calculating $\log M^p$ in terms of p and $\log M$. (*Hint:* Refer to the results from Problem 6.)
8. **Write About It** Explain how you can use the result from Problem 7 and the table from Problem 1 to estimate $\log \frac{1}{8}$.
9. Determine the domain and range of the function $x \mapsto \log x$.
10. **Take It Further** Use the rules that govern the function $x \mapsto \log x$ to find the solution to the following equation.

$$2^x = 5$$

Lesson Overview

GOAL

- Investigate logarithms using a calculator.

Students investigate the LOG button on their calculators and begin to gain insights about the properties of logarithms that lead to the laws of logarithms.

FOR YOU TO EXPLORE
- Core: 1, 2, 3, 4, 5, 6, 7, 9
- Optional: 8
- Extension: 10

MATERIALS
- graph paper
- graphing calculators
- Blackline Master 5.11

HOMEWORK
- Core: 11, 12, 13, 14, 15, 16, 17, 18
- Optional: 19

Launch

Have students get started on the For You to Explore problems right away. Blackline Master 5.11 provides a copy of the table for Problems 1 and 4. If your students are using different types of calculators, you may need to help them figure out where the LOG function is and how to use it. Depending on the calculator, LOG may be accessed through a function library, or there may be a key to access it directly. See the TI-Nspire Handbook on p. 778.

Explore

As students are working, keep track of any conjectures they develop.

For You to Explore

PROBLEM 1 Expect complaints about log 0 being undefined. The hope is students will remember this later when you talk about the restricted domain of the log function, especially when it comes to evaluating multiple solutions to some algebraic equation.

PROBLEM 2 Make sure that students notice that this is the same number they just got for log 6.

PROBLEM 3 The hope is that students notice not only that are the answers to the first three parts identical, but also that the product of the logarithm function inputs is 12 in each case. Some students may figure out, from the way the LOG function is displayed on their calculators, that it is the inverse of the function $y = 10^x$ and use this information to solve the last part, evaluating $10^{1.0792}$. Other students will use trial and error or will guess 12 and check to see if they are right.

PROBLEM 4 If students have trouble here, ask them to calculate $\log 2 + \log 4$ and $\log 2 + \log 5$. They can see these outputs in their table for LOG.

Answers

For You to Explore

1. See back of book.
2. 0.7782
3. **a.** 1.0792 **b.** 1.0792
   c. 1.0792 **d.** 12
4. **a.** 1.1761 **b.** 1.3802
   c. 1.5563 **d.** 1.7993
5. $\log MN = \log M + \log N$
6. **a–e.** Answers may vary in the fourth decimal place.
   a. 1.2041 **b.** 1.5052
   c. 1.8062 **d.** 3.0100
   e. 2.3855
7. $\log M^p = p \cdot \log M$
8. $\frac{1}{8} = 2^{-3}$, so $\log \frac{1}{8} = \log 2^{-3} = -3 \cdot \log 2 = -3 \cdot 0.3010 = -0.9030$.
9. domain: positive real numbers; range: all real numbers
10. 2.3219

PROBLEM 7 Not every student will notice this pattern, but hope that some of them will. Let these students explain what they have noticed and let the rest of the class check to see that it works. The On Your Own exercises rely on students' ability to use this result, so make sure they have it before moving on.

PROBLEM 10 asks students to take the next step and to see how the result of Problem 7 finally gives them a way to find an unknown exponent without using trial and error.

Wrap Up

Go over the For You to Explore core problems. Make sure that students are able to do the calculations correctly. See what they have been able to conjecture about products and powers from their solutions to Problems 5 and 7.

Exercises

HOMEWORK
- Core: 11, 12, 13, 14, 15, 16, 17, 18
- Optional: 19

On Your Own

EXERCISES 11–13 Exercises 11 and 12 are designed to help students notice that log x and 10^x are inverses. They get the chance to explain that conjecture in Exercise 13.

EXERCISE 14 Students need to know that $\log m + \log n = \log mn$..

EXERCISE 16 Some students will remember that if the graph of a function is reflected over the line with equation $y = x$, the resulting image is the graph of the inverse of the function. Others will need to think about what an inverse function does. This tells them that for each point (x, y) on the graph of the function, there is a corresponding point (y, x) on the graph of the inverse. This, of course, produces the same graph as the reflection technique.

EXERCISE 18 If students have trouble with the last part, remind them that they can write a square root as a rational exponent.

Maintain Your Skills

EXERCISE 19 A pattern that some students may notice is that the number of digits in the input is the same as the number of the digits in the greater of the two integers. Encourage students who mention this pattern to investigate further and see if it always holds.

Exercises *Practicing Habits of Mind*

On Your Own

11. You have seen that $\log 10 = 1$. Now calculate each of the following values.

a. $\log 10^2$ **b.** $\log 10^3$ **c.** $\log 10^6$
d. $\log 10^{10}$ **e.** $\log 10^{-3}$

Try evaluating these expressions without using a calculator.

12. Calculate each value.

a. $10^{\log 2}$ **b.** $10^{\log 3}$ **c.** $10^{\log 6}$
d. $10^{\log 10}$ **e.** $10^{\log -3}$

13. Describe the relationship between the functions $x \mapsto \log x$ and $x \mapsto 10^x$. Give examples.

14. Solve each equation for x.

a. $\log \frac{5}{4} + \log 4 = \log x$ **b.** $\log \frac{7}{3} + \log 3 = \log x$
c. $\log \frac{6}{17} + \log 17 = \log x$ **d.** $\log x + \log 2 = \log 5$
e. $\log x + \log 7 = \log 3$ **f.** $\log x = \log 11 - \log 4$

15. Find a rule for calculating $\log \frac{M}{N}$ in terms of $\log M$ and $\log N$.

Refer to the results from Exercise 14.

16. On the same axes, sketch the graphs of $f(x) = 3^x$ and its inverse function.

17. On the same axes, sketch the graphs of $f(x) = \log x$ and its inverse function.

18. Suppose $\log(A) = 1.6$ and $\log(B) = 2.7$. Find each value.

a. $\log AB$ **b.** $\log A^2$ **c.** $\log \frac{1}{A}$
d. $\log \frac{B}{A}$ **e.** $\log AB^2$ **f.** $\log \sqrt{A}$

Maintain Your Skills

19. Find a pair of consecutive integers j and k that satisfy each inequality.
- $j < \log 7 < k$
- $j < \log 70 < k$
- $j < \log 7000 < k$
- $j < \log 143{,}265 < k$

Answers

Exercises

11. a. 2 **b.** 3
c. 6 **d.** 10
e. −3

12. a. 2 **b.** 3
c. 6 **d.** 10
e. undefined

13. They are inverse functions; answers may vary. Sample: Let $f(x) = \log x$ and $g(x) = 10^x$. Then $f(g(2)) = f(10^2) = \log 10^2 = 2$ and $g(f(2)) = g(\log(2)) = 10^{\log 2} = 2$.

14. a. 5 **b.** 7 **c.** 6
d. $\frac{5}{2}$ **e.** $\frac{3}{7}$ **f.** $\frac{11}{4}$

15. $\log \frac{M}{N} = \log M - \log N$

16–17. See back of book.

18. a. 4.3 **b.** 3.2 **c.** −1.6
d. 1.1 **e.** 7 **f.** 0.8

19. 0 and 1; 1 and 2; 3 and 4; 5 and 6

5.12 Defining Logarithms

Until now, you had to solve an equation such as $2^x = 5$ by trial and error. Knowledge that the graph of $y = 2^x$ is increasing can help, but you can only closely approximate the solution by making many guesses. This lesson introduces logarithms, including their definition. It gives an example of how you can use logarithms to solve equations, such as $2^x = 5$, where the variable is in the exponent.

In the last investigation, you learned that exponential functions such as $g(x) = 2^x$ are one-to-one, and therefore have inverse functions. The inverse function of an exponential function is a *logarithmic function.*

Definition

The logarithmic function $x \mapsto \log_b x$ is the inverse function of the exponential function $x \mapsto b^x$.

In the last investigation, you used the notation $L_b(x)$ for logarithmic functions. So, you have actually already seen them. This is just a version of the standard notation.

The logarithmic function is often called the logarithm.

The output $\log_b M$ is the exponent k that solves $b^k = M$. In other words, $\log_b M$ is the power to which you have to raise b in order to get M. So these two statements are equivalent.

$$b^k = M \Leftrightarrow \log_b M = k$$

The base b must be positive and cannot equal 1 in order for $x \mapsto b^x$ to be an exponential function. Therefore, the same restriction applies to logarithmic functions. The base of a logarithm must be positive and cannot equal 1.

Exponential and logarithmic functions are closely related. You can see this by looking at tables and graphs. Consider the function $f(x) = \log_3 x$ and its inverse function $g(x) = 3^x$. The tables for the functions show reversed pairs of values. This is true for any function and its inverse.

x	$g(x) = 3^x$	x	$f(x) = \log_3 x$
-1	$\frac{1}{3}$	$\frac{1}{3}$	-1
0	1	1	0
1	3	3	1
2	9	9	2
3	27	27	3

The two graphs are reflections of each other over the line with equation $y = x$.

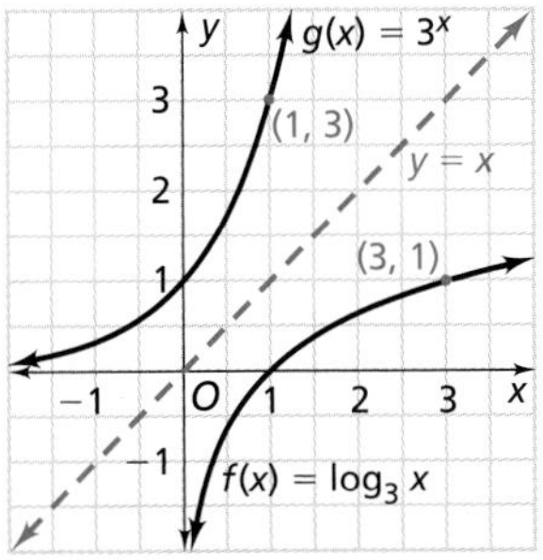

Lesson Overview

GOAL

- Evaluate logarithms of any base using a calculator.

Students have thought about the inverses of exponential functions by using the notation $L_b(x)$ for the inverse of the function b^x, and they have explored the effects of the LOG button on a calculator. In this lesson though, they finally see the standard notation for logarithmic functions. They see how to convert expressions involving logarithms into exponential form, how to use logarithms to solve exponential equations with unknown exponents, and how to evaluate a logarithm of any base by using only the base-10 logarithm and the change-of-base rule. They also use what they know to develop a list of the properties of logarithmic functions.

CHECK YOUR UNDERSTANDING
- Core: 1, 2, 3, 4, 5, 6, 7, 8, 9
- Optional: none
- Extension: 10

MATERIALS
- graph paper
- graphing calculators
- Blackline Master 5.12

HOMEWORK
- Core: 11, 12, 13, 14, 15, 16, 17, 20
- Optional: 18, 21, 22, 23
- Extension: 19

VOCABULARY
- change-of-base rule
- common logarithm, $\log x$
- logarithmic function, $x \mapsto \log_b x$

Launch

Start this lesson by discussing the definition of the *logarithmic function.* Have students translate the informal notation they have already used into standard notation—$L_b(x) \rightarrow \log_b x$. Ask students what b is for the LOG button they experimented with in the Getting Started lesson. Equations such as $\log 100 = 2$ may help students conclude that b for that logarithmic function is 10. Blackline Master 5.12 can be used here.

Explore

Circulate as students work and make note for class discussion of any problems they encounter.

DEFINITION Try to keep the focus on how a logarithm is defined, rather than calculating right away. If students have questions about how to calculate, work those questions back through the definition of a logarithm. If students are having extreme difficulties here, return to Investigation 5B, where they referred to the function $f(x) = \log_2 x$ as $L_2(x)$. The notation sometimes causes problems for students who may expect something that looks like $\log_2 x$ to be inherently difficult.

Example

Have students put away their calculators before doing this example. They should work through the parts of the example before looking at the solutions. The goal is to build students' intuition about approximating logarithms. For each part students should use the definition of a logarithm. For example, to find $\log_5 26$, students need to solve the problem "5 to what power is 26?" This is similar to the work they have been doing throughout this chapter.

For You to Do

Encourage students to do Problem 2 without a calculator to build their estimation skills. This will allow students to expand their "feel" for what these logarithms actually are.

For You to Do

1. Explain why $\log_3 9 = 2$. Find $\log_3 \frac{1}{9}$ and $\log_3 81$.

Facts and Notation

The expression log x without a base generally refers to base 10. This is the common logarithm. In this course, if the base is not given for a logarithm, assume the base is 10.

Not all books or software use log x to mean base 10.

Example

Problem Find the exact value of each expression, if possible. Otherwise, give an approximation.

a. $\log_5 26$ **b.** $\log \frac{1}{10}$ **c.** $\log_4 32$ **d.** $\log_3 -1$

Solution For each expression, write an equivalent expression involving an exponent.

a. If $\log_5 26 = x$, then $5^x = 26$. You cannot find the value of $\log_5 26$ exactly. It is a little greater than 2, since $5^2 = 25$.

b. If $\log \frac{1}{10} = x$, then $10^x = \frac{1}{10}$. You can solve the equation exactly, since $\frac{1}{10}$ is an exact power of 10. The value of $\log \frac{1}{10}$ is exactly -1.

c. If $\log_4 32 = x$, then $4^x = 32$. Both 4 and 32 are powers of 2, so you can find x exactly.

$$4^x = 32$$
$$(2^2)^x = 2^5$$
$$2^{2x} = 2^5$$
$$2x = 5$$
$$x = \frac{5}{2}$$

The value of $\log_4 32$ is exactly $\frac{5}{2}$.

d. If $\log_3 -1 = x$, then $3^x = -1$. This is impossible, since the range of the function $g(x) = 3^x$ is positive real numbers only. That means that the domain of $f(x) = \log_3 x$ is positive real numbers. The value of $\log_3 -1$ does not exist.

Remember...

In this course, if no base is given for a logarithm, assume the base is 10.

Look at the graphs of $f(x) = \log_3 x$ and $g(x) = 3^x$ on the previous page. You can use either graph to show that $\log_3 -1$ does not exist.

For You to Do

2. Put the following numbers in order from least to greatest.

$$\log_{11} 10,\ \log_7 8,\ \log_5 1,\ \log_3 10,\ \log_2 \frac{1}{4}$$

Answers

For You to Do

1. $\log_3 9 = 2$ because $3^2 = 9$; $\log_3 \frac{1}{9} = -2$, $\log_3 81 = 4$

2. $\log_2 \frac{1}{4}$, $\log_5 1$, $\log_{11} 10$, $\log_7 8$, $\log_3 10$

Developing Habits of Mind

Establish a process. Now you can write the solution to $2^x = 5$ using logarithms.

$$\text{If } 2^x = 5, \text{ then } x = \log_2 5.$$

This is useful because it gives an expression for the exact value of x, just as $\sqrt{5}$ is one of the exact solutions of $x^2 = 5$. This process happens frequently in mathematics. You have a useful function, such as the inverse of $x \mapsto 2^x$, that you cannot express in terms of the standard functions at your disposal. So, you invent a new name for this function, in this case $\log_2$. You incorporate it into the toolkit of standard functions. You study its behavior, build it into calculators and computers, and use it until it becomes as familiar as $x \mapsto \sqrt{x}$.

You can find an approximate value for an expression such as $\log_2 5$ by finding other nearby logarithmic outputs with exact values you know. For example, $\log_2 4 = 2$, so $\log_2 5$ must be a bit more than 2.

But this does not help find the value of $\log_2 5$ accurately. Calculators can work with logarithms, but many can only use those with base 10. What can you do? You can argue as follows: Suppose $\log 2 = c$ and $\log 5 = d$. Then

$$10^c = 2 \text{ and } 10^d = 5$$

If $\log_2 5 = x$, then $2^x = 5$ and

$$(10^c)^x = 10^d$$

or

$$10^{cx} = 10^d$$

But then, since exponential functions are one-to-one, you have

$$cx = d$$

$$x = \frac{d}{c} = \frac{\log 5}{\log 2}$$

This is another way to write $x = \log_2 5$. This is a way that calculators can calculate the value of x.

$$x = \log_2 5 = \frac{\log 5}{\log 2} \approx \frac{0.6990}{0.3010} \approx 2.322$$

By using logarithms, you can quickly solve equations that were once unsolvable to any degree of accuracy except by trial and error.

Use the logarithm template to work in any positive base. See the TI-Nspire Handbook, p. 778.

Developing Habits of Mind

If students are working with calculators that allow them to calculate logs to any base, you might reduce the emphasis on this part of the lesson.

THEOREM 5.5 Have students try out this theorem with some examples. Let $b = 2$, $x = 4$, and $y = 16$. For these choices of b, x, and y, the theorem says that $\log_4 16 = \frac{\log_2 16}{\log_2 4}$.

Wrap Up

The Summary is a natural wrap up for this lesson, so you may decide to leave it until after the students have worked through the Check Your Understanding core exercises. The goal is for all of the properties to be clear to the students by the time they see the Summary, and to have the Summary available for them to use as a reference.

Assessment Resources

Lesson Quiz 5.12

1. Identify one point that is on the graph of all logarithmic functions of the form $f(x) = \log_b x$.

2. a. Sketch the graph of $f(x) = \log_3 x$. Include the coordinates of three points on the graph.
   b. Sketch the graph of the inverse function f^{-1} on the same axes.
   c. Find the domain and range of f and the domain and range of f^{-1}.
   d. What is the inverse function of $f(x) = \log_3 x$?

3. Use the change-of-base rule and the LOG key on your calculator to find each value to three decimal places.
   a. $\log_2 18$ b. $\log_3 32$ c. $\log_4 56$ d. $\log_5 27$

4. Find each value. Do not use a calculator.
   a. $\log_4 64$ b. $\log_{\frac{1}{4}} 16$ c. $\log_6 \frac{1}{36}$ d. $\log_{\frac{1}{6}} 216$

Exercises

HOMEWORK
- Core: 11, 12, 13, 14, 15, 16, 17, 20
- Optional: 18, 21, 22, 23
- Extension: 19

Check Your Understanding

EXERCISE 2 Encourage students to do this exercise without using a calculator. Suggest changing the form of each equation to an exponential form rather than a logarithmic form. This technique is helpful as students are able to use their experience with exponents to begin to develop their intuition about logarithms.

EXERCISE 3 is best done without a calculator, but even students who do use a calculator can benefit from rewriting these expressions in exponential form and making sense of what the calculator tells them.

If you carry out the steps above in general for any base, you end up with a useful theorem.

Theorem 5.5 ***Change-of-Base Rule***

If $b, x, y > 0$, and $b, x \neq 1$. then

$$\log_x y = \frac{\log_b y}{\log_b x}$$

You will prove this theorem in the next lesson. The Developing Habits of Mind section on the previous page gives the proof for a specific case.

When working with a calculator, the choice $b = 10$ is often the most practical. The change-of-base rule is the reason why every calculator does not need to have a way to work with logarithms of other bases.

Summary ***Properties of Logarithmic functions***

A logarithmic function $f: \mathbb{R}^+ \rightarrow \mathbb{R}$ is defined as $f(x) = \log_b x$.
- **The base b must be positive and not 1.**
- **The domain of f is $\mathbb{R}^+$, positive real numbers.**
- **The range of f is all real numbers.**
- **The graph of $y = f(x)$ has one x-intercept at $(1, 0)$ and no y-intercepts.**
- **The graph of $y = f(x)$ is increasing when $b > 1$ and decreasing when $0 < b < 1$.**

Exercises *Practicing Habits of Mind*

Check Your Understanding

1. a. Sketch the graphs of $f(x) = \log_2 x$ and its inverse on the same axes.
   b. What is the inverse of $f(x) = \log_2 x$?

2. Which of these statements is true?
   A. $\log_2 9 = 3$
   B. $\log_{16} 4 = 2$
   C. $\log_5 10 > \log_5 9$
   D. $\log_4 0 = 1$

3. Find each value.
   a. $\log_4 2$
   b. $\log_4 2 + \log_4 32$
   c. $\log_4 64$
   d. $\log_9 27$
   e. $\log_9 27 + \log_9 3$
   f. $\log_9 81$

Go Online PHSchool.com

For more information about logarithms, go to **Web Code: bfe-9031**

Answers

Exercises

1. a.

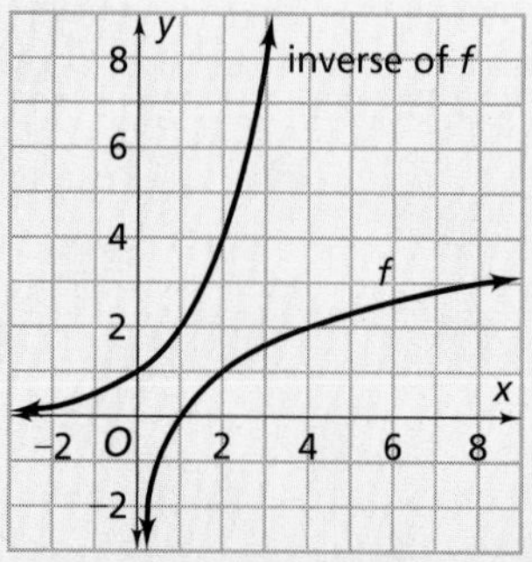

b. $f^{-1}(x) = 2^x$

2. C

3. a. $\frac{1}{2}$ b. 3 c. 3
   d. $\frac{3}{2}$ e. 2 f. 2

4. If $\log_b 0 = x$, then $b^x = 0$. But $b^x = 0$ only when $b = 0$. Since $b = 0$ is not a valid base for logarithms, $\log_b 0$ does not exist.

5. $\log_2 0.1$, $\log_5 \frac{1}{5}$, $\log_{73} 1$, $\log_{100} 10$, $\log 99$, $\log_4 18$, $\log_2 18$

4. **Write About It** Explain why $\log_b 0$ does not exist, no matter what the base is.

5. Put these expressions in order from least to greatest.

$$\log_4 18, \log 99, \log_2 0.1, \log_{100} 10, \log_{73} 1, \log_5 \tfrac{1}{5}, \log_2 18$$

6. Suppose $\log_b 9 = 4$ for some base b.
   a. Write an equation involving b that does not include a logarithm.
   b. Find the exact value of b.

7. Find the value of $3^{\log_3 75}$.

8. Suppose $\log_b 2 = 1.35$ and $\log_b 3 = 2.14$, to two decimal places. Evaluate each expression without finding the value of b.
   a. $b^{1.35}$ b. $b^{2.14}$ c. $b^{3.49}$
   d. $b^{6.42}$ e. $\log_b 6$ f. $\log_b 27$

9. Use the method from the Developing Habits of Mind section to find the solution to $4^x = 25$ to three decimal places.

10. **Take It Further** The value of log 20,000 to four decimal places is 4.3010. Traditionally, the value 4.3010 is considered as two pieces—the characteristic 4, which is the greatest integer less than the number, and the mantissa .3010, which is the decimal part of the number. Experiment to figure out how to interpret these two pieces. For example, if a number M has $\log M = 3.6435$, what does the characteristic 3 tell you about M? What does the mantissa .6435 tell you about M?

Sometimes, people write the mantissa without the decimal point.

On Your Own

11. Explain why $\log_b b = 1$ for any base b.

12. Explain why $\log_b 1 = 0$ for any base b.

13. Suppose $b^x = M$.
   a. If $b^y = M^2$, what is the relationship between y and x?
   b. Find the missing exponent in the equation below.
   $$b^{(\blacksquare)} = M^{10}$$
   c. Explain why this statement is true.
   $$\log_b M^2 = 2 \log_b M$$

14. **Standardized Test Prep** Which of these points is on the graph of $f(x) = \log x$?
   A. (0, 1) B. (100, 2)
   C. (100, 10) D. (2, 0.3)

The equation $\log_2 \frac{a}{b} = n$ relates the frequencies a and b of two notes that are n octaves apart.

6. a. $b^4 = 9$ **b.** $\sqrt{3}$

7. 75

8. a. 2 **b.** 3 **c.** 6
d. 27 **e.** 3.49 **f.** 6.42

9. 2.322

10. See back of book.

11. $b^1 = b$ for any value of b, so $\log_b b = 1$ for any value of b.

12. $b^0 = 1$ for any nonzero value of b, so $\log_b 1 = 0$ for any base b.

13. a. $y = 2x$
b. $10x$ or $5y$
c. By the definition of logarithm, $\log_b M^2 = y$ and $\log_b M = x$. From part (a), $y = 2x$, so $\log_b M^2 = 2 \cdot \log_b M$.

14. B

EXERCISE 4 The reason that the base of a logarithmic or exponential functions is not allowed to be zero is because of expressions such as 0^0. There is no way to make sense of this expression as written, because 0 to any power must be zero and any number raised to the zero power must be one. Since the expression 0^0 must be equal to two different things, you can not allow expressions like this to occur. As students continue in mathematics, they will learn to use limits to approach expressions like 0^0 and make sense of them, just as they will for expressions involving division by zero. For now, though, the base of a logarithm is the base of an exponential function and cannot equal zero.

EXERCISE 5 Encourage students to make sense of the values of logarithms even if they use their calculators and the change-of-base rule to compute these expressions. Students need to develop intuition about approximate values of logarithms if they want to be able to notice errors in calculations.

EXERCISE 7 If you start with an input, apply a function, and then apply the inverse of that function to the result, your final output will be your original input. In other words, inverse functions undo each other. This exercise is designed to help students see that result more concretely for exponential functions and their corresponding logarithmic functions.

EXERCISE 8 should help prepare students to understand the proofs of the laws of logarithms in the next lesson.

EXERCISE 9 Students may be baffled by the fact that the solution is the same. Perhaps someone will try to explain or prove it, but you can demonstrate by the laws of exponents:

$$4^x = 25$$
$$(2^2)^x = 5^2$$
$$(2^x)^2 = 5^2$$

Then either $2^x = 5$ or $2^x = -5$. Since $2^x = -5$ is impossible, it must be true that $2^x = 5$. A simpler version is available once students know the log laws well, since $\log 25 = 2 \log 5$ and $\log 4 = 2 \log 2$. Then you can write the fraction $\frac{\log 25}{\log 4}$ as $\frac{\log 5}{\log 2}$.

EXERCISE 10 may seem irrelevant to students who will never have to look up a logarithm in a table. By recognizing that if $\log X$ has characteristic C, then X has $C + 1$ digits, students may be able to further develop their intuition about the logarithmic function and be better able to recognize errors in calculations.

On Your Own

EXERCISES 11–13 prepare students to prove the laws of logarithms in the next lesson.

EXERCISE 14 The point (2, 0.3) is very close to being on the graph, but it is not, because $\log 2 \approx 0.3010$.

EXERCISE 16 can offer another explanation of why $b = 1$ is an invalid base, since it causes a divide-by-zero error with the change-of-base rule.

EXERCISE 17 is another exercise where students learn more if they do not use a calculator. By converting between logarithmic and exponential form, students will understand the role of the base and input of the logarithm and will be better able to make sense of the proof of the laws of logarithms in the next lesson.

EXERCISE 20 It is necessary to distinguish between solving the equation $b^4 = 9$ and finding b given that $\log_b 9 = 4$. When students change the form of an equation in order to solve it, they may forget about the restrictions present in the original form of the equation.

Maintain Your Skills

EXERCISE 21 Students may not need to complete all the parts to find the reciprocal relationship, which is acceptable: it just means they will do the rest of the exercise faster.

Additional Resources

PRINT RESOURCES	TECHNOLOGY
• Solution Manual	• Interactive Textbook
• Practice Workbook	• TeacherExpress CD-ROM
• Assessment Resources	• ExamView CD-ROM
• Teaching Resources	• PHSchool.com

Additional Practice

1. a. Sketch the graph of $f(x) = \log_2 x$. Include the coordinates of three points on the graph.
   b. Sketch the graph of the inverse function f^{-1} on the same axes.
   c. Find the domain and range of f, and the domain and range of f^{-1}.
   d. What is the inverse function of $f(x) = \log_2 x$?

2. Use the change-of-base rule and the LOG key on your calculator to find each value to three decimal places.
   a. $\log_3 18$ b. $\log_4 32$
   c. $\log_5 56$ d. $\log_6 25$
   e. $\log_7 68$ f. $\log_8 81$

3. Find each value. Do not use a calculator.
   a. $\log_3 27$ b. $\log_3 81$
   c. $\log_3 \frac{1}{9}$ d. $\log_{\frac{1}{3}} 27$
   e. $\log_5 125$ f. $\log_{\frac{1}{5}} \frac{1}{25}$

4. Which is greater, $\log_4 215$ or $\log_9 678$? Explain without relying on a calculator answer.

5. The value of $\log_3 31 + \log_6 228$ is between what two integers?

6. Suppose $\log_b 32{,}456 = 9$. Find the base b.

7. Let $a = \log 4$ and $b = \log 5$. Find each value in terms of a and b.
   a. $\log 20$ b. $\log 1.25$
   c. $\log 125$ d. $\log 400$
   e. $\log \sqrt{5}$ f. $\log 80$

8. Put this list of values in order from least to greatest.
   $\log_2 9$ $\log_3 35$ $\log_4 67$ $\log_5 599$ $\log_6 489$ $\log_7 716$

9. Use logarithms to find the solution to the equation $3^x = 210$ to three decimal places.

Practice: For Lesson 5.12, assign Exercises 1–3.

15. a. Sketch the graph of $f(x) = \log x$. Include the coordinates of three points on the graph.
b. Sketch the graph of the inverse function f^{-1} on the same axes.
c. Find the domain and range of f and the domain and range of f^{-1}.
d. What is the inverse function of $f(x) = \log x$?

Go Online PHSchool.com

For additional practice, go to **Web Code:** bfa-0512

16. Use the change-of-base rule and the LOG key on your calculator to find each value to three decimal places.
a. $\log_4 18$ b. $\log_2 0.1$ c. $\log_{73} 1$
d. $\log_1 9$ e. $\log_3 7$ f. $\log_9 49$

17. Find each value.
a. $\log_2 \frac{1}{8}$ b. $\log_2 8$ c. $\log_4 16$
d. $\log_4 \frac{1}{16}$ e. $\log_{\frac{1}{2}} 8$ f. $\log_{\frac{1}{4}} \frac{1}{16}$

Try to do this without using a calculator!

18. Prove each statement using the definition of logarithm.
a. If $\log_b M = k$, then $\log_b \frac{1}{M} = -k$.
b. $\log_b M = \log_{\frac{1}{b}} \frac{1}{M}$ for any valid base b and $M > 0$.

19. **Take It Further** Exercise 16 suggests that $\log_3 7 = \log_9 49$. Generalize this fact. Then prove it using the definition of logarithm.

20. **What's Wrong Here?** Sharon says there should be two solutions for b in Exercise 6. Sharon explains, "I rewrote the log equation as $b^4 = 9$. Since it's an even exponent, there are two real numbers b that make it true: b is close to plus or minus 1.73. Actually, now that I think about it, I don't need a decimal, it's $\sqrt{3}$ that works. So $b = \pm\sqrt{3}$."

There is only one correct value of b. Explain.

Maintain Your Skills

21. Find each value.
a. $\log_4 2$ b. $\log_2 4$ c. $\log_9 27$
d. $\log_{27} 9$ e. $\log_2 32$ f. $\log_{32} 2$
g. A calculator gives the value of $\log_{10} 2$ as approximately 0.3010. Use this to approximate the value of $\log_2 10$.

22. Find each number to three decimal places.
a. $\log 7.3$ b. $\log 73$
c. $\log 730$ d. $\log (7.3 \times 10^6)$
e. Find $\log 300{,}000$ to four decimal places using the table from Exercise 1 of Lesson 5.11.

Answers

15. a–b. See back of book.
c. domain of f: positive real numbers, range of f: all real numbers, domain of f^{-1}: all real numbers, range of f^{-1}: positive real numbers
d. $f^{-1}(x) = 10^x$

16. a. 2.085 **b.** −3.322
c. 0 **d.** undefined
e. 1.771 **f.** 1.771

17. a. −3 **b.** 3 **c.** 2
d. −2 **e.** −3 **f.** 2

18. a. Rewrite $\log_b M = k$ as $b^k = M$. Then $b^{-k} = \frac{1}{M}$, or $\log_b \frac{1}{M} = -k$.
b. Let $\log_b M = x$ and rewrite this equation as $b^x = M$. Then $(b^x)^{-1} = M^{-1}$, so $\frac{1}{b} = \frac{1}{M}$ or $\left(\frac{1}{b}\right)^x = \frac{1}{M}$, which can be rewritten as $\log_{\frac{1}{b}} \frac{1}{M} = x$. Thus, $\log_b M = \log_{\frac{1}{b}} \frac{1}{M}$.

5.13 Laws of Logarithms

Review the laws of exponents from earlier in this chapter.

Laws of Exponents

Let base $b > 0$, $b \neq 1$, and x and y be real numbers.

The Fundamental Law of Exponents

- $b^{x+y} = b^x \cdot b^y$

Corollaries

- $b^{x-y} = \frac{b^x}{b^y}$
- $b^{xy} = (b^x)^y$

In this lesson you will learn the laws of logarithms, which are restatements of the laws of exponents.

For You to Do

Let $b^x = M$ and $b^y = N$.

1. Find b^{x+y} in terms of M and N.
2. Find b^{x-y} in terms of M and N.
3. Find b^{px} in terms of M and p.

The results from Problems 1–3 follow from the laws of exponents. For example,

$$\text{If } b^x = M \text{ and } b^y = N, \text{ then } b^{x+y} = MN.$$

You can rewrite each of the three equations in the above statement, using the definition of logarithm.

$$\text{If } \log_b M = x \text{ and } \log_b N = y, \text{ then } \log_b MN = x + y.$$

Add the first two statements.

$$\log_b M + \log_b N = x + y$$

Now you have two expressions for $x + y$, so they must be equal.

$$\log_b M + \log_b N = \log_b MN$$

You can restate each of the three laws of exponents in terms of logarithms. This gives you the laws of logarithms.

Lesson Overview

GOAL

- Use logarithms to solve exponential equations.

Students prove the laws of logarithms using the laws of exponents, by converting between expressions involving logarithms and expressions involving exponents. This *change of form* continues to be a useful technique for solving problems. Students also apply the laws of logarithms to solve problems. The lesson also points out some common misuses of the laws of logarithms. Students also work through an example that reminds them to check the solutions to a logarithmic equation by substituting them back into the original equation. Some solutions end up causing negative inputs to a logarithm, and so they are invalid.

CHECK YOUR UNDERSTANDING

- Core: 1, 2, 3, 4, 5, 6, 7, 12
- Optional: 8, 9, 10, 11
- Extension: 13, 14

MATERIALS

- graphing calculators
- Blackline Master 5.13

HOMEWORK

- Core: 15, 16, 17, 18, 19, 20, 21, 22, 23, 26, 28
- Optional: 24, 25a–b, 29
- Extension: 25c, 27

VOCABULARY

- laws of logarithms

Launch

Start this lesson with For You to Do Problems 1–3.

Explore

For You to Do

If students are having trouble, encourage them to pick numerical values for b, x, and y, such as $b = 3$, $x = 5$, and $y = 2$. Then $b^{x+y} = 3^7$, which is equal to MN. Also, $b^{x-y} = 3^3$, which is $\frac{M}{N}$. Doing a few examples like this will help students build the experience they need to work on the general case.

19. $\log_b a = \log_{b^2} a^2$; let $\log_b a = x$ and rewrite this equation as $b^x = a$. Then $(b^x)^2 = a^2$, so $b^{2x} = a^2$ or $(b^2)^x = a^2$, which can be rewritten as $\log_{b^2} a^2 = x$. So, $\log_b a = \log_{b^2} a^2$.

20. Because $b > 0$, $-\sqrt{3}$ cannot be a solution.

21. **a.** $\frac{1}{2}$ **b.** 2 **c.** $\frac{3}{2}$ **d.** $\frac{2}{3}$ **e.** 5 **f.** $\frac{1}{5}$ **g.** about 3.3

22. **a.** 0.863 **b.** 1.863 **c.** 2.863 **d.** 6.863 **e.** 5.4771

For You to Do

1. $b^{x+y} = MN$
2. $b^{x-y} = \frac{M}{N}$
3. $b^{px} = M^p$

Example 1

If your students' calculators support calculations to any base, you do not need to put a lot of emphasis here. Simplify the example in the following way:

$$1000 = 500 \cdot 1.09^n$$
$$2 = 1.09^n$$
$$n = \log_{1.09} 2$$
$$n \approx 8.043$$

This can then be used to explain or even prove the change-of-base rule, because you get two answers: $\log_{1.09} 2$ and also $\frac{\log 2}{\log 1.09}$. Ask students to reconcile the answers.

Laws of Logarithms

Let base $b > 0$, $b \neq 1$ and M and N be positive real numbers.

The Fundamental Law of Logarithms

- $\log_b MN = \log_b M + \log_b N$

Corollaries

- $\log_b \frac{M}{N} = \log_b M - \log_b N$
- $\log_b M^p = p \log_b M$

In other words, a logarithm $g(x) = \log_b x$ satisfies the functional equation $g(xy) = g(x) + g(y)$.

You can prove the laws of logarithms with arguments like the one above, or a set of statements like this proof of the third law.

Proof Let $\log_b M = x$. Then

$b^x = M$	Convert the form.
$(b^x)^p = M^p$	Build M^p.
$b^{px} = M^p$	Use a law of exponents.
$\log_b M^p = px$	Convert the form.
$\log_b M^p = p \log_b M$	Substitute for x.

Convert the form means to change from exponent notation to logarithm notation, or vice versa.

The three laws of logarithms provide the means to solve many equations that you previously had to solve by trial and error.

Example 1

Problem Ariela puts $500 in an investment account. She earns 9% interest per year, compounded annually. How many years will it take to double her initial investment?

Solution The money Ariela invests grows by 9% per year, so after each year, the money invested is multiplied by 1.09. You need to find the number of years it takes for the investment to at least double, so you need to solve the equation below, where n is the number of years.

$$1000 = 500 \cdot 1.09^n$$

Apply the laws of logarithms to find n.

Method 1 Divide through by 500. Then find the base-10 logarithm of each side.

$$1000 = 500 \cdot 1.09^n$$
$$2 = 1.09^n$$
$$\log 2 = \log 1.09^n$$
$$\log 2 = n \log 1.09$$
$$\frac{\log 2}{\log 1.09} = n$$
$$8.043 \approx n$$

Why do you find the base-10 logarithm, and not some other base?

Method 2 Apply the base-10 logarithm first. Then apply the laws of logarithms.

$$1000 = 500 \cdot 1.09^n$$
$$\log 1000 = \log (500 \cdot 1.09^n)$$
$$\log 1000 = \log 500 + \log 1.09^n$$
$$\log 1000 = \log 500 + n \log 1.09$$
$$\log 1000 - \log 500 = n \log 1.09$$
$$\frac{\log 1000 - \log 500}{\log 1.09} = n$$
$$8.043 \approx n$$

Either equation produces the solution $n \approx 8.043$, but this is not the correct answer. Ariela's account compounds annually, so after the end of the eighth year, there is no further interest paid until the ninth year is complete. It will take 9 years to at least double her initial investment, even though the account is very close to \$1000 after 8 years.

The balance at the end of 8 years is $500 \cdot 1.09^8 \approx 996.28$. That is not quite enough.

For Discussion

4. The two methods generate two different expressions for n.

Method 1 $n = \frac{\log 2}{\log 1.09}$ Method 2 $n = \frac{\log 1000 - \log 500}{\log 1.09}$

Is there a way to show these are equivalent using the laws of logarithms? Explain.

Developing Habits of Mind

Use a different process to get the same answer. Method 1 above solves the equation $2 = 1.09^n$ to get $n = \frac{\log 2}{\log 1.09}$. But the definition of logarithms gives another solution: $n = \log_{1.09} 2$. So, you can write the following equation.

$$\log_{1.09} 2 = \frac{\log 2}{\log 1.09}$$

This is an example of the change-of-base rule.

$$\log_x y = \frac{\log_b y}{\log_b x}$$

Here is a quick proof of the change-of-base rule. Let $\log_x y = k$. Then $x^k = y$. Find the base-b logarithm of each side.

$$x^k = y$$
$$\log_b x^k = \log_b y$$
$$k \log_b x = \log_b y$$
$$k = \frac{\log_b y}{\log_b x}$$

Then, since you also know $\log_x y = k$, the proof is complete.

Habits of Mind

Look for relationships. Note that these are the same steps you use to solve a problem involving actual numbers. So your work with numbers basically provides the proof.

Answers

For Discussion

4. The expressions have the same denominators. The numerator in Method 2 is $\log 1000 - \log 500 = \log \frac{1000}{500} = \log 2$, which is the same as the numerator in Method 1.

For Discussion

The two expressions for n have the same denominator, so they are equivalent if the two numerators are equal. Use the law of logarithms that relates the difference of two logs to the log of their quotient.

$$\log 1000 - \log 500 = \log \frac{1000}{500} = \log 2$$

Example 2

An alternative method involves sketching the graph of each side of the equation. Graph $y = \log(x + 7) + \log(x + 22)$ and $y = 2$. Since the graphs only intersect once, there is one value of x that makes the equation true. The intersection point is $(-2, 2)$, so $x = -2$ is the only solution. This method, which will be presented with a different example in the next lesson, can help give students a feel for extraneous solutions that may result from a direct application of the law of logarithms.

Fractions such as $\frac{\log 2}{\log 1.09}$ lead to one of the most common mistakes made with logarithms. It is tempting to look at the corollary

$$\log_b \frac{M}{N} = \log_b M - \log_b N$$

and say that it applies to a fraction like $\frac{\log 2}{\log 1.09}$, so that

$$\frac{\log 2}{\log 1.09} = \log 2 - \log 1.09$$

This is incorrect reasoning. It is also incorrect to cancel the word *log* from the top and bottom of a fraction. It is generally not true that $\frac{\log M}{\log N}$ is equal to $\frac{M}{N}$.

When you solve equations that involve logarithms, it is important to check the solutions for validity. The logarithmic function is only defined for positive real numbers.

Example 2

Problem Find all values of x that solve the equation

$$\log(x + 7) + \log(x + 22) = 2$$

Solution First, rewrite 2 using a logarithm. The base is not given, so by convention it is 10. Since $10^2 = 100$, you have $\log 100 = 2$.

$$\log(x + 7) + \log(x + 22) = \log 100$$

Then use one of the laws of logarithms.

$$\log(x + 7) + \log(x + 22) = \log 100$$
$$\log((x + 7)(x + 22)) = \log 100$$
$$(x + 7)(x + 22) = 100$$

Now solve by factoring or using the quadratic formula.

$$(x + 7)(x + 22) = 100$$
$$x^2 + 29x + 154 = 100$$
$$x^2 + 29x + 54 = 0$$
$$(x + 2)(x + 27) = 0$$

This equation has two solutions, $x = -2$ and $x = -27$. However, consider the domain of the logarithmic function. It can only accept positive inputs. Letting $x = -27$ in the original equation gives the result

$$\log -20 + \log -5 = 2$$

This makes no sense. Neither $\log -20$ nor $\log -5$ exists. So you reject the solution $x = -27$. The solution $x = -2$ is still valid. It gives the result

$$\log 5 + \log 20 = 2$$

All the inputs to the logarithmic function are positive.

Note that x may still be negative. It is the inputs to the logarithmic function that must be positive. Reject any solutions that result in negative inputs to a logarithm.

Laws and Properties of Logarithms

Let base $b > 0$, $b \neq 1$ and M and N be positive real numbers.

The Fundamental Law of Logarithms

- $\log_b MN = \log_b M + \log_b N$

Corollaries

- $\log_b \frac{M}{N} = \log_b M - \log_b N$
- $\log_b M^p = p \log_b M$

Other Properties

- change-of-base rule: $\log_M N = \frac{\log_b N}{\log_b M}$, if $M \neq 1$
- $\log_b 1 = 0$ and $\log_b b = 1$
- $\log_b \frac{1}{N} = -\log_b N$
- $\log_b M = \log_b N \Leftrightarrow M = N$, since the logarithm function is one-to-one.
- $\log_b(b^x) = x = b^{\log_b x}$, since the logarithm and the exponential are inverse functions.

Exercises *Practicing Habits of Mind*

Check Your Understanding

1. Let $\log_b M = 2$ and $\log_b N = 5$. Calculate each value.
   - **a.** $\log_b M^2$
   - **b.** $\log_b MN$
   - **c.** $\log_b \frac{M^3}{N}$
   - **d.** $\log_b (MN)^3$
   - **e.** $\log_b \sqrt{MN}$
2. Find the value of this product.

$$\log_2 3 \cdot \log_3 4 \cdot \log_5 6 \cdot \log_6 25$$

See if you can do this one without a calculator.

3. **What's Wrong Here?** Explain what is wrong with the reasoning in the calculation below. Then determine the correct value.

$$\frac{\log_2 32}{\log_2 8} = \log_2 32 - \log_2 8 = 5 - 3 = 2$$

Answers

Exercises

1. **a.** 4 **b.** 7 **c.** −1 **d.** 21 **e.** $\frac{7}{2}$
2. 4
3. $\frac{\log_2 32}{\log_2 8} \neq \log_2 \frac{32}{8}$, so you cannot apply the rule for $\log_b \frac{M}{N}$ to get $\log_2 32 - \log_2 8$; $\frac{5}{3}$.

Wrap Up

Finish today's lesson by going over as many of the Check Your Understanding core exercises as time allows. As with the previous lesson, you may want to use the summary list to wrap up the lesson, so you may want to wait until students have done the Check Your Understanding exercises before you present the list. You might even ask students to create their own summary of the material in this lesson, and then compare their summaries to the list on this page.

Assessment Resources

Lesson Quiz 5.13

1. The value of $\log_4 39 + \log_7 98$ is between what two integers?
2. Suppose $\log_b 4567 = 11$. Find the base b.
3. Let $a = \log 3$ and $b = \log 7$. Find each value in terms of a and b.
   - **a.** $\log 21$
   - **b.** $\log \frac{7}{3}$
   - **c.** $\log 343$
   - **d.** $\log 147$
   - **e.** $\log \sqrt{7}$
   - **f.** $\log 63$
4. Use logarithms to find the solution to each equation to three decimal places.
   - **a.** $4^x = \frac{1}{64}$
   - **b.** $5^x = 4980$
   - **c.** $8^x = 806$

Exercises

HOMEWORK

- Core: 15, 16, 17, 18, 19, 20, 21, 22, 23, 26, 28
- Optional: 24, 25a–b, 29
- Extension: 25c, 27

Check Your Understanding

EXERCISE 1 pushes students to use the laws of logarithms rather than their calculators, because there are too many variables in play. Throughout this exercise set there are situations in which students will benefit from doing the calculations by hand and manipulating the expressions to practice applying the laws of logarithms. Even if you allow students to use calculators on these exercises, encourage them to make sense of what the calculator tells them. You might suggest that students do the calculations by hand and then use their calculators as a check if they wish.

EXERCISE 3 has a common mistake that was also pointed out in the text of the lesson. There is no way to prevent students from making a mistake like this, but exercises such as this one may help them understand why it was a mistake.

EXERCISE 4 The lesson showed two methods that can be used to do this proof, so encourage students to try them both.

EXERCISE 7 There is more than one possibility here, depending on the steps students use. This problem parallels Example 1 in the lesson.

EXERCISE 8 Students should be able to use the same steps they used to solve the equation in Exercise 7.

EXERCISE 9 There are other possible correct expressions for the exact value of x, depending on the steps students use.

EXERCISE 10 Students should be able to use the same steps they used to solve the equation in Exercise 9.

EXERCISE 12 If necessary, remind students to check their solutions by substituting them back into the original equation. If a solution results in a negative input for a logarithmic function, it must be rejected.

4. Prove the second law of logarithms in two ways.

$$\log_b \frac{M}{N} = \log_b M - \log_b N$$

a. Use the definition.

$$b^x = M \Leftrightarrow \log_b M = x$$

b. Use the Fundamental Law of Logarithms.

$$\log_b MN = \log_b M + \log_b N$$

5. Prove each statement.

a. $\log_b 1 = 0$ **b.** $\log_b b = 1$ **c.** $\log_b \frac{1}{N} = -\log_b N$

6. Due to inflation, the cost of a Big Burger grows by 3% every year. This year a Big Burger costs \$3.99.

a. Write a rule for the function $C(n)$, where $C(n)$ is the cost of a Big Burger n years from now.

b. Using logarithms, find how long, to the nearest year, it will take for the cost of a Big Burger to reach \$20.

7. Find the solution to this equation.

$$2 \cdot 5^x = 7$$

Give an exact answer. Then approximate the answer to three decimal places.

The solutions to the next few exercises will include the logarithmic function in some way.

8. Find the solution to this equation in terms of the constants a, b, and c.

$$a \cdot b^x = c$$

9. Find the solution to this equation.

$$2 \cdot 5^x = 7 \cdot 3^x$$

Give an exact answer. Then approximate the answer to three decimal places.

10. In terms of the constants a, b, c, and d, find the solution to this equation.

$$a \cdot b^x = c \cdot d^x$$

11. In Exercise 21 in Lesson 5.9, you saw that the solution to the equation $6^x = 35$ is the reciprocal of the solution to $35^x = 6$. Use logarithms to explain why this makes sense.

Can you explain it without using logarithms?

12. Find all solutions of each equation.

a. $\log x + \log (x + 1) = \log 6$

b. $\log (x^2 + x) = \log 6$

c. $\log 2x - \log x = \log 2$

d. $\log_2 (x - 3) + \log_2 (x + 3) = 4$

e. $\log_2 (x - 3) - \log_2 (x + 3) = 4$

Answers

4. a. Answers may vary. Sample: Let $b^x = M$ and $b^y = N$ so $x = \log_b M$ and $y = \log_b N$. Then $\log_b \frac{M}{N} = \log_b \frac{b^x}{b^y} = \log_b b^{x-y} = x - y = \log_b M - \log_b N$.

b. Answers may vary. Sample:

$$\begin{aligned}\log_b \frac{M}{N} &= \log_b \left(M \cdot \frac{1}{N}\right)\\ &= \log_b M + \log_b \frac{1}{N}\\ &= \log_b M + \log_b N^{-1}\\ &= \log_b M + (-1) \cdot \log_b N\\ &= \log_b M - \log_b N.\end{aligned}$$

5. a–c. Answers may vary. Samples are given.

a. $b^0 = 1$ for any base b, so $\log_b 1 = 0$

b. $b^1 = b$ for any base b, so $\log_b b = 1$

c. Start with $\log_b \left(N \cdot \frac{1}{N}\right) = \log_b 1$. Rewrite the left side as $\log_b N + \log_b \frac{1}{N}$. The right side is 0, so $\log_b N + \log_b \frac{1}{N} = 0$ and $\log_b \frac{1}{N} = -\log_b N$.

6. a. $C(n) = 3.99 \cdot 1.03^n$

b. 55 yr

7. $\frac{\log 3.5}{\log 5}$; 0.778

8. $\frac{\log \frac{c}{a}}{\log b}$ or $\frac{\log c - \log a}{\log b}$

9. $\frac{\log \frac{7}{2}}{\log \frac{5}{3}}$ or $\frac{\log \frac{2}{7}}{\log \frac{3}{5}}$; 2.452

10. $\frac{\log \frac{c}{a}}{\log \frac{b}{d}}$, $\frac{\log \frac{a}{c}}{\log \frac{d}{b}}$, or $\frac{\log c - \log a}{\log b - \log d}$

11. Answers may vary. Sample: If $6^x = 35$, then $x = \frac{\log 35}{\log 6}$, while if $35^x = 6$, then $x = \frac{\log 6}{\log 35}$; the fractions are reciprocals.

13. Take It Further Suppose $\log 2 = 0.3$ exactly and $\log 3 = 0.5$ exactly. Assume both of these equations are true and prove that $0 = 1$.

14. Take It Further Recall the Rule of 72 from Lesson 5.10, Exercise 17.

Rule of 72 To find the number of years it takes to double an investment's value, divide 72 by the annual percentage interest rate.

Explain why the Rule of 72 gives fairly accurate results for relatively low interest rates (for example, from 6% to 12%).

On Your Own

15. Which is greater, $\log_5 135$ or $\log_7 300$? Explain completely without relying on a calculator answer.

16. Copy and complete this table for $f(x) = \log_3 x$. Use a calculator and the change-of-base rule. Give any approximate answers to four decimal places.

Even if your calculator can work with a base-3 logarithm, use the change-of-base rule here.

x	$\log_3 x$
1	0
2	0.6309
3	■
4	■
5	■
6	■
7	■
8	■
9	■

17. The value of $\log_3 7 + \log_9 81$ is between which two integers?

Try this one without a calculator.

A. 0 and 1
B. 1 and 2
C. 2 and 3
D. 3 and 4

18. Suppose $\log_b 297{,}736 = 7$. Find the base b.

19. Let $a = \log 2$ and $b = \log 3$. Find each value in terms of a and b.

a. $\log 6$
b. $\log 1.5$
c. $\log 27$
d. $\log 200$
e. $\log \sqrt{3}$

Go Online PHSchool.com

For additional practice, go to **Web Code**: bfa-0513

EXERCISE 13 provides students with intuition about why most logarithms are irrational numbers. If students have trouble making progress on this exercise, ask them to evaluate powers of 2 and powers of 3 using the "information" in this exercise (i.e., that $\log 2 = 0.3$ and $\log 3 = 0.5$). Eventually they will find that $\log 2^5 = \log 3^3$.

On Your Own

EXERCISE 16 Blackline Master 5.13 provides a blank copy of the table. After students have completed the table, draw attention to these relationships:

- The output is an integer for inputs $x = 3$ and $x = 9$.
- The output when $x = 6$ is exactly 1 more than the output when $x = 2$.
- The output when $x = 8$ is exactly three times greater than the output when $x = 2$.

Discuss how these relationships relate to the properties of logarithms explored in the lesson.

EXERCISE 17 If students can estimate the value of a logarithm without using a calculator, then they will be able to make sense of what their calculators tell them, and they can spot errors.

EXERCISE 19 By giving their answers in terms of a and b, students are pushed to do the calculations by hand. Students can still figure out how to use a calculator to check their work, but it takes some effort to do so.

12. a. 2
b. −3, 2
c. all real numbers greater than 0
d. 5
e. no solution

13. If $\log 2 = 0.3$ then $5 \cdot \log 2 = 1.5$, and if $\log 3 = 0.5$ then $3 \cdot \log 3 = 1.5$. Then $5 \cdot \log 2 = 3 \cdot \log 3$, so $\log 2^5 = \log 3^3$, which implies that $32 = 27$. Subtracting 27 from each side gives $5 = 0$. Dividing each side by 5 gives $1 = 0$.

14. If r is the annual interest rate, then the situation of doubling an amount A can be written as

$$2A = A\left(1 + \frac{r}{100}\right)^y \text{ or}$$

$$2 = \left(1 + \frac{r}{100}\right)^y.$$

Then $\log 2 = y \cdot \log\left(1 + \frac{r}{100}\right)$

and $y = \dfrac{\log 2}{\log\left(1 + \frac{r}{100}\right)}$.

By letting r take the values 6, 7, 8, 9, 10, 11, and 12, you can calculate the corresponding y-values 11.8957, 10.2448, 9.0065, 8.0432, 7.2725, 6.6419, and 6.1163. These values are very close to the results given by the Rule of 72 (listed in Exercise 17, Lesson 5.10).

15. $\log_5 135$; $5^3 = 125$, so $\log_5 135 > 3$. $7^3 = 343$, so $\log_7 300 < 3$. Thus, $\log_5 135 > \log_7 300$.

16. See back of book.

17. D

18. about 6.0531

19. a. $a + b$
b. $b - a$
c. $3b$
d. $a + 2$
e. $\frac{b}{2}$

EXERCISE 20 A calculator is necessary for this exercise, because the logarithms are too close in value for students to order them with estimates. Every estimate would be "somewhere between 1 and 2."

EXERCISE 25 Students may not notice that parts (a) and (b) of this exercise are very different from one another. Part (a) turns into a linear equation, or can be solved directly. Part (b) is really a quadratic in $\log_2 x$. So for parts (b) and (c), the "hand method" used in Chapter 2 may be very effective here. Students will be able to solve the quadratics that "come from the hands," and then go back and figure out what x must be.

20. Each value below is between 1 and 2. Put them in order from least to greatest.

$$\log_3 7, \log_9 50, \log 60, \log_8 40, \log_{12} 83, \log_2 3.44$$

Be sure to do this exercise with a calculator.

21. **What's Wrong Here?** Explain what is wrong with the reasoning in the calculation below. Then determine the correct value.

$$\log 100 + \log_2 8 = \log 800 \approx 2.903$$

22. Use logarithms to find the solution to the equation $2^x = \frac{1}{1{,}000{,}000}$ to three decimal places.

23. Let $L(h) = 100 \cdot 0.5^h$.

a. If $L(h) = 50$, find h.

b. If $L(h) = 20$, find h.

c. If $L(h) = 10$, find h. How is the answer here related to your answers in parts (a) and (b)?

d. If $L(h) = c$, find h in terms of c.

e. If $L(h) = 1$, find h. How is the answer here related to your answer in part (d)?

24. **Write About It** Is $(\log x)^2$ the same as $\log x^2$? Explain.

25. Find all solutions to each equation.

a. $\log_2 x^2 - 5\log_2 x + 6 = 0$

b. $(\log_2 x)^2 - 5\log_2 x + 6 = 0$

c. **Take It Further** $\log x = 1 - \frac{6}{\log x}$

26. Show that the result $\log_b \frac{1}{N} = -\log_b N$ follows from the second law of logarithms.

27. **Take It Further** The Developing Habits of Mind section, earlier in this lesson, says that it is generally not true that $\frac{\log M}{\log N}$ equals $\frac{M}{N}$. When is it true? Explain.

Maintain Your Skills

28. **Standardized Test Prep** Which of the following expressions is equal to $\log \frac{xy^2}{z}$?

A. $\log x + 2\log y + \log z$

B. $\log x + 2\log y - \log z$

C. $\log z - \log x - 2\log y$

D. $2\log xy - \log z$

Answers

20. $\log_3 7$, $\log_8 40$, $\log 60$, $\log_{12} 83$, $\log_9 50$, $\log_2 3.44$

21. The bases are different, so you cannot apply the rule that the sum of two logarithms is the logarithm of the product; 5.

22. −19.932

23. a. 1 **b.** 2.3219

c. 3.3219; the answer is the sum of the answers to parts (a) and (b).

d. $h = \frac{\log c - 2}{\log 0.5}$

e. 6.6439; if $c = 1$ in part (d), then $\log c = 0$, so $h = \frac{-2}{\log 0.5} \approx -6.6439$.

24. No; $(\log x)^2 = (\log x)(\log x)$, while $\log x^2 = \log x + \log x$.

25. a. 4 **b.** 4, 8

c. no solution

26. Let $M = 1$ in $\log_b \frac{M}{N} = \log_b M - \log_b N$. Then $\log_b \frac{1}{N} = \log_b 1 - \log_b N = 0 - \log_b N = -\log_b N$.

29. The government of Justinia reports that the current population is 10 million. The population is growing at 2.5% per year. Experts report the population will keep growing at this rate. Give the number of years it will take for the population to reach each milestone. Round to two decimal places.

a. 20 million **b.** 30 million
c. 40 million **d.** 60 million
e. 120 million **f.** 240 million

So, a sample answer is 16.43 years.

Historical Perspective

Logarithms used to play a much larger role in second-year algebra courses, because you can use them for arithmetic calculation. Consider the Fundamental Law of Logarithms.

$$\log_b MN = \log_b M + \log_b N$$

You can use it to transform a multiplication problem into an addition problem. To multiply two numbers M and N, you can use base-10 logarithms.

This may seem like a much more complicated way to multiply two numbers, but suppose M and N both have five digits. Adding five-digit numbers by hand is much faster than multiplying five-digit numbers by hand. The other laws of logarithms allow you to reduce division to subtraction and exponentiation to multiplication, which you can then reduce further to addition.

For example, here is how to calculate $\frac{6.453}{2.179}$ using logarithms.

- Call the numerator $M = 6.453$ and the denominator $N = 2.179$.
- Calculate $\log M \approx 0.8098$ and $\log N \approx 0.3383$.
- Subtract: $\log M - \log N \approx 0.4715$.
- This is $\log \frac{M}{N}$, so undo the logarithm: $10^{0.4715} \approx 2.961$.

The result at each step has four significant figures, so the answer is correct to four significant figures. Compare that to the task of dividing these decimals by hand. You reduce the division step to subtraction by using the laws of logarithms.

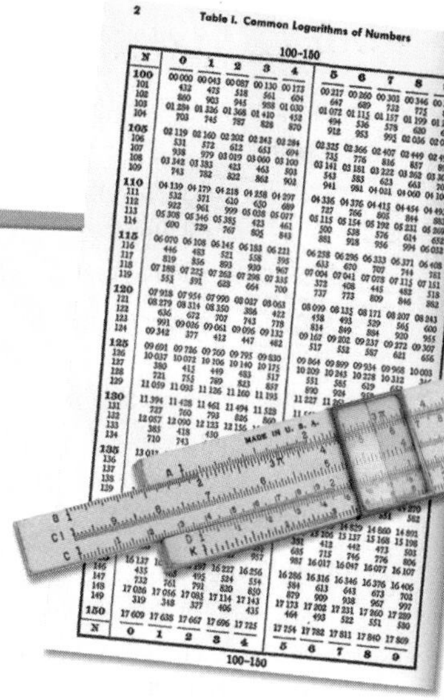

Before the development of pocket calculators, people used logarithm tables and slide rules for complicated arithmetic calculations.

Go Online
PHSchool.com

For more information about logarithms, go to **Web Code:** bfe-8031

27. Answers may vary. Sample: when $M = N$; if $M = N$, then both ratios are equal to 1.

28. B

29. a. 28.07 yr **b.** 44.49 yr
c. 56.14 yr **d.** 72.56 yr
e. 100.63 yr **f.** 128.70 yr

Maintain Your Skills

EXERCISE 29 Students may see the pattern here, that the doubling time is the same throughout; in particular, it takes the same amount of time to get from 20 million to 40 million as it does to get from 60 million to 120 million.

Historical Perspective

Some books have logarithm tables or are entirely made of tables (*Machinery's Mathematical Tables* is a good example). Older mathematics texts probably have logarithm tables in an appendix. If you have one of these books, you might share it with your students, or even use one of the tables to carry out a calculation. If you have a slide rule handy, this would be a good time to bring that out and share it with your students, too.

Additional Resources

PRINT RESOURCES
- Solution Manual
- Practice Workbook
- Assessment Resources
- Teaching Resources

TECHNOLOGY
- Interactive Textbook
- TeacherExpress CD-ROM
- ExamView CD-ROM
- PHSchool.com

Additional Practice

1. a. Sketch the graph of $f(x) = \log_2 x$. Include the coordinates of three points on the graph.
b. Sketch the graph of the inverse function f^{-1} on the same axes.
c. Find the domain and range of f, and the domain and range of f^{-1}.
d. What is the inverse function of $f(x) = \log_2 x$?

2. Use the change-of-base rule and the LOG key on your calculator to find each value to three decimal places.
a. $\log_3 18$ **b.** $\log_4 32$
c. $\log_5 56$ **d.** $\log_6 25$
e. $\log_7 68$ **f.** $\log_8 81$

3. Find each value. Do not use a calculator.
a. $\log_3 27$ **b.** $\log_3 81$
c. $\log_3 \frac{1}{9}$ **d.** $\log_{\frac{1}{3}} 27$
e. $\log_5 125$ **f.** $\log_{\frac{1}{5}} \frac{1}{25}$

4. Which is greater, $\log_4 215$ or $\log_9 678$? Explain without relying on a calculator answer.

5. The value of $\log_3 31 + \log_6 228$ is between what two integers?

6. Suppose $\log_b 32{,}456 = 9$. Find the base b.

7. Let $a = \log 4$ and $b = \log 5$. Find each value in terms of a and b.
a. $\log 20$ **b.** $\log 1.25$
c. $\log 125$ **d.** $\log 400$
e. $\log \sqrt{5}$ **f.** $\log 80$

8. Put this list of values in order from least to greatest.
$\log_2 9$ $\log_3 35$ $\log_4 67$ $\log_5 599$ $\log_6 489$ $\log_7 716$

9. Use logarithms to find the solution to the equation $3^x = 210$ to three decimal places.

Practice: For Lesson 5.13, assign Exercises 4–9.

Lesson Overview

GOAL

- Graph logarithmic functions.

In this lesson, students study the properties of the graphs of logarithmic functions. They learn how to use the change-of-base rule to tabulate or graph a logarithmic function in any base, even if their calculators can work only with base-10 logarithms. Students also use graphs of logarithmic functions to help solve equations.

CHECK YOUR UNDERSTANDING

- Core: 1, 2, 3, 4, 6
- Optional: 5
- Extension: 7

MATERIALS

- CAS (recommended)
- graph paper
- graphing calculators
- Blackline Master 5.14

HOMEWORK

- Core: 8, 9, 10, 11, 13, 15
- Optional: 12, 16
- Extension: 14

Launch

Start today's lesson with the dialog. You might wish to have two students recite the dialog as students follow along with their graphing calculators. Since the dialog shows that two ways of expressing a function give the same graph, you may wish to have students graph the function both ways. Then by hiding one graph and showing the other (and vice versa), students can see that they are identical. See the TI-Nspire Handbook on p. 778 for advice about how to do this. Blackline Master 5.14 can be used here.

Explore

Minds in Action

This dialog serves two purposes: first, to show students how to graph a logarithmic function in any base, and, second, to illustrate the fact that all logarithmic functions are related by a vertical stretch. Stress here that log 3 is just a number, so $\frac{\log x}{\log 3}$ is very similar to $\frac{\log x}{2}$ in its behavior, and students should recognize that as a vertical stretch from working with other functions. This might also be a good time to remind students about the inverse relationship of logarithmic and exponential functions.

5.14 Graphing Logarithmic Functions

This lesson focuses on some properties of the graphs of logarithmic functions. It includes a method for graphing a logarithm for any given base.

Minds in Action — episode 22

Tony wants to know how to graph a logarithmic function.

Tony I've got a question. Exercise 16 in Lesson 5.13 asked us to make a table of values for $f(x) = \log_3 x$. And I can do that.

Sasha So what's your question?

Tony What I want to know is, how do I graph $y = \log_3 x$ on the graphing calculator? Do I have to just enter all these points as data and live with that?

> Assume that Tony's calculator can work with base-10 logarithms only.

Sasha There has to be a way. How did you make the table?

Tony Some of the numbers I can just fill in, like $\log_3 9 = 2$. For the others, I had to use the change-of-base rule.

Sasha Give me an example.

Tony Take 7. To calculate $\log_3 7$, I split it so it's $\log 7$ divided by $\log 3$. I type that on the calculator and I get 1.7712.

Sasha Did you do it the same way each time?

Tony Yes, except the ones that I did in my head. But I could even do those with the change-of-base rule.

Sasha Then that's it. That's how you make the graph. Just take your number x and calculate $\log x$ divided by $\log 3$. That works for any number.

Tony And I can type that in as a function on the calculator! The function is

$$f(x) = \frac{\log x}{\log 3}$$

> You can program this version of Tony's $f(x)$ into your function-modeling language. Define $f(x) = \frac{\log x}{\log 3}$.

Sasha types in the equation.

Sasha Hey, that fraction worked! And the graph goes through the point (9, 2).

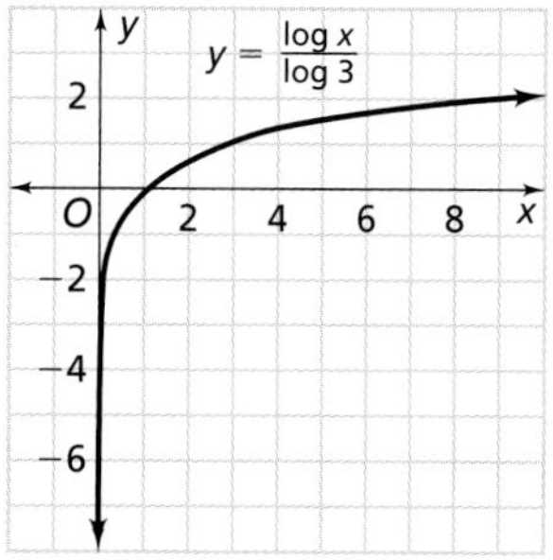

You can graph the logarithm for any base by using the relationship $\log_b x = \frac{\log x}{\log b}$. One interesting consequence of this fact is that the graphs of all logarithmic functions are related to each other by a vertical stretch.

Every one of these functions has the same domain and range. The domain is all positive reals. The range is all real numbers.

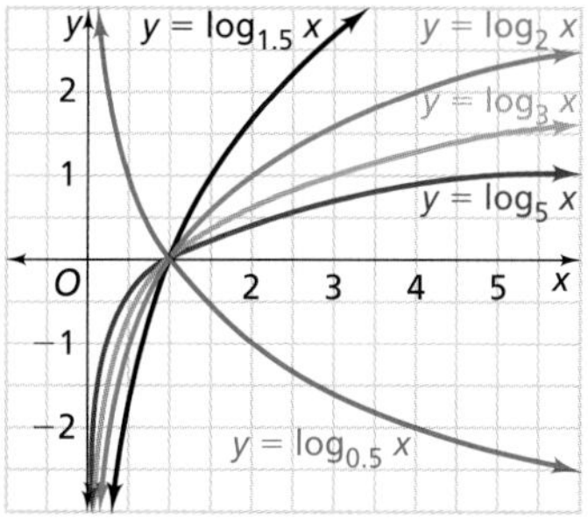

For You to Do

1. Find and graph a function $f(x) = \log_b x$ with a graph that contains the point (2, 5).

Hint: If $y = \log_b x$ contains the point (2, 5), what equation must b solve?

You can use graphs to find the number of solutions of some equations that involve logarithms.

Example

Problem

a. How many solutions are there to the equation $\log_3 (x - 2) + \log_3 x = \log_3 63$?

b. Find all values of x that make $\log_3 (x - 2) + \log_3 x = \log_3 63$ true.

Solution

a. Graph each side of the equation. You can use the equation $y_1 = \frac{\log (x - 2)}{\log 3} + \frac{\log x}{\log 3}$ to graph the left side.
The right side is the horizontal line $y_2 = \frac{\log 63}{\log 3}$.

Plot the two graphs on the same axes.

Each solution to the original equation corresponds to an intersection between the two graphs. The graphs intersect once, so there is one solution.

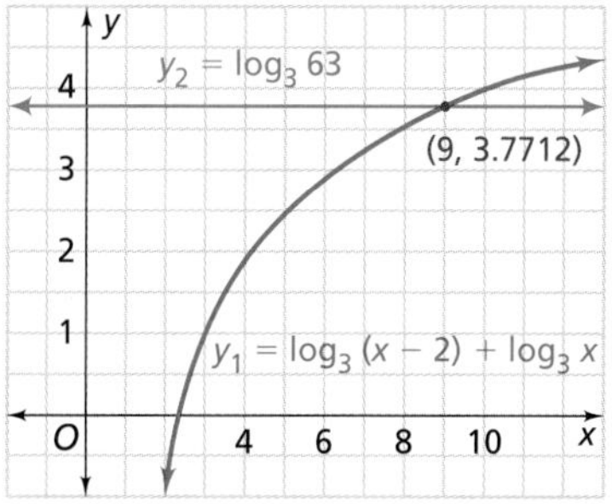

Why is the graph of $y_2 = \frac{\log 63}{\log 3}$ a horizontal line?

Example

If your students' technology allows the input of logarithms to any base, skip the steps that rewrite the equation in terms of base-10 logarithms. As with a similar example in the last lesson, students must check their solutions to find any extraneous results. Graphing the functions makes it clear that there is only one solution to the equation, especially since the graph of y_1 is undefined at $x = -7$.

Wrap Up

As time allows, go over the Check Your Understanding core exercises with your class. Note that most of the exercises for this lesson require students to use a graphing calculator.

Assessment Resources

Lesson Quiz 5.14

1. Use this close-up of the graph of $x \mapsto \log_4 x$ with x between 1.4 and 1.5.
   a. Approximate $\log_4 1.435$.
   b. Approximate the solution to the equation $\log_4 x = 0.28$.

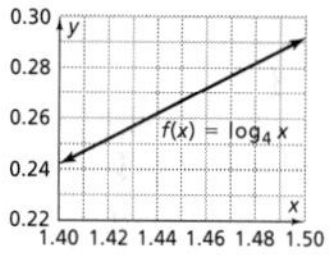

2. If you put money in a bank account at 5% interest per year, the equation $M(n) = 1.05^n$ describes the number of years n it takes to multiply your money by the factor M.
   a. Sketch the graph of $M(n)$.
   b. What is the inverse function of $M(n)$? Graph it on the same axes.
   c. How many years does it take for an amount of money to grow to 5 times its initial value if you invest it at 5% per year?

3. Sketch the graph of $y = \log_5 5^x$. Give another name for a function that is equivalent to $f(x) = \log_5 5^x$. Explain.

Answers

For You to Do

1. $f(x) = \log_{\sqrt[5]{2}} x$

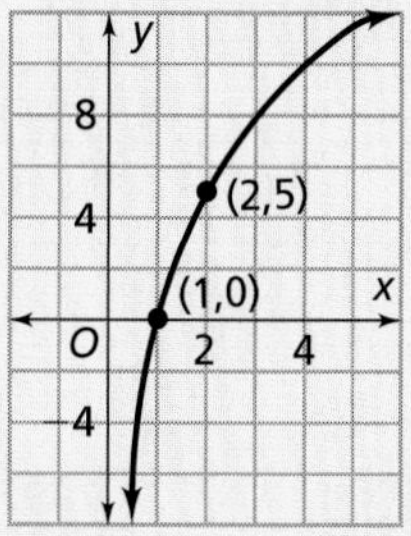

Exercises

HOMEWORK

- Core: 8, 9, 10, 11, 13, 15
- Optional: 12, 16
- Extension: 14

Check Your Understanding

EXERCISE 1 You may wish to demonstrate how the graphing calculator can be used here, but the hope is that most students will prefer to do this exercise using algebra.

EXERCISE 2 Students study the natural logarithm and its base, *e* the Euler constant, in CME Project *Precalculus*.

EXERCISE 3 Remind students that they can zoom in on a graph or use the calculator to locate the intersection points.

EXERCISE 4 may be easier to solve without graphing but instead by substituting greater numbers into both functions and comparing the results. Students might also use a table.

EXERCISES 4 AND 5 highlight a property of logarithm graphs. Logarithmic functions grow slowly for greater values of *x*.

b. Use the laws of logarithms to combine the expressions on the left side. Then build a quadratic equation.

$$\log_3(x-2) + \log_3 x = \log_3 63$$

$$\log_3(x(x-2)) = \log_3 63$$

$$x(x-2) = 63$$

$$x^2 - 2x - 63 = 0$$

$$(x-9)(x+7) = 0$$

The equation gives two solutions, $x = 9$ and $x = -7$. However, the solution $x = -7$ is invalid, since it leads to negative inputs for the logarithms in the original equation. The only solution is $x = 9$.

Exercises *Practicing Habits of Mind*

Check Your Understanding

1. Find all solutions to this equation.

$$\log_2(3x+1) - \log_2(2x-3) = 2$$

2. The **LN** key on a calculator also performs logarithms, but not to base 10. So, $\ln x = \log_b x$ for some unknown base b.
   a. Without using a calculator, determine what $\ln 1$ and $\ln 0$ should be. Then verify your results with a calculator.
   b. Determine the base b as accurately as you can.

3. **a.** Sketch the graphs of $y = \sqrt{x}$ and $y = \log_2 x$ accurately.
   b. How many numbers x make $\sqrt{x} = \log_2 x$ true?

4. As x increases, $\log_2 x$ becomes less than $\sqrt{x}$. Consider the values of $\log_{1.06} x$. Use the graphs of $y = \sqrt{x}$ and $y = \log_{1.06} x$. As x increases, will $\sqrt{x}$ always be less than $\log_{1.06} x$?

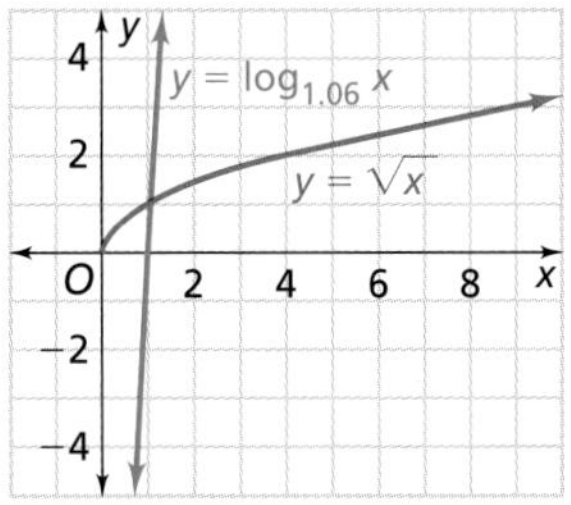

You can locate intersection points on a graph. See the TI-Nspire Handbook, p. 778.

Answers

Exercises

1. 2.6
2. **a.** ln 1 = 0 and ln 0 is undefined.
   b. about 2.71828
3. **a.**

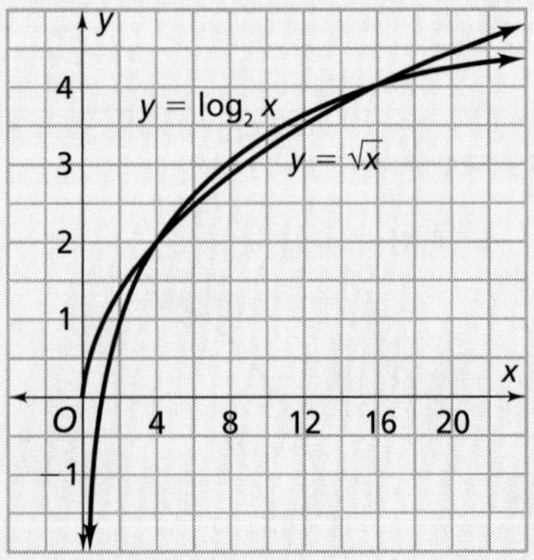

   b. 2
4. no

5. As x increases, $\log_2 x$ becomes less than $\sqrt{x}$. Consider the values of $\sqrt[10]{x}$. Use the graphs of $y = \sqrt[10]{x}$ and $y = \log_2 x$.

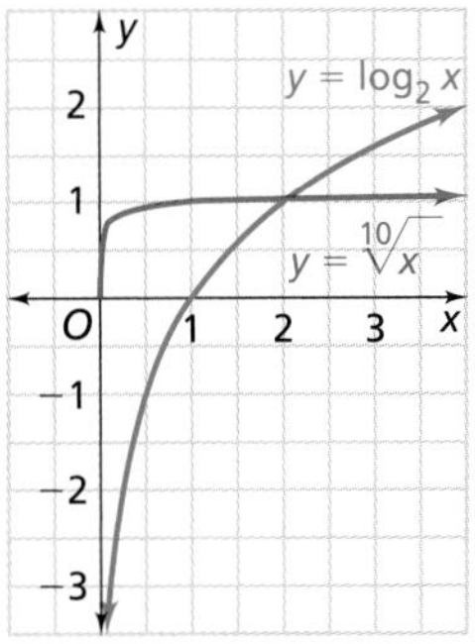

a. As x increases, will $\sqrt[10]{x}$ always be less than $\log_2 x$?

b. As x increases, will $\sqrt[10]{x}$ always be less than $\log_{1.06} x$?

c. As x increases, will $\log_2 x$ always be less than $\log_{1.06} x$?

6. Find the number of solutions to each equation.

a. $\log x^2 = 1$ b. $2 \log x = 1$ c. $\log_3 x = \sqrt{x} - 1$

d. $\log_2 x = 2^x$ e. $\log_{1.4} x = 1.4^x$

7. **Take It Further** The graphs of $y = \log_2 x$ and $y = 2^x$ do not intersect, but the graphs of $y = \log_{1.4} x$ and $y = 1.4^x$ do. For some base b such that $b > 1$, the graphs of $y = \log_b x$ and $y = b^x$ intersect exactly once. Find such a value of b and the intersection point of the two graphs as accurately as you can.

On Your Own

8. Use this detail of the graph of $x \mapsto \log_2 x$ with x between 1.3 and 1.4.

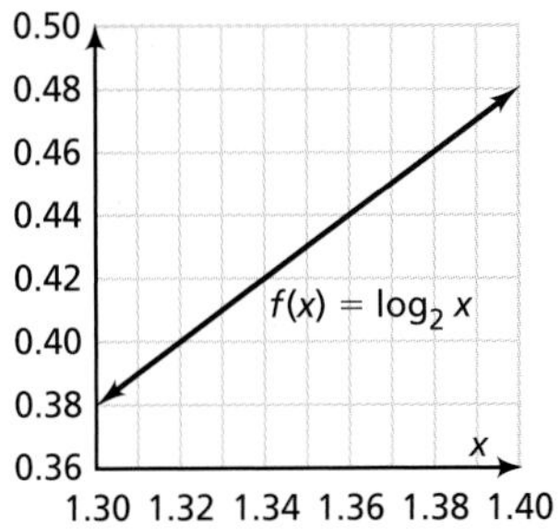

a. Approximate $\log_2 1.383$.

b. Approximate the solution to the equation $\log_2 x = 0.4$.

9. Asako says, "According to one of the laws of logarithms, $\log x^2 = 2 \log x$. So the graphs of $f(x) = \log x^2$ and $g(x) = 2 \log x$ should look exactly the same."

Do you agree or disagree with Asako's statement? Explain.

5. a. yes **b.** yes **c.** yes

6. a. two **b.** one **c.** two

d. zero **e.** two

7. $b \approx 1.4447$, about (2.7183, 2.7183)

8. a. 0.468 **b.** 1.320

9. Disagree; the graphs are not the same because the domain of $f(x) = \log x^2$ is all real numbers except 0, while the domain of $g(x) = 2 \log x$ is only the positive real numbers.

EXERCISE 6 Encourage students to make sense of the number of solutions in each case, if they can, and to predict the result before checking on their calculators.

EXERCISE 7 The actual value of b is $e^{\frac{1}{e}} \approx 1.4446678610098$, where e is the Euler constant (the base of the natural logarithm). The coordinates of the single point of intersection are $(e, e) \approx (2.71828183, 2.71828183)$.

On Your Own

EXERCISE 8 The technique used in this exercise was far more common before calculator usage became standard. A table of logarithms might include only $\log_2 1.3 \approx 0.38$ and $\log_2 1.4 \approx 0.48$, so interpolation would be used to approximate $\log_2 1.383$ or to solve the equation $\log_2 x = 0.4$. While a calculator could be used to verify the approximate solutions students find here, this exercise intends to give students practice with noncalculator interpolation. This topic will be explored further in CME Project *Precalculus,* where the local linearity of functions is used for approximation or to find the equation of a tangent line.

EXERCISE 9 If students have trouble, ask them about the domain of each function or ask them to graph both functions using a calculator.

EXERCISE 13 Students may not naturally investigate whether these two functions have the same domain unless you ask them to investigate or unless they actually graph the functions in the same window.

EXERCISE 14 To complete this exercise, students need to understand how to show that one graph is a translation of another. If each point (x, y) in one graph is mapped to a point $(x + a, y + b)$ in the another graph, then those two graphs are translations of each other. For these two functions, the translation is horizontal, so students just need to show that for a given y-coordinate, the differences of the x-coordinates on the two graphs is a constant.

10. If you put money in a bank account at 6% interest per year, the function below outputs the factor the money in the account has grown by after n years.

$$D(n) = 1.06^n$$

a. Sketch the graph of $D(n)$.

b. What is the inverse function of $D(n)$?

c. On a graphing calculator, graph the inverse function of $D(n)$.

d. How many years does it take for an amount of money to grow to 10 times its initial value if you invest it at 6% per year?

11. Let $f(x) = \log_b x$ with base b between 0 and 1.

a. Graph an example of one such function.

b. Explain why all such functions are decreasing.

12. Show that $f(x) = \log_2 x$ is exactly three times greater than $g(x) = \log_8 x$.

13. a. Sketch the graph of $y = \log 10^x$. Give another name for a function that is equivalent to $f(x) = \log 10^x$. Explain your reasoning.

b. Sketch the graph of $y = 10^{\log x}$. Explain why this graph is not the same as the graph of $y = \log 10^x$.

14. Take It Further

a. For $a > 0$, show that the graph of $f(x) = a \cdot 3^x$ is a translation of the graph of $g(x) = 3^x$.

b. For numbers a and b such that $a > 0$ and $b > 0$, show that the graph of $f(x) = a \cdot b^x$ is a translation of the graph of $g(x) = b^x$. Assume $b \neq 1$.

15. Standardized Test Prep Let $f(x) = \log_4 x$. Suppose the graph of $g(x)$ is a translation of the graph of $f(x)$ two units to the left and one unit down. Which of the following equations is a possible rule for $g(x)$?

A. $g(x) = \log_4 (x - 2) + 1$
B. $g(x) = \log_4 (x - 2) - 1$
C. $g(x) = \log_4 (x + 2) - 1$
D. $g(x) = \log_4 (x - 1) - 2$

Go Online PHSchool.com

For additional practice, go to **Web Code:** bfa-0514

Compare with Exercise 22 from Lesson 5.7.

Answers

10. See back of book.

11. a. Answers may vary. Sample:

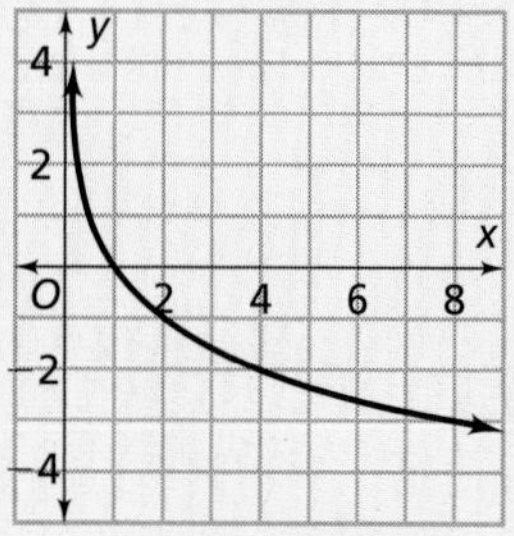

b. Rewrite $y = \log_b x$ as $b^y = x$. Since b is between 0 and 1, as y increases, x decreases, or as x increases, y decreases.

12. Let $y = g(x)$, so $y = \log_8 x$. Then $8^y = x$, so $(2^3)^y = x$ and $2^{3y} = x$. Then $\log_2 x = 3y$. Thus, $f(x) = 3g(x)$.

13. See back of book.

14. a. Answers may vary. Sample: Show there is a number t such that a point (x, y) on

Maintain Your Skills

16. Sketch each graph on the same axes.

a. $y = \log_3 x$ **b.** $y = \log_3 (x - 3)$ **c.** $y = \log_3 (x + 4)$

d. $y = \log_3 x - 3$ **e.** $y = \log_3 x + 4$

f. Explain why the graph of $y = \log_3 (x - 3)$ is not the same as the graph of $y = \log_3 x - 3$.

Go Online
Video Tutor
PHSchool.com

Web Code: bfe-0775

Historical Perspective

In 1938, physicist Frank Benford published a paper describing something he had noticed in scientific data: Numbers started with the digit 1 much more frequently than 2 or 3, and far more frequently than 9. He compiled numeric information from many sources. He found that, on average, just over 30% of numbers started with the digit 1, while fewer than 5% started with the digit 9.

This numeric phenomenon is known as Benford's Law. It works for many sources of data, but not all. For example, it does not work for ZIP codes or telephone numbers, which are assigned to produce an even distribution of initial digits.

So, how do you find the expected frequencies? You use logarithms.

For example, take a number n with a first digit 4. The decimal part of $\log n$ must be between 0.6020 and 0.6990. If Benford's Law is true, then about 9.70% of the numbers observed should start with 4. And this is what actually happens with many sources of data. Numbers starting with 4 are less than one third as common as numbers starting with 1, which occur 30.1% of the time. The diagram at the right shows the relative frequency with which each digit occurs.

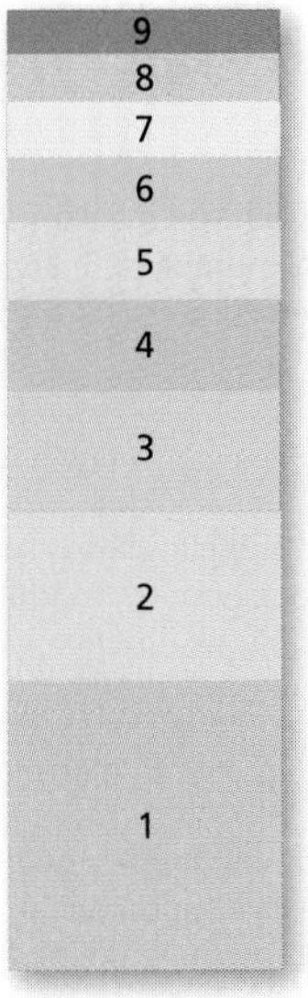

Accountants often use Benford's Law in investigating financial fraud. If the data in a financial report do not come close to the frequencies predicted by Benford's Law, they may be dishonest data.

Go Online
PHSchool.com

For more information about Benford's Law, go to **Web Code:** bfe-9031

the graph of f maps to the point $(x + t, y)$ on the graph of g. Because $a > 0$, you can write a as $3^{\log_3 a}$. Then $f(x) = 3^{\log_3 a} \cdot 3^x = 3^{x + \log_3 a} = g(x + \log_3 a)$. Thus, $t = \log_3 a$.

b. Answers may vary. Sample: Show there is a number t such that a point (x, y) on the graph of f maps to the point $(x + t, y)$ on the graph of g. Because $a, b > 0$, $b \neq 1$, you can write a as $b^{\log_b a}$. Then $f(x) = b^{\log_b a} \cdot b^x = b^{x + \log_b a} = g(x + \log_b a)$. Thus, $t = \log_b a$.

15. C

16. a–e. See back of book.

f. Answers may vary. Sample: The graph of $y = \log_3 (x - 3)$ is a horizontal translation of the graph of $y = \log_3 x$, while the graph of $y = \log_3 x - 3$ is a vertical translation of the graph of $y = \log_3 x$.

Historical Perspective

For interested students, a good project would be to analyze numeric data from a newspaper's stock listings, U.S. Census data, or other source. Students could then compare their results to Benford's predictions, or try to explain why their chosen data does not match the pattern. Some students may comment on the meaning of the word "law" here; Benford's Law is not an actual law in any sense of the word—the name implies about the same "law"-ness as Murphy's Law. But the circumstances that lead to Benford's Law happen often enough to be surprisingly common. The bar that shows the breakdown by digit is divided in the same way a slide rule divides its interval from 1 to 10.

Additional Resources

PRINT RESOURCES
- Solution Manual
- Practice Workbook
- Assessment Resources
- Teaching Resources

TECHNOLOGY
- Interactive Textbook
- TeacherExpress CD-ROM
- ExamView CD-ROM
- PHSchool.com

Additional Practice

1. Use this detail of the graph of $x \mapsto \log_3 x$ with x between 1.4 and 1.5.

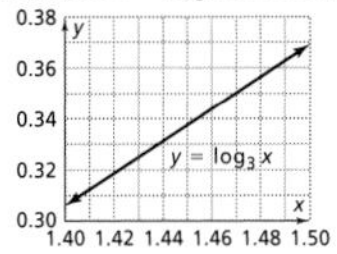

a. Approximate $\log_3 1.456$.
b. Approximate the solution to the equation $\log_3 x = 0.35$.

2. Let $f(x) = \log_b x$ with base b between 1 and 2.
a. Graph an example of one such function.
b. Are all such functions increasing or decreasing? Explain.

3. a. Sketch the graph of $y = \log_2 2^x$.
b. Give another name for a function that is equivalent to $f(x) = \log_2 2^x$. Explain.

4. a. Is $f(x) = \log_3 x$ a one-to-one function? Explain.
b. Is $f(x) = \log_b x$ a one-to-one function, where b is a nonnegative integer? Explain.

5. Find all of the solutions to each equation.
a. $\log_5 (x + 1) = \log_5 8$
b. $\log_5 x + \log_5 (x + 2) = \log_5 8$
c. $\log_5 x^2 = 4$
d. $\log_5 (2x + 1) - \log_5 x = 2$

6. Multiple Choice Without a calculator, determine which of these four numbers is the least.
A. $\log_5 27$ **B.** $\log_6 41$ **C.** $\log_7 63$ **D.** $\log_8 71$

7. Sketch each graph on a linear x-axis and logarithmic y-axis.
a. $y = 3^x$ **b.** $y = 10 \cdot 3^x$ **c.** $y = \left(\frac{1}{2}\right)^x$ **d.** $y = 10 \cdot \left(\frac{1}{2}\right)^x$

Practice: For Lesson 5.14, assign Exercises 1–3.

Lesson Overview

GOAL

- Graph functions using a logarithmic scale.

In this lesson, students experiment with graph paper that has logarithmic scales on one or both axes. They see how familiar graphs look when plotted on this paper, including exponential and logarithmic functions.

This lesson is optional. If time is tight, consider skipping the lesson and moving on to the next chapter.

Logarithmic scales are used in social science, astronomy, finance, and in many other fields. They are used any time that ratios are more useful or descriptive than value change. For example, take the stock market: consider a stock that drops by $2 per share one day. This could be a total disaster, or no big deal—it depends on the original price of the stock, and the ratio of the $2 drop to the original price. This is why financial data is most commonly presented in a logarithmic scale.

In other cases (astronomical data, for example) it may be impossible or impractical to show the data on a linear scale. Showing the distance from the sun to each planet is difficult on a linear scale, since the scale must be huge to show any significant difference in distance for the closer planets. A logarithmic scale may be more appropriate.

Using a logarithmic scale on either or both axes changes what types of functions appear linear. These scales can be useful in taking real data and trying to determine what type of rule best fits the situation.

CHECK YOUR UNDERSTANDING
- Core: 1, 2, 3, 4, 5, 7
- Optional: 6

MATERIALS
- graph paper
- graphing calculators
- log-log graph paper
- semilog graph paper
- Blackline Masters 5.15A–D

HOMEWORK
- Core: 8, 10, 11
- Optional: 9a–b, 12, 14, 15, 16
- Extension: 9c, 13

VOCABULARY
- linear scale
- log-log graph paper
- logarithmic scale
- semilog graph paper

Launch

Start this lesson with the In-Class Experiment. Each student or group will need copies of Blackline Masters 5.15A–D.

5.15 The Logarithmic Scale

You can use different scales for the axes of a graph.

In-Class Experiment

1. Your teacher will give you four pieces of graph paper with the scales on the axes already marked. On the piece with the standard scales, plot the following graphs. On each other piece, plot only the graphs that are straight lines on that set of axes. (*Hint:* The graphs of nonlinear equations can be straight lines when you plot them on axes with different scales. Try to predict which graphs will be straight lines on each piece of graph paper.)

a. $y = x$ **b.** $y = x^2$
c. $y = x^3$ **d.** $y = 2^x$
e. $y = 2 \cdot 3^x$ **f.** $y = 8 \cdot 0.5^x$
g. $y = \log x$ **h.** $y = \log_2 x$

When you measure with a ruler, you use a **linear scale** to keep track of the number of inches, centimeters, yards, or other units you measure. You count by adding: 1 inch, 2 inches, 3 inches . . .

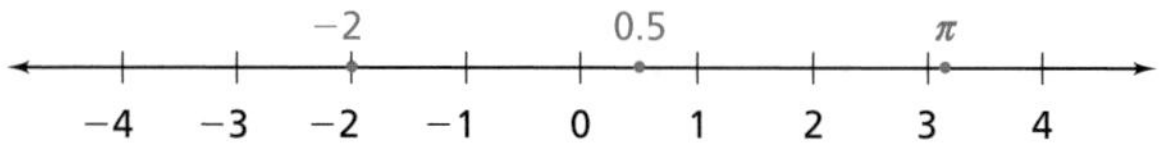

The linear scale is not the only choice. You can also use a **logarithmic scale.** You count by multiplying: 1 unit, 10 units, 100 units, 1000 units . . .

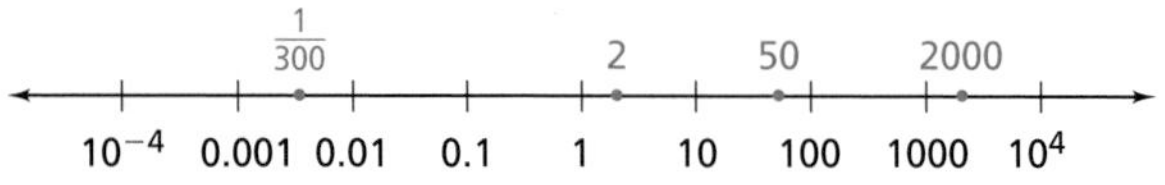

Note that zero and negative numbers do not appear on the logarithmic scale.

You can use a logarithmic scale when working with data that have widely varying values or when relative change is more important than absolute change. Well-known and frequently used logarithmic scales include the pH scale for acidity and the Richter scale for earthquakes.

So, you might consider using a logarithmic scale if a change from 1 to 2 is just as important as a change from 100 to 200. The scale for Benford's Law is logarithmic.

Answers

In-Class Experiment

1. See back of book.

Logarithmic scales are so named because the logarithm outputs of the numbers on the axis increase linearly. For example, the numbers 1, 10, 100, and 1000 are equally spaced. The base-10 logarithms of these numbers are 0, 1, 2, and 3.

Example

Problem The U.S. Census has been taken every 10 years since 1790. It counts the number of people living in the United States. Here are two graphs of the data from the census. One uses a linear scale on both axes. The other uses a logarithmic scale on the y-axis.

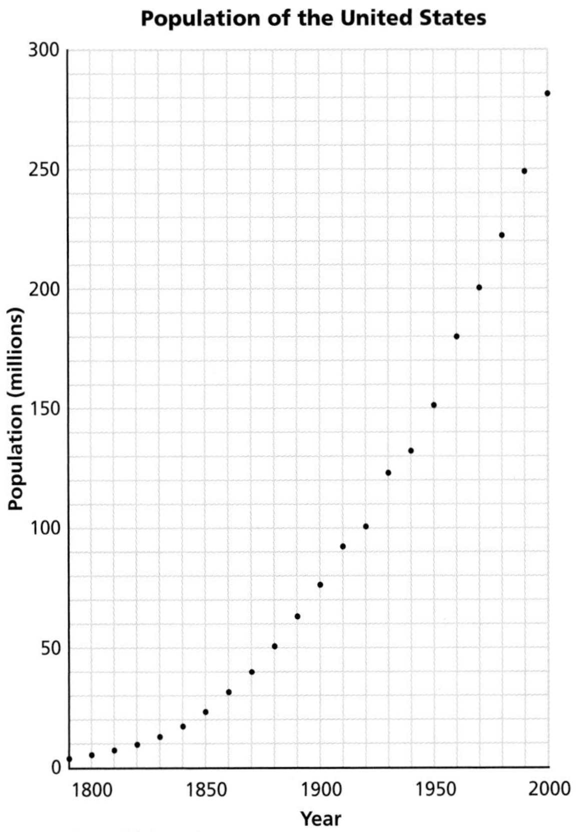

SOURCE: *U.S. Census Bureau*

Explore

In-Class Experiment

Students will notice that different graphs appear to be linear on each type of scale. When the scales on both the x and y axes are linear, only the linear function $y = x$ has a linear graph. When students plot the graphs of these functions on paper with a logarithmic scale on the y-axis, then the exponential functions have graphs that are straight lines. For the logarithmic scale on the x-axis, the logarithm functions have straight-line graphs. Finally, the paper with logarithmic scales on both axes causes the functions that are powers of x to have straight-line graphs. Remind students that this does not mean the graphs suddenly are linear. These "lines" on special papers do not have constant slope, because slope is defined in terms of the coordinates of the points, and these coordinates have not changed. However, such a line can help you estimate the coordinates of other points on the graph of the function. You can also extend the line to find more points.

Example

This example looks at U.S. Census data first on a linear scale and then on a graph with a logarithmic y-axis (sometimes called a "semilog-y" scale). You could provide students with copies of each type of scale and ask them to find and plot the data themselves. If time permits, mention that the grid lines in a log scale are marked very differently from the grid lines in a linear scale; there is a large gap between 10 and 20 million for example, then a smaller gap between 20 and 30 million, and so forth. You could challenge students to determine the relative widths of each of these gaps. Or point out that the gap widths are in the same proportion as the bars used in illustrating Benford's Law in the Historical Perspective in Lesson 5.14.

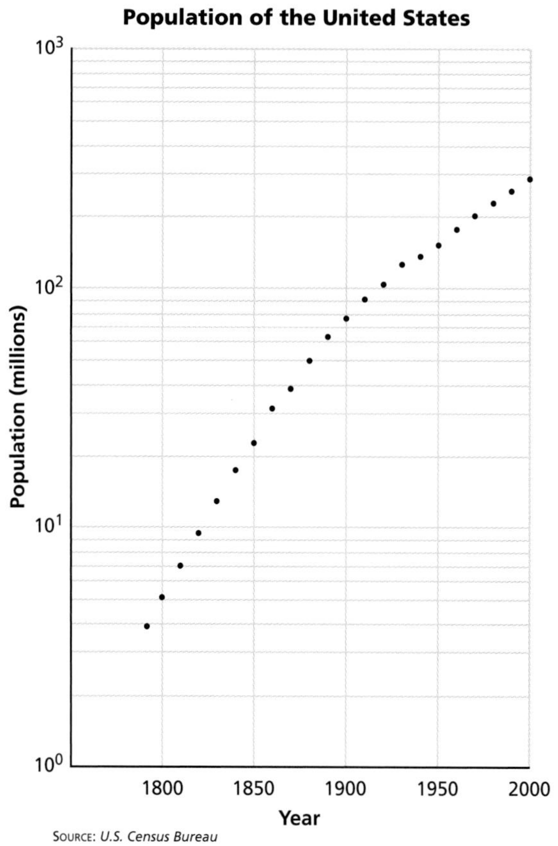

SOURCE: *U.S. Census Bureau*

What information can you gather from each graph?

Solution The graph on a linear scale shows that the population is growing roughly exponentially, since the graph appears similar to the graphs of exponential growth functions you saw earlier in this chapter. One possible observation is that the population for 1940 appears to be slightly lower than might be expected by following the curve. But generally the curve seems to rise consistently. Other observations include the fact that the U.S. population appears to be growing by greater and greater amounts at each census, at least since 1950.

The graph on a logarithmic scale has two portions that appear to be linear. This means that during these two periods the population increased by the same growth factor every n years. In other words, if you compare two populations n years apart, they will have the same ratio as any other pair of populations n years apart.

Habits of Mind

Detect the key characteristics. It is important to remember that the two graphs show the same data. Only the way the data are displayed is different.

The noticeable change in the slope occurs at around 1900. The ratio appears to have changed. This suggests that the U.S. population has grown at a slower rate since 1900. Note that this observation is very difficult to make when viewing the data on a linear scale. This is the advantage of working with a logarithmic scale: ratios between successive outputs, whether equal or different, become immediately visible.

You can also use a logarithmic scale on the x-axis to show the ratios between successive inputs more clearly.

For Discussion

2. The linear scale suggests the U.S. population grew by its greatest amount between 1990 and 2000, but the logarithmic scale suggests the population grew more slowly during that decade than in the past. Is this a contradiction? Explain.

You can use a logarithmic scale on the vertical or the horizontal axis, or on both. Some people prefer to say that you are actually graphing the logarithms of the values when you use this scale.

Graph paper with one logarithmic axis is called *semilog* graph paper. Graph paper with two logarithmic axes is *log-log* graph paper.

Proving the Relationships

The In-Class Experiment and the U.S. Census example both show that when you plot an exponential function using a logarithmic y-axis, the function appears linear. For example, this graph is $y = 3 \cdot 2^x$ plotted with a logarithmic scale on the y-axis.

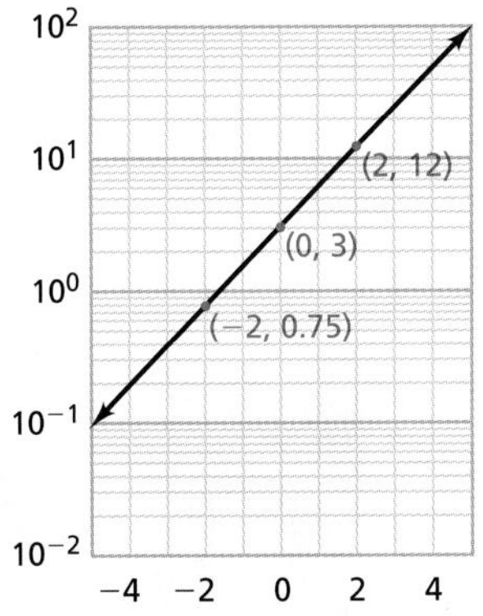

You can prove that the function $y = 3 \cdot 2^x$ should appear as a straight line on a logarithmic scale on the y-axis using the laws of logarithms.

PROVING THE RELATIONSHIPS Students may be surprised that exponential functions appear linear on semilog paper, so be sure they do not get confused about the nature of the functions. They are still exponential, with the same properties, domains, and ranges seen previously. Only the method of graphing has changed, as students graph log y against x instead of y against x. For an exponential function, log y increases linearly, and this graph paper allows it to be displayed as a line. The proof on the next page shows that the graph of log y against x is in a linear form.

Answers

For Discussion

2. No; the two statements are about different quantities. The *amount* of population growth is not the same as the *rate* of population growth. In number of people, the amount of population growth was greater between 1990 and 2000 than in earlier decades, but the rate of growth was lower.

COROLLARY 5.6.1 Show some examples that illustrate Corollary 5.6.1. Since each exponential function appears as a line in this scale, the rules for the number of intersections follow the same rules that lines would follow. You might ask students why the requirement $a_i > 0$ is there: negative values do not appear on a logarithmic y-axis, and two exponential functions will definitely not intersect if their coefficients are of opposite signs (consider, for example, $f_1(x) = 2 \cdot 3^x$ and $f_2(x) = -3 \cdot 2^x$).

Wrap Up

End today's lesson by going over the Check Your Understanding core exercises.

Assessment Resources

Lesson Quiz 5.15

1. Find all solutions to each equation.
   a. $\log_4 (x - 2) = \log_4 9$
   b. $\log_3 x + \log_3 (x - 2) = \log_3 8$
   c. $\log_2 x^3 = 6$
   d. $\log_6 (x + 1) - \log_6 x = 3$

2. **Multiple Choice** Without a calculator, determine which of these four numbers is the greatest.
   A. $\log_5 45$ **B.** $\log_6 54$ **C.** $\log_7 84$ **D.** $\log_8 96$

3. Sketch each graph on a linear x-axis and logarithmic y-axis.
   a. $y = 4^x$ b. $y = 10 \cdot 4^x$

Theorem 5.6

When you use a logarithmic y-axis and a linear x-axis, the graph of an exponential function $y = a \cdot b^x$ with $a > 0$ and $b > 0$ appears as a straight line.

Proof Consider any exponential function $y = a \cdot b^x$ with $a > 0$ and $b > 0$. When you use this scale, you display the logarithms of the y-values. So, calculate $\log y$ in terms of b and x using the laws of logarithms.

$$y = a \cdot b^x$$
$$\log y = \log (a \cdot b^x)$$
$$\log y = \log a + \log b^x$$
$$\log y = \log a + x \log b$$

This may not look like much, but remember that $\log a$ and $\log b$ are just numbers. If $\log a = A$ and $\log b = B$, then $\log y = A + Bx$. This is an equation for a line in the plane. The graph of $\log y$ against x is linear.

Remember...

When making a graph, you choose to graph one thing against another. Here, choosing to graph $\log y$ against x gives a different picture than graphing y against x.

There is an interesting corollary to this theorem. It has to do with two exponential functions graphed on the same set of axes. They appear as lines. Any two lines intersect unless they have the same slope. For example, there is exactly one solution to $2 \cdot 3^x = 8 \cdot 0.5^x$, since they are two lines with different slopes when graphed on this kind of scale. Here is the general statement.

Corollary 5.6.1

The graphs of two exponential functions $f_1(x) = a_1 \cdot b_1{}^x$ and $f_2(x) = a_2 \cdot b_2{}^x$, with all a_i and b_i positive, must intersect exactly once unless $b_1 = b_2$.

This is true no matter what scale you use.

Overall, a logarithmic scale is another way of presenting data, one that stresses proportion instead of magnitude. You can use it to recognize graphically whether a function is exponential or logarithmic, or whether it makes sense to represent a set of data with an exponential or logarithmic function.

The stellar magnitude scale is a logarithmic scale. Brighter stars have lower values on the scale.

Exercises *Practicing Habits of Mind*

Check Your Understanding

The following table gives outputs for $\pi(x)$, the number of prime numbers less than or equal to x. The third column is a measure of the likelihood of choosing a prime among the integers from 1 to x. Out of all the integers from 1 to x, one in every $\frac{x}{\pi(x)}$ will be prime.

x	$\pi(x)$	$\frac{x}{\pi(x)}$
2	1	2
5	3	1.6667
10	4	2.5
50	15	3.3333
100	25	4
1000	168	5.9524
10,000	1229	8.1367
100,000	9592	10.4254
10^{10}	455,052,511	21.9755

For example, $\pi(6) = 3$ for the three primes 2, 3, and 5. This function's name is unrelated to the constant π that you know from studying circles. Amazingly, the primes from 1 to 100 million were calculated in the mid 1800s.

1. According to the table, do prime numbers become more or less frequent among larger integers? Explain.
2. Graph x against $\pi(x)$ using logarithmic x- and y-axes. Is there any observable pattern?
3. Graph x against $\frac{x}{\pi(x)}$ using a logarithmic x-axis and a linear y-axis. Is there any observable pattern?
4. The graph below shows the closing price of a stock from April 1, 2002, through April 1, 2004. Financial graphs use either linear or logarithmic scales on their vertical axis. Which scale does this graph use? Explain.

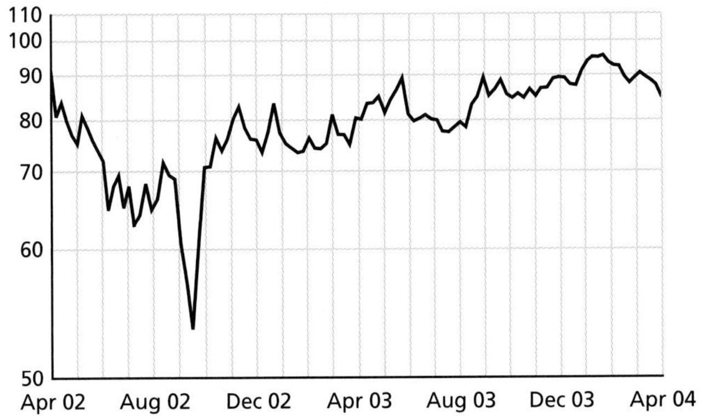

Exercises

HOMEWORK
- Core: 8, 10, 11
- Optional: 9a–b, 12, 14, 15, 16
- Extension: 9c, 13

Check Your Understanding

EXERCISES 1 AND 3 The Prime Number Theorem states that $\frac{x}{\pi(x)}$ (the third column in the table) is approximated by $y = \ln x$. Although your students would not necessarily recognize this graph as the graph of the natural logarithm, because they haven't studied it yet, they should recognize that it is a logarithmic function when they graph it in Exercise 3.

EXERCISES 2 AND 3 Students will find a slight pattern in Exercise 2, but a better pattern is visible in Exercise 3. The observation that $\frac{x}{\pi(x)}$ is approximately a logarithmic function is the Prime Number Theorem. Legendre and Gauss first made this observation over 200 years ago, but the proof took another 100 years. Its methods involve deep work with complex numbers, which is interesting since neither the problem nor the theorem say anything about complex numbers.

Answers

Exercises

1. Less frequent; about 1 out of 10 integers is prime up to 10^5, but only 1 out of 22 is prime up to 10^{10}.

2–3. See back of book.

4. Logarithmic; on the vertical axis, equal differences are not represented by equal distances.

EXERCISE 5 explains the results students saw in the In-Class Experiment at the beginning of this lesson when they graphed logarithmic functions with a linear y scale and a logarithmic x scale.

EXERCISE 6 explains more of the results of the In-Class Experiment. When students graphed $y = x$, $y = x^2$, and $y = x^3$ on log-log paper, the graphs appeared to be straight lines.

EXERCISE 7 relies on students' understanding that the value 0 does not appear on a logarithmic axis. Therefore, the intersection point (0, 0) of the two graphs cannot be plotted on log-log graph paper.

On Your Own

EXERCISE 8 Some students may approach this proof differently. You can show that a function is one-to-one by showing that if $f(a) = f(b)$, then $a = b$. So, in this case, assume that $\log_2 a = \log_2 b$. Then, $\log_2 a - \log_2 b = 0$. Now, you can use the laws of logarithms to write this as $\log_2 \frac{a}{b} = 0$. If the base-2 (or any base) logarithm of a number is 0, then the number is 1. This means that $\frac{a}{b} = 1$ and $a = b$. This proves that the function $f(x) = \log_2 x$ is one-to-one.

5. a. Use Theorem 5.9 as a model to prove the following result.

When you use a logarithmic x-axis and a linear y-axis, the logarithmic function $y = \log_b x$ appears as a straight line.

b. What is the slope of the line in part (a)? Assume that you use the base-10 logarithm for the x-axis.

6. a. Prove the following result.

When you use a logarithmic x-axis and a logarithmic y-axis, the power function $y = a \cdot x^b$ appears as a straight line.

b. What is the slope of the line in part (a)? Assume that you use the base-10 logarithm for both axes.

7. What's Wrong Here? Stephanie graphs $y = x^2$ and $y = 10x^2$ on the same piece of graph paper with both axes logarithmic.

Stephanie says, "Now wait a minute, these look parallel. Parallel lines don't intersect. But I know the graphs of $y = x^2$ and $y = 10x^2$ intersect at the point (0, 0). Shouldn't these intersect too?"

What happened? Why do the graphs not appear to intersect?

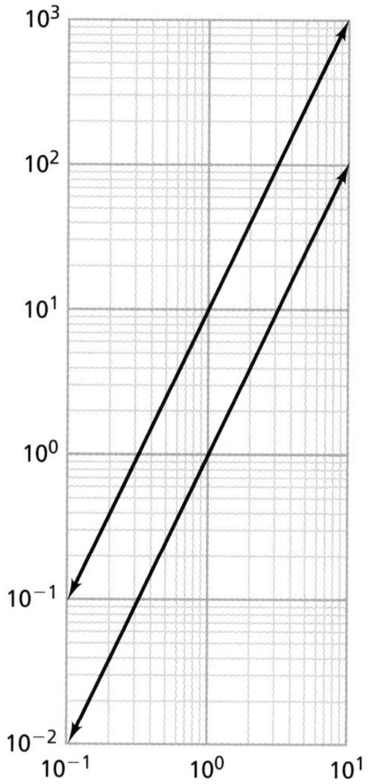

Answers

5. a. Suppose $y = \log_b x$ with $b > 0$, $b \neq 1$. Rewrite the equation as $b^y = x$, and take the logarithm of each side: $\log b^y = \log x$. Then $y \cdot \log b = \log x$, so $y = \frac{1}{\log b} \cdot \log x$. Since $\frac{1}{\log b}$ is a constant, say B, the equation becomes $y = B \cdot \log x$, which is in linear form.

b. $\frac{1}{\log b}$

6. a. If $y = a \cdot x^b$, then $\log y = \log (a \cdot x^b)$. So, $\log y = \log a + b \cdot \log x$. But $\log a$ is a constant, say A, so the equation becomes $\log y = A + b \cdot \log x$, which is in linear form.

b. b

7. The intersection of $y = x^2$ and $y = 10x^2$ is (0, 0). Because there is no value of 0 on the logarithmic axes, the intersection is not shown.

8. Yes. Answers may vary. Sample: If $f(x) = \log_2 x$, then the function $f^{-1}(x) = 2^x$ is its inverse. If a function has an inverse, it must be one-to-one, so $f(x)$ is one-to-one.

9. a–b.

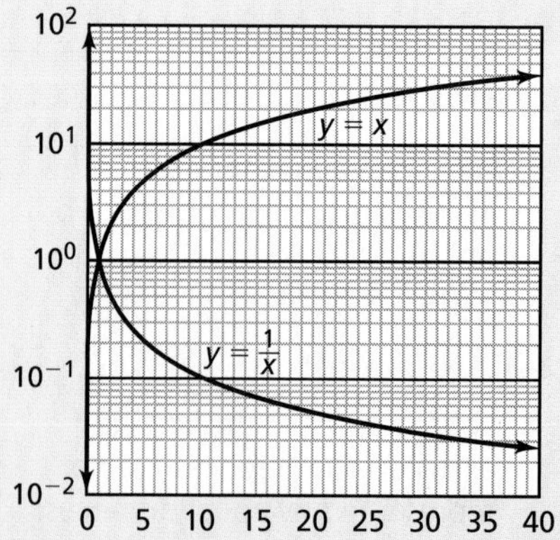

On Your Own

8. Is $f(x) = \log_2 x$ a one-to-one function? Explain.

9. a. Sketch the graph of $y = x$ on a logarithmic y-axis. Describe what the graph looks like.

b. Sketch the graph of $y = \frac{1}{x}$ on the same axes.

c. Take It Further Explain how the two graphs are related and why they are related in this way.

10. Find all solutions to each equation.

a. $\log_3 x = \log_3 7$ **b.** $\log_3 x + \log_3 (x + 1) = \log_3 12$

c. $\log x^2 = 4$ **d.** $\log_5 (x + 1) - \log_5 x = 1$

11. Standardized Test Prep Without a calculator, determine which of these four numbers is the greatest.

A. $\log_4 17$ **B.** $\log_3 27$ **C.** $\log_5 117$ **D.** $\log_2 9$

12. This table includes the frequency for each of the eight A notes on a piano.

Note	Frequency (Hz)
A0	27.5
A1	55
A2	110
A3	220
A4	440
A5	880
A6	1760
A7	3520

Consider the function $F(n)$, where n is the note's octave (0 through 7), and $F(n)$ is the frequency of that note.

a. Is $F(n)$ an exponential function, a logarithmic function, or neither? Explain.

b. Graph $F(n)$. Choose the appropriate graph paper to make the graph of $F(n)$ appear as a straight line.

13. Take It Further Find or graph all the solutions to the equation $x^y = y^x$ with $x > 0$, $y > 0$, and $x \neq y$.

Go Online PHSchool.com

For additional practice, go to Web Code: bfa-0515

Hz (or *hertz*) is a unit measuring cycles per second of a periodic event. In this case, it measures vibrations of a piano string.

EXERCISE 9 These graphs may be difficult for students, especially the behavior when x is between 0 and 1. The graph of $y = x$ will look like $y = \log x$ on a linear scale. If students are having trouble with the complete graph of $y = x$ here, give them some sample fractional values between 0 and 1 to work with. For example, ask them what to plot for $x = \frac{1}{10}$. They should realize that the graph continues "down" forever, since the origin is not on the graph paper! The graph of $y = \frac{1}{x}$ will look like $y = -\log x$ on a linear scale, with the intersection of the graphs at $(1, 10^0)$. For part (c), suggest they rewrite $y = \frac{1}{x}$ as $y = x^{-1}$.

EXERCISE 12 One extension that musically-minded students may appreciate is that the frequency of a musical scale is logarithmic one. When looking at sheet music, each octave takes up the same vertical space, but the frequency of the note actually doubles in each octave. So, while a climbing scale looks linear in sheet music, and will look linear on a logarithmic scale, it will look like an exponential curve if you graph the frequencies of the notes on a linear scale.

EXERCISE 13 Many students will find only the points (2, 4) and (4, 2). As a hint, have them assume $y = kx$ then solve for x and y in terms of k. The solution is $x = \sqrt[k-1]{k}$ and $y = k\sqrt[k-1]{k}$ With $k = 2$ the solution (2, 4) is found, but k can be any number other than 1; this gives a wide range of possible solutions.

13. Solutions are ordered pairs in the form

$$(x, y) = \left(k^{\frac{1}{k-1}}, k^{\frac{k}{k-1}}\right), \text{ for all } k > 0,\ k \neq 1.$$

The graph of $y = x$, when shown using a logarithmic y-axis, looks like the graph of a logarithmic function when that function is shown on a standard coordinate plane.

c. The graphs are reflections of each other over the horizontal line $y = 1$ because they are graphs of functions that are reciprocals. Because the y-axis has a logarithmic scale, the points (a, a) and $\left(a, \frac{1}{a}\right)$ are the same distance from the line $y = 1$. For example, (10, 10) and $(10, 10^{-1})$ are both 1 unit from the line $y = 1$.

10. a. 7 **b.** 3

c. ± 100 **d.** $\frac{1}{4}$

11. D

12. a. Exponential; the ratio of successive outputs is constant.

b.
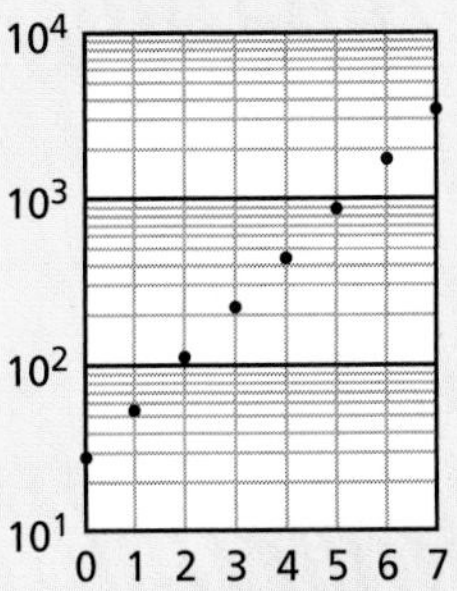

EXERCISE 14 All of these graphs should appear linear. Students should get an understanding that the base of the exponent behaves like the slope of a line, and the coefficient behaves like the *y*-intercept. This can help students understand Corollary 5.6.1. Further exploration can be done here by asking the following questions: What number(s) might you use for the base to produce a graph that appears as a horizontal line? (Answer: 1) As a downward-sloping line? (Answer: $0 < b < 1$)

Additional Resources

PRINT RESOURCES
- Solution Manual
- Practice Workbook
- Assessment Resources
- Teaching Resources

TECHNOLOGY
- Interactive Textbook
- TeacherExpress CD-ROM
- ExamView CD-ROM
- PHSchool.com

Additional Practice

1. Use this detail of the graph of $x \mapsto \log_3 x$ with x between 1.4 and 1.5.

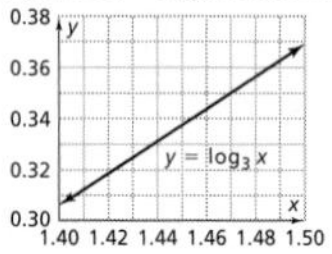

   a. Approximate $\log_3 1.456$.
   b. Approximate the solution to the equation $\log_3 x = 0.35$.

2. Let $f(x) = \log_b x$ with base b between 1 and 2.
   a. Graph an example of one such function.
   b. Are all such functions increasing or decreasing? Explain.

3. a. Sketch the graph of $y = \log_2 2^x$.
   b. Give another name for a function that is equivalent to $f(x) = \log_2 2^x$. Explain.

4. a. Is $f(x) = \log_3 x$ a one-to-one function? Explain.
   b. Is $f(x) = \log_b x$ a one-to-one function, where b is a nonnegative integer? Explain.

5. Find all of the solutions to each equation.
   a. $\log_5 (x + 1) = \log_5 8$
   b. $\log_5 x + \log_5 (x + 2) = \log_5 8$
   c. $\log_5 x^2 = 4$
   d. $\log_5 (2x + 1) - \log_5 x = 2$

6. **Multiple Choice** Without a calculator, determine which of these four numbers is the least.
   A. $\log_5 27$ **B.** $\log_6 41$ **C.** $\log_7 63$ **D.** $\log_8 71$

7. Sketch each graph on a linear x-axis and logarithmic y-axis.
   a. $y = 3^x$ b. $y = 10 \cdot 3^x$ c. $y = \left(\frac{1}{2}\right)^x$ d. $y = 10 \cdot \left(\frac{1}{2}\right)^x$

Practice: For Lesson 5.15, assign Exercises 4–7.

Maintain Your Skills

14. a. Copy and complete the following table.

x	$\log_2 x$	$\log_8 x$
0	■	■
1	■	■
2	■	■
3	■	■
4	■	■
5	■	■
6	■	■
7	■	■
8	■	■
9	■	■
10	■	■

b. A calculator gives the value of $\log_8 23$ as approximately 1.5079. Approximate the value of $\log_2 23$.

15. Sketch each graph on a linear x-axis and logarithmic y-axis.

a. $y = 2^x$ **b.** $y = 10 \cdot 2^x$
c. $y = 1.5^x$ **d.** $y = 10 \cdot 1.5^x$

16. Sketch each graph on a logarithmic x-axis and logarithmic y-axis.

a. $y = x^2$ **b.** $y = x^3$
c. $y = 10x^2$ **d.** $y = 10x^3$

Answers

14–16. See back of book.

Mathematical Reflections

1. a. 5 **b.** 1 **c.** 30 **d.** $\frac{1}{4}$

2. $\log_2 \frac{1}{8}$, $\log_{\frac{1}{2}} 4$, $\log 0.3$, $\log_7 1$, $\log_4 \frac{5}{2}$

3. a. 2 and 3; choose the two consecutive powers of 3 that 17 lies between: $3^2 < 17 < 3^3$ because $9 < 17 < 27$.

b. $N = \log_3 17 = \frac{\log 17}{\log 3} \approx \frac{1.230448921}{0.4771212547} \approx 2.5789$

c. $1 + 2N$

Mathematical Reflections 5C

In this investigation, you learned to evaluate logarithms of any base, to use logarithms in solving exponential equations, and to graph logarithmic functions. These questions will help you summarize what you have learned.

1. Solve each equation for x.
   - **a.** $\log \frac{5}{6} + \log 6 = \log x$
   - **b.** $\log_3 2 + \log_3 \frac{1}{2} = \log_3 x$
   - **c.** $\log 10 \cdot \log x = \log 30$
   - **d.** $\log_2 4 \cdot \log_2 \frac{1}{2} = \log_2 x$
2. Arrange the following numbers in order from least to greatest.
   $$\log_4 \frac{5}{2}, \log_2 \frac{1}{8}, \log 0.3, \log_7 1, \log_{\frac{1}{2}} 4$$
3. Let $N = \log_3 17$.
   - **a.** Find two consecutive integers j and k such that $j < N < k$. Explain how you made your choice.
   - **b.** Show how to use the change-of-base rule to evaluate N on a calculator that can only compute base-10 logarithms.
   - **c.** Express $\log_3 (3 \cdot 17^2)$ in terms of N.
4. Find all values of x that are solutions of the equation $\log (x - 20) + \log (x - 50) = 3$.
5. Let $f(x) = \log_b x$, with $b > 0$ and $b \neq 1$.
   - **a.** What do you know about b if the graph of $y = f(x)$ is increasing? If the graph is decreasing?
   - **b.** For what values of x is $f(x) = 0$?
   - **c.** Give the coordinates of one point on the graph of $f(x)$ without using any variables.
   - **d.** How can you use the graph of $f(x)$ to determine the base b of the logarithm?
6. What are some reasons to use logarithms?
7. What is a logarithmic scale and when do you use it?
8. If you invest \$1000 at 6% interest, compounded annually, how many years will it take until your money grows to \$10,000?

Sand particles with diameters between $\frac{1}{4}$ mm and $\frac{1}{2}$ mm have values between 2 and 1 on the Krumbein scale.

Vocabulary and Notation

In this investigation, you learned these terms and symbols. Make sure you understand what each one means and how to use it.

- **common logarithm, log x**
- **linear scale**
- **logarithmic function, $x \mapsto \log_b x$**
- **logarithmic scale**

Mathematical Reflections

EXERCISES 6–8 At the start of the investigation, you may have assigned these as Questions 1–3 for students to think and write about.

4. 70

5. a. $b > 1$; $0 < b < 1$

b. none

c. (1, 0)

d. Find the point of intersection for the graph of f and the line $y = 1$. The x-coordinate of that point is the base b.

6. Answers may vary. Sample: A logarithm can give an exact solution to an equation in the form $b^x = c$. Logarithms allow you to change a multiplication problem into an addition problem.

7. Answers may vary. Sample: On a logarithmic scale, equal distances between numbers represent equal *ratios* rather than equal *differences*. When plotting data on a logarithmic scale, points that are collinear represent exponential relationships, so a graph drawn using a logarithmic scale can help you identify exponential data and can help you observe patterns in the rate of change.

8. 40 yr

Project Overview

This project explores the functional equation that exponential functions satisfy: $f(x + y) = f(x) \cdot f(y)$. Students start with a very small set of assumptions about this function and try to build an understanding of how any function that satisfies this equation must behave. The level of restriction is pretty surprising, actually.

Functional equations can be found in many places: Exercise 11 gives several examples of functional equations found throughout *Algebra 1* and *Algebra 2*. Several other functional equations are forthcoming, with one example being the rules for $\sin(x + y)$ and $\cos(x + y)$ in trigonometry.

Exercises

EXERCISES 1–3 These exercises slowly build some observations about g. Encourage students to plug in values for x and y to find information about the function. Letting $y = 1$ is a good choice, as this leads to the rule $g(x + 1) = g(x) \cdot b$ (since $g(1) = b$ is given).

EXERCISE 5 Part (b) is a summary exercise that requires students to show that $g(n) = bn$ for all negative integers. They should use a process similar to Exercise 3 to build $g(-2)$, then $g(-3)$, etc.

EXERCISE 8 Part (a) follows from Exercise 7. Students may notice at this point that they are following the same processes followed in Investigation 5A for establishing behaviors such as zero, negative, rational exponents. Students should use the result for

Project: Using Mathematical Habits

Functional Equations

Recall that a functional equation is an equation that relates some values of a function to other values of the function. In other words, the unknowns in a functional equation can be functions.

Suppose $f(x) = b^x$, with $b > 0$ and $b \neq 1$. Then you know that

- $f(1) = b$
- $f: \mathbb{R} \to \mathbb{R}$ is either strictly increasing (for $b > 1$) or strictly decreasing (for $0 < b < 1$)
- $f(x)$ satisfies the functional equation $f(x + y) = f(x) \cdot f(y)$

Conversely, suppose you are given an unknown function $g(x)$. All you know about $g(x)$ is that it satisfies the following three properties.

- $g(1) = b$, with $b > 0$
- $g: \mathbb{R} \to \mathbb{R}$ is strictly increasing
- $g(x)$ satisfies the functional equation $g(x + y) = g(x) \cdot g(y)$

Can you conclude that $g(x) = b^x$, with $b > 1$?

1. Show that $g(0) = 1$. (*Hint:* $0 + 1 = 1$)

2. Show that $b > 1$.

3. Show that each equation is true.

   a. $g(4) = b \cdot g(3)$

   b. $g(4) = b^2 \cdot g(2)$

   c. $g(4) = b^4$

   d. $g(n) = b^n$, for any nonnegative integer n

4. Show that for nonnegative integers m and n, $g(mn) = (g(m))^n$.

5. a. Show that $g(-1) = \frac{1}{b}$. (*Hint:* $1 + (-1) = 0$)

   b. Show that $g(n) = b^n$, for all integers n.

6. Let n be a positive integer. Show that

$$g\left(\left(\tfrac{1}{n}\right)\right)^n = b$$

7. Suppose $n = 4$ and $b = 81$. You know $g\left(\frac{1}{4}\right)$ must be a real number, because you assume that $\mathbb{R}$ is the target of g. From Exercise 6, you know $g\left(\frac{1}{4}\right)$ is a real number satisfying the equation below.

$$\left(g\left(\tfrac{1}{4}\right)\right)^4 = 81$$

So $g\left(\frac{1}{4}\right) = 3$ or -3.

   a. Use the fact that $g(x)$ is increasing to explain why $g\left(\frac{1}{4}\right)$ must equal 3 and not -3.

   b. Andy gives another reason why $g\left(\frac{1}{4}\right)$ must equal 3. He says, "Suppose we set $g\left(\frac{1}{4}\right) = -3$. Then $g\left(\frac{1}{8}\right)$ is not a real number, which doesn't work." Explain Andy's reasoning.

8. a. Show that $g(x) = b^x$ for all rational numbers x.

   b. Show that $g(x) = b^x$ for all real numbers x.

9. Suppose $h(x)$ has all the properties that $g(x)$ has, except that $h(x)$ is strictly decreasing. Show that $h(x) = b^x$ and $0 < b < 1$.

10. Suppose $k(x)$ has all the properties that $g(x)$ has, except that $k(x)$ does not have to be monotonic. Can you still conclude that $k(x) = b^x$?

11. Match each function in column A with a functional equation in column B.

A	B
$x \mapsto 2^x$	$f(a + b) = f(a) + f(b)$
$z \mapsto \lvert z \rvert$	$f(a + b) = f(a) \cdot f(b)$
$z \mapsto \arg z$	$f(ab) = f(a) \cdot f(b)$
$x \mapsto 2x$	$f(ab) = f(a) + f(b)$
$x \mapsto \log_3 x$	

Answers

Project

1. Use $g(x + y) = g(x) \cdot g(y)$ with $x = 1$ and $y = 0$. This gives $g(1 + 0) = g(1) \cdot g(0)$, or $g(1) = g(1) \cdot g(0)$. Since $g(1) = b$, and $b > 0$, you can divide both sides by $g(1)$, resulting in $g(0) = 1$.

2. g is strictly increasing, so since $1 > 0$, $g(1) > g(0)$. Replacing $g(1)$ with b(given) and $g(0)$ with 1 (see part (a)) gives $b > 1$.

3. a. $g(4) = g(1 + 3) = g(1) \cdot g(3) = b \cdot g(3)$

   b. $g(4) = b \cdot g(3) = b \cdot g(1 + 2) = b \cdot [g(1) \cdot g(2)] = b \cdot [b \cdot g(2)] = b^2 \cdot g(2)$

   c. $g(4) = b^2 \cdot g(2) = b^2 \cdot g(1 + 1) = b^2 \cdot g(1) \cdot g(1) = b^2 \cdot b \cdot b = b^4$

   d. Answers may vary. Sample: This proof uses mathematical induction. (i) If $n = 0$, then $g(n) = b^n$ because $g(0) = b^0 = 1$ (from part (a)). (ii) Assume $g(m) = b^m$. Then $g(m + 1) = g(m) \cdot g(1) = b^m \cdot b = b^{m+1}$. Therefore, if the property is true for the integer m, it is also true for the integer $m + 1$. So, since $g(n) = b^n$ is true for $n = 0$, $g(n) = b^n$ for all nonnegative integers n.

4. Because m and n are nonnegative integers, mn is also a nonnegative integer. Then by Exercise 3c, $g(mn) = b^{mn}$ and $g(m) = b^m$. So, $g(mn) = b^{mn} = (b^m)^n = (g(m))^n$.

5–11. See back of book.

Chapter 5

Review

Go Online PHSchool.com

For vocabulary review, go to Web Code: bfj-0551

In **Investigation 5A,** you learned how to

- evaluate expressions involving exponents, including zero, negative, and rational exponents
- find the missing terms in a geometric sequence and make a geometric sequence to interpret expressions involving rational exponents
- convert between exponential and radical forms for rational exponents

The following questions will help you check your understanding.

1. Write each expression as a single power of x. Assume $x \neq 0$.

a. $x^{-2} \cdot x^{-1}$ **b.** $\left(\frac{1}{x}\right)^{-2}$

c. $((x^3)^{-2})^{-5}$ **d.** $\frac{x^4}{x^{-4}}$

e. $(x^6)^0 \cdot x^3$ **f.** $\frac{(x^5)(x^{-2})}{x^{10}}$

2. Find the missing terms in each geometric sequence.

a. 5, 20, ■, ■, ■

b. 6, ■, 24, ■, ■

c. 1, ■, 6, ■

d. 1, ■, ■, 125

e. Use the sequence in part (d) to find $125^{\frac{2}{3}}$.

3. Simplify each expression.

a. $49^{\frac{1}{2}}$ **b.** $81^{\frac{3}{4}}$

c. $8^{-\frac{4}{3}}$ **d.** $\left(\sqrt[4]{16}\right)^5$

In **Investigation 5B,** you learned how to

- graph an exponential function and determine the equation of an exponential function given two points on its graph
- identify an exponential function from the table it generates and use the table to write a closed-form or recursive definition of the function
- evaluate the inverse of the function $y = b^x$, either exactly or by approximation

The following questions will help you check your understanding.

4. a. Suppose f is an exponential function with $f(2) = \frac{9}{2}$ and $f(3) = \frac{27}{2}$. Find $f(x)$.

b. Sketch the graph of $y = f(x)$.

5. Copy this table for the exponential function $g(x)$.

x	$g(x)$	÷
0	−2	■
1	−20	■
2	−200	■
3	−2000	

a. Complete the ratio column and write a recursive definition for $g(x)$.

b. Write a closed-form definition for $g(x)$.

c. Find $g(4)$ and $g(6)$.

6. Let $L_4(x)$ be the inverse of the function $h(x) = 4^x$.

a. Find $L_4(1)$.

b. Find $L_4(64)$.

c. Find $L_4\left(\frac{1}{16}\right)$.

$x = \frac{1}{n}$ to build a result for any rational $x = \frac{m}{n}$. Part (b) is more challenging, and students can use the same argument used in Investigation 5A. Consider assigning this part only to some advanced students.

EXERCISE 11 Even if you are not assigning this project, this is a good exercise to explore, and you might ask students to find more functional equations besides these (or, other functions that satisfy particular functional equations).

Chapter Review

1. a. x^{-3} **b.** x^2 **c.** x^{30}

d. x^8 **e.** x^3 **f.** x^{-7}

2. a. 5, 20, **80**, **320**, **1280**

b. 6, **12**, 24, **48**, **96** or 6, **−12**, 24, **−48**, **96**

c. 1, $\sqrt{6}$, 6, $6\sqrt{6}$ or 1, $-\sqrt{6}$, 6, $-\sqrt{6}$

d. 1, **5**, **25**, 125

e. 25

3. a. 7 **b.** 27 **c.** $\frac{1}{16}$ **d.** 32

4. a. $f(x) = \frac{1}{2} \cdot 3^x$

b.

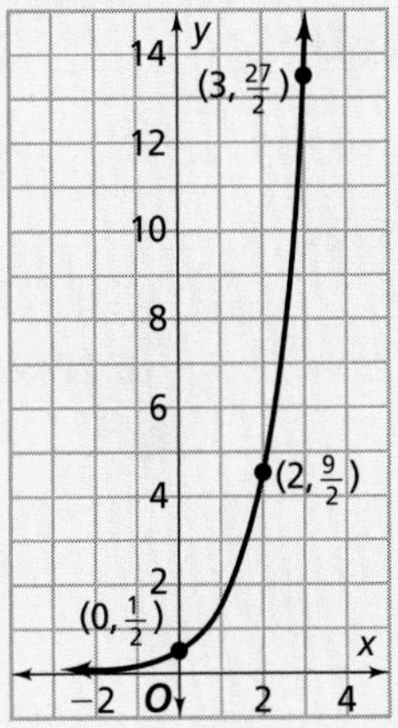

5. a.

x	$g(x)$	÷
0	−2	10
1	−20	10
2	−200	10
3	−2000	

$$g(x) = \begin{cases} -2 & \text{if } x = 0 \\ 10 \cdot g(x-1) & \text{if } x > 0 \end{cases}$$

b. $g(x) = -2 \cdot 10^x$

c. $g(4) = -20{,}000$

$g(6) = -2{,}000{,}000$

6. a. 0 **b.** 3 **c.** −2

In **Investigation 5C,** you learned how to

- evaluate logarithms of any base using a calculator
- use logarithms to solve exponential equations
- graph logarithmic functions

The following questions will help you check your understanding.

7. Arrange the following numbers in order from least to greatest.

$\log_2 16, \log 5, \log_3 8, \log_4 \frac{1}{8}, \log_{\frac{1}{2}} 16$

8. Solve each equation. Give decimal answers to three places.

a. $\log x - \log 5 = \log 15$

b. $\log_2 (x - 1) + \log_2 (x + 1) = 3$

c. $5^x = 7$

d. $3 \cdot 2^x = 20$

9. Let $f(x) = \log_3 x$ and $g(x) = -2x + 3$.

a. Graph $f(x)$ and $g(x)$ on the same set of axes.

b. From the graph, determine the number of solutions to the equation $\log_3 x = -2x + 3$.

c. Use the graph to estimate the solution(s) to $\log_3 x = -2x + 3$.

Answers

7. $\log_{\frac{1}{2}} 16, \log_4 \frac{1}{8}$, $\log 5, \log_3 8, \log_2 16$

8. a. 75 **b.** 3
c. 1.209 **d.** 2.737

9. a.

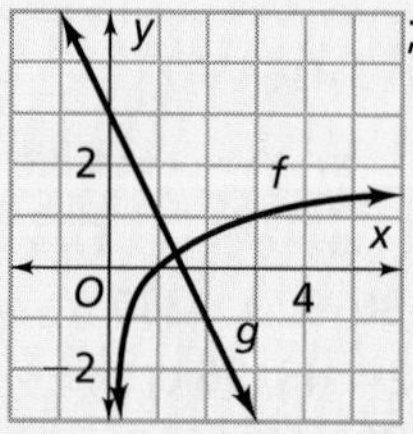

b. one
c. about 1.4

Chapter Test

1. A **2.** D **3.** D **4.** C

Chapter 5 Test

Go Online PHSchool.com — For chapter test, go to Web Code: bfa-0553

Multiple Choice

1. Which of the following expressions is NOT equal to 1?

   A. $(2^3)^{\frac{1}{3}}$ B. $\frac{5^2 \cdot 5^4}{(5^2)^3}$

   C. $3^2 \cdot 3^{-2}$ D. $\left(\frac{1}{2}\right)^{-1} \cdot 2^{-1}$

2. Let $3^m = 2$. Find 3^{m+1}.

   A. 3 B. 4

   C. 5 D. 6

3. Which of the following expressions represents the smallest number?

   A. $25^{\frac{1}{2}}$ B. 4^{-2}

   C. $\log_2 8$ D. $\log_{\frac{1}{2}} 8$

4. Which of the following expressions is NOT equal to $\log_2 (60)$?

   A. $\log_2 10 + \log_2 6$

   B. $\log_2 120 - \log_2 2$

   C. $\log_2 30 \cdot \log_2 2$

   D. $\log_2 12 + \log_2 5$

5. Which point is on the graph of $f(x) = \log_3 x$?

   A. (0, 1) B. (2, 9)

   C. (9, 2) D. (60, 20)

Open Response

6. Copy this table for the exponential function $h(x)$.

   a. Complete the ratio column.

   b. Find a recursive definition for $h(x)$.

   c. Find a closed-form definition for $h(x)$.

   d. Find the exact value of $h(8)$.

x	$h(x)$	÷
0	6	■
1	3	■
2	$\frac{3}{2}$	■
3	$\frac{3}{4}$	■
4	$\frac{3}{8}$	

7. Use the two function definitions below.

$$f(x) = 4^x$$
$$g(x) = \log_4 x$$

   a. Copy and complete each table.

x	$f(x)$
−1	■
0	■
$\frac{1}{2}$	■
1	■
2	■

x	$g(x)$
$\frac{1}{4}$	■
1	■
2	■
4	■

   b. On a single set of axes, sketch the graphs of f and g.

   c. Is the graph of f increasing or decreasing?

   d. Is the graph of g increasing or decreasing?

8. Suppose $N = \log_2 28$.

   a. Find two consecutive integers j and k such that $j < N < k$.

   b. Express $\log_2 7$ in terms of N. (*Hint:* $7 = \frac{28}{4}$)

   c. Find the value of N to three decimal places.

9. Solve each equation. Give exact answers when possible, or round your answer to three decimal places.

   a. $x \cdot 16^{\frac{1}{2}} = 64^{\frac{4}{3}}$

   b. $45 = 5 \cdot 27^x$

   c. $2 \cdot 7^x = 24$

   d. $\log x + \log (x - 2) = \log 8$

10. If you invest $10,000 at 5.5% interest, compounded annually, how many years will it take until your money grows to $15,000?

11. Let $f(x) = b^x$. Explain why $f(m) \cdot f(n) = f(m + n)$.

---

5. C

6. a. See back of book.

b. $h(x) = \begin{cases} 6 & \text{if } x = 0 \\ \frac{1}{2} \cdot h(x-1) & \text{if } x > 0 \end{cases}$

c. $h(x) = 6 \cdot \left(\frac{1}{2}\right)^x$

d. $\frac{3}{128}$

7. a–b. See back of book.

c. increasing

d. increasing

8. a. 4 and 5

b. $N - 2$

c. 4.807

9. a. 64

b. $\frac{2}{3}$

c. $\frac{\log 12}{\log 7} \approx 1.277$

d. 4

10. 8 yr

11. $f(m) \cdot f(n) = b^m \cdot b^n = b^{m+n} = f(m + n)$

Chapter Test

Assessment Resources

Chapter Test page 1

Multiple Choice

1. Which of the following expressions is equal to 1?
   A. $(3^2)^{-2}$
   B. $\frac{3^2}{3^{-2}}$
   C. $3^2 \cdot 3^{-2}$
   D. $3 \cdot \left(\frac{1}{3}\right)^0$

2. Let $3^m = 5$. Find 3^{2m}.
   A. $\frac{10}{3}$
   B. 15
   C. 25
   D. 30

3. Which of the following expressions represents the greatest number?
   A. $9^{\frac{3}{2}}$
   B. 3^{-2}
   C. $\log_2 32$
   D. $\log_{\frac{1}{3}} 9$

4. Which of the following expressions is NOT equal to log 24?
   A. $\log 10 \cdot \log 14$
   B. $\log 48 - \log 2$
   C. $\log 12 + \log 2$
   D. $\log 6 + \log 4$

5. Which point is NOT on the graph of $f(x) = \log_2 x$?
   A. (0, 1)
   B. (4, 2)
   C. (8, 3)
   D. (32, 5)

Chapter Test page 2

Open Response

6. Use the table for the exponential function $h(x)$.
   a. Complete the ratio column.
   b. Find a recursive definition for $h(x)$.
   c. Find a closed-form definition for $h(x)$.
   d. Find the exact value of $h(6)$.

x	$h(x)$	÷
0	3	
1	12	
2	48	
3	192	

7. Use the two function definitions below.
   $f(x) = 9^x$
   $g(x) = \log_9 x$
   a. Complete each table at the right.
   b. On a single set of axes, sketch the graphs of f and g.
   c. Is the graph of f increasing or decreasing?
   d. Is the graph of g increasing or decreasing?

x	$f(x)$
−1	
0	
$\frac{1}{2}$	
1	
2	

x	$g(x)$
$\frac{1}{9}$	
1	
3	
9	

8. Suppose $N = \log_2 10$.
   a. Find two consecutive integers j and k such that $j < N < k$.
   b. Express $\log_2 40$ in terms of N. (*Hint:* $40 = 10 \cdot 4$)
   c. Find the value of N to three decimal places.

9. Solve each equation. Give exact answers when possible, or round your answer to three decimal places.
   a. $x \cdot 27^{\frac{2}{3}} = 81^{\frac{1}{2}}$
   b. $40 = 5 \cdot 16^x$
   c. $5^x = 20$
   d. $\log x + \log 4 = 2$

10. If you invest $5000 at 5% interest, compounded annually, how many years will it take until your money grows to $10,000?

11. What are some reasons to use logarithms?

Also available: Form B

Chapter 6 Graphs and Transformations

In this chapter, students extend the graphing skills they learned in CME Project *Algebra 1* and *Geometry* to include more kinds of graphs. They also learn to recognize transformations of these graphs and to connect translations, scalings, reflections, and affine transformations to their effects on the graphs and their equations. Students learn how to recognize affine transformations of the basic graphs and how to find affine transformations that, when applied to an equation, can transform it into one of the basic graph forms. Then they learn to graph transformed basic graphs by "replacing the axes." In this technique, they use the simple linear relationship between the original variable and the substitution to relabel the axes. Then, by interpreting these graphs, they can locate critical points and describe the transformed graph or make a standard graph of the equation.

Chapter Overview

INVESTIGATION 6A, *Transforming Basic Graphs,* has students transform basic graphs using translations, scalings, and reflections over an axis.

INVESTIGATION 6B, *Affine Transformations,* introduces students to affine transformations, which are compositions of two types of functions, translations T_a, and dilations D_s.

INVESTIGATION 6C, *Graphing Using Affine Transformations,* has students use affine transformations to rewrite an equation in the form of a basic graph, and then graph the equation using the replacing-the-axes method.

For more information on the investigations, see

- Chapter Road Map, pp. 498–499
- Investigation Road Maps, pp. 500, 532, 556

PROJECT The Project near the end of the chapter is optional. You can assign the Project at any time during the chapter depending on how often and how long you feel students should work on it.

DAILY PLANNER DAILY PLANNER DAILY PL

Pacing Suggestions and Materials

Investigation 6A ***Transforming Basic Graphs***

DAY	LESSON	HOMEWORK
1	6.1 Getting Started Core: 1, 2, 3, 4, 5, 8, 9, 10 Optional: 6, 7; Extension: 11	Core: 12, 13, 14, 15, 16, 17, 18, 19, 20 Optional: 21, 22, 23, 24, 25
2	6.2 More Basic Graphs Core: 1, 2, 4, 5, 6, 8 Optional: 3, 7	Core: 9, 10, 11, 12, 13, 14, 15, 17 Optional: 18, 19; Extension: 16
3	6.3 Translating Graphs Core: 1, 2, 3, 4, 6, 7 Optional: 5	Core: 8a–c, 9, 10, 11, 12, 13, 15 Optional: 16; Extension: 8d, 14
4	6.4 Scaling and Reflecting Graphs Core: 1, 2, 3, 4, 6, 7, 9 Optional: 5; Extension: 8	Core: 10, 11, 12, 14, 15 Optional: 13, 16, 19; Extension: 17, 18

Investigation 6B ***Affine Transformations***

DAY	LESSON	HOMEWORK
1	6.5 Getting Started Core: 1, 2, 3, 4, 5 Optional: 6	Core: 7, 8, 9, 10, 11, 12, 13, 14 Optional: 16, 17; Extension: 15
2	6.6 Introducing Affine Transformations Core: 1, 2, 3, 4, 6, 7 Optional: 5, 8	Core: 9, 10, 11, 13, 14, 15, 16, 17 Optional: 12, 18, 19, 20a–b, 21, 22, 23 Extension: 20c
3	6.7 Transforming Equations Core: 1, 2, 3, 4, 6 Optional: none; Extension: 5	Core: 7, 8, 10, 11, 12, 13 Optional: 9, 15, 16; Extension: 14

NOTES	MATERIALS
	• graph paper • graphing calculators
	• graph paper • graphing calculators • Blackline Masters 6.2A–C
	• graph paper • graphing calculators • Blackline Master 6.3A
	• graph paper • graphing calculators • Blackline Masters 6.4A, 6.4B

NOTES	MATERIALS
	• graph paper • graphing calculators

Mathematics Background

MULTI-PURPOSE TOOLS One common thread throughout the CME Project curriculum is the idea that students should not memorize long lists of specialized techniques but rather develop flexible algorithms and tools that are useful in many different contexts. To this end, students add a few new graphs to the list of basic graphs they learned about in *Algebra 1*: exponential graphs, logarithm graphs, and the graphs of $x^2 + y^2 = 1$, $y = x^2 + x$, and $y = x^3 - x$. Then students learn how to recognize transformations of these basic graphs and to associate transformations of a graph with particular kinds of changes to its equation. This skill allows students to graph a wide range of complex equations with a small set of flexible strategies and minimal memorization.

Instead of learning a standard form for each type of basic graph, a method for getting each type of graph into its special form, and then learning to interpret those forms to sketch the graph, students learn general techniques for recognizing which basic graph is appropriate for a given equation. They transform the given equation into one of the basic graph forms and graph these transformed equations.

Students also make connections to previously learned powerful techniques. For example, students know how to make an equation *monic* through a substitution so they can factor it more easily. They use that same technique here as part of the process of transforming an equation into one of the basic graph forms, and they recognize it as a dilation. Students know how to use *completing the square* to solve quadratic equations. In this chapter, they use completing the square to transform an equation and recognize it as a translation. Students have made tables for functions since their earliest study of mathematics, and they use this skill in this chapter to create pairs of number lines that are related by an affine transformation—a function of the form

$$\mathcal{A}_{(a,\, b)}(x) = ax + b$$

In fact, affine transformations are the linear functions that students studied in CME Project *Algebra 1*, considered from a different perspective. In this course, the emphasis is on the algebraic structure of the set of transformations of the form $x \mapsto ax + b$ and whose operation is function composition. Chapter 2 introduced students to the idea of "algebra with functions." In this chapter, they look more closely at this idea.

Students examine translation functions T_a and dilation functions D_s as transformations of the number line, for example, T_4 translates the number to the right by 4 units, and D_5 dilates (stretches) the number line by the factor 5. Thinking about linear functions as transformations helps bring together many of the ideas about graph transformations.

continued on p. 498c

continued from p. 498b

ALGEBRAIC STRUCTURE Like Chapter 3 (Complex Numbers) and Chapter 4 (Linear Algebra), this chapter exposes students to new kinds of algebraic objects—translations, dilations, and affine transformations. By now, when students see these new objects, they should be asking themselves questions like these:

- What operations can you use on these objects?
- Are these objects commutative under this operation?
- What is the identity?
- Do these objects have inverses?

Since translations, dilations, and affine transformations are all functions, the natural operation for students to think about is function composition.

Students prove that translations commute under function composition and that dilations also commute under function composition. Students see parallels to the operations of addition and multiplication in these transformations. They connect the structure of compositions of translations to addition of real numbers and the structure of compositions of dilations to multiplication of real numbers.

However, affine transformations, which are compositions of a translation and a dilation, do not commute under function composition. As with matrices, the fact that affine transformations are not commutative introduces some complexity to calculations involving them, because composing an affine transformation on the left usually produces a different result than composing it on the right. However, many of the ideas that proved useful when dealing with matrices and matrix multiplication prove useful again when dealing with affine transformations. The connections between the two situations will enrich students' understanding of both topics.

Once they know the identity transformation, students can start to think about inverses. Again, there are parallels to the structures of addition and multiplication when considering inverses of translations and dilations, respectively. When thinking about the inverse of an affine transformation—which is itself a composition of a translation and a dilation—students undo the process by undoing each step in reverse order. In an affine transformation, you apply a dilation and then a translation. In the inverse of an affine transformation, you apply the inverse of the translation first and then the inverse of the dilation.

In Lesson 6.10, Advanced Affine Transformations, students delve even deeper into the algebraic structure of affine transformations. They consider what points are fixed by an affine transformation, and then they turn that question inside out to consider what collection of affine transformations

Pacing Suggestions and Materials

Investigation 6C *Graphing Using Affine Transformations*

DAY	LESSON	HOMEWORK
1	6.8 Getting Started Core: 1, 3, 4, 5, 6 Optional: 2	Core: 7, 8, 9, 10, 11 Optional: 12, 13, 14
2	6.9 Replacing the Axes Core: 1, 2, 3, 4, 6, 8, 10 Optional: 5, 7, 9	Core: 11, 14, 15, 18, 20, 21, 22 Optional: 12, 13, 16, 17, 19, 23
3	6.10 Advanced Affine Transformations Core: 1, 2, 5, 6 Optional: 3, 4	Core: 7, 8, 9a–b, 10, 11, 12 Optional: 14; Extension: 9c, 13

	NOTES	MATERIALS
		• CAS (recommended) • graph paper • graphing calculators
		• graph paper • graphing calculators • Blackline Masters 6.8, 6.9A–C
	This is an optional lesson.	• graph paper • graphing calculators • Blackline Master 6.10

fixes a given point. Through this exploration, they also discover conditions under which a particular subset of affine transformations does commute with function composition.

COMPLETING THE SQUARE ON THE CUBIC When students were learning how to solve quadratic equations in CME Project *Algebra 1,* they used the technique of *completing the square*. This transformed an equation of the form $x^2 + bx = c$, which was difficult to solve, into an equation of the form $M^2 = d$. To do this, they figured out the constant term that would make $x^2 + bx$ into a perfect square. By adding $\frac{b^2}{4}$ to both sides of the equation, they ended up with a perfect square on one side and a constant on the other. Their transformed equation was of the form $M^2 = d$, with $M = x + \frac{b}{2}$ and $d = c + \frac{b^2}{4}$. This new equation is much easier to solve. Students also used completing the square as part of their proof of the quadratic formula.

However, students can think of completing the square more generally as the process of getting rid of any term that causes trouble. In a quadratic equation, calculations are much simpler if there is no linear term. So, through a substitution of $M = x + \frac{b}{2}$, which students in this chapter recognize as a translation in x, they transform the original equation into a new equation that has no linear term. Similarly, in a cubic equation (or in fact in an equation of any degree), they can use a translation in x to get rid of the quadratic term.

Students have become familiar with three basic graph forms for cubic equations: $y = x^3$, $y = x^3 + x$, and $y = x^3 - x$. None of these basic graph forms has a quadratic term, so that is the goal of "completing the square" on the cubic: to find the translation substitution that transforms an equation of the form $y = x^3 + ax^2 + bx + c$ into a new equation of the form $N = M^3 + dM$. Students use a general translation $M = T_k(x)$ and then figure out the value of k that eliminates the quadratic term.

Developing Students' Mathematical Habits

Key mathematical habits in this chapter include:

VISUALIZATION Students visualize graphs as transformations of the basic graphs, seeing them as translations, scalings, and reflections or as compositions of these transformations.

MAKING CONNECTIONS Students experiment with changes to an equation and connect the resulting changes in the graph to the type of change in the equation. For example, if every instance of x in the equation of a basic graph is replaced by $x - 4$, the resulting graph is the image of the basic graph after a translation of 4 units to the right—no matter which basic graph they transform in this way.

LOGICAL REASONING When faced with new kinds of functions—translations, dilations, and affine transformations—students ask questions about their algebraic structure, develop conjectures to answer those questions, and use logical reasoning to prove their conjectures.

Chapter Road Map

INVESTIGATION 6A, *Transforming Basic Graphs,* introduces three new graphs that students add to their collection of basic graphs from CME Project *Algebra 1* and the exponential and logarithm graphs that they learned about in Chapter 5. Students practice graphing the basic graphs and transformations of these graphs. Students learn to relate changes to the equation of a basic graph to translations, scalings, and reflections over one of the axes of the graph. In this investigation, students see a transformation as acting on a graph. The new graph is the image of the basic graph after a transformation.

INVESTIGATION 6B, *Affine Transformations,* has students learn how to transform equations into the basic graph forms through compositions of strategic translations and dilations. They make connections between these transformations and the techniques they used to factor and solve quadratic equations in CME Project *Algebra 1*.

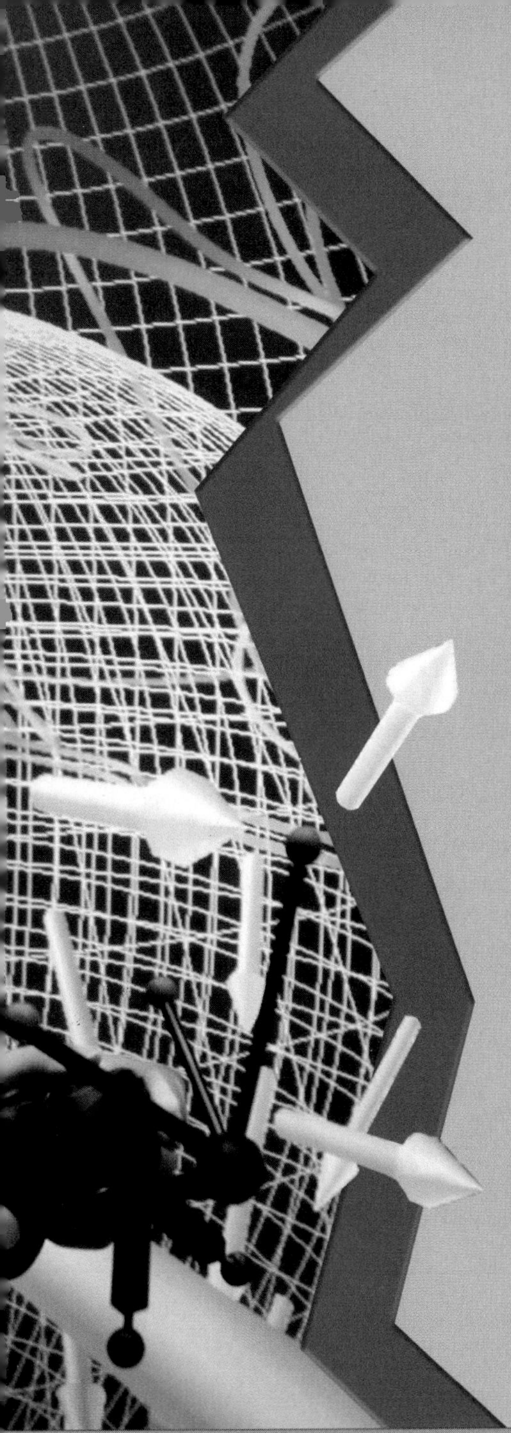

Graphs and Transformations

The field of computer graphics depends heavily on mathematics, because mathematics is the language that computers speak. Computers store drawings as a series of coordinate pairs or triples, along with functions that define relationships and connections between them. In other words, every drawing is a graph.

You can animate a computer drawing using transformations of these graphs.

- Translations produce an identical copy of a drawing in a different location.
- Dilations produce a mathematically similar copy of a drawing that can be larger or smaller than the original.
- Reflections produce a mirror image of a drawing. A line acts as the mirror.
- Rotations produce an identical copy of a drawing that is turned relative to some center of rotation.

In this chapter, you will explore how changes in an equation result in transformations of its graph and how a transformation applied to a graph changes its equation. Computer animators use transformations to make objects appear to move and change shape. They do this either by manipulating the equations that define them or by using tools to change the object directly while the computer keeps track of the calculations. The work you will do in this chapter is at the foundation of computer graphics.

Vocabulary and Notation

- **affine recursive definition**
- **affine transformation, $\mathcal{A}_{(a,\,b)}$**
- **completing the square**
- **dilation, D_s**
- **even function**
- **fixed point**
- **identity transformation**
- **iteration**
- **odd function**
- **reflection transformation**
- **stabilizer, S_x**
- **translation, T_a**
- **unit circle**

INVESTIGATION 6C, *Graphing Using Affine Transformations,* has students connect what they have learned in Investigations 6A and 6B to develop a technique for graphing any equation that they can transform into one of the basic graph forms. They do this by using affine transformation substitutions to "replace the axes" in a basic graph. Then they interpret their graph in its transformed coordinate plane. This represents a new approach to graphing transformations. Instead of changing the graph, students change the perspective from which they view the graph. They see the transformation as acting on the coordinate system rather than on the graph.

Chapter Vocabulary and Notation

The following list gives key vocabulary and notation used in the chapter. Selected new vocabulary and notation items are shown in boldface on the student page.

- affine recursive function, p. 574
- affine transformation, $\mathcal{A}_{(a,\,b)}$, p. 540
- completing the square, p. 546
- dilation, D_s, pp. 534, 537
- even function, p. 510
- fixed point, p. 571
- identity transformation, p. 533
- intercept, p. 511
- iteration, p. 573
- odd function, p. 510
- reflection transformation, p. 534
- replacing-the-axes method, p. 560
- socks and shoes method, p. 542
- stabilizer, S_x, p. 573
- translation, T_a, pp. 533, 536
- unit circle, p. 506

Chapter Technology

CME Project *Algebra 2* assumes that each student has access to a graphing calculator. It also recommends access to a computer algebra system (CAS).

Support for the use of technology is available in the TI-Nspire™ Technology Handbook. See p. 778.

A list of technology used with important concepts in this chapter appears below. Students will need access to the functionality listed to develop complete understanding of these topics.

Function-Modeling Language

LESSON 6.6 Model affine transformations, p. 540.

Graphing Calculator

LESSON 6.1 Graph the absolute value function, p. 501.

LESSON 6.4 Graph equations in two variables, p. 527.

Investigation Overview

In this investigation, students review the basic graphs they studied in CME Project *Algebra 1.* They add a few new graphs to this list—the graphs of exponential and logarithm functions, which they studied in Chapter 5 of this course, and the graphs of the equations $x^2 + y^2 = 1$, $y = x^3 + x$, and $y = x^3 - x$. They analyze how certain changes to an equation affect its graph. They interpret these changes as translations, scalings, and reflections, recalling the work they did with transformations in both CME Project *Algebra 1* and *Geometry.* Students also begin thinking about compositions of transformations. Note that in this investigation, students are thinking of the coordinate system as static and the transformation as producing a new graph that is the image of the basic graph.

You may wish to assign Questions 1–3 for students to think and write about during the investigation.

Learning Goals

- Sketch basic graphs.
- Describe the effect of a translation of one of the basic graphs on both the graph and the equation of the graph.
- Describe the effect of scaling an axis or reflection of one of the basic graphs on both the graph and the equation of the graph.
- Compose transformations and sketch the effect of such a composition on one of the basic graphs.

Habits and Skills

- Visualize variations of the basic graphs under translations, reflections, scalings, and compositions of these transformations.
- Match a transformation of a graph to a corresponding transformation of its equation.
- Analyze the operation of function composition on transformations.

Investigation 6A

Transforming Basic Graphs

In *Transforming Basic Graphs*, you will sketch basic graphs. You will explore the effects, on both the graphs and on their equations of translating, stretching, shrinking, and reflecting the basic graphs.

By the end of this investigation, you will be able to answer questions like these.

1. How are the graphs of $y = x^2$ and $y = (x - 3)^2$ related?

2. What does the graph of $(x + 1)^2 + (y - 4)^2 = 36$ look like?

3. What does the graph of $-2y = x^3 - x$ look like?

You will learn how to

- sketch basic graphs
- describe the effect of a translation of one of the basic graphs on both the graph and the equation of the graph
- describe the effect of scaling an axis or reflection on both the graph and the equation of the graph
- compose transformations and sketch the effect of such a composition

You will develop these habits and skills:

- Visualize variations of the basic graphs under translations, reflections, scaling, and compositions of those transformations.
- Match a transformation of a graph to a corresponding transformation of its equation.
- Analyze the operation of function compositions on transformations.

One image is a stretch of the original figure. The other is a reflection. Can you tell which is which?

Investigation Road Map

LESSON 6.1, *Getting Started,* has students review graphing skills they learned in CME Project *Algebra 1.* They look at collections of related graphs.

LESSON 6.2, *More Basic Graphs,* has students look at a collection of basic graphs from this course and from CME Project *Algebra 1.* They examine the effects on the graphs of certain kinds of changes to the variable in the equation.

LESSON 6.3, *Translating Graphs,* formally introduces translations of the basic graphs. Students learn to recognize an equation of a translated graph.

LESSON 6.4, *Scaling and Reflecting Graphs,* has students extend their understanding of transformations to include scalings and reflections over the x- and y-axes. Students begin to consider compositions of transformations.

6.1 Getting Started

Activating Prior Knowledge
Exploring New Ideas

As you graph equations, you may notice that related equations have similar graphs.

For You to Explore

1. Sketch the graph of $y = x^2$.
2. Here are four equations related to $y = x^2$. Sketch the graph of each equation. Describe how the graph is related to the graph of $y = x^2$.
   a. $y + 5 = x^2$
   b. $y = (x + 5)^2$
   c. $y = x^2 + 5$
   d. $y - 3 = (x + 2)^2$
3. Sketch the graph of $y = x^3$.
4. Here are four equations related to $y = x^3$. Sketch the graph of each equation. Describe how the graph is related to the graph of $y = x^3$.
   a. $y + 5 = x^3$
   b. $y = (x + 5)^3$
   c. $y = x^3 + 5$
   d. $y - 3 = (x + 2)^3$
5. **Write About It** Compare the graphs of $y = x^2$ and $y = x^3$. In particular, address the following questions.
   - What type of symmetry does each graph have?
   - Through which quadrants does each graph pass?
   - How do the graphs compare near the origin? Away from the origin?
6. Sketch the graph of $y = \sqrt{x}$.
7. Here are four equations related to $y = \sqrt{x}$. Sketch the graph of each equation. Describe how the graph is related to the graph of $y = \sqrt{x}$.
   a. $y + 5 = \sqrt{x}$
   b. $y = \sqrt{x + 5}$
   c. $y = \sqrt{x} + 5$
   d. $y - 3 = \sqrt{x + 2}$
8. Sketch the graph of $y = |x|$, the absolute value function.
9. Here are four equations related to $y = |x|$. Sketch the graph of each equation. Describe how the graph is related to the graph of $y = |x|$.
   a. $y + 5 = |x|$
   b. $y = |x + 5|$
   c. $y = |x| + 5$
   d. $y - 3 = |x + 2|$
10. a. Sketch the graph of $y = 3^x$ and $y = \log_3 x$ on the same axes.
    b. How are the two graphs related?
11. **Take It Further** Find three different equations with graphs that pass through the points (6, 0) and (−3, 0).

For help defining the absolute value function, see the TI-Nspire Handbook, p. 778.

Answers

For You to Explore

1–4. See back of book.

5. $y = x^2$ has the y-axis as a line of symmetry, while $y = x^3$ has 180° rotational symmetry about the origin; $y = x^2$ passes through Quadrants I and II, while $y = x^3$ passes through Quadrants I and III; answers may vary. Sample: Near the origin, it is difficult to distinguish between $y = x^2$ and $y = x^3$ for positive x-values, and for negative x-values the graphs look almost like reflections of each other over the x-axis. Away from the origin, $y = x^3$ is steeper than $y = x^2$.

6–10. See back of book.

11. Answers may vary. Sample:
$y = 0,\ y = (x - 6)(x + 3),$
$y = x(x - 6)(x + 3)$

Lesson Overview

GOAL

- Sketch basic graphs.

This lesson asks students to remember some of their basic graphing skills from CME Project *Algebra 1* and *Geometry* by graphing collections of related graphs that push them to remember their work with translations. Decide when you want students to use their graphing calculators in your class. Make sure that students know how to graph a function and how to set the viewing window in their calculators.

FOR YOU TO EXPLORE
- Core: 1, 2, 3, 4, 5, 8, 9, 10
- Optional: 6, 7
- Extension: 11

MATERIALS
- graph paper
- graphing calculators

HOMEWORK
- Core: 12, 13, 14, 15, 16, 17, 18, 19, 20
- Optional: 21, 22, 23, 24, 25

Launch

Have students get started on the For You to Explore problems right away.

Explore

Check that students can translate the information from their graphing calculators onto a hand sketch of the graph. Listen for how students describe related graphs.

For You to Explore

PROBLEM 2 Students often have trouble predicting the direction of a translation. For example, many students might predict that the graph of $y = (x + 5)^2$ is the same as the graph of $y = x^2$, shifted 5 units to the right rather than to the left. Encourage students to predict what the graphs will look like before graphing them on their calculators.

PROBLEM 4 The parts of this problem correspond exactly to the parts of Problem 2, but this time the graph being transformed is $y = x^3$. Problems 7 and 9 show the same transformations on two other graphs. Hope students make connections, noting that when $x + 5$ replaces x in the equation, for example, the new graph is 5 units to the left of the old graph. Students may remember the term *translation* to describe this shift.

PROBLEM 5 Check students' descriptions of the symmetry of these graphs. Are they naming a line of symmetry when they say that a graph has reflection symmetry? Do they recognize rotational symmetry?

Wrap Up

Go over as many of the For You to Explore core problems as time allows. If you plan to assign Problems 8 and 9, make sure that students are able to define and graph the absolute value function on their calculators.

Exercises

HOMEWORK
- Core: 12, 13, 14, 15, 16, 17, 18, 19, 20
- Optional: 21, 22, 23, 24, 25

On Your Own

EXERCISES 12–15 preview the definitions of even and odd functions that students will see in Exercises 4 and 5 of Lesson 6.2.

EXERCISES 12 AND 13 Exercise 12 helps students recognize odd functions by their definition, because it shows the effect of replacing every point (x, y) by the point $(-x, -y)$. In Exercise 13, students think of F and G as a single figure O, and they must identify its symmetry. O has 180° rotational symmetry, which is a characteristic of odd functions.

EXERCISES 14 AND 15 Exercise 14 helps students recognize even functions by their definition, because they see the effect of replacing every point (x, y) by the point $(-x, y)$. In Exercise 15, students must think of figures F and H as a single figure E and identify its symmetry. E has the y-axis as a line of symmetry, which is a characteristic of even functions.

Exercises *Practicing Habits of Mind*

On Your Own

For Exercises 12–15, use this list of instructions.

- Connect endpoints (0, 0) and (3, 3).
- Connect endpoints (2, 2) and (3, 1).
- Connect endpoints (3, 3) and (5, 1).

12. **a.** Follow the instructions to plot figure F.

b. Make a new list of instructions by replacing each point (x, y) in the list above with the point $(-x, -y)$.

c. Follow your new instructions to plot figure G on the same set of axes.

d. Describe how figures F and G are related to each other.

13. Think of figures F and G from Exercise 12 together as a single figure O. What kind of symmetry does figure O have?

14. **a.** Follow the instructions to plot figure F again on a new set of axes.

b. Make a new list of instructions by replacing each point (x, y) in the list with the point $(-x, y)$.

c. Follow your new instructions to plot figure H on the same set of axes.

d. Describe how figures F and H are related to each other.

15. Think of figures F and H from Exercise 14 together as a single figure E. What kind of symmetry does figure E have?

16. Sketch each graph.

a. $y = x^2$ **b.** $y = x^2 + 7$

c. $y = x^2 - 3$ **d.** $y = x^2 - 10$

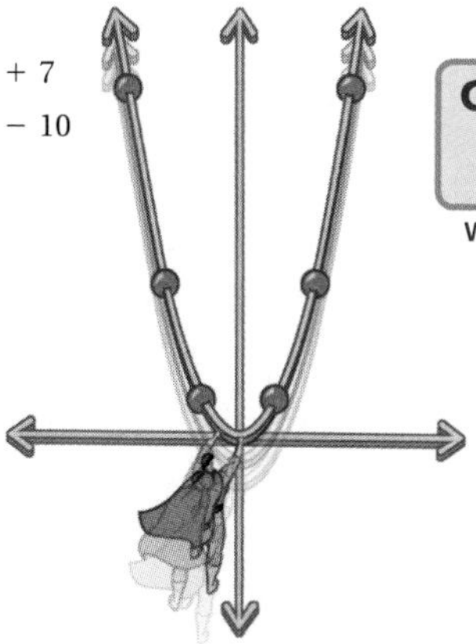

Go Online
Video Tutor
PHSchool.com

Web Code: bfe-0775

Answers

Exercises

12. a, c.

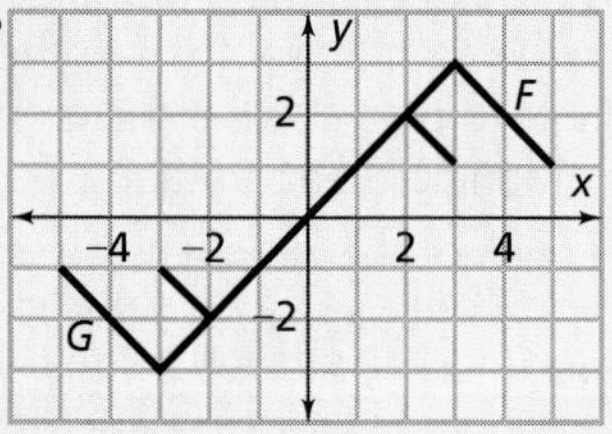

b. Connect (0, 0) and (−3, −3). Connect (−2, −2) and (−3, −1). Connect (−3, −3) and (−5, −1).

d. Figure G is figure F rotated 180° about the origin.

13. 180° rotational symmetry

14. a, c.

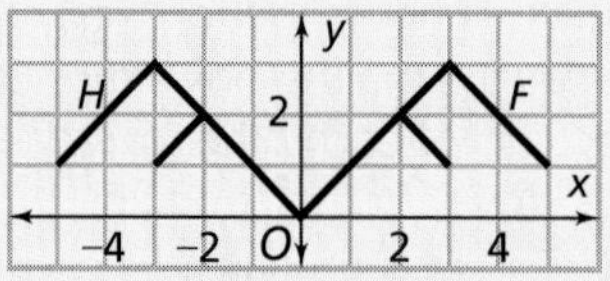

b. Connect (0, 0) and (−3, 3). Connect (−2, 2) and (−3, 1). Connect (−3, 3) and (−5, 1).

d. Figure G is figure F reflected over the y-axis.

15. line symmetry

16. a.

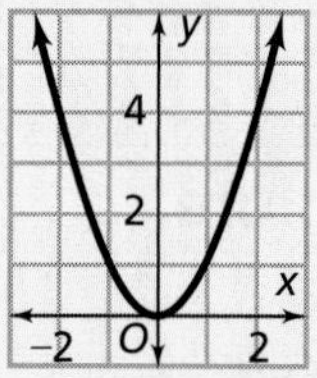

b.

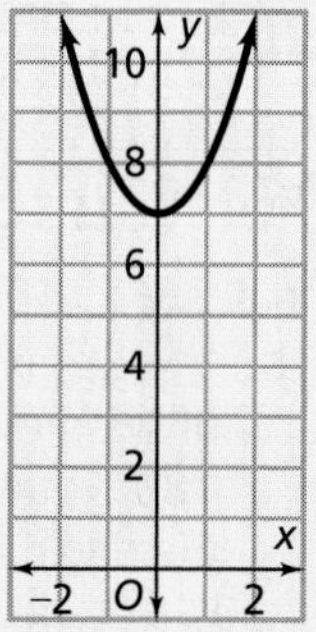

c.

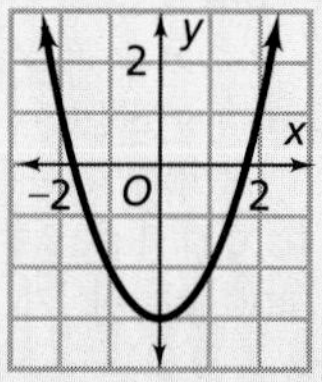

17. **Write About It** Describe the relationship between the graphs of $y = x^2$ and $y = x^2 + C$ for any number C.

18. Sketch each graph.

a. $y = |x|$ **b.** $y = |x| + 7$

c. $y = |x| - 3$ **d.** $y = |x| - 10$

19. **Write About It** Describe the relationship between the graphs of $y = |x|$ and $y = |x| + C$ for any number C.

20. Here are four equations related to $y = 3^x$. Sketch the graph of each equation. Describe how the graph is related to the graph of $y = 3^x$.

a. $y + 5 = 3^x$ **b.** $y = 3^{x+5}$

c. $y = 3^x + 5$ **d.** $y - 3 = 3^{x+2}$

21. **a.** Sketch the graph of $y = \frac{1}{x}$.

b. Explain why the graph never intersects the x-axis or the y-axis.

22. Here are four equations related to $y = \frac{1}{x}$. Sketch the graph of each equation. Describe how the graph is related to the graph of $y = \frac{1}{x}$.

a. $y + 5 = \frac{1}{x}$ **b.** $y = \frac{1}{x + 5}$

c. $y = \frac{1}{x} + 5$ **d.** $y - 3 = \frac{1}{x + 2}$

23. Plot all the points on the xy-plane that are exactly 1 unit from the origin.

You use the capital letter C here to show that C is a parameter rather than one of the variables you are graphing with. It is a value that you can change to produce different graphs. The idea is to see how different values of C change the graph.

Maintain Your Skills

24. Find the solutions to each equation.

a. $5x - 7 = 2x + 5$ **b.** $5 \cdot \frac{x}{3} - 7 = 2 \cdot \frac{x}{3} + 5$

c. $5 \cdot \frac{x}{10} - 7 = 2 \cdot \frac{x}{10} + 5$ **d.** $5 \cdot \frac{x}{100} - 7 = 2 \cdot \frac{x}{100} + 5$

25. Describe what happens to the solutions of an equation when you replace the variable x with $\frac{x}{C}$.

EXERCISE 17 Using one or more parameters, such as the parameter C in this exercise, allows you to think of "classes" of graphs. You can characterize all the graphs of the form $y = x^2 + C$ by noting the *effects* of different values of C on graphs of this form.

Maintain Your Skills

EXERCISE 20 As with the similar exercises in this lesson, students should recognize that the translations apply regardless of the original basic graph. In this case, the basic graph is $y = 3^x$. In parts (a), (c), and (d), the graph shifts vertically. Check that students correctly place the horizontal asymptote (which for the basic graph is the y-axis).

EXERCISE 23 This exercise is the focus of the Minds in Action dialog on page 505, so this is a good exercise to assign here. Some students will move through the exercise very quickly, while others may struggle and only plot the four points that lie on the axes. A point-tester proves useful here: if (x, y) satisfies the requirement, then what rule must it follow? (Answer: $x^2 + y^2 = 1$) Some students may also reason the graph is a circle by definition.

EXERCISE 25 asks students to frame a conjecture from the limited number of examples in Exercise 24. Students should be aware that this does not constitute a proof of this result.

d.

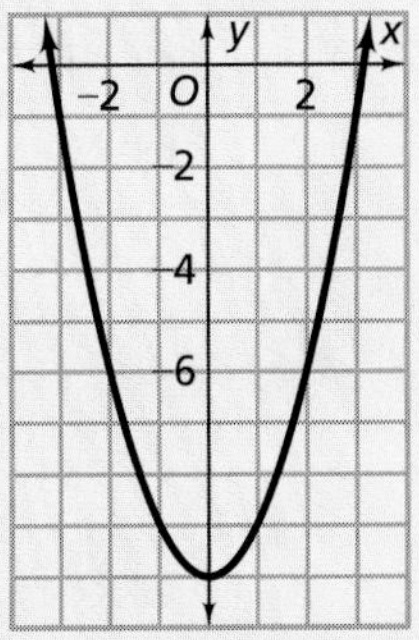

17. $y = x^2 + C$ is $y = x^2$ translated vertically C units. The graph shifts up if $C > 0$, and down if $C < 0$.

18–20. See back of book.

21. a.

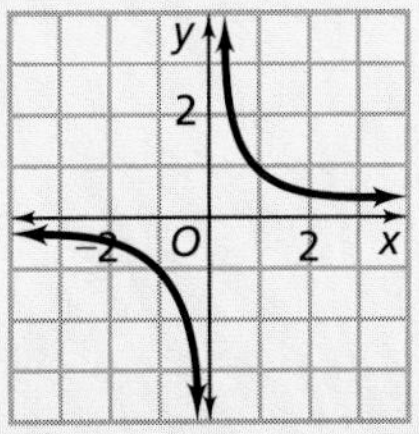

b. The graph never intersects the y-axis because x cannot be zero ($\frac{1}{0}$ is undefined). The graph never intersects the x-axis because y is never zero ($0 = \frac{1}{x}$ has no solution).

22. See back of book.

23.

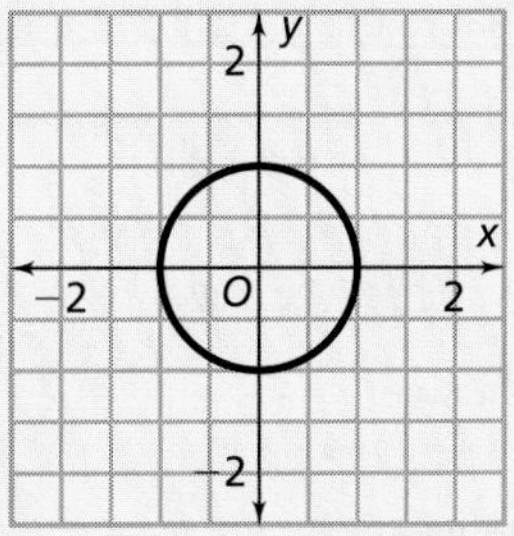

24. a. 4

b. 12

c. 40

d. 400

25. The solutions are multiplied by C.

Lesson Overview

GOAL

- Sketch basic graphs.

This lesson reminds students of the collection of basic graphs that they developed in CME Project *Algebra 1* and earlier in this course. They study three more graphs in detail: the graphs of $x^2 + y^2 = 1$, $y = x^3 + x$, and $y = x^3 - x$.

Students need to remember, as they learned in CME Project *Algebra 1,* that the equation of a graph is a "point-tester" for the graph. In other words, if the coordinates of a point satisfy the equation, then that point is on the graph of the equation.

CHECK YOUR UNDERSTANDING

- Core: 1, 2, 4, 5, 6, 8
- Optional: 3, 7

MATERIALS

- graph paper
- graphing calculators
- Blackline Masters 6.2A–C

HOMEWORK

- Core: 9, 10, 11, 12, 13, 14, 15, 17
- Optional: 18, 19
- Extension: 16

VOCABULARY

- even function
- intercept
- odd function
- unit circle

Launch

Begin today's lesson by going over the basic graphs. You can use Blackline Masters 6.2A and 6.2B to make transparencies to use while reviewing the basic graphs.

Use Lesson 6.1 to judge students' comfort with the eight graphs on these two pages. Do not spend too much time here unless the class seems to require it. If students need more review, list several characteristics of graphs and ask students to identify which of the basic graphs have each characteristic. Characteristics could include:

- passes through Quadrant II (Answer: all)
- passes through Quadrant IV (Answer: none)
- passes through (2, 4) (Answer: $y = x^2$)
- passes through (1, 1) (Answer: $y = x$, $y = \frac{1}{x}$, $y = x^2$, $y = x^3$, $y = \sqrt{x}$, $y = |x|$)
- all y-values are nonnegative (Answer: $y = x^2$, $y = \sqrt{x}$, $y = |x|$, $y = 3^x$)

6.2 More Basic Graphs

You have worked with the graphs of the following equations before, in this course or in your first-year algebra course.

- $y = x$

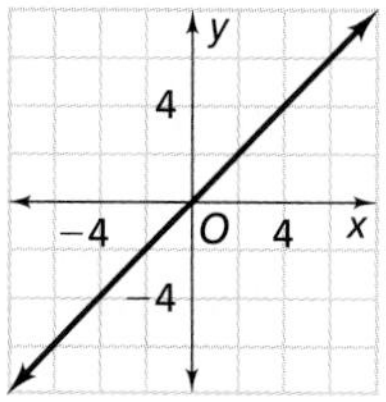

- $y = \frac{1}{x}$

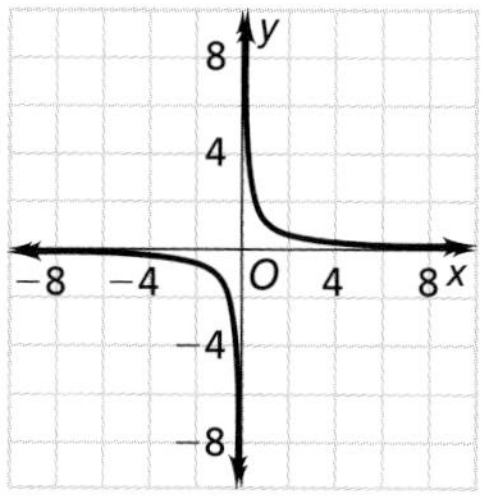

- $y = x^2$

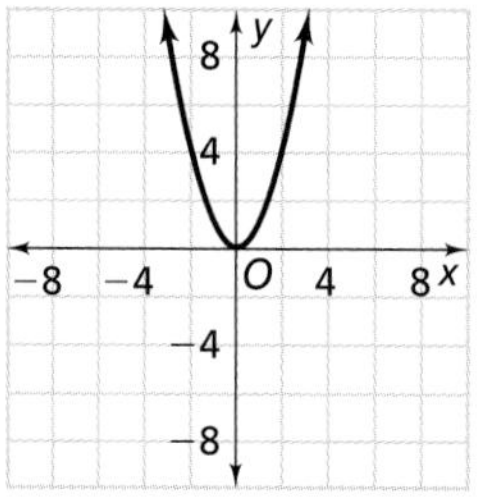

- $y = x^3$

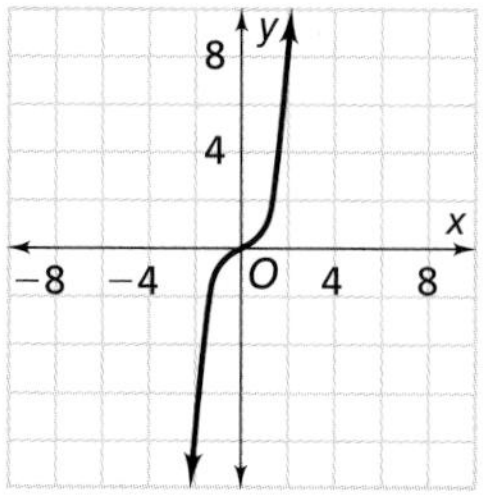

- $y = \sqrt{x}$

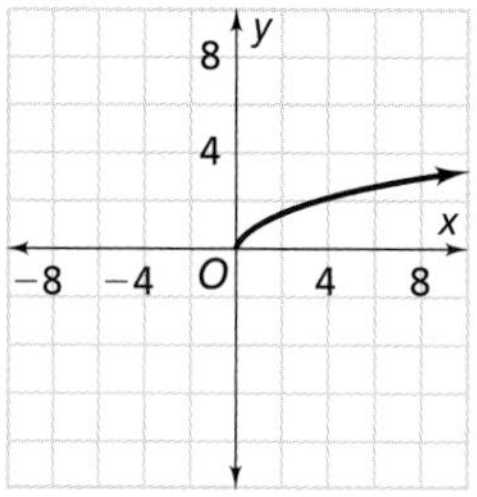

- $y = |x|$

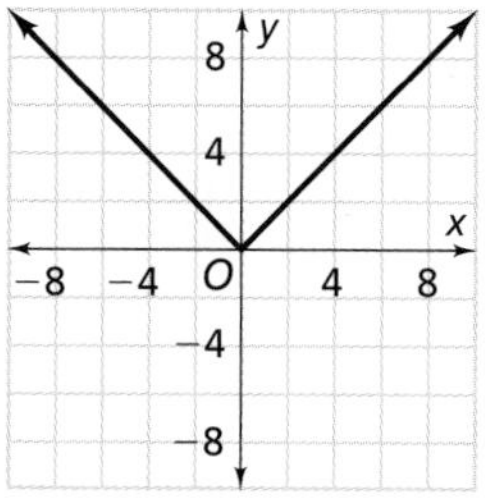

- $y = 3^x$

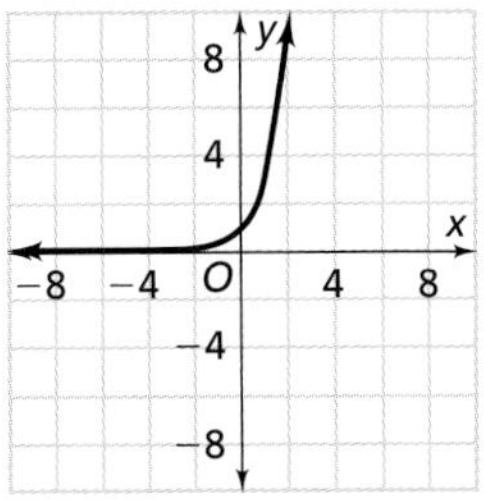

- $y = \log_3 x$

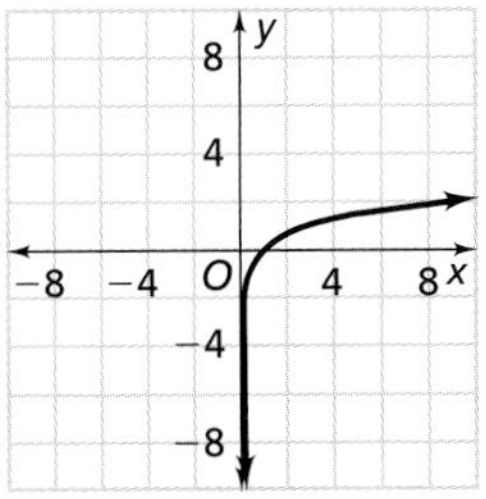

Any graph of $y = b^x$ with $b > 1$ looks similar to the graph of $y = 3^x$. Any graph of $y = \log_b x$ with $b > 1$ looks similar to the graph of $y = \log_3 x$.

You saw in the Getting Started lesson how, by changing these equations slightly, you can translate—move up, down, left, or right—the corresponding graphs without changing their shapes. In this lesson, you will learn three new basic graphs, namely the graphs of the equations $x^2 + y^2 = 1$ and $y = x^3 \pm x$.

The notation $y = x^3 \pm x$ really refers to two different equations: $y = x^3 + x$ and $y = x^3 - x$.

Graphing $x^2 + y^2 = 1$

The graph of the equation $x^2 + y^2 = 1$ is a shape you are familiar with.

Minds in Action — episode 23

Tony and Sasha are working on Exercise 23 from Lesson 6.1.

"Plot all points on the *xy*-plane that are exactly 1 unit from the origin."

Tony Well, there are four obvious ones: (1, 0), (−1, 0), (0, 1), and (0, −1).

Sasha Is there a point that has *x*-coordinate $\frac{1}{2}$?

Tony Well, we would write it $\left(\frac{1}{2}, b\right)$. Then we need to find *b*. And we want its distance to (0, 0) to be 1. What was the distance formula again?

Sasha The distance between the points (x_1, y_1) and (x_2, y_2) is

$$d = \sqrt{(x_1 - x_2)^2 + (y_1 - y_2)^2}$$

Tony Right. So we want

$$\sqrt{\left(\frac{1}{2} - 0\right)^2 + (b - 0)^2} = 1$$

We can get rid of the square root by squaring both sides. So we get

$$\frac{1}{4} + b^2 = 1$$

If we solve for *b*, we get

$$b^2 = \frac{3}{4}$$

$$b = \frac{\sqrt{3}}{2}$$

Sasha Don't forget the negative root.

Explore

Minds in Action

Before working through this dialog, check students' understanding of Exercise 23 from Lesson 6.1. You may be able to skip this dialog if they had little difficulty with that exercise.

The dialog serves as a reminder of the distance formula. You can also use the dialog to talk about the point-tester method of relating graphs and their equations.

Some students may ask how to graph the circle on their graphing calculators. Without going into too much detail, you could teach them how to solve the equation $x^2 + y^2 = 1$ for *y*, which will allow them to enter the equation in two parts.

Tony Oh, right. Thanks. So b is either $\frac{\sqrt{3}}{2}$ or $-\frac{\sqrt{3}}{2}$. Let's see, my calculator says $\frac{\sqrt{3}}{2}$ is about 0.866. So we get two points, (0.5, 0.866) and (0.5, −0.866).

Tony plots the six points they have found so far.

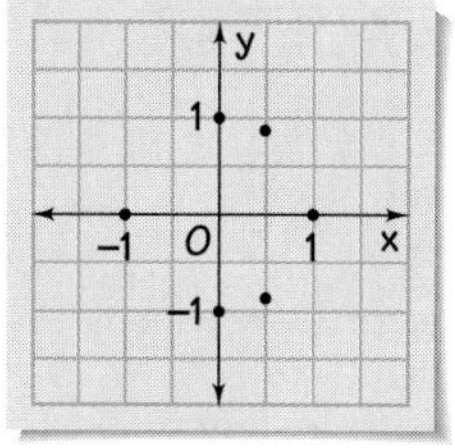

Sasha Hey, shouldn't we also have (−0.5, 0.866) and (−0.5, −0.866) in there?

Tony That makes sense. This picture should be symmetric. So we can also plot (0.866, 0.5), (0.866, −0.5), (−0.866, 0.5), and (−0.866, −0.5), right?

Sasha Yeah, that sounds good.

Sasha plots the six new points.

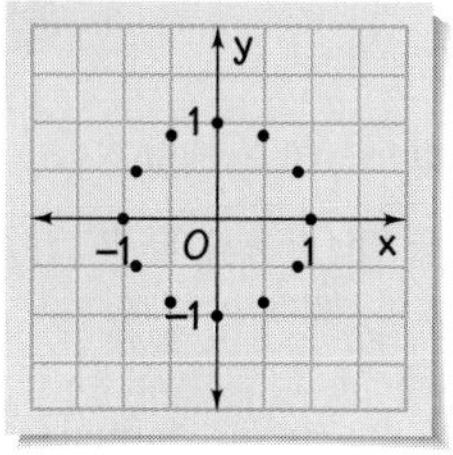

Sasha Hey, it looks like a circle!

Suppose (a, b) is a point on the xy-plane that is exactly 1 unit from the origin. You can write this statement in symbols, using the distance formula.

$$\sqrt{(a-0)^2 + (b-0)^2} = 1$$

One such point is $\left(\frac{1}{2}, \frac{\sqrt{3}}{2}\right)$.

Square both sides and simplify.

$$a^2 + b^2 = 1$$

In other words, the point (a, b) satisfies the equation $x^2 + y^2 = 1$. Conversely, any point (a, b) that satisfies the equation $x^2 + y^2 = 1$ must be exactly 1 unit away from the origin. Therefore, you have just shown that the graph of the equation below is the unit circle.

$$x^2 + y^2 = 1$$

The **unit circle** is a circle of radius 1, centered at the origin.

For You to Do

1. Verify that $\left(\frac{3}{5}, \frac{4}{5}\right)$ is a point on the unit circle.
2. Using the point $\left(\frac{3}{5}, \frac{4}{5}\right)$, find as many other points on the unit circle as you can.

Using the distance formula, you can find an equation of a circle with any center and radius.

Example

Problem

a. Write an equation that describes the set of points that are exactly 1 unit away from $(3, -4)$, and sketch its graph.

b. Write an equation of the circle centered at the origin with radius r.

Solution

a. Using the distance formula as before, you know a point (a, b) is 1 unit away from $(3, -4)$ when

$$\sqrt{(a-3)^2 + (b-(-4))^2} = 1$$

Square both sides and simplify.

$$(a-3)^2 + (b+4)^2 = 1$$

In other words, the desired equation is

$$(x-3)^2 + (y+4)^2 = 1$$

The graph is a circle of radius 1, centered at $(3, -4)$.

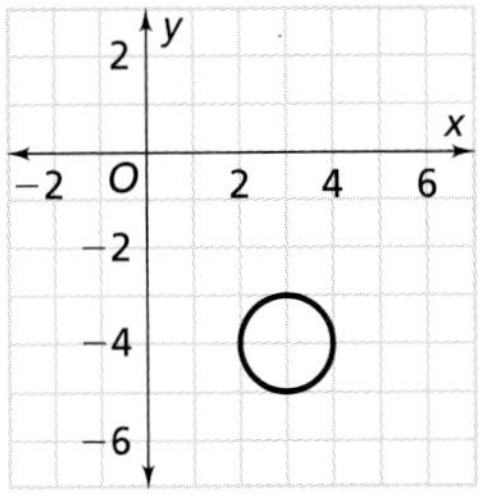

b. A point (a, b) is on a circle centered at the origin when it is r units away from the origin. In symbols,

$$\sqrt{(a-0)^2 + (b-0)^2} = r$$

Square both sides and simplify.

$$a^2 + b^2 = r^2$$

In other words, the desired equation is

$$x^2 + y^2 = r^2$$

Answers

For You to Do

1. $\left(\frac{3}{5}\right)^2 + \left(\frac{4}{5}\right)^2 = \frac{9}{25} + \frac{16}{25} = \frac{25}{25} = 1$, so $\left(\frac{3}{5}, \frac{4}{5}\right)$ is a point on $x^2 + y^2 = 1$.

2. $\left(\frac{3}{5}, -\frac{4}{5}\right)$, $\left(-\frac{3}{5}, \frac{4}{5}\right)$, $\left(-\frac{3}{5}, -\frac{4}{5}\right)$, $\left(\frac{4}{5}, \frac{3}{5}\right)$, $\left(\frac{4}{5}, -\frac{3}{5}\right)$, $\left(-\frac{4}{5}, \frac{3}{5}\right)$, $\left(-\frac{4}{5}, -\frac{3}{5}\right)$

THE EQUATION $y = x^3 + x$ You may want to use Blackline Master 6.2C to display a transparency of the two graphs of $y = x^3 + x$ shown on this page and the two graphs of $y = x^3 - x$ shown in the middle of the next page.

You can describe the thought process presented on these pages as "thinking big-small." If x is big (in absolute value), what happens to the y-value of $y = x^3 + x$? If x is small (in absolute value), what happens to the y-value? Students may think that x^3 should always be the dominant term for the equation $y = x^3 + x$, but (as the graph near the origin shows) the x^3 term becomes less and less important as x gets closer to zero.

This type of thinking will also help students understand the graph of $y = x^3 - x$: when x is big, the graph looks like the graph of $y = x^3$, and when x is small, the graph looks like the graph of $y = -x$. Note that the thought process even works for the graph of $y = x^3$: near the origin, the graph of $y = x^3$ looks like the graph of $y = 0$, a horizontal line (the x-axis).

In general, "thinking big-small" helps prepare students for calculus, where they will examine the behavior of functions for both "big" and "small" values of x. For example, "thinking big" shows that the limit of $f(x) = \frac{\sin x}{x}$ is 0 as x approaches infinity, and "thinking small" shows that the limit is 1 as x approaches 0.

For Discussion

3. If you square both sides of the equation $x = 3$, you introduce solutions that do not satisfy $x = 3$. So, $x^2 = 9$ and $x = 3$ are not equivalent equations.

Explain why the following two equations are equivalent.

$$\sqrt{(a-3)^2 + (b+4)^2} = 1 \text{ and } (a-3)^2 + (b+4)^2 = 1$$

The Equation $y = x^3 + x$

Here is the graph of the equation $y = x^3 + x$.

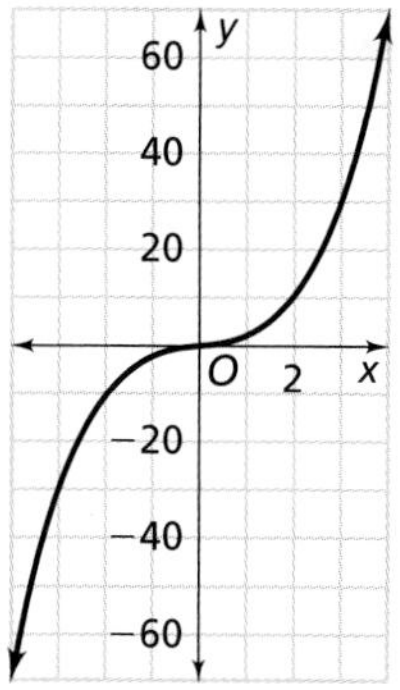

Zoom in on this graph near the origin.

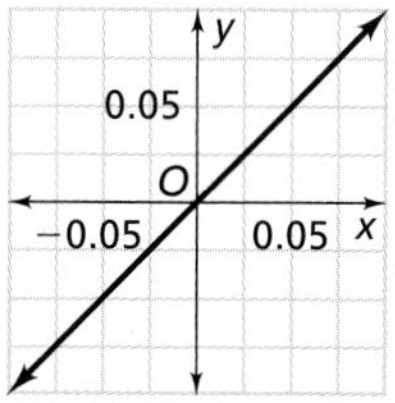

It looks like a straight line with slope 1. In other words, it looks like the graph of $y = x$. Why does it look that way? Well, when x is close to zero, say $x = 0.1$, you have

$$x^3 = (0.1)^3 = 0.001$$

This is very small. Most important, it is much smaller than x itself. Thus, you get

$$\begin{aligned} x^3 + x &= 0.001 + 0.1 \\ &= 0.101 \\ &\approx 0.1 \\ &\approx x \end{aligned}$$

In other words, when x is close to zero, you have

$$x^3 + x \approx x$$

And so the graph of $y = x^3 + x$ looks like the graph of $y = x$ near the origin.

You could also say that when x is small, the term x^3 becomes *negligible* in the expression $x^3 + x$.

Answers

For Discussion

3. In general, for all nonnegative X, $(\sqrt{X})^2 = X$. For all values of a and b, $(a-3)^2 + (b+4)^2$ is nonnegative, so squaring both sides of the equation $\sqrt{(a-3)^2 + (b+4)^2} = 1$ produces the equation $(a-3)^2 + (b+4)^2 = 1$ without introducing any new solutions.

For Discussion

4. Explain why the graph of $y = x^3 + x$ starts to look like the graph of $y = x^3$ far away from the origin, as shown below.

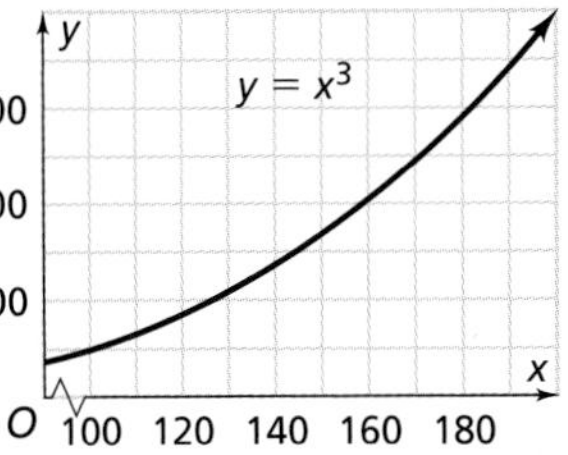

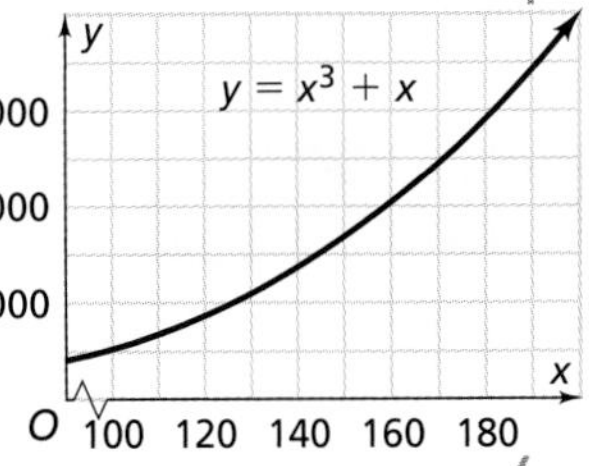

Here is a graph of $y = x^3 - x$.

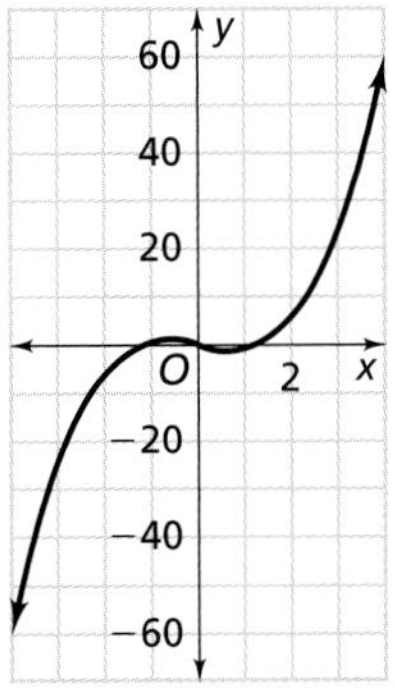

Again, zoom in near the origin.

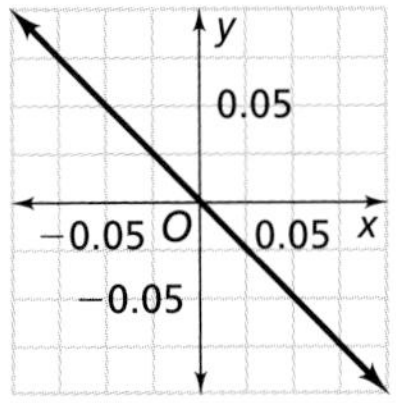

It looks like the graph of $y = -x$. And far away from the origin, the graph of $y = x^3 - x$ starts to resemble the graph of $y = x^3$, as shown below.

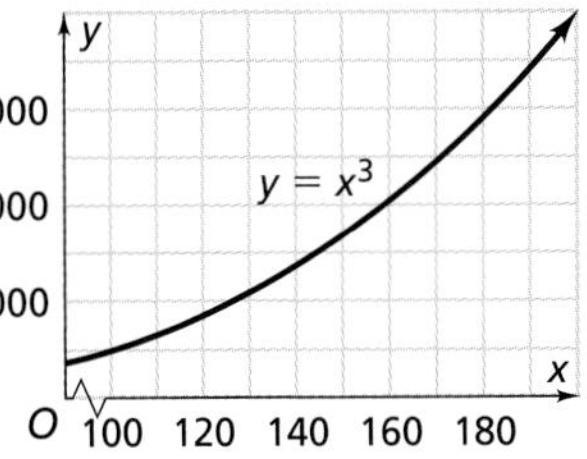

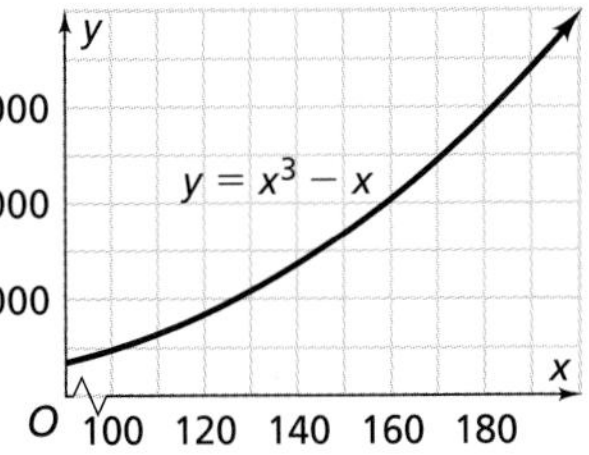

For Discussion

4. Moving away from the origin, x gets larger in absolute value. For a large positive x-value (such as 200), the value of x^3 (8,000,000) is much greater than the value of x, so the x-term has very little effect on the value of $x^3 + x$. A similar argument holds for very small negative x-values (which are large in absolute value). Thus the points (x, x^3) and $(x, x^3 + x)$ are very close to each other for values of x far away from the origin.

Wrap Up

Ask students what the graph of $y = x^3 - 4x$ looks like. As with $y = x^3 - x$, they can think about the y-values for x-values near the origin and far away from the origin.

You may also want students to review the Factor Theorem from Chapter 2 and connect it to finding the x-intercepts of the graph of $y = x^3 - 4x$. By factoring the right side of the equation as $x(x + 2)(x - 2)$, students can identify the roots of $0 = x(x + 2)(x - 2)$ as -2, 0, and 2. Then the x-intercepts of the graph of $y = x^3 - 4x$ are $(-2, 0)$, $(0, 0)$, and $(2, 0)$. Exercises 7 and 11 follow up on this process.

If time allows, go over the Check Your Understanding core exercises.

Assessment Resources

Lesson Quiz 6.2

For Exercises 1 and 2, let $f(x) = x^3$.

1. a. Show that f is an odd function by showing that $f(-x) = -f(x)$.
b. Show that f is an odd function by using the graph of $y = x^3$.

2. a. Explain why the graph of $y = x^3 + x$ resembles the graph of $y = x$ near the origin.
b. Explain why the graph of $y = x^3 + x$ resembles the graph of $y = x^3$ far away from the origin.
c. Find the x-intercepts of the graph of $y = x^3 + x$.

3. Find an equation for each circle.
a. radius 2, center at (0, 0)
b. radius 3, center at (5, −6)
c. radius 5, center at (−1, 4)
d. radius 7, center at (−2, −3)

Exercises

HOMEWORK

- Core: 9, 10, 11, 12, 13, 14, 15, 17
- Optional: 18, 19
- Extension: 16

Check Your Understanding

EXERCISE 3 Explain to students that "rational points" are points with rational *x*- and *y*-coordinates. This exercise shows that you can use Pythagorean triples to generate infinitely many rational points that lie on the unit circle. As an extension, ask students to find general formulas for the *x*- and *y*-coordinates of any such points. (Answer: $x = \frac{m^2 - n^2}{m^2 + n^2}$ and $y = \frac{2mn}{m^2 + n^2}$, where *m* and *n* are rational numbers.)

EXERCISE 6 Some students may classify the graph of $x^2 + y^2 = 1$ as both even and odd. Although this is incorrect because the graph of $x^2 + y^2 = 1$ is not the graph of a function, this graph does display the same symmetries as the graphs of even and odd functions. It has 180° rotational symmetry like an odd function, and it has the *y*-axis as a line of symmetry like an even function.

Exercises *Practicing Habits of Mind*

Check Your Understanding

1. a. Find all points on the graph of $x^2 + y^2 = 1$ with *x*-coordinates equal to $\frac{4}{5}$.

b. Using the point or points you found in part (a), find as many other points on the unit circle as you can.

2. a. Find all points on the graph of $x^2 + y^2 = 1$ with *y*-coordinates equal to $\frac{5}{13}$.

b. Find all points on the graph of $x^2 + y^2 = 1$ with *x*-coordinates equal to $\frac{8}{17}$.

3. Mariko writes down some points on the unit circle with rational coordinates.

Mariko says, "Let's see, so far I've found

$$\left(\frac{3}{5}, \frac{4}{5}\right), \left(\frac{12}{13}, \frac{5}{13}\right), \left(\frac{8}{17}, \frac{15}{17}\right)$$

I've also found all the points I could get from these using the symmetry of the circle. Wait, I recognize those numbers. They're Pythagorean triples! So we can use Pythagorean triples to find rational points on the unit circle."

What does Mariko mean? Explain.

> Here are some other Pythagorean triples.
> - 7, 24, and 25
> - 9, 40, and 41
> - 20, 21, and 29

4. Let $f(x) = x^2$.

a. Show that *f* is an **even function** by showing that $f(-x) = f(x)$.

b. Show that *f* is an even function using the graph of $y = x^2$.

5. Let $f(x) = x^3 + x$.

a. Show that *f* is an odd function by showing that $f(-x) = -f(x)$.

b. Show that *f* is an odd function by using the graph of $y = x^3 + x$.

> A function *f* is an **odd function** if it satisfies $f(-x) = -f(x)$ for all numbers *x* in its domain. In other words, if a point (x, y) is on the graph of *f*, the point $(-x, -y)$ is also on the graph.

6. Classify all of the basic graphs shown in this lesson as graphs of odd functions, even functions, or neither.

Answers

Exercises

1. a. $\left(\frac{4}{5}, \frac{3}{5}\right), \left(\frac{4}{5}, -\frac{3}{5}\right)$

b. $\left(-\frac{4}{5}, \frac{3}{5}\right), \left(-\frac{4}{5}, -\frac{3}{5}\right), \left(\frac{3}{5}, \frac{4}{5}\right), \left(\frac{3}{5}, -\frac{4}{5}\right), \left(-\frac{3}{5}, \frac{4}{5}\right), \left(-\frac{3}{5}, -\frac{4}{5}\right)$

2. a. $\left(\frac{12}{13}, \frac{5}{13}\right), \left(-\frac{12}{13}, \frac{5}{13}\right)$

b. $\left(\frac{8}{17}, \frac{15}{17}\right), \left(\frac{8}{17}, -\frac{15}{17}\right)$

3. If *a*, *b*, and *c* form a Pythagorean triple, then *a*, *b*, and *c* are positive integers that satisfy $a^2 + b^2 = c^2$. Dividing both sides of this equation by c^2 gives $\frac{a^2}{c^2} + \frac{b^2}{c^2} = \frac{c^2}{c^2}$, or $\left(\frac{a}{c}\right)^2 + \left(\frac{b}{c}\right)^2 = 1$. Thus, the point $\left(\frac{a}{c}, \frac{b}{c}\right)$ satisfies the equation of the unit circle, $x^2 + y^2 = 1$, and can be used to generate other points that are on the unit circle.

4. a. $f(-x) = (-x)^2 = x^2 = f(x)$

b. The graph of $y = x^2$ has the *y*-axis as a line of symmetry, so if (x, y) is on the graph, then $(-x, y)$ is also on the graph. Since opposite inputs have the same output, $f(x) = x^2$ is an even function.

5. a. $f(-x) = (-x)^3 + (-x) = -x^3 - x = -(x^3 + x) = -f(x)$

b. The graph of $y = x^3 + x$ has 180° rotational symmetry about the origin, so if (x, y) is on the graph, then $(-x, -y)$ is also on the graph. Since opposite inputs have opposite outputs, $f(x) = x^3 + x$ is an odd function.

6. even functions: $y = x^2$, $y = |x|$; odd functions: $y = x$, $y = \frac{1}{x}$, $y = x^3$, $y = x^3 - x$, $y = x^3 + x$; both: none; neither: $y = \sqrt{x}$, $y = 3^x$, $y = \log_3 x$, $x^2 + y^2 = 1$

7. Explain why the graph of $y = x^3 + x$ has no x-intercept other than the origin.

Remember...

An intercept is a point where a graph intersects one of the axes.

8. **a.** Copy and complete the following table.

x	$x - 3$	$(x - 3)^2$
−1	■	■
0	■	■
1	■	■
2	■	■
3	■	■
4	■	■
5	■	■
6	■	■
7	■	■

b. Using the table from part (a), sketch the graph of $y = (x - 3)^2$.

c. How are the graphs of $y = x^2$ and $y = (x - 3)^2$ related?

On Your Own

9. Let $g(x) = x^3 - x$.

a. Show that g is an odd function by showing that $g(-x) = -g(x)$.

b. Show that g is an odd function by using the graph of $y = x^3 - x$.

10. **a.** Explain why the graph of $y = x^3 - x$ resembles the graph of $y = -x$ near the origin.

b. Explain why the graph of $y = x^3 - x$ resembles the graph of $y = x^3$ far away from the origin.

11. Find the x-intercepts of the graph of $y = x^3 - x$.

12. **a.** Sketch the graph of $y = (x - 3)^3 - (x - 3)$.

b. Find the x-intercepts of the graph of $y = (x - 3)^3 - (x - 3)$.

c. How are the graphs of $y = x^3 - x$ and $y = (x - 3)^3 - (x - 3)$ related?

13. Write an equation for a circle with radius 5, centered at the origin.

14. Write an equation of a circle with radius 5, centered at the point (3, 0).

Go Online
PHSchool.com

For additional practice, go to **Web Code**: bfa-0602

On Your Own

EXERCISE 10 You might ask students to compare the graphs of $y = x^3$, $y = x^3 + x$, and $y = x^3 - x$. They are different from each other near the origin, resembling $y = 0$, $y = x$, and $y = -x$ respectively, but away from the origin, they all look similar.

EXERCISE 12b Encourage students to take advantage of the form of the equation. They can solve the equation $0 = M^3 - M$ for M, and then replace M by $x - 3$ to find x.

Some students may want to multiply out $(x - 3)^3 - (x - 3)$ in order to solve the equation $0 = (x - 3)^3 - (x - 3)$. In that case, they must factor the resulting cubic $x^3 - 9x^2 + 26x - 24$. That task may involve searching for a root and dividing by the corresponding factor to get a quadratic.

Another solution strategy involves recognizing that you can factor out $x - 3$ from each term.

$$0 = (x - 3)[(x - 3)^2 - 1]$$
$$0 = (x - 3)(x^2 - 6x + 9 - 1)$$
$$0 = (x - 3)(x^2 - 6x + 8)$$
$$0 = (x - 3)(x - 4)(x - 2)$$

EXERCISE 14 Some students almost instinctively multiply out and simplify any expression. Use this exercise to discuss again the advantages of different forms for equations. While $(x - 3)^2 + y^2 = 25$ and $x^2 + y^2 - 6x - 16 = 0$ are both correct equations for the circle, many people prefer to use the first form to identify the center and radius and to find intercepts. This form also reveals that this circle is a translation (3 units to the right) of the circle from Exercise 13.

7. $x^3 + x = 0$, or $x(x^2 + 1) = 0$, has only one real root, 0.

8. a. See back of book.

b.

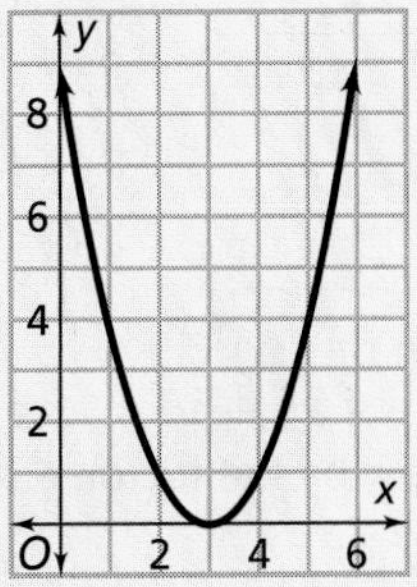

c. The graph of $y = (x - 3)^2$ is the graph of $y = x^2$ translated 3 units to the right.

9. a. $g(-x) = (-x)^3 - (-x) = -x^3 + x = -(x^3 - x) = -g(x)$

b. The graph of $y = x^3 - x$ has 180° rotational symmetry, so if (x, y) is on the graph, then $(-x, -y)$ is also on the graph. Since opposite inputs have opposite outputs, $g(x) = x^3 - x$ is an odd function.

10. a. Near the origin $|x| < 1$, so $|x^3|$ is much less than $|x|$. Thus the x^3-term has very little effect on the value of $x^3 - x$.

b. Far away from the origin x is large in absolute value, so $|x^3|$ is much greater than $|x|$. Thus the x-term has very little effect on the value of $x^3 - x$.

11. (−1, 0), (0, 0), (1, 0)

12. a. See back of book.

b. (2, 0), (3, 0), (4, 0)

c. The graph of $y = (x - 3)^3 - (x - 3)$ is the graph of $y = x^3 - x$ translated 3 units to the right.

13. $x^2 + y^2 = 25$

14. $(x - 3)^2 + y^2 = 25$

EXERCISE 15 Serge's method for finding the equations of these circles will prove useful in Lesson 6.3 where students begin to focus on how changes to an equation affect its graph. Some students will want to use the distance formula to find the equations of these circles. You should encourage them to start with the equation $x^2 + y^2 = r^2$ and use the rules for translations of graphs they studied in CME Project *Algebra 1*. This exercise can serve as a reminder of these rules before students begin Lesson 6.3.

Suggest that students record the result of Exercise 15f, the general equation for a circle.

EXERCISE 16 All the exercises until now have been concerned with translations. This is the first exercise to show a different type of transformation, scaling, which students will study in more detail in Lesson 6.4.

Maintain Your Skills

EXERCISE 19 asks students to draw a conclusion based on their work in Exercise 18. They should be aware that this does not constitute a proof of the result.

Additional Resources

PRINT RESOURCES
- Solution Manual
- Practice Workbook
- Assessment Resources
- Teaching Resources

TECHNOLOGY
- Interactive Textbook
- TeacherExpress CD-ROM
- ExamView CD-ROM
- PHSchool.com

Additional Practice

1. Let $f(x) = x^4 + x^2$.
   a. Show that f is an even function by showing that $f(-x) = f(x)$.
   b. Show that f is an even function by using the graph of $y = x^4 + x^2$.

2. a. Explain why the graph of $y = x^4 + x$ resembles the graph of $y = x$ near the origin.
   b. Explain why the graph of $y = x^4 + x$ resembles the graph of $y = x^4$ far away from the origin.

3. Find the x-intercepts of the graph of $y = x^4 + x$.

4. a. Sketch the graph of $y = (x - 2)^4 + (x - 2)$.
   b. Find the x-intercepts of the graph of $y = (x - 2)^4 + (x - 2)$.
   c. How are the graphs of $y = x^4 + x$ and $y = (x - 2)^4 + (x - 2)$ related?

5. Write an equation for a circle with radius 7, centered at the origin.

6. Write an equation for a circle with radius 7, centered at each given point.
   a. (4, 0)
   b. (1, 3)
   c. (2, −5)
   d. (−1, 2)

7. Find an equation of each circle.
   a. radius 3, center at (2, −6)
   b. radius 4, center at (5, 8)
   c. radius 6, center at (−3, 7)
   d. radius 8, center at (0, −5)
   e. radius 9, center at (6, −1)

8. Find the solutions to each equation.
   a. $x^2 + 7x + 10 = 0$
   b. $(x - 2)^2 + 7(x - 2) + 10 = 0$
   c. $(x - 6)^2 + 7(x - 6) + 10 = 0$
   d. $(x + 3)^2 + 7(x + 3) + 10 = 0$

Practice: For Lesson 6.2, assign Exercises 1–8.

15. Serge takes the following approach to Exercise 14.

Serge says, "Let's see, in Exercise 13, I found an equation of a circle with radius 5, centered at the origin. It was $x^2 + y^2 = 25$.

"Now they're asking for the same circle translated three units to the right. Wait, this is just like the way the graphs of $y = x^2$ and $y = (x - 3)^2$ in Exercise 8 are related! So the equation of the new circle must be $(x - 3)^2 + y^2 = 25$."

Use Serge's method to find an equation of each circle.

a. radius 5, center at (6, 0)
b. radius 4, center at (−3, 0)
c. radius 1, center at (0, −4)
d. radius 1, center at (3, −4)
e. radius 3, center at (−2, 3)
f. radius r, center at (a, b)

16. **Take It Further** Sketch the graph of $(3x)^2 + y^2 = 1$. How is this graph related to the graph of $x^2 + y^2 = 1$?

17. **Standardized Test Prep** Which translation transforms the graph of $y = x^3 + x$ into the graph of $y = (x - 2)^3 + (x - 2)$?

A. 2 units up **B.** 2 units down **C.** 2 units left **D.** 2 units right

Maintain Your Skills

18. Find the solutions to each equation.

a. $x^2 + 5x - 14 = 0$
b. $(x - 3)^2 + 5(x - 3) - 14 = 0$
c. $(x - 5)^2 + 5(x - 5) - 14 = 0$
d. $(x + 2)^2 + 5(x + 2) - 14 = 0$

19. Describe what happens to the solutions of an equation when the variable x is replaced by $x - C$.

Which of the equations $y = \pm x^3$ and $y = x^3 \pm x$ has a graph that resembles this water slide near the origin?

Answers

15. a. $(x - 6)^2 + y^2 = 25$
b. $(x + 3)^2 + y^2 = 16$
c. $x^2 + (y + 4)^2 = 1$
d. $(x - 3)^2 + (y + 4)^2 = 1$
e. $(x + 2)^2 + (y - 3)^2 = 9$
f. $(x - a)^2 + (y - b)^2 = r^2$

16.

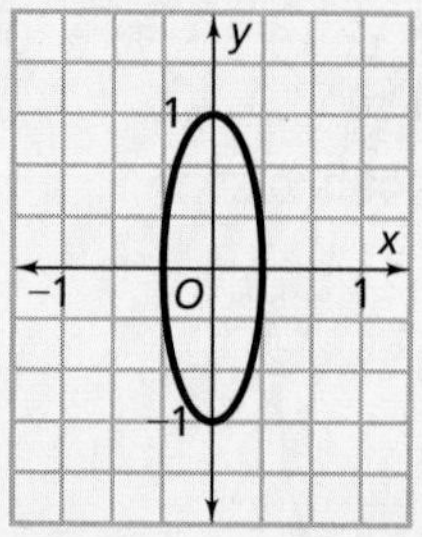

The graph of $(3x)^2 + y^2 = 1$ is the graph of $x^2 + y^2 = 1$ scaled horizontally by the factor $\frac{1}{3}$.

6.3 Translating Graphs

Recall the lumping method of factoring from Chapter 2. You can also use the lumping technique to help you graph equations.

Minds in Action — episode 24

Sasha and Derman are trying to graph the equation $y = (x - 3)^2$.

Derman The equation $y = (x - 3)^2$ looks a lot like $y = x^2$. If I just cover the $x - 3$ part with my hand, it's easier, it is

$$y = M^2$$

Sasha That's pretty neat! And $y = M^2$ is one of the basic graphs we've already seen. Let me start with a table first.

M	y
−3	9
−2	4
−1	1
0	0
1	1
2	4
3	9

Derman Oh, I can graph that . . .

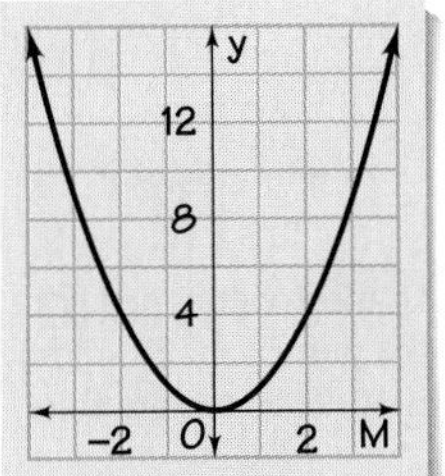

Are we done? I just graphed $y = M^2$, and since $M = x - 3$, is this the graph of $y = (x - 3)^2$?

Sasha Not quite. This is the graph of y against M. For example, the point $(2, 4)$ is on this graph, because when $M = 2$, we have $y = 4$. But what we need is a graph of y against x.

17. D

18. a. −7, 2 **b.** −4, 5
c. −2, 7 **d.** −9, 0

19. The solutions are increased by C.

Lesson Overview

GOAL

- Describe the effect of a translation of one of the basic graphs on both the graph and the equation of the graph.

In the first two lessons of this investigation, students developed conjectures about translating graphs. They are probably confident in predicting that the graph of $y = (x - 5)^2$ will be the same as the graph of $y = x^2$ but shifted 5 units to the right before they start to graph it. This lesson fills in some of the reasons why the graphs are related this way, using the substitution technique—the "hand" method—that students have used in the past to factor polynomials.

CHECK YOUR UNDERSTANDING
- Core: 1, 2, 3, 4, 6, 7
- Optional: 5

MATERIALS
- graph paper
- graphing calculators
- Blackline Master 6.3A

HOMEWORK
- Core: 8a–c, 9, 10, 11, 12, 13, 15
- Optional: 16
- Extension: 8d, 14

Launch

Begin today's lesson with the Minds in Action dialog. If you wish, you can choose students to act out the parts of Sasha and Derman.

Explore

Minds in Action

There are two ways to think of the translation that transforms the graph of $y = x^2$ into the graph of $y = (x - 3)^2$. You can shift the graph 3 units to the right, or you can shift the axes 3 units to the left. This lesson focuses on shifting the graph. In Investigation 6C, the focus will switch to shifting the axes. Students will return to examples like this one and graph the transformed equations by replacing or relabeling the axes.

Like Derman, some students will enjoy using the "hand method" from Chapter 2 here. Cover up the "$x - 3$" with your hand and the equation looks like $y = M^2$. You can apply this to other equations, such as $(x - 3)^2 + (y + 4)^2 = 25$, which can be thought of as $M^2 + N^2 = 25$ by using both hands.

Derman Oh ... When $x = 2$, we have $y = (2 - 3)^2 = 1$, but the point (2, 1) is not on this graph. So what can we do?

Sasha Well, since $M = x - 3$, we can solve for x and get

$$x = M + 3$$

Let me write this in our table.

Sasha includes a new column of x-values in the table.

x = M + 3	M	y
0	−3	9
1	−2	4
2	−1	1
3	0	0
4	1	1
5	2	4
6	3	9

Derman The table has (2, 1) in it! Cool.

Sasha Now we can just ignore the middle column and plot the points (x, y).

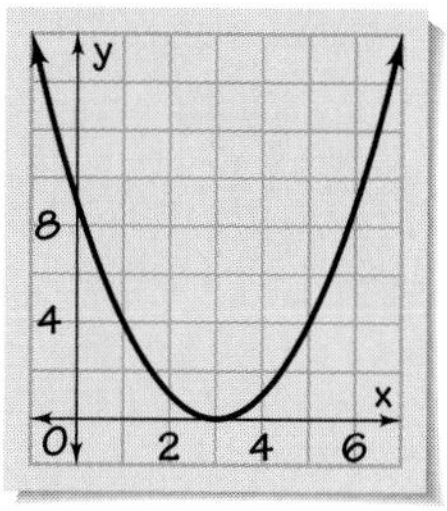

Derman It's the same graph as the graph of $y = M^2$, shifted three units to the right!

Sasha It makes sense, doesn't it? Since $x = M + 3$, the x-values just get shifted to the right by three. For example, the point $(-3, 9)$ on the graph of $y = M^2$ matches up with the point (0, 9) on the graph of $y = (x - 3)^2$.

For Discussion

1. How are the graphs of $y = x^2$ and $y = (x + 5)^2$ related? Explain.

Developing Habits of Mind

Look for relationships In Exercise 18 of Lesson 6.2, you first solved the equation

$$x^2 + 5x - 14 = 0$$

The solutions are $x = -7$ and $x = 2$.

Next, you had to solve

$$(x - 3)^2 + 5(x - 3) - 14 = 0$$

An efficient way of solving this equation is to make the substitution $M = x - 3$. Then you get

$$M^2 + 5M - 14 = 0$$

Its solutions are $M = -7$ and $M = 2$. And since $x = M + 3$, you add three to each solution to get

$$x = -4 \text{ and } x = 5$$

Why does $x = M - 3$?

You can use the same idea to graph the equation $y = (x - 3)^2$. First make the substitution $M = x - 3$ so that $y = M^2$. Any point (M, y) that satisfies $y = M^2$ corresponds to a point (x, y) that satisfies $y = (x - 3)^2$. You can find the corresponding point by sending M to $x = M + 3$. For example, you translate the point $(-3, 9)$ on the graph of $y = M^2$ three units to the right to the point $(0, 9)$ on the graph of $y = (x - 3)^2$.

For Discussion

There are several ways to make sense of this translation. A student might say, "If you replace every instance of x by $x + 5$ in the equation for a graph, you'll end up with x-coordinates that are 5 less in points that satisfy the new equation, because you have to 'make up for' the 5 you're adding." Some students will be comfortable saying things such as, "You move 5 units to the left because that's what's happened every time we've graphed something like this. If you replace every x by $x + 5$, you just have to move 5 units left."

Other students will be struggling with their perception that adding 5 should make you move to the right, but it does not. For these students, it may help to talk about making the substitution $M = x + 5$. The M's are the x-coordinates of points on the basic graph. If you want to find the x-coordinates for the new graph in terms of M, solve the equation $M = x + 5$ for x to get $x = M - 5$. This says that to find each new x-coordinate, subtract 5 from the corresponding old x-coordinate. This kind of logic helps students interpret the equation in a way that matches the direction of the resulting translation with their intuition.

Developing Habits of Mind

Use the "hand method" again to show students the connection between the equations $(x - 3)^2 + 5(x - 3) - 14 = 0$ and $x^2 + 5x - 14 = 0$. This will help them see that any solution of $(x - 3)^2 + 5(x - 3) - 14 = 0$ must be 3 larger than the corresponding solution of $x^2 + 5x - 14 = 0$.

Answers

For Discussion

1. The graph of $y = (x + 5)^2$ is the graph of $y = x^2$ translated 5 units to the left; each point (x, x^2) on the graph of $y = x^2$ corresponds to the point $(x - 5, x^2)$ on the graph of $y = (x + 5)^2$.

Example

You can use Blackline Master 6.3A to guide students through part (a) of the Example.

Part (b) provides a good example of an equation that is almost, but not quite, written in the form of a basic graph. Encourage students to rewrite the equation in the form of the basic graph $N = M^2$—that is, as $(y + 4) = (x - 3)^2$—before trying to describe the horizontal and vertical translations.

Some students will prefer the method described at the end of the example: leave the equation in the form $y = (x - 3)^2 - 4$ and recognize that because the outputs for this equation are 4 less than the outputs for $y = (x - 3)^2$, the graph of $y = (x - 3)^2$ shifts down four units to become the graph $y = (x - 3)^2 - 4$. This method, however, makes some students feel that horizontal and vertical translations do not work the same way. They may ask, "Why does the -4 move the graph down, when the -3 move the graph to the right?" Writing the equation in the form $(y + 4) = (x - 3)^2$ clears up this confusion: it is a $+4$, not a -4, that moves the graph down.

Writing equations in the forms of basic graphs allows students to keep a simpler toolbox of transformations, and prevents them from thinking that horizontal and vertical translations behave differently. In addition, some equations, such as $x^2 + y^2 = 1$, do not easily lend themselves to being written in the "$y =$" form.

Similarly, you can translate graphs vertically (up or down) by making substitutions such as $N = y + 4$. Here are two examples.

Example

Problem Sketch the graph of each equation.

a. $x^2 + (y + 4)^2 = 1$

b. $y = (x - 3)^2 - 4$

Solution

a. With the substitution $N = y + 4$, this equation becomes

$$x^2 + N^2 = 1$$

The graph of this equation is the unit circle, which is a circle of radius 1 centered at the origin. The table at the right shows some points on the unit circle.

x	N
1	0
−1	0
0	1
0	−1

Since $N = y + 4$, solving for y gives

$$y = N - 4$$

Now, include a column of y-values in the table.

x	N	$y = N - 4$
1	0	−4
−1	0	−4
0	1	−3
0	−1	−5

Ignore the middle column and plot the points (x, y).

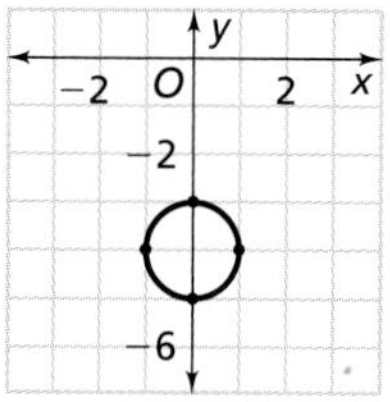

Use these points as the "corner points" of the new circle.

This is the unit circle, translated four units down. The key here is that since $y = N - 4$, you shift the y-values down by four.

Wrap Up

Give students equations of several different graphs that all use the same horizontal and vertical translations. For example, each of the following equations translates a basic graph 5 units to the left and 2 units up.

- $y - 2 = (x + 5)^2$
- $y - 2 = |x + 5|$
- $(x + 5)^2 + (y - 2)^2 = 16$
- $(y - 2)(x + 5) = 1$

If time allows, go over the Check Your Understanding core exercises.

Assessment Resources

Lesson Quiz 6.3

1. Sketch the graph of each equation. Then describe how the graph of each equation is related to the graph of $f(x) = x^2 + x$.
   a. $y = (x + 4)^2 + (x + 4)$
   b. $y - 3 = (x + 4)^2 + (x + 4)$
   c. $y = (x + 4)^2 + x + 7$
   d. $y + 2 = (x - 3)^2 + (x - 3)$

2. **a.** Sketch the graph of $y = -4x$.
   b. Translate the graph of $y = -4x$ four units to the right so that the origin $(0, 0)$ maps to the point $(4, 0)$ in the translated image. Find the equation of this new line.
   c. Translate the graph of $y = -4x$ two units to the left and five units up so that the origin $(0, 0)$ maps to the point $(-2, 5)$ in the translated image. Find the equation of this new line.

3. **a.** Find an equation of the line with slope 2 that contains the point $(5, 3)$.
   b. Find an equation of the line with slope -1.5 that contains the point $(-4, -3)$.

Exercises Practicing Habits of Mind

Check Your Understanding

1. Consider the equation $y = \sqrt{x + 5}$. Let $M = x + 5$.

   a. Copy and complete the following table.

$x = M - 5$	M	$y = \sqrt{M}$
■	0	■
■	1	■
■	4	■
■	9	■
■	16	■
■	25	■

Habits of Mind

Look for relationships. Why are these good choices for values of M?

   b. Using the table from part (a), explain how the graphs of $y = \sqrt{x}$ and $y = \sqrt{x + 5}$ are related.

   c. Sketch the graph of $y = \sqrt{x + 5}$. According to the graph, what are the domain and the range of the function defined by $f(x) = \sqrt{x + 5}$?

2. Sketch the graph of each equation.

   a. $y = |x + 2|$
   b. $(x + 2)^2 + y^2 = 25$
   c. $(y - 3) = \log x$
   d. $y = \frac{1}{x} + 3$

3. Sketch the graph of each equation.

   a. $(y + 1) = |x + 2|$
   b. $(x + 2)^2 + (y - 4)^2 = 25$
   c. $y = \log(x - 5) + 3$
   d. $(x - 2)(y - 3) = 1$

4. **What's Wrong Here?** Walter is working on the following problem. The graph below is a graph of $y = x^3 - x$ translated two units to the right. Find its equation.

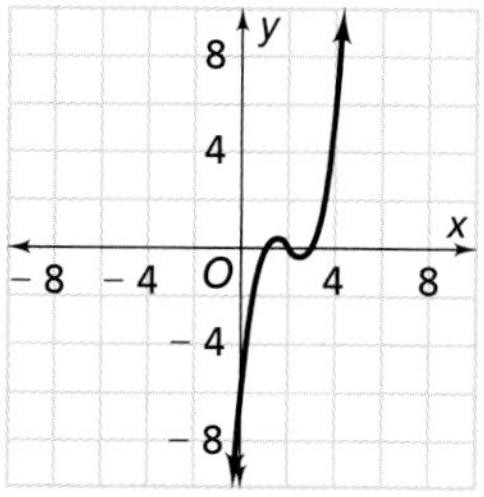

   Walter says, "Since it's two units to the right, I should replace x^3 with $(x - 2)^3$. So the equation I want is $y = (x - 2)^3 - x$."

   Do you agree or disagree with Walter? Explain.

Exercises

HOMEWORK
- Core: 8a–c, 9, 10, 11, 12, 13, 15
- Optional: 16
- Extension: 8d, 14

Check Your Understanding

EXERCISE 1 The square root function is one of the rare functions in this investigation which does not have the entire set of real numbers as its domain. Because of that, it makes sense to examine the effect of a translation on the domain (and range) of this function.

EXERCISES 2 AND 3 ask students to translate many of the basic graphs. Encourage students to predict what each graph will look like before they begin to graph it (either with their calculators or by hand). Taking the time to think out a prediction will help them reinforce their understanding of how a change to an equation will effect a graph.

EXERCISE 3 Part (d) of this exercise may not immediately suggest one of the basic graphs. However, students need to solve this equation for y in order to graph it with their graphing calculators. In the form $y = \frac{1}{x - 2} + 3$, this equation is more evidently a translation of the basic graph of $y = \frac{1}{x}$. Encourage students also to look at the equation in the form $(y - 3) = \frac{1}{x - 2}$. Again, they should recognize it as a translation of $y = \frac{1}{x}$.

Answers

Exercises

1. a.

$x = M - 5$	M	$y = \sqrt{M}$
−5	0	0
−4	1	1
−1	4	2
4	9	3
11	16	4
20	25	5

b. The graph of $y = \sqrt{x + 5}$ is the graph of $y = \sqrt{x}$ translated 5 units to the left.

c.

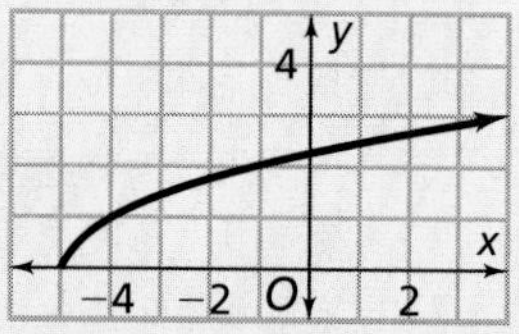

domain: $x \geq -5$, range: $y \geq 0$

2–3. See back of book.

4. Disagree; Walter should have replaced each x in the original equation by $(x - 2)$ to get $y = (x - 2)^3 - (x - 2)$.

5. **a.** Explain how the graphs of the following equations are related.
   - $y = x^3 + 6x^2 + 11x + 7$
   - $y = (x - 2)^3 + 6(x - 2)^2 + 11(x - 2) + 7$

   b. Expand $(x - 2)^3 + 6(x - 2)^2 + 11(x - 2) + 7$.

   c. Using parts (a) and (b), sketch the graph of $y = x^3 + 6x^2 + 11x + 7$.

In Investigation 6B, you will see why you might want to replace x with $x - 2$.

6. **a.** Find the coordinates of the vertex of the parabola with equation $y = (x + 3)^2$.

   b. Find the coordinates of the vertex of the parabola with equation $y - 2 = (x + 3)^2$.

   c. In terms of h and k, find the coordinates of the vertex of the parabola with equation $y = (x + h)^2 + k$.

7. Sketch the graph of each equation.

   a. $y = x^2 + 6x + 9$ **b.** $y = x^2 + 6x + 7$

On Your Own

8. Sketch the graph of each equation.

   a. $y = (x - 2)^3 + (x - 2)$

   b. $y + 1 = (x - 2)^3 + (x - 2)$

   c. $y = (x - 2)^3 + x - 3$

   d. **Take It Further** $y = x^3 - 6x^2 + 13x - 11$

9. Sketch the graph of each equation. Then find the slope of the graph.

   a. $y = 3x$

   b. $y = 3(x - 2)$

   c. $y - 5 = 3(x - 2)$

   d. How are the graphs in parts (a), (b), and (c) related? Explain.

10. **a.** Sketch the graph of $y = \frac{1}{2}x$.

    b. Translate the graph of $y = \frac{1}{2}x$ three units to the right so that the origin (0, 0) maps to the point (3, 0) in the translated image. Find the equation of this new line.

    c. Translate the graph of $y = \frac{1}{2}x$ three units to the right and one unit up so that the origin (0, 0) maps to the point (3, 1) in the translated image. Find the equation of this new line.

Go Online PHSchool.com

For additional practice, go to **Web Code**: bfa-0603

5. a. The graph of the second equation is the graph of the first equation translated 2 units to the right.

b. $x^3 - x + 1$

c. See back of book.

6. a. $(-3, 0)$

b. $(-3, 2)$

c. $(-h, k)$

7. a.

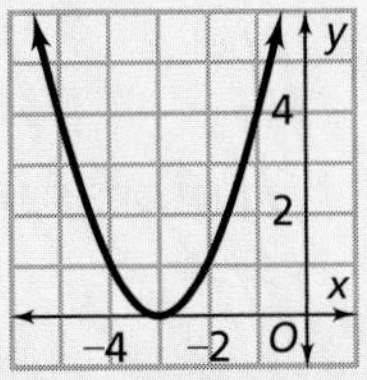

b.

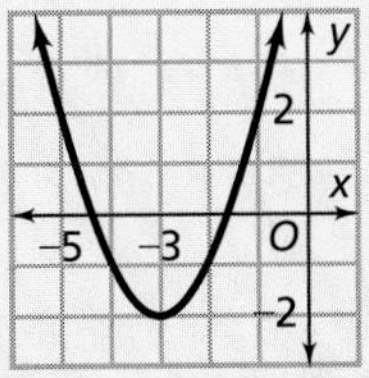

8–10. See back of book.

EXERCISE 5 In Lesson 6.7 of Investigation 6B, students learn how to transform the equation of a general cubic, $y = ax^3 + bx^2 + cx + d$, into a form that reveals it to be a translation of one of the basic cubic graphs, $y = x^3$, $y = x^3 + x$, or $y = x^3 - x$. This exercise shows why such a transformation would be helpful: it makes it easier to sketch the graph of the cubic equation.

EXERCISE 6 Some students may remember that the x-coordinate for the vertex of the parabola $y = ax^2 + bx + c$ is always $\frac{-b}{2a}$. They may think that the most efficient way to solve this exercise is to multiply each equation out, put it in standard form, find the x-coordinate of the vertex from the coefficients of the standard form quadratic, and then substitute that x-value into the equation to find the y-coordinate of the vertex. Of course, this method is possible and will work. However, encourage these students also to think about translations of the basic graph $y = x^2$. Ask them to use the information in each equation to describe the translations that map the basic graph to the graph of the equation. Where do these translations move the vertex of the basic graph?

EXERCISE 7 Encourage students who use only their graphing calculators to produce these sketches to go back and make sense of why these graphs appear the way they do.

On Your Own

EXERCISE 8 Students who were not sure about how to approach part (d) may have begun by using a graphing calculator to see what the graph looks like. It certainly appears to be the same graph as the graphs in parts (b) and (c), but encourage curious students to expand the equation $y = (x - 2)^3 + x - 3$ to see why the graphs are the same.

EXERCISE 9 Depending on their comfort level with translations, some students may still multiply these equations out and simplify them in order to sketch the graphs. A student who rewrites the equation in part (b) as $y = 3x - 6$ will probably describe the graph of this equation as the graph of $y = 3x$ translated 6 units down. A student who leaves the equation in the form $y = 3(x - 2)$ will probably describe the same graph as the graph of $y = 3x$ translated 2 units to the right. This situation, where different translations produce the same result, can be confusing for students.

EXERCISE 11 gives students a new way to think about the task of finding the equation of a line with a given point and slope. They can view the line as the translation of a line with the given slope that passes through the origin. All lines that pass through the origin have equations of the form $y = mx$. Students now know how to change the equation to translate the origin to the given point.

EXERCISE 12 Students see how they can translate a graph of the equation $y = x^2 + 6x + 7$ so that its vertex moves back to the origin. In Investigation 6B, students learn how to start with a general equation for a parabola and use techniques, including completing the square, to write the equation in a form that reveals the transformations that change the basic parabola $y = x^2$ into the given parabola. Students can use this form of the equation for a parabola to read off the coordinates of the vertex of the parabola.

Rather than emphasizing this form as a standard form for students to memorize, hope that students find this form, and all the others like it, useful for identifying transformations of a basic graph.

11. **a.** Find an equation of the line with slope 4 that passes through the point (3, 1).

b. Find an equation of the line with slope $\frac{2}{3}$ that passes through the point $(-2, -1)$.

c. Find an equation of the line with slope m that passes through the point (h, k).

12. The graph of the equation $y = x^2 + 6x + 7$ is a parabola with vertex at $(-3, -2)$.

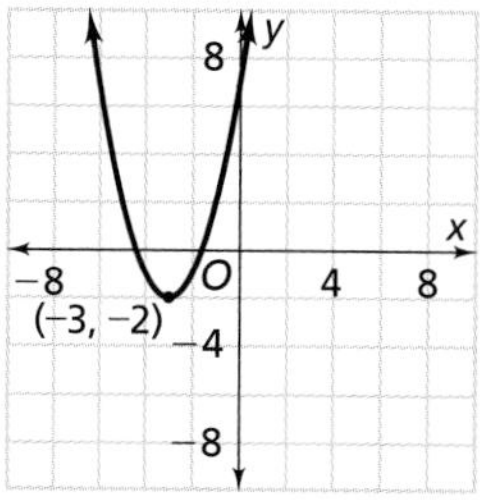

a. How are the graphs of $y = x^2 + 6x + 7$ and $y = (x - 3)^2 + 6(x - 3) + 7$ related? Explain.

b. How are the graphs of $y = (x - 3)^2 + 6(x - 3) + 7$ and $y - 2 = (x - 3)^2 + 6(x - 3) + 7$ related? Explain.

c. Simplify the expression below as much as possible.

$$y - 2 = (x - 3)^2 + 6(x - 3) + 7$$

13. **What's Wrong Here?** Susan is working on Exercise 11.

Susan says, "Let's see, I need a line with slope 4 that passes through the point (3, 1). I can certainly start with $y = 4x$ and translate it to the right three and up one, so that the origin goes to (3, 1). That gives me

$$y - 1 = 4(x - 3)$$

"But I can also take the point (1, 4) on the graph of $y = 4x$ and move that to the point (3, 1). That would mean translating the graph of $y = 4x$ to the right two and down 3, which gives me

$$y + 3 = 4(x - 2)$$

"I get two different answers. So this must mean there are at least two different lines with slope 4 that pass through the point (3, 1)."

Do you agree or disagree with Susan? Explain.

Go Online PHSchool.com

For more information about function transformations, go to Web Code: bfe-9031

Answers

11. a. $y = 4(x - 3) + 1$ or $y = 4x - 11$

b. $y = \frac{2}{3}(x + 2) - 1$ or $y = \frac{2}{3}x + \frac{1}{3}$

c. $y = m(x - h) + k$

12. a. The graph of $y = (x - 3)^2 + 6(x - 3) + 7$ is the graph of $y = x^2 + 6x + 7$ translated 3 units to the right; answers may vary. Sample: In the equation $y = (x - 3)^2 + 6(x - 3) + 7$, each x in the equation $y = x^2 + 6x + 7$ is replaced with $M = x - 3$, so each point on the graph of $y = M^2 + 6M + 7$ corresponds to the point on the graph of $y = x^2 + 6x + 7$ with x-coordinate 3 units less.

b. See back of book.

c. $y = x^2$

13. Disagree; both equations simplify to $y = 4x - 11$.

14. **Take It Further** Derman is thinking about the graph of $y = (x - 3)^2$ again.

Derman thinks, "Instead of translating the graph of $y = x^2$ three units to the right, I can just keep it where it is and shift the coordinate axes three units to the left."

This figure shows the original axes in green and Derman's new axes in purple.

Use the substitution $M = x - 3$ to explain why Derman's method is valid.

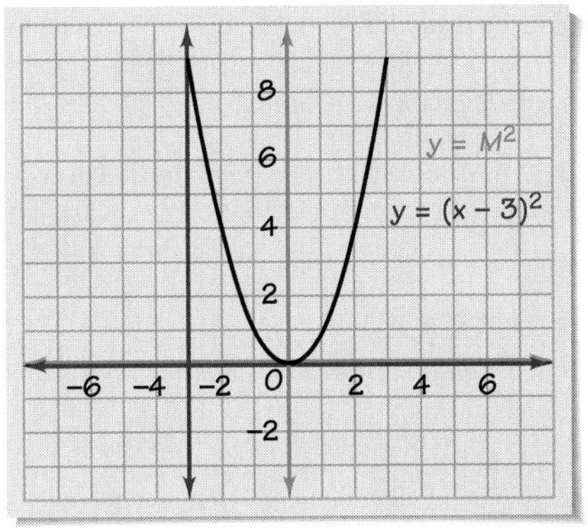

15. **Standardized Test Prep** Which equation has a graph that is a parabola with vertex at $(-1, -2)$?

A. $(y - 2) = (x - 1)^2$ **B.** $(y + 1) = (x - 2)^2$

C. $y = (x - 2)^2 + 1$ **D.** $y = (x + 1)^2 - 2$

Maintain Your Skills

16. **a.** Sketch the graphs of $y = 3^x$ and $y = \log_3 x$. How are the graphs related? Explain why they are related in this way.

Sketch the graphs of each equation. Explain how the graphs for each pair of equations are related to the graphs of $y = 3^x$ and $y = \log_3 x$, respectively. Then explain how the graphs of the two equations are related to each other.

b. $y = 3 \cdot 3^x$ and $y = \log_3 \frac{x}{3}$

c. $y = 9 \cdot 3^x$ and $y = \log_3 \frac{x}{9}$

d. $y = 27 \cdot 3^x$ and $y = \log_3 \frac{x}{27}$

e. $y = 3^n \cdot 3^x$ and $y = \log_3 \frac{x}{3^n}$, for a fixed positive integer n

Habits of Mind

Experiment. What do you find if n is negative?

14. Answers may vary. Sample: Derman thinks of the parabola as $y = M^2$ with the green horizontal axis being the M-axis. When he translates the green M- and y-axes three units left to become the purple x- and y-axes, the M-coordinate of each point on the green horizontal axis is 3 less than its x-coordinate on the purple horizontal axis. That is, $M = x - 3$. So, $y = M^2$ on the green coordinate axes becomes $y = (x - 3)^2$ on the purple coordinate axes.

15. D

16. See back of book.

EXERCISE 14 previews a way of thinking that students will study in detail in Investigation 6C. You can think of a translation either as mapping a graph to a new location on the same set of coordinate axes or as mapping the coordinate axes to a new location in relation to the graph.

EXERCISE 16 There are several ways to look at this exercise. You can use rules of exponents and logarithms to rewrite each pair of new equations in forms that let you recognize their graphs as translations of the basic exponential and logarithm graphs. The basic equations are inverses, so their graphs are reflections of each other over the line $y = x$. Because the new equations translate the basic exponential graph horizontally and the basic logarithm graph vertically by the same amount, the new graphs will still be reflections over the line $y = x$.

You also can show that the equations in each pair are inverses by switching x and y in the exponential equation and solving for y.

Finally, you could look at the graphs of the new equations as vertical and horizontal scalings of the basic graphs, but students are unlikely to use this approach until after Lesson 6.4.

Additional Resources

PRINT RESOURCES
- Solution Manual
- Practice Workbook
- Assessment Resources
- Teaching Resources

TECHNOLOGY
- Interactive Textbook
- TeacherExpress CD-ROM
- ExamView CD-ROM
- PHSchool.com

Additional Practice

1. Sketch the graph of each equation.
   a. $y = (x - 4)^3 + (x - 4)$ **b.** $y - 3 = (x - 1)^3 + (x - 1)$
   c. $y + 1 = (x - 2)^3 + (x - 2)$ **d.** $y = (x - 2)^3 + x - 3$

2. Sketch the graph of each equation. Then find the slope of the graph.
   a. $y = -2x$
   b. $y = -2(x + 1)$
   c. $y + 3 = -2(x + 1)$
   d. How are the graphs in parts (a), (b), and (c) related? Explain.

3. **a.** Sketch the graph of $y = 3x$.
   b. Translate the graph of $y = 3x$ four units to the left so that the origin (0, 0) maps to the point $(-4, 0)$ in the translated image. Find the equation of this new line.
   c. Translate the graph of $y = 3x$ five units to the right and three units down so that the origin (0, 0) is mapped to the point $(5, -3)$ in the translated image. Find the equation of this new line.

4. **a.** Find an equation of the line with slope 3 that contains the point (6, 2).
   b. Find an equation of the line with slope -5 that contains the point $(-4, 3)$.

5. Sketch the graph of each equation.
   a. $y = -x^2$ **b.** $y = -x^3$ **c.** $y = -\frac{1}{x}$
   d. $y = -x^3 + x$ **e.** $y = -x^3 - x$ **f.** $y = -\sqrt{x}$

6. Describe how the graph of each equation is related to the graph of $y = |x|$.
   a. $y = -|x|$ **b.** $y = |5x|$ **c.** $y = -|5x|$ **d.** $y = -\left|\frac{1}{5}x\right|$
   e. $-y = |x|$ **f.** $-5y = |x|$ **g.** $-\frac{y}{5} = |x|$ **h.** $-y = |-x|$

7. Sketch the graph of each equation.
   a. $(2x)^2 + (4y)^2 = 16$
   b. $(2(x - 1))^2 + (4(y + 3))^2 = 16$
   c. $\frac{(x - 1)^2}{9} + \frac{(y + 3)^2}{4} = 1$

Practice: For Lesson 6.3, assign Exercises 1–4.

Lesson Overview

GOALS

- Describe the effect of scaling an axis or reflection of one of the basic graphs on both the graph and the equation of the graph.
- Compose transformations and sketch the effect of such a composition on one of the basic graphs.

Now that students have explored translations, they are ready to look into other transformations: scalings and reflections. Students see what kinds of changes in an equation lead to a scaling or a reflection in a graph. They use a technique similar to the one they used for translations—making a substitution for one of the variables to make an equation look like one of the basic graph forms. Then they look at tables showing coordinates of points after the substitution and use the tables to figure out the coordinates before the substitution. As with translation, it may be difficult for students to make sense of the *direction* of the transformation but through continued experience their instincts will improve. Encourage students to predict what a graph will look like before graphing it on paper or on their calculators.

CHECK YOUR UNDERSTANDING

- Core: 1, 2, 3, 4, 6, 7, 9
- Optional: 5
- Extension: 8

MATERIALS

- graph paper
- graphing calculators
- Blackline Masters 6.4A, 6.4B

HOMEWORK

- Core: 10, 11, 12, 14, 15
- Optional: 13, 16, 19
- Extension: 17, 18

Launch

Begin today's lesson with the Minds in Action dialog.

Explore

Minds in Action

This time, Sasha and Derman use the "hand method" to understand a horizontal stretch, or scaling, of the basic graph $y = x^2$. As with translations in Lesson 6.3, you use substitutions to write the equation in a basic form, and then find the transformations that change the M, N graph into the x, y graph.

6.4 Scaling and Reflecting Graphs

This lesson explores how to change an equation to resize its graph along either axis or reflect its graph over an axis.

Minds in Action — episode 25

Sasha and Derman are trying to graph the equation $y = \left(\frac{x}{3}\right)^2$.

Sasha The equation $y = \left(\frac{x}{3}\right)^2$ looks like $y = x^2$ to me. If I cover $\frac{x}{3}$ with my hand like you did last time, this looks like $y = M^2$...

This time $M = \frac{x}{3}$.

Derman We know this one pretty well.

Derman finds the table and the graph of $y = M^2$ in his notebook.

M	y
−3	9
−2	4
−1	1
0	0
1	1
2	4
3	9

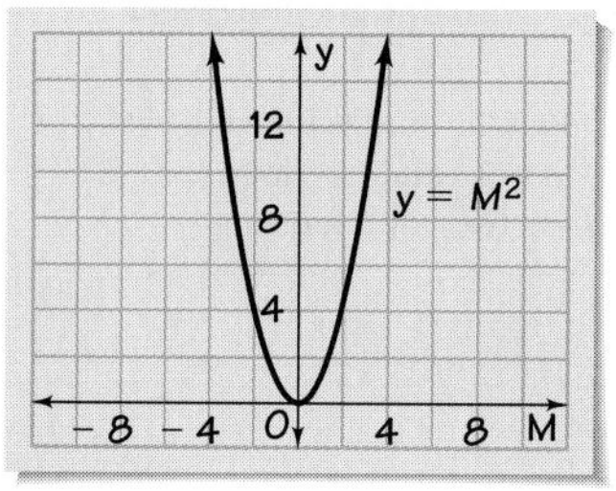

Sasha Great. Now, since $M = \frac{x}{3}$, solving for x gives us

$$x = 3M$$

Can you include this in your table?

Derman adds a column of x-values to his table.

x = 3M	M	y
−9	−3	9
−6	−2	4
−3	−1	1
0	0	0
3	1	1
6	2	4
9	3	9

Derman Oh, I can ignore the middle column and plot the points (x, y).

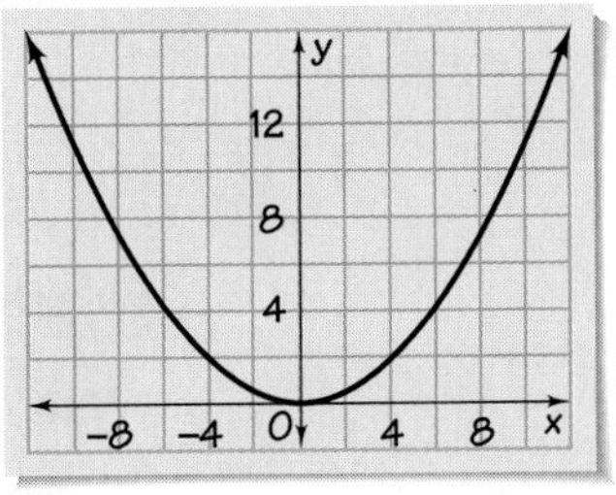

Sasha It looks just like the graph of $y = M^2$, stretched horizontally by a factor of 3.

Derman It makes sense to me. The x-values got tripled. (2, 4) on the graph of $y = M^2$ became (6, 4) on the new graph.

For You to Do

1. How are the graphs of $y = x^2$ and $y = \left(\frac{x}{5}\right)^2$ related?
2. How are the graphs of $y = x^2$ and $y = (5x)^2$ related?

Habits of Mind

Visualize. If $x = 3M$, each jump of one space in M corresponds to a jump of three spaces in x. If you look at a set of points on a graph that are all one unit apart in M, they are three units apart in x.

Lesson 6.4 continues to focus on how an equation transforms a graph. In Investigation 6C, the focus will switch to how the axes can be changed instead. Axes changes more closely match the forms of the equations. Some students may feel when looking at equations like $y = \left(\frac{x}{3}\right)^2$ and $y = (x + 3)^2$ that everything is "backwards"— they think the "divide by 3" in $y = \left(\frac{x}{3}\right)^2$ should make the graph narrower, but the graph of $y = \left(\frac{x}{3}\right)^2$ is actually wider than the graph of $y = x^2$. Likewise, students may feel that the "plus 3" in $y = (x + 3)^2$ should move the graph to the right, but the graph of $y = (x + 3)^2$ is actually to the left of the graph of $y = x^2$. Investigation 6C offers an alternative view: the axes move 3 units to the right, which matches the "plus 3" in the equation.

For You to Do

Using the term *scaling* instead of *stretching* and *shrinking* removes any implication that the resulting image will be bigger or smaller. Some students may describe the graph of $y = (5x)^2$ as the image of the graph of $y = x^2$ after that graph has been "shrunk" by a factor of 5—and for them, the shrunk is what says the factor is $\frac{1}{5}$. Other students may say it was shrunk by the factor $\frac{1}{5}$. If your class has both types of students, the group is in for confusion unless you work together to decide on a way to describe this type of transformation that makes sense to everyone.

Answers

For You to Do

1. The graph of $y = \left(\frac{x}{5}\right)^2$ is the graph of $y = x^2$ scaled horizontally by the factor 5.
2. The graph of $y = (5x)^2$ is the graph of $y = x^2$ scaled horizontally by the factor $\frac{1}{5}$.

Example 1

You can use Blackline Master 6.4A to guide students through Example 1.

You might want to ask students to graph $y = \left(\frac{1}{2}\right)^x$ separately, so they see that its graph is identical to the graph of $y = 2^{-x}$.

As a followup to Example 1, ask students what effect replacing x with $-x$ in the equation $y = x^2$ would have on the graph of this even function.

Developing Habits of Mind

Look for relationships. In Exercise 24 of Lesson 6.1, you solved the equation $5x - 7 = 2x + 5$. The solution is $x = 4$.

Next, you had to solve

$$5 \cdot \frac{x}{3} - 7 = 2 \cdot \frac{x}{3} + 5$$

You can solve this equation by making the substitution $M = \frac{x}{3}$.

$$5M - 7 = 2M + 5$$

The solution to this equation must be $M = 4$. But, since $x = 3M$,

$$x = 3(4) = 12$$

You can also use this idea to graph the equation $y = \left(\frac{x}{3}\right)^2$. Make the substitution $M = \frac{x}{3}$ to get the equation $y = M^2$. And by sending M to $x = 3M$, we find any point (M, y) on the graph of $y = M^2$ corresponds to a point (x, y) on the graph of $y = \left(\frac{x}{3}\right)^2$. For example, the point $(-1, 1)$ that is on the graph of $y = M^2$ gets scaled horizontally by the factor of 3 to the point $(-3, 1)$ on the graph of $y = \left(\frac{x}{3}\right)^2$.

You can use the same substitution technique when dealing with a reflection.

Example 1

Problem Sketch the graph of $y = 2^{-x}$.

Solution With the substitution $M = -x$, this equation becomes

$$y = 2^M$$

Here are the table and graph of this exponential function.

M	y
−3	$\frac{1}{8}$
−2	$\frac{1}{4}$
−1	$\frac{1}{2}$
0	1
1	2
2	4
3	8

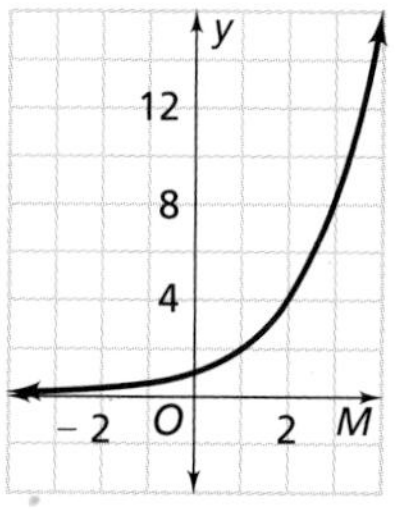

Since $M = -x$, solving for x gives

$$x = -M$$

Now, include a column of x-values in the table.

$x = -M$	M	y
3	−3	$\frac{1}{8}$
2	−2	$\frac{1}{4}$
1	−1	$\frac{1}{2}$
0	0	1
−1	1	2
−2	2	4
−3	3	8

Ignore the middle column and plot the points (x, y).

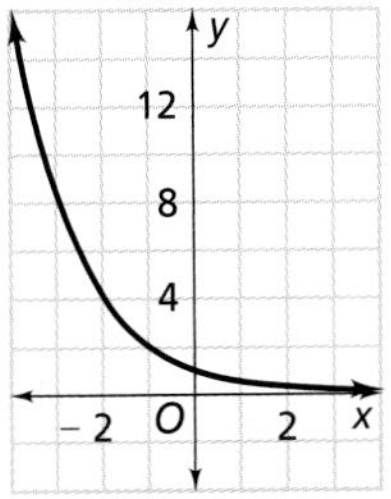

This graph is the same as the graph of $y = 2^M$ reflected over the y-axis. In other words, a point (M, y) on the graph of $y = 2^M$ corresponds to a point (x, y) on the graph of $y = 2^{-x}$, where $x = -M$.

You could also rewrite the equation.

$$y = 2^{-x} = \left(\frac{1}{2}\right)^x$$

Then you could use a relationship that you discovered in Chapter 5: the graph of $y = \left(\frac{1}{n}\right)^x$ is the reflection over the y-axis of the graph of $y = n^x$.

Example 2

You can use Blackline Master 6.4B to guide students through Example 2.

Some students may suggest the substitution $N = -2y - 4$, which also works. However, the simpler substitution $N = -2y$ is more easily interpreted graphically as a vertical reflection and scaling.

The Habits of Mind note near the end of Example 2 asks whether the order in which you carry out the transformations matters. Here, with a scaling and a reflection, the order does not matter; but caution students to take care when composing transformations. For example, a translation 2 units down followed by a reflection over the x-axis is not the same as a reflection over the x-axis followed by a translation 2 units down.

Wrap Up

Finish today's class by going over the Check Your Understanding core exercises as time allows.

Assessment Resources

Lesson Quiz 6.4

1. Sketch the graph of each equation.
   a. $y = \frac{1}{x}$ b. $y = \frac{1}{-x}$ c. $-y = \frac{1}{-x}$
   d. $y = x^3 + x$ e. $y = (-x)^3 + (-x)$ f. $-y = (-x)^3 + (-x)$

2. Describe how the graph of each equation is related to the graph of $y = \sqrt{x}$.
   a. $y = -\sqrt{x}$ b. $y = \sqrt{3x}$ c. $y = -\sqrt{3x}$
   d. $y = -\sqrt{\frac{1}{3}x}$ e. $-y = \sqrt{x}$ f. $-3y = \sqrt{x}$
   g. $-\frac{y}{3} = \sqrt{x}$ h. $-y = -\sqrt{x}$

3. Sketch the graph of each equation.
   a. $x^2 + (-y^2) = 25$ b. $(x + 2)^2 + (y - 3)^2 = 25$
   c. $(3(x + 2))^2 + (2(y - 3))^2 = 25$

Similarly, you can scale graphs vertically, or reflect them over the x-axis, by making substitutions such as $N = -2y$.

Example 2

Problem Sketch the graph of $(x + 1)^2 + (-2y - 4)^2 = 4$.

Solution With the substitution $N = -2y$, this equation becomes

$$(x + 1)^2 + (N - 4)^2 = 4$$

This is a circle of radius 2 with the center at the point $(-1, 4)$. Here is its graph and a table showing some of its points.

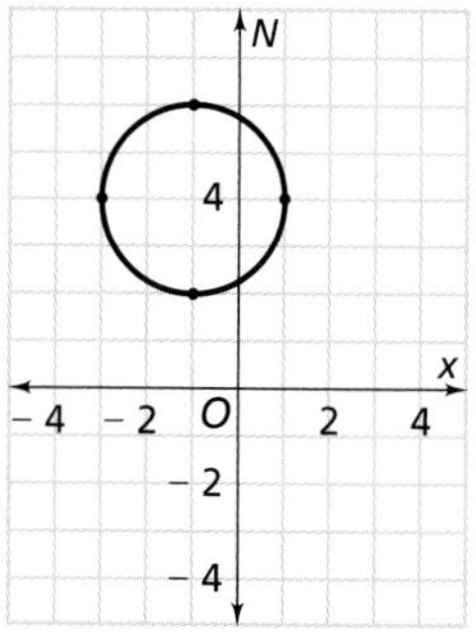

x	N
1	4
−3	4
−1	6
−1	2

Since $N = -2y$, solving for y gives

$$y = -\frac{N}{2}$$

Now, include a column of y-values in the table.

x	N	$y = -\frac{N}{2}$
1	4	−2
−3	4	−2
−1	6	−3
−1	2	−1

Ignore the middle column and plot the points (x, y).

To get this new graph, reflect the original circle over the x-axis and then scale it vertically by a factor of $\frac{1}{2}$. Algebraically, this corresponds to the fact that $y = -\frac{N}{2}$.

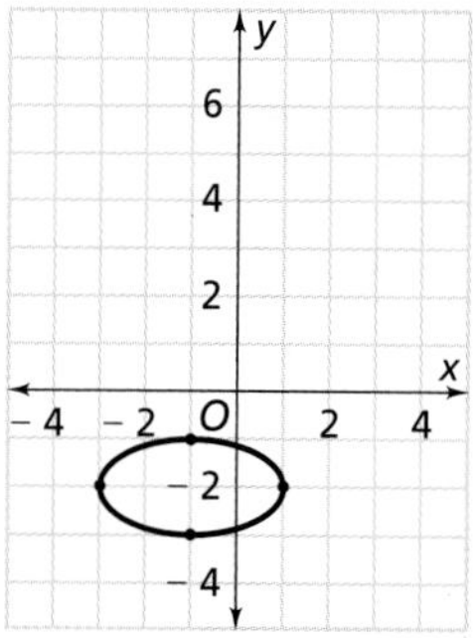

Habits of Mind

Experiment. Could you scale first and then reflect? Does it matter? Explain why or why not.

Answers

Exercises

1. a. See back of book.

b. The y-values for the graph of $5y = x^2 + 1$ are smaller by the factor 5 when compared to the corresponding y-values for the graph of $y = x^2 + 1$, so the graph of $5y = x^2 + 1$ is the graph of $y = x^2 + 1$ scaled vertically by the factor $\frac{1}{5}$.

c.

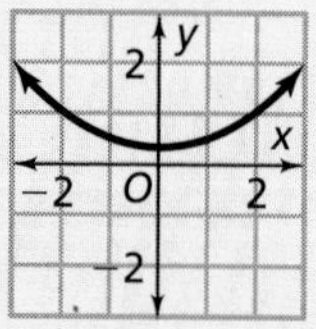

2. See back of book.

3. a.

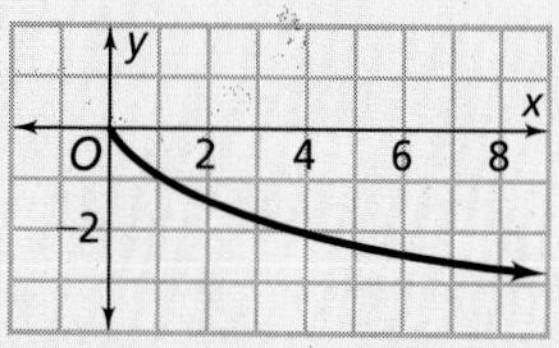

domain: $x \geq 0$, range: $y \leq 0$

Exercises *Practicing Habits of Mind*

Check Your Understanding

1. Consider the equation $5y = x^2 + 1$. Let $N = 5y$.
   a. Copy and complete the following table.
   b. Using the table from part (a), explain how the graphs of $y = x^2 + 1$ and $5y = x^2 + 1$ are related.
   c. Sketch the graph of $5y = x^2 + 1$.

x	$N = x^2 + 1$	$y = \frac{N}{5}$
−2	■	■
−1	■	■
0	■	■
1	■	■
2	■	■
3	■	■

2. Sketch the graph of each equation.
   a. $x^2 + y^2 = 36$ b. $(2x)^2 + y^2 = 36$ c. $x^2 + (3y)^2 = 36$
   d. $(2x)^2 + (3y)^2 = 36$ e. $\left(\frac{x}{2}\right)^2 + \left(\frac{y}{3}\right)^2 = 36$

For help graphing an equation in two variables, see the TI-Nspire Handbook, p. 778.

3. For each function f, sketch the graph of $y = f(x)$. Find the domain and range.
   a. $f(x) = -\sqrt{x}$ b. $f(x) = -3\sqrt{x}$
   c. $f(x) = \sqrt{-3x}$ d. $f(x) = \sqrt{1 - x}$

Hint: $1 - x = -(x - 1)$.

4. This figure shows the basic graph of $y = x^2$ and the graph of another parabola.

   The second parabola is the image of the basic graph after a horizontal scaling by a factor of 2 and a translation of 3 units up and 4 units to the right. What is an equation for the second parabola?

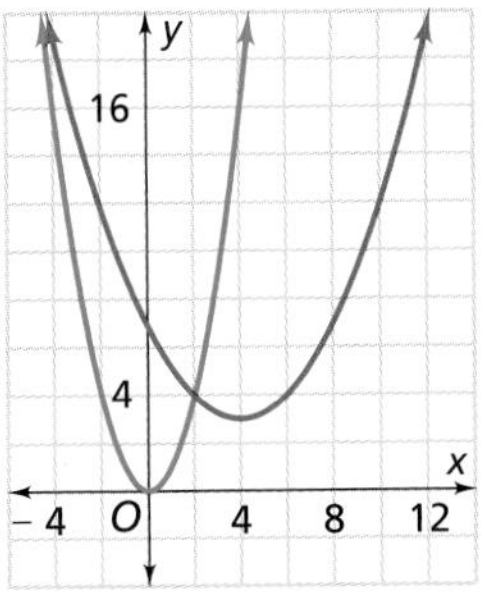

Exercises

HOMEWORK
- Core: 10, 11, 12, 14, 15
- Optional: 13, 16, 19
- Extension: 17, 18

Check Your Understanding

EXERCISE 2 You may wish to check to make sure that students know how to graph equations like these on their graphing calculators. However, if students are using their calculators exclusively to produce these sketches, you may also need to remind them to go back and analyze the effects of the various changes to the equations on the graphs. Ideally, students should be able to predict what the graph will look like before they graph it, either by plotting points or with technology.

EXERCISE 3 As with all of the graphing exercises in this lesson, you should encourage students to predict what each graph will look like before they begin to graph it.

EXERCISE 4 Whenever students are learning a new process, such as graphing a transformed equation of a basic graph, trying to "undo" the process will help them solidify their understanding. This exercise shows students a transformed graph and asks them to figure out how to change the equation of its basic graph to produce this transformation.

b.

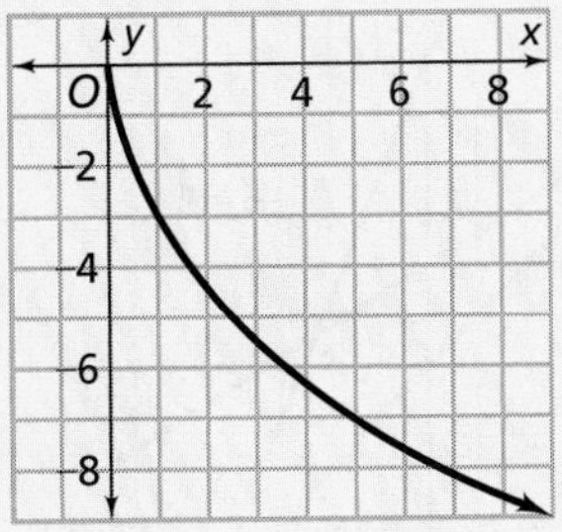

domain: $x \geq 0$, range: $y \leq 0$

c.

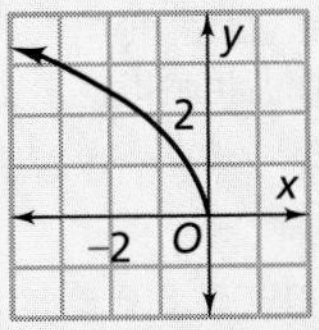

domain: $x \leq 0$, range: $y \geq 0$

d.

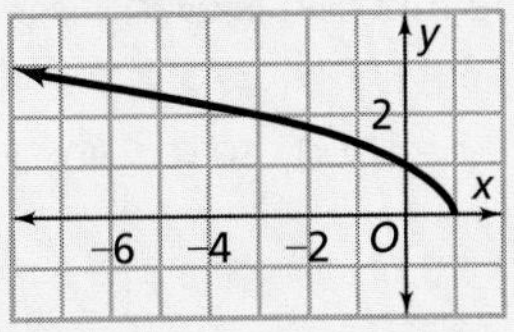

domain: $x \leq 1$, range: $y \geq 0$

4. $y = \left(\frac{1}{2}x - 2\right)^2 + 3$

EXERCISE 5 Students should notice that each of these graphs is identical to its corresponding basic graph. Point out that the basic graphs in parts (a) and (b) are of even functions. Although the equation in part (c) is not a function, its basic graph, $x^2 + y^2 = 1$, does share this property of even functions: a mapping of $(x, y) \mapsto (-x, y)$ sends the original graph onto itself.

EXERCISE 6 Tony's perspective helps when you are trying to recognize an even function by looking at its equation. Sasha's perspective helps when you are looking at a graph of a function and want to determine whether the function is even. Students should become comfortable with both methods.

EXERCISE 7 It is not a coincidence that even powers of x (and sums of even powers) are even functions. Similarly odd powers of x are odd functions. Making this connection may help students identify even and odd polynomial functions.

EXERCISE 9 Notice that vertical and horizontal lines have only one intercept. If you try to write an equation for such a line, for example $y = 3$, in two-intercept form, you cannot. There is no value of a for which $\frac{1}{a}$ equals 0. Similarly, lines that pass through the origin have only one intercept (a, b), where both a and b are 0. This means that you cannot write equations of the form $y = mx$ in two-intercept form.

5. Sketch the graph of each equation.

a. $y = (-x)^2$ **b.** $y = |-x|$ **c.** $(-x)^2 + y^2 = 1$

6. Tony and Sasha are arguing about the definition of an even function.

Tony says, "A function f is even if it has the property that $f(-x) = f(x)$ for all x in its domain."

Sasha says, "No, no. A function f is even if it looks the same when you reflect it over the y-axis."

Do you agree with Sasha or with Tony? Explain.

7. Explain how you can tell *without graphing* that the graph of $y = x^8 + 37x^6 - 71x^2 + 4$ looks the same when you reflect it over the y-axis.

8. **Take It Further** Given any function $f(x)$, explain why the function defined by $g(x) = f(x) + f(-x)$ looks the same when you reflect it over the y-axis.

9. Copy this graph of $x + y = 1$.

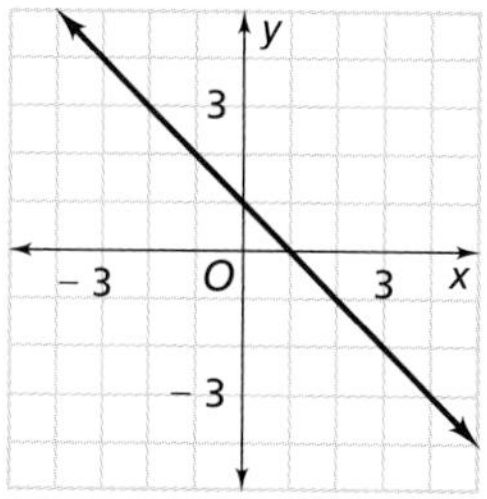

a. Sketch the graph of $\frac{x}{5} + \frac{y}{3} = 1$.

b. Sketch the graph of $\frac{x}{3} + \frac{y}{7} = 1$.

c. Find two points that must be on the graph of $\frac{x}{-17} + \frac{y}{12} = 1$.

d. The equation $\frac{x}{a} + \frac{y}{b} = 1$ is sometimes called the two-intercept form of a line. Explain.

Habits of Mind

Detect the key characteristics. Does every line have an equation of this form?

On Your Own

10. Sketch the graph of each equation.

a. $y = (-x)^3 + (-x)$ **b.** $y = (-x)^3 - (-x)$ **c.** $y = -x^3 - x$

d. $y = -x^3 + x$ **e.** $-y = (-x)^3 + (-x)$ **f.** $-y = (-x)^3 - (-x)$

Answers

5. a.

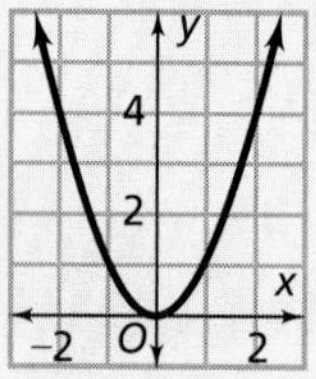

b.

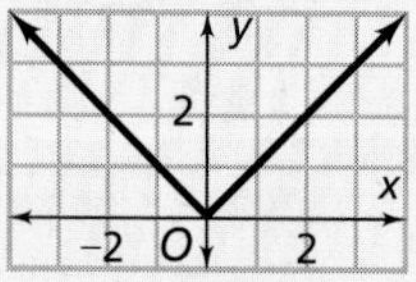

c.

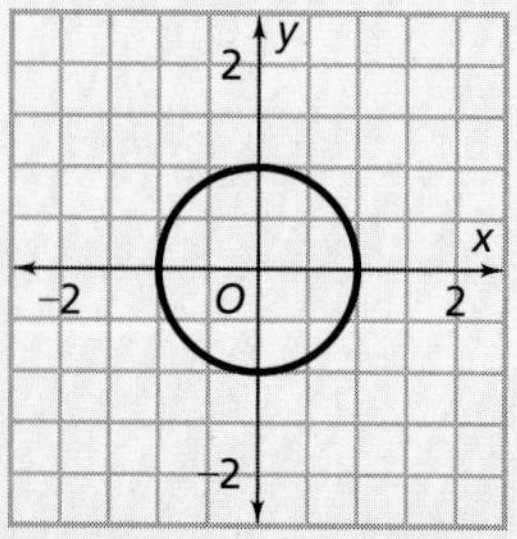

6. Agree with both; the statement $f(-x) = f(x)$ is equivalent to saying the graph of f has the y-axis as a line of symmetry.

7. Because all the exponents are even, the y-values for x and $-x$ are the same, so the function is even.

8. $g(-x) = f(-x) + f(-(-x)) = f(-x) + f(x) = g(x)$, so g is an even function.

9. a–b.

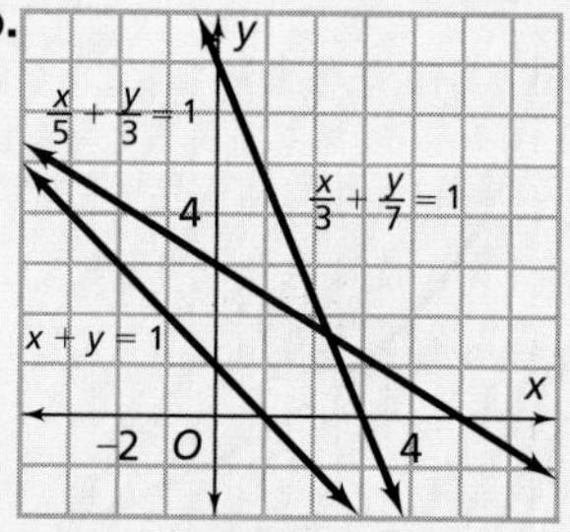

c. Answers may vary. Sample: $(0, 12)$, $(-17, 0)$

d. The intercepts of $\frac{x}{a} + \frac{y}{b} = 1$ are $(0, b)$ and $(a, 0)$.

10. See back of book.

11. Describe how the graph of each equation is related to the graph of $y = \frac{1}{x}$.

a. $y = \frac{1}{-x}$ **b.** $y = \frac{1}{-4x}$ **c.** $y = \frac{4}{-x}$ **d.** $-y = \frac{1}{x}$

e. $-4y = \frac{1}{x}$ **f.** $-\frac{y}{4} = \frac{1}{x}$ **g.** $-y = \frac{1}{-x}$ **h.** $-\frac{y}{4} = \frac{1}{-4x}$

12. This time, Tony, Sasha, and Derman are all arguing about odd functions.

Tony says, "A function f is odd if it has the property that $f(-x) = -f(x)$ for all x in its domain."

Sasha says, "No, no. A function f is odd if its reflection over the y-axis and its reflection over the x-axis look the same."

Derman says, "I always thought that f was odd if rotating its graph 180° around the origin gave you a graph that looked the same as the original."

Do you agree with Tony, Sasha, or Derman? Explain.

13. Explain how the graphs of the following equations are related.

- $(x + 3)^2 + (y - 4)^2 = 1$
- $(-x + 3)^2 + (-y - 4)^2 = 1$

14. Sketch the graph of each equation.

a. $(3x)^2 + (2y)^2 = 36$

b. $(3(x + 1))^2 + (2(y - 4))^2 = 36$

c. $\frac{(x + 1)^2}{4} + \frac{(y - 4)^2}{9} = 1$

15. **Standardized Test Prep** Which equation can you use to graph the reflection of the graph of $y = \sqrt{x - 2} + 3$ over the y-axis?

A. $y = \sqrt{x + 2} - 3$ **B.** $y = \sqrt{x - 2} - 3$

C. $y = \sqrt{-x - 2} + 3$ **D.** $y = \sqrt{-x + 2} + 3$

16. **Write About It** Consider the equation $y = mx$. Its graph is a straight line through the origin. As the slope m increases, the line becomes more steep. On the other hand, you can rewrite the equation as

$$\frac{y}{m} = x$$

Looking at it this way, you can say that as m increases, the line gets scaled vertically.

Are these two ways of visualizing this situation geometrically consistent with each other? Explain.

Go Online PHSchool.com

For additional practice, go to **Web Code:** bfa-0604

On Your Own

EXERCISE 11 Students should note the relationships between the graphs in this exercise. For example, the graphs in parts (a) and (d) look the same, which means that reflecting the graph of $y = \frac{1}{x}$ over the y-axis produces the same result as reflecting it over the x-axis. Algebraically, $f(-x) = -f(x)$, so $y = \frac{1}{x}$ is an odd function.

The graphs for parts (g) and (h) are the graph of $y = \frac{1}{x}$. This means the transformations cancelled each other out. In other words, the transformations come in pairs of inverse transformations.

EXERCISE 12 Some students will see the effect of the mapping $(x, y) \mapsto (-x, -y)$ as a composition of two reflections. Others will see it as a rotation. Both interpretations are correct, because the composition of two reflections over intersecting lines is always a rotation about the intersection of the two lines through an angle that is twice as great as the lesser angle created by the intersecting lines. The two lines here are the x- and y-axes. Their intersection is the origin. The angle formed by the axes measures 90°, so the rotation will be twice 90°, or 180°.

EXERCISE 13 You determine a circle from the coordinates of its center and the magnitude of its radius. A reflection will not change the radius, but it can change the location of the center.

EXERCISE 14 Rather than learning special forms for the equations of ellipses, students learn to think of ellipses as circles under different horizontal and vertical scalings.

EXERCISE 16 Tell students to assume $m > 0$.

11. a–f. Answers may vary. Samples are given.

a. the graph of $y = \frac{1}{x}$ reflected over the y-axis

b. the graph of $y = \frac{1}{x}$ reflected over the y-axis and scaled horizontally by the factor $\frac{1}{4}$

c. the graph of $y = \frac{1}{x}$ reflected over the y-axis and scaled vertically by the factor 4

d. the graph of $y = \frac{1}{x}$ reflected over the x-axis

e. the graph of $y = \frac{1}{x}$ reflected over the x-axis and scaled horizontally by the factor $\frac{1}{4}$

f. the graph of $y = \frac{1}{x}$ reflected over the x-axis and scaled vertically by the factor 4

g. same as the graph of $y = \frac{1}{x}$

h. same as the graph of $y = \frac{1}{x}$

12. Agree with all three; if $f(-x) = -f(x)$, then (x, y) maps to $(-x, -y)$. That mapping is equivalent to a composition of a reflection over the x-axis and a reflection over the y-axis. Those two reflections are equivalent to a 180° rotation about the origin.

13. Answers may vary. Sample: The graph of the second equation is the graph of the first equation after it has been reflected over the y-axis and then over the x-axis.

14. See back of book.

15. C

16. Yes; making a line more steep is the same as increasing the change in y for each unit change in x, which is exactly what happens in a vertical scaling.

EXERCISE 17 previews the process (in reverse) that students will learn in Lesson 6.7.

Additional Resources

PRINT RESOURCES
- Solution Manual
- Practice Workbook
- Assessment Resources
- Teaching Resources

TECHNOLOGY
- Interactive Textbook
- TeacherExpress CD-ROM
- ExamView CD-ROM
- PHSchool.com

Additional Practice

1. Sketch the graph of each equation.
   a. $y = (x - 4)^3 + (x - 4)$ b. $y - 3 = (x - 1)^3 + (x - 1)$
   c. $y + 1 = (x - 2)^3 + (x - 2)$ d. $y = (x - 2)^3 + x - 3$

2. Sketch the graph of each equation. Then find the slope of the graph.
   a. $y = -2x$
   b. $y = -2(x + 1)$
   c. $y + 3 = -2(x + 1)$
   d. How are the graphs in parts (a), (b), and (c) related? Explain.

3. a. Sketch the graph of $y = 3x$.
   b. Translate the graph of $y = 3x$ four units to the left so that the origin (0, 0) maps to the point (−4, 0) in the translated image. Find the equation of this new line.
   c. Translate the graph of $y = 3x$ five units to the right and three units down so that the origin (0, 0) is mapped to the point (5, −3) in the translated image. Find the equation of this new line.

4. a. Find an equation of the line with slope 3 that contains the point (6, 2).
   b. Find an equation of the line with slope −5 that contains the point (−4, 3).

5. Sketch the graph of each equation.
   a. $y = -x^2$ b. $y = -x^3$ c. $y = -\frac{1}{x}$
   d. $y = -x^3 + x$ e. $y = -x^3 - x$ f. $y = -\sqrt{x}$

6. Describe how the graph of each equation is related to the graph of $y = |x|$.
   a. $y = -|x|$ b. $y = |5x|$ c. $y = -|5x|$ d. $y = -\left|\frac{1}{5}x\right|$
   e. $-y = |x|$ f. $-5y = |x|$ g. $-\frac{y}{5} = |x|$ h. $-y = |-x|$

7. Sketch the graph of each equation.
   a. $(2x)^2 + (4y)^2 = 16$
   b. $(2(x - 1))^2 + (4(y + 3))^2 = 16$
   c. $\frac{(x-1)^2}{9} + \frac{(y+3)^2}{4} = 1$

Practice: For Lesson 6.4, assign Exercises 5–7.

17. Take It Further

a. Explain how the graphs of the following equations are related.
- $y = x^3 + 3x^2 + 7x + 13$
- $y = (x - 1)^3 + 3(x - 1)^2 + 7(x - 1) + 13$

b. Expand $(x - 1)^3 + 3(x - 1)^2 + 7(x - 1) + 13$.

c. If you divide the equation $y = x^3 + 4x + 8$ by 8, you get
$$\frac{1}{8}y = \left(\frac{1}{2}x\right)^3 + \left(\frac{1}{2}x\right) + 1$$
Use the second equation to explain how the graph of $y = x^3 + 4x + 8$ is related to the graph of $y = x^3 + x + 1$.

d. Sketch the graph of $y = x^3 + x + 1$.

e. Use parts (a)–(d) to sketch the graph of $y = x^3 + 3x^2 + 7x + 13$.

In Investigation 6B, you will see why you might want to replace x with $x - 1$.

18. Take It Further At home, Derman is thinking about the graph of $y = \left(\frac{x}{3}\right)^2$ again.

Derman thinks, "Instead of scaling the graph of $y = x^2$ horizontally by the factor of 3, I can just keep it where it is and scale the x-axis instead by the factor of $\frac{1}{3}$."

This figure shows the original axes in green and Derman's new axes in purple.

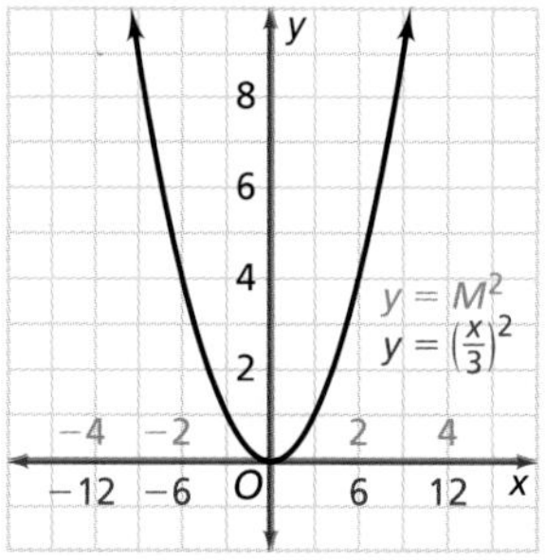

Use the substitution $M = \frac{x}{3}$ to explain why Derman's method is valid.

If the scale factor is greater than 1, the object stretches. If the scale factor is less than 1, the object shrinks.

Maintain Your Skills

19. Determine whether each function is even, odd, or neither.

a. $f(x) = x^2$ b. $f(x) = x^3$ c. $f(x) = x^4$ d. $f(x) = x^5$

e. $f(x) = x^{10}$ f. $f(x) = x^{-1}$ g. $f(x) = x^n$, where n is an integer

Answers

17. a. The graph of the second equation is the graph of the first equation translated 1 unit to the right.

b. $x^3 + 4x + 8$

c. The graph of $y = x^3 + 4x + 8$ is the graph of $y = x^3 + x + 1$ scaled vertically by the factor 8 and horizontally by the factor 2.

d.

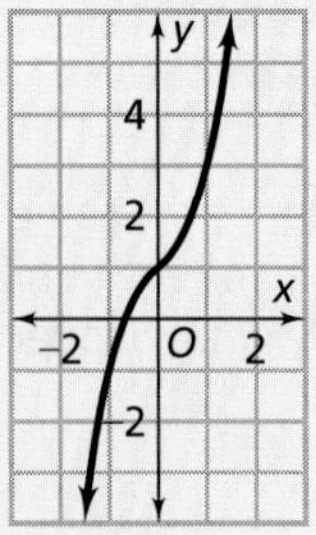

e.

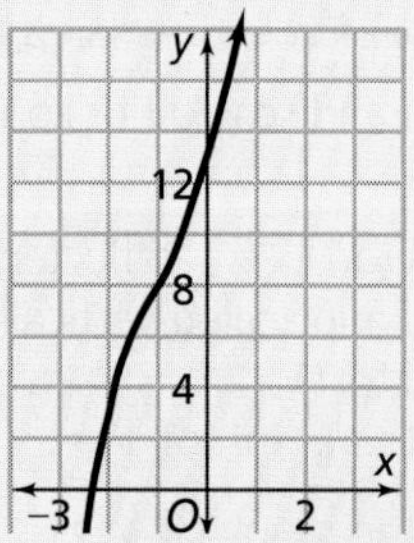

18. Answers may vary. Sample: Derman thinks of the parabola as $y = M^2$ with the green horizontal axis being the M-axis. When he scales the green M-axis by the factor $\frac{1}{3}$ to become the purple x-axis, the M-coordinate of each point on the green horizontal axis is one-third of its x-coordinate on the purple horizontal axis. That is, $M = \frac{x}{3}$. So, $y = M^2$ on the green coordinate axes becomes $y = \left(\frac{x}{3}\right)^2$ on the purple coordinate axes.

19. a. even **b.** odd
c. even **d.** odd
e. even **f.** odd
g. even if $n = 2k$ or odd if $n = 2k + 1$, where k is an integer

Mathematical Reflections 6A

In this investigation, you sketched basic graphs. You learned to relate the effects on a basic graph and on the equation of the graph of a translation, a scaling, or a reflection of the graph. These exercises will help you summarize what you have learned.

1. **a.** Explain what it means for a function to be even, both algebraically and graphically, and give an example of an even function.
   b. Explain what it means for a function to be odd, both algebraically and graphically, and give an example of an odd function.
2. Sketch the graph of $y = |x - 2| + 3$. How is your graph related to the graph of $y = |x|$?
3. Write an equation for a function with a graph that is the graph of $y = x^3$ after a translation 3 units to the left and 1 unit up.
4. Sketch the graph of $\left(\frac{x}{2}\right)^2 + (3y)^2 = 25$. How is your graph related to the graph of $x^2 + y^2 = 25$?
5. Write an equation for a function with a graph that is the graph of $y = \frac{1}{x}$ scaled horizontally by the factor 6.
6. How are the graphs of $y = x^2$ and $y = (x - 3)^2$ related?
7. What does the graph of $(x + 1)^2 + (y - 4)^2 = 36$ look like?
8. What does the graph of $-2y = x^3 - x$ look like?

Vocabulary

In this investigation, you learned these terms. Make sure you understand what each one means and how to use it.

- **even function**
- **odd function**
- **unit circle**

One image is a stretch. The other image is a reflection. $100 question: What does the original figure look like?

Mathematical Reflections

EXERCISES 6–8 At the start of the investigation, you may have assigned these as Questions 1–3 for students to think and write about.

Mathematical Reflections

1. a. Algebraically, a function is even if $f(-x) = f(x)$. Graphically, a function is even if its graph has the y-axis as a line of symmetry; answers may vary. Sample: $y = x^2$

b. Algebraically, a function is odd if $f(-x) = -f(x)$. Graphically, a function is odd if it has 180° rotational symmetry about the origin; answers may vary. Sample: $y = x^3$

2.

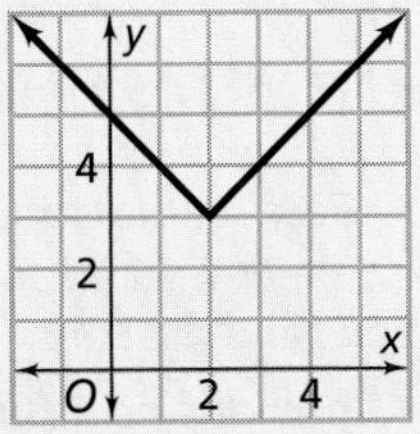

The graph of $y = |x - 2| + 3$ is the graph of $y = |x|$ translated 2 units to the right and 3 units up.

3. $y = (x + 3)^3 + 1$

4.

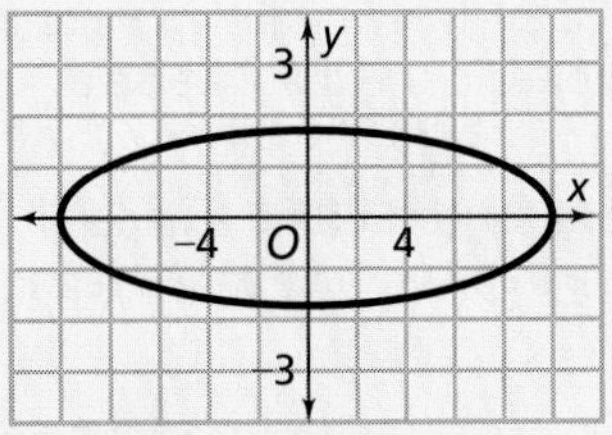

The graph of $\left(\frac{x}{2}\right)^2 + (3y)^2 = 25$ is the graph of $x^2 + y^2 = 25$ scaled horizontally by the factor 2 and vertically by the factor $\frac{1}{3}$.

5. $y = \frac{6}{x}$

6. The graph of $y = (x - 3)^2$ is the graph of $y = x^2$ translated 3 units to the right.

7. a circle with center $(-1, 4)$ and radius 6

8. the graph of $y = x^3 - x$ reflected over the y-axis and scaled vertically by the factor $\frac{1}{2}$

Investigation Overview

In Investigation 6A, students began to see how a change to an equation, such as replacing x by $x - 3$ or by $\frac{x}{2}$, changed its graph. In this investigation, they analyze these changes, translations and dilations (scalings), in a new way. Translations and dilations and any composition of translations and dilations are grouped as *affine transformations*. An affine transformation is a mapping of the form $x \mapsto ax + b$, and is given the notation $\mathcal{A}_{(a,\,b)}$. Rather than just applying such a transformation to the equation for a basic graph to see how the transformation changes a graph, students see how to use an affine transformation to convert the equation of a general graph into one of the basic graph forms. Their goal is to be able to graph many more types of equations, including general cubic equations and ellipses. In Investigation 6C, students will pull everything together and actually graph these more general equations, but for now, students focus on getting the equations into a form that is easy to graph. Along the way, students also examine and analyze the algebraic structure of affine transformations. They look for inverses and the identity, and they test for commutativity. They prove properties of transformations by generalizing from a series of numerical calculations to produce a logical proof.

You may wish to assign Questions 1–3 for students to think and write about during the investigation.

Learning Goals

- Write any composition of translations and dilations as an affine transformation and write any affine transformation as a composition of a dilation and a translation.
- Find the inverse of a dilation, a translation, or an affine transformation and use that inverse as a tool to solve equations.
- Find transformations for converting a general quadratic or cubic into one of the basic graph forms.

Habits and Skills

- Generalize from a series of numerical calculations to produce a proof for a property of transformations.
- Extend the idea of finding an inverse of a function by undoing its steps in reverse order to find the inverse of an affine transformation.
- Find connections between algebraic calculations, such as using substitutions to make an equation monic or to complete the square, and the affine transformations of translation and dilation.

Investigation 6B

Affine Transformations

In *Affine Transformations*, you will continue to work with translations and dilations. You will learn to write the composition of a translation and a dilation as an affine transformation. You will use affine transformations to convert quadratic and cubic equations into the basic graph forms.

By the end of this investigation, you will be able to answer questions like these.

1. Why do dilations commute under function composition?
2. How do you compute the inverse of an affine transformation?
3. How do you transform an equation of the form $y = ax^3 + bx^2 + cx + d$ into one of the equations $y = x^3$, $y = x^3 + x$, or $y = x^3 - x$ by composing dilations and translations?

You will learn how to

- write any composition of translations and dilations as an affine transformation and write any affine transformation as a composition of a dilation and a translation
- find the inverse of a dilation, a translation, or an affine transformation and use that inverse as a tool to solve equations
- find transformations for converting a general quadratic or cubic into one of the basic graph forms

You will develop these habits and skills:

- Generalize from a series of numerical calculations to produce a proof for a property of transformations.
- Extend the idea of finding an inverse of a function by undoing its steps in reverse order to find the inverse of an affine transformation.
- Find connections between algebraic calculations, such as using substitutions to make an equation monic or to complete the square and the affine transformations of translation and dilation.

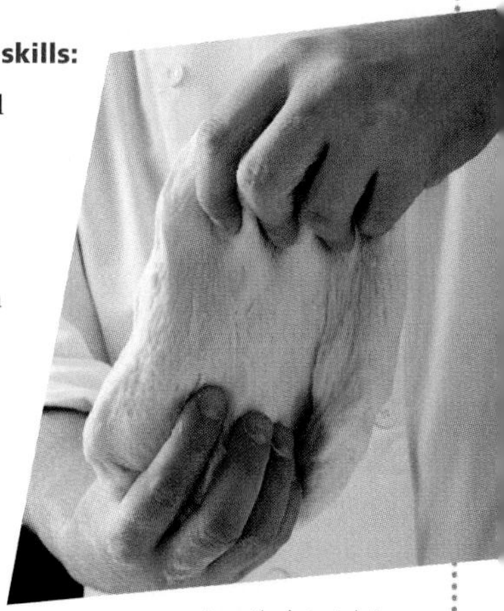

A vertical stretch is an affine transformation.

Investigation Road Map

LESSON 6.5, ***Getting Started,*** has students revisit function composition and work with some new functions, T_n and D_n, that they eventually use as notation for translations and dilations.

LESSON 6.6, ***Introducing Affine Transformations,*** has students begin to examine the algebraic structure (identity, commutativity, inverses, and so on) for the translation and dilation functions they learned about in Lesson 6.5. They also define an *affine transformation* as a composition of a translation and a dilation.

LESSON 6.7, ***Transforming Equations,*** has students learn techniques that allow them to find substitutions that convert any equation of the form $y = ax^2 + bx + c$ into an equation of the form $N = M^2$; also that convert any equation of the form $y = ax^3 + bx^2 + cx + d$ into an equation of one of these forms: $S = R^3$, $S = R^3 + R$, or $S = R^3 - R$.

6.5 Getting Started

Activating Prior Knowledge
Exploring New Ideas

The compositions of some types of functions have special properties.

For You to Explore

Given a real number a, define a function T_a by the formula $T_a(x) = x + a$ for any real number x.

1. a. Compute each value.

   $T_3(2)$ $T_3(5)$ $T_3(-1)$ $T_3(-7)$ $T_3(0)$

   b. Why is T_a called a *translation by a*?

2. a. Compute each value.

   $T_0(2)$ $T_0(5)$ $T_0(-1)$ $T_0(-7)$ $T_0(0)$

   b. Why is T_0 called the **identity transformation**?

Suppose you have two functions, f and g where the target of g matches the domain of f.

As you saw in Chapter 2, you can build a new function $f \circ g$:

$$(f \circ g)(x) = f(g(x))$$

Remember...

You read $f \circ g$ as "f composed with g" or "f circle g." To find $f \circ g(a)$, you apply g to the input a and then apply f to the resulting output.

3. a. Compute each value.

   $(T_3 \circ T_2)(4)$ $(T_3 \circ T_2)(-1)$ $(T_3 \circ T_2)(179)$
   $(T_3 \circ T_2)(\pi)$ $(T_3 \circ T_2)(x)$, in terms of x

   b. Find a such that $T_3 \circ T_2 = T_a$.

4. Two functions $f : \mathbb{R} \to \mathbb{R}$ and $g : \mathbb{R} \to \mathbb{R}$ are defined to be equal if $f(x) = g(x)$ for all real numbers x. Prove that $T_a \circ T_b = T_b \circ T_a$.

In other words, prove that translations are commutative. In general, it is not always true that $f \circ g = g \circ f$.

5. Compute each value.

   a. $(T_{-4} \circ T_4)(3)$
   b. $(T_{-4} \circ T_4)(-2)$
   c. $(T_{-4} \circ T_4)(7)$
   d. $(T_{-4} \circ T_4)(-1)$
   e. $(T_{-4} \circ T_4)(x)$, for any real number x
   f. $(T_4 \circ T_{-4})(x)$, for any real number x

6. **Write About It** Explain how the functions T_a and T_{-a} are related to each other.

Answers

For You to Explore

1. a. 5; 8; 2; −4; 3

   b. Thinking of T_a as mapping the number line onto itself, the output of T_a is the image of the input after a translation. If $a > 0$, the translation is a units to the right, and if $a < 0$, the translation is a units to the left.

2. a. 2; 5; −1; −7; 0

   b. T_0 leaves the input value unchanged.

3. a. 9; 4; 184; $\pi + 5$; $x + 5$

   b. 5

4. $(T_a \circ T_b)(x) = (T_a(T_b(x)) = T_a(x + b) = (x + b) + a = (x + a) + b = T_b(x + a) = (T_b(T_a(x)) = (T_b \circ T_a)(x)$

5. a. 3 b. −2 c. 7
   d. −1 e. x f. x

6. T_a and T_{-a} are inverses because $(T_a \circ T_{-a})(x) = (T_{-a} \circ T_a)(x) = x$.

Lesson Overview

GOAL

- Review function compositions.

This lesson gives students a chance to review function composition, which they studied in Chapter 2. It introduces two new functions:

- T_a, which maps each input x to $x + a$
- D_s, which maps each input x to sx

Students will use this notation throughout the rest of the chapter to describe translations and dilations respectively.

FOR YOU TO EXPLORE
- Core: 1, 2, 3, 4, 5
- Optional: 6

HOMEWORK
- Core: 7, 8, 9, 10, 11, 12, 13, 14
- Optional: 16, 17
- Extension: 15

VOCABULARY
- dilation, D_s
- identity transformation
- reflection transformation
- translation, T_a

Launch

Have students get started on the For You to Explore problems right away.

Explore

As students are working, check on their memory of function composition. Are they working with the notation fluently or is some review in order?

For You to Explore

PROBLEM 2 The function T_a is really a collection of functions, one for each different value of a. It is a standard mathematical question to ask whether there is a particular value of a, call it A, which results in an *identity* function, so that $T_A(x) = x$ for all x. This problem shows that such a value exists and is equal to 0.

PROBLEMS 4 AND 5 ask students to investigate whether the functions T_a and T_b are commutative under function composition and whether a function T_a has an inverse.

PROBLEM 3 gets to the heart of how statements in function algebra are established. Students learn that by performing repeated calculations with numbers, they can sometimes see a pattern that reveals a key property of a function. In this case, the property is $T_a \circ T_b = T_{a+b}$, which students eventually prove as Theorem 6.1 in Lesson 6.6.

PROBLEM 5 The numerical examples in parts (a)–(d) lead to the more general results in parts (e) and (f), and to the even more general result in Problem 6. Students are showing that T_{-4} and T_4 are inverse functions.

Wrap Up

Compare the properties of translation functions T_a to the properties of arithmetic operations. Are translations associative? Are translations commutative? Is there an identity translation? Do translations have inverses? This will prepare students for discussions they will have throughout this investigation.

If time allows, you may want to let students get started on the On Your Own exercises.

Exercises

HOMEWORK

- Core: 7, 8, 9, 10, 11, 12, 13, 14
- Optional: 16, 17
- Extension: 15

On Your Own

EXERCISES 7–13 Students investigate this new group of functions in the same way they investigated the translation functions in the For You to Explore problems.

EXERCISE 9 Some students may have difficulty seeing $-x$ as a reflection of x if they are thinking in terms of the number line rather than the coordinate plane. They might prefer to describe D_{-1} as the "change-the-signs" function, unless you ask a question such as, "What would the line of reflection be if $-x$ is a reflected image of x?"

EXERCISE 10 Students prove the general result, that $D_a \circ D_b = D_{ab}$, as Theorem 6.2 in Lesson 6.2.

EXERCISE 14 Although translations commute under composition and dilations commute under composition, a translation will not commute with a dilation. The order matters when you are working with different types of transformations.

Exercises *Practicing Habits of Mind*

On Your Own

For a nonzero real number s, a function D_s: $\mathbb{R} \to \mathbb{R}$ is defined by the formula $D_s(x) = sx$ for any real number x.

The smooth surface of the water results in a reflection of the city.

7. a. Compute each value.

$D_3(2)$ $D_3(5)$ $D_3(-1)$ $D_3(-7)$ $D_3(0)$

b. Explain why D_s is called a *dilation by s.*

8. a. Compute each value.

$D_1(2)$ $D_1(5)$ $D_1(-1)$ $D_1(-7)$

$D_1(x)$, in terms of x

b. Why is D_1 called the identity transformation?

9. a. Compute each value.

$D_{-1}(2)$ $D_{-1}(5)$ $D_{-1}(-1)$ $D_{-1}(-7)$ $D_{-1}(0)$

b. Why is D_{-1} called the **reflection transformation**?

10. a. Compute each value.

$(D_3 \circ D_2)(4)$ $(D_3 \circ D_2)(-1)$ $(D_3 \circ D_2)(0)$ $(D_3 \circ D_2)(7)$ $(D_3 \circ D_2)(8)$

b. Find k such that $D_3 \circ D_2 = D_k$.

Remember...

It is not usually the case that $f \circ g = g \circ f$. However, dilations commute under composition.

11. Prove that $D_s \circ D_t = D_t \circ D_s$.

12. Compute each value.

a. $(D_{\frac{1}{4}} \circ D_4)(3)$ **b.** $(D_{\frac{1}{4}} \circ D_4)(-2)$

c. $(D_3 \circ D_{\frac{1}{3}})(7)$ **d.** $(D_{\frac{1}{3}} \circ D_3)(-1)$

e. $(D_{\frac{1}{4}} \circ D_4)(x)$, for any real number x

f. $(D_4 \circ D_{\frac{1}{4}})(x)$, for any real number x

13. Write About It Explain how the functions D_s and $D_{\frac{1}{s}}$ are related to each other.

14. Write each function in the form $x \mapsto ax + b$, where a and b are numbers.

a. $T_5 \circ D_2$ **b.** $D_2 \circ T_5$

Answers

7. a. 6; 15; −3; −21; 0

b. Thinking of D_s as mapping the number line onto itself, the output of D_s is the image of the input after a dilation by the factor s (using the origin of the number line as the center of dilation).

8. a. 2; 5; −1; −7; x

b. D_1 leaves the input value unchanged.

9. a. −2; −5; 1; 7; 0

b. Thinking of D_{-1} as mapping the number line onto itself, the output of D_{-1} is the image of the input after a reflection over the origin of the number line.

10. a. 24; −6; 0; 42; 48

b. 6

11. $(D_s \circ D_t)(x) = (D_s(D_t(x)) = D_s(tx) = s(tx) = t(sx) = D_t(sx) = (D_t(D_s(x)) = D_t \circ D_s(x)$

12. a. 3 **b.** −2 **c.** 7 **d.** −1

e. x **f.** x

15. **Take It Further** Suppose r and s are numbers. Show that each function below can be defined by a linear polynomial with coefficients expressed in terms of r and s.

a. $T_r \circ D_s$ **b.** $D_s \circ T_r$

Remember...

A linear polynomial is a polynomial of the form $ax + b$, where the coefficients a and b are numbers.

Maintain Your Skills

16. Use the recursive definition below for a function f.

$$f(n) = \begin{cases} 2 & \text{if } n = 0 \\ T_3\,(f(n-1)) & \text{if } n > 0 \end{cases}$$

a. Copy and complete the following table.

n	$f(n)$
0	2
1	5
2	■
3	■
4	■
5	■
6	■

b. Find a closed form for f.

17. Use the definition below for the linear function $f: \mathbb{R} \rightarrow \mathbb{R}$.

$$f(x) = 2x + 3$$

Find a closed form for each function.

a. $f \circ f$ **b.** $f \circ f \circ f$

c. $f \circ f \circ f \circ f$ **d.** $\underbrace{f \circ f \circ f \circ \cdots \circ f}_{7\ f\text{'s}}$

13. D_4 and $D_{\frac{1}{4}}$ are inverses because $\left(D_4 \circ D_{\frac{1}{4}}\right)(x) = \left(D_{\frac{1}{4}} \circ D_4\right)(x) = x$.

14. a. $x \mapsto 2x + 5$

b. $x \mapsto 2x + 10$

15. a. $(T_r \circ D_s)(x) = T_r(D_s(x)) = T_r(sx) = sx + r$

b. $(D_s \circ T_r)(x) = D_s(T_r(x)) = D_s(x + r) = s(x + r) = sx + sr$

16. a.

n	$f(n)$
0	2
1	5
2	**8**
3	**11**
4	**14**
5	**17**
6	**20**

b. $f(n) = 3n + 2$

17. See back of book.

Maintain Your Skills

EXERCISE 17 Many students may just apply the function seven times to find the closed form for part (d). Others may be able to see that if you apply f n times, the coefficient of x will be 2^n. Finding a closed form for the constant term is a little tougher, but in the next chapter, students learn that it is equal to $3 \cdot \frac{2^n - 1}{2 - 1} = 3(2^n - 1)$.

Lesson Overview

GOAL

- Write any composition of translations and dilations as an affine transformation and write any affine transformation as a composition of a dilation and a translation.

In this lesson, students learn that they can write any composition of the transformation functions introduced in Lesson 6.5—translations, T_a, and dilations, D_s—in the form $x \mapsto ax + b$. This kind of function should be familiar, because students have been working with linear functions since CME Project *Algebra 1*. In this lesson, though, they begin to think about these functions in a new way. Students examine the algebraic structure of these functions under the operation of function composition.

CHECK YOUR UNDERSTANDING
- Core: 1, 2, 3, 4, 6, 7
- Optional: 5, 8

MATERIALS
- graph paper
- graphing calculators

HOMEWORK
- Core: 9, 10, 11, 13, 14, 15, 16, 17
- Optional: 12, 18, 19, 20a–b, 21, 22, 23
- Extension: 20c

VOCABULARY
- affine transformation, $\mathcal{A}_{(a,\,b)}$
- dilation, D_s
- socks and shoes method
- translation, T_a

Launch

Start by asking questions about the properties of dilation functions D_s (and translation functions T_a, if you did not discuss them in the Lesson 6.5 Wrap Up). Are dilations associative? Are dilations commutative? Is there an identity dilation? Do dilations have inverses?

Explore

Developing Habits of Mind

Encourage students to think about the algebraic structure of these new functions. Refer students to Problem 3 in Lesson 6.5, where they discovered that $T_3 \circ T_2 = T_5$. Students should recognize that this statement about the algebra of translation functions has an equivalent statement from the arithmetic of real numbers: $3 + 2 = 5$. Now students will focus on the behavior of the functions, rather than on the arithmetic operation. Still, if at any time students forget the meanings of these functions, use the definitions given on this page along with numeric examples, such as $T_3(4) = 7$ and $(T_3 \circ T_2)(4) = 9$, to help students make sense of the functions.

6.6 Introducing Affine Transformations

Unlike the logarithmic functions in Chapter 5, you are probably familiar with the functions in Lesson 6.5. They are among the first functions you worked with in Algebra 1.

Developing Habits of Mind

Think about functions another way. The function D_5 is just $x \mapsto 5x$, and T_4 is just $x \mapsto x + 4$. These are examples of linear functions, which you have worked with before. However, in this investigation and the next, the perspective on these functions is a bit different.

You will study an algebraic structure, in which transformations of the form $x \mapsto ax + b$ are the objects, and the operation is function composition. Lesson 2.3 introduced you to the idea of algebra with functions. In this lesson, you will look much more closely at this idea.

Think of D_5 and T_4 as transformations of the number line. For example, T_4 translates numbers to the right by 4 units. The function D_5 dilates, or stretches, the number line by a factor of 5. Thinking about linear functions as transformations will help bring together many of the ideas about graph transformations from the previous investigation.

A transformation on $\mathbb{R}$ is a function that maps $\mathbb{R}$ to itself.

Transformations of the form $x \mapsto ax + b$ are called *affine transformations.* An affine transformation can be built from two simpler types of transformation—translations and dilations.

The word *affine* comes from the Latin *affinis*, which means "neighboring" or "related." It is related to the word *affinity*.

Facts and Notation

Let a be a real number. A translation by a is a transformation T_a of $\mathbb{R}$ given by the formula below, for any real number x.

$$T_a(x) = x + a$$

Let s be a nonzero real number. A dilation by s is a transformation D_s of $\mathbb{R}$ given by the formula below, for any real number x.

$$D_s(x) = sx$$

For Discussion

1. Why do you call T_a a translation? Why do you call D_s a dilation?

Answers

For Discussion

1. Thinking of T_a as mapping the number line onto itself, the output of T_a is the image of the input after a translation. If $a > 0$, the translation is a units to the right, and if $a < 0$, the translation is a units to the left. Thinking of D_s as mapping the number line onto itself, the output of D_s is the image of the input after a dilation by the factor s (using the origin of the number line as the center of dilation). If $s < 0$, the dilation includes a reflection over the origin of the number line.

In Problem 3 from Lesson 6.5, you saw that $T_3 \circ T_2 = T_5$. This theorem is the generalization of that result.

Theorem 6.1

Let a and b be real numbers. Then $T_a \circ T_b = T_{a+b}$.

Developing Habits of Mind

Establish a process. Statements like Theorem 6.1 take some getting used to. Here is one way to think about building a proof. This is a series of questions you might ask yourself and steps you might take.

Step 1 What does the claim $T_a \circ T_b = T_{a+b}$ mean? It means that the two functions $T_a \circ T_b$ and T_{a+b} are the same. And what does that mean? It means that they have the same domain and that, given any input, they produce the same output.

Step 2 Try it with numbers. You did this in Exercise 3 of Lesson 6.5. There you showed that

- $(T_3 \circ T_2)(4) = 4 + 5 = T_5(4)$
- $(T_3 \circ T_2)(-1) = -1 + 5 = T_5(-1)$
- $(T_3 \circ T_2)(179) = 179 + 5 = T_5(179)$
- $(T_3 \circ T_2)(\pi) = \pi + 5 = T_5(\pi)$
- $(T_3 \circ T_2)(x) = x + 5 = T_5(x)$, for any number x

This shows that $T_3 \circ T_2 = T_5$. Now generalize this result by replacing 3 and 2 with a and b. That is, show that

- $(T_a \circ T_b)(4) = 4 + a + b = T_{a+b}(4)$
- $(T_a \circ T_b)(-1) = -1 + a + b = T_{a+b}(-1)$
- $(T_a \circ T_b)(179) = 179 + a + b = T_{a+b}(179)$

Here is an example of the computation for $(T_a \circ T_b)(179)$.

$$\begin{aligned}(T_a \circ T_b)(179) &= T_a(T_b(179)) \\ &= T_a(179 + b) \\ &= (179 + b) + a \\ &= 179 + (a + b) \\ &= T_{a+b}(179)\end{aligned}$$

Similarly, you can show that

- $(T_a \circ T_b)(\pi) = \pi + a + b = T_{a+b}(\pi)$
- $(T_a \circ T_b)(x) = x + a + b = T_{a+b}(x)$ for any number x

The last equation does it. If the equation below is true for any number x, then the functions $T_a \circ T_b$ and T_{a+b} are the same.

$$(T_a \circ T_b)(x) = x + a + b = T_{a+b}(x)$$

You can check that the domains of $T_a \circ T_b$ and T_{a+b} are the same. Both domains are the real numbers.

Habits of Mind

Establish a process. There is a rhythm to these calculations. Try to find it. The important thing is that there is nothing special about 179 or -1 or π. The same steps work for any input.

Developing Habits of Mind

Ask students to justify each step of the computation of $(T_a \circ T_b)(179)$, shown in Step 2.

$(T_a \circ T_b)(179) = T_a(T_b(179))$

definition of composition

$= T_a(179 + b)$

definition of T_n

$= (179 + b) + a$

definition of T_n

$= 179 + (a + b)$

commutative and associative properties of addition

$= T_{a+b}(179)$

definition of T_n

For You to Do

PROBLEM 2 Discuss with students why you can omit the steps "$x + a + b = x + b + a$" shown in the proof given below for Problem 2. Because addition of real numbers is commutative, $T_{a+b} = T_{b+a}$; so, by Theorem 6.1, $T_a \circ T_b = T_b \circ T_a$. This reasoning is similar to reasoning used for some of the matrix algebra results in Chapter 4: reduce the matrix arithmetic to element arithmetic that uses real numbers. Here, the algebra of composition of functions T_a and T_b reduces to a problem in real number arithmetic instead. You can have a similar discussion about the proof given for Problem 3.

For Discussion

PROBLEM 4 You might ask your more advanced students to look for a way to rewrite the statement so it becomes true. Students will also explore this question in Exercise 5 and Exercise 22a.

From all your numerical work, you can easily put together the proof.

Proof Given any real number x,

$$\begin{aligned}(T_a \circ T_b)(x) &= T_a(T_b(x)) \\ &= T_a(x + b) \\ &= (x + b) + a \\ &= x + (a + b) \\ &= T_{a+b}(x)\end{aligned}$$

Therefore, $T_a \circ T_b = T_{a+b}$.

Habits of Mind

Check your assumptions. For a complete proof, you need to check that $T_a \circ T_b$ and T_{a+b} have the same domain. But they do, don't they?

For You to Do

2. Prove that, for any real numbers a and b, $T_a \circ T_b = T_b \circ T_a$.

Translations commute under composition.

In Exercise 10 from Lesson 6.5, you saw that $D_3 \circ D_2 = D_6$. This theorem is the generalization of that result.

Theorem 6.2

Let s and t be nonzero real numbers. Then

$$D_s \circ D_t = D_{st}$$

The proof of this theorem is left as an exercise. (See Exercise 3.)

For You to Do

3. Prove that, if s and t are nonzero real numbers, $D_s \circ D_t = D_t \circ D_s$.

Dilations also commute under composition.

For Discussion

4. Do translations and dilations commute with each other? That is, is the equation below true for all real numbers a and $s \neq 0$? Explain.

$$T_a \circ D_s = D_s \circ T_a$$

In Lesson 6.5, you saw that the transformations T_0 and D_1 have the property below for all real numbers x.

$$T_0(x) = D_1(x) = x$$

First of all, this means that $T_0 = D_1$. Moreover, this transformation does not do anything to $\mathbb{R}$. It fixes every number. You met this identity function in Lesson 2.4 as "id."

$$T_0 = D_1 = \text{id}$$

Answers

For You to Do

2. Answers may vary. Sample:
$(T_a \circ T_b)(x) = T_{a+b}(x) =$
$x + a + b = x + b + a =$
$T_{b+a}(x) = (T_b \circ T_a)(x)$

3. Answers may vary. Sample:
$(D_s \circ D_t)(x) = D_{st}(x) =$
$stx = tsx = D_{ts}(x) = (D_s \circ D_t)(x)$

For Discussion

4. No; for example
$(T_2 \circ D_5)(x) = 5x + 2$, but
$(D_5 \circ T_2)(x) = 5(x + 2) =$
$5x + 10$.

In Problem 5 from Lesson 6.5, you saw that for all real numbers x,

$$(T_{-4} \circ T_4)(x) = (T_4 \circ T_{-4})(x) = x$$

So T_{-4} undoes the action of T_4, and vice versa. In other words, T_4 and T_{-4} are inverses of each other: $(T_4)^{-1} = T_{-4}$. This holds in general.

Example 1

Problem Show that $(T_a)^{-1} = T_{-a}$.

Solution In Lesson 2.4, you learned that the inverse of a function f is the function f^{-1} such that $f \circ f^{-1} = \text{id}$.

By Theorem 6.1, you have

$$T_a \circ T_{-a} = T_{a+(-a)} = T_0 = \text{id}$$

Thus, the inverse of T_a is T_{-a}. That is, $(T_a)^{-1} = T_{-a}$.

Habits of Mind

Consider more than one strategy. You can also show that $T_a \circ T_{-a} = \text{id}$ by showing that $T_a \circ T_{-a}$ and id are equal as functions, as you did in the proof of Theorem 6.1. But the theorem allows you to generalize and work completely with function algebra.

For You to Do

5. Show that $(D_s)^{-1} = D_{\frac{1}{s}}$.

Minds in Action episode 26

Tony and Sasha are talking during lunch about what they have learned so far.

Tony So, for translations, we have some properties that seem very familiar.

- $T_a \circ T_b = T_b \circ T_a = T_{a+b}$
- $T_0 = \text{id}$
- $(T_a)^{-1} = T_{-a}$

Sasha These do seem familiar. They seem like the properties of addition with real numbers. And look at the properties of dilations.

- $D_s \circ D_t = D_t \circ D_s = D_{st}$
- $D_1 = \text{id}$
- $(D_s)^{-1} = D_{\frac{1}{s}}$

They seem a lot like multiplication.

For You to Do

5. $D_s \circ D_{\frac{1}{s}} = D_{s \cdot \frac{1}{s}} = D_1 = \text{id}$

Minds in Action

This Minds in Action dialog points out the connections between T_a and addition, and D_s and multiplication. You might not need to spend much time on this, depending on your students' level of success with the problems and exercises in Lesson 6.6 and the other material in this lesson. In any case, use the dialog as a checkpoint before you introduce full affine transformations. You might also ask students to explain why no separate function groups have been defined for subtraction and division.

Wrap Up

Draw students' attention to the two bulleted statements that follow Example 2. In discussing the first statement, emphasize that part (a) of Example 2 does not prove that the composition of any two affine transformations is an affine transformation. In other words, you have not yet proved that affine transformations are closed under function composition. To prove something true, you need much more than a single example. However, to prove something false (as for the second bulleted statement), you need only one counterexample.

Conclude today's lesson by going over the Check Your Understanding core exercises as time allows.

Assessment Resources

Lesson Quiz 6.6

1. a. Solve $2x - 6 = y$ for x in terms of y.
   b. Show that $\left(\mathcal{A}_{(2,\,-6)}\right)^{-1} = \mathcal{A}_{\left(\frac{1}{2},\,3\right)}$.

2. Simplify each composition.
   a. $\mathcal{A}_{(1,\,q)} \circ \mathcal{A}_{(1,\,r)}$
   b. $\mathcal{A}_{(1,\,a)} \circ \mathcal{A}_{(b,\,0)}$
   c. $\left(\mathcal{A}_{(-2,\,5)} \circ \mathcal{A}_{\left(1,\,\frac{1}{2}\right)}\right)^{-1}$
   d. $\left(\mathcal{A}_{\left(1,\,\frac{1}{2}\right)} \circ \mathcal{A}_{(-2,\,5)}\right)^{-1}$

3. Find numbers a and b that satisfy each equation.
   a. $\left(\mathcal{A}_{(3,\,-2)}\right)^{-1} = \mathcal{A}_{(a,\,b)}$
   b. $\left(\mathcal{A}_{(-4,\,1)}\right)^{-1} = \mathcal{A}_{(a,\,b)}$
   c. $\mathcal{A}_{(-1,\,4)} \circ \mathcal{A}_{(a,\,b)} = \mathcal{A}_{(8,\,6)}$
   d. $\mathcal{A}_{(a,\,b)} \circ \mathcal{A}_{(2,\,-5)} = \text{id}$

For Discussion

6. Compare the algebra of translations with the arithmetic of addition. Compare the algebra of dilations with the arithmetic of multiplication.

The composition of two translations is another translation. The composition of two dilations is another dilation. But the composition of a translation and a dilation is an *affine transformation.*

$$\left(T_b \circ D_a\right)(x) = T_b(ax) = ax + b$$

You will use a special notation, $\mathcal{A}_{(a,\,b)}$, to stand for the function $x \mapsto ax + b$.

Go Online PHSchool.com

For information on how affine transformations are used, go to **Web Code: bfe-9031**

Definition

Let a and b be real numbers with $a \neq 0$. An affine transformation by (a, b) is a transformation $\mathcal{A}_{(a,\,b)}$ of $\mathbb{R}$ given by

$$\mathcal{A}_{(a,\,b)} = T_b \circ D_a$$

The following example illustrates what happens when you compose two affine transformations.

Example 2

Problem

a. Simplify $\mathcal{A}_{(2,\,3)} \circ \mathcal{A}_{(-1,\,4)}$.

b. Simplify $\mathcal{A}_{(-1,\,4)} \circ \mathcal{A}_{(2,\,3)}$.

Solution

a. For a real number x, you have

$$\begin{aligned}\left(\mathcal{A}_{(2,\,3)} \circ \mathcal{A}_{(-1,\,4)}\right)(x) &= \mathcal{A}_{(2,\,3)}\left(\mathcal{A}_{(-1,\,4)}(x)\right)\\ &= \mathcal{A}_{(2,\,3)}(-x + 4)\\ &= 2(-x + 4) + 3\\ &= -2x + 11\\ &= \mathcal{A}_{(-2,\,11)}(x)\end{aligned}$$

Therefore, $\mathcal{A}_{(2,\,3)} \circ \mathcal{A}_{(-1,\,4)} = \mathcal{A}_{(-2,\,11)}$.

b. For a real number x, you have

$$\begin{aligned}\left(\mathcal{A}_{(-1,\,4)} \circ \mathcal{A}_{(2,\,3)}\right)(x) &= \mathcal{A}_{(-1,\,4)}\left(\mathcal{A}_{(2,\,3)}(x)\right)\\ &= \mathcal{A}_{(-1,\,4)}(2x + 3)\\ &= -(2x + 3) + 4\\ &= -2x + 1\\ &= \mathcal{A}_{(-2,\,1)}(x)\end{aligned}$$

Therefore, $\mathcal{A}_{(-1,\,4)} \circ \mathcal{A}_{(2,\,3)} = \mathcal{A}_{(-2,\,1)}$.

For help modeling affine transformations, see the TI-Nspire Handbook, p. 778.

Answers

For Discussion

6. Answers may vary. Sample: T_0 is the identity for function composition of translations in the same way that 0 is the additive identity for real numbers. Function composition of translations is commutative in the same way that addition of real numbers is commutative. D_1 is the identity for function composition of dilations in the same way that 1 is the multiplicative identity for real numbers. Function composition of dilations is commutative in the same way that multiplication of real numbers is commutative.

From this example, you can conclude two things:

- This composition of two affine transformations produces another affine transformation.
- Affine transformations do not commute under composition.

You will explore these ideas further in the exercises.

Exercises Practicing Habits of Mind

Check Your Understanding

1. Give another name for the transformation $\mathcal{A}_{(1,\, b)}$.
2. For which values of a and b is $\mathcal{A}_{(a,\, b)}$ a dilation only?
3. Prove Theorem 6.2.
4. Write each transformation in the form $x \mapsto ax + b$.
   a. $(T_3 \circ D_2)(x)$ b. $(D_2 \circ T_3)(x)$ c. $(T_{-5} \circ D_7)(x)$
   d. $(D_7 \circ T_{-5})(x)$ e. $(T_b \circ D_a)(x)$ f. $(D_a \circ T_b)(x)$
5. Find all values of a and b for which
$$T_b \circ D_a = D_a \circ T_b$$
6. Simplify each composition.
   a. $\mathcal{A}_{(2,\,-1)} \circ \mathcal{A}_{(3,\,5)}$ b. $\mathcal{A}_{(3,\,5)} \circ \mathcal{A}_{(2,\,-1)}$
   c. $\mathcal{A}_{(1,\,4)} \circ \mathcal{A}_{(-1,\,3)}$ d. $\mathcal{A}_{(-1,\,3)} \circ \mathcal{A}_{(1,\,4)}$
   e. $\mathcal{A}_{(\frac{1}{2},\,-3)} \circ \mathcal{A}_{(2,\,6)}$ f. $\mathcal{A}_{(2,\,6)} \circ \mathcal{A}_{(\frac{1}{2},\,-3)}$
7. Let $\mathcal{A}_{(a,\,b)} \circ \mathcal{A}_{(c,\,d)} = \mathcal{A}_{(e,\,f)}$. Express e and f in terms of a, b, c, and d.
8. Find numbers a and b that satisfy each equation.
   a. $\mathcal{A}_{(a,\,b)} \circ \mathcal{A}_{(4,\,1)} = \mathcal{A}_{(12,\,11)}$
   b. $\mathcal{A}_{(4,\,3)} \circ \mathcal{A}_{(a,\,b)} = \mathcal{A}_{(20,\,11)}$
   c. $\mathcal{A}_{(a,\,b)} \circ \mathcal{A}_{(2,\,3)} = \text{id}$
   d. $\mathcal{A}_{(2,\,3)} \circ \mathcal{A}_{(a,\,b)} = \text{id}$

Habits of Mind

Experiment. Try it with numbers! For example, give another name for $\mathcal{A}_{(1,\,3)}(x)$ and for $\mathcal{A}_{(1,\,-7)}(x)$.

Habits of Mind

Detect the key characteristics. Why does Exercise 7 show that a composition of two affine transformations is another affine transformation?

In Exercises 8c and 8d, you can write the identity transformation id as $\mathcal{A}_{(1,\,0)}$.

Exercises

1. T_b
2. $a \neq 0,\ b = 0$
3. $(D_s \circ D_t)(x) = D_s(D_t(x)) = D_s(tx) = s(tx) = (st)x = D_{st}(x)$
4. a. $x \mapsto 2x + 3$
   b. $x \mapsto 2x + 6$
   c. $x \mapsto 7x - 5$
   d. $x \mapsto 7x - 35$
   e. $x \mapsto ax + b$
   f. $x \mapsto ax + ab$
5. $b = 0$ or $a = 1$
6. a. $\mathcal{A}_{(6,\,9)}$
   b. $\mathcal{A}_{(6,\,2)}$
   c. $\mathcal{A}_{(-1,\,7)}$
   d. $\mathcal{A}_{(-1,\,-1)}$
   e. $\mathcal{A}_{(1,\,0)}$
   f. $\mathcal{A}_{(1,\,0)}$
7. $e = ac,\ f = ad + b$
8. a. $a = 3,\ b = 8$
   b. $a = 5,\ b = 2$
   c. $a = \frac{1}{2},\ b = -\frac{3}{2}$
   d. $a = \frac{1}{2},\ b = -\frac{3}{2}$

Exercises

HOMEWORK
- Core: 9, 10, 11, 13, 14, 15, 16, 17
- Optional: 12, 18, 19, 20a–b, 21, 22, 23
- Extension: 20c

Check Your Understanding

EXERCISES 1, 2, AND 6 give you a chance to assess whether students understand the new notation for affine transformations and can interpret it correctly.

EXERCISE 2 There are some nuances in this exercise. Some students may want to restrict a further, saying $a > 0$. This is because when a is negative, D_a involves a reflection in addition to the dilation. From a geometric point of view, a transformation with $b = 1$ and $a < 0$ would be both a dilation and a reflection. Some students may not think it is necessary to restrict a at all, because they think of the identity transformation as a dilation—it is just a dilation by a factor of 1.

EXERCISE 6 By providing two counterexamples this exercise proves that affine transformations do not, in general, commute under function composition. However, in the last two parts of the exercise, students see a special case in which two affine transformations do produce the same result through composition in either order. Their composition is the identity transformation, so these two particular affine transformations are inverses of each other. That may lead students to conjecture that two affine transformations commute if and only if they are inverses, but students do not prove anything in this exercise.

EXERCISE 7 Students have shown that the composition of two affine transformations is always another affine transformation. In fact, given the two affine transformations they need to compose (and their order), students can even calculate what affine transformation will result.

EXERCISE 8 Students may notice that the last two parts of this exercise give the same result. This is further evidence for their conjecture that the order of composition does not affect the result for a pair of inverse affine transformations.

On Your Own

EXERCISE 9 gives students food for thought about what kinds of affine transformations do commute under composition. In the first part of the exercise, they see two affine transformations that are equivalent to translations, and those will commute. In part (b), they see two affine transformations that are equivalent to dilations, and those also commute.

EXERCISE 10 There is a relationship between the two parts of this exercise. The equation in part (a) is the affine transformation for which students are finding the inverse in part (b). By solving for x in terms of y, they are "undoing" the equation, and they can read the dilation and translation for the inverse from the result. The coefficient of y gives them the required dilation, and the constant term is the required translation.

EXERCISES 11 AND 12 Students who made the connection in Exercise 10 between solving a linear equation for x in terms of y and finding an inverse affine transformation may have used that method to find the inverses here. In that case, they will have done the work of Exercise 12 already. Students who are still working through the affine transformation notation may be able to make this connection by doing Exercise 12, and then they will have another technique that they can use.

EXERCISE 13 To undo a process, work backwards through each step applying inverses. When you put on your socks and shoes, you have to put the sock on your foot before you put on the shoe. And when you take them off, you have to take off the shoe before you take off the sock. Students can apply the "socks and shoes" method of taking inverses to finding inverses of compositions of any kind of functions. Students have used this same idea to find the inverses of linear functions. For example, consider this description of what happens to an input for the linear function $f(x) = 5x - 3$: first, multiply it by 5 and then subtract 3. To undo this process, just work backwards through each step applying inverses: first add 3 and then divide by 5. This gives $f^{-1}(x) = \frac{(x + 3)}{5}$. As this investigation goes on, students will use this method to find inverses of compositions of affine transformations.

On Your Own

9. Simplify each composition.

a. $\mathcal{A}_{(1,\,m)} \circ \mathcal{A}_{(1,\,n)}$

b. $\mathcal{A}_{(s,\,0)} \circ \mathcal{A}_{(t,\,0)}$

c. $\mathcal{A}_{(1,\,b)} \circ \mathcal{A}_{(a,\,0)}$

d. $\mathcal{A}_{(a,\,0)} \circ \mathcal{A}_{(1,\,b)}$

10. a. Solve $4x + 8 = y$ for x in terms of y.

b. Show that $\left(\mathcal{A}_{(4,\,8)}\right)^{-1} = \mathcal{A}_{\left(\frac{1}{4},\,-2\right)}$.

11. Find numbers c and d that satisfy each equation.

a. $\left(\mathcal{A}_{(2,\,-1)}\right)^{-1} = \mathcal{A}_{(c,\,d)}$

b. $\left(\mathcal{A}_{(3,\,5)}\right)^{-1} = \mathcal{A}_{(c,\,d)}$

c. $\left(\mathcal{A}_{\left(\frac{1}{2},\,-3\right)}\right)^{-1} = \mathcal{A}_{(c,\,d)}$

d. $\left(\mathcal{A}_{(2,\,6)}\right)^{-1} = \mathcal{A}_{(c,\,d)}$

e. $\left(\mathcal{A}_{(a,\,b)}\right)^{-1} = \mathcal{A}_{(c,\,d)}$, for $a \neq 0$

12. Solve each equation for x in terms of y.

a. $2x - 1 = y$

b. $3x + 5 = y$

c. $\frac{x}{2} - 3 = y$

d. $2x + 6 = y$

e. $ax + b = y$, where $a \neq 0$

13. Another way to find the inverse of an affine transformation is to think about it as a composition of a translation and a dilation.

$$\mathcal{A}_{(a,\,b)} = T_b \circ D_a$$

So an input is first dilated by a and then translated by b. The inverse undoes this process, working backward.

$$\left(\mathcal{A}_{(a,\,b)}\right)^{-1} = (D_a)^{-1} \circ (T_b)^{-1}$$

You know how to find the inverse of a dilation and a translation. Then you can write the resulting composition as an affine transformation. Use this method to find each inverse.

a. $\left(\mathcal{A}_{(3,\,4)}\right)^{-1}$ **b.** $\left(\mathcal{A}_{(5,\,1)}\right)^{-1}$ **c.** $\left(\mathcal{A}_{(3,\,2)}\right)^{-1}$

Go Online PHSchool.com

For additional practice, go to **Web Code:** bfa-0606

You can also write the equation $4x + 8 = y$ as $\mathcal{A}_{(4,\,8)}(x) = y$.

When you put on your socks and shoes, which go on first? Which come off first when you take off your socks and shoes?

Answers

9. a. $\mathcal{A}_{(1,\,n+m)}$

b. $\mathcal{A}_{(st,\,0)}$

c. $\mathcal{A}_{(a,\,b)}$

d. $\mathcal{A}_{(a,\,ab)}$

10. See back of book.

11. a. $c = \frac{1}{2}, d = \frac{1}{2}$

b. $c = \frac{1}{3}, d = -\frac{5}{3}$

c. $c = 2, d = 6$

d. $c = \frac{1}{2}, d = -3$

e. $c = \frac{1}{a}, d = -\frac{b}{a}$

12. a. $x = \frac{1}{2}y + \frac{1}{2}$

b. $x = \frac{1}{3}y - \frac{5}{3}$

c. $x = 2y + 6$

d. $x = \frac{1}{2}y - 3$

e. $x = \frac{1}{a}y - \frac{b}{a}$

13. See back of book.

Now that you know how to find the inverse of an affine transformation, you can use these inverses to solve certain equations. But, affine transformations are not commutative under composition. So there is a difference between composing on the left and composing on the right. You need to make your choice strategically.

If you compose both sides of an equation with a function, you have to compose them on the same side to preserve equality.

For example, suppose you want to solve this equation.

$$\mathcal{A}_{(a,\,b)} \circ \mathcal{A}_{(2,\,8)} = \mathcal{A}_{(3,\,-4)}$$

Ideally, you want to isolate the $\mathcal{A}_{(a,\,b)}$ term, so it makes sense to compose each side with the inverse of $\mathcal{A}_{(2,\,8)}$. If you do the composition on the left, this is what you get.

$$(\mathcal{A}_{(2,\,8)})^{-1} \circ \mathcal{A}_{(a,\,b)} \circ \mathcal{A}_{(2,\,8)} = (\mathcal{A}_{(2,\,8)})^{-1} \circ \mathcal{A}_{(3,\,-4)}$$

You can simplify the right side of the equation, but the left side is more complicated than it was before. Because affine transformations are not commutative under composition, you cannot just rearrange the terms. This is what you get if you do the composition on the right.

$$\mathcal{A}_{(a,\,b)} \circ \mathcal{A}_{(2,\,8)} \circ (\mathcal{A}_{(2,\,8)})^{-1} = \mathcal{A}_{(3,\,-4)} \circ (\mathcal{A}_{(2,\,8)})^{-1}$$

For this example, $\mathcal{A}_{(a,\,b)}$ turns out to be $\mathcal{A}_{(\frac{3}{2},\,-8)}$.

Now you can simplify the left side of the equation quite a bit, and the right side is still manageable.

14. Find numbers a and b that satisfy each equation.

a. $\mathcal{A}_{(a,\,b)} \circ \mathcal{A}_{(3,\,4)} = \mathcal{A}_{(9,\,6)}$

b. $\mathcal{A}_{(3,\,4)} \circ \mathcal{A}_{(a,\,b)} = \mathcal{A}_{(13,\,6)}$

c. $\mathcal{A}_{(a,\,b)} \circ \mathcal{A}_{(5,\,1)} = \text{id}$

d. $\mathcal{A}_{(3,\,2)} \circ \mathcal{A}_{(a,\,b)} = \text{id}$

15. Simplify each composition.

a. $(\mathcal{A}_{(2,\,-1)} \circ \mathcal{A}_{(3,\,5)})^{-1}$

b. $(\mathcal{A}_{(3,\,5)})^{-1} \circ (\mathcal{A}_{(2,\,-1)})^{-1}$

c. $(\mathcal{A}_{(\frac{1}{2},\,-3)} \circ \mathcal{A}_{(2,\,6)})^{-1}$

d. $(\mathcal{A}_{(2,\,6)})^{-1} \circ (\mathcal{A}_{(\frac{1}{2},\,-3)})^{-1}$

16. a. Prove that $(\mathcal{A}_{(a,\,b)} \circ \mathcal{A}_{(c,\,d)})^{-1} = (\mathcal{A}_{(c,\,d)})^{-1} \circ (\mathcal{A}_{(a,\,b)})^{-1}$.

b. Make an analogy between the equation in part (a) and the act of putting on your socks and shoes and then taking them off.

14. a. $a = 3, b = -6$

b. $a = \frac{13}{3}, b = \frac{2}{3}$

c. $a = \frac{1}{5}, b = -\frac{1}{5}$

d. $a = \frac{1}{3}, b = -\frac{2}{3}$

15. a. $\mathcal{A}_{(\frac{1}{6},\,-\frac{3}{2})}$

b. $\mathcal{A}_{(\frac{1}{6},\,-\frac{3}{2})}$

c. $\mathcal{A}_{(1,\,0)}$

d. $\mathcal{A}_{(1,\,0)}$

16. a. Using the results of Exercise 7 and Exercise 11e, $(\mathcal{A}_{(a,\,b)} \circ \mathcal{A}_{(c,\,d)})^{-1} = (\mathcal{A}_{(ac,\,ad+b)})^{-1} = \mathcal{A}_{(\frac{1}{ac},\,\frac{-b-ad}{ac})}$. Also,
$(\mathcal{A}_{(c,\,d)})^{-1} \circ (\mathcal{A}_{(a,\,b)})^{-1} =$
$\mathcal{A}_{(\frac{1}{c},\,-\frac{d}{c})} \circ \mathcal{A}_{(\frac{1}{a},\,-\frac{b}{a})} =$
$\mathcal{A}_{(\frac{1}{c}\cdot\frac{1}{a},\,\frac{1}{c}(-\frac{b}{a})+(-\frac{d}{c}))} =$
$\mathcal{A}_{(\frac{1}{ac},\,-\frac{b}{ac}-\frac{d}{c})} = \mathcal{A}_{(\frac{1}{ac},\,\frac{-b-ad}{ac})}$.
Thus, $(\mathcal{A}_{(a,\,b)} \circ \mathcal{A}_{(c,\,d)})^{-1} = (\mathcal{A}_{(c,\,d)})^{-1} \circ (\mathcal{A}_{(a,\,b)})^{-1}$.

b. See back of book.

EXERCISE 14d Some students may recognize immediately that the solution to an equation of the form $\mathcal{A}_{(3,\,2)} \circ \mathcal{A}_{(a,\,b)} = \text{id}$ is $\mathcal{A}_{(a,\,b)} = (\mathcal{A}_{(3,\,2)})^{-1}$, but it is also all right if they need to go through the calculations to realize this.

EXERCISE 15 demonstrates the "socks and shoes" method of finding an inverse of a composition of functions with affine transformations. Students should notice the relationships between parts (a) and (b) and between parts (c) and (d). Encourage them to take advantage of the computations they have already done in Exercises 6 and 11, rather than repeating the work.

EXERCISE 16 is a fairly involved calculation for students who are just coming to understand this new notation, but is a worthwhile process for them to attempt. You might wish to give students a chance to work with a partner so they can check each other's work. Students who have completed Exercise 7 and Exercise 11e may recognize that those results apply here.

EXERCISE 19 Students learn how to find the closed form for the sum of a geometric series in Chapter 7.

EXERCISE 20 asks students to think about the meaning of $\mathcal{A}_{(a,b)}{}^{(n)}$ for n outside its natural domain of the natural numbers. As it happens, the results for $n = 0$, $n = -1$, and $n = \frac{1}{2}$ are exactly what they "ought" to be if you think about a possible meaning for such values of n.

EXERCISE 21 reinforces both the meaning of the $\mathcal{A}_{(a,b)}$ notation for students, and the fact that the order of composition makes a difference when you are composing a dilation and a translation.

EXERCISE 23 If students have trouble starting this exercise, remind them to rewrite $D_3(f(n - a))$ as $3f(n - 1)$. Once they have completed the table, students should recognize f as an exponential function.

17. **Standardized Test Prep** For which values of a and b does $\mathcal{A}_{(a,b)} \circ \mathcal{A}_{(2,4)} = \mathcal{A}_{(6,6)}$?

A. $a = \frac{1}{2},\ b = -2$ **B.** $a = 3,\ b = \frac{3}{2}$

C. $a = 3,\ b = -6$ **D.** $a = 4,\ b = 2$

18. Given a transformation F of $\mathbb{R}$ and a positive integer n, the *nth iterate* $F^{(n)}$ is defined as

$$F^{(n)} = \underbrace{F \circ F \circ \cdots \circ F}_{n \text{ copies of } F}$$

Simplify each transformation.

a. $(\mathcal{A}_{(a,b)})^{(2)}(x)$

b. $(\mathcal{A}_{(a,b)})^{(3)}(x)$

c. $(\mathcal{A}_{(a,b)})^{(4)}(x)$

d. $(\mathcal{A}_{(a,b)})^{(5)}(x)$

19. **a.** Use your work from Exercise 18 to find an expression for $(\mathcal{A}_{(a,b)})^{(n)}$.

b. Suppose $a = 1$. What does your formula from part (a) look like? Why does it make sense?

c. Suppose $b = 0$. What does your formula from part (a) look like? Why does it make sense?

d. Suppose $a \neq 1$. Show that the formula from part (a) simplifies to

$$(\mathcal{A}_{(a,b)})^{(n)} = \mathcal{A}_{\left(a^n,\ b \cdot \frac{a^n - 1}{a - 1}\right)}.$$

Use this famous identity. $(a - 1)(a^{n-1} + a^{n-2} + \cdots + a + 1) = a^n - 1$

20. You showed in Exercise 19d that, for $a \neq 0$ and $n \geq 1$,

$$(\mathcal{A}_{(a,b)})^{(n)}(x) = a^n x + b \cdot \frac{a^n - 1}{a - 1}.$$

a. Substitute $n = 0$ into this equation and simplify. Does your result make sense? Explain.

b. Substitute $n = -1$ into this equation and simplify. How does your result compare to that of Exercise 11e?

c. **Take It Further** Substitute $n = \frac{1}{2}$ into this equation and simplify. Use your result to compute

$$(\mathcal{A}_{(a,b)})^{\left(\frac{1}{2}\right)} \circ (\mathcal{A}_{(a,b)})^{\left(\frac{1}{2}\right)}.$$

Answers

17. C

18. a. $\mathcal{A}_{(a^2,\ ab + b)}(x)$

b. $\mathcal{A}_{(a^3,\ a^2b + ab + b)}(x)$

c. $\mathcal{A}_{(a^4,\ a^3b + a^2b + ab + b)}(x)$

d. $\mathcal{A}_{(a^5,\ a^4b + a^3b + a^2b + ab + b)}(x)$

19. a. $\mathcal{A}_{(a^n,\ a^{n-1}b + a^{n-2}b + \cdots + ab + b)}(x)$

b. $(\mathcal{A}_{(1,b)})^{(n)}(x) = \mathcal{A}_{(1,nb)}(x)$; $\mathcal{A}_{(1,b)}$ is a translation by b units, and applying that translation n times consecutively is the same as a translation by nb units, which is $\mathcal{A}_{(1,nb)}$.

c. $(\mathcal{A}_{(a,0)})^{(n)}(x) = (\mathcal{A}_{(a^n,0)})(x)$; $\mathcal{A}_{(a,0)}$ is a dilation by the factor a, and performing that dilation n times consecutively is equivalent to a dilation by the factor a^n, which is $\mathcal{A}_{(a^n,0)}$.

d. Rewrite the expression in part (a) as $(\mathcal{A}_{(a,b)})^{(n)}(x) = \mathcal{A}_{(a^n,\ b(a^{n-1} + a^{n-2} + \ldots + a + 1))}(x)$.
We know that
$(a - 1)(a^{n-1} + a^{n-2} + \cdots + a + 1) = a^n - 1$, so
$a^{n-1} + a^{n-2} + \cdots + a + 1 = \frac{a^n - 1}{a - 1}$.
Thus, $(\mathcal{A}_{(a,b)})^{(n)}(x) = \mathcal{A}_{\left(a^n,\ b \cdot \frac{a^n - 1}{a - 1}\right)}(x) = a^n x + b \cdot \frac{a^n - 1}{a - 1}$.

20. a. x; yes; performing a transformation 0 times should leave the input value, x, unchanged.

b. $\frac{1}{a}x - \frac{b}{a}$ or $\mathcal{A}_{\left(\frac{1}{a},\ -\frac{b}{a}\right)}$; the results are the same.

c. $a^{\frac{1}{2}}x + b \cdot \frac{a^{\frac{1}{2}} - 1}{a - 1}$; $ax + b$ or $\mathcal{A}_{(a,b)}$

21. Find numbers a and b that satisfy each equation.

a. $\mathcal{A}_{(3, 12)} = T_a \circ D_b$

b. $\mathcal{A}_{(3, 12)} = D_a \circ T_b$

22. If a and b are numbers and $a \neq 0$, show that each equation is true.

a. $T_b \circ D_a = D_a \circ T_{\frac{b}{a}}$

b. $T_b \circ D_a \circ T_{-\frac{b}{a}} = D_a$

Maintain Your Skills

23. Use the definition of function f below.

$$f(n) = \begin{cases} 2 & \text{if } n = 0 \\ D_3(f(n-1)) & \text{if } n > 0 \end{cases}$$

a. Copy and complete the following table.

n	$f(n)$
0	2
1	6
2	■
3	■
4	■
5	■
6	■

b. Find a closed form for f.

Additional Resources

PRINT RESOURCES
- Solution Manual
- Practice Workbook
- Assessment Resources
- Teaching Resources

TECHNOLOGY
- Interactive Textbook
- TeacherExpress CD-ROM
- ExamView CD-ROM
- PHSchool.com

Additional Practice

1. Simplify each composition.

a. $\mathcal{A}_{(1, q)} \circ \mathcal{A}_{(r, 1)}$

b. $\mathcal{A}_{(c, 1)} \circ \mathcal{A}_{(d, 1)}$

c. $\mathcal{A}_{(1, q)} \circ \mathcal{A}_{(r, 0)}$

d. $\mathcal{A}_{(c, 0)} \circ \mathcal{A}_{(d, 0)}$

2. a. Solve $3x - 2 = y$ for x in terms of y.

b. Show that $(\mathcal{A}_{(3, -2)})^{-1} = \mathcal{A}_{(\frac{1}{3}, \frac{2}{3})}$.

3. Find numbers p and q that satisfy each equation.

a. $(\mathcal{A}_{(4, -1)})^{-1} = \mathcal{A}_{(p, q)}$

b. $(\mathcal{A}_{(5, 2)})^{-1} = \mathcal{A}_{(p, q)}$

c. $(\mathcal{A}_{(-2, \frac{1}{2})})^{-1} = \mathcal{A}_{(p, q)}$

d. $(\mathcal{A}_{(3, 6)})^{-1} = \mathcal{A}_{(p, q)}$

4. Use the fact that $(\mathcal{A}_{(a, b)})^{-1} = (D_a)^{-1} \circ (T_b)^{-1}$ to find each inverse below.

a. $(\mathcal{A}_{(6, 3)})^{-1}$

b. $(\mathcal{A}_{(3, -2)})^{-1}$

c. $(\mathcal{A}_{(-4, 2)})^{-1}$

d. $(\mathcal{A}_{(-1, -5)})^{-1}$

5. Find numbers c and d that satisfy each equation.

a. $\mathcal{A}_{(c, d)} \circ \mathcal{A}_{(3, 1)} = \mathcal{A}_{(6, 2)}$

b. $\mathcal{A}_{(3, 1)} \circ \mathcal{A}_{(c, d)} = \mathcal{A}_{(9, 5)}$

c. $\mathcal{A}_{(c, d)} \circ \mathcal{A}_{(4, 5)} = \text{id}$

d. $\mathcal{A}_{(6, 2)} \circ \mathcal{A}_{(c, d)} = \text{id}$

6. Simplify each composition.

a. $(\mathcal{A}_{(6, 3)} \circ \mathcal{A}_{(3, -2)})^{-1}$

b. $(\mathcal{A}_{(3, -2)} \circ \mathcal{A}_{(6, 3)})^{-1}$

c. $(\mathcal{A}_{(-2, \frac{1}{2})} \circ \mathcal{A}_{(3, 1)})^{-1}$

d. $(\mathcal{A}_{(3, 1)} \circ \mathcal{A}_{(-2, \frac{1}{2})})^{-1}$

7. Find numbers p and q that satisfy each equation.

a. $\mathcal{A}_{(2, 8)} = T_p \circ D_q$

b. $\mathcal{A}_{(2, 8)} = D_p \circ T_q$

Practice: For Lesson 6.6, assign Exercises 1–7.

21. a. $a = 12, b = 3$

b. $a = 3, b = 4$

22. a. $(T_b \circ D_a)(x) = T_b(ax) = ax + b$ and $(D_a \circ T_{\frac{b}{a}})(x) = D_a\left(x + \frac{b}{a}\right) = a\left(x + \frac{b}{a}\right) = ax + b$, so $T_b \circ D_a = D_a \circ T_{\frac{b}{a}}$.

b. $(T_b \circ D_a \circ T_{-\frac{b}{a}})(x) = (T_b \circ D_a)\left(x - \frac{b}{a}\right) = T_b(ax - b) = ax - b + b = ax = D_a(x)$

23. a.

n	$f(n)$
0	2
1	6
2	**18**
3	**54**
4	**162**
5	**486**
6	**1458**

b. $f(n) = 2 \cdot 3^n$

Lesson Overview

GOALS

- Find the inverse of a dilation, a translation, or an affine transformation and use that inverse as a tool to solve equations.
- Find transformations for converting a general quadratic or cubic into one of the basic graph forms.

This lesson is optional. If you do not have enough time, you may wish to skip this lesson and move on to Investigation 6C.

In this lesson, students see some techniques for using transformations to convert equations into forms that are easier to graph. For example, students learn to find a composition of dilations and translations to change any equation of the form $y = ax^2 + bx + c$ into a new equation of the form $N = M^2$. Then, in Investigation 6C, students use the basic graph from Investigation 6A together with these transformations to graph the original quadratic equation. Similarly, students convert general cubic equations into one of the basic graph forms from Investigation 6A.

CHECK YOUR UNDERSTANDING
- Core: 1, 2, 3, 4, 6
- Optional: none
- Extension: 5

HOMEWORK
- Core: 7, 8, 10, 11, 12, 13
- Optional: 9, 15, 16
- Extension: 14

VOCABULARY
- completing the square

Launch

In this investigation, students do not graph the functions they are working with. You might, however, want to connect what students are learning in this lesson with what they learned in Investigation 6A. Lead them through the process of sketching the graph of $y = x^2 + 4x - 6$ by first writing the equation in the form $y + 10 = (x + 2)^2$. Use completing the square to do this. When students understand that completing the square on a quadratic leads to an equation in the form of the basic quadratic $y = x^2$, they are ready to move on to the Minds in Action dialog.

Explore

Minds in Action

In this dialog, Tony and Sasha explore the process of using transformations of each axis to rewrite a quadratic equation in the form of the basic quadratic, $y = x^2$. Using compositions of translations T_a and dilations D_s (affine transformations), they determine the transformations to apply in order to transform the quadratic $y = 8x^2 - 2x - 15$ into the form $N = M^2$.

6.7 Transforming Equations

In this lesson, you will transform equations into simpler forms through dilations and translations.

Transforming the Equation $y = ax^2 + bx + c$

You can transform any equation of the form $y = ax^2 + bx + c$ into an equation of the form $N = M^2$.

Minds in Action — episode 27

Tony and Sasha are working on the following problem.

Transform the equation $y = 8x^2 - 2x - 15$ into an equation of the form $N = M^2$ by first making it monic with a dilation and then **completing the square** with a translation.

Tony I don't know about using dilations to make quadratics monic, but I do remember making monic quadratics in Chapter 2. You multiply through by a number that makes the x^2-term a perfect square. It's easiest just to use the coefficient. That gives us $8y = (8x)^2 - 2(8x) - 120$.

We can substitute $P = 8x$ and rewrite it as $8y = P^2 - 2P - 120$.

Sasha But that's a dilation—in x and in y! Look, if $P = D_8(x) = 8x$ and $Q = D_8(y) = 8y$, we have $Q = P^2 - 2P - 120$.

Tony Okay, but completing the square as a translation? I don't know about that one.

Sasha So, let's just complete the square and see. We know how to do that. You look at the $P^2 - 2P$ part of the equation and figure out what constant to add to make it a perfect square. And that's 1, because $P^2 - 2P + 1 = (P - 1)^2$.

Tony Then you go back to the equation and add and subtract that constant so you don't mess things up.

$$Q = P^2 - 2P + 1 - 1 - 120$$
$$Q = (P - 1)^2 - 121$$

Now, how is that a translation?

Sasha Hmm. Oh, if I move the 121 . . .

$$Q + 121 = (P - 1)^2$$

So if $M = T_{-1}(P) = P - 1$ and $N = T_{121}(Q) = Q + 121$, then we have $N = M^2$.

Remember...

A polynomial is monic if the coefficient of its leading term—its term of highest degree—is 1. An equation is monic if the leading term of each variable has coefficient 1.

In this case, you could multiply through by 2 if you wanted to. Explain.

Tony And you know what else? We used affine transformations on x and y as our substitutions!

- $M = (T_{-1} \circ D_8)(x) = \mathcal{A}_{(8,\,-1)}(x)$
- $N = (T_{121} \circ D_8)(y) = \mathcal{A}_{(8,\,121)}(y)$

For You to Do

1. Consider the equation $y = 3x^2 + 4x - 2$. Find a, b, c, and d such that by making the substitutions below, you get the transformed equation $N = M^2$.
   - $M = \mathcal{A}_{(a,\,b)}(x)$
   - $N = \mathcal{A}_{(c,\,d)}(y)$

Now that you can transform an equation of the form $y = ax^2 + bx + c$ into a new equation of the form $y = x^2$, you can use the transformed equation to make other tasks easier. In the next investigation, you will see how this transformed form makes graphing easier. For now, you will learn how to use the transformed form to find the zeros of a quadratic polynomial.

Example 1

Problem Find the roots of the equation $8x^2 - 2x - 15 = 0$.

Solution Tony and Sasha transformed the equation $y = 8x^2 - 2x - 15$ into the form $N = M^2$ with these substitutions.

- $M = \mathcal{A}_{(8,\,-1)}(x)$
- $N = \mathcal{A}_{(8,\,121)}(y)$

To find the zeros of the polynomial $8x^2 - 2x - 15$, you would normally just set $y = 0$ in the equation $y = 8x^2 - 2x - 15$. If you do that here, you get

$$N = \mathcal{A}_{(8,\,121)}(0) = 121$$

And since $N = M^2$, you get

$$M = \pm 11$$

Now you have

$$M = (T_{-1} \circ D_8)(x)$$

Solve for x by taking the inverse.

$$x = (D_{\frac{1}{8}} \circ T_1)(M)$$

Since $M = \pm 11$,

$$x = (D_{\frac{1}{8}} \circ T_1)(\pm 11) = \frac{\pm 11 + 1}{8} = -\frac{5}{4} \text{ or } \frac{3}{2}.$$

The roots of the equation $8x^2 - 2x - 15 = 0$ are $-\frac{5}{4}$ and $\frac{3}{2}$.

Use the "socks-and-shoes" method of taking inverses.

Answers

For You to Do

1. $a = 3$, $b = 2$, $c = 3$, $d = 10$

For You to Do

PROBLEM 1 Begin by multiplying both sides of the equation by 3:

$$3y = 9x^2 + 12x - 6$$
$$3y = (3x)^2 + 4(3x) - 6$$

Now let $P = 3x$ and $Q = 3y$. The equation becomes $Q = P^2 + 4P - 6$. Then complete the square:

$$Q = (P^2 + 4P + 4) - 10$$
$$Q + 10 = (P + 2)^2$$

Letting $M = P + 2$ and $N = Q + 10$ produces an equation in the form $N = M^2$. To find the values of a, b, c, and d, write M and N as affine transformations, which are compositions of translations and dilations:

$$M = (T_2 \circ D_3)(x) = \mathcal{A}_{(3,\,2)}(x)$$
$$N = (T_{10} \circ D_3)(x) = \mathcal{A}_{(3,\,10)}(x)$$

Show students how to check their work by "undoing" these substitutions. Express M and N in terms of x and y, multiply everything out, and combine like terms. The result is the original equation.

$$N = M^2$$
$$3y + 10 = (3x + 2)^2$$
$$3y + 10 = 9x^2 + 12x + 4$$
$$3y = 9x^2 + 12x - 6$$
$$y = 3x^2 + 4x - 2$$

Check Your Understanding Exercise 1 asks students to go through this process for the substitutions Tony and Sasha found in the Minds in Action dialog.

Example 1

There are three steps to this process:

- Use the fact that $y = 0$ to calculate the value of N.
- Use the relationship $N = M^2$ to find the two possible values of M.
- Use each value of M to find a value of x.

This process for finding the roots of a quadratic equation may seem more complicated than using the quadratic formula, but much of what the quadratic formula does is buried inside these calculations. You might follow this example with the generalizations of the process found in Exercises 5 and 9.

Some students will have trouble with the socks and shoes portion of this example. You might remind them of some of the number tricks they encountered in *Algebra 1*. If a number trick tells you to multiply by 8 and then subtract 1, what steps (in what order) undo that two-step process? These are the steps now called $D_{\frac{1}{8}}$ and T_1.

For You to Do

PROBLEM 2 Follow the steps used in Example 1. You might want to show students again how to "unpack" the affine transformation notation into a dilation and a translation. Stress that the order is important here: dilate, then translate—reversing the order with the same numbers produces a different result.

TRANSFORMING THE EQUATION $y = ax^3 + bx^2 + cx + d$ Use the second half of this lesson, on cubics, with more advanced classes. Consider skipping this portion of the lesson unless you are working with a strong group of students.

Minds in Action

The step Sasha takes at the bottom of this page is an interesting one. Her goal is to remove the M^2 term from the equation with an appropriate translation. By using a variable to represent the translation, Sasha can judge the effect of any translation. She uses that information to write an equation she can solve to select the correct translation.

The correct translation is related to one third of the coefficient of the second term. This parallels what happens for quadratics, where the correct translation is related to one half of the coefficient of the second term. Similar translations exist for all higher-degree polynomials as well, allowing any polynomial to be transformed so that its leading coefficient is 1 and its next-degree term is eliminated.

For You to Do

2. Use the transformed equation you found in Problem 1 to find the roots of the equation $3x^2 + 4x - 2 = 0$.

Transforming the Equation $y = ax^3 + bx^2 + cx + d$

You can transform any equation of the form $y = ax^3 + bx^2 + cx + d$ into one of the equations $y = x^3$, $y = x^3 + x$, or $y = x^3 - x$.

Minds in Action episode 28

Sasha and Tony are trying to transform the equation $y = 10x^3 - 9x^2 - 13x + 6$ into one of the basic forms, $S = R^3$, $S = R^3 + R$, or $S = R^3 - R$.

Sasha First, I want to make this equation monic. If I multiply through by 100, I'll make the x^3 term a perfect cube, and that should help.

$$100y = 1000x^3 - 900x^2 - 1300x + 600$$
$$100y = (10x)^3 - 9(10x)^2 - 130(10x) + 600$$

Tony The substitutions we want to make are dilations again. Substituting $Q = D_{100}(y)$ and $P = D_{10}(x)$ makes it monic.

$$Q = P^3 - 9P^2 - 130P + 600$$

To make this into one of the basic other forms, we need to get rid of that quadratic term.

Sasha With the other equation, we did a translation next, but I'm not sure which one will work here.

Tony I know! We can just do a translation by some number k, and then we can pick the k that makes the quadratic term's coefficient 0.

Sasha So if $M = T_k(P) = P + k$, we substitute $P = M - k$ into the equation.

$$\begin{aligned} Q &= P^3 - 9P^2 - 130P + 600 \\ &= (M-k)^3 - 9(M-k)^2 - 130(M-k) + 600 \\ &= M^3 - 3M^2k + 3Mk^2 - k^3 - 9M^2 + 18Mk - \ldots \end{aligned}$$

Wait a minute. All I care about is the M^2 term, and I'm not going to get any more of those at this stage, so here's all I need.

$$-3M^2k - 9M^2 = (-3k - 9)M^2$$

Answers

For You to Do

2. $\frac{-2 \pm \sqrt{10}}{3}$

Tony We want that coefficient to be 0. If $-3k - 9 = 0$, then $k = -3$ and $M = T_{-3}(P) = P - 3$. So let's substitute $P = M + 3$ into $Q = P^3 - 9P^2 - 130P + 600$.

$$\begin{aligned} Q &= (M+3)^3 - 9(M+3)^2 - 130(M+3) + 600 \\ &= M^3 + 9M^2 + 27M + 27 - 9M^2 - 54M - 81 - 130M \\ &\quad - 390 + 600 \\ &= M^3 - 157M + 156 \end{aligned}$$

Sasha No quadratic term! Cool.

Tony And $Q - 156 = M^3 - 157M$, so we can make $N = T_{-156}(Q)$ and have $N = M^3 - 157M$. Oh no, we're not done! How do we make the -157 into a -1 without messing all this up?

Sasha It's got to be another dilation.

Tony and Sasha need a way to scale the equation to make the coefficient of the linear term of $N = M^3 - 157M$ equal to -1 while keeping it monic. This example shows how you can do it.

Example 2

Problem Use a dilation to transform $N = M^3 - 157M$ into an equation of the form $S = R^3 - R$.

Solution Multiply each side of the equation by a cube, say α^3.

$$\begin{aligned} \alpha^3 N &= \alpha^3 M^3 - 157\alpha^3 M \\ &= (\alpha M)^3 - 157\alpha^2(\alpha M) \end{aligned}$$

Then, if $R = D_\alpha(M) = \alpha M$ and $S = D_{\alpha^3}(N) = \alpha^3 N$, the equation becomes

$$S = R^3 - 157\alpha^2 R$$

You want the coefficient of R to be -1.

$$-157\alpha^2 = -1 \Rightarrow \alpha = \frac{1}{\sqrt{157}}$$

You will figure out the value of α shortly.

You can also use $\alpha = -\frac{1}{\sqrt{157}}$, but choosing the positive root often makes the calculations a bit easier.

Example 2

Following Tony's and Sasha's example from the Minds in Action dialog, you can use a variable for the dilation factor. That way, you can judge the effect of any dilation in order to find the correct dilation factor. Here, the goal is to change the coefficient of the R term to -1, so use that fact to write an equation that you can solve for α.

Minds in Action

This Minds in Action dialog summarizes the results of Minds in Action, episode 28, and then includes the results of Example 2. Point out to students that the final substitutions stated by Sasha represent affine transformations—any combination of dilations and translations under composition produces an affine transformation. This allows Tony and Sasha to use one set of clever substitutions to transform the original equation directly into the form $S = R^3 - R$.

For You to Do

PROBLEMS 3–5 This series of problems leads students through the process of converting a general cubic equation into one of the basic graph forms. They can convert the equation in Problem 1 into the equation in Problem 2 and then into the equation in Problem 3. Since students have a starting point for each of the separate steps, they will have checkpoints as they work through this complex process.

For an alternate solution, begin by multiplying both sides of the equation by 2. Here is what that would look like:

$$2y = (2x)^3 - 15(2x)^2 + 59(2x) + 30$$

The substitutions are $P = 2x$ and $Q = 2y$ for the monic equation

$$Q = P^3 - 15P^2 + 59P + 30$$

Most students will use the substitutions shown in the Problem 3 answer at the bottom of this page, so these are the ones that For You to Do Problems 4 and 5 continue with. Encourage interested students to continue this alternate solution.

Minds in Action episode 29

Tony and Sasha continue trying to transform the equation $y = 10x^3 - 9x^2 - 13x + 6$ *into* $S = R^3 - R$.

Tony Let's figure out where we are and see if we can answer the original question.

Sasha So we started with $y = 10x^3 - 9x^2 - 13x + 6$.

To make that monic, we substituted $P = D_{10}(x)$ and $Q = D_{100}(y)$.

And we had

$$Q = P^3 - 9P^2 - 130P + 600$$

Tony Then, to get rid of the quadratic term, we figured out what translation would work, and substituted $M = T_{-3}(P) = (T_{-3} \circ D_{10})(x)$ and $N = T_{-156}(Q) = (T_{-156} \circ D_{100})(y)$.

And we got

$$N = M^3 - 157M$$

Sasha Then, to make the coefficient of M equal -1, we found $\alpha = \frac{1}{\sqrt{157}}$ and we substituted $R = D_\alpha(M) = (D_\alpha \circ T_{-3} \circ D_{10})(x)$ and $S = D_{\alpha^3}(N) = (D_{\alpha^3} \circ T_{-156} \circ D_{100})(y)$.

We ended up with $S = R^3 - R$.

Tony Finally!

You should also note that, as with the quadratic equation, you can substitute your expressions for R and S in terms of x and y into the equation $S = R^3 - R$. By multiplying terms out and combining like terms, you can get back to your original cubic equation.

For You to Do

For Problems 3–5, give both the requested substitutions and the resulting equation.

3. Find substitutions that transform the equation $y = 4x^3 - 30x^2 + 59x + 15$ into a monic equation.
4. The equation $y = x^3 - 30x^2 + 236x + 240$ is already monic. Find substitutions that transform it into an equation without a quadratic term.
5. The equation $y = x^3 - 64x$ is already monic and has no quadratic term. Find substitutions that transform it into an equation of the form $S = R^3 - R$.

Answers

For You to Do

3. $P = D_4(x)$, $Q = D_{16}(y)$;
   $Q = P^3 - 30P^2 + 236P + 240$
4. $M = T_{-10}(x)$, $N = T_{-600}(y)$;
   $N = M^3 - 64M$
5. $R = D_{\frac{1}{8}}(x)$, $S = D_{\frac{1}{512}}(x)$;
   $S = R^3 - R$

Developing Habits of Mind

Extend the process. Can you find the zeros of the cubic polynomial below in the same way you found the zeros of the quadratic polynomial in Example 1?

$$10x^3 - 9x^2 - 13x + 6$$

Well, begin by setting $y = 0$. Then you have

$$S = (D_{\alpha^3} \circ T_{-156} \circ D_{100})(0) = -156\alpha^3$$

And since $S = R^3 - R$, you get

$$R^3 - R + 156\alpha^3 = 0$$

Once you solve that equation for R, you can use the relationship below to find the values of x.

$$x = (D_\alpha \circ T_{-3} \circ D_{10})^{-1}(R)$$

This gives you the zeros of the original polynomial $10x^3 - 9x^2 - 13x + 6$.

But solving an equation such as $R^3 - R + 156\alpha^3 = 0$ is no simple task. In later math courses, you may study how to solve equations of the form $R^3 \pm R + D = 0$, where D is a constant.

Exercises *Practicing Habits of Mind*

Check Your Understanding

1. Recall the work Tony and Sasha did in Minds in Action episode 27. By making the substitutions $M = \mathcal{A}_{(8,\,-1)}(x)$ and $N = \mathcal{A}_{(8,\,121)}(y)$, they transformed the equation $y = 8x^2 - 2x - 15$ into the equation $N = M^2$. Substitute $M = \mathcal{A}_{(8,\,-1)}(x)$ and $N = \mathcal{A}_{(8,\,121)}(y)$ into $N = M^2$. Then solve for y in terms of x.

What should you get for y?

2. Consider the equation $y = 9x^2 + 12x - 5$.
   - **a.** Find a, b, c, and d such that, by making the substitutions $M = \mathcal{A}_{(a,\,b)}(x)$ and $N = \mathcal{A}_{(c,\,d)}(y)$, you transform the equation to $N = M^2$.
   - **b.** Let $y = 0$. Find, in order, the value or values of N, M, and x.
   - **c.** Find the roots of $9x^2 + 12x - 5 = 0$.

3. Repeat Exercise 2 using the equation $y = 2x^2 + 4x + 5$.

Exercises

1. $y = 8x^2 - 2x - 15$

2. a. $a = 9, b = 6, c = 9, d = 81$

b. $N = 81, M = \pm 9,$ $x = \frac{1}{3}$ or $-\frac{5}{3}$

c. $\frac{1}{3}, -\frac{5}{3}$

3. a. $a = 2, b = 2, c = 2, d = -6$

b. $N = -6$, no real values for M or x

c. no real roots

Wrap Up

Discuss Exercises 5 and 9, which have students solve general monic and nonmonic quadratics. The results should look familiar to students, since they are the results of the quadratic formula. Students may be interested to see these results coming from a completely different direction.

Finish today's lesson by going over the Check Your Understanding core exercises as time allows.

Assessment Resources

Lesson Quiz 6.7

1. Complete the square of the equation $y = x^2 + 4x - 9$.

2. Consider the equation $y = x^2 + 6x - 5$. Find a, b, c, and d such that, by making the substitutions below, you get the transformed equation $N = M^2$.
   - $M = \mathcal{A}_{(a,\,b)}(x)$
   - $N = \mathcal{A}_{(c,\,d)}(y)$

3. Consider the equation $y = 7x^2 + 6x - 5$.
   - **a.** Find a, b, c, and d such that, by making the substitutions below, you get the transformed equation $N = M^2$.
     - $M = \mathcal{A}_{(a,\,b)}(x)$
     - $N = \mathcal{A}_{(c,\,d)}(y)$
   - **b.** Let $y = 0$. Find, in order, the value or values of N, M, and x.
   - **c.** Find the roots of the equation $7x^2 + 6x - 5 = 0$.

Exercises

HOMEWORK

- Core: 7, 8, 10, 11, 12, 13
- Optical: 9, 15, 16
- Extension: 14

Check Your Understanding

EXERCISE 1 The result of this exercise is the original equation that Tony and Sasha started with, before they made any substitutions.

EXERCISE 2c Some students may choose to find the roots to the equation $9x^2 + 12x - 5 = 0$ by using the quadratic formula rather than trusting the substitutions they found in part (a). This approach is fine and gives them a nice check of their work.

EXERCISES 4 AND 5 Part (c) of Exercise 4 requires students to figure out that they need to use a fraction to complete the square. This is a warm up for Exercise 5, in which students work through an example of completing the square for a general monic quadratic equation.

EXERCISE 5 It is helpful for some students, as they work with expressions involving a lot of variables, to write out specific goals, such as "Solve for k in terms of b and c," or to have a numerical example side-by-side with the general problem so that they can do the steps in parallel.

EXERCISE 6 Students may get confused about the substitutions. If they use the variables M and N for their first set of substitutions, part (a) works out fine, but in part (b) they will not yet be finished. They will need to choose new variables for their second set of substitutions, and then interpret their answer. In part (a), if they do not assume that one substitution will suffice (which their experience will have shown to be a good guess), they may not know how to proceed when they get the result they want from the first set of substitutions. In the end, it is important for students to learn that they can use any variables. There is nothing magic about the choices of P, Q, M, N, and α. The text is consistent, where possible, so that students are able to follow the calculations more easily. In their own work, though, students can choose any variable names they like.

On Your Own

EXERCISE 8 Even if students do not notice that they do not need to complete the square in this exercise, they will not run into trouble. They will add and subtract 36 and come out with the same results.

4. For each equation, complete the square. That is, write it in the form below for some numbers k and D.

$$y = (x + k)^2 + D$$

a. $y = x^2 + 6x + 5$ **b.** $y = x^2 - 4x + 1$ **c.** $y = x^2 + 5x + 7$

5. Take It Further Consider the equation $y = x^2 + bx + c$.

a. If $M = T_k(x)$, then $x = T_{-k}(M) = M - k$.

Substitute $x = M - k$ into $y = x^2 + bx + c$. Find the value of k such that the coefficient of M is 0.

b. Use the value of k you found in part (a). Substitute $x = M - k$ into $y = x^2 + bx + c$. Simplify as much as possible.

c. Write the equation you found in part (b) in the form

$$y = (x + k)^2 + D$$

where D is some number. Find D in terms of b and c.

6. For each equation, find a, b, c, and d such that, by making the substitutions below, you get a transformed equation of the form $N = M^3$, $N = M^3 + M$, or $N = M^3 - M$.

- $M = \mathcal{A}_{(a,b)}(x)$ • $N = \mathcal{A}_{(c,d)}(y)$

a. $y = x^3 + 6x^2 + 11x + 7$ **b.** $y = x^3 + 3x^2 + 7x + 13$

On Your Own

7. Consider the equation $y = 5x^2 + 6x - 7$.

a. Find a, b, c, and d such that, by making the substitutions below, you get the transformed equation $N = M^2$.

- $M = \mathcal{A}_{(a,b)}(x)$ • $N = \mathcal{A}_{(c,d)}(y)$

b. Let $y = 0$. Find, in order, the value or values of N, M, and x.

c. Find the roots of the equation $5x^2 + 6x - 7 = 0$.

Go Online PHSchool.com

For additional practice, go to Web Code: bfa-0607

8. Repeat Exercise 7 using the equation $y = 9x^2 - 12x + 4$.

9. Consider the equation $y = ax^2 + bx + c$, with $a \neq 0$.

a. Find e, f, g, and h such that, by making the substitutions below, you get the transformed equation $N = M^2$.

- $M = \mathcal{A}_{(e,f)}(x)$ • $N = \mathcal{A}_{(g,h)}(y)$

b. Let $y = 0$. Find, in order, the value or values of N, M, and x.

c. Find the roots of the equation $ax^2 + bx + c = 0$.

What should x be when $y = 0$?

Answers

4. a. $y = (x + 3)^2 + (-4)$

b. $y = (x + (-2))^2 + (-3)$

c. $y = \left(x + \frac{5}{2}\right)^2 + \frac{3}{4}$

5. a. $\frac{b}{2}$

b. $y = M^2 - \frac{b^2}{4} + c$

c. $y = \left(x + \frac{b}{2}\right)^2 + \left(-\frac{b^2}{4} + c\right)$; $D = -\frac{b^2}{4} + c$

6. a. $a = 1, b = 2, c = 1, d = -1$

b. $a = \frac{1}{2}, b = \frac{1}{2}, c = \frac{1}{8}, d = -1$

7. a. $a = 5, b = 3, c = 5, d = 44$

b. $N = 44$, $M = \pm 2\sqrt{11}$, $x = \frac{\pm 2\sqrt{11} - 3}{5}$

c. $\frac{\pm 2\sqrt{11} - 3}{5}$

8–9. See back of book.

10. **Standardized Test Prep** What are the roots of the equation $2x^2 + 7x + 5 = 0$?

A. $x = -\frac{9}{2}$ and $x = 7$
B. $x = -\frac{7}{2}$ and $x = -\frac{3}{2}$
C. $x = -\frac{5}{2}$ and $x = -1$
D. $x = -\frac{3}{2}$ and $x = \frac{7}{2}$

11. Consider the equation $y = x^3 + bx^2 + cx + d$.
If $M = T_k(x)$, then $x = T_{-k}(M) = M - k$.
Substitute $x = M - k$ into $y = x^3 + bx^2 + cx + d$. Find the value of k such that the coefficient of M^2 is 0.

12. Consider this equation.
$$y = \left(M - \frac{b}{3}\right)^3 + b\left(M - \frac{b}{3}\right)^2 + c\left(M - \frac{b}{3}\right) + d$$
Expand the right side to get
$$y = M^3 + \left(-\frac{b^2}{3} + c\right)M + \text{(a number)}$$
a. Even before you expand the right side, why should you expect the quadratic term to vanish?
b. Given the equation $y = x^3 + bx^2 + cx + d$, you know that it transforms into one of the forms $N = M^3$, $N = M^3 + M$, or $N = M^3 - M$.
How can you tell which form from the coefficients b and c?
c. Given the equation $y = ax^3 + bx^2 + cx + d$, you know that it transforms into one of the forms $N = M^3$, $N = M^3 + M$, or $N = M^3 - M$.
How can you tell which form from the coefficients a, b, and c?

For Exercises 13 and 14, describe the substitutions required to transform each equation into one of the equations $N = M^3$, $N = M^3 + M$, or $N = M^3 - M$.

13. $y = 8x^3 - 6x^2 + 2x - 1$

14. **Take It Further** $y = ax^3 + bx^2 + cx + d$

Maintain Your Skills

15. Compute each composition.
a. $\mathcal{A}_{(2, 3)} \circ T_4 \circ \left(\mathcal{A}_{(2, 3)}\right)^{-1}$
b. $\mathcal{A}_{(3, -7)} \circ T_{-3} \circ \left(\mathcal{A}_{(3, -7)}\right)^{-1}$
c. $\mathcal{A}_{(-1, 8)} \circ T_5 \circ \left(\mathcal{A}_{(-1, 8)}\right)^{-1}$
d. $\mathcal{A}_{(-5, 12)} \circ T_{-2} \circ \left(\mathcal{A}_{(-5, 12)}\right)^{-1}$

16. Given an affine transformation $\mathcal{A}_{(a, b)}$ and a translation T_r, show that the composition below is a translation.
$$\mathcal{A}_{(a, b)} \circ T_r \circ \left(\mathcal{A}_{(a, b)}\right)^{-1}$$

10. C

11. $\frac{b}{3}$

12. See back of book.

13. The substitutions $M = (D_{\frac{1}{2}} \circ T_{-2} \circ D_8)(x) = \mathcal{A}_{(4, -1)}$ and $N = (D_{\frac{1}{8}} \circ T_{48} \circ D_{64})(y) = \mathcal{A}_{(8, 6)}$ transform the equation into $N = M^3 + M$.

14. See back of book.

15. a. T_8 **b.** T_{-9} **c.** T_{-5} **d.** T_{10}

16. Using the result from Lesson 6.6, Exercise 11e,
$(\mathcal{A}_{(a, b)} \circ T_r \circ (\mathcal{A}_{(a, b)})^{-1})(x) =$
$(\mathcal{A}_{(a, b)} \circ T_r)(\mathcal{A}_{(\frac{1}{a}, -\frac{b}{a})}) =$
$(\mathcal{A}_{(a, b)} \circ T_r)\left(\frac{1}{a}x - \frac{b}{a}\right) =$
$\mathcal{A}_{(a, b)}\left(\frac{1}{a}x + \frac{ar - b}{a}\right) =$
$a\left(\frac{1}{a}x + \frac{ar - b}{a}\right) + b =$
$x + ar = T_{ar}$.

EXERCISES 11 AND 12 Assign these two exercises together so that students can use the results of Exercise 11 to answer the question asked in part (a) of Exercise 12.

EXERCISE 12 Some students may want to memorize the result of this exercise. Do not overemphasize the importance of this result. Being able to predict the final form does not really help you transform a general cubic equation into one of the basic graph forms.

EXERCISE 13 Some students may think they can substitute $P = 2x$, since the coefficient of x^3 is already a perfect cube, and the other terms have even coefficients. This does not work, however, because the coefficient of x^2 is not a multiple of 4.

EXERCISE 14 is a challenge for those students who really enjoy complex calculations.

Maintain Your Skills

EXERCISES 14 AND 15 You may find that some students derive (or have memorized) a formula for $(\mathcal{A}_{(a, b)})^{-1}$ and use that in Exercises 14 and 15. That is an efficient strategy.

Additional Resources

PRINT RESOURCES
- Solution Manual
- Practice Workbook
- Assessment Resources
- Teaching Resources

TECHNOLOGY
- Interactive Textbook
- TeacherExpress CD-ROM
- ExamView CD-ROM
- PHSchool.com

Additional Practice

1. For each equation, complete the square. That is, write it in the form $y = (x + k)^2 + D$ for some numbers k and D.
a. $y = x^2 + 8x + 11$
b. $y = x^2 + 12x + 21$
c. $y = x^2 + 7x + 5$

2. Consider the equation $y = 3x^2 + 4x - 5$.
a. Find a, b, c, and d such that, by making the substitutions below, you get the transformed equation $N = M^2$.
- $M = \mathcal{A}_{(a, b)}(x)$
- $N = \mathcal{A}_{(c, d)}(y)$

b. Let $y = 0$. Find, in order, the value or values of N, M, and x.
c. Find the roots of the equation $3x^2 + 4x - 5 = 0$.

3. Repeat Exercise 1 using the equation $y = 4x^2 + 12x + 9$.

4. Consider the equation $y = x^3 + bx^2 + cx + d$.
If $M = T_k(x)$, then $x = T_{-k}(M) = M - k$. Substitute $x = M - k$ into $y = x^3 + bx^2 + cx + d$.
a. Find the value of k such that the coefficient of M^2 is 1.
b. Find the value of k such that the coefficient of M^2 is 0.

5. Consider this equation.
$$y = \left(M - \frac{b}{2}\right)^3 + b\left(M - \frac{b}{2}\right)^2 + c\left(M - \frac{b}{2}\right) + d$$
a. Without expanding the right side, explain whether the quadratic term will vanish.
b. Expand the right side to confirm your answer to part (a).

6. Consider the equation $y = 2x^3 - 3x^2 + 2x - 2$.
Describe the substitutions required to transform the equation into an equation of the form $N = M^3 + M$.

Practice: For Lesson 6.7, assign Exercises 1–6.

Mathematical Reflections

EXERCISES 6–8 At the start of the investigation, you may have assigned these as Questions 1–3 for students to think and write about.

Mathematical Reflections 6B

In this investigation, you learned to write any composition of translations and dilations as an affine transformation and find the inverse of a dilation, a translation, or an affine transformation. These exercises will help you summarize what you have learned.

1. Write each composition as a single affine transformation, $\mathcal{A}_{(a,\,b)}$.

a. $T_3 \circ T_{-1} \circ T_5$ **b.** $D_{-4} \circ D_2 \circ D_{-3}$ **c.** $D_{-4} \circ T_3$

d. $T_3 \circ D_{-4}$ **e.** $T_3 \circ D_{-3} \circ (T_3)^{-1}$ **f.** $(D_{-4})^{-1} \circ T_5 \circ D_{-4}$

2. Write each expression as a single affine transformation, $\mathcal{A}_{(a,\,b)}$.

a. $(\mathcal{A}_{(2,\,5)})^{-1}$ **b.** $(\mathcal{A}_{(-3,\,4)})^{-1}$ **c.** $\mathcal{A}_{(-3,\,4)} \circ \mathcal{A}_{(2,\,5)}$

d. $\mathcal{A}_{(2,\,5)} \circ \mathcal{A}_{(-3,\,4)}$ **e.** $(\mathcal{A}_{(2,\,5)} \circ \mathcal{A}_{(-3,\,4)})^{-1}$

f. Write an equation that relates $(\mathcal{A}_{(2,\,5)})^{-1}$, $(\mathcal{A}_{(-3,\,4)})^{-1}$, and $(\mathcal{A}_{(2,\,5)} \circ \mathcal{A}_{(-3,\,4)})^{-1}$.

3. Consider the equation $y = 3x^2 + 10x + 7$. Find a, b, c, and d such that, by making the substitutions $M = \mathcal{A}_{(a,\,b)}(x)$ and $N = \mathcal{A}_{(c,\,d)}(y)$, you get the transformed equation $N = M^2$.

4. The substitutions $M = \mathcal{A}_{(6,\,-5)}(x)$ and $N = \mathcal{A}_{(4,\,1)}(y)$ transform a certain quadratic equation into the equation $N = M^2$.

a. Substitute $M = \mathcal{A}_{(6,\,-5)}(x)$ and $N = \mathcal{A}_{(4,\,1)}(y)$ into $N = M^2$. Solve for y in terms of x to find the original equation.

b. Let $y = 0$ in the equation you found in part (a). Find, in order, the corresponding value or values of N, M, and x.

5. For $y = x^3 - 3x^2 + 12x + 17$, find a, b, c, and d such that, by making the substitutions $R = \mathcal{A}_{(a,\,b)}(x)$ and $S = \mathcal{A}_{(c,\,d)}(y)$, you get a transformed equation of the form $S = R^3$, $S = R^3 + R$, or $S = R^3 - R$.

6. Why do dilations commute under function composition?

7. How do you compute the inverse of an affine transformation?

8. How do you transform an equation of the form $y = ax^3 + bx^2 + cx + d$ into one of the equations $y = x^3$, $y = x^3 + x$, or $y = x^3 - x$ by composing dilations and translations?

Vocabulary and Notation

In this investigation, you learned these terms and symbols. Make sure you understand what each one means and how to use it.

- **affine transformation, $\mathcal{A}_{(a,\,b)}$**
- **completing the square**
- **dilation, D_s**
- **identity transformation**
- **reflection transformation**
- **translation, T_a**

Answers

Mathematical Reflections

1. a. $\mathcal{A}_{(1,\,7)}$ **b.** $\mathcal{A}_{(24,\,0)}$

c. $\mathcal{A}_{(-4,\,-12)}$ **d.** $\mathcal{A}_{(-4,\,3)}$

e. $\mathcal{A}_{(-3,\,12)}$ **f.** $\mathcal{A}_{\left(1,\,-\frac{5}{4}\right)}$

2. a. $\mathcal{A}_{\left(\frac{1}{2},\,-\frac{5}{2}\right)}$ **b.** $\mathcal{A}_{\left(-\frac{1}{3},\,\frac{4}{3}\right)}$

c. $\mathcal{A}_{(-6,\,-11)}$ **d.** $\mathcal{A}_{(-6,\,13)}$

e. $\mathcal{A}_{\left(-\frac{1}{6},\,\frac{13}{6}\right)}$

f. $(\mathcal{A}_{(2,\,5)} \circ \mathcal{A}_{(-3,\,4)})^{-1} = (\mathcal{A}_{(-3,\,4)})^{-1} \circ (\mathcal{A}_{(2,\,5)})^{-1}$

3. $a = 3, b = 5, c = 3, d = 4$

4. a. $y = 9x^2 - 15x + 6$

b. $N = 1, M = \pm 1, x = 1$ or $\frac{2}{3}$

5. $a = \frac{1}{3}, b = -\frac{1}{3}, c = \frac{1}{27}, d = -1$

6. $D_a \circ D_b = D_{ab}$ and $D_b \circ D_a = D_{ba}$. Because multiplication of real numbers is commutative, $ab = ba$, so $D_{ab} = D_{ba}$. Thus, $D_a \circ D_b = D_b \circ D_a$.

7. $(\mathcal{A}_{(a,\,b)})^{-1} = \mathcal{A}_{\left(\frac{1}{a},\,-\frac{b}{a}\right)}$

8. First, find the dilations that will make the equation monic. Then, use a translation to eliminate the quadratic term and have an equation in the form $N = M^3 + aM$. If $a \neq \pm 1$, use a dilation to make $a = \pm 1$, resulting in an equation of the form $S = R^3 \pm R$.

Chapter 6

Mid-Chapter Test

Go Online PHSchool.com — For a mid-chapter test, go to Web Code: bfa-0652

Multiple Choice

1. Which translation transforms the graph of $y = x^2$ to the graph of $y = (x + 4)^2$?
   - A. 4 units up
   - B. 4 units down
   - C. 4 units left
   - D. 4 units right

2. What is the vertex of the parabola with equation $y - 4 = (x + 1)^2$?
   - A. $(1, 4)$
   - B. $(-1, 4)$
   - C. $(1, -4)$
   - D. $(-1, -4)$

3. Use the definitions of functions f and g below.

   $$f(x) = x^2 + 4x$$
   $$g(x) = x^3 + 4x$$

   Which of the following statements are true?

   I. f is an even function.
   II. f is an odd function.
   III. g is an even function.
   IV. g is an odd function.

   - A. I and IV
   - B. II and III
   - C. I only
   - D. IV only

4. For a nonzero real number s, the formula $D_s(x) = sx$ defines a function $D_s: \mathbb{R} \to \mathbb{R}$. What is $(D_2 \circ D_{-3})(5)$?
   - A. -30
   - B. -5
   - C. $-\frac{5}{6}$
   - D. 30

5. Which affine transformation is equal to $\mathcal{A}_{(2, 4)} \circ \mathcal{A}_{(-1, 3)}$?
   - A. $\mathcal{A}_{(1, 12)}$
   - B. $\mathcal{A}_{(-2, 7)}$
   - C. $\mathcal{A}_{(-2, 10)}$
   - D. $\mathcal{A}_{(-2, 12)}$

Open Response

6. a. Find all points on the unit circle $x^2 + y^2 = 1$ with x-coordinate $\frac{7}{25}$.
   b. Use your answer to find six more points on the unit circle.

7. a. Sketch a graph of $y = x^3 - x$.
   b. Write an equation for a function having a graph that is the graph of $y = x^3 - x$ after a translation 5 units to the right and 2 units down. Sketch the graph.
   c. Write an equation for a function having a graph that is the graph of $y = x^3 - x$ scaled horizontally by a factor of 3. Sketch the graph.

8. a. Sketch the graph of $y + 1 = 2|x - 4|$. How is your graph related to the graph of $y = |x|$?
   b. Sketch the graph of $\left(\frac{x}{2}\right)^2 + (y - 3)^2 = 25$. How is your graph related to the graph of $x^2 + y^2 = 25$?

9. Write each expression as a single affine transformation $\mathcal{A}_{(a, b)}$.
   a. $D_3 \circ T_1$
   b. $T_1 \circ D_3$
   c. $D_2 \circ D_{-2} \circ T_6$
   d. $T_4 \circ (D_2)^{-1}$
   e. $(\mathcal{A}_{(2, 6)})^{-1}$
   f. $\mathcal{A}_{(2, -4)} \circ \mathcal{A}_{(-3, 5)}$

10. Consider the equation $y = 2x^2 + 6x - 3$. Find a, b, c, and d such that, by making the substitutions below, you get the transformed equation $N = M^2$.
    - $M = \mathcal{A}_{(a, b)}(x)$
    - $N = \mathcal{A}_{(c, d)}(y)$

11. What does the graph of $-2y = x^3 - x$ look like?

Mid-Chapter Test

Assessment Resources

Mid-Chapter Test page 1 of 2

Multiple Choice

1. Which translation transforms the graph of $y = x^2$ to the graph of $y - 3 = x^2$?
   A. 3 units up
   B. 3 units down
   C. 3 units left
   D. 3 units right

2. What is the center of the circle with equation $(x + 2)^2 + (y - 5)^2 = 16$?
   A. $(2, 5)$
   B. $(2, -5)$
   C. $(-2, 5)$
   D. $(-2, -5)$

3. Use the definitions of functions f and g below.

   $$f(x) = x^4 + x^2$$
   $$g(x) = x^3 + 2x$$

   Which of the following statements are true?
   I. f is an even function. II. f is an odd function.
   III. g is an even function. IV. g is an odd function.

   A. I and IV
   B. II and III
   C. I only
   D. IV only

4. For a nonzero real number s, the formula $D_s(x) = sx$ defines a function $D_s: \mathbb{R} \to \mathbb{R}$. What is $(D_3 \circ D_{-4})(-2)$?
   A. -24
   B. -12
   C. -6
   D. 24

5. Which affine transformation is equal to $\mathcal{A}_{(5, -1)} \circ \mathcal{A}_{(2, -4)}$?
   A. $\mathcal{A}_{(7, -5)}$
   B. $\mathcal{A}_{(10, 5)}$
   C. $\mathcal{A}_{(7, 21)}$
   D. $\mathcal{A}_{(10, -21)}$

Also available: Form B

Mid-Chapter Test

1. C 2. B 3. D
4. A 5. C

6. a. $\left(\frac{7}{25}, \frac{24}{25}\right), \left(\frac{7}{25}, -\frac{24}{25}\right)$
   b. $\left(-\frac{7}{25}, \frac{24}{25}\right), \left(-\frac{7}{25}, -\frac{24}{25}\right), \left(\frac{24}{25}, \frac{7}{25}\right), \left(\frac{24}{25}, -\frac{7}{25}\right), \left(-\frac{24}{25}, \frac{7}{25}\right), \left(-\frac{24}{25}, -\frac{7}{25}\right)$

7. See back of book.

8. a.

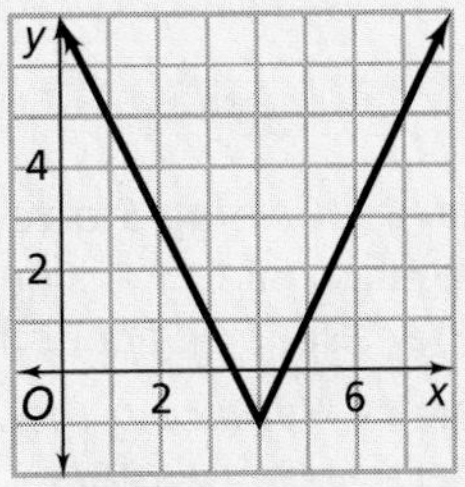

Answers may vary. Sample: The graph of $y + 1 = 2|x - 4|$ is the graph of $y = |x|$ scaled vertically by the factor 2 and translated 4 units to the right and 1 unit down.

b.

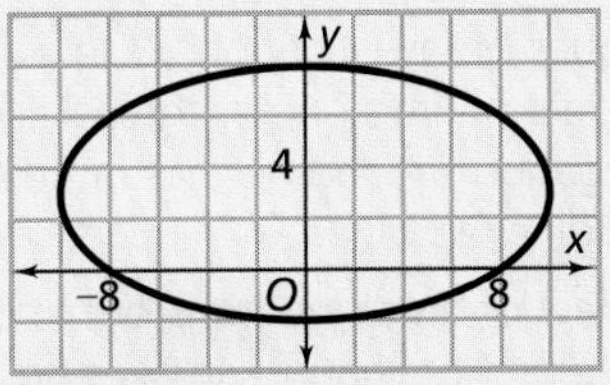

The graph of $\left(\frac{x}{2}\right)^2 + (y - 3)^2 = 25$ is the graph of $x^2 + y^2 = 25$ scaled horizontally by the factor 2 and translated 3 units up.

9. a. $\mathcal{A}_{(3, 3)}$ b. $\mathcal{A}_{(3, 1)}$
   c. $\mathcal{A}_{(-4, -24)}$ d. $\mathcal{A}_{(\frac{1}{2}, 4)}$
   e. $\mathcal{A}_{(\frac{1}{2}, -3)}$ f. $\mathcal{A}_{(-6, 6)}$

10. $a = 2, b = 3, c = 2, d = 15$

11. Answers may vary. Sample: The graph of $-2y = x^3 - x$ is the graph of $y = x^3 - x$ reflected over the x-axis and scaled vertically by the factor $\frac{1}{2}$.

Investigation Overview

This investigation connects the ideas of the first two investigations. Students transform an equation into one of the basic graph forms and then graph it using a new approach. In Investigation 6A, students saw a transformation as acting on a basic graph to produce a new graph on the standard coordinate axes. In this investigation, students view a transformation as acting on the *coordinate axes*.

Instead of scaling a graph, students dilate the coordinate axes. This changes the size of the units that measure horizontal or vertical distances, so that points on the graph have new coordinates corresponding to these new units. Similarly, translations of the coordinate axes create a coordinate system with its origin in a new location, so that points on the graph have new coordinates corresponding to this change in the location of the origin. Students interpret graphs that show paired coordinate systems—old and new—and describe how the basic graphs look from a transformed point of view. They use these paired-coordinate-system graphs to identify critical points on a transformed graph. By making connections between the methods of Investigations 6A and 6C, students develop a more robust understanding of how transformations act on graphs, coordinate systems, and equations.

Students also continue to explore the algebraic structure of affine transformations by thinking about fixed points, and about collections of affine transformations for which a particular point is fixed.

You may wish to assign Questions 1–3 for students to think and write about during the investigation.

Learning Goals

- Use the techniques of Investigation 6B to transform an equation into one of the basic graph forms of Investigation 6A and use the information to graph the original equation.
- Describe the effect of an affine transformation on an axis and the effect of changes in axes on the graph of an equation.
- Identify the fixed points of an affine transformation and the set of affine transformations that fix a particular point.

Habits and Skills

- Visualize transformations both as operations on graphs and as operations on coordinate axes.
- Make connections between transformations on graphs and on coordinate axes.
- Think algebraically to further examine the structure of the set of affine transformations.

Investigation 6C

Graphing Using Affine Transformations

In *Graphing Using Affine Transformations*, you will use what you learned about affine transformations in the previous investigation to graph equations.

By the end of this investigation, you will be able to answer questions like these.

1. How do you use the replacing-the-axes method to sketch the graph of $y = x^3 + 3x^2 - x + 4$?
2. How do you use the replacing-the-axes method to explain the relationship between the graphs of $y = x^2$ and $y = (x - 3)^2$?
3. What is the fixed point for $\mathcal{A}_{(5,\,3)}$?

You will learn how to

- use the techniques of Investigation 6B to transform an equation into one of the basic graph forms of Investigation 6A and use the information to graph the original equation
- describe the effect of an affine transformation on an axis and the effect of changes in axes on the graph of an equation
- identify the fixed points of an affine transformation and the set of affine transformations that fix a particular point

You will develop these habits and skills:

- Visualize transformations both as operations on graphs and as operations on coordinate axes.
- Make connections between transformations on graphs and on coordinate axes.
- Think algebraically to further examine the structure of the set of affine transformations.

You can use a dilation to relate the miles-per-hour scale and the kilometers-per-hour scale on the speedometer.

Investigation Road Map

LESSON 6.8, *Getting Started,* has students review techniques they used in Investigation 6B to transform equations into forms they graphed in Investigation 6A. They also think about the effects of transformations on a number line.

LESSON 6.9, *Replacing the Axes,* has students use techniques for transforming number lines to transform coordinate axes. Students see how such a transformation changes the coordinates of points on the graph of an equation. Rather than thinking of the transformation as applied to the graph, they think of it as applied to the axes.

LESSON 6.10, *Advanced Affine Transformations,* explores other applications of affine transformations. Students think about the fixed point(s) of an affine transformation and about the set of affine transformations for which a particular point is fixed. They also consider affine recursive definitions of functions.

6.8 Getting Started

Activating Prior Knowledge
Exploring New Ideas

You can use number lines to show the result of an affine transformation.

For You to Explore

For each equation in Problems 1 and 2, find *a*, *b*, *c*, and *d* such that, by making the substitutions $M = \mathcal{A}_{(a,\,b)}(x)$ and $N = \mathcal{A}_{(c,\,d)}(y)$, you get the transformed equation $N = M^2$.

1. a. $y = 2x^2 - 12x + 17$ **b.** $y = -x^2 + 2x + 3$

2. a. $y = 3x^2 - 14x + 10$ **b.** $y = -\frac{1}{4}x^2 + 6x + 8$

3. Write each expression in the form $(x - h)^2 + k$.

a. $x^2 + 4x$ **b.** $x^2 - 6x$ **c.** $x^2 + 5x$ **d.** $x^2 + 3x$

4. Write each equation in the form $(x - h)^2 + (y - k)^2 = r^2$.

a. $x^2 + y^2 + 4x = 0$ **b.** $x^2 + y^2 - 6x + 4y - 12 = 0$

c. $x^2 + y^2 + 5x = 0$ **d.** $x^2 + y^2 + 3x + 5y - \frac{1}{2} = 0$

5. Suppose $M = T_{-3}(x) = x - 3$. Then $x = T_3(M) = M + 3$.

Explain how the pair of number lines below shows the relationship between *M* and *x*.

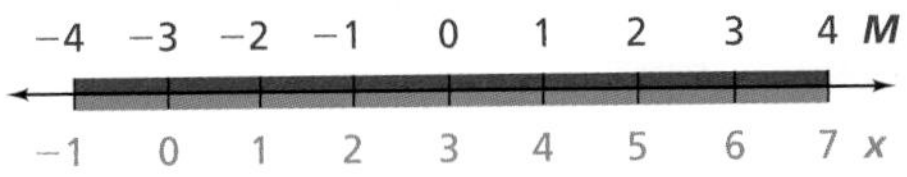

6. For each expression, solve for *x* in terms of *M*. Then draw a pair of number lines like the one in Problem 5 showing the relationship between *M* and *x*.

a. $M = T_4(x)$ **b.** $M = T_{-2}(x)$ **c.** $M = T_{\frac{3}{2}}(x)$ **d.** $M = T_0(x)$

e. If $M = T_a(x)$, describe how the number lines for *M* and *x* are related.

Answers

For You to Explore

1. a. $a = 2, b = -6, c = 2, d = 2$

b. $a = -1, b = 1, c = -1, d = 4$

2. a. $a = 3, b = -7, c = 3, d = 19$

b. $a = -\frac{1}{4}, b = 3, c = -\frac{1}{4}, d = 11$

3. a. $(x - (-2))^2 + (-4)$

b. $(x - 3)^2 + (-9)$

c. $\left(x - \left(-\frac{5}{2}\right)\right)^2 + \left(-\frac{25}{4}\right)$

d. $\left(x - \left(-\frac{3}{2}\right)\right)^2 + \left(-\frac{9}{4}\right)$

4. a. $(x - (-2))^2 + (y - 0)^2 = 2^2$

b. $(x - 3)^2 + (y - (-2))^2 = 5^2$

c. $\left(x - \left(-\frac{5}{2}\right)\right)^2 + (y - 0)^2 = \left(\frac{5}{2}\right)^2$

d. $\left(x - \left(-\frac{3}{2}\right)\right)^2 + \left(y - \left(-\frac{5}{2}\right)\right)^2 = 3^2$

5–6. See back of book.

Lesson Overview

GOALS

- Use the techniques of Investigation 6B to transform an equation into one of the basic graph forms of Investigation 6A.
- Describe the effect of an affine transformation on an axis.

In this lesson, students review what they have learned in Investigations 6A and 6B and think about the effect of an affine transformation on a number line. This prepares them to apply transformations to the coordinate axes.

FOR YOU TO EXPLORE
- Core: 1, 3, 4, 5, 6
- Optional: 2

HOMEWORK
- Core: 7, 8, 9, 10, 11
- Optional: 12, 13, 14

MATERIALS
- CAS (recommended)
- graph paper
- graphing calculators
- Blackline Master 6.8

Launch

Use Problem 1 to review what students learned in Lesson 6.7. If you skipped Lesson 6.7, then skip Problems 1 and 2 for this Getting Started lesson.

Explore

For You to Explore

PROBLEMS 3 AND 4 Some algebra texts have students memorize these forms to use when graphing parabolas and circles. In CME Project *Algebra 2*, students use substitutions like the ones in Problems 1 and 2 to transform equations into basic graph forms. In this investigation, they learn to use these substitutions to graph parabolas and circles by transforming the coordinate axes.

PROBLEM 5 It may seem as though asking students to think about transforming the axes rather than transforming a particular graph makes the task of graphing more difficult. However, there are some advantages. If you look at the paired *M*- and *x*-values in this picture of related axes, they form an input-output table for the function $M = T_3(x)$. Students who have been doing well with algebraic calculation but have had trouble visualizing graphs may find this kind of representation particularly helpful, because they can see the numerical relationships between the coordinates of the *M*- and *x*-axes.

PROBLEM 6 Blackline Master 6.8 provides number lines to be used as a transparency or a handout.

Encourage students to start with the same *M*-axis every time and show the changes in the *x*-axis. This may seem backwards to them, but remind students

continued on p. 558

continued from p. 557

that in Investigation 6B, they worked to transform equations in x and y that were not in a basic graph form into equations in variables like N and M, which were in basic graph form. In this investigation they will start with a basic graph in the coordinate system of the substitution variables and convert the coordinates to the xy-coordinate system.

Students may still have trouble predicting the direction of the translation and be surprised that if $M = T_a(x)$, then the M-axis is the image of the x-axis after a translation of a units to the *left* for $a > 0$. However, the fact that the M- and x-values form an input-output table for the function $M = T_a(x)$ should allow students to draw the correct picture. Then they should be able to describe the translation correctly even if their intuition is not yet helpful in predicting the direction.

Wrap Up

Go over the For You to Explore core problems with your class. Pay special attention to how students interpret Problems 5 and 6.

Exercises

HOMEWORK
- Core: 7, 8, 9, 10, 11
- Optional: 12, 13, 14

Exercises *Practicing Habits of Mind*

On Your Own

7. Suppose $M = D_2(x) = 2x$. Then $x = D_{\frac{1}{2}}(M) = \frac{M}{2}$. Explain how the pair of number lines below shows the relationship between M and x.

−4	−3	−2	−1	0	1	2	3	4	**M**
−2	$-\frac{3}{2}$	−1	$-\frac{1}{2}$	0	$\frac{1}{2}$	1	$\frac{3}{2}$	2	*x*

8. For each expression, solve for x in terms of M. Then draw a pair of number lines showing the relationship between M and x.

a. $M = D_3(x)$ **b.** $M = D_{\frac{1}{2}}(x)$ **c.** $M = D_{-1}(x)$ **d.** $M = D_{-\frac{1}{2}}(x)$

e. If $M = D_s(x)$, describe how the number lines for M and x are related.

9. Suppose $M = \mathcal{A}_{(2,\,-3)}(x) = 2x - 3$. Then $x = \mathcal{A}_{(\frac{1}{2},\,\frac{3}{2})}(M) = \frac{1}{2}M + \frac{3}{2}$.

Explain how the pair of number lines below shows the relationship between M and x.

−4	−3	−2	−1	0	1	2	3	4	**M**
$-\frac{1}{2}$	0	$\frac{1}{2}$	1	$\frac{3}{2}$	2	$\frac{5}{2}$	3	$\frac{7}{2}$	*x*

10. For each equation, solve for x in terms of M. Then draw a pair of number lines like the one in Exercise 9 showing the relationship between M and x.

a. $M = \mathcal{A}_{(3,\,-1)}(x)$ **b.** $M = \mathcal{A}_{(\frac{1}{4},\,2)}(x)$

c. $M = \mathcal{A}_{(-1,\,-3)}(x)$ **d.** $M = \mathcal{A}_{(-\frac{1}{2},\,\frac{3}{2})}(x)$

11. For each equation, solve for x in terms of M. Then draw a pair of number lines like the one in Exercise 9 showing the relationship between M and x.

a. $M = (\mathcal{A}_{(3,\,-1)})^{-1}(x)$ **b.** $M = \left(\mathcal{A}_{(\frac{1}{4},\,2)}\right)^{-1}(x)$

c. $M = (\mathcal{A}_{(-1,\,-3)})^{-1}(x)$ **d.** $M = \left(\mathcal{A}_{(-\frac{1}{2},\,\frac{3}{2})}\right)^{-1}(x)$

Answers

Exercises

7. Answers may vary. Sample: Each value on the x number line is one-half the corresponding value on the M number line.

8. a. $x = \frac{M}{3}$

−3	−2	−1	0	1	2	3	*M*
−1	$-\frac{2}{3}$	$-\frac{1}{3}$	0	$\frac{2}{3}$	$\frac{1}{3}$	1	*x*

b. $x = 2M$

−3	−2	−1	0	1	2	3	*M*
−6	−4	−2	0	2	4	6	*x*

c. $x = -M$

−3	−2	−1	0	1	2	3	*M*
3	2	1	0	−1	−2	−3	*x*

d. $x = -2M$

−3	−2	−1	0	1	2	3	*M*
6	4	2	0	−2	−4	−6	*x*

e. The x number line is the image of the M number line after a dilation (centered at 0) by the factor s. If $s < 0$, then the dilation includes a reflection over 0.

9. Answers may vary. Sample: For each value on the M number line, the corresponding value on the x number line is $\frac{1}{2}M + \frac{3}{2}$.

10. a. $x = \frac{1}{3}M + \frac{1}{3}$

−3	−2	−1	0	1	2	3	*M*
$-\frac{2}{3}$	$-\frac{1}{3}$	0	$\frac{1}{3}$	$\frac{2}{3}$	1	$\frac{4}{3}$	*x*

b. $x = 4M - 8$

−3	−2	−1	0	1	2	3	*M*
−20	−16	−12	−8	−4	0	4	*x*

c. $x = -M - 3$

−3	−2	−1	0	1	2	3	*M*
0	−1	−2	−3	−4	−5	−6	*x*

d. $x = -2M + 3$

−3	−2	−1	0	1	2	3	*M*
9	7	5	3	1	−1	−3	*x*

12. Simplify each expression using the socks-and-shoes method of taking inverses.

a. $(T_3 \circ D_2)^{-1}$ b. $(D_2 \circ T_3)^{-1}$ c. $(T_{-3} \circ D_{\frac{1}{2}})^{-1}$ d. $(D_{\frac{1}{2}} \circ T_{-3})^{-1}$

Write each inverse as a single affine transformation $\mathcal{A}_{(a,\, b)}$. See Exercise 13 from Lesson 6.6 for the meaning of the socks-and-shoes method.

Maintain Your Skills

13. Expand the right side of each equation.

a. $y = (x - 1)^3 + 3(x - 1)^2 - (x - 1) + 4$

b. $y = (x + 2)^3 - 6(x + 2)^2 - 4(x + 2) + 1$

c. $y = (x - 2)^3 + 6(x - 2)^2 + 4(x - 2) + 1$

d. $y = (x + 1)^3 - 3(x + 1)^2 + 2(x + 1) + 4$

Go Online
Video Tutor
PHSchool.com

Web Code: bfe-0775

14. What is the coefficient of x^2 if you expand the following expression and write it as a polynomial in x?

$$\left(x - \frac{b}{3}\right)^3 + b\left(x - \frac{b}{3}\right)^2 + c\left(x - \frac{b}{3}\right) + d$$

On Your Own

EXERCISE 9 Also ask your students to describe the transformations that relate the M number line to the x number line. This may be difficult for them. In this case, when students think about translating to the left or right, they must think about the size of step, because 1 unit is not the same size on both axes. A unit on the M-axis is half the size of a unit on the x-axis. Suggest that students first describe the necessary dilation and then use the new size of step to describe the translation.

Students may question whether they should describe the dilation or translation first. They can do it correctly either way, but they must pay attention to the location of the center of the dilation. When transforming number lines, students should assume the center of dilation is the origin. Later on, when students think about the effect transforming the coordinate axes has on a graph, they must keep this fact in mind. The center of the dilation has an impact on how the coordinates of the points on the graph change.

EXERCISE 11 Hope that students recognize, either through logic or repeated calculation, that if $M = (\mathcal{A}_{(a,\, b)})^{-1}(x)$, then $x = aM + b$.

Maintain Your Skills

EXERCISE 14 Students who are not using CAS to expand this polynomial should think strategically. Rather than multiplying everything out, they should just consider where the x^2 terms come from and use their knowledge of binomial expansions.

11. a. $x = 3M - 1$

M	−3	−2	−1	0	1	2	3
x	−10	−7	−4	−1	2	5	8

b. $x = \frac{1}{4}M + 2$

M	−3	−2	−1	0	1	2	3
x	$\frac{5}{4}$	$\frac{3}{2}$	$\frac{7}{4}$	2	$\frac{9}{4}$	$\frac{5}{2}$	$\frac{11}{4}$

c. $x = -M - 3$

M	−3	−2	−1	0	1	2	3
x	0	−1	−2	−3	−4	−5	−6

d. $x = -\frac{1}{2}M + \frac{3}{2}$

M	−3	−2	−1	0	1	2	3
x	3	$\frac{5}{2}$	2	$\frac{3}{2}$	1	$\frac{1}{2}$	0

12. a. $\mathcal{A}_{\left(\frac{1}{2},\, -\frac{3}{2}\right)}$ **b.** $\mathcal{A}_{\left(\frac{1}{2},\, -3\right)}$

c. $\mathcal{A}_{(2,\, 6)}$ **d.** $\mathcal{A}_{(2,\, 3)}$

13. a. $x^3 - 4x + 7$ **b.** $x^3 - 16x - 23$

c. $x^3 - 8x + 9$ **d.** $x^3 - x + 4$

14. 0

Lesson Overview

GOALS

- Use the techniques of Investigation 6B to transform an equation into one of the basic graph forms of Investigation 6A and use the information to graph the original equation.
- Describe the effect of an affine transformation on an axis and the effect of changes in axes on the graph of an equation.

In this lesson, students learn to graph transformations of the basic graph functions using the "replacing-the-axes" method. This allows them to use the process of transforming equations they learned about in Investigation 6B to graph many more general equations by replacing the axes in a basic graph with a set of transformed axes.

CHECK YOUR UNDERSTANDING
- Core: 1, 2, 3, 4, 6, 8, 10
- Optional: 5, 7, 9

MATERIALS
- graph paper
- graphing calculators
- Blackline Masters 6.8, 6.9A–C

HOMEWORK
- Core: 11, 14, 15, 18, 20, 21, 22
- Optional: 12, 13, 16, 17, 19, 23

VOCABULARY
- "replacing-the-axes" method

Launch

You can use Blackline Master 6.8 to make transparencies or handouts of blank number lines to use in this lesson.

Begin today's lesson by going over the process presented here for using number lines to represent the affine transformation $M = \mathcal{A}_{(2,\,-3)}(x)$. Students worked on this kind of problem in Lesson 6.8, so you will have some idea of how deeply you need to cover this material. If they showed a good understanding of this process in the previous lesson, start right in with the Minds in Action dialog on p. 562.

6.9 Replacing the Axes

In this lesson, you will learn how you can use affine transformations to translate, scale, and reflect graphs with the "replacing-the-axes" method. In Investigation 6B, you found a way to transform equations into the basic forms. This resulted in a substitution such as $M = \mathcal{A}_{(2,\,-3)}(x)$.

For You to Do

For $M = \mathcal{A}_{(2,\,-3)}(x)$, show that each equation is true.

1. $x = (T_{\frac{3}{2}} \circ D_{\frac{1}{2}})(M)$
2. $x = (D_{\frac{1}{2}} \circ T_3)(M)$

You can use this affine transformation to create a pair of number lines that shows the relationship between the two variables.

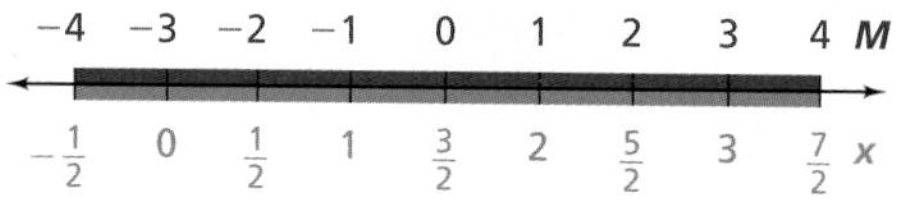

To describe this relationship in terms of translations and dilations, you might say that you dilated the M number line by the factor 2 and then translated it $\frac{3}{2}$ units left. This sequence of number lines shows that process.

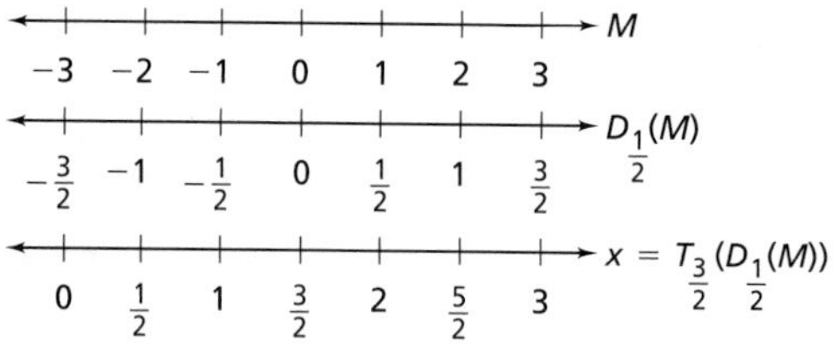

Habits of Mind

Look for relationships. Notice that $D_{\frac{1}{2}}$ multiplies numbers by $\frac{1}{2}$. From a geometric viewpoint, the result is a dilation of the number line by the factor 2.

Each value on the $D_{\frac{1}{2}}(M)$ number line is half the corresponding value on the M number line. As a result, a unit on the $D_{\frac{1}{2}}(M)$ number line is twice as long as a unit on the M number line. You can think of the $D_{\frac{1}{2}}(M)$ number line as the image of the M number line after a dilation by the factor 2.

Answers

For You to Do

1. $M = 2x - 3$, so $x = \frac{1}{2}M + \frac{3}{2} = T_{\frac{3}{2}}\left(\frac{1}{2}M\right) = (T_{\frac{3}{2}} \circ D_{\frac{1}{2}})(M)$.
2. $M = 2x - 3$, so $x = \frac{1}{2}M + \frac{3}{2} = \frac{1}{2}\left(M + 3\right) = D_{\frac{1}{2}}(M + 3) = (D_{\frac{1}{2}} \circ T_3)(M)$.

Since $x = T_{\frac{3}{2}}(D_{\frac{1}{2}}(M)) = D_{\frac{1}{2}}(M) + \frac{3}{2}$, each value on the x number line is $\frac{3}{2}$ more than the corresponding value on the $D_{\frac{1}{2}}(M)$ number line. This means that the x number line is the image of the $D_{\frac{1}{2}}(M)$ number line after a translation of $\frac{3}{2}$ units to the left. You can check that corresponding values of M and x satisfy the equation $M = \mathcal{A}_{(2, -3)}(x)$.

You can also think of the transformation from the M number line to the x number line as a translation followed by a dilation. This sequence of number lines shows that process.

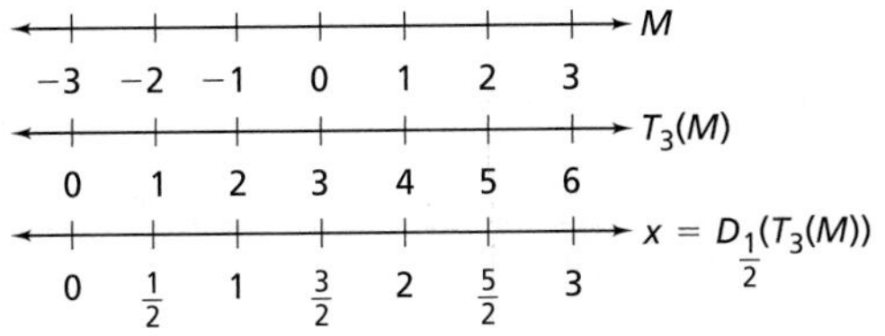

Notice that the number line for $T_3(M)$ is the image of the number line for M after a translation 3 units to the left. The number line for $x = D_{\frac{1}{2}}(T_3(M))$ is the image of the number line for $T_3(M)$ after a dilation by the factor 2.

Even though you follow a different process, the resulting pair of number lines for M and x is the same. You will use affine transformations on coordinate axes to graph some rather complicated equations.

Explore

Consider discussing with students the effects of each transformation on the number line. For the M number line shown on this page, the translation T_3 adds 3 to each number; but notice that on the resulting $T_3(M)$ number line, each number appears to have moved left 3 units. For the $T_3(M)$ number line, the dilation $D_{\frac{1}{2}}$ multiplies each number by one half; but notice that on the resulting x number line the distance between 0 and 1 appears to have doubled.

Students can use these ideas to think about the "directions" of transformations of graphs: for example, the graph of $(x - 3)^2 + (2y)^2 = 16$ will be a circle of radius 4 units, with the x-axis translated 3 units to the left and the y-axis dilated (stretched) by the factor 2.

Minds in Action

You can use Blackline Masters 6.8 and 6.9A–C to make transparencies to use as you go over this dialog with your class. If you wish, you can use a color marker to emphasize which set of axes is which. Start by showing the curve with the M- and y-axes (Blackline Master 6.9A). Then place the x-axis transparency (Blackline Master 6.9B) on top when Derman adds the new labels. Have your students label several points with their (x, y) coordinates, and then use those points on the blank set of x- and y-axes (Blackline Master 6.9C) to make a sketch like Derman's.

Outside of this course, a replacing-the-axes graph may not be considered a final answer. Help your students recognize these situations. For example, if a question on a standardized test asks for a graph of $y = \sqrt{\frac{1}{4}x + 2}$ as part of an open-response item, the test evaluator will expect to see a sketch like Derman's in the standard xy-coordinate system. However, students can use a replacing-the-axes graph to generate points for their standard-axes graph. Make sure students understand that, outside of this course, most people will not have Sasha's eye for interpreting a replacing-the-axes graph.

Minds in Action episode 30

Sasha and Derman are trying to graph the equation $y = (2x - 3)^2$.

Sasha Okay, if we set $M = 2x - 3$, then this equation turns into $y = M^2$, which is a parabola. Here are its table and graph.

M	y
−3	9
−2	4
−1	1
0	0
1	1
2	4
3	9

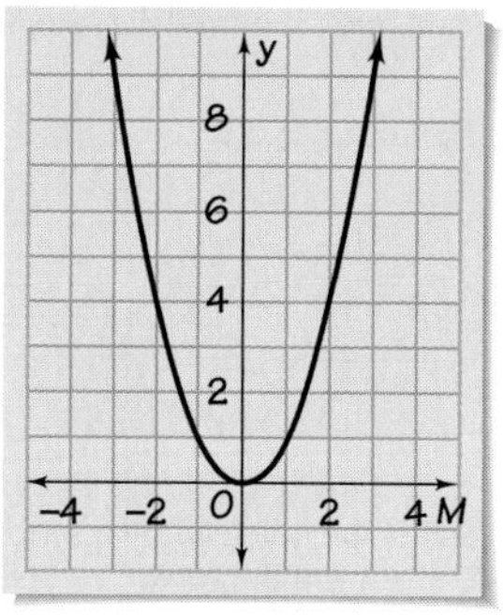

Derman We already have a pair of number lines showing the relationship $M = \mathcal{A}_{(2, -3)}(x)$.

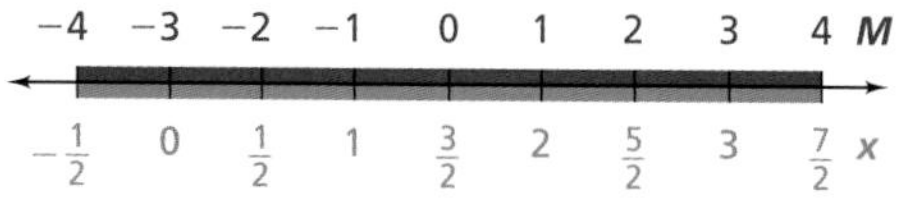

We can use this relationship to show the labels for x that correspond to each value of M, right on the graph!

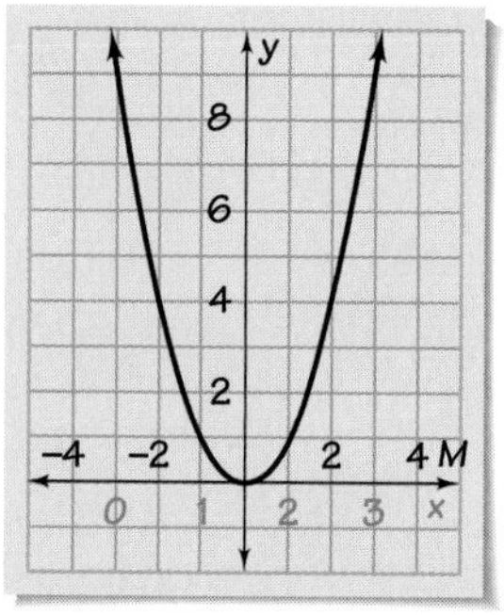

Sasha With these new labels, we can figure out the (x, y) coordinates of lots of points on the graph of the parabola. For instance, we know its vertex is $\left(\frac{3}{2}, 0\right)$ and its line of symmetry has equation $x = \frac{3}{2}$. We can label as many points as we want.

Derman But wait. Doesn't the graph change at all?

Sasha Well, no, it is different. A graph is just a picture that lets us read off information about an equation. The picture itself tells us nothing about the equation unless we look at the axes. I can tell you anything you want to know about the pairs that satisfy the equation by looking at this picture. I can tell you if an (M, y) does or does not satisfy the equation, and I can do the same for an (x, y) pair. I just have to be careful that I read the information from the correct axes.

Derman But I can use this picture and all the points we found to make the usual kind of picture.

Derman makes a quick sketch.

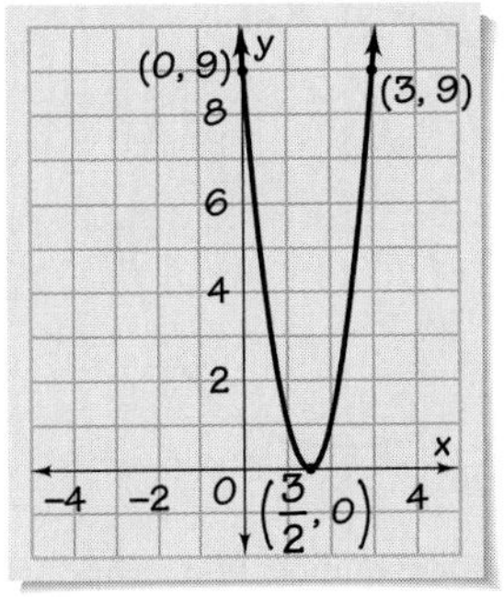

Sasha Sure, if that makes you feel better. But you can also learn to use the graph of y against M to get everything you can get from your graph. Try it. You'll get used to it.

For You to Do

Using the replacing-the-axes method, sketch the graph of each equation. You can stop at the replacing-the-axes graph if you want to, but be sure to label several points with their (x, y) coordinates. If you like, you can also make a sketch like Derman's, showing the graph in the xy-plane.

3. $y = |3x - 1|$
4. $y = \sqrt{\frac{1}{4}x + 2}$

As the following examples show, you can also transform a graph by replacing the vertical axis or by replacing both the horizontal and the vertical axes.

For You to Do

PROBLEMS 3 AND 4 If students want to see a sketch like Derman's, showing one of these graphs in a standard xy-coordinate system, remind them that they can use their graphing calculators to do this. By comparing their replacing-the-axes graphs with the graphs they can see on their calculators, students will better understand how to interpret the information contained in a replacing-the-axes graph.

Answers

For You to Do

3.

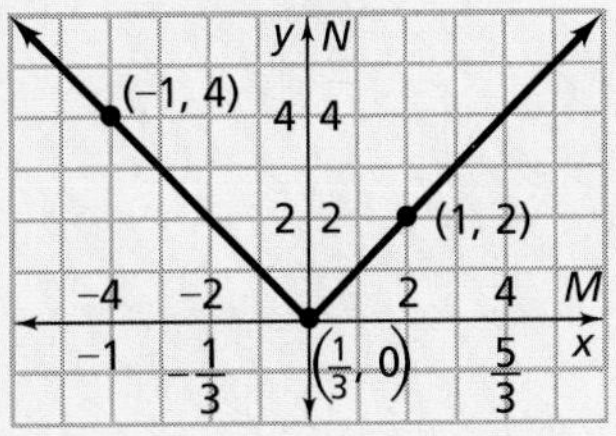

4.

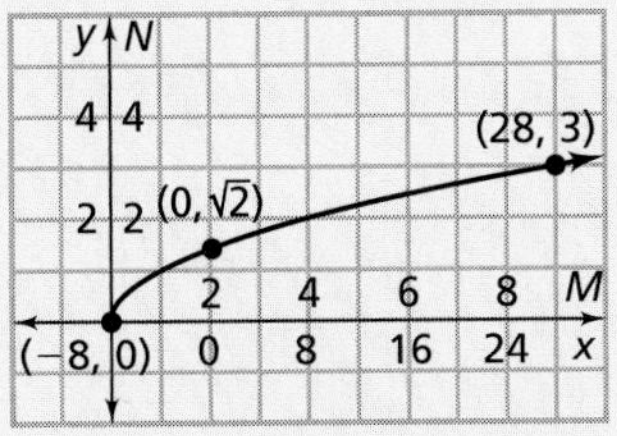

Example

Some students may be able to interpret the final graphs in the Example better if they also include a more traditional set of x- and y-axes. Normally, the x-axis is the line with equation $y = 0$ and the y-axis is the line with equation $x = 0$. Here is the circle from part (a) with these axes shown as dashed lines.

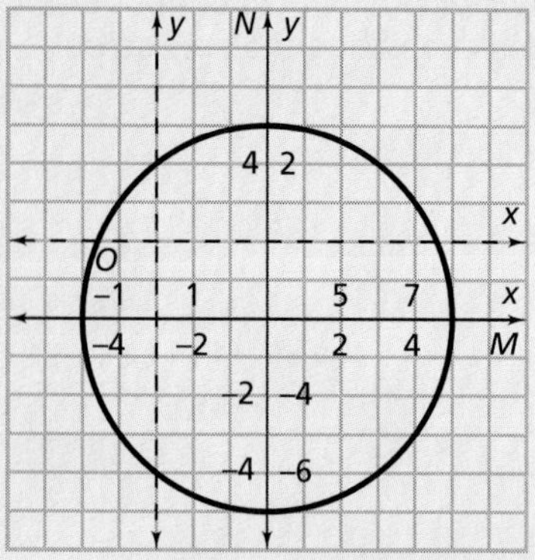

This graph may help students who have been having trouble seeing this circle as having been translated down and to the right from the basic graph. In the final graph shown in the student text the circle has not moved relative to the M- and N-axes. You can describe this change of viewpoint by saying that when you think of the circle as having equation $N^2 + M^2 = 5$, you are standing at the point (0, 0) in the MN-plane. When you think of the circle as having equation $(x - 3)^2 + (y + 2)^2 = 5^2$, you are standing at the point (0, 0) in the xy-plane.

Example

Problems Sketch the graph of each equation.

a. $x^2 + y^2 - 6x + 4y - 12 = 0$ **b.** $y = 2x^2 - 12x + 17$

Solutions

a. In Problem 4b of Lesson 6.8, you rewrote this equation as

$$(x - 3)^2 + (y + 2)^2 = 5^2$$

With the substitutions $M = x - 3$ and $N = y + 2$, the equation becomes

$$M^2 + N^2 = 5^2$$

The graph of this equation is a circle of radius 5 centered at the origin.

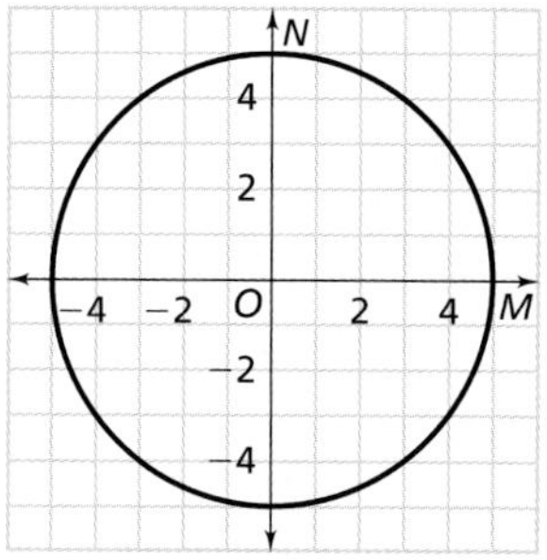

Since $M = x - 3$, you know $x = M + 3$. The pair of number lines below shows the relationship between M and x.

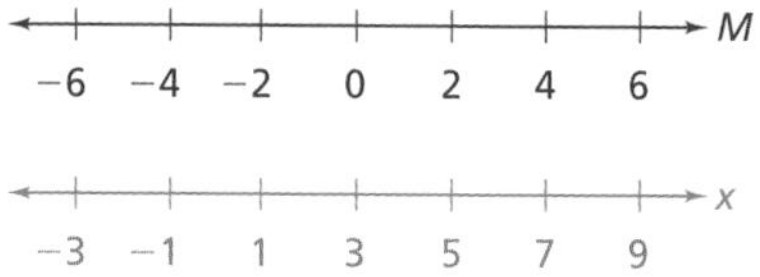

Likewise, $N = y + 2$ implies $y = N - 2$. The following pair of number lines relates N and y.

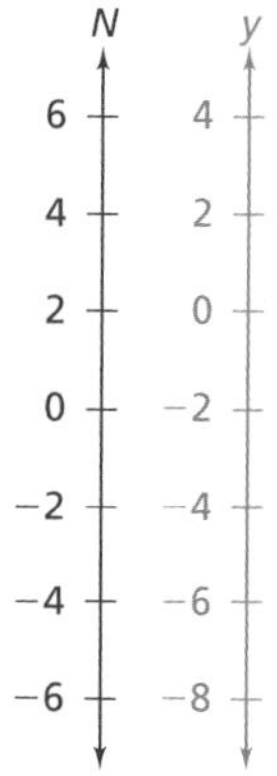

Using the graph of $M^2 + N^2 = 5^2$, replace the M-axis with the x-axis, and replace the N-axis with the y-axis.

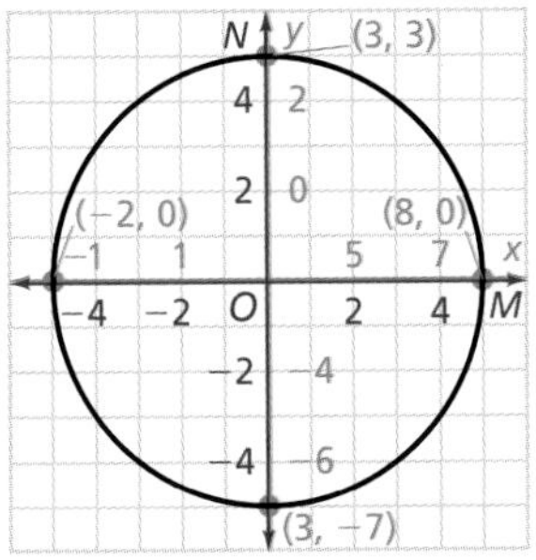

The resulting circle is centered at the point $(3, -2)$. Its radius is still 5. Note that the x-axis is the image of the M-axis translated to the left by three units. The y-axis is the image of the N-axis translated up by two units.

As a consequence, the graph of the circle $(x - 3)^2 + (y + 2)^2 = 5^2$ is the image of the basic circle of radius 5 translated three units to the right and two units down.

b. In Problem 1a from Lesson 6.8, you found that the following substitutions transform $y = 2x^2 - 12x + 17$ into $N = M^2$.

- $M = \mathcal{A}_{(2,\,-6)}(x)$
- $N = \mathcal{A}_{(2,\,2)}(y)$

The graph of $N = M^2$ is just the basic parabola shown below.

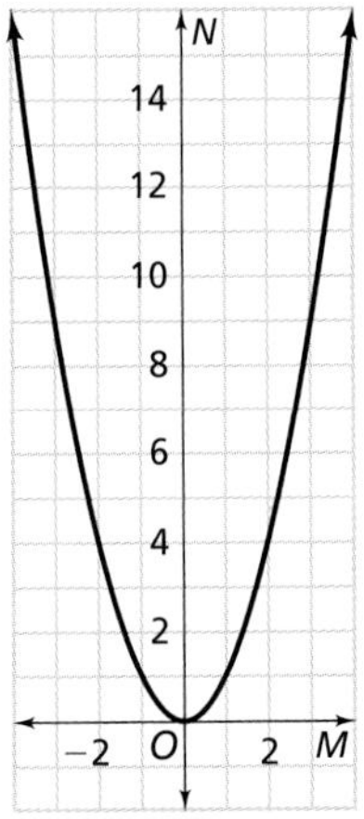

You have

$$
\begin{aligned}
x &= (\mathcal{A}_{(2,\,-6)})^{-1}(M) \\
&= \mathcal{A}_{(\frac{1}{2},\,3)}(M) \\
&= \tfrac{1}{2}M + 3
\end{aligned}
$$

PART (b) Here is the final graph of the parabola (see the graph at the bottom of the next page of the student text), with the "ordinary" x- and y-axes shown as dashed lines.

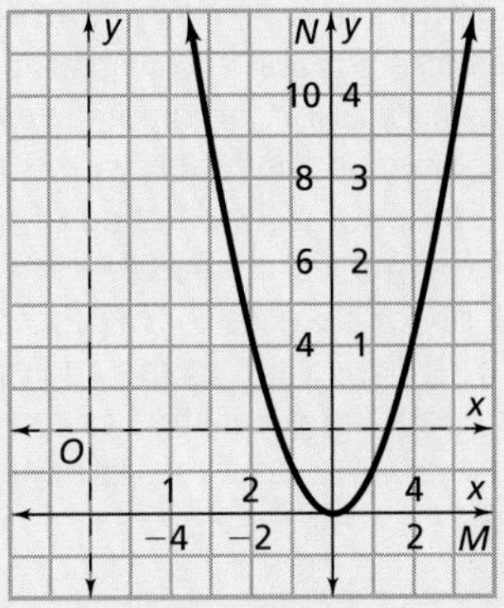

Notice that in this graph, you can "see" the translation of the parabola but not the scaling. The changes in shape caused by the dilations are not apparent, because the length of each unit in the xy-plane is twice the length of a unit in the MN-plane. Here are graphs of $N = M^2$ and $y = 2x^2 - 12x + 17$ drawn using units of the same length for both coordinate systems.

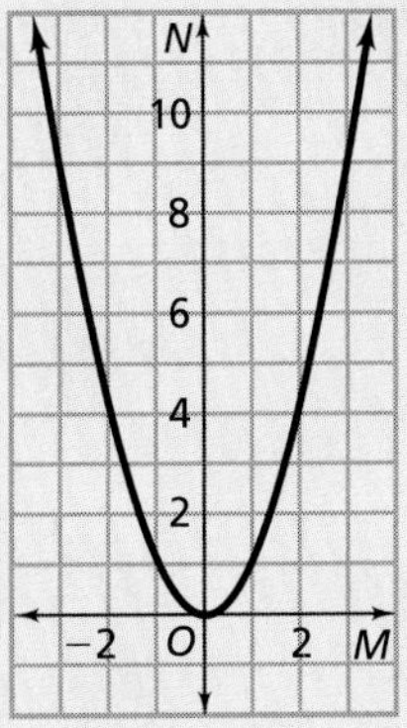

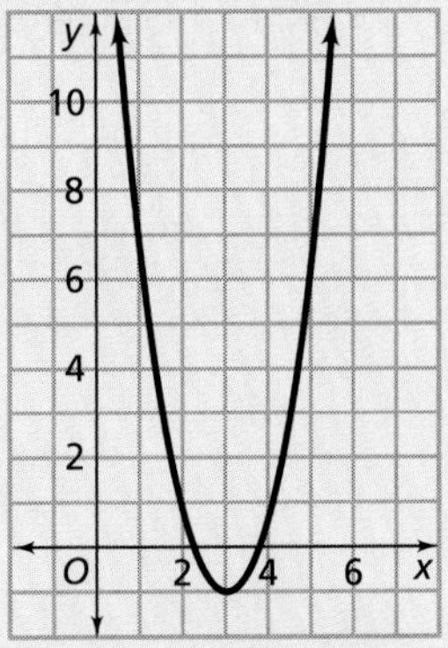

With the two sets of coordinate axes drawn at the same scale, you can see that the parabola in the xy-plane is stretched vertically and shrunk horizontally, compared to the parabola in the MN-plane. The two parabolas are not scaled copies of each other; they are not mathematically similar. Expect students to have difficulty interpreting graphs from two different perspectives and thinking about the impact a change in the coordinate system has on the actual graph. This takes practice. Remind students that they can see these two graphs by graphing $y = x^2$ and $y = 2x^2 - 12x + 17$ on their graphing calculators.

Wrap Up

Finish today's lesson by going over some of the Check Your Understanding core exercises with your class. The goal now is for students to be able to produce a correct graph showing an original and a transformed set of coordinate axes and to label several points on the graph with their (x, y) coordinates. Students' interpretation of these pictures evolve as they gain more experience, so give them plenty of chances to try describing the relationship of a final graph to the appropriate basic graph. Using graphing calculators to compare the graphs before and after the transformations will also help students.

Assessment Resources

Lesson Quiz 6.9

1. Sketch the graph of each equation. Use the replacing-the-axes method.
   a. $y = \frac{1}{5x - 1}$
   b. $(5x - 1)(y - 2) = 1$
   c. $y = 10^{5x-1}$
   d. $y + 2 = 10^{5x-1}$

2. a. Sketch the graph of $y = (-x)^5$ using the replacing-the-axes method.
   b. How are the number lines for $M = D_{-1}(x)$ and x related?
   c. Using your answer from part (b), explain why the graph of $y = (-x)^5$ is the image of the graph of $y = x^5$ after a reflection over the y-axis.

3. a. Sketch the graph of $y = (x - 3)^3$ using the replacing-the-axes method.
   b. How are the number lines for $M = T_{-3}(x)$ and x related?
   c. Using your answer from part (b), explain why you get the graph of $y = (x - 3)^3$ by translating the graph of $y = x^3$ three units to the right.

The pair of number lines shows the relationship between M and x.

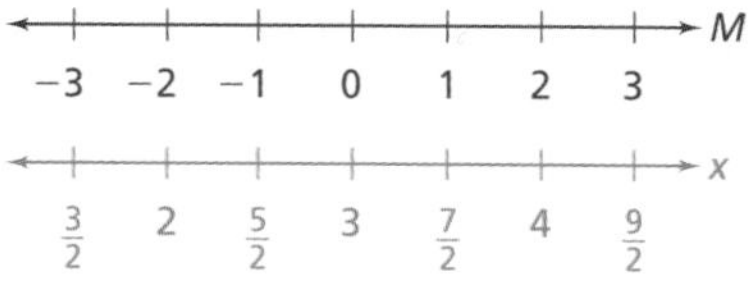

You also know that $N = (T_2 \circ D_2)(y)$, and the socks-and-shoes method of taking inverses gives

$$y = (D_{\frac{1}{2}} \circ T_{-2})(N) = \frac{1}{2}(N - 2)$$

So the following pair of number lines relates N and y.

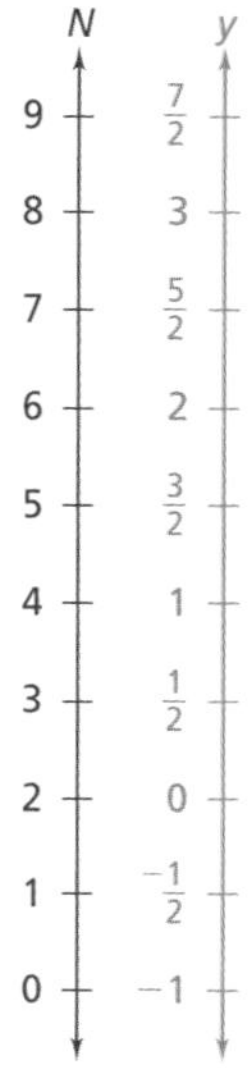

Using the graph of $N = M^2$, replace the M-axis with the x-axis, and replace the N-axis with the y-axis.

The resulting parabola has its vertex at the point $(3, -1)$. The graph shows that the units on both the x- and y-axes are twice as big as those on the M- and N-axes.

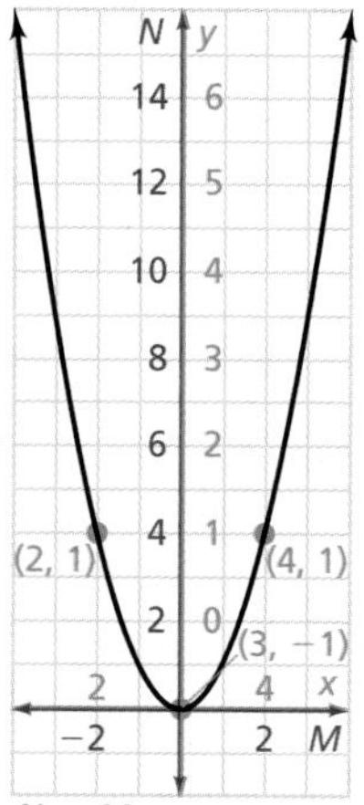

$N = M$
$y = 2x^2 - 12x + 12$

The usual graph of $y = 2x^2 - 12x + 17$ is the image of the basic parabola graph after horizontal and vertical scaling by a factor $\frac{1}{2}$ followed by a translation 3 units to the right and 1 unit down.

Answers

Exercises

1. a. If $M = -2x + 1$, then

$$x = -\frac{1}{2}M + \frac{1}{2} =$$

$$T_{\frac{1}{2}}\left(-\frac{1}{2}M\right) = (T_{\frac{1}{2}} \circ D_{-\frac{1}{2}})(M).$$

b.

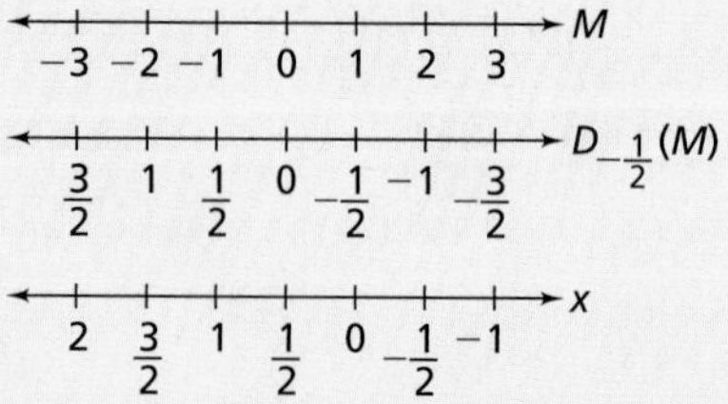

Exercises *Practicing Habits of Mind*

Check Your Understanding

For Exercises 1 and 2, suppose $M = -2x + 1$.

1. a. Show that $x = (T_{\frac{1}{2}} \circ D_{-\frac{1}{2}})(M)$.

b. Copy and label the number lines for $D_{-\frac{1}{2}}(M)$ and x.

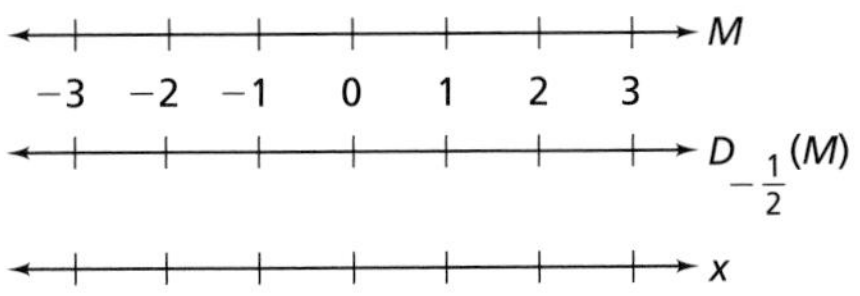

c. Describe the relationship between the number lines in each pair.

M and $D_{-\frac{1}{2}}(M)$ $\quad$ $D_{-\frac{1}{2}}(M)$ and x $\quad$ M and x

2. a. Show that $x = (D_{-\frac{1}{2}} \circ T_{-1})(M)$.

b. Copy and label the number lines for $T_{-1}(M)$ and x.

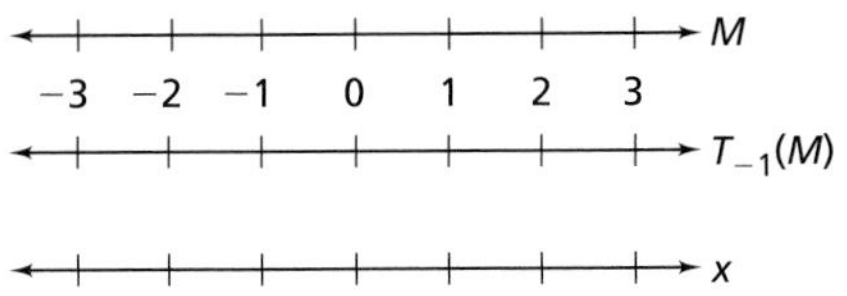

c. Describe the relationship between the number lines in each pair.

M and $T_{-1}(M)$ $\quad$ $T_{-1}(M)$ and x $\quad$ M and x

3. The figure shows the graph of $N = M^2$, but the corresponding x- and y-axes are not labeled.

The equation of this parabola in x and y is $y = 3x^2 + 2x - 1$.

a. Find the substitutions that transform the equation $y = 3x^2 + 2x - 1$ into $N = M^2$.

b. Copy the figure to the right and label the x- and y-axes to show these substitutions. Show the (x, y) coordinates of several points on the graph.

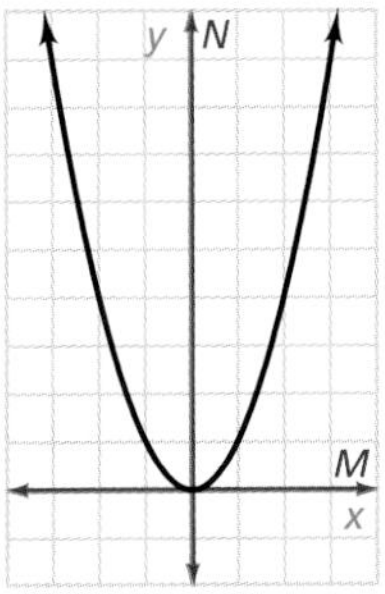

c. The $D_{-\frac{1}{2}}(M)$ number line is the image of the M number line reflected over 0 and dilated by the factor 2; the x number line is the image of the $D_{-\frac{1}{2}}(M)$ number line translated $\frac{1}{2}$ unit to the right; the x number line is the image of the M number line reflected over 0, dilated by the factor 2, and translated $\frac{1}{2}$ unit to the right.

2. See back of book.

3. a. $M = \mathcal{A}_{(3,\,1)}(x)$, $N = \mathcal{A}_{(3,\,4)}(y)$

b.

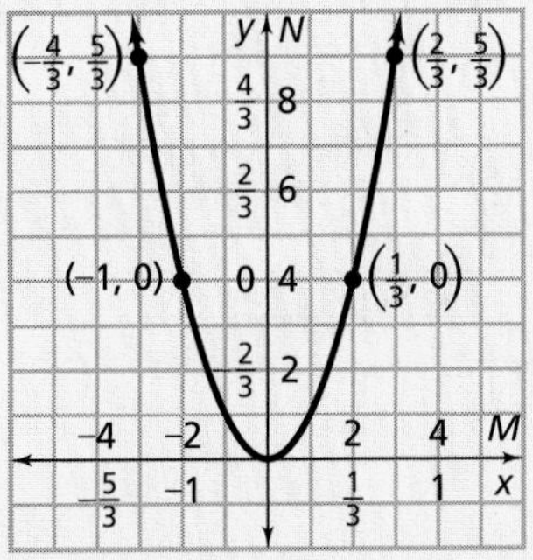

Exercises

HOMEWORK

- Core: 11, 14, 15, 18, 20, 21, 22
- Optional: 12, 13, 16, 17, 19, 23

Check Your Understanding

EXERCISES 1 AND 2 Students describe the relationship between a pair of number lines in various ways. They do not have to describe the actual steps they took to get from one number line to the other, but check that their descriptions result in a correct correspondence between the two number lines.

EXERCISE 2 Here students see that two completely different sets of steps lead to the same pair of number lines. Students may use many different methods to make paired number lines as they continue through this exercise set, and they may not always go through a series of steps like the ones shown in Exercises 1 and 2. For example, some students might write $(\mathcal{A}_{(-2,\,1)})^{-1}(M) = \mathcal{A}_{\left(-\frac{1}{2},\,\frac{1}{2}\right)}(M) = x$ and use that relationship to find corresponding x-values for M-values. Others might use the socks and shoes method of taking inverses and say $x = (D_{-\frac{1}{2}} \circ T_{-1})(M)$. Others might say, "If $M = -2x + 1$, then $x = \frac{-M + 1}{2}$," and use that relationship. Still others might say, "First I find the image of the M-axis after a translation of 1 unit to the right and then I find the image of that image after a dilation by the factor -2." Any method that the student understands and that produces consistently correct results is fine.

EXERCISE 3 In part (a), students should use the techniques they learned in Lesson 6.7. If you skipped that lesson, give students the correct substitutions:

$$M = \mathcal{A}_{(3,\,1)}(x) \text{ and } N = \mathcal{A}_{(3,\,4)}(y)$$

In part (b), like Derman in the Minds in Action dialog, some students will also want to draw a graph in the xy-plane. They may be bothered by the idea that now the graph of every quadratic seems to be the graph of $y = x^2$. Point out that their graphs are not the graphs of $y = x^2$—they are graphs of $N = M^2$. Suggest that students think of this as looking at the graph in a different window on a graphing calculator's screen.

EXERCISE 5 This exercise is a lot like Exercise 3, except here, the affine transformations have already been given. If time permits, show students how to find those transformations by rewriting the equation as $2y = 4x^2 + 12x + 10$, and then making the substitutions $Q = 2y$ and $P = 2x$ before completing the square.

EXERCISES 6–9 Students may choose to sketch some of these graphs using the techniques from Investigation 6A. In such cases, you will not see the paired coordinate axes, and the shape of the graph you see may differ from that of the basic graph. Graphs produced using the techniques of Investigation 6A are like the graphs graphing calculators produce. Check that students answering in this way are not dependent on their calculators and are able to produce the graphs by hand. Encourage these students to try out the replacing-the-axes method.

EXERCISE 10 shows why it is important either to think carefully about how to interpret the information on a replacing-the-axes graph or to use the information from such a graph to sketch a graph in the standard x, y plane. In any case, a replacing-the-axes graph that involves dilation will not show (directly) the shape of the graph.

4. Write About It In Exercises 1 and 2, $x = \mathcal{A}_{(-\frac{1}{2}, \frac{1}{2})}(M)$.

You wrote $\mathcal{A}_{(-\frac{1}{2}, \frac{1}{2})}$ as a composition of translations and dilations in two different ways.

$$\mathcal{A}_{(-\frac{1}{2}, \frac{1}{2})} = T_{\frac{1}{2}} \circ D_{-\frac{1}{2}} = D_{-\frac{1}{2}} \circ T_{-1}$$

Are there other ways to decompose $\mathcal{A}_{(-\frac{1}{2}, \frac{1}{2})}$ into translations and dilations? Explain.

5. a. Confirm that the substitutions below transform the equation $y = 2x^2 + 6x + 5$ into the equation $N = M^2$. (To do this, write expressions for M and N in terms of x and y and plug them into the equation $N = M^2$. Multiply everything out and simplify your answer.)

$M = \mathcal{A}_{(2, 3)}(x) \qquad N = \mathcal{A}_{(2, -1)}(y)$

b. Sketch the graph of $y = 2x^2 + 6x + 5$ using the substitutions above and the replacing-the-axes method. Label several points on your graph with their (x, y) coordinates.

In Exercises 6–9, you will sketch some graphs. You can use any method, but try to use the replacing-the-axes method on at least two of the exercises, just to get used to it.

6. Sketch the graph of $y = 9x^2 + 12x - 5$. You may find your work from Exercise 2 in Lesson 6.7 helpful. Label several points on your graph with their (x, y) coordinates.

7. Sketch the graph of $y = -\frac{1}{4}x^2 + 6x + 8$. You may find your work from Problem 2b in Lesson 6.8 helpful. Label several points on your graph with their (x, y) coordinates.

8. Sketch the graph of each equation. Label several points on each graph with their (x, y) coordinates.

a. $(x + 5)^2 + y^2 = 9$ **b.** $(-2x + 1)^2 + y^2 = 9$

c. $(x - 1)^2 + (-y + 4)^2 = 9$ **d.** $(x + 2)^2 + (4y - 16)^2 = 9$

9. Sketch the graph of each equation. Label several points on each graph with their (x, y) coordinates.

a. $y = \sqrt{x + 5}$ **b.** $y = \sqrt{-2x + 1}$

c. $y = -\sqrt{x - 1} + 4$ **d.** $y = \frac{1}{4}\sqrt{x + 2} + 4$

10. What's Wrong Here? Greg says that all of the graphs he drew in Exercise 8 are circles. Greg explains, "When using the replacing-the-axes method, I keep the original circle $M^2 + N^2 = 9$ where it is and just relabel the axes. The resulting graph has the same shape as the graph of $M^2 + N^2 = 9$, which is a circle of radius 3. So they must all be circles, too."

Do you agree with Greg? Explain.

Answers

4. Yes; answers may vary. Sample: You can use more than two transformations. For example, $\mathcal{A}_{(-\frac{1}{2}, \frac{1}{2})} = D_{\frac{1}{2}} \circ T_1 \circ D_{-1}$.

5. a. $M = 2x + 3$ and $N = 2y - 1$, so $N = M^2$ becomes $2y - 1 = (2x + 3)^2$, or $2y - 1 = 4x^2 + 12x + 9$. Then $2y = 4x^2 + 12x + 10$, so $y = 2x^2 + 6x + 5$.

b.

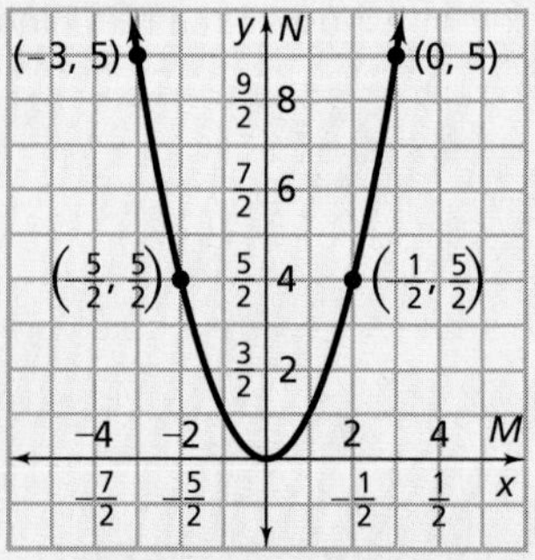

6.

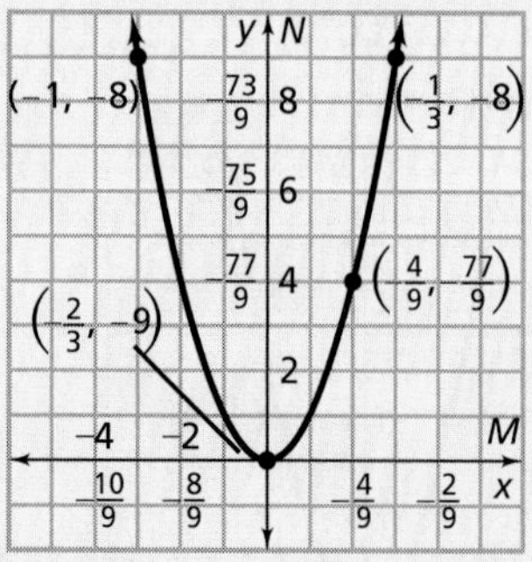

7–9. See back of book.

10. Disagree; answers may vary. Sample: If you scale the graph of a circle horizontally and vertically by factors with different absolute values, the distances between the transformed intercepts are no longer equal and the transformed graph is no longer a circle. So, the graphs for Exercises 8b and 8d are not circles.

On Your Own

In Exercises 11–16, you will sketch some graphs. You can use any method, but try to use the replacing-the-axes method on some of the exercises, just to get used to it.

11. Sketch the graph of each equation. You may find your work from Exercise 6 in Lesson 6.7 helpful.

a. $y = x^3 + 6x^2 + 11x + 7$ **b.** $y = x^3 + 3x^2 + 7x + 13$

12. Sketch the graph of $y = 8x^3 - 6x^2 + 2x - 1$. You may find your work from Exercise 13 in Lesson 6.7 helpful.

13. Sketch the graph of each equation.

a. $y = 2x - 3$ **b.** $y - 1 = 2x - 3$

c. $-y + 1 = 2x - 3$ **d.** $2y - 3 = 2x - 3$

14. Sketch the graph of each equation.

a. $y = \frac{1}{2x - 3}$ **b.** $(2x - 3)(y - 1) = 1$

c. $(2x - 3)(-y + 1) = 1$ **d.** $(2x - 3)(2y - 3) = 1$

15. Sketch the graph of each equation.

a. $y = 10^{2x-3}$ **b.** $y - 1 = 10^{2x-3}$

c. $-y + 1 = 10^{2x-3}$ **d.** $2y - 3 = 10^{2x-3}$

16. Sketch the graph of each equation.

a. $2y - 3 = \log x$ **b.** $2y - 3 = \log (x - 1)$

c. $2y - 3 = \log (-x + 1)$ **d.** $2y - 3 = \log (2x - 3)$

17. Explain how the graphs in Exercises 15 and 16 are related to each other.

18. a. Sketch the graph of $y = (x - 3)^2$ using the replacing-the-axes method.

b. How are the number lines for $M = T_{-3}(x)$ and x related?

c. Using your answer from part (b), explain why you get the graph of $y = (x - 3)^2$ by translating the graph of $y = x^2$ three units to the right.

19. a. Sketch the graph of $y = \sqrt{2x}$ using the replacing-the-axes method.

b. How are the number lines for $M = D_2(x)$ and x related?

c. Using your answer from part (b), explain why you get the graph of $y = \sqrt{2x}$ by scaling the graph of $y = \sqrt{x}$ horizontally by the factor $\frac{1}{2}$.

Go Online PHSchool.com

For additional practice, go to Web Code: bfa-0609

On Your Own

EXERCISE 11 Encourage students to describe the graphs in terms of transformations of the corresponding basic graph. For example, in part (a), the graph of $y = x^3 + 6x^2 + 11x + 7$ is the image of the basic graph $y = x^3 - x$ after a translation of two units to the right and one unit down. Students can use their graphing calculators to graph both the given equation and its basic graph. Comparing the locations and shapes of the graphs will help students interpret their replacing-the-axes pictures.

EXERCISE 13 Students have difficulty with affine transformations of linear equations, because there are an infinite number of affine transformations that can map one particular line onto a specific target line. To see why this is so, imagine the two lines. If they have different slopes, a dilation in x and y of one of the lines can result in an image that has the same slope as the target line. Then choose any point on the image line. A translation in x and y can map that point onto any point on the target line, producing an image identical to the target line.

EXERCISE 18C Students may still have trouble explaining why the graph is where it is even though they can successfully graph it. The why behind the direction of a translation is extraordinarily difficult for students to understand.

EXERCISE 19C Even students who are successful in drawing the graph may have trouble explaining why it behaves the way it does.

11–16. See back of book.

17. The graphs in corresponding parts of Exercises 15 and 16 are reflections of each other over the line $y = x$.

18. a.

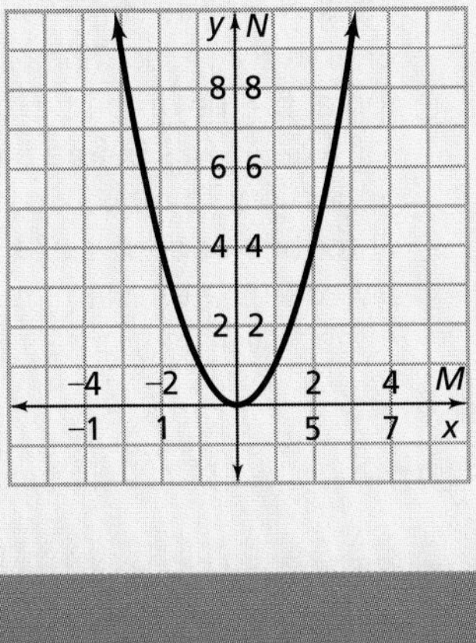

b. Answers may vary. Sample: The x number line is the image of the M number line translated 3 units to the left.

c. Answers may vary. Sample: Translating the M-axis 3 units to the left means that each point on the parabola is now three units to the right of where is was before the translation. For example, the vertex, which was at (0, 0), is now at (3, 0), 3 units to the right of (0, 0).

19. a.

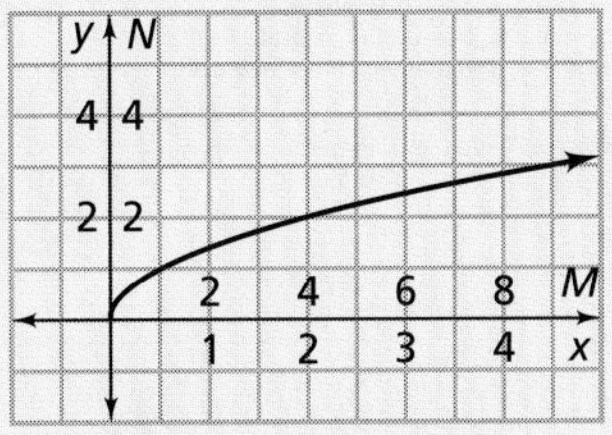

b. Answers may vary. Sample: The x number line is the M number line after a dilation by the factor 2.

c. Answers may vary. Sample: Dilating the M-axis by the factor 2 makes the length of a unit on the x-axis twice as long as the length of a unit on the y-axis. On a coordinate system with units of the same length on both axes, the x-coordinate of each point on the graph of $y = \sqrt{2x}$ will be one half the x-coordinate of the corresponding point on the graph of $y = \sqrt{x}$, which is a scaling of the graph by the factor $\frac{1}{2}$.

Maintain Your Skills

EXERCISE 23 asks students to think in a new way about affine transformations. In effect, the exercise asks students to find the one value that all affine transformations of the form $\mathcal{A}_{(p,\,-\frac{p}{2})}$ map to 0. This entire class of affine transformations maps $\frac{1}{2}$ to 0. In Lesson 6.10, students examine the question of what point a given affine transformation maps to itself, and then, for any given value x, what kinds of affine transformations map x to itself.

Additional Resources

PRINT RESOURCES
- Solution Manual
- Practice Workbook
- Assessment Resources
- Teaching Resources

TECHNOLOGY
- Interactive Textbook
- TeacherExpress CD-ROM
- ExamView CD-ROM
- PHSchool.com

Additional Practice

In Exercises 1–3, sketch the graph of each equation. Use any method, but try using the replacing-the-axes method on some of the exercises.

1. a. $y = 3x + 2$
   b. $y - 2 = 3x + 2$
   c. $-y - 2 = 3x + 2$
   d. $2y + 3 = 3x + 2$

2. a. $y = \frac{1}{3x + 2}$
   b. $(3x + 2)(y + 1) = 1$
   c. $(3x + 2)(-y - 1) = 1$
   d. $(3x + 2)(3y + 2) = 1$

3. a. $y = 10^{3x+2}$
   b. $y + 1 = 10^{3x+2}$
   c. $-y - 1 = 10^{3x+2}$
   d. $3y + 2 = 10^{3x+2}$

4. a. Sketch the graph of $y = (x + 4)^2$ using the replacing-the-axes method.
   b. How are the number lines for $M = T_4(x)$ and x related?
   c. Using your answer from part (b), explain why you get the graph of $y = (x + 4)^2$ by translating the graph of $y = x^2$ four units to the left.

5. a. Sketch the graph of $y = (3x)^3$ using the replacing-the-axes method.
   b. How are the number lines for $M = D_{\frac{1}{3}}(x)$ and x related?
   c. Using your answer from part (b), explain why you get the graph of $y = (3x)^3$ by scaling the graph of $y = x^3$ horizontally by the factor $\frac{1}{3}$.

6. a. Sketch the graph of $y = -|x|$ using the replacing-the-axes method.
   b. How are the number lines for $N = D_{-1}(y)$ and y related?
   c. Using your answer from part (b), explain why the graph of $y = -|x|$ is the image of the graph of $y = |x|$ after a reflection over the x-axis.

7. Sketch the graph of $y = 8x^3 - 12x^2 + 8x - 2$ using the replacing-the-axes method.

Practice: For Lesson 6.9, assign Exercises 1–7.

20. a. Sketch the graph of $y = \left|\frac{1}{2}x\right|$.
b. How are the number lines for $M = D_{\frac{1}{2}}(x)$ and x related?
c. Using your answer from part (b), explain why you get the graph of $y = \left|\frac{1}{2}x\right|$ by scaling the graph of $y = |x|$ horizontally by the factor of 2.

21. a. Sketch the graph of $y = (-x)^3$ using the replacing-the-axes method.
b. How are the number lines for $M = D_{-1}(x)$ and x related?
c. Using your answer from part (b), explain why the graph of $y = (-x)^3$ is the image of the graph of $y = x^3$ after reflection over the y-axis.

22. Standardized Test Prep Which description best fits the graph of $(y - 7)^2 = -(x + 3)^2 + 25$?
A. a parabola with vertex $(-3, 7)$
B. a circle with center $(-3, 7)$
C. a square with side length 5 units
D. a circle with radius 25 units

Maintain Your Skills

23. For each affine transformation $\mathcal{A}_{(a,\,b)}$, find all x such that $\mathcal{A}_{(a,\,b)}(x) = 0$.
a. $\mathcal{A}_{(2,\,-1)}$ **b.** $\mathcal{A}_{(4,\,-2)}$ **c.** $\mathcal{A}_{(6,\,-3)}$
d. $\mathcal{A}_{(-1,\,\frac{1}{2})}$ **e.** $\mathcal{A}_{(-3,\,\frac{3}{2})}$

Answers

20. a–b. See back of book.
c. Answers may vary. Sample: Dilating the M-axis by the factor $\frac{1}{2}$ makes the length of a unit on the x-axis half the length of a unit on the y-axis. On a coordinate system with units of the same length on both axes, the x-coordinate of each point on the graph of $y = \left|\frac{1}{2}x\right|$ will be twice the x-coordinate of the corresponding point on the graph of $y = |x|$, which is a scaling of the graph by the factor 2.

21. a–b. See back of book.
c. Answers may vary. Sample: Reflecting the M-axis over 0 makes the x-coordinate of each point on the graph the opposite of what it was before the reflection. To make x-coordinates into their opposites in a standard xy-coordinate system, reflect the graph over the y-axis.

22. B

23. a–e. $\frac{1}{2}$

6.10 Advanced Affine Transformations

This lesson focuses on properties and applications of affine transformations.

In-Class Experiment

1. Find all x such that $\mathcal{A}_{(2,3)}(x) = x$.
2. Find all x such that $\mathcal{A}_{(1,3)}(x) = x$.
3. Find all x such that $\mathcal{A}_{(1,0)}(x) = x$.

Fixed Points

Given an affine transformation $\mathcal{A}_{(a,b)}$, you are often interested in finding the values of x that are unchanged by $\mathcal{A}_{(a,b)}$. This gives rise to the following definition.

Definition

Let $\mathcal{A}_{(a,b)}$ be an affine transformation. A number x is a fixed point of $\mathcal{A}_{(a,b)}$ if $\mathcal{A}_{(a,b)}(x) = x$.

For Discussion

4. Which affine transformations have no fixed points?

The center of the potter's wheel is a fixed point.

In-Class Experiment

1. -3
2. no solution
3. all real numbers

For Discussion

4. $\mathcal{A}_{(1,b)}$ for $b \neq 0$

Lesson Overview

GOAL

- Identify the fixed points of an affine transformation and the set of affine transformations that fix a particular point.

This optional lesson gives students gives the opportunity to further examine the algebraic structure of affine transformations. Students think about fixed points of a given affine transformation, and about classes of affine transformations that all fix a certain point. Students also learn to find closed forms for repeated iterations of affine transformations. Much of the work they do in this lesson previews work they will do in Chapter 7.

CHECK YOUR UNDERSTANDING
- Core: 1, 2, 5, 6
- Optional: 3, 4

MATERIALS
- graph paper
- graphing calculators
- Blackline Master 6.10

HOMEWORK
- Core: 7, 8, 9a–b, 10, 11, 12
- Optional: 14
- Extension: 9c, 13

VOCABULARY
- affine recursive function
- fixed point
- iteration
- stabilizer, S_x

Launch

Begin today's lesson with the In-Class Experiment.

Explore

In-Class Experiment

The three problems correspond to the three possibilities for the number of solutions of a linear equation in one variable: 0, 1, or infinitely many.

PROBLEM 1 Some students will try different values of x, perhaps "homing in" on the correct value, -3. Others will see that $\mathcal{A}_{(2,3)}(x) = 2x + 3$, and set up the equation $2x + 3 = x$.

PROBLEM 2 Students may again try to "home in" on the correct value, but should find that any value gives an output 3 greater than the input. Once students recognize that $\mathcal{A}_{(1,3)}(x)$ is actually $T_3(x)$, they should realize there is no solution.

PROBLEM 3 Let students come up with several different answers before they realize why any number x will work in this equation.

For Discussion

PROBLEM 4 In-Class Experiment Problem 2 should provide a clue. Students may also remember their discussions of the fixed points of transformations in CME Project *Geometry,* from which they learned that translations of the plane have no fixed points.

Minds in Action

Stop the dialog after Sasha says "I think I see a pattern." Give students a chance to try to figure out what comes next. If they do, you might be able to have students finish off this dialog themselves, skip For You To Do Problem 5, and go directly to the summary at the top of the next page.

If students prefer to try the calculations shown in the dialog with numbers, write out the expressions but do not simplify them. For example, you might write $5^3 \cdot 7 + 5^2 \cdot 7 + 5 \cdot 7 + 7$, instead of actually performing the calculation. This will help students see the patterns.

Minds in Action episode 31

Sasha and Tony are working on Exercise 19 from Lesson 6.6.

Tony We need to come up with a formula for $(\mathcal{A}_{(a,b)})^{(n)}$.

Sasha Let's try it for small values of n, like $n = 2$.

Tony Okay. The composition formula says $\mathcal{A}_{(a,b)} \circ \mathcal{A}_{(c,d)} = \mathcal{A}_{(ac,\, ad+b)}$. So we get

$$\begin{aligned}(\mathcal{A}_{(a,b)})^{(2)} &= \mathcal{A}_{(a,b)} \circ \mathcal{A}_{(a,b)} \\ &= \mathcal{A}_{(a^2,\, ab+b)}\end{aligned}$$

Remember... This formula is from Exercise 7 of Lesson 6.6.

Sasha Great. Let's use this result to compute the next one.

$$\begin{aligned}(\mathcal{A}_{(a,b)})^{(3)} &= \mathcal{A}_{(a,b)} \circ (\mathcal{A}_{(a,b)})^{(2)} \\ &= \mathcal{A}_{(a,b)} \circ \mathcal{A}_{(a^2,\, ab+b)} \\ &= \mathcal{A}_{(a^3,\, a(ab+b)+b)} \\ &= \mathcal{A}_{(a^3,\, a^2b+ab+b)}\end{aligned}$$

Tony Let me try one more.

$$\begin{aligned}(\mathcal{A}_{(a,b)})^{(4)} &= \mathcal{A}_{(a,b)} \circ (\mathcal{A}_{(a,b)})^{(3)} \\ &= \mathcal{A}_{(a,b)} \circ \mathcal{A}_{(a^3,\, a^2b+ab+b)} \\ &= \mathcal{A}_{(a^4,\, a(a^2b+ab+b)+b)} \\ &= \mathcal{A}_{(a^4,\, a^3b+a^2b+ab+b)}\end{aligned}$$

Sasha I think I see a pattern. Let me double-check.

Sasha writes in her notebook.

Sasha Yup, I got $(\mathcal{A}_{(a,b)})^{(5)} = \mathcal{A}_{(a^5,\, a^4b+a^3b+a^2b+ab+b)}$.

Tony And I bet we get $(\mathcal{A}_{(a,b)})^{(6)} = \mathcal{A}_{(a^6,\, a^5b+a^4b+a^3b+a^2b+ab+b)}$.

Sasha That's right! And in general, we have

$$\begin{aligned}(\mathcal{A}_{(a,b)})^{(n)} &= \mathcal{A}_{(a^n,\, a^{n-1}b+a^{n-2}b+\cdots+ab+b)} \\ &= \mathcal{A}_{(a^n,\, b(a^{n-1}+a^{n-2}+\cdots+a+1))}\end{aligned}$$

Tony We can do even better. Remember? When $a \neq 1$, we know

$$a^{n-1} + a^{n-2} + \cdots + a + 1 = \frac{a^n - 1}{a - 1}$$

Sasha So when $a \neq 1$, we get $(\mathcal{A}_{(a,b)})^{(n)}(x) = a^n x + b \cdot \frac{a^n - 1}{a - 1}$, just as the exercise says!

For You to Do

5. Using Tony's result for $(\mathcal{A}_{(a,b)})^{(4)}$, show that $(\mathcal{A}_{(a,b)})^{(5)} = \mathcal{A}_{(a^5,\, a^4b+a^3b+a^2b+ab+b)}$.

This is the calculation Sasha wrote in her notebook.

Here is a summary of the results from Lesson 6.6 and the dialog above.

Answers

For You to Do

5. $$\begin{aligned}(\mathcal{A}_{(a,b)})^{(5)} &= \mathcal{A}_{(a,b)} \circ (\mathcal{A}_{(a,b)})^{(4)} \\ &= \mathcal{A}_{(a,b)} \circ \mathcal{A}_{(a^4,\, a^3b+a^2b+ab+b)} \\ &= \mathcal{A}_{(a^5,\, a(a^3b+a^2b+ab+b)+b)} \\ &= \mathcal{A}_{(a^5,\, a^4b+a^3b+a^2b+ab+b)}\end{aligned}$$

Summary *Affine Transformation Formulas*

- **Composition:**

  $\mathcal{A}_{(a,\ b)} \circ \mathcal{A}_{(c,\ d)} = \mathcal{A}_{(e,\ f)}$, **where e = ac and f = ad + b**

- **Inverse:**

  $(\mathcal{A}_{(a,\ b)})^{-1} = \mathcal{A}_{\left(\frac{1}{a},\ -\frac{b}{a}\right)}$

- **Iteration: For $a \neq 1$ and positive integer n,**

  $(\mathcal{A}_{(a,\ b)})^{(n)} = \mathcal{A}_{\left(a^n,\ b \cdot \frac{a^n - 1}{a - 1}\right)}$

This means that $(\mathcal{A}_{(a,\ b)})^{(n)}(x) = a^n(x) + b \cdot \frac{a^n - 1}{a - 1}$.

Stabilizers

In the In-Class Experiment, you had to find all numbers x that the affine transformation $\mathcal{A}_{(2,\ 3)}$ fixes. The only value that worked was $x = -3$. Now change the perspective a bit. Suppose you have a number, such as $x = -3$, and have to find all affine transformations $\mathcal{A}_{(a,\ b)}$ that fix x. Of course, $\mathcal{A}_{(2,\ 3)}$ is one such transformation. But there are many others—for example, the identity transformation $\mathcal{A}_{(1,\ 0)}$ fixes all points, so it certainly fixes $x = -3$. The following transformations all fix $x = -3$.

- $\mathcal{A}_{(3,\ 6)}(-3) = 3(-3) + 6 = -3$
- $\mathcal{A}_{(5,\ 12)}(-3) = 5(-3) + 12 = -3$
- $\mathcal{A}_{\left(\frac{1}{2},\ -\frac{3}{2}\right)}(-3) = \frac{1}{2}(-3) - \frac{3}{2} = -3$

For You to Do

6. Find at least three more affine transformations $\mathcal{A}_{(a,\ b)}$ that fix $x = -3$. Can you characterize all such transformations?

To *characterize* something means to list its properties (or characteristics) so that another person could recognize it if he or she saw it.

Definition

Let x be a real number. Then the stabilizer of x, denoted S_x, is the set of all affine transformations that fix x.

$$S_x = \{\mathcal{A}_{(a,\ b)} \text{ such that } \mathcal{A}_{(a,\ b)}(x) = x\}$$

For example, the discussion above shows that S_{-3} contains the affine transformations $\mathcal{A}_{(2,\ 3)}$, $\mathcal{A}_{(1,\ 0)}$, $\mathcal{A}_{(3,\ 6)}$, $\mathcal{A}_{(5,\ 12)}$, $\mathcal{A}_{\left(\frac{1}{2},\ -\frac{3}{2}\right)}$, and perhaps many more.

For Discussion

7. Which affine transformation is in S_x for all values of x?

For You to Do

6. Answers may vary. Sample: $\mathcal{A}_{(1,\ 0)}$, $\mathcal{A}_{(2,\ 3)}$, $\mathcal{A}_{(4,\ 9)}$; $\mathcal{A}_{(a,\ 3a-3)}$

For Discussion

7. $\mathcal{A}_{(1,\ 0)}$

AFFINE TRANSFORMATION FORMULAS You can use Blackline Master 6.10 to make a transparency or a handout of this summary of important formulas.

STABILIZERS Some students will confuse fixed point and stabilizers. Point out the differences.

To find fixed points (numbers), you begin with a particular affine transformation and look for points (x-values) that do not change under that transformation. Any affine transformation other than the identity transformation has at most one fixed point.

To find a stabilizer (a set of transformations), you begin with a particular point (number) and look for affine transformations that fix that point. Any affine transformation that has this number as a fixed point is part of that number's stabilizer. A stabilizer always contains an infinite number of affine transformations. Note that For Discussion Problem 7 shows students that the identity transformation is in every stabilizer.

For Discussion

PROBLEMS 8 AND 9 If students are not sure how to start, encourage them to write out the first several outputs for each function.

Example

To help students see the pattern, use the method of "calculating without simplifying." Write

$$\begin{aligned} f(1) &= 2(1) + 3 \\ f(2) &= 2(2(1) + 3) + 3 \\ &= 2^2 \cdot 1 + 2 \cdot 3 + 3 \\ f(3) &= 2(2^2 \cdot 1 + 2 \cdot 3 + 3) + 3 \\ &= 2^3 \cdot 1 + 2^2 \cdot 3 + 2 \cdot 3 + 3 \end{aligned}$$

Students should be able to generalize this pattern to find a formula. Like Tony's and Sasha's result in the Minds in Action dialog, this result also uses the summation formula

$$1 + a + a^2 + \cdots + a^{n-1} = \frac{a^n - 1}{a - 1}$$

This formula will continue to be important in Chapter 7, where students will learn about summation notation and the sum of a geometric series. Stress this formula here if you get the chance.

Wrap Up

Finish today's lesson by going over the Check Your Understanding core exercises as time allows.

Assessment Resources

Lesson Quiz 6.10

1. a. Show that $\mathcal{A}_{(-3,\,-8)}$ and $\mathcal{A}_{(4,\,6)}$ are in S_{-2}.
   b. Without simplifying, show that $\mathcal{A}_{(-3,\,-8)} \circ \mathcal{A}_{(4,\,6)}$ and $\mathcal{A}_{(4,\,6)} \circ \mathcal{A}_{(-3,\,-8)}$ are both in S_{-2}.
   c. Show that $(\mathcal{A}_{(-3,\,-8)})^{-1}$ and $(\mathcal{A}_{(4,\,6)})^{-1}$ are both in S_{-2}.
   d. Now simplify $\mathcal{A}_{(-3,\,-8)} \circ \mathcal{A}_{(4,\,6)}$ and $\mathcal{A}_{(4,\,6)} \circ \mathcal{A}_{(-3,\,-8)}$. What do you observe?

2. Show that each transformation is in S_{-3}.
   a. $T_{-3} \circ D_5 \circ (T_{-3})^{-1}$
   b. $T_{-3} \circ D_3 \circ (T_{-3})^{-1}$
   c. $T_{-3} \circ D_{-1} \circ (T_{-3})^{-1}$
   d. $T_{-3} \circ D_a \circ (T_{-3})^{-1}$

3. Use the affine recursive definition $f(n) = \begin{cases} 1 & \text{if } n = 0 \\ \mathcal{A}_{(-4,\,-1)} f(n-1) & \text{if } n > 0 \end{cases}$.
   a. Compute $(\mathcal{A}_{(-4,\,-1)})^{(3)}(x)$.
   b. Explain why $f(3) = (\mathcal{A}_{(-4,\,-1)})^{(3)} f(0)$.
   c. Use your answers from parts (a) and (b) to compute $f(3)$.

Affine Recursive Definition

Recall the following functions from Exercise 16 in Lesson 6.5 and Exercise 23 in Lesson 6.6.

- $f(n) = \begin{cases} 2 & \text{if } n = 0 \\ T_3\,(f(n-1)) & \text{if } n > 0 \end{cases}$
- $f(n) = \begin{cases} 2 & \text{if } n = 0 \\ D_3\,(f(n-1)) & \text{if } n > 0 \end{cases}$

Definition

Let $\mathcal{A}_{(a,\,b)}$ be an affine transformation of $\mathbb{R}$ and let p be a number. Then a recursive definition of the form below is an affine recursive definition.

$$f(n) = \begin{cases} p & \text{if } n = 0 \\ \mathcal{A}_{(a,\,b)}(f(n-1)) & \text{if } n > 0 \end{cases}$$

For Discussion

Find a closed form for each function in terms of a and b.

8. $f(n) = \begin{cases} 5 & \text{if } n = 0 \\ T_b\,(f(n-1)) & \text{if } n > 0 \end{cases}$
9. $f(n) = \begin{cases} 5 & \text{if } n = 0 \\ D_a\,(f(n-1)) & \text{if } n > 0 \end{cases}$

Example

Problem Consider the function below.

$$f(n) = \begin{cases} 1 & \text{if } n = 0 \\ \mathcal{A}_{(2,\,3)}\,(f(n-1)) & \text{if } n > 0 \end{cases}$$

Compute $f(5)$.

Solution Compute terms of the sequence in succession.

$$\begin{aligned} f(1) &= \mathcal{A}_{(2,\,3)}(f(0)) = 2(1) + 3 = 5 \\ f(2) &= \mathcal{A}_{(2,\,3)}(f(1)) = 2(5) + 3 = 13 \\ f(3) &= \mathcal{A}_{(2,\,3)}(f(2)) = 2(13) + 3 = 29 \\ f(4) &= \mathcal{A}_{(2,\,3)}(f(3)) = 2(29) + 3 = 61 \\ f(5) &= \mathcal{A}_{(2,\,3)}(f(4)) = 2(61) + 3 = 125 \end{aligned}$$

Therefore, $f(5) = 125$.

Habits of Mind

Consider more than one strategy. Is there a more efficient approach?

Answers

For Discussion

8. $f(n) = 5 + nb$
9. $f(n) = 5a^n$

Exercises *Practicing Habits of Mind*

Check Your Understanding

1. Find all the fixed points of each affine transformation.

   a. $\mathcal{A}_{(4,\,-2)}$ b. $\mathcal{A}_{(-2,\,4)}$ c. $\mathcal{A}_{(-10,\,22)}$

   d. $\mathcal{A}_{(a,\,0)}$ e. $\mathcal{A}_{(1,\,-3)}$ f. $\mathcal{A}_{(a,\,b)}$

2. Determine which affine transformations $\mathcal{A}_{(a,\,b)}$ have the following number of fixed points: exactly one, more than one, or zero.

3. Find all affine transformations $\mathcal{A}_{(a,\,b)}$ such that $(\mathcal{A}_{(a,\,b)})^{-1} = \mathcal{A}_{(a,\,b)}$.

4. Find all affine transformations $\mathcal{A}_{(a,\,b)}$ such that $(\mathcal{A}_{(a,\,b)})^{(n)} = \mathcal{A}_{(a,\,b)}$ for all $n \geq 1$.

5. **What's Wrong Here?** Larry is solving the equation $3x + 7 = 3x - 2$ using affine transformations.

   Larry says, "Let's see, I first rewrite it as $\mathcal{A}_{(3,\,7)}(x) = \mathcal{A}_{(3,\,-2)}(x)$.

   Then I apply $(\mathcal{A}_{(3,\,7)})^{-1} = \mathcal{A}_{(\frac{1}{3},\,-\frac{7}{3})}$ to each side. I get

   $$x = (\mathcal{A}_{(\frac{1}{3},\,-\frac{7}{3})} \circ \mathcal{A}_{(3,\,-2)})(x)$$
   $$= \mathcal{A}_{(1,\,-3)}(x)$$

   So x is a fixed point of $\mathcal{A}_{(1,\,-3)}$. But wait, I just did Exercise 1e, and I know that $\mathcal{A}_{(1,\,-3)}$ has no fixed point!"

   Where did Larry go wrong?

6. Find S_5. In other words, find all affine transformations $\mathcal{A}_{(a,\,b)}$ such that $\mathcal{A}_{(a,\,b)}(5) = 5$.

On Your Own

7. **Standardized Test Prep** Which point is a fixed point of $\mathcal{A}_{(3,\,34)}$?

   A. -17 B. -3 C. 0 D. 34

8. a. Show that $\mathcal{A}_{(3,\,-4)}$ and $\mathcal{A}_{(-5,\,12)}$ are in S_2.

   b. Without simplifying, show that $\mathcal{A}_{(3,-4)} \circ \mathcal{A}_{(-5,\,12)}$ and $\mathcal{A}_{(-5,\,12)} \circ \mathcal{A}_{(3,\,-4)}$ are both in S_2.

   c. Show that $(\mathcal{A}_{(3,\,-4)})^{-1}$ and $(\mathcal{A}_{(-5,\,12)})^{-1}$ are both in S_2.

   d. Now simplify $\mathcal{A}_{(3,-4)} \circ \mathcal{A}_{(-5,\,12)}$ and $\mathcal{A}_{(-5,\,12)} \circ \mathcal{A}_{(3,\,-4)}$. What do you observe?

Go Online
PHSchool.com

For additional practice, go to **Web Code:** bfa-0610

You can do this without actually computing the inverses.

Exercises

HOMEWORK
- Core: 7, 8, 9a–b, 10, 11, 12
- Optional: 14
- Extension: 9c, 13

Check Your Understanding

EXERCISE 1 Some students may want to memorize the formula for the fixed point of an affine transformation, but that formula is not likely to have much further application. Point out that calculating a fixed point is not difficult. However, even if it seems inefficient, allow students to use the formula.

EXERCISE 2 summarizes the results of Exercise 1 and serves to emphasize that the only affine transformation that fixes more than one point is the identity transformation, $\mathcal{A}_{(1,\,0)}$.

EXERCISE 3 Interested students may wonder why linear equations with x-coefficient -1 are their own inverses. The graph of the inverse of a function is the image of the graph of the function after reflection over the line with equation $y = x$. Because the line with equation $y = x$ has slope 1, any line with slope -1 is perpendicular to it. So, if a line is perpendicular to a line of reflection, the reflection maps that line to itself.

EXERCISE 4 You may need to give students the idea of looking first for functions where $(\mathcal{A}_{(a,\,b)})^2 = \mathcal{A}_{(a,\,b)}$.

On Your Own

EXERCISES 8 AND 9 Exercise 8 may lead to many conjectures. For example, if $\mathcal{A}_{(a,\,b)}$ and $\mathcal{A}_{(c,\,d)}$ are in S_n for some n, then $\mathcal{A}_{(a,\,b)} \circ \mathcal{A}_{(c,\,d)}$ and $\mathcal{A}_{(c,\,d)} \circ \mathcal{A}_{(a,\,b)}$ are both in S_n, and $(\mathcal{A}_{(a,\,b)})^{-1}$ is also in S_n. Students will use their steps from these calculations to prove these conjectures in Exercise 9.

Exercises

1. a. $\frac{2}{3}$ b. $\frac{4}{3}$ c. 2

   d. $a = 1$: all real numbers, $a \neq 1$: 0

   e. none

   f. $a = 1$ and $b = 0$: all real numbers, $a = 1$ and $b \neq 0$: none, $a \neq 1$: $\frac{-b}{a-1}$

2. exactly one: $\mathcal{A}_{(a,\,b)}$ where $a \neq 1$; more than one: $\mathcal{A}_{(a,\,b)}$ where $a = 1$ and $b = 0$; zero: $\mathcal{A}_{(a,\,b)}$ where $a = 1$ and $b \neq 0$

3. $\mathcal{A}_{(1,\,0)}$ and $\mathcal{A}_{(-1,\,b)}$ where b is any real number

4. $\mathcal{A}_{(1,\,0)}$

5. Larry just needs to use his result to draw the correct conclusion. The fact that $\mathcal{A}_{(1,\,-3)}$ has no fixed point implies that the original equation, $3x + 7 = 3x - 2$, has no solution.

6. $\mathcal{A}_{(a,\,5-5a)}$

7. A

8. See back of book.

EXERCISE 11 Remind students of what it means for a transformation to be in S_3: if 3 goes in, then 3 comes out! This will help them understand why the particular transformations listed here are all in S_3. The translation $(T_3)^{-1}$ maps 3 to 0, where any dilation D_a has no effect; then T_3 maps 0 back to 3 again. Students may be interested to know that any transformation in the stabilizer S_3 can be written in the form shown in part (e). This method allows students to find the general form of the transformations in any particular stabilizer.

EXERCISE 13 uses a method similar to Euclid's method for finding the sum of a geometric series, so this exercise serves as a bridge to Investigation 7A. It also follows closely the Example at the end of this lesson. Finding the closed form for $\sigma(n)$ is the most challenging part here—see the teaching notes for the Example for some ideas on how to approach this.

Additional Resources

PRINT RESOURCES
- Solution Manual
- Practice Workbook
- Assessment Resources
- Teaching Resources

TECHNOLOGY
- Interactive Textbook
- TeacherExpress CD-ROM
- ExamView CD-ROM
- PHSchool.com

Additional Practice

1. Find all affine transformations $\mathcal{A}_{(a,\, b)}$ that satisfy each equation below.
   a. $\mathcal{A}_{(a,\, b)}(-2) = -2$
   b. $\mathcal{A}_{(a,\, b)}(4) = 4$

2. a. Show that $\mathcal{A}_{(2,\, -3)}$ and $\mathcal{A}_{(-4,\, 15)}$ are in S_3.
   b. Without simplifying, show that $\mathcal{A}_{(2,\, -3)} \circ \mathcal{A}_{(-4,\, 15)}$ and $\mathcal{A}_{(-4,\, 15)} \circ \mathcal{A}_{(2,\, -3)}$ are both in S_3.
   c. Show that $(\mathcal{A}_{(2,\, -3)})^{-1}$ and $(\mathcal{A}_{(-4,\, 15)})^{-1}$ are both in S_3.
   d. Now simplify $\mathcal{A}_{(2,\, -3)} \circ \mathcal{A}_{(-4,\, 15)}$ and $\mathcal{A}_{(-4,\, 15)} \circ \mathcal{A}_{(2,\, -3)}$. What do you observe?

3. a. Show that $\mathcal{A}_{(-1,\, -8)}$ and $\mathcal{A}_{(3,\, 8)}$ are in S_{-4}.
   b. Without simplifying, show that $\mathcal{A}_{(-1,\, -8)} \circ \mathcal{A}_{(3,\, 8)}$ and $\mathcal{A}_{(3,\, 8)} \circ \mathcal{A}_{(-1,\, -8)}$ are both in S_{-4}.
   c. Show that $(\mathcal{A}_{(-1,\, -8)})^{-1}$ and $(\mathcal{A}_{(3,\, 8)})^{-1}$ are both in S_{-4}.

4. Show that each transformation is in S_2.
   a. $T_2 \circ D_5 \circ (T_2)^{-1}$
   b. $T_2 \circ D_3 \circ (T_2)^{-1}$
   c. $T_2 \circ D_{-1} \circ (T_2)^{-1}$
   d. $T_2 \circ D_a \circ (T_2)^{-1}$

5. Use the affine recursive definition below.
$$f(n) = \begin{cases} 1 & \text{if } n = 0 \\ \mathcal{A}_{(3,\, -2)} f(n-1) & \text{if } n > 0 \end{cases}$$
   a. Compute $(\mathcal{A}_{(3,\, -2)})^{(4)}(x)$.
   b. Explain why $f(4) = (\mathcal{A}_{(3,\, -2)})^{(4)}(f(0))$.
   c. Use your answers from parts (a) and (b) to compute $f(4)$.

6. On the xy-plane, plot all points (a, b) such that $\mathcal{A}_{(a,\, b)}$ is in each given stabilizer.
   a. S_2
   b. S_{-3}
   c. S_5

Practice: For Lesson 6.10, assign Exercises 1–6.

9. Suppose $\mathcal{A}_{(a,\, b)}$ and $\mathcal{A}_{(c,\, d)}$ are in S_x.

a. Show that $\mathcal{A}_{(a,\, b)} \circ \mathcal{A}_{(c,\, d)}$ is in S_x. **b.** Show that $(\mathcal{A}_{(a,\, b)})^{-1}$ is in S_x.

c. Take It Further Show that if $\mathcal{A}_{(a,\, b)}$ and $\mathcal{A}_{(c,\, d)}$ are in S_x, then
$$\mathcal{A}_{(a,\, b)} \circ \mathcal{A}_{(c,\, d)} = \mathcal{A}_{(c,\, d)} \circ \mathcal{A}_{(a,\, b)}$$

10. Find S_0. What special name do you use for this transformation?

11. Show that each transformation is in S_3.

a. $T_3 \circ D_4 \circ (T_3)^{-1}$ **b.** $T_3 \circ D_{-1} \circ (T_3)^{-1}$ **c.** $T_3 \circ D_2 \circ (T_3)^{-1}$

d. $T_3 \circ D_a \circ (T_3)^{-1}$ **e.** Explain why $T_x \circ D_a \circ (T_x)^{-1}$ is in S_x.

12. Use the affine recursive definition below.
$$f(n) = \begin{cases} 1 & \text{if } n = 0 \\ \mathcal{A}_{(2,\, 3)}(f(n-1)) & \text{if } n > 0 \end{cases}$$

a. Compute $(\mathcal{A}_{(2,\, 3)})^{(5)}(x)$.

b. Explain why $f(5) = (\mathcal{A}_{(2,\, 3)})^{(5)}(f(0))$.

c. Use your answers from parts (a) and (b) to compute $f(5)$.

13. Take It Further Consider the function below.
$$g(n) = \begin{cases} 2 & \text{if } n = 0 \\ D_3(g(n-1)) & \text{if } n > 0 \end{cases}$$
Your goal is to find a closed form for the sum
$$\sigma(n) = g(0) + g(1) + g(2) + \cdots + g(n)$$

a. Explain why $3\sigma(n-1) = g(1) + g(2) + \cdots + g(n)$.

b. Explain why the following equation is true.
$$\sigma(n) = g(0) + 3\sigma(n-1)$$
$$= \mathcal{A}_{(3,\, 2)}(\sigma(n-1))$$

c. Compute $\sigma(10)$. Verify your result by computing the sum below directly.
$$\sigma(10) = g(0) + g(1) + g(2) + \cdots + g(10)$$

d. Find a closed form for $\sigma(n)$.

Maintain Your Skills

14. On the xy-plane, plot all points (a, b) such that $\mathcal{A}_{(a,\, b)}$ is in S_{-4}.

Answers

9. a. $(\mathcal{A}_{(a,\, b)} \circ \mathcal{A}_{(c,\, d)})(x) = \mathcal{A}_{(a,\, b)}(\mathcal{A}_{(c,\, d)}(x)) = \mathcal{A}_{(a,\, b)}(x) = x$

b–c. See back of book.

10. $\mathcal{A}_{(a,\, 0)}$; dilations

11. See back of book.

12. a. $\mathcal{A}_{(32,\, 93)}$

b. The recursion step applies $\mathcal{A}_{(2,\, 3)}$ to the previous output, so computing $f(5)$ involves applying $\mathcal{A}_{(2,\, 3)}$ five times, with the result of $(\mathcal{A}_{(2,\, 3)})^{(5)}(f(0))$.

c. 125

13. a–b. See back of book.

c. 177,146

d. $\sigma(n) = 3^{n+1} - 1$

14.

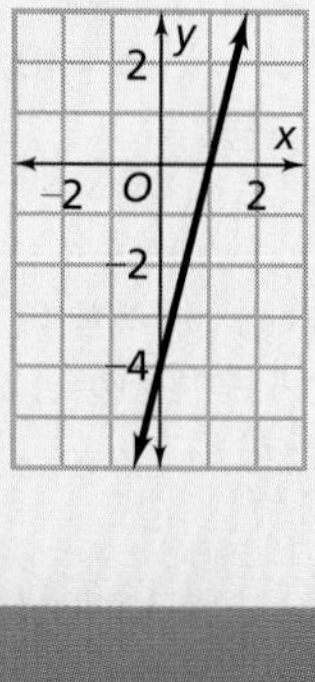

Mathematical Reflections 6C

In this investigation, you transformed an equation into one of the basic graph forms, described the effect of an affine transformation on an axis, and identified the fixed points of an affine transformation. These exercises will help you summarize what you have learned.

1. For each equation, copy and complete the pair of number lines showing the relationship between M and x.

   a. $M = T_4(x)$

   b. $M = D_{\frac{1}{3}}(x)$

   c. $M = \mathcal{A}_{(-1,\,2)}(x)$

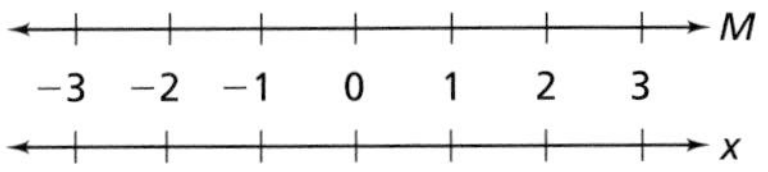

2. For each number-line pair you made in Exercise 1, describe the number line for x as a transformation of the number line for M.

3. Sketch the graph of $(2x - 1)^2 + (y + 3)^2 = 16$. Label several points on your sketch with their (x, y) coordinates. Then describe the graph as a transformation of the basic graph of $x^2 + y^2 = 16$.

4. The substitutions below transform the equation $y = -x^2 + 6x - 7$ into the equation $S = R^2$.

   $R = \mathcal{A}_{(1,\,-3)}(x) \qquad S = \mathcal{A}_{(-1,\,2)}(y)$

   a. Confirm that the substitutions work by replacing R and S with expressions in x and y in the equation $S = R^2$ and simplifying.

   b. Sketch the graph of $y = -x^2 + 6x - 7$. Label several points on your graph with their (x, y) coordinates.

   c. Describe your graph from part (b) as a transformation of the basic graph of $y = x^2$.

5. Find at least four affine transformations that have 6 as a fixed point.

6. How do you use the replacing-the-axes method to sketch the graph of $y = x^3 + 3x^2 - x + 4$?

7. How do you use the replacing-the-axes method to explain the relationship between the graphs of $y = x^2$ and $y = (x - 3)^2$?

8. What is the fixed point for $\mathcal{A}_{(5,\,3)}$?

The transformation you use to convert from °C to °F has a fixed point at −40°.

Vocabulary and Notation

In this investigation, you learned these terms and this symbol. Make sure you understand what each one means and how to use it.

- **affine recursive definition**
- **fixed point**
- **iteration**
- **stabilizer, S_x**

Mathematical Reflections

EXERCISES 6–8 At the start of the investigation, you may have assigned these as Questions 1–3 for students to think and write about.

Mathematical Reflections

1. See back of book.
2. **a.** The x number line is the image of the M number line translated 4 units to the right.

   b. The x number line is the image of the M number line dilated by the factor $\frac{1}{3}$.

   c. The x number line is the image of the M number line reflected over 0 and translated 2 units to the right.
3. See back of book.
4. **a.** Substitute $R = x - 3$ and $S = -y + 2$ into $S = R^2$ and simplify.

   $$-y + 2 = (x - 3)^2$$
   $$-y + 2 = x^2 - 6x + 9$$
   $$-y = x^2 - 6x + 7$$
   $$y = -x^2 + 6x - 7$$

   b–c. See back of book.
5. Answers may vary. Sample: $\mathcal{A}_{(-1,\,12)}$, $\mathcal{A}_{(0,\,6)}$, $\mathcal{A}_{(1,\,0)}$, $\mathcal{A}_{(2,\,-6)}$

6–7. See back of book.

8. $-\frac{3}{4}$

Project

This project introduces the idea of a mathematical *group*. Since the properties that define a group are familiar to your students, this can be an accessible project even though it resembles an introduction to abstract algebra. If you want to discuss with your students the definition of a group before they start the exercises, see the Exercise 6 note on the next page. Students who complete this project will get a lot of practice with function composition, finding inverses for functions, and understanding mathematical definitions and notation.

As usual, you can choose to assign the project to your entire class or to make it optional. Students can work individually, in pairs, or in small groups to complete it.

EXERCISE 3 Watch for students confusing the order of operations. Some students may assume commutativity works, which is why the functions were chosen to show that, in general, function composition is not a commutative operation. Depending on your expectations for the project, you may want to ask students to write out all their algebra work in completing the table. Some students may opt for a CAS, which also gives opportunity to talk about how some CAS answers, such as $-(x - 1)$ or $\frac{x}{x-1}$, are equivalent to some of the functions used here.

EXERCISE 5 Encourage students not to use the identity function as one of the choices, since it makes the exercise easier and less interesting.

Project Using Mathematical Habits

A Group of Functions

In Chapter 2, you learned that the function $f(x) = x$ is the identity function under the operation of composition. If $f(x) = x$ and g is any function, then $(f \circ g)(x) = g(x) = (g \circ f)(x)$.

Since $f(x) = x$ is the identity function, two functions g and h are inverse functions if $g \circ h = f = h \circ g$.

1. Give some examples of the use of *identity* and *inverse* in other mathematical contexts. Explain how the usage is similar to the usage with functions.

   Consider the following six functions.

   $a(x) = \frac{1}{x}$

   $b(x) = \frac{1}{1 - x}$

   $c(x) = 1 - \frac{1}{x}$

   $d(x) = 1 - x$

   $e(x) = 1 + \frac{1}{x - 1}$

   $f(x) = x$

2. Determine which of the six functions is equivalent to each composition.

   a. $e \circ f$

   b. $a \circ a$

   c. $b \circ e$

   d. $e \circ b$

   e. $b \circ a \circ a$

3. Copy and complete the following table with the results of composing the six functions. The first function is the row, and the second function is the column. Some entries have been filled in to help you get started.

$\circ$	a	b	c	d	e	f
a	■	d	■	■	■	■
b	e	■	■	■	■	■
c	■	■	■	■	a	■
d	■	■	■	■	■	■
e	■	■	d	■	■	■
f	■	■	■	■	■	■

4. Find the inverse function of each function *a* through *f*.

5. A set of elements under a binary operation $\diamond$ has the associative property if, for any elements *m*, *n*, and *p*,

   $$(m \diamond n) \diamond p = m \diamond (n \diamond p)$$

   Pick three functions from Exercise 1, not including *f*, to test whether the associative property holds for those functions under composition. For example, you might check to see if $(a \circ b) \circ d = a \circ (b \circ d)$. Pay attention to the order of operations.

Answers

Project

1. Answers may vary. Sample: Identity: 0 is called the identity for the real numbers under the operation of addition. This means that for all real a, $0 + a = a = a + 0$, which shows that for addition of real numbers, 0 behaves the same way that f behaves for composition of functions: $(f \circ g)(x) = g(x) = (g \circ f)(x)$. Inverse: a and $-a$ are called inverses for the real numbers under the operation of addition. This means that for all real a, $a + (-a) = 0 = -a + a$, which shows that for addition of real numbers, a and $-a$ behave in the same way that inverse functions g and h behave under composition: $(g \circ h)(x) = f(x) = (h \circ g)(x)$.

2. a. *e* **b.** *f* **c.** *d* **d.** *a* **e.** *b*

3.

$\circ$	a	b	c	d	e	f
a	f	d	e	b	c	a
b	e	c	f	a	d	b
c	d	f	b	e	a	c
d	c	e	a	f	b	d
e	b	a	d	c	f	e
f	a	b	c	d	e	f

4. *a*, *d*, *e*, and *f* are their own inverses. *b* and *c* are inverses of each other.

5. Answers may vary. Sample: Using the three functions *a*, *b*, and *d*, the six possible orders of composing the functions all satisfy the associative property.

6. a. Closure: the set must be closed under the binary operation.

Associative property: the associative property must hold for all combinations of three elements under the binary operation.

Identity: the set must contain an identity element for the operation.

Inverses: every element in the set must have an inverse element in the set.

6. a. What four properties does a set need to have for it to be a group under a binary operation?

b. Do you think that the six functions in Exercise 1 form a group under composition? Explain.

c. A group is Abelian if it has the property of commutivity. Do you think that the six functions from Exercise 1 form an Abelian group under composition? Explain.

7. The order of an element in a group is the lowest number of copies of the element you need to operate together to get the identity element. For example, the order of *a* is 2, since $a \circ a = f$ and *f* is the identity element. Find the order of the functions *b* through *f* under the operation of composition.

8. Consider an equilateral triangle. There are six ways that you can map the triangle to itself.

- Reflect it around any of the three lines of symmetry (3 mappings).
- Rotate it 120° clockwise (1 mapping).
- Rotate it 120° counterclockwise (1 mapping).
- Leave the triangle the way it is (1 mapping).

Build a table for the operation "then," which means doing one of the mappings and then doing another of the mappings. For example, one output should be the result of doing a specific reflection and then doing a 120° rotation. (*Hint:* You can make a cutout of an equilateral triangle and label the three points.)

Is it possible to build this table to be the same as the table you completed in Exercise 3? If so, do it. If not, explain why not.

9. Consider a regular hexagon. There are six ways that you can map this hexagon onto itself while preserving its orientation. (*Hint:* In order to preserve orientation, you cannot reflect the hexagon.)

Build a table for the operation "then" as defined in Exercise 8. Is it possible to build this table to be the same as the one you completed in Exercise 3? If so, do it. If not, explain why not.

EXERCISE 6 Ask students to search out the definition of a group in mathematics. A *group* is a set *G* with a binary operation that satisfies the following four properties:

- Closure: For all *a, b* in *G*, the result of $a \diamond b$ is also in *G*.
- Associativity: For all *a, b*, and *c* in *G*, $(a \diamond b) \diamond c = a \diamond (b \diamond c)$.
- Identity element: There exists an element e in *G* such that for all *a* in *G*, $e \diamond a = a \diamond e = a$.
- Inverse element: For each *a* in *G*, there exists an element *b* in *G* such that $a \diamond b = b \diamond a = e$, where e is the identity element.

Then you can discuss the definition with the class and come up with some examples. Have students consider the set of the whole numbers under the operation of addition. Under addition, the set is closed, it is associative, and it has identity 0, but there are no additive inverses. It is not a group. However, students should see that if you include negative numbers—in other words, if the set is the integers—then you do have a group. That is likely to be as much formal structure as you need to establish.

EXERCISE 7 Order is one way to distinguish between two different groups with the same number of elements. Two groups that are isomorphic, that is having equivalent operations, must have the same number of elements of each order.

EXERCISES 8 AND 9 serve as jumping-off points for further exploration.

b. Yes; Exercise 3 shows that the six functions are closed under composition and that *f* is the identity element. Exercise 4 shows that each of the six functions has an inverse within the set of functions. Exercise 5 gives evidence (but not a complete proof) that that the six functions possess the associative property under composition.

c. No; answers may vary. Sample: The table in Exercise 3 shows that, for example, $a \circ b \neq b \circ a$.

7. See back of book.

8.

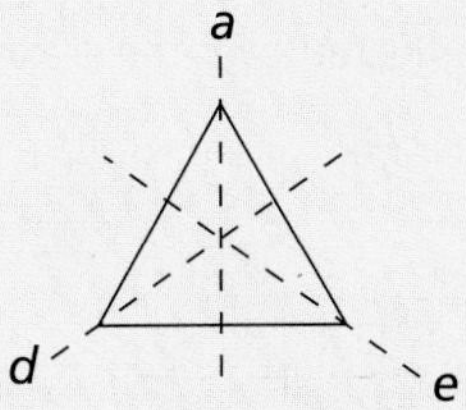

Answers may vary. Sample: In the following table, the six mappings of the equiangular triangle correspond to the letters $a-f$, as follows:

a = reflect over line of symmetry *a*

b = rotate 120° clockwise

c = rotate 120° counterclockwise

d = reflect over line of symmetry *d*

e = reflect over the line of symmetry *e*

f = leave the triangle as it is

then	a	b	c	d	e	f
a	f	d	e	b	c	a
b	e	c	f	a	d	b
c	d	f	b	e	a	c
d	c	e	a	f	b	d
e	b	a	d	c	f	e
f	a	b	c	d	e	f

Yes; the table above is the same as the table in Exercise 3.

9. See back of book.

Answers

Chapter Review

1. a.

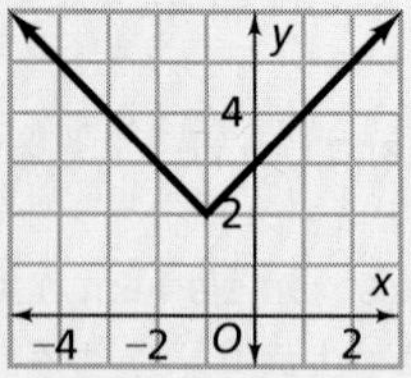

The graph of $y - 2 = |x + 1|$ is the graph of $y = |x|$ translated 1 unit to the left and 2 units up.

b.

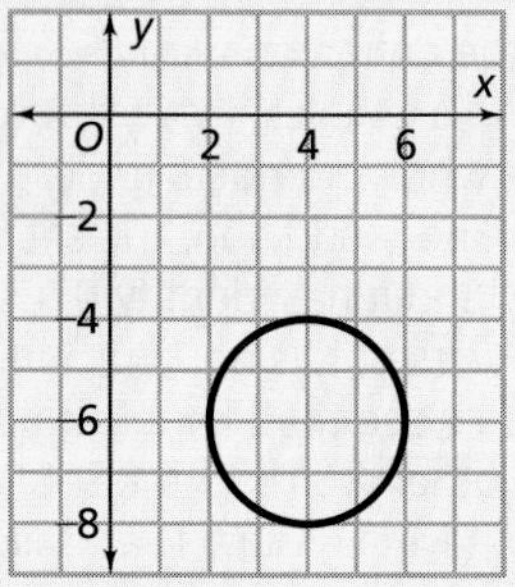

The graph of $(x - 4)^2 + (y + 6)^2 = 4$ is the graph of $x^2 + y^2 = 4$ translated 4 units to the right and 6 units down.

2. a.

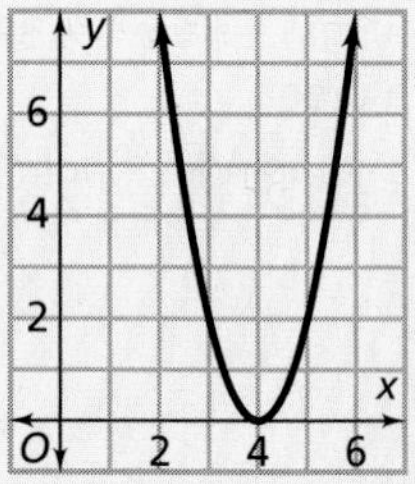

The graph of $\frac{y}{2} = (x - 4)^2$ is the graph of $y = x^2$ scaled vertically by the factor 2 and translated 4 units to the right.

b.

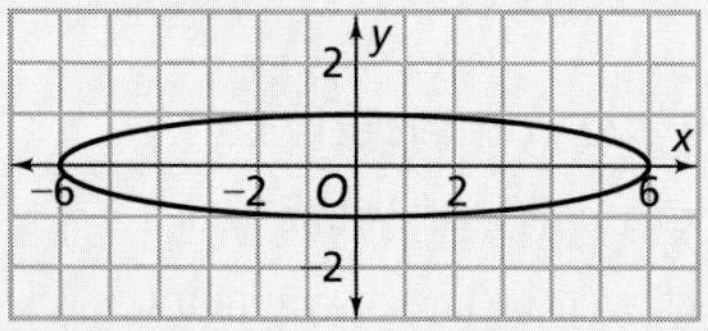

The graph of $\left(\frac{x}{3}\right)^2 + (2y)^2 = 4$ is the graph of $x^2 + y^2 = 4$ scaled horizontally by the factor 3 and vertically by the factor $\frac{1}{2}$.

c.

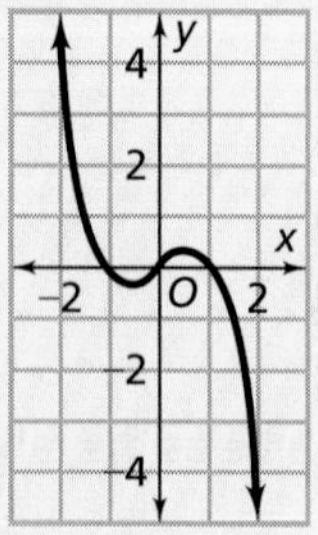

Answers may vary. Sample: The graph of $y = (-x)^3 - (-x)$ is the graph of $y = x^3 - x$ reflected over the y-axis.

3. $y + 7 = \left|\frac{x + 3}{2}\right|$

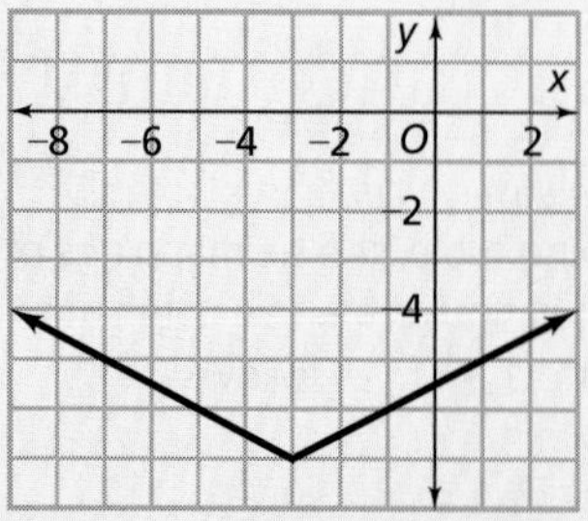

4. a. $\mathcal{A}_{(3,\,4)}$
b. $\mathcal{A}_{(-1,\,-4)}$
c. $\mathcal{A}_{(1,\,-7)}$
d. $\mathcal{A}_{\left(\frac{1}{7},\,0\right)}$
e. $\mathcal{A}_{(-6,\,-11)}$
f. $\mathcal{A}_{\left(-\frac{1}{2},\,4\right)}$

5. a. $a = 5, b = -37$
b. $a = 4, b = 2$

6. $a = 5, b = -2, c = 5, d = -26$

Chapter 6

Review

Go Online PHSchool.com

For vocabulary review, go to Web Code: bfj-0651

In **Investigation 6A** you learned how to

- sketch the basic graphs
- relate the effect of a translation of a basic graph on both the graph and the equation of the graph
- relate the effect of a scale or reflection of a basic graph on both the graph and the equation of the graph
- compose transformations and sketch the effect of a composition on one of the basic graphs

The following questions will help you check your understanding.

1. a. Sketch the graph of $y - 2 = |x + 1|$. How is your graph related to the graph of $y = |x|$?

b. Sketch the graph of $(x - 4)^2 + (y + 6)^2 = 4$. How is your graph related to the graph of $x^2 + y^2 = 4$?

2. a. Sketch the graph of $\frac{y}{2} = (x - 4)^2$. How is your graph related to the graph of $y = x^2$?

b. Sketch the graph of $\left(\frac{x}{3}\right)^2 + (2y)^2 = 4$. How is your graph related to the graph of $x^2 + y^2 = 4$?

c. Sketch the graph of $y = (-x)^3 - (-x)$. How is your graph related to the graph of $y = x^3 - x$?

3. Suppose you scale the graph of $y = |x|$ horizontally by the factor 2 and then translate the graph 3 units left and 7 units down. Write an equation to describe the resulting graph and sketch the graph of the equation.

In **Investigation 6B** you learned how to

- write any composition of translations and dilations as an affine transformation and write any affine transformation as a composition of a dilation and a translation
- find the inverse of a dilation, a translation, or an affine transformation and use inverses as a tool to solve equations
- find transformations to convert a general quadratic or cubic into one of the basic graph forms

The following questions will help you check your understanding.

4. Write each composition or inverse as a single affine transformation $\mathcal{A}_{(a,\,b)}$.

a. $T_4 \circ D_3$
b. $D_{-1} \circ T_6 \circ T_{-2}$
c. $(T_7)^{-1}$
d. $(D_7)^{-1}$
e. $\mathcal{A}_{(2,\,-1)} \circ \mathcal{A}_{(-3,\,-5)}$
f. $(\mathcal{A}_{(-2,\,8)})^{-1}$

5. Find a and b that satisfy each equation.

a. $\mathcal{A}_{(a,\,b)} \circ \mathcal{A}_{(3,\,9)} = \mathcal{A}_{(15,\,8)}$
b. $\mathcal{A}_{(4,\,-1)} \circ \mathcal{A}_{(a,\,b)} = \mathcal{A}_{(16,\,7)}$

6. Consider the equation $y = 5x^2 - 4x + 6$. Find a, b, c, and d such that, by making the substitutions below, you get the transformed equation $N = M^2$.

- $M = \mathcal{A}_{(a,\,b)}(x)$
- $N = \mathcal{A}_{(c,\,d)}(y)$

In **Investigation 6C** you learned how to

- use the techniques from Investigation 6B to transform an equation into one of the basic graph forms from Investigation 6A and use the information to graph the original equation
- describe the effect of an affine transformation on an axis and the effect of changes in axes on the graph of an equation
- identify the fixed points of an affine transformation and the set of affine transformations that fix a particular point.

The following questions will help you check your understanding.

7. For each equation, sketch a pair of number lines showing the relationship between M and x. Then describe the number line for x as a transformation of the number line for M.

a. $M = T_2(x)$

b. $M = D_4(x)$

c. $M = \mathcal{A}_{\left(\frac{1}{4}, -2\right)}(x)$

8. Use the replacing-the-axes method to sketch the graph of $2y + 1 = \sqrt{3x - 4}$. Label the three points on your sketch that have (M, N) coordinates $(0, 0)$, $(1, 1)$, and $(4, 2)$ with their corresponding (x, y) coordinates. Then, describe the graph as a transformation of the basic graph of $y = \sqrt{x}$.

9. Find all the fixed points of each affine transformation.

a. $\mathcal{A}_{(2, -3)}$ **b.** $\mathcal{A}_{(-3, 2)}$

c. $\mathcal{A}_{\left(\frac{2}{3}, 4\right)}$ **d.** $\mathcal{A}_{(1, 6)}$

7. a.

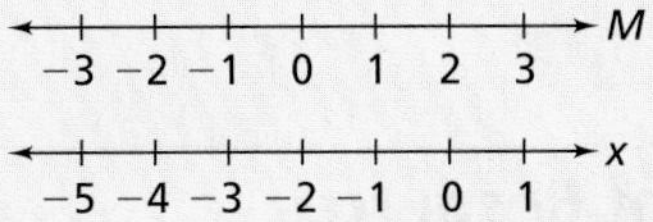

The x number line is the image of the M number line translated 2 units to the right.

b.

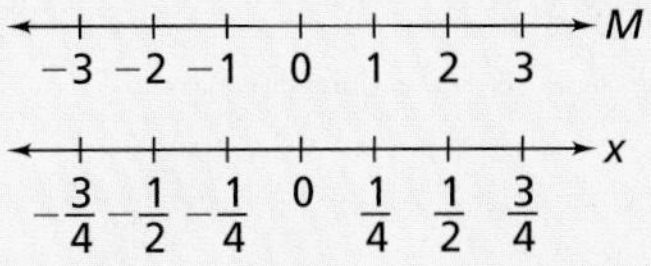

The x number line is the image of the M number line dilated by the factor 4.

c.

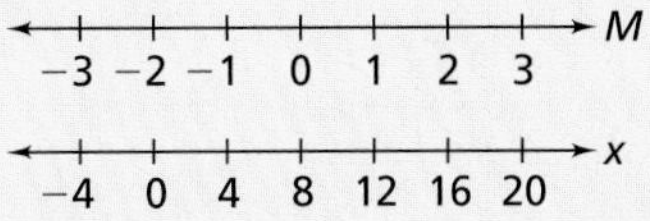

Answers may vary. Sample: The x number line is the image of the M number line translated 2 units to the right and then dilated by the factor $\frac{1}{4}$.

8.

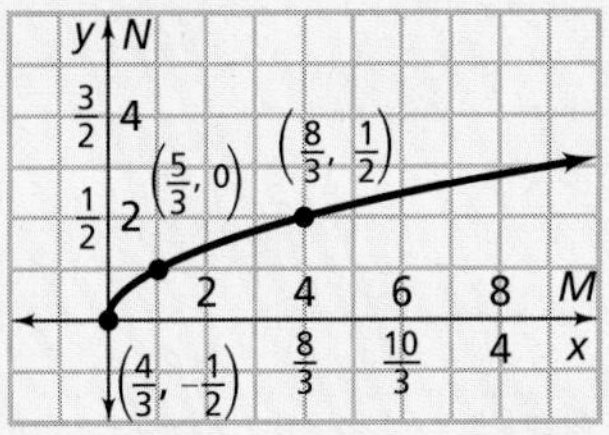

The graph of $2y + 1 = \sqrt{3x - 4}$ is the graph of $y = \sqrt{x}$ scaled horizontally by the factor $\frac{1}{3}$ and vertically by the factor $\frac{1}{2}$, and translated $\frac{4}{3}$ units to the right and $\frac{1}{2}$ unit down.

9. a. 3 **b.** $\frac{1}{2}$ **c.** 12 **d.** none

Chapter Test

Assessment Resources

Chapter Test | **page 1 of 2**

Multiple Choice

1. Which equation describes the graph of $y = x^2$ after a translation 3 units to the right and 2 units up?
   A. $y + 2 = (x - 3)^2$
   B. $y - 2 = (x - 3)^2$
   C. $y + 2 = (x + 3)^2$
   D. $y - 2 = (x + 3)^2$

2. Which equation describes the graph of $y = x^3$ after a horizontal scale by a factor of 2?
   A. $y = 2x^3$
   B. $y = \frac{x^3}{2}$
   C. $y = (2x)^3$
   D. $y = \left(\frac{x}{2}\right)^2$

3. Find the value of $\left(T_3 \circ D_5 \circ D_{\frac{1}{4}}\right)(8)$.
   A. 2
   B. $\frac{15}{4}$
   C. 13
   D. 30

4. Simplify $\mathcal{A}_{(3,\,-8)} \circ \mathcal{A}_{\left(\frac{4}{3},\,2\right)}$.
   A. $\mathcal{A}_{(-4,\,-2)}$
   B. $\mathcal{A}_{\left(-\frac{13}{3},\,-16\right)}$
   C. $\mathcal{A}_{(4,\,-2)}$
   D. $\mathcal{A}_{(4,\,-6)}$

5. Which of the following affine transformations has a fixed point of 4?
   A. $\mathcal{A}_{(5,\,16)}(x)$
   B. $\mathcal{A}_{(4,\,-12)}(x)$
   C. $\mathcal{A}_{(3,\,1)}(x)$
   D. $\mathcal{A}_{(1,\,4)}(x)$

Also available: Form B

Chapter 6 Test

Go Online PHSchool.com — For a chapter test, go to Web Code: bfa-0653

Multiple Choice

1. Which equation describes the graph of $x^2 + y^2 = 4$ after a translation 2 units to the right and 7 units down?

A. $(x - 2)^2 + (y - 7)^2 = 4$

B. $(x + 2)^2 + (y - 7)^2 = 4$

C. $(x - 2)^2 + (y + 7)^2 = 4$

D. $(x + 7)^2 + (y - 2)^2 = 4$

2. Which equation describes the graph of $y = \frac{1}{x}$ after a horizontal scale by the factor 4?

A. $y = \frac{4}{x}$

B. $y = \frac{x}{4}$

C. $y = 4x$

D. $y = x + 4$

3. Find the value of $D_3 \circ T_{-2} \circ D_{\frac{1}{2}}(8)$.

A. 5

B. 6

C. 12

D. 13

4. Simplify $\mathcal{A}_{(-4,\,1)} \circ \mathcal{A}_{\left(\frac{1}{4},\,-1\right)}$.

A. $\mathcal{A}_{\left(-4,\,-\frac{1}{4}\right)}$

B. $\mathcal{A}_{\left(-\frac{13}{4},\,-1\right)}$

C. $\mathcal{A}_{(-1,\,0)}$

D. $\mathcal{A}_{(-1,\,5)}$

5. Which of the following affine transformations does NOT have a fixed point of 3?

A. $\mathcal{A}_{(-3,\,12)}(x)$

B. $\mathcal{A}_{\left(-\frac{1}{2},\,\frac{9}{2}\right)}(x)$

C. $\mathcal{A}_{(2,\,3)}(x)$

D. $\mathcal{A}_{(3,\,-6)}(x)$

Open Response

6. Sketch the graph of each equation. How is each graph related to the corresponding basic graph?

a. $y - 1 = (2x)^2$

b. $y = \left(\frac{x}{2}\right)^3 - \frac{x}{2}$

c. $2y = |x - 5|$

d. $y = 2^{x+1}$

7. Write each composition or inverse as a single affine transformation.

a. $D_5 \circ (D_2)^{-1} \circ T_{-4}$

b. $\mathcal{A}_{\left(\frac{2}{3},\,-8\right)} \circ \mathcal{A}_{(6,\,-2)}$

c. $\left(\mathcal{A}_{(4,\,8)}\right)^{-1}$

8. Find a and b that satisfy each equation.

a. $\mathcal{A}_{(a,\,b)} \circ \mathcal{A}_{(-1,\,3)}(x) = \mathcal{A}_{(-2,\,-4)}(x)$

b. $\mathcal{A}_{(4,\,-6)} \circ \mathcal{A}_{(a,\,b)}(x) = \mathcal{A}_{(12,\,3)}(x)$

9. For each equation, find an equation for x in terms of M. Then sketch a pair of number lines showing the relationship between M and x.

a. $M = T_{-5}(x)$

b. $M = D_{10}(x)$

c. $M = \mathcal{A}_{(2,\,-6)}(x)$

10. Use the replacing-the-axes method to sketch the graph of $\frac{y}{2} = (3x + 2)^3 + (3x + 2)$. Label three points on your sketch with their (x, y) coordinates. Then describe the graph as a transformation of $y = x^3 + x$.

11. What does the graph of $(x + 1)^2 + (y - 4)^2 = 36$ look like?

Answers

Chapter Test

1. C

2. A

3. B

4. D

5. C

6. See back of book.

7. a. $\mathcal{A}_{\left(\frac{5}{2},\,-10\right)}$

b. $\mathcal{A}_{\left(4,\,-\frac{28}{3}\right)}$

c. $\mathcal{A}_{\left(\frac{1}{4},\,-2\right)}$

8. a. $a = 1,\ b = -7$

b. $a = 3,\ b = \frac{9}{4}$

9. a. $x = M + 5$

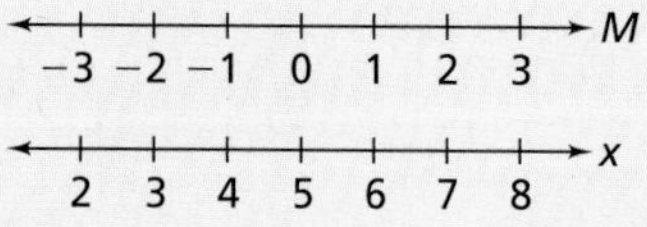

b. $x = \frac{M}{10}$

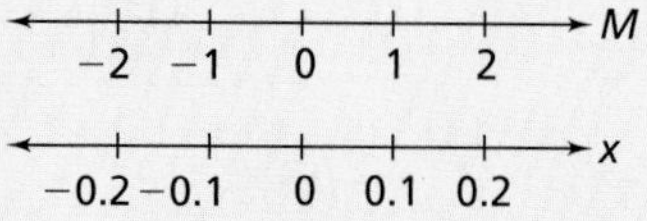

c. $x = \frac{1}{2}M + 3$

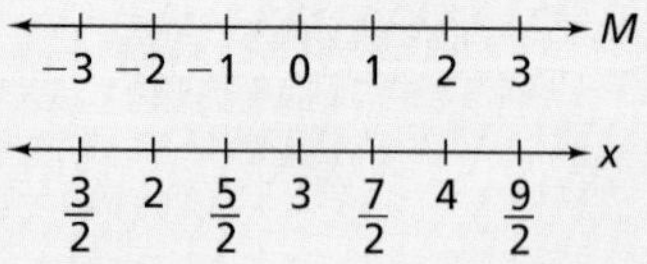

Chapter 6

Cumulative Review

Multiple Choice

1. Simplify the following expression.

$$\frac{x^{-5}y^{-9}}{x^{-11}y^{-7}}$$

A. $\frac{x^{-16}}{y^{-16}}$ **B.** $\frac{y^2}{x^6}$

C. $\frac{x^6}{y^2}$ **D.** x^6y^2

2. If $4^x = 32$, then which number is equal to 4^{4x}?

A. 4^5 **B.** 4^{10}

C. 2^5 **D.** 2^{10}

3. Place the following numbers in order from least to greatest.

12^{-1} $9^{\frac{3}{2}}$ $\left(\frac{2}{3}\right)^{-1}$ $\log_2 8$

A. $12^{-1}, 9^{\frac{3}{2}}, \left(\frac{2}{3}\right)^{-1}, \log_2 8$

B. $12^{-1}, \left(\frac{2}{3}\right)^{-1}, \log_2 8, 9^{\frac{2}{3}}$

C. $9^{\frac{3}{2}}, \log_2 8, \left(\frac{2}{3}\right)^{-1}, 12^{-1}$

D. $\left(\frac{2}{3}\right)^{-1}, 9^{\frac{3}{2}}, 12^{-1}, \log_2 8$

4. Which of the following expressions is equivalent to $\log 45$?

A. $\log 9 + \log 5$ **B.** $\log 15 - \log 3$

C. $\log 20 + \log 25$ **D.** $\log 100 - \log 55$

5. Which of the following points lies on the graph of $f(x) = \log_4 x$?

A. (4, 1) **B.** (0, 1)

C. (2, 16) **D.** (8, 2)

For Exercises 6 and 7, determine which equation describes the given transformation.

6. $y = x^3$ after a translation 4 units left and 5 units down

A. $y = (x - 4)^3 + 5$

B. $y = (x - 4)^3 - 5$

C. $y = (x + 4)^3 + 5$

D. $y = (x + 4)^3 - 5$

7. $y = |x|$ after a horizontal scaling by the factor $\frac{1}{3}$ and a reflection over the x-axis

A. $y = 3|x|$ **B.** $y = -3|x|$

C. $y = \frac{1}{3}|x|$ **D.** $y = -\frac{1}{3}|x|$

For Exercises 8 and 9, simplify each composition.

8. $(T_2 \circ D_4 \circ D_{\frac{1}{2}})(6)$

A. 9 **B.** 11

C. 13 **D.** 14

9. $\mathcal{A}_{(4,\,-6)} \circ \mathcal{A}_{(\frac{1}{2},\,3)}$

A. $\mathcal{A}_{(8,\,6)}$ **B.** $\mathcal{A}_{(2,\,6)}$

C. $\mathcal{A}_{(6,\,2)}$ **D.** $\mathcal{A}_{(-2,\,-6)}$

10. Which affine transformation has a fixed point of 5?

A. $\mathcal{A}_{(2,\,-5)}$ **B.** $\mathcal{A}_{(5,\,-1)}$

C. $\mathcal{A}_{(-3,\,5)}$ **D.** $\mathcal{A}_{(-1,\,2)}$

Cumulative Review

Assessment Resources

Quarter Test — page 1

Multiple Choice

1. Which of the following expressions is equal to 1?

A. $(5^2)^{-2}$ **B.** $\frac{5^{-2}}{5^2}$ **C.** $5^2 \cdot 5^{-2}$ **D.** $5 \cdot \left(\frac{1}{5}\right)^0$

2. Which of the following expressions represents the greatest number?

A. $9^{\frac{3}{2}}$ **B.** $\left(\frac{1}{3}\right)^{-2}$ **C.** $\log_2 32$ **D.** $\log_{\frac{1}{2}} 16$

3. Which of the following expressions is NOT equal to $\log 24$?

A. $\log 8 \cdot \log 3$ **B.** $\log 72 - \log 3$

C. $\log 4 + \log 6$ **D.** $\log 12 + \log 2$

4. Which of the following expressions represents the greatest number?

A. $\log_7 54$ **B.** $\log_6 49$

C. $\log_5 104$ **D.** $\log_8 85$

5. Find the value of $\left(T_5 \circ D_2 \circ D_{\frac{1}{2}}\right)(8)$.

A. 40 **B.** 13

C. 11 **D.** 4

6. Simplify $\mathcal{A}_{(4,-5)} \circ \mathcal{A}_{\left(\frac{1}{2},9\right)}$.

A. $\mathcal{A}_{(-5,9)}$ **B.** $\mathcal{A}_{(2,-4)}$

C. $\mathcal{A}_{(2,4)}$ **D.** $\mathcal{A}_{(2,31)}$

7. Which of the following affine transformations has a fixed point of 5?

A. $\mathcal{A}_{(2,-5)}(x)$ **B.** $\mathcal{A}_{(5,-2)}(x)$

C. $\mathcal{A}_{(3,10)}(x)$ **D.** $\mathcal{A}_{(6,-4)}(x)$

Open Response

8. Use the sequence below.

8, □, □, □, 2048, . . .

a. Find the missing terms if the sequence is arithmetic.

b. Find the missing terms if the sequence is geometric.

10.

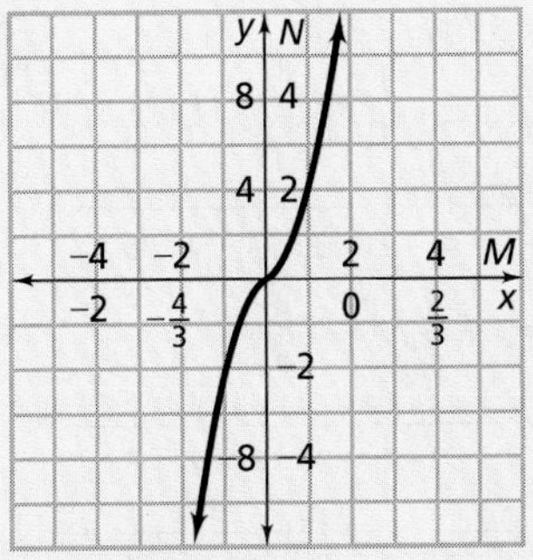

The graph of $\frac{y}{2} = (3x + 2)^3 + (3x + 2)$ is the graph of $y = x^3 + x$ scaled vertically by the factor 2 and horizontally by the factor $\frac{1}{3}$, and translated by $\frac{2}{3}$ unit left.

11. The graph of $(x + 1)^2 + (y - 4)^2 = 36$ is a circle with center $(-1, 4)$ and radius 6.

Cumulative Review

1. C

2. B

3. B

4. A

5. A

6. D

7. B

8. D

9. B

10. A

Quarter Test — page 2

9. Solve each equation. Give exact answers when possible, or round your answer to three decimal places.

a. $x \cdot 16^{-\frac{3}{2}} = 8^{\frac{2}{3}}$
b. $11^x = 15$
c. $18 = 2 \cdot 81^x$
d. $\log 4x + \log 5 = 3$

10. Use the two function definitions below.

$$f(x) = 3^x$$
$$g(x) = \log_3 x$$

a. Complete each table at the right.
b. On a single set of axes, sketch the graphs of *f* and *g*.

x	f(x)
−1	
0	
$\frac{1}{2}$	
1	
2	

x	g(x)
$\frac{1}{3}$	
1	
3	
9	

11. If you invest $12,000 at 4% interest, compounded annually, how many years will it take until your money doubles in value?

12. Sketch the graph of each equation. How is each graph related to its corresponding basic graph?

a. $2y = \frac{1}{x+4}$
b. $y + 3 = |4x|$
c. $y = (x+2)^2 - 5$
d. $(x-1)^2 + (2y)^2 = 16$

13. Find numbers *a* and *b* that satisfy each equation.

a. $(\mathcal{A}_{(a,\,b)} \circ \mathcal{A}_{(3,\,6)})(x) = \mathcal{A}_{(9,\,-4)}(x)$
b. $(\mathcal{A}_{(4,\,-5)} \circ \mathcal{A}_{(a,\,b)})(x) = \mathcal{A}_{(-4,\,-1)}(x)$

14. Consider the equation $y = 3x^2 + 2x + 1$. Find numbers *a*, *b*, *c*, and *d* such that, by making the substitutions below, you get the transformed equation $N = M^2$.

- $M = \mathcal{A}_{(a,\,b)}(x)$
- $N = \mathcal{A}_{(c,\,d)}(y)$

15. a. Sketch the graph of $y = (-x)^3$ using the replacing-the-axes method.
b. In part (a), how are the number lines for *M* and *x* related?
c. Sketch the graph of $y = (x+2)^2 - 3$ using the replacing-the-axes method.
d. In part (c), how are the number lines for *M* and *x* related? How are the number lines for *N* and *y* related?

Open Response

11. a. Copy and complete this ratio table for the exponential function $g(x)$.

x	g(x)	÷
0	−3	■
1	6	■
2	−12	■
3	24	

b. Find a recursive definition for the function.

c. Find a closed-form definition for $g(x)$.

d. Find the exact value of $g(5)$.

12. Let $f(x) = 6^x$ and $g(x) = \log_6 x$.

a. Copy and complete each table.

x	f(x)
−2	■
−1	■
0	■
1	■
2	■

x	g(x)
$\frac{1}{36}$	■
$\frac{1}{6}$	■
1	■
6	■
36	■

b. Sketch the graphs of *f* and *g* on the same axes.

c. Is the graph of *f* increasing or decreasing? Explain.

d. Is the graph of *g* increasing or decreasing? Explain.

13. Suppose $N = \log_3 15$.

a. Find two consecutive integers *j* and *k* such that $j < N < k$.

b. Express $\log_3 45$ in terms of *N*.

c. Find the value of *N* to three decimal places.

14. Solve each equation. Give exact answers when possible, or round your answers to three decimal places.

a. $3^x = 48$

b. $x \cdot 8^3 = 16^2$

c. $\log 2x + \log 8 = 3$

15. If you invest $3000 at 6% interest compounded annually, how many years will it take until your money triples in value?

16. Sketch the graph of each equation. Then describe how each graph is related to its corresponding basic graph.

a. $y = \frac{1}{x+3} - 4$

b. $y - 5 = -|x|$

c. $2y = (x-5)^2$

d. $(x-5)^2 + (y+3)^2 = 16$

17. Write each expression as a single affine transformation $\mathcal{A}_{(a,\,b)}$.

a. $(T_{-4})^{-1} \circ D_8 \circ D_7$

b. $\mathcal{A}_{(-2,\,3)} \circ \mathcal{A}_{(4,\,-7)}$

c. $(\mathcal{A}_{(4,\,5)})^{-1}$

18. Find numbers *a* and *b* such that the following equations are true.

a. $\mathcal{A}_{(a,\,b)} \circ \mathcal{A}_{(2,\,1)} = \mathcal{A}_{(-4,\,9)}$

b. $\mathcal{A}_{(2,\,-3)} \circ \mathcal{A}_{(a,\,b)} = \mathcal{A}_{(7,\,1)}$

19. For each equation below, do the following.

Solve for *x* in terms of *M*. Then draw a pair of number lines showing the relationship between *M* and *x*.

a. $M = T_6(x)$

b. $M = D_{\frac{1}{2}}(x)$

c. $M = \mathcal{A}_{(-3,\,5)}(x)$

Answers

11. a.

x	g(x)	÷
0	−3	−2
1	6	−2
2	−12	−2
3	24	

b. $g(x) = \begin{cases} -3 & \text{if } x = 0 \\ -2(g(x-1)) & \text{if } x > 0 \end{cases}$

c. $g(x) = -3(-2)^x$

d. 96

12. a–b. See back of book.

c. Increasing; as *x* increases, $f(x) = 6^x$ increases.

d. Increasing; as *x* increases, $f(x) = \log_6 x$ increases.

13. a. $j = 2, k = 3$ **b.** $N + 1$ **c.** 2.465

14. a. 3.524 **b.** $\frac{1}{2}$ **c.** 62.5

15. 19 years

16. See back of book.

17. a. $\mathcal{A}_{(56,\,4)}$ **b.** $\mathcal{A}_{(-8,\,17)}$

c. $\mathcal{A}_{(\frac{1}{4},\,-\frac{5}{4})}$

18. a. $a = -2, b = 11$

b. $a = \frac{7}{2}, b = 2$

19. a. $x = M - 6$

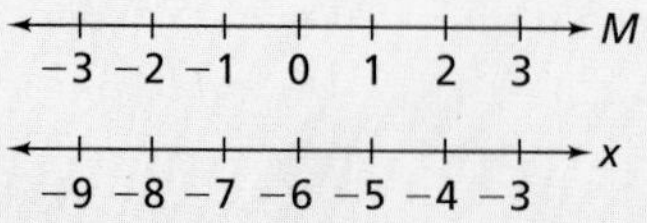

b. $x = 2M$

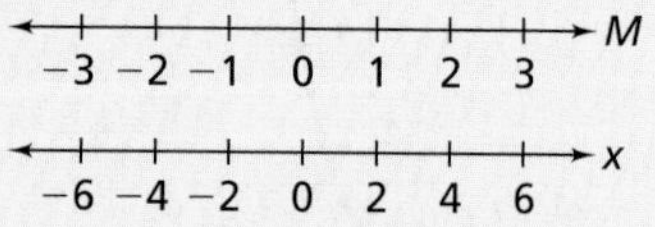

c. $x = -\frac{1}{3}M + \frac{5}{3}$

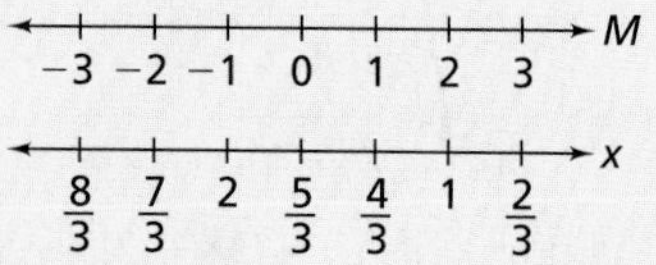

20. **a.** Use the replacing-the-axes method to sketch the graph of $4y + 4 = (x + 2)^2$. Label three points with their (x, y) coordinates.

b. Describe the graph as a transformation of $y = x^2$.

21. Find all fixed points of the affine transformation $\mathcal{A}_{(4,\,7)}$.

22. Multiply and simplify the following expression.

$$\sqrt{5} \cdot \sqrt{-20}$$

23. Let $z = 5 - 4i$. What is $-z + \bar{z}$?

24. Let $z = 3\sqrt{3} + 3i$ and $w = -2i$.

a. Find zw.

b. On the complex plane, graph z, w, and zw.

c. Find the magnitudes and directions of z, w, and zw.

25. Rewrite the following matrix in row-reduced echelon form.

$$\left(\begin{array}{cc|c} 4 & -6 & -3 \\ 0 & -8 & 5 \end{array}\right)$$

26. Let $A = \begin{pmatrix} 0 & -1 & -7 \\ 5 & 4 & 3 \end{pmatrix}$, $B = \begin{pmatrix} 4 & -2 \\ 2 & 0 \end{pmatrix}$, and $C = \begin{pmatrix} 3 & 6 \\ -9 & -2 \end{pmatrix}$.

If possible, find the following.

a. $B + C$

b. AC

c. CB

d. A^{-1}

e. B^{-1}

27. Find a polynomial function in normal form for $f(x)$ that agrees with the following table.

Input, x	Output, $f(x)$
0	5
1	9
2	17

28. Let $p(x) = x^3 + 2x^2 - 5x + 10$.

a. Find the quotient and remainder when $p(x)$ is divided by $x + 4$.

b. Use your answer to part (a) to find $p(-4)$.

29. Use the table below to write a recursive definition for $a(n)$.

Input, n	Output, $a(n)$
0	−5
1	−2
2	1
3	4
4	7

20. a.

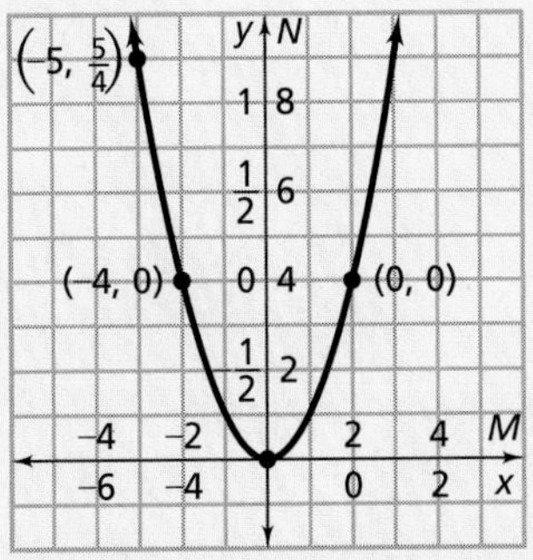

b. The graph of $4y + 4 = (x + 2)^2$ is the graph of $y = x^2$ scaled vertically by the factor $\frac{1}{4}$ and translated 2 units to the left and 1 unit down.

21. $-\frac{7}{3}$

22. $10i$

23. $8i$

24. a. $6 - 6i\sqrt{3}$

b. See back of book.

c. z: magnitude = 6, direction = 30°

w: magnitude = 2, direction = 270°

zw: magnitude = 12, direction = 300°

25. $\left(\begin{array}{cc|c} 1 & 0 & -1.6875 \\ 0 & 1 & -0.625 \end{array}\right)$

26. a. $\begin{pmatrix} 7 & 4 \\ -7 & 2 \end{pmatrix}$

b. not possible

c. $\begin{pmatrix} 24 & -6 \\ -32 & 18 \end{pmatrix}$

d. not possible

e. $\begin{pmatrix} 0 & \frac{1}{2} \\ -\frac{1}{2} & 1 \end{pmatrix}$

27. $f(x) = 2x^2 + 2x + 5$

28. a. quotient: $x^2 - 2x + 3$, remainder: -2

b. -2

29. $a(n) = \begin{cases} -5 & \text{if } n = 0 \\ a(n-1) + 3 & \text{if } n > 0 \end{cases}$

Chapter 7 Sequences and Series

The CME Project has taken a different approach from the way most textbooks present sequences and series for the first time. Usually, a text starts with arithmetic sequences, and then geometric sequences, followed by arithmetic and geometric series, followed by infinite geometric series, and then maybe some sigma notation. Students may come away with a stash of formulas such as $t_n = t_1 + (n - 1)d$ and a set of heuristics for when to apply them, but they do not necessarily have an understanding of where sequences and series fit in with the rest of the mathematics they have learned.

In CME Project field tests, the developers started with something similar to this standard introduction to sequences and series, but they soon realized that another approach was not only possible but more natural from the students' point of view. The end result of that realization is this chapter.

Chapter Overview

INVESTIGATION 7A, *The Need to Sum,* has students learn Gauss's method and Euclid's method as techniques to find closed-form rules to match the Σ column for a particular table. They also visualize sums geometrically and learn Σ notation.

INVESTIGATION 7B, *Sum Identities,* has students build a toolbox of identities in order to evaluate definite sums and to find closed-form rules for indefinite sums.

INVESTIGATION 7C, *Arithmetic and Geometric Sequences and Series,* defines arithmetic and geometric sequences and series. Students learn how to determine when a geometic sequence has a limit and how to find it.

INVESTIGATION 7D, *Pascal's Triangle and the Binomial Theorem,* has students pull together many of the threads of the chapter in an examination and analysis of Pascal's Triangle.

For more information on the investigations, see

- Chapter Road Map, pp. 586–587
- Investigation Road Maps, pp. 588, 606, 628, 660

PROJECT The Project near the end of the chapter is optional. You can assign the Project at any time during the chapter depending on how often and how long you feel students should work on it.

DAILY PLANNER DAILY PLANNER DAILY PL

Pacing Suggestions and Materials

Investigation 7A *The Need to Sum*

DAY	LESSON	HOMEWORK
1	7.1 Getting Started Core: 1, 2, 3, 4, 5 Optional: none	Core: 6, 7, 8, 9, 11, 12, 13 Optional: 10, 14
2	7.2 Gauss's Method and Euclid's Method Core: 1, 2, 4, 5, 6 Optional: 3, 7	Core: 8, 9, 10, 13, 14 Optional: 12, 15; Extension: 11
3	7.3 Ways to Visualize Sums Core: 1, 3, 4, 5 Optional: 6; Extension: 2	Core: 7, 8, 9a–c Optional: 10, 11; Extension: 9d
4	7.4 The Σ Notation Core: 1, 2, 3, 4a–b, 5 Optional: none; Extension: 4c	Core: 6a–b, 7, 8 Optional: 9; Extension: 6c

Investigation 7B *Sum Identities*

DAY	LESSON	HOMEWORK
1	7.5 Getting Started Core: 1, 2 Optional: none	Core: 3, 4 Optional: none
2	7.6 Definite and Indefinite Sums Core: 1, 2, 3 Optional: none	Core: 4, 5, 6, 7, 8, 9, 10 Optional: 11
3	7.7 Σ Identities Core: 1, 2, 3 Optional: none	Core: 4, 5, 6a, 7, 9, 10, 11, 13, 14 Optional: 8a, 12, 15; Extension: 6b, 8b
4	7.8 Tables and Figurate Numbers Core: 1, 2, 3 Optional: none	Core: 4, 5, 6, 7, 8, 9 Optional: 10, 11, 12, 13

NOTES	MATERIALS
	• CAS (recommended) • graphing calculators • spreadsheet software
	• graphing calculators • spreadsheet software
	• graph paper • graphing calculators • paper • scissors • spreadsheet software • Blackline Master 7.3
	• graphing calculators • Blackline Master 7.4

NOTES	MATERIALS
	• graphing calculators • Blackline Master 7.5
	• CAS (recommended) • graphing calculators • spreadsheet software
	• CAS (recommended) • graphing calculators • spreadsheet software • Blackline Masters 7.7A, 7.7B
	• graphing calculators • Blackline Master 7.8

Mathematics Background

REALLY NOTHING NEW A driving principle behind the development of the CME Project curriculum has been, "Do not introduce new things if you do not have to." That principle is evident in this course's treatment of sequences and series.

For example, you can think of $f(n) = 2n + 3$ as a linear function with the real numbers as its domain. However, if you restrict the domain of this function to the nonnegative integers, you can also think of $f(n)$ as an arithmetic sequence. The traditional idea of a sequence as a list of numbers is just a list of the outputs of this restricted-domain function in sequence: 3, 5, 7, 9, ... Students can also think of this as the output column from an input-output table for $f(n)$. Similarly, you can think of $g(n) = 3 \cdot 2^n$ as an exponential function with the real numbers as its domain, but if you restrict the domain to the nonnegative integers, then you can think of $g(n)$ as a geometric sequence. Sequences are not a new thing—they are functions, and input-output tables are still a relevant and useful representation. This pair of input-output tables shows the sequences $f(n)$ and $g(n)$. A third column shows the defining feature of each type of sequence. Arithmetic sequences have a constant difference between successive outputs; geometric series have a constant ratio between successive outputs.

Input	$f(n)$	$\Delta = f(n+1) - f(n)$
0	3	2
1	5	2
2	7	2
3	9	2
4	11	2
5	13	

n	$g(n)$	$\frac{g(n+1)}{g(n)}$
0	3	2
1	6	2
2	12	2
3	24	2
4	48	2
5	96	

Students have been using tables like these since Chapter 1. They are not new. Making a table like this for a sequence expressed as a list remakes the unfamiliar task of finding a closed form for a sequence into the extremely familiar task of finding a function to match an input-output table. CME Project *Algebra 2* does not use subscripts to refer to terms in a sequence. It stays with the more familiar notation, $f(n)$.

continued on p. 586c

continued from p. 586b

This chapter does introduce a new kind of column to include with an input-output table, though—the Σ column. Students keep track of a running total for the outputs of the function (terms in the sequence) in this column. Here is an example for the sequences $f(n)$ and $g(n)$.

n	$f(n)$	Σ
0	3	3
1	5	8
2	7	15
3	9	24
4	11	35
5	13	48

n	$g(n)$	Σ
0	3	3
1	6	9
2	12	21
3	24	45
4	48	93
5	96	189

In each case, this new column is the output column for another function, and this new function is the series associated with the sequence for each table. A series is just a running total of the outputs in an input-output table. An arithmetic series is the result of summing an arithmetic sequence, and a geometric series is the result of summing a geometric sequence. A series, arithmetic or geometric, is just another function in a table for which students can find a closed form. It is really nothing new.

Now, of course, there are new things to notice in Σ tables. Students see connections to the difference table work they did in Chapter 1, such as the fact that the $f(n)$ or $g(n)$ column is the Δ column for the Σ column. They find properties of the Σ table that correspond to the hockey stick and up-and-over properties of difference tables. As a consequence, students should be comfortable with the idea that the closed form representation for the series associated with an arithmetic series must be a quadratic polynomial, because that series is a function with a constant second difference. Students have not found closed forms for geometric series before, but they can, with familiar techniques, write a recursive rule for such a series. With a few new steps, they can convert that recursive form into a closed form. Everything is familiar, with some new terminology. Students can approach the new material with confidence.

FEWER FORMULAS TO MEMORIZE Another object of the CME Project approach to sequences and series is to pare down the list of formulas that students need to memorize by making connections. One of the most important connections to make is that Σ behaves linearly, which boils down to two simple rules:

$$\sum_{k=0}^{n} (f(k) + g(k)) = \sum_{k=0}^{n} f(k) + \sum_{k=0}^{n} g(k)$$

$$\sum_{k=0}^{n} af(k) = a\sum_{k=0}^{n} f(k)$$

In words, the "sigma of the sum is the sum of the sigmas" and "factors come out."

Pacing Suggestions and Materials

Investigation 7C *Arithmetic and Geometric Sequences and Series*

DAY	LESSON	HOMEWORK
1	7.9 Getting Started Core: 1, 2, 3 Optional: 4	Core: 5, 6, 7 Optional: 8, 9
2	7.10 Arithmetic Sequences and Series Core: 1, 2, 3, 4, 5, 7 Optional: 6, 8	Core: 9, 11, 12, 13, 14, 15, 16, 17, 20 Optional: 10, 18, 19, 21, 23; Extension: 22
3	7.11 Geometric Sequences and Series Core: 1, 2, 4, 5 Optional: 3	Core: 6, 7, 10, 11, 12, 14, 15, 16, 17 Optional: 8a–d, 9, 12, 18, 19, 20, 21; Extension: 8e
4	7.12 Limits Core: 1, 2 Optional: none	Core: 3, 5, 7 Optional: 4, 6, 8; Extension: 9
5	7.13 Repeating Decimals Core: 1, 2 Optional: none	Core: 3, 4, 5, 6 Optional: none

Investigation 7D *Pascal's Triangle and the Binomial Theorem*

DAY	LESSON	HOMEWORK
1	7.14 Getting Started Core: 1, 2, 3, 4, 5 Optional: none	Core: 6, 7, 8 Optional: 9, 10
2	7.15 Pascal's Triangle Core: 1, 2 Optional: none	Core: 3, 4, 5 Optional: 7; Extension: 6
3	7.16 The Binomial Theorem Core: 1, 2, 3 Optional: none	Core: 4, 5, 6, 7 Optional: 8, 9

NOTES	MATERIALS
	• graphing calculators • Blackline Master 7.9
	• graphing calculators • Blackline Master 7.10
You may wish to spend two days on this lesson. See the Lesson Overview notes for suggestions on how to cover the lesson over two days.	• CAS (recommended) • graph paper • graphing calculators • spreadsheet software • Blackline Master 7.11
	• graphing calculators • Blackline Master 7.12
	• graphing calculators

NOTES	MATERIALS
	• CAS (recommended) • graphing calculators • Blackline Master 7.14
	• CAS (recommended) • graphing calculators • Blackline Masters 7.15A, 7.15B
	• CAS (recommended) • graphing calculators • Blackline Masters 7.15A, 7.16

Students have examined most of the new operations they have encountered in this course to see whether they behave linearly, so it should make sense to them to examine Σ for these properties.

There are a few other critical formulas to learn, including the formula for the sum of the first n integers, which students derive using Gauss's method, and the formula for the sum of the first n powers of a constant, which students derive using Euclid's method. Students receive a list of formulas for the sums of powers, but they will use only the sum of the squares formula regularly in this course. Students will derive the formulas for the sums of powers in CME Project *Precalculus*.

That makes a total of *five* formulas that students will be able, with a little adaptation, to apply to almost every situation they encounter in this chapter.

LIMITS The other big idea that a chapter on sequences and series needs to deal with is limits. This course treats limits informally and looks at limits only as one variable gets arbitrarily large. This approach lays the groundwork for the more formal definitions and proofs that students encounter in calculus. Here is an example that shows the CME Project approach.

The domain of the function $f(n) = \frac{1}{2^n}$ is the real numbers. This means that the domain includes arbitrarily large values of n, but does not include $n = \infty$, because ∞ is not a real number. You might say that the limit as n gets larger (often written as $n \to \infty$) is 0, because you are dividing 1 by greater numbers. So the quotient must decrease but also stay positive. Suppose a student does not believe you and challenges you: "I bet you cannot show me an n that brings you within $t = 0.000001$ of 0." You can accept the challenge and show the student that $\frac{1}{2^{20}} = \frac{1}{1048576} \approx 0.0000009537$.

The student might respond with an even smaller t, but you can always come back with an n that brings the value of $f(n)$ within t of the limit 0—no matter how small t gets. Eventually, the student will have to believe you.

Here is the informal definition. A function $f(n)$ has a limit L as n approaches infinity *if* for any tiny number t there exists an n great enough so that $|f(n) - L| < t$.

This is a very informal argument, but it does include all the elements of a formal epsilon-delta proof. When students encounter the formal proofs, they will be able to relate to the process by thinking back to this "challenge and answer" idea.

Students apply this process of passing to the limit to the task of finding sums of infinite geometric series. The closed form for such a sum includes the form $\frac{1 - r^n}{1 - r}$, where r is the ratio between the terms of the geometric sequence associated with this series. To determine whether a limit exists for the

continued on p. 586

continued from p. 586d

geometric series, students factor out the constant part of this term, $\frac{1}{1-r}$, and look at the remaining factor, $1 - r^n$. If $r < 1$ this factor will approach 1 as n increases. That is because for $r < 1$, r^n is decreasing. If you subtract smaller numbers from 1, the difference gets closer to 1. That means that, for series with $r < 1$, as n gets arbitrarily large, $\frac{1-r^n}{1-r}$ approaches $\frac{1}{1-r}$.

Developing Students' Mathematical Habits

Key mathematical habits in this chapter include:

VISUALIZING SUMS Using pictures of arrays of squares and dots, students make sense of the closed forms for various sums.

REASONING ABOUT LINEARITY Students verify that the $\sum$ operation meets the functional equation requirements of linearity—$\sum(f + g) = \sum f + \sum g$ and $\sum(kf) = k \cdot \sum f$.

PASSING TO THE LIMIT Through experiment and reasoning, students develop their intuition about the process of finding a limit of a function as one variable gets arbitrarily large.

Chapter Vocabulary and Notation

The following list gives key vocabulary and notation used in the chapter. Selected new vocabulary and notation items are shown in boldface on the student page.

- arithmetic sequence, p. 633
- arithmetic series, p. 634
- associated series, p. 634
- Bernoulli's formulas, p. 616
- Binomial Theorem, p. 668
- common difference, p. 663
- common ratio, p. 640
- constant difference, p. 631
- definite sum, p. 610
- Euclid's method, p. 594
- figurate numbers, p. 622
- Gauss's method, p. 594
- geometric sequence, p. 640
- geometric series, p. 640
- identity, p. 611
- indefinite sum, p. 610
- index, p. 602
- limit, p. 649
- Pascal's Triangle, p. 663
- repeating decimal, p. 657
- sequence, p. 632
- series associated with f, p. 611
- term, p. 632
- $\sum$ (sigma), p. 590
- $\sum_{k=0}^{n} f(k)$ (summation), p. 602
- $\binom{n}{k}$, p. 663

Chapter 7

Investigations at a Glance

Chapter Road Map

INVESTIGATION 7A, *The Need to Sum,* introduces the $\sum$ table and presents Gauss's method and Euclid's method as techniques that allow students to find closed-form rules to match the $\sum$ column for a particular table. Students also visualize sums geometrically and learn $\sum$ notation.

INVESTIGATION 7B, *Sum Identities,* has students build a toolbox of identities in order to evaluate definite sums and to find closed-form rules for indefinite sums. They verify the linearity of the $\sum$ operation, and they use that information, together with the Bernoulli formulas for sums of powers, to evaluate sums of polynomials. Students also meet the figurate numbers, such as the triangular numbers, and they use their new techniques to write closed-form rules for them.

Sequences and Series

If you win \$1,000,000 in a state lottery, it is often buried in the contest rules that the prize is not really a check for \$1,000,000. Instead, it is \$50,000 a year for 20 years. Is your prize really worth \$1,000,000?

No, it is not. If you got the \$1,000,000 at the time you won the lottery, you might be able to invest it safely for at least a 6% return. That would give you not just \$50,000 a year, but \$60,000 a year, and not just for 20 years, but forever!

So your prize is not worth \$1,000,000. How much is it worth? What is its present value? To find the present value of the lottery prize, assuming you invest it at an interest rate of 6%, you can compute this sum.

$$50{,}000 + 50{,}000\left(\frac{1}{1.06}\right) + 50{,}000\left(\frac{1}{1.06}\right)^2 + \cdots + 50{,}000\left(\frac{1}{1.06}\right)^{19}$$

That expression is an example of a geometric series. You can write it more compactly.

$$\sum_{k=0}^{19} 50{,}000\left(\frac{1}{1.06}\right)^k$$

And even though it is not really worth \$1,000,000, you can see why the lottery does not advertise a big $\sum_{k=0}^{19} 50{,}000\left(\frac{1}{1.06}\right)^k$ prize. It is just not as impressive!

Vocabulary and Notation

- arithmetic sequence
- arithmetic series
- definite sum
- geometric sequence
- geometric series
- identity
- Pascal's triangle
- repeating decimal
- sequence
- series associated with f
- indefinite sum
- limit
- $\sum_{k=0}^{n} f(k)$ (summation)

Chapter Technology

CME Project *Algebra 2* assumes that each student has access to a graphing calculator. It also recommends access to a computer algebra system (CAS).

Support for the use of the technology is available in the TI-Nspire™ Technology Handbook. See p. 778.

A list of technology used with important concepts in this chapter appears below. Students will need access to the functionality listed to develop complete understanding of these topics.

Computer Algebra System

LESSON 7.4 Evaluate finite and indefinite sums, p. 603.

LESSON 7.7 Evaluate finite and indefinite sums, p. 615.

LESSON 7.10 Evaluate an indefinite sum, p. 638.

LESSON 7.16 Expand binomials, p. 670. Help determine coefficients in a binomial expansion, p. 670.

Function-Modeling Language

LESSON 7.4 Model functions with $\sum$ notation, p. 602.

LESSON 7.11 Model a monthly payment function, p. 641.

Spreadsheet Software

LESSON 7.1 Make a summation column, p. 591.

LESSON 7.6 Tabulate a series associated with a function, p. 611.

INVESTIGATION 7C, ***Arithmetic and Geometric Sequences and Series,*** defines arithmetic and geometric sequences and series. Through geometric series, students gain further insight into the monthly payment context they first encountered in Chapter 1. Students learn how to determine when a geometric series has a limit and how to find it. They apply this knowledge to the task of converting repeating decimals to exact fractions.

INVESTIGATION 7D, ***Pascal's Triangle and the Binomial Theorem,*** pulls together many of the threads of the chapter in an examination and analysis of Pascal's Triangle. Students see the pattern of the triangle entries in binomial expansions. The Binomial Theorem is stated and applied.

Investigation Overview

This investigation introduces students to the idea that sometimes a function is actually the sum of the outputs of another function. In Chapter 1, students made difference tables for various functions. These tables have an added column that lists the differences between successive outputs to a standard input-output table. Students learned to find a rule for the entries in this difference column in terms of the inputs to the original function. Similarly, in this investigation, students make sum tables by adding a column to an input-output table for a function showing the running total of the outputs. They write rules for the entries to these sum columns in terms of the inputs to the original function.

You may wish to assign Questions 1–3 for students to think and write about during the investigation.

Learning Goals

- Make a sum table for a function and write a closed-form rule for the sum column where appropriate.
- Use Gauss's method to find the sum of a sequence with a constant difference between successive terms.
- Use Euclid's method to find the sum of a sequence with a constant ratio between successive terms.
- Expand $\sum$ notation or convert an expanded sum back to $\sum$ notation.

Habits and Skills

- Reason logically to undrstand how both Gauss's method and Euclid's method work, and choose which method to use for finding a particular sum.
- Visualize a sum geometrically to make sense of an algebraic pattern.
- Generalize a result from a series of numerical examples.

Investigation 7A

The Need to Sum

In *The Need to Sum,* you will explore sums. You will add a sum column to tables and find function rules to match the sum column. You will learn methods to calculate sums more easily.

By the end of this investigation, you will be able to answer questions like these.

1. Describe Gauss's method for summing all integers from 1 to n.
2. Find a formula for $\sum_{j=0}^{n} 2^j$ in terms of n.
3. Evaluate $\sum_{j=1}^{5} 4j$.

You will learn how to

- make a sum table for a function and write a closed-form rule for the sum column where appropriate
- use Gauss's method to find the sum of a sequence with a constant difference between successive terms
- use Euclid's method to find the sum of a sequence with a constant ratio between successive terms
- expand $\sum$ notation or convert an expanded sum back to $\sum$ notation

You will develop these habits and skills:

- Reason logically to understand how both Gauss's method and Euclid's method work, and choose which method to use for finding a particular sum.
- Visualize a sum geometrically to make sense of an algebraic pattern.
- Generalize a result from a series of numerical examples.

You can use $\sum$ notation to describe sums with patterns, such as the total volume of successively smaller slices of watermelon.

Investigation Road Map

LESSON 7.1, *Getting Started,* has students begin to think about the running total of a column of function outputs as a function in its own right. They include this total column in an input-output table, marking it as $\sum$, and find closed-form rules to describe it.

LESSON 7.2, *Gauss's Method and Euclid's Method,* introduces Gauss's method for finding the sum of a sequence of numbers with a common difference between successive terms. Students also learn Euclid's method for finding the sum of a sequence of numbers with a common ratio between successive terms.

LESSON 7.3, *Ways to Visualize Sums,* has students use geometric visualization to model sums and make sense of algebraic patterns.

LESSON 7.4, *The $\sum$ Notation,* formalizes $\sum$ notation. Students practice expanding $\sum$ notation and converting an expanded sum into $\sum$ notation.

7.1 Getting Started

Activating Prior Knowledge
Exploring New Ideas

For some problems, you need to look at the sums of all the outputs as well as the individual outputs.

For You to Explore

Emile got a letter in the mail saying that a wealthy relative had left him an inheritance. At a meeting the next week, a lawyer read the following statement.

To Emile, because he likes math problems, I leave a choice. He can have one of two inheritances. He must make his choice before leaving the office today.

Option 1 A starting amount of \$10,000 and then, for the next 26 years, an annual payment at the end of each year that is \$1000 more than the amount he received the previous year.

For each option, there is a total of 27 payments.

Option 2 A starting amount of one cent and then, for the next 26 years, an annual payment at the end of each year that is twice the amount he received in the previous year.

Luckily, Emile brought his calculator to the meeting.

1. Suppose $f(n)$ is the amount of money Emile gets in Year n under Option 1 and $g(n)$ is the amount of money he gets in Year n under Option 2. Year 0 is the year in which Emile chooses one of the options and gets his first payment.
   a. Find closed-form rules for $f(n)$ and $g(n)$.
   b. For what values of n is $f(n) < g(n)$?
   c. For what values of n is $f(n) > g(n)$?

Habits of Mind

Check your units. When you compare the two functions, do not forget that you probably calculated f in dollars and g in cents.

2. Suppose $F(n)$ is the total amount of money Emile has received after n years under Option 1, and $G(n)$ is the total amount of money he has received after n years under Option 2.
   a. Make a table of values for $F(n)$ with inputs 0 through 5.
   b. Make a table of values for $G(n)$ with inputs 0 through 5.
   c. For what values of n is $F(n) < G(n)$?
   d. For what values of n is $F(n) > G(n)$?
3. a. Write a closed-form rule for $F(n)$.
   b. Write a closed-form rule for $G(n)$.
4. If you were Emile, which option would you choose? Explain.

Answers

For You to Explore

1. a. $f(n) = 10{,}000 + 1000n$; $g(n) = (0.01)2^n$
   b. $n \geq 22$
   c. $n < 22$ (or $n \leq 21$)
2. a–b. See back of book.
   c. $n \geq 25$
   d. $n \leq 24$
3. a. $F(n) = 500n^2 + 10{,}500n + 10{,}000$
   b. $G(n) = (0.01) \cdot (2^{n+1} - 1)$
4. Answers may vary. Sample: If you expect to live at least 25 more years, and if the relative's estate has enough money, the better choice would be Option 2.

Lesson Overview

GOAL

- Make a sum table for a function and write a closed-form rule for the sum column where appropriate.

In this lesson, students are introduced to a few contexts in which it makes sense to keep track of a running total. As always in a Getting Started lesson, there is no need to formalize these ideas today. Students meet these ideas throughout this chapter. In fact, this whole investigation should give students a lot of informal experience with sequences and series. Later in the chapter they encounter a more formal approach.

FOR YOU TO EXPLORE
- Core: 1, 2, 3, 4, 5
- Optional: none

MATERIALS
- CAS (recommended)
- graphing calculators
- spreadsheet software

HOMEWORK
- Core: 6, 7, 8, 9, 11, 12, 13
- Optional: 10, 14

VOCABULARY
- Σ

Launch

Have students get started on the For You to Explore problems. If they have a spreadsheet application that they can use, encourage them to tabulate the different inheritance options for the full 26-year term of the inheritance.

Explore

As students are working, assess how much review they need on writing closed-form rules to match entries in a table. This is something they will need to do throughout the investigation. Have them verbalize what they remember, and write some of their answers on the board. For example, you might hear something such as, "If you're multiplying by the same number every time, it's going to be an exponential function," or "This is just linear, because there is a constant difference."

For You to Explore

PROBLEM 2 If students have difficulty answering the question about when $F(n) < G(n)$ and when $F(n) > G(n)$, encourage them to do the next problem first. After they have written a closed-form rule, it should be easier to decide.

PROBLEM 4 Some students who look at Problem 4 say there is no clear answer. As long as students analyze the situation correctly, their answer is correct no matter what choice they make.

PROBLEM 5 helps you decide how much you want to review finding a polynomial rule to match a table.

Wrap Up

Wrap up by asking students to give a linear function rule and build a table with a Σ column for that rule. Then, see if students can determine the rule for the Σ column (which should be a quadratic). Go over the For You to Explore problems as time allows.

Exercises

HOMEWORK

- Core: 6, 7, 8, 9, 11, 12, 13
- Optional: 10, 14

On Your Own

EXERCISE 6 Watch out for students arguing that the game is unfair simply because Maggie loses more than she gains on these seven moves. It is definitely possible for Maggie to be ahead after 7 moves, if enough odd numbers are rolled. A second question to ask here is, "On average, how far behind will Maggie be after 7 rolls?" (Answer: 3.5 chips) On each roll, she could gain 9 chips $(1 + 3 + 5)$ and lose 12 chips $(2 + 4 + 6)$. So, on an average turn, she will lose $\frac{3}{6} = \frac{1}{2}$ of a chip.

Here is a table from Chapter 1, with a new column labeled Σ. The numbers in the Σ column are just the running totals of the outputs.

A closed-form rule for the Σ column in this case is $n \mapsto (n + 1)^2$.

n	$f(n)$	Σ
0	1	1
1	3	4
2	5	9
3	7	16
4	9	25
5	11	36

The symbol Σ is based on the capital Greek letter *sigma*. In mathematics, you often use Σ to stand for "sum."

5. a. Copy the table at the right. Add a Σ column to the table.

b. Find a closed-form rule for the Σ column.

n	$h(n)$
0	0
1	2
2	4
3	6
4	8
5	10

Exercises *Practicing Habits of Mind*

On Your Own

6. Ken and Maggie both start with 50 chips. One of them rolls a number cube. If the number is even, Maggie gives Ken that many chips. If the number is odd, Ken gives Maggie that many chips.

The table shows how many chips Maggie gains for each roll. If she loses chips, she records this as a negative gain.

a. Copy Maggie's table. Add a column that shows how many chips she has after each move.

b. Is this a fair game? Explain.

Maggie's Table

Roll	Gain
1	5
2	=2
3	=4
4	3
5	=6
6	1
7	=6

Answers

5. a.

n	$h(n)$	Σ
0	0	0
1	2	2
2	4	6
3	6	12
4	8	20
5	10	30

b. $\Sigma = n^2 + n$

Exercises

6. a.

Roll	Gain	Total
1	5	55
2	−2	53
3	−4	49
4	3	52
5	−6	46
6	1	47
7	−6	41

b. Answers may vary. Sample: Maggie is generally losing chips as they play, so the game is not fair.

7.

n	$t(n)$	Σ
0	1	1
1	9	10
2	90	100
3	900	1000
4	9000	10,000

$\Sigma = 10^n$

For Exercises 7–9, copy each table. Add a Σ column. Find a closed-form rule for the Σ column.

You can use a spreadsheet to make Σ columns. See the TI-Nspire Handbook, p. 778.

7.

n	$t(n)$
0	1
1	9
2	90
3	900
4	9000

8.

n	$h(n)$
0	5
1	5
2	5
3	5
4	5

9.

n	$g(n)$
0	−1
1	1
2	3
3	5
4	7
5	9

10. At the beginning of a bus route, 10 people get on the bus. At the first stop, 3 more people get on. At the second stop, 2 people get off and 5 others get on. At the third stop, 1 person gets off. At the next stop, 3 get off and 4 get on. At the next stop, 2 get on and 5 get off. At the next stop, 3 get on. How many passengers are on the bus?

11. A bakery manager asks employees to keep at least 6 dozen muffins in the display case at all times. The counter clerk has to keep track of the sales as well as how many muffins the baker brings out from the kitchen. Copy the table below. Add a Σ column to answer the questions.

Time	Baked or Bought	Amount
6:00 A.M.	Baked	144
6:10 A.M.	Bought	12
6:25 A.M.	Bought	2
6:45 A.M.	Bought	24
7:00 A.M.	Bought	5
7:15 A.M.	Baked	24
7:30 A.M.	Bought	36
8:15 A.M.	Baked	12
8:25 A.M.	Bought	6
8:30 A.M.	Bought	24

a. What was the total number of muffins in the case after the 8:30 A.M. count?

b. Did the clerk ever allow the total muffin count to go below the manager's requirement? If so, when?

EXERCISE 8 Some students may be making connections to the difference tables of Chapter 1. The difference tables showed the "running total" as the function value and the difference between successive terms in the Δ column. Here the roles are reversed; the function value is the difference between successive terms in the Σ column.

EXERCISE 10 shows students that they are familiar with the idea of keeping a running total. Some students may also have experience with balancing a checkbook or keeping track of a simple inventory (as in the next exercise).

8.

n	$h(n)$	Σ
0	5	5
1	5	10
2	5	15
3	5	20
4	5	25

$\Sigma = 5n + 5$ or $5(n + 1)$

9.

n	$g(n)$	Σ
0	−1	−1
1	1	0
2	3	3
3	5	8
4	7	15
5	9	24

$\Sigma = n^2 - 1$

10. 16

11.

Time	Baked or Bought	Amount	Σ
6:00 A.M.	Baked	144	144
6:10 A.M.	Bought	12	132
6:25 A.M.	Bought	2	130
6:45 A.M.	Bought	24	106
7:00 A.M.	Bought	5	101
7:15 A.M.	Baked	24	125
7:30 A.M.	Bought	36	89
8:15 A.M.	Baked	12	101
8:25 A.M.	Bought	6	95
8:30 A.M.	Bought	24	71

a. 71

b. yes; 8:30

EXERCISE 13 Students are not expected to find a closed form for $H(n)$ here, but they should be able to work with $h(n)$, and then build a table similar to the ones used earlier to calculate the values of $H(n)$. It is possible that a few astute students will find a closed form for $H(n)$. If this comes up, do not spend time on it—the topic will come up again later in the chapter.

Maintain Your Skills

EXERCISE 14 This exercise should remind students of some rules about the Δ operation that they learned in Chapter 1. Specifically, the difference column for $H(n)$ is constant, so $H(n)$ can be represented by a linear function. The difference column for $F(n)$ is linear, so $F(n)$ can be represented by a quadratic function. The difference column for $T(n)$ remains exponential.

Suppose that in Problem 1, the will gives Emile a third option.

Option 3 There is a starting amount of \$0 and then, for the next 26 years, an annual payment at the end of each year that is the square of the year (1, 2, and so on) times \$100.

12. Suppose $h(n)$ is the amount of money Emile gets in Year n under Option 3.

a. What is a closed form for $h(n)$?

b. Compare $h(n)$ to the functions $f(n)$ and $g(n)$ from Problem 1. For what values of n is each inequality true?

$h(n) < f(n)$

$h(n) > f(n)$

$h(n) < g(n)$

$h(n) > g(n)$

13. Suppose $H(n)$ is the total amount of money Emile gets after n years under Option 3. For what values of n is each inequality true?

a. $H(n) < F(n)$

b. $H(n) > F(n)$

c. $H(n) < G(n)$

d. $H(n) > G(n)$

Maintain Your Skills

14. Copy and complete the following difference tables. Write a closed-form rule for each function.

n	$F(n)$	Δ
0	1	■
1	4	■
2	9	■
3	16	■
4	25	■
5	36	

n	$T(n)$	Δ
0	1	■
1	10	■
2	100	■
3	1000	■
4	10,000	■
5	10,0000	

n	$H(n)$	Δ
0	5	■
1	10	■
2	15	■
3	20	■
4	25	■
5	30	

Answers

12. a. $h(n) = 100n^2$

b. $h(n) < f(n)$ if $n < 17$;
$h(n) > f(n)$ if $n > 16$;
$h(n) < g(n)$ if $n > 22$;
$h(n) > g(n)$ if $n < 23$.

13. a. $H(n) < F(n)$ for all 26 years.

b. $H(n)$ is never greater than $F(n)$.

c. $H(n) < G(n)$ if $n > 24$.

d. $H(n) > G(n)$ if $n < 25$.

14. See back of book.

7.2 Gauss's Method and Euclid's Method

Many stories are told about the mathematician Carl Friedrich Gauss. According to one story, one of his teachers gave Gauss and some classmates a problem to keep them busy for a while. The teacher asked the students to add all of the integers from 1 to 100. In just a few moments, Gauss wrote the number 5050 on his paper, and he was right!

Minds in Action episode 32

For her history class, Sasha is doing a project about Gauss's life.

Sasha So, Gauss had to solve the following problem.

Add up the integers from 1 to 100.

He probably did something like this.

You can write the sum two ways.

$$S = 1 + 2 + 3 + 4 + \cdots + 100$$

$$S = 100 + 99 + 98 + 97 + \cdots + 1$$

Add the first numbers of each sum together, then the second numbers, then the third ones, and so on, and you'll get

	S	=	1	+	2	+	3	+	4	+	$\cdots$	+	100
	↓		↓		↓		↓		↓				↓
+	S	=	100	+	99	+	98	+	97	+	$\cdots$	+	1
	$2S$	=	101	+	101	+	101	+	101	+	$\cdots$	+	101

There are one hundred 101's altogether, so

$$2S = 100 \cdot 101$$

$$S = 5050$$

Some people believe that he just added all the numbers up in his head.

For You to Do

Gauss found a way to add up the first 100 integers. Use his method to find the following sums.

1. Add up all integers from 1 to 371, inclusive.
2. Add up all integers from 0 to 789, inclusive.

For You to Do

1. 69,006 **2.** 311,655

Lesson Overview

GOALS

- Use Gauss's method to find the sum of a sequence with a constant difference between successive terms.
- Use Euclid's method to find the sum of a sequence with a constant ratio between successive terms.

This lesson introduces Gauss's method for finding the sum of an arithmetic sequence of numbers. In Gauss's method, students write the sum in two ways—forward and backward. They add the two versions and get an expression for twice the sum they are looking for in which a single number is added to itself repeatedly. Through experience, they come to understand what that number is and how many times it will appear for any particular arithmetic sequence.

Then, students see Euclid's method for finding the sum of a geometric sequence of numbers, which is similar but involves multiplication rather than addition. In Euclid's method, students multiply the sum by this constant ratio and subtract the original sum from this product. Many terms cancel out in this subtraction, and students are able to find an expression for the original sum in the process.

During class, it is important that students understand not only how to use each method but also how to decide which method to use for a particular sum.

CHECK YOUR UNDERSTANDING
- Core: 1, 2, 4, 5, 6
- Optional: 3, 7

MATERIALS
- graphing calculators
- spreadsheet software

HOMEWORK
- Core: 8, 9, 10, 13, 14
- Optional: 12, 15
- Extension: 11

VOCABULARY
- Gauss's method
- Euclid's method

Launch

Ask students to find the sum $1 + 2 + \cdots + 100$ any way they want. Give a very short time limit, about one minute, and see if anyone gets it. Then have students read the Minds in Action section.

Explore

Minds in Action

Gauss's method can be used for any arithmetic series. Watch for students assuming it only works for sums that start with 0 or 1, or for consecutive numbers. A good follow-up is Exercise 4, which asks for sums of odd and even integers.

Example

Show the steps here; then show a second example, such as $1 + 5 + 25 + 125 + 625$, where students will need to figure out what exponents to use. If students are catching on right away, switch to $1 + r + r^2 + r^3 + r^4$ and get as close to the general form as possible.

For You to Do

The sum in Problem 3 has a constant ratio of 2 between successive terms. When you subtract S from $2S$, you get $S = -1 + 2^{13} = 8191$. In Problem 4, the constant ratio between successive terms is 5. When you subtract S from $5S$, you get $S = \frac{-5^3 + 5^9}{4} = 488{,}250$.

Wrap Up

Have students develop and share a description of each of the summation methods in their own words and describe how to recognize which method to use for a particular sum. Then, go over the Check Your Understanding core exercises as time allows.

Assessment Resources

Lesson Quiz 7.2

1. Let $g(n) = \left(\frac{1}{5}\right)^0 + \left(\frac{1}{5}\right)^1 + \left(\frac{1}{5}\right)^2 + \left(\frac{1}{5}\right)^3 + \cdots + \left(\frac{1}{5}\right)^n$. Make a table for g starting with the initial term $g(0) = \left(\frac{1}{5}\right)^0 = 1$. Find a closed form for $g(n)$.

2. Use Gauss's method to add up the integers in each range.
   a. 3 to 11, inclusive
   b. 32 to 37, inclusive
   c. −6 to 50, inclusive

3. Use Euclid's method to find each sum.
   a. $5^2 + 5^3 + 5^4 + \cdots + 5^{10}$
   b. $2 \cdot 5^2 + 2 \cdot 5^3 + 2 \cdot 5^4 + \cdots + 2 \cdot 5^{10}$
   c. $0.3 + (0.3)^2 + (0.3)^3 + \cdots + (0.3)^{10}$

Gauss's method allows you to add up certain kinds of lists of numbers. The method works when the numbers add up in the same way forward and backward. Not all sequences of numbers have this property.

For example, suppose $g(n) = 3^n$. A table for g looks fairly regular.

n	$g(n)$
0	$3^0 = 1$
1	$3^1 = 3$
2	$3^2 = 9$
3	$3^3 = 27$
4	$3^4 = 81$
5	$3^5 = 243$

How would you add up all the outputs of g between 1 and, say, 3^5? You might try Gauss's method.

$$S = 1 + 3 + 3^2 + 3^3 + 3^4 + 3^5$$

$$S = 3^5 + 3^4 + 3^3 + 3^2 + 3 + 1$$

$$\begin{array}{rcccccccccccccc} & S & = & 1 & + & 3 & + & 9 & + & 27 & + & 81 & + & 243 \\ & \downarrow & & \downarrow & & \downarrow & & \downarrow & & \downarrow & & \downarrow & & \downarrow \\ + & S & = & 243 & + & 81 & + & 27 & + & 9 & + & 3 & + & 1 \\ \hline & 2S & = & 244 & + & 84 & + & 36 & + & 36 & + & 84 & + & 244 \end{array}$$

These sums are not all the same, so Gauss's trick does not work. What can you do?

Example

Problem Add up the numbers $3^0 + 3^1 + 3^2 + 3^3 + 3^4 + 3^5$.

Solution About B.C. 300, the Greek mathematician Euclid described a way of adding numbers like the outputs of g. Today's algebraic version of **Euclid's method** is to multiply the whole sum by 3. Since each output is 3 times the previous one, this shifts things over.

$$\begin{array}{rcccccccccccccc} S & = & 3^0 & + & 3^1 & + & 3^2 & + & 3^3 & + & 3^4 & + & 3^5 & & \\ 3S & = & & & 3^1 & + & 3^2 & + & 3^3 & + & 3^4 & + & 3^5 & + & 3^6 \end{array}$$

Now subtract the top sum from the bottom one.

$$\begin{array}{rrcccccccccccccc} & 3S & = & & & 3^1 & + & 3^2 & + & 3^3 & + & 3^4 & + & 3^5 & + & 3^6 \\ - & S & = & -3^0 & - & 3^1 & - & 3^2 & - & 3^3 & - & 3^4 & - & 3^5 & & \\ \hline & 2S & = & -3^0 & & & & & & & & & & & + & 3^6 \end{array}$$

Almost everything cancels. You get the following result.

$$2S = -1 + 3^6$$

$$S = \frac{3^6 - 1}{2} = 364$$

Euclid described his method in Book IX, Proposition 35 of *Elements*. He based his demonstration on the theory of proportions.

Answers

For You to Do

3. 8191 **4.** 488,250

Exercises

1. a. $S = \frac{n(n + 1)}{2}$

b. $S = \frac{n(n + 1)}{2}$

c. $S = \frac{(n - 1) \cdot n}{2}$

2. a. 6 **b.** 30 **c.** 250,500

3. a. 16 **b.** 49 **c.** 250,000

4. a. $S = n(n + 1)$

b. $S = (n + 1)^2$

5. a. 65,504 **b.** 196,512

c. ≈ 5.862 **d.** $1 - \frac{1}{10^{10}} \approx 1$

e. ≈ 0.664

6. a. Answers may vary. Sample: $1 + 2 + 3 + \cdots + 10 = 55$; $2 + 4 + 6 + \cdots + 22 = 132$; $4 + 7 + 10 + \cdots + 31 = 175$; Gauss's method works

For You to Do

Use Euclid's method to find each sum.

3. $1 + 2 + 2^2 + 2^3 + \cdots + 2^{12}$ **4.** $5^3 + 5^4 + 5^5 + 5^6 + 5^7 + 5^8$

Exercises *Practicing Habits of Mind*

Check Your Understanding

1. Use Gauss's method to find a formula for each sum.

a. Add up all the integers from 0 to n.

b. Add up all the integers from 1 to n.

c. Add up all the integers from 0 to $n - 1$.

2. Add up the even integers in each range.

a. 0 to 4, inclusive **b.** 0 to 10, inclusive **c.** 0 to 1000, inclusive

3. Add up the odd integers in each range.

a. 1 to 7, inclusive **b.** 1 to 13, inclusive **c.** 1 to 999, inclusive

4. Find a formula for each sum.

a. the even integers from 0 to $2n$ **b.** the odd integers from 1 to $2n + 1$

5. Use Euclid's method to find each sum.

a. $2^5 + 2^6 + 2^7 + \cdots + 2^{15}$

b. $3 \cdot 2^5 + 3 \cdot 2^6 + 3 \cdot 2^7 + \cdots + 3 \cdot 2^{15}$

c. $\frac{9}{10} + \left(\frac{9}{10}\right)^2 + \left(\frac{9}{10}\right)^3 + \cdots + \left(\frac{9}{10}\right)^{10}$

d. $\frac{9}{10} + \frac{9}{10^2} + \frac{9}{10^3} + \cdots + \frac{9}{10^{10}}$

e. $1 - \frac{1}{2} + \left(\frac{1}{2}\right)^2 - \left(\frac{1}{2}\right)^3 + \cdots - \left(\frac{1}{2}\right)^7$

6. **Write About It**

a. Give three sequences of numbers for which Gauss's method works. What do they have in common?

b. Give three sequences of numbers for which Euclid's method works. What do they have in common?

7. Suppose r is some number. Find a formula for each sum.

a. $1 + r + r^2 + \cdots + r^n$ **b.** $a + ar + ar^2 + \cdots + ar^n$

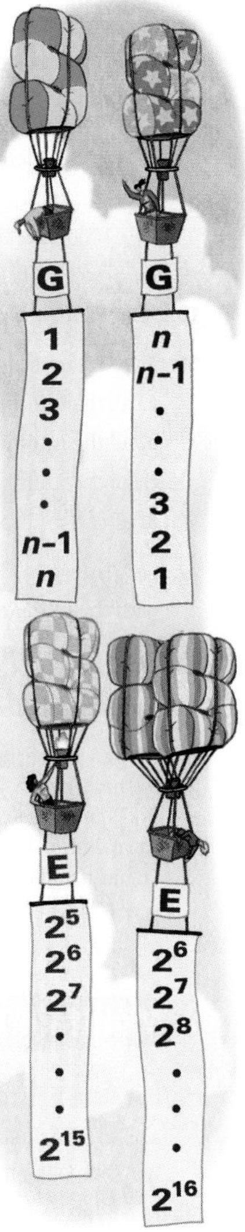

Exercises

HOMEWORK

- Core: 8, 9, 10, 13, 14
- Optional: 12, 15
- Extension: 11

Check Your Understanding

EXERCISE 1 If students do not notice the relationships between the sums they are being asked to compute in the exercise, you may wish to point it out in discussion.

EXERCISE 2 Students may feel that it is overkill to use Gauss's method on the short sums in the first two parts. As long as they are able to work out the last part of the exercise, that is fine. Otherwise, encourage them to try the method when they already know the answer, so that they can see how it works in the larger case.

EXERCISE 3 Working through the smaller cases using Gauss's method may help students who are having trouble with the larger case.

EXERCISE 4 If students are having trouble, you might suggest they look back at the numerical examples in the previous exercises.

EXERCISE 5 The last part of this exercise asks students to evaluate an alternating sum. If they see that the ratio between successive terms is negative, the rest of the method should be the same as in the other parts.

EXERCISE 6 Some students may make a further connection and say that Gauss's method works for terms generated by a linear function and Euclid's method works for terms generated by an exponential function.

EXERCISE 7 Euclid's method is likely to be less familiar to students, so it is important for them to draw on their experience with numerical examples to figure out how to do these general cases.

when there is a constant difference between successive terms.

b. Answers may vary. Sample: $2 + 4 + 8 + \cdots + 64 = 126$; $5 + 10 + 20 + 40 + \cdots + 640 = 1275$; $4 + 12 + 36 + \cdots + 4 \cdot 3^{100} = 2 \cdot 3^{101} - 2 \approx 3.09 \cdot 10^{48}$; Euclid's method works when there is a constant ratio between successive terms.

7. a. $S = \frac{r^{n+1} - 1}{r - 1}$

b. $S = a \cdot \frac{r^{n+1} - 1}{r - 1}$

On Your Own

EXERCISE 8 Some students may also find these sums by finding the sum from, for example, 0 to 4 and multiplying it by -1.

EXERCISE 9 Students could take their formula for the sum of the integers from 0 to n and multiply it by -1.

EXERCISE 13 Some students may notice that $g(n)$ from this exercise is just $f(n) + 1$ for $f(n)$ from Exercise 12.

Maintain Your Skills

EXERCISE 15 There are a couple of tricky points in the general case. First, students must find a way to write the initial sum S in both directions that allows them to see $2S$ as the sum of a lot of equal terms. Then they need to figure out how many terms there are. Encourage students to check their expressions in the general case with the numerical examples they have already done.

Additional Resources

PRINT RESOURCES
- Solution Manual
- Practice Workbook
- Assessment Resources
- Teaching Resources

TECHNOLOGY
- Interactive Textbook
- TeacherExpress CD-ROM
- ExamView CD-ROM
- PHSchool.com

Additional Practice

1. Add up all the integers in each range.
   a. -6 to 0, inclusive
   b. -12 to 0, inclusive
   c. -500 to 0, inclusive

2. Find a formula for the sum of the integers from $-2n$ to 0.

3. Adapt a formula or formulas to find the sum of the integers from -20 to 16.

4. Find a formula for each sum.
   a. all the multiples of 2 from 0 to n
   b. all the multiples of 4 from 0 to $2n$
   c. all the multiples of 6 from 0 to $3n$
   d. all the multiples of k from 0 to $\frac{1}{2}kn$

5. Let $g(n) = \left(\frac{1}{3}\right)^0 + \left(\frac{1}{3}\right)^1 + \left(\frac{1}{3}\right)^2 + \left(\frac{1}{3}\right)^3 + \cdots + \left(\frac{1}{3}\right)^n$. Make a table for g starting with the initial term $g(0) = \left(\frac{1}{3}\right)^0 = 1$. Find a closed form for $g(n)$.

6. Use Gauss's method to add up the integers in each range.
   a. 2 to 8, inclusive
   b. 40 to 45, inclusive
   c. -3 to 60, inclusive
   d. -35 to 120, inclusive

7. Use Euclid's method to find each sum.
   a. $3^3 + 3^4 + 3^5 + \cdots + 3^{12}$
   b. $2 \cdot 3^3 + 2 \cdot 3^4 + 2 \cdot 3^5 + \cdots + 2 \cdot 3^{12}$
   c. $\frac{7}{10} + \left(\frac{7}{10}\right)^2 + \left(\frac{7}{10}\right)^3 + \cdots + \left(\frac{7}{10}\right)^{10}$

Practice: For Lesson 7.2, assign Exercises 1–7.

On Your Own

Go Online PHSchool.com
For additional practice, go to **Web Code**: bfa-0702

8. Add up all the integers in each range.
   a. -4 to 0, inclusive
   b. -10 to 0, inclusive
   c. -1000 to 0, inclusive
9. Find a formula for the sum of the integers from $-n$ to 0.
10. Adapt a formula or formulas to find the sum of the integers from -10 to 8.
11. **Take It Further** Find a formula for each sum.
    a. all the multiples of 3 from 0 to $3n$
    b. all the multiples of 5 from 0 to $5n$
    c. all the multiples of 7 from 0 to $7n$
    d. all the multiples of k from 0 to kn
12. Let $f(n) = \left(\frac{1}{2}\right)^1 + \left(\frac{1}{2}\right)^2 + \left(\frac{1}{2}\right)^3 + \cdots + \left(\frac{1}{2}\right)^n$. Make a table for f starting with the initial term $f(1) = \frac{1}{2}$. Find a closed form for $f(n)$.
13. Let $g(n) = \left(\frac{1}{2}\right)^0 + \left(\frac{1}{2}\right)^1 + \left(\frac{1}{2}\right)^2 + \left(\frac{1}{2}\right)^3 + \cdots + \left(\frac{1}{2}\right)^n$. Make a table for g starting with the initial term $g(0) = \left(\frac{1}{2}\right)^0 = 1$. Find a closed form for $g(n)$.
14. **Standardized Test Prep** Rod went to a party. The host asked each guest to shake hands with every other guest exactly once. The next morning Rod's mother asked him how many guests attended the party. He forgot the number, but he remembered the host announced there had been 78 handshakes. How many guests attended the party?
    A. 10 **B.** 11 **C.** 12 **D.** 13

Maintain Your Skills

15. Use Gauss's method to add up the integers in each range.
    a. 3 to 5, inclusive
    b. 55 to 60, inclusive
    c. 5 to 80, inclusive
    d. -7 to 150, inclusive
    e. -31 to 131, inclusive
    f. n to m, inclusive

Go Online Video Tutor PHSchool.com
Web Code: bfe-0775

Answers

8. a. -10 **b.** -55 **c.** $-500{,}500$

9. $S = -\frac{n(n+1)}{2}$

10. -19

11. a. $S = \frac{3n(n+1)}{2}$

b. $S = \frac{5n(n+1)}{2}$

c. $S = \frac{7n(n+1)}{2}$

d. $S = \frac{kn(n+1)}{2}$

12.

n	$f(n)$
1	$\frac{1}{2}$
2	$\frac{3}{4}$
3	$\frac{7}{8}$
4	$\frac{15}{16}$
5	$\frac{31}{32}$
n	$\frac{2^n-1}{2^n}$

$f(n) = \frac{2^n - 1}{2^n}$

7.3 Ways to Visualize Sums

Many people like to think in images. Here are two In-Class Experiments that help you "see" what is going on with Gauss's and Euclid's methods.

In-Class Experiment

Suppose $f(n) = n$. The diagram at the right represents the first five outputs of f. The outputs are the number of squares in the towers.

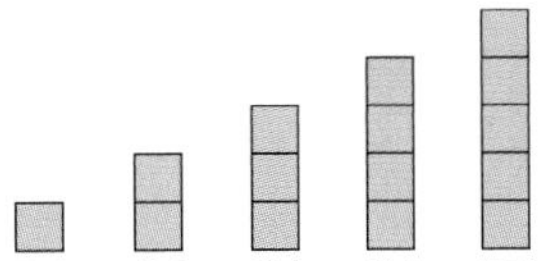

$f(1)$ $f(2)$ $f(3)$ $f(4)$ $f(5)$

Now you want to add these up, so you can think of pushing the towers together to form a staircase. Then you want to count the number of blocks that make up the staircase.

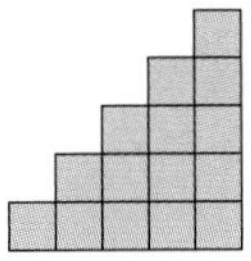

Step 1 Make two copies of the staircase above. Cut out the two copies of the staircase, made up of the blocks that you want to count. For now, just draw diagrams for the staircase that goes from $f(1)$ to $f(5)$.

Step 2 Flip one of the copies.

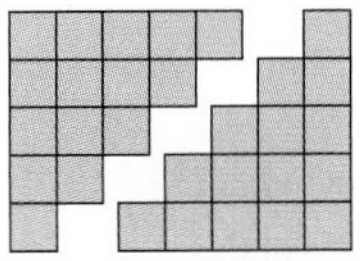

Step 3 Push them together to make a rectangle.

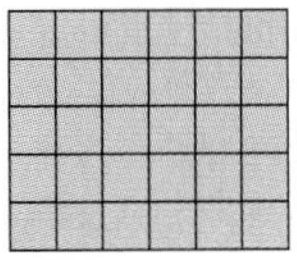

1. Find the height and length of the resulting rectangle. What is its area?
2. How many blocks are in the original staircase?
3. Use the staircase method to find $1 + 2 + 3 + 4 + 5 + 6$.

Lesson Overview

GOAL

- Expand $\sum$ notation.

Students use pictures and paper-tearing to represent sums in this lesson. Their experiences may make the results they get for the sums less abstract than the results they obtained through Gauss's method and Euclid's method. This concrete understanding is especially important as students try to think about the limit of the paper-tearing process as the number of trials approaches infinity.

CHECK YOUR UNDERSTANDING
- Core: 1, 3, 4, 5
- Optional: 6
- Extension: 2

MATERIALS
- graph paper
- graphing calculators
- paper
- scissors
- spreadsheet software
- Blackline Master 7.3

HOMEWORK
- Core: 7, 8, 9a–c
- Optional: 10, 11
- Extension: 9d

Launch

Begin this lesson with the In-Class Experiment. Blackline Master 7.3 provides two copies of the shapes described in the experiment.

Explore

In-Class Experiment

The results here are not limited to this form of staircase $(1 + 2 + 3 + \cdots)$. You could give another example $(2 + 6 + 10 + 14 + 18$ is one) where the "staircase" still works but the steps look different. If students finish quickly, ask them to find the general form for the rule $1 + 2 + 3 + \cdots + n$. Advanced students will get this using the staircases.

13.

n	$g(n)$
0	1
1	$\frac{3}{2}$
2	$\frac{7}{4}$
3	$\frac{15}{8}$
4	$\frac{31}{16}$
5	$\frac{63}{32}$
n	$\frac{2^{n+1}-1}{2^n}$

$g(n) = \frac{2^{n+1} - 1}{2^n}$

14. D

15. a. 12 **b.** 345
c. 3230 **d.** 11,297
e. 8150 **f.** $\frac{(m - n + 1)(m + n)}{2}$

In-Class Experiment

1. height 5, length 6, area 30
2. 15
3. 21

In-Class Experiment

Focus students' attention on the sum of the areas of the rectangles they place on the desk. After several steps, students will want to stop adding the areas of rectangles on their desks, and may switch to subtracting the area of the one rectangle in their hands from the area of the original piece of paper.

At the end of the experiment, you could also ask students what happens if they continue the process "forever." This leads to the sum of an infinite number of terms:

$$\frac{1}{2} + \frac{1}{4} + \frac{1}{8} + \cdots + \frac{1}{2^n} + \cdots = 1$$

The area of the rectangle in your hand will drop as close to 0 as desired, and the area of the rectangles on the table will grow as close to 1 as desired. This is the focus of Exercise 2, but if the situation is right, bring it up here.

Euclid's method applies to functions in which each output is a multiple of the previous one, such as $f(n) = 3^n$. If that multiple is between 0 and 1, you can picture what is going on by ripping up a piece of paper.

Remember...

The function $f(n) = 3^n$ is an exponential function.

In-Class Experiment

Get a piece of paper. Call the area of the paper 1.

Step 1 Take your piece of paper and fold it in half. Cut it into two pieces.

Step 2 Place one half on the desk in front of you. Keep the other half in your hand.

Step 3 Repeat Steps 1 and 2 using just the piece of paper that is in your hand now.

Repeat this process a few more times.

4. After doing Steps 1 and 2 three times, you have one rectangle in your hand and three on the desk.

a. What is the area of each rectangle?

b. What is the sum of the areas of the rectangles on the desk?

Remember...

The area of the original sheet was 1.

5. After doing Steps 1 and 2 eight times, you have one rectangle in your hand and eight on the desk.

a. What is the area of each rectangle?

b. What is the sum of the areas of the rectangles on the desk?

6. After doing Steps 1 and 2 n times, you have one rectangle in your hand and n rectangles on the desk.

a. What is the area of each rectangle?

b. What is the sum of the areas of the rectangles on the desk?

Answers

In-Class Experiment

4. a. $\frac{1}{8}$ in hand; $\frac{1}{2}, \frac{1}{4}, \frac{1}{8}$ on desk

b. $\frac{7}{8}$

5. a. $\frac{1}{2^8}$ or $\frac{1}{256}$ in hand; $\frac{1}{2}, \frac{1}{4}, \frac{1}{8}, \frac{1}{16}, \frac{1}{32}, \frac{1}{64}, \frac{1}{128}, \frac{1}{256}$ on desk

b. $\frac{255}{256}$

6. a. $\frac{1}{2^n}$ in hand; $\frac{1}{2}, \frac{1}{2^2}, \ldots, \frac{1}{2^n}$ on desk

b. $\frac{2^n - 1}{2^n}$

Developing Habits of Mind

Consider more than one strategy. There are two useful ways to visualize the algebraic pattern that results when you find the product below.

$$P = (1 - x)(1 + x + x^2 + x^3 + x^4)$$

One is the telescoping sum model and the other is the shifting model.

The telescoping method works as follows.

$$\begin{aligned} P &= (1 - x)(1 + x + x^2 + x^3 + x^4) \\ &= (1 - x) + (x - x^2) + (x^2 - x^3) + (x^3 - x^4) + (x^4 - x^5) \\ &= 1 - x + x - x^2 + x^2 - x^3 + x^3 - x^4 + x^4 - x^5 \\ &= 1 + (-x + x) + (-x^2 + x^2) + (-x^3 + x^3) + (-x^4 + x^4) - x^5 \\ &= 1 - x^5 \end{aligned}$$

The terms telescope as shown.

The shifting method works as follows.

$$\begin{aligned} P &= 1(1 + x + x^2 + x^3 + x^4) - x(1 + x + x^2 + x^3 + x^4) \\ &= 1 + x + x^2 + x^3 + x^4 - (x + x^2 + x^3 + x^4 + x^5) \\ &= 1 - x^5 \end{aligned}$$

Shift and subtract.

Remember...

You saw and used the general identity in Chapter 2.

Habits of Mind

Detect the key characteristics. Each method corresponds to a different application of the Distributive Property.

Exercises *Practicing Habits of Mind*

Check Your Understanding

1. Referring to the second In-Class Experiment, Cori says, "If I add the areas of all these rectangles, I will never have a sum of more than the area of the piece of paper I started with."

   David replies, "That can't be right! If you repeat the process more times, you'll get more rectangles and the total area will grow."

   Who do you think is correct? Explain.

Exercises

1. Answers may vary. Sample: Cori is correct that the sum is never more than the whole sheet. David is correct that the total area of the rectangles on the desk increases, although by smaller and smaller amounts.

Developing Habits of Mind

"Telescoping" refers to the way that terms cancel each other out in the sum. Students may enjoy the mental picture of a hand-held long scope that retracts to a small piece. Looking for telescoping is a good habit when working with this type of sum, since it can reduce a complicated problem to an easier one. The "shifting method" shown here aligns well with Euclid's method for summation.

Wrap Up

Go over as many of the Check Your Understanding core exercises as time allows. Do not get bogged down in discussion around Exercise 2. The concept of infinity is a difficult one for most people, and it may take some time for students to work around their own mental conflicts in thinking about limits.

Assessment Resources

Lesson Quiz 7.3

1. The diagram represents the first four outputs for a function s.
   a. Make a table for s, including a Σ column.
   b. Find a closed form for $s(n)$.
   c. Use a "cut and paste" argument to find a closed form for the Σ column.

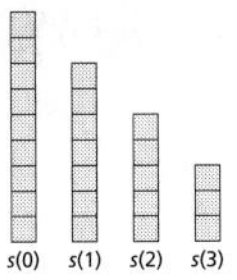

2. What is a closed form for the following sum?

$$\frac{1}{4} + \frac{1}{16} + \frac{1}{64} + \cdots + \frac{1}{4^n}$$

3. Find each sum.
   a. $1 + \frac{2}{3} + \left(\frac{2}{3}\right)^2 + \left(\frac{2}{3}\right)^3 + \cdots + \left(\frac{2}{3}\right)^{10}$
   b. $1 + 5 + 5^2 + 5^3 + \cdots + 5^8$

Exercises

HOMEWORK

- Core: 7, 8, 9a–c
- Optional: 10, 11
- Extension: 9d

Check Your Understanding

EXERCISE 2 asks students to think informally about the limit as n approaches infinity of the expression $1 - \frac{1}{2^n}$. From their own experience with the actual paper, students can understand that the fraction in the expression (the area of the paper in their hands) is getting smaller and that, as n approaches infinity, the fraction is approaching zero. However, the argument that if Emma continues the process "forever" then eventually all the paper will be on the desk can be disturbing. Let students know that as they continue to study limits in mathematics they will eventually be able to make more sense of this process.

EXERCISE 3 Some of your students may decide to find the closed form first and then use that to calculate the sums in the numerical part of the exercise. Others will find the numericals helpful in deriving the general form.

EXERCISE 6 Although this is a short exercise, make sure to cover it when reviewing. Each of these forms will be seen frequently when working with geometric series, and it is important for students to recognize that these forms are really identical. The first form is typically used when $r < 1$, and the second is typically used when $r > 1$. It is an interesting aside to note that the formula breaks down when $r = 1$, and to look at what should happen then (the fraction becomes $\frac{0}{0}$, which could be any number).

2. Take It Further When Emma does the second In-Class Experiment, she puts half of the paper (area = 1) on the table and keeps half for herself. She then cuts in half the piece that she kept, and again puts half on the table and keeps half for herself. Now, suppose that Emma repeats this process forever and ever. Explain why this suggests the following.

$$\frac{1}{2} + \frac{1}{4} + \frac{1}{8} + \frac{1}{16} + \frac{1}{32} + \frac{1}{64} + \cdots = 1$$

3. Use the staircase method to calculate each sum.

a. $1 + 2 + 3 + \cdots + 23 + 24$ **b.** $1 + 2 + 3 + \cdots + 55 + 56$

c. $1 + 2 + 3 + \cdots + 79 + 80$ **d.** $1 + 2 + 3 + \cdots + 122 + 123$

e. Use the staircase method to find a closed form for the following sum.

$$1 + 2 + 3 + \cdots + (n - 2) + (n - 1) + n$$

4. Expand each product.

a. $(1 - r)(1 + r)$ **b.** $(1 - r)(1 + r + r^2)$

c. $(1 - r)(1 + r + r^2 + r^3)$

d. $(1 - r)(1 + r + r^2 + r^3 + \cdots + r^n)$

Exercise 4 was more than just an exercise in algebraic calculation. The results give you the following identity.

$$(1 - r)(1 + r + r^2 + r^3 + \cdots + r^n) = 1 - r^{n+1}$$

You can divide both sides by $1 - r$.

$$1 + r + r^2 + r^3 + \cdots + r^n = \frac{1 - r^{n+1}}{1 - r}$$

This is an algebraic identity. It holds for any value of r that is allowed, which means all values of r such that $r \neq 1$. This formula allows you to add up certain sequences of numbers without working through the details of Euclid's method each time.

Remember... You saw this identity in Chapter 2.

5. Use the formula above to find each sum.

a. $1 + \frac{2}{3} + \left(\frac{2}{3}\right)^2 + \left(\frac{2}{3}\right)^3 + \cdots + \left(\frac{2}{3}\right)^8$

b. $1 + \frac{1}{4} + \left(\frac{1}{4}\right)^2 + \left(\frac{1}{4}\right)^3 + \cdots + \left(\frac{1}{4}\right)^8$

c. $1 + 10 + 10^2 + 10^3 + \cdots + 10^{10}$

6. Show that $\frac{1 - r^{n+1}}{1 - r}$ is the same as $\frac{r^{n+1} - 1}{r - 1}$.

Habits of Mind

Make strategic choices. When would it be more convenient to use the $1 - r$ form? When would the $r - 1$ form be more convenient? Explain.

On Your Own

7. Standardized Test Prep What is the sum $1 + \frac{3}{4} + \left(\frac{3}{4}\right)^2 + \left(\frac{3}{4}\right)^3 + \left(\frac{3}{4}\right)^4$ rounded to two decimal places?

A. 2.15 **B.** 2.73 **C.** 3.05 **D.** 3.29

Answers

2. Answers may vary. Sample: The area of the piece of paper in her hand keeps getting smaller and smaller, so the area of the "rest" of the paper gets closer to the starting area of 1.

3. a. 300
b. 1596
c. 3240
d. 7626
e. $\frac{n(n + 1)}{2}$

4. a. $1 - r^2$
b. $1 - r^3$
c. $1 - r^4$
d. $1 - r^{n+1}$

5. a. ≈ 2.92
b. ≈ 1.33
c. 11,111,111,111

6. $\frac{1 - r^{n+1}}{1 - r} = \frac{-1}{-1} \cdot \frac{1 - r^{n+1}}{1 - r} = \frac{-1 + r^{n+1}}{-1 + r} = \frac{r^{n+1} - 1}{r - 1}$

7. C

8. The diagram below represents the first four outputs for a function s.

a. Make a table for s, including a Σ column.

b. Find a closed form for $s(n)$.

c. Use a "cut and paste" argument to find a closed form for the Σ column.

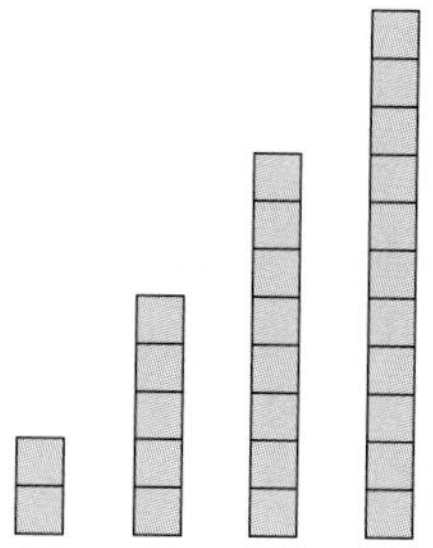

9. Use any piece of paper. Call its area 1. Follow these steps.

Step 1 Fold the paper in your hand into thirds. Cut it into 3 pieces.

Step 2 Put one piece in Pile 1, put one piece in Pile 2, and keep one piece in your hand.

Step 3 Repeat Steps 1 and 2 with just the piece of paper that is in your hand.

Repeat this process a few more times.

This is similar to, but not exactly the same as, the last cutting activity you did.

a. After completing Steps 1 and 2 twice, you have two pieces of paper in each stack. What is the area of the paper in your hand? What is the sum of the areas of the rectangles in each pile?

b. After completing Steps 1 and 2 three times, what is the area of the paper in your hand? What is the sum of the areas of the rectangles in each pile?

c. After completing Steps 1 and 2 n times, what is the area of the paper in your hand? What is the sum of the areas of the rectangles in each pile?

d. Take It Further Suppose you could do this process infinitely many times. Estimate the sum of the areas of the rectangles in each pile.

10. What is a closed form for $\frac{1}{3} + \frac{1}{9} + \frac{1}{27} + \cdots + \frac{1}{3^n}$?

Maintain Your Skills

11. Find each sum.

a. $1 + 2 + 1$

b. $1 + 2 + 3 + 2 + 1$

c. $1 + 2 + 3 + 4 + 3 + 2 + 1$

d. $1 + 2 + 3 + 4 + 5 + 4 + 3 + 2 + 1$

e. $1 + 2 + \cdots + 23 + 24 + 25 + 24 + 23 + \cdots + 2 + 1$

f. $1 + 2 + 3 + \cdots + (n - 1) + n + (n - 1) + 3 + 2 + 1$

8. a.

n	$s(n)$	Σ
0	2	2
1	5	7
2	8	15
3	11	26

b. $s(n) = 3n + 2$

c. $S(n) = \frac{(n+1)(3n+4)}{2}$

9. a. $\frac{1}{9}$ in hand, $\frac{4}{9}$ in pile 1, $\frac{4}{9}$ in pile 2

b. $\frac{1}{27}$ in hand, $\frac{13}{27}$ in pile 1, $\frac{13}{27}$ in pile 2

c. $\frac{1}{3^n}$ in hand, $\frac{\frac{1}{2}(3^n - 1)}{3^n}$ in pile 1, $\frac{\frac{1}{2}(3^n - 1)}{3^n}$ in pile 2

d. 0 in hand, $\frac{1}{2}$ in pile 1, $\frac{1}{2}$ in pile 2

10. $\frac{1}{2}\left(1 - \frac{1}{3^n}\right)$ or $\frac{1}{2}\left(1 - \left(\frac{1}{3}\right)^n\right)$

11. a. 4 **b.** 9 **c.** 16 **d.** 25 **e.** 625 **f.** n^2

On Your Own

EXERCISES 9 AND 10 Exercise 9 gives students an opportunity to understand the similar experiment they did in class at greater depth. You might want to encourage students to evaluate their explanation of what is going on by trying out their explanation on someone not in this class.

If you assign Exercise 10, you should also assign Exercise 9 so that students will have a concrete reference.

Maintain Your Skills

EXERCISE 11 Many students will see the pattern in the sums but will have difficulty explaining why it works that way. Encourage them to visualize the sums as patterns of blocks. Some students will find graph paper cutouts helpful.

Additional Resources

PRINT RESOURCES
- Solution Manual
- Practice Workbook
- Assessment Resources
- Teaching Resources

TECHNOLOGY
- Interactive Textbook
- TeacherExpress CD-ROM
- ExamView CD-ROM
- PHSchool.com

Additional Practice

1. The following picture represents the first four outputs for a function r.

a. Make a table for r, including a Σ column.

b. Find a closed form for $r(n)$.

c. Use a "cut and paste" argument to find a closed form for the Σ column.

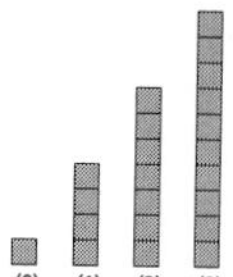

2. What is a closed form for $\frac{1}{6} + \frac{1}{36} + \frac{1}{216} + \cdots + \frac{1}{6^n}$?

3. Use any piece of paper. Call its area 1. Follow these steps.

Step 1 Fold the paper in your hand into fourths. Cut it into 4 pieces.

Step 2 Put one piece in Pile 1, put one piece in Pile 2, put one piece in Pile 3, and keep one piece in your hand.

Step 3 Repeat Steps 1 and 2 with just the piece of paper that is in your hand.

Repeat this process a few more times.

a. After completing Steps 1 and 2 twice, you have two pieces of paper in each stack. What is the area of the paper in your hand? What is the sum of the areas of the rectangles in each pile?

b. After completing Steps 1 and 2 three times, what is the area of the paper in your hand? What is the sum of the areas of the rectangles in each pile?

c. After completing Steps 1 and 2 n times, what is the area of the paper in your hand? What is the sum of the areas of the rectangles in each pile?

4. In Exercise 3, you cut paper in fourths. Use Σ notation to describe the sum of the areas of the pieces of paper in each pile on the table after you complete the steps the following number of times.

a. 12 times **b.** n times **c.** infinitely many times

5. Use your calculator to find the sum of the areas of the pieces of paper on the table after you complete the steps in Exercise 3 twelve times.

6. Evaluate each sum.

a. $\sum_{n=1}^{5} 3n - 5$ **b.** $\sum_{n=5}^{9} 3n - 5$ **c.** $\sum_{j=0}^{4} j(2j - 1)$

d. $\sum_{j=1}^{6} -3j + 2$ **e.** $\sum_{k=0}^{5} 3k^2$ **f.** $\sum_{j=1}^{16} 2$

Practice: For Lesson 7.3, assign Exercises 1–3.

Lesson Overview

GOAL

- Expand $\sum$ notation or convert an expanded sum back to $\sum$ notation.

This lesson formalizes $\sum$ notation. Students learn to use the symbol $\sum$ as a shorthand notation to describe the sum of a sequence. They practice expanding $\sum$ notation and converting an expanded sum into $\sum$ notation.

CHECK YOUR UNDERSTANDING
- Core: 1, 2, 3, 4a–b, 5
- Optional: none
- Extension: 4c

MATERIALS
- CAS (recommended)
- graphing calculators
- spreadsheet software
- Blackline Master 7.4

HOMEWORK
- Core: 6a–b, 7, 8
- Optional: 9
- Extension: 6c

VOCABULARY
- index
- sequence
- term
- $\sum_{k=0}^{n} f(k)$ (summation)

Launch

Begin this lesson by going over $\sum$ notation with your class. Some students are initially confused by an index i, because they are used to using i as $\sqrt{-1}$ when working with complex numbers. You may also want to remind students of the definitions of arithmetic sequence and geometric sequence that they learned in Chapter 5. Once students have a good idea about the notation, have them work through the Example. Blackline Master 7.4 can be used with the Example.

Explore

Circulate while students work and have them verbalize their thinking.

Example

Decide for yourself if you want students to work with the $\sum$ notation on their calculators (if the calculators support it; the TI-Nspire supports this notation among its templates). There is definitely some benefit to having students do some of these sums by hand, so they recognize that the $\sum$ notation is just that: "shorthand" notation that provides a compact way of writing the sum of the terms of sequence. Also, point out that the result of a $\sum$ calculation should be a single number, the sum of all the terms.

One thing to watch out for is the frequent use of the letter i as an indexing letter. Some students may confuse this with the use of i as the imaginary unit from Chapter 3. These uses are coincidental; i, j, and k are the most frequently used letters for indices.

7.4 The $\sum$ Notation

You have been looking at ways to find sums—to add up sequences of numbers. You have already used the symbol $\sum$ to describe sums in a table. You can also use this symbol as a shorthand notation to describe the sum of a sequence.

For now, think of a *sequence* as a list of numbers. The elements of this list are *terms*.

Example

Problem Find the sum of $2i$ as i goes from 1 to 4, that is, $\sum_{i=1}^{4} 2i$.

Solution
$$\sum_{i=1}^{4} 2i = 2 \cdot 1 + 2 \cdot 2 + 2 \cdot 3 + 2 \cdot 4 = 2 + 4 + 6 + 8 = 20$$

Problem Find the sum of $2k + 3$ as k goes from 0 to 5, that is, $\sum_{k=0}^{5} (2k + 3)$.

Solution
$$\sum_{k=0}^{5} (2k+3) = (2 \cdot 0 + 3) + (2 \cdot 1 + 3) + (2 \cdot 2 + 3) + (2 \cdot 3 + 3) + (2 \cdot 4 + 3) + (2 \cdot 5 + 3) = 3 + 5 + 7 + 9 + 11 + 13 = 48$$

Problem Find the sum of 2^k as k goes from 0 to 5, that is, $\sum_{k=0}^{5} 2^k$.

Solution
$$\sum_{k=0}^{5} 2^k = 2^0 + 2^1 + 2^2 + 2^3 + 2^4 + 2^5 = 1 + 2 + 4 + 8 + 16 + 32 = 63$$

You can model functions with $\sum$ notation. See the TI-Nspire Handbook, p. 778.

This is a general form of the notation.

$$\sum_{k=0}^{n} f(k) = f(0) + f(1) + \cdots + f(n)$$

final value → n; function to sum → $f(k)$; **index** variable → k; starting value → 0

Go Online PHSchool.com

For more information about sigma notation, go to **Web Code:** bfe-9031

For You to Do

Write each sum using $\sum$ notation.

1. $2 + 4 + 6 + 8 + 10 + 12 + 14 + 16 + 18 + 20$

2. $1 + 4 + 9 + 16 + 25$

Answers

For You to Do

1. $\sum_{i=1}^{10} 2i = 110$

2. $\sum_{i=1}^{5} i^2 = 55$

Exercises *Practicing Habits of Mind*

Check Your Understanding

1. Evaluate each sum.
   a. $\sum_{j=0}^{6} (3j + 4)$
   b. $\sum_{i=1}^{324} 1$
   c. $\sum_{i=0}^{4} i$
   d. $\sum_{i=12}^{45} i$

Shorthand allows you to write sentences more easily. Σ notation allows you to write sums more easily.

2. Ms. Take wrote Exercise 1 on the board. When Robin copied part (a), he accidentally changed all the *j*'s to *i*'s. Will Robin still get the correct answer? Explain.

3. Write each sum using Σ notation.
   a. $1 + 4 + 9 + 16 + 25 + \ldots + n^2$
   b. $1 + 1 + 1 + 1 + 1 + 1$
   c. $1 + 2 + 3 + 4 + 5 + 6 + 7 + 8 + 9 + 10$

4. In Exercise 2 from Lesson 7.3, Emma cuts sheets of paper in half. Use Σ notation to describe the sum of the areas of the pieces of paper on the table after Emma completes the steps the given number of times.
   a. 10 times
   b. *n* times
   c. **Take It Further** infinitely many times

Habits of Mind

Experiment. In Exercises 4 and 5, you have to picture cutting the paper 10 times. Can you actually cut it 10 times?

5. Use your calculator to find the sum of the areas of the paper on the table after Emma completes the steps 10 times.

Exercises

1. a. 91 b. 324
   c. 10 d. 969
2. Yes; answers may vary. Sample: After you substitute values for the placeholder, the placeholder does not appear in the sequence.
3. a. $\sum_{i=1}^{n} i^2$ b. $\sum_{i=1}^{6} 1$
   c. $\sum_{i=1}^{10} i$
4. a. $\sum_{i=1}^{10} \frac{1}{2^i}$
   b. $\sum_{i=1}^{n} \frac{1}{2^i}$
   c. $\sum_{i=1}^{\infty} \frac{1}{2^i}$
5. $\frac{1023}{1024} \approx 0.999023438$

Wrap Up

To end this lesson, go over the Check Your Understanding core exercises. Exercises 1 and 3 are critical to check because they assess students' ability to expand summation notation and to write a specific sequence of numbers in summation notation.

Assessment Resources

Lesson Quiz 7.4

1. Evaluate each sum.
   a. $\sum_{n=1}^{5} (2n - 5)$ b. $\sum_{n=5}^{9} (2n - 5)$ c. $\sum_{k=0}^{5} k(k + 2)$
2. Write each sum using Σ notation.
   a. $1 + 8 + 27 + 64 + \cdots + n^3$
   b. $1 + 3 + 5 + 7 + 9 + \cdots + 31$
3. Elsie cuts a sheet of paper with area 1 into fifths. She puts four of the pieces in four piles on a table. She cuts the remaining piece into fifths and again puts four of the pieces in the four piles on the table. She repeats this process a few more times.
   Use Σ notation to describe the sum of the areas of the pieces of paper on the table after Elsie completes the steps the given number of times.
   a. 3 times
   b. *n* times

Exercises

HOMEWORK
- Core: 6a–b, 7, 8
- Optional: 9
- Extension: 6c

Check Your Understanding

EXERCISE 1 Check this exercise to be sure that students understand how to expand summation notation.

EXERCISE 3 In part (b) of this exercise, students can choose any starting value and ending value for their index that have a difference of 5, because this will result in 6 terms for the sequence.

EXERCISE 4 Students who have seen limit notation before may use it in part (c), writing something similar to this:

$$\lim_{n\to\infty} \sum_{j=1}^{n} \frac{1}{2^j}$$

Additional Resources

PRINT RESOURCES
- Solution Manual
- Practice Workbook
- Assessment Resources
- Teaching Resources

TECHNOLOGY
- Interactive Textbook
- TeacherExpress CD-ROM
- ExamView CD-ROM
- PHSchool.com

Additional Practice

1. The following picture represents the first four outputs for a function r.
   a. Make a table for r, including a Σ column.
   b. Find a closed form for $r(n)$.
   c. Use a "cut and paste" argument to find a closed form for the Σ column.

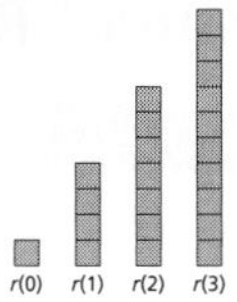

2. What is a closed form for $\frac{1}{6} + \frac{1}{36} + \frac{1}{216} + \cdots + \frac{1}{6^n}$?

3. Use any piece of paper. Call its area 1. Follow these steps.
   Step 1 Fold the paper in your hand into fourths. Cut it into 4 pieces.
   Step 2 Put one piece in Pile 1, put one piece in Pile 2, put one piece in Pile 3, and keep one piece in your hand.
   Step 3 Repeat Steps 1 and 2 with just the piece of paper that is in your hand.
   Repeat this process a few more times.
   a. After completing Steps 1 and 2 twice, you have two pieces of paper in each stack. What is the area of the paper in your hand? What is the sum of the areas of the rectangles in each pile?
   b. After completing Steps 1 and 2 three times, what is the area of the paper in your hand? What is the sum of the areas of the rectangles in each pile?
   c. After completing Steps 1 and 2 n times, what is the area of the paper in your hand? What is the sum of the areas of the rectangles in each pile?

4. In Exercise 3, you cut paper in fourths. Use Σ notation to describe the sum of the areas of the pieces of paper in each pile on the table after you complete the steps the following number of times.
   a. 12 times b. n times c. infinitely many times

5. Use your calculator to find the sum of the areas of the pieces of paper on the table after you complete the steps in Exercise 3 twelve times.

6. Evaluate each sum.
   a. $\sum_{n=1}^{5} 3n - 5$ b. $\sum_{n=5}^{9} 3n - 5$ c. $\sum_{j=0}^{4} j(2j - 1)$
   d. $\sum_{j=1}^{6} -3j + 2$ e. $\sum_{k=0}^{5} 3k^2$ f. $\sum_{j=1}^{16} 2$

Practice: For Lesson 7 .4, assign Exercises 4–6.

On Your Own

6. For Exercise 9 in Lesson 7.3, you cut paper in thirds. Use Σ notation to describe the sum of the areas of the pieces of paper in each pile on the table after you complete the steps the given number of times.
   a. 10 times
   b. n times
   c. **Take It Further** infinitely many times

7. Use your calculator to find the sum of the areas of the pieces of paper on the table after you complete the steps 10 times.

8. **Standardized Test Prep** Which of the following sums is equivalent to $3 + 5 + 7 + 9 + 11 + 13 + 15 + 17 + 19$?
   A. $\sum_{i=1}^{9} (2i + 1)$
   B. $\sum_{i=1}^{19} (2i - 1)$
   C. $1 + \sum_{i=1}^{9} 2i$
   D. $2 \cdot \sum_{i=0}^{8} (i + 3)$

Go Online PHSchool.com
For additional practice, go to **Web Code:** bfa-0704

Maintain Your Skills

9. Evaluate each sum. Look for patterns and general methods.
   a. $\sum_{j=1}^{4} (5j - 1)$ b. $\sum_{j=4}^{10} (5j - 1)$
   c. $\sum_{k=1}^{4} (5k - 1)$ d. $\sum_{i=0}^{6} 2i$
   e. $\sum_{k=1}^{6} k(k + 1)$ f. $\sum_{i=0}^{15} 1$
   g. $\sum_{i=0}^{16} 1$ h. $\sum_{i=1}^{15} 1$

Habits of Mind
Look for patterns. While evaluating a sum, see if you can use sums you have already evaluated. Which sums can you find using Gauss's method? Which can you find using Euclid's? Which can you find using arithmetic or other methods?

Answers

6. a. $\sum_{i=1}^{10} \frac{1}{3^i}$
   b. $\sum_{i=1}^{n} \frac{1}{3^i}$
   c. $\sum_{i=1}^{\infty} \frac{1}{3^i}$

7. $\frac{29{,}524}{59{,}049} \approx 0.499991532$

8. A

9. a. 46 b. 238 c. 46 d. 42
   e. 112 f. 16 g. 17 h. 15

Mathematical Reflections 7A

In this investigation, you learned to make a sum table for a function, write closed-form rules for the sum column, and use Σ notation. You used Gauss's method to find the sum of a sequence with constant differences and Euclid's method to find the sum of a sequence with constant ratios. These exercises will help you summarize what you have learned.

1. Copy and complete the following sum table. Find a closed-form rule for the Σ column.

n	*g*(*n*)	Σ
0	=3	■
1	1	■
2	5	■
3	9	■
4	13	■
5	17	■

$\sum_{i=1}^{4}\left(\frac{1}{2^6}\right) = \frac{15}{16}$

2. Let $S = \frac{1}{3} + \frac{2}{3} + \frac{4}{3} + \cdots + \frac{256}{3}$.

a. Explain why you can use Euclid's method to find the sum S.

b. Find S using Euclid's method. Show your work.

3. Write an expression in Σ notation for the sum in Exercise 2.

4. Find each sum.

a. odd integers 3 to 33, inclusive

b. powers of 4 from 4^0 to 4^{11}

5. Find each sum.

a. $\sum_{i=1}^{8}\left(\frac{1}{2}\right)^i$ **b.** $\sum_{k=0}^{8}(9 - 3k)$

6. Describe Gauss's method for summing all integers from 1 to n.

7. Find a formula for $\sum_{j=0}^{n} 2^j$ in terms of n.

8. Evaluate $\sum_{j=1}^{5} 4j$.

Vocabulary and Notation

In this investigation, you learned these terms and symbols. Make sure you understand what each one means and how to use it.

- **Euclid's method**
- **Gauss's method**
- **index**
- $\sum_{k=0}^{n} f(k)$ **(summation)**

Mathematical Reflections

EXERCISES 6–8 At the start of the investigation, you may have assigned these as Questions 1–3 for students to think and write about.

Mathematical Reflections

1.

n	*g*(*n*)	Σ
0	−3	−3
1	1	−2
2	5	3
3	9	12
4	13	25
5	17	42

$\Sigma = 2n^2 - n - 3$

2. a. There is a constant ratio of 2 between successive terms, so you can use Euclid's method.

b. $2S = \frac{2}{3} + \frac{4}{3} + \frac{8}{3} + \cdots + \frac{512}{3}$

$S = \frac{1}{3} + \frac{2}{3} + \frac{4}{3} + \cdots + \frac{256}{3}$

$S = \frac{512}{3} - \frac{1}{3} = \frac{511}{3} = 170.\overline{3}$

3. $S = \sum_{i=0}^{8} \frac{2^i}{3}$

4. a. 288 **b.** 5,592,405

5. a. $\frac{225}{226}$ **b.** −27

6. Gauss's method works when there is a constant difference between successive terms. First write the sum with the addends in increasing order and then write them in decreasing order. Add the two equations together to get a new equation equal to twice the sum where there are n terms equal to $(n + 1)$. So the sum is equal to $\frac{n(n + 1)}{2}$.

7. $\sum_{j=0}^{n} 2^j = 2^{n+1} - 1$

8. 60

Investigation Overview

In this investigation, students combine and extend much of their work from the previous investigation. They see how more complicated sums are built from simpler sums and how to use this insight to evaluate these sums. They also develop a list of identities that act as a "bag of tricks" that they can use to evaluate many different kinds of sums. They find closed-form expressions for indefinite sums, including Bernoulli's formulas for sums of powers and those for the figurate numbers, and for the series associated with a given function.

You may wish to assign Questions 1–3 for students to think and write about during the investigation.

Learning Goals

- Find closed-form expressions for indefinite sums and use them to evaluate definite sums.
- Develop a list of $\sum$ identities and recognize situations in which you can apply them.
- Find closed-form expressions for the series associated with a function.

Habits and Skills

- Visualize a complicated sum as a combination of different simpler sums.
- Generalize the steps in calculating definite sums to find a closed form for an indefinite sum.
- Reason logically using a recursive definition of a function to develop a closed-form definition.

Investigation 7B

Sum Identities

In *Sum Identities*, you will evaluate definite sums and find closed-form formulas for indefinite su ms. You will learn identities that help you simplify sums. You will also use sums and these identities to find functions that agree with tables.

By the end of this investigation, you will be able to answer questions like these.

1. What is $\sum_{k=0}^{25}(k + 6^k)$?

2. What is a recursive rule for the series associated with $f(n) = 3n + 6$ having initial term $f(0)$?

3. What is a closed form for the following recursive rule?

$$f(n) = \begin{cases} 5 & \text{if } n = 0 \\ f(n-1) + 2n^2 + 3n + 2 & \text{if } n > 0 \end{cases}$$

You will learn how to

- find closed-form expressions for indefinite sums and use them to evaluate definite sums
- develop a list of $\sum$ identities and recognize situations in which you can apply them
- find closed-form expressions for the series associated with a function

You will develop these habits and skills:

- Visualize a complicated sum as a combination of different simpler sums.
- Generalize the steps in calculating definite sums to find a closed form for an indefinite sum.
- Reason logically using a recursive definition of a function to develop a closed-form definition.

To complete the stack, she needs $(4 + 3 + 2 + 1)$ cups.

Investigation Road Map

LESSON 7.5, *Getting Started,* has students look back at tables and sums from Investigation 7A to prepare for a discussion of general summation techniques.

LESSON 7.6, *Definite and Indefinite Sums,* introduces a method for calculating the sum of the form $ax + b$, which combines Gauss's method and Euclid's method and the idea that "the sigma of a sum is the sum of the sigmas."

LESSON 7.7, *$\sum$ Identities,* has students collect all of the $\sum$ identities they have developed or conjectured so far, along with Bernoulli's formulas for the sums of powers. They use them to evaluate some more complicated sums.

LESSON 7.8, *Tables and Figurative Numbers,* has students use difference tables to find recursive definitions for functions. Then they use summation techniques to develop closed-form definitions from the recursive ones.

7.5 Getting Started

Activating Prior Knowledge
Exploring New Ideas

Look for patterns as you do the following problems.

For You to Explore

1. Copy and complete each table.

a.

n	$f(n)$	Σ
0	−2	■
1	3	■
2	8	■
3	13	■
4	18	■
5	23	■

b.

n	$g(n)$	Σ
0	0	■
1	2	■
2	4	■
3	6	■
4	8	■
5	10	■

c.

n	$f(n) + g(n)$	Σ
0	−2	■
1	5	■
2	■	■
3	■	■
4	■	■
5	■	■

d.

n	$2f(n)$	Σ
0	−4	■
1	6	■
2	■	■
3	■	■
4	■	■
5	■	■

e.

n	$3g(n)$	Σ
0	0	■
1	6	■
2	■	■
3	■	■
4	■	■
5	■	■

f.

n	$f(n)\ g(n)$	Σ
0	0	■
1	6	■
2	■	■
3	■	■
4	■	■
5	■	■

2. Calculate each sum.

a. $\sum_{j=1}^{5} 1$ b. $\sum_{j=1}^{5} j$ c. $\sum_{j=1}^{5} 2j$ d. $\sum_{j=1}^{5} 3j$

e. $2\sum_{j=1}^{5} j$ f. $3\sum_{j=1}^{5} j$ g. $\sum_{j=1}^{5} (j+1)$ h. $\sum_{j=1}^{5} j^2$

i. $\left(\sum_{j=1}^{5} j\right)^2$ j. $\sum_{j=6}^{10} j$ k. $\sum_{j=1}^{10} j$

Answers

For You to Explore

1. See back of book.

2. a. 5 **b.** 15 **c.** 30
d. 45 **e.** 30 **f.** 45
g. 20 **h.** 55 **i.** 225
j. 40 **k.** 55

Lesson Overview

GOAL

- Warm up to the ideas of the investigation.

Students should notice two important patterns in this lesson:

- $\Sigma(f + g) = \Sigma f + \Sigma g$
- $\Sigma cf = c\Sigma f$, for any constant c

These patterns will help students write general summation formulas in this investigation by building on the rules they already know. As always in a Getting Started lesson, there is no need to formalize these ideas today. Students meet these ideas throughout this chapter.

FOR YOU TO EXPLORE
- Core: 1, 2
- Optional: none

MATERIALS
- graphing calculators
- Blackline Master 7.5

HOMEWORK
- Core: 3, 4
- Optional: none

Launch

Have students get started right away on Problems 1 and 2 and then discuss Problem 1. Blackline Master 7.5 provides blank copies of the tables from Problem 1.

Explore

As students are working, note any conjectures that students are expressing. For example, students may develop the "factors come out" identity by looking at pairs of problems such as 2(c) and 2(e).

For You to Explore

PROBLEM 1 Your students may think about this problem from a mathematical perspective and ask questions such as, "Is the Σ column of the product of the two functions equal to the product of the Σ columns of each function on its own?" If questions like this come up in your class, highlight them in your discussion of the problem.

PROBLEM 2 provides a second opportunity to find patterns while practicing the use of Σ notation. The answer to part (c) equals the answer to part (e), and is double the answer for part (b). The answer to part (g) is the sum of the answers to parts (a) and (b). The sum of the answers to parts (b) and (j) equals the answer to part (k). This last pattern is not used as frequently as the others, but some students will find it interesting and easy to verify using the definition of Σ.

Wrap Up

Go over the For You to Explore problems and discuss any student conjectures.

Exercises

HOMEWORK
- Core: 3, 4
- Optional: none

Maintain Your Skills

EXERCISE 4 If you think about this exercise from a calculus perspective, you can see that it shows (in this discrete environment) why a constant of integration is necessary. All these functions have the same "derivative," but when you integrate, or sum, that derivative, you get a result that is off by a constant each time (except in the first case where $f(0) = 0$).

Exercises *Practicing Habits of Mind*

On Your Own

3. Tony is filling in a table like those in Problem 1.

n	q(n)	Σ
0	5	5
1	8	13
2	11	24
3	14	38
4	17	55
5	20	75

Tony says, "I can tell that $q(n)$ is linear. And I think Σ is a quadratic function of the inputs."

a. Show that $q(n)$ is a linear function.

b. Show that in this table, Σ is a quadratic function of the inputs.

c. Is it true that the Σ column in a table of any linear function is quadratic? Explain.

Maintain Your Skills

4. a. Copy and complete each table. The numbers in the Σ column are just the running totals of the outputs in the Δ column.

n	(n)	Δ	Σ
0	0	1	1
1	1	3	4
2	4	■	■
3	9	■	■
4	16	■	■
5	25		

n	g(n)	Δ	Σ
0	1	■	■
1	2	■	■
2	5	■	■
3	10	■	■
4	17	■	■
5	26		

n	h(n)	Δ	Σ
0	5	■	■
1	6	■	■
2	9	■	■
3	14	■	■
4	21	■	■
5	30		

b. What is going on here?

Answers

Exercises

3. a. $q(n) = 3n + 5$, which is linear.

b. The first differences in the Σ column are 8, 11, 14, 17, 20, so the second differences are 3, 3, 3, 3. Since the second differences of the Σ column are constant, Σ is quadratic.

c. Yes, because the differences of the function column are the second differences of the Σ column.

4. a.

n	f(n)	Δ	Σ
0	0	1	1
1	1	3	4
2	4	5	9
3	9	7	16
4	16	9	25
5	25		

n	g(n)	Δ	Σ
0	1	1	1
1	2	3	4
2	5	5	9
3	10	7	16
4	17	9	25
5	26		

n	h(n)	Δ	Σ
0	5	1	1
1	6	3	4
2	9	5	9
3	14	7	16
4	21	9	25
5	30		

b. The functions have different values at $n = 0$, but they have identical differences and so identical Σ columns.

7.6 Definite and Indefinite Sums

You have already learned at least two methods for finding certain kinds of sums. Using Gauss's method, Euclid's method, and a few new methods that you will learn in this investigation, you can solve very complicated sums.

Minds in Action **episode 33**

Sasha and Derman are working on evaluating $\sum_{i=1}^{25}(3i + 2)$.

Derman I've got this one. $5 + 8 + 11 + 14 + \cdots$

Sasha Derman, we *could* figure out the 25 numbers and add them up. But let's try arranging the terms differently instead of writing out the whole list.

Sasha starts writing on the board.

$$\sum_{i=1}^{25}(3i + 2) = (3 \cdot 1 + 2) + (3 \cdot 2 + 2) + (3 \cdot 3 + 2) + (3 \cdot 4 + 2) + \cdots + (3 \cdot 25 + 2)$$

Sasha Now rearrange the numbers, grouping all the "3 ×" terms together and all the 2's together.

$$(3 \cdot 1 + 3 \cdot 2 + 3 \cdot 3 + 3 \cdot 4 + \cdots + 3 \cdot 25) + \underbrace{2 + 2 + \cdots + 2}_{25\ 2\text{'s}}$$

Factor out a 3 from the first part of the sum.

$$3(1 + 2 + 3 + 4 + \cdots + 25) + \underbrace{2 + 2 + \cdots + 2}_{25\ 2\text{'s}}$$

Derman I get it! You have three times the sum of the integers from 1 to 25, plus 25 two's.

- The sum of the integers from 1 to 25 is $\frac{25 \cdot 26}{2}$.
- 25 two's is $25 \cdot 2$ or 50.

So, the sum is $3 \cdot \frac{25 \cdot 26}{2} + 25 \cdot 2$, which simplifies to 1025.

You can summarize Sasha's method this way.

- Collect all the terms with a common factor of 3, factor out the 3, and use Gauss's method.
- Collect all the 2's, figure out how many there will be, and multiply.

Lesson Overview

GOAL

- Find closed-form expressions for indefinite sums and use them to evaluate definite sums.

In this lesson, students learn a method that allows them to compute sums where the terms are of the form $ax + b$ by a combination of Gauss's method and Euclid's method and grouping the elements of the sum. This lesson also introduces students to indefinite sums, and defines the series associated with f as a function defined on the nonnegative integers that produces outputs equal to the "running total" of the output of f. In other words, it generates the Σ column for that function.

CHECK YOUR UNDERSTANDING
- Core: 1, 2, 3
- Optional: none

MATERIALS
- CAS (recommended)
- graphing calculators
- spreadsheet software

HOMEWORK
- Core: 4, 5, 6, 7, 8, 9, 10
- Optional: 11

VOCABULARY
- definite sum
- identity
- indefinite sum
- series associated with f

Launch

Ask students to write out the first few terms and the last few terms in the summation $\sum_{i=1}^{25}(3i + 2)$. Then continue with the Minds in Action dialog.

Explore

Example

Note that this Example relies on students knowing the formula for the sum of the first n integers, $\frac{n(n+1)}{2}$. If any students are unclear about this formula, go through the "staircase" reasoning for the sum or use Gauss's method to establish it again. Students reading this example must be able to jump from $(1 + 2 + \cdots + n)$ to $\frac{n(n+1)}{2}$, and this may not be completely clear to everyone. Point out to students that the collecting of terms here is the same collecting that Sasha did. In fact, there is nothing different in this Example except that the number 25 has been replaced by the variable n.

While CAS technology can be used here, it is good to give students the experience of building the indefinite sum by hand. Later, a CAS could be used for more complicated examples.

For You to Do

Use Sasha's method to evaluate each sum.

1. $\sum_{k=1}^{30}(3k+2)$

2. $\sum_{k=1}^{13}3^k$

3. $\sum_{k=0}^{10}(f(k)+g(k))$, where $f(n) = 5n - 1$ and $g(n) = 2n + 3$

4. $\sum_{k=0}^{12}f(k)$, where $f(n) = 5n - 1$

Write out each sum and rearrange it so that you can use the method of Gauss or the method of Euclid.

In all the problems so far, you knew where to start summing and where to stop. Sums like that are **definite sums.** Sometimes you have an **indefinite sum,** such as $\sum_{k=1}^{n}(3k+2)$, where n is a variable.

With an indefinite sum, you cannot find a number equal to the sum, but you can find a closed-form expression for it.

Example

Problem Find a closed form for $\sum_{k=1}^{n}(3k+2)$.

Solution

$$\begin{aligned}\sum_{k=1}^{n}(3k+2) &= (3\cdot 1+2)+(3\cdot 2+2)+\ldots+(3\cdot n+2)\\ &= (3\cdot 1+3\cdot 2+3\cdot 3+3\cdot 4+\cdots+3\cdot n) + \underbrace{2+2+\cdots+2}_{n\ 2\text{'s}}\\ &= 3(1+2+\ldots+n)+2n\\ &= 3\,\frac{n(n+1)}{2}+2n\\ &= \frac{3n^2+7n}{2}\end{aligned}$$

What good are indefinite sums? Well, if you can find a closed form for one, you can just plug numbers into that closed form to get values for many definite sums. For example, you know

$$\sum_{k=1}^{n}(3k+2) = \frac{3n^2+7n}{2}$$

So you can say with certainty that

$$\sum_{k=1}^{20}(3k+2) = \frac{3\cdot 20^2+7\cdot 20}{2} = 670$$

Answers

For You to Do

1. 1455

2. 2,391,483

3. 407

4. 377

You can also use indefinite sums to define new functions from old ones.

Definition

Given a function f having a domain that contains the nonnegative integers, the series associated with f is the function defined on nonnegative integers by

$$F(n) = \sum_{k=0}^{n} f(k) = f(0) + f(1) + f(2) + \cdots + f(n)$$

If you use a spreadsheet, you can make a summation column to tabulate the associated series. See the TI-Nspire Handbook, p. 778.

So, the series associated with f is a running total of the outputs of f. For example, in Exercise 3 from Lesson 7.5, the Σ column gives the outputs for the series associated with the function q.

Definition

An identity is a statement that two expressions that may seem different are actually equivalent under the basic rules of algebra.

Minds in Action episode 34

Derman is looking at his solutions to Exercise 2 in Lesson 7.5.

Derman I found that my answers to a lot of these were the same. For instance, $\sum_{j=1}^{5} 2j = 2\left(\sum_{j=1}^{5} j\right)$. I wonder if it's true for any n that $\sum_{j=1}^{n} 2j$ is the same as $2\left(\sum_{j=1}^{n} j\right)$?

Sasha You mean, you wonder if you've found an identity?

In the Check Your Understanding exercises, you will get to investigate this very question, and others like it.

Minds in Action

Students should have found several cases of matched results (see the notes for Problem 2 in Lesson 7.5). Rather than read through the dialog, have students use their matching results to suggest patterns that might be identities. Raise the question of whether these patterns are true in general, or are true only for specific cases.

Wrap Up

You may wish to split up the parts of Exercise 1 between different groups of students and then discuss the results as a class. Ask: Which of the statements are identities? How did you go about proving that a statement is or is not an identity? You may need to remind students that no number of examples showing that a statement is true is enough to prove that it is an identity, although even one example that shows the statement to be false is enough to prove that it is *not* an identity.

Assessment Resources

Lesson Quiz 7.6

1. Find a closed form for the series associated with each given function.
   a. function g, where $g(x) = 5x + 1$
   b. function f, where $f(x) = -3x + 4$

2. Find a closed form for each sum.
   a. $\left(\sum_{k=0}^{n} 5k\right) + 1$
   b. $\left(\sum_{k=0}^{n} -3k\right) + 4$

3. Find each sum.
   a. $\sum_{k=0}^{6} 8$
   b. $\sum_{k=1}^{7} 8$
   c. Find a closed form for $\sum_{k=1}^{n} 8$.
   d. Find a closed form for $\sum_{k=0}^{n-1} 8$.

Exercises

HOMEWORK
- Core: 4, 5, 6, 7, 8, 9, 10
- Optional: 11

Check Your Understanding

EXERCISE 1 Do not be too concerned if students are having trouble with this exercise right now. In the next lesson, they see the ideas here presented formally as a group of Σ identities. They will have another chance to understand how to verify them.

EXERCISE 2 With these paired exercises involving sums of the same function but with different starting and stopping points, students see the effects of changes to these parameters and develop a motivation for understanding indefinite sums.

EXERCISE 3 gives students another opportunity to notice that for $a < b < c$,

$$\sum_{j=a}^{c} f(j) = \sum_{j=a}^{b} f(j) + \sum_{j=b+1}^{c} f(j)$$

Exercises *Practicing Habits of Mind*

Check Your Understanding

1. Consider the statements below. Some of them are identities. Others are not, even though they may look as though they are true. Explore the statements and discover exactly which are identities and which are not.

In these exercises, n is some integer.

a. $\sum_{k=1}^{n} 2k \stackrel{?}{=} 2\sum_{k=1}^{n} k$

b. $\sum_{k=0}^{n} 2f(k) \stackrel{?}{=} 2\sum_{k=0}^{n} f(k)$

c. $\sum_{k=1}^{n} k^2 \stackrel{?}{=} \left(\sum_{k=1}^{n} k\right)^2$

d. $\sum_{k=0}^{n} k \stackrel{?}{=} \frac{n(n+1)}{2}$

e. $\sum_{k=1}^{n} k \stackrel{?}{=} \frac{n(n+1)}{2}$

f. $\sum_{k=0}^{n} 1 \stackrel{?}{=} n + 1$

g. $\sum_{k=1}^{n} 1 \stackrel{?}{=} n$

h. $\sum_{k=1}^{n} 1^2 \stackrel{?}{=} \left(\sum_{k=1}^{n} 1\right)^2$

i. $\sum_{k=0}^{n} g(k)f(k) \stackrel{?}{=} \left(\sum_{k=0}^{n} g(k)\right) \times \left(\sum_{k=0}^{n} f(k)\right)$

j. $\sum_{k=0}^{n} r^k \stackrel{?}{=} \frac{r^{n+1} - 1}{r - 1}$, where $r \neq 1$

k. $\sum_{k=0}^{n} (f(k) + g(k)) \stackrel{?}{=} \sum_{k=0}^{n} f(k) + \sum_{k=0}^{n} g(k)$

2. Use Sasha's method from the dialog to evaluate the two sums in each part.

a. $\sum_{k=1}^{16} (3k + 2)$, $\sum_{k=0}^{16} (3k + 2)$

b. $\sum_{k=1}^{13} 2 \cdot 3^k$, $\sum_{k=0}^{6} 2 \cdot 3^k$

c. $\sum_{k=0}^{12} (f(k) - g(k))$, $\sum_{j=5}^{12} f(j)$, where $f(n) = 5n - 1$ and $g(n) = 2n + 3$

3. Find each sum.

a. $\sum_{k=1}^{5} (2k - 1)$

b. $\sum_{k=1}^{10} (2k - 1)$

c. $\sum_{k=6}^{10} (2k - 1)$

d. Find a closed form for $\sum_{k=1}^{n} (2k - 1)$.

e. Use the closed form for $\sum_{k=1}^{n} (2k - 1)$ to calculate $\sum_{k=1}^{1000} (2k - 1)$.

Or find a closed form for the series associated with $x \mapsto 2x - 1$.

Answers

Exercises

1. a. yes **b.** yes **c.** no
d. yes **e.** yes **f.** yes
g. yes **h.** no **i.** no
j. yes **k.** yes

2. a. 440; 442
b. 4,782,966; 2186
c. 182; 332

3. a. 25
b. 100
c. 75
d. $\sum_{k=1}^{n} (2k - 1) = n^2$
e. 1,000,000

On Your Own

4. Find a closed form for the series associated with the function f, where $f(x) = 5x - 1$.
5. Use the closed form from Exercise 4 to find each sum.
   a. $\sum_{k=0}^{23} (5k - 1)$
   b. $\sum_{k=0}^{7} (5k - 1)$
6. Find a closed form for $\left(\sum_{k=0}^{n} 5k\right) - 1$.
7. Find each sum.
   a. $\sum_{k=0}^{5} 7$
   b. $\sum_{k=1}^{6} 7$
   c. Find a closed form for $\sum_{k=1}^{n} 7$.
   d. Find a closed form for $\sum_{k=0}^{n-1} 7$.
8. Suppose a and b are numbers. What is a closed form for $\sum_{k=1}^{n} (ak + b)$, in terms of a and b?
9. Find each sum.
   a. $\sum_{k=0}^{4} 9 \cdot 10^k$
   b. $\sum_{k=0}^{12} 9 \cdot 10^k$
   c. $\sum_{k=5}^{12} 9 \cdot 10^k$
   d. Find a closed form for $\sum_{k=0}^{n} 9 \cdot 10^k$.
10. **Standardized Test Prep** Which expression is a closed form for $\sum_{k=0}^{n} \left(\frac{2}{3}\right)^k$?
   A. $\dfrac{1 - \left(\frac{2}{3}\right)^{n+1}}{3}$
   B. $3\left(1 - \left(\frac{2}{3}\right)^{n+1}\right)$
   C. $3 - \left(\frac{1}{3}\right)^{n+1}$
   D. $\dfrac{\left(\frac{2}{3}\right)^{n+1} - 1}{\frac{1}{3}}$

Go Online PHSchool.com

For additional practice, go to **Web Code:** bfa-0706

If you wanted to be fancy, you might restate the question as "Find a closed form for the series associated with the affine map $\mathcal{A}_{(a,\,b)}$."

Maintain Your Skills

11. Consider the statements below. Some of them are identities. Others are not, even though they may look as though they are true. Explore the statements and discover which are identities and which are not.
   a. $\sum_{k=1}^{m} f(k) + \sum_{k=m+1}^{n} f(k) \stackrel{?}{=} \sum_{k=1}^{n} f(k)$, where $m < n$
   b. $\sum_{k=1}^{n} ck^2 \stackrel{?}{=} c\sum_{k=1}^{n} k^2$, where c is any real number
   c. $\sum_{k=1}^{n} k(k+1) \stackrel{?}{=} \sum_{k=1}^{n} k^2 + \sum_{k=1}^{n} k$
   d. $\sum_{k=1}^{n} k(k+1) \stackrel{?}{=} \left(\sum_{k=1}^{n} k\right) \times \left(\sum_{k=1}^{n} (k+1)\right)$

In these exercises, m and n are integers.

4. $\sum_{k=0}^{n} (5k - 1) = \dfrac{(n+1)(5n-2)}{2}$
5. a. 1356
   b. 132
6. $\left(\sum_{k=0}^{n} 5k\right) - 1 = 5 \cdot \dfrac{n(n+1)}{2} - 1$
7. a. 42
   b. 42
   c. $7n$
   d. $7n$
8. $\sum_{k=1}^{n} (ak + b) = \dfrac{an(n+1)}{2} + bn$
9. a. 99,999
   b. 9,999,999,999,999
   c. 9,999,999,900,000
   d. $\sum_{k=0}^{n} 9 \cdot 10^k = 10^{n+1} - 1$
10. B
11. a. yes
    b. yes
    c. yes
    d. no

On Your Own

EXERCISE 5 Notice that the indices start at $k = 0$. Some students will have built a closed form for the series starting with $k = 1$. This will cause their answers to be 1 greater than the correct answers for each part.

EXERCISE 6 Ask students why this question is not identical to the one in Exercise 4 and specifically how the -1 affects the answer.

EXERCISE 8 This is the generalization of the preceding exercises. If students have trouble, ask them to use specific numbers for any or all of a, b, and n.

EXERCISE 9 Encourage students to look for a relationship between the answers in this exercise and the starting and stopping points for the index in each sum.

Additional Resources

PRINT RESOURCES	TECHNOLOGY
• Solution Manual	• Interactive Textbook
• Practice Workbook	• TeacherExpress CD-ROM
• Assessment Resources	• ExamView CD-ROM
• Teaching Resources	• PHSchool.com

Additional Practice

1. Find a closed form for the series associated with the function g, where $g(x) = 3x - 2$.
2. Use the closed form from Exercise 1 to find each sum.
   a. $\sum_{k=0}^{21} (3k - 2)$
   b. $\sum_{k=0}^{9} (3k - 2)$
3. Find a closed form for the series associated with the function f, where $f(x) = -2x + 1$.
4. Use the closed form from Exercise 3 to find each sum.
   a. $\sum_{k=0}^{21} (-2k + 1)$
   b. $\sum_{k=0}^{9} (-2k + 1)$
5. Find a closed form for each sum.
   a. $\left(\sum_{k=0}^{n} 3k\right) - 2$
   b. $\left(\sum_{k=0}^{n} -2k\right) + 1$
6. Find each sum.
   a. $\sum_{k=0}^{7} 5$
   b. $\sum_{k=1}^{8} 5$
   c. Find a closed form for $\sum_{k=1}^{n} 5$.
   d. Find a closed form for $\sum_{k=0}^{n-1} 5$.
7. Suppose a and b are numbers. What is a closed form for $\sum_{k=1}^{n} k(a + b)$, in terms of a and b?
8. Find each sum.
   a. $\sum_{k=0}^{5} 3 \cdot 5^k$
   b. $\sum_{k=0}^{14} 3 \cdot 5^k$
   c. $\sum_{k=6}^{14} 3 \cdot 5^k$
   d. Find a closed form for $\sum_{k=0}^{a} 3 \cdot 5^k$.

Practice: For Lesson 7.6, assign Exercises 1–8.

Lesson Overview

GOAL

- Develop a list of $\sum$ identities and recognize situations in which you can apply them.

This lesson begins with a theorem listing various $\sum$ identities that students will use to find more complicated sums. They see the techniques they used in the preceding lesson more formally expressed as identities. They also apply Bernoulli's formulas for the sums of powers to both definite and indefinite sums.

CHECK YOUR UNDERSTANDING
- Core: 1, 2, 3
- Optional: none

MATERIALS
- CAS (recommended)
- graphing calculators
- spreadsheet software
- Blackline Masters 7.7A, 7.7B

HOMEWORK
- Core: 4, 5, 6a, 7, 9, 10, 11, 13, 14
- Optional: 8a, 12, 15
- Extension: 6b, 8b

VOCABULARY
- Bernoulli's formulas

Launch

Begin this lesson by going over the list of identities in Theorem 7.1. Note any of these that students in your class have already discovered for themselves. You may wish to use Blackline Master 7.7A here.

7.7 $\sum$ Identities

Take stock of what you have done so far. There are several $\sum$ identities that are so useful that you can list them in a theorem and refer to them by name. You have seen most of these in Exercise 1 of Lesson 7.6. And, as you go on, you will add to this list.

Theorem 7.1

The following are identities.

- **Factors come out.**

$$\sum_{k=0}^{n} cf(k) = c \times \sum_{k=0}^{n} f(k), \text{ where } c \text{ is any real number}$$

- **The sigma of a sum is the sum of the sigmas.**

$$\sum_{k=0}^{n} (f(k) + g(k)) = \sum_{k=0}^{n} f(k) + \sum_{k=0}^{n} g(k)$$

- **Splitting up a sum**

$$\sum_{k=0}^{n} f(k) = \sum_{k=0}^{m} f(k) + \sum_{k=m+1}^{n} f(k), \text{ where } 0 < m < n$$

- **Add a bunch of ones.**

$$\sum_{k=0}^{n} 1 = n + 1 \text{ or } \sum_{k=1}^{n} 1 = n$$

- **Think Gauss.**

$$\sum_{k=0}^{n} k = \frac{n(n+1)}{2}$$

- **Think Euclid.**

$$\sum_{k=0}^{n} r^k = \frac{r^{n+1} - 1}{r - 1}$$

Habits of Mind

Detect the key characteristics. You can use the first two identities together under the name *linearity*.

It is a good idea to put these identities on a poster or in your notes.

For Discussion

1. Why are the "add a bunch of ones" identities different depending on whether the summation starts at $k = 0$ or $k = 1$?
2. How does a change of starting point from $k = 0$ to $k = 1$ affect the identities listed above as "Think Gauss" and "Think Euclid"?

Answers

For Discussion

1. Answers may vary. Sample: There are $k + 1$ values from 0 to k, but only k values from 1 to k.
2. There is no change to "Think Gauss" because $\sum_{k=0}^{0} k = \frac{n(n+1)}{2} = 0$. There is a change to "Think Euclid" because $\sum_{k=0}^{0} r^k = \frac{r-1}{r-1} = 1$.

Example

Problem Evaluate $\sum_{k=0}^{8} (3k + 2)$.

Solution You can calculate it this way.

$$\sum_{k=0}^{8} (3k + 2) = \sum_{k=0}^{8} 3k + \sum_{k=0}^{8} 2 \text{ (The sigma of a sum is the sum of the sigmas.)}$$

$$= 3\sum_{k=0}^{8} k + 2\sum_{k=0}^{8} 1 \text{ (Factors come out.)}$$

$$= 3\frac{8 \cdot (8 + 1)}{2} + 2 \cdot (8 + 1) \text{ (Gauss and add a bunch of ones.)}$$

$$= 108 + 18 = 126$$

Problem Find a closed form for $\sum_{k=0}^{n} (3k + 2)$.

Solution

$$\sum_{k=0}^{n} (3k + 2) = \sum_{k=0}^{n} 3k + \sum_{k=0}^{n} 2 \text{ (The sigma of a sum is the sum of the sigmas.)}$$

$$= 3\sum_{k=0}^{n} k + 2\sum_{k=0}^{n} 1 \text{ (Factors come out.)}$$

$$= 3\frac{n(n + 1)}{2} + 2(n + 1) \text{ (Gauss and add a bunch of ones.)}$$

This is an example of an indefinite sum.

The last expression in the solution above is a fine way to represent the closed form for the sum. If you want, however, you can transform it even more.

$$\sum_{k=0}^{n} (3k + 2) = 3\frac{n(n + 1)}{2} + 2(n + 1)$$

$$= \frac{3n(n + 1) + 4(n + 1)}{2}$$

$$= \frac{(n + 1)(3n + 4)}{2}$$

Notice that if you substitute $n = 8$ in this formula, you get 126. This agrees with the earlier result. And, you can use this formula for the indefinite sum to do other definite sums, such as the following.

$$\sum_{k=0}^{205} (3k + 2) = \frac{(205 + 1)(3 \cdot 205 + 4)}{2} = 63{,}757$$

Habits of Mind

Use a different process to get the same answer. Your CAS can evaluate finite and indefinite sums. See the TI-Nspire Handbook on p. 778. But it is important to know how to use the sigma identities to break down complicated sums into simpler ones. Besides, why should the calculator have all the fun?

For You to Do

Evaluate each sum.

3. $\sum_{k=1}^{30} (3k - 2)$

4. $\sum_{k=1}^{n} (6k - 4)$, in terms of n

Explore

Example

Encourage students to use methods as similar as possible on the two problems in the Example. If they can evaluate the sum in the first problem, they should be ready for the generalization in the second problem just by replacing 8 with n. Point out to students that in either case, the summation rule for the first n integers is what drives this.

For You to Do

3. 1335

4. $3n^2 - n$

BERNOULLI'S FORMULAS You might ask students to find the degree and leading coefficient of each of Bernoulli's formulas. Students may have noticed earlier that the sum of the first n integers was quadratic, but they will notice a clear pattern when they see that the sum of the first n squares is cubic, and the sum of the first n cubes is quartic. You may wish to use Blackline Master 7.7B here.

With a strong class, you might pause to revisit the method of Lagrange interpolation, which could be used here to establish these formulas once enough data is known. For example, the sum of the first n squares includes (0, 0), (1, 1), (2, 5), and (3, 14). With this information, plus the knowledge that the result is a cubic, it is possible to derive the formula given in this development.

Jakob Bernoulli (1654–1705) was a member of a remarkable Swiss family that produced many mathematicians and scientists. Jakob studied the formulas for the sums of powers. These sums are the series associated with the functions $x \mapsto x^m$ for positive integers m. Johan Faulhaber published them in his 1631 work *Academia Algebrae.*

Jakob Bernoulli

These sums are

$$\sum_{k=0}^{n} k = 0 + 1 + 2 + 3 + \cdots + n$$
$$\sum_{k=0}^{n} k^2 = 0^2 + 1^2 + 2^2 + 3^2 + \cdots + n^2$$
$$\sum_{k=0}^{n} k^3 = 0^3 + 1^3 + 2^3 + 3^3 + \cdots + n^3$$
$$\sum_{k=0}^{n} k^4 = 0^4 + 1^4 + 2^4 + 3^4 + \cdots + n^4$$
$$\vdots$$
$$\sum_{k=0}^{n} k^m = 0^m + 1^m + 2^m + 3^m + \cdots + n^m$$

You have seen a closed form for the first sum. Bernoulli studied all such sums. His definitive results were published in his book *Ars Conjectandi* in 1713, after his death. The coefficients in these formulas are related to an important sequence called the Bernoulli numbers. This book calls these formulas **Bernoulli's formulas** in his honor. Here are just the first few of the formulas Bernoulli gave.

$$\sum_{k=0}^{n} k = \frac{n(n+1)}{2}$$
$$\sum_{k=0}^{n} k^2 = \frac{n(n+1)(2n+1)}{6}$$
$$\sum_{k=0}^{n} k^3 = \frac{n^2(n+1)^2}{4}$$
$$\sum_{k=0}^{n} k^4 = \frac{n(n+1)(2n+1)(3n^2+3n-1)}{30}$$
$$\sum_{k=0}^{n} k^5 = \frac{n^2(n+1)^2(2n^2+2n-1)}{12}$$

It is useful to add these formulas to your list of Σ identities.

Bernoulli liked to brag that he could find the sum of the tenth powers of the first thousand numbers in less than 10 minutes. He would have been amazed at how his methods have continued to evolve over the last 300 years. A calculator uses Bernoulli's formulas and can find the sum of the first thousand tenth powers in seconds.

$$\sum_{k=0}^{1000} k^{10} = 91{,}409{,}924{,}241{,}424{,}243{,}424{,}241{,}924{,}242{,}500$$

None of this would have been possible without the work of mathematicians such as Bernoulli.

For You to Do

Use Bernoulli's formulas to evaluate each sum.

5. $\sum_{j=1}^{45}(4j+3)$

6. $\sum_{k=0}^{100}(2k^2+1)$

Find a formula for each series.

7. $\sum_{j=1}^{n}(4j+3)$

8. $\sum_{j=0}^{n}(4j+3)$

Exercises *Practicing Habits of Mind*

Check Your Understanding

1. Evaluate $\sum_{k=1}^{50}5(k+1)$.

2. Evaluate each sum using the method in the example.

a. $\sum_{k=0}^{16}(3k-2)$ **b.** $\sum_{k=0}^{13}\left(\frac{1}{2}\right)^k$ **c.** $\sum_{k=1}^{13}\left(\frac{1}{2}\right)^k$

3. Suppose $f(n)=5n-1$ and $g(n)=2n+3$. Evaluate each sum.

a. $\sum_{k=0}^{12}f(k)$ **b.** $\sum_{k=0}^{12}(f(k)+g(k))$

c. $\sum_{k=0}^{12}(3f(k)+g(k))$ **d.** $\sum_{j=5}^{12}f(j)$

Answers

For You to Do

5. 4275

6. 676,801

7. $\sum_{j=1}^{n}(4j+3)=4\cdot\frac{n(n+1)}{2}+3n$

8. $\sum_{j=0}^{n}(4j+3)=$ $4\cdot\frac{n(n+1)}{2}+3(n+1)$

Exercises

1. 6625

2. a. 374
b. 1.99988
c. 0.99988

3. a. 377
b. 572
c. 1326
d. 332

Wrap Up

As time allows, go over some of the Check Your Understanding core exercises. Parts (a) and (b) of Exercise 2 might be a good place to start, because they will allow you to make sure students understand how to sum polynomial expressions and exponential expressions.

Assessment Resources

Lesson Quiz 7.7

1. Use the Σ identities to evaluate each sum.

a. $\sum_{k=1}^{7}(3k-4)$ **b.** $\sum_{k=1}^{n}(3k-4)$

c. $\sum_{k=0}^{6}(2^k-1)$ **d.** $\sum_{k=0}^{n}(2^k-1)$

2. Use Bernoulli's formulas to evaluate each sum.

a. $\sum_{k=1}^{40}2k(k+3)(k-1)$ **b.** $\sum_{k=1}^{100}(5k^2+k-4)$

3. Find a formula for each indefinite sum.

a. $\sum_{k=1}^{n}k(k+2)(k-1)$ **b.** $\sum_{k=1}^{n}(k+2)(k+3)$

Exercises

HOMEWORK

- Core: 4, 5, 6a, 7, 9, 10, 11, 13, 14
- Optional: 8a, 12, 15
- Extension: 6b, 8b

Check Your Understanding

EXERCISE 1 Check for students writing the 5 directly outside right away. These students are doing something more thoughtful than just expanding the expression to get $5k+5$. Some students will do this exercise by Gauss's method, writing out the terms. This is fine, but make sure to demonstrate the solution method that uses the formula for the sum of the first n integers.

EXERCISE 3 Point out to students that they can evaluate the sum for $f(k)$ and $g(k)$, and then use the results for parts (b) and (c). For part (d), note that the sum from 5 to 12 is the sum from 0 to 12 minus the sum from 0 to 5.

On Your Own

EXERCISE 5 In part (c) and again in Exercise 7c, a simple way to find the sum is to change the variable and the index. You can rewrite $\sum_{k=1}^{11} f(k-1)$ as $\sum_{j=0}^{10} f(j)$ and the sum becomes one you have already found. If students do not see how to do this on their own, you may want to demonstrate this useful technique.

EXERCISE 6 You can also use the idea of a difference table for $t(n)$ to find $g(n)$, but to do this, you would need to realize that if $t(n)$ is the running total, then the differences between successive terms for $t(n)$ give you $f(n)$. The Δ column in the table below matches $g(n) = 2n - 2$, which gives you the correct function. The trick is, that if you then make a running total for Δ, you do not get $t(n)$!

n	$t(n) = n^2 - 3n$	Δ	Σ
0	0	−2	−2
1	−2	0	−2
2	−2	2	0
3	0	4	4
4	4	6	10
5	10	8	18

As you can see in the table, when you record the running total of the differences of the running total, you get $t(n+1)$. This complexity is likely to throw students for a loop, so you may want to guide them to work backwards as in the solution for this exercise and for Exercise 8.

EXERCISE 7 You might choose to assign only parts (a) and (c) here. Parts (a) and (c) are one example of how the same sum can be written in more than one way, depending on the reference of the variable. In both cases the sum is $g(0) + g(1) + \cdots + g(10)$. Part (b) is difficult without recognizing that the sum from 5 to 10 is the sum from 0 to 10 minus the sum from 0 to 4.

On Your Own

Go Online PHSchool.com

For additional practice, go to **Web Code:** bfa-0707

4. Use the Σ identities in Theorem 7.1 to evaluate each sum.

a. $\sum_{j=1}^{12} (5j - 1)$ **b.** $\sum_{j=7}^{12} (5j - 1)$ **c.** $\sum_{j=1}^{n} (5j - 1)$

d. $\sum_{j=0}^{7} 2^j$ **e.** $\sum_{j=0}^{7} 3 \cdot 2^j$ **f.** $\sum_{j=0}^{n} 3 \cdot 2^j$

Suppose you have a mystery function f, and all you know is a formula for its associated series.

$$\sum_{k=0}^{n} f(k) = n^2 - 3n$$

5. Find each sum.

a. $\sum_{k=0}^{10} f(k)$ **b.** $\sum_{k=5}^{10} f(k)$ **c.** $\sum_{k=1}^{11} f(k-1)$ **d.** $\sum_{k=0}^{10} (3f(k) + 5^k)$

6. a. Find a polynomial g that agrees with f for all integers $n > 0$.

b. Take It Further Is there more than one polynomial g that works? Explain.

Suppose you have a mystery function g, and all you know is a formula for this indefinite sum.

$$\sum_{k=0}^{n} g(k) = 2n^2 - 5n$$

7. Find each sum.

a. $\sum_{k=0}^{10} g(k)$ **b.** $\sum_{k=5}^{10} g(k)$

c. $\sum_{k=1}^{11} g(k-1)$ **d.** $\sum_{k=0}^{10} (3g(k) + 7^k)$

8. a. Find a polynomial h that agrees with g for all integers $n > 0$.

b. Take It Further Is there more than one polynomial h that works? Explain.

9. What is the sum of all the multiples of 3 that are greater than 1 and less than 1000?

10. Use Bernoulli's formulas to evaluate each sum.

a. $\sum_{k=1}^{30} k(k+1)(k+2)$ **b.** $\sum_{k=1}^{100} (3k^2 + 5k - 7)$

Answers

4. a. 378 **b.** 279

c. $\frac{5n^2 + 3n}{2}$ **d.** 255

e. 765 **f.** $3(2^{n+1} - 1)$

5. a. 70 **b.** 66

c. 70 **d.** 12,207,241

6. a. $g(n) = 2n - 4$

b. No; there is only one polynomial g because it has to agree with *all* the outputs for $n > 0$, not just a finite number of outputs.

7. a. 150

b. 138

c. 150

d. 329,554,907

8. a. $g(n) = 4n - 7$

b. No; there is only one polynomial g because it has to agree with *all* the outputs for $n > 0$, not just a finite number of outputs.

9. 166,833

10. a. 245,520

b. 1,039,600

11. Find a formula for each indefinite sum.

a. $\sum_{k=0}^{n} k(k+1)$ b. $\sum_{k=0}^{n} k(k+1)(k+2)$

c. $\sum_{k=0}^{n} k(k+1)(k+2)(k+3)$

12. Evaluate each definite sum.

a. $\sum_{j=12}^{45} (4j+3)$ b. $5 + 9 + 13 + 17 + 21 + \cdots + 201$

c. $\sum_{k=1}^{36} k(k+1)$ d. $1 - 2 + 3 - 4 + 5 - \cdots - 1000$

e. $1 - 2 + 4 - 8 + 16 - \cdots + 1024$

13. Use Bernoulli's formulas to evaluate each sum.

a. $\sum_{k=1}^{5} 2k^3$ b. $\sum_{k=1}^{30} (k-1)^3$ c. $\sum_{k=1}^{30} (k+1)^3$ d. $\sum_{k=7}^{30} (k+2)^3$

14. **Standardized Test Prep** Which of the following closed-form formulas can you use to find the sum of all perfect squares less than or equal to 100?

A. $\dfrac{n(n-1)^2}{2}$ B. $\dfrac{10^3\left(1 - \left(\frac{1}{10}\right)^{n+1}\right)}{3}$

C. $\dfrac{n(n+1)(2n+1)}{6}$ D. $\dfrac{n^2(n+1)^2}{4}$

Maintain Your Skills

15. a. Copy and complete each table. The numbers in the Σ column are just the running totals of the outputs in the Δ column.

n	$f(n)$	Δ	Σ
0	0	2	2
1	2	4	6
2	6	■	■
3	12	■	■
4	20	■	■
5	30		

n	$g(n)$	Δ	Σ
0	1	■	■
1	3	■	■
2	7	■	■
3	13	■	■
4	21	■	■
5	31		

n	$h(n)$	Δ	Σ
0	5	■	■
1	7	■	■
2	11	■	■
3	17	■	■
4	25	■	■
5	35		

b. What is going on here?

11. a. $\dfrac{n(n+1)(n+2)}{3}$

b. $\dfrac{n(n+1)(n+2)(n+3)}{4}$

c. $\dfrac{n(n+1)(n+2)(n+3)(n+4)}{5}$

12. a. 3978

b. 5150

c. 16,872

d. −500

e. 683

13. a. 450

b. 189,225

c. 246,015

d. 277,488

14. C

15. a. See back of book.

b. The functions have different values at $n = 0$, but they have identical differences and so identical Σ columns.

EXERCISE 11 is a good exercise for students to use their CAS to reduce some of the computational overload. To evaluate an indefinite sum on a CAS, just input a variable for the stopping point of the index. (See the TI-Nspire Handbook on p. 778 for more details.)

EXERCISE 13 One technique for finding these sums is changing the variables and indices. For example, $\sum_{k=1}^{30} (k-1)^3$ can be rewritten as $\sum_{j=0}^{29} (j)^3$. This is a strategy that you may wish to demonstrate for your class.

Maintain Your Skills

EXERCISE 15 is similar to Exercise 4 from Lesson 7.5. If you discussed that exercise in class, you can use this exercise to assess student understanding of the discussion.

Additional Resources

PRINT RESOURCES
- Solution Manual
- Practice Workbook
- Assessment Resources
- Teaching Resources

TECHNOLOGY
- Interactive Textbook
- TeacherExpress CD-ROM
- ExamView CD-ROM
- PHSchool.com

Additional Practice

1. Use the Σ identities to evaluate each sum.

a. $\sum_{k=1}^{9} (4k-3)$ b. $\sum_{k=5}^{9} (4k-3)$ c. $\sum_{k=1}^{n} (4k-3)$

d. $\sum_{k=0}^{6} 3^k$ e. $\sum_{k=0}^{6} 2 \cdot 3^k$ f. $\sum_{k=0}^{n} 2 \cdot 3^k$

For Exercises 2–4, suppose you have a mystery function s, and all you know is a formula for its associated series.

$$\sum_{k=0}^{n} s(k) = 3n^2 - 2n$$

2. Find each sum.

a. $\sum_{k=0}^{10} s(k)$ b. $\sum_{k=1}^{10} s(k)$ c. $\sum_{k=1}^{5} s(k-1)$ d. $\sum_{k=0}^{10} (2s(k) + 3^k)$

3. Find a polynomial r that agrees with s for all integers $n > 0$.

4. Is there more than one polynomial r that works? Explain.

5. What is the sum of all the multiples of 6 that are greater than 1 and less than 1000?

6. Use this recursive definition of the function f.

$$f(n) = \begin{cases} 16 & \text{if } n = 0 \\ f(n-1) + 3n - 2 & \text{if } n > 0 \end{cases}$$

Find a closed-form definition for a function F that agrees with f.

7. Use the table at the right for a function t.

a. Complete the Δ column. Use it to find a recursive formula for $t(n)$.

b. Find a closed-form definition for a function T that agrees with your function t.

n	$t(n)$	Δ
0	6	
1	7	
2	10	
3	15	

8. Use this recursive definition of the function r.

$$r(n) = \begin{cases} 1 & \text{if } n = 0 \\ r(n-1) + 3^n & \text{if } n > 0 \end{cases}$$

a. Express $r(n)$ as a sum of powers of 3.

b. Find a closed-form definition for a function R that agrees with r.

Practice: For Lesson 7.7, assign Exercises 1–5.

Lesson Overview

GOAL

- Find closed-form expressions for the series associated with a function.

In this lesson, students use the difference tables from Chapter 1 to find a recursive definition for a function, and then use the summation techniques they have learned to convert this recursive definition into a closed-form definition.

CHECK YOUR UNDERSTANDING
- Core: 1, 2, 3
- Optional: none

MATERIALS
- graphing calculators
- Blackline Master 7.8

HOMEWORK
- Core: 4, 5, 6, 7, 8, 9
- Optional: 10, 11, 12, 13

VOCABULARY
- figurate number

Launch

You might begin this lesson by writing the table for $g(n)$ on the board and asking students to construct a difference table for the function and find a recursive definition that agrees with the table. Use this activity as an opportunity to assess how much review of these Chapter 1 techniques your students need. Then go over the solution given in the text.

7.8 Tables and Figurate Numbers

In Chapter 1, you looked at tables like this one.

n	$g(n)$
0	7
1	8
2	10
3	13

Remember...

In Chapter 2, you studied Lagrange Interpolation, a method for fitting a function to any table. This lesson develops another method.

Your goal was to find a function that agreed with the table. Finding a closed-form function that agrees with a table is not always easy. But sometimes it is fairly easy to find a recursively defined function. For example, you can add a Δ column.

As you saw in Chapter 2, there are many functions (even polynomial functions) that agree with this table.

n	$g(n)$	Δ
0	7	1
1	8	2
2	10	3
3	13	

This leads to a function g, defined on positive integers, that agrees with the table above.

$$g(n) = \begin{cases} 7 & \text{if } n = 0 \\ g(n-1) + n & \text{if } n > 0 \end{cases}$$

You can sometimes use the ideas in this investigation to find a closed form for recursively defined functions. You can call this method *unstacking*.

You can "unstack" the nesting dolls until you reach the smallest doll.

Example

Problem Find a closed-form definition for a function G, defined on all of $\mathbb{R}$, that agrees with g.

Solution

Step 1 Calculate $g(5)$ the way a computer would.

$$g(5) = g(4) + 5 \quad \text{but } g(4) = g(3) + 4 \quad \text{so}$$

$$\begin{aligned} &= g(3) + 4 + 5 \\ &= g(2) + 3 + 4 + 5 \\ &= g(1) + 2 + 3 + 4 + 5 \\ &= g(0) + 1 + 2 + 3 + 4 + 5 \\ &= 7 + 1 + 2 + 3 + 4 + 5 \end{aligned}$$

So $g(5) = 7 + 1 + 2 + 3 + 4 + 5$.

Step 2 Now, write $g(6)$ and $g(7)$ in the same form, just to get in the rhythm of the calculation.

Step 3 So, you can also write $g(n)$ using Σ notation.

$$g(n) = 7 + 1 + 2 + 3 + \cdots + n = 7 + \sum_{k=1}^{n} k$$

Step 4 Use Gauss's method to write $\sum_{k=1}^{n} k$ in a closed form.

Step 5 Now you can write a closed form for $G(n)$.

Habits of Mind

Make a connection. This is just the hockey stick property of difference tables from Chapter 1.

For You to Do

1. Complete the missing calculations in the Example above.

Answers

For You to Do

1. Step 2:
$g(6) = 7 + 1 + 2 + 3 + 4 + 5 + 6$;
$g(7) = 7 + 1 + 2 + 3 + 4 + 5 + 6 + 7$

Step 4: $\sum_{k=1}^{n} k = \frac{k(k+1)}{2}$

Step 5: $G(n) = 7 + \frac{n(n+1)}{2} = \frac{n(n+1)+14}{2} = \frac{n^2}{2} + \frac{n}{2} + 7$

Explore

Example

Take students through all the steps, and be sure they understand the rhythm of the calculation (Step 2) before generalizing. You might ask them to write out the calculation of $g(8)$. Once the closed-form rule for $G(n)$ is found, test it with the values found so far, and then have students determine $G(100)$ or some other value that would have been difficult to calculate without the closed form.

The For Discussion section on the next page is a step up, so consider first working through another example, such as $h(n) = h(n-1) + 2n + 5$ with $h(0) = 1$. See if students recognize that the summation involves the expression in the recursive rule (here, it would be the sum of $2k + 5$). The step up to an example involving the sum of squares can stop some students, so try to point out that the next For Discussion section uses the same process, just with an additional formula applied for the sum of squares.

FIGURATE NUMBERS There may be some confusion about how to form a diagram for a pentagonal or hexagonal number. If you start by extending the two sides from the lower left corner, students should recognize what to do. Also, point out that each side of the nth pentagon has n dots. You may wish to use Blackline Master 7.8 here.

This is not a very important topic, just an example of a recursive rule in action, so you could consider skipping it or keeping the focus on triangular or square numbers. If you choose to not cover this section in class, you might assign it as reading if you intend to assign Exercises 10 and 11.

Wrap Up

If time allows go over the Check Your Understanding core exercises. Ask students to generate a recursive rule such as the ones seen in Exercises 1–4. Then bounce the rule back to the class to see if they can find a closed-form function to match the recursive rule.

Assessment Resources

Lesson Quiz 7.8

1. Use this recursive definition of the function f.

$$f(n) = \begin{cases} 6 & \text{if } n = 0 \\ f(n-1) + 2n - 1 & \text{if } n > 0 \end{cases}$$

Find a closed-form definition for a function F that agrees with f.

2. Use the table at the right for a function t.
   a. Fill in the Δ column. Use it to find a recursive formula for $t(n)$.
   b. Find a closed-form definition for a function T that agrees with your function t.

n	$t(n)$	Δ
0	20	
1	19	
2	15	
3	6	

3. Use this recursive definition of the function r.

$$r(n) = \begin{cases} 10 & \text{if } n = 0 \\ r(n-1) + 2^n & \text{if } n > 0 \end{cases}$$

   a. Express $r(n)$ as a sum of powers of 2.
   b. Find a closed-form definition for a function R that agrees with r.

For Discussion

Tony is looking for a closed-form function $F(n)$ that agrees with the function $f(n)$ below.

$$f(n) = \begin{cases} 3 & \text{if } n = 0 \\ f(n-1) + 6n^2 + 2n + 5 & \text{if } n > 0 \end{cases}$$

Tony says, "After I unstacked $f(n)$, I ended up with

$$F(n) = 3 + 6\sum_{k=1}^{n} k^2 + 2\sum_{k=1}^{n} k + 5\sum_{k=1}^{n} 1."$$

Sasha circles the coefficients and draws some arrows.

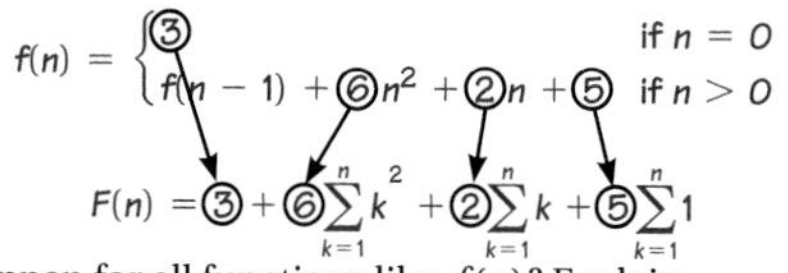

2. Does this happen for all functions like $f(n)$? Explain.
3. Find a closed form for f.

Figurate Numbers

Since the time of the Pythagoreans, around 500 B.C., people have classified numbers according to geometric shapes. The diagrams below show examples of **figurate numbers.** The triangular numbers are the numbers of dots needed to make up the equilateral triangles shown below.

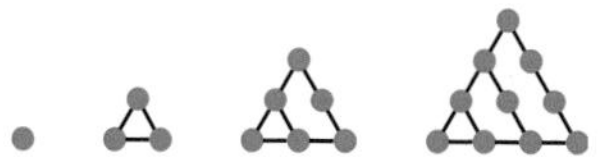

The square numbers are the numbers of dots needed to make up the squares shown below.

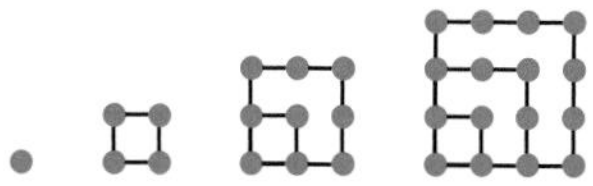

And there are pentagonal numbers, hexagonal numbers, and so on.

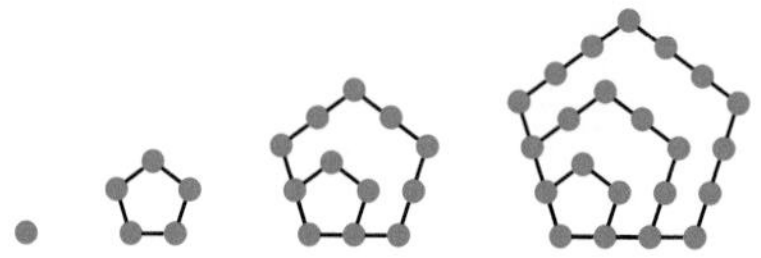

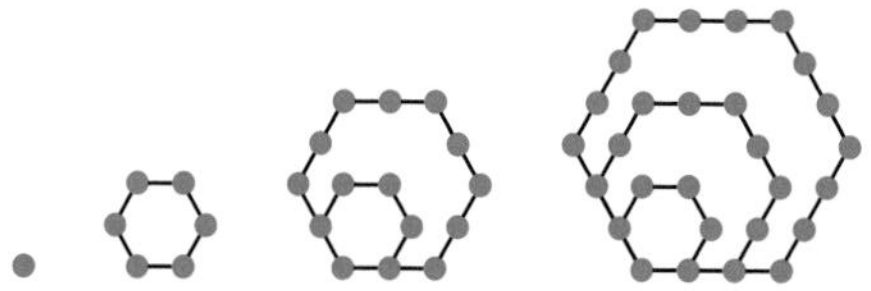

Go Online PHSchool.com

For more information about figurative numbers, go to **Web Code:** bfe-9031

Answers

For Discussion

2. Yes; if the second line of a recursive definition is the previous value plus a polynomial function of n, then a closed-form function is the value for $n = 0$ plus the "unstacked" form of the polynomial.
3. $f(n) = 2n^3 + 4n^2 + 7n + 3$

For You to Do

You can use the recursive definition below to find the nth triangular number.

$$t(n) = \begin{cases} 1 & \text{if } n = 1 \\ t(n-1) + n & \text{if } n > 1 \end{cases}$$

4. Verify that this recursive formula is correct for the diagrams above.

5. Find a closed form for the triangular numbers.

Exercises *Practicing Habits of Mind*

Check Your Understanding

In these exercises, *a closed-form definition for a function* means a closed-form definition for a function defined on all of $\mathbb{R}$. Also, *a closed-form definition for a function H that agrees with h* means a closed-form definition for a function H that agrees with h for all nonnegative integers.

1. Use the recursive definition for the function h below.

$$h(n) = \begin{cases} 3 & \text{if } n = 0 \\ h(n-1) + n & \text{if } n > 0 \end{cases}$$

Find a closed-form definition for a function H that agrees with h.

2. This table shows values of a function q.

n	$q(n)$	Δ
0	32	■
1	34	■
2	38	■
3	44	

a. Find a recursively defined formula for $q(n)$ that agrees with the table.

b. Find a closed-form definition for a function Q that agrees with your function from part (a).

3. Find a closed form for this recursive definition.

$$s(n) = \begin{cases} 1 & \text{if } n = 1 \\ s(n-1) + (2n-1) & \text{if } n > 1 \end{cases}$$

For You to Do

4. $t(1) = 1$, $t(2) = 3$, $t(3) = 6$, $t(4) = 10$; these values agree with the four triangular numbers shown.

5. $t(n) = \frac{n(n+1)}{2}$

Exercises

1. $H(n) = \frac{n^2 + n + 6}{2}$

2. a. $q(n) = \begin{cases} 3 & \text{if } n = 0 \\ q(n-1) + 2n & \text{if } n > 0 \end{cases}$

b. $Q(n) = n(n + 1) + 32$

3. $S(n) = n^2$

Exercises

HOMEWORK
- Core: 4, 5, 6, 7, 8, 9
- Optional: 10, 11, 12, 13

Check Your Understanding

EXERCISE 1 This exercise parallels the Example very closely, since only the constant term has changed. If students get stuck, ask them to follow each of the steps in the Example and see how they do.

EXERCISE 3 is a nice proof of the fact that the sum of the first n odd numbers is equal to n^2. There are also many visual proofs of this fact. For example, the diagram below that shows that $1 + 3 + 5 + 7 + 9 + 11 = 36$.

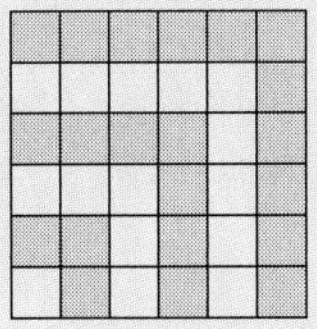

Assign Exercise 3 if you plan on also assigning Exercise 4.

On Your Own

EXERCISE 4 If you assign this exercise, make sure that you assigned Exercise 3.

EXERCISE 5 Some students will get stuck here trying to decide whether the summing term is n^2 or $(n+1)^2$. Encourage them to try an example; since $s(1) = s(0) + 1$, whatever rule they use has to give 1 when $s = 1$. This should help students to get $s(n) = s(n-1) + n^2$. As a challenge to advanced students, you could ask them to find more than one recursive rule that generates the table, then the closed-form rule for each.

EXERCISE 7 uses the hockey stick property of difference tables. Keep an eye out for students who can calculate $g(5)$ without calculating $g(4)$. As with the other exercises, some students may be stumped by whether it should be $g(n) = g(n-1) + (n+4)$ or $g(n) = g(n-1) + (n+5)$. The sample value $g(1) = 17$ should help them.

On Your Own

Go Online PHSchool.com

For additional practice, go to **Web Code:** bfa-0708

4. Use this recursive definition of the function m.

$$m(n) = \begin{cases} 28 & \text{if } n = 0 \\ m(n-1) + 2n - 1 & \text{if } n > 0 \end{cases}$$

Find a closed-form definition for a function M that agrees with the function m.

5. Copy this table for a function s.

n	$s(n)$	Δ
0	7	■
1	8	■
2	12	■
3	21	

a. Complete the Δ column. Use it to find a recursive formula for $s(n)$.

b. Find a closed-form definition for a function S that agrees with your function s.

6. Use this recursive definition of a function t.

$$t(n) = \begin{cases} 1 & \text{if } n = 0 \\ t(n-1) + 2^n & \text{if } n > 0 \end{cases}$$

a. Express $t(n)$ as a sum of powers of 2.

b. Find a closed-form definition for a function T that agrees with t.

7. This table for some function g has a Δ column. Nina spilled ink over most of the $g(n)$ column.

n	$g(n)$	Δ
1	12	5
2		6
3		7
4		8
5		

a. What is $g(5)$?

b. How did you find it?

c. Find a recursive formula for $g(n)$.

d. Find a closed-form definition for a function G that agrees with g.

Answers

4. $M(n) = n^2 + 28$

5. a.

n	$s(n)$	Δ
0	7	1
1	8	4
2	12	9
3	21	

$$s(n) = \begin{cases} 7 & \text{if } n = 0 \\ s(n-1) + n^2 & \text{if } n > 0 \end{cases}$$

b. $S(n) = \frac{n(n+1)(2n+1)}{6} + 7$ or

$S(n) = \frac{2n^3 + 3n^2 + n + 42}{6}$

6. a. $t(n) = \sum_{k=0}^{n} 2^k$

b. $T(n) = 2^{n+1} - 1$

7. a. 38

b. Answers may vary. Sample: $g(5) = g(1)$ plus the sum of the differences $5 + 6 + 7 + 8$, so $g(5) = 12 + 5 + 6 + 7 + 8 = 38$.

c.

$$g(n) = \begin{cases} 12 & \text{if } n = 1 \\ g(n-1) + (n+3) & \text{if } n > 1 \end{cases}$$

d. $G(n) = \frac{n^2 + 7n + 16}{2}$

8. Standardized Test Prep Which of the following expressions is a closed-form rule for the recursively defined function below?

$$f(n) = \begin{cases} 5 & \text{if } n = 0 \\ f(n-1) + 8n^3 & \text{if } n > 0 \end{cases}$$

A. $8n^3(n+1)^2$ B. $5 + 4n(n+1)$

C. $8n^38n^3(n+1)^2$ D. $5 + 2n^2(n+1)^2$

9. a. Find two triangular numbers that are also square numbers.

b. Are there more than two such numbers?

10. a. Find a recursive formula $p(n)$ to describe the pentagonal numbers.

b. Find a closed-form definition for a function P to describe the pentagonal numbers.

11. a. Find a recursive formula $h(n)$ to describe the hexagonal numbers.

b. Find a closed-form formula $H(n)$ to describe the hexagonal numbers.

Maintain Your Skills

12. Let $T(n)$ be a formula for the nth triangular number. Show that $T(n-1) + T(n) = S(n)$. In other words, show that if you add two consecutive triangular numbers, you get a square number.

Here is a picture of the tetrahedral numbers. Notice that each level is made up of a triangular number of dots.

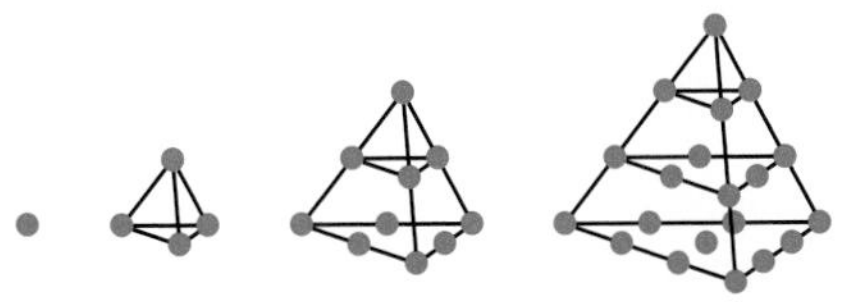

Let $T(n)$ be the nth triangular number. You can use the recursive formula below for the tetrahedral numbers.

$$a(n) = \begin{cases} 1 & \text{if } n = 1 \\ a(n-1) + T(n) & \text{if } n > 1 \end{cases}$$

13. a. Find a recursive definition for $a(n)$ that does not depend on $T(n)$.

b. Find a closed-form function definition for a function A that agrees with the tetrahedral numbers at positive integers.

Go Online
Video Tutor
PHSchool.com
Web Code: bfe-0775

Additional Resources

PRINT RESOURCES
- Solution Manual
- Practice Workbook
- Assessment Resources
- Teaching Resources

TECHNOLOGY
- Interactive Textbook
- TeacherExpress CD-ROM
- ExamView CD-ROM
- PHSchool.com

Additional Practice

1. Use the Σ identities to evaluate each sum.

a. $\sum_{k=1}^{9}(4k-3)$ b. $\sum_{k=5}^{9}(4k-3)$ c. $\sum_{k=1}^{n}(4k-3)$

d. $\sum_{k=0}^{6}3^k$ e. $\sum_{k=0}^{6}2\cdot 3^k$ f. $\sum_{k=0}^{n}2\cdot 3^k$

For Exercises 2–4, suppose you have a mystery function s, and all you know is a formula for its associated series.

$$\sum_{k=0}^{n} s(k) = 3n^2 - 2n$$

2. Find each sum.

a. $\sum_{k=0}^{10}s(k)$ b. $\sum_{k=1}^{10}s(k)$ c. $\sum_{k=1}^{5}s(k-1)$ d. $\sum_{k=0}^{10}(2s(k)+3^k)$

3. Find a polynomial r that agrees with s for all integers $n > 0$.

4. Is there more than one polynomial r that works? Explain.

5. What is the sum of all the multiples of 6 that are greater than 1 and less than 1000?

6. Use this recursive definition of the function f.

$$f(n) = \begin{cases} 16 & \text{if } n = 0 \\ f(n-1) + 3n - 2 & \text{if } n > 0 \end{cases}$$

Find a closed-form definition for a function F that agrees with f.

7. Use the table at the right for a function t.

a. Complete the Δ column. Use it to find a recursive formula for $t(n)$.

b. Find a closed-form definition for a function T that agrees with your function t.

n	$t(n)$	Δ
0	6	
1	7	
2	10	
3	15	

8. Use this recursive definition of the function r.

$$r(n) = \begin{cases} 1 & \text{if } n = 0 \\ r(n-1) + 3^n & \text{if } n > 0 \end{cases}$$

a. Express $r(n)$ as a sum of powers of 3.

b. Find a closed-form definition for a function R that agrees with r.

Practice: For Lesson 7.8, assign Exercises 6–8.

13. a. Replace $T(n)$ with $\frac{n(n+1)}{2}$ to get

$$a(n) = \begin{cases} 1 & \text{if } n = 1 \\ a(n-1) + \frac{n(n+1)}{2} & \text{if } n > 1 \end{cases}$$

b. $A(n) = \frac{n(n+1)(n+2)}{6}$

8. D

9. a. $t(1) = 1$, $t(8) = 36$

b. yes; $t(49) = 1225$

10. a.

$$p(n) = \begin{cases} 1 & \text{if } n = 1 \\ p(n-1) + (3n-2) & \text{if } n > 1 \end{cases}$$

b. $P(n) = \frac{3n^2 - n}{2}$

11. a.

$$h(n) = \begin{cases} 1 & \text{if } n = 1 \\ h(n-1) + (4n-3) & \text{if } n > 1 \end{cases}$$

b. $H(n) = 2n^2 - n$

12. $T(n-1) + T(n)$

$= \frac{(n-1)n}{2} + \frac{n(n+1)}{2}$

$= \frac{n^2 - n + n^2 + n}{2}$

$= \frac{2n^2}{2} = n^2$

Mathematical Reflections

EXERCISES 6–8 At the start of the investigation, you may have assigned these as Questions 1–3 for students to think and write about.

Mathematical Reflections 7B

In this investigation, you learned to find closed-form definitions for indefinite sums and to use the definitions to evaluate definite sums, develop and use $\sum$ identities, and find closed-form expressions for the series associated with a function. These questions will help you summarize what you have learned.

1. Evaluate each sum.

a. $\sum_{k=2}^{21}(2k - 4)$ **b.** $\sum_{k=3}^{10}(2 \cdot 5^k)$

2. Find a closed form for each indefinite sum.

a. $\sum_{k=0}^{n}(2k - 4)$ **b.** $\sum_{k=0}^{n}(2 \cdot 5^k)$

3. Suppose you know $\sum_{j=0}^{n} f(j) = 3n^2 + 4$ for a mystery function f.

a. Copy and complete the table at the right for f.

b. Find a polynomial g that agrees with f for all integers $n > 0$.

n	$h(n)$	Σ
0	5	5
1	8	■
2	■	30
3	■	■
4	■	■
5	■	■

4. Find a closed form for the series associated with $h(n) = 3 - 8n$, having initial term $h(0)$.

5. a. Explain why you can write the $\sum$ identity "Think Euclid" as $\sum_{k=0}^{n} r^k = \frac{1 - r^{n+1}}{1 - r}$.

b. Find a closed form for $\sum_{k=2}^{n} r^k$.

6. What is $\sum_{k=0}^{25}(k + 6^k)$?

7. What is a recursive rule for the series associated with $f(n) = 3n + 6$, having initial term $f(0)$?

8. What is a closed form for the following recursive rule?

$$f(n) = \begin{cases} 5 & \text{if } n = 0 \\ f(n-1) + 2n^2 + 3n + 2 & \text{if } n > 0 \end{cases}$$

Vocabulary

In this investigation, you learned these terms. Make sure you understand what each one means and how to use it.

- **Bernoulli's formulas**
- **definite sum**
- **figurate number**
- **identity**
- **indefinite sum**
- **series associated with *f***

Answers

Mathematical Reflections

1. a. 380 **b.** 24,414,000

2. a. $(n + 1)(n - 4)$ or $n^2 - 3n - 4$

b. $\frac{5^{n+1} - 1}{2}$

3. a.

n	$f(n)$	Σ
0	4	4
1	3	7
2	9	16
3	15	31
4	21	52
5	27	79

b. $g(n) = 6n - 3$

4. $H(n) = -4n^2 - n + 3$

5. a. $\frac{r^{n+1} - 1}{r - 1} \cdot \frac{-1}{-1} = \frac{-r^{n+1} + 1}{-r + 1} = \frac{1 - r^{n+1}}{1 - r}$

b. $\sum_{k=2}^{n} r^k = \frac{r^{n+1} - r^2}{r - 1}$

6. 34,116,345,635,915,641,976

7.

$$F(n) = \begin{cases} 6 & \text{if } n = 0 \\ F(n-1) + (3n + 6) & \text{if } n > 0 \end{cases}$$

8. $F(n) = \frac{4n^3 + 15n^2 + 23n + 30}{6}$

Chapter 7

Mid-Chapter Test

Go Online PHSchool.com

For a mid-chapter test, go to **Web Code:** bfa-0752

Multiple Choice

1. What is the value of the following sum?
$1 + \frac{1}{10} + \left(\frac{1}{10}\right)^2 + \left(\frac{1}{10}\right)^3 + \cdots + \left(\frac{1}{10}\right)^6$
   A. 1 **B.** 1.111111
   C. 0.111111 **D.** 0.999999

2. Use Σ notation to write the sum
$1 + 2 + 4 + 8 + \cdots + 128$.
   A. $\sum_{k=0}^{7} 2^k$
   B. $\sum_{k=1}^{128} k$
   C. $\sum_{k=1}^{64} 2k$
   D. $\sum_{k=0}^{64} 2k$

3. What is the value of the sum $\sum_{j=3}^{n} (2j - 1)$?
   A. 12 **B.** 14
   C. 21 **D.** 25

4. What is the value of the sum $\sum_{k=1}^{n} 3$?
   A. $3 + k$ **B.** $3k$
   C. $3n$ **D.** $3n + 3$

5. Use the table below to find $h(2)$.

n	$h(n)$	Σ
0	5	5
1	8	■
2	■	30

   A. 6 **B.** 8
   C. 11 **D.** 17

Open Response

6. **a.** Find the sum of the integers from -5 to 75, inclusive.
   b. Find the sum: $5^0 + 5^1 + 5^2 + \cdots + 5^{12}$.

7. Copy and complete the following sum table. Find a closed-form rule for the Σ column.

n	$f(n)$	Σ
0	3	■
1	5	■
2	7	■
3	9	■
4	11	■
5	13	■

8. Evaluate each sum.
   a. $\sum_{k=6}^{8} (10k + 4)$ **b.** $\sum_{k=0}^{10} (3k - 1)$
   c. $\sum_{k=0}^{20} (k^2 + 2)$ **d.** $\sum_{k=5}^{18} (k^3)$

9. Find a closed-form rule for each indefinite sum.
   a. $\sum_{k=0}^{n} (5k + 3)$
   b. $\sum_{k=0}^{n} (3k^2 + k)$

10. What is a closed-form rule for the following recursive rule?
$$G(n) = \begin{cases} 3 & \text{if } n = 0 \\ G(n-1) + n^2 + 4 & \text{if } n > 0 \end{cases}$$

11. What is a recursive rule for the series associated with $f(n) = 3n + 6$, having initial term $f(0)$?

Mid-Chapter Test

Mid-Chapter Test page 1 of 2

Multiple Choice

1. What is the value of the following sum?
$2 + \frac{1}{2} + \left(\frac{1}{2}\right)^2 + \left(\frac{1}{2}\right)^3 + \cdots + \left(\frac{1}{2}\right)^8$
   A. 1.99609
   B. 2.99219
   C. 2.99609
   D. 3

2. Use Σ notation to write the sum $4 + 8 + 12 + \cdots + 80$.
   A. $\sum_{k=1}^{80} k$ **B.** $\sum_{k=1}^{80} 4k$
   C. $\sum_{k=1}^{20} 4^k$ **D.** $\sum_{k=1}^{20} 4k$

3. What is the value of the sum $\sum_{k=5}^{7} (k^2 + k)$?
   A. 56
   B. 74
   C. 86
   D. 128

4. What is the value of the sum $\sum_{k=1}^{n} (2 + k)$?
   A. $3n$
   B. $\frac{n^2 + n + 4}{2}$
   C. $\frac{n^2 + 5n}{2}$
   D. $2n + k$

5. Use the table at the right to find $h(2)$.
   A. 4
   B. 5
   C. 11
   D. 15

n	$h(n)$	Σ
0	1	1
1	3	
2		15

Also available: Form B

Mid-Chapter Test

1. B
2. A
3. C
4. C
5. D
6. **a.** 2835
   b. 305,175,781

7.

n	$f(n)$	Σ
0	3	3
1	5	8
2	7	15
3	9	24
4	11	35
5	13	48

$\Sigma = n^2 + 4n + 3$

8. **a.** 222
   b. 154
   c. 2912
   d. 29,141

9. **a.** $\sum_{k=0}^{n} (5k + 3) = \frac{5n^2 + 11n + 6}{2}$
   b. $\sum_{k=0}^{n} (3k^2 + k) = n(n+1)^2$

10. $G(n) = \frac{n^3}{3} + \frac{n^2}{2} + \frac{25n}{6} + 3$

11. $F(n) = \begin{cases} 6 & \text{if } n = 0 \\ F(n-1) + (3n + 6) & \text{if } n > 0 \end{cases}$

Investigation Overview

In this investigation, students formalize much of their earlier work. Students define arithmetic and geometric sequences and series formally. They find closed-form expressions for sequences and series and relationships among them. Through geometric series, students study limits. Even though limits are defined only informally, students touch on many important ideas as they prepare for a more formal study of this topic. Students also look into repeating decimals as a special kind of geometric series and convert the decimals to exact fractions.

You may wish to assign Questions 1–3 for students to think and write about during the investigation.

Learning Goals

- Find a closed-form representation for an arithmetic sequence and its associated series.
- Find a closed-form representation for a geometric sequence and its associated series.
- Determine whether a geometric sequence has a limit, and if it does, how to find the limit.
- Convert a repeating decimal into an exact fraction.

Habits and Skills

- Visualize arithmetic and geometric series to better understand their behavior.
- Think about extreme cases as values of n become very large or terms in a sequence become very small.
- Reason logically to understand, write, and analyze proofs.

Investigation 7C

Arithmetic and Geometric Sequences and Series

In *Arithmetic and Geometric Sequences and Series,* you will explore the properties of arithmetic and geometric sequences. You will also investigate the series associated with arithmetic and geometric sequences.

By the end of this investigation, you will be able to answer questions like these.

1. What is an arithmetic sequence?
2. What is a geometric series?
3. How do you write the repeating decimal 0.121212121 . . . as a fraction?

You will learn how to

- find a closed-form representation for an arithmetic sequence and its associated series
- find a closed-form representation for a geometric sequence and its associated series
- determine whether a geometric sequence has a limit, and if it does, how to find the limit
- convert a repeating decimal into an exact fraction

You will develop these habits and skills:

- Visualize arithmetic and geometric series to better understand their behavior.
- Think about extreme cases as values of n become very large or as terms in a sequence become very small.
- Reason logically to understand, write, and analyze proofs.

You can use a geometric sequence with common ratio $\frac{1}{2}$ to model the number of teams in each round of a single-elimination tournament.

Investigation Road Map

LESSON 7.9, *Getting Started,* reminds students that linear functions have a constant difference between successive terms, and exponential functions have a common ratio between terms.

LESSON 7.10, *Arithmetic Sequences and Series,* formally defines arithmetic sequence and arithmetic series.

LESSON 7.11, *Geometric Sequences and Series,* formally defines geometric sequence and geometric series.

LESSON 7.12, *Limits,* has students study limits informally.

LESSON 7.13, *Repeating Decimals,* has students evaluate the logic in a common technique for converting repeating decimals to fractions and practice the technique.

7.9 Getting Started

Activating Prior Knowledge
Exploring New Ideas

Recall the difference tables you made in Chapter 1.

For You to Explore

You have seen these two tables before.

1. a. Make a difference table for each function.
   b. Describe functions K and L as completely as you can.

Table K

n	$K(n)$
0	3
1	8
2	13
3	18
4	23

Table L

m	$L(m)$
0	3
1	9
2	15
3	21
4	27

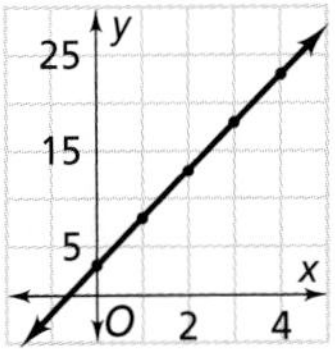

Graph of Table K

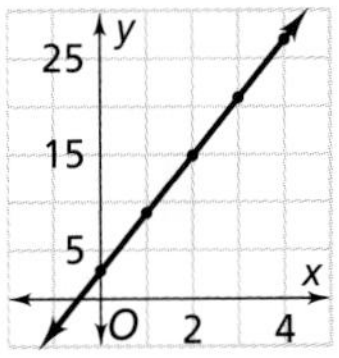

Graph of Table L

2. Thor and Pandora are bouncing a ball. Thor drops the ball from a height of 2 meters. Each time it bounces, Pandora measures the height of the bounce. The following table shows the results of this experiment.

Number of Bounces	Height (m)
0	2.00
1	1.68
2	1.41
3	1.19
4	1.00
5	0.84
6	0.71

Does the ball ever stop bouncing?

a. Find a recursive rule for determining the height of a bounce based on the previous height.
b. How high would the ball bounce on its 100th bounce? Do you think Pandora would be able to measure this height?

Answers

For You to Explore

1. a. See back of book.
   b. Answers may vary. Sample: $K(n)$ and $L(m)$ are both linear; $K(n) = 5n + 3$ and $L(m) = 6m + 3$.

2. a.

$$h(n) = \begin{cases} 2 & \text{if } n = 0 \\ h(n-1) \cdot 0.84 & \text{if } n > 0 \end{cases}$$

   b. $h(100) = 2 \cdot 0.84^{100} \approx 0.000000054$ m; that height is too small to manually measure.

Lesson Overview

GOAL

- Warm up to the ideas of the investigation.

The exercises in this lesson remind students of some familiar sequences of numbers and of the difference table properties of linear functions. As always in a Getting Started lesson, there is no need to formalize these ideas today. Students meet these ideas throughout this chapter.

FOR YOU TO EXPLORE
- Core: 1, 2, 3
- Optional: 4

MATERIALS
- graphing calculators
- Blackline Master 7.9

HOMEWORK
- Core: 5, 6, 7
- Optional: 8, 9

VOCABULARY
- common ratio
- constant difference

Launch

Have students get started on the For You to Explore problems right away. They should complete Problem 1 quite quickly, and may or may not have trouble with the others. Expect this Getting Started to last less than a full class period.

Explore

As students are working, assess their memory of linear and exponential functions to see what you may need to review.

For You to Explore

PROBLEM 2 Some students may get stymied here, looking first for a linear pattern (there is not one); then building a Δ^2 column and looking for a pattern there. Ask them to look at the situation again: is it reasonable for a ball to bounce 0.4 meters less each time? This should jump-start students to look for a decaying exponential function similar to some seen in Chapter 5. Blackline Master 7.9 provides a copy of the table.

PROBLEM 3 Some students may protest (with reason) that the height of the room is actually the limiting factor for Lisa's stack. She would not be able to build the entire triangular stack 75 cans high because it would be more than 31 feet high. You can extend the problem for these students by asking them to figure out how many cans there would be in the top row of a truncated triangle (a trapezoid) if Lisa's ceiling is 8 feet high, or how large a row she could start with on the bottom to fit an entire triangular stack in her room.

Wrap Up

Go over the For You to Explore core problems. If time allows, make a list with your class of what they remember about linear and exponential functions. Ask students to give examples of other rules or situations corresponding to the results they found in each of Problems 1–3. This should help them as they head toward the lessons in this investigation.

3. Lisa is collecting soda cans to win a contest. She is storing her soda cans in her bedroom by making a stack like the one shown here. If she begins with a base of 75 soda cans (the number of cans that will fit across the length of her room), how many cans will she have in her finished stack?

4. Find the missing terms in each sequence. The ratio between each term and the previous one is constant. For each sequence, find this common ratio.

a. 1, 2, 4, ■, 16, ■, ■, . . .

b. 1, −2, 4, ■, 16, ■, ■, . . .

c. 1, −1, 1, ■, ■, ■, . . .

d. 2, 6, 18, ■, ■, . . .

e. 4, 16, $\frac{1}{4}$, ■, ■, . . .

f. −1, $\frac{2}{3}$, $-\frac{4}{9}$, ■, . . .

Look back at Problem 4 from Lesson 5.1. How does this exercise compare to that one?

Answers

3. 2850 cans

4. a. 8, 32, 64; $r = 2$

b. −8, −32, 64; $r = -2$

c. −1, 1, −1; $r = -1$

d. 54, 162; $r = 3$

e. $\frac{1}{16}$, $\frac{1}{64}$; $r = \frac{1}{4}$

f. $\frac{8}{27}$; $r = -\frac{2}{3}$

Exercises *Practicing Habits of Mind*

On Your Own

5. Suppose a snail moves 5 inches up a tree every day and 2 inches down the tree every night. In the morning of Day 0, the snail starts on the ground.

a. Write a function for the snail's height in the morning and another function for the snail's height in the evening.

b. Does either of these functions have a constant Δ column? Explain.

c. If the tree is 40 feet tall, on what day does the snail reach the top?

6. The function $F(n)$ has a constant difference. Copy and complete the following table.

n	$F(n)$	Δ
0	8	■
1	■	■
2	■	■
3	■	■
4	12	

7. A health club charges $70 for the first month's membership fee and reduces the monthly fee by $2 each month after that. What is the total membership fee for an entire year?

Maintain Your Skills

8. How many multiples of 9 are between each pair of numbers?

a. 2 and 22 **b.** 2 and 62 **c.** 2 and 1000

d. 2 and n, where n is some integer greater than 2

9. How many multiples of 3 are strictly between each pair of numbers?

a. 2 and 22 **b.** 45 and 62 **c.** 45 and 1000

d. integers m and n, where n is greater than m

Exercises

HOMEWORK
- Core: 5, 6, 7
- Optional: 8, 9

On Your Own

EXERCISE 5 You might consider assigning only part (c), which makes this exercise more difficult, since most students will not see that the snail reaches the top of the tree near the end of Day 12. This is a chance for the student who sees why the answer is Day 12, and not Day 13, to shine.

EXERCISE 6 Some of your students may notice that finding the constant difference is really the same as finding the slope between the two points (4, 12) and (0, 8). That is a nice mathematical connection that shows understanding of what the slope of a line is.

Maintain Your Skills

EXERCISE 9 In solving the general case for multiples of 3 between m and n, there are some subtleties in defining the "endpoints" of the list of multiples. If either of the numbers is a multiple of 3, you would not want to include it in your list because the exercise specifies you are counting only multiples that are strictly between the two values.

9. a. 7

b. 5

c. 318

d. Using the notation $\lfloor A \rfloor$ for the greatest integer less than or equal to A, the number of multiples is $\left\lfloor \frac{n-1}{3} \right\rfloor - \left\lfloor \frac{m}{3} \right\rfloor$.

Exercises

5. a. A.M.: $h(n) = 3n$;
P.M.: $g(n) = 3n + 5$

b. Both have the constant difference 3.

c. day 12

6.

n	$F(n)$	Δ = constant
0	8	1
1	9	1
2	10	1
3	11	1
4	12	

7. $708

8. a. 2

b. 6

c. 111

d. the greatest integer less than or equal to $\frac{n}{9}$

Lesson Overview

GOAL

- Find a closed-form representation for an arithmetic sequence and its associated series.

In this lesson, the terms *arithmetic sequence* and *arithmetic series* are formally defined. Students will recognize arithmetic sequences from Chapter 5 and as the list of outputs of a linear function. They should be familiar with the idea that such sequences have a common difference between successive terms. Earlier in this chapter, students saw that Σ tables for linear functions have quadratic closed forms. Now that they see the outputs of the Σ column as the series associated with that linear function, this result still holds. Keep in mind that students will be familiar with most of the tasks they are asked to do in this lesson, but they will not be familiar with the terminology used to describe those tasks.

CHECK YOUR UNDERSTANDING

- Core: 1, 2, 3, 4, 5, 7
- Optional: 6, 8

MATERIALS

- CAS (recommended)
- graphing calculators
- Blackline Master 7.10

HOMEWORK

- Core: 9, 11, 12, 13, 14, 15, 16, 17, 20
- Optional: 10, 18, 19, 21, 23
- Extension: 22

VOCABULARY

- arithmetic sequence
- arithmetic series
- associated series
- common difference
- sequence
- term

Launch

Begin this lesson by going over the definitions in the text. Ask your students to describe the arithmetic sequences in Tony's work by naming the initial term and the common difference. Then continue to the For You to Do problems.

Explore

Minds in Action

Reviewing what students came up with for Problem 1 from the Getting Started lesson should cover more than what is found in this quick Minds in Action. You might point out that the tables are given for a very specific domain, and there is no information to guarantee that the function is valid for other inputs, or that the pattern continues any further than the table.

7.10 Arithmetic Sequences and Series

Until now, a sequence has been a list of numbers. Another way to think about a **sequence** is as a function with a domain that is the set of nonnegative integers. So sequences are nothing new. If the domain of a function is {0, 1, 2, 3, 4, 5, . . . }, then it is a sequence. For example, the function defined by $f(n) = 2n^2 + 3n + 5$ is a sequence, if you restrict its domain. You can then list the outputs of the function "in sequence."

$$\{f(0), f(1), f(2), f(3), f(4), \ldots\} = \{5, 10, 19, 32, 49, \ldots\}$$

The outputs of the function are the **terms** of the sequence. In this case, the initial term is 5, the next term is 10, and the fourth term is 32.

In this example, $f(0)$ is the initial term. Sometimes, you want the domain to be all integers n that are greater than 1, and then the initial term is $f(1)$.

Habits of Mind

Detect the key characteristics. In Chapter 2, you saw that to define a function, you must specify the domain. If the domain is the nonnegative integers, the function is a sequence.

Minds in Action — episode 35

Tony is working on Problem 1 from Lesson 7.9.

Tony $K(m)$ and $L(m)$ have a lot in common.

Table K

m	K(m)	Δ
0	3	5
1	8	5
2	13	5
3	18	5
4	23	

Table L

m	L(m)	Δ
0	3	6
1	9	6
2	15	6
3	21	6
4	27	

There's a constant difference of 5 in Table K.

There's a constant difference of 6 in Table L.

The two functions are defined on the set {0, 1, 2, 3, 4}.

Functions like $K(m)$ and $L(m)$ are special sequences called *arithmetic sequences*. They are defined by the property that their Δ columns are constant.

The constant value of an arithmetic sequence's Δ column is the *common difference d* for that sequence. The formal definition is on the following page.

When you use *arithmetic* as an adjective, the accent is on the third syllable: arithMETIC.

Definitions

A sequence is an **arithmetic sequence** if

- its domain is the set of integers $n \geq 0$
- there is a number d, the **common difference** for the sequence, such that

$$f(n) = f(n-1) + d \text{ for all integers } n > 0$$

Habits of Mind

Detect the key characteristics. How does this definition compare to the definition in Lesson 5.4? You can also call arithmetic sequences *linear sequences.* Do their graphs suggest why? Is there an algebraic reason?

Examples of Arithmetic Sequences

Initial term	d	Sequence	Formula and Domain
$a(0) = 3$	3	3, 6, 9, 12, . . .	$a(n) = 3(n+1)$ for all $n \geq 0$
$b(1) = 10$	-1	10, 9, 8, 7, . . .	$b(n) = 11 - n$ for all $n \geq 1$
$w(3) = 180$	180	180, 360, 540, . . .	$w(n) = 180(n-2)$ for all $n \geq 3$

For You to Do

1. In an arithmetic sequence, $f(0) = 8$ and $f(1) = 12$. Write out the first several terms of such a sequence. Is there any other arithmetic sequence with first term 8 and second term 12?

You can denote the terms of a sequence by subscripts $t_0, t_1, t_2, \ldots$ Here, the ninth term is t_8. Explain.

2. Suppose r is an arithmetic sequence with $r(5) = 8$ and $r(12) = 29$.
   - **a.** What is the common difference?
   - **b.** Find $r(9)$.
   - **c.** Find a closed form for r.
   - **d.** Is 78,209,756 a term of r? If so, what term is it? If not, explain why you think it is not.
3. Give two different examples of an arithmetic sequence with common difference 0. How would you describe an arithmetic sequence with common difference 0?

For Discussion

4. Suppose f is an arithmetic sequence with initial term $f(0) = a$ and common difference d. Find a closed form for $f(n)$ in terms of a and d.
5. Suppose g is an arithmetic sequence with initial term $g(1) = b$ and common difference d. Find a closed form for $g(n)$ in terms of b and d.

Habits of Mind

Establish a process. It might help you to make a table for the sequence.

For You to Do

When students try to express why they are sure no other sequence would meet the requirements in Problem 1, they may say something such as, "If you know two points, you know the function." Help them clarify what they mean by making sure they understand that arithmetic sequences are generated by linear functions and that linear functions can be completely determined by two input-output pairs. Not all functions can be completely determined by two input-output pairs.

Answers

For You to Do

1. 8, 12, 16, 20, 24, . . . ; that is the only arithmetic sequence that fits the conditions.
2. **a.** 3
   b. 20
   c. $r(n) = 3n - 7$
   d. Yes, $r(26{,}069{,}921) = 78{,}209{,}756$.
3. Answers may vary. Sample: 5, 5, 5, 5, . . . ; 1, 1, 1, 1, . . . ; in general, the sequence is $a, a, a, a, \ldots$.

For Discussion

4. $f(n) = a + nd$
5. $g(n) = b + (n-1)d$

Example

If students are having trouble here, write out the first few terms very specifically:

$3 + (3 + 5) + (3 + 5 + 5) + (3 + 5 + 5 + 5) + (3 + 5 + 5 + 5 + 5)$

Students should realize they are counting the threes and fives.

Wrap Up

As time allows, go over the Check Your Understanding core exercises.

Assessment Resources

Lesson Quiz 7.10

1. Suppose a is an arithmetic sequence with initial term $a(1) = 9$ and common difference of -2.
   a. Find $a(11)$.
   b. Find a closed form for a.
   c. Is -381 a term of a? If so, what term is it? If not, explain why not.

2. a. Show that the average of any three consecutive odd integers is equal to the middle number.
   b. Show that the average of any three consecutive even integers is equal to the middle number.

3. In an arithmetic sequence with a difference d, the product of the third term and d is -90. The sum of the third and fifth terms is 26. Find the first five terms in this sequence.

Arithmetic Series

Every arithmetic sequence has an associated arithmetic series.

Remember...

If f is any function, the function defined on nonnegative integers by $n \mapsto \sum_{k=0}^{n} f(k)$ is the series associated with f.

Definition

If the sequence t is an arithmetic sequence with initial term $t(0)$, the associated series T defined on integers n, such that $n \geq 0$ by $T(n) = \sum_{k=0}^{n} t(k)$ is an arithmetic series.

Example

Problem Consider the arithmetic sequence in Table K. The initial terms is $f(0) = 3$. The common difference is 5. A closed form is $f(n) = 3 + 5n$.

Find a closed form for $F(n) = \sum_{k=0}^{n} f(k)$.

Solution

$$\sum_{k=0}^{n} (3 + 5k) = \sum_{k=0}^{n} 3 + \sum_{k=0}^{n} 5k$$
$$= 3(n + 1) + 5 \cdot \frac{n(n + 1)}{2}$$
$$= \frac{(5n + 6)(n + 1)}{2}$$

For You to Do

Here is Table L again.

n	$L(m)$	Σ
0	3	■
1	9	■
2	15	■
3	21	■
4	27	■

6. Copy the table and complete the Σ column.
7. Find a closed form for the sequence.
8. Find a closed form for the series.

Answers

For You to Do

6. Table L

m	$L(m)$	Σ
0	3	3
1	9	12
2	15	27
3	21	48
4	27	75

7. $L(m) = 3 + 6m$
8. $\Sigma = 3m^2 + 6m + 3$

Exercises

1. $\frac{4}{n - 1}$
2. Yes; $\frac{1}{6}, \frac{1}{3}, \frac{1}{2}, \frac{2}{3}, \frac{5}{6}, 1, \ldots$
3. Yes; 1, 3, π; any multiple of the difference between 3 and π cannot equal a multiple of the difference between 1 and 3.
4. a.

n	$q(n)$	Σ
0	9	9
1	15	24
2	21	45
3	27	72
4	33	105

$q(n) = 6n + 9$;
$Q(n) = 3n^2 + 12n + 9$

Exercises Practicing Habits of Mind

Check Your Understanding

1. In an arithmetic sequence, the first term is 8 and the nth term is 12. Find the common difference.

2. Can the numbers 1, $\frac{1}{2}$, and $\frac{1}{3}$ belong to the same arithmetic sequence? If so, give an example of such a sequence. If not, explain why not.

3. Can you find three numbers that cannot all belong to the same arithmetic sequence? If so, give an example. If not, explain why not.

4. For each table,
   - Copy the table and complete the Σ column.
   - Find a closed form for the sequence.
   - Find a closed form for the series.

a.

n	$q(n)$	Σ
0	9	■
1	15	■
2	21	■
3	27	■
4	33	■

b.

n	$p(n)$	Σ
0	12	■
1	7	■
2	2	■
3	−3	■
4	−8	■

5. In an arithmetic sequence, $f(0) = 8$ and $f(2) = 12$. Write the first several terms of such a sequence. Is there any other arithmetic sequence with first term 8 and third term 12?

6. Consider the arithmetic sequence g with $g(0) = 2$ and common difference 3.
   a. Write the first four terms of g.
   b. Write the first four terms of the series G associated with g.
   c. Find closed forms for $g(n)$ and for the associated series $G(n)$.

7. For each sequence with the given initial term and constant difference,
   - tabulate the sequence and the associated series
   - find closed forms for the sequence and the associated series

   a. $t(0) = 5, d = 9$ **b.** $h(0) = 7, d = -4$ **c.** $t(0) = 6, d = \frac{1}{2}$

Exercises

HOMEWORK
- Core: 9, 11, 12, 13, 14, 15, 16, 17, 20
- Optional: 10, 18, 19, 21, 23
- Extension: 22

Check Your Understanding

EXERCISE 2 Many students will say "no" since the differences between these numbers are not equal. Point out to students that the terms need not be consecutive. The number lines students built in *Algebra 1* make an arithmetic sequence that includes all three numbers!

EXERCISE 3 You may need to suggest that students try an irrational number in their sequence, such as π or $\sqrt{2}$.

EXERCISE 4 Some students may use Chapter 1 techniques to find the closed-form rules to match the series. This is acceptable, but they will find it more time-consuming than using their new summation techniques. Encourage them to write the series as a sum and use the identities from this chapter.

EXERCISES 4 AND 8 Blackline Master 7.10 provides blank copies of the tables.

b.

n	$p(n)$	Σ
0	12	12
1	7	19
2	2	21
3	−3	18
4	−8	10

$p(n) = 12 - 5n$;
$P(n) = -\frac{5}{2}n^2 + \frac{19}{2}n + 12$

5. 8, 10, 12, 14, 16, . . .; there is no other arithmetic sequence with the same first and third terms.

6. a. 2, 5, 8, 11, 14, . . .
b. 2, 7, 15, 26, 40, . . .
c. $g(n) = 2 + 3n$;
$G(n) = \frac{3}{2}n^2 + \frac{7}{2}n + 2$

7. a.

n	$t(n)$	Σ
0	5	5
1	14	19
2	23	42
3	32	74
4	41	115

$t(n) = 5 + 9n$;
$T(n) = \frac{9}{2}n^2 + \frac{19}{2}n + 5$

b.

n	$h(n)$	Σ
0	7	7
1	3	10
2	−1	9
3	−5	4
4	−9	−5

$h(n) = 7 - 4n$; $H(n) = -2n^2 + 5n + 7$

7. c.

n	$t(n)$	Σ
0	6	6
1	6.5	12.5
2	7	19.5
3	7.5	27
4	8	35

$t(n) = 6 + \frac{1}{2}n$; $T(n) = \frac{1}{4}n^2 + \frac{25}{4}n + 6$

EXERCISE 8 Although it is a good exercise for students to compute this general form, it would not really be useful for them to memorize this result and use it as a formula. It does give them a way to immediately find a closed form for the series associated with a linear function. However, by going through the process when you ask them to find such a closed form, they learn a great deal more about what the series associated with a function is (and not just a linear function). They also learn how to find a closed form for such a series.

8. Let $f(n) = a + dn$, where a is the initial term and d is the common difference.

a. Copy and complete this table in terms of a and d.

n	$f(n)$	Σ
0	a	■
1	$a + d$	■
2	■	$3a + 3d$
3	■	■
4	■	■
5	■	■

b. Find a closed form for the series associated with f.

On Your Own

9. Suppose f is an arithmetic sequence with initial term $f(0) = 3$ and common difference 6.

a. Find $f(8)$.

b. Find a closed form for f.

c. Is 78,209,756 a term of f? If so, what term is it? If not, explain why not.

Go Online PHSchool.com

For additional practice, go to **Web Code:** bfa-0710

10. How would you describe the arithmetic sequence with initial term $f(0) = 1$ and common difference 1?

11. Show that the average of any three consecutive integers is equal to the middle number.

The diameters, in inches, of the cake's layers are part of an arithmetic sequence with initial term 6 and common difference 2.

Answers

8. a.

n	$f(n)$	Σ
0	a	a
1	$a + d$	$2a + d$
2	$a + 2d$	$3a + 3d$
3	$a + 3d$	$4a + 6d$
4	$a + 4d$	$5a + 10d$
5	$a + 5d$	$6a + 15d$

b. $F(n) = \frac{1}{2}(n + 1)(2a + nd)$

9. a. 51

b. $f(n) = 3 + 6n$

c. No; $f(13{,}034{,}958) = 78{,}209{,}751$ and $f(13{,}034{,}959) = 78{,}209{,}757$, so 78,209,756 is not a term of f.

10. Answers may vary. Sample: The sequence is 1, 2, 3, 4, ...

11. If the integers are n, $n + 1$, and $n + 2$, then the average is $\frac{n + (n + 1) + (n + 2)}{3} = \frac{3n + 3}{3} = n + 1$, which is the middle number.

12. Consider an arithmetic sequence t. Show that any term $t(n)$ is the average of the one before it, $t(n-1)$, and the one after it, $t(n+1)$.

> In other words, in an arithmetic sequence, each term starting with the second one is the arithmetic mean of the preceding term and the following term. That is where the name "arithmetic sequence" comes from.

13. Below is an illustration of the first three pyramidal numbers. Each layer is a square.

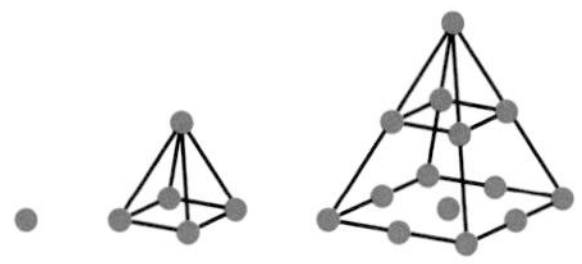

a. Use this illustration to list the first five pyramidal numbers.

b. What series does the total number of dots in each figure represent? Is this series an arithmetic series? Explain.

> You count the dots here.

c. Find the closed form for the number of dots n in a pyramid that is n rows high.

d. How many dots are in a pyramid ten levels high?

14. An arithmetic sequence with terms $a_1, a_2, \dots, a_5$ satisfies both $a_1 + a_3 + a_5 = -12$ and $a_1a_3a_5 = 80$. Find the terms in this sequence.

> Some of these exercises have more than one solution.

15. In an arithmetic sequence with a difference d, the product of the second term and d is 30. The sum of the third and fifth terms is 32. Find the first three terms in this sequence.

16. Give an example of a sequence with a Δ column that is an arithmetic sequence. Find a closed form for your sequence.

17. Give an example of a sequence with a Σ column that is an arithmetic sequence. Find a closed form for your sequence.

18. Can the Σ column of an arithmetic sequence ever be arithmetic? Explain.

19. The sum of the first and fifth terms of an arithmetic sequence is $\frac{5}{3}$. The product of the third and fourth terms of the same sequence is $\frac{65}{72}$. Find the sum of the first 17 terms of this sequence.

20. **Standardized Test Prep** Let $G(n) = \sum_{k=0}^{n} g(k)$, where $g(n) = 5 - 3n$. What is the value of $G(3)$?

A. -4 **B.** -3 **C.** -1 **D.** 2

On Your Own

EXERCISE 12 Students may use the general formula for a term of an arithmetic sequence to do this exercise, and that formula will work. A different choice, however, can make the work much simpler: let $t(n) = x$. Then $t(n-1)$ must equal $x - d$ for the common difference d, and $t(n+1)$ must equal $x + d$. The algebra wraps itself up more nicely than if using $t(n) = an + d$.

EXERCISE 13 The fact that this is not an arithmetic series should be found fairly quickly. You could ask an extension question here: if terms 1, 5, 14 are part of an arithmetic series, what would its next few terms be? Students could use common differences (4 and 9) to get the next term, 28, followed by $28 + 19 = 47$.

EXERCISE 14 relies on the result of Exercise 12. This is a very difficult exercise unless students notice that a_1, a_3, and a_5 also form an arithmetic sequence. Then $a_3 = -4$ and a_5 can be written as $-4 + 2d$ with $a_1 = -4 - 2d$, leading to the two possible values of d. Otherwise, students will have a more difficult time and are likely to get one of the answers by guesswork. Since the exercise does not specify the sequence is increasing, there are two possible answers. The equation for d gives both values (-3 and 3) and both are valid.

EXERCISE 16 All you need to do to write a sequence with a Δ column that is an arithmetic sequence is to use the series associated with any arithmetic sequence.

12. Answers may vary. Sample: If d is the common difference and $t(n) = k$, then $t(n-1) = k - d$ and $t(n+1) = k + d$. The average of $k - d$ and $k + d$ is

$$\frac{(k-d)+(k+d)}{2} = \frac{2k}{2} = k,$$

which is $t(n)$.

13. a. 1, 5, 14, 30, 55

b. $1^2 + 2^2 + 3^2 + \dots + n^2 = \sum_{k=1}^{n} k^2$. The series is not an arithmetic series because the differences in the terms are 4, 9, 16, 25, ..., which are not constant.

c. $\sum_{k=1}^{n} k^2 = \frac{n(n+1)(2n+1)}{6}$

d. 385

14. 2, -1, -4, -7, -10, -13, ... or -10, -7, -4, -1, 2, 5, ...

15. 1, 6, 11, 21, ... or 7, 10, 13, 16, 19, ...

16. Answers may vary. Sample: for the sequence 1, 4, 9, 16, 25, 36, ..., the Δ values are 3, 5, 7, 9, 11, ..., which is an arithmetic sequence. A closed form is $f(n) = n^2$.

17. Answers may vary. Sample: For the sequence 3, 3, 3, 3, ..., the Σ values are 3, 6, 9, 12, ..., which is an arithmetic sequence. A closed form for the sequence is $f(n) = 3$.

18. Yes, if $d = 0$ then the sequence is arithmetic and its Σ values are arithmetic.

19. $\frac{119}{3}$

20. D

EXERCISE 21 involves parsing some fairly complex instructions, but it should be accessible to students once they figure out what they are being asked.

EXERCISE 22 Some students may be confused by the question here. It takes them through the first few terms of g, namely $g(1) = 1$, $g(2) = 3 \cdot 2 = 6$, and $g(3) = 5 \cdot 3 = 15$. Students should see pretty quickly that $g(n) = (2n - 1)n$, which follows up on the result of Exercise 21, $s(n) = 2n - 1$. Once the summation is established, methods presented in Investigation 7B should be applied: the sum is twice the sum of the first n squares minus the sum of the first n integers.

Additional Resources

PRINT RESOURCES	TECHNOLOGY
• Solution Manual	• Interactive Textbook
• Practice Workbook	• TeacherExpress CD-ROM
• Assessment Resources	• ExamView CD-ROM
• Teaching Resources	• PHSchool.com

Additional Practice

1. Suppose a is an arithmetic sequence with initial term $a(0) = 5$ and common difference -7.
   a. Find $a(9)$
   b. Find a closed form for a.
   c. Is -1878 a term of a? If so, what term is it? If not, explain why not.

2. An arithmetic sequence with terms $a_1, a_2, a_3, \dots, a_6$ satisfies both $a_2 + a_4 + a_6 = 30$ and $a_2a_4a_6 = 640$. Find the terms in this sequence.

3. In an arithmetic sequence with a difference d, the product of the second term and d is -48. The sum of the third and fifth terms is 8. Find the first five terms in this sequence.

4. Find $g(10)$ for each geometric sequence.
   a. $g(1) = 12, r = -2$
   b. $g(1) = -4, r = \frac{3}{2}$
   c. $g(2) = 8, g(6) = 32$

5. Write a closed-form definition for a function that generates each sequence in Exercise 4.

6. Candice makes a resolution to do sit-ups every day. Suppose Candice does 10 sit-ups every day this week. She challenges herself to increase the number of sit-ups 20% each week. How many sit-ups will Candice do after each given week?
   a. week 5 b. week 12 c. week w

7. What price can Herb afford to pay for a car if he can put $1000 down and pay $550 per month on a 4-year, 3% loan?

8. A basketball drops from a height of 30 feet. After each bounce, the ball bounces to $\frac{2}{3}$ its previous height.
   a. How high does the ball bounce after 10 bounces?
   b. What is the total distance the ball travels downward after 10 bounces?
   c. What is the total distance the ball travels upward after 10 bounces?
   d. Find the total distance the ball travels upward and downward after 100 bounces.

Practice: For Lesson 7.10, assign Exercises 1–3.

Use this array for Exercises 21 and 22.

$$\begin{array}{cccccccc} 1 & 2 & 3 & 4 & 5 & \cdots & k \\ 2 & 2 & 3 & 4 & 5 & \cdots & k \\ 3 & 3 & 3 & 4 & 5 & \cdots & k \\ 4 & 4 & 4 & 4 & 5 & \cdots & k \\ 5 & 5 & 5 & 5 & 5 & \cdots & k \\ \vdots & \vdots & \vdots & \vdots & \vdots & \ddots & \\ k & k & k & k & k & & k \end{array}$$

21. You can continue the pattern of numbers above indefinitely down and to the right. Let $S(n)$ be the number of entries that are less than or equal to n in this array.

So $S(2) = 4$ because there are one 1 and three 2's for a total of 4 entries.

a. Find a sequence $s(n)$ such that $S(n) = \sum_{k=1}^{n} s(k)$. Is s an arithmetic sequence? Explain.

b. Find a closed form for $S(n)$.

22. Take It Further Let $G(n)$ be the sum of all of the entries in the array above that are less than or equal to n.

So $G(2) = 2 + 2 + 2 + 1 = 7$. It is the sum of the one 1 and the three 2's.

a. Find a sequence $g(n)$ such that $G(n) = \sum_{k=1}^{n} g(k)$. Is g an arithmetic sequence? Explain.

b. Find a closed form for $G(n)$.

Maintain Your Skills

23. Suppose t is the sequence given by $t(n) = (n + 1)2^n$.

a. Make a table for t for $n = 0$ through $n = 5$.

b. Add a column to the table for the values of the ratio $\frac{t(n)}{t(n-1)}$.

c. Is t an arithmetic sequence? Is the definition of each of its terms as $t(n) = (n + 1)2^n$ enough to decide? Explain.

d. Find a closed form for $\sum_{k=0}^{n} t(k)$.

To evaluate the indefinite sum, see the TI-Nspire Handbook, p. 778.

Answers

21. a. $s(n) = 2n - 1$; $s(n)$ is an arithmetic sequence because the common difference is 2.

b. $S(n) = n^2$

22. a. $g(n) = (2n - 1)n$ or $g(n) = 2n^2 - n$; $g(n)$ is not an arithmetic sequence because the differences between terms increase.

b. $G(n) = \frac{n(n + 1)(4n - 1)}{6}$

23.a–b.

n	$t(n)$	$\frac{t(n)}{t(n-1)}$
0	1	
1	4	4
2	12	3
3	32	$2.\overline{6}$
4	80	2.5
5	192	2.4

c. No; no; if $t(n) = (n + 1)2^n$, then $t(n + 1) - t(n) = 2^n(n + 3)$, which is not constant.

d. $\sum_{k=0}^{n} (k + 1) \cdot 2^k = 2n \cdot 2^n + 1$

7.11 Geometric Sequences and Series

There are other types of sequences and series besides arithmetic sequences and series.

In-Class Experiment

Rolf was writing down the recursive formula for an arithmetic sequence g with initial term $g(0) = 1$ and common difference 2. As a result of a slip of a pen, he came up with the following definition.

$$g(n) = \begin{cases} 1 & \text{if } n = 0 \\ g(n-1) \cdot 2 & \text{if } n > 0 \end{cases}$$

1. **a.** Make a table and write down a few entries for g.
   b. Is g an arithmetic sequence? Explain.
   c. Write a closed form for $g(n)$.
2. **a.** Add a Δ column to the table for g. Describe a pattern in the Δ column.
   b. Add a Σ column to the table for g. Describe a pattern in the Σ column.
3. **a.** Add a ratio column to the table for g.

n	$g(n)$	Ratio $\frac{g(n+1)}{g(n)}$
0	1	$\frac{2}{1} = 2$
1	2	■
2	4	■
3	■	■
4	■	■

   b. Describe a pattern in the ratio column.

Remember...

Instead of what you must add to one output to get the next one, this column gives what you must multiply each output by to get the next one.

Functions like the ones that Rolf built and that Thor and Pandora recorded in Exercise 2 from Lesson 7.9 are *geometric sequences*. To be a geometric sequence, a function has to have two properties.

- It is a sequence, meaning a function defined on the nonnegative integers.
- The ratio column is constant.

Lesson Overview

GOAL

- Find a closed-form representation for a geometric sequence and its associated series.

You may wish to spend two days on this lesson. This lesson introduces students to geometric sequences and series. A geometric sequence has the nonnegative integers as its domain and a constant ratio between successive terms. A geometric series is the function that generates the running totals for a geometric sequence. By seeing the monthly payment function from Chapter 1 as a geometric series, students are able to explain why the monthly payment on a loan turns out to be a linear function of the cost of the car.

To give students a chance to understand this result for themselves two days may be needed. One way to divide the lesson is to cover the definitions of *geometric sequence* and *geometric series* and to introduce the monthly payment result on the first day. You could ask the students to come up with their own ideas about why the payment should be a linear function of the cost of the car as homework. Begin the second day by asking some students to present their results and start off a class discussion of Theorem 7.2 and the Check Your Understanding core exercises.

CHECK YOUR UNDERSTANDING

- Core: 1, 2, 4, 5
- Optional: 3

MATERIALS

- CAS (recommended)
- graph paper
- graphing calculators
- spreadsheet software
- Blackline Master 7.11

HOMEWORK

- Core: 6, 7, 10, 11, 12, 14, 15, 16, 17
- Optional: 8a–d, 9, 12, 18, 19, 20, 21
- Extension: 8e

VOCABULARY

- geometric sequence
- geometric series

Launch

Start this lesson with the In-Class Experiment. You may wish to use Blackline Master 7.11 here.

In-Class Experiment

Here is the table for Problems 1–3.

n	$g(n)$	Δ	Σ	$\frac{g(n+1)}{g(n)}$
0	1	1	1	$\frac{2}{1} = 2$
1	2	2	3	$\frac{4}{2} = 2$
2	4	4	7	$\frac{8}{4} = 2$
3	8	8	15	$\frac{16}{8} = 2$
4	16	16	31	$\frac{32}{16} = 2$
5	32			

1. **a.** See the first two columns of the table.
   b. No; there is no common difference.
   c. $g(n) = 2^n$

2.a-b. See the Δ and Σ columns of the table; answers may vary. Samples are given.
   a. The Δ column is the same as the $g(n)$ column.
   b. The nth entry of the Σ column is 1 less than the $(n+1)$st entry of the Δ column.

3. **a.** See the fifth column of the table.
   b. Each ratio is equivalent to 2.

Explore

For You to Do

PROBLEM 4 Many students will not see that there are two possible values for $t(4)$. Encourage the use of the common ratio: if $t(3) = 100$ and the common ratio is r, what is $t(4)$? If $t(5) = 10{,}000$ and the common ratio is r, what is $t(4)$? This gives the equation $100r = \frac{10000}{r}$, which leads to the equation $r^2 = 100$ and the two possible values of $t(4)$. The same tactic works for all three parts.

Here is a formal definition.

Definitions

A sequence is a **geometric sequence** if

- its domain is the integers $n \geq 0$
- there is a number $r \neq 0$, called the **common ratio,** such that

$f(n) = r \cdot f(n-1)$ for all integers $n > 0$

Compare this definition with the definition of arithmetic sequence in Lesson 7.10.

Examples of Geometric Sequences

Initial Term	r	Sequence	Formula and Domain
$a(0) = 3$	3	3, 9, 27, 81, . . .	$a(n) = 3^{n+1}$ for all $n \geq 0$
$b(1) = 1$	-1	1, −1, 1, −1, . . .	$b(n) = (-1)^{n-1}$ for all $n \geq 1$
$c(0) = 8$	$\frac{1}{2}$	8, 4, 2, 1, . . .	$c(n) = \frac{8}{(2^n)}$ for all $n \geq 0$

For You to Do

4. Suppose t is a geometric sequence.

a. If $t(3) = 100$ and $t(5) = 10{,}000$, what is $t(4)$?

b. If $t(3) = 100$ and $t(5) = 4$, what is $t(4)$?

c. If $t(n-1) = a$ and $t(n+1) = b$, what is $t(n)$?

There could be more than one possibility for $t(4)$.

5. Write down the first four terms of a geometric sequence g with the given initial term and common ratio.

a. $g(0) = 5$, $r = 2$

b. $g(0) = 5$, $r = -2$

c. $g(0) = 5$, $r = 1$

d. $g(0) = 5$, $r = \frac{1}{2}$

Geometric Series

Just as an arithmetic sequence has an associated arithmetic series, a geometric sequence has an associated *geometric series.*

Definition

If the sequence g is a geometric sequence with initial term $g(0)$, the associated series $G(n) = \sum_{k=0}^{n} g(n)$ is a **geometric series.**

Answers

For You to Do

4. a. 1000 or −1000

b. 20 or −20

c. $\sqrt{ab}$ or $-\sqrt{ab}$

5. a. 5, 10, 20, 40

b. 5, −10, 20, −40

c. 5, 5, 5, 5

d. 5, $\frac{5}{2}$, $\frac{5}{4}$, $\frac{5}{8}$

For You to Do

6. $t(n) = 3 \cdot 2^n$

$$t(n) = \begin{cases} 3 & \text{if } n = 0 \\ t(n-1) \cdot 2 & \text{if } n > 0 \end{cases}$$

7. $T(n) = 3(2^{n+1} - 1)$

$$T(n) = \begin{cases} 3 & \text{if } n = 0 \\ T(n-1) + 3 \cdot 2^n & \text{if } n > 0 \end{cases}$$

8. Show that $T(n)$ and $2T(n-1) + 3$ are equivalent:

$$\begin{aligned} &2T(n-1) + 3 \\ &= 2 \cdot 3(2^{n-1+1} - 1) + 3 \\ &= 3[2(2^n - 1) + 1] \\ &= 3(2^{n+1} - 2 + 1) \\ &= 3(2^{n+1} - 1) \\ &= T(n) \end{aligned}$$

9. 1,572,861

For You to Do

Suppose you have a table for a geometric sequence t. You can make a table for the series associated with t by adding a Σ column.

n	$t(n)$	Σ
0	3	3
1	6	9
2	12	21
3	24	45
4	48	93
5	96	189

6. Find both closed and recursive forms for t.
7. Find both closed and recursive forms for the associated series $T(n) = \sum_{k=0}^{n} t(k)$.
8. Show that $T(n) = 2T(n-1) + 3 = \mathcal{A}_{(2,3)}(T(n-1))$.
9. What is $\sum_{k=0}^{18} t(k)$?

Habits of Mind

Consider more than one strategy. Can you use Problem 8 to find a closed form for T?

Monthly Payments

In Lesson 1.11, you experimented with the monthly payment on a loan, modeled by a balance function like the one below.

$$b(n, m) = \begin{cases} 10{,}000 & \text{if } n = 0 \\ \left(1 + \frac{0.05}{12}\right)b(n-1, m) - m & \text{if } n > 0 \end{cases}$$

Suppose you have the following parameters.

- The amount borrowed is \$10,000.
- The interest rate is 5%.
- Payments are made at the end of each month.

Then $b(n, m)$ gives you the balance on the loan at the end of n months, with a monthly payment of m dollars.

For Discussion

10. Review the construction of this function and why it does what we say it does. Model it in your function-modeling language and experiment with it. You might want to introduce two more inputs for the initial amount of the loan and the interest rate so that you can control these things.

To model the monthly payment function b, see the TI-Nspire Handbook, p. 778.

MONTHLY PAYMENTS Depending on how much work you did on the payment formulas in Chapter 1, consider stopping this lesson after the For You to Do section. Much of the development here parallels the development of the monthly payment formula, the Chapter 1 Project. If you skip the portion on monthly payments, also skip Exercises 5, 12, and 13.

For Discussion

10. The beginning of the loan is when $n = 0$, and so the principal is \$10,000. To calculate the balance after n months with a monthly payment of m, start by finding the interest accrued over the previous month. Since the annual interest rate is 5%, the monthly interest rate is $\frac{5\%}{12}$, or $\frac{0.05}{12}$. If the current balance is $b(n, m)$, then the previous month's balance is $b(n-1, m)$, and therefore the interest accrued over that month is $\frac{0.05}{12}b(n-1, m)$. This interest is added to the previous balance to bring the current balance to $\frac{0.05}{12}b(n-1, m) + b(n-1, m)$, or $\left(1 + \frac{0.05}{12}\right)b(n-1, m)$. Finally, subtract the monthly payment of m to find the current balance of $\left(1 + \frac{0.05}{12}\right)b(n-1, m) - m$. Check students' models.

For You to Do

It may have been a while since your class thought about this function, so take it apart with them and ask them to explain the role of each part. For example, they need to remember that what the b function calculates is the balance remaining on the loan at the end of the month. The interest is added on, and the monthly payment is subtracted off. Have them show you where each of these things is done in the definition of the function.

You might choose to stop the lesson here, and as homework, have students work through the proof of Theorem 7.2 and the For Discussion problem that follows it.

For You to Do

Revisit Exercise 6 from Lesson 1.11.

Suppose you want to pay off a car loan in 36 months. Pick an interest rate and keep it constant. Investigate how the monthly payment changes with the cost of the car.

11. Make a table like the one below and complete it.

Cost of Car (thousands of dollars)	Monthly Payment
10	■
11	■
12	■
13	■
14	■
15	■
16	■
17	■
18	■
⋮	⋮

12. Find either a closed-form or a recursive definition for a function that agrees with your table. Build a model of your function.

13. Use your model to find the monthly payment on a \$26,000 car loan.

If this function works for all inputs, you can use it to calculate the monthly payment in terms of the cost of the car in thousands of dollars.

It appears that the Δ column for this table is constant. That is, it seems that the monthly payment is a linear function of the cost of the car. You can use geometric series to see why.

Suppose you borrow C dollars at an interest rate of i, where i is a decimal so that you can calculate with it. Then the recursive definition below gives the more general function b.

$$b(n, m) = \begin{cases} C & \text{if } n = 0 \\ \left(1 + \frac{i}{12}\right)b(n-1, m) - m & \text{if } n > 0 \end{cases}$$

Notice that $\left(1 + \frac{i}{12}\right)$ is a constant. You can cover it up with your hand and deal with it as if it is one piece q.

$$\text{Let } q = \left(1 + \frac{i}{12}\right).$$

So your function definition looks like this.

$$b(n, m) = \begin{cases} C & \text{if } n = 0 \\ q \cdot b(n-1, m) - m & \text{if } n > 0 \end{cases}$$

Notice that $b(n, m) = A_{(q, -m)}(b(n-1, m))$.

Answers

For You to Do

11. See back of book.

12. Answers may vary. Sample: If A is the amount of the loan, r is the annual interest rate, and y is the number of years of the loan, then a closed-form function for the monthly payment P is

$$P = \frac{A \cdot \frac{r}{12} \cdot \left(1 + \frac{r}{12}\right)^{12y}}{\left(1 + \frac{r}{12}\right)^{12y} - 1}.$$

13. Answers may vary. Sample: For $A = \$26{,}000$, $r = 7.5\%$, and $y = 3$, $P = \$808.76$.

Unstack this definition and look for some regularity in the calculation.

$$
\begin{aligned}
b(n, m) &= q \cdot b(n-1, m) - m \\
&= q(q \cdot b(n-2, m) - m) - m = q^2 \cdot b(n-2, m) - qm - m \\
&= q^2(q \cdot b(n-3, m) - m) - qm - m \\
&= q^3 \cdot b(n-3, m) - q^2 m - qm - m \\
&\vdots \\
&= q^n \cdot b(0, m) - q^{n-1}m - q^{n-2}m - \cdots - q^2 m - qm - m \\
&= C \cdot q^n - m(q^{n-1} + q^{n-2} + \cdots + q^2 + q + 1)
\end{aligned}
$$

The last series is geometric. Summing it, you get

$$b(n, m) = Cq^n - m\frac{q^n - 1}{q - 1}$$

Setting $b(n, m)$ equal to 0 gives an explicit relationship between m and the cost of the car.

$$m = C\frac{(q-1)q^n}{q^n - 1}$$

You can state the general result as a theorem.

Theorem 7.2

If you take out a loan for C dollars for n months at an interest rate of i, then the equation below gives the monthly payment.

$$m = C \cdot \frac{(q-1)q^n}{q^n - 1}$$

where n is the term of the loan and

$$q = 1 + \frac{i}{12}$$

For Discussion

14. Why does this theorem say that the monthly payment is a linear function of the amount borrowed? If you write that linear function as $m = aC + b$, what is a? What is b?

THEOREM 7.2 Begin the second day of the lesson by discussing this theorem and students' understanding of the argument that leads to it. You may wish to have one or two students present their work. Some students may find experimentally (using graphs) that $C = 0$ produces an m of 0. In other words, if the cost of the car is 0, then the monthly payment should also be 0.

For Discussion

14. Answers may vary. Sample: If, for example, you double the amount borrowed, then you will double the amount that you have to pay each month. If you triple the amount borrowed, then the monthly payment triples. This describes a linear relationship between the monthly payment and the amount borrowed. More precisely, if $m = aC + b$, then $a = \frac{(q-1)q^n}{q^n - 1}$ and $b = 0$.

Wrap Up

Finish up this lesson by going over the Check Your Understanding core exercises as time allows.

Assessment Resources

Lesson Quiz 7.11

1. Find $g(12)$ for each geometric sequence. Then find a closed-form definition for a function that generates each sequence.
   a. $g(1) = 15, r = -\frac{1}{3}$ b. $g(1) = -6, r = \frac{5}{2}$
2. Anthony loves to swim. He challenges himself with a fitness plan. He starts with 10 laps of the pool every day this week. He will increase the distance he swims by 10% each week. How many laps per day will Anthony do after each given week? Round to the nearest lap.
   a. week 6 b. week 15 c. week w
3. A tennis ball drops from a height of 20 feet. After each bounce, the ball bounces to $\frac{3}{4}$ its previous height.
   a. How high does the tennis ball bounce after 8 bounces?
   b. What is the total distance the ball travels downward after 8 bounces?
   c. What is the total distance the ball travels upwards after 8 bounces?
   d. Find the total distance the ball travels upward and downward after 100 bounces.

Exercises

HOMEWORK

- Core: 6, 7, 10, 11, 12, 14, 15, 16, 17
- Optional: 8a–d, 9, 12, 18, 19, 20, 21
- Extension: 8e

Check Your Understanding

EXERCISE 1 Students need to pay attention to whether they can determine the sign of the ratio when they are given two terms in the sequence. If you discuss this exercise in class, you might wish to have students articulate the conditions that leave the sign of the ratio undetermined.

EXERCISE 3 Be sure that students consider ratios or differences that are fractional or negative, if they do not think of these cases.

On Your Own

EXERCISE 6 If time is a factor, you do not need to assign all the parts of this exercise.

Exercises *Practicing Habits of Mind*

Check Your Understanding

1. Find $g(7)$ for each geometric sequence.

a. $g(1) = 5, r = 2$ **b.** $g(1) = 5, r = -2$ **c.** $g(1) = 5, r = 1$

d. $g(1) = 5, r = \frac{1}{2}$ **e.** $g(5) = 18, g(6) = 9$ **f.** $g(3) = 12, g(5) = 30$

g. $g(6) = 6, g(8) = 54$ **h.** $g(5) = 6, g(9) = 54$

2. Can a sequence be geometric and arithmetic at the same time? Explain.

3. **Write About It** Write at least four pairs of sequences. A pair will consist of an arithmetic sequence a and a geometric sequence g with the same initial term and the common difference of a equal to the common ratio of g. For example,

$$a_1 = 2, 5, 8, 11, 14, \ldots$$

$$g_1 = 2, 6, 18, 54, 162, \ldots$$

Both sequences have initial term 2. The common difference for the arithmetic series a is 3. The common ratio for geometric series g is 3.

Compare the behavior of sequences in each pair. Do both sequences increase or decrease?

> Make sure you have first terms, common differences, and common ratios with various signs and values.

4. Let $s(n) = 5 \cdot \left(\frac{1}{2}\right)^n$.

a. Find a formula for $\sum_{i=0}^{n} s(i)$. **b.** Use the formula to find $\sum_{i=0}^{15} s(i)$.

5. Rosita took out a loan for a car that cost \$11,000. She paid \$1000 down and got a 4% interest rate.

a. If the term of the loan is 36 months, what is the monthly payment?

b. If Rosita pays \$500 per month, which is more than the minimum monthly payment, how long will it take her to pay off the car?

On Your Own

6. Write a closed-form definition for a function that generates each sequence in Exercise 1.

> That is, write a formula for $g(n)$.

7. **Standardized Test Prep** Suppose $a(n)$ is a geometric sequence with initial term $a(0) = 6$ and common ratio $\frac{3}{2}$. What is the value of $a(5)$?

A. $\frac{15}{2}$ **B.** $\frac{243}{32}$ **C.** $\frac{27}{2}$ **D.** $\frac{729}{16}$

Answers

Exercises

1. a. 320 **b.** 320 **c.** 5 **d.** $\frac{5}{64}$
e. 4.5 **f.** 75 **g.** ± 18 **h.** 18

2. Yes; any constant sequence such as 3, 3, 3, 3, ... has a constant difference (0) and a constant ratio (1), so it is both arithmetic and geometric.

3. See back of book.

4. a. See back of book.
b. ≈ 9.999847

5. a. \$295.24 **b.** 21 months

6. a. $g(n) = 5 \cdot 2^{n-1}$
b. $g(n) = 5 \cdot (-2)^{n-1}$
c. $g(n) = 5 \cdot 1^{n-1}$ or $g(n) = 5$
d–g. See back of book.
h. $g(n) = \frac{2\sqrt{3}}{9} \cdot \left(-\sqrt{3}\right)^n$ or $g(n) = -\frac{2\sqrt{3}}{9} \cdot \left(-\sqrt{3}\right)^n$

7. D

8. Draw a square. Connect the midpoints of the sides of this square to form another square. Connect the midpoints of the sides of the second square to form the next one. You can continue to make more squares in this pattern.

   a. If the side length of the first square you draw is 1, what is the side length of the second square? Of the third square?

   b. Do these lengths form a geometric sequence? Explain. If they do, what are the first term and the common ratio of this geometric sequence?

   c. If the area of the first square you draw is 1, what is the area of the second square? Of the third square?

   d. Do these areas form a geometric sequence? Explain. If they do, what are the first term and the common ratio of this geometric sequence? If they do not, what kind of a sequence do they form?

   e. **Take It Further** Prove that connecting the midpoints of the sides of a square really gives you another square.

Go Online PHSchool.com

For additional practice, go to **Web Code**: bfa-0711

9. a. Turn a blank piece of $8\frac{1}{2}$ in.-by-11 in. paper lengthwise and draw a 45° angle in the bottom left corner of the paper.

   b. Draw a small square, $\frac{1}{2}$ in. on each side, with one side on the horizontal side of the angle and a vertex on the other side of the angle.

   c. Extend the right side of this square vertically until it intersects the sloping side of the 45° angle. Draw a second square with this segment as its left side, as shown.

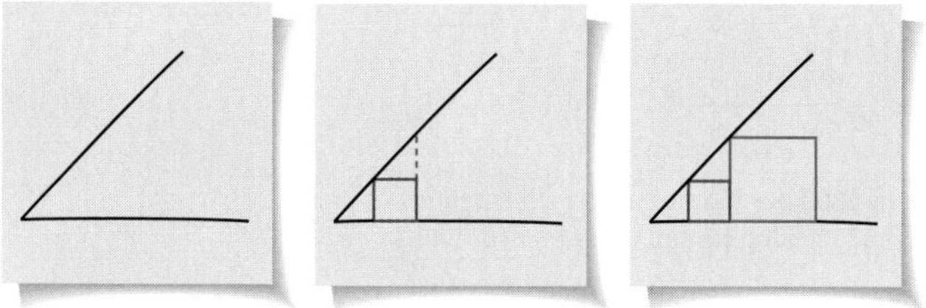

   d. Continue the process to draw two more squares.

   e. What are the lengths of the sides of the four squares?

   f. Find at least two geometric sequences in the diagram.

10. An old tale tells of a king who was tricked into paying an outrageous amount for a favor. The king was to pay by placing 1 grain of rice on the first square of a chessboard, 2 on the second square, 4 on the third square, 8 on the fourth square, and keep doubling the amount this way until all 64 squares had rice. The king thought this might take several pounds of rice.

   a. How many grains of rice would the king place on the last (64th) square?

   b. In all, how many grains of rice would the king place on the chessboard?

   c. If there are 8000 grains of rice in a pound, how many pounds of rice did the king have to pay for the favor?

EXERCISE 8 Some students will get stuck on part (a) if they do not remember or recognize that this construction gives an isosceles right triangle in each corner. You might want to show them how the second square is constructed, indicating the right triangle that can be used to find the side length. It may be better still to show that in each new square, the old side length is now a diagonal. This can allow students to pick up on the pattern more quickly, and especially to notice that the third square has side length $\frac{1}{2}$. Part (e) is not especially difficult and gives students an opportunity to review relationships they learned in *Geometry*. This part is not essential to the exercise, so you might not need to spend much time discussing it.

EXERCISE 10 There are many possible extensions for this exercise. How many tons of rice would you need? How big a pile of rice would you need if you wanted to fill a cylindrical tank with a diameter of 5 feet? Depending on your students' interest, you can take this exercise in many directions.

8.

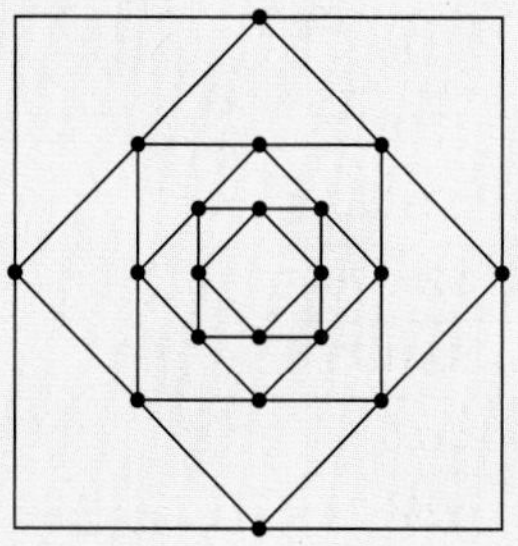

a. $\frac{\sqrt{2}}{2}; \frac{1}{2}$

b. Yes, the first term is 1 and the common ratio is $\frac{\sqrt{2}}{2}$.

c. $\frac{1}{2}, \frac{1}{4}$

d. Yes; the first term is 1 and the common ratio is $\frac{1}{2}$.

e. See back of book.

9. a–d. See back of book.

e. $\frac{1}{2}$ in., 1 in., 2 in., 4 in.

f. sides of the squares: $\frac{1}{2}, 1, 2, 4, \ldots$; areas of the squares: $\frac{1}{4}, 1, 4, 16, \ldots$

10. a. $2^{63} \approx 9.22 \cdot 10^{18}$

b. $\sum_{i=0}^{63} 2^i = 2^{64} - 1 \approx 1.84 \cdot 10^{19}$

c. $\approx 2.3 \cdot 10^{15}$

EXERCISES 10 AND 11 are both examples that demonstrate the power of exponential growth. This situation may be less familiar to students, and so, more intriguing.

EXERCISE 12 Students may assume there is a linear pattern here, but it should emerge quickly that the values of *m* do not form either an arithmetic or a geometric sequence. If time permits, give some higher values of *r* so that students can see the effects of the higher interest rate. These same kinds of rates apply to any savings or annuity account as well as to credit cards. Lowering the interest rate on any loan can have a huge effect in the long run.

EXERCISE 14 Check how students are solving part (d). Some may want just to calculate the terms and add them up, but the numbers are deliberately messy here in order to encourage use of the geometric series formula.

11. Suppose you make up a joke. On Day 1, you tell your two best friends. They cannot stop laughing. The next day (Day 2), each of them tells two people, who also love the joke. On Day 3, the four people who heard the joke the day before all tell two new people. And so it continues. Each day, everyone who heard the joke yesterday tells two people who have never heard the joke. How quickly does the joke spread?

a. How many people hear the joke for the first time on the 8th day?

b. In all, how many people have heard the joke by the end of the 8th day?

c. How long would it take all the students in your school to hear the joke?

d. How long would it take all the students in your town or city to hear the joke?

e. How long would it take everyone in the world to hear the joke?

You can also model the spread of disease with geometric series, but the spread of jokes is more pleasant to think about.

Assume there are about 6 billion people in the world.

12. Jaden wants to get a 3-year loan of $9000. He wants to know what monthly payment to expect for different interest rates.

a. Copy and complete this table showing the monthly payments *m* for different interest rates *r*.

r	*m*
0%	■
1%	■
2%	■
3%	■
4%	■
5%	■

b. If Jaden can afford to pay $300 per month, what is the greatest interest rate (to one tenth of a percent) that he can accept for his loan?

13. What price can Hector afford to pay for a car if he can put $1500 down and pay $500 per month on a 5-year, 4% loan?

14. To keep from getting in a rut, many athletes challenge themselves. Suppose Michelle runs 5 miles this week. She gives herself this challenge. In any week, she will never run a shorter distance than she did the week before, and she will try to increase her distance 10% each week.

a. How far will Michelle run next week?

b. How far will she run the week after next?

c. Michelle plans to run in a marathon 33 weeks from now. How far will she run the week before the marathon?

d. What total mileage will Michelle run between now and the week prior to the marathon, if she keeps her pact?

Answers

11. a. 256 people

b. 511 people

c–e. Answers may vary. Sample: Find the smallest integer *n* so that $2^{n+1} - 1 \geq S$, where *S* is the number of people in the group.

12. a.

r	*m*
0%	$250
1%	$253.87
2%	$257.78
3%	$261.73
4%	$265.72
5%	$269.74

b. 12%

Do you remember this exercise from Lesson 7.1?

A wealthy relative left Emile an inheritance. The will read as follows.

To Emile, because he likes math problems, I leave a choice. He can have one of two inheritances.

Option 1 A starting amount of $10,000 with an annual payment at the end of each year that is $1000 more than the amount he received the previous year, for the next 26 years

Option 2 A starting amount of one cent with an annual payment at the end of each year that is twice the amount he received in the previous year, for the next 26 years

Year 0 is the year in which Emile chooses an option and gets his first payment.

To find the total Emile gets under Option 1, you can sum an arithmetic series. After 26 years, he will get

$$10{,}000 + 11{,}000 + 12{,}000 + 13{,}000 + \cdots + (10{,}000 + 1{,}000n)$$

To find the total Emile gets under Option 2, you can sum a geometric series. After 26 years, he will get

$$0.01 + 0.02 + 0.04 + 0.08 + \cdots + (0.01) \cdot 2^n$$

15. a. What is n? That is, what is the last term you would add in each series?

b. Sum the arithmetic series to find the total Emile gets with Option 1.

c. Sum the geometric series to find the total Emile gets with Option 2.

Remember Thor and Pandora? They dropped a ball from a height of 2 meters and measured the height of each bounce. The following table shows the results of this experiment.

Number of Bounces	Height (m)
0	2.00
1	1.68
2	1.41
3	1.19
4	1.00
5	0.84
6	0.71

One question you might ask is what total distance the ball travels in, say, 100 bounces? The problem is more complicated than it might seem at first. Exercises 16–20 will help you answer this question.

EXERCISE 15 The exercise as presented is primarily a review of the situation discussed in the For You to Explore section from Lesson 7.1. For an alternative approach, ask students to find rules in terms of n instead of just calculating the sums for $n = 26$. Then, use a graphing calculator to look at the graphs of the functions for Option 1 and Option 2. As expected, Option 1 has a huge lead for a long time, but Option 2 catches up nicely!

13. about $28,650

14. a. at least 5.5 mi

b. at least 6.05 mi

c. almost 96 mi

d. about 1005.7 mi

15. a. The last value of n is 26, so the last term you would add for Option 1 is $10{,}000 + 26 \cdot 1000$ or $36,000; the last term you would add for Option 2 is $(0.01) \cdot 2^{26}$ or $671,088.64.

b. $621,000

c. $1,342,177.27

EXERCISES 16–18 take students through the calculation of this geometric series, including finding the common ratio of the sequence. When reviewing these exercises, remind students of the following identity:

$$1 + x + x^2 + \cdots + x^{100} = \frac{x^{101} - 1}{x - 1} = \frac{1 - x^{101}}{1 - x}$$

The second form might be preferred, since the common ratio x is less than 1. Here, that same identity is doubled.

EXERCISE 20 is meant to feed into the next lesson on limits. The total distance for 100 bounces and 1000 bounces is almost identical. Some students may recognize that x^n is getting very close to 0, to the point where it could be removed from the calculation entirely, leaving the rule for the infinite series, $\frac{a}{1 - r}$.

Additional Resources

PRINT RESOURCES
- Solution Manual
- Practice Workbook
- Assessment Resources
- Teaching Resources

TECHNOLOGY
- Interactive Textbook
- TeacherExpress CD-ROM
- ExamView CD-ROM
- PHSchool.com

Additional Practice

1. Suppose a is an arithmetic sequence with initial term $a(0) = 5$ and common difference -7.
   a. Find $a(9)$
   b. Find a closed form for a.
   c. Is -1878 a term of a? If so, what term is it? If not, explain why not.

2. An arithmetic sequence with terms $a_1, a_2, a_3, \ldots, a_6$ satisfies both $a_2 + a_4 + a_6 = 30$ and $a_2 a_4 a_6 = 640$. Find the terms in this sequence.

3. In an arithmetic sequence with a difference d, the product of the second term and d is -48. The sum of the third and fifth terms is 8. Find the first five terms in this sequence.

4. Find $g(10)$ for each geometric sequence.
   a. $g(1) = 12, r = -2$
   b. $g(1) = -4, r = \frac{3}{2}$
   c. $g(2) = 8, g(6) = 32$

5. Write a closed-form definition for a function that generates each sequence in Exercise 4.

6. Candice makes a resolution to do sit-ups every day. Suppose Candice does 10 sit-ups every day this week. She challenges herself to increase the number of sit-ups 20% each week. How many sit-ups will Candice do after each given week?
   a. week 5   b. week 12   c. week w

7. What price can Herb afford to pay for a car if he can put \$1000 down and pay \$550 per month on a 4-year, 3% loan?

8. A basketball drops from a height of 30 feet. After each bounce, the ball bounces to $\frac{2}{3}$ its previous height.
   a. How high does the ball bounce after 10 bounces?
   b. What is the total distance the ball travels downward after 10 bounces?
   c. What is the total distance the ball travels upward after 10 bounces?
   d. Find the total distance the ball travels upward and downward after 100 bounces.

Practice: For Lesson 7.11, assign Exercises 4–8.

16. First, just think about the distance the ball falls. Do not worry about the distance it travels bouncing up. When the ball first drops, it falls 2 meters. How far does it fall after the first bounce? After the second bounce? After the third bounce?

17. You saw that the bounce height was actually close to a geometric sequence. So you can rewrite your answers above as 2 meters, $2x$ meters, $2x^2$ meters, and $2x^3$ meters. What is the common ratio x?

18. To find the distance the ball falls in 100 bounces, you have to find this sum.

$$2 + 2x + 2x^2 + 2x^3 + \cdots + 2x^{100}$$

The value of x is whatever you found in Exercise 16. What is the sum?

19. What is the total distance the ball travels upward? Use any method you like to find out that total distance.

20. Find the total distance the ball travels upward and downward. Do you think your answer would be different if you calculated the distance for 1000 bounces instead? Explain.

Maintain Your Skills

21. Zeno starts 24 feet from a wall. He jumps half the distance to the wall. Then he jumps halfway across the remaining distance to the wall. Then he jumps half of that.

a. How far does Zeno travel after 3 jumps? How far is he from the wall?

b. How far does Zeno travel after 6 jumps? How far is he from the wall?

c. How far does Zeno travel after n jumps? How far is he from the wall?

d. Will Zeno ever get to the wall if he keeps up this "jumping halfway" scheme?

This is a variation on a famous problem known as Zeno's paradox, named for a Greek mathematician who lived in the 400's B.C.

Answers

16. 1.68 m; 1.41 m; 1.19 m

17. 0.84

18. 12.5 m

19. 10.5 m

20. 23 m; the bounces get smaller and smaller, so the total distance after 1000 bounces would still be 23 m.

21. a. 21 ft; 3 ft

b. 23.625 ft; 0.375 ft

c. $24\left(1 - \left(\frac{1}{2}\right)^n\right)$ ft; $\frac{24}{2^n}$ ft

d. No, he will never reach the wall, but he will get closer than any particular distance.

7.12 Limits

For some sequences and series, as the input values increase, the output values get closer and closer to a certain number.

In-Class Experiment

1. Suppose $f(n) = \frac{1}{2^n}$, and f is defined on the integers n such that $n \geq 1$.

n	$f(n)$
1	$\frac{1}{2^1} = \frac{1}{2}$
2	$\frac{1}{2^2} = \frac{1}{4}$
3	$\frac{1}{2^3} = \frac{1}{8}$
4	$\frac{1}{2^4} = \frac{1}{16}$
5	$\frac{1}{2^5} = \frac{1}{32}$

a. How large do you have to make n to be sure that $f(n)$ is within 0.1 of 0?

b. How large do you have to make n to ensure that $f(n)$ is within 0.01 of 0?

c. How large do you have to make n to ensure that $f(n)$ is within 0.001 of 0?

2. Copy the table above and add a Σ column. Use it to answer these questions.

a. Suppose $F(n)$ is the series associated with f.

$$F(n) = \sum_{k=1}^{n} f(k) = \frac{1}{2} + \frac{1}{4} + \frac{1}{8} + \cdots + \frac{1}{2^n}$$

Find a closed form for $F(n)$.

b. How large do you have to make n to be sure that $F(n)$ is within 0.1 of 1?

c. How large do you have to make n to ensure that $F(n)$ is within 0.01 of 1?

d. How large do you have to make n to ensure that $F(n)$ is within 0.001 of 1?

You say that the sequence in Problem 1 of the In-Class Experiment has a **limit**, or ultimate value, of 0. This means that if you make n large enough, you can make $f(n)$ as close as you want to 0.

Similarly, the series in Problem 2 has a limit of 1. If you make n large enough, you can make $F(n)$ as close as you want to 1.

In-Class Experiment

1. a. $n = 4$ **b.** $n = 7$ **c.** $n = 10$

2.

n	$f(n)$	Σ
1	$\frac{1}{2^1} = \frac{1}{2}$	$\frac{1}{2}$
2	$\frac{1}{2^2} = \frac{1}{4}$	$\frac{3}{4}$
3	$\frac{1}{2^3} = \frac{1}{8}$	$\frac{7}{8}$
4	$\frac{1}{2^4} = \frac{1}{16}$	$\frac{15}{16}$
5	$\frac{1}{2^5} = \frac{1}{32}$	$\frac{31}{32}$

a. $F(n) = 1 - \frac{1}{2^n}$

b. 4

c. 7

d. 10

Lesson Overview

GOAL

- Determine whether a geometric sequence has a limit and, if it does, how to find the limit.

In this lesson, *limit* is informally defined in this way: a function $f(n)$ has a limit L if you can guarantee that for any small distance d from L, you can find an input e large enough so that $f(e)$ is within d of L. Students are given various functions and numerical values with which to experiment, and they develop their intuition about limits.

CHECK YOUR UNDERSTANDING
- Core: 1, 2
- Optional: none

MATERIALS
- graphing calculators
- Blackline Master 7.12

HOMEWORK
- Core: 3, 5, 7
- Optional: 4, 6, 8
- Extension: 9

VOCABULARY
- limit

Launch

Begin the lesson with the In-Class Experiment.

Explore

You may wish to have students work in pairs or in small groups.

In-Class Experiment

The idea of ensuring that $f(n)$ is within *any* given distance of 0 is necessary for limits. Some students think that as long as the value of an expression keeps getting closer to a number, that number is the limit, but this is not quite true. $f(n) = \frac{1}{2^n}$ is also getting closer and closer to -1 as n increases, but there are many numbers x that can be chosen for which it is impossible to ensure that $f(n)$ will always be within x of -1. But, for *all* $x > 0$, it is possible to choose n to ensure that $f(n)$ is within x of 0. You may wish to use Blackline Master 7.12 here.

For Discussion

Have groups share their answers with the class.

Minds in Action

Derman's mindset here is that if the terms are approaching *something*, the something must be the limit. One way to convince students otherwise is to use a rule such as $h(n) = \frac{1}{5^n} + \frac{1}{1{,}000{,}000}$.

If students make a table similar to Tony's they may want to conclude that the limit of $h(n)$ is 0, as the function appears to approach 0. However if students use very large values of n, they will see that $h(n)$ does not approach 0.

For Discussion

3. In Problem 1, is there any value of n for which $f(n) = 0$? In what sense is 0 a limit for the sequence?

4. In Problem 2, is there any value of n for which $F(n) = 1$? In what sense is 1 a limit for the series?

5. Can a sequence ever have more than one limit? Explain.

Minds in Action   episode 36

Tony, Sasha, and Derman are working on the following questions.

Question 1 Suppose g is a geometric sequence with first term $g(0) = 1$ and common ratio $\frac{1}{5}$. Does g have a limit? If so, what is it?

Question 2 Using the same function g, does the associated series have a limit? If so, what is it?

Sasha Let's try making a table for g, so we can see what's going on.

Tony I've already filled in values up to $n = 3$.

n	$g(n)$
0	1
1	$\frac{1}{5}$
2	$\frac{1}{25}$
3	$\frac{1}{125}$

Derman Look—the outputs get smaller and smaller! They seem to approach 0, so I guess that's the limit.

Sasha It's not enough to say "they seem to approach 0." In order to say that the limit of the sequence is 0, we have to show that we can get as close as we want to 0. I mean, if we pick any number close to 0, we then have to find an n such that $g(n)$ is even closer to 0 than our number.

Tony Yes, look at this.

To get within 0.1 of 0, let $n = 2$.

$$g(2) = \left(\frac{1}{5}\right)^2 = \frac{1}{25} < 0.1$$

To get within 0.01 of 0, let $n = 3$.

$$g(3) = \left(\frac{1}{5}\right)^3 = \frac{1}{125} < 0.01$$

To get within 0.001 of 0, let $n = 5$.

$$g(5) = \left(\frac{1}{5}\right)^5 = \frac{1}{3125} < 0.001$$

Since you can get as close as you want to 0 by making n large enough, 0 is the limit of the sequence.

Answers

For Discussion

3. No; if n increases, the value of $\frac{1}{2^n}$ gets closer and closer to 0.

4. No; as n increases, the value of $F(n)$ gets closer to 1.

5. No; answers may vary. Sample: There can be *subsequences* that respectively approach different limits; for example, let $f(n) = \frac{1}{n}$ for odd n, and $f(n) = 1 - \frac{1}{n}$ for even n. Then $f(n)$ has one subsequence approaching 0 and another approaching 1, but the *entire* sequence cannot approach two different numbers.

Derman Look—it seems that for every three steps in this process, we get another two places of accuracy. If that's true, I'm sure that the terms of the sequence converge to 0.

Sasha OK, so what's the answer to Question 2? I think we should find a formula for the associated series. We have $g(n) = \left(\frac{1}{5}\right)^n$, so we can write out $G(n)$ like this.

$$\begin{aligned} G(n) &= \sum_{k=0}^{n} g(k) \\ &= \sum_{k=0}^{n} \left(\tfrac{1}{5}\right)^k \\ &= \frac{1 - \left(\frac{1}{5}\right)^{n+1}}{1 - \frac{1}{5}} \\ &= \frac{1}{1 - \frac{1}{5}}\left(1 - \left(\tfrac{1}{5}\right)^{n+1}\right) \\ &= \frac{1}{\frac{4}{5}}\left(1 - \left(\tfrac{1}{5}\right)^{n+1}\right) \\ &= \tfrac{5}{4}\left(1 - \left(\tfrac{1}{5}\right)^{n+1}\right) \end{aligned}$$

Derman Then I'll use the fact that $G(n) = \frac{5}{4}\left(1 - \left(\frac{1}{5}\right)^{n+1}\right)$ to fill in a Σ column.

n	g(n)	Σ
0	1	$\frac{5}{4}\left(1 - \frac{1}{5}\right)$
1	$\frac{1}{5}$	$\frac{5}{4}\left(1 - \frac{1}{25}\right)$
2	$\frac{1}{25}$	$\frac{5}{4}\left(1 - \frac{1}{125}\right)$
3	$\frac{1}{125}$	$\frac{5}{4}\left(1 - \frac{1}{625}\right)$
4	$\frac{1}{625}$	$\frac{5}{4}\left(1 - \frac{1}{3125}\right)$

Tony Well, $1 - \frac{1}{25}$ is within 0.1 of 1, $1 -$ is within 0.01 of 1, and $1 - \frac{1}{3125}$ is within 0.001 of 1. Now it's clear that as n gets larger, the factor $\left(1 - \left(\frac{1}{5}\right)^{n+1}\right)$ gets closer and closer to 1. It's equal to 1 minus a tiny number.

Sasha Right, so you can get as close as anyone wants to $\frac{5}{4}$ by making n large enough. So the limit of the series is $\frac{5}{4}$.

Habits of Mind

Look for relationships. If g is a geometric sequence with first term $g(0) = a$ and common ratio r, then $g(n) = ar^n$, and

$$\sum_{k=0}^{n} g(k) = a\sum_{k=0}^{n} r^k = a\left(\frac{1 - r^{n+1}}{1 - r}\right)$$

You can rewrite this as $\frac{a}{1-r}(1 - r^{n+1})$.

This is equivalent to the "Think Euclid" identity multiplied by the constant a.

For You to Do

The r values given here lead to series that converge quickly. You may want your students to try some other values as well, such as $r = \frac{2}{3}$ or $r = -\frac{5}{7}$.

Wrap Up

As time allows, have students work on the Check Your Understanding exercises and share their solutions.

Assessment Resources

Lesson Quiz 7.12

1. For each geometric sequence described, do the following.
   - Write the first five terms of the sequence.
   - Write the first five terms of the series associated with the sequence.
   - Decide if the series will have a limit.
   - If the series does have a limit, find that number.

   a. first term 26, common ratio $\frac{5}{2}$ **b.** first term 15, common ratio -0.3

2. You can line up squares shown in the diagram to make an infinite staircase. The first square is 1 by 1. The second square is $\frac{3}{5}$ by $\frac{3}{5}$. Each successive square is $\frac{3}{5}$ the base and height of the previous square.

   a. Find the area of the staircase.
   b. Find the perimeter of the staircase.

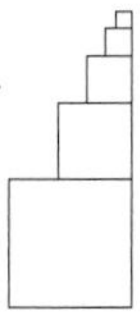

For You to Do

Suppose $a = 12$. Pick three values for r from this list.

$$2, \frac{1}{2}, \frac{1}{3}, -1, -3, -\frac{1}{2}, -\frac{1}{3}, \frac{3}{8}, \frac{9}{8}, 10$$

6. For each r-value you select, decide whether the following series has a limit.

$$\sum_{k=0}^{n} g(k) = \frac{12}{1-r}(1 - r^{n+1})$$

7. If it does, say what the limit is. If it does not, explain why not.

8. If $r = 1$, what happens with the formula? Does the series have a limit? Explain.

For Discussion

9. Explain how you can tell, just based on the value of r, if a geometric series has a limit.

10. Can an arithmetic series have a limit? Does the limit depend on the first term, the common difference, or both? Explain.

Exercises *Practicing Habits of Mind*

Check Your Understanding

1. For each geometric sequence described, do the following.

- Write the first four terms of the sequence.
- Write the first four terms of the series associated with the sequence.
- Decide if the series has a limit.
- If the series does have a limit, give that number.

a. first term 7 and common ratio $\frac{2}{9}$

b. first term 100 and common ratio $\frac{1}{2}$

c. first term $\frac{3}{4}$ and common ratio 2

d. first term 1 and common ratio 1

Answers

For You to Do

6. $\sum_{k=0}^{n} g(k)$ has a limit if $|r| < 1$.

7. The following table gives the limits for the series with r values between -1 and 1.

r	Limit
$\frac{1}{2}$	24
$\frac{1}{3}$	18
$-\frac{1}{2}$	8
$-\frac{1}{3}$	9
$\frac{3}{8}$	19.2

If $r > 1$, then r^{n+1} grows larger without bound as n increases, so the series also increases without bound. If $r < -1$, then r^{n+1} oscillates between larger and larger positive numbers and smaller and smaller negative numbers, so the series does not approach any one number. If $r = -1$, then the series becomes $12 - 12 + 12 - 12 + 12 - \dots$, so the sum oscillates between 12 and 0 and thus the series has no limit.

8. The formula is undefined. If $r = 1$, then $\sum_{k=0}^{n} g(k) = (n + 1) \cdot 12$. The series does not have a limit. The value of $\sum_{k=0}^{n} g(k)$ will increase as n increases.

For Discussion

9. If $|r| < 1$, a geometric series has a limit.

10. The only arithmetic series that has a limit is the series associated with the sequence 0, 0, 0, 0, ...

2. Pat and Sam are out for some exercise. They start off on a mile-long path. Sam starts walking at a steady rate. Pat starts running twice as fast as Sam walks. Pat runs to the end of the mile, runs back to Sam, turns around and runs to the end of the mile, turns around and runs to Sam, and so on. All the while Sam walks steadily along, laughing at Pat.

When Sam reaches the end of the mile-long path, how far has Pat run?

On Your Own

3. The diagrams below show the first three stages of the Koch curve. The segment of Stage 0 gets replaced by four segments, each $\frac{1}{3}$ the length of the original segment and arranged as shown in Stage 1. The same rule applies to each segment of Stage n as you pass to Stage $n + 1$.

Stage 0

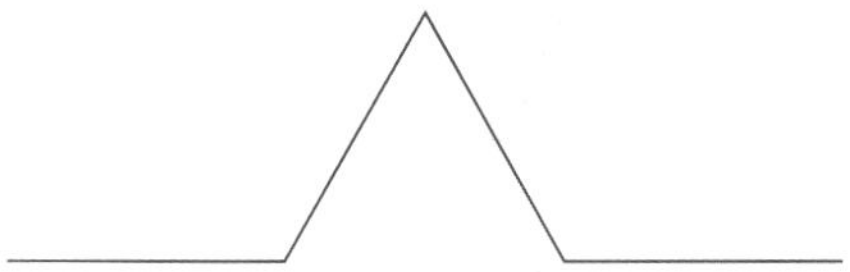

Stage 1

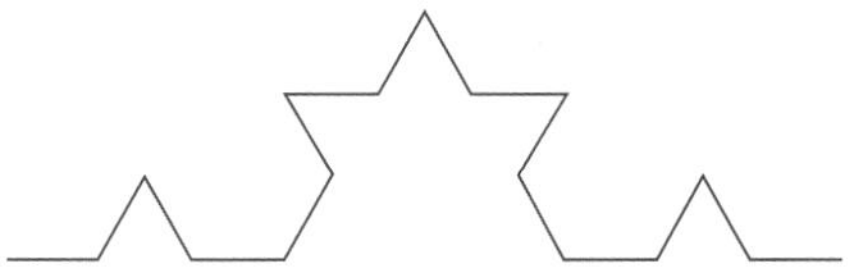

Stage 2

a. Draw the next stage.

b. Assume you start with length 1 at Stage 0. Find the length of the curve at Stages 1–3.

c. Find a closed form for the length of the curve at stage n.

d. Does the perimeter have a limit? That is, as n increases, does the perimeter of Stage n approach some fixed number, or does it increase without bound?

Go Online PHSchool.com

For additional practice, go to **Web Code**: bfa-0712

Exercises

HOMEWORK
- Core: 3, 5, 7
- Optional: 4, 6, 8
- Extension : 9

Check Your Understanding

EXERCISE 2 There is an even simpler solution to this exercise. If Pat is running twice as fast as Sam, how far does Pat run in the time it takes Sam to walk a mile? (Answer: 2 miles) It does not matter that Pat is turning; she is running in a straight line.

On Your Own

EXERCISE 3 Although the length of this curve increases without bound, it is contained in a limited area of the plane even as the number of stages approaches infinity. It is a fractal, an object with a fractional dimension. A line is one dimensional, area is two dimensional, and this curve with its infinite length in a finite area of the plane is somewhere between the two. At each stage, a unit length is replaced by 4 sections each of length $\frac{1}{3}$, so the Koch curve (at its limit) has dimension $\frac{4}{3}$.

Exercises

1. a.

n	$t(n)$	$T(n)$
1	7	7
2	$7 \cdot \left(\frac{2}{9}\right) = \frac{14}{9}$	$8\frac{5}{9}$
3	$7 \cdot \left(\frac{2}{9}\right)^2 = \frac{28}{81}$	$8\frac{73}{81}$
4	$7 \cdot \left(\frac{2}{9}\right)^3 = \frac{56}{729}$	$8\frac{713}{729}$

$T(n)$ has a limit, which is 9.

b.

n	$t(n)$	$T(n)$
1	100	100
2	$100 \cdot \frac{1}{2} = 50$	150
3	$100 \cdot \left(\frac{1}{2}\right)^2 = 25$	175
4	$100 \cdot \left(\frac{1}{2}\right)^3 = 12.5$	187.5

$T(n)$ has a limit, which is 200.

c–d. See back of book.

2. 2 mi

3. a.

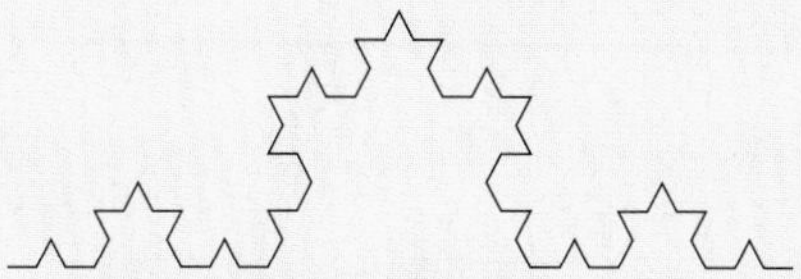

b. The lengths of the ends of Stages 0, 1, 2, and 3 are 1, $\frac{4}{3}$, $\frac{16}{9}$, and $\frac{64}{27}$, respectively.

c. $\ell(n) = \left(\frac{4}{3}\right)^n$

d. The perimeter does not have a limit.

EXERCISE 5 Students may get stuck on this exercise if they do not think of a way to organize the information they have into sums. Suggesting splitting the perimeter into left, right, top, and bottom may be all they need to get started.

4. You can close the shape at each stage by adding line segments. The diagram below shows closed shapes for Stage 1 and Stage 2. Then you can find the area within the curve.

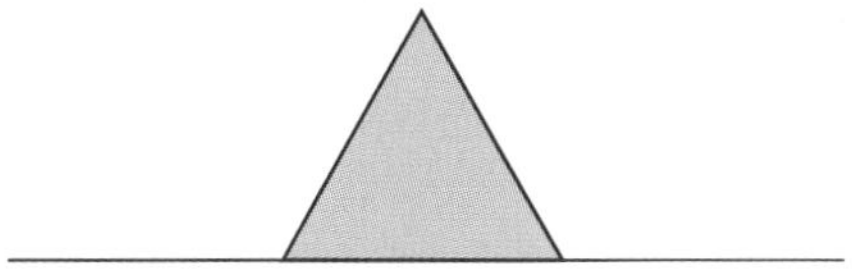

Area of Stage 1

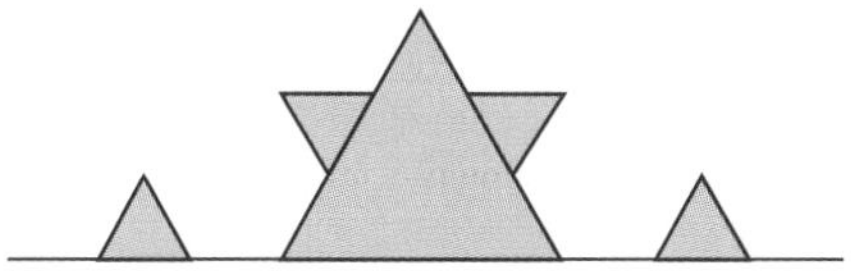

Area of Stage 2

Assume that for Stage 1 above, the area is 1 square unit.

a. Find the area within the curve at Stages 2–4.

b. What is the area at Stage n?

c. Does the area have a limit? That is, as n increases, does the area of Stage n approach some fixed number, or does it increase without bound?

5. You can line up the squares shown in the diagram below on the left to make an infinite staircase, shown below on the right. The first square is 1 by 1. The second square is $\frac{2}{3}$ by $\frac{2}{3}$. Each successive square is $\frac{2}{3}$ the height of the previous square.

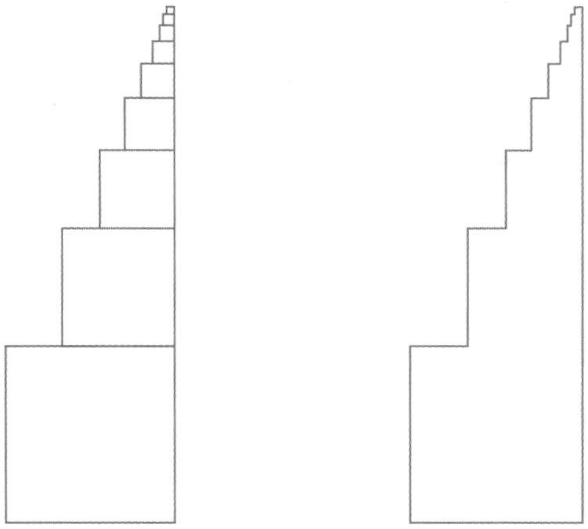

a. Find the area of the staircase. **b.** Find the perimeter of the staircase.

Answers

4. a. The areas at the end of Stages 1, 2, 3, and 4 are 1, $\frac{13}{9}$, $\frac{133}{81}$, and $\frac{1261}{729}$, respectively.

b. $\frac{9}{5}\left(1 - \left(\frac{4}{9}\right)^n\right)$

c. Yes, the limit is $\frac{9}{5}$.

5. a. $\frac{9}{5}$ square units

b. 8 units

6. To make the figure at the right, you connect the midpoints of the sides of a square of area 1 to form an inner square. You shade two opposite corners. You then repeat the process for the smaller square. Suppose you repeat this process an infinite number of times. Use a geometric series to find the total area of the shaded region. Does your answer make sense?

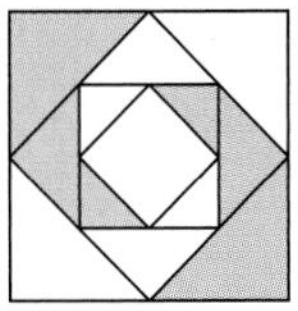

7. **Standardized Test Prep** What is the limit of the following geometric series?

$$1 + \frac{3}{5} + \frac{9}{25} + \frac{27}{125} + \frac{81}{625} + \cdots$$

A. $\frac{3}{2}$ **B.** 2 **C.** $\frac{5}{2}$ **D.** 3

Maintain Your Skills

8. Achilles and the tortoise run a race. Since Achilles is a faster runner (in fact, he can run 10 times faster than the tortoise), he gives the tortoise a 10-meter head start.

During the time it takes Achilles to run 10 meters, the tortoise covers 1 meter. Thus, the tortoise now has a 1-meter lead. During the time it takes Achilles to run another 1 meter, the tortoise runs 0.1 meter. Thus, the tortoise still has a 0.1-meter lead.

As Achilles runs the next 0.1 meter of the race, the tortoise goes 0.01 meter. Therefore, as small as the lead may be, the tortoise is still ahead in the race.

Does this mean Achilles never catches up to the tortoise? Explain.

9. **Take It Further** Suppose you divide a 3 inch-by-3 inch square into nine smaller squares and shade the center square. You then partition each unshaded square into nine squares and shade their centers. If you continue this process forever, how much area is shaded? (Note: The figures below are not full size.)

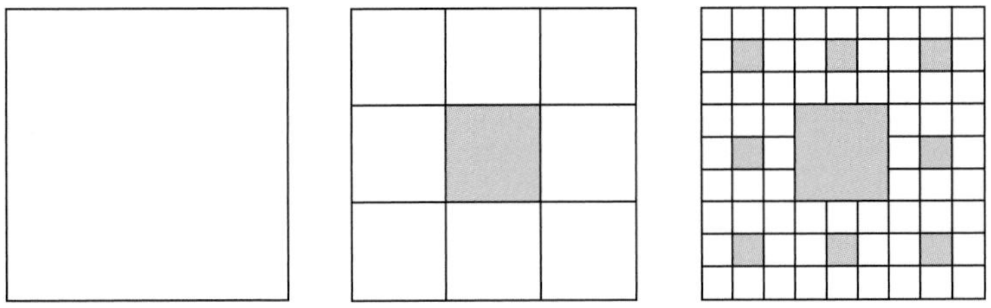

6. $\frac{1}{2}$; answers may vary. Sample: After you draw an inner square, you shade half of what is outside that inner square. By repeating this without end, you shade half of the original square.

7. C

8. Achilles *will* catch the tortoise. (An analogy is the second hand of a clock "catching up" to the minute hand.)

9. At each stage you leave $\frac{8}{9}$ of the original square unshaded. Since $\left(\frac{8}{9}\right)^n$ approaches 0 as n gets larger and larger, the entire area of the square gets shaded as n increases.

Maintain Your Skills

EXERCISE 8 A version of this exercise appears in the Douglas Hofstadter book *Gödel, Escher, Bach: an Eternal Golden Braid*, which may be an interesting read here, in part because it takes the form of a dialog among Achilles, the Tortoise, and Zeno, who tries to explain his paradox. There are many mathematically-oriented dialogs in the book.

EXERCISE 9 This shape is a famous fractal called the Sierpinski carpet. Often students are amazed by the result, but it is forced by the way area is removed. Students may also be amazed that an infinite number of points are never removed by this process, but these points do not form any measurable area.

Additional Resources

PRINT RESOURCES
- Solution Manual
- Practice Workbook
- Assessment Resources
- Teaching Resources

TECHNOLOGY
- Interactive Textbook
- TeacherExpress CD-ROM
- ExamView CD-ROM
- PHSchool.com

Additional Practice

1. For each geometric sequence described below, do the following.
   - Write the first five terms of the sequence.
   - Write the first five terms of the series associated with the sequence.
   - Decide if the series has a limit.
   - If the series does have a limit, give that number.

   a. first term 12, common ratio $\frac{2}{3}$ b. first term 6, common ratio -2
   c. first term 16, common ratio 0.4 d. first term -15, common ratio 1.5

2. The diagrams at the right show the first three stages of a variation of the Koch curve. The segment of Stage 0 gets replaced by five segments, each $\frac{1}{3}$ the length of the original segment and arranged as shown in Stage 1. The same rule applies to each segment of Stage n as you pass to Stage $n + 1$.
   a. Draw Stage 3.
   b. Assume you start with length 1 at Stage 0. Find the length of the curve at Stages 1–3.
   c. Find a closed form for the length of the curve at Stage n.
   d. Does the perimeter have a limit? Explain.

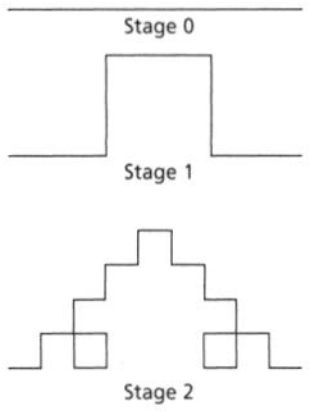

3. You can line up squares shown in the first diagram at the right to make an infinite staircase, shown in the second diagram at the right. The first square is 1 by 1. The second square is $\frac{3}{4}$ by $\frac{3}{4}$. Each successive square is $\frac{3}{4}$ the base and height of the previous square.
   a. Find the area of the staircase.
   b. Find the perimeter of the staircase.

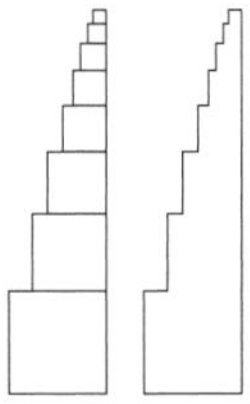

4. Consider the repeating decimal 0.045045045045 . . .
   a. What is the initial term a?
   b. What is the common ratio r?
   c. Write this repeating decimal as a fraction.

5. Write each repeating decimal as a fraction.
   a. 0.7878787878 . . . b. 0.3939393939 . . . c. 0.0210210210 . . .
   d. 0.1717171717 . . . e. 0.6363636363 . . . f. 0.3453453453 . . .

Practice: For Lesson 7.12, assign Exercises 1–3.

Lesson Overview

GOAL

- Convert a repeating decimal into an exact fraction.

Students learn to see repeating decimals as geometric series and to use their understanding of the limits of geometric series to convert repeating decimals into exact fractions. They also examine the logic of a commonly-taught technique for converting repeating decimals into fractions. They see some of the subtleties inherent in the logic behind it. This is a short lesson, so you might have time to do some chapter review.

CHECK YOUR UNDERSTANDING
- Core: 1, 2
- Optional: none

MATERIALS
- graphing calculators

HOMEWORK
- Core: 3, 4, 5, 6
- Optional: none

VOCABULARY
- repeating decimal

Launch

Have the class read through the introduction and work on the For You to Do problems.

Explore

For You to Do

Students generally will already "know" that $0.\overline{2}$ is $\frac{2}{9}$. But the result here should be a very convincing argument of why it is true: 0.2222 can be written as $\frac{2}{9}$ multiplied by something close to 1; 0.22222 can be written as $\frac{2}{9}$ multiplied by something even closer to 1, etc. This argument can help with an inevitable question (Exercise 6i in this lesson): why should $0.\overline{9}$ be equal to 1? These same arguments apply. If students are convinced about limits, then they will agree that the terms of the sequence 0.999, 0.9999, 0.99999, ... get as close to 1 as desired; therefore $0.\overline{9}$ must equal 1.

7.13 Repeating Decimals

You have learned the following two things in this investigation.

- If g is a geometric sequence $g(n) = a \cdot r^n$, then the formula for the associated series is

$$G(n) = \sum_{k=0}^{n} g(k) = \frac{a}{1-r}(1 - r^{n+1})$$

- If the common ratio of a geometric sequences is between -1 and 1—that is, $-1 < r < 1$—then the associated series has a limit. That limit is $\frac{a}{1-r}$.

Remember...

If $|r| < 1$, then as n gets very large, $|r^{n+1}|$ gets very small. In fact, it gets arbitrarily close to 0. So the factor of $(1 - r^{n+1})$ gets very close to 1. If $(1 - r^{n+1})$ is very close to 1, then $G(n)$ is very close to $\frac{a}{1-r}$.

Some decimals are geometric series. You can use the above facts to find fractions equivalent to them. For example, the decimal 0.2222 is

$$\frac{2}{10} + \frac{2}{100} + \frac{2}{1000} + \frac{2}{10{,}000} = \frac{2}{10} + \frac{2}{10^2} + \frac{2}{10^3} + \frac{2}{10^4}$$

$$= \frac{2}{10} + \frac{2}{10}\left(\frac{1}{10}\right) + \frac{2}{10}\left(\frac{1}{10}\right)^2 + \frac{2}{10}\left(\frac{1}{10}\right)^3$$

This is the sum of four terms of a geometric sequence with first term $\frac{2}{10}$ and common ratio $\frac{1}{10}$. You can use the formula below for the sum of $n + 1$ terms of a geometric series to get a fraction equivalent to 0.2222.

$$\left(\frac{a}{1-r}\right)(1 - r^{n+1})$$

Why are there $n + 1$ terms?

For You to Do

1. Think about the sequence that represents 0.2222.
   a. What is the initial term a?
   b. What is the common ratio r?
   c. What is n?
   d. Use the formula above to find a fraction equivalent to 0.2222.
2. Show that the following equations are true.

$$0.22222 = \frac{2}{9}\left(1 - \left(\frac{1}{10}\right)^5\right)$$

$$0.222222 = \frac{2}{9}\left(1 - \left(\frac{1}{10}\right)^6\right)$$

3. What is the limit of this sequence?

$$\{0.2, 0.22, 0.222, 0.2222, 0.22222, 0.222222, \ldots\}$$

Remember...

When you write 0.222 . . . or $0.\overline{2}$, what you mean is the limit of the sequence.

Answers

For You to Do

1. a. $\frac{2}{10}$
   b. $\frac{1}{10}$
   c. 4
   d. $\frac{1111}{5000}$
2. Answers may vary. Sample:
   $\frac{2}{9}(1 - (0.1)^5)$
   $= \frac{2}{9}(1 - 0.00001)$
   $= \frac{2}{9}(0.99999) = 0.22222;$
   $\frac{2}{9}(1 - (0.1)^6)$
   $= \frac{2}{9}(1 - 0.000001)$
   $= \frac{2}{9}(0.999999) = 0.222222$
3. $\frac{2}{9}$

Developing Habits of Mind

Think about it another way. This is another way to think about **repeating decimals.** What you really want in Problem 3 above is the infinite decimal 0.222 . . . . Call this x. Then

$$10x = 2.22222\ldots$$
$$x = 0.22222\ldots$$

Subtract. You get $9x = 2$, so $x = \frac{2}{9}$.

What the argument really says is if 0.2222 . . . stands for anything, it has to stand for a number that when multiplied by 10, gives two more than itself. That is the 2.22222. . . . The only number with this property is $\frac{2}{9}$.

The important point is that the repeating decimal stands for something in the first place. Suppose you have an infinite string of 9's to the left of the decimal place.

$$\ldots 999999.00\ldots$$

See where this leads you. In these calculations, make the decimal point large, as in 9**.**0, so it is distinct from an ordinary decimal point.

Let $x = \ldots 9999.000\ldots$

Then

$$x = \ldots 99999.000\ldots$$
$$10x = \ldots 99990.000\ldots$$

Subtract. You get $-9x = 9$, so $x = -1$.

That cannot be right. So a string of 9's to the left of the decimal point does not name a real number. You cannot call it x and do algebra with it.

This trick does, in fact, work. You can use it to convert repeating decimals to fractions. But it rests on some properties of limits that you will not learn until you study calculus.

To be safe, use geometric series when dealing with repeating decimals. For example, think of the decimal 0.12121212 . . . as a series with first term $\frac{12}{100}$ and common ratio $\frac{1}{100}$.

Sometimes you can only successfully complete an action by going in a certain direction.

Developing Habits of Mind

This multiply-and-subtract method is a standard way of finding the fraction for a repeating decimal. For example, it works with $x = \frac{1}{11} = 0.09090909\ldots$ by multiplying x by 100. The multiplier is always a power of 10, the power being the number of repeated digits. Note that this method only works for real numbers, so there has to be a second convincing argument that the number exists in the first place. For numbers such as $0.22222\ldots$, the sequence of finite decimals leading toward it converge to $\frac{2}{9}$, therefore it makes sense to say $0.2222\ldots = \frac{2}{9}$.

Wrap Up

Discuss with the class the ideas presented in Developing Habits of Mind. See if they can identify the flaw in the argument. Then have them work on the Check Your Understanding exercises.

Assessment Resources

Lesson Quiz 7.13

1. Consider the repeating decimal 0.35353535 . . .
   a. What is the initial term a?
   b. What is the common ratio r?
   c. Write this repeating decimal as a fraction.
2. Consider the repeating decimal 0.035035035035 . . .
   a. What is the initial term a?
   b. What is the common ratio r?
   c. Write this repeating decimal as a fraction.
3. Write the repeating decimal 0.1616161616 . . . as a fraction.
4. Write the repeating decimal 0.116116116116116 . . . as a fraction.

Exercises

HOMEWORK
- Core: 3, 4, 5, 6
- Optional: none

Check Your Understanding

EXERCISE 2 The last two parts ask students to think about where the geometric sequence starts. In part (c), students can make an adjustment to the first term, but the sequence is still clear. In part (d), though, the sequence does not start with the first digits after the decimal; it starts later.

On Your Own

EXERCISE 4 Infinitely repeating decimals are in the set of real numbers, and one way to see this is by locating the number on the number line. For example, 0.272727... is between 0.272 and 0.273. However, Shannon's series is not a real number, because you cannot find an upper bound for the sum to fence it on the real number line; there is not such an upper bound. There is not even an upper bound for the terms of her series.

Additional Resources

PRINT RESOURCES
- Solution Manual
- Practice Workbook
- Assessment Resources
- Teaching Resources

TECHNOLOGY
- Interactive Textbook
- TeacherExpress CD-ROM
- ExamView CD-ROM
- PHSchool.com

Additional Practice

1. For each geometric sequence described below, do the following.
   - Write the first five terms of the sequence.
   - Write the first five terms of the series associated with the sequence.
   - Decide if the series has a limit.
   - If the series does have a limit, give that number.

   a. first term 12, common ratio $\frac{2}{3}$ b. first term 6, common ratio -2
   c. first term 16, common ratio 0.4   d. first term -15, common ratio 1.5

2. The diagrams at the right show the first three stages of a variation of the Koch curve. The segment of Stage 0 gets replaced by five segments, each $\frac{1}{3}$ the length of the original segment and arranged as shown in Stage 1. The same rule applies to each segment of Stage n as you pass to Stage $n + 1$.
   a. Draw Stage 3.
   b. Assume you start with length 1 at Stage 0. Find the length of the curve at Stages 1–3.
   c. Find a closed form for the length of the curve at Stage n.
   d. Does the perimeter have a limit? Explain.

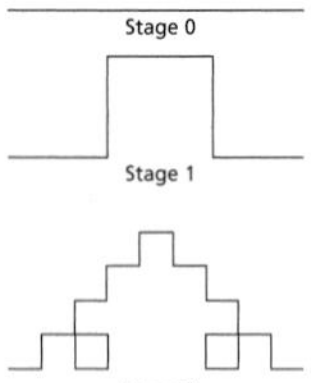

3. You can line up squares shown in the first diagram at the right to make an infinite staircase, shown in the second diagram at the right. The first square is 1 by 1. The second square is $\frac{3}{4}$ by $\frac{3}{4}$. Each successive square is $\frac{3}{4}$ the base and height of the previous square.
   a. Find the area of the staircase.
   b. Find the perimeter of the staircase.

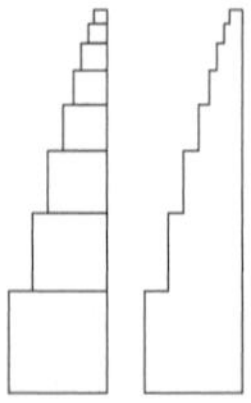

4. Consider the repeating decimal 0.045045045045 . . .
   a. What is the initial term a?
   b. What is the common ratio r?
   c. Write this repeating decimal as a fraction.

5. Write each repeating decimal as a fraction.
   a. 0.7878787878 . . .   b. 0.3939393939 . . .   c. 0.0210210210 . . .
   d. 0.1717171717 . . .   e. 0.6363636363 . . .   f. 0.3453453453 . . .

Practice: For Lesson 7.13, assign Exercises 4 and 5.

Exercises *Practicing Habits of Mind*

Check Your Understanding

1. Consider the repeating decimal 0.123123123. . . .
- **a.** What is the initial term a?
- **b.** What is the common ratio r?
- **c.** Write this repeating decimal as a fraction.

2. Write each repeating decimal as a fraction.
- **a.** 0.121212 . . .
- **b.** 0.807807807 . . .
- **c.** 0.0123123123 . . .
- **d.** 0.075123123123 . . .

On Your Own

3. Write each repeating decimal as a fraction.
- **a.** 0.09090909 . . .
- **b.** 0.0370370370 . . .
- **c.** 0.0522222 . . .

Go Online PHSchool.com
For additional practice, go to **Web Code:** bfa-0713

4. Shannon says, "I know the series $1 + 2 + 4 + 8 + \cdots$ keeps increasing. But if I call it x, watch what happens.

$$2x = 2 + 4 + 8 + 16 + \cdots$$
$$x = 1 + 2 + 4 + 8 + \cdots$$

Subtract and I get $x = -1$."

Shannon is confused. What would you say to help?

5. **Standardized Test Prep** Which fraction is equivalent to the repeating decimal $0.25714\overline{714}$?

A. $\frac{8563}{33,300}$ **B.** $\frac{25,689}{99,000}$

C. $\frac{25,714}{99,900}$ **D.** $\frac{25,714}{99,999}$

Maintain Your Skills

6. Write each repeating decimal as a fraction.
- **a.** 0.111 . . . **b.** 0.222 . . . **c.** 0.333 . . .
- **d.** 0.444 . . . **e.** 0.555 . . . **f.** 0.666 . . .
- **g.** 0.777 . . . **h.** 0.888 . . . **i.** 0.999 . . .

Answers

Exercises

1. a. $a = 0.123$
b. $r = 0.001$
c. $\frac{123}{999}$ $\left(\text{or } \frac{41}{333}\right)$

2. a. $\frac{12}{99}$ $\left(\text{or } \frac{4}{33}\right)$
b. $\frac{807}{999}$ $\left(\text{or } \frac{269}{333}\right)$
c. $\frac{123}{9990}$ $\left(\text{or } \frac{41}{3330}\right)$
d. $\frac{75,048}{999,000}$ $\left(\text{or } \frac{3127}{41,625}\right)$

3. a. $\frac{9}{99}$ $\left(\text{or } \frac{1}{11}\right)$
b. $\frac{37}{999}$ $\left(\text{or } \frac{1}{27}\right)$
c. $\frac{47}{900}$

4. The series $1 + 2 + 3 + 4 + \ldots$ does not have a finite value, so it was not possible to "call it x."

5. A

6. See back of book.

Mathematical Reflections 7C

In this investigation, you learned to find closed forms for arithmetic and geometric sequences and their associated series. The following exercises will help you summarize what you have learned.

1. An arithmetic sequence s has second term 8 and fifth term 1.
   a. Explain why there is only one sequence that meets these requirements.
   For the sequence, find each of the following.
   b. the common difference c. the 28th term d. a closed form
2. An arithmetic sequence g has $g(0) = -10$ and common difference 4.
   a. Make a Σ table for $g(n)$ for n-values 0 through 5.
   b. Find a closed form for the sequence.
   c. Find a closed form for the associated series.
3. Repeat Exercise 1 replacing *arithmetic sequence* with *geometric sequence*. In part (b), replace *common difference* with *common ratio*.
4. Repeat Exercise 2 replacing *arithmetic sequence* with *geometric sequence* and *common difference* with *common ratio*.
5. Derman wins a "million-dollar" prize, which he knows is not really worth \$1,000,000. Instead of a check for \$1,000,000, he is going to get \$50,000 per year for 20 years. He wants to know what the present value of his prize is.
   a. Use $\sum_{k=0}^{19} 50{,}000\left(\frac{1}{1.06}\right)^k$ to find the present value. Assume a 6% interest rate.
   b. Suppose Derman is able to invest his money with an 8% rate of return. Would the present value of his prize be more or less than the amount you found for a 6% rate? Find the new present value to check your estimate. Explain why the interest rate affects the present value in the way it does.
6. What is an arithmetic sequence?
7. What is a geometric series?
8. How do you write the repeating decimal 0.121212121 . . . as a fraction?

Vocabulary

In this investigation, you learned these terms. Make sure you understand what each one means and how to use it.

- **arithmetic sequence**
- **arithmetic series**
- **common difference**
- **common ratio**
- **geometric sequence**
- **geometric series**
- **limit**
- **repeating decimal**
- **sequence**
- **term**

Mathematical Reflections

1. a. The common difference is $-\frac{7}{3}$ so the first term is $\frac{31}{3}$, and there is only one arithmetic sequence with those characteristics.

b. $-\frac{7}{3}$ **c.** $-\frac{158}{3}$

d. $s(n) = \frac{1}{3}(31 - 7n)$

2. a. The entries for the $g(n)$ column are $-10, -6, -2, 2, 6, 10$ so the entries for the Σ column are $-10, -16, -18, -16, -10, 0$.

b. $g(n) = -10 + 4n$

c. $G(n) = 2n^2 - 8n - 10$

3. a. $r^3 = \frac{1}{8}$ so $r = \frac{1}{2}$, and the first term is 16; there is exactly one geometric sequence that begins 16, 8, 4, ...

b. $r = \frac{1}{2}$ **c.** $\frac{1}{8{,}388{,}608}$

d. $s(n) = 16 \cdot \left(\frac{1}{2}\right)^n$

4–8. See back of book.

Mathematical Reflections

EXERCISES 6–8 At the start of the investigation, you may have assigned these as Questions 1–3 for students to think and write about.

Investigation Overview

This investigation gives students a chance to apply what they have learned about sequences and series to the investigation of patterns in Pascal's Triangle. Then it presents the Binomial Theorem.

You may wish to assign Questions 1–3 for students to think and write about during the investigation.

Learning Goals

- Generate Pascal's Triangle and evaluate the nth row, kth column entry as $\binom{n}{k}$.
- Notice and explain patterns in Pascal's Triangle.
- Use the Binomial Theorem for expanding expressions of the form $(a + b)^n$.

Habits and Skills

- Seek invariants or regularity in calculation to develop a conjecture.
- Reason logically to prove conjectures.
- Apply previous results in new contexts.

Investigation 7D

Pascal's Triangle and the Binomial Theorem

In *Pascal's Triangle and the Binomial Theorem*, you will explore the patterns in Pascal's Triangle. You will find patterns in the triangle and learn how the numbers in the triangle are related to powers of polynomials.

By the end of this investigation, you will be able to answer questions like these.

1. What is the sum of the entries of the tenth row of Pascal's Triangle?
2. What is the expanded form of $(2d + 7)^8$?
3. What is the coefficient of x^7y^3 in the expansion of $(x + y)^{10}$?

You will learn how to

- generate Pascal's Triangle and evaluate the nth row, kth column entry as $\binom{n}{k}$
- notice and explain patterns in Pascal's Triangle
- use the Binomial Theorem for expanding expressions of the form $(a + b)^n$

You will develop these habits and skills:

- Seek invariants or regularity in calculation to develop a conjecture.
- Reason logically to prove conjectures.
- Apply previous results in new contexts.

There are $\binom{30}{2}$ ways to choose 2 socks from a pile of 30 socks.

Investigation Road Map

LESSON 7.14, *Getting Started,* has students start looking for patterns in a simple table, where each column is the Σ of the column before. They also look for patterns in the expansion of binomials.

LESSON 7.15, *Pascal's Triangle,* formally introduces Pascal's Triangle. Students learn how to generate it and start looking for and explaining patterns in the triangle.

LESSON 7.16, *The Binomial Theorem,* states the Binomial Theorem, relating the coefficients in the expansion of a binomial raised to a power and the entries in Pascal's Triangle.

7.14 Getting Started

Activating Prior Knowledge
Exploring New Ideas

You can find many patterns in the sums of sums and in the powers of polynomials.

For You to Explore

For Problems 1–5, use this big, but simple, table.

n	$f(n)$	Σ	$\Sigma\Sigma$	$\Sigma\Sigma\Sigma$	$\Sigma\Sigma\Sigma\Sigma$
1	1	■	■	■	■
2	2	■	■	■	■
3	3	■	■	■	■
4	4	■	■	■	■
5	5	■	■	■	■
6	6	■	■	■	■
7	7	■	■	■	■
8	8	■	■	■	■
9	9	■	■	■	■
10	10	■	■	■	■

1. Copy and complete the table.
2. Find, describe, and explain several patterns in your table.
3. Find a closed form for f.
4. a. What is $\sum_{k=1}^{7} f(k)$?

   b. What is $\sum_{k=1}^{1000} f(k)$? Explain.

   c. Find a closed form for $\sum_{k=1}^{n} f(k)$.
5. a. Find a closed form for the $\Sigma\Sigma$ column.

   b. Find a closed form for the $\Sigma\Sigma\Sigma$ column.

   c. Where have you seen these closed forms before? What can you predict as a closed form for the $\Sigma\Sigma\Sigma\Sigma$ column?

Answers

For You to Explore

1. See back of book.
2. Answers may vary. Sample: Σ lists the triangular numbers.
3. $f(n) = n$
4. a. 28

   b. $\sum_{k=1}^{1000} (f(k))$ is the sum of the numbers from 1 to 1000, which is $\frac{1000(1001)}{2} = 500{,}500$.

   c. $\sum_{k=1}^{n} f(k) = \frac{n(n+1)}{2}$
5. a. $\Sigma\Sigma = \frac{n(n+1)(n+2)}{6}$

   b. $\Sigma\Sigma\Sigma = \frac{n(n+1)(n+2)(n+3)}{24}$

   c. See back of book.

Lesson Overview

GOAL

- Warm up to the ideas of the investigation.

In this lesson, students are given several different contexts and asked to look for patterns and to try to explain the patterns they see. As always in a Getting Started lesson, there is no need to formalize these ideas today. Students will meet all of the ideas again throughout the investigation.

FOR YOU TO EXPLORE
- Core: 1, 2, 3, 4, 5
- Optional: none

MATERIALS
- CAS (recommended)
- graphing calculators
- Blackline Master 7.14

HOMEWORK
- Core: 6, 7, 8
- Optional: 9, 10

Launch

Have students get started on the For You to Explore problems right away.

Explore

As students are working, you might wish to keep track of any patterns they find on the board.

For You to Explore

PROBLEMS 1–5 Blackline Master 7.14 provides a blank copy of the table to be completed.

PROBLEM 1 Some of your students may recognize Pascal's Triangle in this table.

PROBLEM 2 There are so many patterns present in Pascal's Triangle that shelves of books have been written about them. Encourage any student that comes up with a pattern you have not seen before to write it out and present it to the class.

PROBLEM 5 Students who have seen binomial coefficients before (or who have used that form in their investigations of Pascal's Triangle) may be expecting to see them here, but could be a little baffled. They may have seen the formula $\binom{n}{k} = \frac{n!}{(n-k)!k!}$, but here the Σ column shows $\binom{n+1}{2}$ and the $\Sigma\Sigma$ column shows $\binom{n+2}{3}$. This makes sense only if you can see the relationship between the rows and columns in this table and the rows and columns of Pascal's Triangle. In the Σ column, every number is the third entry in a row of Pascal's Triangle starting with row 2, and in the $\Sigma\Sigma$ column, every number is the fourth entry in a row of Pascal's Triangle starting with row 3.

Wrap Up

Give students an opportunity to describe the patterns they have found and to talk about why they think the pattern would continue. If students have made a connection to the factorial function or even if they have noticed the products of consecutive integers, you might follow up on that.

Exercises

HOMEWORK
- Core: 6, 7, 8
- Optional: 9, 10

On Your Own

EXERCISE 6 Some students may recognize the coefficients of these expanded polynomials as the diagonals of the chart in Problem 1. Students familiar with Pascal's Triangle may also recognize it more easily here than in the chart.

EXERCISE 8 Some students may still instinctively start multiplying these expressions out by hand, or will just use their CAS. That is fine, but encourage them to go back to their results for Exercise 6 and confirm that by substituting $\frac{1}{4}r$ for a and $\frac{3}{4}s$ for b, they still get the terms they expect.

Maintain Your Skills

EXERCISE 10 Interested students have enough background to prove this result.

Exercises *Practicing Habits of Mind*

On Your Own

6. Expand each expression.

a. $(a + b)^2$ **b.** $(a + b)^3$

c. $(a + b)^4$ **d.** $(a + b)^5$

e. $(a + b)^6$ **f.** What patterns do you observe?

7. Use your result from Exercise 6c to expand $(M + N)^4$, where $M = 2d$ and $N = 7$.

8. Expand each expression.

a. $\left(\frac{1}{4}r + \frac{3}{4}s\right)^2$ **b.** $\left(\frac{1}{4}r + \frac{3}{4}s\right)^3$

c. $\left(\frac{1}{4}r + \frac{3}{4}s\right)^4$ **d.** $\left(\frac{1}{4}r + \frac{3}{4}s\right)^5$

Habits of Mind

Look for patterns. Use the answer to each part to help you with the next one.

Maintain Your Skills

9. a Find the first five powers of 99.

b. What patterns do you notice?

10. Tony is looking at differences of cubes. He says, "Let's see.

$$1^3 - 0^3 = 1 - 0 = 1$$

$$2^3 - 1^3 = 8 - 1 = 7$$

$$3^3 - 2^3 = 27 - 8 = 19$$

$$4^3 - 3^3 = 64 - 27 = 37$$

"I'm going to make a Σ table for these differences and see what happens."

n	$(n+1)^3 - n^3$	Σ
0	1	1
1	7	8

Use Tony's idea to find the sum of the first 20 differences of cubes starting with $1^3 - 0^3$. The last one is $20^3 - 19^3$.

Answers

Exercises

6. a. $a^2 + 2ab + b^2$

b. $a^3 + 3a^2b + 3ab^2 + b^3$

c. $a^4 + 4a^3b + 6a^2b^2 + 4ab^3 + b^4$

d. $a^5 + 5a^4b + 10a^3b^2 + 10a^2b^3 + 5ab^4 + b^5$

e. $a^6 + 6a^5b + 15a^4b^2 + 20a^3b^3 + 15a^2b^4 + 6ab^5 + b^6$

f. Answers may vary. Sample: The coefficients form a palindrome, the first and last coefficients are 1, the second and second-to-last coefficients are the exponent of $(a + b)$.

7. $16d^4 + 224d^3 + 1176d^2 + 2744d + 2401$

8. a. $\frac{1}{16}r^2 + \frac{3}{8}rs + \frac{9}{16}s^2$

b. $\frac{1}{64}r^3 + \frac{9}{64}r^2s + \frac{27}{64}rs^2 + \frac{27}{64}s^3$

7.15 Pascal's Triangle

This triangular table below is **Pascal's Triangle.** It is a very famous triangle, named after mathematician Blaise Pascal, who is known for his studies of the relationships in the triangle.

$$
\begin{array}{ccccccccccccc}
 & & & & & & 1 & & & & & & \\
 & & & & & 1 & & 1 & & & & & \\
 & & & & 1 & & 2 & & 1 & & & & \\
 & & & 1 & & 3 & & 3 & & 1 & & & \\
 & & 1 & & 4 & & 6 & & 4 & & 1 & & \\
 & 1 & & 5 & & 10 & & 10 & & 5 & & 1 & \\
1 & & 6 & & 15 & & 20 & & 15 & & 6 & & 1 \\
\vdots & & \vdots & & \vdots & & \vdots & & \vdots & & \vdots & & \vdots
\end{array}
$$

Pascal's Triangle shows up in many different areas of mathematics, including combinatorics. You will spend some time getting familiar with it and finding some of the many beautiful patterns it contains. You will also use it in other parts of this book, and in other mathematics courses throughout your life. An interesting thing to do with Pascal's Triangle is to see how many different patterns you can see in the rows and the columns of the triangle.

Some people might even call it fun!

For Discussion

1. If you have seen Pascal's Triangle before, discuss anything you remember about it. What do the numbers represent?
2. What patterns can you find in the entries of Pascal's Triangle?
3. Describe in words how to find any entry in Pascal's Triangle.
4. Describe how Pascal's Triangle is related to the table in this investigation's Getting Started lesson.

You can label the entries of Pascal's Triangle with their row and column numbers, this way.

$$\binom{n}{k}$$

The horizontal entries are the rows. The diagonals are the columns. Usually you number the first column and the first row 0.

The top number n is the row number, starting with 0.

The bottom number k is how far you go across in a row, starting with 0. So you label the entries in the sixth row this way.

row number (starting at 0)

$$\binom{n}{k}$$

column number (starting at 0)

c. $\frac{1}{256}r^4 + \frac{3}{64}r^3s + \frac{27}{128}r^2s^2 + \frac{27}{64}rs^3 + \frac{81}{256}s^4$

d. $\frac{1}{1024}r^5 + \frac{15}{1024}r^4s + \frac{45}{512}r^3s^2 + \frac{135}{512}r^2s^3 + \frac{405}{1024}rs^4 + \frac{243}{1024}s^5$

9–10. See back of book.

For Discussion

1. Answers may vary. Sample: The numbers are the coefficients of the terms of $(a + b)^n$.
2. Answers may vary. Sample: The first and last entries in each row are 1. The second and second-to-last entries of the nth row are n (if $n = 0$ for the top row). The sum of the numbers in row n is 2^n.
3. To find any entry, add the two numbers closest to it in the preceding row.
4. Except for the first column, the columns in Problem 1 of Lesson 17.14 are the "angled columns" of Pascal's Triangle.

Lesson Overview

GOALS

- Generate Pascal's Triangle and evaluate the nth row and the kth column entry as $\binom{n}{k}$.
- Notice and explain patterns in Pascal's Triangle.

In this lesson, students are introduced to Pascal's Triangle. They identify the entries in the nth row and kth column as $\binom{n}{k}$. They look for and discuss patterns in the triangle, including a variant of the now familiar hockey stick property.

CHECK YOUR UNDERSTANDING
- Core: 1, 2
- Optional: none

MATERIALS
- (CAS recommended)
- graphing calculators
- Blackline Masters 7.15A, 7.15B

HOMEWORK
- Core: 3, 4, 5
- Optional: 7
- Extension: 6

VOCABULARY
- Pascal's Triangle
- $\binom{n}{k}$

Launch

Distribute to each student one copy of Blackline Master 7.15A, and three copies of Blackline Master 7.15B. Begin this lesson by introducing Pascal's Triangle. Continue with For Discussion.

Explore

For Discussion

Some students may have learned about Pascal's Triangle only as a pattern of numbers. Others will have had brief introductions to the Binomial Theorem and know that you can "read off" the coefficients in a binomial expansion from the triangle. Still others will have learned that each entry $\binom{n}{k}$ in the triangle tells you how many ways there are to choose a subset of k objects from a set of n objects. There are many possibilities here, so let students share what they already know.

Most students will describe how to generate the table by adding the two entries above a cell starting with a single 1 and assuming a value of 0 for any cells above and around that 1. Others may have seen this formula for calculating the entries:

$$\binom{n}{k} = \frac{n!}{(n-k)!k!}$$

Do not worry if the formula does not come up. You will not cover it explicitly in this investigation, and all of the exercises can be completed without it.

For You to Do

A few students may already know how to find these values on a calculator, but that is not the intent here. Students should be able to answer all these questions without a calculator. Have students look for more patterns. They should notice that every number appears as $\binom{n}{1}$, only the triangular numbers appear as $\binom{n}{2}$, and numbers are greater in the middle of a row. See if students discover any other patterns before continuing.

Wrap Up

As time allows, go over the Check Your Understanding exercises with your class.

Assessment Resources

Lesson Quiz 7.15

1. Evaluate each sum.

a. $\sum_{k=0}^{3}\binom{3}{k}$ **b.** $\sum_{k=0}^{10}\binom{10}{k}$

c. $\sum_{k=0}^{12}\binom{12}{k}$

2. Find the values of m and n that satisfy each equation.

a. $\binom{13}{6}=\binom{12}{6}+\binom{12}{m}$ **b.** $\binom{60}{12}=\binom{m}{12}+\binom{m}{n}$

3. a. Using sentences, describe three different patterns that you found in Pascal's Triangle.

b. For each pattern in part (a), draw a section of Pascal's Triangle to demonstrate the pattern.

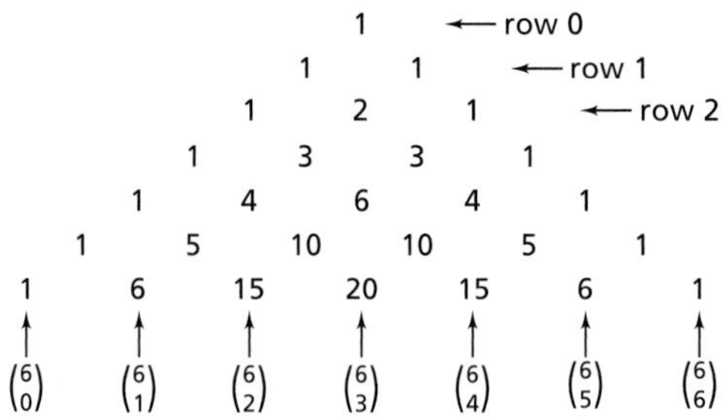

For You to Do

5. Find the value of each entry in the triangle.

a. $\binom{17}{1}$ **b.** $\binom{14}{14}$ **c.** $\binom{19}{0}$

6. Find all n and k such that $\binom{n}{k} = 15$.

Pascal's Triangle seems to have a kind of hockey stick property. If you draw a hockey stick on the triangle, the sum of the numbers on the handle is equal to the number on the tip.

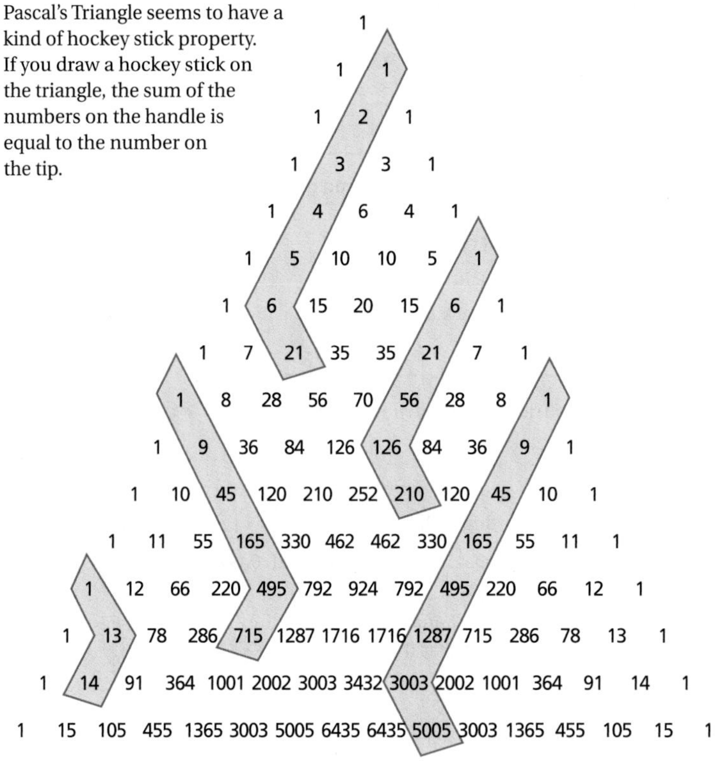

Answers

For You to Do

5. a. 17

b. 1

c. 1

6. $\binom{6}{2}$ or $\binom{6}{4}$

For Discussion

7. It has to start at a 1.

8. no

9. It has to point down.

10. Answers may vary. Sample: Any number N is the sum of the two numbers A and B above it. If the "heel" of the hockey stick is the number A, then the rest of the stick has the numbers that sum to B.

For Discussion

7. Does the hockey stick have to start on a one, or can it start anywhere in the triangle?
8. Does it matter if the hockey stick points left or right?
9. Does it matter if the hockey stick points up or down?
10. Explain the hockey stick property based on how you construct Pascal's Triangle.

For You to Do

11. Write the hockey stick property as an identity involving sums and the numbers $\binom{n}{k}$.

Exercises *Practicing Habits of Mind*

Check Your Understanding

1. Evaluate each sum.

   a. $\sum_{k=0}^{5}\binom{5}{k}$ b. $\sum_{k=0}^{6}\binom{6}{k}$ c. $\sum_{k=0}^{7}\binom{7}{k}$ d. $\sum_{k=0}^{n}\binom{n}{k}$

2. **Write About It** Explain why you get the sum you found in part (d) of Exercise 1. Think about how you get the numbers in Pascal's Triangle, or about what you know they represent.

On Your Own

3. Investigate the number of odd numbers in each row of Pascal's Triangle. If you continued the triangle out to row 64, how many odd numbers would you find in this row? In row 100? Explain.

Remember...
You start counting at row 0, so row 100 is really the 101st row you write down.

Exercises

HOMEWORK
- Core: 3, 4, 5
- Optional: 7
- Extension: 6

Check Your Understanding

EXERCISE 1 This pattern is one that many students may already have seen, and it will be explored in more depth in CME Project *Precalculus*.

On Your Own

EXERCISE 3 has a pattern that is difficult to find. It is a fascinating pattern, partially because it is hard to justify why the pattern works. Students will need at least the first 16 rows to find the pattern, and probably more. This exercise can be assigned in tandem with Exercise 4, but note that both are quite involved and will take some time to complete either in or out of class.

For You to Do

11. $\binom{n}{k} = \sum_{i=0}^{k}\binom{n-k-1+i}{i}$

Exercises

1. a. 32 or 2^5 **b.** 64 or 2^6
c. 128 or 2^7 **d.** 2^n

2. Answers may vary. Sample: Each element in row $(n - 1)$ contributes twice to row n, so the sum of entries in row n is twice the sum of entries in row $(n - 1)$.

3. There are 2 odd numbers in row n if n is a power of 2; there are 8 odd numbers in row 100.

EXERCISE 4 Students may not figure out right away that they do not need to know the actual numbers in Pascal's Triangle to complete this exercise; let them discover this. This is the reason the hexagons are so small in the diagram; they are deliberately too small for more than a single digit. Students should begin to generate some "color math" corresponding to things such as $1 + 2 = 0$ in mod 3 (the system of remainders when dividing by 3). The patterns that emerge are fractal in nature, and if students do not bring it up, point out that many larger or smaller versions of the same pattern can be found in the grid.

4. Make three copies of the diagram below. Write in the values of Pascal's Triangle on your copies. You will use your copies to explore patterns in Pascal's Triangle.

Go Online
PHSchool.com
For additional practice, go to **Web Code:** bfa-0715

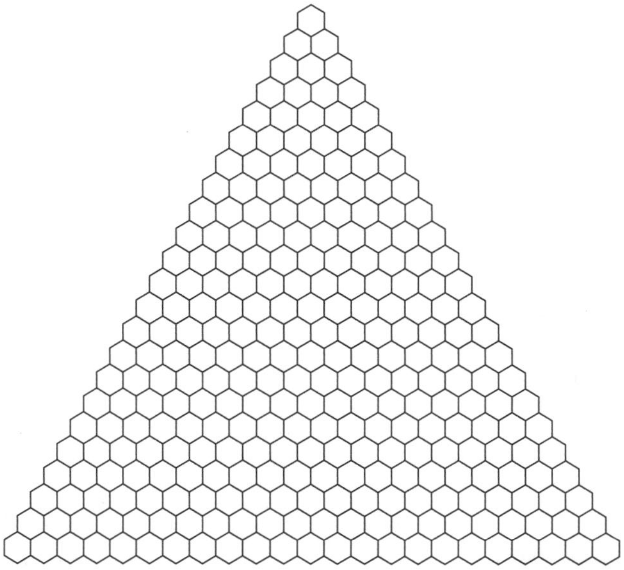

a. On one copy, color the odd numbers one color and the even numbers another color. Describe the patterns you find.

b. You can divide the integers up into three categories when you divide them by 3: those that leave a remainder of 1, those that leave a remainder of 2, and those that can be divided evenly by 3. On the second copy of the diagram, color each of these kinds of numbers a different color. Describe the patterns you find.

c. If you divide integers by 4, how many different kinds of numbers do you get? On the third copy of the diagram, color each of them a different color. Describe the patterns you find.

5. **Standardized Test Prep** The following list gives the first eight entries in the 15th row of Pascal's Triangle.

1 15 105 455 1365 3003 5005 6435

What is the value of $\binom{17}{6}$ in Pascal's Triangle?

A. 6188 **B.** 8008 **C.** 12,376 **D.** 19,448

Answers

4. Students' descriptions of patterns may vary.

a–c. See back of book.

5. C

6. **Take It Further** In Lesson 7.14, you found the closed forms for f, $\sum f$, $\sum\sum f$, and $\sum\sum\sum f$, where $f(n) = 1$. You can see these functions along diagonals in Pascal's Triangle.

Find a closed form for $\underbrace{\sum\sum\sum\sum \dots \sum}_{k \text{ times}} f(n)$.

f, $\sum f$, $\sum\sum f$, $\sum\sum\sum f$, $\sum\sum\sum\sum f$

1
1 1
1 2 1
1 3 3 1
1 4 6 4 1
1 5 10 10 5 1
1 6 15 20 15 6 1
1 7 21 35 35 21 7 1
1 8 28 56 70 56 28 8 1
1 9 36 84 126 126 84 36 9 1
1 10 45 120 210 252 210 120 45 10 1
1 11 55 165 330 462 462 330 165 55 11 1
1 12 66 220 495 792 924 792 495 220 66 12 1
1 13 78 286 715 1287 1716 1716 1287 715 286 78 13 1
1 14 91 364 1001 2002 3003 3432 3003 2002 1001 364 91 14 1
1 15 105 455 1365 3003 5005 6435 6435 5005 3003 1365 455 105 15 1

Maintain Your Skills

7. Find the values of m and n that satisfy each equation.

a. $\binom{9}{4} = \binom{8}{4} + \binom{8}{m}$
b. $\binom{3}{2} = \binom{2}{2} + \binom{2}{m}$
c. $\binom{14}{8} = \binom{13}{8} + \binom{13}{m}$
d. $\binom{100}{15} = \binom{m}{15} + \binom{m}{n}$

Go Online Video Tutor
PHSchool.com
Web Code: bfe-0775

6. $\underbrace{\sum\sum\sum\sum \cdots \sum}_{k \text{ times}} f(n) =$
$\binom{n+k}{k+1}$ or $\binom{n+k}{n-1}$

7. **a.** $m = 3$ or $m = 5$
b. $m = 1$
c. $m = 7$ or $m = 6$
d. $m = 99$; $n = 14$ or $n = 85$

EXERCISE 6 The factored form of each result will be needed in order to see the general pattern. This should be available on a CAS, or through solid use of factoring techniques and root-guessing. The factored forms of each of the four found in Lesson 7.14 should be enough to get the general rule.

Maintain Your Skills

EXERCISE 7 Ask students to point to where each of these values is found in Pascal's Triangle, and which sum gives the value. Part (d) is nearly a generalization to the full result, $\binom{n}{k} = \binom{n-1}{k-1} + \binom{n-1}{k}$.

Additional Resources

PRINT RESOURCES
- Solution Manual
- Practice Workbook
- Assessment Resources
- Teaching Resources

TECHNOLOGY
- Interactive Textbook
- TeacherExpress CD-ROM
- ExamView CD-ROM
- PHSchool.com

Additional Practice

1. Evaluate each sum.
a. $\sum_{k=0}^{4} \binom{4}{k}$ b. $\sum_{k=0}^{8} \binom{8}{k}$ c. $\sum_{k=0}^{9} \binom{9}{k}$ d. $\sum_{k=0}^{11} \binom{11}{k}$

2. Investigate the number of even numbers in each row of Pascal's Triangle. If you continued the triangle out to row 60, how many even numbers would you find in this row? In row 90? Explain.

3. Find values of m and n that satisfy each equation.
a. $\binom{10}{5} = \binom{9}{5} + \binom{9}{m}$ b. $\binom{6}{2} = \binom{5}{2} + \binom{5}{m}$
c. $\binom{15}{6} = \binom{14}{6} + \binom{14}{m}$ d. $\binom{50}{10} = \binom{m}{10} + \binom{m}{n}$

For Exercises 4–7, use the diagram below.

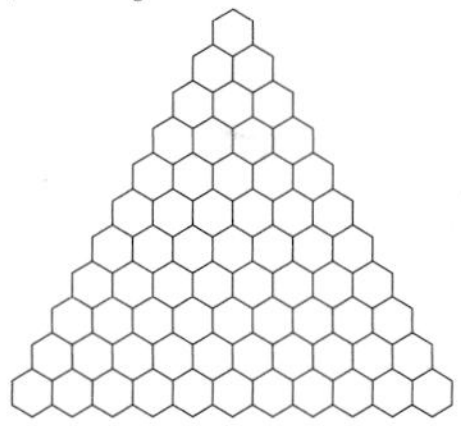

4. Write in the values of Pascal's Triangle. Describe how you can generate each row from the previous row.

5. How many entries are in the nth row?

6. a. Find the sum of each of the first five rows. What is the pattern?
b. What is the sum of the entries of the 11th row?

7. What is the value of $\binom{15}{9}$ in Pascal's Triangle?

Practice: For Lesson 7.15, assign Exercises 1–7.

Lesson Overview

GOAL

- Use the Binomial Theorem for expanding expressions of the form $(a + b)^n$.

This lesson states the Binomial Theorem, which relates the entries in the nth row of Pascal's Triangle to the coefficients of the expansion of $(a + b)^n$. It gives an informal argument to justify the theorem. You will also find a Historical Perspective that outlines some of the history of Pascal's Triangle.

CHECK YOUR UNDERSTANDING
- Core: 1, 2, 3
- Optional: none

MATERIALS
- CAS (recommended)
- graphing calculators
- Blackline Masters 7.15A, 7.16

HOMEWORK
- Core: 4, 5, 6, 7
- Optional: 8, 9

VOCABULARY
- Binomial Theorem

Launch

Begin this lesson by reviewing notes about Exercise 6 in Lesson 7.14. There students expanded expressions of the form $(a + b)^n$ leading to Theorem 7.3. Rather than just write out the result for $(a + b)^3$, you might ask students how the expansion could be performed. Rewriting this as $(a + b)(a + b)^2$ can give some insight about why the binomial coefficients emerge. The diagrams in the Developing Habits of Mind section may also help here, as multiplying by $(a + b)$ can be pictured the same way. You may wish to use Blackline Masters 7.15A and 7.16 here.

7.16 The Binomial Theorem

In Exercise 6 of Lesson 7.14, you found some of these expansions.

$(a + b)^0 = 1$

$(a + b)^1 = a + b$

$(a + b)^2 = a^2 + 2ab + b^2$

$(a + b)^3 = a^3 + 3a^2b + 3ab^2 + b^3$

$(a + b)^4 = a^4 + 4a^3b + 6a^2b^2 + 4ab^3 + b^4$

$(a + b)^5 = a^5 + 5a^4b + 10a^3b^2 + 10a^2b^3 + 5ab^4 + b^5$

$(a + b)^6 = a^6 + 6a^5b + 15a^4b^2 + 20a^3b^3 + 15a^2b^4 + 6ab^5 + b^6$

Compare the coefficients of these polynomials to the entries of Pascal's Triangle.

```
            1
          1   1
        1   2   1
      1   3   3   1
    1   4   6   4   1
  1   5  10  10   5   1
1   6  15  20  15   6   1
```

In fact, you find the coefficients for any binomial expansion $(a + b)^n$ in Pascal's triangle. The Binomial Theorem states this relationship.

Theorem 7.3 The Binomial Theorem

For $n \geq 0$,

$$(a+b)^n = \binom{n}{0}a^nb^0 + \binom{n}{1}a^{n-1}b^1 + \binom{n}{2}a^{n-2}b^2 + \cdots + \binom{n}{k}a^{n-k}b^k + \ldots + \binom{n}{n-1}a^1b^{n-1} + \binom{n}{n}a^0b^n$$

Go Online PHSchool.com

For examples of using the Binomial Theorem, go to **Web Code: bfe-9031**

You must admit, this connection is rather unexpected! But, as is usually the case in mathematics, it is no coincidence. The real question to ask is, "Why is there a connection?"

Developing Habits of Mind

Establish a process. To see why this pattern holds, look closely at an example—multiplication by $(x + 1)$. Suppose you want to expand

$$(x + 1)(x^5 + 3x^4 + 7x^3 + 2x^2 + x + 1)$$

By the Distributive Property, this equals

$$x \cdot (x^5 + 3x^4 + 7x^3 + 2x^2 + x + 1) + 1 \cdot (x^5 + 3x^4 + 7x^3 + 2x^2 + x + 1)$$
$$= (x^6 + 3x^5 + 7x^4 + 2x^3 + x^2 + x) + (x^5 + 3x^4 + 7x^3 + 2x^2 + x + 1)$$
$$= x^6 + 4x^5 + 10x^4 + 9x^3 + 3x^2 + 2x + 1$$

Notice that the original polynomial has these coefficients.

1 3 7 2 1 1

To find the coefficients of the product, you can simply add Pascal-style, as follows.

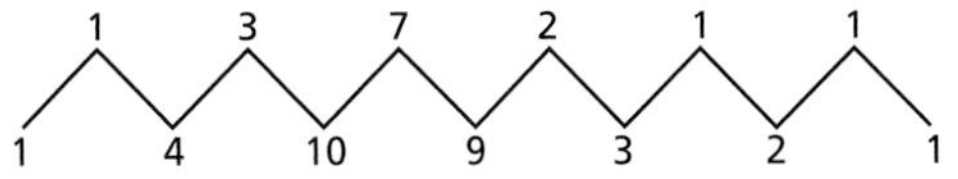

You should convince yourself why this method works. Look at another example. Suppose you want to expand

$$(x + 1)(7x^4 + 2x^3 + x^2 + 3x + 1)$$

You can obtain the coefficients of the product as follows.

So the product is

$$7x^5 + 9x^4 + 3x^3 + 4x^2 + 4x + 1$$

For Discussion

1. Use the discussion above to explain why the fifth row of Pascal's Triangle gives the coefficients of $(x + 1)^5$, assuming that you know that the fourth row gives the coefficients of $(x + 1)^4$. (*Hint:* $(x + 1)^5 = (x + 1)(x + 1)^4$, and you already know what $(x + 1)^4$ looks like.)

Answers

For Discussion

1. Answers may vary. Sample: When you multiply the expanded form of $(x + 1)^4$ by $(x + 1)$, the coefficient of x^5 is 1 and the constant term is 1; for each exponent r from $n - 1$ to 1, the coefficient of the term with that exponent is the sum of the original coefficient plus 1 times the coefficient of the term with exponent $(r - 1)$.

Explore

Developing Habits of Mind

Use the diagram presented here to perform a second expansion:

$$(a + b)(7a^4 + 2a^3b + a^2b^2 + 3ab^3 + b^4)$$

The expansion gives the same coefficients as the expansion in the lower middle of this page. This can give students another way of latching onto the Binomial Theorem, seeing it work for more than just expansions of $(x + 1)$.

For Discussion

When you are multiplying

$$(a + b)^4 = a^4 + 4a^3b + 6a^2b^2 + 4ab^3 + b^4$$

by $a + b$ to get $(a + b)^5$, each of the terms in $(a + b)^4$ contributes to *two* terms in the new expansion. For example, you will multiply $6a^2b^2$ by both a and b, so it contributes to the a^3b^2 term and also to the a^2b^3 term. That is why you show two lines coming out of each coefficient in the previous expansion, contributing their coefficients to the sum that is the coefficient in the new expansion.

Wrap Up

As time allows, discuss the Check Your Understanding exercises with your class.

Assessment Resources

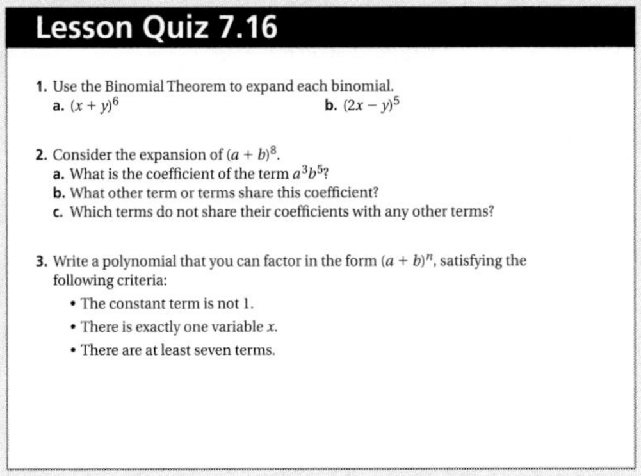
Lesson Quiz 7.16

1. Use the Binomial Theorem to expand each binomial.
   a. $(x + y)^6$ **b.** $(2x - y)^5$

2. Consider the expansion of $(a + b)^8$.
   a. What is the coefficient of the term a^3b^5?
   b. What other term or terms share this coefficient?
   c. Which terms do not share their coefficients with any other terms?

3. Write a polynomial that you can factor in the form $(a + b)^n$, satisfying the following criteria:
   - The constant term is not 1.
   - There is exactly one variable x.
   - There are at least seven terms.

Exercises

HOMEWORK
- Core: 4, 5, 6, 7
- Optional: 8, 9

Check Your Understanding

EXERCISE 1 Part (b) is more challenging because of the coefficient 2 in the second term. It may prove helpful to write this expression as $((x) + (2y))^5$ so that students realize that they replace each a with x and each b with $2y$ in the Binomial Theorem. Ask students to compute each coefficient of the expanded polynomial.

On Your Own

EXERCISE 4 This property, that the alternating sum of any row (other than row 0) is 0, is, of course, due to the way that Pascal's Triangle is constructed. Once you have the first row with an alternating sum of 0, the rest will have to also have alternating sum 0. In row 1, $1 - 1 = 0$, so start there. Each of the 1's in row 1 contributes once to a positive term in the alternating sequence of the row below and once to a negative term. The next row will also have alternating sum 0. Each of its terms contributes to one positive and one negative term in the row below, and so on.

Exercises *Practicing Habits of Mind*

Check Your Understanding

1. Use the Binomial Theorem to expand each binomial. Use your CAS to verify your answers.

a. $(x + y)^7$ **b.** $(x + 2y)^5$

2. Consider the expansion of $(a + b)^8$.

a. What is the coefficient of the term a^3b^5?

b. What other term or terms share this coefficient?

c. Which terms do not share their coefficients with any other terms?

3. Determine the coefficient of each term below in the expansion of $(x + y)^{10}$.

a. x^3y^7 **b.** xy^9 **c.** x^5y^5

You certainly should use your CAS to help evaluate these, but do not ask it to find all 11 terms! Use what you know, too, so the CAS does not have to do everything.

On Your Own

4. Compute the alternating sum below.

$$\binom{5}{0} - \binom{5}{1} + \binom{5}{2} - \binom{5}{3} + \binom{5}{4} - \binom{5}{5}$$

This is the alternating sum of the numbers in the fifth row of Pascal's Triangle. What is the sum if the row number n is 6 instead of 5? If n is 11 instead of 5?

5. Write a polynomial that you can factor in the form $(a + b)^n$, satisfying the following criteria:
- The constant term is not 1.
- There is exactly one variable x.
- There are at least five terms.

6. Simplify $(\sqrt{3} + \sqrt{2})^{100}(\sqrt{3} - \sqrt{2})^{100}$.

7. Standardized Test Prep What is the coefficient of the x^3 term in the expansion of $(a + b)^n$, where $a = 2x$, $b = -1$, and $n = 4$?

A. -32 **B.** -4 **C.** 24 **D.** 21

Go Online PHSchool.com
For additional practice, go to **Web Code:** bfa-0716

Answers

Exercises

1. a. $x^7 + 7x^6y + 21x^5y^2 + 35x^4y^3 + 35x^3y^4 + 21x^2y^5 + 7xy^6 + y^7$

b. $x^5 + 10x^4y + 40x^3y^2 + 80x^2y^3 + 80xy^4 + 32y^5$

2. a. 56 **b.** a^5b^3

c. entry $\binom{8}{4}$

3. a. 120 **b.** 10 **c.** 252

4. 0; 0; 0

5. Answers may vary. Sample: $x^4 - 8x^3 + 24x^2 - 32x + 16 = (x - 2)^4$

6. 1

7. A

Maintain Your Skills

8. Write About It Look at the pattern in the powers of 11.

$$11^2 = 121$$
$$11^3 = 1331$$
$$11^4 = 14{,}641$$

Look at this more closely. You have $11^4 = 11^3 \times 11$, and since $11^3 = 1331$, you get

$$\begin{array}{r} 1\,3\,3\,1 \\ \times \quad\;\; 1\,1 \\ \hline 1\,3\,3\,1 \\ 1\,3\,3\,1\;\; \\ \hline 1\,4\,6\,4\,1 \end{array}$$

Or you can calculate Pascal-style.

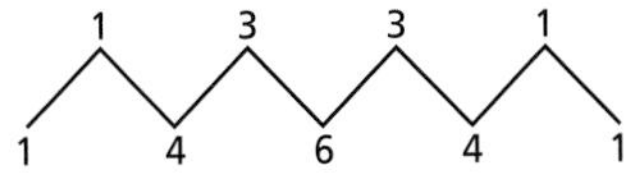

Now you may be tempted to conclude that $11^5 = 15{,}101{,}051$, but, in fact, $11^5 = 161{,}051$. What went wrong? Did anything really go wrong here?

9. a. Write out the first 7 powers of 101.

b. Write out the first 7 powers of 1001.

Go Online
PHSchool.com

For more information on Pascal's Triangle, go to **Web Code:** bfe-8031

Historical Perspective

Pascal's Triangle gets its name from Blaise Pascal, a famous French mathematician who wrote *Traité du triangle arithmétique* in 1654. Pascal showed many uses of the triangle and proved many things about its number patterns. He was not, however, the first person to discover or write about the triangle. The triangle was known in India as early as 1068—nearly 600 years before Pascal wrote his *Traité*. A mathematician named Bhattotpala used it to compute combinations of as many as sixteen things. The triangle was also known in China, probably as early as 1100, when Chia Hsien used something similar for finding binomial coefficients. It was certainly known there by 1303, when Chu Shih-Chieh used the triangle at the right.

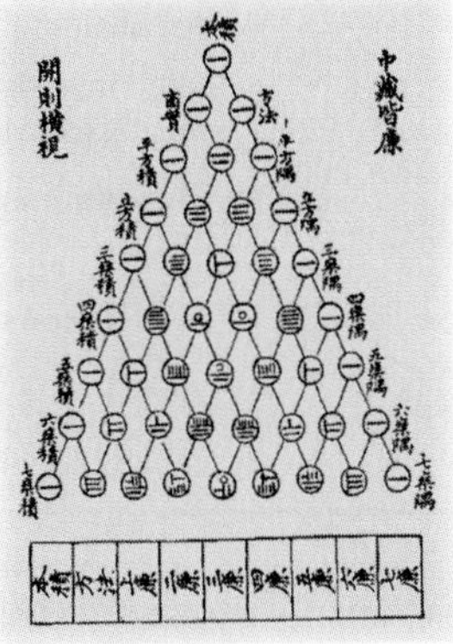

The triangle of Chu Shih-Chieh

8. Answers may vary. Sample: Adding the "Pascal's Triangle" way resulted in two 2-digit numbers $(4 + 6 = 10, 6 + 4 = 10)$, and the numbers 5, 10, 10 in the ten thousands, thousands, and hundreds places should have been rewritten as 6, 1, 0, giving the result 161,051.

9. a. 101; 10,201; 1,030,301; 104,060,401; 10,510,100,501; 1,061,520,150,601; 107,213,535,210,701

b. 1001; 1,002,001; 1,003,003,001; 1,004,006,004,001; 1,005,010,010,005,001; 1,006,015,020,015,006,001; 1,007,021,035,035,021,007,001

Maintain Your Skills

EXERCISE 8 Expect students to have difficulty explaining this in words. It has probably been a long time since they thought deeply about place value. Terms like "carry" and "regroup" will vary depending on students' mathematics background.

EXERCISE 9 Students notice that the digits in these powers are the entries in Pascal's Triangles with some zeros between them. In the powers of 101, each number appears in a two-digit "block," while in the powers of 1001, each number appears in a three-digit "block."

Additional Resources

PRINT RESOURCES
- Solution Manual
- Practice Workbook
- Assessment Resources
- Teaching Resources

TECHNOLOGY
- Interactive Textbook
- TeacherExpress CD-ROM
- ExamView CD-ROM
- PHSchool.com

Additional Practice

1. Use the Binomial Theorem to expand each binomial. Use your CAS to verify your answers.
   a. $(2x + y)^8$ b. $(x + 3y)^6$
   c. $(2x - 3y)^8$ d. $(3x - 4y)^6$

2. Consider the expansion of $(a + b)^9$.
   a. What is the coefficient of the term a^4b^5?
   b. What other term or terms share this coefficient?
   c. Which terms do not share their coefficients with any other terms?

3. Determine the coefficient of each term below in the expansion of $(x - y)^{12}$.
   a. x^3y^9 b. x^5y^7 c. x^6y^6

4. Determine the coefficient of each term below in the expansion of $(2x + 5y)^{12}$.
   a. x^3y^9 b. x^5y^7 c. x^6y^6

5. a. Compute the alternating sum below.
   $$\binom{7}{0} - \binom{7}{1} + \binom{7}{2} - \binom{7}{3} + \binom{7}{4} - \binom{7}{5} + \binom{7}{6}$$
   b. This is the alternating sum of the numbers in the seventh row of Pascal's Triangle. What is the sum if the row number n is 8 instead of 7? If n is 9? If n is 10?

6. Write a polynomial that you can factor in the form $(a - b)^n$, satisfying the following criteria:
   - The constant term is not 1.
   - There is exactly one variable x.
   - There are at least five terms.

7. Simplify each expression.
   a. $(\sqrt{2} + \sqrt{5})^{50}(\sqrt{2} - \sqrt{5})^{50}$
   b. $(\sqrt{3} + \sqrt{6})^{100}(\sqrt{3} - \sqrt{6})^{100}$

Practice: For Lesson 7.16, assign Exercises 1–7.

Mathematical Reflections

EXERCISES 6–8 At the start of the investigation, you may have assigned these as Questions 1–3 for students to think and write about.

Mathematical Reflections 7D

In this investigation, you learned to generate Pascal's Triangle, to find and explain patterns in Pascal's Triangle, and to use the Binomial Theorem to expand expressions. These exercises will help you summarize what you have learned.

1. Give an example of the hockey stick property of Pascal's Triangle in which the sum on the tip is 20.
2. Find all values of m that satisfy each equation.
   a. $\binom{m}{1} = 27$ **b.** $\binom{24}{m} = 1$
   c. $\binom{m}{31} = 32$ **d.** $\binom{m}{4} + \binom{m}{5} = \binom{19}{5}$
3. Make an input-output table for the function $b(n) = \binom{n}{2}$ for $n = 2$ to $n = 6$. Find a polynomial function $p(n)$ that matches your table for $b(n)$, even if you continue the table.
4. Multiply $(x + 1)(5x^5 + 3x^4 - 2x^3 + 4x^2 + 6x - 7)$.
5. You can factor the polynomial below into the form $(a + b)^5$.
   $$32x^5 - 80x^4 + cx^3 - 40x^2 + 10x - 1$$
   Find a, b, and c.
6. What is the sum of the entries of the tenth row of Pascal's Triangle?
7. What is the expanded form of $(2d + 7)^8$?
8. What is the coefficient of x^7y^3 in the expansion of $(x + y)^{10}$?

Vocabulary and Notation

In this investigation, you learned this term and this symbol. Make sure you understand what each one means and how to use it.

- **Pascal's Triangle**
- $\binom{n}{k}$ **(the nth row, kth column entry of Pascal's triangle)**

If you have 30 socks and 6 of them are striped, the probability of randomly choosing a matching pair of striped socks is $\binom{6}{2} \div \binom{30}{2}$.

Answers

Mathematical Reflections

1. $1 + 3 + 6 + 10 = 20$

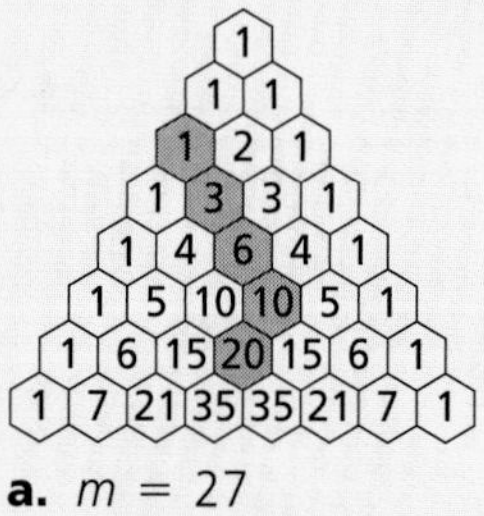

2. a. $m = 27$
b. $m = 0$ or $m = 24$
c. $m = 32$
d. $m = 18$

3.

Input	Output
2	1
3	3
4	6
5	10
6	15

$p(n) = \frac{(n-1)n}{2}$ or
$p(n) = \frac{1}{2}n^2 - \frac{1}{2}n$

4. $5x^6 + 8x^5 + x^4 + 2x^3 + 10x^2 - x - 7$

5. $a = 2x$, $b = -1$, $c = 80$

6. 1024

7. $256d^8 + 7168d^7 + 87{,}808d^6 + 614{,}656d^5 + 2{,}689{,}120d^4 + 7{,}529{,}536d^3 + 13{,}176{,}688d^2 + 13{,}176{,}688d + 5{,}764{,}801$

8. 120

Project: Using Mathematical Habits

The Line of Best Fit Contains the Centroid

The goal of this project is for you to prove Conjecture 1.1 from Lesson 1.9 of Investigation 1B.

For any set of data, the line of best fit contains the balance point.

As often happens in mathematics, it is easier to prove a related result. Exercises 3, 4, and 8 from Lesson 1.8 suggested a fascinating property:

Suppose you have a set of data points and you pick some number a. Then, the line with slope a that best fits the data is the one that contains the balance point $(\bar{x}, \bar{y})$ *of the data.*

You experimented with this idea in Investigation 1B, and you helped Tony verify it for a given data set and slopes 0, 1, 2, and 3. The first goal of this project is to prove that it is true in general.

Proofs of this kind often involve a careful analysis of an algebraic expression. In this case, the expression is for the calculation of the sum of the squares of the errors. A good algebraic habit is to carry out the calculations in numerical examples, keeping track of your steps. You did this in Lesson 1.8. A good next step is to make the slope a variable, keeping the same numerical data. After that, you can make the data itself variable. This kind of "ramping up" from numbers to variables is typical of how you develop many proofs in algebra.

For a numerical example to get started, go back to the data from Exercise 2 from Lesson 1.8. It has probably been quite a while since you first found a line of best fit for a data set, so take some time to go through the process.

Input	Output
1	3
2	4.5
3	8.1
4	8

1. Find the centroid of the data.

Next, you and Tony looked at all the lines of slope 3 and completed this table to find the one that minimized the error for this data set.

2. Copy and complete this table.

Data vs. Line Fit: $y = 3x + b$

Input	Output	Predicted	Error
1	3	$3 \cdot 1 + b$	$3 - (3 + b) = -b$
2	4.5	■	■
3	8.1	■	■
4	8	■	■

3. Write an expression for the sum of the squares of the errors. Simplify it to a quadratic expression in b.

Project

Use this project with an individual, a small group, or your whole class. If you are planning to include line of best fit calculations in your final exam, this can be a nice review of that process as well as a chance to use Σ notation in another context. It is also a nice wrap up of their work on regression lines, because it gives students the opportunity to derive the actual formula that their calculators use to find the line of best fit for a data set. You may want to remind students that although the project asks them to do the calculations by hand, they can still use their calculators as a check. Students should also be capitalizing on their calculator's function definition and algebraic expansion features to save time.

You may want to have students check the formula they derive in Exercise 16 with another data set as part of their write up. If only a small group of your students have done this project, you may also want to provide them an opportunity to present their results to the rest of the class. If your entire class does this project, you could have them turn in Exercises 15 and 16 as a write up.

Project

1. (2.5, 5.9)

2.

Input	Output	Predicted	Error
1	3	$3 \cdot 1 + b$	$3 - (3 \cdot 1 + b) = -b$
2	4.5	$3 \cdot 2 + b$	$4 \cdot 5 - (3 \cdot 2 + b) = -1 \cdot 5 - b$
3	8.1	$3 \cdot 3 + b$	$8 \cdot 1 - (3 \cdot 3 + b) = -0.9 - b$
4	8	$3 \cdot 4 + b$	$8 - (3 \cdot 4 + b) = -4 - b$

3. $(-b)^2 + (-1.5 - b)^2 + (-0.9 - b)^2 + (-4 - b)^2 = 4b^2 + 12.8b + 19.06$

EXERCISE 4 uses the quadratic formula with the coefficients p, q, and r to avoid confusion with the a and b, which are used as the coefficients of the line of best fit. This may confuse some students at first.

4. A quadratic expression

$$px^2 + qx + r$$

takes on its minimum or maximum value at $x = -\frac{q}{2p}$.

a. Why does $x = -\frac{q}{2p}$ produce the minimum or maximum value?

b. How can you tell whether $x = -\frac{q}{2p}$ produces a minimum or maximum?

c. What value of b minimizes the sum of the squares of the errors you found in the previous exercise?

5. Find the equation for the line of slope 3 that is the best fit for the data. Does the centroid satisfy this equation? Explain.

You might try to carry out the same calculation with other slopes. You did this for slopes 0, 1, and 2 in Exercise 4 from Lesson 1.8.

To get more into the rhythm of the calculation, try it with some other slopes, say 4, 5, and 6. In each case, check that (2.5, 5.9) is on the best line with that slope.

Once you are comfortable with the calculations, you can carry out the process in general for any slope a.

6. Copy and complete this table.

Data vs. Line Fit: $y = ax + b$

Input	Output	Predicted	Error
1	3	$a \cdot 1 + b$	$3 - (a \cdot 1 + b) = 3 - a - b$
2	4.5	■	■
3	8.1	■	■
4	8	■	■

7. Show that the sum of squares of the errors is

$$(3 - a - b)^2 + (4.5 - 2a - b)^2 + (8.1 - 3a - b)^2 + (8 - 4a - b)^2$$

Instead of squaring the four trinomials, look back at what happened with the numbers. The slope a is constant, so you can think of each term that you are squaring as a binomial.

$$((3 - a) - b)^2 + ((4.5 - 2a) - b)^2 + ((8.1 - 3a) - b)^2 + ((8 - 4a) - b)^2$$

If you square each term, you get

$$\begin{aligned}&(3 - a)^2 - 2(3 - a)b + b^2\\ &+ (4.5 - 2a)^2 - 2(4.5 - 2a)b + b^2\\ &+ (8.1 - 3a)^2 - 2(8.1 - 3a)b + b^2\\ &+ (8 - 4a)^2 - 2(8 - 4a)b + b^2\end{aligned}$$

Think about gathering up all the like terms, basically by "adding down."

An important habit in algebra is to predict the form of the result of a calculation without having to carry it out. The resulting expression will be a quadratic in b. The coefficient of b^2 will be 4 (look at the last column). The coefficient of b will be the sum of all the expressions in the middle column. And the constant term will be the sum of all the expressions in the left-most column.

Answers

4. **a.** The parabola's vertex is on its line of symmetry; the graph of $x = -\frac{q}{2p}$.
b. If $p > 0$, then $-\frac{q}{2p}$ is a minimum. If $p < 0$, then $-\frac{q}{2p}$ is a maximum.
c. -1.6

5. $y = 3x - 1.6$; yes; $5.9 = 3 \cdot (2.5) - 1.6$

6.

Input	Output	Predicted	Error
1	3	$a \cdot 1 + b$	$3 - (a \cdot 1 + b) = 3 - a - b$
2	4.5	$a \cdot 2 + b$	$4.5 - (a \cdot 2 + b) = 4.5 - 2a - b$
3	8.1	$a \cdot 3 + b$	$8.1 - (a \cdot 3 + b) = 8.1 - 3a - b$
4	8	$a \cdot 4 + b$	$8 - (a \cdot 4 + b) = 8 - 4a - b$

7. Check students' work.

EXERCISE 9 It is important that students notice the sudden reappearance of $\overline{x}$ and $\overline{y}$ in this equation.

But to find the value of b that minimizes the quadratic, you do not care what the constant term is. You just take the negative of the coefficient of b and divide it by twice the coefficient of b^2.

The coefficient of b is

$$-2(3 - a) + 2(4.5 - 2a) + 2(8.1 - 3a) + 2(8 - 4a) = -2((3 + 4.5 + 8.1 + 8) - (1 + 2 + 3 + 4)a)$$

Notice how the sum of the x-values $(1 + 2 + 3 + 4)$ and the sum of the y-values $(3 + 4.5 + 8.1 + 8)$ show up in the calculation. Rather than simplifying this expression further, leave it like this—it will reveal more of what is going on behind the scenes.

The quadratic in b looks like this.

$$4b^2 - 2((3 + 4.5 + 8.1 + 8) - (1 + 2 + 3 + 4)a)b + \text{something}$$

You know that the minimum value for this expression occurs when

$$b = -\frac{\text{the coefficient of } b}{2 \cdot \text{the coefficient of } b^2}$$

8. Find an expression in a for the value of b that minimizes the sum of the squares of the errors.

9. Find the equation of the line of best fit with slope a and show that the centroid is on this line, no matter what a is.

Everything so far has used the data in the table from Exercise 1. But the evidence suggests that the key to the proof is that the equation of the line with slope a that best fits any data set is

$$y = ax + (\overline{y} - \overline{x}a)$$

where $(\overline{x}, \overline{y})$ is the centroid for the data. If this were the case, you would be in business—you can show that $(\overline{x}, \overline{y})$ satisfies the equation

$$y = ax + (\overline{y} - \overline{x}a)$$

So the next step is to ramp up to any set of data, say

$$\{(x_1, y_1), (x_2, y_2), \ldots, (x_n, y_n)\}$$

Just follow what you did before.

10. Copy and complete this error table.

Data vs. Line Fit: $y = ax + b$

Input	Output	Predicted	Error
x_1	y_1	$ax_1 + b$	$y_1 - (ax_1 + b) = (y_1 - ax_1) - b$
x_2	y_2	■	■
x_3	y_3	■	■
⋮	⋮	⋮	⋮
x_n	y_n	■	■

Once you get the rhythm, the process becomes automatic.

8. $b = 5.9 - 2.5a$

9. $y = ax + (5.9 - 2.5a)$; $5.9 = a(2.5) + (5.9 - 2.5a)$; $5.9 = 5.9$

10.

Input	Output	Predicted	Error
x_1	y_1	$ax_1 + b$	$y_1 - (ax_1 + b) = (y_1 - ax_1) - b$
x_2	y_2	$ax_2 + b$	$y_2 - (ax_2 + b) = (y_2 - ax_2) - b$
x_3	y_3	$ax_3 + b$	$y_3 - (ax_3 + b) = (y_3 - ax_3) - b$
⋮	⋮	⋮	⋮
x_n	y_n	$ax_n + b$	$y_n - (ax_n + b) = (y_n - ax_n) - b$

EXERCISE 16 Students who wish to may find it beneficial to work through a calculation using numbers first before ramping up to the generic data set. For example, they could use the data set from this project with the equation for the line of best fit $y = ax + (5.9 - 2.5a)$ or $y = 5.9 + a(x - 2.5)$.

11. Write an expression for the sum of the squares of the errors in Σ notation.

If you square each term in your sum, you get

$$\begin{aligned}&(y_1 - ax_1)^2 - 2(y_1 - ax_1)b + b^2\\&+ (y_2 - ax_2)^2 - 2(y_2 - ax_2)b + b^2\\&\quad\vdots\\&+ (y_n - ax_n)^2 - 2(y_n - ax_n)b + b^2\end{aligned}$$

Or

$$\sum_{i=1}^{n}((y_i - ax_i)^2 - 2(y_i - ax_i)b + b^2)$$

Again, think about gathering up all the like terms, basically by "adding down."

12. The sum of the squares of the errors will be a quadratic in b.

a. What is the coefficient of b^2 in this quadratic?

b. What is the coefficient of b in Σ notation?

13. To find the value of b that minimizes the quadratic, you do not care what the constant term is. Just take the negative of the coefficient of b and divide it by twice the coefficient of b^2.

Show that the best value for b is when

$$b = -\frac{-2\left(\sum_{i=1}^{n} y_i - \left(\sum_{i=1}^{n} x_i\right)a\right)}{2 \cdot n}$$
$$= \bar{y} - \bar{x}a$$

So, the equation of the best line with slope a is

$$y = ax + (\bar{y} - \bar{x}a)$$

14. Show that $(\bar{x}, \bar{y})$ satisfies $y = ax + (\bar{y} - \bar{x}a)$.

You are now in a position to prove Conjecture 1.1, by showing that the line of best fit for a set of data points contains the centroid of the data.

You can reason that, for reasonable data sets, there is one (and exactly one) line that best fits the data. You can prove this by generalizing the technique in Lesson 1.9. So you can argue that the line of best fit has some slope. For all lines of that slope, by the result you just proved, the best one contains the centroid.

15. In your own words, write out a proof of Conjecture 1.1.

16. Take It Further Now you know that the line of best fit has equation

$$y = ax + (\bar{y} - \bar{x}a)$$

for some slope a. You can go through the method of Lesson 1.9 with a generic slope and actually get a formula for the slope of the line of best fit—the one your calculator uses. Try it.

Answers

11. $\sum_{i=1}^{n}((y_1 - ax_4) - b)^2$

12. a. n

b. $\sum_{i=1}^{n}(-2(y_i - ax_i)) =$

$$-2\left(\sum_{i=1}^{n} y_i - \left(\sum_{i=1}^{n} x_i\right)a\right)$$

13. $nb^2 - 2\left(\sum_{i=1}^{n} y_i - \left(\sum_{i=1}^{n} x_i\right)a\right)b + \text{constant}$

is the quadratic. So

$$b = -\frac{-2\left(\sum_{i=1}^{n} y_i - \left(\sum_{i=1}^{n} x_i\right)a\right)}{2 \cdot n} =$$

$$-\frac{-\sum_{i=1}^{n} y_i + \left(\sum_{i=1}^{n} x_i\right)a}{n}$$

$$= \frac{\sum_{i=1}^{n} y_i}{n} - \frac{\sum_{i=1}^{n} x_i}{n} \cdot a$$

$$= \bar{y} - \bar{x}a$$

14. $\bar{y} = a\bar{x} + (\bar{y} - \bar{x}a)$

$\bar{y} = a\bar{x} - a\bar{x} + \bar{y}$

$\bar{y} = \bar{y}$

15. Check student's work.

16. Check students' work.

Chapter 7

Review

Go Online PHSchool.com — For vocabulary review, go to **Web Code:** bfj-0751.

In **Investigation 7A,** you learned how to

- make a sum table for a function and write a closed-form rule for the sum column where appropriate
- use Gauss's method to find the sum of a sequence with a constant difference between successive terms
- use Euclid's method to find the sum of a sequence with a constant ratio between successive terms
- expand Σ notation or convert an expanded sum back to Σ notation

The following exercises will help you check your understanding.

1. Copy and complete the following sum table. Find a closed-form rule for the Σ column.

n	$g(n)$	Σ
0	1	■
1	2	■
2	6	■
3	18	■
4	37	■
5	61	■

2. Suppose $S = 3 + 6 + \cdots + 96$.

a. If there is a constant difference between successive terms, what is the value of S? Use Gauss's method.

b. If there is a constant ratio between successive terms, what is the value of S? Use Euclid's method.

3. a. Evaluate $\sum_{j=0}^{3} 3^j$.

b. Evaluate $\sum_{k=1}^{5} (k + 2)$.

c. Use Σ notation to write an expression for $S = \frac{1}{2} + 1 + \frac{3}{2} + 2 + \cdots + 6$.

In **Investigation 7B,** you learned how to

- find closed-form expressions for indefinite sums and use them to evaluate definite sums
- develop a list of Σ identities and recognize situations in which you can apply them
- find closed-form expressions for the series associated with a function

The following exercises will help you check your understanding.

4. Use the definitions below.

$$S(n) = \sum_{k=0}^{n} (4 - 3k)$$

$$T(n) = \sum_{k=0}^{n} \left(\tfrac{1}{2}\right)^k$$

a. Find a closed form for $S(n)$.

b. Find a closed form for $T(n)$.

c. Use the closed form for $S(n)$ to find $\sum_{k=0}^{100} (4 - 3k)$.

d. Use the closed form for $T(n)$ to find $\sum_{k=0}^{4} \left(\tfrac{1}{2}\right)^k$.

5. Find a closed form for the series associated with $g(n) = 4 - 5n$, with initial term $g(0)$.

Chapter Review

1.

n	$g(n)$	Σ
0	1	1
1	2	3
2	6	9
3	18	27
4	54	81
5	162	243

$\Sigma = 3^n$

2. a. 1584 **b.** 189

3. a. 40 **b.** 25 **c.** $\sum_{j=1}^{12} \frac{j}{2}$

4. a. $S(n) = \frac{-3n^2 + 5n + 8}{2}$

b. $T(n) = 2 - \left(\frac{1}{2}\right)^n$

c. −14,746

d. $\frac{31}{16}$

5. $G(n) = \frac{-5n^2 + 3n + 8}{2}$

In **Investigation 7C,** you learned how to

- find a closed-form representation for an arithmetic sequence and its associated series
- find a closed-form representation for a geometric sequence and its associated series
- determine whether a geometric sequence has a limit, and if it does, how to find it
- convert a repeating decimal into an exact fraction

The following exercises will help you check your understanding.

6. Suppose f is a sequence with initial term $f(0) = 5$.

n	$f(n)$	Σ
0	5	5
1	■	■
2	■	■
3	■	■
4	■	■
5	■	■

a. • Copy and complete the table if f is an arithmetic sequence with a constant difference of 2.

- Find a closed form for the sequence.
- Find a closed form for the series $F(n) = \sum_{k=0}^{n} f(k)$.
- Find $f(10)$ and $F(10)$.

b. • Copy and complete the table if f is a geometric sequence with a constant ratio of 2.

- Find a closed form for the sequence.
- Find a closed form for the series $F(n) = \sum_{k=0}^{n} f(k)$.
- Find $f(10)$ and $F(10)$.

7. For each geometric sequence t, do the following:

- Write the first four terms of the sequence.
- Find $T(0)$, $T(1)$, $T(2)$, and $T(3)$, where $T(n) = \sum_{k=0}^{n} t(k)$ is the series associated with the sequence.
- Decide if the series has a limit.
- If the series does have a limit, find it.

a. first term 10 and common ratio $\frac{1}{10}$

b. second term 3 and fifth term $\frac{81}{8}$

8. Write each repeating decimal as a fraction.

a. 0.151515...

b. 0.100100100...

In **Investigation 7D,** you learned how to

- generate Pascal's Triangle and write the nth row, kth column entry as $\binom{n}{k}$
- notice and explain patterns in Pascal's Triangle
- use the Binomial Theorem to expand expressions of the form $(a + b)^n$

The following exercises will help you check your understanding.

9. a. Make a copy of Pascal's Triangle through Row 5.

b. On your copy, show two examples of the hockey stick property in which the sum on the tip is 10.

c. Find the value of $\binom{4}{2} + \binom{5}{4}$.

10. a. What is the expanded form for $(3x + 2)^5$?

b. What is the coefficient of x^2y^4 in the expansion of $(x + 2y)^6$?

Answers

6. a.

n	$f(n)$	Σ
0	5	5
1	7	12
2	9	21
3	11	32
4	13	45
5	15	60

$f(n) = 2n + 5$; $F(n) = n^2 + 6n + 5$; $f(10) = 25$, $F(10) = 165$

b.

n	$f(n)$	Σ
0	5	5
1	10	15
2	20	35
3	40	75
4	80	155
5	160	315

$f(n) = 5 \cdot 2^n$; $F(n) = 5(2^{n+1} - 1)$; $f(10) = 5120$, $F(10) = 10{,}235$

7. a. 10, 1, $\frac{1}{10}$, $\frac{1}{100}$; 10, 11, 11.1, 11.11; the series does have a limit; it is $\frac{100}{9}$.

b. 2, 3, $\frac{9}{2}$, $\frac{27}{4}$; 2, 5, $9\frac{1}{2}$, $16\frac{1}{4}$; the series does not have a limit.

8. a. $\frac{15}{99}$ or $\frac{5}{33}$ **b.** $\frac{100}{999}$

9. a–b. See back of book.

c. 11

10. a. $243x^5 + 810x^4 + 1080x^3 + 720x^2 + 240x + 32$

b. 240

Chapter 7

Test

Go Online PHSchool.com

For a chapter test, go to Web Code: bfa-0753.

Multiple Choice

1. What is the sum of the odd integers from 7 to 55, inclusive?

   A. 62 B. 775
   C. 850 D. 1550

2. Suppose $\binom{j}{1} = 5$. What is j?

   A. 0 B. 4
   C. 5 D. 6

3. Which number is equivalent to 0.999 . . . ?

   A. 0 B. $\frac{1}{9}$
   C. $\frac{999}{1000}$ D. 1

4. In an arithmetic sequence, the second term is 9 and the eighth term is 33. What is the third term?

   A. 4 B. 12
   C. 13 D. 17

5. What is the coefficient of x^4y^5 in the expansion of $(x + y)^9$?

   A. $\binom{5}{4}$
   B. $\binom{4}{5}$
   C. $\binom{9}{1}$
   D. $\binom{9}{5}$

Open Response

6. Find each sum.

   a. $\sum_{k=0}^{10} (7 - 4k)$
   b. $\sum_{j=0}^{8} \left(\frac{1}{3}\right)^j$
   c. $\sum_{k=3}^{12} 4k$

7. Find a closed form for each indefinite sum.

   a. $\sum_{k=0}^{n} (6k + 2)$ b. $\sum_{k=0}^{n} (k^2 + 1)$

8. Find a recursive rule and a closed-form rule for the series associated with $h(n) = 4 - 6n$, having initial term $h(0)$.

9. A geometric sequence h has $h(0) = 18$ and common ratio $\frac{1}{3}$.

   a. Make a Σ table for $h(n)$ for $n = 0$ through $n = 4$.
   b. Find a closed form for the sequence.
   c. Find a closed form for the associated series.

10. You can factor the polynomial below into the form $(a + b)^7$.

    $$x^7 - 14x^6 + 84x^5 + cx^4 + 560x^3 - 672x^2 + 448x - 128$$

    Find a, b, and c.

11. What is a geometric series?

Chapter Test

Assessment Resources

Chapter Test page 1 of 2

Multiple Choice

1. What is the sum of the even integers from 10 to 100, inclusive?
   A. 1375
   B. 2475
   C. 2530
   D. 5060

2. Suppose $\binom{10}{k} = 10$. What is k?
   A. 0 or 10
   B. 1 or 9
   C. 0 or 9
   D. 1 or 10

3. Which number is equivalent to 0.111 . . . ?
   A. 0
   B. $\frac{111}{1000}$
   C. $\frac{1}{9}$
   D. 1

4. In an arithmetic sequence, the second term is 12 and the tenth term is 52. What is the fifth term?
   A. 5
   B. 27
   C. 32
   D. 40

5. What is the coefficient of x^3y^7 in the expansion of $(x + y)^{10}$?
   A. $\binom{3}{7}$
   B. $\binom{7}{3}$
   C. $\binom{10}{3}$
   D. $\binom{10}{7}$

Also available: Form B

Chapter Test

1. B
2. C
3. D
4. C
5. D
6. a. -143 b. $\frac{9841}{6561} \approx 1.49992$
   c. 300
7. a. $\sum_{k=0}^{n} (6k + 2) = 3n^2 + 5n + 2$
   b. $\sum_{k=0}^{n} (k^2 + 1) = \frac{2n^3 + 3n^2 + 7n + 6}{6}$
8. $$H(n) = \begin{cases} 4 & \text{if } n = 0 \\ H(n-1) + (4 - 6n) & \text{if } n > 0 \end{cases}$$
   $H(n) = -3n^2 + n + 4$
9. a. The entries in the $h(n)$ column are 18, 6, 2, $\frac{2}{3}$, $\frac{2}{9}$, so the entries in the Σ column are 18, 24, 26, $26\frac{2}{3}$, $26\frac{8}{9}$.
   b. $h(n) = 18 \cdot \left(\frac{1}{3}\right)^n$
   c. $H(n) = 27 - 3^{2-n}$
10. $a = x$, $b = -2$, $c = -280$
11. Answers may vary. Sample: A geometric series is the accumulating sum of the terms of a geometric sequence.

Chapter 8 Introduction to Trigonometry

Students were first introduced to trigonometry in CME Project *Geometry*, in which the trigonometric functions sine, cosine, and tangent were defined as ratios of sidelengths in right triangles. This approach had the effect of restricting the domain of the trigonometric functions to angle measures θ, with $0° < \theta < 90°$. In this chapter, that domain is extended to any angle measure by relating sine and cosine (and so, tangent) to coordinates of points on the unit circle. Students also graph sine, cosine, and tangent as a function of angle measure. They see the relationship between these graphs and the unit circle definitions. They also verify familiar trigonometric identities, such as $\sin(90° - \theta) = \cos\theta$ and $\sin^2\theta + \cos^2\theta = 1$ for the new domain. Then students prove new identities, such as the Angle-Sum Identities.

Chapter Overview

INVESTIGATION 8A, *Trigonometric Functions,* has students extend the domains of the sine, cosine, and tangent functions to any angle.

INVESTIGATION 8B, *Graphs of Trigonometric Functions,* has students graph the sine, cosine, and tangent functions and use the graphs to explore properties of the functions.

INVESTIGATION 8C, *Applications to Triangles,* has students apply trigonometry to find missing side lengths and angle measures in triangles.

For more information on the investigations, see

- Chapter Road Map, pp. 680–681
- Investigation Road Maps, pp. 688, 714, 736

PROJECT The Project near the end of the chapter is optional. You can assign the Project at any time during the chapter depending on how often and how long you feel students should work on it.

Mathematics Background

EXTENSION As in previous work with extension, such as the extension of the set of real numbers into the set of complex numbers, you let students into the process of how and why the domain of the trigonometric functions can be expanded to angle measures that are not possible in a right triangle. They understand that you make choices about how to extend the domain strategically in order to preserve key properties of the functions.

Pacing Suggestions and Materials

Reviewing Key Ideas

DAY	LESSON	HOMEWORK
1	8.0 Right Triangle Trigonometry Core: 1, 2, 3, 4, 5 Optional: none; Extension: 6	Core: 7, 8, 9, 10, 11, 12, 13, 14 Optional: 16, 17; Extension: 15

Investigation 8A *Trigonometric Functions*

DAY	LESSON	HOMEWORK
1	8.1 Getting Started Core: 1, 2, 4, 5, 6, 8, 9 Optional: 3, 7; Extension: 10	Core: 11, 13, 14, 16, 17 Optional: 12, 15, 18, 19, 20
2	8.2 Extending the Domain, Part 1 Core: 1, 2, 4, 5, 7 Optional: 3, 6	Core: 8, 9, 10, 11, 12, 13 Optional: 14; Extension: 15
3	8.3 Extending the Domain, Part 2 Core: 1, 2, 3, 4, 7 Optional: 5, 6, 8; Extension: 8b	Core: 9, 10, 11, 12, 13, 17, 19, 20 Optional: 14, 15, 16, 18a; Extension: 18b
4	8.4 The Pythagorean Identity Core: 1, 2, 3, 4, 5 Optional: 6	Core: 8, 11, 12, 13, 14 Optional: 7, 9, 10
5	8.5 Solving Trigonometric Equations Core: 1, 2, 3, 4, 5a–b Optional: 6, 7, 8; Extension: 5c	Core: 9, 10, 11, 14, 17 Optional: 12, 13, 15a–c, 18a–d Extension: 15d, 16, 18f

Investigation 8B *Graphs of Trigonometric Functions*

DAY	LESSON	HOMEWORK
1	8.6 Getting Started Core: 1, 2, 3, 4, 5 Optional: none	Core: 6, 7, 8, 9, 10 Optional: 12; Extension: 11
2	8.7 Graphing Cosine and Sine Core: 1, 2, 3, 4, 5, 6, 7, 9, 10 Optional: none; Extension: 8	Core: 11, 12, 13, 14, 15, 16, 17, 18 Optional: 19, 20, 21
3	8.8 Graphing the Tangent Function Core: 1, 2, 3, 4, 5, 7 Optional: 6, 8	Core: 9, 10, 11, 12, 14 Optional: 15; Extension: 13
4	8.9 The Angle-Sum Identities Core: 1, 2, 3 Optional: 5, 6; Extension: 4, 7	Core: 8, 9, 10, 11, 13, 14, 16, 17 Optional: 12; Extension: 15

NOTES	MATERIALS
This lesson reviews right triangle trigonometry and is optional.	• graphing calculators

NOTES	MATERIALS
If necessary, precede this lesson with the review of right triangle trigonometry in Lesson 8.0.	• graph paper • graphing calculators • Blackline Masters 8.1A, 8.1B
	• graph paper • graphing calculators • Blackline Master 8.1A
	• graph paper • graphing calculators • Blackline Masters 8.1A, 8.3
	• graph paper • graphing calculators • Blackline Master 8.1A
	• graph paper • graphing calculators

NOTES	MATERIALS
	• graph paper • graphing calculators
	• graph paper • graphing calculators • Blackline Masters 8.7A, 8.7B
	• graph paper • graphing calculators • Blackline Masters 8.7A, 8.8A, 8.8B
This lesson is optional, but critical for students continuing to precalculus.	• graph paper • graphing calculators • Blackline Master 8.9

This chapter introduces students to a context in which they visualize an observer standing at the origin of a coordinate plane and facing in the direction of its positive *x*-axis. This observer watches another person who begins walking along the unit circle, which is a circle of radius 1 centered at the origin, in a counterclockwise direction, starting at the point $(1, 0)$. The observer does not move away from the origin but does turn to watch. The angle through which the observer turns is related to the coordinates of the walker's position on the unit circle. The observer can turn through any angle, positive or negative, but every angle is immediately related to a specific right triangle—the triangle created by dropping a perpendicular to the *x*-axis from the walker's position.

Students see that for any angle, they can find the coordinates of the walker's position, and that for any position of the walker, they can give several candidates for the angle through which the observer may have turned to watch the walker. For example, if the angle is 300°, the right triangle associated with this angle forms a 60° angle with the x-axis, so the horizontal distance from the origin to the walker's position is $\frac{1}{2}$, and the vertical distance from the origin to the walker's position is $\frac{\sqrt{3}}{2}$. Since the walker is in Quadrant IV, the *x*-coordinate of the walker's location is positive, and the y-coordinate is negative. When the observer has turned through an angle of 300°, the walker must be at the point $\left(\frac{1}{2}, -\frac{\sqrt{3}}{2}\right)$. However, if the walker's position is known to be $\left(\frac{1}{2}, -\frac{\sqrt{3}}{2}\right)$, then students understand that the observer may have turned any number of complete circles and then turned a further 300°. It is also possible that the walker moved in a clockwise direction, which would make the observer's angle measurement negative. This means that for the position $\left(\frac{1}{2}, -\frac{\sqrt{3}}{2}\right)$, any angle of the form $300° + k \cdot 360°$ with k any integer, could be the angle through which the observer has turned.

Once this connection has been made, the sine and cosine functions for any angle are defined to be the coordinates of the unit circle that correspond to that angle. Students see that this definition gives the same values for acute angles as the right triangle definition, and then they verify that identities that were true in right triangle trigonometry still hold under this new definition. This process of choosing a new definition strategically, so that critical properties still hold, lets students understand the reasons why mathematicians in the past made the choices they did. Instead of presenting students with a new definition of the trigonometric functions in a new domain, they are invited to make sense of the choice of the definition by relating it to their previous work.

continued on page 680c

continued from page 680b

In CME Project *Precalculus*, a further adjustment is made to the definitions of the trigonometric functions. Rather than inputting the measure of the central angle in degrees, students begin inputting the measure of the intercepted arc in radians. In other words, instead of inputting the angle through which the observer has turned, students input the distance the walker has walked. This approach makes the sine function, for example, into a genuine function of a real-valued variable, which will be necessary for some more advanced work in trigonometry, including calculus and Fourier analysis.

INVERSE TRIGONOMETRIC FUNCTIONS Students also begin to rethink their understanding of the inverse trigonometric functions in this new context. In right triangle trigonometry, the trigonometric functions are all one-to-one. Over the domain $0° < \theta < 90°$, there is only one solution to an equation such as $\sin \theta = \frac{1}{2}$.

However, in the extended domain, the trigonometric functions are not one-to-one. Students have faced a problem like this before, with the square root function. Since the function $y = x^2$ is not one-to-one, it does not have an inverse. However, if you consider only $x \geq 0$, $y = x^2$ is one-to-one over that restricted domain, and its inverse is $y = \sqrt{x}$. Similarly, the trigonometric functions in their extended domain are not one-to-one. By experimentation with inverse trigonometric functions on their calculators, students discover the values that are returned for inverse sine, cosine, and tangent. Inverse sine and inverse tangent, for example, return angles in the range $-90° \leq x \leq 90°$ while inverse cosine returns angles $0° \leq x \leq 180°$. Students then decide how to interpret these results to solve problems. Just as the solution to the equation $x^2 = 3$ is not simply $x = \sqrt{3}$, but rather $x = \pm\sqrt{3}$, the solution to the equation $\sin x = \frac{\sqrt{2}}{2}$ is not $x = \sin^{-1}\left(\frac{\sqrt{2}}{2}\right) = 45°$ (which is the only value returned by a calculator), but rather $x = 45° + j \cdot 360°$ or $135° + k \cdot 360°$ with j and k integers.

Pacing Suggestions and Materials

Investigation 8C *Applications to Triangles*

DAY	LESSON	HOMEWORK
1	8.10 Getting Started Core: 1, 2, 3, 4, 5 Optional: none; Extension: 6	Core: 7, 8, 9, 10, 11, 12 Optional: 13
2	8.11 The Area of a Triangle Core: 1, 2, 3, 4 Optional: 5a, 6, 7; Extension: 5b	Core: 8, 9, 10, 11, 12, 14, 16 Optional: 13, 15, 17
3	8.12 The Law of Sines Core: 1, 2, 3, 4, 7, 8 Optional: 5, 6; Extension: 9	Core: 10, 11, 12, 13, 14, 15, 16, 17 Optional: 19; Extension: 18
4	8.13 The Law of Cosines Core: 1, 2, 3, 4, 6, 7 Optional: 8a; Extension: 5, 8b	Core: 9, 10, 11, 12, 13, 14, 15, 17 Optional: 18; Extension: 16, 19
5	8.14 Heron's Formula Core: 1, 2, 5 Optional: 3, 4	Core: 6, 7a–b, 8, 9, 10 Optional: 11, 13; Extension: 7c, 12

NOTES	MATERIALS
	• geometry software • graphing calculators • protractors • rulers
	• geometry software • graphing calculators • protractors • rulers • Blackline Master 8.11
	• geometry software • graph paper • graphing calculators • Blackline Master 8.12
	• CAS (recommended) • graphing calculators • Blackline Masters 8.13A, 8.13B
This lesson is optional.	• geometry software • graphing calculators • Blackline Master 8.14

REPRESENTATIONS Now that students have extended the domain of the trigonometric functions to any angle measure, it makes sense to graph a function such as $y = \sin x$. This graph gives new insights about the properties of the sine function. Students can see clearly the periodic nature of the function. They may have already made sense of this by realizing that as the walker continues around and around the unit circle, the walker's position will pass over a particular set of coordinates once on each circuit. For example, there are two occasions on each trip around the circle where the walker's position has a y-coordinate equal to $-\frac{1}{2}$. But there are not only two solutions to the equation $\sin x = -\frac{1}{2}$. When students look at the graph of the sine function, they can see that the line $y = -\frac{1}{2}$ has an infinite number of intersections with the graph of sine. By working back and forth between the graph of the function and its relationship to the coordinates of points on the unit circle, students make connections and increase their understanding of the behavior of this function.

Students can see symmetry in the graph of the function $y = \cos x$ which helps them understand why $\cos x = \cos -x$. The y-axis is a line of symmetry for the graph, and reflection over this line maps a point (x, y) to the point $(-x, y)$. Students also see that the graph of $y = \cos x$ looks like the graph of $y = \sin x$, shifted 90° to the left. This realization can help students make sense of the relationships that exist between these two functions, including identities such as $\sin(90° - \theta) = \cos\theta$.

As students analyze the graphs of the trigonometric functions, they are given many opportunities to think about when the function is positive or negative, when it is increasing or decreasing, and what happens to a function like $y = \tan x$ when it approaches a value where the tangent is undefined. However, the graphs are not a replacement for the unit circle representation. The unit circle helps students make sense of identities such as $\sin^2\theta + \cos^2\theta = 1$ and allows students to prove other identities using the ideas of geometry. The more connections students can make between the unit circle and the graphs of the trigonometric functions, the more robust their understanding of these functions will be.

Developing Students' Mathematical Habits

Key mathematical habits in this chapter include:

EXTENSION By extending the domain of the trigonometric functions in a way that preserves key properties, students make sense of the choices made. They think carefully about the consequences of a new definition, including the fact that the tangent function will sometimes be undefined.

LOGICAL REASONING Students prove theorems and establish identities using ideas of algebra and of geometry. They develop coherent chains of reasoning and begin to develop strategies for choosing results that will lead to a desired conclusion.

VISUALIZATION Students move flexibly between the unit circle representation and graphs of the trigonometric functions, choosing which representation to use depending on context.

Chapter Road Map

INVESTIGATION 8A, *Trigonometric Functions,* has students extend the domains of the trigonometric functions sine, cosine, and tangent so that they can be evaluated for any angle, not just for an acute angle as part of a right triangle. As usual, they do this extension mathematically, reasoning about its effect on previously proven results.

INVESTIGATION 8B, *Graphs of Trigonometric Functions,* has students graph the sine, cosine, and tangent functions and use this new representation to develop insights about the functions. They examine periodicity and symmetry. They use these facts to prove trigonometric identities, concluding with an optional lesson that proves the Angle-Sum Identities that are critical as they continue to precalculus.

Introduction to Trigonometry

Trigonometry, at first glance, seems to be about triangles. With further study, you will see that it is also about waves and oscillations. When you graph $y = \sin x$ on your calculator and look at the function for $-720° \leq x \leq 720°$ and $-2 \leq y \leq 2$, you see a wave. This wave has properties in common with many natural systems such as a weight on a spring, a swinging pendulum, or a vibrating string on a musical instrument. You can use the sine function to describe movement in these systems.

In fact, Joseph Fourier, a French engineer, found a method for writing virtually any periodic function as a combination of sine and cosine functions. The entire graph of a periodic function consists of copies of one portion of the graph laid end to end. Light, sound, and even molecules in a solid move as waves. Trigonometry is at the heart of such diverse sciences as acoustics, optics, chemistry, seismology, meteorology, and electrical engineering.

Vocabulary and Notation

- **cosine, $\cos\theta$**
- **discontinuity**
- **Heronian triangle**
- **Law of Cosines**
- **Law of Sines**
- **period**
- **periodic function**
- **sine, $\sin\theta$**
- **standard position**
- **tangent, $\tan\theta$**
- **trigonometric equation**

INVESTIGATION 8C, *Applications to Triangles,* has students apply the trigonometry they have learned to finding missing side lengths and angle measures in triangles. They revisit and expand on topics from CME Project *Geometry*, including finding the area of a triangle given two sides and their included angle, the Law of Sines, and the Law of Cosines. Then they prove Heron's Formula, which computes the area of a triangle given only its side lengths.

Chapter Vocabulary and Notation

The following list gives key vocabulary and notation used in the chapter. Selected new vocabulary and notation items are shown in boldface on the student page.

- ambiguous case, p. 753
- cosine, $\cos\theta$, pp. 682, 694, 698
- discontinuity, p. 723
- Heronian triangle, p. 768
- included angle, p. 747
- included side, p. 747
- Law of Cosines, p. 754
- Law of Sines, p. 747
- period, p. 721
- periodic function, p. 699
- sine, $\sin\theta$, pp. 682, 694, 698
- solve a triangle, p. 750
- standard position, p. 696
- tangent, $\tan\theta$, pp. 682, 694, 698
- trigonometric equation, p. 710

Chapter Technology

CME Project *Algebra 2* assumes that each student has access to a graphing calculator. It also recommends access to a computer algebra system (CAS).

Support for the use of technology is available in the TI-Nspire™ Technology Handbook. See p. 778.

A list of technology used with important concepts in this chapter appears below. Students will need access to the functionality listed to develop complete understanding of these topics.

Graphing Calculator

LESSON 8.2 Set to degree mode and approximate values for cos 70° and sin 70°, p. 692.

LESSON 8.3 Find the cosine of various angle measures, pp. 698, 699.

LESSON 8.7 Approximate angle measures for which the cosine is –0.4, p. 718. Graph $y = \sin x$, p. 719. Check a sketch of the graph of $k(x) = \cos 2x$, p. 720.

LESSON 8.13 Find the inverse of a matrix, p. 763.

LESSON 8.15 Find measures of acute angles in right triangles given two side lengths, p. 685. Find the sine, cosine, and tangent of various angle measures, p. 687.

Lesson Overview

GOAL

- Review right angle trigonometry.

This optional lesson is intended as a quick review of right triangle trigonometry. If your students have not seen this material before, you may want to refer to Investigation 6B in CME Project *Geometry* for a more basic introduction.

In right angle trigonometry, the functions sine, cosine, and tangent are defined strictly as the ratio of side lengths in right triangles, with respect to one of the acute angles in the triangle. The definitions are based on the fact that all right triangles that also have one pair of their nonright angles congruent are similar, so ratios of side lengths between pairs of similar triangles and among side lengths with similar triangles are contant. This lesson reviews how to evaluate sine, cosine, and tangent when you know at least two side lengths of a right triangle and how to use inverse trigonometric functions to find unknown angle measures. In the exercises, students will review the ratios of side lengths in 30°-60°-90° and 45°-45°-90° triangles.

CHECK YOUR UNDERSTANDING
- Core: 1, 2, 3, 4, 5
- Optional: none
- Extension: 6

MATERIALS
- graphing calculators

HOMEWORK
- Core: 7, 8, 9, 10, 11, 12, 13, 14
- Optional: 16, 17
- Extension: 15

VOCABULARY
- sine, sin θ
- cosine, cos θ
- tangent, tan θ

8.0 Right Triangle Trigonometry

Activating Prior Knowledge
Reviewing Key Ideas

In geometry, you learned about similarity and the AA Theorem: Two triangles are similar if two pairs of corresponding angles have the same measure.

If two triangles have two pairs of corresponding angles with the same measure, the third pair of angles also has the same measure, because the sum of the measures of the angles in a triangle is 180°.

If two right triangles have one pair of acute angles with the same measure, then they are similar. The ratio of any two side lengths in one of the triangles is the same as the ratio of the corresponding side lengths in the other triangle.

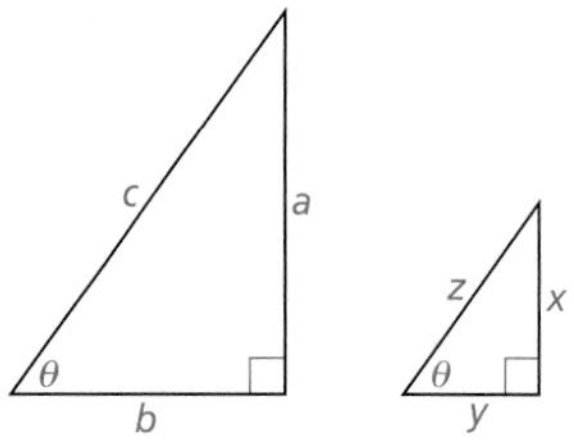

$$\frac{a}{c} = \frac{x}{z}$$

$$\frac{b}{c} = \frac{y}{z}$$

$$\frac{a}{b} = \frac{x}{y}$$

These ratios are determined by the marked angle in the triangle. In other words, each ratio is a function of the given angle. It helps to refer to the three sides of the triangle in terms of their position from the perspective of this angle. There are the leg opposite the angle, the leg adjacent to the angle, and the hypotenuse.

Which side is which depends on which angle you are talking about. The side opposite one acute angle is adjacent to the other. The hypotenuse does not change.

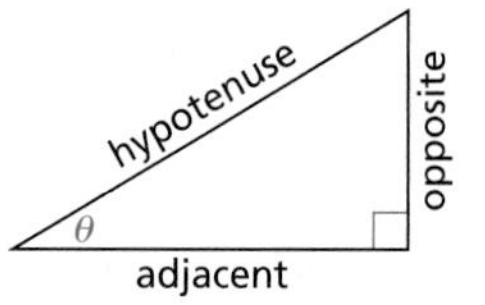

The three ratios are functions of the angle θ. Since they are helpful in many problems, they have standard names.

Definitions

The sine of an acute angle θ is the ratio of the opposite side to the hypotenuse in any right triangle that has θ as an acute angle. It is denoted by sin θ.

The cosine of an acute angle θ is the ratio of the adjacent side to the hypotenuse. It is denoted by cos θ.

The tangent of an acute angle θ is the ratio of the opposite side to the adjacent side. It is denoted by tan θ.

Here are those ratios again, written in the form of equations.

$$\sin\theta = \frac{\text{opposite}}{\text{hypotenuse}}$$

$$\cos\theta = \frac{\text{adjacent}}{\text{hypotenuse}}$$

$$\tan\theta = \frac{\text{opposite}}{\text{adjacent}}$$

Calculators have keys for all three of these functions. They also have keys for their inverse functions, which allow you to calculate an angle if you know its sine, cosine, or tangent.

Example 1

Problem A wheelchair ramp should not incline at an angle steeper than 5°. You are building a ramp next to a staircase that rises a total of 2 feet. How long will the ramp be if the angle is 5°?

Solution The picture below shows what the ramp would look like.

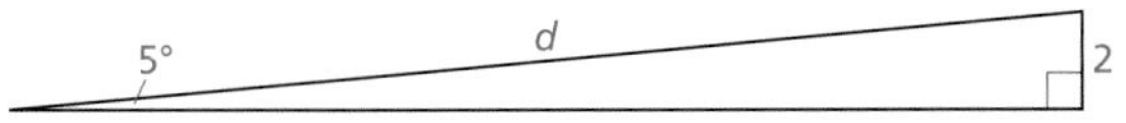

The hypotenuse and the side opposite the 5° angle are involved, so it is simplest to use the sine function. You know the angle measure, and that the length of the opposite side is 2. The hypotenuse is the unknown d.

$$\sin 5^\circ = \frac{2}{d}$$

Solve for d: $d = \frac{2}{\sin 5^\circ}$. You can use a calculator to find that $d \approx 23$ feet.

A 5° angle is quite small. How does the length of the ramp compare with the horizontal distance from the end of the ramp to the building?

For You to Do

1. For safety, a ladder manufacturer recommends that you should place a ladder's base a minimum distance from the wall.This distance is at least one foot for every 6 feet of ladder length. How high on the wall can a 20-foot ladder reach if the base is at the minimum distance from the wall?

Launch

Begin by asking students to read the introductory material and definitions. Then proceed to Example 1.

Answers

For You to Do

1. about 19.7 ft

Explore

For Discussion

Point out to students that it is fairly easy to calculate with the numbers in the example. This is the exception rather than the rule.

Example 2

Problem For some angle θ, $\cos\theta = \frac{3}{5}$. Find $\sin\theta$ and $\tan\theta$.

Solution

Method 1 You can use any right triangle with this angle θ, so pick one that has convenient side lengths. Since the ratio given is $\frac{3}{5}$, set up a right triangle with a side of length 3 adjacent to angle θ and a hypotenuse of length 5.

Method 1 gives exact answers.

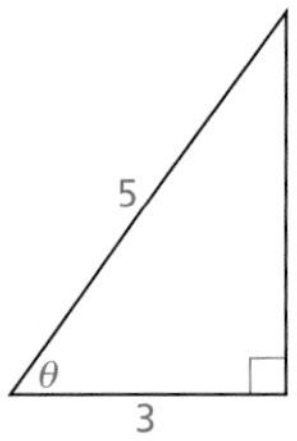

You can find the length of the remaining side with the Pythagorean Theorem or by recognizing the famous 3-4-5 right triangle. Since the third side's length is 4, you know the other ratios.

$$\sin\theta = \frac{\text{opposite}}{\text{hypotenuse}} = \frac{4}{5}$$

$$\tan\theta = \frac{\text{opposite}}{\text{adjacent}} = \frac{4}{3}$$

Method 2 Use the inverse function to find the angle θ.

Method 2 gives approximate answers.

$$\cos\theta = \frac{3}{5} \Rightarrow \theta = \cos^{-1}\left(\frac{3}{5}\right)$$

The angle θ is approximately 53.130°. Once you know θ, you can find the other ratios with your calculator.

$$\sin 53.130° \approx 0.8000$$

$$\tan 53.130° \approx 1.3333$$

These values are very close to the exact fractions $\frac{4}{5}$ and $\frac{4}{3}$ you found using Method 1.

For Discussion

2. For this example, it seems that Method 1 gives more accurate answers, more quickly. Can you think of a situation in which Method 2 might be necessary?

Answers

For Discussion

2. Answers may vary. Sample: If the two given lengths are not part of a Pythagorean triple, then it may take more steps to use Method 1 to find the third side of the triangle.

Developing Habits of Mind

Look for relationships. You can express the Pythagorean Theorem using sine and cosine. Consider the triangle drawn at the right. The Pythagorean Theorem tells you that for this triangle,

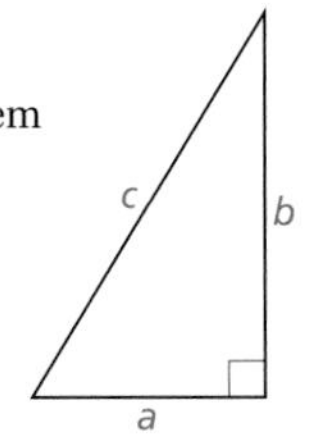

$$a^2 + b^2 = c^2$$

Divide each side by c^2.

$$\frac{a^2}{c^2} + \frac{b^2}{c^2} = 1$$

The trigonometric functions define $\cos\theta$ as $\frac{a}{c}$ and $\sin\theta$ as $\frac{b}{c}$. So,

$$(\cos\theta)^2 + (\sin\theta)^2 = 1$$

The parentheses can get in the way. The exponent is frequently moved to appear next to the function name.

$$\cos^2\theta + \sin^2\theta = 1$$

You read this equation as "cosine squared theta plus sine squared theta equals 1." It is one of the most fundamental relationships in trigonometry.

How far is the point ($\cos\theta$, $\sin\theta$) from the origin?

Exercises *Practicing Habits of Mind*

Check Your Understanding

1. A right triangle has a 40° angle and hypotenuse of length 10. Find the triangle's perimeter to two decimal places.

2. A right triangle has legs of lengths 20 and 21.

a. What is the area of this triangle?

b. How long is the hypotenuse?

c. Draw an accurate picture of this triangle. Estimate the acute angle measures.

d. Using a calculator, find the measure of each acute angle to the nearest degree.

3. In a right triangle, the value of $\cos\theta$ is $\frac{8}{17}$. Find the values of $\sin\theta$ and $\tan\theta$ exactly (without decimal approximations).

Wrap Up

Finish the lesson by going over the core Check Your Understanding exercises.

Exercises

HOMEWORK

- Core: 7, 8, 9, 10, 11, 12, 13, 14
- Optional: 16, 17
- Extension: 15

Check Your Understanding

EXERCISE 1 If students have trouble getting started, ask them to draw a picture of the triangle and use variables for the side lengths they do not know. Then they can write expressions for sin 40° and cos 40° in terms of the variables.

Exercises

1. 24.09

2. a. 210

b. 29

c.

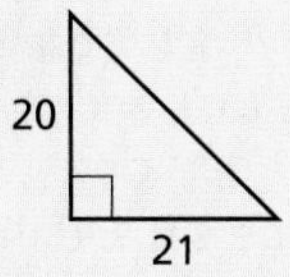

Each angle measures about 45°.

d. 46°, 44°

3. $\sin\theta = \frac{15}{17}$, $\tan\theta = \frac{15}{8}$

EXERCISE 4 This identity will eventually be used as the definition of the tangent function, with the added restriction that $\tan\theta$ is only defined for angles for which $\cos\theta \neq 0$.

EXERCISE 6 is a nice review of the ratios of side lengths in a 30°-60°-90° triangle. You may need to help students see that there are three cases to examine.

On Your Own

EXERCISE 7 introduces a result that will be critical when the students start working with the unit circle.

EXERCISE 8 Students will use this identity extensively throughout the chapter.

EXERCISE 9 If you discuss this exercise, mention that the result from Exercise 8 applies here. You may also want to tell students that they will be responsible for knowing the values of sine, cosine, and tangent in 30°-60°-90° and 45°-45°-90° triangles. See Exercise 10.

EXERCISE 11 asks students to think beyond the domain that has been established for the trigonometric functions. This situation is undefined because a right triangle cannot have a second 90° angle. Students will need to reason by continuity, thinking about what happens to the trigonometric ratios as one of the legs of the triangle gets shorter.

EXERCISE 12 Point out that the answers to these questions will be different after students learn new definitions for the trigonometric functions in Investigation 8A. Students will have to answer the same questions again there.

4. Show that for any angle measure θ such that $0° < \theta < 90°$,

$$\tan\theta = \frac{\sin\theta}{\cos\theta}$$

5. For some angle θ, $\sin\theta$ is exactly $\frac{1}{4}$. Find the exact value of $\cos\theta$ for this angle by drawing a right triangle.

6. **Take It Further** A right triangle has a 30° angle and one side length that is 12. Find all possible values for the area of the triangle.

On Your Own

7. A right triangle has an angle θ and a hypotenuse of length 1. Find the lengths of the other two sides in terms of θ.

8. Explain why it is true that for any angle θ, $0° < \theta < 90°$,

$$\sin\theta = \cos(90° - \theta)$$

Remember... Angles with measure θ and $90° - \theta$ are complementary. Hence the name cosine.

9. Use this triangle to find the exact values of sine, cosine, and tangent for 30° and 60°.

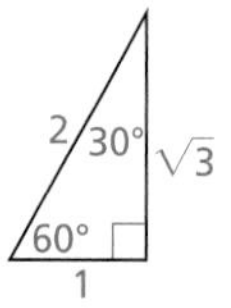

θ	$\sin\theta$	$\cos\theta$	$\tan\theta$
30°	■	■	■
60°	■	■	■

10. Use this triangle to find the exact values of sine, cosine, and tangent for 45°.

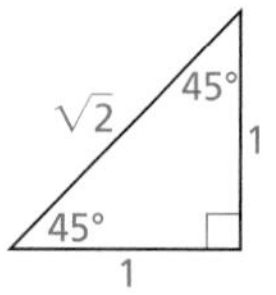

θ	$\sin\theta$	$\cos\theta$	$\tan\theta$
45°	■	■	■

11. Derman wants to extend the domain of sine and cosine so that he can give a value for $\sin 90°$ and $\cos 90°$. What are good values for Derman to pick? Explain.

12. a. What are the largest and smallest possible values for $\sin\theta$? Explain.

b. What are the largest and smallest possible values for $\cos\theta$? Explain.

c. What are the largest and smallest possible values for $\tan\theta$? Explain.

For Exercise 12, assume $0° < \theta < 90°$.

Answers

4. $\sin\theta = \frac{\text{opp}}{\text{hyp}}$ and $\cos\theta = \frac{\text{adj}}{\text{hyp}}$, so

$$\frac{\sin\theta}{\cos\theta} = \frac{\frac{\text{opp}}{\text{hyp}}}{\frac{\text{adj}}{\text{hyp}}} = \frac{\text{opp}}{\text{adj}} = \tan\theta.$$

5. $\frac{\sqrt{15}}{4}$

6. $72\sqrt{3} \approx 124.71$, $24\sqrt{3} \approx 41.57$, or $18\sqrt{3} \approx 31.18$

7. $\sin\theta$, $\cos\theta$

8. Answers may vary. Sample: In a right triangle, if one acute angle is θ then the other is $(90° - \theta)$. Also, the side opposite θ is the side adjacent to the $(90° - \theta)$ angle. So, $\sin\theta = \frac{\text{side opp } \theta}{\text{hyp}} = \frac{\text{side adj. to } (90° - \theta)}{\text{hyp}} = \cos(90° - \theta)$.

9.

θ	$\sin\theta$	$\cos\theta$	$\tan\theta$
30°	$\frac{1}{2}$	$\frac{\sqrt{3}}{2}$	$\frac{\sqrt{3}}{3}$
60°	$\frac{\sqrt{3}}{2}$	$\frac{1}{2}$	$\sqrt{3}$

10.

θ	$\sin\theta$	$\cos\theta$	$\tan\theta$
45°	$\frac{\sqrt{2}}{2}$	$\frac{\sqrt{2}}{2}$	1

11. As θ gets closer to 90°, the length of the opposite side gets closer to the length of the hypotenuse and the length of the adjacent side gets closer to 0. So $\sin 90° = 1$ and $\cos 90° = 0$.

12. a. The largest value is 1 and the smallest is 0. As θ gets close to 90°, $\sin\theta$ gets close to 1, and as θ gets close to 0, $\sin\theta$ gets close to 0.

b. The largest value is 1 and the smallest is 0. As θ gets close to 90°, $\cos\theta$ gets close to 0, and as θ gets close to 0, $\cos\theta$ gets close to 1.

c. The smallest value is 0 and there is no largest value. Since $\tan\theta = \frac{\sin\theta}{\cos\theta}$, this value would be 0 when $\sin\theta = 0$. The value of $\tan\theta$ would get very large as the value of

13. For each triangle, find $\sin\theta$, $\cos\theta$, and $\tan\theta$.

a.

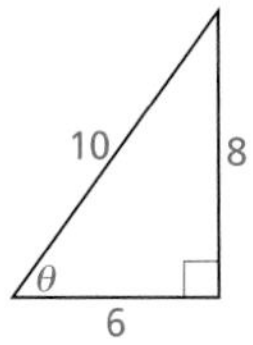

b.

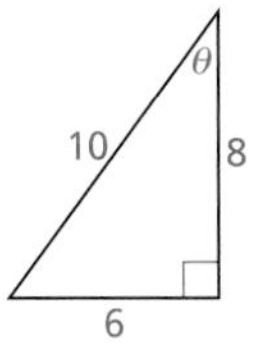

c.

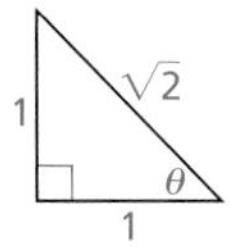

d.

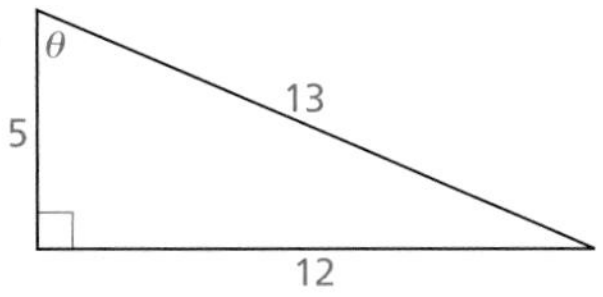

14. **What's Wrong Here?** Trent sees $\triangle TRI$.

Trent says, "So side TI is 10 and angle T is 70°, that means I can find side RI by using sine of 70°. So I know $\sin 70^\circ = \frac{RI}{10}$."

What is wrong with Trent's reasoning?

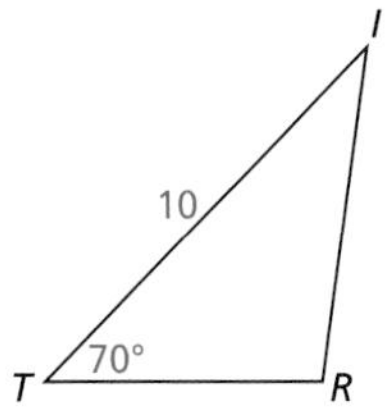

15. **Take It Further** Prove that for any angle θ such that $0^\circ < \theta < 90^\circ$, $\tan(90^\circ - \theta) = \frac{1}{\tan\theta}$.

Maintain Your Skills

16. Copy the following table. Use a calculator to complete it for the sine, cosine, and tangent of angles in increments of 10°. Find each value to three decimal places.

θ	$\sin\theta$	$\cos\theta$	$\tan\theta$
10°	■	■	■
20°	■	■	■
30°	■	■	■
40°	■	■	■
50°	■	■	■
60°	■	■	■
70°	■	■	■
80°	■	■	■

Habits of Mind

Look for relationships. Review Exercise 8.

17. Explain why $\sin 10^\circ$ and $\cos 80^\circ$ are equal.

EXERCISE 14 points out a common misconception among students beginning to study trigonometry.

Maintain Your Skills

EXERCISE 16 is similar to an exercise later in the chapter that prepares students to graph the sine, cosine, and tangent functions.

the denominator $\cos\theta$ gets close to 0.

13. a. $\sin\theta = \frac{4}{5}$, $\cos\theta = \frac{3}{5}$, $\tan\theta = \frac{4}{3}$

b. $\sin\theta = \frac{3}{5}$, $\cos\theta = \frac{4}{5}$, $\tan\theta = \frac{3}{4}$

c. $\sin\theta = \cos\theta = \frac{\sqrt{2}}{2}$, $\tan\theta = 1$

d. $\sin\theta = \frac{12}{13}$, $\cos\theta = \frac{5}{13}$, $\tan\theta = \frac{12}{5}$

14. You do not know that $\triangle TRI$ is a right triangle.

15. In a right triangle, with acute angles θ and $(90^\circ - \theta)$, let a be the side opposite θ, which is also the side adjacent to $(90^\circ - \theta)$. Let b be the side adjacent to θ, which is also the side opposite $(90^\circ - \theta)$. So if $\tan\theta = \frac{a}{b}$, then

$$\tan(90^\circ - \theta) = \frac{b}{a} = \frac{1}{\frac{a}{b}} = \frac{1}{\tan\theta}.$$

16.

θ	$\sin\theta$	$\cos\theta$	$\tan\theta$
10°	0.174	0.985	0.176
20°	0.342	0.940	0.364
30°	0.500	0.866	0.577
40°	0.643	0.766	0.839
50°	0.766	0.643	1.192
60°	0.866	0.500	1.732
70°	0.940	0.342	2.747
80°	0.985	0.174	5.671

17. Answers may vary. Sample: They are equal because $10^\circ + 80^\circ = 90^\circ$, and 10° and 80° are the acute angles of the same right triangle. The side adjacent to 80° is the side opposite 10°, so $\cos 80^\circ = \sin 10^\circ$.

Investigation Overview

Students have previously defined the trigonometric functions of sine, cosine, and tangent only as ratios of side lengths in right triangles. These functions could be evaluated only for angles θ such that $0° < \theta < 90°$. Now, students use a special context to rethink their understanding of these functions—an observer at the origin paired with a person walking around the unit circle. The observer starts out looking in the direction of the positive x-axis and turns to watch the walker, who begins at the point $(1, 0)$ and walks along the unit circle in a counterclockwise direction. Students see the coordinates of the walker's position at any moment as related to the angle through which the observer has turned. This relationship is formalized into new definitions for sine, cosine, and tangent that can be evaluated for any angle. For an angle θ in standard position, its left side intersects the unit circle at the point $(\cos \theta, \sin \theta)$, and $\tan \theta$ is defined to be $\frac{\sin \theta}{\cos \theta}$, where $\cos \theta \neq 0$.

You may wish to assign Questions 1–3 for students to think and write about during the investigation.

Learning Goals

- Use right triangle trigonometry to find the coordinates of a person walking on the unit circle, given an angle through which an observer has turned.
- Evaluate the sine, cosine, and tangent functions for any angle.
- Solve equations involving trigonometric functions.

Habits and Skills

- Visualize relationships between coordinates of a point on the unit circle and the angle that an observer at the origin must turn through to look at that point.
- Extend the sine, cosine, and tangent functions carefully, in order to preserve key properties.
- Use logical reasoning to find all possible solutions to a trigonometric equation.

Investigation 8A

Trigonometric Functions

In *Trigonometric Functions*, you will explore the relationships between points on a circle with radius 1 centered at the origin and angles with vertex at the origin. You will learn how to find the sine, cosine, and tangent of angles of any measure.

By the end of this investigation, you will be able to answer questions like these.

1. How can you extend the definitions of sine, cosine, and tangent to any angle, not just acute angles?
2. If an angle is in Quadrant IV, what can you say about the sign of its sine, cosine, and tangent?
3. What is the relationship between the equation of the unit circle and the Pythagorean Identity?

You will learn how to

- use right triangle trigonometry to find the coordinates of a person walking on the unit circle, given an angle through which an observer has turned
- evaluate the sine, cosine, and tangent functions for any angle
- solve equations involving trigonometric functions

You will develop these habits and skills:

- Visualize relationships between coordinates of a point on the unit circle and the angle that an observer at the origin must turn through to look at that point.
- Extend the sine, cosine, and tangent functions carefully, in order to preserve key properties.
- Use logical reasoning to find all possible solutions of a trigonometric equation.

As this drawbridge rises, the angle it forms with the river increases. The right end traces part of a circle.

Investigation Road Map

LESSON 8.1, *Getting Started,* has students explore what happens when one person stands at the origin and turns to watch another person walking counterclockwise around the unit circle.

LESSON 8.2, *Extending the Domain, Part 1,* has students evaluate the sine and cosine functions for angles between 0° and 360°.

LESSON 8.3, *Extending the Domain, Part 2,* extends the domain of the trigonometric functions to negative angles and angles greater than 360°.

LESSON 8.4, *The Pythagorean Identity,* has students use their new definitions and the unit circle to prove the Pythagorean Identity.

LESSON 8.5, *Solving Trigonometric Equations,* has students solve more complex trigonometric equations using factoring techniques.

8.1 Getting Started

Activating Prior Knowledge
Exploring New Ideas

The values of trigonometric functions are related to the coordinates of points on a circle with radius 1 centered at the origin.

For You to Explore

Olivia watches Paul walk around a circle. The circle's radius is 1 meter. Olivia stands at the center, and Paul begins walking counterclockwise. Consider a coordinate grid, with Olivia standing at the origin and Paul starting at the point (1, 0).

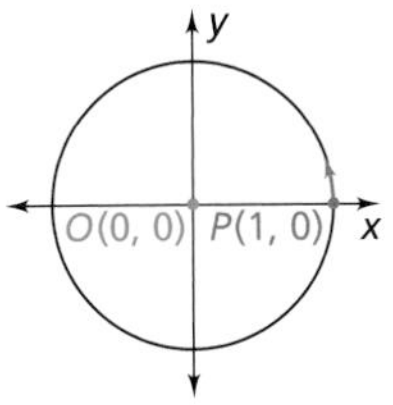

Remember...
This circle, with center (0, 0) and radius 1, is the unit circle.

As Paul walks, Olivia watches Paul and keeps track of the angle she has turned. For example, when Olivia has turned 70°, the situation looks like this.

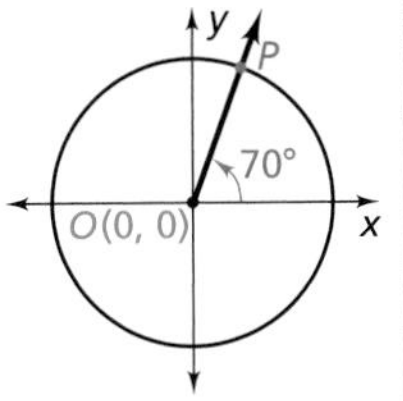

1. a. Explain why the distance between Olivia and Paul is always 1.
   b. Suppose Paul is at a point with coordinates (x, y). Write an equation in x and y to express the fact that Paul is 1 unit away from (0, 0).
2. Find the coordinates of Paul's location when Olivia has turned 70°. Round to three decimal places.
3. Find the lengths of the other two sides of this triangle.
4. Find the coordinates of Paul's location when Olivia has turned 45°.
   (*Hint:* Your work in Problem 3 should be helpful here.)

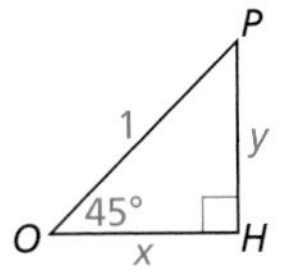

5. Find the coordinates of Paul's location when Olivia has turned 90°.

Draw a diagram. You do not need to use triangles this time.

6. a. Explain why Paul will pass through the point $\left(\frac{3}{5}, \frac{4}{5}\right)$.
   b. When Paul is at $\left(\frac{3}{5}, \frac{4}{5}\right)$, find the angle Olivia has turned to the nearest degree.
7. **Write About It** Describe how the y-coordinate of Paul's location changes as Olivia's angle increases.

Answers

For You to Explore

1. **a.** The distance between Paul and Olivia is always the length of the radius, which is 1.
   b. $x^2 + y^2 = 1$
2. (0.342, 0.940)
3. $x = y = \frac{\sqrt{2}}{2}$
4. $\left(\frac{\sqrt{2}}{2}, \frac{\sqrt{2}}{2}\right)$
5. (0, 1)
6. **a.** Answers may vary. Sample: The ordered pair $\left(\frac{3}{5}, \frac{4}{5}\right)$ satisfies the equation $x^2 + y^2 = 1$.
   b. 53°
7. Answers may vary. Sample: The y-coordinate starts at 0 when Olivia's angle is 0°, increases to 1 as her angle increases to 90°, decreases to −1 as her angle increases to 270°, and then increases to 0 as her angle increases to 360°. This pattern will repeat from 360° to 720°, from 720° to 1080°, and so on.

Lesson Overview

GOAL

- Warm up to the ideas of the investigation.

This Getting Started lesson introduces a context for extending the domains of the trigonometric functions. It should also remind students of their work in the complex plane in Chapter 3 for finding the direction of a complex number. As always in a Getting Started lesson, there is no need to formalize these ideas today. Students meet all the ideas again throughout the investigation.

FOR YOU TO EXPLORE
- Core: 1, 2, 4, 5, 6, 8, 9
- Optional: 3, 7
- Extension: 10

MATERIALS
- graph paper
- graphing calculators
- Blackline Masters 8.1A, 8.1B

HOMEWORK
- Core: 11, 13, 14, 16, 17
- Optional: 12, 15, 18, 19, 20

Launch

With your class, read the description of how Olivia stands at the origin and watches Paul walk around the unit circle. Then let students get started on the problems.

Explore

As students are working, make sure they know the equation for the unit circle and are able to find the coordinates and angles they need. If necessary, you may wish to demonstrate how to use the calculator to do some of the calculations.

For You to Explore

PROBLEM 1 It is critically important for the chapter that students know that the unit circle's equation is $x^2 + y^2 = 1$. Expect students to recognize it almost immediately. Check that they can solve this exercise and understand the solution. Blackline Master 8.1A provides a unit circle.

PROBLEM 2 If students are not sure how to get started, suggest they draw a picture. You might also suggest that this exercise is similar to finding the $a + bi$ form of a complex number when you know its magnitude and direction.

PROBLEMS 4 AND 5 Look at students' results for Problems 4 and 5. Make sure they have the idea before they attempt the big table in Problem 8.

PROBLEM 6 This problem is the first in this chapter that asks students to find an unknown angle. You might relate it to finding the direction of a complex number.

PROBLEMS 8 AND 9 The data from Problem 8 give students many points for this graph, but they should think carefully about how to connect these points. Encourage students to go back to the description of Paul and Olivia and the unit circle. Let students develop their own strategies. Some students might use visual estimates for angles not in the table; others might include angles related to the 30°-60°-90° triangle as new data points. You can use Blackline Master 8.1B as a transparency or a handout.

PROBLEM 9 In this book, "between 0° and 360°" means the graph should show all points from 0° to 360°, including 0° and 360°.

EXERCISE 10 If your students are ready to tackle this question, you might want to ask them to consider some interim angle measurements, such as 361°, 450°, and 540°, etc. That should help them think to figure out how many complete revolutions 10,000° is.

Wrap Up

End the lesson by going over Problems 8 and 9. Encourage students to think about how to connect on the graph the points that come from the table. Ask: Will there be straight segments connecting the points or curves? How could you find out?

Exercises

HOMEWORK

- Core: 11, 13, 14, 16, 17
- Optional: 12, 15, 18, 19, 20

On Your Own

EXERCISES 11 AND 16 Exercise 16 asks students to graph Paul's *x*-coordinate as a function of Olivia's angle. The table in Exercise 11 should help students decide what sort of curve they should use to connect the points from the table in Problem 8.

8. Copy and complete this table, giving the coordinates of Paul's location when Olivia has turned each angle.

Angle	Coordinates	Angle	Coordinates
0°	(1, 0)	270°	■
45°	■	315°	■
90°	■	360°	■
135°	■	405°	■
180°	(−1, 0)	450°	■
225°	■		

9. The *y*-coordinate of Paul's position is a function of the angle through which Olivia has turned. Make a coordinate grid labeled like the one below. Draw the graph of the function for angles between 0° and 360°.

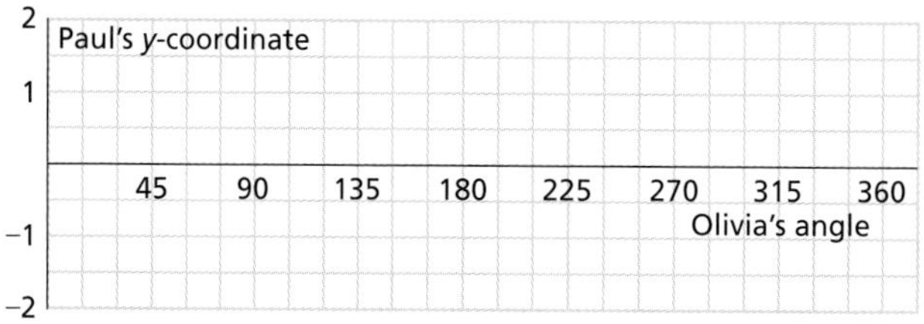

10. **Take It Further** Find the coordinates of Paul's location when Olivia has turned 10,000°. Calculate to three decimal places.

Exercises *Practicing Habits of Mind*

On Your Own

11. Copy and complete this table, giving the coordinates of Paul's location when Olivia has turned through each angle. Find each answer to three decimal places.

Angle	Coordinates	Angle	Coordinates
0°	(1, 0)	50°	■
10°	■	60°	■
20°	■	70°	■
30°	■	80°	■
40°	■	90°	(0, 1)

Answers

8–9. See back of book.

10. (0.174, −0.985)

Exercises

11. See back of book.

12. Find the magnitude and argument of each complex number.

a. $3 + 4i$

b. $\frac{3}{5} + \frac{4}{5}i$

c. $-5 + 12i$

d. $-\frac{5}{13} + \frac{12}{13}i$

Approximate the arguments to the nearest degree.

13. Which of these points is on the unit circle $x^2 + y^2 = 1$?

A. $\left(\frac{1}{2}, -\frac{1}{2}\right)$

B. $(1, -1)$

C. $\left(-\frac{5}{13}, \frac{12}{13}\right)$

D. $\left(\frac{2}{3}, -\frac{4}{5}\right)$

14. a. Find the coordinates of Paul's location to three decimal places when Olivia has turned 130°.

b. Find the coordinates of Paul's location to three decimal places when Olivia has turned 230°.

15. Describe how the x-coordinate of Paul's location varies as Olivia's angle increases.

16. In Problem 9, you graphed Paul's y-coordinate as a function of the angle Olivia had turned. Now graph Paul's x-coordinate as a function of the angle Olivia has turned.

Include the points (0, 1) and (180, −1).

17. Find the coordinates of Paul's location to three decimal places when Olivia has turned 430°.

18. Suppose a and b are real numbers and $z = a + bi$, a complex number. If $|z| = 2$ and $\arg z = 120°$, find a and b.

Maintain Your Skills

19. Draw the graphs of each pair of equations on the same axes. Find the number of intersections of the two graphs.

a. $x^2 + y^2 = 1$, $x = 0.5$

b. $x^2 + y^2 = 1$, $x = 0.9$

c. $x^2 + y^2 = 1$, $x = 1$

d. $x^2 + y^2 = 1$, $x = 1.3$

Go Online Video Tutor
PHSchool.com
Web Code: bfe-0775

20. Draw the graphs of each pair of equations on the same axes. Find the number of intersections of the two graphs.

a. $x^2 + y^2 = 1$, $y = 0.5$

b. $x^2 + y^2 = 1$, $y = -0.5$

c. $x^2 + y^2 = 1$, $y = -0.9$

d. $x^2 + y^2 = 1$, $y = -1$

12. a. magnitude 5, argument ≈ 53°
b. magnitude 1, argument ≈ 53°
c. magnitude 13, argument ≈ 113°
d. magnitude 1, argument ≈ 113°

13. C

14. a. $(-0.643, 0.766)$
b. $(-0.643, -0.766)$

15. Answers may vary. Sample: The x-coordinate starts at 1 when Olivia's angle is 0°, decreases to 0 as her angle increases to 90°, decreases to −1 as her angle increases to 180°, increases to 0 as her angle increases to 270°, and increases to 1 as her angle increases to 360°. This pattern will repeat from 360° to 720°, from 720° to 1080°, and so on.

16. See back of book.

17. $(0.342, 0.940)$

18. $a = -1$, $b = \sqrt{3}$

19–20. See back of book.

EXERCISE 12 is review, but it reminds students that they already have a way to relate angles with coordinates.

EXERCISE 14 Some students may discover that you can use sine and cosine to find the coordinates for these angles. If that is the case in your class, have students share their result in the upcoming lesson.

EXERCISE 17 The goal here is to let students discover the relationships between angles greater than 360° and corresponding angles less than 360°. Eventually, your students will all understand why only angles from 0° to 360° are necessary for a complete understanding of the behavior of the sine, cosine, and tangent functions.

EXERCISE 18 Students solved exercises similar this one in Chapter 3. Here, they start to see the relationship between the trigonometric functions and complex numbers, a connection they will continue to explore in CME Project *Precalculus.*

Maintain Your Skills

EXERCISES 19 AND 20 reinforce the fact that for most values between −1 and 1, there are two angles (between 0° and 360°) with that sine or cosine value. In other words, there are two possible values for $\sin^{-1} x$ when considering angles between 0 and 360 (except when $x = 1$ or $x = -1$). Similarly, there are two possible values between 0 and 360 for $\cos^{-1} x$.

Lesson Overview

GOAL

- Use right triangle trigonometry to find the coordinates of a person walking on the unit circle, given an angle through which an observer has turned.

Students use their visualization of Olivia standing at the origin and turning to watch Paul walk around the unit circle to extend the domains of the trigonometric functions. Until now, students have been able only to evaluate these functions for angles $0° < \theta < 90°$, because sine, cosine, and tangent were defined as ratios of side lengths in right triangles.

Now, however, students can drop a perpendicular to the x-axis from Paul's position P to form a right triangle. That triangle has an angle at O, sometimes referred to as the *reference angle* that is related to the actual angle θ through which Olivia has turned. The cosine and sine of this reference angle determine the side lengths of the right triangle for this point P, and with appropriate signs for the quadrant in which P lies, determine the coordinates of P.

The domains of cosine and sine are extended to any angle by choosing their values to be equal to the coordinates of the point P. In other words, when an angle θ is positioned with its vertex at the origin, with one of its sides lying along the positive x-axis so that it opens out counterclockwise from that fixed side, the values of $\cos\theta$ and $\sin\theta$ are defined to be the x- and y-coordinates, respectively, of the point P where its other side intersects the unit circle.

CHECK YOUR UNDERSTANDING
- Core: 1, 2, 4, 5, 7
- Optional: 3, 6

MATERIALS
- graph paper
- graphing calculators
- Blackline Master 8.1A

HOMEWORK
- Core: 8, 9, 10, 11, 12, 13
- Optional: 14
- Extension: 15

VOCABULARY
- cosine, $\cos\theta$
- sine, $\sin\theta$
- standard position
- tangent, $\tan\theta$

Launch

Start this lesson by having students describe the methods they used in the Getting Started lesson to determine the coordinates of Paul's position P on the unit circle in terms of the angle θ through which Olivia has turned while watching Paul. Then have them work through the Example. You can use Blackline Master 8.1A to guide students through the Example and to discuss the definitions of sine and cosine.

8.2 Extending the Domain, Part 1

Right now, you can only find the sine, cosine, or tangent of an angle if the angle has measure between 0° and 90°, since these functions have been defined as ratios of sides in a right triangle. By following Olivia and Paul around their circle, you can extend the domain of these trigonometric functions to include all angles from 0° to 360°. Here is how.

The position of the hammer at the moment of release is related to the angle the athlete has rotated.

Consider the situation in Lesson 8.1. Suppose Paul has moved along the circle, and Olivia has turned through an angle of 70°.

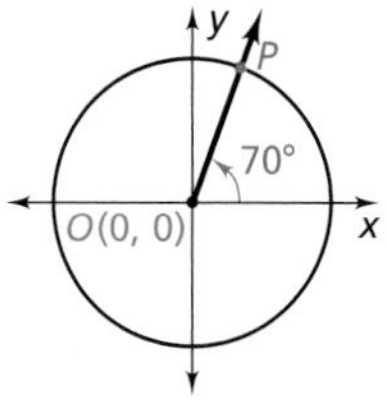

The 70° angle Olivia has turned is part of a right triangle with vertices at O and P. You complete the triangle by dropping an altitude from point P to the x-axis.

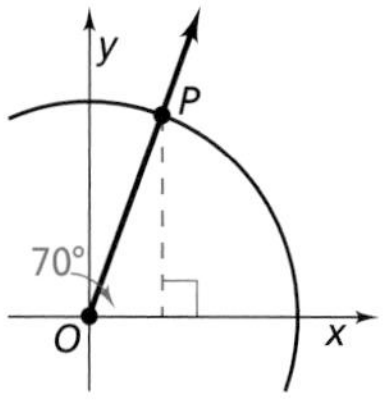

The hypotenuse of this right triangle has length 1, so the horizontal leg has length $\cos 70°$ and the vertical leg has length $\sin 70°$. The coordinates of point P are $(\cos 70°, \sin 70°)$.

You can find the approximate values of cos 70° and sin 70° on a calculator. Note that calculators typically have more than one way to measure angles. Refer to the TI-Nspire Handbook on p. 778 to see how to check that your calculator is in degree mode.

In fact, this works for any angle in Quadrant I. Angles with measures between 0° and 90° are in Quadrant I. If the angle at the origin is θ, the coordinates of point P are $(\cos\theta, \sin\theta)$.

In the other quadrants, you can draw right triangles to find Paul's coordinates, but one or both of the coordinates will be negative.

Example

Problem Find Paul's coordinates when Olivia has turned 210°.

Solution First, draw a diagram for the situation. The angle is in Quadrant III, so both coordinates will be negative. To find the exact coordinates, draw an altitude from P to the x-axis.

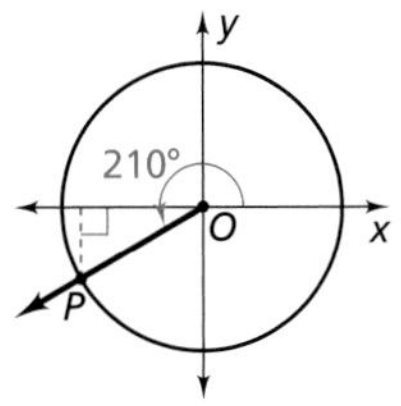

You can use sine and cosine to find the side lengths in this triangle. The triangle has a 30° angle at the origin, so it is a 30-60-90 triangle with hypotenuse length 1. Because this is a special right triangle, you can write exact expressions for its side lengths without using a calculator.

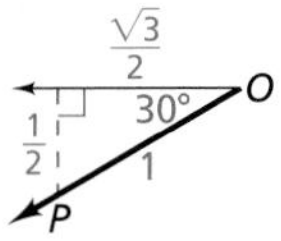

The side opposite the 30° angle has length $\frac{1}{2}$, and the side opposite the 60° angle has length $\frac{\sqrt{3}}{2}$.

To determine the coordinates of point P, use the side lengths of the triangle. Note that both coordinates are negative, since P is in Quadrant III. The coordinates of point P are $\left(-\frac{\sqrt{3}}{2}, -\frac{1}{2}\right)$.

Remember...

The values $\frac{1}{2}$ and $\frac{\sqrt{3}}{2}$ come up often in trigonometry.

For Discussion

1. Why does the hypotenuse of the triangle in the Example have length 1?
2. Find another angle in Quadrant III where you can find the coordinates of point P exactly without including a trigonometric function or using a calculator.

The unit circle gives you a way to extend the domain of sine and cosine.

Habits of Mind

Give an exact answer. Finding coordinates exactly means to use a rational number written as a fraction or an expression involving rational numbers and square roots. For example, $\cos 45° = \frac{\sqrt{2}}{2}$ is exact. But 0.707107 is an approximation of $\frac{\sqrt{2}}{2}$.

Explore

Example

Students followed a similar procedure when working with the argument of complex numbers in Chapter 3. At the time, they looked at vectors with any magnitude. You can look at the analysis here as considering vectors with unit length.

The question of "exactness" of answers is complicated. cos (20°) is an exact value, but because it involves a trigonometric function, it is hard to know how big it is or where it would fit on a number line. So, you might type it into a calculator, which would return a decimal approximation for this exact number. You can see how great this decimal is, and the approximation is accurate enough for almost any purpose. but this is a fairly subtle observation.

Answers

For Discussion

1. The hypotenuse is a radius of the circle, which is 1.
2. Answers may vary. Samples: If the angle is 225°, the coordinates are $\left(-\frac{\sqrt{2}}{2}, -\frac{\sqrt{2}}{2}\right)$. 240° also works, with coordinates $\left(-\frac{1}{2}, \frac{\sqrt{3}}{2}\right)$.

Wrap Up

If time allows, go over the Check Your Understanding core exercises.

Assessment Resources

Lesson Quiz 8.2

1. For each angle, draw the angle in standard position. Find the sine, cosine, and tangent of the angle.
   a. 210° **b.** 135°
   c. 300° **d.** 330°

2. Explain why each statement is true.
   a. $\sin 120^\circ = -\sin 240^\circ$
   b. $\cos 20^\circ = \sin 70^\circ$

3. Let $\theta = 60^\circ$. Find each value.
   a. $\cos 2\theta$
   b. $2 \cdot \sin\theta \cdot \cos\theta$

4. Find a formula for all values of θ such that the given equation is true.
   a. $\sin\theta = 0$ **b.** $\cos\theta = 0$ **c.** $\tan\theta = 0$

Definitions

Let θ be an angle centered at the origin and measured counterclockwise from the positive x-axis. The left side of θ intersects the graph of $x^2 + y^2 = 1$ (the unit circle) in exactly one point.

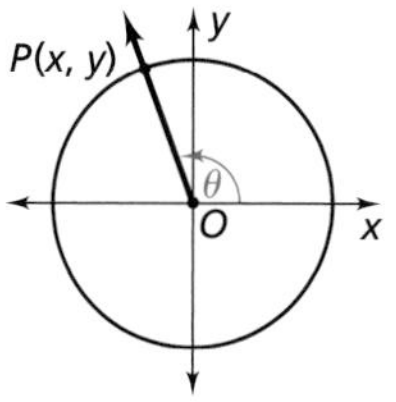

$\cos\theta = x$
$\sin\theta = y$

The cosine of angle θ is the x-coordinate of this intersection.

The sine of angle θ is the y-coordinate of this intersection.

This is the same as the situation with Olivia and Paul. You measure angles in the same way you measured the direction (or argument) of complex numbers in Chapter 3.

Remember...

The coordinates of a point P on the unit circle are $(\cos\theta, \sin\theta)$.

This definition is the one calculators use. For example, a calculator gives $\cos 180^\circ = -1$.

For You to Do

3. Is $\sin 280^\circ$ positive or negative? Answer without using a calculator.

4. In which quadrants is cosine negative?

For acute angles θ, one of the properties of the tangent function is that

$$\tan\theta = \frac{\sin\theta}{\cos\theta}$$

Since you now have a definition for the sine and cosine of any angle, you can use the above formula to extend the domain of the tangent function to any angle, as well. For example, you can say that

$$\tan 120^\circ = \frac{\sin 120^\circ}{\cos 120^\circ} = \frac{\frac{\sqrt{3}}{2}}{-\frac{1}{2}} = -\sqrt{3}$$

Now you have a tentative definition. If θ is any angle, define $\tan\theta$ by the rule

$$\tan\theta = \frac{\sin\theta}{\cos\theta}$$

Answers

For You to Do

3. negative

4. Quadrants II and III

Developing Habits of Mind

Check your definition. Why is this definition only tentative? The formula $\tan\theta = \frac{\sin\theta}{\cos\theta}$ is valid only for $0 \le \theta < 90$, but is often used to define $\tan\theta$ for any angle.

In mathematics, it often happens that you can have a functional equation $\left(\text{in this case, } \tan\theta = \frac{\sin\theta}{\cos\theta}\right)$ that is valid for certain values (in this case, for $0 \le \theta < 90$). Sometimes the right side of the equation makes sense for many more values, so you define the left side for those additional values.

When you do this, you have to be careful. In the case of $\tan\theta = \frac{\sin\theta}{\cos\theta}$, you have to check two things:

- Does the right side make sense for all angles θ? Clearly, the numerator and denominator do, but does the fraction?
- You originally defined the left side of the equation to be "opposite over adjacent" for acute angles θ. Does this still make sense for angles with measure greater than 90°?

For Discussion

5. As a class, discuss the two bullet points above and make a more precise definition of the tangent function.

Habits of Mind

Represent a function. To define a function, you have to give its domain.

Exercises *Practicing Habits of Mind*

Check Your Understanding

1. **What's Wrong Here?** Jo says that $\sin 45°$ should be $\frac{1}{2}$. Jo explains, "Well, $\sin 0° = 0$ and $\sin 90° = 1$. The same is true for cosine, except reversed. Halfway between, they should both be $\frac{1}{2}$." Use the unit circle to explain what is wrong with Jo's reasoning.
2. A complex number $w = a + bi$ has $|w| = 1$ and $\arg w = 70°$. Find a and b to three decimal places.

Exercises

HOMEWORK
- Core: 8, 9, 10, 11, 12, 13
- Optional: 14
- Extension: 15

Check Your Understanding

EXERCISE 1 The 45°-45°-90° triangle is probably a clearer way to refute Jo's argument for most students.

For Discussion

5. Answers may vary. Sample:

$$\tan\theta = \frac{\sin\theta}{\cos\theta} \text{ if } \cos\theta \ne 0$$

Exercises

1. Answers may vary. Sample: If Jo's reasoning were correct, then the point $\left(\frac{1}{2}, \frac{1}{2}\right)$ should be on the unit circle and satisfy the equation $x^2 + y^2 = 1$. However, $\left(\frac{1}{2}\right)^2 + \left(\frac{1}{2}\right)^2 \ne 1$, so the point $\left(\frac{1}{2}, \frac{1}{2}\right)$ is not on the circle.
2. $a = 0.342$, $b = 0.940$

EXERCISE 4 You might suggest that students graph (or visualize) a few specific examples.

EXERCISE 6 asks students to recall work from Chapter 3 on complex numbers. Essentially, students should describe the class of complex numbers whose magnitude is 1, which is all complex numbers on the unit circle.

EXERCISE 7 In this lesson, students may consider only angles between 0° and 360° as possible solutions, depending on how you have handled the class discussion. That is acceptable, because Lesson 8.3 explicitly extends the domains of the trigonometric functions to include any angle.

On Your Own

EXERCISE 8 is a good exercise to check students' understanding of the lesson.

3. What complex number has magnitude 1 and direction 210°?

4. **Write About It** Write an identity that gives the relationship between the two expressions.

a. $\cos\theta$ and $\cos(\theta + 180°)$

b. $\sin\theta$ and $\sin(\theta + 180°)$

c. $\tan\theta$ and $\tan(\theta + 180°)$

5. Find each value.

a. $(\cos 150°)^2 + (\sin 150°)^2$

b. $(\cos 52.696°)^2 + (\sin 52.696°)^2$

6. **Write About It** Suppose you know a complex number has magnitude 1, but you do not know its direction. Describe, with some examples, where that complex number can be located.

7. a. Find a formula for all values of θ such that $\sin\theta = 0$.

b. Find a formula for all values of θ such that $\cos\theta = 0$.

c. Find a formula for all values of θ such that $\tan\theta = 0$.

On Your Own

Remember...

An angle is in **standard position** when its vertex is at the origin and one of its sides lies along the positive *x*-axis. The angle opens counterclockwise from this fixed side.

8. For each angle, draw the angle in standard position. Find the sine, cosine, and tangent of the angle.

a. 210°

b. 330°

c. 40°

d. 320°

e. 360°

9. **Standardized Test Prep** If $\sin\theta = 0.57358$ and $\tan\theta = 0.70021$, what is $\cos\theta$?

A. 0.40163 **B.** 0.81915 **C.** 1.22077 **D.** 1.27379

Answers

3. $-\frac{\sqrt{3}}{2} - \frac{1}{2}i \approx -0.866 - 0.5i$

4. a. $\cos\theta = -\cos(\theta + 180°)$

b. $\sin\theta = -\sin(\theta + 180°)$

c. $\tan\theta = \tan(\theta + 180°)$

5. a. 1

b. 1

6. If the magnitude of a complex number is 1, such as i or $-i$, then it must lie on the unit circle.

7. a. $\theta = 180° \cdot k$, where k is an integer.

b. $\theta = 90° + 180° \cdot k$, where k is an integer.

c. $\theta = 180° \cdot k$, where k is an integer.

8. See back of book.

9. B

10. For each angle in the table, find the cosine, sine, cosine squared, and sine squared. Look for rules and relationships that allow you to find the results more quickly.

θ	$\cos\theta$	$\sin\theta$	$\cos^2\theta$	$\sin^2\theta$
0°	■	0	■	0
30°	$\frac{\sqrt{3}}{2}$	■	$\frac{3}{4}$	■
45°	■	$\frac{\sqrt{2}}{2}$	■	$\frac{1}{2}$
60°	■	■	■	■
90°	0	1	0	1
120°	■	■	■	■
135°	■	■	■	■
150°	■	$\frac{1}{2}$	■	$\frac{1}{4}$
180°	■	■	■	■
210°	■	■	■	■
225°	$-\frac{\sqrt{2}}{2}$	■	■	$\frac{1}{2}$
240°	■	■	■	■
270°	0	■	■	■
300°	■	■	■	■
315°	■	■	■	■
330°	■	■	■	■
360°	1	■	■	■

11. Explain why $\sin 310° = -\sin 50°$.

12. Let $\theta = 150°$. Find each value.
   a. $\sin 2\theta$
   b. $2 \cdot \sin\theta \cdot \cos\theta$

13. Find a formula for all values of θ such that the given equation is true.
   a. $\sin\theta = 1$
   b. $\cos\theta = 1$
   c. $\tan\theta = 1$

Remember...

The notation $\cos^2 x$ means $(\cos x)^2$. You use this notation primarily for ease of reading. You read $\cos^2 x$ as "cosine squared of x."

Go Online PHSchool.com

For additional practice, go to **Web Code:** bfa-0802

14. a. Find the magnitude and direction of $-6\sqrt{3} + 6i$.
   b. What complex number has magnitude 10 and direction 30°?
   c. What complex number has magnitude 1 and direction 60°?

Maintain Your Skills

15. **Take It Further** Find the value of θ in each equation.
   a. $\cos\theta + i\sin\theta = (\cos 40° + i\sin 40°)(\cos 50° + i\sin 50°)$
   b. $\cos\theta + i\sin\theta = (\cos 40° + i\sin 40°)(\cos 20° + i\sin 20°)$
   c. $\cos\theta + i\sin\theta = (\cos 40° + i\sin 40°)(\cos 80° + i\sin 80°)$
   d. $\cos\theta + i\sin\theta = (\cos 45° + i\sin 45°)^2$

10. See back of book.

11. Answers may vary. Sample: Since 310° is the same as −50° on the unit circle, we know that $\sin 310° = \sin(-50°)$. And because −50° is in Quadrant IV, where sine is negative, $\sin(-50°) = -\sin 50°$. So, $\sin 310° = -\sin 50°$.

12. a. $-\frac{\sqrt{3}}{2}$ **b.** $-\frac{\sqrt{3}}{2}$

13. a. $\theta = 90° + 360° \cdot k$, where k is an integer.
b. $\theta = 360° \cdot k$, where k is an integer.
c. $\theta = 45° + 180° \cdot k$, where k is an integer.

14. a. magnitude = 12, direction = 150°
b. $5\sqrt{3} + 5i$
c. $\frac{1}{2} + \frac{\sqrt{3}}{2}i$

15. a. 90° **b.** 60°
c. 120° **d.** 90°

EXERCISE 12 gives students a single case of one of the trigonometric identities they prove later in this chapter.

EXERCISE 13 Some students may not consider angles that are not between 0° and 360°, depending on whether you have discussed these angles in your class.

Maintain Your Skills

EXERCISE 15 In CME Project *Precalculus,* students explore cis notation for complex numbers. Using that notation simplifies arithmetic of complex numbers, helps prove addition formulas for sine and cosine (demonstrated by parts a through c), and is the basis for DeMoivre's Theorem (demonstrated by part d).

Additional Resources

PRINT RESOURCES
- Solution Manual
- Practice Workbook
- Assessment Resources
- Teaching Resources

TECHNOLOGY
- Interactive Textbook
- TeacherExpress CD-ROM
- ExamView CD-ROM
- PHSchool.com

Additional Practice

1. For each angle, draw the angle in standard position. Find the sine, cosine, and tangent of the angle.
   a. 120° b. 315° c. 240° d. 60°

2. Explain why each statement is true.
   a. $\sin 210° = -\sin 150°$ b. $\cos 30° = \sin 60°$

3. Let $\theta = 120°$. Find each value.
   a. $\cos 2\theta$ b. $2 \cdot \sin\theta \cdot \cos\theta$

4. Find a formula for all values θ of such that the given equation is true.
   a. $\sin\theta = -1$ b. $\cos\theta = -1$ c. $\tan\theta = -1$

5. Find the value of the cosine, sine, and tangent of each angle.
   a. −45° b. −60°

6. Express each value as a sine or cosine of an acute angle.
   a. $\sin 125°$ b. $\cos 260°$
   c. $\sin 310°$ d. $\cos(-130°)$

7. Express each value as a sine or cosine of θ.
   a. $\sin(90° - \theta)$ b. $\cos(90° - \theta)$
   c. $\sin(90° + \theta)$ d. $\cos(90° + \theta)$
   e. $\sin(360° - \theta)$ f. $\cos(360° - \theta)$
   g. $\sin(360° + \theta)$ h. $\cos(360° + \theta)$

8. Is this statement true or false? Explain.
   For any two angles a and b, $\sin(a - b) = \sin a - \sin b$ and $\cos(a - b) = \cos a - \cos b$.

9. Suppose an angle θ is unknown, but it is between 125° and 175°. Determine whether each expression is *positive* or *negative*.
   a. $\sin\theta$ b. $\cos\theta$
   c. $\tan\theta$ d. $\sin^2\theta + \cos^2\theta$

10. Find an angle θ, not equal to 45°, that satisfies each equation.
   a. $\cos\theta = \cos 45°$ b. $\sin\theta = \sin 45°$ c. $\tan\theta = \tan 45°$

Practice: For Lesson 8.2, assign Exercises 1–4.

Lesson Overview

GOAL

- Evaluate the sine, cosine, and tangent functions for any angle.

In this lesson, students formally extend the domain of the trigonometric functions to angles measuring less than 0° and more than 360°. Your students may already feel capable of evaluating trigonometric functions for such angles, so the definitions will be what they expect.

CHECK YOUR UNDERSTANDING
- Core: 1, 2, 3, 4, 7
- Optional: 5, 6, 8a
- Extension: 8b

MATERIALS
- graph paper
- graphing calculators
- Blackline Masters 8.1A, 8.3

HOMEWORK
- Core: 9, 10, 11, 12, 13, 17, 19, 20
- Optional: 14, 15, 16, 18a
- Extension: 18b

VOCABULARY
- cosine, cos θ
- periodic function
- sine, sin θ
- tangent, tan θ

Launch

Start today's lesson with the For You to Do.

Explore

For You to Do

The way the exposition continues, the expected angle is of the form $20 + 360n$ for integer values of n. But, as students saw in the exercises from Lesson 8.2, they also could choose 340° (or −20°). If students choose these angles, have them hold onto their thought. It comes back in the Developing Habits of Mind section later in the lesson.

8.3 Extending the Domain, Part 2

In the last lesson, you learned the meaning of cosine, sine, and tangent for values from 0° to 360°. This lesson extends the definitions to all real numbers.

For You to Do

1. Using a calculator, find cos 20°, cos 380°, and cos 1100°. Find another angle that produces the same value for the cosine.

The table in Exercise 10 from Lesson 8.2 only goes from 0° to 360°. The reason is that turning through any angle larger than 360° returns you to an angle between 0° and 360°. The coordinates after turning through a 20° angle are the same as the coordinates after turning 360° + 20° = 380° or 720° + 20° = 740°. It makes sense, then, to define the cosine of 740° to be the same as the cosine of 20°.

Two numbers that differ by a multiple of 360 are *congruent modulo 360*. *Modulo* means "except for." The numbers 20 and 380 are the same, except for 360.

The same goes for negative angle measures: An angle of −35° puts you at the same place on the unit circle as an angle of 325°. So it makes sense to say that sin (−35°) = sin 325°.

With this extension, you can find the sine or cosine for any angle measure from the set of real numbers. For an angle θ with measure outside of $0° < \theta < 360°$, simply find another angle that is between 0° and 360° but has the same coordinates on the unit circle. You can use almost exactly the same definition as the one in Lesson 8.2 to extend the definition to any angle measure.

Habits of Mind

Experiment. Will the tangent of any angle be the same as the tangent of an angle between 0° and 360°?

Definitions

Let θ be an angle centered at the origin and measured from the positive x-axis. The terminal side of θ intersects the graph of $x^2 + y^2 = 1$ (the unit circle) in exactly one point.

The cosine of angle θ is the x-coordinate of this intersection.

The sine of angle θ is the y-coordinate of this intersection.

The tangent of angle θ is $\frac{\sin\theta}{\cos\theta}$, whenever $\cos\theta \neq 0$.

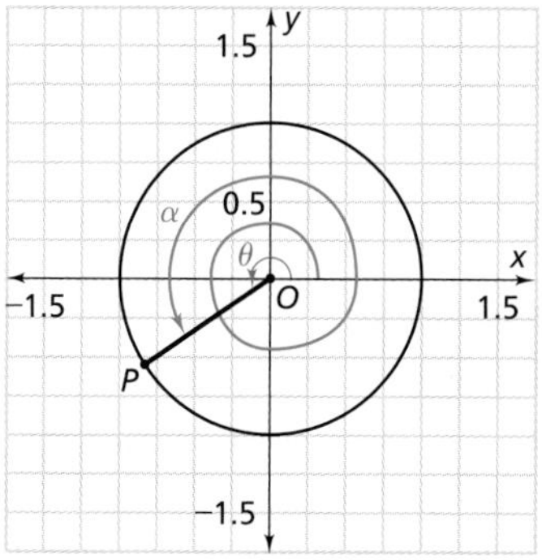

$P = (\cos\theta, \sin\theta) = (\cos\alpha, \sin\alpha)$

One side of θ passes through (1, 0). This is its initial side. The other side is the terminal side. When are these two sides the same ray?

Answers

For You to Do

1. cos 20° = 0.940,
cos 380° = 0.940,
cos 1100° = 0.940; answers may vary. Samples: −340°, 740°

For You to Do

2. Using a calculator, find cos 20°, cos 160°, cos 200°, and cos 340°.

Theorem 8.1

If n is an integer and x is an angle in degrees,

- $\cos(x + 360n) = \cos x$
- $\sin(x + 360n) = \sin x$

For Discussion

3. The functions sine and cosine are periodic with period 360°. What does this mean? Is the tangent function a **periodic function**?

Developing Habits of Mind

Visualize. In Chapter 3, you learned how to calculate the direction of complex numbers. You noticed that the direction of $4 + 3i$ is related to the direction of $-4 + 3i$, $-4 - 3i$, and $4 - 3i$.

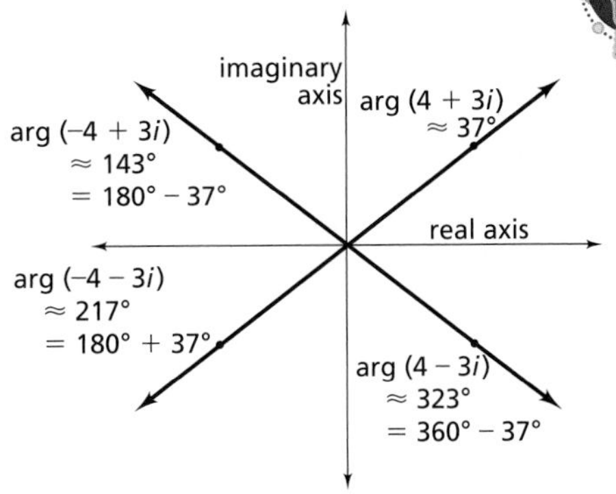

This is the same picture you see now in the unit circle. Each quadrant has a related angle with coordinates that are the same, except for a sign.

For example, if you know the cosine and sine of a 20° angle, you automatically know the cosine and sine of a 160° angle, as well as a 200° angle and a 340° angle, and many other angles.

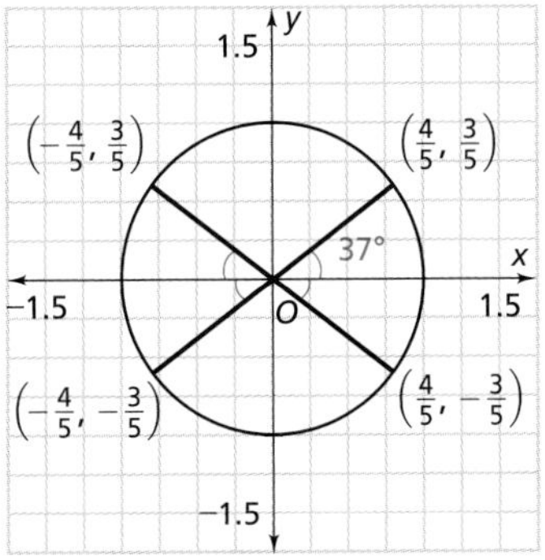

Habits of Mind

Look for relationships. Equations like $\cos x = -\cos(180° - x)$ express a symmetry of the cosine function.

For Discussion

When your students discuss what it means for a function to be periodic, they will likely say things such as, "You keep getting the same values." Help them bring some precision to this definition. One analogy that is helpful is to relate periodicity to wallpaper patterns. You can also demonstrate periodicity with graphs of the functions on transparency paper. Another clarifying question to ask is, "Could you also say that these functions have period 720°?" This brings up the issue of minimal period, the smallest section of a function that repeats. Make sure students know that just because two values of sine or cosine have the same value does not mean that the interval between them is the period of the function. sin 30° = sin 150°, but the period of the sine function is not 120°.

Developing Habits of Mind

You can use Blackline Masters 8.3 and 8.1A for this section.

For You to Do

2. cos 20° = 0.940,
cos 160° = −0.940,
cos 200° = −0.940,
cos 340° = 0.940

For Discussion

3. It means that the values of the sine and cosine functions repeat every 360°. The tangent function repeats every 180°, so it is periodic with period 180°.

Example

This Example helps students see that the definitions they learned in geometry for triangle trigonometry give them all the values they need for any angle measure. As they work through the exercises, they will develop a rhythm of dropping a perpendicular to the *x*-axis, then working on the triangle, and finally figuring out the correct sign. You can use Blackline Master 8.1A as a transparency to guide students through the Example.

Wrap Up

Wrap up the lesson by going over the Example and giving students some time to work on the Check Your Understanding core exercises.

Assessment Resources

Lesson Quiz 8.3

1. Find the value of the cosine, sine, and tangent of each angle.
   a. $-120°$ b. $-225°$

2. Express each value as a sine or cosine of an acute angle.
   a. $\sin 115°$ b. $\cos 290°$ c. $\sin 210°$ d. $\cos(-150°)$

3. Suppose an angle θ is unknown, but it is between $190°$ and $245°$. Determine whether each expression is *positive* or *negative*.
   a. $\sin\theta$ b. $\cos\theta$ c. $\tan\theta$ d. $\sin^2\theta + \cos^2\theta$

4. Find an angle θ, not equal to $60°$, that satisfies each equation.
   a. $\cos\theta = \cos 60°$
   b. $\sin\theta = \sin 60°$
   c. $\tan\theta = \tan 60°$

Knowing about the signs of the coordinates in each quadrant will help you decide quickly about whether the cosine, sine, or tangent of an angle is positive or negative. For example, in Quadrant I, cosine is positive and sine is positive. Therefore, tangent is positive.

Habits of Mind

Look for relationships. If you are familiar with angles in Quadrant I, then you can handle any other angle using these relationships.

For You to Do

Find the sign of the sine, cosine, and tangent for angles in each quadrant.

4. Quadrant II

5. Quadrant III

6. Quadrant IV

Example

Problem Express each value as the value of the sine or cosine of an acute angle.

a. $\cos 150°$

b. $\sin 460°$

c. $\sin 290°$

Solution It helps to draw the angles on the unit circle:

a. The coordinates of *P* are $(\cos 150°, \sin 150°)$. That means that $m\angle POC = 30°$. Imagine $\triangle QOD \cong \triangle POC$ in the first quadrant, oriented as in the graph. Then $m\angle DOQ = 30°$, so $OD = \cos 30°$. But $OC = OD$, and the *x*-coordinate of *P* is the opposite of *OD*. In other words, $\cos 150° = -\cos 30°$. Since $\cos 30° = \frac{\sqrt{3}}{2}$, $\cos 150° = -\frac{\sqrt{3}}{2}$.

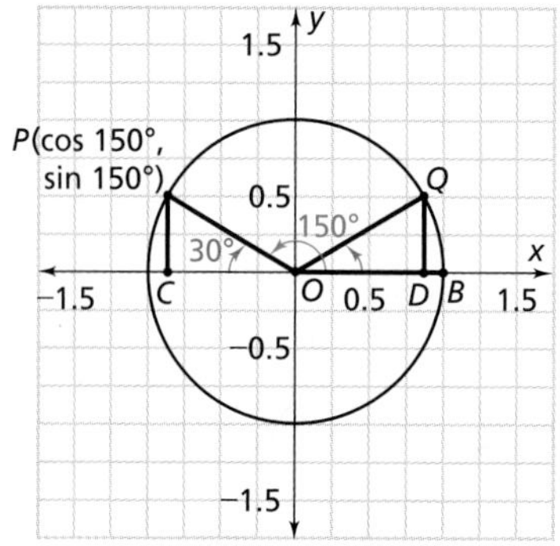

b. Note that $\sin 460°$ is the same as $\sin 100°$, since traveling around the circle $460°$ is the same as making one complete revolution $(360°)$ with an additional $100°$. Now draw a graph like the one above and convince yourself that $\sin 100° = \sin 80°$.

Answers

For You to Do

4. Sine is positive, cosine is negative, and tangent is negative.

5. Sine is negative, cosine is negative, and tangent is positive.

6. Sine is negative, cosine is positive, and tangent is negative.

c. The graph shows that $\sin 290° = -\sin 70°$.

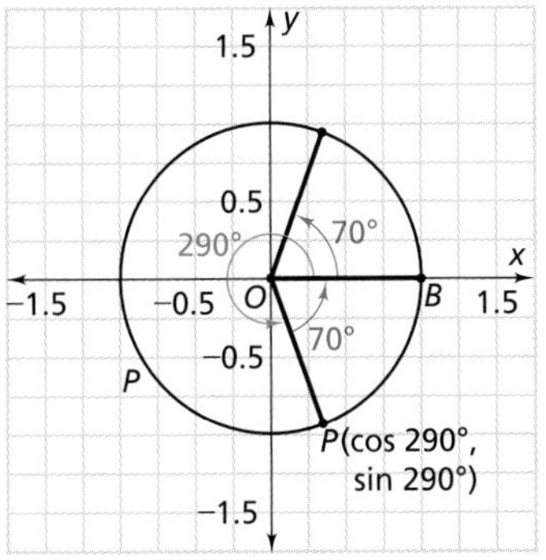

Habits of Mind

Generalize. Convince yourself that $\sin(-x) = \sin x$ for any angle measure x.

Exercises *Practicing Habits of Mind*

Check Your Understanding

1. **Write About It** Explain why $\sin 160° = \sin 20°$ but $\cos 160° = -\cos 20°$.
2. Suppose $\sin\theta = \frac{20}{29}$ for some angle θ.
   a. In what quadrants can θ be located?
   b. Find both possible values for $\cos\theta$.
   c. Find both possible values for $\tan\theta$.
3. Find an angle θ for which $\tan\theta > 100$, or explain why no such angle exists.
4. **What's Wrong Here?** Herb wants to calculate $\cos(-60°)$. He says, "I know that $\cos 60°$ is $\frac{1}{2}$. So $\cos(-60°)$ should just be the negative. The answer is $-\frac{1}{2}$."
   What is wrong with Herb's reasoning? What is the correct value of $\cos(-60°)$?
5. List the following values in order from least to greatest.
   $\tan 70°$ $\sin 120°$ $\cos 120°$ $\cos 720°$ $\tan 110°$ $\sin 210°$
6. Find the two angles between 0° and 360° for which $\sin\theta + \sin(180° - \theta) = 1$.

HABITS OF MIND The drawing of the unit circle is usually sufficient for convincing students that $\sin(-x) = -\sin x$. In the graph for part (c) of the Example, you can draw a vertical line with equation $x = \cos 70$, and it intersects the circle in two points. The distances of those points from the x-axis have to be equal, since the triangles are congruent, so one has a positive value, the other a negative. You can then move the vertical line back and forth to cover all points on the circle.

Exercises

HOMEWORK
- Core: 9, 10, 11, 12, 13, 17, 19, 20
- Optional: 14, 15, 16, 18a
- Extension: 18b

Check Your Understanding

EXERCISE 2 If students have trouble getting started, you might remind them that trigonometric functions were originally defined as side lengths of right triangles. Have them start by drawing the triangle for this situation. Then, when they have found the lengths of all of its sides, ask them to place that triangle in the unit circle.

EXERCISE 3 Students can use the inverse tangent function on their calculator to solve this exercise, but remind them to make sense of the answer they get. You can extend this by asking students to find the maximum and minimum values for tangent. They will find, informally, that the value of tangent approaches infinity as an angle increases to 90° and that the value of tangent approaches negative infinity as an angle decreases to 90°.

EXERCISE 4 You can extend this exercise by asking whether $\sin -\theta = -\sin\theta$ or $\tan -\theta = -\tan\theta$.

EXERCISE 5 If you assign this exercise, challenge students to do it first without a calculator by making sense of the order. Then allow them to use their calculators to check.

EXERCISE 6 Remind students that "between 0° and 360°" includes the angles that measure 0° and 360°.

Exercises

1. Answers may vary. Sample: 160° is in Quadrant II and 20° is in Quadrant I. Since $\sin\theta$ is positive in both quadrants, $\sin 160° = \sin 20°$. Since $\cos\theta$ is positive in Quadrant I and negative in Quadrant II, then $\cos 160° = -\cos 20°$.

2. a. I or II **b.** $\cos\theta = \pm\frac{21}{29}$

c. $\tan\theta = \pm\frac{20}{21}$

3. Answers may vary. Sample: $\theta \approx 89.5°$

4. Answers may vary. Sample: Since −60° intersects the unit circle in Quadrant IV, the cosine will be positive. In general, $\cos(-\theta) = \cos\theta$. So $\cos(-60°) = \cos 60° = \frac{1}{2}$.

5. $\tan 110°$; $\cos 120° = \sin 210°$; $\sin 120°$; $\cos 720°$; $\tan 70°$

6. 30°, 150°

EXERCISE 7 If students have trouble with part (f), suggest that they draw a triangle. Remind students that since these functions were originally defined in right triangles, that representation may still have value in certain situations. It is a good approach to try if they are stuck.

On Your Own

EXERCISE 10 is a good assessment of students' understanding of the use of reference angles and how to determine the sign of a trigonometric function from the quadrant in which the angle lies.

EXERCISE 11 Parts (d)–(f) ask students to relate trigonometric functions of complementary angles. Relating these situations back to triangles helps students remember that $\sin\theta = \cos(90^\circ - \theta)$ and $\cos\theta = \sin(90^\circ - \theta)$.

EXERCISE 12 is an important exercise if you plan to cover Lesson 8.9 on the angle-sum identities. Students should recognize there that the most obvious first-guess formula does not work.

7. Given that $\sin 50^\circ \approx 0.7660$ and $\cos 50^\circ \approx 0.6428$, find each value to four decimal places.

a. $\sin 130^\circ$ **b.** $\cos 130^\circ$
c. $\cos 230^\circ$ **d.** $\sin 310^\circ$
e. $\cos^2 230^\circ + \sin^2 230^\circ$ **f.** $\sin 40^\circ$

You do not need a calculator for any of the parts of this exercise.

8. a. There is a relationship between $\tan^2\theta$ and $\frac{1}{\cos^2\theta}$. Find the relationship by calculating each expression for several angles.

b. Take It Further Prove that this relationship holds for any angle θ, as long as $\tan\theta$ is defined.

On Your Own

9. Find the values of $\cos(-30^\circ)$, $\sin(-30^\circ)$, and $\tan(-30^\circ)$.

10. Express each value as a sine or cosine of an acute angle.

a. $\sin 400^\circ$ **b.** $\cos 400^\circ$ **c.** $\cos 300^\circ$
d. $\sin 315^\circ$ **e.** $\sin(-100^\circ)$

11. Express each value as a sine or cosine of θ.

a. $\sin(180^\circ - \theta)$ **b.** $\cos(180^\circ - \theta)$ **c.** $\sin(180^\circ + \theta)$
d. $\cos(180^\circ + \theta)$ **e.** $\sin(270^\circ - \theta)$ **f.** $\cos(270^\circ - \theta)$
g. $\sin(270^\circ + \theta)$ **h.** $\cos(270^\circ + \theta)$

Habits of Mind

Use what you know. There is no need to memorize these identities. You can reconstruct them by looking at the unit circle.

12. Is this statement true or false? Explain.

For any two angles a and b, $\sin(a + b) = \sin a + \sin b$ and $\cos(a + b) = \cos a + \cos b$.

This statement says that addition is distributive over the sine and cosine functions. But maybe it is not!

13. Suppose an angle θ is unknown, but it is between 300° and 350°. Determine whether each expression is positive or negative.

a. $\cos\theta$ **b.** $\sin\theta$ **c.** $\tan\theta$
d. $\cos^2\theta + \sin^2\theta$ **e.** $\tan^3\theta$

14. What is the value of $\cos 120^\circ + \sin 120^\circ$?

A. 0 **B.** $\frac{\sqrt{3} - 1}{2}$ **C.** 1 **D.** $\frac{\sqrt{3} + 1}{2}$

Answers

7. a. 0.7660 **b.** −0.6428
c. −0.6428 **d.** −0.7660
e. 1 **f.** 0.6428

8. a. $\tan^2\theta = \frac{1}{\cos^2\theta} - 1$ or

$\tan^2\theta + 1 = \frac{1}{\cos^2\theta}$

b. $\tan^2\theta + 1 = \frac{\sin^2\theta}{\cos^2\theta} + 1 = \frac{\sin^2\theta}{\cos^2\theta} + \frac{\cos^2\theta}{\cos^2\theta} = \frac{\sin^2\theta + \cos^2\theta}{\cos^2\theta} = \frac{1}{\cos^2\theta}$.

So, $\tan^2\theta = \frac{1}{\cos^2\theta} - 1$ or

$\tan^2\theta + 1 = \frac{1}{\cos^2\theta}$.

9. $\cos(-30^\circ) = \frac{\sqrt{3}}{2}$, $\sin(-30^\circ) = -\frac{1}{2}$, $\tan(-30^\circ) = -\frac{\sqrt{3}}{3}$

10. a. $\sin 40^\circ$ **b.** $\cos 40^\circ$
c. $\cos 60^\circ$ **d.** $-\sin 45^\circ$
e. $-\sin 80^\circ$

11–13. See back of book.

14. B

15. Find this sum: $\sin 60^\circ + \sin 120^\circ + \sin 180^\circ + \cdots + \sin 360^\circ$.

16. For which angles between 0° and 360° can you find the sine and cosine exactly without using a calculator or an approximation?

17. Suppose θ is an angle in Quadrant II with $\sin \theta = \frac{35}{37}$.
   a. Find the value of $\cos \theta$.
   b. Find the value of $\tan \theta$.
   c. Suppose θ is between 0° and 360°. Find θ to the nearest degree.

18. a. There is a relationship between $\frac{1}{\tan^2 \theta}$ and $\frac{1}{\sin^2 \theta}$. Find the relationship by calculating each expression for several angles.
   b. **Take It Further** Prove that this relationship holds for any angle θ, as long as $\tan \theta$ is defined and $\tan \theta$ and $\sin \theta$ are not equal to 0.

19. **Standardized Test Prep** Lindsay has a four-function calculator (+, −, ×, ÷). She also has a printed table showing values of $\sin \theta$ for values of θ from 0° to 90° in increments of 1°. Which formula will allow her to use this table and her calculator to compute the values of $\cos \theta$ for several different angles between 0° and 90°?
   A. $\cos \theta = 1 - \sin \theta$ B. $\cos \theta = \sin (90 - \theta)$ C. $\cos \theta = -\sin \theta$
   D. No relation exists between $\cos \theta$ and $\sin \theta$ for values of θ between 0° and 90°.

The missing terms all follow the arithmetic sequence set up by 60, 120, and 180.

Go Online PHSchool.com

For additional practice, go to **Web Code**: bfa-0803

Maintain Your Skills

20. Find an angle θ, not equal to 30°, that satisfies each equation.
   a. $\cos \theta = \cos 30^\circ$ b. $\sin \theta = \sin 30^\circ$ c. $\tan \theta = \tan 30^\circ$
   d. Describe how you can find ten other angles θ such that $\cos \theta = \cos 30^\circ$.

15. 0

16. 0°, 30°, 45°, 60°, 90°, 120°, 135°, 150°, 180°, 210°, 225°, 240°, 270°, 300°, 315°, 330°, 360°

17. a. $-\frac{12}{37}$ **b.** $-\frac{35}{12}$ **c.** 109°

18. a. $\frac{1}{\tan^2\theta} = \frac{1}{\sin^2\theta} - 1$

b. $\frac{1}{\tan^2 \theta} = \frac{1}{\left(\frac{\sin^2 \theta}{\cos^2 \theta}\right)} = \frac{\cos^2 \theta}{\sin^2 \theta} = \frac{\cos^2 \theta + (\sin^2 \theta - \sin^2 \theta)}{\sin^2 \theta} = \frac{1 - \sin^2 \theta}{\sin^2 \theta} = \frac{1}{\sin^2 \theta} - \frac{\sin^2 \theta}{\sin^2 \theta} = \frac{1}{\sin^2 \theta} - 1$

19. B

20. a. 330° **b.** 150°
c. 210°
d. Use the relationship $\cos \theta = \cos (\theta + k \cdot 360^\circ)$ where k is an integer, and, in this case, $\theta = 30^\circ$.

EXERCISE 15 Students who use a calculator may say that the sum is very close to zero. However, if you encourage students to make sense of this sum by graphing on the unit circle, they will see that each positive value of sine has a corresponding negative value and that the sum must equal exactly zero.

EXERCISE 16 Remind students that "between 0° and 360°" includes the angles that measure 0° and 360°.

EXERCISE 17 Some of your students may be comfortable assuming the identity $\sin^2 \theta + \cos^2 \theta = 1$ without a formal proof. Others may use the idea that all the points $(\cos \theta, \sin \theta)$ are on the unit circle which has equation $x^2 + y^2 = 1$. Still others may need to go back to the right triangle definitions to find the third side length of the triangle.

Additional Resources

PRINT RESOURCES
- Solution Manual
- Practice Workbook
- Assessment Resources
- Teaching Resources

TECHNOLOGY
- Interactive Textbook
- TeacherExpress CD-ROM
- ExamView CD-ROM
- PHSchool.com

Additional Practice

1. For each angle, draw the angle in standard position. Find the sine, cosine, and tangent of the angle.
   a. 120° b. 315° c. 240° d. 60°
2. Explain why each statement is true.
   a. $\sin 210^\circ = -\sin 150^\circ$ b. $\cos 30^\circ = \sin 60^\circ$
3. Let $\theta = 120^\circ$. Find each value.
   a. $\cos 2\theta$ b. $2 \cdot \sin \theta \cdot \cos \theta$
4. Find a formula for all values θ of such that the given equation is true.
   a. $\sin \theta = -1$ b. $\cos \theta = -1$ c. $\tan \theta = -1$
5. Find the value of the cosine, sine, and tangent of each angle.
   a. −45° b. −60°
6. Express each value as a sine or cosine of an acute angle.
   a. sin 125° b. cos 260°
   c. sin 310° d. cos (−130°)
7. Express each value as a sine or cosine of θ.
   a. $\sin (90^\circ - \theta)$ b. $\cos (90^\circ - \theta)$
   c. $\sin (90^\circ + \theta)$ d. $\cos (90^\circ + \theta)$
   e. $\sin (360^\circ - \theta)$ f. $\cos (360^\circ - \theta)$
   g. $\sin (360^\circ + \theta)$ h. $\cos (360^\circ + \theta)$
8. Is this statement true or false? Explain.
   For any two angles a and b, $\sin (a - b) = \sin a - \sin b$ and $\cos (a - b) = \cos a - \cos b$.
9. Suppose an angle θ is unknown, but it is between 125° and 175°. Determine whether each expression is *positive* or *negative.*
   a. $\sin \theta$ b. $\cos \theta$
   c. $\tan \theta$ d. $\sin^2 \theta + \cos^2 \theta$
10. Find an angle θ, not equal to 45°, that satisfies each equation.
   a. $\cos \theta = \cos 45^\circ$ b. $\sin \theta = \sin 45^\circ$ c. $\tan \theta = \tan 45^\circ$

Practice: For Lesson 8.3, assign Exercises 5–10.

Lesson Overview

GOAL

- Evaluate the sine, cosine, and tangent functions for any angle.

In this lesson, students prove that $\sin^2 \theta + \cos^2 \theta = 1$ for all angles θ. Up until now, they have only proven this identity for acute angles. It is likely that many of your students have already been using this result without a formal proof, and their personal justifications will help them formalize their conjecture.

CHECK YOUR UNDERSTANDING
- Core: 1, 2, 3, 4, 5
- Optional: 6

MATERIALS
- graph paper
- graphing calculators
- Blackline Master 8.1A

HOMEWORK
- Core: 8, 11, 12, 13, 14
- Optional: 7, 9, 10

Launch

To start the lesson, you might write the Pythagorean Identity on the board and ask students to tell you whether it is true for all angles and why they think so. After some initial discussion, have them work in groups to prove it. For You to Do Problem 1 assigns the proof.

You can use Blackline Master 8.1A to guide students through the proof of the Pythagorean Identity and the Example.

Explore

For You to Do

Have students share their proofs and their thinking with the class.

8.4 The Pythagorean Identity

While solving Exercise 10 in Lesson 8.2, you may have noticed the following equation is true for all angles between 0° and 360°.

$$\cos^2 \theta + \sin^2 \theta = 1$$

Since then, you have extended the domain for sine and cosine to include all angles. Does the identity still hold? Happily, it does.

Theorem 8.2 The Pythagorean Identity

If α is any angle, then

$$\cos^2 \alpha + \sin^2 \alpha = 1$$

The symbol α is the Greek letter alpha. You pronounce it AL fuh.

Proof For any angle α, $\cos \alpha$ and $\sin \alpha$ are the coordinates of the point P on the unit circle, where the left side of α intersects the unit circle.

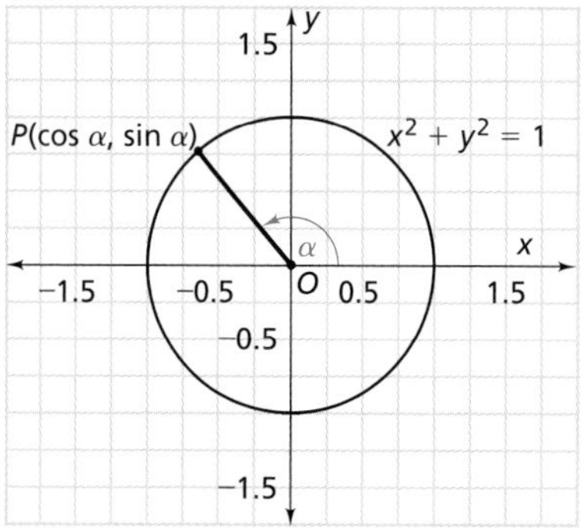

There are several ways to see that the sum of the squares of the coordinates of P is 1.

Method 1 The equation of the unit circle is $x^2 + y^2 = 1$, and the coordinates of P satisfy this equation.

Method 2 The distance from P to the origin is 1.

Method 3 Drop a perpendicular from P to the x-axis and use the Pythagorean Theorem.

For You to Do

1. Pick one of the methods above (or one of your own) and finish the proof of Theorem 8.2.

Answers

For You to Do

1. Answers may vary. Samples: $(x, y) = (\cos \alpha, \sin \alpha)$; substituting into $x^2 + y^2 = 1$ gives $\cos^2 \alpha + \sin^2 \alpha = 1$. The distance from P to $(0, 0)$ is 1, so $\sqrt{(\cos \alpha - 0)^2 + (\sin \alpha - 0)^2} = 1$. Then $\sqrt{\cos^2 \alpha + \sin^2 \alpha} = 1$ or $\cos^2 \alpha + \sin^2 \alpha = 1$. Dropping a perpendicular from P to the x-axis, the legs of the right triangle are $\cos \alpha$ and $\sin \alpha$, so $\cos^2 \alpha + \sin^2 \alpha = 1$.

Example

Problem If $\sin\gamma = \frac{1}{2}$, find $\cos\gamma$.

Solution Think of $(\cos\gamma, \sin\gamma)$ as a point P on the unit circle. Then $\sin\gamma$ is the y-coordinate of P. How many points have a y-coordinate of $\frac{1}{2}$ on the unit circle?

In Exercise 20a from Lesson 8.1, you saw that there are two points on the unit circle with y-coordinate $\frac{1}{2}$. The x-coordinates of these two points are precisely the values of $\cos\gamma$ for which $\sin\gamma = \frac{1}{2}$.

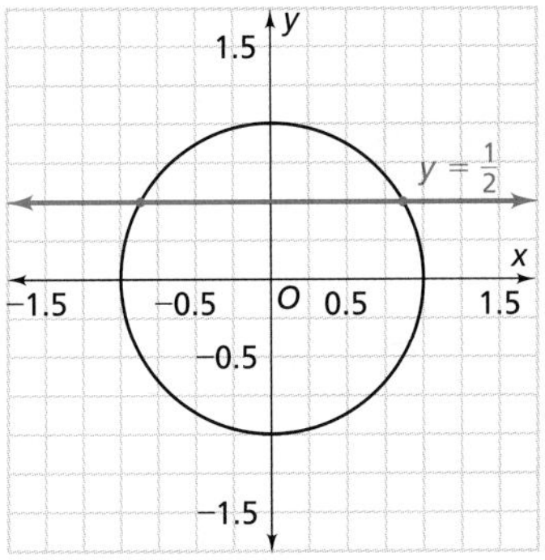

To find the two intersection points, you can do one of two equivalent things.

Method 1 In the equation $x^2 + y^2 = 1$, substitute $y = \frac{1}{2}$ and solve for x.

$$x^2 + \left(\tfrac{1}{2}\right)^2 = 1$$
$$x^2 + \frac{1}{4} = 1$$
$$x^2 = \frac{3}{4}$$
$$x = \pm\sqrt{\frac{3}{4}} = \pm\frac{\sqrt{3}}{2}$$

Method 2 Use the Pythagorean Identity.

$$\cos^2\gamma + \sin^2\gamma = 1$$

Substitute $\sin\gamma = \frac{1}{2}$.

$$\cos^2\gamma + \left(\tfrac{1}{2}\right)^2 = 1$$
$$\cos^2\gamma + \frac{1}{4} = 1$$
$$\cos^2\gamma = \frac{3}{4}$$
$$\cos\gamma = \pm\sqrt{\frac{3}{4}} = \pm\frac{\sqrt{3}}{2}$$

The symbol γ is the Greek letter gamma. You pronounce it GAM uh.

Methods 1 and 2 really are the same. On the unit circle, if (x, y) is the point where a radius that forms an angle γ with the x-axis intersects the circle, then $\cos\gamma = x$ and $\sin\gamma = y$.

Habits of Mind

Consider more than one solution. If you ask your calculator for $\sin^{-1}(0.5)$, it will probably return 30°. It is true that $\sin 30° = 0.5$, but is that the only solution for γ? The calculator picks its values for $\sin^{-1}$ from a restricted domain.

For You to Do

2. Solve $\sin\gamma = \frac{1}{2}$ for γ.

For You to Do

2. $30° + 360° \cdot k$ or $150° + 360° \cdot k$, where k is an integer

Example

As the middle side-column note indicates, the two methods are really the same. They are presented as two separate methods to give students time to become comfortable with the fact that any point P on the unit circle has coordinates $(\cos\theta, \sin\theta)$, where θ is the angle from the positive x-axis to the ray $\overrightarrow{OP}$ (where O is the origin).

HABITS OF MIND As discussed in the side-column note, the standard for most calculators is to return values for $\sin^{-1}$ in the range $[-90°, 90°]$, $\cos^{-1}$ in the range $[0°, 180°]$, and $\tan^{-1}$ in the range $(-90°, 90°]$. The terms *arcsin*, *arccos*, and *arctan* are sometimes used to avoid confusion with reciprocal functions.

Wrap Up

Finish the lesson by going over some of the Check Your Understanding core exercises.

Assessment Resources

Lesson Quiz 8.4

1. Suppose $\sin x = -\frac{\sqrt{3}}{2}$ and x is an angle between 0° and 360°.
   a. Find all possible values of x.
   b. Find all possible values of $\cos x$.
   c. Find all possible values of $\cos^2 x$.

For Exercises 2 and 3, solve each equation or each system for $0 \le x \le 360°$.

2. $\cos x = -\frac{\sqrt{2}}{2}$

3. $\begin{cases} \cos x = \frac{\sqrt{2}}{2} \\ \sin x > 0 \end{cases}$

Exercises

HOMEWORK
- Core: 8, 11, 12, 13, 14
- Optional: 7, 9, 10

Check Your Understanding

EXERCISES 3 AND 4 Assign Exercise 3 only if you also assign Exercise 4.

EXERCISES 6 AND 7 Exercise 6 is a nice review of calculations with complex numbers. Assign this exercise if you plan to assign Exercise 7, which asks students to prove the general case.

Exercises *Practicing Habits of Mind*

Check Your Understanding

1. Suppose $\sin q = 0.72$ and q is in the second quadrant. Find the approximate value of $\cos q$. Then find the measure of angle q to the nearest degree.

2. Suppose $\cos x = \frac{1}{2}$ and x is an angle between 0° and 360°.
  a. Find all possible values of x.
  b. Find all possible values of $\sin x$.
  c. Find all possible values of $\sin^2 x$.

3. Graph both equations on the same axes.

$$x^2 + y^2 = 1$$
$$y = 0.6$$

4. Find all solutions to the system of equations in Exercise 3.

5. Suppose $\cos x = 0.6$ and x is an angle between 0° and 360°.
  a. Find all possible values of x.
  b. Find all possible values of $\sin x$.
  c. Find all possible values of $\sin^2 x$.

Approximate to one decimal place if necessary.

6. Suppose that $z = \cos 30° + i \sin 30°$. Show that $\frac{1}{z} = \bar{z}$.

Remember...
The notation $\bar{z}$ means the complex conjugate of z.

On Your Own

7. Suppose that $z = \cos\theta + i\sin\theta$. Show that $\frac{1}{z} = \bar{z}$.

8. Solve each equation or system for $0 \le x \le 360°$.
  a. $\sin x = \frac{\sqrt{2}}{2}$
  b. $\begin{cases} \sin x = \frac{\sqrt{2}}{2} \\ \cos x > 0 \end{cases}$
  c. $\begin{cases} \sin x = \frac{\sqrt{2}}{2} \\ \cos x < 0 \end{cases}$
  d. $\begin{cases} \sin x = -\frac{\sqrt{2}}{2} \\ \cos x < 0 \end{cases}$

Answers

Exercises

1. $\cos q \approx -0.69$; $m\angle q \approx 134°$

2. a. 60°, 300° **b.** $\pm\frac{\sqrt{3}}{2}$ **c.** $\frac{3}{4}$

3.

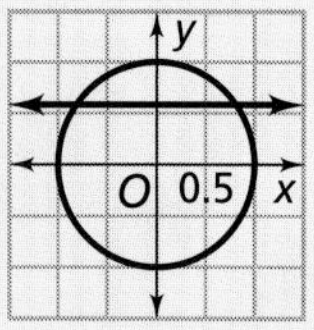

4. (0.8, 0.6), (−0.8, 0.6)

5. a. 53.1°, 306.9° **b.** ±0.8
  c. 0.64

6. Answers may vary. Sample:

$$\frac{1}{z} = \frac{1}{\cos 30° + i \sin 30°} = \frac{1}{\frac{\sqrt{3}}{2} + \frac{1}{2}i}$$
$$= \frac{1}{\frac{\sqrt{3}}{2} + \frac{1}{2}i} \cdot \frac{\frac{\sqrt{3}}{2} - \frac{1}{2}i}{\frac{\sqrt{3}}{2} - \frac{1}{2}i} = \frac{\frac{\sqrt{3}}{2} - \frac{1}{2}i}{\frac{3}{4} + \frac{1}{4}}$$
$$= \frac{\sqrt{3}}{2} - \frac{1}{2}i = \cos 30° - i \sin 30°$$
$$= \bar{z}$$

7. If $z = \cos\theta + i\sin\theta$, then
$$z\bar{z} = (\cos\theta + i\sin\theta)(\cos\theta - i\sin\theta)$$
$$= \cos^2\theta + \sin^2\theta = 1. \text{ So } \bar{z} = \frac{1}{z}.$$

8. a. 45°, 135°
  b. 45°
  c. 135°
  d. 225°

9. Find ten pairs of rational numbers (a, b) such that $a^2 + b^2 = 1$.

10. **Write About It** The Pythagorean Identity says that, if θ is any angle, $\cos^2\theta + \sin^2\theta = 1$.

Suppose you have numbers a and b such that $a^2 + b^2 = 1$. Is there an angle θ such that $\sin\theta = a$ and $\cos\theta = b$? Explain.

11. **a.** Show that $\tan^2 30° = \frac{1}{\cos^2 30°} - 1$.

b. If α is any angle, is the equation below true? Explain.

$$\tan^2\alpha = \frac{1}{\cos^2\alpha} - 1$$

Alpha is the first letter of the Greek alphabet. The alpha wolf is the leader of the pack.

12. **a.** Calculate $\cos^2 30° - \sin^2 30°$.

b. Calculate $\cos^4 30° - \sin^4 30°$.

c. Verify that $\cos^2\theta - \sin^2\theta = \cos^4\theta - \sin^4\theta$ for a new choice of θ.

Pick a θ, any θ.

d. Prove that for any angle θ, it must be true that

$$\cos^2\theta - \sin^2\theta = \cos^4\theta - \sin^4\theta.$$

13. **Standardized Test Prep** If $\cos\theta = \frac{1}{3}$ and $0° < \theta < 90°$, what is the value of $\sin\theta$?

A. $\frac{2}{3}$ **B.** $\frac{4}{9}$

C. $\frac{2\sqrt{2}}{3}$ **D.** $\frac{8}{9}$

Go Online
PHSchool.com

For additional practice, go to **Web Code**: bfa-0804

On Your Own

EXERCISE 9 Students should recognize that the pairs of rational numbers they find form Pythagorean triples with the number 1.

EXERCISE 10 Students may get hung up on the possible combinations of positive and negative values of a and b, since both variables are squared. You can point them to the figure in the Developing Habits of Mind in Lesson 8.3 to help them see that all the combinations are accounted for.

EXERCISE 11 shows students that although the Pythagorean Identity involves only sine and cosine, there are implications for tangent as well. You may be more familiar with this identity in the form $\tan^2\alpha = \sec^2\alpha - 1$ where $\sec\alpha$ is the secant function, which is equal to $\frac{1}{\cos\alpha}$ for any angle where $\cos\alpha \neq 0$.

EXERCISE 12 asks students to think of factoring in a new context.

9. Answers may vary. Sample: $(\pm 1, 0), (0, \pm 1), \left(\pm\frac{3}{5}, \pm\frac{4}{5}\right), \left(\pm\frac{4}{5}, \pm\frac{3}{5}\right), \left(\pm\frac{5}{13}, \pm\frac{12}{13}\right), \left(\pm\frac{12}{13}, \pm\frac{5}{13}\right)$, and in general, $\left(\pm\frac{a}{c}, \pm\frac{b}{c}\right)$, where a, b, and c form a Pythagorean triple.

10. Yes, if a and b are real numbers and $a^2 + b^2 = 1$, then (b, a) is on the unit circle and $b = \cos\theta$ and $a = \sin\theta$.

11. a. Answers may vary. Sample: $\tan 30° = \frac{\sqrt{3}}{3}$ and $\cos 30° = \frac{\sqrt{3}}{2}$, so $\frac{1}{\cos^2 30°} - 1$

$= \frac{1}{\left(\frac{\sqrt{3}}{2}\right)^2} - 1 = \frac{1}{\left(\frac{3}{4}\right)} - 1$

$= \frac{4}{3} - \frac{3}{3} = \frac{1}{3} = \frac{3}{9}$

$= \left(\frac{\sqrt{3}}{3}\right)^2 = \tan^2 30°$.

b. No; however if $\cos\alpha \neq 0$, then $\frac{1}{\cos^2\alpha} - 1 = \frac{1}{\cos^2\alpha} - \frac{\cos^2\alpha}{\cos^2\alpha} = \frac{1 - \cos^2\alpha}{\cos^2\alpha} = \frac{\cos^2\alpha + \sin^2\alpha - \cos^2\alpha}{\cos^2\alpha} = \frac{\sin^2\alpha}{\cos^2\alpha} = \tan^2\alpha$.

12. a. $\frac{1}{2}$

b. $\frac{1}{2}$

c. Answers may vary. Sample: $\cos^2 45° - \sin^2 45° = \left(\frac{\sqrt{2}}{2}\right)^2 - \left(\frac{\sqrt{2}}{2}\right)^2 = 0$ and $\cos^4 45° - \sin^4 45° = \left(\frac{\sqrt{2}}{2}\right)^4 - \left(\frac{\sqrt{2}}{2}\right)^4 = 0$.

d. $\cos^4\theta - \sin^4\theta$
$= (\cos^2\theta + \sin^2\theta)(\cos^2\theta - \sin^2\theta)$
$= (1)(\cos^2\theta - \sin^2\theta)$
$= (\cos^2\theta - \sin^2\theta)$

13. C

Maintain Your Skills

EXERCISE 14 Encourage your students to use common sense to remember the values of trigonometric functions for special angles. 30°, 45°, and 60° are the special angles in the first quadrant, so they all have positive sines, cosines, and therefore tangents. Your students likely remember what the values of the trigonometric functions are, but may not remember which value goes with which function and angle.

One way is to remember this ordering: $\frac{\sqrt{1}}{2} < \frac{\sqrt{2}}{2} < \frac{\sqrt{3}}{2}$. Then you can look at the unit circle and see that 30° has the greatest *x*-coordinate of the three and the least *y*-coordinate. This tells you that $\cos 30° = \frac{\sqrt{3}}{2}$ and $\sin 30° = \frac{1}{2}$. Divide to get $\tan 30° = \frac{\sqrt{3}}{3}$. Similarly 45° has the "middle" *x*- and *y*-coordinates, and 60° will have the least *x*-coordinate and greatest *y*-coordinate for the three special angles.

Additional Resources

PRINT RESOURCES
- Solution Manual
- Practice Workbook
- Assessment Resources
- Teaching Resources

TECHNOLOGY
- Interactive Textbook
- TeacherExpress CD-ROM
- ExamView CD-ROM
- PHSchool.com

Additional Practice

1. Solve each equation or each system for $0 \le x \le 360°$.
   a. $\sin x = \frac{\sqrt{3}}{2}$
   b. $\cos x = -\frac{\sqrt{3}}{2}$
   c. $\begin{cases} \sin x = \frac{\sqrt{3}}{2} \\ \cos x > 0 \end{cases}$
   d. $\begin{cases} \cos x = -\frac{\sqrt{3}}{2} \\ \sin x < 0 \end{cases}$

2. a. Show that $\frac{1}{\tan^2 45°} + 1 = \frac{1}{\sin^2 45°}$.
   b. If α is any angle, is the equation below true? Explain.
   $$\frac{1}{\tan^2 \alpha} + 1 = \frac{1}{\sin^2 \alpha}$$

3. a. Calculate $\sin^2 45° - \cos^2 45°$.
   b. Calculate $\sin^4 45° - \cos^4 45°$.
   c. Verify that $\sin^2 \theta - \cos^2 \theta = \sin^4 \theta - \cos^4 \theta$ for a new choice of θ.
   d. Prove that for any angle θ, it must be true that $\sin^2 \theta - \cos^2 \theta = \sin^4 \theta - \cos^4 \theta$.

4. Find all solutions to each equation for $0 \le x \le 360°$.
   a. $2 \sin x + 1 = 0$
   b. $2 \cos^2 x - 1 = 0$
   c. $\tan x + 1 = 0$
   d. $-\sqrt{2} \cos x + 1 = 2$

5. Find all solutions to each equation for $0 \le x \le 360°$.
   a. $\sin x \tan x - \frac{\sqrt{2}}{2} \tan x = 0$
   b. $4 \sin^2 x - 1 = 0$
   c. $2 \sin^2 x = 2 + \cos x$
   d. $2 \cos^2 x - \cos x - 1 = 0$

6. For what values of α between 0° and 360° is the following equation true?
   $$\sin^2 \alpha + 2 \sin \alpha + 1 = 0$$

7. Solve the equation $\sin x \cos x - \cos x = 0$ for x, where $0 \le x \le 360°$.

Practice: For Lesson 8.4, assign Exercises 1–3.

Maintain Your Skills

14. Copy and complete the table without using a calculator.

θ	$\cos \theta$	$\sin \theta$	$\tan \theta$
0°	■	0	■
30°	$\frac{\sqrt{3}}{2}$	■	$\frac{1}{\sqrt{3}}$
45°	■	$\frac{\sqrt{2}}{2}$	1
60°	■	■	■
90°	0	1	■
120°	■	■	■
135°	■	■	■
150°	■	$-\frac{1}{2}$	■
180°	■	■	■
210°	■	■	■
225°	$-\frac{\sqrt{2}}{2}$	■	■
240°	■	■	■
270°	0	■	■
300°	■	■	■
315°	■	■	■
330°	■	■	■
360°	1	■	■

You have done much of the work for this table before.

Answers

14. See back of book.

8.5 Solving Trigonometric Equations

You solve equations with trigonometric functions in much the same way you solve other equations.

Minds in Action episode 37

Tony and Sasha are trying to solve the equation $5 \cos x + 6 = 9$ for x between $0°$ and $360°$.

Tony I'm not sure what to do with the $\cos x$.

Sasha It's like in Chapter 2, when we lumped things.

Sasha goes to the board and covers up the $\cos x$ with her hand.

5 c✋x + 6 = 9

Sasha See? Now it looks like it's saying "5 times something plus 6 is 9."

So, let z stand for $\cos x$, for the time being, and solve

$$5z + 6 = 9$$

Tony I know how to do that. You get $z = \frac{3}{5} = 0.6$.

Sasha But z is just an alias for $\cos x$, so our equation is $\cos x = 0.6$.

Tony And I know how to do that, too. In fact, we have already done it in Exercise 5 in the last lesson. You just use the inverse cosine button and get $53.13°$. That's an approximation, I know.

Sasha Yes, but that's not the only answer. Look:

Sasha draws on the board.

Sasha See? Cosine is the x-coordinate, and there are two points on the unit circle with x-coordinate 0.6. One has a central angle of about $53.13°$.

Tony And the other is $-53.13°$.

Sasha Or, if you want your angles to measure between $0°$ and $360°$, the second angle is about $306.87°$.

Sasha replaces z with $\cos x$ in the equation $z = 0.6$.

Habits of Mind

Make strategic choices. What happens when you allow angles with measure greater than $360°$?

Lesson Overview

GOAL

- Solve equations involving trigonometric functions.

Students have already solved some trigonometric equations by finding the value of an angle in a right triangle when they know the sidelengths. In this lesson, though, they will take that work further. Rather than restricting their solutions to acute angles, they find all the solutions between $0°$ and $360°$, and solve more complex equations that require factoring.

CHECK YOUR UNDERSTANDING
- Core: 1, 2, 3, 4, 5a–b
- Optional: 6, 7, 8
- Extension: 5c

MATERIALS
- graph paper
- graphing calculators

HOMEWORK
- Core: 9, 10, 11, 14, 17
- Optional: 12, 13, 15a–c, 18a–e
- Extension: 15d, 16, 18f

VOCABULARY
- trigonometric equation

Launch

Start the lesson with the dialog. You may wish to have two students act out the dialog for the class.

Explore

Minds in Action

Many students may be unsure how to proceed when they see trigonometric equations. The presence of the $\cos x$ in the equation may confuse them. The hand method, which students first saw in CME Project *Algebra 1,* allows them to convert the equation temporarily to a form that looks more familiar. To refresh students' memory, you may want to remind them of how they used this method before to solve nonmonic quadratic equations. For example:

$$4x^2 + 10x + 6 = 0$$

$$(2x)^2 + 5(2x) + 6 = 0 \quad \text{Let } z = 2x.$$

$$z^2 + 5z + 6 = 0 \quad \text{Factor.}$$

$$(z + 2)(z + 3) = 0 \quad \text{Substitute } 2x \text{ back in for } z.$$

$$(2x + 2)(2x + 3) = 0$$

So $x = -1$ or $x = -\frac{3}{2}$.

Eventually, students may become comfortable enough with these equations that they do not need the substitution step.

For You to Do

Make sure that students see that although the calculator gives them the same angle as in the dialog, the second solution is different. Sine is positive in Quadrants I and II, and cosine is positive in Quadrants I and IV.

Wrap Up

Have students work through the Check Your Understanding exercises. Review Exercises 4 and 6, as they follow the Example directly, and several homework exercises are similar.

Assessment Resources

Lesson Quiz 8.5

1. Find all solutions to each equation for $0 \le x \le 360°$.
   a. $\sin x \cos x - \frac{\sqrt{2}}{2} \cos x = 0$
   b. $4 \cos^2 x - 1 = 0$
   c. $2 \cos^2 x = 2 + \sin x$
   d. $2 \tan^2 x - 2 = 0$

2. For what values of α between 0° and 360° is the following equation true?

$$\cos^2 \alpha - 2 \cos \alpha - 1 = 0$$

3. Solve the equation $2 \cos x \sin x - \sin x = 0$ for x, where $0 \le x \le 360°$.

Exercises

HOMEWORK

- Core: 9, 10, 11, 14, 17
- Optional: 12, 13, 15a–c, 18a–e
- Extension: 15d, 16, 18f

For You to Do

1. Solve $5 \sin x + 3 = 7$ for x between 0° and 360°.

Developing Habits of Mind

Look for patterns. The lumping idea is often used to solve trigonometric equations that look like ordinary algebraic equations.

For example, the trigonometric equation below is a quadratic equation in $\sin x$.

$$10 \sin^2 x - 3 \sin x = 4$$

That is, if you let $z = \sin x$, the equation becomes

$$10z^2 - 3z = 4$$

You can solve this with the methods of Chapter 2. When you find two values for z, replace z with $\sin x$. Then solve for x.

A **trigonometric equation** is an equation that involves trigonometric functions.

For You to Do

2. Solve the equation $10 \sin^2 x - 3 \sin x = 4$ for x, where $0° \le x \le 360°$.

Exercises *Practicing Habits of Mind*

Check Your Understanding

1. Suppose $\sin x = \sin 50°$. Find all possible values of x.
2. a. Find, to the nearest degree, the two angles between 0° and 360° that make $\sin x = 0.6$.
   b. Find, to the nearest degree, the two angles between 0° and 360° that make $\sin x = -0.6$.

Answers

For You to Do

1. 53.1°, 126.9°
2. 53.1°, 126.9°, 210°, 330°

Exercises

1. $x = 50° + 360° \cdot k$ or $x = 130° + 360° \cdot k$, where k is an integer
2. a. 37°, 143°
   b. 217°, 323°

3. a. Find, to the nearest degree, all angles between 0° and 360° that make $\cos x = 0.8$.

b. Find, to the nearest degree, all angles between 0° and 360° that make $\cos x = -1.2$.

4. Find all solutions to each equation for $0° \le x \le 360°$.

a. $3 \cos x + 4 = 0$
b. $6 \sin x - 1 = 3$
c. $4 \sin^2 x = 1$
d. $4 \sin^2 x = 4 \sin x + 3$

5. a. Find, to the nearest degree, all angles between 0° and 360° that make $\sin x = \cos x$.

b. Find, to the nearest degree, all angles between 0° and 360° that make $\sin x = -\cos x$.

c. **Take It Further** Find, to the nearest degree, all angles between 0° and 360° that make $\sin x = \tan x$.

6. Solve the equation $6 \cos^2 x + \sin x - 5 = 0$ for x, where $0° \le x \le 360°$. (*Hint:* $\cos^2 x + \sin^2 x = 1$)

7. Suppose z is a complex number and $\arg z = \theta$. Use geometry to show that $z + \overline{z} = 2|z| \cos \theta$.

8. In the isosceles triangle below, $OA = OB = 1$ and $m\angle O = 36°$. Show that $z = 2 \cos 72°$.

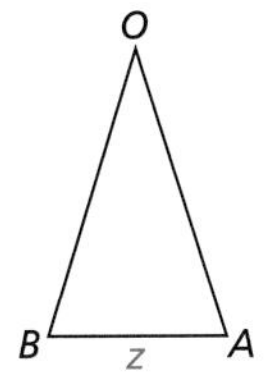

Habits of Mind

Detect the key characteristics. What is special about the parallelogram that has vertices 0, z, $z + \overline{z}$, and $\overline{z}$?

On Your Own

9. Find all solutions to each equation for $0° \le x \le 360°$.

a. $5 \cos x + 4 = 0$
b. $\sqrt{2} \sin x - 1 = 3$
c. $4 \cos^2 x = 1$
d. $4 \cos^2 x = 4 \cos x + 3$

10. Find all solutions to each equation for $0° \le x \le 360°$.

a. $2 \cos x + 1 = 0$
b. $\tan x - 1 = 0$
c. $1 - 3 \sin x + 2 \sin^2 x = 0$
d. $2 \cos^2 x - 5 \cos x = 2$

11. For what values of α between 0° and 360° is the following equation true?

$$2 \sin^2 \alpha + 5 \cos \alpha = 2$$

Go Online PHSchool.com

For additional practice, go to **Web Code:** bfa-0805

3. a. 37°, 323°
b. no solution

4. a. no solution
b. 41.8°, 138.2°
c. 30°, 150°, 210°, 330°
d. 210°, 330°

5. a. 45°, 225°
b. 135°, 315°
c. 0°, 180°, 360°

6. 30°, 150°, 199.47°, 340.53°

7. Using the Parallelogram Law from Chapter 3, you find that the vertices of the parallelogram formed by z and $\overline{z}$ are (0, 0), (a, b), $(a, -b)$, and $(2a, 0)$. So $z + \overline{z} = 2a$. Also, if $\arg z = \theta$, then $\cos \theta = \frac{a}{|z|}$ (because a is the value of the x-coordinate and $|z|$ is the distance from the origin to z). So $a = |z| \cos \theta$ and $2a = 2|z| \cos \theta$.

8–10. See back of book.

11. 90°, 270°

Check Your Understanding

EXERCISE 3 By asking students to find an angle for an impossible value of cosine, this exercise reminds students of the limited range of outputs for sine and cosine. There are several ways for students to make sense of this restricted range.

- Coordinates of a point on the unit circle can never be greater than 1 or less than −1. Cosine and sine are defined as being equal to the x- and y-coordinates of these points.
- The graph of cosine or sine "waves" up and down between the lines $y = 1$ and $y = -1$, touching them at its high and low points.
- The sine and cosine functions were originally defined as ratios of legs in a right triangle to the hypotenuse. Since the legs are always shorter than the hypotenuse (except in the strange collapsed case of the 0°-90°-90° right triangle), this ratio is always less than or equal to 1. In the expanded definitions of sine and cosine, these ratios sometimes have a negative sign, but their absolute value is always less than or equal to 1.

EXERCISE 4 Make sure that students correctly interpret error messages from their calculators when computing inverse trigonometric functions. Make sure that they are able to find all the angles x so that $0 \le x < 360°$, not just the value returned by their calculators.

EXERCISE 5 If students are not sure how to approach equations involving both sine and cosine, you might ask what happens to the tangent function when $\sin x = \cos x$. To find values of x where $\sin x = \tan x$, you can suggest that students rewrite the equation using only sine and cosine.

EXERCISE 7 Suggest that students graph this situation in the complex plane and use the graph to find the sum using the Parallelogram Law. To help them write the sum using trigonometric functions, ask them to find an expression for a that uses the fact that $\arg z = \theta$.

EXERCISE 8 Remind students that since the trigonometric functions were originally defined for right triangles, it might be useful to make some right triangles by dropping an altitude. Students will also have to either remember or reobserve the fact that the altitude to the base of an isosceles triangle is also a bisector of that base.

On Your Own

EXERCISE 9 To find all possible solutions, students will need to remember both that there are usually two solutions to equations of the form $x^2 = a$ and that there are usually two solutions between 0° and 360° to equations of the form $\cos x = b$. This means that $\cos^2 \theta = a$ may have as many as four solutions between 0° and 360°.

EXERCISE 11 begins with an equation involving both sine and cosine. If necessary, remind students to use the Pythagorean Identity to rewrite this equation in terms of only one trigonometric function.

EXERCISE 13 Students may benefit from sketching a picture of the complex numbers.

EXERCISE 14 You may wish to give your students the hint that they can factor this polynomial by grouping.

EXERCISE 15 The first part of this exercise calls fairly heavily on students' recollections of CME Project *Geometry*.

EXERCISE 16 This equation is nearly identical to the one in the Minds in Action dialog. Students can follow the same procedure, except at the end, they substitute back cos 2*x* instead of cos *x*. The difficulty comes in deciding what the final step should be, and making sure that all possible answers are included. In fact, there are four answers, not just two.

Additional Resources

PRINT RESOURCES
- Solution Manual
- Practice Workbook
- Assessment Resources
- Teaching Resources

TECHNOLOGY
- Interactive Textbook
- TeacherExpress CD-ROM
- ExamView CD-ROM
- PHSchool.com

Additional Practice

1. Solve each equation or each system for $0 \le x \le 360°$.

   a. $\sin x = \frac{\sqrt{3}}{2}$ b. $\cos x = -\frac{\sqrt{3}}{2}$

   c. $\begin{cases} \sin x = \frac{\sqrt{3}}{2} \\ \cos x > 0 \end{cases}$ d. $\begin{cases} \cos x = -\frac{\sqrt{3}}{2} \\ \sin x < 0 \end{cases}$

2. a. Show that $\frac{1}{\tan^2 45°} + 1 = \frac{1}{\sin^2 45°}$.

   b. If α is any angle, is the equation below true? Explain.
   $$\frac{1}{\tan^2 \alpha} + 1 = \frac{1}{\sin^2 \alpha}$$

3. a. Calculate $\sin^2 45° - \cos^2 45°$.
   b. Calculate $\sin^4 45° - \cos^4 45°$.
   c. Verify that $\sin^2\theta - \cos^2\theta = \sin^4\theta - \cos^4\theta$ for a new choice of θ.
   d. Prove that for any angle θ, it must be true that $\sin^2\theta - \cos^2\theta = \sin^4\theta - \cos^4\theta$.

4. Find all solutions to each equation for $0 \le x \le 360°$.
   a. $2\sin x + 1 = 0$
   b. $2\cos^2 x - 1 = 0$
   c. $\tan x + 1 = 0$
   d. $-\sqrt{2}\cos x + 1 = 2$

5. Find all solutions to each equation for $0 \le x \le 360°$.
   a. $\sin x \tan x - \frac{\sqrt{2}}{2}\tan x = 0$
   b. $4\sin^2 x - 1 = 0$
   c. $2\sin^2 x = 2 + \cos x$
   d. $2\cos^2 x - \cos x - 1 = 0$

6. For what values of α between 0° and 360° is the following equation true?
   $$\sin^2\alpha + 2\sin\alpha + 1 = 0$$

7. Solve the equation $\sin x\cos x - \cos x = 0$ for x, where $0 \le x \le 360°$.

Practice: For Lesson 8.5, assign Exercises 4–7.

12. Find or approximate the complex number on the unit circle that has each argument. Write your answers in $a + bi$ form.

a. 20° **b.** 330° **c.** −30° **d.** 100° **e.** 227° **f.** 75°

13. For each complex number z, find arg z.

a. $z = \frac{4}{5} + \frac{3}{5}i$ **b.** $z = \frac{3}{5} + \frac{4}{5}i$ **c.** $z = -\frac{3}{5} - \frac{4}{5}i$ **d.** $z = -\frac{4}{5} + \frac{3}{5}i$

14. Solve the equation $2\sin^3 x - \sin^2 x - 2\sin x + 1 = 0$ for x, where $0° \le x \le 360°$.

15. In the isosceles triangle below, $OA = OB = 1$ and $m\angle O = 36°$. $\overline{BC}$ bisects $\angle OBA$.

See Exercise 8.

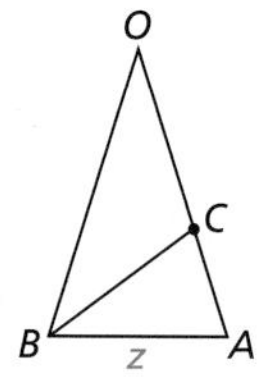

Habits of Mind
Look for relationships. There are similar triangles in the figure.

a. Show that $1 - z^2 = z$.

b. Use the result of part (a) to find an exact value for z.

c. Use parts (a) and (b) and the result of Exercise 8 to find an exact value for cos 72°.

d. **Take It Further** Find an exact value for sin 72°.

16. **Take It Further** Solve the equation $5\cos 2x + 6 = 9$, where $0° \le x \le 360°$.

17. **Standardized Test Prep** Solve, to the nearest hundredth of a degree, $\tan x - 10 = -\tan x$ for $-90° < x < 90°$.

A. −80° **B.** 1.37° **C.** 78.69° **D.** 84.29°

Maintain Your Skills

18. Here is a graph of the unit circle with a line ℓ that intersects the circle at the points $A(0, -1)$ and $P(a, b)$.

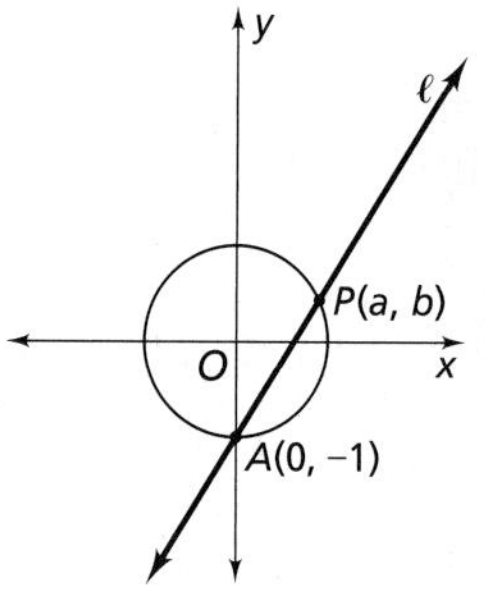

Find the coordinates of P for each slope of ℓ.

a. 1 **b.** 2 **c.** $\frac{3}{2}$

d. 4 **e.** $\frac{6}{5}$

f. **Take It Further** $\frac{r}{s}$

Answers

12. a. $0.940 + 0.342i$

b. $\frac{\sqrt{3}}{2} - \frac{1}{2}i$

c. $\frac{\sqrt{3}}{2} - \frac{1}{2}i$

d. $-0.174 + 0.985i$

e. $-0.682 - 0.731i$

f. $0.259 + 0.966i$

13. a. 36.87° **b.** 53.13°
c. 233.13° **d.** 143.13°

14. 30°, 90°, 150°, 270°

15. a. Answers may vary. Sample: $\triangle OAB$ and $\triangle BAC$ are similar by AA similarity and $\triangle COB$ is isosceles. Also, $AB = BC = z$ and. So, $\frac{OB}{BA} = \frac{BA}{AC}$ or $\frac{1}{z} = \frac{z}{AC}$, so $AC = z^2$. But $AC = 1 - OC = 1 - z$, so $z^2 = 1 - z$, or $1 - z^2 = z$.

b. $\frac{-1 + \sqrt{5}}{2}$ **c.** $\frac{-1 + \sqrt{5}}{4}$

d. $\sqrt{\frac{5 + \sqrt{5}}{8}}$

16–18. See back of book.

Mathematical Reflections 8A

In this investigation, you learned how to evaluate the sine, cosine, and tangent functions for any angle and to solve equations involving trigonometric equations. These questions will help you summarize what you have learned.

1. A line through the origin forms a 30° angle with the x-axis. What are the coordinates of the points where this line intersects the graph of the unit circle?

2. Sketch each angle in standard position. Find its sine, cosine, and tangent.

a. 150° **b.** 315° **c.** 240°

3. Find five solutions to the equation $\sin x = -1$.

4. For some angle θ, $\sin \theta = \frac{12}{13}$.

a. Find all possible values for $\cos \theta$.

b. Find all possible values for $\tan \theta$.

c. Find a possible θ between 0° and 360° to the nearest tenth of a degree.

5. Solve the following equation for α between 0° and 360°.

$$10 \cos^2 \alpha + \cos \alpha - 3 = 0$$

6. How can you extend the definitions of sine, cosine, and tangent to any angle, not just acute angles?

7. If an angle is in Quadrant IV, what can you say about the sign of its sine, cosine, and tangent?

8. What is the relationship between the equation of the unit circle and the Pythagorean Identity?

Vocabulary and Notation

In this investigation, you learned these terms and symbols. Make sure you understand what each one means and how to use it.

- **cosine, cos θ**
- **periodic function**
- **sine, sin θ**
- **standard position**
- **tangent, tan θ**
- **trigonometric equation**

The tip of the wiper moves along a circle as the wiper rotates.

Mathematical Reflections

EXERCISES 6–8 At the start of the investigation, you may have assigned these as Questions 1–3 for students to think and write about.

Mathematical Reflections

1. $\left(\frac{\sqrt{3}}{2}, \frac{1}{2}\right), \left(-\frac{\sqrt{3}}{2}, -\frac{1}{2}\right)$ or $\left(-\frac{\sqrt{3}}{2}, \frac{1}{2}\right), \left(\frac{\sqrt{3}}{2}, -\frac{1}{2}\right)$

2. a.

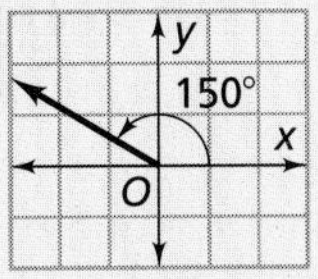

$\sin 150° = \frac{1}{2}$, $\cos 150° = -\frac{\sqrt{3}}{2}$, $\tan 150° = -\frac{\sqrt{3}}{3}$

b.

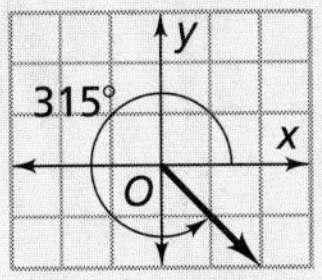

$\sin 315° = -\frac{\sqrt{2}}{2}$, $\cos 315° = \frac{\sqrt{2}}{2}$, $\tan 315° = -1$

c. See back of book.

3–8. See back of book.

Investigation Overview

In this investigation, students examine the graphs of the trigonometric functions—sine, cosine, and tangent—over their new domains. They see that the functions are periodic. They use the graphs together with the unit circle to prove trigonometric identities, including the Angle-Sum Identities.

You may wish to assign Questions 1–3 for students to think and write about during the investigation.

Learning Goals

- Sketch graphs of sine, cosine, and tangent.
- Use the graphs of trigonometric functions to solve problems.
- Prove and use trigonometric identities.

Habits and Skills

- Visualize relationships between graphs of trigonometric functions.
- Choose the appropriate representation—graph or unit circle—to understand and develop trigonometric identities.
- Reason logically to prove trigonometric identities.

Investigation 8B

Graphs of Trigonometric Functions

In *Graphs of Trigonometric Functions*, you will sketch the graphs of the sine, cosine, and tangent functions. You can use these graphs to explore trigonometric identities.

By the end of this investigation, you will be able to answer questions like these.

1. What do the graphs of the sine and cosine functions look like?
2. Why does the tangent function have a period of 180°?
3. What is a simple rule for finding the value of $\cos(90° + \theta)$?

You will learn how to

- sketch graphs of the sine, cosine, and tangent
- use the graphs of trigonometric functions to solve problems
- prove and use trigonometric identities

You will develop these habits and skills:

- Visualize relationships between graphs of trigonometric functions.
- Choose the appropriate representation—graph or unit circle—to understand and develop trigonometric identities.
- Reason logically to prove trigonometric identities.

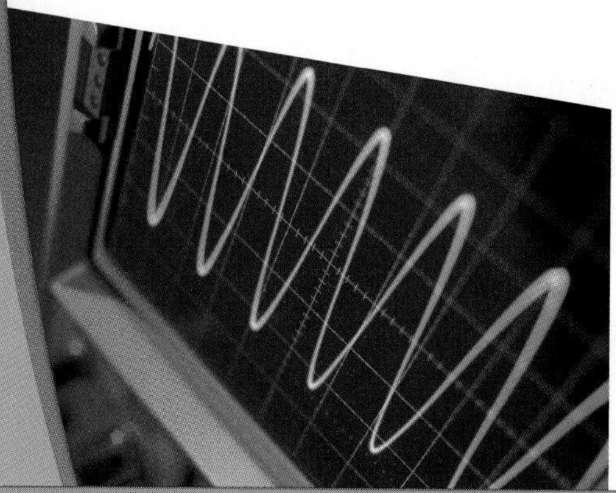

An oscilloscope displays voltage as a function of time. The graph is a sine wave.

Investigation Road Map

LESSON 8.6, ***Getting Started,*** has students begin the work of graphing trigonometric functions by using tables of values for special triangles. They use the graphs to think about some new kinds of questions.

LESSON 8.7, ***Graphing Cosine and Sine,*** has students graph sine and cosine formally. They use the graphs and the unit circle to find solutions to trigonometric equations and to prove some trigonometric identities.

LESSON 8.8, ***Graphing the Tangent Function,*** formally examines the graph of the tangent function and shows students a new way to visualize the numerical value of the tangent as a length related to the unit circle.

LESSON 8.9, ***The Angle-Sum Identities,*** collects several identities that students have proven.

8.6 Getting Started

Activating Prior Knowledge
Exploring New Ideas

The graphs of the sine, cosine, and tangent functions show the periodic nature of these functions.

For You to Explore

An exact value for a trigonometric function is an expression that may include square roots. If you use your calculator, it may return a decimal approximation and not an exact value.

1. Find the exact values of $\cos 30°$ and $\sin 30°$.
2. Find the exact values of $\cos 45°$ and $\sin 45°$.
3. Calculate each value.
   a. $\cos^2 30°$
   b. $\sin^2 30°$
   c. $\cos^2 45°$
   d. $\sin^2 45°$
   e. $\cos^2 30° + \sin^2 30°$
   f. $\cos^2 45° + \sin^2 45°$
4. Describe how the cosine and sine of 60° are related to the cosine and sine of 30°.
5. Describe how the cosine and sine of 150° are related to the cosine and sine of 30°.

Exercises *Practicing Habits of Mind*

On Your Own

6. Use the information from Exercise 14 in Lesson 8.4 to draw a graph of $y = \cos x$ for $0° \le x \le 360°$.
7. Use the graph of $y = \cos x$ to answer this question: Is $\cos 230°$ greater or less than $\cos 190°$?
8. Use the information from Exercise 14 in Lesson 8.4 to draw a graph of the function $y = \sin x$ for $0° \le x \le 360°$.

Answers

For You to Explore

1. $\cos 30° = \frac{\sqrt{3}}{2}$, $\sin 30° = \frac{1}{2}$
2. $\cos 45° = \sin 45° = \frac{\sqrt{2}}{2}$
3. a. $\frac{3}{4}$ b. $\frac{1}{4}$ c. $\frac{1}{2}$
   d. $\frac{1}{2}$ e. 1 f. 1
4. $\cos 60° = \sin 30°$; $\sin 60° = \cos 30°$
5. $\cos 150° = -\cos 30°$; $\sin 150° = \sin 30°$

Exercises

6.

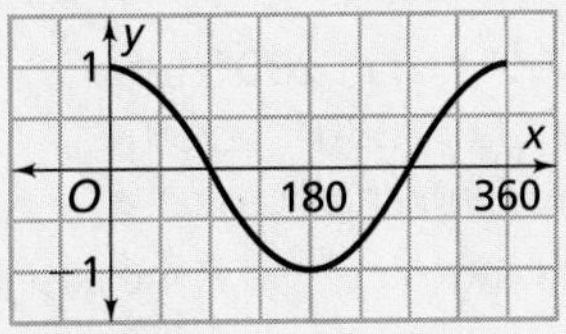

7. $\cos 230° > \cos 190°$
8. See back of book.

Lesson Overview

GOAL

- Sketch graphs of sine, cosine, and tangent.

In this lesson, students re-examine relationships between particular values of trigonometric functions and graph the sine and cosine functions. As always in a Getting Started lesson, there is no need to formalize these ideas today. Students meet all the ideas again throughout the investigation.

FOR YOU TO EXPLORE
- Core: 1, 2, 3, 4, 5
- Optional: none

MATERIALS
- graph paper
- graphing calculators

HOMEWORK
- Core: 6, 7, 8, 9, 10
- Optional: 12
- Extension: 11

Launch

Have students get started on the For You to Explore problems right away. Students with advanced calculators that display exact values for trigonometric functions may make it through the problems in no time. You may want to ask students to do the work first without their calculators.

Explore

If some students finish the For You to Explore problems, you might ask them to fill out a table like the one in Exercise 14 of Lesson 8.4.

For You to Explore

PROBLEMS 1 AND 2 Remind students that they need to be able to give exact values for trigonometric functions related to the special right triangles. They should also be able to give exact values for functions of angles that are multiples of 90°. These values are the anchor points in their graphs of the trigonometric functions.

PROBLEM 3 is both practice with special values and a reminder of the Pythagorean Identity.

PROBLEM 4 It might be easier for students to see the relationship between the sine and cosine of complementary angles if they use a right triangle representation.

PROBLEM 5 is a specific case of the identities $\cos(180° - \theta) = -\cos\theta$ and $\sin(180° - \theta) = \sin\theta$. These identities are also a specific case of the general Angle-Sum Identities.

Wrap Up

Go over the For You to Explore problems and discuss patterns in the table of trigonometric function values. Make sure students either have a copy of this table or thoroughly understand how to fill it in, as they will need it for Exercises 6 and 8.

Exercises

HOMEWORK

- Core: 6, 7, 8, 9, 10
- Optional: 12
- Extension: 11

On Your Own

EXERCISES 7 AND 9 ask students to use the graph to compare two values directly. Some students may try to develop numerical approximations (especially if they attempt Exercise 11), but this is not necessary to answer the question.

EXERCISE 10 asks students to compare values that are 180° apart in the x-direction. One technique is to make a strip of paper that is 180° "wide," as measured on the graph, and then to compare the values of the sine function at the two ends.

EXERCISE 11 The exercises do not ask students to graph the tangent function. Some students may attempt to make a graph to answer the question. Others may use the table from Exercise 14 in Lesson 8.4 and spot a general trend of data. Another way to show which is greater is to realize that $\tan \theta$ is the slope of the line from the origin to the point $(\cos \theta, \sin \theta)$, so students can draw a unit circle and compare the respective slopes.

9. Use the graph of $y = \sin x$ to answer this question: Is $\sin 230°$ greater or less than $\sin 190°$?

10. Find and describe a relationship between $\sin \theta$ and $\sin (180° + \theta)$.

11. **Take It Further** Which is greater, $\tan 190°$ or $\tan 230°$? Determine the answer without a calculator. Justify your answer.

Maintain Your Skills

12. For each complex number, calculate the magnitude and direction.

a. $3 + 2i$ **b.** $(3 + 2i)^2$ **c.** $1 + 2i$

d. $(1 + 2i)^2$ **e.** $-\frac{8}{17} + \frac{15}{17}i$ **f.** $\left(-\frac{8}{17} + \frac{15}{17}i\right)^2$

g. z^2, where z has magnitude 5 and direction 100°

Calculate the direction to the nearest tenth of a degree.

13. Here is the table you completed in Lesson 8.4, Exercise 14. What patterns can you find in each column?

θ	$\cos \theta$	$\sin \theta$	$\tan \theta$
0°	1	0	0
30°	$\frac{\sqrt{3}}{2}$	$\frac{1}{2}$	$\frac{1}{\sqrt{3}}$
45°	$\frac{\sqrt{2}}{2}$	$\frac{\sqrt{2}}{2}$	1
60°	$\frac{1}{2}$	$\frac{\sqrt{3}}{2}$	$\sqrt{3}$
90°	0	1	undefined
120°	$-\frac{1}{2}$	$\frac{\sqrt{3}}{2}$	$-\sqrt{3}$
135°	$-\frac{\sqrt{2}}{2}$	$\frac{\sqrt{2}}{2}$	-1
150°	$-\frac{\sqrt{3}}{2}$	$\frac{1}{2}$	$-\frac{1}{\sqrt{3}}$
180°	-1	0	0
210°	$-\frac{\sqrt{3}}{2}$	$-\frac{1}{2}$	$\frac{1}{\sqrt{3}}$
225°	$-\frac{\sqrt{2}}{2}$	$-\frac{\sqrt{2}}{2}$	1
240°	$-\frac{1}{2}$	$-\frac{\sqrt{3}}{2}$	$\sqrt{3}$
270°	0	-1	undefined
300°	$\frac{1}{2}$	$-\frac{\sqrt{3}}{2}$	$-\sqrt{3}$
315°	$\frac{\sqrt{2}}{2}$	$-\frac{\sqrt{2}}{2}$	-1
330°	$\frac{\sqrt{3}}{2}$	$-\frac{1}{2}$	$-\frac{1}{\sqrt{3}}$
360°	1	0	0

Answers

9. $\sin 230° < \sin 190°$

10. $\sin (180° + \theta) = -\sin \theta$ or $\sin \theta = -\sin (180° + \theta)$

11. $\tan 190° < \tan 230°$; for $190° \le \theta \le 230°$, $|\sin \theta|$ is increasing and $|\cos \theta|$ is decreasing, so $\left|\frac{\sin \theta}{\cos \theta}\right|$ is increasing. Both $\sin \theta$ and $\cos \theta$ are negative for $190° \le \theta \le 230°$, so $\left|\frac{\sin \theta}{\cos \theta}\right| = \frac{\sin \theta}{\cos \theta}$.

12. a. magnitude $\sqrt{13}$, direction 33.7°

b. magnitude 13, direction 67.4°

c. magnitude $\sqrt{5}$, direction 63.4°

d. magnitude 5, direction 126.9°

e. magnitude 1, direction 118.1°

f. magnitude 1, direction 236.1°

g. magnitude 25, direction 200°

13. Answers may vary. Sample: Cosine is positive in the first quadrant, negative in the second, negative in the third, and positive in the fourth. Sine is positive in the first and second quadrants and negative

8.7 Graphing Cosine and Sine

In Lesson 8.3, you extended the domain of sine and cosine to all of ℝ. This means that you can graph sin x or cos x against x on a Cartesian graph. One way to do this is to use the completed table on the facing page.

Remember...

ℝ is the set of real numbers.

Consider the sine function first. Notice that the second column in the table starts at 0, climbs to 1, then retreats backs to 0, plunges to -1, and then climbs back up to 0.

For You to Do

1. To get a feeling for the relative sizes, rewrite the sine values as decimal approximations.

Once you get the decimal approximations, you can plot points. If you use your calculator to get decimal approximations for even more sines, you will end up with a graph that looks like this.

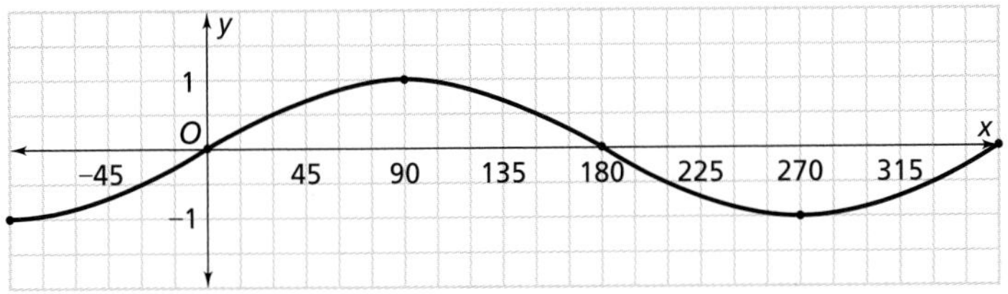

For Discussion

2. Use the fact that sine is periodic to extend the graph to $-360° \leq x \leq 720°$.

For You to Do

3. Sketch the graph of $y = \cos x$ for $-360° \leq x \leq 720°$. Describe how the graph of $y = \cos x$ is related to the graph of $y = \sin x$.

Habits of Mind

Visualize. Because of the symmetry of the graphs, there are many ways to describe this relationship.

Along with the unit circle, the graphs of sine and cosine give you a toolkit that will help you think about the properties of the trigonometric functions.

Lesson Overview

GOAL

- Sketch graphs of sine, cosine, and tangent.

In the On Your Own exercises for the Getting Started lesson, you asked students to sketch graphs for the sine and cosine functions. Now those are graphs are examined in greater detail. Students think about the periodic nature of the graphs, how to use the graphs to solve problems, and how to relate the graphs to what they already know about the unit circle.

CHECK YOUR UNDERSTANDING

- Core: 1, 2, 3, 4, 5, 6, 7, 9, 10
- Optional: none
- Extension: 8

MATERIALS

- graph paper
- graphing calculators
- Blackline Masters 8.7A, 8.7B

HOMEWORK

- Core: 11, 12, 13, 14, 15, 16, 17, 18
- Optional: 19, 20, 21

VOCABULARY

- period

Launch

Begin class with For You to Do Problem 1. Blackline Master 8.7A provides a copy of the table.

Explore

For Discussion

Discuss what it means for a function to be periodic and how to determine the period of such a function. Although it is more correct to talk about the *minimal* period, it is likely that your students will automatically consider the shortest repeating section as the period rather than considering longer sections. If students do not bring it up, you may want to ask them to relate the idea of the period of 360° for the sine function back to the unit circle. You can use Blackline Master 8.7B as a transparency.

in the third and fourth. Tangent is positive in the first quadrant, negative in the second, positive in the third, and negative in the fourth.

For You to Do

1. Decimal approximations for sin θ are 0, 0.5, 0.71, 0.87, 1, 0.87, 0.71, 0.5, 0, −0.5, −0.71, −0.87, −1, −0.87, −0.71, −0.5, 0.

For Discussion

2.

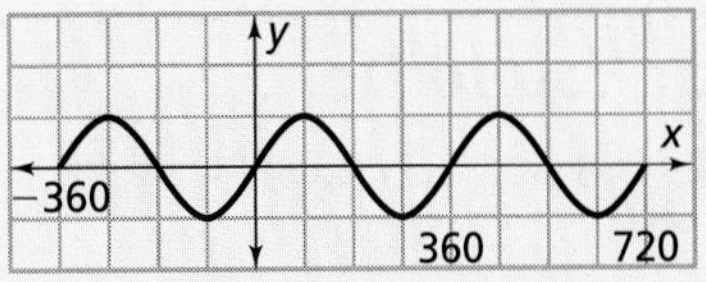

For You to Do

3. See back of book.

Example

If students do not see the connection between the two methods, you can present a visual that links the unit circle representation (Method 2) with the graph of the trigonometric function (Method 1). You can use Blackline Master 8.7B as a transparency.

The comparison using $y = \sin x$ is clearer. As you slowly trace a point from (1, 0) counterclockwise, trace a corresponding point along the graph of $y = \sin x$. The y-heights are always the same. This makes sense, since on the unit circle, the y-height is the y-coordinate of the point, which is $\sin \theta$, and on the graph of $y = \sin x$ the y-height is $\sin x$.

Example

Problem For how many values of α between 0° and 360° is $\cos \alpha = -0.4$? What are they, approximately?

Solution There are two ways to think about this.

Method 1 Use the graph of the function $\cos x = y$. Just as on the graph of any function, the output at x is the y-height above or below x on the graph. So, to find α such that $\cos \alpha = -0.4$, find the intersections of the graphs of $y = -0.4$ and $y = \cos x$.

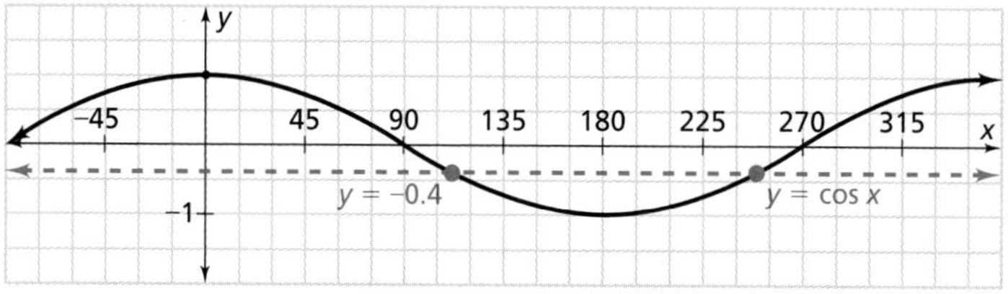

There are two such intersections in the interval $0° \leq x \leq 360°$. And it looks as if the intersections occur at $x \approx 110°$ and $x \approx 250°$. So, $\cos \alpha = -0.4$ for $\alpha \approx 110°$ and $\alpha \approx 250°$.

Method 2 Use the unit circle. On the unit circle, an angle of measure α with vertex at the origin and with initial side containing (1, 0) cuts the circle with its terminal side at $(\cos \alpha, \sin \alpha)$. If you want $\cos \alpha$ to be -0.4, you want to look on the unit circle for points with x-coordinate equal to -0.4.

Once again, we see that there are two such angles between 0° and 360°. They are approximately 110° and 250°.

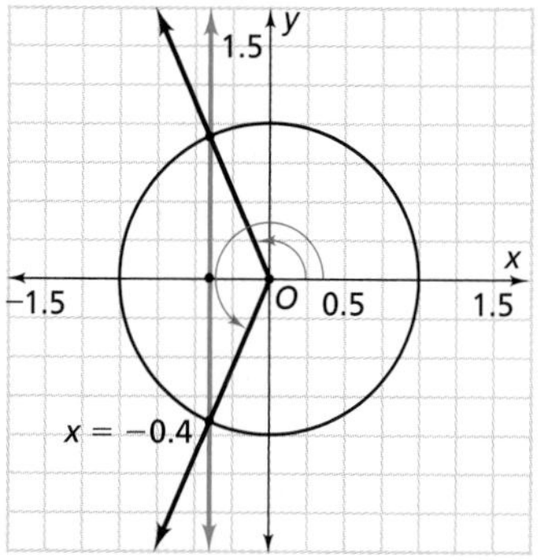

two angles with cosine −0.4

Go Online PHSchool.com

For animated sine and cosine graphs, go to **Web Code**: bfe-9031

For You to Do

4. Use your calculator's $\cos^{-1}$ key to get better approximations of the angles with cosine -0.4. Round to three decimal places.

Answers

For You to Do

4. 113.578°, 246.422°

For You to Do

5. Answers may vary. Sample: $\cos 20° = \cos(-20°)$ because the graph of $y = \cos x$ is symmetric over the y-axis; yes, $\cos x = \cos(-x)$ for all values of x.

Developing Habits of Mind

Consider more than one strategy. These two ways of thinking—using the graphs and using the unit circle—complement each other in many ways. The graph, because of its symmetry, is useful for discovering interesting things like the fact that $\cos 20^\circ = \cos(-20^\circ)$. But the proof of such a fact usually relies on the geometry of the unit circle.

The unit circle is ideal for figuring out exact values for things like $\sin 240^\circ$, because you can use what you know from geometry. The graph is ideal for finding qualitative facts, such as the number of solutions to $\sin x = 0.7$.

For You to Do

5. Explain why $\cos 20^\circ = \cos(-20^\circ)$. Is it always true that $\cos x = \cos(-x)$?

For Discussion

For each question, decide whether it is a good idea to use the unit circle, the graph, or both. Then answer each question.

6. How many solutions are there to $|\sin x| = 1$ for $-360^\circ \le x \le 360^\circ$?
7. Find the solutions to $|\sin x| = 1$ for $-360^\circ \le x \le 360^\circ$.
8. Find a formula for all solutions of $|\sin x| = 1$.

Exercises *Practicing Habits of Mind*

Check Your Understanding

1. The values of $\sin 50^\circ$ and $\sin(-50^\circ)$ are related.
   a. Use the unit circle to describe and illustrate this relationship.
   b. Use the graph of $y = \sin x$ to describe and illustrate this relationship.
2. **What's Wrong Here?** Derman uses his graphing calculator to sketch the graph of $y = \sin x$. As is his custom, he sets the window so that x and y go from -10 to 10. He is surprised by what he sees. Describe what Derman sees. How can he fix the problem?

To help Derman, see the TI-Nspire Handbook, p. 778.

For Discussion

6. 4
7. $-270^\circ, -90^\circ, 90^\circ, 270^\circ$
8. $x = 90^\circ + k \cdot 180^\circ$, where k is an integer

Exercises

1. a. The points on the unit circle that represent $\sin 50^\circ$ and $\sin(-50^\circ)$ have opposite y-values. So, $\sin 50^\circ = -\sin(-50^\circ)$.
   b. The y-values for $x = 50^\circ$ and $x = -50^\circ$ on the graph of $y = \sin x$ are opposites. So, $\sin 50^\circ = -\sin(-50^\circ)$.
2. Answers may vary. Sample: Derman sees only a portion of $y = \sin x$, and all the y-values are close to the x-axis. He should reset his window so that $-360 \le x \le 360$ and $-2 \le y \le 2$.

For You to Do

Students will work through a similar argument for the graph of $y = \sin x$ in Exercise 1.

For Discussion

PROBLEM 6 is probably easiest to answer with a graph, but it could just be a graph of $y = \sin x$ and you could visualize what the absolute value does to the graph. There are four solutions.

PROBLEM 7 To figure out *where* the sine function has absolute value 1, students might be more comfortable using the unit circle, because they can just locate angles with corresponding points on the y-axis.

Wrap Up

You may want to go over Exercise 2, because it is important for students to figure out how to set the graphing window of their calculator to get useful graphs of trigonometric functions. See the TI-Nspire Handbook on page 778 for more advice on doing this. As time allows, go over other core Check Your Understanding exercises.

Assessment Resources

Lesson Quiz 8.7

1. Draw a picture to explain why $\cos(180^\circ + x) = -\cos x$.
2. Sketch the graph of $f(x) = \cos x - \sin x$ for at least two periods.
3. Below are the graphs of $y = \sin x$ and $y = -0.6$ on the same axes. Find all values of x between 0° and 360° that solve the equation $\sin x = -0.6$, to the nearest degree.

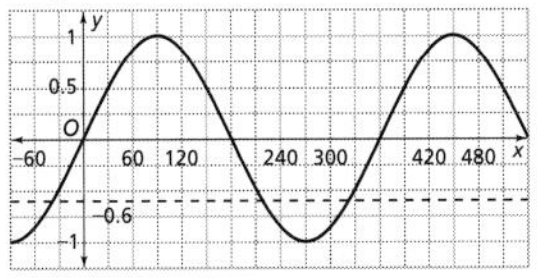

Exercises

HOMEWORK
- Core: 11, 12, 13, 14, 15, 16, 17, 18
- Optional: 19, 20, 21

Check Your Understanding

EXERCISE 1 Encourage students to use both representations. They can use one to check the other.

EXERCISE 2 Check to see that students know how to set the graphing window on their calculators to make useful graphs of trigonometric functions.

EXERCISE 5 Students will not have a way of explaining why this graph appears to be the same as the graph of cosine until the lesson on Angle-Sum Identities, but we hope this exercise piques their interest.

EXERCISE 6 Students may have a better idea of why this graph appears to be the same as the graph of sine, because they have probably noticed that the graph of cosine is a translation of the graph of sine.

EXERCISE 8 Some students may not expect the factor of 2 to affect the period of the graph, but encourage them to look at the graph generated by their calculator and make sense of it for themselves.

EXERCISE 9 Some students may solve this by thinking about where the line $y = x$ intersects the unit circle.

On Your Own

EXERCISES 11 AND 12 will be referred to in the lesson on Angle-Sum Identities. Cosine is an even function, and sine is an odd function.

3. Sketch the graph of $f(x) = \cos(x + 360°)$. Describe why the graph looks the way it does.

4. a. How many x-intercepts does the graph of $y = \cos x$ have?

b. Explain why the cosine function cannot be a polynomial function.

c. Where is the tangent function undefined? Explain.

Consider the entire graph, not just a small section.

5. Sketch the graph of $f(x) = \sin(30° + x) + \sin(30° - x)$.

6. Sketch the graph of $g(x) = \cos(x - 90°)$.

7. Here are the graphs of $y = \sin x$ and $y = 0.6$ on the same axes.

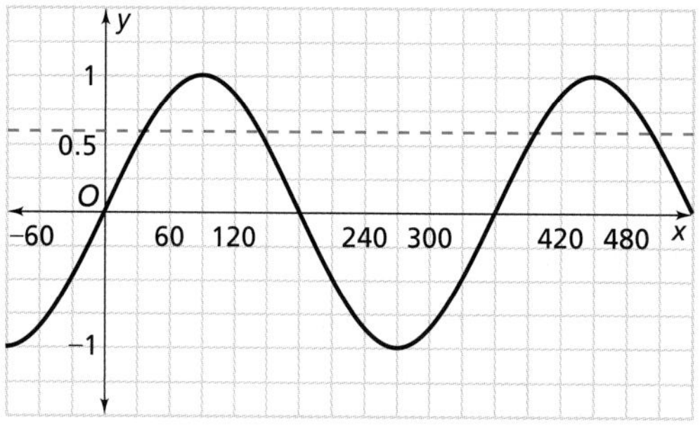

The least positive value of x that solves $\sin x = 0.6$ is about 53°. Find the next two values of x, to the nearest degree, that solve the equation.

8. **Take It Further** Sketch the graph of $k(x) = \cos 2x$ without the aid of a graphing calculator. Then use a calculator to check your work.

9. a. Sketch the graphs of $f(x) = \cos x$ and $g(x) = \sin x$ on the same axes.

b. Use the graphs to find two angles θ for which $\sin\theta = \cos\theta$.

10. a. For each angle θ you found in Exercise 9, find $\tan\theta$.

b. If $\sin\theta = \cos\theta$, prove that $\tan\theta = 1$.

On Your Own

11. Draw a picture to explain why $\cos(-\theta) = \cos\theta$.

12. Draw a picture to explain why $\sin(-\theta) = -\sin\theta$.

13. Sketch the graph of $s(x) = \cos^2 x + \sin^2 x$.

14. **Standardized Test Prep** Which function has the same graph as $y = \sin x$?

A. $y = 180° + \cos x$ **B.** $y = -\sin x$

C. $y = \sin(x + 360°)$ **D.** $y = 2\sin x$

Habits of Mind

Make strategic choices. For Exercises 11 and 12, should you draw a unit circle or a graph? You decide.

Answers

3.

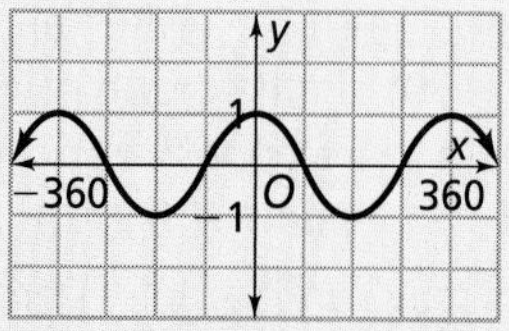

The graph looks like $y = \cos x$ because $\cos(x + 360°) = \cos x$.

4. a. There are infinitely many x-intercepts of $y = \cos x$.

b. A polynomial function must have a finite degree and a finite number of x-intercepts, so the cosine function cannot be written as a polynomial function.

c. The tangent function, $\frac{\sin\theta}{\cos\theta}$, is undefined when $\cos\theta = 0$, that is when $\theta = 90° + k \cdot 180°$, where k is an integer.

5–14. See back of book.

15. Below are the graphs of $y = \cos x$ and $y = 0.8$ on the same axes. The least positive value of x that solves $\cos x = 0.8$ is about 37°. Find the next two values of x that solve the equation, to the nearest degree.

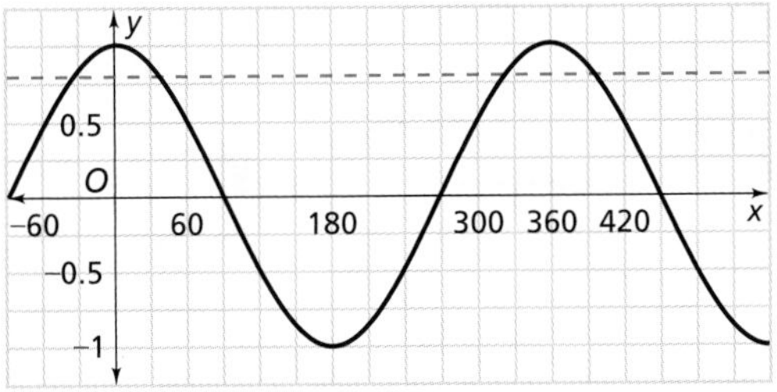

16. Use the unit circle or graphs to illustrate that each identity is true for all θ.

a. $\sin(180° - \theta) = \sin\theta$
b. $\cos(180° - \theta) = -\cos\theta$
c. $\sin(180° + \theta) = -\sin\theta$
d. $\cos(360° - \theta) = \cos\theta$
e. $\sin\theta = \cos(\theta - 90°)$
f. $\cos\theta = -\sin(\theta - 90°)$

17. Sketch the graph of $h(x) = -\sin x$ for at least two periods.

18. Describe the graph of $h(x) = -\sin x$ as a translation of the graph of $g(x) = \sin x$.

19. Sketch an accurate graph of each function.

a. $j(x) = \cos^2 x - \sin^2 x$
b. $r(x) = \cos 2x$
c. $k(x) = \cos^4 x - \sin^4 x$

Go Online PHSchool.com

For additional practice, go to **Web Code:** bfa-0807

A **period** is a full cycle of the wave: up, down, and back again. It is the smallest piece that you can repeat over and over to produce the entire graph.

Maintain Your Skills

20. The graph below in black shows a portion of the graph of $y = \cos x$. Find the coordinates of each marked point.

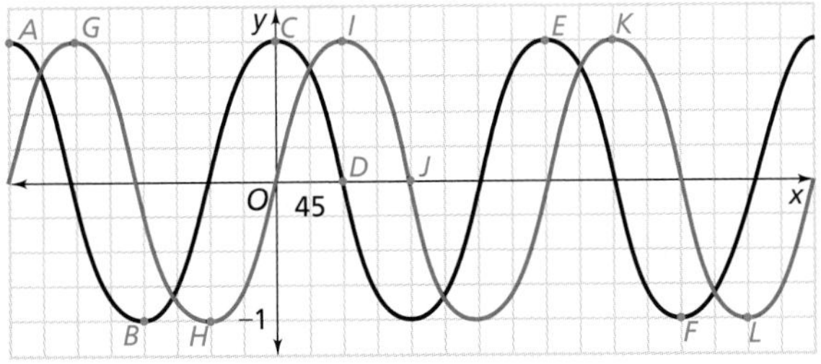

21. The graph above in red shows a portion of the graph of $y = \sin x$. Find the coordinates of each marked point.

15. 323°, 397°

16–17. See back of book.

18. Answers may vary. Sample: The graph of $h(x) = -\sin x$ is a translation of $g(x) = \sin x$ by 180° to the right or left.

19. a–c. The graphs of $y = \cos^2 x - \sin^2 x$, $y = \cos 2x$, and $y = \cos^4 x - \sin^4 x$ are identical.

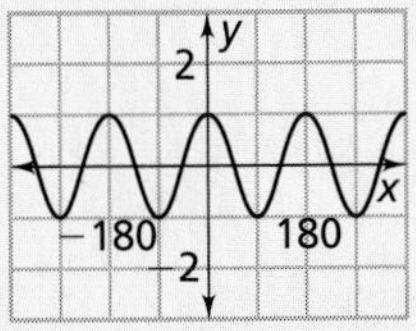

20. $A = (-360°, 1)$, $B = (-180°, -1)$, $C = (0°, 1)$, $D = (90°, 0)$, $E = (360°, 1)$, $F = (540°, -1)$

21. $G = (-270°, 1)$, $H = (-90°, -1)$, $I = (90°, 1)$, $J = (180°, 0)$, $K = (450°, 1)$, $L = (630°, -1)$

EXERCISE 16 These are all specific cases of the Angle-Sum Identities.

EXERCISE 19 Students who work this exercise along with Exercise 8 may be intrigued by the fact that the graphs appear identical. Indeed, they are the same function. An earlier exercise showed that $\cos^4 x - \sin^4 x = \cos^2 x - \sin^2 x$, and this is one of the formulas for $\cos 2x$ that students will learn later.

Maintain Your Skills

EXERCISES 20 AND 21 are meant to reinforce the identity $\sin x = \cos(x - 90°)$, since each point on the sine wave is translated 90 degrees to the right from a corresponding point on the cosine wave.

Additional Resources

PRINT RESOURCES
- Solution Manual
- Practice Workbook
- Assessment Resources
- Teaching Resources

TECHNOLOGY
- Interactive Textbook
- TeacherExpress CD-ROM
- ExamView CD-ROM
- PHSchool.com

Additional Practice

1. Draw a picture to explain why $\sin\theta = \cos(\theta + 90°)$.

2. Sketch the graph of $f(x) = \cos^2 x - \sin^2 x$.

3. Below are the graphs of $y = \cos x$ and $y = 0.4$ on the same axes. The least positive value of x that solves $\cos x = 0.4$ is about 66°. Find all values of x between 0° and 360° that solve the equation, to the nearest degree.

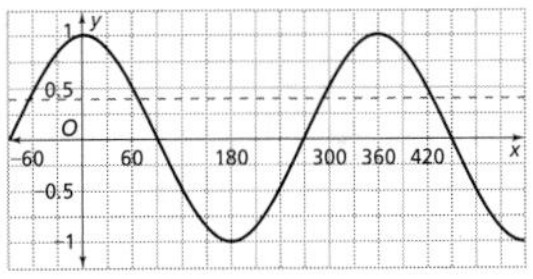

4. a. Sketch the graph of $f(x) = -\cos x$ for at least two periods.
b. Describe the graph of $f(x) = -\cos x$ as a translation of the graph of $g(x) = \cos x$.

5. Give two different explanations for why the tangent function is positive in Quadrant I, but negative in Quadrant IV.

6. a. Sketch the graph of $y = \tan x$.
b. Approximate the solutions to the equation $\tan x = 3$.
c. Approximate the solutions to the equation $\tan x = -3$.

7. a. Sketch the graph of $f(x) = -\tan x$ for at least two periods.
b. Describe the graph of $f(x) = -\tan x$ as a transformation of the graph of $g(x) = \tan x$.

8. Explain how the graph of the tangent function suggests that $\tan(180° - x) = \tan x$.

Practice: For Lesson 8.7, assign Exercises 1–4.

Lesson Overview

GOALS

- Sketch graphs of sine, cosine, and tangent.
- Use the graphs of trigonometric functions to solve problems.

Students build the graph of $y = \tan x$, giving special consideration to what happens to the value of tangent as it approaches its undefined values. They also learn a way to represent tangent in the coordinates of a point associated with the angle and the unit circle as they have done for sine and cosine: Visualize a line tangent to the unit circle at the point $(1, 0)$. Students prove that the line through the origin and the point P associated with the angle θ on the unit circle intersects this tangent line in a point T with coordinates $(1, \tan \theta)$.

CHECK YOUR UNDERSTANDING

- Core: 1, 2, 3, 4, 5, 7
- Optional: 6, 8

MATERIALS

- graph paper
- graphing calculators
- Blackline Masters 8.7A, 8.8A, 8.8B

HOMEWORK

- Core: 9, 10, 11, 12, 14
- Optional: 15
- Extension: 13

VOCABULARY

- discontinuity

Launch

You might begin this lesson by asking students what they predict the graph of the tangent function will look like. Write the definition of the function $\tan x = \frac{\sin x}{\cos x}$ on the board to help students think about how the function behaves. After recording students' predictions, move on to the Developing Habits of Mind section.

8.8 Graphing the Tangent Function

You have extended the definition of tangent to $\tan x = \frac{\sin x}{\cos x}$, whenever $\cos x \neq 0$. In other words, tangent is defined for all real numbers except odd multiples of 90°. In this lesson, you will build the graph of $y = \tan x$. First, however, note this interesting way to picture the tangent.

Developing Habits of Mind

Visualize. Why do you call it *tangent*? The diagrams below show a tangent to the unit circle at (1, 0). The angle x is shown in each of the four quadrants.

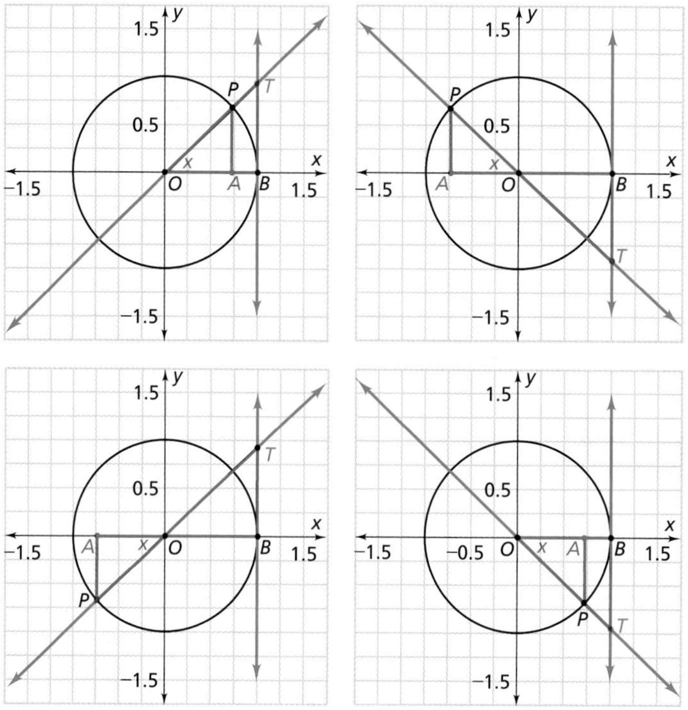

In each case, $\triangle POA \sim \triangle TOB$, so $\frac{TB}{OB} = \frac{PA}{OA}$.

But $OB = 1$, so $TB =$ the length of the tangent $= \frac{PA}{OA}$.

You can use this to show that the coordinates of T are $(1, \tan x)$. So you measure $\tan x$ along the tangent.

For Discussion

1. Finish the argument above by showing that the coordinates of T are $(1, \tan x)$.
2. What happens when the angle is 90° or 270°?

Check the signs.

For You to Do

3. What happens to $\tan x$ for values of x close to, but slightly less than, 90°?
4. What happens to $\tan x$ for values of x close to, but slightly greater than, 90°?

Along with the definition of the tangent function, some other information may help you think about the shape of the graph of $y = \tan x$.

The familiar completed table below shows some values of $\tan \theta$.

θ	$\cos \theta$	$\sin \theta$	$\tan \theta$
0°	1	0	0
30°	$\frac{\sqrt{3}}{2}$	$\frac{1}{2}$	$\frac{1}{\sqrt{3}}$
45°	$\frac{\sqrt{2}}{2}$	$\frac{\sqrt{2}}{2}$	1
60°	$\frac{1}{2}$	$\frac{\sqrt{3}}{2}$	$\sqrt{3}$
90°	0	1	undefined
120°	$-\frac{1}{2}$	$\frac{\sqrt{3}}{2}$	$-\sqrt{3}$
135°	$-\frac{\sqrt{2}}{2}$	$\frac{\sqrt{2}}{2}$	-1
150°	$-\frac{\sqrt{3}}{2}$	$\frac{1}{2}$	$-\frac{1}{\sqrt{3}}$
180°	-1	0	0
210°	$-\frac{\sqrt{3}}{2}$	$-\frac{1}{2}$	$\frac{1}{\sqrt{3}}$
225°	$-\frac{\sqrt{2}}{2}$	$-\frac{\sqrt{2}}{2}$	1
240°	$-\frac{1}{2}$	$-\frac{\sqrt{3}}{2}$	$\sqrt{3}$
270°	0	-1	undefined
300°	$\frac{1}{2}$	$-\frac{\sqrt{3}}{2}$	$-\sqrt{3}$
315°	$\frac{\sqrt{2}}{2}$	$-\frac{\sqrt{2}}{2}$	-1
330°	$\frac{\sqrt{3}}{2}$	$-\frac{1}{2}$	$-\frac{1}{\sqrt{3}}$
360°	1	0	0

Habits of Mind

Detect the key characterisitics. Notice that the tangent function is undefined for some angles. This happens when you try to divide by 0. Look at what happens close to these points of **discontinuity.**

Answers

For Discussion

1. Answers may vary. Sample: $TB = \frac{PA}{OA} = \tan x$, so the coordinates of T, which are (OB, BT), can be rewritten as $(1, \tan x)$.
2. The value of OA is 0, so the value of $TB = \frac{PA}{OA}$ is undefined.

For You to Do

3. If x is slightly less than 90°, $\tan x$ is a very large positive number.
4. If x is slightly greater than 90°, $\tan x$ is negative with a very large absolute value.

Explore

In-Class Experiment

Blackline Master 8.7A provides a copy of the completed trigonometric function table. Blackline Master 8.8A provides a blank graph for students to complete.

Wrap Up

Check students' graph of the tangent function. Blackline Master 8.8B shows the completed tangent graph. You can use it as a transparency. Then have students continue on to the core Check Your Understanding exercises. Go over as many of these exercises as time allows.

Assessment Resources

Lesson Quiz 8.8

1. a. What is the domain of the tangent function? Give a complete answer, not just one for angles from 0° to 360°.
   b. What is the range of the tangent function?

2. a. Sketch the graph of $y = \tan x$.
   b. Approximate the solutions to the equation $\tan x = 2.5$.
   c. Approximate the solutions to the equation $\tan x = -2.5$.

3. a. Use the graph of $y = \tan x$ to sketch an accurate graph of $\tan(90° - x)$.
   b. How does $\tan(90° - x)$ relate to $y = \frac{1}{\tan x}$? Explain.

The discussion and graphs in Developing Habits of Mind show that $\tan x$ is the coordinate of a point related to x.

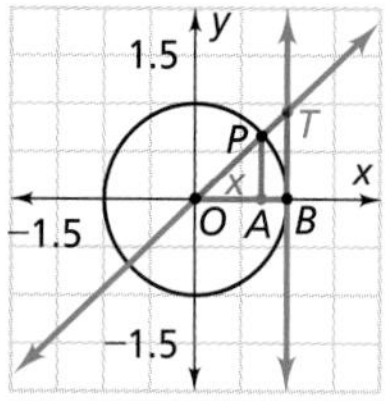

$T(1, \tan x)$

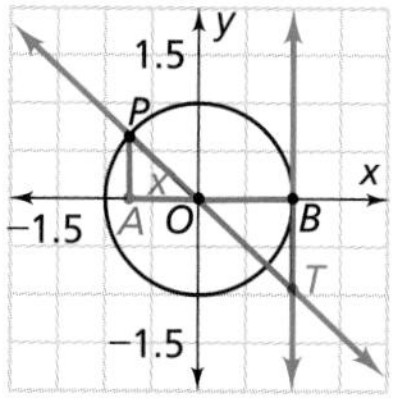

$T(1, \tan x)$

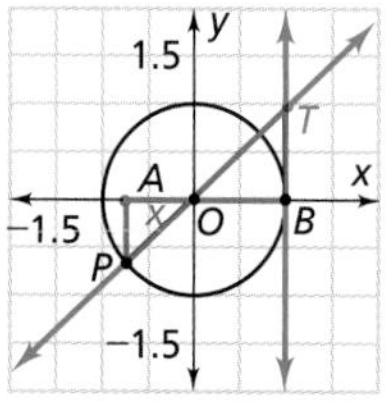

$T(1, \tan x)$

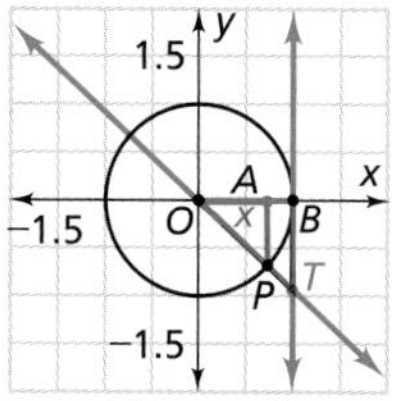

$T(1, \tan x)$

In-Class Experiment

5. Use these ideas or any other information you have to carefully draw the graph of $y = \tan x$. Label the coordinates of all points you plot.

For Discussion

6. Explain why the tangent function is periodic. What is its period?

The periods of the traffic lights are set to manage the flow of traffic.

Answers

In-Class Experiment

5. Check students' graphs for coordinate labels.

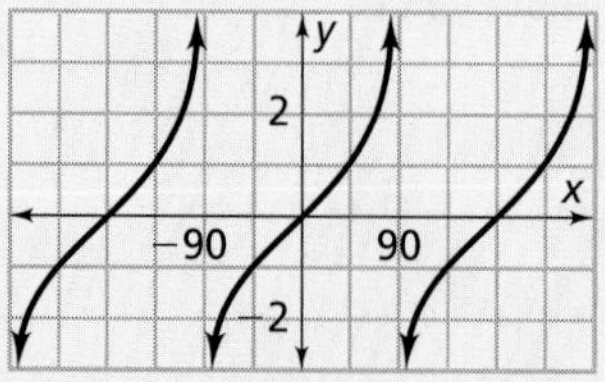

For Discussion

6. The tangent function is periodic because it has a set of y-values that repeat regularly; 180°.

Exercises

1. a.

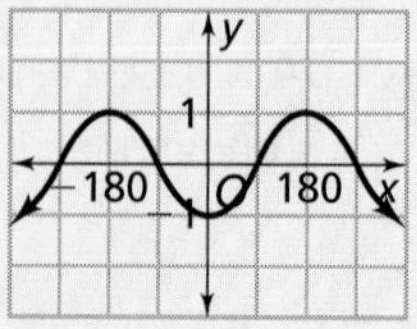

Exercises *Practicing Habits of Mind*

Check Your Understanding

1. **a.** Explain why $\cos(180^\circ + \theta) = -\cos\theta$.
   b. Explain why $\sin(180^\circ + \theta) = -\sin\theta$.
2. Use the results from Exercise 1 to explain why $\tan(180^\circ + \theta) = \tan\theta$.
3. Suppose θ is in Quadrant I and $\tan\theta = \frac{2}{3}$.
   a. Draw a right triangle in the unit circle to indicate the location of θ.
   b. Find the exact values of $\sin\theta$ and $\cos\theta$.
4. Suppose θ is in Quadrant I and $\tan\theta = \frac{2}{3}$.
   a. Find the value of $\tan(90^\circ + \theta)$ in terms of $\tan\theta$.
   b. Suppose that ℓ is a line. Show that the slope of ℓ is the tangent of the angle ℓ makes with the positive x-axis.
   c. Show that two lines are perpendicular if and only if their slopes are negative reciprocals.
5. As stated at the beginning of this lesson, cosine is equal to 0 for odd multiples of 90°. Explain why this is true.
6. Find the argument of each complex number to the nearest degree.
   a. $4 + i$
   b. $(4 + i)^2$
   c. $-1 + 4i$
   d. $(-1 + 4i)^2$
7. Find each angle to the nearest degree.
   a. θ is in Quadrant I, and $\tan\theta = \frac{1}{4}$.
   b. θ is in Quadrant I, and $\tan\theta = \frac{8}{15}$.
   c. θ is in Quadrant II, and $\tan\theta = -4$.
   d. θ is in Quadrant III, and $\tan\theta = \frac{8}{15}$.
8. **a.** Calculate $(x + yi)^2$ and write the results in the form ■ + ■i.
   b. Suppose $\tan\theta = \frac{y}{x}$. Find an expression for $\tan 2\theta$, the tangent of twice the given angle.

From the graph, $\cos(180^\circ + \theta)$ and $-\cos\theta$ are equal for any given θ, so $\cos(180^\circ + \theta) = -\cos\theta$.

b.

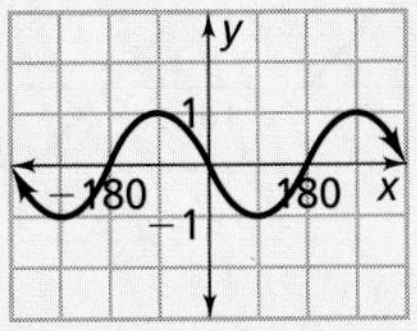

From the graph, $\sin(180^\circ + \theta)$ and $-\sin\theta$ are equal for any given θ, so $\sin(180^\circ + \theta) = -\sin\theta$.

2. $\tan(180^\circ + \theta) = \dfrac{\sin(180^\circ + \theta)}{\cos(180^\circ + \theta)} = \dfrac{-\sin\theta}{-\cos\theta} = \tan\theta$

3. a.

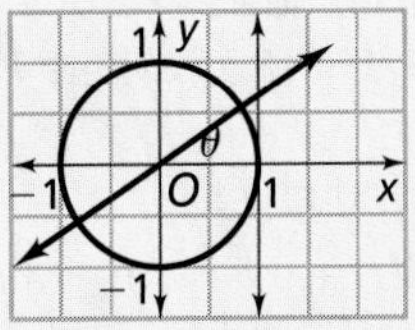

b. $\sin\theta = \dfrac{2\sqrt{13}}{13}$, $\cos\theta = \dfrac{3\sqrt{13}}{13}$

4–8. See back of book.

Exercises

HOMEWORK
- Core: 9, 10, 11, 12, 14
- Optional: 15
- Extension: 13

Check Your Understanding

EXERCISES 1 AND 2 help students see why the period of the tangent function is different than the periods of sine and cosine. In Exercise 2, remind students to think back to the definition of tangent if they are having trouble.

EXERCISE 3 There are other ways to approach this exercise. Some students may use the fact that the triangle with legs 1 and $\frac{2}{3}$ and hypotenuse $\frac{\sqrt{13}}{3}$ is similar to the triangle with legs $\cos x$, $\sin x$, and hypotenuse 1, and compute exact values of $\sin x$ and $\cos x$ by comparing ratios of corresponding sides between the two triangles.

EXERCISE 4 Rather than using the "unique parallel" argument to cover lines that do not pass through the origin or intersect at the origin, some students may use the idea that a translation does not change the slope of a line. They may translate their lines (or their intersection) to the origin.

EXERCISE 7 helps students gain experience interpreting the inverse tangent function on their calculator. It returns only values between −90° and 90°, so for angles in Quadrants II and III, students need to think about the unit circle or the graph of tangent to find the correct angle.

EXERCISE 8 gives a way to think about producing a formula for $\tan 2\theta$. In the next lesson, students learn a different proof of this trigonometric identity.

On Your Own

EXERCISE 11 encourages students to use the graph of the tangent function as a tool for estimating solutions to simple trigonometric equations. This activity helps students understand more concretely the results their calculators produce.

EXERCISE 13 This graph is not the same as the graph of $y = \cot x$. The cotangent function, $y = \cot x$, is equal to $\frac{1}{\tan x}$ only where $\tan x$ has a defined value (and where it is nonzero). Cotangent is formally defined as $\frac{\cos x}{\sin x}$.

Maintain Your Skills

EXERCISE 15 is a preview of Lesson 8.9, an example of the rule $\sin(a + b) = \sin a \cos b + \cos a \sin b$.

Additional Resources

PRINT RESOURCES
- Solution Manual
- Practice Workbook
- Assessment Resources
- Teaching Resources

TECHNOLOGY
- Interactive Textbook
- TeacherExpress CD-ROM
- ExamView CD-ROM
- PHSchool.com

Additional Practice

1. Draw a picture to explain why $\sin\theta = \cos(\theta + 90°)$.

2. Sketch the graph of $f(x) = \cos^2 x - \sin^2 x$.

3. Below are the graphs of $y = \cos x$ and $y = 0.4$ on the same axes. The least positive value of x that solves $\cos x = 0.4$ is about 66°. Find all values of x between 0° and 360° that solve the equation, to the nearest degree.

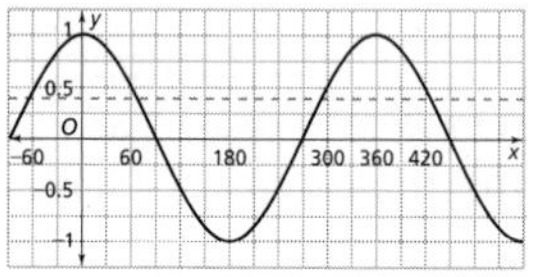

4. a. Sketch the graph of $f(x) = -\cos x$ for at least two periods.
   b. Describe the graph of $f(x) = -\cos x$ as a translation of the graph of $g(x) = \cos x$.

5. Give two different explanations for why the tangent function is positive in Quadrant I, but negative in Quadrant IV.

6. a. Sketch the graph of $y = \tan x$.
   b. Approximate the solutions to the equation $\tan x = 3$.
   c. Approximate the solutions to the equation $\tan x = -3$.

7. a. Sketch the graph of $f(x) = -\tan x$ for at least two periods.
   b. Describe the graph of $f(x) = -\tan x$ as a transformation of the graph of $g(x) = \tan x$.

8. Explain how the graph of the tangent function suggests that $\tan(180° - x) = \tan x$.

Practice: For Lesson 8.8, assign Exercises 5–8.

On Your Own

9. **Write About It** Give two different explanations for why the tangent function is positive in Quadrant III but negative in Quadrant II.

10. a. What is the domain of the tangent function? Give a complete answer, not just one for angles from 0° to 360°.
    b. What is the range of the tangent function?

Go Online PHSchool.com
For additional practice, go to **Web Code:** bfa-0808

This graph of $y = \tan x$ may be helpful for Exercises 11–13.

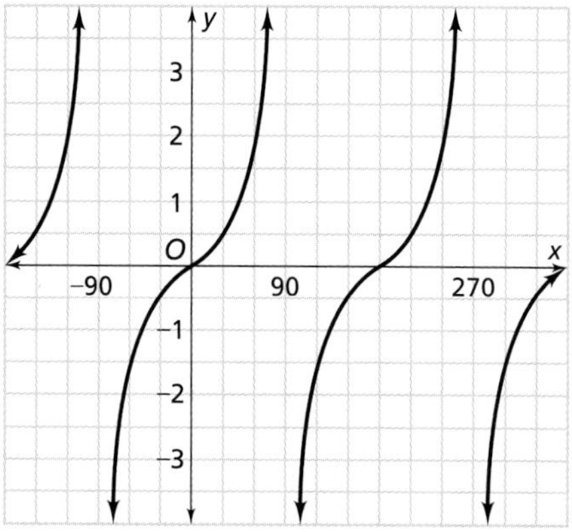

11. a. Approximate the solutions to the equation $\tan x = 2$.
    b. Approximate the solutions to the equation $\tan x = -2$.

12. Explain how the graph of the tangent function suggests that $\tan(180° + x) = \tan x$.

13. **Take It Further** Use the graph of $y = \tan x$ to sketch an accurate graph of the function $y = \frac{1}{\tan x}$.

Habits of Mind
Experiment. Where is tangent undefined?

14. **Standardized Test Prep** Use the equation $\tan(A + B) = \frac{\tan A + \tan B}{1 - (\tan A)(\tan B)}$. What is the value of $\tan 2\theta$ if $\tan\theta = \frac{1}{2}$?

A. $\frac{3}{4}$ **B.** 1 **C.** $\frac{4}{3}$ **D.** 2

Maintain Your Skills

15. For each angle θ, calculate $\sin(120° + \theta)$.
    a. $\theta = 0°$ b. $\theta = 30°$ c. $\theta = 60°$ d. $\theta = 90°$
    e. Suppose $\sin(120° + \theta) = A\cos\theta + B\sin\theta$. Find the values of A and B.

Answers

9. See back of book.

10. a. all real numbers except $90° + k \cdot 180°$, where k is an integer
    b. all real numbers

11. a. $x \approx 65° + k \cdot 180°$, where k is an integer
    b. $x \approx 115° + k \cdot 180°$, where k is an integer

12. The graph of $y = \tan x$ shows that it is periodic with period 180°, so $\tan(180° + x) = \tan x$.

13.

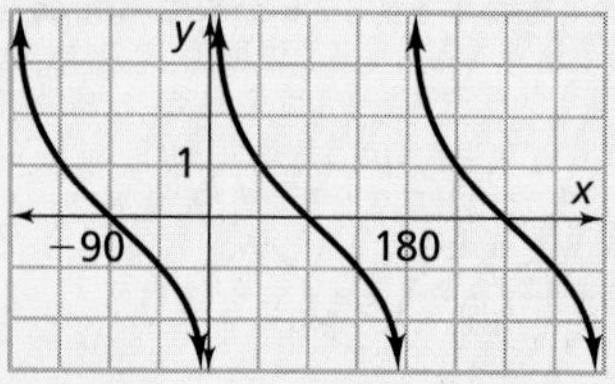

14. C

15. a. $\frac{\sqrt{3}}{2}$ b. $\frac{1}{2}$
    c. 0 d. $-\frac{1}{2}$
    e. $A = \frac{\sqrt{3}}{2}$, $B = -\frac{1}{2}$

8.9 The Angle-Sum Identities

If you look back at the results of some of the problems you have solved in this chapter, you can see a thread that has woven its way through many of them. For example, Exercise 16 from Lesson 8.7 and Exercises 1 and 2 from Lesson 8.8 give some interesting identities.

For all x:

- $\sin(180° - x) = \sin x$
- $\cos(180° - x) = -\cos x$
- $\cos(360° - x) = \cos x$
- $\sin x = \cos(x - 90°)$
- $\cos x = -\sin(x - 90°)$
- $\cos(180° + x) = -\cos x$
- $\sin(180° + x) = -\sin x$
- $\tan(180° + x) = \tan x$

All of these identities have the same form. They give an alternate expression for $f(a + b)$, where f is a trigonometric function and a and b are numbers. Usually when you see a collection of identities with the same form, there are a few general identities lurking in the background that tie all the special identities together.

Habits of Mind

Look for relationships. For example, $25 - 9 = (5 + 3)(5 - 3)$, $49 - 25 = (7 + 5)(7 - 5)$, and $x^2 - 1 = (x - 1)(x + 1)$ are all special cases of the general identity $a^2 - b^2 = (a + b)(a - b)$. An important part of algebra is looking for general identities that yield many special ones.

For You to Do

Derman says, "I bet $\sin(\alpha + \beta) = \sin\alpha + \sin\beta$ for all numbers α and β."

1. Help Derman see that this is not an identity.
2. Do any values of α and β make Derman's equation work? If so, find them.
3. Is $\cos(\alpha + \beta) = \cos\alpha + \cos\beta$ an identity for all α and β? Explain.

Can you find a function f such that $f(a + b) = f(a) + f(b)$ for all numbers a and b?

So, Derman's try at a formula for $\sin(\alpha + \beta)$, while simple, is not correct. The purpose of this lesson is to come up with formulas for $\sin(\alpha + \beta)$ and $\cos(\alpha + \beta)$ that are true for all values of α and β. The main result is the following theorem.

Lesson Overview

GOAL

- Prove and use trigonometric identities.

In this lesson, students look back at several identities they have proven and realize that many of them are of the same form: writing a simpler expression for a trigonometric function of the sum of two angles. They see how all these identities can be expressed with a much smaller set of general identities for the sine and cosine of a sum. You expose them to three different ideas for proving the general result: using rotated triangles, coordinate geometry, and complex numbers. Encourage them to take one of the ideas and work through the proof to understand it completely. This lesson is optional because it is not core material that students need to complete this course, but the material in this lesson will be extremely helpful for students continuing on to precalculus.

CHECK YOUR UNDERSTANDING

- Core: 1, 2, 3
- Optional: 5, 6
- Extension: 4, 7

MATERIALS

- graph paper
- graphing calculators
- Blackline Master 8.9

HOMEWORK

- Core: 8, 9, 10, 11, 13, 14, 16, 17
- Optional: 12
- Extension: 15

Launch

Start this lesson by making sure that students see how all of the identities can be thought of as Angle-Sum Identities. You can use Blackline Master 8.9. Then go on to the For You to Do problems.

For You to Do

1. Answers may vary. Sample: Let $\alpha = 45°$ and $\beta = 45°$. Then $\sin(45° + 45°) = \sin 90° = 1$, but $\sin 45° + \sin 45° = \frac{\sqrt{2}}{2} + \frac{\sqrt{2}}{2} = \sqrt{2}$, and $1 \neq \sqrt{2}$.
2. Answers may vary. Sample: $\alpha = 90°$, $\beta = 0°$
3. No; let $\alpha = 45°$ and $\beta = 45°$. Then $\cos(45° + 45°) = \cos 90° = 0$, but $\cos 45° + \cos 45° = \frac{\sqrt{2}}{2} + \frac{\sqrt{2}}{2} = \sqrt{2}$, and $0 \neq \sqrt{2}$.

Explore

One way to cover this lesson is to state Theorem 8.3 and then assign the Pick a Proof as a take-home assignment. Students could work on this task independently or in groups outside of class for a few days. They should decide which proof to study and then write it up in their own words. You may wish to devote some class time to having groups share their write-ups.

PROOF 1 (ROTATED TRIANGLES) The steps for working through cosine are similar. You can start with the same images to get $\alpha + \beta$. The cosine of $\alpha + \beta$ is the x-coordinate of B, which is the length of $\overline{OJ}$.

***Theorem 8.3** Angle-Sum Identities*

For all α and β,

- $\cos(\alpha + \beta) = \cos\alpha\cos\beta - \sin\alpha\sin\beta$
- $\sin(\alpha + \beta) = \sin\alpha\cos\beta + \cos\alpha\sin\beta$

Identities that involve functions, such as $\cos(\alpha + \beta) = \cos\alpha\cos\beta - \sin\alpha\sin\beta$ or $\log_2 ab = \log_2 a + \log_2 b$, are functional equations.

Pick a Proof

This time, you will find the formula and build the proof. In this section, there are three sketches of a derivation for the formulas you want. Your job is to pick a method, study it, and write it up in your own words. You will fill in all the missing steps and explain all the statements.

Habits of Mind

Work like a mathematician. An important part of learning mathematics is learning to read mathematics and to fill in the gaps for yourself.

Proof 1 (Rotated Triangles) This derivation uses the unit circle definitions of sine and cosine. Here you will look at sine. (You can look at cosine on your own.) In the graph below, $AD = \sin\alpha$ and $BK = \sin\beta$.

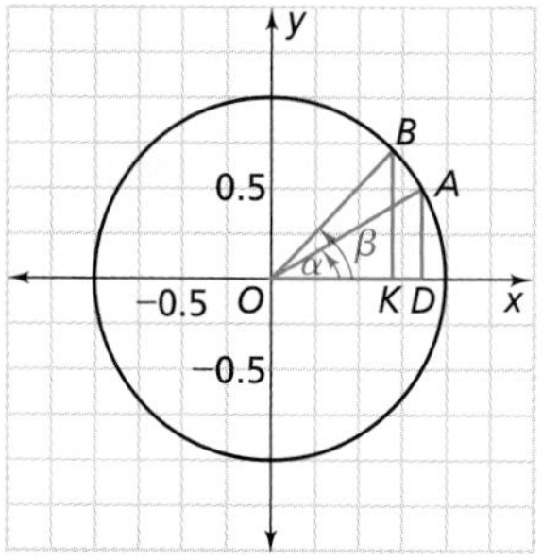

You want a picture of $\sin(\alpha + \beta)$. To get an $\alpha + \beta$ in the picture, rotate $\triangle OBK$ upward through an angle of α.

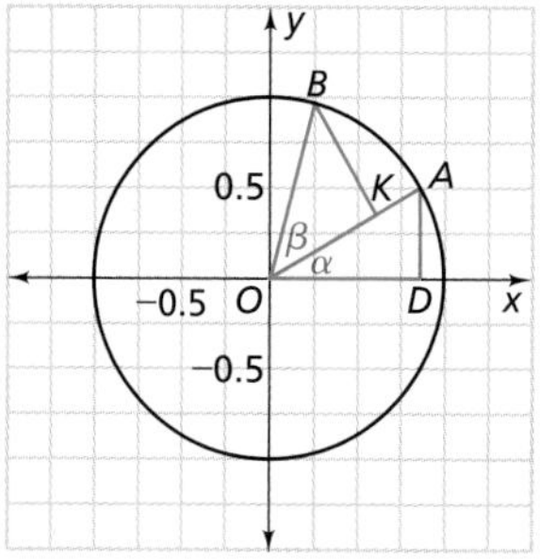

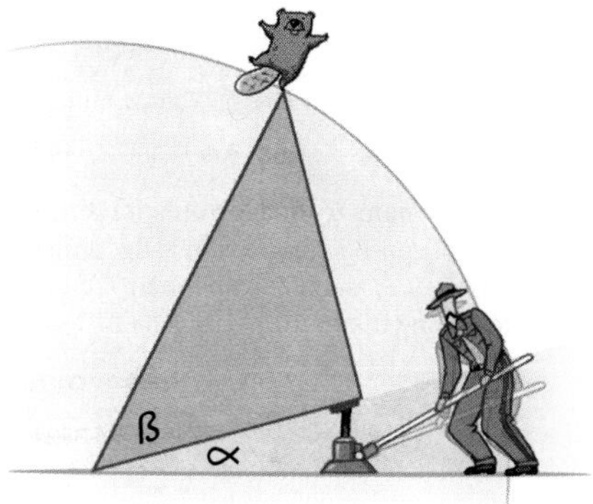

The sine of $\alpha + \beta$ is the y-height of B—the length of the perpendicular from B to the x-axis. Copy the diagram below. Make sure the segments are parallel and perpendicular to the appropriate axes.

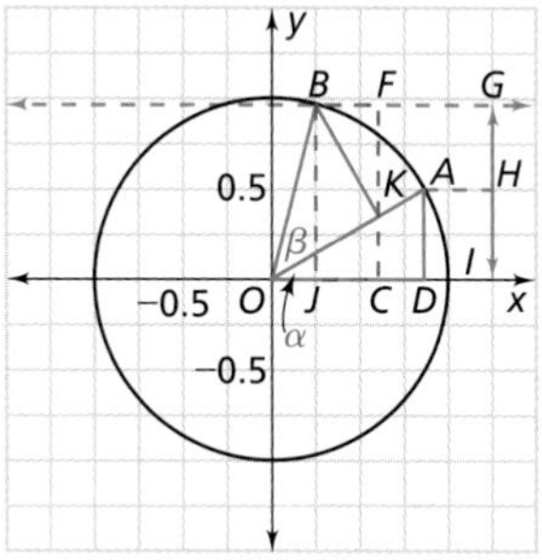

Here is where the work really starts. You need to justify these basic steps.

Step 1 $BJ = \sin(\alpha + \beta)$, $BK = \sin\beta$, and $AD = \sin\alpha$.

Step 2 Also, $KO = \cos\beta$ and $DO = \cos\alpha$.

Step 3 $\sin(\alpha + \beta) = IH + HG$

Step 4 $IH = KC$

Step 5 Now, to get KC, prove that $\triangle KCO \sim \triangle ADO$, so

$$\frac{KC}{KO} = \frac{AD}{AO}$$

Step 6 Use Steps 1 and 2 to conclude that

$$\frac{KC}{\cos\beta} = \frac{\sin\alpha}{1}$$

So, $KC = \sin\alpha\cos\beta$.

Step 7 Next, show $GH = FK$.

Step 8 To get FK, prove that $\triangle FKB \sim \triangle DOA$, so

$$\frac{FK}{BK} = \frac{DO}{AO}$$

Step 9 Use Steps 1 and 2 to conclude that

$$\frac{FK}{\sin\beta} = \frac{\cos\alpha}{1}$$

So $FK = \sin\beta\cos\alpha$.

Step 10 Now comes the grand finale. Combine Steps 3, 6, and 9 to conclude that

$$\sin(\alpha + \beta) = \sin\alpha\cos\beta + \cos\alpha\sin\beta$$

Step 11 To complete your proof, use the same diagram to prove that

$$\cos(\alpha + \beta) = \cos\alpha\cos\beta - \sin\alpha\sin\beta$$

In your description, you might want to explain why the same formulas work if α and β are in other quadrants. You can also show how some of the facts from the beginning of the lesson follow from your formulas.

Justification of steps:

Step 1: For BJ and AD, the equality stems from the basic unit circle definitions. $BK = \sin\beta$, because the rotated triangle is congruent to the original triangle.

Step 2: $KO = \cos\beta$ for the same reason—the basic unit circle definition, and the fact that $\triangle OBK$ was rotated up from the x-axis.

Step 3: By the basic unit circle definitions, $\cos(\alpha + \beta) = BJ$. $\overline{IG} \parallel \overline{BJ}$, and $\overline{BG} \parallel$ the x-axis, so B and G have the same y-height. Thus, $BJ = IG$. H is on $\overline{IG}$, so $IH + HG = IG$.

Step 4: $IH = KC$ because H was selected to have the same y-height as K.

Step 5: $\triangle KCO \sim \triangle ADO$ by AA, since they both have right angles (at C and D) and both share the angle with measure α at O.

Step 6: Simple substitution and the fact that $\overline{AO}$ is a radius of the unit circle, thus $AO = 1$.

Step 7: $IG = CF$ by construction. So $IH + HG = CK + KF$. But $IH = CK$, also by construction. Thus, $HG = KF$.

Step 8: $\triangle FKB \sim \triangle DOA$ by AA.

- Both triangles have right angles (at D and F).
- $\angle FKB \cong \angle DOA$, since $\angle FKB$ is complementary to $\angle CKO$ (because $m\angle FKB + m\angle CKO + m\angle BKO = 180$, and $m\angle BKO = 90$, by construction). Also, $\angle CKO$ is complementary to $\angle KOC$ (they are the two acute angles in a right triangle). And, by construction, $m\angle KOC = m\angle DOA$.

Step 9: Simple substitution.

Step 10: Substitution again.

Step 11:

- $\cos(\alpha + \beta) = OJ$
- $OJ = OC - CJ$, so $\cos(\alpha + \beta) = OC - CJ$.
- Since $\triangle KCO \sim \triangle ADO$ (from Step 5 above), $\frac{OC}{OK} = \frac{OD}{OA} \Rightarrow \frac{OC}{\cos\beta} = \frac{\cos\alpha}{1} \Rightarrow OC = \cos\alpha\cos\beta$
- Since $\triangle FKB \sim \triangle DOA$ (from Step 8 above), $\frac{OC}{OK} = \frac{OD}{OA} \Rightarrow \frac{BF}{\sin\beta} = \frac{\sin\alpha}{1} \Rightarrow BF = \sin\alpha\sin\beta$
- $BF = CJ$, since $\overline{BF} \parallel \overline{CJ}$, and $\overline{BJ} \parallel \overline{CF}$ (by construction) and $\overline{BF} \perp \overline{BJ}$. So quadrilateral $BFCJ$ is a rectangle.
- $CJ = \sin\alpha\sin\beta$

  Thus, by substitution, $\cos(\alpha + \beta) = \cos\alpha\cos\beta - \sin\alpha\sin\beta$.

PROOF 2 (COORDINATE GEOMETRY) Point out to students that the point S is not necessarily at the point (0, 1), even though it appears to be in the diagram. Make sure that students understand that they must prove each step, rather than relying on the diagram.

Justification of steps:

Step 1: The slope of $\overline{OA}$ is $\frac{s}{r}$, and the slope of $\overline{OH}$ is $\frac{-r}{s}$. Since $\frac{s}{r} \cdot \frac{-r}{s} = -1$, $\overline{OA} \perp \overline{OH}$. Both r and s are positive, since (r, s) is in the first quadrant. Thus the point $(-s, r)$ is in the second quadrant, since the x-coordinate is negative and the y-coordinate is positive.

Step 2: Q is a point on $\overline{OH}$, so its coordinates are $k(-s, r)$ where k is between 0 and 1. Since (a, b) is on the unit circle and is in the first quadrant, both a and b are between 0 and 1. Thus, $b(-s, r) = (-bs, br)$ is a point on $\overline{OH}$. Similarly, R is a point on $\overline{OA}$, so its coordinates are $k(r, s)$, where k is between 0 and 1. a is between 0 and 1, so $a(r, s) = (ar, as)$ is a point on $\overline{OA}$.

Step 3: $S = Q + R = (-bs, br) + (ar, as) = (ar - bs, as + br)$

Step 4:

$$\begin{aligned} |S| &= \sqrt{(ar - bs)^2 + (as + br)^2} \\ &= \sqrt{a^2r^2 - 2arbs + b^2s^2 + a^2s^2 + 2asbr + b^2r^2} \\ &= \sqrt{a^2(r^2 + s^2) + b^2(r^2 + s^2)} \\ &= \sqrt{(a^2 + b^2)(r^2 + s^2)} \\ &= \sqrt{a^2 + b^2} \cdot \sqrt{r^2 + s^2} \\ &= |B| \cdot |A| = 1 \cdot 1 = 1 \end{aligned}$$

Step 5: $OK = a$, and $OR = \sqrt{(ar)^2 + (as)^2} = \sqrt{a^2(r^2 + s^2)} = \sqrt{a^2}\sqrt{r^2 + s^2} = a \cdot 1 = a$, so $\overline{OK} \cong \overline{OR}$. Also, $OB = OS = 1$, so $\overline{OB} \cong \overline{OS}$. Thus, by the Hypotenuse-Leg Theorem (if the hypotenuse and a leg of one right triangle are congruent to the hypotenuse and a leg of another right triangle, then the triangles are congruent), $\triangle OSR \cong \triangle OBK$.

Step 6: Since S is on the unit circle, and the angle between the x-axis and $\overline{OS}$ is $\alpha + \beta$, then the coordinates of S are $(\cos(\alpha + \beta), \sin(\alpha + \beta))$.

Step 7: Thus, $\cos(\alpha + \beta) = ar - bs$, and $\sin(\alpha + \beta) = as + br$. Since $a = \cos\beta$, $b = \sin\beta$, $r = \cos\alpha$, and $s = \sin\alpha$, you have proved the formulas.

Proof 2 (Coordinate Geometry) This derivation uses ideas from basic algebra (slope), geometry (coordinates and vectors), and Chapter 4 of this book.

The setup is in the graph below. In this picture of the unit circle, $(r, s) = (\cos\alpha, \sin\alpha)$, and $(a, b) = (\cos\beta, \sin\beta)$.

The segment $\overline{HO}$ is perpendicular to $\overline{AO}$. The coordinates of H are $(-s, r)$.

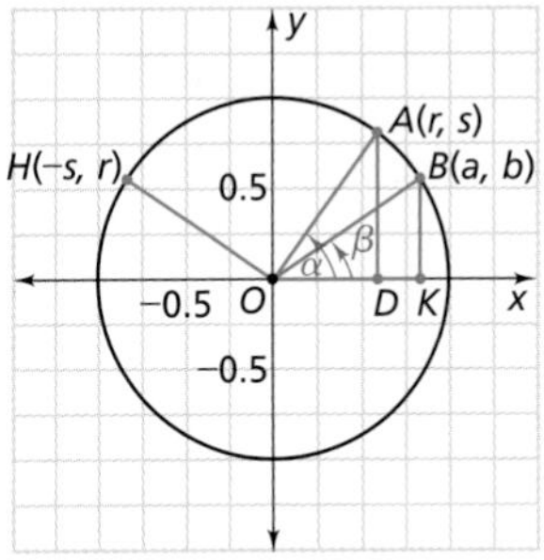

Step 1 Explain why the coordinates of H are $(-s, r)$.

Copy the graph. Now draw in some lines. Pick Q along $\overline{HO}$ such that $QO = BK$. Pick R along $\overline{AO}$ such that $RO = KO$. Then draw a line through Q parallel to $\overline{OA}$ and a line through R parallel to $\overline{OH}$. These segments intersect at S.

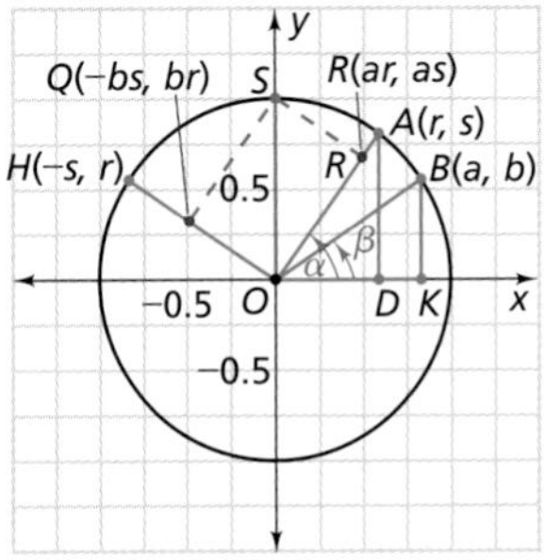

Step 2 Show that $Q = (-bs, br)$ and $R = (ar, as)$.

Step 3 Show that $S = (ar - bs, as + br)$.

Step 4 Show that S is on the circle by showing that it is 1 unit from O.

Step 5 Show that $\triangle OSR \cong \triangle OBK$. Then $m\angle SOR = \beta$ and $m\angle SOK = \alpha + \beta$.

Step 6 So, the coordinates of S are $(\cos(\alpha + b), \sin(\alpha + b))$.

Step 7 Combine steps 3 and 6 to get your formulas.

In your description, you might want to explain why the same formulas work if α and β are in other quadrants. You can also show how some of the facts from the beginning of the lesson follow from your formulas.

Remember...

You can use the distance formula.

Proof 3 (Complex Numbers) In Chapter 3, you saw a derivation of the fact that when you multiply two complex numbers, the length of the product is the product of the lengths of the factors. The argument (direction) of the product is the sum of the arguments of both factors.

Fact 1 $|zw| = |z| \cdot |w|$ **Fact 2** $\arg zw = \arg z + \arg w$

Step 1 Look back at this derivation in Chapter 3 and summarize it as part of your description.

The basic idea of this proof is to think of points on the unit circle in the complex plane. So, instead of $(\cos\alpha, \sin\alpha)$ and $(\cos\beta, \sin\beta)$, think of $z = \cos\alpha + i\sin\alpha$ and $w = \cos\beta + i\sin\beta$.

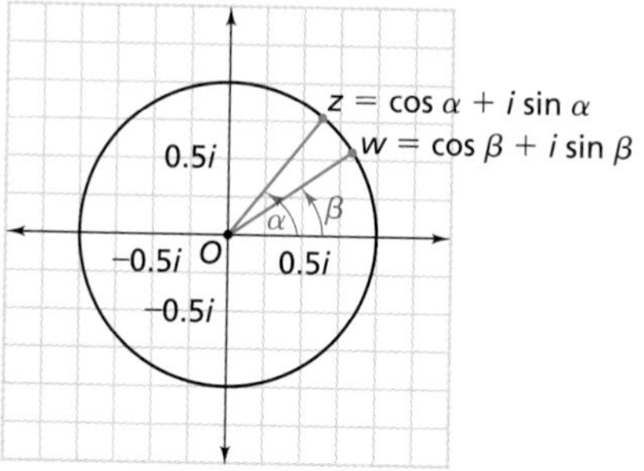

The idea is to write zw in two ways.

Step 2 Show that $|zw| = 1$. Then zw is on the unit circle.

If zw is on the unit circle, it is of the form $\cos x + i\sin x$ for some angle x. But what is the angle? By Fact 2 above, it is the sum of the angles of z and w.

$$zw = \cos(\alpha + \beta) + i\sin(\alpha + \beta)$$

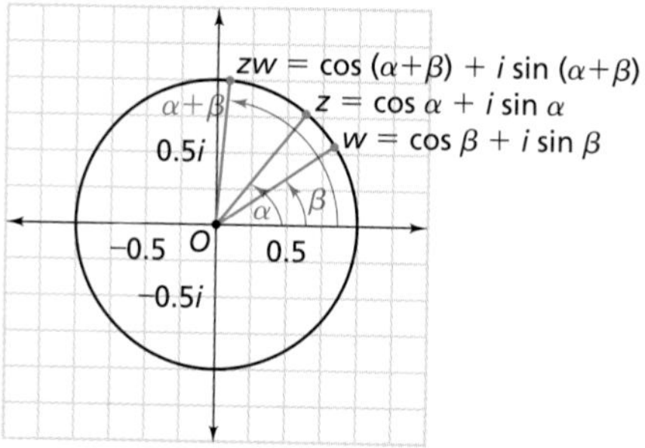

Step 3 Multiply $z = \cos\alpha + i\sin\alpha$ by $w = \cos\beta + i\sin\beta$, using the usual rules for multiplying complex numbers, to show that

$$zw = (\cos\alpha\cos\beta - \sin\alpha\sin\beta) + i(\sin\alpha\cos\beta + \cos\alpha\sin\beta)$$

Step 4 Combine the results from Steps 2 and 3 to get your formulas.

In your description, you might want to explain why the same formulas work if α and β are in other quadrants. You can also show how some of the facts from the beginning of the lesson follow from your formulas.

PROOF 3 (COMPLEX NUMBERS) Justification of steps:

Step 1: Suppose $z = (a, b)$. By the unit circle definition of trigonometric functions, $a = \cos\alpha$ and $b = \sin\alpha$. But, since z is on the complex plane, $z = a + bi$. So, by substitution, $z = \cos\alpha + i\sin\alpha$. A similar argument shows $w = \cos\beta + i\sin\beta$.

Step 2: By Fact 1, $|zw| = |z| \cdot |w|$. Since both z and w are on the unit circle,

$$|z| = |w| = 1, \text{ so } |zw| = 1.$$

Step 3: $(\cos\alpha + i\sin\alpha)(\cos\beta + i\sin\beta) = \cos\alpha\cos\beta + i\cos\alpha\sin\beta + i\sin\alpha\sin\beta + i^2\sin\alpha\sin\beta = (\cos\alpha\cos\beta - \sin\alpha\sin\beta) + i(\cos\alpha\sin\beta + \sin\alpha\sin\beta)$

Step 4: Since $\cos(\alpha + \beta) + i\sin(\alpha + \beta) = (\cos\alpha\cos\beta - \sin\alpha\sin\beta) + i(\cos\alpha\sin\beta + \sin\alpha\sin\beta)$, the real parts are equal and the imaginary parts are equal. The two equations yield the two formulas.

Wrap Up

Give students time to work on the Check Your Understanding core exercises, and go over in class as many as time allows.

Assessment Resources

Lesson Quiz 8.9

1. **Multiple Choice** Which expression is equal to $\sin(180° - \theta)$?
   A. $\sin\theta$ **B.** $-\sin\theta$ **C.** $\cos\theta$ **D.** $-\cos\theta$

2. Use an angle-sum identity to find an exact value for each expression.
   a. $\sin 75°$ **b.** $\cos 105°$

3. Simplify each expression.
   a. $\sin(360° - x)$ **b.** $\cos(180° + x)$ **c.** $\sin(90° + x)$

4. Rewrite each expression in the form $A\cos\theta + B\sin\theta$.
   a. $\cos(30° - \theta)$ **b.** $\cos(45° - \theta)$
   c. $\sin(210° + \theta)$ **d.** $\sin(315° + \theta)$

Exercises

HOMEWORK
- Core: 8, 9, 10, 11, 13, 14, 16, 17
- Optional: 12
- Extension: 15

Check Your Understanding

EXERCISE 1 The goal here is for students to see that you can derive the Pythagorean Identity from the Angle-Sum Identity. This is a reminder about the identity rather than a significant finding, but students may be pleasantly surprised when it pops up.

EXERCISE 2 demonstrates the versatility of the Angle-Sum Identities. Rather than memorizing many different identities, it is easier to memorize just two and use them to derive the other more specific cases.

EXERCISE 3 It is important for students who work both Exercise 1c and 3a to confirm that both methods give the same answer, because the two results look so different. cos 15° has to have only one value, or cosine would not be a function.

EXERCISES 6 AND 7 If you assign Exercise 7, you should also assign this Exercise 6 so students will have some experience with specific cases before tackling the general proof.

Exercises Practicing Habits of Mind

Check Your Understanding

1. One identity for cosine is

$$\cos(a - b) = \cos a \cos b + \sin a \sin b$$

   a. Use Exercises 11 and 12 from Lesson 8.7 to derive this formula.
   b. What happens in this identity if $a = b$? Evaluate the left and right sides separately.
   c. Use this identity to find an exact value for cos 15°.

$45 - 30 = 15$

2. Prove each identity by making appropriate substitutions into the angle-sum identities.
   a. $\cos 2x = \cos^2 x - \sin^2 x$
   b. $\sin 2x = 2 \sin x \cos x$
   c. $\cos 2x = 2\cos^2 x - 1$

Habits of Mind

Visualize. Check your results from Exercise 18 in Lesson 8.7.

3. From the identity in Exercise 2c, you know $\cos 30^\circ = 2\cos^2 15^\circ - 1$. Also, $\cos 30^\circ = \frac{\sqrt{3}}{2}$. So if you let $z = \cos 15^\circ$, this equation becomes

$$\frac{\sqrt{3}}{2} = 2z^2 - 1$$

   a. Use this equation to find an exact value for cos 15°.
   b. Compare your answer with the answer to Exercise 1c. Are they equal? Explain.

4. **Take It Further** Use the angle-sum identities to develop formulas for $\cos 3x$ and $\sin 3x$ in terms of $\cos x$ and $\sin x$.

5. Find a complex number z such that

$$z^2 = \frac{1}{2} + i\frac{\sqrt{3}}{2}$$

6. Here is an interesting fact about the sine function.

$$\sin 10^\circ + \sin 50^\circ = \sin 70^\circ$$

   a. Find the values of sin 10°, sin 50°, and sin 70° to four decimal places. Then verify that the above equation is approximately true.
   b. For some acute angle x, $\sin 20^\circ + \sin 40^\circ = \sin x$. Find x.
   c. For some acute angle x, $\sin 5^\circ + \sin 55^\circ = \sin x$. Find x.

7. **Take It Further** Find a general result from the examples in Exercise 6. Prove it using angle-sum identities.

Answers

Exercises

1. a. $\cos(-x) = \cos x$ and $\sin(-x) = -\sin x$. So, $\cos(a - b) = \cos(a + (-b)) = \cos a \cos(-b) - \sin a \sin(-b) = \cos a \cos b - (\sin a)(-\sin b) = \cos a \cos b + \sin a \sin b$.

b. If $a = b$, then $\cos(a - b) = \cos 0^\circ = 1$ and $\cos a \cos b + \sin a \sin b = \cos^2 a + \sin^2 a = 1$.

c. $\frac{\sqrt{2} + \sqrt{6}}{4}$

2. a. $\cos(2x) = \cos(x + x) = \cos x \cos x - \sin x \sin x = \cos^2 x - \sin^2 x$

b. $\sin(2x) = \sin(x + x) = \sin x \cos x + \cos x \sin x = 2 \sin x \cos x$

c. $\cos 2x = \cos^2 x - \sin^2 x = \cos^2 x - (1 - \cos^2 x) = \cos^2 x - 1 + \cos^2 x = 2\cos^2 x - 1$

3–7. See back of book.

On Your Own

8. Which expression is equal to $\cos(90^\circ - \theta)$?

A. $\cos\theta$ **B.** $-\cos\theta$ **C.** $\sin\theta$ **D.** $-\sin\theta$

9. Derive a formula for $\sin(\alpha - \beta)$ in terms of sine and cosine of α and β.

10. Use the angle-sum identities to prove the following identities.

$$\cos(180^\circ + \theta) = -\cos\theta$$
$$\sin(180^\circ + \theta) = -\sin\theta$$

11. Simplify each expression.

a. $\sin(360^\circ + x)$ **b.** $\sin(90^\circ + x)$ **c.** $\cos(90^\circ + x)$
d. $\sin(90^\circ - x)$ **e.** $\sin(180^\circ - x)$

12. Match each function in List A with its functional equation in List B.

A	B
$x \mapsto 2^x$	$f(a+b) = f(a) + f(b)$
$z \mapsto \lvert z \rvert$	$f(a+b) = f(a)f(b)$
$z \mapsto \arg z$	$f(ab) = f(a)f(b)$
$x \mapsto 2x$	$f(ab) = f(a) + f(b)$
$x \mapsto \log_3 x$	

13. Use the angle-sum identities to find another expression for $\tan(45^\circ + x)$.

14. Use the angle-sum identities to find a rule for $\tan(x + y)$ in terms of $\tan x$ and $\tan y$.

15. Take It Further Use your derivation of the formulas in Theorem 8.3, adjusting the diagrams if necessary, to justify the formulas for $\cos(a - b)$ and $\sin(a - b)$.

16. Standardized Test Prep If $\cos 2A = \frac{5}{8}$, what is the value of $\frac{1}{(\cos^2 A) - (\sin^2 A)}$?

A. −4.57 **B.** 0.31 **C.** 1.6 **D.** 4

Go Online PHSchool.com
For additional practice, go to Web Code: bfa-0809

The matching is not one-to-one.

Maintain Your Skills

17. Rewrite each expression in the form $A\cos\theta + B\sin\theta$.

a. $\sin(30^\circ + \theta)$ **b.** $\sin(45^\circ + \theta)$ **c.** $\sin(60^\circ + \theta)$
d. $\sin(120^\circ + \theta)$ **e.** $\sin(150^\circ + \theta)$

Go Online Video Tutor PHSchool.com
Web Code: bfe-0775

8. C

9. $\sin(\alpha - \beta) = \sin\alpha\cos\beta - \cos\alpha\sin\beta$

10. $\cos(180^\circ + \theta) = \cos 180^\circ \cos\theta - \sin 180^\circ \sin\theta = (-1)(\cos\theta) - (0)\sin\theta = -\cos\theta$; $\sin(180^\circ + \theta) = \sin 180^\circ \cos\theta + \cos 180^\circ \sin\theta = 0 \cdot \cos\theta + (-1)\cdot\sin\theta = -\sin\theta$

11. a. $\sin x$ **b.** $\cos x$
c. $-\sin x$ **d.** $\cos x$
e. $\sin x$

12. $x \mapsto 2^x$ matches $f(a+b) = f(a)\cdot f(b)$.

$z \mapsto |z|$ matches $f(ab) = f(a)\cdot f(b)$.

$z \mapsto \arg z$ matches $f(ab) = f(a) + f(b)$.

$x \mapsto 2x$ matches none of these.

$x \mapsto \log_3 x$ matches $f(ab) = f(a) + f(b)$.

13. Answers may vary. Sample: $\frac{\sin x + \cos x}{\cos x - \sin x}$

14–17. See back of book.

On Your Own

EXERCISES 9–11 are all examples of specific identities that result directly from the Angle-Sum Identities.

EXERCISE 12 asks students to think about algebraic properties of functions in much the same way as they have been thinking about the additive properties of trigonometric functions during this lesson.

EXERCISE 14 You may want to give students the hint that dividing by $\cos x \cdot \cos y$ will help.

Maintain Your Skills

EXERCISE 17 is about promoting practice with exact values for the special angles. You might point out the relationship between this and the Maintain Your Skills exercise from Lesson 8.8, which considered only $\sin(120^\circ + \theta)$. Students now have a way of finding A and B directly using the formula from this lesson.

Additional Resources

PRINT RESOURCES
- Solution Manual
- Practice Workbook
- Assessment Resources
- Teaching Resources

TECHNOLOGY
- Interactive Textbook
- TeacherExpress CD-ROM
- ExamView CD-ROM
- PHSchool.com

Additional Practice

1. **Multiple Choice** Which expression is equal to $\sin(90^\circ - \theta)$?
   A. $\sin\theta$
   B. $-\sin\theta$
   C. $\cos\theta$
   D. $-\cos\theta$
2. Derive a formula for $\cos(\alpha - \beta)$ in terms of the sine and cosine of α and β.
3. Use the angle-sum identities to prove each identity.
   a. $\cos(180^\circ - \theta) = -\cos\theta$
   b. $\sin(180^\circ - \theta) = \sin\theta$
4. Simplify each expression.
   a. $\cos(360^\circ + x)$
   b. $\cos(90^\circ - x)$
   c. $\sin(x - 180^\circ)$
   d. $\sin(270^\circ + x)$
5. Use the angle-sum identities to find another expression for $\tan(135^\circ - x)$.
6. Use the angle-sum identities to find a rule for $\tan(x - y)$ in terms of $\tan x$ and $\tan y$.
7. Rewrite each expression in the form $A\cos\theta + B\sin\theta$.
   a. $\cos(30^\circ + \theta)$
   b. $\cos(45^\circ + \theta)$
   c. $\cos(60^\circ + \theta)$
   d. $\cos(120^\circ + \theta)$
   e. $\cos(150^\circ + \theta)$
8. Use the identity $\cos 2x = 2\cos^2 x - 1$ to find an exact value for $\cos 22.5^\circ$. (*Hint:* $\cos 45^\circ = \frac{\sqrt{2}}{2}$)

Practice: For Lesson 8.9, assign Exercises 1–8.

Mathematical Reflections

EXERCISES 6–8 At the start of the investigation, you may have assigned these as Questions 1–3 for students to think and write about.

Mathematical Reflections 8B

In this investigation, you learned how to use the graphs of trigonometric functions to solve problems and to prove and use trigonometric identities. These questions will help you summarize what you have learned.

1. Sketch a graph of $y = \cos x$ for $90° \le x \le 180°$. Label five points on your graph with exact coordinates.
2. For each interval below, state whether $\sin x$ is *positive* or *negative* in the interval and whether its value is increasing or decreasing as x increases through the interval.
   a. $0° < x < 90°$
   b. $90° < x < 180°$
   c. $180° < x < 270°$
   d. $270° < x < 360°$
3. Sketch a picture of the unit circle. Use it to locate and label points with coordinates ($\cos 210°$, $\sin 210°$) and (1, $\tan 210°$).
4. Sketch a graph of $y = \tan x$ that shows two periods of the function.
5. Simplify each expression.
   a. $\sin(270° - x)$
   b. $\cos(180° - x)$
6. What do the graphs of the sine and cosine functions look like?
7. Why does the tangent function have a period of 180°?
8. What is a simple rule for finding the value of $\cos(90° + \theta)$?

Vocabulary

In this investigation, you learned these terms. Make sure you understand what each one means and how to use it.

- **discontinuity**
- **period**

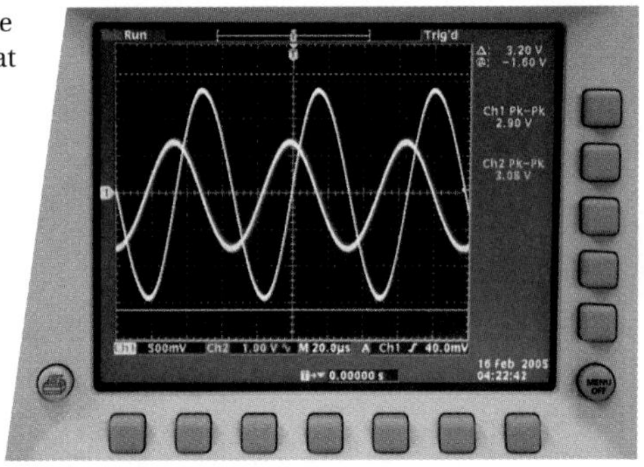

These two sine waves have the same period.

Answers

Mathematical Reflections

1. Answers may vary. Sample:

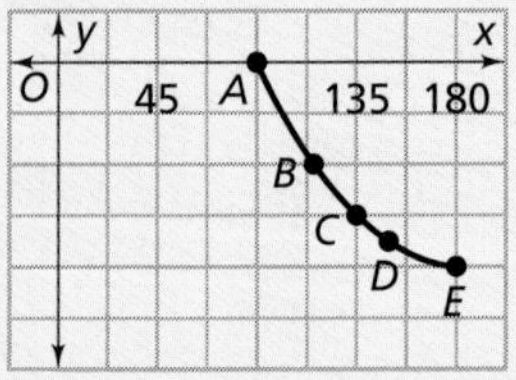

$A(90, 0)$, $B\left(120, -\frac{1}{2}\right)$, $C\left(135, -\frac{\sqrt{2}}{2}\right)$, $D\left(150, -\frac{\sqrt{3}}{2}\right)$, $E(180, -1)$

2. **a.** positive, increasing
   b. positive, decreasing
   c. negative, decreasing
   d. negative, increasing

3. 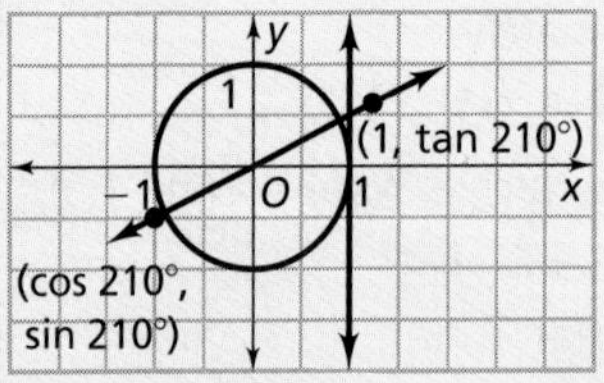

4. 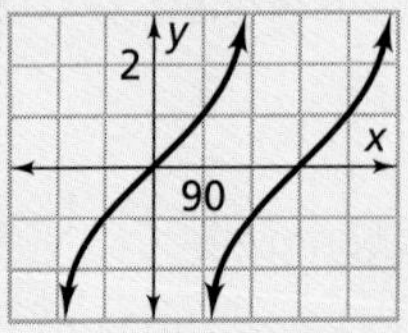

5. **a.** $-\cos x$ **b.** $-\cos x$

6. Answers may vary. Sample: The graphs of the sine and cosine functions are periodic curves with the same period, 360°, a maximum of 1, a minimum of −1, and $\sin(90° + x) = \cos x$.

7. Answers may vary. Sample: The tangent function is equal to the slope of the line passing through the origin and the point $P(\cos\theta, \sin\theta)$ on the unit circle. The ray OP forms an angle θ measured counterclockwise from the positive x-axis. Point $Q(-\cos\theta, -\sin\theta)$ is also on this line. The ray OQ

Chapter 8

Mid-Chapter Test

Go Online PHSchool.com — For a mid-chapter test, go to Web Code: bfa-0852

Multiple Choice

1. Which point is on the unit circle $x^2 + y^2 = 1$?

A. $(-1, 1)$

B. $\left(\frac{1}{4}, \frac{3}{4}\right)$

C. $\left(\frac{4}{5}, -\frac{4}{5}\right)$

D. $\left(\frac{2}{3}, \frac{2}{5}\right)$

2. If $\cos\theta = 0$, then which could NOT be the value of θ?

A. 90°

B. 180°

C. 270°

D. 450°

3. Suppose $\sin 80° = a$ and $\cos 80° = b$. Which expression is equal to $\sin 260°$?

A. $-a$

B. a

C. b

D. $a^2 + b^2$

4. Simplify $\cos^2 60° + \sin^2 60°$.

A. $\cos^2 120°$

B. $\sin^2 120°$

C. 0

D. 1

5. How many solutions does the equation $\cos x = -0.4$ have for $-90° \le x \le 180°$?

A. 0

B. 1

C. 2

D. 3

Open Response

6. Write each expression as the sine or cosine of an acute angle.

a. $\sin 145°$

b. $\cos 260°$

c. $\cos 740°$

d. $\sin(-78°)$

7. Write each expression as some factor of the sine or cosine of α.

a. $\sin(180° + \alpha)$

b. $\cos(360° - \alpha)$

8. Suppose $\cos\theta = \frac{3}{5}$ and θ is an angle between 0° and 360°.

a. Find all possible values of $\sin\theta$.

b. Find all possible values of $\tan\theta$.

c. Find all possible values of θ to the nearest tenth.

9. Find all solutions of each equation for $0° \le x \le 360°$.

a. $2\cos x - 1 = 0$

b. $2\cos^2 x - 1 = 0$

c. $2\sin^2 x - 3\sin x = 5$

10. Graph $y = \sin x$ for $-90° \le x \le 270°$. Label five points on your graph with exact coordinates.

11. If an angle is in Quadrant IV, what do you know about the sign of its sine, cosine, and tangent?

Mid-Chapter Test

Assessment Resources

Mid-Chapter Test

Multiple Choice

1. Which point is NOT on the unit circle $x^2 + y^2 = 1$?
A. $(-1, 0)$ **B.** $\left(\frac{2}{3}, \frac{2}{5}\right)$ **C.** $\left(\frac{1}{2}, \frac{\sqrt{3}}{2}\right)$ **D.** $\left(-\frac{3}{5}, -\frac{4}{5}\right)$

2. If $\sin\theta = 0$, then which could NOT be the value of θ?
A. −180° **B.** 0° **C.** 90° **D.** 360°

3. Suppose $\sin 10° = a$ and $\cos 10° = b$. Which expression is equal to $\cos 350°$?
A. $-a$ **B.** a **C.** b **D.** $-b$

4. Simplify $\cos^2 45° + \sin^2 45°$.
A. 0 **B.** 1 **C.** $\cos 90°$ **D.** $\sin^2 45°$

5. How many solutions does the equation $\sin x = 0.6$ have for $-90° \le x \le 270°$?
A. 0 **B.** 1 **C.** 2 **D.** 3

Open Response

6. Write each expression as the sine or cosine of an acute angle.
a. $\cos 205°$ **b.** $\sin 290°$ **c.** $\cos(-100°)$ **d.** $\sin 95°$

7. Write each expression as some factor of the sine or cosine of α.
a. $\sin(180° - \alpha)$ **b.** $\cos(270° + \alpha)$

8. Suppose $\cos\theta = -\frac{7}{25}$ and θ is an angle between 0° and 360°.
a. Find all possible values of $\sin\theta$.
b. Find all possible values of $\tan\theta$.
c. Find all possible values of θ to the nearest tenth.

9. Find all solutions of each equation for $0° \le x < 360°$.
a. $2\sin x + 1 = 0$ **b.** $4\cos^2 x - 3 = 0$
c. $2\cos^2 x + 3\cos x + 1 = 0$

10. Graph $y = \cos x$ for $-90° \le x \le 270°$. Label five points on your graph with exact coordinates.

11. What is a simple rule for finding the value of $\cos(90° + \theta)$?

Also available: Form B

forms an angle $\theta + 180°$ measured counterclockwise from the positive x-axis. The slopes (and thus the tangents for these angles) for θ and $180° + \theta$ must be the same, because they are the slopes of the same line.

8. $-\sin\theta$

Mid-Chapter Test

1. C

2. B

3. A

4. D

5. B

6. a. $\sin 35°$ **b.** $-\cos 80°$
c. $\cos 20°$ **d.** $-\sin 78°$

7. a. $-\sin\alpha$ **b.** $\cos\alpha$

8. a. $\pm\frac{4}{5}$ **b.** $\pm\frac{4}{3}$
c. 53.1°, 306.9°

9. a. 60°, 300°
b. 45°, 135°, 225°, 315°
c. 270°

10. Answers may vary. Sample:

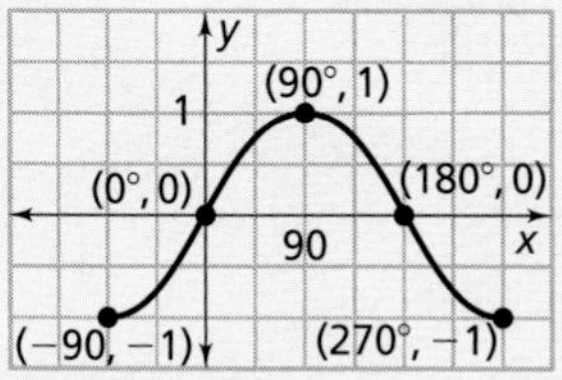

11. Sine is negative, cosine is positive, and tangent is negative.

Investigation Overview

In the previous two investigations, students extended the domains of the trigonometric functions to include any angle, and they used the unit circle and the graphs of the trigonometric functions to prove identities in this extended domain. Now they combine these results to use the trigonometric functions to solve triangles—in other words, find any unknown side lengths and angle measures. With this goal in mind, they prove the Law of Sines and the Law of Cosines as well as Heron's Formula for the area of a triangle.

You may wish to assign Questions 1–3 for students to think and write about during the investigation.

Learning Goals

- Solve a triangle—find all of its side lengths and angle measures—given enough information.
- State and use the Law of Sines.
- State and use the Law of Cosines.
- State and use Heron's Formula.

Habits and Skills

- Analyze given information to choose a solution strategy.
- Reason logically to understand and produce a mathematical proof.
- Reason by continuity to examine extreme cases.

Investigation 8C

Applications to Triangles

In *Applications to Triangles*, you will use what you know about trigonometric functions to find the side lengths, angle measures, and areas of triangles.

By the end of this investigation, you will be able to answer questions like these.

1. What information do you need to find all of a triangle's side lengths and angle measures?
2. What information do you need to find the area of a triangle?
3. A triangle has sides of length 5, 8, and 10. What is the measure of its largest angle?

You will learn how to

- solve a triangle—find all of its side lengths and angle measures—given enough information
- state and use the Law of Sines
- state and use the Law of Cosines
- state and use Heron's Formula

You will develop these habits and skills:

- Analyze given information to choose a solution strategy.
- Reason logically to understand and produce a mathematical proof.
- Reason by continuity to examine extreme cases.

You can use triangle relationships to measure the width of the glacier.

Investigation Road Map

LESSON 8.10, *Getting Started,* presents the task of finding unknown side lengths and angle measures in triangles.

LESSON 8.11, *The Area of a Triangle,* has students develop a formula for the area of a triangle given two side lengths and their included angle.

LESSON 8.12, *The Law of Sines,* introduces and proves the Law of Sines. Students use this result to solve triangles.

LESSON 8.13, *The Law of Cosines,* introduces and proves the Law of Cosines. Students use this result to solve triangles.

LESSON 8.14, *Heron's Formula,* introduces and proves Heron's Formula for finding the area of a triangle given three side lengths.

8.10 Getting Started

Activating Prior Knowledge
Exploring New Ideas

You can use trigonometry to get the information you need to find the area of a triangle.

For You to Explore

1. **Write About It** Here is a triangle.

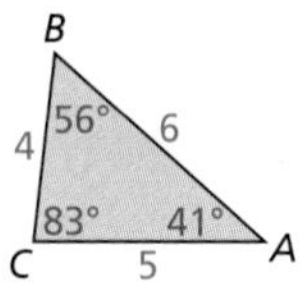

Describe some measurements you could use to find the area of the triangle.

2. In $\triangle ABC$, $AC = 10$, $BC = 12$, and $\angle C$ measures 50°.

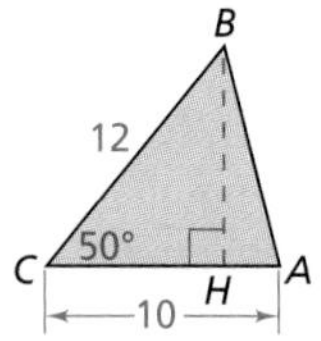

a. Find the length of the altitude $\overline{BH}$.

b. Find the area of $\triangle ABC$.

c. Find the length of side $\overline{AB}$.

3. In $\triangle XYZ$, $XZ = 10$, $YZ = 12$, and $\angle Z$ measures 100°.

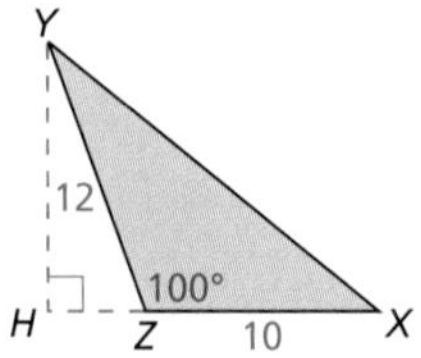

a. Find the length of the altitude $\overline{YH}$.

b. Find the area of $\triangle XYZ$.

c. Find the length of side $\overline{XY}$.

Answers

For You To Explore

1. To find the area, you need to know the height of the triangle. You can find the height by drawing an altitude from any vertex perpendicular to the opposite side and using the sine function for the angle opposite the altitude you drew.

2. **a.** 9.19
b. 45.96
c. 9.47

3. **a.** 11.82
b. 59.1
c. 16.9

Lesson Overview

GOAL

- Warm up to the ideas of the investigation.

This lesson challenges students to use what they have learned about trigonometry to find unknown side lengths and angle measures in triangles. They develop and test their own strategies. There is often more than one way to approach a problem. As always in a Getting Started lesson, there is no need to formalize these ideas today.

FOR YOU TO EXPLORE
- Core: 1, 2, 3, 4, 5
- Optional: none
- Extension: 6

MATERIALS
- geometry software
- graphing calculators
- protractors
- rulers

HOMEWORK
- Core: 7, 8, 9, 10, 11, 12
- Optional: 13

Launch

Let students get started on the For You to Explore problems. Most students should remember the formula for the area of a triangle, $A = \frac{1}{2}bh$. Try to avoid giving students the formula outright, as the first few problems nudge students toward remembering the correct formula.

Explore

While students are working, keep track of any techniques they develop that you would like to bring up when you discuss the problems.

For You to Explore

PROBLEM 1 The goal here is to see whether students recall the area formula for a triangle $A = \frac{1}{2}bh$. A few students may decide that all the measurements they need are already there and think about applying trigonometry to find the altitude without making further measurements.

PROBLEM 2 The hope is that students will recall that the formula for the area of a triangle is $A = \frac{1}{2}bh$. If they do not, you can remind them by drawing a rectangle around the triangle and showing that the area of the triangle is half the area of the rectangle. Of course, you will also want to make sure that your students remember how to find the area of a rectangle.

PROBLEM 3 See if students use $\angle YZH$ to calculate the altitude, or whether they are already comfortable enough with trigonometric functions of obtuse angles to use $\angle YZX$ directly.

PROBLEM 4 previews the Hinge Theorem, which students prove in Lesson 8.12.

PROBLEM 5 As usual in mathematics, it is easier to show that something is false than that it is true. Encourage students to look for counterexamples. If they believe that something is true, it may help them find an argument to show it; if they believe it is false, they might find an example that proves them correct.

PROBLEM 6 You might suggest that students restrict themselves to isosceles triangles. It will be easier for them to find the area of this type of triangle and to hold the area and perimeter fixed while changing the side lengths of the triangle.

Wrap Up

Go over as many of the problems as time allows. Discuss and compare the different strategies that students used.

Exercises

HOMEWORK

- Core: 7, 8, 9, 10, 11, 12
- Optional: 13

4. In $\triangle PQR$, $PR = 10$, $QR = 12$, and $\angle R$ measures 130°.

a. Draw an accurate diagram of $\triangle PQR$. Use your diagram to answer the next two questions.

b. Which triangle has a greater perimeter, $\triangle PQR$ or $\triangle XYZ$ from Exercise 3?

c. Which triangle has a larger area, $\triangle PQR$ or $\triangle XYZ$ from Exercise 3?

Remember...

The perimeter of a polygon is the sum of its side lengths.

5. Determine whether each statement is true or false. Justify your answers with a diagram.

a. The longest side in a triangle is opposite its largest angle.

b. In $\triangle ABC$, if $\overline{AC}$ and $\overline{BC}$ stay the same length but angle C increases in size, side $\overline{AB}$ increases in length.

c. In $\triangle ABC$, if $\overline{AC}$ and $\overline{BC}$ stay the same length but $\overline{AB}$ increases in length, the area of $\triangle ABC$ increases.

d. Two triangles with the same perimeter must have the same area.

6. **Take It Further** Suppose two triangles have the same perimeter and the same area. Must the triangles be congruent? Justify your answer.

Exercises *Practicing Habits of Mind*

On Your Own

7. Suppose $\sin \theta = \sin 50°$ and θ is between 0° and 360°. What are the possible values of θ?

8. Suppose $\cos \theta = \cos 50°$ and θ is between 0° and 360°. What are the possible values of θ?

9. Which statement is true?

A. $\cos 70° = \cos 110°$

B. $\sin 70° = \sin 110°$

C. $\tan 70° = \tan 110°$

D. $\sin 70° = -\sin 110°$

Answers

4. a.

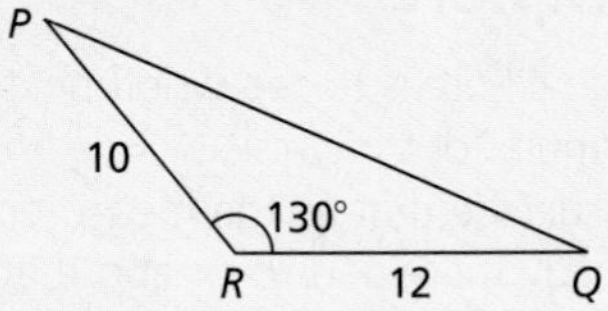

b. $\triangle PQR$

c. $\triangle XYZ$

5. a. True; answers may vary. Sample:

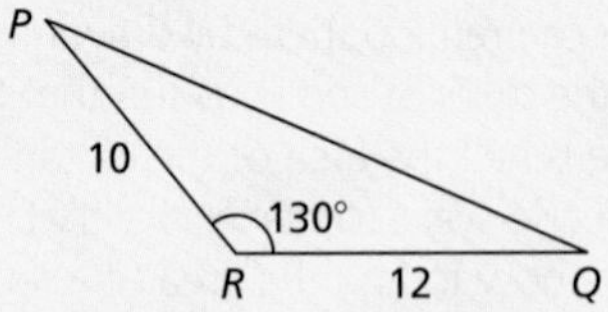

b. True; answers may vary. Sample:

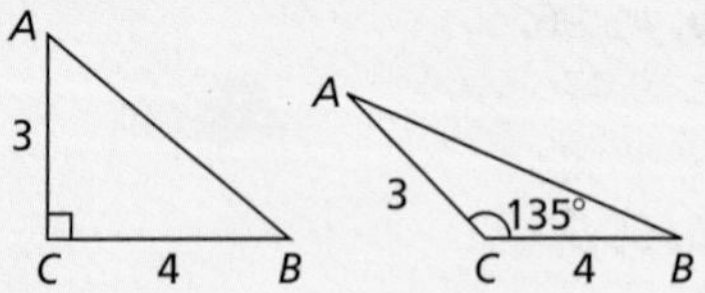

c. False, the area of the triangle increases as $\angle C$ goes from 0° to 90°, then decreases as $\angle C$ increases beyond 90°; answers may vary. Sample:

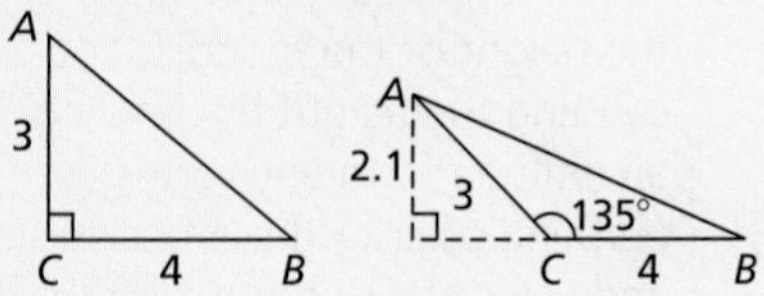

10. Jan lives 5 miles away from Paul. Paul lives 8 miles away from Dwayne.

a. What is the shortest possible distance between Jan's and Dwayne's houses? Draw a diagram to represent this situation.

b. What is the longest possible distance between Jan's and Dwayne's houses? Draw a diagram to represent this situation.

c. Is it possible for the distance between Jan's and Dwayne's houses to be 10 miles? If so, draw a diagram to represent the situation.

11. Consider the labeled diagram below.

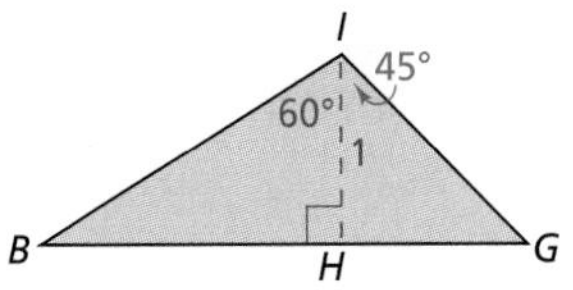

a. Find all missing lengths.

b. Use any method to find the area of $\triangle BIG$.

12. The diagram below gives variables for the side lengths of $\triangle ABC$.

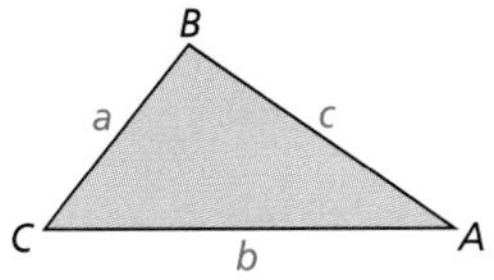

Find at least two different expressions for the area of $\triangle ABC$ in terms of its side lengths and angle measures.

Maintain Your Skills

13. For each set of three lengths, determine whether or not they can be the side lengths of a triangle.

a. 8, 6, 10	**b.** 8, 6, 12	**c.** 8, 6, 14
d. 8, 6, 16	**e.** 8, 6, 9	**f.** 8, 6, 5
g. 8, 6, 3	**h.** 8, 6, 2	**i.** 8, 6, 1

On Your Own

EXERCISE 10 Reminds students about the Triangle Inequality.

EXERCISE 11 You will revisit this diagram in the next lesson. Expect students to solve this exercise by finding the area of each smaller triangle. This exercise may also serve as a reminder of 30°-60°-90° and 45°-45°-90° triangle facts.

EXERCISE 12 previews the next lesson on finding the area of a triangle with limited information.

Maintain Your Skills

EXERCISE 13 is another exercise that reminds students of the Triangle Inequality.

d. False; answers may vary. Sample:

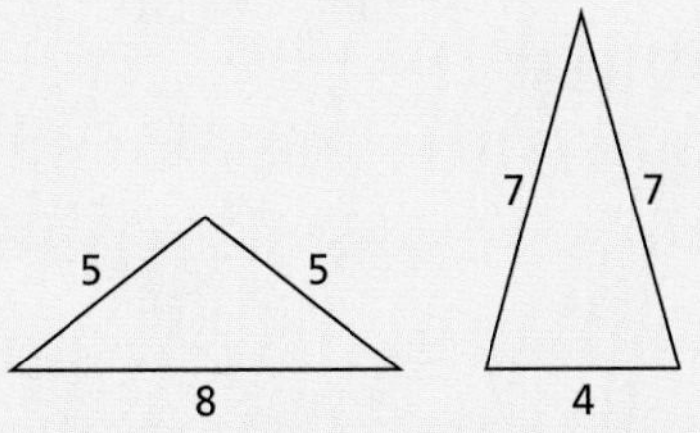

6. No; a triangle with side lengths 29, 29, and 40 and a triangle with side lengths 37, 37, and 24 have the same perimeters, 98, and areas, 420, but they are not congruent.

7. 50°, 130°

8. 50°, 310°

9. B

10. a. 3 miles;

b. 13 miles;

c. Yes;

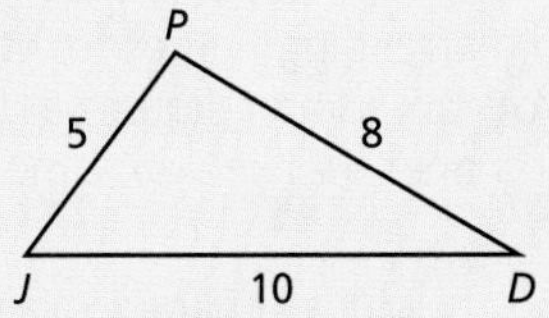

11. a. $BH = \sqrt{3}$, $BI = 2$, $HG = 1$, $IG = \sqrt{2}$, $BG = 1 + \sqrt{3}$

b. $\frac{\sqrt{3} + 1}{2}$

12. any two of the following expressions: $\frac{1}{2}bc \sin A$, $\frac{1}{2}ac \sin B$, $\frac{1}{2}ab \sin C$

13. a. yes	**b.** yes	**c.** no
d. no	**e.** yes	**f.** yes
g. yes	**h.** no	**i.** no

Lesson Overview

GOAL

- Solve a triangle—find all its side lengths and angle measures—given enough information.

In this lesson, students apply trigonometry to the problem of finding an unknown altitude in a triangle in order to find its area. They develop a formula that gives the area of any triangle given two side lengths and their included angle. Then they use that formula to prove the Angle-Sum Identity for sine.

CHECK YOUR UNDERSTANDING
- Core: 1, 2, 3, 4
- Optional: 5a, 6, 7
- Extension: 5b

MATERIALS
- geometry software
- graphing calculators
- protractors
- rulers
- Blackline Master 8.11

HOMEWORK
- Core: 8, 9, 10, 11, 12, 14, 16
- Optional: 13, 15, 17

Launch

Begin this lesson by reviewing the area formula for a triangle, if necessary. If it did not come up in discussion during the Getting Started lesson, you might ask students how they could find the altitude of a triangle if it is not part of the given information. Bring in the idea of using trigonometry to find this length if students do not mention it.

Explore

In CME Project *Geometry,* students experimented with cutting and rearranging figures to work through area formulas. You can use the figures at the start of this lesson for a brief overview of some of those experiments.

The exposition on the student page explains the first figure. For the second figure, the formula works as follows.

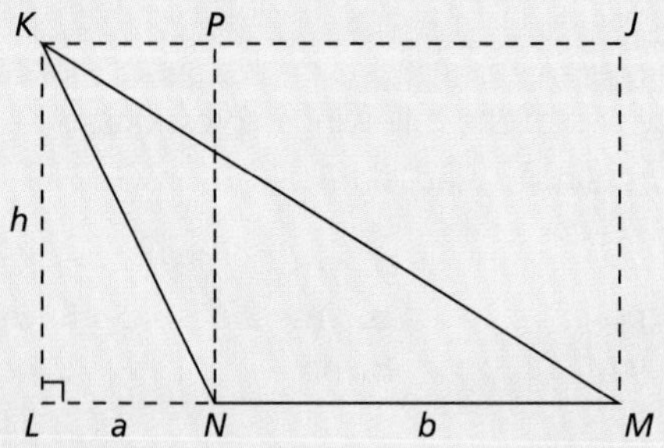

area of $\triangle KNM$ = area of $\triangle KLM$ − area of $\triangle KLN$

8.11 The Area of a Triangle

In geometry, you learned the area formulas for many shapes, including triangles. For example, a right triangle is half of a rectangle.

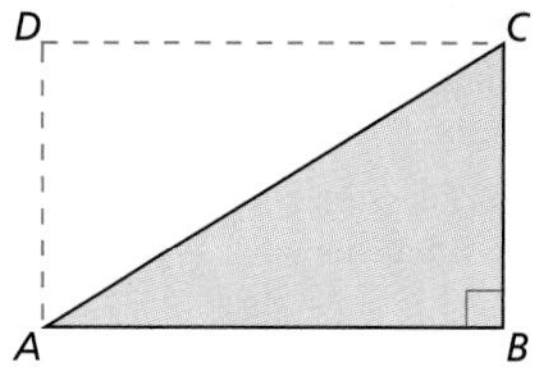

The area of this triangle is $A = \frac{1}{2}bh$, since it is equal to exactly half the rectangle's area. The same applies to any triangle. Its area is half the product of its base and height.

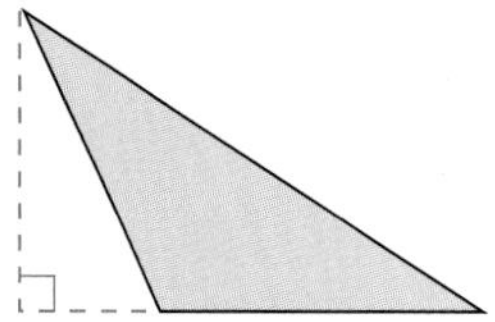

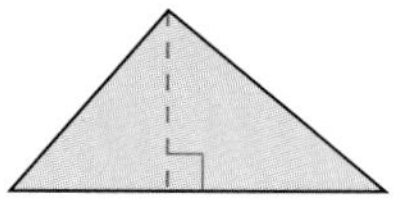

Remember...

The height is always measured perpendicular to the base. You can use any side of the triangle as the base.

You can often use trigonometry to find the height of a triangle when it is unknown.

Example

Problem In $\triangle BCU$, $BC = 10$, $UC = 12$, and $\angle C$ measures 50°. Find an expression for the exact area of this triangle. Then approximate the area to two decimal places.

Solution First, sketch the triangle. Here is an accurate sketch of $\triangle BCU$, including the altitude drawn to side $\overline{UC}$.

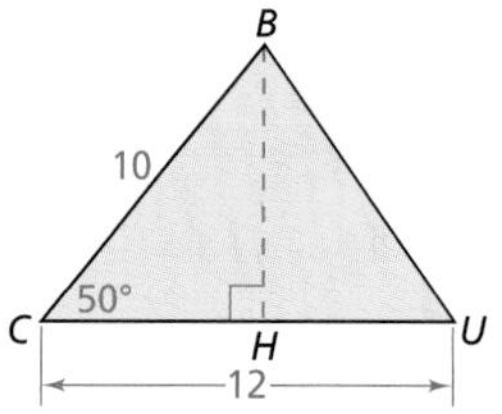

The area is $A = \frac{1}{2}bh$, and the base is 12. So $A = \frac{1}{2} \cdot 12 \cdot h$.

Find h by recognizing the right triangle BCH. The missing side h is opposite the 50° angle. You know the length of the hypotenuse. Use the sine ratio.

$$\sin 50^\circ = \frac{h}{10}$$

The exact value of h is $10 \sin 50^\circ$. The area is $\frac{1}{2} \cdot 12 \cdot 10 \sin 50^\circ$. This simplifies to $A = 60 \sin 50^\circ$, which is approximately 45.96.

For You to Do

1. Follow the same process as in the Example, but drop the altitude to the side of length 10. What happens?

You can generalize the process in the Example. Consider $\triangle ABC$ with no numbered sides.

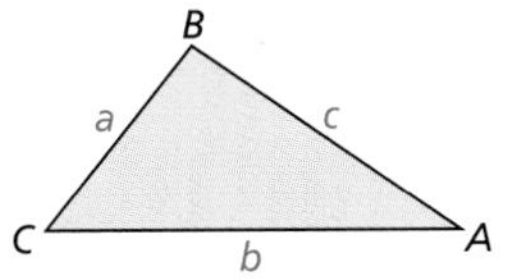

Drop the altitude to the side of length b. One expression for the altitude's length is $a \sin C$. Then the area of the triangle is $\frac{1}{2}ab \sin C$. Since a triangle has three altitudes, there are three possible area formulas.

Theorem 8.4 Area of a Triangle

For $\triangle ABC$ with $AB = c$, $AC = b$, and $BC = a$, the area of the triangle is equal to the expressions below.

$$\frac{1}{2}ab \sin C = \frac{1}{2}bc \sin A = \frac{1}{2}ac \sin B$$

What measurements can you use to calculate the area of this triangular lot?

Answers

For You To Do

1. You get $h = 12 \sin 50^\circ$ and $A = \frac{1}{2}(10)h = \frac{1}{2}(10)(12 \sin 50^\circ) = 60 \sin 50^\circ = 45.96$, which is the same as the Example.

The altitude with length h forms the right triangle $\triangle KLM$ with base $(a + b)$. The area of rectangle $JKLM$ is $(a + b)h$, so the area of $\triangle KLM$ is $\frac{1}{2}(a + b)h$. The area of rectangle $PKLN$ is ah, so the area of $\triangle KLN$ is $\frac{1}{2}ah$. Thus,

$$\text{area of } \triangle KNM = \frac{1}{2}(a = b)h - \frac{1}{2}ah = \frac{1}{2}bh$$

In the third figure, if you split the rectangle at the altitude, you can swap the two sides left to right.

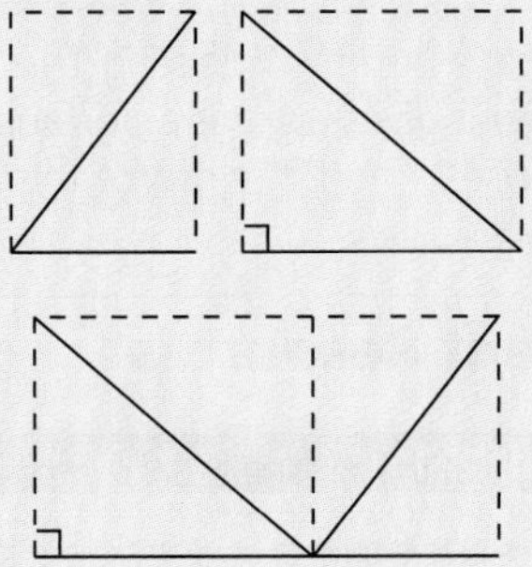

The resulting figure has a triangle that is congruent to the original triangle (now upside down). That triangle represents the "added space" in the original picture that makes a rectangle from the triangle.

Another way to look at it is that the altitude splits the larger rectangle into two pieces. Each one is then shown as part of a larger rectangle. The sum of the areas of those two rectangles is the area of the larger rectangle, so the area of the original triangle is the sum of half the area of the left rectangle and half the area of the right rectangle, which equals half the area of the larger rectangle. Two sides of that rectangle have length equal to the base of the triangle, and the other two sides have length equal to the altitude of the triangle.

Developing Habits of Mind

Theorem 8.4 gives a general purpose formula for area, which covers the basic formula $A = \frac{1}{2}bh$ that students have known for some time. The case where the angle is right shows how the formula simplifies back to the basic formula.

Wrap Up

Summarize the lesson by reviewing Theorem 8.4 and discussing how it gives a general formula for any triangle. Exercises 1 and 2 reinforce this theorem.

Assessment Resources

Lesson Quiz 8.11

1. In $\triangle BAT$, $BA = 22$ and $AT = 13$. Find the maximum possible area for this triangle.

2. **Multiple Choice** Which statement is true?
   A. $\cos 35^\circ = \cos 55^\circ$
   B. $\cos 35^\circ = \cos^2 55^\circ$
   C. $\cos 35^\circ = \sin^2 55^\circ$
   D. $\cos 35^\circ = \sin 55^\circ$

3. Use the diagram of an isosceles triangle with legs of length 5.
   a. Find the area of $\triangle DOG$ using the rule $A = \frac{1}{2}bh$.
   b. Find the area of $\triangle DOG$ using $\angle O$.
   c. Write a formula for $\sin 2x$ by using your results from parts (a) and (b).

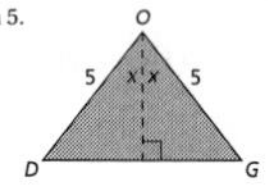

Developing Habits of Mind

Visualize. Angle C is acute in all the diagrams used to show that the area is $\frac{1}{2}ab \sin C$. But $\angle C$ might not be acute. It could be right or obtuse. What is the area formula then?

If $\angle C$ is a right angle, the triangle looks like this.

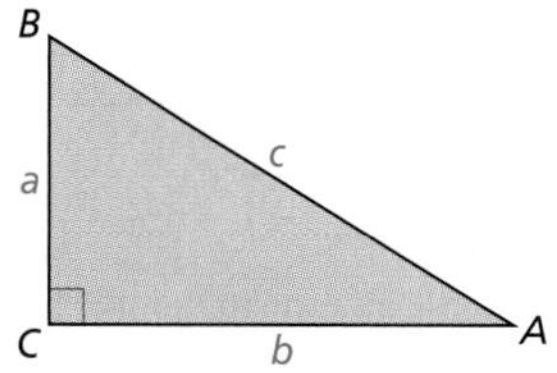

$$\text{area} = \frac{1}{2}ab$$

Since this is a right triangle, the area is $\frac{1}{2}ab$. But $\sin 90^\circ = 1$, so this is also equal to $\frac{1}{2}ab \sin C$. The formula covers the case when $\angle C$ is a right angle.

If $\angle C$ is obtuse, the triangle looks like this.

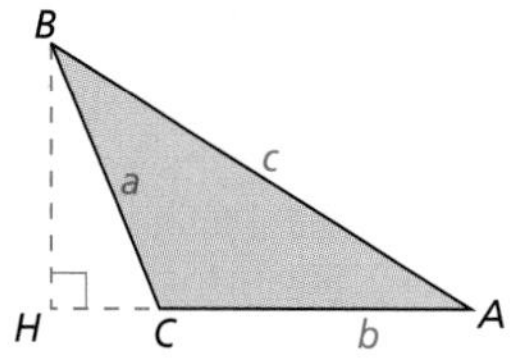

$$\text{area} = \frac{1}{2}ab \sin (180^\circ - m\angle C)$$

To find the altitude, you use the sine of $\angle BCH$. This angle is the supplement of $\angle ACB$. If $\angle ACB$ measures θ, $\angle BCH$ measures $(180^\circ - \theta)$. Then the altitude is $a \sin (180^\circ - \theta)$.

Earlier, however, you learned that $\sin (180^\circ - \theta) = \sin \theta$. So, the sine of $\angle ACB$ is the same as the sine of $\angle BCH$. The area is $\frac{1}{2}ab \sin C$, even for obtuse triangles.

Remember...

See, for example, Exercise 11 from Lesson 8.9.

The formula for the area of the triangle leads to an elegant proof of the formula for $\sin (a + b)$. Consider this diagram.

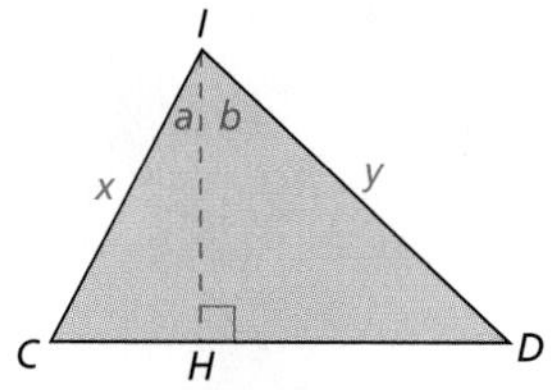

Now, what is the area of $\triangle CID$? There are two ways to find it.

- First, look at $\triangle CID$ as a whole. The area is $\frac{1}{2}xy\sin(a+b)$.
- Second, consider $\triangle CIH$ and $\triangle DIH$ separately. Within $\triangle CIH$, $CH = x\sin a$ and $IH = y\cos b$. The area of $\triangle CIH$ is $\frac{1}{2}(x\sin a)(y\cos b) = \frac{1}{2}xy\sin a\cos b$. Similarly, the area of $\triangle DIH$ is $\frac{1}{2}xy\cos a\sin b$.

The sum of the areas of the two smaller triangles is equal to the area of the larger triangle.

$$\frac{1}{2}xy\sin(a+b) = \frac{1}{2}xy\sin a\cos b + \frac{1}{2}xy\cos a\sin b$$
$$\frac{1}{2}xy\sin(a+b) = \frac{1}{2}xy(\sin a\cos b + xy\cos a\sin b)$$
$$\sin(a+b) = \sin a\cos b + \cos a\sin b$$

This expression for $\sin(a+b)$ is the one you found in Investigation 8B. All the proof uses is the rule for the area of a triangle and the definitions of sine and cosine for right triangles.

For Discussion

2. When finding the area of $\triangle CIH$, why did you write it as $y\cos b$ and not $x\cos a$? Both are equal, so what purpose is there in using one instead of the other?

Exercises Practicing Habits of Mind

Check Your Understanding

1. Use the diagram of $\triangle EFG$ below.

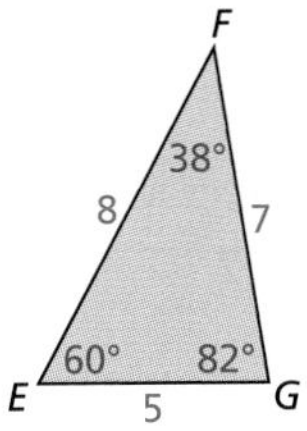

Find at least two different ways to calculate the area of $\triangle EFG$.

Answers

For Discussion

2. The purpose was to end up with a familiar formula for $\sin(a+b)$.

Exercises

1. Answers may vary. Sample: You can use $\frac{1}{2}(8)(5\sin 60°)$ or $\frac{1}{2}(5)(7\sin 82°)$ to find the area.

Exercises

HOMEWORK
- Core: 8, 9, 10, 11, 12, 14, 16
- Optional: 13, 15, 17

Check Your Understanding

EXERCISE 1 Expect that students will drop altitudes and use the techniques demonstrated in the lesson, but look for students who use Heron's Formula here. It was first introduced in the Project in Chapter 2. You will remind students of it in this investigation. Students are not very likely to use it; if anyone does, be sure to refer to their work when you go over these exercises.

EXERCISE 2 Although this exercise gives students an exact value for sin 150°, you might reassure them that you are not going to require them to remember it.

EXERCISES 3 AND 7 are a sequence of problems that lead students toward the idea that the area of a series of regular n-gons inscribed in a circle of radius 1 approachs the area of the circle—π. This is, historically, one of the ways in which mathematicians approximated π. Although many of these exercises are marked as optional, you may want to assign the entire series so that students get a chance to see this result for themselves. It would be especially helpful if students had access to geometry software to reduce the amount of calculation.

EXERCISE 6 Blackline Master 8.11 provides a copy of the table for students to complete.

2. Use the diagram from Exercise 11 in Lesson 8.10.

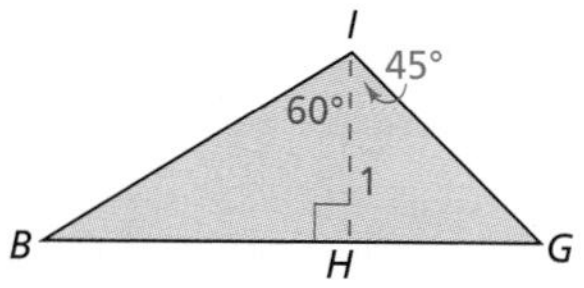

a. Use the formula $A = \frac{1}{2}bh$ to find the exact area of $\triangle BIG$.

b. Use the formula $A = \frac{1}{2}ab\sin C$ along with the measure of angle I to write another expression for the area of $\triangle BIG$.

c. Use the two expressions for the area of $\triangle BIG$ to find the exact value of sin 105°.

3. Find the area of a regular pentagon inscribed in a circle of radius 1.

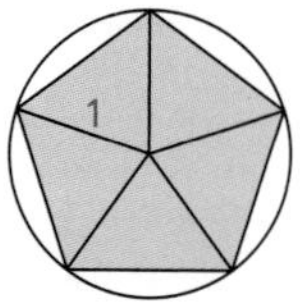

4. Find the exact area and perimeter of a regular hexagon inscribed in a circle of radius 1.

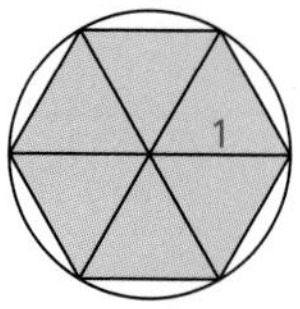

5. Here is a regular decagon (10-sided figure) inscribed in a circle of radius 1.

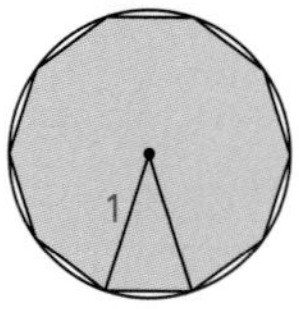

a. Approximate the area of the decagon to four decimal places.

b. **Take It Further** Find an exact value for the area of the decagon that involves no trigonometric functions.

6. a. Write an expression for the area of a regular n-gon (n-sided figure) inscribed in a circle of radius 1.

b. Copy and complete this table for the function $A(n)$, the area of the n-gon. Find all values to four decimal places.

Sides, n	Area, $A(n)$
4	2
5	■
6	■
10	■
12	■
20	■
30	■
50	■
100	■
360	■

Answers

2. a. $\frac{\sqrt{3}+1}{2}$ **b.** $\sqrt{2}\sin 105°$

c. $\frac{\sqrt{6}+\sqrt{2}}{4}$

3. $\frac{5}{2}\sin 72° \approx 2.38$

4. $A = \frac{3\sqrt{3}}{2}$, $P = 6$

5. a. 2.9389 **b.** $\frac{5\sqrt{10-2\sqrt{5}}}{4}$

6. a. $\frac{n}{2} \cdot \sin\left(\frac{360°}{n}\right)$

b.

Sides n	Area $A(n)$
4	2
5	2.3776
6	2.5981
10	2.9389
12	3
20	3.0902
30	3.1187
50	3.1333
100	3.1395
360	3.1414

7. **Write About It** Use your completed table from Exercise 6. Describe what happens to the area of the n-gons as the number of sides increases. Explain why this happens.

On Your Own

8. In $\triangle MIB$, $MI = 12$ and $IB = 10$. Find the maximum possible area for this triangle.

9. Which statement is true?

   A. $\cos 20^\circ = \cos 70^\circ$ **B.** $\cos 20^\circ = \cos^2 70^\circ$

   C. $\cos 20^\circ = \sin^2 70^\circ$ **D.** $\cos 20^\circ = \sin 70^\circ$

10. Use this diagram of an isosceles triangle with legs of length 1.

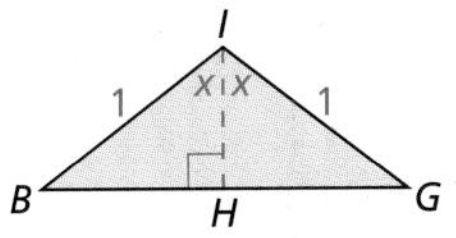

   a. Find the area of $\triangle BIG$ using the rule $A = \frac{1}{2}bh$.

   b. Find the area of $\triangle BIG$ using $\angle I$.

   c. Write a formula for $\sin 2x$ by using the two expressions for the area of $\triangle BIG$.

You will have to find the base and height in terms of x first.

11. **a.** Can one side of a triangle be ten times as long as each of the other sides? Explain.

   b. Can one angle in a triangle be ten times as large as each of the other angles?

12. Use this diagram of $\triangle ONE$.

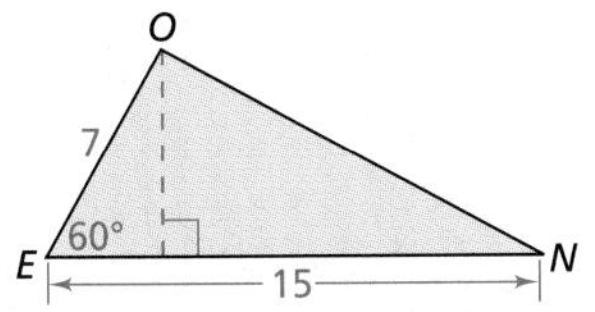

   a. Explain why there can be only one such $\triangle ONE$.

   b. Find the length of side $\overline{ON}$.

Habits of Mind

Establish a process. Keep track of your steps!

13. Use what you have learned in this lesson to find area formulas for each figure.

   a. a parallelogram **b.** a rhombus

Remember...

A rhombus is a parallelogram with all four sides equal in length.

7. As n increases, the polygon approaches a circle with radius 1, so the area approaches π.

8. 60

9. D

10. a. $\sin x \cos x$ **b.** $\frac{1}{2}\sin(2x)$

c. $\sin(2x) = 2 \sin x \cos x$

11. a. No; the sides cannot have lengths x, x, and $10x$ because $x + x < 10x$, and the sum of any two sides of a triangle must be greater than the third side.

b. Yes; it is possible for the angles of a triangle to be x, x, and $10x$; that would be 15°, 15°, and 150°.

12. a. Any other triangle with the same SAS would be congruent by SAS.

b. 13

13. a. If a parallelogram has adjacent sides a and b and the angle formed by the sides is θ, then $A = ab \sin \theta$.

b. If a rhombus has side length a, then $A = a^2 \sin \theta$.

On Your Own

EXERCISE 8 Drawing multiple triangles or making models may help students visualize this optimization problem, but the simplest way to do the problem is to use the area formula $\frac{1}{2}ab \sin C$. If $a = 10$ and $b = 12$, then the area of this triangle is $60 \sin C$. So now the question is, what is the maximum value of $\sin C$? Students learned from the graph of $y = \sin x$ that $\max(\sin C) = 1$. You can note that the only possible angle measurement for C is 90°.

EXERCISES 9 AND 10 The goal of Exercise 9 is to remind students that $\cos x = \sin(90 - x)$ for Exercise 10.

EXERCISE 11 emphasizes that, although there is a relationship between the measure of an angle and the length of the side opposite it, the relationship is not direct.

EXERCISE 12 Once they have the Law of Sines, students are able to continue with the same given information to determine every angle in the triangle.

EXERCISE 14 is a good reminder to students that they have to evaluate any assumptions they make about expressions involving trigonometric functions carefully. Most other functions with which students have dealt behave in a more "predictable" way. They might have one or two points where they "change direction" from increasing to decreasing, but the sine and cosine functions have infinitely many such points.

EXERCISE 15 Students need to recall here that sin x is greatest when x is 90°, or that since sin x is the y-coordinate of a point on the unit circle, it can never be greater than 1.

Additional Resources

PRINT RESOURCES
- Solution Manual
- Practice Workbook
- Assessment Resources
- Teaching Resources

TECHNOLOGY
- Interactive Textbook
- TeacherExpress CD-ROM
- ExamView CD-ROM
- PHSchool.com

Additional Practice

1. In $\triangle TOM$, $TO = 15$ and $OM = 18$. Find the maximum possible area for this triangle.

2. **Multiple Choice** Which statement is true?
   A. $\cos 25° = \cos 65°$ **B.** $\cos 25° = \cos^2 65°$
   C. $\cos 25° = \sin 65°$ **D.** $\cos 25° = \sin^2 65°$

3. Use this diagram of an isosceles triangle with legs of length 3.

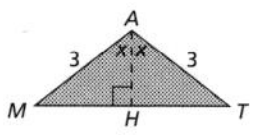

   a. Find the area of $\triangle MAT$ using the rule $A = \frac{1}{2}bh$.
   b. Find the area of $\triangle MAT$ using $\angle A$.
   c. Write a formula for sin $2x$ by using the two expressions for the area of $\triangle MAT$.

4. Use this diagram of $\triangle CAR$.

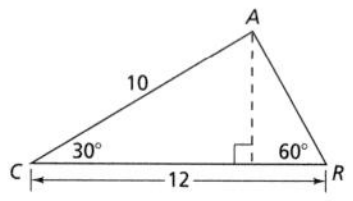

   a. Explain why there can be only one such $\triangle CAR$.
   b. Find the length of side $\overline{AR}$.

5. Verify that the Law of Sines is valid for a 45-45-90 right triangle.

6. In $\triangle ABC$, $AB = 14$, $AC = 9$, and $\angle B$ measures 35°.
   a. According to the Law of Sines, what is the value of sin C to three decimal places?
   b. Find all possible measures of $\angle C$ to the nearest degree.
   c. Find all possible measures of $\angle A$ and all possible lengths of side $\overline{BC}$.

7. In $\triangle ABC$, $AB = 14$, $AC = 9$, and $\angle C$ measures 35°.
   a. According to the Law of Sines, what is the value of sin B to three decimal places?
   b. Find all possible measures of $\angle B$ to the nearest degree.
   c. Find all possible measures of $\angle A$ and all possible lengths of side $\overline{BC}$.

Practice: For Lesson 8.11, assign Exercises 1–4.

14. **What's Wrong Here?** Derman thinks he has found two different formulas for the area of a parallelogram.

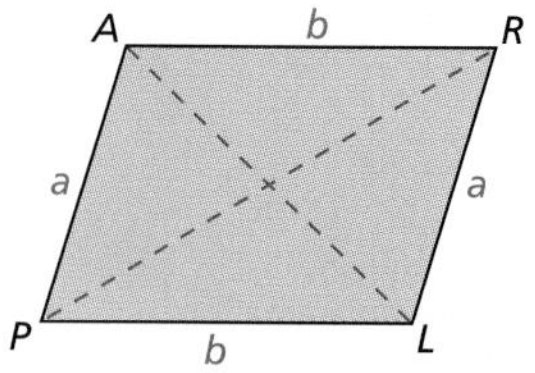

Derman says, "If I cut along one diagonal, I get that the area is $ab \sin P$, but if I cut along the other diagonal, I get that the area is $ab \sin L$. That doesn't seem possible—the areas should be the same. Angle L looks larger than angle P, so isn't sin L greater than sin P?"

What is wrong with Derman's reasoning? Are both area formulas correct?

15. A rhombus has perimeter 36. What is the largest possible area it could have?

16. **Standardized Test Prep** A triangle has a side that is 8 cm long and a side that is 12 cm long. The included angle measures 65°. To the nearest hundredth, what is the area of the triangle?

A. 24 cm^2 **B.** 40.57 cm^2 **C.** 43.50 cm^2 **D.** 81.14 cm^2

Go Online PHSchool.com
For additional practice, go to **Web Code:** bfa-0811

Maintain Your Skills

17. Each set of three lengths forms a triangle. Determine whether the triangle is acute, right, or obtuse.

a. 8, 6, 10 **b.** 8, 6, 12 **c.** 8, 6, 13 **d.** 8, 6, 9
e. 8, 6, 8 **f.** 8, 6, 7 **g.** 8, 6, 6 **h.** 8, 6, 5

Answers

14. Derman's reasoning is incorrect because the fact that the sine of one angle is bigger than the sine of another angle does not imply that the angle is bigger; both area formulas are correct because in a parallelogram, any two adjacent angles are supplementary. So, $P = 180° - L$ and $\sin L = \sin(180° - L) = \sin P$.

15. 81

16. C

17. a. right
b. obtuse
c. obtuse
d. acute
e. acute
f. acute
g. acute
h. acute

8.12 The Law of Sines

In the last lesson, you learned to find the area of a triangle using the rule $A = \frac{1}{2}ab \sin C$, where a and b are two side lengths and C is the angle between those sides. This lesson introduces the Law of Sines, which you can prove using that formula. The Law of Sines relates the side lengths in a triangle to their corresponding angle measures.

Remember...

You call the angle between two given sides the included angle. Similarly, you call the side between two given angles the included side.

For Discussion

1. If one angle in a triangle is twice as large as another, is the corresponding side twice as long? Give an example to justify your answer.
2. Can one side of a triangle be ten times as long as each of the other sides? Can one angle in a triangle be ten times as large as each of the other angles? Explain.

There is a correspondence between sides and angles in a triangle, but not a direct one. For example, it is possible for one angle in a triangle to be many times larger than both of the other angles (say, a triangle with angles 10°, 15°, and 165°). But it is not possible for one side of a triangle to be many times larger than both other sides. Still, the longest side in a triangle is opposite the largest angle, so there is a relationship.

That relationship is the **Law of Sines.**

Theorem 8.5 *Law of Sines*

Given $\triangle ABC$ with corresponding side lengths a, b, and c,

$$\frac{a}{\sin A} = \frac{b}{\sin B} = \frac{c}{\sin C}$$

You can write the Law of Sines with the numerators and denominators switched.

$$\frac{\sin A}{a} = \frac{\sin B}{b} = \frac{\sin C}{c}$$

It is true in either form. Work through Exercise 6 to see why you might want to use the form with $\frac{c}{\sin C}$.

Proof Consider $\triangle ABC$.

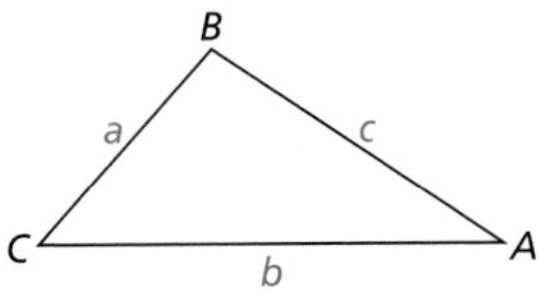

You can write the area of this triangle in three different ways. Choose two.

$$\text{area} = \frac{1}{2}ac \sin B \quad \text{and} \quad \text{area} = \frac{1}{2}bc \sin A$$

For Discussion

1. No; answers may vary. Sample: The ratio of the sides opposite the 30° and 60° angles in a 30° – 60° – 90° right triangle is $1 : \sqrt{3}$, so the side opposite the 60° angle is $\sqrt{3}$ times as long, not twice as long.
2. No, the sides cannot have lengths x, x, and $10x$ because $x + x < 10x$, and the sum of any two sides of a triangle must be greater than the third side; yes, it is possible for the angles of a triangle to be x, x, and $10x$; the angles could be 15°, 15°, and 150°.

Lesson Overview

GOAL

- State and use the Law of Sines.

In this lesson, students formalize their intuitions about the relationship between the lengths of sides in a triangle and the measure of the angle opposite the sides. Although they know that the largest side in a triangle is opposite the largest angle, they also know that if you make an angle twice as big, it does not make the side twice as long. They use different expressions for the area of a triangle—obtained using techniques from the previous lesson—to prove the Law of Sines. Then they see how to apply this result to solve triangles.

CHECK YOUR UNDERSTANDING

- Core: 1, 2, 3, 4, 7, 8
- Optional: 5, 6
- Extension: 9

MATERIALS

- geometry software
- graph paper
- graphing calculators
- Blackline Master 8.12

HOMEWORK

- Core: 10, 11, 12, 13, 14, 15, 16, 17
- Optional: 19
- Extension: 18

VOCABULARY

- ambiguous case
- included angle
- included side
- Law of Sines
- solve a triangle

Launch

Begin the lesson with For Discussion Problems 1 and 2.

Explore

For Discussion

PROBLEM 1 Students may bring up examples of triangles that have one angle that is twice the measure of another. The 30°-60°-90° and 45°-45°-90° triangles are both such triangles, and students are already familiar with them. You may want to remind students that all it takes is a single counterexample to disprove a statement.

PROBLEM 2 was already posed in Exercise 11 from Lesson 8.11. If you assigned this exercise as homework, your students have already had a chance to think about it. It is possible for one of the angles in a triangle to be a lot larger than the other two, as long as the three angle measures sum to 180°. However, it is not possible for one of the sides of a triangle to be a much greater than both of the others. This is because of the Triangle Inequality, which states that the sum of any two side lengths in a triangle must be greater than the length of the third side. This means that if you have sides measuring n and $10n$, the third side must have length greater than $11n$.

Developing Habits of Mind

Make sure students understand the side note. Some students may be confused, expecting that since 60° is twice the size of 30°, the side opposite 60° must be twice as long as the side opposite 30°. As the side note points out, the sines of the angles are compared, not the measures of the angles.

A triangle cannot have two different areas, so these expressions must be equal.

$$\frac{1}{2}ac\sin B = \frac{1}{2}bc\sin A$$

You can cancel the factors of $\frac{1}{2}$ and c from each side. You know $c \neq 0$ since it is a side length.

$$a\sin B = b\sin A$$
$$\frac{a}{\sin A} = \frac{b}{\sin B}$$

Use the starting point $\frac{1}{2}ac\sin B = \frac{1}{2}ab\sin C$ to obtain the relationship $\frac{b}{\sin B} = \frac{c}{\sin C}$. This completes the proof.

Developing Habits of Mind

Look for relationships. The Law of Sines is useful whenever you know a side and its opposite angle measure. For one thing, it puts a limit on how long the other sides in the triangle can be. Suppose you know $a = 10$ and $\angle A$ measures 50°. Then

$$\frac{a}{\sin A} \approx 13.05$$

The Law of Sines says that this also equals $\frac{b}{\sin B}$. Since $\sin B$ cannot be greater than 1, b cannot be greater than 13.05.

You can rewrite the proportions in the Law of Sines to discover more facts. Here is one way.

$$\frac{a}{b} = \frac{\sin A}{\sin B}$$

This proportion answers the For Discussion problem. If one side of a triangle is twice as long as another side, the sine of the angle opposite the longer side is twice as great.

Note that this does not say that the angle itself is twice as large.

You can see this in a 30-60-90 right triangle.

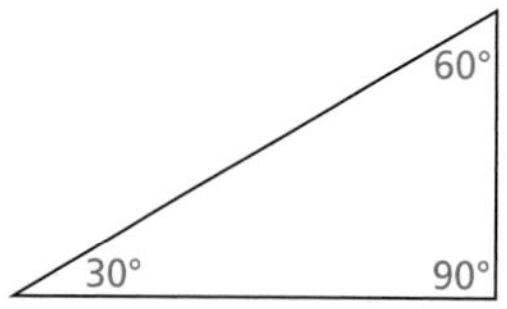

The side opposite the right angle is twice as long as the side opposite the 30° angle. The Law of Sines confirms this: $\sin 90^\circ = 1$ and $\sin 30^\circ = \frac{1}{2}$.

Example

Problem Find all remaining side lengths and angle measures in this triangle.

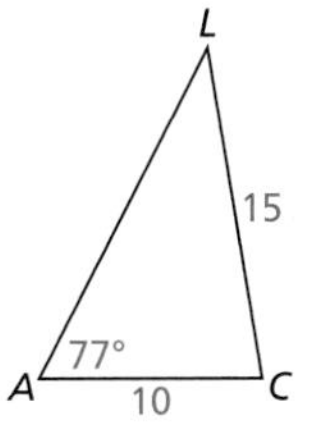

> $\triangle LAC$ is not to scale. It could be acute, right, or obtuse.

Solution You know the measure of $\angle A$ and the length of its opposite side. Use the Law of Sines.

$$\frac{a}{\sin A} = \frac{\ell}{\sin L} = \frac{c}{\sin C}$$

The variables a, ℓ, and c are the side lengths opposite angles A, L, and C. Fill in the known information.

$$\frac{15}{\sin 77^\circ} = \frac{10}{\sin L} = \frac{c}{\sin C}$$

Use the first two equal expressions and solve for $\sin L$.

$$\sin L = \frac{10 \sin 77^\circ}{15} \approx 0.6496$$

A calculator gives $\sin^{-1}(0.6496)$ as approximately 40.5°. Note, though, that this is not the only angle with sine about 0.6496. The other angle is $180^\circ - 40.5^\circ = 139.5^\circ$.

So, are there two possible measures of $\angle L$? No, the 139.5° angle is impossible, since there is a 77° angle in the triangle. The measure of $\angle L$ must be less than 103°.

That means $\angle L$ measures 40.5°, and $\angle C$ measures 62.5°.

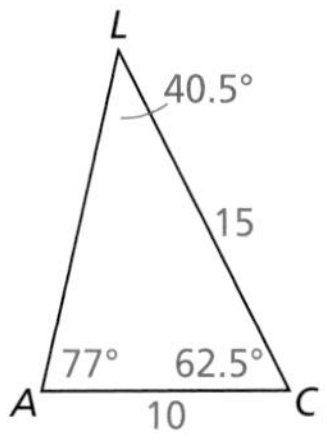

Then use the Law of Sines again to find c.

$$\frac{15}{\sin 77^\circ} = \frac{c}{\sin 62.5^\circ}$$

This gives $c \approx 13.66$. Now you know all the side lengths and angle measures.

Habits of Mind

Check your work. This is an important check. Note that there is no other reason to reject the second angle. If both angles are possible, so be it. There would then be two cases to look at for the rest of the solution.

Example

You might want to reinforce the idea of checking work at opportune points when working through problems. Otherwise, students may do lots of extra work working through a problem using alternatives they could have dismissed right away.

You can use Blackline Master 8.12 to guide students through the Example.

For You to Do

Work together as a class to find a complete proof. You may need to hint that students can handle the obtuse case separately. One way is to sketch a graph of the sine function. Help students understand that, when working with obtuse angles, an angle with greater measure does not necessarily have a greater sine value.

You may also need to discuss how students can begin their proof with a statement such as, "If A is the smallest angle in a triangle and C is the largest . . ." without losing its generality—its application to every possible triangle. Tell students that they can begin by drawing any triangle. They can label the triangle so that A is the smallest angle, C is the largest, and B is the one that is left. The statement tells them how to label any triangle.

Wrap Up

If you do not complete the proof of the Hinge Theorem in class, you may want to assign it as homework or clear up the details at the beginning of your next class. If you have time, go over some of the Check Your Understanding core exercises.

Assessment Resources

Lesson Quiz 8.12

1. Find all the remaining side lengths and angle measures of the triangle at the right. Round answers to the nearest tenth, if necessary.

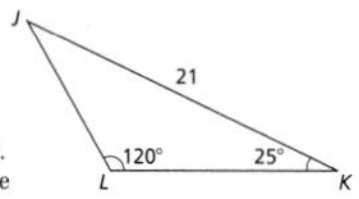

2. In $\triangle ABC$, $AB = 16$, $AC = 14$, and $\angle B$ measures 50°.
   a. According to the Law of Sines, what is the value of sin C to three decimal places?
   b. Find all possible measures of $\angle C$ to the nearest degree.
   c. Find all possible measures of $\angle A$ and all possible lengths of side $\overline{BC}$.

3. In $\triangle ABC$, $AB = 16$, $AC = 14$, and $\angle C$ measures 50°.
   a. According to the Law of Sines, what is the value of sin B to three decimal places?
   b. Find all possible measures of $\angle B$ to the nearest degree.
   c. Find all possible measures of $\angle A$ and all possible lengths of side $\overline{BC}$.

Exercises

HOMEWORK

- Core: 10, 11, 12, 13, 14, 15, 16, 17
- Optional: 19
- Extension: 18

Check Your Understanding

EXERCISE 1 By now, students should be comfortable with the fact that the maximum possible value for sin x is 1, but remind them to make sure that a 90° angle would make sense in the context of the rest of the situation. In this case, a 90° angle is possible.

Note that you need at least three pieces of information about a triangle before you can use the Law of Sines to solve for the rest. And not all groups of three pieces will do. For example, if you only know the three side lengths, you have all the numerators and none of the denominators. So, the Law of Sines helps in solving triangles, but sometimes you need a different method. You will learn another method in the next lesson.

To *solve a triangle* just means to find its side lengths and angle measures. The example's direction line could have been "Solve $\triangle ALC$."

For You to Do

3. Use the Law of Sines to prove the Hinge Theorem: In a triangle, the longest side is opposite the largest angle and the shortest side is opposite the smallest angle.

Exercises *Practicing Habits of Mind*

Check Your Understanding

Figures of triangles in this lesson are not to scale. Do not assume anything about the size of angles or the relative lengths of the sides of a triangle.

1. In $\triangle MIB$, $MI = 12$. This side is opposite a 30° angle. Find the maximum possible side length that this triangle can have.

For Exercises 2 and 3, find all the remaining side lengths and angle measures of the triangle. Round answers to one decimal place if necessary.

How can you apply the Law of Sines in Exercise 3? You need a side and an opposite angle.

2. 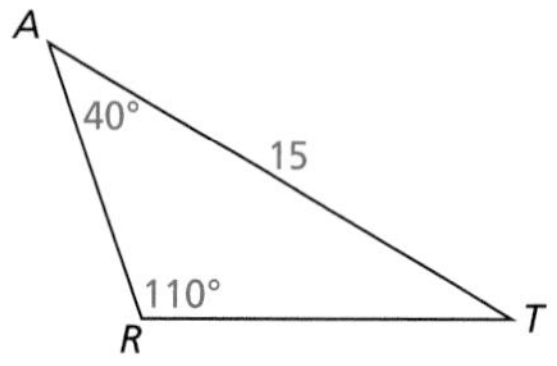

3. 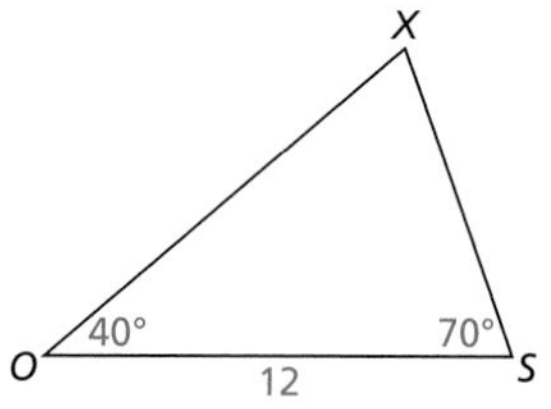

Answers

For You To Do

3. Answers may vary. Sample: In an acute or right triangle, all the angles are less than or equal to 90°. If A is the smallest angle and C is the largest angle, then $\sin A \leq \sin B \leq \sin C$ because $y = \sin x$ increases as x goes from 0° to 90°. Using the Law of Sines, you can write $a = b \cdot \frac{\sin A}{\sin B} = c \cdot \frac{\sin A}{\sin C}$. Both of the sine ratios in this equation are less than or equal to 1, so you know that $a \leq b$ and $a \leq c$. So a is the smallest side. You can also write $c = a \cdot \frac{\sin C}{\sin A} = b \cdot \frac{\sin C}{\sin B}$. Both of the sine ratios in this equation are greater than or equal to 1, so c is the largest side of the triangle.

In an obtuse triangle, the greatest side is opposite the obtuse angle, and each of the other two angles is less than 90°, so the proof for acute and right triangles above can be applied.

4. Use the triangle below. Find the two possible measures of $\angle K$. Explain why there are two possible answers.

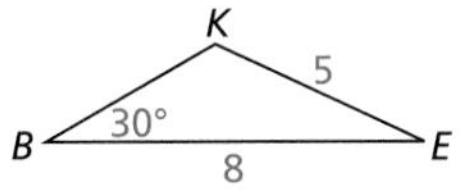

5. **Write About It** What do Exercises 2, 3, and 4 suggest about triangle congruence?

6. You can draw a circle through any three noncollinear points. Draw a circle through the vertices of a triangle such as $\triangle ABC$ below. Draw diameter $\overline{AD}$. Connect points B and D.

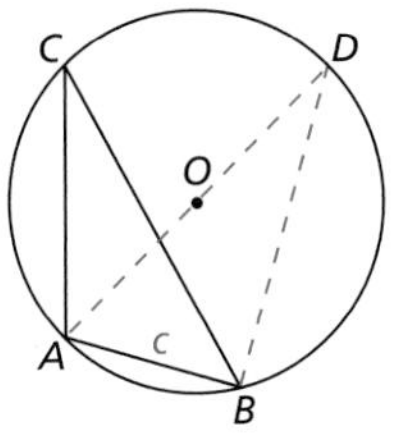

   a. Why is $\angle ABD$ a right angle?

   b. Explain why $\angle C$ and $\angle D$ are congruent.

   c. Explain why $\sin C = \sin D$.

   d. Show that the diameter $\overline{AD}$ has length $\frac{c}{\sin C}$.

7. Copy the diagram below. Drop an altitude from any vertex of the triangle. Find two expressions for the length of the altitude. Use these expressions to prove the Law of Sines.

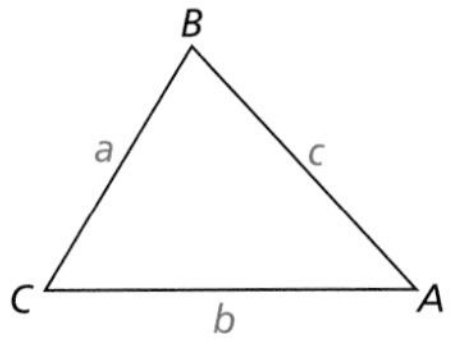

You can state the result of Exercise 6 as part of the Law of Sines: In a triangle, the ratio of any side to the sine of its opposite angle is the diameter of a circle circumscribing the triangle.

EXERCISE 2 is an example where AAS is given. Since all triangles with two angles and the corresponding nonincluded side congruent are congruent by AAS, there is one possible solution for this triangle.

EXERCISE 3 is an example where ASA is given. Since all triangles with two angles and the included side congruent are congruent by ASA, there is one possible solution for this triangle.

EXERCISE 4 is an example where SSA is given. SSA does not guarantee congruence, so there are two possible solution for this triangle.

EXERCISE 5 asks students to summarize the results of Exercises 2–4.

EXERCISE 7 results in a second proof of the Law of Sines.

Exercises

1. 24
2. $m\angle T = 30°$, $RT = 10.3$, $AR = 8.0$
3. $m\angle X = 70°$, $XS = 8.2$, $XO = 12$
4. $m\angle K = 53.1°$ or $126.9°$; there are two solutions for $\sin K = 0.8$.
5. The situations in Exercises 2 and 3 are AAS and ASA, and those situations result in a unique triangle, so they are congruence theorems. The situation in Exercise 4 is SSA, and that situation results in two triangles, so it is not a congruence theorem.

6–7. See back of book.

EXERCISES 8 AND 9 Exercise 8 is a specific numerical example of the generic calculation in Exercise 9. If you assign Exercise 9, make sure you also assign Exercise 8.

EXERCISE 9 Students who solve this exercise have proved the Law of Cosines, perhaps with the expression in some other form. The most difficult piece here is students' recognition of the divided lengths of the cut side. Another numeric example may help, but this result is proved in the following lesson.

On Your Own

EXERCISE 12 motivates the Law of Cosines, which is proved in the next lesson. It gives a situation in which the Law of Sines is not enough to solve the triangle.

8. Use the diagram of $\triangle TWO$ below. Find the length of $\overline{TW}$. Keep track of your steps!

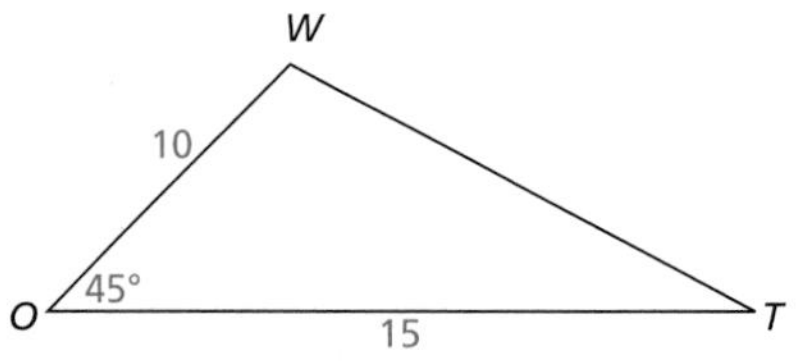

9. **Take It Further** Use the diagram of $\triangle ABC$ below. Find the length of side $\overline{AB}$ in terms of a, b, and $\angle C$.

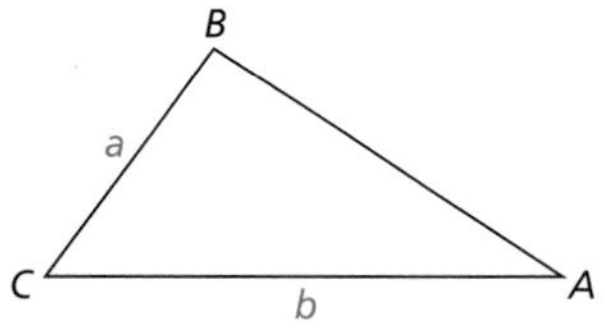

On Your Own

10. Verify that the Law of Sines is valid for a 30-60-90 right triangle.

11. Verify that the Law of Sines is valid for a 45-45-90 right triangle.

12. In $\triangle ABC$, $AB = 7$, $AC = 15$, and $\angle A$ measures 60°. What happens if you try to use the Law of Sines to find the other sides and angles in this triangle?

13. **Standardized Test Prep** You are given $\triangle ABC$ with $AB = 14$ cm, $AC = 10$ cm, and $m\angle C = 110°$. What is the length of $\overline{BC}$?

A. 4.82 cm

B. 5.10 cm

C. 6.96 cm

D. 7.38 cm

Go Online PHSchool.com

For additional practice, go to **Web Code:** bfa-0812

Answers

8. $TW = \sqrt{325 - 150\sqrt{2}}$

9. $AB = \sqrt{a^2 + b^2 - 2ab\cos C}$

10. Answers may vary. Sample: The sides 1, $\sqrt{3}$, and 2 are opposite the angles with measures 30°, 60°, and 90°, so $\frac{1}{\sin 30°} = 2$, $\frac{\sqrt{3}}{\sin 60°} = 2$, $\frac{2}{\sin 90°} = 2$.

11. Answers may vary. Sample: The sides 1, 1, and $\sqrt{2}$ are opposite the angles with measures 45°, 45° and 90°, so $\frac{1}{\sin 45°} = \sqrt{2}$ and $\frac{\sqrt{2}}{\sin 90°}\sqrt{2}$.

12. To use the Law of Sines, you need to know a side and the angle opposite that side. There is not enough information for this exercise, so you cannot use the Law of Sines.

13. C

14. a. $\sin C = 0.771$

b. 50°, 130°

c. $m\angle A = 90°$ or 10°; $BC = 15.6$ or 2.7

The case in which you know two side lengths and a nonincluded angle measure of a triangle is the "ambiguous case." Exercises 14–18 explore this situation.

14. In $\triangle ABC$, $AB = 12$, $AC = 10$, and $\angle B$ measures 40°.

a. According to the Law of Sines, what is the value of sin C to three decimal places?

b. Find all possible measures of $\angle C$ to the nearest degree.

c. Find all possible measures of $\angle A$ and all possible lengths of side $\overline{BC}$.

15. In $\triangle ABC$, $AB = 12$, $AC = 10$, and $\angle C$ measures 40°.

a. According to the Law of Sines, what is the value of sin B to three decimal places?

b. Find all possible measures of $\angle B$ to the nearest degree.

c. Find all possible measures of $\angle A$ and all possible lengths of side $\overline{BC}$.

16. In $\triangle ABC$, $AB = 12$, $AC = 10$, and $\angle B$ measures 70°.

a. According to the Law of Sines, what is the value of sin C to three decimal places?

b. Find all possible measures of $\angle C$ to the nearest degree.

c. Find all possible measures of $\angle A$ and all possible lengths of side $\overline{BC}$.

17. Write About It Tyler says that if the given angle in an ambiguous-case problem is obtuse, then there can be only one solution. Do you agree? Explain.

18. Take It Further For the information given in an ambiguous-case problem, there can be 0, 1, or 2 possible triangles. Determine the conditions on the sides and angle that produce these possible outcomes.

Maintain Your Skills

19. For each set of measurements for $\triangle ABC$, find the remaining side lengths and angle measures.

a. $BC = 10$, $\angle A$ measures 30°, and $\angle B$ measures 45°.

b. $BC = 20$, $\angle A$ measures 30°, and $\angle B$ measures 45°.

c. $AC = 10$, $\angle A$ measures 30°, and $\angle B$ measures 45°.

d. $AC = 10$, $\angle A$ measures 30°, and $\angle B$ measures 60°.

e. $AC = 10$, $\angle A$ measures 30°, and $\angle B$ measures 120°.

Go Online Video Tutor
PHSchool.com
Web Code: bfe-0775

15. a. $\sin B = 0.536$

b. $m\angle B = 32°$ or $148°$

c. Answers may vary. Sample: If $m\angle B = 148°$, then $m\angle A = -8°$, which is not possible. So $m\angle A$ must be 108°, and $BC = 17.8$.

16. a. $\sin C = 1.128$, which is impossible.

b. no solution

c. no solution

17. No; there is no solution if the side opposite the given angle is less than or equal to the side adjacent to the given angle.

18. Assume that you are given angle A, and sides a and b with a opposite $\angle A$ in the triangle. If $\angle A$ is acute and if $a < b \sin A$, then there is no solution. If $a = b \sin A$, there will be one solution. If $a > b \sin A$ there will be two solutions. If $\angle A$ is right or obtuse, and if $a > b$, there is one solution. If $a \leq b$, there are no solutions.

19. See back of book.

EXERCISE 15 Students may not notice until they start calculating angle A that there is a problem with one of the measures of angle B, and that there should only be one solution. Let this happen.

EXERCISE 16 This time, the given information does not give any viable triangles. Again, let students discover this for themselves.

Additional Resources

PRINT RESOURCES
- Solution Manual
- Practice Workbook
- Assessment Resources
- Teaching Resources

TECHNOLOGY
- Interactive Textbook
- TeacherExpress CD-ROM
- ExamView CD-ROM
- PHSchool.com

Additional Practice

1. In $\triangle TOM$, $TO = 15$ and $OM = 18$. Find the maximum possible area for this triangle.

2. Multiple Choice Which statement is true?

A. $\cos 25° = \cos 65°$ **B.** $\cos 25° = \cos^2 65°$
C. $\cos 25° = \sin 65°$ **D.** $\cos 25° = \sin^2 65°$

3. Use this diagram of an isosceles triangle with legs of length 3.

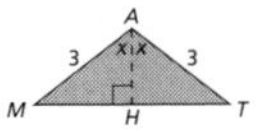

a. Find the area of $\triangle MAT$ using the rule $A = \frac{1}{2}bh$.

b. Find the area of $\triangle MAT$ using $\angle A$.

c. Write a formula for $\sin 2x$ by using the two expressions for the area of $\triangle MAT$.

4. Use this diagram of $\triangle CAR$.

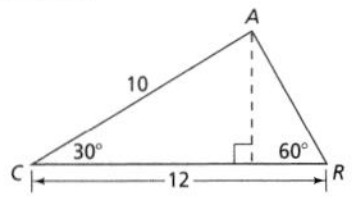

a. Explain why there can be only one such $\triangle CAR$.

b. Find the length of side $\overline{AR}$.

5. Verify that the Law of Sines is valid for a 45-45-90 right triangle.

6. In $\triangle ABC$, $AB = 14$, $AC = 9$, and $\angle B$ measures 35°.

a. According to the Law of Sines, what is the value of sin C to three decimal places?

b. Find all possible measures of $\angle C$ to the nearest degree.

c. Find all possible measures of $\angle A$ and all possible lengths of side $\overline{BC}$.

7. In $\triangle ABC$, $AB = 14$, $AC = 9$, and $\angle C$ measures 35°.

a. According to the Law of Sines, what is the value of sin B to three decimal places?

b. Find all possible measures of $\angle B$ to the nearest degree.

c. Find all possible measures of $\angle A$ and all possible lengths of side $\overline{BC}$.

Practice: For Lesson 8.12, assign Exercises 5–7.

Lesson Overview

GOAL

- State and use the Law of Cosines.

In the last lesson, students were able to solve many triangles, but there were a few situations that did not work. If they knew two sides and the included angle, or if they knew all three sides and no angles, they could not use the Law of Sines to solve the triangle. In this lesson, students will prove the Law of Cosines, which will give them the tool they need to solve the triangles they could not in the previous lesson.

CHECK YOUR UNDERSTANDING

- Core: 1, 2, 3, 4, 6, 7
- Optional: 8a
- Extension: 5, 8b

MATERIALS

- CAS (recommended)
- graphing calculators
- Blackline Masters 8.13A, 8.13B

HOMEWORK

- Core: 9, 10, 11, 12, 13, 14, 15, 17
- Optional: 18, 20
- Extension: 16, 19

VOCABULARY

- Law of Cosines

Launch

Begin this lesson with the Minds in Action dialog. You might ask two students to read the parts of Sasha and Derman.

Explore

Minds in Action

Go over this dialog carefully in class. For students who have difficulty remembering the Law of Cosines, this dialog provides them with a way to derive it on their own from information they may already remember well.

After going over the dialog, you can use Blackline Master 8.13A as a transparency.

8.13 The Law of Cosines

In the last lesson, you learned the Law of Sines. It relates the side lengths of a triangle to their corresponding angle measures. In this lesson, you will learn the **Law of Cosines.** If you know two side lengths of a triangle and the measure of their included angle, the Law of Cosines can help you find the length of the third side. Alternatively, if you know three side lengths of a triangle, you can use the Law of Cosines to figure out the measure of any angle in the triangle.

Minds in Action — episode 38

Derman and Sasha are looking at $\triangle ONE$.

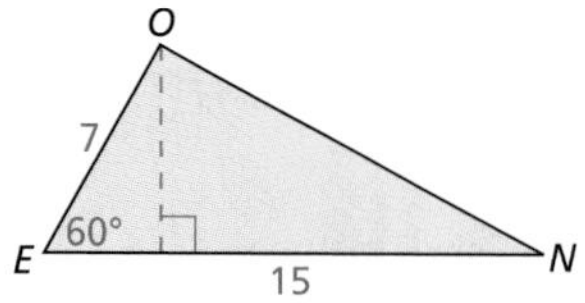

Sasha We need to find the length of side $\overline{ON}$.

Derman Can't we just use that $a^2 + b^2 = c^2$ theorem? We know the two sides, so let's just find the length of the third. $(ON)^2 = 7^2 + 15^2$. So ON is about 16.55.

Sasha The Pythagorean Theorem only works for right triangles!

Derman Oh, right. Well, there are two right triangles in our drawing. Too bad we don't know the height of the dotted line.

What right triangles is Derman talking about?

Sasha We can figure that out. We can at least figure out the length of the legs of each triangle, using sine and cosine.

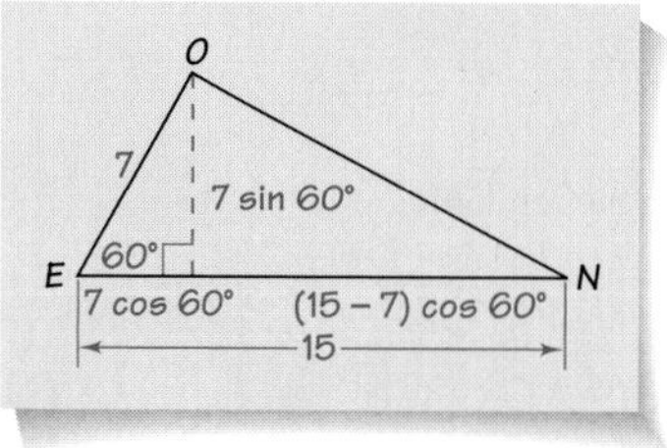

Derman Now we can use the Pythagorean Theorem to find ON. It looks messy, though.

They write down their steps.

$$\begin{aligned}(ON)^2 &= (7 \sin 60°)^2 + (15 - 7 \cos 60°)^2 \\ &= 49 \sin^2 60° + 225 - 2 \cdot 15 \cdot 7 \cos 60° + 49 \cos^2 60°\end{aligned}$$

Sasha I wonder if we can simplify this a bit.

Derman Hey. There's 49 times sine squared, and 49 times cosine squared, and they're even the same angle. I'm going to combine those and see what happens.

$$\begin{aligned}(ON)^2 &= 49\,(\sin^2 60^\circ + \cos^2 60^\circ) + 225 - 210 \cos 60^\circ \\ &= 49 + 225 - 210 \cos 60^\circ \\ &= 274 - 210\left(\tfrac{1}{2}\right) \\ &= 169\end{aligned}$$

Derman Wow! $ON = 13$.

Sasha Very smooth.

For You to Do

1. Find the length of side $\overline{TW}$ in the triangle below.

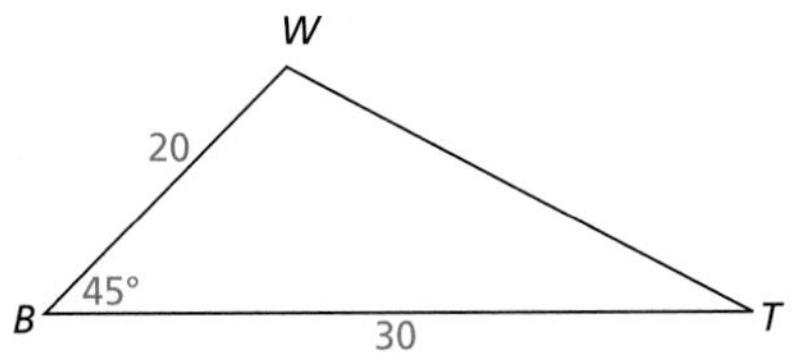

Sasha and Derman found the following equation.

$$c^2 = 49 + 225 - 210 \cos 60^\circ$$

They can rewrite the equation this way.

$$(ON)^2 = 7^2 + 15^2 - 2 \times 7 \times 15 \cos 60^\circ$$

In fact, a similar relationship holds for any triangle with sides of length *a*, *b*, and *c*.

Theorem 8.6 The Law of Cosines

Given $\triangle ABC$ with corresponding side lengths *a*, *b*, and *c*,

$$c^2 = a^2 + b^2 - 2ab \cos C$$

The following proof of the Law of Cosines closely follows what Derman and Sasha did in the dialog. There are three possible situations, depending on whether $\angle C$ is acute, right, or obtuse.

Answers

For You To Do

1. 21.2 units

PROOF You can do an alternate proof using information from Chapter 3 *Complex Numbers*.

In Chapter 3, students learned that if z is any complex number, $z + \overline{z}$ is a real number. Using the polar form of a complex number makes this analysis simpler. Students will see polar form in CME Project *Precalculus.* However, once students know a little trig, they can say more.

You can say that 0, z, $z + \overline{z}$, and $\overline{z}$ form a rhombus, and then $z + \overline{z} = 2|z|\cos\theta$ where $\theta = \arg z$.

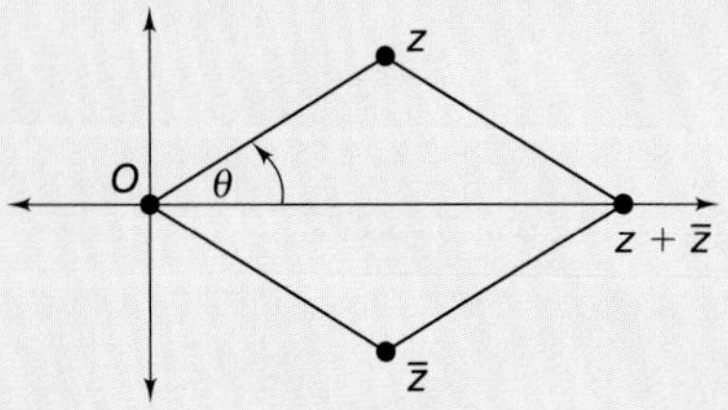

Using the multiplication rule, you can show that, if z and w are any complex numbers and if α is the angle between z and w, then

$$\arg z\overline{w} = \arg z - \arg w = \alpha$$

So, suppose z and w are complex numbers and the angle between them is α.

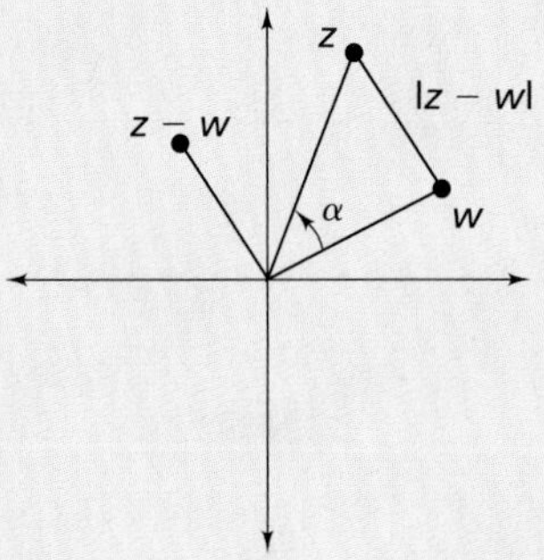

Then

$$\begin{aligned}
|z - w|^2 &= (z - w)\overline{(z - w)} \\
&= (z - w)(\overline{z} - \overline{w}) \\
&= z\overline{z} - z\overline{w} - w\overline{z} + w\overline{w} \\
&= z\overline{z} - (z\overline{w} + \overline{z\overline{w}}) + w\overline{w} \\
&= |z|^2 - 2|z\overline{w}|\cos\alpha + |w|^2 \\
&= |z|^2 - 2|zw|\cos\alpha + |w|^2
\end{aligned}$$

That is the Law of Cosines.

Case 2: You may want to reinforce the concept that the Law of Cosines is a more general statement of the Pythagorean Theorem. In other words, as Case 2 shows, the Pythagorean Theorem is just a special case of the Law of Cosines.

Proof Case 1: Suppose $\angle C$ is an acute angle. Let $\triangle ABC$ be the triangle below.

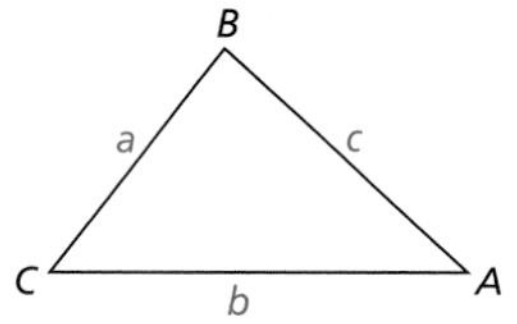

As Sasha did for her triangle, you can write down much more information about this triangle.

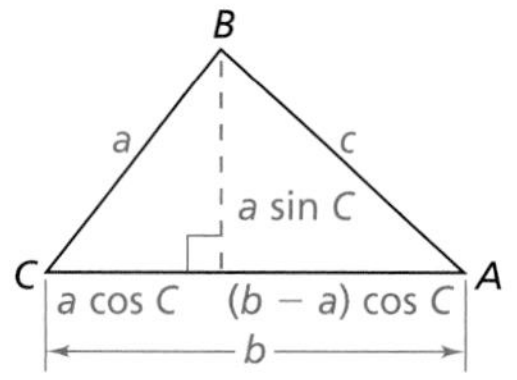

Now find c^2 by using the Pythagorean Theorem and the triangle on the right.

$$\begin{aligned}
c^2 &= (a\sin C)^2 + (b - a\cos C)^2 \\
&= a^2\sin^2 C + b^2 - 2ab\cos C + a^2\cos^2 C \\
&= a^2(\sin^2 C + \cos^2 C) + b^2 - 2ab\cos C \\
&= a^2 + b^2 - 2ab\cos C
\end{aligned}$$

Case 2: Suppose $\angle C$ is a right angle. Let $\triangle ABC$ be the triangle below.

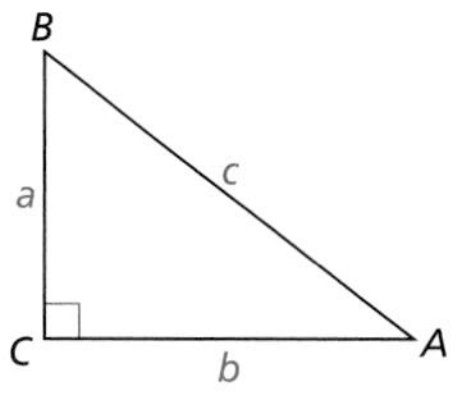

Since C is a right angle, by the Pythagorean Theorem $c^2 = a^2 + b^2$. Also, $\cos C = 0$. So, $c^2 = a^2 + b^2 + (\text{anything})\cos C$.

In particular, $c^2 = a^2 + b^2 - 2ab\cos C$ is true.

Case 3: Suppose $\angle C$ is an obtuse angle. Let $\triangle ABC$ be the triangle below.

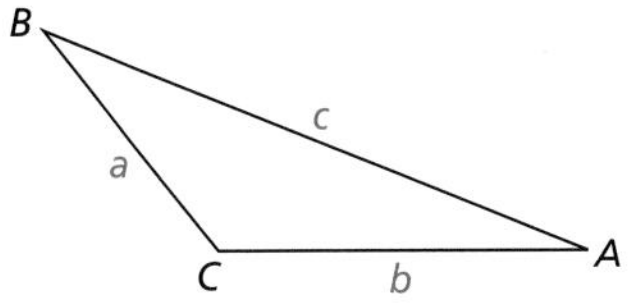

You can extend side $\overline{AC}$ to meet the altitude.

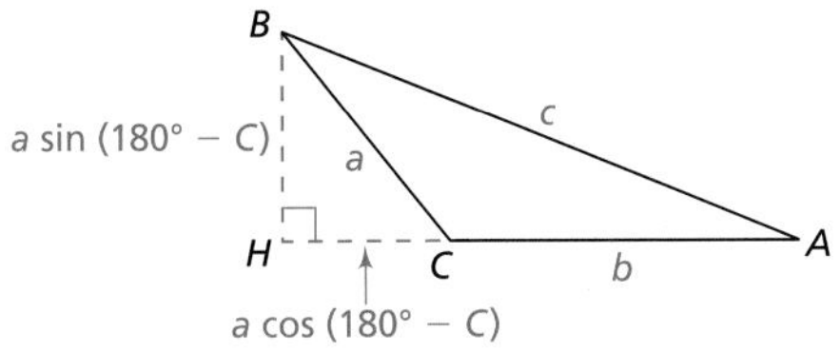

You know that $\sin(180° - C) = \sin C$ and $\cos(180° - C) = -\cos C$. So, you can relabel the diagram to use $\angle C$.

Why is the length of the altitude $a \sin(180° - C)$? Why does $CH = a \cos(180° - C)$?

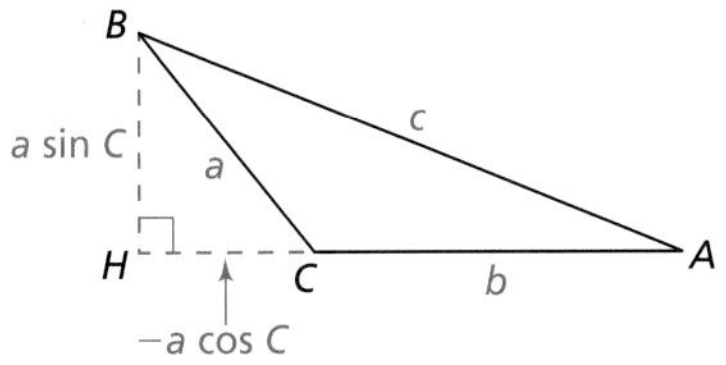

Note that the length $-a \cos C$ is positive, since $\cos C$ is negative. Use the Pythagorean Theorem again. The length along the base is the sum of the two lengths b and $-a \cos C$.

$$\begin{aligned} c^2 &= (a \sin C)^2 + (b + (-a \cos C))^2 \\ &= a^2 \sin^2 C + b^2 - 2ab \cos C + a^2 \cos^2 C \\ &= a^2 (\sin^2 C + \cos^2 C) + b^2 - 2ab \cos C \\ &= a^2 + b^2 - 2ab \cos C \end{aligned}$$

Separating a proof into cases is similar to sorting your laundry into whites and colors.

GEOMETRIC PROOF OF THE LAW OF COSINES This proof of the Law of Cosines is actually a generalization of Euclid's proof of the Pythagorean Theorem. It is optional. Go through this with your class if you wish to revisit some material from geometry. There are a few questions left open in the presented proof, which are answered below.

- The blue rectangle is constructed to have base b and height $a \cos C$, so its area is $ab \cos C$.
- The green rectangle is constructed to have base a and height $b \cos C$, so its area is also $ab \cos C$.
- $\triangle CAI \cong \triangle FAB$ by SAS. $FA = CA = b$, $AB = AI = c$, and $m\angle FAB = m\angle CAI = m\angle A + 90$.
- Rectangle $AIQS$ and triangle CAI share base $\overline{AI}$ and have height $IQ = b \cos A$, so the area of the rectangle is twice that of the triangle. Similarly, rectangle $FAMT$ and triangle FAB share base $\overline{FA}$ and have height $FM = c \cos A$, so again, the rectangle has twice the area of the triangle.

The Law of Cosines looks very much like the Pythagorean Theorem. The only difference is the little correction of $-2ab \cos C$. This suggests that you can find a different proof using only ideas from geometry.

Habits of Mind

Look for relationships. You can think of the Law of Cosines as a generalization of the Pythagorean Theorem, since it includes the Pythagorean Theorem as a special case.

Proof Suppose you have $\triangle ABC$.

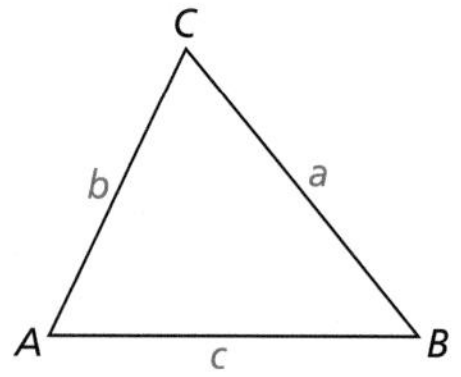

You can draw in squares with areas a^2, b^2, and c^2.

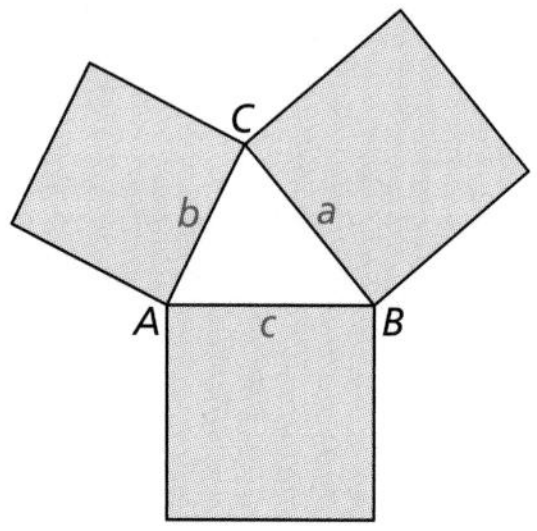

You want to find a way to describe c^2 in terms of a^2 and b^2. The diagram below shows the three altitudes of the triangle.

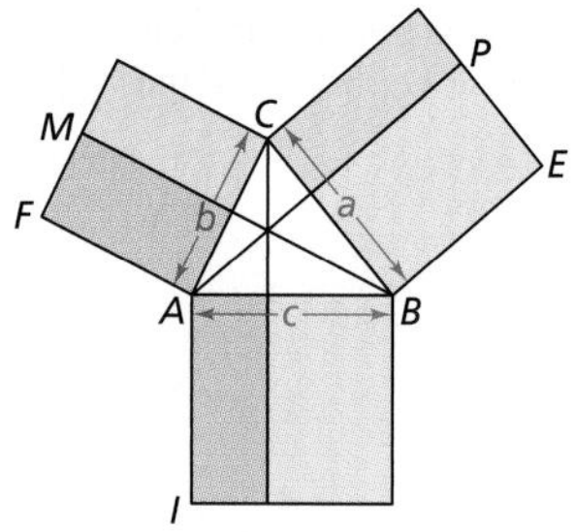

The area of each green rectangle is $ab \cos C$.

If you can show the purple rectangles have the same area and the yellow rectangles have the same area, then

$$c^2 = \text{purple} + \text{yellow} = b^2 - \text{green} + a^2 - \text{green}$$

In other words,

$$c^2 = a^2 + b^2 - 2ab \cos C$$

To show that the purple rectangles have the same area, you have to be a little tricky. Consider the diagram below.

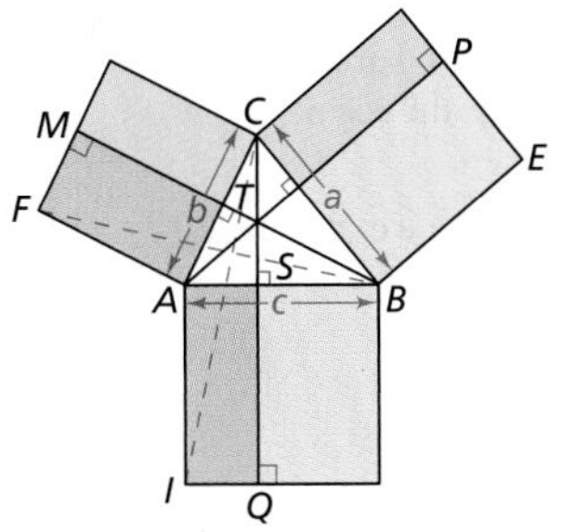

Triangles *CAI* and *FAB* are congruent.

Figure out why $\triangle CAI \cong \triangle FAB$.

The area of rectangle *AIQS* is twice the area of $\triangle CAI$. The area of rectangle *FAMT* is twice the area of $\triangle FAB$.

So rectangles *AIQS* and *FAMT* have the same area.

You can use a similar argument to show that the yellow rectangles have the same area. This proves the result.

For Discussion

2. Use the Law of Cosines to find all the angle measures of this triangle.

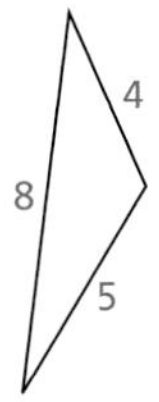

Answers

For Discussion

2. 24°, 31°, 125°

For Discussion

Make sure that students realize that there are cases in which three pieces of information may not be enough. Given two sides and a nonincluded angle, there may be one unique solution, but there may also be two different solutions or no solution. Even with SSS, if the three side lengths do not satisfy the Triangle Inequality there is no solution. AAA, however, is not enough to determine a triangle. Two triangles with every pair of corresponding angles congruent are similar, but if you do not know any side lengths, you cannot determine any side lengths. You can determine ratios between side lengths, but that would not solve the triangle!

You can use Blackline Master 8.13B as a transparancy or a handout to summarize For Discussion Problem 5.

Property	Can you solve the triangle?
SSS	yes, using the Law of Cosines
SSA	there may be 0, 1, or 2 solutions
SAS	yes, using the Law of Cosines
ASA	yes, using the Law of Sines
AAS	yes, using the Law of Sines
AAA	no

Wrap Up

You may want to revisit your discussion about solving triangles after students have worked on Exercise 6. The key idea is that they understand the Law of Cosines and its relationship to the Pythagorean Theorem.

Assessment Resources

Lesson Quiz 8.13

1. **Multiple Choice** In $\triangle BLT$, $BL = 12$, $LT = 5$, and $\angle L$ measures 60°. Which value is the exact length of side $\overline{BT}$?
   - **A.** $\sqrt{54.5}$
   - **B.** 10
   - **C.** $\sqrt{109}$
   - **D.** 13

2. A triangle has side lengths 9, 13, and 16. Find the measure of the largest angle in the triangle to the nearest tenth of a degree.

3. Let θ be an angle between 180° and 360°. Determine whether each statement is *true* or *false*.
   - **a.** $\cos\theta > 0$
   - **b.** $\sin\theta < 0$
   - **c.** $\sin^2\theta = 1 - \cos^2\theta$
   - **d.** $\cos\theta = \sqrt{1 - \sin^2\theta}$

Developing Habits of Mind

Consider more than one strategy. The For Discussion problem above required you to use the Law of Cosines in a slightly different way. Since you know the three side lengths, the only unknown is the cosine of the given angle.

You can rewrite the Law of Cosines to solve for the cosine of the angle.

$$c^2 = a^2 + b^2 - 2ab\cos C$$
$$2ab\cos C = a^2 + b^2 - c^2$$
$$\cos C = \frac{a^2 + b^2 - c^2}{2ab}$$

Use this form when you know the three side lengths and need to find the angle measure. You get the cosine of the angle. The $\cos^{-1}$ function on a calculator can give you the angle's approximate measure.

You may recall that the Law of Sines produces two possible angle measures when you know the sine. If $\sin\theta = 0.8$, the angle may be 53° or 127°. This does not happen with the Law of Cosines. If $\cos\theta = 0.8$, the angle is either 37° or 323°. An angle of 323° is impossible in a triangle!

This means that if you are faced with the option of using either the Law of Sines or the Law of Cosines, you might consider using the Law of Cosines. Its answers are always unique.

For You to Do

3. Find the missing side length and angle measures in the triangle below.

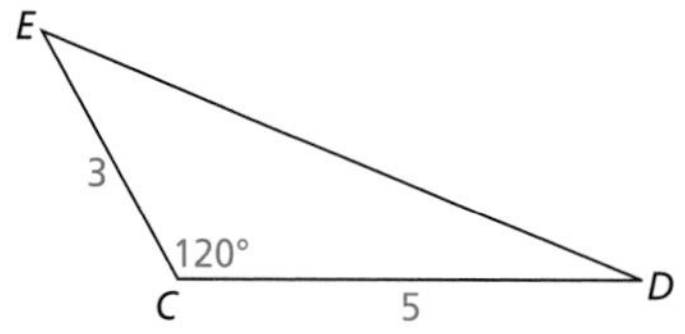

4. Find the measures of all three angles in the triangle below.

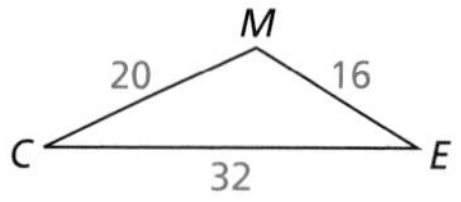

For Discussion

5. You have learned that if you know all three side lengths of a triangle, you can figure out the angle measures. If you have all three angle measures, can you figure out the side lengths? Explain.

Answers

For You to Do

3. $ED = 7$, $m\angle E = 38.2°$, $m\angle D = 21.8°$

4. $m\angle C = 24.1°$, $\angle E = 30.8°$, $m\angle M = 125.1°$

For Discussion

5. No; if you know all three angle measures, you cannot determine any of the sides, but you could find the ratios of pairs of sides.

Exercises

1. $\sqrt{a^2 + b^2 - 2ab\cos C}$

2. $|a - b| < AB < a + b$

3. $5 < OT < 7$

4. $1 < AU < 5$

5. $\sqrt{119} < FB < 13$

6. a. Use the Law of Cosines to find one angle. Then use the Law of Cosines or the Law of Sines to find a second angle. Subtract the sum of the angles from 180° to find the third angle.

Exercises Practicing Habits of Mind

Check Your Understanding

1. In $\triangle ABC$, $BC = a$ and $AC = b$. Write an expression for the length of side $\overline{AB}$ in terms of a, b, and the cosine of $\angle C$.
2. For $\triangle ABC$ from Exercise 1, use the properties of the cosine function to find upper and lower bounds on the length of side $\overline{AB}$. Your answers should be expressed in terms of a and b.

It is possible to find expressions here that do not involve a square root. Try to figure it out!

3. In $\triangle OBT$, $OB = 3$, $BT = 4$, and $\angle B$ is obtuse. What can you say about the length of side $\overline{OT}$?
4. In $\triangle ACU$, $AC = 3$, $CU = 4$, and $\angle C$ is acute. What can you say about the length of side $\overline{AU}$?
5. **Take It Further** $\triangle FMB$ is acute, with $FM = 12$ and $MB = 5$. Find the range of possible lengths for side $\overline{FB}$.
6. **Write About It** There are six possible combinations of three pieces of information about a triangle. For each combination below, explain how you can find the remaining side lengths and angle measures, or explain why you cannot find them.
   a. SSS (three side lengths)
   b. SAS (two side lengths and the measure of the included angle)
   c. SSA (two side lengths and the measure of a nonincluded angle)
   d. AAS (two angle measures and the length of a nonincluded side)
   e. ASA (two angle measures and the length of the included side)
   f. AAA (three angle measures)
7. A triangle has side lengths 13, 14, and 15.
   a. Find the cosine of each angle in this triangle.
   b. Which is the largest angle, the one with the greatest cosine or the one with the least cosine?
   c. Suppose you draw an altitude to the side of length 14. Find the length of the altitude.
   d. What is the area of this triangle?
8. Suppose all the side lengths of $\triangle ABC$ are integers.
   a. Explain why $\cos C$ must be rational.
   b. **Take It Further** Show that you can write an expression for the area of $\triangle ABC$ in the form $x\sqrt{y}$, where x is rational and y is an integer.

b. Use the Law of Cosines to find the third side. Then use the Law of Cosines or the Law of Sines to find a second angle. Subtract the sum of the angles from 180° to find the third angle.

c. Use the Law of Sines to find the angle opposite the other given side (there may be 0, 1, or 2 values). Subtract the sum of the angles from 180° to find the third angle. Use the Law of Sines or the Law of Cosines to find the third side length.

d. Subtract the sum of the angles from 180° to find the third angle. Use the Law of Sines or the Law of Cosines to find the lengths of the other two sides.

e. Subtract the sum of the angles from 180° to find the third angle. Use the Law of Sines to find a second side. Use the Law of Sines or the Law of Cosines to find the length of the third side.

f. This cannot be solved. The triangle will not be unique because you are not given the length of a side.

7–8. See back of book.

Exercises

HOMEWORK

- Core: 9, 10, 11, 12, 13, 14, 15, 17
- Optional: 18, 20
- Extension: 16, 19

Check Your Understanding

EXERCISE 2 If students do not see how they could start here, have them do some of the On Your Own exercises, especially Exercise 10.

Some students will not remember to include the absolute value around $|a - b|$, and that is acceptable. Just point it out, and they will realize why it is necessary.

This is a key exercise in this lesson, since it shows you can use the Law of Cosines to prove the Triangle Inequality. The bounds established here are the same ones that are implied by the Triangle Inequality.

EXERCISE 3 The purpose here is to recognize that in an obtuse triangle, $c^2 > a^2 + b^2$.

EXERCISE 4 Students realize that in an acute triangle, $c^2 < a^2 + b^2$.

EXERCISE 5 If students say that the lower bound is $FB > 7$, ask them to calculate the angles when $FB = 8$ using Law of Cosines. They will notice that something went wrong.

EXERCISE 6 gives students a chance to summarize the results of For Discussion Problem 5 in their own words.

EXERCISE 7 Students confirm their previous work on the Hinge Theorem here, showing that the largest side is opposite the largest angle and the smallest side is opposite the smallest angle.

EXERCISE 8 is a nice exercise if you would like students to think about the impact of restricting the side lengths in a triangle to rational values and the implications that has on the values of the cosine and the area.

On Your Own

EXERCISE 9 Point out to students that the first and last options are impossible in a triangle, due to the Triangle Inequality.

EXERCISE 11 Again, by looking at the upper and lower bounds from the Law of Cosines, students see the values they would get from the Triangle Inequality.

EXERCISE 13 In thinking carefully about the possibilities for the smallest angle in a triangle, students are bringing together many results and reasoning visually.

EXERCISE 14 It is subtle, but the last statement requires $\sin\theta > 0$, which is true based on the angle measure. Students will use this identity in the next lesson.

EXERCISE 16 Some calculators allow students to solve this problem with brute force, but the goal is for it to be solved through clever use of the angle formulas (or, perhaps, clever use of altitudes within a triangle).

On Your Own

Go Online PHSchool.com

For additional practice, go to Web Code: bfa-0813

9. In $\triangle MLT$, $ML = 10$, $LT = 3$, and $\angle L$ measures 60°. Which number is the exact length of side $\overline{MT}$?

A. 7 **B.** $\sqrt{79}$ **C.** $\sqrt{139}$ **D.** 13

10. In $\triangle ABC$, $BC = 10$ and $AC = 3$. Write an expression for the length of side $\overline{AB}$ in terms of the cosine of $\angle C$.

11. For $\triangle ABC$ from Exercise 10, use the properties of the cosine function. Find the upper and lower bounds of the length of side $\overline{AB}$.

12. A triangle has sides of length 12, 15, and 10. Find the measure of the smallest angle in the triangle to the nearest degree.

13. In $\triangle FOM$, $FO = 12$, $OM = 20$, and $\angle O$ measures 60°.

a. Explain why $\angle O$ cannot be the smallest angle in the triangle.

b. Use the Law of Cosines and the Law of Sines to find the measure of the smallest angle in the triangle to the nearest degree.

14. Let θ be an angle between 0° and 180°. Determine whether each statement is true or false.

a. $\cos\theta > 0$ **b.** $\sin\theta > 0$

c. $\sin^2\theta = 1 + \cos^2\theta$ **d.** $\sin\theta = \sqrt{1 - \cos^2\theta}$

15. A triangle has side lengths 7, 10, and 12.

a. Find the angles in the triangle to the nearest degree.

b. Use the diagram at the right. Find x and h.

c. Find the area of the triangle.

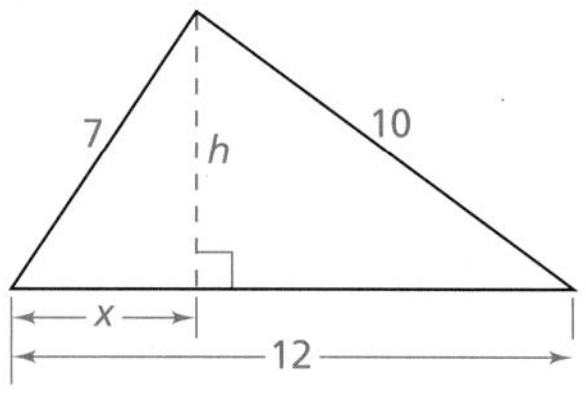

16. **Take It Further** The cosines of two angles of a triangle are $\frac{4}{5}$ and $\frac{5}{13}$. Find the exact cosine of the third angle.

17. **Standardized Test Prep** What is the measure of the smallest angle in a triangle with side lengths 5, 7, and 8 inches?

A. 17.19° **B.** 34.38° **C.** 38.21° **D.** 60.00°

Answers

9. B

10. $\sqrt{109 - 60\cos C}$

11. $7 < AB < 13$

12. 42°

13. a. If $\angle O$ is the smallest angle, the measures of angles F and M would be greater than 60°. But the sum of the angles in a triangle cannot be greater than 180°. So $\angle O$ cannot be the smallest angle.

b. $m\angle M = 37°$

14. a. false **b.** true

c. false **d.** true

15. a. The angles opposite the sides of length 7, 10, and 12 are 36°, 56°, and 88°, respectively.

b. $h = 5.83$, $x = 3.87$

c. 34.98

16. $\frac{16}{65}$

17. C

18. The diagram below shows $\triangle ABC$ with altitude $\overline{CD}$.

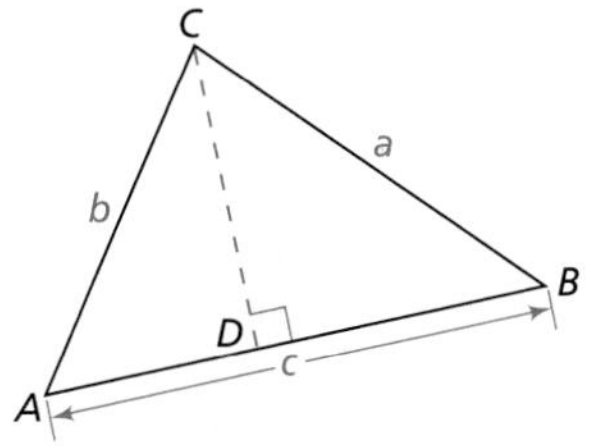

a. Show that $b \cos A + a \cos B = c$.

b. Use a similar diagram to show that $c \cos A + a \cos C = b$.

c. Show that $c \cos B + b \cos C = a$.

19. **Take It Further** Solve the system of equations below for $\begin{pmatrix} \cos A \\ \cos B \\ \cos C \end{pmatrix}$.

$$\begin{pmatrix} b & a & 0 \\ c & 0 & a \\ 0 & c & b \end{pmatrix} \begin{pmatrix} \cos A \\ \cos B \\ \cos C \end{pmatrix} = \begin{pmatrix} c \\ b \\ a \end{pmatrix}$$

This gives you another proof of the Law of Cosines.

This system comes from Exercise 18. For help in finding the inverse of a matrix, see the TI-Nspire Handbook, p. 778.

Maintain Your Skills

20. For each set of measurements for $\triangle ABC$, calculate the length of side $\overline{AB}$ to two decimal places.

a. $AC = 13$, $BC = 8$, and $\angle C$ measures 1°.

b. $AC = 13$, $BC = 8$, and $\angle C$ measures 10°.

c. $AC = 13$, $BC = 8$, and $\angle C$ measures 50°.

d. $AC = 13$, $BC = 8$, and $\angle C$ measures 90°.

e. $AC = 13$, $BC = 8$, and $\angle C$ measures 130°.

f. $AC = 13$, $BC = 8$, and $\angle C$ measures 170°.

g. $AC = 13$, $BC = 8$, and $\angle C$ measures 179°.

h. Describe what happens to the length of side $\overline{AB}$ as $\angle C$ increases from 1° to 179°.

18. See back of book.

19. $\cos A = \frac{c}{2b} + \frac{b}{2c} - \frac{a^2}{2bc}$

$\cos B = \frac{c}{2a} - \frac{b^2}{2ac} + \frac{a}{2c}$

$\cos C = -\frac{c^2}{2ab} + \frac{b}{2a} + \frac{a}{2b}$

You can rewrite those equations as

$a^2 = b^2 + c^2 - 2bc \cos A$

$b^2 = a^2 + c^2 - 2ac \cos B$

$c^2 = a^2 + b^2 - 2ab \cos C$

20. a. 5.00
b. 5.31
c. 9.96
d. 15.26
e. 19.15
f. 20.92
g. 21.00
h. AB increases from 5 to 21.

EXERCISE 18 sets up the system of equations that students solve in Exercise 19.

EXERCISE 19 Some of your students may be interested in this very different proof of the Law of Cosines. You may also want to assign this exercise to remind students of their work with matrices.

Maintain Your Skills

EXERCISE 20 provides calculation practice with the Law of Cosines, but it also reinforces the idea that you could use the Law of Cosines to prove the Triangle Inequality.

Additional Resources

PRINT RESOURCES
- Solution Manual
- Practice Workbook
- Assessment Resources
- Teaching Resources

TECHNOLOGY
- Interactive Textbook
- TeacherExpress CD-ROM
- ExamView CD-ROM
- PHSchool.com

Additional Practice

1. In $\triangle PAT$, $PA = 21$, $AT = 27$, and $\angle A$ measures 120°. Find the exact length of side $\overline{PT}$.

2. In $\triangle DEF$, $EF = 15$ and $DF = 7$. Write an expression for the length of side $\overline{DE}$ in terms of the cosine of $\angle F$.

3. For $\triangle DEF$ in Exercise 2, use the properties of the cosine function to find the upper and lower bounds of the length of side $\overline{DE}$.

4. In $\triangle TUB$, $TU = 14$, $UB = 23$, and $\angle U$ measures 80°.
a. Explain why $\angle U$ cannot be the smallest angle in the triangle.
b. Use the Law of Cosines and the Law of Sines to find the measure of the smallest angle in the triangle to the nearest degree.

5. A triangle has side lengths 9, 13, and 15.

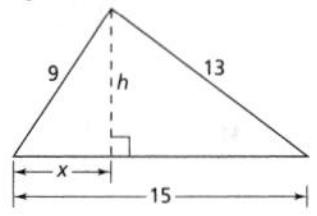

a. Find the angles in the triangle to the nearest tenth of a degree.
b. Use the diagram above. Find x and h.
c. Find the area of the triangle.

6. Suppose $\triangle CAT$ is isosceles with sides of length 14 and base of length 4.
a. Find the area of $\triangle CAT$. Use any method.
b. Find the area of $\triangle CAT$ using Heron's Formula.

7. **Multiple Choice** Which set of three lengths forms a Heronian triangle?
A. 3, 4, 5
B. 2, 6, 7
C. 12, 14, 15
D. 9, 10, 17

8. The isosceles triangle with side lengths 5, 5, and 6 is Heronian. Its area is 12. Find some more Heronian triangles that are isosceles.

Practice: For Lesson 8.13, assign Exercises 1–5.

Lesson Overview

GOAL

- State and use Heron's Formula.

Although this lesson is optional, it is a chance to bring together a lot of the results that students have developed during this course. Students prove Heron's Formula, which gives the area of a triangle in terms of its side lengths. They practice various skills in algebra, including factoring, and look at this proof from two perspectives—one rooted in algebra and the other in trigonometry.

CHECK YOUR UNDERSTANDING
- Core: 1, 2, 5
- Optional: 3, 4

MATERIALS
- geometry software
- graphing calculators
- Blackline Master 8.14

HOMEWORK
- Core: 6, 7a–b, 8, 9, 10
- Optional: 11, 13
- Extension: 7c, 12

VOCABULARY
- Heronian triangle

Launch

Start class with For You to Do Problem 1.

Explore

This lesson presents two different proofs of Heron's Formula. You may want to work through one of the proofs with your students as part of the lesson and have them study the other on their own. A second choice is to have students work in groups on key parts of each proof and then work through both proofs as a class, consulting the groups as appropriate. You could also ask students to read and work through both proofs as part of their homework. Students may have worked through the the first proof in the Project for Chapter 2. If so, you can review this proof here, or choose to skip it and focus on the second proof.

You can use Blackline Master 8.14 to guide students through the proofs.

8.14 Heron's Formula

For any three given side lengths, there is at most one triangle. That means that given the three side lengths, you should be able to find all the angle measures in the triangle, and its area.

The side lengths 10, 50, and 100 cannot form a triangle.

For You to Do

1. A triangle has side lengths 16, 25, and 31. Use the Law of Cosines to find the angles in this triangle to the nearest degree. Then use any of the angles and the two sides next to the angle to find the area of the triangle.

The Greek mathematician Heron developed a formula for the area of a triangle based only on its side lengths. In this lesson, you will see two proofs of Heron's Formula. The first proof uses algebra. You may have worked through this proof in the Chapter 2 project. The second proof uses trigonometry. Look for similarities between the proofs.

Theorem 8.7* *Heron's Formula

Given a triangle with side lengths *a*, *b*, and *c*, the area of the triangle is

$$A = \sqrt{s(s-a)(s-b)(s-c)}$$

where *s* is the semiperimeter $\frac{a+b+c}{2}$.

For You to Do

2. Use Heron's Formula to find the area of a triangle with side lengths 16, 25, and 31. Find *s* first. Does the value for the area you get using the formula agree with the answer you got in Problem 1 above?

The two proofs of Heron's Formula rely on the known area formulas for triangles. The diagram for the first proof looks remarkably like the one you used to prove the Law of Cosines.

Proof 1 Draw a $\triangle ABC$. Label the side lengths. Drop an altitude to side $\overline{AB}$.

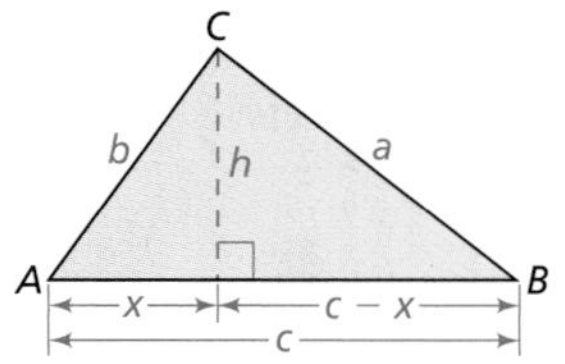

Answers

For You to Do

1. 31°, 53°, 96°; 199

2. 199; yes

The area of the triangle is $A = \frac{1}{2}ch$. So, the task is to find h in terms of a, b, and c. Apply the Pythagorean Theorem to the right triangles formed by the altitude.

$$h^2 + x^2 = b^2$$
$$h^2 + (c - x)^2 = a^2$$

You can rewrite the second equation as $h^2 + c^2 - 2cx + x^2 = a^2$. Then subtract the first equation from the second to find an expression for x.

$$(h^2 + c^2 - 2cx + x^2) - (h^2 + x^2) = a^2 - b^2$$
$$c^2 - 2cx = a^2 - b^2$$
$$c^2 + b^2 - a^2 = 2cx$$
$$\frac{c^2 + b^2 - a^2}{2c} = x$$

Now that you have a formula for x, you can use the first equation to find h.

$$h^2 = b^2 - x^2$$
$$h^2 = b^2 - \left(\frac{c^2 + b^2 - a^2}{2c}\right)^2$$
$$h^2 = \frac{(4b^2c^2 - (c^2 + b^2 - a^2)^2)}{4c^2}$$

This looks unmanageable, but the key to success is recognizing that the numerator of the right side is a difference of squares.

$$h^2 = \frac{(2bc)^2 - (c^2 + b^2 - a^2)^2}{4c^2}$$
$$h^2 = \frac{(2bc + c^2 + b^2 - a^2)(2bc - c^2 - b^2 + a^2)}{4c^2}$$
$$h^2 = \frac{((b + c)^2 - a^2)(a^2 - (b - c)^2)}{4c^2}$$

And there are even *more* differences of squares. You can factor again to find a final formula for h^2 and then find h.

$$h^2 = \frac{(b + c + a)(b + c - a)(a + b - c)(a - b + c)}{4c^2}$$
$$h = \frac{\sqrt{(b + c + a)(b + c - a)(a - b + c)(a + b - c)}}{2c}$$

The area of the triangle is $A = \frac{1}{2}ch$. Substitute for h. You can cancel c in the numerator and denominator.

$$A = \frac{\sqrt{(b + c + a)(b + c - a)(a - b + c)(a + b - c)}}{4}$$

Pushing the 4 inside the square root as a 16 gives Heron's Formula.

$$A = \sqrt{s(s - a)(s - b)(s - c)}$$

You will explain this last step further in the exercises.

The first proof relies primarily on algebra, but some of the work involved closely resembles the Law of Cosines. You can also use the Law of Cosines in a second proof.

THEOREM 8.7 This formula is also commonly written as

$$A = \frac{\sqrt{(a + b + c)(a + b - c)(b + c - a)(c + a - b)}}{4}$$

At one point in Proof 1, students will see the formula written this way. The formula using the semiperimeter is typically preferred because it is simpler to write (and thus remember), but watch out for students who forget the proper formula for s: Emphasize that s is the *semi*perimeter, so it is half the perimeter.

Wrap Up

As time allows, go over some of the Check Your Understanding core exercises. You may already have covered the result of Exercise 5 while going over Proof 1 of Heron's Formula, so you may not need to assign it now.

Assessment Resources

Lesson Quiz 8.14

1. Use Heron's Formula to find the area of a triangle with side lengths 10, 13, and 15.

2. Suppose $\triangle RAP$ is equilateral with $AP = 15$.
   a. Find the area of $\triangle RAP$. Use any method.
   b. Find the area of $\triangle RAP$ using Heron's Formula.
   c. Use Heron's Formula to show that the formula $A = \frac{x^2\sqrt{3}}{4}$ gives the area of an equilateral triangle with sides of length x.

3. **Multiple Choice** Which sets of three lengths form a Heronian triangle?
   I. 3, 4, 6　　II. 6, 8, 10
   III. 7, 7, 12　　IV. 13, 14, 15
   A. I and III　**B.** II and IV　**C.** III only　**D.** IV only

4. Can an equilateral triangle be Heronian? Explain.

Proof 2 The formula $A = \frac{1}{2}ab\sin C$ gives the area of $\triangle ABC$. A handy formula already exists for the cosine of C in terms of side lengths. Use the Law of Cosines and solve for $\cos C$.

$$\cos C = \frac{a^2 + b^2 - c^2}{2ab}$$

You can use the relationship $\cos^2\theta + \sin^2\theta = 1$ here. Exercise 14 in Lesson 8.13 gives the following identity for angles between 0° and 180°.

$$\sin\theta = \sqrt{1 - \cos^2\theta}$$

Use this identity to rewrite the formula for the area of the triangle.

$$A = \frac{1}{2}ab\sin C = \frac{1}{2}ab\sqrt{1 - \cos^2 C}$$

Now swap in the formula for cosine and work inside the square root.

$$\begin{aligned} A &= \frac{1}{2}ab\sqrt{1 - \cos^2 C} \\ &= \frac{1}{2}ab\sqrt{1 - \left(\frac{a^2 + b^2 - c^2}{2ab}\right)^2} \\ &= \frac{1}{2}ab\sqrt{\frac{(2ab)^2 - (a^2 + b^2 - c^2)^2}{(2ab)^2}} \\ &= \frac{1}{4}\sqrt{(2ab)^2 - (a^2 + b^2 - c^2)^2} \end{aligned}$$

The remainder of the work under the square root is the same as the work in Proof 1, with a different ordering of the variables. You factor in two steps. Both times you find differences of squares.

If you start with the area as $\frac{1}{2}bc\sin A$, you actually end up with the same ordering of the variables as in Proof 1.

$$\begin{aligned} A &= \frac{1}{4}\sqrt{(2ab + a^2 + b^2 - c^2)(2ab - a^2 - b^2 + c^2)} \\ &= \frac{1}{4}\sqrt{((a + b)^2 - c^2)(c^2 - (a - b)^2)} \\ &= \frac{1}{4}\sqrt{(a + b + c)(a + b - c)(c + a - b)(c - a + b)} \end{aligned}$$

The algebra of the two proofs is quite similar, although the means to get there differs. Since you derived the Law of Cosines using a diagram similar to the one in the first proof, it is not surprising to find similar steps in the two proofs.

You can use Heron's Formula to find the area of the triangular sails. How can you find the area of the quadrilateral sails?

Answers

Exercises

1. **a.** $s = \frac{x + 14}{2}$
   b. $A(x) = \frac{1}{4}\sqrt{(x+14)(-x+14)(x-2)(x+2)}$
   c. 2, 14
   d. The maximum of $A(x)$ is 24 when $x = 10$.

Exercises *Practicing Habits of Mind*

Check Your Understanding

1. In $\triangle QED$, $QE = 6$ and $ED = 8$.
   - **a.** Suppose the remaining side length is x. Write a formula for the semiperimeter s in terms of x.
   - **b.** Write a formula for $A(x)$, the area of $\triangle QED$ in terms of x.
   - **c.** Find the zeros of $A(x)$.
   - **d.** Find the maximum value of $A(x)$ and the value of x that produces it.
2. In $\triangle QEU$, $QE = 6$. The triangle's perimeter is 18.
   - **a.** Suppose $QU = x$. Find the length of $\overline{EU}$ in terms of x.
   - **b.** Write a formula for $A(x)$, the area of $\triangle QEU$ in terms of x.
   - **c.** Find the zeros of $A(x)$.
   - **d.** Find the maximum value of $A(x)$ and the value of x that produces it.
3. Find the area of this quadrilateral.

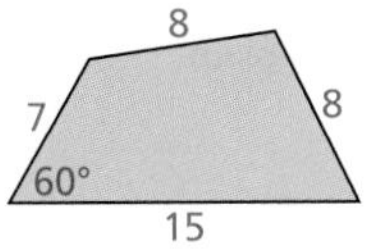

4. Peter thinks there is another way to draw the quadrilateral in Exercise 3 given only its marked side lengths and angle measure. He says the quadrilateral might be concave instead.
   - **a.** What does *concave* mean? Draw an example of a concave quadrilateral.
   - **b.** Could this quadrilateral be concave? If so, find its area. If not, explain why not.

Exercises

HOMEWORK
- Core: 6, 7a–b, 8, 9, 10
- Optional: 11, 13
- Extension: 7c, 12

Check Your Understanding

EXERCISE 1 Expect students to use a graphing calculator once they have the rule for $A(x)$. This exercise can be time consuming. The goal is for students to recognize that the right triangle is the one with the greatest area for two given side lengths, a fact they should know from the area formula $\frac{1}{2}ab \sin C$.

EXERCISE 2 will probably require a graphing calculator. This time, the goal is to show that the equilateral triangle has the greatest area given a specific perimeter.

EXERCISES 3 AND 4 If you assign Exercise 3, also assign Exercise 4 so that students can realize that SSSSA is not quite enough to determine a quadrilateral. Students can also consider what is involved in considering a concave case.

EXERCISE 4 Peter can be right in other cases. This is similar to the SSA case for triangles—for quadrilaterals, SSSSA is nearly, but not quite, enough.

2. a. $12 - x$
b. $A(x) = \sqrt{27(9 - x)(-3 + x)}$
c. 3, 9
d. The maximum of $A(x) \approx 15.6$ when $x = 6$.

3. 75.8

4. a. Answers may vary. Sample: A concave polygon has at least one diagonal that contains points outside the polygon.

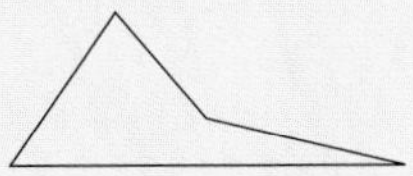

b. No; if you collapse the center of the triangle without changing any of the other measurements, the result is not a quadrilateral.

EXERCISE 5 Depending on how thoroughly you went over Proof 1 in class, you may not need to assign this exercise. If students were to study the proofs of Heron's Formula independently, this is a nice point for them to investigate and figure out on their own.

On Your Own

EXERCISE 6 It is important for students to see how Heron's Formula, in effect, has the Triangle Inequality embedded in it. If a triangle has a real area, no side can have a length that is greater than or equal to the semiperimeter.

$$a < \frac{a+b+c}{2}$$
$$2a < a+b+c$$
$$a < b+c$$

EXERCISES 7 AND 10 If you assign Exercise 10, you should also assign Exercise 7.

EXERCISE 10 may give students a hint for finding their own Heronian triangles.

EXERCISE 12 is a good question to assign to students who have computer programming skills. The matching triples are very hard to find otherwise.

5. Proof 1 in the lesson gives the formula below.

$$A = \frac{\sqrt{(b+c+a)(b+c-a)(a-b+c)(a+b-c)}}{4}$$

You can rewrite this formula as

$$A = \sqrt{s(s-a)(s-b)(s-c)}$$

where $s = \frac{a+b+c}{2}$.

a. Show that the two expressions below are equal.

$$\frac{\sqrt{(b+c+a)(b+c-a)(a-b+c)(a+b-c)}}{4}$$

$$\sqrt{\frac{b+c+a}{2}\cdot\frac{b+c-a}{2}\cdot\frac{a-b+c}{2}\cdot\frac{a+b-c}{2}}$$

b. Show the remaining steps you need to write the formula in the following form.

$$A = \sqrt{s(s-a)(s-b)(s-c)}$$

On Your Own

6. **Write About It** What happens when you try to use Heron's Formula to find the area of a triangle with sides of length 12, 25, and 11? Explain.

7. Suppose $\triangle ABT$ is equilateral with $AT = 10$.

a. Find the area of $\triangle ABT$. Use any method.

b. Find the area of $\triangle ABT$ using Heron's Formula.

c. **Take It Further** Use Heron's Formula to show that the formula below gives the area of an equilateral triangle with sides of length x.

$$A = \frac{x^2\sqrt{3}}{4}$$

A **Heronian triangle** is a triangle with integer side lengths and integer area.

8. Which sets of three lengths form a Heronian triangle?

a. 7, 10, 12

b. 6, 8, 9

c. 10, 15, 20

d. 10, 17, 21

9. **Standardized Test Prep** Which set of three lengths does NOT form a Heronian triangle?

A. 10, 13, 13 **B.** 9, 12, 16 **C.** 15, 37, 44 **D.** 5, 29, 30

10. Prove that an equilateral triangle cannot be Heronian.

Habits of Mind

Make strategic choices. You have seen Heron's Formula in several forms in this lesson. Some forms may be more helpful than others.

Go Online PHSchool.com

For information about Super Heron Triangles, go to **Web Code:** bfe-9031

Answers

5. a. The denominator 4 is outside the radical. You can move the denominator into the radical and change it to 16, which can be expressed as a denominator 2 for each of the four factors.

b. If $a+b+c = 2s$, then $b+c-a = 2s-2a$; $a-b+c = 2s-2b$; $a+b-c = 2s-2c$. Therefore $\frac{a+b+c}{2} = s$, $\frac{b+c-a}{2} = s-a$, $\frac{a+c-b}{2} = s-b$, and $= s-c$. Then substitute each expression above into the second expression in part (a) to get the expression $\sqrt{s(s-a)(s-b)(s-c)}$.

6. The factors inside the radical result in an imaginary number. So, the lengths 12, 25, and 11 cannot form a triangle.

7. a–b. $25\sqrt{3}$

c. $s = 1.5x$, so

$$\begin{aligned}\text{Area} &= \sqrt{1.5x(0.5x)(0.5x)(0.5x)}\\ &= \sqrt{0.1875x^4}\\ &= \sqrt{x^4}\cdot\sqrt{0.0625}\cdot\sqrt{3}\\ &= 0.25x^2\sqrt{3} = \frac{x^2\sqrt{3}}{4}\end{aligned}$$

8. d

9. B

10. The area of an equilateral triangle with side x is $\frac{x^2\sqrt{3}}{4}$. If x is an integer, then $\frac{x^2\sqrt{3}}{4}$ is irrational, so an equilateral triangle cannot be Heronian.

11. Use the two right triangles below to form a Heronian triangle.

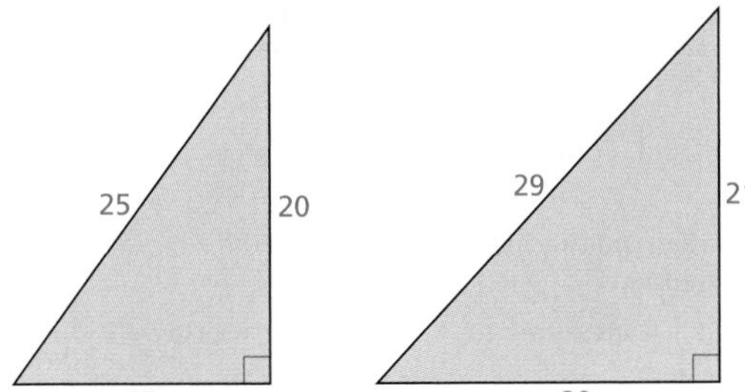

12. Take It Further The triangle with side lengths 13, 14, and 15 is Heronian. Its area is 84. Find some more Heronian triangles with side lengths that are consecutive integers.

Maintain Your Skills

13. In a triangle with side lengths 5 and 12, the third side can be any real number between 7 and 17.

a. Copy and complete this table for $A(c)$, the area of the triangle with sides 5, 12, and c. Find each answer to two decimal places.

c	$A(c)$
7	■
8	■
9	■
10	■
11	■
12	■
13	■
14	■
15	■
16	■
17	■

b. What value of c appears to give the maximum area $A(c)$? Explain.

Go Online PHSchool.com

For additional practice, go to **Web Code**: bfa-0814

Habits of Mind

Look for relationships. How do you know that the length of the third side must be between 7 and 17?

Additional Resources

PRINT RESOURCES
- Solution Manual
- Practice Workbook
- Assessment Resources
- Teaching Resources

TECHNOLOGY
- Interactive Textbook
- TeacherExpress CD-ROM
- ExamView CD-ROM
- PHSchool.com

Additional Practice

1. In $\triangle PAT$, $PA = 21$, $AT = 27$, and $\angle A$ measures 120°. Find the exact length of side $\overline{PT}$.

2. In $\triangle DEF$, $EF = 15$ and $DF = 7$. Write an expression for the length of side $\overline{DE}$ in terms of the cosine of $\angle F$.

3. For $\triangle DEF$ in Exercise 2, use the properties of the cosine function to find the upper and lower bounds of the length of side $\overline{DE}$.

4. In $\triangle TUB$, $TU = 14$, $UB = 23$, and $\angle U$ measures 80°.
   a. Explain why $\angle U$ cannot be the smallest angle in the triangle.
   b. Use the Law of Cosines and the Law of Sines to find the measure of the smallest angle in the triangle to the nearest degree.

5. A triangle has side lengths 9, 13, and 15.

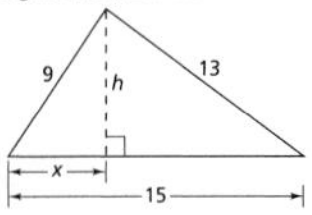

   a. Find the angles in the triangle to the nearest tenth of a degree.
   b. Use the diagram above. Find x and h.
   c. Find the area of the triangle.

6. Suppose $\triangle CAT$ is isosceles with sides of length 14 and base of length 4.
   a. Find the area of $\triangle CAT$. Use any method.
   b. Find the area of $\triangle CAT$ using Heron's Formula.

7. **Multiple Choice** Which set of three lengths forms a Heronian triangle?
   A. 3, 4, 5
   B. 2, 6, 7
   C. 12, 14, 15
   D. 9, 10, 17

8. The isosceles triangle with side lengths 5, 5, and 6 is Heronian. Its area is 12. Find some more Heronian triangles that are isosceles.

Practice: For Lesson 8.14, assign Exercises 6–8.

11. When you match the two legs of length 20 together to form a new triangle, the height is 20 and its base measures $15 + 21 = 36$. Its other two sides measure 25 and 29. The area of the new triangle is $A = \frac{1}{2}(20)(36) = 360$, so it is a Heronian triangle.

12. Answers may vary. Samples: 3, 4, 5; 51, 52, 53; 193, 194, 195; 723, 724, 725; 2701, 2702, 2703

13. a.

c	$A(c)$
7	0
8	14.52
9	20.40
10	24.54
11	27.50
12	29.34
13	30
14	29.23
15	26.53
16	20.66
17	0

b. 13; when $c = 13$, the sides, 5, 12, and 13, form a right triangle.

Mathematical Reflections

EXERCISES 6–8 At the start of the investigation, you may have assigned these as Questions 1–3 for students to think and write about.

Mathematical Reflections 8C

In this investigation, you learned to solve a triangle. You also proved and used the Law of Sines, the Law of Cosines, and Heron's Formula. These questions will help you summarize what you have learned.

1. In $\triangle DOG$, $DG = 10$, $GO = 8$, and $\angle G$ measures 20°. Find the area of $\triangle DOG$.
2. Find the missing angle measures and side lengths for $\triangle DOG$ from Exercise 1. Give all possible solutions.
3. In $\triangle PIG$, $PI = 7$, $GI = 8$, and $\angle G$ measures 40°. Solve the triangle. Give all possible solutions.
4. In $\triangle CAT$, $CA = 6$, $AT = 4$, and $CT = 8$. Find the angle measures of the triangle.
5. Find the area of $\triangle CAT$ from Exercise 4.
6. What information do you need to find all of a triangle's side lengths and angle measures?
7. What information do you need to find the area of a triangle?
8. A triangle has sides of length 5, 8, and 10. What is the measure of its largest angle?

Vocabulary

In this investigation, you learned these terms. Make sure you understand what each one means and how to use it.

- **Heronian triangle**
- **Law of Cosines**
- **Law of Sines**

You can use triangle relationships to measure how the glacier changes over time.

Answers

Mathematical Reflections

1. 13.7
2. $DO = 3.7$, $m\angle O \approx 112°$, $m\angle D \approx 48°$
3. If $m\angle P = 47.3°$, then $m\angle I = 92.7°$ and $PG = 10.9$. If $m\angle P = 132.7°$, then $m\angle I = 7.3°$ and $PG = 1.4$.
4. $m\angle C \approx 29°$, $m\angle A \approx 104°$, $m\angle T \approx 47°$
5. 11.6
6. You need SSS (with the three lengths satisfying the Triangle Inequality), SAS, AAS, or ASA. If you have SSA, there may be 0, 1, or 2 possible triangles.
7. You need SSS (with the three lengths satisfying the Triangle Inequality), SAS, AAS, or ASA. If you have SSA, there may be 0, 1, or 2 possible triangles.
8. 97.9°

Project: Using Mathematical Habits

Brahmagupta's Formula

In the 600s, the Indian mathematician Brahmagupta found a generalization of Heron's Formula. It applies to cyclic quadrilaterals. A cyclic quadrilateral is a quadrilateral with four vertices that are all on the same circle. This is not true for most quadrilaterals.

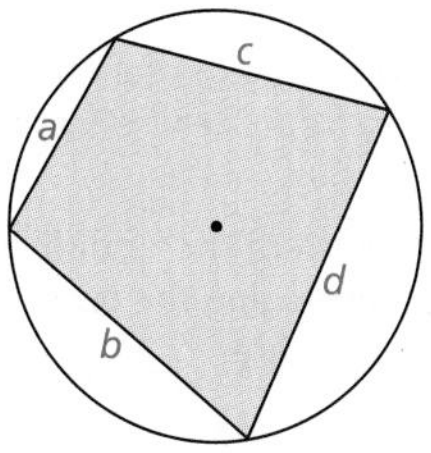

His formula relates the area of the quadrilateral to the lengths of its sides.

Theorem 8.8 ***Brahmagupta's Formula***

Given a cyclic quadrilateral with side lengths *a*, *b*, *c*, and *d* the area of the quadrilateral is

$$A = \sqrt{(s-a)(s-b)(s-c)(s-d)}$$

where *s* is the semiperimeter $s = \frac{a+b+c+d}{2}$.

The goal of this project is for you to work through a proof of the theorem. You will write up the proof in your own words and supply reasons for the major steps.

1. Show that the opposite angles of a cyclic quadrilateral are supplementary. Two angles are supplementary if their measures sum to 180°.

2. Call one of the angles in the cyclic quadrilateral α. Let e be the length of the diagonal in the diagram.

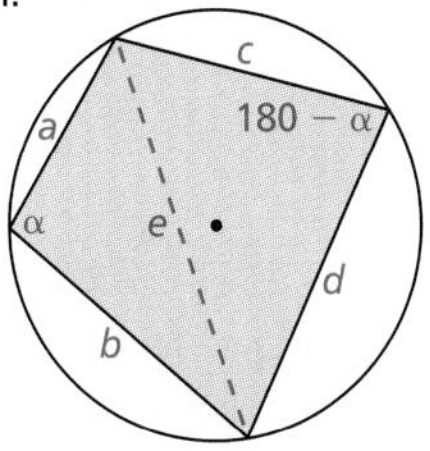

Let *A* be the area of the quadrilateral. Find expressions for the areas of the two triangles and add them to get a formula for *A*.

$$A = \frac{1}{2}(ab + cd)\sin\alpha$$

You can solve the equation for sin α.

$$\frac{2A}{ab + cd} = \sin\alpha$$

Project

1. The measure of an inscribed angle is half of the measure of its intercepted arc. The sum of the intercepted arcs for the opposite angles is 360°, so the sum of the measures of the opposite angles is 180°. So, the angles are supplementary.

2. area of the triangle on the left = $\frac{1}{2}ab\sin\alpha$

   area of the triangle on the right = $\frac{1}{2}cd\sin\alpha$

Project

As always with a project, there are several options. You can do this as a class and work on some or all of the questions together. Or, assign the questions to groups or individuals as homework. If students work on the Project outside of class, you may want to allow them to prepare individual or group reports.

In this particular Project, the text states most of what is necessary to prove Brahmagupta's Formula. Students will read the mathematics, figure it out, and write up the results in their own words, making the proof their own.

If you do the Project in class, you may want to assign Problems 10 and 11 as homework so students can summarize the results. If only some students work on the Project, you may want to give them an opportunity to present their findings to the class.

PROBLEMS 3 AND 4 There is a factor of $ab + cd$ that shows up in the expression for cos α and the expression for sin α. This looks like a job for the Pythagorean Identity! (Or at least some form of it.) Because the expressions for sine and cosine have so much in common, encourage students to look for terms that will cancel or combine.

Answers

3. $e^2 = a^2 + b^2 - 2ab\cos\alpha$ and
$e^2 = c^2 + d^2 - 2cd\cos(180° - \alpha)$;
$a^2 + b^2 - 2ab\cos\alpha$
$= c^2 + d^2 + 2cd\cos\alpha$.
Then $a^2 + b^2 - c^2 - d^2 = 2ab\cos\alpha + 2cd\cos\alpha = 2(ab + cd)\cos\alpha$, and $\cos\alpha = \frac{a^2 + b^2 - c^2 - d^2}{2(ab + cd)}$.

4. $\left(\frac{a^2 + b^2 - c^2 - d^2}{2(ab + cd)}\right)^2 = \cos^2\alpha = 1 - \sin^2\alpha$
$= 1 - \left(\frac{2A}{ab + cd}\right)^2$

5. Rewrite the first expression and the last expression in the equation in Exercise 4, using $4(ab + cd)^2$ as a common denominator: $\frac{(a^2 + b^2 - c^2 - d^2)^2}{4(ab + cd)^2} = \frac{4(ab + cd)^2}{4(ab + cd)^2} - \frac{16A^2}{4(ab + cd)^2}$. Then $\frac{4(ab + cd)^2 - (a^2 + b^2 - c^2 - d^2)^2}{4(ab + cd)^2} = \frac{16A^2}{4(ab + cd)^2}$. The numerators must be equal, so $16A^2 = 4(ab + cd)^2 - (a^2 + b^2 - c^2 - d^2)^2$.

6. $4(ab + cd)^2 - (a^2 + b^2 - c^2 - d^2)^2 =$
$(a + b + c - d)(a + b - c + d)$
$(c + d - a + b)(c + d + a - b)$

7. Rewrite the end of Exercise 6 as
$16A^2 = (-a + b + c + d) \cdot$
$(a - b + c + d) \cdot (a + b - c + d) \cdot$
$(a + b + c - d)$. Divide both sides by 16 to get $A^2 = \frac{-a + b + c + d}{2} \cdot \frac{a - b + c + d}{2} \cdot \frac{a + b - c + d}{2} \cdot \frac{a + b + c - d}{2}$.

Note that $\frac{-a + b + c + d}{2} = \frac{2s - 2a}{2} = s - a$, $\frac{a - b + c + d}{2} = \frac{2s - 2b}{2} = s - b$, $\frac{a + b - c + d}{2} = \frac{2s - 2c}{2} = s - c$, and $\frac{a + b + c + -d}{2} = \frac{2s - 2d}{2} = s - d$. So $A^2 = (s - a)(s - b)(s - c)(s - d)$ and $A = \sqrt{(s - a)(s - b)(s - c)(s - d)}$.

8. Let $d = 0$ so that the cyclic quadrilateral becomes an inscribed triangle. Then $s - d = s$ and $A = \sqrt{s(s - a)(s - b)(s - c)}$.

3. Now apply the Law of Cosines to each triangle to find expressions for e^2, where e is the length of the diagonal in the diagram. Set these expressions equal to each other. Show that

$$a^2 + b^2 - c^2 - d^2 = 2(ab + cd)\cos\alpha$$

Conclude that

$$\frac{a^2 + b^2 - c^2 - d^2}{2(ab + cd)} = \cos\alpha$$

There is a factor of $ab + cd$ that shows up in both the expression for $\cos\alpha$ and the expression for $\sin\alpha$. This is a good place to use the Pythagorean Identity or at least some form of it. Because the expressions for sine and cosine have so much in common, maybe you can cancel or combine some of the terms in their squares.

4. Use the fact that $\cos^2\alpha = 1 - \sin^2\alpha$ to write the following equation.

$$\left(\frac{a^2 + b^2 - c^2 - d^2}{2(ab + cd)}\right)^2 = 1 - \left(\frac{2A}{ab + cd}\right)^2$$

5. Rearrange the result of Exercise 4 to get the equation below.

$$\frac{4(ab + cd)^2 - (a^2 + b^2 - c^2 - d^2)^2}{4(ab + cd)^2} = \frac{16A^2}{4(ab + cd)^2}$$

So

$$16A^2 = 4(ab + cd)^2 - (a^2 + b^2 - c^2 - d^2)^2.$$

6. The rest is factoring. Factor the right side of the equation from Exercise 5 as a difference of two squares.

Then factor each of the resulting factors some more. Try rearranging the terms so that you see some perfect squares.

7. Now you should have an equation like this.

$$16A^2 = (-a + b + c + d)(a - b + c + d) \cdot$$
$$(a + b - c + d)(a + b + c - d)$$

Put it all together to get Brahmagupta's Formula.

8. **Write About It** Explain how you can use Brahmagupta's Formula to prove Heron's Formula.

Chapter Review

1. a. $\left(-\frac{1}{2}, -\frac{\sqrt{3}}{2}\right)$

b. 293°

2. a.

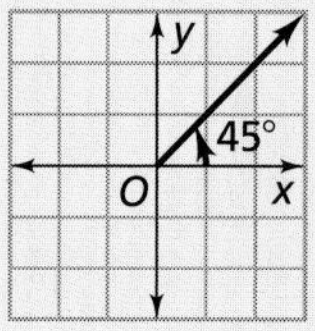

$\sin 45° = \frac{\sqrt{2}}{2}$, $\cos 45° = \frac{\sqrt{2}}{2}$,
$\tan 45° = 1$

b.

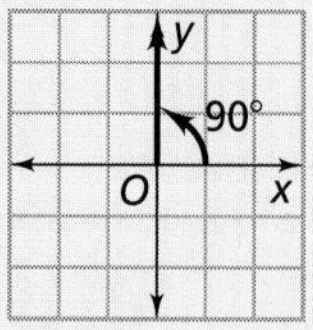

$\sin 90° = 1$, $\cos 90° = 0$, and $\tan 90°$ is undefined.

c.

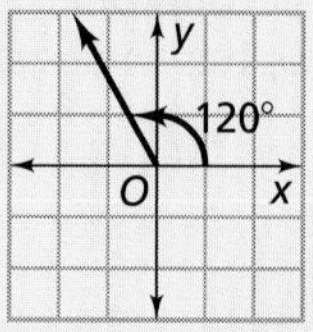

Chapter 8 Review

Go Online PHSchool.com — For additional practice, go to Web Code: bfj-0851

In **Investigation 8A,** you learned how to

- use right triangle trigonometry to find the coordinates of a person walking on the unit circle, given an angle through which an observer has turned
- evaluate the sine, cosine, and tangent functions for any angle
- solve equations involving trigonometric equations

The following questions will help you check your understanding.

1. Paul walks on the unit circle starting at the point (1, 0), in a counterclockwise direction. Olivia is the observer standing at the origin.

a. Find the coordinates of Paul's location when Olivia has turned 240°.

b. When Paul is at the point $\left(\frac{5}{13}, -\frac{12}{13}\right)$ for the first time, find the angle Olivia has turned to the nearest degree.

2. Sketch each angle in standard position. Find its sine, cosine, and tangent.

a. 45°

b. 90°

c. 120°

d. 180°

e. 210°

f. 330°

3. Solve each equation for α between 0° and 360°.

a. $\sin \alpha - 1 = 0$

b. $2 \sin \alpha = \sqrt{2}$

c. $4 \cos^2 \alpha - 1 = 0$

d. $3 \cos^2 \alpha + 2 \cos \alpha = 1$

In **Investigation 8B,** you learned how to

- sketch the graphs of sine, cosine, and tangent
- use the graphs of trigonometric functions to solve problems
- prove and use trigonometric identities

The following questions will help you check your understanding.

4. a. Copy and complete the table.

x	$\sin x$
0°	■
30°	■
45°	■
90°	■
120°	■
180°	■
210°	■
240°	■
270°	■
315°	■

b. Sketch a graph of $y = \sin x$ for $0° \le x \le 360°$. On your graph, label the points that you found for $x = 30°$, $x = 90°$, $x = 120°$, $x = 270°$, and $x = 315°$.

5. a. Sketch a graph of $y = \tan x$ for $0° \le x \le 360°$.

b. Use the graph of $y = \tan x$ to determine the number of solutions to the equation below for $0° \le x \le 360°$.

$$\tan x = \frac{1}{2}$$

c. Use $x = \tan^{-1} \frac{1}{2}$ to find all values of x for $0° \le x \le 360°$ to the nearest degree.

$\sin 120° = \frac{\sqrt{3}}{2}$, $\cos 120° = -\frac{1}{2}$, $\tan 120° = -\sqrt{3}$

d.

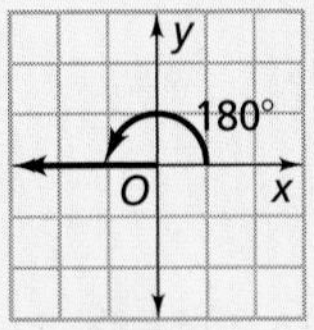

$\sin 180° = 0$, $\cos 180° = -1$, $\tan 180° = 0$

e.

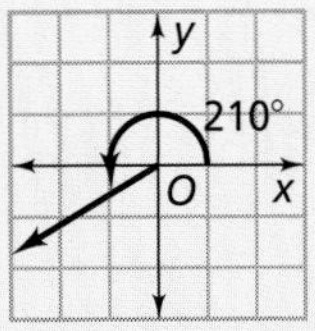

$\sin 210° = -\frac{1}{2}$, $\cos 210° = -\frac{\sqrt{3}}{2}$, $\tan 210° = \frac{\sqrt{3}}{3}$

f.

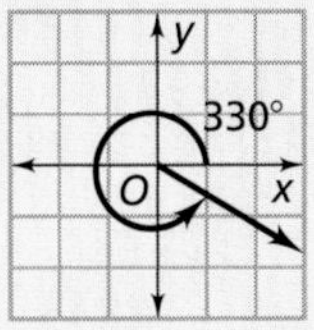

$\sin 330° = -\frac{1}{2}$, $\cos 330° = \frac{\sqrt{3}}{2}$, $\tan 330° = -\frac{\sqrt{3}}{3}$

3. a. 90°

b. 45°, 135°

c. 60°, 120°, 240°, 300°

d. 70.5°. 180°, 289.5°

4. a.

x	$\sin x$
0°	0
30°	$\frac{1}{2}$
45°	$\frac{\sqrt{2}}{2}$
90°	1
120°	$\frac{\sqrt{3}}{2}$
180°	0
210°	$-\frac{1}{2}$
240°	$-\frac{\sqrt{3}}{2}$
270°	−1
315°	$-\frac{\sqrt{2}}{2}$

b.

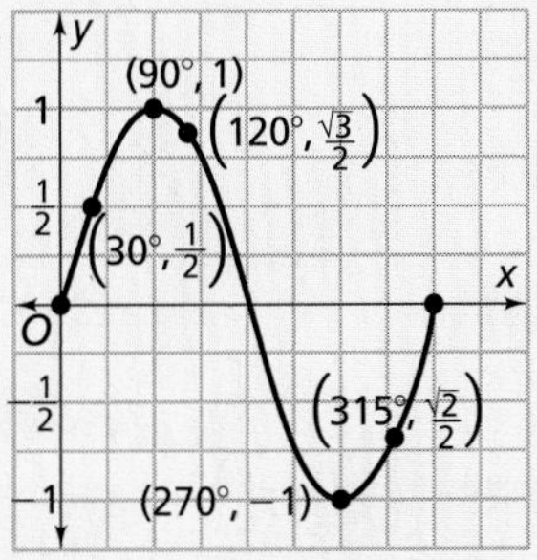

5. a.

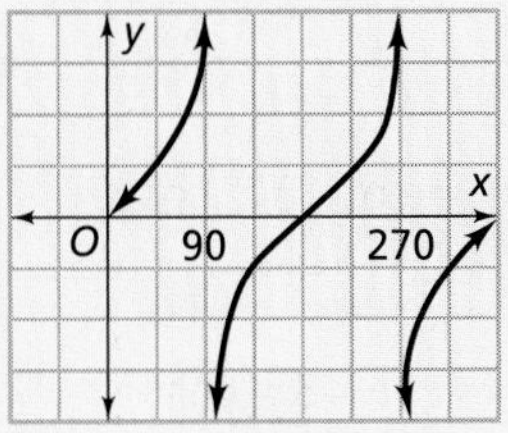

b. two

c. 27°, 207°

6. Use the angle-sum identities to prove each identity.

a. $\cos(180^\circ + x) = -\cos x$

b. $\sin(180^\circ + x) = -\sin x$

c. $\tan(180^\circ + x) = \tan x$

In **Investigation 8C** you learned how to

- solve a triangle
- state and use the Law of Sines
- state and use the Law of Cosines
- state and use Heron's Formula

The following questions will help you check your understanding.

7. In $\triangle ABC$, $AB = 6$, $\angle A = 50°$, and $\angle B = 60°$.

a. Find all remaining side lengths and angle measures in this triangle to the nearest tenth.

b. Find the area of $\triangle ABC$ to the nearest tenth by drawing the altitude $\overline{CH}$ from $\angle C$ to side $\overline{AB}$.

8. In $\triangle DEF$, $DE = 12$, $EF = 10$, and $DF = 9$.

a. Find the angle measure of the largest angle of this triangle to the nearest degree.

b. Find the area of this triangle using Heron's Formula.

9. For each set of equations about $\triangle GHI$, find all possible values for the measure of $\angle G$.

a. $GH = 3$, $GI = 8$, and $HI = 7$

b. $GI = 8$, $HI = 7$, and $m\angle H = 50^\circ$

c. $GI = 18$, $HI = 21$, $m\angle H = 52^\circ$

d. $GI = 6$, $HI = 7$, and $m\angle H = 75^\circ$

Answers

6. a. $\cos(180^\circ + x) = \cos 180^\circ \cos x - \sin 180^\circ \sin x = (-1)(\cos x) - (0)(\sin x) = -\cos x$

b. $\sin(180^\circ + x) = \sin 180^\circ \cos x + \cos 180^\circ \sin x = (0)(\cos x) + (-1)(\sin x) = -\sin x$

c. $\tan(180^\circ + x) = \dfrac{\sin(180^\circ + x)}{\cos(180^\circ + x)} = \dfrac{-\sin x}{-\cos x} = \tan x$

7. a. $m\angle C = 70^\circ$, $AC = 5.5$, $BC = 4.9$

b. 12.7

8. a. $m\angle F = 78^\circ$

b. 44

9. a. 60°

b. 42°

c. 67°, 113°

d. no solution

Chapter Test

1. D

2. B

3. B

4. B

5. D

6. a.

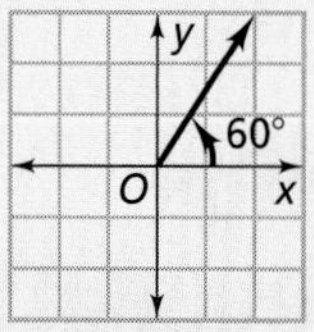

$\sin 60^\circ = \frac{\sqrt{3}}{2}$, $\cos 60^\circ = \frac{1}{2}$, $\tan 60^\circ = \sqrt{3}$

b.

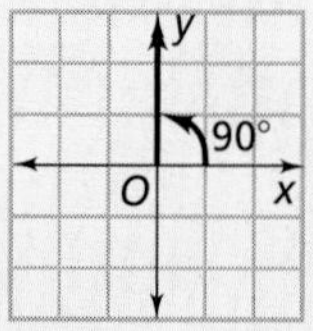

$\sin 90^\circ = 1$, $\cos 90^\circ = 0$, and $\tan 90^\circ$ is undefined.

Chapter 8 Test

Go Online PHSchool.com For chapter test, go to Web Code: bfa-0853

Multiple Choice

1. If $\cos\theta > 0$ and $\sin\theta < 0$, then θ is in which quadrant?
   A. I B. II
   C. III D. IV

2. For some angle α in Quadrant II, $\sin\alpha = \frac{15}{17}$. What is $\cos\alpha$?
   A. $-\frac{15}{17}$ B. $-\frac{8}{17}$
   C. $\frac{8}{17}$ D. 1

3. For the interval $90^\circ < x < 180^\circ$, is $\sin x$ positive or negative? Is the value of $\sin x$ increasing or decreasing as x increases through the interval?
   A. positive, increasing
   B. positive, decreasing
   C. negative, increasing
   D. negative, decreasing

4. Which is equal to $\cos 200^\circ$?
   A. $\cos 20^\circ$ B. $-\cos 20^\circ$
   C. $\sin 20^\circ$ D. $-\sin 20^\circ$

5. In $\triangle ABC$, $AB = 5$, $BC = 9$, and $AC = 8$. What is the area of $\triangle ABC$?
   A. $\sqrt{22}$ B. 11
   C. $11\sqrt{6}$ D. $6\sqrt{11}$

Open Response

6. Sketch each angle in standard position. Find its sine, cosine, and tangent. Give exact values, if possible. Otherwise, round to the nearest hundredth.
   a. 60° b. 90°
   c. 150° d. 289°

7. Solve each equation for $0^\circ \le \theta \le 360^\circ$.
   a. $2\sin\theta + 1 = 0$
   b. $2\cos^2\theta - 1 = 0$
   c. $3\cos^2\theta - 5\cos\theta + 2 = 0$

8. Simplify each expression.
   a. $\sin(180^\circ - x)$
   b. $\cos(180^\circ + x)$
   c. $\sin(270^\circ + x)$

9. a. Sketch a graph of $y = \cos x$ for $0^\circ \le x \le 450^\circ$.
   b. Use your graph to determine the number of solutions to the equation $\cos x = \frac{1}{2}$.
   c. Find all solutions to $\cos x = \frac{1}{2}$ for $0^\circ \le x \le 450^\circ$.

10. For each set of information about $\triangle ABC$, find all the missing side lengths to the nearest tenth and angle measures to the nearest degree.
    a. $AB = 16$, $BC = 12$, and $AC = 8$
    b. $m\angle A = 34^\circ$, $BC = 5$, and $AC = 7$

11. What information do you need about a triangle to find its area?

Chapter Test

Assessment Resources

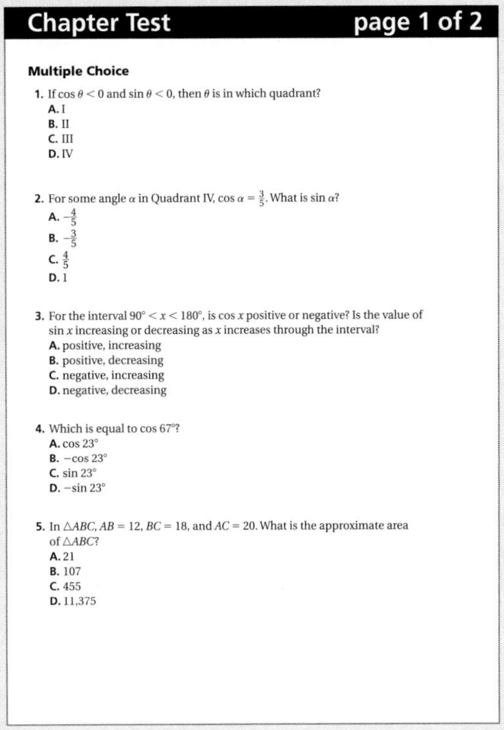
Chapter Test page 1 of 2

Multiple Choice

1. If $\cos\theta < 0$ and $\sin\theta < 0$, then θ is in which quadrant?
   A. I
   B. II
   C. III
   D. IV

2. For some angle α in Quadrant IV, $\cos\alpha = \frac{3}{5}$. What is $\sin\alpha$?
   A. $-\frac{4}{5}$
   B. $-\frac{3}{5}$
   C. $\frac{4}{5}$
   D. 1

3. For the interval $90^\circ < x < 180^\circ$, is $\cos x$ positive or negative? Is the value of $\sin x$ increasing or decreasing as x increases through the interval?
   A. positive, increasing
   B. positive, decreasing
   C. negative, increasing
   D. negative, decreasing

4. Which is equal to $\cos 67^\circ$?
   A. $\cos 23^\circ$
   B. $-\cos 23^\circ$
   C. $\sin 23^\circ$
   D. $-\sin 23^\circ$

5. In $\triangle ABC$, $AB = 12$, $BC = 18$, and $AC = 20$. What is the approximate area of $\triangle ABC$?
   A. 21
   B. 107
   C. 455
   D. 11,375

Also available: Form B

9. a. 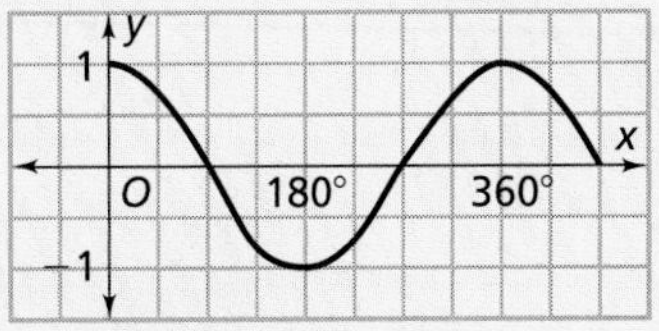

   b. three solutions
   c. $60^\circ, 300^\circ, 420^\circ$

10. a. $m\angle A = 47^\circ$, $m\angle B = 29^\circ$, $m\angle C = 104^\circ$
    b. If $m\angle B = 52^\circ$, then $m\angle C = 94^\circ$ and $AB = 8.9$. If $m\angle B = 128^\circ$, then $m\angle C = 18^\circ$ and $AB = 2.7$.

11. Answers may vary. Sample: You can find the area if you know SSS, SAS, ASA, or AAS, as well as SSA if a triangle exists.

c. 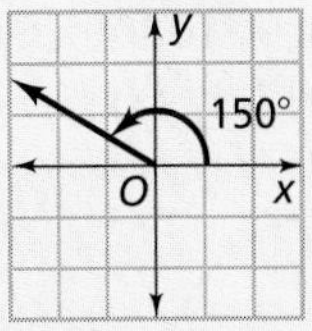

$\sin 150^\circ = \frac{1}{2}$, $\cos 150^\circ = -\frac{\sqrt{3}}{2}$, $\tan 150^\circ = -\frac{\sqrt{3}}{3}$

d. 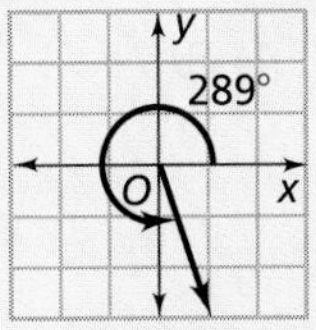

$\sin 289^\circ = -0.95$, $\cos 289^\circ = 0.33$, $\tan 289^\circ = -2.90$

7. a. $210^\circ, 330^\circ$
   b. $45^\circ, 135^\circ, 225^\circ, 315^\circ$
   c. $0^\circ, 48^\circ, 312^\circ$

8. a. $\sin x$
   b–c. $-\cos x$

Cumulative Review

Assessment Resources

Quarter Test — page 1 of 2

Multiple Choice

1. What is the sum of the even integers from 24 to 110, inclusive?
   A. 134
   B. 2881
   C. 2948
   D. 5829

2. Which number is equivalent to 0.232323 . . . ?
   A. 0.232
   B. $\frac{23}{99}$
   C. $\frac{116}{500}$
   D. $\frac{2323}{10{,}000}$

3. In an arithmetic sequence, the third term is 18 and the eighth term is 53. What is the fifth term?
   A. 7
   B. 25
   C. 32
   D. 46

4. If $\cos\theta < 0$ and $\sin\theta > 0$, then θ is in which quadrant?
   A. I
   B. II
   C. III
   D. IV

5. Which is equal to $\sin(-32°)$?
   A. $-\sin 32°$
   B. $\sin 32°$
   C. $-\cos 32°$
   D. $\cos 32°$

6. In $\triangle ABC$, $AB = 18$, $BC = 21$, and $AC = 27$. What is the approximate area of $\triangle ABC$?
   A. 33
   B. 189
   C. 243
   D. 283.5

Chapter 8

Cumulative Review

Multiple Choice

1. What is the sum of the odd integers from 9 to 101, inclusive?
   A. 1242 B. 2484
   C. 2538 D. 5076

2. If $\binom{20}{k} = 1$, what is k?
   A. 0 B. 1
   C. 19 D. 20

3. What is a rational expression for 0.131313 . . . ?
   A. $\frac{1}{13}$ B. $\frac{13}{87}$
   C. $\frac{13}{99}$ D. $\frac{13}{100}$

4. In an arithmetic sequence, the third term is 18 and the eighth term is 576. What is the sixth term?
   A. 112 B. 352
   C. 464 D. 688

5. What is the coefficient of x^4y^8 in the expansion of $(x + y)^{12}$?
   A. $\binom{8}{4}$ B. $\binom{12}{4}$
   C. $\binom{12}{8}$ D. $\binom{16}{12}$

6. If $\cos\theta > 0$ and $\sin\theta < 0$, which quadrant is θ in?
   A. I B. II
   C. III D. IV

7. For some angle α in Quadrant IV, $\cos\alpha = \frac{5}{13}$. What is $\sin\alpha$?
   A. $\frac{5}{12}$ B. $-\frac{5}{12}$
   C. $\frac{12}{13}$ D. $-\frac{12}{13}$

8. As x increases through the interval $-90° < x < 90°$, is $\cos\alpha$ positive or negative? Is the value of $\sin\alpha$ increasing or decreasing?
   A. positive, increasing
   B. positive, decreasing
   C. negative, increasing
   D. negative, decreasing

9. What is the value of $\cos 42°$?
   A. $\cos 48°$ B. $-(\cos 48°)$
   C. $\sin 48°$ D. $-\sin 48°$

10. In $\triangle ABC$, $AB = 16$, $BC = 23$, and $AC = 21$. What is the approximate area of $\triangle ABC$?
    A. 41 B. 81
    C. 163 D. 1654

Open Response

11. Find each sum.
    a. $\sum_{k=1}^{10} (3k - 1)$
    b. $\sum_{k=0}^{4} 6(-2)^k$

12. Find a closed-form rule for the following indefinite sum.
    $$\sum_{k=0}^{n} (6k + 4)$$

13. Find a recursive rule and a closed-form rule for the series defined by $h(n) = 6n + 2$, with initial term $h(0)$.

14. A geometric sequence g has $g(0) = 8$ and common ratio $\frac{3}{2}$.
    a. Create a summation table for $g(n)$ for $n = 0$ through $n = 4$.
    b. Find a closed-form rule for the sequence.

Answers

1. C
2. A
3. C
4. B
5. C
6. D
7. D
8. A
9. C
10. C
11. a. 155
    b. 66
12. $(n + 1)(3n + 4)$
13. $\sum_{k=0}^{n} h(k) = H(n) = \begin{cases} 2 & \text{if } n = 0 \\ H(n-1) + 6n + 2 & \text{if } n > 0 \end{cases}$

$\sum_{k=0}^{n} h(k) = (n + 1)(3n + 2)$

14. a.

n	$g(n)$
0	8
1	12
2	18
3	27
4	$\frac{81}{2}$

b. $g(n) = 8 \cdot \left(\frac{3}{2}\right)^n$

15. $243x^5 - 810x^4y + 1080x^3y^2 - 720x^2y^3 + 240xy^4 - 32y^5$

16. a.

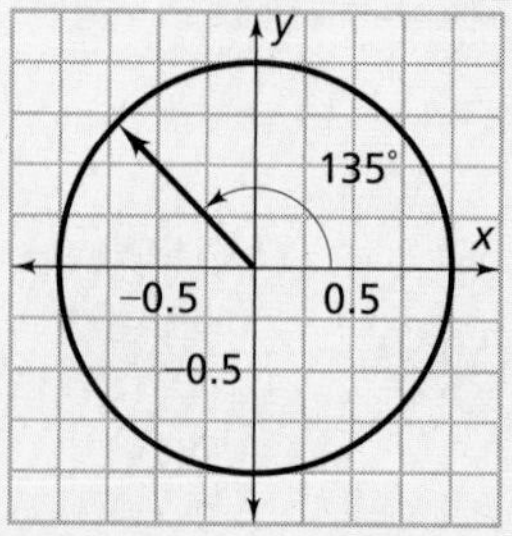

$\sin 135° = \frac{\sqrt{2}}{2}$, $\cos 135° = -\frac{\sqrt{2}}{2}$, $\tan 135° = -1$

15. Use Pascal's Triangle to expand $(3x - 2y)^5$.

16. Sketch each angle in standard position and find its sine, cosine, and tangent. Give exact values if possible.

a. $135°$ b. $300°$

17. Solve each equation over $0° \le \theta \le 360°$.

a. $\cos\theta + 1 = 0$ b. $\sqrt{2}\sin\theta + 1 = 0$

c. $\sin^2\theta - 3\theta + 2 = 0$

18. Simplify each expression

a. $\cos(360° - x)$ b. $\sin(90° - x)$

c. $\sin(180° - x)$

19. Write each expression as the sine or cosine of an acute angle.

a. $\sin 135°$ b. $\cos 330°$

c. $\tan 240°$

20. Suppose $\sin\theta = -\frac{12}{13}$ and θ is an angle in the interval $0° \le \theta \le 360°$.

a. Find all possible values of $\cos\theta$.

b. Find all possible values of $\tan\theta$.

c. Find all possible values of θ to the nearest tenth.

21. Find the center and radius of the circle with equation $(x - 3)^2 + (y + 4)^2 = 36$.

22. Determine whether the function $g(x) = 2x^3 - x$ is even, odd, or neither.

23. Describe the translation of $y = x^3$ to $y + 2 = (x + 1)^3$.

24. a. Write an equation for a function with a graph that is the graph of $y = x^2$ stretched vertically by a factor of $\frac{1}{2}$ and translated up 3 units.

b. Sketch the graph.

25. Write each expression as a single affine transformation.

a. $D_5 \circ T_{-3}$ b. $D_2 \circ D_6 \circ T_3$

c. $\mathcal{A}_{(3,\,-2)} \circ \mathcal{A}_{(6,\,3)}$

26. Simplify each expression.

a. $8^{-\frac{5}{3}}$ b. $\frac{x^{-3}y^{-7}}{x^{-5}y^{-1}}$

27. You are given the sequence 15, ■, ■, 120.

a. Find the missing terms if the sequence is arithmetic.

b. Find the missing terms if the sequence is geometric.

28. Find the inverse of each function.

a. $f(x) = 5^x$ b. $g(x) = \log_3 x$

29. Find the solution to the following system.

$$2x + 3y = 12$$
$$-3x - y = 3$$

30. Find the dot product.

$(2, -1, 5) \cdot (6, -2, 0)$

31. Simplify each expression.

a. $\sqrt{40} \cdot \sqrt{-5}$ b. $(3 - 2i)^2$

32. Find the magnitude of $6 + 2i$.

33. Suppose $f(x) = -2x + 4$. If possible, find a function $g(x)$ such that $f \circ g(x) = x$.

34. Find the line of best fit for the data set.

x	y
−1	4
2	7
4	10
7	14

Assessment Resources

End-of-Year Test page 1 of 4

Multiple Choice

1. What is the balance point of the data set below?

x	y
1	3
2	4
5	2
8	5

A. (16, 14) B. (8, 7) C. (4, 3.5) D. (3.5, 3)

2. Suppose the function b represents the balance of a loan at the end of month n.

$$b(n) = \begin{cases} 10{,}000 & \text{if } n = 0 \\ \frac{12.05}{12} \cdot b(n-1) - 300 & \text{if } n > 0 \end{cases}$$

Which of the following statements about b is NOT true?
A. The original amount of the loan is $10,000.
B. The balance of the loan at the end of one month is $9700.
C. The interest rate is 5%.
D. The monthly payment is $300.

3. Consider the definitions for the functions f and g below.

$$f(x) = 6x + 1$$
$$g(x) = -2x + 5$$

What is the value of $f \circ g(3)$?
A. −33 B. −19 C. −5 D. 0

4. Factor the polynomial $6x^2 - 7x - 20$.
A. $(3x + 5)(2x - 4)$ B. $(6x + 5)(x - 4)$
C. $(6x - 5)(x + 4)$ D. $(3x + 4)(2x - 5)$

5. What is the magnitude of $z = 2 + 3i$?
A. $\sqrt{5}$ B. $\sqrt{13}$ C. 5 D. 6

6. A polynomial equation with real coefficients has −5 and $4 - 2i$ as two of its solutions. Which of the following is another solution?
A. 5 B. $-2 + 4i$ C. $4 + 2i$ D. $-4 + 2i$

Also available: Form B

b.

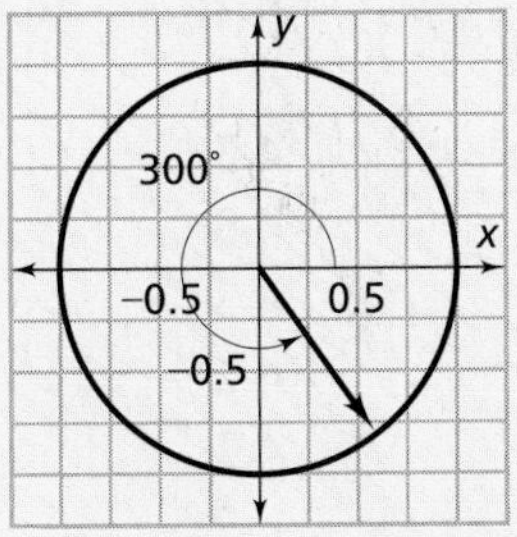

$\sin 300° = -\frac{\sqrt{3}}{2}$, $\cos 300° = \frac{1}{2}$, $\tan 300° = -\sqrt{3}$

17. a. 180° **b.** 225°, 315° **c.** 90°

18. a. $\cos x$ **b.** $\cos x$ **c.** $\sin x$

19. a. $\sin 45°$ **b.** $\cos 30°$ **c.** $\tan 60°$

20. a. $\pm\frac{5}{13}$ **b.** $\pm\frac{12}{5}$ **c.** 247.4°, 292.6°

21. center: (3, −4); radius: 6

22. odd

23. one unit left, two units down

24. a. $y = \frac{1}{2}x^2 + 3$

b.

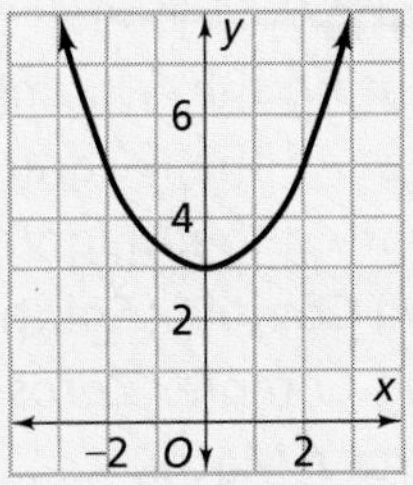

25. a. $\mathcal{A}_{(5,\,-15)}$ **b.** $\mathcal{A}_{(12,\,36)}$ **c.** $\mathcal{A}_{(18,\,7)}$

26. a. 2^{-5} **b.** x^2y^{-6}

27. a. 50, 85 **b.** 30, 60

28. a. $f^{-1}(x) = \log_5 x$ **b.** $g^{-1}(x) = 3^x$

29. $x = -3, y = 6$

30. 14

31. a. $10i\sqrt{2}$ **b.** $5 - 12i$

32. $2\sqrt{10}$

33. $g(x) = -\frac{1}{2}x + 2$

34. $y = 1.26x + 4.96$

TI-Nspire™ Technology Handbook

Recognizing how to use technology to support your mathematics is an important habit of mind. Although the use of technology in this course is independent of any particular hardware or software, this handbook gives examples of how you can apply the TI-Nspire™ handheld technology.

Handbook Contents

Setting the Handheld to Degree Mode, Lesson 8.2

1. Press ctrl [home]. Choose **File** and then **Document Settings**. Press enter.

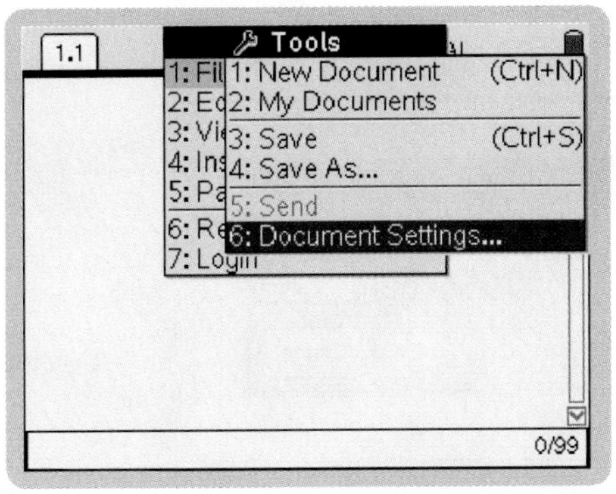

2. Tab down to the **Angle** menu. Press ▽ until **Degree** is highlighted. Press enter enter.

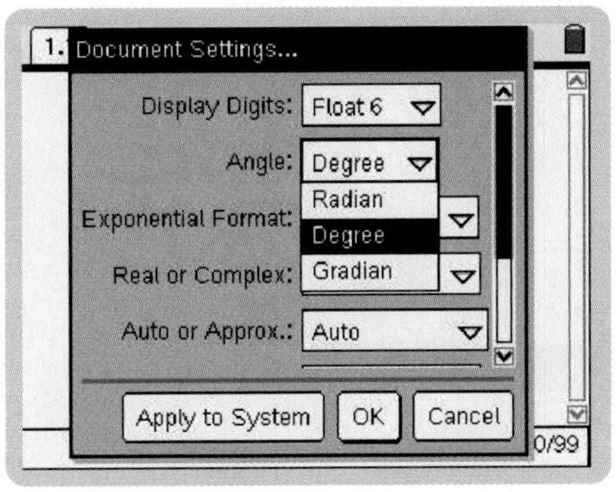

Modeling a Function, Lessons 1.2, 2.2

1. Choose **Define** from the **Actions** menu (or type D E F I N E).

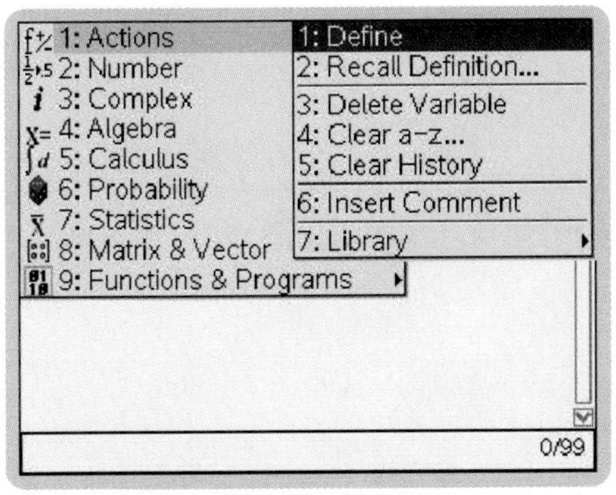

2. Type the function. Press enter.

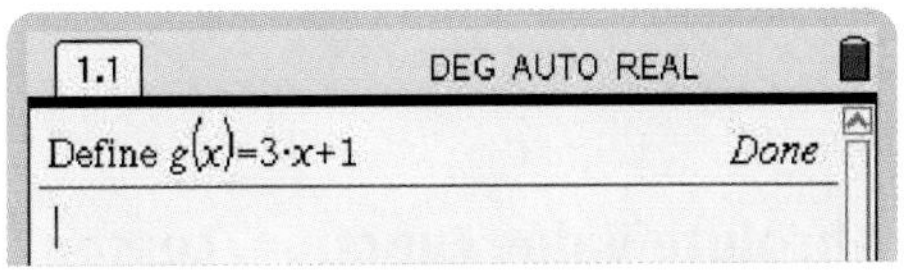

Modeling a Recursive Function I, Lessons 1.2, 5.8

1. Choose **Define** from the **Actions** menu. Name the function by typing B (N) =. Press ctrl × to open the Templates palette. Select [piecewise template]. Press enter.

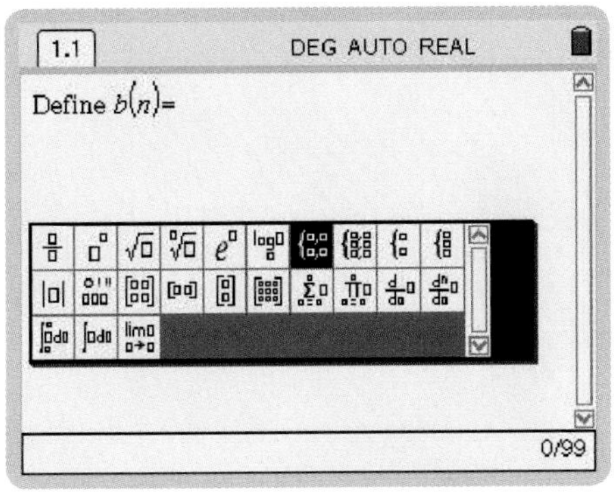

2. Enter the function. Press tab to move from box to box. Press enter when done.

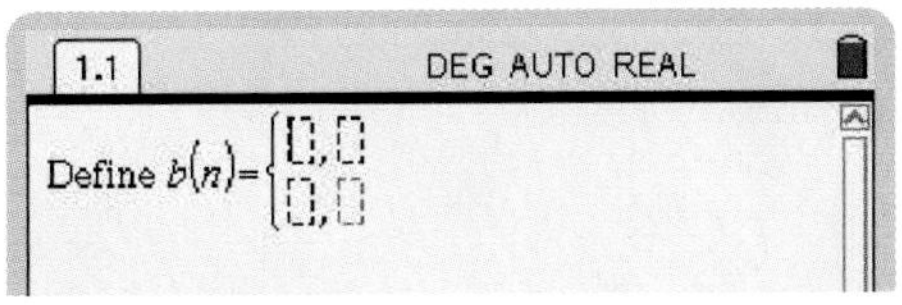

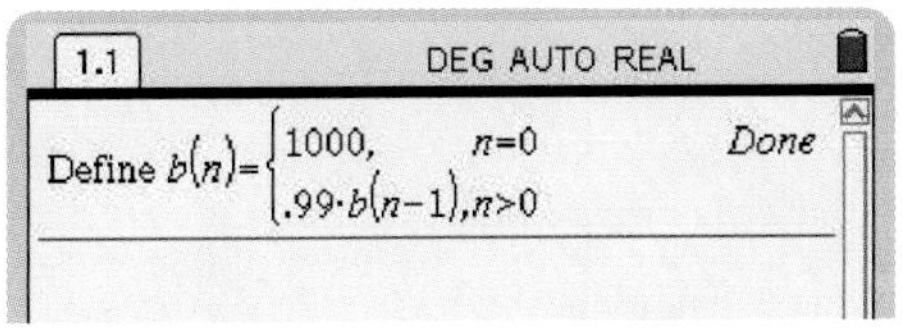

Modeling a Recursive Function II, Lesson 1.10

1. Choose **Define** from the **Actions** menu. Name the function by typing G (N) =. Press (ctrl) (x) to open the Templates palette. Select [piecewise template]. Press (enter).

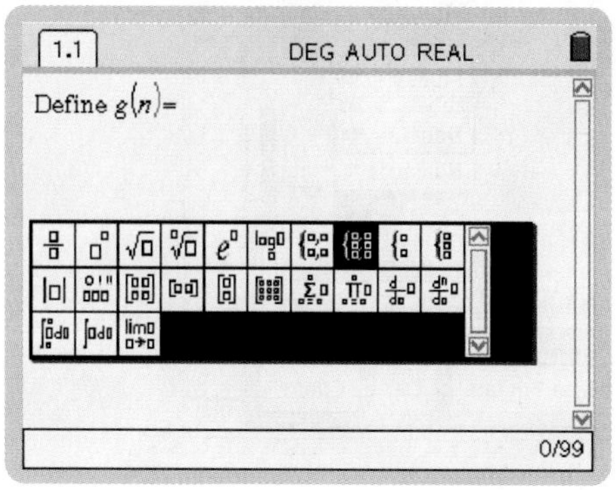

2. Select the number of pieces in the definition. Press (enter).

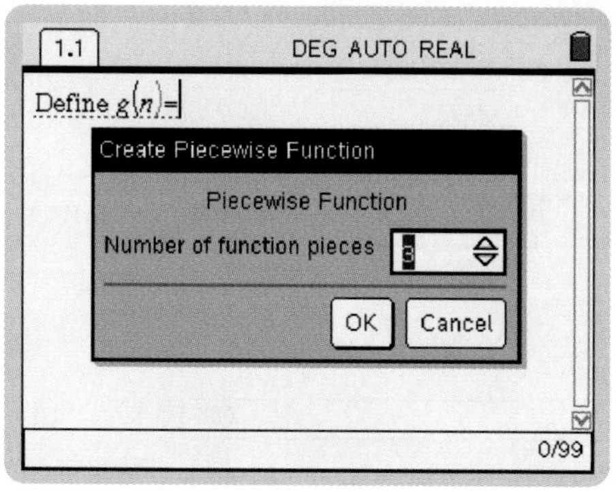

3. Enter the function. Press (tab) to move from box to box. Press (enter) when done.

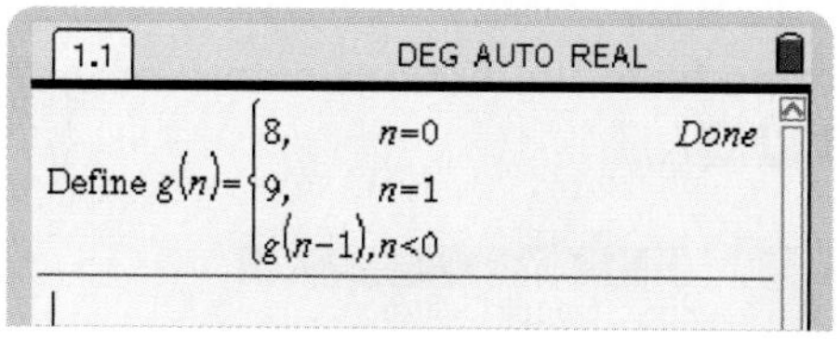

Modeling an Absolute Value Function, Lesson 6.1

1. Choose **Define** from the **Actions** menu. Name the function by typing F (N) =. Press (ctrl) (x) to open the Templates palette. Select [absolute value template]. Press (enter).

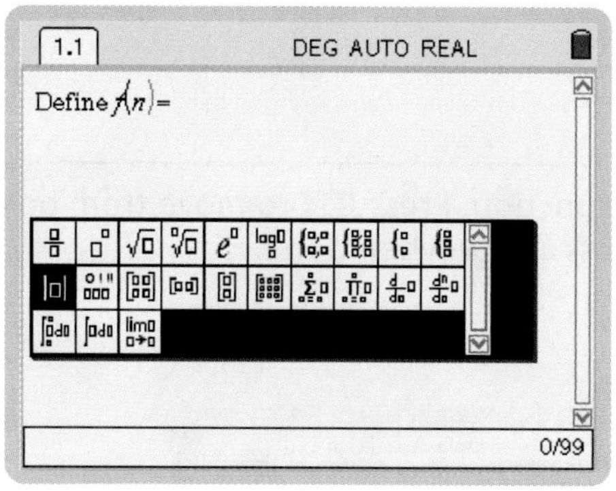

2. Enter the function. Press (enter) when done.

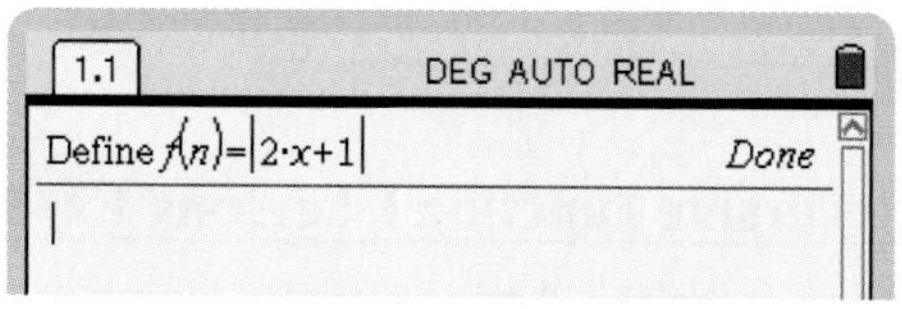

Modeling a Monthly Payment Function, Lessons 1.11, 7.11

1. Choose **Define** from the **Tools** menu. Name the function by typing B (N , C , I , M) = . Press ctrl ⊠ to open the Templates palette. Select [piecewise template]. Press enter.

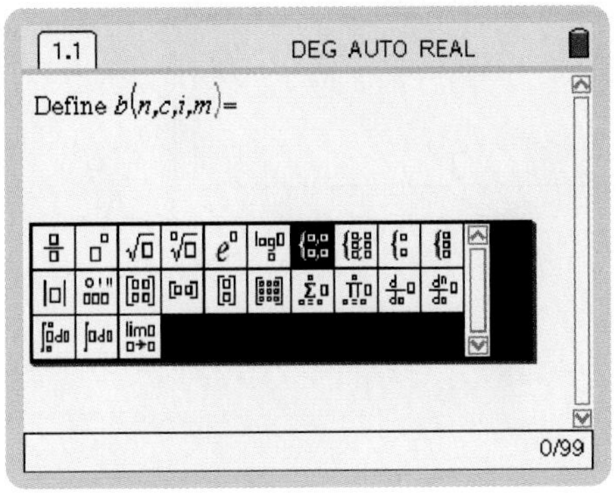

2. Enter the function. Press tab to move from box to box. Press enter when done.

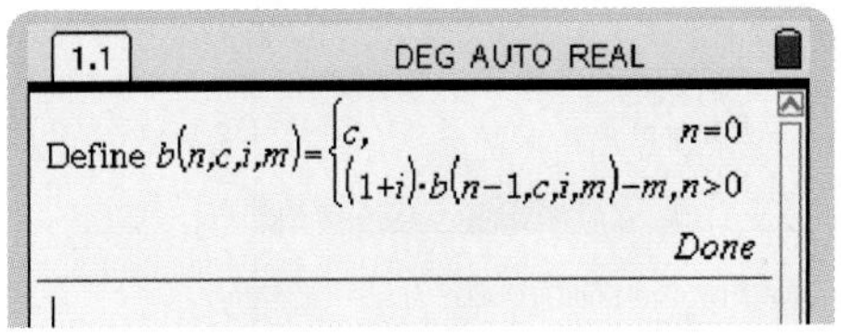

3. Enter values for the number of months, the initial principal, the interest rate, and the monthly payment. Press enter to calculate the current balance.

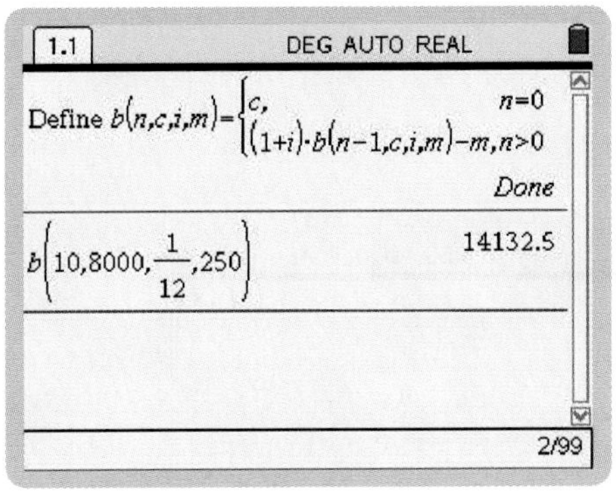

Using the Logarithm Template, Lesson 5.12

1. Press ctrl ⊠ to open the Templates palette. Select [log template]. Press enter.

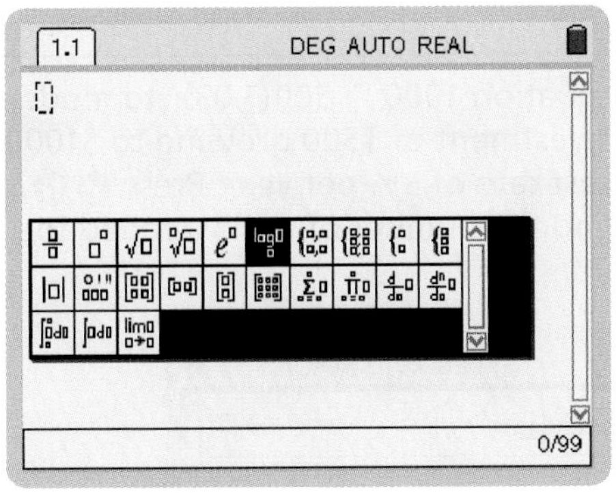

2. Press tab to move from box to box. Press enter when done.

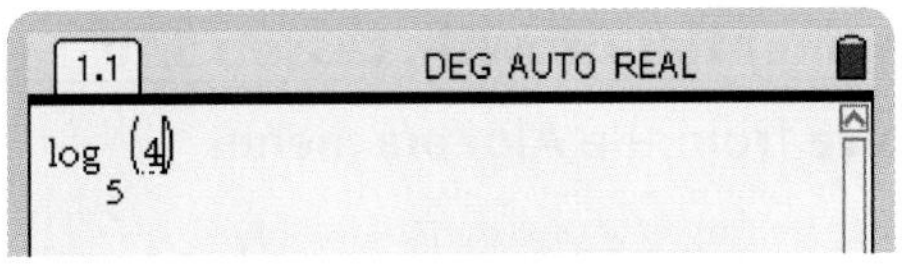

Using Sigma Notation, Lessons 7.4, 7.7, 7.10

1. Choose **Sum** in the **Calculus** menu.

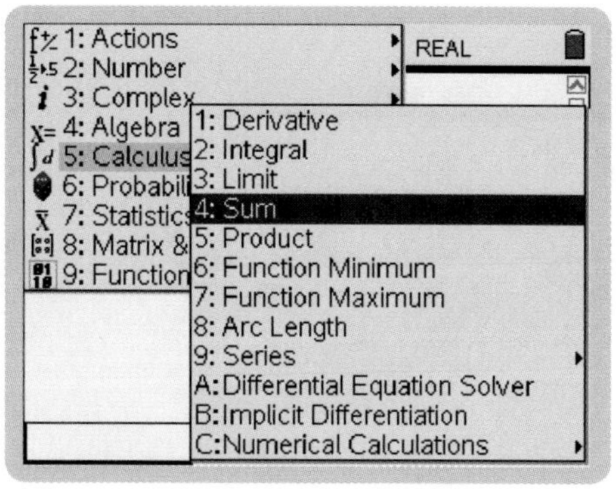

2. Press **tab** to move from box to box. Type the upper limit, the lower limit, and the expression for the sequence. Press **enter**.

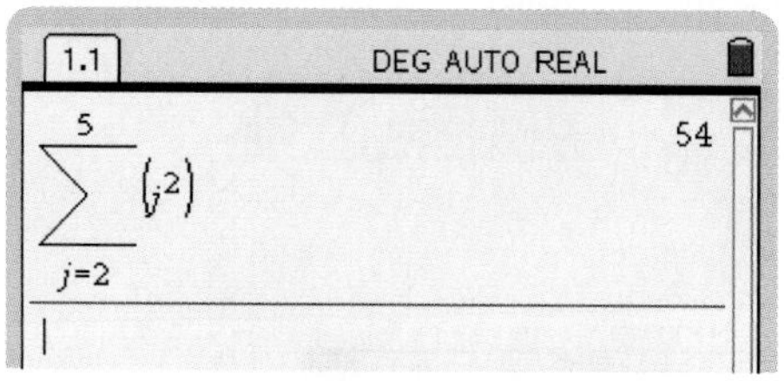

3. To evaluate an indefinite sum, Choose **Sum** in the **Calculus** menu.

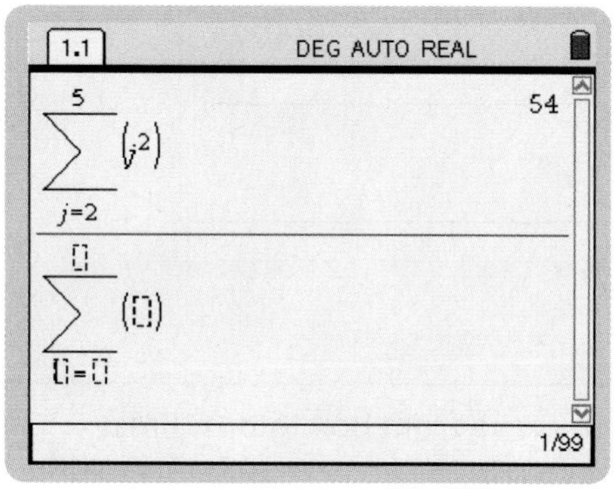

4. Press **tab** to move from box to box. Use a variable for the upper limit, and an integer for the lower limit. Type an expression for the sequence using the upper limit variable. Press **enter** to evaluate the sum.

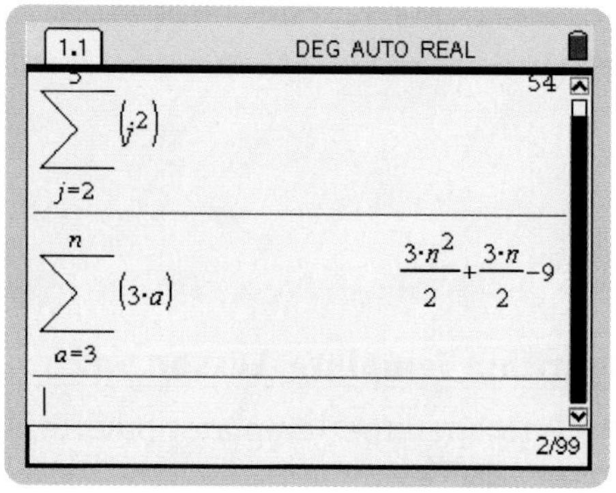

Modeling Exponential Growth, Lesson 5.10

1. Choose **Solve** from the **Algebra** menu.

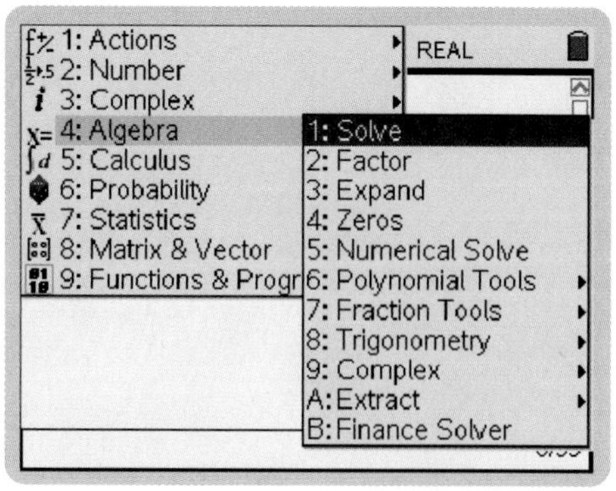

2. Type the equation $1000 = 500(1.03)^n$ to model an initial investment of \$500 growing to \$1000 at an interest rate of 3% per year. Press **ctrl** **N**, **enter** to find the number of years needed to reach \$1000.

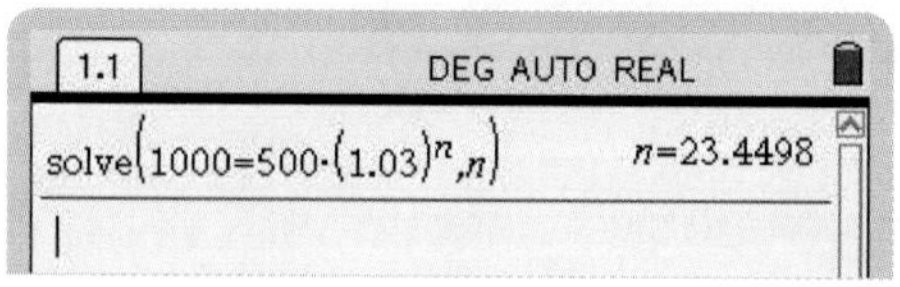

Modeling an Affine Transformation, Lesson 6.6

1. Choose **Delete Variable** from the **Actions** menu. Type A , B enter to delete two variables to use in the affine transformation.

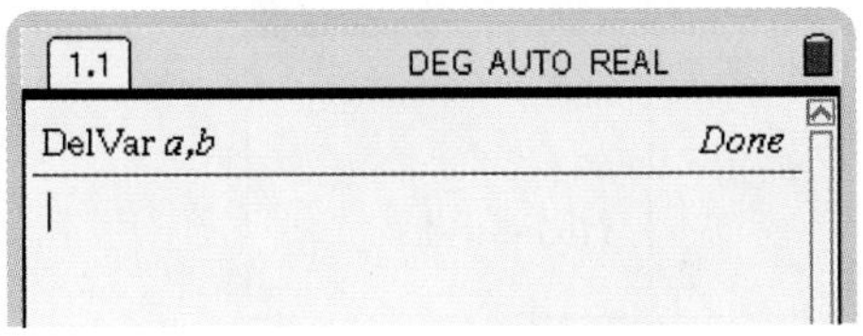

2. Define the function $m(x,a,b) = ax + b$.

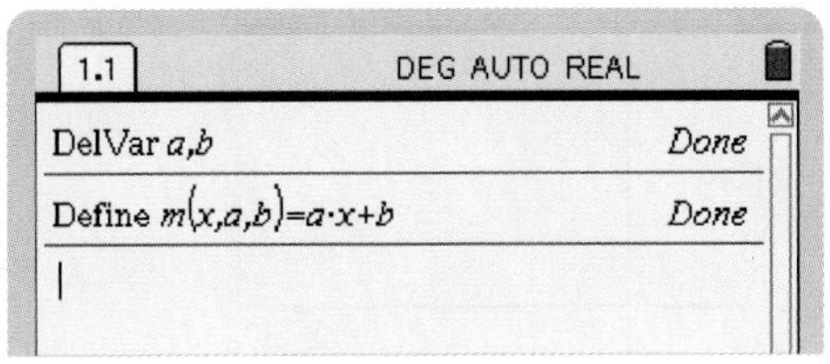

3. To define the affine transformation $x \mapsto \mathcal{A}_{(3,4)}(x)$, define $f(x)$ as $m(x,3,4)$.

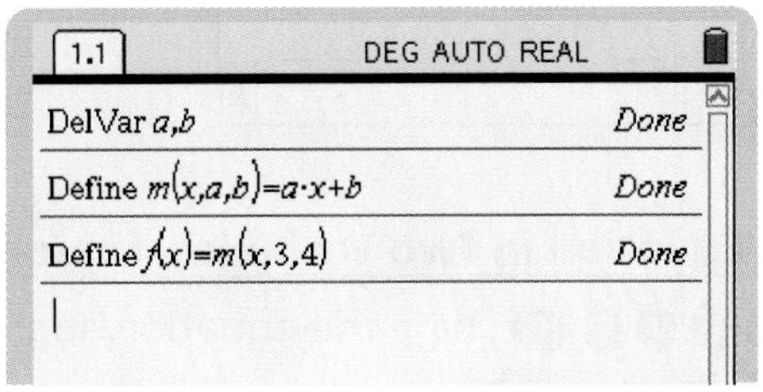

Graphing an Equation, Lesson 2.2

1. Use the **Text** tool in the **Actions** menu. Type the equation on the screen. Press enter.

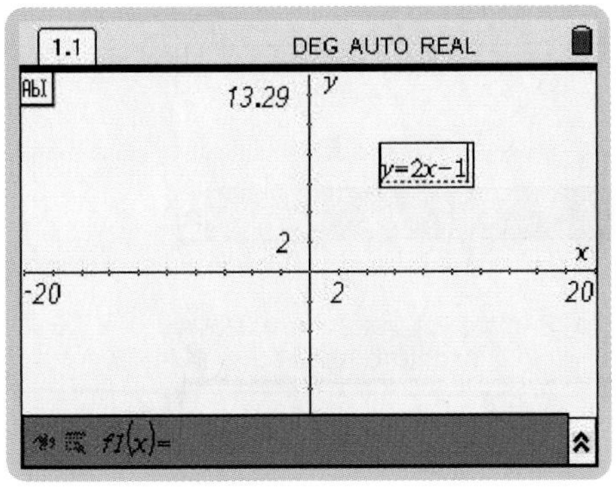

2. Place the cursor on the equation. Press ctrl to grab the equation. Drag it to an axis. Press enter.

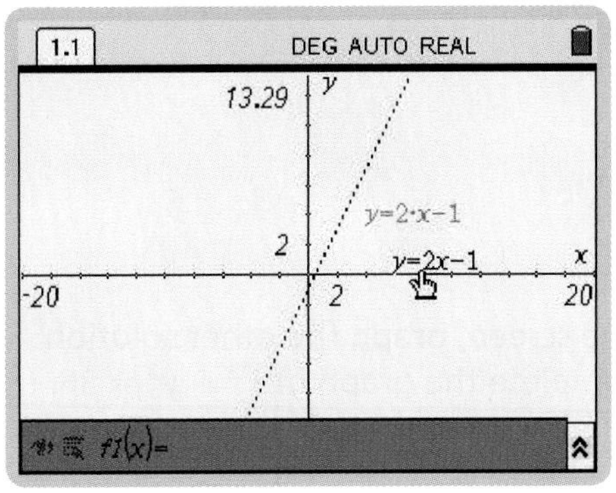

Graphing a Function, Lesson 2.2

1. Tab down to the entry line at the bottom of the screen. Type an expression in *x*.

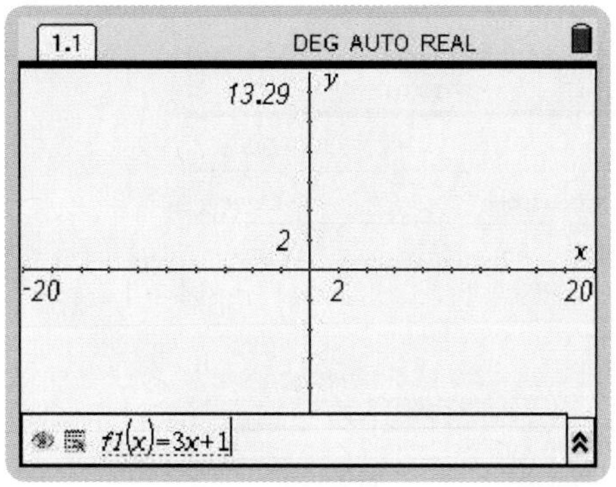

2. Press enter.

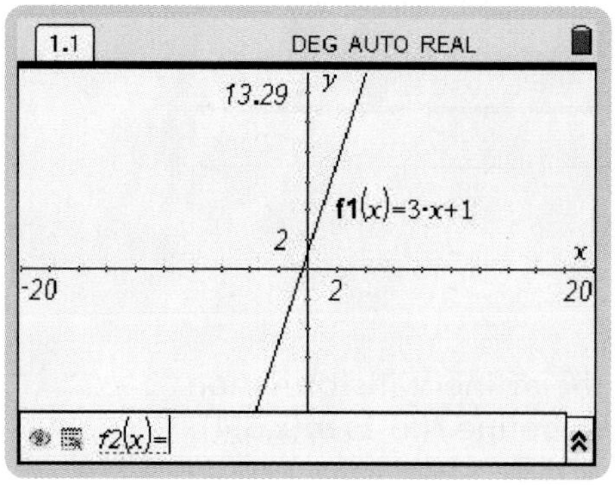

Graphing an Equation in Two Variables, Lesson 6.4

1. Type S O L V E (. Type the equation and then , Y. Press enter.

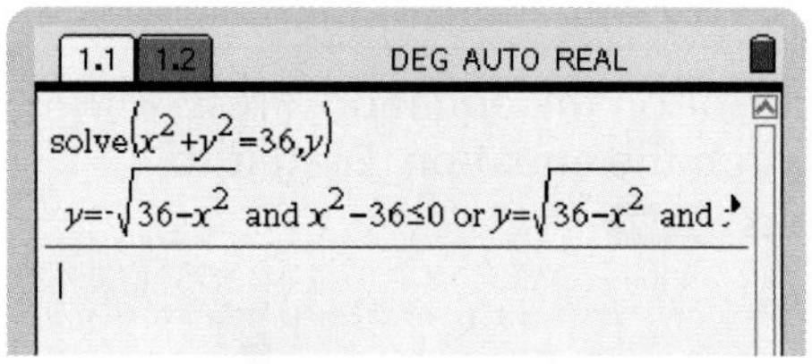

2. In a graphing screen, graph one of the solutions for *y*.

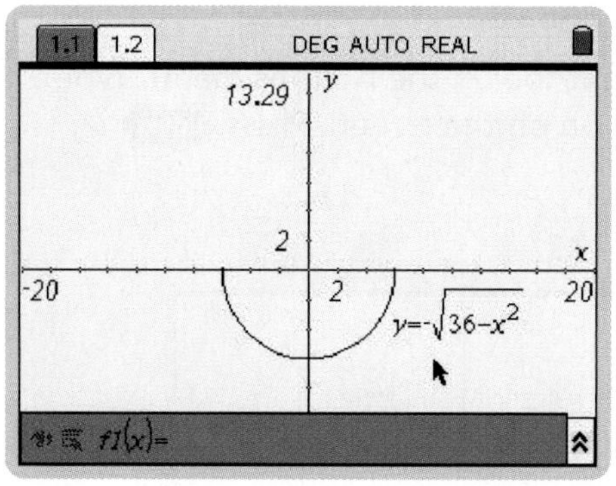

3. In the same screen, graph the other solution for *y* to complete the graph of $x^2 + y^2 = 36$.

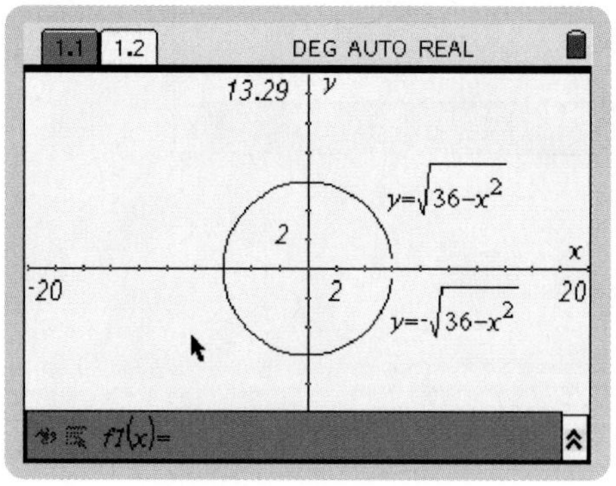

Finding the Intersection of Two Graphs, Lessons 5.7, 5.14

1. Choose **Intersection Point(s)** from the **Points & Lines** menu.

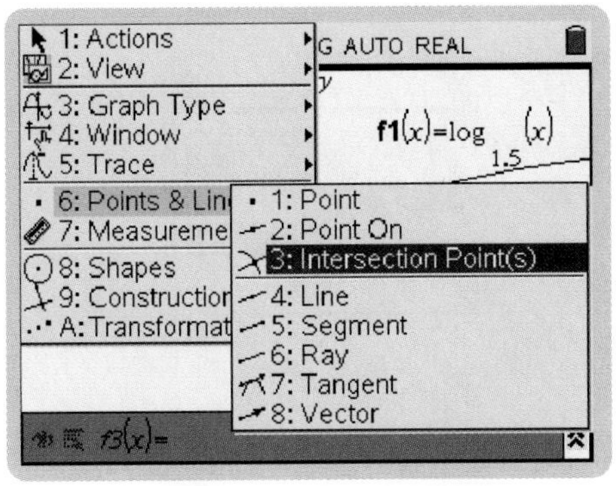

2. Place the cursor on one graph. Press **enter**.

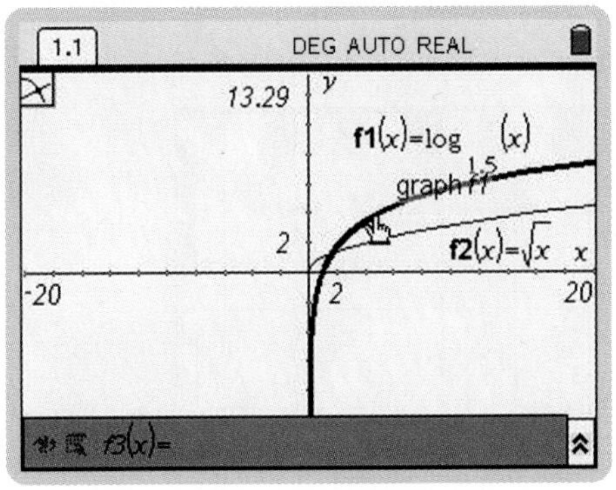

3. Place the cursor on the other graph. Press **enter**.

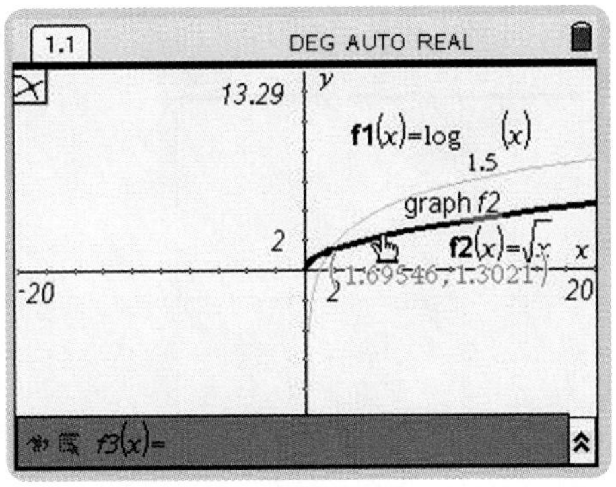

4. Move the cursor to drag the coordinates of the point of intersection. Press **enter** to anchor the coordinates.

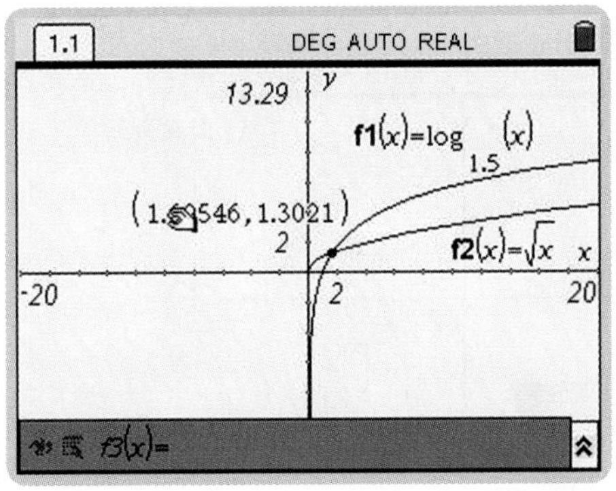

Using Zoom—Trig to View the Graph of a Trigonometric Function, Lesson 8.7

1. Choose **Zoom–Trig** from the **Window** menu.

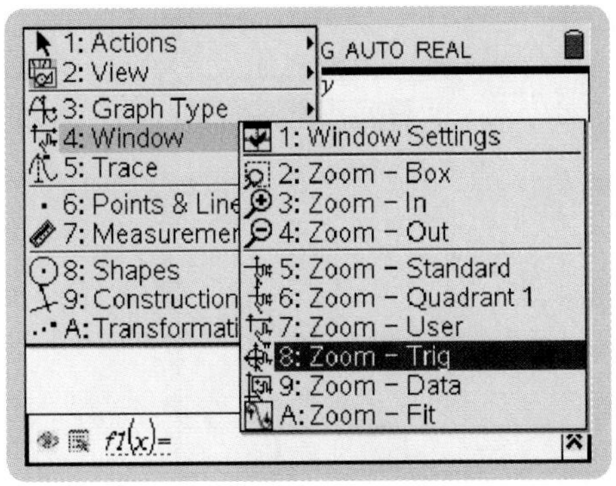

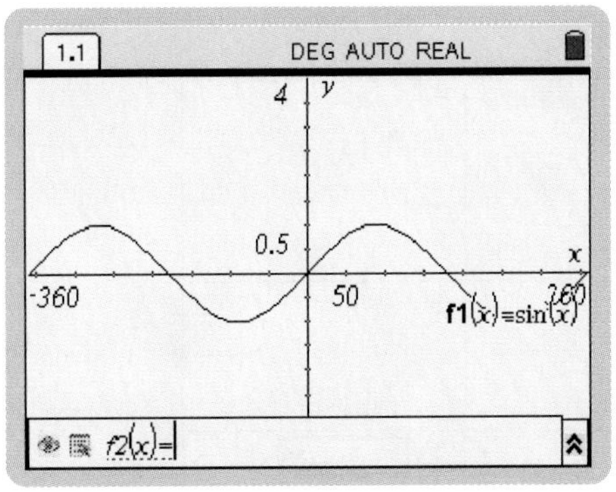

Finding the Line of Best Fit I, Lesson 1.8

1. Name the first two columns of a spreadsheet *a* and *b*. Enter the *x*-coordinates of your points in column *a* and the *y*-coordinates in column *b*.

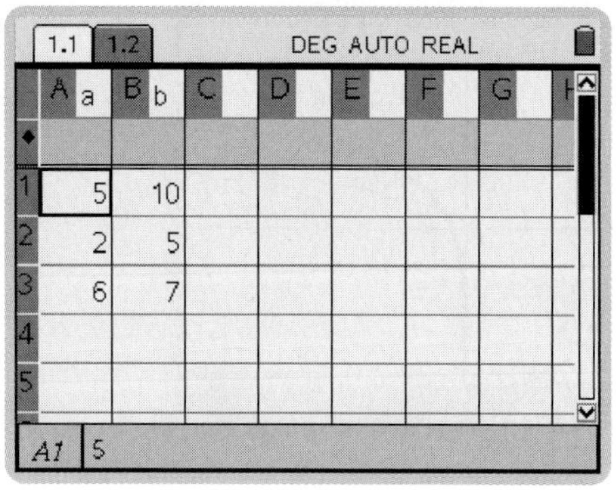

2. Navigate to the Graphs & Geometry application. Choose **Scatter Plot** from the **Graph Type** menu.

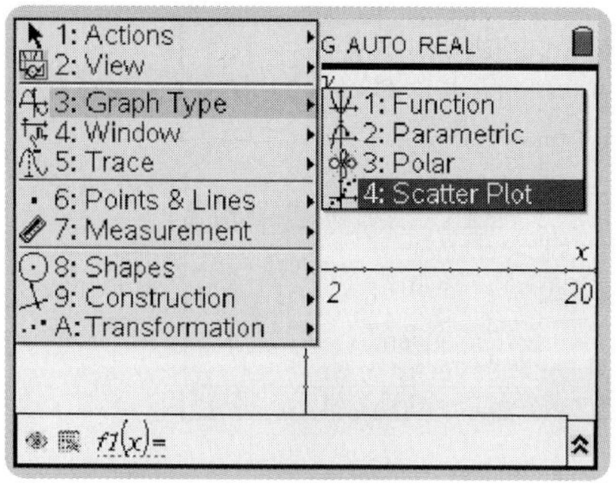

3. Press **enter** to select from among a list of possible *x*-values. Select *a*. Press **enter**.

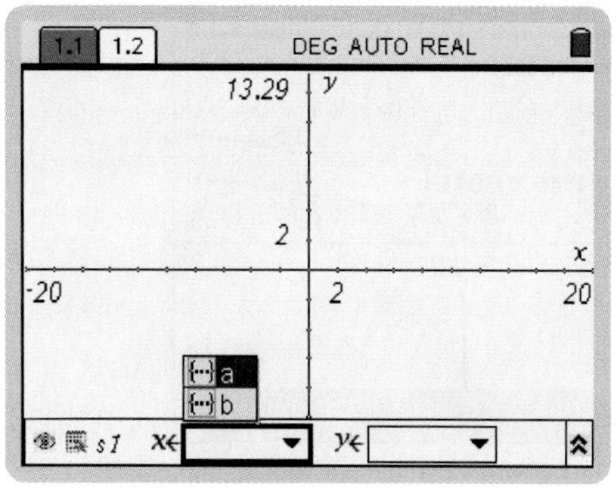

4. Press **tab** and then **enter** to select from among a list of possible *y*-values.

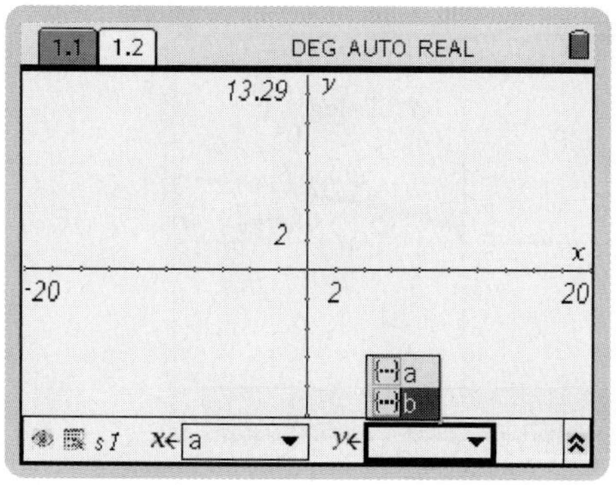

5. Select *b*. Press **enter** to view a scatter plot of the selected data.

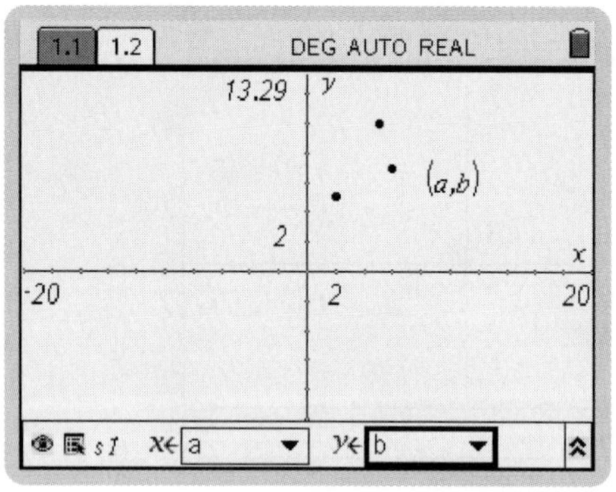

6. Choose **Function** from the **Graph Type** menu.

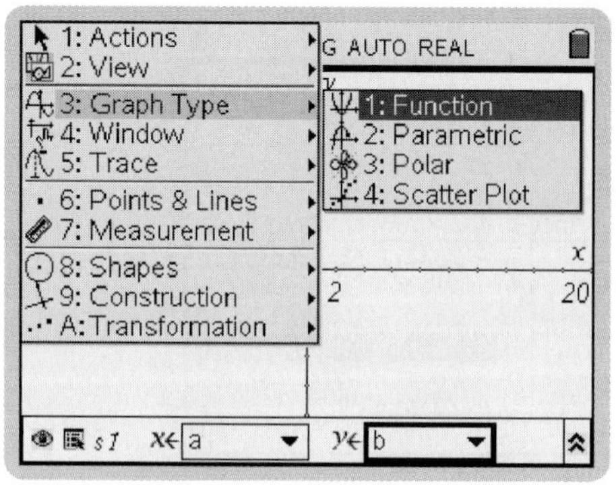

Finding the Line of Best Fit I, (continued)

7. Graph any linear function. Here the function is $f(x) = 2$.

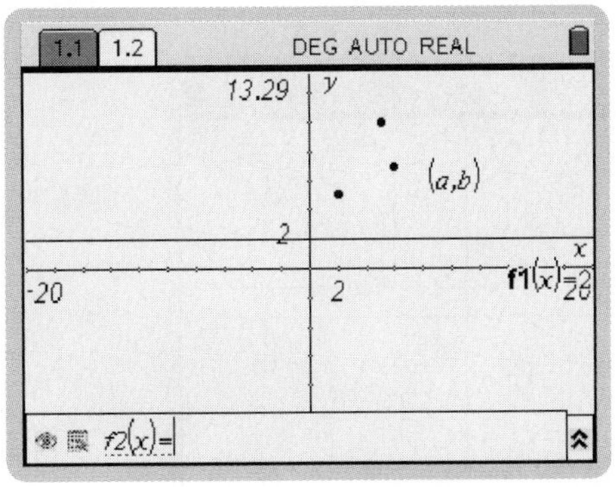

8. Choose **Parallel** from the **Constructions** menu.

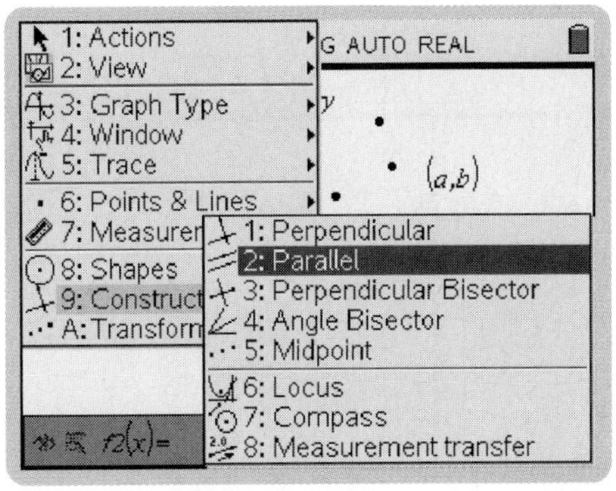

9. Select a scatter-plot point with the cursor. Press **enter**. Select the *y*-axis. Press **enter** to construct a vertical line that passes through the point.

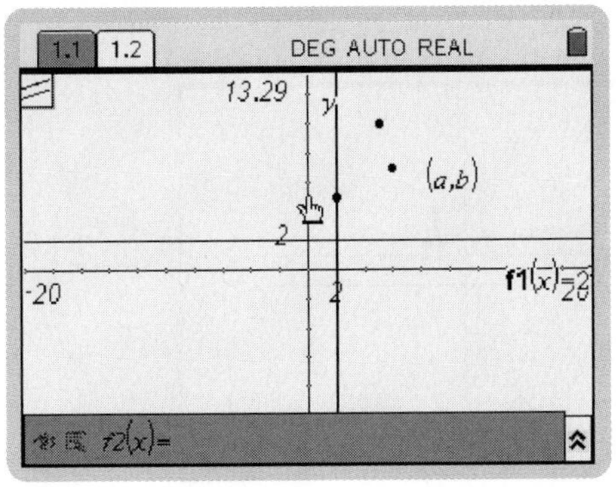

10. Choose **Segment** from the **Points & Lines** menu.

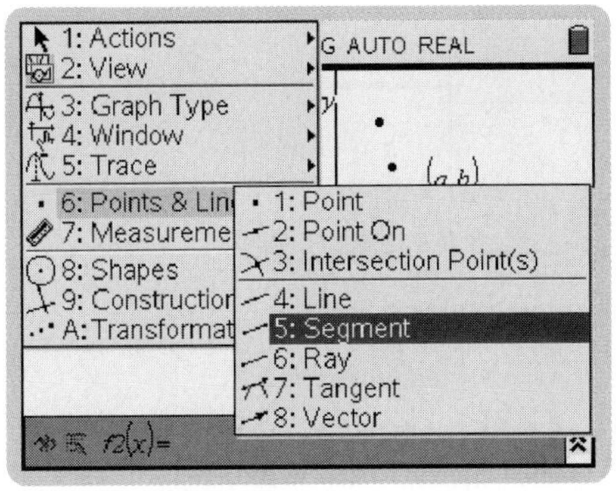

11. Select the point (Step 9) again. Press **enter**. Select the intersection point of its vertical line and the graph of the linear function. Press **enter** to construct a segment between the two points.

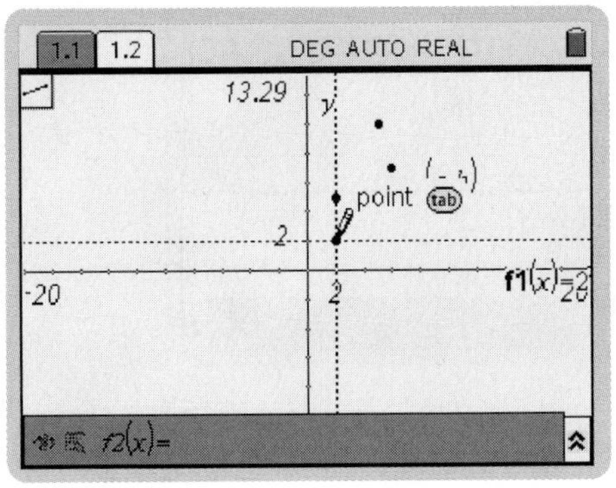

12. Choose **Hide/Show** from the **Actions** menu.

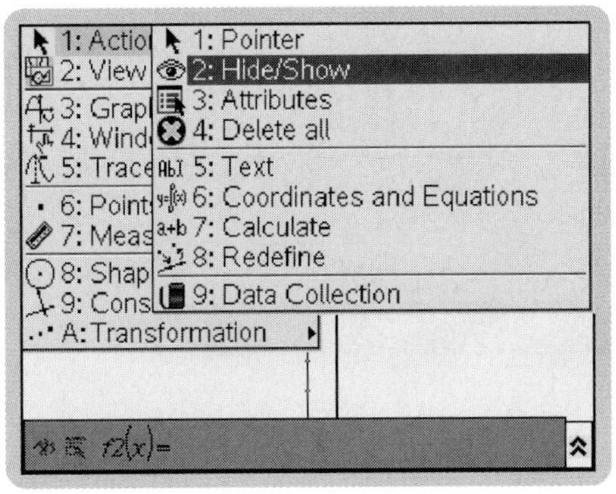

Finding the Line of Best Fit I, (continued)

13. Select the vertical line (not the segment). Press **enter** to hide it. Press **esc** to exit the Hide/Show tool.

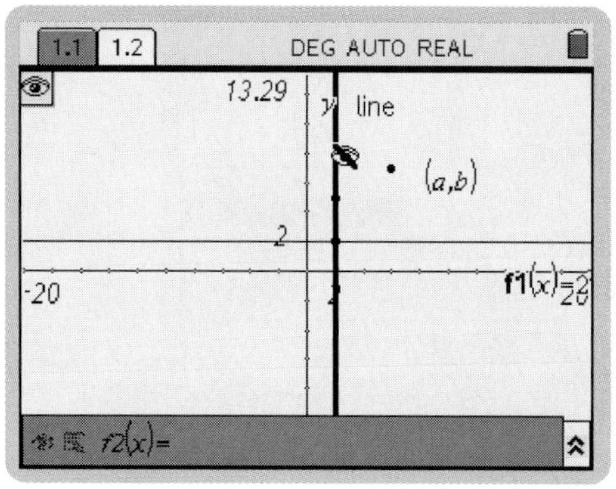

14. Repeat Steps 8–13 for the other points.

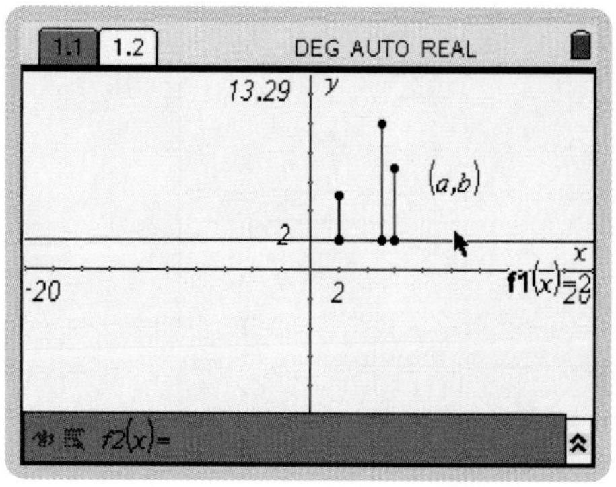

15. Choose **Length** from the **Measurement** menu.

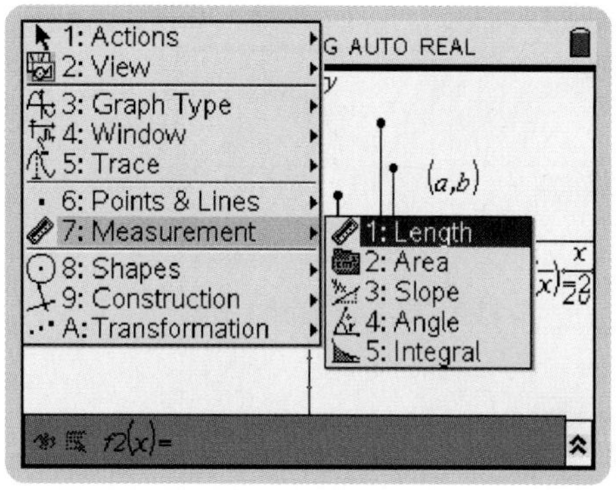

16. Select a segment. Press **enter**. Drag the measurement to the desired location on the screen. Press **enter** to anchor it.

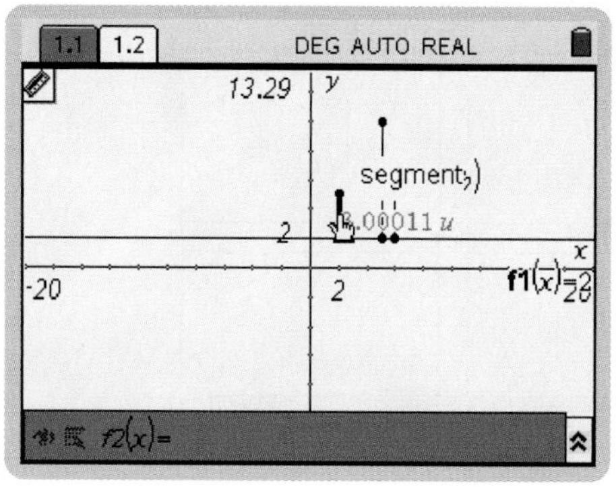

17. Repeat Step 16 for the other segments.

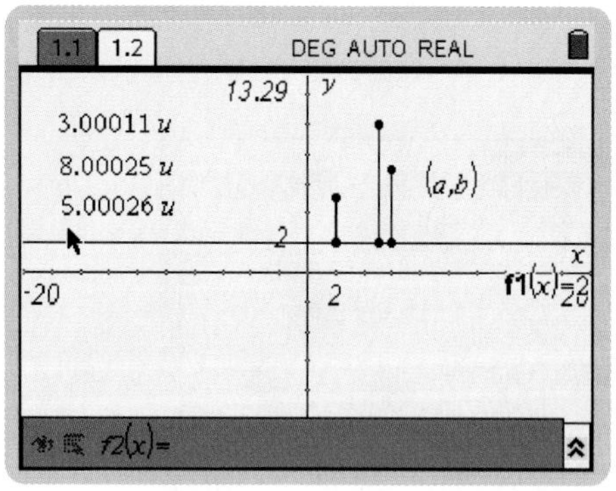

18. Choose **Text** from the **Actions** menu. Write $i^2 + k^2 + l^2$ on the screen.

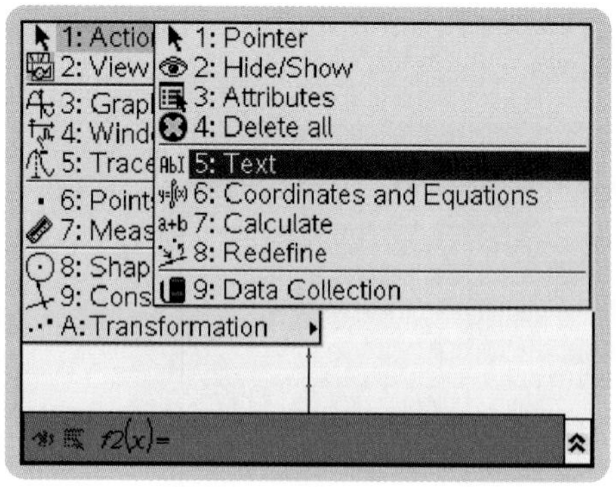

Finding the Line of Best Fit I, (continued)

19. Choose **Calculate** from the **Actions** menu.

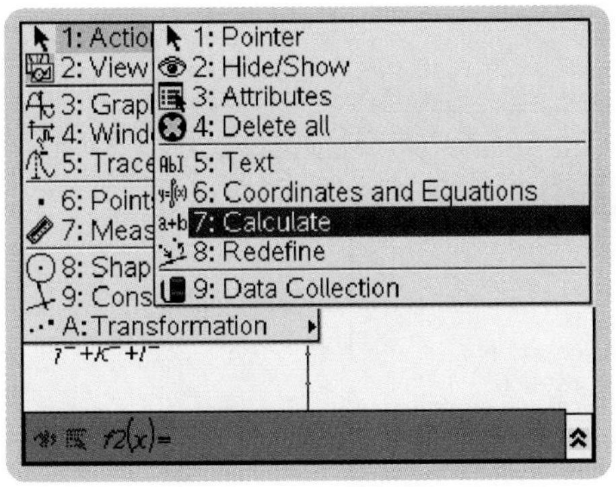

20. Position the cursor on $i^2 + k^2 + l^2$. Press **enter**.

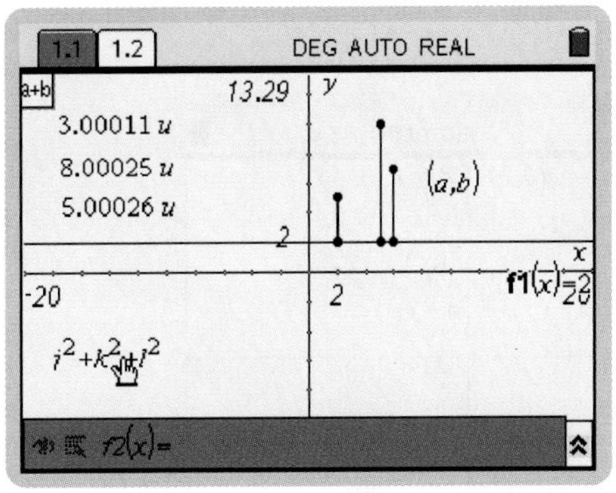

21. Select a value for each variable. Position the cursor over the respective length measurements and press **enter**.

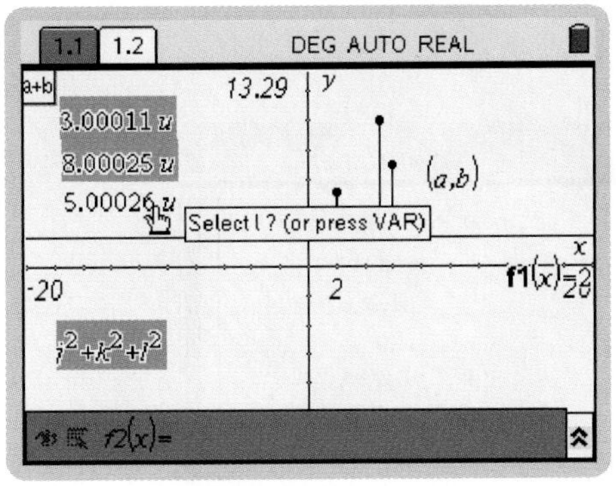

22. Drag the result of the calculation to the desired location. Press **enter** to anchor it. Press **esc** to exit the Text tool.

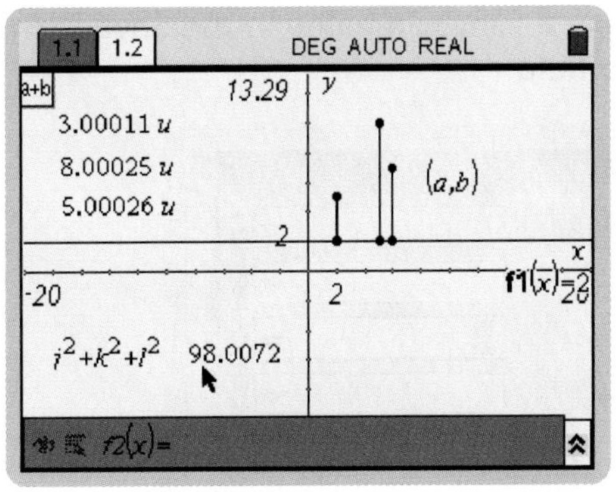

23. Use arrow keys to navigate to the horizontal line. Press **ctrl** to grab it. Drag the line to rotate and translate the line.

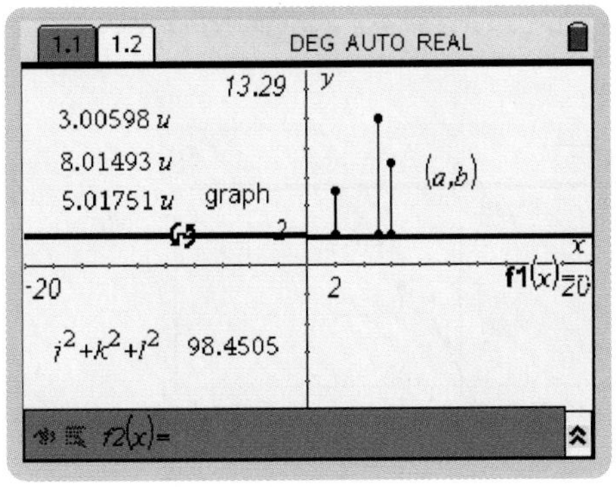

24. Move the line to make the sum of the squares of the segment lengths as small as possible. The line with the least value of $i^2 + k^2 + l^2$ is the line of best fit.

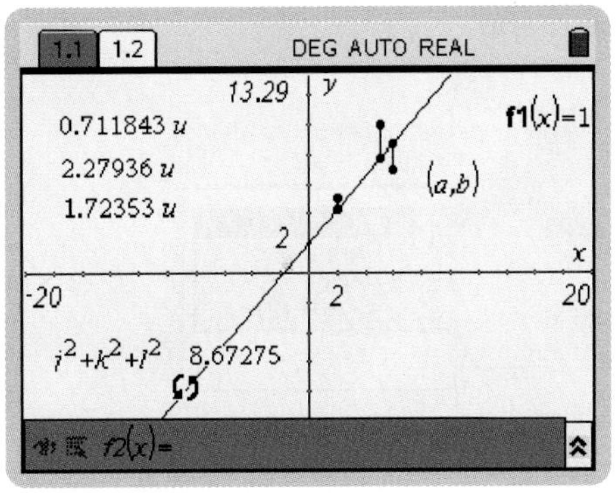

Finding the Line of Best Fit II, Lesson 1.8

1. Make a scatter plot of the data you wish to use.

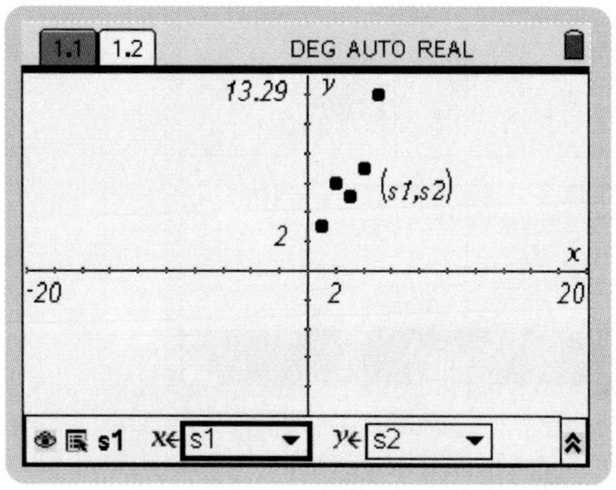

2. Navigate to the calculator application. Choose **Stat Calculations** from the **Statistics** menu. Choose **Linear Regression (mx + b)**. Press **enter**.

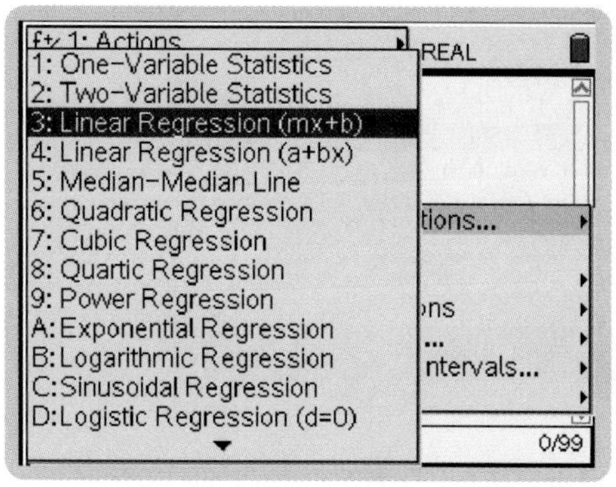

3. Select the data to use in the **X List** and **Y List** fields. Press **tab** to navigate between fields. Select a function name in the **Save RegEqn to** field.

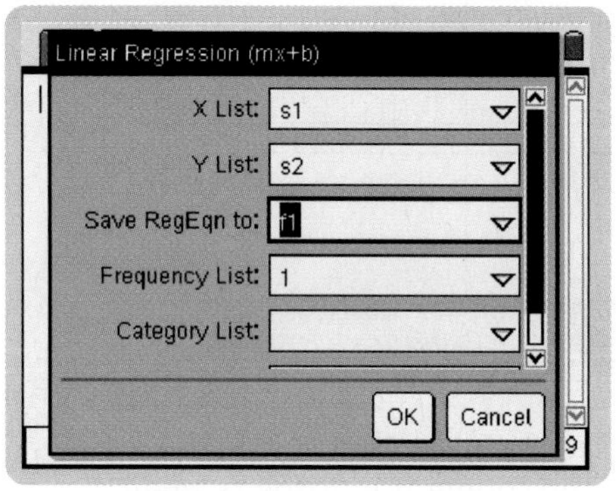

4. Press **enter** to show a summary of the linear regression.

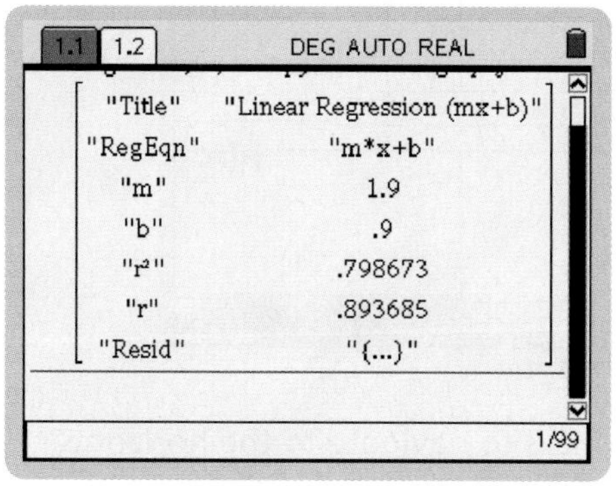

5. Navigate to the Graphs & Geometry application. Choose **Function** from the **Graph Type** menu.

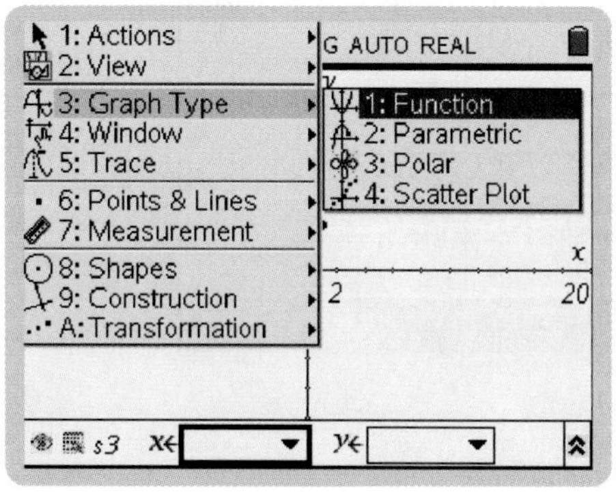

6. Press **tab** to navigate to the function entry line. Press ▲ to navigate to the linear regression function. Press **enter** to draw its graph.

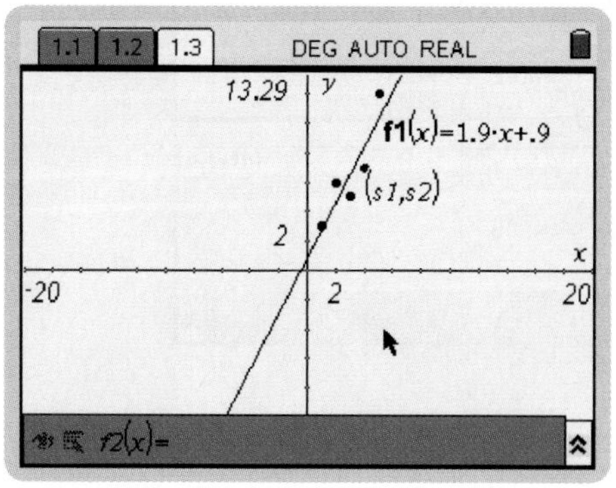

Finding the Quadratic Curve of Best Fit, Lesson 1.8

1. Navigate to the Calculator application. Choose **Stat Calculations** from the **Statistics** menu. Choose **Quadratic Regression**. Press enter.

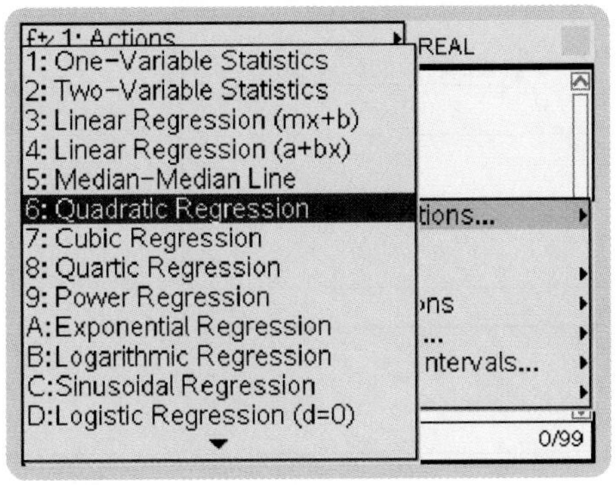

2. Select the data to use in the **X List** and **Y List** fields. Press tab to navigate between fields. Select a function name in the **Save RegEqn to** field.

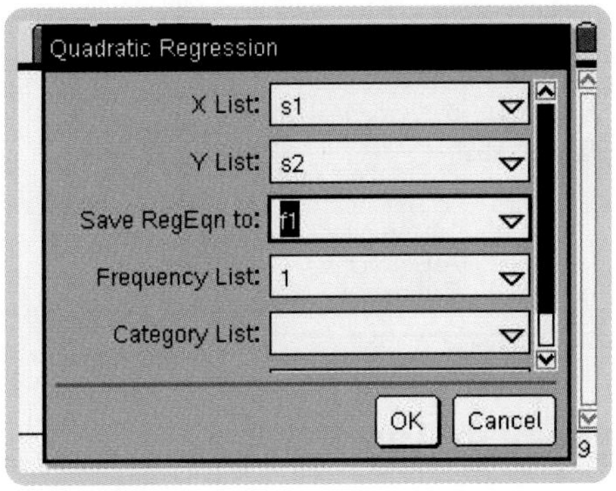

3. Press enter to show a summary of the quadratic regression. Navigate to the Graphs & Geometry application. Choose **Function** from the **Graph Type** menu.

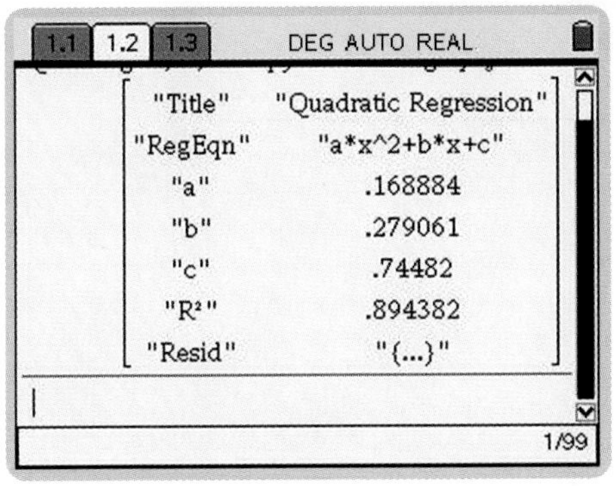

4. Press tab to navigate to the function entry line. Press △ to navigate to the quadratic regression function. Press enter to draw its graph.

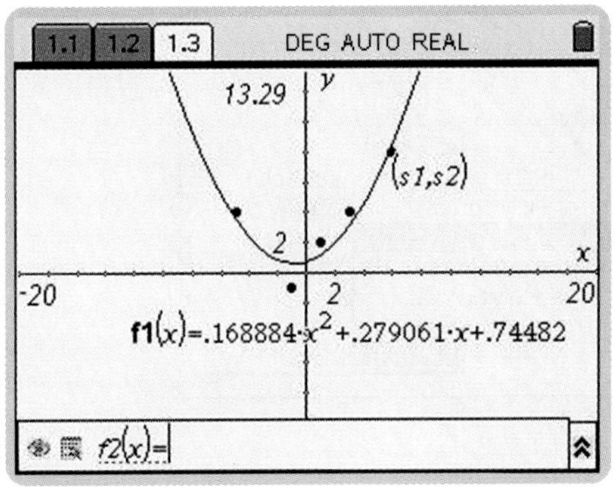

Making a Function Table, Lesson 2.2

1. Choose **Add Function Table** from the **View** menu . . .

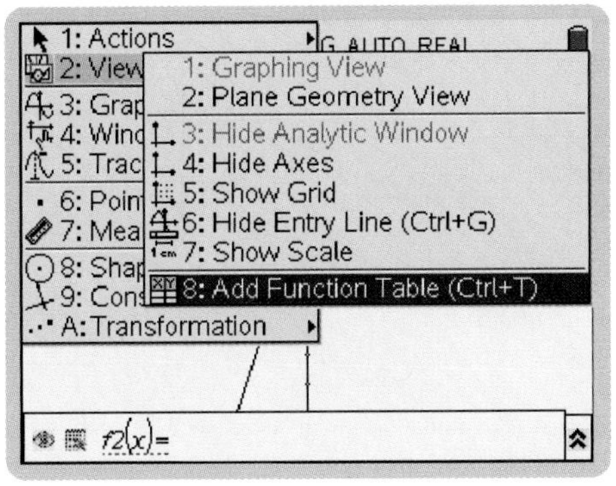

2. . . . to show a function table on the right side of the screen.

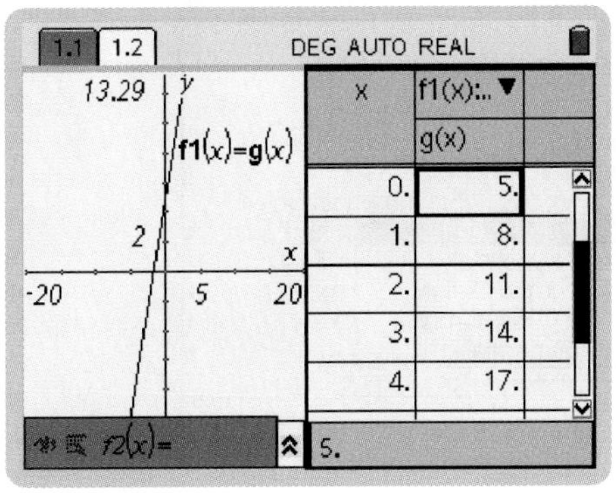

Expanding a Product of Polynomials, Lesson 3.10

1. Choose **Expand** from the **Algebra** menu.

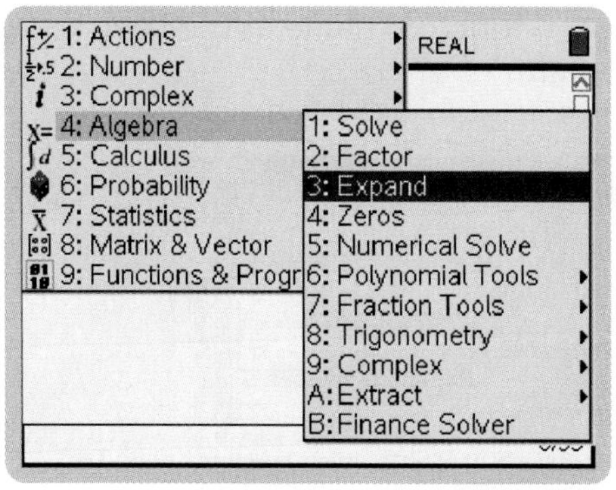

2. Type a product of polynomials. Press **enter**.

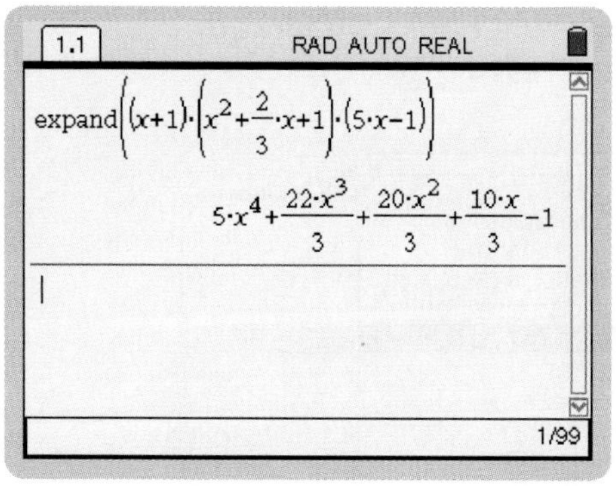

Dividing Polynomials, Lesson 2.9

1. Choose **Polynomial Tools** from the **Algebra** menu. Choose **Quotient of Polynomial**.

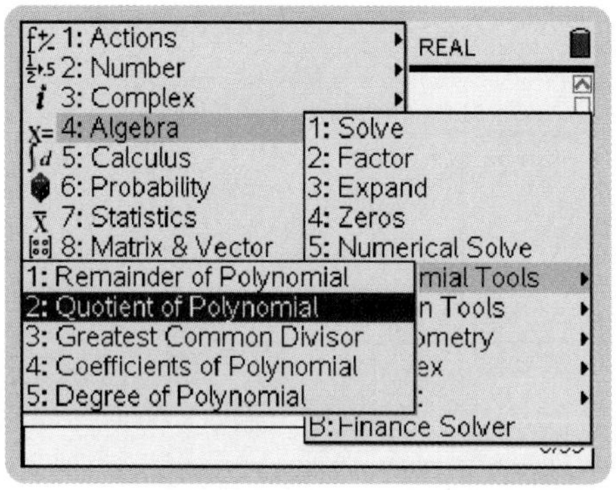

2. Type the polynomial to divide and then ⁄. Type the polynomial you are dividing by. Press **enter** to show the quotient without remainder.

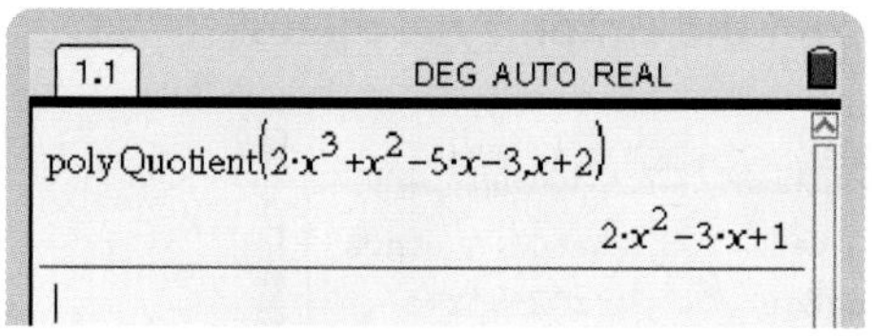

3. Choose **Polynomial Tools** from the **Algebra** menu. Choose **Remainder of Polynomial**.

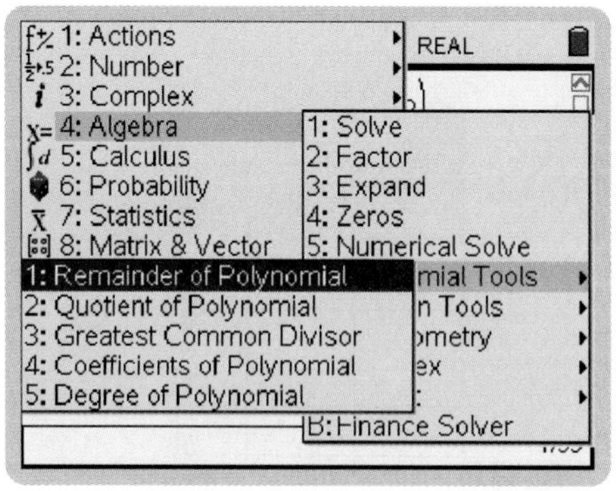

4. Type the polynomial to divide and then ⁄. Type the polynomial you are dividing by. Press **enter** to find the remainder after dividing the polynomials.

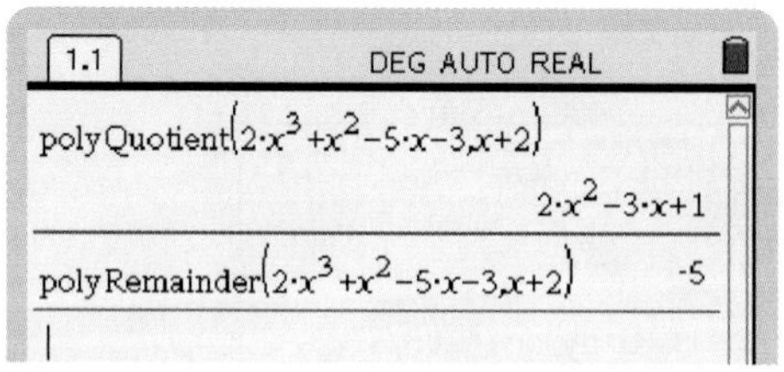

Factoring a Polynomial, Lesson 2.12

1. Choose **Factor** from the **Algebra** menu.

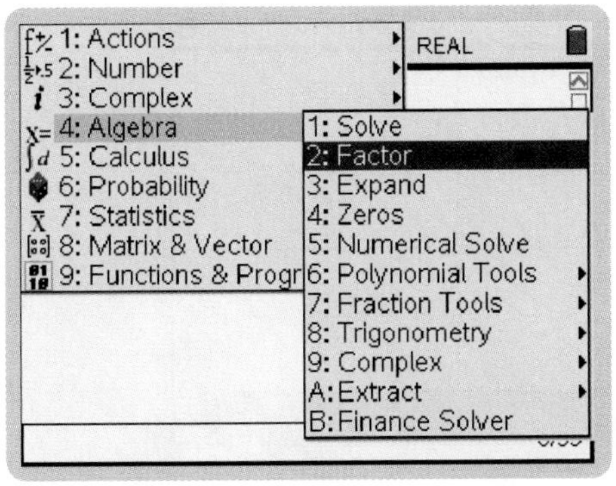

2. Type the polynomial to be factored. Press **enter**.

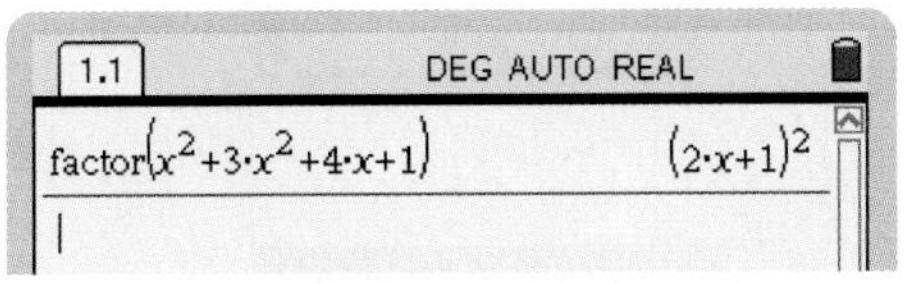

Calculating the Argument of a Complex Number, Lesson 3.9

1. Choose **Polar Angle** from the **Complex** menu.

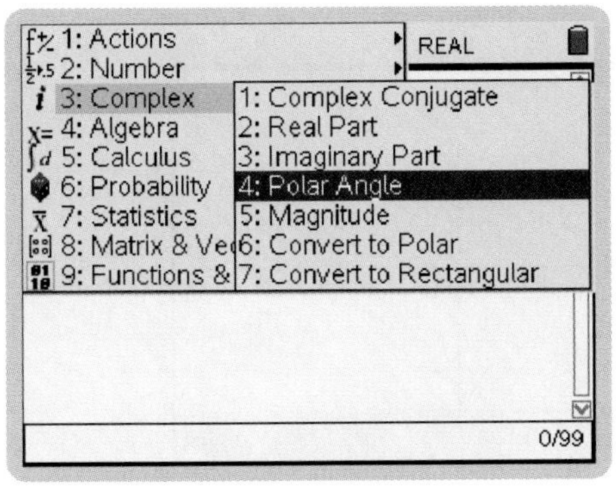

2. Type the complex number. Press **enter**.

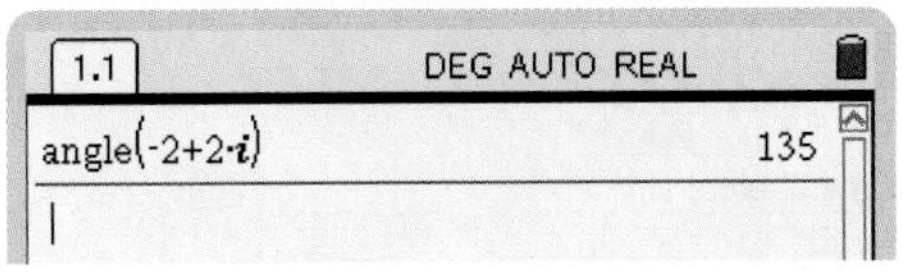

Calculating the Magnitude of a Complex Number, Lesson 3.9

1. Choose **Magnitude** from the **Complex** menu.

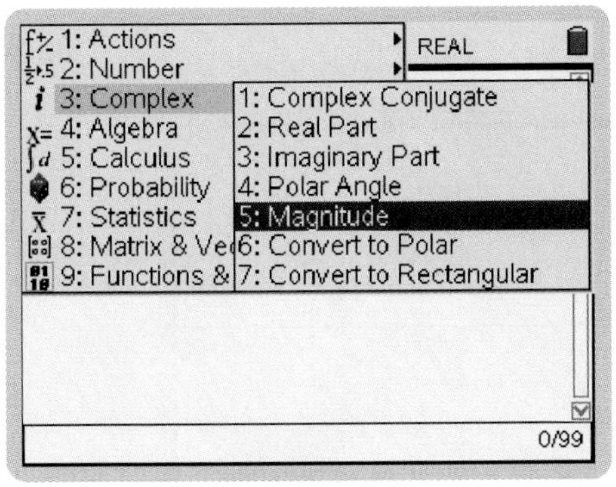

2. Type the complex number. Press **enter**.

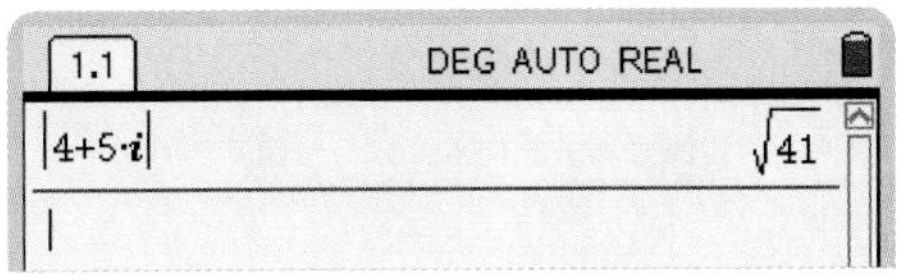

Calculating the Magnitude of a Complex Number Graphically, Lesson 3.9

1. Choose **Point** from the **Points & Lines** menu.

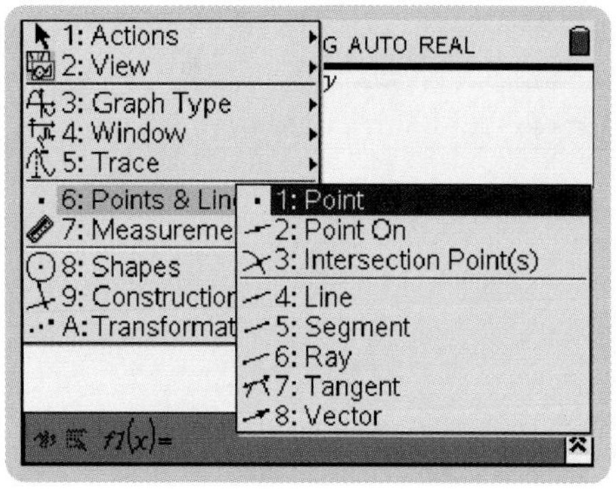

2. Press **enter** to place a point on the graphing screen.

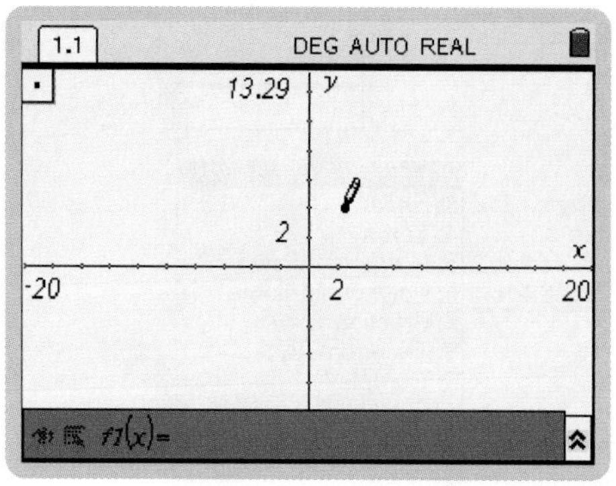

3. Choose **Coordinates and Equations** from the **Actions** menu.

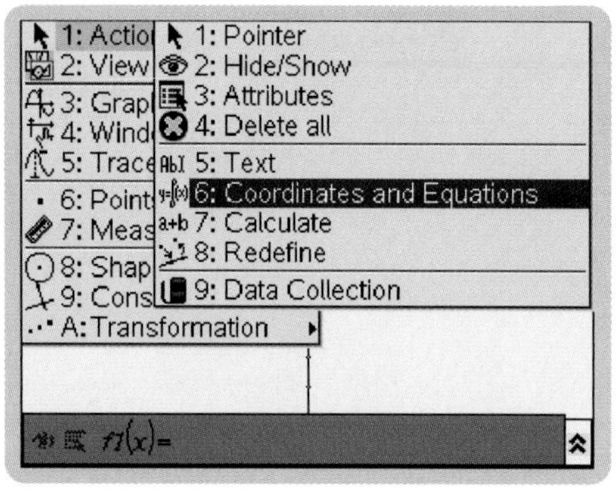

4. Select the point. Press **enter**. Drag the coordinates to the desired location. Press **enter**. Press **esc** to exit the Coordinates and Equations tool.

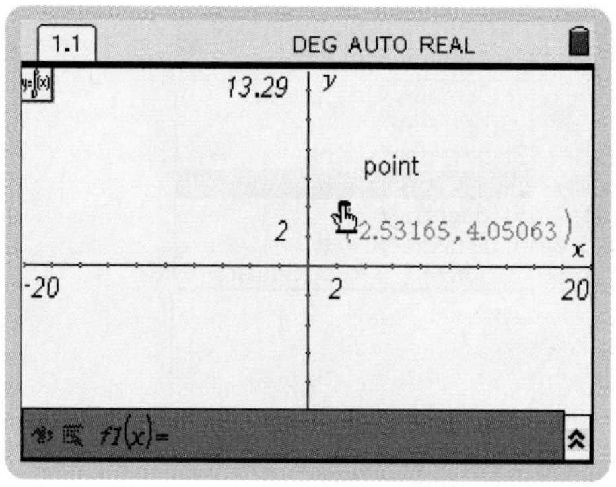

5. Double click on the first coordinate. Replace the existing number with the real part of the complex number. The point moves to reflect the new coordinates.

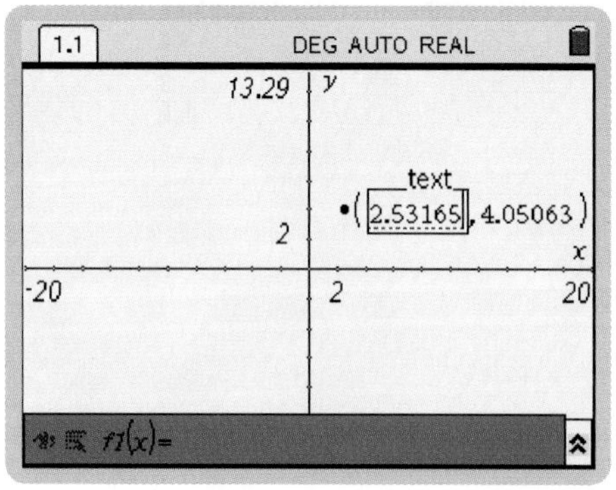

6. Replace the second coordinate with the imaginary part.

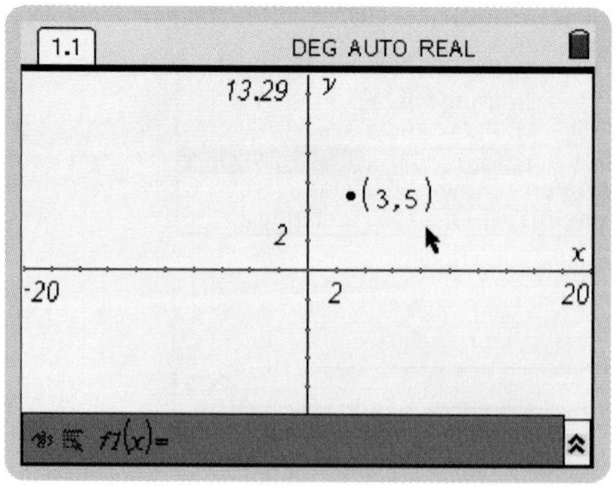

Calculating the Magnitude of a Complex Number Graphically (continued)

7. Choose **Vector** from the **Points & Lines** menu.

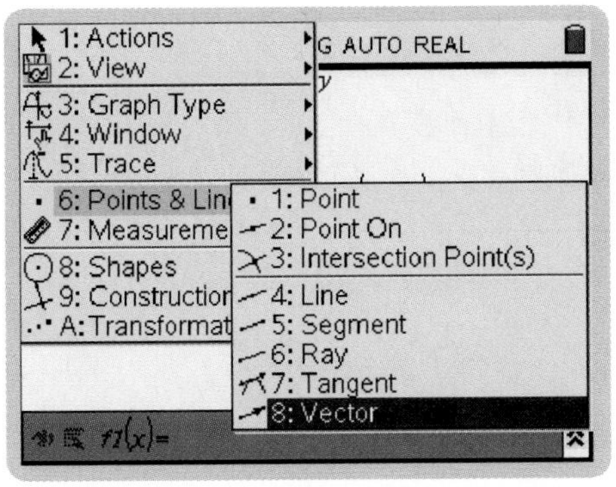

8. Select the origin. Press enter to set the tail of the vector.

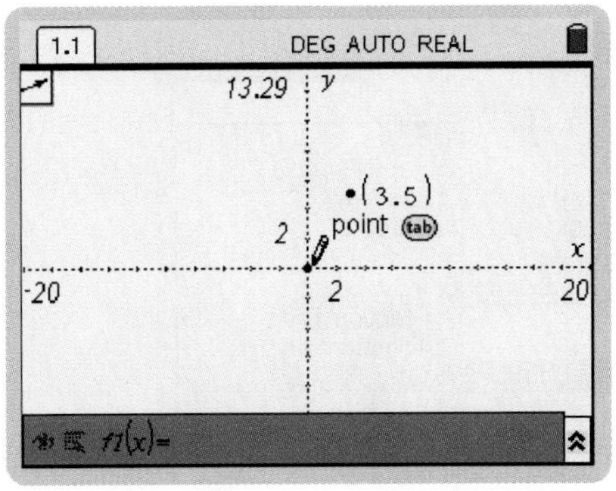

9. Select the point. Press enter to set the head of the vector.

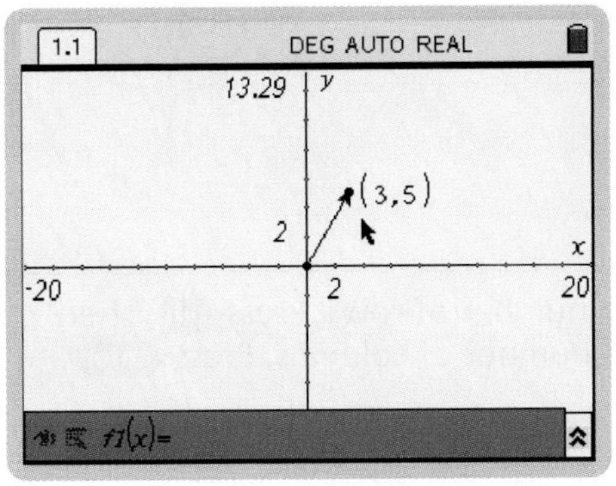

10. Choose **Length** from the **Measurement** menu.

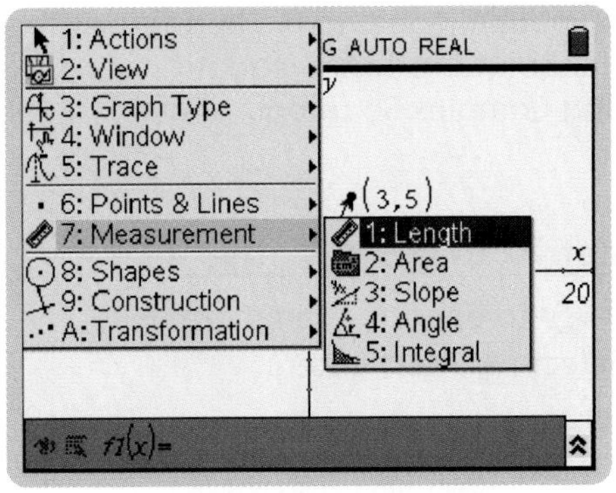

11. Select the vector. Press enter.

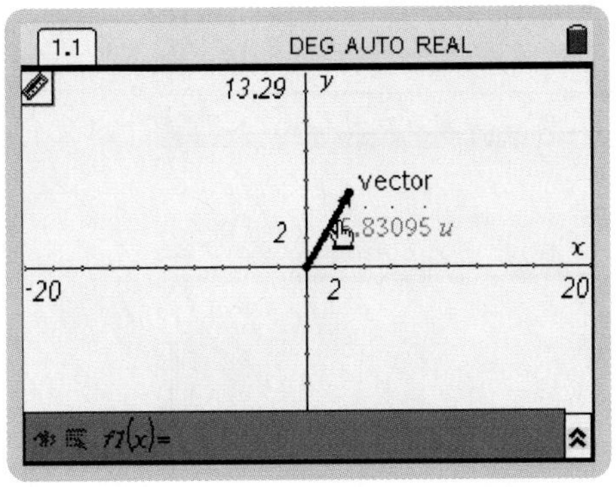

12. Drag the length measurement to the desired location. Press enter to anchor it. This is the magnitude of the complex number.

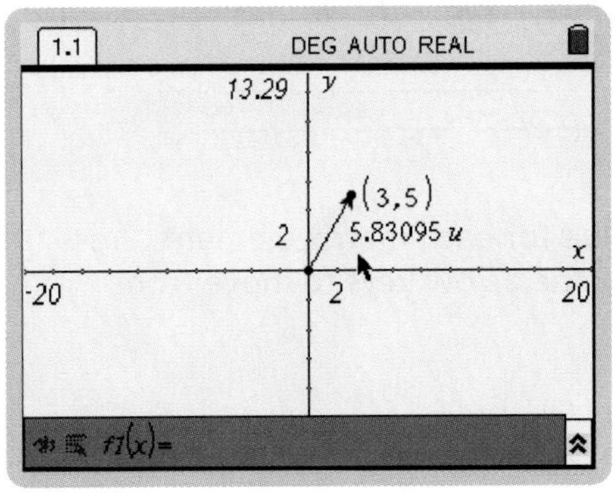

Finding Complex Solutions, Lesson 3.8

1. Choose **Complex** from the **Algebra** menu. Choose **Solve**.

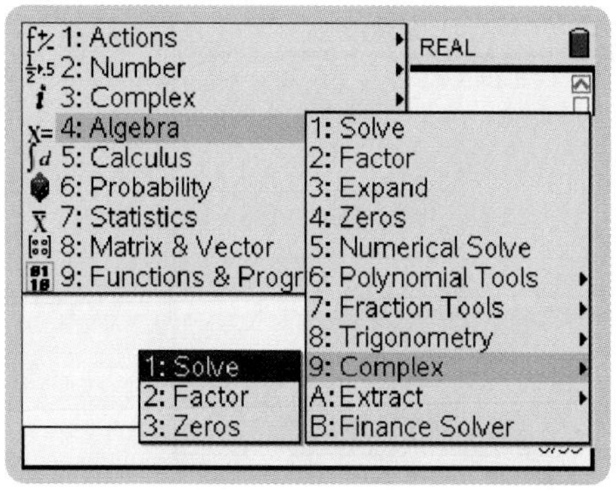

2. Type the equation and then ,. Type the variable to solve for. Press enter.

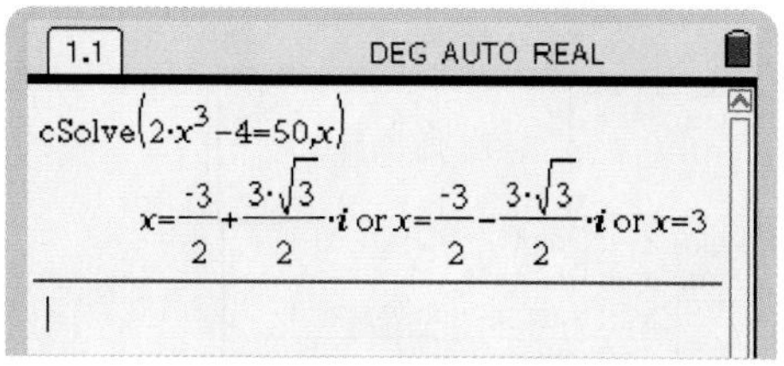

Finding Complex Zeros, Lesson 3.12

1. To find the complex roots of a polynomial, set the polynomial equal to 0. Then find the complex solutions to the equation. (See Finding Complex Solutions, above.)

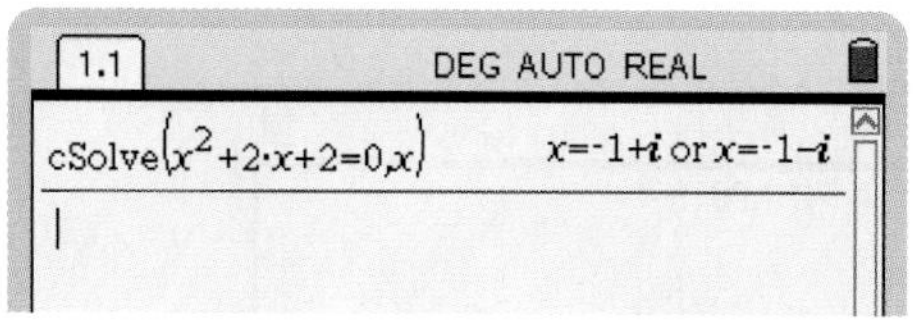

Entering a Matrix, Lesson 4.7

1. Press ctrl ✕ to open the template palette. Select ▦. Press enter.

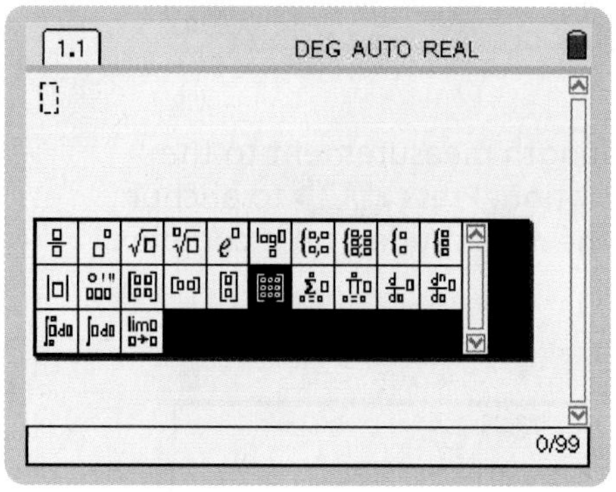

2. Select the number of rows. Press tab. Then select the number of columns. Press enter.

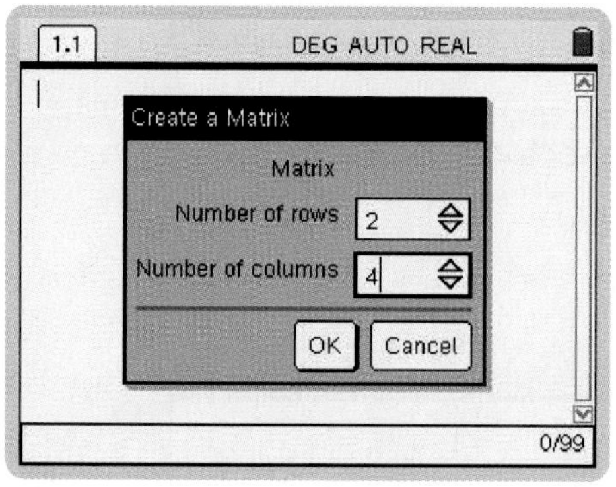

3. Type a value for each matrix element. Press tab or use the arrow keys to move from box to box.

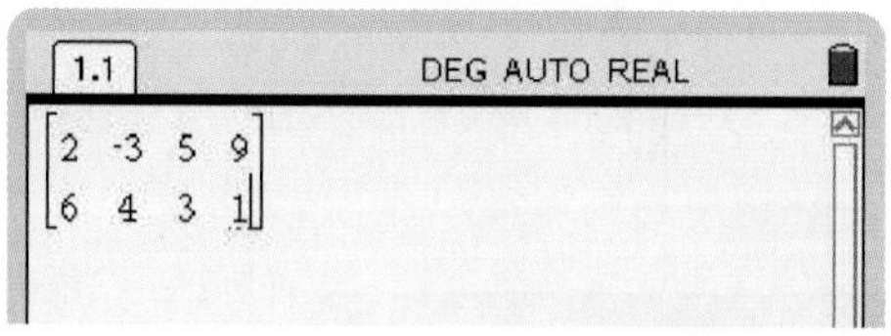

Adding or Subtracting Matrices, Lesson 4.7

1. Enter a matrix. Press + or −. Enter a second matrix. Press enter.

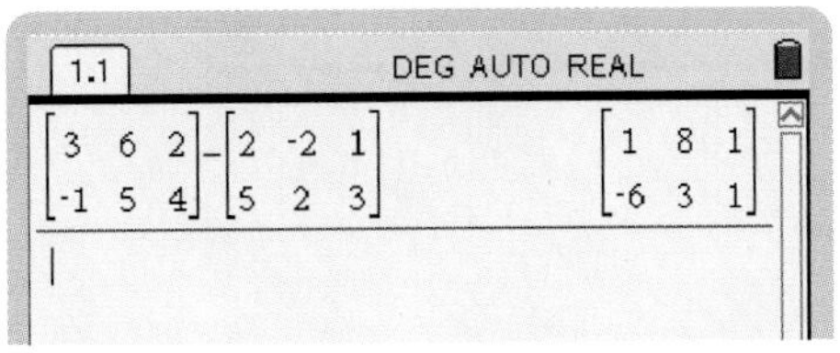

2. If the matrices do not have the same dimensions, you see this image.

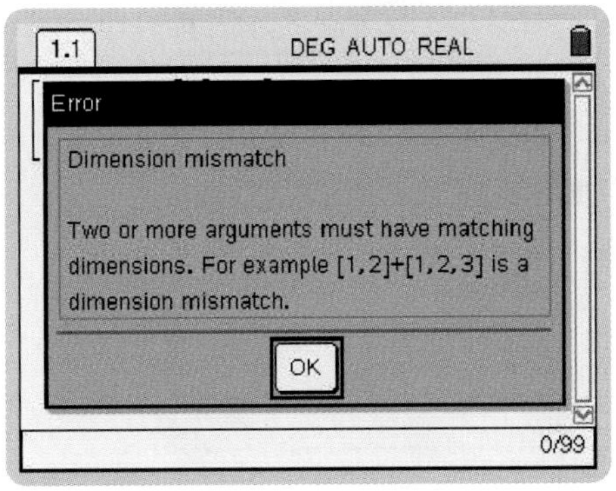

Multiplying Matrices, Lesson 4.7

1. Enter a matrix. Press ×. Enter a second matrix. Press enter.

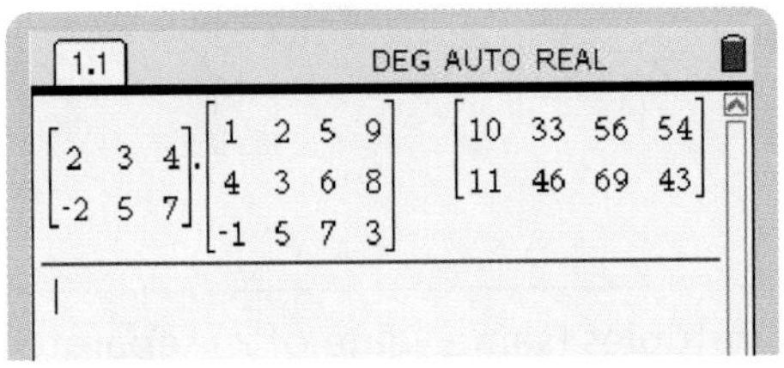

2. If the number of columns of the first matrix does not equal the number of rows of the second matrix, you see this image.

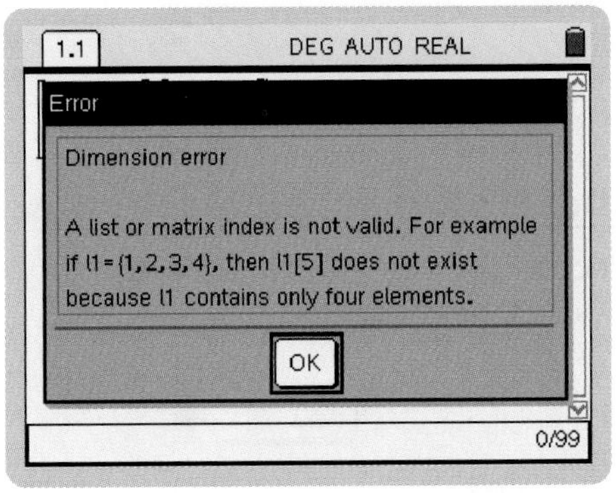

Finding the Inverse of a Matrix, Lesson 4.8

1. Enter a square matrix. Press ^ (−) 1 enter.

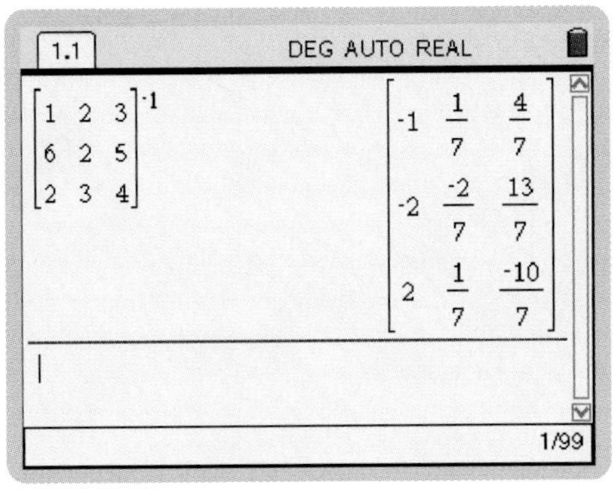

2. If the matrix has no inverse, you see this image.

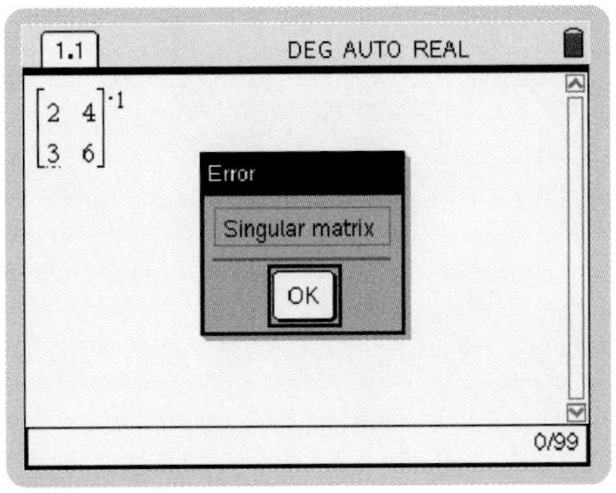

Using the rref Command, Lesson 4.3

1. Choose **Reduced Row-Echelon** Form from the **Matrix & Vector** menu.

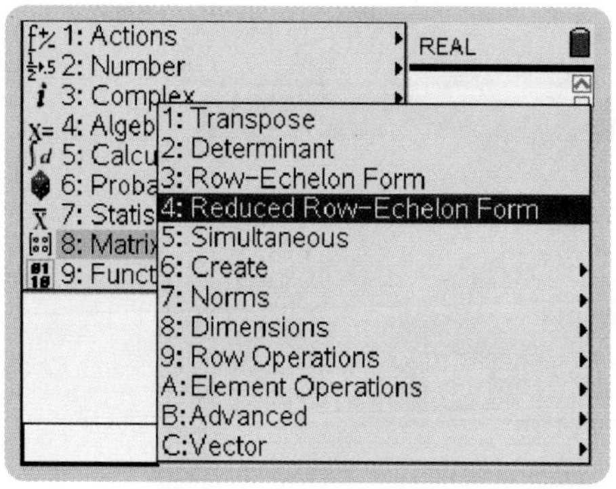

2. Enter a matrix. Press enter.

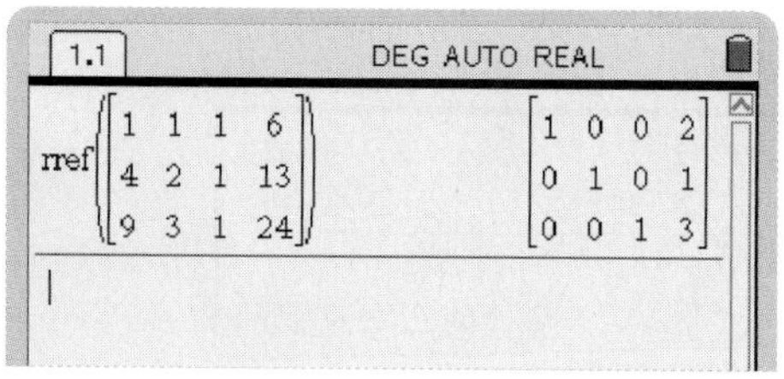

Adding or Subtracting *n*-tuples, Lesson 4.7

1. Press ctrl (. Enter *n*-tuple elements separated by commas.

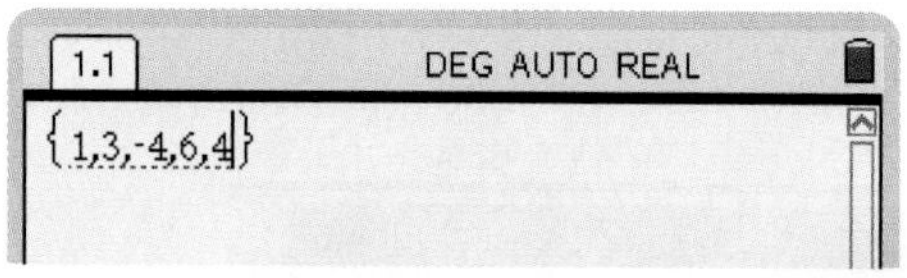

2. Press + or −. Then enter a second *n*-tuple (same *n* value as the first). Press enter.

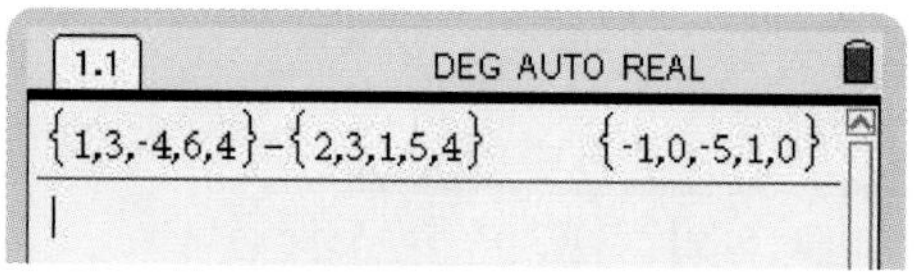

Finding the Dot Product of Two *n*-tuples, Lesson 4.7

1. Choose **Vector** from the **Matrix & Vector** menu. Choose **Dot Product**.

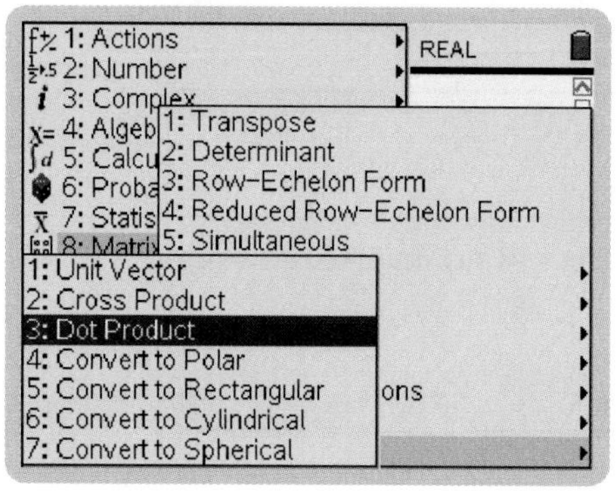

2. Enter two *n*-tuples (same value of *n*) separated by a comma. Press enter.

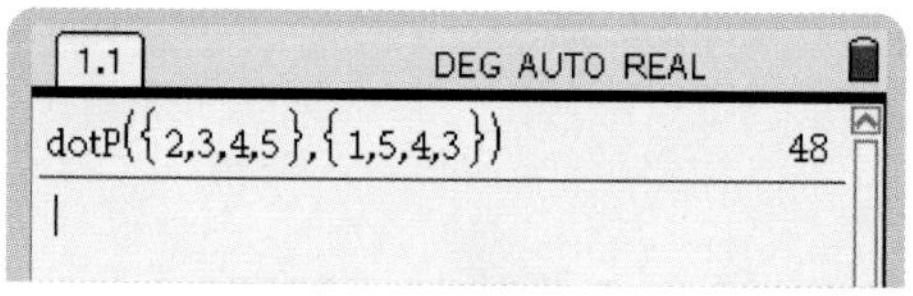

Using a Spreadsheet to Make a Summation Column, Lesson 7.1, 7.6

1. In column A, make an index column with 1 in the first row, 2 in the second row, and so on. In column B, enter the data to be summed. In cell C1, type = S U M (B ctrl (, ctrl " A ctrl " 1 , A 1. Press enter.

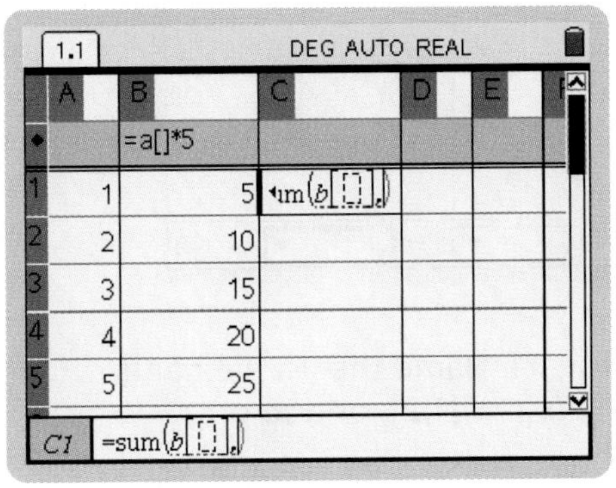

2. Move the cursor back to cell C1. Choose **Fill Down** from the **Data** menu.

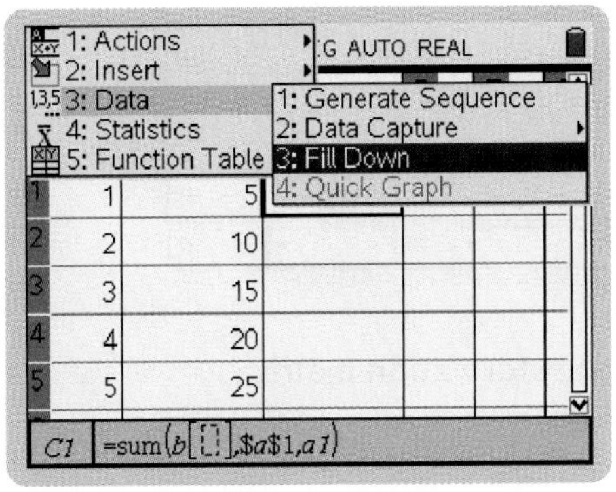

3. Press ▽ to extend highlighted cells to match the last data cell in column B. Press enter.

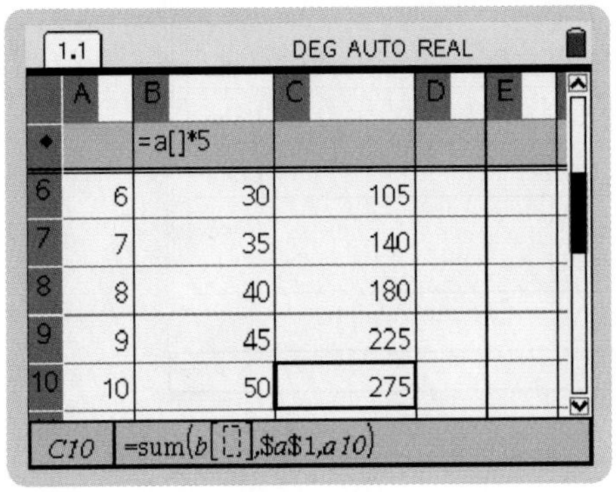

Using a Matrix to Transform Points, Lesson 4.11

1. Define a 2-by-*n* matrix to model a set of *n* points. The first row consists of the *x*-coordinates, and the second row consists of the corresponding *y*-coordinates. Define lists of the *x*-coordinates and *y*-coordinates, in order.

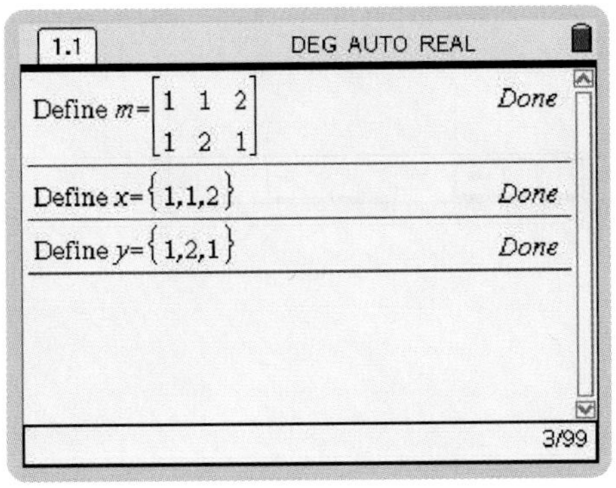

2. Navigate to the Graphs & Geometry application. Choose **Scatter Plot** from the **Graph Type** menu.

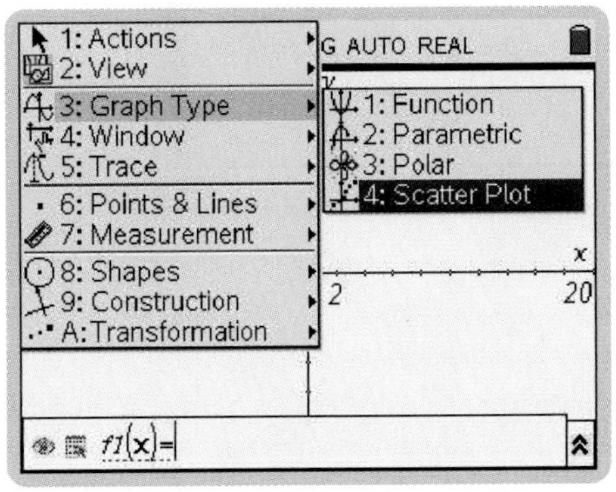

Using a Matrix to Transform Points (continued)

3. Select the data lists from Step 1 as the *x*- and *y*-values.

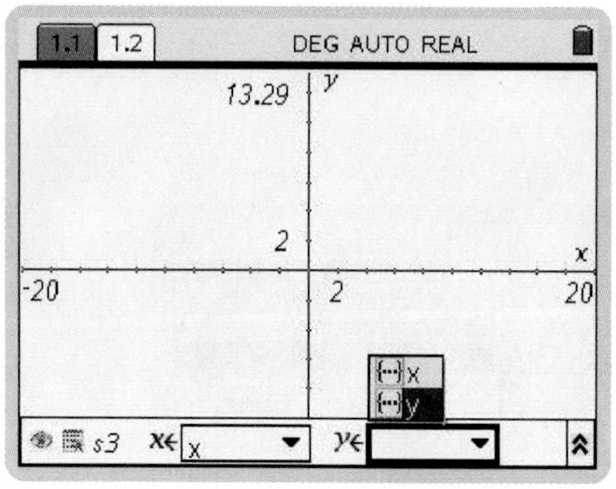

4. Press **enter** to see the points you will transform using a 2-by-2 matrix.

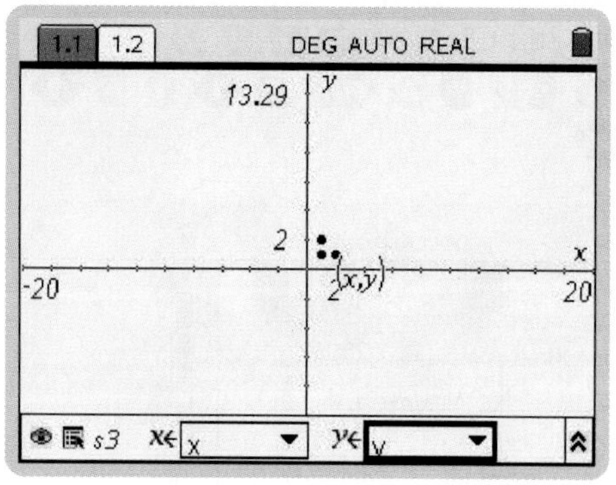

5. Define a transformation matrix *s*.

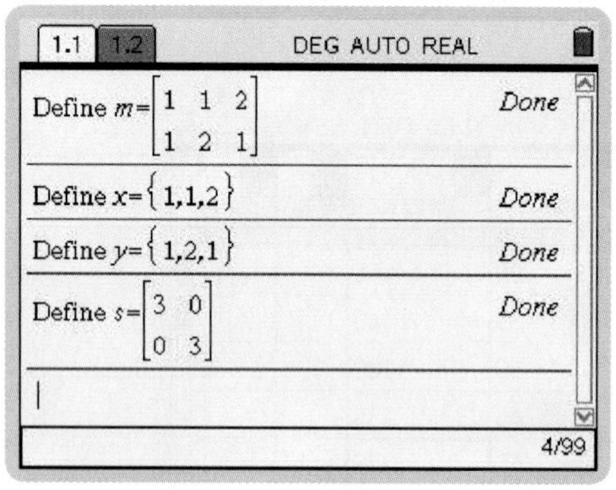

6. Define a list, *x*1. Name the list elements $(s \cdot m)[1,1]$, $(s \cdot m)[1,2]$, and so on.

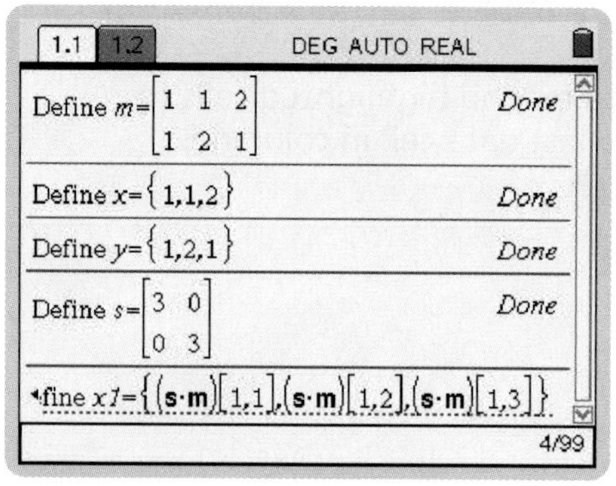

7. Define a list, *y*1. Name the list elements $(s \cdot m)[2,1]$, $(s \cdot m)[2,2]$, and so on.

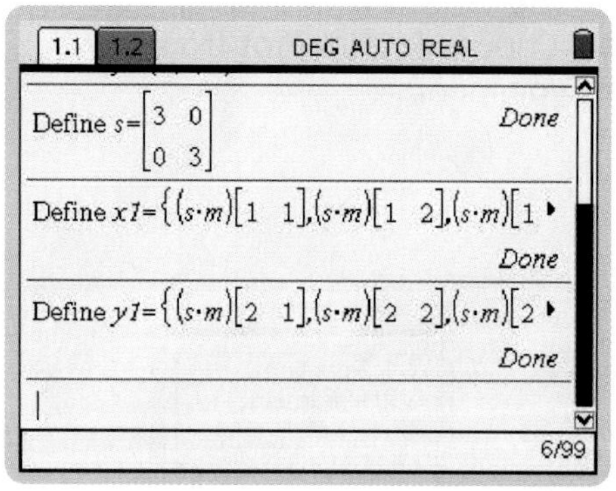

8. Make a scatter plot using *x*1 for the *x*-values and *y*1 for the *y*-values. The result is the original points transformed by the matrix *s*.

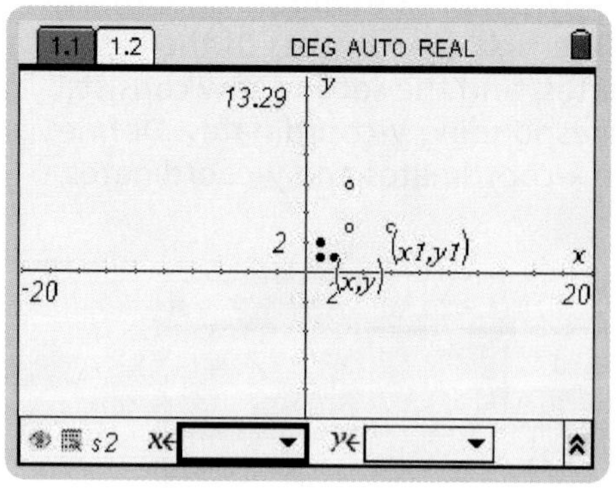

Using a Matrix to Transform Points (continued)

9. For a second transformation, press ▲ in the calculator screen until you highlight the definition of *s*. Press **enter** to copy it to the entry line.

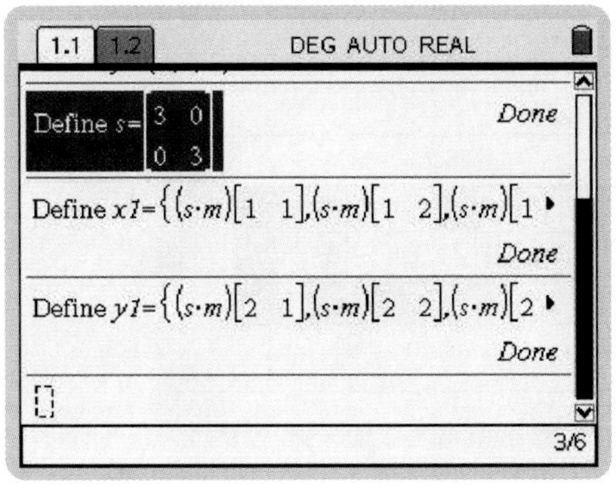

10. Use the arrow keys to change the values in *s*. Press **enter**.

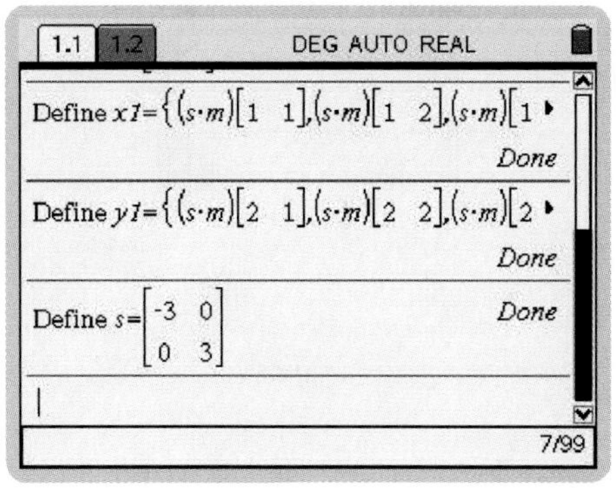

11. Press ▲ in the calculator screen until you highlight the definition of *x*1. Press **enter** to copy it to the entry line. Press **enter**.

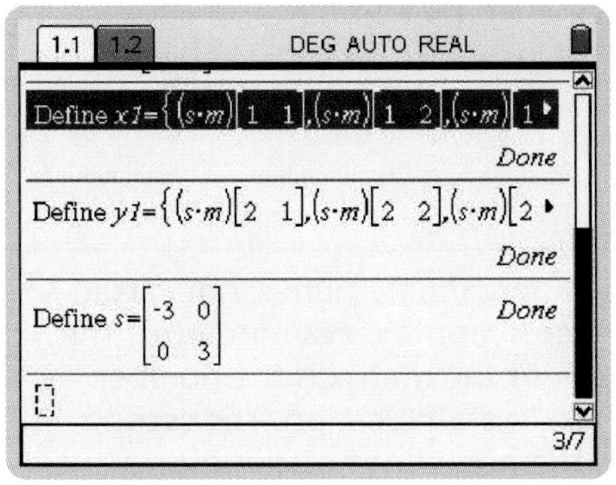

12. Repeat Step 11 with the definition of *y*1.

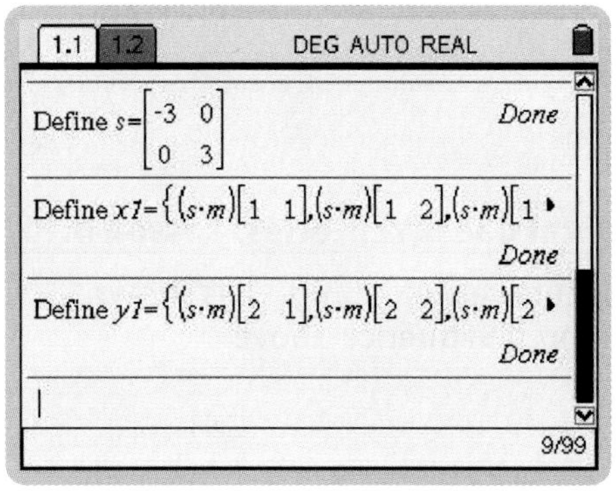

13. Navigate to the scatter plot from Step 8 to view the new transformation.

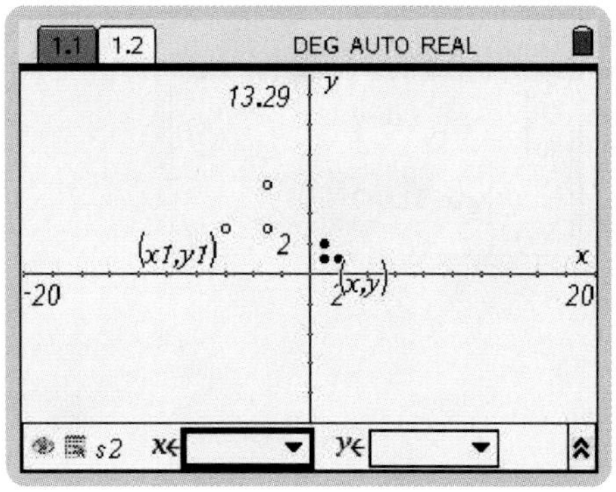

Modeling a Sequence, Lesson 4.10

1. Choose **Define** from the **Actions** menu. Press M =. Enter the matrix shown. Press enter.

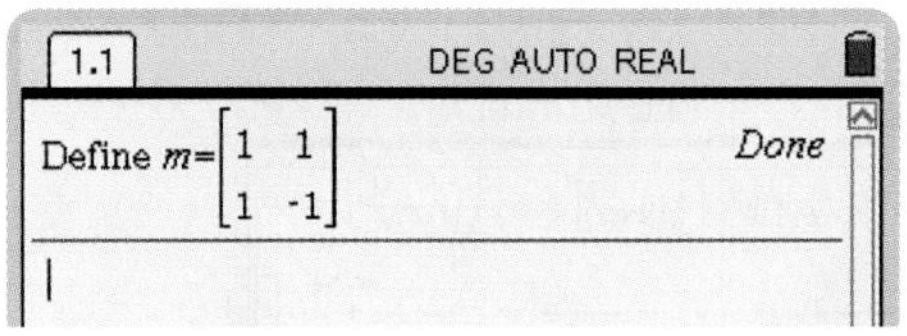

2. Choose **Define** from the **Actions** menu. Press S =. Press ctrl × to open the template palette. Select the piecewise template. Press enter.

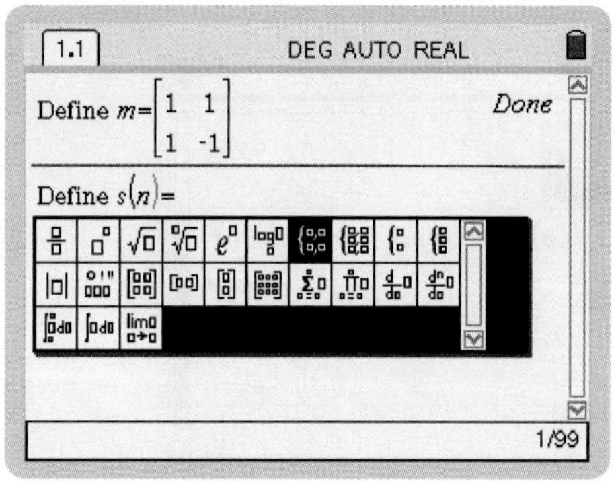

3. Enter the 2-by-1 matrix in the first box as shown. Complete the rest of the function. Press enter.

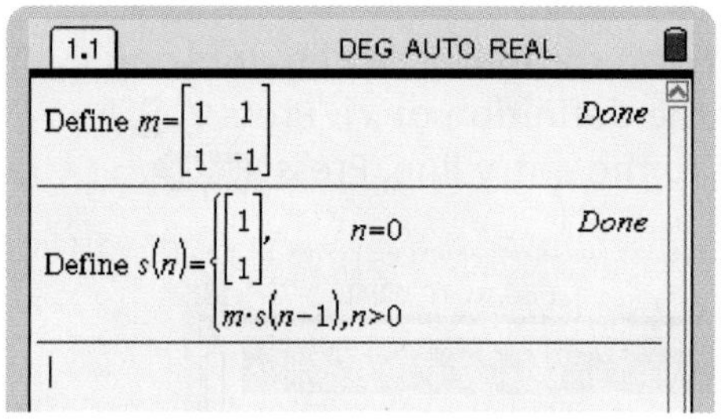

Modeling Rental Car Inventories, Lesson 4.10

1. Define a recursive function $g(x)$ as shown. See **Modeling a Sequence** above.

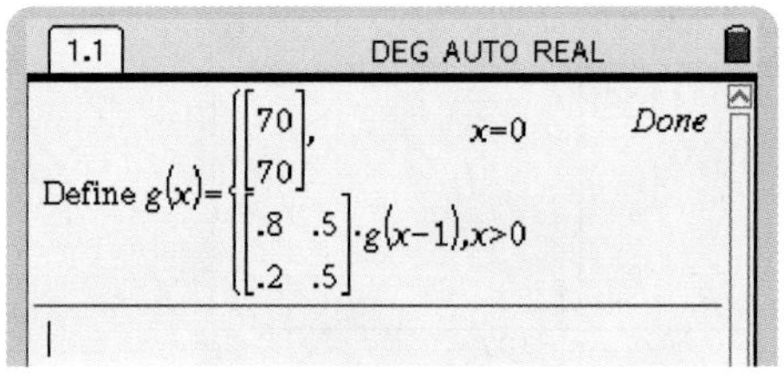

3. To find the approximate number of cars in each lot after n months, evaluate $g(n)$. The first element of the matrix is the number of cars in the Boston location. The second element is the number of cars in the Cambridge location.

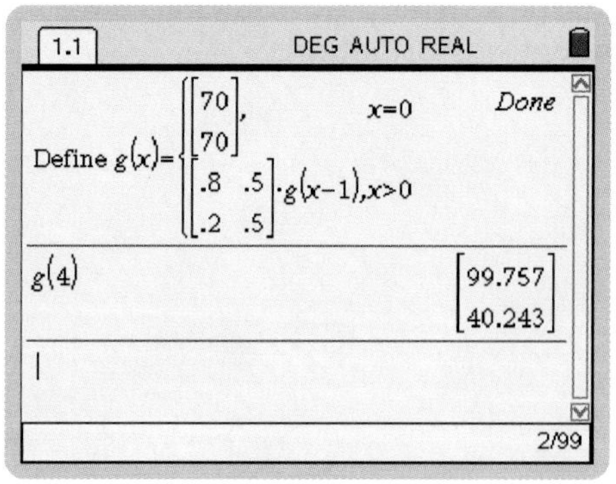

Tables

Table 1 Math Symbols

Symbol	Meaning
...	and so on
$=$	is equal to
$\approx$	is approximately equal to
$\neq$	is not equal to
$>$	is greater than
$\geq$	is greater than or equal to
$<$	is less than
$\leq$	is less than or equal to
$\pm$	plus or minus
$\mapsto$	which gives, leads to, maps to
n^2	n squared
a^{-m}	$\frac{1}{a^m}, a \neq 0$
a^0	1
$a^{\frac{1}{n}}$	$\sqrt[n]{a}$
$a^{\frac{p}{q}}$	$(\sqrt[q]{a})^p$
$\sqrt{x}$	nonnegative square root of x
$\sqrt[n]{r}$	nth root of r
Δ	difference (delta)
$\Leftrightarrow$	if and only if
A	point A
A'	image of A, A prime
$\overleftrightarrow{AB}$	line through A and B
$\overline{AB}$	segment from A to B
AB	length of $\overline{AB}$
$\angle A$	angle A
$\angle ABC$	angle with sides $\overrightarrow{BA}$ and $\overrightarrow{BC}$
$m\angle A$	measure of angle A
$^\circ$	degree(s)
$\log_b x$	logarithm of x, base b
$\arg z$	argument
$\triangle ABC$	triangle with vertices A, B, and C
π	pi, the ratio of the circumference of a circle to its diameter
$a:b, \frac{a}{b}$	ratio of a to b
$\sin\theta$	sine of θ
$\cos\theta$	cosine of θ
$\tan\theta$	tangent of θ
$\sin^{-1}x$	inverse sine of x
$\cos^{-1}x$	inverse cosine of x
$\tan^{-1}x$	inverse tangent of x
$n!$	n factorial
$\binom{n}{k}$	the nth row, kth column entry of Pascal's triangle
$\sum_{n=1}^{5}$	summation notation
$f^{-1}(x)$	inverse of function f
$g \circ f(x)$	$g(f(x))$
$x \mapsto y$	x maps to y
$\mathbb{N}$	set of natural numbers
$\mathbb{Z}$	set of integers
$\mathbb{Q}$	set of rational numbers
$\mathbb{R}$	set of real numbers
i	$\sqrt{-1}$
$a + bi$	complex number
$\bar{z}$	conjugate
$\lvert z \rvert$	magnitude of a complex number
I	identity matrix
A^{-1}	inverse of matrix A
0	zero matrix
$\mathcal{A}_{(a,b)}$	affine transformation
S_x	stabilizer
T_a	translation
D_s	dilation

Table 2 Measures

	United States Customary	Metric
Length	12 inches (in.) = 1 foot (ft)	10 millimeters (mm) = 1 centimeter (cm)
	36 in. = 1 yard (yd)	100 cm = 1 meter (m)
	3 ft = 1 yard	1000 mm = 1 meter
	5280 ft = 1 mile (mi)	1000 m = 1 kilometer (km)
	1760 yd = 1 mile	
Area	144 square inches (in.^{2}) = 1 square foot (ft^2)	100 square millimeters (mm^2) = 1 square centimeter (cm^2)
	9 ft^2 = 1 square yard (yd^2)	10,000 cm^2 = 1 square meter (m^2)
	43,560 ft^2 = 1 acre (a)	10,000 m^2 = 1 hectare (ha)
	4840 yd^2 = 1 acre	
Volume	1728 cubic inches (in.^{3}) = 1 cubic foot (ft^3)	1000 cubic millimeters (mm^3) = 1 cubic centimeter (cm^3)
	27 ft^3 = 1 cubic yard (yd^3)	1,000,000 cm^3 = 1 cubic meter (m^3)
Liquid Capacity	8 fluid ounces (fl oz) = 1 cup (c)	1000 milliliters (mL) = 1 liter (L)
	2 c = 1 pint (pt)	1000 L = 1 kiloliter (kL)
	2 pt = 1 quart (qt)	
	4 qt = 1 gallon (gal)	
Weight and Mass	16 ounces (oz) = 1 pound (lb)	1000 milligrams (mg) = 1 gram (g)
	2000 pounds = 1 ton (t)	1000 g = 1 kilogram (kg)
		1000 kg = 1 metric ton
Temperature	32°F = freezing point of water	0°C = freezing point of water
	98.6°F = normal body temperature	37°C = normal body temperature
	212°F = boiling point of water	100°C = boiling point of water
Time	60 seconds (s) = 1 minute (min)	365 days = 1 year (yr)
	60 minutes = 1 hour (h)	52 weeks (approx.) = 1 year
	24 hours = 1 day (d)	12 months = 1 year
	7 days = 1 week (wk)	10 years = 1 decade
	4 weeks (approx.) = 1 month (mo)	100 years = 1 century

Table 3 Formulas From Geometry

You may need geometric formulas as you work through your algebra book. Here are some perimeter, area, and volume formulas.

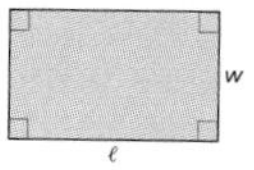

$P = 2\ell + 2w$
$A = \ell w$

Rectangle

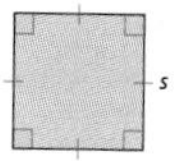

$P = 4s$
$A = s^2$

Square

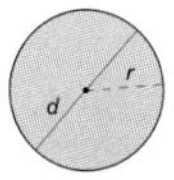

$C = 2\pi r$ or $C = \pi d$
$A = \pi r^2$

Circle

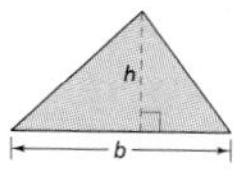

$A = \frac{1}{2}bh$

Triangle

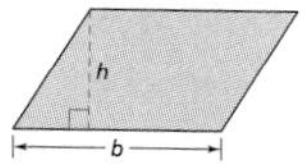

$A = bh$

Parallelogram

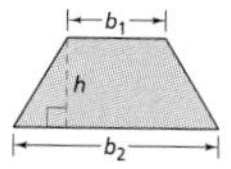

$A = \frac{1}{2}(b_1 + b_2)h$

Trapezoid

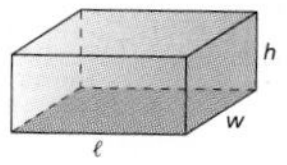

$V = Bh$
$V = \ell wh$

Rectangular Prism

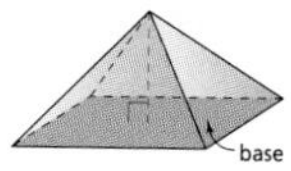

$V = \frac{1}{3}Bh$

Pyramid

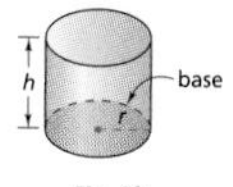

$V = Bh$
$V = \pi r^2 h$

Cylinder

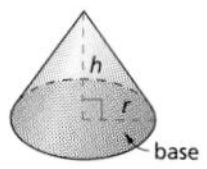

$V = \frac{1}{3}Bh$
$V = \frac{1}{3}\pi r^2 h$

Cone

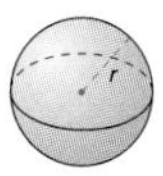

$V = \frac{4}{3}\pi r^3$

Sphere

Properties and Theorems

Chapter 1

Theorem 1.1, p. 18
You can match an input-output table having constant differences with a linear function. The slope of the graph of the function is the constant difference in the table.

Theorem 1.2, p. 18
If $f(x) = ax + b$ is a linear function, its differences are constant.

Theorem 1.3, p. 32
For any quadratic function $p(x) = ax^2 + bx + c$, the second differences are constant. The constant second difference is $2a$, twice the coefficient of the squared term.

Theorem 1.4, p. 34
If a table has constant second differences, there is some quadratic function that agrees with the table.

Theorem 1.5 *Invariance Under Translation*, p. 56
Suppose a and b are fixed numbers and you have a set of data labeled (x, y). If you perform the transformation $(x, y) \mapsto (x + a, y + b)$ on the data set, the lines of best fit for the two data sets will have the same slope.

Conjecture 1.1, p. 62
For any set of data, the line of best fit contains the balance point.

Chapter 2

Theorem 2.0 *The Zero Product Property*, p. 92
If a and b are real numbers with a product of 0, then either a or b (or both) must be 0.

Theorem 2.1, p. 121
Suppose $f: A \rightarrow B$ is one-to-one. Then
- $f^{-1}: B \rightarrow A$ is one-to-one
- $(f^{-1})^{-1} = f$

***Euclidean Property*, p. 150**
Given positive integers a and b, there are unique nonnegative integers q (the quotient) and r (the remainder) such that
- $b = a \cdot q + r$
- $0 \le r < a$

***Euclidean Property for Polynomials*, p. 150**
Given polynomials $f(x)$ and $g(x)$, there are unique polynomials $q(x)$ (the quotient) and $r(x)$ (the remainder) such that
- $f(x) = g(x) \cdot q(x) + r(x)$
- $\deg(r(x)) < \deg(g(x))$

Theorem 2.2 *The Remainder Theorem*, p. 151
If you divide a polynomial $f(x)$ by $x - a$, where a is a number, the remainder is the number $f(a)$.

Theorem 2.3 *The Factor Theorem*, p. 155
Suppose $f(x)$ is a polynomial. Then the number a is a root of the equation $f(x) = 0$ if and only if $x - a$ is a factor of $f(x)$.

Corollary 2.3.1, p. 156
A polynomial of degree n can have at most n distinct real-number zeros.

Corollary 2.3.2, p. 156
If two polynomials of degree n agree at $n + 1$ inputs, they are identical.

Corollary 2.3.3, p. 157
A polynomial of degree n is completely determined by its output values for $n + 1$ inputs.

Theorem 2.4, p. 169
The following identities show the factoring for the difference of cubes and the sum of cubes.
- $x^3 - y^3 = (x - y)(x^2 + xy + y^2)$
- $x^3 + y^3 = (x + y)(x^2 - xy + y^2)$

Theorem 2.5, p. 174
The following are identities.
- $(x + y)^3 = x^3 + 3x^2y + 3xy^2 + y^3$
- $(x - y)^3 = x^3 - 3x^2y + 3xy^2 - y^3$

Chapter 3

Theorem 3.1, p. 213
If a, b, c, and d are real numbers, then $a + bi = c + di$ only when $a = c$ and $b = d$.

Theorem 3.2, p. 235
Suppose $z = a + bi$ and $w = c + di$ are complex numbers. Then, on the complex plane, the numbers 0, z, w, and $z + w$ form the vertices of a parallelogram.

Theorem 3.3 *Multiplication by i*, p. 237
If z is a complex number, iz is obtained from z by rotating it 90° counterclockwise about the origin.

Theorem 3.4 *Magnitude and Conjugates*, p. 242
The magnitude $|z|$ of a complex number is given by $|z| = \sqrt{z\bar{z}}$.

Theorem 3.5, p. 256
Given complex numbers z and w, the following statements are true.
- $|zw| = |z| \cdot |w|$
- $\arg zw = \arg z + \arg w$

Theorem 3.6, p. 263
Suppose that z and w are complex numbers. Then the following statements are true.

$$\bar{z} + \bar{w} = \overline{z + w}$$

When you add conjugates, the result is the conjugate of the sum of the original numbers.

$$\bar{z} \cdot \bar{w} = \overline{zw}$$

When you multiply conjugates, the result is the conjugate of the product of the original numbers.

$$(\bar{z})^2 = \overline{z^2}$$

When you square a conjugate, the result is the conjugate of the square of the original number. If z is a real number, then $\bar{z} = z$.

Theorem 3.7 *Polynomials and Conjugates*, p. 264
For any polynomial f with real coefficients and any complex number z, $\overline{f(z)} = f(\bar{z})$.

Corollary 3.7.1 *Conjugate Pairs*, p. 264
If f is a polynomial with real coefficients, and $f(z) = 0$, then $f(\bar{z}) = 0$.

Chapter 4

Theorem 4.1, p. 325
Suppose matrix A represents a system where the z's are linear combinations of y's. Suppose B represents a system where these y's are linear combinations of x's. Then, by substitution, the z's are linear combinations of the x's, and the matrix that represents this system is the product AB.

Chapter 5

Theorem 5.1 *The Fundamental Law of Exponents*, p. 401
If b and c are positive integers, then

$$a^b \cdot a^c = a^{b+c}$$

Corollary 5.1.1, p. 402
If b and c are positive integers with $b > c$ and $a \neq 0$, then

$$\frac{a^b}{a^c} = a^{b-c}$$

Corollary 5.1.2, p. 402
For all numbers a and positive integers b and c,

$$(a^b)^c = a^{bc}$$

Lemma 5.1, p. 429
Let $b > 1$ and let x be a positive rational number. Then $b^x > 1$.

Theorem 5.2, p. 429
If $b > 1$, then the function $f(x) = b^x$ is strictly increasing on rational-number inputs. In other words, if s and t are rational numbers such that $s > t$, then $f(s) > f(t)$.

Lemma 5.2, p. 433
Let $0 < b < 1$ and let x be a positive number. Then $b^x < 1$.

Theorem 5.3, p. 433
Let $0 < b < 1$. Then the function $f(x) = b^x$ is strictly decreasing on rational-number inputs.

Theorem 5.4 *One-to-One Property for Exponential Functions*, p. 452
If f is an exponential function, then f is one-to-one.

Corollary 5.4.1, p. 452
If $b > 0$, $b \neq 1$, and $b^x = b^y$, then $x = y$.

Theorem 5.5 *Change-of-Base Rule*, p. 466
If $b, x, y > 0$, and $b, x, y \neq 1$, then

$$\log_x y = \frac{\log_b y}{\log_b x}$$

Theorem 5.6, p. 488
When you use a logarithmic y-axis and a linear x-axis, the graph of an exponential function $y = a \cdot b^x$ with $a > 0$ and $b > 0$ appears as a straight line.

Corollary 5.6.1, p. 488
The graphs of two exponential functions $f_1(x) = a \cdot b_1^{\,x}$ and $f_2(x) = a_2 \cdot b_2^{\,x}$, with all a_i and b_i positive, must intersect exactly once, unless $b_1 = b_2$.

Chapter 6

Theorem 6.1, p. 537
Let a and b be real numbers. Then

$$T_a \circ T_b = T_{a+b}$$

Theorem 6.2, p. 538
Let s and t be nonzero real numbers. Then

$$D_s \circ D_t = D_{st}$$

Chapter 7

Theorem 7.1, p. 614
The following are identities.
- Factors come out.
  $$\sum_{k=0}^{n} cf(k) = c \times \sum_{k=0}^{n} f(k)$$
  where c is any number
- The sigma of a sum is the sum of the sigmas.
  $$\sum_{k=0}^{n} (f(k) + g(k)) = \sum_{k=0}^{n} f(k) + \sum_{k=0}^{n} g(k)$$
- Splitting up a sum
  $$\sum_{k=0}^{n} f(k) = \sum_{k=0}^{m} f(k) + \sum_{k=m+1}^{n} f(k)$$
  where $0 < m < n$
- Add a bunch of ones.
  $$\sum_{k=0}^{n} 1 = n + 1 \text{ or } \sum_{k=1}^{n} 1 = n$$
- Think Gauss.
  $$\sum_{k=0}^{n} k = \frac{n(n+1)}{2}$$
- Think Euclid.
  $$\sum_{k=0}^{n} r^k = \frac{r^{n+1} - 1}{r - 1}$$

Theorem 7.2, p. 643
If you take a loan for C dollars for n months at an interest rate of i, then the equation below gives the monthly payment.

$$m = C \cdot \frac{(q-1)q^1}{q^n - 1}$$

where n is the term of the loan and $q = 1 + \frac{i}{12}$.

Theorem 7.3 *The Binomial Theorem*, p. 668
For $n \ge 0$,

$$(a+b)^n = \binom{n}{0}a^n b^0 + \binom{n}{1}a^{n-1}b^1 + \binom{n}{2}a^{n-2}b^2 + \cdots + \binom{n}{k}a^{n-k}b^k + \cdots + \binom{n}{n-1}a^1 b^{n-1} + \binom{n}{n}a^0 b^n$$

Chapter 8

Theorem 8.1, p. 699
If n is an integer and x is an angle in degrees,
- $\cos(x + 360n) = \cos x$
- $\sin(x + 360n) = \sin x$

Theorem 8.2 *The Pythagorean Identity*, p. 704
If α is any angle, then $\cos^2 \alpha + \sin^2 \alpha = 1$.

Theorem 8.3 *Angle-Sum Identities*, p. 728
For all α and β,
- $\cos(\alpha + \beta) = \cos\alpha\cos\beta - \sin\alpha\sin\beta$
- $\sin(\alpha + \beta) = \sin\alpha\cos\beta + \cos\alpha\sin\beta$

Theorem 8.4 *Area of a Triangle*, p. 741
For $\triangle ABC$ with $AB = c$, $AC = b$, and $BC = a$, the area of the triangle is equal to the expressions below.

$$\frac{1}{2}ab\sin C = \frac{1}{2}bc\sin A = \frac{1}{2}ac\sin B$$

Theorem 8.5 *Law of Sines*, p. 747
Given $\triangle ABC$ with corresponding side lengths a, b, and c,

$$\frac{a}{\sin A} = \frac{b}{\sin B} = \frac{c}{\sin C}$$

Theorem 8.6 *The Law of Cosines*, p. 755
Given $\triangle ABC$ with corresponding side lengths a, b, and c,

$$c^2 = a^2 + b^2 - 2ab\cos C$$

Theorem 8.7 *Heron's Formula*, p. 764
Given a triangle with side lengths a, b, and c, the area of the triangle is

$$A = \sqrt{s(s-a)(s-b)(s-c)}$$

where s is the semiperimeter $\frac{a+b+c}{2}$.

Theorem 8.8 *Brahmagupta's Formula*, p. 771
Given a cyclic quadrilateral with side lengths a, b, c, and d, the area of the quadrilateral is

$$A = \sqrt{(s-a)(s-b)(s-c)(s-d)}$$

where s is the semiperimeter $s = \frac{a+b+c+d}{2}$.

Glossary

A

absorbing state (p. 381) An absorbing state in a probability transition matrix brings an end to an infinite situation.

absolute value of a complex number (p. 243) The absolute value, or magnitude, of a complex number is its distance from the origin on the complex number plane.

absolute value of a real number (p. 52) The absolute value of a real number is its distance from the origin on the number line.

additive inverse (p. 120) The additive inverse, or opposite, of any number a is $-a$.

affine recursive definition (p. 574) Let $\mathcal{A}_{(a,\,b)}$ be an affine transformation of $\mathbb{R}$ and let p be a number. Then a recursive definition of the form below is an affine recursive definition.

$$f(n) = \begin{cases} p & \text{if } n = 0 \\ \mathcal{A}_{(a,\,b)}(f(n-1)) & \text{if } n > 0 \end{cases}$$

affine transformation (p. 540) Let a and b be real numbers with $a \neq 0$. An affine transformation by (a, b) is a transformation $\mathcal{A}_{(a,\,b)}$ of $\mathbb{R}$ given by $\mathcal{A}_{(a,\,b)} = T_b \circ D_a$.

argument (p. 247) *Argument* is another term used for direction of a complex number vector. The notation is arg z.

arithmetic mean (p. 636) The arithmetic mean of any two numbers is their sum divided by two.

arithmetic sequence (pp. 412, 633) A sequence is an arithmetic sequence if its domain is the set of integers $n \geq 0$, and there is a number d, the common difference, for the sequence such that $f(n) = f(n-1) + d$ for all integers $n > 0$.

arithmetic series (p. 634) If the sequence t is an arithmetic sequence with initial term $t(0)$, the associated series T defined on integers n, such that $n \geq 0$ by $T(n) = \sum_{k=0}^{n} t(k)$ is an arithmetic series.

augmentation line (p. 292) An augmentation line is the vertical bar in an augmented matrix that separates the coefficients from the constants.

augmented matrix (p. 292) An augmented matrix contains the coefficients and constants from a system of equations.

B

balance point (p. 44) The balance point $(\overline{x}, \overline{y})$ is the point with x-coordinate that is the average of the x-coordinates in a table and with y-coordinate that is the average of the y-coordinates in the table.

base (p. 428) In the exponential function $f(x) = a \cdot b^x$, b is the base.

Bernoulli's formulas (p. 616) Bernoulli's formulas give closed-form sums for series associated with the functions $x \mapsto x^m$ for positive integers m. For example, $\sum_{k=0}^{n} k = \frac{n(n+1)}{2}$, and $\sum_{k=0}^{n} k^2 = \frac{n(n+1)(2n = 1)}{6}$.

binary operation (p. 110) A binary operation takes two inputs and produces one output.

C

centroid (p. 43) Centroid is another term for balance point. It is most commonly used in geometry.

circle (p. 290) A circle is a set of all points in a plane at a distance r from a given point. The standard form of the equation of a circle with center (h, k) and radius r is $(x-h)^2 + (y-k)^2 = r^2$.

circumcenter (p. 226) The circumcenter of a polygon is the center of the circle that contains the vertices of the polygon.

closed-form definition (p. 9) A closed-form definition of a function uses direct calculation to find an output for any input.

coefficient (p. 90) The coefficient is the numerical factor in a monomial.

coefficient matrix (p. 292) When representing a system of equations with a matrix equation, the matrix containing the coefficients of the system is the coefficient matrix.

collinear (p. 44) Points are collinear if they lie on the same line.

combination (p. 671) Any unordered selection of r objects from a set of n objects is a combination. The number of combinations of n objects taken r at a time is ${}_nC_r = \frac{n!}{r!(n-r)!}$ for $0 \leq r \leq n$.

common difference (p. 633) The common difference for a sequence is a number d such that $f(n) = f(n-1) + d$ for all $n > 0$.

common logarithm (p. 464) A common logarithm is a logarithm that uses base 10. You can write the common logarithm $\log_{10} y$ as $\log y$.

common ratio (p. 640) The common ratio for a sequence is a number $r \neq 0$ such that $f(n) = r \cdot f(n-1)$ for all integers $n > 0$.

completing the square (p. 546) Completing the square is a process for converting a quadratic equation into a perfect square trinomial.

complex conjugate (p. 269) The complex numbers $a + bi$ and $a - bi$ are complex conjugates.

complex numbers (p. 212) The system of complex numbers $\mathbb{C}$ consists of all expressions in the form $a + bi$ with the following properties.

- a and b are real numbers.
- $i^2 = -1$
- You can use addition and multiplication as if $a + bi$ were a polynomial.

complex plane (p. 229) The complex plane is used to represent a complex number geometrically. The real-number part of the number is located on the horizontal axis and the imaginary part on the vertical axis.

composite function (p. 110) For two functions $f: A \rightarrow B$ and $g: B \rightarrow C$, the composite function meets the following conditions.

- $g \circ f: A \rightarrow C$
- $g \circ f(x) = g(f(x))$

concurrent lines (p. 58) Concurrent lines all intersect at the same point.

conjugate (p. 218) Number pairs of the form $a + bi$ and $a - bi$ are conjugates. The symbol $\overline{z}$ represents the conjugate of z.

converge (p. 651) When the outputs of an iteration get closer and closer to a number, the iteration converges to that number.

cosine (pp. 694, 698) The cosine function, $y = \cos\theta$, matches the measure θ of an angle in standard position with the x-coordinate of a point on the unit circle. This point is where the terminal side of the angle intersects the unit circle.

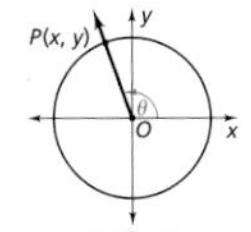

$\cos\theta = x$
$\sin\theta = y$

cubic function (p. 35) A cubic function is a polynomial in which the highest-degree term is cubed.

D

definite sum (p. 610) A definite sum is a summation with numbers for starting and ending values.

degree of a monomial (p. 90) The degree of a monomial is the sum of the exponents of each variable in the monomial.

degree of a polynomial (p. 90) The degree of a polynomial is the largest degree of any of its terms.

determinant (p. 340) The determinant of a 2×2 matrix $\begin{pmatrix} a & b \\ c & d \end{pmatrix}$ is the real number $ad - bc$.

difference of cubes (p. 169) A difference of cubes is an expression of the form $x^3 - y^3$. It can be factored as $(x - y)(x^2 + xy + y^2)$.

difference table (p. 10) A difference table shows the difference between consecutive outputs. It can help show patterns that lead to recursive definitions.

dilation (p. 536) A dilation is a transformation that changes the size of a figure. A dilation by s is a transformation D_s of $\mathbb{R}$ given by the formula $D_s(x) = sx$ for any real number x.

dimension (p. 292) The dimensions of a matrix tell the number of rows and columns. A matrix with m rows and n columns has dimensions $m \times n$.

direction of a complex number (p. 244) The direction of a complex number z is the angle measured from the positive real axis in a counterclockwise direction.

discontinuity (p. 723) A point of discontinuity in a graph occurs whenever the function is undefined at that point.

domain (p. 104) The domain of a function is the set of all inputs. *See* **function**.

dot product (p. 315) The dot product is an operation over two n-tuples that returns a real number. If $A = (a_1, a_2, \ldots, a_n)$ and $B = (b_1, b_2, \ldots, b_n)$ then the dot product $A \cdot B$ is the real number $a_1b_1 + a_2b_2 + \ldots + a_nb_n$.

E

elimination (p. 286) Elimination is a method for solving a system of equations by using addition, subtraction, and multiplication to find an equation in one variable that can be solved.

equal functions (p. 105) Two functions f and g are equal functions if both of these conditions are satisfied.

- f and g have the same domain.
- $f(a) = g(a)$ for every a in the common domain.

error (p. 48) Error is the difference between the actual value and the predicted value.

Euclid's method (p. 594) Euclid's method tells how to find the sum of a sequence with a constant ratio.

evaluate (p. 9) To evaluate an expression, substitute numbers for the variables in the expression and follow the order of operations.

even function (p. 510) A function f is an even function if it satisfies $f(x) = f(-x)$ for all numbers x in its domain. If point (x, y) is on the graph of f, the point $(-x, y)$ is also on the graph.

exponential decay (p. 436) Given $f(x) = a \cdot b^x$, if $0 < b < 1$, the function shows exponential decay.

exponential equations (p. 460) An equation of the form $b^{cx} = a$, where the exponent includes a variable, is an exponential equation. You can solve an exponential equation by taking the logarithm of each side of the equation.

exponential function (p. 428) An exponential function is a function f that you can write in the form $f(x) = a \cdot b^x$, where $a \neq 0$, $b > 0$, and $b \neq 1$.

exponential growth (p. 436) Given $f(x) = a \cdot b^x$, if $b > 1$, the function $f(x)$ shows exponential growth.

F

factorial function (p. 78) The factorial function is defined by the recursive function

$$f(n) = \begin{cases} 1 & \text{if } n = 0 \\ n \cdot f(n-1) & \text{if } n > 0 \end{cases}$$

factoring (p. 155) Factoring is rewriting an expression as the product of its factors.

figurate numbers (p. 622) Figurate numbers tell the number of dots needed to make a series of regular geometric shapes of increasing size. Examples of figurate numbers include the triangular, square, and pentagonal numbers.

fixed point (p. 571) Let $\mathcal{A}_{(a,\,b)}$ be an affine transformation. A number x is a fixed point of $\mathcal{A}_{(a,\,b)}$ if $\mathcal{A}_{(a,\,b)}(x) = x$.

function (p. 104) A function from set A to set B is a pairing between A and B such that each element in A pairs with exactly one element of B. A is the *domain* of f. B is the *target* of f. The set of objects in B that are paired with objects in A is the *range* of f.

function notation (p. 96) You read the function notation $f(x)$ as "f of x" or "a function of x." Note that $f(x)$ does *not* mean "f times x."

functional equation (p. 445) A functional equation is an equation with unknowns that are functions.

Fundamental Theorem of Algebra (p. 215) If $P(x)$ is a polynomial of degree $n \geq 1$ with complex coefficients, then $P(x) = 0$ has at least one complex root.

G

Gaussian Elimination (p. 294) Gaussian elimination is an algorithm that transforms the matrix of any given system of linear equations through a sequence of other matrices, ending in a final matrix form from which the solution to the corresponding system is obvious.

Gauss's method (p. 594) Gauss's method tells how to find the sum of a sequence with a constant difference.

geometric sequence (pp. 413, 640) A sequence is a geometric sequence if its domain is the integers $n \geq 0$, and there is a number $r \neq 0$, called the common ratio, such that $f(n) = r \cdot f(n-1)$ for all integers $n > 0$.

geometric series (p. 640) If a sequence g is a geometric sequence with initial term $g(0)$, the associated series $G(n) = \sum_{k=0}^{n} g(n)$ is a geometric series.

H

Heronian triangle (p. 768) A Heronian triangle is a triangle with integer side lengths and integer area.

hockey stick property (p. 17) The hockey stick property states that, in a difference table, an output is the sum of all of the differences above it to the right and the single output at the top of the table.

hypotenuse (p. 225) The hypotenuse of a right triangle is the side opposite the right angle. It is always the longest side in a right triangle.

I

***i* (p. 208)** The imaginary number i is defined as the number with square -1. So $i^2 = -1$ and $i = \sqrt{-1}$.

identity (p. 611) An identity is a statement that two expressions that may seem different are actually equivalent under the basic rules of algebra.

identity function (p. 119) The identity function on a set is the function id that simply returns its input.

identity matrix (pp. 296, 338) An identity matrix is a square matrix with all entries 0 except for 1's along the main diagonal from the top left to the bottom right. Multiplying a matrix by an identity matrix will result in the original matrix.

identity transformation (p. 533) An identity transformation leaves all inputs unchanged.

image (p. 356) An image is a figure obtained by a transformation of a preimage.

imaginary number (p. 229) An imaginary number is any number of the form $a + bi$, where $b \neq 0$.

indefinite sum (p. 610) An indefinite sum is a summation with a variable for the ending value of the index.

index (p. 602) The index of a summation indicates the range of the variable.

intercept (p. 203) An intercept is a point where a graph crosses either the x- or y-axis.

interest (p. 72) Interest is the amount of money paid regularly at a particular rate for the use of money lent.

initial side (of an angle) (p. 698) When an angle is in standard position, the side along the x-axis is the initial side of the angle, and the side not along the x-axis is the terminal side of the angle.

inverse function (f^{-1}) (p. 119) Suppose f is a one-to-one function with domain A and range B. The inverse function f^{-1} is a function with these properties:

- f^{-1} has domain B and range A.
- For all x in B, $f(f^{-1}(x)) = x$, or alternatively, $f \circ f^{-1} = \text{id}$.

inverse matrix (A^{-1}) (p. 339) The inverse of matrix A is a matrix M such that $AM = I$. You write it as A^{-1}.

irrational numbers (p. 201) Irrational numbers cannot by expressed as the quotient of integers.

iteration (p. 573) An iteration is a repeated calculation that uses the previous result in the next calculation.

L

Lagrange interpolation (p. 135) Lagrange interpolation is a method of finding a polynomial to fit a data set.

Law of Cosines (p. 755) Given $\triangle ABC$ with corresponding side lengths a, b, and c, $c^2 = a^2 + b^2 - 2ab\cos C$.

Law of Sines (p. 747) Given $\triangle ABC$ with corresponding side lengths a, b, and c, $\frac{a}{\sin A} = \frac{b}{\sin B} = \frac{c}{\sin C}$.

leg (p. 228) The legs in a right triangle are the sides adjacent to the right angle.

limit (p. 649) A limit is a value a series or summation converges to as the input values increase.

line of best fit (p. 62) Given a set of data, the line of best fit is the line that minimizes the sum of the squares of the errors. It minimizes the mean squared error.

linear combination (p. 323) A linear combination of variables is a sum of multiples of the variables.

linear function (p. 18) A linear function is a function of the form $x \mapsto ax + b$ for some numbers a and b.

linear scale (p. 484) A linear scale increases by a constant amount.

logarithm (p. 463) A logarithm of a positive number y to the base b is defined as follows: If $y = b^x$, then $\log_b y = x$. If a base is not given, it is assumed to be 10. The logarithmic function is often called the logarithm.

logarithmic function (p. 463) The logarithmic function $x \mapsto \log_b x$ is the inverse function of the exponential function $x \mapsto b^x$.

logarithmic scale (p. 484) A logarithmic scale increases by a common multiple.

M

magnitude of a complex number (p. 242) The magnitude of the complex number z, denoted by $|z|$, is the distance between the complex number and (0, 0) in the complex plane. In other words, $|z|$ is the length of the vector that represents z.

matrix (p. 292) A matrix is a rectangular array of numbers written within brackets. A matrix with m horizontal rows and n vertical columns is an $m \times n$ matrix.

matrix equation (p. 328) A matrix equation is an equation in which the variable is a matrix.

matrix multiplication (p. 324) Let A have as many columns as B has rows. Say, A is $m \times n$ and B is $n \times p$. Let the rows of A be called $R_1, R_2, \ldots, R_m$. Let the columns of B be called $C_1, C_2, \ldots, C_p$. The product AB is defined to be the $m \times p$ matrix for which the entry ij is the dot product $R_i \cdot C_j$.

$$AB = \begin{pmatrix} R_1 \cdot C_1 & R_1 \cdot C_2 & \cdots & R_1 \cdot C_p \\ R_2 \cdot C_1 & R_2 \cdot C_2 & \cdots & R_2 \cdot C_p \\ \vdots & \vdots & \ddots & \vdots \\ R_m \cdot C_1 & R_m \cdot C_2 & \cdots & R_m \cdot C_p \end{pmatrix}$$

matrix transformation (p. 360) A transformation is called a matrix transformation if it can be expressed in the form $X \mapsto AX$, where A is a 2×2 matrix and points X are represented as column vectors $\begin{pmatrix} x \\ y \end{pmatrix}$ so that they can be multiplied by matrices on the left.

mean (p. 43) The sum of the data values divided by the number of data values.

mean absolute error (p. 55) The mean absolute error is the average of the absolute values of the differences between the line of best fit and the actual data points.

mean squared error (p. 55) The mean squared error is the average of the squares of the differences between the line of best fit and the actual data points.

median (p. 59) The median is the middle value in a data set. If the data set contains an even number of values, the median is the mean of the two middle values.

mode (p. 59) The mode is the most frequently occurring value (or values) in a set of data.

monic (p. 124) A monic polynomial is a polynomial with a leading coefficient of one.

monomial (p. 90) A monomial is an expression that you can write as a product of a nonzero number and one or more variables, each raised to a nonnegative integer exponent.

monotonic (p. 446) A function is monotonic if it either increases or decreases over its domain.

multiplicative inverse (p. 120) The multiplicative inverse, or reciprocal, of any nonzero number a is $\frac{1}{a}$.

N

***n* factorial ($n!$) (p. 79)** For any positive integer n, $n!$ is the product of all of the integers between n and 1. $0! = 1$.

***n*-tuple (p. 315)** An n-tuple is a string of n numbers.

***n*th root (p. 419)** For any real numbers a and b, and any positive integer n, if $a^n = b$, then a is the nth root of b.

natural domain (p. 97) The natural domain of a function is the largest set of inputs for which a function produces an output.

natural numbers (p. 201) The natural numbers, or counting numbers, are 1, 2, 3, . . . and are represented by the symbol $\mathbb{N}$.

negative exponent (a^{-m}) (p. 407) If $a \neq 0$ and m is a positive integer, then $a^{-m} = \frac{1}{a^m}$.

normal form (p. 91) A polynomial is in normal form if it contains no parenthesis, like terms have been combined, and the degrees of the terms go from highest to lowest.

O

odd function (p. 510) A function f is an odd function if it satisfies $f(-x) = -f(x)$ for all numbers x in its domain. If the point (x, y) is on the graph of f, the point $(-x, -y)$ is also on the graph.

one-to-one (p. 117) A function is one-to-one if its outputs are unique. That is, a function f is one-to-one if $f(r) = f(s)$ only when $r = s$.

opposite (p. 120) The opposite, or additive inverse, of any number a is $-a$.

outlier (p. 46) An outlier is an item of data with a substantially different value from the rest of the items in the data set.

P

parabola (p. 519) A parabola is the graph of a quadratic function.

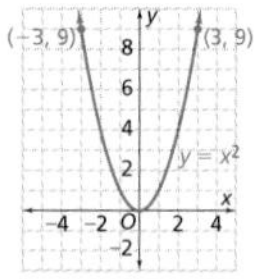

Pascal's Triangle (p. 663) Pascal's triangle is a pattern that can be used to find combinations of n things taken k at a time. Each entry can be labeled $\binom{n}{k}$, where n is the row number and k is the column number.

```
            1
          1   1
        1   2   1
      1   3   3   1
    1   4   6   4   1
  1   5  10  10   5   1
1   6  15  20  15   6   1
```

period (p. 721) A period of a periodic function is one complete pattern of y-values.

periodic function (p. 699) A periodic function repeats a pattern of y-values at regular intervals.

polynomial (p. 90) A polynomial is a sum of monomials.

polynomial function (p. 38) A polynomial function is a function defined on $\mathbb{R}$ by a polynomial.

probability transition matrix (p. 379) A probability transition matrix is a matrix that shows the probabilities of moving from one state or position to another.

Q

$\mathbb{Q}$ (p. 181) $\mathbb{Q}$ is the set of all rational numbers.

quadratic formula (p. 169) A quadratic equation written in standard form $ax^2 + bx + c = 0$, can be solved using the quadratic formula.

$$x = \frac{-b \pm \sqrt{b^2 - 4ac}}{2a}$$

quadratic function (p. 31) A quadratic function is a function defined by a polynomial of degree 2.

quartic (p. 176) A quartic polynomial is a fourth-degree polynomial.

quotient (p. 150) Given positive integers a and b, there are nonnegative integers q (the quotient) and r (the remainder) such that $b = a \cdot q + r$ and $0 \le r < a$. Given polynomials $f(x)$ and $g(x)$, there are unique polynomials $q(x)$ (the quotient) and $r(x)$ (the remainder) such that $f(x) = g(x) \cdot q(x) + r(x)$ and $\deg(r(x)) < \deg(g(x))$.

R

$\mathbb{R}$ (p. 102) $\mathbb{R}$ is the set of all real numbers.

radius (p. 97) The radius r of a circle is the distance between the center of the circle and any point on the circumference.

range (p. 104) The range of a function is the set of objects that are paired with objects from the domain. *See* **function**.

rational exponent ($a^{\frac{p}{q}}$) (p. 420) For integers p and q with $q > 0$, if $a^{\frac{1}{q}}$ is a real number, then $a^{\frac{p}{q}} = \left(a^{\frac{1}{q}}\right)^p = \left(\sqrt[q]{a}\right)^p$.

rational expression (p. 184) A rational expression is a ratio of two expressions.

reciprocal (p. 120) The reciprocal, or multiplicative inverse, of any nonzero number a is $\frac{1}{a}$.

recursive definition (p. 9) A recursive definition of a function gives an output in terms of previous outputs.

reflection (p. 356) A reflection, or flip, is a transformation that maps a point in the plane to its mirror image, using a specific line as a mirror.

reflection transformation (p. 534) A reflection transformation on a function returns the opposite of the input.

relation (p. 104) A relation is any pairing between two sets A and B.

remainder (p. 150) Given positive integers a and b, there are nonnegative integers q (the quotient) and r (the remainder) such that $b = a \cdot q + r$ and $0 \le r < a$. Given polynomials $f(x)$ and $g(x)$, there are unique polynomials $q(x)$ (the quotient) and $r(x)$ (the remainder) such that $f(x) = g(x) \cdot q(x) + r(x)$ and $\deg(r(x)) < \deg(g(x))$.

repeating decimal (p. 657) A repeating decimal is a decimal that has a set of digits that repeat infinitely many times.

roots of unity (p. 271) The solutions to $x^n = 1$ are roots of unity. They will all have magnitude 1 and a direction n times the direction of x.

rotation (p. 237) A rotation is a transformation that turns a figure about a fixed point called the center of rotation.

row-reduced echelon form (rref) (p. 295) A matrix in row-reduced echelon form is the final matrix in an Gaussian elimination. There will be an identity matrix to the left of the augmentation line.

S

scalar multiplication (p. 309) Multiplying a matrix by a number (called a scalar) is scalar multiplication.

sequence (p. 632) A sequence is a function with a domain that is the set of nonnegative integers.

series associated with f (p. 611) Given a function having a domain that contains the nonnegative integers, the series associated with f is the function defined on nonnegative integers by

$$F(n) = \sum_{k=0}^{n} f(k) = f(0) + f(1) + f(2) + \cdots + f(n)$$

sine (pp. 694, 698) The sine function, $y = \sin\theta$, matches the measure θ of an angle in standard position with the y-coordinate of a point on the unit circle. This point is where the terminal side of the angle intersects the unit circle.

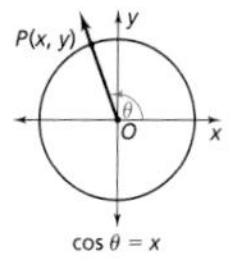

$\cos\theta = x$
$\sin\theta = y$

slope (p. 15) Slope is the ratio of the change in the y-coordinates to the change in the x-coordinates.

square matrix (p. 346) A square matrix is a matrix with equal numbers of columns and rows.

stabilizer (p. 573) Let x be a real number. Then the stabilizer of x, denoted S_x, is the set of all affine transformations that fix x.

standard error (p. 55) The standard error is a measure of error involving the square root of the mean squared error.

standard position (of an angle) (p. 696) An angle is in standard position when its vertex is at the origin and one of its sides lies along the positive x-axis. The angle opens counterclockwise from this fixed side.

steady state (p. 373) A steady state occurs when a variable in a system settles to a constant value.

strictly decreasing (p. 430) A function f is strictly decreasing if for any s and t such that $s > t$, then $f(s) < f(t)$.

strictly increasing (p. 429) A function f is strictly increasing if for any s and t such that $s > t$, then $f(s) > f(t)$.

substitution (p. 286) Substitution is a method for solving a system of equations by replacing one variable with an equivalent expression containing the other variable(s).

sum of cubes (p. 169) A sum of cubes is an expression of the form $x^3 + y^3$. It factors as $(x + y)(x^2 - xy + y^2)$.

summation notation (p. 602) The general form of summation notation is $\sum_{k=0}^{n} f(k) = f(0) + f(1) + \cdots f(n)$, where k is the index variable, 0 is the starting value, and n is the final value. You can use summation notation as a shorthand notation to describe the sum of a sequence.

T

tangent (p. 698) The tangent of angle θ is $\frac{\sin\theta}{\cos\theta}$, whenever $\cos\theta \neq 0$.

target (p. 104) In a function f from A to B, B is the target of f. *See* **function**.

term of a sequence (p. 632) Each number in a sequence is a term.

terminal side (of an angle) (p. 698) When an angle is in standard position, the side along the x-axis is the initial side of the angle, and the side not along the x-axis is the terminal side of the angle.

terms of a polynomial (p. 90) Each monomial in a polynomial is a term.

transition matrix (p. 373) A transition matrix is used to model changes from one time period, or state, to another.

transformation (p. 536) A transformation is a change made to a figure. Four types of transformations are translations, rotations, reflections, and dilations.

translation (p. 536) A translation is a transformation that slides a graph or figure horizontally, vertically, or both without changing the size or shape of the graph. A translation by a is a transformation T_a of $\mathbb{R}$ given by the formula $T_a(x) = x + a$ for any real number x.

triangular numbers (p. 14) The triangular numbers are numbers determined by how many dots are needed to form a triangle with n dots on a side. The number of dots in a triangular pattern with n dots on a side is the nth triangular number.

trigonometric equation (p. 710) A trigonometric equation is an equation that involves trigonometric functions.

trigonometric identities (p. 714) A trigonometric identity is a trigonometric equation that is true for all values except those for which an expression on either side of the equal sign is undefined.

U

unit circle (p. 506) The unit circle has a radius of 1 unit and its center at the origin of the coordinate plane.

unit fraction exponent (p. 419) The expression $a^{\frac{1}{n}}$ is defined, when possible, as the real nth root of a.

$$a^{\frac{1}{n}} = \sqrt[n]{a}$$

up-and-over property (p. 17) The up-and-over property states that, in a difference table, an output is the sum of the two numbers above it: the output directly above and the difference above and to the right.

V

variable (p. 53) A variable is a symbol, usually a letter, that represents one or more variables.

vector (p. 234) A vector is any quantity that has magnitude and direction. It is represented as an arrow from the origin to a point.

vertex of a parabola (p. 519) The vertex of a parabola is the point at which the parabola intersects the line of symmetry. The y-value of the vertex is the maximum or minimum value of the function.

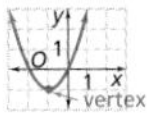

X

$x \mapsto y$ (p. 100) $x \mapsto y$ is read as "x maps to y." This uses arrow notation to represent a function.

x-intercept (p. 284) The point at which a line crosses the x-axis (or the x-coordinate of that point) is an x-intercept.

Y

y-intercept (p. 428) The point at which a line crosses the y-axis (or the y-coordinate of that point) is a y-intercept.

Z

$\mathbb{Z}$ (p. 163) $\mathbb{Z}$ is the set of all integers.

zero exponent (a^0) (p. 407) If $a \neq 0$, then $a^0 = 1$.

zero matrix (p. 329) The zero matrix 0, or $0_{m \times n}$, is the $m \times n$ matrix with elements that are all zeros. It is the additive identity matrix for the set of all $m \times n$ matrices.

zeros of a function (p. 123) The zeros of a function j are the numbers a that make $j(a) = 0$.

Selected Answers

Selected Answers

Chapter 1
Lesson 1.1
On Your Own
3–18. Answers may vary. Samples are given.
3. $E(n) = 2n + 3$ **8.** $J(n) = 2n^2$
12. $N(n) = (n + 3)^2$ **16.** $R(n) = n^3$
18. $T(n) = 3^n$

Lesson 1.2
Check Your Understanding
1.

Input, n	Output, $B(n)$	Δ
0	0	2
1	2	4
2	6	6
3	12	8
4	20	

2a. no **b.** no **c.** yes **d.** no **3a.** no **b.** yes **c.** yes **d.** no
4.

Input	Output	Δ
0	5	6
1	11	**8**
2	19	10
3	**29**	15
4	**44**	

5.

Input	Output	Δ
0	**6**	3
1	**9**	3
2	**12**	3
3	**15**	3
4	18	

6.

Input	Output	Δ
0	5	−3
1	**2**	**15**
2	17	**−13**
3	**4**	−5
4	−1	

7a. $f(1) = 1 \cdot f(0) = 1 \cdot 1 = 1$
$f(2) = 2 \cdot f(1) = 2 \cdot 1 = 2$
$f(3) = 3 \cdot f(2) = 3 \cdot 2 = 6$
$f(4) = 4 \cdot f(3) = 4 \cdot 6 = 24$
$f(5) = 5 \cdot f(4) = 5 \cdot 24 = 120$
$f(6) = 6 \cdot f(5) = 6 \cdot 120 = 720$
b. $f(n) = n!$
8a.

Input	Output
0	2
1	6
2	**10**
3	**14**
4	**18**

b–c.

Input	Output
0	2
1	6
2	**18**
3	**54**
4	**162**

d. see part (a) **9.** Answers may vary. Sample: Tables E, F, and G have a constant difference in the difference table; Tables I, J, and K include an x^2 term in the rule.

On Your Own
10.

Side Length	Number of Dots	Δ
0	0	**1**
1	1	**2**
2	3	**3**
3	6	**4**
4	10	**5**
5	15	

11a. $T(n) = T(n - 1) + n$
12a. The differences are all a.

Lesson 1.3
Check Your Understanding
1.

Input	Output	Δ
0	−7	**3**
1	−4	**3**
2	−1	**3**
3	2	**3**
4	5	**3**
5	8	

2. $f(n) = \begin{cases} -7 & \text{if } n = 0 \\ f(n-1) + 3 & \text{if } n > 0 \end{cases}$
3. $g(n) = 3n - 7$ **4a.** 23 **b.** 23.3 for closed form rule; the recursive rule cannot be applied if n is not a nonnegative integer. **5.** The differences are −6, 6, −6, and 6, which are not constant.
6.

n	$p(n)$	Δ
0	3	$-\frac{7}{4}$
1	$\frac{5}{4}$	$-\frac{7}{4}$
2	$-\frac{1}{2}$	$-\frac{7}{4}$
3	$-\frac{9}{4}$	$-\frac{7}{4}$
4	−4	

7. $p(10) = -\frac{29}{2}$; $p(100) = -172$; $p(263) = -\frac{1829}{4}$ **8.** D
9a.

n	$F(n)$	Δ
0	1	**0**
1	1	**1**
2	2	**1**
3	3	**2**
4	5	**3**
5	8	**5**
6	13	

b. The differences are the same as the outputs except that $\Delta_1 = 0$ and $\Delta_n = F(n - 1)$ for $n > 0$. **c.** $F(10) = 89$

On Your Own
14a.

n	$D(n)$	Δ
0	1	**1**
1	2	**2**
2	4	**4**
3	8	**8**
4	16	**16**
5	32	**32**
6	64	

b. The differences are directly related to the output. They are the same. $D(n + 1) - D(n) = D(n)$. They will never get to constant differences
17. −1.5

Lesson 1.4
Check Your Understanding
1a. $\frac{7}{2}$ **b.** $-\frac{1}{2}$ **c.** $f(n) = \frac{7}{2}n - \frac{1}{2}$ **2a.** $\frac{7}{2}$
b. $y = \frac{7}{2}x - \frac{1}{2}$ or $2y = 7x - 1$ **3.** The slope for (0, −12) and (3, 5) is $\frac{17}{3}$, and the slope for (3, 5) and (4, 10) is 5, so one line cannot contain all three points. **4.** No; the difference for the last two outputs is 5, but using that as the constant difference, you would expect the point (0, −10), so the table does not have a constant difference. **5.** $a = -1, b = -26$
6. $f(n) = \frac{n}{2} - 2$ **7a.** 2 **b.** −18
7c. $f(n) = 5n - 33$
8. The differences are 1, 3, 5, and 7. Since those differences are not constant, the table cannot match a linear function.
9.

x	$K(x)$	Δ	Δ^2
0	1	1	2
1	2	3	**2**
2	5	**5**	**2**
3	10	7	
4	17		

On Your Own
10a. −5 **b.** $a = -1$
12a.
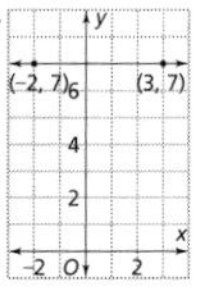

b. 0
17.

w	$R(w)$	Δ	Δ^2	Δ^3
0	0	1	6	**6**
1	1	**7**	**12**	**6**
2	8	19	**18**	**6**
3	27	**37**	24	6
4	64	61	30	**6**
5	125	91	**36**	
6	216	**127**		
7	343			

Lesson 1.5
Check Your Understanding
1. $y(n) = 5n^2 + 3n - 2$
2. $y(n) = -3n^2 + 15n + 10$
3.

w	$R(w)$	Δ	Δ^2	Δ^3
0	0	1	6	**6**
1	1	**7**	**12**	**6**
2	8	19	**18**	**6**
3	27	**37**	24	6
4	64	61	30	**6**
5	125	91	**36**	
6	216	**127**		
7	343			

4.

x	$m(x)$	Δ	Δ^2	Δ^3
0	4	**−3**	**34**	**30**
1	1	**31**	**64**	**30**
2	32	**95**	**94**	**30**
3	127	**189**	**124**	**30**
4	316	**313**	**154**	**30**
5	629	**467**	**184**	
6	1096	**651**		
7	1747			

5a. The column for Δ^3 should be constant. **b.** The constant third difference is 6 times the leading coefficient. **6.** Yes; for any table with constant third differences, calculate $f(x + 1) - f(x)$ and show that the result can be put into Sasha's form. **7.** The Δ column begins $a + b + c$, $7a + 3b + c$, $19a + 5b + c$; the Δ^2 column begins $6a + 2b$, $12a + 2b$, $18a + 2b$; the Δ^3 column begins $6a$, $6a$, $6a$.
8a. $x = 3, x = 5, x = 6$
b. $x^3 - 14x^2 + 63x - 90$
9.

x	$v(x)$	Δ	Δ^2	Δ^3
0	90	50	−22	6
1	−40	28	−16	6
2	−12	12	−10	6
3	0	2	−4	6
4	2	−2	2	6
5	0	0	8	
6	0	8		
7	8			

10. $y = 10x^2 - 23x + 7$ **11a.** No, the third differences are not constant. **b.** Except for the left column, each cell is equal to the cell that is one to the right and one down.
12. $f(n) = 2n^3 - 5n^2 + n - 3$

On Your Own
17. None of the first, second, or third differences are constant, so the table is not a linear, quadratic, or cubic function. **18.** The values of Rule 4 match the five input-output pairs in the table.

Lesson 1.6
On Your Own
8a. 86 **9a.** Answers will vary. Sample: More

people are living in the western regions of the country. **10a.** For each pair of points the slope is 3, so the points lie on a line. **b.** $y = 3x + 4$
12a. 5.9

Lesson 1.7
Check Your Understanding
1a. Answers may vary. Samples: $y = 2x$, $y = x + 3$, $y = 6$ **b.** $7x + 5y = 51$
2a–b.
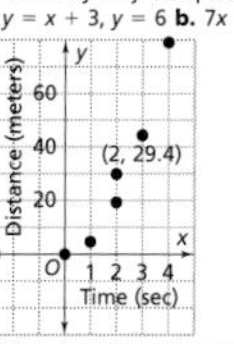

b. (2, 29.4) **c.** No; the points seem to lie on a curve, not a line.
3a-b.
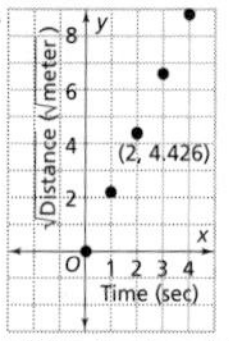

b. (2, 4.426) **c.** Yes, the points seem to lie on a line.
4.
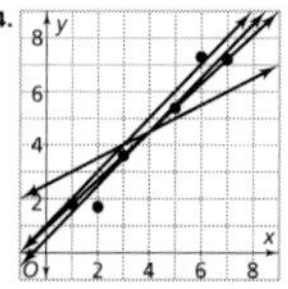

Lines (c) and (d) seem to fit the data.
5a. (667, −93) **b.** (629, 6) **6.** For 1900–1960: (1929, 233.2); a linear function is $f(x) = -0.5(x - 1929) + 233.3$. For 1960–2000: (1980, 216); a linear function is $f(x) = 216$. The two functions fit the data better than the single function $f(x) = -0.34x + 892.1$.

a. Using $f(x) = -0.5(x - 1929) + 233.3$ for the dates prior to 1960, $f(1916) \approx 240$, $f(1940) \approx 228$, $f(1944) \approx 226$.
b. Using $f(x) = 216$ for dates after 1960, $f(2623) = 216$.

On Your Own
7a. no **b.** below **9a.** The balance point is (4, 4.5); an equation is $y = x + 0.5$ or $y = 0.9x + 0.9$. **b.** For line (c), the sum of the errors is 0 and for line (d) the sum of the errors is 0. **11a.** 14 sixes **b.** mean: 3.5; median: 3; mode: 3 **13a.** Data vs. Line Fit: $y = 333.4476x - 26.2917$

Hours x	Actual Yeast Density, y	Predicted Yeast Density, y	Error
0	9.6	−26.3	35.9
1	18.3	7.2	11.1
2	29.0	40.6	−11.6
3	47.2	74.1	−26.9
4	71.1	107.5	−36.4
5	119.1	141.0	−21.9
6	174.6	174.4	−0.2
7	257.3	207.8	49.5

Lesson 1.8
Check Your Understanding
1. A **2a.** A **b.** For $y = 3x - 1$: sum of errors is −2.4; mean absolute error is 1.15; mean squared error is 2.565. For $y = -x + 8.4$: sum of errors is 1; mean absolute error is 2.9; mean squared error is 8.855.
3a.

Input	Output	Predicted	Error
1	3	$3 \cdot 1 + b = 3 + b$	$3 - (3 + b) = -b$
2	4.5	$3 \cdot 2 + b = 6 + b$	$4.5 - (6 + b) = -1.5 - b$
3	8.1	$3 \cdot 3 + b = 9 + b$	$8.1 - (9 + b) = -0.9 - b$
4	8	$3 \cdot 4 + b = 12 + b$	$-4 - b$

b. $4b^2 + 12.8b + 19.06$ **c.** −1.6
d. $y = 3x - 1.6$ **4a.** $y = x + 3.4$
b. $y = 2x + 0.9$ **c.** $y = 5.9$
5.

Slope	Equation of Best Line
0	$y = 5.9$
1	$y = x + 3.4$
2	$y = 2x + 0.9$
3	$y = 3x - 1.6$

As the slope increases by 1, the constant term decreases by 2.5.

On Your Own

6. Table 1.

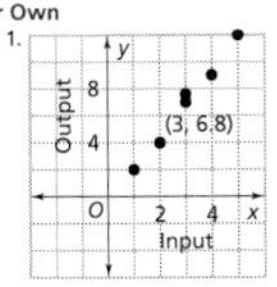

Table 2.

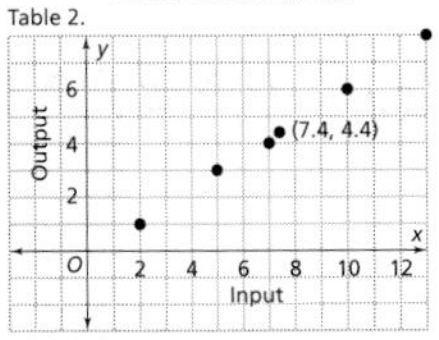

Table 3.

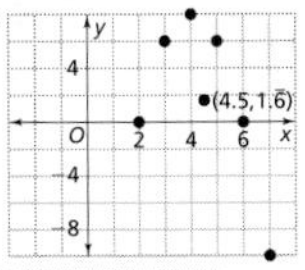

Table 4.

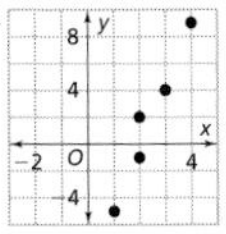

Tables 1, 2, and 4 show a linear trend.
7a. (3, 6.8) **9a.** 1.25 **10a.** 1.32

Lesson 1.9
Check Your Understanding
1. Table 1: $y = 4x - 7$; Table 2: $y = 4x - 19$; Table 3: $y = 12x - 5$; Table 4: $y = 12x - 29$
2. $y = 1.86x + 1.25$ **3a.** $y = 53.69x - 85.36$
b. quadratic: $y = 7.56x^2 - 14.35x + 28.04$; exponential: $y = 13.9 \cdot 1.55^x$; the quadratic has the smaller mean squared error.

On Your Own

5. Table 1

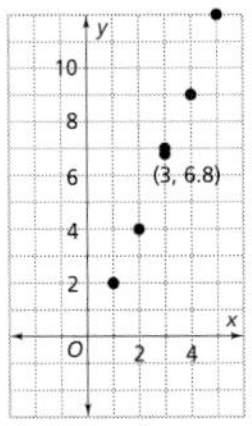

6. Table 1: (3, 6.8) **7.** Table 1: $y = 2.5x - 0.7$

Lesson 1.10
On Your Own

10.

n	$t(n)$
0	1
1	3
2	9
3	27
4	81
5	243
6	729
7	2187
8	6561
9	19,683
10	54,049

$t(n) = 3^n$; $t(103) \approx 1.39 \times 10^{49}$, $t(104) \approx 4.17 \times 10^{49}$, $t(245) \approx 7.8 \times 10^{116}$.

11.

n	$j(n)$
0	1
1	4
2	9
3	16
4	25
5	36
6	49
7	64
8	81
9	100
10	121

$j(n) = (n + 1)^2$; $j(103) = 10{,}816$, $j(104) = 11{,}025$, $j(245) = 60{,}516$.

13.

n	$d(n)$
0	1
1	1
2	2
3	6
4	24
5	120
6	720
7	5040
8	40,320
9	362,880
10	3,628,800

$d(n) = \begin{cases} 1 & \text{if } n = 0 \\ n \cdot d(n-1) & \text{if } n > 0 \end{cases}$

Lesson 1.11
Check Your Understanding
1. \$6390.74 **2.** no **3a.** \$269.74 **b.** \$250.51 **c.** \$207.26 **4.** \$8341.43 **5.** about 0.9%

On Your Own
7. Answers may vary. Sample: For cars that cost less than \$33,200, you would pay less over the life of the loan if you chose the rebate deal. For cars that cost more than \$33,200, you would pay less if you chose the low interest rate deal. The deals are the same if the car costs \$33,200.

Lesson 1.12
Check Your Understanding

1.

n	$g(n)$
2	2
3	3
4	4
5	5
6	6
7	7
8	8
9	9
10	10

$g(n) = n$

2.

n	$h(n)$
3	6
4	12
5	20
6	30
7	42
8	56
9	72
10	90

$h(n) = n(n - 1)$ **3.** $k(n) = \frac{n!}{(n-4)!}$
4. $q(n) = (n!)^2$ **5a.** 1 **b.** 2 **c.** 4

On Your Own

6a. 8 **7.** $f(n) = \begin{cases} 2 & \text{if } n = 1 \\ n \cdot f(n-1) & \text{if } n > 1 \end{cases}$

10a.

n	$r(n)$
1	1
2	3
3	6
4	10
5	15

b. $r(n) = \begin{cases} 1 & \text{if } n = 1 \\ r(n-1) + n & \text{if } n > 1 \end{cases}$

c. $r(n) = \frac{n(n+1)}{2}$

12a.

n	$t(n)$
1	3
2	15
3	105
4	945
5	10,395

b. $t(n) = \begin{cases} 2 & \text{if } n = 1 \\ t(n-1) \cdot (2n+1) & \text{if } n > 1 \end{cases}$

Chapter 2

Lesson 2.0
Check Your Understanding
1a. no **b.** no **c.** yes **d.** yes **e.** no **2a.** 2 **b.** 27
3. $g(n) = n^3$ **4a.** $x^3 + x^2 + x + 1$
b. $x^7 + x^6 + x^5 + x^4 + x^3 + x^2 + x + 1$
c. $x^{15} + x^{14} + \ldots + x^2 + x + 1$
d. $x^{31} + x^{30} + \ldots + x^2 + x + 1$ **5a.** 3, 4
b. −20, 4 **c.** 4, 6

On Your Own
6a. 0 **b.** $f(1) = 0$, so $(x - 1)$ is a factor of $f(x)$.
8a. $f(3) = 16$ **b.** $x^2 + 4x - 21$
11a. deg (fg) = deg (f) + deg (g)

Lesson 2.1
On Your Own
6a. no **7a.** Answers may vary. Sample: −3 and 3 **8b.** 5 **9b.**10

Lesson 2.2
Check Your Understanding
1a. all real numbers ≤ 1296

b.

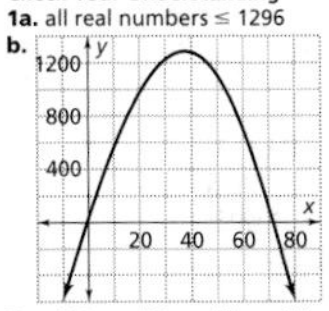

2a. $A(x) = x(72 - x)$ **b.** positive numbers less than 72 **c.** positive numbers less than or equal to 1296

d.

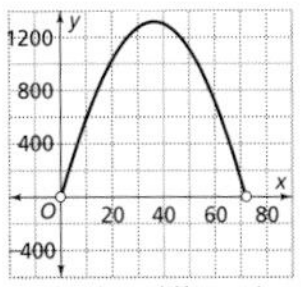

3. No; they have different domains and ranges.

4a.

Input	Output
0	3
1	8
2	13
3	18
4	23
5	28

b. H: all real numbers; K: all nonnegative integers **c.** No; they have different domains and ranges. **5a.** all nonnegative real numbers **b.** all nonnegative real numbers **6a.** domain is $\mathbb{R}^2$ and the target is $\mathbb{R}$ **b.** Answers may vary. Sample: (0, 4), (6, 0), (3, 2), or any solution of $b = \frac{12 - 2a}{3}$

c.

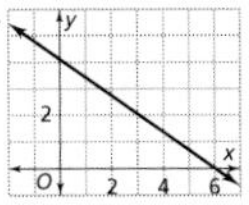

7a. $f(3) = 27$, $f(-3) = 27$ **b.** 2, −2 **c.** 63
d. $f(x + 1) = 3(x + 1)^2 = 3(x^2 + 2x + 1) = 3x^2 + 6x + 3$ **e.** $6x + 3$ **f.** 63 **8a.** 5 **b.** 5
c. 10 **d.** A **e.** $2x + 1$ **f.** $6x + 3$ **g.** $20x + 10$
h. $2x + 11$ **i.** $6x + 13$ **9a.** all real numbers ≤ 6

b.

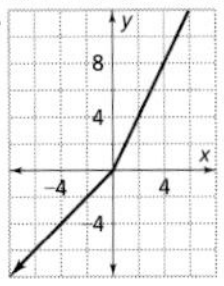

On Your Own
14a. domain: all real numbers; target: all real numbers; range: $f(x) \geq \frac{-49}{24}$ **b.** domain: $x \geq 3$; target: all real numbers; range: all nonnegative real numbers **15a.** 12
d. $z^2 - 4z - 6$ **16a.** $-\frac{1}{3}$ **17a.** 4096 **18b.** false

Lesson 2.3
Check Your Understanding
1a. 9 **b.** 16 **c.** 35 **d.** 35 **e.** 46 **f.** 144
2a. $g \circ f(x) = 10x + 16$ **b.** $f \circ g(x) = 10x + 5$
3a. $A = \pi r^2$ **b.** $A = 16\pi t^2$ **4a.** $f \circ g(x) =$ $f \circ g(x) = x^2 + 3$; $g \circ f(x) = x^2 + 3$
b. $f \circ g(x) = 2x - 7$; $g \circ f(x) = 2x - 7$
c. $f \circ g(x) = (x - 4)^3$; $g \circ f(x) = (x - 4)^3$
d. Sample: The function takes any input and produces that same value as the output.
5. $g(x) = \frac{x + 1}{3}$ **6.** $g(x) = \frac{x - 3}{2}$
7a. $g(x) = 2x^2 - 2$ **b.** $g(x) = \frac{4x^2 + 1}{2x + 5}$
8a. $f \circ g(x) = acx + ad + b$, $g \circ f(x) = acx + bc + d$ **b.** $ad + b = bc + d$ or $\frac{a}{c} = \frac{b - 1}{d - 1}$ **9.** $a = 2$, $b = 3$ or $a = -2$, $b = -9$

On Your Own
12c. $a^2 - 9a + 20$ **g.** 4 or 5 **13a.** x^2

Lesson 2.4
Check Your Understanding
1a. Yes; $f^{-1}(x) = x$ **b.** Yes; $g^{-1}(x) = \frac{1}{x}$ **c.** No; $h(x) = x^2$ is not one-to-one. **d.** Yes; $k^{-1}(x) = x$ **e.** No; $l(x) = x^3 - x$ is not one-to-one. **f.** Yes; $m^{-1}(x) = x^2$ with $x \geq 0$. **g.** No; $n(x) = |x|$ is not one-to-one. **2a.** (5, 1) **b.** Answers may vary. Sample: Reflect the graph over the line $y = x$. **c.** Answers may vary. Sample: Each graph represents a one-to-one function, and if you reflect either graph over the line $y = x$, you get the other graph. **3a.** $x \leq 6$

b.

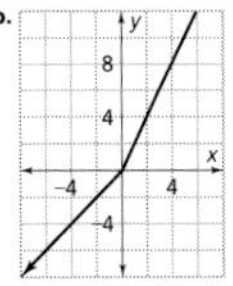

c. Answers may vary. Sample:
$f(x) = \begin{cases} x & \text{if } x < 0 \\ 2x & \text{if } x \geq 0 \end{cases}$ **d.** Answers may vary.

Sample: $f(x) = \begin{cases} x & \text{if } x < 0 \\ 2x & \text{if } 0 \leq x \leq 6 \\ -x & \text{if } x > 6 \end{cases}$

4a. Answers may vary. Sample: $x > 0$
b. $f^{-1}(x) = \sqrt{x}$ **5a.** the numbers 1, 5, 9, 13

b.

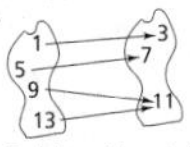

c. Each input is matched to a unique output. **d.** $t(x)$ does not have an inverse because it contains (9, 11) and (13, 11). To make it a function, change one of the output 11's to a number other than 3, 7, or 11. **6.** $f^{-1}(x) = \frac{x}{x - 1}$ **7.** Yes, $h = j^{-1}$. **8a.** $g \circ f(x) = 25x^2 - 85x + 30$ **b.** $5x^2 - 17x + 6$
c. The graphs are identical parabolas. **d.** The zeros of each are $\frac{2}{5}$ and 3. **9.** False; Answers may vary. Sample: See Exercise 6, in which $f(x) = f^{-1}(x) = \frac{x}{x - 1}$.

On Your Own
10. a and d **14a.** $m^{-1}(x) = \frac{x - 3}{5}$
16a. $g \circ f(x) = 125x^3 - 300x^2 - 275x + 150$

Lesson 2.5
On Your Own
10a. $A = 6$, $B = -2$, $C = 3$ **12a.** The $f(x)$ values are −5, −2, 1, 4, 7, 10, 13, and 16; the $g(x)$ values are 499, −2, −55, 4.7, −46, 13, 520. **13a.** Answers may vary. Sample: $g(x) = 5$ (or any polynomial function for which $g(2) = 5$).

Lesson 2.6
Check Your Understanding
1. $f(x) = 6x^2 - 22x + 28$
2. $f(x) = 9x - 7$ **3.** $f(x) = 4x^2 - 3x + 1$
4. $f(x) = x^3 + 3x^2 + 5x - 8$ **5a.** $A = 1$, $B = 21$, $C = 9$, $D = 1$ **b.** yes **6.** Answers may vary. Sample: As in Exercise 18 in Lesson 2.5, when $A = -3$, $B = 1$, and $C = 2$, the final coefficient of x^2 was 0 so the equation was linear. Whenever the coefficient of the leading term is 0, the degree will be smaller than expected.

On Your Own
10. greatest degree: 4; least degree: 0
11. Answers may vary. Sample:
$h(x) = (x - 1)(x - 2)(x - 3)(x - 4)$
$= x^4 - 10x^3 + 35x^2 - 50x + 24$

Lesson 2.7

Check Your Understanding

1. The graphs intersect at (1, 4), (2, 6), and (3, 8). **2.** $j(x) = 2x + 2 + T(x - 1)(x - 2)(x - 3)$ where T is a polynomial or a constant. **3a.** $f(x) = 2x - 1$; the next term is 7. **b.** Answers may vary. Sample: For the rule $g(x) = 2x - 1 + (x - 1)(x - 2)(x - 3)$, the next term $g(4)$ is 13. **c.** $g(x) = 2x - 1 + 2(x - 1)(x - 2)(x - 3)$ or $g(x) = 2x^3 - 12x^2 + 24x - 13$ **d.** $g(x) = 2x - 1 - (x - 1)(x - 2)(x - 3)$ or $g(x) = -x^3 + 6x^2 - 9x + 5$ **4a.** $f(4) = 8$ if $f(x) = 2x$ **b.** $f(4) = 10$ if $f(x) = 2x + \frac{1}{3}(x - 1)(x - 2)(x - 3)$ or $f(x) = \frac{x^3}{3} - 2x^2 + \frac{17}{3}x - 2$ **c.** $f(4) = 80$ if $f(x) = 2x + 12(x - 1)(x - 2)(x - 3)$ or $f(x) = 12x^3 - 72x^2 + 134x - 72$ **d.** $f(4) = 0$ if $f(x) = 2x + \frac{4}{3}(x - 1)(x - 2)(x - 3)$ or $f(x) = -\frac{4}{3}(x^3 + 8x^2 - \frac{38}{3}x + 8)$ **5a.** 3 points **b.** 6 points **c.** $(n + 1)$ points

On Your Own

8. Answers may vary. Sample: $p(x) = 4 - x^2 - 3x(x - 1)(x - 2)(x - 3)$ The graphs intersect at (0, 4), (1, 3), (2, 0), and (3, −5). **11a.** Yes; a sample is $f(x) = 3(x - 2)^2$.

Lesson 2.8

On Your Own

8a. 1 and −3 **9.** $x^3 - a^3$

Lesson 2.9

Check Your Understanding

1a. quotient: $x^2 - 3$; remainder: 0 **b.** 0 **2.** 3 **3.** −1 **4.** 0 **5a.** Answers may vary. Sample: 8 **b.** Answers may vary. Samples: 113 and 218, or any number of the form $8 + 105n$, where n is a nonnegative integer. **6a.** Answers may vary. Sample: $f(x) = 2x^2 - 3x + 7$ **b.** Answers may vary. Sample: any polynomial of the form $g(x) = 2x^2 - 3x + 7 + p(x)(x - 3)(x - 5)(x - 7)$, where $p(x)$ is a polynomial

On Your Own

8a. 26 **9a.** 11 **10a.** 8

Lesson 2.10

Check Your Understanding

1. By Corollary 2.4, a polynomial of degree 2 can have at most 2 real roots. **2a.** Checking 5 values, $P(0) = R(0) = -2$, $P(1) = R(1) = -2$, $P(-1) = R(-1) = -2$, $P(\sqrt{2}) = R(\sqrt{2}) = 0$, and $P(-\sqrt{2}) = R(-\sqrt{2}) = 0$. So $P(x) = R(x)$. **b.** Checking 3 values, $P(1) = R(1) = 0$, $P(0) = R(0) = 0$, $P(-1) = R(-1) = 0$, but $P(2) \neq R(2)$. So $P(x) \neq R(x)$. **c.** Checking three values, $P(-3) = R(-3) = -7$, $P(0) = R(0) = 2$, $P(-2) = R(-2) = -6$. So $P(x) = R(x)$. **3.** −5 **4.** $a = 7$, $b = 1$ **5.** −3, −1, 1, 2 **6.** Answers may vary. Sample: Checking 3 values, for $x = 1$ both sides are 2; for $x = 3$ both sides are 2, and for $x = 2$ both sides are −1. So the expressions are equivalent. **7.** Answers may vary. Sample: Checking 3 values, for $x = 1$ both sides are 20; for $x = 3$ both sides are 12; and for $x = 6$ both sides are 60. So the two expressions are equivalent. **8.** $P(x) = 1$

On Your Own

12a. $f(2) = 0$, so $(x - 2)$ is a factor of $f(x)$. **b.** $g(x) = \frac{f(x)}{x - 2} = 3x^3 - 6x^2 + x - 2$ and $g(2) = 0$, so $x - 2$ is a factor of $g(x)$.

Lesson 2.11

On Your Own

5a. $(x + 1)(x + 5)$ **d.** It doesn't factor; there are no rational numbers with sum 10 and product −20. **6a.** $x^3 - 1$ **7c.** $(x - 2)(x^2 + 2x + 4)$ **f.** $(2x + 1)(4x^2 - 2x + 1)$ **i.** $x(x^2 + 3x + 3)$

Lesson 2.12

Check Your Understanding

1a. $(3x + 7)(3x - 1)$ **b.** $(2x - 7)(3x - 5)$ **c.** $(3x - 1)(5x + 7)$ **d.** $(9x - 1)(x + 7)$ **e.** $-(9x + 1)(2x + 7)$ **f.** $-(9x + 1)(2x - 7)$ **g.** $(3x + 1)(3x - 1)(x^2 + 7)$ **h.** $(5 - 2x)(5 + 2x)$ **i.** $x(9x + 1)(2x - 7)$ **2a.** $(3x + 7y)(3x - y)$ **b.** $(2x - 7y)(3x - 5y)$ **c.** $(3x - a)(5x + 7a)$ **d.** $(9x - b)(x + 7b)$ **e.** $-(9x + a)(2x + 7a)$ **f.** $-(9x + y)(2x - 7y)$ **g.** $(5y + 2x)(5y - 2x)$ **h.** $x(9x + y)(2x - 7y)$

On Your Own

3d. $(2x + 5)(2x + 1)$ **e.** $(2x + 1)(2x - 1)(x^2 - 3)$ **5a.** $z^2 = 2$

Lesson 2.13

Check Your Understanding

1. Expand the left sides: $(x + y)^3 = (x + y)(x^2 + 2xy + y^2) = x^3 + 3x^2y + 3xy^2 + y^3$, and $(x - y)^3 = (x - y)(x^2 - 2xy + y^2) = x^3 - 3x^2y + 3xy^2 - y^3$ **2a.** $(x - 4)(x^2 + 4x + 16)$ **b.** $(x + 4)(x^2 - 4x + 16)$ **c.** $(3x - 4)(9x^2 + 12x + 16)$ **d.** $(3x - 4)(9x^2 - 12x + 16)$ **e.** $(x - 3)(x^2 - 2x + 21)$ **f.** $(2x + 1)(4x^2 - 20x + 37)$ **g.** $(x + 3)(x - 3)(x + 3)$ **h.** $(x + a)(x - a)(x + a)$ **i.** $(-2x - 1)(4x + 1)$ **j.** $(x - y + z)(x + y - z)$ **k.** $(x - 2)(x - 7)(x + 5)$ **l.** $(x - 2y)(x - 7y)(x + 5y)$

m. $(x + 1)(x^2 - x + 1)$ **3.** Multiply each term by 25 to get $125x^3 + 75x^2 + 75x - 50$; that can be rewritten as $(5x)^3 + 3(5x)^2 + 15(5x) - 50$, which can be factored as $25(5x - 2)(x^2 + x + 1)$. Divide by 25 to get $(5x - 2)(x^2 + x + 1)$.

On Your Own

4l. $(x - 2)(x^2 - x + 1)$ **5.** $(x - 4)(x^2 + 4x + 1)$

Lesson 2.14

Check Your Understanding

1a. $(x^2 + 2)(x^2 - 3)$ **b.** $(x - 1)(x^2 + x + 1)(x - 2)(x^2 + 2x + 4)$ **c.** $(x^2 + 4)(x + 2)(x - 2)$ **d.** $(x^2 - 2)(x^4 + 2x^2 + 4)$ **e.** $(x^2 + 4y^2)(x + 2y)(x - 2y)$ **f.** $(x^2 + 2)(x^4 - 2x^2 + 4)$ **g.** $(x^2 + x - 4)(x^2 - x - 4)$ **h.** $(x^2 + x + 1)(x^2 - x + 1)$ **2a.** $(x - 1 - \sqrt{5})(x - 1 + \sqrt{5})$ **b.** $\left(x - 0.5 - \frac{\sqrt{5}}{2}\right)\left(x - 0.5 + \frac{\sqrt{5}}{2}\right)$ **3a.** Answers may vary. Sample: $x^2 - 4x + 1$ **b.** Answers may vary. Sample: $x^2 - 4x + 1$ **c.** $x^4 - 10x^2 + 1 = 0$ **4.** yes; Sample: $x^2 - \frac{1}{4} = (x - \frac{1}{2})(x + \frac{1}{2})$

On Your Own

5e. $(x^2 - x + 5)(x^2 + x + 5)$ **6a.** 49 **c.** 81

Lesson 2.15

Check Your Understanding

1a. $\frac{3}{x}$ **b.** $x - y$ **c.** $\frac{x - y}{x + y}$ **d.** $\frac{1}{x^2 + 1}$ **e.** $\frac{2x - 3}{3x - 2}$ **f.** $\frac{(x + 1)(x^2 + 1)}{x^2 + x + 1}$ **2.** $f(x) = \frac{(2x - 3)(x + 2)}{(3x - 2)(x + 2)}$ and $g(x) = \frac{2x - 3}{3x - 2}$. The graph of $f(x)$ will have a "hole" at $f(-2)$, or (−2, 0.875), since $f(-2)$ is undefined. The graph of $g(x)$ will not have a hole, since $g(-2)$ is defined. **3a.** 1 **b.** $\frac{1}{(x - a)(x - b)}$ **4a.** $\frac{2x^2 - 10x + 1}{3(x - 1)(x - 4)}$ **b.** $\frac{-x^2 + 12x + 9}{x(x - 3)(x + 3)}$ **c.** 0 **5.** $A = -\frac{1}{2}$, $B = \frac{1}{2}$

On Your Own

6c. $x^3 + 1$ **7a.** $\frac{x^2 + 1}{x^2 - 1}$

Chapter 3

Lesson 3.1

On Your Own

9a. 102 **14c.** $\frac{3}{2}$ and $\frac{1}{2}$

Lesson 3.2

Check Your Understanding

1a. 4, 6 **b.** 10 **c–g.** no solution **h.** 1 **2a.** no additional solutions **b.** 0 **c.** −6, −4 **d–h.** no additional solutions **3a–c.** no additional solutions **d.** $\frac{1}{4}, \frac{1}{6}$ **e–h.** no additional solutions **4a–d.** no additional solutions **e.** $\sqrt{10}, -\sqrt{10}$ **f–h.** no additional solutions **5a–e.** no additional solutions **f.** $\sqrt{-10}, -\sqrt{-10}$ **g.** $\frac{-1 \pm \sqrt{-3}}{2}$ **h.** $\frac{-1 \pm \sqrt{-3}}{2}$ **6a.** 2 **b.** 1 **c.** 0 **d.** 2

7a.

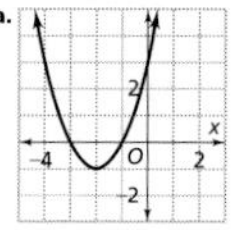

x-intercepts (−3, 0), (−1, 0), y-intercept (0, 3)

b.

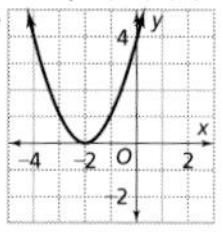

x-intercept (−2, 0), y-intercept (0, 4)

c.

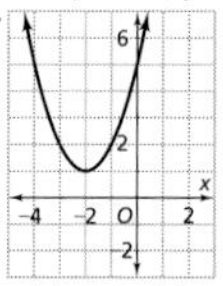

no x-intercept, y-intercept (0, 5)

d.

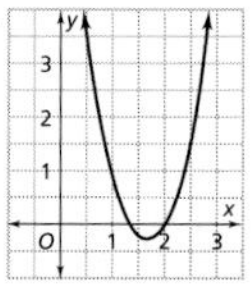

x-intercepts $(\frac{4}{3}, 0)$, (2, 0), y-intercept (0, 8)

8a. 0 **b.** If $f(x) = x^2 - 2x + 2$, then $f(1 + i) = 0$ (by Exercise 8a). **9a.** $a(0) = 2$, $a(1) = 0$, $a(2) = 6$, $a(3) = 0$, $a(4) = 18$, $a(5) = 0$, $a(6) = 54$ **b.** $a(10) = 486$, $a(101) = 0$ **c.** No; Answers may vary. Sample: $a(n) = 0$ for all odd values of n, and since there are an infinite number of odd positive integers, $a(n)$ cannot be a polynomial. **10a.** rational **b.** irrational **c.** irrational **d.** $f(0) = 2$, $f(1) = 2$, $f(2) = 6$, $f(3) = 14$, $f(4) = 34$, $f(5) = 82$, $f(6) = 198$ **e.** Answers may vary. Sample: $x^2 - 2x - 1 = 0$ **f.** Answers may vary. Sample: $2 \cdot f(n - 1) + f(n - 2)$

$$\begin{aligned} &= 2[(1 + \sqrt{2})^{n-1} + (1 - \sqrt{2})^{n-1}] \\ &\quad + (1 + \sqrt{2})^{n-2} + (1 - \sqrt{2})^{n-2} \\ &= 2(1 + \sqrt{2})^{n-1} + (1 + \sqrt{2})^{n-2} \\ &\quad + 2(1 - \sqrt{2})^{n-1} + (1 - \sqrt{2})^{n-2} \\ &= (1 + \sqrt{2})^{n-2}[2(1 + \sqrt{2}) + 1] \\ &\quad + (1 + \sqrt{2})^{n-2}[2(1 - \sqrt{2}) + 1] \\ &= (1 + \sqrt{2})^{n-2}[(3 + 2\sqrt{2})] + \\ &\quad (1 - \sqrt{2})^{n-2}[(3 - 2\sqrt{2})] \\ &= (1 + \sqrt{2})^{n-2}(1 + \sqrt{2})^2 \\ &\quad + (1 - \sqrt{2})^{n-2}(1 - \sqrt{2})^2 \\ &= (1 + \sqrt{2})^n + (1 - \sqrt{2})^n \\ &= f(n) \end{aligned}$$

11a. $g(0) = 2$, $g(1) = 4$, $g(2) = 6$, $g(3) = 4$, $g(4) = -14$, $g(5) = -76$, $g(6) = -234$ **b.** $(2 + \sqrt{-1})^2 = 4 + (-1) + 4\sqrt{-1} = 3 + 4\sqrt{-1}$ **c.** Answers may vary. Sample: $x^2 - 4x + 5 = 0$ **d.** $4g(n - 1) - 5g(n - 2)$

$$\begin{aligned} &= 4(2 + \sqrt{-1})^{n-1} + 4(2 - \sqrt{-1})^{n-1} \\ &\quad - 5(2 + \sqrt{-1})^{n-2} - 5(2 - \sqrt{-1})^{n-2} \\ &= (2 + \sqrt{-1})^{n-2}[4(2 + \sqrt{-1}) - 5] \\ &\quad + (2 - \sqrt{-1})^{n-2}[4(2 - \sqrt{-1}) - 5] \\ &= (2 + \sqrt{-1})^{n-2}(8 + 4\sqrt{-1} - 5) \\ &\quad + (2 - \sqrt{-1})^{n-2}(8 - 4\sqrt{-1} - 5) \\ &= (2 + \sqrt{-1})^{n-2}(3 + 4\sqrt{-1}) \\ &\quad + (2 - \sqrt{-1})^{n-2}(3 - 4\sqrt{-1}) \\ &= (2 + \sqrt{-1})^{n-2}(2 + \sqrt{-1})^2 \\ &\quad + (2 - \sqrt{-1})^{n-2}(2 - \sqrt{-1})^2 \\ &= (2 + \sqrt{-1})^n + (2 - \sqrt{-1})^n \\ &= g(n) \end{aligned}$$

On Your Own

12. Answers may vary. Samples are given. **a.** $(-10) - (-20) = 10$, $(-10)(-20) = 200$ **b.** $\frac{5}{4} \cdot \frac{4}{5} = 1$, $\frac{5}{4} + \frac{3}{4} = 2$ **d.** $(1 + \sqrt{-2}) + (1 - \sqrt{-2}) = 2$, $\sqrt{-1} \cdot \sqrt{-1} = -1$ **15c.** The sum is 2, and the product is −2.

Lesson 3.3

Check Your Understanding

1a. $a^2 - b^2$ **b.** $a^2 - 2b^2$ **c.** $a^2 - 3b^2$ **d.** $a^2 - cb^2$ **e.** $a^2 + b^2$

2.

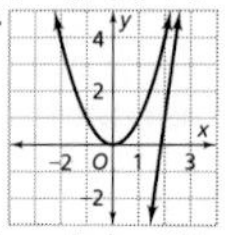

The graphs do not intersect. **3a.** $3 \pm \sqrt{-2}$ **b.** The sum is 6, and the product is 11. **4.** Yes; Answers may vary. Sample: The Quadratic Formula gives the solutions to any quadratic equation. **5.** $\sqrt{34} = 5.83$ and $-\sqrt{34} = -5.83$ **6.** No; 0 is nonnegative and has only one number whose square is 0. **7.** Answers may vary. Sample: $x^3 - 5x^2 + 8x - 6 = (x - 3)(x^2 - 2x + 2) = 0$, and the solutions to $x^2 - 2x + 2 = 0$ are $1 + \sqrt{-1}$ and $1 - \sqrt{-1}$. **8a.** 5 **b.** 8 **c.** 6

On Your Own

9a. −6 **e.** $-3 + 2\sqrt{-3}$ **11b.** $7 + 9\sqrt{-1}$ **c.** $23 + 15\sqrt{-1}$ **13a.** $x^3 - 8 = (x - 2)(x^2 + 2x + 4)$

Lesson 3.4

Check Your Understanding

1a. $12 + i$ **b.** $25 + 21i$ **c.** $10 + 0i$ **d.** $29 + 0i$ **e.** $6 + 6i$ **f.** $0 + 20i$ **2a.** 6 **b.** 34 **c.** −14 **d.** 53 **e.** 24 **f.** 169 **3a.** $(a - bi)$ **b.** $(a + bi) + (a - bi) = a + a + (b - b)i = 2a$, and if a is real, $2a$ is also real. **c.** $(a + bi)(a - bi) = a^2 - b^2i^2 + abi - abi = a^2 + b^2$, and if a and b are real, $a^2 + b^2$ is also real. **d.** when $a = 0$ in $a + bi$ and $a - bi$ **e.** when $a = 0$ and $b = 0$ **4.** No; Derman is wrong because a and b must be real numbers in $a + bi$. **5.** $4 - 7i$ **6a.** Yes; the opposite of $2 + 3i$ is $-2 - 3i$. **b.** All complex numbers have opposites. **7.** If $z = a + bi$, then $z^2 + \overline{z}^2 = (a + bi)^2 + (a - bi)^2 = (a^2 + 2abi - b^2) + (a^2 - 2abi - b^2) = 2a^2 - 2b^2$, which is a real number. **8a.** $x^2 - 6x + 13 = 0$ **b.** $x^2 - 6x + 13 = 0$ **c.** $(x^2 - 6x + 13)(x^2 - 2x + 26) = 0$ **d.** $(x^2 - 2x + 26)(x^2 + 2x + 26) = 0$ **e.** $x^2 - 2x + 4 = 0$ **f.** $x - (\sqrt{2} + \sqrt{3}) = 0$, or $x^4 - 10x^2 + 1 = 0$ **g.** $x^2 - (2\sqrt{2})x + 5 = 0$

On Your Own

10a. $-i$ **b.** 1 **11a.** $3 + 3i$ **d.** $3 \pm 5i$ **13.** Answers may vary. Samples are given. **a.** $1 + i$ **14a.** $(x + i)(x - i) = x^2 - i^2 + xi - xi = x^2 - (-1) = x^2 + 1$

Lesson 3.5

Check Your Understanding

1. $z + \overline{z}$ is a real number. **2a.** $-2i$ **b.** 7 **c.** $\overline{z + w} = \overline{7 + 2i} = 7 - 2i$, and $\overline{z} + \overline{w} = -2i + 7 = 7 - 2i$, so they are equal. **3a.** $\overline{z} = a - bi$, and $\overline{w} = c - di$ **b.** $\overline{z + w} = \overline{(a + c) + (b + d)i} = (a + c) - (b + d)i$; $\overline{z} + \overline{w} = (a - bi) + (c - di) = (a + c) - (b + d)i$ **4a.** $3 - 2i$ **b.** $3 + 2i$ **c.** $7 + 3i$ **d.** $7 + 3i$ **e.** $22 + 7i$ **f.** $22 + 7i$ **g.** 6 **h.** 41 **5a.** $4 - 7i$ **b.** $\frac{7}{5} + \frac{6}{5}i$ **c.** $4 + 0i$ **d.** $\frac{4}{5} + \frac{3}{5}i$ **e.** $\frac{4}{5} - \frac{3}{5}i$ **f.** $\frac{ac + bd}{a^2 + b^2} + \frac{ad - bc}{a^2 + b^2}i$ **6a.** $-9 + 38i$ **b.** $-9 - 38i$ **c.** $37 + 50i$ **d.** $37 - 50i$ **e.** $1 + 76i$ **f.** $1 - 76i$ **7.** If $z = a + bi$ and $w = c + di$, then $\overline{zw} = \overline{(ac - bd) + (ad + bc)i} = (ac - bd) - (ad + bc)i$, and $(\overline{z})(\overline{w}) = (a - bi)(c - di) = (ac - bd) + (-ad - bc)i = (ac - bd) - (ad + bc)i$. **8a.** $z + \overline{z} = (a + bi) + (a - bi) = 2a$ **b.** $z\overline{z} = (a + bi)(a - bi) = a^2 - b^2i^2 + (ab - ab)i = a^2 + b^2$ **9a.** $a = 7$, $b = 5$ or $a = 7$, $b = -5$ **b.** $7 + 5i$, $7 - 5i$

On Your Own

10a. $\frac{1}{2} - \frac{1}{2}i$ **12a.** −1 **g.** $9 - 40i$ **16a.** $(a + bi)^2 = a^2 + abi + abi + b^2i^2 = (a^2 - b^2) + (2ab)i$

Lesson 3.6

On Your Own

7a. $\sqrt{17}$ **8a.** 17 **d.** 85 **9a.** 14.04° **10a.** $4\sqrt{2}$ **d.** $2\sqrt{2}$ **11a.** $A(8, 0)$, $B(8, 8)$

Lesson 3.7

Check Your Understanding

1a–d.

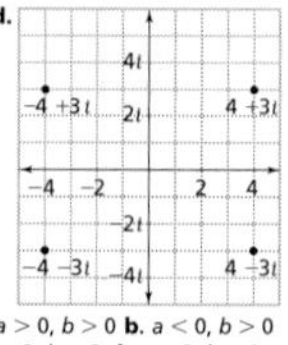

2a. $a > 0, b > 0$ **b.** $a < 0, b > 0$ **c.** $a < 0, b < 0$ **d.** $a > 0, b < 0$

3a.

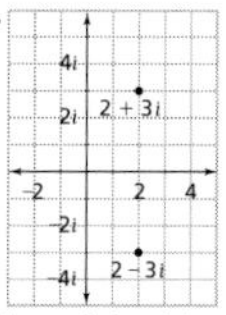

b. The sum is 4, and the product is 13.

4a.

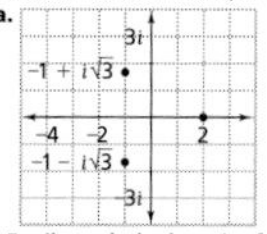

b. Equilateral; the length of each side of the triangle is 2. **c.** The sum is 0, and the product is 8. **5.** Answers may vary. Sample: $1 + i$, $1 - i$, $-1 - i$, $-1 + i$

6a–f.

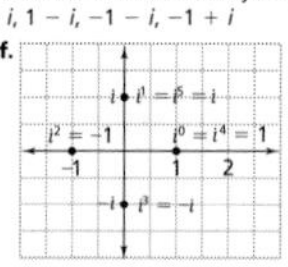

On Your Own

8a–d.

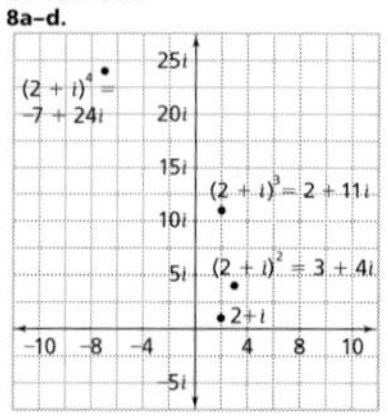

9a.

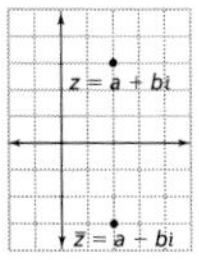

b.

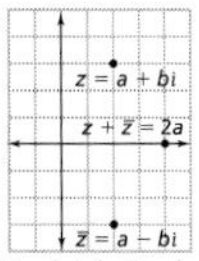

10c. $-3 + i$, $-3 - i$

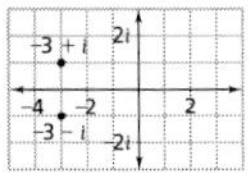

11a. $\pm i$, ± 1

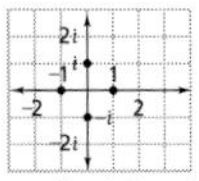

13a. $w = 2 - i$, $2w = 4 - 2i$, $3w = 6 - 3i$

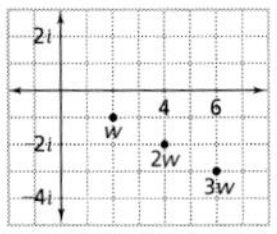

Lesson 3.8

Check Your Understanding

1a.

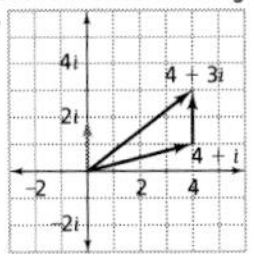

b.

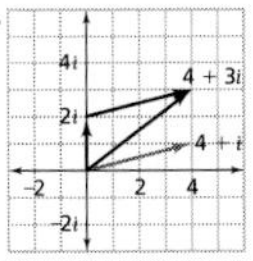

c.

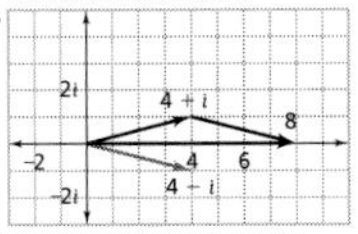

d.

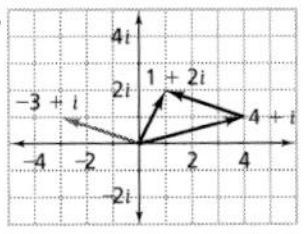

e.

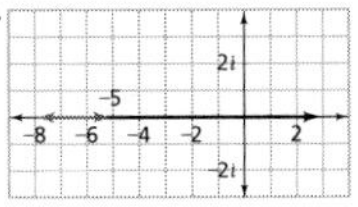

2a.

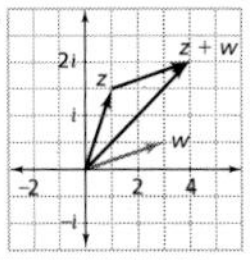

b.

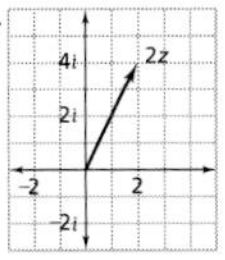

c.

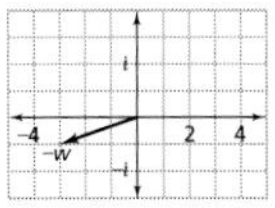

d.

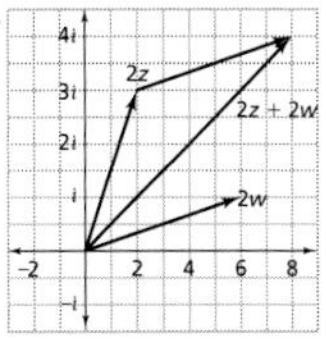

e.

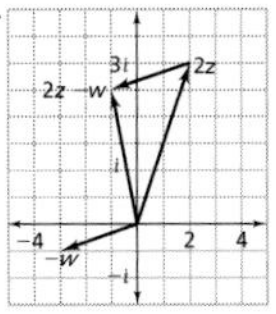

f.

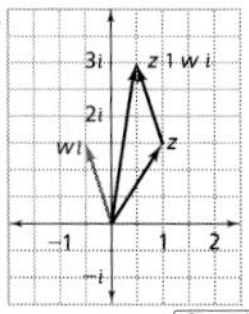

3. $z = a + bi$ is $\sqrt{a^2 + b^2}$ units from the origin, and $iz = -b + ai$ is $\sqrt{b^2 + a^2}$ units from the origin. The distances are equal.

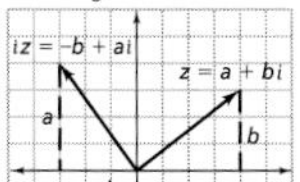

4a. $\sqrt{17}$ b. $\sqrt{5}$ c. $\sqrt{13}$ d. $\sqrt{61}$ 5a. 17 b. 5 c. 13 d. 61

6a. 65, 17, 80 b. rotated 180°

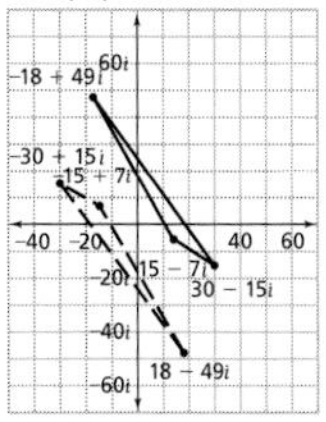

c. rotated 90°

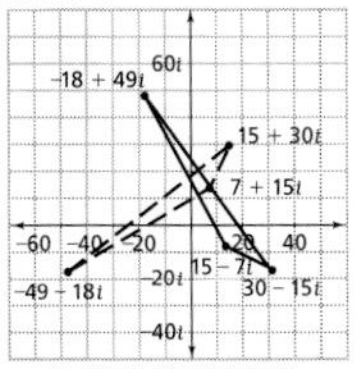

7a.

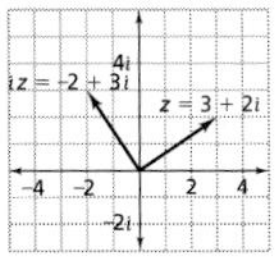

b.

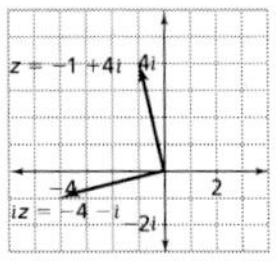

c.

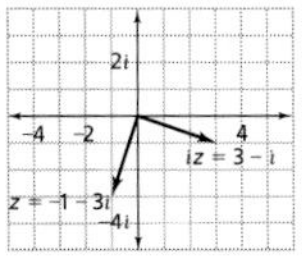

d.

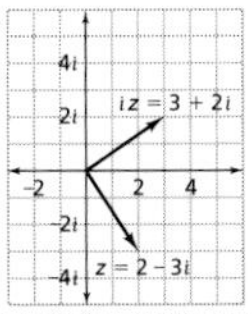

8a. a rotation of 180° about the origin

b. a rotation of 270° counterclockwise about the origin 9. Answers may vary. Samples are given. a. Points; the vertices of a square are points.

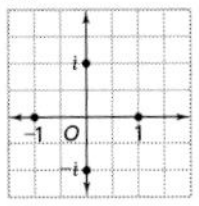

b. Vectors; you use vectors to illustrate the parallelogram law.

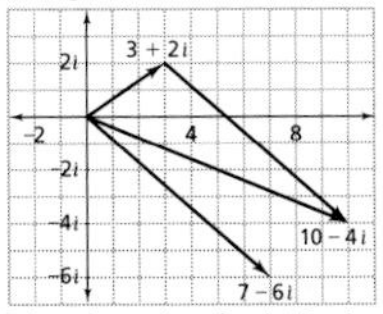

c. Points; the vertices of each triangle are points.

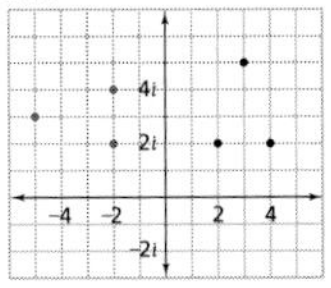

d. Vectors; distances can be represented by vectors.

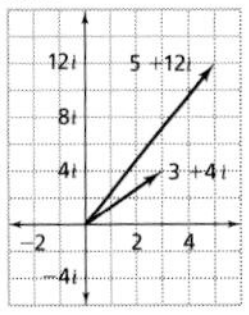

On Your Own

10.

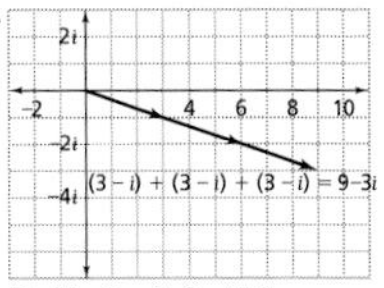

13. $5 + 3i$, $-6 - 4i$, $2 - 7i$, 8

15a. $(1 + i)z = \sqrt{2}i$

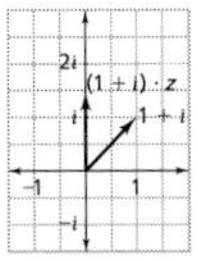

Lesson 3.9

Check Your Understanding

1a. 5, 37° b. 5, 323° c. 5, 143° d. 5, 217°

2a. $|w| = 2\sqrt{2}$, arg $w = 45°$ b. $|w| = 2\sqrt{2}$, arg $w = 315°$ c. $|w| = 2\sqrt{2}$, arg $w = 135°$ d. $|w| = 2\sqrt{2}$, arg $w = 225°$ 3. Answers may vary. Samples are given. a. 40° b. 140° c. 320° d. 220° 4. The magnitude is doubled, and the direction stays the same. 5. The property holds for complex numbers. 6a. $|z| = 2$; arg $z = 90°$ $|z^2| = 4$; arg $z^2 = 180°$ b. $|z| = \sqrt{2}$; arg $z = 135°$ $|z^2| = 2$; arg $z^2 = 270°$ c. $|z| = \sqrt{17}$; arg $z \approx 14°$ $|z^2| = 17$; arg $z^2 \approx 28°$ d. $|z| = \sqrt{17}$; arg $z \approx 166°$ $|z^2| = 17$; arg $z^2 \approx 332°$

7a. $\frac{1}{z} = \frac{1}{2} - \frac{1}{2}i$

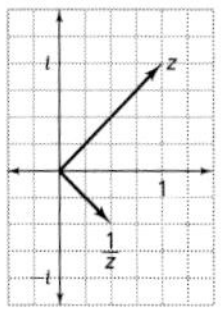

b. $\frac{1}{z} = \frac{2}{5} - \frac{1}{5}i$

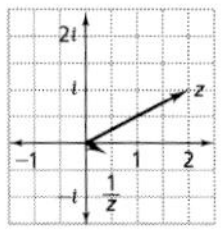

c. $\frac{1}{z} = \frac{1}{4} - \frac{\sqrt{3}}{4}i$

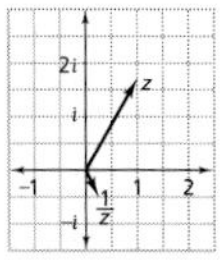

d. $\frac{1}{z} = -\frac{1}{2} + \frac{1}{2}i$

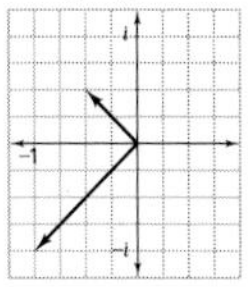

8a. $|z| = \sqrt{2}$, arg $z = 45°$; $\left|\frac{1}{z}\right| = \frac{\sqrt{2}}{2}$, arg $\frac{1}{z}$ $= 315°$ b. $|z| = \sqrt{5}$, arg $z = 27°$; $\left|\frac{1}{z}\right| = \frac{\sqrt{5}}{5}$,

arg $\frac{1}{z}$ = 333° **c.** $|z| = 2$, arg $z = 60°$; $\left|\frac{1}{z}\right| = \frac{1}{2}$, arg $\frac{1}{z} = 300°$ **d.** $|z| = \sqrt{2}$, arg $z = 225°$; $\left|\frac{1}{z}\right| = \frac{\sqrt{2}}{2}$, arg $\frac{1}{z} = 135°$
9a. $5\left(\frac{4}{5} + \frac{3}{5}i\right)$ **b.** $13\left(\frac{5}{13} + \frac{12}{13}i\right)$ **c.** $\sqrt{2}\left(\frac{\sqrt{2}}{2} + \frac{\sqrt{2}}{2}i\right)$ **d.** $\sqrt{2}\left(\frac{\sqrt{2}}{2} - \frac{\sqrt{2}}{2}i\right)$ **e.** $\sqrt{13}\left(\frac{2\sqrt{13}}{13} + \frac{3\sqrt{13}}{13}i\right)$ **f.** $2\left(-\frac{1}{2} + \frac{\sqrt{3}}{2}i\right)$
10. For $z = a + bi$ with $|z| = k$, rewrite z as $z = k\left(\frac{a}{k} + \frac{b}{k}i\right)$. Then k is a positive real number and the magnitude of $\frac{a}{k} + \frac{b}{k}i$ is $\sqrt{\frac{a^2}{k^2} + \frac{b^2}{k^2}} = \sqrt{\frac{a^2 + b^2}{k^2}} = \sqrt{\frac{k^2}{k^2}} = 1$.

On Your Own
12c. 2, 240°
14a–b.

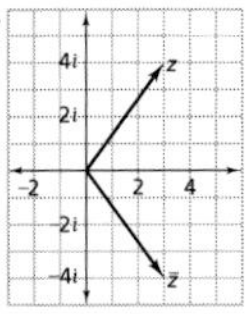

16a. 0° **b.** 26.565° **17a.** $|z| = \sqrt{5}$, $|w| = \sqrt{10}$, $|zw| = 5\sqrt{2}$

Lesson 3.10
On Your Own
8.

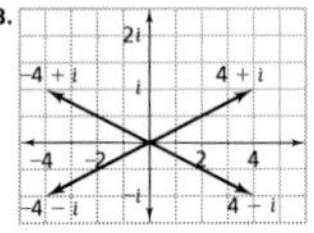

a. 14° **9a.** 30° **10b.** $-1 - 5i$ **d.** $-5 + 12i$

Lesson 3.11
Check Your Understanding
1a. magnitude 9, direction 240° **b.** magnitude 27, direction 0° **c.** $x^2 + 3x + 9 = 0$
2. Answers may vary. Sample: For z^2, square the magnitude and double the direction. For z^3, cube the magnitude and triple the direction. For z^n raise the magnitude to the nth power and multiply the direction by n.
3. options b, c, or d
4.

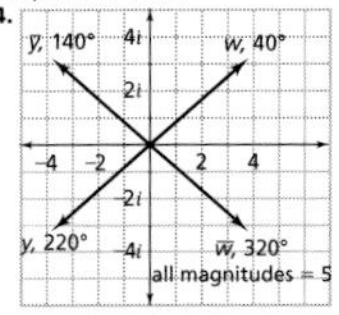

5a. magnitude $5\sqrt{2}$, direction 355° **b.** magnitude $5\sqrt{2}$, direction 355° **c.** $yz = (-w)(-x) = wx$ **6.** Answers may vary. Sample: The magnitude is about (3.5)(4.5) = 16, and the direction is about 50° + 110° = 160° **7.** The magnitude of the product is the product of the magnitudes. The direction of the product is the sum of the directions, but subtract 360° if necessary to express the angle between 0° and 360°.
8a.

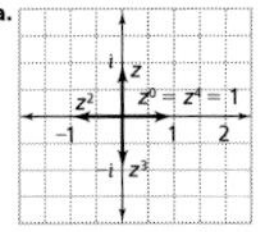

Consecutive powers of i rotate 90° counterclockwise; if you raise $z = i$ to the nth power, you multiply the direction, 90°, by n, and there is no change to the magnitude. So consecutive powers of i rotate 90° counterclockwise.
b.

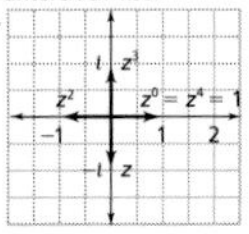

Consecutive powers of $-i$ rotate 90° clockwise; if you raise $z = -i$ to the nth power, you multiply the direction, 270°, by n, and there is no change to the magnitude. So consecutive powers of $-i$ rotate 270°

counterclockwise, which is equivalent to rotating by 90° clockwise.
c.

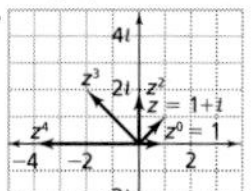

Consecutive powers of $1 + i$ rotate 45° counterclockwise, with the magnitudes increasing by a factor of $\sqrt{2}$; if you raise $z = 1 + i$ to the nth power, you multiply the direction, 45°, by n, and you raise the magnitude, $\sqrt{2}$, to the nth power. So consecutive powers of $1 + i$ rotate 45° counterclockwise, and increase the magnitude by a factor of $\sqrt{2}$.
d.

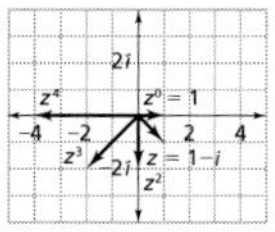

The powers of $1 - i$ rotate 45° clockwise, with the magnitudes increasing by a factor of $\sqrt{2}$; if you raise $z = 1 - i$ to the nth power, you multiply the direction, 315°, by n, and you raise the magnitude, $\sqrt{2}$, to the nth power. So consecutive powers of $1 - i$ rotate 315° counterclockwise (which is equivalent to rotating by 45° clockwise), and increase the magnitude by a factor of $\sqrt{2}$.
e.

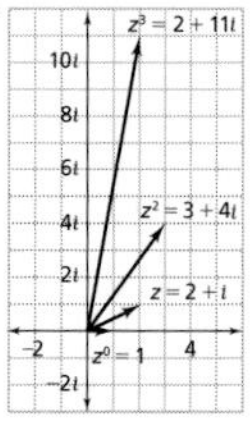

The powers of $2 + i$ rotate about 26.6° counterclockwise, with the magnitudes increasing by a factor of $\sqrt{5}$; if you raise $z = 2 + i$ to the nth power, you multiply the direction, 26.6°, by n, and you raise the magnitude, $\sqrt{5}$, to the nth power. So consecutive powers of $2 + i$ rotate 26.6° counterclockwise, and increase the magnitude by a factor of $\sqrt{5}$.
f.

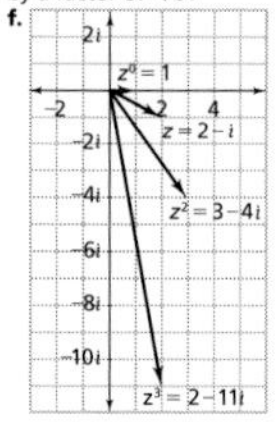

The powers of $2 - i$ rotate about 26.6° clockwise, with the magnitudes increasing by a factor of $\sqrt{5}$; if you raise $z = 2 - i$ to the nth power, you multiply the direction, 333.4°, by n and you raise the magnitude, $\sqrt{5}$, to the nth power. So consecutive powers of $2 - i$ rotate 333.4° counterclockwise (which is equivalent to rotating by 26.6° clockwise), and increase the magnitude by a factor of $\sqrt{5}$.

On Your Own
9. a, c, d, and e must have magnitude 1.
10a.

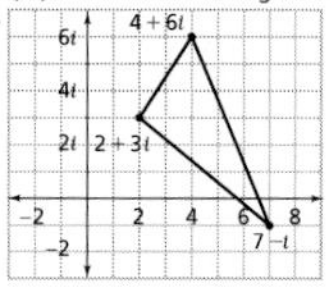

b.

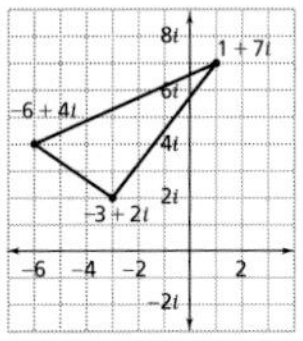

11a. Answers may vary. Sample: $1 + i$, $5 + 5i$
13a. Answers may vary. Sample:

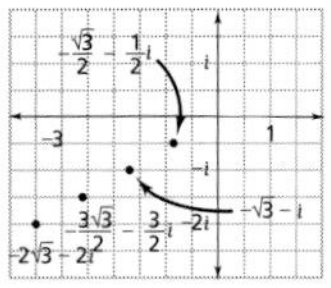

16a. $\frac{7}{5} + \frac{1}{5}i$

Lesson 3.12
Check Your Understanding
1a. $x = -2$ **b.** $x = 1 \pm 3i$ **2.** $x^2 - 8x + 17 = 0$ **3.** $x^3 - 15x^2 + 73x - 119 = 0$ **4a.** $g(-1 + 2i) = (-1 + 2i)^3 - 4(-1 + 2i)^2 - 7(-1 + 2i) - 30 = (11 - 2i) - (-12 - 16i) - (-7 + 14i) - 30 = 0$ So $(-1 + 2i)$ is a root of $g(x)$. **b.** $-1 - 2i$, 6
5a. $f(3 + i) = (3 + i)^2 - (8 + 6i) = (8 + 6i) - (8 + 6i) = 0$, so $3 + i$ is a solution. **b.** No; The equation does not have real coefficients, which is a requirement for the conjugate to be a root. When you test $x = 3 - i$, it does not make the equation true. **6.** All the complex roots come in pairs, $a + bi$ and $a - bi$, and the product of each pair of complex roots is $a^2 + b^2$, which is positive. Since the product of all the roots is the product of the complex roots and the real roots, then that product is positive if and only if the product of the real roots is positive.

On Your Own
7a. $|z| = \sqrt{26}$, arg $z = 11.3°$; $|w| = \sqrt{13}$, arg $w = 56.3°$ **10a.** 0 **c.** $1 - 3i$ **13a.** Answers may vary. Sample: $x^3 + 37x + 212 = 0$ **14a.** 0 **b.** 0

Lesson 3.13
Check Your Understanding
1a. $(w^2)^n = w^{2n} = (w^n)^2 = 1^2 = 1$
b. $(w^k)^n = w^{nk} = (w^n)^k = 1^k = 1$
2.

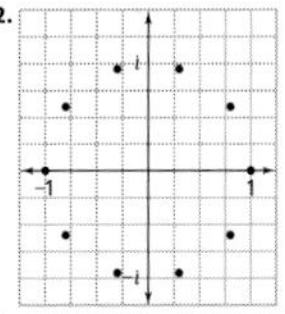

3a.

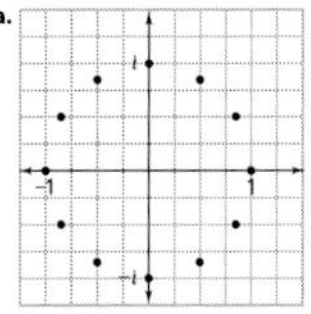

b. Yes; Answers may vary. Sample: the magnitude of $-\frac{1}{2} - \frac{\sqrt{3}}{2}i$ is $\sqrt{\frac{1}{4} + \frac{3}{4}} = 1$ and the direction is 240°, and that is one of the solutions shown in part (a).
4a.

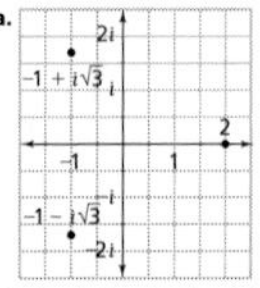

b. Each solution to $x^3 = 8$ is doubled in magnitude. **5.** $\frac{\sqrt{2}}{2} + \frac{\sqrt{2}}{2}i$, $-\frac{\sqrt{2}}{2} - \frac{\sqrt{2}}{2}i$
6a. Answers may vary. Sample: $\frac{\sqrt{3}}{2} + \frac{1}{2}i$

b. $-i$, $\frac{\sqrt{3}}{2} + \frac{1}{2}i$, $\frac{\sqrt{3}}{2} - \frac{1}{2}i$

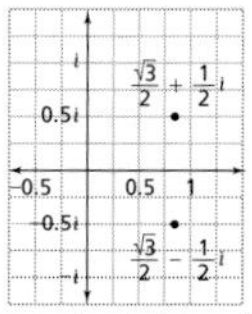

c. Rotate the solutions to $x^3 = 1$ 30° counterclockwise to get the solutions to $x^3 = i$. **7.** 0 **8.** Yes; complex roots of polynomials come in conjugate pairs.
9a.

Equation	Number of New Roots
$x = 1$	1
$x^2 = 1$	1
$x^3 = 1$	2
$x^4 = 1$	2
$x^5 = 1$	4
$x^6 = 1$	2
$x^7 = 1$	6
$x^8 = 1$	4
$x^9 = 1$	6
$x^{10} = 1$	4

b. Answers may vary. Sample: Beginning with $x^3 = 1$, the number of new roots is even.

On Your Own
11. 18 sides **12a.** $|z| = 1$, arg $z = 60°$ **13a.** The magnitudes are 1, and the directions are 0°, 45°, 90°, 135°, 180°, 225°, 270°, and 315°.

Chapter 4
Lesson 4.1
On Your Own
7. $x = \frac{16}{5}$, $y = -\frac{9}{5}$ **9.** $p(1) = 4$ so $a + b = 4$; $p(3) = 2$ so $3a + b = 2$; $a = -1$ and $b = 5$ so $p(x) = -x + 5$. **12a.** The two equations represent the same line, so any point on $x + 2y = 3$ is a solution to the system. **b.** The two equations represent parallel lines, so the system has no solution.

Lesson 4.2
Check Your Understanding
1. (2, 1, −1) **2.** (2, 1, −1) **3.** (2, 1, −1)
4. (2, 1, −1) **5.** $a = \frac{1}{2}$, $b = \frac{1}{2}$, $c = 0$.

On Your Own
8. (−4, 1, −1, 2) **9.** The system has no solution.

Lesson 4.3
Check Your Understanding
1a. $x - y + 2z = 5$, $2x - 3y + z = 3$, $x + 7z = 16$
b. $\left(\begin{array}{ccc|c} 1 & 0 & 0 & 2 \\ 0 & 1 & 0 & 1 \\ 0 & 0 & 1 & 2 \end{array}\right)$ or $(x, y, z) = (2, 1, 2)$
2. $\left(\begin{array}{ccc|c} 1 & 0 & 0 & -\frac{1}{2} \\ 0 & 1 & 0 & \frac{1}{2} \\ 0 & 0 & 1 & 1 \end{array}\right)$
3. Yes, $\left(\begin{array}{ccc|c} 1 & 0 & 0 & 1 \\ 0 & 1 & 0 & -1 \\ 0 & 0 & 1 & 2 \end{array}\right)$ represents the same solution.
4. $\left(\begin{array}{ccc|c} 1 & 0 & 0 & 1 \\ 0 & 1 & 0 & -1 \\ 0 & 0 & 1 & 2 \end{array}\right) \xrightarrow[(1)+(3)]{(1)+(2)} \left(\begin{array}{ccc|c} 1 & 1 & 1 & 2 \\ 0 & 1 & 0 & -1 \\ 0 & 0 & 1 & 2 \end{array}\right) \xrightarrow{(2)+2(3)} \left(\begin{array}{ccc|c} 1 & 1 & 1 & 2 \\ 0 & 1 & 2 & 3 \\ 0 & 0 & 1 & 2 \end{array}\right)$; then reverse the steps shown in the middle of page 517 to get $A = \left(\begin{array}{ccc|c} 1 & 1 & 1 & 2 \\ 2 & -1 & 1 & 5 \\ 1 & 2 & 3 & 5 \end{array}\right)$.
5. Answers may vary. Sample: Adding a positive multiple is the same as subtracting the same multiple with the opposite sign(s).
6. $\left(\begin{array}{cc|c} 1 & 0 & 1 \\ 0 & 1 & -2 \end{array}\right)$
7. $a = -\frac{7}{2}$, $b = \frac{8}{3}$ **8a.** Each equation in the system is a line in the xy-plane, and the intersection of the lines is the solution to the system. **b.** The solution represents m lines in the xy-plane; if the lines have point(s) in common, that point or points is the solution to the system. **c.** Each equation represents a plane in 3-space; the common intersection of

the m planes (if it exists) is the solution to the system.

On Your Own

12. $f(x) = 2x - 2$ **13.** $(2, 0, 4)$
15. $x + 2y + 2z = 3$, $x - \frac{1}{2}y - \frac{1}{2}z = 1$, $x + \frac{1}{3}y + \frac{1}{6}z = 1$ **19.** 4 in. by 6 in. by 8 in.

Lesson 4.4

On Your Own

7.

	A	B	C	D	E
EUR	0.6	0.25	0.3	0.3	1.3
US	4.6	3.3	1.4	2.2	0.4
ASIA	0.3	0.15	1.3	4.5	0.1

8a.

	A	B	C	D	E
EUR	1	0.5	0	1	6
US	2	−0.5	2	3	0
ASIA	−1	−0.5	8	11	−1

b.

A	B	C	D	E
2	−0.5	10	15	5

c.

EUR	8.5
US	6.5
ASIA	16.5

10. 1239 mi

Lesson 4.5

Check Your Understanding

1a. 2×3 **b.** 2 **c.** 4 **d.** 6 **e.** There is no 3rd row.

2a. $\begin{pmatrix} 3 \\ 6 \\ 11 \\ 18 \end{pmatrix}$ **b.** $\begin{pmatrix} 3 & 5 & 9 & 17 \end{pmatrix}$ **3a.** $a_{ij} = i + j$
b. $b_{ij} = 2(i - 1) + j$ **c.** $c_{ij} = (i + j - 1)^i$
4a. $A + B = (c_{ij})$, where $c_{ij} = a_{ij} + b_{ij}$.
b. $A - B = (c_{ij})$, where $c_{ij} = a_{ij} - b_{ij}$.
c. $k \cdot A = (c_{ij})$, where $c_{ij} = k \cdot a_{ij}$.

5. $3 \cdot \begin{pmatrix} 6 \\ 8 \\ 10 \end{pmatrix} = \begin{pmatrix} 18 \\ 24 \\ 30 \end{pmatrix}$ or
$3 \cdot \begin{pmatrix} 6 & 8 & 10 \end{pmatrix} = \begin{pmatrix} 18 & 24 & 30 \end{pmatrix}$
6. $\begin{pmatrix} 271 & 282 & 233 \\ 365 & 362 & 340 \end{pmatrix}$ This is matrix addition.
7. The matrices cannot be added term-by-term; the teacher could change the percent information to point information, then find the means of the entries in the matrices.

On Your Own

9. $\begin{pmatrix} 1 & 2 & 3 & 4 \\ 1 & 4 & 9 & 16 \end{pmatrix}$ **10a.** $\begin{pmatrix} 1 & 0 & 0 & 0 \\ 0 & 1 & 0 & 0 \\ 0 & 0 & 1 & 0 \\ 0 & 0 & 0 & 1 \end{pmatrix}$

12. matrix addition

Lesson 4.6

Check Your Understanding

1. In Lesson 4.4, Exercises 5, 6, 10, and 11 were dot products. **2a.** 32 **b.** 32 **c.** 32 **d.** 32 **e.** 32
f. The dot product is not defined. **3a.** 25
b. $a^2 + b^2$ **c.** 29 **4a.** $(0, 0)$ **b.** $(0, 0)$ **c.** $(0, 0, 0, 0)$
5. For any n-tuple X, there is a unique n-tuple $Z = (0, 0, \dots, 0)$ such that $X + Z = X$.
6a. 0 **b.** Answers may vary. Sample: Rewrite the expression as $(1 + 0 - 1, 0 + 2 - 2, 1 + 1 - 2) \cdot (x, y, z) = (0, 0, 0) \cdot (x, y, z) = 0$.

7.
$$\begin{aligned}(A + B) \cdot (A + B) &= (A + B) \cdot A + (A + B) \cdot B \\ &= A \cdot A + B \cdot A + A \cdot B + B \cdot B \\ &= A \cdot A + A \cdot B + A \cdot B + B \cdot B \\ &= A \cdot A + 2A \cdot B + B \cdot B\end{aligned}$$

8.
$$\begin{aligned}(A + B) \cdot (A - B) &= A \cdot (A - B) + B \cdot (A - B) \\ &= A \cdot A - A \cdot B + B \cdot A - B \cdot B \\ &= A \cdot A - A \cdot B + A \cdot B - B \cdot B \\ &= A \cdot A - B \cdot B\end{aligned}$$

9. If X is the n-tuple $(x_1, x_2, \dots, x_n)$, then $(-1)X = (-1)(x_1, x_2, \dots, x_n) = (-x_1, -x_2, \dots, -x_n)$. Then $X + (-1)X = (0, 0, \dots, 0)$ so $-1(X) = -X$.
10. We know that $A \cdot (kB) = k(A \cdot B) = (kA) \cdot B$, so $A \cdot ((-1)B) = A \cdot (-B)$ by Exercise 9, and $A \cdot (-B) = -(A \cdot B) = (-A) \cdot B$.

On Your Own

13. No **14a.** 0 **b.** 0 **c.** 0 **d.** 0 The Zero Product Property, that if a product is zero then at least one of the factors is zero, does not hold for dot products. **18a.** $(-1, -2)$ **b.** $(-x, -y)$
c. $(-1, -2, 3, -\pi)$

Lesson 4.7

Check Your Understanding

1a. $\begin{pmatrix} a & b \\ c & d \end{pmatrix}$ **b.** $\begin{pmatrix} a & b \\ c & d \end{pmatrix}$ **c.** $\begin{pmatrix} 2a & -3b \\ 2c & -3d \end{pmatrix}$
d. $\begin{pmatrix} 2a & 2b \\ -3b & -3d \end{pmatrix}$

2a.

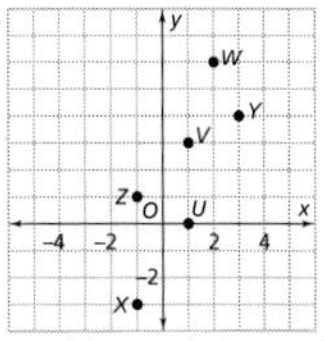

b. $AU = \begin{pmatrix} 1 \\ 0 \end{pmatrix}$, $AV = \begin{pmatrix} 1 \\ -3 \end{pmatrix}$, $AW = \begin{pmatrix} 2 \\ -6 \end{pmatrix}$,
$AX = \begin{pmatrix} -1 \\ 3 \end{pmatrix}$, $AY = \begin{pmatrix} 3 \\ -4 \end{pmatrix}$, $AZ = \begin{pmatrix} -1 \\ -1 \end{pmatrix}$

c.

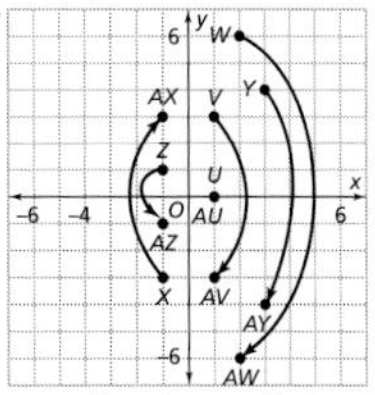

Corresponding points are reflections of each other over the x-axis.
d. $BU = \begin{pmatrix} 0 \\ 1 \end{pmatrix}$, $BV = \begin{pmatrix} -3 \\ 1 \end{pmatrix}$, $BW = \begin{pmatrix} -6 \\ 2 \end{pmatrix}$,
$BX = \begin{pmatrix} 3 \\ -1 \end{pmatrix}$, $BY = \begin{pmatrix} -4 \\ 3 \end{pmatrix}$, $BZ = \begin{pmatrix} -1 \\ -1 \end{pmatrix}$
Each point in part (d) is a rotation of the original point by 90° counterclockwise.
3a. $\begin{pmatrix} 2 \\ 5 \\ 3 \end{pmatrix}$ **b.** $\begin{pmatrix} 6 \\ 15 \\ 9 \end{pmatrix}$ **c.** $\begin{pmatrix} 5 & 3 & 1 \end{pmatrix}$ **d.** $\begin{pmatrix} -4 & -1 & 2 \end{pmatrix}$
e. $\begin{pmatrix} 0 & 0 \\ 0 & 0 \\ 0 & 0 \end{pmatrix}$ **f.** $\begin{pmatrix} 0 & 0 \\ 0 & 0 \\ 0 & 0 \end{pmatrix}$ **4a.** $p = x - y$, $q = 3x - 2y$ **b.** $2a + b = 3$, $4a + 3b = 5$, $6b = 7$
5a. $\begin{pmatrix} x \\ y \\ z \end{pmatrix} = \begin{pmatrix} 2 & -3 & 4 \\ -1 & 2 & \pi \\ 7 & -4 & -2 \end{pmatrix}\begin{pmatrix} u \\ v \\ w \end{pmatrix}$

b. $\begin{pmatrix} p \\ q \end{pmatrix} = \begin{pmatrix} 2 & 3 & -4 \\ 1 & -3 & 0 \end{pmatrix}\begin{pmatrix} x \\ y \\ z \end{pmatrix}$ **c.** $\begin{pmatrix} y_1 \\ y_2 \\ y_3 \end{pmatrix} = x\begin{pmatrix} 3 \\ -1 \\ 4 \end{pmatrix}$
6a. possible **b.** not possible **c.** possible **d.** not possible **e.** possible **f.** not possible **g.** possible **h.** not possible **7.** Answers may vary.
8a. Matrix B must have 3 rows. **b.** Matrix B must have 2 columns. **c.** Matrix B must have 3 rows and 2 columns. **9.** any square matrix
10. any square matrix
11. $z_1 = 8x_1 + x_2$, $z_2 = -6x_1 - 7x_2$
12. To add down the columns, you can multiply on the left by a 1×3 matrix of 1's. To add across columns, you can multiply on the right by a 5×1 matrix of 1's.
13a. $\begin{pmatrix} 5 & 10 \\ 1 & 1 \end{pmatrix}\begin{pmatrix} 200 & 150 & 50 \\ 100 & 100 & 85 \end{pmatrix} = \begin{pmatrix} 2000 & 1750 & 1100 \\ 300 & 250 & 135 \end{pmatrix}$
b. $\begin{pmatrix} 2000 & 1750 & 1100 \\ 300 & 250 & 135 \end{pmatrix}\begin{pmatrix} 1 \\ 1 \\ 1 \end{pmatrix} = \begin{pmatrix} 3850 \\ 685 \end{pmatrix}$
14. $BA = \begin{pmatrix} 2 & 1 & 3 \\ 3 & 4 & 2 \\ 2 & 2 & 1 \end{pmatrix}\begin{pmatrix} 0.3 & 0.5 \\ 0.3 & 0.2 \\ 0.3 & 0.3 \end{pmatrix} = \begin{pmatrix} 1.8 & 2.1 \\ 2.7 & 2.9 \\ 1.5 & 1.7 \end{pmatrix}$

On Your Own

15. $\begin{pmatrix} a & b & c \\ d & e & f \\ g & h & i \end{pmatrix}$, $\begin{pmatrix} a & b & c \\ d & e & f \\ g & h & i \end{pmatrix}$
19a. $AB + AC = \begin{pmatrix} 0 \\ 2 \end{pmatrix} + \begin{pmatrix} 11 \\ 25 \end{pmatrix} = \begin{pmatrix} 11 \\ 27 \end{pmatrix}$
b. $A(B + C) = \begin{pmatrix} 1 & 2 \\ 3 & 4 \end{pmatrix}\begin{pmatrix} 5 \\ 3 \end{pmatrix} = \begin{pmatrix} 11 \\ 27 \end{pmatrix}$
21a. $\begin{pmatrix} -3 & -26 \\ -7 & -58 \end{pmatrix}$ **b.** $\begin{pmatrix} -3 & -26 \\ -7 & -58 \end{pmatrix}$
25a. 29 g protein, 49.5 g fat, 260 g carbohydrates **b.** The problem (and solution) can be written as $\begin{pmatrix} 2 & 0.5 & 0.2 \\ 3 & 1 & 0.5 \\ 5 & 10 & 3 \end{pmatrix}\begin{pmatrix} 9 \\ 20 \\ 5 \end{pmatrix} = \begin{pmatrix} 29 \\ 49.5 \\ 260 \end{pmatrix}$.

Lesson 4.8

Check Your Understanding

1. $\begin{pmatrix} x \\ y \\ z \end{pmatrix} = \begin{pmatrix} 1 \\ -1 \\ 2 \end{pmatrix}$

2. $\begin{pmatrix} a \\ b \\ c \\ d \end{pmatrix} = \begin{pmatrix} 0 \\ \frac{1}{2} \\ \frac{1}{2} \\ 0 \end{pmatrix}$

3a. The two lines $x + 2y = 1$ and $2x + 4y = 1$ are parallel, so the system has no solution.
b. Gaussian Elimination results in $\left(\begin{array}{cc|c} 1 & 2 & 1 \\ 0 & 0 & -1 \end{array}\right)$, and the second row indicates that the system has no solution. **c.** The inverse does not exist $(ad - bc = 0)$. **4.** Answers may vary. Sample: To solve $AX = B$, find A^{-1} and write $A^{-1}AX = A^{-1}B$ or $X = A^{-1}B$.
5. $MA = \begin{pmatrix} 1 & 0 & 0 \\ 0 & 0 & 1 \end{pmatrix}\begin{pmatrix} 1 & 0 \\ 3 & 4 \\ 0 & 1 \end{pmatrix} = \begin{pmatrix} 1 & 0 \\ 0 & 1 \end{pmatrix}$ and
$AM = \begin{pmatrix} 1 & 0 \\ 3 & 4 \\ 0 & 1 \end{pmatrix}\begin{pmatrix} 1 & 0 & 0 \\ 0 & 0 & 1 \end{pmatrix} = \begin{pmatrix} 1 & 0 \\ 3 & 4 \\ 0 & 1 \end{pmatrix}$, so $MA \neq AM$.
6. $AM = \begin{pmatrix} 1 & 2 \\ 3 & 4 \end{pmatrix}\begin{pmatrix} -2 & 1 \\ \frac{3}{2} & -\frac{1}{2} \end{pmatrix} =$
$\begin{pmatrix} -2 + 3 & 1 - 1 \\ -6 + 6 & 3 - 2 \end{pmatrix} = \begin{pmatrix} 1 & 0 \\ 0 & 1 \end{pmatrix} = I$
7. No, zero is a real number but it does not have an inverse.
8. No; for example, $\begin{pmatrix} 3 & -1 \\ -2 & 2 \end{pmatrix}\begin{pmatrix} 1 \\ 1 \end{pmatrix} = \begin{pmatrix} 2 \\ 0 \end{pmatrix}$ and $\begin{pmatrix} 1 \\ 1 \end{pmatrix} \neq \begin{pmatrix} 2 \\ 0 \end{pmatrix}$.

On Your Own

10. Using $M = \begin{pmatrix} 2 & 0.5 & 0.2 \\ 3 & 1 & 0.5 \\ 5 & 10 & 3 \end{pmatrix}$, the system is $M\begin{pmatrix} m \\ p \\ c \end{pmatrix} = \begin{pmatrix} 30 \\ 50 \\ 120 \end{pmatrix}$. Then $\begin{pmatrix} m \\ p \\ c \end{pmatrix} = M^{-1}\begin{pmatrix} 30 \\ 50 \\ 120 \end{pmatrix} = \begin{pmatrix} 12.\overline{8} \\ -3.\overline{1} \\ 28.\overline{8} \end{pmatrix}$. But the value $p = -3.\overline{1}$ indicates that there is no solution.
11. If $\begin{pmatrix} a & b \\ c & d \end{pmatrix}\begin{pmatrix} x \\ y \end{pmatrix} = \begin{pmatrix} x \\ y \end{pmatrix}$, then $ax + by = x$ and $cx + dy = y$. The only values of a, b, c, and d that satisfy both equations simultaneously are $a = 1$, $b = 0$, $c = 0$, and $d = 1$ or $\begin{pmatrix} 1 & 0 \\ 0 & 1 \end{pmatrix}$.
12. $\begin{pmatrix} x & y \\ z & w \end{pmatrix} = \begin{pmatrix} -2 & 1 \\ \frac{3}{2} & -\frac{1}{2} \end{pmatrix}$

Lesson 4.9

Check Your Understanding

1a. $I = \begin{pmatrix} 1 & 0 \\ 0 & 1 \end{pmatrix}$ **b.** $I = \begin{pmatrix} 1 & 0 & 0 \\ 0 & 1 & 0 \\ 0 & 0 & 1 \end{pmatrix}$
2. If $A = B$, then by substitution $AB = AA = BA$, so square matrices commute with themselves under multiplication. Also, $AA^2 = AAA = A^2A$ because matrix multiplication is associative.
3. Answers may vary. Sample: Matrix multiplication is not always commutative, so $A(B + C) \neq (B + C)A$. Therefore we need a distributive property for $A(B + C)$ and another distributive property for $(B + C)A$.
4a. $B = \begin{pmatrix} -2c \\ c \end{pmatrix}$ for any value of c.
b. $B = \begin{pmatrix} -2c & -2d \\ c & d \end{pmatrix}$ for any values of c and d.
5. Line 1: OK, by the definition of squaring; Line 2: OK; distribute the second factor $(X + Y)$ over the two terms of the first factor; Line 3: OK; distributive property; Line 4: OK, by the definition of squaring; Line 5: wrong because $XY \neq YX$. The last line should be $X^2 + XY + YX + Y^2$. **6.** yes **7.** Since A^{-1} exists and $AB = AC$, $A^{-1}(AB) = A^{-1}(AC)$. Then $(A^{-1}A)B = (A^{-1}A)C$ or $B = C$. **8.** Answers may vary. Sample: When you multiply a square matrix M by its appropriate identity matrix, there is only one element in each row of M that results in a nonzero term, and that is the same whether the identity is to the left or to the right of M.

On Your Own

9. Answers may vary. Sample: $A + A = 1A + 1A = (1 + 1)A = 2A$ **10.** Answers may vary. Sample: From Exercise 5, $(X + Y)^2 = X^2 + XY + YX + Y^2$. Substituting I for Y gives us $(X + I)^2 = X^2 + XI + IX + I^2 = X^2 + 2X + I$. **13a.** For a zero matrix Z and another matrix B, $ZB = Z$. Since $ZB \neq I$ for any B, matrix Z cannot have an inverse.

Lesson 4.10

On Your Own

9b.

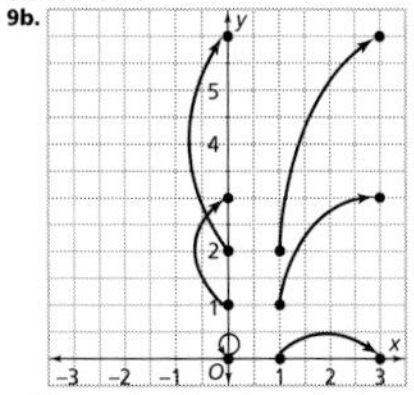

c. The mapping dilates line and polygons by a factor of 3, with the origin as the centre of the dilation.

11a. The images are $\begin{pmatrix} -2 \\ -1 \end{pmatrix}$, $\begin{pmatrix} 1 \\ 2 \end{pmatrix}$, $\begin{pmatrix} 0 \\ 0 \end{pmatrix}$, and $\begin{pmatrix} -x \\ -y \end{pmatrix}$, respectively. **b.** $M = \begin{pmatrix} -1 & 0 \\ 0 & -1 \end{pmatrix}$

Lesson 4.11

Check Your Understanding

1a. $(x, y) \mapsto (-x, y)$, which is a reflection over the y-axis. **b.** $(x, y) \mapsto (y, x)$, which is a reflection over the line $y = x$.

2. $A^{-1} = \begin{pmatrix} \frac{1}{2} & 0 \\ 0 & \frac{1}{2} \end{pmatrix}$; $A^{-1}\begin{pmatrix} x \\ y \end{pmatrix} = \begin{pmatrix} \frac{1}{2} & 0 \\ 0 & \frac{1}{2} \end{pmatrix}\begin{pmatrix} x \\ y \end{pmatrix} = \begin{pmatrix} \frac{1}{2}x \\ \frac{1}{2}y \end{pmatrix}$

3. $A^2 = \begin{pmatrix} 4 & 0 \\ 0 & 4 \end{pmatrix}$, so $A^2\begin{pmatrix} x \\ y \end{pmatrix} = \begin{pmatrix} 4x \\ 4y \end{pmatrix}$;
$A^{-2} = \begin{pmatrix} \frac{1}{4} & 0 \\ 0 & \frac{1}{4} \end{pmatrix}$, so $A^{-2}\begin{pmatrix} x \\ y \end{pmatrix} = \begin{pmatrix} \frac{1}{4}x \\ \frac{1}{4}y \end{pmatrix}$.
4. $M\begin{pmatrix} a \\ b \end{pmatrix} = \begin{pmatrix} c & -d \\ d & c \end{pmatrix}\begin{pmatrix} a \\ b \end{pmatrix} = \begin{pmatrix} ac - bd \\ ad + bc \end{pmatrix}$, or M maps the point $a + bi$ to $ac - bd + (ad + bc)i = (a + bi)(c + di)$. **5.** The result of the matrix is to reflect each point over the line $y = \frac{1}{2}x$.
6. The mapping $X \mapsto M^{-1}X$ reflects a preimage over the line $y = \frac{1}{2}x$; $M^{-1} = \begin{pmatrix} \frac{3}{5} & \frac{4}{5} \\ \frac{4}{5} & -\frac{3}{5} \end{pmatrix}$ so $M^{-1} = M$. **7a.** If a point is on the line $y = -2x$, then its image is also on that line. **b.** 90°
c. $(2t)s + t(-2s) = 0$ **8.** A reflection scales by 1 in the direction of the line of reflection (points on this line are not moved) and scales by −1 in the perpendicular direction identified in exercise 7. **9a.** 180° (counterclockwise) rotation
b. $R^2 = \begin{pmatrix} -1 & 0 \\ 0 & -1 \end{pmatrix}$, so $R^2\begin{pmatrix} x \\ y \end{pmatrix} = \begin{pmatrix} -x \\ -y \end{pmatrix}$.
c. 270° counterclockwise rotation
d. $R^3 = \begin{pmatrix} 0 & 1 \\ -1 & 0 \end{pmatrix}$, so $R^3\begin{pmatrix} x \\ y \end{pmatrix} = \begin{pmatrix} y \\ -x \end{pmatrix}$.
e. $R^4 = \begin{pmatrix} 1 & 0 \\ 0 & 1 \end{pmatrix}$, which is the same as a (clockwise) rotation of 360° **10a.** $x + y = kx$, $2x = ky$; $(1 - k)x + y = 0$, $2x - ky = 0$
b. $k = 2$, $k = -1$ **c.** If $k = 2$, the equations are $-x + y = 0$ and $2x - 2y = 0$; the solution to that system is any point on the line $y = x$. If $k = -1$, the equations are $2x + y = 0$ and $2x + y = 0$; the solution to that system is any point on the line $y = -2x$. **11.** Answers may vary. Sample: Using the technique from Exercise 10 results in the proportion $\frac{-2.7 - k}{-1.4} = \frac{2.1}{2.2 - k}$; solving that proportion gives $k = -2$ or $k = \frac{3}{2}$. The value $k = -2$ results in a system of equations with a solution of all points on the line $y = \frac{1}{2}x$. The value $k = \frac{3}{2}$ results in a system of equations with a solution of all points on the line $y = 3x$.

12. $M = \begin{pmatrix} 0 & -1 \\ -1 & 0 \end{pmatrix}$ **13.** $M = \begin{pmatrix} \frac{\sqrt{2}}{2} & -\frac{\sqrt{2}}{2} \\ \frac{\sqrt{2}}{2} & \frac{\sqrt{2}}{2} \end{pmatrix}$
14. Answers may vary.

On Your Own

15. $X \mapsto A^{-1}X$ dilates the plane by a factor of $\frac{1}{3}$ horizontally and by a factor of $\frac{1}{2}$ vertically; $A^{-1} = \begin{pmatrix} \frac{1}{3} & 0 \\ 0 & \frac{1}{2} \end{pmatrix}$. **16.** Answers may vary. Sample: Using the general point $\begin{pmatrix} x \\ y \end{pmatrix}$, $\begin{pmatrix} 0 & -1 \\ 1 & 0 \end{pmatrix}\begin{pmatrix} x \\ y \end{pmatrix} = \begin{pmatrix} -y \\ x \end{pmatrix}$, and the distance from

the origin to $\begin{pmatrix} x \\ y \end{pmatrix}$ or to $\begin{pmatrix} -y \\ x \end{pmatrix}$ is $\sqrt{x^2 + y^2}$.
19a. $(-12, -6)$ **b.** $(-2.5, 2.5)$
24a. The images are $(0, -1)$, $(-1, 0)$, $(-1, -1)$, $(-1, 1)$, $(-y, -x)$. **b.** $\begin{pmatrix} 0 & -1 \\ -1 & 0 \end{pmatrix}$

Lesson 4.12
Check Your Understanding

1. Rewriting $MA = A$ as $\begin{pmatrix} 0.8 & 0.5 \\ 0.2 & 0.5 \end{pmatrix}\begin{pmatrix} b \\ c \end{pmatrix} = \begin{pmatrix} b \\ c \end{pmatrix}$, then $A = \begin{pmatrix} 100 \\ 40 \end{pmatrix}$.
2. Answers may vary. Sample: Refer to the TI-Nspire Handbook, p. 778 to see how to calculate each expression. **3a.** For the cars that start at location A, 70% of them are returned to A, 20% are returned to B, and 10% are returned to C. For the cars that start at location B, 20% of them are returned to A, 50% are returned to B, and 30% are returned to C. For the cars that start at location C, 30% of them are returned to A, 10% are returned to B, and 60% are returned to C. **b.**
$M = \begin{pmatrix} 0.7 & 0.2 & 0.3 \\ 0.2 & 0.5 & 0.1 \\ 0.1 & 0.3 & 0.6 \end{pmatrix}$
c. $P(2) = \begin{pmatrix} 130 \\ 74 \\ 96 \end{pmatrix}$, $P(3) = \begin{pmatrix} 134.6 \\ 72.6 \\ 92.8 \end{pmatrix}$; the distribution seems to settle at about $\begin{pmatrix} 138 \\ 73 \\ 89 \end{pmatrix}$.
4a. Answers may vary. Sample: We know that $X(n) = \begin{pmatrix} f(n) \\ f(n-1) \end{pmatrix}$. Also, $\begin{pmatrix} 1 & 1 \\ 1 & 0 \end{pmatrix}\begin{pmatrix} f(n-1) \\ f(n-2) \end{pmatrix} = \begin{pmatrix} f(n-1) + f(n-2) \\ f(n-1) \end{pmatrix}$. But $f(n-1) + f(n-2) = f(n)$ by definition, so $\begin{pmatrix} f(n-1) + f(n-2) \\ f(n-1) \end{pmatrix} = \begin{pmatrix} f(n) \\ f(n-1) \end{pmatrix}$. So the transitive property of equality lets us conclude that $X(n) = \begin{pmatrix} 1 & 1 \\ 1 & 0 \end{pmatrix}\begin{pmatrix} f(n-1) \\ f(n-2) \end{pmatrix}$ or $X(n) = \begin{pmatrix} 1 & 1 \\ 1 & 0 \end{pmatrix} X(n-1)$. **b.** Let $M = \begin{pmatrix} 1 & 1 \\ 1 & 0 \end{pmatrix}$. Then $X(9) = \begin{pmatrix} f(10) \\ f(9) \end{pmatrix} = M^9X(0) = \begin{pmatrix} 55 & 34 \\ 34 & 31 \end{pmatrix}\begin{pmatrix} 1 \\ 1 \end{pmatrix} = \begin{pmatrix} 89 \\ 55 \end{pmatrix}$, or $f(10) = 89$. **5.** For $n > 1$, $Y(n) = \begin{pmatrix} g(n) \\ g(n-1) \end{pmatrix}$; $Y(n+1) = \begin{pmatrix} 3 & -4 \\ 1 & 0 \end{pmatrix} Y(n)$. **6.** $h(n+1) = 2h(n) - 3h(n-1) + 4h(n-2)$

On Your Own

7. The transition matrix is $\begin{pmatrix} 0.97 & 0.02 \\ 0.03 & 0.98 \end{pmatrix}$; the migrations stabilize with 120 million people in the east and 180 million people in the west. **9a.** Answers may vary. Sample: A car rental agency has 2 locations. For cars rented at A, 60% return to A and 40% return to B. For cars rented at B, 25% return to A and 75% return to B. **b.** $X = (100, 160)$

Lesson 4.13
Check Your Understanding
1a. $\frac{1}{4}$ **b.** $\frac{1}{4}$ **c.** $\frac{1}{2}$ **2a.** This cannot be answered using a matrix because the matrix does not describe how to move one vertex counterclockwise in 2 steps. **b.** $\frac{5}{16}$ **c.** $\frac{3}{8}$ **3a.** This cannot be answered using a matrix because the matrix does not describe how to move one vertex counterclockwise in 2 steps. **b.** $\frac{13}{36}$ **c.** $\frac{5}{18}$
4. Answers may vary. Sample: Probabilities cannot be negative; each column represents *all* the possibilities for a particular situation, so the sum of the entries in a column must be 1.
5. The weather transition matrix is $\begin{pmatrix} 0.6 & 0.7 \\ 0.4 & 0.3 \end{pmatrix}$.
a. 0.64 **b.** 0.636 **c.** 0.636 **d.** 0.636 **e.** 0.636
6a. $\begin{pmatrix} 0.8 & 0.1 \\ 0.2 & 0.9 \end{pmatrix}$ **b.** 0.343 **c.** 0.671
7. The matrix is $\begin{pmatrix} 0 & \frac{1}{2} & 0 \\ \frac{1}{2} & 0 & 0 \\ \frac{1}{2} & \frac{1}{2} & 0 \end{pmatrix}$.
(1) $\frac{1}{2}$ (2) 0.696 (3) $\frac{1}{16}$

On Your Own

8. $M^3 = \begin{pmatrix} 0.344 & 0.328 & 0.328 \\ 0.328 & 0.344 & 0.328 \\ 0.328 & 0.328 & 0.344 \end{pmatrix}$, $M^4 = \begin{pmatrix} 0.366 & 0.332 & 0.332 \\ 0.332 & 0.336 & 0.332 \\ 0.332 & 0.332 & 0.336 \end{pmatrix}$; in the long run, all the entries will be 0.333, regardless of the starting vertex. **13a.** 0.625 **b.** 0.312

Chapter 5

Lesson 5.1
On Your Own
6a. no **c.** yes **f.** no **7a.** No; $2^{10} + 2^2 \neq 2^{10+2}$. This sum cannot be written as a single power of 2. **c.** Yes; $2^{10} \cdot 2^2 = 2^{10+2} = 2^{12}$ **h.** Yes; $4 \cdot 2^{10} = 2^2 \cdot 2^{10} = 2^{2+10} = 2^{12}$

Lesson 5.2
Check Your Understanding
1. $(ab)^n = \underbrace{(ab) \cdot (ab) \cdot \cdots \cdot (ab)}_{n \text{ copies of } ab} = \underbrace{(a \cdot a \cdot \cdots \cdot a)}_{n \text{ copies of } a} \underbrace{(b \cdot b \cdot \cdots \cdot b)}_{n \text{ copies of } b} = a^n \cdot b^n$
2. $\frac{3^{11}}{3^5} = \frac{3 \cdot 3 \cdot 3 \cdot 3 \cdot 3 \cdot 3 \cdot 3 \cdot 3 \cdot 3 \cdot 3 \cdot 3}{3 \cdot 3 \cdot 3 \cdot 3 \cdot 3} = \frac{3 \cdot 3 \cdot 3 \cdot 3 \cdot 3}{3 \cdot 3 \cdot 3 \cdot 3 \cdot 3} \cdot \frac{3 \cdot 3 \cdot 3 \cdot 3 \cdot 3 \cdot 3}{1} = 1 \cdot 3^6 = 3^6$
3. Corollary 5.2:
$$\frac{a^b}{a^c} = \frac{\overbrace{(a \cdot a \cdot \cdots \cdot a)}^{b \text{ copies of } a}}{\underbrace{(a \cdot a \cdot \cdots \cdot a)}_{c \text{ copies of } a}} = \frac{\overbrace{(a \cdot a \cdot \cdots \cdot a)}^{c \text{ copies of } a}}{\underbrace{(a \cdot a \cdot \cdots \cdot a)}_{c \text{ copies of } a}} \cdot \frac{\overbrace{(a \cdot a \cdot \cdots \cdot a)}^{b-c \text{ copies of } a}}{1} = 1 \cdot a^{b-c} = a^{b-c}$$
Corollary 5.3: $(a^b)^c =$
$$\underbrace{\overbrace{(a \cdot a \cdot \cdots \cdot a)}^{b \text{ copies of } a} \cdot \overbrace{(a \cdot a \cdot \cdots \cdot a)}^{b \text{ copies of } a} \cdot \cdots \cdot \overbrace{(a \cdot a \cdot \cdots \cdot a)}^{b \text{ copies of } a}}_{c \text{ copies of } a^b} = \underbrace{a \cdot a \cdot \cdots \cdot a}_{bc \text{ copies of } a} = a^{bc}$$
4a. Yes; $3^{14} + 3^{14} + 3^{14} = 3 \cdot 3^{14} = 3^1 + 3^{14} = 3^{1+14} = 3^{15}$ **b.** No; $(3^6)^9 = 3^{6 \cdot 9} = 3^{54} \neq 3^{15}$
c. Yes; $(3^{10})(3^5) = 3^{10+5} = 3^{15}$
d. No; $(3^3)(3^5) = 3^{3+5} = 3^8 \neq 3^{15}$
e. No; $(3^{15})(3^1) = 3^{15+1} = 3^{16} \neq 3^{15}$
f. Yes; $(3^5)(3^5)(3^5) = 3^{5+5+5} = 3^{15}$
g. No; $3^9 + 3^6 \neq 3^{9+6}$. This sum cannot be written as a single power of 3. **h.** Yes; $(3^5)^3 = 3^{5 \cdot 3} = 3^{15}$ **i.** Yes; $(3^3)^5 = 3^{3 \cdot 5} = 3^{15}$
j. Yes; $9(3^{13}) = (3^2)(3^{13}) = 3^{2+13} = 3^{15}$
k. No; $(3^5)^{10} = 3^{5 \cdot 10} = 3^{50} \neq 3^{15}$ **l.** Yes; $(3^1)^{15} = 3^{1 \cdot 15} = 3^{15}$ **5.** Answers may vary. Sample: M^3N, $\frac{M^6}{N^3}$ **6.** Each time you multiply a power of x from the first factor by a power of x from the second factor, you can use the Fundamental Law of Exponents to find the exponent to place on x in the resulting term of the product. **7.** 3^{31} **8a.** 3 **b.** 5 **c.** $\frac{6}{5}$ **d.** 3
9. $f(n) = 3 \cdot 5^n$ **10.** mean: 11,111; median: $5 \cdot 10^2$ or 500 **11a.** 10 **b.** $\frac{9y^5}{8}$ **c.** $2x^4$ **d.** $\frac{1}{8}$
12a. ± 4 **b.** 2

On Your Own
13a. 1000 **b.** 1,000,000,000,000 **d.** 16
f. 10,000 **17.** about 2,000,000 **18a.** No; $\frac{2^6}{2^2} = 2^{6-2} = 2^4 \neq 2^3$ **d.** Yes; $\frac{(2^2)^5}{2^7} = \frac{2^{2 \cdot 5}}{2^7} = \frac{2^{10}}{2^7} = 2^{10-7} = 2^3$ **22a.** x^{12} **g.** x^8

Lesson 5.3
Check Your Understanding
1a. Yes; $\left(\frac{1}{7}\right)^{10} = (7^{-1})^{10} = 7^{-1 \cdot 10} = 7^{-10}$
b. No; $7^{-4} \cdot 7^{-3} = 7^{-4+(-3)} = 7^{-7} \neq 7^{-10}$
c. No; $(7^{13})(7^{-6}) = 7^{13+(-6)} = 7^7 \neq 7^{-10}$
d. Yes; $\frac{7^3}{7^{13}} = 7^{3-13} = 7^{-10}$ **e.** No; $\frac{7^2}{7^3 \cdot 7^4 \cdot 7^4} = \frac{7^2}{7^{3+4+4}} = \frac{7^2}{7^{11}} = 7^{2-11} = 7^{-9} \neq 7^{-10}$
f. No; $\frac{1}{7^{-10}} = 7^{-(-10)} = 7^{10} \neq 7^{-10}$
g. No; $7^5 \cdot 7^{-2} = 7^{5+(-2)} = 7^3 \neq 7^{-10}$
h. Yes; $\left(\frac{1}{7^2}\right)^5 = (7^{-2})^5 = 7^{(-2) \cdot 5} = 7^{-10}$
i. No; $(7^5)^{-15} = 7^{5 \cdot (-15)} = 7^{-75} \neq 7^{-10}$
j. Yes; $(7^5)^{-2} = 7^{5 \cdot (-2)} = 7^{-10}$
k. Yes; $(7^{-2})^5 = 7^{-2 \cdot 5} = 7^{-10}$ **l.** Yes; $\frac{1}{7^{10}} = 7^{-10}$ **2.** $10^{-2} \cdot 10^3 = \frac{1}{10^2} \cdot \frac{10^3}{1} = \frac{10^3}{10^2} = 10^{3-2} = 10^1$ **3.** $a^b \cdot a^c = a^{b+c}$:
If $b = 0$, then $a^b \cdot a^c = a^0 \cdot a^c = a^c$ and $a^{b+c} = a^{0+c} = a^c$. $\frac{a^b}{a^c} = a^{b-c}$ $(b > c)$:
If $c = 0$, then $\frac{a^b}{a^c} = \frac{a^b}{a^0} = \frac{a^b}{1} = a^b$ and $a^{b-c} = a^{b-0} = a^b$. $(a^b)^c = a^{bc}$: If $b = 0$, then $(a^b)^c = (a^0)^c = 1^c = 1$ and $a^{bc} = a^{0 \cdot c} = a^0 = 1$.
4a. 6 **b.** $\frac{2}{3}$ **c.** 4 **d.** 8 **e.** 1 **f.** $2^{\frac{1}{2}}$ or $\sqrt{2}$ **5.** 1
6. 0.75×10^7h; 1.53×10^9h; 0.89×10^{11}h
7a. 16, 8, 4, **2**, **1**, $\frac{1}{2}$, ... **b.** 2, **6**, 18, **54**, **162**, **486**, ... **c.** 1, a, a^2, a^3, a^4, a^5, ...
d. b^6, b^3, 1, b^{-3}, b^{-6}, b^{-9}, ...
e. c^{10}, c^8, c^6, c^4, c^2, 1, ...
8a. $h(x) = 2 \cdot 5^x$ **b.** $h(x) = \frac{2}{125}, \frac{2}{25}, \frac{2}{5}$

9. $(2^3)(2^{-3}) = 2^{3+(-3)} = 2^0 = 1$

On Your Own
10a. 2 **e.** -3 **14a.** $3^{2x} + 2 + 3^{-2x}$ **15b.** z^{-27}
16b. $\frac{1}{9}$ **f.** 3

Lesson 5.4
Check Your Understanding
1a. 0, 3, 6, **9**, **12**, **15**, ... **b.** 0, **6**, **12**, **18**, **24**, 30, ... **c.** 1, **21**, **41**, **61**, 81, **101**, ... **d.** 5, **1**, **−3**, −7, **−11**, **−15**, **−19** ... **2.** There are five "steps" from 0 to 30, so the third step, 18, is three fifths of the way from 0 to 30. **3a.** 2, −6, 18, **−54**, **162**, **−486**, ... **b.** 1, i, −1, $-i$, **1**, i, ... **c.** 1, $\sqrt{5}$, 5, $5\sqrt{5}$, **25**, $25\sqrt{5}$, ... **d.** 1, **5**, **25**, 125, **625**, ... **e.** 1, $\sqrt{3}$, **3**, $3\sqrt{3}$, 9, $9\sqrt{3}$, **27**, ... **4.** There are three "steps" from 1 to 125, so the second step, 25, is two thirds of the way from 1 to 125. **5a.** $\frac{a+b}{2}$ **b.** $\sqrt{ab}$

6a.

(a, b)	$\frac{a+b}{2}$	$\sqrt{ab}$
(1, 2)	1.5	1.4142
(2, 5)	**3.5**	**3.1623**
(4, 1)	**2.5**	**2**
(3, 3)	**3**	**3**
(6, 9)	**7.5**	**7.3485**
(8, 10)	**9**	**8.9443**
(7, 7)	**7**	**7**

b. $\frac{a+b}{2}$; Answers may vary. Sample: The square of any real number is positive, so $(a-b)^2 \geq 0$. Then, $a^2 - 2ab + b^2 \geq 0$, $a^2 + 2ab + b^2 \geq 4ab$, $\frac{a^2 + 2ab + b^2}{4} \geq ab$, and $\frac{(a+b)^2}{4} \geq ab$. Taking the square root of each side (since $a, b > 0$) gives $\frac{a+b}{2} \geq \sqrt{ab}$. **7.** Yes; the missing terms could be 2, 4, 8, or −2, 4, −8.
8. $64^{\frac{2}{3}} = 16$, $625^{\frac{1}{4}} = 5$ **9a.** 4 **b.** 3 **c.** 3 **d.** 16

On Your Own
10a. 81 **b.** 27 **12a.** Balance: 546.36, 562.75, 579.64, 597.03 **13a.** 5 **17a.** $\frac{2}{3}$ **b.** 6

Lesson 5.5
Check Your Understanding
1a. a little more than 6 **b.** Answers may vary. Sample: a little more than 222 **2a.** 3 **b.** 32 **c.** 49 **d.** 9 **3a.** Answers may vary. Sample: $a = 32$, $b = 4$ **b.** Yes; if $a^{\frac{2}{5}} = b$, then $\left(a^{\frac{2}{5}}\right)^5 = b^5$, which simplifies to $a^2 = b^5$.
4. $1^{\frac{p}{q}} = (1^p)^{\frac{1}{q}} = 1^{\frac{1}{q}} = \sqrt[q]{1} = 1$
5. The graph is made up of points from the horizontal lines $y = 1$ and $y = -1$. It consists of the points $(x, 1)$ when x is an even integer and $(x, -1)$ when x is an odd integer. If x is not an integer, the output is sometimes defined (for example, $(-1)^{\frac{1}{3}} = -1$) and sometimes not defined (for example, $(-1)^{\frac{1}{2}}$ is not a real number). **6a.** $a(b(9)) = 9$, $b(a(7)) = 7$ **b.** No; Answers may vary. Sample: It is not always true that $b(a(x)) = x$. For example, $b(a(-7)) = b(49) = 7$. **7.** If $a, b, c, d, \ldots$ is an arithmetic sequence, then $b = a + k$, $c = a + 2k$, $d = a + 3k, \ldots$, for some number k. Then $10^b = 10^{a+k} = 10^a \cdot 10^k$, $10^c = 10^{a+2k} = 10^a \cdot 10^{2k}$, and $10^d = 10^{a+3k} = 10^a \cdot 10^{3k}$. Thus $10^a, 10^b, 10^c, 10^d, \ldots$ is a geometric sequence with the common ratio 10^k.

On Your Own
10. ± 3, $\pm 3i$ **11a.** 3
15a.

x	$f(x) = x^3$	$g(x) = x^{\frac{1}{3}}$
−8	−512	−2
−2	**−8**	**−1.256**
−1	**−1**	**−1**
$-\frac{1}{2}$	**−0.125**	**−0.794**
$-\frac{1}{8}$	**−0.002**	**−0.5**
0	**0**	**0**
$\frac{1}{8}$	**0.002**	**0.5**
$\frac{1}{2}$	**0.125**	**0.794**
1	**1**	**1**
2	**8**	**1.256**
8	**512**	**2**

Lesson 5.6
On Your Own
11a. $\pm\sqrt{5}$ **b.** 2.32
12.
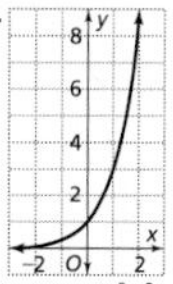

15a. outputs: $\frac{3}{4}, \frac{3}{2}$, 3, 6, 12
16b. $L(h) = 100 \cdot \left(\frac{1}{2}\right)^h$

Lesson 5.7
Check Your Understanding
1a. $f(x) = -3 \cdot 2^x$ **b.** $f(x) = 3 \cdot \left(\frac{1}{2}\right)^x$
c. $f(x) = 3 \cdot 2^x$ **d.** $f(x) = 3 \cdot 5^x$
2a. $f(x) = 12 \cdot \left(\frac{1}{2}\right)^x$ **b.** $f(x) = 48 \cdot \left(\frac{1}{2}\right)^x$
3a. Answers may vary. Sample: $f(x) = 2 \cdot 6^x$, $g(x) = 8 \cdot 3^x$ **b.** $f(x) = a \cdot \left(\sqrt{\frac{72}{a}}\right)^x$
4. Lemma: The proof uses the fact that b^x is strictly decreasing for nonnegative integer inputs. Let $x = \frac{p}{q}$ for some positive integers p and q, and then suppose that $b^{\frac{1}{q}} \geq 1$. Then $b = (b^{\frac{1}{q}})^q \geq 1^q = 1$, which implies $b \geq 1$. But this contradicts the hypothesis of the lemma that $b < 1$. Thus $b^{\frac{1}{q}} < 1$, and therefore $b^x = (b^{\frac{p}{q}}) = (b^{\frac{1}{q}})^p < 1^p = 1$. So, $b^x < 1$.
Theorem: Let s and t be rational numbers such that $s > t$. Then $s - t > 0$, so (using the Lemma) $b^{s-t} < 1$. Since $b^t > 0$, multiplying both sides of the inequality by b^t does not reverse the inequality symbol. So,
$b^{s-t} \cdot b^t < 1 \cdot b^t$
$b^{s-t+t} < b^t$
$b^s < b^t$
Thus, if $s > t$, then $f(s) < f(t)$, which means that f is strictly decreasing on rational number inputs.
5. Answers may vary. Sample: If $f(x) = 2^x$, then $f(-x) = 2^{-x} = \frac{1}{2^x} = \left(\frac{1}{2}\right)^x = g(x)$.
6. 2.807 **7.** 2.807
8a.
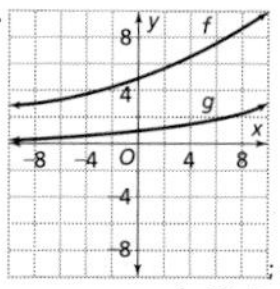

; no
b. one **9a.** 4 **b.** Yes; $\left(2^{\sqrt{2}}\right)^{\sqrt{2}} = 2^{\sqrt{2} \cdot \sqrt{2}} = 2^2 = 4$ **10.** Answers may vary. Sample: A calculator gives error messages because b^a is not defined for $b < 0$.

On Your Own
11. $f(0) = a \cdot b^0 = a \cdot 1 = a$, so the graph contains $(0, a)$. **13a.** \$4.11, \$4.23
15. $2 < \sqrt{6} < 3$, so $3^2 < 3^{\sqrt{6}} < 3^3$ or $9 < 3^{\sqrt{6}} < 27$. **18a.** outputs: $\frac{1}{4}, -\frac{1}{2}$, 1, −2, 4, −8

Lesson 5.8
Check Your Understanding
1a. $A(n) = 18 \cdot \left(\frac{1}{3}\right)^n$ **b.** $B(x) = -2 \cdot (4)^n$
c. No exponential function fits the table because the ratio between consecutive outputs is not constant. **d.** $D(z) = \frac{1}{3} \cdot 6^z$
2a. $A(n) = \begin{cases} 18 & \text{if } n = 0 \\ \frac{1}{3} \cdot A(n-1) & \text{if } n > 0 \end{cases}$
b. $B(x) = \begin{cases} -2 & \text{if } x = 0 \\ 4 \cdot B(x-1) & \text{if } x > 0 \end{cases}$
c. not an exponential function
d. $D(z) = \begin{cases} \frac{1}{3} & \text{if } z = 0 \\ 6 \cdot D(z-1) & \text{if } z > 0 \end{cases}$
3. $q(x) = 12{,}500 \cdot \left(\frac{1}{5}\right)^x$ **4.** Disagree; a value of $-\frac{1}{5}$ for b is not possible because the base of an exponential function must be positive.
5. Answers may vary. Sample: $f(x) = 2x + 16$; $f(x) = (10 \cdot 2^{\frac{3}{5}})(2^{\frac{1}{5}})^x$ **6a.** $a = 100$, $b = 3^{\frac{1}{5}}$

b.

x	$T(x)$	$\div$
0	100	≈**1.246**
1	≈**124.57**	≈**1.246**
2	≈**155.18**	≈**1.246**
3	≈**193.32**	≈**1.246**
4	≈**240.82**	≈**1.246**
5	300	

7a. \$16,000; \$12,800; \$10,240 **b.** $V(n) = 20{,}000 \cdot (0.8)^n$ **c.** Yes; $V(14) = \$879.61$, so after 14 yr the car will be worth less than \$1000.

8. $y = y_1^{\frac{-x_2}{x_1 - x_2}} \cdot y_2^{\frac{x_1}{x_1 - x_2}} \cdot \left(\left(\frac{y_1}{y_2}\right)^{\frac{1}{x_1 - x_2}}\right)^x$

On Your Own

10. $M(n) = 24, 36, 54, 81$; $M(n) = 16 \cdot \left(\frac{3}{2}\right)^n$, $M(n) = \begin{cases} 16 & \text{if } n = 0 \\ \frac{3}{2} \cdot M(n-1) & \text{if } n > 0 \end{cases}$

12b. $y = -5^{\frac{1}{4}} \cdot \left(5^{\frac{1}{4}}\right)^x$ or $y = -5^{\frac{x+1}{4}}$

Lesson 5.9

Check Your Understanding

1. Multiply a by the power b^x. **2.** Divide C by the power b^x. **3.** Find the $\frac{1}{x}$ power of the quotient $C \div a$. **4.** Find $C \div a$, and then find the power of b that results in the value $C \div a$.

5a.

x	$f(x) = 2^x$
0	1
1	2
1.5850	3
2	4
2.3219	5
2.5850	6
	7
3	8
3.1700	9
3.3219	10

b. 2.8074

6a. $f(x + y) = \frac{f(x) \cdot f(y)}{a}$ **b.** $f(x - y) = a \cdot \frac{f(x)}{f(y)}$ **c.** $f(xy) = a^{1-y} \cdot (f(x))^y$ **7a.** 3.162 **b.** $\sqrt{10}$ **c.** \$4743.42 **8a.** 2.154 **b.** $\sqrt[3]{10}$ **c.** \$6962.38

9. If $x = 1$, then $x^y = 1$ for all real number values of y; if $x = -1$, then $x^y = 1$ for all even values of y, or for all fractions $\frac{p}{q}$ where p and q are relatively prime and p is even; if $y = 0$, then $x^y = 1$ for all values of x except $x = 0$.

On Your Own

10a. 2 **d.** no solution **12a.** 11.9 yr

13.

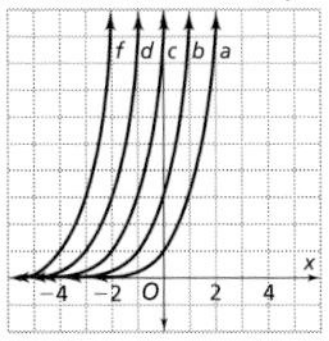

The graphs are all horizontal translations of each other. Answers may vary. Sample: Each function can be written in the form $F(x) = 3^{x+n}$, which represents a horizontal translation of $a(x) = 3^x$. For example, $c(x) = 9 \cdot 3^x = 3^2 + 3^x = 3^{2+x}$, so the graph of $c(x) = 3^{x+2}$ is a horizontal translation of two units to left of the graph of $a(x) = 3^x$. **16a.** Plan 1: 2 yr, Plan 2: 3 yr

Lesson 5.10

Check Your Understanding

1. domain: positive real numbers, range: all real numbers **2a.** 2 **b.** 0 **c.** 6 **d.** 3 **e.** −2 **3a.** 1.1610 **b.** 1.5 **c.** 2.6610 **d.** 0.3390

4.

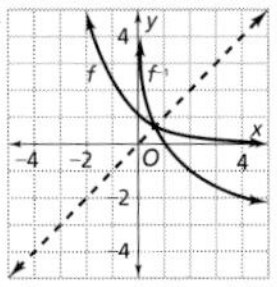

5a. the mean of $f(3)$ and $f(5)$ **b.** the mean of $f(5)$ and $f(7)$ **c.** the mean of $f(-4)$ and $f(-2)$ **d.** the mean of $f(x)$ and $f(y)$

6a.

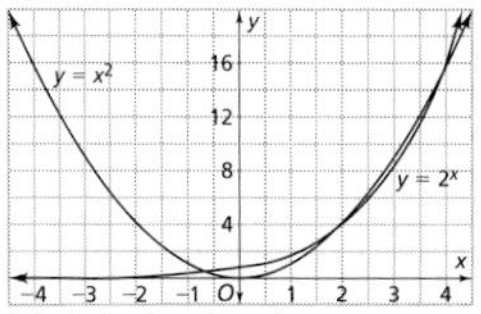

b. 3 solutions **7.** no **8a.** no **b.** no **c.** yes **9.** $b \approx 1.4$; about (2.7, 2.7)

On Your Own

10. Yes; $L_2(x)$ is the inverse of $f(x) = 2^x$. Since $f(x)$ is one-to-one, its inverse is one-to-one.

12.

x	$L_2(x)$
1	0
2	1
3	1.5850
4	2
5	2.3219
6	2.5850
7	2.8074
8	3
9	3.1699

13b. $8^{\frac{1}{3}} = 2$, so $L_8(2) = \frac{1}{3}$. **15.** 8 yr

Lesson 5.11

On Your Own

11a. 2 **12a.** 2 **14a.** 5 **d.** $\frac{5}{2}$

16.

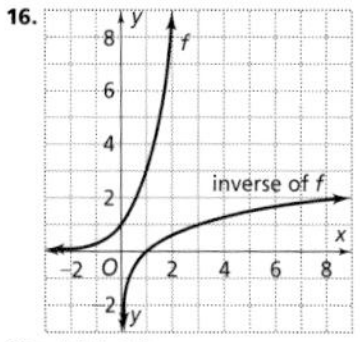

18a. 4.3 **b.** 3.2

Lesson 5.12

Check Your Understanding

1a.

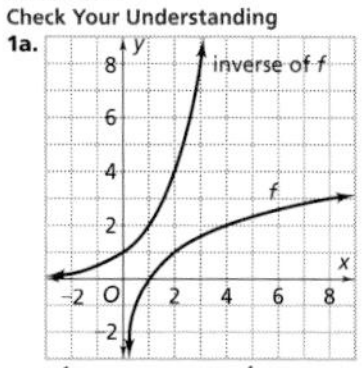

b. $f^{-1}(x) = 2^x$ **2.** C **3a.** $\frac{1}{2}$ **b.** 3 **c.** 3 **d.** $\frac{3}{2}$ **e.** 2 **f.** 2 **4.** If $\log_b 0 = x$, then $b^x = 0$. But $b^x = 0$ only when $b = 0$. Since $b = 0$ is not a valid base for logarithms, $\log_b 0$ does not exist. **5.** $\log_2 0.1$, $\log_5 \frac{1}{5}$, $\log_{73} 1$, $\log_{100} 10$, $\log 99$, $\log_4 18$, $\log_2 18$ **6a.** $b^4 = 9$ **b.** $\sqrt{3}$ **7.** 75 **8a.** 2 **b.** 3 **c.** 6 **d.** 27 **e.** 3.49 **f.** 6.42 **9.** 2.322 **10.** Answers may vary. Sample: The characteristic of $\log M$ is a good indicator of the size of the number M. For example, if $\log M = 3.6435$, then the characteristic 3 means M is between $10^3 = 1000$ and $10^4 = 10{,}000$. The mantissa of $\log M$ is always the logarithm of the number between 1 and 10 that $10^{\text{characteristic}}$ is multiplied by to get M. For example, the number 0.6465 in $\log M = 3.6435$ tells us that $10^{0.6435}$ is the number that must be multiplied by 10^3 to get M. The mantissa in combination with the characteristic provides a way to find M from a logarithm table that gives logarithms of numbers between 1 and 10.

On Your Own

12. $b^0 = 1$ for any nonzero value of b, so $\log_b 1 = 0$ for any base b. **13a.** $y = 2x$ **16a.** 2.085

Lesson 5.13

Check Your Understanding

1a. 4 **b.** 7 **c.** −1 **d.** 21 **e.** $\frac{7}{2}$ **2.** 4 **3.** $\frac{\log_2 32}{\log_2 8} \neq \log_2 \frac{32}{8}$, so you cannot apply the rule for $\log_b \frac{M}{N}$ to get $\log_2 32 - \log_2 8$; $\frac{5}{3}$.

4a. Answers may vary. Sample: Let $b^x = M$ and $b^y = N$ so $x = \log_b M$ and $y = \log_b N$. Then $\log_b \frac{M}{N} = \log_b \frac{b^x}{b^y} = \log_b b^{x-y} = x - y = \log_b M - \log_b N$.

b. Answers may vary. Sample: $\log_b \frac{M}{N} = \log_b \left(M \cdot \frac{1}{N}\right) = \log_b M + \log_b \frac{1}{N} = \log_b M + \log_b N^{-1} = \log_b M + (-1) \cdot \log_b N = \log_b M - \log_b N$. **5a–c.** Answers may vary. Samples are given. **a.** $b^0 = 1$ for any base b, so $\log_b 1 = 0$. **b.** $b^1 = b$ for any base b, so $\log_b b = 1$. **c.** Start with $\log_b (N \cdot \frac{1}{N}) = \log_b 1$. Rewrite the left side as $\log_b N + \log_b \frac{1}{N}$. The right side is 0, so $\log_b N + \log_b \frac{1}{N} = 0$ and $\log_b \frac{1}{N} = -\log_b N$. **6a.** $C(n) = 3.99 \cdot 1.03^n$ **b.** 55 yr **7.** $\frac{\log 3.5}{\log 5}$; 0.778 **8.** $\frac{\log \frac{c}{a}}{\log b}$ or $\frac{\log c - \log a}{\log b}$ **9.** $\frac{\log \frac{7}{2}}{\log \frac{5}{3}}$; 2.452 **10.** $\frac{\log \frac{c}{a}}{\log \frac{b}{d}}$ or $\frac{\log c - \log a}{\log b - \log d}$

11. Answers may vary. Sample: If $6^x = 35$, then $x = \frac{\log 35}{\log 6}$, while if $35^x = 6$ then $x = \frac{\log 6}{\log 35}$; the fractions are reciprocals. **12a.** 2 **b.** −3, 2 **c.** all real numbers greater than 0 **d.** 5 **e.** no solution **13.** If $\log 2 = 0.3$ then $5 \cdot \log 2 = 1.5$, and if $\log 3 = 0.5$ then $3 \cdot \log 3 = 1.5$. Then $5 \cdot \log 2 = 3 \cdot \log 3$, so $\log 2^5 = \log 3^3$, which implies that $32 = 27$. Subtracting 27 from each side gives $5 = 0$. Dividing each side by 5 gives $1 = 0$. **14.** If r is the annual interest rate, then the situation of doubling an amount A can be written as $2A = A\left(1 + \frac{r}{100}\right)^y$ or $2 = \left(1 + \frac{r}{100}\right)^y$. Then $\log 2 = y \cdot \log\left(1 + \frac{r}{100}\right)$ and $y = \frac{\log 2}{\log\left(1 + \frac{r}{100}\right)}$. By letting r take the values 6, 7, 8, 9, 10, 11, and 12, you can calculate the corresponding y-values 11.8957, 10.2448, 9.0065, 8.0432, 7.2725, 6.6419, and 6.1163. These values are very close to the results given by the Rule of 72 (listed in Exercise 17, Lesson 5.10).

On Your Own

15. $\log_5 135$; $5^3 = 125$, so $\log_5 135 > 3$. $7^3 = 343$, and $\log_7 300 < 3$. Thus, $\log_5 135 > \log_7 300$. **16.** $\log_3 x = 1$, 1.2619, 1.4650, 1.6309, 1.7712, 1.8928, 2 **17.** D **19a.** $a + b$ **23a.** 1

Lesson 5.14

Check Your Understanding

1. 2.6 **2a.** $\ln 1 = 0$; $\ln 0$ is undefined. **b.** about 2.71728.

3a.

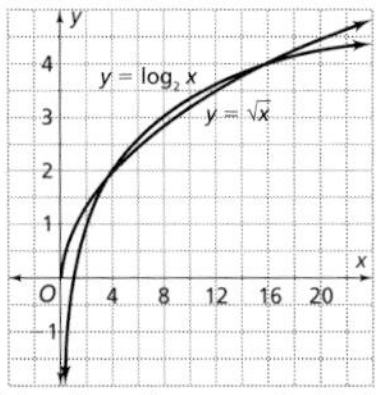

b. 2 **4.** no **5a.** yes **b.** yes **c.** yes **6a.** 1 **b.** 1 **c.** 2 **d.** 0 **e.** 2 **7.** $b \approx 1.4447$, intersect at about (2.7183, 2.7183)

On Your Own

8a. 0.468 **9.** Disagree; the graphs are not the same because the domain of $f(x) = \log x^2$ is all real numbers except 0, while the domain of $g(x) = 2 \log x$ is only the positive real numbers.

10a.

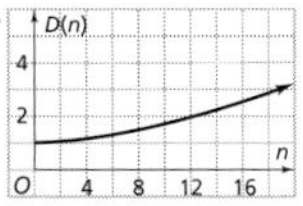

13a.

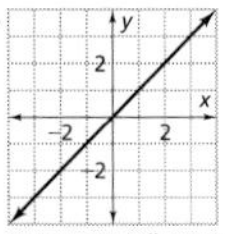

$y = x$; since $\log 10^x = x$ for all real numbers x, the graph of $y = \log 10^x$ is the same as the graph of $y = x$.

Lesson 5.15

Check Your Understanding

1. Less frequent; about 1 out of 10 integers are prime up to 10^5, but only 1 out of 22 are prime up to 10^{10}.

2.

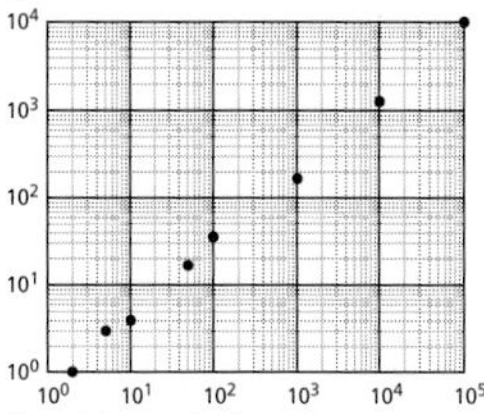

The points appear to lie on a line.

3.

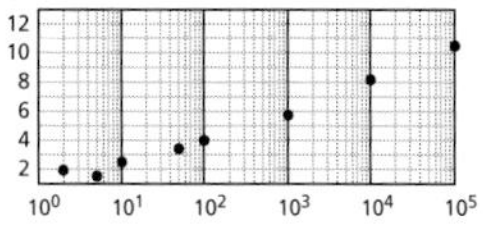

The points appear to lie on a line, especially as the values of x get larger. **4.** Logarithmic; on the vertical axis, equal differences are not represented by equal distances.

5a. Suppose $y = \log_b x$ with $b > 0$, $b \neq 1$. Rewrite the equation as $b^y = x$, and take the logarithm of each side: $\log b^y = \log x$. Then $y \cdot \log b = \log x$, so $y = \frac{1}{\log b} \cdot \log x$. Since $\frac{1}{\log b}$ is a constant, say B, the equation becomes $y = B \cdot \log x$, which is in linear form. **b.** $\frac{1}{\log b}$

6a. If $y = a \cdot x^b$, then $\log y = \log (a \cdot x^b)$. So, $\log y = \log a + b \cdot \log x$. But $\log a$ is a constant, say A, so the equation becomes $\log y = A + b \cdot \log x$, which is in linear form. **b.** b **7.** The intersection of $y = x^2$ and $y = 10x^2$ is (0, 0). Because there is no value of 0 on the logarithmic axes, the intersection is not shown.

On Your Own

9a–b.

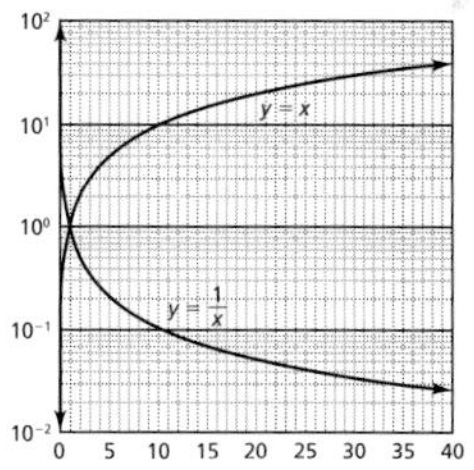

The graph of $y = x$, when shown using a logarithmic y-axis, looks like the graph of a logarithmic function when that function is shown on a standard coordinate plane. **10b.** 3 **c.** ±100 **12a.** Exponential; the ratio of successive outputs is constant.

Chapter 6

Lesson 6.1

On Your Own

12a, c.

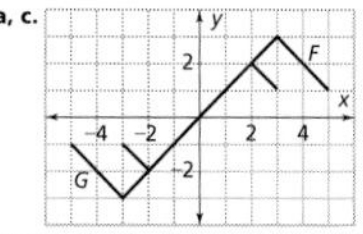

b. Connect (0, 0) and (−3, −3). Connect (−2, −2) and (−3, −1). Connect (−3, −3) and (−5, −1). **d.** Figure G is figure F rotated 180° about the origin. **13.** 180° rotational symmetry

16b.
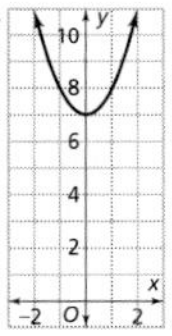

18c.
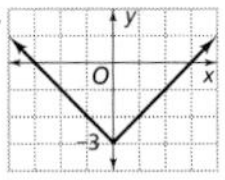

20a.
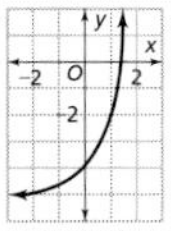

It is the graph of $y = 3^x$ translated 5 units down.

22c.
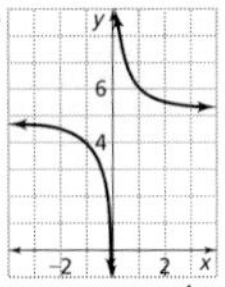

It is the graph of $y = \frac{1}{x}$ translated 5 units up.

Lesson 6.2
Check Your Understanding

1a. $\left(\frac{4}{5}, \frac{3}{5}\right), \left(\frac{4}{5}, -\frac{3}{5}\right)$
b. $\left(-\frac{4}{5}, \frac{3}{5}\right), \left(-\frac{4}{5}, -\frac{3}{5}\right), \left(\frac{3}{5}, \frac{4}{5}\right), \left(\frac{3}{5}, -\frac{4}{5}\right), \left(-\frac{3}{5}, \frac{4}{5}\right), \left(-\frac{3}{5}, -\frac{4}{5}\right)$ **2a.** $\left(\frac{12}{13}, \frac{5}{13}\right), \left(-\frac{12}{13}, \frac{5}{13}\right)$
b. $\left(\frac{8}{17}, \frac{15}{17}\right), \left(\frac{8}{17}, -\frac{15}{17}\right)$ **3.** If a, b, and c form a Pythagorean triple, then a, b, and c are positive integers that satisfy $a^2 + b^2 = c^2$. Dividing both sides of this equation by c^2 gives $\frac{a^2}{c^2} + \frac{b^2}{c^2} = \frac{c^2}{c^2}$, or $\left(\frac{a}{c}\right)^2 + \left(\frac{b}{c}\right)^2 = 1$. Thus, the point $\left(\frac{a}{c}, \frac{b}{c}\right)$ satisfies the equation of the unit circle, $x^2 + y^2 = 1$, and can be used to generate other points that are on the unit circle.
4a. $f(-x) = (-x)^2 = x^2 = f(x)$ **b.** The graph of $y = x^2$ has the y-axis as a line of symmetry, so if (x, y) is on the graph, then $(-x, y)$ is also on the graph. Since opposite inputs have the same output, $f(x) = x^2$ is an even function.
5a. $f(-x) = (-x)^3 + (-x) = -x^3 - x = -(x^3 + x) = -f(x)$ **b.** The graph of $y = x^3 + x$ has 180° rotational symmetry about the origin, so if (x, y) is on the graph, then $(-x, -y)$ is also on the graph. Since opposite inputs have opposite outputs, $f(x) = x^3 + x$ is an odd function. **6.** even functions: $y = x^2, y = |x|$; odd functions: $y = x, y = \frac{1}{x}, y = x^3, y = x^3 - x, y = x^3 + x$; both: none; neither: $y = \sqrt{x}, y = b^x, y = log_b x, x^2 + y^2 = 1$
7. $x^3 + x = 0$, or $x(x^2 + 1) = 0$, has only one real root, 0.

8a.

x	$x–3$	$(x–3)^2$
−1	−4	16
0	−3	9
1	−2	4
2	−1	1
3	0	0
4	1	1
5	2	4
6	3	9
7	4	16

b.
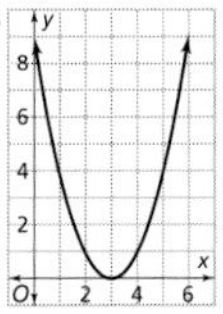

c. The graph of $y = (x - 3)^2$ is the graph of $y = x^2$ translated 3 units to the right.

On Your Own

10a. Near the origin $|x| < 1$, so $|x^3|$ is much less than $|x|$. Thus the x^3-term has very little effect on the value of $x^3 - x$. **11.** $(-1, 0)$, $(0, 0)$, $(1, 0)$

12a.
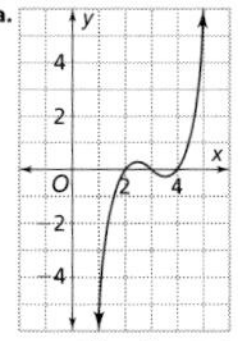

15a. $(x - 6)^2 + y^2 = 25$ **b.** $(x + 3)^2 + y^2 = 16$

Lesson 6.3
Check Your Understanding

1a.

$x = M - 5$	M	$y = \sqrt{M}$
−5	0	0
−4	1	1
−1	4	2
4	9	3
11	16	4
20	25	5

b. The graph of $y = \sqrt{x + 5}$ is the graph of $y = \sqrt{x}$ translated 5 units to the left.

c.
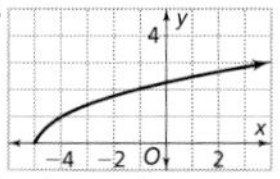

domain: $x \geq -5$, range: $y \geq 0$

2a.
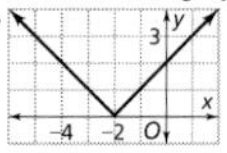

b.
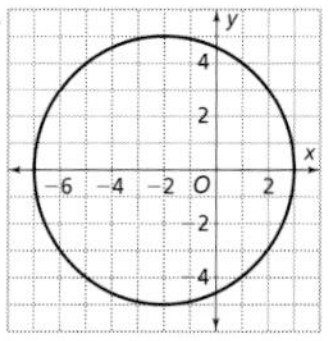

c.
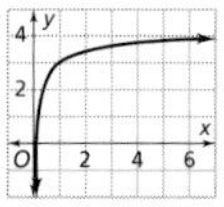

d.
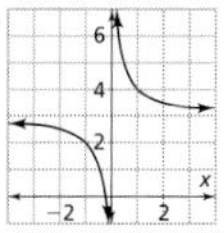

3a.
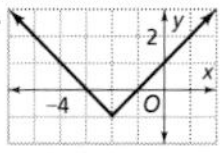

b.
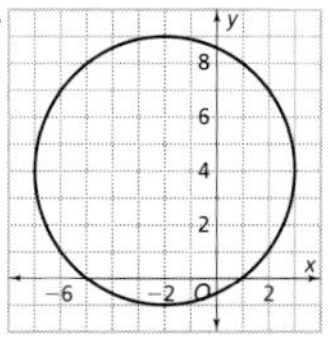

c.
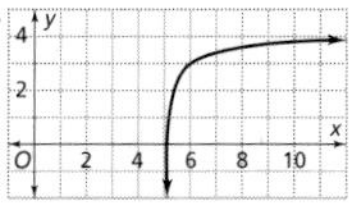

d.
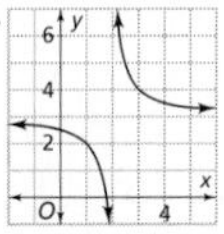

4. Disagree; Walter should have replaced each x in the original equation by $(x - 2)$ to get $y = (x - 2)^3 - (x - 2)$. **5a.** The graph of the second equation is the graph of the first equation translated 2 units to the right.
b. $x^3 - x + 1$

c.
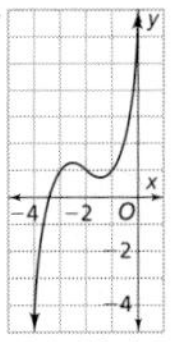

6a. $(-3, 0)$ **b.** $(-3, 2)$ **c.** $(-h, k)$

7a.
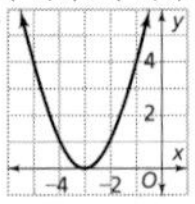

b.
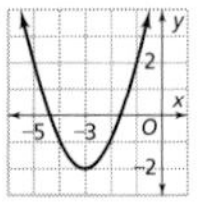

On Your Own

8a.
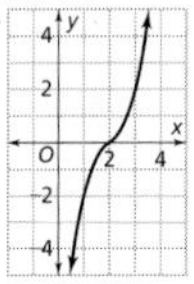

9a.
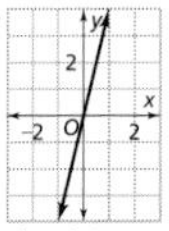

The slope is 3.
11a. $y = 4(x - 3) + 1$ or $y = 4x - 11$
12a. The graph of $y = (x - 3)^2 + 6(x - 3) + 7$ is the graph of $y = x^2 + 6x + 7$ translated 3 units to the right; Answers may vary. Sample: In the equation $y = (x - 3)^2 + 6(x - 3) + 7$, each x in the equation $y = x^2 + 6x + 7$ is replaced by $M = x - 3$, so each point on the graph of $y = M^2 + 6M + 7$ corresponds to the point on the graph of $y = x^2 + 6x + 7$ with x-coordinate 3 units less.

Lesson 6.4
Check Your Understanding

1a.

x	$N = x^2 + 1$	$y = \frac{N}{5}$
−2	5	1
−1	2	$\frac{2}{5}$
0	1	$\frac{1}{5}$
1	2	$\frac{2}{5}$
2	5	1
3	10	2

b. The y-values for the graph of $5y = x^2 + 1$ are smaller by the factor 5 when compared to the corresponding y-values for the graph of $y = x^2 + 1$, so the graph of $5y = x^2 + 1$ is the graph of $y = x^2 + 1$ scaled vertically by the factor $\frac{1}{5}$.

c.
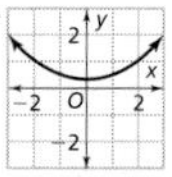

2a.
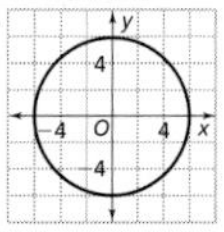

b.
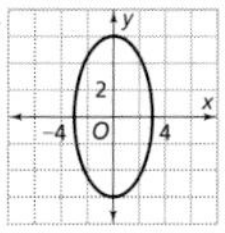

c.
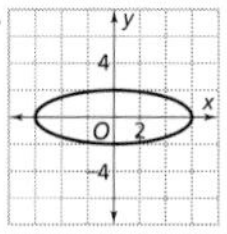

d.
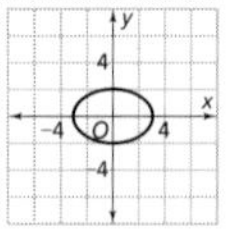

e.
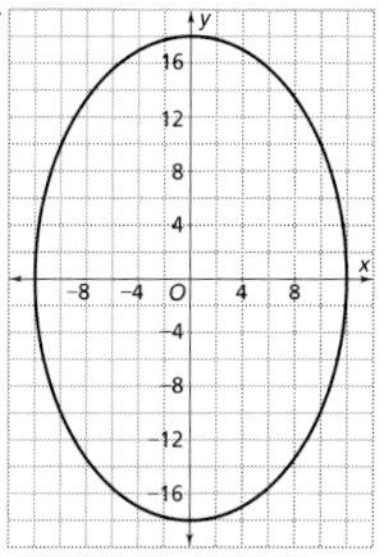

3a.
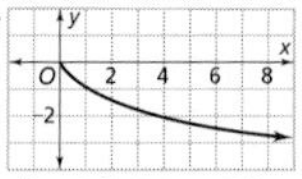

domain: $x \geq 0$, range: $y \leq 0$

b.
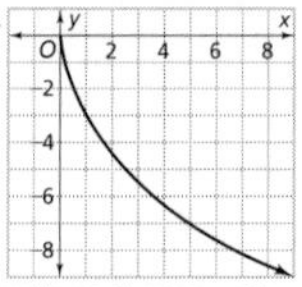

domain: $x \geq 0$, range: $y \leq 0$

c.
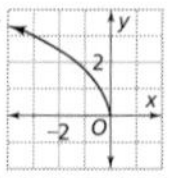

domain: $x \leq 0$, range: $y \geq 0$

d.

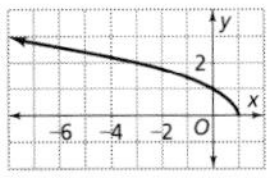

domain: $x \le 1$, range: $y \ge 0$

4. $y = \left(\frac{1}{2}x - 2\right)^2 + 3$

5a.

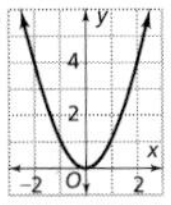

b.

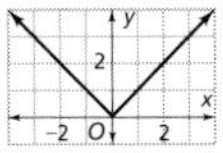

c.

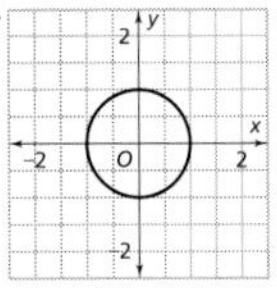

6. Agree with both; the statement $f(-x) = f(x)$ is equivalent to saying the graph of f has the y-axis as a line of symmetry.
7. Because all the exponents are even the y-values for x and $-x$ are the same, so the function is even. **8.** $g(-x) = f(-x) + f(-(-x)) = f(-x) + f(x) = g(x)$, so g is an even function.

9a–b.

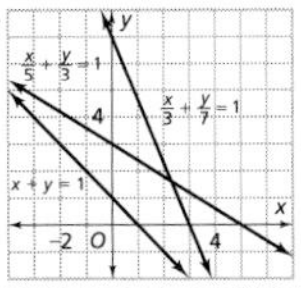

c. Answers may vary. Sample: (0, 12), (−17, 0)
d. The intercepts of $\frac{x}{a} + \frac{y}{b} = 1$ are $(0, b)$ and $(a, 0)$.

On Your Own

10a.

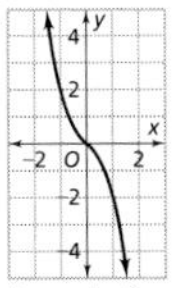

11a. the graph of $y = \frac{1}{x}$ reflected over the y-axis **c.** the graph of $y = \frac{1}{x}$ reflected over the y-axis and scaled vertically by the factor 4
13. Answers may vary. Sample: The graph of the second equation is the graph of the first equation after it has been reflected over the y-axis and then over the x-axis.

Lesson 6.5

On Your Own

7a. 6; 15; −3; −21; 0 **b.** Thinking of D_s as mapping the number line onto itself, the output of D_s is the image of the input after a dilation by the factor s (using the origin of the number line as the center of dilation).
10a. 24; −6; 0; 42; 48 **12a.** 3 **14a.** $x \mapsto 2x + 5$
17a. $(f \circ f)(x) = 4x + 9$

Lesson 6.6

Check Your Understanding

1. T_b **2.** $a \neq 0$, $b = 0$
3. $(D_s \circ D_t)(x) = D_s(D_t(x)) = D_s(tx) = s(tx) = (st)x = D_{st}(x)$ **4a.** $x \mapsto 2x + 3$
b. $x \mapsto 2x + 6$ **c.** $x \mapsto 7x - 5$ **d.** $x \mapsto 7x - 35$
e. $x \mapsto ax + b$ **f.** $x \mapsto ax + ab$ **5.** $b = 0$ or $a = 1$ **6a.** $\mathcal{A}_{(6,\,9)}$ **b.** $\mathcal{A}_{(6,\,2)}$ **c.** $\mathcal{A}_{(-1,\,7)}$
d. $\mathcal{A}_{(-1,\,-1)}$ **e.** $\mathcal{A}_{(1,\,0)}$ **f.** $\mathcal{A}_{(1,\,0)}$ **7.** $e = ac$, $f = ad + b$ **8a.** $a = 3$, $b = 8$ **b.** $a = 5$, $b = 2$
c. $a = \frac{1}{2}$, $b = -\frac{3}{2}$ **d.** $a = \frac{1}{2}$, $b = -\frac{3}{2}$

On Your Own

10a. $x = \frac{1}{4}y - 2$ **b.** $\left(\mathcal{A}_{(4,\,8)} \circ \mathcal{A}_{(\frac{1}{4},\,-2)}\right)(x) = \mathcal{A}_{(4,\,8)}\left(\mathcal{A}_{(\frac{1}{4},\,-2)}(x)\right) = \mathcal{A}_{(4,\,8)}\left(\frac{1}{4}x - 2\right) = 4\left(\frac{1}{4}x - 2\right) + 8 = x - 8 + 8 = x$, and $\left(\mathcal{A}_{(\frac{1}{4},\,-2)} \circ \mathcal{A}_{(4,\,8)}\right)(x) = \mathcal{A}_{(\frac{1}{4},\,-2)}\left(\mathcal{A}_{(4,\,8)}(x)\right) = \mathcal{A}_{(\frac{1}{4},\,-2)}(4x + 8) = \frac{1}{4}(4x + 8) - 2 = x + 2 - 2 = x$. Thus, $\mathcal{A}_{(4,\,8)}$ and $\mathcal{A}_{(\frac{1}{4},\,-2)}$ are inverses, so $(\mathcal{A}_{(4,\,8)})^{-1} = \mathcal{A}_{(\frac{1}{4},\,-2)}$. **11a.** $c = \frac{1}{2}$, $d = \frac{1}{2}$
13a. $\mathcal{A}_{(\frac{1}{3},\,-\frac{4}{3})}$ **14a.** $a = 3$, $b = -6$

15a. $\mathcal{A}_{(\frac{1}{6},\,-\frac{3}{2})}$ **18a.** $\mathcal{A}_{(a^2,\,ab+b)}(x)$

Lesson 6.7

Check Your Understanding

1. $y = 8x^2 - 2x - 15$ **2a.** $a = 9$, $b = 6$, $c = 9$, $d = 81$ **b.** $N = 81$, $M = \pm 9$, $x = \frac{1}{3}$ or $-\frac{5}{3}$ **c.** $\frac{1}{3}, -\frac{5}{3}$ **3a.** $a = 2$, $b = 2$, $c = 2$, $d = -6$ **b.** $N = -6$, no real values for M or x
c. no real roots **4a.** $y = (x + 3)^2 + (-4)$
b. $y = (x + (-2))^2 + (-3)$ **c.** $y = \left(x + \frac{5}{2}\right)^2 + \frac{3}{4}$
5a. $\frac{b}{2}$ **b.** $y = M^2 - \frac{b^2}{4} + c$
c. $y = \left(x + \frac{b}{2}\right)^2 + \left(-\frac{b^2}{4} + c\right)$; $D = -\frac{b^2}{4} + c$
6a. $a = 1$, $b = 2$, $c = 1$, $d = -1$ **b.** $a = \frac{1}{2}$, $b = \frac{1}{2}$, $c = \frac{1}{8}$, $d = -1$

On Your Own

9a. $e = a$, $f = \frac{b}{2}$, $g = a$, $h = \frac{b^2 - 4ac}{4}$
11. $\frac{b}{3}$ **12a.** The equation shown is the result of substituting $\left(M - \frac{b}{3}\right)$ into the equation $y = x^3 + bx^2 + cx + d$. In Exercise 11, we found that $\frac{b}{3}$ is the value of k for which the substitution of $(M - k)$ into the equation $y = x^3 + bx^2 + cx + d$ makes the coefficient of M^2 0.

Lesson 6.8

Exercises

On Your Own

7. Answers may vary. Sample: Each value on the x number line is one-half the corresponding value on the M number line.
8c. $x = -M$

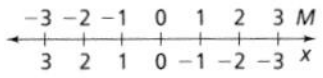

9. Answers may vary. Sample: For each value on the M number line, the corresponding value on the x number line is $\frac{1}{2}M + \frac{3}{2}$.
11a. $x = 3M - 1$

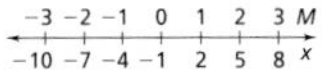

12a. $\mathcal{A}_{(\frac{1}{2},\,\frac{-3}{2})}$

Lesson 6.9

Check Your Understanding

1a. If $M = -2x + 1$, then $x = -\frac{1}{2}M + \frac{1}{2} = T_{\frac{1}{2}}\left(-\frac{1}{2}M\right) = \left(T_{\frac{1}{2}} \circ D_{-\frac{1}{2}}\right)(M)$.

b.

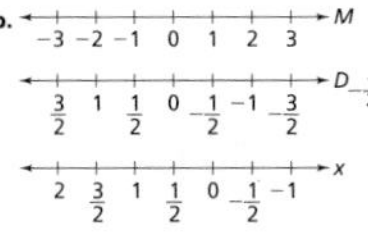

c. The $D_{-\frac{1}{2}}(M)$ number line is the image of the M number line reflected over 0 and dilated by the factor 2; the x number line is the image of the $D_{-\frac{1}{2}}(M)$ number line translated $\frac{1}{2}$ unit to the right; the x number line is the image of the M number line reflected over 0, dilated by the factor 2, and translated $\frac{1}{2}$ unit to the right.
2a. If $M = -2x + 1$, then $x = -\frac{1}{2}M + \frac{1}{2} = -\frac{1}{2}(M - 1) = D_{-\frac{1}{2}}(M - 1) = \left(D_{-\frac{1}{2}} \circ T_{-1}\right)(M)$.

b.

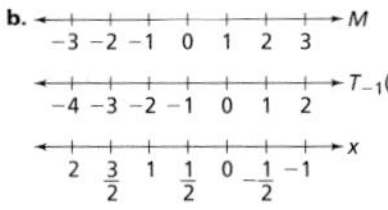

c. The $T_{-1}(M)$ number line is the image of the M number line translated 1 unit to the right; the x number line is the image of the $T_{-1}(M)$ number line reflected over 0 and dilated by the factor 2; the x number line is the image of the M number line translated 1 unit right, reflected over 0, and dilated by the factor 2.
3a. $M = \mathcal{A}_{(3,\,1)}(x)$, $N = \mathcal{A}_{(3,\,4)}(y)$

b.

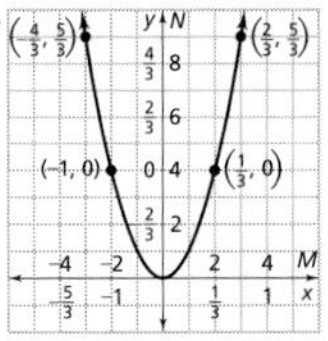

4. Yes; Answers may vary. Sample: You can use more than two transformations. For example, $\mathcal{A}_{(-\frac{1}{2},\,\frac{1}{2})} = D_{\frac{1}{2}} \circ T_1 \circ D_{-1}$.

5a. $M = 2x + 3$ and $N = 2y - 1$, so $N = M^2$ becomes $2y - 1 = (2x + 3)^2$, or $2y + 1 = 14x^2 + 12x + 9$. Then $2y = 4x^2 + 12x + 10$, so $y = 2x^2 + 6x + 5$.

b.

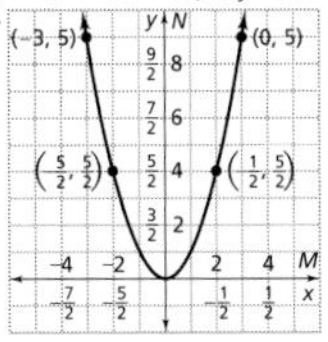

6.

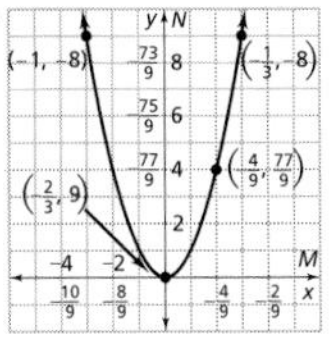

7.

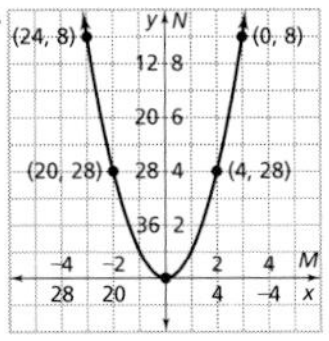

8a.

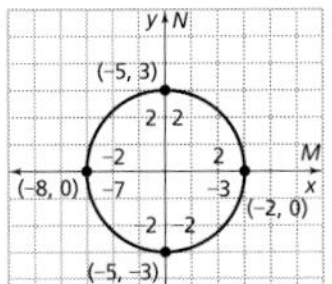

b.

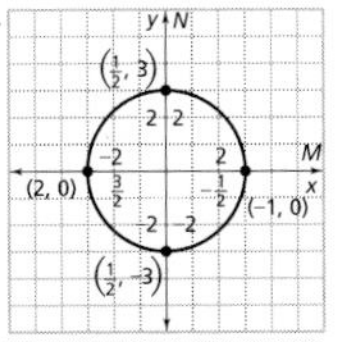

c.

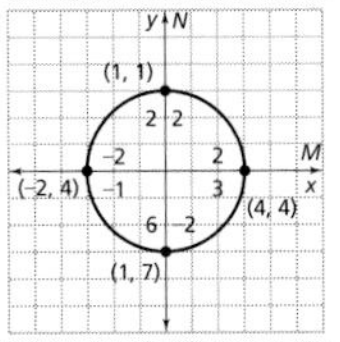

d.

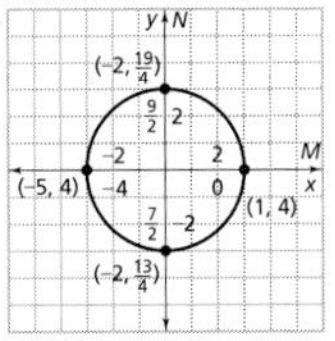

9a.

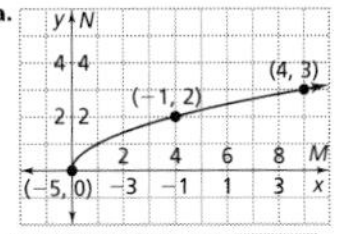

b.

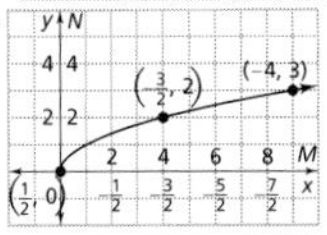

c.

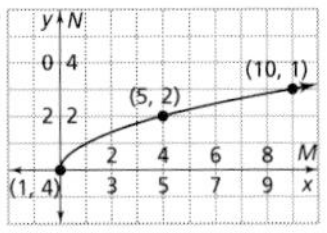

d.

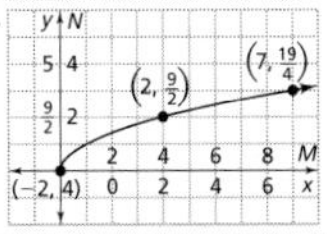

10. Disagree; Answers may vary. Sample: If you dilate the graph of a circle horizontally and vertically by factors with different absolute values, the distances between the transformed intercepts are no longer equal and the transformed graph is no longer a circle. So, the graphs for Exercises 8b and 8d are not circles.

On Your Own

11a.

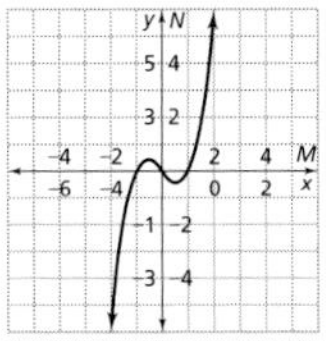

13b.

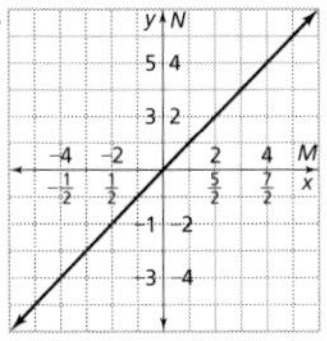

14a.

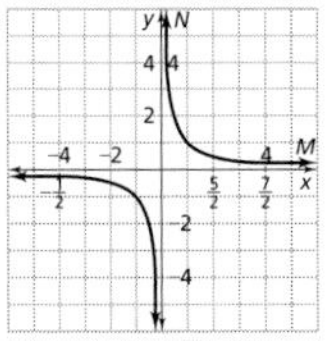

15a.

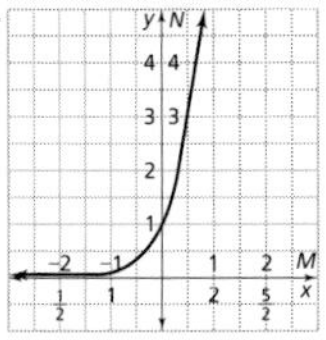

16a.
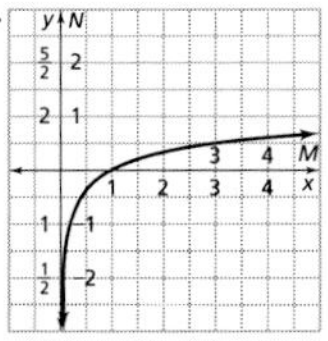

20a.
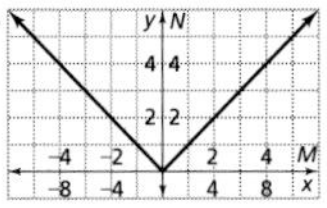

Lesson 6.10
Check Your Understanding
1a. $\frac{2}{3}$ **b.** $\frac{4}{3}$ **c.** 2 **d.** $a = 1$: all real numbers, $a \neq 1$: 0 **e.** none **f.** $a = 1$ and $b = 0$: all real numbers, $a = 1$ and $b \neq 0$: none, $a \neq 1$: $\frac{-b}{a-1}$
2. exactly one: $\mathcal{A}_{(a,\,b)}$ where $a \neq 1$; more than one: $\mathcal{A}_{(a,\,b)}$ where $a = 1$ and $b = 0$; zero: $\mathcal{A}_{(a,\,b)}$ where $a = 1$ and $b \neq 0$ **3.** $\mathcal{A}_{(1,\,0)}$ and $\mathcal{A}_{(-1,\,b)}$ where b is any real number **4.** $\mathcal{A}_{(1,\,0)}$
5. Larry just needs to use his result to draw the correct conclusion. The fact that $A_{(1,\,-3)}$ has no fixed point implies that the original equation, $3x + 7 = 3x - 2$, has no solution.
6. $\mathcal{A}_{(a,\,5-5a)}$

On Your Own
8a. $\mathcal{A}_{(3,\,-4)}(2) = 3(2) - 4 = 2$, $\mathcal{A}_{(-5,\,12)}(2) = -5(2) + 12 = 2$ **b.** $\left(\mathcal{A}_{(3,\,-4)} \circ \mathcal{A}_{(-5,\,12)}\right)(2) = \mathcal{A}_{(3,\,-4)}(\mathcal{A}_{(-5,\,12)}(2)) = \mathcal{A}_{(3,\,-4)}(2) = 2$, $(\mathcal{A}_{(-5,\,12)} \circ \mathcal{A}_{(3,\,-4)})(2) = \mathcal{A}_{(-5,\,12)}(\mathcal{A}_{(3,\,-4)}(2)) = \mathcal{A}_{(-5,\,12)}(2) = 2$
c. Answers may vary. Sample: $(\mathcal{A}_{(3,\,-4)})^{-1}(2) = \mathcal{A}_{(\frac{1}{3},\,\frac{4}{3})}(2) = 2\left(\frac{2}{3}\right) + \frac{4}{3} = \frac{2}{3} + \frac{4}{3} = \frac{6}{3} = 2$, $(\mathcal{A}_{(-5,\,12)})^{-1}(2) = \mathcal{A}_{(-\frac{1}{5},\,\frac{12}{5})}(2) = 2\left(-\frac{1}{5}\right) + \frac{12}{5} = -\frac{2}{5} + \frac{12}{5} = \frac{10}{5} = 2$
11a. $T_3 \circ D_4 \circ (T_3)^{-1}(3) = T_3 \circ D_4(0) = T_3(0) = 3$, so the original composite is in S_3.
12a. $\left(\mathcal{A}_{(2,3)}\right)^{(5)} = \mathcal{A}\left(2^5, 3 \cdot \frac{2^5-1}{2-1}\right) = \mathcal{A}_{(32,\,93)}$

Chapter 7
Lesson 7.1
On Your Own
6a.

Roll	Gain	Total
1	5	55
2	−2	53
3	−4	49
4	3	52
5	−6	46
6	1	47
7	−6	41

7.

n	$t(n)$	Σ
0	1	1
1	9	10
2	90	100
3	900	1000
4	9,000	10,000

$\sum = 10^n$ **12a.** $h(n) = 100n^2$

Lesson 7.2
Check Your Understanding
1a. $S = \frac{n(n+1)}{2}$ **b.** $S = \frac{n(n+1)}{2}$
c. $S = \frac{(n-1) \cdot n}{2}$ **2a.** 6 **b.** 30 **c.** 250,500
3a. 16 **b.** 49 **c.** 250,000 **4a.** $S = n(n+1)$
b. $S = (n+1)^2$ **5a.** 65,504 **b.** 196,512
c. ≈5.862 **d.** $1 - \frac{1}{10^{10}} \approx 1$ **e.** ≈0.664
6a. Answers may vary. Sample: $1 + 2 + 3 + \cdots + 10 = 55$; $2 + 4 + 6 + \cdots + 22 = 132$; $4 + 7 + 10 + \cdots + 31 = 175$; Gauss's method works when there is a constant difference between successive terms. **b.** Answers may vary. Sample: $2 + 4 + 8 + \cdots + 64 = 126$; $5 + 10 + 20 + 40 + \cdots + 640 = 1275$; $4 + 12 + 36 + \cdots + 4 \cdot 3^{100} = 2 \cdot 3^{101} - 2 \approx 3.09 \cdot 10^{48}$; Euclid's method works when there is a constant ratio between successive terms. **7a.** $S = \frac{r^{n+1} - 1}{r - 1}$
b. $S = a \cdot \frac{r^{n+1} - 1}{r - 1}$

On Your Own
8a. −10 **10.** −19
12.

n	$f(n)$
1	$\frac{1}{2}$
2	$\frac{3}{4}$
3	$\frac{7}{8}$
4	$\frac{15}{16}$
5	$\frac{31}{32}$
n	$\frac{2^n-1}{2^n}$

$f(n) = \frac{2^n - 1}{2^n}$

Lesson 7.3
Check Your Understanding
1. Answers may vary. Sample: Cori is correct that the sum is never more than the whole sheet. David is correct that the total area of the rectangles on the desk increases, although by smaller and smaller amounts. **2.** Answers may vary. Sample: The area of the piece of paper in her hand keeps getting smaller and smaller, so the area of the "rest" of the paper gets closer to the starting area of 1. **3a.** 300
b. 1596 **c.** 3240 **d.** 7626 **e.** $\frac{n(n+1)}{2}$ **4a.** $1 - r^2$
b. $1 - r^3$ **c.** $1 - r^4$ **d.** $1 - r^{n+1}$ **5a.** ≈2.92
b. ≈1.33 **c.** 11,111,111,111 **6.** $\frac{1 - r^{n+1}}{1 - r} = \frac{-1}{-1} \cdot \frac{1 - r^{n+1}}{1 - r} = \frac{-1 + r^{n+1}}{-1 + r} = \frac{r^{n+1} - 1}{r - 1}$

On Your Own
8a.

n	$s(n)$	Σ
0	2	2
1	5	7
2	8	15
3	11	26

b. $s(n) = 3n + 2$ **9a.** $\frac{1}{9}$ in hand, $\frac{4}{9}$ in pile 1, $\frac{4}{9}$ in pile 2

Lesson 7.4
Check Your Understanding
1a. 91 **b.** 324 **c.** 10 **d.** 969 **2.** Yes; Answers may vary. Sample: After you substitute values for the placeholder, the placeholder does not appear in the sequence.
3a. $\sum_{i=1}^{n} n^2$ **b.** $\sum_{i=1}^{6} 1$ **c.** $\sum_{i=1}^{10} i$ **4a.** $\sum_{i=1}^{10} \frac{1}{2^i}$ **b.** $\sum_{i=1}^{n} \frac{1}{2^i}$
c. $\sum_{i=1}^{\infty} \frac{1}{2^i}$ **5.** $\frac{1023}{1024} \approx 0.999023438$

On Your Own
6a. $\sum_{i=1}^{10} \frac{1}{3^i}$ **7.** $\frac{29{,}524}{59{,}049} \approx 0.499991532$

Lesson 7.5
On Your Own
3a. $q(n) = 3n + 5$, which is linear.

Lesson 7.6
Check Your Understanding
1a. yes **b.** yes **c.** no **d.** yes **e.** yes **f.** yes **g.** yes **h.** no **i.** no **j.** yes **k.** yes **2a.** 440; 442 **b.** 4,782,966; 2186 **c.** 182; 332 **3a.** 25 **b.** 100
c. 75 **d.** $\sum_{k=1}^{n} (2k - 1) = n^2$ **e.** 1,000,000

On Your Own
4. $\sum_{k=0}^{n} (5k - 1) = \frac{(n+1)(5n-2)}{2}$ **7a.** 42
9a. 99,999

Lesson 7.7
Check Your Understanding
1. 6625 **2a.** 374 **b.** 1.99988 **c.** 0.99988 **3a.** 377 **b.** 572 **c.** 1326 **d.** 332

On Your Own
4e. 765 **5a.** 70 **b.** 66 **c.** 70 **d.** 12,207,241
10b. 1,039,600 **11a.** $\frac{n(n+1)(n+2)}{3}$ **13a.** 450

Lesson 7.8
Check Your Understanding
1. $H(n) = \frac{n^2 + n + 6}{2}$
2a. $q(n) = \begin{cases} 32 & \text{if } n = 0 \\ q(n-1) + 2n & \text{if } n > 0 \end{cases}$
b. $Q(n) = n(n+1) + 32$ **3.** $S(n) = n^2$

On Your Own
5a.

n	$s(n)$	Δ
0	7	1
1	8	4
2	12	9
3	21	

$s(n) = \begin{cases} 7 & \text{if } n = 0 \\ s(n-1) + n^2 & \text{if } n > 0 \end{cases}$

6a. $t(n) = \sum_{k=0}^{n} 2^k$

10a. $p(n) = \begin{cases} 1 & \text{if } n = 1 \\ p(n-1) + (3n-2) & \text{if } n > 1 \end{cases}$
b. $P(n) = \frac{3n^2 - n}{2}$

Lesson 7.9
On Your Own
5a. A.M.: $h(n) = 3n$; P.M.: $g(n) = 3n + 5$
7. $708

Lesson 7.10
Check Your Understanding
1. $\frac{4}{n-1}$ **2.** Yes; $\frac{1}{6}, \frac{1}{3}, \frac{1}{2}, \frac{2}{3}, \frac{5}{6}, 1, \ldots$ **3.** Yes; 1, 3, π; Any multiple of the difference between 3 and π cannot equal a multiple of the difference between 1 and 3.
4a.

n	$q(n)$	Σ
0	9	9
1	15	24
2	21	45
3	27	72
4	33	105

$q(n) = 6n + 9$;
$Q(n) = 3n^2 + 2n + 9$
b.

n	$p(n)$	Σ
0	12	12
1	7	19
2	2	21
3	−3	18
4	−8	10

$p(n) = 12 - 5n$; $P(n) = -\frac{5}{2}n^2 + \frac{19}{2}n + 12$
5. 8, 10, 12, 14, 16, . . . ; there is no other arithmetic sequence with the same 0th and 2nd terms. **6a.** 2, 5, 8, 11, 14, . . . **b.** 2, 7, 15, 26, 40, . . . **c.** $g(n) = 2 + 3n$; $G(n) = \frac{3}{2}n^2 + \frac{7}{2}n + 2$
7a.

n	$t(n)$	Σ
0	5	5
1	14	19
2	23	42
3	32	74
4	41	115

$t(n) = 5 + 9n$; $T(n) = \frac{9}{2}n^2 + \frac{19}{2}n + 5$

b.

n	$h(n)$	Σ
0	7	7
1	3	10
2	−1	9
3	−5	4
4	−9	−5

$h(n) = 7 - 4n$; $H(n) = -2n^2 + 5n + 7$
c.

n	$t(n)$	Σ
0	6	6
1	6.5	12.5
2	7	19.5
3	7.5	27
4	8	35

$t(n) = 6 + \frac{1}{2}n$; $T(n) = \frac{1}{4}n^2 + \frac{25}{4}n + 6$
8a.

n	$f(n)$	Σ
0	a	a
1	$a + d$	$2a + d$
2	$a + 2d$	$3a + 3d$
3	$a + 3d$	$4a + 6d$
4	$a + 4d$	$5a + 10d$
5	$a + 5d$	$6a + 15d$

b. $F(n) = \frac{1}{2}(n+1)(2a + nd)$

On Your Own
11. If the integers are n, $n + 1$, and $n + 2$, then the average is $\frac{n + (n+1) + (n+2)}{3} = \frac{3n+3}{3} = n + 1$, which is the middle number.
13a. 1, 5, 14, 30, 55 **15.** 1, 6, 11, 21, . . . or 7, 10, 13, 16, 19, . . . **16.** Answers may vary. Sample: for the sequence 1, 4, 9, 16, 25, 36, . . . , the Δ values are 3, 5, 7, 9, 11, . . . , which is an arithmetic sequence. A closed form is $f(n) = n^2$.

Lesson 7.11
Check Your Understanding
1a. 320 **b.** 320 **c.** 5 **d.** $\frac{5}{64}$ **e.** 4.5 **f.** 75 **g.** ±18 **h.** 18 **2.** Yes; Any constant sequence such as 3, 3, 3, 3, . . . has a constant difference (0) and a constant ratio (1), so it is both arithmetic and geometric. **3.** Answers may vary. Sample:

$a_1 = 2, 4, 6, 8, \ldots$ and $g_1 = 2, 4, 8, 16, 32, \ldots$, the common difference is greater than 1 and the terms of the sequence increase, the common ratio is greater than 1, if the first term is positive the terms will increase, if the first term is negative the terms will decrease; $a_2 = 1, 2, 3, 4, 5, \ldots$ and $g_2 = 1, 1, 1, 1, 1, \ldots$, the common difference is 1 and the terms of the sequence increase, the common ratio is 1 and the terms of the sequence remain constant; $a_3 = 6, 5, 4, 3, 2, \ldots$ and $g_3 = 6, -6, 6, -6, 6, \ldots$ the common difference is negative 1 and the terms of the sequence decrease, the common ratio is −1, the terms will alternate between positive and negative values with the same absolute value; $a_4 = 5, 2, -1, -4, -7, \ldots$ and $g_4 = 5, -15, 45, -135, 405, \ldots$ the common difference is less than −1 and the terms of the sequence decrease, the common ratio is less than −1, the terms will alternate between positive and negative values; $a_5 = 10, 9.5, 9, 8.5, 8, 7.5, \ldots$ and $g_5 = 10, 5, \frac{5}{2}, \frac{5}{4}, \frac{5}{8}, \ldots$, the common difference is between 0 and 1, and the terms of the sequence decrease, the common ratio is between 0 and 1, if the first term is positive the terms will decrease towards zero, if the first term is negative the terms will increase towards zero

4a. $\sum_{i=0}^{n} 5 \cdot \left(\frac{1}{2}\right)^n = -10\left[\left(\frac{1}{2}\right)^{n+1} - 1\right]$ or $\sum_{i=0}^{n} 5 \cdot \left(\frac{1}{2}\right)^n = 10\left[1 - \left(\frac{1}{2}\right)^{n+1}\right]$ **b.** ≈9.999847
5a. $295.24 **b.** 21 months

On Your Own
6a. $g(n) = 5 \cdot 2^{n-1}$ **e.** $g(n) = 576 \cdot \left(\frac{1}{2}\right)^n$
8.
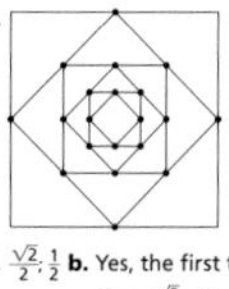

a. $\frac{\sqrt{2}}{2}; \frac{1}{2}$ **b.** Yes, the first term is 1 and the common ratio is $\frac{\sqrt{2}}{2}$. **10a.** $2^{63} \approx 9.22 \cdot 10^{18}$
13. about $28,650 **14a.** at least 5.5 mi

Lesson 7.12
Check Your Understanding
1a.

n	$t(n)$	$T(n)$
1	7	7
2	$7 \cdot \left(\frac{2}{9}\right) = \frac{14}{9}$	$8\frac{5}{9}$
3	$7 \cdot \left(\frac{2}{9}\right)^2 = \frac{28}{81}$	$8\frac{73}{81}$
4	$7 \cdot \left(\frac{2}{9}\right)^3 = \frac{56}{729}$	$8\frac{713}{729}$

$T(n)$ has a limit, which is 9.
b.

n	$t(n)$	$T(n)$
1	100	100
2	$100 \cdot \frac{1}{2} = 50$	150
3	$100 \cdot \left(\frac{1}{2}\right)^2 = 25$	175
4	$100 \cdot \left(\frac{1}{2}\right)^3 = 12.5$	187.5

$T(n)$ has a limit, which is 200.
c.

n	$t(n)$	$T(n)$
1	$\frac{3}{4}$	$\frac{3}{4}$
2	$\frac{3}{4} \cdot 2 = \frac{3}{2}$	$2\frac{1}{4}$
3	$\frac{3}{4} \cdot 2^2 = 3$	$5\frac{1}{4}$
4	$\frac{3}{4} \cdot 2^3 = 6$	$11\frac{1}{4}$

$T(n)$ does not have a limit.
d.

n	$t(n)$	$T(n)$
1	1	1
2	1	2
3	1	3
4	1	4

$T(n)$ does not have a limit.
2. 2 miles (she is traveling twice as fast, so in the same time period she will travel twice as far).

On Your Own
3a.

b. The lengths of the ends of Stages 0, 1, 2, and 3 are 1, $\frac{4}{3}$, $\frac{16}{9}$, and $\frac{64}{27}$, respectively.
5a. $\frac{9}{5}$ square units

Lesson 7.13
Check Your Understanding
1a. $a = 0.123$ **b.** $r = 0.001$ **c.** $\frac{123}{999}$ (or $\frac{41}{333}$)
2a. $\frac{12}{99}$ (or $\frac{4}{33}$) **b.** $\frac{807}{999}$ (or $\frac{269}{333}$) **c.** $\frac{123}{9990}$ (or $\frac{41}{3330}$)
d. $\frac{75{,}048}{999{,}000}$ (or $\frac{3127}{41{,}625}$)

On Your Own
4. The series $1 + 2 + 3 + 4 + \ldots$ does not have a finite value, so it was not possible to "call it x."

Lesson 7.14
On Your Own
6a. $(a + b)^2 = a^2 + 2ab + b^2$
b. $(a + b)^3 = a^3 + 3a^2b + 3ab^2 + b^3$
8a. $\frac{1}{16}r^2 + \frac{3}{8}rs + \frac{9}{16}s^2$ **b.** $\frac{1}{64}r^3 + \frac{9}{64}r^2s + \frac{27}{64}rs^2 + \frac{27}{64}s^3$

Lesson 7.15
Check Your Understanding
1a. 32 or 2^5 **b.** 64 or 2^6 **c.** 128 or 2^7 **d.** 2^n
2. Answers may vary. Sample: Each element in row $(n - 1)$ contributes twice to row n, so the sum of entries in row n is twice the sum of entries in row $(n - 1)$.

Lesson 7.16
Check Your Understanding
1a. $(x + y)^7 = x^7 + 7x^6y + 21x^5y^2 + 35x^4y^3 + 35x^3y^4 + 21x^2y^5 + 7xy^6 + y^7$
b. $(x + 2y)^5 = x^5 + 10x^4y + 40x^3y^2 + 80x^2y^3 + 80xy^4 + 32y^5$ **2a.** 56 **b.** a^5b^3
c. entry $\binom{8}{4}$ **3a.** 120 **b.** 10 **c.** 252

On Your Own
4. 0; 0; 0

Chapter 8
Lesson 8.0
Check Your Understanding
1. 24.09 **2a.** 210 **b.** 29

c.
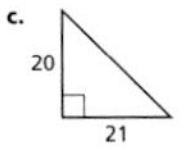

Each angle measures about 45°. **d.** 46°, 44°
3. $\sin\theta = \frac{15}{17}$, $\tan\theta = \frac{15}{8}$ **4.** $\sin\theta = \frac{\text{opp}}{\text{hyp}}$ and $\cos\theta = \frac{\text{adj}}{\text{hyp}}$, so $\frac{\sin\theta}{\cos\theta} = \frac{\frac{\text{opp}}{\text{hyp}}}{\frac{\text{adj}}{\text{hyp}}} = \frac{\text{opp}}{\text{adj}} = \tan\theta$.
5. $\frac{\sqrt{15}}{4}$ **6.** $72\sqrt{3} \approx 124.71$, $24\sqrt{3} \approx 41.57$, or $18\sqrt{3} \approx 31.2$

On Your Own
9.

θ	$\sin\theta$	$\cos\theta$	$\tan\theta$
30°	$\frac{1}{2}$	$\frac{\sqrt{3}}{2}$	$\frac{\sqrt{3}}{3}$
60°	$\frac{\sqrt{3}}{2}$	$\frac{1}{2}$	$\sqrt{3}$

12a. The largest value is 1 and the smallest is 0. As θ gets close to 90°, $\sin\theta$ gets close to 1, and as θ gets close to 0, $\sin\theta$ gets close to 0. **13a.** $\sin\theta = \frac{4}{5}$, $\cos\theta = \frac{3}{5}$, $\tan\theta = \frac{4}{3}$ **14.** You do not know that $\triangle TRI$ is a right triangle.

Lesson 8.1
On Your Own
11.

Angle	Coordinates
0°	(1, 0)
10°	(0.985, 0.174)
20°	(0.940, 0.342)
30°	(0.866, 0.5)
40°	(0.766, 0.643)
50°	(0.643, 0.766)
60°	(0.5, 0.866)
70°	(0.342, 0.940)
80°	(0.174, 0.985)
90°	(0, 1)

12a. magnitude 5, argument ≈ 53°
15. Answers may vary. Sample: The x-coordinate starts at 1 when Olivia's angle is 0°, decreases to 0 as her angle increases to 90°, decreases to −1 as her angle increases to 180°, increases to 0 as her angle increases to 270°, and increases to 1 as her angle increases to 360°. This pattern will repeat from 360° to 720°, from 720° to 1080°, and so on.
18. $a = -1$, $b = \sqrt{3}$

Lesson 8.2
Check Your Understanding
1. Answers may vary. Sample: If Jo's reasoning were correct, then the point $\left(\frac{1}{2}, \frac{1}{2}\right)$ should be on the unit circle and satisfy the equation $x^2 + y^2 = 1$. However, $\left(\frac{1}{2}\right)^2 + \left(\frac{1}{2}\right)^2 \neq 1$, so the point $\left(\frac{1}{2}, \frac{1}{2}\right)$ is not on the circle. **2.** $a = 0.342$, $b = 0.940$ **3.** $-\frac{\sqrt{3}}{2} - \frac{1}{2}i \approx -0.866 - 0.5i$ **4a.** $\cos\theta = -\cos(\theta + 180°)$
b. $\sin\theta = -\sin(\theta + 180°)$
c. $\tan\theta = \tan(\theta + 180°)$ **5a.** 1 **b.** 1 **6.** If the magnitude of a complex number is 1, such as i or $-i$, then it must lie on the unit circle.
7a. $\theta = 180° \cdot k$, where k is an integer.
b. $\theta = 90° + 180° \cdot k$, where k is an integer.
c. $\theta = 180° \cdot k$, where k is an integer.

On Your Own
8a.
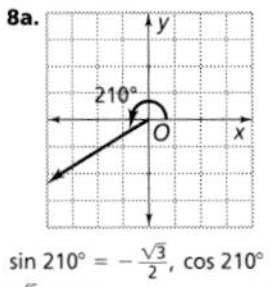

$\sin 210° = -\frac{\sqrt{3}}{2}$, $\cos 210° = -\frac{1}{2}$, $\tan 210° = \frac{\sqrt{3}}{3}$ **11.** Answers may vary. Sample: Since 310° is the same as −50° on the unit circle, we know that $\sin 310° = \sin(-50°)$. And because −50° is in Quadrant IV, where sine is negative, $\sin(-50°) = -\sin 50°$. So, $\sin 310° = -\sin 50°$.
12a. $-\frac{\sqrt{3}}{2}$

Lesson 8.3
Check Your Understanding
1. Answers may vary. Sample: 160° is in Quadrant II and 20° is in Quadrant I. Since $\sin\theta$ is positive in both quadrants, $\sin 160° = \sin 20°$. Since $\cos\theta$ is positive in Quadrant I and negative in Quadrant II, then $\cos 160° = -\cos 20°$. **2a.** I or II **b.** $\cos\theta = \pm\frac{21}{29}$
c. $\tan\theta = \pm\frac{20}{21}$ **3.** Answers may vary. Sample: $\theta \approx 89.5°$ **4.** Answers may vary. Sample: Since −60° intersects the unit circle in Quadrant IV, the cosine will be positive. In general, $\cos(-\theta) = \cos\theta$. So $\cos(-60°) = \cos 60° = \frac{1}{2}$.
5. tan 110°; cos 120° = sin 210°; sin 120°; cos 720°; tan 70° **6.** 30°, 150° **7a.** 0.7660
b. −0.6428 **c.** −0.6428 **d.** −0.7660 **e.** 1
f. 0.6428 **8a.** $\tan^2\theta = \frac{1}{\cos^2\theta} - 1$ or $\tan^2\theta + 1 = \frac{1}{\cos^2\theta}$ **b.** $\tan^2\theta + 1 = \frac{\sin^2\theta}{\cos^2\theta} + 1 = \frac{\sin^2\theta}{\cos^2\theta} + \frac{\cos^2\theta}{\cos^2\theta} = \frac{\sin^2\theta + \cos^2\theta}{\cos^2\theta} = \frac{1}{\cos^2\theta}$.
So, $\tan^2\theta = \frac{1}{\cos^2\theta} - 1$ or $\tan^2\theta + 1 = \frac{1}{\cos^2\theta}$.

On Your Own
9. $\cos(-30°) = \frac{\sqrt{3}}{2}$, $\sin(-30°) = -\frac{1}{2}$, $\tan(-30°) = -\frac{\sqrt{3}}{3}$ **10a.** sin 40° **d.** −sin 45°
11a. $\sin\theta$ **f.** $-\sin\theta$ **13a.** positive **c.** negative
17a. $-\frac{12}{37}$

Lesson 8.4
Check Your Understanding
1. $\cos q \approx -0.69$; $m\angle q \approx 134°$
2a. 60°, 300° **b.** $\pm\frac{\sqrt{3}}{2}$ **c.** $\frac{3}{4}$
3.
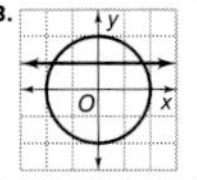

4. (0.8, 0.6), (−0.8, 0.6) **5a.** 53.1°, 306.9°
b. ±0.8 **c.** 0.64 **6.** Answers may vary. Sample:
$\frac{1}{z} = \frac{1}{\cos 30° + i\sin 30°} = \frac{1}{\frac{\sqrt{3}}{2} + \frac{1}{2}i} = \frac{1}{\frac{\sqrt{3}}{2} + \frac{1}{2}i} \cdot \frac{\frac{\sqrt{3}}{2} - \frac{1}{2}i}{\frac{\sqrt{3}}{2} - \frac{1}{2}i} = \frac{\frac{\sqrt{3}}{2} - \frac{1}{2}i}{\frac{3}{4} + \frac{1}{4}} = \frac{\sqrt{3}}{2} - \frac{1}{2}i = \bar{z}$

On Your Own
8a. 45°, 135° **11a.** Answers may vary. Sample: $\tan 30° = \frac{\sqrt{3}}{3}$ and $\cos 30° = \frac{\sqrt{3}}{2}$, so $\frac{1}{\cos^2 30°} - 1 = \frac{1}{\left(\frac{\sqrt{3}}{2}\right)^2} - 1 = \frac{1}{\frac{3}{4}} - 1 = \frac{4}{3} - \frac{3}{3} = \frac{1}{3} = \frac{3}{9} = \left(\frac{\sqrt{3}}{3}\right)^2 = \tan^2 30°$. **12a.** $\frac{1}{2}$

Lesson 8.5
Check Your Understanding
1. $x = 50° + 360° \cdot k$, where k is an integer.
2a. 37°, 143° **b.** 217°, 323° **3a.** 37°, 323°
b. no solution **4a.** no solution **b.** 41.8°, 138.2°
c. 30°, 150°, 210°, 330° **d.** 210°, 330° **5a.** 45°, 225° **b.** 135°, 315° **c.** 0°, 180°, 360° **6.** 30°, 150°, 199.47°, 340.53° **7.** Using the Parallelogram Law from Chapter 3, you find the vertices of the parallelogram formed by z and $\bar{z}$ are (0, 0), (a, b), $(a, -b)$, and $(2a, 0)$. So $z + \bar{z} = 2a$. Also, if $\arg z = \theta$, then $\cos\theta = \frac{a}{|z|}$ (because a is the value of the x-coordinate and

$|z|$ is the distance from the origin to z). So $a = |z|\cos\theta$ and $2a = 2|z|\cos\theta$. **8.** Drop a perpendicular from O to $\overline{AB}$ to form two congruent right triangles with acute angles 18° and 72°, legs $\frac{z}{2}$ and $\frac{z\sqrt{3}}{2}$, and hypotenuse 1.
Then $\cos 72° = \frac{\text{adjacent}}{\text{hypotenuse}} = \frac{z}{2}$, so
$z = 2 \cdot \cos 72°$.

On Your Own
10b. 45°, 225° **12a.** $0.940 + 0.342i$
e. $-0.682 - 0.731i$ **13a.** 36.87°

Lesson 8.6
On Your Own
6.
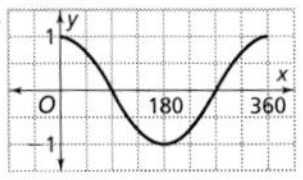

7. cos 230° > cos 190°

Lesson 8.7
Check Your Understanding
1a. The points on the unit circle that represent sin 50° and sin (−50°) have opposite y-values. So, $\sin 50° = -\sin(-50°)$. **b.** The y-values for $x = 50°$ and $x = -50°$ on the graph of $y = \sin x$ are opposites. So, $\sin 50° = -\sin(-50°)$.
2. Answers may vary. Sample: Derman sees only a portion of $y = \sin x$, and all the y-values are close to the x-axis. He should reset his window so that $-360 \le x \le 360$ and $-2 \le y \le 2$.
3.
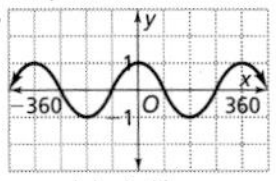

The graph looks like $y = \cos x$ because $\cos(x + 360°) = \cos x$. **4a.** There are infinitely many x-intercepts of $y = \cos x$.
b. A polynomial function must have a finite degree and a finite number of x-intercepts, so the cosine function cannot be written as a polynomial function. **c.** The tangent function, $\frac{\sin\theta}{\cos\theta}$, is undefined when $\cos\theta = 0$, that is when $\theta = 90° + k \cdot 180°$, where k is an integer.

5.
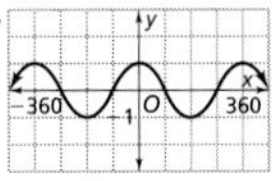

6.
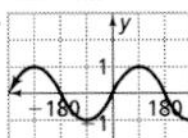

7. 127°, 413°
8.
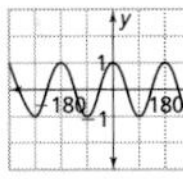

9a.
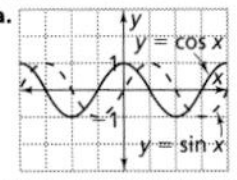

b. Answers may vary. Sample: 45°, 225°. Any angle of the form $45° + k \cdot 180°$, where k is an integer. **10a.** 1 **b.** $\tan\theta = \frac{\sin\theta}{\cos\theta}$ and if $\sin\theta = \cos\theta$, then the tangent must be 1.

On Your Own
11. Answers may vary. Sample:
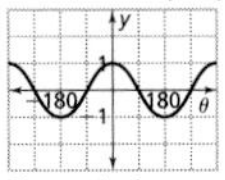

The graph of $y = \cos\theta$ is symmetric about the y-axis, so $\cos(-\theta) = \cos\theta$. **16.** Answers may vary. Samples:
a.
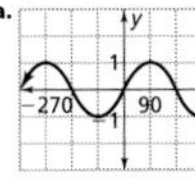

From the graph, $\sin x$ and $\sin(180° - x)$ are equal for any given x, so $\sin(180° - x) = \sin x$.

17. Answers may vary. Sample:
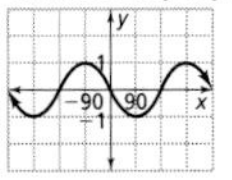

Lesson 8.8
Check Your Understanding
1a.
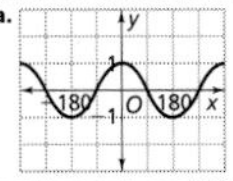

From the graph, $\cos(180° + x)$ and $-\cos x$ are equal for any given x, so $\cos(180° + x) = -\cos x$.
b.
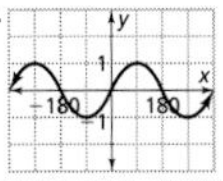

From the graph, $\sin(180° + x)$ and $-\sin x$ are equal for any given x, so $\sin(180° + x) = -\sin x$.
2. $\tan(180° + x) = \frac{\sin(180° + x)}{\cos(180° + x)} = \frac{-\sin x}{-\cos x} = \tan x$
3a.
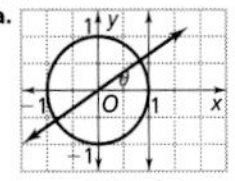

b. $\sin\theta = \frac{2\sqrt{13}}{13}$, $\cos\theta = \frac{3\sqrt{13}}{13}$
4a. $\tan(90° + \theta) = -\frac{3}{2} = -\frac{1}{\tan\theta}$ **b.** Answers may vary. Sample: The slope of the line is $\frac{y}{x}$, which is the same as the tangent of the angle formed by the line and the positive x-axis.
c. Answers may vary. Sample: If two perpendicular lines intersect at the origin and are not the x- and y-axes, and if (a, b) is a point on one line, then $(-b, a)$ is a point on the other line. So the slopes are $\frac{b}{a}$ and $-\frac{a}{b}$, which are negative reciprocals. Now suppose two lines have slopes that are negative reciprocals $\frac{b}{a}$ and $-\frac{a}{b}$. Using the results of Exercise 4a, $\tan(90° + \theta) = -\frac{1}{\tan\theta}$. If the line through (a, b) forms an angle of θ with the positive x-axis, then the line through $(-b, a)$ forms an angle of $(\theta + 90°)$, so the two lines are perpendicular. **5.** Answers may vary. Sample: $\cos\theta$ is 0 for $\theta = 90° + k \cdot 180°$, where k is an integer. We can rewrite $90 + 180k$ as $90(1 + 2k)$. The values $2k + 1$ are the odd integers, so the values $90°(1 + 2k)$ are the odd multiples of 90°. **6a.** 14° **b.** 28° **c.** 104° **d.** 208°
7a. 14° **b.** 28° **c.** 104° **d.** 208°
8a. $(x^2 - y^2) + (2xy)i$ **b.** $\frac{2xy}{x^2 - y^2}$

On Your Own
10a. All real numbers except $90° + k \cdot 180°$, where k is an integer **11a.** $x \approx 65° + k \cdot 180°$, where k is an integer.

Lesson 8.9
Check Your Understanding
1a. $\cos(-x) = \cos x$ and $\sin(-x) = -\sin x$.
So, $\cos(a - b) = \cos(a + (-b)) =$
$\cos a\cos(-b) - \sin a\sin(-b) =$
$\cos a\cos b - (\sin a)(-\sin b) =$
$\cos a\cos b + \sin a\sin b$. **b.** If $a = b$, then
$\cos(a - b) = \cos 0° = 1$ and
$\cos a\cos b + \sin a\sin b = \cos^2 a + \sin^2 a = 1$.
c. $\frac{\sqrt{2} + \sqrt{6}}{4}$ **2a.** $\cos(2x) = \cos(x + x) = \cos x\cos x - \sin x\sin x = \cos^2 x - \sin^2 x$
b. $\sin(2x) = \sin(x + x) = \sin x\cos x + \cos x\sin x = 2\sin x\cos x$ **c.** $\cos 2x = \cos^2 x - \sin^2 x = \cos^2 x - (1 - \cos^2 x) = \cos^2 x - 1 + \cos^2 x = 2\cos^2 x - 1$ **3a.** $\frac{\sqrt{2 + \sqrt{3}}}{2}$
b. Yes; if $A = \frac{\sqrt{2 + \sqrt{3}}}{2}$, then $4A = 2\sqrt{2 + \sqrt{3}}$ and $(4A)^2 = (4)(2 + \sqrt{3}) = 8 + 4\sqrt{3}$. If $B = \frac{\sqrt{2} + \sqrt{6}}{4}$, then $4B = \sqrt{6} + \sqrt{2}$ and $(4B)^2 = 6 + 2\sqrt{12} + 2 = 8 + 2\sqrt{4} \cdot \sqrt{3} = 8 + 4\sqrt{3}$. So, $\frac{\sqrt{2 + \sqrt{3}}}{2} = \frac{\sqrt{2} + \sqrt{6}}{4}$.
4. $\cos 3x = \cos^3 x - 3\sin^2 x\cos x$, $\sin 3x = 3\sin x\cos^2 x - \sin^3 x$ **5.** $\frac{\sqrt{3}}{2} + \frac{1}{2}i$
6a. sin 10° = 0.1736, sin 50° = 0.7660, and sin 70° = 0.9397; sin 10° + sin 50° = 0.1736 + 0.7660 = 0.9396, which is about 0.9397. **b.** 80° **c.** 65°
7. $\sin x + \sin(60° - x) = \sin(60° + x)$; to prove that result, the left side is $\sin x + \sin(60° - x) = \sin x + (\sin 60°)(\cos x) - (\cos 60°)(\sin x) = \sin x + \left(\frac{\sqrt{3}}{2}\right)(\cos x) - \left(\frac{1}{2}\right)(\sin x) = \left(\frac{1}{2}\right)(\sin x) + \left(\frac{\sqrt{3}}{2}\right)(\cos x)$. The right

side is $(\sin 60°)(\cos x) + (\cos 60°)(\sin x) =$ $\left(\frac{\sqrt{3}}{2}\right)(\cos x) + \left(\frac{1}{2}\right)(\sin x)$. The two sides are equal, so $\sin x + \sin(60° - x) = \sin(60° + x)$.

On Your Own

8. C **11a.** $\sin x$ **d.** $\cos x$ **12.** $x \mapsto 2^x$ matches $f(a + b) = f(a) \cdot f(b)$.

Lesson 8.10

On Your Own

7. 50°, 130° **9.** B

10a. 3 miles;

11a. $BH = \sqrt{3}$, $BI = 2$, $HG = 1$, $IG = \sqrt{2}$, $BG = 1 + \sqrt{3}$

Lesson 8.11

Check Your Understanding

1. Answers may vary. Sample: You can use $\frac{1}{2}(8)(5 \sin 60°)$ or $\frac{1}{2}(5)(7 \sin 82°)$ to find the area. **2a.** $\frac{\sqrt{3} + 1}{2}$ **b.** $\sqrt{2} \sin 105°$ **c.** $\frac{\sqrt{6} + \sqrt{2}}{4}$

3. $\frac{5}{2} \sin 72° \approx 2.38$ **4.** $A = \frac{3\sqrt{3}}{2}$, $P = 6$

5a. 2.9389 **b.** $\frac{5\sqrt{10 - 2\sqrt{5}}}{4}$ **6a.** $\frac{n}{2} \cdot \sin\left(\frac{360°}{n}\right)$

b.

Sides n	Area $A(n)$
4	2
5	2.3776
6	2.5981
10	2.9389
12	3
20	3.0902
30	3.1187
50	3.1333
100	3.1395
360	3.1414

7. As n increases, the polygon approaches a circle with radius 1, so the area approaches π.

On Your Own

8. 60 **10a.** $\sin x \cos x$ **11a.** No; the sides cannot have lengths x, x, and $10x$ because $x + x < 10x$, and the sum of any two sides of a triangle must be greater than the third side. **12a.** Any other triangle with the same SAS would be congruent by SAS.

Lesson 8.12

Check Your Understanding

1. 24 **2.** $m\angle S = 30°$, $RS = 10.3$, $AR = 8.0$

3. $m\angle W = 70°$, $WS = 8.2$, $WO = 12$

4. $m\angle K = 53.1°$ or $126.9°$; there are two solutions for $\sin K = 0.8$. **5.** The situations in Exercises 2 and 3 are AAS and ASA, and those situations result in a unique triangle, so they are congruence theorems. The situation in Exercise 4 is SSA, and that situation results in two triangles, so it is not a congruence theorem.

6.

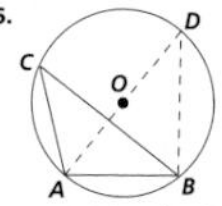

a. $\angle ABD$ is inscribed in a semicircle, so it is a right angle. **b.** $\angle C$ and $\angle D$ intercept the same arc, $\overset{\frown}{AB}$, so they are congruent.
c. $m\angle C = m\angle D$, so $\sin C = \sin D$ **d.** We know $\frac{c}{\sin C} = \frac{AD}{\sin \angle ABD}$. $\angle ABD$ is a right angle, so $\sin \angle ABD = 1$. Thus $AD = \frac{c}{\sin C}$.

7.

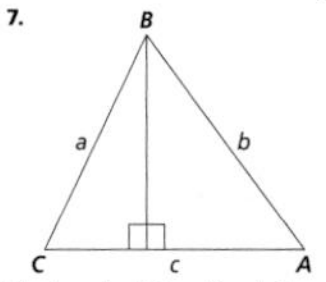

The length of the altitude from vertex B is $a \sin C$ or $c \sin A$. Therefore the area of the triangle is $\frac{1}{2} a \sin C \cdot c$ or $\frac{1}{2} c \sin A \cdot c$. The expressions are equal, so $\frac{1}{2} a \sin C \cdot c = \frac{1}{2} c \sin A \cdot c$, and $a \sin C = c \sin A$. Then $\frac{a}{\sin A} = \frac{c}{\sin C}$. By using a different altitude you can make a similar argument to prove $\frac{a}{\sin A} = \frac{b}{\sin B}$. Therefore $\frac{a}{\sin A} = \frac{b}{\sin B} = \frac{c}{\sin C}$.

8. $TW = \sqrt{325 - 150\sqrt{2}}$

9. $AB = \sqrt{a^2 + b^2 - 2ab \cos C}$

On Your Own

10. Answers may vary. Sample: The sides 1, $\sqrt{3}$, and 2 are opposite the angles with measures 30°, 60°, and 90°, so $\frac{1}{\sin 30°} = 2$, $\frac{\sqrt{3}}{\sin 60°} = 2$, $\frac{2}{\sin 90°} = 2$. **12.** To use the Law of Sines, you need to know a side and the angle opposite that side. There is not enough information for this exercise, so you cannot use the Law of Sines. **14a.** $\sin C = 0.771$
b. 50°, 130° **c.** $m\angle A = 90°$ or $10°$; $BC = 15.6$ or 2.7

Lesson 8.13

Check Your Understanding

1. $\sqrt{a^2 + b^2 - 2ab \cos C}$

2. $|a - b| < AB < a + b$ **3.** $5 < OT < 7$

4. $1 < AU < 5$ **5.** $\sqrt{119} < FB < 13$

6a. Use the Law of Cosines to find one angle. Then use the Law of Cosines or the Law of Sines to find a second angle. Subtract the sum of the angles from 180° to find the third angle. **b.** Use the Law of Cosines to find the third side. Then use the Law of Cosines or the Law of Sines to find a second angle. Subtract the sum of the angles from 180° to find the third angle. **c.** Use the Law of Sines to find the angle opposite the other given side (there may be 0, 1, or 2 values). Subtract the sum of the angles from 180° to find the third angle. Use the Law of Sines or the Law of Cosines to find the third side length. **d.** Subtract the sum of the angles from 180° to find the third angle. Use the Law of Sines to find a second side. Use the Law of Sines or the Law of Cosines to find the length of the third side. **e.** Subtract the sum of the angles from 180° to find the third angle. Use the Law of Sines to find a second side. Use the Law of Sines or the Law of Cosines to find the length of the third side. **f.** This cannot be solved. The triangle will not be unique because you are not given the length of a side. **7a.** The cosines opposite the sides of length 13, 14, and 15 are 0.6, 0.5077, and 0.3846, respectively.
b. The largest angle has the smallest cosine.
c. 12 **d.** 84 **8a.** $\cos C = \frac{a^2 + b^2 - c^2}{2ab}$, and the numerator and denominator must be integers, so $\cos C$ must be rational. **b.** The area of a triangle can be written as $\frac{1}{2}ab \sin C$. We know that ab is an integer, and part a showed that $\cos C$ is rational. So $\frac{1 - \cos^2 C}{4} = \frac{\sin^2 C}{4}$ is rational. Therefore $\sqrt{\frac{\sin^2 C}{4}} = \frac{1}{2} \sin C$ is the square root of a rational number. So the area of a triangle, $\frac{1}{2}ab \sin C$ or $ab \cdot \frac{1}{2} \sin C$, is the product of an integer times the square root of a rational number.

On Your Own

12. 42° **13a.** If $\angle O$ is the smallest angle, the measures of angles F and M would be greater than 60°. But the sum of the angles in a triangle cannot be greater than 180°. So $\angle O$ cannot be the smallest angle. **14a.** false
15a. The angles opposite the sides of length 7, 10, and 12 are 36°, 56°, and 88°, respectively.

Lesson 8.14

Check Your Understanding

1a. $s = \frac{x + 14}{2}$ **b.** $A(x) = \frac{1}{4}\sqrt{(x + 14)(-x + 14)(x - 2)(x + 2)}$ **c.** 2, 14
d. The maximum of $A(x)$ is 24 when $x = 10$.
2a. $12 - x$ **b.** $A(x) = \sqrt{27(9 - x)(-3 + x)}$
c. 3, 9 **d.** The maximum of $A(x) \approx 15.6$ when $x = 6$. **3.** 75.8

4a.

b. No; if you fold the figure on its diagonal, you do not get a concave quadrilateral.
5a. The denominator 4 is outside the radical. You can move the denominator into the radical and change it to 16, which can be expressed as a denominator 2 for each of the four factors. **b.** If $a + b + c = 2s$, then $b + c - a = 2s - 2a$; $a - b + c = 2s - 2b$; $a + b - c = 2s - 2c$. Therefore $\frac{a + b + c}{2} = s$, $\frac{b + c - a}{2} = s - a$, $\frac{a + c - b}{2} = s - b$, and $\frac{a + b - c}{2} = s - c$. Then substitute each expression above into the second expression in part (a) to get the expression $\sqrt{s(s - a)(s - b)(s - c)}$.

On Your Own

7a. $25\sqrt{3}$ **8.** D

Additional Answers

Chapter 1

Lesson 1.1 pp. 5–7

For You to Explore

2a.

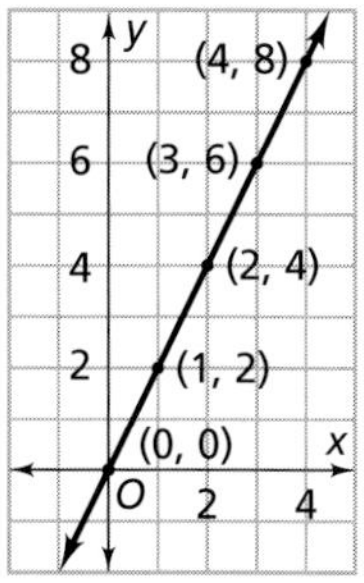

Lesson 1.2 pp. 8–15

Exercises **6.**

Input	Output	Δ
0	5	−3
1	**2**	**15**
2	17	**−13**
3	**4**	−5
4	−1	

8a. and d.

Input	Output
0	2
1	6
2	**10**
3	**14**
4	**18**

b–c.

Input	Output
0	2
1	6
2	**18**
3	**54**
4	**162**

13a.

Input, x	Output, $ax^2 + bx + c$	Δ
0	c	$\mathbf{a + b}$
1	$a + b + c$	$\mathbf{3a + b}$
2	$4a + 2b + c$	$\mathbf{5a + b}$
3	$9a + 3b + c$	$\mathbf{7a + b}$
4	$16a + 4b + c$	$\mathbf{9a + b}$
5	$25a + 5b + c$	

Lesson 1.3 pp. 16–21

For You to Do **4.** If $f(x) = ax + b$, then $f(1) = a + b$, $f(2) = 2a + b$, $f(3) = 3a + b$, $f(4) = 4a + b$, and so on. The differences are $a, a, a, \ldots$, which are constant. **5.** In Table H, the output 23 is equal to the first output, 3, plus the four Δ values of 5: $3 + 4(5) = 23$. **6.** The hockey stick property says that any output value O_n is equal to the initial output value, O_1, plus n times the constant difference. So $f(n) = f(0) + n\Delta$.

Exercises **1.**

Input	Output	Δ
0	−7	**3**
1	−4	**3**
2	−1	**3**
3	2	
4	5	

9a.

n	$F(n)$	Δ
0	1	**0**
1	1	**1**
2	2	**1**
3	3	**2**
4	5	**3**
5	8	**5**
6	13	

14a.

n	$D(n)$	Δ
0	1	**1**
1	2	**2**
2	4	**4**
3	8	**8**
4	16	**16**
5	32	**32**
6	64	

18b.

Input	Output	Δ
0	$-\frac{3}{2}$	$\frac{1}{6}$
1	$-\frac{4}{3}$	$\frac{1}{6}$
2	$-\frac{7}{6}$	$\frac{1}{6}$
3	−1	$\frac{1}{6}$
4	$-\frac{5}{6}$	

Lesson 1.5 pp. 29–38

Exercises

21a.

x	$f(x)$
0	14
1	6
2	0
3	−4
4	−6
5	−6

b.

x	$g(x)$
0	78
1	60
2	44
3	30
4	18
5	8

c.

x	$h(x)$
0	0
1	−8
2	−14
3	−18
4	−20
5	−20

d.

x	$j(x)$
0	9
1	0
2	−3
3	0
4	9
5	24

e. Answers may vary. Sample: $k(x) = (x - 5)(x - 6)$

x	$k(x)$
0	30
1	20
2	12
3	6
4	2
5	0

f. Answers may vary. Sample: $m(x) = 4x(x - 1)(x - 2)$

x	$m(x)$
0	0
1	0
2	0
3	24
4	96
5	240

22a.

x	$f(x)$
0	0
1	3
2	6
3	9
4	12

b.

x	$g(x)$
0	0
1	4
2	8
3	12
4	16

c.

x	$h(x)$
0	0
1	3
2	8
3	15
4	24

d.

x	$j(x)$
0	0
1	2
2	4
3	12
4	32

e. Answers may vary. Sample: $k(x) = 3x + x(x - 1)(x - 2)(x - 3)(x - 4)$

x	$k(x)$
0	0
1	3
2	6
3	9
4	12

Additional Answers

Lesson 1.6 pp. 41–45

Exercises 16. Step 2:

$x - \bar{x}$	$y - \bar{y}$
42.3	−40.3
−8.7	19.7
−14.7	7.7
29.3	−28.3
−24.7	−37.3
42.3	−33.3
−20.7	35.7
−24.7	38.7
−22.7	26.7
2.3	10.7

Lesson 1.7 pp. 46–52

Exercises 8a. See Figure 1.

12a. See Figure 2.

13a. See Figure 3.

15a.

x	$f(x)$
0	1
1	4
2	7
3	10
4	13

17a.

x	$f(x)$
0	0
1	1
2	4
3	9
4	16

c. (2, 6)

16a.

x	$f(x)$
0	4
1	7
2	10
3	13
4	16

b–c.

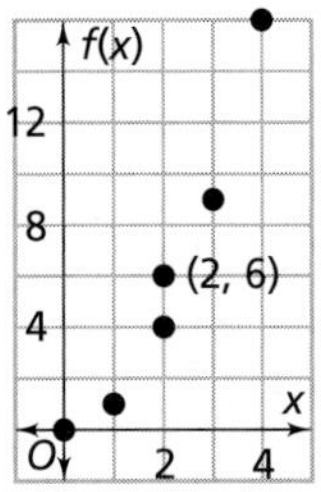

18b–c.

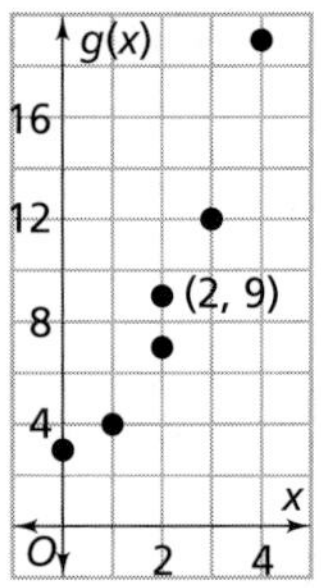

c. (2, 9)

Lesson 1.8 pp. 53–59

Exercises 3a. See Figure 4.

Figure 1

Data vs. Line Fit: $y = 0.5x + 2.5$

Input	Actual	Predicted: $y = 0.5x + 2.5$	Error: Actual – Predicted
1	1.8	3	−1.2
2	1.7	3.5	−1.8
3	3.6	4	−0.4
5	5.4	5	0.4
6	7.3	5.5	1.8
7	7.2	6	1.2

Data vs. Line Fit: $y = 0.9x + 0.9$

Input	Actual	Predicted: $y = 0.9x + 0.9$	Error: Actual – Predicted
1	1.8	1.8	0
2	1.7	2.7	−1
3	3.6	3.6	0
5	5.4	5.4	0
6	7.3	6.3	1
7	7.2	7.2	0

Data vs. Line Fit: $y = x + 0.5$

Input	Actual	Predicted: $y = x + 0.5$	Error: Actual – Predicted
1	1.8	1.5	0.3
2	1.7	2.5	−0.8
3	3.6	3.5	0.1
5	5.4	5.5	−0.1
6	7.3	6.5	0.8
7	7.2	7.5	−0.3

Figure 2

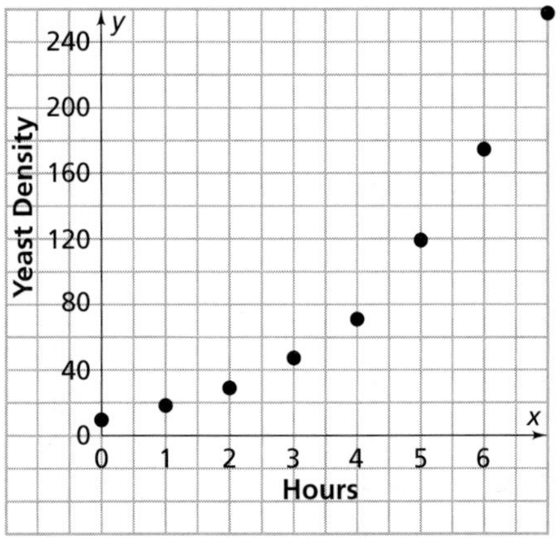

Figure 3

Data vs. Line Fit: $y = 33.4476x - 26.2917$

Hours, x	Actual Yeast Density, y	Predicted Yeast Density, y	Error
0	9.6	−26.3	35.9
1	18.3	7.2	11.1
2	29.0	40.6	−11.6
3	47.2	74.1	−26.9
4	71.1	107.5	−36.4
5	119.1	141.0	21.9
6	174.6	174.4	0.2
7	257.3	207.8	49.5

Figure 4

Input	Output	Predicted	Error
1	3	$3 \cdot 1 + b = 3 + b$	$3 - (3 + b) = -b$
2	4.5	$3 \cdot 2 + b = 6 + b$	$4.5 - (6 + b) = -1.5 - b$
3	8.1	$3 \cdot 3 + b = 9 + b$	$8.1 - (9 + b) = -0.9 - b$
4	8	$3 \cdot 4 + b = 12 + b$	$8 - (12 + b) = -4 - b$

6–7. Table 1

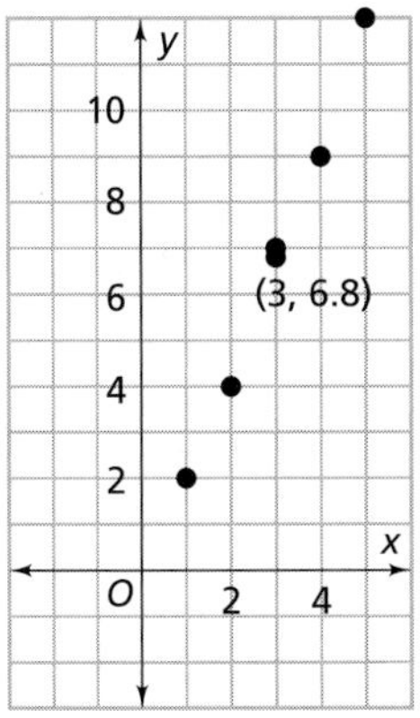

Table 2

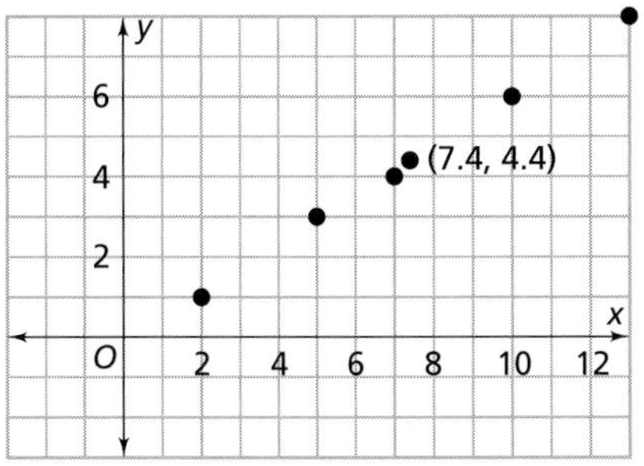

Table 3

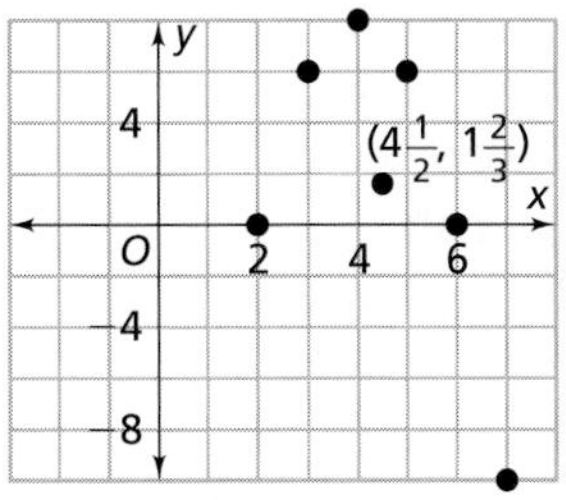

Table 4

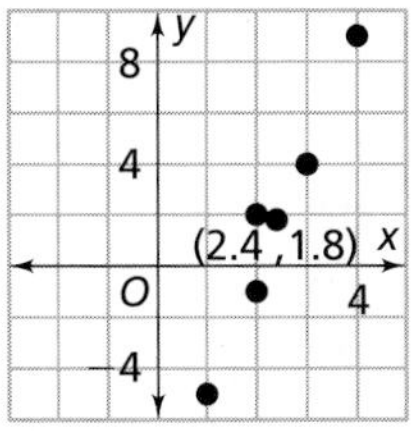

Lesson 1.9 **pp. 60–65**

For You to Do 1. See Figure 5.

Exercises

5. Table 1

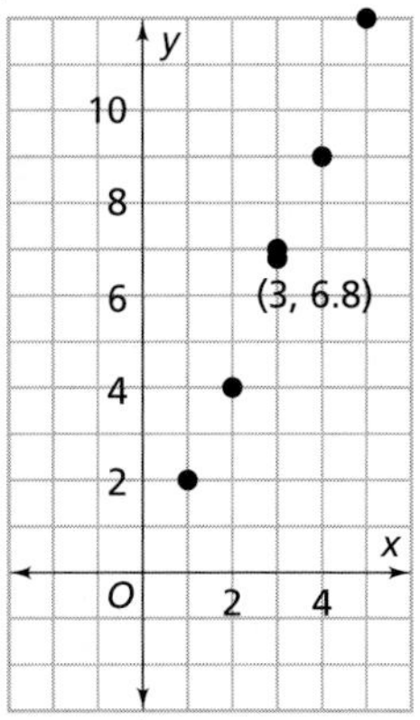

Table 2

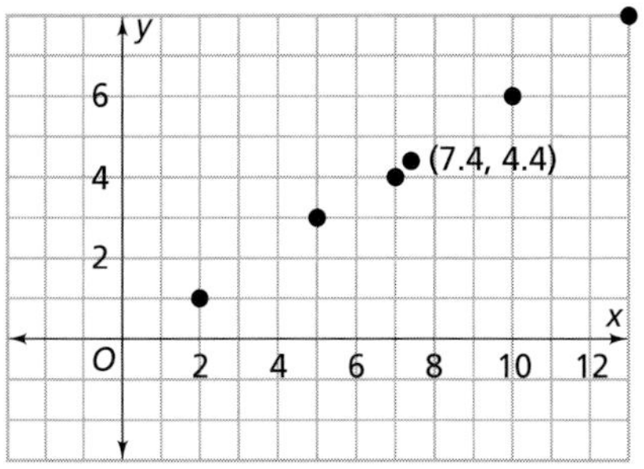

Figure 5

Data vs. Line Fit: $y = m(x - 11) = 37.4$

Months	Pounds	Predicted	Error
5	18	$m(5 - 11) + 37.4$ $= -6m + 37.4$	$18 - (-6m + 37.4)$ $= 6m - 19.4$
2	2	$m(2 - 11) + 37.4$ $= -9m + 37.4$	$2 - (-9m + 37.4)$ $= 9m - 35.4$
15	54	$m(15 - 11) + 37.4$ $= 4m + 37.4$	$54 - (4m + 37.4)$ $= -4m + 16.6$
10	39	$m(10 - 11) + 37.4$ $= m + 37.4$	$39 - (-m + 37.4)$ $= m + 1.6$
18	65	$m(18 - 11) + 37.4$ $= 7m + 37.4$	$65 - (7m + 37.4)$ $= -7m + 27.6$
8	25	$m(8 - 11) + 37.4$ $= -3m + 37.4$	$25 - (-3m + 37.4)$ $= 3m - 12.4$
5	12	$m(5 - 11) + 37.4$ $= -6m + 37.4$	$12 - (-6m + 37.4)$ $= 6m - 25.4$
13	41	$m(13 - 11) + 37.4$ $= 2m + 37.4$	$41 - (2m + 37.4)$ $= -2m + 3.6$
23	72	$m(23 - 11) + 37.4$ $= 12m + 37.4$	$72 - (12m + 37.4)$ $= -12m + 34.6$
11	46	$m(11 - 11) + 37.4$ $= 37.4$	$46 - 37.4$ $= 8.6$

Table 3

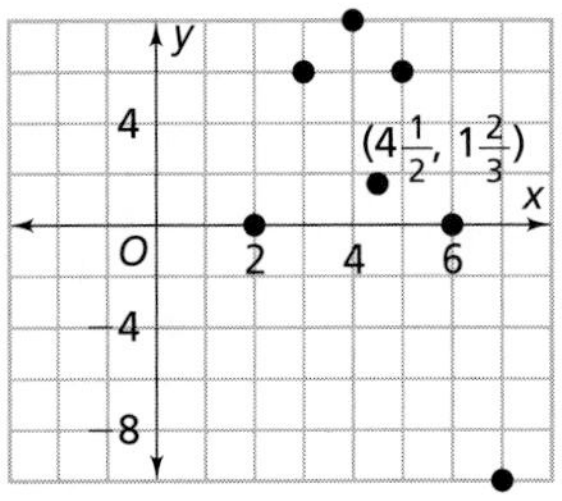

Table 4

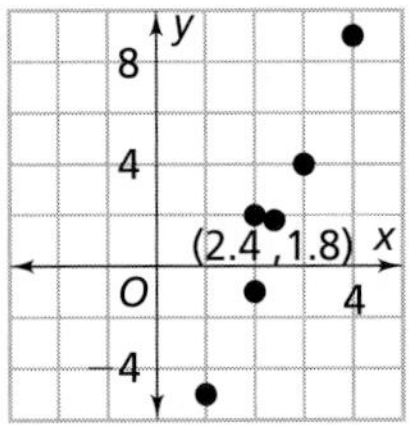

Tables 1, 2, and 4 show a linear trend.

13a. $(x_1 - x_2)^2 = 2(x_1^2 + x_2^2) - (x_1 + x_2)^2$
$= 2x_1^2 + 2x_2^2 - (x_1^2 + 2x_1x_2 + x_2^2)$
$= x_1^2 - 2x_1x_2 + x_2^2$
$= (x_1 - x_2)^2$

b. $(x_1 - x_2)^2 + (x_1 - x_3)^2 + (x_2 - x_3)^2 = 3((x_1)^2 + (x_2)^2 + (x_2)^2 + (x_3)^2) - (x_1 + x_2 + x_3)^2$
$= 3((x_1)^2 + (x_2)^2 + (x_3)^2) - (x_1^2 + x_2^2 + x_3^2 + 2x_1x_2 + 2x_1x_3 + 2x_2x_3)$
$= 2((x_1)^2 + (x_2)^2 + (x_3)^2) - (2x_1x_2 + 2x_1x_3 + 2x_2x_3)$
$= (x_1^2 - 2x_1x_2 + x_2^2) + (x_1^2 - 2x_1x_3 + x_3^2) + (x_2^2 - 2x_2x_3 + x_3^2)$
$= (x_1 - x_2)^2 + (x_1 - x_3)^2 + (x_2 - x_3)^2$

c. Following the pattern in part (b), the right side is $3x_1^2 + 3x_2^2 + 3x_3^2 + 3x_4^2 - 2(x_1x_2 + x_1x_3 + x_1x_4 + x_2x_3 + x_2x_4 + x_3x_4) = (x_1 - x_2)^2 + (x_1 - x_3)^2 + (x_1 - x_4)^2 + (x_2 - x_3)^2 + (x_2 - x_4)^2 + (x_3 - x_4)^2$, which is the same as the left side. **14.** The next identity would have 5 terms involving x_1, x_2, x_3, x_4, and x_5, where the left side is the sum of the squares of the differences of terms and the right side is 5 times the sum of the squares of the terms, minus the square of the sum of the terms. For the general identity, the left side is the sum of squares, where each square is the difference of two terms; the right side is n times the sum of the squares of the terms, minus the square of the sum of the terms.

Lesson 1.10 **pp. 69–71**

For You to Explore

1.

n	$g(n)$
0	5
1	12
2	19
3	26
4	33
5	40
6	47
7	54
8	61
9	68
10	75

$g(n) = 7n + 5$; $g(103) = 726$, $g(104) = 733$, $g(245) = 1720$

2.

n	$t(n)$
0	1
1	2
2	4
3	8
4	16
5	32
6	64
7	128
8	256
9	512
10	1024

$t(n) = 2^n$; $t(103) \approx 1.014 \times 10^{31}$, $t(104) \approx 2.028 \times 10^{31}$, $t(245) \approx 5.65 \times 10^{73}$

3.

n	$j(n)$
0	0
1	1
2	4
3	9
4	16
5	25
6	36
7	49
8	64
9	81
10	100

$j(n) = n^2$; $j(103) = 10{,}609$, $j(104) = 10{,}816$, $j(245) = 60{,}025$

4.

n	$k(n)$
0	0
1	2
2	6
3	12
4	20
5	30
6	42
7	56
8	72
9	90
10	110

$k(n) = n(n + 1)$; $k(103) = 10{,}712$, $k(104) = 10{,}920$, $k(245) = 60{,}270$

Exercises

5.

n	$l(n)$
0	0
1	1
2	3
3	6
4	10
5	15
6	21
7	28
8	36
9	45
10	55

$l(n) = \frac{n(n + 1)}{2}$; $l(103) = 5356$, $l(104) = 5460$, $l(245) = 30{,}135$

6. $a(n) = \begin{cases} 6 & \text{if } n = 0 \\ a(n - 1) + 3 & \text{if } n > 0 \end{cases}$

Input	Output
0	6
1	9
2	12
3	15
4	18
5	21
6	24
7	27
8	30
9	33
10	36

7. $b(n) = \begin{cases} 7 & \text{if } n = 0 \\ b(n-1) + 4 & \text{if } n > 0 \end{cases}$

Input	Output
0	7
1	11
2	15
3	19
4	23
5	27
6	31
7	35
8	39
9	43
10	47

8.

$c(n) = \begin{cases} 7 & \text{if } n = 0 \\ c(n-1) + 4n + 7 & \text{if } n > 0 \end{cases}$

Input	Output
0	7
1	18
2	33
3	52
4	75
5	102
6	133
7	168
8	207
9	250
10	297

9.

n	$g(n)$
0	0
1	1
2	2
3	3
4	4
5	5
6	6
7	7
8	8
9	9
10	10

$g(n) = n$; $g(103) = 103$, $g(104) = 104$, $g(245) = 245$

10.

n	$t(n)$
0	1
1	3
2	9
3	27
4	81
5	243
6	729
7	2187
8	6561
9	19,683
10	59,049

$t(n) = 3^n$; $t(103) \approx 1.39 \times 10^{49}$, $t(104) \approx 4.17 \times 10^{49}$, $t(245) \approx 7.85 \times 10^{116}$

11.

n	$j(n)$
0	1
1	4
2	9
3	16
4	25
5	36
6	49
7	64
8	81
9	100
10	121

$j(n) = (n + 1)^2$; $j(103) = 10,816$, $j(104) = 11,025$, $j(245) = 60,516$

12.

n	$k(n)$
0	0
1	0
2	1
3	4
4	10
5	20
6	35
7	56
8	84
9	120
10	165

$k(n) = \frac{1}{6}(n^3 - n)$; $k(103) = 182,104$, $k(104) = 187,460$, $k(245) = 2,450,980$

13. $d(n) = \begin{cases} 1 & \text{if } n = 0 \\ n \cdot d(n-1) & \text{if } n > 0 \end{cases}$

n	$d(n)$
0	1
1	1
2	2
3	6
4	24
5	120
6	720
7	5040
8	40,320
9	362,880
10	3,628,800

14.

n	$f(n)$
0	1
1	1
2	2
3	3
4	5
5	8
6	13
7	21
8	34
9	55
10	89

Lesson 1.11 **pp. 72–76**

Exercises 6a. Answers may vary. Sample: Students' tables should show that the 36th payment would bring the balance to $0 or less. For 7% interest, here is the table.

Cost of car (dollars)	Monthly Payment
10,000	308.77
11,000	339.65
12,000	370.53
13,000	401.40
14,000	432.28
15,000	463.15
16,000	494.03
17,000	524.91
18,000	555.78

Lesson 1.12 pp. 77–80

Exercises

1.

n	$g(n)$
2	2
3	3
4	4
5	5
6	6
7	7
8	8
9	9
10	10

$g(n) = n$

2.

n	$h(n)$
3	6
4	12
5	20
6	30
7	42
8	56
9	72
10	90

$h(n) = n(n - 1)$

Mathematical Reflections p. 81

2. $a(n) = \begin{cases} 3 & \text{if } n = 0 \\ a(n-1) + 5 & \text{if } n > 0 \end{cases}$

Input	Output
0	3
1	8
2	13
3	18
4	23
5	28
6	33
7	38
8	43
9	48
10	53

3.

$b(n) = \begin{cases} 3 & \text{if } n = 0 \\ b(n-1) + 5n + 3 & \text{if } n > 0 \end{cases}$

Input	Output
1	11
2	24
3	42
4	65
5	93
6	126
7	164
8	207
9	255
10	308

4.

n	$b(n)$
1	11,660.00
2	11,318.30
3	10,974.89
4	10,629.77
5	10,282.91
6	9,934.33
7	9584.00
8	9231.92
9	8878.08
10	8522.47

a. \$12,000; 6% **b.** 33

Test pp. 86–87

7.

n	$m(n)$
0	4
1	1
2	−2
3	−5
4	−8
5	−11
6	−14
7	−17
8	−20
9	−23
10	−26

$m(n) = -3n + 4$; $m(80) = -236$

Chapter 2

Lesson 2.0 pp. 90–95

Exercises **16a.** $a^2 - b^2$ **b.** $a^3 - b^3$ **c.** $a^4 - b^4$ **d.** $a^5 - b^5$ **e.** $(a - b)(a^n + a^{n-1}b + a^{n-2}b^2 + \cdots + ab^{n-1} + b^n) = a^n - b^n$ **17a.** $1 - x^2$ **b.** $1 + x^3$ **c.** $1 - x^4$ **d.** $(1 + x) \cdot (1 - x + x^2 - x^3 + \cdots + (-1)^n x^n) = 1 + (-1)^n x^{n+1}$

Lesson 2.1 pp. 97–99

For You to Explore **1a.** 12 **b.** 0.75 **c.** 0.75 **d.** 0 **e.** It cannot be evaluated because division by 0 is undefined. **f.** 5 **g.** 5 **h.** It cannot be evaluated in the real number system because SQRT(−5) is not a real number. **i.** 5 **j.** 1 **k.** August 17 **l.** "3" does not have a birthday. **m.** 5 **n.** 7 **o.** The SQRT of a birthday does not have a meaning. **p.** The square root of a negative value is not a real number. **q.** 0.5 **r.** 2 **s.** 0.5 **t.** $\frac{1}{0}$ is undefined, so 0 does not have a reciprocal.

Exercises **8f.**

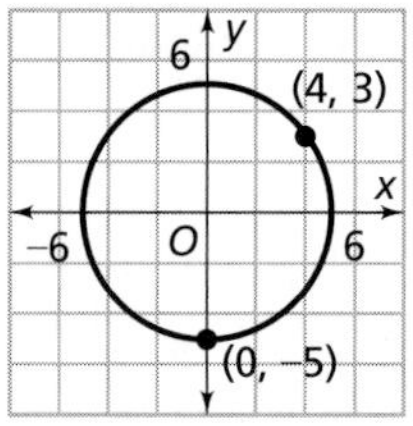

9a. 0 **b.** 10 **c.** 10 **d.** 0 **e.** −6 **f.** All real numbers such that $z = -\sqrt{a^2 + b^2}$; answers may vary. Sample: (3, 4, −5).

Lesson 2.2 pp. 100–108

Exercises **11a.** Answers may vary. Check students' work. **b.** Answers may vary. Check students' work. **c.** Yes, each input in the domain results in a unique output. **12a.** $\mathbb{R}^2$; $\mathbb{R}$ **b.** Answers may vary. Samples: (0, 5), (5, 0), (±3, ±4) **c.** (0, 0)

d.

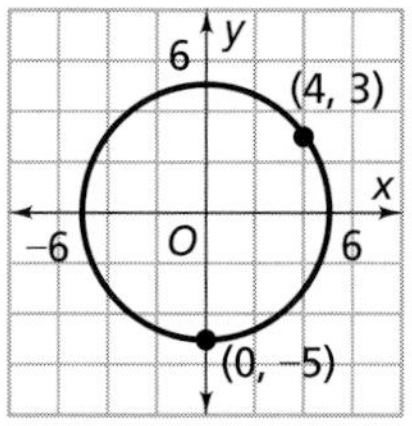

e. $\mathbb{R}^+$; $N(a, b) \geq 0$ for all real numbers a and b, since $a^2 \geq 0$ and $b^2 \geq 0$. **13.** The domain of f includes negative values, but the domain of t does not. **14a.** domain: all real numbers; target: all real numbers; range: $f(x) \geq \frac{-49}{24}$ **b.** domain: $x \geq 3$; target: all real numbers; range: all nonnegative real numbers **c.** domain: $x > 3$; target: all real numbers; range: all positive real numbers **d.** domain: all nonzero real numbers; target: all real numbers; range: all real numbers **e.** domain: all real numbers; target: all real numbers; range: all real numbers **f.** domain: all real numbers; target: all ordered pairs of real numbers; range: all ordered pairs of the form (x, x^3) **g.** domain: all ordered pairs of real numbers; target: all ordered pairs of real numbers; range: all ordered pairs of real numbers

Lesson 2.3 pp. 109–114

Exercises **20a.** $g(x) = x - 3$ **b.** $g(x) = x + 3$ **c.** $g(x) = \frac{x - 5}{3}$ **d.** $g(x) = \frac{x + 5}{3}$ **e.** $g(x) = \frac{x - 5}{2}$ **f.** $g(x) = \frac{x - B}{A}$ **21a.** $g(x) = x - 3$

b. $g(x) = x + 3$ **c.** $g(x) = \frac{x-5}{3}$
d. $g(x) = \frac{x+5}{3}$ **e.** $g(x) = \frac{x-5}{2}$
f. $g(x) = \frac{x-B}{A}$

Lesson 2.4 **pp. 115–124**

Exercises 17. Answers may vary. Sample: $g(x) = 7x$ **18a.** Answers may vary. The graph must always rise as it goes to the right. **b.** Yes; if the function is increasing, then any horizontal line can intersect the graph in at most one point. **19a.** 43 **b.** 10 **c.** 15 **d.** 0 **e.** 289 **f.** −162.3 **g.** 43 **20a.** $4r + 3$ **b.** $16r + 15$ **c.** $64r + 63$ **d.** $256r + 255$ **e.** $1024r + 1023$ **f.** $16{,}777{,}216r + 16{,}777{,}215$

Mathematical Reflections **p. 125**

4c. Check students' graphs. **d.** The zeros of h are -6, -4, and 2; the zeros of f are $\frac{-3}{2}$, -1, and $\frac{1}{2}$. **5.** Answers may vary. Sample: A function is a correspondence between an input set and an output set such that no two values of the output set correspond to the same value of the input set. **6.** Answers may vary. Sample: You can form a string of functions, under the condition that the output of each function can be an input of the function to its left. **7.** $f^{-1}(x) = \frac{x-7}{3}$

Lesson 2.5 **pp. 127–130**

Exercises 16a. $A = 3$, $B = -1$, $C = 0$
b. $f(x) = 2x^2 - 8x + 6$
c.

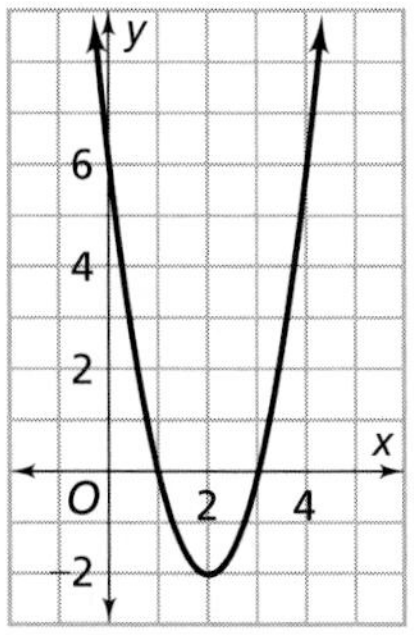

d. minimum $= -2$; no maximum
17a. $A = -3$, $B = -1$, $C = 0$
b. $f(x) = -4x^2 + 22x - 18$
c.

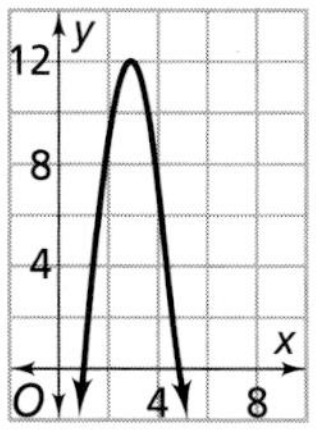

d. no minimum; maximum $= 12.25$
18a. $A = -3$, $B = 1$, $C = 2$
b. $f(x) = -12x + 42$
c.

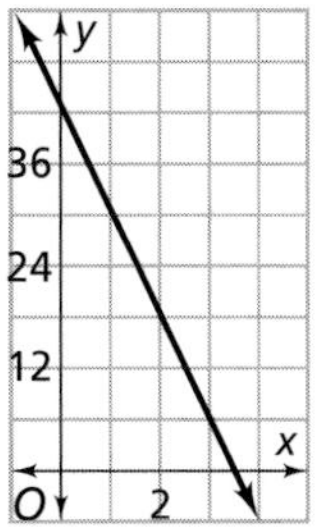

d. There is no maximum or minimum.

Lesson 2.7 **pp. 139–143**

Exercises 7. Answers may vary. Sample: $q(x) = 3x - 1 - 4x(x-1)(x-2) \cdot (x-3)(x-4)$ The graphs intersect at (0, −1), (1, 2), (2, 5), (3, 8), and (4, 11). **8.** Answers may vary. Sample: $p(x) = 4 - x^2 - 3x(x-1)(x-2) \cdot (x-3)$ The graphs intersect at (0, 4), (1, 3), (2, 0), and (3, −5). **9.** Answers may vary. Sample: $q(x) = 4 - x^2 - 7x(x-1)(x-2)(x-3)(x-4)$ The graphs intersect at (0, 4), (1, 3), (2, 0), (3, −5), and (4, −12).
15e. $x^6 - 21x^5 + 175x^4 - 735x^3 + 1624x^2 - 1764x + 720$
f. $x^7 - 28x^6 + 322x^5 - 1960x^4 + 6769x^3 - 13{,}132x^2 + 13{,}068x - 5040$
g. $x^8 - 36x^7 + 546x^6 - 4536x^5 + 22{,}449x^4 - 67{,}284x^3 + 118{,}124x^2 - 109{,}584x + 40{,}320$

Lesson 2.10 **pp. 155–160**

Exercises 6. Answers may vary. Sample: Checking any three values, for $x = 1$ both sides are 2; for $x = 3$ both sides are 2, and for $x = 2$ both sides are -1. So the expressions are equivalent. **7.** Answers may vary. Sample: Checking any three values, for $x = 1$ both sides are 20; for $x = 3$ both sides are 12; and for $x = 6$ both sides are 60. So the two expressions are equivalent. **8.** $P(x) = 1$ **9.** −8
10. $a = 10$, $b = 4$ **11.** −3, −2, 2
12a. $f(2) = 0$, so $(x-2)$ is a factor of $f(x)$. **b.** $g(x) = \frac{f(x)}{x-2} = 3x^3 - 6x^2 + x - 2$ and $g(2) = 0$, so $x - 2$ is a factor of $g(x)$. **c.** Since $x - 2$ is a factor of $g(x)$, and $f(x) = (x-2) \cdot g(x)$, then $f(x) = (x-2)(x-2) \cdot r(x)$ for some $r(x)$, and $(x-2)^2$ is a factor of $f(x)$.

14a. Using the definition of $f(x)$, $f(r) = a_nr^n + a_{n-1}r^{n-1} + \cdots + a_1r + a_0$. So $f(x) - f(r) = a_n(x^n - r^n) + a_{n-1}(x^{n-1} - r^{n-1}) + \cdots + a_1(x - r)$. Since each term is of the form $x^k - r^k$, every term contains a factor $(x - r)$. Therefore $f(x) - f(r) = (x - r) \cdot g(x)$ and $(x - r)$ is a factor of $f(x) - f(r)$.
b. $g(x) = (a_n)x^{n-1} + (a_nr + a_{n-1})x^{n-2} + (a_nr^2 + a_{n-1}r + a_{n-2})x^{n-3} + \cdots + (a_nr^{n-1} + a_{n-1}r^{n-2} + \cdots + a_1)$
18a. $(x^2 + 1)(x-2)(x-3)(x-4)$
b. $(x^2 + 1)(x-3)(x-4)$
c. $(x^2 + 1)(x-1)(x-2)(x-4)$
d. $(x^2 + 1)(x-1)(x-2)(x-3)$
e. $(x^2 + 1)(x-4)$ **f.** $x^2 + 1$
19a.

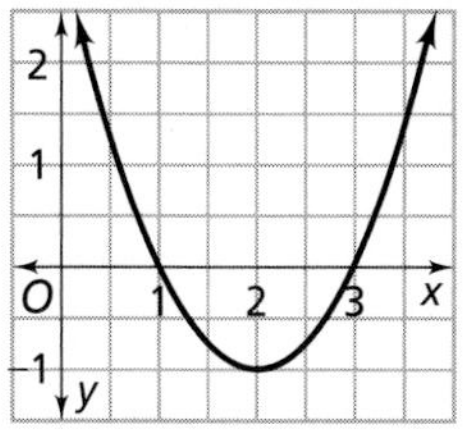

b.

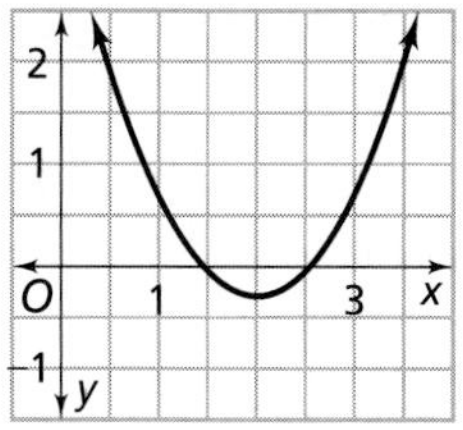

c.

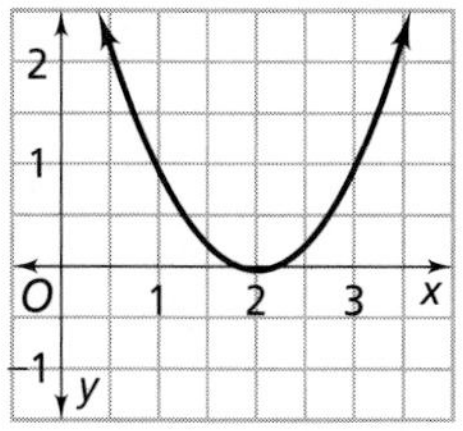

d.

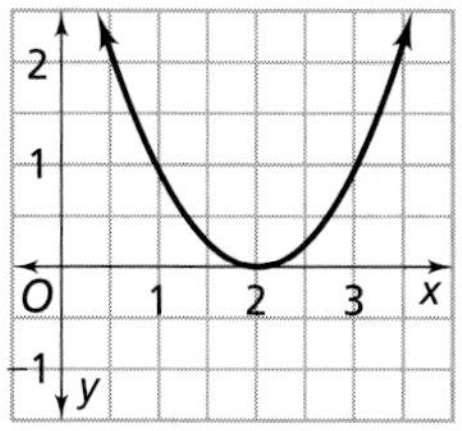

e.

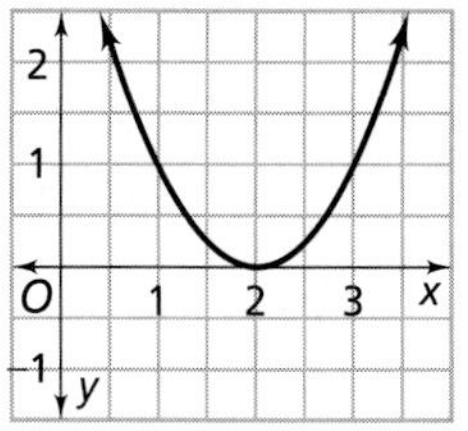

Lesson 2.11 **pp. 163–164**

For You to Explore 4. Answers may vary. Sample: For $x^2 - 6x - 3 = 0$, the sum of the roots is -6 and the product of the roots is -3. If $\alpha + \beta = -6$ and $\alpha \cdot \beta = -3$, then α and β satisfy the two conditions for the roots, so α and β are the roots of $x^2 - 6x - 3 = 0$.
7a. $(x - 1)(x^2 + x + 1)$
b. $(x + 1)(x^2 - x + 1)$
c. $(x - 2)(x^2 + 2x + 4)$
d. $(x + 2)(x^2 - 2x + 4)$
e. $(2x - 1)(4x^2 + 2x + 1)$
f. $(2x + 1)(4x^2 - 2x + 1)$
g. $(x - a)(x^2 + ax + a^2)$
h. $(x + a)(x^2 - ax + a^2)$
i. $x(x^2 + 3x + 3)$ **j.** $x(x^2 - 3x + 3)$
8. Answers may vary. Sample: If p and q are the roots, then $x^2 - 10x + 7 = (x - p)(x - q)$ so $x^2 - 10x + 7 = x^2 - (p + q)x + pq$. Comparing the like terms, $p + q = 10$ and $pq = 7$.
12a. $(x + 3)(x - 3)$
b. $(2x + 3)(2x - 3)$
c. $(3 + x)(3 - x)$
d. $(x + 4)(x - 2)$
e. $2x + 1$
f. $(x^2 + x + 1)(x^2 - x + 1)$
g. $(x^2 - x + 1)(x^4 + x^3 + 3x^2 + x + 1)$ **h.** $3x^4 + 3x^2 + 1$

Lesson 2.12 **pp. 165–168**

Exercises 3a. $(4x - 1)(x - 3)$
b. $(2x - 1)(2x - 3)$
c. $(2x + 3)(2x - 1)$
d. $(2x + 5)(2x + 1)$
e. $(2x + 1)(2x - 1)(x^2 - 3)$
f. $(2x - 1)(2x - 3)(x^2 - 2x - 2)$
g. $(x^6 - 6x^5 + 15x^4 - 20x^3 + 15x^2 - 6x - 2)(2x^3 - 6x^2 + 6x - 3)(2x^3 - 6x^2 + 6x - 1)$
h. $(x^2 - x + 1)(x^2 + x + 1)$

9. Answers may vary. Samples are given. **a.** $x^2 - 56x + 343 = 0$
b. $2x^2 + 77x - 1029 = 0$
c. $x^2 + 11x - 42 = 0$
d. $x^2 + 11x - 63 = 0$
e. $x^2 + 11x - 105 = 0$

Lesson 2.13 **pp. 169–175**

Exercises 1. Expand the left sides: $(x + y)^3 = (x + y)(x^2 + 2xy + y^2) = x^3 + 3x^2y + 3xy^2 + y^3$, and $(x - y)^3 = (x - y)(x^2 - 2xy + y^2) = x^3 - 3x^2y + 3xy^2 - y^3$
2.a. $(x - 4)(x^2 + 4x + 16)$
b. $(x + 4)(x^2 - 4x + 16)$
c. $(3x - 4)(9x^2 + 12x + 16)$
d. $(3x + 4)(9x^2 - 12x + 16)$
e. $(x - 3)(x^2 + 6x + 21)$
f. $(2x + 1)(4x^2 - 20x + 37)$
g. $(x + 3)(x - 3)(x + 3)$
h. $(x + a)(x - a)(x + a)$
i. $(-2x - 1)(4x + 1)$
j. $(x - y + z)(x + y - z)$
k. $(x - 2)(x - 7)(x + 5)$
l. $(x - 2y)(x - 7y)(x + 5y)$
m. $(x + 1)(x^2 - x + 1)$
3. Multiply each term by 25 to get $125x^3 + 75x^2 + 75x - 50$; that can be rewritten as $(5x)^3 + 3(5x)^2 + 15(5x) - 50$, which can be factored as $25(5x - 2)(x^2 + x + 1)$. Divide by 25 to get $(5x - 2)(x^2 + x + 1)$.

Mathematical Reflections **p. 187**

2a. $(x - 5)(x^2 + 5x + 25)$
b. $(x + 5)(x^2 - 5x + 25)$
c. $(3x - 4)(9x^2 + 12x + 16)$
d. $(3x + 4)(9x^2 - 12x + 16)$
e. $(x - 4)(x^2 + x + 7)$
f. $(2x)(4x^2 - 18x + 27)$
g. $(x - 3)(x + 3)(x + 3)$
h. $(x - 3)(x^2 - x + 1)$
i. $(-x + 1)(3x + 1)(5x^2 + 4x + 1)$
j. $(x - y + z)(x + y - z)$
3a. $(7x^2 + 6)(5x^2 + 7)$
b. $(3x^3 + 5)(2x^3 - 3)$
c. $(x^2 + 9)(x + 3)(x - 3)$
d. $(x^2 - 3)(x^4 + 3x^2 + 9)$
e. $(x + 1)(x - 1)(2x + 1)(2x - 1)$
f. $(x^2 - x + 3)(x^2 + x + 3)$

Chapter 3

Lesson 3.1 **pp. 199–200**

For You to Explore 5a. The sum is 12, the product is 35, and the sum of the squares is 74. **b.** The sum is 12, the product is 32, and the sum of the squares is 80. **c.** The sum is 12, the product is 33, and the sum of the squares is 78. **d.** The sum is -12, the product is 32, and the sum of the squares is 80. **e.** The sum is 0, the product is -25, and the sum of the squares is 50. **f.** The sum is 0, the product is -10, and the sum of the squares is 20. **g.** The sum is -8, the product is -33, and the sum of the squares is 130.

Lesson 3.2 **pp. 201–205**

Exercises
7a.
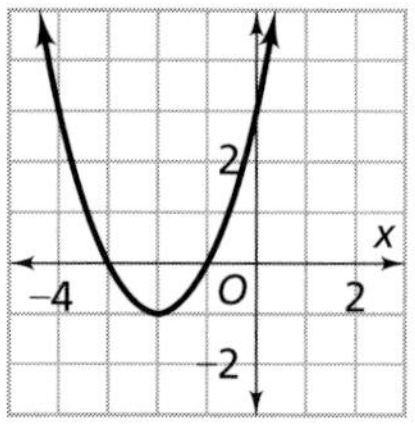

x-intercepts $(-3, 0)$, $(-1, 0)$, y-intercept (0, 3)
b.
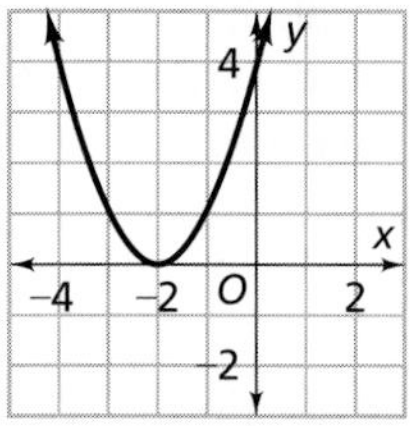

x-intercept $(-2, 0)$, y-intercept (0, 4)
c.
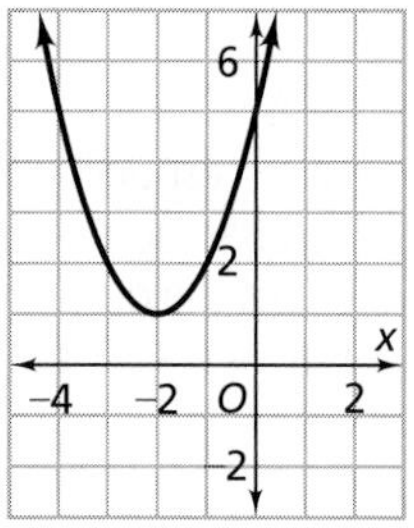

no x-intercept, y-intercept (0, 5)
d.
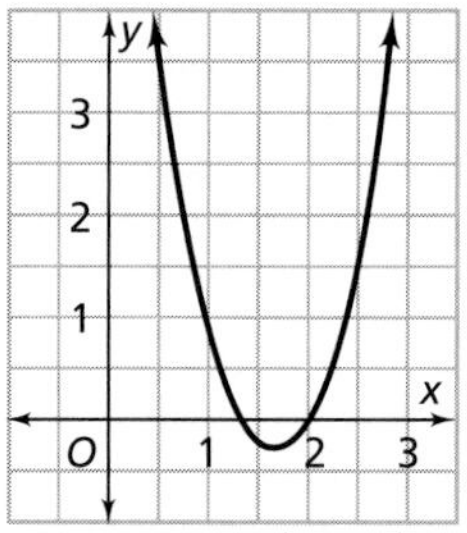

x-intercepts $\left(\frac{4}{3}, 0\right)$, (2, 0), y-intercept (0, 8)
9a. $a(0) = 2$, $a(1) = 0$, $a(2) = 6$, $a(3) = 0$, $a(4) = 18$, $a(5) = 0$, $a(6) = 54$ **b.** $a(10) = 486$, $a(101) = 0$ **c.** No; answers may vary. Sample: $a(n) = 0$ for all odd values of n, and since there are an infinite number of odd positive integers, $a(n)$ cannot be a polynomial. **10a.** rational **b.** irrational **c.** irrational
d. $f(0) = 2$, $f(1) = 2$, $f(2) = 6$, $f(3) = 14$, $f(4) = 34$, $f(5) = 82$, $f(6) = 198$ **e.** Answers may vary. Sample: $x^2 - 2x - 1 = 0$
f. Answers may vary. Sample: $2 \cdot f(n - 1) + f(n - 2)$

$= 2[(1 + \sqrt{2})^{n-1} + (1 - \sqrt{2})^{n-1}]$
$+ (1 + \sqrt{2})^{n-2} + (1 - \sqrt{2})^{n-2}$
$= 2(1 + \sqrt{2})^{n-1} + (1 + \sqrt{2})^{n-2}$
$+ 2\,(1 - \sqrt{2})^{n-1} + (1 - \sqrt{2})^{n-2}$
$= (1 + \sqrt{2})^{n-2}\,[2(1 + \sqrt{2}) + 1]$
$+ (1 + \sqrt{2})^{n-2}\,[2(1 - \sqrt{2}) + 1]$
$= (1 + \sqrt{2})^{n-2}\,[(3 + 2\sqrt{2})]$
$+ (1 - \sqrt{2})^{n-2}\,[(3 - 2\sqrt{2})$
$= (1 + \sqrt{2})^{n-2}(1 + \sqrt{2})^2$
$+ (1 - \sqrt{2})^{n-2}(1 - \sqrt{2})^2$
$= (1 + \sqrt{2})^n + (1 - \sqrt{2})^n = f(n)$

11a. $g(0) = 2, g(1) = 4, g(2) = 6,$ $g(3) = 4, g(4) = -14,$ $g(5) = -76, g(6) = -234$
b. $(2 + \sqrt{-1})^2 = 4 + (-1) + 4\sqrt{-1} = 3 + 4\sqrt{-1}$ **c.** Answers may vary. Sample: $x^2 - 4x + 5 = 0$
d. $4g(n - 1) - 5g(n - 2)$
$= 4(2 + \sqrt{-1})^{n-1} + 4(2 - \sqrt{-1})^{n-1}$
$- 5(2 + \sqrt{-1})^{n-2} - 5(2 - \sqrt{-1})^{n-2}$
$= (2 + \sqrt{-1})^{n-2}\,[4(2 + \sqrt{-1}) - 5]$
$+ (2 - \sqrt{-1})^{n-2}\,[4(2 - \sqrt{-1}) - 5]$
$= (2 + \sqrt{-1})^{n-2}(8 + 4\sqrt{-1} - 5)$
$+ (2 - \sqrt{-1})^{n-2}(8 - 4\sqrt{-1} - 5)$
$= (2 + \sqrt{-1})^{n-2}(3 + 4\sqrt{-1})$
$+ (2 - \sqrt{-1})^{n-2}(3 - 4\sqrt{-1})$
$= (2 + \sqrt{-1})^{n-2}(2 + \sqrt{-1})^2$
$+ (2 - \sqrt{-1})^{n-2}(2 - \sqrt{-1})^2$
$= (2 + \sqrt{-1})^n + (2 - \sqrt{-1})^n$
$= g(n)$

Lesson 3.4 **pp. 212–217**

Exercises 10a. $-i$ **b.** 1 **c.** $i^5 = i$, $i^6 = -1, i^7 = -i, i^8 = 1$ **d.** -1 **e.** $-i$
11a. $3 + 3i$ **b.** $9 + i$ **c.** $\pm 3i$
d. $3 \pm 5i$

Lesson 3.5 **pp. 218–222**

Exercises
8a. $z + \bar{z} = (a + bi) + (a - bi) = 2a$
b. $z\bar{z} = (a + bi)(a - bi) = a^2 - b^2i^2 + (ab - ab)i = a^2 + b^2$
9a. $a = 7, b = 5$ or $a = 7, b = -5$
b. $7 + 5i, 7 - 5i$ **10a.** $\frac{1}{2} - \frac{1}{2}i$
b. $\frac{1}{2} + \frac{1}{2}i$ **c.** $\frac{2}{13} - \frac{3}{13}i$
d. $\frac{5}{61} - \frac{6}{61}i$ **16a.** $(a + bi)^2 = a^2 + abi + abi + b^2i^2 = (a^2 - b^2) + (2ab)i$ **b.** $(a^2 + b^2)^2 = a^4 + 2a^2b^2 + b^4$; $(a^2 - b^2)^2 + (2ab)^2 = a^4 - 2a^2b^2 + b^4 + 4a^2b^2 = a^4 + 2a^2b^2 + b^4$ **c.** $a^2 + b^2 = 13$, $a^2 - b^2 = 5$, $2ab = 12$ **18.** Using the quadratic formula, one root is $\frac{-b}{2a} + \frac{\sqrt{b^2 - 4ac}}{2a}$. If the root is $m + ni$, then $m = -\frac{b}{2a}$ and $ni = \frac{\sqrt{b^2 - 4ac}}{2a}$. But $\frac{-b}{2a} - \frac{\sqrt{b^2 - 4ac}}{2a}$ also is a root, and you can write it as $m - ni$. So if $z = m + ni$ is one root of a quadratic polynomial, then $\bar{z} = m - ni$ is also a root.

19a. $\frac{17}{5} - \frac{6}{5}i$ **b.** $\frac{17}{5} + \frac{6}{5}i$
c. $-\frac{9}{13} + \frac{19}{13}i$ **d.** $-\frac{9}{13} - \frac{19}{13}i$
e. $2 + i$ **f.** $2 - i$ **20a.** 1 **b.** $\frac{4}{13}$ **c.** $\frac{5}{13}$
d. If $z = a + bi$, then $\frac{1}{z} = \frac{1}{a + bi} = \frac{a - bi}{a^2 + b^2}$ and $\frac{1}{\bar{z}} = \frac{1}{a - bi} = \frac{a + bi}{a^2 + b^2}$, so $\frac{1}{z} + \frac{1}{\bar{z}} = \frac{2a}{a^2 + b^2}$, which is a real number.

Lesson 3.7 **pp. 229–233**

Exercises **10a.** $-1, -5$

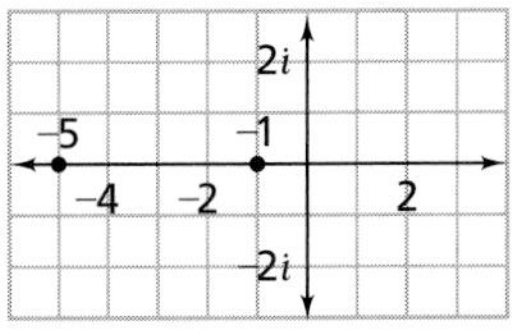

b. $-2, -4$

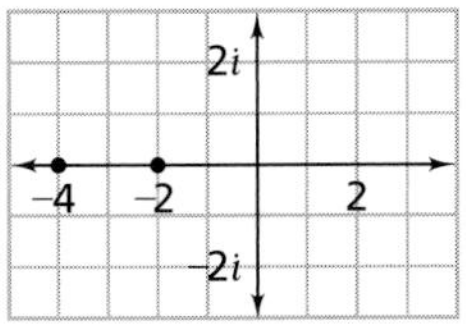

c. $-3 + i, -3 - i$

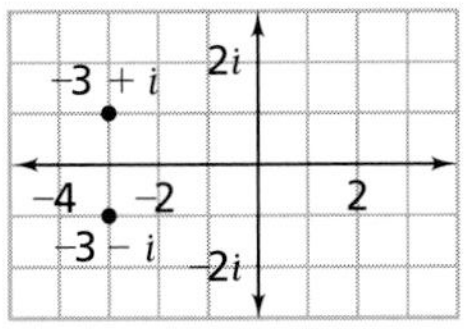

d. $-3 + 2i, -3 - 2i$

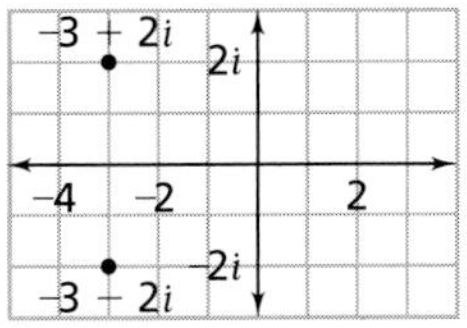

e. $-3 + 3i, -3 - 3i$

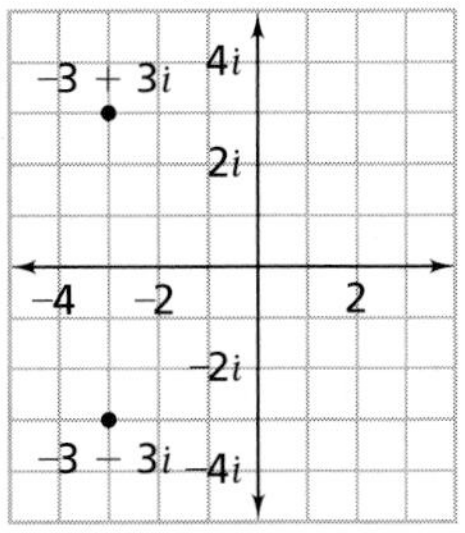

11a. $\pm i, \pm 1$

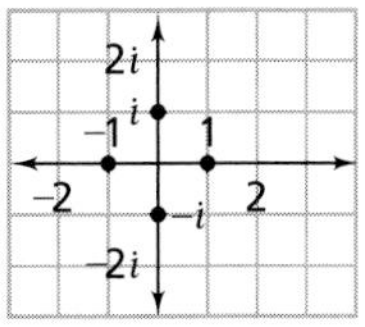

b. $\pm 2i, \pm 2$

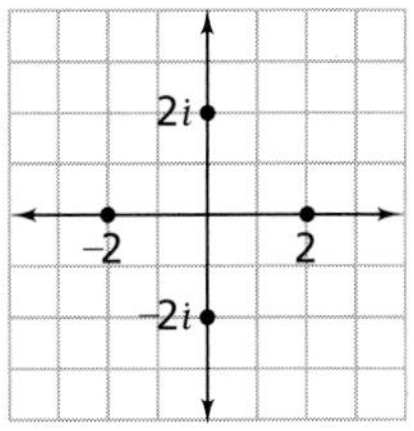

c. $\pm 3i, \pm 3$

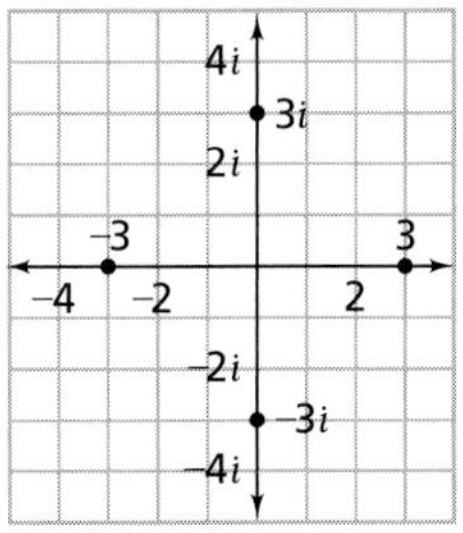

d. $\pm 4i, \pm 4$

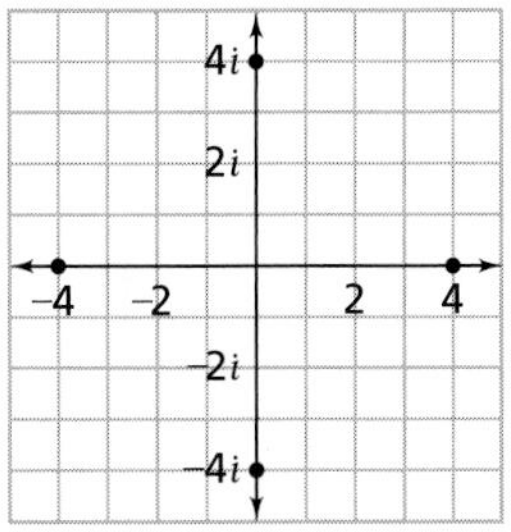

12a–f.

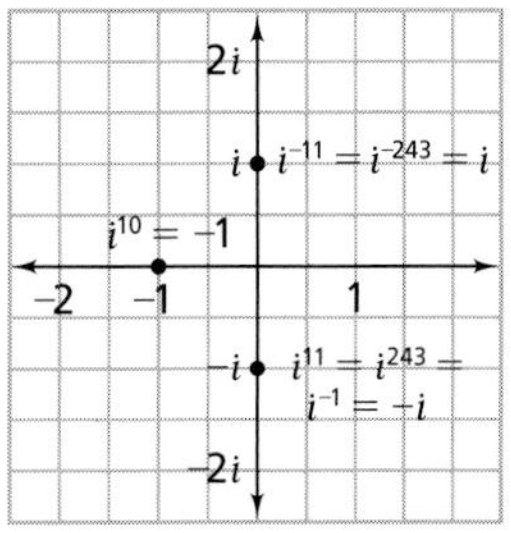

13a. $w = 2 - i$, $2w = 4 - 2i$, $3w = 6 - 3i$

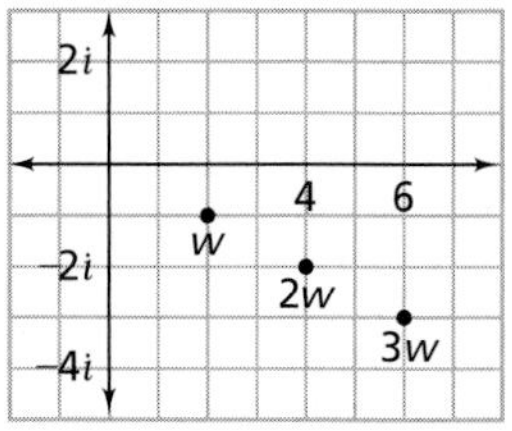

b. $z + w = 5$, $z + 2w = 7 - i$, $z + 3w = 9 - 2i$

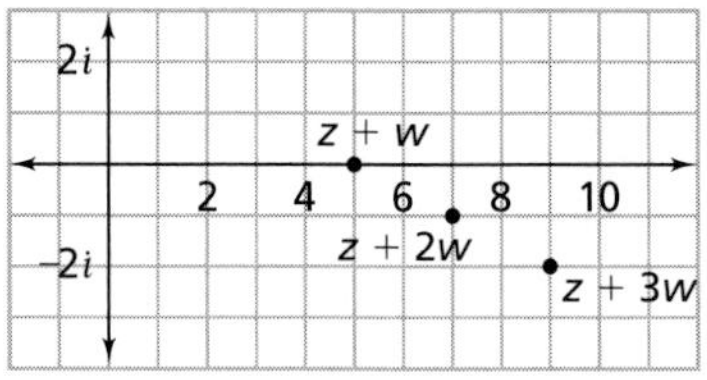

c. $\overline{w} = 2 + i$, $\overline{2w} = 4 + 2i$, $\overline{3w} = 6 + 3i$

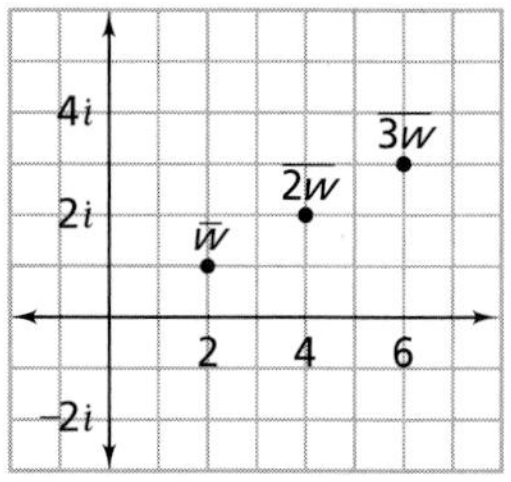

d. $\overline{z + w} = 5$, $\overline{z + 2w} = 7 + i$, $\overline{z + 3w} = 9 + 2i$

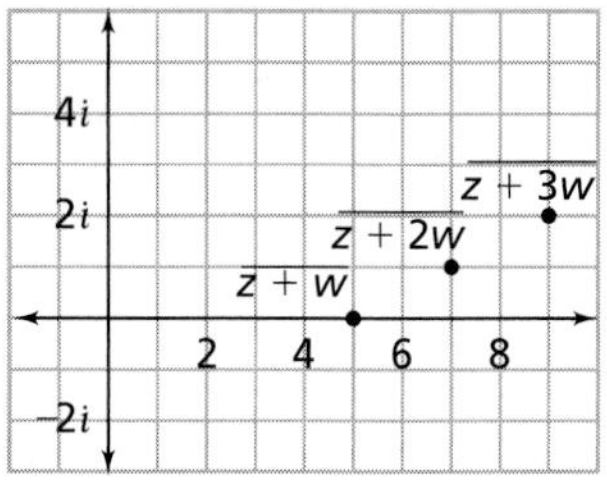

16a–e.

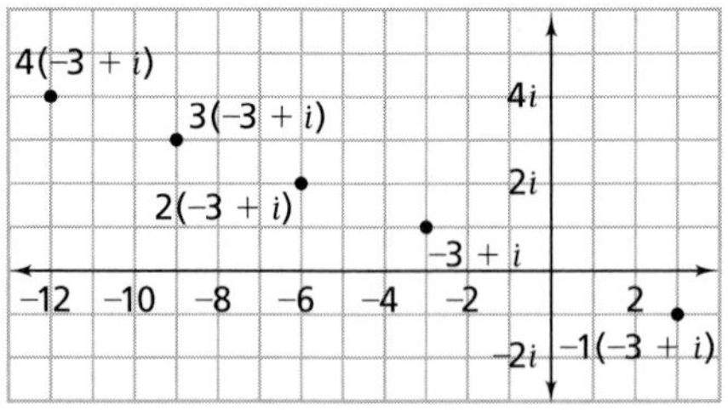

17a. $3 + 5i$ **b.** $-5 + 3i$ **c.** $-3 - 5i$ **d.** $5 - 3i$ **e.** $3 + 5i$

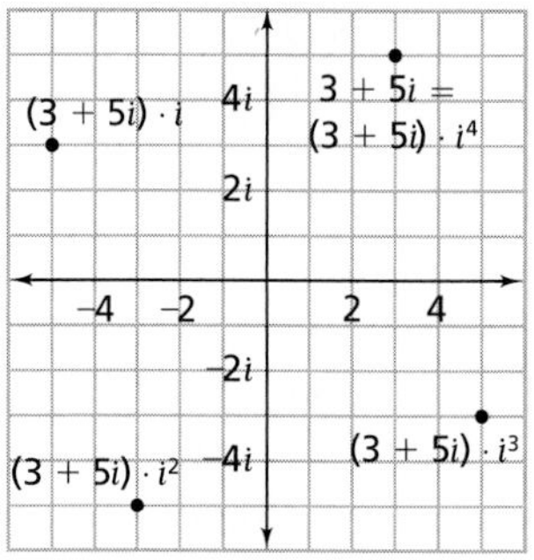

Lesson 3.8 **pp. 234–241**

In-Class Experiment

6. $z = -3 - 4i$, $iz = 4 - 3i$

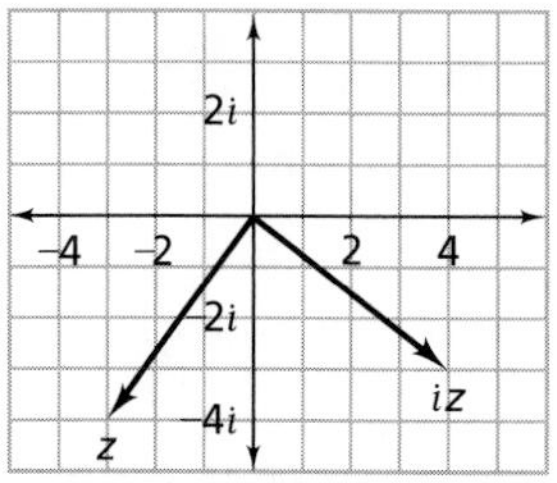

The graph of iz is a rotation of z by 90° counterclockwise about the origin.

Exercises 2a.

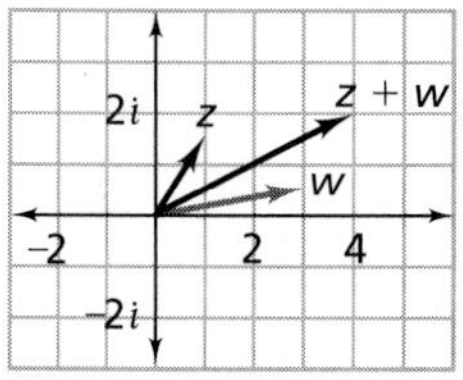

b.

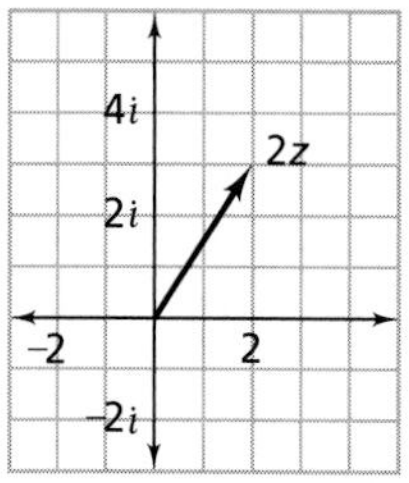

c.

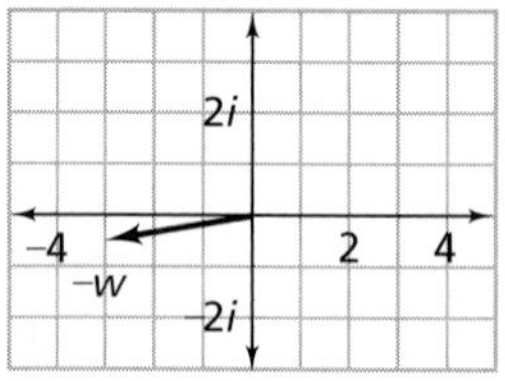

d.

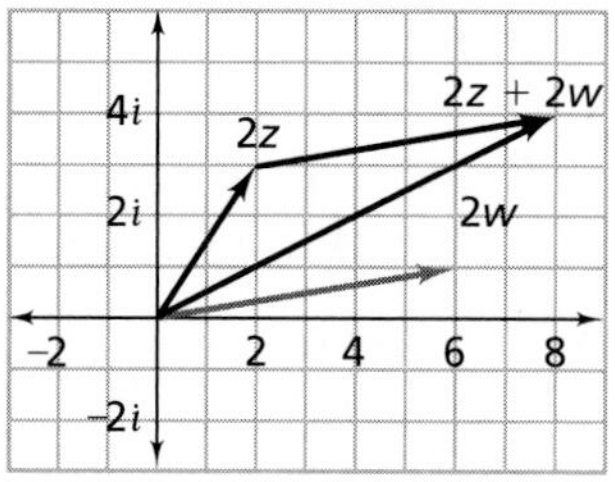

e.

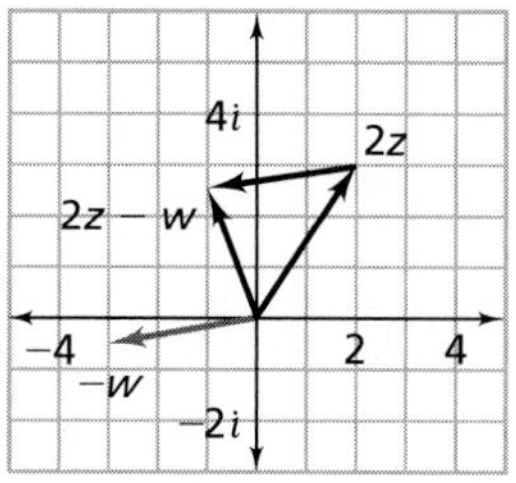

f.

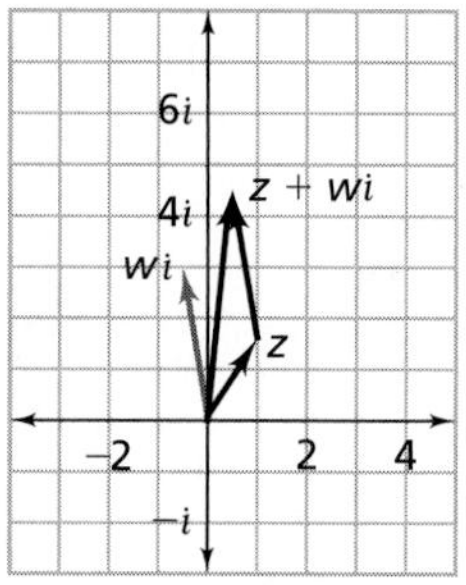

7a.

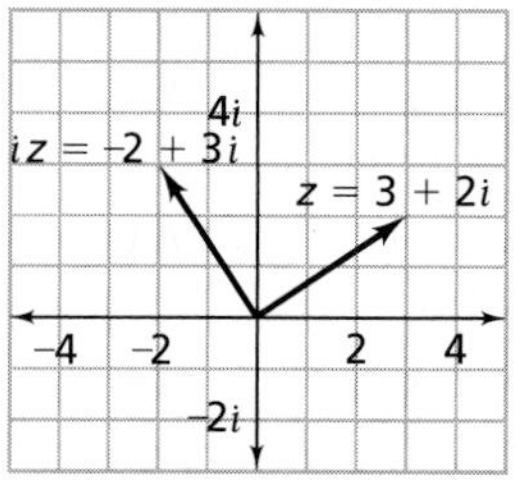

b.

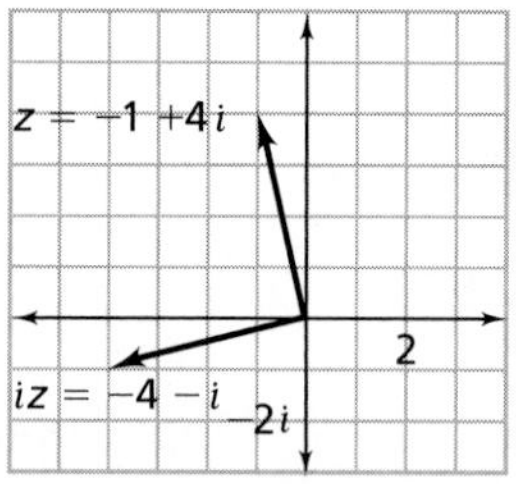

c.

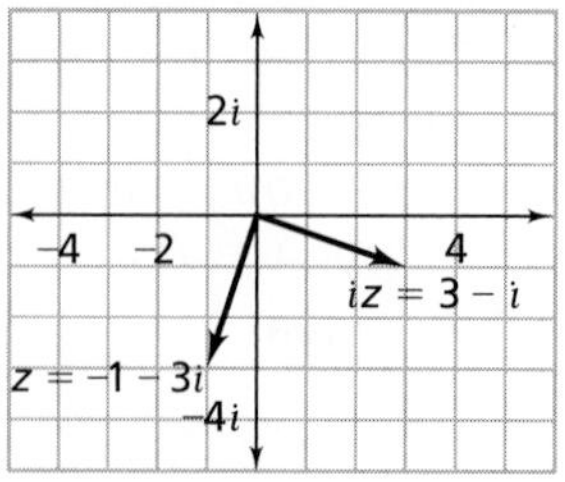

d.

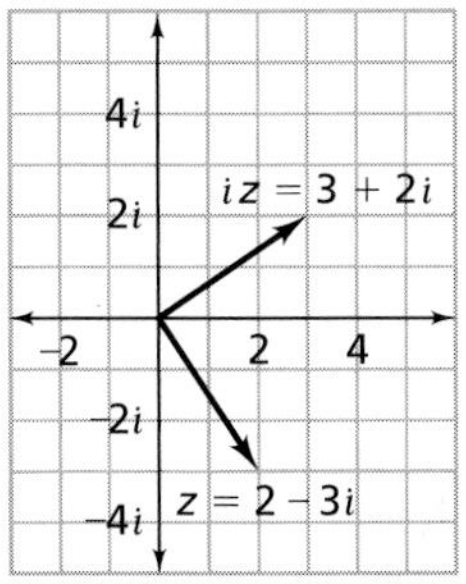

9. Answers may vary. Samples are given.

a. Points; the vertices of a square are points.

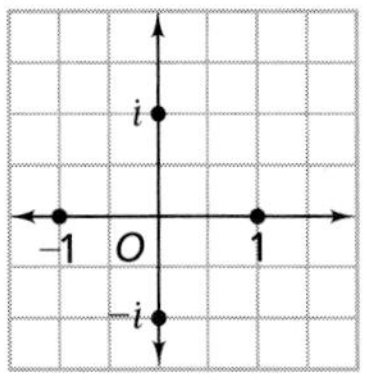

b. Vectors; you use vectors to illustrate the parallelogram law.

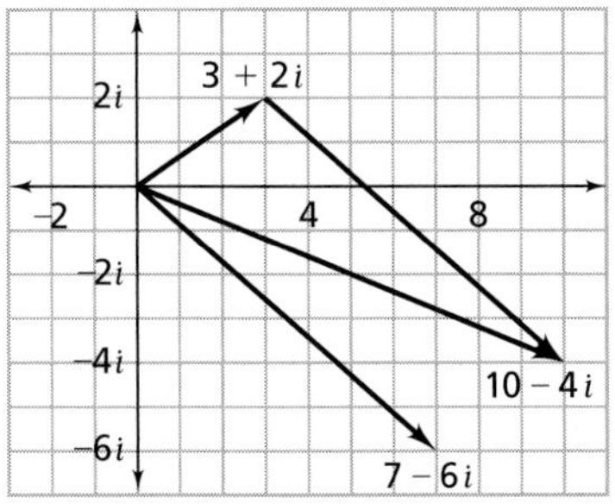

c. Points; the vertices of each triangle are points.

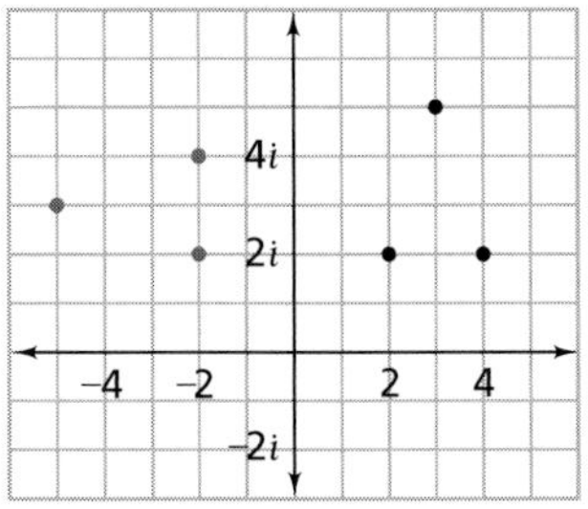

d. Vectors; distances can be represented by vectors.

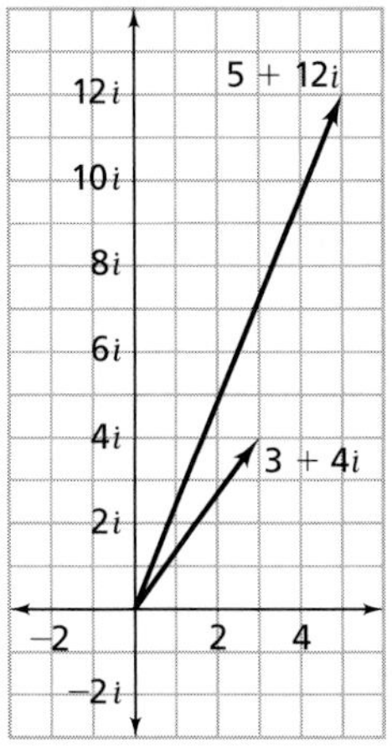

15a. $(1 + i)z = \sqrt{2}i$

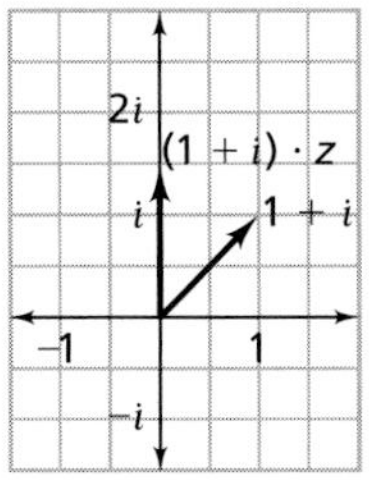

b. $(3 + 5i)z = -\sqrt{2} + 4\sqrt{2}i$

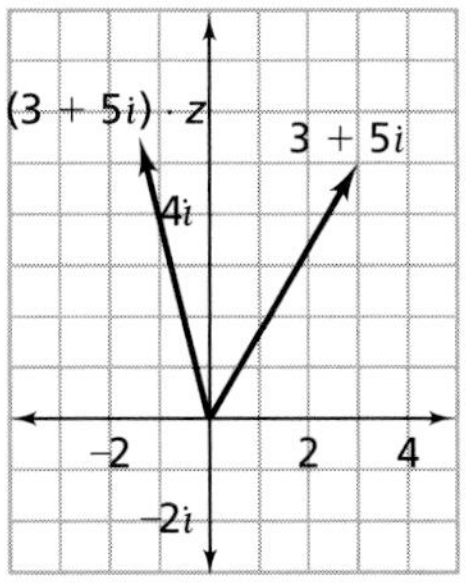

c. $(-2 + i)z = -\frac{3\sqrt{2}}{2} - \frac{\sqrt{2}}{2}i$

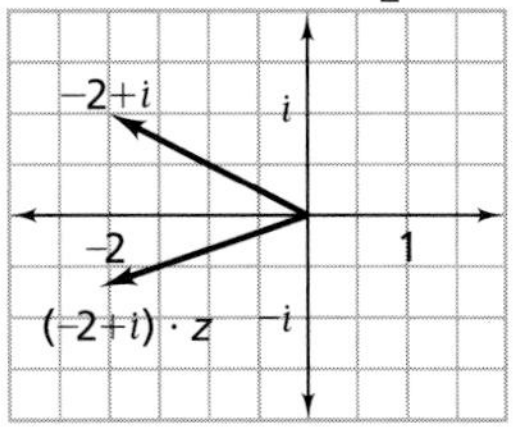

d. $(-3 - 4i)z = \frac{\sqrt{2}}{2} - \frac{7\sqrt{2}}{2}i$

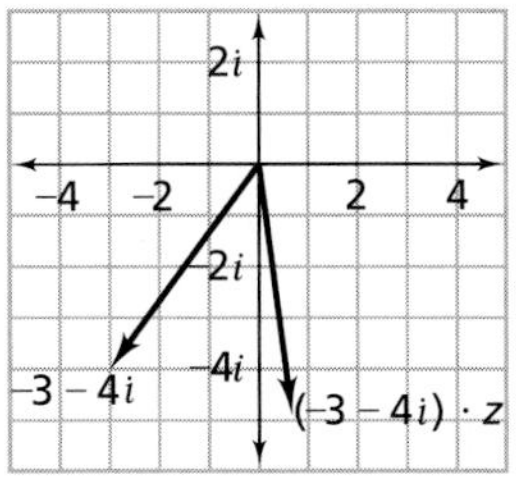

18a. $zw = -1 + 7i$

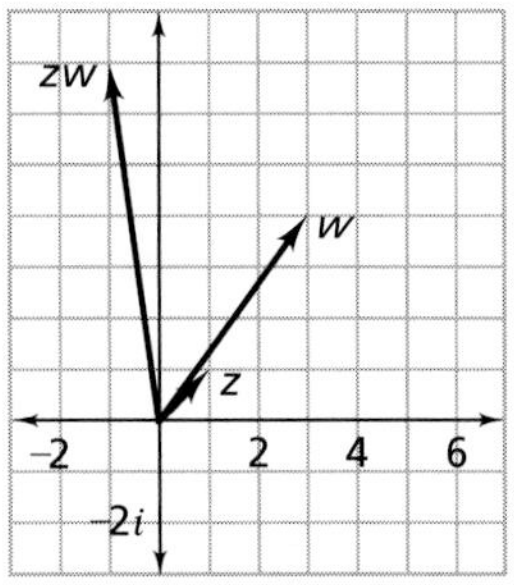

b. $zw = -7 + i$

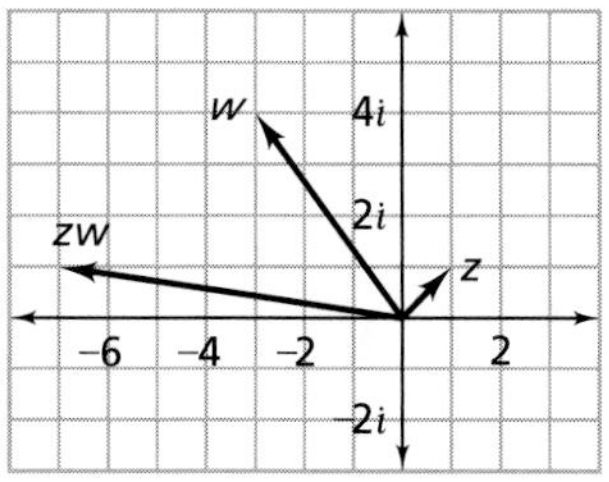

c. $zw = -17 + 7i$

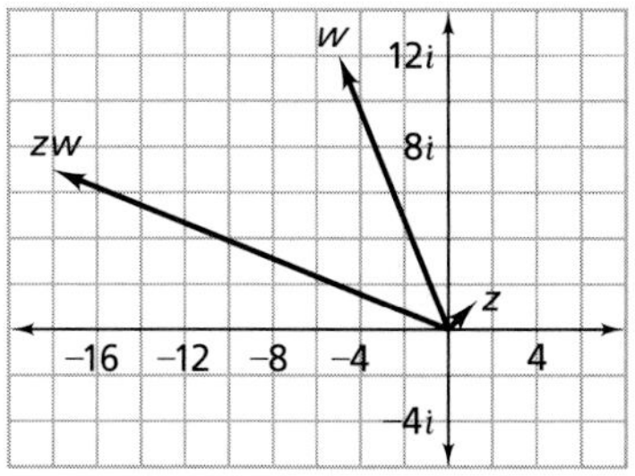

d. $zw = 7 + 7i$

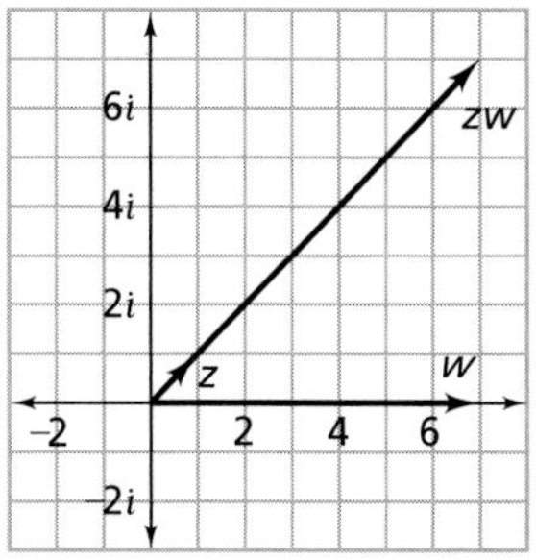

e. $zw = -3 + 3i$

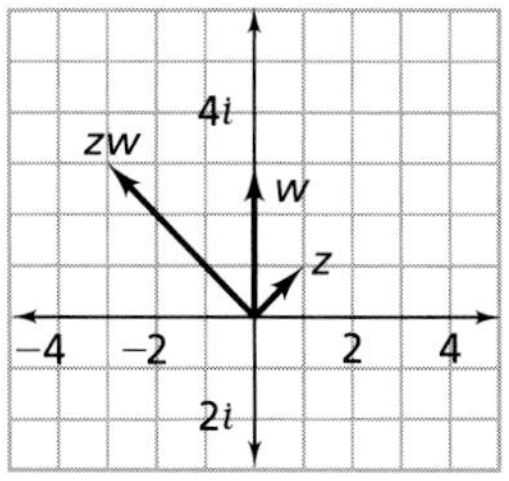

Lesson 3.9 **pp. 242–249**

Exercises **7a.** $\frac{1}{z} = \frac{1}{2} - \frac{1}{2}i$

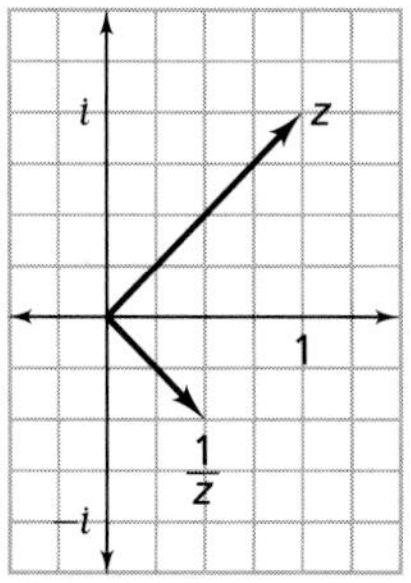

b. $\frac{1}{z} = \frac{2}{5} - \frac{1}{5}i$

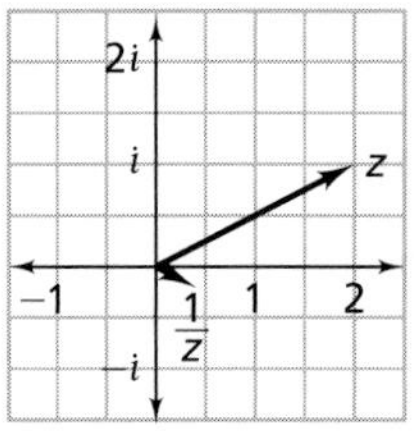

c. $\frac{1}{z} = \frac{1}{4} - \frac{\sqrt{3}}{4}i$

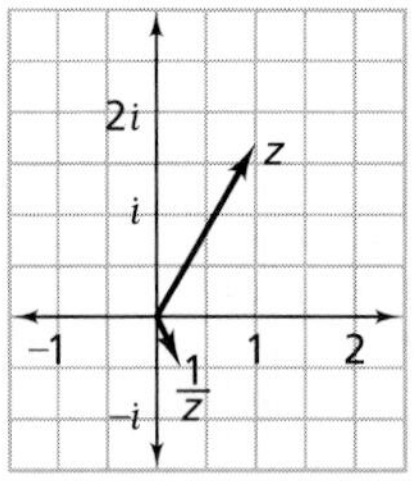

d. $\frac{1}{z} = -\frac{1}{2} + \frac{1}{2}i$

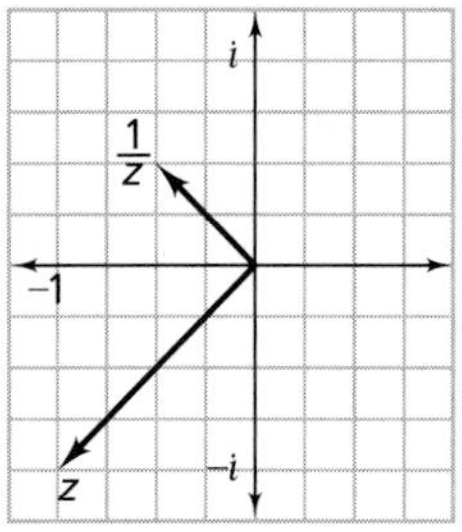

8a. $|z| = \sqrt{2}$, $\arg z = 45°$;

$\left|\frac{1}{z}\right| = \frac{\sqrt{2}}{2}$, $\arg \frac{1}{z} = 315°$

b. $|z| = \sqrt{5}$, $\arg z = 27°$;

$\left|\frac{1}{z}\right| = \frac{\sqrt{5}}{5}$, $\arg \frac{1}{z} = 333°$

c. $|z| = 2$, $\arg z = 60°$;

$\left|\frac{1}{z}\right| = \frac{1}{2}$, $\arg \frac{1}{z} = 300°$

d. $|z| = \sqrt{2}$, $\arg z = 225°$;

$\left|\frac{1}{z}\right| = \frac{\sqrt{2}}{2}$, $\arg \frac{1}{z} = 135°$

9a. $5\left(\frac{4}{5} + \frac{3}{5}i\right)$

b. $13\left(\frac{5}{13} + \frac{12}{13}i\right)$

c. $\sqrt{2}\left(\frac{\sqrt{2}}{2} + \frac{\sqrt{2}}{2}i\right)$

d. $\sqrt{2}\left(\frac{\sqrt{2}}{2} - \frac{\sqrt{2}}{2}i\right)$

e. $\sqrt{13}\left(\frac{2\sqrt{13}}{13} + \frac{3\sqrt{13}}{13}i\right)$

f. $2\left(-\frac{1}{2} + \frac{\sqrt{13}}{2}i\right)$

10. For $z = a + bi$ with $|z| = k$, rewrite z as $z = k\left(\frac{a}{k} + \frac{b}{k}i\right)$. Then k is a positive real number and the magnitude of $\frac{a}{k} + \frac{b}{k}i$ is $\sqrt{\frac{a^2}{k^2} + \frac{b^2}{k^2}} = \sqrt{\frac{a^2 + b^2}{k^2}} = \sqrt{\frac{k^2}{k^2}} = 1$.

17a. $|z| = \sqrt{5}$, $|w| = \sqrt{10}$, $|zw| = 5\sqrt{2}$

b. $|z| = \sqrt{5}$, $|w| = \sqrt{13}$, $|zw| = \sqrt{65}$

c. $|z| = 5$, $|w| = 3$, $|zw| = 15$

d. $|z| = \sqrt{5}$, $|w| = \frac{\sqrt{5}}{5}$, $|zw| = 1$

18a. $|z| \cdot |w| = |z \cdot w|$

b. Answers may vary. Sample: From Theorem 3.4, $|zw| = \sqrt{zw \cdot \overline{zw}} = \sqrt{z \cdot w \cdot \overline{z} \cdot \overline{w}} = \sqrt{z \cdot \overline{z} \cdot w \cdot \overline{w}} = \sqrt{z \cdot \overline{z}} \cdot \sqrt{w \cdot \overline{w}} = |z| \cdot |w|$

19a. 2 **b.** 5 **c.** 10 **d.** 50 **e.** 13 **f.** Answers may vary. Sample: $(5 + 2i)^2 = 21 + 20i$

Mid-Chapter Test p. 251

10a. $1 - i\sqrt{3}$ **b.** $2 + 2i\sqrt{3}$

c. $-2 + 2i\sqrt{3}$

d.

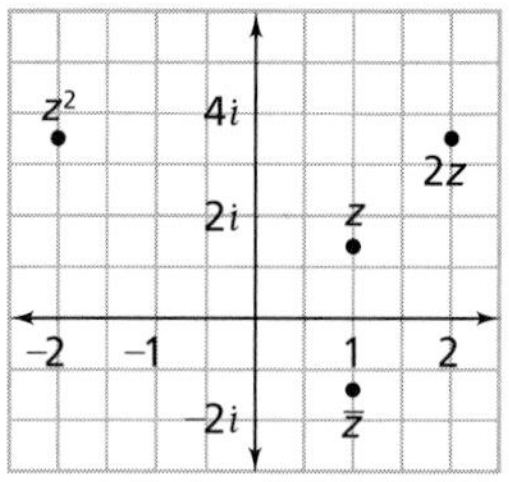

e.

Vector	Magnitude	Direction
z	2	60°
$\overline{z}$	2	300°
$2z$	4	60°
z^2	4	120°

Lesson 3.10 pp. 253–254

For You to Explore

3.

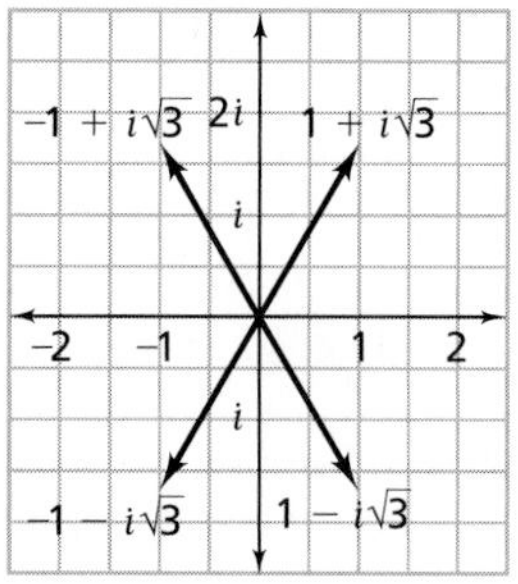

a. 60° **b.** 120° **c.** 240° **d.** 300°

4. $(ac - bd)^2 + (bc + ad)^2$
$= (a^2c^2 - 2abcd + b^2d^2) + (b^2c^2 + 2abcd + a^2d^2)$
$= a^2c^2 + b^2d^2 + b^2c^2 + a^2d^2$
$= a^2c^2 + a^2d^2 + b^2c^2 + b^2d^2$
$= a^2(c^2 + d^2) + b^2(c^2 + d^2)$
$= (a^2 + b^2)(c^2 + d^2)$

5a. $(x - r)(x - s)(x - t) = x^3 - (r + s + t)x^2 + (rs + rt + st)x - rst$

b. $a = -(r + s + t)$

c. $b = rs + rt + st$

d. $c = -rst$ **6a.** $f(2 + i) = 6 - 7i$, $f(2 - i) = 6 + 7i$, so they are conjugates. **b.** $f(4 + i) = 4 + 13i$, $f(4 - i) = 4 - 13i$, so they are conjugates. **c.** $f(-1 + 3i) = 80$, $f(-1 - 3i) = 80$, so they are conjugates. **d.** $f(3 + i) = 0$, so $f(3 - i) = 0$. **7a.** $x = \frac{-1 + \sqrt{5}}{4} \pm \frac{\sqrt{10 + 2\sqrt{5}}}{4}i$ or about $0.309 \pm 0.951i$

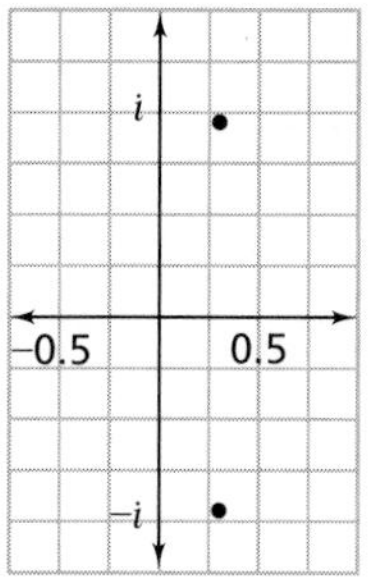

b. $x = \frac{-1 - \sqrt{5}}{4} \pm \frac{\sqrt{10 - 2\sqrt{5}}}{4}i$ or about $-0.809 \pm 0.588i$

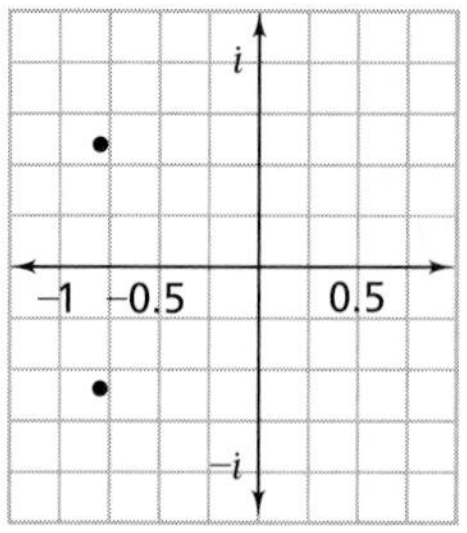

c. $(x-1)\left(x^2+\left(\frac{1+\sqrt{5}}{2}\right)x+1\right)\cdot\left(x^2+\left(\frac{1-\sqrt{5}}{2}\right)x+1\right)=$
$(x-1)(x^4+x^3+x^2+x+1)=$
x^5-1

Lesson 3.11 **pp. 255–262**

For You to Do 6. When you multiply by $2+i$, the magnitude is multiplied by $\sqrt{5}$,and the argument is increased by 26.6° counterclockwise; when you multiply by $-i$, there is no change to the magnitude, and the argument is increased by 270° counterclockwise; when you multiply by -1, there is no change to the magnitude, and the argument is increased by 180°. **Exercises 1a.** magnitude 9, direction 240° **b.** magnitude 27, direction 0° **c.** $x^2+3x+9=0$ **2.** Answers may vary. Sample: For z^2, square the magnitude and double the direction. For z^3, cube the magnitude and triple the direction. For z^n, raise the magnitude to the *n*th power and multiply the direction by *n*.

8a.

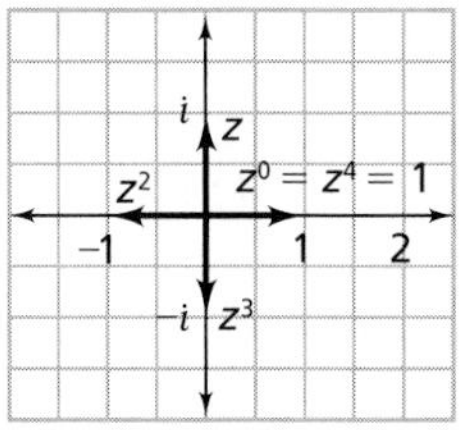

Consecutive powers of *i* rotate 90° counterclockwise; if you raise $z=i$ to the *n*th power, you multiply the direction, 90°, by *n*, and there is no change to the magnitude. So consecutive powers of *i* rotate 90° counterclockwise.

b.

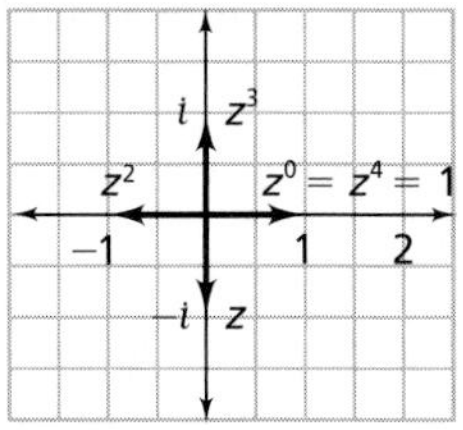

Consecutive powers of $-i$ rotate 90° clockwise; if you raise $z=-i$ to the *n*th power, you multiply the direction, 270°, by *n*, and there is no change to the magnitude. So consecutive powers of $-i$ rotate 270° counterclockwise, which is equivalent to rotating by 90° clockwise.

c.

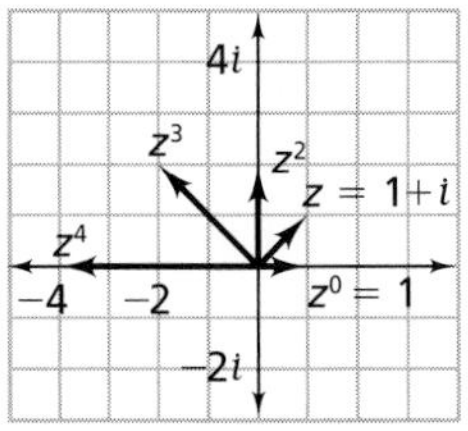

Consecutive powers of $1+i$ rotate 45° counterclockwise, with the magnitudes increasing by the factor $\sqrt{2}$; if you raise $z=1+i$ to the *n*th power, you multiply the direction, 45°, by *n*, and you raise the magnitude, $\sqrt{2}$, to the *n*th power. So consecutive powers of $1+i$ rotate 45° counterclockwise and increase the magnitude by the factor $\sqrt{2}$.

d.

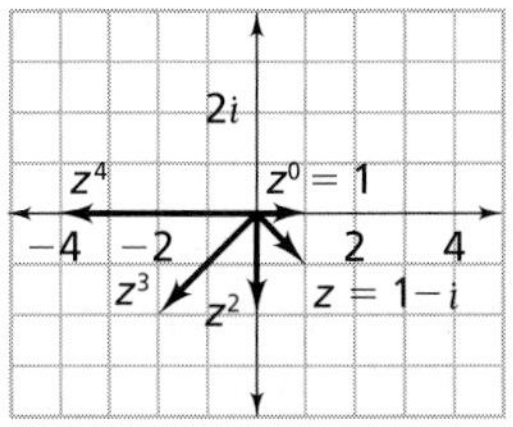

The powers of $1-i$ rotate 45° clockwise, with the magnitudes increasing by the factor $\sqrt{2}$; if you raise $z=1-i$ to the *n*th power, you multiply the direction, 315°, by *n*, and you raise the magnitude, $\sqrt{2}$, to the *n*th power. So consecutive powers of $1-i$ rotate 315° counterclockwise (which is equivalent to rotating by 45° clockwise), and increase the magnitude by the factor $\sqrt{2}$.

e.

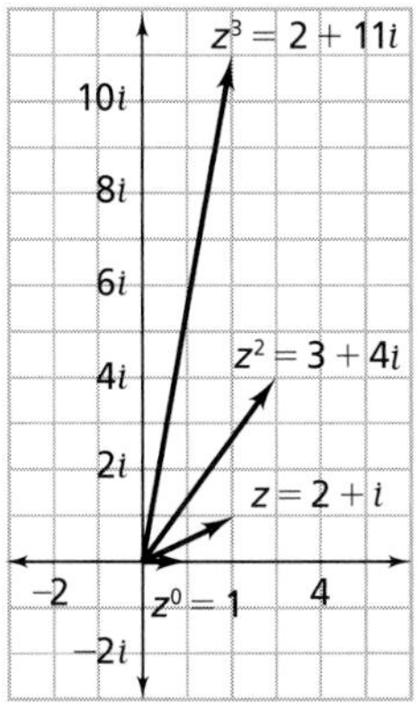

The powers of $2+i$ rotate about 26.6° counterclockwise, with the magnitudes increasing by the factor $\sqrt{5}$; if you raise $z=2+i$ to the *n*th power, you multiply the direction, 26.6°, by *n*, and you raise the magnitude, $\sqrt{5}$, to the *n*th power. So consecutive powers of $2+i$ rotate 26.6° counterclockwise, and increase the magnitude by the factor $\sqrt{5}$.

f.

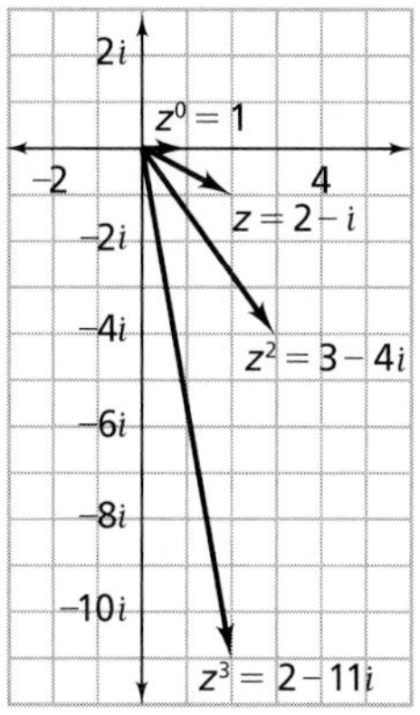

The powers of $2-i$ rotate about 26.6° clockwise, with the magnitudes increasing by the factor $\sqrt{5}$; if you raise $z=2-i$ to the *n*th power, you multiply the direction, 333.4°, by *n* and you raise the magnitude, $\sqrt{5}$, to the *n*th power. So consecutive powers of $2-i$ rotate 333.4° counterclockwise (which is equivalent to rotating by 26.6° clockwise), and increase the magnitude by the factor $\sqrt{5}$.

10a.

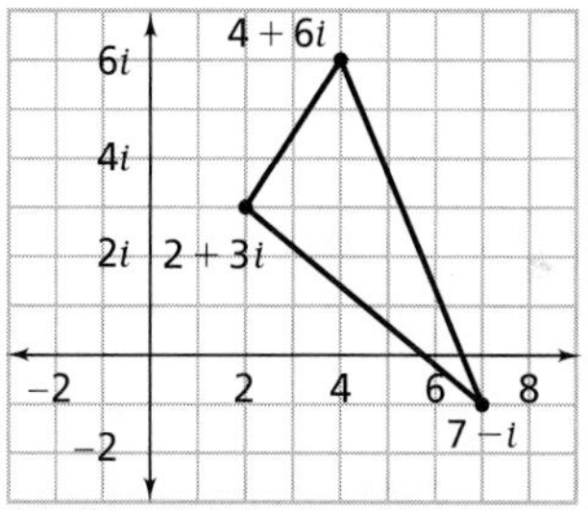

b.

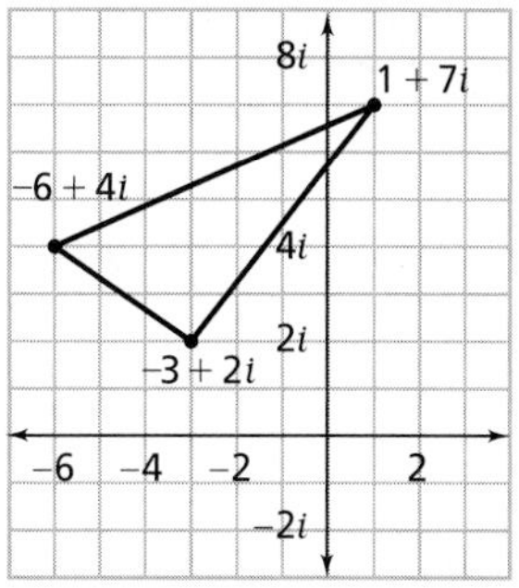

c.

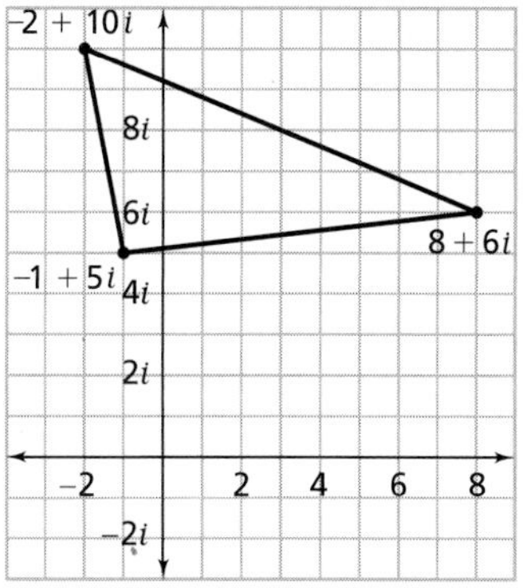

d.

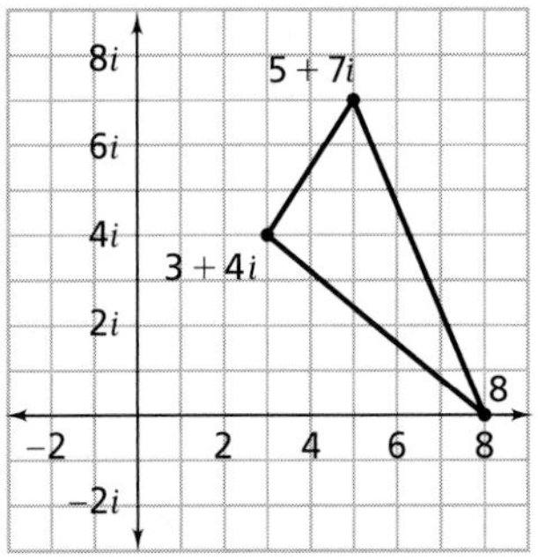

18a.

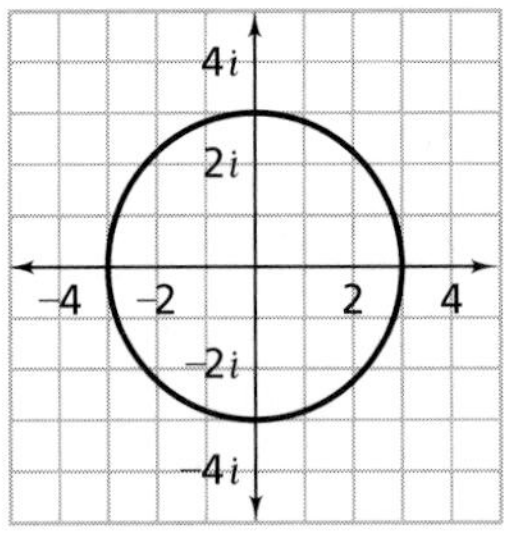

b.

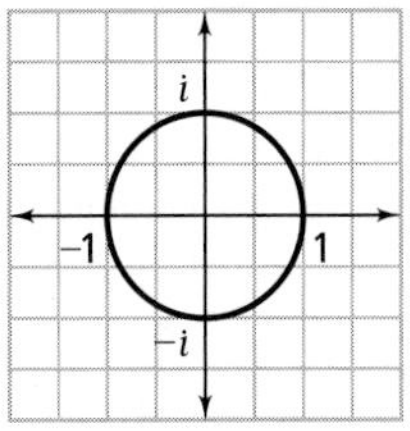

c.

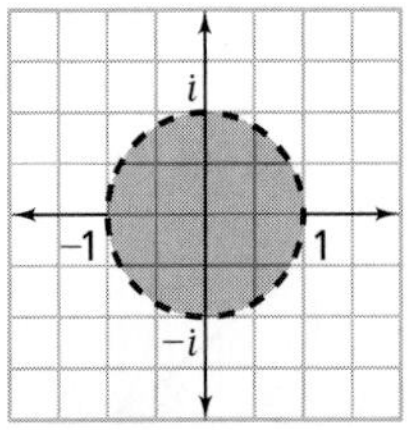

d.

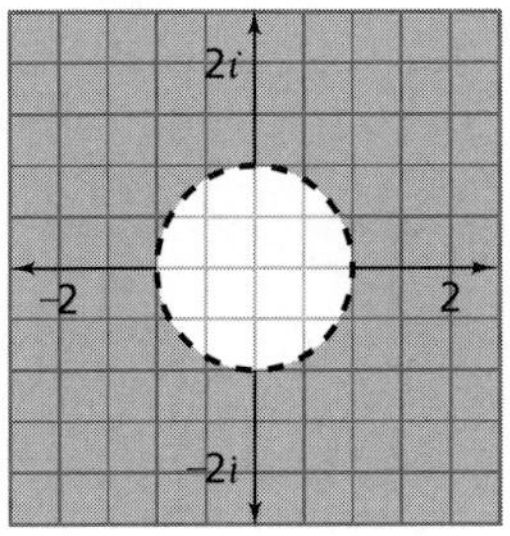

e.

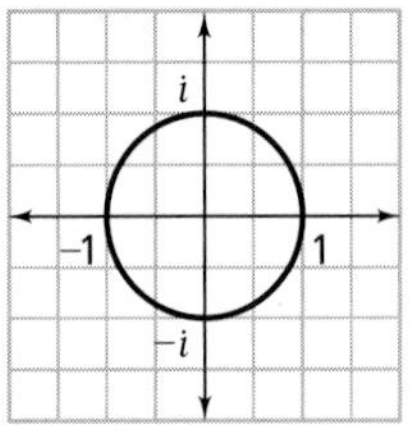

f.

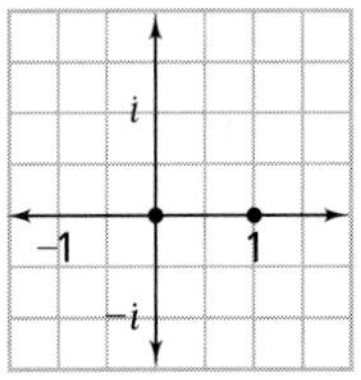

g.

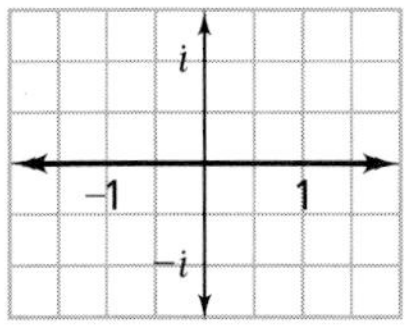

h.

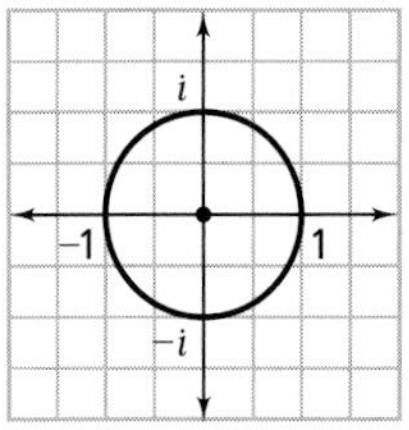

Chapter 4

Lesson 4.3 pp. 291–300

Exercises 26. Answers may vary. Samples are given. **a.** $\left(\begin{array}{cc|c} 1 & 0 & -2 \\ 0 & 1 & 3 \end{array}\right)$

b. $\left(\begin{array}{cc|c} 1 & -2 & -8 \\ 0 & 0 & -3 \end{array}\right)$ **c.** $\left(\begin{array}{cc|c} 1 & -2 & -2 \\ 0 & 0 & 0 \end{array}\right)$

d. $\left(\begin{array}{ccc|c} 1 & 0 & -1 & 1 \\ 0 & 1 & 2 & 2 \\ 0 & 0 & 0 & 0 \end{array}\right)$ **e.** $\left(\begin{array}{ccc|c} 1 & 0 & -1 & 1 \\ 0 & 1 & 2 & 2 \\ 0 & 0 & 0 & 0 \end{array}\right)$

f. $\left(\begin{array}{ccc|c} 1 & 0 & -1 & 0 \\ 0 & 1 & 2 & 0 \\ 0 & 0 & 0 & 1 \end{array}\right)$ **g.** $\left(\begin{array}{ccc|c} 1 & 0 & -1 & 0 \\ 0 & 1 & 2 & 0 \\ 0 & 0 & 0 & 1 \end{array}\right)$

h. $\left(\begin{array}{ccc|c} 1 & -2 & 0 & -2 \\ 0 & 0 & 1 & 3 \\ 0 & 0 & 0 & 0 \end{array}\right)$

i. $\left(\begin{array}{ccc|c} 1 & -2 & 0 & -2 \\ 0 & 0 & 1 & 3 \\ 0 & 0 & 0 & 0 \end{array}\right)$ **j.** $\left(\begin{array}{ccc|c} 1 & 3 & 0 & -2 \\ 0 & 0 & 1 & 3 \\ 0 & 0 & 0 & 0 \end{array}\right)$

k. $\left(\begin{array}{ccc|c} 1 & 3 & 0 & -2 \\ 0 & 0 & 1 & 3 \\ 0 & 0 & 0 & 0 \end{array}\right)$ **l.** $\left(\begin{array}{ccc|c} 1 & 0 & 0 & 2 \\ 0 & 1 & -1 & 3 \\ 0 & 0 & 0 & 0 \end{array}\right)$

m. $\left(\begin{array}{ccc|c} 1 & 0 & 0 & 2 \\ 0 & 1 & -1 & 3 \\ 0 & 0 & 0 & 0 \end{array}\right)$

n. $\left(\begin{array}{ccc|c} 1 & 0 & 0 & 2 \\ 0 & 1 & 0 & -1 \\ 0 & 0 & 1 & 3 \end{array}\right)$

o. $\left(\begin{array}{ccc|c} 1 & 0 & 0 & 2 \\ 0 & 1 & 0 & -1 \\ 0 & 0 & 1 & 3 \end{array}\right)$

p. $\left(\begin{array}{cccc|c} 1 & 0 & 3 & 0 & 1 \\ 0 & 1 & 3 & 0 & 2 \\ 0 & 0 & 0 & 1 & 3 \\ 0 & 0 & 0 & 0 & 0 \end{array}\right)$

q. $\left(\begin{array}{cccc|c} 1 & 0 & 0 & 3 & 1 \\ 0 & 1 & 0 & -1 & -2 \\ 0 & 0 & 1 & -2 & -1 \\ 0 & 0 & 0 & 0 & 0 \end{array}\right)$

r. $\left(\begin{array}{ccccc|c} 1 & -2 & 3 & 0 & 1 & 4 \\ 0 & 0 & 0 & 1 & 3 & 5 \end{array}\right)$

Lesson 4.4 pp. 303–307

Exercises 7.

Sales (millions of units)

	A	B	C	D	E
Europe	0.6	0.25	0.3	0.3	1.3
United States	4.6	3.3	1.4	2.2	0.4
Asia	0.3	0.15	1.3	4.5	0.1

9a.

Sales (millions of cars)

	A	B	C	D	E
Europe	0.42	0.21	0.21	0.21	1.05
United States	2.1	1.575	0.63	1.05	0.315
Asia	0.21	0.105	0.84	3.675	0.105

Multiply each entry in the table of passenger car sales by 1.05.

b.

Sales (millions of cars)

	A	B	C	D	E
Europe	0.4	0.206	0.2	0.21	1.02
United States	2.0	1.545	0.6	1.05	0.306
Asia	0.2	0.103	0.8	3.675	0.102

Multiply the values in the D column by 1.05, multiply the values in the B column by 1.03, multiply the values in the E column by 1.02, and multiply the values in the other columns by 1.0.

c.

Sales (millions of cars)

	A	B	C	D	E
Europe	0.396	0.198	0.198	0.198	0.99
United States	2.02	1.515	0.606	1.01	0.303
Asia	0.212	0.106	0.848	3.71	0.106

Multiply the values in the Asia row by 1.06, in the U.S. row by 1.01, and in the Europe row by 0.99. **15a.** −47; the 20th entry is $10 - 19(3)$. **b.** Answers may vary. Sample: It is a row matrix of twenty numbers; the first entry is 10 and each subsequent entry is 3 less than the previous entry. **c.** Answers may vary. Sample: Each entry is the product $[10 - (n - 1)3][2n]$, which can be rewritten as $26n - 6n^2$. The question asks to find the sum of the values of $26n - 6n^2$ for the values of n from 1 to 20.

Lesson 4.6 **pp. 315–322**

Exercises 14a. 0 **b.** 0 **c.** 0 **d.** 0 The Zero Product Property, that if a product is zero then at least one of the factors is zero, does not hold for dot products. **15.** Answers may vary. Sample: If we represent each ordered pair in Exercise 13 as a vector, then the vectors in each pair are perpendicular. In general, two vectors are perpendicular if and only if their dot product is zero. **16a.** Answers may vary. Sample: Solutions are (1, 2), (5, 0) or any ordered pair (x, y) such that $x + 2y = 5$. **b.** Answers may vary. Sample: $(1, 2) \cdot (3, 6) = 15$, $(5, 0) \cdot (3, 6) = 15$; $x + 2y = 3 + 2(6) = 15$ **c.** Answers may vary. Sample: Solutions are (5, 0), (3, 1), or any ordered pair (x, y) such that $2x + 4y = 10$ (or $x + 2y = 5$). **d.** Answers may vary. Sample: A is any ordered pair on the line $y = -\frac{1}{2}x + \frac{5}{2}$. **20.** If $A = (a_1, a_2, \dots a_n)$, $B = (b_1, b_2, \dots, b_n)$, and $C = (c_1, c_2, \dots, c_n)$, then $A \cdot (B \pm C) = A \cdot (b_1 \pm c_1, b_2 \pm c_2, \dots, b_n \pm c_n) = (a_1(b_1 \pm c_1), a_2(b_2 \pm c_2) + \cdots + a_n(b_n \pm c_n)) = (a_1b_1 \pm a_1c_1, a_2b_2 \pm a_2c_2 + \cdots + a_nb_n \pm a_nc_n) = A \cdot B \pm A \cdot C$.

Lesson 4.7 **pp. 323–336**

Exercises

2a.

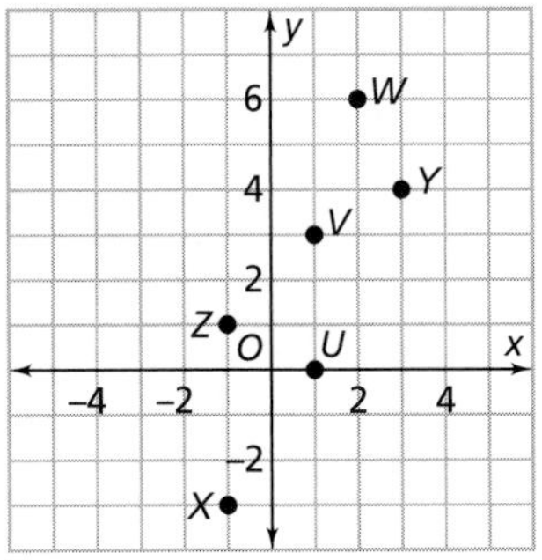

b. $AU = \begin{pmatrix} 1 \\ 0 \end{pmatrix}$, $AV = \begin{pmatrix} 1 \\ -3 \end{pmatrix}$, $AW = \begin{pmatrix} 2 \\ -6 \end{pmatrix}$, $AX = \begin{pmatrix} -1 \\ 3 \end{pmatrix}$, $AY = \begin{pmatrix} 3 \\ -4 \end{pmatrix}$, $AZ = \begin{pmatrix} -1 \\ -1 \end{pmatrix}$

c.

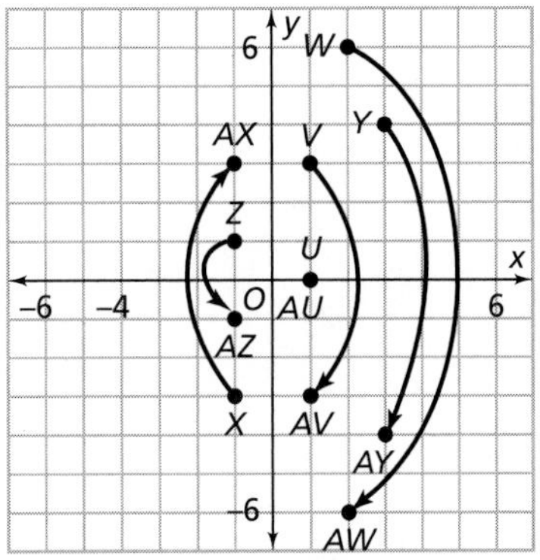

Corresponding points are reflections of each other over the x-axis.

d. $BU = \begin{pmatrix} 0 \\ 1 \end{pmatrix}$, $BV = \begin{pmatrix} -3 \\ 1 \end{pmatrix}$, $BW = \begin{pmatrix} -6 \\ 2 \end{pmatrix}$, $BX = \begin{pmatrix} 3 \\ -1 \end{pmatrix}$, $BY = \begin{pmatrix} -4 \\ 3 \end{pmatrix}$, $BZ = \begin{pmatrix} -1 \\ -1 \end{pmatrix}$; each point is a rotation of the original point by 90° counterclockwise. **23.** Use M as the original matrix.

a. $(1 \quad 1)M = (316 \quad 303 \quad 286)$

b. $M\begin{pmatrix} 1 \\ 1 \\ 1 \end{pmatrix} = \begin{pmatrix} 438 \\ 467 \end{pmatrix}$

c. Answers may vary. Sample:

$$((1, 1)M)\begin{pmatrix} 1 \\ 1 \\ 1 \end{pmatrix} = 905$$

$$(1, 1)\left(M\begin{pmatrix} 1 \\ 1 \\ 1 \end{pmatrix}\right) = 905$$

24. Let S be the matrix for the original year. **a.** Using scalar multiplication, $1.05S$ is the matrix for the following year.

b. $S\begin{pmatrix} 1 & 0 & 0 & 0 & 0 \\ 0 & 1.03 & 0 & 0 & 0 \\ 0 & 0 & 1 & 0 & 0 \\ 0 & 0 & 0 & 1.05 & 0 \\ 0 & 0 & 0 & 0 & 1.02 \end{pmatrix}$

c. $\begin{pmatrix} 0.99 & 0 & 0 \\ 0 & 1.01 & 0 \\ 0 & 0 & 1.06 \end{pmatrix}S$

25a. 74.5 g protein, 50.2 g fat, 128.4 g carbohydrates **b.** The problem (and solution) can be written as

$$\begin{pmatrix} 5.5 & 0.5 & 3 \\ 5.5 & 0.03 & 0.02 \\ 0.1 & 6 & 1.5 \end{pmatrix}\begin{pmatrix} 9 \\ 20 \\ 5 \end{pmatrix} = \begin{pmatrix} 74.5 \\ 50.2 \\ 128.4 \end{pmatrix}.$$

26a. Using m, p, and c for the numbers of ounces of meat, potatoes, and cabbage, respectively, the system of equations is $5.5m + 0.5p + 3c = 45$, $5.5m + 0.03p + 0.02c = 35$, $0.1m + 6p + 1.5c = 100$.

b. $\begin{pmatrix} 5.5 & 0.5 & 3 \\ 5.5 & 0.03 & 0.02 \\ 0.1 & 6 & 1.5 \end{pmatrix}\begin{pmatrix} m \\ p \\ c \end{pmatrix} = \begin{pmatrix} 45 \\ 35 \\ 100 \end{pmatrix}$

33a. $(4 \quad 5 \quad 6)$ **b.** $(-7 \quad -8 \quad -9)$

c. $\begin{pmatrix} 0 & 0 & 0 \\ 0 & 0 & 0 \\ 4 & 5 & 6 \end{pmatrix}$ **d.** $\begin{pmatrix} 7 & 8 & 9 \\ 4 & 5 & 6 \\ 1 & 2 & 3 \end{pmatrix}$

34. $EA = (-4 \quad -4)$, $FA = (0 \quad 0)$, $GA = \begin{pmatrix} -4 & -4 \\ 0 & 0 \end{pmatrix}$

Lesson 4.8 **pp. 337–342**

Exercises 8. No; for example,

$\begin{pmatrix} 3 & -1 \\ -2 & 2 \end{pmatrix}\begin{pmatrix} 1 \\ 1 \end{pmatrix} = \begin{pmatrix} 2 \\ 0 \end{pmatrix}$ and $\begin{pmatrix} 1 \\ 1 \end{pmatrix} \neq \begin{pmatrix} 2 \\ 0 \end{pmatrix}$.

9. Using $M = \begin{pmatrix} 2 & 0.5 & 0.2 \\ 3 & 1 & 0.5 \\ 5 & 10 & 3 \end{pmatrix}$, the system is $M\begin{pmatrix} m \\ p \\ c \end{pmatrix} = \begin{pmatrix} 30 \\ 50 \\ 150 \end{pmatrix}$. Then

$$\begin{pmatrix} m \\ p \\ c \end{pmatrix} = M^{-1}\begin{pmatrix} 30 \\ 50 \\ 150 \end{pmatrix} = \begin{pmatrix} 12.\overline{2} \\ 2.\overline{2} \\ 22.\overline{2} \end{pmatrix}.$$

10. Using $M = \begin{pmatrix} 2 & 0.5 & 0.2 \\ 3 & 1 & 0.5 \\ 5 & 10 & 3 \end{pmatrix}$, the system is $M\begin{pmatrix} m \\ p \\ c \end{pmatrix} = \begin{pmatrix} 30 \\ 50 \\ 120 \end{pmatrix}$. Then

$$\begin{pmatrix} m \\ p \\ c \end{pmatrix} = M^{-1}\begin{pmatrix} 30 \\ 50 \\ 120 \end{pmatrix} = \begin{pmatrix} 12.\overline{8} \\ -3.\overline{1} \\ 28.\overline{8} \end{pmatrix}.$$

But the value $p = -3.\overline{1}$ indicates that there is no solution.

11. If $\begin{pmatrix} a & b \\ c & d \end{pmatrix}\begin{pmatrix} x \\ y \end{pmatrix} = \begin{pmatrix} x \\ y \end{pmatrix}$, then $ax + by = x$ and $cx + dy = y$. The only values of a, b, c, and d that satisfy both equations simultaneously are $a = 1$, $b = 0$, $c = 0$, $d = 1$ or $\begin{pmatrix} 1 & 0 \\ 0 & 1 \end{pmatrix}$.

Mathematical Reflections p. 352

3. $F(G + H) = \begin{pmatrix} 1 & -1 \\ 2 & 0 \end{pmatrix}\begin{pmatrix} -3 & 2 \\ -2 & 4 \end{pmatrix} = \begin{pmatrix} -1 & -2 \\ -6 & 4 \end{pmatrix}$ and $FG + FH = \begin{pmatrix} -3 & -3 \\ -6 & 2 \end{pmatrix} + \begin{pmatrix} 2 & 1 \\ 0 & 2 \end{pmatrix} = \begin{pmatrix} -1 & -2 \\ -6 & 4 \end{pmatrix}$.

4. $JK \neq KJ$; $JK = \begin{pmatrix} 2 & 1 & -1 \\ 0 & -4 & 2 \\ 6 & -5 & 1 \end{pmatrix}$ and $KJ = \begin{pmatrix} 2 & -4 \\ 3 & -3 \end{pmatrix}$.

Lesson 4.10 pp. 355–359

For You to Explore 1a. The values of $s(n)$ and $t(n)$ for $n = 0$ to $n = 8$ are 1, 2, 2, 4, 4, 8, 8, 16, 16 and 1, 0, 2, 0, 4, 0, 8, 0, 16, respectively. When n is even, $s(n) = t(n) = 2^{\frac{n}{2}}$; when n is odd, $s(n) = 2^{\frac{n+1}{2}}$ and $t(n) = 0$.
b. If n is odd, $S(n) = MS(n - 1) = \begin{pmatrix} 1 & 1 \\ 1 & -1 \end{pmatrix}\begin{pmatrix} 2^{\frac{n-1}{2}} \\ 2^{\frac{n-1}{2}} \end{pmatrix} = \begin{pmatrix} 2^{\frac{n+1}{2}} \\ 0 \end{pmatrix}$, and if n is even, $S(n) = MS(n - 1) = \begin{pmatrix} 1 & 1 \\ 1 & -1 \end{pmatrix}\begin{pmatrix} 2^{\frac{n}{2}} \\ 0 \end{pmatrix} = \begin{pmatrix} 2^{\frac{n}{2}} \\ 2^{\frac{n}{2}} \end{pmatrix}$.
c. Use mathematical induction.
(i) $S(1) = MS(0)$, so it is true for $n = 1$.
(ii) Assume it is true for $n - 1$, or $S(n - 1) = M^{n-1}S(0)$. Then $S(n) = MS(n - 1) = M(M^{n-1}S(0)) = (M^n)S(0)$, so it is true for n. Both parts of mathematical induction are satisfied, so $S(n) = (M^n)S(0)$ for all positive integers n.
d. $M = \begin{pmatrix} 1 & 1 \\ 1 & -1 \end{pmatrix}$, $M^2 = \begin{pmatrix} 2 & 0 \\ 0 & 2 \end{pmatrix}$, $M^3 = \begin{pmatrix} 2 & 2 \\ 2 & -2 \end{pmatrix}$, $M^4 = \begin{pmatrix} 4 & 0 \\ 0 & 4 \end{pmatrix}$, $M^5 = \begin{pmatrix} 4 & 4 \\ 4 & -4 \end{pmatrix}$

4a.

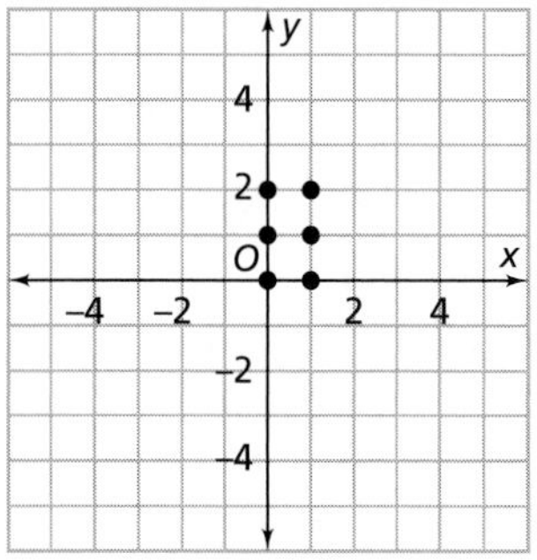

b.

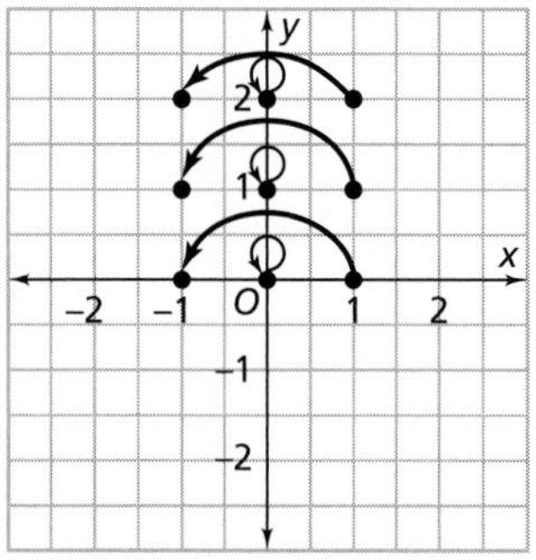

c. The mapping reflects lines or polygons over the y-axis. **d.** It reflects the plane over the y-axis. **e.** Answers may vary. Sample: The pattern will be reflected over the y-axis.

Exercises

9a.

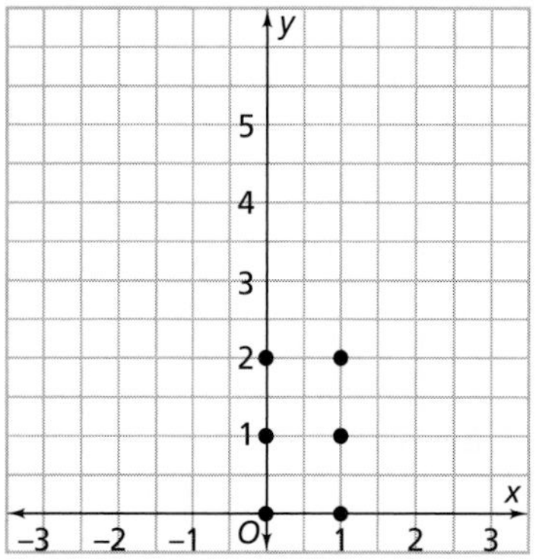

b.

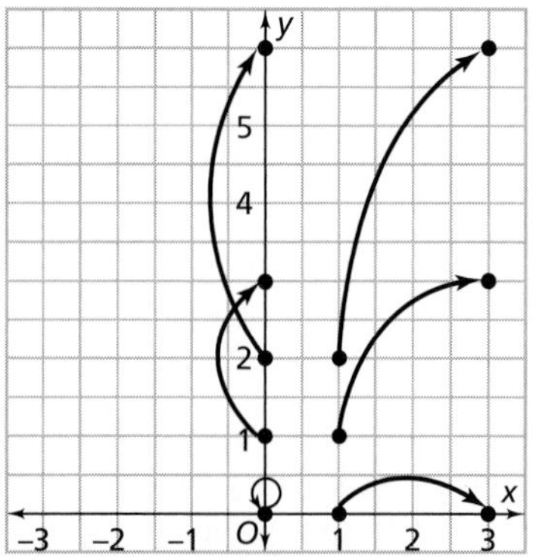

c. The mapping dilates lines and polygons by the factor 3, with the origin as the center of the dilation. **d.** M dilates the plane by the factor 3, with the center at the origin. **e.** The pattern will be dilated by the factor 3, centered at the origin. **f.** The mapping produces a scale drawing with scale factor 3. **16a.** $B^2 = \begin{pmatrix} 2 & 1 \\ 1 & 1 \end{pmatrix}$ **b.** $B^3 = \begin{pmatrix} 3 & 2 \\ 2 & 1 \end{pmatrix}$ **c.** $B^4 = \begin{pmatrix} 5 & 3 \\ 3 & 2 \end{pmatrix}$, $B^5 = \begin{pmatrix} 8 & 5 \\ 5 & 3 \end{pmatrix}$, $B^6 = \begin{pmatrix} 13 & 8 \\ 8 & 5 \end{pmatrix}$; the entries are Fibonacci numbers, or $B^n = \begin{pmatrix} F_{n+1} & F_n \\ F_n & F_{n-1} \end{pmatrix}$.
d. The first few ordered pairs are $\begin{pmatrix} 2 \\ 1 \end{pmatrix}, \begin{pmatrix} 3 \\ 2 \end{pmatrix}, \begin{pmatrix} 5 \\ 3 \end{pmatrix}, \begin{pmatrix} 8 \\ 5 \end{pmatrix}, \begin{pmatrix} 13 \\ 8 \end{pmatrix}$; in general, $S(n) = \begin{pmatrix} F_{n+3} \\ F_{n+2} \end{pmatrix}$. **e.** $s_0 = t_0 = 1$; $s_{n+1} = s_n + t_n$, $t_{n+1} = s_n$

Mathematical Reflections pp. 387–388

1a.

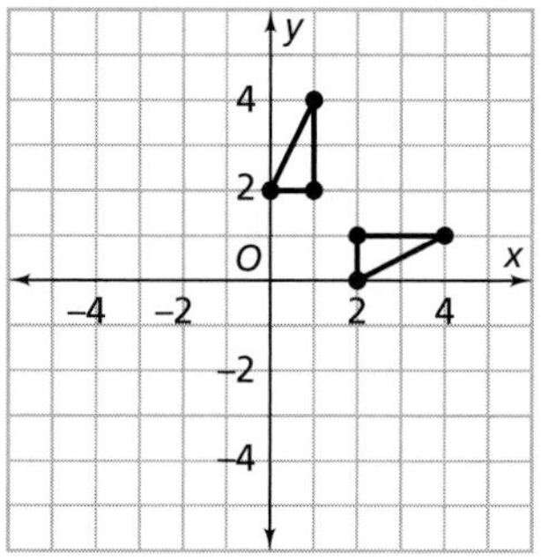

b. $(x, y) \mapsto (y, x)$, which is a reflection in the line $y = x$. **2.** $\begin{pmatrix} 0 & 1 \\ -1 & 0 \end{pmatrix}$

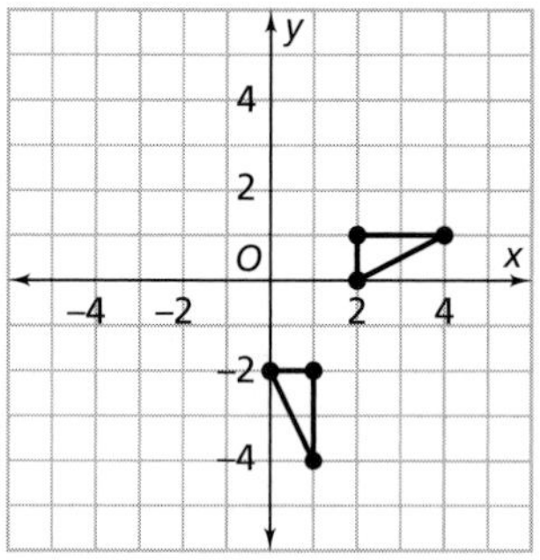

Cumulative Review pp. 394–395

8a. $z \cdot w = -4 + 4\sqrt{3}i$
b.

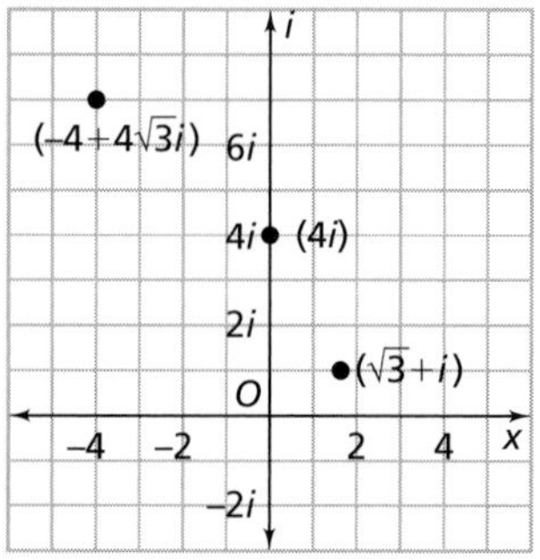

c. z: magnitude = 2, direction 30°
w: magnitude = 4, direction 90°
$z \cdot w$: magnitude = 8, direction 120°

22.

Input, n	Output, $a(n)$	Δ	Δ^2
0	5	4	1
1	9	**5**	1
2	**14**	**6**	1
3	**20**	**7**	
4	**27**		

27a. $81x^2 - 49y^2 = (9x + 7y) \cdot (9x - 7y)$ **b.** $64x^3 + 27y^3 = (4x + 3y)(16x^2 - 12xy + 9y^2)$
30a. $5x^2 + -16x + 12 = (5x - 6) \cdot (x - 2)$ **b.** $6x^2 + 21x + 9 = 3(2x + 1)(x + 3)$ **c.** $9x^4 - 35x^2 - 4 = (9x^2 + 1)(x + 2)(x - 2)$

Chapter 5

Lesson 5.1 pp. 399–400

For You to Explore

1.

Input, n	Output, $f(n)$
6	64
5	32
4	16
3	8
2	**4**
1	**2**
0	**1**
−1	$\mathbf{\frac{1}{2}}$
−2	$\mathbf{\frac{1}{4}}$
−3	$\mathbf{\frac{1}{8}}$

Exercises

8.

Input, n	Output, $g(n)$
5	243
4	81
3	27
2	**9**
1	**3**
0	**1**
−1	$\mathbf{\frac{1}{3}}$
−2	$\mathbf{\frac{1}{9}}$
−3	$\mathbf{\frac{1}{27}}$

Lesson 5.2 pp. 401–405

Exercises **3.** See Figure 6

Lesson 5.3 pp. 406–411

Exercises **8b.**

x	$h(x)$
−3	$\mathbf{\frac{2}{125}}$
−2	$\mathbf{\frac{2}{25}}$
−1	$\mathbf{\frac{2}{5}}$
0	2
1	10
2	50
3	250
4	1250

Lesson 5.4 pp. 412–417

Exercises

6a.

(a, b)	$\frac{a+b}{2}$	$\sqrt{ab}$
(1, 2)	1.5	1.4142
(2, 5)	**3.5**	**3.1623**
(4, 1)	**2.5**	**2**
(3, 3)	**3**	**3**
(6, 9)	**7.5**	**7.3485**
(8, 10)	**9**	**8.9443**
(7, 7)	**7**	**7**

b. $\frac{a+b}{2}$; answers may vary. Sample: The square of any real number is positive, so $(a - b)^2 \geq 0$. Then,

$$a^2 - 2ab + b^2 \geq 0$$
$$a^2 + 2ab + b^2 \geq 4ab$$
$$\frac{a^2 + 2ab + b^2}{4} \geq ab$$
$$\frac{(a+b)^2}{4} \geq ab$$

Taking the square root of each side (since $a, b > 0$), gives $\frac{a+b}{2} \geq \sqrt{ab}$.

12a.

Years	Balance (dollars)
0	500.00
1	515.00
2	530.00
3	**546.36**
4	**562.75**
5	**579.64**
6	**597.03**

Figure 6

3. Corollary 5.2:

$$\frac{a^b}{a^c} = \frac{\overbrace{(a \cdot a \cdot \cdots \cdot a)}^{b \text{ copies of } a}}{\underbrace{(a \cdot a \cdot \cdots \cdot a)}_{c \text{ copies of } a}}$$

$$= \frac{\overbrace{(a \cdot a \cdot \cdots \cdot a)}^{c \text{ copies of } a}}{\underbrace{(a \cdot a \cdot \cdots \cdot a)}_{c \text{ copies of } a}} \cdot \frac{\overbrace{(a \cdot a \cdot \cdots \cdot a)}^{(b-c) \text{ copies of } a}}{1}$$

$$= 1 \cdot a^{b-c} = a^{b-c}$$

Corollary 5.3:

$$(a^b)^c = \underbrace{\overbrace{(a \cdot a \cdot \cdots \cdot a)}^{b \text{ copies of } a} \cdot \overbrace{(a \cdot a \cdot \cdots \cdot a)}^{b \text{ copies of } a} \cdot \cdots \cdot \overbrace{(a \cdot a \cdot \cdots \cdot a)}^{b \text{ copies of } a}}_{c \text{ copies of } a^b}$$

$$= \underbrace{a \cdot a \cdot \cdots \cdot a}_{bc \text{ copies of } a} = a^{bc}$$

Lesson 5.5 pp. 418–422

Exercises

15a.

x	$f(x) = x^3$	$g(x) = x^{\frac{1}{3}}$
-8	-512	-2
-2	-8	-1.26
-1	-1	-1
$-\frac{1}{2}$	-0.125	-0.794
$-\frac{1}{8}$	-0.002	-0.5
0	0	0
$\frac{1}{8}$	0.002	0.5
$\frac{1}{2}$	0.125	0.794
1	1	1
2	8	1.26
8	512	2

b.

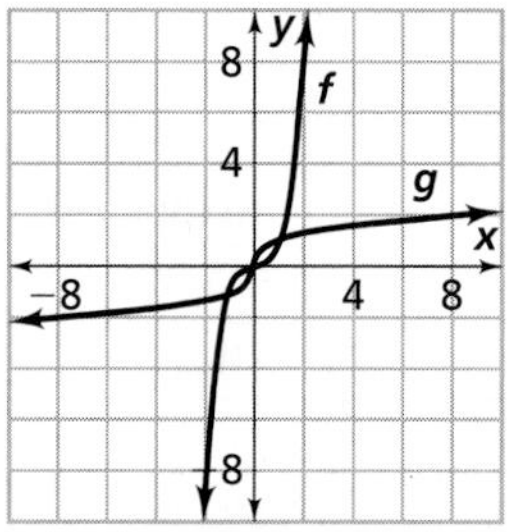

c. They are reflections of each other over the line $y = x$. **d.** 3

Lesson 5.6 pp. 425–427

For You to Explore

1.

Input	Output	Δ
0	1	3
1	4	3
2	7	3
3	10	3
4	13	3
5	16	

2.

Input	Output	Δ
0	1	0
1	1	2
2	3	4
3	7	6
4	13	8
5	21	

3.

Input	Output	Δ
0	1	2
1	3	6
2	9	18
3	27	54
4	81	162
5	243	

4.

Input	Output	Δ
0	3	12
1	15	60
2	75	300
3	375	1500
4	1875	7500
5	9375	

5.

Input	Output	Δ
0	1	$-\frac{1}{2}$
1	$\frac{1}{2}$	$-\frac{1}{4}$
2	$\frac{1}{4}$	$-\frac{1}{8}$
3	$\frac{1}{8}$	$-\frac{1}{16}$
4	$\frac{1}{16}$	$-\frac{1}{32}$
5	$\frac{1}{32}$	

7a.

Input	Output	÷
0	1	4
1	4	1.75
2	7	1.43
3	10	1.3
4	13	1.23
5	16	

b. The numbers get closer to 1.

8. Problem 2:

Input	Output	÷
0	1	1
1	1	3
2	3	2.33
3	7	1.86
4	13	1.62
5	21	

Problem 3:

Input	Output	÷
0	1	3
1	3	3
2	9	3
3	27	3
4	81	3
5	243	

Problem 4:

Input	Output	÷
0	3	5
1	15	5
2	75	5
3	375	5
4	1875	5
5	9375	

Problem 5:

Input	Output	÷
0	1	$\frac{1}{2}$
1	$\frac{1}{2}$	$\frac{1}{2}$
2	$\frac{1}{4}$	$\frac{1}{2}$
3	$\frac{1}{8}$	$\frac{1}{2}$
4	$\frac{1}{16}$	$\frac{1}{2}$
5	$\frac{1}{32}$	

Exercises

15b.

Input, a	Output, $g(a)$
-2	$\frac{15}{2}$
-1	15
0	30
1	60
2	120

c.

Input, a	Output, $h(a)$
0	$\frac{1}{5}$
1	1
2	5
3	25
4	125

d.

Input, a	Output, $j(a)$
−1	**81**
0	**27**
1	**9**
2	**3**
3	**1**

Lesson 5.7 pp. 428–435
Exercises

8a.

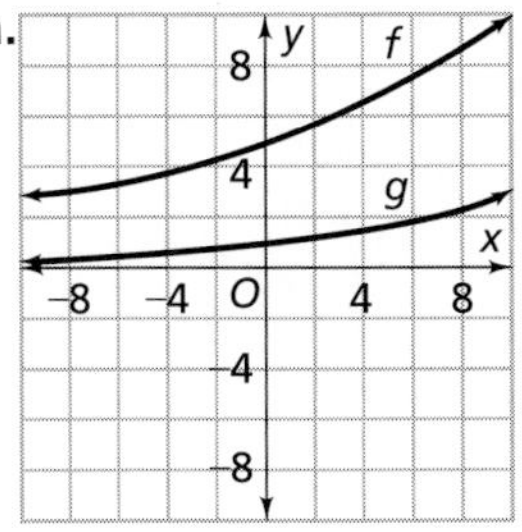

no

b. one

Lesson 5.10 pp. 451–457

Exercises **6.** see Figure 7

12.

x	$L_2(x)$
1	0
2	1
3	1.5850
4	**2**
5	**2.3219**
6	**2.5850**
7	**2.8074**
8	**3**
9	**3.1699**

13c.

x	$L_8(x)$
1	0
2	0.3333
3	0.5283
4	**0.6667**
5	**0.7740**
6	**0.8617**
7	**0.9358**
8	1
9	**1.0566**

16.

APR	Years to Double
3%	**23**
4%	**18**
5%	**14**
6%	12
7%	**10**
8%	**9**
9%	**8**
10%	**7**
11%	**7**
12%	**6**

Mid-Chapter Test p. 459

6b.

x	$h(x)$	÷
0	3	**2**
1	6	**2**
2	12	**2**
3	**24**	**2**
4	**48**	**2**
5	**96**	

9b.

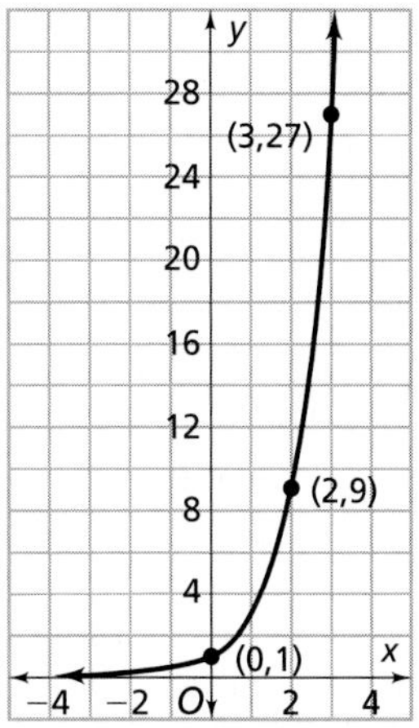

d.

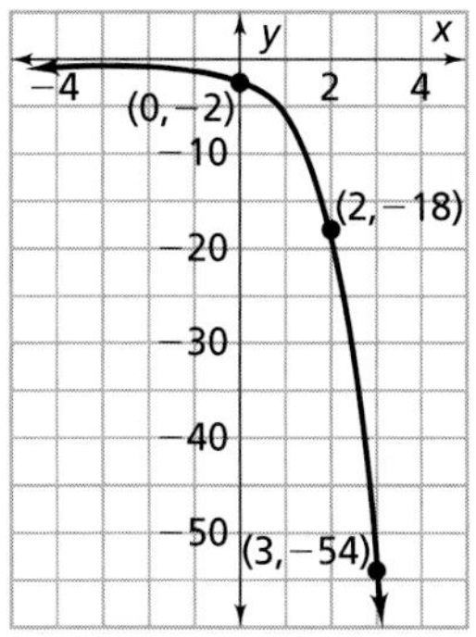

Lesson 5.11 pp. 461–462
For You to Explore

1.

x	log x
0	**undefined**
1	**0**
2	**0.3010**
3	**0.4771**
4	**0.6021**
5	**0.6990**
6	**0.7782**
7	**0.8451**
8	**0.9031**
9	**0.9542**
10	**1**

Figure 7

6a.

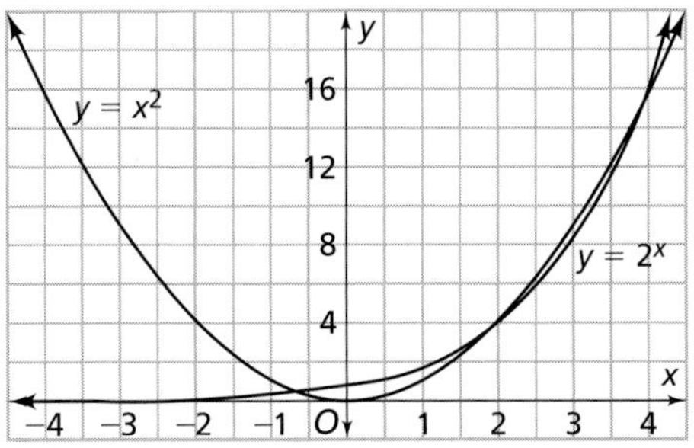

Exercises

16.

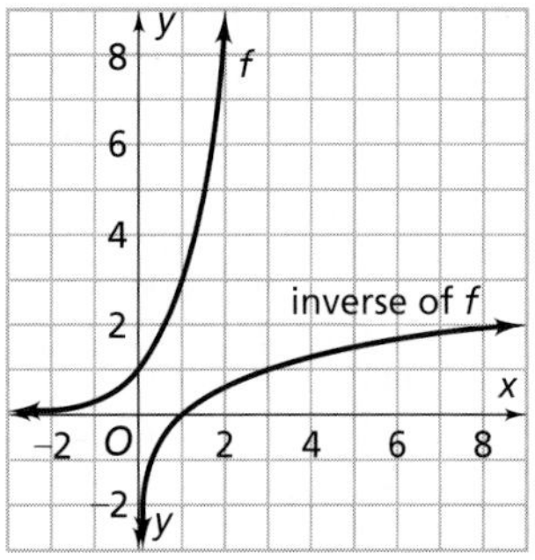

17.

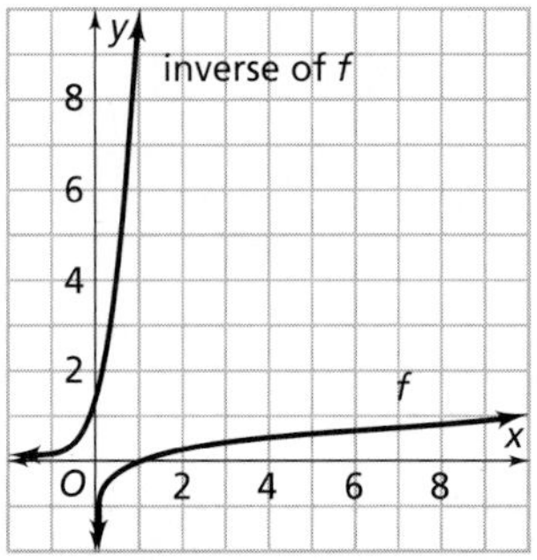

Lesson 5.12 **pp. 463–468**

Exercises 10. Answers may vary. Sample: The characteristic of log M is a good indicator of the size of the number M. For example, if $\log M = 3.6435$, then the characteristic 3 means M is between $10^3 = 1000$ and $10^4 = 10{,}000$. The mantissa of log M is always the logarithm of the number between 1 and 10 that $10^{\text{characteristic}}$ is multiplied by to get M. For example, the number 0.6465 in $M = 3.6435$ tells us that $10^{0.6435}$ is the number that must be multiplied by 10^3 to get M. The mantissa in combination with the characteristic provides a way to find M from a logarithm table that gives logarithms of numbers between 1 and 10.

15a–b.

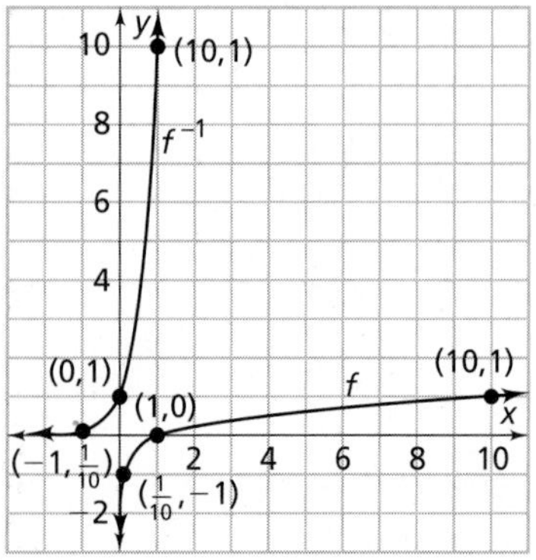

Lesson 5.13 **pp. 469–477**

Exercises 16.

x	$\log_3 x$
1	0
2	0.6309
3	**1**
4	**1.2619**
5	**1.4650**
6	**1.6309**
7	**1.7712**
8	**1.8928**
9	**2**

Lesson 5.14 **pp. 478–483**

Exercises

10a.

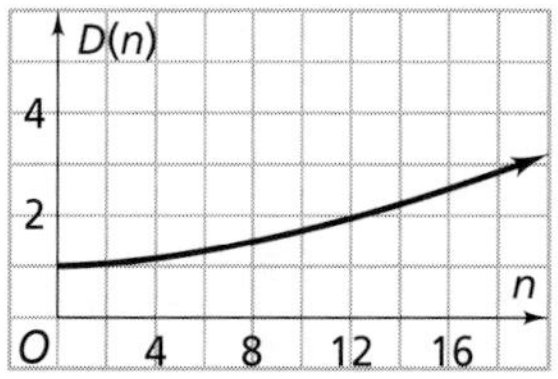

b. $D^{-1}(n) = \log_{1.06} n,\ n \geq 1$

c.

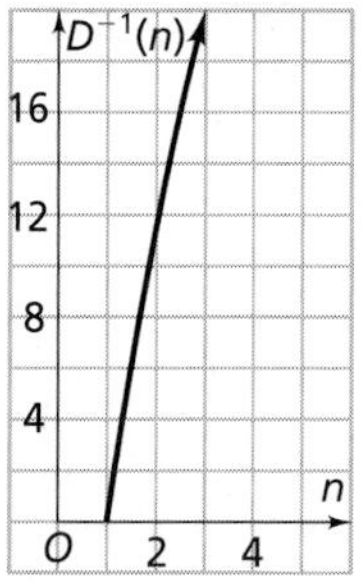

d. about 40 yr

13a.

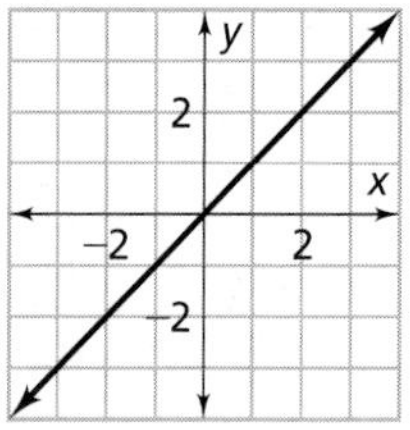

$y = x$; since $\log 10^x = x$ for all real numbers x, the graph of $y = \log 10^x$ is the same as the graph of $y = x$.

b.

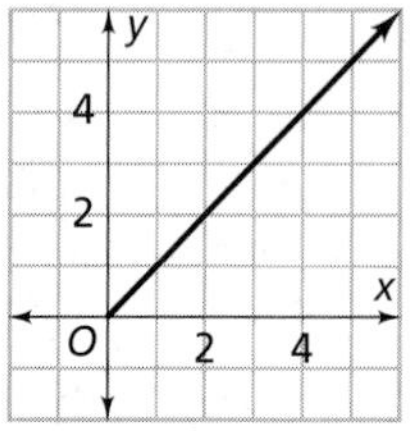

The domain of $y = 10^{\log x}$ is all positive real numbers, so it is equivalent to $y = x$ only for positive values of x. The domain of $y = \log 10^x$ is all real numbers, so it is equivalent to $y = x$ for all real values of x.

16a–e.

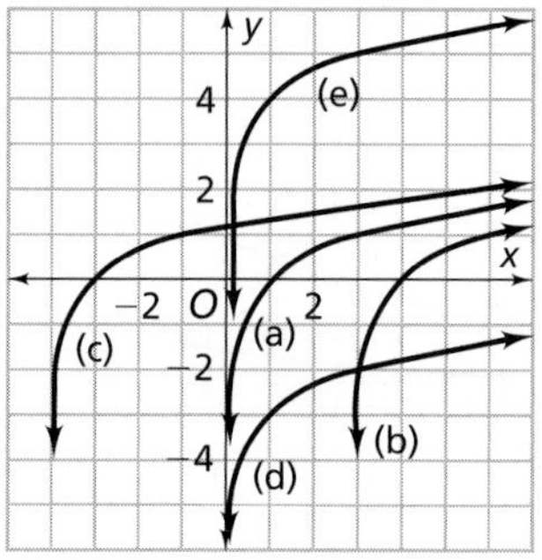

Lesson 5.15 **pp. 484–492**

In-Class Experiment 1. See Figure 8.

Exercises

2.

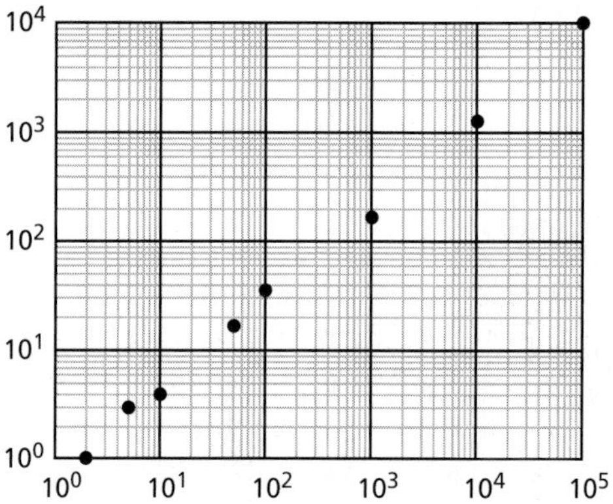

The points appear to lie on a line.

3.

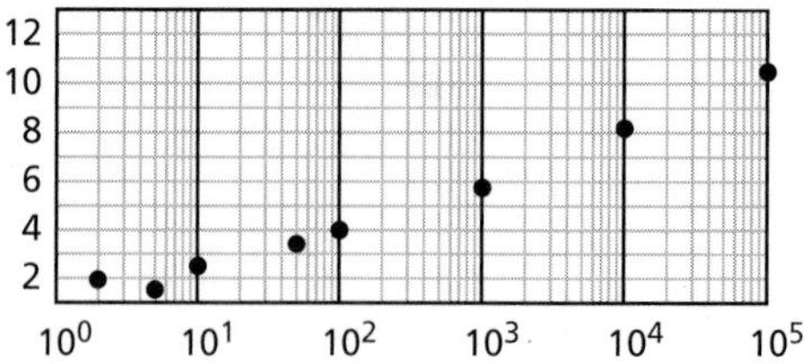

The points appear to lie on a line, especially as the values of x get greater.

14a.

x	$\log_2 x$	$\log_8 x$
0	undefined	undefined
1	0	0
2	1	$\frac{1}{3}$
3	1.5850	0.5283
4	2	$\frac{2}{3}$
5	2.3219	0.7740
6	2.5850	0.8617
7	2.8074	0.9358
8	3	1
9	3.1699	1.0566
10	3.3219	1.1073

b. 4.5237

15a–d.

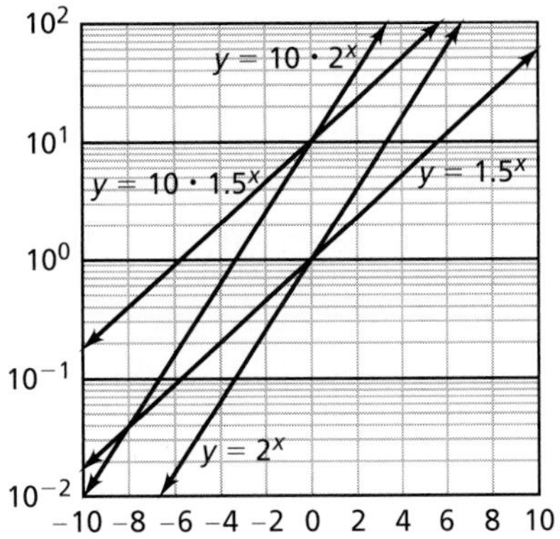

16a–d.

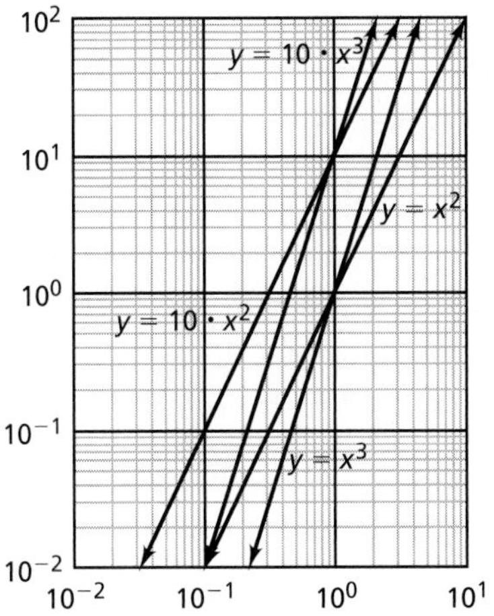

Figure 8

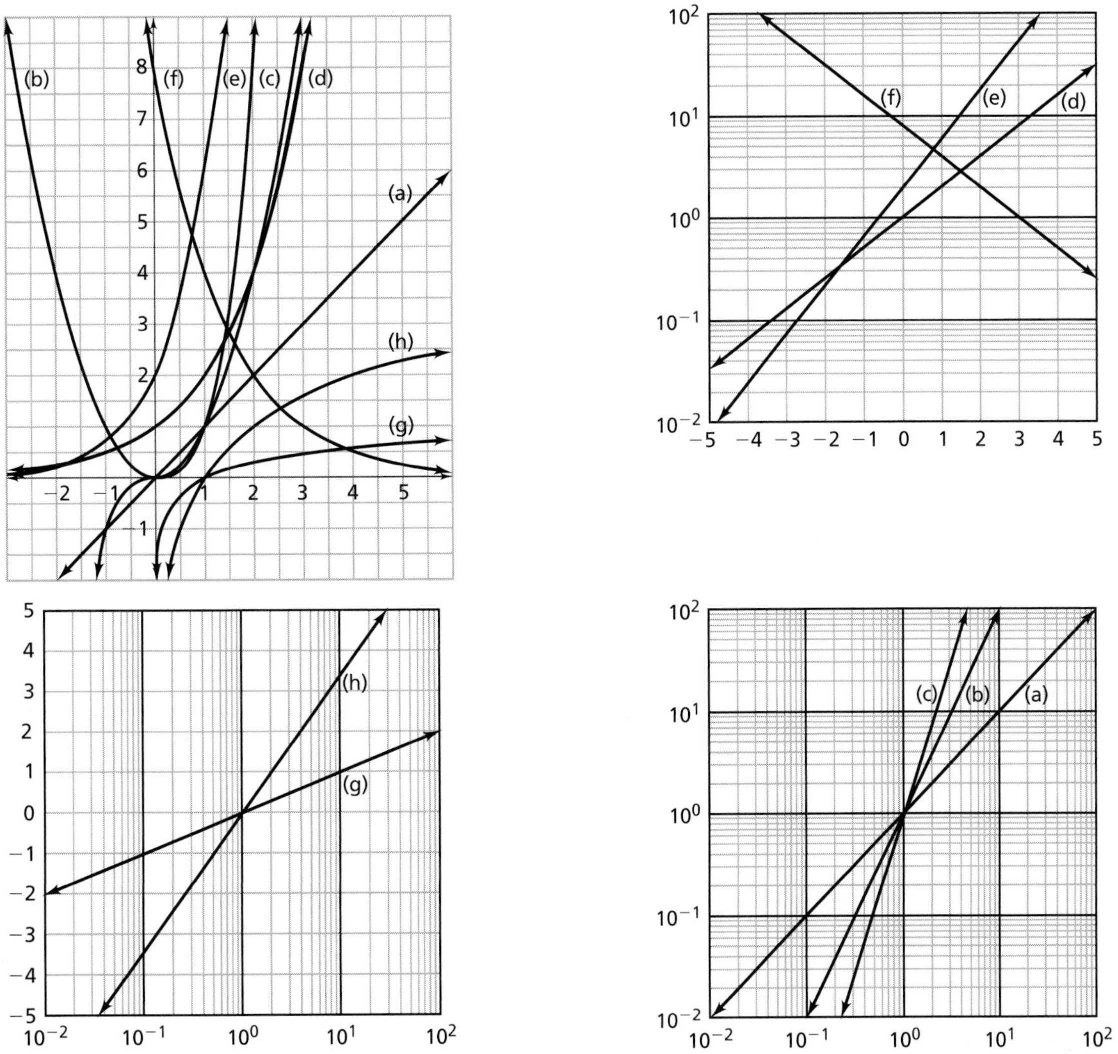

5a. $g(0) = g(1 + (-1)) = g(1) \cdot g(-1)$. We know $g(0) = 1$ and $g(1) = b$, so $1 = b \cdot g(-1)$ and therefore, $g(-1) = \frac{1}{b}$. **b.** We know $g(n) = b^n$ for all nonnegative integers n. To prove it is true for negative integers, use mathematical induction.

(i) If $n = -1$, then $g(n) = g(-1) = \frac{1}{b} = b^{-1}$. So $g(n) = b^n$ for $n = -1$.

(ii) Assume $g(n) = b^n$ for some negative integer m. Then $g(m - 1) = g(m) \cdot g(-1) = b^m \cdot \frac{1}{b} = b^m \cdot b^{-1} = b^{m-1}$.

Therefore, if the property is true for the negative integer m, it is also true for the negative integer $m - 1$. So, since $g(n) = b^n$ is true for $n = -1$, $g(n) = b^n$ for all negative integers n. Putting that result together with Exercise 3d, $g(n) = b^n$ for all integers.

6. $\left(g\left(\frac{1}{n}\right)\right)^n$

$$= \overbrace{g\left(\tfrac{1}{n}\right) \cdot g\left(\tfrac{1}{n}\right) \cdot \cdots \cdot g\left(\tfrac{1}{n}\right)}^{n \text{ copies of } g\left(\frac{1}{n}\right)}$$

$$= \overbrace{b^{\frac{1}{n}} \cdot b^{\frac{1}{n}} \cdot \cdots \cdot b^{\frac{1}{n}}}^{n \text{ copies of } b^{\frac{1}{n}}}$$

$$= g\left(\tfrac{1}{n} \cdot n\right) = g(1) = b$$

7a. $g(x)$ is increasing and $g(0) = 1$. So $g\left(\frac{1}{4}\right) > 1$, which means $g\left(\frac{1}{4}\right)$ cannot be -3. **b.** $g\left(\frac{1}{4}\right) = g\left(\frac{1}{8} + \frac{1}{8}\right) = g\left(\frac{1}{8}\right) \cdot g\left(\frac{1}{8}\right) = \left(g\left(\frac{1}{8}\right)\right)^2$. So $g\left(\frac{1}{8}\right)$ is the square root of $g\left(\frac{1}{4}\right)$, and if $g\left(\frac{1}{4}\right)$ is a negative number, then $g\left(\frac{1}{8}\right)$ would not be a real number.

8a. If m and n are integers, $n \neq 0$, then $g\left(\frac{m}{n}\right) = g\left(\frac{1}{n} \cdot m\right) = \left(g\left(\frac{1}{n}\right)\right)^m = \left(b^{\frac{1}{n}}\right)^m = b^{\frac{m}{n}}$.

b. For any real x there are rational numbers p and q such that $p < x < q$. Then since $g(x)$ is strictly increasing, $g(p) < g(x) < g(q)$, which means $b^p < g(x) < b^q$. By choosing p and q closer and closer to x, $g(x)$ gets closer and closer to b^x and thus can be defined to be b^x for any real value of x.

9. Go through the same steps that were used in Exercises 1–8 to prove that $g(x) = b^x$. The proof that $h(0) = 1$ is the same as for $g(0) = 1$. Then to show that $0 < b < 1$, note that h is strictly decreasing means that since $0 < 1$, $h(1) < h(0)$, so $b < 1$. Thus $0 < b < 1$. The remainder of the proof is similar to the proof for $g(x) = b^x$ but note that in proving that the definition extends to all real numbers x, when x is between rational numbers p and q, $h(q) < h(x) < h(p)$.

10. If $k(x)$ is not monotonic, then we cannot prove $b > 1$ or $0 < b < 1$, and we will not be able to extend the definition of $k(x) = b^x$ for real-number values of x. **11.** $x \mapsto 2^x$ and $f(a + b) = f(a) \cdot f(b)$; $z \mapsto |z|$ and $f(ab) = f(a) \cdot f(b)$; $z \mapsto \arg z$ and $f(ab) = f(a) + f(b)$; $x \mapsto 2x$ and $f(a + b) = f(a) + f(b)$; $x \mapsto \log_3 x$ and $f(ab) = f(a) + f(b)$

6a.

x	$h(x)$	÷
0	6	$\frac{1}{2}$
1	3	$\frac{1}{2}$
2	$\frac{3}{2}$	$\frac{1}{2}$
3	$\frac{3}{4}$	$\frac{1}{2}$
4	$\frac{3}{8}$	

7a.

x	$f(x)$
−1	$\frac{1}{4}$
0	1
$\frac{1}{2}$	2
1	4
2	16

x	$g(x)$
$\frac{1}{4}$	−1
1	0
2	$\frac{1}{2}$
4	1

b.

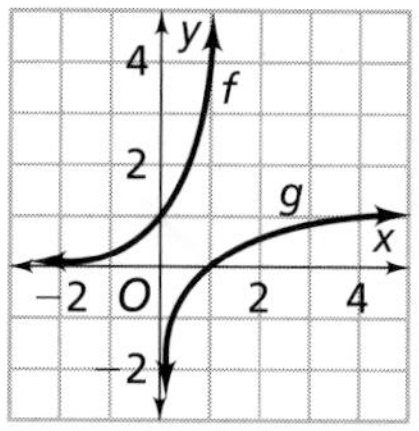

Chapter 6

Lesson 6.1 pp. 501–503

For You to Explore

1.

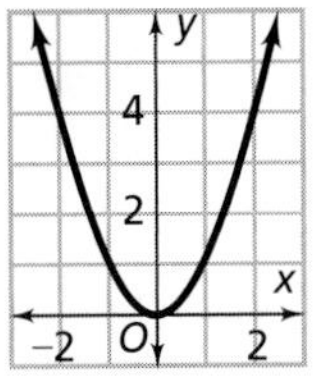

2a.

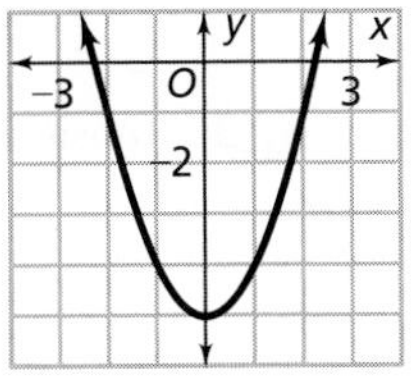

It is the graph of $y = x^2$ translated 5 units down.

b.

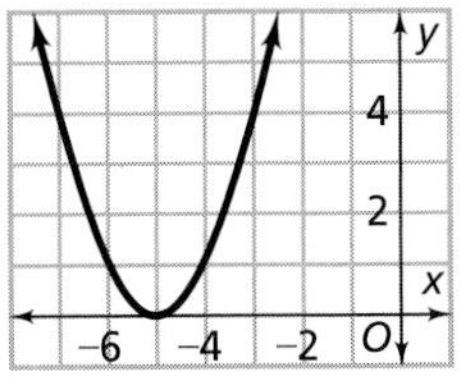

It is the graph of $y = x^2$ translated 5 units to the left.

c.

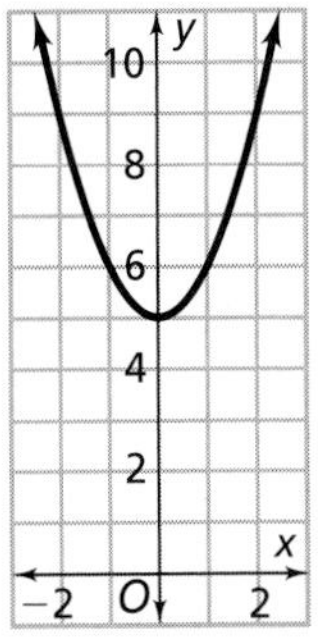

It is the graph of $y = x^2$ translated 5 units up.

d.

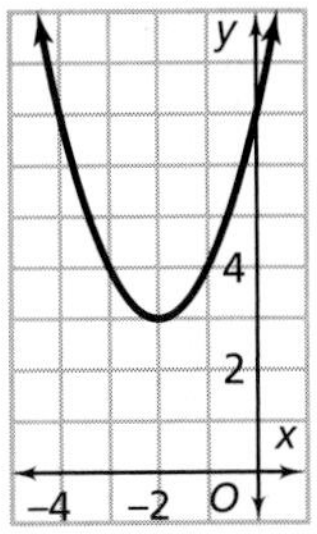

It is the graph of $y = x^2$ translated 2 units to the left and 3 units up.

3.

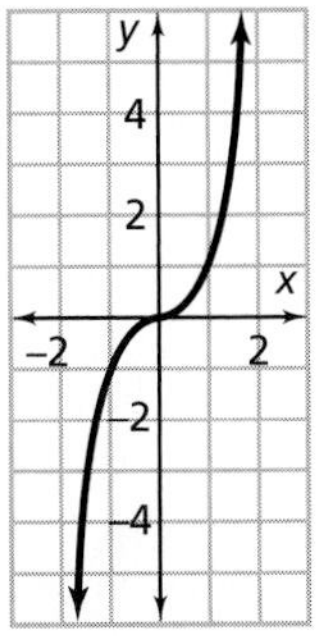

4a.

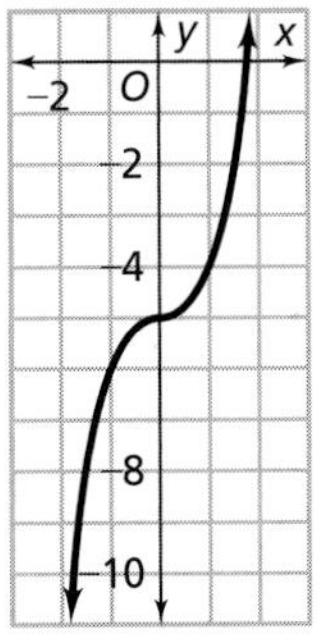

It is the graph of $y = x^3$ translated 5 units down.

b.

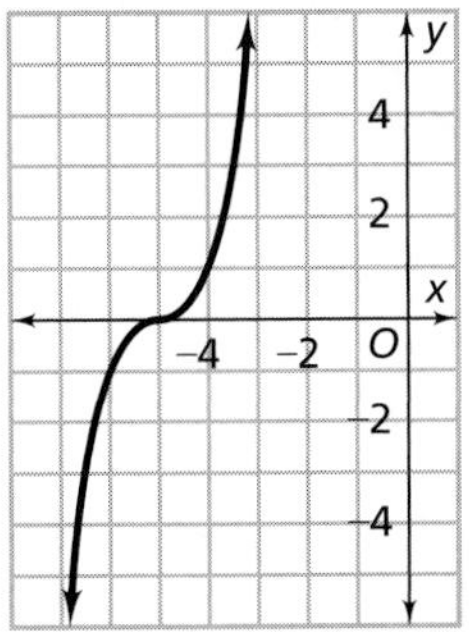

It is the graph of $y = x^3$ translated 5 units to the left.

c.

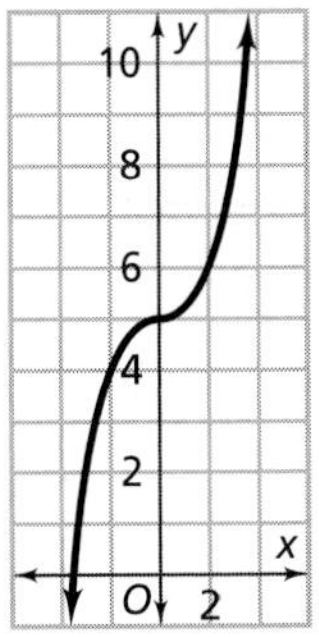

It is the graph of $y = x^3$ translated 5 units up.

d.

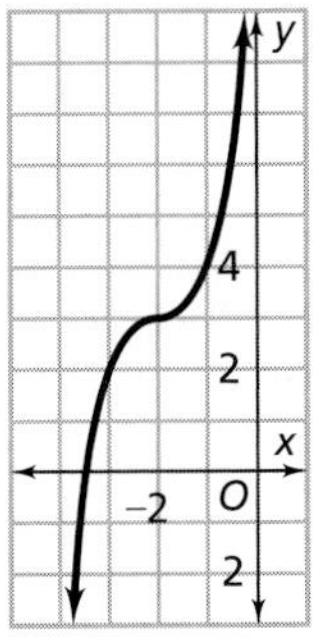

It is the graph of $y = x^3$ translated 2 units to the left and 3 units up.

6.

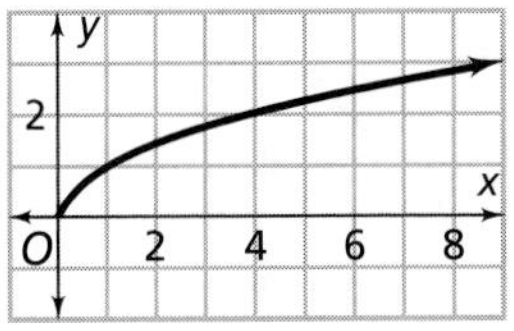

7a.

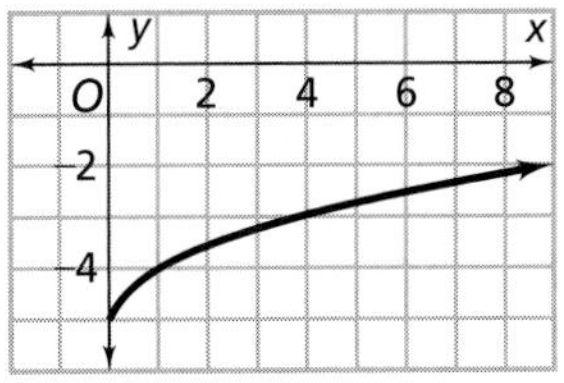

It is the graph of $y = \sqrt{x}$ translated 5 units down.

b.

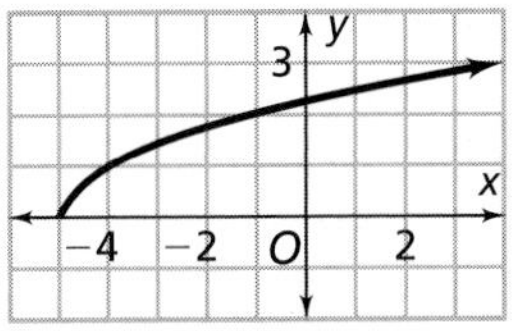

It is the graph of $y = \sqrt{x}$ translated 5 units to the left.

c.

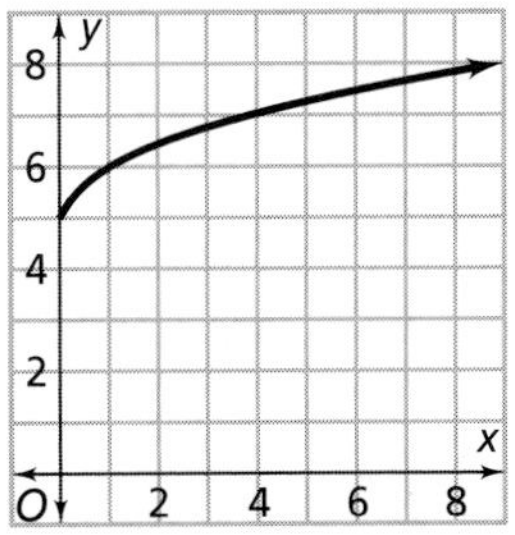

It is the graph of $y = \sqrt{x}$ translated 5 units up.

d.

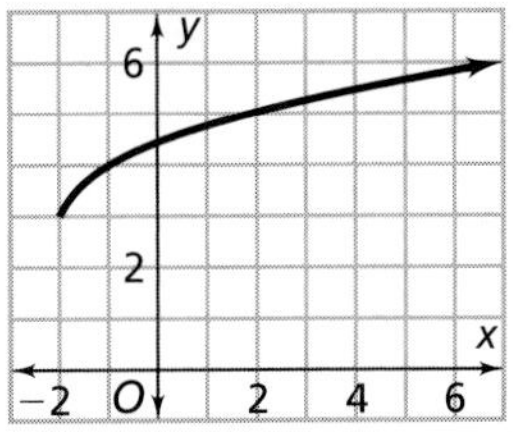

It is the graph of $y = \sqrt{x}$ translated 2 units to the left and 3 units up.

Additional Answers

8. 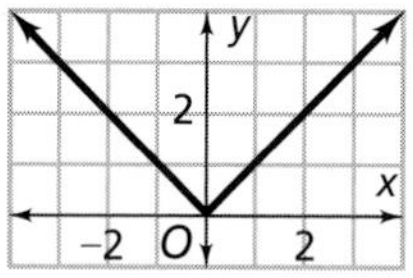

9a. 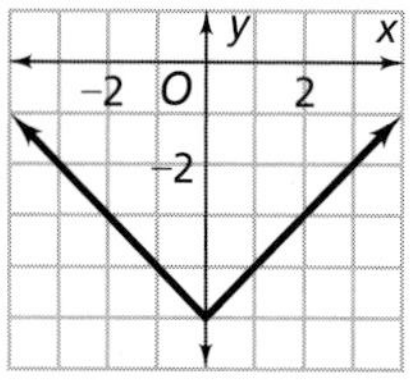

It is the graph of $y = |x|$ translated 5 units down.

b. 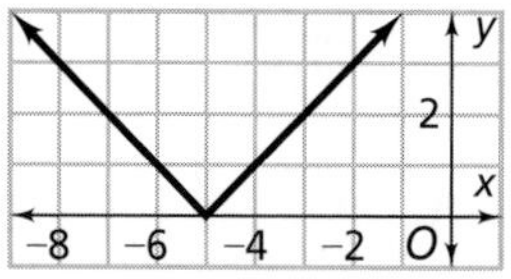

It is the graph of $y = |x|$ translated 5 units to the left.

c. 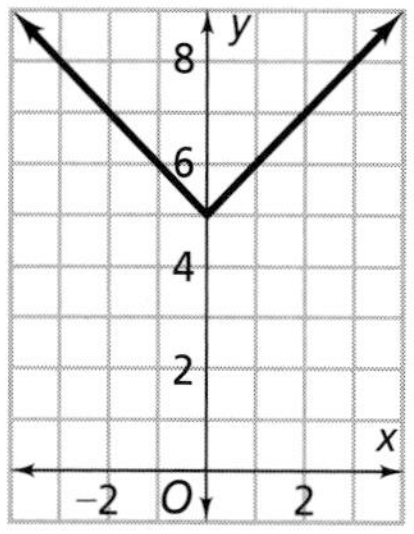

It is the graph of $y = |x|$ translated 5 units up.

d. 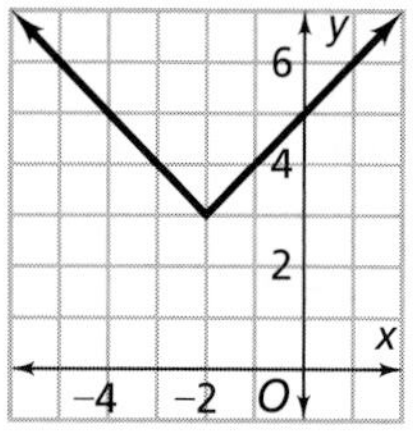

It is the graph of $y = |x|$ translated 2 units to the left and 3 units up.

10a. 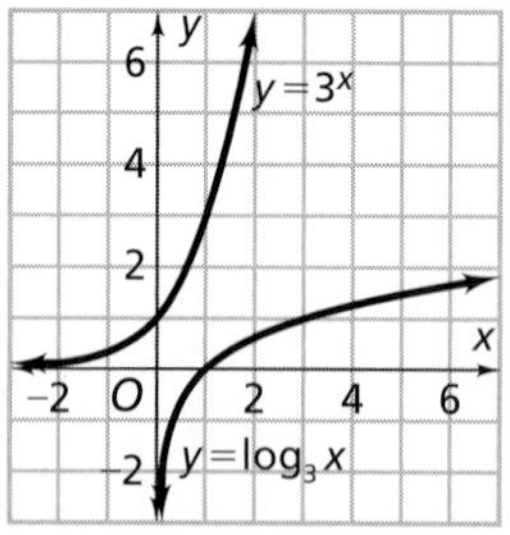

b. They are reflections of each other over the line given by $y = x$.

Exercises **18a.** 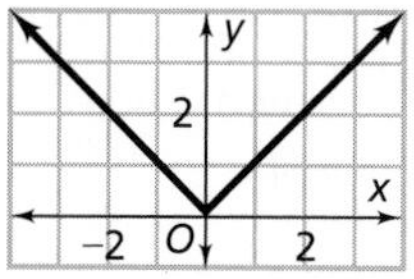

b. 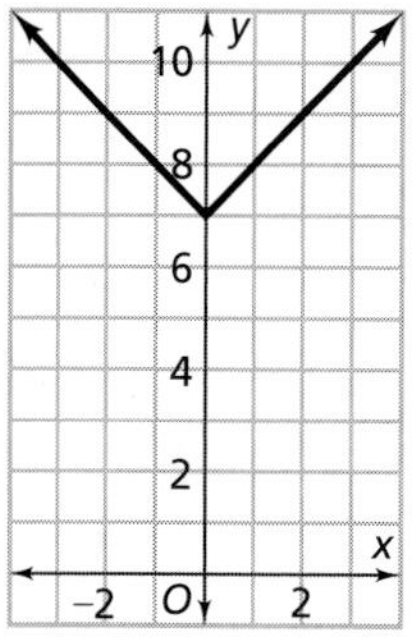

c. 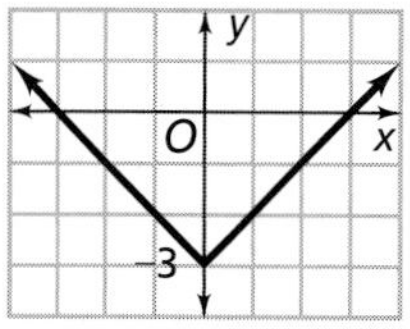

d. 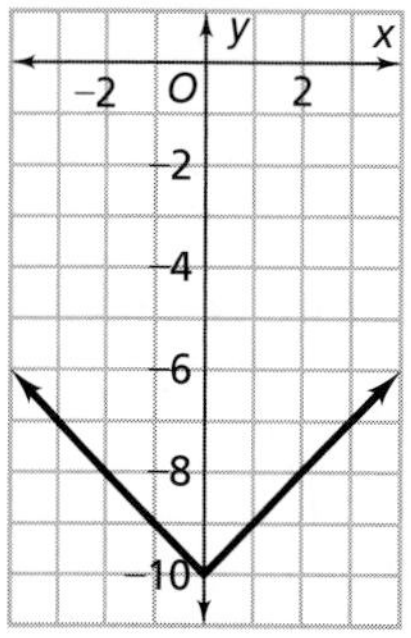

19. $y = |x| + C$ is $y = |x|$ translated vertically C units. The graph shifts up if $C > 0$, and down if $C < 0$.

20a. 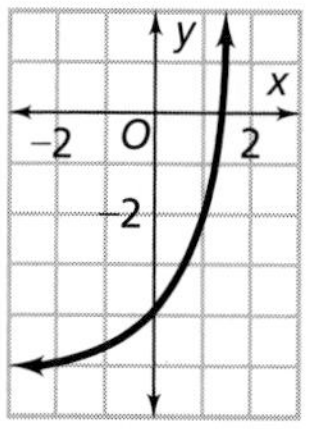

It is the graph of $y = 3^x$ translated 5 units down.

b. 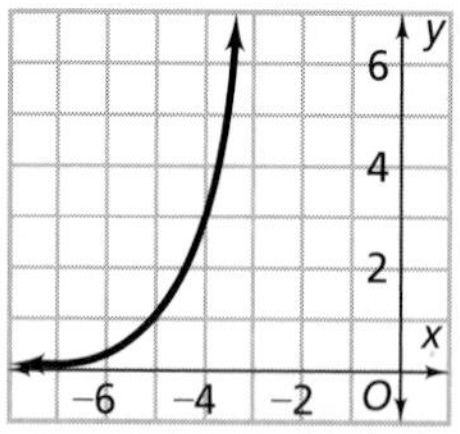

It is the graph of $y = 3^x$ translated 5 units left.

c. 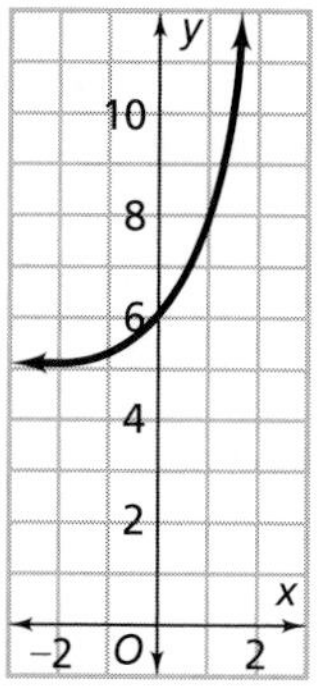

It is the graph of $y = 3^x$ translated 5 units up.

d. 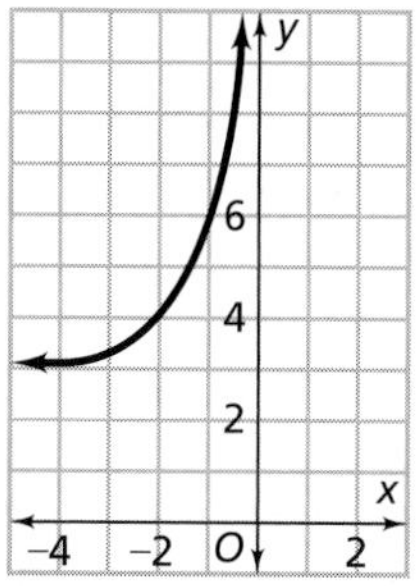

It is the graph of $y = 3^x$ translated 2 units to the left and 3 units up.

22a. 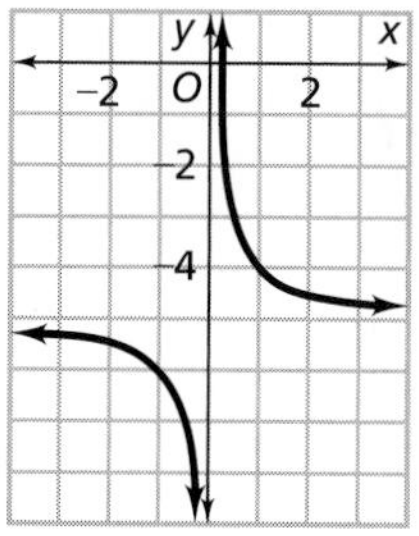

It is the graph of $y = \frac{1}{x}$ translated 5 units down.

b. 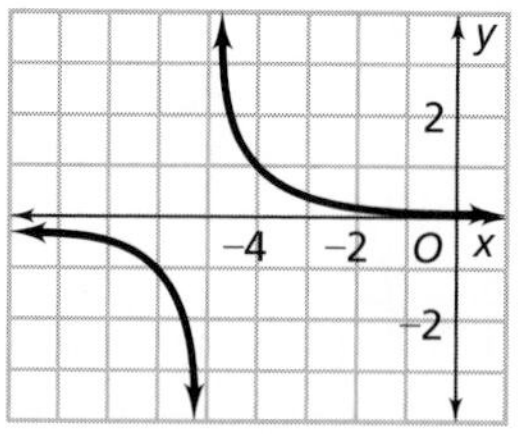

It is the graph of $y = \frac{1}{x}$ translated 5 units to the left.

c. 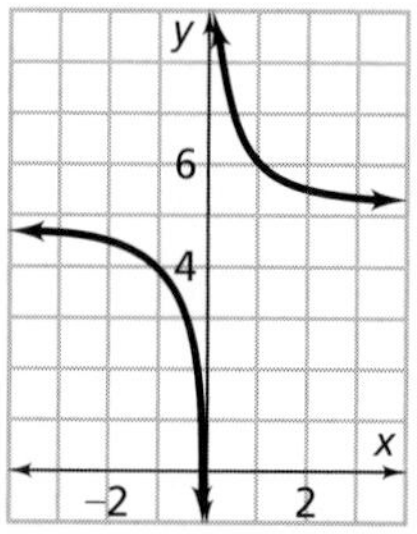

It is the graph of $y = \frac{1}{x}$ translated 5 units up.

d.

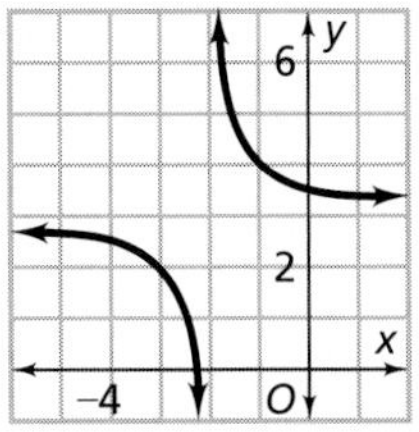

It is the graph of $y = \frac{1}{x}$ translated 2 units to the left and 3 units up.

Lesson 6.2 **pp. 504–512**

Exercises 8a.

x	$x - 3$	$(x - 3)^2$
−1	−4	16
0	−3	9
1	−2	4
2	−1	1
3	0	0
4	1	1
5	2	4
6	3	9
7	4	16

12a.

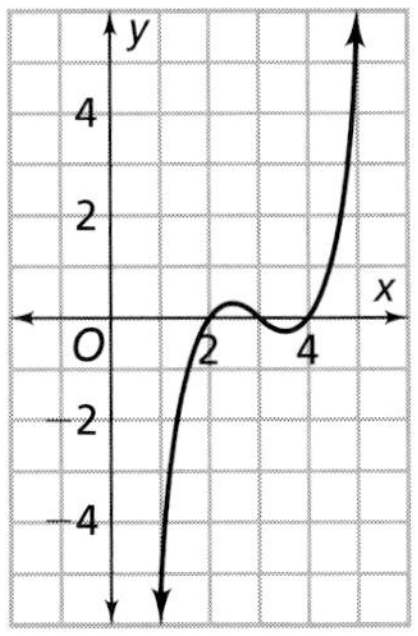

Lesson 6.3 **pp. 513–521**

Exercises 2a.

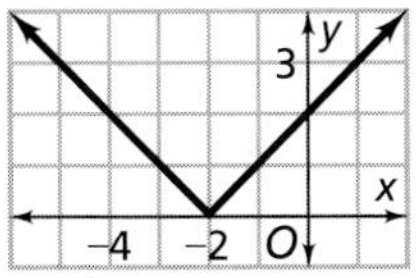

b.

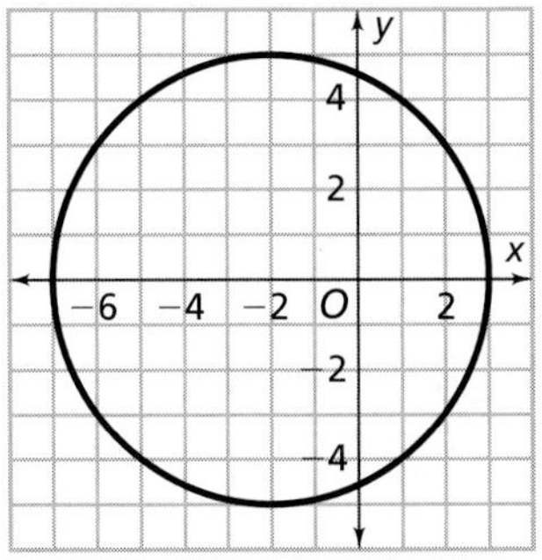

c.

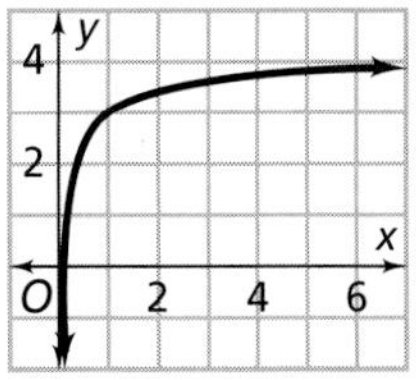

d.

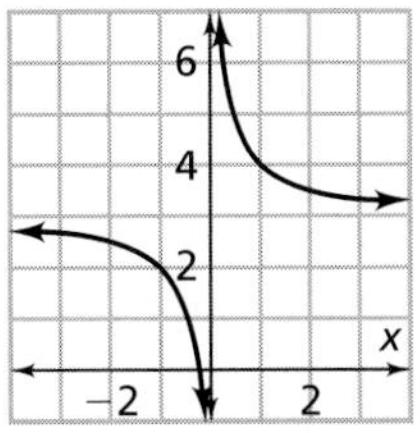

3a.

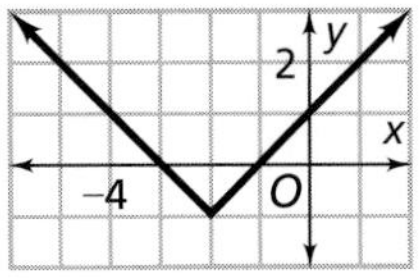

b.

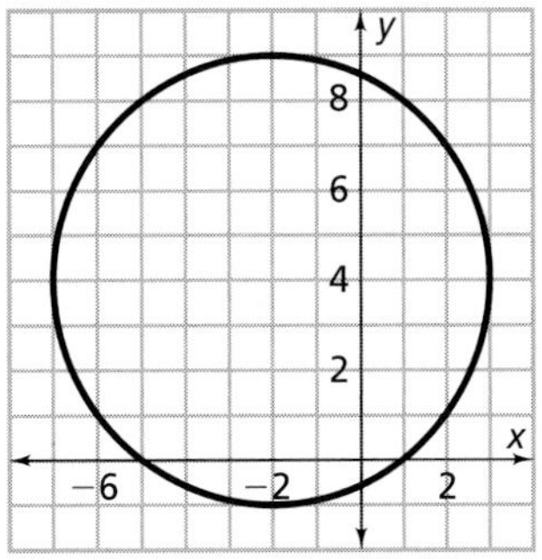

c.

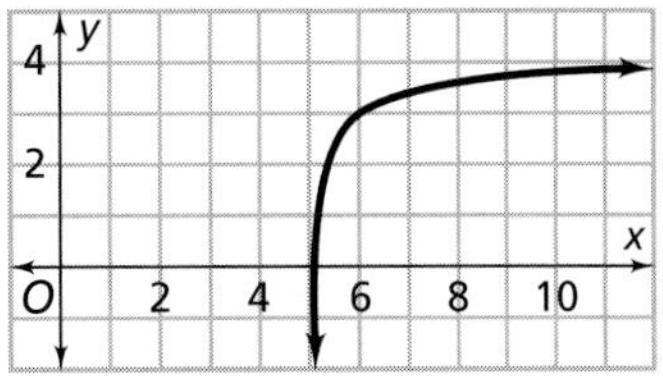

d.

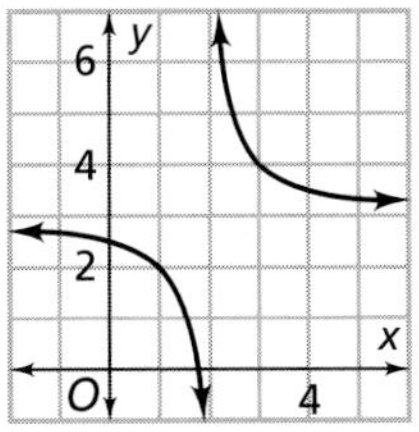

5c.

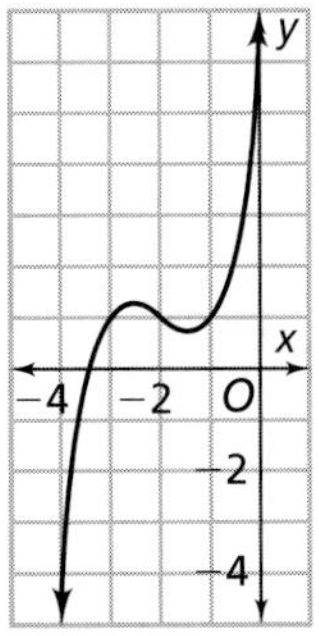

8a.

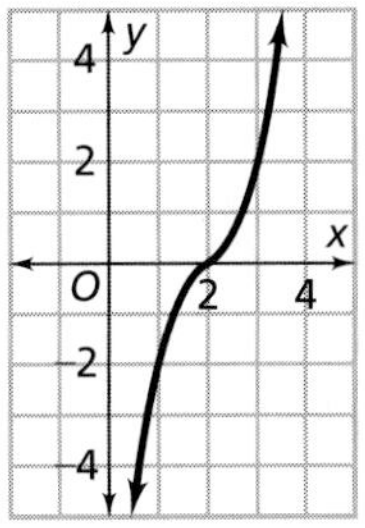

b.

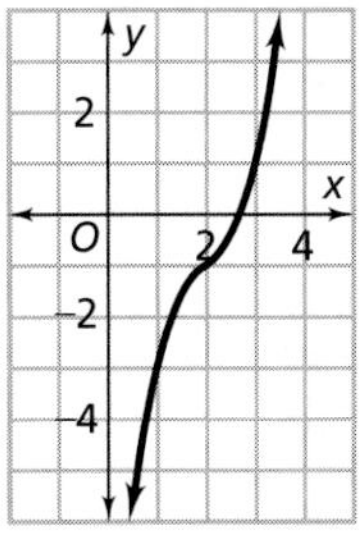

c.

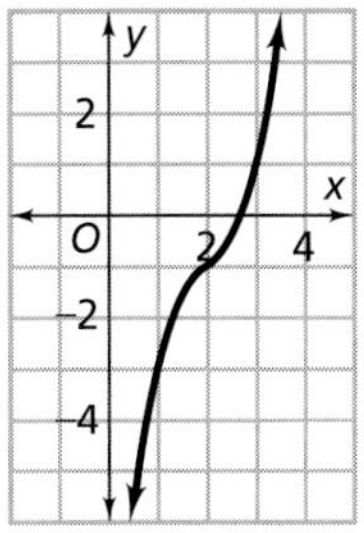

d.

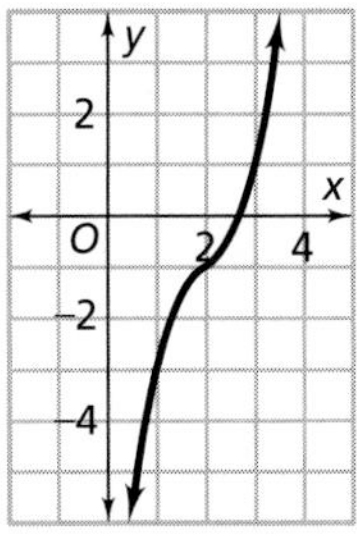

9a.

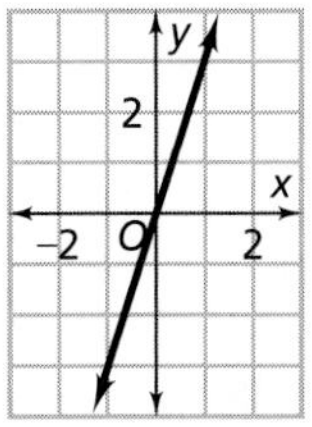

The slope is 3.

b.

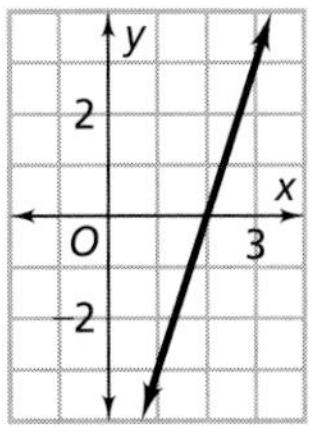

The slope is 3.

c.

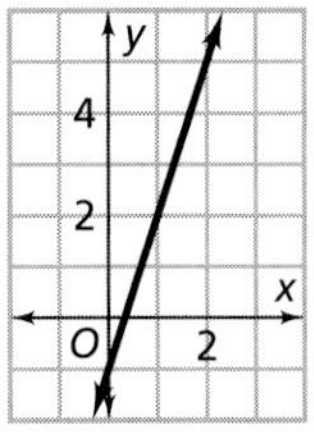

The slope is 3.

d. The graphs are parallel lines. The line in part (b) is the line in part (a) translated 2 units to the right. The line in part (c) is the line in part (b) translated 5 units up.

10a.

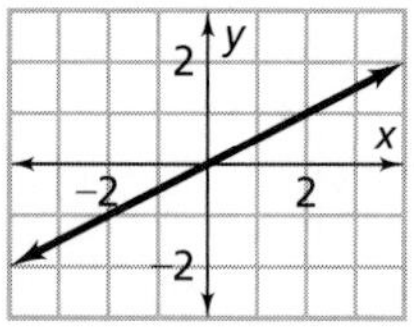

b.

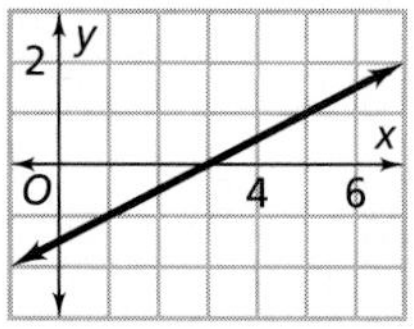

$y = \frac{1}{2}(x - 3)$

c.

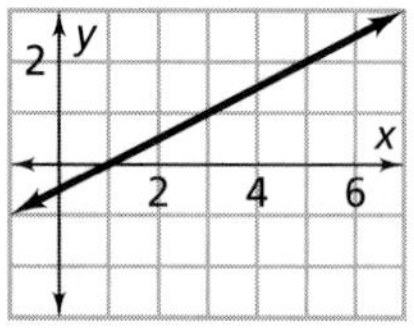

$y = \frac{1}{2}(x - 3) + 1$

12b. The graph of $y - 2 = (x - 3)^2 + 6(x - 3) + 7$ is the graph of $y = (x - 3)^2 + 6(x - 3) + 7$ translated 2 units up; answers may vary. Sample: In the equation $y - 2 = (x - 3)^2 + 6(x - 3) + 7$, the y in the equation $y = (x - 3)^2 + 6(x - 3) + 7$ is replaced by $N = y - 2$, so each point of the graph of $N = (x - 3)^2 + 6(x - 3) + 7$ corresponds to the point on the graph of $y = (x - 3)^2 + 6(x - 3) + 7$ with y-coordinate 2 units less.

16a.

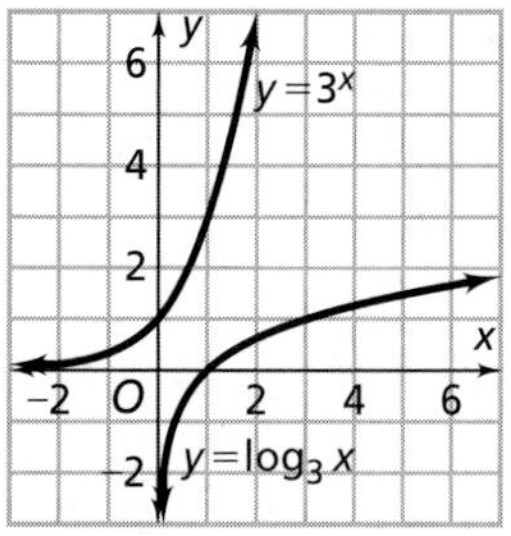

The graphs are reflections of each other over the line given by $y = x$, because $y = 3^x$ and $y = \log_3 x$ are inverse functions.

b.

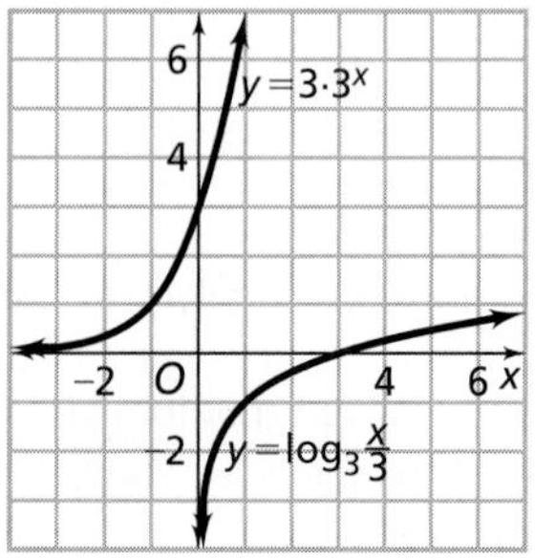

Because $3 \cdot 3^x = 3^{x+1}$, the graph of $y = 3 \cdot 3^x$ is the graph of $y = 3^x$ translated 1 unit to the left. Because $\log_3 \frac{x}{3} = \log_3 x - \log_3 3 = \log_3 x - 1$, the graph of $y = \log_3 \frac{x}{3}$ is the graph of $y = \log_3 x$ translated 1 unit down. The new graphs are reflections of each other over the line given by $y = x$, because $y = 3 \cdot 3^x$ and $y = \log_3 \frac{x}{3}$ are inverse functions.

c.

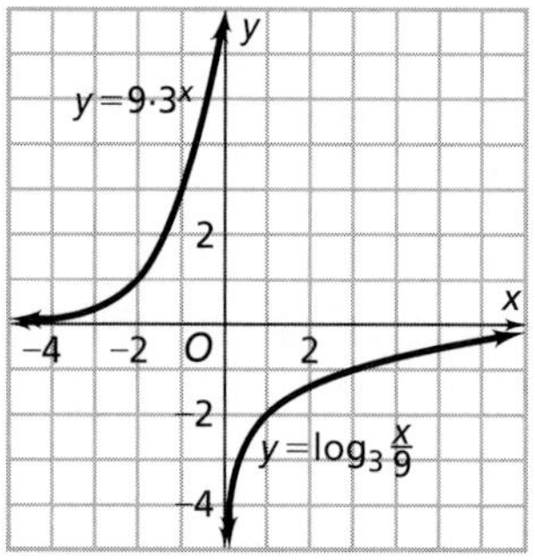

Because $9 \cdot 3^x = 3^{x+2}$, the graph of $y = 9 \cdot 3^x$ is the graph of $y = 3^x$ translated 2 units to the left. Because $\log_3 \frac{x}{9} = \log_3 x - \log_3 9 = \log_3 x - 2$, the graph of $y = \log_3 \frac{x}{9}$ is the graph of $y = \log_3 x$ translated 2 units down. The new graphs are reflections of each other over the line given by $y = x$, because $y = 9 \cdot 3^x$ and $y = \log_3 \frac{x}{9}$ are inverse functions.

d.

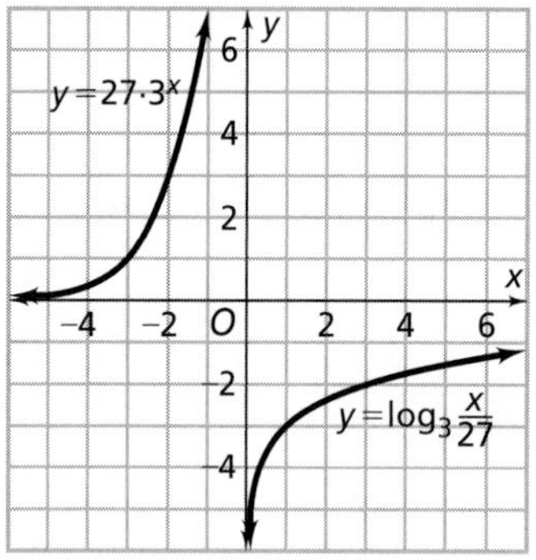

Because $27 \cdot 3^x = 3^{x+3}$, the graph of $y = 27 \cdot 3^x$ is the graph of $y = 3^x$ translated 3 units to the left. Because $\log_3 \frac{x}{27} = \log_3 x - \log_3 27 = \log_3 x - 3$, the graph of $y = \log_3 \frac{x}{27}$ is the graph of $y = \log_3 x$ translated 3 units down. The new graphs are reflections of each other over the line given by $y = x$, because $y = 27 \cdot 3^x$ and $y = \log_3 \frac{x}{27}$ are inverse functions.

e. Because $3^n \cdot 3^x = 3^{x+n}$, the graph of $y = 3^n \cdot 3^x$ is the graph of $y = 3^x$ translated n units to the left. Because $\log_3 \frac{x}{3^n} = \log_3 x - \log_3 3^n = \log_3 x - n$, the graph of $y = \log_3 \frac{x}{3^n}$ is the graph of $y = \log_3 x$ translated n units down. The new graphs are reflections of each other over the line given by $y = x$, because given by $y = 3^n \cdot 3^x$ and $y = \log_3 \frac{x}{3^n}$ are inverse functions.

Lesson 6.4 pp. 522–530

Exercises **1a.**

x	$N = x^2 + 1$	$y = \frac{N}{5}$
−2	5	1
−1	2	$\frac{2}{5}$
0	1	$\frac{1}{5}$
1	2	$\frac{2}{5}$
2	5	1
3	10	2

2a.

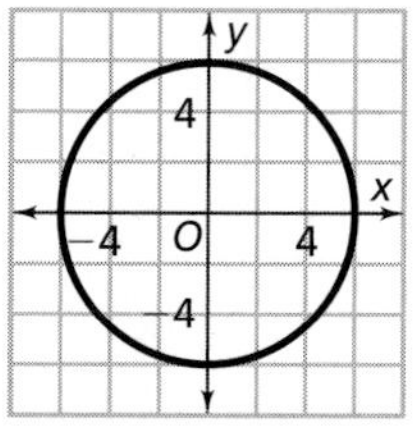

b.

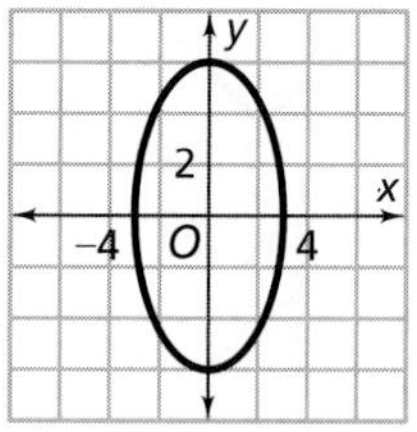

c.

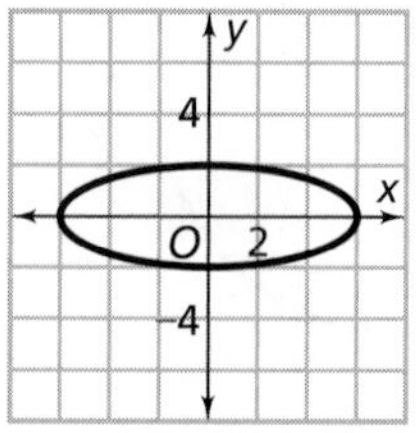

d.

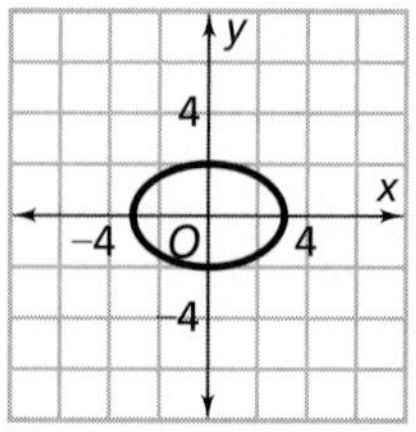

e.
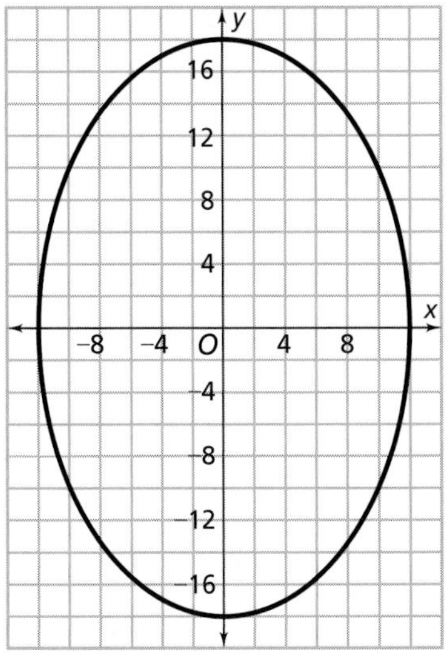

10a.
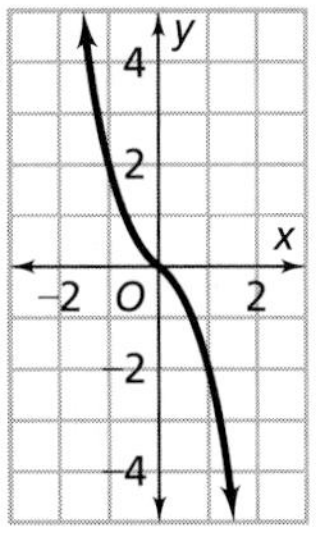

b.
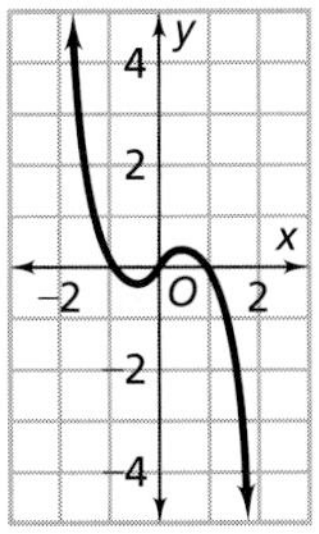

c.
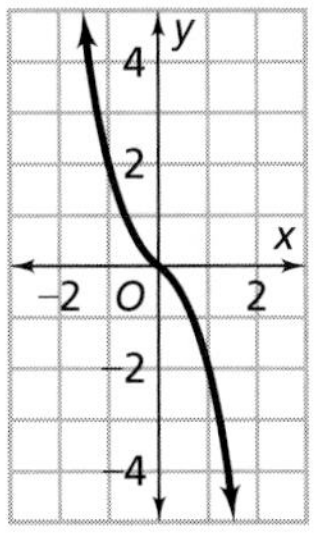

d.
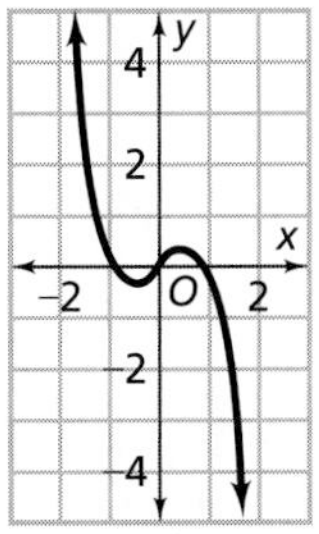

e.
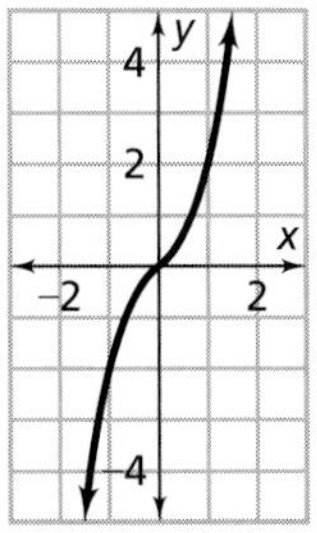

f.
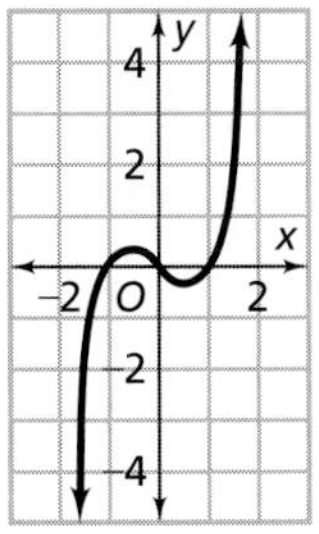

14a.
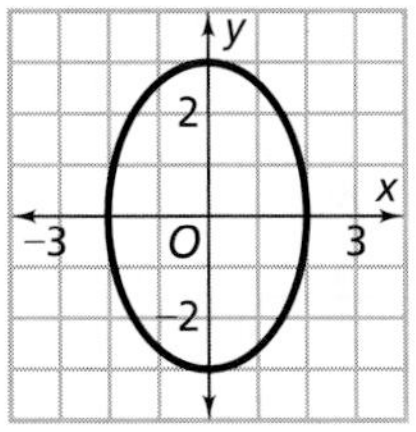

b.
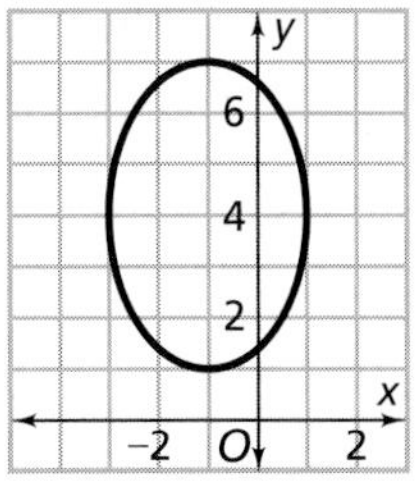

c.
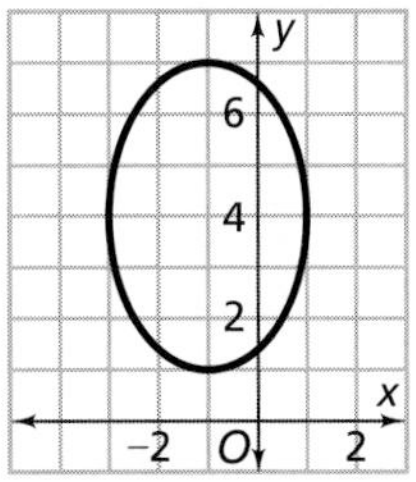

Lesson 6.5 **pp. 533–535**

Exercises 17a. $(f \circ f)(x) = 4x + 9$
b. $(f \circ f \circ f)(x) = 8x + 21$
c. $(f \circ f \circ f \circ f)(x) = 16x + 45$
d. $(f \circ f \circ f \circ f \circ f \circ f \circ f)(x) = 128x + 381$

Lesson 6.6 **pp. 536–545**

Exercises 10a. $x = \frac{1}{4}y - 2$

b. $(\mathcal{A}_{(4,\,8)} \circ \mathcal{A}_{(\frac{1}{4},\,-2)})(x)$
$= \mathcal{A}_{(4,\,8)}(\mathcal{A}_{(\frac{1}{4},\,-2)}(x))$
$= \mathcal{A}_{(4,\,8)}\left(\frac{1}{4}x - 2\right)$
$= 4\left(\frac{1}{4}x - 2\right) + 8$
$= x - 8 + 8 = x$
$(\mathcal{A}_{(\frac{1}{4},\,-2)} \circ \mathcal{A}_{(4,\,8)})(x)$
$= \mathcal{A}_{(\frac{1}{4},\,-2)}(\mathcal{A}_{(4,\,8)}(x))$
$= \mathcal{A}_{(\frac{1}{4},\,-2)}(4x + 8)$
$= \frac{1}{4}(4x + 8) - 2$
$= x + 2 - 2$
$= x$
Thus, $\mathcal{A}_{(4,\,8)}$ and $\mathcal{A}_{(\frac{1}{4},\,-2)}$ are inverses, so $(\mathcal{A}_{(4,\,8)})^{-1} = \mathcal{A}_{(\frac{1}{4},\,-2)}$.

13a. $\mathcal{A}_{(\frac{1}{3},\,-\frac{4}{3})}$ **b.** $\mathcal{A}_{(\frac{1}{5},\,-\frac{1}{5})}$ **c.** $\mathcal{A}_{(\frac{1}{3},\,-\frac{2}{3})}$
16b. If $\mathcal{A}_{(c,\,d)}$ is putting on your socks and $\mathcal{A}_{(a,\,b)}$ is putting on your shoes, then the composition $\mathcal{A}_{(a,\,b)} \circ \mathcal{A}_{(c,\,d)}$ represents putting on first your socks and then your shoes. The equation in part (a) shows that to undo this process, you first take off your shoes (represented by $(\mathcal{A}_{(a,\,b)})^{-1}$) and then take off your socks (represented by $(\mathcal{A}_{(c,\,d)})^{-1}$).

Lesson 6.7 **pp. 546–553**

Exercises
8a. $a = 9, b = -6, c = 9, d = 0$
b. $N = 0, M = 0, x = \frac{2}{3}$ **c.** $\frac{2}{3}$
9a. $e = a, f = \frac{b}{2}, g = a,$
$h = \frac{b^2 - 4ac}{4}$
b. $N = \frac{b^2 - 4ac}{4}$,
$M = \frac{\pm\sqrt{b^2 - 4ac}}{2}$,
$x = \frac{-b \pm \sqrt{b^2 - 4ac}}{2a}$
c. $\frac{-b \pm \sqrt{b^2 - 4ac}}{2a}$
12a. The equation shown is the result of substituting $(M - \frac{b}{3})$ into the equation $y = x^3 + bx^2 + cx + d$. Exercise 11 showed that $\frac{b}{3}$ is the value of k for which the substitution of $(M - k)$ into the equation $y = x^3 + bx^2 + cx + d$ makes the coefficient of M^2 zero. **b.** In part (a), the coefficient of the M-term simplifies to $\frac{3c - b^2}{3}$. Positive, zero, or negative values give a transformed equation in the form $N = M^3 + M$, $N = M^3$, or $N = M^3 - M$, respectively.
c. The coefficient of the M-term will be $\frac{3(ac) - b^2}{3}$. Positive, zero, or negative values of that expression give a transformed equation in the form $N = M^3 + M$, $N = M^3$, or $N = M^3 - M$, respectively.
14. If $3ac = b^2$, then the substitutions $M = \left(T_{\frac{b}{3}} \circ D_a\right)(x)$ and $N = \left(T_{\frac{9abc - 2b^3 - 27a^2d}{27}} \circ D_a\right)(y)$ transform the equation into $N = M^3$. If $3ac \neq b^2$, then the substitutions $M = \left(D_\alpha \circ T_{\frac{b}{3}} \circ D_a\right)(x)$ and $N = \left(D_{\alpha^3} \circ T_{\frac{9abc - 2b^3 - 27a^2d}{27}} \circ D_{a^2}\right)(y)$ transform the equation into $N = M^3 + M$ or $N = M^3 - M$, where $\alpha = \frac{1}{\sqrt{\left|ca - \frac{1}{3}b^2\right|}}$.

Additional Answers

Mid-Chapter Test p.555

7a.

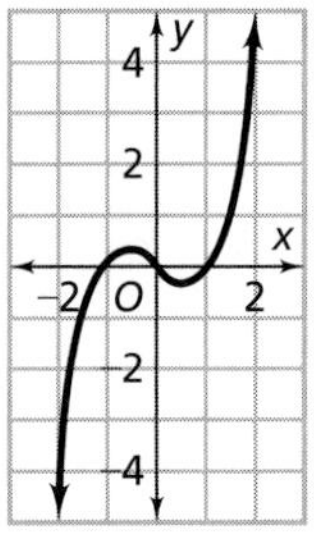

b. $y + 2 = (x - 5)^3 - (x - 5)$

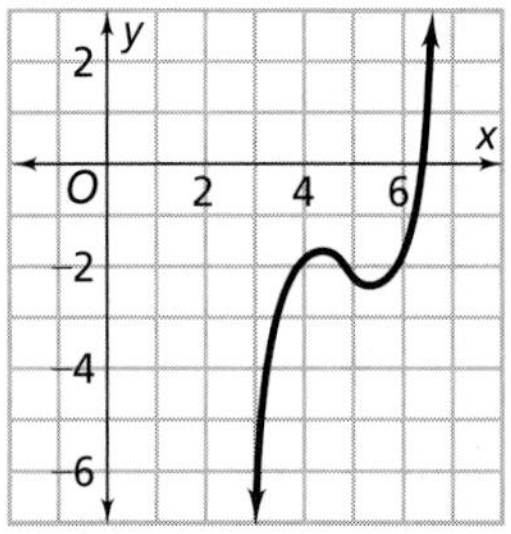

c. $y = \left(\frac{x}{3}\right)^3 - \left(\frac{x}{3}\right)$

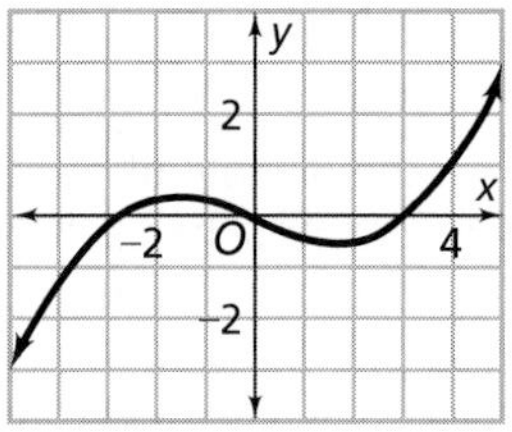

Lesson 6.8 pp. 557–559

For You to Explore 5. Answers may vary. Sample: Each value on the x number line is 3 more than the corresponding value on the M number line.

6a. $x = M - 4$

M	−3	−2	−1	0	1	2	3
x	−7	−6	−5	−4	−3	−2	−1

b. $x = M + 2$

M	−3	−2	−1	0	1	2	3
x	−1	0	1	2	3	4	5

c. $x = M - \frac{3}{2}$

M	−3	−2	−1	0	1	2	3
x	$-\frac{9}{2}$	$-\frac{7}{2}$	$-\frac{5}{2}$	$-\frac{3}{2}$	$-\frac{1}{2}$	$\frac{1}{2}$	$\frac{3}{2}$

d. $x = M$

M	−3	−2	−1	0	1	2	3
x	−3	−2	−1	0	1	2	3

e. Answers may vary. Sample: The x number line is the image of the M number line after a translation by a units. If $a > 0$, the translation is to the right, and if $a < 0$, the translation is to the left.

Lesson 6.9 pp. 560–570

Exercises 2a. If $M = -2x + 1$, then $x = -\frac{1}{2}M + \frac{1}{2} = -\frac{1}{2}(M - 1) = D_{-\frac{1}{2}}(M - 1) = (D_{-\frac{1}{2}} \circ T_{-1})(M)$.

b.

M	−3	−2	−1	0	1	2	3
$T_{-1}(M)$	−4	−3	−2	−1	0	1	2
x	2	$\frac{3}{2}$	1	$\frac{1}{2}$	0	$-\frac{1}{2}$	−1

c. The $T_{-1}(M)$ number line is the image of the M number line translated 1 unit to the right; the x number line is the image of the $T_{-1}(M)$ number line reflected over 0 and dilated by the factor 2; the x number line is the image of the M number line translated 1 unit right, reflected over 0, and dilated by the factor 2.

7.

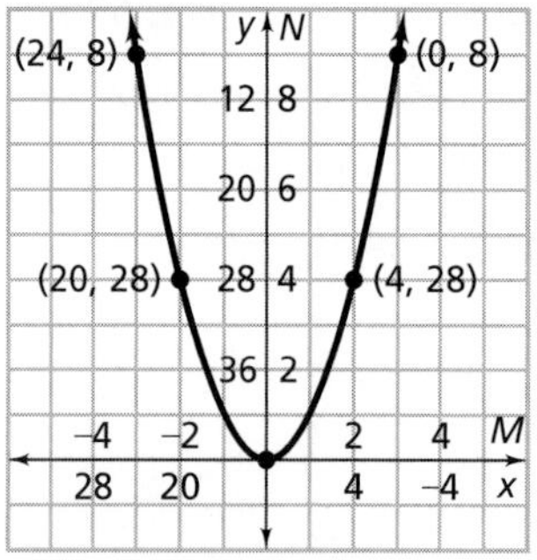

8a.

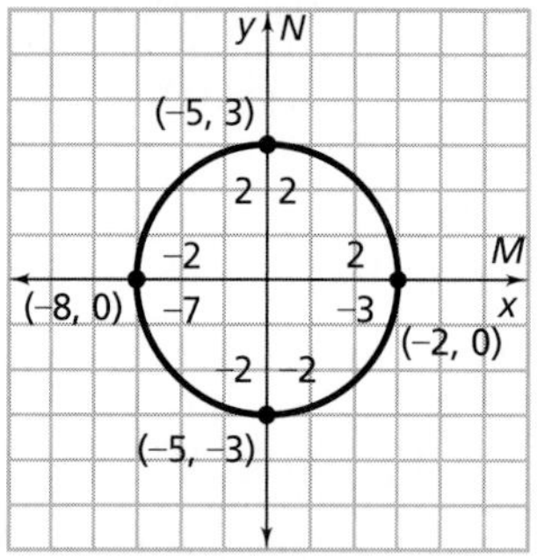

b.

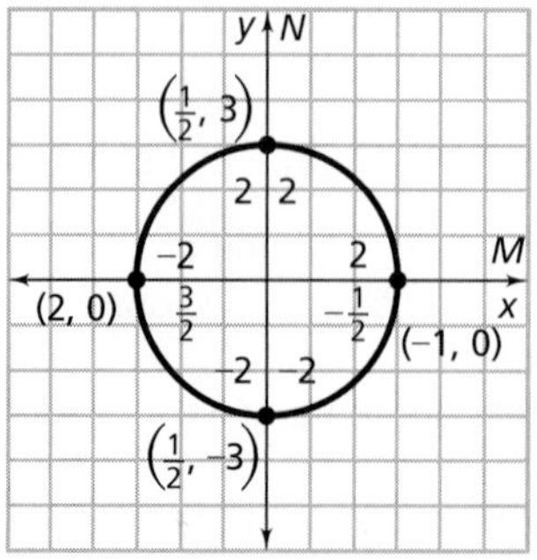

c.

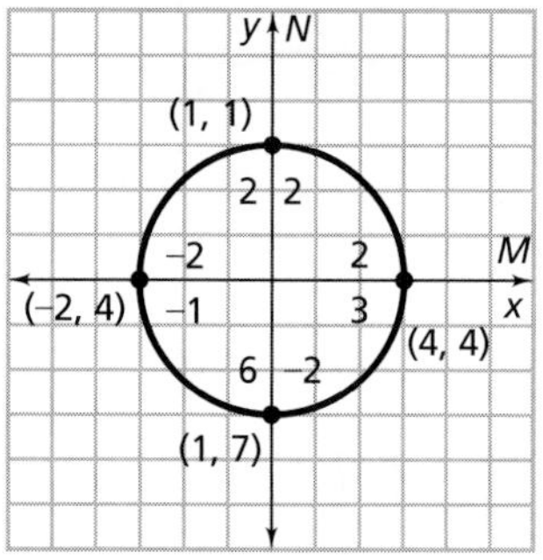

d.

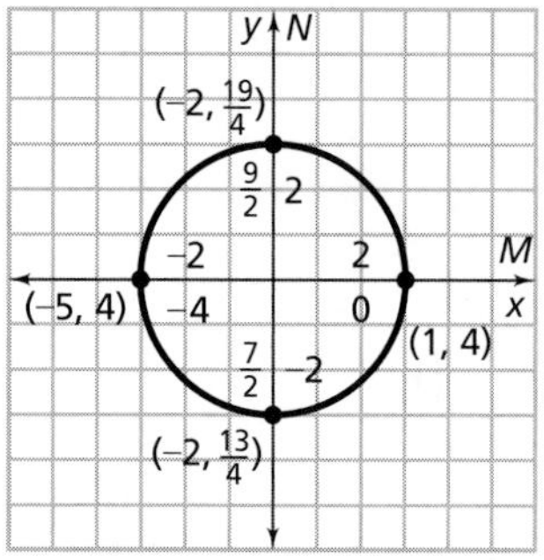

9a.

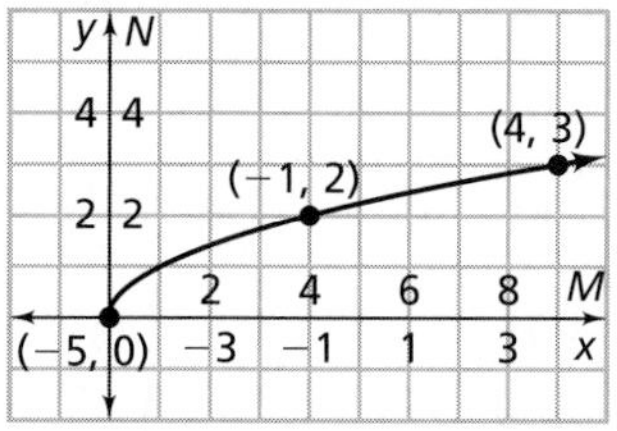

b.

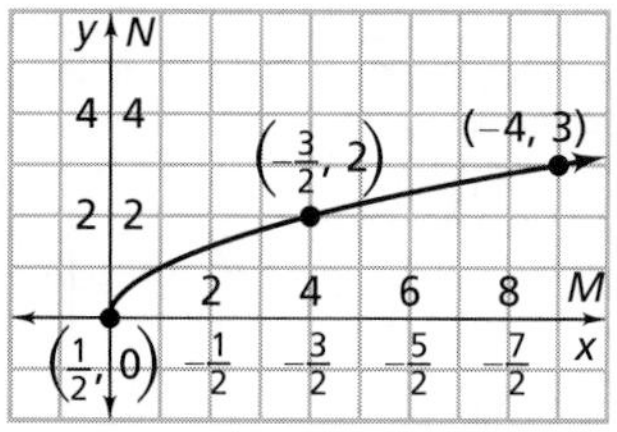

c.

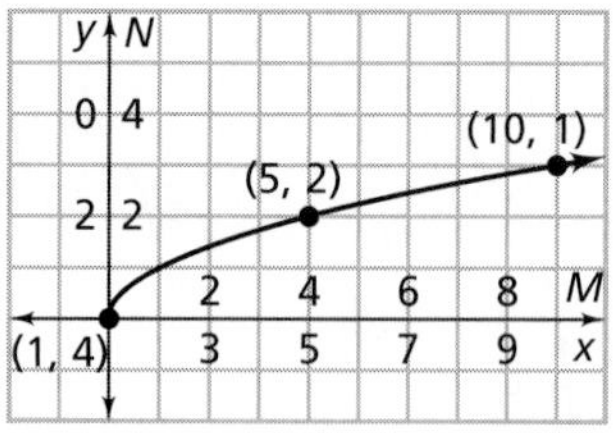

d.

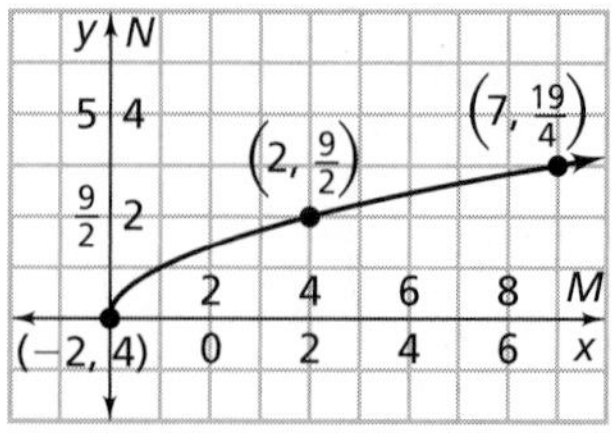

11a.

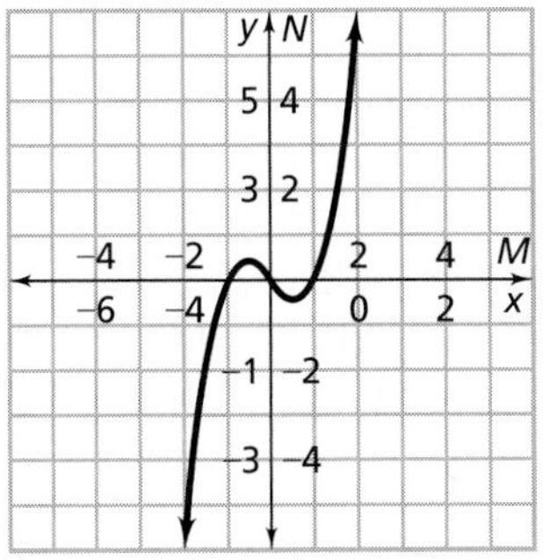

b.

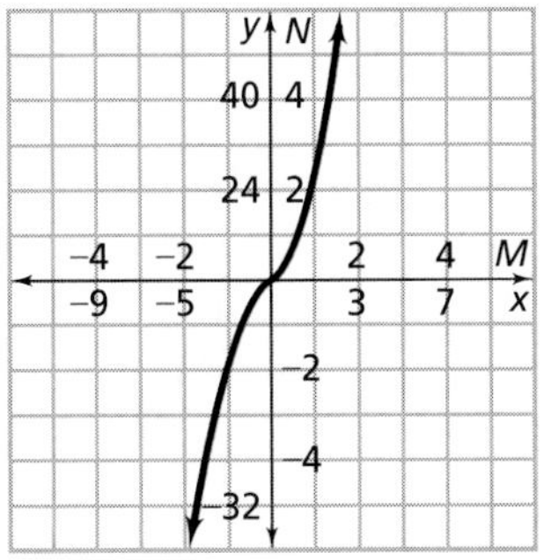

12.

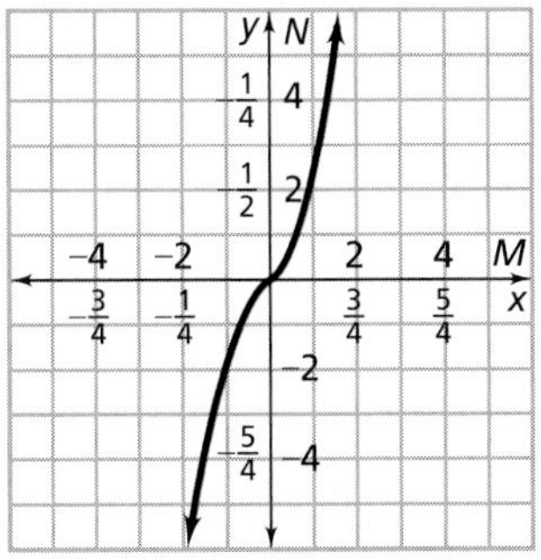

13a.

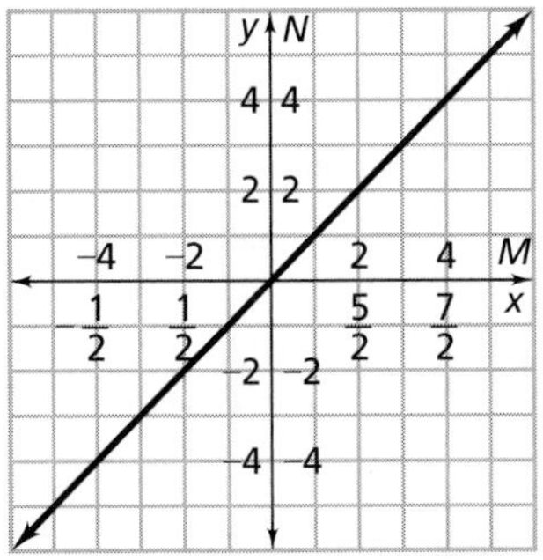

b.

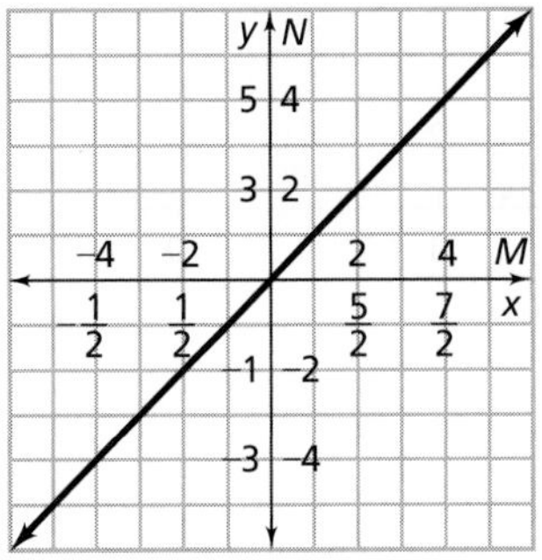

c.

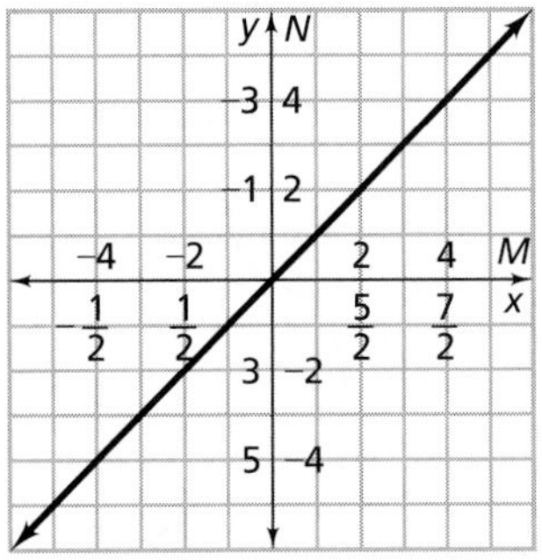

d.

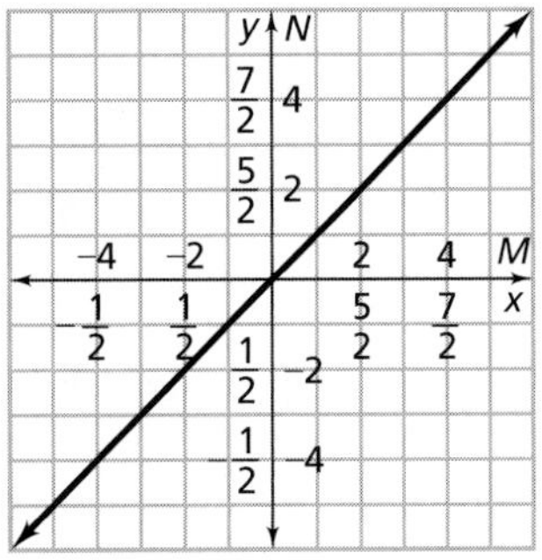

14a.

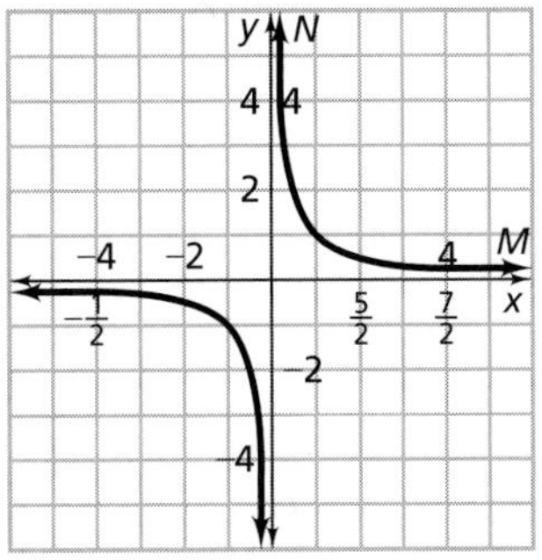

b.

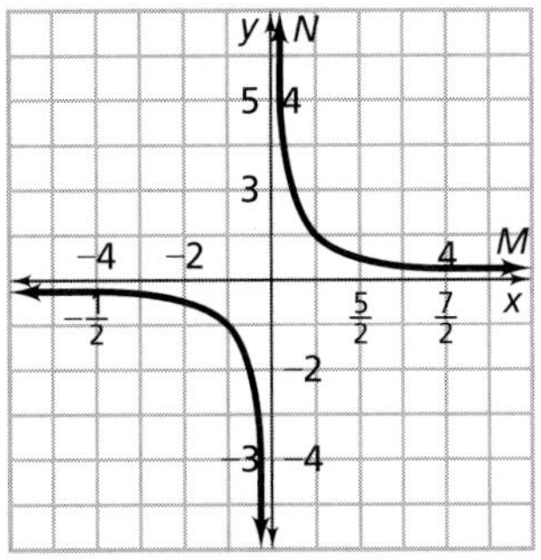

c.

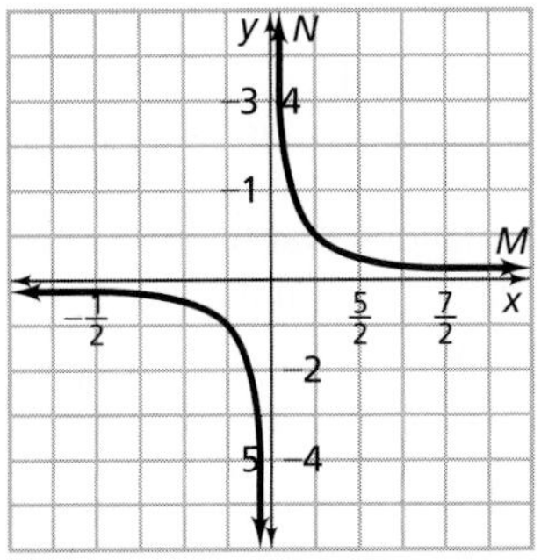

d.

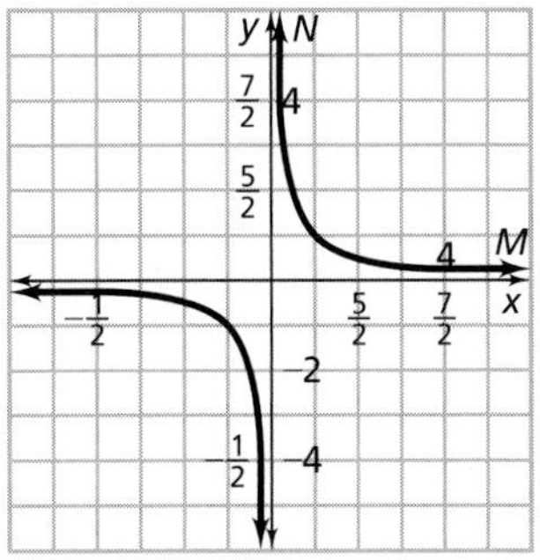

15a.

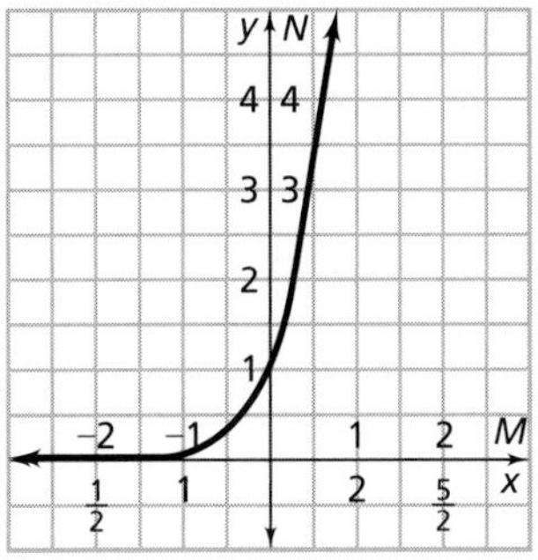

b.

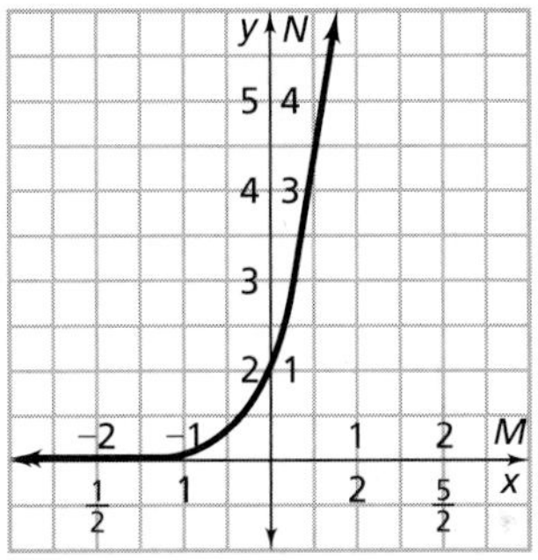

c.

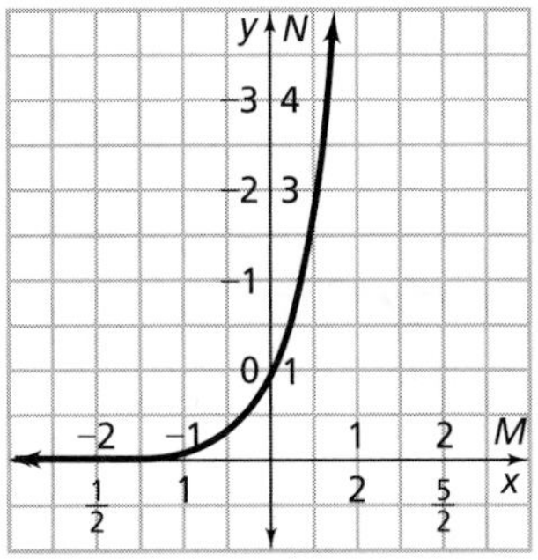

d.

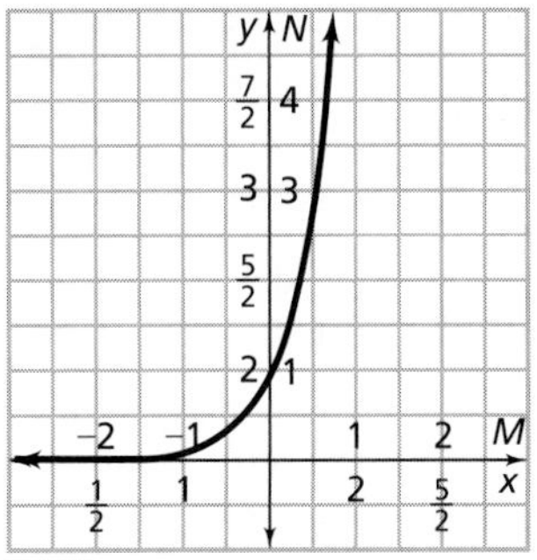

Additional Answers

16a.
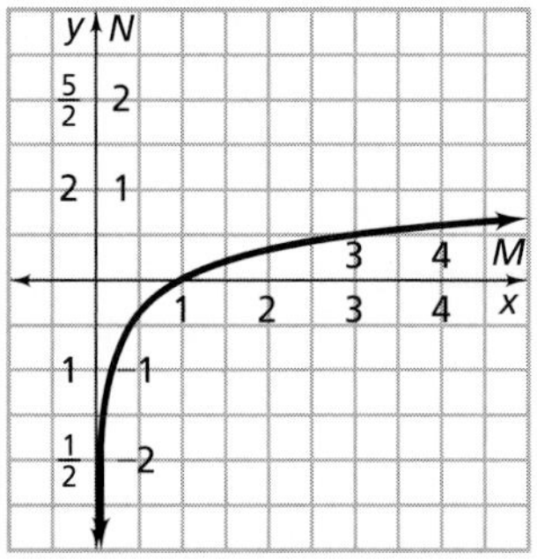

b.
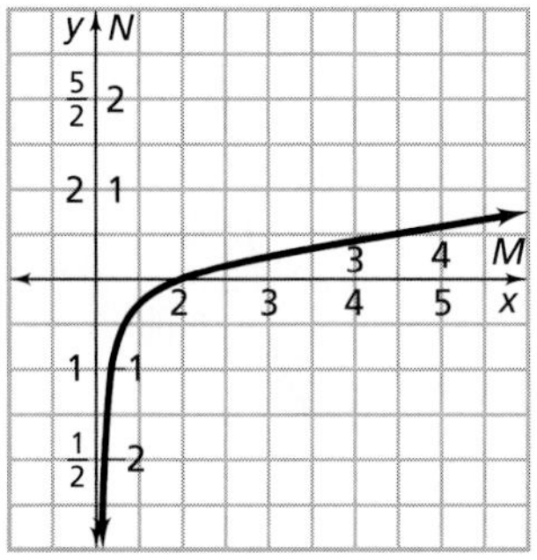

c.
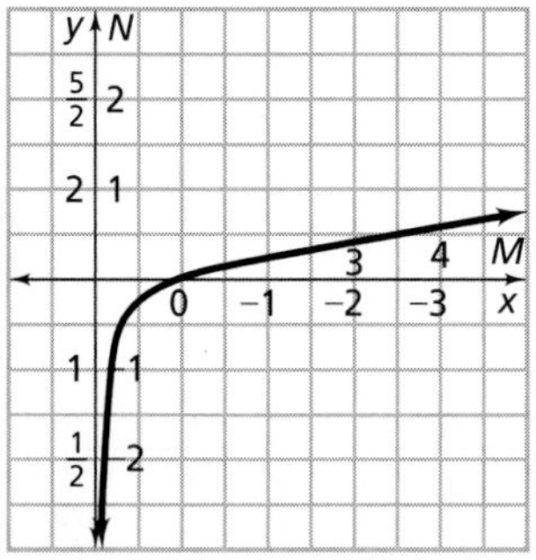

d.
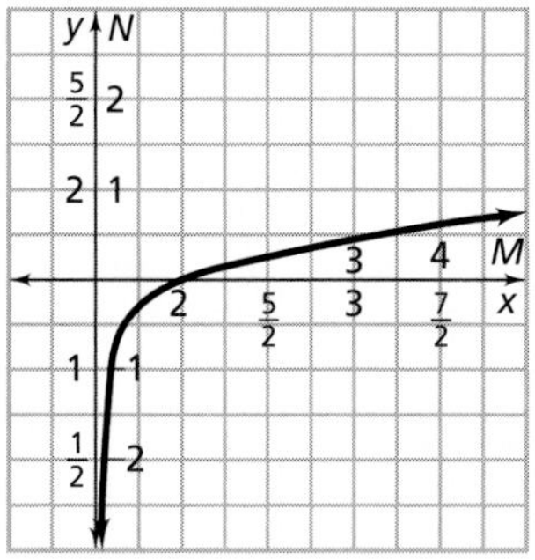

20a.
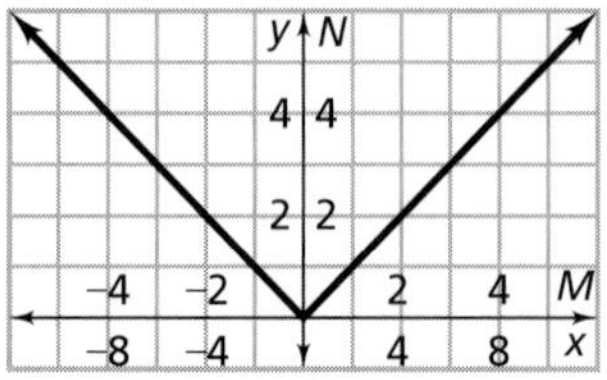

b. Answers may vary. Sample: The x number line is the M number line after a dilation by the factor $\frac{1}{2}$.

21a.
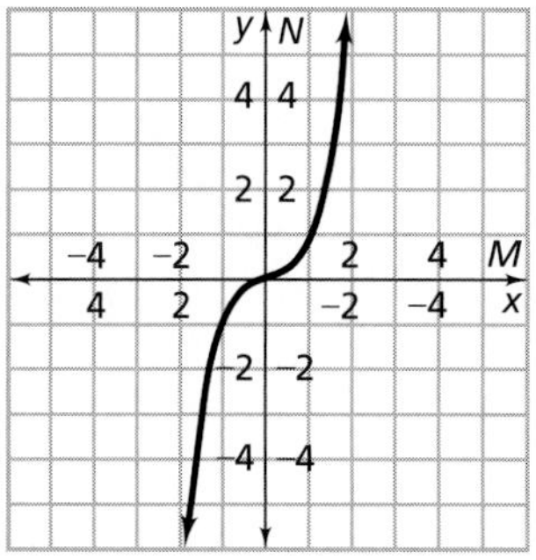

b. Answers may vary. Sample: The x number line is the same as the M number line after a reflection over 0.

Lesson 6.10 pp. 571–576

Exercises

8a. $\mathcal{A}_{(3,\,-4)}(2) = 3(2) - 4 = 2$
$\mathcal{A}_{(-5,\,12)}(2) = -5(2) + 12 = 2$

b. $(\mathcal{A}_{(3,\,-4)} \circ \mathcal{A}_{(-5,\,12)})(2)$
$= \mathcal{A}_{(3,\,-4)}(\mathcal{A}_{(-5,\,12)}(2))$
$= \mathcal{A}_{(3,\,-4)}(2)$
$= 2$

$(\mathcal{A}_{(-5,\,12)} \circ \mathcal{A}_{(3,\,-4)})(2)$
$= \mathcal{A}_{(-5,\,12)}(\mathcal{A}_{(3,\,-4)}(2))$
$= \mathcal{A}_{(-5,\,12)}(2)$
$= 2$

c. Answers may vary. Sample:
$(\mathcal{A}_{(3,\,-4)})^{-1}(2)$
$= \mathcal{A}_{\left(\frac{1}{3},\,\frac{4}{3}\right)}(2)$
$= 2\left(\frac{1}{3}\right) + \frac{4}{3}$
$= \frac{2}{3} + \frac{4}{3} = \frac{6}{3} = 2$
$(\mathcal{A}_{(-5,\,12)})^{-1}(2)$
$= \mathcal{A}_{\left(-\frac{1}{5},\,\frac{12}{5}\right)}(2)$
$= 2\left(-\frac{1}{5}\right) + \frac{12}{5}$
$= -\frac{2}{5} + \frac{12}{5} = \frac{10}{5} = 2$

d. $\mathcal{A}_{(-15,\,32)}$, $\mathcal{A}_{(-15,\,32)}$; the results of the two compositions are equal, which leads to a conjecture that affine transformations that fix the same point may be commutative under composition.

9b. Answers may vary. Sample:
$(\mathcal{A}_{(a,\,b)})^{-1}(x) =$
$\mathcal{A}_{\left(\frac{1}{a},\,-\frac{b}{a}\right)}(x) = \frac{x}{a} - \frac{b}{a} =$
$\frac{x-b}{a} = \frac{ax+b-b}{a} = \frac{ax}{a} = x$

c. $(\mathcal{A}_{(c,\,d)} \circ \mathcal{A}_{(a,\,b)})(x) =$
$\mathcal{A}_{(c,\,d)}(\mathcal{A}_{(a,\,b)}(x)) =$
$\mathcal{A}_{(c,\,d)}(x) = x$, and combining this result with part (a) shows that
$(\mathcal{A}_{(a,\,b)} \circ \mathcal{A}_{(c,\,d)}) = (\mathcal{A}_{(c,\,d)} \circ \mathcal{A}_{(a,\,b)})$

11a. $(T_3 \circ D_4 \circ (T_3)^{-1})(3) =$
$(T_3 \circ D_4)(0) = T_3(0) = 3$

b. $(T_3 \circ D_{-1} \circ (T_3)^{-1})(3) =$
$(T_3 \circ D_{-1})(0) = T_3(0) = 3$

c. $(T_3 \circ D_2 \circ (T_3)^{-1})(3) =$
$(T_3 \circ D_2)(0) = T_3(0) = 3$

d. $(T_3 \circ D_a \circ (T_3)^{-1})(3) =$
$(T_3 \circ D_a)(0) = T_3(0) = 3$

e. In general, $(T_x)^{-1}(x) = 0$, so
$(T_x \circ D_a \circ (T_x)^{-1})(x) =$
$(T_x \circ D_a)(0) = T_x(0) = x.$

13a. $3\sigma(n-1) = 3(g(0) + g(1) + g(2) + \cdots + g(n-1)) =$
$3(2 + 2 \cdot 3 + 2 \cdot 3^2 + \cdots + 2 \cdot 3^{n-1}) =$
$2 \cdot 3 + 2 \cdot 3^2 + \cdots + 2 \cdot 3^n =$
$g(1) + g(2) + \cdots + g(n)$

b. Because
$g(0) + g(1) + g(2) + \cdots + g(n) = \sigma(n)$,
$g(1) + g(2) + \cdots + g(n) = \sigma(n) - g(0)$, so the equation in part (a) becomes $3\sigma(n-1) = \sigma(n) - g(0)$ or $\sigma(n) = g(0) + 3\sigma(n-1)$.
Replacing $g(0)$ with 2 gives
$\sigma(n) = 3\sigma(n-1) + 2 = \mathcal{A}_{(3,\,2)}(\sigma(n-1))$.

Mathematical Reflections p. 577

1a.
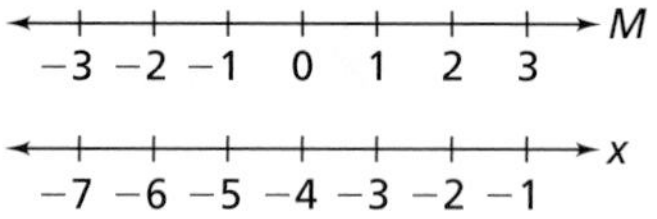

b.
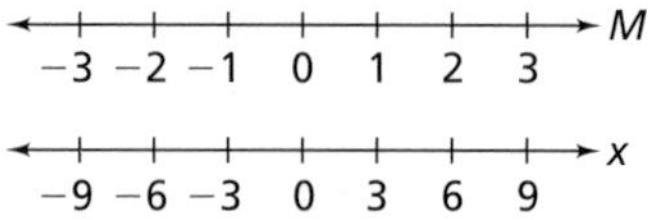

c.
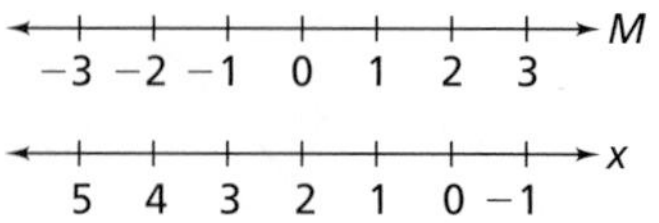

3.

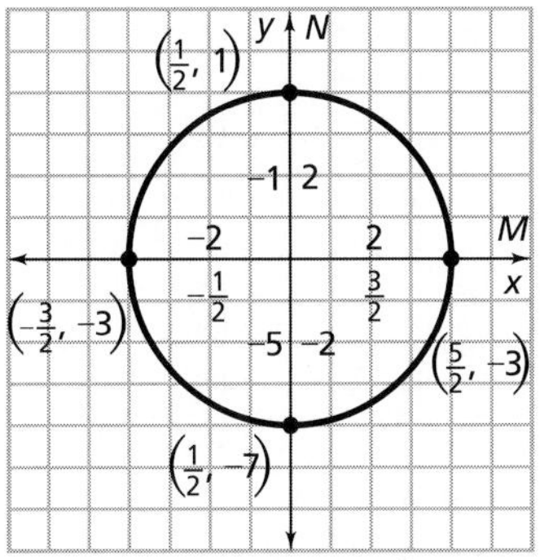

The graph of $(2x - 1)^2 + (x + 3)^2 = 16$ is the image of the graph of $x^2 + y^2 = 16$ scaled horizontally by the factor $\frac{1}{2}$ and translated $\frac{1}{2}$ unit to the right and 3 units down.

4b.

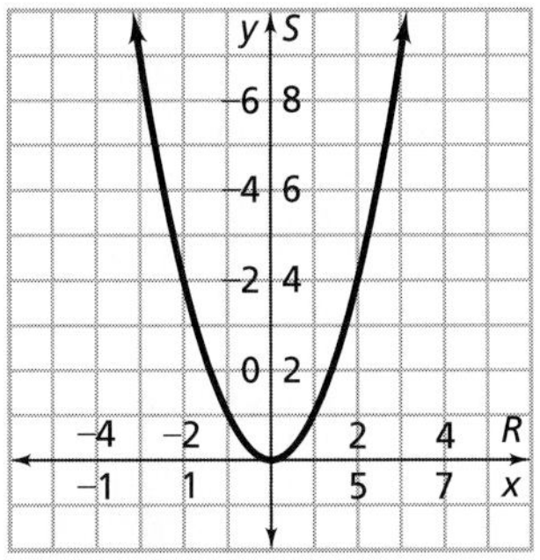

c. The graph of $y = -x^2 + 6x - 7$ is the graph of $y = x^2$ reflected over the x-axis and translated 3 units to the right and 2 units up. **6.** Find the substitutions $R = \mathcal{A}_{\left(\frac{1}{2}, \frac{1}{2}\right)}$ and $S = \mathcal{A}_{\left(\frac{1}{8}, -\frac{7}{8}\right)}$ that transform the equation into the form $S = R^3 - R$. Graph $S = R^3 - R$ in an RS-coordinate system and then use the equations $R = \frac{1}{2}x + \frac{1}{2}$ and $S = \frac{1}{8}y - \frac{7}{8}$ (solved for x and for y) to relabel the scales on the R- and S-axes with the corresponding x- and y-values. **7.** Answers may vary. Sample: See the graph for Lesson 6.9, Exercise 18. The x-coordinate of each point on the graph is 3 more than its corresponding M-coordinate, while the point's y-coordinate is the same as its corresponding N-coordinate. This means that the graph of $y = (x - 3)^2$ is the graph of $y = x^2$ translated 3 units to the right.

Project pp. 578–579

7.

Function	Order
a	2
b	3
c	3
d	2
e	2
f	1

9. Answers may vary. Sample: In the following table, the six mappings of the regular hexagon correspond to the letters a–f as follows:

a = rotate 60° clockwise
b = rotate 120° clockwise
c = rotate 180° clockwise
d = rotate 240° clockwise
e = rotate 300° clockwise
f = leave the hexagon as it is

then	a	b	c	d	e	f
a	b	c	d	e	f	a
b	c	d	e	f	a	b
c	d	e	f	a	b	c
d	e	f	a	b	c	d
e	f	a	b	c	d	e
f	a	b	c	d	e	f

No; answers may vary. Sample: The set of hexagon mappings has an element (a = rotate 60° clockwise) that is of order 6. There is no element of order 6 in the set of functions used in Exercise 3, so the two tables cannot be built to be the same.

Test p. 582

6a.

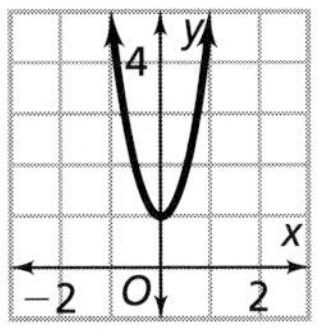

The graph of $y - 1 = (2x)^2$ is the graph of $y = x^2$ scaled horizontally by the factor $\frac{1}{2}$ and translated 1 unit up.

b.

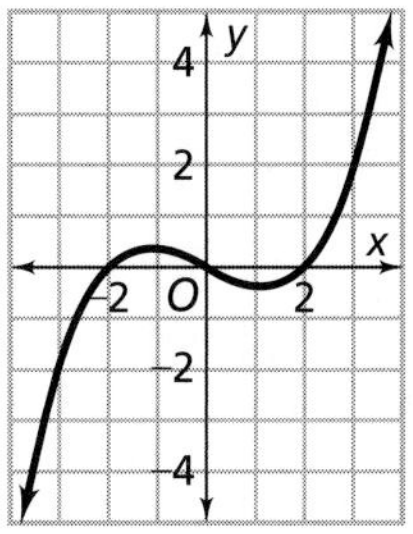

The graph of $y = \left(\frac{x}{2}\right)^3 - \frac{x}{2}$ is the graph of $y = x^3 - x$ scaled horizontally by the factor 2.

c.

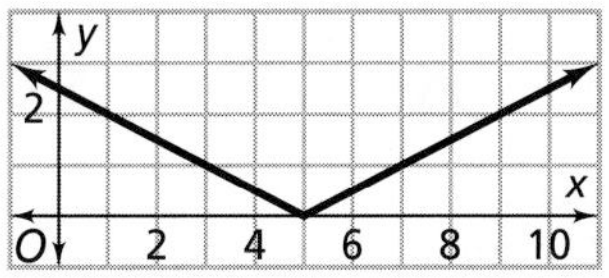

The graph of $2y = |x - 5|$ is the graph of $y = |x|$ scaled vertically by the factor $\frac{1}{2}$ and translated 5 units to the right.

d.

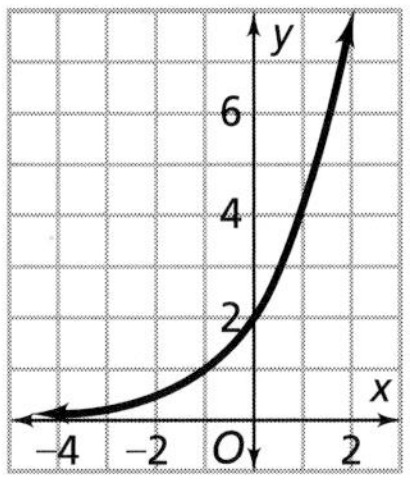

The graph of $y = 2^{x+1}$ is the graph of $y = 2^x$ translated 1 unit to the left.

Cumulative Review pp. 583–585

12a.

x	f(x)
−2	$\frac{1}{36}$
−1	$\frac{1}{6}$
0	1
1	6
2	36

x	g(x)
$\frac{1}{36}$	−2
$\frac{1}{6}$	−1
1	0
6	1
36	2

b.

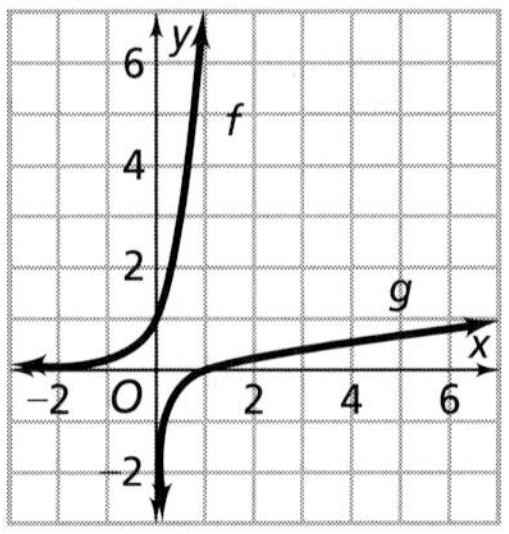

16a. 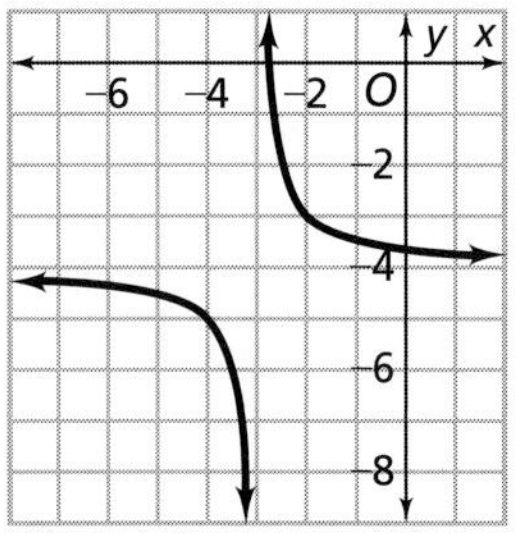

The graph of $y = \frac{1}{x+3} - 4$ is the graph of $y = \frac{1}{x}$ translated 3 units to the left and 4 units down.

b. 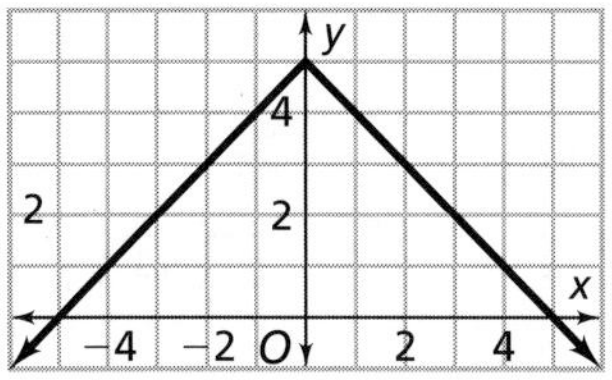

Answers may vary. Sample: The graph of $y - 5 = -|x|$ is the graph of $y = |x|$ reflected over the x-axis and translated 5 units up.

c. 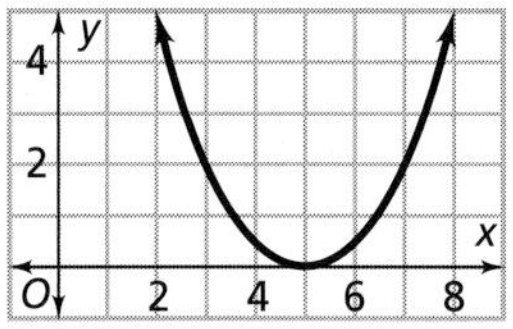

The graph of $2y = (x - 5)^2$ is the graph of $y = x^2$ scaled vertically by the factor $\frac{1}{2}$ and translated 5 units to the right.

d. 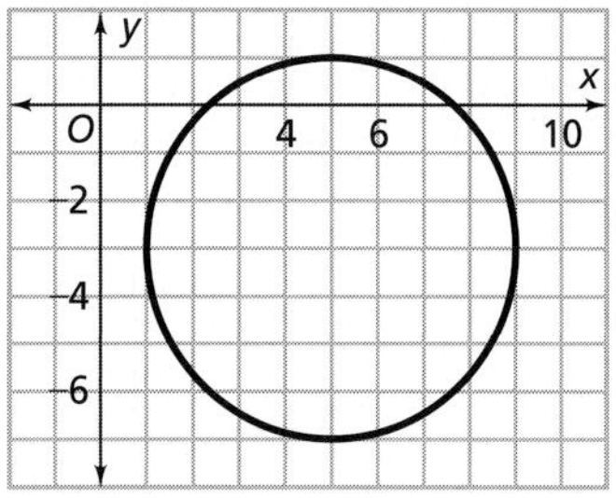

The graph of $(x - 5)^2 + (y + 3)^2 = 16$ is the graph of $x^2 + y^2 = 16$ translated 5 units to the right and 3 units down.

24b. 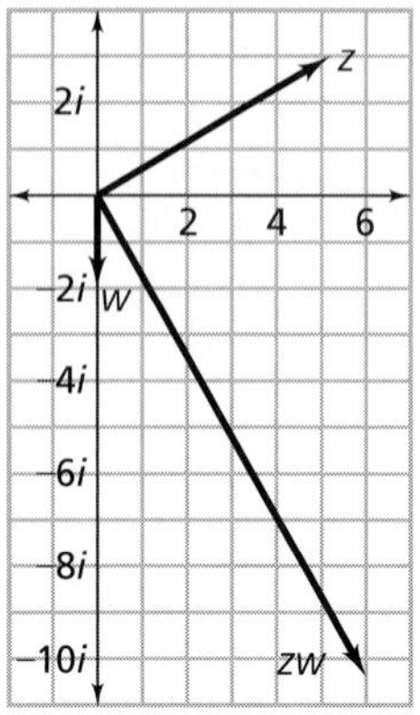

Chapter 7

Lesson 7.1 pp. 589–592

For You to Explore

2a–b.

End of year	$F(n)$	$G(n)$
0	10,000	0.01
1	21,000	0.03
2	33,000	0.07
3	46,000	0.15
4	60,000	0.31
5	75,000	0.63

Exercises **14.**

n	$F(n)$	Δ
0	1	3
1	4	5
2	9	7
3	16	9
4	25	11
5	36	

$F(n) = (n + 1)^2$

n	$T(n)$	Δ
0	1	9
1	10	90
2	100	900
3	1000	9000
4	10,000	90,000
5	100,000	

$T(n) = 10^n$

n	$H(n)$	Δ
0	5	5
1	10	5
2	15	5
3	20	5
4	25	5
5	30	

$H(n) = 5(n + 1)$

Lesson 7.5 pp. 607–608

For You to Explore

1a.

n	$f(n)$	Σ
0	−2	−2
1	3	1
2	8	9
3	13	22
4	18	40
5	23	63

b.

n	$g(n)$	Σ
0	0	0
1	2	2
2	4	6
3	6	12
4	8	20
5	10	30

c.

n	$f(n) + g(n)$	Σ
0	−2	−2
1	5	3
2	12	15
3	19	34
4	26	60
5	33	93

d.

n	$2f(n)$	Σ
0	−4	−4
1	6	2
2	16	18
3	26	44
4	36	80
5	46	126

e.

n	$3g(n)$	Σ
0	0	0
1	6	6
2	12	18
3	18	36
4	24	60
5	30	90

f.

n	$f(n) \cdot g(n)$	Σ
0	0	0
1	6	6
2	32	38
3	78	116
4	144	260
5	230	490

Lesson 7.7 pp. 614–619

Exercises 15a.

n	$f(n)$	Δ	Σ
0	0	2	2
1	2	4	6
2	6	6	12
3	12	8	20
4	20	10	30
5	30		

n	$g(n)$	Δ	Σ
0	1	2	2
1	3	4	6
2	7	6	12
3	13	8	20
4	21	10	30
5	31		

n	$h(n)$	Δ	Σ
0	5	2	2
1	7	4	6
2	11	6	12
3	17	8	20
4	25	10	30
5	35		

Lesson 7.9 pp. 629–631

For You to Explore 1a. Table K:

n	$K(n)$	Δ
0	3	5
1	8	5
2	13	5
3	18	5
4	23	

Table L:

m	$L(m)$	Δ
0	3	6
1	9	6
2	15	6
3	21	6
4	27	

Lesson 7.11 pp. 639–648

For You to Do 11. Answers may vary. Sample: For an interest rate of 7.5%:

Cost of Car (thousands of dollars)	Monthly Payment
10	311.06
11	342.17
12	373.27
13	404.38
14	435.49
15	466.59
16	497.70
17	528.81
18	559.91

Exercises 3. Answers may vary. Sample: $a_1 = 2, 4, 6, 8, \dots$ and $g_1 = 2, 4, 8, 16, 32, \dots$. The common difference is greater than 1 and the terms of the sequence increase; the common ratio is greater than 1, so if the first term is positive the terms will increase, and if the first term is negative the terms will decrease. $a_2 = 1, 2, 3, 4, 5, \dots$ and $g_2 = 1, 1, 1, 1, 1, \dots$. The common difference is 1 and the terms of the sequence increase; the common ratio is 1 and the terms of the sequence remain constant. $a_3 = 6, 5, 4, 3, 2, \dots$ and $g_3 = 6, -6, 6, -6, 6, \dots$. The common difference is –1 and the terms of the sequence decrease; the common ratio is –1, and the terms will alternate between positive and negative values with the same absolute value. $a_4 = 5, 2, -1, -4, -7, \dots$ and $g_4 = 5, -15, 45, -135, 405, \dots$. The common difference is less than –1 and the terms of the sequence decrease; the common ratio is less than –1, so the terms will alternate between positive and negative values. $a_5 = 10, 10.5, 11, 11.5, 12, \dots$ and $g_5 = 10, 5, \frac{5}{2}, \frac{5}{4}, \frac{5}{8}, \dots$. The common difference is between 0 and 1, and the terms of the sequence increase; the common ratio is between 0 and 1, so if the first term is positive the terms will decrease toward zero, and if the first term is negative the terms will increase toward zero.

4a. $\sum_{i=0}^{n} 5 \cdot \left(\frac{1}{2}\right)^n = -10\left(\left(\frac{1}{2}\right)^{n+1} - 1\right)$ or $\sum_{i=0}^{n} 5 \cdot \left(\frac{1}{2}\right)^n = 10\left(1 - \left(\frac{1}{2}\right)^{n+1}\right)$
6d. $g(n) = 10 \cdot \left(\frac{1}{2}\right)^n$
e. $g(n) = 576 \cdot \left(\frac{1}{2}\right)^n$
f. $g(n) = 0.96\sqrt{10}\left(\frac{\sqrt{10}}{2}\right)^n$
g. $g(n) = \frac{2}{243} \cdot 3^n$ or $g(n) = \frac{2}{243} \cdot (-3)^n$ **8e.** Answers may vary. Sample: After you connect the four midpoints of the sides, you have four isosceles right triangles at the corners of the original square. They are congruent by SAS, so the sides of the "inside figure" are congruent. Each isosceles right triangle has acute angles of 45°, so each of the four angles of the "inside figure" is 90°. Therefore the "inside figure" is a square.
9a–d.

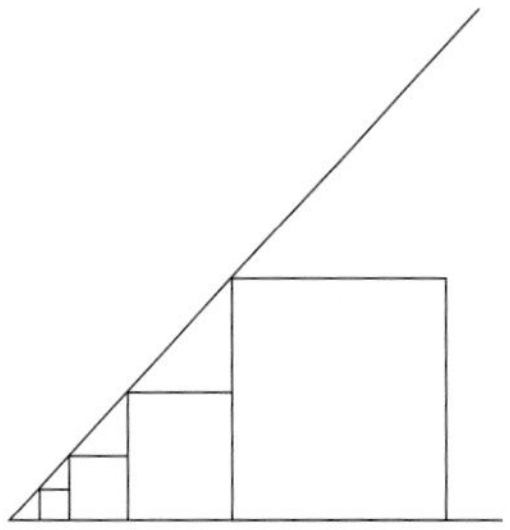

Lesson 7.12 pp. 649–655

Exercises 1c.

n	$t(n)$	$T(n)$
1	$\frac{3}{4}$	$\frac{3}{4}$
2	$\frac{3}{4} \cdot 2 = \frac{3}{2}$	$2\frac{1}{4}$
3	$\frac{3}{4} \cdot 2^2 = 3$	$5\frac{1}{4}$
4	$\frac{3}{4} \cdot 2^3 = 6$	$11\frac{1}{4}$

$T(n)$ does not have a limit.

d.

n	$t(n)$	$T(n)$
1	1	1
2	1	2
3	1	3
4	1	4

$T(n)$ does not have a limit.

Lesson 7.13 pp. 656–658

For You to Do 6a. $\frac{1}{9}$ **b.** $\frac{2}{9}$ **c.** $\frac{3}{9}$ or $\frac{1}{3}$ **d.** $\frac{4}{9}$ **e.** $\frac{5}{9}$ **f.** $\frac{6}{9}$ or $\frac{2}{3}$ **g.** $\frac{7}{9}$ **h.** $\frac{8}{9}$ **i.** $\frac{9}{9}$ or 1

Mathematical Reflections p. 659

4a.

n	$g(n)$	Σ
0	−10	−10
1	−40	−50
2	−160	−210
3	−640	−850
4	−2560	−3410
5	−10,240	−13,650

b. $g(n) = -10 \cdot 4^n$ **c.** $G(n) = -\frac{10}{3} \cdot \left(4^{n+1} - 1\right)$ **5a.** $\approx$ \$607,906 **b.** The present value would be about \$530,180. **6.** An arithmetic sequence is a function with domain the nonnegative integers and which has a constant difference between successive terms. **7.** A geometric series is the sum of its associated geometric sequence with domain the nonnegative integers and which has a constant ratio between successive terms. **8.** If $N = 0.121212\dots$, then $100N = 12.121212\dots$. Subtracting, $99N = 12$ and $N = \frac{12}{99}$ or $\frac{4}{33}$.

Lesson 7.14 pp. 661–662

For You to Explore

1. See Figure 9. **5c.** Answers may vary. Sample: The numerators are products of consecutive numbers, and each denominator is the factorial of the number of factors in the numerator; $\Sigma\Sigma\Sigma\Sigma = \frac{n(n+1)(n+2)(n+3)(n+4)}{120}$.

Exercises 9a. $99^1 = 99$; $99^2 = 9801$; $99^3 = 970{,}299$; $99^4 = 96{,}059{,}601$; $99^5 = 9{,}509{,}900{,}499$ **b.** Answers may vary. Sample: The first digit is 9; the second digit adds 9 each time; the third digit is 0; the last digit is 9 (if the exponent is odd) or 1 (if the exponent is even).

10.

n	$(n+1)^3 - n^3$	Σ
0	1	1
1	7	8
2	19	27
3	37	64
4	61	125
5	91	216
6	127	343
7	169	512
8	217	729
9	271	1000
10	331	1331
11	397	1728
12	469	2197
13	547	2744
14	631	3375
15	721	4096
16	817	4913
17	919	5832
18	1027	6859
19	1141	8000

A closed form for the Σ column is $(n + 1)^3$.

Lesson 7.15 **pp. 663–667**

Exercises 4a–c. See Figure 10

Review **pp. 677–678**

9a–b. See Figure 11

Chapter 8

Lesson 8.1 **pp. 689–691**

For You to Explore

8.

Angle	Coordinates
0°	(1, 0)
45°	$\left(\frac{\sqrt{2}}{2}, \frac{\sqrt{2}}{2}\right)$
90°	(0, 1)
135°	$\left(-\frac{\sqrt{2}}{2}, \frac{\sqrt{2}}{2}\right)$
180°	(−1, 0)
225°	$\left(-\frac{\sqrt{2}}{2}, \frac{\sqrt{2}}{2}\right)$
270°	(0, −1)
315°	$\left(\frac{\sqrt{2}}{2}, \frac{\sqrt{2}}{2}\right)$
360°	(1, 0)
405°	$\left(\frac{\sqrt{2}}{2}, \frac{\sqrt{2}}{2}\right)$
450°	(0, 1)

9. See Figure 12.

Exercises

11.

Angle	Coordinates
0°	(1, 0)
10°	(0.985, 0.174)
20°	(0.940, 0.342)
30°	(0.866, 0.5)
40°	(0.766, 0.643)
50°	(0.643, 0.766)
60°	(0.5, 0.866)
70°	(0.342, 0.940)
80°	(0.174, 0.985)
90°	(0, 1)

16. See Figure 13.

19a.

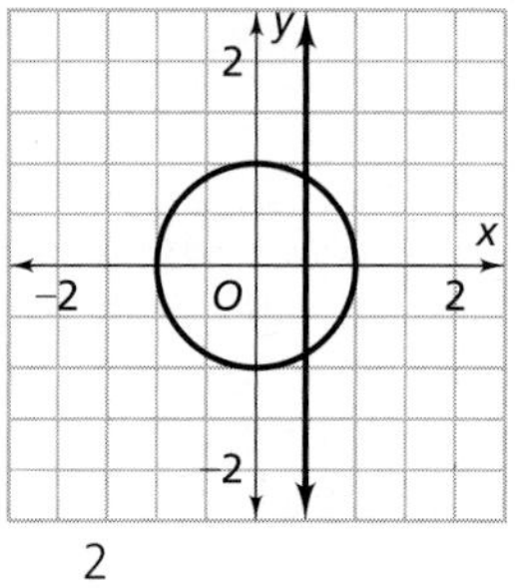

Figure 9

n	$f(n)$	Σ	$\Sigma\Sigma$	$\Sigma\Sigma\Sigma$	$\Sigma\Sigma\Sigma\Sigma$
1	1	1	1	1	1
2	2	3	4	5	6
3	3	6	10	15	21
4	4	10	20	35	56
5	5	15	35	70	126
6	6	21	56	126	252
7	7	28	84	210	462
8	8	36	120	330	792
9	9	45	165	495	1287
10	10	55	220	715	2002

Figure 10a

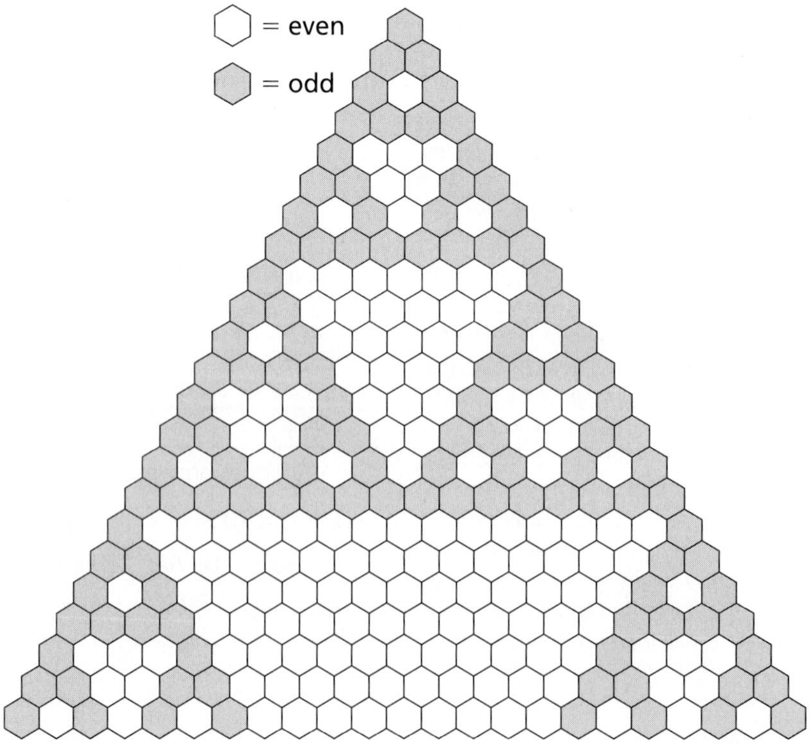

Figure 10b

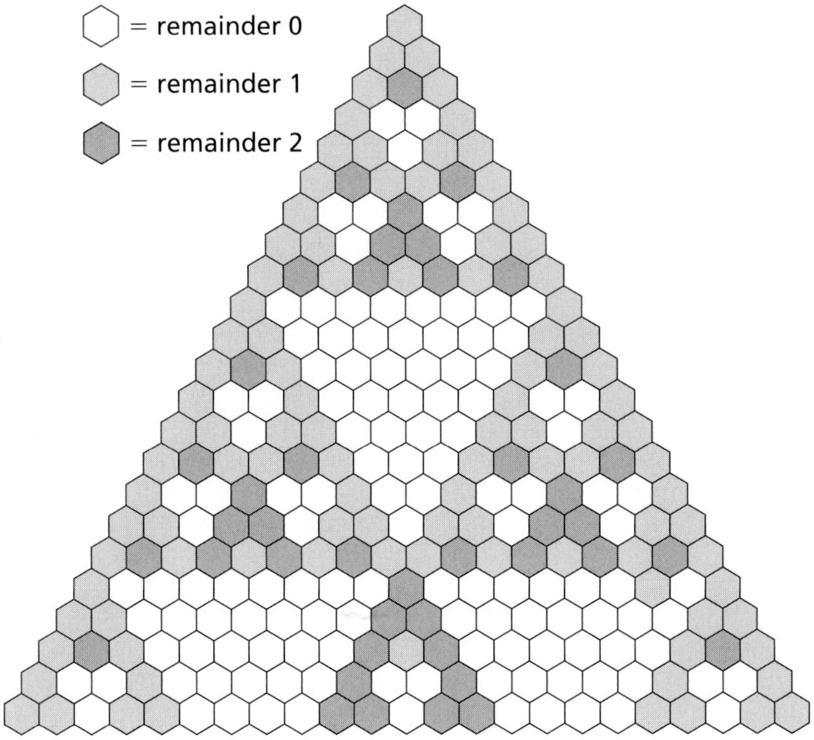

Figure 11

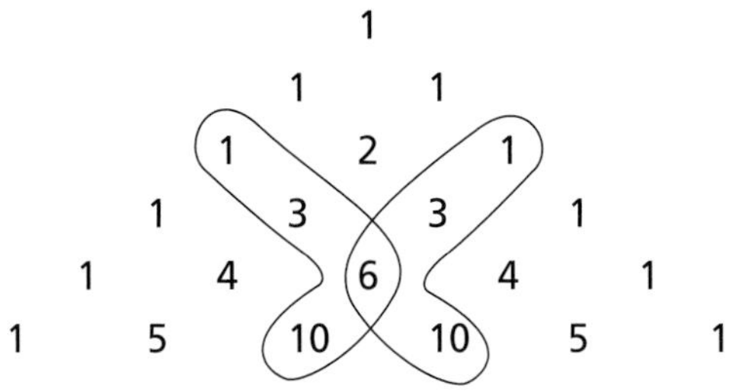

Figure 12

9.

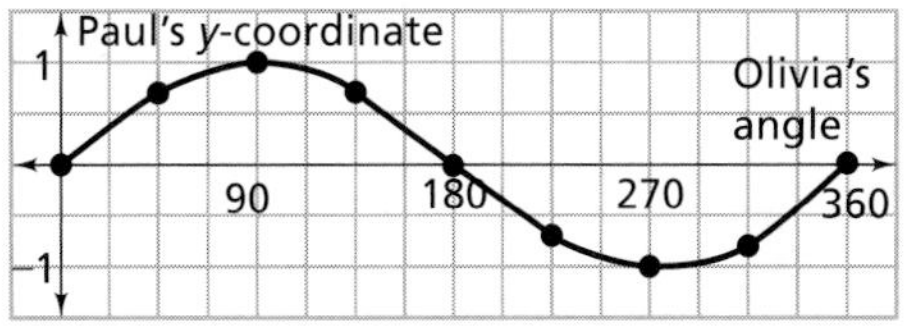

Figure 13

16.

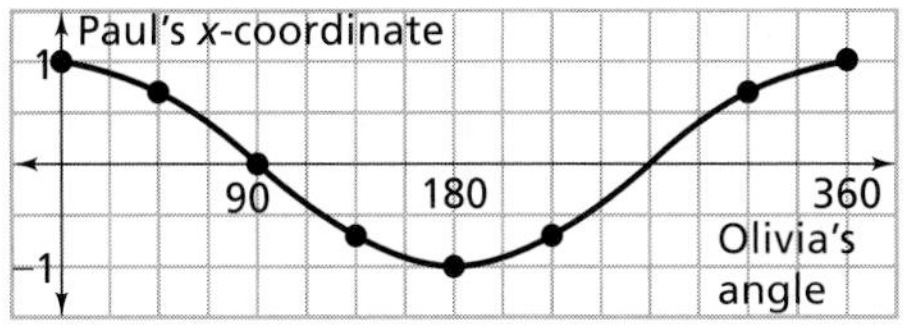

Figure 10c

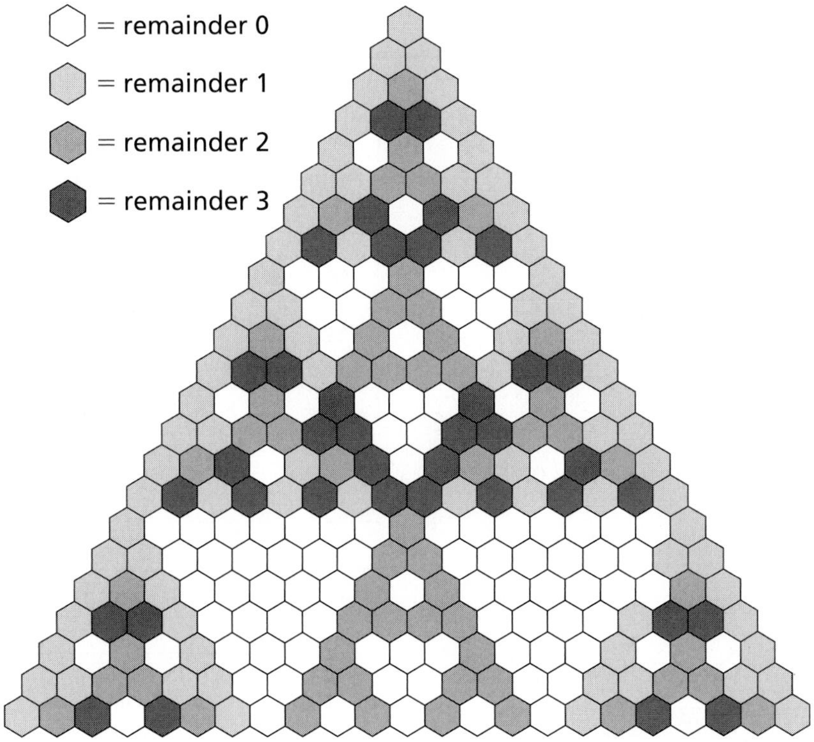

b.

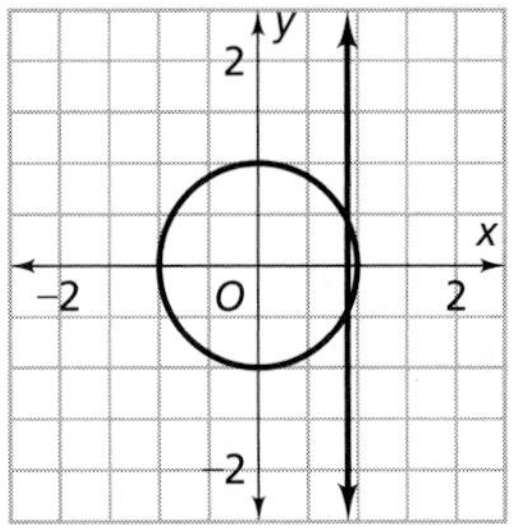

2

c.

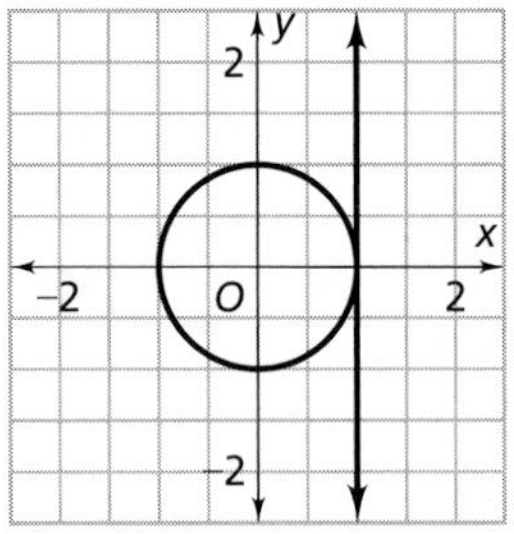

1

d.

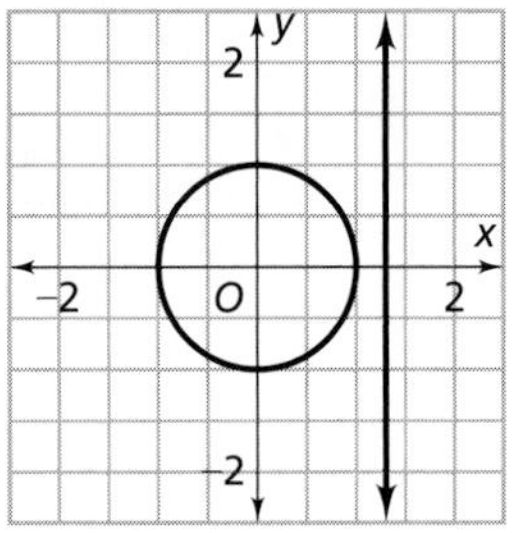

0

20a.

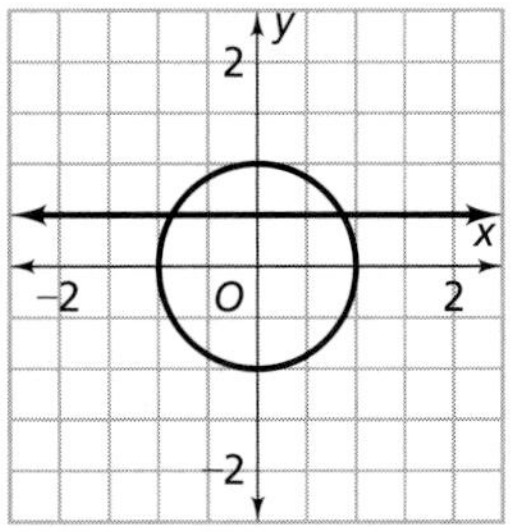

2

b.

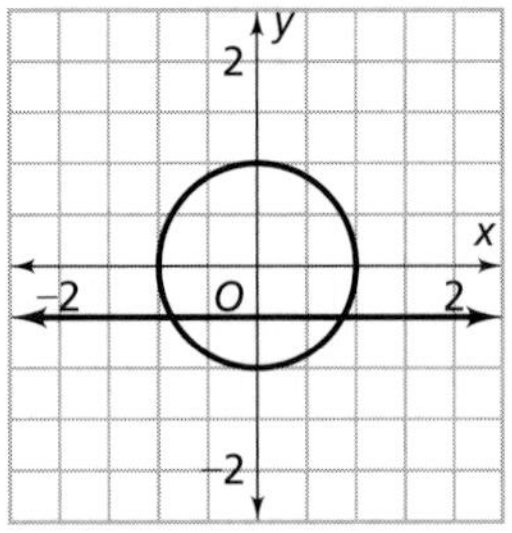

2

c.

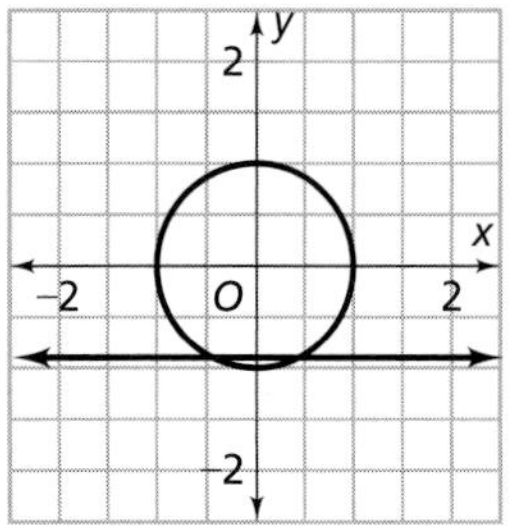

2

d.

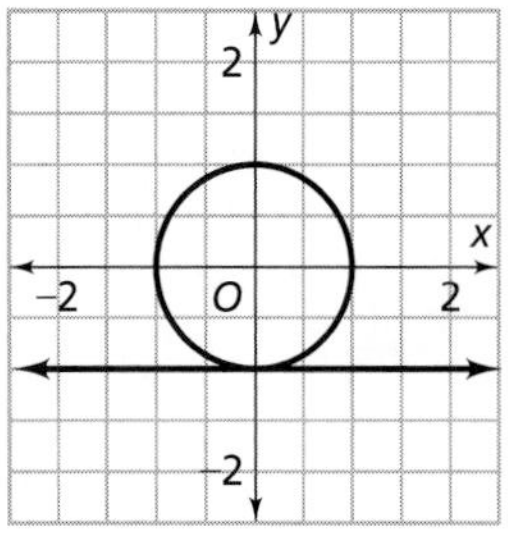

1

Lesson 8.2 pp. 692–697

Exercises

8. a.

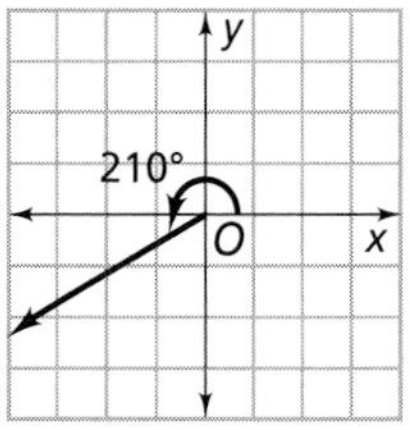

$\sin 210° = -\frac{1}{2}$, $\cos 210° = -\frac{\sqrt{3}}{2}$, $\tan 210° = \frac{\sqrt{3}}{3}$

b.

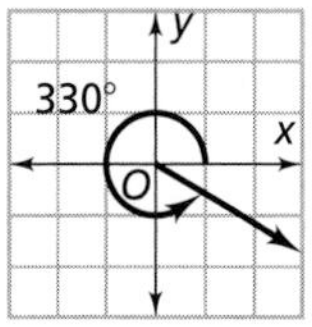

$\sin 330° = -\frac{1}{2}$, $\cos 330° = \frac{\sqrt{3}}{2}$, $\tan 330° = -\frac{\sqrt{3}}{3}$

c.

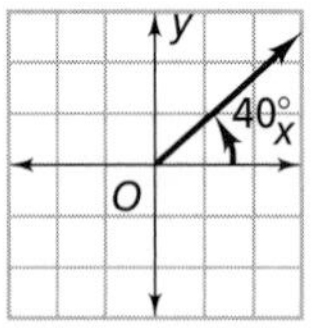

$\sin 40° \approx 0.643$, $\cos 40° \approx 0.766$, $\tan 40° \approx 0.839$

d.

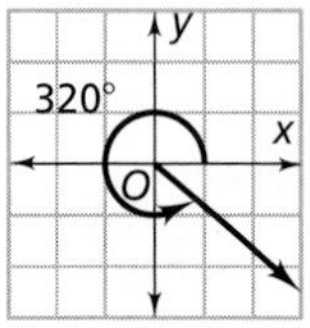

$\sin 320° \approx -0.643$,
$\cos 320° \approx 0.766$,
$\tan 320° \approx -0.839$

e.

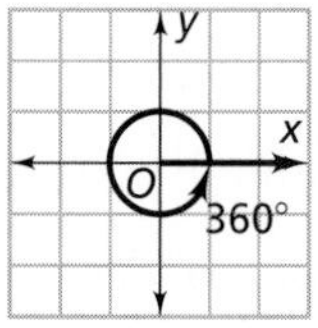

$\sin 360° = 0$, $\cos 360° = 1$, $\tan 360° = 0$

10. See Figure 14.

Lesson 8.3 pp. 698–703

Exercises

11a. $\sin \theta$ **b.** $-\cos \theta$ **c.** $-\sin \theta$ **d.** $-\cos \theta$ **e.** $-\cos \theta$ **f.** $-\sin \theta$ **g.** $-\cos \theta$ **h.** $\sin \theta$

12. False. Answers may vary. Sample: Let $a = 30°$ and $b = 60°$. Then $\sin(a + b) = \sin 90° = 1$, but $\sin 30° + \sin 60° = \frac{1}{2} + \frac{\sqrt{3}}{2} \neq 1$. Also $\cos(a + b) = \cos 90° = 0$, but $\cos 30° + \cos 60° = \frac{\sqrt{3}}{2} + \frac{1}{2} \neq 0$.

13a. positive **b.** negative **c.** negative **d.** positive **e.** negative

Lesson 8.4 pp. 704–708

Exercises

14.

θ	$\cos\theta$	$\sin\theta$	$\tan\theta$
0°	1	0	0
30°	$\frac{\sqrt{3}}{2}$	$\frac{1}{2}$	$\frac{1}{\sqrt{3}}$
45°	$\frac{\sqrt{2}}{2}$	$\frac{\sqrt{2}}{2}$	1
60°	$\frac{1}{2}$	$\frac{\sqrt{3}}{2}$	$\sqrt{3}$
90°	0	1	Undefined
120°	$-\frac{1}{2}$	$\frac{\sqrt{3}}{2}$	$-\sqrt{3}$
135°	$-\frac{\sqrt{2}}{2}$	$\frac{\sqrt{2}}{2}$	−1
150°	$-\frac{\sqrt{3}}{2}$	$-\frac{1}{2}$	$-\frac{\sqrt{3}}{3}$
180°	−1	0	0
210°	$-\frac{\sqrt{3}}{2}$	$-\frac{1}{2}$	$\frac{\sqrt{3}}{3}$
225°	$-\frac{\sqrt{2}}{2}$	$-\frac{\sqrt{2}}{2}$	1
240°	$-\frac{1}{2}$	$-\frac{\sqrt{3}}{2}$	$\sqrt{3}$
270°	0	−1	Undefined
300°	$\frac{1}{2}$	$-\frac{\sqrt{3}}{2}$	$-\sqrt{3}$
315°	$\frac{\sqrt{2}}{2}$	$-\frac{\sqrt{2}}{2}$	−1
330°	$\frac{\sqrt{3}}{2}$	$-\frac{1}{2}$	$-\frac{\sqrt{3}}{3}$
360°	1	0	0

Lesson 8.5 pp. 709–712

Exercises

8. Drop a perpendicular from O to $\overline{AB}$ to form two congruent right triangles, each with shorter leg $\frac{z}{2}$. $m\angle B = 72°$.

$\cos 72° = \frac{\text{adjacent}}{\text{hypotenuse}} = \frac{\frac{z}{2}}{1} = \frac{z}{2}$, so $z = 2 \cdot \cos 72°$. **9a.** 143.13°, 216.87° **b.** no solution **c.** 60°, 120°, 240°, 300° **d.** 120°, 240° **10a.** 120°, 240° **b.** 45°, 225° **c.** 30°, 90°, 150° **d.** 110.54°, 249.46° **16.** 26.57°, 206.57°, 153.43°, 333.43° **17.** C

18a. (1, 0) **b.** $\left(\frac{4}{5}, \frac{3}{5}\right)$
c. $\left(\frac{12}{13}, \frac{5}{13}\right)$ **d.** $\left(\frac{8}{17}, \frac{15}{17}\right)$
e. $\left(\frac{60}{61}, \frac{11}{61}\right)$ **f.** $\left(\frac{2rs}{r^2 + s^2}, \frac{r^2 - s^2}{r^2 + s^2}\right)$

Mathematical Reflections p. 713

2c.

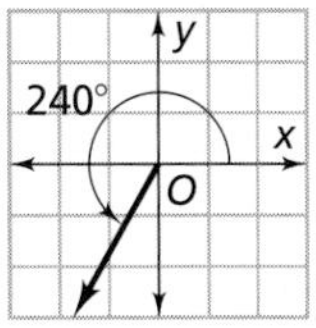

$\sin 240° = -\frac{\sqrt{3}}{2}$, $\cos 240° = -\frac{1}{2}$, $\tan 240° = \sqrt{3}$

3. −450°, −90°, 270°, 630°, 990°, any answer of the form $-90° + 360° \cdot k$ **4a.** $\pm\frac{5}{13}$ **b.** $\pm\frac{12}{5}$ **c.** 67.4°, 112.6° **5.** 60°, 126.87°, 233.13°, 300° **6.** For any point (x, y) on the unit circle, define $\cos \theta = x$, $\sin \theta = y$, and $\tan \theta = \frac{\sin \theta}{\cos \theta}$. **7.** Sine is negative, cosine is positive, and tangent is negative. **8.** The equation of the unit circle, $x^2 + y^2 = 1$, can be rewritten as $\cos^2 \theta + \sin^2 \theta = 1$, which is the Pythagorean Identity.

Lesson 8.6 pp. 715–716

Exercises

8.

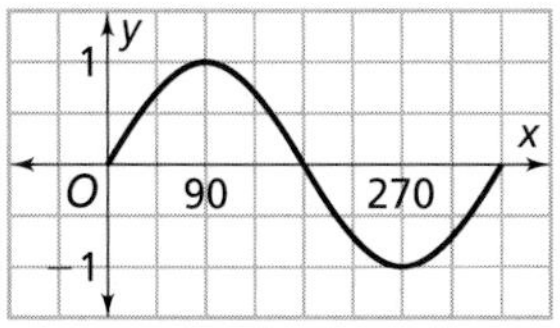

Lesson 8.7 pp. 717–721

For You to Do

3.

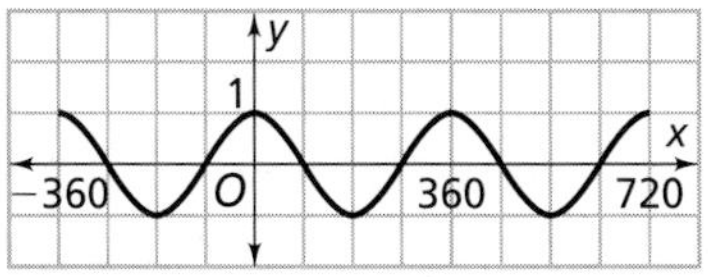

The graph of $y = \cos x$ is a translation of the graph of $y = \sin x$.

Exercises

5.

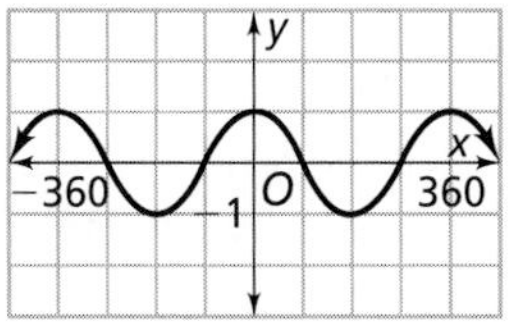

Figure 14

θ	$\cos \theta$	$\sin \theta$	$\cos^2\theta$	$\sin^2\theta$
0°	1	0	1	0
30°	$\frac{\sqrt{3}}{2}$	$\frac{1}{2}$	$\frac{3}{4}$	$\frac{1}{4}$
45°	$\frac{\sqrt{2}}{2}$	$\frac{\sqrt{2}}{2}$	$\frac{1}{2}$	$\frac{1}{2}$
60°	$\frac{1}{2}$	$\frac{\sqrt{3}}{2}$	$\frac{1}{4}$	$\frac{3}{4}$
90°	0	1	0	1
120°	$-\frac{1}{2}$	$\frac{\sqrt{3}}{2}$	$\frac{1}{4}$	$\frac{3}{4}$
135°	$-\frac{\sqrt{2}}{2}$	$\frac{\sqrt{2}}{2}$	$\frac{1}{2}$	$\frac{1}{2}$
150°	$-\frac{\sqrt{3}}{2}$	$\frac{1}{2}$	$\frac{3}{4}$	$\frac{1}{4}$
180°	−1	0	1	0
210°	$-\frac{\sqrt{3}}{2}$	$-\frac{1}{2}$	$\frac{3}{4}$	$\frac{1}{4}$
225°	$-\frac{\sqrt{2}}{2}$	$-\frac{\sqrt{2}}{2}$	$\frac{1}{2}$	$\frac{1}{2}$
240°	$-\frac{1}{2}$	$-\frac{\sqrt{3}}{2}$	$\frac{1}{4}$	$\frac{3}{4}$
270°	0	−1	0	1
300°	$\frac{1}{2}$	$-\frac{\sqrt{3}}{2}$	$\frac{1}{4}$	$\frac{3}{4}$
315°	$\frac{\sqrt{2}}{2}$	$-\frac{\sqrt{2}}{2}$	$\frac{1}{2}$	$\frac{1}{2}$
330°	$\frac{\sqrt{3}}{2}$	$-\frac{1}{2}$	$\frac{3}{4}$	$\frac{1}{4}$
360°	1	0	1	0

6.
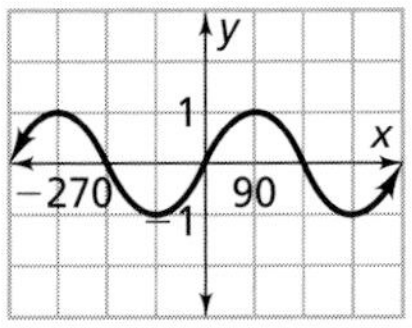

7. $\sin x = 0.6$ for $x = 37°$, $143°$, $397°$

8.
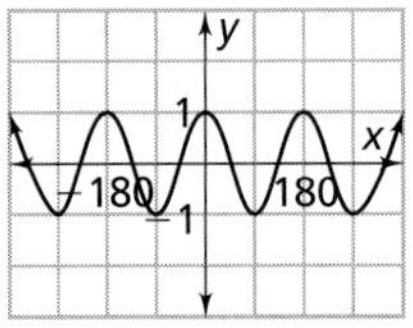

9a.
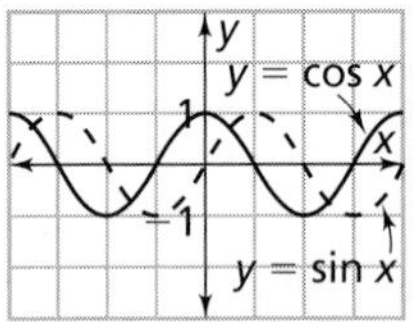

b. Answers may vary. Sample: 45°, 225°; any angle of the form $45° + k \cdot 180°$, where k is an integer

10a. 1 **b.** $\tan\theta = \frac{\sin\theta}{\cos\theta}$ and if $\sin\theta = \cos\theta$, then the tangent must be 1. **11.** Answers may vary. Sample:
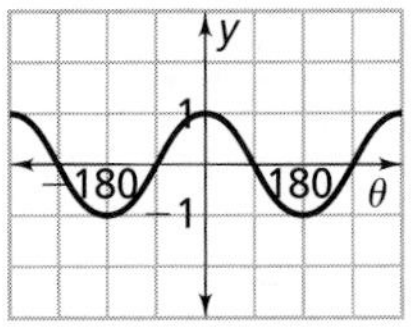

The graph of $y = \cos\theta$ is symmetric about the y-axis, so $\cos(-\theta) = \cos\theta$.

12. Answers may vary. Sample:
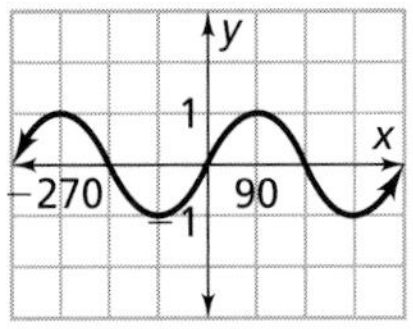

You can see from the graph of $y = \sin\theta$ that the y-values for $\sin\theta$ and $\sin(-\theta)$ are opposites for any given θ. So, $\sin(-\theta) = -\sin\theta$.

13.
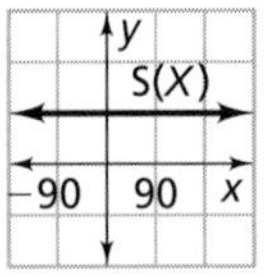

14. C

16. Answers may vary. Samples:

a.
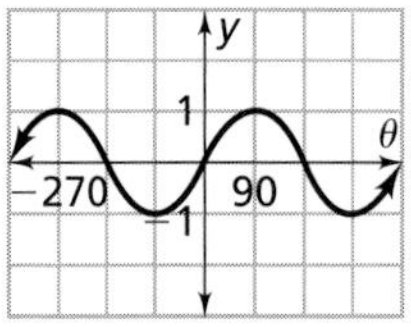

From the graph, $\sin\theta$ and $\sin(180° - \theta)$ are equal for any given θ, so $\sin(180° - \theta) = \sin\theta$.

b.
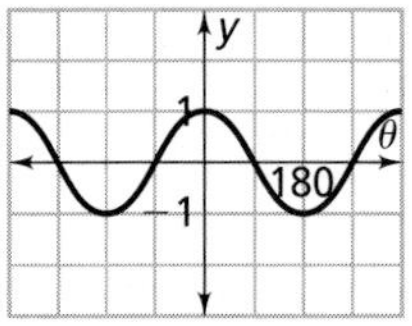

From the graph, $\cos(180° - \theta)$ and $-\cos\theta$ are equal for any given θ, so $\cos(180° - \theta) = -\cos\theta$.

c.
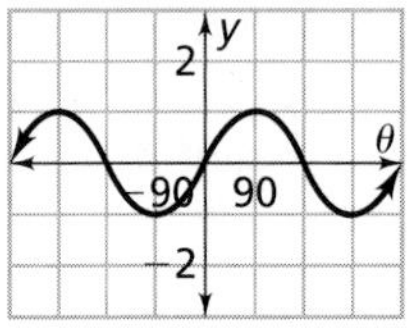

From the graph, $\sin(180° + \theta)$ and $-\sin\theta$ are equal for any given θ, so $\sin(180° + \theta) = -\sin\theta$.

d.
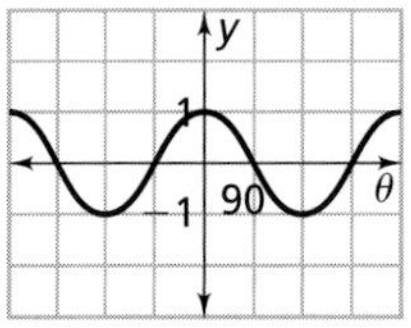

From the graph, $\cos(360° - \theta)$ and $\cos\theta$ are equal for any given θ, so $\cos(360° - \theta) = \cos\theta$.

e.
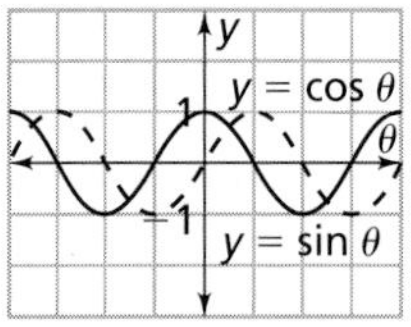

From the graph, $\sin\theta$ and $\cos(\theta - 90°)$ are equal for any given θ, so $\sin\theta = \cos(\theta - 90°)$.

f.
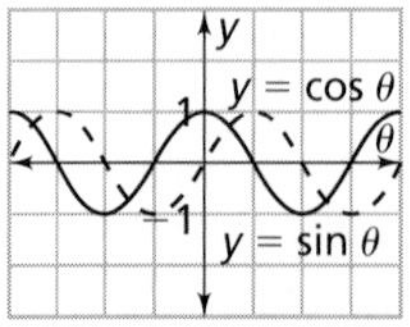

From the graph, $\cos\theta$ and $-\sin(\theta - 90°)$ are equal for any given θ, so $\cos\theta = -\sin(\theta - 90°)$.

17. Answers may vary. Sample:
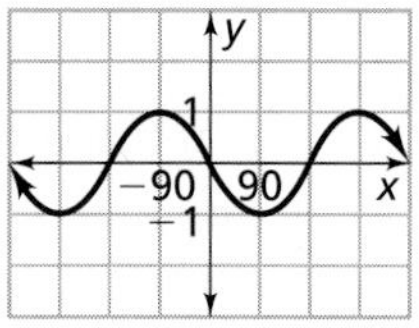

Lesson 8.8 pp. 722–726

Exercises

4a. $\tan(90° + \theta) = -\frac{3}{2} = -\frac{1}{\tan\theta}$
b. Answers may vary. Sample: The slope of the line is $\frac{y}{x}$, which is the same as the tangent of the angle formed by the line and the positive x-axis.
c. Answers may vary. Sample: If two perpendicular lines intersect at the origin and are not the x- and y-axes, and if (a, b) is a point on one line, then $(-b, a)$ is a point on the other line. So the slopes are $\frac{b}{a}$ and $-\frac{a}{b}$, which are negative reciprocals. Now suppose two lines have slopes that are negative reciprocals $\frac{b}{a}$ and $-\frac{a}{b}$. Using the results of Exercise 4a, $\tan(90° + \theta) = -\frac{1}{\tan\theta}$, if the line through (a, b) forms an angle of θ with the positive x-axis, then the line through $(-b, a)$ forms an angle of $(\theta + 90°)$, so the two lines are perpendicular.
5. Answers may vary. Sample: $\cos\theta$ is 0 for $\theta = 90° + k \cdot 180°$, where k is an integer. You can rewrite $90 + 180k$ as $90(1 + 2k)$. The values $2k + 1$ are the odd integers, so the values $90°(1 + 2k)$ are the odd multiples of 90°. **6a.** 14° **b.** 28° **c.** 104° **d.** 208° **7a.** 14° **b.** 28° **c.** 104° **d.** 208° **8a.** $(x^2 - y^2) + (2xy)i$ **b.** $\frac{2xy}{x^2 - y^2}$ **9.** Answers may vary. Sample: $\tan x = \frac{\sin x}{\cos x}$, and in Quadrant III both $\sin x$ and $\cos x$ have the same sign, but in Quadrant II they have different signs. So $\tan x$ is positive in Quadrant III and negative in Quadrant II. A second explanation is that if θ is in Quadrant II, the line through the origin at angle θ will intersect the tangent drawn to the unit circle at (1, 0) at the point $(1, \tan\theta)$ in Quadrant IV. So $\tan\theta$ must be negative. If θ is in Quadrant III, the line through the origin at angle θ will intersect the tangent line in Quadrant I, so $\tan\theta$ is positive.

Lesson 8.9 pp. 727–733

Exercises

3a. $\frac{\sqrt{2+\sqrt{3}}}{2}$

b. Yes; if $A = \frac{\sqrt{2+\sqrt{3}}}{2}$, then $4A = 2\sqrt{2+\sqrt{3}}$ and $(4A)^2 = (4)(2+\sqrt{3}) = 8 + 4\sqrt{3}$. If $B = \frac{\sqrt{2}+\sqrt{6}}{4}$, then $4B = \sqrt{6}+\sqrt{2}$ and $(4B)^2 = 6 + 2\sqrt{12} + 2 = 8 + 2\sqrt{4}\cdot\sqrt{3} = 8 + 4\sqrt{3}$. So, $\frac{\sqrt{2+\sqrt{3}}}{2} = \frac{\sqrt{2}+\sqrt{6}}{4}$.

4. $\cos 3x = \cos^3 x - 3\sin^2 x \cos x$, $\sin 3x = 3\sin x\cos^2 x - \sin^3 x$

5. $\frac{\sqrt{3}}{2} + \frac{1}{2}i$ **6a.** $\sin 10° = 0.1736$, $\sin 50° = 0.7660$, and $\sin 70° = 0.9397$; $\sin 10° + \sin 50° = 0.1736 + 0.7660 = 0.9396$, which is about 0.9397. **b.** 80° **c.** 65°

7. $\sin x + \sin(60° - x) = \sin(60° + x)$; to prove that result, the left side is $\sin x + \sin(60° - x) = \sin x + (\sin 60°)(\cos x) - (\cos 60°)(\sin x) = \sin x + \left(\frac{\sqrt{3}}{2}\right)\cdot(\cos x) - \left(\frac{1}{2}\right)(\sin x) = \left(\frac{1}{2}\right)(\sin x) + \left(\frac{\sqrt{3}}{2}\right)(\cos x)$. The right side is $(\sin 60°)(\cos x) + (\cos 60°)(\sin x) = \left(\frac{\sqrt{3}}{2}\right)(\cos x) + \left(\frac{1}{2}\right)(\sin x)$.
The two sides are equal, so $\sin x + \sin(60° - x) = \sin(60° + x)$.

14. $\tan(x+y) = \frac{\tan x + \tan y}{1 - \tan x \cdot \tan y}$

15. Answers may vary. Sample: $\cos(a+b) = \cos a\cos b - \sin a\sin b$. So, $\cos(a-b) = \cos(a+(-b)) = \cos a\cos(-b) - \sin a\sin(-b) = \cos a\cos b - (\sin a)(-\sin b) = \cos a\cos b + \sin a\sin b$. Also, $\sin(a+b) = \sin a\cos b + \cos a\sin b$. So $\sin(a-b) = \sin(a+(-b)) = \sin a\cos(-b) + \cos a\sin(-b) = \sin a\cos b + (\cos a)(-\sin b) = \sin a\cos b - \cos a\sin b$.

16. C **17a.** $\frac{1}{2}\cos\theta + \frac{\sqrt{3}}{2}\sin\theta$

b. $\frac{\sqrt{2}}{2}\cos\theta + \frac{\sqrt{2}}{2}\sin\theta$

c. $\frac{\sqrt{3}}{2}\cos\theta + \frac{1}{2}\sin\theta$

d. $\frac{\sqrt{3}}{2}\cos\theta + \left(-\frac{1}{2}\right)\sin\theta$

e. $\frac{1}{2}\cos\theta + \left(-\frac{\sqrt{3}}{2}\right)\sin\theta$

Lesson 8.12 pp. 747–753

Exercises

6.

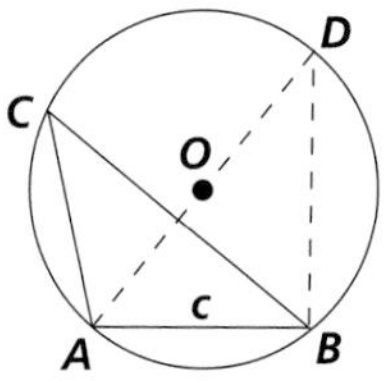

a. $\angle ABD$ is inscribed in a semicircle, so it is a right angle. **b.** $\angle C$ and $\angle D$ intercept the same arc, AB, so they are congruent. **c.** $m\angle C = m\angle D$, so $\sin C = \sin D$ **d.** You know $\frac{c}{\sin C} = \frac{c}{\sin D} = \frac{AD}{\sin\angle ABD}$. $\angle ABD$ is a right angle, so $\sin\angle ABD = 1$. Thus $AD = \frac{c}{\sin C}$.

7.

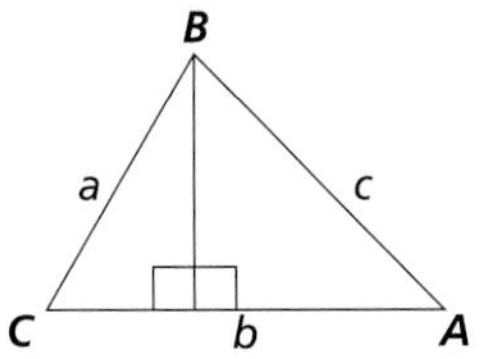

The length of the altitude from vertex B is $a\sin C$ or $c\sin A$. Therefore the area of the triangle is $\frac{1}{2}a\sin C\cdot b$ or $\frac{1}{2}c\sin A\cdot b$. The expressions are equal, so $a\sin C = c\sin A$. Then $\frac{a}{\sin A} = \frac{c}{\sin C}$. By using a different altitude you can make a similar argument to prove $\frac{a}{\sin A} = \frac{b}{\sin B}$. Therefore $\frac{a}{\sin A} = \frac{b}{\sin B} = \frac{c}{\sin C}$.

19a. $AC \approx 14.1$, $AB \approx 19.3$, $m\angle C = 105°$ **b.** $m\angle C = 105°$, $AB \approx 38.6$, $AC \approx 28.3$

c. $m\angle C = 105°$, $AB \approx 13.7$, $BC \approx 7.1$

d. $m\angle C = 90°$, $AB \approx 11.5$, $BC \approx 5.8$

e. $m\angle C = 30°$, $AB \approx 5.8$, $BC \approx 5.8$

Lesson 8.13 pp. 754–763

Exercises

7a. The cosines opposite the sides of length 13, 14, and 15 are 0.6, 0.5077, and 0.3846, respectively. **b.** The largest angle has the least cosine. **c.** 12

d. 84 **8a.** $\cos C = \frac{a^2 + b^2 - c^2}{2ab}$, and the numerator and denominator must be integers, so $\cos C$ must be rational.

b. The area of a triangle can be written as $\frac{1}{2}ab\sin C$. We know that ab is an integer, and part (a) showed that $\cos C$ is rational. So $\frac{1-\cos^2 C}{4} = \frac{\sin^2 C}{4}$ is rational. Therefore $\sqrt{\frac{\sin^2 C}{4}} = \frac{1}{2}\sin C$ is the square root of a rational number. So the area of a triangle, $\frac{1}{2}ab\sin C$ or $ab\cdot\frac{1}{2}\sin C$, is the product of an integer times the square root of a rational number.

18a. Answers may vary. Sample: $\cos A = \frac{AD}{b}$ and $\cos B = \frac{BD}{a}$, so $c = AD + BD = b\cos A + a\cos B$. **b.** Label the existing diagram so the base is $\overline{CA}$ and the altitude is $\overline{BD}$. Then $\cos C = \frac{CD}{a}$, $\cos A = \frac{AD}{c}$, and $b = CD + AD = a\cos C + c\cos A$. **c.** Label the existing diagram so the base is $\overline{BC}$ and the altitude is $\overline{AD}$. Then $\cos C = \frac{CD}{b}$, $\cos B = \frac{BD}{c}$, and $a = CD + BD = b\cos C + c\cos B$.

Index

Teacher Edition entries appear in blue type.

D

H

I

K

L

P

Q

R

Acknowledgments

Staff Credits

The Pearson people on the CME Project team—representing design, editorial, editorial services, digital product development, publishing services, and technical operations—are listed below. Bold type denotes the core team members.

Ernest Albanese, Scott Andrews, Carolyn Artin, Michael Avidon, Margaret Banker, Suzanne Biron, Beth Blumberg, Stacie Cartwright, Carolyn Chappo, Casey Clark, Bob Craton, Sheila DeFazio, Patty Fagan, **Frederick Fellows**, **Patti Fromkin**, Paul J. Gagnon, Cynthia Harvey, Gillian Kahn, Jonathan Kier, Jennifer King, Elizabeth Krieble, Sara Levendusky, Lisa Lin, Clay Martin, **Carolyn McGuire**, Rich McMahon, Eve Melnechuk, **Hope Morley**, Jen Paley, Mairead Reddin, Marcy Rose, Rashid Ross, Carol Roy, Jewel Simmons, Ted Smykal, Kara Stokes, Richard Sullivan, Tiffany Taylor-Sullivan, Catherine Terwilliger, Mark Tricca, Lauren Van Wart, Paula Vergith, **Joe Will**, **Kristin Winters**, Allison Wyss

Additional Credits

Gina Choe, Cynthia Metallides, Christine Nevola, Lillian Pelaggi, Deborah Savona

Cover Design and Illustration
9 Surf Studios

Cover Photography
Alamy/RubberBall

Illustration
Kerry Cashman, Rich McMahon, Deborah Savona, Ted Smykal

Photography
Table of Contents: vi, Visuals Unlimited/Joe McDonald; **ix,** Corbis; **x,** Alamy/Kevin Schafer; **xi,** Getty Images/Allan Baxter.

Chapter 1: Pages 2–3, Corbis/Don Mason/RM; **4,** Visuals Unlimited/Joe McDonald; **9,** Kara Stokes; **20l,** Merrill Education; **20r,** Carolyn Chappo; **27,** Photo Researchers, Inc.; **39,** A. & J. Visaoe/Peter Arnold, Inc.; **45,** Super Stock; **51,** Carolyn Chappo; **59,** Jupiter Images/Manfred Kage; **64,** Alamy/Wim Wiskerke; **68,** Corbis/LIII K.; **71,** Fundamental Photographs; **81,** Corbis; **82,** Alamy/Steven May.

Chapter 2: Page 88–89, Corbis/William Sallaz; **96,** NewsCom/James Baigrie; **111,** Newscom/Sipa; **112,** Alamy; **126,** Animals Animals/Richard Shiell; **130,** Getty/ML Harris; **136,** AP Images/Charles Krupa; **135,** Granger; **144,** Dreamstime; **146,** iStockphoto; **153,** iStockphoto; **161,** Alamy/Ellen McKnight; **162,** Newscom/Bo Rader; **165,** Corbis/Dirk Anschütz; **165,** SuperStock/PhotoDisc; **178,** Getty Images/S. Meltzer; **183,** iStockphoto; **189,** Corbis/Arcaid.

Chapter 3: Pages 196–197, Kris Northern; **198,** Corbis/Camille Flammarion; **205l,** North Wind; **205r,** Granger; **218,** Carolyn Chappo; **224,** Photo Researchers/Mehau Kulyk; **238,** Getty Images/Eric Feferberg; **244,** Veer; **250,** Photo Researchers/Gregory Sams; **252,** Dr. Bahman Kalantari; **260t,** Photo Researchers/Gusto; **260b,** NewsCom; **267,** Carolyn Chappo; **269,** Alamy/Ilene MacDonald; **275,** Dr. Bahman Kalantari.

Chapter 4: Pages 280–281, Peter Arnold/Jochen Tack; **282,** Getty Images/Al Bello; **291,** Corbis; **301,** Corbis/Anthony John West; **302,** Alamy/RubberBall; **330,** Corbis/George Shelley; **341 both,** AP Images/Dave Bowman; **348,** Getty Images/Christian Lagereek; **352,** Alamy/RubberBall; **354,** istockphoto.com/Sharon Shimoni; **375,** Minden Pictures; 387, istockphoto/Mark Evans; **390,** Newscom/Stacey Wescott.

Chapter 5: Pages 396–397 both, Getty Images/Craig Mitchelldyer; **398,** Corbis/A. Inden; **411,** Photo Researchers Inc./Andrew Syred; **423,** Corbis/Arctic-Images; **424,** Alamy/David Lyons; **435,** Veer; **448,** AP Images/Richard Drew; **460,** Alamy/Kevin Schafer; **467,** istockphoto.com; **477** Dreamstime; **488,** Photo Researchers/Eckhard Slawik; **493,** Veer.

Chapter 6: Pages 498–499, Newscom/Yoshikaza Tsuno; **500,** Dreamstime; **512,** Dreamstime; **517,** John Moore; **531,** Dreamstime; **532,** Alamy/Foodcollection; **534,** Getty Images/Allan Baxter; **536,** Corbis/William Whitehurst; **556,** Corbis/William Whitehurst; **571,** Alamy/Magdalena Rehova; **577,** Alamy/Stock Images.

Chapter 7: Pages 586–587, Getty Images/Ian Mckinnell; **616,** North Wind; **588,** Corbis/Tobbe; **603,** Dreamstime; **605,** John Moore; **606,** Newscom; **620,** Dreamstime; **628,** AP Images/Ann Heisenfelt; **636,** Alamy; **657,** Alamy/Dusty Dingo; **660,** John Moore; **672,** John Moore; **674–675,** NewsCom/ZUMA.

Chapter 8: Pages 680–681, Alamy/Michael Jenner; **688,** Getty Images/Joe Sohm; **692,** AP Images/Sue Ogrocki; **707,** Alamy/John Pitcher; **713,** istockphoto; **714,** Photo Researchers; **734,** Alamy; **724,** Getty Images/Grant V. Faint; **736,** Newscom/Benjamin M. Arnao; **741,** Getty Images/Bruce Dale; **757,** Getty Images/Howard Shooter; **766,** AP Images/Matt Ferguson; **770,** Newscom/Benjamin M. Arnao.

Text Acknowledgments
Grateful acknowledgment is made to the following for copyrighted material:
40, 46, 66, "Gold Medal Times (in seconds) from the Men's 1500-Meter Run" from *Sports Illustrated 2007 Almanac.* Copyright © 2006 Time Inc. Home Entertainment.

Note: Every effort has been made to locate the copyright owner of material reprinted in this component. Omissions brought to our attention will be corrected in subsequent editions.